ROTHMANS FOOTBALL YEARBOOK 1995-96

Rothmans

EDITOR: JACK ROLLIN
ASSISTANT EDITOR: GLENDA ROLLIN

HEADLINE

First published in 1995
by HEADLINE BOOK PUBLISHING

10 9 8 7 6 5 4 3 2 1

Cover photographs: (top left) Steve Bould (Arsenal) and Jürgen Klinsmann (Tottenham Hotspur)—*Colorsport*; (bottom left) Alan Shearer (Blackburn Rovers)—*Colorsport*; (top right) Robert Lee (Newcastle United)—*Action Images*; (bottom right) Maurizio Gaudino (Manchester City) and Andy Cole (Manchester United)—*Colorsport*.

British Library Cataloguing in Publication Data
Rothmans Football Yearbook.—1995–96
1. Association Football—Serials
796.334'05

ISBN 0 7472 1413 1 (hardback)
0 7472 7823 7 (softback)

Typeset by BPC Whitefriars Ltd,
Tunbridge Wells

Printed and bound in Great Britain by
BPC Hazell Books Ltd
Member of BPC Ltd

HEADLINE BOOK PUBLISHING
A division of Hodder Headline PLC
338 Euston Road
London NW1 3BH

CONTENTS

INTERNATIONAL FOOTBALL

EUROPEAN FOOTBALL

NON-LEAGUE FOOTBALL

INFORMATION AND RECORDS

INTRODUCTION

The 26th Edition of Rothmans Yearbook includes an up-to-date list of all qualifying results in the 1996 European Championship, the finals of which will be held in England next summer. There are goalscorers, teams, times of goals, attendances and referees for the competition.

On the domestic scene there is a radical change in the presentation of players for the 92 English League clubs (*see page 33*). The new Players Directory includes all previous items of information in an easy-to-read A-Z guide. There are now four pages for each English club in the FA Carling Premiership and Endsleigh Insurance League. Again squad numbers have been ignored, the more familiar 1 to 11, 12, 14 and 15 (representing the goalkeeper substitute) have been utilised.

Information which previously featured on the sixth club page has now been moved elsewhere, with both the Managers and Did You Know sections now separately listed, while other data has been incorporated into the extended page two. As a consequence of this, the club badge has been moved to the top of the third club page and the fourth one in this section now features initials of the players making appearances in 1994-95.

The performances of British clubs in Europe are monitored and special articles include those on the Football Trust, Football and the Law, Referees and the work of Football in the Community. Also the special work carried out by Chaplains to clubs is again included.

Amateur, schools, university and women's football plus coverage of non-league soccer, awards, records and the International Directory of all member countries in FIFA are among the regular items.

Transfer fees are given where known. When two clubs have differed as to the amount of a record move, the lower figure has been quoted in both instances. Also the date when a player is signed often varies from one given as his registration.

The Editor would also like to thank Alan Elliott for the Scottish section, Norman Barrett for the Milestones Diary and Ian Vosper for the Obituaries. Thanks are also due to John English who provided his usual painstaking and conscientious reading of the proofs. Appreciation, too, for the fine editorial assistance of Christine Forrest.

The Editor would like to pay tribute to the various organisations who have helped to make this edition complete, especially Sheila Andrew of the Football League, Mike Foster of the FA Premier League and the secretaries of all the FA Premier, Football League and Scottish League clubs for their kind co-operation. The ready availability of Football League secretary David Dent and his staff to answer queries was as usual most appreciated especially Chris Hull and thanks are due in equal measure to the Scottish Football League as well as Adrian Cook and Neil Harrison of the FA Premier League.

ACKNOWLEDGEMENTS

The Editor would also like to express his appreciation of the following individuals and organisations for their co-operation: Glynis Firth, Sandra Whiteside, Lorna Parnell, Debbie Birch (all from the Football League), David C. Thompson of the Scottish League, Alan Dick, Malcolm Brodie, Bob Hennessy, Peter Hughes (English Schools FA), W.P. Goss (AFA), Ken Scott for Vauxhall Conference information, Rev. Nigel Sands, Edward Grayson, Ken Goldman and Andy Howland.

Special thanks are due to Lorraine Jerram of Headline Book Publishing Ltd for her constant support, unflagging patience, sincerity, understanding and appreciation.

Finally sincere thanks to Allan Wyatt, David Prebble and Trevor Stevens and the production staff at BPC Whitefriars for their efforts in the production of this book which was much appreciated throughout the year.

DON ALDRIDGE

A few days after the 25th edition went to press, Don Aldridge, a valued Rothmans contributor over many years, died in hospital following a short illness. He had completed his work on the book before being taken ill. Formerly editor of the FA News, he was, until shortly before his death also responsible for editing programmes at Wembley Stadium. A first-class researcher, his other speciality was successfully harrassing errant organisations for their Rothmans copy.

EDITORIAL

Two days after Eric Cantona's infamous Bruce Lee impression at Crystal Palace, one of those early morning radio programmes cuttingly posed the rhetorical question: "How can you bring soccer into disrepute". Then you know the image of the game is flawed.

That was not the end of the problem. There was the disaster in Dublin and as a result of this, all English teams playing abroad have been designated as 'high risk' affairs. Allegations of managers accepting 'bungs', players accused of involvement in fixing matches, it seemed that the list of scandal was endless. Greed and corruption would appear to be widespread.

All this is so sad, particularly when the game is making strenuous efforts to improve its stature. Ground redevelopments, the unsung work of the various supporters organisations, the Football Trust, Football in the Community programmes, signs of closer liaison between the authorities and the fans, encouragement of families at football etc., all point to the positive aspect of our national sport.

Alas football's answer to the outbreaks of hooliganism is that it is society's problem. But the game is a crucial part of the fabric of many people's leisure activities and those connected with the game cannot divorce themselves from what is happening in the world. More importantly, how we have allowed events to drift to a degree with which we are dissatisfied, affects each and everyone of us.

In an era when there is a proliferation of bad language and violence on television, we can scarcely be surprised when a minority of spectators fail to observe the decencies at matches. The human species may have become wretched and miserable; advanced in technology, but forever slipping back on a moral plane. Parental responsibility is probably politically incorrect, but it is necessary. No one should underestimate the pressures of raising children in present circumstances, but when it is often abrogated completely or at best privatised, only a total re-think can alter the situation.

After all if we want to foster family enclosures at football, there will have to be sufficient numbers to make it viable.

While numbers of spectators and the standard of behaviour they display must play a leading role in the future, there are other statistics to be noted. While the FA Carling Premiership showed a further welcome increase in attendances at matches in 1994-95, there was a less encouraging set of figures for goalscoring.

Going back to 1924-25 when the offside law was about to be changed, the number of goals scored in the then First Division had fallen to 1,192. The following season under the new rules, it had increased to 1,703. In 1994-95 it was just 1,195, the same figure as in 1993-94.

Perhaps we have come to expect fewer goals in the modern era of tighter defences and the danger is that there will be a panic towards implementing the type of idea, like the kick-in experiment which had to be seen to be disapproved, that will further erode the standing of the beautiful game.

Bill Shankly's oft quoted remarks about life and death and football were much nearer the truth than we might have imagined. The best evidence is that while death is likely to strike just once, losing matches is a certainty more than once.

The game of life has few enough free kicks but frequent penalties. One must gratefully accept the former and face the latter with as much dignity as possible. But then is sudden death preferable to penalties...?

ROTHMANS FOOTBALL HONOURS

BIRMINGHAM CITY FOOTBALL CLUB. Though the midland club were regularly involved in the transfer market during the 1994-95 season, and called upon the services of more players than any other in the four English divisions -37 in all -they could reflect on a successful outcome and a double which produced the Second Division championship and the Auto Windscreens Shield Trophy. Ebullient manager Barry Fry shuffled his pack shrewdly enough to bring promotion and the crowds flocked to St Andrews. Indeed the attendance for their final at Wembley was bettered there by just one other during the entire season and that for the FA Cup Final itself, as City fans alone accounted for well over 40,000 spectators.

MATTHEW LE TISSIER. Discovered while touring with the Guernsey Under-15's, he was once the youngest Southampton player to score a hat-trick. While he has delved deeply into his resources to contrive goals from various angles and positions, it is his inherent flair and vision which has made him one of the most gifted of present day players, despite just a handful of full England international opportunities. Last season he did much to stifle the cry that consistency was not one of his attributes. His almost unerring accuracy from the penalty spot is also confirmed: he has never failed to hit the target and only once in March 1993 did he have a shot saved in 36 overall attempts.

BRYAN ROBSON. The 1994-95 season must have seemed like a fairy story come true for Middlesbrough and Bryan Robson. Striving to regain their Premier League status and with a newly-installed player-manager anxious to prove himself, they emerged as worthy champions of the Endsleigh Insurance First Division. Now they are taking their place among the elite and about to settle into a new £6 million home. Robson's first season at the helm was all that he might have wished for himself and his calculated moves into the transfer arena were well-judged and rewarding. He also succeeded in overcoming injury problems to combine his demanding midfield role with well executed off-field duties.

JOE ROYLE. That Joe Royle would won day become manager of Everton was possibly not the wildest of dreams for anyone to contemplate. Merseyside born, he had been their youngest senior debutant at only 16 years of age in 1966. In ten seasons he scored 119 League and Cup goals for the club and won England honours in their colours. After playing spells elsewhere, he became Oldham Athletic's manager in 1982 and was generally acknowledged to have distinguished himself in their cause. Taking over at Goodison Park last season when Everton were staring relegation in the face, he put the smiles back with his commitment and enthusiasm, banishing fear of the drop and adding the FA Cup as an endorsement of his fine efforts.

ALAN SHEARER. The Geordie who came south to make his name and then move to the north-west, Alan Shearer is probably best described as an old-fashioned leader of the attack, who in a previous era would have contributed 40 or 50 goals a season. That in 1994-95 with Blackburn Rovers he equalled the record for the FA Premier League with 34 goals, merely emphasises his value among tighter modern defences. In only his second game for Southampton, he scored three goals to become the youngest to do so in a First Divison game. Accuracy on the ground and in the air, the ability to initiate attacks and clinically finish them off, has earned him international honours for England. Another personal milestone: his 100th League goal on 18 March.

WOKING FOOTBALL CLUB. Under the astute managership of Geoff Chapple, Woking have become one of the most consistent teams outside the four English divisions in recent years, consolidating their position in the Vauxhall Conference, enjoying spirited FA Cup runs and achieving the unusual feat of winning the FA Trophy in successive years 1994 and 1995. The club's ambitions do not lie dormant there, however, for there are advance plans to break into the Football League once suitable headquarters have been prodcued. Importantly the Cards have an excellent deal with the local Council. In addition to their Cup triumph in 1994-95, they were well in the hunt for championship honours in the League, finishing a creditable second in the final analysis.

AN EXCLUSIVE GOALSCORING CLUB

Hat-tricks are few and far between—last season there were less than 75 in Premier and Endsleigh League matches. Players scoring four or more goals in League football are naturally very rare. Usually less than five players manage four goals in a single match and last season just one player—Andy Cole of Manchester United—scored five, the first five in the top division since 1983.
Since the Football League was formed in 1888, there have been over 440,000 goals scored. A list of players scoring six goals or more in a single league match will take up far less room. The following players belong to this rather exclusive 'club'.

Name	**Club**	**Date**	**Goals Scored**	
Southworth	Everton	30/12/1893	Six	WBA
Capes Adr.	Bolton W	21/1/1895	Six	Walsall
McCairns	Grimsby T	11/4/1896	Six	Leicester F
Glover	Southport	22/10/1921	Six	Grimsby T
Duncan	Leicester C	25/12/1924	Six	Port Vale
Page	Burnley	10/4/1926	Six	Birmingham
Walsh	Bristol C	15/1/1927	Six	Gillingham
Cookson	WBA	17/9/1927	Six	Blackpool
Waring	Tranmere R	7/1/1928	Six	Durham C
Chandler	Leicester C	20/10/1928	Six	Portsmouth
Watson	West Ham U	9/2/1929	Six	Leeds U
Keetley	Doncaster R	16/2/1929	Six	Ashington
Whitehurst	Bradford C	6/3/1929	Seven	Tranmere R
Tippett	Rochdale	21/4/1930	Six	Hartlepool U
Cheesemuir	Gillingham	26/4/1930	Six	Merthyr T
Simpson	Crystal Palace	4/10/1930	Six	Exeter C
Bacon	Reading	3/4/1931	Six	Stoke C
Keetley	Lincoln C	16/1/1932	Six	Halifax T
Littlewood	Port Vale	24/9/1932	Six	Chesterfield
Drake	Arsenal	14/12/1935	Seven	Aston Villa
Bell	Tranmere R	26/12/1935	Nine	Oldham Ath
Payne	Luton T	13/4/1936	Ten	Bristol R
Hartson	Mansfield T	23/1/1937	Seven	Hartlepool U
Henson	Bradford PA	29/1/1938	Six	Blackburn R
Hunt	Sheffield W	19/11/1938	Six	Norwich C
Shackleton	Newcastle U	5/10/1946	Six	Newport Co
Graver	Lincoln C	29/9/1951	Six	Crewe Alex
Gemmell	Oldham Ath	19/1/1952	Seven	Chester
Briggs	Blackburn R	5/2/1955	Seven	Bristol R
Coleman	Stoke C	23/2/1957	Seven	Lincoln C
Lister	Oldham Ath	26/12/1962	Six	Southport
Hurst	West Ham U	19/10/1968	Six	Sunderland

This represents 32 occasions out of almost 150,000 League games since 1888. And the last time some 27 years ago.

The Association of Football Statisticians.

NUMBER OF PLAYERS SENT OFF IN ENGLISH LEAGUE MATCHES 1946–47 TO 1994–95

1946–47	12	1963–64	45	1980–81	107
1947–48	5	1964–65	46	1981–82	133
1948–49	10	1965–66	46	1982–83	221
1949–50	14	1966–67	50	1983–84	152
1950–51	7	1967–68	48	1984–85	165
1951–52	14	1968–69	51	1985–86	185
1952–53	15	1969–70	37	1986–87	193
1953–54	14	1970–71	28	1987–88	195
1954–55	13	1971–72	36	1988–89	172
1955–56	20	1972–73	83	1989–90	161
1956–57	15	1973–74	76	1990–91	202
1957–58	27	1974–75	97	1991–92	244
1958–59	20	1975–76	89	1992–93	226
1959–60	19	1976–77	100	1993–94	233
1960–61	18	1977–78	98	1994–95	314
1961–62	25	1978–79	108		
1962–63	35	1979–80	111		

MILESTONES DIARY 1994–95

June 1994

Spurs banished from Cup and docked 12pts in League . . . Celtic sack Lou Macari . . . 5-goal Oleg . . . Maradona chucked out of World Cup

13 FIFA deny Irish claims that players would not be allowed water during World Cup matches, maintaining that instructions insist only that they come to the touchline to drink.

14 Found guilty of financial irregularities, Spurs receive swingeing punishments from the FA - banishment from next season's FA Cup, 12 points deducted at the start of the Premiership season, and £600,000 fine. The Diadora League will be the first in the world to operate FIFA's 'kick-in' experiment.

15 Spurs chairman Alan Sugar accuses FA of a personal vendetta against him. Rangers complete the signing of Danish international Brian Laudrup from Fiorentina for 'quite a lot less than £3m', and Middlesbrough sign Villa's U-21 defender Neil Cox for £1m.

16 Celtic sack Lou Macari after less than 8 months in charge, citing his failure to move to Scotland as a major reason. Joao Havelange is re-elected FIFA president unopposed.

17 Holders Germany beat Bolivia 1-0 in the opening World Cup match (Chicago 3.00pm).

18 A Ray Houghton goal gives Ireland victory over Italy in their first World Cup match.

20 Hearts' new chairman Chris Robinson performs his first duty - sacking manager Sandy Clark.

21 Millwall are found guilty of misconduct regarding the pitch invasion in the play-off against Derby last month, but instead of the feared ground closure for the 6th time they receive a suspended (until December) punishment of two games behind closed doors, 3 League points deducted and a £100,000 fine to be imposed in the event of further serious misconduct.

22 Man City complete the signing of defender Nicky Summerbee, son of their former star Mike, from Swindon for £1.5m. In the World Cup, FIFA general secretary Sepp Blatter is unhappy about two things - some of the refereeing and Jack Charlton's attitude.

24 Ireland manager Jack Charlton is involved in row with FIFA official over delay in substitution of John Aldridge, who goes on to score a vital goal in their 2-1 defeat by Mexico.

25 Jack Charlton is banned by FIFA disciplinary committee from the touchline for Ireland's last group match and is fined £10,000, as is the Irish FA, and John Aldridge is fined £1,250, for the altercation during the game against Mexico.

27 Germany's manager Bertie Vogts sends Stefan Effenberg home from the World Cup after the aptly named midfielder shows his middle finger to German fans in their stuttering 3-2 victory over S.Korea.

28 Despite the sensational World Cup record of 5 goals achieved by Oleg Salenko in their 6-1 thrashing of Cameroon, Russia go out. Sweden striker Martin Dahlin, who has 3 goals to his credit, turns down a transfer from Borussia to Everton at the last moment after two weeks of negotiations.

29 FIFA announce that a World Cup player has tested positive for drugs, but refuse to name him or his country until the second sample is analysed.

30 FIFA drop a bombshell - the player whose second sample has now tested positive is Diego Maradona, and the Argentina captain is expelled from the tournament. Argentina are not punished, however, and even though they lose their evening match to Bulgaria, they go through to the 2nd round. Leeds sign Carlton Palmer from Sheff Wed for £2.6m and intend to use him in defence.

July

Colombian captain assassinated after own goal . . . Ireland out of World Cup . . . Blackburn sign Chris Sutton for record £5m . . . Brazil win 4th World Cup . . . Spurs sign World Cup stars Dumitrescu and Klinsmann

1 Maradona determines to fight possible life ban. Fans in Ireland have so far raised more than £100,000 to pay Jack Charlton's World Cup fine, but any money collected will go to charity.

2 Andreas Escobar, captain of the disappointingly eliminated Colombian team, is gunned down in a Medellin car park after his return home, apparently because of the own goal he scored in the match they lost to the USA.

4 The Irish World Cup bubble is burst as two defensive mistakes hand Holland a 2-0 victory in Orlando.

6 The FA Appeals Board reduce Tottenham's 12-point deduction to 6 points, but increase their fine from £600,000 to £1.5m and maintain their ban from next season's FA Cup. FIFA's disciplinary committee suspend Brazil left-back Leonardo for 4 matches, which rules him out of the World Cup finals.

8 FIFA president Joao Havelange denies there has been a FIFA conspiracy against Diego Maradona to wreck his career after the Argentine had failed a drug test.

9 Kilmarnock block Celtic's attempt to lure player-manager Tommy Burns back to Parkhead.

10 Norwich chairman Robert Chase announces that uncapped striker Chris Sutton is available at a British record £5m, provided the deal is ratified by next Friday (15th).

11 Man Utd bow out of the chase for Norwich's Chris Sutton, leaving Blackburn and Arsenal as favourites for his signature.

12 After studying video evidence, FIFA hand Italy's defender Mauro Tassotti an 8-game suspension and a £10,000 fine for elbowing Luis Enrique of Spain in the face, an off-the-ball incident that escaped punishment on the field. Kilmarnock's Tommy Burns is appointed Celtic manager.

13 Man Utd star Eric Cantona, working for French TV, is arrested at the Rose Bowl and misses the Brazil-Sweden semi-final after a scuffle with a Press Box official, but is released without being charged. In Norwich, Chris Sutton is arrested and spends a night in a police cell after an incident involving damage to a car outside a night club. Leeds agree a club record of £3m for Genoa's Czech international striker Tomas Skuhravy. Dutch winger Bryan Roy completes his £2.5m signing for Forest. Spurs keeper Erik Thorstvedt has a shoulder operation and will be out till October. Alex McLeish is confirmed as Motherwell manager.

14 Brazilian criminal Peralta, the mastermind behind the theft 9 years ago of the Jules Rimet Trophy - won outright by the last Brazilian team to reach the World Cup final (in 1970) and believed to have been melted down - is recaptured after 8 years on the run. Arsenal withdraw from the race for Chris Sutton, leaving the field to Blackburn.

15 Blackburn complete the signing of Chris Sutton from Norwich for £5m - at a reputed weekly salary of £12,000 - £1m more than the previous British record paid by Rangers for Duncan Ferguson.

17 Brazil become the first country to win 4 World Cups, beating Italy on penalties after a 0-0 draw.

20 In the draw for the new-style European Cup, seeded Man Utd find themselves in the same group as Barcelona, with a possible return clash with Galatasaray, who knocked them out last season.

21 Liverpool's new assistant manager is old-boy Doug Livermore, who resigned from Spurs earlier in the week.

22 England will play the USA in a friendly at Wembley on 7 September. Premiership debutants Leicester sign Notts County midfielder Mark Draper, the fee to go to tribunal.

25 Liverpool transfer-list midfielder Don Hutchison after his third disciplinary lapse in a year. Blackburn's David Batty will be out for about 3 months with a broken bone in his foot.

26 Spurs captain Gary Mabbutt, now fully recovered from the effects of John Fashanu's elbow, announces that he will not be taking legal action. Richard Thompson quits as chairman of QPR, retaining his controlling interest and his seat on the board, while director Peter Ellis takes his place. Peter Johnson is confirmed as Everton chairman. The proposed £3m transfer of Czech international Tomas Skuhravy from Genoa to Leeds has collapsed.

27 Ossie Ardiles finally gets to spend some of the £9m promised him by chairman Alan Sugar, as Spurs agree a fee with Steaua Bucharest of £2.6m for Romanian World Cup star Ilie Dumitrescu. Liverpool manager Roy Evans gets tough with his players after their 4-1 defeat by 1st Div Bolton in a friendly, pulling defenders Mark Wright and Julian Dicks out of the squad to tour Germany, the former for his 'attitude', the latter for his 'fitness'. Extrovert US World Cup defender Alexi Lalas punctures Coventry's hopes by signing for Padova, and will be the first American to play in the Italian League. A 10-day tournament is planned in England next summer called Euro 95, in which the 1996 European Championship hosts will compete with Brazil, Japan and 3 other countries.

28 Ardiles loses out in his quest for Brazilian World Cup defender Marcio Santos, who joins Fiorentina in Italy for about £2m. Former Chelsea manager Ian Porterfield leaves Zambia to take over as coach for Saudi Arabia.

29 Spurs' spending spree gathers momentum with the acquisition of German star World Cup striker Jurgen Klinsmann, 30, from Monaco for £2m.

August

West Ham discard Billy Bonds . . . Bruce Grobbelaar goes to Southampton . . . Spurs fraud inquiry dropped . . . Celtic fined for poaching manager . . . Rangers' early exit from Coca-Cola Cup

1 Wolves winger Tony Daley needs a cartilage op and will miss the start of the season. Scarborough sack manager Steve Wicks after 9 months. Liverpool defender Torben Piechnik returns to Denmark.

2 Everton sign unsettled Spurs midfielder Vinny Samways, 25, for £2.2m.

3 PSV Eindhoven sign teenage Brazilian international striker Ronaldo from Cruzeiro for £4m.

4 Wimbledon striker John Fashanu goes to Villa in a surprise £1.35m deal.

5 Man Utd tell Paul Ince to sign a new contract or leave the club. Arsenal announce record profits of £5.63m for a turnover of £21.5m, with commercial profits overtaking gate receipts for the first time. Bournemouth sack manager Tony Pulis. Former Newcastle midfielder Terry Hibbitt dies of cancer at 46.

6 Man United's Eric Cantona is sent off in the Ibrox pre-season tournament. Sampdoria beat Newcastle 3-1 in the final. Sheff Wed complete the signing of Romanian World Cup defender Dan Petrescu for £1.3m from Genoa.

7 Arsenal beat Napoli 1-0 to win the Makita tournament.

8 The dreadlocked Cobi Jones, US World Cup winger, joins Coventry for a fee to be agreed with the USSF, who hold his registration.

9 In the UEFA Cup Preliminary Round, Aberdeen draw away and Motherwell win 3-0 at home, but the Welsh and Irish clubs in action all lose.

10 After 27 years at Upton Park as player, coach and manager, Billy Bonds is asked to step down, with his place being taken by his assistant Harry Redknapp, who earlier in the week turned down the Bournemouth job. Newcastle complete the signing of Belgian World Cup defender Philippe Albert from Anderlecht for £2.6m. Rangers lose their preliminary round 1st leg European Cup tie 2-0 at AEK Athens, while Galatasaray's 5-1 victory over Avenir Beggen in Luxembourg virtually sets up another meeting with Man Utd. Hearts transfer-list captain Craig Levein and Graeme Hogg, who were sent off for fighting in a friendly against Raith, Hogg having to be stretchered off. Mario Zagalo takes over as Brazil coach for the third time.

11 Chelsea sign former England midfielder David Rocastle from Man City for £1.25m. Keeper Bruce Grobbelaar leaves Liverpool after 13 years to sign for Southampton. Newcastle fail to get a work permit for US keeper Brad Friedel.

12 The fraud inquiry into bribery allegations at Spurs involving England manager Terry Venables is finally dropped, removing also the clouds hanging over Brian Clough and Frank McLintock. Eric Cantona, who was fined 2 weeks' wages (£20,000) by Man Utd, is banned for 3 matches, while the Broadcast Advertising Clearance Centre ban, for being offensive, a Nike advert featuring Cantona making a 'four-letter boast' about his 'dirty tricks' on the field.

13 The English season starts with a full Endsleigh League programme but not the Premiership, and 10 players are dismissed, all in Divs 2 and 3. Hibs make the best start in the Scottish Premier with a 5-0 home win over Cup-winners Dundee Utd, whose manager Ivan Golac condemns referee Joe Timmins for sending off Alex Cleland - 9 players are booked, 6 of them from United. Motherwell's Rab Shannon is sent off at Ibrox and in the 5 Premier League matches 26 players are cautioned. The initial reaction to kick-ins in the Diadora League is unfavourable, and St Albans City general manager Allan Cockram threatens his players with substitution and fines if any opt for them.

14 Man Utd beat Blackburn 2-0 in the Charity Shield, Cantona scoring his 3rd penalty in consecutive games at Wembley. World Cup referee Philip Don flourishes 7 yellow cards.

15 Spurs will not start the season 6 points behind the rest of the Premiership, but will have the points deducted after the completion of the programme. Brechin City player-manager Ian Redford resigns as the result of their 5-1 home defeat by Meadowbank on Saturday.

16 Twelve players are sent off in 21 1st-round Coca-Cola Cup ties. Newcastle and Man Utd chairmen, Sir John Hall and Martin Edwards, launch scathing attacks on PFA chief Gordon Taylor for his claim that English clubs are bringing foreigners in to the detriment of national interests.

17 Apart from Aberdeen, who need a late goal to scrape through against Stranraer at Pittodrie, all the big guns in Scotland ease through the Coca-Cola Cup 2nd round, Rangers winning 6-1 at Arbroath, where Duncan Ferguson hits 3.

18 The Scottish League fine Celtic a record £100,000 for poaching Kilmarnock manager Tommy Burns. Sheff Wed sign full-back Ian Nolan from Tranmere for £1.5m.

19 Paul Ince finally re-signs for Man Utd, on a 3-year contract. A tribunal decides Leicester must pay Notts County £1.25m for midfielder Mark Draper.

20 The Premiership start is marked by a 6-1 Liverpool win at Palace. Champions Man Utd beat QPR 2-0, both sides finishing with 10 men. Jurgen Klinsmann scores in Spurs' 4-3 win at Hillsborough. Wendy Toms is the Football League's first female linesman, officiating at the Torquay-Carlisle match in Div 3. After only two games, Rangers are the only 100% side in the Scottish Premier.

21 Newcastle begin their Premiership programme with a 3-1 win at Leicester.

22 Man Utd draw 1-1 at Forest. Newcastle's Peter Beardsley and Palace's Ray Wilkins expect to be out for several weeks with cheekbone and foot fractures, respectively.

23 Aberdeen make a shock exit from the UEFA Cup in the Preliminary Round, losing on away goals to Skonto Riga (Latvia) after a 1-1 draw at Pittodrie, but Motherwell steam through 7-1 on aggregate over Havnar Boltfelag in the Faroes. Of the Irish and Welsh sides, only Linfield progress. Man Utd fine Paul Ince and he is warned about conduct in the Charity Shield match in which he 'overdid' celebrations after scoring. £5m Chris Sutton scores his first for Blackburn in their 3-0 Premiership defeat of Leicester.

24 FIFA slap their second 15-month ban on Diego Maradona since 1991, for testing positive for drugs during the World Cup in June. AEK Athens win 1-0 at Ibrox to put Rangers out of the European Cup in the Preliminary Round. Newcastle beat Coventry 4-0 to go top of the Premiership after two games, on goal difference above Spurs, for whom Klinsmann scores both goals in their 2-1 defeat of Everton. Other 100% teams, Liverpool and Chelsea do not have a game. Barcelona fine Brazilian star Romario £50,000 for returning 3 weeks late from the World Cup. Sheff Utd have 3 players sent off at Bramall Lane in an Anglo-Italian Cup match against Udinese.

25 Sligo Rovers reach the 1st round of the Cup-Winners' Cup with a 3-2 aggregate victory over Floriana of Malta, but Barry Town and Bangor City are hammered out.

26 Norwich sign Man City forward Mike Sheron for £1m.

27 Chairman Alan Sugar states that England coach Terry Venables is still persona non grata at Spurs, after manager Ossie Ardiles had yesterday said he was welcome. Newcastle go 2pts clear in the Premiership after beating Southampton 5-1, Spurs losing 1-0 at home to Man Utd. Chris Sutton scores a hat-trick in Blackburn's 4-0 defeat of Coventry. Leicester are still pointless. Everton complete the £3m signing of Nigeria's World Cup striker Daniel Amokachi, 21, from Bruges. Hibs go top of the Scottish Premier on goal difference over Celtic, whose 2-0 win at Ibrox ruins Rangers 100% record.

28 Liverpool retain their 100% Premiership record after 2 matches as Robbie Fowler hits all 3 in their 3-0 win over Arsenal.

29 West Ham sign Liverpool's troubled midfielder Don Hutchison for £1.5m. The Scottish FA fine Dundee £10,000 for their poor disciplinary record, doubling last year's similar punishment.

30 Terry Venables, who brings John Barnes back into the England reckoning and introduces Newcastle midfielder Robert Lee into the squad for the match with USA, dismisses as outrageous Alan Sugar's claims that he hired a PR company to stage a demonstration against the Spurs chairman. Forest go top of the Premiership with a 2-1 win at Everton, and Klinsmann scores another 2 for Spurs who move up to 3rd with a 3-1 win at Ipswich.

31 Newcastle go back to the Premiership summit with a 3-1 win at West Ham, while both Chelsea and Liverpool maintain their 100% records. There are shocks galore in the Scottish Coca-Cola Cup as Rangers go down 2-1 at home to Falkirk and Premier clubs Hearts, Motherwell and Kilmarnock all go out to Div 1 sides.

September
Littlewoods to sponsor FA Cup . . . Liverpool spend £7m on two defenders . . . Billy Wright of England and Wolves dies . . . Newcastle win first 6 in Premiership . . . Blackburn out of UEFA Cup

1 The FA Cup is to be sponsored in a 4-year deal with Pools giants Littlewoods out of which Wembley will take a considerable - though undisclosed - share. The competition will be called, officially, 'The FA Cup, sponsored by Littlewoods Pools'. Liverpool pay Coventry £3.75m for Irish World Cup central defender Phil Babb, who becomes the most expensive defender in British football. Mel Machin, 49, former Man City manager, takes over the job at Bournemouth, replacing Tony Pulis.

2 Liverpool take spending on their central defence to nearly £7m in 24 hours as John Scales joins them from Wimbledon for £3m. Two Div 3 managers are sacked, Kenny Hibbit of Walsall and Kenny Swain of Wigan. UEFA fine AEK Athens £25,000 for the violent behaviour of their fans at their European Cup match with Rangers in August.

3 Billy Wright, former England and Wolves captain, first man to win 100 caps, dies at 70. There are no Premier division matches because of England and Scotland's midweek matches. Preston, the last English team to play on 'plastic', beat Lincoln 4-0 in the first match on their new grass pitch.

6 Venables gives Newcastle's Barry Venison his first England cap, against the USA tomorrow. An exchange deal sees striker Tony Cottee back at West Ham together with an undisclosed sum, while David Burrows returns to Merseyside, to Everton.

7 Ireland and Scotland enjoy good away victories over Latvia and Finland respectively in European Championship qualifiers, while Wales beat Albania, but N.Ireland go down 2-1 at home to Portugal. Alan Shearer scores both goals in England's comfortable 2-0 defeat of the USA at Wembley. Vinny Jones takes over the Wimbledon captaincy from transfer-seeking Dean Holdsworth.

8 Stoke and manager Joe Jordan agree to part company. Spurs' profits last season slumped to less than £0.9m from £3.4m the previous year owing largely to the big FA fine and a deficit on transfer deals.

9 Spurs take their summer spending on foreign stars to £7.5m with the signing for £2.9m from Dutch side PSV of another Romanian World Cup star, central defender Gheorge Popescu, 26, while Sheff Wed complete the signing, from the same club, of Sweden's midfielder Klas Ingesson for £2m. Man Utd get £2m for striker Dion Dublin from Coventry, double what they paid Cambridge Utd in 1992 for a player who has started only 4 League games for them. Celtic break their club record by paying £1.75m for Motherwell midfielder Phil O'Donnell. Hartlepool manager of less than a year John MacPhail is sacked. Man City's new youth coach Neil McNab is banned for 5 weeks for abusing the referee after his first game in charge. National captain Eric Cantona is in trouble with the French Football Federation for his belligerent attitude to the French press in midweek.

10 Newcastle make it 5 wins out of 5 with a 4-2 victory at St James' Park to destroy Chelsea's 100% record, and Liverpool lose theirs when they are surprisingly held at Anfield 0-0 by West Ham, who have Tony Cottee sent off after 55min. This leaves Newcastle with the only 100% record in the League. Wimbledon's new captain Vinnie Jones is sent off, but they notch their first win as Leicester lose two players and the match 2-1 - all in the first half.

11 Pre-publication extracts from Terry Venables' autobiography reopen the dispute with Spurs chairman Alan Sugar. Leeds beat Man Utd 2-1 at Elland Road, their first victory over the champions for 13 matches that go back to the early 1980s.

13 Newcastle make a sensational return to Europe after 17 years with a brilliant 5-0 victory in the UEFA Cup over Royal Antwerp in Belgium, midfielder Robert Lee hitting a hat-trick, but Blackburn lose on their European debut 1-0 at home to Trelleborgs of Sweden.

14 Man Utd enjoy a convincing 4-2 win at Old Trafford over IFK Gothenburg in their first Champions League Group A match. Notts Co sack manager Mick Walker. Archie Gemmill and John McGovern are confirmed as the new managerial team at Rotherham in place of Phil Henson, who becomes chief executive.

15 Paul Merson scores 2 as Arsenal begin their defence of the Cup-Winners' Cup with a 3-1 victory over Omonia Nicosia in Cyprus, while Chelsea beat Czech side Viktoria Zizkov 4-2. Dundee Utd beat Tatran Presov of Slovakia 3-2 at Tannadice Park. In the UEFA Cup, Villa return from Milan 1-0 down to Inter. Everton's long-drawn-out efforts to sign Brazilian star Muller collapse at Goodison when they refuse to pay his annual tax bill. Assistant manager Russell Slade moves up to take the vacant manager's post at Notts Co. Hereford manager Greg Downs leaves by mutual agreement and assistant John Layton takes over.

17 With Newcastle engaged tomorrow, Forest miss their chance to sneak top spot in the Premiership when they only draw at The Dell, and Man Utd beat Liverpool 2-0 to go 3rd. The last two pointless teams in the League, Bournemouth and Chester of Div 2, draw 1-1. Celtic are still the only unbeaten side in the Scottish Premier League, but a home draw with bottom club Kilmarnock allows Rangers to go top.

18 Newcastle beat Arsenal 3-2 at Highbury to make it 6 out of 6 and take a 4-pt lead in the Premiership over Blackburn, who win 2-1 at Chelsea.

20 In Coca-Cola Cup 2nd round first-leg matches, three Div 3 sides enjoy home wins over Premiership clubs, Barnet 1-0 over Man City with a goal by Dougie Freedman in 27sec, Walsall 2-1 over West Ham, and Lincoln 1-0 over Palace. Premiership bottom club Everton lose 3-2 at home to Div 1 Portsmouth. Dane Whitehouse scores 3 for Sheff Utd in their 5-1 victory at Stockport. Raith reach the semi-finals of the Scottish Coca-Cola Cup.

21 Wednesday night thrills in the Coca-Cola Cup include Jurgen Klinsmann's hat-trick in Spurs' 6-3 win at Watford, the 1-0 home defeat of Leeds by Mansfield, 4th from bottom of the League, and Div 1 Bolton's 3-0 win at Ipswich. Arsenal away to Hartlepool and Villa at home to Wigan make their 2nd legs redundant with 5-0 victories. Leicester go down 1-0 at Brighton of Div 2. Man Utd manager Alec Ferguson, controversially fielding a largely inexperienced young side at Port Vale, justifies his

selection with a 2-1 victory despite going behind in the first minute. In the Scottish Coca-Cola Cup, Div 1 Airdrie, who win 2-1 at Hibs, reach the semi-finals along with Celtic and Aberdeen. Injury-plagued Gary Lineker will retire from Japanese football in November and join the BBC.

22 As Terry Venables launches his autobiography, Alan Sugar says he will not be allowed into the Spurs ground until he apologises for 'slagging' Sugar off and stops suing for wrongful dismissal.

23 Liverpool spoil Newcastle's 100% record in the Premiership with a 1-1 draw at St James' Park. The other two unbeaten sides win to move within 2pts of the leaders, Blackburn beating Villa 3-1 and Forest winning 4-1 at Spurs. Man Utd go down to a shock 3-2 defeat at Ipswich. Newcastle finally sign striker Paul Kitson from Derby for £2.25 after prolonged negotiations. Celtic go back to the top of the Scottish Premier.

27 Blackburn, costing some £27m, go out of the UEFA Cup to a team of Swedish part-timers as Trelleborgs, playing most of the second half with 10 men, score 5min from time to earn a draw and win 3-2 on aggregate. It's a different story at St James' Park, where Andy Cole is the hat-trick man this time as the Magpies slam Antwerp 5-2 for a 10-2 aggregate. But the European hero of the night is Fabrizi Ravanelli, who scores all 5 as Juventus thrash CSKA Sofia 5-1 (7-4 on agg). In the Coca-Cola Cup, Swindon stage a splendid recovery with a 4-1 win at Charlton after extra time and a 5-4 aggregate victory, Norwegian striker Jan-Aage Fjortoft scoring 3. Belgium and Holland will co-host the European Championship in 2000.

28 Man Utd come through their intimidating Euro tie in Turkey unscathed with a 0-0 draw against Galatasaray and lead Group A as Gothenburg beat Barcelona 2-1. After two matches, the only 100% sides are Paris St Germain and Ajax Amsterdam. Holders AC Milan beat Salzburg 3-0 but face an inquiry after the Austrian keeper is hit by a bottle from the crowd. In the UEFA Cup, Motherwell lose 2-0 at home to Borussia Dortmund and go out 3-0 on aggregate. Transfer-listed Hearts players Craig Levein and Graeme Hogg are now banned for 10 matches by the SFA for their violent brawl in a friendly last month.

29 Villa beat Inter Milan on penalties after a nail-biting 1-0 victory and go through to the 2nd Round of the UEFA Cup. Chelsea earn a safe passage in the Cup-Winners' Cup with a goalless away draw, while Arsenal ease through 6-1 on aggregate. Lou Macari is appointed manager of Stoke for the second time. Portsmouth defender Andy Awford is out for the season with a multiple fracture of his leg sustained last night in a Div 1 match at West Brom.

30 Man Utd announce pre-tax profits of £10.7m to the year ending 31 July.

October

Tony Adams captains England . . . Raich Carter dies . . . John Aldridge scores goal No.400 . . . English fair play earns extra UEFA Cup place . . . Terry Venables again attacked in *Panorama*

1 Thursday's European victors Arsenal and Villa lose at home in the Premiership, the latter 2-0 to Newcastle, who extend their lead to 5pts as Blackburn lose their unbeaten record at Norwich. In Palace's first win of the season and first League victory at Highbury, Ian Wright scores his 100th goal for Arsenal against his old club. Steve McManaman hits a second-half hat-trick as Liverpool beat Sheff Wed 4-1. In the Scottish Premier, Rangers regain the lead from Celtic.

2 Forest go 2nd in the Premiership, 2pts behind Newcastle, with a 3-2 win over QPR.

3 Terry Venables makes Arsenal's Tony Adams captain of England for the first time, in the absence of injured David Platt, and includes Newcastle's in-form midfielder Robert Lee in his squad for the game against Romania, but there is controversy about the omission of Andy Cole, who feels his manager Kevin Keegan has exaggerated his shin-splints injury to the England coach. Leicester PRO Alan Birchenall strongly criticises the referee over the PA system at Filbert Street at half-time after the dismissal of a player from each side in the 2-2 draw with Coventry. Bottom Premiership club Everton sign two Glasgow Rangers players on loan - Ian Durrant for 1 month, after his transfer collapsed when he failed a medical, and £4m striker Duncan Ferguson for 3 months.

4 Lowly Div 3 club Mansfield knock Leeds out of the Coca-Cola Cup, holding them 0-0 at Field Mill to retain their 1-0 advantage from the 1st leg. Watford embarrass Spurs with a 3-2 win at White Hart Lane but lose 8-6 on aggregate.

5 Three Premiership teams go out of the Coca-Cola Cup to Div 1 sides - Everton to Portsmouth, Leicester to Brighton and Ipswich to Bolton - while Man City and West Ham reverse their 1st-leg deficits against Barnet and Walsall respectively. Matt Le Tissier scores all 4 for Southampton as they beat Huddersfield 5-0 on aggregate.

6 The FA have sent videos of matches to referees asking for comments on certain incidents they are unhappy with.

8 Forest draw 3-3 at Man City to climb to within a point of Newcastle, who play tomorrow.

9 Newcastle retain their unbeaten record in the Premiership with a late goal from Steve Howey to draw 1-1 with Blackburn at St James' Park, but Peter Beardsley has to withdraw from the England squad with a thigh strain. Liverpool's Steve McManaman replaces the injured Darren Anderton in the squad.

10 Raich Carter, legendary England, Sunderland and Derby inside-forward, dies at 80.

11 Liverpool's Jamie Redknapp scores a hat-trick for England Under-21s as they beat Austria 3-1 in Kapfenberg in Group 6 of the European U-21 Championship, but club-mate Robbie Fowler is sent off for dissent. Wales U-21s lose 1-0 in Moldova. Northampton play their last match at the County Ground. Wimbledon sign Nigerian striker Efan Ekoku from Norwich for £1m.

12 Robert Lee keeps Venables' unbeaten record intact with the equaliser in England's 1-1 draw with Romania at Wembley, in which Matt Le Tissier also makes his debut. In European Championship qualifiers, Scotland and Ireland enjoy easy wins against Faroe Is and Liechtenstein respectively and N.Ireland a splendid 2-1 victory in Austria, but a depleted Wales are beaten 3-2 in Moldova.

14 UEFA dock AC Milan 2pts from their Champions League total for the bottle-throwing incident but allow the result, a 3-0 win over Casino Salzburg, to stand. They must also play their next two home matches in the tournament at least 185 miles from Milan.

15 A Peter Beardsley goal in the 89th minute gives Newcastle a 1-0 win at Palace, their 5th away victory out of 5, and stretches their Premiership lead to 5pts. Blackburn beat Liverpool 3-2 to go 2nd, above Forest who play on Monday. Man City hold out for a 2-1 win at QPR despite playing the last 14min with 9 men and a replacement keeper. Everton, still winless, lose 2-0 at home to Coventry and are 4pts adrift at the bottom. John Aldridge scores the 400th goal of his career in a hat-trick for Tranmere. Celtic, beaten at Hearts, lose the last unbeaten record in the Scottish Premier.

17 Forest beat Wimbledon 3-1 and close the gap at the top to 3pts. West Brom sack manager Keith Burkinshaw after exactly a year of his 4-year contract.

18 In the UEFA Cup 2nd round, Newcastle are pegged back from 3-0 at St James' Park by 2 late goals from Athletic Bilbao, while Villa incur a 1-0 deficit to Trabzonspor in Turkey. Everton reveal they are paying Rangers £35,000 a week for the loan of Duncan Ferguson in addition to his wages (probably £5,000 a week).

19 Lee Sharpe earns Man Utd a 2-2 draw with Barcelona in a classic at Old Trafford and they retain their lead in Group A on goal difference over IFK, who beat Galatasaray 1-0. Paris retain their 100% record in Group B. The FA reduce to a caution the sending-off of Spurs defender Kevin Scott against QPR 11 days ago after seeing a video of the incident and asking the referee to reconsider.

20 Holders Arsenal come away from Copenhagen with a 2-1 edge over Brondby in the 2nd round of the Cup-Winners' Cup, but Chelsea are held 0-0 at home by Austria Vienna. Alan Buckley leaves Grimsby to become the new West Brom manager, their 11th in 13 years. After 13 mostly unhappy months at Anfield, full-back Julian Dicks moves back to West Ham.

21 The first UEFA Fair Play Ranking List, produced from club and national fixtures, recognizes England, Norway and Luxembourg for their sportsmanlike conduct, and the three associations are awarded an extra place in next season's UEFA Cup, upping England's contingent to 4. But the winner of the Coca-Cola Cup will cease to qualify in 3 years' time - unless the domestic championship has been limited to 34 matches (18-team league). Rangers striker Duncan Ferguson's court hearing on an assault charge is postponed till 9 Jan, so he will be able to complete his loan period with Everton.

22 Newcastle and Forest both win, so the gap at the top of the Premiership is still 2pts. Spurs suffer another heavy defeat, 5-2 at Man City, and Everton are still stranded at the bottom after their 4th straight defeat, 1-0 at Palace, puts more pressure on manager Mike Walker.

23 Referee Gerald Ashby has Kenny Dalglish fuming when he awards Man Utd a penalty and sends off Henning Berg just before half time, enabling Cantona to equalise from the spot and United eventually to win 4-2, ruining Blackburn's 100% home record and jumping above them into 3rd place. Ian Wright hits both of Arsenal's goals in their 2-1 defeat of Coventry, making it his 10th consecutive game on Arsenal's scoresheet to beat their record set in 1931 by David Jack, but his 7th booking of the season earns him a 3-match ban and a groin injury puts him out at half-time.

24 The Football League decide not to fine Man Utd for fielding weakened teams in their 2nd round Coca-Cola ties, and are to recommend that clubs involved in European competition should be exempt in future until the 3rd round.

25 In the Coca-Cola Cup 3rd round, Kevin Gallen scores for QPR after 13sec, but in-form Man City come away from Loftus Road with a 4-3 win. In the semi-final of the Scottish equivalent at Perth, Raith beat Airdrie 5-4 on penalties to reach their first final since 1948-49.

26 Notts Co humiliate Spurs 3-0 in the Coca-Cola Cup, any chance Spurs had of clawing back an early 2-0 deficit disappearing when Dumitrescu is sent off after 36min - the knives are out for manager Ossie Ardiles. In the big tie of the round, at St James' Park, Newcastle beat an again under-strength Man Utd 2-0 with goals in the last 10min. Celtic central defender Brian O'Neil scores in extra time against Aberdeen at Ibrox to take them into the Scottish Coca-Cola Cup final.

27 FIFA decree that from next season all member countries' domestic leagues must employ the 3pts for a win system. In FIFA's distribution of the 8 extra places for the 1998 World Cup finals in France, the zones Europe, Africa and Asia/Oceania have been allotted two places each, and South America and Concacaf one each.

28 Newcastle's Andy Cole is sidelined for a month to rest his troublesome shin splints.

29 Saturday sees the clash of the top 4 in the Premiership and something has to give - it turns out to be the last two unbeaten records in the League, as Newcastle go down 2-0 at Old Trafford and Forest 2-0 at home to Blackburn. The positions stay the same, but now there are only 6pts between 1st and 5th, as Liverpool win 3-1 at Ipswich to come into contention with still a game in hand. Spurs beat West Ham 3-1, but there seems little hope for manager Ossie Ardiles, who has to face a board meeting on Thursday. Beleaguered Mike Walker at Everton is in a similar position, as they grab a rare point at Goodison from Arsenal, but Albion Rovers' victory in the Scots Div 3 leaves the Toffeemen as the only team in Britain without a win. In Div 2, Linton Brown hits a 7min 2nd-half hat-trick as Hull blast Crewe 7-1. With Rangers playing tomorrow, Hibs and Motherwell overtake them at the top of the Scottish Premier.

30 Rangers beat Celtic 3-1 at Parkhead to go back on top in Scotland.

31 New allegations of financial chicanery are levelled at England coach Terry Venables in a second BBC *Panorama* investigation, which accuses him of unlawfully obtaining over £430,000 which he used in connection with purchasing Tottenham shares. QPR's Les Ferdinand, back after a 3-match suspension, punctures Liverpool's revival with a late winner at Loftus Road.

November

Ossie Ardiles and Mike Walker out, Gerry Francis and Joe Royle in . . . Bruce Grobbelaar in bribe allegations . . . Ron Atkinson out, Brian Little in . . . Paul Merson confesses to drug, drink and gambling problems . . . Raith Rovers win Coca-Cola Cup

1 Inevitably, Ossie Ardiles is sacked from the Spurs job, learning the news last night at chairman Alan Sugar's home, and assistant manager Steve Perryman becomes caretaker manager. Ardiles had 3 years of his contract to run, and should get over £500,000 in compensation. The FA stand by Terry Venables despite allegations on *Panorama*. Villa and Newcastle both go out of the UEFA Cup on away goals. Everton chalk up their first Premiership win, 1-0 over West Ham at Goodison, but is it too late for Mike Walker?

2 Man Utd are humbled and outclassed 4-0 by Barcelona at the Nou Camp as World Cup stars Stoichkov and Romario run riot, and with Gothenburg winning in Turkey, United are now 3rd in their group of the Champions League with an awful lot to do. Paris qualify for the last 8. In the Premiership, Blackburn win 1-0 at Sheff Wed to go 2nd. On the managerial front, QPR's Gerry Francis was expected to resign because the offer of the post of chief executive (with full control over transfers) to former star Rodney Marsh would compromise the manager's job - but he doesn't. Villa chairman Doug Ellis goes on air to give his manager a vote of confidence - which must have Ron Atkinson worried. And Derby fans turn on manager Roy McFarland after the Rams lose 2-1 at home to improving Reading.

3 Both London clubs get through to the 3rd round of the Cup-Winners' Cup, Arsenal getting a fright at Highbury as Brondby draw 2-2 but winning 4-3 on aggregate, and Chelsea winning on away goals. QPR back down over Marsh and won't accept Francis's resignation. Former Spurs manager David Pleat, now with Luton, has talks at White Hart Lane.

5 At the top of the Premiership, Newcastle and Blackburn both win.

6 Man Utd put their Barcelona defeat behind them and win 2-1 at Villa to go 3rd in the Premiership.

7 Forest and Newcastle play out an entertaining goalless draw at the City Ground, so the Magpies extend their lead over Blackburn in the Premiership to 3pts. The Premier League launch a code to prevent the practice of managers moving to another club without the consent of their employers. Paul Gascoigne has some pins removed and sets a spring comeback target.

8 The sensational claim published in the *Sun* that Southampton keeper Bruce Grobbelaar has taken bribes to fix matches almost obscures the news of Mike Walker's sacking as Everton manager. Ironically, the two clubs, Everton and Spurs, who have been fined in the last year for seducing managers from other clubs, have now given those managers the chop within a week of each other. Southend chairman Vic Jobson warns that 16 clubs are about to serve notice on the Football League to form an elite First Division attached to the FA Premiership.

9 The Grobbelaar bribe allegations, which go back to 1992 and refer to specific matches involving former club Liverpool as well as Southampton and involve Malaysian betting syndicates, have caused a furore, and the FA promise a swift investigation. Meanwhile Liverpool take advantage of their game in hand, beating Chelsea 3-1 to move up to 3rd in the Premiership, 4pts behind Newcastle. In Coca-Cola Cup replays, all three home teams reach the 4th round, Arsenal, Swindon and Norwich, who come back from 2-0 down to beat Tranmere 4-2. Rangers draw at Hearts to take a 3pt lead in the Scottish Premier. Dutch star Ruud Gullit leaves AC Milan after 2 months and returns to Sampdoria.

10 While hysteria mounts over the Grobbelaar 'scandal', with the police to open an inquiry and the accused denying any wrongdoing as he flies out to play for Zimbabwe, Aston Villa sack manager Ron Atkinson and Everton appoint their former star striker Joe Royle. Meanwhile, a most significant move is made at the top end of the Premiership, Man Utd using their game in hand to thrash neighbours City 5-0 at Old Trafford (Kanchelskis 3) - their biggest ever derby win - to go 2nd, just 2pts behind Newcastle. FA chairman Sir Bert Millichip is appointed to FIFA's World Cup Organising Committee. Newcastle's uncapped defender Steve Howey is drafted into the England squad in place of the injured Tony Adams.

11 David Pleat decides not to join Spurs as general manager and Gerry Francis, now granted his release from QPR, is the new favourite for the job. Villa are fined £9,000 for the pitch invasion after their UEFA Cup defeat by Trabzonspor, who are fined £6,000. The FA inform FIFA that Bruce Grobbelaar will not be suspended pending a hearing, and FIFA clear him to play for Zimbabwe.

12 With no Premier games, the 1st Round of the FA Cup takes centre stage, and Enfield and Kingstonian are non-League conquerors of League sides Cardiff and Brighton respectively. Paul Miller scores 4 in Bristol Rovers' 5-0 win at Bath, Ashley Ward 3 in Crewe's 7-1 thrashing of Gresley, and Martin Foyle 3 in Div 1 Port Vale's 6-0 beating of Hartlepool. Barnet come back from a 3-0 half-time deficit at Underhill to draw 4-4 with Woking. Sheff Utd chairman Reg Brealey announces at half-time in their 2-1 victory over Derby that the club is up for sale.

13 More giant-killing in the FA Cup as Marlow - 3rd from bottom of the Diadora League - knock out neighbours Oxford United with 2 goals from John Caesar.

14 After studying documents and videos provided by the *Sun* and coming to the conclusion that there is a case to answer, the FA charge Bruce Grobbelaar with offences relating to match-fixing, but do not suspend him and stress that he is innocent until proved guilty. Bristol City sack manager Russell Osman.

15 Gerry Francis signs a one-year rolling contract as manager of Spurs, making his first act to dispense with the services of caretaker-manager Steve Perryman, while Ray Wilkins takes over at former club QPR as player-manager. Joe Jordan also returns to manage a former club, Bristol City. Newcastle suffer another injury blow, midfielder Scott Sellars out for 6-8 weeks after a knee op. Sheff Wed

captain Des Walker is banned for 3 matches and fined £1,200, having been found guilty of misconduct regarding his dismissal at Ipswich.

16 Terry Venables' gamble on Dennis Wise pays off as the Chelsea forward is instrumental in England's 1-0 victory over African champions Nigeria at Wembley in a friendly in which Newcastle's Steve Howey and Liverpool's Neil Ruddock win their first caps and Steve McManaman wins his as a 25min sub. In European Championship qualifiers, Wales are humiliated 5-0 in Georgia, but no less so than Italy, who go down 2-1 at home to Croatia, or Belgium, held at home by Macedonia. The Republic beat N.Ireland 4-0 in Belfast, but Scotland can only draw 1-1 with Russia at Hampden Park. Oldham striker Graeme Sharp is appointed player-manager of the club.

17 Leicester chairman Martin George demands £1.5m compensation from Villa if they want his manager Brian Little and two assistants. Quashing rumours, Football League president Gordon McKeag states that neither the FA nor the Premier League would sanction the formation of a 2nd Division. As a result of the 3rd meeting with referees, players and managers, the Premier League announce a plan designed to cut out the two-footed tackle and provide more consistency in the application of the laws, especially the punishments for tackles from behind and player dissent.

19 With most of Saturday's interest elsewhere, Man Utd beat Palace 3-0 at Old Trafford to go top of the Premiership, a point in front of Blackburn, who win 3-1 at Ipswich, and Newcastle, who go down 3-2 at Wimbledon and lose 1st place for the first time since the start of the season. Wimbledon captain Vinnie Jones is sent off again, 15min from time. The media crowd into The Dell, where Bruce Grobbelaar puts on an immaculate performance, watches Paul Dickov put a penalty over his bar and sees Southampton beat Arsenal 1-0. Elsewhere, the new managers have a mixed day, Gerry Francis watching Spurs stage a magnificent recovery from 3-0 down to managerless Villa at White Hart Lane only for Dean Saunders to spoil it with a last-minute winner, while his old side QPR, now under Ray Wilkins, beat Leeds 3-2. In Scotland, Falkirk draw with Rangers at Ibrox fielding a debut-making goalkeeper - for his 21st club in England and Scotland - 42-year-old John Burridge.

20 Leicester, under reluctant manager Brian Little, lose 1-0 at home to Man City and stay 2nd from bottom of the Premiership. In the crucial Div 1 clash at Ayresome Park, Middlesbrough beat Wolves 1-0 to take their place at the top.

21 Joe Royle could not have wished for a better start at Goodison as Everton - with keeper Neville Southall making a record 35th Merseyside derby appearance and on-loan striker Duncan Ferguson scoring his first goal for the club - beat Liverpool 2-0 and climb off the bottom of the Premiership. John Lyall, manager of 2nd-bottom club Ipswich, is ominously given a vote of confidence by chairman John Kerr. Div 1 Swindon sack manager John Gorman.

22 Leicester manager Brian Little resigns for 'personal' reasons. In FA Cup 1st round replays, non-League Hitchin and Woking beat League opposition, Hereford (4-2) and Barnet (1-0) respectively, but Yeading come a 7-1 cropper at Colchester. Bury need penalties to beat Bishop Auckland, and Fulham extra time to account for Ashford 5-3. Bobby Davison scores a 10sec goal in Rotherham's 3-0 win over York.

23 Man Utd, with Paul Ince sent off late on, go down 3-1 in Gothenburg and only Barcelona's shock 2-1 defeat by Galatasaray leaves the Reds with just a chance of reaching the knock-out stage of the European Cup. Ajax clinch their place in the last 8, beating AC Milan - whose home tie is played in Trieste - 2-0, and the Italian club must win their remaining game to go through. Managerless Leicester lift themselves off the bottom of the Premiership by beating Arsenal 2-1.

25 Arsenal's England international Paul Merson, 26, confesses in the *Daily Mirror* that he has been taking cocaine for about a year, has been on 8-hour drinking binges and has amassed huge gambling debts: the FA's first reaction is to provide help rather than take immediate disciplinary action, while his club also promise total support. Spurs may be allowed to play in the Cup after all, as the independent arbiters studying their punishment for irregular payments rule that an FA commission must reassess the penalties imposed. Brian Little is named as Villa's new manager. Meanwhile, the FA, in the shape of chief executive Graham Kelly and England coach Terry Venables, unveil a far-reaching plan for raising the standards of English football, including the creation of a post for a technical director in charge of long-term strategy. Man Utd announce an £11.45m trading profit. In Scotland, Rangers beat Aberdeen to boost their lead over Motherwell to 4pts, at least until tomorrow.

26 Blackburn go top of the Premiership after beating QPR 4-0 helped by an Alan Shearer hat-trick, while Man Utd draw 0-0 at Highbury and to compound a week's misery have Mark Hughes sent off near the end.

27 Raith Rovers of Scottish Div 1 win their first major trophy, beating Celtic 6-5 on penalties after a 2-2 draw at Ibrox to take the Coca-Cola Cup and leave the Glasgow giants 5 years without one.

28 More grief for Arsenal as the Premier League look into allegations in a book published in Denmark that a top official received payment as part of the John Jensen transfer deal in 1992; other Scandinavian transfers are also being looked into. Man City's midfielder Steve McMahon is appointed Swindon player-manager. Cardiff sack manager Eddie May, and Rochdale Dave Sutton.

29 Brian Laws is the new manager of Grimsby.

30 Ian Rush celebrates his 600th appearance for Liverpool by scoring a hat-trick as they win 3-1 at Blackburn in the 4th round of the Coca-Cola Cup. Forest and West Ham both suffer two-goal home defeats to Div 1 sides, Millwall and, inevitably, Bolton, respectively. A goal down at half-time, Palace come back to smash Villa 4-1, while Steve Morrow scores in Arsenal's 2-0 win over Sheff Wed at Highbury - his only other goal for Arsenal having been the winner against the same side in the 1993 final. The Scottish FA and League agree a £10.5m deal with Sky TV for the screening of 17 League and Cup matches a season.

December

Paul Merson escapes punishment . . . John Lyall forced out at Ipswich . . . Man Utd out of European Cup . . . Spurs reinstated . . . George Graham 'bung' allegations . . . Everton sign Duncan Ferguson for £4m . . . John Jensen scores for Arsenal!

1 After a meeting with Paul Merson and club and PFA representatives, the FA decide to take no action against the errant Arsenal forward, although he must undergo a 4-6 week rehabilitation programme away from home. On the basis of a long-dead Welsh grandfather, Watford-born Vinnie Jones of Wimbledon is drafted into the Welsh international squad. Martin O'Neill turns down the Leicester job to stay with Wycombe.

2 Preston manager John Beck resigns rather than change his notorious long-ball game, and his assistant Gary Peters is appointed in his place. Arsenal captain Tony Adams has an Achilles op and will be out for 2 months, while striker Ian Wright's goal against Newcastle in September is validated by the Premier League giving him a club record of scoring in 12 consecutive League and Cup matches.

3 Blackburn's splendid 3-0 win at Wimbledon keeps them a point ahead of Man Utd in the Premiership, but Newcastle slip back again, 4pts adrift, after losing 4-2 at Spurs, where Teddy Sheringham hits 3. Brian Little's immediate return to Leicester with his new club Aston Villa brings a 1-1 draw - and a constant stream of abuse from the fans directed at the former manager. Chris Waddle comes on as a 75th-min sub for Sheff Wed, his first League appearance of the year after a long-term injury. In Div 1, new Swindon player-manager Steve McMahon is sent off in his first match as his side lose 2-0 at Southend. In Scotland, Div 1 bottom club Stranraer are hammered 8-1 at leaders Airdrie after scoring in the 1st minute, but create a Scottish League record - 4 players in one team sent off, the maximum before a referee must abandon the match.

4 Rangers go 4pts clear in Scotland, beating Dundee Utd 3-0 at Tannadice.

5 Under increasing pressure from the fans, manager of bottom club Ipswich, John Lyall, resigns after 4 years and coach Paul Goddard becomes caretaker manager. The PFA, having spent a year and £100,000 compiling a report on coaching, condemn FA director of coaching Charles Hughes and his 'formula football'. Altrincham, of the Vauxhall Conference, who were drawn against 'Tottenham or bye' in the 3rd round of the Cup, will be compensated if Spurs are not reinstated and the tie at White Hart Lane does not take place.

7 Despite a stirring 4-0 victory over Galatasaray with a scratch side containing several fledglings, Man Utd are out of the European Cup. Barcelona only draw at home to Gothenburg but it is enough to see them through. Milan get their win, 1-0, at Salzburg to scrape through despite their 2pt penalty.

8 'Green Flag' will be plastered all over England's training kit in the next 4 years after a sponsorship deal is agreed with the parent company of National Breakdown.

9 It's Spurs 2 the FA 0 and they're still playing - Spurs have been reinstated in the Cup and their 6pt Premiership penalty annulled by the investigating tribunal, who feel that it was unreasonable to impose any penalty other than a fine, and this might still be reduced. UEFA want to stage experimental matches with two referees.

10 The Premiership's major contenders Blackburn and Man Utd both win 3-2. Rangers begin to draw clear in Scotland, their 2-1 win at Kilmarnock extending their lead to 7pts over Motherwell, beaten at home by Aberdeen.

11 Reports that Arsenal manager George Graham has been under investigation by the IR have again brought to the surface accusations regarding Scandinavian players signing for English clubs - specifically that Graham is alleged to have received a secret payment of £285,000 via a Norwegian agent from the £1.57m transfer of John Jensen in 1992 - although Graham denies he has profited from any transfers. Former Scotland striker Frank McAvennie, now with St Mirren, admits he took cocaine when with West Ham. Scottish football enters its first official winter shut-down, with clubs not due to play again till Boxing Day.

12 FIFA president Joao Havelange, not for the first time, comes under attack for his dictatorial ways, with UEFA chief Lennart Johansson threatening UEFA's secession, now backed by Peter Velappan of the Asian Football Confederation, who resents the autocratic manner in which at FIFA's October meeting all the general secretaries of the continental confederations except the S.American one were excluded from the executive committee - Havelange having resorted to photocopying lists of the new members personally, distributing them, and then immediately declaring the meeting closed.

13 Everton sign their on-loan striker Duncan Ferguson from Rangers for £4m despite the fact that the controversial Scottish international has a 12-match suspension hanging over his head, pending the resolution of an alleged criminal assault. Plymouth manager Peter Shilton is given 4 matches to improve the team's performances and 7 days to answer the club solicitor's letter regarding an unpaid tax bill Plymouth are being pressed for by the IR. Newcastle's Andy Cole and Liverpool's Rob Fowler, as substitute, make their goalscoring marks at B-international level as England beat Ireland 2-0 at Anfield. Non-League Enfield win their FA Cup replay at Torquay 1-0.

14 Wales suffer their 3rd successive defeat in the Euro Championship qualifiers, going down 3-0 at Cardiff to Bulgaria despite the debut of adopted Vinnie Jones. Mark McGhee decides to wrench himself away from promotion-chasing Reading and take his chance as manager of relegation-haunted Leicester. Billy Ayre resigns after just 4 months with the League's bottom club Scarborough. Portsmouth are refused planning permission for the projected new stadium.

15 The Premier League's 3-man commission begins its inquiry into the Scandinavian 'bung' allegations, examining evidence and documents from Arsenal. Hampshire County Council refuse Southampton permission to buy land at Stoneham to build a new stadium.

17 Premiership leaders Blackburn, after 7 straight League wins, are held 0-0 at Leicester but go 2pts clear of Man Utd, who not only lose their 100% home record but suffer their first defeat at Old

Trafford, 2-1 to Forest, conceding their first League goals at home since 4 April. With their goalless draw at Goodison with Spurs, Everton set a club record 7th game without conceding a goal. The Plymouth board warn manager Peter Shilton before their Div 2 game at Brentford that he faces the sack unless they collect 8pts from the next 4 matches - they lose 7-0.

18 As the FA commission inquiry widens to cover 23 transfers, further revelations appear to stick the knife deeper into Arsenal manager George Graham's back, in that he is said to have admitted during Thursday's meeting with the commission handing over more than £400,000 to Arsenal, not just the £285,000 allegedly received from Norwegian agent Rune Hauge for the Jensen deal. Other allegations are published implying that Graeme Souness received similar 'bungs' while with both Rangers and Liverpool. On the football pitch, Scotland suffer a crucial defeat in Athens, going down to an 18th-min penalty by group leaders Greece. Ray McHale, sacked last year, is back as Scarborough manager.

19 Beleaguered manager George Graham receives unanimous backing from the Arsenal board. Steve Coppell, a member of the FA's 3-man investigating commission, is to remain despite calls from Graham for his withdrawal in the light of comments published that appeared to prejudge the issue. Merthyr chairman John Reddy claims to have encountered 'foul and abusive language' from chief executive Alun Evans when presenting a petition on behalf of 25 clubs calling for a vote of no confidence in the FA of Wales Council. Another 10 footballers are arrested in Malaysia. bringing the total to nearly 40 detained as the police wrap up their two-year probe into match-fixing - a 'cottage industry' said by Mr Peter Velappan, Asian Football Confederation chief, to be worth more than £300m a year in South-East Asia.

20 PFA's Gordon Taylor says that Forest captain Stuart Pearce is going to apologise for allegedly racist remarks made to Man Utd's Paul Ince. League Managers' Association chairman Howard Wilkinson defends Steve Coppell against calls for him to resign from the FA commission, suggesting his comments 'reflected a hypothetical outcome to a hypothetical question'. Liverpool's Stig Bjornebye, who was signed from Norwegian club Rosenborg for £600,000 in 1992, says he will be paying a reported £33,000 tax bill, 40% of the sum allegedly received from agent Rune Hauge's company.

21 Man City reach the Coca-Cola Cup quarter-finals with a shock 2-0 replay win at Newcastle. FIFA admit that transfer irregularities have become a world problem, but new regulations concerning the registration of agents that come into force on Jan 1 will bring some order. Orient chairman Tony Wood says he will listen to any reasonable offer for the club.

22 Spurs manager Gerry Francis transfer-lists Romanian star Ilie Dumitrescu. Villa and Sheff Wed complete an exchange deal that takes midfielder Ian Taylor to Villa Park for £700,000 rated striker Guy Whittingham and £300,000.

24 George Burley resigns as manager of Colchester.

26 Boxing Day away wins for Blackburn, 3-1 at Man City, and Man Utd, 3-2 at Chelsea, maintain the status quo at the top of the Premiership. Joe Royle suffers his first serious setback as Everton go down 4-1 at home to Sheff Wed, for whom new boy Whittingham scores 2. High scoring in Div 3 includes Mansfield's 7-1 thrashing of Hereford and Carlisle's 5-1 victory at Hartlepool which takes them 8pts clear of 2nd club Bury. Rangers retain their 7pt lead over Motherwell in Scotland, with the rest dropping further behind. Celtic set an unwanted club record with their 11th League game without a win when they chalk up their 7th successive draw.

27 Only 4 Premiership clubs are asked to play two days running, and only Forest produce a goal as they beat Norwich. The Endsleigh League offers almost a full programme again, and in Div 3 Mansfield make it 12 goals in 2 days with a 5-2 win at Scarborough.

28 With Blackburn's home match against Leeds postponed because of a mini-monsoon, Man Utd miss their chance to go top as they are held 1-1 at home by lowly Leicester. Villa provide new manager Brian Little with his first win in 7 games, beating Chelsea 3-0. George Burley, who made exactly 500 appearances for Ipswich, is appointed manager and watches the team chosen by caretaker-manager Paul Goddard go down 2-0 to Arsenal at Portman Road.

29 Northampton sack manager John Barnwell.

30 Spurs loan Ilie Dumitrescu to Spanish club Sevilla for the rest of the season.

31 John Jensen scores for Arsenal! The Danish midfielder who has become a cult figure at Highbury for his inability to score in 97 games, and whose transfer in 1992 is currently giving his manager much grief, finally puts the ball in the net with a spectacular effort, but QPR spoil the show and run out 3-1 winners. Blackburn win 1-0 at Palace to take a 3pt lead in the Premiership as Man Utd draw 2-2 at Southampton. Birmingham go top of Div 2, thrashing Blackpool 7-1 after being a goal down. Rangers win 3-1 at their nearest challengers Motherwell to open up a 10pt lead in Scotland. Bristol Rovers mourn the death of their only England international, Geoff Bradford, 67.

January

Wrexham knock Ipswich out of Cup . . . £7 million Cole for Man Utd . . . Cantona goes berserk - suspended for season . . . Death in Genoa . . . Romario World Player of the Year

1 UEFA offer places in the UEFA Cup for semi-finalists in the long-established (1953) but peripheral Inter Toto Cup, a summer competition geared to accommodate 64 clubs, and the FA apply for 4 places, while most western European countries continue to abstain.

2 An Alan Shearer hat-trick (including 2 pens) gives Blackburn a 4-2 win over West Ham and a 6pt lead in the Premiership over Man Utd, who play tomorrow.

3 Man Utd beat Coventry 2-0, the second a penalty for the incident that sees central defender Steve Pressley dismissed. FIFA announce that official bids for the 2002 World Cup have been lodged by Japan, Mexico and S.Korea.

4 Plymouth suspend manager Peter Shilton for up to 2 weeks for his failure to meet the deadline set for repayment of a tax debt esimated at about £50,000. Celtic hold Rangers 1-1 at Ibrox.

5 In a letter to all members of the FA Council, FA chairman Sir Bert Millichip stresses that the FA remain the power in English football whatever some Premiership moguls might be hinting at.
6 Villa sign Tommy Johnson and Gary Charles from Derby for £2.9m. Southampton pay a club record £1.2m for Chelsea's Neil Shipperley. On the eve of Arsenal's Cup tie at the New Den, Ian Wright accuses the Millwall fans of racism.
7 Ipswich, who lose 2-1 at 2nd Div Wrexham, are the only Premiership side to go down to lower-division opposition in today's 3rd round FA Cup ties, although Leeds' equaliser comes in the last 5 minutes of their 1-1 draw at Walsall. All four non-League sides go out without scoring a goal. In Scotland, Rangers increase their lead to 12pts in the Premier despite only drawing at Partick. Celtic pay Dutch club NAC Breda £1.2m for striker Pierre van Hooijdonk.
8 In the big Cup match, Blackburn hold Newcastle 1-1 at St James'.
9 FA Cup holders Man Utd win 2-0 at Sheff Utd after the home side have midfielder Charlie Hartfield dismissed in the 13th minute. Leeds pay a club record £3.4m for Frankfurt's Ghanaian striker Anthony Yeboah, top Bundesliga scorer for the last two seasons. Malaysian officials identify a 50-year-old blind man with no knowledge of football as the mastermind behind their match-fixing scandal.
10 Man Utd manager Alex Ferguson brings off a sensational coup, signing striker Andy Cole from rivals Newcastle for a British record fee of £7m - £6m plus N.Ireland winger Keith Gillespie. Mike Pejic, manager for only 7 months, leaves struggling Div 2 side Chester. Ian Atkins takes over at Northampton.
11 In the Coca-Cola Cup quarter-finals, Liverpool beat Arsenal 1-0, Bolton claim another Premiership scalp with a 1-0 victory over Norwich, and Palace slam 4 goals past Man City without reply, including 3 in the last 10min. Swindon beat Millwall 3-1 in the other tie, and respective managers Steve McMahon and Mick McCarthy have to be separated by the police and admonished by the referee in the 2nd half. Peter Shilton and Plymouth part in confusion, the club chairman Don McCauley insisting he resigned, Shilton's solicitors claiming he did not.
12 Howard Kendall takes charge at struggling Notts Co, replacing Russell Slade, who stays as assistant manager. Plymouth appoint caretaker manager Steve McCall in Peter Shilton's place, while Colchester appoint former player Steve Wignall as manager and Mick Docherty takes over at Rochdale.
13 In an emotional press conference, a tearful Paul Merson, discharged today from an addiction clinic, admits to being an alcoholic, apart from being addicted to gambling, although the FA confirm that cocaine abuse was a 'minimal problem'. Meanwhile his club Arsenal pay Luton £2m (rising to £2.5m) for 19-year-old Welsh striker John Hartson and also sign Ipswich striker Chris Kiwomya, offering half the £2m asking fee, and a Premier League inquiry team investigating the George Graham 'kickback' allegations spend three hours interviewing Norwegian agent Rune Hauge.
14 Blackburn extend their Premiership lead to 6pts over Man Utd with equal games played, beating Forest 3-0, while Ipswich's first ever win at Anfield dents Liverpool's title aspirations. A last-minute goal from Stuart McCall gives Rangers a 3-2 win at Falkirk and a 14pt lead in the Scottish Premier.
15 Man Utd, by agreement without newly signed Andy Cole, are held 1-1 by Newcastle at St James' and have Mark Hughes stretchered off with damaged knee ligaments, dashing Everton's immediate expectations of securing his services. The Football Writers' Association celebrate the birthday of Sir Stanley Matthews (80 on 1 Feb).
16 Leeds veteran Gordon Strachan, 37, retires from first-team football to concentrate on coaching. Leicester complete the £1m signing of Norwich striker Mark Robins.
17 In 3rd-round FA Cup replays, Leeds beat Walsall 5-2 thanks to a hat-trick by South African striker Phil Masinga who comes on as a sub in extra-time, and 2nd Div Swansea win 2-1 at 1st Div leaders Middlesbrough.
18 An eventful evening of Cup replays sees Newcastle win 2-1 at Blackburn, Millwall shock Arsenal 2-0 at gloom-laden Highbury, Liverpool scrape through 2-0 on penalties over Birmingham at Anfield and Man City welcomed former manager Howard Kendall back to Maine Road by thrashing his new side Notts Cty 5-2, German striker Uwe Rosler snaffling 4.
20 Steve Nicol leaves Liverpool after 13 years to join Notts Co as player-coach on a free transfer.
21 Torrential rain washes out all but 16 English League fixtures. In Scotland, where only 3 matches, all in the lower divisions, are lost, Rangers beat Hearts 1-0 to stay 14pts ahead, while Motherwell drop back to 3rd after a 6-1 thrashing at Dundee Utd.
22 Man Utd beat Blackburn 1-0 at Old Trafford to move within 2pts of them at the top of the Premiership, but have played one more game. More embarrassment for Arsenal as *The Mail on Sunday* alleges a 'secret kickback' of £145,000 paid to a 'mysterious Swiss company' out of the transfer of Pal Lyderson from Norwegian club IK Start in September 1991.
23 West Ham's relegation worries are not helped by the dismissals of Alvin Martin and Tim Breacker in their 2-0 defeat by Sheff Wed at Upton Park. New Zealander Linda Black, 36, is the first woman to referee a men's international, officiating in New Zealand's 2-1 defeat of Denmark's Olympic side.
24 Everton earn a goalless draw at Anfield and Liverpool manager Roy Evans criticises their 'tough tactics'. Celtic's £8.9m share issue is oversubscribed, making it £21m raised in 10 months.
25 Eric Cantona really goes over the top this time - sent off at Selhurst Park for kicking Richard Shaw, he leaps the barrier with a two-footed attack on a spectator and then wades in with fists before he can be dragged away. Palace earn a 1-1 draw which leaves Man Utd still 1pt behind Blackburn, having played 2 more games, both home fixtures. Wimbledon manager Joe Kinnear calls the ref a cheat after their 2-1 defeat at Newcastle. Jurgen Klinsmann is carried off after a rash aerial challenge from Mark Bosnich outside the area, but the Villa keeper goes unpunished and Spurs lose 1-0. A

transfer tribunal sets Chris Kiwomya's fee at £1.25m (rising to a maximum £1.55m after 60 first-team appearances), Arsenal having offered £0.5m, while Ipswich asked for £2.5m. Paul Merson makes his comeback in Arsenal's reserves.

26 The 'Cantona affair' takes up an extraordinary amount of media space and time, as the errant Man Utd star is given 14 days by the FA to answer their charges, but his club have not yet spoken. The police receive a complaint from the Palace fan involved in the incident, and will also interview United captain Paul Ince, who was allegedly involved in a separate scuffle. Five players in France, 4 from Bordeaux, are suspended for up to 2 months for fighting in a Div 1 match last week at St Etienne. Former Spurs and West Brom player Vic Buckingham dies at 79.

27 Man Utd suspend Cantona from the rest of the season's first-team games and fine him the maximum 2 weeks' wages (about £20,000), while in France Cantona is stripped of the national team captaincy and dropped for the season. The Palace fan involved, season-ticket holder 20-year-old Matthew Simmons (who, it is revealed, has a conviction for assault with intent to rob), is banned from the club for the rest of the season.

28 In the FA Cup 4th round, Man Utd recover their composure to beat 2nd Div Wrexham 5-2 at Old Trafford despite going a goal down, while they go 4pts behind in the Premiership as Blackburn, still with a game in hand, beat Ipswich 4-1, Alan Shearer scoring a hat-trick. Other Cup results include Newcastle's 3-0 defeat of Swansea, Paul Kitson scoring all 3, and Palace's 2-1 win at Forest. Burnley hold Liverpool 0-0 at Turf Moor, and Leicester win 1-0 at Portsmouth, who have two men sent off including keeper Alan Knight. At the New Den, 3 policemen are taken to hospital and 5 arrests are made as trouble flares up between respective fans during Millwall's 0-0 draw with Chelsea. With the leaders Birmingham's game postponed, Brentford go top of Div 2, beating Cambridge 6-0, all the goals coming in the last 25min, 4 in the last 10. In the 3rd round of Scottish Cup, holders Dundee Utd are held 0-0 at home by 2nd Div Clyde, Kilmarnock likewise by Morton, while Huntly win the non-League clash 7-0 against Burntisland Shipyard, 7 ties being snowed off.

29 All 3 FA Cup ties go to Premiership sides playing away to Div 1 clubs, Spurs leading the way with a 4-1 win at Sunderland, who lose defender Gary Bennett after 49min for handling on the line. The Genoa v AC Milan fixture in Italy is abandoned at half-time because of crowd trouble caused by the death of a Genoa fan in a stabbing incident before the start.

30 The FA appoint Don Howe full-time Technical Co-ordinator on a 2-year contract, and he will be responsible for overseeing England's progress at all levels and co-ordinating the development of techniques and tactics. Everton complete the signing of defender Earl Barrett from Villa for £1.7m. Arsenal striker Ian Wright is banned for 4 matches and fined a record £1,000 for accumulating 41 penalty points, and Fulham midfielder Terry Hurlock, on 51pts, has a 4-match ban extended to 6. Italian sports authorities cancel events scheduled for next Sunday in deference to the death of the fan killed yesterday.

31 Vauxhall Labour MP Kate Hoey's call for an independent inquiry into the 'backhanders, bungs and fixes' of football is rejected by Sports Minister Iain Sproat, who feels confident that the FA can deal with the problem. West Ham's Alvin Martin has his sending-off against Sheff Wed on Saturday cancelled, as referee Paul Danson, after studying the video, allows the FA to rescind his decision. Cambridge terminate the contract of Billy Manuel, sent off on Saturday for the 3rd time in 6 games. FIFA name Brazil's Romario Player of the Year after a poll of national team coaches.

February

Sir Stanley Matthews 80 . . . Aberdeen sack manager Willie Miller . . . Rioting as Millwall knock Chelsea out of Cup . . . Cantona attacks ITN reporter in Guadeloupe . . . Dublin international abandoned after England fans riot . . . Arsenal sack George Graham

1 Paul Merson makes his return for Arsenal after his enforced rehabilitation, coming on at Highbury for the last 15min of the 0-0 draw with AC Milan in the 1st leg of the European Super Cup. In the two Premiership games to survive the weather, 14 players are booked, and Blackburn's keeper Tim Flowers is dismissed after 2min of their 1-1 draw with Leeds at Ewood Park, both goals coming from disputed penalties, and referee Rodger Gifford is attacked by a fan at the end of the game. Blackburn go 5pts ahead of Man Utd in the Premiership. In the other match, Everton have two players sent off, their new signing Earl Barrett and Barry Horne, before going down 2-0 to Newcastle at St James' Park in a match that sees David Elleray brandish his yellow card 12 times to 10 different players. Sir Stanley Matthews, never booked in his long career, celebrates his 80th birthday. Former Liverpool chairman Sir John Smith dies at 74. Portsmouth sack manager Jim Smith and replace him with Terry Fenwick.

4 Andy Cole's first goal for Man Utd is enough to give his new club victory over Villa and take them to within 2pts of Blackburn, who play tomorrow. Is there no end to Arsenal's woes? Tony Adams and John Hartson are sent off at Hillsborough as they lose 3-1 to Sheff Wed. Bolton slam rivals Wolves 5-1 to go top of Div 1 as leaders Middlesbrough are beaten 1-0 at home by Reading, another promotion challenger. Despite being held at home by lowly Dundee Utd, Rangers increase their lead of the Scottish Premier League to 15pts as Hibs go down at home to bottom club Partick.

5 A comprehensive 3-1 defeat by Spurs at White Hart Lane leaves Blackburn only 2pts ahead of Man Utd, who are now favourites to retain the Premiership title.

6 Terry Venables looks to his old club Spurs for new talent, promoting Nick Barmby and Sol Campbell to the senior squad for next week's international in Dublin. Aberdeen sack manager Willie Miller, with them since he joined the club as a player in 1971. Jimmy Allen, former Portsmouth, Villa and England defender, dies at 85.

7 Chelsea captain Dennis Wise is found guilty of assaulting a taxi driver and faces possible prison; the FA drop him from the England squad, but Chelsea will keep him in tomorrow's Cup side. Liverpool beat Burnley 1-0 at Anfield in their 4th round FA Cup replay.

8 AC Milan beat Arsenal 2-0 in the return tie to win the European Super Cup. Millwall beat Chelsea on penalties in their 4th round FA Cup replay at Stamford Bridge, where some of the worst scenes witnessed in recent years take place, with fans fighting on the pitch and in the stands at the finish, and two dozen police horses needed to keep rival fans apart - 11 policemen are injured and 38 arrests made. In other replays, Wolves beat Sheff Wed on penalties - with Chris Waddle missing a vital sudden-death spot-kick to bring back unwanted World Cup '90 memories, and Southampton enjoy an easy passage, beating Luton 6-0. Man United's suspended French striker Eric Cantona is involved in further controversy, allegedly completing a Caribbean family holiday instead of turning up for a police interview. English clubs earn an extra place in next season's UEFA Cup because of their prominence in the fair-play ranking list. Sacked Portsmouth manager Jim Smith will take over from Steve Coppell as chief executive of the League Managers' Association on 1 April.

9 The police attach no blame to Chelsea for yesterday's Cup tie riots, stating that their security arrangements could not be faulted.

10 Peter Shilton signs for Wimbledon as keeper cover.

11 Eric Cantona hits the front pages again, as well as, allegedly, an ITN reporter trying to film him on the holiday island of Guadeloupe, with a repeat of the 'kung-fu kick' that felled a Crystal Palace fan two weeks ago. With Blackburn playing tomorrow, Man Utd go top with a flourish, winning the Maine Road local derby 3-0. Villa slam 7 past Wimbledon after going a goal down, Tommy Johnson hitting 3. The pressure builds on manager George Graham, who has to deny reports that he is going to quit, as Arsenal are held at home by bottom club Leicester and Ian Selley breaks a leg. Bad weather and waterlogged pitches see 12 English games called off and another 8 in Scotland.

12 Blackburn restore their 2pt Premiership lead with a 3-1 win over Sheff Wed, who have keeper Kevin Pressman sent off after 44min. Swindon beat Bolton 2-1 in the 1st leg of their Coca-Cola Cup semi-final. Rangers suffer a rare defeat in the Scottish Premier, 2-0 by lowly Aberdeen under new manager Roy Aitken. Keeper Ian Walker is the fifth Spurs player in Terry Venables' England squad, drafted in to replace injured Tim Flowers.

13 As Eric Cantona's lawyer announces that he is to sue ITN over the Guadeloupe incident for 'invasion of privacy', Man Utd manager Alex Ferguson comes out strongly in support of his player.

14 Coventry manager Phil Neal loses his job after just 15 months. Arsenal sign Dutch winger Glenn Helder from Vitesse Arnhem for £2m.

15 Rioting England soccer followers, in what is thought to have been an orchestrated incident, bring shame on their country and force the Dublin friendly to be abandoned after 27min, with Ireland leading 1-0; there are 43 arrests and 20 people are taken to hospital. A last-minute goal gives Liverpool a 1-0 lead from their Coca-Cola Cup semi-final 1st leg against Palace at Anfield. Ron Atkinson takes over as manager at Coventry.

16 Reactions to last night's Dublin riot: the FA launch an inquiry and call on true fans to identify the troublemakers; FIFA president Joao Havelange supports England's right to retain Euro '96; Ireland manager Jack Charlton pleads for the game to be put back on; and the National Football Intelligence Unit blame the Irish authorities for not heeding the warnings and detailed briefings sent to them more than a week ago.

18 In the FA Cup 5th round, Everton slam Norwich 5-0, and the visitors' captain Jon Newsome becomes the 289th player sent off this season, an English record. Millwall go out at last to their third London Premiership opponents when QPR's Clive Wilson converts a disputed last-minute penalty. Hibs beat Motherwell 2-0 in the big clash of the Scottish Cup 4th round, while Aberdeen lose 2-0 to Div 2 leaders Stenhousemuir.

19 Holders Man Utd score twice in the first 4min and a 2nd half goal from the fit-again Mark Hughes eases them to a 3-1 win over Leeds in the Cup.

20 Behind-the-scenes reports emerge that the Premier League Commission have found Arsenal manager George Graham guilty of taking a 'bung' - a cut of some £285,000 from the John Jensen transfer - and have made their finding known to the club directors. Thanks to the FA's 'hooligan hotline', at least 40 Dublin riot suspects are claimed to have been identified. Another shock in the Scottish Cup - Hearts knock Rangers out by 4-2.

21 Arsenal sack manager George Graham as a result of the Premier League Commission findings for failing to 'act in the best interests of the club', and Graham promises to 'vigorously contest' his dismissal; 7 hours later, under assistant manager Stewart Houston who has been offered the job as caretaker, Arsenal beat Forest 1-0, their first League win at Highbury for 4 months. After being questioned at South Norwood police station, Man United's Eric Cantona is charged with common assault over the infamous incident at Crystal Palace. Peterborough keeper John Keeley, 33, has quit the game because of verbal abuse from supporters..

22 Man Utd enjoy a comprehensive 2-0 victory at Carrow Road, while leaders Blackburn struggle to beat Wimbledon 2-1 at Ewood Park. At the other end of the Premiership table, Leicester scrape themselves off the bottom with 3 goals in the last 13 minutes for a 4-4 draw at Villa Park, enough to take them above Ipswich, 2-0 losers at Maine Road. Several matches are off because of rain and snow, including both Coca-Cola Cup semi-final 2nd legs. Southend manager Peter Taylor has been told to take a month's holiday, and it is thought he will return in a coaching capacity.

23 Premier League chief executive Rick Parry confirms the leaked reports concerning the George Graham inquiry, namely that the Arsenal manager received a total of £425,500 from agent Rune Hauge, and had returned this plus £40,000 interest to the club; Parry warns that Graham is not the only culprit. Ex-Lincoln manager Steve Thompson takes over at Southend.

24 An FA disciplinary ruling on the Cantona incident at Selhurst Park extends his ban until 30 Sep (worldwide) and fines him £10,000; Man Utd confirm the player intends to remain with them.

25 Blackburn stretch their Premiership lead to 3pts but fail to take full advantage of Man United's defeat at Everton, being held at home by Norwich.

28 Chelsea lose their Cup-Winners' Cup quarter-final 1st leg 1-0 at Bruges. Liverpool win their 5th round Cup replay 2-0 at Wimbledon.

March

Chris Armstrong fails drugs test . . . Man Utd beat Ipswich 9-0 . . . Three outfield subs . . . Paul Ince charged with common assault . . . Grobbelaar, Fashanu and Segers arrested . . . Cantona jail sentence reduced to community service . . .

1 In a thrill-packed Cup replay at the Dell, 2nd-half sub Ronnie Rosenthal pulls Spurs back from a 2-0 deficit, completes his hat-trick to put them ahead in extra time and the final result is Southampton 2 Spurs 6.. Mike Walker wins his case against Everton for breach of contract, having been sacked with 32 months still to run, damages to be assessed later. With Mexico withdrawing, only Japan and S.Korea are left as applicants to host the 2002 World Cup finals.

2 A 1-1 draw against Auxerre at Highbury in the Cup-Winners' Cup leaves Arsenal with a stiff task in the 2nd leg. David Burrows joins Coventry for £1.1m after only 6 months at Everton. Darlington sack manager Alan Murray.

3 Palace striker Chris Armstrong, it is revealed, failed a random drugs test on 23 Jan in which traces of cannabis were found, and will have to undergo counselling. Boxing and snooker promoter Barry Hearn agrees to buy a controlling interest in ailing Orient. The FA warn players not to take their shirts off when celebrating a goal.

4 Man Utd run riot against Ipswich to the tune of 9-0, a Premiership record, with 5 from Andy Cole, and although Blackburn squeeze a 1-0 win at Villa Park to maintain their 3pts Premiership lead, the overall result switches goal advantage to the champions. In a relegation battle at Filbert Street, Leicester claw back a 2-goal deficit after Everton are reduced to 9 men, having had Vinny Samways and Duncan Ferguson sent off. Ex-ref Ken Aston claims he was offered £25,000 by a Far Eastern syndicate for addresses and telephone numbers of Premiership referees and players. New Laws passed by the International Board at Turnberry, Scotland, include provision for 3 subs (including keeper or not) and rewording of the offside law to prevent penalising a player not interfering with play; there will also be an experiment with time-outs in a FIFA tournament in the next 12 months.

6 Graeme Souness has started libel proceedings against the *Today* newspaper for allegations concerning Torben Piechnik's transfer to Liverpool in 1992. MP David Mellor makes a scathing TV attack on the Belgian police for their indiscriminate use of water cannon and riot squads to control fans at the Bruges-Chelsea European tie last week and is bluntly dismissive not only of Bruges' ground but of the Belgian nation.

7 A late Steve Bruce goal at Wimbledon gives Man Utd a 1-0 win and the Premiership lead on goal difference over Blackburn, who now have a game in hand, and leaves Wimbledon manager Joe Kinnear, ordered off the bench, fuming at the referee for the dismissal of Alan Kimble shortly before the goal. The FA finally charge sacked Arsenal manager with misconduct over the Scandinavian transfers and the police charge Man United's Paul Ince with common assault over an incident alleged to have occurred at Selhurst Park after the infamous Cantona foray into the front stalls.

8 Blackburn beat Arsenal 3-1 to go back on top of the Premiership. Bolton win a stirring Coca-Cola Cup semi-final against Swindon after going 2-0 down on aggregate, with 3 goals in the last half hour, and in the final they will meet Liverpool, 1-0 victors at Palace (2-0 agg).

9 Wimbledon manager Joe Kinnear bans himself from the touchline.

10 Aston Villa pay Blackburn £1m for Under-21 defender Alan Wright. Bolton take on Peter Shilton as their third keeper till the end of the season.

11 Spurs march into the FA Cup semi-finals with a 2-1 victory at Anfield, Jurgen Klinsmann scoring a late winner after Liverpool had initially gone ahead. In the other tie Palace are held 1-1 at home by 1st Div Wolves. A late Alan Shearer equaliser gives Blackburn a point at Coventry and takes them 4 clear of Man Utd, who now have a game in hand. Rangers are held at home by Falkirk but still lead the Scottish Premier by 16pts.

12 Both home sides go through to the FA Cup semi-finals, Everton beating Newcastle 1-0, Man Utd beating QPR 2-0. Hearts reach the Scottish Cup semis, beating holders Dundee Utd 2-1.

13 The FA clear Palace striker Chris Armstrong to resume playing. Wimbledon manager Joe Kinnear is charged with bringing the game into disrepute.

14 In melodramatic raids, three footballers are arrested on claims of match-fixing by a Far-Eastern syndicate - Bruce Grobbelaar (Southampton), John Fashanu (Villa) and Hans Segers (Wimbledon) - and, together with Fashanu's wife Melissa Kassa-Mapsi and London-based Malaysian businessman Heng Suan Lim, are held overnight at separate police stations in Hampshire. Chelsea beat Bruges 2-0 (agg 2-1) to reach the Cup-Winners' Cup semis. In the Premiership, Palace climb out of the bottom 4 with a 2-1 win over Sheff Wed, Chris Armstrong scoring on his return, and a Peter Ndlovu hat-trick gives Coventry a 3-2 victory at Anfield. Dundee Utd part company with manager Ivan Golac.

15 All five arrested yesterday by police investigating match-fixing allegations are released after questioning. Man United's title hopes take a knock as Spurs hold them to a 0-0 draw at Old Trafford. Blackburn sign Southampton's Irish international defender Jeff Kenna for £1.5m.

16 A spectacular Ian Wright goal at Auxerre is enough to put Arsenal into the Cup-Winners' Cup semis. Sampdoria beat Porto on penalties, but David Platt, sent off 4 minutes from the end of extra time, will miss both semi-final legs. FIFA cancel the World Youth Championships to be held in Nigeria owing to concern over security, and will probably transfer the competition to Qatar.

18 Blackburn, with Alan Shearer scoring his 100th League goal, beat Chelsea 2-1 after going behind early on and go 6pts ahead of Man Utd, who play tomorrow. Rangers lose 2-1 at Hearts and their Scottish Premier lead is cut to 12pts by Motherwell, who have a game in hand.

19 Man Utd go down 2-0 to Liverpool, a severe blow to their Premiership ambitions. Relegation-threatened Swindon gain an invaluable win at West Brom by 5-2, twice coming from

behind, with all the goals scored in the 2nd half. Notts Co beat Ascoli 2-1 in the Anglo-Italian Cup final at Wembley.

20 Terry Venables leaves Paul Ince, facing a court appearance this week, out of his England squad for the Uruguay game, as well as the 'out of form' Matt Le Tissier, while both Ian Walker and Nick Barmby of Spurs and Jamie Redknapp of Liverpool are in. Another Spurs man, central defender Colin Calderwood, is a surprise inclusion in the Scottish squad for the Euro qualifier in Moscow.

21 Liverpool sign Millwall's Dublin-born winger Mark Kennedy, 18, for £1.5m, with another £0.5m linked to appearances. Middlesbrough win 1-0 at Sunderland to go top of Div 1.

22 Crystal Palace outclass Wolves 4-1 in their FA Cup 6th round replay at Molineux, with 2 goals from a rampant Chris Armstrong. Man Utd beat Arsenal 3-0 to cut Blackburn's Premiership lead to 3pts, but have now played one game more. Southampton, with 3 goals in the last 5min, beat Newcastle 3-1, but remain in the bottom 4. Gordon Strachan rejoins his old Man Utd boss Ron Atkinson to become assistant at Coventry, with a clause in his contract that he will be offered the manager's job in 1997.

23 Eric Cantona is bailed pending appeal after being sentenced by Croydon magistrates to 2 weeks' jail for his assault on a spectator at Selhurst Park on 25 Jan. Man Utd team-mate Paul Ince, who pleaded 'not guilty' to an assault charge at the same game, is bailed to his trial on 25 May. Clydebank and former Scotland and Rangers winger Davie Cooper, 39, dies in hospital after collapsing yesterday with a brain haemorrhage while making a coaching video. Man United striker Andy Cole is called up to replace the injured Alan Shearer in the England squad. Blackburn sign £1.5m-rated Dutch midfielder Richard Witschge on loan. Middlesbrough sign Swindon's Norwegian striker Jan Aage Fjortoft for £1.3m.

24 The Palace fan, Matthew Simmons, attacked by Eric Cantona pleads not guilty to charges of using threatening behaviour and is remanded on bail by Croydon magistrates until 23 May.

25 With no Premiership soccer, the spotlight is on Div 1, where gameless Middlesbrough stay top as Tranmere lose and Bolton draw away from home. Only 5pts now cover the top 6 teams. In 30 Endsleigh League matches only Div 3 Gillingham, who have been in receivership for 2 months, score more than 2 goals, beating fellow-strugglers Exeter 3-0.

26 Middlesbrough, with player-manager Bryan Robson scoring his first goal for the club, beat Port Vale 3-0 to extend their Div 1 lead to 4pts.

27 In a European U-21 group match, England beat Ireland 2-0 in Dublin in front of 6,000 spectators, marshalled by some 700 stewards and police, none of whom are troubled. Charlton suspend two teenagers who failed random drug tests, both Dean Chandler and Lee Bowyer admitting taking cannabis.

28 Man United's half-yearly accounts show a pre-tax profit of £7.3m but throw up a mystery in that winger Keith Gillespie, a supposed £1m makeweight in the Andy Cole deal with Newcastle, is valued at only £0.25m. Former Dundee Utd player and coach Billy Kirkwood takes over as manager.

29 As England and Uruguay play out a disappointing 0-0 draw at Wembley, Nick Barmby and Andy Cole win their first caps as 2nd-half subs. In Euro Championship matches, Ireland miss their chance to go top of Gp 6, held frustratingly to a 1-1 draw in Dublin by N.Ireland, Wales's 3-1 defeat in Bulgaria leaves them bottom of Gp 7, and Scotland manage a 0-0 draw away to Russia. Peter Reid replaces Mick Buxton in charge of struggling Sunderland, their fifth managerial change in little over 3 years, his position to be reviewed in the summer. Plymouth manager Steve McCall, in charge less than 3 months, resigns.

30 Man Utd captain Steve Bruce will miss the FA Cup semi against Palace because of a 41-pt suspension. Cardiff team manager and director Terry Yorath, a member of a consortium trying to buy the club, resigns. Sporting impresario Barry Hearn takes over officially as Orient chairman. Gillingham chairman Bernard Baker quits. Millwall chairman Reg Burr, the recipient of death threats against his family, will step down at the end of the season.

31 Eric Cantona wins his appeal against his jail sentence, receiving 120 hours' community service instead, and a subsequent press conference is reduced to farce by his pseudo-philosophic utterances. Stockport's Uruguayan manager Danny Bergara is sacked after 6 years in the job, reportedly after an altercation with chairman Brendan Elwood. Eddie May returns to take charge of Cardiff 4 months after being sacked.

April

Owls' record 7-1 home defeat . . . Liverpool win Coca-Cola Cup . . . Palace fan killed in brawl . . . Alan Shearer PFA Player of Year . . . Paul Gascoigne makes his comeback . . . Roy Keane in stamping incident . . . Leicester and Ipswich relegated . . . 7th Championship running for Rangers . . . Seaman saves 3 penalties to put Arsenal in Euro final . . . Graham Taylor spat at . . . Klinsmann Footballer of the Year . . . Carlisle win Div 3 title

1 Blackburn go 6pts clear again in the Premiership with an important 2-1 victory at Everton. Forest shatter Sheff Wed 7-1 at Hillsborough, the Owls' heaviest ever home defeat. Notts Co, beaten at home 3-1 by Barnsley and now 4pts adrift at the bottom of Div 1, sack manager Howard Kendall after only 10 weeks - not because of the results but for the way the club was being run. In the Scottish Premier, a 1-0 defeat at home to Kilmarnock leaves Aberdeen in deep relegation trouble.

2 Bolton put up a brave fight at Wembley but lose 2-1 to Liverpool in a Coca-Cola Cup final graced by two outstanding goals from Steve McManaman. Man Utd stutter again in the Championship race, held 0-0 at home by Leeds, and are 5pts behind Blackburn who have a game in hand.

3 The FA complete another sponsorship package, this time with brewers Carlsberg for £5m, which includes what will now be called the FA Carlsberg Vase. Cambridge Utd sack manager Gary Johnson, putting former West Ham defender Tommy Taylor in temporary charge.

4 A 1-0 victory at QPR gives Blackburn an 8pt lead over Man Utd at the top of the Premiership and, with only 6 games to go, the title is theirs for the taking. Partick's 3-1 defeat of Hearts pushes Aberdeen to bottom spot in the Scottish Premier.

5 Liverpool spoil Bruce Grobbelaar's emotional return to Anfield and to football, beating Southampton 3-1. Leeds' Ghanaian striker Anthony Yeboah scores a hat-trick as they crush hapless Ipswich 4-0 and send the East Anglians to the bottom. Middlesbrough lose 1-0 at Oldham, but remain 4pts clear in Div 1. But Bolton win 1-0 at Swindon, whose player-manager Steve McMahon is sent off for the second time, to go 3rd, 4pts behind with 2 games in hand, despite having Mixu Paatelainen sent off in the last minute. But the most sensational dismissal is that of the club's PA announcer Pete Lewis, whose half-time criticism of the referee earns him a warning from a senior police officer followed by the sack from the club.

6 In the Cup-Winners' Cup semis, Chelsea crash 3-0 to Real Zaragoza in Spain, where some of their fans rip up and throw seats at police during the match, while Arsenal will take a slender 3-2 lead to Italy as Sampdoria rally after central defender Steve Bould gives the Gunners a 2-0 half-time lead.

7 Hibs' veteran keeper Jim Leighton saves an Andy Walker penalty to earn them a 0-0 draw with Celtic and a replay in their Scottish Cup semi at Ibrox. Disgraced 1993 European Cup winners Marseille hit a new low - no longer able to pay their debts, they are placed into receivership.

8 Div 1 Airdrie reach the Scottish Cup final, beating Hearts with a goal from Englishman Steve Cooper on his first visit to Hampden. Rangers' 3-2 victory over a desperate Aberdeen takes them out of reach of all challengers except 4th-placed Celtic. In England, Leicester lose 1-0 at Sheff Wed, which means, barring miracles, they are relegated to Div 1. Chester, bottom of Div 2, are the first club to be relegated.

9 In the first FA Cup semi at Leeds, Everton surprise Spurs to the tune of 4-1, Nigerian striker Daniel Amokachi coming on by mistake for Paul Rideout and scoring 2 late goals to make sure Spurs get no further in the competition they were originally banned from. Later in the day Man Utd have to come back twice, once in extra time, at Villa Park to force a 2-2 draw and a replay against Palace. It later emerges that a Palace fan, Paul Nixon, was killed by a coach while trying to escape from a brawl between rival fans at a pub 8 miles from Villa Park before the match. Alan Shearer (Blackburn) is voted PFA Player of the Year, Robbie Fowler (Liverpool), Young Player of the Year. In Italy, Paul Gascoigne lasts the full 90min in his comeback after a year out through injury, helping Lazio to a 2-0 win over Reggiana.

10 The 6 South Yorkshire police officers who claimed their career was ruined by the trauma suffered in witnessing the 1989 Hillsborough disaster fail to win damages against their own chief constable at Sheffield High Court.

11 Celtic beat Hibs 3-1 in their replayed Scottish Cup semi.

12 Man Utd beat Palace 2-0 in the Cup semi replay, but Roy Keane, who has 7 stitches in an ankle gash at half-time, may miss the final after being red-carded for stamping on Gareth Southgate; Palace's Darren Patterson is also sent off for getting into the argument. Newport AFC, Caernarfon and Colwyn Bay win their restraint of trade action as the High Court reject FA of Wales claims that banning them from playing from Welsh bases was necessary to protect the Konica League representation in Europe.

13 The FA charge yesterday's culprits Keane and Patterson with bringing the game into disrepute. West Ham climb out of the relegation frame with a 3-0 win over Wimbledon, and send Leicester back to Div 1 in the process.

14 In Friday night matches, a late Klinsmann equaliser for Spurs at Selhurst Park robs Palace of vital points they need in their fight against relegation, while fellow strugglers Everton and Man City both notch valuable wins, condemning Ipswich to relegation.

15 Man Utd show they still have title - and double - aspirations with a 4-0 victory at Leicester to go within 6pts of Blackburn, who are stunned by a last-minute Brian Deane goal at Elland Road that gives Leeds a draw; only 5 matches remain. In Div 1 Steve Bull scores his 200th League goal in Wolves' 3-2 defeat at Charlton. In Div 2, Orient lose 2-0 at Swansea and are relegated. In Scotland, Aberdeen gain on the clubs directly above them with a 2-0 win over Celtic - handing the title to Rangers, their 7th in succession. Forfar clinch promotion from Div 3.

17 The Easter Monday fixtures expose jangling nerves in the Premiership race as Man Utd apparently blow their outside chance when held 0-0 at Old Trafford by Chelsea, but then in the evening Blackburn lose 3-2 at home to Man City - so the gap is reduced to 5pts. Newcastle lose 2-1 at home to Leeds, their first Premiership defeat at St James' since Jan '94. Arsenal win 4-0 at Villa, who are now in serious trouble, only 1pt above Palace in the relegation zone but having played 2 games more. Norwich lose at Spurs and look doomed, 3rd from bottom with only 3 games left, while Palace's 1-0 win at QPR gives them new hope. In Div 1, Tranmere's hopes of the automatic promotion spot take a nose-dive with a 5-0 defeat at Derby, who appear to have left their effort too late to win a play-off spot. In Div 3, leaders Carlisle suffer their first home defeat, 1-0 to lowly Hartlepool, but are still 8pts clear at the top.

18 Dundee Utd win at Partick in an important Scottish relegation battle, but Aberdeen lose 2-1 at Motherwell and are now 4pts adrift. Terry Venables includes 13 uncapped Premiership players in the 19-strong England squad for next week-end's get-together, including central midfielders Jamie Redknapp (Liverpool), Garry Flitcroft (Man City) and Mark Draper (Leicester). Middlesbrough lose their British Steel sponsorship because their new stadium is being built from cheaper German steel.

19 Ajax impressively beat Bayern Munich 5-2 (5-2 agg) to reach the final of the European Cup, where they will play AC Milan. England captain David Platt signs for another year with Sampdoria.

20 David Seaman is Arsenal's hero in their Cup-Winners' Cup semi as he makes 3 penalty saves in a shoot-out against Sampdoria after Stefan Schwarz had kept Arsenal in the game with a late goal to make the aggregate score 5-5. In the final, Arsenal will play Real Zaragoza, who, although losing 3-1 to a courageous Chelsea at Stamford Bridge, win the tie 4-3. Blackburn take another shaky step towards the Premiership title with a 2-1 win at home to Palace and now go 8pts clear - they need 5pts from their last 3 games. Former Coventry striker Keith Houchen takes over at Hartlepool from David McCreery, who resigned when told his contract would not be renewed in the summer, and former Welsh international Kevin Ratcliffe becomes caretaker manager of Chester, Derek Mann stepping down to become youth development officer. Billy Bonds rejects an offer to take over at Orient, who have sacked their joint managers John Sitton and Chris Turner.

21 Bolton miss a chance of going top of Div 1 when they lose 2-1 at Reading.

22 There are no Saturday Premier games in England or Scotland. A 1-1 draw at Barnsley gives Middlesbrough a 3pt lead in Div 1 and ensures them at least a play-off place. After his side draw 3-3 at Sheff Utd, Wolves manager Graham Taylor tries unsuccessfully to make a citizen's arrest on a spectator who spits on him. At the bottom, Bristol City lose 1-0 at Watford and are relegated - along with Burnley, who go down 2-1 to Portsmouth at Turf Moor. In Div 2, jittery leaders Brentford manage to beat Cardiff 2-0 and send the Welshmen down. Chelsea's Robert Fleck has been banned from receiving Cup final tickets for 5 years.

23 A crowd of 76,000 see Birmingham make history with an extra-time sudden-death victory over Carlisle in the final of the Auto Windscreens Shield, sub Paul Tait making the score 1-0 in the 103rd minute. The safety officer at Bramall Lane, Tom Broomhead, criticises Wolves manager Graham Taylor for trying to grab a spectator who spat on him, but the former England manager is unrepentant.

24 The FA charge Birmingham's Paul Tait with bringing the game into disrepute for revealing an offensive T-shirt during the celebrations of his sudden-death winner at Wembley yesterday. Spurs veteran midfielder Micky Hazard, 35, has been forced to retire because of a persistent back problem.

25 Blackburn's unfortunate Paul Warhurst breaks a leg in a reserve-team work-out.

26 In Euro Championship qualifiers, Wales are the only British Isles team not to win, but their performance takes pride of place - an improbable 1-1 draw with Germany in Dusseldorf that takes them off bottom spot in Gp 7 and deprives the Germans of their 100% record. Ireland's important 1-0 victory over Portugal in Dublin takes them to the top of Gp 6, above their hitherto 100% opponents, while N.Ireland's 1-0 win in Latvia takes them into 3rd place. Scotland should have recorded more than a 2-0 victory from their away tie with San Marino. The only domestic match was of great significance, Birmingham beating Brentford 2-0 to leapfrog above them on goals at the top of Div 2 with a game in hand. The Sheff Utd supporter, Robert Hollister, who spat at Graham Taylor is released on bail after being questioned by police and travels to Wolverhampton to apologise in person to the Wolves manager.

27 Ill-advised verbal utterances cost Wimbledon personnel - manager Joe Kinnear a £1,500 fine and a touchline ban for recent remarks about two referees, and midfielder Vinnie Jones a £1,750 fine for comments after the game at Newcastle. Fulham midfielder Terry Hurlock, having become the first player to register 61 disciplinary points in a season since the present system started 21 years ago, is fined £400 and banned for 4 matches. Spurs youth team coach Pat Holland takes over as manager of Orient.

28 Eric Cantona signs a new 3-year contract with Man Utd rather than accept an offer from Inter-Milan.

29 Jurgen Klinsmann, who scores Spurs' equaliser in the 1-1 draw at Highbury, his 28th goal of the season, is voted Footballer of the Year. Palace and Norwich dig themselves into deeper relegation trouble, both losing 2-1 at home, to Forest and Liverpool respectively, and Villa's 1-0 defeat at Leeds leaves them on the precipice. An angry protest outside Carrow Road after Norwich's defeat, in which two police officers are injured, leads to 13 arrests and 5 charges for public order offences. Derby decide to part company with manager Roy McFarland in the wake of their home defeat by in-form Southend. All 4 relegation places are now decided as Portsmouth, having done for Burnley last week, repeat the dose at Swindon, whose 2-0 defeat sends them down. Sunderland's draw at Burnley ensures their safety. Nerve-ends are showing in Div 2, where leaders Birmingham lose a 2-goal lead and are lucky to salvage a point from their home game with Brighton, Brentford go down 2-1 at home to lowly Bournemouth, and Huddersfield's draw at struggling Cambridge now puts them out of the running for the automatic promotion place. Carlisle clinch the Div 3 title with a 1-0 win at Colchester. In Scotland, Aberdeen's 2-1 victory at Hearts enables them to make ground on their relegation rivals.

30 Blackburn's shock 2-0 defeat at relegation-haunted West Ham suddenly leaves their 8pt Premiership lead looking vulnerable as Man Utd now have 2 games in hand. While Div 1 leaders Middlesbrough almost clinch automatic promotion with a 2-1 win over Luton in the last match they will play at Ayresome Park, Tranmere blow their chances of that luxury in their 5-1 defeat at West Brom, where Lee Ashcroft hits a hat-trick and the visitors have defender David Higgins sent off in the 45th minute. Meanwhile at Tranmere's ground, Arsenal beat Liverpool 3-2 in the FA Women's Cup final. H.E. Bert McGhee, 77, former Sheff Wed chairman (1975-90), dies.

May

Robson's Middlesbrough promoted . . . Norwich go down . . . Arsenal beaten in Cup-Winners' Cup final . . . Klinsmann to leave Spurs . . . Dundee Utd relegated . . . Blackburn win the Premiership . . . Everton win Cup, Man Utd miss out twice . . . Owls sack Trevor Francis . . . Crewe win Fair Play trophy . . . Ajax win European Cup . . . Celtic win Scottish Cup . . . Bolton promoted . . . Ted Drake dies . . . Chelsea sign Ruud Gullit

1 Despite having 6 first-choice players suspended or injured, Man Utd keep up the pressure on Blackburn with an inspired 3-2 victory at Coventry, Andy Cole scoring twice.

2 Birmingham, held at home 0-0 by Bradford, miss their first chance to clinch promotion from Div 2, while Bournemouth's 3-0 victory over Shrewsbury ensures their survival and at the same time the relegation of both Cambridge and Plymouth.

3 The Premiership relegation battle is the Wednesday night focus, and home draws for West Ham, Everton and Villa bring important points in view of Palace's 3-1 defeat by Southampton. Bolton's failure to get more than a draw at Stoke hands Middlesbrough the Div 1 title and promotion.

4 A 0-0 draw at Bury is enough for Walsall to clinch the second automatic promotion place to Div 2. Jurgen Klinsmann signs a boot deal with Reebok worth £3m over 4 years, but has not yet decided whether to stay with Spurs next season.

6 One of the two remaining Premiership relegation spots is filled when Norwich suffer their 7th successive defeat, 2-1 at Leeds. Palace keep their hopes alive by beating West Ham 1-0, and Villa by beating Liverpool 2-0. A 1-0 win over Man City ensures Forest 3rd or 4th place and a spot in next season's UEFA Cup. Div 1 is playing tomorrow, but the Div 2 programme is completed, with Birmingham finally clinching the title, winning 2-1 at Huddersfield, where one person is injured and several arrested as rival fans clash before the match. Aberdeen win their crucial home match with Dundee Utd to leapfrog above them at the bottom of the Scottish Premier with one round of matches left. Greenock Morton clinch promotion from Div 2, Montrose from Div 3. Noel Brotherston, 38, former N.Ireland winger, dies suddenly from a heart attack in Blackburn.

7 David May, the defender acquired from Blackburn last summer, scores a 5th-minute goal that is enough to beat Sheff Wed and take Man Utd to within 2pts of the leaders with 2 games to play. One fan is killed and several seriously injured when they fall from a stand after a railing collapses at the Jose de Alvalade stadium, home ground of Sporting Lisbon, before the match with Bobby Robson's Porto; Porto's 1-0 victory clinches the Portuguese title.

8 Blackburn clear their penultimate hurdle, beating Newcastle 1-0 in their last home match with a typical far-post header from Alan Shearer after 28min - his 36th goal of the season - but may have to win at Anfield to clinch the Premiership.

9 The 3 Premiership evening games all have a bearing on relegation, Coventry and Everton winning respectively at Spurs and Ipswich to ensure safety, but Palace losing at Leeds to leave themselves on the precipice.

10 Arsenal are cruelly defeated in the Cup-Winners' Cup final 2-1 by Real Zaragoza with the last kick of extra time, as keeper David Seaman, hero of their semi-final penalty shoot-out, is beaten by a brilliant, speculative 40-yard looping shot from former Spurs midfielder Nayim. Man Utd take the Premiership struggle right down to the wire as Denis Irwin converts a late penalty to give them a 2-1 victory over Southampton at Old Trafford. West Ham, who entertain United in their last match next Sunday, beat Liverpool, who entertain Blackburn, by 3-0 to ensure safety.

11 The 'Will he?, Won't he?' saga of Jurgen Klinsmann is finally resolved when Spurs' inspirational striker confirms he is going back to Germany, to join Bayern Munich, but the good news, revealed in another press conference, is that manager Gerry Francis is staying. Villa join Rangers in a £5m bid for Paul Gascoigne.

12 Chelsea director Matthew Harding, who has already committed more than £7m to the club in the last 18 months, buys the freehold of Stamford Bridge from the Royal Bank of Scotland for £16.5m, but neither takes nor wants control of the club.

13 Saturday sees the completion of the Scottish programme, with Dundee Utd, beaten 1-0 at home by Celtic, relegated, and Aberdeen having to play off with Div 1 runners-up Dunfermline, as Raith claim the title with a goalless draw at Hamilton. In Div 2, Dumbarton win 2-0 at Stirling to pip them for the second promotion place.

14 Blackburn win the Carling Premiership, their first Championship for 81 years, despite losing 2-1 at Liverpool, as Man Utd are held 1-1 by West Ham at Upton Park; Blackburn chief Kenny Dalglish thus joins Herbert Chapman and Brian Clough in managing two clubs to the Championship. Palace are relegated after a brave fight at Newcastle, but Wednesday's and Villa's positive results would have consigned them to Div 1 anyway. Chelsea player-manager Glenn Hoddle marks the end of an era as he celebrates his last game with a 2-1 victory over Arsenal at Stamford Bridge. At White Hart Lane, Jurgen Klinsmann, captain for the day, fails to get the goal the Spurs fans wanted, but he is given a standing ovation at the end and the 1-1 draw is sufficient for Leeds to clinch a UEFA Cup place. In Div 1 play-offs, runners-up Reading gain a comprehensive 3-1 1st-leg victory at Tranmere, while Wolves will take a 2-1 lead to Bolton.

15 Palace manager Alan Smith, publicly at loggerheads with his chairman, Ron Noades, for much of the season, is finally sacked. Man Utd win the FA Youth Cup final on penalties from Spurs after Terry Cooke puts them level on aggregate in the last seconds of normal time.

16 As expected, Man City fire manager Brian Horton after 21 months - he is the 12th Premier League manager to get the chop this season, the 52nd League manager to part company with a total of 43 clubs. Mark Kennedy, 18, is called into the Irish senior squad only 2 months after his £2m transfer from Millwall to Liverpool. AC Milan sign Paris SG's Liberian striker George Weah for £5m, with the player getting £1.5m over the 2-year contract.

17 Luckless England keeper David Seaman breaks an ankle playing for Arsenal on their Far Eastern tour. Parma beat fellow Italians Juventus 2-1 on aggregate to win the UEFA Cup. Ilie Dumitrescu, on loan to Sevilla, is returning to Spurs because the Spanish club will not pay the £2m asking fee. Two goals by John McGinlay against Wolves, the second in extra time, put Bolton through to the final of the Div 1 play-offs against Reading. In Div 2, Huddersfield beat Brentford on penalties, while Bristol Rovers beat Crewe on away goals. Chesterfield, with 3 goals in extra time, win their Div 3 play-off 6-3 on aggregate against Mansfield - who have 2 players sent off - and will play Bury at Wembley.

18 Man United's Ukrainian winger Andrei Kanchelskis, who has not played in the team since returning from international duty in April suffering from a stomach problem, announces he no longer wants to play for Alex Ferguson. Aberdeen appoint Roy Aitken as their new manager.

20 Having averted relegation, Joe Royle's Everton win the Cup with a Paul Rideout goal after 30min to deprive Man Utd of their second trophy in a week. Sheff Wed announce that manager Trevor Francis's contract has been terminated by mutual agreement with still a year to run.

21 Wrexham beat Cardiff 2-1 in the National Stadium to win the Welsh Cup for a record 23rd time. Scotland play a goalless draw with Japan in Hiroshima, both teams having a man sent off and Scotland finishing with 9 men.

22 The consortium taking over Cardiff City replace manager Eddie May with Colin Murphy. Arsenal return home from their tour of China and Hong Kong with young midfielder Ray Parlour in disgrace, having been fined around £170 by a Hong Kong court after an incident in which a taxi driver was injured. An arbitration tribunal orders Celtic to pay Kilmarnock £200,000 compensation for poaching manager Tommy Burns and his assistant last year. Graeme Souness returns to the game, agreeing to manage Turkish club Galatasaray on a 1-year contract worth a reported £0.5m. Barcelona complete the £2.8m signing of Spurs' Romanian defender Gica Popescu.

23 Paul Gascoigne is back in England's international squad for the upcoming Umbro Cup, while Ray Parlour is dropped from the U-21s for his misdemeanours in Hong Kong. Southampton manager Alan Ball, one of only 9 Premiership managers to keep their job this season, is given a new 3-year contract. Crewe win the Bobby Moore Fair Play Trophy for the second year running, with only 89 disciplinary points.

24 Ajax lift the European Cup for the 4th time, beating holders AC Milan 1-0 with an 86th-min goal from 18-year-old Patrick Kluivert. Man United's Paul Ince is cleared of threatening behaviour and assaulting a fan. UEFA alter the method of qualifying direct into next season's Champions League, which means Blackburn, as English champions, are seeded 5th and will not have to pre-qualify.

25 UEFA threaten to ban all English clubs from their competitions if the FA do not persuade 3 teams to take part in the Inter Toto Cup. Paul Ince withdraws from the England squad after consultation with Terry Venables, who replaces him with Liverpool's Jamie Redknapp. Aberdeen beat Dunfermline 3-1 to win their play-off 6-2 on aggregate and remain in the Premier League.

26 Man United's Roy Keane is fined a further £5,000 for his red-card offence in the Cup semi replay against Palace, the FA deciding to make a special case of the incident. Everton's uncapped defender David Unsworth, 21, replaces the injured Tony Adams in the England squad.

27 Celtic beat Airdrie 1-0 to win the Scottish Cup, their first major trophy for 6 years, with a goal scored by Dutchman Pierre van Hooijdonk. Chesterfield beat Bury 2-0 in the Div 3 play-off final.

28 Huddersfield beat Bristol Rovers 2-1 in the Div 2 play-off final.

29 The English domestic season, one of the most troubled in the history of the game, concludes with a stirring Wembley final, as Bolton, 2-0 down at half-time, come back to beat Reading 4-3 after extra time to win the Div 1 play-offs and return to the top division after 15 years in the wilderness. Former Sunderland defender Tom Gilbert, only 36, collapses and dies while coaching.

30 Euro '96 matches that go to extra time will be decided by sudden death, or, failing that, penalties. Former Southampton, Arsenal and England centre-forward and Chelsea manager Ted Drake dies at 82. Bobby Stokes, scorer of Southampton's winning goal in the 1976 Cup final, dies of natural causes at the age of 44.

31 Chelsea manager Glenn Hoddle pulls off an audacious coup, signing 32-year-old Dutch goalscoring midfielder Ruud Gullit from Sampdoria on a free transfer; the former shining star of Holland and AC Milan is set to receive about £1.5m over 2 years and play as a sweeper. Sheff Wed, Spurs and Wimbledon have agreed to play in the unpopular Inter Toto Cup.

June

Irish setbacks in Euro qualifiers . . . £6m Ferdinand for Newcastle . . . Bruce Rioch Arsenal's new manager . . . England no match for Brazil in Umbro Cup

2 Chelsea captain Dennis Wise wins his appeal against a 3-month prison sentence for attacking a taxi driver, but receives scathing criticism from the judge and is not awarded costs. Bristol City midfielder Martin Kuhl is banned from driving for 18 months as a result of a near miss with a police car and being over twice the legal alcohol limit. It appears that the 3 clubs persuaded to take part in the Inter Toto Cup have been promised £250,000 each, and the Premier League are demanding £50,000 from each of the other Premiership clubs to fund the entrants.

3 Ireland suffer a severe setback to their Euro '96 qualifying campaign as they are held to a shock 0-0 draw in Liechtenstein. England put up an embarrassing performance at Wembley in the opening match of the Umbro Cup, just scraping a 2-1 win over Japan with a late penalty by captain David Platt, albeit with a makeshift side including 4 new caps - defenders Gary Neville (Man Utd), David Unsworth (Everton) and John Scales (Liverpool) and striker Stan Collymore (Forest); Paul Gascoigne, on his way to Rangers to confirm his end-of-the-month transfer from Lazio, comes on as a 68th-min sub. Newcastle sign England full-back Warren Barton from Wimbledon for £4m (plus £1m after 50 games)

4 Brazil beat Sweden 1-0 at Villa Park in the Umbro Cup.
5 Neil Warnock, manager of promoted Huddersfield, resigns. Notts Co appoint a managerial partnership - Colin Murphy as general manager, Steve Thompson responsible for team affairs.
6 Brazil brush Japan aside 3-0 in the Umbro Cup with a masterly display of football, while their Under-21s beat England 2-0 in the Toulon Tournament. Bobby Robson accepts that his contract with Porto cannot be broken and declines a £2m offer from Arsenal.
7 Newcastle sign England striker Les Ferdinand, 28, from QPR for £6m, 10% of which will go to Diadora League club Hayes. A poor night for British clubs in the Euro Championship sees Wales return to the bottom of Gp 7 after losing 1-0 at home to Georgia and having Vinnie Jones sent off for stamping on an opponent, N.Ireland blow their chances in Gp 6 with a 2-1 home defeat by Latvia, and Scotland making a meal of their 2-0 win away to the Faroes in Gp 8, where Russia show how it should be done, winning 7-0 in San Marino. Germany lose 3-2 to Gp 7 runaway leaders Bulgaria after leading 2-0, but the biggest shock is Luxembourg's 1-0 defeat of the Czechs.
8 Arsenal appoint Bolton's Bruce Rioch as their new manager. Two goals in the last 2min, including a spectacular equaliser from Darren Anderton, give England a lucky draw against a superior Swedish side in the Umbro Cup at Elland Road. Former manager Steve Coppell returns to Palace as technical director. Paul Ince is stunned by Man United's decision to accept a reported offer of £8m from Inter-Milan.
10 England beat Nigeria 3-2 to reach the quarter-finals of the Women's World Championships.
11 Ireland stutter to a disastrous 3-1 defeat in Dublin by Austria after taking a 65th-min lead and their once odds-on chances of qualifying for Euro '96 take a nose-dive. Brazil come back from 1-0 down with a fluent display to beat England 3-1 at Wembley and win the Umbro Cup. UEFA back the joint Holland-Belgium bid to host Euro 2000.
12 Last season's Spurs love affair with Jurgen Klinsmann looks like ending in acrimony as the German striker accuses chairman Alan Sugar (who reportedly wants him suspended until FIFA have investigated their contractual dispute) of attempting to sour his relationship with English supporters. England and Scotland are beaten in the semis of the Toulon U-21 Tournament by France and Brazil respectively.

Jack Rollin about to receive a Rothmans Award of a crystal decanter from the then Arsenal manager George Graham to mark the 25th edition of Rothmans Football Yearbook. In the background, Master of Ceremonies Jim Rosenthal.

Review of the season

Blackburn Rovers may not have been the most scintillating championship winners of all time, but there was an admirable balance and adaptability about a team which was maintained despite several forced and unforced changes. Moreover, they fully deserved to celebrate their first title success for 81 years.

The key roles were undoubtedly found in defence and attack with centre-back Colin Hendry and striker Alan Shearer outstanding. Hendry intelligently covered large areas of ground at the rear, organising on the ground and commanding in the air, while Shearer effectively kept the attack flowing as well as contributing 34 goals. He was well supported by £5 million capture Chris Sutton and these two accounted for all but 31 of Blackburn's League total.

Oddly enough Blackburn lost both matches to their nearest rivals from Old Trafford. On 23 October they crashed 4-2 at home and were lying fourth at the time of the defeat. However this proved to be something of a spur, as they embarked on a run of 12 unbeaten games which took them into first place. The sequence was ended — by United! This time they went down to a single goal defeat at Old Trafford.

Blackburn called upon the services of 21 different players during the season. Shearer was the only ever present in the ranks, Hendry and Tim Sherwood each missed four matches, Henning Berg and Chris Sutton two each, while Graeme Le Saux and Tim Flowers were absent on three occasions.

Shearer scored three hat-tricks and ten penalties, Sutton one treble. At the back, United's success in scoring four times against the Blackburn defence was an isolated event; no other team in the Premiership managed to score as many in one game, though the Mancunian connection across at Manchester City was responsible for a 3-2 win at Ewood Park in the middle of April, a reverse which then gave United some cause for hope that they might still catch their opponents.

Blackburn failed to score in just five games, three of these finishing as goalless draws. The defence produced 16 clean sheets, eight at home and eight away. Their highest wins were 4-0 against both Coventry and Queens Park Rangers. Significantly, they did not have more than a two-match gap without a win.

Arguably the biggest disappointment of the season was the failure to reach beyond the first round in the UEFA Cup, though this might well have proved a blessing in their ultimate aim of the championship title.

Manager Kenny Dalglish was always mindful of using the full width of the pitch in his preferred 4-4-2 formation and though he did not have a large pool of players on whom to call, one or two judicious moves into the transfer market at crucial moments proved well justified. The club owed much to the money lavished on it by millionaire Jack Walker, but the overall approach by everyone connected with Blackburn proved a winning formula. Yet in some respects, the last game of the season became almost anti-climatic.

Manchester United had to win at West Ham and hope Liverpool defeated Blackburn at Anfield. A draw would have been enough for Blackburn, who took the lead, lost it and the game in the last seconds, only for news to filter through almost immediately that United had only managed a draw themselves.

Six days later, Manchester United were to lose the FA Cup Final. Over the season they could point to the loss of the suspended Eric Cantona, injuries to wingers Andrei Kanchelskis and Ryan Giggs, plus loss of form elsewhere in the team for failure to retain the title. At Old Trafford they were practically invincible. Peter Schmeichel conceded just two goals there, Gary Walsh letting in the other two in the United's only home defeat 2-1 to Nottingham Forest on 17 December. All told, United boasted 24 clean sheets.

Forest, in fact, were 11 points behind in third place. Stan Collymore scored freely for a team who often looked the most attractive the League. They finished the season in style: 13 games unbeaten. Collymore joined Liverpool in the summer for an English record £8.5 million, his new team having finished a respectable fourth and winners of the Coca-Cola Cup. Their attitude in the final match of the season against Blackburn was both a credit to themselves and the competition as a whole. Top scorer Robbie Fowler hit the fastest Premier League hat-trick in five minutes against Arsenal in August.

Leeds made several useful signings from Africa, the most successful of them being Tony Yeboah, the Ghana international striker from Germany, but Newcastle United fell away after a perfect start and the sale of Andy Cole to Manchester United. Tottenham Hotspur improved after the psychological barrier of points deduction was removed and German striker Jurgen Klinsmann enjoyed his brief season in English football.

Attractive Queens Park Rangers ended the campaign in eighth place, their highest all season and Wimbledon tailed off after causing several notable upsets. Southampton equalled the number of draws in the Premier League and seven of their 18 came in successive matches. A spell of ten games ending in mid-February upset Chelsea and Arsenal, who had a mid-table look all season, did best in Europe, just failing to retain the Cup-Winners' Cup.

Disappointing Sheffield Wednesday even suffered their heaviest home defeat when losing 7-1 to Nottingham Forest on April Fools' Day, but West Ham made up six places in the last two months to avoid relegation. A change of manager had a dramatic effect on Everton's season and they climbed to 15th themselves in the latter stages. Any inflated hopes that Coventry had ended from early December with 11 matches without a win. Manchester City had similar problems around the same time and showed inconsistency in attack, while Aston Villa contrived only one win in the last 11 matches.

However, the four relegated clubs were Crystal Palace, Norwich City, Leicester City and Ipswich Town. Palace scraped only 34 goals and went nine successive games without scoring even one. Norwich plummeted with only one win from their last 20, Leicester were never out of the bottom two from November and Ipswich produced fewest points, the heaviest defeat-9-0 at Manchester United -and more reverses than anyone else.

Middlesbrough justifiably emerged as champions of the Endsleigh First Division, finishing with only one defeat in their last ten. But the play-off system dealt cruelly to second placed Reading, who reached the final against Bolton Wanderers at Wembley to become involved in one of the most exciting matches of the 1994-95 season. They led 2-0, missed a penalty and were beaten 4-3 in extra time. Third placed Bolton, who had finished as runners-up to Liverpool in the Coca-Cola Cup, had incredibly failed to score more than one goal in any of their last 13 League games in the regular season.

Wolverhampton Wanderers were handicapped by drawing seven of their last nine matches and losing one of the other two, while Tranmere failed to win any of the last five. Barnsley, as high as third on Boxing Day, were unable to stay the course, Watford had little to show for 20 clean sheets and Sheffield United, fourth on 18 March, managed only one other win. Derby also faltered with a single victory among the last seven games, Grimsby were fourth on 3 December and a late revival for Stoke only took them to half-way.

Millwall reached the fifth round of both major cup competitions, yet had one run of ten in the League without a win and nine without defeat. Southend won eight of their last 12, Oldham scored them freely and conceded goals just as easily, Charlton Athletic were as high as sixth by the end of October and Luton snatched just one win from the final ten games.

Alan Shearer turns to acknowledge the cheers of Blackburn supporters at Anfield after his opening goal against Liverpool. Though Rovers were beaten by a last minute goal from Jamie Redknapp, Manchester United's failure to win at West Ham was enough for Blackburn to take the title. (Action Images)

Matt Le Tissier avoids Norwich City's tackling duo of Jon Newsome (left) and Ian Crook. Both Southampton matches with Norwich were drawn last season. In fact the Saints were the draw specialists of the Premiership, while Le Tissier was their inspiration. (Colorsport)

Inconsistency prevented Port Vale from making any substantial impact, but Portsmouth showed a second-half improvement after a string of nine matches without victory.

West Bromwich were handicapped by having to play their first five games away because of ground improvements and had to struggle up to reach even 19th. Sunderland hauled themselves out of trouble following the appointment of Peter Reid as manager, but it was relegation for Swindon Town, Burnley, Bristol City and Notts County.

Swindon's season collapsed having been as high as fifth on 29 October. Burnley's leaky defence prevented the opposition from scoring only four times, Bristol City won one of their last 11 as did Notts County, whose consolation was winning the Anglo-Italian Cup.

Birmingham City survived one stumbling period to lose just once in the last third of the season and as Second Division champions were excellently supported. Brentford failed in the play-offs but had a free-scoring attacking duo in Nicky Forster and Robert Taylor, while the defence produced 22 clean sheets, 14 of them at home.

Crewe Alexandra were also unable to overcome the play-offs, despite finishing strongly with ten undefeated games and a similar fate befell Bristol Rovers with one defeat in the last 15. However, fifth placed Huddersfield Town, who had slipped slightly after a splendid opening when they suffered just one defeat in 15 -and that on their debut at the new ground -came through to join Birmingham in promotion.

Wycombe Wanderers' hopes were dashed with five successive scoreless games in March, Oxford United failed to live up to early-season promise as did Hull who were fourth on 5 November. York City improved too late for the play-offs, and Swansea City never appeared to mount a serious challenge of their own. Goalkeeper Roger Freestone even converted a late season penalty. Injury to Kevin Francis and his subsequent move to Birmingham affected Stockport County and Blackpool in spite of reaching fifth on several occasions, lacked consistency.

Wrexham were unable to improve on 13th place despite having in Gary Bennett, the country's leading goalscorer. Bradford City had a good opening spell and a poor late one, Peterborough went 12 games without a win at the turn of the year and Brighton were never as convincing after the transfer of Kurt Nogan to Burnley. Rotherham United hovered just above the relegation zone as did Shrewsbury Town, but Bournemouth showed distinct improvement in the New Year.

Jan Aage Fjortoft (right), Middlesbrough's late season capture from Swindon Town at £1.3 million, celebrates Alan Moore's goal on the way towards the Ayresome Park club winning a place back in the top echelon. (Action Images)

The five clubs demoted were Cambridge United, Plymouth Argyle, Cardiff City, Chester City and Leyton Orient. Cambridge never recovered from a run of ten games without a win, Plymouth had a wretched start with only two points from a possible 21, Cardiff were never higher than 19th, Chester had a disastrous sequence of 16 games without a win from November and Leyton Orient lost their last nine games.

At one stage, Carlisle United seemed capable of breaking several records in Division Three. They suffered only their second defeat of the season on 18 February losing 1-0 at Preston and twice had crowds of over 12,000. They were joined in automatic promotion by Walsall, who produced several strong runs of consecutive wins.

Third placed Chesterfield were able to give some logic to the play-offs and owed much to their defence which enjoyed 22 clean sheets. Bury themselves managed one fewer, but lost out to Chesterfield at Wembley despite a late run of 11 games without defeat. Preston, back on grass, again found the play-offs too difficult but had improved under a new manager. Free-scoring Mansfield were third on 11 March but had some defensive frailties.

Scunthorpe, as high as fifth in January, also missed out on the play-offs as did Fulham, whose best sequence was one of ten unbeaten matches, starting on New Year's Eve. Doncaster Rovers were as high as third on 10 December but they too faltered along with Colchester fifth in February after winning 1-0 at Barnet, who had been hit by eight games without a win prior to the New Year.

Lincoln had a mid-table look throughout the season, though they were the last to fail to score a goal at home, Torquay never improved after a fine beginning and Wigan were never higher than 12th all season. Rochdale's lack of scoring power was evident after a useful start and 16th place was as high as Hereford managed all season.

Northampton were never higher than one place lower than this, but were well supported at their new ground from the middle of October. Hartlepool pulled themselves together after a run of 12 games without a win, Gillingham's financial position never kept them far from the bottom and Darlington won only one of their last 14 games.

Scarborough completed a club record 16 matches without a win ending in January and Exeter, who also faced serious financial problems, finished last after a run of 16 unsuccessful games of their own at the end of the season. They escaped demotion as Vauxhall Conference champions Macclesfield had been informed much earlier that their ground did not meet Football League requirements, despite providing Chester with a home two years earlier!

INTRODUCTION TO THE CLUB SECTION

For the first time since Rothmans Football Yearbook was originally formulated, this edition introduces a complete change in the way in which players in the 92 League clubs are presented. Instead of the names appearing under the club with whom they were last with in the previous season, there is an A-Z of all such players (see pages 404-532). However, in an easy-to-read guide, the name of the player's last club is indicated in black. All other aspects of the players' details are kept intact as in previous editions.

Because of this alteration to the club section, this now comprises four instead of six pages. The first page again features the team photograph depicting those players and officials taken at the beginning of the 1994-95 season. On the second page which gives historical and record details for each club, the information which was previously to be found on the sixth page of this section is now incorporated here. As a result of this, the club badge has been moved to page three while page four has an added piece of information with the initials of all players appearing for that club during the 1994-95 season.

Again, the third and fourth pages give a complete record of the League season, including date, venue, opponents, result, half-time score, League position, goalscorers, attendance and complete line-ups, including substitutes where used, for every League game in the 1994-95 season. Once again, squad numbers have been ignored; those used are familar ones, 1-11, 12, 14 and 15. The No. 15 represents the substitute goalkeeper. Players replaced are respectively given a light type figure, an italic one with a bold italic for the goalkeeper. These two pages also include consolidated lists of goalscorers for the club in League, Coca-Cola and FA Cup matches and a summary of results in these two main domestic cups.

Due to the increase in the number of matches played on Sundays, the League positions shown after every League result takes into consideration the final standings on this day. Full holiday programmes are also recorded, but the position after mid-week fixtures will not normally be updated. Attendance figures quoted for each Endsleigh Insurance League game are those which appeared in the Press at the time. But those in the FA Carling Premiership are official. The attendance statistics published on pages 574 and 575 are those officially issued by the Football League at the end of the season. However, the figures for each League games are those used in conjunction with the Daily Telegraph and Jack Rollin's weekly statistics in that newspaper.

In the totals at the top of each column on page four, substitute appearances are listed separately by the '+', but have been amalgamated in the totals which feature in the player's historical section in the directory mentioned above. Thus these appearances include those as substitute. In fact the players directory again features those whose names appear on the FA Premier League and Football League's 'Retained' list, which is published at the end of May. Each player's height and weight where known, plus birth place, birth date and source together with total League goals and appearances for each club he has represented can be found as in previous editions. The player's details remain under the club which retain him at the end of the season. An asterisk * by a player's name indicates that he was given a free transfer at the end of the 1994-95 season, a dagger against a name means that he is a non-contract player, a double dagger indicates that the player's registration was cancelled during the season and a SS indicates either a Trainee or an Associated Schoolboy who has made FA Premier League or Football League apperances. Appearances by players in the play-offs are not included in their career totals.

There is also a directory of all League club managers and a separate section with new stories in the 'Did you know' series.

ARSENAL 1994-95 *Back row (left to right):* Pat Rice (Youth Team Coach), Gary Lewin (Physio), Lee Harper, Steve Morrow, Paul Merson, Martin Keown, Andy Linighan, David Seaman, Nigel Winterburn, Alan Smith, Scott Marshall, Ray Parlour, Alan Miller, Stewart Houston (First Team Coach), George Armstrong (Reserve Team Coach).
Front row: Steve Bould, Stefan Schwarz, David Hillier, Kevin Campbell, Jimmy Carter, Eddie McGoldrick, Ian Wright, George Graham (Manager), Tony Adams, John Jensen, Paul Davis, Lee Dixon, Paul Dickov, Ian Selley, Mark Flatts.

FA Premiership ARSENAL

Arsenal Stadium, Highbury, London N5 1BU. Telephone: (0171) 226 0304. Box Office: (0171) 354 5404. Commercial and Marketing (0171) 359 0808. Recorded information on (0171)359 0131. Clubline: 0891 20 20 20. Mail Order (0171) 354 8397.

Ground capacity: 38,500 all seated.

Record attendance: 73,295 v Sunderland, Div 1, 9 March 1935.

Record receipts: £392,726.50 v Sampdoria, European Cup-Winners Cup, semi-final first leg, 6 April 1995.

Pitch measurements: 110yd × 71yd.

Chairman: P. D. Hill-Wood. ***Vice-Chairman:*** D. Dein.

Directors: Sir Robert Bellinger CBE, DSC, R. G. Gibbs, C. E. B. L. Carr, R. C. S. Carr, D. D. Fiszman.

Managing Director: K. J. Friar.

Manager: Bruce Rioch. ***Assistant Manager/Coach:*** Stewart Houston.

Physio: Gary Lewin. ***Reserve Coach:*** George Armstrong. ***Youth Coach:*** Pat Rice.

Secretary: K. J. Friar. ***Assistant Secretary:*** David Miles. ***Commercial Manager:*** John Hazell. ***Marketing Manager:*** Phil Carling.

Year Formed: 1886. ***Turned Professional:*** 1891. ***Ltd Co.:*** 1893.

Previous Names: 1886, Dial Square; 1886–91, Royal Arsenal; 1891–1914, Woolwich Arsenal.

Club Nickname: 'Gunners'.

Previous Grounds: 1886–87, Plumstead Common; 1887–88, Sportsman Ground; 1888–90, Manor Ground; 1890–93, Invicta Ground; 1893–1913, Manor Ground; 1913, Highbury.

Foundation: Formed by workers at the Royal Arsenal, Woolwich in 1886 they began as Dial Square (name of one of the workshops) and included two former Nottingham Forest players Fred Beardsley and Morris Bates. Beardsley wrote to his old club seeking help and they provided the new club with a full set of red jerseys and a ball. The club became known as the "Woolwich Reds" although their official title soon after formation was Woolwich Arsenal.

First Football League game: 2 September, 1893, Division 2, v Newcastle U (h) D 2-2 – Williams; Powell, Jeffrey; Devine, Buist, Howat; Gemmell, Henderson, Shaw (1), Elliott (1), Booth.

Record League Victory: 12–0 v Loughborough T, Division 2, 12 March 1900 – Orr; McNichol, Jackson; Moir, Dick (2), Anderson (1); Hunt, Cottrell (2), Main (2), Gaudie (3), Tennant (2).

Record Cup Victory: 11–1 v Darwen, FA Cup, 3rd rd, 9 January 1932 – Moss; Parker, Hapgood; Jones, Roberts, John; Hulme (2), Jack (3), Lambert (2), James, Bastin (4).

Record Defeat: 0–8 v Loughborough T, Division 2, 12 December 1896.

Most League Points (2 for a win): 66, Division 1, 1930–31.

Most League Points (3 for a win): 83, Division 1, 1990–91.

Most League Goals: 127, Division 1, 1930–31.

Highest League Scorer in Season: Ted Drake, 42, 1934–35.

Most League Goals in Total Aggregate: Cliff Bastin, 150, 1930–47.

Most Capped Player: Kenny Sansom, 77 (86), England.

Most League Appearances: David O'Leary, 558, 1975–93.

Record Transfer Fee Received: £2,000,000 from Leeds U for David Rocastle.

Record Transfer Fee Paid: £7,500,000 to Internazionale for Dennis Bergkamp, June 1995.

Football League Record: 1893 Elected to Division 2; 1904–13 Division 1; 1913–19 Division 2; 1919–92 Division 1; 1992– FA Premier League.

Honours: *Football League:* Division 1 – Champions 1930–31, 1932–33, 1933–34, 1934–35, 1937–38, 1947–48, 1952–53, 1970–71, 1988–89, 1990–91; Runners-up 1925–26, 1931–32, 1972–73; Division 2 – Runners-up 1903–04. *FA Cup:* Winners 1930, 1936, 1950, 1971, 1979, 1993; Runners-up 1927, 1932, 1952, 1972, 1978, 1980. *Double performed:* 1970–71. *Football League Cup:* Winners 1987, 1993; Runners-up 1968, 1969, 1988. **European Competitions:** *Fairs Cup:* 1963–64, 1969–70 (winners), 1970–71; *European Cup:* 1971–72, 1991–92; *UEFA Cup:* 1978–79, 1981–82, 1982–83; *European Cup-Winners' Cup:* 1979–80 (runners-up), 1993–94 (winners), 1994–95 (runners-up).

Colours: Red shirts with white sleeves, white shorts, red and white hooped stockings. **Change colours:** Navy shirts with teal sleeves, navy shorts, navy and teal hooped stockings.

ARSENAL 1994–95 LEAGUE RECORD

Match No.	*Date*		*Venue*	*Opponents*	*Result*		*H/T Score*	*Lg. Pos.*	*Goalscorers*	*Attendance*
1	Aug	20	H	Manchester C	W	3-0	2-0	—	Campbell, Coton (og), Wright	38,368
2		23	A	Leeds U	L	0-1	0-0	—		34,318
3		28	A	Liverpool	L	0-3	0-3	14		30,017
4		31	H	Blackburn R	D	0-0	0-0	—		37,629
5	Sept	10	A	Norwich C	D	0-0	0-0	12		17,768
6		18	H	Newcastle U	L	2-3	1-2	15	Adams, Wright	36,819
7		25	A	West Ham U	W	2-0	1-0	14	Adams, Wright	18,495
8	Oct	1	H	Crystal Palace	L	1-2	0-2	14	Wright	34,136
9		8	A	Wimbledon	W	3-1	1-0	12	Wright, Smith, Campbell	10,842
10		15	H	Chelsea	W	3-1	1-1	11	Wright 2, Campbell	38,234
11		23	H	Coventry C	W	2-1	2-0	9	Wright 2	31,725
12		29	A	Everton	D	1-1	1-1	10	Schwarz	32,005
13	Nov	6	H	Sheffield W	D	0-0	0-0	10		33,705
14		19	A	Southampton	L	0-1	0-0	11		15,201
15		23	A	Leicester C	L	1-2	1-2	—	Wright (pen)	20,774
16		26	H	Manchester U	D	0-0	0-0	12		38,301
17	Dec	3	A	Nottingham F	D	2-2	0-1	12	Keown, Davis	21,662
18		12	A	Manchester C	W	2-1	2-0	—	Smith, Schwarz	20,500
19		17	H	Leeds U	L	1-3	0-1	11	Linighan	38,100
20		26	H	Aston Villa	D	0-0	0-0	11		34,452
21		28	A	Ipswich T	W	2-0	1-0	9	Wright, Campbell	22,047
22		31	H	QPR	L	1-3	0-1	13	Jensen	32,393
23	Jan	2	A	Tottenham H	L	0-1	0-1	13		28,747
24		14	H	Everton	D	1-1	1-1	13	Wright	34,743
25		21	A	Coventry C	W	1-0	0-0	11	Hartson	14,557
26		24	H	Southampton	D	1-1	1-0	—	Hartson	27,213
27	Feb	4	A	Sheffield W	L	1-3	1-2	11	Linighan	23,468
28		11	H	Leicester C	D	1-1	0-0	12	Merson	31,373
29		21	H	Nottingham F	W	1-0	0-0	—	Kiwomya	35,441
30		25	A	Crystal Palace	W	3-0	2-0	8	Merson, Kiwomya 2	17,063
31	Mar	5	H	West Ham U	L	0-1	0-1	9		36,295
32		8	A	Blackburn R	L	1-3	0-2	—	Morrow	23,452
33		19	A	Newcastle U	L	0-1	0-0	13		35,611
34		22	A	Manchester U	L	0-3	0-2	—		43,623
35	Apr	1	H	Norwich C	W	5-1	3-1	10	Hartson 2, Dixon, Merson, Newman (og)	36,942
36		8	A	QPR	L	1-3	0-1	12	Adams	16,341
37		12	H	Liverpool	L	0-1	0-0	—		38,036
38		15	H	Ipswich T	W	4-1	1-0	10	Merson, Wright 3	36,818
39		17	A	Aston Villa	W	4-0	2-0	10	Hartson 2, Wright 2 (1 pen)	32,005
40		29	H	Tottenham H	D	1-1	0-0	10	Wright (pen)	38,377
41	May	4	H	Wimbledon	D	0-0	0-0	—		32,822
42		14	A	Chelsea	L	1-2	1-1	12	Hartson	29,542

Final League Position: 12

GOALSCORERS

League (52): Wright 18 (3 pens), Hartson 7, Campbell 4, Merson 4, Adams 3, Kiwomya 3, Linighan 2, Schwarz 2, Smith 2, Davis 1, Dixon 1, Jensen 1, Keown 1, Morrow 1, own goals 2.
Coca-Cola Cup (11): Dickov 3, Wright 3, Adams 1, Campbell 1, Merson 1, Morrow 1, Smith 1.
FA Cup (0).

Seaman D.A. 31	Dixon L.M. 39	Winterburn N. 39	Schwarz S. 34	Bould S.A. 30 + 1	Adams T.A. 27	Campbell K.J. 19 + 4	Wright I.E. 30 + 1	Smith A.M. 17 + 2	Merson P.C. 24	Jensen J. 24	Keown M.R. 24 + 7	Dickov P. 4 + 5	Linighan A. 13 + 7	Davis P. 3 + 1	Selley I. 10 + 3	Parlour R. 22 + 8	McGoldrick E.J.P. 9 + 2	Hillier D. 5 + 4	Carter J.W.C. 2 + 1	Morrow S.J. 11 + 4	Bartram V.L. 11	Flatts M. 1 + 2	Shaw P. — + 1	Hughes S.J. 1	Clarke A.J. — + 1	Hartson J. 14 + 1	Kiwomya C.M. 5 + 9	Helder G. 12 + 1	McGowan G.G. 1	*Match No.*
1	2	3	4	5	6	7	8	9	*10*	11	12	14																		1
1	2	3	4	5	6	7	8	9	10	11	12																			2
1	2	3	4		6	7	8	9	*10*	11	5		12	14																3
1	2	3	4		*6*	7	8	9	10	11	5	12	14																	4
1	2	3	4		6	9	8	12			5				7	10	11													5
1	2	3	4		6	12	8	9	10	7	5				14	*11*														6
1	2	3	4		6		8	9	10		5		12	11	7															7
1	2	3	4		6	12	8	9	10				5	11	7															8
1	2	3	4	5	6	10	8	9		7						11		12												9
1	2	3	4	5	6	10	8	9		7	12				14	11														10
1	2	3	4	5		10	8	9			6				7	11	12													11
1		*3*	4		6	8		9	10	7	5		12		14	11	2													12
1		3	4	5	6	12		9			2	10			7	8	11													13
1	2	3	4	5	6	9					10	8			7		11		12											14
1	2	3	4	5		12	8				10	9	6		7				11	14										15
1	2	3		5	6		8	9		7	14	12					11		10	4										16
	2	3	4	5		9					6			10		11		7			1	8	12							17
	2	3	4	5		8		9		7	6					11				10	1									18
	2	3	4	5		8		*9*		7	6		12			11				10	1	14								19
	2	3	4	5		9					6	8				11				10	1	12		7						20
	2	3	4	5		10	*8*	9		7	6	14	12			11					1									21
	2	3	4	5		10	8	9		7	6					11					1				12					22
1	2	3	4	5		9	8	12		7			6		10	11														23
1	2	3	4				8			7	5		6			*11*		10		12						9	14			24
1	2		4	5		7	*8*				11		6			12		10		3						9	14			25
1	2		4	5			8			7	*3*		6			11		14		10						9	12			26
1	2	3			6	8			10	7	12		5		*4*	14										9	11			27
1	2	3			6				10	*4*	12		5		7	14	11									9	8			28
1	2	3	4	5					10	7			6				11										9	8		29
1	2	3	4	5					10	7			6			14	11			*12*							9	8		30
	2	3	4	5			8		10	7			6			11				12	1						14	*9*		31
	2	3	4	14	6		12		10				*5*			11				7	1					9		8		32
	2	3		5	6		8		10	7						12	14			4	1					*9*		11		33
	2	3		5	6		8		10		7					11				4	1						9	12		34
	2	3		5	6		8		10		12							4		7	1					*9*	14	11		35
1	2	3	4	5	6		8		10									14		*7*						9	12	11		36
1		3	4	5	6		8		*10*		7					14	2	11								12		9		37
1	2	3	4	5	6		*8*		10		7					12										9	14	11		38
1	2	3	4	5	6		*8*		10		7					11		12								9	14			39
1	2	3	4	5	6		8		10		7					12										9		11		40
1	2	3			6		8		10	7			5			4										9	12	11		41
1	2			5	6		8		10	7		12	14			4										9		11	*3*	42

Coca-Cola Cup

Second Round	Hartlepool U (a)	5-0
	(h)	2-0
Third Round	Oldham Ath (a)	0-0
	(h)	2-0
Fourth Round	Sheffield W (h)	2-0
Fifth Round	Liverpool (a)	0-1

FA Cup

Third Round	Millwall (a)	0-0
	(h)	0-2

ASTON VILLA 1994–95 *Back row (left to right):* David Farrell, Ugo Ehiogu, Paul McGrath, John Fashanu, Shaun Teale, Andy Townsend, Garry Parker.
Centre row: Jim Walker, Graham Fenton, Guy Whittingham, Nigel Spink, Mark Bosnich, Michael Oakes, Bryan Small, Earl Barrett, Jim Barron.
Front row: Dwight Yorke, Nii Lamptey, Ray Houghton, Kevin Richardson, Ron Atkinson, Dean Saunders, Dalian Atkinson, Phil King, Steve Staunton.
(Photograph: Mike Smith)

FA Premiership ASTON VILLA

Villa Park, Trinity Rd, Birmingham B6 6HE. Telephone: (0121) 327 2299. Fax: (0121) 322 2107. Commercial Dept: (0121) 327 5399. Clubcall: 0891 121148. Ticketline: 0891 121848. Ticket office: (0121) 327 5353. Club shop: (0121) 327 2800.

Ground capacity: 40,310.

Record attendance: 76,588 v Derby Co, FA Cup 6th rd, 2 March 1946.

Record receipts: £1,005,402 Manchester U v Crystal Palace, FA Cup semi-final, 9 April 1995.

Pitch measurements: 115yd × 75yd.

President: H. J. Musgrove. ***Chairman:*** H. D. Ellis.

Directors: J. A. Alderson, Dr D. H. Targett, P. D. Ellis.

Manager: Brian Little. ***Assistant Manager:*** Allan Evans. ***First Team Coach:*** John Gregory.

Secretary: Steven Stride. ***Director of Youth:*** Peter Withe.

Physio: Jim Walker. ***Youth Coach:*** Tony McAndrew. ***Chief Scout:*** Malcolm Beard. ***Fitness Consultant:*** Paul Barron.

Commercial Manager: Abdul Rashid.

Year Formed: 1874. ***Turned Professional:*** 1885. ***Ltd Co.:*** 1896.

Previous Grounds: 1874–76, Aston Park; 1876–97, Perry Barr; 1897, Villa Park.

Club Nickname: 'The Villans'.

Foundation: Cricketing enthusiasts of Villa Cross Wesleyan Chapel, Aston, Birmingham decided to form a football club during the winter of 1873–74. Football clubs were few and far between in the Birmingham area and in their first game against Aston Brook St. Mary's Rugby team they played one half rugby and the other soccer. In 1876 they were joined by a Scottish soccer enthusiast George Ramsay who was immediately appointed captain and went on to lead Aston Villa from obscurity to one of the country's top clubs in a period of less than 10 years.

First Football League game: 8 September, 1888, Football League, v Wolverhampton W, (a) D 1-1 – Warner; Cox, Coulton; Yates, H. Devey, Dawson; A. Brown, Green (1), Allen, Garvey, Hodgetts.

Record League Victory: 12–2 v Accrington S, Division 1, 12 March 1892 – Warner; Evans, Cox; Harry Devey, Jimmy Cowan, Baird; Athersmith (1), Dickson (2), John Devey (4), L. Campbell (4), Hodgetts (1).

Record Cup Victory: 13–0 v Wednesbury Old Ath, FA Cup, 1st rd, 30 October 1886 – Warner; Coulton, Simmonds; Yates, Robertson, Burton (2); R. Davis (1), A. Brown (3), Hunter (3), Loach (2), Hodgetts (2).

Record Defeat: 1–8 v Blackburn R, FA Cup, 3rd rd, 16 February 1889.

Most League Points (2 for a win): 70, Division 3, 1971–72.

Most League Points (3 for a win): 78, Division 2, 1987–88.

Most League Goals: 128, Division 1, 1930–31.

Highest League Scorer in Season: 'Pongo' Waring, 49, Division 1, 1930–31.

Most League Goals in Total Aggregate: Harry Hampton, 215, 1904–15.

Most Capped Player: Paul McGrath, 45 (76), Republic of Ireland.

Most League Appearances: Charlie Aitken, 561, 1961–76.

Record Transfer Fee Received: £5,500,000 from Bari for David Platt, August 1991.

Record Transfer Fee Paid: £3,500,000 to Partizan Belgrade for Savo Milosevic, June 1995.

Football League Record: 1888 Founder Member of the League; 1936–38 Division 2; 1938–59 Division 1; 1959–60 Division 2; 1960–67 Division 1; 1967–70 Division 2; 1970–72 Division 3; 1972–75 Division 2; 1975–87 Division 1; 1987–88 Division 2; 1988–92 Division 1; 1992– FA Premier League.

Honours: *FA Premier League:* – Runners-up 1992–93. *Football League:* Division 1 – Champions 1893–94, 1895–96, 1896–97, 1898–99, 1899–1900, 1909–10, 1980–81; Runners-up 1888–89, 1902–03, 1907–08, 1910–11, 1912–13, 1913–14, 1930–31; 1932–33, 1989–90; Division 2 – Champions 1937–38, 1959–60; Runners-up 1974–75, 1987–88; Division 3 – Champions 1971–72. *FA Cup:* Winners 1887, 1895, 1897, 1905, 1913, 1920, 1957; Runners-up 1892, 1924. *Double Performed:* 1896–97. *Football League Cup:* Winners 1961, 1975, 1977, 1994; Runners-up 1963, 1971. **European Competitions:** *European Cup:* 1981–82 (winners), 1982–83; *UEFA Cup:* 1975–76, 1977–78, 1983–84, 1990–91, 1993–94, 1994–95. *World Club Championship:* 1982; European Super Cup: 1982–83 (winners).

Colours: Claret body, sky blue sleeves, sky blue collar with trim, white shorts, claret stockings with sky blue top. **Change colours:** Dark blue body, sky blue trim & collar, sky blue shorts, dark blue stockings, sky blue top.

ASTON VILLA F.C.

PREPARED

ASTON VILLA 1994–95 LEAGUE RECORD

Match No.	Date		Venue	Opponents	Result		H/T Score	Lg. Pos.	Goalscorers	Attendance
1	Aug	20	A	Everton	D	2-2	0-1	—	Fashanu, Saunders	35,552
2		24	H	Southampton	D	1-1	1-0	—	Saunders	24,179
3		27	H	Crystal Palace	D	1-1	0-0	12	Staunton	23,305
4		29	A	Coventry C	W	1-0	1-0	—	Yorke	12,218
5	Sept	10	H	Ipswich T	W	2-0	1-0	9	Staunton, Saunders	22,241
6		17	A	West Ham U	L	0-1	0-0	8		18,326
7		24	A	Blackburn R	L	1-3	0-1	9	Ehiogu	22,694
8	Oct	1	H	Newcastle U	L	0-2	0-0	12		29,960
9		8	A	Liverpool	L	2-3	1-2	14	Whittingham, Staunton	32,158
10		15	H	Norwich C	D	1-1	0-0	16	Saunders	22,468
11		22	H	Nottingham F	L	0-2	0-1	16		29,217
12		29	A	QPR	L	0-2	0-1	19		16,073
13	Nov	6	H	Manchester U	L	1-2	1-1	19	Atkinson	32,136
14		9	A	Wimbledon	L	3-4	2-1	—	Parker, Saunders 2	6221
15		19	A	Tottenham H	W	4-3	3-1	19	Atkinson, Fenton 2, Saunders	26,899
16		27	H	Sheffield W	D	1-1	1-0	19	Atkinson	25,082
17	Dec	3	A	Leicester C	D	1-1	0-1	19	Whittingham	20,896
18		10	H	Everton	D	0-0	0-0	20		29,678
19		19	A	Southampton	L	1-2	0-1	—	Houghton	13,874
20		26	A	Arsenal	D	0-0	0-0	20		34,452
21		28	H	Chelsea	W	3-0	2-0	19	Sinclair (og), Yorke, Taylor	32,901
22		31	A	Manchester C	D	2-2	0-1	20	Brightwell I (og), Saunders	22,513
23	Jan	2	H	Leeds U	D	0-0	0-0	19		35,038
24		14	H	QPR	W	2-1	1-0	18	Fashanu, Ehiogu	26,578
25		21	A	Nottingham F	W	2-1	1-0	14	Fashanu, Saunders	24,598
26		25	H	Tottenham H	W	1-0	1-0	—	Saunders	40,017
27	Feb	4	A	Manchester U	L	0-1	0-1	14		43,795
28		11	H	Wimbledon	W	7-1	4-1	11	Reeves (og), Johnson 3, Saunders 2 (1 pen), Yorke	23,982
29		18	A	Sheffield W	W	2-1	2-0	9	Saunders 2	24,063
30		22	H	Leicester C	D	4-4	2-0	—	Saunders, Staunton, Yorke, Johnson	30,825
31		25	A	Newcastle U	L	1-3	1-1	11	Townsend	34,637
32	Mar	4	H	Blackburn R	L	0-1	0-1	11		40,114
33		6	H	Coventry C	D	0-0	0-0	—		26,186
34		18	H	West Ham U	L	0-2	0-1	15		28,682
35	Apr	1	A	Ipswich T	W	1-0	0-0	13	Swailes (og)	15,895
36		4	A	Crystal Palace	D	0-0	0-0	—		12,949
37		15	A	Chelsea	L	0-1	0-1	16		17,015
38		17	H	Arsenal	L	0-4	0-2	16		32,005
39		29	A	Leeds U	L	0-1	0-0	18		32,973
40	May	3	H	Manchester C	D	1-1	1-0	—	Ehiogu	30,133
41		6	H	Liverpool	W	2-0	2-0	15	Yorke 2	40,154
42		14	A	Norwich C	D	1-1	1-0	18	Staunton	19,374

Final League Position: 18

GOALSCORERS

League (51): Saunders 15 (1 pen), Yorke 6, Staunton 5, Johnson 4, Atkinson 3, Ehiogu 3, Fashanu 3, Fenton 2, Whittingham 2, Houghton 1, Parker 1, Taylor 1, Townsend 1, own goals 4.
Coca-Cola Cup (10): Atkinson 3, Lamptey 3, Saunders 1, Townsend 1, Whittingham 1, Yorke 1.
FA Cup (2): Saunders 1, Yorke 1.

Bosnich M.J. 30	Richardson K. 18 + 1	Staunton S. 34 + 1	Townsend A.D. 32	McGrath P. 36 + 4	Ehiogu U. 38 + 1	Houghton R.J. 19 + 7	Fashanu J. 11 + 2	Saunders D.N. 39	Parker G.S. 12 + 2	Yorke D. 33 + 4	King P.G. 13 + 3	Atkinson D.R. 11 + 5	Barrett E.D. 24 + 1	Spink N.P. 12 + 1	Teale S. 28	Lamptey N. 1 + 5	Fenton G.A. 7 + 10	Whittingham G. 4 + 3	Small B. 5	Boden C.D. — + 1	Taylor I.K. 22	Johnson T. 11 + 3	Charles G.A. 14 + 2	Carr F.A. — + 2	Wright A. 8	*Match No.*
1	2	3	4	5	6	7	8	9	10	11	12															1
1	2		4	5	6	7	8	9	*10*	11	3	12	14													2
1	6	3	11	5	4	7	8	9		12		10	2													3
1	6	11	10	5	4		8	9		7	3		2													4
	6	11	10	5	4		8	9		7	3	12	2	1												5
1	6	3	10		5	7	8	9		11		12	2		4											6
1	6	3	8	5	7			9		11		10	2		4	*12*	14									7
		12	8	5	4	7			6	11	3		2	1		14	*9*	10								8
1		3	8	5	4	7		9	6	11	12		2			14		10								9
1	6	11		5	4	12		9	8	7	3	*10*	2					14								10
		6	8	5	4	7		9	12	11	*3*		2	1			10	14								11
1	6	3	8	5	4			9	11	7			2			10	12									12
	6	11	8	5	4	7		9	14	12	3	10	2	1												13
1	12		8	5	4	7		*9*	6	11	3	10	2				14									14
1	6			5	4	7		9	8		3	10	2			12	11									15
1	6			5	4	7		9	8		3	10	2				11	12								16
				12	5	7		9	6		*11*		2	1	4		8	10	3	14						17
	6				5	7			8		11		2	1	4	12	9	10	3							18
	6			5		7	8	9	10	12	11		2	1	4				3							19
	6	3	10	12	5	7	8	9					2	1	4						11					20
	6	3	8	12	5	7		9		11			2	1	4						10					21
	6	*3*	8	12	5	7	14	9		11			2	1	4						10					22
	6	3		5	8	7	12	9		11			2	1	4						10					23
1		3		5	6	12	8	9		7			2		4						10	11				24
1		3		5	6	12	8	9		7			2		4						10	*11*	14			25
1		3	8	5	6	12		9		7			2		4						10	11	14			26
1		6	11	5		12	*8*	9		7					4				3		10	14	2			27
1		6	11	5				9		7					4				3		10	8	2			28
1		6	11	5	4			9		7					3						10	8	2			29
1		6	11	5	4			9		*7*		12			3						10	8	2	14		30
1		6	11	5	4			9		7		12			3						10	8	2			31
1		6	11	5	4	12		9		7					3		14				10	*8*	2			32
1		6		5	4	7		9		11					3		12				10	8	2	14		33
1		6	11	5	14	12		9		*7*					4						10	8	2		3	34
1		11	7	5	6			9		12		*8*			4		14				10		2		3	35
1		11	8	5	6					7		9			4		12				10		2		3	36
1		6	11	5	2			9		7		*8*			4		12				10	14			3	37
1		3	11	5	2			9		7		10			4						6	8				38
1		11	8	5	6			9		7				15	4		12				10		2		3	39
1		11	8	5	6			9		7					4						10		2		3	40
1		11	8	5	6			9		7					4		12				10		2		3	41
		11	8	5	6			*9*		7	12			1	4		10					14	2		3	42

Coca-Cola Cup

Second Round	Wigan Ath (h)	5-0
	(a)	3-0
Third Round	Middlesbrough (h)	1-0
Fourth Round	Crystal Palace (a)	1-4

FA Cup

Third Round	Barnsley (a)	2-0
Fourth Round	Manchester C (a)	0-1

BARNET 1994–95 *Back row (left to right):* Shaun Gale, Mark Cooper, Carl Hoddle, Alan Walker, Tim Alexander, Lee Hodges, Linvoy Primus, Geoff Cooper.
Centre row: Terry Bullivant (Coach), Laird Budge (Kit Manager), Gary Smith, Mark Newson, Paul Newell, Gary Phillips, Dougie Freedman, David McDonald, Barry Frankham (Physio).
Front row: Micky Tomlinson, Terry Gibson, Peter Scott, Ray Clemence (Manager), Paul Wilson, Robert Mutchell, Louis Affor.

Division 3 **BARNET**

Underhill Stadium, Barnet Lane, Barnet, Herts EN5 2BE. Telephone: (0181) 441 6932. Fax: (0181)447 0655. Credit Card Bookings: (0181)441 1677.

Ground capacity: 3924.

Record attendance: 11,026 v Wycombe Wanderers. FA Amateur Cup 4th Round 1951–52.

Record Receipts: £31,202 v Portsmouth FA Cup 3rd Round 5th January 1991.

Pitch measurements: 112yd × 72yd.

Chairman: A. Kleanthous. ***Vice-Chairman:*** D. J. Buchler FCA. ***Chief Executive:*** D. B. Edwards OBE.

Directors: S. Glynne, F. Higgins FCA.

Manager: Ray Clemence MBE. ***Player-Manager:*** Gary Phillips. ***Physio:*** David Mott.

Coach: Terry Bullivant. ***Secretary:*** Miss P. J. Sawford. ***Sales and Commercial Manager:*** Brian Wheeler. ***Marketing Manager:*** Tessa Bills.

Year Formed: 1888. ***Turned Professional:*** 1965. ***Ltd Co:***

Club Nickname: The Bees.

Previous Names: 1906–19 Barnet Alston FC.

Previous Grounds: Queens Road (1888–1901) Totteridge Lane (1901–07).

Foundation: Barnet Football Club was formed in 1888, disbanded in 1901. A club known as Alston Works FC was then formed and in 1906 changed its name to Barnet Alston FC. In 1912 it combined with The Avenue to become Barnet and Alston.

First Football League game: 17 August, 1991, Division 4, v Crewe Alex (h) L 4-7 – Phillips; Blackford, Cooper (Murphy), Horton, Bodley (Stein), Johnson, Showler, Carter (2), Bull (2), Lowe, Evans.

Record League Victory: 6–0 v Lincoln C (away), Division 4, 4 September 1991 – Pape; Poole, Naylor, Bodley, Howell, Evans (1), Willis (1), Murphy (1), Bull (2), Lowe, Showler (1 og).

Record Defeat: 1–5 v York C, Division 3, 13 March 1993.

Most League Points (3 for a win): 79, Division 3, 1992–93.

Most League Goals: 81, Division 4, 1991–92.

Highest League Scorer in Season: Gary Bull, 20, Division 4, 1991–92.

Most League Goals in Total Aggregate: Gary Bull 37, 1991–93.

Most League Appearances: Gary Phillips, 117, 1991–95.

Record Transfer Fee Received: £350,000 from Wimbledon for Andy Clarke, February 1991.

Record Transfer Fee Paid: £40,000 to Barrow for Kenny Lowe, January 1991 and £40,000 to Runcorn for Mark Carter, February 1991.

Football League Record: Promoted to Division 4 from GMVC 1991; 1991–92 Division 4; 1992–93 Division 3; 1993–94 Division 2; 1994– Division 3.

Honours: *Football League:* best season 24th, Division 2, 1993–94. *FA Amateur Cup:* Winners 1946. *GM Vauxhall Conference:* Winners 1990–91. *FA Cup:* best season; never past 3rd rd. *League Cup:* never past 2nd rd.

Colours: Amber and black striped shirts, black shorts, black stockings. **Change colours:** Green and white striped shirts, green shorts, green stockings.

BARNET 1994–95 LEAGUE RECORD

Match No.	Date	Venue	Opponents	Result	H/T Score	Lg. Pos.	Goalscorers	Attendance
1	Aug 13	H	Scunthorpe U	L 1-2	0-2	—	Cooper	2208
2	20	A	Scarborough	W 1-0	0-0	14	Cooper	1471
3	27	H	Preston NE	W 2-1	0-0	7	Freedman, Hodges	2441
4	30	A	Hartlepool U	W 1-0	1-0	—	Freedman	2095
5	Sept 3	A	Wigan Ath	W 2-1	1-1	3	Cooper, Wilson (pen)	1438
6	10	H	Doncaster R	D 0-0	0-0	5		2625
7	13	H	Rochdale	W 6-2	4-1	—	Freedman 4, Cooper, Gale	1688
8	17	A	Scunthorpe U	L 0-1	0-0	3		2481
9	24	A	Torquay U	W 2-1	2-0	3	Newson, Hodges	3280
10	Oct 1	H	Fulham	D 0-0	0-0	3		3579
11	8	H	Hereford U	D 2-2	1-1	3	Newson, Hodges	2116
12	15	A	Northampton T	D 1-1	0-0	4	Freedman	7461
13	22	A	Carlisle U	L 0-4	0-1	5		6155
14	29	H	Chesterfield	W 4-1	2-1	4	Freedman 2, McMahon, Dyche (og)	2130
15	Nov 5	A	Lincoln C	W 2-1	1-1	4	Cooper, Freedman	2741
16	19	H	Bury	D 1-1	1-0	4	McMahon	3006
17	26	A	Darlington	W 1-0	0-0	4	Gregan (og)	2157
18	Dec 10	H	Scarborough	W 3-1	0-0	4	Wilson (pen), Cooper, Freedman	1988
19	17	A	Preston NE	L 0-1	0-0	4		6429
20	26	A	Walsall	L 0-4	0-2	5		5392
21	27	H	Gillingham	W 1-0	0-0	4	Freedman	3074
22	31	A	Mansfield T	L 0-3	0-1	4		2891
23	Jan 14	A	Colchester U	D 1-1	1-0	6	Hodges	3706
24	24	H	Carlisle U	L 0-2	0-0	—		2413
25	Feb 4	H	Darlington	L 2-3	0-2	10	Walker, Cooper	2034
26	14	A	Chesterfield	L 0-2	0-0	—		2978
27	18	H	Colchester U	L 0-1	0-1	11		2242
28	25	A	Fulham	L 0-4	0-3	12		6195
29	28	H	Exeter C	D 1-1	1-0	—	Gibson	1325
30	Mar 4	H	Torquay U	W 2-0	1-0	11	Freedman, Gale	1816
31	11	A	Doncaster R	D 1-1	0-0	12	Freedman	1979
32	14	A	Bury	L 0-3	0-3	—		2380
33	18	H	Hartlepool U	W 4-0	1-0	10	Freedman 3, Tomlinson	1557
34	25	H	Wigan Ath	D 1-1	1-1	11	Freedman	2362
35	Apr 1	A	Rochdale	D 2-2	1-1	11	Freedman 2	1834
36	4	H	Lincoln C	W 2-1	1-1	—	Freedman, Wilson (pen)	1616
37	8	H	Mansfield T	D 2-2	1-1	9	Cooper 2	2115
38	15	A	Gillingham	L 1-2	1-2	10	Freedman	3448
39	17	H	Walsall	L 1-3	1-2	11	Inglethorpe	2078
40	22	A	Exeter C	W 2-1	1-0	11	Inglethorpe, Cooper	1903
41	29	H	Northampton T	L 2-3	1-2	11	Freedman, Inglethorpe	2796
42	May 6	A	Hereford U	L 2-3	1-3	11	Cooper, Freedman	2069

Final League Position: 11

GOALSCORERS

League (56): Freedman 24, Cooper M 11, Hodges 4, Inglethorpe 3, Wilson 3 (3 pens), Gale 2, McMahon 2, Newson 2, Gibson 1, Tomlinson 1, Walker 1, own goals 2.
Coca-Cola Cup (7): Freedman 5, Cooper M 2.
FA Cup (4): Cooper 2, Hodges 1, McMahon 1.

Phillips G.C. 27	McDonald D.H. 35	Gale S.M. 25 + 2	Hoddle C. 26 + 4	Walker A. 21	Newson M.J. 29 + 1	Tomlinson M.L. 21 + 6	Freedman D.A. 42	Hodges L.L. 32 + 2	Cooper M.D. 32 + 2	Wilson P.R. 35 + 1	Scott P.R. 23 + 5	Primus L.S. 39	Alexander T.M. 2 + 2	Haynes J.L.A. 2 + 4	Carmichael M. 2 + 1	Mutchell R.D. 7 + 1	McMahon G.J. 10	Newell P.C. 15	Hamlet A.G. 3	Smith G.N. 3 + 1	Adams K.C. 2 + 2	Gibson T.B. 4 + 8	Watson K.E. 13	Inglethorpe A.M. 5 + 1	Thomas G.A. 6 + 1	Brady M.J. — + 1	Cooper G.V. 1	*Match No.*
1	2	3	4	5	6	7	8	9	10	11	12																	1
1	2	3	4	5		7	8	9	10	11	12	6																2
1	2	3	4	5		7	8	9	10	11		6																3
1	2	3	4	5		7	8	9	10	11	12	*6*	14															4
1	2	3	4	*5*		7	8	9	10	11	12	6	14															5
1	2	3	4			7	8	9	10	11		6	5															6
1	2	3	4			7	8	9	10	11	12	6	5	14														7
1	2	3	4	5	12		8	9		11	10	6		7														8
1	2	3	4		5		8	9		11	7	6		12	10													9
1	2	3	4		5	12	8	9		11	10	6			7													10
1	2		4		5	7	8	9	12	11	10	6				3												11
1	2	3	*4*		5	7	8	9	10	11		6		12	14													12
1	2	3	4		5	12	8	9	10	11		6					7											13
1	2		4	3	5		8	9	10		11	6					7											14
1			4	2	5		8	9	10		11	6				3	7											15
1	2		4	3	5		8		10	9	11	6				12	7											16
	2		4	5		10	8			9	11	6		12		3	7	1										17
	2		4	3	5		8		10	9	11	6					7	1										18
	2		4	3	5		8	12	10	9	11	6					7	1										19
	2		*4*	3	5	14	8	9	10	12	11	6					7	1										20
	2				5	12	8	4	10	9	11	6				3	7	1										21
						12	8	4		9		6		11		*3*	7	1	2	10	14						5	22
			4	5		7	8	9		11		6				3		1	2	10								23
	2		4	5		7	8	9	10	11		6				3		1				12						24
	2		4	5		7	8	9	10	11	3	6						1				12						25
	2		4	5		7	8	9	10	11	3	6						1				12						26
1	2	14		5	3	7	8	9	10		*11*	6										12	4					27
1	2	7	11	5	3		8	9	10			6											4					28
1	2	3			5		8	9	10	11		6										7	4					29
1	2	3	12		5		*8*	9	14	11	10	6										7	4					30
1		3		2	5	12	8	9		11	10	6										7	4					31
1		3		5	2	7	8			10	11	6								12		9	4					32
1	2	3	12		5	9	*8*		10	11		6								7	14		4					33
1	2	3	7		5	9	8		10	11		6											4	12				34
1	2	3			5	9	8		10	11	7	6										12	4					35
1	2	*3*			5	7	8		10	11	9	6										12	4		14			36
1	2	3			5	7	8	12	10	11		6										14	9		4			37
		2	12		5		8	9	10	11		6						1					4	7	3			38
	2	3			5		8	9	10		11							1				12	4	7	6			39
	2	3	12		5		8	9	10		11							1			4			7	6			40
	2	12			5		8	9	10	3	11	4						1						7	6			41
					5		8	9	10	11		6						1	2		4			7	3	12		42

Coca-Cola Cup

First Round	Leyton Orient (h)	4-0
	(a)	1-1
Second Round	Manchester C (h)	1-0
	(a)	1-4

FA Cup

First Round	Woking (h)	4-4
	(a)	0-1

BARNSLEY 1994–95 *Back row (left to right):* Chris Jackson, Richard Hanby, Steve Davis, Lee Butler, Dean Fearon, Gerry Taggart, Dave Watson, Adrian Moses, Andy Rammell, Glynn Hurst.
Centre row: Malcolm Shotton (Reserve Team Coach), Eric Winstanley (First Team Coach), Darren Field, Gary Fleming, Andy Payton, Andy Liddell, Nicky Eaden, Mark Burton, Troy Bennett, David Brooke, Simon Bochenski, Scott Jones, Norman Rimmington (Kit Manager), Steve Stafford (Physio).
Front row: Glynn Snodin, Martin Bullock, Brendan O'Connell, Danny Wilson (Player/Manager), Neil Redfearn, Darren Sheridan, Owen Archdeacon, Mark Feeney.

Division 1 **BARNSLEY**

Oakwell Ground, Grove St, Barnsley, South Yorkshire S71 1ET. Telephone:(01226) 295353. Fax: (01226) 201000. Clubcall: 0891 121152. Commercial Office: (01226) 286718.

Ground capacity: 19,101.

Record attendance: 40,255 v Stoke C, FA Cup 5th rd, 15 February 1936.

Record receipts: Not disclosed.

Pitch measurements: 110yd × 75yd.

President: Arthur Raynor. ***Chairman:*** J. A. Dennis.

Directors: C. B. Taylor (Vice-Chairman), C. H. Harrison, M. R. Hayselden, J. N. Kelly, S. M. Hall, I. D. Potter.

Player-Manager: Danny Wilson.

First Team Coach: Eric Winstanley. ***Physio:*** Stephen Redmond.

General Manager/Secretary: Michael Spinks. ***Lotteries Manager:*** Gerry Whewall. ***Marketing Manager:*** Ian Davies.

Year Formed: 1887. ***Turned Professional:*** 1888. ***Ltd Co.:*** 1899.

Previous Name: Barnsley St Peter's, 1887–97.

Club Nickname: 'The Tykes', 'Reds' or 'Colliers'.

Foundation: Many clubs owe their inception to the church and Barnsley are among them, for they were formed in 1887 by the Rev. T. T. Preedy, curate of Barnsley St. Peter's and went under that name until it was dropped in 1897 a year before being admitted to the Second Division of the Football League.

First Football League game: 1 September, 1898, Division 2, v Lincoln C (a) L 0-1 – Fawcett; McArtney, Nixon; King, Burleigh, Porteous; Davis, Lees, Murray, McCullough, McGee.

Record League Victory: 9–0 v Loughborough T, Division 2, 28 January 1899 – Greaves; McCartney, Nixon; Porteous, Burleigh, Howard; Davis (4), Hepworth (1), Lees (1), McCullough (1), Jones (2). 9–0 v Accrington S, Division 3 (N), 3 February 1934 – Ellis; Cookson, Shotton; Harper, Henderson, Whitworth; Spence (2), Smith (1), Blight (4), Andrews (1), Ashton (1).

Record Cup Victory: 6–0 v Blackpool, FA Cup, 1st rd replay, 20 January 1910 – Mearns; Downs, Ness; Glendinning, Boyle (1), Utley; Bartrop, Gadsby (1), Lillycrop (2), Tufnell (2), Forman. 6–0 v Peterborough U, League Cup, 1st rd, 2nd leg, 15 September 1981 – Horn; Joyce, Chambers, Glavin (2), Banks, McCarthy, Evans, Parker (2), Aylott (1), McHale, Barrowclough (1).

Record Defeat: 0–9 v Notts Co, Division 2, 19 November 1927.

Most League Points (2 for a win): 67, Division 3 (N), 1938–39.

Most League Points (3 for a win): 74, Division 2, 1988–89.

Most League Goals: 118, Division 3 (N), 1933–34.

Highest League Scorer in Season: Cecil McCormack, 33, Division 2, 1950–51.

Most League Goals in Total Aggregate: Ernest Hine, 123, 1921–26 and 1934–38.

Most Capped Player: Gerry Taggart, 35, Northern Ireland.

Most League Appearances: Barry Murphy, 514, 1962–78.

Record Transfer Fee Received: £1,500,000 from Nottingham F for Carl Tiler, May 1991.

Record Transfer Fee Paid: £310,000 to Celtic for Andy Payton, November 1993.

Football League Record: 1898 Elected to Division 2; 1932–34 Division 3 (N); 1934–38 Division 2; 1938–39 Division 3 (N); 1946–53 Division 2; 1953–55 Division 3 (N); 1955–59 Division 2; 1959–65 Division 3; 1965–68 Division 4; 1968–72 Division 3; 1972–79 Division 4; 1979–81 Division 3; 1981–92 Division 2; 1992– Division 1.

Honours: *Football League:* best season: 3rd, Division 2, 1914–15, 1921–22; Division 3 (N) – Champions 1933–34, 1938–39, 1954–55; Runners-up 1953–54; Division 3 – Runners-up 1980–81; Division 4 – Runners-up 1967–68; Promoted 1978–79. *FA Cup:* Winners 1912; Runners-up 1910. *Football League Cup:* best season: 5th rd, 1982.

Colours: Red shirts, white shorts, red stockings. **Change colours:** Navy and turquoise striped shirts, black shorts, black stockings.

BARNSLEY 1994–95 LEAGUE RECORD

Match No.	*Date*		*Venue*	*Opponents*	*Result*		*H/T Score*	*Lg. Pos.*	*Goalscorers*	*Attendance*
1	Aug	13	H	Derby Co	W	2-1	2-1	—	Rammell 2	8737
2		20	A	Charlton Ath	D	2-2	0-0	3	Payton, Davis	8171
3		27	H	Reading	L	0-2	0-1	11		4771
4		30	A	Port Vale	L	1-2	0-1	—	O'Connell	7228
5	Sept	3	A	Burnley	W	1-0	0-0	10	Payton	11,968
6		10	H	Watford	D	0-0	0-0	12		4251
7		13	H	Notts Co	D	1-1	0-0	—	Rammell	3928
8		17	A	Sunderland	L	0-2	0-0	18		16,145
9		24	A	Oldham Ath	L	0-1	0-0	21		7941
10	Oct	1	H	Swindon T	W	2-1	1-0	18	Redfearn 2	3911
11		8	H	Southend U	D	0-0	0-0	19		3659
12		16	A	Sheffield U	D	0-0	0-0	20		12,317
13		22	H	WBA	W	2-0	1-0	16	O'Connell, Redfearn	5082
14		29	A	Luton T	W	1-0	0-0	9	Rammell	7212
15	Nov	1	A	Tranmere R	L	1-6	0-2	—	Rammell	5592
16		5	H	Stoke C	W	2-0	1-0	7	O'Connell, Sheridan	5117
17		19	A	Millwall	W	1-0	1-0	9	Liddell	7040
18		26	H	Bolton W	W	3-0	2-0	6	Eaden, Davis, Redfearn	8507
19	Dec	3	A	WBA	L	1-2	0-1	9	Jackson	13,921
20		7	H	Bristol C	W	2-1	1-1	—	Liddell, Archdeacon	4305
21		10	H	Charlton Ath	W	2-1	1-0	5	Redfearn, Liddell	5465
22		17	A	Derby Co	L	0-1	0-0	6		13,205
23		26	H	Grimsby T	W	4-1	2-1	3	Payton 3, Liddell	8669
24		27	A	Portsmouth	L	0-3	0-3	4		6751
25		31	H	Wolverhampton W	L	1-3	1-2	7	Redfearn (pen)	9207
26	Jan	14	H	Luton T	W	3-1	0-0	6	Redfearn, Liddell 2	4808
27	Feb	4	A	Bristol C	L	2-3	0-0	9	Rammell, Wilson	6408
28		11	H	Tranmere R	D	2-2	1-1	9	Rammell, Redfearn	5506
29		18	A	Bolton W	L	1-2	0-2	10	Liddell	12,463
30		21	H	Millwall	W	4-1	1-0	—	Redfearn 2, Payton 2	4733
31		25	A	Swindon T	D	0-0	0-0	9		8158
32	Mar	7	H	Burnley	W	2-0	1-0	—	Taggart, Payton	5537
33		11	A	Reading	W	3-0	1-0	7	O'Connell, Taggart, Payton	7556
34		14	A	Middlesbrough	D	1-1	0-1	—	Payton	19,655
35		18	H	Port Vale	W	3-1	2-0	7	Liddell 2, Sheridan	6878
36		21	A	Watford	L	2-3	0-1	—	Liddell 2	6883
37		24	H	Sunderland	W	2-0	0-0	—	Shotton, Payton	7803
38	Apr	1	A	Notts Co	W	3-1	1-1	7	O'Connell, Wilson, Liddell	6834
39		8	A	Wolverhampton W	D	0-0	0-0	6		26,385
40		12	A	Stoke C	D	0-0	0-0	—		10,752
41		15	H	Portsmouth	W	1-0	0-0	5	Payton	6825
42		17	A	Grimsby T	L	0-1	0-1	6		7277
43		22	H	Middlesbrough	D	1-1	0-1	6	Liddell	11,711
44		29	H	Sheffield U	W	2-1	1-1	6	O'Connell 2	10,844
45	May	2	H	Oldham Ath	D	1-1	1-1	—	Taggart	9838
46		7	A	Southend U	L	1-3	0-1	6	Redfearn	6425

Final League Position: 6

GOALSCORERS

League (63): Liddell 13, Payton 12, Redfearn 11 (1 pen), O'Connell 7, Rammell 7, Taggart 3, Davis 2, Sheridan 2, Wilson 2, Archdeacon 1, Eaden 1, Jackson 1, Shotton 1.
Coca-Cola Cup (3): Redfearn 2, Taggart 1.
FA Cup (0).

Watson D.N. 37	Eaden N.J. 44 + 1	Fleming J.G. 46	Wilson D.J. 34	Taggart G.P. 41	Bishop D.C. 7 + 1	O'Connell B. 44 + 1	Redfearn N.D. 37 + 2	Rammell A.V. 17 + 7	Payton A.P. 38 + 5	Snodin G. 11 + 3	Davis S.P. 34 + 2	Liddell A.M. 31 + 8	Bullock M.J. 17 + 12	Jackson C.D. 7 + 1	Sheridan D.S. 35	Archdeacon O.D. 6 + 3	Butler L.S. 9	Moses A.P. 3 + 1	Shotton M. 8	Hurst G. — + 2	*Match No.*
1	2	3	4	5	6	7	8	9	10	11											1
1	2	3	4	5	6	7	8	9	10	11	12										2
1	2	3	4	5		7	8	9	10	11	6	12	14								3
1	2	*3*	4	5	6	7	8	9	10	11	12		14								4
1	2	3	4	5		7	8	9	10	11	6										5
1	2	3	4	5		7	8	9	10	11	6	12									6
1	2	3	4	5		7	8	9	10	11	6	12									7
1		3	4	5	2	7	8	9	10	11	6	12									8
1	14	3	4	5	*2*	7	8	9	10	11	6	12									9
1	2	3	4	5	6		8		10	11		7	12	9							10
1	2	3	4	5		7	8	12	10		6	14		9	11						11
1	2	3	4	5		7	8	9	10		6				11						12
1	2	3	4	5		7	8	9	10		6				11						13
1	2	3	4	5		7	8	9	10		6				11						14
1	2	3	4	5		7	8	9	*10*		6	12			11	14					15
1	2	3	4	5		7	8				6	10		9	11						16
	2	3	*4*	5		7	8		12		6	10		9	11	14	1				17
	2	3		5		7	8		12		6	10		9	11	4	1				18
	2	3		5		7	8		14		6	10	12	9	11	4	1				19
	2	3		5		7	8		14		6	10	12	*9*	11	4	1				20
	2	3		5		7	8		9		6	10			11	4	1				21
	2	3		5		7	8		9		6	10	12		11	4	1				22
	2	3		5		7	8		9		6	10	4		11		1				23
	2	3		*5*	14	7	8	12	9		6	10	4		11		1				24
	2	3			5	7	8	12	9		6	10	4		11		1				25
1	2	3	4			7	8	9			6	10			11			5			26
1	2	3	4			7	8	9				10	12		11			5	6		27
1	2	3	4	5		7	8	9	14			*10*	12		11				6		28
1	2	*3*	4	5		7	8		9	14	6	10	12		11						29
1	2	3	4	5		7	*8*		9	14	6	10	12		11						30
1	2	3	4	5		7	8		9		6	10	12		11						31
1	2	3	4	5		7	*8*		9	14	6	10	12		11						32
1	2	3	4	5		7			9		6	10	8		11						33
1	2	3	4	5		7			9		6	10	8		11	12					34
1	2	3	4	5		7		12	9			10	8		11	*6*		14			35
1	2	3	4	5		7		12	9			10	8		11			6			36
1	2	3	4	5		7			9			10	8		11				6		37
1	2	3	4	5		7			9			10	8		11				6		38
1	2	3	4	5		7	12		9			10	8		11				6		39
1	2	3	4	5		7		12	9			10	8		11				6		40
1	2	3	4	5		7	12		9	11	6	10	8								41
1	2	3		5		7	4	12	9		6	10	8		11						42
1	2	3				7	4		9		6	10	8		11				5	12	43
1	2	3				7	4		9		6	10	8		11				5		44
1	2	3		5		7	8		9		6	*10*	4	12	11					14	45
1	2	3	*4*	5		12	8	10	9		6	14	7		11						46

Coca-Cola Cup

First Round	Darlington (a)		2-2
		(h)	0-0
Second Round	Newcastle U (a)		1-2
		(h)	0-1

FA Cup

Third Round	Aston Villa (h)	0-2

BIRMINGHAM CITY 1994–95 *Back row (left to right):* Neil McDairmid (Physio), Danny Wallace, Paul Tait, Kenny Lowe, Miguel De Souza, Steve McGavin, Chris Whyte, Peter Shearer, Paul Harding, Richard Scott, Lil Fuccillo (Chief Scout).
Centre row: Kevan Broadhurst (Coach), Andy Saville, Dave Barnett, Dave Regis, Ian Bennett, Richard Dryden, Liam Daish, Harry Willis, David Howell (Coach).
Front row: Jose Dominguez, Louie Donowa, Gary Cooper, John Frain, Mark Ward (Player Coach), Barry Fry (Manager), Edwin Stein (Assistant Manager), Scott Hiley, Steve Claridge, Paul Moulden, Neil Doherty.

Division 1 BIRMINGHAM CITY

St Andrews, Birmingham B9 4NH. Telephone: (0121) 772 0101. Fax: (0121) 766 7866. Lottery Office/Souvenir Shop: (0121) 772 1245. Clubcall: 0891 121188. Club Soccer Shop: (0121) 766 8274.

Ground capacity: 25,936.

Record attendance: 66,844 v Everton, FA Cup 5th rd, 11 February 1939.

Record receipts: £230,000 v Aston Villa, Coca Cola Cup 2nd rd 1st leg, 21 September 1993.

Pitch measurements: 115yd × 75yd.

Directors: J. F. Wiseman (Chairman), K. R. Brady (Managing Director), D. Sullivan, D. Gold, R. Gold, B. Gold, H. Brandman, A. G. Jones.

Manager: Barry Fry. ***Assistant Manager:*** Edwin Stein. ***Coach:*** David Howell. ***Physio:*** N. McDiarmid. ***Commercial Manager:*** Allan Robson.

Secretary: A. G. Jones BA, MBA.

Year Formed: 1875. ***Turned Professional:*** 1885. ***Ltd Co.:*** 1888.

Previous Names: 1875–88, Small Heath Alliance; 1888, dropped 'Alliance'; became Birmingham 1905; became Birmingham City 1945.

Club Nickname: 'Blues'.

Previous Grounds: 1875, waste ground near Arthur St; 1877, Muntz St, Small Heath; 1906, St Andrews.

Foundation: In 1875 cricketing enthusiasts who were largely members of Trinity Church, Bordesley, determined to continue their sporting relationships throughout the year by forming a football club which they called Small Heath Alliance. For their earliest games played on waste land in Arthur Street, the team included three Edden brothers and two James brothers.

First Football League game: 3 September, 1892, Division 2, v Burslem Port Vale (h) W5-1 – Charsley; Bayley, Speller; Ollis, Jenkyns, Devey; Hallam (1), Edwards (1), Short (1), Wheldon (2), Hands.

Record League Victory: 12–0 v Walsall T Swifts, Division 2, 17 December 1892 – Charnley; Bayley, Jones; Ollis, Jenkyns, Devey; Hallam (2), Walton (3), Mobley (3), Wheldon (2), Hands (2). 12–0 v Doncaster R, Division 2, 11 April 1903 – Dorrington; Goldie, Wassell; Beer, Dougherty (1), Howard; Athersmith (1), Leonard (3), McRoberts (1), Wilcox (4), Field (1). Aston. (1 og).

Record Cup Victory: 9–2 v Burton W, FA Cup, 1st rd, 31 October 1885 – Hedges; Jones, Evetts (1); F. James, Felton, A. James (1); Davenport (2), Stanley (4), Simms, Figures, Morris (1).

Record Defeat: 1–9 v Sheffield W, Division 1, 13 December 1930 and v Blackburn R, Division 1, 5 January 1895.

Most League Points (2 for a win): 59, Division 2, 1947–48.

Most League Points (3 for a win): 89, Division 2, 1994–95.

Most League Goals: 103, Division 2, 1893–94 (only 28 games).

Highest League Scorer in Season: Joe Bradford, 29, Division 1, 1927–28.

Most League Goals in Total Aggregate: Joe Bradford, 249, 1920–35.

Most Capped Player: Malcolm Page, 28, Wales.

Most League Appearances: Frank Womack, 491, 1908–28.

Record Transfer Fee Received: £975,000 from Nottingham F for Trevor Francis, February 1979.

Record Transfer Fee Paid: £800,000 to Southend U for Ricky Otto, December 1994.

Football League Record: 1892 elected to Division 2; 1894–96 Division 1; 1896–1901 Division 2; 1901–02 Division 1; 1902–03 Division 2; 1903–08 Division 1; 1908–21 Division 2; 1921–39 Division 1; 1946–48 Division 2; 1948–50 Division 1; 1950–1955 Division 2; 1955–65 Division 1; 1965–72 Division 2; 1972–79 Division 1; 1979–80 Division 2; 1980–84 Division 1; 1984–1985 Division 2; 1985–86 Division 1; 1986–89 Division 2; 1989–92 Division 3; 1992–94 Division 1; 1994–95 Division 2; 1995– Division 1.

Honours: *Football League:* Division 1 best season: 6th, 1955–56; Division 2 – Champions 1892–93, 1920–21, 1947–48, 1954–55, 1994–95; Runners-up 1893–94, 1900–01, 1902–03, 1971–72, 1984–85.Division 3 Runners-up 1991–92. *FA Cup:* Runners-up 1931, 1956. *Football League Cup:* Winners 1963. *Leyland Daf Cup:* Winners 1991. *Auto Windscreens Shield:* Winners 1995. **European Competitions:** *European Fairs Cup:* 1955–58, 1958–60 (runners-up), 1960–61 (runners-up), 1961–62.

Colours: Blue shirts, white shorts, blue and white hooped stockings. **Change colours:** All red.

BIRMINGHAM CITY 1994–95 LEAGUE RECORD

Match No.	Date	Venue	Opponents	Result		H/T Score	Lg. Pos.	Goalscorers	Attendance
1	Aug 13	A	Leyton Orient	L	1-2	1-1	—	Claridge	7578
2	20	H	Chester C	W	1-0	1-0	14	Donowa	12,188
3	27	A	Swansea C	W	2-0	0-0	10	Claridge 2	5797
4	30	H	Wycombe W	L	0-1	0-0	—		14,305
5	Sept 3	H	Plymouth Arg	W	4-2	2-0	8	Regis 2, Wallace, Tait	13,202
6	10	A	Oxford U	D	1-1	0-0	11	Claridge	8077
7	13	A	Rotherham U	D	1-1	0-1	—	Bull	3799
8	18	H	Peterborough U	W	4-0	3-0	6	Bull 2, Tait, Dominguez	10,600
9	24	H	Hull C	D	2-2	1-1	9	Claridge (pen), Dominguez	12,192
10	Oct 1	A	Wrexham	D	1-1	0-1	9	Claridge	6002
11	8	H	Huddersfield T	D	1-1	1-1	9	Bull	15,265
12	15	A	Brighton & HA	W	1-0	0-0	9	Donowa	11,004
13	22	A	Brentford	W	2-1	1-0	9	Shearer, Ward	7779
14	29	H	Bristol R	W	2-0	2-0	6	Bull, Claridge	15,886
15	Nov 1	H	Crewe Alex	W	5-0	3-0	—	Hunt 3, Donowa, Claridge	14,212
16	5	A	Shrewsbury T	W	2-0	1-0	3	Bull, Hunt	5942
17	19	H	Bournemouth	D	0-0	0-0	3		15,477
18	26	A	Stockport Co	W	1-0	0-0	3	Hunt	5577
19	Dec 10	A	Chester C	W	4-0	2-0	2	Daish, Claridge, McGavin, Lowe	3946
20	17	H	Leyton Orient	W	2-0	1-0	2	Donowa 2	20,022
21	26	H	Cambridge U	D	1-1	1-0	2	Otto	20,098
22	28	A	Cardiff C	W	1-0	0-0	—	Otto	7420
23	31	H	Blackpool	W	7-1	3-1	1	Bradshaw (og), Donowa 2, Claridge 2, Lowe, Parris	18,025
24	Jan 2	A	Bradford C	D	1-1	0-1	1	Cooper	10,539
25	14	A	York C	L	0-2	0-1	1		6828
26	Feb 4	H	Stockport Co	W	1-0	0-0	1	Dinning (og)	17,160
27	11	A	Crewe Alex	L	1-2	0-1	3	Donowa	6359
28	18	H	York C	W	4-2	2-0	3	Francis 2, Otto, Shearer	14,846
29	21	A	Bournemouth	L	1-2	0-1	—	Francis	6024
30	25	H	Wrexham	W	5-2	1-2	2	Francis 2, Shearer, Otto, Donowa	18,884
31	Mar 4	A	Hull C	D	0-0	0-0	3		9854
32	11	H	Swansea C	L	0-1	0-1	4		16,191
33	18	A	Wycombe W	W	3-0	2-0	4	Shearer, Claridge, Evans (og)	7289
34	21	H	Oxford U	W	3-0	1-0	—	Francis, Claridge, Daish	19,781
35	25	A	Peterborough U	D	1-1	0-0	3	Shearer	8796
36	29	A	Bristol R	D	1-1	0-1	—	Claridge	8010
37	Apr 1	H	Rotherham U	W	2-1	0-1	3	Francis, Shearer	16,077
38	4	A	Blackpool	D	1-1	1-1	—	Claridge	4494
39	11	H	Shrewsbury T	W	2-0	1-0	—	Claridge 2	18,366
40	15	H	Cardiff C	W	2-1	1-1	2	Tait, Ward (pen)	17,455
41	17	A	Cambridge U	L	0-1	0-0	3		5317
42	19	A	Plymouth Arg	W	3-1	0-0	—	Whyte, Claridge 2	8550
43	26	H	Brentford	W	2-0	0-0	—	Francis, Daish	25,581
44	29	H	Brighton & HA	D	3-3	2-1	1	Dominguez, Shearer, Ward	19,006
45	May 2	H	Bradford C	D	0-0	0-0	—		25,139
46	6	A	Huddersfield T	W	2-1	0-0	1	Claridge, Tait	18,775

Final League Position: 1

GOALSCORERS

League (84): Claridge 20 (1 pen), Donowa 9, Francis 8, Shearer 7, Bull 6, Hunt 5, Otto 4, Tait 4, Daish 3, Dominguez 3, Ward 3 (1 pen), Lowe 2, Regis 2, Cooper 1, McGavin 1, Parris 1, Wallace 1, Whyte 1, own goals 3.
Coca-Cola Cup (4): Claridge 1 (pen), Daish 1, McGavin 1, Saville 1.
FA Cup (7): McGavin 3, Shearer 2, Cooper 1, Otto 1.

Bennett I.M. 46	Hiley S.P. 9	Dryden R.A. 3	Ward M.W. 41	Shearer P.A. 20 + 3	Whyte C.A. 31	Lowe K. 4 + 3	Claridge S.E. 41 + 1	Saville A.V. 3 + 7	Willis R.C. 1 + 2	Donowa B.L. 21 + 10	Regis D. 4 + 2	Dominguez J.M.M. 12 + 18	Frain J.W. 6 + 1	Daish L.S. 37	Harding P. 5 + 1	Doherty N. 3 + 5	Scott R.P. 5	De Souza J.M. 4 + 4	Tait P.R. 18 + 7	Wallace D.L. 4 + 2	Small B. 3	Bull G.W. 10	Poole G.J. 34	Hunt J.R. 18 + 2	McGavin S.J. 10 + 5	Barnett D. 31	Cooper G. 26	Howell D.C. 2	Otto R. 18 + 6	Parris G. 1 + 1	Bodley M.J. 3	Francis K.D.M. 15	Robinson S.E. 5 + 1	Webb M.L. — + 1	Williams P.A. 8 + 3	Hendon I.M. 4	*Match No.*
1	2	3	4	5	6	7	*8*	9	10	11	12	14																									1
1	2		4		5		8	9		7		12	3	6	10	11																					2
1	2		4		5		8	9		11	12	14		6	10		3	*7*																			3
1	2		4		5		8	12		14	9	*11*		6			3	7	10																		4
1	2		*4*		5		8			12	9	14		6	7		3		10	11																	5
1			*4*		5		8		12		9	14		6	7		2		10	11	3																6
1		4			5		8		12		9	14	3		7		2		10	*11*		6															7
1		5	4		6		8					14			12				10	*11*	3	9	2	7													8
1			4		5		8					11		6					*10*	12	3	9	2	7	14												9
1			4				8					11	3	6				12	*10*	14		9	2	7		5											10
1			*4*	11			8			12		10	3	6				14				9	2	7		5											11
1			4	11			8			12				6				10				9	2	7		5	3										12
1			4	11	3		8			10		12		6								9	2	7		5											13
1			4	11	3		*8*			10		12		6								9	2	7	14	5											14
1			4	11	3		8			10		12		6								*9*	2	7	14	5											15
1			4	11	3		*8*			10		12		6								9	2	7	14	5											16
1			4	11	3		8			12		10		6					14				2	7	*9*	5											17
1			4	11	3		8			10		12		6					14				2	7	*9*	5											18
1					3	12	8			7		*10*		6		14			11				2		9	5	4										19
1			4		3	12	8	14		7				6		11							2		*9*	5	10										20
1			4		3	12	8	14		7													2		*9*	5	11	6	10								21
1			4		3		8									7		9					2			5	11	6	10								22
1			4		*3*	9	8			7				6									2		12	5	11		10	14							23
1			4			*10*	8			7				6		14		12					2		9	5	3			11							24
1			4			11	8			7			12	6				14					2		*9*	5	3		10								25
1			4		2		8			7		12							11							5	3		10		6	9					26
1			4	12	3					7		14		6					11				2			5	*8*		10			9					27
1			4	12				14		7									11				2		*8*	5	3		10		6	9					28
1			4	12				14		7									11				2		*8*	5	3		10		6	9					29
1			4	11	3			12		7		*10*		6									2			5	8		14			9					30
1				11	3		8	12		*7*				6					4				2			5			10			9	14				31
1			4		3		8							6		12			11				2		*9*	5			10				7	14			32
1			4	11			8							6									2			5	3		12			9	7		10		33
1			4	11			8							6		12							2			5	3		14			9	*7*		10		34
1			*4*	11			8							6		12			14				2			5	3		10			9			7		35
1				11	3		12					14							6				2				4		10			9	*7*		8	5	36
1	2		4	11	3		8					12		6										7					*10*			9			14	5	37
1				11			8					12		6					4					7		5	3		14			9			*10*	2	38
1	2		4	11			8					7		6					12							5	3		10			*9*			14		39
1			4				8			12		7		6					*11*				2	14		5	3		10						9		40
1	2		4				8			12		7		6									11	14		5	3		10						*9*		41
1			4		5		8					12	3	6									2	*7*			10		14			9	11				42
1			*4*	11			8			12				6					14				2	7		5	3		10			9					43
1	2		4	*11*	5		8			12		9		6					14					7			3		10								44
1			4		5		8			9		*10*		6					11				2	7			3		12						14		45
1			4		5		8			12			3	6					14				2	7			11								*10*	9	46

Coca-Cola Cup

First Round	Shrewsbury T (a)	1-2
	(h)	2-0
Second Round	Blackburn R (a)	0-2
	(h)	1-1

FA Cup

First Round	Slough (a) (at Birmingham)	4-0
Second Round	Scunthorpe U (h)	0-0
	(a)	2-1
Third Round	Liverpool (h)	0-0
	(a)	1-1

BLACKBURN ROVERS 1994–95 *Back row (left to right):* Peter Thorne, Mark Atkins, Paul Harford, Frank Talia, Tim Flowers, Matt Dickins, Bobby Mimms, Seamus Given, Nicky Marker, Andy Morrison, Chris Malone.
Centre row: Tony Parkes, Jason Wilcox, Stuart Ripley, Henning Berg, Tim Sherwood, Tony Gale, Ian Pearce (First Team Coach), Chris Sutton, Colin Hendry, Mike Newell, Paul Warhurst, Alan Shearer, Danny Goodall, Mike Pettigrew (Physio).
Front row: Gary Tallon, Wayne Gill, Kevin Gallacher, Graeme Le Saux, Richard Brown, Ray Harford (Assistant Manager), Kenny Dalglish (Manager), Robbie Slater, Lee Makel, David Batty, Alan Wright, Paul Ainscough.
(Photograph: Action Images)

FA Premiership **BLACKBURN ROVERS**

Ewood Park, Blackburn BB2 4JF. Telephone: (01254) 698888. Fax: (01254) 671042. Ticket Office: (01254) 696767. Club Shop-Mail Order: (01254) 672137.

Ground capacity: 31,089.

Record attendance: 61,783 v Bolton W, FA Cup 6th rd, 2 March, 1929.

Record receipts: £333,067 v Liverpool, Coca-Cola Cup 4th rd, 30 November 1994.

Pitch measurements: 115yd × 72yd.

Chairman: R. D. Coar BSC. ***Vice-Chairman:*** R. L. Matthewman. ***Directors:*** K. C. Lee, I. R. Stanners, G. R. Root FCMA.

Director of Football: Kenny Dalglish MBE. ***Manager:*** Ray Harford. ***Physio:*** Steve Foster. ***Coach:*** Tony Parkes.

Commercial Manager: Ken Beamish.

Secretary: John W. Howarth FAAI.

Year Formed: 1875. ***Turned Professional:*** 1880. ***Ltd Co.:*** 1897.

Club Nickname: Rovers.

Previous Grounds: 1875/6, all matches played away; 1876, Oozehead Ground; 1877, Pleasington Cricket Ground; 1878, Alexandra Meadows; 1881, Leamington Road; 1890, Ewood Park.

Foundation: It was in 1875 that some Public School old boys called a meeting at which the Blackburn Rovers club was formed and the colours blue and white adopted. The leading light was John Lewis, later to become a founder of the Lancashire FA, a famous referee who was in charge of two FA Cup Finals, and a vice-president of both the FA and the Football League.

First Football League game: 15 September, 1888, Football League, v Accrington (h) D 5-5 – Arthur; Beverley, James Southworth; Douglas, Almond, Forrest; Beresford (1), Walton, John Southworth (1), Fecitt (1), Townley (2).

Record League Victory: 9–0 v Middlesbrough, Division 2, 6 November 1954 – Elvy; Suart, Eckersley; Clayton, Kelly, Bell; Mooney (3), Crossan (2), Briggs, Quigley (3), Langton (1).

Record Cup Victory: 11–0 v Rossendale, FA Cup 1st rd, 13 October 1884 – Arthur; Hopwood, McIntyre; Forrest, Blenkhorn, Lofthouse; Sowerbutts (2), J. Brown (1), Fecitt (4), Barton (3), Birtwistle (1).

Record Defeat: 0–8 v Arsenal, Division 1, 25 February 1933.

Most League Points (2 for a win): 60, Division 3, 1974–75.

Most League Points (3 for a win): 89, FA Premier League, 1994–95.

Most League Goals: 114, Division 2, 1954–55.

Highest League Scorer in Season: Ted Harper, 43, Division 1, 1925–26.

Most League Goals in Total Aggregate: Simon Garner, 168, 1978–92.

Most Capped Player: Bob Crompton, 41, England.

Most League Appearances: Derek Fazackerley, 596, 1970–86.

Record Transfer Fee Received: £900,000 from Aston Villa for Alan Wright, March 1995.

Record Transfer Fee Paid: £5,000,000 to Norwich C for Chris Sutton, July 1994.

Football League Record: 1888 Founder Member of the League; 1936–39 Division 2; 1946–48 Division 1; 1948–58 Division 2; 1958–66 Division 1; 1966–71 Division 2; 1971–75 Division 3; 1975–79 Division 2; 1979–80 Division 3; 1980–92 Division 2; 1992– FA Premier League.

Honours: *FA Premier League:* – Champions 1994–95; Runners-up 1993–94. *Football League:* Division 1 – Champions 1911–12, 1913–14; Division 2 – Champions 1938–39; Runners-up 1957–58; Division 3 – Champions 1974–75; Runners-up 1979–80. *FA Cup:* Winners 1884, 1885, 1886, 1890, 1891, 1928; Runners-up 1882, 1960. *Football League Cup:* Semi-final 1962, 1993. *Full Members' Cup:* Winners 1987. **European Competitions:** *UEFA Cup:* 1994–95.

Colours: Blue and white halved shirts, white shorts with blue trim, blue stockings with white trim. **Change colours:** Red and black shirts, red shorts, black and red stockings.

BLACKBURN ROVERS 1994–95 LEAGUE RECORD

Match No.	Date	Venue	Opponents	Result		H/T Score	Lg. Pos.	Goalscorers	Attendance
1	Aug 20	A	Southampton	D	1-1	0-1	—	Shearer	14,209
2	23	H	Leicester C	W	3-0	1-0	—	Sutton, Berg, Shearer	21,050
3	27	H	Coventry C	W	4-0	0-0	2	Sutton 3, Wilcox	21,657
4	31	A	Arsenal	D	0-0	0-0	—		37,629
5	Sept 10	H	Everton	W	3-0	2-0	3	Shearer 2 (1 pen), Wilcox	26,548
6	18	A	Chelsea	W	2-1	1-0	2	Johnsen (og), Sutton	17,513
7	24	H	Aston Villa	W	3-1	1-0	2	Shearer 2 (1 pen), Sutton	22,694
8	Oct 1	A	Norwich C	L	1-2	1-1	3	Sutton	18,146
9	9	A	Newcastle U	D	1-1	0-0	3	Shearer (pen)	34,344
10	15	H	Liverpool	W	3-2	0-1	2	Atkins, Sutton 2	30,263
11	23	H	Manchester U	L	2-4	1-1	4	Warhurst, Hendry	30,260
12	29	A	Nottingham F	W	2-0	1-0	4	Sutton 2	22,131
13	Nov 2	A	Sheffield W	W	1-0	0-0	—	Shearer	24,207
14	5	H	Tottenham H	W	2-0	1-0	2	Wilcox, Shearer (pen)	26,933
15	19	A	Ipswich T	W	3-1	2-1	2	Sutton, Sherwood, Shearer	17,607
16	26	H	QPR	W	4-0	1-0	1	Sutton, Shearer 3 (1 pen)	21,302
17	Dec 3	A	Wimbledon	W	3-0	0-0	1	Atkins, Wilcox, Shearer	12,341
18	10	H	Southampton	W	3-2	2-0	1	Atkins, Shearer 2	23,372
19	17	A	Leicester C	D	0-0	0-0	1		20,559
20	26	A	Manchester C	W	3-1	2-1	1	Shearer, Atkins, Le Saux	23,387
21	31	A	Crystal Palace	W	1-0	0-0	1	Sherwood	14,232
22	Jan 2	H	West Ham U	W	4-2	1-1	1	Shearer 3 (2 pens), Le Saux	25,503
23	14	H	Nottingham F	W	3-0	0-0	1	Warhurst, Wilcox, Chettle (og)	27,510
24	22	A	Manchester U	L	0-1	0-0	1		43,742
25	28	H	Ipswich T	W	4-1	2-0	1	Shearer 3 (1 pen), Sherwood	21,325
26	Feb 1	H	Leeds U	D	1-1	1-0	—	Shearer (pen)	28,561
27	5	A	Tottenham H	L	1-3	0-1	1	Sherwood	28,124
28	12	H	Sheffield W	W	3-1	2-1	1	Sherwood, Atkins, Shearer	22,223
29	22	H	Wimbledon	W	2-1	2-1	—	Shearer, Atkins	20,586
30	25	H	Norwich C	D	0-0	0-0	1		25,579
31	Mar 4	A	Aston Villa	W	1-0	1-0	1	Hendry	40,114
32	8	H	Arsenal	W	3-1	2-0	—	Shearer 2 (1 pen), Le Saux	23,452
33	11	A	Coventry C	D	1-1	0-1	1	Shearer	18,556
34	18	H	Chelsea	W	2-1	2-1	1	Shearer, Sherwood	25,490
35	Apr 1	A	Everton	W	2-1	2-1	1	Sutton, Shearer	37,905
36	4	A	QPR	W	1-0	0-0	—	Sutton	16,508
37	15	A	Leeds U	D	1-1	1-0	1	Hendry	39,426
38	17	H	Manchester C	L	2-3	2-1	1	Shearer, Hendry	27,851
39	20	H	Crystal Palace	W	2-1	0-0	—	Kenna, Gallacher	28,005
40	30	A	West Ham U	L	0-2	0-0	1		24,202
41	May 8	H	Newcastle U	W	1-0	1-0	—	Shearer	30,545
42	14	A	Liverpool	L	1-2	1-0	1	Shearer	40,014

Final League Position: 1

GOALSCORERS

League (80): Shearer 34 (10 pens), Sutton 15, Atkins 6, Sherwood 6, Wilcox 5, Hendry 4, Le Saux 3, Warhurst 2, Berg 1, Gallacher 1, Kenna 1, own goals 2.
Coca-Cola Cup (6): Sutton 3, Shearer 2, Wilcox 1.
FA Cup (2): Sutton 2.

Flowers T.D. 39	Berg H. 40	Le Saux G.P. 39	Slater R. 12 + 6	Hendry E.C.J. 38	Gale A.P. 15	Ripley S.E. 36 + 1	Sherwood T.M. 38	Shearer A. 42	Sutton C.R. 40	Wilcox J.M. 27	Warhurst P. 20 + 7	Pearce I.A. 22 + 6	Atkins M.N. 30 + 4	Newell M.C. 2 + 10	Wright A. 4 + 1	Mimms R.A. 3 + 1	Kenna J.J. 9	Batty D. 4 + 1	Gallacher K.W. 1	Witschge R. 1	Match No.
1	2	3	4	5	6	7	8	9	10	11											1
1	2	3	4	5	6	7	8	9	*10*	11	12	14									2
1		3	4	5	*6*	7	8	9	10	11	2	14	12								3
1	2	3	4	5	6	7	8	9	10	11	12										4
1	2	3	4	5	6	7	8	9	*10*	11		12	14								5
1	2	3	4	5	6	7	8	9	10		12		11								6
1	2	3		5	6	7	4	9	10	11	12		8								7
1	2	3	12	5		7	4	9	10	11	6		8								8
1	2	3		5		7	4	9	10	11	6		8								9
1	2	3		5	4	7		9	10	11	6		8								10
1	2	3	12	5	*6*	7		9	10	11	4	14	8								11
1	2	3		5		7	4	9	10	11	6	12	8								12
1	2	3		5	6	7	8	9	10	11	4										13
1	2	3		5	6	7	8	9	10	11	4										14
1		3	11		6	7	4	9	10		2	5	8								15
1	6	3	11			7	4	9	10		2	5	8	12	14						16
1	6	3		5		7	4	9	10	11	2		8								17
1	6	3	12	5		7	4	9	*10*	11	2		8	14							18
1	2	3			6	7	4	9	10	11		5	8								19
1	2	3		5	6	7	4	9	10	11			8								20
1	2	3		5		7	4	9	10	11		6	8								21
1	2	3		5	6	7	4	*9*	10	11	12		8	14							22
1	2		7	5				9	10	11	4	6	8	12	3						23
1	2	3		5			4	9	10	*11*	6	14	8	12	7						24
1	2	3	7	5			8	9	*10*	11	4	6	12	14							25
1	2	3		5			4	9	10	11	7	6	*8*			15					26
	2			5		7	4	9	10	11	8	6	12	14	3	1					27
	2		11	5			4	9	10		7	6	8		3	1					28
	2	3	11	5		12	4	9			7	6	8	10		1					29
1	2	3		5		7	4	9		11	12	6	8	10							30
1	2	3		5		7	4	9	10	11		6	8								31
1	2	3		5		7	4	9	*10*	11	12	6	8	14							32
1	2	3	12	5		7	4	9	*10*		11	6	8	14							33
1	2	11		5		7	4	9	10			6	8				3				34
1	2	11		5		7	4	9	10			6	8				3				35
1	2	11		5		7	4	9	10			6	8				3				36
1	2	11		5		7	4	9	10			6	8				3				37
1	2	11		5		7	4	9	10			6	8				3	12			38
1	5	3	12			7		9	10			6	8				2	4	11		39
1	2	6		5		7	8	9	10					12			3	4		11	40
1	2	11	12	5		7	8	9	10			6					3	4			41
1	2	11		5		7	8	9	10			6					3	4			42

Coca-Cola Cup

Second Round	Birmingham C (h)	2-0
	(a)	1-1
Third Round	Coventry C (h)	2-0
Fourth Round	Liverpool (h)	1-3

FA Cup

Third Round	Newcastle U (a)	1-1
	(h)	1-2

BLACKPOOL 1994–95 *Back row (left to right):* Stuart Parkinson, Graeme Craggs, Andy Watson, Kevin Sheedy, Paul Symons, Ian Gore, Mitch Cook, Jonathan Sunderland, Mike Davies, Lee Thorpe, Jamie Sheppard.

Centre row: Fred O'Donoghue (Youth Liaison Scout), Tony Rodwell, Bryan Griffiths, Paul Stoneman, Tony Ellis, Jamie Murphy, David Thompson, Melvin Capleton, Les Sealey, Lee Martin, Phil Horner, Darren Bradshaw, David Burke, Andy Gouck, Neil Mitchell, Steve Redmond (Physio).

Front row: Mark Bonner, Phil Brown, Bobby Saxton (Chief Scout/Coach), Sam Allardyce (Manager), Billy Bingham (Director of Football), Neil Bailey (Youth Team Coach), Chris Beech, James Quinn.

Division 2 **BLACKPOOL**

Bloomfield Rd Ground, Blackpool FY1 6JJ. Telephone: (01253) 404331. Fax: (01253) 405011. Clubcall: 0891 121648.

Ground capacity: 10,337.

Record attendance: 38,098 v Wolverhampton W, Division 1, 17 September 1955.

Record receipts: £72,949 v Tottenham H, FA Cup 3rd rd, 5 January 1991.

Pitch measurements: 112yd × 74yd.

President: C. A. Sagar BEM.

Chairman: Owen J. Oyston. ***Deputy Chairman:*** Mrs V. Oyston.

Managing Director: Mrs G. Bridge.

Directors: G. Warburton, J. Wilde MBE, W. Bingham MBE.

Manager: Sam Allardyce.

Secretary: Carol Banks.

Commercial Manager: Geoffrey Warburton.

Coach: Neil Bailey. ***Physio:*** Stephen Redmond.

Year Formed: 1887. ***Turned Professional:*** 1887. ***Ltd Co.:*** 1896.

Previous Name: 'South Shore' combined with Blackpool in 1899, twelve years after the latter had been formed on the breaking up of the old 'Blackpool St John's' club.

Club Nickname: 'The Seasiders'.

Previous Grounds: 1887, Raikes Hall Gardens; 1897, Athletic Grounds; 1899, Raikes Hall Gardens; 1899, Bloomfield Road.

Foundation: Old boys of St. John's School who had formed themselves into a football club decided to establish a club bearing the name of their town and Blackpool FC came into being at a meeting at the Stanley Arms Hotel in the summer of 1887. In their first season playing at Raikes Hall Gardens, the club won both the Lancashire Junior Cup and the Fylde Cup.

First Football League game: 5 September, 1896, Division 2, v Lincoln C (a) L 1-3 – Douglas; Parr, Bowman; Stuart, Stirzaker, Norris; Clarkin, Donnelly, R. Parkinson, Mount (1), J. Parkinson.

Record League Victory: 7–0 v Preston NE (away), Division 1, 1 May 1948 – Robinson; Shimwell, Crosland; Buchan, Hayward, Kelly; Hobson, Munro (1), McIntosh (5), McCall, Rickett (1).

Record Cup Victory: 7–1 v Charlton Ath, League Cup, 2nd rd, 25 September 1963 – Harvey; Armfield, Martin; Crawford, Gratrix, Cranston; Lea, Ball (1), Charnley (4), Durie (1), Oakes (1).

Record Defeat: 1–10 v Small Heath, Division 2, 2 March 1901 and v Huddersfield T, Division 1, 13 December 1930.

Most League Points (2 for a win): 58, Division 2, 1929–30.

Most League Points (3 for a win): 86, Division 4, 1984–85.

Most League Goals: 98, Division 2, 1929–30.

Highest League Scorer in Season: Jimmy Hampson, 45, Division 2, 1929–30.

Most League Goals in Total Aggregate: Jimmy Hampson, 247, 1927–38.

Most Capped Player: Jimmy Armfield, 43, England.

Most League Appearances: Jimmy Armfield, 568, 1952–71.

Record Transfer Fee Received: £750,000 from QPR for Trevor Sinclair, August 1993.

Record Transfer Fee Paid: £200,000 to Crystal Palace for Andy Preece, June 1995.

Football League Record: 1896 Elected to Division 2; 1899 Failed re-election; 1900 Re-elected; 1900–30 Division 2; 1930–33 Division 1; 1933–37 Division 2; 1937–67 Division 1; 1967–70 Division 2; 1970–71 Division 1; 1971–78 Division 2; 1978–81 Division 3; 1981–85 Division 4; 1985–90 Division 3; 1990–92 Division 4; 1992– Division 2.

Honours: *Football League:* Division 1 – Runners-up 1955–56; Division 2 – Champions 1929–30; Runners-up 1936–37, 1969–70; Division 4 – Runners-up 1984–85. *FA Cup:* Winners 1953; Runners-up 1948, 1951. *Football League Cup:* Semi-final 1962. *Anglo-Italian Cup:* Winners 1971; Runners-up 1972.

Colours: Tangerine shirts with navy and white trim, white shorts, tangerine stockings with navy blue tops. **Change colours:** Navy and sky blue stripes, navy shorts, navy stockings.

BLACKPOOL 1994–95 LEAGUE RECORD

Match No.	Date		Venue	Opponents	Result		H/T Score	Lg. Pos.	Goalscorers	Attendance
1	Aug	13	H	Huddersfield T	L	1-4	0-2	—	Gouck	8343
2		20	A	Bournemouth	W	2-1	1-1	13	Ellis 2	3098
3		27	H	Shrewsbury T	W	2-1	0-1	9	Horner, Ellis (pen)	4428
4		31	A	Bristol R	D	0-0	0-0	—		3762
5	Sept	3	A	Crewe Alex	L	3-4	2-2	12	Beech, Watson, Griffiths (pen)	4915
6		10	H	Cardiff C	W	2-1	0-1	10	Brown, Ellis (pen)	4189
7		13	H	Brighton & HA	D	2-2	2-2	—	Brown, Beech	3438
8		17	A	Brentford	L	2-3	1-0	13	Horner, Quinn	4157
9		24	H	Wrexham	W	2-1	0-0	10	Brown 2 (1 pen)	5015
10	Oct	1	A	Rotherham U	W	2-0	2-0	7	Quinn, Ellis	3517
11		8	A	Hull C	L	0-1	0-1	10		3829
12		15	H	Bradford C	W	2-0	0-0	8	Ellis, Watson	6156
13		22	H	Swansea C	W	2-1	2-0	8	Ellis (pen), Watson	4911
14		29	A	Plymouth Arg	W	2-0	1-0	5	Ellis, Watson	6285
15	Nov	1	A	Oxford U	L	2-3	1-1	—	Watson 2	5610
16		5	H	Leyton Orient	W	2-1	1-1	6	Ellis, Watson	4653
17		19	A	Chester C	L	0-2	0-1	6		3114
18		26	H	Wycombe W	L	0-1	0-0	8		4846
19	Dec	10	H	Bournemouth	W	3-1	2-1	6	Ellis 2, Mitchell	3847
20		17	A	Huddersfield T	D	1-1	0-0	8	Watson	11,536
21		26	A	York C	L	0-4	0-2	11		4542
22		27	H	Stockport Co	L	1-2	0-1	12	Mitchell	5745
23		31	A	Birmingham C	L	1-7	1-3	13	Bradshaw	18,025
24	Jan	2	H	Peterborough U	W	4-0	1-0	12	Quinn 2, Watson, Ellis	3692
25		7	A	Cardiff C	W	1-0	1-0	8	Watson	3467
26		14	H	Cambridge U	L	2-3	1-1	9	Mellon, Murphy	4076
27		28	H	Plymouth Arg	W	5-2	0-1	7	Watson 2, Ellis, Mellon 2	3599
28	Feb	4	A	Wycombe W	D	1-1	0-1	8	Quinn	6380
29		7	A	Leyton Orient	W	1-0	1-0	—	Watson	3301
30		11	H	Oxford U	W	2-1	0-0	6	Gouck, Quinn	5206
31		18	A	Cambridge U	D	0-0	0-0	6		3192
32		21	H	Chester C	W	3-1	2-1	—	Mitchell, Alsford (og), Mellon (pen)	4649
33		25	H	Rotherham U	D	2-2	1-1	5	Mitchell, Ellis	5043
34		28	A	Swansea C	L	0-1	0-0	—		2308
35	Mar	4	A	Wrexham	W	1-0	0-0	5	Watson	4251
36		7	H	Crewe Alex	D	0-0	0-0	—		5859
37		11	A	Shrewsbury T	D	0-0	0-0	6		4261
38		18	H	Bristol R	L	0-2	0-0	7		4484
39		25	H	Brentford	L	1-2	0-2	8	Brown	4663
40	Apr	1	A	Brighton & HA	D	2-2	1-1	10	Ellis, Watson	7157
41		4	H	Birmingham C	D	1-1	1-1	—	Quinn	4494
42		15	A	Stockport Co	L	2-3	0-2	11	Quinn 2	5021
43		18	H	York C	L	0-5	0-3	—		3517
44		22	A	Peterborough U	L	0-1	0-0	13		5716
45		29	A	Bradford C	W	1-0	1-0	12	Ellis	5036
46	May	6	H	Hull C	L	1-2	1-1	12	Ellis	4251

Final League Position: 12

GOALSCORERS

League (64): Ellis 17 (3 pens), Watson 15, Quinn 9, Brown 5 (1 pen), Mellon 4 (1 pen), Mitchell 4, Beech 2, Gouck 2, Horner 2, Bradshaw 1, Griffiths 1 (pen), Murphy 1, own goal 1.
Coca-Cola Cup (3): Brown 1, Ellis 1, Quinn 1.
FA Cup (0).

Sealey L.J. 7	Brown P. 28 + 3	Burke D.I. 23	Bonner M. 9 + 8	Horner P.M. 33 + 1	Gore I.G. 3 + 1	Rodwell A. 7 + 2	Gouck A.S. 35 + 4	Bamber J.D. 2	Ellis A.J. 40	Griffiths B.K. 12 + 2	Quinn S.J. 37 + 4	Gibson C.J. 1 + 1	Briggs G. 1	Beech C.S. 25 + 3	Stoneman P. 4	Watson A.A. 24 + 9	Cook M. 4 + 2	Thompson D. 17	Moore N. 7	Martin L.B. 31	Thorpe L.A. — + 1	Mitchell N.N. 25 + 5	Bradshaw D.S. 26	Capleton M.D.R. 8 + 2	Murphy J.A. 6	Mellon M.J. 26	Sunderland J. — + 2	Morrison A.C. 18	Davies M.J. 1	Rowett G. 17	Darton S.R. 18	Lydiate J.L. 11	Parkinson S.G. — + 1	Match No.
1	2	3	4	5	6	7	8	9	10	11	12	14																						1
1	2	3		4	6	12			10	11	9	8	5	7																				2
1	2	3		4		7	11	9	10		8			6	5																			3
1	2	3	4	6		7	11		10	12	9			8	5																			4
1	2	3	14	4	6	7	11			12	9			8	5	10																		5
1	2			4		7	11		10		9			8			3	5	6															6
1	2		12	4		7	11			10	9			8			3	5	6															7
	2		6	4	12	7	11			10	9			8			3		5	1	14													8
	2			4					10	11	9			8	7		3	5	6	1		12												9
	2	3		4		12	7		10		9			8			14	5	6	1		11												10
	2	3		4			7			10	9			8		12	14	5	6	1		11												11
	2	3	12	5			4		10	11	9			8		7			6	1														12
	2	3		6			12		10	11	9			8		7		5		1			4											13
	2	3		6					10	11	12			8		9		5		1		7	4											14
	2	3		6					10	11				8		9		5		1		7	4											15
	2	3		6					10	11				8		9		5		1		7	4											16
	2	3	8	6			12		10	11	14					9		5		1		7	4	15										17
		3	11	6					10		9							5				7	8	1	2	4	12							18
		3	7	6			12		10		9					14		5				11		1	2	8		4						19
		3	7	6					10		9					12		5				11		1	2	8		4						20
	12	3	7	6			14		10					4		9		5				11		1	2	8								21
	2	3		6			7		10					4		9		5				11		1		8								22
	2	3		12			4		10		7					9						11	6	1	5	8								23
	2	3					11		10		7			4		9				1			6			8		5						24
	2	3		6			11		10		7			4		9				1		12				8		5						25
				6			11		10		7			4		9				1		12			3	8		5	2					26
				6			11		10		7					9				1			4			8		5		2	3			27
				4			11		10		7					9				1			6			8		5		2	3			28
				4			11		10		7					9				1		12	6			8		5		2	3			29
				4			11		10		7					9				1			6			8		5		2	3			30
	12		14	4			11				7					9				1		10	6			8		5		2	3			31
	6		12	4			11				7					9		5		1		10				8				2	3			32
	6		12	4			11		10		7							5		1		9				8				2	3			33
			12	4			11		10		7					9				1		5	6			8				2	3			34
			4				11		10		7					9				1			6			8				2	3	5		35
			12				11		10		7					9				1		14	6			8		4		2	3	5		36
							11		10		7			12						1		9	6			8		4		2	3	5		37
							11		10		7			12						1		9	6			8		4		2	3	5		38
	2			5			8		10		9			4		12				1		11	6							7	3		14	39
	2						8		10		9			4		12				1		11	6							7	3	5		40
	14						8		10		9			4		12				1		11	6					7		2	3	5		41
							7		10		9					12				1		11	6			8		4		2	3	5		42
							7		10		9					12						11	6	1		8		4		2	3	5		43
	2						7		10		9			12		14						11	6	1		8		4			3	5		44
	2	3					11		10		12			7		9				1			6			8		4				5		45
	2	3					11		10					4		9				1		7	6	15		8	12					5		46

Coca-Cola Cup
First Round — Chesterfield (h) 1-2
(a) 2-4

FA Cup
First Round — Preston NE (a) 0-1

BOLTON WANDERERS 1994–95 *Back row (left to right):* Mark Winstanley, Andy Mason, Jason Lydiate, Mark Seagraves, Scott Green.
Third row: Jason McAteer, David Lee, Aidan Davison, Keith Branagan, Jimmy Phillips, Owen Coyle.
Second row: Ewan Simpson (Physio), Steve Carroll (Reserve Team Manager), Stuart Whittaker, Neil Fisher, Andy McKay, Gary Martindale, Neil McDonald, Tony Kelly, Colin Todd (Coach), Ian McNeil (Chief Scout)
Front row: Andy Roscoe, Alan Thompson, John McGinlay, Bruce Rioch (Manager), Alan Stubbs, Nicky Spooner, Mark Patterson.

FA Premiership **BOLTON WANDERERS**

Burnden Park, Bolton BL3 2QR. Telephone: (01204) 389200. Fax: (01204) 382334. Ticket Office: (01204) 521101. Ticket Office Fax: (01204) 392474. Commercial Dept: (01204) 24518.

Ground capacity: 20,500.

Record attendance: 69,912 v Manchester C, FA Cup 5th rd, 18 February 1933.

Record receipts: £159,290.50 v Swindon T, Coca-Cola Cup semi-final, 8 March 1995.

Pitch measurements: 113yd × 76yd.

President: Nat Lofthouse.

Chairman: G. Hargreaves.

Directors: P. A. Gartside, G. Ball, G. Seymour, G. Warburton, W. B. Warburton, B. Scowcroft.

Team Manager: Roy McFarland. ***Assistant Manager:*** Colin Todd. ***Physio:*** E. Simpson.

Chief Executive & Secretary: Des McBain. ***Commercial Manager:*** T. Holland.

Year Formed: 1874. ***Turned Professional:*** 1880. ***Ltd Co.:*** 1895.

Previous Name: 1874–77, Christ Church FC; 1877 became Bolton Wanderers.

Club Nickname: 'The Trotters'.

Previous Grounds: Park Recreation Ground and Cockle's Field before moving to Pike's Lane ground 1881; 1895, Burnden Park.

Foundation: In 1874 boys of Christ Church Sunday School, Blackburn Street, led by their master Thomas Ogden, established a football club which went under the name of the school and whose president was Vicar of Christ Church. Membership was 6d (two and a half pence). When their president began to lay down too many rules about the use of church premises, the club broke away and formed Bolton Wanderers in 1877, holding their earliest meetings at the Gladstone Hotel.

First Football League game: 8 September, 1888, Football League, v Derby C (h), L 3-6 – Harrison; Robinson, Mitchell; Roberts, Weir, Bullough, Davenport (2), Milne, Coupar, Barbour, Brogan (1).

Record League Victory: 8–0 v Barnsley, Division 2, 6 October 1934 – Jones; Smith, Finney; Goslin, Atkinson, George Taylor; George T. Taylor (2), Eastham, Milsom (1), Westwood (4), Cook. (1 og).

Record Cup Victory: 13–0 v Sheffield U, FA Cup, 2nd rd, 1 February 1890 – Parkinson; Robinson (1), Jones; Bullough, Davenport, Roberts; Rushton, Brogan (3), Cassidy (5), McNee, Weir (4).

Record Defeat: 1–9 v Preston NE, FA Cup 2nd rd, 10 December 1887.

Most League Points (2 for a win): 61, Division 3, 1972–73.

Most League Points (3 for a win): 90, Division 2, 1992–93.

Most League Goals: 96, Division 2, 1934–35.

Highest League Scorer in Season: Joe Smith, 38, Division 1, 1920–21.

Most League Goals in Total Aggregate: Nat Lofthouse, 255, 1946–61.

Most Capped Player: Nat Lofthouse, 33, England.

Most League Appearances: Eddie Hopkinson, 519, 1956–70.

Record Transfer Fee Received: £550,000 from Celtic for Andy Walker, July 1994.

Record Transfer Fee Paid: £450,000 to Leeds U for Chris Fairclough, July 1995.

Football League Record: 1888 Founder Member of the League; 1899–1900 Division 2; 1900–03 Division 1; 1903–05 Division 2; 1905–08 Division 1; 1908–09 Division 2; 1909–10 Division 1; 1910–11 Division 2; 1911–33 Division 1; 1933–35 Division 2; 1935–64 Division 1; 1964–71 Division 2; 1971–73 Division 3; 1973–78 Division 2; 1978–80 Division 1; 1980–83 Division 2; 1983–87 Division 3; 1987–88 Division 4; 1988–92 Division 3; 1992–93 Division 2; 1993–95 Division 1; 1995– FA Premier League.

Honours: *Football League:* Division 1 best season: 3rd, 1891–92, 1920–21, 1924–25, 1994–95; Division 2 – Champions 1908–09, 1977–78; Runners-up 1899–1900, 1904–05, 1910–11, 1934–35, 1992–93; Division 3 – Champions 1972–73. *FA Cup:* Winners 1923, 1926, 1929, 1958; Runners-up 1894, 1904, 1953. *Football League Cup:* Runners-up 1995. *Freight Rover Trophy:* Runners-up 1986. *Sherpa Van Trophy:* Winners 1989.

Colours: White shirts, navy blue shorts, blue stockings. **Change colours:** Dark/sky blue shirts, navy blue shorts, blue stockings.

BOLTON WANDERERS 1994–95 LEAGUE RECORD

Match No.	Date	Venue	Opponents	Result	H/T Score	Lg. Pos.	Goalscorers	Attendance
1	Aug 13	A	Grimsby T	D 3-3	2-1	—	Paatelainen 2, McGinlay (pen)	8393
2	20	H	Bristol C	L 0-2	0-1	17		12,127
3	27	A	Middlesbrough	L 0-1	0-1	19		19,570
4	30	H	Millwall	W 1-0	0-0	—	Patterson	9519
5	Sept 3	H	Stoke C	W 4-0	1-0	9	McGinlay (pen), McAteer 2, Paatelainen	11,515
6	10	A	Sheffield U	L 1-3	0-1	15	McGinlay	14,116
7	13	A	Luton T	W 3-0	1-0	—	McGinlay 2, Sneekes	5764
8	17	H	Portsmouth	D 1-1	1-0	10	McGinlay	11,284
9	24	A	Southend U	L 1-2	1-0	12	Sneekes	4507
10	Oct 1	H	Derby Co	W 1-0	0-0	8	McGinlay	12,015
11	8	A	Burnley	D 2-2	1-0	9	McGinlay, Coleman	16,687
12	16	H	Oldham Ath	D 2-2	2-0	10	Paatelainen, Lee	11,106
13	22	A	Port Vale	D 1-1	0-0	12	Green	10,003
14	29	H	Watford	W 3-0	1-0	7	Paatelainen, McGinlay 2 (1 pen)	10,483
15	Nov 1	H	Swindon T	W 3-0	1-0	—	Coleman, Thompson, De Freitas	10,046
16	5	A	Charlton Ath	W 2-1	1-0	5	Sneekes 2	9793
17	19	H	Notts Co	W 2-0	1-0	3	De Freitas, Paatelainen	11,698
18	23	A	Wolverhampton W	L 1-3	1-0	—	Paatelainen	25,903
19	26	A	Barnsley	L 0-3	0-2	4		8507
20	Dec 6	H	Port Vale	W 1-0	0-0	—	Patterson	10,324
21	10	A	Bristol C	W 1-0	1-0	4	Patterson	6144
22	17	H	Grimsby T	D 3-3	1-2	3	Coyle 2, Lee	10,522
23	26	A	Sunderland	D 1-1	0-0	5	Paatelainen	19,758
24	27	H	Tranmere R	W 1-0	1-0	2	Thompson	16,782
25	31	A	WBA	L 0-1	0-1	6		18,184
26	Jan 2	H	Reading	W 1-0	1-0	4	Coleman	14,705
27	14	A	Watford	D 0-0	0-0	3		9113
28	21	H	Charlton Ath	W 5-1	2-1	3	McGinlay 2, McAteer, Coyle, Paatelainen	10,516
29	Feb 4	H	Wolverhampton W	W 5-1	2-1	1	Sneekes, Coleman, Phillips, Coyle, Thompson	16,964
30	7	A	Notts Co	D 1-1	0-0	—	Coyle	7553
31	18	H	Barnsley	W 2-1	2-0	1	Thompson, Sneekes	12,463
32	26	A	Derby Co	L 1-2	1-0	3	McAteer	11,003
33	Mar 4	H	Southend U	W 3-0	1-0	3	Thompson, Lee, McAteer	10,766
34	11	H	Middlesbrough	W 1-0	1-0	3	Paatelainen	18,370
35	19	A	Millwall	W 1-0	0-0	2	McGinlay	6103
36	22	H	Sheffield U	D 1-1	1-1	—	Stubbs	16,756
37	25	A	Portsmouth	D 1-1	1-0	2	Paatelainen	7765
38	Apr 5	A	Swindon T	W 1-0	0-0	—	Thompson	8100
39	8	H	WBA	W 1-0	0-0	3	Thompson	16,207
40	11	H	Luton T	D 0-0	0-0	—		13,619
41	14	A	Tranmere R	L 0-1	0-1	—		14,959
42	17	H	Sunderland	W 1-0	0-0	2	McGinlay	15,030
43	21	A	Reading	L 1-2	0-1	—	Lee	13,223
44	29	A	Oldham Ath	L 1-3	1-2	3	McGinlay	11,901
45	May 3	A	Stoke C	D 1-1	1-1	—	McGinlay	15,557
46	7	H	Burnley	D 1-1	0-0	3	Paatelainen	16,853

Final League Position: 3

GOALSCORERS

League (67): McGinlay 16 (3 pens), Paatelainen 12, Thompson 7, Sneekes 6, Coyle 5, McAteer 5, Coleman 4, Lee 4, Patterson 3, De Freitas 2, Green 1, Phillips 1, Stubbs 1.
Coca-Cola Cup (15): McGinlay 4, Lee 2, McAteer 2, Paatelainen 2, Thompson 2, Sneekes 1, Stubbs 1, own goal 1.
FA Cup (1): Sneekes 1.

Branagan K.G. 43	McDonald N.R. 4	Phillips J.N. 46	McAteer J.W. 41 + 2	Lydiate J.L. 17 + 1	Stubbs A. 37 + 2	Lee D.M. 35 + 4	Patterson M.A. 23 + 3	Paatelainen M. 43 + 1	McGinlay J. 34 + 3	Thompson A. 34 + 3	Coyle O.C. 8 + 11	Sneekes R. 37 + 1	Kernaghan A.N. 9 + 2	Fisher N.J. 10 + 1	De Freitas F. 7 + 6	Kelly A.G. 4	Spooner N.M. 1	Coleman S. 22	Green S.P. 26 + 5	Whitaker S. — + 1	Davison A.J. 3 + 1	Seagraves M. 13	Bergsson G. 8	Dreyer J.B. 1 + 1	Shilton P.L. — + 1	*Match No.*
1	2	3	4	5	6	7	8	9	10	*11*	12	14														1
1	*2*	3	4		6	7	8	9	10	14	12	11	5													2
1		3	4	2	6		11	9	12			8	5	7	10											3
1		3	4	2	6		11	9	12			8	5	7	10											4
1		3	4	2	6			9	10			8	5	7		11										5
1		*3*	4	2	6			9	10	14	12	8	5	7		11										6
1		3	4	2	6			9	10			8	5	7		11										7
1		3	4	2	6	12		9	10			8	5	7		11										8
1		3	4	2	6	11		*9*	10	5		8	12	7	14											9
1		3	4	2		11		9	10	5		8	6	7												10
1		3	4	2		11		9	10	*5*		8		12	14		6	7								11
1		3	4	2		11		9	10	5		8	12	7				6								12
1		3	4			11		9	10	5		8	2	*7*	12			6	14							13
1		3		2		11	4	9	10	5		8						6	7							14
1		3	12	2		11	4	9		5	14	8			*10*			7	6							15
1		3	12	2		11	4	9		5	14	8			*10*			7	6							16
1		3		2	12	11	4	9		5	14	8			*10*			7	6							17
1		3		2	12	11	4	9		5	14	8			*10*			7	6							18
1		3	11	2	4	12		9	10	*5*	14	8						7	6							19
1		3	4		6	7	11	9	10			8						5	2							20
1		3	4		6	7	11	9	10		12	8						5	2							21
1		3	4		6	7	11	9		12	10	8						5	2							22
1		3	4		6	7		9		11	10	8						5	2							23
1		3	4		6	7	8	9	10	11	12							5	2							24
1		3	4		6	7	12	9	10	11		8						5	2							25
1		3	4		6	7	9	12	10		11	*8*						5	2	14						26
1		3	4		6	7		9	10	11		8						5	2							27
1		3	4	14	6	7		9	10	11	*12*	8						5	2							28
1		3	4		6	7		9		11	10	8						5	2							29
1		3	4		6	7		9		11	10	8			12			5	2		15					30
1		3	4		6	7		9	10	11		8						5	2							31
		3	4		6	7	12	9	*10*	11		8			14			5	2		1					32
1		3	4		6	7	8		10	11	9								2			5				33
1		3	4		6	12	8	9	10	11		7							2			5				34
1	8	3	4		6			9	10	11		7							2			5				35
1		3	4		6	7		9	10	11		8							2			5				36
1	8	3	4		6	12		9		11	10	7							2			5				37
1		3	4		6	7	8	9	10	11									12			5	2			38
1		3	4		6	7	8	9	*10*	11					14				12			5	2			39
1		3	4		6			9	12	11		8			10				7			5	2			40
1		3	4		6	7	12	9	10	11		8										5	2			41
1		3	4		6	7	11	9	10			8							12			5	2	14		42
1		3	4		6	7	8		10	11	9											5		2		43
1		3	4		6	7	8	9	10	11												5	2			44
		3	4		6	7	8	9	10	11									12		1	5	2		15	45
		3	4		6	7	8	9	10	11									2		1		5			46

Coca-Cola Cup

Second Round	Ipswich T (a)	3-0
	(h)	1-0
Third Round	Sheffield U (a)	2-1
Fourth Round	West Ham U (a)	3-1
Fifth Round	Norwich C (h)	1-0
Semi-final	Swindon T (a)	1-2
	(h)	3-1
Final at Wembley	Liverpool	1-2

FA Cup

Third Round	Portsmouth (a)	1-3

AFC BOURNEMOUTH 1994–95 *Back row (left to right):* Sean O'Driscoll (Physio/Player), Chris Leadbitter, Mark Morris, Michael McElhatton, Robert Murray.
Centre row: Steve Hardwick (Physio), Gary Chivers, Scott Mean, Neil Moss, Ian Andrews, Alex Watson, Steve Fletcher, John Williams (Youth Manager).
Front row: Mark O'Connor, Kevin Russell, Steve Cotterill, Mel Machin (Manager), Warren Aspinall, Adrian Pennock, Russell Beardsmore.

Division 2 AFC BOURNEMOUTH

Dean Court Ground, Bournemouth, Dorset BH7 7AF. Telephone: (01202) 395381. Fax: (01202) 309797.

Ground capacity: 11,880.

Record attendance: 28,799 v Manchester U, FA Cup 6th rd, 2 March 1957.

Record receipts: £33,723 v Manchester U, FA Cup 3rd rd, 7 January 1984.

Pitch measurements: 112yd × 75yd.

Chairman: K. Gardiner.

Directors: B. E. Willis (vice-chairman), G. M. C. Hayward, E. G. Keep, C. W. Legg, N. Hayward.

Secretary: K. R. J. MacAlister.

Manager: Mel Machin. ***First Team Coach:*** John Williams. ***Youth Team Coach:*** Sean O'Driscoll. ***Physio:*** Steve Hardwick. ***Commercial Manager:*** Terry Lovell.

Year Formed: 1899. ***Turned Professional:*** 1912. ***Ltd Co.:*** 1914.

Previous Names: Boscombe St Johns, 1890–99; Boscombe FC, 1899–1923; Bournemouth & Boscombe Ath FC, 1923–71.

Club Nickname: 'Cherries'.

Previous Grounds: 1899–1910, Castlemain Road, Pokesdown; 1910, Dean Court.

Foundation: There was a Bournemouth FC as early as 1875, but the present club arose out of the remnants of the Boscombe St John's club (formed 1890). The meeting at which Boscombe FC came into being was held at a house in Gladstone Road in 1899. They began by playing in the Boscombe and District Junior League.

First Football League game: 25 August, 1923, Division 3(S), v Swindon T (a), L 1-3 – Heron; Wingham, Lamb; Butt, C. Smith, Voisey; Miller, Lister (1), Davey, Simpson, Robinson.

Record League Victory: 7–0 v Swindon T, Division 3 (S), 22 September 1956 – Godwin; Cunningham, Keetley; Clayton, Crosland, Rushworth; Siddall (1), Norris (2), Arnott (1), Newsham (2), Cutler (1). 10–0 win v Northampton T at start of 1939–40 expunged from the records on outbreak of war.

Record Cup Victory: 11–0 v Margate, FA Cup, 1st rd, 20 November 1971 – Davies; Machin (1), Kitchener, Benson, Jones, Powell, Cave (1), Boyer, MacDougall (9 incl. 1p), Miller, Scott (De Garis).

Record Defeat: 0–9 v Lincoln C, Division 3, 18 December 1982.

Most League Points (2 for a win): 62, Division 3, 1971–72.

Most League Points (3 for a win): 97, Division 3, 1986–87.

Most League Goals: 88, Division 3 (S), 1956–57.

Highest League Scorer in Season: Ted MacDougall, 42, 1970–71.

Most League Goals in Total Aggregate: Ron Eyre, 202, 1924–33.

Most Capped Player: Gerry Peyton, 7 (33), Republic of Ireland.

Most League Appearances: Sean O'Driscoll, 423, 1984–95.

Record Transfer Fee Received: £800,000 from Everton for Joe Parkinson, March 1994.

Record Transfer Fee Paid: £210,000 to Gillingham for Gavin Peacock, August 1989.

Football League Record: 1923 Elected to Division 3 (S). Remained a Third Division club for record number of years until 1970; 1970–71 Division 4; 1971–75 Division 3; 1975–82 Division 4; 1982–87 Division 3; 1987–90 Division 2; 1990– 92 Division 3; 1992– Division 2.

Honours: *Football League:* Division 3 – Champions 1986–87; Division 3 (S) – Runners-up 1947–48. Promotion from Division 4 1970–71 (2nd), 1981–82 (4th). *FA Cup:* best season: 6th rd, 1957. *Football League Cup:* best season: 4th rd, 1962, 1964. *Associate Members' Cup:* Winners 1984.

Colours: Red shirts with black 4″ stripe, black shorts, black stockings. **Change colours:** Blue shirts, with black 4″ stripe, white shorts, white stockings.

AFC BOURNEMOUTH 1994–95 LEAGUE RECORD

Match No.	Date	Venue	Opponents	Result	H/T Score	Lg. Pos.	Goalscorers	Attendance
1	Aug 13	A	Wrexham	L 0-2	0-2	—		3580
2	20	H	Blackpool	L 1-2	1-1	21	Cotterill	3098
3	27	A	Rotherham U	L 0-4	0-0	24		2306
4	30	H	Peterborough U	L 0-3	0-2	—		2649
5	Sept 3	H	York C	L 1-4	0-3	24	Aspinall (pen)	3181
6	10	A	Stockport Co	L 0-1	0-0	24		4054
7	13	A	Leyton Orient	L 2-3	1-1	—	Aspinall, Leadbitter	2536
8	17	H	Chester C	D 1-1	0-1	24	Leadbitter	3025
9	24	H	Cardiff C	W 3-2	1-1	23	Beardsmore 2, Aspinall (pen)	3177
10	Oct 1	A	Hull C	L 1-3	1-2	23	Aspinall	3056
11	8	A	Shrewsbury T	L 0-3	0-1	24		3684
12	15	H	Brentford	L 0-1	0-1	24		4411
13	22	H	Bradford C	L 2-3	1-2	24	Mean (pen), Morris	3037
14	29	A	Huddersfield T	L 1-3	0-2	24	Jones	11,251
15	Nov 2	A	Brighton & HA	D 0-0	0-0	—		5631
16	5	H	Cambridge U	W 1-0	0-0	24	Robinson	3272
17	19	A	Birmingham C	D 0-0	0-0	24		15,477
18	26	H	Oxford U	L 0-2	0-1	24		4277
19	Dec 10	A	Blackpool	L 1-3	1-2	24	Jones	3847
20	16	H	Wrexham	L 1-3	1-1	—	Hughes (og)	2505
21	26	A	Bristol R	L 1-2	0-1	24	Pennock	6913
22	27	H	Crewe Alex	D 1-1	1-0	24	Beardsmore	3325
23	31	A	Wycombe W	D 1-1	1-0	24	Robinson	5990
24	Jan 2	H	Swansea C	W 3-2	2-1	23	Fletcher 2, Pennock	3816
25	7	A	Bradford C	W 2-1	0-0	22	Robinson, Leadbitter (pen)	5426
26	14	H	Plymouth Arg	D 0-0	0-0	22		4913
27	21	A	Cambridge U	D 2-2	0-1	22	Pennock, McElhatton	2834
28	28	H	Huddersfield T	L 0-2	0-0	22		4427
29	Feb 4	A	Oxford U	W 3-0	2-0	21	Jones 2, Fletcher	5473
30	11	H	Brighton & HA	L 0-3	0-2	21		5247
31	18	A	Plymouth Arg	W 1-0	1-0	21	McElhatton	5435
32	21	H	Birmingham C	W 2-1	1-0	—	Jones, Mean	6024
33	25	H	Hull C	L 2-3	2-3	21	Jones, Pennock	4345
34	Mar 4	A	Cardiff C	D 1-1	1-1	20	Fletcher	3008
35	7	A	York C	L 0-1	0-0	—		2301
36	11	H	Rotherham U	D 1-1	0-0	20	Morris	5666
37	18	A	Peterborough U	D 0-0	0-0	21		4495
38	21	H	Stockport Co	W 2-0	1-0	—	Fletcher, Jones	2892
39	25	A	Chester C	D 1-1	0-0	20	Fletcher	1618
40	Apr 1	H	Leyton Orient	W 2-0	1-0	20	Pennock, Holland	4118
41	8	H	Wycombe W	W 2-0	1-0	20	Mean 2 (2 pens)	8615
42	15	A	Crewe Alex	L 0-2	0-1	20		3906
43	18	H	Bristol R	W 2-0	1-0	—	Morris, Jones	7020
44	22	A	Swansea C	L 0-1	0-0	20		2664
45	29	A	Brentford	W 2-1	0-0	19	Mean, Jones	10,079
46	May 2	H	Shrewsbury T	W 3-0	3-0	—	Robinson 2, Mean	10,737

Final League Position: 19

GOALSCORERS

League (49): Jones 9, Fletcher 6, Mean 6 (3 pens), Pennock 5, Robinson 5, Aspinall 4 (2 pens), Beardsmore 3, Leadbitter 3 (1 pen), Morris 3, McElhatton 2, Cotterill 1, Holland 1, own goal 1.
Coca-Cola Cup (3): Cotterill 2, Russell 1.
FA Cup (4): Jones 1, McElhatton 1, Morris 1, Russell 1.

Moss N.G. 8	O'Driscoll S.M. 10	O'Connor M.A. 11 + 2	Morris M.J. 38	Watson A.F. 16 + 6	Leadbitter C.J. 25 + 2	Beardsmore R.P. 43	Aspinall W. 8 + 1	Fletcher S.M. 37 + 3	Cotterill S. 8	Russell K.J. 13	Mean S. 32 + 8	Reeve J.M. 2 + 5	McElhatton M.T. 13 + 14	Murray R.J. 28 + 3	Andrews I.E. 38	Russell L. 3	Town D.E. — + 5	Williams G.J. — + 1	Barfoot S.J. — + 2	Brooks S. 1	Ferrett C.A. — + 1	Young N.A. 32	Chivers G.P.S. 5	Pennock A.B. 31	Scully A.D.T. 6 + 4	Jones S.G. 27 + 3	Robinson S. 30 + 2	Vincent J.R. 8	Wells D. — + 1	Brissett J.C. 24 + 1	Holland M.R. 9 + 7	Strong S.G. — + 1	*Match No.*
1	2	3	4	5	6	7	8	9	10	11	12																						1
1	2	3	4	5	6	7		9	10	11	8	12																					2
1	2	3	4	5	6	7		9	10	11	8																						3
1	2	3	4	*5*	6	7	12	9	10	11			8	14																			4
1	2	3			8	7	6	5	10	11	12	14	4	*9*																			5
	2	3			11	7	8	6	10	4	12		5		1	9	14																6
	2	3		5	11		8	6	10	9	12	14	*7*		1	4																	7
		3		5	11	7		6	10	9	8	12	2		1	4		14															8
	2	3		5	11	7	9	6		10	8		4		1																		9
	2	3		5	11	7	9	6		10	8	12	*4*		1				14														10
	2			5	11	7	9	6			8	10	4		1				12	*3*	14												11
			4	5		7	*9*	12			8	10	14		1							2	3	6	11								12
			4			7		12			8		14	*5*	1							2	3	6	11	9	10						13
			4		6	7		5		9	8				1							2	3		11	10	12						14
			4	5	6	7				11	8				1							2	3		12	10	9						15
			4	5	6	7					8		12	14	1							2	3		11	10	9						16
			4	5	6	7					8		12		1							3		2	11	10	9						17
				5	6	7					8			12	1							2		4	11	10	9	3					18
		12	4	5	6	7					8				1							*2*		11	14	10	9	3					19
1			4	5		7				11	8											2		6	12	10	*9*	3	15				20
			4		6	7		12						5	1							2		11	14	10	*9*	3		8			21
		12	4		8	7		*10*						5	1		14					2		6			9	3		11			22
			4		9	7		10			12		14	5	1							2		6			8	3		*11*			23
			4		*9*	7		10			12			5	1							2		6		14	8	3		11			24
			4		9	7		10						5	1							2		6		12	8	3		11			25
		3	4	12				10			9		7	5	1							2		6		14	8			11			26
			4	12		3		10			9		14	5	1							2		6		7	8			11			27
			4		9	3		10					12	5	1							2		6		7	8			*11*	14		28
			4		9	3		10					12	5	1							2		6		7	8				11		29
			4		9	3		10			12			5	1							2		6		7	8			14	11		30
			4			3		10			12		2	5	1									6		9	8			11	7		31
1			4	12		3		10			6		2	5												9	8			11	7		32
1			*4*	12				10			6		2	5			14					3		8		9				11	7		33
			4			3		10			*6*		12	5	1							2		8		9	14			11	7		34
			4			3		10			6		12	5	1							2		8		9				11	7		35
			4	12	14	3		10			6			5	1							2		9			8			11	7		36
			4		12	3		10			6			5	1							2		9			8			11	7		37
			4			3		10			6		12	5	1							2		8		9	7			11			38
			4			3		10			6			5	1		12					2		7		9	8			11	14		39
			4			3		10			6			5	1							2		7		9	8			11	12		40
			4			3		10			6			5	1							2		7		9	8			11	12		41
			4			3		10			6			5	1		12					2		7		9	*8*			11	14		42
			4			3		10			6		12	5	1							2		7		9	8			11			43
			4	12		3		10			6		*2*	5	1									7		9	8			11	14		44
			4			3		10			6		12	5	1							2		7		9	*8*			11	14		45
			4			3		10			6		12	5	1							2		7		*9*	8			11		14	46

Coca-Cola Cup

First Round	Northampton T (h)	2-0
	(a)	1-0
Second Round	Chelsea (a)	0-1
	(h)	0-1

FA Cup

First Round	Worthing (h)	3-1
Second Round	Plymouth Arg (a)	1-2

BRADFORD CITY 1994–95 *Back row (left to right):* Leena Stocks (Physio), Wayne Jacobs, Chris Kamara, Neil Tolson, John Taylor, Ian Bowling, Paul Tomlinson, Lee Sinnott, Dean Richards, Des Hamilton, Paul Showler, Steve Smith (Youth Development Officer).
Front row: Wayne Benn, Gary Robson, Lee Power, Gavin Oliver, Lennie Lawrence (Manager), Lee Duxbury, George Shipley (Assistant Manager), Paul Jewell, Richard Liburd, Neil Grayston, Shaun Murray.

Division 2 BRADFORD CITY

The Pulse Stadium, Bradford BD8 7DY. Telephone: (01274) 306062 (Office). Fax: (01274) 307457.

Ground capacity: 14,359.

Record attendance: 39,146 v Burnley, FA Cup 4th rd, 11 March 1911.

Record receipts: £74,213 v Sheffield W, Coca-Cola Cup 2nd rd 2nd leg, 4 October 1994.

Pitch measurements: 110yd × 73yd.

Chairman: Geoffrey Richmond. ***Vice-Chairman:*** David Thompson FCA.

Directors: David Richmond, Elizabeth Richmond, Terry Goddard.

Manager: Lennie Lawrence. ***Assistant Manager:*** Chris Kamara.

Youth Coach: Steve Smith. ***Physio:*** S. Redmond.

Secretary: Shaun A. Harvey. ***Commercial Manager:*** Allan Gilliver.

Year Formed: 1903. ***Turned Professional:*** 1903. ***Ltd Co.:*** 1908.

Club Nickname: 'The Bantams'.

Foundation: Bradford was a rugby stronghold around the turn of the century but after Manningham RFC held an archery contest to help them out of financial difficulties in 1903, they were persuaded to give up the handling code and turn to soccer. So they formed Bradford City and continued at Valley Parade. Recognising this as an opportunity of spreading the dribbling code in this part of Yorkshire, the Football League immediately accepted the new club's first application for membership of the Second Division.

First Football League game: 1 September, 1903, Division 2, v Grimsby T (a), L 0-2 – Seymour; Wilson, Halliday; Robinson, Millar, Farnall; Guy, Beckram, Forrest, McMillan, Graham.

Record League Victory: 11–1 v Rotherham U, Division 3 (N), 25 August 1928 – Sherlaw; Russell, Watson; Burkinshaw (1), Summers, Bauld; Harvey (2), Edmunds (3), White (3), Cairns, Scriven (2).

Record Cup Victory: 11–3 v Walker Celtic, FA Cup, 1st rd (replay), 1 December 1937 – Parker; Rookes, McDermott; Murphy, Mackie, Moore; Bagley (1), Whittingham (1), Deakin (4 incl. 1p), Cooke (1), Bartholomew (4).

Record Defeat: 1–9 v Colchester U, Division 4, 30 December 1961.

Most League Points (2 for a win): 63, Division 3 (N), 1928–29.

Most League Points (3 for a win): 94, Division 3, 1984–85.

Most League Goals: 128, Division 3 (N), 1928–29.

Highest League Scorer in Season: David Layne, 34, Division 4, 1961–62.

Most League Goals in Total Aggregate: Bobby Campbell, 121, 1981–84, 1984–86.

Most Capped Player: Harry Hampton, 9, Northern Ireland.

Most League Appearances: Cec Podd, 502, 1970–84.

Record Transfer Fee Received: £1,850,000 from Wolverhampton W for Dean Richards, June 1995.

Record Transfer Fee Paid: £300,000 to Bristol R for John Taylor, July 1994.

Football League Record: 1903 Elected to Division 2; 1908–22 Division 1; 1922–27 Division 2; 1927–29 Division 3 (N); 1929–37 Division 2; 1937–61 Division 3; 1961–69 Division 4; 1969–72 Division 3; 1972–77 Division 4; 1977–78 Division 3; 1978–82 Division 4; 1982–85 Division 3; 1985–90 Division 2; 1990–92 Division 3; 1992– Division 2.

Honours: *Football League:* Division 1 best season: 5th, 1910–11; Division 2 – Champions 1907–08; Division 3 – Champions 1984–85; Division 3 (N) – Champions 1928–29; Division 4 – Runners-up 1981–82. *FA Cup:* Winners 1911 (first holders of the present trophy). *Football League Cup:* best season: 5th rd, 1965, 1989.

Colours: Claret and amber striped shirts, black shorts, black stockings. **Change colours:** Light blue shirts and shorts, blue stockings.

BRADFORD CITY 1994–95 LEAGUE RECORD

Match No.	Date		Venue	Opponents	Result		H/T Score	Lg. Pos.	Goalscorers	Attendance
1	Aug	13	A	Chester C	W	4-1	1-0	—	Jewell 3, Taylor	4459
2		20	H	Leyton Orient	W	2-0	1-0	3	Jewell 2	7473
3		27	A	Plymouth Arg	W	5-1	4-0	1	Jewell 3, Shutt 2	6469
4		30	H	Oxford U	L	0-2	0-1	—		9005
5	Sept	3	H	Wycombe W	W	2-1	1-0	3	Jewell, Shutt	8010
6		10	A	Swansea C	D	0-0	0-0	5		3445
7		13	A	Wrexham	W	1-0	1-0	—	Jewell	4179
8		17	H	York C	D	0-0	0-0	3		8670
9		24	H	Huddersfield T	L	3-4	0-1	3	Jewell, Kamara, Taylor	11,300
10	Oct	1	A	Cambridge U	L	1-4	1-2	6	Liburd	3338
11		8	H	Brighton & HA	W	2-1	1-0	6	Kamara, Taylor	6970
12		15	A	Blackpool	L	0-2	0-0	7		6156
13		22	A	Bournemouth	W	3-2	2-1	7	Kamara, Jewell, Huxford	3037
14		30	H	Cardiff C	L	2-3	1-2	10	Murray, Perry (og)	5937
15	Nov	2	H	Brentford	W	1-0	1-0	—	Jewell	4105
16		5	A	Bristol R	L	0-4	0-2	9		4247
17		19	H	Crewe Alex	L	0-2	0-2	11		5520
18		26	A	Shrewsbury T	W	2-1	1-0	9	Sinnott, Murray	3776
19	Dec	10	A	Leyton Orient	D	0-0	0-0	10		2553
20		17	H	Chester C	D	1-1	1-0	12	Taylor	4555
21		26	A	Rotherham U	L	1-3	0-3	13	Taylor	5400
22		28	H	Hull C	W	1-0	0-0	—	Taylor	7312
23		31	A	Stockport Co	W	2-1	1-0	9	Shutt, Taylor	4613
24	Jan	2	H	Birmingham C	D	1-1	1-0	9	Taylor	10,539
25		7	H	Bournemouth	L	1-2	0-0	10	Young (og)	5426
26		14	A	Peterborough U	D	0-0	0-0	11		4400
27	Feb	4	H	Shrewsbury T	D	1-1	1-0	12	Jacobs	4817
28		7	H	Bristol R	W	2-1	1-0	—	Murray, Verveer	4243
29		11	A	Brentford	L	3-4	1-1	11	Robson, Murray, Power	6019
30		18	H	Peterborough U	W	4-2	2-0	10	Taylor 2, Youds 2	4806
31		21	A	Crewe Alex	W	1-0	0-0	—	Taylor	4214
32		25	H	Cambridge U	D	1-1	0-0	8	Jewell	6075
33	Mar	4	A	Huddersfield T	D	0-0	0-0	9		17,404
34		11	H	Plymouth Arg	W	2-0	0-0	10	Power 2 (1 pen)	5399
35		18	A	Oxford U	L	0-1	0-0	12		5363
36		21	H	Swansea C	L	1-3	0-1	—	Richards	4417
37		25	A	York C	D	0-0	0-0	12		5431
38		28	A	Cardiff C	W	4-2	1-2	—	Tolson 2, Murray, Showler	2560
39	Apr	1	H	Wrexham	D	1-1	1-1	11	Showler	4461
40		4	A	Wycombe W	L	1-3	0-3	—	Hamilton	4522
41		8	H	Stockport Co	L	1-2	1-0	12	Youds	3927
42		15	A	Hull C	L	0-2	0-2	13		4368
43		17	H	Rotherham U	L	0-3	0-2	14		3535
44		29	H	Blackpool	L	0-1	0-1	14		5036
45	May	2	A	Birmingham C	D	0-0	0-0	—		25,139
46		6	A	Brighton & HA	L	0-1	0-0	14		7701

Final League Position: 14

GOALSCORERS

League (57): Jewell 14, Taylor 11, Murray 5, Shutt 4, Kamara 3, Power 3 (1 pen), Youds 3, Showler 2, Tolson 2, Hamilton 1, Huxford 1, Jacobs 1, Liburd 1, Richards 1, Robson 1, Sinnott 1, Verveer 1, own goals 2.
Coca-Cola Cup (6): Taylor 2, Duxbury 1, Murray 1, Richards 1, Shutt 1.
FA Cup (3): Power 1, Richards 1, Tolson 1.

Tomlinson P. 37	Benn W. 8 + 2	Jacobs W.G. 38	Robson G. 22 + 1	Sinnott L. 16	Richards D.I. 30	Shutt C.S. 28 + 4	Kamara C. 22 + 1	Taylor J.P. 35 + 1	Jewell P. 32 + 6	Murray S. 38 + 3	Duxbury L.E. 19 + 1	Liburd R.J. 9	Hamilton D.V. 23 + 7	Power L.M. 12 + 15	Tolson N. 4 + 6	Oliver G.R. 11	Huxford R.J. 33	Bowling I. 6	Dow A. 5	Showler P. 17 + 6	Scargill W. 1	Petterson A.K. 3	Mitchell G.L. 26	Youds E.P. 17	Verveer E. 9	Stabb C.J. 1	Johnson I. 1 + 1	Midgley C.S. — + 3	Grayston N.J. 3	*Match No.*
1	2	3	4	5	6	7	8	9	10	11	12																			1
1		3	8	5	6	7	12	9	10	11	4	2																		2
1		3		5	6	7	8	9	10	11	4	2																		3
1		3		5	6	7	8	9	10	*11*	4	2	12	14																4
1		3		5	6	7	8	9	10	11	4	2																		5
1		3		5	6	7	8	9	10	11	4	2	12																	6
1		3		5	6		8	9	10	11	4	2		7	12															7
1		3		5	6	7	8	9	10	11	4	2		12																8
1	5	3			6	7	8	9	10	11	4	2		12	14															9
1	12	3				7	8	9	10	11	4	2		*6*	14	5														10
1	12	3	6			7	8	9	10		4		*11*	14		5	2													11
			6			7	8	9	10	11	4			12		5	2	1	3											12
1				5	6	7	8	9	10	11	4			12			2		3											13
1				5	6	7	8	9	10	11	4		14	12			2		3											14
1				5			8	9	10		4		7		12	6	2		3	11										15
1				5			8	9	*10*	12	4		7		14	6			3	11	2									16
1		3		6	5	12	8	14			4		7	*9*	10		2			11										17
1		3		5	6	7		9	10	11	4			12		8	2													18
	8	3		5	6	7		9		11	4			10			2			12		1								19
	8	3		5	6	7		9		11	4		12	*10*	14		2					1								20
	8	3	4		6	7		9		11			10				2					1	5							21
1		3	4			7		9	10	11			8			6	2			12			5							22
1		3			6	7		9	10	11			8			4	2						5							23
1		3			6	7		9	10	11			8			4	2			12			5							24
1		3	8		6	7		9	10	11			12			4	2			14			5							25
1		3	8		6	7		9	10	11			12			4	2						5							26
1		3	4		6	7		9	10	11			8							12			5	2						27
1		3	8		6			9	12	11			7	14						*10*			5	2	4					28
1		3	*4*		6			9	12	11			7	14			2						5	10	8					29
1		3			6			9		11			7				2			8			5	10	4					30
1		3	4		6			9	12	11							2			7			5	10	8					31
1		3	4		6			9	12	*11*				14			2			7			5	10	8					32
1		3	4		6			9					11				2			7			5	10	8					33
1		3	4		6	12		9		*11*			10	14			2			7			5		8					34
1		3			6	12		9		14			11	10			2			7			5	4	*8*					35
1		3	12		6			9	14				7	10			2			11			5	4	*8*					36
1		3	6			9			10	11			7		8		2						5	4						37
1		3	4			9			10	11			*7*	12	8		2			14			5	6						38
1		3	4			9	*6*		12	11			14	10	8		2			7			5							39
1		3	4			12	9		8	10			11				2			7			5			6				40
1		3	4			9	8		*10*	12			11	14			2			7			5	6						41
		3	4			9	8		10	7			*11*	12			2	1					5	6			14			42
		3	4				8		10	7				9			2	1					5	6			11	12		43
	4						8		10	11				9			2	1		7			5	6				12	3	44
	4								10	11			8	9			2	1		7			5	6					3	45
	4								10	11			8	9			2	1		7			5	6				12	3	46

Coca-Cola Cup

First Round	Grimsby T (h)	2-1
	(a)	2-1
Second Round	Sheffield W (a)	1-2
	(h)	1-1

FA Cup

First Round	Scunthorpe U (h)	1-1
	(a)	2-3

BRENTFORD 1994–95 *Back row (left to right):* Robert Taylor, Simon Ratcliffe, David Thompson, Alan Judge, Tamar Fernandes, Kevin Dearden, Shane Westley, Barry Ashby, Jamie Bates.

Centre row: Bob Booker (Youth Team Manager), Kevin Lock (Assistant Manager), David McGhee, Robert Peters, Paul Smith, Ian Benjamin, Corey Campbell, Gus Hurdle, Billy Manuel, Carl Hutchings, Roy Johnson (Physio), Neil Mason (Physio).

Front row: Martin Grainger, Brian Statham, Darren Annon, Denny Mundee, David Webb (Manager), Nick Forster, Craig Ravenscroft, Paul Stephenson, Lee Harvey.

Division 2 **BRENTFORD**

Griffin Park, Braemar Rd, Brentford, Middlesex TW8 0NT. Telephone: (0181) 847 2511. Fax: (0181) 568 9940. Commercial Dept: (0181) 560 6062. Press Office: (0181) 574 3047. Clubcall: 0891 21108.

Ground capacity: 13,870.

Record attendance: 39,626 v Preston NE, FA Cup 6th rd, 5 March 1938.

Record receipts: £79,838 v Tottenham H, Coca Cola Cup 2nd rd 2nd leg, 7 October 1992.

Pitch measurements: 111yd × 74yd.

President: W. Wheatley. ***Deputy President:*** E. White.

Chairman: M. M. Lange.

Directors: B. Evans, J. Herting, E. J. Radley-Smith MS, FRCS, LRCP, D. Tana.

Chief Executive: Keith Loring.

Manager: David Webb. ***Assistant Manager:*** Kevin Lock.

Youth Team Manager: Bob Booker.

Community Officer: Lee Doyle.

Secretary: Polly Kates.

Press Officer/Programme Editor: Eric White (0181)–574 3047. ***Safety officer:*** Jill Dawson.

Year Formed: 1889. ***Turned Professional:*** 1899. ***Ltd Co.:*** 1901.

Club Nickname: 'The Bees'.

Previous Grounds: 1889–91, Clifden Road; 1891–95, Benns Fields, Little Ealing; 1895–98, Shotters Field; 1898–1900, Cross Road, S. Ealing; 1900–04, Boston Park; 1904, Griffin Park.

Foundation: Formed as a small amateur concern in 1889 they were very successful in local circles. They won the championship of the West London Alliance in 1893 and a year later the West Middlesex Junior Cup before carrying off the Senior Cup in 1895. After winning both the London Senior Amateur Cup and the Middlesex Senior Cup in 1898 they were admitted to the Second Division of the Southern League.

First Football League game: 28 August, 1920, Division 3, v Exeter C (a), L 0-3 – Young; Rosier, Hodson; Amos, Levitt, Elliott; Henery, Morley, Spredbury, Thompson, Smith.

Record League Victory: 9–0 v Wrexham, Division 3, 15 October 1963 – Cakebread; Coote, Jones; Slater, Scott, Higginson; Summers (1), Brooks (2), McAdams (2), Ward (2), Hales (1). (1 og).

Record Cup Victory: 7–0 v Windsor & Eton (away), FA Cup, 1st rd, 20 November 1982 – Roche; Rowe, Harris (Booker), McNichol (1), Whitehead, Hurlock (2), Kamara, Bowles, Joseph (1), Mahoney (3), Roberts.

Record Defeat: 0–7 v Swansea T, Division 3 (S), 8 November 1924 and v Walsall, Division 3 (S), 19 January 1957.

Most League Points (2 for a win): 62, Division 3 (S), 1932–33 and Division 4, 1962–63.

Most League Points (3 for a win): 85, Division 2, 1994–95.

Most League Goals: 98, Division 4, 1962–63.

Highest League Scorer in Season: Jack Holliday, 38, Division 3 (S), 1932–33.

Most League Goals in Total Aggregate: Jim Towers, 153, 1954–61.

Most Capped Player: John Buttigieg, (63), Malta.

Most League Appearances: Ken Coote, 514, 1949–64.

Record Transfer Fee Received: £720,000 from Wimbledon for Dean Holdsworth, August 1992.

Record Transfer Fee Paid: £275,000 to Chelsea for Joe Allon, November 1992.

Football League Record: 1920 Original Member of Division 3; 1921–33 Division 3 (S); 1933–35 Division 2; 1935–47 Division 1; 1947–54 Division 2; 1954–62 Division 3 (S); 1962–63 Division 4; 1963–66 Division 3; 1966–72 Division 4; 1972–73 Division 3; 1973–78 Division 4; 1978–92 Division 3; 1992–93 Division 1; 1993– Division 2.

Honours: *Football League:* Division 1 best season: 5th, 1935–36; Division 2 – Champions 1934–35; Division 3 – Champions 1991–92; Division 3 (S) – Champions 1932–33; Runners-up 1929–30, 1957–58; Division 4 – Champions 1962–63. *FA Cup:* best season: 6th rd, 1938, 1946, 1949, 1989. *Football League Cup:* best season: 4th rd, 1983. *Freight Rover Trophy;* Runners-up 1985.

Colours: Red and white vertical striped shirts, red shorts, red stockings. **Change colours:** Blue shirts, dark blue shorts, dark blue stockings.

BRENTFORD 1994–95 LEAGUE RECORD

Match No.	*Date*		*Venue*	*Opponents*	*Result*		*H/T Score*	*Lg. Pos.*	*Goalscorers*	*Atten-dance*
1	Aug	13	A	Plymouth Arg	W	5-1	3-1	—	Smith, Forster 2, Stephenson, Taylor	7976
2		20	H	Peterborough U	L	0-1	0-1	11		5516
3		27	A	Stockport Co	W	1-0	1-0	7	Taylor	4399
4		30	H	Rotherham U	W	2-0	1-0	—	Taylor, Forster	4031
5	Sept	3	H	Wrexham	L	0-2	0-2	7		5820
6		10	A	Wycombe W	L	3-4	1-1	13	Taylor, Stephenson, Cousins (og)	6847
7		13	A	York C	L	1-2	1-1	—	Taylor	2836
8		17	H	Blackpool	W	3-2	0-1	11	Forster, Smith, Grainger (pen)	4157
9		24	A	Crewe Alex	W	2-0	1-0	8	Forster, Taylor	3839
10	Oct	1	H	Shrewsbury T	W	1-0	1-0	5	Taylor	4556
11		8	H	Bristol R	W	3-0	2-0	5	Forster 2, Taylor	5330
12		15	A	Bournemouth	W	1-0	1-0	4	Forster	4411
13		22	H	Birmingham C	L	1-2	0-1	5	Ward (og)	7779
14		29	A	Cambridge U	D	0-0	0-0	7		3102
15	Nov	2	A	Bradford C	L	0-1	0-1	—		4105
16		5	H	Hull C	L	0-1	0-0	10		5455
17		19	A	Huddersfield T	L	0-1	0-0	13		10,889
18		26	H	Brighton & HA	W	2-1	0-1	11	Ashby, Ansah	4728
19	Dec	10	A	Peterborough U	D	2-2	1-2	12	Taylor, Forster	4102
20		17	H	Plymouth Arg	W	7-0	2-0	9	Annon, Smith, Taylor 2, Forster, Mundee, Harvey	4492
21		26	H	Leyton Orient	W	3-0	3-0	8	Mundee, Ratcliffe, Forster	6125
22		27	A	Chester C	W	4-1	3-1	6	Forster 3, Grainger	2266
23		31	H	Oxford U	W	2-0	1-0	5	Forster, Taylor	7125
24	Jan	2	A	Cardiff C	W	3-2	2-0	5	Harvey, Forster, Taylor	5235
25		14	H	Swansea C	D	0-0	0-0	5		7211
26		21	A	Hull C	W	2-1	0-0	2	Mundee, Grainger	3823
27		28	H	Cambridge U	W	6-0	0-0	1	Taylor 2, Forster, Grainger (pen), Bailey 2	6390
28	Feb	4	A	Brighton & HA	D	1-1	1-0	2	Bailey	9499
29		11	H	Bradford C	W	4-3	1-1	1	Mundee, Taylor, Grainger (pen), Forster	6019
30		17	A	Swansea C	W	2-0	1-0	—	Forster 2	3935
31		21	H	Huddersfield T	D	0-0	0-0	—		9562
32		25	A	Shrewsbury T	L	1-2	1-1	1	Forster	4570
33	Mar	4	H	Crewe Alex	W	2-0	1-0	2	Mundee, Taylor	7143
34		7	A	Wrexham	D	0-0	0-0	—		2834
35		11	H	Stockport Co	W	1-0	1-0	1	Taylor	6513
36		18	A	Rotherham U	W	2-0	2-0	1	Forster, Abrahams	2968
37		21	H	Wycombe W	D	0-0	0-0	—		9530
38		25	A	Blackpool	W	2-1	2-0	2	Bates, Taylor	4663
39	Apr	1	H	York C	W	3-0	1-0	1	Grainger, Forster, Taylor	6474
40		8	A	Oxford U	D	1-1	1-1	2	Taylor	7800
41		15	H	Chester C	D	1-1	0-1	3	Abrahams	8020
42		17	A	Leyton Orient	W	2-0	1-0	1	Bates, Forster	4459
43		22	H	Cardiff C	W	2-0	0-0	1	Grainger (pen), Taylor	8268
44		26	A	Birmingham C	L	0-2	0-0	—		25,581
45		29	H	Bournemouth	L	1-2	0-0	2	Abrahams	10,079
46	May	6	A	Bristol R	D	2-2	0-1	2	McGhee, Taylor	8501

Final League Position: 2

GOALSCORERS

League (81): Forster 24, Taylor 23, Grainger 7 (4 pens), Mundee 5, Abrahams 3, Bailey 3, Smith 3, Bates 2, Harvey 2, Stephenson 2, Annon 1, Ansah 1, Ashby 1, McGhee 1, Ratcliffe 1, own goals 2.
Coca-Cola Cup (4): Parris 1, Smith 1, Stephenson 1, Taylor 1.
FA Cup (3): Annon 1, Grainger 1, Taylor 1.

Fernandes T.H. 3 + 1	Hurdle A.A.J. 7 + 2	Hutchings C.E. 38 + 1	Westley S.L.M. 15 + 1	Bates J. 38	Smith P.W. 35	Parris G. 5	Harvey L.D. 24 + 1	Taylor R.A. 43	Forster N.M. 46	Stephenson P. 34	Dearden K.C. 43	Annon D.C. 9 + 1	Ashby B.J. 40	Mundee D.W.J. 22 + 17	Grainger M.R. 36 + 1	Statham B. 26 + 10	Ratcliffe S. 24 + 1	Benjamin I.T. 1	Ravenscroft C. 1	Ansah A. 2 + 1	Hooker J.W. — + 1	McGhee D. 1 + 6	Bailey D.L. 6	Abrahams P. 7 + 3	Match No.
1	2	3	4	5	6	7	8	9	10	11															1
	2	3	4	5	6	7	8	9	10	11	1	12													2
	2	3		4	6	7	8	9	10	11	1		5	12											3
	2	3		4	6	7		9	10	11	1		5	8											4
	2	3		4	6	7	12	9	10	11	1		5	8	14										5
	2	7		4	6		8	9	10	11	1		5	12	3										6
		7		4	6		8	9	10	11	1		5		3	2	12								7
		7	14	4	6		8		10	11	1		5	12	3	2		9							8
		7	4		6		8	9	10	11	1		5	12	3	2									9
		7	4		6		8	9	10		1		5	12	3	2			11						10
	12	7		4	6		8	9	10	11	1		5	14	3	2									11
15		7	4		6		8	9	10	11	1		5	12	3	2									12
		7	4		6		8	9	10	11	1		5	12	3	2									13
1			4		6		8	9	10	11			5		3	2	7								14
			4		6		8	9	10	11	1		5	12	3	2	7								15
			4		6		8	9	10		1		5	12	3	2	7			11					16
	12	7	4		6		8	9	10		1		5		3	2				11					17
			4	7	6		8	9	10		1	11	5	12	3	2				14					18
1	3			4	6		8	9	10			7	5	11		2					12				19
		2		4	6		8	9	10		1	11	5	12	3		7								20
		2		4			8	9	10		1	7	5	11	3		6								21
		2		4			8	9	10		1	7	5	11	3		6								22
		2	4	5			8	9	10		1	7		11	3	12	6								23
		2	4	5			8	9	10		1	7		11	3	12	6								24
		2		4			8	9	10		1	7	5	11	3	12	6								25
		2		4			8	9	10		1	7	5	11	3	12	6					14			26
		2		4				9	10	7	1		5	11	3	12	6						8		27
		2		4				9	10	7	1		5	11	3	12	6					14	8		28
		2		4				9	10	7	1		5	11	3	12	6						8		29
		2		4				9	10	7	1		5	11	3		6						8		30
		2		4					10	11	1		5	9	3	12	6					7	8		31
		2		4	6				10	11	1		5	9	3	12	7					14	8		32
		2		4	6			9	10	11	1		5	8	3	12	7								33
		2	4	5	6			9	10	11	1			8		3	7								34
		2	4	5	6			9	10	11	1			8		3	7								35
		2		4	6			9	10	7	1		5		3	8								11	36
		2		4	6			9	10	7	1		5	11	3	8								12	37
		2		4	6			9	10	7	1		5	12	3	8								11	38
		2		4	6			9	10	7	1		5		3	8								11	39
		2		4	6			9	10	7	1		5	12	3	8								11	40
		2		4	6			9	10	7	1		5	12	3	8						14		11	41
				4	6			9	10	11	1		5	8	3	2	7								42
		12		4	6			9	10	11	1		5	8	3	2	7							14	43
				4	6			9	10	11	1		5	8	3	2	7							12	44
		3		4	6			9	10	7	1		5	12		2	8					14		11	45
		3		4	6			9	10	7	1		5	12		2	8					14		11	46

Coca-Cola Cup

First Round	Colchester U (a)	2-0
	(h)	2-0
Second Round	Tranmere R (a)	0-1
	(h)	0-0

FA Cup

First Round	Cambridge U (a)	2-2
	(h)	1-2

BRIGHTON AND HOVE ALBION 1994–95 *Back row (left to right):* George Petchey (Youth Development Officer), Junior McDougald, Nicky Bisset, Simon Funnell, Nicky Rust, Paul McCarthy, Mark Ormerod, Mark Fox, Kevin McGarrigle, Ross Yorke-Johnson, Malcolm Stuart (Physio).
Third row: Gerry Ryan (Assistant Manager), Stuart Munday, Danny Simmonds, Stuart Tuck, Stuart Myall, Steven Scott, Jeffrey Minton, Nicky Henderson, Lee MacAulay, John Ryan, Jimmy Case (Player/Coach).
Second row: John Crumplin, Kurt Nogan, Ian Chapman, Steve Foster, Liam Brady (Manager), Raphael Meade, Colin Pates, Robert Codner, Dean Wilkins.
Front row: Philip Andrews, Robert Cox, Garrett Doyle, Ian Earles, Simon Fox, Kerry Mayo, Jay Pickering, Danny Smith, Anthony Tilley, Tim Whitehouse.

Division 2 BRIGHTON & HOVE ALBION

Goldstone Ground, Newtown Rd, Hove, East Sussex BN3 7DE. Telephone: (01273) 778855 (all departments). Fax: (01273) 321095. Recorded information (team & ticket news etc): Seagull Line 0891 800609.

Ground capacity: 16,254.

Record attendance: 36,747 v Fulham, Division 2, 27 December 1958.

Record receipts: £109,615.65 v Crawley T, FA Cup 3rd rd, 4 January 1992.

Pitch measurements: 111yd × 74yd.

Directors: G. A. Stanley (Chairman), W. Archer, R. A. Bloom, B. E. Clarke, P. Kent, D. Sizen, D. Stanley, D. Sullivan.

Manager: Liam Brady. ***Assistant Manager:*** Gerry Ryan.

Secretary: Derek Allan. ***Chief Executive/Deputy Chairman:*** David Bellotti.

Coach: Jimmy Case. ***Physio:*** Malcolm Stuart.

Promotions Executive: Ray Woodford.

Year Formed: 1901. ***Turned Professional:*** 1901. ***Ltd Co.:*** 1904.

Previous Grounds: 1901, County Ground; 1902, Goldstone Ground.

Club Nickname: 'The Seagulls'.

Foundation: A professional club Brighton United was formed in November 1897 at the Imperial Hotel, Queen's Road, but folded in March 1900 after less than two seasons in the Southern League at the County Ground. An amateur team, Brighton & Hove Rangers was then formed by some prominent United supporters and after one season at Withdean, decided to turn semi-professional and play at the County Ground. Rangers were accepted into the Southern League but then also folded June 1901. John Jackson the former United manager organised a meeting at the Seven Stars public house, Ship Street on 24 June 1901 at which a new third club Brighton & Hove United was formed. They took over Rangers' place in the Southern League and pitch at County Ground. The name was changed to Brighton & Hove Albion before a match was played because of objections by Hove FC.

First Football League game: 28 August, 1920, Division 3, v Southend U (a), L 0-2 – Hayes; Woodhouse, Little; Hall, Comber, Bentley; Longstaff, Ritchie, Doran, Rodgerson, March.

Record League Victory: 9–1 v Newport C, Division 3 (S), 18 April 1951 – Ball; Tennant (1p), Mansell (1p); Willard, McCoy, Wilson; Reed, McNichol (4), Garbutt, Bennett (2), Keene (1). 9–1 v Southend U, Division 3, 27 November 1965 – Powney; Magill, Baxter; Leck, Gall, Turner; Gould (1), Collins (1), Livesey (2), Smith (3), Goodchild (2).

Record Cup Victory: 10–1 v Wisbech, FA Cup, 1st rd, 13 November 1965 – Powney; Magill, Baxter; Collins (1), Gall, Turner; Gould, Smith (2), Livesey (3), Cassidy (2), Goodchild (1). (1 og).

Record Defeat: 0–9 v Middlesbrough, Division 2, 23 August 1958.

Most League Points (2 for a win): 65, Division 3 (S), 1955–56 and Division 3, 1971–72.

Most League Points (3 for a win): 84, Division 3, 1987–88.

Most League Goals: 112, Division 3 (S), 1955–56.

Highest League Scorer in Season: Peter Ward, 32, Division 3, 1976–77.

Most League Goals in Total Aggregate: Tommy Cook, 114, 1922–29.

Most Capped Player: Steve Penney, 17, Northern Ireland.

Most League Appearances: 'Tug' Wilson, 509, 1922–36.

Record Transfer Fee Received: £900,000 from Liverpool for Mark Lawrenson, August 1981.

Record Transfer Fee Paid: £500,000 to Manchester U for Andy Ritchie, October 1980.

Football League Record: 1920 Original Member of Division 3; 1921–58 Division 3 (S); 1958–62 Division 2; 1962–63 Division 3; 1963–65 Division 4; 1965–72 Division 3; 1972–73 Division 2; 1973–77 Division 3; 1977–79 Division 2; 1979–83 Division 1; 1983–87 Division 2; 1987–88 Division 3; 1988– Division 2.

Honours: *Football League:* Division 1 best season: 13th, 1981–82; Division 2 – Runners-up 1978–79; Division 3 (S) – Champions 1957–58; Runners-up 1953–54, 1955–56; Division 3 – Runners-up 1971–72, 1976–77, 1987–88; Division 4 – Champions 1964–65. *FA Cup:* Runners-up 1983. *Football League Cup:* best season: 5th rd, 1979.

Colours: Blue and white striped shirts, blue shorts, white stockings. **Change colours:** All yellow.

BRIGHTON & HOVE ALBION 1994–95 LEAGUE RECORD

Match No.	Date		Venue	Opponents	Result		H/T Score	Lg. Pos.	Goalscorers	Attendance
1	Aug	13	A	Swansea C	D	1-1	0-1	—	Nogan (pen)	4640
2		20	H	Plymouth Arg	D	1-1	0-0	16	Chamberlain	8309
3		27	A	Wrexham	L	1-2	0-1	17	McDougald	3339
4		31	H	York C	W	1-0	0-0	—	Nogan (pen)	6996
5	Sept	3	H	Leyton Orient	W	1-0	0-0	10	Nogan	8581
6		10	A	Chester C	W	2-1	1-0	8	Nogan 2	2063
7		13	A	Blackpool	D	2-2	2-2	—	Bissett, Chamberlain	3438
8		17	H	Oxford U	D	1-1	1-0	10	Nogan	9970
9		24	H	Cambridge U	W	2-0	1-0	6	McDougald, Nogan	8280
10	Oct	1	A	Huddersfield T	L	0-3	0-1	11		10,321
11		8	A	Bradford C	L	1-2	0-1	13	McDougald	6970
12		15	H	Birmingham C	L	0-1	0-0	14		11,004
13		22	A	Bristol R	L	0-3	0-2	15		4107
14		29	H	Rotherham U	D	1-1	0-1	15	Smith	6734
15	Nov	2	H	Bournemouth	D	0-0	0-0	—		5631
16		5	A	Cardiff C	L	0-3	0-0	17		5004
17		19	H	Peterborough U	L	1-2	1-2	18	Codner	6445
18		26	A	Brentford	L	1-2	1-0	18	Chapman	4728
19	Dec	10	A	Plymouth Arg	W	3-0	0-0	17	Codner 2, Akinbiyi	6091
20		17	H	Swansea C	D	1-1	0-1	18	Codner	6817
21		26	A	Wycombe W	D	0-0	0-0	17		7085
22		27	H	Shrewsbury T	W	2-1	0-1	16	McDougald, Akinbiyi	7290
23		31	A	Hull C	D	2-2	1-1	17	Minton, Akinbiyi	5099
24	Jan	2	H	Stockport Co	W	2-0	0-0	15	Minton, Akinbiyi	8842
25		14	A	Crewe Alex	L	0-4	0-1	17		4286
26	Feb	4	H	Brentford	D	1-1	0-1	17	Bates (og)	9499
27		11	A	Bournemouth	W	3-0	2-0	16	Minton 2, McDougald	5247
28		14	H	Bristol R	L	1-2	1-0	—	Chapman	5232
29		18	H	Crewe Alex	L	0-1	0-1	17		6986
30		21	A	Peterborough U	L	1-2	0-1	—	McDougald	3870
31		25	H	Huddersfield T	D	0-0	0-0	18		7751
32	Mar	4	A	Cambridge U	W	2-0	1-0	18	Chapman, Myall	3856
33		7	A	Leyton Orient	W	3-0	1-0	—	Minton, McDougald, Fox M	2983
34		11	H	Wrexham	W	4-0	0-0	15	Byrne J, McCarthy, Parris, McDougald	7514
35		15	H	Cardiff C	D	0-0	0-0	—		6956
36		18	A	York C	L	0-1	0-1	15		2915
37		22	H	Chester C	W	1-0	1-0	—	McDougald	5979
38		25	A	Oxford U	D	0-0	0-0	15		6725
39		28	A	Rotherham U	L	3-4	1-3	—	Byrne J, Byrne P, Myall	2316
40	Apr	1	H	Blackpool	D	2-2	1-1	15	McCarthy, Byrne J	7157
41		8	H	Hull C	W	1-0	0-0	15	McDougald	6038
42		15	A	Shrewsbury T	D	1-1	1-1	16	Byrne J	3597
43		19	H	Wycombe W	D	1-1	1-0	—	Parris	8094
44		22	A	Stockport Co	L	0-2	0-1	16		3789
45		29	A	Birmingham C	D	3-3	1-2	16	Munday, Storer, Chapman	19,006
46	May	6	H	Bradford C	W	1-0	0-0	16	Munday	7701

Final League Position: 16

GOALSCORERS

League (54): McDougald 10, Nogan 7 (2 pens), Minton 5, Akinbiyi 4, Byrne J 4, Chapman 4, Codner 4, Chamberlain 2, McCarthy 2, Munday 2, Myall 2, Parris 2, Bissett 1, Byrne P 1, Fox M 1, Smith 1, Storer 1, own goal 1.
Coca-Cola Cup (10): Nogan 5, McDougald 2, Chamberlain 1, McCarthy 1, Munday 1.
FA Cup (1): Codner 1.

Rust N.C.I. 44	Munday S.C. 18 + 13	Pates C.G. 15 + 1	Chapman I.R. 38 + 2	Foster S.B. 38	McCarthy P.J. 37	Minton J.T. 37 + 2	McDougald D.E. 37 + 4	Nogan K. 26	Codner R.A.G. 21 + 2	Wilkins D.M. 11 + 3	Chamberlain M.V. 12 + 7	Bissett N. 12	Case J.R. 9	Simmonds D.B. 2 + 2	Smith P. 35 + 3	Tuck S.G. 18 + 5	Funnell S.P. — + 1	Meade R.J. — + 3	Kerr S. 2	Stapleton F.A. 1 + 1	Andrews P.D. — + 5	Myall S.T. 23 + 4	Akinbiyi A.P. 7	McGarrigle K. 16 + 1	Parris G. 18	Fox M.S. 4 + 5	Byrne J.F. 14	Byrne P. 8	Fox S.M. 1 + 1	Storer S.J. 2	*Match No.*
1	2	3	4	5	6	7	8	9	10	11																					1
1	2	3	4	5	6	7	8	9	10	11	12																				2
1		3		5	6	11	8	9	10		7	2	4	12																	3
1		3		5	6	11	8	9	*10*	12	7	2	4	14																	4
1		6	12	5		*10*	8	9	14		7		4	11	2	3															5
1		3	*11*	5		12	8	9	10		7	6	4		2	14															6
1		3	11	5		8		9	10		7	6	*4*		2	12	14														7
1	12	3	11	5		8		9	10	4	*7*	6			2			14													8
1	12	3	11	5		7	8	9	*10*	4		6			2			14													9
1	4		11	5		7	8	9	10			6			2	3		12													10
1		12	11		5	7	8	9	10			6		4	2	3															11
1	10	3	*11*		5	7	8	9			12	6	4		2	14															12
1	12	3	*11*	5	6	10	8	9			7	2	4			14															13
1	12	3	11	5	6	7	8	9	10		14	*2*			4																14
	7	3	11	*5*	6		8	9	10		12	2			4				1	14											15
	4	5	12		6	7	*8*	9	10		14				2	3			1	11											16
1	12	5	11		6	4	8	9	10		*7*				2	3					14										17
1			3		6	4		9	10	11					2	5						7	8								18
1	11		3		6	4		9	10						2	5						7	8	12							19
1			3		6	4	12	9	10	11					2	5						7	8								20
1	12		3	5	6	4		9	10	11					2							7	8								21
1			3	5	6		12	9	10	11	14		4		*2*							7	8								22
1	4		3	5	6	10	12	9		*11*					2	14						7	8								23
1			3	5	6	11	12	9	*10*	14			4		2							7	8								24
1	2		3	5	6	4	8	9	10	11	12											7									25
1	12		11	5	6	10	8	9			4				2	3						7									26
1			11	5	6	10	8				9				2	3					12	7			4						27
1	12		11	5	6	10	8			14	*9*				2	3						7			4						28
1	12		3	5	6	10	8		14	11	*9*				2							7			4						29
1	11		3	5	6	10	8								2						12	7			4	9					30
1	12		3	5	6	10	9								2						14	7		11	4		*8*				31
1			3	5	6	10	9								2							7		11	4		8				32
1			3	5	6	10	9								2							7		11	4	12	8				33
1	12		3	5	6		9								2							*7*		11	4	14	8	10			34
1	2		3	5	6	12	9								14							*7*		11	4		8	10			35
1	2		3	5	6		9															7		11	4	12		10	8		36
1	2		3	5	6		9								12									11	4	7	8	10			37
1	2		3	5	6		9															7		11	4	8		10	12		38
1	2		3	5	6		9								12							*7*		11	4	14	8	10			39
1				5	6	*10*	9								2	3						12		11	4	14	8	7			40
1				5	6	10	9								2	3								11	4		8	7			41
1	7			5	6	10	9								2	3						12		11	4		8				42
1	12			5	6	10	9								2	3						7		11	4		8				43
1	5		3			10	9								2	6					12	7		11		4	8				44
1	4		3	5		10	9								2	6						12		11			8			7	45
1	12		*3*	5		10	9								2	6						14		11	4		8			7	46

Coca-Cola Cup

First Round	Wycombe W	(h)	2-1
		(a)	3-1
Second Round	Leicester C	(h)	1-0
		(a)	2-0
Third Round	Swindon T	(h)	1-1
		(a)	1-4

FA Cup

First Round	Kingstonian (a)	1-2

BRISTOL CITY 1994–95 *Back row (left to right):* Marvin Harriott, Scott Partridge, Stuart Duffin, Colin Loss, Mike Wyatt, Ian Brown, Rodney McAree, Junior Bent.
Centre row: Russell Osman (Manager), Clive Whitehead (First Team Coach), Martin Scott, Jason Fowler, Scott Paterson, Wayne Allison, Keith Welch, Richard Rowe, Henry McKop, Paul Milsom, Matt Hewlett, Leroy Rosenior (Reserve Team Coach), Buster Footman (Physio).
Front row: Tony Fawthrop (Assistant Manager), Liam Robinson, Matt Bryant, Brian Tinnion, Stuart Munro, Mark Shail, Dave Martin, Ian Baird, Rob Edwards, Gerry Sweeney (Coach).

Division 2 BRISTOL CITY

Ashton Gate, Bristol BS3 2EJ. Telephone: (0117) 962812 (5 lines). Fax: (0117) 9639574. Commercial: (0117) 9633876. Shop: (0117) 9538566. Clubcall: 0891 121176. Supporters Club: (0117) 9665554. Community Dept: (0117) 9664685.

Ground capacity: 20,000 approx.

Record attendance: 43,335 v Preston NE, FA Cup 5th rd, 16 February 1935.

Record receipts: £148,282 v Everton, FA Cup 4th rd, 29 January 1995.

Pitch measurements: 115yd × 75yd.

Chairman: D. A. Russe. ***Vice-Chairman:*** M. Fricker.

Directors: J. Clapp, D. Coller, S. Davidson, R. Neale, G. Williams. ***Commercial Manager:*** John Cox.

Manager: Joe Jordan. ***Assistant Manager:*** John Gorman.

Physio: H. Footman. ***Secretary:*** Jean Harrison. ***Commercial Manager:*** John Cox.

Year Formed: 1894. ***Turned Professional:*** 1897. ***Ltd Co.:*** 1897. BCFC (1982) PLC.

Previous Name: Bristol South End 1894–97.

Club Nickname: 'Robins'.

Previous Grounds: 1894, St John's Lane; 1904, Ashton Gate.

Foundation: The name Bristol City came into being in 1897 when the Bristol South End club, formed three years earlier, decided to adopt professionalism and apply for admission to the Southern League after competing in the Western League. The historic meeting was held at The Albert Hall, Bedminster. Bristol City employed Sam Hollis from Woolwich Arsenal as manager and gave him £40 to buy players. In 1901 they merged with Bedminster, another leading Bristol club.

First Football League game: 7 September, 1901, Division 2, v Blackpool (a) W 2-0 – Moles; Tuft, Davies; Jones, McLean, Chambers; Bradbury, Connor, Boucher, O'Brien (2), Flynn.

Record League Victory: 9–0 v Aldershot, Division 3 (S), 28 December 1946 – Eddols; Morgan, Fox; Peacock, Roberts, Jones (1); Chilcott, Thomas, Clark (4 incl. 1p), Cyril Williams (1), Hargreaves (3).

Record Cup Victory: 11–0 v Chichester C, FA Cup, 1st rd, 5 November 1960 – Cook; Collinson, Thresher; Connor, Alan Williams, Etheridge; Tait (1), Bobby Williams (1), Atyeo (5), Adrian Williams (3), Derrick. (1 og).

Record Defeat: 0–9 v Coventry C, Division 3 (S), 28 April 1934.

Most League Points (2 for a win): 70, Division 3 (S), 1954–55.

Most League Points (3 for a win): 91, Division 3, 1989–90.

Most League Goals: 104, Division 3 (S), 1926–27.

Highest League Scorer in Season: Don Clark, 36, Division 3 (S), 1946–47.

Most League Goals in Total Aggregate: John Atyeo, 314, 1951–66.

Most Capped Player: Billy Wedlock, 26, England.

Most League Appearances: John Atyeo, 597, 1951–66.

Record Transfer Fee Received: £1,750,000 from Newcastle U for Andy Cole, March 1993.

Record Transfer Fee Paid: £500,000 to Arsenal for Andy Cole, July 1992.

Football League Record: 1901 Elected to Division 2; 1906–11 Division 1; 1911–22 Division 2; 1922–23 Division 3 (S); 1923–24 Division 2; 1924–27 Division 3 (S); 1927–32 Division 2; 1932–55 Division 3 (S); 1955–60 Division 2; 1960–65 Division 3; 1965–76 Division 2; 1976–80 Division 1; 1980–81 Division 2; 1981–82 Division 3; 1982–84 Division 4; 1984–90 Division 3; 1990–92 Division 2; 1992– Division 1.

Honours: *Football League:* Division 1 – Runners-up 1906–07; Division 2 – Champions 1905–06; Runners-up 1975–76; Division 3 (S) – Champions 1922–23, 1926–27, 1954–55; Runners-up 1937–38; Division 3 – Runners-up 1964–65, 1989–90. *FA Cup:* Runners-up 1909. *Football League Cup:* Semi-final 1971, 1989. *Welsh Cup:* Winners 1934. *Anglo-Scottish Cup:* Winners 1978. *Freight Rover Trophy:* Winners 1986; Runners-up 1987.

Colours: Red shirts, white shorts, red and white stockings. **Change colours:** Green, black, red repeat hooped shirts, black shorts with red trim, green stockings with black trim.

BRISTOL CITY FC

BRISTOL CITY 1994–95 LEAGUE RECORD

Match No.	Date	Venue	Opponents	Result	H/T Score	Lg. Pos.	Goalscorers	Attendance
1	Aug 13	H	Sunderland	D 0-0	0-0	—		11,127
2	20	A	Bolton W	W 2-0	1-0	4	Baird, Allison	12,127
3	27	H	Port Vale	D 0-0	0-0	8		8588
4	30	A	Burnley	D 1-1	0-1	—	Allison	11,067
5	Sept 3	A	Charlton Ath	L 2-3	0-1	16	Allison 2	9019
6	10	H	Notts Co	W 2-1	1-1	10	Bent, Scott (pen)	6670
7	13	H	Derby Co	L 0-2	0-1	—		8029
8	17	A	Southend U	L 1-2	0-1	17	Baird	3663
9	24	H	Middlesbrough	L 0-1	0-0	20		8642
10	Oct 1	A	Luton T	W 1-0	0-0	17	Baird	6633
11	8	H	Millwall	W 1-0	0-0	13	Baird	7499
12	15	A	Reading	L 0-1	0-0	16		9389
13	22	A	Grimsby T	L 0-1	0-0	20		4024
14	29	H	Portsmouth	D 1-1	1-0	21	Scott (pen)	7238
15	Nov 1	H	Wolverhampton W	L 1-5	1-2	—	Baird	10,401
16	5	A	Sheffield U	L 0-3	0-2	22		11,568
17	20	H	Swindon T	W 3-2	0-0	22	Bent, Allison 2	9086
18	26	A	Oldham Ath	L 0-2	0-0	22		7277
19	Dec 3	H	Grimsby T	L 1-2	0-0	23	Partridge	6030
20	7	A	Barnsley	L 1-2	1-1	—	Bent	4305
21	10	H	Bolton W	L 0-1	0-1	23		6144
22	17	A	Sunderland	L 0-2	0-0	23		11,661
23	26	A	WBA	L 0-1	0-0	23		21,071
24	27	H	Stoke C	W 3-1	0-0	23	Bryant, Allison 2	8500
25	31	A	Tranmere R	L 0-2	0-2	23		7439
26	Jan 2	H	Watford	D 0-0	0-0	23		9423
27	14	A	Portsmouth	D 0-0	0-0	23		8803
28	21	H	Sheffield U	W 2-1	0-0	23	Gayle (og), Shail	10,211
29	Feb 4	H	Barnsley	W 3-2	0-0	22	Dryden, Bryant, Allison	6408
30	11	A	Wolverhampton W	L 0-2	0-1	22		25,451
31	15	A	Swindon T	W 3-0	1-0	—	Bent, Fleck, Bryant	9881
32	18	H	Oldham Ath	D 2-2	2-1	20	Allison 2	7851
33	25	H	Luton T	D 2-2	0-1	21	Owers, Bent	7939
34	Mar 4	A	Middlesbrough	L 0-3	0-1	21		17,371
35	7	H	Charlton Ath	W 2-1	1-0	—	Kuhl, Tinnion	6118
36	11	A	Port Vale	L 1-2	1-1	21	Owers	7646
37	18	H	Burnley	D 1-1	1-0	22	Partridge	6717
38	21	A	Notts Co	D 1-1	0-0	—	Baird	5692
39	25	H	Southend U	D 0-0	0-0	21		6159
40	Apr 1	A	Derby Co	L 1-3	1-2	21	Allison	14,555
41	8	H	Tranmere R	L 0-1	0-1	23		6723
42	15	A	Stoke C	L 1-2	1-1	23	Shail	10,172
43	17	H	WBA	W 1-0	0-0	23	Bent	8777
44	22	A	Watford	L 0-1	0-0	23		7190
45	29	H	Reading	L 1-2	0-1	23	Tinnion	9474
46	May 7	A	Millwall	D 1-1	1-1	23	Allison	8805

Final League Position: 23

GOALSCORERS

League (42): Allison 13, Baird 6, Bent 6, Bryant 3, Owers 2, Partridge 2, Scott 2 (2 pens), Shail 2, Tinnion 2, Dryden 1, Fleck 1, Kuhl 1, own goal 1.
Coca-Cola Cup (0).
FA Cup (3): Baird 1, Bent 1, Tinnion 1.

Welch K.J. 44	Harriott M.L. 19	Scott M. 18	Shail M.E.D. 37 + 1	Bryant M. 37	Fowler J.K.G. 10 + 3	McAree R.J. 4 + 2	Bent J.A. 40 + 1	Baird I.J. 28 + 9	Allison W. 37	Edwards R.W. 29 + 1	Partridge S.M. 14 + 19	Munro S. 29 + 2	Loss C.P. 3 + 2	Brown I.O. — + 1	McKop H.G. — + 1	Tinnion B. 33 + 2	Simpson F. 4	Seal D. 5 + 4	Wyatt M.J. 1 + 2	Humphries M. 4	Paterson S. 2 + 1	Kite P.D. 2	Hansen V. 29	Parris G. 6	Watson K.E. 1 + 1	Owers G. 21	Dryden R.A. 15 + 4	Kuhl M. 17	Fleck R. 10	Flatts M. 4 + 2	Martin D. 3 + 1	Hewlett P.M. — + 1	Match No.
1	2	3	4	5	6	7	8	9	10	11	12																						1
1	2	3	4	5	6	7	8	9	10	11	12	14																					2
1	2	3	4	5	6		8	9	10	11	12		7	14																			3
1	2	3	4	5	6		8	9	10	11	12		7																				4
1	2	3	4	5	6		8	9	10	11	12		7																				5
1	2	3	4	5	6		8	9	10	11	7		12		14																		6
1	2	3	4	5	6		8	9	10	11	7		12																				7
1	2	3	4	5			8	9		11	7					6	10																8
1	2	3	4	5		7	8	9		11	12					6	10																9
1	2	3	4	5			8	9		11	12	6				10	7																10
1	2	3	4	5		11		9			12	6				10	7	8	14														11
1	2		4	5				9	10	11	12	7				6		8		3													12
1	2		4	5		12		9	10	11	14	7				6		8		3													13
1	2	3	4	5			7	9	10	11	8	12				6		14															14
1			4	5	12		7	9		11		3				6		8		2	10												15
1	2		4	5	6		12	9		11	14							8	7	3	10												16
	2	3		5	6		8		10	11	7					9						1	4										17
	2	3	4		7	12	8		10	11	9					6						1	5										18
1		3	4	5	12		8		10	11	9					6								2	7								19
1	2	3	4				8	9	10	11	12					6							5	7									20
1	2	3	4				8	9	10	11	12					6							5	7	14								21
1		3	4				8	9	10	11	6	2				12							5	7									22
1			4	5			8	9	10		12	3				6							2	7		11							23
1			4	5			8	9	10		12	3				6							2	7		11	14						24
1			4	5			8	9	10		12	3				6							2			11		7					25
1			4	5			8	9	10	11		3				6		12					2					7					26
1			4	5			8	12	10			3				6							2			11	14	7	9				27
1			4	5			8		10	7	12					6							2			11	3		9				28
1				5			8	12	10			3				6							2			11	4	7	9				29
1			4	5			8	12	10			3				6							2			11		7	9				30
1			4	5			8	12	10			3				6							2			11		7	9				31
1			4	5			8	12	10			3				6							2			11	14	7	9				32
1				5			8		10			3				6							2			11	4	7	9				33
1			4	5			8	12	10			3				6							2			11	14	7	9				34
1				5			8	12	10			3				6							2			11	4	7	9				35
1			12	5			8		10			3				6		14					2			11	4	7	9				36
1				5			8	9		6	10	3							12				2			11	4	7					37
1				5			8	9		7	10	3				6							2			11	4						38
1				5			8	9		7	10	3				6							2			11	4			12			39
1			4				8	9	10			3				6							2			11	5	7		12			40
1			4				8		10		12	3				6							2			11	5	7		9			41
1			4				8	12	10	14		3				6							2			11	5			9	7		42
1			4				8		10	6	12	3											2			11	5	7		9	14		43
1			4				8	12	10		9	3				14							2			11	5	7		6			44
1			4	8	12				10	11	9	3				6		14					2				5				7		45
1				4				9	10	11	6	3									12		2				5	8			7	14	46

Coca-Cola Cup

Second Round	Notts Co (h)	0-1
	(a)	0-3

FA Cup

Third Round	Stoke C (h)	0-0
	(a)	3-1
Fourth Round	Everton (h)	0-1

BRISTOL ROVERS 1994–95 *Back row (left to right):* Ian Wright, Billy Clark, Andy Tillson, Ian McLean, Gareth Taylor, Marcus Browning, Tom White, Lee Maddison.
Third row: Ian Alexander, Justin Channing, Gary Waddock, Marcus Law, Brian Parkin, Paul Hardyman, David Pritchard, Marcus Stewart.
Second Row: Roy Dolling (Youth Development Manager), Keith James (Physio), Dennis Booth (Assistant Manager), John Ward (Manager), Steve Cross (Reserve Team Manager), Tony Gill (Youth Coach), Ray Kendall (Kit Manager), Terry Connor (Community Officer).
Front Row: Lee Archer, Paul Tovey, Andrew Gurney, Mike Davis, Martin Paul, Worrell Sterling, Matt Hayfield.

Division 2 — BRISTOL ROVERS

Twerton Park, Twerton, Bath, BA2 1DB. Telephone: (0117) 352508. Fax: (0117) 353477. Training Ground: (0117) 861743. Match Day Ticket Office: (01225) 312327. Offices: Avonfields House, Somerdale, Keynsham, Bristol BS18 2DJ. (0117) 9869999. Pirates Hotline: 0891 338345. Fax: (0117) 9864030. Community Office: (0117) 9860809.

Ground capacity: 8943.

Record attendance: 9464 v Liverpool, FA Cup 4th rd, 8 February 1992 (Twerton Park). 38,472 v Preston NE, FA Cup 4th rd, 30 January 1960 (Eastville).

Record receipts: £62,480 v Liverpool, FA Cup 4th rd, 8 February 1992.

Pitch measurements: 110yd × 75yd.

President: Marquis of Worcester.

Vice-Presidents: Dr W. T. Cussen, A. I. Seager, H. E. L. Brown, R. Redmond.

Chairman: D. H. A. Dunford. ***Vice-Chairman:*** G. M. H. Dunford.

Directors: R. Craig, B. Andrews, V. Stokes.

Manager: John Ward. ***Assistant Manager:***–.

Reserve Team Manager: Steve Cross. ***Physio:*** Keith James. ***Youth Team Coach:*** Tony Gill. ***Commercial Manager:*** R. Miller.

Secretary: Ian Wilson. ***Assistant Secretary:*** I. I. Wilson. ***Office Manager:*** Mrs Angela Mann.

Year Formed: 1883. ***Turned Professional:*** 1897. ***Ltd Co.:*** 1896.

Previous Names: 1883, Black Arabs; 1884, Eastville Rovers; 1897, Bristol Eastville Rovers; 1898, Bristol Rovers.

Club Nickname: 'Pirates'.

Previous Grounds: Purdown, Three Acres, Ashley Hill, Rudgeway, Eastville.

Foundation: Bristol Rovers were formed at a meeting in Stapleton Road, Eastville, in 1883. However, they first went under the name of the Black Arabs (wearing black shirts). Changing their name to Eastville Rovers in their second season, they won the Gloucestershire Senior Cup in 1888–89. Original members of the Bristol & District League in 1892, this eventually became the Western League and Eastville Rovers adopted professionalism in 1897.

First Football League game: 28 August, 1920, Division 3, v Millwall (a) L 0-2 – Stansfield; Bethune, Panes; Boxley, Kenny, Steele; Chance, Bird, Sims, Bell, Palmer.

Record League Victory: 7–0 v Brighton & HA, Division 3 (S), 29 November 1952 – Hoyle; Bamford, Geoff Fox; Pitt, Warren, Sampson; McIlvenny, Roost (2), Lambden (1), Bradford (1), Peterbridge (2). (1 og). 7–0 v Swansea T, Division 2, 2 October 1954 – Radford; Bamford, Watkins; Pitt, Muir, Anderson; Petherbridge, Bradford (2), Meyer, Roost (1), Hooper (2). (2 og). 7–0 v Shrewsbury T, Division 3, 21 March 1964 – Hall; Hillard, Gwyn Jones; Oldfield, Stone (1), Mabbutt; Jarman (2), Brown (1), Biggs (1p), Hamilton, Bobby Jones (2).

Record Cup Victory: 6–0 v Merthyr Tydfil, FA Cup, 1st rd, 14 November 1987 – Martyn; Alexander (Dryden), Tanner, Hibbitt, Twentyman, Jones, Holloway, Meacham (1), White (2), Penrice (3) (Reece), Purnell.

Record Defeat: 0–12 v Luton T, Division 3 (S), 13 April 1936.

Most League Points (2 for a win): 64, Division 3 (S), 1952–53.

Most League Points (3 for a win): 93, Division 3, 1989–90.

Most League Goals: 92, Division 3 (S), 1952–53.

Highest League Scorer in Season: Geoff Bradford, 33, Division 3 (S), 1952–53.

Most League Goals in Total Aggregate: Geoff Bradford, 245, 1949–64.

Most Capped Player: Neil Slatter, 10 (22), Wales.

Most League Appearances: Stuart Taylor, 545, 1966–80.

Record Transfer Fee Received: £1,000,000 from Crystal Palace for Nigel Martyn, November 1989.

Record Transfer Fee Paid: £370,000 to QPR for Andy Tillson, November 1992.

Football League Record: 1920 Original Member of Division 3; 1921–53 Division 3 (S); 1953–62 Division 2; 1962–74 Division 3; 1974–81 Division 2; 1981–90 Division 3; 1990– 92 Division 2. 1992–93 Division 1; 1993– Division 2.

Honours: *Football League:* Division 2 best season: 4th, 1994–95; Division 3 (S) – Champions 1952–53; Division 3 – Champions 1989–90; Runners-up 1973–74. *FA Cup:* best season: 6th rd, 1951, 1958. *Football League Cup:* best season: 5th rd, 1971, 1972.

Colours: Blue and white quartered shirts, white shorts, blue stockings. **Change colours:** Green shirts, black shorts, black stockings.

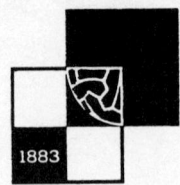

BRISTOL ROVERS 1994–95 LEAGUE RECORD

Match No.	Date	Venue	Opponents	Result		H/T Score	Lg. Pos.	Goalscorers	Atten-dance
1	Aug 13	A	Peterborough U	D	0-0	0-0	—		5695
2	20	H	York C	W	3-1	1-1	8	Clark, Miller, Stewart	3957
3	27	A	Wycombe W	D	0-0	0-0	11		5895
4	31	H	Blackpool	D	0-0	0-0	—		3762
5	Sept 3	H	Stockport Co	D	2-2	2-1	13	Tillson, Archer	4263
6	10	A	Rotherham U	W	3-0	3-0	12	Miller 2, Wilder (og)	2596
7	13	A	Swansea C	D	0-0	0-0	—		3226
8	17	H	Wrexham	W	4-2	1-0	7	Clark 2, Taylor, Miller	4441
9	24	A	Shrewsbury T	L	0-1	0-1	11		4596
10	Oct 1	H	Crewe Alex	D	2-2	0-2	12	Taylor 2	4862
11	8	A	Brentford	L	0-3	0-2	15		5330
12	15	H	Cardiff C	D	2-2	0-1	13	Channing, Clark	3936
13	22	H	Brighton & HA	W	3-0	2-0	12	Stewart, Miller 2	4107
14	29	A	Birmingham C	L	0-2	0-2	12		15,886
15	Nov 1	A	Cambridge U	D	1-1	0-0	—	Tillson	2328
16	5	H	Bradford C	W	4-0	2-0	12	Stewart 2, Oliver (og), Browning	4247
17	19	A	Hull C	W	2-0	1-0	10	Stewart 2	4450
18	26	H	Huddersfield T	D	1-1	1-1	12	Miller	5679
19	Dec 10	A	York C	W	3-0	1-0	9	Skinner, Stewart 2	3094
20	17	H	Peterborough U	W	3-1	0-1	7	Stewart 2 (1 pen), Gurney	4635
21	26	H	Bournemouth	W	2-1	1-0	7	Miller, Stewart	6913
22	31	H	Chester C	W	3-0	2-0	8	Archer 2, Stewart	5629
23	Jan 14	H	Oxford U	W	3-2	0-2	8	Taylor, Miller, Stewart	5875
24	Feb 4	A	Huddersfield T	D	1-1	1-0	9	Sterling	10,389
25	7	A	Bradford C	L	1-2	0-1	—	Heggs	4243
26	14	A	Brighton & HA	W	2-1	0-1	—	Stewart, Archer	5232
27	18	A	Oxford U	D	0-0	0-0	8		6349
28	25	A	Crewe Alex	L	1-2	0-2	11	Miller	4222
29	Mar 1	H	Hull C	L	0-2	0-1	—		3707
30	4	H	Shrewsbury T	W	4-0	1-0	10	Taylor, Archer, Browning, Miller (pen)	4338
31	7	A	Stockport Co	L	1-2	1-1	—	Miller	3580
32	11	H	Wycombe W	W	1-0	1-0	11	Taylor	5118
33	15	H	Cambridge U	W	2-1	2-1	—	Miller, Taylor	3734
34	18	A	Blackpool	W	2-0	0-0	6	Miller, Skinner	4484
35	22	H	Rotherham U	W	2-0	0-0	—	Taylor, Clark	4420
36	25	A	Wrexham	D	1-1	1-0	5	Archer	3170
37	29	H	Birmingham C	D	1-1	1-0	—	Whyte (og)	8010
38	Apr 1	H	Swansea C	W	1-0	0-0	4	Taylor	7062
39	4	A	Plymouth Arg	D	1-1	0-1	—	Miller	6743
40	8	A	Chester C	D	0-0	0-0	4		2241
41	11	A	Leyton Orient	W	2-1	1-0	—	Miller, Channing	2338
42	15	H	Plymouth Arg	W	2-0	0-0	4	Taylor, Wright	7068
43	18	A	Bournemouth	L	0-2	0-1	—		7020
44	22	H	Leyton Orient	W	1-0	0-0	4	Clark	4838
45	29	A	Cardiff C	W	1-0	0-0	4	Stewart	5462
46	May 6	H	Brentford	D	2-2	1-0	4	Taylor 2	8501

Final League Position: 4

GOALSCORERS

League (70): Miller 16 (1 pen), Stewart 15 (1 pen), Taylor 12, Archer 6, Clark 6, Browning 2, Channing 2, Skinner 2, Tillson 2, Gurney 1, Heggs 1, Sterling 1, Wright 1, own goals 3.
Coca-Cola Cup (2): Stewart 1, Tillson 1.
FA Cup (8): Millar 4, Stewart 4.

Parkin B. 40	Pritchard D.M. 43	Maddison L.R. 12 + 2	Channing J.A. 35 + 5	Clark W.R. 42	Tillson A. 40	Sterling W.R. 46	Stewart M.P. 26 + 1	Paul M.L. 2 + 3	Skinner J. 38	Archer L. 32 + 10	Browning M.T. 31 + 10	Taylor G.K. 23 + 16	Gurney A.R. 35 + 3	Miller P. 41 + 1	Waddock G.P. 1	Wright I.M. 6 + 1	Law M.W. 2	Davis M.V. — + 2	McLean I. — + 1	Collett A.A. 4	Hardyman P.G.T. 1 + 4	Heggs C.S. 2 + 3	White T.M. 4	Match No.
1	2	3	4	5	6	7	8	9	10	*11*	12	14												1
1	2		4	5	6	7	9		10	11	12		3	8										2
1	2		4	5	6	7	*9*		10	11	12	14	3	8										3
1	2		4	5	6	7				11		9	3	8	10									4
1	2		4	5	6	7			10	11	12	9	3	8										5
1	2		4	5	6	7		12	10	11		9	3	8										6
1	2		4	5	6	7			10	11		9	3	8										7
1	2		4	5	6	7			10	11		9	3	8										8
1	2		*4*	5	6	7			10	11	12	9	3	8		14								9
1	2	12	4	5		7			*10*	11	14	9	3	8		6								10
	2	12	4	5		7		*8*	10	11	9		3			6	1	14						11
	2	3	4	5	6	7			*10*	11	8	9	14				1		12					12
	2		4	5	6	7	9		10		11	12	3	8						1				13
	2		4	5	6	7	9		*10*	14	11	12	3	8						1				14
	2		4	5	6	7	9		10		11		3	8						1				15
	2		4	5	6	7	9		10	12	11	14	3	*8*						1				16
1	2		4	5	6	7	9	14	*10*	12	11	8	3											17
1	2			5	6	7	9		10	11	4	12	3	8										18
1	2			5	6	7	9		10	11	4		3	8							12			19
1			2	5		7	9		10	11	4		3	8		6					12			20
1		3		5		7	9		10	*11*	4	12	2	8		6					14			21
1	*2*			5	6	7	9		10	11	4	12	3	8							14			22
1			2	5	6	7	9	12		11	4	14	3	8							*10*			23
1	2		11	5	6	7			10		4	12	3	8								9		24
1	2		11		6	7			10		4	12	3	8								9	5	25
1	2		8		5	7	9			11	6	12	3	*10*								14	4	26
1	2		10		6	7	*9*			11	4	12	3	8								14	5	27
1	2		10		6	7	*9*			11	4	8	3	12								14	5	28
1	2		10	6	5	7	9		11	12	4		3	8										29
1	2			5	6	7			10	11	4	9	3	8				12						30
1	2		12	5	6	7			10	11	4	9	3	8										31
1	2			5	6	7			10	11	4	9	3	8										32
1	2		12	5	6	7			10	11	4	9	3	8										33
1	2		12	5	6	7			10	11	4	9	3	8										34
1	2	3	12	5	6	7			10	11	4	9		8										35
1	2	3	12	5	6	7			10	11	4	9		8										36
1	2	3	4	5	6	7	9		10	11		12		8										37
1	2	3	4	5	6	7	9		*10*	11	12	14		8										38
1	2	3	4	5	6	7	9			11	10			8										39
1	2	3	4	5	6	7	9			11	*10*	14	12	8										40
1	2	3	10	5	6	7	9			*12*	4	11	14	8										41
1	2	3	4	5		7	*9*		10	12	14	11		8		6								42
1	2	3	11	5		7			10	12	4	9		8		6								43
1	2		*11*	5	6	7	12		10	14	4	9	3	8										44
1	2		11	5	6	7	4		10	12	14	*9*	3	8										45
1	2		*11*	5	6	7	4		10	12	14	9	3	8										46

Coca-Cola Cup

First Round	Port Vale (h)	1-3
	(a)	1-1

FA Cup

First Round	Bath C (a)	5-0
Second Round	Leyton Orient (a)	2-0
Third Round	Luton T (a)	1-1
	(h)	0-1

BURNLEY 1994–95 *Back row (left to right):* Andy Farrell, Mark Winstanley, Nathan Peel, Wayne Russell, Marlon Beresford, Mark Monington, John Pender, Tony Philliskirk.
Centre row: Harry Wilson (Reserve Team Coach), Paul Wilson, David Eyres, Adrian Randall, Anthony McCluskey, Paul Smith, Andrew Bannister, Richard Livingstone, Wayne Dowell, John Mullin, Glen Davis, Matthew Taylor, Adrian Heath, Graham Lancashire, Andy Jones (Physio).
Front row: Terry Pashley (Youth Team Coach), Liam Robinson, Chris Vinnicombe, Ted McMinn, Gary Parkinson, Mr Jimmy Mullen (Manager), Steve Davis, Mr Brian Miller (Chief Scout), Chris Brass, Paul Weller, John Deary, Warren Joyce, Clive Middlemass (Assistant Manager).

Division 2 BURNLEY

Turf Moor, Burnley BB10 4BX. Telephone: (01282) 427777. Fax: (01282) 428938. Clubcall: 0891 121153. Credit Card Ticket Sales: (0645) 101010.

Ground capacity: 22,966.

Record attendance: 54,775 v Huddersfield T, FA Cup 3rd rd, 23 February 1924.

Record receipts; £150,000 v Liverpool, FA Cup 4th rd, 28 January 1995.

Pitch measurements: 114yd × 72yd.

Chairman: F. J. Teasdale.

Vice-Chairman: Dr R. D. Iven MRCS (Eng), LRCP (Lond), MRCGP.

Directors: B. Dearing LLB, B. Rothwell JP, C. Holt,R. Blakeborough.

Manager: Jimmy Mullen. ***Assistant Manager:*** Clive Middlemass.

Secretary: Mark Blackbourne. ***Coaches:*** Harry Wilson, Terry Pashley.

Commercial Manager: T. Skelly. ***Physio:*** Andy Jones.

Year Formed: 1882. ***Turned Professional:*** 1883. ***Ltd Co.:*** 1897.

Previous Name: 1881–82, Burnley Rovers.

Club Nickname: 'The Clarets'.

Previous Grounds: 1881, Calder Vale; 1882, Turf Moor.

Foundation: The majority of those responsible for the formation of the Burnley club in 1881 were from the defunct rugby club Burnley Rovers. Indeed, they continued to play rugby for a year before changing to soccer and dropping "Rovers" from their name. The changes were decided at a meeting held in May 1882 at the Bull Hotel.

First Football League game: 8 September, 1888, Football League, v PNE (a), L 2-5 – Smith; Lang, Bury, Abrams, Friel, Keenan, Brady, Tait, Poland (1), Gallocher (1), Yates.

Record League Victory: 9–0 v Darwen, Division 1, 9 January 1892 – Hillman; Walker, McFettridge, Lang, Matthews, Keenan, Nicol (3), Bowes, Espie (1), McLardie (3), Hill (2).

Record Cup Victory: 9–0 v Crystal Palace, FA Cup, 2nd rd (replay) 10 February 1909 – Dawson; Barron, McLean; Cretney (2), Leake, Moffat; Morley, Ogden, Smith (3), Abbott (2), Smethams (1). 9–0 v New Brighton, FA Cup, 4th rd, 26 January 1957 – Blacklaw; Angus, Winton; Seith, Adamson, Miller; Newlands (1), McIlroy (3), Lawson (3), Cheesebrough (1), Pilkington (1). 9–0 v Penrith FA Cup, 1st rd, 17 November 1984 – Hansbury; Miller, Hampton, Phelan, Overson (Kennedy), Hird (3 incl. 1p), Grewcock (1), Powell (2), Taylor (3), Biggins, Hutchison.

Record Defeat: 0–10 v Aston Villa, Division 1, 29 August 1925 and v Sheffield U, Division 1, 19 January 1929.

Most League Points (2 for a win): 62, Division 2, 1972–73.

Most League Points (3 for a win): 83, Division 4, 1991–92.

Most League Goals: 102, Division 1, 1960–61.

Highest League Scorer in Season: George Beel, 35, Division 1, 1927–28.

Most League Goals in Total Aggregate: George Beel, 178, 1923–32.

Most Capped Player: Jimmy McIlroy, 51 (55), Northern Ireland.

Most League Appearances: Jerry Dawson, 522, 1907–28.

Record Transfer Fee Received: £300,000 from Everton for Martin Dobson, August 1974, and from Derby Co for Leighton James, November 1975.

Record Transfer Fee Paid: £250,000 to Bristol C for Liam Robinson, August 1994 and £250,000 to Brighton & HA for Kurt Nogan, February 1995.

Football League Record: 1888 Original Member of the Football League; 1897–98 Division 2; 1898–1900 Division 1; 1900–13 Division 2; 1913–30 Division 1; 1930–47 Division 2; 1947–71 Division 1; 1971–73 Division 2; 1973–76 Division 1; 1976–80 Division 2; 1980–82 Division 3; 1982–83 Division 2; 1983–85 Division 3; 1985–92 Division 4; 1992–94 Division 2; 1994–95 Division 1; 1995– Division 2.

Honours: *Football League:* Division 1 – Champions 1920–21, 1959–60; Runners-up 1919–20, 1961–62; Division 2 – Champions 1897–98, 1972–73; Runners-up 1912–13, 1946–47; Division 3 – Champions 1981–82. Division 4 – Champions 1991–92. Record 30 consecutive Division 1 games without defeat 1920–21. *FA Cup:* Winners 1914; Runners-up 1947, 1962. *Football League Cup:* semi-final 1961, 1969, 1983. *Anglo-Scottish Cup:* Winners 1979. *Sherpa Van Trophy:* Runners-up 1988. **European Competitions;** *European Cup:* 1960–61. *European Fairs Cup:* 1966–67.

Colours: Claret shirts with sky blue sleeves, white shorts and stockings. **Change colours:** Yellow shirts with black pinstripe, yellow shorts, yellow stockings with black band.

BURNLEY 1994–95 LEAGUE RECORD

Match No.	Date		Venue	Opponents	Result		H/T Score	Lg. Pos.	Goalscorers	Attendance
1	Aug	13	A	Middlesbrough	L	0-2	0-2	—		23,343
2		20	H	Stoke C	D	1-1	1-0	20	Davis	15,331
3		27	A	Oldham Ath	L	0-3	0-0	23		11,310
4		30	H	Bristol City	D	1-1	1-0	—	Robinson	11,067
5	Sept	3	H	Barnsley	L	0-1	0-0	23		11,968
6		10	A	Luton T	W	1-0	1-0	21	Robinson	6911
7		14	A	Millwall	W	3-2	0-0	—	Winstanley 2, Robinson	7375
8		17	H	Wolverhampton W	L	0-1	0-0	21		17,766
9		24	A	WBA	L	0-1	0-0	22		13,539
10	Oct	1	H	Tranmere R	D	1-1	0-1	22	Eyres (pen)	12,427
11		8	H	Bolton W	D	2-2	0-1	22	Davis, Deary	16,687
12		15	A	Sunderland	D	0-0	0-0	22		17,700
13		22	A	Charlton Ath	W	2-1	0-0	21	Davis, Robinson	9436
14		29	H	Notts Co	W	2-1	1-0	18	Eyres (pen), Hoyland	12,876
15	Nov	1	H	Watford	D	1-1	0-1	—	Eyres	11,739
16		5	A	Reading	D	0-0	0-0	21		8150
17		20	H	Sheffield U	W	4-2	1-1	15	Robinson, Hoyland, Gayle, Davis	11,475
18		23	A	Swindon T	D	1-1	0-1	—	Gayle	7654
19		26	A	Grimsby T	D	2-2	0-1	15	Davis, Parkinson	7084
20	Dec	10	A	Stoke C	L	0-2	0-0	18		13,040
21		18	H	Middlesbrough	L	0-3	0-1	20		12,049
22		31	H	Southend U	W	5-1	2-0	19	Saville, Gayle, Bressington (og), Davis, Robinson	10,561
23	Jan	2	A	Portsmouth	L	0-2	0-1	20		9097
24		14	A	Notts Co	L	0-3	0-0	22		8702
25		21	H	Reading	L	1-2	0-2	22	Parkinson	9841
26	Feb	4	H	Swindon T	L	1-2	0-1	23	Harrison	10,960
27		11	A	Watford	L	0-2	0-0	23		9297
28		18	H	Grimsby T	L	0-2	0-1	23		10,511
29		21	A	Sheffield U	L	0-2	0-1	—		13,349
30		25	A	Tranmere R	L	1-4	0-1	24	Garnett (og)	9909
31	Mar	4	H	WBA	D	1-1	0-0	24	Robinson	11,885
32		7	A	Barnsley	L	0-2	0-1	—		5537
33		11	H	Oldham Ath	W	2-1	1-0	24	Nogan, Vinnicombe	11,620
34		15	A	Derby Co	L	0-4	0-1	—		13,922
35		18	A	Bristol C	D	1-1	0-1	24	Eyres	6717
36		21	H	Luton T	W	2-1	0-0	—	Mullin, Harrison	9551
37		24	A	Wolverhampton W	L	0-2	0-1	—		25,703
38		28	H	Port Vale	W	4-3	1-1	—	Nogan, Randall, Shaw, Sandeman (og)	10,058
39	Apr	1	H	Millwall	L	1-2	0-1	23	Shaw	10,454
40		4	H	Charlton Ath	W	2-0	1-0	—	Eyres, Shaw	10,045
41		8	A	Southend U	L	1-3	0-2	22	Nogan	5027
42		15	H	Derby Co	W	3-1	2-0	22	Eyres, Shaw, Davis	11,534
43		17	A	Port Vale	L	0-1	0-1	22		9663
44		22	H	Portsmouth	L	1-2	0-1	22	Eyres	10,666
45		29	H	Sunderland	D	1-1	1-1	21	Eyres (pen)	15,121
46	May	7	A	Bolton W	D	1-1	0-0	22	Philliskirk	16,853

Final League Position: 22

GOALSCORERS

League (49): Eyres 8 (3 pens), Davis 7, Robinson 7, Shaw 4, Gayle 3, Nogan 3, Harrison 2, Hoyland 2, Parkinson 2, Winstanley 2, Deary 1, Mullin 1, Philliskirk 1, Randall 1, Saville 1, Vinnicombe 1, own goals 3.
Coca-Cola Cup (4): Robinson 2, Gayle 1, Joyce 1.
FA Cup (8): Eyres 2 (2 pens), Heath 2, Deary 1, Gayle 1, Randall 1, Robinson 1.

Beresford M. 40	Parkinson G. 42 + 1	Vinnicombe C. 29	Davis S.M. 43	Winstanley M.A. 44	Joyce W.G. 4 + 1	Harper A. 27	Deary J.S. 12 + 4	Heath A.P. 21 + 6	Robinson S.L. 29 + 10	McMinn K.C. 17 + 5	Lancashire G. — + 1	Gayle J. 7 + 7	Harrison G.R. 16 + 3	Russell W.L. 6 + 2	Eyres D. 38 + 1	Randall A.J. 32	Philliskirk A. 7 + 6	Hoyland J.W. 30	Francis J.A. — + 2	Dowell W.A. 5	Mullin J. 6 + 6	Armstrong C. 4	Saville A.V. 3 + 1	Brass C.P. 2 + 3	Pender J.P. 5	Stewart P.A. 6	Peel N.J. — + 3	Nogan K. 11 + 4	Thompson S.J. 12	Shaw P. 8 + 1	*Match No.*
1	2	3	4	5	6	7	8	9	10	11	12																				1
1	2	3	4	5	6	7	12	9	10	11		8																			2
1	3		4	5	6	7	12	9	10	11		8	2	15																	3
1	2	3	4	5	6	7		9	10	11		8	12																		4
1	2	3	4	5	14	*6*	8	12	10	7		9			11																5
	2	3	4	5		7		9	10	11			8	1		6															6
1	2	3	4	5		7	6	9	10	11			8																		7
1	2	3	4	5		7	6	9	*10*	11			8		12		14														8
1	2	3	4	5		7	12	9	10	*8*			6		11		14														9
1	2	3	4	5		6		9	10	7			8		11		12														10
1	*2*	3	4	5			9		10	7		12	14		11	6	8														11
1	2	3		5		7	9	12	10			14			11	6	*8*	4													12
1	2	3	4	5		7	9		10						11	6		8													13
1	2	3	4	5		7	9	12	10						11	6		8													14
1	2	3	4	5		7	*9*	12	10						11	6	14	8													15
1	2	*3*	4	5		7	9	8	10			12			11	6			14												16
1	2		4	5		7		8	10			12			11	6		9		3											17
1	2		4	5		7		8	10			12			11	6		9		3											18
1	2		4	5		7		8	*10*			12			11	6		9	14	3											19
1	2		4	5		7		8	10			9			11	*6*	12	3			14										20
1	2		4	5		7		8	*10*			12			11	6		9		3	14										21
1	2		4	5			11	8	10	12		9	6									3	7								22
1	2		4	5			11	8	9				*6*	15	10		12					*3*	7	14							23
1	2		4	5		7	12	8	10	14					3	*6*		11					9								24
	2		4	5		7			10	12		9		1	11	6		8				*3*	14								25
1	2		4	5		7			*10*	12			14		11	6		8			9	3									26
1	2			5		7		9	10	12			6		3			8			11				4						27
1	3			5				12	14	7			*2*		11	6		8			10				4	9					28
1	2		4	5		7		9					6		3			8			11					10	12				29
1	2		4			7		9	12				6		3			5								10		11	8		30
1	2		4			7		12	14						11	6		5		*3*						9		10	8		31
1	2	3	4	5											11	6		7								9	12	10	8		32
1	2	3	4	5											11	6		7								9		10	8		33
1	2	3	4	5											11	6		7			9						12	10	8		34
	12	3	4	5					14				2	1	11	6		7							10			*9*	8		35
		3	4	5					7				2	1	11	6					12				10			9	8		36
		3	4	5					*10*				2	1	11	6		7						12				9	8	14	37
		3	4	5									2	1	11	6		10			14			12				*9*	8	7	38
1	2		4	5					12						11	6		10			14			3				*9*	8	7	39
1	2	3	4	5					12	11					9	6		10											8	7	40
1	2	3	4	5					12	11					9	6		10						8				14		*7*	41
1	2	3	4	5					12	7					11	6	9	10												8	42
1	2	3	4	5					12						11	6	9	10							8			14		*7*	43
1	2	3	4	5					12	7					11	6	*9*	10										14		8	44
1	2	3	4	5						7					11	6	9	10			12							14		*8*	45
1	2	3	4	5											11	6	9				7							8	10		46

Coca-Cola Cup

First Round	York C (h)	1-0
	(a)	2-2
Second Round	Liverpool (a)	0-2
	(h)	1-4

FA Cup

First Round	Shrewsbury T (h)	2-1
Second Round	Chester C (a)	2-1
Third Round	Cambridge U (a)	4-2
Fourth Round	Liverpool (h)	0-0
	(a)	0-1

BURY 1994–95 *Back row (left to right):* Peter Reid, Mark Sertori, David Pugh, Ryan Cross, John Paskin, Tony Kelly.
Centre row: Alan Raw (Physio), Stan Ternent (Assistant Manager), Lee Anderson, Ian Hughes, Ian Stevens, Lee Bracey, Chris Lucketti, Nick Daws, Tony Rigby, Cliff Roberts (Coach), Walter Joyce (Youth Development Officer).
Front row: Mark Carter, Michael Jackson, Ronnie Mauge, Mike Walsh (Manager), Jimmy Mulligan, Roger Stanislaus, Lenny Johnrose.

Division 3 **BURY**

Gigg Lane, Bury BL9 9HR. Telephone: (0161) 764 4881. Fax:(0161) 764 5521. Commercial Dept: (0161) 705 2144. Clubcall: 0898 121197. Community Programme: (0161) 797 5423. Social Club: (0161) 764 6771.

Ground capacity: 12,000 (unofficial).

Record attendance: 35,000 v Bolton W, FA Cup 3rd rd, 9 January 1960.

Record receipts: £37,000 v Bolton W, Division 3 play-off, 19 May 1991.

Pitch measurements: 112yd × 72yd.

Chairman: T. Robinson. ***Vice-Chairman:*** Canon J. R. Smith MA.

Directors: C. H. Eaves, J. Smith, F. Mason.

Manager: Mike Walsh. ***Coaches:*** Stan Ternent and Cliff Roberts. ***Physio:*** Alan Raw. ***Youth Development:*** W. Joyce.

Assistant Secretary: J. Neville. ***Commercial Manager:*** Neville Neville.

Year Formed: 1885. ***Turned professional:*** 1885. ***Ltd Co.:*** 1897. ***Club Nickname:*** 'Shakers'.

Club Sponsors: Birthdays.

Foundation: A meeting at the Waggon & Horses Hotel, attended largely by members of Bury Wesleyans and Bury Unitarians football clubs, decided to form a new Bury club. This was officially formed at a subsequent gathering at the Old White Horse Hotel, Fleet Street, Bury on April 24, 1885.

First Football League game: 1 September, 1894, Division 2, v Manchester C (h) W 4-2 – Lowe; Gillespie, Davies; White, Clegg, Ross; Wylie, Barbour (2), Millar (1), Ostler (1), Plant.

Record League Victory: 8–0 v Tranmere R, Division 3, 10 January 1970 – Forrest; Tinney, Saile; Anderson, Turner, McDermott; Hince (1), Arrowsmith (1), Jones (4), Kerr (1), Grundy. (1 og).

Record Cup Victory: 12–1 v Stockton, FA Cup, 1st rd (replay), 2 February 1897 – Montgomery; Darroch, Barbour; Hendry (1), Clegg, Ross (1); Wylie (3), Pangbourn, Millar (4), Henderson (2), Plant. (1 og).

Record Defeat: 0–10 v Blackburn R, FA Cup, preliminary round, 1 October 1887 and v West Ham U, Milk Cup, 2nd rd, 2nd leg, 25 October 1983.

Most League Points (2 for a win): 68, Division 3, 1960–61.

Most League Points (3 for a win): 84, Division 4, 1984–85.

Most League Goals: 108, Division 3, 1960–61.

Highest League Scorer in Season: Craig Madden, 35, Division 4, 1981–82.

Most League Goals in Total Aggregate: Craig Madden, 129, 1978–86.

Most Capped Player: Bill Gorman, 11 (13), Republic of Ireland and (4), Northern Ireland.

Most League Appearances: Norman Bullock, 506, 1920–35.

Record Transfer Fee Received: £375,000 from Southampton for David Lee, October 1991.

Record Transfer Fee Paid: £175,000 to Shrewsbury T for John McGinlay, July 1990.

Football League Record: 1894 Elected to Division 2; 1895–1912 Division 1; 1912–24 Division 2; 1924–29 Division 1; 1929–57 Division 2; 1957–61 Division 3; 1961–67 Division 2; 1967–68 Division 3; 1968–69 Division 2; 1969–71 Division 3; 1971–74 Division 4; 1974–80 Division 3; 1980–85 Division 4; 1985– Division 3.

Honours: *Football League:* Division 1 best season: 4th, 1925–26; Division 2 – Champions 1894–95; Runners-up 1923–24; Division 3 – Champions 1960–61; Runners-up 1967–68. *FA Cup:* Winners 1900, 1903. *Football League Cup:* Semi-final 1963.

Colours: White shirts, royal blue shorts, royal blue stockings. **Change colours:** Navy/red shirts, white shorts, navy/red stockings.

BURY 1994–95 LEAGUE RECORD

Match No.	Date		Venue	Opponents	Result		H/T Score	Lg. Pos.	Goalscorers	Attendance
1	Aug	13	H	Rochdale	L	0-1	0-0	—		3230
2		20	A	Exeter C	W	4-0	3-0	10	Carter 3, Jackson	2164
3		27	H	Hartlepool U	W	2-0	1-0	6	Carter 2 (1 pen)	2145
4		30	H	Preston NE	D	0-0	0-0	—		3623
5	Sept	3	A	Mansfield T	W	2-0	1-0	5	Carter, Paskin	2576
6		10	H	Scunthorpe U	W	2-0	1-0	3	Johnrose, Carter	2540
7		13	H	Doncaster R	W	2-0	1-0	—	Pugh, Paskin	2395
8		17	A	Rochdale	W	3-0	0-0	2	Carter, Paskin 2	3748
9		24	H	Chesterfield	W	2-1	1-1	1	Pugh, Carter	3031
10	Oct	1	A	Colchester U	L	0-1	0-0	2		3286
11		8	A	Darlington	W	2-0	0-0	2	Carter, Pugh	2352
12		15	H	Lincoln C	W	2-0	2-0	1	Johnrose, Pugh	3139
13		22	H	Gillingham	W	3-2	2-0	1	Carter (pen), Paskin 2	2976
14		29	A	Walsall	W	1-0	0-0	1	Pugh (pen)	5255
15	Nov	5	H	Scarborough	W	1-0	0-0	1	Johnrose	3016
16		19	A	Barnet	D	1-1	0-1	2	Mulligan	3006
17		26	H	Fulham	D	0-0	0-0	2		3323
18	Dec	10	H	Exeter C	D	0-0	0-0	2		2876
19		17	A	Hartlepool U	L	1-3	0-2	2	Daws	1746
20		26	H	Wigan Ath	D	3-3	2-2	2	Lucketti, Carter, Matthews	3616
21		27	A	Carlisle U	L	0-3	0-1	2		12,242
22	Jan	14	H	Hereford U	D	1-1	1-0	4	Carter	2708
23	Feb	4	A	Fulham	L	0-1	0-0	5		3941
24		18	A	Hereford U	L	0-1	0-1	9		1827
25		25	H	Colchester U	W	4-1	1-0	7	Stant, Hughes, Betts (og), Lucketti	2484
26		28	H	Torquay U	W	3-1	1-0	—	Kelly T, Lucketti, Stant	2241
27	Mar	4	A	Chesterfield	D	0-0	0-0	5		4429
28		7	A	Northampton T	W	5-0	1-0	—	Pugh 3 (1 pen), Kelly T, Stant	4208
29		11	A	Scunthorpe U	L	2-3	1-1	5	Pugh, Mulligan	2767
30		14	H	Barnet	W	3-0	3-0	—	Rigby, Stant, Johnrose	2380
31		18	A	Preston NE	L	0-5	0-2	5		9626
32		21	A	Scarborough	W	2-1	1-1	—	Pugh 2	1744
33		25	H	Mansfield T	D	2-2	1-0	4	Kelly T, Pugh (pen)	4188
34	Apr	1	A	Doncaster R	W	2-1	0-1	4	Stant 2	2485
35		4	A	Gillingham	D	1-1	1-1	—	Lancaster	2945
36		8	A	Torquay U	D	2-2	1-1	4	Stant 2	1969
37		15	H	Carlisle U	W	2-0	0-0	4	Stant, Jackson	5507
38		18	A	Wigan Ath	W	3-0	1-0	—	Stant 2, Paskin	2531
39		22	H	Northampton T	W	5-0	1-0	4	Daws, Pugh 2 (1 pen), Rigby, Paskin	2921
40		29	A	Lincoln C	W	3-0	2-0	4	Pugh 2, Stant	3928
41	May	4	H	Walsall	D	0-0	0-0	—		6790
42		6	H	Darlington	W	2-1	1-1	4	Carter (pen), Stant	3612

Final League Position: 4

GOALSCORERS

League (73): Pugh 16 (4 pens), Carter 14 (3 pens), Stant 13, Paskin 8, Johnrose 4, Kelly T 3, Lucketti 3, Daws 2, Jackson 2, Mulligan 2, Rigby 2, Hughes 1, Lancaster 1, Matthews 1, own goal 1.
Coca-Cola Cup (3): Carter 1 (pen), Rigby 1, own goal 1.
FA Cup (5): Johnrose 1, Lucketti 1, Paskin 1, Rigby 1, Stanislaus 1.

Kelly G.A. 38	Cross R. 11 + 1	Stanislaus R.E.P. 33	Mauge R.C. 14 + 4	Lucketti C.J. 39	Jackson M.J. 24	Mulligan J. 9 + 6	Carter M.C. 21 + 5	Hulme K. 24 + 4	Reid P. 1	Pugh D. 42	Daws N.J. 30 + 4	Paskin W.J. 15 + 11	Johnrose L. 23 + 3	Rigby A.A. 24 + 6	Matthewson T. 18	Bracey L.M.I. 4 + 2	Sertori M.A. — + 2	Kelly A.O.N. 19 + 3	Hughes I. 19 + 4	De Souza J.M. 2 + 1	Matthews N. 2	Stant P. 19 + 1	Bimson S.J. 19	Lancaster D. 3 + 2	Rowe R.C. 1 + 2	Woodward A.S. 8	Match No.
1	2	3	4	5	6	7	8	9	10	11	*12*	14															1
1	2	3	4	5	6	7	8	9		11		12	10														2
1	2	3	4	5	6	7	8	*9*		11		14	12	10													3
1	2	3	4	5	6	7	8	9		11		12	14	*10*													4
1	2	3	4	5		7	8	9		11		12	10	14	6												5
		3	*4*	5	2	7	8	9		11		12	10		6	1	14										6
		3		5	2	7	8	9		11	4	12	10		6	1											7
1		3	4	5	2		8	*9*		11	12	7	10	14	6												8
1		3		5	2		8	9		11	4	7	10	12	6												9
1		3		5	2		8	9		11	4	7	10	12	6												10
1		3		5	2		8	9		11	4	7	10		6			12									11
1		3		5	2		8			11	4	7	10	9	6		12										12
1	2	3		5			8	12		11	4	7	10	9	6												13
1	2	3		5		*12*	8	9		11	4		10	7	6				14								14
1		3		5	2	8		9		11	4		10	7	6			12									15
1	2	3	10	5		12				11	4	9	8	7	6	15											16
1	2	3	10	5				8		11		9	4		6			7		12							17
1		3		5	*2*		12			11	10		4	14	6			7	9	8							18
1		3		5	2		8			11	4		10	12	6				7	9							19
1		3	4	5	2		8			11	14		10	*7*	6				12		9						20
1	12	3	4	5	2		8			11	6		10						7		9						21
1	2	3	4			12	8	7		11		9	10		6				5								22
1		3	4	5	2		8			11	12	*9*	10					7	6			14					23
1	2			5				12		11		8	10	4				7	6			9	3				24
1		2		5				12		11	10	8		4				7	6			9	3				25
1		2		5						11	10	8		4				7	6			9	3				26
1		2	12	5				14		11	10	*8*		4				7	6			9	3				27
1		2	12	5		14		8		11	*10*			4				7	6			9	3				28
1		2		5		12		8		11	10			4				7	6			9	3				29
1		2		5		7	14			11	10		12	4					6			9	3	*8*			30
1		2			7			8		11	10			4	5				6			9	3	12			31
1		2		5				8		11	10			4		15		12	6			*9*	3		7		32
1		2		5			12	8		11	10			*4*				7	6			9	3		14		33
1		2		5						11	4		10					7	6			9	3	8			34
				5			12			11	4		10			1		7	6			9	3	8	14	2	35
			12	5			*8*			11	4			10		1		7	6			9	3	14		2	36
1				5	6			8		11	4	12		10				7				9	3			2	37
1			*4*	5	6			8		11	10	12						7	14			9	3			2	38
1				5	6			8		11	4	12		10				7				9	3			2	39
1				5	6			8		11	4	12		10				7	14			9	3			*2*	40
1				5	6	12				11	10	8		4				7				9	3			2	41
1			12		6	14	*8*			11	4			10				7	5			9	3			2	42

Coca-Cola Cup

First Round	Hartlepool U (h)	2-0
	(a)	1-5

FA Cup

First Round	Bishop Auckland (a)	0-0
	(h)	1-1
Second Round	Crewe Alex (a)	2-1
Third Round	Tranmere R (h)	2-2
	(a)	0-3

CAMBRIDGE UNITED 1994–95 *Back row (left to right):* Craig Middleton, Darran Hay, Ollie Morah, Mick Heathcote, Steve Butler, Michael Danzey, Jody Craddock, Simon Livett, Kevin Bartlett, Danny Granville.

Centre row: Ken Steggles (Physio), Roger Parker (Kit Manager), Kofi Nyamah, Andy Jeffrey, Jon Sheffield, John Filan, Micah Hyde, John Fowler, Efon Elad, Paul Ashworth (Youth Development Officer).

Front row: Tommy Taylor (Youth Team Manager), Hakan Hayrettin, Carlo Corazzin, Matthew Joseph, Gary Johnson (Manager), Dean Barrick, Junior Hunter, Jon Rattle, Danny O'Shea (Player/Coach).

Division 3 **CAMBRIDGE UNITED**

Abbey Stadium, Newmarket Rd, Cambridge, CB5 8LN. Telephone: (01223) 566500. Fax: (01223) 566502. Abbey Update: 0891 555885.

Ground capacity: 9667.

Record attendance; 14,000 v Chelsea, Friendly, 1 May 1970.

Record receipts: £86,308 v Manchester U, Rumbelows Cup 2nd rd 2nd leg, 9 October 1991.

Pitch measurements: 110yd × 74yd.

Chairman: R. H. Smart. ***Vice-Chairman:*** R. F. Hunt. ***Directors:*** G. Harwood, J. Howard, R. Hunt, G. Lowe, R. Summerfield.

Manager: Tommy Taylor. ***Assistant Manager:*** Paul Clark. ***Youth Manager:*** Peter Braybrook.

Physio: Ken Steggles.

Secretary: Steve Greenall. ***Commercial Manager:*** John Holmes. ***Stadium Manager:*** Ian Darler.

Year Formed: 1919. ***Turned Professional:*** 1946. ***Ltd Co.:*** 1948.

Club Nickname: The 'U's'.

Previous Name: Abbey United until 1949.

Foundation: The football revival in Cambridge began soon after World War II when the Abbey United club (formed 1919) decided to turn professional and in 1949 changed their name to Cambridge United. They were competing in the United Counties League before graduating to the Eastern Counties League in 1951 and the Southern League in 1958.

First Football League game: 15 August, 1970, Division 4, v Lincoln C (h) D 1-1 – Roberts; Thompson, Meldrum (1), Slack, Eades, Hardy, Leggett, Cassidy, Lindsey, McKinven, Harris.

Record League Victory: 6–0 v Darlington, Division 4, 18 September 1971 – Roberts; Thompson, Akers, Guild, Eades, Foote, Collins (1p), Horrey, Hollett, Greenhalgh (4), Phillips. (1 og). 6–0 v Hartlepool, Division 4, 11 February 1989 – Vaughan; Beck, Kimble, Turner, Chapple (1), Daish, Clayton, Holmes, Taylor (3 incl. 1p), Bull (1), Leadbitter (1).

Record Cup Victory: 5–1 v Bristol C, FA Cup, 5th rd, second replay, 27 February 1990 – Vaughan; Fensome, Kimble, Bailie (O'Shea), Chapple, Daish, Cheetham (Robinson), Leadbitter (1), Dublin (2), Taylor (1), Philpott (1).

Record Defeat: 0–6 v Aldershot, Division 3, 13 April 1974 and v Darlington, Division 4, 28 September 1974 and v Chelsea, Division 2, 15 January 1983.

Most League Points (2 for a win): 65, Division 4, 1976–77.

Most League Points (3 for a win): 86, Division 3, 1990–91.

Most League Goals: 87, Division 4, 1976–77.

Highest League Scorer in Season: David Crown, 24, Division 4, 1985–86.

Most League Goals in Total Aggregate: Alan Biley, 74, 1975–80.

Most Capped Player: Tom Finney, 7 (15), Northern Ireland.

Most League Appearances: Steve Spriggs, 416, 1975–87.

Record Transfer Fee Received: £1,000,000 from Manchester U for Dion Dublin, August 1992.

Record Transfer Fee Paid: £190,000 to Luton T for Steve Claridge, November 1992.

Football League Record: 1970 Elected to Division 4; 1973–74 Division 3; 1974–77 Division 4; 1977–78 Division 3; 1978–84 Division 2; 1984–85 Division 3; 1985–90 Division 4; 1990–91 Division 3; 1991–92 Division 2; 1992–93 Division 1; 1993– 95 Division 2; 1995– Division 3.

Honours: *Football League:* Division 2 best season: 5th, 1991–92; Division 3 – Champions 1990–91; Runners-up 1977–78; Division 4 – Champions 1976–77. *FA Cup:* best season: 6th rd, 1990, 1991. *Football League Cup:* 5th rd, 1993.

Colours: Amber & black striped shirts, black shorts with amber & black trim, black & amber stockings. **Change colours:** Patterned white & sky blue shirts, royal blue shorts, royal blue stockings.

CAMBRIDGE UNITED 1994–95 LEAGUE RECORD

Match No.	*Date*		*Venue*	*Opponents*	*Result*		*H/T Score*	*Lg. Pos.*	*Goalscorers*	*Atten-dance*
1	Aug	13	A	Wycombe W	L	0-3	0-1	—		5782
2		20	H	Stockport Co	L	3-4	1-2	18	Joseph, Morah, Corazzin	3163
3		27	A	Oxford U	L	0-1	0-1	22		5513
4		30	H	Chester C	W	2-1	0-0	—	Barrick, Corazzin	2520
5	Sept	3	H	Rotherham U	W	2-1	1-0	15	Corazzin 2	2885
6		10	A	Leyton Orient	D	1-1	0-0	15	Morah	3699
7		13	A	Plymouth Arg	D	0-0	0-0	—		3824
8		17	H	Swansea C	L	1-3	1-2	18	Granville	2795
9		24	A	Brighton & HA	L	0-2	0-1	20		8280
10	Oct	1	H	Bradford C	W	4-1	2-1	18	Corazzin, Lillis, Butler 2	3338
11		8	H	Wrexham	L	1-2	0-0	18	Corazzin	3221
12		15	A	Huddersfield T	L	1-3	1-0	19	Butler	10,742
13		22	A	Cardiff C	L	1-3	1-1	20	Jeffrey	3580
14		29	H	Brentford	D	0-0	0-0	21		3102
15	Nov	1	H	Bristol R	D	1-1	0-0	—	Corazzin	2328
16		5	A	Bournemouth	L	0-1	0-0	22		3272
17		19	H	Shrewsbury T	W	3-1	1-1	21	Butler 2, Lillis	2748
18		26	A	Crewe Alex	L	2-4	0-1	21	Corazzin 2	3636
19	Dec	10	A	Stockport Co	L	1-2	0-0	21	Butler	3903
20		16	H	Wycombe W	D	2-2	1-1	—	Butler, Corazzin	3713
21		26	A	Birmingham C	D	1-1	0-1	20	Otto (og)	20,098
22		28	H	York C	W	1-0	0-0	—	Corazzin	3285
23		31	A	Peterborough U	D	2-2	1-1	18	Lillis 2	7412
24	Jan	2	H	Hull C	D	2-2	0-2	18	Hay 2	3569
25		14	A	Blackpool	W	3-2	1-1	18	Butler, Corazzin 2	4076
26		17	H	Cardiff C	W	2-0	1-0	—	Corazzin, Butler (pen)	2460
27		21	H	Bournemouth	D	2-2	1-0	17	Butler 2	2834
28		28	A	Brentford	L	0-6	0-0	17		6390
29	Feb	4	H	Crewe Alex	L	1-2	0-0	18	Corazzin	3339
30		18	H	Blackpool	D	0-0	0-0	19		3192
31		21	A	Shrewsbury T	D	1-1	1-0	—	Hay	3200
32		25	A	Bradford C	D	1-1	0-0	19	Jeffrey	6075
33	Mar	4	H	Brighton & HA	L	0-2	0-1	19		3856
34		7	A	Rotherham U	L	0-1	0-1	—		2208
35		11	H	Oxford U	L	1-2	0-1	19	Corazzin	3558
36		15	A	Bristol R	L	1-2	1-2	—	Kyd	3734
37		18	A	Chester C	W	3-1	3-0	19	Corazzin 2, Butler	1720
38		21	H	Leyton Orient	D	0-0	0-0	—		3048
39		24	A	Swansea C	L	0-1	0-1	—		4007
40	Apr	1	H	Plymouth Arg	D	1-1	0-0	19	Butler (pen)	3913
41		8	H	Peterborough U	W	2-0	1-0	19	Joseph, Butler	5828
42		15	A	York C	L	0-2	0-1	19		3278
43		17	H	Birmingham C	W	1-0	0-0	19	Heathcote	5317
44		22	A	Hull C	L	0-1	0-0	19		3483
45		29	H	Huddersfield T	D	1-1	1-1	20	Granville	5188
46	May	6	A	Wrexham	W	1-0	1-0	20	Corazzin	3172

Final League Position: 20

GOALSCORERS

League (52): Corazzin 19, Butler 14 (2 pens), Lillis 4, Hay 3, Granville 2, Jeffrey 2, Joseph 2, Morah 2, Barrick 1, Heathcote 1, Kyd 1, own goal 1.
Coca-Cola Cup (2): Barrick 1, Craddock 1.
FA Cup (8): Butler 4 (2 pens), Lillis 2, Barrick 1, Hay 1.

Filan J.R. 16	Hunter A.J. 23 + 3	Barrick D. 44	Craddock J.D. 38	Heathcote M. 24	O'Shea D.E. 30 + 1	Hyde M. 18 + 9	Elad D.E. 2 + 1	Butler S. 35 + 2	Corazzin G.M. 45 + 1	Nyamah K. 5 + 4	Morah O. 8 + 6	Fowler J.A. 12 + 4	Rattle J.P. 6	Joseph M.N.A. 39	Livett S.R. 2	Danzey M.J. 7 + 4	Kyd M.R. 10 + 9	Granville D.P. 11 + 5	Lillis J.W. 14 + 5	Rush D. 2	Hayrettin H. 15 + 2	Walker R.K. 5	Hay D.A. 7 + 19	Jeffrey A.S. 25 + 3	Manuel W.A.J. 10	Sheffield J. 28	Campbell D.A. 1	Campbell J. 12	Lomas A. 2	Pack L.J. 3	Thompson D.G. 7	*Match No.*
1	2	3	4	5	6	7	8	9	10	*11*	12	14																				1
1	2	3	4	5	6	7	14	9	10		12		8	*11*																		2
1	2	3	4	5	12	6	8	14	10	*11*	9	7																				3
1	2	3	4		5				10		9	7	11		6	8	12															4
1	2	3	4		5	12			10		9	7	11		6	*8*	14															5
1	2	3	4		5	12			10		9	7	11				14	*6*	8													6
1	2	3	4		5	12			10		14	7	11					6	*8*	9												7
1	2	3	4		5	12			10		14	7	*11*	8				6		9												8
1	2	3	4		5	14		9	10		12	*7*		11							6	8										9
1	2	3	4		5	12		9	10	14				11					*7*		6	8										10
1	2	3	4		5			9	10	14				11			12		7		*6*	8										11
1		3	4		5			9	10	*2*				11		6		14	7			8	12									12
1	4	3			5			*9*	10					11		6		12	7			8	14	2								13
1	6	3	4		5			9	10			12		11				7						2	8							14
1	2	3	4		5	12		9	10			6		*11*				7					14		8							15
1	2	3	4		5	6		9	10			12		11				7					14		8							16
		3	4		5	6		9	10			12		2					8				11		7	1						17
		3	4		5	6		9	10	14		7		2					*8*				11	12		1						18
	2	3	4			6		9	10					8					12				11	5	7	1						19
	2	3	4			6		9	10					8					12				11	5	7	1						20
	2	3	4		6	8		9	10					*11*				14	12					5	7	1						21
	2	3	4		6	9			11					10				12	*8*				14	5	7	1						22
	2	3	4		6	8			10			7		11					9				12	5		1						23
	2	3	4		6	9		12	10			*7*		11					8				14	5		1						24
		3	4	5	6	7		9	10					11					8				12	2		1						25
	12	3	4	5	6	7		9	10					11					*8*				14	2		1						26
		3	4	5	6			9	10		7			11					12				14	2	*8*	1						27
		3	4	5	*6*			9	10		7			11									14	12	8	1	2					28
		3	4			6		9	10					2		5		7			8		12	11		1						29
		3	4	5		7		9	10			8		2							6		12	11		1						30
	7	3	4	5					10		*9*			2			14		12		6		8	11		1						31
	7	3	4	5				9	10		12			2			14				6		*8*	11		1						32
		3	4	5				9	10		7			2			8				6		12	11		1						33
		3	4	5	6	12		9	10					2			8				*7*		14	11		1						34
			4	5	6	14		9	12					2			8		10				7	11		1		3				35
		3		5	6			9	10					2			8	11					12	4		1		7				36
		3	4	5	6			9	10					2			*8*	11			12		14					7	1			37
		3		5	6			9	10					2			8				7		12	14				4	1	*11*		38
		3		5		4		9	10					2			8				7		12			1		6		11		39
	12			5		*7*		9	10	14				2			*8*				6					1		3		11	4	40
		3		5				9	10	8				2		6	12							11		1		7			4	41
		3	4	5				9	10	*8*				2		14	12							11		1		7			6	42
	12	3	*4*	5					10					2		14	9				8			11		1		7			6	43
		3		5				9	10							2	6	12			8			11		1		7			4	44
		3		5				9	10					2		12	14	*6*			8			11		1		7			4	45
		3	4	5				9	10					2		12		8			14			*11*		1		7			6	46

Coca-Cola Cup

First Round	Portsmouth (a)	0-2
	(h)	2-3

FA Cup

First Round	Brentford (h)	2-2
	(a)	2-1
Second Round	Peterborough U (a)	2-0
Third Round	Burnley (h)	2-4

CARDIFF CITY 1994–95 *Back row (left to right):* Carl Dale, Derek Brazil, Andy Scott, Wayne Fereday
Centre row: Gavin Tait (Youth Development Officer), Jimmy Goodfellow (Physio), Mark Aizlewood (Player Coach), Paul Millar, Lee Baddeley, David Williams, Jason Perry, Steve Williams, Nick Richardson, Scott Young, Gary Thompson, Harry Parsons (Kit Manager).
Front row: Damon Searle, Nathan Wigg, Charlie Oatway, Terry Yorath (Manager), Ryan Nicholls, Darren Adams, Anthony Bird.

Division 3 **CARDIFF CITY**

Ninian Park, Cardiff CF1 8SX. Telephone: (01222) 398636. Fax: (01222) 341148. Newsline: 0891 888603.

Ground capacity: 20,284.

Record attendance: 61,566, Wales v England, 14 October 1961.

Club record: 57,893 v Arsenal, Division 1, 22 April 1953.

Record receipts: £141,756 v Manchester C, FA Cup 4th rd, 29 January 1994.

Pitch measurements: 114yd × 78yd.

Directors: R. Wright, W. Dixon, D. Henderson, J. Oliver, S. Williams.

Secretary: Jim Finney.

Manager: Eddie May.

Physio: Jimmy Goodfellow. ***Coach:*** Eddie May.

Year Formed: 1899. ***Turned Professional:*** 1910. ***Ltd Co.:*** 1910.

Previous Names: 1899–1902, Riverside; 1902–08, Riverside Albion; 1908, Cardiff City.

Club Nickname: 'Bluebirds'.

Previous Grounds: Riverside, Sophia Gardens, Old Park and Fir Gardens. Moved to Ninian Park, 1910.

Foundation: Credit for the establishment of a first class professional football club in such a rugby stronghold as Cardiff, is due to members of the Riverside club formed in 1899 out of a cricket club of that name. Cardiff became a city in 1905 and in 1908 the local FA granted Riverside permission to call themselves Cardiff City.

First Football League game: 28 August, 1920, Division 2, v Stockport C (a) W 5-2 – Kneeshaw; Brittain, Leyton; Keenor (1), Smith, Hardy; Grimshaw (1), Gill (2), Cashmore, West, Evans (1).

Record League Victory: 9–2 v Thames, Division 3 (S), 6 February 1932 – Farquharson; E. L. Morris, Roberts; Galbraith, Harris, Ronan; Emmerson (1), Keating (1), Jones (1), McCambridge (1), Robbins (5).

Record Cup Victory: 8–0 v Enfield, FA Cup, 1st rd, 28 November 1931 – Farquharson; Smith, Roberts; Harris (1), Galbraith, Ronan; Emmerson (2), Keating (3); O'Neill (2), Robbins, McCambridge.

Record Defeat: 2–11 v Sheffield U, Division 1, 1 January 1926.

Most League Points (2 for a win): 66, Division 3 (S), 1946–47.

Most League Points (3 for a win): 86, Division 3, 1982–83.

Most League Goals: 93, Division 3 (S), 1946–47.

Highest League Scorer in Season: Stan Richards, 30, Division 3 (S), 1946–47.

Most League Goals in Total Aggregate: Len Davies, 128, 1920–31.

Most Capped Player: Alf Sherwood, 39 (41), Wales.

Most League Appearances: Phil Dwyer, 471, 1972–85.

Record Transfer Fee Received: £300,000 from Sheffield U for Nathan Blake, February 1994.

Record Transfer Fee Paid: £180,000 to San Jose Earthquakes for Godfrey Ingram, September 1982.

Football League Record: 1920 Elected to Division 2; 1921–29 Division 1; 1929–31 Division 2; 1931–47 Division 3 (S); 1947–52 Division 2; 1952–57 Division 1; 1957–60 Division 2; 1960–62 Division 1; 1962–75 Division 2; 1975–76 Division 3; 1976–82 Division 2; 1982–83 Division 3; 1983–85 Division 2; 1985–86 Division 3; 1986–88 Division 4; 1988–90 Division 3; 1990–92 Division 4; 1992–93 Division 3; 1993–95 Division 2; 1995– Division 3.

Honours: *Football League:* Division 1 – Runners-up 1923–24; Division 2 – Runners-up 1920–21, 1951–52, 1959–60; Division 3 (S) – Champions 1946–47; Division 3 – Champions 1992–93. Runners-up 1975–76, 1982–83; Division 4 – Runners-up 1987–88. *FA Cup:* Winners 1927 (only occasion the Cup has been won by a club outside England); Runners-up 1925. *Football League Cup:* Semi-final 1966. *Welsh Cup:* Winners 21 times. *Charity Shield:* 1927. European Competitions: *European Cup-Winners' Cup:* 1964–65, 1965–66, 1967–68, 1968–69, 1969–70, 1970–71, 1971–72, 1973–74, 1974–75, 1976–77, 1977–78, 1988–89, 1991–92, 1992–93, 1993–94.

Colours: Blue shirts, blue shorts, blue stockings. **Change colours:** Yellow shirts, navy shorts, navy stockings.

CARDIFF CITY 1994–95 LEAGUE RECORD

Match No.	Date	Venue	Opponents	Result		H/T Score	Lg. Pos.	Goalscorers	Attendance
1	Aug 13	A	Stockport Co	L	1-4	1-1	—	Stant	5139
2	20	H	Oxford U	L	1-3	1-2	20	Stant	7281
3	27	A	York C	D	1-1	0-0	19	Millar	2861
4	30	H	Wrexham	D	0-0	0-0	—		4903
5	Sept 3	H	Swansea C	D	1-1	0-1	21	Richardson	5523
6	10	A	Blackpool	L	1-2	1-0	21	Richardson	4189
7	13	A	Chester C	W	2-0	0-0	—	Stant, Aizlewood	1671
8	17	H	Plymouth Arg	L	0-1	0-0	21		5674
9	24	A	Bournemouth	L	2-3	1-1	22	Scott, Griffith	3177
10	Oct 1	H	Peterborough U	L	1-2	1-1	22	Fereday	4225
11	8	H	Crewe Alex	L	1-2	1-0	22	Stant	4126
12	15	A	Bristol R	D	2-2	1-2	22	Millar, Richardson	3936
13	22	H	Cambridge U	W	3-1	1-1	22	Stant 3	3580
14	30	A	Bradford C	W	3-2	3-1	20	Millar 2 (1 pen), Stant	5937
15	Nov 1	A	Leyton Orient	L	0-2	0-0	—		2558
16	5	H	Brighton & HA	W	3-0	0-0	19	Baddeley, Stant 2	5004
17	19	A	Wycombe W	L	1-3	0-1	20	Stant	5391
18	25	H	Hull C	L	0-2	0-2	—		4226
19	Dec 10	A	Oxford U	L	0-1	0-1	20		6181
20	17	H	Stockport Co	D	1-1	0-0	21	Dale	3448
21	26	A	Shrewsbury T	W	1-0	0-0	19	Stant (pen)	4933
22	28	H	Birmingham C	L	0-1	0-0	—		7420
23	31	A	Rotherham U	L	0-2	0-1	20		3064
24	Jan 2	H	Brentford	L	2-3	0-2	21	Stant, Bird	5235
25	7	H	Blackpool	L	0-1	0-1	21		3467
26	14	H	Huddersfield T	D	0-0	0-0	21		3808
27	17	A	Cambridge U	L	0-2	0-1	—		2460
28	Feb 4	A	Hull C	L	0-4	0-2	22		3903
29	18	A	Huddersfield T	L	1-5	0-4	22	Brazil	10,035
30	21	H	Wycombe W	W	2-0	0-0	—	Dale, Richardson	3024
31	25	A	Peterborough U	L	1-2	1-1	22	Dale	4226
32	Mar 4	H	Bournemouth	D	1-1	1-1	22	Dale	3008
33	7	A	Swansea C	L	1-4	0-3	—	Wigg	3943
34	11	H	York C	L	1-2	1-2	22	Griffith	2689
35	15	A	Brighton & HA	D	0-0	0-0	—		6956
36	18	A	Wrexham	W	3-0	1-0	22	Nicholls, Griffith, Humes (og)	3023
37	25	A	Plymouth Arg	D	0-0	0-0	22		5611
38	28	H	Bradford C	L	2-4	2-1	—	Perry, Millar	2560
39	Apr 1	H	Chester C	W	2-1	1-0	22	Dale, Millar	4405
40	4	H	Leyton Orient	W	2-1	0-0	—	Bird 2	4324
41	8	H	Rotherham U	D	1-1	1-0	22	Griffith	6412
42	15	A	Birmingham C	L	1-2	1-1	22	Millar	17,455
43	17	H	Shrewsbury T	L	1-2	0-1	22	Bird	4677
44	22	A	Brentford	L	0-2	0-0	22		8268
45	29	H	Bristol R	L	0-1	0-0	22		5462
46	May 6	A	Crewe Alex	D	0-0	0-0	22		4382

Final League Position: 22

GOALSCORERS

League (46): Stant 13 (1 pen), Millar 7 (1 pen), Dale 5, Bird 4, Griffith 4, Richardson 4, Aizlewood 1, Baddeley 1, Brazil 1, Fereday 1, Nicholls 1, Perry 1, Scott 1, Wigg 1, own goal 1.
Coca-Cola Cup (3): Stant 2, Oatway 1.
FA Cup (0).

Williams S.D. 6	Evans T. 7	Scott A.M. 13	Aizlewood M. 17	Perry J. 34	Oatway A.P.D. 27 + 3	Griffith C. 31 + 7	Richardson N.J. 32 + 1	Stant P. 19	Bird A. 7 + 12	Fereday W. 26 + 1	Brazil D.M. 26 + 4	Dale C. 33 + 2	Williams D. 40	Millar W.P. 25 + 10	Adams D.S. 4 + 2	Young S. 15 + 7	Thompson G.L. 11 + 2	Searle D.P. 32	Baddeley L.M. 33 + 3	McLean I. 4	Ramsey P. 11	Wigg N.M. 18 + 1	Evans D.A. 4 + 8	Nicholls R. 6 + 6	Honor C. 10	Pearson J.S. 12	Vick L. 2	Milsom P.J. 1 + 2	Match No.
1	2	3	4	5	6	7	8	9	*10*	11	12	14																	1
	2		4	5	6		8	9	10	*11*	3	14	1	7	12														2
	2	3			6	7	8		9	11	5	10	1	12		4													3
	2	3			6	7	8		12	11	5	10	1	9		4													4
	2	3	4		6	7	8				5	10	1	12			9	11	14										5
	2	3	4		7	*11*	8	9			6	10	1	12			14			5									6
		3	4	6	7	11	8	9	12		2	10	1							5									7
		3	4	6	7	11	8		12		2	10	1				9		14	*5*									8
	2	3	4	6	7	11	8					10	1	14		12	*9*		5										9
			4	2	6	8	12	9	14	11		*10*	1	7				3	5										10
			4	5	6	7	8	9		11	2		1		10			3					12						11
				6	4	7	8	9		*11*	2		1	14	10			3	5				12						12
		3		6	4	7		9		11	2	10	1	8					5										13
		3		6	4	7		9		11	2	10	1	8					5										14
		3		6	4	7		9		11	2	10	1	8					5										15
		3		6	*4*	8		9	12	11	2		1	10					5		7	14							16
			4	6	8	12		9					1	11		2	10	3	5		7								17
			4		6	12	8	9	14		5		1	*11*		2	10	3			7								18
					4	12	8	9		14	6	7	1	*11*		2	10	3	5										19
			6		4			9		11		8	1	12		2	10	3	5		7								20
				6	4	12		9		11		8	1					3	5	2	7		10						21
				6	*4*	11		9		2		8	1	12		14		3	5		7		10						22
				6	4	12		9	14	2		8	1	11		7		3	5				*10*						23
		11		6	4			9	12	*2*		8	1			14	10	3	5		7								24
				6	8	11				*2*		9	1			12	10	3	5		7		14	4					25
				6	8				14	2		11	1	12	*9*		10	3	5		7			4					26
				6	4	12			14			8	1	11	9	2	*10*	3	5		7								27
			4				8			11		7	1			12	14	3	5		6			10	2	*9*			28
			4				10			2	6	8	1	12				3	5			11			7	9			29
			4	6		12	10			11		8	1					3	5			7			2	9			30
				6			10			11	4	8	1					3	5			7	9		2				31
			4	6			10			11	14	8	1					*3*	5			7	12		2	9			32
			4	6		8	10			11	12		1	14				3	5			7			2	*9*			33
				6		4	10			3	12		1	11					5			7		14	*2*	9	8		34
				6		4	10			3			1	11		12			5			7		14	2	9	*8*		35
				6		4	10						1	11		5		3				7		8	2	9			36
				6		4	10				2		1	11		5		3	12			7		8		*9*		14	37
				6		4	10						1	11		5		3				7		8	2	9		12	38
				6		11	8		12		2	10	1	7				3	5			*4*		14		9			39
				6		11	8		12		2	10	1	7				3	5			4		14		9			40
				6		11	8		9		2	10	1	7				3	5			*4*	12	14					41
1				6		11	8		9		2	10		7		12		3	5			4							42
1						11	8		*9*		2	10		7		6		3	5			4	12	14					43
1					12	11	8		9		2	10		7	14	*6*		3	5			4							44
1					12	11	10				2	8		7		6		3	5			4	14					*9*	45
1				6	12	11	8				2	10		*9*		7		3	5			4	14						46

Coca-Cola Cup
First Round — Torquay U (h) — 1-0
(a) — 2-4

FA Cup
First Round — Enfield (a) — 0-1

CARLISLE UNITED 1994–95 *Back row (left to right):* David Reeves, Tony Hopper, Jeff Thorpe, Tony Gallimore, Paul Murray, Rory Delap, Richard Prokas, Dave Burgess, Dean Walling. *Centre row:* Peter Hampton (Physio/Coach), David Wilkes (Youth/Reserves Coach), Darren Edmondson, Jamie Robinson, Paul Conway, Tony Caig, Tony Elliott, John Pearson, Derek Mountfield, David Currie, Mick Wadsworth (Director of Coaching), Mervyn Day (Coach).
Front row: Neil Dalton, Joe Joyce (Player Coach), Simon Davey, Albert Doweck (Director), Barry Chaytow (Vice Chairman), Michael Knighton (Chairman & Chief Executive), Bob McKnight (Director), Rod Thomas, Ian Arnold, Shane Reddish.

Division 2 **CARLISLE UNITED**

Brunton Park, Carlisle CA1 1LL. Telephone: (01228) 26237. Fax: (01228) 30138. Commercial Dept: (01228) 24014. Information Line: 0891 230011.

Record attendance: 27,500 v Birmingham C, FA Cup 3rd rd, 5 January 1957 and v Middlesbrough, FA Cup 5th rd, 7 February 1970.

Record receipts: £104,410 v Sunderland, FA Cup 3rd rd replay, 18 January 1994.

Ground capacity: 13,288 (will increase to 17,500).

Pitch measurements: 117yd × 72yd.

Directors: M Knighton (Chairman), B. Chaytow, R. McKnight, A. Doweck.

Director of Coaching: Mick Wadsworth ***Player-Coach:*** Joe Joyce. ***Coach:*** Mervyn Day.

Physio: Peter Hampton.

Commercial Manager: Martin Hudson.

Acting Secretary: A. Ritchie.

Year Formed: 1903. ***Ltd Co.:*** 1921.

Previous Grounds: 1903–5, Milholme Bank; 1905–9, Devonshire Park; 1909– Brunton Park.

Previous Name: Shaddongate United.

Club Nickname: 'Cumbrians' or 'The Blues'.

Foundation: Carlisle United came into being in 1903 through the amalgamation of Shaddongate United and Carlisle Red Rose. The new club was admitted to the Second Division of the Lancashire Combination in 1905–06, winning promotion the following season.

First Football League game: 25 August, 1928, Division 3(N), v Accrington S (a) W 3-2 – Prout; Coulthard, Cook; Harrison, Ross, Pigg; Agar, Hutchison, McConnell (1), Ward (1), Watson. 1 o.g.

Record League Victory: 8–0 v Hartlepools U, Division 3 (N), 1 September 1928 – Prout; Smiles, Cook; Robinson (1) Ross, Pigg; Agar (1), Hutchison (1), McConnell (4), Ward (1), Watson. 8–0 v Scunthorpe United, Division 3 (N), 25 December 1952 – MacLaren; Hill, Scott; Stokoe, Twentyman, Waters; Harrison (1), Whitehouse (5), Ashman (2), Duffett, Bond.

Record Cup Victory: 6–1 v Billingham Synthonia, FA Cup, 1st rd, 17 November 1956 – Fairley; Hill, Kenny; Johnston, Waters, Thompson; Mooney, Broadis (1), Ackerman (2), Garvie (3), Bond.

Record Defeat: 1–11 v Hull C, Division 3 (N), 14 January 1939.

Most League Points (2 for a win): 62, Division 3 (N), 1950–51.

Most League Points (3 for a win): 91, Division 3, 1994–95.

Most League Goals: 113, Division 4, 1963–64.

Highest League Scorer in Season: Jimmy McConnell, 42, Division 3 (N), 1928–29.

Most League Goals in Total Aggregate: Jimmy McConnell, 126, 1928–32.

Most Capped Player: Eric Welsh, 4, Northern Ireland.

Most League Appearances: Alan Ross, 466, 1963–79.

Record Transfer Fee Received: £275,000 from Vancouver Whitecaps for Peter Beardsley, April 1981.

Record Transfer Fee Paid: £121,000 to Notts Co for David Reeves, December 1993.

Football League Record: 1928 Elected to Division 3 (N); 1958–62 Division 4; 1962–63 Division 3; 1963–64 Division 4; 1964–65 Division 3; 1965–74 Division 2; 1974–75 Division 1; 1975–77 Division 2; 1977–82 Division 3; 1982–86 Division 2; 1986–87 Division 3; 1987–92 Division 4; 1992–95 Division 3; 1995– Division 2.

Honours: *Football League:* Division 1 best season: 22nd, 1974–75; Promoted from Division 2 (3rd) 1973–74; Division 3 – Champions 1964–65, 1994–95; Runners-up 1981–82; Division 4 – Runners-up 1963–64. *FA Cup:* 6th rd 1975. *Football League Cup:* Semi-final 1970. *Auto Windscreens Shield:* Runners-up 1995.

Colours: Blue shirts, white shorts, blue stockings. **Change colours:** Red shirts, green shorts, white stockings.

CARLISLE UNITED 1994–95 LEAGUE RECORD

Match No.	Date		Venue	Opponents	Result		H/T Score	Lg. Pos.	Goalscorers	Attendance
1	Aug	13	H	Wigan Ath	W	2-1	1-0	—	Reeves, Walling	6231
2		20	A	Torquay U	D	1-1	0-0	5	Reeves	3506
3		27	H	Scarborough	W	2-0	2-0	4	Mountfield, Reeves	5720
4		30	A	Walsall	W	2-1	1-1	—	Reeves 2	3610
5	Sept	3	A	Scunthorpe U	W	3-2	0-2	1	Gallimore, Thorpe 2	3217
6		10	H	Exeter C	W	1-0	1-0	1	Thomas	6213
7		13	H	Mansfield T	W	2-1	0-0	—	Thomas, Currie	6136
8		17	A	Wigan Ath	W	2-0	0-0	1	Edmondson, Reeves	3003
9		24	A	Northampton T	L	1-2	0-1	2	Reeves	3508
10	Oct	1	H	Darlington	W	2-1	0-1	1	Gallimore (pen), Walling	6100
11		8	A	Lincoln C	D	1-1	0-0	1	Reeves	3097
12		15	H	Colchester U	D	0-0	0-0	2		5817
13		22	H	Barnet	W	4-0	1-0	2	Reeves, Conway, Davey, Thomas	6155
14		29	A	Fulham	W	3-1	2-0	2	Reeves, Mountfield, Conway	5563
15	Nov	5	H	Rochdale	W	4-1	1-0	2	Davey 2, Reeves, Edmondson	5984
16		19	A	Hereford U	W	1-0	1-0	1	Conway	2531
17		26	H	Doncaster R	D	1-1	0-0	1	Walling	7781
18	Dec	10	H	Torquay U	W	1-0	1-0	1	Thomas	5141
19		17	A	Scarborough	W	2-1	1-1	1	Gallimore (pen), Currie	1910
20		26	A	Hartlepool U	W	5-1	1-0	1	Mountfield, Conway, Reeves 2, Gallimore (pen)	3854
21		27	H	Bury	W	3-0	1-0	1	Currie, Conway, Reeves	12,242
22		31	A	Gillingham	W	1-0	0-0	1	Walling	3682
23	Jan	14	H	Preston NE	D	0-0	0-0	1		10,684
24		21	A	Rochdale	D	1-1	0-0	1	Walling	3289
25		24	A	Barnet	W	2-0	0-0	—	Currie, Davey	2413
26		28	H	Fulham	D	1-1	1-1	1	Thomas	6891
27	Feb	4	A	Doncaster R	D	0-0	0-0	1		3587
28		11	H	Hereford U	W	1-0	1-0	1	Gallimore (pen)	5676
29		18	A	Preston NE	L	0-1	0-1	1		11,867
30		25	A	Darlington	W	2-0	1-0	1	Thomas, Reeves	3992
31	Mar	4	H	Northampton T	W	2-1	2-0	1	Walling 2	6755
32		11	A	Exeter C	D	1-1	1-1	1	Reeves	2673
33		18	H	Walsall	W	2-1	0-1	1	Reeves 2	7769
34		25	H	Scunthorpe U	W	2-1	0-0	1	Aspinall, Hayward	6704
35	Apr	1	A	Mansfield T	W	2-1	1-1	1	Prokas, Thorpe	5197
36		4	H	Chesterfield	D	1-1	0-0	—	Robinson	8478
37		8	H	Gillingham	W	2-0	2-0	1	Thorpe, Hayward	6786
38		15	A	Bury	L	0-2	0-0	1		5507
39		17	H	Hartlepool U	L	0-1	0-1	1		10,242
40		29	A	Colchester U	W	1-0	0-0	1	Reeves	3333
41	May	2	A	Chesterfield	W	2-1	1-1	—	Reeves 2	7283
42		6	H	Lincoln C	L	1-3	0-1	1	Conway	12,412

Final League Position: 1

GOALSCORERS

League (67): Reeves 21, Walling 7, Conway 6, Thomas 6, Gallimore 5 (4 pens), Currie 4, Davey 4, Thorpe 4, Mountfield 3, Edmondson 2, Hayward 2, Aspinall 1, Prokas 1, Robinson 1.
Coca-Cola Cup (3): Reeves 2, Walling 1.
FA Cup (8): Conway 2, Reeves 2, Currie 1, Davey 1, Mountfield 1, Walling 1.

Caig A. 40	Joyce J.P. 17 + 4	Gallimore A.M. 40	Walling D.A. 41	Mountfield D.N. 30 + 1	Edmondson D.S. 36 + 2	Thomas R.C. 36	Currie D.N. 38	Reeves D. 42	Davey S. 25	Reddish S. 2	Thorpe J.R. 7 + 21	Pearson J.S. — + 1	Prokas R. 37 + 2	Peacock L.A. 2 + 5	Valentine P. 9	Robinson J. 6 + 8	Arnold I. 1 + 3	Lowe K. 1 + 1	Murray P. 2 + 3	Conway P.J. 24	Peters R.A.A. 5 + 3	Delap R.J. 2 + 1	Elliott A.R. 2 + 1	Aspinall W. 6 + 1	Hayward S.L. 9	Hopper T. 2 + 3	*Match No.*
1	2	3	4	5	6	7	*8*	9	10	11	12	14															1
1	2	3	4	5	6	7	8	9		10	12		11														2
1	2	3	4	5	6	7	8	9	10		12		11	14													3
1	2	3	4		6	7	8	9	10		12		*11*		5	14											4
1	2	3	4		6	7	*8*	9	10		12		11		5	14											5
1	2	3	4		12	7	*8*	9	10		6		11		5		14										6
1	2	3	4		6	7	8	9	10		12		11		5												7
1	2	3	4		6	7	8	9	10		12		11		5												8
1	2	3	4	6	12	7	8	9	10				14		5			*11*									9
1	2	3	4		6	7	8	9	10		12		11		5		14										10
1	2	3	4	12	6	7	*8*	9	10		14		11		5												11
1	2	3	4		*6*	7		9	10				11	12	5		8	14									12
1			4	5	2	7	8	9	10		12		11						3	6							13
1		3	4	5	2	7	8	9	10				11							6							14
1		3	4	5	2	7	8	9	10				11				12		14	*6*							15
1	12	3	4	5	2	7	8	9	10				11							6							16
1		3	4	5	2	7	8	9	10				11							6							17
1		3	4	5	2	7	8	9					11							6	10						18
1		3	4	5	2	7	*8*	9			12		11							6	10		15				19
1	12	3	4	5	2		*8*	9			7		11							6	10	14					20
1		3	4	5	2	7	8	9	10		12		11							6							21
		3	4	5	2		8	9	10		7		11							6	12		1				22
1		3	4	5	2	7	8	9	10		12		11							6							23
1		3	4	5	2	7	8	9	10		12		11							6							24
1	2	3	4	5		7	8	9	10				11			12				6							25
1		3	4	5	2	7	8	9	10		12		11							6							26
1		3	4	5	2	7	8	9	10				11			12				6							27
1		3	4	5	2	7	8	9	10				11							6	12						28
1		3	4	5	2	7	8	9	10				12						11	*6*	14						29
1		3	4	5	2	7	8	9					11			12				10	6						30
1		3	4	5	*2*	7	8	9			12		11			14				10	6						31
1		3	4	5	2	7	8	9			12		11							10				6			32
1		3	4	5	2		8	9			12		11							10				6	7		33
1		3		5	2		*8*	9			14		11	12		4				10				6	7		34
1	2	3	4	5		7	8	9			12		11	14										*6*	10		35
1	*11*	3	4		2	7		9			8			6		5			12						10	14	36
1	12		4	5	2	*7*		9			8		11	6		3									10	14	37
1	2	3	4	5			8	9			7		11			12						10				6	38
1	2	3	4	5		7	8	9					11			12								*6*	10	14	39
1	12	3	4		2	7	8	9			14		11			5				6					10		40
		3	4		2			9			11			14		5			12			7	1	*6*	10	8	41
1		3	4		2	7	8	9					11			5				6				12	10		42

Coca-Cola Cup

First Round	Rotherham U (a)	0-1
	(h)	3-1
Second Round	QPR (h)	0-1
	(a)	0-2

FA Cup

First Round	Guiseley (a) (at Bradford)	4-1
Second Round	Darlington (h)	2-0
Third Round	Sunderland (a)	1-1
	(h)	1-3

CHARLTON ATHLETIC 1994–95 *Back row (left to right):* Scott McGleish, Steve Brown, Richard Rufus, Mike Ammann, Mike Salmon, Andy Petterson, Carl Leaburn, Dean Chandler, Danny Mills.

Centre row: Jimmy Hendry (Physio), Lee Bowyer, Shaun Newton, Mickey Bennett, Paul Sturgess, Phil Chapple, Kim Grant, David Whyte, Mark Robson, Paul Linger, Neil Banfield (Youth Development Officer).

Front row: Paul Mortimer, Alan Pardew, Garry Nelson, Alan McLeary, Keith Peacock (Reserve Team Coach), Steve Gritt (Player/Manager), Alan Curbishley (Player/Manager), Stuart Balmer, Colin Walsh, Peter Garland, John Robinson.

(Photograph: Tom Morris)

Division 1 CHARLTON ATHLETIC

The Valley, Floyd Road, Charlton, London SE7 8BL. Telephone: (0181) 293 4567. Fax: (0181) 293 5143. Box Office: (0181) 858 5888. Clubcall 0891 121146.

Ground capacity: 15,000.

Record attendance: 75,031 v Aston Villa, FA Cup 5th rd, 12 February 1938 (at The Valley).

Record receipts: £114,618.70 v Liverpool (at Selhurst Park), Division 1, 23 January 1988.

Pitch measurements: 110yd × 73yd.

President: R. D. Collins.

Chairman: M. A. Simons. ***Vice-Chairman:*** R. A. Murray.

Directors: R. N. Alwen, G. P. Bone, S. T. Clarke, R. D. Collins, J. T. T. Fuller, M. C. Stevens, D. G. Ufton.

Manager: Alan Curbishley.

Reserve team manager: Keith Peacock. ***Youth Team Manager:*** Neil Banfield. ***Youth Development Officer:*** Steve Watts. ***Physio:*** Jimmy Hendry.

Secretary: Chris Parkes.

Marketing Manager: Steve Dixon.

Year Formed: 1905. ***Turned Professional:*** 1920. ***Ltd Co.:*** 1919.

Club Nickname: 'Addicks'.

Previous Grounds: 1906, Siemen's Meadow; 1907, Woolwich Common; 1909, Pound Park; 1913, Horn Lane; 1920, The Valley; 1923, Catford (The Mount); 1924, The Valley; 1985 Selhurst Park; 1991 Upton Park; 1992 The Valley.

Foundation: The club was formed on 9 June 1905, by a group of 14 and 15-year-old youths living in streets by the Thames in the area which now borders the Thames Barrier. The club's progress through local leagues was so rapid that after the First World War they joined the Kent League where they spent a season before turning professional and joining the Southern League in 1920. A year later they were elected to the Football League's Division 3 (South).

First Football League game: 27 August, 1921, Division 3(S), v Exeter C (h) W 1-0 – Hughes; Mitchell, Goodman; Dowling (1), Hampson, Dunn; Castle, Bailey, Halse, Green, Wilson.

Record League Victory: 8–1 v Middlesbrough, Division 1, 12 September 1953 – Bartram; Campbell, Ellis; Fenton, Ufton, Hammond; Hurst (2), O'Linn (2), Leary (1), Firmani (3), Kiernan.

Record Cup Victory: 7–0 v Burton A, FA Cup, 3rd rd, 7 January 1956 – Bartram; Campbell, Townsend; Hewie, Ufton, Hammond; Hurst (1), Gauld (1), Leary (3), White, Kiernan (2).

Record Defeat: 1–11 v Aston Villa, Division 2, 14 November 1959.

Most League Points (2 for a win): 61, Division 3 (S), 1934–35.

Most League Points (3 for a win): 77, Division 2, 1985–86.

Most League Goals: 107, Division 2, 1957–58.

Highest League Scorer in Season: Ralph Allen, 32, Division 3 (S), 1934–35.

Most League Goals in Total Aggregate: Stuart Leary, 153, 1953–62.

Most Capped Player: John Hewie, 19, Scotland.

Most League Appearances: Sam Bartram, 583, 1934–56.

Record Transfer Fee Received: £750,000 from Newcastle U for Robert Lee, September 1992.

Record Transfer Fee Paid: £600,000 to Chelsea for Joe McLaughlin, August 1989.

Football League Record: 1921 Elected to Division 3 (S); 1929–33 Division 2; 1933–35 Division 3 (S); 1935–36 Division 2; 1936–57 Division 1; 1957–72 Division 2; 1972–75 Division 3; 1975–80 Division 2; 1980–81 Division 3; 1981–86; Division 2; 1986–90 Division 1; 1990–92 Division 2; 1992– Division 1.

Honours: *Football League:* Division 1 – Runners-up 1936–37; Division 2 – Runners-up 1935–36, 1985–86; Division 3 (S) – Champions 1928–29, 1934–35; Promoted from Division 3 (3rd) 1974–75, 1980–81. *FA Cup:* Winners 1947; Runners-up 1946. *Football League Cup:* best season: 4th rd, 1963, 1966, 1979. *Full Members Cup:* Runners-up 1987.

Colours: Red shirts, white shorts, red stockings. **Change colours:** White shirts, black shorts, white stockings.

CHARLTON ATHLETIC 1994–95 LEAGUE RECORD

Match No.	Date	Venue	Opponents	Result		H/T Score	Lg. Pos.	Goalscorers	Attendance
1	Aug 13	A	Oldham Ath	L	2-5	2-2	—	Whyte, Robinson	8924
2	20	H	Barnsley	D	2-2	0-0	16	Whyte, Chapple	8171
3	27	A	Portsmouth	D	1-1	1-1	18	Nelson	10,566
4	30	H	Sheffield U	D	1-1	1-1	—	Brown (pen)	8678
5	Sept 3	H	Bristol C	W	3-2	1-0	14	Mortimer, Whyte 2	9019
6	10	A	Grimsby T	W	1-0	0-0	8	Robson	3970
7	14	A	Stoke C	L	2-3	0-2	—	Nelson, Whyte	10,643
8	17	H	Swindon T	W	1-0	1-0	8	Whyte	9794
9	24	A	Notts Co	D	3-3	1-2	7	Nelson 2, Whyte	5726
10	Oct 1	H	Watford	W	3-0	0-0	6	Nelson, Grant, Whyte	8169
11	8	H	Reading	L	1-2	0-1	6	Robson	10,544
12	15	A	Port Vale	W	2-0	0-0	6	Chapple, Whyte	7707
13	22	H	Burnley	L	1-2	0-0	6	Whyte	9436
14	29	A	Derby Co	D	2-2	1-1	6	Grant 2	12,588
15	Nov 1	A	Sunderland	D	1-1	0-1	—	Grant	14,085
16	5	H	Bolton W	L	1-2	0-1	10	Brown (pen)	9793
17	13	H	WBA	D	1-1	1-0	11	Grant	10,876
18	19	A	Tranmere R	D	1-1	1-0	11	Nelson	7567
19	26	H	Middlesbrough	L	0-2	0-1	16		10,019
20	Dec 10	A	Barnsley	L	1-2	0-1	19	Mortimer	5465
21	17	H	Oldham Ath	W	2-0	0-0	17	Whyte, Jones	8970
22	26	H	Southend U	W	3-1	0-1	16	Whyte, Leaburn 2	9525
23	28	A	Wolverhampton W	L	0-2	0-2	—		26,738
24	Jan 1	H	Millwall	D	1-1	0-1	16	Robinson	10,655
25	2	A	Luton T	W	1-0	1-0	15	Whyte	7642
26	14	H	Derby Co	L	3-4	3-1	17	Whyte, Pardew, Robson	9389
27	21	A	Bolton W	L	1-5	1-2	17	Whyte	10,516
28	Feb 5	A	WBA	W	1-0	0-0	14	Nelson	12,084
29	11	H	Sunderland	W	1-0	0-0	12	Whyte	12,380
30	18	A	Middlesbrough	L	0-1	0-1	12		16,301
31	21	H	Tranmere R	L	0-1	0-0	—		11,860
32	Mar 4	H	Notts Co	W	1-0	1-0	14	Mortimer	13,638
33	7	A	Bristol C	L	1-2	0-1	—	Pardew	6118
34	11	H	Portsmouth	W	1-0	1-0	13	Leaburn	9443
35	18	A	Sheffield U	L	1-2	0-0	13	Pardew	11,862
36	21	H	Grimsby T	W	2-1	1-1	—	Robinson, Balmer	9601
37	25	A	Swindon T	W	1-0	0-0	12	Grant	9106
38	Apr 1	H	Stoke C	D	0-0	0-0	13		10,008
39	4	A	Burnley	L	0-2	0-1	—		10,045
40	8	A	Millwall	L	1-3	1-2	14	Balmer	9506
41	15	H	Wolverhampton W	W	3-2	1-1	14	Whyte, Walsh, Mortimer	10,922
42	18	A	Southend U	L	1-2	0-0	—	Whyte	6397
43	22	H	Luton T	W	1-0	0-0	13	Whyte	10,867
44	29	H	Port Vale	D	1-1	1-1	13	Brown	12,596
45	May 2	A	Watford	L	0-2	0-0	—		6024
46	7	A	Reading	L	1-2	0-1	15	Chandler	12,137

Final League Position: 15

GOALSCORERS

League (58): Whyte 19, Nelson 7, Grant 6, Mortimer 4, Brown 3 (2 pens), Leaburn 3, Pardew 3, Robinson 3, Robson 3, Balmer 2, Chapple 2, Chandler 1, Jones 1, Walsh 1.
Coca-Cola Cup (4): Nelson 2, Whyte 2.
FA Cup (0).

Salmon M.B. 20	Brown S.B. 42	Sturgess P.C. 23	Mortimer P.H. 26	Chapple P.R. 21	McLeary A.T. 22	Robinson J.R.C. 16 + 5	Nelson G.P. 21 + 6	Pardew A.S. 22 + 2	Whyte D.A. 36 + 2	Walsh C.D. 23 + 5	Grant K.T. 14 + 12	Robson M.A. 40	Garland P.J. 6 + 4	Linger P.H. 3 + 5	Ammann M.A. 18 + 1	Newton S.O. 10 + 16	Balmer S.M. 28 + 1	Petterson A.K. 8 + 1	Jones K.A. 31	Leaburn C.W. 22 + 5	Bowyer L.D. 5	McGleish S. — + 6	Bennett M.R. 9 + 5	Rufus R.R. 27 + 1	Hovi T.H. — + 2	Stuart J.C. 12	Chandler D.A.R. 1	Match No.
1	2	3	4	5	6	7	8	9	10	11	12																	1
1	2	3	4	5	6	7	8	9	10			*11*	12	14	15													2
	2	3	4	5	6	7	8		10		12	*11*	9		1	14												3
	2	3	*4*	5	6	7	8		10		12	11	9		1		14											4
	2	3	4	5	6		8		10	14	12	*11*	9		1	7												5
	2	3	4	5	6		8		10	14	12	*11*	9		1	7												6
	2	3		5	6		8	14	10	4	12	11	*9*		1	7												7
	2	3		5			8	12	10	9		*11*				7	6	1	4	14								8
	2	3		5			8		10	*9*	12	11	14			7	6	1	4									9
	2	3		5			8		10	9	12	11				14	6	1	*4*		7							10
	2	3		5			8		10	*9*	12	11				14	6	1	4		7							11
	2	3		5					10	9	8	11					6	1	4		7	12						12
	2	3		5					10	9	8	11					6	1	4		7	12						13
	2	3		5	6	*11*			10	9	8				1	12			4				7	14				14
	2	3		5	6	11		10		9	*8*			14	1	12							7	4				15
	2	3		9	6	*11*		10			8	7			1	14			4	12				5				16
	2	3			6		10	4		11	8	7			1	12				9				5				17
	2	3			6		10			11	8	7			1	12			4	9				5				18
	2	3			6		10		12	*11*	8	7			1	14			4	9				5				19
	2	3	11		6		12		10						1	7	8		4	9				5				20
1	2	3	11		6				10	12		7					8		4	9				5				21
1	2	3	11		6		14		10	12		7					*8*		4	9				5				22
1	*2*		3	5	6		12		10	11		7					8		4	9			14					23
1			3	5	6	8	12		10	*11*		7				14			4	9			2					24
1	2		4	5	6	8	12	11	10			7								9			3					25
1	2		*3*	5	6		12	8	10	11		7								9			4		14			26
	2		3		6		8	9	10	11	12	7			1								4	5	14			27
1	2		11				8	9	*10*			7					6		4			14	12	5		3		28
1	2					12	*8*	9	10			7					6		4			14	11	5		3		29
1	2					12	8	9	10			7					6		4			14	*11*	5		3		30
1	2					12	*8*	9	10			7					6		4	14			11	5		3		31
1	2		*11*			12	8	9	10			7					6		4	14				5		3		32
1	2		11			12	8	9	10			7					6		4	14				5		*3*		33
1	2		3			11		9	10			7				12	6		4	8				5				34
1			3	2		11		9	10	4	12	7					6			8				5				35
1	2		3			11		9			10	*7*		12		14	6		4	8				5				36
1	*2*		3			11		9			10	7		12		14	6		4	8				5				37
1	2		3			11		9	12		10	*7*				14	6		4	8				5				38
1	2		3			11		9			*10*	7				12	6	15	4	8			14	5				39
		3	7		*2*	11		9		12	10			4			6	1		8			14	5				40
	2		11					9	10	4		7			1	12	6			8				5		3		41
	2								10	11	8	7	12	9	1	5	6		4							3		42
	2		11						10	9		7			1		6		4	8		12		5		3		43
	2								10	9		7	12		1	11	6		4	8				5		3		44
	2								10	9			11	12	1	7	6		4	8				5		3		45
									10		12	7		*11*		2		1	4	8	9		14	5		3	6	46

Coca-Cola Cup
Second Round — Swindon T (a) 3-1; (h) 1-4

FA Cup
Third Round — Chelsea (a) 0-3

CHELSEA 1994–95 *Back row (left to right):* David Collyer (Youth Development Officer), Anthony Barness, Neil Shipperley, Nigel Spackman, Michael Duberry, Jacob Kjeldbjerg, Erland Johnsen, Paul Furlong, Paul Hughes, Craig Norman, Mustafa Izzett, Gwyn Williams (Chief Scout/Youth Development Officer).

Centre row: Eddie Niedzwiecki (Reserve Team Manager), Bob Ward (Physio), Scott Minto, Darren Barnard, Zeke Rowe, Andy Myers, Kevin Hitchcock, Dmitri Kharine, Nick Colgan, Steve Clarke, Terry Skiverton, David Hopkin, Craig Burley, Graham Rix (Youth Team Manager), Terry Byrne (Kit Manager/Club Masseur).

Front row: Eddie Newton, Andy Dow, Gareth Hall, Mark Stein, Dennis Wise, Glenn Hoddle (Manager), Peter Shreeves (Assistant Manager), Gavin Peacock, David Rocastle, Robert Fleck, John Spencer, Frank Sinclair

(Photograph: Action Images)

FA Premiership **CHELSEA**

Stamford Bridge, London SW6 1HS. Telephone: (0171) 385 5545. Fax: (0171) 381 4831. Clubcall: 0891 121159. Ticket News and Promotions: 0891 121011. Ticket credit card service: (0171) 386 7799.

Ground capacity: 31,791 (during ground development); 41,000 (eventually).

Record attendance: 82,905 v Arsenal, Division 1, 12 Oct 1935.

Record receipts: £465,324 v Manchester U, FA Premier League, 11 September 1993.

Pitch measurements: 110yd × 74yd.

President: G. M. Thomson.

Chairman: K. W. Bates.

Directors: C. Hutchinson (Managing), Y. S. Todd, M. Harding.

Team Manager: Glenn Hoddle. ***Assistant Manager:*** Peter Shreeves.

Physio: Michael Banks. ***Reserve Team Manager:*** Eddie Niedzwiecki.

Company Secretary/Director: Yvonne Todd. ***Match Secretary:*** Keith Lacy. ***Commercial Manager:*** Carole Phair.

Year Formed: 1905. ***Turned Professional:*** 1905. ***Ltd Co.:*** 1905.

Club Nickname: 'The Blues'.

Foundation: Chelsea may never have existed but for the fact that Fulham rejected an offer to rent the Stamford Bridge ground from Mr. H. A. Mears who had owned it since 1904. Fortunately he was determined to develop it as a football stadium rather than sell it to the Great Western Railway and got together with Frederick Parker, who persuaded Mears of the financial advantages of developing a major sporting venue. Chelsea FC was formed in 1905, and when admission to the Southern League was denied, they immediately gained admission to the Second Division of the Football League.

First Football League game: 2 September, 1905, Division 2, v Stockport C (a) L 0-1 – Foulke; Mackie, McEwan; Key, Harris, Miller; Moran, J.T. Robertson, Copeland, Windridge, Kirwan.

Record League Victory: 9–2 v Glossop N E, Division 2, 1 September 1906 – Byrne; Walton, Miller; Key (1), McRoberts, Henderson; Moran, McDermott (1), Hilsdon (5), Copeland (1), Kirwan (1).

Record Cup Victory: 13–0 v Jeunesse Hautcharage, ECWC, 1st rd 2nd leg, 29 September 1971 – Bonetti; Boyle, Harris (1), Hollins (1p), Webb (1), Hinton, Cooke, Baldwin (3), Osgood (5), Hudson (1), Houseman (1).

Record Defeat: 1–8 v Wolverhampton W, Division 1, 26 September 1953.

Most League Points (2 for a win): 57, Division 2, 1906–07.

Most League Points (3 for a win): 99, Division 2, 1988–89.

Most League Goals: 98, Division 1, 1960–61.

Highest League Scorer in Season: Jimmy Greaves, 41, 1960–61.

Most League Goals in Total Aggregate: Bobby Tambling, 164, 1958–70.

Most Capped Player: Ray Wilkins, 24 (84), England.

Most League Appearances: Ron Harris, 655, 1962–80.

Record Transfer Fee Received: £2,200,000 from Tottenham H for Gordon Durie, July 1991.

Record Transfer Fee Paid: £2,300,000 to Norwich C for Robert Fleck, July 1992.

Football League Record: 1905 Elected to Division 2; 1907–10 Division 1; 1910–12 Division 2; 1912–24 Division 1; 1924–30 Division 2; 1930–62 Division 1; 1962–63 Division 2; 1963–75 Division 1; 1975–77 Division 2; 1977–79 Division 1; 1979–84 Division 2; 1984–88 Division 1; 1988–89 Division 2; 1989–92 Division 1; 1992– FA Premier League.

Honours: *Football League:* Division 1 – Champions 1954–55; Division 2 – Champions 1983–84, 1988–89; Runners-up 1906–7, 1911–12, 1929–30, 1962–63, 1976–77. *FA Cup:* Winners 1970; Runners-up 1915, 1967, 1994. *Football League Cup:* Winners 1965; Runners-up 1972. *Full Members' Cup:* Winners 1986. *Zenith Data Systems Cup:* Winners 1990. **European Competitions:** *European Fairs Cup:* 1958–60, 1965–66, 1968–69; *European Cup-Winners' Cup:* 1970–71 (winners), 1971–72, 1994–95.

Colours: Royal blue, amber shirts, royal blue, white shorts, white stockings. **Change colours:** Graphite, tangerine and navy shirts, tangerine, navy and graphite shorts, tangerine, navy and graphite stockings.

CHELSEA 1994–95 LEAGUE RECORD

Match No.	Date	Venue	Opponents	Result	H/T Score	Lg. Pos.	Goalscorers	Atten-dance
1	Aug 20	H	Norwich C	W 2-0	1-0	—	Sinclair, Furlong	23,098
2	27	A	Leeds U	W 3-2	1-2	7	Wise (pen), Spencer 2	32,212
3	31	H	Manchester C	W 3-0	1-0	—	Peacock, Wise, Vonk (og)	21,740
4	Sept 10	A	Newcastle U	L 2-4	2-2	7	Peacock, Furlong	34,435
5	18	H	Blackburn R	L 1-2	0-1	7	Spencer	17,513
6	24	A	Crystal Palace	W 1-0	0-0	5	Furlong	16,064
7	Oct 2	H	West Ham U	L 1-2	0-0	7	Furlong	18,696
8	8	H	Leicester C	W 4-0	2-0	6	Spencer 2, Peacock, Shipperley	18,397
9	15	A	Arsenal	L 1-3	1-1	7	Wise	38,234
10	23	H	Ipswich T	W 2-0	0-0	7	Wise, Shipperley	15,068
11	29	A	Sheffield W	D 1-1	1-0	7	Wise	25,356
12	Nov 6	H	Coventry C	D 2-2	0-1	8	Spencer, Kjeldbjerg	17,090
13	9	A	Liverpool	L 1-3	1-3	—	Spencer	32,855
14	19	A	Nottingham F	W 1-0	1-0	7	Spencer	22,092
15	23	A	Tottenham H	D 0-0	0-0	—		27,037
16	26	H	Everton	L 0-1	0-1	8		28,115
17	Dec 3	A	Southampton	W 1-0	0-0	7	Furlong	14,404
18	10	A	Norwich C	L 0-3	0-2	8		18,246
19	18	H	Liverpool	D 0-0	0-0	8		27,050
20	26	H	Manchester U	L 2-3	0-1	9	Spencer (pen), Newton	31,139
21	28	A	Aston Villa	L 0-3	0-2	10		32,901
22	31	H	Wimbledon	D 1-1	0-0	10	Furlong	16,009
23	Jan 14	H	Sheffield W	D 1-1	1-0	12	Spencer	17,285
24	21	A	Ipswich T	D 2-2	0-0	12	Stein, Burley	17,619
25	25	H	Nottingham F	L 0-2	0-1	—		17,890
26	Feb 4	A	Coventry C	D 2-2	2-2	12	Stein, Spencer (pen)	13,423
27	11	H	Tottenham H	D 1-1	0-1	13	Wise	30,812
28	25	A	West Ham U	W 2-1	0-1	13	Burley, Stein	21,500
29	Mar 5	H	Crystal Palace	D 0-0	0-0	13		14,130
30	8	A	Manchester C	W 2-1	1-1	—	Stein 2	21,880
31	11	H	Leeds U	L 0-3	0-2	11		20,174
32	18	A	Blackburn R	L 1-2	1-2	14	Stein	25,490
33	22	A	QPR	L 0-1	0-0	—		15,103
34	Apr 1	H	Newcastle U	D 1-1	1-0	15	Peacock	22,987
35	10	A	Wimbledon	D 1-1	1-0	—	Sinclair	7022
36	12	H	Southampton	L 0-2	0-2	—		16,739
37	15	H	Aston Villa	W 1-0	1-0	14	Stein	17,015
38	17	A	Manchester U	D 0-0	0-0	14		43,728
39	29	H	QPR	W 1-0	0-0	12	Sinclair	21,704
40	May 3	A	Everton	D 3-3	1-1	—	Furlong 2, Hopkin	33,180
41	6	A	Leicester C	D 1-1	1-1	12	Furlong	18,140
42	14	H	Arsenal	W 2-1	1-1	11	Furlong, Stein	29,542

Final League Position: 11

GOALSCORERS

League (50): Spencer 11 (2 pens), Furlong 10, Stein 8, Wise 6 (1 pen), Peacock 4, Sinclair 3, Burley 2, Shipperley 2, Hopkin 1, Kjeldbjerg 1, Newton 1, own goal 1.
Coca-Cola Cup (2): Peacock 1, Rocastle 1.
FA Cup (4): Peacock 1, Sinclair 1, Spencer 1, Stein 1.

Kharine D.V. 31	Clarke S. 29	Sinclair F.M. 35	Kjeldbjerg J. 23	Johnsen E. 33	Spackman N. 36	Rocastle D.C. 26 + 2	Shipperley N.J. 6 + 4	Furlong P.A. 30 + 6	Peacock G.K. 38	Wise D.F. 18 + 1	Newton E.J.I. 22 + 8	Hoddle G. 3 + 9	Spencer J. 26 + 3	Barness A. 10 + 2	Lee D.J. 9 + 5	Hall G.D. 4 + 2	Hopkin D. 7 + 8	Myers A. 9 + 1	Hitchcock K. 11 + 1	Burley C.W. 16 + 9	Minto S.C. 19	Stein M.E.S. 21 + 3	Rix G. — + 1	Match No.
1	2	3	4	5	6	7	*8*	9	10	11	12	14												1
1	2	3	4	5	6	7		9	10	11	12		8											2
1	2	3	4	5	6	7		9	10	11	12		8											3
1	2	3	4	5	6	7		9	10	11	12	14	8											4
1	2	3	4	5	6	7		9	10	11	12		8											5
1	2	3	4	5	6	7		9	10		11		8											6
1	2	3	4	5		7	12	9	10		6		8	11	14									7
1	2	3	4	5	6	7	14	9	10	11	12		*8*											8
1	2	3	4	5	6	7	12	9	10	11	8													9
1			4	5		7	8	*9*	10	11	6			3	12	2	14							10
1			4	5	6	7	9			11	8			3		2	10	12						11
			4	5	6	7	9				11		8	2			10	3	1	12				12
			4	5	6	7	*9*			11	10		8	2			12	3	1	14				13
1			4	5	6	7	12		10	11	9		*8*	2						14	3			14
1		5	4		6	7	*9*			11	10		8	2	14					12	3			15
1		5	4		6			12	10	11	9	14	8	2						*7*	3			16
1		5	4		6			12	10	11	9		*8*	2			14			7	3			17
1		4		5	6			9	10	11	7		8	2						12	3			18
1		4		5	6	7		9	10	11	2	8		12							3	14		19
1	2	4		5	6			9	10		12	7	8					3		*11*		14		20
1	2	6		5	11			9	10		8		7					3		4		12		21
1	2	3	4	5	6			8	10		11	12	7									9		22
1	2	6	4	5	11			8	10		12		7								3	9		23
1		6	4	5	*11*			8	10		2		7				12			14	3	9		24
1		4		5	6			8	10	12	11		7							2	3	9		25
1	2	6		5	8	12		14	10	11			7							4	3	*9*		26
1	2	6				7		12	10	11	4	14	8		5						3	9		27
1	2			5		7		12	10		6		8		4				15	11	3	9		28
	2	6		5	4	12			10		7		8					3	1	11		9		29
	2	6		5		7		8	10		4						12	3	1	11		9		30
	2	6		5		7		8	10		4			14			12	*3*	1	11		9		31
	2	6		5	4	7		8	10						12	14		3	1	11		9		32
	2			5	6	7		8	10			12			4			3	1	11		9		33
	2	6		5	4	11		8	10				*7*				14		1	12	3	9		34
		6	4		5			8	10				12			2	11		1	7	3	9		35
1	2	6	4		*5*			12	10				8		14		11			7	3	9		36
1	2	3	*4*	5	11	7		8	10				12		6	14						9		37
	2	6		5	11	7		8	10				12		4	3			1	14		9		38
1	2	6		5	11	7		8	10			12			4		14				3	9		39
1	2	6			5			8	10			12			4		7			11	3	9		40
	2	6			5			8	10			12			4		7		1	11	3	9		41
1	2	6			5			8	10			*7*			4		*11*			12	3	9	14	42

Coca-Cola Cup

Second Round	Bournemouth (h)	1-0
	(a)	1-0
Third Round	West Ham U (a)	0-1

FA Cup

Third Round	Charlton Ath (h)	3-0
Fourth Round	Millwall (a)	0-0
	(h)	1-1

CHESTER CITY 1994–95 *Back row (left to right):* Iain Cannon, Don Page, Jason Burnham, Julian Aisford, Dave Feigate, Spencer Whelan, Ray Newland, Chris Lightfoot, Andy Milner, Leroy Chambers, Brett Bariow.
Centre row: Dave Turner, Gary Shelton, Roger Preece, Eddie Bishop, Kevin Ratcliffe, Mike Pejic, Dave Flitcroft, Iain Jenkins, Stuart Rimmer, John Murphy.
Front row: Ian Bold, Greg Briggs, Philip Wood, Steven Spence, Roy Sweeney, Greg Brown, Steven Moss.

Division 3 **CHESTER CITY**

The Deva Stadium, Bumpers Lane, Chester, CH1 4LT. Telephone: (01244) 371376, 371809. Fax: (01244) 390265. Commercial: (01244) 390243.

Ground capacity: 6000.

Record attendance: 20,500 v Chelsea, FA Cup 3rd rd (replay), 16 January, 1952 (at Sealand Road).

Record receipts: £30,609 v Sheffield W, FA Cup 4th rd, 31 January 1987.

Pitch measurements: 115yd × 78yd.

Club Patron: Duke of Westminster.

Chairman: M. S. Guterman. ***Director:*** I. G. Morris. ***Manager:*** Kevin Ratcliffe. ***General Manager:*** Bill Wingrove.

Secretary: Derek Barber JP, AMITD. ***Physio:*** Derek Mann.

Year Formed: 1884. ***Turned Professional:*** 1902. ***Ltd Co.:*** 1909.

Previous Name: Chester until 1983.

Club Nickname: 'Blues' and 'City'.

Previous Grounds: Faulkner Street; Old Showground; 1904, Whipcord Lane; 1906, Sealand Road; 1990, Moss Rose Ground, Macclesfield; 1992, The Stadium, Bumpers Lane.

Foundation: All students of soccer history have read about the medieval games of football in Chester, but the present club was not formed until 1884 through the amalgamation of King's School Old Boys with Chester Rovers. For many years Chester were overshadowed in Cheshire by Northwich Victoria and Crewe Alexandra who had both won the Senior Cup several times before Chester's first success in 1894–95.

First Football League game: 2 September, 1931, Division 3(N), v Wrexham (a) D 1-1 – Johnson; Herod, Jones; Keeley, Skitt, Reilly; Thompson, Ranson, Jennings (1), Cresswell, Hedley.

Record League Victory: 12–0 v York C, Division 3 (N), 1 February 1936 – Middleton; Common, Hall; Wharton, Wilson, Howarth; Horsman (2), Hughes, Wrightson (4), Cresswell (2), Sargeant (4).

Record Cup Victory: 6–1 v Darlington, FA Cup, 1st rd, 25 November 1933 – Burke; Bennett, Little; Pitcairn, Skitt, Duckworth; Armes (3), Whittam, Mantle (2), Cresswell (1), McLachlan.

Record Defeat: 2–11 v Oldham Ath, Division 3 (N), 19 January 1952.

Most League Points (2 for a win): 56, Division 3 (N), 1946–47 and Division 4, 1964–65.

Most League Points (3 for a win): 84, Division 4, 1985–86.

Most League Goals: 119, Division 4, 1964–65.

Highest League Scorer in Season: Dick Yates, 36, Division 3 (N), 1946–47.

Most League Goals in Total Aggregate: Stuart Rimmer, 110, 1985–88, 1991–95.

Most Capped Player: Bill Lewis, 7 (30), Wales.

Most League Appearances: Ray Gill, 408, 1951–62.

Record Transfer Fee Received: £300,000 from Liverpool for Ian Rush, May 1980.

Record Transfer Fee Paid: £94,000 to Barnsley for Stuart Rimmer, August 1991.

Football League Record: 1931 Elected Division 3 (N); 1958–75 Division 4; 1975–82 Division 3; 1982–86 Division 4; 1986–92 Division 3; 1992–93 Division 2; 1993–94 Division 3; 1994–95 Division 2; 1995– Division 3.

Honours: *Football League:* Division 3 – Runners-up 1993–94; Division 3 (N) – Runners-up 1935–36; Division 4 – Runners-up 1985–86. *FA Cup:* best season: 5th rd, 1977, 1980. *Football League Cup:* Semi-final 1975. *Welsh Cup:* Winners 1908, 1933, 1947. *Debenhams Cup:* Winners 1977.

Colours: Blue and white striped shirts, blue shorts, blue stockings. **Change colours:** Jade and black striped shirts, black shorts, black stockings.

CHESTER CITY 1994–95 LEAGUE RECORD

Match No.	Date	Venue	Opponents	Result	H/T Score	Lg. Pos.	Goalscorers	Attendance
1	Aug 13	H	Bradford C	L 1-4	0-1	—	Milner	4459
2	20	A	Birmingham C	L 0-1	0-1	22		12,188
3	27	H	Huddersfield T	L 1-2	0-1	23	Bishop	2895
4	30	A	Cambridge U	L 1-2	0-0	—	Page	2520
5	Sept 3	A	Hull C	L 0-2	0-1	23		3615
6	10	H	Brighton & HA	L 1-2	0-1	23	Page	2063
7	13	H	Cardiff C	L 0-2	0-0	—		1671
8	17	A	Bournemouth	D 1-1	1-0	23	Lightfoot	3025
9	24	A	Plymouth Arg	L 0-1	0-1	24		5329
10	Oct 1	H	Oxford U	W 2-0	1-0	24	Hackett, Priest	2324
11	8	H	Swansea C	D 2-2	1-1	23	Page (pen), Shelton	2186
12	15	A	Leyton Orient	L 0-2	0-1	23		3309
13	22	A	York C	L 0-2	0-1	23		2820
14	30	H	Wrexham	D 1-1	1-0	23	Hackett	4974
15	Nov 2	H	Stockport Co	W 1-0	0-0	—	Shelton	2400
16	5	A	Peterborough U	L 0-2	0-1	23		4610
17	19	H	Blackpool	W 2-0	1-0	23	Milner, Page	3114
18	26	A	Rotherham U	L 0-2	0-0	23		2947
19	Dec 10	H	Birmingham C	L 0-4	0-2	23		3946
20	17	A	Bradford C	D 1-1	0-1	23	Milner	4555
21	26	A	Crewe Alex	L 1-2	1-0	23	Page (pen)	5428
22	27	H	Brentford	L 1-4	1-3	23	Richardson	2266
23	31	A	Bristol R	L 0-3	0-2	23		5629
24	Jan 7	H	York C	L 0-4	0-0	24		1844
25	14	A	Shrewsbury T	L 0-1	0-0	24		3879
26	28	H	Peterborough U	D 1-1	0-0	24	Hackett	1501
27	31	H	Wycombe W	L 0-2	0-2	—		1524
28	Feb 4	H	Rotherham U	D 4-4	3-2	24	Hackett, Rimmer, Milner, Preece	1794
29	11	A	Stockport Co	D 2-2	2-0	24	Preece, Dinning (og)	4405
30	14	A	Wrexham	D 2-2	1-2	—	Bishop (pen), Milner	5698
31	18	H	Shrewsbury T	L 1-3	0-1	24	Bishop (pen)	2720
32	21	A	Blackpool	L 1-3	1-2	—	Milner	4649
33	25	A	Oxford U	L 0-1	0-0	24		4930
34	Mar 4	H	Plymouth Arg	W 1-0	1-0	24	Rimmer	1823
35	11	A	Huddersfield T	L 1-5	1-3	24	Booth (og)	9606
36	18	H	Cambridge U	L 1-3	0-3	24	Milner	1720
37	22	A	Brighton & HA	L 0-1	0-1	—		5979
38	25	H	Bournemouth	D 1-1	0-0	24	Jackson	1618
39	28	H	Hull C	L 1-2	0-0	—	Lightfoot	1191
40	Apr 1	A	Cardiff C	L 1-2	0-1	24	Hackett	4405
41	8	H	Bristol R	D 0-0	0-0	24		2241
42	15	A	Brentford	D 1-1	1-0	24	Lightfoot	8020
43	17	H	Crewe Alex	L 0-1	0-0	24		3054
44	22	A	Wycombe W	L 1-3	1-2	24	Whelan	5284
45	29	H	Leyton Orient	W 1-0	0-0	23	Bishop	1596
46	May 6	A	Swansea C	W 1-0	1-0	23	Milner	2065

Final League Position: 23

GOALSCORERS

League (37): Milner 8, Hackett 5, Page 5 (2 pens), Bishop 4 (2 pens), Lightfoot 3, Preece 2, Rimmer 2, Shelton 2, Jackson 1, Priest 1, Richardson 1, Whelan 1, own goals 2.
Coca-Cola Cup (2): Chambers 1, Whelan 1.
FA Cup (3): Alsford 1, Milner 1, Page 1.

Felgate D.W. 37 + 1	Jenkins I. 40	Burnham J.J. 22 + 2	Ratcliffe K. 23	Alsford J. 32 + 3	Whelan S.R. 23	Flitcroft D.J. 20 + 12	Rimmer S.A. 22 + 3	Preece R. 42 + 1	Milner A.J. 32 + 4	Chambers L.D. 6 + 7	Page D.R. 22 + 8	Lightfoot C.I. 26 + 2	Bishop E.M. 16 + 3	Newland R.J. 9 + 1	Anthrobus S.A. 7	Hackett G.S. 30 + 5	Priest C. 22 + 2	Shelton G. 31 + 2	Jackson P.A. 32	Murphy J.J. — + 5	Richardson N.J. 6	Aunger G.E. 1 + 4	Tolson N. 3 + 1	Gardiner M.C. 2 + 1	*Match No.*
1	2	3	4	5	6	7	*8*	9	10	11	12	14													1
1	2	3	4	9	5	12	*10*	6	7	14	11		8												2
	2	3	4	5	11	7		6	9	12	*8*		14	1	10										3
	2	3	4	8	5	7		6	*9*	14	11	12		1	10										4
1	2	3		4	5			6		12	11	9	8	15	10	7									5
	2	3		4	5						11	9	8	1	10	7	6								6
	2	3		4	5	8			12	14	11	9		1	10	7	6								7
	2	3		4	5					12	11	9		1	10	7	8	6							8
	2	3		4	5	14		12		10	7	9		1	11		*8*	6							9
	2		3	4		12		7			10	9		1		11	8	6	5						10
1	2		3	4		12		7	14		10	*9*				11	8	6	5						11
	2		3			9		7	12		10	4		1		11	8	6	5						12
1	2		4			12		9	14	*7*	10	5				11	8	6	3						13
1	2		3	4		12		9		*7*	10					11	8	6	5	14					14
1	2		3	4		12		9		*7*	10					11	8	6	5	14					15
1	2		3	4		12		9		*7*	10					11	8	6	5	14					16
1	2		3	4		8	12	9	7		10					11		6	5						17
1	2		3	4		8	12	9	7		*10*					11		6	5	14					18
1	2	3		4		8		9		12	*10*	7				11		6	5	14					19
1			3	4				2	7		10	9				11		6	5		8	12			20
1			3	4				2	7		10	9				11		6	5		8	12			21
1			3	4				2	7		12	9				11		6	5		8	10			22
1			3	4				2	7		*10*	9	11			12		6	5		8	14			23
1	2		3	4				7	11			9	12					*6*	5		8	14	10		24
1	3			2		7		4	9		12	6	14			*11*			5		8		10		25
1	3			2		7	12	4	9			6	8			11			5				10		26
1	3			2		7	10	4	*9*			6	8			11		12	5				14		27
1	3			2			10	4	9		12	6	8			11		7	5						28
1	2		3	5			10	4	9		12	6	8			*11*	14	7							29
1	3	12		5		7	*10*	2	9		14	6	11				8	4							30
1	3			2		7	10	4	9			6	11				8		5						31
1	2		3	5		12	10	7	9			4	8				11		6						32
1	2	12	3		6	7	10	4	9							11	*8*	14	5						33
1	2		3		5	12	10	4			9					11	7	8	6					14	34
1		3	6	2	5		10	4	9		12					14	7	8						*11*	35
15		3		2	6	12	10	4	9					*1*		11	14	7	5					*8*	36
1	2	3		12	6		10	4	9							11	7	8	5						37
1	2	3			6		10	4	9							11	7	8	5						38
1	2	3			6	12	10	4	9			8				11	7		5						39
1	2	3			6	8	10	4	9		12	5				11	7								40
1	2	3			6		10	4	9							11	7	8	5						41
1	2	3		12	6	7	10	4	9			5	11					8							42
1	2	3			6	7	10	4	9				11			12		8	5						43
1	2	3		12	6	7	10	4	*9*				11			14		8	5						44
1	2	3			6	7	10	4	9				11					8	5						45
1	2	3			6	7	10	4	9				11			12		8	5						46

Coca-Cola Cup

First Round	Lincoln C (a)	0-2
	(h)	2-3

FA Cup

First Round	Witton Alb (h)	2-0
Second Round	Burnley (h)	1-2

CHESTERFIELD 1994–95 *Back row (left to right):* Dave Moss, Kevin Davies, Mick Leonard, Lyndly Brocklehurst, Chris Marples, Nicky Law, Darren Carr.
Third row: Mark Jules, Wayne Fairclough, Lee Rogers, Andy Morris, Sean Dyche, Darren Roberts, Steve Spooner, Steve Norris.
Second row: Steve Williams, Chris Perkins, Jamie Hewitt, Kevin Randall (Assistant Manager), John Duncan (Manager), Dave Rushbury (Physio), Tony Dennis, Michael Cheetham, Tom Curtis.
Front row: Andrew Kuchta, Lee Ashton, Richard Hopkinson.

Division 2 CHESTERFIELD

Recreation Ground, Chesterfield S40 4SX. Telephone: (01246) 209765. Fax: (01246) 556799. Commercial Dept: (01246) 231535.

Ground capacity: 8880.

Record attendance: 30,968 v Newcastle U, Division 2, 7 April 1939.

Record receipts: £45,000 v Mansfield T, Division 3 play-off semi-final, 17 May 1995.

Pitch measurements: 113yd × 71yd.

President: His Grace the Duke of Devonshire MC, DL, JP.

Chairman: J. Norton Lea. ***Vice-Chairman:*** B. W. Hubbard.

Directors: R. F. Pepper, M. L. Warner.

Manager: John Duncan.

Physio: Dave Rushbury. ***Assistant Manager:*** Kevin Randall.

Secretary: Mrs N. J. Bellamy. ***Commercial Manager:*** Jim Brown.

Year Formed: 1866. ***Turned Professional:*** 1891. ***Ltd Co:*** 1871.

Previous Names: Chesterfield Town.

Club Nickname: 'Blues' or 'Spireites'.

Foundation: Chesterfield are fourth only to Stoke, Notts County and Nottingham Forest in age for they can trace their existence as far back as 1866, although it is fair to say that they were somewhat casual in the first few years of their history playing only a few friendlies a year. However, their rules of 1871 are still in existence showing an annual membership of 2s (10p), but it was not until 1891 that they won a trophy (the Barnes Cup) and followed this a year later by winning the Sheffield Cup, Barnes Cup and the Derbyshire Junior Cup.

First Football League game: 2 September, 1899, Division 2, v Sheffield W (a) L 1-5 – Hancock; Pilgrim, Fletcher; Ballantyne, Bell, Downie; Morley, Thacker, Gooing, Munday (1), Geary.

Record League Victory: 10–0 v Glossop, Division 2, 17 January 1903 – Clutterbuck; Thorpe, Lerper; Haig, Banner, Thacker; Tomlinson (2), Newton (1), Milward (3), Munday (2), Steel (2).

Record Cup Victory: 5–0 v Wath Ath (away), FA Cup, 1st rd, 28 November 1925 – Birch; Saxby, Dennis; Wass, Abbott, Thompson; Fisher (1), Roseboom (1), Cookson (2), Whitfield (1), Hopkinson.

Record Defeat: 0–10 v Gillingham, Division 3, 5 September 1987.

Most League Points (2 for a win): 64, Division 4, 1969–70.

Most League Points (3 for a win): 91, Division 4, 1984–85.

Most League Goals: 102, Division 3 (N), 1930–31.

Highest League Scorer in Season: Jimmy Cookson, 44, Division 3 (N), 1925–26.

Most League Goals in Total Aggregate: Ernie Moss, 161, 1969–76, 1979–81 and 1984–86.

Most Capped Player: Walter McMillen, 4 (7), Northern Ireland.

Most League Appearances: Dave Blakey, 613, 1948–67.

Record Transfer Fee Received: £200,000 from Wolverhampton W for Alan Birch, August 1981.

Record Transfer Fee Paid: £150,000 to Carlisle U for Phil Bonnyman, March 1980.

Football League Record: 1899 Elected to Division 2; 1909 failed re-election; 1921–31 Division 3 (N); 1931–33 Division 2; 1933–36 Division 3 (N); 1936–51 Division 2; 1951–58 Division 3 (N); 1958–61 Division 3; 1961–70 Division 4; 1970–83 Division 3; 1983–85 Division 4; 1985–89 Division 3; 1989–92 Division 4; 1992–95 Division 3; 1995– Division 2.

Honours: *Football League:* Division 2 best season: 4th, 1946–47; Division 3 (N) – Champions 1930–31, 1935–36; Runners-up 1933–34; Division 4 – Champions 1969–70, 1984–85. *FA Cup:* best season: 5th rd, 1933, 1938, 1950. *Football League Cup:* best season: 4th rd, 1965. *Anglo-Scottish Cup:* Winners 1981.

Colours: Blue shirts, white shorts, blue stockings. **Change colours:** Green and white striped shirts, navy shorts, navy stockings.

CHESTERFIELD 1994–95 LEAGUE RECORD

Match No.	Date		Venue	Opponents	Result		H/T Score	Lg. Pos.	Goalscorers	Attendance
1	Aug	13	H	Scarborough	L	0-1	0-1	—		3099
2		20	A	Rochdale	L	1-4	0-1	17	Norris	2122
3		27	H	Mansfield T	L	0-1	0-0	19		4210
4		30	A	Wigan Ath	W	3-2	2-1	—	Robertson (og), Morris, Moss	1231
5	Sept	3	A	Hartlepool U	W	2-0	0-0	11	Morris, Moss	2173
6		10	H	Walsall	D	0-0	0-0	12		3027
7		13	H	Exeter C	W	2-0	1-0	—	Davies, Norris	2136
8		17	A	Scarborough	W	1-0	1-0	10	Curtis	1475
9		24	A	Bury	L	1-2	1-1	12	Davies	3031
10	Oct	1	H	Torquay U	W	1-0	0-0	9	Burton (og)	2465
11		8	A	Colchester U	W	3-0	1-0	8	Davies, Moss, Morris	3476
12		15	H	Darlington	D	0-0	0-0	6		2836
13		22	H	Fulham	D	1-1	1-0	7	Roberts	2860
14		29	A	Barnet	L	1-4	1-2	9	Hewitt	2130
15	Nov	5	H	Hereford U	W	1-0	1-0	7	Norris	2448
16		19	A	Gillingham	D	1-1	1-0	7	Davies	2722
17		26	H	Preston NE	W	1-0	0-0	7	McAuley	3191
18	Dec	10	H	Rochdale	D	2-2	2-1	7	Hewitt 2	2457
19		18	A	Mansfield T	L	2-4	0-2	7	Davies, Robinson	3519
20		26	H	Doncaster R	W	2-0	1-0	7	Robinson 2	4226
21		27	A	Northampton T	W	3-2	2-1	7	Moss 2, Madden	6329
22		31	H	Lincoln C	W	1-0	0-0	5	Robinson	3325
23	Jan	8	A	Fulham	D	1-1	1-0	4	Moss	3927
24		14	H	Scunthorpe U	W	3-1	3-0	3	Lormor, Moss 2	3245
25		24	A	Hereford U	W	2-0	1-0	—	Lormor, Davies	1673
26	Feb	4	A	Preston NE	D	0-0	0-0	3		8544
27		11	H	Gillingham	W	2-0	2-0	2	Lormor, Law	3070
28		14	H	Barnet	W	2-0	0-0	—	Moss, Davies	2978
29		18	A	Scunthorpe U	W	1-0	0-0	2	Robinson	3566
30		25	A	Torquay U	D	3-3	1-1	2	Lormor, Davies 2	3236
31	Mar	4	H	Bury	D	0-0	0-0	2		4429
32		11	A	Walsall	W	3-1	1-0	2	Carr, Lormor, Howard	6219
33		18	H	Wigan Ath	D	0-0	0-0	2		3808
34		25	H	Hartlepool U	W	2-0	1-0	2	Lormor 2 (1 pen)	4125
35	Apr	1	A	Exeter C	W	2-1	0-0	2	Davies, Morris	2144
36		4	A	Carlisle U	D	1-1	0-0	—	Moss	8478
37		8	A	Lincoln C	W	1-0	1-0	2	Robinson	5141
38		15	H	Northampton T	W	3-0	1-0	2	Morris 2, Robinson	4884
39		17	A	Doncaster R	W	3-1	1-1	2	Robinson, Carr, Curtis	4796
40		29	A	Darlington	W	1-0	1-0	2	Lormor	3387
41	May	2	H	Carlisle U	L	1-2	1-1	—	Davies	7283
42		6	H	Colchester U	D	2-2	1-1	3	Lormor 2 (1 pen)	4133

Final League Position: 3

GOALSCORERS

League (62): Davies 11, Lormor 10 (2 pens), Moss 10, Robinson 8, Morris 6, Hewitt 3, Norris 3, Carr 2, Curtis 2, Howard 1, Law 1, McAuley 1, Madden 1, Roberts 1, own goals 2.
Coca-Cola Cup (8): Cheetham 1, Curtis 1, Davies 1, Jules 1, Morris 1, Moss 1, Norris 1, Perkins 1.
FA Cup (0).

Marples C. 21	Hewitt J.R. 38	Rogers L.J. 39	Fairclough W.R. 12 + 1	Carr D. 35	Law N. 35	Curtis T. 39 + 1	Norris S.M. 5 + 2	Davies K.C. 41	Moss D. 27 + 5	Cheetham M.M. 5	Perkins C.P. 17 + 1	Roberts D.A. 4 + 7	Spooner S.A. 6 + 1	Marshall D. — + 1	Morris A.D. 21 + 5	Hill D.M. 3	Jules M.A. 10 + 13	Madden L.D. 10	Reddish S. 2 + 1	Dyche S.M. 22	McAuley S. 1	Beasley A. 20 + 1	Robinson P.J. 22	Howard J. 1 + 11	Lormor A. 23	Narbett J.V. 2 + 1	Bibbo S. — + 1	Stewart W.I. 1	*Match No.*
1	2	3	4	5	6	7	*8*	9	10	11	12	14																	1
1	2	3	4	5		7	8	9		11	6		10	12															2
1	2	3	4	5	6	7	8	9		10					11														3
1	2	3		5	6	7		9	10						8	4	11												4
1	2	3		5	6	7		9	10						8	4	11												5
1	2	3		5	6	7		9	10			12	14		8	4	*11*												6
1	2	3		5	6	7	12	9				10	11		8			4											7
1	2	3		5	6	7		9	10			12	11		8			4											8
1	2	3	14	5	6	7		9	10			12	4		8		*11*												9
1	2			5	6	7		10				8	4		9		11	3	12										10
1		3	2		6	7		8	10			12	*4*		9		14	5	11										11
1	2	3	6			7		8	*10*			12			9		14	5	4	11									12
1	2	3	6	5		7		8	12	*10*	4	9					14			11									13
1	2	3	6	5		7		8	10		4				9		12			11									14
1	2	3	6	5		7	8				4	10			9					11									15
1		3	6	5		7	8	9	10		4						11			2									16
	11	3	7	5	6			8			4				9					2	10	1							17
	2	3			6		12	8	10		4						14	5		*11*		1	7	9					18
	2	3			6	12		9	10	*8*	4	14						5		11		1	7						19
1	2	3		5	6	4		9	10								12			11			7		8				20
1	2			5	6	4		8	10								12	3		11			7		9				21
1	2		5		6	4		8	10		3						12			11			7		9				22
1	2	3		5	6	4		8	10								12			11			7		9				23
1	2	3		5	6	4		8	10								12			11		15	7		9				24
	2	3		5	*6*	4		8							10		12			11		1	7		9	14			25
	2	3		5	6	4		8	10						12					11		1	7		9				26
	2	3		5	6	4		8	10						12					11		1	7		9				27
	2	3		5	6	4		8	10						12					11		1	7		9				28
	2	3		5	6	4		8	10		11											1	7		9				29
	2	3		5	6	4		8	10								11					1	7	12	9				30
	2	3		5	6	4		8	10						12					11		*1*	7		9		15		31
	2	3		5	6	4		8	10								7			11		1		12	9				32
	2	3		5	6	4		*8*	10								12			11				14	9	7		1	33
		3			6	4		8			*2*				10		12	5		11		1		14	9	7			34
		3			6	4		8							10		2	5		11		1	7	12	9				35
	2	3		5	6	4		8	12						10		*11*					1	7	14	9				36
	2	3		5	6	4		8	10		11											1	7	12	9				37
	2	3		5	6	4		8	12		11				10							1	7	14	*9*				38
	2	3		5	6	4		8			11				10							1	7		9				39
	2	3		5	6	4		*8*	12		11				10							1	7	14	9				40
	2	3		5	6	4		8	10		11				12							1	7	14	*9*				41
	2	3	6	5		4		*8*	12		11				10							1	7	14	9				42

Coca-Cola Cup

First Round	Blackpool (a)	2-1
	(h)	4-2
Second Round	Wolverhampton W (h)	1-3
	(a)	1-1

FA Cup

First Round	Scarborough (h)	0-0
	(a)	0-2

COLCHESTER UNITED 1994–95 *Back row (left to right):* Steve Whitton (Player/Coach), Chris Fry, Scott Walters, Paul Champ, Steve Brown, Andy Partner, David Schultz, Peter Cawley, Tony English, Tim Allpress, Paul Abrahams, Brian Owen (Physio).
Front row: Simon Betts, Danny Roberts, Neil Butler, Justin Gentle, John Cheesewright, George Burley (Manager), Carl Emberson, Steve Ball, Mark Kinsella, Christian Hyslop, Justin Booty.

Division 3 COLCHESTER UNITED

Layer Rd Ground, Colchester, Essex CO2 7JJ. Telephone: (01206) 574042. Fax: (01206) 48700. Club Shop: (01206) 561180. Soccer Centre: (01206) 571581. Commercial Dept: (01206) 574042.

Ground capacity: 7190.

Record attendance: 19,072 v Reading, FA Cup 1st rd, 27 Nov, 1948.

Record receipts: £26,330 v Barrow, GM Vauxhall Conference, 2 May 1992.

Pitch measurements: 110yd × 71yd.

Patron: The Mayor of Colchester.

Directors: Gordon Parker (Chairman), Peter Heard (vice-chairman), John Worsp, Peter Powell.

Manager: Steve Wignall. ***Player-Coach:*** Steve Whitton. ***Youth Coach:*** Steve Foley.

Physio: Brian Owen. ***Consultant Physio:*** Ray Cole.

Secretary: Sue Smith.

Commercial Manager: Marie Partner. ***Lottery Manager:*** Liz Blacknall.

Year Formed: 1937. ***Turned Professional:*** 1937. ***Ltd Co.:*** 1937.

Club Nickname: 'The U's'.

Foundation: Colchester United was formed in 1937 when a number of enthusiasts of the much older Colchester Town club decided to establish a professional concern as a limited liability company. The new club continued at Layer Road which had been the amateur club's home since 1909.

First Football League game: 19 August, 1950, Division 3(S), v Gillingham (a) D 0-0 – Wright; Kettle, Allen; Bearryman, Stewart, Elder; Jones, Curry, Turner, McKim, Church.

Record League Victory: 9–1 v Bradford C, Division 4, 30 December 1961 – Ames; Millar, Fowler; Harris, Abrey, Ron Hunt; Foster, Bobby Hunt (4), King (4), Hill (1), Wright.

Record Cup Victory: 7–1 v Yeovil T (away), FA Cup, 2nd rd (replay), 11 December 1958 – Ames; Fisher, Fowler; Parker, Milligan, Hammond; Williams (1), McLeod (2), Langman (4), Evans, Wright.

Record Defeat: 0–8 v Leyton Orient, Division 4, 15 October 1989.

Most League Points (2 for a win): 60, Division 4, 1973–74.

Most League Points (3 for a win): 81, Division 4, 1982–83.

Most League Goals: 104, Division 4, 1961–62.

Highest League Scorer in Season: Bobby Hunt, 37, Division 4, 1961–62.

Most League Goals in Total Aggregate: Martyn King, 131, 1959–65.

Most Capped Player: None.

Most League Appearances: Micky Cook, 613, 1969–84.

Record Transfer Fee Received: £100,000 from Birmingham C for Steve McGavin, January 1994.

Record Transfer Fee Paid: £40,000 to Lokeren for Dale Tempest, August 1987.

Football League Record: 1950 Elected to Division 3(S); 1958–61 Division 3; 1961–62 Division 4; 1962–65 Division 3; 1965–66 Division 4; 1966–68 Division 3; 1968–74 Division 4; 1974–76 Division 3, 1976–77 Division 4; 1977–81 Division 3; 1981–90 Division 4; 1990–92 GM Vauxhall Conference; 1992– Division 3.

Honours: *Football League:* Division 3(S) best season: 3rd , 1956–57; Division 4 – Runners-up 1961–62. *FA Cup* best season: 1971, 6th rd (record for a Fourth Division club shared with Oxford United and Bradford City). *Football League Cup:* best season 5th rd 1975. *GM Vauxhall Conference winners* 1991–92. *FA Trophy winners* 1992.

Colours: Blue and white striped shirts, white shorts, white stockings. **Change colours:** White shirts, black shorts black stockings white trim.

COLCHESTER UNITED FC

COLCHESTER UNITED 1994–95 LEAGUE RECORD

Match No.	Date	Venue	Opponents	Result	H/T Score	Lg. Pos.	Goalscorers	Attendance
1	Aug 13	H	Torquay U	L 1-3	1-2	—	Kinsella	3175
2	20	A	Mansfield T	L 0-2	0-0	18		2247
3	27	H	Doncaster R	L 0-3	0-2	21		2320
4	30	A	Exeter C	L 0-1	0-1	—		1804
5	Sept 3	A	Scarborough	W 1-0	0-0	20	Dennis	1494
6	10	H	Hartlepool U	W 1-0	0-0	18	Whitton	2428
7	13	H	Walsall	W 3-2	0-1	—	Kinsella 2, Whitton	2239
8	17	A	Torquay U	D 3-3	0-1	12	Whitton, Brown, Dennis	3390
9	24	A	Darlington	W 3-2	2-1	11	Whitton 2, Brown	2260
10	Oct 1	H	Bury	W 1-0	0-0	8	Cawley	3286
11	8	H	Chesterfield	L 0-3	0-1	9		3476
12	15	A	Carlisle U	D 0-0	0-0	11		5817
13	22	H	Preston NE	W 3-1	1-0	9	Brown 2, Whitton	3015
14	29	A	Wigan Ath	W 2-1	2-0	6	Kinsella, Fry	1621
15	Nov 5	H	Gillingham	D 2-2	1-2	6	Fry, Kinsella	3817
16	19	A	Rochdale	D 0-0	0-0	6		1903
17	26	H	Scunthorpe U	W 4-2	2-0	6	Brown, Abrahams 2, Whitton	2904
18	Dec 10	H	Mansfield T	D 1-1	1-0	6	Fry	3016
19	16	A	Doncaster R	W 2-1	0-0	—	Cawley, Brown	2460
20	26	H	Northampton T	L 0-1	0-1	6		5064
21	27	A	Fulham	W 2-1	1-1	6	Kinsella, Blake (og)	4243
22	31	H	Hereford U	D 2-2	0-2	7	Stoneman, Whitton	3322
23	Jan 10	A	Preston NE	L 1-2	0-1	—	Fry	6377
24	14	H	Barnet	D 1-1	0-1	8	Putney	3706
25	28	H	Wigan Ath	L 0-1	0-0	11		3067
26	Feb 4	A	Scunthorpe U	W 4-3	2-3	9	Locke, English, Thompson 2	2748
27	11	H	Rochdale	D 0-0	0-0	7		3080
28	18	A	Barnet	W 1-0	1-0	5	Asaba	2242
29	21	A	Lincoln C	L 0-2	0-0	—		1969
30	25	A	Bury	L 1-4	0-1	9	Fry	2484
31	Mar 4	H	Darlington	W 1-0	1-0	7	Asaba	6055
32	11	A	Hartlepool U	L 1-3	1-2	9	Fry	1371
33	18	H	Exeter C	W 3-1	1-0	8	Thompson, Betts (pen), Lock	2375
34	25	H	Scarborough	L 0-2	0-0	8		3025
35	Apr 1	A	Walsall	L 0-2	0-0	9		3622
36	8	A	Hereford U	L 0-3	0-2	11		1669
37	11	A	Gillingham	W 3-1	0-1	—	Betts (pen), Thompson 2	3328
38	15	H	Fulham	W 5-2	4-1	8	Cheetham, English, Caesar, Fry 2	3448
39	17	A	Northampton T	D 1-1	0-1	8	Whitton	5011
40	22	H	Lincoln C	L 1-2	1-1	9	McCarthy	2654
41	29	H	Carlisle U	L 0-1	0-0	10		3333
42	May 6	A	Chesterfield	D 2-2	1-1	10	Whitton, Putney (pen)	4133

Final League Position: 10

GOALSCORERS

League (56): Whitton 10, Fry 8, Brown 6, Kinsella 6, Thompson 5, Abrahams 2, Asaba 2, Betts 2 (2 pens), Cawley 2, Dennis 2, English 2, Putney 2 (1 pen), Caesar 1, Cheetham 1, Lock 1, Locke 1, McCarthy 1, Stoneman 1, own goal 1.
Coca-Cola Cup (0).
FA Cup (11): Abrahams 3, Whitton 3, Brown 2, Kinsella 2, English 1.

Cheesewright J. 23	Culling G. 2	Dalli J. 1	English A.K. 33	Caesar G. 39	Dennis J.A. 32 + 1	Fry C.D. 24 + 9	Brown S.R. 26 + 2	Whitton S.P. 36	Kinsella M.A. 42	Abrahams P. 20 + 8	Allpress T.J. 3 + 8	Davis A. 4	Burley G. 5 + 2	Putney T.A. 28	Partner A.N. — + 1	Cawley P. 23	Allen L.G. — + 2	Betts S.R. 34 + 1	Locke A.S. 20 + 2	Stoneman P. 3	Emberson C.W. 19 + 1	Thompson N. 5 + 8	Lock A.C. — + 3	Asaba C. 9 + 3	Gibbs P. 8 + 1	Williams M.K. 3	McCarthy A.P. 10	Cheetham M.M. 8 + 1	Reinelt R.S. 2 + 3	*Match No.*
1	2	3	4	5	6	7	8	9	10	11	12																			1
1	2		6	5	7	12	9	10	8	11	4	3																		2
1				5	6		8	9	10	11	4	3	2	7																3
1				*5*	6	12	8	9	10	11	4	3	2	7	14															4
1			2	5	6	12	8	9	10	11		3		7		4														5
1			3	5	6		8	9	10	11			2	7		4	12													6
1			3	5	6		8	9	10	11			2	7		4		12												7
1			3	5	6		8	9	10	11			12	7		4		2												8
1			3	5	6	*11*	8	9	10					7		4	12	2	14											9
1			3	5	6		8	9	10	11						4		2	7											10
1			3	5	6	12	8	9	10	*11*			14			4		2	7											11
1			3	5	*6*	11	8	9	10	12				7		4		2	14											12
1			3	5		11	8	9	10	12				7		4		2	6											13
1			3	5	12	*11*	8	9	10	14				7		4		2	6											14
1			3	5		11	8	9	10	12				7		4		2	6											15
1			3	5	6	12	8	9	10	11						4		2	7											16
1			3	5			8	9	10	11				7		4		2	6											17
1				5	3	7	8	9	10	11						4		2	6											18
1				*5*	11	7	8	9	10	12	14		2			4		3	6											19
1			3	5	4	12	8	9	10	11				7				2	6											20
1			3		4	11	8	9	10	12	14			7				2	6	5										21
1			3			11	8	9	10	12	14			7		4		2	6	5										22
1			3	5	6	12	8	9	10	11				7		4		2			15									23
			3	5	8	12			10	11				7		4		2	6		1	9								24
				5	8		12		10	11				7		4		2	6	3	1	*9*	14							25
			2	5	8	7	11	9	10							4		3	6		1	12								26
			3	5	*6*	7	8	9	10	12	14					4		2			1	11								27
			4	5	6	7		9	10	*11*	12							3	2		1	14		8						28
			4	5	6	7			10	11								3	2		1	9	12	8						29
			4	5	6	7			10	11	12			8				3	2		1			9						30
				5	6	7	12	9	10					8		4		3	2		1			11						31
				5	6	7	*8*		10		12					4		2			1	14		9	3	11				32
			4		6	7			10									2			1	8	12	9	3	11	5			33
			4	6				9	10					7				2			1	12		8	3	*11*	5	14		34
			3	5	6			9	10									2	8		1			11			4	7		35
			3	5	6	12		11	10					8				2			1	14		*9*			4	7		36
			8	5		7		9	2					6				3			1	12			*11*		4	10	14	37
			8	5		7		*9*	2					6				3			1	12			11		4	10	14	38
			8	5		7		9	2					6				3			1	14		12	*11*		4	10		39
			8	5		7		9	2					6				*3*			1			12	11		4	10	14	40
				5	6	7		11	2					8							1			12	3		4	10	9	41
				5	6	7		11	2					8				3			1				12		4	10	9	42

Coca-Cola Cup

First Round	Brentford (h)	0-2
	(a)	0-2

FA Cup

First Round	Yeading (a)	2-2
	(h)	7-1
Second Round	Exeter C (a)	2-1
Third Round	Wimbledon (a)	0-1

COVENTRY CITY 1994–95 *Back row (left to right):* Jason Smith, David Busst, Mick Harford, Jim Blythe (Goalkeeping Coach), Steve Sims (Youth Development Officer), Tim Exeter (Fitness Coach), John Williams, Steve Morgan, Julian Darby.
Centre row: George Dalton (Physio), Brian Roberts (Reserve Team Manager), Paul Williams, Tony Sheridan, Stewart Robson, Jamie Barnwell-Edinboro, Jonathan Gould, Steve Ogrizovic, Martin Davies, Tim Blake, Marcus Hall, Gavin O'Toole, Sandy Robertson, Trevor Gould (Youth Team Manager), Bert Edwards (Recruitment Officer).
Front row: Willie Boland, Brian Borrows, Roy Wegerle, Leigh Jenkinson, Mick Quinn, Mick Brown (Assistant Manager), Phil Neal (Manager), Phil Babb, David Rennie, Sean Flynn, Peter Ndlovu, Ally Pickering.
(Photograph: Action Images)

FA Premiership **COVENTRY CITY**

Highfield Road Stadium, King Richard Street, Coventry CV2 4FW. Telephone: (01203) 223535. Fax: (01203) 630318. Ticket Office Fax: (01203) 258856. Sales & Marketing: (01203) 633823. Clubcall: 0891 121166.

Ground capacity: 23,500.

Record attendance: 51,455 v Wolverhampton W, Division 2, 29 April 1967.

Record receipts: £250,065.38 v Manchester U, FA Premiership, 1 May 1995 (£216,126 actual receipts excluding season tickets).

Pitch measurements: 110yd × 75yd.

Life President: Derrick H. Robbins.

Chairman: B. A. Richardson. ***Deputy Chairman:*** M. C. McGinnity.

Directors: E. W. Grove, A. M. Jepson, J. F. W Reason, P. D. H. Robins.

Secretary: Graham Hover.

Manager: Ron Atkinson. ***Assistant Manager:*** Gordon Strachan. ***Physio:*** George Dalton.

Sales & Marketing Manager: Mark Jones.

Club Statistician: Jim Brown.

Year Formed: 1883. ***Turned Professional:*** 1893. ***Ltd Co.:*** 1907.

Previous Names: 1883–98, Singers FC; 1898, Coventry City FC.

Club Nickname: 'Sky Blues'.

Previous Grounds: Binley Road, 1883–87; Stoke Road, 1887–99; Highfield Road, 1899–.

Foundation: Workers at Singer's cycle factory formed a club in 1883. The first success of Singers' FC was to win the Birmingham Junior Cup in 1891 and this led in 1894 to their election to the Birmingham and District League. Four years later they changed their name to Coventry City and joined the Southern League in 1908 at which time they were playing in blue and white quarters.

First Football League game: 30 August, 1919, Division 2, v Tottenham H (h) L 0-5 – Lindon; Roberts, Chaplin, Allan, Hawley, Clarke, Sheldon, Mercer, Sambrooke, Lowes, Gibson.

Record League Victory: 9–0 v Bristol C, Division 3 (S), 28 April 1934 – Pearson; Brown, Bisby; Perry, Davidson, Frith; White (2), Lauderdale Bourton (5), Jones (2), Lake.

Record Cup Victory: 7–0 v Scunthorpe U, FA Cup, 1st rd, 24 November 1934 – Pearson; Brown, Bisby; Mason, Davidson, Boileau; Birtley (2), Lauderdale (2), Bourton (1), Jones (1), Liddle (1).

Record Defeat: 2–10 v Norwich C, Division 3 (S), 15 March 1930.

Most League Points (2 for a win): 60, Division 4, 1958–59 and Division 3, 1963–64.

Most League Points (3 for a win): 63, Division 1, 1986–87.

Most League Goals: 108, Division 3 (S), 1931–32.

Highest League Scorer in Season: Clarrie Bourton, 49, Division 3 (S), 1931–32.

Most League Goals in Total Aggregate: Clarrie Bourton, 171, 1931–37.

Most Capped Player: Dave Clements, 21 (48), Northern Ireland and Ronnie Rees, 21 (39) Wales.

Most League Appearances: George Curtis, 486, 1956–70.

Record Transfer Fee Received: £3,600,000 from Liverpool for Phil Babb, September 1994.

Record Transfer Fee Paid: £1,950,000 to Manchester U for Dion Dublin, September 1994.

Football League Record: 1919 Elected to Division 2; 1925–26 Division 3 (N); 1926–36 Division 3 (S); 1936–52 Division 2; 1952–58 Division 3 (S); 1958–59 Division 4; 1959–64 Division 3; 1964–67 Division 2; 1967–92 Division 1; 1992– FA Premier League.

Honours: *Football League:* Division 1 best season: 6th, 1969–70; Division 2 – Champions 1966–67; Division 3 – Champions 1963–64; Division 3 (S) – Champions 1935–36; Runners-up 1933–34; Division 4 – Runners-up 1958–59. *FA Cup:* Winners 1987. *Football League Cup:* best season: Semi-final 1981, 1990. **European Competitions:** *European Fairs Cup:* 1970–71.

Colours: All Sky blue. **Change colours:** Purple and mauve striped shirts with gold pinstripe, purple and gold shorts, gold stockings with purple trim.

COVENTRY CITY 1994–95 LEAGUE RECORD

Match No.	Date	Venue	Opponents	Result	H/T Score	Lg. Pos.	Goalscorers	Attendance
1	Aug 20	H	Wimbledon	D 1-1	0-0	—	Busst	11,005
2	24	A	Newcastle U	L 0-4	0-3	—		34,163
3	27	A	Blackburn R	L 0-4	0-0	21		21,657
4	29	H	Aston Villa	L 0-1	0-1	—		12,218
5	Sept 10	A	QPR	D 2-2	1-2	20	Cook, Dublin	11,398
6	17	H	Leeds U	W 2-1	0-0	18	Dublin, Cook (pen)	15,383
7	24	H	Southampton	L 1-3	1-1	20	Dublin	11,798
8	Oct 3	A	Leicester C	D 2-2	1-1	—	Wegerle, Dublin	19,372
9	10	H	Ipswich T	W 2-0	1-0	—	Wark (og), Cook (pen)	9509
10	15	A	Everton	W 2-0	2-0	14	Dublin, Wegerle	28,219
11	23	A	Arsenal	L 1-2	0-2	15	Wegerle (pen)	31,725
12	29	H	Manchester C	W 1-0	0-0	13	Dublin	15,802
13	Nov 2	H	Crystal Palace	L 1-4	1-2	—	Dublin	10,729
14	6	A	Chelsea	D 2-2	1-0	15	Dublin, Ndlovu	17,090
15	19	H	Norwich C	W 1-0	0-0	13	Jones	11,891
16	26	A	West Ham U	W 1-0	0-0	10	Busst	17,251
17	Dec 3	H	Liverpool	D 1-1	0-1	10	Flynn	21,032
18	10	A	Wimbledon	L 0-2	0-2	16		7349
19	17	H	Newcastle U	D 0-0	0-0	12		17,237
20	26	H	Nottingham F	D 0-0	0-0	12		19,116
21	28	A	Sheffield W	L 1-5	1-3	15	Ndlovu (pen)	26,056
22	31	H	Tottenham H	L 0-4	0-1	17		19,965
23	Jan 3	A	Manchester U	L 0-2	0-1	—		43,120
24	14	A	Manchester C	D 0-0	0-0	17		20,232
25	21	H	Arsenal	L 0-1	0-0	19		14,557
26	25	A	Norwich C	D 2-2	1-1	—	Dublin, Jenkinson	14,024
27	Feb 4	H	Chelsea	D 2-2	2-2	20	Flynn, Burley (og)	13,423
28	11	A	Crystal Palace	W 2-0	0-0	17	Jones, Dublin	12,076
29	18	H	West Ham U	W 2-0	1-0	13	Ndlovu, Marsh	17,563
30	25	H	Leicester C	W 4-2	2-0	12	Flynn 2, Marsh, Ndlovu	20,650
31	Mar 4	A	Southampton	D 0-0	0-0	12		14,505
32	6	A	Aston Villa	D 0-0	0-0	—		26,186
33	11	H	Blackburn R	D 1-1	1-0	12	Dublin	18,556
34	14	A	Liverpool	W 3-2	2-0	—	Ndlovu 3 (1 pen)	27,183
35	18	A	Leeds U	L 0-3	0-1	10		29,179
36	Apr 1	H	QPR	L 0-1	0-0	12		15,751
37	15	H	Sheffield W	W 2-0	1-0	12	Dublin, Ndlovu	15,733
38	17	A	Nottingham F	L 0-2	0-2	15		26,253
39	May 1	H	Manchester U	L 2-3	1-1	—	Ndlovu, Pressley	21,858
40	6	A	Ipswich T	L 0-2	0-0	18		12,342
41	9	A	Tottenham H	W 3-1	1-0	—	Ndlovu 2 (1 pen), Dublin	24,930
42	14	H	Everton	D 0-0	0-0	16		21,787

Final League Position: 16

GOALSCORERS

League (44): Dublin 13, Ndlovu 11 (3 pens), Flynn 4, Cook 3 (2 pens), Wegerle 3 (1 pen), Busst 2, Jones 2, Marsh 2, Jenkinson 1, Pressley 1, own goals 2.
Coca-Cola Cup (5): Dublin 2, Darby 1, Flynn 1, Wegerle 1.
FA Cup (4): Ndlovu 2, Dublin 1, Wegerle 1 (pen).

Ogrizovic S. 33	Borrows B. 33 + 2	Morgan S. 26 + 2	Busst D.J. 20	Rennie D. 28	Babb P.A. 3	Darby J.T. 27 + 2	Jenkinson L. 10 + 1	Flynn S. 32	Quinn M. 3 + 3	Boland W.J. 9 + 3	Wegerle R.C. 21 + 5	Cook P.A. 33 + 1	Pickering A.G. 27 + 4	Williams J.N. 1 + 6	Dublin D. 31	Jones C. 16 + 5	Gillespie G.T. 2 + 1	Ndlovu P. 28 + 2	Pressley S. 18 + 1	Marsh M.A. 15	Hall M.T.J. 2 + 3	Richardson K. 14	Gould J.A. 7	Burrows D. 11	Robertson A. — + 1	Strachan G.D. 5	Filan J.R. 2	Williams P.R. 5	Match No.
1	2	3	4	5	6	7	8	9	10	11	12	14																	1
1	2	3	4	5		7	8	6	10	12	9	11	14																2
1	2	3	4	5	6	7		11	10		9	8		12															3
1	2	3	4	5	6	7		9		11	10	8		12															4
1		3	6	5		7	10	11		12	8	4	2	14	9														5
1		3	6	5		7		10		11		4	2		9	8													6
1		3	6	5		7		10		11	12	4	2		9	8	14												7
1	12	3	6			7		11			10	4	2		9	8	5												8
1		3	6	5		7		11			10	4	2		9	8		12											9
1		3	6	5		7		11			10	4	2		9	8													10
1	12	3	6	5		7		11			10		2		9	8		14	4										11
1	2		6	5		7		11			10	4	3		9			8											12
1	3	12	6	5		7		4		11	10		2		9	14		8											13
1	2	3	6			7					10	4			9	11		8	5										14
1	2	3	6			7		11				4			9	10		8	5										15
1	2	3	6			7	12	11				4			9	10		8	5										16
1	2	3	6			7	10	9				4	12			11		8	5										17
1	2	3	6			7		9			10	4		12		11		8	5										18
1	2	3	6			7		9		12	10	4				11		8	5										19
1	2	3	6			7		9	12		10	4	14			11		8	5										20
1	2	3				7		9	12		10	4	14			11	6	8	5										21
1	2	3				7		9	12		8	4	5			11				10	14							6	22
1		3				12	11	7			8	4	2		9	14			5	10								6	23
1	2	3				7	11	4							9			8	5	10								6	24
1	2			5		7	11				8	4	3		9	12				10								6	25
1	2			5		7	11				12	4	3		9			8		10								6	26
1	2	6		5			11	7			12		3		9			8	4	10									27
1	2	3		5		12		7					6		9	11		8	4	10									28
1	2	3		5				11				7	6		9			8		10		4							29
1	2	3		5				11				7	6		9			8		10		4							30
	2			5				11				7	6		9			8		10		4	1	3					31
	2			5				7		11		10	6		9			8				4	1	3					32
	2			5				7		11			6		9			8	12	10		4	1	3					33
	6			5						11		7	2		9			8		10		4	1	3					34
	6	12		5				9		11		7	2	14				8		10		4	1	3					35
1				5				11				7	2		9			8	6	10		4		3	12				36
1	6										10	11	2	12	9			8	5		14	4		3		7			37
1	6										12	7	2	11	9			8	5	10	14	4		3					38
	2			5							10	11			9			8	6		3	4	1			7			39
	2			5								11			9	12		8	6		10	4	1	3		7			40
	6			5		11					10		2		9	12		8				4		3		7	1		41
	6			5		11	10						2		9			8				4		3		7	1		42

Coca-Cola Cup

Second Round	Wrexham (a)	2-1
	(h)	3-2
Third Round	Blackburn R (a)	0-2

FA Cup

Third Round	WBA (h)	1-1
	(a)	2-1
Fourth Round	Norwich C (h)	0-0
	(a)	1-3

CREWE ALEXANDRA 1994–95 *Back row (left to right):* Phil Clarkson, Gus Wilson, Anthony Hughes, Steve Macauley, Danny Collier, Dele Adebola, Anthony Woodward, Rob Savage, Steve Walters.
Centre row: John Fleet (Kit Man), Steve Holland (Youth Coach), Billy Barr, Wayne Collins, Francis Tierney, Mark Smith, Ian Wilkinson, Mark Gayle, Ashley Ward, Shaun Smith, Rob Edwards, Neil Baker (Assistant Manager).
Front row: Mark Gardiner, Martyn Booty, Neil Lennon, Darren Rowbotham, Dario Gradi (Manager), Steve Garvey, Gareth Whalley, Danny Murphy, Richard Annan.
(Photograph: Steve Finch L.R.P.S.)

Division 2 CREWE ALEXANDRA

Football Ground, Gresty Rd, Crewe, CW2 6EB. Telephone: (01270) 213014.

Ground capacity: 6000.

Record attendance: 20,000 v Tottenham H, FA Cup 4th rd, 30 January 1960.

Record receipts: £41,093 v Liverpool, FA Cup 3rd rd, 6 January 1992.

Pitch measurements: 112yd × 74yd.

President: N. Rowlinson.

Chairman: J. Bowler. ***Vice-Chairman:*** N. Hassall.

Directors: K. Potts, D. Rowlinson, R. Clayton, J. McMillan, E. Weetman, J. R. Holmes, D. Gradi.

Manager: Dario Gradi.

Secretary/Commercial Manager: Mrs Gill Palin.

Year Formed: 1877. ***Turned Professional:*** 1893. ***Ltd Co.:*** 1892.

Club Nickname: 'Railwaymen'.

Foundation: Crewe Alexandra played cricket and probably rugby before they decided to form a football club in 1877. They took the name "Alexandra" after Princess Alexandra. Crewe's first trophy was the Crewe and District Cup in 1887 and it is worth noting that they reached the semi-finals of the FA Cup the following year.

First Football League game: 3 September, 1892, Division 2, v Burton Swifts (a) L 1-7 – Hickton; Moore, Cope; Linnell, Johnson, Osborne; Bennett, Pearson (1), Bailey, Barnett, Roberts.

Record League Victory: 8–0 v Rotherham U, Division 3 (N), 1 October 1932 – Foster; Pringle, Dawson; Ward, Keenor (1), Turner (1); Gillespie, Swindells (1), McConnell (2), Deacon (2), Weale (1).

Record Cup Victory: 7–1 v Gresley R, FA Cup, 1st rd, 12 November 1994 – Smith M; Booty, Smith S (1), Wilson, Macauley, Whalley, Garvey (1), Collins, Ward (3), Lennon, Rowbotham (2).

Record Defeat: 2–13 v Tottenham H, FA Cup 4th rd replay, 3 February 1960.

Most League Points (2 for a win): 59, Division 4, 1962–63.

Most League Points (3 for a win): 83, Division 2, 1994–95.

Most League Goals: 95, Division 3 (N), 1931–32.

Highest League Scorer in Season: Terry Harkin, 35, Division 4, 1964–65.

Most League Goals in Total Aggregate: Bert Swindells, 126, 1928–37.

Most Capped Player: Bill Lewis, 12 (30), Wales.

Most League Appearances: Tommy Lowry, 436, 1966–78.

Record Transfer Fee Received: £600,000 from Liverpool for Rob Jones, October 1991.

Record Transfer Fee Paid: £80,000 to Barnsley for Darren Foreman, March 1990.

Football League Record: 1892 Original Member of Division 2; 1896 Failed re-election; 1921 Re-entered Division 3 (N); 1958–63 Division 4; 1963–64 Division 3; 1964–68 Division 4; 1968–69 Division 3; 1969–89 Division 4; 1989–91 Division 3; 1991–92 Division 4; 1992–94 Division 3; 1994– Division 2.

Honours: *Football League:* Division 2 best season: 3rd, 1994–95. *FA Cup:* best season: semi-final 1888. *Football League Cup:* best season: 3rd rd, 1975, 1976, 1979, 1993. *Welsh Cup:* Winners 1936, 1937.

Colours: Red shirts, white shorts, red stockings. **Change colours:** Blue and green shirts, white shorts, blue stockings.

CREWE ALEXANDRA 1994–95 LEAGUE RECORD

Match No.	Date		Venue	Opponents	Result		H/T Score	Lg. Pos.	Goalscorers	Attendance
1	Aug	13	A	York C	W	2-1	0-0	—	Macauley 2	4420
2		20	H	Rotherham U	W	3-1	2-0	4	Rowbotham, Tierney, Ward	3505
3		27	A	Peterborough U	W	5-1	3-0	2	Rowbotham 2, Collins, Smith S (pen), Ward	4579
4		30	H	Stockport Co	W	2-1	0-0	—	Booty, Collins	5050
5	Sept	3	H	Blackpool	W	4-3	2-2	1	Garvey, Smith S (pen), Barr, Booty	4915
6		10	A	Wrexham	L	0-1	0-0	1		6399
7		13	A	Oxford U	L	1-2	0-2	—	Savage	6499
8		17	H	Wycombe W	L	1-2	0-2	5	Walters	4466
9		24	H	Brentford	L	0-2	0-1	7		3839
10	Oct	1	A	Bristol R	D	2-2	2-0	8	Ward, Garvey	4862
11		8	A	Cardiff C	W	2-1	0-1	7	Ward, Edwards	4126
12		15	H	Shrewsbury T	W	1-0	1-0	6	Ward	4296
13		22	H	Huddersfield T	D	3-3	3-2	6	Garvey, Macauley, Edwards	5352
14		29	A	Hull C	L	1-7	0-2	9	Ward	4694
15	Nov	1	A	Birmingham C	L	0-5	0-3	—		14,212
16		5	H	Swansea C	L	1-2	0-1	11	Smith S (pen)	3242
17		19	A	Bradford C	W	2-0	2-0	8	Ward, Adebola	5520
18		26	H	Cambridge U	W	4-2	1-0	6	Smith S (pen), Collins 2, Ward	3636
19	Dec	10	A	Rotherham U	D	2-2	2-0	8	Collins, Lennon	2907
20		16	H	York C	W	2-1	2-0	—	Adebola, Lennon	3432
21		26	H	Chester C	W	2-1	0-1	6	Adebola, Lennon	5428
22		27	A	Bournemouth	D	1-1	0-1	7	Collins	3325
23		31	H	Leyton Orient	W	3-0	0-0	6	Clarkson, Murphy, Bellamy (og)	3792
24	Jan	2	A	Plymouth Arg	L	2-3	2-1	7	Murphy, Clarkson	6802
25		7	A	Huddersfield T	W	2-1	1-1	6	Smith S, Collins	11,466
26		14	H	Brighton & HA	W	4-0	1-0	3	Adebola, Collins, Smith S, Clarkson	4286
27	Feb	4	A	Cambridge U	W	2-1	0-0	4	Murphy, Collins	3339
28		11	H	Birmingham C	W	2-1	1-0	4	Clarkson, Murphy	6359
29		18	A	Brighton & HA	W	1-0	1-0	4	Savage	6986
30		21	H	Bradford C	L	0-1	0-0	—		4214
31		25	H	Bristol R	W	2-1	2-0	4	Adebola, Murphy	4222
32	Mar	4	A	Brentford	L	0-2	0-1	4		7143
33		7	A	Blackpool	D	0-0	0-0	—		5859
34		11	H	Peterborough U	L	1-3	0-2	5	Rowbotham	3983
35		18	A	Stockport Co	L	1-3	0-1	5	Lennon	4946
36		21	H	Wrexham	L	1-3	0-0	—	Smith S (pen)	3632
37		25	A	Wycombe W	D	0-0	0-0	7		6288
38	Apr	1	H	Oxford U	W	3-2	1-2	6	Rowbotham, Smith S, Adebola	3928
39		8	A	Leyton Orient	W	4-1	2-1	6	Whalley, Rowbotham, Tierney, Lennon	2797
40		15	H	Bournemouth	W	2-0	1-0	6	Collins, Tierney	3906
41		17	A	Chester C	W	1-0	0-0	5	Tierney	3054
42		22	H	Plymouth Arg	D	2-2	2-1	7	Lennon, Adebola	3786
43		25	A	Swansea C	W	1-0	1-0	—	Clarkson	2600
44		29	A	Shrewsbury T	W	2-1	2-1	5	Collins, Barr	4381
45	May	2	H	Hull C	W	3-2	2-2	—	Macauley, Clarkson, Adebola	3870
46		6	H	Cardiff C	D	0-0	0-0	3		4382

Final League Position: 3

GOALSCORERS

League (80): Collins 11, Adebola 8, Smith S 8 (5 pens), Ward 8, Clarkson 6, Lennon 6, Rowbotham 6, Murphy 5, Macauley 4, Tierney 4, Garvey 3, Barr 2, Booty 2, Edwards 2, Savage 2, Walters 1, Whalley 1, own goal 1.
Coca-Cola (2): Garvey 1, Ward 1.
FA Cup (8): Ward 4, Rowbotham 2, Garvey 1, Smith S 1.

Smith M.A. 22 + 2	Booty M.J. 44	Gardiner M.C. 9 + 2	Wilson E. 20 + 1	Macauley S.R. 43	Barr W.J. 29 + 5	Tierney F. 13 + 7	Walters S.P. 8 + 3	Ward A.S. 16	Whalley G. 40	Rowbotham D. 20 + 1	Adebola B. 25 + 5	Smith G.S. 45	Garvey S.H. 22 + 6	Gayle M.S.R. 24 + 1	Collier D.J. 3 + 2	Collins W.A. 38 + 2	Murphy D.B. 20 + 15	Savage R.W. 5 + 1	Edwards R. 8 + 9	Lennon N.F. 31	Clarkson P.I. 19 + 4	McCarthy A.P. 2	Woodward A.S. — + 2	*Match No.*
1	2	3	4	5	6	7	8	9	10	11	12													1
1	2	3		5	6	7	8	9	10	11		4	12											2
	2			5	6	7		*9*	10	11	12	4		1	3	8	14							3
	2			5	6			9	10	11		3	7	1	4	8	12							4
	2			5	6		12	9	3	11		4	7	1		8	10							5
	2			5	6		4		10	11		3	7	1	12	8		*9*	14					6
	2			5	6		4	9	10			3	7	1		8	12	11						7
	2			5	6		4	9	10			3	7	1	12		8	*11*	14					8
	2	10			6		4	9			14	3	7	1	*5*	8	12		11					9
15	2	10		5	6			9	4	11		3	7	*1*		8	12							10
	2		4	5				9	6	11		3	7	1		8	10		12					11
15	2		4	5	12		14	*9*		11		3	7	*1*		8	10		6					12
	2		4	5					6	11	9	3	7	1		8	12		10					13
	2		4	5			12	9	*6*	11	14	3	7	1		8	10							14
	2		4	5		12	8	9	6	11		3		1		14	10			*7*				15
	2		4	5			8	9	*6*	11		3	12	1		14	10			7				16
1	2		4	5				9	6		11	3	7			8				10				17
1	2		4	5				9	6		11	3	7			8				10				18
1	2		4	5					6		11	3	7			8				10	9			19
1	2	12	4	5					6		11	3	7			8				10	9			20
1	2		4						6		11	3	7			8	12			10	*9*	5	14	21
1	2	6	4								11	3	7			*8*	12	14		10	9	5		22
1	2	6	4	5	12	14						3	*7*			8	11			10	9			23
1	2	6	4	5	12	7						3				8	11		14	10	*9*			24
1	2		4	5					6		9	3		15		8	7		11	10	12			25
1	2		4	5	12				6		9	3				8	7			10	11			26
1	2		4	5	12	14			6		9	3				8	*7*			10	11			27
1	2			5	4	8			6		9	3	12				7			10	11			28
1	2			5	4	12			6			3	8				7	9		10	11			29
1	2			5	4	12			6			3	8				7	*9*		10	11		14	30
1	2			5	4				6		*9*	3	12			8	7		14	10	11			31
1			2	5	4	12			6		9	3				8	7		14	10	*11*			32
1	2			5	4				6		9	3				8	7		11	10	12			33
1	*2*		14	5	4				6	12		3				8	7		11	10	9			34
1			4	5	2				6	9	14	3	12			8			7	10	*11*			35
1	2			5	4				6	11	9	3	12			8			7	10				36
	2			5	4				6	11	9	3	7	1		8	12			10				37
	2			5	4	12			6	*11*	9	3	7	1		8				10	14			38
	2			5	4	7			6	11	9	3		1		8	12			10				39
	2	12		5	4	7			6	*11*	9	3		1		8	14			10				40
	2			5	4	7			6	11	9	3		1		8	12			10				41
	2	6		5	4	7					9	3		1		8	12		14	10	*11*			42
	2	10		5	4	7			6		9	3		1		8			12		11			43
	2			5	4	7			6		9	3		1		8	12			10	11			44
	2			5	4	7			6		9	3		1		8	12			10	11			45
	2			5	4	7			6		*9*	3		1		8	11		12	10	14			46

Coca-Cola Cup

First Round	Wigan Ath (h)	2-1
	(a)	0-3

FA Cup

First Round	Gresley R (h)	7-1
Second Round	Bury (h)	1-2

CRYSTAL PALACE 1994–95 *Back row (left to right):* Paul Sparrow, Glen Little, Eric Smith, Eddie Dixon.
Third row: Kevin Hall, Brian Launders, George Ndah, Darren Patterson, Andrew Preece, Ian Cox, Andy Thorn, Bobby Bowry, Ricky Newman, Jamie Vincent, Anthony Scully
Second row: Spike Hill, David Kemp, Bruce Dyer, Ray Wilkins, Damian Matthew, Dean Gordon, Jimmy Glass, Nigel Martyn, Richard Shaw, Darren Pitcher, Paul Williams, Ray Lewington, Peter McLean.
Front row: John Salako, John Humphrey, Chris Armstrong, Ron Noades, Alan Smith, Gareth Southgate, Chris Coleman, Simon Rodger, Eric Young.

Division 1 CRYSTAL PALACE

Selhurst Park, London SE25 6PU. Telephone: (0181) 653 1000. Fax: (0181) 771 5311. Lottery Office: (0181) 771 9502. Club Shop: (0181) 653 5584. Dial-A-Seat Ticketline: (0181) 771 8841. Palace Publications: (0181) 771 8299. Fax: (0181) 653 6312. Palace Clubline: 0891 400 333. Palace Ticket Line: 0891 400 334 (normal 0891 charges apply for these services).

Ground capacity: 26,400.

Record attendance: 51,482 v Burnley, Division 2, 11 May 1979.

Record receipts: £327,124 v Manchester U, FA Premier League, 21 April 1993 (League); £336,583 v Chelsea, Coca-Cola Cup 5th rd, 6 January 1993.

Pitch measurements: 110yd × 74yd.

Chairman: R. G. Noades.

Directors: R. G. Noades (Chairman and Managing), B. Coleman OBE, A. S. C. De Souza, M. E. Lee, S. Hume-Kendall, P. H. J. Norman, R. E. Anderson, V. E. Murphy, C. L. Noades, S. R. Ebbs MS, FRCS, D. A. Miller, P. L. Morley CBE, JP.

Technical Director: Steve Coppell. ***First Team Coaches:*** Ray Lewington, Peter Nicholas. ***Physio:*** Peter McClean.

Company Secretary: Doug Miller. ***Club Secretary:*** Mike Hurst. ***Assistant Secretary:*** Terry Byfield. ***Sales and Marketing Manager:*** Mike Ryan.

Year Formed: 1905. ***Turned Professional:*** 1905. ***Ltd Co.:*** 1905.

Club Nickname: 'The Eagles'.

Club Sponsor: TDK.

Previous Grounds: 1905, Crystal Palace; 1915, Herne Hill; 1918, The Nest; 1924, Selhurst Park.

Foundation: There was a Crystal Palace club as early as 1861 but the present organisation was born in 1905 after the formation of a club by the company that controlled the Crystal Palace (the building that is), had been rejected by the FA who did not like the idea of the Cup Final hosts running their own club. A separate company had to be formed and they had their home on the old Cup Final ground until 1915.

First Football League game: 28 August, 1920, Division 3, v Merthyr T (a) L 1-2 – Alderson; Little, Rhodes; McCracken, Jones, Feebury; Bateman, Conner, Smith, Milligan (1), Whibley.

Record League Victory: 9–0 v Barrow, Division 4, 10 October 1959 – Rouse; Long, Noakes; Truett, Evans, McNichol; Gavin (1), Summersby (4 incl. 1p), Sexton, Byrne (2), Colfar (2).

Record Cup Victory: 8–0 v Southend U, Rumbelows League Cup, 2nd rd (1st leg), 25 September 1990 – Martyn; Humphrey (Thompson (1)), Shaw, Pardew, Young, Thorn, McGoldrick, Thomas, Bright (3), Wright (3), Barber (Hodges (1)).

Record Defeat: 0–9 v Burnley, FA Cup, 2nd rd replay, 10 February 1909 and 0–9 v Liverpool, Division 1, 12 September 1990.

Most League Points (2 for a win): 64, Division 4, 1960–61.

Most League Points (3 for a win): 90, Division 1, 1993–94.

Most League Goals: 110, Division 4, 1960–61.

Highest League Scorer in Season: Peter Simpson, 46, Division 3 (S), 1930–31.

Most League Goals in Total Aggregate: Peter Simpson, 153, 1930–36.

Most Capped Player: Eric Young, 19 (20), Wales.

Most League Appearances: Jim Cannon, 571, 1973–88.

Record Transfer Fee Received: £4,500,000 from Tottenham H for Chris Armstrong, June 1995.

Record Transfer Fee Paid: £1,800,000 to Sunderland for Marco Gabbiadini, September 1991.

Football League Record: 1920 Original Members of Division 3; 1921–25 Division 2; 1925–58 Division 3 (S); 1958–61 Division 4; 1961–64 Division 3; 1964–69 Division 2; 1969–73 Division 1; 1973–74 Division 2; 1974–77 Division 3; 1977–79 Division 2; 1979–81 Division 1; 1981–89 Division 2; 1989–92 Division 1; 1992–93 FA Premier League; 1993–94 Division 1; 1994–95 FA Premier League; 1995– Division 1.

Honours: *Football League:* Division 1 – Champions 1993–94; 3rd 1990–91; Division 2 – Champions 1978–79; Runners-up 1968–69; Division 3 – Runners-up 1963–64; Division 3 (S) – Champions 1920–21; Runners-up 1928–29, 1930–31, 1938–39; Division 4 – Runners-up 1960–61. *FA Cup:* best season: Runners-up 1990. *Football League Cup:* best season; semi-final 1993, 1995. *Zenith Data System Cup:* Winners: 1991.

Colours: Red and blue shirts, red shorts, red stockings. **Change colours:** White shirts, red or blue shorts, red or blue stockings.

CRYSTAL PALACE 1994–95 LEAGUE RECORD

Match No.	Date	Venue	Opponents	Result	H/T Score	Lg. Pos.	Goalscorers	Attendance
1	Aug 20	H	Liverpool	L 1-6	0-3	—	Armstrong	18,084
2	24	A	Norwich C	D 0-0	0-0	—		19,015
3	27	A	Aston Villa	D 1-1	0-0	18	Southgate	23,305
4	30	H	Leeds U	L 1-2	0-1	—	Gordon	14,453
5	Sept 10	A	Manchester C	D 1-1	1-1	17	Dyer	19,971
6	17	H	Wimbledon	D 0-0	0-0	21		12,366
7	24	H	Chelsea	L 0-1	0-0	21		16,064
8	Oct 1	A	Arsenal	W 2-1	2-0	17	Salako 2	34,136
9	8	A	West Ham U	L 0-1	0-0	19		16,959
10	15	H	Newcastle U	L 0-1	0-0	20		17,739
11	22	H	Everton	W 1-0	0-0	17	Preece	15,026
12	29	A	Leicester C	W 1-0	1-0	16	Preece	20,022
13	Nov 2	A	Coventry C	W 4-1	2-1	—	Preece 2, Salako, Newman	10,729
14	5	H	Ipswich T	W 3-0	1-0	11	Newman, Armstrong, Salako	13,450
15	19	A	Manchester U	L 0-3	0-2	12		43,788
16	26	H	Southampton	D 0-0	0-0	13		14,186
17	Dec 3	A	Sheffield W	L 0-1	0-1	15		21,930
18	11	A	Liverpool	D 0-0	0-0	13		30,972
19	17	H	Norwich C	L 0-1	0-0	16		12,473
20	26	H	QPR	D 0-0	0-0	17		16,699
21	27	A	Tottenham H	D 0-0	0-0	—		27,730
22	31	H	Blackburn R	L 0-1	0-0	18		14,232
23	Jan 2	A	Nottingham F	L 0-1	0-0	18		21,326
24	14	H	Leicester C	W 2-0	2-0	16	Newman, Ndah	12,707
25	21	A	Everton	L 1-3	0-1	17	Coleman	23,734
26	25	H	Manchester U	D 1-1	0-0	—	Southgate	18,224
27	Feb 4	A	Ipswich T	W 2-0	0-0	16	Dowie, Gordon (pen)	15,361
28	11	H	Coventry C	L 0-2	0-0	18		12,076
29	25	H	Arsenal	L 0-3	0-2	19		17,063
30	Mar 5	A	Chelsea	D 0-0	0-0	20		14,130
31	14	H	Sheffield W	W 2-1	0-1	—	Armstrong, Dowie	10,964
32	18	A	Wimbledon	L 0-2	0-1	19		8835
33	Apr 1	H	Manchester C	W 2-1	1-0	19	Armstrong, Patterson	13,451
34	4	H	Aston Villa	D 0-0	0-0	—		12,949
35	14	H	Tottenham H	D 1-1	1-0	—	Armstrong	18,068
36	17	A	QPR	W 1-0	0-0	19	Dowie	14,227
37	20	A	Blackburn R	L 1-2	0-0	—	Houghton	28,005
38	29	H	Nottingham F	L 1-2	0-1	19	Dowie	16,335
39	May 3	A	Southampton	L 1-3	1-2	—	Southgate	15,151
40	6	H	West Ham U	W 1-0	0-0	19	Armstrong	18,224
41	9	A	Leeds U	L 1-3	0-2	—	Armstrong	30,963
42	14	A	Newcastle U	L 2-3	0-3	19	Armstrong, Houghton	35,626

Final League Position: 19

GOALSCORERS

League (34): Armstrong 8, Dowie 4, Preece 4, Salako 4, Newman 3, Southgate 3, Gordon 2 (1 pen), Houghton 2, Coleman 1, Dyer 1, Ndah 1, Patterson 1.
Coca-Cola Cup (12): Armstrong 5, Southgate 2, Dyer 1, Gordon 1, Pitcher 1, Preece 1, Salako 1.
FA Cup (15): Armstrong 5, Dowie 4, Salako 2, Coleman 1, Gordon 1 (pen), Ndah 1, Pitcher 1.

Martyn A.N. 37	Pitcher D.E.J. 21 + 4	Gordon D.D. 38 + 3	Southgate G. 42	Young E. 13	Coleman C. 35	Rodger S.L. 4	Wilkins R.C. 1	Armstrong C.P. 40	Preece A.P. 17 + 3	Salako J.A. 39	Bowry R. 13 + 5	Dyer B.A. 7 + 9	Patterson D.J. 22	Shaw R.E. 41	Newman R.A. 32 + 3	Cox I.G. 1 + 10	Matthew D. 2 + 2	Ndah G.E. 5 + 7	Launders B.T. 1 + 1	Humphrey J. 19 + 2	Williams P.A. 2 + 2	Wilmot R.J. 5 + 1	Dowie I. 15	Houghton R.J. 10	Match No.
1	2	3	4	5	6	7	8	9	*10*	11	12	14													1
1		3	4		6	7		9		11	8	*10*	2	5	12	14									2
1	12	3	4		6	*7*		9		11		10	2	5	8	14									3
1		3	4		6	7		9	10	11		8	2	5	12										4
1		2	4		6			9		11		7	3	5	8		10								5
1	2	3	4		6			9		11		7		5	8		10	12							6
1		2	4		6			9		11		12	3	5	8			10	7						7
1		2	4		6			9		11	7		3	5	8			10							8
1		3	4		6			9		11	7	12	*2*	5	8			10	14						9
1		3	4		6			9	10	11	7			5	8					2					10
1	12	3	4		6			9	10	11	7			5	8					2					11
1	12	3	4		6			9	10	11	7			5	8					2					12
1		3	4		6			9	10	11			2	5	8					7					13
1		3	4		6			9	10	11	7			5	8					2					14
1		3	4		6			9	10	11	12		2	5	8					7					15
1		3	4		6			9	10	11	7	12		5	8					2					16
1		3	4		6			9	10	11	7			5	8			12		2					17
1	6	3	4					9	10	11	7			5	8					2					18
1	14	3	4		6			9	10	11	7	12		*5*	8					2					19
1		3	4		6			9	10	11				5	8	7				2	12				20
1	10	3	4		6			9		11	7		2	5	8						12				21
1		3	4		6			9	10				2	5	8			12		7	11				22
1	10	3	4		6			9					2	5	8			12		7	11	15			23
1	10	3	4		6			9	12	11				5	8			7		2					24
1	10	3	4		6			9		11				5	8			12		2			7		25
1	10	3	4		6			9	12	11			2	5	8								7		26
1	10	3	4		6			9		11	12		2	5	8								7		27
1	10	3	4		6				12	11	7		2	5				8					9		28
1	10	3	4		6			9		11		12	2	5	*8*		14			7					29
1	7	3	4	*6*					10	11			2	5	8		14	12					9		30
1	2	12	4	6	3			9	10	11				5	8								7		31
1	2	12	4	6	3			9	10	11				5	*8*					14			7		32
1	10		4	6	3			9		*11*		7	2	5		14		12						8	33
1	10	12	4	6	3			9		11		7	2	5		14								8	34
	10	3	4	6				9		*11*			2	5	12	14						1	7	8	35
		3	4	6	5			9		11	14			2	7	*12*						1	10	8	36
		11	4	6	3			9					2	5	7	14				*12*		1	10	8	37
		3	4		6			9		11	14			5	*7*	12				2		1	10	8	38
	10	3	4	6				9		11		12		5						2		1	7	8	39
1	10	3	4	6				9		11				5						2			7	8	40
1	10	3	4	6				9		11		12	2	5		14							7	*8*	41
1	2	3	4	6				9		11		12		5	*10*	14							7	8	42

Coca-Cola Cup

Second Round	Lincoln C (a)	0-1
	(h)	3-0
Third Round	Wimbledon (a)	1-0
Fourth Round	Aston Villa (h)	4-1
Fifth Round	Manchester C (h)	4-0
Semi-final	Liverpool (a)	0-1
	(h)	0-1

FA Cup

Third Round	Lincoln C (h)	5-1
Fourth Round	Nottingham F (a)	2-1
Fifth Round	Watford (a)	0-0
	(h)	1-0
Sixth Round	Wolverhampton W (h)	1-1
	(a)	4-1
Semi-final	Manchester U at Villa Park	2-2
	Replay at Villa Park	0-2

DARLINGTON 1994–95 *Back row (left to right):* Darren Collier, Mike Pollitt, Ryan Scott.
Third row: Matty Appleby, Robbie Painter, Steve Gaughan, Andy Crosby, Sean Gregan, Adam Reed, Ian Banks.
Second row: Simon Shaw, Paul Cross, Nigel Carnel (Physio), Alan Murray, Eddie Kyle, Paul Olsson, Bernie Slaven.
Front row: Gary Himsworth, Peter Kirkham, Robert Blake, Andy Ripley, Gary Chapman, Paul Mattison.

Division 3 DARLINGTON

Feethams Ground, Darlington, DL1 5JB. Telephone: (01325) 465097. Fax: (01325) 381377.

Ground capacity: 7046.

Record attendance: 21,023 v Bolton W, League Cup 3rd rd, 14 November 1960.

Record receipts: £32,300 v Rochdale, Division 4, 11 May 1991.

Pitch measurements: 110yd × 74yd.

President: A. Noble.

Chairman: S. Weeks. ***Vice-Chairman:*** G. Hodgson.

Director: S. Morgon.

Directors of Coaching: David Hodgson, Jim Platt. ***Coach:*** J. Hope.

Chief Executive: T. D. Hughes.

Secretary: S. Morgon. ***Physio:*** Nigel Carnell.

Year Formed: 1883. ***Turned Professional:*** 1908. ***Ltd Co.:*** 1891.

Club Nickname: 'The Quakers'.

Foundation: A football club was formed in Darlington as early as 1861 but the present club began in 1883 and reached the final of the Durham Senior Cup in their first season, losing to Sunderland in a replay after complaining that they had suffered from intimidation in the first. The following season Darlington won this trophy and for many years were one of the leading amateur clubs in their area.

First Football League game: 27 August, 1921, Division 3(N), v Halifax T (h) W 2-0 – Ward; Greaves, Barbour; Dickson (1), Sutcliffe, Malcolm; Dolphin, Hooper (1), Edmunds, Wolstenholme, Winship.

Record League Victory: 9–2 v Lincoln C, Division 3 (N), 7 January 1928 – Archibald; Brooks, Mellen; Kelly, Waugh, McKinnell; Cochrane (1), Gregg (1), Ruddy (3), Lees (3), McGiffen (1).

Record Cup Victory: 7–2 v Evenwood T, FA Cup, 1st rd, 17 November 1956 – Ward; Devlin, Henderson; Bell (1p), Greener, Furphy; Forster (1), Morton (3), Tulip (2), Davis, Moran.

Record Defeat: 0–10 v Doncaster R, Division 4, 25 January 1964.

Most League Points (2 for a win): 59, Division 4, 1965–66.

Most League Points (3 for a win): 85, Division 4, 1984–85.

Most League Goals: 108, Division 3 (N), 1929–30.

Highest League Scorer in Season: David Brown, 39, Division 3 (N), 1924–25.

Most League Goals in Total Aggregate: Alan Walsh, 90, 1978–84.

Most Capped Player: None.

Most League Appearances: Ron Greener, 442, 1955–68.

Record Transfer Fee Received: £200,000 from Leicester C for Jim Willis, December 1991.

Record Transfer Fee Paid: £95,000 to Motherwell for Nick Cusack, January 1992.

Football League Record: 1921 Original Member Division 3 (N); 1925–27 Division 2; 1927–58 Division 3 (N); 1958–66 Division 4; 1966–67 Division 3; 1967–85 Division 4; 1985–87 Division 3; 1987–89 Division 4; 1989–90 GM Vauxhall Conference; 1990–91 Division 4; 1991– Division 3.

Honours: *Football League:* Division 2 best season: 15th, 1925–26; Division 3 (N) – Champions 1924–25; Runners-up 1921–22; Division 4 Champions 1990–91 – Runners-up 1965–66. *FA Cup:* best season: 3rd rd, 1911, 5th rd, 1958. *Football League Cup:* best season: 5th rd, 1968. *GM Vauxhall Conference:* Champions 1989–90.

Colours: Black and white. **Change colours:** All red.

DARLINGTON 1994–95 LEAGUE RECORD

Match No.	*Date*	*Venue*	*Opponents*	*Result*	*H/T Score*	*Lg. Pos.*	*Goalscorers*	*Attendance*
1	Aug 13	H	Preston NE	D 0-0	0-0	—		3800
2	20	A	Hartlepool U	L 0-1	0-0	16		3035
3	27	H	Exeter C	W 2-0	0-0	13	Gaughan, Painter	1861
4	30	A	Mansfield T	W 1-0	0-0	—	Gaughan	2427
5	Sept 3	A	Doncaster R	D 0-0	0-0	9		2967
6	10	H	Torquay U	W 2-1	1-1	8	Painter, Gaughan	2161
7	13	H	Scunthorpe U	L 1-3	1-2	—	Painter	2181
8	17	A	Preston NE	W 3-1	1-0	7	Appleby, Olsson, Chapman	8884
9	24	H	Colchester U	L 2-3	1-2	9	Chapman, Himsworth	2260
10	Oct 1	A	Carlisle U	L 1-2	1-0	12	Painter	6100
11	8	H	Bury	L 0-2	0-0	14		2352
12	15	A	Chesterfield	D 0-0	0-0	13		2836
13	22	H	Hereford U	W 3-1	0-0	11	Gregan, Olsson, Painter	1996
14	29	A	Gillingham	L 1-2	1-1	13	Painter	2785
15	Nov 5	H	Walsall	D 2-2	1-0	13	Painter, Gregan	2186
16	19	A	Wigan Ath	L 1-4	1-2	15	Worboys	1785
17	26	H	Barnet	L 0-1	0-0	16		2157
18	Dec 10	H	Hartlepool U	L 1-2	1-1	16	Burgess (og)	3193
19	17	A	Exeter C	W 2-0	1-0	15	Gaughan, Worboys	2338
20	26	H	Scarborough	W 1-0	1-0	14	Slaven	2958
21	27	A	Lincoln C	L 1-3	1-1	15	Slaven	2964
22	31	H	Northampton T	W 4-1	1-0	13	Slaven, Banks, Gaughan, Shaw	2250
23	Jan 7	A	Hereford U	D 0-0	0-0	13		2237
24	14	H	Fulham	D 0-0	0-0	13		2113
25	Feb 4	A	Barnet	W 3-2	2-0	14	Worboys 2, Gaughan	2034
26	11	H	Wigan Ath	L 1-3	0-1	15	Worboys	1780
27	18	A	Fulham	L 1-3	0-1	15	Slaven	3864
28	21	H	Gillingham	W 2-0	0-0	—	Slaven, Painter	1548
29	25	H	Carlisle U	L 0-2	0-1	16		3992
30	Mar 4	A	Colchester U	L 0-1	0-1	16		6055
31	11	A	Torquay U	L 0-1	0-0	16		2332
32	14	A	Walsall	L 0-2	0-1	—		3154
33	18	H	Mansfield T	D 0-0	0-0	16		1613
34	21	A	Rochdale	L 0-2	0-0	—		1471
35	25	H	Doncaster R	L 0-2	0-0	16		2017
36	Apr 1	A	Scunthorpe U	L 1-2	1-1	17	Olsson	2449
37	8	A	Northampton T	L 1-2	0-1	18	Painter	4496
38	15	H	Lincoln C	D 0-0	0-0	17		1664
39	18	A	Scarborough	L 1-3	0-1	—	Olsson	2182
40	22	H	Rochdale	W 4-0	2-0	17	Worboys (pen), Gaughan 2, Himsworth	1886
41	29	H	Chesterfield	L 0-1	0-1	19		3387
42	May 6	A	Bury	L 1-2	1-1	20	Reed	3612

Final League Position: 20

GOALSCORERS

League (43): Painter 9, Gaughan 8, Worboys 6 (1 pen), Slaven 5, Olsson 4, Chapman 2, Gregan 2, Himsworth 2, Appleby 1, Banks 1, Reed 1, Shaw 1, own goal 1.
Coca-Cola Cup (2): Cross 1, Slaven 1.
FA Cup (3): Worboys 2, Slaven 1.

Pollitt M.F. 40	Appleby M.W. 35 + 1	Cross P. 13	Crosby A. 35	Gregan S.M. 22 + 3	Banks I.F. 39	Slaven B. 24 + 2	Painter P.R. 34 + 4	Gaughan S.E. 39 + 2	Olsson P. 42	Mattison P. 4 + 6	Himsworth G.P. 32 + 6	Chapman G.A. 19 + 14	Reed A.M. 34 + 4	Collier D. 2	Taylor M.S. 8	Worboys G. 24 + 3	Kirkham P.J. 3 + 1	Shaw S.R. 9 + 3	Blake R.J. 3 + 6	Bolton N.A. 1 + 1	Match No.
1	2	3	4	5	6	7	8	9	10	11	12										1
1	2	3	5	*6*	4	7	8	9	10		12	11	14								2
1	2	3	5			7	8	9	10		11	4	6								3
1	2	3	5		4	7	8	9	10			11	6								4
1	2	3	5		4	7	8	9	10		12	11	6								5
1	2	3	5		4	7	8	9	10	14	*12*	11	6								6
1	2	3	5		4	7	8	9	10		12	11	6								7
1	2	3	5		4		8	9	10		7	11	6								8
1	2	3	5		4	12	8	9	10		7	11	6								9
1	2	3	5	6	4	7	8	9	10		11	12									10
1	2	3	5	6	4	7		9	10	12	11	8	14								11
1	2	3	5	6	4		8	9	10	7		11	12								12
		3	5	6	4	12	8	9	10	14	7	11	2	1							13
	2		5	6	4	7	8	9	10		11	12		1	3						14
1	2		5	6	4		8	9	10		11		12		3	7					15
1	2			6	4		8	9	10		7		5		3	11					16
1	2			6	4	7	8	12	10		11		5		3	9					17
1	2		5		4	7	8	12	10		11	14	6		3	*9*					18
1	2		5		4	7	8	11	10		12	14	6		3	9					19
1			5		4	7	8	*11*	10	14	2	12	6		3	9					20
1			5		4	7	8	*11*	10	14	2	12	6		3	9					21
1	2		5		*4*	7		8	10		3	12	6			9	11	14			22
1	2		5	12	4	7	8	11	*10*		3	14	6			9					23
1	2		5		4		8	11	10		3		6			9	7				24
1	2		5	12	4	7	8	11	10		3	14	6			9					25
1	2		5		4	7	8	11	10		3	12	6			9					26
1	2		5	3	4	7	8	11	10			12	6			9					27
1			5	3		7	8	11	10		4	2	6			9					28
1	12		5	3		7	8	11	10		4	2	6			9					29
1	2			5	4	7	8	11	10		3	9						6	12		30
1	2				4		8	11	10		3	12	5			9	*7*	6	14		31
1	2		5		4		8	11	10		3	12	6			*9*		7	14		32
1			5	2	4		*8*	11	10	7	3	12	6			14			9		33
1			5	2	4	7	12		10	*8*	3		6			11		14	9		34
1	7		5	2	4		8	11	10		3		6			*9*		12		14	35
1	7		5	2	4		8	11	10		3		6			9			12		36
1	7			5	4		*8*	11	10	12	3		6			9		2	14		37
1	7			5	4			11	10		3	9	6			12		2	8		38
1	7			5	4			11	10		3	9	6			12	14	*2*		8	39
1	7		5		*4*		12	11	10		3	8	6			9		2	14		40
1	7		5	12	4		14	11	10		3	*8*	6			9		2			41
1	7		5	3	4		12	11	10			8	6			9		2			42

Coca-Cola Cup

First Round	Barnsley (h)	2-2
	(a)	0-0

FA Cup

First Round	Hyde (a)	3-1
Second Round	Carlisle U (a)	0-2

DERBY COUNTY 1994–95 *Back row (left to right):* Jason Kavanagh, Darren Wassall, Michael Forsyth, Craig Short, Paul Williams, Shane Nicholson, Martin Kuhl.
Centre row: Billy McEwan (Coach), Alan Durban (Assistant Manager), Steve Hayward, Mark Stallard, Martin Taylor, Steve Sutton, Tommy Johnson, John Harkes, Gary Charles, Gordon Guthrie (Physio).
Front row: Dean Sturridge, Paul Simpson, Marco Gabbiadini, Roy McFarland (Manager), Gordon Cowans, Paul Kitson, Mark Pembridge.

Division 1 **DERBY COUNTY**

Baseball Ground, Shaftesbury Crescent, Derby DE3 8NB. Telephone: (01332) 340505. Fax: (01332) 293514. Ramtique Sports Shop: (01332) 292081. Clubcall: 0891 121187.

Ground capacity: 19,500 (15,000 seated).

Record attendance: 41,826 v Tottenham H, Division 1, 20 September 1969.

Record receipts: £146,651 v Aston Villa, FA Cup 4th rd, 5 February 1992.

Pitch measurements: 110yd × 71yd.

President:

Chairman: L. V. Pickering. ***Vice-Chairman:*** P. J. Gadsby.

Directors: J. N. Kirkland, A. S. Webb.

Manager: Jim Smith. ***Chief Scout:*** Alan Durban.

Coach: Billy McEwan. ***Physio:*** Gordon Guthrie.

Secretary: Lance Luckhurst. ***Commercial Manager:*** Colin Tunnicliffe.

Year Formed: 1884. ***Turned Professional:*** 1884. ***Ltd Co.:*** 1896.

Club Nickname: 'The Rams'.

Previous Grounds: 1884–95, Racecourse Ground; 1895, Baseball Ground.

Foundation: Derby County was formed by members of the Derbyshire County Cricket Club in 1884, when football was booming in the area and the cricketers thought that a football club would help boost finances for the summer game. To begin with, they sported the cricket club's colours of amber, chocolate and pale blue, and went into the game at the top immediately entering the FA Cup.

First Football League game: 8 September, 1888, Football League, v Bolton W (a) W 6-3 – Marshall; Latham, Ferguson, Williamson; Monks, W. Roulstone; Bakewell (2), Cooper (2), Higgins, H. Plackett, L. Plackett (2).

Record League Victory: 9–0 v Wolverhampton W, Division 1, 10 January 1891 – Bunyan; Archie Goodall, Roberts; Walker, Chalmers, Roulston (1); Bakewell, McLachlan, Johnny Goodall (1), Holmes (2), McMillan (5). 9–0 v Sheffield W, Division 1, 21 January 1899 – Fryer; Methven, Staley; Cox, Archie Goodall, May; Oakden (1), Bloomer (6), Boag, McDonald (1), Allen. (1 og).

Record Cup Victory: 12–0 v Finn Harps, UEFA Cup, 1st rd 1st leg, 15 September 1976 – Moseley; Thomas, Nish, Rioch (1), McFarland, Todd (King), Macken, Gemmill, Hector (5), George (3), James (3).

Record Defeat: 2–11 v Everton, FA Cup 1st rd, 1889–90.

Most League Points (2 for a win): 63, Division 2, 1968–69 and Division 3 (N), 1955–56 and 1956–57.

Most League Points (3 for a win): 84, Division 3, 1985–86 and Division 3, 1986–87.

Most League Goals: 111, Division 3 (N), 1956–57.

Highest League Scorer in Season: Jack Bowers, 37, Division 1, 1930–31 and Ray Straw, 37 Division 3 (N), 1956–57.

Most League Goals in Total Aggregate: Steve Bloomer, 292, 1892–1906 and 1910–14.

Most Capped Player: Peter Shilton, 34 (125), England.

Most League Appearances: Kevin Hector, 486, 1966–78 and 1980–82.

Record Transfer Fee Received: £2,900,000 from Liverpool for Dean Saunders, July 1991.

Record Transfer Fee Paid: £2,500,000 to Notts Co for Craig Short, September 1992.

Football League Record: 1888 Founder Member of the Football League; 1907–12 Division 2; 1912–14 Division 1; 1914–15 Division 2; 1915–21 Division 1; 1921–26 Division 2; 1926–53 Division 1; 1953–55 Division 2; 1955–57 Division 3 (N); 1957–69 Division 2; 1969–80 Division 1; 1980–84 Division 2; 1984–86 Division 3; 1986–87 Division 2; 1987–91 Division 1; 1991–92 Division 2; 1992– Division 1.

Honours: *Football League:* Division 1 – Champions 1971–72, 1974–75; Runners-up 1895–96, 1929–30, 1935–36; Division 2 – Champions 1911–12, 1914–15, 1968–69, 1986–87; Runners-up 1925–26; Division 3 (N) Champions 1956–57; Runners-up 1955–56. *FA Cup:* Winners 1946; Runners-up 1898, 1899, 1903. *Football League Cup:* Semi-final 1968. *Texaco Cup:* 1972. **European Competitions:** *European Cup:* 1972–73, 1975–76; *UEFA Cup:* 1974–75, 1976–77. *Anglo-Italian Cup:* Runners-up 1993.

Colours: White shirts, black shorts, white stockings. **Change colours:** All Petrol blue.

DERBY COUNTY 1994–95 LEAGUE RECORD

Match No.	Date		Venue	Opponents	Result		H/T Score	Lg. Pos.	Goalscorers	Attendance
1	Aug	13	A	Barnsley	L	1-2	1-2	—	Pembridge	8737
2		20	H	Luton T	D	0-0	0-0	19		13,060
3		27	A	Millwall	L	1-4	0-1	21	Sturridge	8809
4		31	H	Middlesbrough	L	0-1	0-1	—		14,659
5	Sept	3	H	Grimsby T	W	2-1	1-0	21	Charles, Pembridge	12,027
6		11	A	Swindon T	D	1-1	1-1	20	Kitson	9054
7		13	A	Bristol C	W	2-0	1-0	—	Kitson, Carsley	8029
8		17	H	Oldham Ath	W	2-1	1-0	11	Carsley, Short	13,746
9		25	H	Stoke C	W	3-0	2-0	6	Hodge, Gabbiadini, Charles	11,782
10	Oct	1	A	Bolton W	L	0-1	0-0	8		12,015
11		8	H	Watford	D	1-1	0-1	11	Hodge	13,413
12		16	A	Southend U	L	0-1	0-0	15		4218
13		23	A	Notts Co	D	0-0	0-0	18		6389
14		29	H	Charlton Ath	D	2-2	1-1	16	Short, Johnson	12,588
15	Nov	2	H	Reading	L	1-2	0-1	—	Gabbiadini	10,585
16		6	A	Portsmouth	W	1-0	0-0	17	Gabbiadini	5507
17		12	A	Sheffield U	L	1-2	0-0	18	Simpson (pen)	15,001
18		19	H	Port Vale	W	2-0	1-0	14	Johnson 2	13,357
19		27	A	Wolverhampton W	W	2-0	1-0	11	Johnson, Stallard	22,768
20	Dec	3	H	Notts Co	D	0-0	0-0	13		14,278
21		11	A	Luton T	D	0-0	0-0	14		6400
22		17	H	Barnsley	W	1-0	0-0	10	Johnson	13,205
23		26	A	Tranmere R	L	1-3	0-1	14	Johnson	11,581
24		31	A	Sunderland	D	1-1	0-0	15	Johnson	13,979
25	Jan	2	H	WBA	D	1-1	0-1	16	Trollope	16,035
26		14	A	Charlton Ath	W	4-3	1-3	13	Short, Gabbiadini 2, Stallard	9389
27		22	H	Portsmouth	W	3-0	0-0	8	Simpson 3	11,143
28	Feb	4	H	Sheffield U	L	2-3	1-1	12	Williams, Kavanagh	15,882
29		11	A	Reading	L	0-1	0-1	13		8834
30		21	A	Port Vale	L	0-1	0-0	—		9387
31		26	H	Bolton W	W	2-1	0-1	12	Yates, Mills	11,003
32	Mar	4	A	Stoke C	D	0-0	0-0	13		13,462
33		7	A	Grimsby T	W	1-0	0-0	—	Pembridge	5310
34		11	H	Millwall	W	3-2	1-1	10	Pembridge, Trollope, Gabbiadini	12,490
35		15	H	Burnley	W	4-0	1-0	—	Mills, Trollope, Simpson (pen), Gabbiadini	13,922
36		18	A	Middlesbrough	W	4-2	3-0	8	Mills 2, Pembridge, Gabbiadini	18,168
37		22	H	Swindon T	W	3-1	1-1	—	Simpson (pen), Pembridge, Mills	16,839
38		25	A	Oldham Ath	L	0-1	0-1	8		7696
39	Apr	1	H	Bristol C	W	3-1	2-1	8	Gabbiadini, Williams, Wrack	14,555
40		8	H	Sunderland	L	0-1	0-1	8		15,442
41		12	H	Wolverhampton W	D	3-3	1-1	—	Simpson 2 (1 pen), Gabbiadini	16,040
42		15	A	Burnley	L	1-3	0-2	8	Trollope	11,534
43		17	H	Tranmere R	W	5-0	2-0	7	Pembridge 2, Mills, Williams, Gabbiadini	13,957
44		22	A	WBA	D	0-0	0-0	7		15,265
45		29	H	Southend U	L	1-2	0-2	7	Mills	12,528
46	May	7	A	Watford	L	1-2	0-1	9	Pembridge	8492

Final League Position: 9

GOALSCORERS

League (66): Gabbiadini 11, Pembridge 9, Simpson 8 (4 pens), Johnson 7, Mills 7, Trollope 4, Short 3, Williams 3, Carsley 2, Charles 2, Hodge 2, Kitson 2, Stallard 2, Kavanagh 1, Sturridge 1, Wrack 1, Yates 1.
Coca-Cola Cup (5): Gabbiadini 2, Simpson 1, Stallard 1, Williams 1.
FA Cup (0).

Taylor M.J. 12	Charles G.A. 18	Forsyth M.E. 21 + 1	Hayward S.L. 3	Short C.J. 37	Williams P.D. 37	Cowans G.S. 17	Gabbiadini M. 30 + 2	Kitson P. 8	Pembridge M.A. 27	Simpson P.D. 37 + 5	Harkes J.A. 29 + 4	Wassall D.P. 25 + 7	Johnson T. 14	Nicholson S.M. 15	Kuhl M. 9	Kavanagh J.C. 20 + 5	Sturridge D.C. 7 + 5	Hodge S.B. 10	Stallard M. 13 + 3	Carsley L.K. 22 + 1	Davies W. 1 + 1	Sutton S.J. 19 + 1	Trollope P.J. 23 + 1	Wrack D. 2 + 14	Sutton W.F. 3 + 3	Yates D.R. 11	Mills R.L. 16	Hoult R. 15	Boden C.D. 4 + 2	Ashbee I. 1	Cooper K.L. — + 1	*Match No.*
1	2	3	4	5	6	7	8	9	10	11	12	14																				1
1	2	3	4	5		7	12	9	10	11		6	8																			2
1	2	5	8			7		*9*	10	11		6		3	4	12	14															3
1	2	3		5		*7*		9	10	11		6				12	8	4	14													4
1	2	3		5		7		9	10	12	11	6					8	4														5
1	2	3		5	6	7	8	9	10									4		11												6
1	2	3		5	6	7	8	9	10	12								4		11												7
1	2	3		5	6	7	8	9	10	12	14							4		*11*												8
1	2	3		5	6	7	8		10	12	14		9					4		*11*												9
1	2	3		5	6	7			10	9	*11*	12					8	4		14												10
1	2	3			6	7			10		11	5					8	4			9											11
1	2	3		5	6	7			10	*12*	11	14					8	4		9		15										12
	2	3		5	6	7					11		10				9	4	12	8		1										13
	2	3		5	6	7	10			11		4	9							8		1										14
	2	3		5	6	7	10			11		4	9							8		1										15
	2	3		5	6	7	10			11			9		4	12				8		1										16
	2	*3*			6	7	10			11		5	9		4	12			14	8		1										17
				5	6					11	7		9	3	4	2			10	8		1										18
				5	6					11	7		9	3	4	2			10	8		1										19
				5	6					11	7		9	3	4	2			10	8		1										20
				5	6					11	7		9		4	2	3		10	8		1										21
		3			6					11	7	5	9		4	2			10	8		1	12									22
	2				6		12			11	7	5	9		4	3			10	8		1										23
		3		5	6						7	12	9	4		2			10	8		1	11	14								24
				5	6					11	7			3		2			10	8	12	1	4	9								25
		6		5			10			11		7		3		2			9	8		1	4									26
		3		2			11			7		5		4		6			10			1	9	12	8							27
		12		5	6		10			11		7		3		2			9			1	4	14	*8*							28
				5	6		10			11		12		3		*7*			*9*	8		1	4	14		2						29
				5	6		10			11	12	2		3					*9*	8		1	7	14		4						30
				5			10			11	7			3		2				8			4	12		6	9	1				31
				5			10		8	11	7	12		3		2							4			6	9	1				32
				5			10		8	11	7	2		3									4			6	9	1				33
				5	6		10		*8*	11	7	12		3									4	14		2	9	1				34
				5	6		10		8	11	7	3											4	12	14	*2*	9	1				35
				5	6		10		8	11	7	3											4	12		2	9	1				36
				5	6		10		8	11	7	3											4	12		2	9	1				37
				5	6		10		8	11	7	3				12							4	14		2	*9*	1				38
					6		10		8	11	7	3				5	12						4	14		*2*	9	1				39
					6		10		8	*11*	7	3				5	12						4	2			9	1	14			40
				5	6		10		8	11	7	3				2							4				9	1				41
				5	6		10		8	*11*	7	3				2							4	12			9	1	14			42
				5	6		10		8	11	7	3											4		12		9	1	2			43
				5	6		10		8	11	7	3											4	12			9	1	2			44
					6		10		8	11	7					5	12						4		14		9	1	2	*3*		45
					6		10		8	7	2					5	12					1	4		*3*		9		11		14	46

Coca-Cola Cup

Second Round	Reading (a)	1-3
	(h)	2-0
Third Round	Portsmouth (a)	1-0
Fourth Round	Swindon T (a)	1-2

FA Cup

Third Round	Everton (a)	0-1

DONCASTER ROVERS 1994–95 *Back row (left to right):* Lee Warren, Graeme Jones, Sam Kitchen, Russ Wilcox, Andy Beasley, Perry Suckling, Paul Marquis, David Roche, Gary Brabin, Ryan Kirby.
Centre row: Andy Sibson, Nicky Limber, Lee Thew, Scott Maxfield, Khristian Hoy, Sean Parrish, Steve Harper, James Lawrence, Warren Hackett.
Front row: Gudmunder Torfason, Steve Gallen, James Meara, Jimmy Golze (Youth Coach), George Smith (Assistant Manager/Coach), Sammy Chung (Team Manager), Steve Beaglehole (Youth Manager), Darren Finlay, Paul Williams, Chris Swailes.

Division 3 DONCASTER ROVERS

Belle Vue Ground, Doncaster, DN4 5HT. Telephone: (01302) 539441. Fax: (01302) 539679.

Ground capacity: 7794.

Record attendance: 37,149 v Hull C, Division 3 (N), 2 October 1948.

Record receipts: £22,000 v QPR, FA Cup 3rd rd, 5 January 1985.

Pitch measurements: 110yd × 76yd.

Chairman: –. ***Directors:*** K. Haran, C. Dunn, L. Mabbett, J. Richardson.

Manager: Sammy Chung. ***Coach:*** John McClelland.

Secretary: Mrs K. J. Oldale. ***Physio:*** Phil McLoughlin. ***Youth Team Coach:*** Jim Golze.

Commercial Executive: Terry Burdass.

Year Formed: 1879. ***Turned Professional:*** 1885. ***Ltd Co.:*** 1905 and 1920.

Club Nickname: 'Rovers'.

Previous Grounds: 1880–1916, Intake Ground; 1920–22, Benetthorpe Ground; 1922, Low Pasture, Belle Vue.

Foundation: In 1879 Mr. Albert Jenkins got together a team to play a game against the Yorkshire Institution for the Deaf. The players stuck together as Doncaster Rovers joining the Midland Alliance in 1889 and the Midland Counties League in 1891.

First Football League game: 7 September, 1901, Division 2, v Burslem Port Vale (h) D 3-3 – Eggett; Simpson, Layton; Longden, Jones, Wright; Langham, Murphy, Price, Goodson (2), Bailey (1).

Record League Victory: 10–0 v Darlington, Division 4, 25 January 1964 – Potter; Raine, Meadows; Windross (1), White, Ripley (2); Robinson, Book (2), Hale (4), Jeffrey, Broadbent (1).

Record Cup Victory: 7–0 v Blyth Spartans, FA Cup, 1st rd, 27 November 1937 – Imrie; Shaw, Rodgers; McFarlane, Bycroft, Cyril Smith; Burton (1), Kilourhy (4), Morgan (2), Malam, Dutton.

Record Defeat: 0–12 v Small Heath, Division 2, 11 April 1903.

Most League Points (2 for a win): 72, Division 3 (N), 1946–47.

Most League Points (3 for a win): 85, Division 4, 1983–84.

Most League Goals: 123, Division 3 (N), 1946–47.

Highest League Scorer in Season: Clarrie Jordan, 42, Division 3 (N), 1946–47.

Most League Goals in Total Aggregate: Tom Keetley, 180, 1923–29.

Most Capped Player: Len Graham, 14, Northern Ireland.

Most League Appearances: Fred Emery, 417, 1925–36.

Record Transfer Fee Received: £250,000 from QPR for Rufus Brevett, February 1991.

Record Transfer Fee Paid: £60,000 to Stirling Albion for John Philliben, March 1984.

Football League Record: 1901 Elected to Division 2; 1903 Failed re-election; 1904 Re-elected; 1905 Failed re-election; 1923 Re-elected to Division 3 (N); 1935–37 Division 2; 1937–47 Division 3 (N); 1947–48 Division 2; 1948–50 Division 3 (N); 1950–58 Division 2; 1958–59 Division 3; 1959–66 Division 4; 1966–67 Division 3; 1967–69 Division 4; 1969–71 Division 3; 1971–81 Division 4; 1981–83 Division 3; 1983–84 Division 4; 1984–88 Division 3; 1988– 92 Division 4; 1992– Division 3.

Honours: *Football League:* Division 2 best season: 7th, 1901–02; Division 3 (N) Champions 1934–35, 1946–47, 1949–50; Runners-up 1937–38, 1938–39; Division 4 – Champions 1965–66, 1968–69; Runners-up 1983–84. Promoted 1980–81 (3rd). *FA Cup:* best season: 5th rd, 1952, 1954, 1955, 1956. *Football League Cup:* best season: 5th rd, 1976.

Colours: All red. **Change colours:** All blue.

Doncaster Rovers Football Club Ltd.
(Founded 1879)

DONCASTER ROVERS 1994–95 LEAGUE RECORD

Match No.	Date	Venue	Opponents	Result	H/T Score	Lg. Pos.	Goalscorers	Attendance
1	Aug 13	A	Hereford U	W 1-0	1-0	—	Jones	3076
2	20	H	Northampton T	W 1-0	1-0	2	Jones	2194
3	27	A	Colchester U	W 3-0	2-0	1	Jones, Donaldson 2	2320
4	30	H	Fulham	D 0-0	0-0	—		3003
5	Sept 3	H	Darlington	D 0-0	0-0	4		2967
6	10	A	Barnet	D 0-0	0-0	6		2625
7	13	A	Bury	L 0-2	0-1	—		2395
8	16	H	Hereford U	W 3-0	2-0	—	Brabin, Thew, Harper	1938
9	24	H	Preston NE	W 2-1	0-0	4	Harper, Brabin	3321
10	Oct 1	A	Rochdale	L 0-2	0-0	5		2445
11	8	H	Wigan Ath	W 5-3	3-1	4	Roche (pen), Brabin 2, Harper 2	2060
12	15	A	Scarborough	D 2-2	0-2	5	Roche 2 (2 pens)	1641
13	22	A	Mansfield T	W 1-0	0-0	3	Jones (pen)	2988
14	29	H	Torquay U	W 3-0	0-0	3	Hackett, Jones, Lawrence	2697
15	Nov 5	A	Exeter C	W 5-1	4-0	3	Parrish 2, Turner, Harper, Jones	2813
16	19	H	Hartlepool U	W 3-0	1-0	3	Brabin, Harper, Meara	2507
17	26	A	Carlisle U	D 1-1	0-0	3	Lawrence	7781
18	Dec 10	A	Northampton T	D 0-0	0-0	3		4538
19	16	H	Colchester U	L 1-2	0-0	—	Brabin	2460
20	26	A	Chesterfield	L 0-2	0-1	4		4226
21	27	H	Scunthorpe U	D 1-1	1-0	5	Bryan	3852
22	31	A	Walsall	L 0-1	0-0	6		4561
23	Jan 10	H	Mansfield T	L 0-2	0-0	—		2577
24	14	A	Lincoln C	L 0-1	0-0	9		2771
25	28	A	Torquay U	W 1-0	0-0	8	Hackett	2852
26	31	H	Exeter C	W 1-0	0-0	—	Brabin	1611
27	Feb 4	H	Carlisle U	D 0-0	0-0	4		3587
28	7	H	Gillingham	L 1-2	1-1	—	Schofield	1740
29	18	H	Lincoln C	W 3-0	1-0	4	Wilcox, Finlay, Harper	2291
30	25	H	Rochdale	L 0-1	0-1	5		2246
31	Mar 4	A	Preston NE	D 2-2	1-0	6	Jones, Wilcox	9624
32	11	H	Barnet	D 1-1	0-0	7	Harper	1979
33	18	A	Fulham	W 2-0	1-0	7	Jones, Parrish	4031
34	21	A	Hartlepool U	L 1-2	0-2	—	Jones	1354
35	25	A	Darlington	W 2-0	0-0	7	Wilcox (pen), Brabin	2017
36	Apr 1	H	Bury	L 1-2	1-0	7	Wilcox (pen)	2485
37	8	H	Walsall	L 0-2	0-1	8		2368
38	15	A	Scunthorpe U	W 5-0	3-0	7	Norbury 3, Warren, Harper	4366
39	17	H	Chesterfield	L 1-3	1-1	7	Jones	4796
40	22	A	Gillingham	L 2-4	2-3	8	Norbury, Warren	2826
41	29	H	Scarborough	W 1-0	0-0	7	Jones	1710
42	May 6	A	Wigan Ath	L 2-3	0-0	9	Jones, Norbury	1576

Final League Position: 9

GOALSCORERS

League (58): Jones 12 (1 pen), Harper 9, Brabin 8, Norbury 5, Wilcox 4 (2 pens), Parrish 3, Roche 3 (3 pens), Donaldson 2, Hackett 2, Lawrence 2, Warren 2, Bryan 1, Finlay 1, Meara 1, Schofield 1, Thew 1, Turner 1.
Coca-Cola Cup (3): Jones 1, Swailes 1, Torfason 1.
FA Cup (1): Jones 1.

Suckling P.J. 9	Kitchen D.E. 7 + 1	Hackett W.J. 39	Brabin G. 27 + 1	Wilcox R. 37	Swailes C.W. 32	Lawrence J.H. 14 + 2	Thew L. 15 + 6	Jones G.A. 25 + 7	Finlay D.J. 6 + 2	Parrish S. 25	Kirby R. 41 + 1	Donaldson O.M. 7 + 2	Torfason G. 1 + 3	Harper S.J. 31 + 2	Meara J.S. 14 + 1	Williams D.P. 33 + 2	Warren L.A. 10 + 4	Roche D. 19 + 1	Williams D.A. 1	Marquis P.R. 1 + 1	Turner A.P. 4	Schofield J.D. 25 + 2	Norbury M.S. 17 + 5	Bryan M.L. 5	Maxfield S. 10	Williams P.L. 6 + 1	Hoy K. — + 1	Measham I. 1	Match No.
1	2	3	4	5	6	7	8	*9*	10	11	12	14																	1
1		3	4	5	6	7	8	9			2	12	10	11															2
1		3		5	6	7	8	9		11	2	10	12		4	15													3
		3		5	6	7		9		11	2	*10*	12	14	4	1	8												4
		3	14	5	6	7		9		11	2	10	12		*4*	1	8												5
		3	4	5	6	7	12	9		11	2	10				1		8											6
		3	4	5	6		7	9		*11*	2	10		14		1	12	8											7
		3	4	5	6		7			11	2	10		9		1		8											8
		3	4	5	6		7	12		11	2			9		1		8	10										9
		3	4		6		7	9		11	2			10		1		8		5									10
		3	4	5	6		7	9	11		2			10		1		8		12									11
		3	4	5	6	12	7			11	2			10		1		8			9								12
		3	4	5	6	7		12		11	2			10		1		8			9								13
		3	4	5	6	7		12		11	2			10		1		8			9								14
		3	4	5	6	7		12		11	2			10		1		8			9								15
		3	4	5	6	7		12		11	2			10	9	1						8							16
		3	4	5	6	7		12		*11*	2	10			8	1						14	9						17
		3		5	6	7		9		11	2				8	1						12	10	4					18
		3	4	5	6		12				2			9	11	1						8	10	7					19
		3	4	5	6	12	14				2			*10*	11	1						8	9	7					20
	6		4	5		7	11		10		2					1	12					8		9	3				21
	6	3	4	5		7	11		12		2					1		10				8		9					22
	5	3	4		6		7			11	2			9	12	1		10				8	14						23
		3			6		7	12	4	11	2			9	5	1	14	10				8							24
		3	4	5	6			9			2			7		1		10				8	12		11				25
		3	4	5	6			9			2			7		1		10				8	12		11				26
		3		5	6			9		11	2			7	4	1		10				8	12						27
		3		5	6		11				2			7	4	1	12	10				8	9						28
1				5	6				11		2			7	4							8	9		3	10			29
1				5	6		12		11		2			7	4							8	9		3	10			30
1		3	4	5	6			9		11	2			7								8	10						31
1		3	4	5	6			9		11	2			7		15		12				8	10						32
		3	4		6		12	9		11	2			7		1		5				8	10						33
		3	4		6			9		11	2			7		1		5				8	10						34
	6	3	4	5				9		11	2			7		1	10					8							35
	6	3		5			12	9		11	2			7		1	4					8	10						36
	6	3		5			11	9			2			7		1	4					8	12			10			37
		3		5				9			2			7		1	4					8	10		6	11	12		38
		3		5				9			2			7		1	4					8	10		6	11			39
		3		5				9	12		2			7		1	4					8	10		6	11			40
1		3	4	5				9			2			7			11					8	10		6	12			41
1	12	3		5				9			2				11		4					8	10		6			7	42

Coca-Cola Cup

First Round	Wrexham (h)	2-4
	(a)	1-1

FA Cup

First Round	Huddersfield T (h)	1-4

EVERTON 1994–95 *Back row (left to right):* Gary Ablett, Graham Stuart, John Ebbrell, Gary Rowett, Joe Parkinson, Matt Jackson, Paul Rideout, Andy Hinchcliffe, Paul Holmes, Neil Moore.
Centre row: Jim Martin (Kit Manager), Jim Gabriel (Reserve Team Coach), Duncan Ferguson, Vinny Samways, Jason Kearton, Neville Southall, Stephen Reeves, Tony Grant, Chris Priest, Willie Donachie (First Team Coach), Les Helm (Physiotherapist).
Front row: David Unsworth, Stuart Barlow, Barry Horne, Anders Limpar, Joe Royle (Manager), Dave Watson, David Burrows, Daniel Amokachi, Brett Angell.

FA Premiership **EVERTON**

Goodison Park, Liverpool L4 4EL. Telephone: (0151) 521 2020. Fax: (0151) 523 9666. Ticket Infoline: 0891 121599. Clubcall 0891 121199. Dial-A-Seat Service: (0151) 525 1231.

Ground capacity: 39,655.

Record attendance: 78,299 v Liverpool, Division 1, 18 September 1948.

Record receipts: £330,000 v Liverpool, FA Premiership, 21 November 1994.

Pitch measurements: 112yd × 78yd.

Chairman: Peter R. Johnson.

Directors: Sir Desmond Pitcher, Clifford Finch, Richard Hughes, Sir Philip Carter CBE, Dr. David M. Marsh, Keith Tamlin, David Newton, Bill Kenwright, Arthur Abercromby, John C. Suenson–Taylor.

Manager: Joe Royle. ***Assistant Manager:*** Willie Donachie. ***Coach:*** Jimmy Gabriel.

Physio: Les Helm.

Secretary: Michael J. Dunford.

Commercial Manager: Andrew Watson. ***Sales Promotion Manager:*** Colum Whelan.

Year Formed: 1878. ***Turned Professional:*** 1885. ***Ltd Co.:*** 1892.

Previous Name: St Domingo FC, 1878–79.

Club Nickname: 'The Toffees'.

Previous Grounds: 1878, Stanley Park; 1882, Priory Road; 1884, Anfield Road; 1892, Goodison Park.

Foundation: St. Domingo Church Sunday School formed a football club in 1878 which played at Stanley Park. Enthusiasm was so great that in November 1879 they decided to expand membership and changed the name to Everton playing in black shirts with a white sash and nicknamed the "Black Watch". After wearing several other colours, royal blue was adopted in 1901.

First Football League game: 8 September, 1888, Football League, v Accrington (h) W 2-1 – Smalley; Dick, Ross; Holt, Jones, Dobson; Fleming (2), Waugh, Lewis, E. Chadwick, Farmer.

Record League Victory: 9–1 v Manchester C, Division 1, 3 September 1906 – Scott; Balmer, Crelley; Booth, Taylor (1), Abbott (1); Sharp, Bolton (1), Young (4), Settle (2), George Wilson. 9–1 v Plymouth Arg, Division 2, 27 December 1930 – Coggins; Williams, Cresswell; McPherson, Griffiths, Thomson; Critchley, Dunn, Dean (4), Johnson (1), Stein (4).

Record Cup Victory: 11–2 v Derby Co, FA Cup, 1st rd, 18 January 1890 – Smalley; Hannah, Doyle(1); Kirkwood, Holt (1), Parry; Latta, Brady (3), Geary (3), Chadwick, Millward (3).

Record Defeat: 4–10 v Tottenham H, Division 1, 11 October 1958.

Most League Points (2 for a win): 66, Division 1, 1969–70.

Most League Points (3 for a win): 90, Division 1, 1984–85.

Most League Goals: 121, Division 2, 1930–31.

Highest League Scorer in Season: William Ralph 'Dixie' Dean, 60, Division 1, 1927–28 (All-time League record).

Most League Goals in Total Aggregate: William Ralph 'Dixie' Dean, 349, 1925–37.

Most Capped Player: Neville Southall, 81, Wales.

Most League Appearances: Neville Southall, 494, 1981–95.

Record Transfer Fee Received: £2,750,000 from Barcelona for Gary Lineker, July 1986.

Record Transfer Fee Paid: £4,000,000 to Rangers for Duncan Ferguson, December 1994.

Football League Record: 1888 Founder Member of the Football League; 1930–31 Division 2; 1931–51 Division 1; 1951–54 Division 2; 1954–92 Division 1; 1992– FA Premier League.

Honours: *Football League:* Division 1 – Champions 1890–91, 1914–15, 1927–28, 1931–32, 1938–39, 1962–63, 1969–70, 1984–85, 1986–87; Runners-up 1889–90, 1894–95, 1901–02, 1904–05, 1908–09, 1911–12, 1985–86; Division 2 Champions 1930–31; Runners-up 1953–54. *FA Cup:* Winners 1906, 1933, 1966, 1984, 1995; Runners-up 1893, 1897, 1907, 1968, 1985, 1986, 1989. *Football League Cup:* Runners-up 1977, 1984. *League Super Cup:* Runners-up 1986. *Simod Cup:* Runners-up 1989. *Zenith Data System Cup:* Runner-up 1991. **European Competitions:** *European Cup:* 1963–64, 1970–71. *European Cup-Winners' Cup:* 1966–67, 1984–85 (winners). *European Fairs Cup:* 1962–63, 1964–65, 1965–66. *UEFA Cup:* 1975–76, 1978–79, 1979–80.

Colours: Blue shirts, white shorts, black/blue hooped stockings. **Change colours:** White shirts, black shorts, black stockings.

EVERTON 1994–95 LEAGUE RECORD

Match No.	Date	Venue	Opponents	Result	H/T Score	Lg. Pos.	Goalscorers	Atten-dance
1	Aug 20	H	Aston Villa	D 2-2	1-0	—	Stuart, Rideout	35,552
2	24	A	Tottenham H	L 1-2	0-2	—	Rideout	24,553
3	27	A	Manchester C	L 0-4	0-0	20		19,867
4	30	H	Nottingham F	L 1-2	0-1	—	Rideout	26,689
5	Sept 10	A	Blackburn R	L 0-3	0-2	22		26,548
6	17	H	QPR	D 2-2	2-1	22	Amokachi, Rideout	27,291
7	24	H	Leicester C	D 1-1	0-0	22	Ablett	28,015
8	Oct 1	A	Manchester U	L 0-2	0-1	22		43,803
9	8	A	Southampton	L 0-2	0-1	22		15,163
10	15	H	Coventry C	L 0-2	0-2	22		28,219
11	22	A	Crystal Palace	L 0-1	0-0	22		15,026
12	29	H	Arsenal	D 1-1	1-1	22	Unsworth	32,005
13	Nov 1	H	West Ham U	W 1-0	0-0	—	Ablett	28,353
14	5	A	Norwich C	D 0-0	0-0	22		18,377
15	21	H	Liverpool	W 2-0	0-0	—	Ferguson, Rideout	39,866
16	26	A	Chelsea	W 1-0	1-0	20	Rideout	28,115
17	Dec 5	H	Leeds U	W 3-0	1-0	—	Rideout, Ferguson, Unsworth (pen)	25,906
18	10	A	Aston Villa	D 0-0	0-0	18		29,678
19	17	H	Tottenham H	D 0-0	0-0	19		32,813
20	26	H	Sheffield W	L 1-4	1-2	19	Ferguson	37,089
21	31	H	Ipswich T	W 4-1	1-1	19	Ferguson, Rideout 2, Watson	25,667
22	Jan 2	A	Wimbledon	L 1-2	1-2	20	Rideout	9506
23	14	A	Arsenal	D 1-1	1-1	20	Watson	34,743
24	21	H	Crystal Palace	W 3-1	1-0	18	Ferguson 2, Rideout	23,734
25	24	A	Liverpool	D 0-0	0-0	—		39,505
26	Feb 1	A	Newcastle U	L 0-2	0-0	—		34,465
27	4	H	Norwich C	W 2-1	1-0	18	Stuart, Rideout	23,295
28	13	A	West Ham U	D 2-2	1-1	—	Rideout, Limpar	21,081
29	22	A	Leeds U	L 0-1	0-0	—		30,793
30	25	H	Manchester U	W 1-0	0-0	16	Ferguson	40,011
31	Mar 4	A	Leicester C	D 2-2	2-0	17	Limpar, Samways	20,447
32	8	A	Nottingham F	L 1-2	1-1	—	Barlow	24,526
33	15	H	Manchester C	D 1-1	0-1	—	Unsworth (pen)	28,485
34	18	A	QPR	W 3-2	0-1	17	Barlow, McDonald (og), Hinchcliffe	14,488
35	Apr 1	H	Blackburn R	L 1-2	1-2	18	Stuart	37,905
36	14	H	Newcastle U	W 2-0	1-0	—	Amokachi 2	34,628
37	17	A	Sheffield W	D 0-0	0-0	17		27,880
38	29	H	Wimbledon	D 0-0	0-0	17		31,567
39	May 3	H	Chelsea	D 3-3	1-1	—	Hinchcliffe, Ablett, Amokachi	33,180
40	6	H	Southampton	D 0-0	0-0	17		36,851
41	9	A	Ipswich T	W 1-0	0-0	—	Rideout	14,940
42	14	A	Coventry C	D 0-0	0-0	15		21,787

Final League Position: 15

GOALSCORERS

League (44): Rideout 14, Ferguson 7, Amokachi 4, Ablett 3, Stuart 3, Unsworth 3 (2 pens), Barlow 2, Hinchcliffe 2, Limpar 2, Watson 2, Samways 1, own goal 1.
Coca-Cola Cup (3): Samways 1, Stuart 1 (pen), Watson 1.
FA Cup (13): Amokachi 2, Jackson 2, Rideout 2, Stuart 2, Ferguson 1, Hinchcliffe 1, Limpar 1, Parkinson 1, Watson 1.

Southall N. 41	Jackson M.A. 26 + 3	Ablett G.I. 26	Ebbrell J.K. 26	Watson D. 38	Unsworth D.G. 37 + 1	Samways V. 14 + 5	Stuart G.C. 20 + 8	Cottee A.R. 3	Rideout P.D. 25 + 4	Limpar A. 19 + 8	Parkinson J.S. 32 + 2	Angell B.A.M. 3 + 1	Hinchcliffe A.G. 28 + 1	Burrows D. 19	Amokachi D. 17 + 1	Snodin I. 2 + 1	Holmes P. 1	Rowett G. 2	Barlow S. 7 + 4	Durrant I. 4 + 1	Ferguson D. 22 + 1	Horne B. 31	Kearton J.B. 1	Grant A.J. 1 + 4	Barrett E.D. 17	Match No.
1	2	3	4	5	6	7	8	9	10	11	12															1
1	2	3	4	5	6	7	8	9	10		*11*	12	14													2
1	2	3	4	5	6	7	8	9	10	12	11															3
1	2		4	5	6	7	8		10	11		9	3													4
1	2		4	5	6	7	8		10	11				3	9											5
1	2		4	5	6	7	8		10	11				3	9	12										6
1		4		5	6	7	8					10		3	9	11	2									7
1				5	6	7	8				4		11	3	9	2		10	12							8
1	2			*5*	6	7	12		10		4		11	3	9			8		14						9
1	2	5			6	7	12				4			3	9					11	10	8				10
1	2	5			6	7	8				12			3	9					11	10	4				11
1	2	5			6		8		12	14	4			3	9					*11*	10	7				12
1	2	6		5			*8*		12	14	4			3	9					11	10	7				13
1	2	4		5	6		8		10	12	11			3							9	7				14
1	2	3	4	5	6				12	14	8		11		*9*						10	7				15
1	2	4		5	6				10	11	8		3								9	7				16
1	2	3	4	5	6		12		10		8		11								9	7				17
	2		4	5	6				10	7	8		11	3							9		1			18
1	2		4	5	6				10	12	8		11	3					9			7				19
1	2		4	5	6		12		10	7			11	3							9	8				20
1	2		4	5	6				10		8		11	3							9	7				21
1	2		4	5	6				10		8		11	3					12		9	7				22
1	2		4	5	6				10		8		11	3							9	7				23
1	2		4	5	6				10		8		11	3							9	7				24
1	2		4	5	6				10		8		11	3							9	7				25
1	2		4	5	6	12	9			7	10			11								8		14	3	26
1		3	4	5	6	12	9		10		8		11									7			2	27
1		3	4	5	6		8		10	12			11								9	7			2	28
1		6	4	5			12		10	11	8		3								9	7			2	29
1			4	5	6	12				11	8		3						10		9	7			2	30
1	12			5	6	7	14			*11*	4		3						10		9	8			2	31
1		3		5	6	7	12			11	4								10		9	8			2	32
1		*6*	4	5	12		14			11	8		3						10		9	7			2	33
1	12	6	4	5						11		*10*	3		14				9			7		8	2	34
1	2	6		5			8				11		3		9				10			7		12	4	35
1		3		5	6		8			7	4		11		9							10		12	2	36
1	12	3		5	6				10	7	4		11								*9*	8		14	2	37
1		3		5	6		10		12	7	4		11		9							8			2	38
1		3		5	6		8		10		4		11		9				12			7			2	39
1		3	4	5	6	12			10	14	8		*11*		9							7			2	40
1		3	4	5	6	12			10	7			11		*9*				14			8			2	41
1	5	3	4		6	7	8			11	10				9						12				2	42

Coca-Cola Cup

Second Round	Portsmouth	(h)	2-3
		(a)	1-1

FA Cup

Third Round	Derby Co (h)	1-0
Fourth Round	Bristol C (a)	1-0
Fifth Round	Norwich C (h)	5-0
Sixth Round	Newcastle U (h)	1-0
Semi-final	Tottenham H at Elland Road	4-1
Final at Wembley	Manchester U	1-0

EXETER CITY 1994–95 *Back row (left to right):* Mark Gavin, Mark Cooper, David Cooper, Anthony Thirlby, Gary Rice, Martin Phillips, Danny Bailey, Micky Ross, Jason Minett.
Centre row: Russell Coughlin, Ronnie Robinson, Peter Whiston, Mark Came, Peter Fox, Robbie Turner, Andy Woodman, Stuart Storer, Scott Daniels, Jonathan Richardson, Richard Pears, Jonathan Brown.
Front row: Michele Cecere, Mike Chapman (Physio), Trevor Morgan, Terry Cooper (Manager), George Kent, Mark Radfort (YTS Manager), Colin Anderson.

Division 3 **EXETER CITY**

St James Park, Exeter EX4 6PX. Telephone: (01392) 54073. Fax: (01392) 425885. Training Ground: (01395) 232784.

Ground capacity: 10,570.

Record attendance: 20,984 v Sunderland, FA Cup 6th rd (replay), 4 March 1931.

Record receipts: £59,862.98 v Aston Villa, FA Cup 3rd rd 8 January 1994.

Pitch measurements: 114yd × 73yd.

Honorary President: W. C. Hill.

Chairman: A. I. Doble.

Directors: P. Carter, M. Couch, S. W. Dawe, L. G. Vallance, M. Shelbourne.

Manager: Peter Fox. ***Assistant Manager/Coach:*** Trevor Morgan. ***Physio:*** Mike Chapman.

Secretary: Margaret Bond. ***Company Secretary:*** P. Carter.

Commercial Manager: –.

Year Formed: 1904. ***Turned Professional:*** 1908. ***Ltd Co.:*** 1908.

Club Nickname: 'The Grecians'.

Foundation: Exeter City was formed in 1904 by the amalgamation of St. Sidwell's United and Exeter United. The club first played in the East Devon League and then the Plymouth & District League. After an exhibition match between West Bromwich Albion and Woolwich Arsenal was held to test interest as Exeter was then a rugby stronghold, Exeter City decided at a meeting at the Red Lion Hotel to turn professional in 1908.

First Football League game: 28 August, 1920, Division 3, v Brentford (h) W 3-0 – Pym; Coleburne, Feebury (1p); Crawshaw, Carrick, Mitton; Appleton, Makin, Wright (1), Vowles (1), Dockray.

Record League Victory: 8–1 v Coventry C, Division 3 (S), 4 December 1926 – Bailey; Pollard, Charlton; Pullen, Pool, Garrett; Purcell (2), McDevitt, Blackmore (2), Dent (2), Compton (2). 8–1 v Aldershot, Division 3 (S), 4 May 1935 – Chesters; Gray, Miller; Risdon, Webb, Angus; Jack Scott (1), Wrightson (1), Poulter (3), McArthur (1), Dryden (1). (1 og).

Record Cup Victory: 9–1 v Aberdare, FA Cup 1st rd, 26 November 1927 – Holland; Pollard, Charlton; Phoenix, Pool, Gee; Purcell (2), McDevitt, Dent (4), Vaughan (2), Compton (1).

Record Defeat: 0–9 v Notts Co, Division 3 (S), 16 October 1948 and v Northampton T, Division 3 (S), 12 April 1958.

Most League Points (2 for a win): 62, Division 4, 1976–77.

Most League Points (3 for a win): 89, Division 4, 1989–90.

Most League Goals: 88, Division 3 (S), 1932–33.

Highest League Scorer in Season: Fred Whitlow, 33, Division 3 (S), 1932–33.

Most League Goals in Total Aggregate: Tony Kellow, 129, 1976–78, 1980–83, 1985–88.

Most Capped Player: Dermot Curtis, 1 (17), Eire.

Most League Appearances: Arnold Mitchell, 495, 1952–66.

Record Transfer Fee Received: £500,000 from Rangers for Chris Vinnicombe, November 1989.

Record Transfer Fee Paid: £65,000 to Blackpool for Tony Kellow, March 1980.

Football League Record: 1920 Elected Division 3; 1921–58 Division 3 (S); 1958–64 Division 4; 1964–66 Division 3; 1966–77 Division 4; 1977–84 Division 3; 1984–90 Division 4; 1990–92 Division 3; 1992–94 Division 2; 1994– Division 3.

Honours: *Football League:* Division 3 best season: 8th, 1979–80; Division 3 (S) – Runners-up 1932–33; Division 4 – Champions 1989–90; Runners-up 1976–77. *FA Cup:* best season: 6th rd replay, 1931. *Football League Cup:* never beyond 4th rd. *Division 3 (S) Cup:* Winners 1934.

Colours: Red and white striped shirts, black shorts, red stockings. **Change colours:** Blue and white striped shirts, blue shorts, blue stockings.

EXETER CITY 1994–95 LEAGUE RECORD

Match No.	Date	Venue	Opponents	Result	H/T Score	Lg. Pos.	Goalscorers	Attendance
1	Aug 13	A	Lincoln C	L 0-2	0-2	—		3439
2	20	H	Bury	L 0-4	0-3	22		2164
3	27	A	Darlington	L 0-2	0-0	22		1861
4	30	H	Colchester U	W 1-0	1-0	—	Bailey	1804
5	Sept 3	H	Gillingham	W 3-0	2-0	14	Cooper M 2, Dunne (og)	2241
6	10	A	Carlisle U	L 0-1	0-1	17		6213
7	13	A	Chesterfield	L 0-2	0-1	—		2136
8	17	H	Lincoln C	W 1-0	0-0	15	Thirlby	2180
9	24	A	Mansfield T	D 1-1	0-0	14	Morgan	2468
10	Oct 1	H	Hartlepool U	W 2-1	1-1	14	Gavin, Cooper M	2390
11	8	H	Northampton T	D 0-0	0-0	15		3015
12	15	A	Fulham	L 0-4	0-2	16		4314
13	22	H	Scunthorpe U	D 2-2	1-1	15	Came, Cecere	2511
14	29	A	Preston NE	W 1-0	1-0	14	Cecere	6808
15	Nov 5	H	Doncaster R	L 1-5	0-4	15	Turner	2813
16	19	A	Walsall	L 0-1	0-1	16		3629
17	26	H	Scarborough	W 5-2	2-1	14	Cecere 2, Gavin, Phillips, Storer	2179
18	Dec 10	A	Bury	D 0-0	0-0	15		2876
19	17	H	Darlington	L 0-2	0-1	16		2338
20	26	H	Torquay U	L 1-2	1-0	16	Storer	5538
21	27	A	Hereford U	L 0-3	0-2	17		2567
22	Jan 7	A	Scunthorpe U	L 0-3	0-2	18		2463
23	14	H	Rochdale	D 0-0	0-0	17		2316
24	31	A	Doncaster R	L 0-1	0-0	—		1611
25	Feb 4	A	Scarborough	W 2-0	1-0	17	Anderson, Pears	1512
26	18	A	Rochdale	W 1-0	1-0	17	Cooper M	1945
27	21	H	Wigan Ath	L 2-4	1-2	—	Richardson, Cecere	2370
28	25	A	Hartlepool U	D 2-2	1-1	18	Cecere, Thirlby	1440
29	28	A	Barnet	D 1-1	0-1	—	Cooper M	1325
30	Mar 4	H	Mansfield T	L 2-3	1-1	18	Phillips, Minett (pen)	2458
31	11	H	Carlisle U	D 1-1	1-1	18	Brown	2673
32	18	A	Colchester U	L 1-3	0-1	19	Cecere	2375
33	21	H	Preston NE	L 0-1	0-0	—		2057
34	25	A	Gillingham	L 0-3	0-2	21		3332
35	Apr 1	H	Chesterfield	L 1-2	0-0	21	Brown	2144
36	4	H	Walsall	L 1-3	0-1	—	Cecere	1551
37	8	A	Wigan Ath	L 1-3	0-2	21	Cecere	1417
38	15	H	Hereford U	D 1-1	0-1	21	Cecere	2083
39	18	A	Torquay U	D 0-0	0-0	—		4155
40	22	H	Barnet	L 1-2	0-1	21	Cooper M	1903
41	29	H	Fulham	L 0-1	0-0	22		3388
42	May 6	A	Northampton T	L 1-2	0-1	22	Minett (pen)	6734

Final League Position: 22

GOALSCORERS

League (36): Cecere 10, Cooper M 6, Brown 2, Gavin 2, Minett 2 (2 pens), Phillips 2, Storer 2, Thirlby 2, Anderson 1, Bailey 1, Came 1, Morgan 1, Pears 1, Richardson 1, Turner 1, own goal 1.
Coca-Cola Cup (2): Cecere 1, Turner 1.
FA Cup (2): Cecere 1, Morgan 1.

Woodman A.J. 6	Daniels S. 6 + 1	Anderson C.R. 21	Cooper M.N. 31 + 9	Came M.R. 32	Richardson J.D.P. 38	Storer S.J. 21 + 2	Coughlin R. 23 + 2	Turner R.P. 10 + 1	Ross M.P. 1	Gavin M.W. 37	Thirlby A.D. 20 + 7	Brown J. 32 + 5	Rice G.J. 5 + 5	Bailey D.S. 14	Phillips M.J. 18 + 6	Cecere M.J. 27 + 1	Pears R.J. 12 + 7	Fox P.D. 31	Minett J. 38	Robinson R. 16 + 1	Morgan T.J. 4 + 5	Bellotti R.C. 1 + 1	Barrett M.J. 4	Cooper D.B.E. 14	Match No.
1	2	3	4	5	6	7	8	*9*	10	11	12	14													1
1	2		12	5				9		11	8	6	3	4	7	*10*	14								2
			7	5	6	12				11	8	14	3	4		9	*10*	1	2						3
		3	9	5	6	7	10			11	8	12		4				1	2						4
			9	5	6	7	10			11	8			4	12			1	2	3					5
			9	5	6	7	10				8	11	12	4				1	2	3					6
			9	5	6	7	10			11	8	4	14		12			1	2	3					7
				5	6	7	10			11	8	4				12		1	2	3	9				8
			10		6	7	5	9			8	4	11					1	2	3	12				9
		10	4	5	6		7	9		11	*8*	12						1	2	3	14				10
			4	5		7	10	9		11	8	6						1	2	3	12				11
			4	5	6	7	10	9		11	8							1	2	3					12
1			4	5		7	10	9		11	8	3				6			2						13
1			4	5	6	7	10	9		11						8			2	3					14
1			4	5	6	7	10	12		11		3	14		*8*	9			2						15
			12	5	6		8	9		11	7	3		4	14	10		1	2						16
1			12		6	7	*10*	*9*		11		3	14	4	5	8			2			15			17
	10		9	5	6	7	8			11		3		4					2	12		1			18
	12		*9*	5	6	7				11	8	3		4					2	10	14		1		19
		8	12	5	6	7				11		10		4					2	3	9		1		20
	5	8	10		6	7				11				4	12		9		2	3			1		21
	5	10	8		6	7				11				4		3			2	9			1		22
	5	10	8		6	7				9		12		4		*11*	14	1	2	3					23
		3	8	5	6	7	4			11		9				10	12	1	2						24
		4	8	5	6	7				11	12	3				10	9	1	2						25
		4	8	5	6					11	7	3			12	10	9	1	2						26
		4	8	5	6	12				11	7	3			14	10	*9*	1	2						27
			8		6		4			11	12	2			7	10	9	1		5	14			3	28
			8		6		4			11	12	5			7	10	9	1	2					3	29
			8		6		4			11	12	9			7	10		1	2	5				3	30
			12	5	6					11	8	4			7	10	9	1	2					3	31
		4	12	5						11	10	6			7	8	9	1	2					3	32
		4	12	5	6					11	*10*	9			7	8	14	1	2					3	33
		4	12	5	6					11		8			7	10		1	2		9			3	34
		4	8	5	6		12				11	10			7		14	1	2		*9*			3	35
		4	8	5	6					11		9			7	10		1	2					3	36
		4	8	5	6							11	12		7	10	9	1	2					3	37
		4	8		6		11				12	2	3	9	7	10		1						5	38
		4		5	6		8			11		9			7	10	12	1	2					3	39
			12	5	6		4			11		8			7	10	9	1	2					3	40
		3	8	5	6		12			11	14	4			7	10	*9*	1	2						41
		10	9		6					11		4	3		7	8	12	1	2					5	42

Coca-Cola Cup

First Round	Swansea C (h)		2-2
		(a)	0-2

FA Cup

First Round	Crawley (h)	1-0
Second Round	Colchester U (h)	1-2

FULHAM 1994–95 *Back row (left to right):* Micky Adams (Player/Coach), Chris Smith (Physio), Julian Hails, Duncan Jupp, Robert Haworth, Michael Mison, Jim Stannard, Lee Harrison, Terry Angus, Glen Thomas, Alan Cork, Martin Ferney, Len Walker (Assistant Manager).
Front row: Danny Bolt, Martin Thomas, Gary Bazil, John Marshall, Kevin Moore, Ian Branfoot (Manager), Simon Morgan, Ara Bedrossian, Robbie Herrera, Nicky Andrews, Terry Hurlock.

Division 3 **FULHAM**

Craven Cottage, Stevenage Rd, Fulham, London SW6 6HH. Telephone: (0171) 736 6561. Fax: (0171) 731 7047. Call Line: 0891 440044.

Ground capacity: 14,969.

Record attendance: 49,335 v Millwall, Division 2, 8 October 1938.

Record receipts: £80,247 v Chelsea, Division 2, 8 October 1983.

Pitch measurements: 110yd × 75yd.

Chief Executive: R.J. Summers.

Chairman: Jimmy Hill.

Directors: W. F. Muddyman (vice-chairman), C. A. Swain, A. Muddyman, T. Wilson, D. E. Shrimpton.

Manager: Ian Branfoot. ***Assistant Manager:*** Len Walker.

Player-Coach: Micky Adams. ***Physio:*** Chris Smith. ***Community Officer:*** Gary Mulcahey.

Club Secretary: Mrs Janice O'Doherty.

Commercial Manager: Ken Myers.

Year Formed: 1879. ***Turned Professional:*** 1898. ***Ltd Co.:*** 1903. ***Reformed:*** 1987.

Club Nickname: 'Cottagers'.

Previous Name: 1879–88, Fulham St Andrew's.

Previous Grounds: 1879 Star Road, Fulham; c.1883 Eel Brook Common, 1884 Lillie Road; 1885 Putney Lower Common; 1886 Ranelagh House, Fulham; 1888 Barn Elms, Castelnau; 1889 Purser's Cross (Roskell's Field), Parsons Green Lane; 1891 Eel Brook Common; 1891 Half Moon, Putney; 1895 Captain James Field, West Brompton; 1896 Craven Cottage.

Foundation: Churchgoers were responsible for the foundation of Fulham, which first saw the light of day as Fulham St. Andrew's Church Sunday School FC in 1879. They won the West London Amateur Cup in 1887 and the championship of the West London League in its initial season of 1892–93. The name Fulham had been adopted in 1888.

First Football League game: 3 September, 1907, Division 2, v Hull C (h) L 0-1 – Skene; Ross, Lindsay; Collins, Morrison, Goldie; Dalrymple, Freeman, Bevan, Hubbard, Threlfall.

Record League Victory: 10–1 v Ipswich T, Division 1, 26 December 1963 – Macedo; Cohen, Langley; Mullery (1), Keetch, Robson (1); Key, Cook (1), Leggat (4), Haynes, Howfield (3).

Record Cup Victory: 6–0 v Wimbledon (away), FA Cup, 1st rd (replay), 3 December 1930 – Iceton; Gibbon, Lilley; Oliver, Dudley, Barrett; Temple, Hammond (1), Watkins (1), Gibbons (2), Penn (2). 6–0 v Bury, FA Cup, 3rd rd, 7 January 1938 – Turner; Bacuzzi, Keeping; Evans, Dennison, Tompkins; Higgins, Worsley, Rooke (6), O'Callaghan, Arnold.

Record Defeat: 0–10 v Liverpool, League Cup 2nd rd, 1st leg, 23 September 1986.

Most League Points (2 for a win): 60, Division 2, 1958–59 and Division 3, 1970–71.

Most League Points (3 for a win): 78, Division 3, 1981–82.

Most League Goals: 111, Division 3 (S), 1931–32.

Highest League Scorer in Season: Frank Newton, 43, Division 3 (S), 1931–32.

Most League Goals in Total Aggregate: Gordon Davies, 159, 1978–84, 1986–91.

Most Capped Player: Johnny Haynes, 56, England.

Most League Appearances: Johnny Haynes, 594, 1952–70.

Record Transfer Fee Received: £333,333 from Liverpool for Richard Money, May 1980.

Record Transfer Fee Paid: £150,000 to Orient for Peter Kitchen, February 1979, and to Brighton & HA for Teddy Maybank, December 1979.

Football League Record: 1907 Elected to Division 2; 1928–32 Division 3 (S); 1932–49 Division 2; 1949–52 Division 1; 1952–59 Division 2; 1959–68 Division 1; 1968–69 Division 2; 1969–71 Division 3; 1971–80 Division 2; 1980–82 Division 3; 1982–86 Division 2; 1986–92 Division 3; 1992–94 Division 2; 1994– Division 3.

Honours: *Football League:* Division 1 best season: 10th, 1959–60; Division 2 – Champions 1948–49; Runners-up 1958–59; Division 3 (S) – Champions 1931–32; Division 3 – Runners-up 1970–71. *FA Cup:* Runners-up 1975. *Football League Cup:* best season: 5th rd, 1968, 1971.

Colours: White shirts, red and black trim, black shorts, white stockings red and black trim. **Change colours:** Red and black halved shirts, white shorts, black stockings with red trim.

FULHAM 1994–95 LEAGUE RECORD

Match No.	*Date*		*Venue*	*Opponents*	*Result*		*H/T Score*	*Lg. Pos.*	*Goalscorers*	*Attendance*
1	Aug	13	H	Walsall	D	1-1	0-1	—	Moore	5308
2		20	A	Scunthorpe U	W	2-1	1-1	6	Cork 2	3165
3		27	H	Wigan Ath	W	2-0	1-0	5	Morgan, Cork	4241
4		30	A	Doncaster R	D	0-0	0-0	—		3003
5	Sept	3	A	Torquay U	L	1-2	1-2	8	Moore	4739
6		10	H	Preston NE	L	0-1	0-0	10		5001
7		13	H	Scarborough	L	1-2	1-2	—	Hails	2729
8		17	A	Walsall	L	1-5	0-3	17	Brazil	3378
9		24	H	Hereford U	D	1-1	0-1	15	Brazil	3740
10	Oct	1	A	Barnet	D	0-0	0-0	17		3579
11		8	A	Rochdale	W	2-1	0-1	16	Brazil, Hurlock	2573
12		15	H	Exeter C	W	4-0	2-0	12	Stallard 3, Morgan	4314
13		22	A	Chesterfield	D	1-1	0-1	12	Moore	2860
14		29	H	Carlisle U	L	1-3	0-2	15	Morgan	5563
15	Nov	5	A	Northampton T	W	1-0	1-0	12	Adams	7366
16		19	H	Lincoln C	D	1-1	1-0	13	Adams	3955
17		26	A	Bury	D	0-0	0-0	11		3323
18	Dec	10	H	Scunthorpe U	W	1-0	1-0	8	Morgan	3358
19		17	A	Wigan Ath	D	1-1	0-1	10	Marshall	1791
20		26	A	Gillingham	L	1-4	0-1	12	Morgan	4677
21		27	H	Colchester U	L	1-2	1-1	13	Hamill	4243
22		31	A	Hartlepool U	W	2-1	1-1	12	Cusack, Brazil	1698
23	Jan	2	H	Mansfield T	W	4-2	1-1	12	Hamill, Cusack, Blake, Thomas M	4091
24		8	H	Chesterfield	D	1-1	0-1	11	Brazil	3927
25		14	A	Darlington	D	0-0	0-0	12		2113
26		28	A	Carlisle U	D	1-1	1-1	12	Walling (og)	6891
27	Feb	4	H	Bury	W	1-0	0-0	12	Thomas M	3941
28		14	H	Northampton T	D	4-4	2-1	—	Morgan 2, Adams (pen), Hamill	3423
29		18	H	Darlington	W	3-1	1-0	8	Adams 2, Hamill	3864
30		25	H	Barnet	W	4-0	3-0	6	Cusack, Marshall, Morgan, Hamill	6195
31	Mar	4	A	Hereford U	D	1-1	1-0	8	Jupp	2895
32		11	A	Preston NE	L	2-3	1-1	10	Jupp, Blake (pen)	8601
33		18	H	Doncaster R	L	0-2	0-1	11		4031
34		25	H	Torquay U	W	2-1	0-1	9	Adams, Cusack	4941
35	Apr	1	A	Scarborough	L	1-3	0-0	10	Adams	2050
36		8	H	Hartlepool U	W	1-0	0-0	10	Blake	3465
37		11	A	Lincoln C	L	0-2	0-1	—		2932
38		15	A	Colchester U	L	2-5	1-4	11	Morgan, Mison	3448
39		17	H	Gillingham	W	1-0	0-0	10	Morgan	3612
40		22	A	Mansfield T	D	1-1	0-1	10	Morgan	2861
41		29	A	Exeter C	W	1-0	0-0	9	Brazil	3388
42	May	6	H	Rochdale	W	5-0	3-0	8	Cusack 3, Thomas M, Brazil	4342

Final League Position: 8

GOALSCORERS

League (60): Morgan 11, Adams 7 (1 pen), Brazil 7, Cusack 7, Hamill 5, Blake 3 (1 pen), Cork 3, Moore 3, Stallard 3, Thomas M 3, Jupp 2, Marshall 2, Hails 1, Hurlock 1, Mison 1, own goal 1.
Coca-Cola Cup (5): Haworth 2, Moore 2, Blake 1.
FA Cup (9): Adams 4 (2 pens), Hamill 2, Blake 1, Cork 1, Morgan 1.

Stannard J. 36	Morgan S.C. 42	Marshall J.P. 25 + 2	Mison M. 17 + 7	Moore K.T. 31	Thomas G.A. 7	Thomas M.R. 21 + 2	Bedrossian A. 3	Cork A.G. 11 + 4	Brazil G.N. 30 + 2	Herrera R. 26 + 1	Haworth R.J. 3 + 7	Jupp D.A. 35 + 1	Ferney M.J. 5 + 2	Hurlock T.A. 27	Hails J. 6 + 2	Angus T.N. 21 + 2	Adams M.R. 18 + 3	Blake M.C. 34 + 1	Stallard M. 4	Finnigan A. 7 + 4	Cusack N.J. 26 + 1	Harrison L.D. 6 + 1	Hamill R. 18 + 5	Bartley C.A. 1	Gregory J.G. — + 1	Bolt D.A. 2	Match No.
1	2	3	4	5	6	7	8	9	10	11	12	14															1
1	2	7	4	5	6			9	10	3	11	8	12														2
1	2	7	11	5	6			9	10	3		8		4	12												3
1	2	7	11	5	6				10			8		4	9	3											4
1	2	7	11	5	6			9	10		12	8		4	14		3										5
1	2	7		5	6			9	10		12	8		4	11		3										6
1	2	12	7	5	6	14		9	10			8		4	11		*3*										7
1	2	7		5		*6*		9	10	3	12	8		4	11			14									8
1	2	7	4	5				9	12	3		8					10	6	11								9
1	6	3	4			11	7		10		14			8		12		5	9	2							10
1	6		8			11	7		10		12	2		4		3		5	9								11
1	8		7	5		11			10			2		4		3		6	9								12
1	8		7	5					10		9	2		4	*11*	3	12	6		14							13
1	8		7	5					10		9	2		4	*11*	3	12	6		14							14
1	8	4	7					12	10	3						5	11	6		2	9						15
1	8	10	7	5						3		2		4			11	6			9	15					16
1	8	7		5				10		3		2		4			11	6			9						17
1	8	7		5				11	10	3		2		4				6			9		12				18
1	8	7	4	5					10	3		2	12					6			9		11				19
1	8		12	5					10	3		2	7	4		14		6			9		11				20
1	8			5					10			2		4		3		6		7	9		11				21
1	8			5		7			10			2		4		3		6			9		11				22
1	8			5		7			10	12		2		4		3		6			9		11				23
1	8			5		7			10	3	12	2		4				6			9		11				24
1	8			5		7			10	3			4					6		2	9		11				25
1	8			5		7			10				4			3		6		2	9		11				26
1	8	4		5		7			10			2				3		6			9		11				27
1	8	4		5		7			10			2				3	12	6			9		11				28
1	8	4				7				3		2				5	10	6		12	9		11				29
1	8	4	12			7				3		2				5	*10*	6		14	9		11				30
1	8	7	12						14	3		2		4		5	*10*	6			9		11				31
1	8	7	10					12		3		2		4		5		6			9		11				32
1	8	7		5		12				3		2		4			10	6			9		11				33
1	8			5		7				3		2		4			10	6			9		11				34
1	8	11		5		7						2		4		3	10	6			9		12				35
	8	7		5				12		3		2		4			10	6				1	11	*9*	15		36
	8	12		5		7		9		3		2		4			10	6			14	1	*11*				37
	8	7	12	5				14	*11*	3		2		4			10	6			9	1					38
	8	7	12			4			*11*	3		2				5	10	6			9	1	14				39
1	8		4			7			11	3		2				5	10	6			9		12				40
	8		12			7			11	3			4			5		6		2	9	1				10	41
	8		12			7			11	3			4			5		6		2	9	1	14			*10*	42

Coca-Cola Cup

First Round	Luton T (a)	1-1
	(h)	1-1
Second Round	Stoke C (h)	3-2
	(a)	0-1

FA Cup

First Round	Ashford T (a)	2-2
	(h)	5-3
Second Round	Gillingham (a)	1-1
	(h)	1-2

GILLINGHAM 1994–95 *Back row (left to right):* Andy Ramage, Paul Hague, Tony Butler, Steve Banks, Lee Osborne, Scott Barrett, Robin Trott, Andy Arnott, Lee Palmer.
Third row: Paul Baker, Sam Comer, Danny Lander, Lee Spiller, Marc Hills, Neil Smillie (Coach), Kevin Clifford, Scott Clarke, Paul Wilson, Lee Quigley, Javed Mughal (Physio).
Second row: Joe Dunne, Richard Carpenter, Paul Watson, Robert Reinelt, Mike Flanagan (Manager), Richard Green, Gary Micklewhite, Neil Smith, Scott Lindsey.
Front row: Lee Williams, Richard Corbyn, Karl Emerick, John Carney, Danny Francis, Mark Barnes, Lee Bacon, Adam Flanagan, Paul Sykes.

Division 3 **GILLINGHAM**

Priestfield Stadium, Gillingham, ME7 4DD. Telephone: (01634) 851854/576828. Fax: (01634) 850986.

Ground capacity: 10,412.

Record attendance: 23,002 v QPR, FA Cup 3rd rd 10 January 1948.

Record receipts: £80,184 v Sheffield W, FA Cup 3rd rd, 7 January 1995.

Pitch measurements: 114yd × 75yd.

President: J. W. Leech. ***Vice-Presidents:*** G. B. Goodere, G. V. W. Lukehurst.

Chairman: A. Smith.

Directors: M. G. Lukehurst, Mrs. V. Smith.

Manager: Tony Pulis. ***Coach:*** Gary Micklewhite.

Physio: Javed Mughal.

Acting Secretary: S. Close. ***Commercial Manager:*** M. Ling.

Year Formed: 1893. ***Turned Professional:*** 1894. ***Ltd Co.:*** 1893.

Club Nickname: 'The Gills'.

Previous Name: New Brompton, 1893–1913.

Foundation: The success of the pioneering Royal Engineers of Chatham excited the interest of the residents of the Medway Towns and led to the formation of many clubs including Excelsior. After winning the Kent Junior Cup and the Chatham District League in 1893, Excelsior decided to go for bigger things and it was at a meeting in the Napier Arms, Brompton, in 1893 that New Brompton FC came into being as a professional concern, securing the use of a ground in Priestfield Road.

First Football League game: 28 August, 1920, Division 3, v Southampton (h) D 1-1 – Branfield; Robertson, Sissons; Battiste, Baxter, Wigmore; Holt, Hall, Gilbey (1), Roe, Gore.

Record League Victory: 10–0 v Chesterfield, Division 3, 5 September 1987 – Kite; Haylock, Pearce, Shipley (2) (Lillis), West, Greenall (1), Pritchard (2), Shearer (2), Lovell, Elsey (2), David Smith (1).

Record Cup Victory: 10–1 v Gorleston, FA Cup, 1st rd, 16 November 1957 – Brodie; Parry, Hannaway; Riggs, Boswell, Laing; Payne, Fletcher (2), Saunders (5), Morgan (1), Clark (2).

Record Defeat: 2–9 v Nottingham F, Division 3 (S), 18 November 1950.

Most League Points (2 for a win): 62, Division 4, 1973–74.

Most League Points (3 for a win): 83, Division 3, 1984–85.

Most League Goals: 90, Division 4, 1973–74.

Highest League Scorer in Season: Ernie Morgan, 31, Division 3 (S), 1954–55 and Brian Yeo, 31, Division 4, 1973–74.

Most League Goals in Total Aggregate: Brian Yeo, 135, 1963–75.

Most Capped Player: Tony Cascarino, 3 (56), Republic of Ireland.

Most League Appearances: John Simpson, 571, 1957–72.

Record Transfer Fee Received: £300,000 from Tottenham H for Peter Beadle, June 1992.

Record Transfer Fee Paid: £102,500 to Tottenham H for Mark Cooper, October 1987.

Football League Record: 1920 Original Member of Division 3; 1921 Division 3 (S); 1938 Failed re-election; Southern League 1938–44; Kent League 1944–46; Southern League 1946–50; 1950 Re-elected to Division 3 (S); 1958–64 Division 4; 1964–71 Division 3; 1971–74 Division 4; 1974–89 Division 3; 1989–92 Division 4; 1992– Division 3.

Honours: *Football League:* Division 3 best season: 4th, 1978–79, 1984–85; Division 4 – Champions 1963–64; Runners-up 1973–74. *FA Cup:* best season: 5th rd, 1970. *Football League Cup:* best season: 4th rd, 1964.

Colours: Blue shirts, white shorts, white stockings. **Change colours:** Red shirts, white shorts, red stockings.

GILLINGHAM 1994–95 LEAGUE RECORD

Match No.	Date		Venue	Opponents	Result		H/T Score	Lg. Pos.	Goalscorers	Attendance
1	Aug	13	H	Hartlepool U	D	0-0	0-0	—		2956
2		20	A	Wigan Ath	W	3-0	1-0	4	Foster, Reinelt, Watson	1514
3		27	H	Rochdale	D	1-1	0-1	9	Butler	3015
4		30	A	Scunthorpe U	L	0-3	0-0	—		2098
5	Sept	3	A	Exeter C	L	0-3	0-2	16		2241
6		10	H	Scarborough	W	3-1	1-0	9	Palmer, Ritchie, Baker	2414
7		13	H	Preston NE	L	2-3	2-2	—	Smith, Baker	2555
8		17	A	Hartlepool U	L	0-2	0-1	16		1756
9		24	A	Walsall	L	1-2	0-1	17	Micklewhite	3654
10	Oct	1	H	Mansfield T	L	0-2	0-1	20		2555
11		8	H	Torquay U	W	1-0	1-0	17	Pike	2439
12		15	A	Hereford U	L	1-2	0-1	19	Arnott	2472
13		22	A	Bury	L	2-3	0-2	20	Pike 2 (1 pen)	2976
14		29	H	Darlington	W	2-1	1-1	17	Pike, Smillie	2785
15	Nov	5	A	Colchester U	D	2-2	2-1	17	Reinelt, Pike	3817
16		19	H	Chesterfield	D	1-1	0-1	17	Reinelt	2722
17		26	A	Lincoln C	D	1-1	0-0	17	Arnott	2919
18	Dec	10	H	Wigan Ath	L	0-1	0-0	19		2257
19		17	A	Rochdale	L	1-2	0-2	19	Foster	1665
20		26	H	Fulham	W	4-1	1-0	18	Reinelt, Micklewhite, Foster 2	4677
21		27	A	Barnet	L	0-1	0-0	18		3074
22		31	H	Carlisle U	L	0-1	0-0	19		3682
23	Jan	14	A	Northampton T	L	0-2	0-0	21		5529
24	Feb	4	H	Lincoln C	D	0-0	0-0	20		4196
25		7	A	Doncaster R	W	2-1	1-1	—	Pike 2	1740
26		11	A	Chesterfield	L	0-2	0-2	19		3070
27		18	H	Northampton T	W	3-1	1-0	19	Ramage, Green, Foster	4075
28		21	A	Darlington	L	0-2	0-0	—		1548
29		25	A	Mansfield T	L	0-4	0-1	20		3182
30	Mar	4	H	Walsall	L	1-3	0-0	20	Foster	3669
31		11	A	Scarborough	D	0-0	0-0	21		1949
32		18	H	Scunthorpe U	D	2-2	0-1	20	Foster, Pike	2459
33		25	H	Exeter C	W	3-0	2-0	19	Foster, Pike (pen), Butler	3332
34	Apr	1	A	Preston NE	D	1-1	0-1	19	Dunne	9100
35		4	H	Bury	D	1-1	1-1	—	Brown	2945
36		8	A	Carlisle U	L	0-2	0-2	19		6786
37		11	H	Colchester U	L	1-3	1-0	—	Watson	3328
38		15	H	Barnet	W	2-1	2-1	18	Brown, Pike	3448
39		17	A	Fulham	L	0-1	0-0	19		3612
40		22	H	Doncaster R	W	4-2	3-2	18	Kirby (og), Pike 3	2826
41		29	H	Hereford U	D	0-0	0-0	17		4208
42	May	6	A	Torquay U	L	1-3	0-1	19	Stamps (og)	2638

Final League Position: 19

GOALSCORERS

League (46): Pike 13 (2 pens), Foster 8, Reinelt 4, Arnott 2, Baker 2, Brown 2, Butler 2, Micklewhite 2, Watson 2, Dunne 1, Green 1, Palmer 1, Ramage 1, Ritchie 1, Smillie 1, Smith 1, own goals 2.
Coca-Cola Cup (0).
FA Cup (6): Pike 4 (1 pen), Reinelt 2.

Barrett S. 4	Dunne J.J. 35	Palmer L.J. 10	Micklewhite G. 33 + 2	Green R.E. 37	Butler P.A. 31 + 2	Smillie N. 15	Smith N.J. 32 + 1	Foster A.M. 27 + 2	Arnott A.J. 24 + 4	Watson P.D. 39	Ramage A.W. 8 + 5	Baker D.P. 7 + 1	Reinelt R.S. 18 + 9	Carpenter R. 26 + 3	Wilson P.A.F. — + 2	Banks S. 38	Watts G.S. 2 + 1	Ritchie P. 5	Kennedy A.J. — + 2	Trott R.F. 7 + 2	Pike C. 26 + 1	Hutchinson I.N. 1 + 4	Bodley M.J. 6 + 1	Lindsey S. 11 + 1	Knott G.R. 5	Freeman D.B.A. — + 2	Martin E.J. 7	Brown S.R. 8	*Match No.*
1	2	3	4	5	6	7	8	9	*10*	11	12	14																	1
1	2	3	4	5	6		8	9		11		10	7																2
1	2	3	4	5	6		8	*9*	12	11		10	7	14															3
1	2	3	4	5	6		8		9	11		*10*	7	12	14														4
	2		4	5	6	11	8		9	3			7	12	14	1	*10*												5
	2	3		5	6		8			11		9	7	4		1		10											6
	2	3	*12*	5	6		8			11		9	7	4		1		10	14										7
	2			5	6		8			11		9	7	4		1		10	12	3									8
	2		7	5	6	11	8			3		9	12	4		1		10											9
	2	3	7	5	6		8			11			12	4		1		10			9								10
	2	3	7	5	6		8		12	11			10	4		1	14				*9*								11
	2	3	7	5	6		8		12	11			10	*4*		1	9					14							12
	2	3	7	5	6		*8*		12	11	14		10	4		1					9								13
	2		7	5	6	11	8			3			10	4		1					9								14
	2		7	5	6	11			8	3			10	4		1					9	12							15
	2		7		6	11	12	8	5	3			10	4		1				14	9								16
			7			11	2	8	5	3			10	4		1					9	12	6						17
			12		5	11	7	9	2	3			8	4		1					10		6						18
			7	5	*6*	11	8	9	2	3			12	4		1					10		14						19
			7	6	5		8	9	2				11	4		1					10		3						20
			7	6	5		8	9	2				11	4		1						10	3						21
			7	6	5		8	9	2				11	4		1					10	12	*3*	14					22
			7	6	5		8	9	2	11			12	4		1					10		3						23
	2		7	5		11		10		3	4		12			1				6	9			8					24
	2		7	5		11		9		3	4					1				6	10			8					25
	2		7	5		11		9		3	4		12			1				6	10			8					26
	2		8	5	11			10		3	4					1				6	9				7				27
	2		7	5	8			10		3	4		12			1				6	9				11				28
	2		7	5	6			9	8	11	4		12			1				3	10								29
	7		8	5	*6*		4	10	2	3			12			1					9				11	14			30
	7		8	5	6		4	10	2	3	12					1					9				11				31
	2		8	5	6		4	10		3				7		1					9				11	12			32
	2		8	5	6		4	10		11				7		1					9						3		33
	4			5				10	6	11	8			7		1					9			2			3		34
	7		8	5				10	6	11				4		1								2			3	9	35
	7			5	12		4	*10*	6	11				8		1					14			2			3	9	36
	2		8	5			4	10	6	11				7		1											3	9	37
	7			5		11	4		6	3	12			8		1					10			2				9	38
	7			5		11	4	10	6	3	12			8		1				14				*2*				9	39
	7		8	5	12		4	14	*6*	11						1					9			2			3	10	40
	7		8		5		4	10	6	11						1								2			3	9	41
	7				5	11	4	12	6	3	8					1					10			2				9	42

Coca-Cola Cup

First Round	Reading (h)	0-1
	(a)	0-3

FA Cup

First Round	Heybridge S (a)	2-0
Second Round	Fulham (h)	1-1
	(a)	2-1
Third Round	Sheffield W (h)	1-2

GRIMSBY TOWN 1994–95 *Back row (left to right):* Paul Groves, Paul Futcher, Steve Livingstone, Graham Rodger, Mark Lever, Peter Handyside, Neil Woods, Joby Gowshall, Clive Mendonca.

Centre row: Richard O'Kelly (Youth Coach), Tony Rees, Jim Dobbin, John Cook, Jimmy Neil, Paul Crichton, Rhys Wilmot, Simon Buckley, Jack Lester, Paul Agnew, Gary Croft, Paul Mitchell (Physio), Arthur Mann (Reserve Coach).

Front row: Darren Lambert, Tommy Watson, David Gilbert, Alan Buckley (Manager), Gary Childs, John McDermott, Kevin Jobling.

Division 1 **GRIMSBY TOWN**

Blundell Park, Cleethorpes, South Humberside DN35 7PY. Telephone: (01472) 697111. Fax: (01472) 693665. Clubcall: 0891 121576.

Ground capacity: 8,500 (approx).

Record attendance: 31,657 v Wolverhampton W, FA Cup 5th rd, 20 February 1937.

Record receipts: £119,799 v Aston Villa, FA Cup 4th rd, 29 January 1994.

Pitch measurements: 111yd × 75yd.

Presidents: T. J. Lindley, T. Wilkinson.

Chairman: W. H. Carr. ***Vice-Chairman:*** T. A. Aspinall.

Directors: P. W. Furneaux, G. Lamming, J. Mager.

Manager: Brian Laws. ***Assistant Manager:*** Kenny Swain.

Youth Team Coach: John Cockerill.

Company Secretary: Ian Fleming. ***Commercial Manager:*** Tony Richardson.

Lottery Manager: T. E. Harvey.

Physio: Paul Mitchell.

Year Formed. 1878. ***Turned Professional:*** 1890. ***Ltd Co.:*** 1890.

Previous Name: Grimsby Pelham.

Club Nickname: 'The Mariners'.

Previous Grounds: Clee Park; Abbey Park.

Foundation: Grimsby Pelham FC as they were first known, came into being at a meeting held at the Wellington Arms in September 1878. Pelham is the family name of big landowners in the area, the Earls of Yarborough. The receipts for their first game amounted to 6s. 9d. (approx. 39p). After a year, the club name was changed to Grimsby Town.

First Football League game: 3 September, 1892, Division 2, v Northwich Victoria (h) W 2-1 – Whitehouse; Lundie, T. Frith; C. Frith, Walker, Murrell; Higgins, Henderson, Brayshaw, Riddoch (2), Ackroyd.

Record League Victory: 9–2 v Darwen, Division 2, 15 April 1899 – Bagshaw; Lockie, Nidd; Griffiths, Bell (1), Nelmes; Jenkinson (3), Richards (1), Cockshutt (3), Robinson, Chadburn (1).

Record Cup Victory: 8–0 v Darlington, FA Cup, 2nd rd, 21 November 1885 – G. Atkinson; J. H. Taylor, H. Taylor; Hall, Kimpson, Hopewell; H. Atkinson (1), Garnham, Seal (3), Sharman, Monument (4).

Record Defeat: 1–9 v Arsenal, Division 1, 28 January 1931.

Most League Points (2 for a win): 68, Division 3 (N), 1955–56.

Most League Points (3 for a win): 83, Division 3, 1990–91.

Most League Goals: 103, Division 2, 1933–34.

Highest League Scorer in Season: Pat Glover, 42, Division 2, 1933–34.

Most League Goals in Total Aggregate: Pat Glover, 182, 1930–39.

Most Capped Player: Pat Glover, 7, Wales.

Most League Appearances: Keith Jobling, 448, 1953–69.

Record Transfer Fee Received: £650,000 from Sunderland for Shaun Cunnington, July 1992.

Record Transfer Fee Paid: £150,000 to Blackpool for Paul Groves, August 1992.

Football League Record: 1892 Original Member Division 2; 1901–03 Division 1; 1903 Division 2; 1910 Failed re-election; 1911 re-elected Division 2; 1920–21 Division 3; 1921–26 Division 3 (N); 1926–29 Division 2; 1929–32 Division 1; 1932–34 Division 2; 1934–48 Division 1; 1948–51 Division 2; 1951–56 Division 3 (N); 1956–59 Division 2; 1959–62 Division 3; 1962–64 Division 2; 1964–68 Division 3; 1968–72 Division 4; 1972–77 Division 3; 1977–79 Division 4; 1979–80 Division 3; 1980–87 Division 2; 1987–88 Division 3; 1988–90 Division 4; 1990–91 Division 3; 1991– 92 Division 2; 1992– Division 1.

Honours: *Football League:* Division 1 best season: 5th, 1934–35; Division 2 – Champions 1900–01, 1933–34; Runners-up 1928–29; Division 3 (N) – Champions 1925–26, 1955–56; Runners-up 1951–52; Division 3 – Champions 1979–80; Runners-up 1961–62; Division 4 – Champions 1971–72; Runners-up 1978–79; 1989–90. *FA Cup:* Semi-finals, 1936, 1939. *Football League Cup:* best season: 5th rd, 1980, 1985. *League Group Cup:* Winners 1982.

Colours: Black and white striped shirts, black shorts, white stockings. **Change colours:** Red and blue striped shirts, blue shorts, red stockings.

GRIMSBY TOWN 1994–95 LEAGUE RECORD

Match No.	Date		Venue	Opponents	Result		H/T Score	Lg. Pos.	Goalscorers	Attendance
1	Aug	13	H	Bolton W	D	3-3	1-2	—	Mendonca 3 (1 pen)	8393
2		20	A	Watford	D	0-0	0-0	13		6324
3		27	H	Tranmere R	W	3-1	2-0	6	Livingstone 2, Groves	4087
4		30	A	Sunderland	D	2-2	1-1	—	Childs, Mendonca (pen)	15,788
5	Sept	3	A	Derby Co	L	1-2	0-1	13	Mendonca	12,027
6		10	H	Charlton Ath	L	0-1	0-0	17		3970
7		13	H	Port Vale	W	4-1	1-0	—	Woods, Mendonca 2, Gilbert	3216
8		17	A	WBA	D	1-1	0-1	12	Shakespeare	14,496
9		24	A	Swindon T	L	2-3	1-1	14	Woods, Groves	8219
10	Oct	1	H	Portsmouth	W	2-0	1-0	11	Mendonca (pen), Woods	4172
11		8	H	Sheffield U	D	0-0	0-0	14		8930
12		15	A	Wolverhampton W	L	1-2	1-1	17	Groves	24,447
13		22	H	Bristol C	W	1-0	0-0	11	Childs	4024
14		29	A	Southend U	D	0-0	0-0	13		5086
15	Nov	1	A	Luton T	W	2-1	0-0	—	Gilbert 2	5839
16		5	H	Middlesbrough	W	2-1	2-0	6	Woods, Dobbin	8488
17		12	H	Millwall	W	1-0	0-0	5	Woods	5261
18		19	A	Stoke C	L	0-3	0-2	6		12,055
19		26	H	Burnley	D	2-2	1-0	7	Woods, Gilbert	7084
20	Dec	3	A	Bristol C	W	2-1	0-0	4	Gilbert, Childs	6030
21		10	H	Watford	D	0-0	0-0	8		6288
22		17	A	Bolton W	D	3-3	2-1	8	Woods, Jobling, Groves	10,522
23		26	A	Barnsley	L	1-4	1-2	9	Woods	8669
24		27	H	Oldham Ath	L	1-3	0-2	13	Woods	6958
25		31	A	Reading	D	1-1	1-0	13	Shakespeare	8526
26	Jan	14	H	Southend U	W	4-1	1-1	10	Shakespeare, Groves, Woods, Croft	3915
27		21	A	Middlesbrough	D	1-1	0-0	9	Woods	15,360
28		28	H	Notts Co	W	2-1	1-0	7	Woods, Mendonca	5161
29	Feb	4	A	Millwall	L	0-2	0-1	8		7397
30		11	H	Luton T	W	5-0	2-0	8	Dobbin, Gilbert, Woods, Watson 2	4615
31		18	A	Burnley	W	2-0	1-0	7	Mendonca 2	10,511
32		21	H	Stoke C	D	0-0	0-0	—		6384
33		25	A	Portsmouth	L	1-2	1-1	7	Rodger	8274
34	Mar	4	H	Swindon T	D	1-1	1-0	7	Watson	4934
35		7	H	Derby Co	L	0-1	0-0	—		5310
36		11	A	Tranmere R	L	0-2	0-2	9		15,810
37		19	H	Sunderland	W	3-1	1-0	9	Livingstone 2, Forrester	5697
38		21	A	Charlton Ath	L	1-2	1-1	—	Childs	9601
39		25	H	WBA	L	0-2	0-1	10		7393
40	Apr	1	A	Port Vale	W	2-1	2-0	9	Livingstone, Laws	7150
41		8	H	Reading	W	1-0	0-0	9	Livingstone	4519
42		15	A	Oldham Ath	L	0-1	0-1	10		6757
43		17	H	Barnsley	W	1-0	1-0	9	Woods	7277
44		22	A	Notts Co	W	2-0	1-0	9	Livingstone, Reece (og)	5286
45		29	H	Wolverhampton W	D	0-0	0-0	9		10,112
46	May	6	A	Sheffield U	L	1-3	1-2	10	Livingstone	14,323

Final League Position: 10

GOALSCORERS

League (62): Woods 14, Mendonca 11 (3 pens), Livingstone 8, Gilbert 6, Groves 5, Childs 4, Shakespeare 3, Watson 3, Dobbin 2, Croft 1, Forrester 1, Jobling 1, Laws 1, Rodger 1, own goal 1.
Coca-Cola Cup (2): Gilbert 1, Groves 1.
FA Cup (0).

Crichton P.A. 43	Jobling K.A. 37 + 1	Croft G. 44	Futcher P. 6 + 1	Lever M. 31	Shakespeare C.R. 16 + 3	Watson T.R. 20 + 1	Gilbert D.J. 40	Livingstone S. 29 + 5	Mendonca C.P. 21 + 1	Groves P. 46	Agnew P. 7 + 3	Lester J. 1 + 6	Handyside P.D. 34 + 1	Woods N.S. 33 + 4	Childs G.P.C. 18 + 7	Dobbin J. 35 + 3	McDermott J. 8 + 4	Rodger G. 20 + 1	Laws B. 6 + 10	Forrester J. 7 + 2	Fickling A. 1	Pearcey J.K. 3	Match No.
1	2	3	4	5	6	7	8	9	10	11	12												1
1		2	4	5	6		8	9	10	11	3		7	12									2
1		2	4	5	6		8	9	10	11	3	12			7								3
1	3	2	4	5	6		8	9	10	11			12	14	7								4
1	3	2	4	5	6		8	9	10	11	12			14	7								5
1		2		5	6		8		10	11	3		4	9	7	12							6
1		2		5	6		8	12	10	11	3		4	9	7								7
1		2		5	6		8	12	10	11	3		4	9	7	14							8
1		2		5	6		8	12	10	11	3		4	9		7							9
1	12	2		5	6		8		10	11	3		4	9		7							10
1	3	2		5	6	8			10	11		12	4	9		7							11
1	3	2	12	5	6	8		10		11			4	9	14	7							12
1	3	2		5	6	7		9		11			4	10	12	8							13
1	3	2		5		7	11	9		6			4	10		8							14
1	3	2		5		7	11	9		6	12		4	10		8							15
1	3	2		5		7	11	9		6			4	10		8							16
1	3	2		5		7	11	9		6			4	10		8							17
1	3	2		5		7	11	9		6			4	10	12	8	14						18
1	3	2		5			11	9		6			4	10	7	8							19
1	3	2		5			11	9		6		12	4	10	7	8		14					20
1	3	2					11	9		6			4	10	7	8	12	5					21
1	3	2					11	9		6			4	10	7	8	12	5					22
1	3	2			12		11	9		6		14	4	10	7	8	5						23
1		3	5		12	7	11		14	6		9	4	10		8	2						24
1		3			8	7	11		9	6		12	4	10			2	5					25
1	2	3			8	7	11		9	6			4	10				5					26
1	2	3		5		7	11	12	10	6			4	9		8	14						27
1	2	3		5		7	11		10	6			4	9		8			12				28
1	2	3		5		7	11		10	6			4	9	12	8			14				29
1	3			5		7	11		10	6			4	9	12	8	2		14				30
1	3					7	11		10	6			4	9		8	2	5	12				31
1	3	2				7	11		10	6			4	9		8		5	12				32
1	3	11				7		12	10	6			4	9		8	2	5	14				33
1	3	11				7			10	6			4	9		8	2	5					34
1	3	11				12	10	9		6			4		7	8	2	5	14				35
1	3	2					11	9		6			4		7	8		5	12	10			36
1	3	2					11	9		6			4		7	8		5		10			37
1	3	2					11	9		6			4		7	8		5	12	10			38
1	3	2		4	12		11	9		6					7	8		5	14	10			39
1	3	11		4				9		6					7	8		5	2	10			40
1	3	7		4			11	9		6		12				8		5	2	10			41
1	3	7					11	9		6				12		8		5	2	10	4		42
1	3	7		4			11	10		6				9	12	8		5	2	14			43
	3	7		4			11	10		6				9		8		5	2			1	44
	3	7		4			11	10		6				9	12	8		5	2			1	45
	3	2		4	8		11	10		6				9	7	12		5		14		1	46

Coca-Cola Cup
First Round — Bradford C (a) 1-2
(h) 1-2

FA Cup
Third Round — Norwich C (h) 0-1

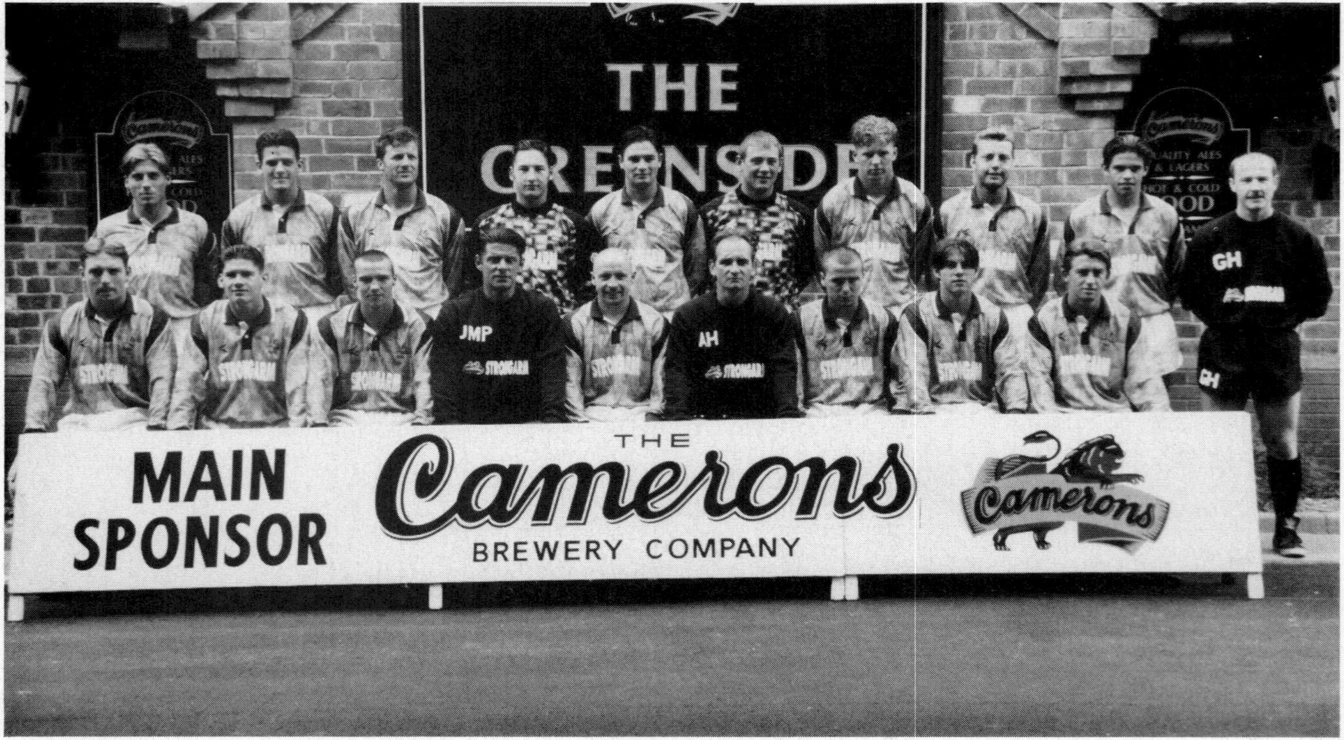

HARTLEPOOL UNITED 1994–95 *Back row (left to right):* Nicky Southall, Phil Gilchrist, Keith Houchen, Steven Jones, Ian McGuckin, Brian Horne, Matty Hyson, Jason Ainsley, Paul Thompson, Gary Henderson (Physio).

Front row: Scott Garrett, Chris Lynch, Denny Ingram, John MacPhail (Manager), Brian Honour, Alan Hay (Assistant Manager), Anthony Skedd, Stephen Halliday, Keith Oliver.

Division 3 HARTLEPOOL UNITED

The Victoria Ground, Clarence Road, Hartlepool, TS24 8BZ. Telephone: (01429) 272584. Commercial Dept: (01429) 222077. Fax: (01429) 863007. Football in the Community: (01429) 862595.

Ground capacity: 7985.

Record attendance: 17,426 v Manchester U, FA Cup 3rd rd, 5 January 1957.

Record receipts: £42,300 v Tottenham H, Rumbelows Cup, 2nd rd 2nd leg, 9 October 1990.

Pitch measurements: 110yd × 75yd.

President: E. Leadbitter.

Chairman: H. Hornsey.

Directors: A. Bamford, D. Jukes.

Manager: Keith Houchen. ***Coach:*** Mick Tait.

Youth/Reserve Coach: Eric Gates. ***Physio:*** Gary Henderson. ***Commercial Manager:*** Frank Baggs. ***Secretary:*** Stuart Bagnall.

Year Formed: 1908. ***Turned Professional:*** 1908. ***Ltd Co.:*** 1908.

Club Nickname: 'The Pool'.

Previous Names: Hartlepools United until 1968; Hartlepool until 1977.

Foundation: The inspiration for the launching of Hartlepool United was the West Hartlepool club which won the FA Amateur Cup in 1904–05. They had been in existence since 1881 and their Cup success led in 1908 to the formation of the new professional concern which first joined the North-Eastern League. In those days they were Hartlepools United and won the Durham Senior Cup in their first two seasons.

First Football League game: 27 August, 1921, Division 3(N), v Wrexham (a) W 2-0 – Gill; Thomas, Crilly; Dougherty, Hopkins, Short; Kessler, Mulholland (1), Lister (1), Robertson, Donald.

Record League Victory: 10–1 v Barrow, Division 4, 4 April 1959 – Oakley; Cameron, Waugh; Johnson, Moore, Anderson; Scott (1), Langland (1), Smith (3), Clark (2), Luke (2). (1 og).

Record Cup Victory: 6–0 v North Shields, FA Cup, 1st rd, 30 November 1946 – Heywood; Brown, Gregory; Spelman, Lambert, Jones; Price, Scott (2), Sloan (4), Moses, McMahon.

Record Defeat: 1–10 v Wrexham, Division 4, 3 March 1962.

Most League Points (2 for a win): 60, Division 4, 1967–68.

Most League Points (3 for a win): 82, Division 4, 1990–91.

Most League Goals: 90, Division 3 (N), 1956–57.

Highest League Scorer in Season: William Robinson, 28, Division 3 (N), 1927–28 and Joe Allon, 28, Division 4, 1990–91.

Most League Goals in Total Aggregate: Ken Johnson, 98, 1949–64.

Most Capped Player: Ambrose Fogarty, 1 (11), Republic of Ireland.

Most League Appearances: Wattie Moore, 447, 1948–64.

Record Transfer Fee Received: £300,000 from Chelsea for Joe Allon, August 1991.

Record Transfer Fee Paid: £60,000 to Barnsley for Andy Saville, March 1992.

Football League Record: 1921 Original Member of Division 3 (N); 1958–68 Division 4; 1968–69 Division 3; 1969–91 Division 4; 1991–92 Division 3; 1992–94 Division 2; 1994– Division 3.

Honours: *Football League:* Division 3 best season: 22nd, 1968–69; Division 3 (N) – Runners-up 1956–57. *FA Cup:* best season: 4th rd, 1955, 1978, 1989, 1993. *Football League Cup,* best season: 4th rd, 1975.

Colours: Blue and white striped shirts. **Change colours:** Red shirts with white trim.

HARTLEPOOL UNITED 1994–95 LEAGUE RECORD

Match No.	Date	Venue	Opponents	Result	H/T Score	Lg. Pos.	Goalscorers	Attendance
1	Aug 13	A	Gillingham	D 0-0	0-0	—		2956
2	20	H	Darlington	W 1-0	0-0	9	Lynch	3035
3	27	A	Bury	L 0-2	0-1	14		2145
4	30	H	Barnet	L 0-1	0-1	—		2095
5	Sept 3	H	Chesterfield	L 0-2	0-0	18		2173
6	10	A	Colchester U	L 0-1	0-0	20		2428
7	13	A	Northampton T	D 1-1	0-0	—	Halliday	2466
8	17	H	Gillingham	W 2-0	1-0	18	Houchen, Walsh (pen)	1756
9	24	H	Lincoln C	L 0-3	0-3	19		1419
10	Oct 1	A	Exeter C	L 1-2	1-1	21	Halliday	2390
11	8	A	Mansfield T	L 0-2	0-1	21		2545
12	15	H	Preston NE	W 3-1	2-1	20	Houchen, Ainsley, Foster	2002
13	22	H	Walsall	D 1-1	1-1	19	Houchen	1704
14	29	A	Scunthorpe U	D 0-0	0-0	20		2624
15	Nov 5	H	Wigan Ath	L 0-1	0-1	20		1683
16	19	A	Doncaster R	L 0-3	0-1	22		2507
17	26	H	Rochdale	W 1-0	1-0	19	Sloan	1387
18	Dec 10	A	Darlington	W 2-1	1-1	17	Southall, Houchen	3193
19	17	H	Bury	W 3-1	2-0	17	Houchen 3	1746
20	26	H	Carlisle U	L 1-5	0-1	17	Caig (og)	3854
21	27	A	Torquay U	D 2-2	1-1	16	Southall (pen), Thompson	3172
22	31	H	Fulham	L 1-2	1-1	16	Southall (pen)	1698
23	Jan 14	H	Scarborough	D 3-3	0-1	16	Thompson 2, Sloan	1784
24	28	H	Scunthorpe U	L 1-4	0-1	17	Thompson	1660
25	Feb 4	A	Rochdale	L 0-1	0-1	19		1848
26	18	A	Scarborough	D 2-2	1-1	21	McGuckin, Houchen	1517
27	21	A	Hereford U	L 0-1	0-0	—		1685
28	25	H	Exeter C	D 2-2	1-1	21	Houchen, McGuckin	1440
29	28	A	Wigan Ath	L 0-2	0-1	—		1452
30	Mar 4	A	Lincoln C	L 0-3	0-0	21		6477
31	7	A	Walsall	L 1-4	1-1	—	McGuckin	3314
32	11	H	Colchester U	W 3-1	2-1	20	Southall 3 (2 pens)	1371
33	18	A	Barnet	L 0-4	0-1	21		1557
34	21	H	Doncaster R	W 2-1	2-0	—	Houchen 2	1354
35	25	A	Chesterfield	L 0-2	0-1	20		4125
36	Apr 1	H	Northampton T	D 1-1	1-0	20	Houchen	2113
37	8	A	Fulham	L 0-1	0-0	20		3465
38	15	H	Torquay U	D 1-1	0-0	20	Henderson	1770
39	17	A	Carlisle U	W 1-0	1-0	20	Houchen	10,242
40	22	H	Hereford U	W 4-0	0-0	19	Holmes 2, Henderson 2	1596
41	29	A	Preston NE	L 0-3	0-2	20		9129
42	May 6	H	Mansfield T	W 3-2	1-0	18	Halliday 3	3049

Final League Position: 18

GOALSCORERS

League (43): Houchen 13, Southall 6 (4 pens), Halliday 5, Thompson 4, Henderson 3, McGuckin 3, Holmes 2, Sloan 2, Ainsley 1, Foster 1, Lynch 1, Walsh 1 (pen), own goal 1.
Coca-Cola Cup (5): Southall 2, Houchen 1, Thompson 1, own goal 1.
FA Cup (0).

Horne B. 41	Ingram S.D. 35	Sweeney P.M. 1	Gilchrist P.A. 23	McGuckin T.I. 34	Oliver K. 18	Ainsley J. 14 + 1	Sloan S.M. 26 + 3	Houchen K.M. 32	Honour B. 1	Southall L.N. 37	Skedd A.S. 17 + 6	Thompson P.D.Z. 24 + 4	Lynch C.J. 8 + 3	Halliday S.W. 19 + 9	Hyson M.A. 1 + 4	Tait M.P. 20	Garrett S. — + 1	Gourlay A.M. — + 1	Burgess D.J. 11	Walsh A. 4	McCreery D. 7 + 2	Foster W.P. 4	Cook M. 22 + 2	Reddish S. 23	MacPhail J. 6	Daughtry P.W. 14 + 1	Peverell N.J. — + 1	Jones S. 1 + 1	Sunley M. 1 + 1	Henderson D.M. 12	Holmes S.P. 5	Homer C. 1	Match No.
1	2	3	4	5	6	7	8	9	10	11																							1
1	2		4	5	6		8	9		11	3	7	10	12																			2
1	2		4	5		6		9		11	3	7	10	8	12																		3
1	2		4	5	6			9		11	3	7	10	8	12																		4
1	2		4	*5*	6	8		9		11	3	7	10	12	14																		5
1	2		4		6	8	11	9			*3*	7	10		12	5	14																6
1	2		4		6	8	11	9				7	3	10		5		12															7
1			4	5	6		11	9				7	12	10		8			2	3													8
1			4	5	6			9			14	7	12	10	*11*	8			2	3													9
1	8		4	5	6	11	12	9				7		10					2	3													10
1	8		4	5	6	11	14	9		7		12		10					2	*3*													11
1	3		4	5		6	7	9		11									2		8	10											12
1	3		4	5		6	7	9		11		12							2		8	10											13
1	3		4	5		6	7	9		11									2		8	10											14
1	3		4	5		6	*7*	9		11	14	12							2		8	10											15
1	10		4	5		*6*	9			11		7		12					2		14		3	8									16
1			4				10			11	6	9		12					2				3	8	5	7							17
1			4	5			10	9		11	6					8			2				3			7							18
1	2		4	5			10	9		11	6					8							3			7							19
1	2		4				10			11	6	9		12		5							3	8		7							20
1	2		4			8	10			11		9				6							3		5	7							21
1	2		4	5		8	10			11	3	9				6										7	12						22
1	2			5			*10*			11		9		12		6							3	8	4	7		15					23
	2			5			10			11		9		12		6							3	8	4	7		1					24
1	2		4	5		12	10			11		9		14		6							3	8		7							25
1	2			5			10	9		11	14	4				6					12		3	8		7							26
1	2			5			10	9		11		4				6							3	8		7							27
1	2			5			10	9		11	12	4		14		6							3	8		7							28
1	*2*			5			10	9		11	12			7		6							3	8	4				14				29
1					4		10	9		11				7		6							3	8	5				2				30
1				5	4		10			11	12			7		6					8		3	2						9			31
1				5	8			9		11				7		6							3	2						10	4		32
1	2			5				9		11				7									3	6		8				10	4		33
1	8			5			12	9		11	3			7		*6*								2		14				10	4		34
1	6			5				9		11	3	4		7										2		8				10			35
1	6			5				9		11	3	4		7							8		12	2						10			36
1	9									11	10	4	12	7							8		3	2						5		6	37
1	6				4		10	9		11	3	8		7									12	2						5			38
1	2			5	4			9		11	3												7	8						10	6		39
1	2			5	4			9		11			3										7	8						10	6		40
1	2			5	4			9		11	3	12		10									7	8						6			41
1	6			5	4			9		11			3	8									7	2						10			42

Coca-Cola Cup

First Round	Bury (a)	0-2
	(h)	5-1
Second Round	Arsenal (h)	0-5
	(a)	0-2

FA Cup

First Round	Port Vale (a)	0-6

HEREFORD UNITED 1994–95 *Back row (left to right):* Richard Wilkins, Michael Gonzague, Howard Clark, Chris Pike, Chris MacKenzie, Tony Pennock, Brian Thomas, Tony James, Gareth Davies, Paul Eversham.
Front row: Phil Preedy, Tim Steele, John Layton (Assistant Manager), Dean Smith, Greg Downs (Manager), Andy Reece, Nicky Cross.

Division 3 **HEREFORD UNITED**

Edgar Street, Hereford, HR4 9JU. Telephone: (01432) 276666. Fax: (01432) 341359.

Ground capacity: 9022.

Record attendance: 18,114 v Sheffield W, FA Cup 3rd rd, 4 January 1958.

Record receipts: £72,840 v Manchester U, FA Cup 4th rd, 28 January 1990.

Pitch measurements: 110yd × 74yd.

Chairman: P. S. Hill FRICS. ***Vice-Chairman:*** M. B. Roberts.

Directors: J. W. T. Duggan, D. H. Vaughan, R. A. Fry, J. Simmons, K. Benjamin (Assoc).

Manager: ***Assistant Manager:*** Dick Bate.

Physio: S. Shakesaft. ***Coach:*** S. Ritchie.

Secretary: J. Fennessy. ***Commercial Manager:*** M. Tranter.

Year Formed: 1924. ***Turned Professional:*** 1924. ***Ltd Co.:*** 1939.

Club Nickname: 'United'.

Foundation: A number of local teams amalgamated in 1924 under the chairmanship of Dr. E. W. Maples to form Hereford United and joined the Birmingham Combination. They graduated to the Birmingham League four years later.

First Football League game: 12 August, 1972, Division 4, v Colchester U (a) L 0-1 – Potter; Mallender, Naylor; Jones, McLaughlin, Tucker; Slattery, Hollett, Owen, Radford, Wallace.

Record League Victory: 6–0 v Burnley (away), Division 4, 24 January 1987 – Rose; Rodgerson, Devine, Halliday, Pejic, Dalziel, Harvey (1p), Wells, Phillips (3), Kearns (2), Spooner.

Record Cup Victory: 6–1 v QPR, FA Cup, 2nd rd, 7 December 1957 – Sewell; Tomkins, Wade; Masters, Niblett, Horton (2p); Reg Bowen (1), Clayton (1), Fidler, Williams (1), Cyril Beech (1).

Record Defeat: 1-7 v Mansfield T, Division 3, 26 December 1994.

Most League Points (2 for a win): 63, Division 3, 1975–76.

Most League Points (3 for a win): 77, Division 4, 1984–85.

Most League Goals: 86, Division 3, 1975–76.

Highest League Scorer in Season: Dixie McNeil, 35, 1975–76.

Most League Goals in Total Aggregate: Stewart Phillips, 93, 1980–88, 1990–1.

Most Capped Player: Brian Evans, 1 (7), Wales.

Most League Appearances: Mel Pejic, 412, 1980–92.

Record Transfer Fee Received: £440,000 from QPR for Darren Peacock, December 1990.

Record Transfer Fee Paid: £80,000 to Walsall for Dean Smith, June 1994.

Football League Record: 1972 Elected to Division 4; 1973–76 Division 3; 1976–77 Division 2; 1977–78 Division 3; 1978–92 Division 4; 1992– Division 3.

Honours: *Football League:* Division 2 best season: 22nd, 1976–77; Division 3 – Champions 1975–76; Division 4 – Runners-up 1972–73. *FA Cup:* best season: 4th rd, 1972, 1977, 1982, 1990. *Football League Cup:* best season: 3rd rd, 1975. *Welsh Cup:* Winners 1990.

Colours: White and black striped shirts, black shorts, black stockings. **Change colours:** Red and black striped shirts, white shorts, white stockings.

HEREFORD UNITED 1994–95 LEAGUE RECORD

Match No.	*Date*	*Venue*	*Opponents*	*Result*	*H/T Score*	*Lg. Pos.*	*Goalscorers*	*Attendance*
1	Aug 13	H	Doncaster R	L 0-1	0-1	—		3076
2	20	H	Preston NE	L 0-2	0-0	21		3039
3	27	H	Walsall	D 0-0	0-0	18		3004
4	30	A	Scarborough	L 1-3	0-1	—	Clark	1490
5	Sept 3	A	Rochdale	W 3-1	1-0	17	Preedy, James, White	2258
6	10	H	Wigan Ath	L 1-2	1-0	19	White	2771
7	13	H	Torquay U	D 1-1	1-0	—	White	2153
8	16	A	Doncaster R	L 0-3	0-2	—		1938
9	24	A	Fulham	D 1-1	1-0	21	White	3740
10	Oct 1	H	Scunthorpe U	W 2-1	1-1	18	Cross, White	2267
11	8	A	Barnet	D 2-2	1-1	18	White, Reece	2116
12	15	H	Gillingham	W 2-1	1-0	17	Cross, Davis	2472
13	22	A	Darlington	L 1-3	0-0	17	Cross	1996
14	29	H	Lincoln C	L 0-3	0-1	19		2485
15	Nov 5	A	Chesterfield	L 0-1	0-1	19		2448
16	19	H	Carlisle U	L 0-1	0-1	21		2531
17	26	A	Northampton T	W 3-1	0-0	18	Pick, Reece (pen), White	5148
18	Dec 10	A	Preston NE	L 2-4	0-3	20	Reece, Cross	6581
19	17	A	Walsall	L 3-4	2-1	20	Cross, James, White	3652
20	26	A	Mansfield T	L 1-7	0-1	21	Wilkins	2887
21	27	H	Exeter C	W 3-0	2-0	20	Lyne, Cross, Wilkins	2567
22	31	A	Colchester U	D 2-2	2-0	18	Brough, Whitton (og)	3322
23	Jan 7	H	Darlington	D 0-0	0-0	19		2237
24	14	A	Bury	D 1-1	0-1	19	Reece (pen)	2708
25	24	H	Chesterfield	L 0-2	0-1	—		1673
26	28	A	Lincoln C	L 0-2	0-0	19		2545
27	Feb 4	H	Northampton T	W 2-1	1-1	18	Lloyd, White	2365
28	11	A	Carlisle U	L 0-1	0-1	18		5676
29	18	H	Bury	W 1-0	1-0	18	Lloyd	1827
30	21	H	Hartlepool U	W 1-0	0-0	—	White	1685
31	25	A	Scunthorpe U	L 0-1	0-1	17		2193
32	Mar 4	H	Fulham	D 1-1	0-1	17	Pick	2895
33	18	H	Scarborough	W 2-1	0-0	17	Smith 2 (1 pen)	1479
34	25	H	Rochdale	D 0-0	0-0	17		1954
35	29	A	Wigan Ath	D 1-1	0-0	—	Pounder	1492
36	Apr 1	A	Torquay U	W 1-0	1-0	16	White	2410
37	8	H	Colchester U	W 3-0	2-0	16	White 2, Smith	1669
38	15	A	Exeter C	D 1-1	1-0	16	White	2083
39	17	H	Mansfield T	D 0-0	0-0	16		2743
40	22	A	Hartlepool U	L 0-4	0-0	16		1596
41	29	A	Gillingham	D 0-0	0-0	16		4208
42	May 6	H	Barnet	W 3-2	3-1	16	White, Pounder, Lloyd	2069

Final League Position: 16

GOALSCORERS

League (45): White 15, Cross 6, Reece 4 (2 pens), Lloyd 3, Smith 3 (1 pen), James 2, Pick 2, Pounder 2, Wilkins 2, Brough 1, Clark 1, Davis 1, Lyne 1, Preedy 1, own goal 1.
Coca-Cola Cup (2): White 2.
FA Cup (4): Lyne 2, Pick 1, White 1.

Pennock A. 13 + 2	Reece A.J. 35 + 2	Preedy P. 15 + 1	Davies G.M. 26 + 2	Smith D. 35	James A.C. 18	Wilkins R.J. 34 + 1	Pick G. 23 + 6	Cross N.J. 24 + 4	Clark H.W. 17 + 1	Steele T.W. 4 + 1	Downs G. 2 + 1	Clarke D.B. 3 + 2	Davis M.V. 1	White S.J. 31 + 5	Mackenzie C.N. 21 + 1	Pounder A.M. 23 + 5	Pike C. 2 + 2	Gonzague M. 2 + 1	Williams C.J. — + 2	Eversham P.J. 3 + 2	Lyne N.G.F. 27 + 4	Sheffield J. 8	Fishlock M.E. 12 + 2	Farrington M.A. — + 1	Llewellyn A.D. 3 + 1	Brough J.R. 16 + 2	Lloyd K. 24	Warner R.M. 15 + 1	Brownrigg A.D. 8	Gregory D. 2	Henderson D.M. 5	Stoker G. 10	Reeve J.M. — + 5	Hall L. — + 1	*Match No.*
1	2	3	4	5	6	7	8	9	*10*	11	12	14																							1
1	2	3	4	5	6	7	12	9		11	8		10																						2
1	6	11	*12*	4	5	7		10	2	8	3			9					14																3
1	4	11	3	5	6	7		9	2			*8*		10	15																				4
1	12	*3*		5	6	7	4	9	2					10		8	11	14																	5
1	4		3	5	6	7		9	2					10		8	11		12																6
	4		3	5	6	7		9	2					10	1	8	12			11	14														7
	4	3		5	6		12	*9*	2	7				10			14			8	11	1													8
	4	3	11	5	6	7	8	9	2					10							12	1													9
	4	11		5	6	12	8	9	2					10						7		1	3												10
	4	11		5	6	7	8	9	2					10								1	3												11
	4	11	12	5	6	7	*8*	9	2					10								1	3	14											12
	4	11	5		6		8	9						10		7		2		12		1	3												13
	4	11	5		6	8		9						10		7		*2*		14	12	1	3												14
	4	11	5		6	8		9						10		7					12	1	3		*2*	14									15
1	6	14	5	4		8	11	9						12		7					10		3			*2*									16
1	2		5	4		8	11							9		7					10		6			12	3								17
1	2		*11*	4	6		8	12						9		7					10		5		14		3								18
1	4	11		5	6	7		8						9							10				2		3								19
1	4	*11*		5	6	7	12	8						9		14					10				2		3								20
	4			5		7	11	8							1	12					10					9	3	2	6						21
	4		7	5			11	8							1	12					10					9	3	2	6						22
	4			5			11		7	12				8	1						10					9	3	2	6						23
15	4			5		7	*11*	12						10	1						9					8	3	2	6						24
	4			5		7		11	*6*					12	1	14					10					9	3	2		8					25
1	4		2	5		6		12						14							10					9	3	7		*8*	11				26
	4		8	5		7								10	1						11						3	2	6		9				27
	4		8			7	12							10	1	14					11					5	*3*	2	6		9				28
	4		8			7								12	1	11					9					5	3	2	6		10				29
	4		8			7								12	1	11					10					5	3	2	6		9				30
	4		8	5		7		9							1	11					10					6	3	2							31
	4		8	5		7	12	14	*3*					9	1	11					10					6		2							32
15			8	5		7	12	9	14						*1*	11					10		3			6		*2*				4			33
			8	5		7	4	*9*						10	1	11							12			6	3					2	14		34
1				5		7	4							9		11					10		3			6	8					2	12		35
			8	5		7	4							9	1	11					10		12			6	*3*					2	14		36
			8	5		7	4							9	1	11					10		3				6	12				2			37
	12		8	5		7	4							9	1	11					*10*						6	3				2	14		38
	6		8	5			4					12		9	1	11					10						3	2				7			39
	4			5			8		6			2		*9*	1	11					10						3					7	14	12	40
	4			5		7	8		6					9	1	11					10						3					2			41
	4					7	8		6			3		9	1	11					10						5					2			42

Coca-Cola Cup

First Round	WBA (h)	0-0
	(a)	1-0
Second Round	Nottingham F (a)	1-2
	(h)	0-0

FA Cup

First Round	Hitchin (h)	2-2
	(a)	2-4

HUDDERSFIELD TOWN 1994–95 *Back row (left to right):* Jon Whitney, Michael Midwood, Rodney Rowe, Robbie Ryan, Kevin Blackwell, Steve Francis, Chris Billy, Gary Glayton, Stephen Payne, Simon Collins.
Centre row: Mick Jones (Assistant Manager), Richard Logan, Jonathan Dyson, Kevin Gray, Pat Scully, Peter Jackson, Andrew Booth, Graham Mitchell, Ronnie Jepson, Dave Wilson (Physio).
Front row: Simon Trevitt, Simon Baldry, Tom Cowan, Phil Starbuck, Neil Warnock (Manager), Darren Bullock, Iain Dunn, Paul Robinson, Paul Reid.

Division 1 HUDDERSFIELD TOWN

The Alfred McAlpine Stadium, Leeds Rd, Huddersfield HD1 6PX. Telephone: (01484) 420335. Fax: (01484) 515122. Ticket Office: (01484) 424444. Club Shop: (01484) 534867. Recorded Information: 0891 121635.

Ground capacity: 19,500.

Record attendance: 67,037 v Arsenal, FA Cup 6th rd, 27 February 1932 (at new ground): 18,775 v Birmingham C, Division 2, 6 May 1995.

Record receipts: £89,081 v Arsenal, Coca-Cola Cup, 2nd rd lst leg, 21 September 1993 (at new ground): £110,850 v Southampton, Coca-Cola Cup, 20 September 1994.

Pitch measurements: 115yd × 76yd.

Chairman: D. G. Headey.

Directors: M. Asquith, D. Taylor, R. Whiteley.

Associate Director: T. J. Cherry.

Manager: Brian Horton. ***Assistant Managers:*** David Moss, Dennis Booth.

Secretary: Alan D. Sykes. ***Commercial Manager:*** Alan Stevenson. ***Chief Executive:*** Paul Fletcher.

Physio: Dave Wilson.

Year Formed: 1908. ***Turned Professional:*** 1908. ***Ltd Co.:*** 1908.

Club Nickname: 'The Terriers'.

Foundation: A meeting, attended largely by members of the Huddersfield & District FA, was held at the Imperial Hotel in 1906 to discuss the feasibility of establishing a football club in this rugby stronghold. However, it was not until a man with both the enthusiasm and the money to back the scheme came on the scene, that real progress was made. This benefactor was Mr. Hilton Crowther and it was at a meeting at the Albert Hotel in 1908, that the club formally came into existence with a capital of £2,000 and joined the North-Eastern League.

First Football League game: 3 September, 1910, Division 2, v Bradford PA (a) W 1-0 – Mutch; Taylor, Morris; Beaton, Hall, Bartlett; Blackburn, Wood, Hamilton (1), McCubbin, Jee.

Record League Victory: 10–1 v Blackpool, Division 1, 13 December 1930 – Turner; Goodall, Spencer; Redfern, Wilson, Campbell; Bob Kelly (1), McLean (4), Robson (3), Davies (1), Smailes (1).

Record Cup Victory: 7–1 v Chesterfield (away), FA Cup, 3rd rd, 12 January 1929 – Turvey; Goodall, Wadsworth; Evans, Wilson, Naylor: Jackson (1), Kelly, Brown (3), Cumming (2), Smith. (1 o.g).

Record Defeat: 1–10 v Manchester C, Division 2, 7 November 1987.

Most League Points (2 for a win): 66, Division 4, 1979–80.

Most League Points (3 for a win): 82, Division 3, 1982–83.

Most League Goals: 101, Division 4, 1979–80.

Highest League Scorer in Season: Sam Taylor, 35, Division 2, 1919–20; George Brown, 35, Division 1, 1925–26.

Most League Goals in Total Aggregate: George Brown, 142, 1921–29 and Jimmy Glazzard, 142, 1946–56.

Most Capped Player: Jimmy Nicholson, 31 (41), Northern Ireland.

Most League Appearances: Billy Smith, 520, 1914–34.

Record Transfer Fee Received: £375,000 from Southampton for Simon Charlton, June 1993.

Record Transfer Fee Paid: £250,000 to Bradford C for Lee Duxbury, December 1994.

Football League Record: 1910 Elected to Division 2; 1920–52 Division 1; 1952–53 Division 2; 1953–56 Division 1; 1956–70 Division 2; 1970–72 Division 1; 1972–73 Division 2; 1973–75 Division 3; 1975–80 Division 4; 1980–83 Division 3; 1983–88 Division 2; 1988–92 Division 3; 1992–95 Division 2; 1995– Division 1.

Honours: *Football League:* Division 1 – Champions 1923–24, 1924–25, 1925–26; Runners-up 1926–27, 1927–28, 1933–34; Division 2 – Champions 1969–70; Runners-up 1919–20, 1952–53; Division 4 – Champions 1979–80. *FA Cup:* Winners 1922; Runners-up 1920, 1928, 1930, 1938. *Football League Cup:* Semi-final 1968. *Autoglass Trophy:* Runners-up 1994.

Colours: Blue and white striped shirts, white shorts, white stockings. **Change colours:** White shirts with black sleeves, black shorts, white stockings.

HUDDERSFIELD TOWN 1994–95 LEAGUE RECORD

Match No.	Date	Venue	Opponents	Result		H/T Score	Lg. Pos.	Goalscorers	Attendance
1	Aug 13	A	Blackpool	W	4-1	2-0	—	Reid 2, Jepson 2	8343
2	20	H	Wycombe W	L	0-1	0-1	12		13,334
3	27	A	Chester C	W	2-1	1-0	8	Booth, Dunn	2895
4	30	H	Leyton Orient	W	2-1	0-1	—	Booth, Reid	8552
5	Sept 3	H	Oxford U	D	3-3	1-2	5	Booth, Starbuck (pen), Bullock	10,122
6	10	A	Plymouth Arg	W	3-0	2-0	4	Booth 3	5464
7	13	A	Peterborough U	D	2-2	1-2	—	Dunn 2	5316
8	17	H	Stockport Co	W	2-1	1-1	2	Booth 2	9526
9	24	A	Bradford C	W	4-3	1-0	2	Booth 2, Jepson, Reid	11,300
10	Oct 1	H	Brighton & HA	W	3-0	1-0	1	Booth, Reid, Logan	10,321
11	8	A	Birmingham C	D	1-1	1-1	1	Bullock	15,265
12	15	H	Cambridge U	W	3-1	0-1	1	Jepson 2 (1 pen), Dunn	10,742
13	22	A	Crewe Alex	D	3-3	2-3	1	Jepson, Billy, Booth	5352
14	29	H	Bournemouth	W	3-1	2-0	1	Booth, Jepson, Scully	11,251
15	Nov 1	H	Wrexham	W	2-1	1-0	—	Bullock, Billy	9639
16	5	A	York C	L	0-3	0-2	1		6345
17	19	H	Brentford	W	1-0	0-0	1	Jepson	10,889
18	26	A	Bristol R	D	1-1	1-1	2	Jepson (pen)	5679
19	Dec 10	A	Wycombe W	L	1-2	1-0	4	Jepson	6790
20	17	H	Blackpool	D	1-1	0-0	4	Booth	11,536
21	26	A	Hull C	L	0-1	0-0	4		10,220
22	27	H	Rotherham U	W	1-0	1-0	4	Booth	15,557
23	31	A	Swansea C	D	1-1	0-0	4	Booth	5438
24	Jan 2	H	Shrewsbury T	W	2-1	1-1	2	Jepson, Duxbury	12,748
25	7	H	Crewe Alex	L	1-2	1-1	2	Booth	11,466
26	14	A	Cardiff C	D	0-0	0-0	2		3808
27	28	A	Bournemouth	W	2-0	0-0	2	Jepson, Duxbury	4427
28	Feb 4	H	Bristol R	D	1-1	0-1	3	Booth	10,389
29	11	A	Wrexham	W	2-1	0-1	2	Booth, Jepson	5894
30	18	H	Cardiff C	W	5-1	4-0	2	Booth, Cowan, Jepson, Reid, Crosby	10,035
31	21	A	Brentford	D	0-0	0-0	—		9562
32	25	A	Brighton & HA	D	0-0	0-0	3		7751
33	28	H	York C	W	3-0	1-0	—	Jepson, Bullock, Crosby	10,468
34	Mar 4	H	Bradford C	D	0-0	0-0	1		17,404
35	7	A	Oxford U	L	1-3	0-0	—	Dyson	7160
36	11	H	Chester C	W	5-1	3-1	2	Cowan, Jepson, Booth 3	9606
37	18	A	Leyton Orient	W	2-0	0-0	2	Dunn, Jepson (pen)	3177
38	21	H	Plymouth Arg	W	2-0	1-0	—	Dyson, Booth	12,099
39	25	A	Stockport Co	W	2-1	1-0	1	Jepson (pen), Gannon (og)	5383
40	Apr 1	H	Peterborough U	L	1-2	0-1	2	Bullock	11,324
41	8	H	Swansea C	W	2-0	1-0	1	Crosby 2	10,105
42	15	A	Rotherham U	D	1-1	0-0	1	Booth	6687
43	17	H	Hull C	D	1-1	0-0	2	Sinnott	12,402
44	22	A	Shrewsbury T	L	1-2	0-2	3	Jepson (pen)	4758
45	29	A	Cambridge U	D	1-1	1-1	3	Booth	5188
46	May 6	H	Birmingham C	L	1-2	0-0	5	Bullock	18,775

Final League Position: 5

GOALSCORERS

League (79): Booth 26, Jepson 19 (5 pens), Bullock 6, Reid 6, Dunn 5, Crosby 4, Billy 2, Cowan 2, Duxbury 2, Dyson 2, Logan 1, Scully 1, Sinnott 1, Starbuck 1 (pen), own goal 1.
Coca-Cola Cup (4): Jepson 2, Reid 1, Scully 1.
FA Cup (4): Booth 1, Bullock 1, Dunn 1, Jepson 1.

Francis S.S. 43	Billy C.A. 30 + 7	Cowan T. 37	Starbuck P.M. 4 + 5	Scully P.J. 38	Mitchell G.L. 11 + 1	Baldry S. 8 + 3	Bullock D.J. 39	Booth A.D. 45 + 1	Jepson R.F. 36 + 5	Reid P.R. 42	Dyson J.P. 23 + 5	Dunn I.G.W. 13 + 26	Logan R.A. 24 + 3	Trevitt S. 20 + 1	Whitington C. 1	Gray K.J. 5	Crosby G. 16 + 3	Blackwell K.P. 3 + 1	Williams P.R. 9	Short C.M. 6	Sinnott L. 25	Duxbury L.E. 26	Clayton G. — + 2	Moulden P.A. — + 2	Collins S. 2 + 2	Match No.
1	2	3	4	5	6	7	8	9	10	11	12	14														1
1	2	3	4	5	6	7	8	9	10	11		12														2
1	2	3	10	5		7	8	9		11	6	12	4	14												3
1	2	3		5		7	8	9		11	6	12	4		10											4
1	2	3	7		12	14	8	9		11	6	10	4			5										5
1	2	3		5	6	7	8	9	14	11	12	10	4													6
1	2	3		5	6	7	8	9		11	12	10	4													7
1	2	3	12	5		7	8	9	14	11	6	10	4													8
1	2	3	12	5			8	9	14	11	6	10	4	7												9
1		3	12	5			8	9	10	11	6		4	2			7									10
1		3		5			8	9	10	11	6		4	2			7	15								11
		3	12	5			8	9	10	11	6	14	4	2			7	1								12
	7	3	14	5			8	9	10	11	6	12	4	2				1								13
1	7	3		5	6		8	9	10	11		12	4	2			14									14
1	7	3		5	6		8	9	10	11			4	2												15
1	7	3		5	6		8	9	10	11	4	14	12	2												16
1	7			5	6		8	9	10	11		12	4	2					3							17
	7			5	6		8	9	10	11			4	2				1	3							18
1	7	3			6		8	9	10	11		14	12	2		5	4									19
1	7	3			6		8	9	10	11		14	4	2		5	12									20
1	12	3		5			8	9	10	11		14	4							2	6	7				21
1	7	3						9	10	11	5	12	4							2	6	8				22
1	7	3						9	12	11	5	10	4							2	6	8	14			23
1	7	3						9	10	11	5	12	4							2	6	8				24
1		3				7	4	9	10	11	5	12					14			2	6	8				25
1	12	3		5				14	10	11		9	4				7			2	6	8				26
1	7	3		5				9	10			12	4	2			11				6	8				27
1	7	3		5				9	10			12	4	2			11				6	8	14			28
1		3		5			4	9	10	11				2			7				6	8				29
1	12	3		5			4	9	10	11		14		2			7				6	8				30
1		3		5			4	9	10	11				2			7				6	8				31
1	12	3		5			4	9	10	11		14		2			7				6	8				32
1	2	3		5			4	9	10	11	14	12					7				6	8				33
1	2	3		5			4	9	10	11		12					7				6	8				34
1	2	3		5			4	9	10	11	14	12					7				6	8				35
1	7	3		5		14	4	9	10	11	2	12									6	8				36
1				5			4	9	10	11	2	7							3		6	8				37
1				5		12	4	9	10	11	2	7							3		6	8				38
1	12			5			4	9	10	11	2	7				6			3			8				39
1	12			5			4	9	10	11	2	7							3		6	8		14		40
1	7						4	9	12	11	2					5	10		3		6	8				41
1	7			5			4	9		11	2	12	14				10		3		6	8				42
1	7			5			4	9	10	11	2	12							3		6	8			14	43
1	7	3		5				9	10	11	2	12	4								6	8			14	44
1		3		5			4	9	10			11		2							6	8			7	45
1	12	3		5			4	9	10			11		2							6	8		14	7	46

Coca-Cola Cup

First Round	Scunthorpe U (a)		1-2
	(h)		3-0
Second Round	Southampton (h)		0-1
	(a)		0-4

FA Cup

First Round	Doncaster R (a)	4-1
Second Round	Lincoln C (a)	0-1

HULL CITY 1994–95 *Back row (left to right):* David Mail, Gary Hobson, Chris Hargreaves, Steve Wilson, Rob Dewhurst, Alan Fettis, Neil Allison, Graeme Atkinson, Matthew Edeson.
Centre row: Billy Legg (Under-16s Manager), Jamie Cass, Dean Windass, Neil Mann, Simon Dakin, Richard Peacock, Jimmy Graham, Brian Mitchell, Bernard Ellison (Chief Scout/Youth Team Manager), Jeff Radcliffe (Physio).
Front row: Steve Moran, Linton Brown, Greg Abbott, Terry Dolan (Manager), Jeff Lee (Assistant Manager), Craig Lawford, Chris Lee, Adam Lowthorpe.

Division 2 **HULL CITY**

Boothferry Park, Hull HU4 6EU. Telephone: (01482) 351119. Fax: (01482) 565752. Commercial Manager: (01482) 566050. Football in the Community Office: (01482) 565088.

Ground capacity: 16,564.

Record attendance: 55,019 v Manchester U, FA Cup 6th rd, 26 February 1949.

Record receipts: £79,604 v Liverpool FA Cup, 5th rd, 18 February 1989.

Pitch measurements: 115yd × 75yd.

President: T. C. Waite FIMI, MIRTE.

Honorary Vice-President: D. Robinson, H. Bermitz, J. Johnson BA, DPA.

Vice-Presidents: R. Beercock, K. Davis, N. Howe, R. Booth, A. Fetiveau, W. Law.

Chairman: M. W. Fish MCA. ***Vice-Chairman:*** R. M. Chetham.

Directors: G. H. C. Needler MA, FCA, .

Manager: Terry Dolan. ***Assistant Manager:*** Jeff Lee.

Secretary: M. W. Fish. ***Physio:*** Jeff Radcliffe MCSP, SRP.

Commercial Manager: Simon Cawkhill. ***Stadium Manager:*** John Cooper.

Ticket Office/Gate Manager: Wilf Rogerson. ***Hon. Medical Officers:*** G. Hoyle, MBCHB, FRCS, Dr. B. Kell, MBBS.

Year Formed: 1904. ***Turned Professional:*** 1905. ***Ltd Co.:*** 1905.

Club Nickname: 'The Tigers'.

Previous Grounds: 1904, Boulevard Ground (Hull RFC); 1905, Anlaby Road (Hull CC); 1944/5 Boulevard Ground; 1946, Boothferry Park.

Foundation: The enthusiasts who formed Hull City in 1904 were brave men indeed. More than that they were audacious for they immediately put the club on the map in this Rugby League fortress by obtaining a three-year agreement with the Hull Rugby League club to rent their ground! They had obtained quite a number of conversions to the dribbling code, before the Rugby League forbade the use of any of their club grounds by Association Football clubs. By that time, Hull City were well away having entered the FA Cup in their initial season and the Football League, Second Division after only a year.

First Football League game: 2 September, 1905, Division 2, v Barnsley (h) W 4-1 – Spendiff; Langley, Jones; Martin, Robinson, Gordon (2); Rushton, Spence (1), Wilson (1), Howe, Raisbeck.

Record League Victory: 11–1 v Carlisle U, Division 3 (N), 14 January 1939 – Ellis; Woodhead, Dowen; Robinson (1), Blyth, Hardy; Hubbard (2), Richardson (2), Dickinson (2), Davies (2), Cunliffe (2).

Record Cup Victory: 8–2 v Stalybridge Celtic (away), FA Cup, 1st rd, 26 November 1932 – Maddison; Goldsmith, Woodhead; Gardner, Hill (1), Denby; Forward (1), Duncan, McNaughton (1), Wainscoat (4), Sargeant (1).

Record Defeat: 0–8 v Wolverhampton W, Division 2, 4 November 1911.

Most League Points (2 for a win): 69, Division 3, 1965–66.

Most League Points (3 for a win): 90, Division 4, 1982–83.

Most League Goals: 109, Division 3, 1965–66.

Highest League Scorer in Season: Bill McNaughton, 39, Division 3 (N), 1932–33.

Most League Goals in Total Aggregate: Chris Chilton, 195, 1960–71.

Most Capped Player: Terry Neill, 15 (59), Northern Ireland.

Most League Appearances: Andy Davidson, 520, 1952–67.

Record Transfer Fee Received: £750,000 from Middlesbrough for Andy Payton, November 1991.

Record Transfer Fee Paid: £200,000 to Leeds U for Peter Swan, March 1989.

Football League Record: 1905 Elected to Division 2; 1930–33 Division 3 (N); 1933–36 Division 2; 1936–49 Division 3 (N); 1949–56 Division 2; 1956–58 Division 3 (N); 1958–59 Division 3; 1959–60 Division 2; 1960–66 Division 3; 1966–78 Division 2; 1978–81 Division 3; 1981–83 Division 4; 1983–85 Division 3; 1985–91 Division 2; 1991– 92 Division 3; 1992– Division 2.

Honours: *Football League:* Division 2 best season: 3rd, 1909–10; Division 3 (N) – Champions 1932–33, 1948–49; Division 3 – Champions 1965–66; Runners-up 1958–59; Division 4 – Runners-up 1982–83. *FA Cup:* best season: Semi-final 1930. *Football League Cup:* best season: 4th, 1974, 1976, 1978. *Associate Members' Cup:* Runners-up 1984.

Colours: Black and amber striped shirts, black shorts, amber stockings with two black hoops and black turnover. **Change colours:** White and jade.

HULL CITY 1994–95 LEAGUE RECORD

Match No.	Date	Venue	Opponents	Result	H/T Score	Lg. Pos.	Goalscorers	Attendance
1	Aug 13	A	Oxford U	L 0-4	0-4	—		5485
2	20	H	Swansea C	L 0-2	0-0	24		3797
3	27	A	Leyton Orient	D 1-1	0-0	21	Brown	3243
4	30	H	Plymouth Arg	W 2-0	0-0	—	Mann, Lee	3384
5	Sept 3	H	Chester C	W 2-0	1-0	14	Brown, Windass	3615
6	10	A	Peterborough U	L 1-2	1-1	17	Peacock	5044
7	13	A	Wycombe W	W 2-1	1-0	—	Dakin, Abbott	4626
8	17	H	Rotherham U	L 0-2	0-2	16		4431
9	24	A	Birmingham C	D 2-2	1-1	17	Windass (pen), Peacock	12,192
10	Oct 1	H	Bournemouth	W 3-1	2-1	14	Brown, Dewhurst, Atkinson	3056
11	8	H	Blackpool	W 1-0	1-0	12	Gouck (og)	3829
12	15	A	Wrexham	D 2-2	1-0	11	Lawford, Windass	3418
13	22	A	Shrewsbury T	W 3-2	2-0	11	Peacock, Dewhurst, Lawford	3685
14	29	H	Crewe Alex	W 7-1	2-0	8	Windass 2, Peacock, Brown 3, Dewhurst	4694
15	Nov 1	H	York C	W 3-0	3-0	—	Brown, Windass, Lawford	6551
16	5	A	Brentford	W 1-0	0-0	4	Dewhurst	5455
17	19	H	Bristol R	L 0-2	0-1	5		4450
18	25	A	Cardiff C	W 2-0	2-0	—	Brown, Windass (pen)	4226
19	Dec 10	A	Swansea C	L 0-2	0-1	5		4903
20	17	H	Oxford U	W 3-1	2-1	5	Windass 2, Fettis	4884
21	26	H	Huddersfield T	W 1-0	0-0	5	Peacock	10,220
22	28	A	Bradford C	L 0-1	0-0	—		7312
23	31	H	Brighton & HA	D 2-2	1-1	7	Brown, Windass	5099
24	Jan 2	A	Cambridge U	D 2-2	2-0	6	Brown, Windass	3569
25	7	H	Shrewsbury T	D 2-2	0-2	7	Windass (pen), Cox	4369
26	14	A	Stockport Co	L 0-4	0-1	7		4516
27	21	H	Brentford	L 1-2	0-0	7	Joyce	3823
28	Feb 4	H	Cardiff C	W 4-0	2-0	7	Ormondroyd 2, Brown, Joyce	3903
29	18	H	Stockport Co	D 0-0	0-0	9		4576
30	25	A	Bournemouth	W 3-2	3-2	9	Ormondroyd 2, Mann	4345
31	Mar 1	A	Bristol R	W 2-0	1-0	—	Brown, Ormondroyd	3707
32	4	H	Birmingham C	D 0-0	0-0	8		9854
33	11	H	Leyton Orient	W 2-0	1-0	7	Dewhurst, Joyce	4519
34	18	A	Plymouth Arg	L 1-2	1-2	9	Ormondroyd	4839
35	21	H	Peterborough U	D 1-1	1-1	—	Breen (og)	4609
36	25	A	Rotherham U	L 0-2	0-1	11		3692
37	28	A	Chester C	W 2-1	0-0	—	Abbott, Lund	1191
38	Apr 1	H	Wycombe W	D 0-0	0-0	9		5054
39	4	A	York C	L 1-3	0-1	—	Windass	4612
40	8	A	Brighton & HA	L 0-1	0-0	11		6038
41	15	H	Bradford C	W 2-0	2-0	10	Windass 2 (1 pen)	4368
42	17	A	Huddersfield T	D 1-1	0-0	8	Dewhurst	12,402
43	22	H	Cambridge U	W 1-0	0-0	9	Dewhurst	3483
44	29	H	Wrexham	W 3-2	2-1	9	Dewhurst, Lund, Windass	3683
45	May 2	A	Crewe Alex	L 2-3	2-2	—	Abbott, Lund	3870
46	6	A	Blackpool	W 2-1	1-1	8	Windass (pen), Fettis	4251

Final League Position: 8

GOALSCORERS

League (70): Windass 17 (5 pens), Brown 12, Dewhurst 8, Ormondroyd 6, Peacock 5, Abbott 3, Joyce 3, Lawford 3, Lund 3, Fettis 2, Mann 2, Atkinson 1, Cox 1, Dakin 1, Lee 1, own goals 2.
Coca-Cola Cup (2): Lee 1, Peacock 1.
FA Cup (0).

Fettis A. 27 + 1	Dakin S.M. 19 + 2	Graham J. 39	Allison N.J. 11 + 2	Dewhurst R.M. 41	Abbott G.S. 22 + 4	Peacock R.J. 28 + 9	Lee C. 42 + 3	Hargreaves C. 13 + 8	Windass D. 43 + 1	Lawford C.B. 25 + 6	Hobson G. 35 + 1	Brown L. 32 + 1	Lowthorpe A. 21 + 1	Atkinson G. 7 + 2	Mann N. 29 + 2	Mail D. 10 + 4	Wilson S.L. 20	Wallace R.G. 7	Cox P.R. 5	Joyce W.G. 9	Ormondroyd I. 10	Lund G.J. 11	Edeson M.K. — + 3	Fewings P.J. — + 2	Match No.
1	2	3	4	5	6	7	*8*	9	10	11	12	14													1
1		3		5		7	8	6	10	11	4	9	2	12											2
1		3		5		7	8		10	12	4	9	2	11	6										3
1		3		5			8		10	11	4	9	2	7	6										4
1		3		5	12	14	8		10	11	4	9	2	*7*	6										5
1		3		5		7	8		10	11	4	9	2	12	6										6
1	7	3		5	6		8		10			9	2	11		4									7
1	*7*	3		5	6	14	8	12	10			9	2	11		4									8
1		3		5	6	7	8	9	10		4			11		2									9
	2	3		5	6	7	8	10			4	9		11			1								10
	2	3		5		7	8	10		11	4	9			6		1								11
	2	3		5		7	8	10	12	11	4	9			6		1								12
		3		5		7	8	12	10	11	4	9	2		6		1								13
		3		5	14	7	*8*	12	10	11	4	9	2		6		1								14
		3		5	14	7	8	12	10	11	4	9	*2*		6		1								15
	2	3		5		7	8	12	10	11	4	9			6		1								16
	2	3		5	14		8	*7*	10	11	4	9			6	12	1								17
	2	3		5	6	7	8		10	11	4	9					1								18
	2	3	12	5	6	7	8		10	11	4	9			14		1								19
12		3			6	7			10	11	4	9			8		1	2	5						20
		3		5	6	7	12		10	11	4	9			8		1	2							21
		3		*5*	6	7	8	12	10	11	4	9				14	1	2							22
		3			6	7	12		10	11	4	9			8		1	2	5						23
		3				7	6	12	10	11	4	9			8		1	2	5						24
		3				7	6	12	10	11	*4*	9			8	14	1	2	5						25
		3		7		12	6		10	11		9			8	4	1	2	5						26
1		3		5			6	9	10	11	4		2		8					7					27
1		3	6	5		12	14		10		4	9	2		*8*					7	11				28
1		3	6	5			2		10		4	9			8					7	11				29
1		3	6	5			2		10		4	9			8					7	11				30
1		3	6	5			2		10		4	9			8					7	11				31
1		3	6	5		12	2		10		4	9			8					7	11				32
1		3	6	5		12	2		10		4	9			8					7	11				33
1	4	*3*	6	5		12	2		10	14		9			8					7	11				34
1		3	6	5		8	2		10	12	4	9								7	11				35
	12	3	6	5	*8*	7	2		10	14	4						1				11	9			36
	4	*3*		5	8		2		10	14			12		7	6	1				11	9			37
1	5	3			8	12	2		10	14	4		*11*		7	6						9			38
1	5	*3*		6	8		7		10	11	4		2		12	14						9			39
1				5	8	12	7		10	3	6		2		11	4						9			40
1	12			5	6	7	8		10	3	4		2		*11*							9	14		41
1	4			5	6	7	8	11	10				2			3						9			42
1	4			5	6	7	8	11	10				2			3						9	12		43
1	4		12	5	6	7	8	11	10				2			3						9			44
1	4		3	5	6	7	8	11	10				2									9		12	45
8	4			5	*6*	7	2	11	10				3				1					9	12	14	46

Coca-Cola Cup

First Round	Scarborough (h)	2-1
	(a)	0-2

FA Cup

First Round	Lincoln C (h)	0-1

IPSWICH TOWN 1994–95 *Back row (left to right):* Geraint Williams, Neil Gregory, David Gregory, Antony Vaughan, Adam Tanner, James Scowcroft, Phil Whelan, Claus Thomsen, Steve Palmer, Eddie Youds, Gavin Johnson, John Wark.

Centre row: Gary Thompson, Graham Connell, Peter Mortley, Kenneth Weston, Clive Baker, Craig Forrest, Philip Morgan, Graham Mansfield, Gavin Dolby, Matthew Weston, Leo Cotterell, David Pirie.

Front row: Mick Stockwell, Lee Norfolk, Lee Durrant, Ian Marshall, Stuart Slater, Paul Mason, David Linighan, Steve Sedgley, Neil Thompson, Frank Yallop, Chris Kiwomya, Simon Milton.

Division 1 IPSWICH TOWN

Portman Road, Ipswich, Suffolk IP1 2DA. Telephone: (01473) 219211 (4 lines). Fax: (01473) 226835. Ticket office: (01473) 221133. Sales & Marketing Dept: (01473) 212202.

Ground capacity: 22,559.

Record attendance: 38,010 v Leeds U, FA Cup 6th rd, 8 March 1975.

Record receipts: £105,950 v AZ 67 Alkmaar, UEFA Cup Final 1st leg, 6 May 1981.

Pitch measurements: 112yd × 70yd.

Chairman: John Kerr MBE.

President: P. M. Cobbold. ***Vice-President:*** J. M. Sangster.

Directors: K. H. Brightwell, P. Hope-Cobbold, J. Kerridge, R. Moore, D. Sheepshanks, H. Smith.

Manager: George Burley. ***Assistant Manager:*** Dale Roberts. ***Coaches:*** Bryan Klug, Paul Goddard. ***Youth Team Coach:*** Peter Trevivian. ***Chief Scout:*** C. Woods. ***Director of Coaching:*** C. Suggett.

Physio: D. Bingham.

Secretary: David C. Rose.

Commercial Manager: C. Turner. ***Sales & Promotions Manager:*** Mike Noye.

Year Formed: 1878. ***Turned Professional:*** 1936. ***Ltd Co.:*** 1936.

Club Nickname: 'Blues' or 'Town'.

Foundation: Considering that Ipswich Town only reached the Football League in 1938, many people outside of East Anglia may be surprised to learn that this club was formed at a meeting held in the Town Hall as far back as 1878 when Mr. T. C. Cobbold, MP, was voted president. Originally it was the Ipswich Association FC to distinguish it from the older Ipswich Football Club which played rugby. These two amalgamated in 1888 and the handling game was dropped in 1893.

First Football League game: 27 August, 1938, Division 3(S), v Southend U (h) W 4-2 – Burns; Dale, Parry; Perrett, Fillingham, McLuckie; Williams, Davies (1), Jones (2), Alsop (1), Little.

Record League Victory: 7–0 v Portsmouth, Division 2, 7 November 1964 – Thorburn; Smith, McNeil; Baxter, Bolton, Thompson; Broadfoot (1), Hegan (2), Baker (1), Leadbetter, Brogan (3). 7–0 v Southampton, Division 1, 2 February 1974 – Sivell; Burley, Mills (1), Morris, Hunter, Beattie (1), Hamilton (2), Viljoen, Johnson, Whymark (2), Lambert (1) (Woods). 7–0 v WBA, Division 1, 6 November 1976 – Sivell; Burley, Mills, Talbot, Hunter, Beattie (1), Osborne, Wark (1), Mariner (1) (Bertschin), Whymark (4), Woods.

Record Cup Victory: 10–0 v Floriana, European Cup, Prel. rd, 25 September 1962 – Bailey; Malcolm, Compton; Baxter, Laurel, Elsworthy (1); Stephenson, Moran (2), Crawford (5), Phillips (2), Blackwood.

Record Defeat: 1–10 v Fulham, Division 1, 26 December 1963.

Most League Points (2 for a win): 64, Division 3 (S), 1953–54 and 1955–56.

Most League Points (3 for a win): 84, Division 1, 1991–92.

Most League Goals: 106, Division 3 (S), 1955–56.

Highest League Scorer in Season: Ted Phillips, 41, Division 3 (S), 1956–57.

Most League Goals in Total Aggregate: Ray Crawford, 203, 1958–63 and 1966–69.

Most Capped Player: Allan Hunter, 47 (53), Northern Ireland.

Most League Appearances: Mick Mills, 591, 1966–82.

Record Transfer Fee Received: £1,900,000 from Tottenham Hotspur for Jason Dozzell, August 1993.

Record Transfer Fee Paid: £1,000,000 to Tottenham H for Steve Sedgley, June 1994.

Football League Record: 1938 Elected to Division 3 (S); 1954–55 Division 2; 1955–57 Division 3 (S); 1957–61 Division 2; 1961–64 Division 1; 1964–68 Division 2; 1968–86 Division 1; 1986–92 Division 2; 1992–95 FA Premier League; 1995– Division 1.

Honours: *Football League:* Division 1 – Champions 1961–62; Runners-up 1980–81, 1981–82; Division 2 – Champions 1960–61, 1967–68, 1991–92; Division 3 (S) – Champions 1953–54, 1956–57. *FA Cup:* Winners 1978. *Football League Cup:* best season: Semi-final 1982, 1985, *Texaco Cup:* 1973. **European Competitions:** *European Cup:* 1962–63. *European Cup-Winners' Cup:* 1978–79. *UEFA Cup:* 1973–74, 1974–75, 1975–76, 1977–78, 1979–80, 1980–81 (winners), 1981–82, 1982–83.

Colours: Blue shirts, white shorts, blue stockings. **Change colours:** Red shirts, thin black stripe, black shorts, red stockings.

IPSWICH TOWN 1994–95 LEAGUE RECORD

Match No.	Date	Venue	Opponents	Result	H/T Score	Lg. Pos.	Goalscorers	Attendance
1	Aug 20	H	Nottingham F	L 0-1	0-1	—		18,763
2	23	A	Wimbledon	D 1-1	0-1	—	Milton	6341
3	27	A	QPR	W 2-1	1-0	9	Yates (og), Guentchev	12,456
4	30	H	Tottenham H	L 1-3	0-3	—	Kiwomya	22,430
5	Sept 10	A	Aston Villa	L 0-2	0-1	16		22,241
6	19	H	Norwich C	L 1-2	1-1	—	Wark (pen)	17,405
7	24	H	Manchester U	W 3-2	2-0	15	Mason 2, Sedgley	22,553
8	Oct 1	A	Southampton	L 1-3	0-0	16	Marshall	13,266
9	10	A	Coventry C	L 0-2	0-1	—		9509
10	16	H	Sheffield W	L 1-2	0-1	21	Wark	12,825
11	23	A	Chelsea	L 0-2	0-0	21		15,068
12	29	H	Liverpool	L 1-3	0-1	21	Paz	22,379
13	Nov 1	H	Leeds U	W 2-0	1-0	—	Sedgley, Williams	15,354
14	5	A	Crystal Palace	L 0-3	0-1	20		13,450
15	19	H	Blackburn R	L 1-3	1-2	20	Thomsen	17,607
16	26	A	Newcastle U	D 1-1	0-0	22	Thomsen	34,459
17	Dec 3	H	Manchester C	L 1-2	0-2	22	Mason	13,754
18	10	A	Nottingham F	L 1-4	1-4	22	Thomsen	21,340
19	16	H	Wimbledon	D 2-2	1-1	—	Milton, Sedgley	11,282
20	26	A	West Ham U	D 1-1	0-1	22	Thomsen	20,562
21	28	H	Arsenal	L 0-2	0-1	22		22,047
22	31	A	Everton	L 1-4	1-1	22	Sedgley	25,667
23	Jan 2	H	Leicester C	W 4-1	1-0	21	Kiwomya 2, Tanner, Yallop	15,817
24	14	A	Liverpool	W 1-0	1-0	21	Tanner	32,733
25	21	H	Chelsea	D 2-2	0-0	21	Slater, Wark (pen)	17,619
26	28	A	Blackburn R	L 1-4	0-2	21	Wark (pen)	21,325
27	Feb 4	H	Crystal Palace	L 0-2	0-0	21		15,361
28	22	A	Manchester C	L 0-2	0-0	—		21,430
29	25	H	Southampton	W 2-1	0-1	21	Mathie, Chapman	15,788
30	28	H	Newcastle U	L 0-2	0-2	—		18,639
31	Mar 4	A	Manchester U	L 0-9	0-3	21		43,804
32	8	A	Tottenham H	L 0-3	0-2	—		24,930
33	20	A	Norwich C	L 0-3	0-0	—		17,510
34	Apr 1	H	Aston Villa	L 0-1	0-0	21		15,895
35	5	A	Leeds U	L 0-4	0-4	—		28,565
36	11	H	QPR	L 0-1	0-0	—		11,736
37	15	A	Arsenal	L 1-4	0-1	22	Marshall	36,818
38	17	H	West Ham U	D 1-1	1-0	22	Thomsen	18,882
39	29	A	Leicester C	L 0-2	0-0	22		15,248
40	May 6	H	Coventry C	W 2-0	0-0	22	Marshall, Pressley (og)	12,342
41	9	H	Everton	L 0-1	0-0	—		14,940
42	14	A	Sheffield W	L 1-4	0-1	22	Mathie	30,307

Final League Position: 22

GOALSCORERS

League (36): Thomsen 5, Sedgley 4, Wark 4 (3 pens), Kiwomya 3, Marshall 3, Mason 3, Mathie 2, Milton 2, Tanner 2, Chapman 1, Guentchev 1, Paz 1, Slater 1, Williams 1, Yallop 1, own goals 2.
Coca-Cola Cup (0).
FA Cup (1): Linighan 1.

Forrest C.L. 36	Stockwell M.T. 14 + 1	Yallop F.W. 41	Mason P.D. 19 + 2	Wark J. 26	Youds E.P. 9 + 1	Williams D.G. 38	Slater S.I. 22 + 5	Milton S.C. 19 + 6	Marshall I.P. 14 + 4	Kiwomya C.M. 13 + 2	Guentchev B.L. 11 + 5	Linighan D. 31 + 1	Johnson G. 14 + 3	Sedgley S.P. 26	Palmer S.L. 10 + 2	Paz A. 13 + 4	Thomsen C. 31 + 2	Cotterell L.S. — + 2	Vaughan A.J. 10	Gregory D.S. — + 1	Whelan P.J. 12 + 1	Gregory N.R. 1 + 2	Tanner A.D. 9 + 1	Chapman L.R. 9 + 7	Thompson N. 9 + 1	Mathie A. 13	Norfolk L.R. 1 + 2	Swailes C.W. 4	Baker C.E. 2	Ellis K.E. 1	Morgan P.J. 1	Wright R.I. 3	*Match No.*
1	2	3	4	5	6	7	8	9	10	11	12																						1
1	2	3	4	5		7	8	9	10	11		6																					2
1	2	3	4	5		7	8	9		11	10	6																					3
1	2	3	4	5		7	8	9		11	10	6																					4
1	2	3	4	5		7	8	9	12	11	10	6																					5
1		2		5		7	8	9	10	11	12	6	3	4																			6
1		2	4	5		7		12			14	6	3	8	9	*10*	11																7
1		2	4	*5*		7			12		10	6	3	8	9		11	14															8
1		2		5		7	8			10		6	3	4	9		11	12															9
1		2		5	12	7		4			8		3	6	9	10	11																10
1	12	2			5	7		9			8			6	4	*10*	11		3	14													11
1	2				5	7					8	12	6	4	9	10	11		3														12
1	2	3			5	7		12		14	*9*	6		8		10	11				4												13
1	2	3			5	7		12		14	*9*	6		8		10	11				4												14
1		2	4		5	7		12	9			6		8		10	11				3												15
1		2	4		5	7	12		9			6		8		10	11				3												16
1		2	4		5	7	12				9	*6*	14	8		10	11				3												17
1		2	4			7	12	14		9		*6*	3	8		10	11				5												18
1		2	4			7		8		10				6		12	11		3		5	9											19
1		2	4	5		7	12	10		9				8			11		3		6												20
1		2	*4*	5		7		8		9	12		10		14		11		3		6												21
1		2	4	*5*			12			9	10	6		7	8		11		3		14												22
1		2	*4*				8			9		6		7	12		11		3		5	14	10										23
1		2		5		7	8					6	3	4		10	11						9										24
1		2		5		7	8					6	3	4		10	11						9	12									25
1		2		5		7	8						12	4			11		3		6		9	10									26
1		2		5		7	8						*11*	4		14	12		6				9	10	3								27
1		2		5		7	8					6	9	4		12	11		*3*					10	14								28
1		2		5					*8*			6	4	7		12							11	10	3	9	14						29
1		2	12	5			8					6		4									9	10	3	7	11						30
1		2		5		7	8		12			6		4	11									10	3	9							31
1		2			5	7		8	14			6		4		*10*	12						9	11	3								32
1		2		5		6	8	7	9								11				4			12	3	10							33
1		2		5		6	8	7	9								11								3	10		4					34
1		2				7	8	4			12	6					11							10	3	9		5					35
1	2	4				6	8		9			5			7		11							12	3	10							36
	2	4				6	8	12	9			5			10		11							14		*7*			1	3			37
	2	3	12	5		6	8	7	*9*			4					11							14		10			1				38
		2		5		4	8	7	9			6	3				11									10					1		39
	2	3	4	5		7			9			6					11						*8*	12		10	14					1	40
	2	3	4			7		9	*10*			6	12				11							14		8		5				1	41
	2	3	4			7		9				*6*					11					14	12	10		8		5				1	42

Coca-Cola Cup

Second Round	Bolton W (h)	0-3
	(a)	0-1

FA Cup

Third Round	Wrexham (a)	1-2

LEEDS UNITED 1994–95 *Back row (left to right):* David White, Carlton Palmer, John Lukic, David Wetherall, Mark Beeney, Brian Deane, Gary McAllister.
Centre row: Mike Hennigan (Assistant Manager), Lucas Radebe, Mark Tinkler, Kevin Sharp, John Pemberton, Philemon Masinga, Chris Fairclough, Noel Whelan, Nigel Worthington, David O'Leary, Geoff Ladley (Physio).
Front row: Gary Kelly, Gary Speed, Gordon Strachan, Howard Wilkinson (Manager), Tony Dorigo, Rod Wallace, Jamie Forrester.

FA Premiership **LEEDS UNITED**

Elland Road, Leeds LS11 0ES. Telephone: (0113) 2716037 (4 lines). Fax: (0113) 2720370. Ticket Office: (0113) 710710. Clubcall: 0891 121181.

Ground capacity: 40,000.

Record attendance: 57,892 v Sunderland, FA Cup 5th rd (replay), 15 March 1967.

Record receipts: £314,063 v Oldham Ath, FA Cup 4th rd, 28 January 1995.

Pitch measurements: 117yd × 72yd.

President: The Right Hon The Earl of Harewood LLD.

Executive Directors: L. H. Silver OBE (Chairman); P. J. Gilman (Vice-chairman); W. J. Fotherby (Managing).

Directors: J. W. G. Marjason, R. Barker, M. Bedford, E. Carlile, R. Feldman, A. Hudson, P. Ridsdale, K. J. Woolmer.

Manager: Howard Wilkinson. ***Assistant Manager:*** Mick Hennigan.

Company/Club Secretary: Nigel Pleasants.

General Manager: Alan Roberts.

Coaches: Paul Hart, Peter Gunby, David Williams, Robin Wray, Eddie Gray.

Physios: Geoff Ladley, Alan Sutton.

Commercial Manager: Bob Baldwin.

Year Formed: 1919, as Leeds United after disbandment (by FA order) of Leeds City (formed in 1904). ***Turned Professional:*** 1920. ***Ltd Co.:*** 1920.

Club Nickname: 'United'.

Foundation: Immediately the Leeds City club (founded in 1904) was wound up by the FA in October 1919, following allegations of illegal payments to players, a meeting was called by a Leeds solicitor, Mr. Alf Masser, at which Leeds United was formed. They joined the Midland League playing their first game in that competition in November 1919. It was in this same month that the new club had discussions with the directors of a virtually bankrupt Huddersfield Town who wanted to move to Leeds in an amalgamation. But Huddersfield survived even that crisis.

First Football League game: 28 August, 1920, Division 2, v Port Vale (a) L 0-2 – Down; Duffield, Tillotson; Musgrove, Baker, Walton; Mason, Goldthorpe, Thompson, Lyon, Best.

Record League Victory: 8–0 v Leicester C, Division 1, 7 April 1934 – Moore; George Milburn, Jack Milburn; Edwards, Hart, Copping; Mahon (2), Firth (2), Duggan (2), Furness (2), Cochrane.

Record Cup Victory: 10–0 v Lyn (Oslo), European Cup, 1st rd 1st leg, 17 September 1969 – Sprake; Reaney, Cooper, Bremner (2), Charlton, Hunter, Madeley, Clarke (2), Jones (3), Giles (2) (Bates), O'Grady (1).

Record Defeat: 1–8 v Stoke C, Division 1, 27 August 1934.

Most League Points (2 for a win): 67, Division 1, 1968–69.

Most League Points (3 for a win): 85, Division 2, 1989–90.

Most League Goals: 98, Division 2, 1927–28.

Highest League Scorer in Season: John Charles, 42, Division 2, 1953–54.

Most League Goals in Total Aggregate: Peter Lorimer, 168, 1965–79 and 1983–86.

Most Capped Player: Billy Bremner, 54, Scotland.

Most League Appearances: Jack Charlton, 629, 1953–73.

Record Transfer Fee Received: £2,700,000 from Blackburn Rovers for David Batty, October 1993.

Record Transfer Fee Paid: £3,400,000 to Eintracht Frankfurt for Tony Yeboah, January 1995.

Football League Record: 1920 Elected to Division 2; 1924–27 Division 1; 1927–28 Division 2; 1928–31 Division 1; 1931–32 Division 2; 1932–47 Division 1; 1947–56 Division 2; 1956–60 Division 1; 1960–64 Division 2; 1964–82 Division 1; 1982–90 Division 2; 1990–92 Division 1; 1992– FA Premier Division.

Honours: *Football League:* Division 1 – Champions 1968–69, 1973–74, 1991–92; Runners-up 1964–65, 1965–66, 1969–70, 1970–71, 1971–72; Division 2 – Champions 1923–24, 1963–64, 1989–90; Runners-up 1927–28, 1931–32, 1955–56. *FA Cup:* Winners 1972; Runners-up 1965, 1970, 1973. *Football League Cup:* Winners 1968. **European Competitions:** *European Cup:* 1969–70, 1974–75 (runners-up), 1992–93. *European Cup-Winners' Cup:* 1972–73 (runners-up). *European Fairs Cup:* 1965–66, 1966–67 (runners-up), 1967–68 (winners), 1968–69, 1970–71 (winners). *UEFA Cup:* 1971–72, 1973–74, 1979–80.

Colours: All white with yellow and blue trim. **Change colours:** Blue and green striped shirts, blue shorts, green stockings.

LEEDS UNITED 1994–95 LEAGUE RECORD

Match No.	Date	Venue	Opponents	Result		H/T Score	Lg. Pos.	Goalscorers	Attendance
1	Aug 20	A	West Ham U	D	0-0	0-0	—		18,610
2	23	H	Arsenal	W	1-0	0-0	—	Whelan	34,318
3	27	H	Chelsea	L	2-3	2-1	10	Masinga, Whelan	32,212
4	30	A	Crystal Palace	W	2-1	1-0	—	White, Whelan	14,453
5	Sept 11	H	Manchester U	W	2-1	1-0	6	Wetherall, Deane	39,120
6	17	A	Coventry C	L	1-2	0-0	6	Speed	15,383
7	26	A	Sheffield W	D	1-1	1-1	—	McAllister	23,227
8	Oct 1	H	Manchester C	W	2-0	1-0	6	Whelan 2	30,938
9	8	A	Norwich C	L	1-2	0-0	9	Wallace	17,390
10	15	H	Tottenham H	D	1-1	0-1	9	Deane	39,362
11	24	H	Leicester C	W	2-1	1-0	—	McAllister, Whelan	28,479
12	29	A	Southampton	W	3-1	0-1	6	Maddison (og), Wallace 2	15,202
13	Nov 1	A	Ipswich T	L	0-2	0-1	—		15,354
14	5	H	Wimbledon	W	3-1	3-1	6	Wetherall, Speed, White	27,246
15	19	A	QPR	L	2-3	0-2	6	McDonald (og), Deane	17,416
16	26	H	Nottingham F	W	1-0	0-0	6	Whelan	37,709
17	Dec 5	A	Everton	L	0-3	0-1	—		25,906
18	10	H	West Ham U	D	2-2	2-1	7	Worthington, Deane	28,987
19	17	A	Arsenal	W	3-1	1-0	6	Masinga 2, Deane	38,100
20	26	H	Newcastle U	D	0-0	0-0	6		39,337
21	31	H	Liverpool	L	0-2	0-1	8		38,468
22	Jan 2	A	Aston Villa	D	0-0	0-0	7		35,038
23	14	H	Southampton	D	0-0	0-0	8		28,869
24	24	H	QPR	W	4-0	2-0	—	Masinga 2, White, Deane	28,750
25	Feb 1	A	Blackburn R	D	1-1	0-1	—	McAllister (pen)	28,561
26	4	A	Wimbledon	D	0-0	0-0	7		10,211
27	22	H	Everton	W	1-0	0-0	—	Yeboah	30,793
28	25	A	Manchester C	D	0-0	0-0	6		22,892
29	Mar 4	H	Sheffield W	L	0-1	0-1	7		33,774
30	11	A	Chelsea	W	3-0	2-0	7	Yeboah 2, McAllister	20,174
31	15	A	Leicester C	W	3-1	1-1	—	Yeboah 2, Palmer	20,068
32	18	H	Coventry C	W	3-0	1-0	6	Yeboah, Gould (og), Wallace	29,179
33	22	A	Nottingham F	L	0-3	0-3	—		26,299
34	Apr 2	A	Manchester U	D	0-0	0-0	6		43,712
35	5	H	Ipswich T	W	4-0	4-0	—	Yeboah 3, Speed	28,565
36	9	A	Liverpool	W	1-0	1-0	6	Deane	37,454
37	15	H	Blackburn R	D	1-1	0-1	6	Deane	39,426
38	17	A	Newcastle U	W	2-1	2-1	6	McAllister (pen), Yeboah	35,626
39	29	H	Aston Villa	W	1-0	0-0	6	Palmer	32,973
40	May 6	H	Norwich C	W	2-1	0-1	6	McAllister (pen), Palmer	31,981
41	9	H	Crystal Palace	W	3-1	2-0	—	Yeboah 2, Wetherall	30,963
42	14	A	Tottenham H	D	1-1	0-1	5	Deane	33,040

Final League Position: 5

GOALSCORERS

League (59): Yeboah 12, Deane 9, Whelan 7, McAllister 6 (3 pens), Masinga 5, Wallace 4, Palmer 3, Speed 3, Wetherall 3, White 3, Worthington 1, own goals 3.
Coca-Cola Cup (0).
FA Cup (10): Masinga 4, Wetherall 2, Deane 1, Palmer 1, White 1, Yeboah 1.

Lukic J. 42	Kelly G. 42	Worthington N. 21 + 6	Palmer C.L. 39	Wetherall D. 38	Strachan G.D. 5 + 1	White D. 18 + 5	Wallace R.S. 30 + 2	Deane B.C. 33 + 2	McAllister G. 41	Speed G.A. 39	Masinga P. 15 + 7	Whelan N. 18 + 5	Fairclough C.H. 1 + 4	Pemberton J.M. 22 + 5	Tinkler M.R. 3	Radebe L. 9 + 3	Dorigo A.R. 28	Yeboah A. 16 + 2	Couzens A.J. 2 + 2	Sharp K. — + 2	*Match No.*
1	2	3	4	5	6	7	8	9	10	11	12										1
1	2	3	4	5	6	7	8		10	11	9	12									2
1	2	3	4	5		7	8		6	11	9	10									3
1	2	3	4	5		7	8		6	11	9	10	12								4
1	2	3	4	5		7	8	12	6	11	*9*	10	14								5
1	2	3	4	5	7		8		6	11	*9*	10	12	14							6
1	2	3	4	5			8	9	10	11	7	12			*6*	14					7
1	2	3	4	6			8	9	10	11		7	5	12							8
1	2	11	4	5			8	9	6	7		*10*	12	14			3				9
1	2	11	4	5			8	9	6	7		10		12			3				10
1	2	11	4	5			8	9	6	7		10					3				11
1	2	11	4	5			8	9	6	7		10				12	3				12
1	2	3	4	5		7	8	9	6	11	12	10									13
1	2	3	4	5		7	8	9	6	11	12	10				14					14
1	2	3	4	5		12	8	9	6	11		10				*7*					15
1	2		4	5		7	8	9	6	11	12	*10*		14			3				16
1	2		4	5		7	8	9	6	11		10					3				17
1	2	11	4	5	7	12		9	6			10			8		3				18
1	2		4	5		12		9		11	8	10		6		7	3				19
1	2	12	4	5	14	7			8	11	*9*	10		6			3				20
1	2	12		5	*7*	14			8	11	9	10		6		4	3				21
1	2	3		5		7	12	9	10	11	8			6		4					22
1	2	3	4	5		7	12	9	10	11	14			6		*8*					23
1	2	3	4	5		7		9	10	11	8			6				12			24
1	2	12	4			7		9	10	11	*8*			6		5	3	14			25
1	2	11	4			7		9	10		8			6		5	3				26
1	2	12		5		7			10	11	8			6		4	3	9			27
1	2	6	4	5		7		12	10	11	8						3	9			28
1	2		4	5			8	9	10	11	12			6			3	7			29
1	2		4	5			8	9	10	11				6			3	7			30
1	2		4	5			8	9	10	11				6			3	7			31
1	2		4				8	9	10	11					6	5	3	7	12		32
1	2		4			12	8	9	10	11				6			3	7	5		33
1	2	12	4	5			8	*9*	10			14		6			3	7	11		34
1	2		4	5			8	9	10	11				6			3	7	12		35
1	2		4	5			8	9	10	11				6			3	7			36
1	2		4	5			8	9	10	11		12		6			3	7			37
1	2	12	4	5		7		9	10	11	14			6			3	*8*			38
1	2		4	5			8	9	10	11				6			3	7			39
1	2		4	5			*8*	9	10	11		12		6			3	7		14	40
1	2		4	5			8	9	10	11				6			3	7			41
1	2		4	5			8	9	10	11				6			3	7		12	42

Coca-Cola Cup

Second Round	Mansfield T (h)	0-1
	(a)	0-0

FA Cup

Third Round	Walsall (a)	1-1
	(h)	5-2
Fourth Round	Oldham Ath (h)	3-2
Fifth Round	Manchester U (a)	1-3

LEICESTER CITY 1994–95 *Back row (left to right):* Sam McMahon, Jimmy Willis, Scott Eustace, Brian Carey, Steve Walsh, Ian Ormondroyd, Iwan Roberts, Gary Coatsworth, Ian Thompson, Richard Smith, Ian Blyth.

Centre row: Neil Lewis, David Speedie, Colin Gibson, Gary Mills, Nicky Mohan, Russell Hoult, Kevin Poole, Gavin Ward, David Oldfield, Steve Thompson, Lee Philpott, Colin Hill, Neil Maisey.

Front row: Mark Draper, David Lowe, Simon Grayson, Julian Joachim, Allan Evans (Assistant Manager), Brian Little (Manager), John Gregory (First Team Coach), Steve Agnew, Mike Whitlow, Phil Gee, Mark Blake.

Division 1 **LEICESTER CITY**

City Stadium, Filbert St, Leicester LE2 7FL. Telephone: (0116) 2555000 and (0116) 2854000. Fax: (0116) 2470585. Ticket Office: (0116) 2915232. Club Shop: (0116) 2559455. Ticket line: 0891 121028. Clubcall: 0891 121185.

Ground capacity: 22,517.

Record attendance: 47,298 v Tottenham H, FA Cup 5th rd, 18 February 1928.

Record receipts: £200,613 v Liverpool, FA Premiership, 26 December 1994.

Pitch measurements: 112yd × 75yd.

President: K. R. Brigstock.

Chairman: Martin George. ***Vice-Chairman:*** Tom Smeaton.

Chief Executive: Barrie Pierpoint.

Directors: J. M. Elsom FCA, R. W. Parker, J. E. Sharp, T. W. Shipman, W. K. Shooter FCA.

Manager: Mark McGhee. ***Assistant Manager:*** Colin Lee. ***First Team Coach:*** Mike Hickman.

Youth Team Coach: David Nish.

Football Secretary: Ian Silvester.

Company Secretary: Steve Kind.

Head of Publicity/Press Officer: Paul Mace.

Physio: Alan Smith. ***General Sales Manager:*** Charles Rayner.

Year Formed: 1884.

Club Nickname: 'Fiberts' or 'Foxes'.

Previous Grounds: 1884, Victoria Park; 1887, Belgrave Road; 1888, Victoria Park; 1891, Filbert Street.

Previous Name: 1884–1919, Leicester Fosse.

Foundation: In 1884 a number of young footballers who were mostly old boys of Wyggeston School, held a meeting at a house on the Roman Fosse Way and formed Leicester Fosse FC. They collected 9d (less than 4p) towards the cost of a ball, plus the same amount for membership. Their first professional, Harry Webb from Stafford Rangers, was signed in 1888 for 2s 6d (12p) per week, plus travelling expenses.

First Football League game: 1 September, 1894, Division 2, v Grimsby T (a) L 3-4 – Thraves; Smith, Bailey; Seymour, Brown, Henrys; Hill, Hughes, McArthur (1), Skea (2), Priestman.

Record League Victory: 10–0 v Portsmouth, Division 1, 20 October 1928 – McLaren; Black, Brown; Findlay, Carr, Watson; Adcock, Hine (3), Chandler (6), Lochhead, Barry (1).

Record Cup Victory: 8–1 v Coventry C (away), League Cup, 5th rd, 1 December 1964 – Banks; Sjoberg, Norman (2); Roberts, King, McDerment; Hodgson (2), Cross, Goodfellow, Gibson (1), Stringfellow (2). (1 og).

Record Defeat: 0–12 (as Leicester Fosse) v Nottingham F, Division 1, 21 April 1909.

Most League Points (2 for a win): 61, Division 2, 1956–57.

Most League Points (3 for a win): 77, Division 2, 1991–92.

Most League Goals: 109, Division 2, 1956–57.

Highest League Scorer in Season: Arthur Rowley, 44, Division 2, 1956–57.

Most League Goals in Total Aggregate: Arthur Chandler, 259, 1923–35.

Most Capped Player: John O'Neill, 39, Northern Ireland.

Most League Appearances: Adam Black, 528, 1920–35.

Record Transfer Fee Received: £3,250,000 from Aston Villa for Mark Draper, July 1995.

Record Transfer Fee Paid: £1,250,000 to Notts Co for Mark Draper, July 1994.

Football League Record: 1894 Elected to Division 2; 1908–09 Division 1; 1909–25 Division 2; 1925–35 Division 1; 1935–37 Division 2; 1937–39 Division 1; 1946–54 Division 2; 1954–55 Division 1; 1955–57 Division 2; 1957–69 Division 1; 1969–71 Division 2; 1971–78 Division 1; 1978–80 Division 2; 1980–81 Division 1; 1981–83 Division 2; 1983–87 Division 1; 1987–92 Division 2; 1992–94 Division 1; 1994–95 FA Premier League; 1995– Division 1.

Honours: *Football League:* Division 1 – Runners-up 1928–29; Division 2 – Champions 1924–25, 1936–37, 1953–54, 1956–57, 1970–71, 1979–80; Runners-up 1907–08. *FA Cup:* Runners-up 1949, 1961, 1963, 1969. *Football League Cup:* Winners 1964; Runners-up 1965. **European Competitions:** *European Cup-Winners' Cup:* 1961–62.

Colours: All blue. **Change colours:** All gold.

LEICESTER CITY 1994–95 LEAGUE RECORD

Match No.	Date	Venue	Opponents	Result	H/T Score	Lg. Pos.	Goalscorers	Attendance
1	Aug 21	H	Newcastle U	L 1-3	0-0	—	Joachim	20,048
2	23	A	Blackburn R	L 0-3	0-1	—		21,050
3	27	A	Nottingham F	L 0-1	0-1	22		21,601
4	31	H	QPR	D 1-1	0-1	—	Gee	18,695
5	Sept 10	A	Wimbledon	L 1-2	1-2	21	Lowe	7683
6	17	H	Tottenham H	W 3-1	1-0	20	Joachim 2, Lowe	21,300
7	24	A	Everton	D 1-1	0-0	18	Draper	28,015
8	Oct 3	H	Coventry C	D 2-2	1-1	—	Roberts 2	19,372
9	8	A	Chelsea	L 0-4	0-2	20		18,397
10	15	H	Southampton	W 4-3	2-0	18	Blake 2, Roberts, Carr	20,020
11	24	A	Leeds U	L 1-2	0-1	—	Blake	28,479
12	29	H	Crystal Palace	L 0-1	0-1	20		20,022
13	Nov 5	A	West Ham U	L 0-1	0-0	21		18,780
14	20	H	Manchester C	L 0-1	0-1	21		19,006
15	23	H	Arsenal	W 2-1	2-1	—	Seaman (og), Lowe	20,774
16	26	A	Norwich C	L 1-2	1-0	21	Draper	20,657
17	Dec 3	H	Aston Villa	D 1-1	1-0	21	Gee	20,896
18	10	A	Newcastle U	L 1-3	0-1	21	Oldfield	34,400
19	17	H	Blackburn R	D 0-0	0-0	21		20,559
20	26	H	Liverpool	L 1-2	0-0	21	Roberts	21,393
21	28	A	Manchester U	D 1-1	0-0	21	Whitlow	43,789
22	31	H	Sheffield W	L 0-1	0-1	21		20,624
23	Jan 2	A	Ipwich T	L 1-4	0-1	22	Roberts	15,817
24	14	A	Crystal Palace	L 0-2	0-2	22		12,707
25	25	A	Manchester C	W 1-0	0-0	—	Robins	21,007
26	Feb 4	H	West Ham U	L 1-2	1-2	22	Robins	20,375
27	11	A	Arsenal	D 1-1	0-0	22	Draper	31,373
28	22	A	Aston Villa	D 4-4	0-2	—	Robins, Roberts, Lowe 2	30,825
29	25	A	Coventry C	L 2-4	0-2	22	Lowe, Roberts	20,650
30	Mar 4	H	Everton	D 2-2	0-2	22	Draper, Roberts	20,447
31	8	A	QPR	L 0-2	0-0	—		10,189
32	11	H	Nottingham F	L 2-4	1-1	22	Lowe, Draper	20,423
33	15	H	Leeds U	L 1-3	1-1	—	Roberts	20,068
34	18	A	Tottenham H	L 0-1	0-0	22		30,851
35	Apr 1	H	Wimbledon	L 3-4	1-0	22	Robins, Willis, Lawrence	15,489
36	5	H	Norwich C	W 1-0	0-0	—	Parker	15,992
37	8	A	Sheffield W	L 0-1	0-1	21		22,551
38	15	H	Manchester U	L 0-4	0-2	21		21,281
39	17	A	Liverpool	L 0-2	0-0	21		36,012
40	29	H	Ipswich T	W 2-0	0-0	21	Whitlow, Lowe	15,248
41	May 6	H	Chelsea	D 1-1	1-1	21	Willis	18,140
42	14	A	Southampton	D 2-2	0-1	21	Parker, Robins	15,101

Final League Position: 21

GOALSCORERS

League (45): Roberts 9, Lowe 8, Draper 5, Robins 5, Blake 3, Joachim 3, Gee 2, Parker 2, Whitlow 2, Willis 2, Carr 1, Lawrence 1, Oldfield 1, own goal 1.
Coca-Cola Cup (0).
FA Cup (3): Roberts 2, Oldfield 1.

Ward G.J. 6	Grayson S.N. 34	Whitlow M. 28	Mohan N. 23	Smith R.G. 10 + 2	Hill C.F. 24	Joachim J.K. 11 + 4	Blake M.A. 26 + 4	Walsh S. 5	Agnew S.M. 7 + 4	Draper M.A. 39	Roberts I.W. 32 + 5	Thompson S.J. 16 + 3	Willis J.A. 29	Poole K. 36	Philpott L. 19 + 4	Lowe D.A. 19 + 10	Mills G.R. 1	Gee P. 3 + 4	Lewis N.A. 13 + 3	Carey B.P. 11 + 1	Carr F.A. 12 + 1	Oldfield D.C. 8 + 6	Ormondroyd I. 6	Lawrence J.H. 9 + 8	Robins M.G. 16 + 1	Galloway M. 4 + 1	Parker G.S. 14	Heskey E. 1	McMahon S.K. — + 1	*Match No.*
1	2	3	4	5	6	7	*8*	9	10	11	12	14																		1
1	2	3	4		*6*	7	8	9	10	11	12	14	5																	2
	2	*3*	4	5		7	8		10	11	9	12	6	1	14															3
		3	4	2					10		9	8	5	1	11	7	6	12												4
	2					12	8		14	6	10		5	1	11	9			*3*	4	7									5
	2		4			9	8		14	6	10		5	1	*11*	12			3		7									6
	2		4			9	8			6	10		5	1	11				3		7									7
	2		4	12		9	8		14	6	10		5	1	11				*3*		7									8
	2	3	4	12		9	8			6	10		5	1	*11*	14					7									9
1	2	4					8			6	10		5		11	*9*		14	3		7	12								10
1	2	5	4			9	8			6	10				*11*	12			3		7	14								11
1	2	5	4			9	8			6	10				11	12			3		*7*	14								12
1	2	5	4				8			6	10				11	9			3		7									13
	2	3		5				9		6	12	8	4	1		10					7	14	*11*							14
		3	4				2	9		6		8	5	1		10						7	11							15
		3	4				2	9		6		8	5	1		10		12				7	11							16
		3	4		5	12	2			6	14	8		1				*9*			7	10	11							17
	7	3	4		5	12	2			6		8		1	11			9			14	10								18
	7	3			4	12	2			6		8	5	1	11			9				10								19
	2	3			4		10		14	6	12	*8*	5	1	11						7	9								20
	2	3			4		12		9	6	10	8	5	1	11	14						*7*								21
	2	3			4		12		9	6	10	8	5	1	11	14						*7*								22
	2	3			4				7	6	10	8	5	1	12	*9*			11			14								23
			4	2	5		9			6	10	8		1	3	12						14	*11*	7						24
	2		4	3	5		11			6	10	8		1										7	9					25
	2		4	3	5					6	10	8		1	11									12	9	7				26
	2	3		*5*	4					6	10	8		1	11				12					7	9	14				27
	2	3			4					6	10	8	5	1		14			*12*						9	7	11			28
	2				4					6	10		5	1		8			3						9	7	11			29
	2				4					6	10		5	1		8			3					12	9	7	11			30
			4	2			5			6	9			1	3	8		12						7			10	11		31
			4	2			11			6	10			1	12	8			3	5				7	9					32
	2		4				7			*6*	*10*			1	14	8			3	5				12	9		11			33
	2		4				3			*7*	*10*		5	1		8			12	6				14	9		11			34
	7	3	4		*6*								2	1		8				5			11	14	9		10		12	35
	2	3			4						10		5	1		8				6				7	9		11			36
	2	3			4		12			7	10		5	1		8				*6*				14	9		11			37
	2	3			4		12			6	10		5	1		*8*				14				7	9		11			38
	2	3			4		8			7	10		5	1						6				12	9		11			39
		3			4		2			7	10		5	1		8				6				12	9		11			40
	3				4	7				8	10		5	1		12				6				2	9		11			41
	2	3			4	9				8	10		5	1		12				*6*				7	14		11			42

Coca-Cola Cup
Second Round — Brighton & HA (a) 0-1
(h) 0-2

FA Cup
Third Round — Enfield (h) 2-0
Fourth Round — Portsmouth (a) 1-0
Fifth Round — Wolverhampton W (a) 0-1

LEYTON ORIENT 1994–95 *Back row (left to right):* Danny Carter, Darren Purse, Colin West, Glenn Cockerill, Mark Warren, Barry Lakin.
Centre row: Tony Flynn, Andy Gray, Kevin Austin, Paul Heald, Gary Bellamy, Terry Howard, Andy Taylor.
Front row: Gary Barnett, Mark Dempsey, Chris Turner, Ian Hendon, John Sitton, Ian Bogie, Vaughan Ryan.

Division 3 LEYTON ORIENT

Leyton Stadium, Brisbane Road, Leyton, London E10 5NE. Telephone: (0181) 539 2223/4. Fax: (0181) 539 4390. Clubcall: 0891 121150.

Ground capacity: 17,065 (7,171 seats).

Record attendance: 34,345 v West Ham U, FA Cup 4th rd, 25 January 1964.

Record receipts: £87,867.92 v West Ham U, FA Cup 3rd rd, 10 January 1987.

Pitch measurements: 110yd × 80yd.

Chairman: Barry Hearn.

Directors: D. L. Weinrabe, Tony Wood, Harry Linney, V. Marsh, J. Goldsmith FR, BA.

Team Manager: Pat Holland. ***Assistant Manager:*** Tom Cunningham. ***Physio:*** A. Taylor.

Secretary: David Burton. ***Asst. Sec.:*** Mrs Sue Tilling. ***Commercial Manager:*** Frank Woolf.

Year Formed: 1881. ***Turned Professional:*** 1903. ***Ltd Co.:*** 1906.

Club Nickname: 'The O's'.

Previous Names: 1881–86, Glyn Cricket and Football Club; 1886–88, Eagle Football Club; 1888–98, Orient Football Club; 1898–1946, Clapton Orient; 1946–66, Leyton Orient; 1966–87, Orient.

Previous Grounds: Glyn Road, 1884–96; Whittles Athletic Ground, 1896–1900; Millfields Road, 1900–30; Lea Bridge Road, 1930–37.

Foundation: There is some doubt about the foundation of Leyton Orient, and, indeed, some confusion with clubs like Leyton and Clapton over their early history. As regards the foundation, the most favoured version is that Leyton Orient was formed originally by members of Homerton Theological College who established Glyn Cricket Club in 1881 and then carried on through the following winter playing football. Eventually many employees of the Orient Shipping Line became involved and so the name Orient was chosen in 1888.

First Football League game: 2 September, 1905, Division 2, v Leicester Fosse (a) L 1-2 – Butler; Holmes, Codling; Lamberton, Boden, Boyle; Kingaby (1), Wootten, Leigh, Evenson, Bourne.

Record League Victory: 8–0 v Crystal Palace, Division 3 (S), 12 November 1955 – Welton; Lee, Earl; Blizzard, Aldous, McKnight; White (1), Facey (3), Burgess (2), Heckman, Hartburn (2). 8–0 v Rochdale, Division 4, 20 October 1987 – Wells; Howard, Dickenson (1), Smalley (1), Day, Hull, Hales (2), Castle (Sussex), Shinners (2), Godfrey (Harvey), Comfort (2). 8–0 v Colchester U, Division 4, 15 October 1988 – Wells; Howard, Dickenson, Hales (1p), Day (1). Sitton (1), Baker (1), Ward, Hull (3). Juryeff, Comfort (1).

Record Cup Victory: 9–2 v Chester, League Cup, 3rd rd, 15 October 1962 – Robertson; Charlton, Taylor; Gibbs, Bishop, Lea; Deeley (1), Waites (3), Dunmore (2), Graham (3), Wedge.

Record Defeat: 0–8 v Aston Villa, FA Cup 4th rd, 30 January 1929.

Most League Points (2 for a win): 66, Division 3 (S), 1955–56.

Most League Points (3 for a win): 75, Division 4, 1988–89.

Most League Goals: 106, Division 3 (S), 1955–56.

Highest League Scorer in Season: Tom Johnston, 35, Division 2, 1957–58.

Most League Goals in Total Aggregate: Tom Johnston, 121, 1956–58, 1959–61.

Most Capped Player: John Chiedozie, 8 (10), Nigeria.

Most League Appearances: Peter Allen, 432, 1965–78.

Record Transfer Fee Received: £600,000 from Notts Co for John Chiedozie, August 1981.

Record Transfer Fee Paid: £175,000 to Wigan Ath for Paul Beesley, October 1989.

Football League Record: 1905 Elected to Division 2; 1929–56 Division 3 (S); 1956–62 Division 2; 1962–63 Division 1; 1963–66 Division 2; 1966–70 Division 3; 1970–82 Division 2; 1982–85 Division 3; 1985–89 Division 4; 1989–92 Division 3; 1992–95 Division 2; 1995– Division 3.

Honours: *Football League:* Division 1 best season: 22nd, 1962–63; Division 2 – Runners-up 1961–62; Division 3 – Champions 1969–70; Division 3 (S) – Champions 1955–56; Runners-up 1954–55. *FA Cup:* Semi-final 1978. *Football League Cup:* best season: 5th rd, 1963.

Colours: Red shirts with white pinstripe, white shorts, red stockings. **Change colours:** Blue and yellow.

LEYTON ORIENT 1994–95 LEAGUE RECORD

Match No.	Date	Venue	Opponents	Result		H/T Score	Lg. Pos.	Goalscorers	Attendance
1	Aug 13	H	Birmingham C	W	2-1	1-1	—	Purse, Bogie	7578
2	20	A	Bradford C	L	0-2	0-1	15		7473
3	27	H	Hull C	D	1-1	0-0	14	Gray	3243
4	30	A	Huddersfield T	L	1-2	1-0	—	Purse	8552
5	Sept 3	A	Brighton & HA	L	0-1	0-0	19		8581
6	10	H	Cambridge U	D	1-1	0-0	19	West	3699
7	13	H	Bournemouth	W	3-2	1-1	—	Cockerill, West 2 (2 pens)	2536
8	17	A	Shrewsbury T	L	0-3	0-3	19		3560
9	24	A	Oxford U	L	2-3	0-0	19	Hague, Howard	5814
10	Oct 1	H	Plymouth Arg	L	0-2	0-2	21		4140
11	8	A	Wycombe W	L	1-2	0-1	20	Gray	5668
12	15	H	Chester C	W	2-0	1-0	20	Cockerill, West	3309
13	22	A	Rotherham U	L	0-2	0-1	21		2700
14	29	H	Stockport Co	L	0-1	0-0	22		3267
15	Nov 1	H	Cardiff C	W	2-0	0-0	—	Purse, West	2558
16	5	A	Blackpool	L	1-2	1-1	21	West	4653
17	19	H	York C	L	0-1	0-0	22		3532
18	26	A	Peterborough U	D	0-0	0-0	22		5114
19	Dec 10	H	Bradford C	D	0-0	0-0	22		2553
20	17	A	Birmingham C	L	0-2	0-1	22		20,022
21	26	A	Brentford	L	0-3	0-3	22		6125
22	27	H	Swansea C	L	0-1	0-1	22		3259
23	31	A	Crewe Alex	L	0-3	0-0	22		3792
24	Jan 7	H	Rotherham U	D	0-0	0-0	23		2796
25	14	A	Wrexham	L	1-4	0-1	23	Bogie (pen)	6616
26	28	A	Stockport Co	L	1-2	0-1	23	West	4250
27	Feb 4	H	Peterborough U	W	4-1	2-0	23	Warren 3, West	3447
28	7	H	Blackpool	L	0-1	0-1	—		3301
29	18	H	Wrexham	D	1-1	1-0	23	Cockerill	3135
30	21	A	York C	L	1-4	1-2	—	Cockerill	2926
31	25	A	Plymouth Arg	L	0-1	0-0	23		5173
32	Mar 4	H	Oxford U	D	1-1	1-0	23	West	4052
33	7	H	Brighton & HA	L	0-3	0-1	—		2983
34	11	A	Hull C	L	0-2	0-1	23		4519
35	18	H	Huddersfield T	L	0-2	0-0	23		3177
36	21	A	Cambridge U	D	0-0	0-0	—		3048
37	25	H	Shrewsbury T	W	2-1	1-1	23	Austin, Gray	2724
38	Apr 1	A	Bournemouth	L	0-2	0-1	23		4118
39	4	A	Cardiff C	L	1-2	0-0	—	McGleish	4324
40	8	H	Crewe Alex	L	1-4	1-2	23	Austin	2797
41	11	H	Bristol R	L	1-2	0-1	—	Dempsey	2338
42	15	A	Swansea C	L	0-2	0-2	23		3277
43	17	H	Brentford	L	0-2	0-1	23		4459
44	22	A	Bristol R	L	0-1	0-0	23		4838
45	29	A	Chester C	L	0-1	0-0	24		1596
46	May 6	H	Wycombe W	L	0-1	0-0	24		4698

Final League Position: 24

GOALSCORERS

League (30): West 9 (2 pens), Cockerill 4, Gray 3, Purse 3, Warren 3, Austin 2, Bogie 2 (1 pen), Dempsey 1, Hague 1, Howard 1, McGleish 1.
Coca-Cola Cup (1): Cockerill 1.
FA Cup (3): Carter 1, Gray 1, West 1.

Heald P.A. 45	Warren M.W. 24 + 7	Austin K. 39	Purse D.J. 37 + 1	Hendon I.M. 29	Lakin B. 17 + 5	Barnett G.L. 15 + 12	Ryan V.W. 6 + 1	Bogie I. 28 + 3	West C. 27 + 3	Dempsey M.A. 43	Gray A. 13 + 12	Cockerill G. 32 + 1	Howard T. 27	Carter D.S. 25 + 4	Martin J.A. 1 + 3	Hague P. 17 + 1	Bellamy G. 32	Brooks S. 8 + 1	Wilkie G. 10 + 1	Read P. 11	McGleish S. 4 + 2	Turner C.R. 1	Barry G. 5 + 1	Perifimou C. 3 + 1	Rufus M.M. 5 + 2	Shearer L.S. 2	*Match No.*
1	2	3	4	5	6	7	*8*	9	10	11	12	14															1
1		3	4	5	12	7	6	14	10	11		8	2	*9*													2
1		3	4	5	12			6	10	11	9	8	2	7													3
1	14	3	4	2	12		6	*7*	10	11	9	8	5														4
1	2	3	4		6	12	7		10	11	*9*	8	5	14													5
1		3	4	2	6		7		10	11	*9*	8	5	12	14												6
1		3	4	2		12	7		10	11	*9*	8	5	6	14												7
1		3	*4*	2	7		12		10	11		8	5	6	9	14											8
1		3	4	2	7				10	*11*	12	8	6	9	14	5											9
1		3	4		7	12		14	10	11	9	8	2	*6*		5											10
1	12	3	14		7			6	10	11	9	8	2			*5*	4										11
1		3	9	5	7			6	10	11		8	2	12			4										12
1	12	3	9	5	7			6	10	11			2	8			4										13
1		3	9	5	7	12		6	10	11			2	8			4										14
1		3	9	5	7	12		6	10	11			2	8			4										15
1	2	3	*9*		7	12		6	10	11	14	8	5				4										16
1		3		2	12	7		6	10	11	9	8	5				4										17
1		3		2	12	7		6	10	11	9	8	5				4	14									18
1		3	5		7	12		6		11	14	8	2	9			4	*10*									19
1	12		5	2	8	7		6		11	14		3	9			4	10									20
1	12			2				6		11	7	8	3	9		5	4	10									21
1	10			2		12		6		11	7	8	3	9		5	4										22
1	10	3	5			12		6		11	7	8	*2*	9			4		14								23
1	*9*	3	4			7		6		11	14	8	2	12		5		10									24
1	9	3	4	8				6	12	11			2	7		5		10									25
1			5	2				12	10	11	9	8	3	7			4	6									26
1	10		5	2	6			9	12	11		8	3	7			4										27
1	10		5	2	6			9	12	11		8	3	7			4										28
1	9	3	5	2		12		6	10	11		8		7			4										29
1	9	3	5	2				6	10	11		8		7			4										30
1	9	3	5	2				6	10	11		8		7			4										31
1	12	3	5	2				6	*10*	11	14	8		7			4			9							32
1	10	3	5	2		7		6		11		8					4			9	12						33
	12	3	5	2				6	10	11		8					4			9	7	1					34
1	9	3		2	7			6	10	11		8				5	4										35
1	*9*			2		12		6	10	11	14	8				5			4		7		3				36
1	*9*	3	4			12			10	11	14	8				5			6		7		2				37
1	9	3	4			8				11						5	7		6	10	12		2				38
1	9	3	4			8					12					5	7			10	6		2	*11*	14		39
1	10	3	4							11	12	8				5	7		6	9			2				40
1	10	3	4			*8*				11	12						5		2	9			14	7	6		41
1	10	3				8				11						5	4		2	9				7	6		42
1	10	3				7				11				8			4		2	9					6	5	43
1		3	9			8				11				7		5	4		2	10					6		44
1	2	3	9			7								11		5	6	4	8	10					12		45
1	2	3	9			7										5	6	4	8					12	11	10	46

Coca-Cola Cup

First Round	Barnet (a)	0-4
	(h)	1-1

FA Cup

First Round	Tiverton (a)	3-1
Second Round	Bristol R (h)	0-2

LINCOLN CITY 1994–95 *Back row (left to right):* Steve Williams, Neil Matthews, Colin Greenall, Nicky Platnauer, Mark Smith, John Schofield, Alan Johnson, Grant Brown, Trevor Hebberd.
Centre row: Billy Ayre, Ben Dixon, David Johnson, Sean Dunphy, Andy Leaning, Matt Carbon, Steve Parkinson, Udo Onwere, Sam Ellis (Manager).
Front row: Paul Smith, Dean West, Tony Daws, Steve Mardenborough, Steve Foley, David Puttnam, David Hill, Darren Huckerby

Division 3 **LINCOLN CITY**

Sincil Bank, Lincoln LN5 8LD. Telephone: (01522) 522224. Fax: (01522) 520564. Commercial: (01522) 536966. Community Officer: (01522) 539671.

Ground capacity: 10,918.

Record attendance: 23,196 v Derby Co, League Cup 4th rd, 15 November 1967.

Record receipts: £44,184.46 v Everton, Coca-Cola Cup 2nd rd 1st leg, 21 September 1993.

Pitch measurements: 110yd × 75yd.

Hon. Life Presidents: V. C. Withers, D. W. L. Bocock.

President: H. Dove.

Chairman: K. J. Reames. ***Vice-Chairman:*** G. R. Davey (and Managing).

Directors: H. C. Sills, J. Hicks, Mrs E. C. Reames, N. Woolsey, C. J. Thomas.

Hon. Consultant Surgeon: Mr Brian Smith. ***Hon. Club Doctor:*** Nick Huntley.

Secretary: Phil Hough.

Manager: Sam Ellis. ***Assistant Manager:*** Frank Lord. ***Physio:*** Mark Riley. ***Commercial Manager:*** G. R. Davey.

Year Formed: 1883. ***Turned Professional:*** 1892. ***Ltd Co.:*** 1892.

Club Nickname: 'The Red Imps'.

Previous Grounds: 1883, John O'Gaunt's; 1894, Sincil Bank.

Foundation: Although there was a Lincoln club as far back as 1861, the present organisation was formed in 1883 winning the Lincolnshire Senior Cup in only their fourth season. They were Founder members of the Midland League in 1889 and that competition's first champions.

First Football League game: 3 September, 1892, Division 2, v Sheffield U (a) L 2-4 – W. Gresham; Coulton, Neill; Shaw, Mettam, Moore; Smallman, Irving (1), Cameron (1), Kelly, J. Gresham.

Record League Victory: 11–1 v Crewe Alex, Division 3 (N), 29 September 1951 – Jones; Green (1p), Varney; Wright, Emery, Grummett (1); Troops (1), Garvey, Graver (6), Whittle (1), Johnson (1).

Record Cup Victory: 8–1 v Bromley, FA Cup, 2nd rd, 10 December 1938 – McPhail; Hartshorne, Corbett; Bean, Leach, Whyte (1); Hancock, Wilson (1), Ponting (3), Deacon (1), Clare (2).

Record Defeat: 3–11 v Manchester C, Division 2, 23 March 1895.

Most League Points (2 for a win): 74, Division 4, 1975–76.

Most League Points (3 for a win): 77, Division 3, 1981–82.

Most League Goals: 121, Division 3 (N), 1951–52.

Highest League Scorer in Season: Allan Hall, 42, Division 3 (N), 1931–32.

Most League Goals in Total Aggregate: Andy Graver, 144, 1950–55 and 1958–61.

Most Capped Player: David Pugh, 3 (7), Wales and George Moulson, 3, Republic of Ireland.

Most League Appearances: Tony Emery, 402, 1946–59.

Record Transfer Fee Received: £250,000 plus increments from Blackburn R for Matt Dickins, March 1992.

Record Transfer Fee Paid: £63,000 to Leicester City for Grant Brown, January 1990.

Football League Record: 1892 Founder member of Division 2. Remained in Division 2 until 1920 when they failed re-election but also missed seasons 1908–09 and 1911–12 when not re-elected. 1921–32 Division 3 (N); 1932–34 Division 2; 1934–48 Division 3 (N); 1948–49 Division 2; 1949–52 Division 3 (N); 1952–61 Division 2; 1961–62 Division 3; 1962–76 Division 4; 1976–79 Division 3; 1979–81 Division 4; 1981–86 Division 3; 1986–87 Division 4; 1987–88 GM Vauxhall Conference; 1988–92 Division 4; 1992– Division 3.

Honours: *Football League:* Divison 2 best season: 5th, 1901–02; Division 3 (N) – Champions 1931–32, 1947–48, 1951–52; Runners-up 1927–28, 1930–31, 1936–37; Division 4 – Champions 1975–76; Runners-up 1980–81. *FA Cup:* best season: 1st rd of Second Series (5th rd equivalent), 1887, 2nd rd (5th rd equivalent), 1890, 1902. *Football League Cup:* best season: 4th rd, 1968. *GM Vauxhall Conference:* Champions 1987–88.

Colours: Red and white striped shirts, black shorts, red stockings with white trim. **Change colours:** Jade shirts, black shorts, jade stockings.

LINCOLN CITY 1994–95 LEAGUE RECORD

Match No.	Date	Venue	Opponents	Result		H/T Score	Lg. Pos.	Goalscorers	Attendance
1	Aug 13	H	Exeter C	W	2-0	2-0	—	Daws, Johnson D (pen)	3439
2	20	A	Walsall	L	1-2	0-1	11	West	3813
3	27	H	Torquay U	L	1-2	1-1	15	Daley	3154
4	30	A	Rochdale	L	0-1	0-1	—		1974
5	Sept 3	A	Preston NE	L	0-4	0-0	19		8337
6	10	H	Mansfield T	W	3-2	1-1	14	Daley, West, Puttnam	2575
7	13	H	Wigan Ath	W	1-0	0-0	—	Schofield	2030
8	17	A	Exeter C	L	0-1	0-0	13		2180
9	24	A	Hartlepool U	W	3-0	3-0	13	West, Greenall, Puttnam	1419
10	Oct 1	H	Northampton T	D	2-2	1-2	13	Brown, Puttnam	3248
11	8	H	Carlisle U	D	1-1	0-0	12	Bannister	3097
12	15	A	Bury	L	0-2	0-2	15		3139
13	22	H	Scarborough	W	2-0	1-0	13	Bannister (pen), Daley	2396
14	29	A	Hereford U	W	3-0	1-0	11	Matthews, Daley, Puttnam	2485
15	Nov 5	H	Barnet	L	1-2	1-1	11	Matthews	2741
16	19	A	Fulham	D	1-1	0-1	12	Bannister (pen)	3955
17	26	H	Gillingham	D	1-1	0-0	10	West	2919
18	Dec 10	H	Walsall	D	1-1	1-1	11	Brown	2717
19	17	A	Torquay U	L	1-2	0-1	14	Daws	2004
20	26	A	Scunthorpe U	L	0-2	0-0	15		4785
21	27	H	Darlington	W	3-1	1-1	12	Johnson D, Carbon 2	2964
22	31	A	Chesterfield	L	0-1	0-0	14		3325
23	Jan 14	H	Doncaster R	W	1-0	0-0	15	Daws (pen)	2771
24	28	H	Hereford U	W	2-0	0-0	13	Hill, Carbon	2545
25	Feb 4	A	Gillingham	D	0-0	0-0	15		4196
26	7	A	Scarborough	D	1-1	1-0	—	Daws (pen)	1217
27	18	A	Doncaster R	L	0-3	0-1	14		2291
28	21	H	Colchester U	W	2-0	0-0	—	Bannister, Johnson D.	1969
29	25	A	Northampton T	L	1-3	0-1	13	Greenall	4821
30	Mar 4	H	Hartlepool U	W	3-0	0-0	12	Bannister, Carbon, Daws (pen)	6477
31	11	A	Mansfield T	L	2-6	0-1	13	Daws, Brown	3396
32	18	H	Rochdale	D	2-2	2-0	13	West, Johnson D	2939
33	25	H	Preston NE	D	1-1	1-0	14	West	5487
34	Apr 1	A	Wigan Ath	W	1-0	1-0	13	Hill	1696
35	4	A	Barnet	L	1-2	1-1	—	Carbon	1616
36	8	H	Chesterfield	L	0-1	0-1	14		5141
37	11	H	Fulham	W	2-0	1-0	—	Carbon, Hill	2932
38	15	A	Darlington	D	0-0	0-0	13		1664
39	17	H	Scunthorpe U	D	3-3	2-2	12	Carbon, Greenall, Williams	3330
40	22	A	Colchester U	W	2-1	1-1	12	Bannister, Huckerby	2654
41	29	H	Bury	L	0-3	0-2	12		3928
42	May 6	A	Carlisle U	W	3-1	1-0	12	Bannister, Huckerby, Daws	12,412

Final League Position: 12

GOALSCORERS

League (54): Bannister 7 (2 pens), Carbon 7, Daws 7 (3 pens), West 6, Johnson D 4 (1 pen), Daley 4, Puttnam 4, Brown 3, Greenall 3, Hill 3, Huckerby 2, Matthews 2, Schofield 1, Williams 1.
Coca-Cola Cup (6): Johnson D 2 (1 pen), Schofield 2, Carbon 1, West 1.
FA Cup (3): Bannister 1, Greenall 1, Johnson D 1.

Hoult R. 15	Schofield J.D. 12	Platnauer N.R. 13	Hebberd T.N. 20 + 5	Greenall C.A. 39	Brown G.A. 39	West D. 41	Onwere U.A. 7 + 1	Daley P. 19 + 1	Daws A. 20 + 6	Johnson D.A. 23 + 1	Johnson A.K. 24 + 1	Matthews N. 17 + 6	Carbon M.P. 30 + 3	Puttnam D.P. 8 + 9	Foley S. 15 + 1	Bannister G. 25 + 4	Lucas R. 4	Hill D.M. 25 + 1	Leaning A.J. 21	Dixon B. 17 + 1	Smith P.M. 15 + 2	Williams S.R. 3 + 3	Sherwood S. 6 + 1	Huckerby D.C. 4 + 2	Match No.
1	2	3	4	5	6	7	8	9	*10*	11	12	14													1
1	2	3	4	5	6	7		9		11	8	12	10												2
1	2	3	4	5	6	7		9		11	8		10												3
1	2	3	12	5	6	7	4	9	14	11	8		*10*												4
1	2	3	12	5	6	7	4	9		11	8		*10*	14											5
1	2	3		5	6	7		9		11	8			10	4										6
1	2	3	12	5	6	7		9		11	8			10	4										7
1	2	3		5	6	7		9		11	8			10	4	12									8
1	2	3		5	6	7	8						11	10	4	9									9
1	2	3	12	5	6	7	8	14					*11*	10	4	9									10
1	2	3	4	5	6	7	8	9			11		12			10									11
1	2		12	5	6	7	8	*9*					11	14	4	10	3								12
1			7	5	6	2		9			3		11	12	4	10	8								13
1			4	5	6	2		9			3	8		11		10	7	12							14
1			4	5	6	2		9			3	8	12			10	7	11							15
			8	5	6	2		9			3	7	12		4	10		11	1						16
			8	5	6	2		9	14	12	3	7			4	*10*		11	1						17
			8	5	6	2		9	12	*10*	3	7	4			14		11	1						18
			4	5	6	2		9	8	10		7		12		14		*11*	1	3					19
			8	5	6	2		9	10		3		4	12	7	11			1						20
			7	5	6	2		9	14	11	3		4	*10*	12	8			1						21
			8		6	2	12		14	10	3		4	11	7	*9*			1	5					22
			4			2			10	11	3		9		8			7	1	5	6				23
			4		6	2			10	7	3		9		8			11	1	5	12				24
			4	5	6	2			10	7	3	9			8			11	1		12				25
				5	6	2			10	7	3	9			8			11	1		4				26
				5	6	2			10	7	3	*9*	8					11	1	12	4	14			27
			10	5	6	2				7	3		8			12		11	1		4	9			28
			8	5	6	2				7	3		9			10		11	1		4				29
			8	5	6	2			12	7			9			10		11	1	3	4				30
				5	6	2			8	7		12	9			10		11	1	3	4				31
				5	6	2			8	7		12	9			10		11	1	3	4				32
				5	6	2			10	7		12	9			8		11	1	3	4				33
				5	6	2			10			7	9	12		8		11	*1*	3	4		15		34
				5	6	2			10			7	9	12		*8*		11		3	4		1	14	35
				5	6	2			10			7	9	12		8		11		3	4		1		36
				5	6	2			8			7	9			10		11		3	4		1		37
				5	6	2			8			7	9			10		11		3	4	12	1	14	38
				5	*6*	2			8			12	9			10		11		3	4	14	1	7	39
		4		5					8			7	9			10		11		3		6	1	2	40
				5	6	2			8			7	9	12				11	1	3		4		10	41
		4		5		2			8			7	9			6		11	1	3				10	42

Coca-Cola Cup

First Round	Chester C (h)	2-0
	(a)	3-2
Second Round	Crystal Palace (h)	1-0
	(a)	0-3

FA Cup

First Round	Hull C (a)	1-0
Second Round	Huddersfield T (h)	1-0
Third Round	Crystal Palace (a)	1-5

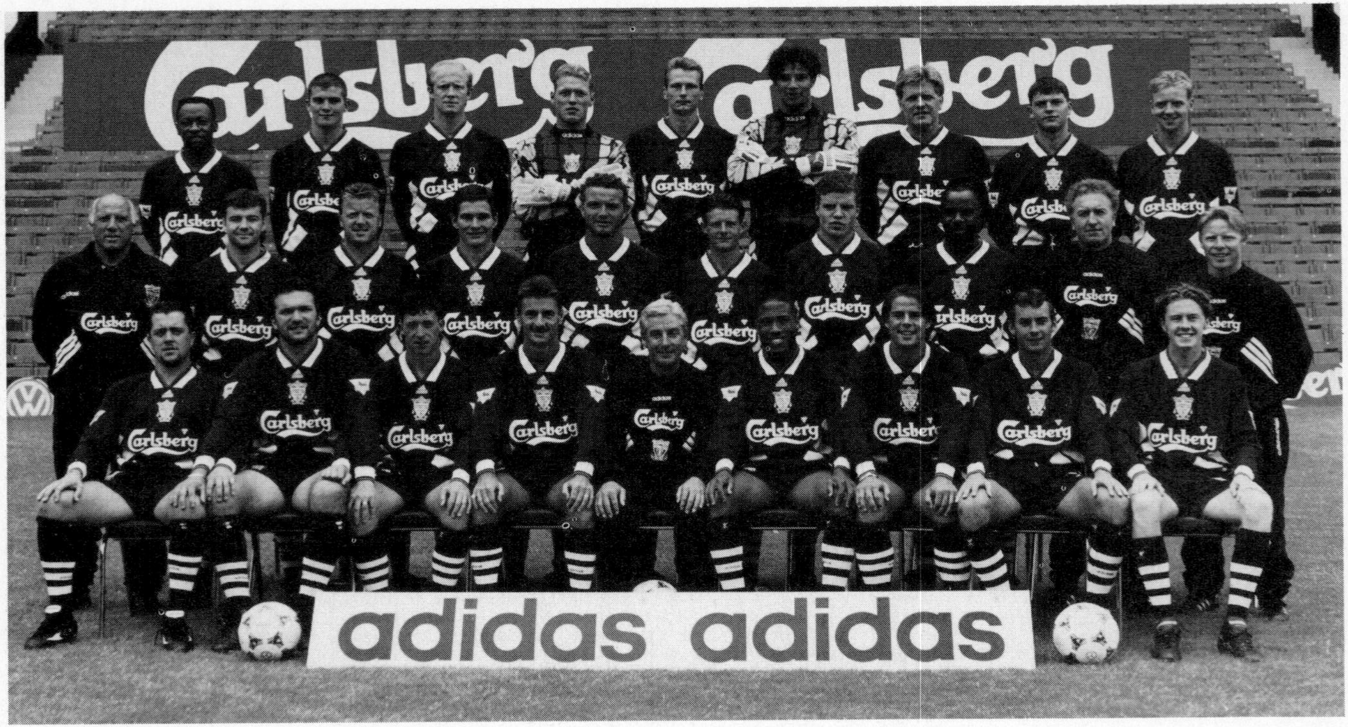

LIVERPOOL 1994–95 *Back row (left to right):* Mark Walters, Dominic Matteo, Mark Wright, Michael Stensgaard, Torben Piechnik, David James, Jan Molby, Phil Charnock, Rob Jones.
Centre row: Ronnie Moran (Coach), Steve Harkness, Steve Nicol, Nigel Clough, Paul Stewart, Lee Jones, Stig Bjornebye, Michael Thomas, Doug Livermore (Assistant Manager), Sammy Lee (Coach).
Front row: Julian Dicks, Neil Ruddock, Robbie Fowler, Ian Rush, Roy Evans (Team Manager), John Barnes, Jamie Redknapp, Don Hutchison, Steve McManaman.

FA Premiership **LIVERPOOL**

Anfield Road, Liverpool L4 0TH. Telephone: (0151) 263 2361. Fax: (0151) 260 8813. Clubcall: 0891 121184. Ticket and Match Information: (0151) 260 9999 (24-hour service) or (0151) 260 8680 (office hours) Credit Card Bookings.

Ground Capacity: 41,000.

Record attendance: 61,905 v Wolverhampton W, FA Cup 4th rd, 2 February 1952.

Record receipts: £445,000 v Tottenham H, FA Cup 6th rd, 11 March 1995.

Pitch measurements: 110yd × 74yd.

Chairman: D. R. Moores.

Directors:J. T. Cross, N. White FSCA, T. D. Smith, T. W. Saunders, P. B. Robinson, K. E. B. Clayton FCA.

Vice-Presidents: C. J. Hill, H. E. Roberts, W. D. Corkish FCA, R. Paisley OBE, HON MSC.

Team Manager: Roy Evans. ***Assistant Manager:*** Doug Livermore. ***Coach:*** Ronnie Moran.
Physio: Mark Leather.

Chief Executive/General Secretary: Peter B. Robinson. ***Commercial Manager:*** Mike Turner.

Year Formed: 1892. ***Turned Professional:*** 1892. ***Ltd Co.:*** 1892.

Club Nickname: 'Reds' or 'Pool'.

Foundation: But for a dispute between Everton FC and their landlord at Anfield in 1892, there may never have been a Liverpool club. This dispute persuaded the majority of Evertonians to quit Anfield for Goodison Park, leaving the landlord, Mr. John Houlding, to form a new club. He originally tried to retain the name "Everton" but when this failed, he founded Liverpool Association FC on 15 March, 1892.

First Football League game: 2 September, 1893, Division 2, v Middlesbrough Ironopolis (a) W 2-0 – McOwen; Hannah, McLean; Henderson, McQue (1), McBride; Gordon, McVean (1), M. McQueen, Stott, H. McQueen.

Record League Victory: 10–1 v Rotherham T, Division 2, 18 February 1896 – Storer; Goldie, Wilkie; McCarthy, McQueen, Holmes; McVean (3), Ross (2), Allan (4), Becton (1), Bradshaw.

Record Cup Victory: 11–0 v Stromsgodset Drammen, ECWC 1st rd 1st leg, 17 September 1974 – Clemence; Smith (1), Lindsay (1p), Thompson (2), Cormack (1), Hughes (1), Boersma (2), Hall, Heighway (1), Kennedy (1), Callaghan (1).

Record Defeat: 1–9 v Birmingham C, Division 2, 11 December 1954.

Most League Points (2 for a win): 68, Division 1, 1978–79.

Most League Points (3 for a win): 90, Division 1, 1987–88.

Most League Goals: 106, Division 2, 1895–96.

Highest League Scorer in Season: Roger Hunt, 41, Division 2, 1961–62.

Most League Goals in Total Aggregate: Roger Hunt, 245, 1959–69.

Most Capped Player: Ian Rush, 65 (71), Wales.

Most League Appearances: Ian Callaghan, 640, 1960–78.

Record Transfer Fee Received: £2,750,000 from Juventus for Ian Rush, June 1986.

Record Transfer Fee Paid: £8,500,000 to Nottingham F for Stan Collymore, June 1995.

Football League Record: 1893 Elected to Division 2; 1894–95 Division 1; 1895–96 Division 2; 1896–1904 Division 1; 1904–05 Division 2; 1905–54 Division 1; 1954–62 Division 2; 1962–92 Division 1; 1992– FA Premier Division.

Honours: *Football League:* Division 1 – Champions 1900–01, 1905–06, 1921–22, 1922–23, 1946–47, 1963–64, 1965–66, 1972–73, 1975–76, 1976–77, 1978–79, 1979–80, 1981–82, 1982–83, 1983–84, 1985–86, 1987–88, 1989–90 (Liverpool have a record number of 18 League Championship wins); Runners-up 1898–99, 1909–10, 1968–69, 1973–74, 1974–75, 1977–78, 1984–85, 1986–87, 1988–89, 1990–91; Division 2 – Champions 1893–94, 1895–96, 1904–05, 1961–62. *FA Cup:* Winners 1965, 1974, 1986, 1989, 1992; Runners-up 1914, 1950, 1971, 1977, 1988; *Football League Cup:* Winners 1981, 1982, 1983, 1984, 1995; Runners-up 1978, 1987. *League Super Cup:* Winners 1986. **European Competitions:** *European Cup:* 1964–65, 1966–67, 1973–74, 1976–77 (winners), 1977–78 (winners), 1978–79, 1979–80, 1980–81 (winners), 1981–82, 1982–83, 1983–84 (winners), 1984–85 (runners-up); *European Cup-Winners' Cup:* 1965–66 (runners-up), 1971–72, 1974–75, 1992–93; *European Fairs Cup:* 1967–68, 1968–69, 1969–70, 1970–71; *UEFA Cup:* 1972–73 (winners), 1975–76 (winners), 1991–92; *Super Cup:* 1977 (winners), 1978, 1984; *World Club Championship:* 1981 (runners-up).

Colours: All red. **Change colours:** White and green.

LIVERPOOL 1994–95 LEAGUE RECORD

Match No.	Date	Venue	Opponents	Result		H/T Score	Lg. Pos.	Goalscorers	Attendance
1	Aug 20	A	Crystal Palace	W	6-1	3-0	—	Molby (pen), McManaman 2, Fowler, Rush 2	18,084
2	28	H	Arsenal	W	3-0	3-0	5	Fowler 3	30,017
3	31	A	Southampton	W	2-0	1-0	—	Fowler, Barnes	15,190
4	Sept 10	H	West Ham U	D	0-0	0-0	4		30,907
5	17	A	Manchester U	L	0-2	0-0	5		43,740
6	24	A	Newcastle U	D	1-1	0-0	6	Rush	34,435
7	Oct 1	H	Sheffield W	W	4-1	0-1	5	McManaman 2, Walker (og), Rush	31,493
8	8	H	Aston Villa	W	3-2	2-1	4	Ruddock, Fowler 2	32,158
9	15	A	Blackburn R	L	2-3	1-0	5	Fowler, Barnes	30,263
10	22	H	Wimbledon	W	3-0	2-0	5	McManaman, Fowler, Barnes	31,139
11	29	A	Ipswich T	W	3-1	1-0	5	Barnes, Fowler 2	22,379
12	31	A	QPR	L	1-2	0-1	—	Barnes	18,295
13	Nov 5	H	Nottingham F	W	1-0	1-0	5	Fowler	33,329
14	9	H	Chelsea	W	3-1	3-1	—	Fowler 2, Ruddock	32,855
15	21	A	Everton	L	0-2	0-0	—		39,866
16	26	H	Tottenham H	D	1-1	1-0	4	Fowler (pen)	35,007
17	Dec 3	A	Coventry C	D	1-1	1-0	4	Rush	21,032
18	11	H	Crystal Palace	D	0-0	0-0	4		30,972
19	18	A	Chelsea	D	0-0	0-0	5		27,050
20	26	A	Leicester C	W	2-1	0-0	4	Fowler (pen), Rush	21,393
21	28	H	Manchester C	W	2-0	0-0	3	Phelan (og), Fowler	38,122
22	31	A	Leeds U	W	2-0	1-0	3	Redknapp, Fowler	38,468
23	Jan 2	H	Norwich C	W	4-0	2-0	3	Scales, Fowler 2, Rush	34,709
24	14	H	Ipswich T	L	0-1	0-1	3		32,733
25	24	H	Everton	D	0-0	0-0	—		39,505
26	Feb 4	A	Nottingham F	D	1-1	0-1	4	Fowler	25,418
27	11	H	QPR	D	1-1	0-1	4	Scales	35,996
28	25	A	Sheffield W	W	2-1	1-1	4	Barnes, McManaman	31,964
29	Mar 4	H	Newcastle U	W	2-0	0-0	4	Fowler, Rush	39,300
30	14	H	Coventry C	L	2-3	0-2	—	Molby (pen), Burrows (og)	27,183
31	19	H	Manchester U	W	2-0	1-0	4	Bruce (og), Redknapp	38,906
32	22	A	Tottenham H	D	0-0	0-0	—		31,988
33	Apr 5	H	Southampton	W	3-1	1-1	—	Rush 2, Fowler (pen)	29,881
34	9	H	Leeds U	L	0-1	0-1	5		37,454
35	12	A	Arsenal	W	1-0	0-0	—	Fowler	38,036
36	14	A	Manchester C	L	1-2	1-1	—	McManaman	27,055
37	17	H	Leicester C	W	2-0	0-0	4	Fowler, Rush	36,012
38	29	A	Norwich C	W	2-1	1-1	4	Harkness, Rush	21,843
39	May 2	A	Wimbledon	D	0-0	0-0	—		12,041
40	6	A	Aston Villa	L	0-2	0-2	4		40,154
41	10	A	West Ham U	L	0-3	0-1	—		22,446
42	14	H	Blackburn R	W	2-1	0-1	4	Barnes, Redknapp	40,014

Final League Position: 4

GOALSCORERS

League (65): Fowler 25 (3 pens), Rush 12, Barnes 7, McManaman 7, Redknapp 3, Molby 2 (2 pens), Ruddock 2, Scales 2, Harkness 1, own goals 4.
Coca-Cola Cup (16): Rush 6, Fowler 4, McManaman 2, Redknapp 2, Clough 1, Scales 1.
FA Cup (6): Barnes 2, Fowler 2, Redknapp 1, Rush 1.

James D.B. 42	Jones R.M. 31	Bjornebye S.I. 31	Nicol S. 4	Molby J. 12 + 2	Ruddock N. 37	McManaman S. 40	Redknapp J.F. 36 + 5	Rush I.J. 36	Barnes J.C.B. 38	Fowler R.B. 42	Thomas M.L. 16 + 7	Scales J.R. 35	Babb P.A. 33 + 1	Clough N.H. 3 + 7	Jones P.L. — + 1	Harkness S. 8	Walters M.E. 7 + 11	Matteo D. 2 + 5	Wright M. 5 + 1	Kennedy M. 4 + 2	*Match No.*
1	2	3	4	5	6	7	8	9	10	11	12										1
1	2	3	4	5	6	7	8	9	10	11	12										2
1	2	3	4	5	6	7	8	9	10	11											3
1	2	3		5	6	7	8	9	10	11		4									4
1	2	3		5	6	7	8	9	10	11		4	12								5
1	2	3		8	6	7		9	10	11		4	5	12							6
1	2	3	4	8	6	7	12	9	10	11			5								7
1	2	3		8	6	7	12	9	10	11		4	5								8
1	2	3		8	6	7	12	9	10	11		4	5								9
1	2	3			6	7	8	9	10	*11*		4	5	12	14						10
1	2	3			6	7	8	9	10	11		4	5								11
1	2	3		12	6	7	8	9	10	11		4	5								12
1	2	3		12	6	7	8	9	10	11		4	5								13
1	2	3		4	6	7	8	9	10	11			5								14
1	2	3		8	6	7	12	9	10	11		4	5								15
1	2	3			6	7	8	9	10	11	12	4	5								16
1		2			6	7	8	9		11	10	4	5			3	12				17
1		2			6		8		10	11	7	4	5	9		3	12				18
1		3			6		8	9	10	11	2	4	5				7				19
1	2	3			6	7	8	9	10	11	12	4	5								20
1	2	3			6	7	8	9	10	11		4	5								21
1	2	3			6	7	8	9	10	11		4	5								22
1	2	3			6	7	8	9	10	11		4	5								23
1	2	3			6	7	8	9		11	10	4	5				12				24
1	2	3			6	7	8	9	10	11		4	5								25
1	2				6	7	8	9	10	11	12	4	5				14	*3*			26
1	2	*3*			6	7	12	9	10	11	8	4	5				14				27
1	2	3				7	6		10	9	8	4	5				11	12			28
1	2				6	7	4	9	10	11	12	5	3				8				29
1	2	3		5	6	7	8	9		11	10	4					12				30
1		3			6	7	8	9	*10*	11	14	4	5				12		2		31
1	2	3			6	7	8			11	9	4	5	12			10				32
1	2	3			6	7	8	9	10	11		4	5				12				33
1	2				6	7	4	9	10	11		5	3				8			12	34
1	*2*				6	7	4		10	8	9	5	3				12		14	11	35
1					6	7	4	9	10	8	5		3	12				14	2	11	36
1					6	7	4	9	10	8	2			12		3			5	11	37
1						7	8	9	10	*11*	2	4	5	12		3	14		6		38
1					6	7	4	9	10	11	2	5				3	8	12			39
1						7	4	9	10	11	2	5		12		3	*8*	14	6		40
1						7	8		10	11	2	4	5	9		6	12	*3*		14	41
1						7	6		10	8	2	4	5	9		3		12		11	42

Coca-Cola Cup

Second Round	Burnley (h)	2-0
	(a)	4-1
Third Round	Stoke C (h)	2-1
Fourth Round	Blackburn R (a)	3-1
Fifth Round	Arsenal (h)	1-0
Semi-final	Crystal Palace (h)	1-0
	(a)	1-0
Final at Wembley	Bolton W	2-1

FA Cup

Third Round	Birmingham C (a)	0-0
	(h)	1-1
Fourth Round	Burnley (a)	0-0
	(h)	1-0
Fifth Round	Wimbledon (h)	1-1
	(a)	2-0
Sixth Round	Tottenham H (h)	1-2

LUTON TOWN 1994–95 *Back row (left to right):* Tony Adcock, Des Linton, Mitchell Thomas, Juergen Sommer, Marvin Johnson, David Greene, John Hartson.
Centre row: Clive Goodyear (Physio), Martin Williams, Richard Harvey, Julian James, Kerry Dixon, Aaron Skelton, Scott Oakes, Dwight Marshall, John Moore (Coach).
Front row: Ceri Hughes, Scott Houghton, David Preece, David Pleat (Manager), Trevor Peake, Tony Thorpe, Paul Telfer.

Division 1 LUTON TOWN

Kenilworth Road Stadium, 1 Maple Rd, Luton, Beds. LU4 8AW. Telephone: (01582) 411622. Ticket Office: (01582) 416976. Credit Hotline: (01582) 30748 (24 hrs). Banqueting: (01582) 411526. Clubcall: 0891 121123.

Ground capacity: 9975.

Record attendance: 30,069 v Blackpool, FA Cup 6th rd replay, 4 March 1959.

Record receipts: £115,541.20 v West Ham U, FA Cup 6th rd, 23 March 1994.

Pitch measurements: 110yd × 72yd.

Chairman & Managing Director: D. A. Kohler BSC (HONS), ARICS.

Directors: C. S. Bassett, C. T. F. Green, N. S. Terry.

Secretary: Cherry Newbery.

Commercial Manager: Kathy Leather.

Manager: Terry Westley. ***Assistant Manager:*** Mick McGiven. ***Coaches:*** Wayne Turner, John Moore.

Physio: Clive Goodyear.

Year Formed: 1885. ***Turned Professional:*** 1890. ***Ltd Co.:*** 1897.

Club Nickname: 'The Hatters'.

Previous Grounds: 1885, Excelsior, Dallow Lane; 1897, Dunstable Road; 1905, Kenilworth Road.

Foundation: Formed by an amalgamation of two leading local clubs, Wanderers and Excelsior a works team, at a meeting in Luton Town Hall in April 1885. The Wanderers had three months earlier changed their name to Luton Town Wanderers and did not take too kindly to the formation of another Town club but were talked around at this meeting. Wanderers had already appeared in the FA Cup and the new club entered in its inaugural season.

First Football League game: 4 September, 1897, Division 2, v Leicester Fosse (a) D 1-1 – Williams; McCartney, McEwen; Davies, Stewart, Docherty; Gallacher, Coupar, Birch, McInnes, Ekins (1).

Record League Victory: 12–0 v Bristol R, Division 3 (S), 13 April 1936 – Dolman; Mackey, Smith; Finlayson, Nelson, Godfrey; Rich, Martin (1), Payne (10), Roberts (1), Stephenson.

Record Cup Victory: 9–0 v Clapton, FA Cup, 1st rd (replay after abandoned game), 30 November 1927 – Abbott; Kingham, Graham; Black, Rennie, Fraser; Pointon, Yardley (4), Reid (2), Woods (1), Dennis (2).

Record Defeat: 0–9 v Small Heath, Division 2, 12 November 1898.

Most League Points (2 for a win): 66, Division 4, 1967–68.

Most League Points (3 for a win): 88, Division 2, 1981–82.

Most League Goals: 103, Division 3 (S), 1936–37.

Highest League Scorer in Season: Joe Payne, 55, Division 3 (S), 1936–37.

Most League Goals in Total Aggregate: Gordon Turner, 243, 1949–64.

Most Capped Player: Mal Donaghy, 58 (91), Northern Ireland.

Most League Appearances: Bob Morton, 494, 1948–64.

Record Transfer Fee Received: £2,500,000 from Arsenal for John Hartson, January 1995.

Record Transfer Fee Paid: £850,000 to Odense for Lars Elstrup, August 1989.

Football League Record: 1897 Elected to Division 2; 1900 Failed re-election; 1920 Division 3; 1921–37 Division 3 (S); 1937–55 Division 2; 1955–60 Division 1; 1960–63 Division 2; 1963–65 Division 3; 1965–68 Division 4; 1968–70 Division 3; 1970–74 Division 2; 1974–75 Division 1; 1975–82 Division 2; 1982– Division 1.

Honours: *Football League:* Division 1 best season: 7th, 1986–87; Division 2 – Champions 1981–82; Runners-up 1954–55, 1973–74; Division 3 – Runners-up 1969–70; Division 4 – Champions 1967–68; Division 3 (S) – Champions 1936–37; Runners-up 1935–36. *FA Cup:* Runners-up 1959. *Football League Cup:* Winners 1988; Runners-up 1989. *Simod Cup:* Runners-up 1988.

Colours: White shirts with blue sleeves with white and orange trim, blue collar with orange trim, blue shorts with orange and white trim, blue and white hooped stockings with orange trim. **Change colours:** Black and orange vertical striped shirts, with black collar and orange trim, black shorts with orange stripe down side, black stockings with orange turnover.

LUTON TOWN 1994–95 LEAGUE RECORD

Match No.	Date	Venue	Opponents	Result	H/T Score	Lg. Pos.	Goalscorers	Attendance
1	Aug 13	H	WBA	D 1-1	0-1	—	Oakes	8640
2	20	A	Derby Co	D 0-0	0-0	14		13,060
3	27	H	Southend U	D 2-2	1-0	17	Hartson, Hughes	5918
4	30	A	Tranmere R	L 2-4	0-0	—	Hughes, Hartson	5480
5	Sept 3	A	Port Vale	W 1-0	0-0	15	Marshall	8541
6	10	H	Burnley	L 0-1	0-1	18		6911
7	13	H	Bolton W	L 0-3	0-0	—		5764
8	17	A	Watford	W 4-2	3-2	16	Oakes, Dixon, Telfer 2	8880
9	24	A	Millwall	D 0-0	0-0	16		7150
10	Oct 1	H	Bristol C	L 0-1	0-0	20		6633
11	9	A	Stoke C	W 2-1	1-0	18	Marshall, Preece	11,712
12	15	H	Middlesbrough	W 5-1	3-0	11	Wilkinson (og), Marshall 2, Preece, Hartson	8412
13	22	A	Sheffield U	W 3-1	1-1	7	Gayle (og), James, Dixon	13,317
14	29	H	Barnsley	L 0-1	0-0	10		7212
15	Nov 1	H	Grimsby T	L 1-2	0-0	—	Oakes	5839
16	5	A	Wolverhampton W	W 3-2	1-0	8	Preece, Marshall, Dixon	26,749
17	12	A	Oldham Ath	D 0-0	0-0	8		7907
18	19	H	Portsmouth	W 2-0	1-0	8	Dixon, Preece	8214
19	26	A	Swindon T	W 2-1	1-1	5	Dixon, Oakes	9455
20	Dec 3	H	Sheffield U	L 3-6	0-2	8	Hartson, Gayle (og), Johnson (pen)	8516
21	11	H	Derby Co	D 0-0	0-0	10		6400
22	18	A	WBA	L 0-1	0-1	12		14,392
23	26	A	Reading	D 0-0	0-0	12		11,623
24	27	H	Sunderland	W 3-0	2-0	9	Oakes 2, Hartson	8953
25	31	A	Notts Co	W 1-0	0-0	8	Telfer	6249
26	Jan 2	H	Charlton Ath	L 0-1	0-1	8		7642
27	14	A	Barnsley	L 1-3	0-0	11	Dixon	4808
28	Feb 4	H	Oldham Ath	W 2-1	1-0	10	Marshall 2	6903
29	11	A	Grimsby T	L 0-5	0-2	10		4615
30	18	H	Swindon T	W 3-0	1-0	9	Horlock (og), Marshall 2	6595
31	21	A	Portsmouth	L 2-3	1-0	—	Telfer, James	7363
32	25	A	Bristol C	D 2-2	1-0	10	Oakes 2	7939
33	Mar 4	H	Millwall	D 1-1	1-0	10	Marshall	6864
34	7	H	Port Vale	W 2-1	0-0	—	Telfer, Dixon	5947
35	11	A	Southend U	L 0-3	0-1	11		4558
36	18	H	Tranmere R	W 2-0	1-0	10	James, Biggins	6660
37	21	A	Burnley	L 1-2	0-0	—	Marshall	9551
38	26	H	Watford	D 1-1	1-0	11	Telfer	7984
39	Apr 4	H	Wolverhampton W	D 3-3	2-0	—	Telfer 2, Taylor	9651
40	8	H	Notts Co	W 2-0	1-0	12	Telfer, Oakes (pen)	6482
41	11	A	Bolton W	D 0-0	0-0	—		13,619
42	15	A	Sunderland	D 1-1	1-0	11	Taylor	17,292
43	17	H	Reading	L 0-1	0-1	11		8717
44	22	A	Charlton Ath	L 0-1	0-0	12		10,867
45	30	A	Middlesbrough	L 1-2	0-1	16	Taylor	23,903
46	May 7	H	Stoke C	L 2-3	1-0	16	Harvey, Waddock	8252

Final League Position: 16

GOALSCORERS

League (61): Marshall 11, Oakes 9 (1 pen), Telfer 9, Dixon 7, Hartson 5, Preece 4, James 3, Taylor 3, Hughes 2, Biggins 1, Harvey 1, Johnson 1 (pen), Waddock 1, own goals 4.
Coca-Cola Cup (2): Marshall 1, Oakes 1.
FA Cup (3): Biggins 1, Hartson 1, Marshall 1.

Sommer J.P. 37	James J.C. 42	Johnson M.A. 46	Skelton A.M. 3 + 2	Greene D.M. 7 + 1	Peake T. 46	Telfer P.N. 45 + 1	Oakes S.J. 37 + 6	Dixon K.M. 23 + 6	Preece D.W. 42	Houghton S.A. 1	Linton D.M. 5 + 5	Marshall D.W. 36 + 9	Hughes C.M. 8 + 1	Hartson J. 11 + 9	Thomas M.A. 33 + 3	Woodsford J.M. 1 + 6	Waddock G.P. 40	Thorpe A. — + 4	Allen P.K. 4	Williams M.K. — + 2	Adcock A.C. — + 2	Harvey R.G. 9 + 3	Biggins W. 6 + 1	Matthews R. 6 + 5	Davis K.G. 9	Taylor J.P. 9	Match No.
1	2	3	4	5	6	7	8	9	10	*11*	12	14															1
1	2	3		5	6	7		9	10		4	8	11														2
1	2	3		5	6	7	8	12	10			*11*	4	9	14												3
1	2	3	4	5	6	7	8		10			12	11	9													4
1	2	3	4	5	6	7	11	9	*10*			8			12	14											5
1	2	3		*5*	6	7	11	12	10			8		9	14		4										6
1	2	3			6	7	8	9	10		12	14		*11*	5		4										7
1	2	3			6	7	8	9	10			11			5		4										8
1	2	3			6	7	8	9	10			11		12	5		4										9
1	2	3			6	7	8	9	10			11	14	12	*5*		4										10
1	2	3			6	7	12		10			11	8	9	5		4										11
1	2	3			6	7	12		10			11	8	9	5		4										12
1	2	3			6	7	12	9	10			11	8		5		4										13
1	2	3			6	7	12	14	10			11	8	9	5		*4*										14
1	2	3			6	7	12		10			11	8	9	5		4										15
1	2	3			6	7	8	9	10			11		12	5		4										16
1	2	3			6	7	8	9	10			11		12	5		4										17
1	2	3			6	7	8	9	10			11			5		4	12									18
1	2	3			6	7	8	9	10		11			12	5		4										19
1	2	3			6	7	8	9	10		*11*	12		14	5		4										20
1	2	3			6	7	8	9	10			14		12	5		4		*11*								21
1	2	3			6	7	8	9	10			11		12	5				4								22
1	2	3			6	7	12	*9*	10			11		14	5		4		8								23
1	2	3	12		6	7	8		10			*11*		9	5		4			14							24
1	2	3			6	7	8		10			11		9	5		4				12						25
1	2	3			6	7	8					11		9	5		4		10		12						26
1	2	3	12		6	7	8	9				11			5		4					10					27
1	2	3			6	7	8	9				11			5		4	12					10				28
1	2	3			6	12	8	*9*	7			11			5	14	4						10				29
1	2	3			6	7	8	12	10			*11*			5	14	4						9				30
1	2	3			6	7	*8*	9	10			11			5	12	4					14					31
1	2	3			6	7	8	9	10			11			5		4			12							32
1	2	3			6	7	8	12	10			11			5		*4*						9	14			33
1	2	3			6	7	8	12	10			11			5		*4*						9	14			34
1	2	3			6	7	8	9				11			5		4						12	10			35
1	2	3			6	7	8		10			11			5		4						9	12			36
1	2	3			6	7		9	10			11			*5*	12	4					14		8			37
	2	3			6	7			10			11					4	12				5		8	1	9	38
	2	3			6	7	8		10			11				12	4					5			1	9	39
	2	3			6	7	8		10		12	*11*					4					5		14	1	9	40
	2	3			6	7	8		10		12	14					4					5		11	1	9	41
		3		12	6	7	8		10		2	14					4					5		*11*	1	9	42
	2	3			6	7	8		10		12	11					*4*					5		14	1	9	43
		3		2	6	7	8		10			12			5		4					14		*11*	1	9	44
		3			6	7	8		10		2	11					4	12				5			1	9	45
		2			6	7	8		10			12			5	11	4					3			1	9	46

Coca-Cola Cup

First Round	Fulham (h)	1-1
	(a)	1-1

FA Cup

Third Round	Bristol R (h)	1-1
	(a)	1-0
Fourth Round	Southampton (h)	1-1
	(a)	0-6

MANCHESTER CITY 1994–95 *Back row (left to right):* Nick Summerbee, Ian Brightwell, Rae Ingram, Adie Mike, Andy Hill, Alan Kernaghan, David Kerr, Mike Sheron, Alphonse Groenendijk, Garry Flitcroft.

Centre row: Les Chapman (Reserve Team Manager), David Moss (Assistant Manager), Paul Lake, Steve Lomas, Michael Vonk, Martyn Margetson, Tony Coton, Andy Dibble, David Brightwell, Niall Quinn, Uwe Rosler, Eamonn Salmon (Physio), Tony Book (Reserve Team Coach).

Front row: Peter Beagrie, Michael Quigley, Carl Griffiths, Richard Edghill, Steve McMahon, Brian Horton (Manager), Keith Curle, Fitzroy Simpson, Jonathan Foster, Terry Phelan, Paul Walsh.

FA Premiership **MANCHESTER CITY**

Maine Road, Moss Side, Manchester M14 7WN. Telephone: (0161) 226 1191/2. Fax: (0161) 227 9418. Ticket Office: (0161) 226 2224. Dial-A-Seat: (0161) 227 9229. Development Office: (0161) 226 3143. Clubcall: 0891 121191. Ticketcall: 0891 121591.

Ground capacity: 28,053.

Record attendance: 84,569 v Stoke C, FA Cup 6th rd, 3 March 1934 (British record for any game outside London or Glasgow).

Record receipts: £512,235 Manchester U v Oldham Ath, FA Cup semi-final replay, 13 April 1994.

Pitch measurements: 117yd × 78yd.

Chairman: F. H. Lee. ***Vice-Chairman:*** F. Pye. ***Managing Director:*** C. J. Barlow.

Directors: I. L. G. Niven, A. Thomas, J. G. Dunkerley, W. A. Miles, G. Doyle, B. Turnbull, J. Greibach, D. A. Holt, A. M. Lewis, G. J. Grant, B. Jervis.

General Secretary: J. B. Halford. ***Commercial Manager:*** G. Durbin.

Manager: Alan Ball. ***Assistant Manager:***Asa Hartford. ***First Team Coach:*** Tony Book.
Physio: Eamonn Salmon. ***Youth Team Coach:*** Neil McNab.

Year Formed: 1887 as Ardwick FC; 1894 as Manchester City.

Turned Professional: 1887 as Ardwick FC. ***Ltd Co.:*** 1894. ***Club Nickname:*** Blues The Citizens.

Previous Names: 1887–94, Ardwick FC (formed through the amalgamation of West Gorton and Gorton Athletic, the latter having been formed in 1880).

Previous Grounds: 1880–81, Clowes Street; 1881–82, Kirkmanshulme Cricket Ground; 1882–84, Queens Road; 1884–87, Pink Bank Lane; 1887–1923, Hyde Road (1894–1923, as City); 1923, Maine Road.

Foundation: Manchester City was formed as a Limited Company in 1894 after their predecessors Ardwick had been forced into bankruptcy. However, many historians like to trace the club's lineage as far back as 1880 when St. Mark's Church, West Gorton added a football section to their cricket club. They amalgamated with Gorton Athletic in 1884 as Gorton FC. Because of a change of ground they became Ardwick in 1887.

First Football League game: 3 September, 1892, Division 2, v Bootle (h) W 7-0 – Douglas; McVickers, Robson; Middleton, Russell, Hopkins; Davies (3), Morris (2), Angus (1), Weir (1), Milarvie.

Record League Victory: 10–1 Huddersfield T, Division 2, 7 November 1987 – Nixon; Gidman, Hinchcliffe, Clements, Lake, Redmond, White (3), Stewart (3), Adcock (3), McNab (1) Simpson.

Record Cup Victory: 10–1 v Swindon T, FA Cup, 4th rd, 29 January 1930 – Barber; Felton, McCloy; Barrass, Cowan, Heinemann; Toseland, Marshall (5), Tait (3), Johnson (1), Brook (1).

Record Defeat: 1–9 v Everton, Division 1, 3 September 1906.

Most League Points (2 for a win): 62, Division 2, 1946–47.

Most League Points (3 for a win): 82, Division 2, 1988–89.

Most League Goals: 108, Division 2, 1926–27.

Highest League Scorer in Season: Tommy Johnson, 38, Division 1, 1928–29.

Most League Goals in Total Aggregate: Tommy Johnson, 158, 1919–30.

Most Capped Player: Colin Bell, 48, England.

Most League Appearances: Alan Oakes, 565, 1959–76.

Record Transfer Fee Received: £1,700,000 from Tottenham H for Paul Stewart, June 1988.

Record Transfer Fee Paid: £2,500,000 to Wimbledon for Keith Curle, August 1991.

Football League Record: 1892 Ardwick elected founder member of Division 2; 1894 Newly-formed Manchester C elected to Division 2; Division 1 1899–1902, 1903–09, 1910–26, 1928–38, 1947–50, 1951–63, 1966–83, 1985–87, 1989–92; Division 2 1902–03, 1909–10, 1926–28, 1938–47, 1950–51, 1963–66, 1983–85, 1987–89; 1992– FA Premier League.

Honours: *Football League:* Division 1 – Champions 1936–37, 1967–68; Runners-up 1903–04, 1920–21, 1976–77; Division 2 – Champions 1898–99, 1902–03, 1909–10, 1927–28, 1946–47, 1965–66; Runners-up 1895–96, 1950–51, 1987–88. *FA Cup:* Winners 1904, 1934, 1956, 1969; Runners-up 1926, 1933, 1955, 1981. *Football League Cup:* Winners 1970, 1976; Runners-up 1974. **European Competitions:** *European Cup:* 1968–69. *European Cup-Winners' Cup:* 1969–70 (winners), 1970–71. *UEFA Cup:* 1972–73, 1976–77, 1977–78, 1978–79.

Colours: Sky blue shirts, white shorts, white stockings. **Change colours:** Red and black striped shirts, black shorts, black stockings with white top.

MANCHESTER CITY 1994–95 LEAGUE RECORD

Match No.	Date	Venue	Opponents	Result		H/T Score	Lg. Pos.	Goalscorers	Attendance
1	Aug 20	A	Arsenal	L	0-3	0-2	—		38,368
2	24	H	West Ham U	W	3-0	2-0	—	Walsh, Beagrie, Rosler	19,150
3	27	H	Everton	W	4-0	0-0	6	Rosler 2, Walsh 2	19,867
4	31	A	Chelsea	L	0-3	0-1	—		21,740
5	Sept 10	H	Crystal Palace	D	1-1	1-1	10	Walsh	19,971
6	17	A	Sheffield W	D	1-1	1-0	10	Walsh	26,585
7	24	H	Norwich C	W	2-0	0-0	7	Quinn, Rosler	21,031
8	Oct 1	A	Leeds U	L	0-2	0-1	11		30,938
9	8	H	Nottingham F	D	3-3	1-1	11	Quinn 2, Lomas	23,150
10	15	A	QPR	W	2-1	0-0	8	Flitcroft, Walsh	13,631
11	22	H	Tottenham H	W	5-2	3-1	8	Walsh 2, Quinn, Lomas, Flitcroft	25,473
12	29	A	Coventry C	L	0-1	0-0	9		15,802
13	Nov 5	H	Southampton	D	3-3	0-1	9	Walsh 2, Beagrie	21,589
14	10	A	Manchester U	L	0-5	0-2	—		43,738
15	20	A	Leicester C	W	1-0	1-0	8	Quinn	19,006
16	26	H	Wimbledon	W	2-0	1-0	7	Flitcroft, Rosler	21,131
17	Dec 3	A	Ipswich T	W	2-1	2-0	6	Flitcroft, Rosler	13,754
18	12	H	Arsenal	L	1-2	0-2	—	Simpson	20,500
19	17	A	West Ham U	L	0-3	0-2	9		17,286
20	26	H	Blackburn R	L	1-3	1-2	10	Quinn	23,387
21	28	A	Liverpool	L	0-2	0-0	11		38,122
22	31	H	Aston Villa	D	2-2	1-0	11	Rosler 2	22,513
23	Jan 2	A	Newcastle U	D	0-0	0-0	11		34,437
24	14	H	Coventry C	D	0-0	0-0	11		20,232
25	25	H	Leicester C	L	0-1	0-0	—		21,007
26	Feb 4	A	Southampton	D	2-2	1-1	13	Kernaghan, Flitcroft	14,902
27	11	H	Manchester U	L	0-3	0-0	14		26,368
28	22	H	Ipswich T	W	2-0	0-0	—	Quinn, Rosler	21,430
29	25	H	Leeds U	D	0-0	0-0	15		22,892
30	Mar 4	A	Norwich C	D	1-1	0-0	15	Simpson	16,266
31	8	H	Chelsea	L	1-2	1-1	—	Gaudino	21,880
32	15	A	Everton	D	1-1	1-0	—	Gaudino	28,485
33	18	H	Sheffield W	W	3-2	1-2	12	Rosler 2, Walsh	23,355
34	21	A	Wimbledon	L	0-2	0-0	—		5268
35	Apr 1	A	Crystal Palace	L	1-2	0-1	16	Rosler	13,451
36	11	A	Tottenham H	L	1-2	0-0	—	Rosler	27,410
37	14	H	Liverpool	W	2-1	1-1	—	Summerbee, Gaudino	27,055
38	17	A	Blackburn R	W	3-2	1-2	12	Curle (pen), Rosler, Walsh	27,851
39	29	H	Newcastle U	D	0-0	0-0	13		27,389
40	May 3	A	Aston Villa	D	1-1	0-1	—	Rosler	30,133
41	6	A	Nottingham F	L	0-1	0-1	13		28,882
42	14	H	QPR	L	2-3	1-1	17	Quinn, Curle (pen)	27,850

Final League Position: 17

GOALSCORERS

League (53): Rosler 15, Walsh 12, Quinn 8, Flitcroft 5, Gaudino 3, Beagrie 2, Curle 2 (2 pens), Lomas 2, Simpson 2, Kernaghan 1, Summerbee 1.
Coca-Cola Cup (11): Quinn 2, Rosler 2, Summerbee 2, Walsh 2, Beagrie 1, Curle 1 (pen), Lomas 1.
FA Cup (9): Rosler 5, Beagrie 1, Brightwell D 1, Gaudino 1, Walsh 1.

Coton A.P. 22 + 1	Hill A.R. 10 + 3	Phelan T. 26 + 1	McMahon S. 6 + 1	Curle K. 31	Vonk M.C. 19 + 2	Summerbee N. 39 + 2	Walsh P.A. 39	Rosler U. 29 + 2	Flitcroft G.W. 37	Beagrie P.S. 33 + 4	Quinn N.J. 24 + 11	Brightwell I.R. 29 + 1	Lomas S.M. 18 + 2	Edghill R.A. 14	Griffiths C.B. — + 2	Mike A.R. 1 + 1	Dibble A. 14 + 1	Tracey S.P. 3	Brightwell D.J. 9	Kernaghan A.N. 18 + 4	Simpson F. 10 + 6	Kerr D.W. 2	Foster J.C. 9 + 2	Gaudino M. 17 + 3	Burridge J. 3 + 1	Thomas S.L. — + 2	*Match No.*
1	2	3	4	5	6	7	8	9	*10*	11	12	14															1
1		*3*	4	5	6	7	8	9	10	11	12	2	14														2
1			4	5	6	7	8	9	10	11	12	2	3														3
1			4	5	6	7	8	9	10	11	12	2	3														4
1		3	4	5	6	7	8		10	11	9	2															5
1	5		4		6	7	8	9		11	12	3	10	2													6
1	12	3		5		7	8	*9*	4	11	10	6	14	2													7
1	2	3	12		6	7			4	11	9	5	10		14	*8*											8
	5	3				7	8		4	11	9	6	10	2			1										9
15	12	3		5		7	8		4	11	9	6	10	2			1										10
		3		5		7	8		4	11	9	6	10	2			1										11
	2	3			6	7	8		4	11	9	5	10					1									12
	2	3			6	7	8		4	11	9	5	10			12		1									13
		3			6	7	8		4	11	9	5	10	2				1									14
	2			5		7	8	12	4	11	9	6	10				1		3								15
	2			5		7	8	12	4	11	9	6	10				1		3	14							16
				5		7	*8*	10	4	11	9	6		2			1		3	12	14						17
				5		7	8	10	4	*11*	9	6	3				1			12	14	2					18
					12	7	8	11	4		9	6	10				1		*3*	5		2	14				19
		12				7		10	4	11	9	6	3				1			5			2	8			20
		3			12	7	8	9	4	11		6	2				1			5				10			21
		3				7	8	9	4	11		6	10				1			5			2				22
		3			6	7	8	9	4	11			10				1			5	12		2				23
		3		5		2	8	9	10	11							1		6	4	12			7			24
				5	6	2	8	9	10	11	12	4					1		3					7			25
1				5	6	2	8	9	10	11		7					15		3	4				12			26
1				5		2	8	9	10	11	12	6							3	4				7			27
1		3		5		2	*8*	9	10	11	12	6								4	14			7			28
1	2	3		5	6	7					10	8								4	11			9			29
1	12	3		5	*6*	2	8				9	10			14					4	11			7			30
1		3		5		2	8	9		11	12	6								4	10			7			31
1		3		5	6		8	9		11	10	2									4		12	7			32
1		3		5	6	2	8	9	10	11											4			7			33
1		3		5	6	12	8	9	10	11	14										4		2	7			34
1				5	6	12	8	9	10	11									3	4			2	7			35
1	4	3		5		7	8	9	10		12			2									6	11			36
1		*3*		5		7	8	9	4	12	10			2						14			6	11			37
1				5		7	8	9	4	12	10			3						6	11		2				38
1		3		5		7	8	9	4	12	10			2						6	*11*			14	15		39
		3		5		7	8	*9*	4	12	10			2						6	11			14	1		40
				5		2	8		10	11	9			3						4	6			7	1	12	41
				5		7	*8*	9	4		10			2						6	12		3	11	1	14	42

Coca-Cola Cup

Second Round	Barnet (a)	0-1
	(h)	4-1
Third Round	QPR (a)	4-3
Fourth Round	Newcastle U (h)	1-1
	(a)	2-0
Fifth Round	Crystal Palace (a)	0-4

FA Cup

Third Round	Notts County (a)	2-2
	(h)	5-2
Fourth Round	Aston Villa (h)	1-0
Fifth Round	Newcastle U (a)	1-3

MANCHESTER UNITED 1994–95 *Back row (left to right):* Lee Sharpe, Eric Cantona, Peter Schmeichel, Gary Walsh, Gary Pallister, Dion Dublin.
Centre row: Norman Davies (Kit Manager), Andrei Kanchelskis, Ryan Giggs, Chris Casper, Nicky Butt, David May, Roy Keane, David Fevre (Physio).
Front row: Brian McClair, Mark Hughes, Steve Bruce, Alex Ferguson, Brian Kidd, Paul Ince, Denis Irwin, Paul Parker.

FA Premiership MANCHESTER UNITED

Old Trafford, Manchester M16 0RA. Telephone: (0161) 872 1661. Fax: (0161) 876 5502. Ticket and Match Information: (0161) 872 0199. Membership Enquiries: (0161) 872 5208. Souvenir shop: (0161) 872 3398.

Ground capacity: 30,000 (all-seater – at start of season due to re-development).

Record attendance: 76,962 Wolverhampton W v Grimsby T, FA Cup semi-final. 25 March 1939.

Club record: 70,504 v Aston Villa, Division 1, 27 December 1920.

Record receipts: £529,827.50 v Leeds U, FA Cup 5th rd, 19 February 1995.

Pitch measurements: 116yd × 76yd.

Chairman/Chief Executive: C. M. Edwards.

Directors: J. M. Edelson, Sir Bobby Charlton CBE, E. M. Watkins LL.M., R. L. Olive, R. P. Launders.

Manager: Alex Ferguson CBE. ***Assistant Manager:*** Brian Kidd.

Secretary: Kenneth Merrett. ***Commercial Manager:*** Danny McGregor.

Year Formed: 1878 as Newton Heath LYR; 1902, Manchester United.

Turned Professional: 1885. ***Ltd Co.:*** 1907.

Previous Name: Newton Heath, 1880–1902.

Club Nickname: 'Red Devils'.

Previous Grounds: 1880–93, North Road, Monsall Road; 1893, Bank Street; 1910, Old Trafford (played at Maine Road 1941–49).

Foundation: Manchester United was formed as comparatively recently as 1902 after their predecessors, Newton Heath, went bankrupt. However, it is usual to give the date of the club's foundation as 1878 when employees of the Lancashire and Yorkshire Railway Company formed Newton Heath L and YR. Cricket and Football Club. They won the Manchester Cup in 1886 and as Newton Heath FC were admitted to the Second Division in 1892.

First Football League game: 3 September, 1892, Division 1, v Blackburn R (a) L 3-4 – Warner; Clements, Brown; Perrins, Stewart, Erentz; Farman (1), Coupar (1), Donaldson (1), Carson, Mathieson.

Record League Victory (as Newton Heath): 10–1 v Wolverhampton W, Division 1, 15 October 1892 – Warner; Mitchell, Clements; Perrins, Stewart (3), Erentz; Farman (1), Hood (1), Donaldson (3), Carson (1), Hendry (1).

Record League Victory (as Manchester U): 9–0 v Ipswich T, FA Premiership, 4 March 1995 – Schmeichel; Keane (1) (Sharpe), Irwin, Bruce (Butt), Kanchelskis, Pallister, Cole (5), Ince (1), McClair, Hughes (2), Giggs.

Record Cup Victory: 10–0 v RSC Anderlecht, European Cup, Prel. rd (2nd leg), 26 September 1956 – Wood; Foulkes Byrne; Colman, Jones, Edwards; Berry (1), Whelan (2), Taylor (3), Viollet (4), Pegg.

Record Defeat: 0–7 v Blackburn R, Division 1, 10 April 1926 and v Aston Villa, Division 1, 27 December 1930 and v Wolverhampton W. Division 2, 26 December 1931.

Most League Points (2 for a win): 64, Division 1, 1956–57.

Most League Points (3 for a win): 92, FA Premier League, 1993–94.

Most League Goals: 103, Division 1, 1956–57 and 1958–59.

Highest League Scorer in Season: Dennis Viollet, 32, 1959–60.

Most League Goals in Total Aggregate: Bobby Charlton, 199, 1956–73.

Most Capped Player: Bobby Charlton, 106, England.

Most League Appearances: Bobby Charlton, 606, 1956–73.

Record Transfer Fee Received: £7,000,000 from Internazionale for Paul Ince, June 1995.

Record Transfer Fee Paid: £6,250,000 to Newcastle U for Andy Cole, January 1995.

Football League Record: 1892 Newton Heath elected to Division 1; 1894–1906 Division 2; 1906–22 Division 1; 1922–25 Division 2; 1925–31 Division 1; 1931–36 Division 2; 1936–37 Division 1; 1937–38 Division 2; 1938–74 Division 1; 1974–75 Division 2; 1975–92 Division 1; 1992– FA Premier League.

Honours: *FA Premier League:* – Champions 1992–93, 1993–94; Runners-up 1994–95. *Football League:* Division 1 – Champions 1907–8, 1910–11, 1951–52, 1955–56, 1956–57, 1964–65, 1966–67; Runners-up 1946–47, 1947–48, 1948–49, 1950–51, 1958–59, 1963–64, 1967–68, 1979–80, 1987–88, 1991–92. Division 2 – Champions 1935–36, 1974–75; Runners-up 1896–97, 1905–06, 1924–25, 1937–38. *FA Cup:* Winners 1909, 1948, 1963, 1977, 1983, 1985, 1990, 1994; Runners-up 1957, 1958, 1976, 1979, 1995. *Football League Cup:* Winners 1992, 1983 (Runners-up), 1991 (Runners-up), 1994 (Runners-up). **European Competitions:** *European Cup:* 1956–57 (s-f), 1957–58 (s-f), 1965–66 (s-f), 1967–68 (winners), 1968–69 (s-f), 1993–94, 1994–95. *European Cup-Winners' Cup:* 1963–64, 1977–78, 1983–84, 1990–91 (winners). 1991–92. *European Fairs Cup:* 1964–65. *UEFA Cup:* 1976–77, 1980–81, 1982–83, 1984–85, 1992–93. *World Club Championship:* 1968. *Super Cup:* 1991 (winners).

Colours: Red shirts, white shorts, black stockings. **Change colours:** Black shirts, black shorts, black stockings.

MANCHESTER UNITED 1994–95 LEAGUE RECORD

Match No.	Date	Venue	Opponents	Result		H/T Score	Lg. Pos.	Goalscorers	Attendance
1	Aug 20	H	QPR	W	2-0	0-0	—	Hughes, McClair	43,214
2	22	A	Nottingham F	D	1-1	1-1	—	Kanchelskis	22,072
3	27	A	Tottenham H	W	1-0	0-0	3	Bruce	24,502
4	31	H	Wimbledon	W	3-0	1-0	—	Cantona, McClair, Giggs	43,440
5	Sept 11	A	Leeds U	L	1-2	0-1	5	Cantona (pen)	39,120
6	17	H	Liverpool	W	2-0	0-0	4	Kanchelskis, McClair	43,740
7	24	A	Ipswich T	L	2-3	0-2	4	Cantona, Scholes	22,553
8	Oct 1	H	Everton	W	2-0	1-0	4	Kanchelskis, Sharpe	43,803
9	8	A	Sheffield W	L	0-1	0-1	5		32,616
10	15	H	West Ham U	W	1-0	1-0	4	Cantona	43,795
11	23	A	Blackburn R	W	4-2	1-1	3	Cantona (pen), Kanchelskis 2, Hughes	30,260
12	29	H	Newcastle U	W	2-0	1-0	3	Pallister, Gillespie	43,795
13	Nov 6	A	Aston Villa	W	2-1	1-1	3	Ince, Kanchelskis	32,136
14	10	H	Manchester C	W	5-0	2-0	—	Cantona, Kanchelskis 3, Hughes	43,738
15	19	H	Crystal Palace	W	3-0	2-0	1	Irwin, Cantona, Kanchelskis	43,788
16	26	A	Arsenal	D	0-0	0-0	2		38,301
17	Dec 3	H	Norwich C	W	1-0	1-0	2	Cantona	43,789
18	10	A	QPR	W	3-2	2-1	2	Scholes 2, Keane	18,948
19	17	H	Nottingham F	L	1-2	0-1	2	Cantona	43,744
20	26	A	Chelsea	W	3-2	1-0	2	Hughes, Cantona (pen), McClair	31,139
21	28	H	Leicester C	D	1-1	0-0	2	Kanchelskis	43,789
22	31	A	Southampton	D	2-2	0-1	2	Butt, Pallister	15,204
23	Jan 3	H	Coventry C	W	2-0	1-0	—	Scholes, Cantona (pen)	43,120
24	15	A	Newcastle U	D	1-1	1-0	2	Hughes	34,471
25	22	H	Blackburn R	W	1-0	0-0	2	Cantona	43,742
26	25	A	Crystal Palace	D	1-1	0-0	—	May	18,224
27	Feb 4	H	Aston Villa	W	1-0	1-0	2	Cole	43,795
28	11	A	Manchester C	W	3-0	0-0	2	Ince, Kanchelskis, Cole	26,368
29	22	A	Norwich C	W	2-0	2-0	—	Ince, Kanchelskis	21,824
30	25	A	Everton	L	0-1	0-0	2		40,011
31	Mar 4	H	Ipswich T	W	9-0	3-0	2	Keane, Cole 5, Hughes 2, Ince	43,804
32	7	A	Wimbledon	W	1-0	0-0	—	Bruce	18,224
33	15	H	Tottenham H	D	0-0	0-0	—		43,802
34	19	A	Liverpool	L	0-2	0-1	2		38,906
35	22	H	Arsenal	W	3-0	2-0	—	Hughes, Sharpe, Kanchelskis	43,623
36	Apr 2	H	Leeds U	D	0-0	0-0	2		43,712
37	15	A	Leicester C	W	4-0	2-0	2	Sharpe, Cole 2, Ince	21,281
38	17	H	Chelsea	D	0-0	0-0	2		43,728
39	May 1	A	Coventry C	W	3-2	1-1	—	Scholes, Cole 2	21,858
40	7	H	Sheffield W	W	1-0	1-0	2	May	43,868
41	10	H	Southampton	W	2-1	1-1	—	Cole, Irwin (pen)	43,479
42	14	A	West Ham U	D	1-1	0-1	2	McClair	24,783

Final League Position: 2

GOALSCORERS

League (77): Kanchelskis 14, Cantona 12 (4 pens), Cole 12, Hughes 8, Ince 5, McClair 5, Scholes 5, Sharpe 3, Bruce 2, Irwin 2 (1 pen), Keane 2, May 2, Pallister 2, Butt 1, Giggs 1, Gillespie 1.
Coca-Cola Cup (4): Scholes 2, McClair 1, May 1.
FA Cup (16): Irwin 4 (1 pen), Bruce 2, Hughes 2, McClair 2, Pallister 2, Cantona 1, Giggs 1, Sharpe 1, own goal 1.

Schmeichel P.B. 32	May D. 15 + 4	Irwin J.D. 40	Bruce S.R. 35	Sharpe L.S. 26 + 2	Pallister G.A. 42	Kanchelskis A. 25 + 5	Ince P.E.C. 36	McClair B.J. 35 + 5	Hughes L.M. 33 + 1	Giggs R.J. 29	Parker P.A. 1 + 1	Keane R.M. 23 + 2	Cantona E. 21	Walsh G. 10	Scholes P. 6 + 11	Butt N. 11 + 11	Gillespie K.R. 3 + 6	Davies S.I. 3 + 2	Pilkington K.W. — + 1	Neville G.A. 16 + 2	Cole A. 17 + 1	Neville P.J. 1 + 1	Beckham D.R.J. 2 + 2	Match No.
1	2	3	4	*5*	6	7	8	9	10	11	12	14												1
1	2	3	4	5	6	7	8	9	10	11		12												2
1	2	3	4	5	6	7	8	9	10	11														3
1	2	3	4	5	6	8		9	10	11			7											4
1	2	3	4	12	6	5	8	*9*	10	11			7			14								5
1	2	3	4	5	6	7	8	12	10	11			9											6
		2	4	3	6	7	8	*9*		11		5	10	1	12	14								7
1	2	3	4	5	6	11	8	12	10			9	7											8
1	12	3	4	5	6		8	9	10		2	7			14		*11*							9
1	2	3	4	5	6	7	8		10	11			9			12								10
1		3	4	5	6	7	8	12	10			2	9			11								11
1		3	4		6	5	8	9	10	11		2	7				12							12
		3	4		6	5	8	12		11		2	9	1	7	10	14							13
1		3	4		6	5	8	9	10	11		2	7		12									14
1	4	3			6	5	8	9	10				7		14		12	*11*	15	2				15
	4	3			6	5	8	9	10				7	1		12	*11*	14		2				16
	4	3			6	*5*	8	9	10				7	1		14	12	11		2				17
		3	4		6	7	8	9				5		1	10	14	12	*11*		2				18
		3	4		6	*5*	8	9	10	11		2	7	1		12				14				19
		3	4		6	12	*8*	9	10	11		2	7	1		5				14				20
		3	4		6	5		9	10	11		8	7	1	12					2				21
	2		4		6			9	10	11		5	7	1		8	12			3				22
		3	4		6			12		11		8	7	1	9	10	5			2				23
1	12	3	4	5	6			9	*10*	11		2	7		14	8								24
1		3	4	5	6	12	8	9		11		2	7								10			25
1	4	3		5	6	12	8	9		11		2	7								10			26
1	12	3	4	5	6	14	8	9		*11*					7					2	10			27
1	12	3	4	5	6	7	8	9		11					14						10	*2*		28
1			4	3	6	5	8	9	10	11		2									7			29
1		2	4	3	6	12	8	9	10	11		5									7			30
1		3	*4*	12	6	5	8	9	10	11		2				14					7			31
1		3	4	5	6		8	9	10	11										2	7			32
1		2	4	3	6	5	8	9	10	11						12					7			33
1		2	4	3	6	7	8	9	10	11		*5*				14					12			34
1		3	4	5	6	7	8		10	11		2									9			35
1		3			6		8	9	10	11		5								2	7		4	36
1		3	4	*5*	6		8	9	10						12	11				2	7		14	37
1		3	4		6		8	9	10						12	11		14		2	7		*5*	38
1	4	3		5	6			9	10						11	7				2	8		12	39
1	*4*	3		5	6		8	9	10						11	12				2	7	14		40
1		3	4	5	6		8	9	10						12	11				2	7			41
1		3	4	5	6		8	9	12			*10*			14	11				2	7			42

Coca-Cola Cup

Second Round	Port Vale (a)	2-1
	(h)	2-0
Third Round	Newcastle U (a)	0-2

FA Cup

Third Round	Sheffield U (a)	2-0
Fourth Round	Wrexham (h)	5-2
Fifth Round	Leeds U (h)	3-1
Sixth Round	QPR (h)	2-0
Semi-final	Crystal Palace at Villa Park	2-2
Replay at Villa Park		2-0
Final at Wembley	Everton	0-1

MANSFIELD TOWN 1994–95 *Back row (left to right):* Chris Timons, Stewart Hadley, Darren Ward, Paul Holland, Jason Pearcey, Simon Ireland, Lee Howarth.
Centre row: Chris Kerry, Kevin Noteman, Dean Marrows, Lee Wilkinson, Kevin Lampkin, Gary Castledine, Brendan Aspinall.
Front row: Steve Wilkinson, Ian Barraclough, Adey Boothroyd, Barry Statham (Physio), Andy King (Manager), Keith Alexander (Reserve and Youth Team Coach), Steve Parkin, Paul Fleming, Iffy Onoura.

Division 3 MANSFIELD TOWN

Field Mill Ground, Quarry Lane, Mansfield, NG18 5DA. Telephone: (01623) 23567. Fax: (01623) 25014. Marketing: (01623) 658070. Football in the Community: (01623) 25197.

Ground capacity: 7073.

Record attendance: 24,467 v Nottingham F, FA Cup 3rd rd, 10 January 1953.

Record receipts: £46,915 v Sheffield W, FA Cup 3rd rd, 5 January 1991.

Pitch measurements: 115yd × 70yd.

Chairman/Chief Executive: Keith Haslam.

Directors: K. Walker, Mrs M. Haslam. ***Associate Directors:*** T. Hewson, D. Wardman, K. Woodcock, S. Whetton.

Manager: Andy King.

Physio: Barry Statham.

Community Scheme Organiser: D. Bentley Tel: (01623) 25197.

Secretary: Mick Horton. ***Marketing Manager:*** L. Smith.

Year Formed: 1910. ***Turned Professional:*** 1910. ***Ltd Co.:*** 1921.

Previous Name: Mansfield Wesleyans 1891–1910.

Club Nickname: 'The Stags'.

Foundation: Many records give the date of Mansfield Town's formation as 1905. But the present club did not come into being until 1910 when the Mansfield Wesleyans (formed 1891) and playing in the Notts and District League, decided to spread their wings and changed their name to Mansfield Town, joining the new Central Alliance in 1911.

First Football League game: 29 August, 1931, Division 3(S), v Swindon T (h) W 3-2 – Wilson; Clifford, England; Wake, Davis, Blackburn; Gilhespy, Readman (1), Johnson, Broom (2), Baxter.

Record League Victory: 9–2 v Rotherham U, Division 3 (N), 27 December 1932 – Wilson; Anthony, England; Davies, S. Robinson, Slack; Prior, Broom, Readman (3), Hoyland (3), Bowater (3).

Record Cup Victory: 8–0 v Scarborough (away), FA Cup, 1st rd, 22 November 1952 – Bramley; Chessell, Bradley; Field, Plummer, Lewis; Scott, Fox (3), Marron (2), Sid Watson (1), Adam (2).

Record Defeat: 1–8 v Walsall, Division 3 (N), 19 January 1933.

Most League Points (2 for a win): 68, Division 4, 1974–75.

Most League Points (3 for a win): 81, Division 4, 1985–86.

Most League Goals: 108, Division 4, 1962–63.

Highest League Scorer in Season: Ted Harston, 55, Division 3 (N), 1936–37.

Most League Goals in Total Aggregate: Harry Johnson, 104, 1931–36.

Most Capped Player: John McClelland, 6 (53), Northern Ireland.

Most League Appearances: Rod Arnold, 440, 1970–83.

Record Transfer Fee Received: £500,000 from Middlesbrough for Simon Coleman, September 1989.

Record Transfer Fee Paid: £80,000 to Leicester C for Steve Wilkinson, September 1989.

Football League Record: 1931 Elected to Division 3 (S); 1932–37 Division 3 (N); 1937–47 Division 3 (S); 1947–58 Division 3 (N); 1958–60 Division 3; 1960–63 Division 4; 1963–72 Division 3; 1972–75 Division 4; 1975–77 Division 3; 1977–78 Division 2; 1978–80 Division 3; 1980–86 Division 4; 1986–91 Division 3; 1991–92 Division 4; 1992–93 Division 2; 1993– Division 3.

Honours: *Football League:* Division 2 best season: 21st, 1977–78; Division 3 – Champions 1976–77; Division 4 – Champions 1974–75; Division 3 (N) – Runners-up 1950–51. *FA Cup:* best season: 6th rd, 1969. *Football League Cup:* best season: 5th rd, 1976. *Freight Rover Trophy:* Winners 1987.

Colours: Amber and blue striped shirts, blue shorts, white stockings. **Change colours:** Green with purple trim shirts, green shorts, purple stockings.

MANSFIELD TOWN 1994–95 LEAGUE RECORD

Match No.	Date	Venue	Opponents	Result		H/T Score	Lg. Pos.	Goalscorers	Attendance
1	Aug 20	H	Colchester U	W	2-0	0-0	13	Holland, Hadley	2247
2	27	A	Chesterfield	W	1-0	0-0	8	Hadley	4210
3	30	H	Darlington	L	0-1	0-0	—		2427
4	Sept 3	H	Bury	L	0-2	0-1	15		2576
5	10	A	Lincoln C	L	2-3	1-1	15	Wilkinson, Noteman	2575
6	13	A	Carlisle U	L	1-2	0-0	—	Hadley	6136
7	17	H	Northampton T	D	1-1	0-0	19	Holland	2557
8	24	H	Exeter C	D	1-1	0-0	18	Howarth	2468
9	Oct 1	A	Gillingham	W	2-0	1-0	15	Holland, Wilkinson	2555
10	8	H	Hartlepool U	W	2-0	1-0	13	Holland, Wilkinson	2545
11	11	A	Northampton T	W	1-0	1-0	—	Wilkinson	4993
12	15	A	Torquay U	L	1-2	1-1	10	Peters	2800
13	22	H	Doncaster R	L	0-1	0-0	14		2988
14	29	A	Rochdale	D	3-3	2-1	12	Hadley, Noteman (pen), Wilkinson	1968
15	Nov 5	H	Preston NE	L	1-2	1-2	14	Hadley	2602
16	19	A	Scunthorpe U	W	4-3	0-1	11	Holland, Hadley, Noteman, Peters	2975
17	26	H	Walsall	L	1-3	0-2	13	Wilkinson	2733
18	Dec 10	A	Colchester U	D	1-1	0-1	14	Wilkinson	3016
19	18	H	Chesterfield	W	4-2	2-0	11	Campbell, Wilkinson 3	3519
20	26	H	Hereford U	W	7-1	1-0	10	Donaldson 2, Baraclough, Hadley, Howarth, Ireland, Wilkinson	2887
21	27	A	Scarborough	W	5-2	2-1	8	Donaldson 2, Baraclough, Wilkinson, Noteman	1926
22	31	H	Barnet	W	3-0	1-0	8	Donaldson 2, Ireland	2891
23	Jan 2	A	Fulham	L	2-4	1-1	8	Baraclough, Hadley	4091
24	10	A	Doncaster R	W	2-0	0-0	—	Hadley 2	2577
25	14	H	Wigan Ath	W	4-3	1-0	5	Holland, Peters, Wilkinson, Doolan	2618
26	21	A	Preston NE	L	1-2	1-1	5	Lampkin	8448
27	Feb 4	A	Walsall	L	0-1	0-0	8		4369
28	18	A	Wigan Ath	W	4-0	2-0	7	Holland 2, Hadley 2	1884
29	21	H	Scunthorpe U	W	1-0	0-0	—	Wilkinson	3079
30	25	H	Gillingham	W	4-0	1-0	3	Holland, Ireland, Parkin, Wilkinson	3182
31	Mar 4	A	Exeter C	W	3-2	1-1	4	Wilkinson 2, Onuora	2458
32	7	H	Rochdale	D	1-1	0-1	—	Wilkinson	2931
33	11	H	Lincoln C	W	6-2	1-0	3	Noteman 2 (1 pen), Hadley, Onuora 3	3396
34	18	A	Darlington	D	0-0	0-0	4		1613
35	25	A	Bury	D	2-2	0-1	5	Onuora, Wilkinson	4188
36	Apr 1	H	Carlisle U	L	1-2	1-1	5	Lampkin	5197
37	8	A	Barnet	D	2-2	1-1	5	Wilkinson, Phillips (og)	2115
38	15	H	Scarborough	W	3-2	2-2	5	Ireland, Wilkinson, Hadley	2931
39	17	A	Hereford U	D	0-0	0-0	6		2743
40	22	H	Fulham	D	1-1	1-0	5	Peters	2861
41	29	H	Torquay U	D	2-2	1-1	6	Onuora, Wilkinson	3216
42	May 6	A	Hartlepool U	L	2-3	0-1	6	Ireland, Onuora	3049

Final League Position: 6

GOALSCORERS

League (84): Wilkinson 22, Hadley 14, Holland 9, Onuora 7, Donaldson 6, Noteman 6 (2 pens), Ireland 5, Peters 4, Baraclough 3, Howarth 2, Lampkin 2, Campbell 1, Doolan 1, Parkin 1, own goal 1.
Coca-Cola Cup (4): Wilkinson 3, Ireland 1.
FA Cup (7): Holland 3, Aspinall 1, Donaldson 1, Hadley 1, Ireland 1.

Ward D. 35	Boothroyd A.N. 35 + 1	Baraclough I.R. 36	Holland P. 33	Howarth L. 39 + 1	Aspinall B.J. 13 + 7	Ireland S.P. 38 + 2	Parkin S.J. 22	Wilkinson S.J. 41	Hadley S. 28 + 11	Fleming P. 2	Noteman K.S. 27 + 5	Timons C. 4 + 2	Castledine G.J. 3 + 7	Alexander K. — + 2	Doolan J. 21 + 3	Frain D. 4 + 2	Peters M. 25 + 1	Hoyle C.R. 4 + 1	Pearcey J.K. 3	Trinder J.L. 4 + 3	Campbell J. 3	Pearson J.S. — + 2	Donaldson O.M. 4	Lampkin K. 22 + 1	Elad E. — + 2	Onuora I. 10 + 4	Walker R.N. 4	Sherlock P.G. 1 + 1	Clifford M.R. 1	Williams M.J. — + 1	*Match No.*
1	2	3	4	5	6	7	8	9	10	11	12																				1
1	2		4	5	6	7	8	9	10	3	11	12																			2
1	2		4	5	6	7	8	9	10		11	3	12	14																	3
1	2		4	5	6	7	8	9	10		*11*		12		3	14															4
1	3		4	5	6	7	8	9	10		12				2	11															5
1	2	3	4	5	6	7		9	12		*11*		14		8	10															6
1	2	3	4	5	6	7		9	10		11				8	12															7
1	2	3	4	5	6	7		9	10		11		12			8															8
1	2	3	4	5		7		9	10		11					8	6														9
1	2	3	4	5.		7		9			11				10		6	8													10
	2	3	4	5		7		9	12		11	14			10		6	8	1												11
	2	3		5	12	7		9	8		11		4		10		6		1												12
	2	3	4	5		7		9	12		11		*8*		10		6	14	1												13
1	2	3	4	5		7		9	8		11		12		10		6														14
1	2	3	4	5				9	10		11		7				6	8													15
1		3	4	5	12	7	8	9	10		11						6	2		15											16
1	2	3	4	5		12		9	10		*11*	6			8						7	14									17
1	2	3	4		6	7		9			*11*	5	12		8					15	10	14									18
1	2	3	4		5	7		9			11			12	10		6				8										19
1	2	3		5	12	7		9	10		11						6			15			8	4							20
	2	3		5	6	7		9	10		11									1			8	4							21
	2	3	4	5	12	7		9	10		11		14							1			8	*6*							22
	2	3	4	5	12	7		9	10		*11*						14			1			8	6							23
1	2	3	4	5		7	8	9	10						12		6							11							24
1	2		4	5	12	7		9	10		11				3		6							8							25
1	2	3	4	5	12	7		9	10		14				*11*		6							8							26
1	2	3	4	5		7	8	9	10								6							11	12						27
1		3	*4*	5	2	7	8	9	10								6							11	12	14					28
1		3	4	5		7	8	9	10						2		6							11							29
1		3	4	5		7	8	9	*10*		12				2		6							11		14					30
1		3	4	5		7	8	9	*10*		12				2		6							11		14					31
1	12	3	4	5		7	8	9	*10*						2		6							11		14					32
1	2	3		5		7	*8*	9	12		11				14		6							4		10					33
1	2	3		5			8	9	11						7		6							4		10					34
1	2	3		5		7	8	9	12		11													4		10	6				35
1	2	3		5		12	8	9	14		11				7									4		10	6				36
1	2	3	*4*	5		7	8	9	12						14									11		10	6				37
1	2	11	4	5		7	8	9	12								6							14		10	*3*				38
1	2	3		5		7	8	9	12		11						6							4		10					39
1	2	3	4	5		7	8	9	12								6							11		10					40
1	2	3	4	5		7	8	9	12								6							*11*		10		14			41
				12	6	7			9		11	5			3					1				4		10		8	*2*	14	42

Coca-Cola Cup		
First Round	Rochdale (a)	2-1
	(h)	1-0
Second Round	Leeds U (a)	1-0
	(h)	0-0
Third Round	Millwall (h)	0-2

FA Cup		
First Round	Northwich V (h)	3-1
Second Round	Halifax T (a)	0-0
	(h)	2-1
Third Round	Wolverhampton W (h)	2-3

MIDDLESBROUGH 1994–95 *Back row (left to right):* Andy Todd, Jamie Pollock, Derek Whyte, Steve Vickers, Nigel Pearson, Paul Wilkinson, Robbie Mustoe.
Centre row: Chris Morris, Curtis Fleming, Michael Barron, Ben Roberts, Steve Pears, Andy Collett, Craig Hignett, Graham Kavanagh, Alan Moore.
Front row: Mark Nile (Senior Physio), John Hendrie, Neil Cox, Bryan Robson (Player-Manager), John Pickering (First Team Coach), Viv Anderson (Assistant Manager), Clayton Blackmore, Tommy Wright, Tommy Johnson (Physio).

FA Premiership MIDDLESBROUGH

Cellnet Riverside Stadium, Middlesbrough, Cleveland TS3 6RS. Telephone: (01642) 227227. Fax: (01642) 252532. Boro Livewire: 0891 424200.

Ground capacity: 30,000.

Record attendance: 53,596 v Newcastle U, Division 1, 27 December 1949.

Record receipts: £200,351 v Newcastle U, Coca Cola Cup 2nd rd 2nd leg, 7 October 1992.

Pitch measurements: 115yd × 75yd.

Chairman: S. Gibson.

Directors: G. Cooke, R. Corbidge, G. Fordy.

Chief Executive/Secretary: Keith Lamb.

Manager: Bryan Robson. ***Assistant Manager:*** Viv Anderson.

Physio: Bob Ward. ***Coach:*** John Pickering. ***Commercial Director:*** Graham Fordy.

Youth Development Officer: Ron Bone.

Year Formed: 1876. ***Turned Professional:*** 1889; became amateur 1892, and professional again, 1899. ***Ltd Co:*** 1892.

Club Nickname: 'Boro'.

Previous Grounds: 1877, Old Archery Ground, Albert Park; 1879, Breckon Hill; 1882, Linthorpe Road Ground; 1903, Ayresome Park; 1995, Cellnet Riverside Stadium.

Foundation: A previous belief that Middlesbrough Football Club was founded at a tripe supper at the Corporation Hotel has proved to be eroneous. In fact, members of Middlesbrough Cricket Club were responsible for forming it at a meeting in the gymnasium of the Albert Park Hotel in 1875.

First Football League game: 2 September, 1899, Division 2, v Lincoln C (a) L 0-3 – Smith; Shaw, Ramsey; Allport, McNally, McCracken; Wanless, Longstaffe, Gettins, Page, Pugh.

Record League Victory: 9–0 v Brighton & HA, Division 2, 23 August 1958 – Taylor; Bilcliff, Robinson; Harris (2 pens), Phillips, Walley; Day, McLean, Clough (5), Peacock (2), Holliday.

Record Cup Victory: 9–3 v Goole T, FA Cup, 1st rd, 9 January 1915 – Williamson; Haworth, Weir; Davidson, Cook, Malcolm; Wilson, Carr (3), Elliott (3), Tinsley (3), Davies.

Record Defeat: 0–9 v Blackburn R, Division 2, 6 November 1954.

Most League Points (2 for a win): 65, Division 2, 1973–74.

Most League Points (3 for a win): 94, Division 3, 1986–87.

Most League Goals: 122, Division 2, 1926–27.

Highest League Scorer in Season: George Camsell, 59, Division 2, 1926–27 (Second Division record).

Most League Goals in Total Aggregate: George Camsell, 326, 1925–39.

Most Capped Player: Wilf Mannion, 26, England.

Most League Appearances: Tim Williamson, 563, 1902–23.

Record Transfer Fee Received: £2,300,000 from Manchester United for Gary Pallister, August 1989.

Record Transfer Fee Paid: £1,300,000 to Swindon T for Jan-Aage Fjortoft, March 1995.

Football League Record: 1899 Elected to Division 2; 1902–24 Division 1; 1924–27 Division 2; 1927–28 Division 1; 1928–29 Division 2; 1929–54 Division 1; 1954–66 Division 2; 1966–67 Division 3; 1967–74 Division 2; 1974–82 Division 1; 1982–86 Division 2; 1986–87 Division 3; 1987–88 Division 2; 1988–89 Division 1; 1989–92 Division 2; 1992–93 FA Premier League; 1993–95 Division 1; 1995– FA Premier League.

Honours: *Football League:* Division 1 – Champions 1994–95. Division 2 – Champions 1926–27, 1928–29, 1973–74; Runners-up 1901–02, 1991–92. Division 3 – Runners-up 1966–67, 1986–87. *FA Cup:* best season: 6th rd, 1936, 1947, 1970, 1975, 1977, 1978; old last eight 1901, 1904. *Football League Cup:* Semi-final 1976. *Amateur Cup:* Winners 1895, 1898, *Anglo-Scottish Cup:* Winners 1976.

Colours: Red and white. **Change colours:** Royal blue and black.

MIDDLESBROUGH 1994–95 LEAGUE RECORD

Match No.	Date	Venue	Opponents	Result	H/T Score	Lg. Pos.	Goalscorers	Attendance
1	Aug 13	H	Burnley	W 2-0	2-0	—	Hendrie 2	23,343
2	20	A	Southend U	W 2-0	1-0	1	Hendrie 2	5722
3	27	H	Bolton W	W 1-0	1-0	1	Wilkinson	19,570
4	31	A	Derby Co	W 1-0	1-0	—	Blackmore	14,659
5	Sept 3	A	Watford	D 1-1	1-0	1	Blackmore	9478
6	11	H	Sunderland	D 2-2	0-1	1	Moore, Pearson	19,578
7	14	H	WBA	W 2-1	1-1	—	Mustoe, Hignett (pen)	14,878
8	17	A	Port Vale	L 1-2	1-0	2	Pollock	10,313
9	25	A	Bristol C	W 1-0	0-0	2	Hendrie	8642
10	Oct 1	H	Millwall	W 3-0	0-0	2	Hendrie, Wilkinson, Beard (og)	17,229
11	8	H	Tranmere R	L 0-1	0-0	2		18,497
12	15	A	Luton T	L 1-5	0-3	4	Whyte	8412
13	23	A	Portsmouth	D 0-0	0-0	3		7281
14	29	H	Swindon T	W 3-1	1-0	2	Cox, Hendrie, Wilkinson (pen)	17,328
15	Nov 1	H	Oldham Ath	W 2-1	0-1	—	Moore, Hignett	15,929
16	5	A	Grimsby T	L 1-2	0-2	2	Hignett (pen)	8488
17	20	H	Wolverhampton W	W 1-0	0-0	1	Hendrie	19,953
18	26	A	Charlton Ath	W 2-0	1-0	1	Hendrie, Pollock	10,019
19	Dec 3	H	Portsmouth	W 4-0	2-0	1	Wilkinson 2, Hignett 2	17,185
20	6	A	Reading	D 1-1	0-0	—	Wilkinson (pen)	10,301
21	10	H	Southend U	L 1-2	0-1	1	Hendrie	16,843
22	18	A	Burnley	W 3-0	1-0	1	Hendrie 3	12,049
23	26	A	Sheffield U	D 1-1	0-0	1	Hignett	20,693
24	28	H	Notts Co	W 2-1	2-1	—	Hignett, Pearson	21,558
25	31	A	Stoke C	D 1-1	1-1	1	Vickers	15,914
26	Jan 15	A	Swindon T	L 1-2	1-1	1	Hignett	8888
27	21	H	Grimsby T	D 1-1	0-0	1	Mustoe	15,360
28	Feb 4	H	Reading	L 0-1	0-0	3		17,982
29	18	H	Charlton Ath	W 1-0	1-0	3	Fuchs	16,301
30	21	A	Wolverhampton W	W 2-0	0-0	—	Vickers, Fuchs	27,611
31	26	A	Millwall	D 0-0	0-0	2		7247
32	Mar 4	H	Bristol C	W 3-0	1-0	2	Fuchs 3	17,371
33	7	H	Watford	W 2-0	1-0	—	Mustoe, Fuchs	16,630
34	11	A	Bolton W	L 0-1	0-1	2		18,370
35	14	H	Barnsley	D 1-1	1-0	—	Moreno	19,655
36	18	H	Derby Co	L 2-4	0-3	3	Fuchs, Pollock	18,168
37	21	A	Sunderland	W 1-0	0-0	—	Pollock	16,501
38	26	H	Port Vale	W 3-0	2-0	1	Fuchs, Robson, Vickers	17,401
39	Apr 1	A	WBA	W 3-1	0-1	1	Pollock, Raven (og), Moore	20,256
40	5	A	Oldham Ath	L 0-1	0-0	—		11,024
41	8	H	Stoke C	W 2-1	1-1	1	Pearson, Moore	20,867
42	15	A	Notts Co	D 1-1	0-0	1	Fuchs	9377
43	17	H	Sheffield U	D 1-1	1-1	1	Fjortoft	23,225
44	22	A	Barnsley	D 1-1	1-0	1	Fjortoft	11,711
45	30	H	Luton T	W 2-1	1-0	1	Hendrie 2	23,903
46	May 7	A	Tranmere R	D 1-1	0-1	1	Fjortoft	16,377

Final League Position: 1

GOALSCORERS

League (67): Hendrie 15, Fuchs 9, Hignett 8 (2 pens), Wilkinson 6 (2 pens), Pollock 5, Moore 4, Fjortoft 3, Mustoe 3, Pearson 3, Vickers 3, Blackmore 2, Cox 1, Moreno 1, Robson 1, Whyte 1, own goals 2.
Coca-Cola Cup (8): Wilkinson 3, Hendrie 1, Hignett 1, Moore 1, Mustoe 1, Pollock 1.
FA Cup (2): Hendrie 1, Moore 1.

Miller A.J. 41	Cox N.J. 39 + 1	Fleming C. 21	Vickers S. 44	Pearson N.G. 33	Blackmore C.G. 26 + 4	Robson B. 21 + 1	Pollock J. 41	Wilkinson P. 27 + 4	Hendrie J.G. 37 + 2	Moore A. 35 + 2	Mustoe R. 24 + 3	Whyte D. 36	Hignett C. 19 + 7	Pears S. 5	Moreno J. 6 + 8	Kavanagh G.A. 5 + 2	Wright T.E. 1	Todd A.J.J. 5	Morris C.B. 14 + 1	Fuchs U. 13 + 2	Stamp P.L. 1 + 2	O'Halloran K. 1	Anderson V.A. 2	Fjortoft J.A. 8	Freestone C.M. — + 1	Liddle C. 1	*Match No.*
1	2	3	4	5	6	7	8	9	10	11																	1
1	2	3	4	5	6	7	8	9	10	11																	2
1	2	3	4	5	6	7	8	9	10	11	12																3
1	2	3	4	5	6	7	8	9	10	11	12																4
1	2	3		5	6	7	8	9	10	11		4															5
1	2	3	4	5	6	7	8	9	10	11			12														6
1	2	3	4	*5*	14	7	8	9	10	11	12		6														7
	2	3	4				8	9	10	11	7	5	6	1													8
	2	3	4				8	9	10	11	7	5	6	1													9
	2	3	4		6		8	9	10		7	5	11	1	12												10
	2	3	4		6		8	9	10		7	5	11	1	12												11
	2	3	4		6		8	9	10			5	7	1		12	11										12
1	2	3	4		6		8	9	10			5	12		11			7									13
1	2	3	4		6		8	9	10	11		5	12					7									14
1	2	3	4		6		8	9	10	11		5	12					7									15
1	2		4		3		8	9	10	11		5	7					6									16
1	2		4		12		8	9	10	11	6	5	7						3								17
1	2		4	6			8	9	10		7	5	11						3								18
1	2		4				8	9	10	11	6	5	7		12				3								19
1	2		4	6			8	9	10	12	11	5	7						3								20
1	7		4	5	12			9	10	11	6	3			14			*8*	2								21
1	2	3	4	6		7		9	10	11	8	5															22
1	2	3	4	6		7		9	10	11		5	12			8											23
1	2	3		6			8	9	10	11	4	5	7						12								24
1		3	4	5		7	8	9	10		6		11						2								25
1		3	4	5			8		10	11	7	6	9			12			2								26
1		3	4	5	7		8	9	10	12	6		11						2								27
1			4	5		12	8	9	10	11	6	3	*7*						2	14							28
1			4	5	6	7	8			11	10	3							2	9							29
1			4	5	6	7	8			11	10	3							2	9							30
1	14		4	5	6	7	*8*	12		11	10	3							2	9							31
1	2		*4*	5	6	7		12		11	10	3	14		8					9							32
1	2		4	5	6		7			11	10	3			8					9							33
1	2		4	5	6	7	8		11		10	3			14					9	12						34
1	2		4	5			8	12	14	11	6	3	*7*		10					9							35
1	2		4	5		7	8		10	11	6				12					9		3					36
1	2		4	5		7	8		10	11	6	3								9							37
1	2		4	5	6	7	8		10	11		3			12					9							38
1	2		4		6	7	8			11		3								9			5	10			39
1	2		4	5	6	7	8	12		11		3	14							9				10			40
1	2		4	5	12		8		10	*11*		3	7		14	6								9			41
1	2		4	5			8		11			3	7		*10*	6				14	12			9			42
1	2		4	5	6		8		12	11		3				7				9				10			43
1	2		4		6		8		10	11						7			3				5	9			44
1	2		4	5	6	7	8		10	11		3												9			45
1	2		4	5					10			6			11				3		7			9	12	8	46

Coca-Cola Cup

Second Round	Scarborough (a)	4-1
	(h)	4-1
Third Round	Aston Villa (a)	0-1

FA Cup

Third Round	Swansea C (a)	1-1
	(h)	1-2

MILLWALL 1994–95 *Back row (left to right):* John Kerr, Mark Kennedy, Dave Mitchell, Jon Goodman, Greg Berry, Tony McCarthy, Kenny Cunningham, Clive Allen.
Centre row: Keith Johnstone (Physio), Ken Barry (Kit Manager), Keith Stevens, Pat Van Den Hauwe, Kasey Keller, Tim Carter, Richard Huxford, Dave Savage, Ian McDonald (Coach), Peter Melville (Physio).
Front row: Andy May, Andy Roberts, Mark Beard, Alex Rae, Ian Evans (First Team Coach), Mick McCarthy (Manager), Phil Barber, Jermaine Wright, Ian Dawes, Ben Thatcher.

Division 1 MILLWALL

Millwall Football & Athletic Company (1985) plc, The Den, Zampa Road, Bermondsey SE16 3LN. Telephone: (0171) 232 1222. Ticket Office: (0171) 231 9999. Club Shop: (0171) 231 5881. Fax: (0171) 231 3663.

Ground capacity: 20,146 (all-seater).

Record Attendance: 20,093 v Arsenal, FA Cup 3rd rd, 10 January 1994.

Record Receipts: (to be advised).

Pitch measurements: 100 metres × 68m.

President: Lord Mellish of Bermondsey.

Chairman: Peter W. Mead. ***Directors:*** R. I. Burr, J. D. Burnige, B. E. Mitchell, Cllr. David Sullivan, J. M. R. Berardo.

Chief Executive Secretary: Graham Hortop. ***Assistant Secretary:*** Yvonne Haines.

Manager: Mick McCarthy. ***First Team Coach:*** Ian Evans.

Reserve Team Coach: Ian McDonald. ***Youth Team Coach:*** Tom Walley. ***Chief Scout:*** Ron Howard. ***Youth Development Officer:*** Allen Batsford. ***Physio:*** Keith Johnstone. ***Hon. Medical Officer:*** Dr. Daniel Baron.

Sales & Promotions Manager: Mike Sullivan. ***Commercial Manager:*** Billy Neil.
Marketing Manager: D. Frazer.

Year Formed: 1885. ***Turned Professional:*** 1893. ***Ltd Co.:*** 1894.

Previous Names: 1885, Millwall Rovers; 1889, Millwall Athletic.

Club Nickname: 'The Lions'.

Previous Grounds: 1885, Glengall Road, Millwall; 1886, Back of 'Lord Nelson'; 1890, East Ferry Road; 1901, North Greenwich; 1910, The Den, Cold Blow Lane; 1993, The Den, Bermondsey.

Foundation: Formed in 1885 as Millwall Rovers by employees of Morton & Co, a jam and marmalade factory in West Ferry Road. The founders were predominantly Scotsmen. Their first headquarters was the The Islanders pub in Tooke Street, Millwall. Their first trophy was the East End Cup in 1887.

First Football League game: 28 August, 1920, Division 3, v Bristol R (h) W 2-0 – Lansdale; Fort, Hodge; Voisey (1), Riddell, McAlpine; Waterall, Travers, Broad (1), Sutherland, Dempsey.

Record League Victory: 9–1 v Torquay U, Division 3 (S), 29 August 1927 – Lansdale; Tilling, Hill; Amos, Bryant (3), Graham; Chance, Hawkins (3), Landells (1), Phillips (2), Black. 9–1 v Coventry C, Division 3 (S), 19 November 1927 – Lansdale; Fort, Hill; Amos, Collins (1), Graham; Chance, Landells (4), Cock (2), Phillips (2), Black.

Record Cup Victory: 7–0 v Gateshead, FA Cup, 2nd rd, 12 December 1936 – Yuill; Ted Smith, Inns; Brolly, Hancock, Forsyth; Thomas (1), Mangnall (1), Ken Burditt (2), McCartney (2), Thorogood (1).

Record Defeat: 1–9 v Aston Villa, FA Cup 4th rd, 28 January 1946.

Most League Points (2 for a win): 65, Division 3 (S), 1927–28 and Division 3, 1965–66.

Most League Points (3 for a win): 90, Division 3, 1984–85.

Most League Goals: 127, Division 3 (S), 1927–28.

Highest League Scorer in Season: Richard Parker, 37, Division 3 (S), 1926–27.

Most League Goals in Total Aggregate: Teddy Sheringham, 93, 1984–91.

Most Capped Player: Eamonn Dunphy, 22 (23), Republic of Ireland.

Most League Appearances: Barry Kitchener, 523, 1967–82.

Record Transfer Fee Received: £2,300,000 from Liverpool for Mark Kennedy, March 1995.

Record Transfer Fee Paid: £800,000 to Derby Co for Paul Goddard, December 1989.

Football League Record: 1920 Original Members of Division 3; 1921 Division 3 (S); 1928–34 Division 2; 1934–38 Division 3 (S); 1938–48 Division 2; 1948–58 Division 3 (S); 1958–62 Division 4; 1962–64 Division 3; 1964–65 Division 4; 1965–66 Division 3; 1966–75 Division 2; 1975–76 Division 3; 1976–79 Division 2; 1979–85 Division 3; 1985–88 Division 2; 1988–90 Division 1; 1990–92 Division 2; 1992– Division 1.

Honours: *Football League:* Division 1 best season: 7th 1992–93; Division 2 – Champions 1987–88; Division 3 (S) – Champions 1927–28, 1937–38; Runners-up 1952–53; Division 3 – Runners-up 1965–66, 1984–85; Division 4 – Champions 1961–62; Runners-up 1964–65. *FA Cup:* Semi-final 1900, 1903, 1937 (first Division 3 side to reach semi-final). *Football League Cup:* best season: 5th rd, 1974, 1977, 1995. *Football League Trophy:* Winners 1983.

Colours: Blue shirts, white shorts, blue stockings. **Change colours:** Green and white shirts, green shorts, green stockings.

MILLWALL 1994–95 LEAGUE RECORD

Match No.	Date		Venue	Opponents	Result		H/T Score	Lg. Pos.	Goalscorers	Attendance
1	Aug	13	H	Southend U	W	3-1	1-0	—	Mitchell, Goodman, Tilson (og)	8283
2		20	A	Sunderland	D	1-1	1-0	2	Rae	17,296
3		27	H	Derby Co	W	4-1	1-0	2	Rae, Kerr 3	8809
4		30	A	Bolton W	L	0-1	0-0	—		9519
5	Sept	3	A	Reading	D	0-0	0-0	5		8715
6		10	H	WBA	D	2-2	1-1	7	Goodman 2	8378
7		14	H	Burnley	L	2-3	0-0	—	Savage, Rae (pen)	7375
8		17	A	Tranmere R	L	1-3	1-1	15	Roberts	6243
9		24	H	Luton T	D	0-0	0-0	15		7150
10	Oct	1	A	Middlesbrough	L	0-3	0-0	19		17,229
11		8	A	Bristol C	L	0-1	0-0	21		7499
12		15	H	Stoke C	D	1-1	1-0	21	Goodman	7856
13		22	A	Wolverhampton W	D	3-3	1-1	22	Goodman 2, Cadette	25,059
14		29	H	Sheffield U	W	2-1	0-0	22	Kennedy (pen), Cadette	8445
15	Nov	2	H	Portsmouth	D	2-2	2-1	—	Goodman, Rae	7108
16		5	A	Swindon T	W	2-1	0-0	18	Goodman, Kennedy	9311
17		12	A	Grimsby T	L	0-1	0-0	19		5261
18		19	H	Barnsley	L	0-1	0-1	20		7040
19		26	A	Port Vale	L	1-2	0-0	20	Kennedy	8016
20	Dec	4	H	Wolverhampton W	W	1-0	0-0	20	Mitchell	8025
21		10	H	Sunderland	W	2-0	0-0	15	Kennedy, Mitchell	7698
22		17	A	Southend U	W	1-0	1-0	15	Cadette	5833
23		26	A	Notts Co	W	1-0	0-0	13	Mitchell	6758
24		27	H	Watford	W	2-1	0-0	10	Rae (pen), Cadette	12,289
25	Jan	1	A	Charlton Ath	D	1-1	1-0	11	Rae	10,655
26		3	H	Oldham Ath	D	1-1	0-1	—	Rae (pen)	7438
27		14	A	Sheffield U	D	1-1	1-0	12	Beard	12,650
28	Feb	4	H	Grimsby T	W	2-0	1-0	11	Kennedy, Roberts	7397
29		21	A	Barnsley	L	1-4	0-1	—	Webber	4733
30		26	H	Middlesbrough	D	0-0	0-0	13		7247
31	Mar	1	H	Swindon T	W	3-1	0-0	—	Rae 2, Van Blerk	5950
32		4	A	Luton T	D	1-1	0-1	11	Mitchell	6864
33		8	H	Reading	W	2-0	1-0	—	Oldfield, Williams (og)	7546
34		11	A	Derby Co	L	2-3	1-1	12	Rae, Mitchell	12,490
35		15	A	Portsmouth	L	2-3	1-1	—	Oldfield, Witter	6032
36		19	H	Bolton W	L	0-1	0-0	12		6103
37		22	A	WBA	L	0-3	0-1	—		11,782
38		25	H	Tranmere R	W	2-1	0-0	13	Dixon, Roberts	7470
39	Apr	1	A	Burnley	W	2-1	1-0	11	Oldfield 2	10,454
40		5	H	Port Vale	L	1-3	0-2	—	Oldfield	5260
41		8	H	Charlton Ath	W	3-1	2-1	11	McRobert, Thatcher, Dixon	9506
42		14	A	Watford	L	0-1	0-1	—		6907
43		19	H	Notts Co	D	0-0	0-0	—		5471
44		22	A	Oldham Ath	W	1-0	0-0	11	Savage	6319
45		29	A	Stoke C	L	3-4	2-2	11	Dixon, Webber, Oldfield	9111
46	May	7	H	Bristol C	D	1-1	1-1	12	Dixon	8805

Final League Position: 12

GOALSCORERS

League (60): Rae 10 (3 pens), Goodman 8, Mitchell 6, Oldfield 6, Kennedy 5 (1 pen), Cadette 4, Dixon 4, Kerr 3, Roberts 3, Savage 2, Webber 2, Beard 1, McRobert 1, Thatcher 1, Van Blerk 1, Witter 1, own goals 2.
Coca-Cola Cup (8): Berry 2, Goodman 2, Kennedy 2, Cadette 1, Mitchell 1.
FA Cup (3): Beard 1, Kennedy 1, Savage 1.

Keller K. 44	Cunningham K.E. 15	Thatcher B.D. 38 + 2	May A.M. 14 + 2	McCarthy A.P. 12	Roberts A.J. 44	Savage D. 31 + 6	Rae A. 38	Mitchell D.S. 23 + 5	Goodman J. 15	Kennedy M. 28 + 2	Beard M. 24 + 7	Kerr J. 7 + 7	Chapman D.G. 4 + 8	Huxford R.J. — + 1	Van Den Hauwe P.W. 4	Van Blerk J. 24 + 3	Carter T.D. 2	Connor J.R. 1	Witter A.J. 26 + 1	Cadette R.R. 12 + 4	Dawes I.R. 12 + 2	Stevens K.H. 20	Kelly A.G. 1 + 1	Webber D. 19 + 3	Berry G.J. 4 + 5	Beckford J.N. 6 + 3	Edwards A.M. 3 + 1	McRobert L. 4 + 3	Oldfield D.C. 16 + 1	Joseph R. 5	Dixon K.M. 9	Taylor S.J. 1 + 5	Forbes S. — + 1	*Match No.*
1	2	3	4	5	6	7	8	*9*	10	11	12	14																						1
1	2	3	4	5	6	7	8	9	10	11		12																						2
1	2	3	4	5	6	7	8	*9*	10	11	12	14																						3
1	2	3		5	6	7	8		10	11		9	4																					4
1	2	3		5	6	7	8		10	11	12	9	4	14																				5
1	2	3		5	6	7	8		10	11		9	4																					6
1	2	3		5	6	7	8	12	10	11	14	*9*	4																					7
1	2	3		5	6	7	8	9	10	11		12			4	14																		8
1	2	3		5	6	7	8	*9*	10	11		12			4	14																		9
1		3		5	6	7	8		10	11	2	9	14		*4*	12																		10
	2	3		5	6	12	8	*10*		11	7	9	14			4	1																	11
1	2	3			6	7	8	12	10	11								4	*5*	9	14													12
1	2	3			6	7		*9*	10	11	12				4				5	14	8													13
1	2				4	7		12	10	11	3								5	9	8	6												14
1	2				4	7	3	12	10	*11*	14								5	9	8	6												15
1	2	8			4	7	3	12	10	*11*									5	9	14	6												16
1		8			4		3	10		11	2								5	9	7	6	12											17
1		8			4	7	3	10		11	2								5	9			6	12										18
1		3			4	7	8	10		11	2								5	9		6			12									19
1		3			4		8	10		11	2								5	12	7	6			9									20
1		3			4	12	8	10		11	2								5	14	7	6			*9*									21
1					4		8	10		*11*			14			3			5	9	2	6			12	7								22
1					4		8	10		*11*			12			3			5	9	2	6		14		7								23
1		3			4	7	8	10			2					11			5	9		6		12										24
1		3			4	7	8	10				12	14			11			5	9	2			6										25
1		3			4		8			12	14	10				11			5	9	2			6		7								26
1					4	12	8	10		11	7		14			3					2	6		5			*9*							27
1		6			4	12	8	10		*11*	7					3			5		2					14	9							28
1		3	*8*	11	4	7					2	12				10			5					6			9	14						29
1		3			4	7	8				2					11			5					6		10		12	9					30
1		3	12		4	7	8				2					11			5					6		10	14		*9*					31
1		3	4			7	8	10								11			5					6		12			9	2				32
1		3	4			7	8	10		12						11			5					6		14			*9*	2				33
		12	7		4	14	8	10		*11*						3	1		5					6					9	2				34
1		12	2		4	7	8	10		11						3			5					6					9					35
1		3	12		4	7		10		11	2					8			5			6							9					36
1		3			4	10					7					11			12			6		5	9				8	2				37
1		3	10		4	12					7					11						6		5	14				*8*	2	9			38
1		3	10		4	7					2		12			11						6		5					8		9			39
1		3	10		4						2		12						6					5	11	7			9		8	14		40
1		3	10		4		*7*				2					11								5	12			6	8		9	14		41
1		3	7		4		10				2					11						6		5				12	*8*		9	14		42
1			*2*		4	7	8									3						6		5	12			11	14		9	10		43
1		3			4	7	8				2					11						6		5					10		9			44
1		3			4	7	8				2									12		6		5				*11*	10		9	14		45
1		3			4		8				2					11			5			*6*						7	10		9	12	14	46

Coca-Cola Cup

Second Round	Sunderland (h)	2-1
	(a)	1-1
Third Round	Mansfield T (a)	2-0
Fourth Round	Nottingham F (a)	2-0
Fifth Round	Swindon T (a)	1-3

FA Cup

Third Round	Arsenal (h)	0-0
	(a)	2-0
Fourth Round	Chelsea (h)	0-0
	(a)	1-1
Fifth Round	QPR (a)	0-1

NEWCASTLE UNITED 1994–95 *Back row (left to right):* Chris Holland, Nicos Papavasliou, Alan Neilson, Nathan Murray, Stephen Harper, Mike Jeffrey, Alex Mathie, Jason Drysdale, Malcolm Allen.

Centre row: Paul Ferris (Assistant Physio), Derek Fazackerley (First Team Coach), Scott Sellars, Lee Clark, Steve Howey, Mike Hooper, Steve Watson, Pavel Srnicek, Philippe Albert, Marc Hottiger, Steve Guppy, Robbie Elliott, Jeff Clarke (Reserve Team Coach), Derek Wright (Physio).

Front row: Barry Venison, John Beresford, Andy Cole, Peter Beardsley, Terry McDermott (Assistant Manager), Kevin Keegan (Manager), Arthur Cox (Coach), Paul Bracewell, Ruel Fox, Robert Lee, Darren Peacock.

FA Premiership **NEWCASTLE UNITED**

St James' Park, Newcastle-upon-Tyne NE1 4ST. Telephone: (0191) 232 8361. Club Fax: (0191) 232 9875. Lottery Office: (0191) 230 2861. Commercial Dept: (0191) 232 3050. Ticket Office Hotline: (0191) 261 1571. Club Shop: (0191) 261 6357. Club Shop Mail Order Answering Service: (0191) 232 4080. Football in the Community Scheme: (0191) 261 9715. Conference and Banqueting: (0191) 222 1860. Clubcall: 0891 121590. Clubcall Main Line: 0891 121190. Ticket Line: 0891 121590. Club Shop numbers: St James' Park Club Shop: (0191) 261 6357. Metro Centre Club Shop: (0191) 461 0000. Eldon Square Club Shop: (0191) 230 0808. Travel Club: (0191) 2211000. Junior Magpies: (0191) 232 2571. Lottery Office: (0191) 230 2861.

Ground capacity: 36,649.

Record attendance: 68,386 v Chelsea, Division 1, 3 Sept 1930.

Record receipts: £359,112.12 v Swansea C, FA Cup 4th rd, 28 January 1995.

Pitch measurements: 110yd × 73yd (subject to alteration).

President: T. L. Bennett.

Chairman: Sir John Hall.

Vice-Chairman: W. F. Shepherd. ***Chief Executive:*** A. O. Fletcher.

Directors: D. S. Hall, R. Jones, T. L. Bennett.

Manager: Kevin Keegan. ***Assistant Manager:*** Terry McDermott.

Coach: Jeff Clarke. ***Physios:*** Derek Wright, Paul Ferris.

General Manager/Secretary: R. Cushing.

Assistant Secretary: A. Toward. ***Marketing Control:*** Trevor Garwood.

Year Formed: 1881. ***Turned Professional:*** 1889. ***Ltd Co.:*** 1890.

Club Nickname: 'Magpies'.

Previous Names: Stanley 1881; Newcastle East End 1882–1892.

Previous Grounds: South Byker, 1881; Chillingham Road, Heaton, 1886 to 1892.

Foundation: It stemmed from a newly formed club called Stanley in 1881. In October 1882 they changed their name to Newcastle East End to avoid confusion with Stanley in Co. Durham. Shortly afterwards another club Rosewood merged with them. Newcastle West End had been formed in August 1882 and they played on a ground which is now St. James' Park. In 1889, West End went out of existence after a bad run and the remaining committee men invited East End to move to St. James' Park. They accepted and at a meeting in Bath Lane Hall in 1892, changed their name to Newcastle United.

First Football League game: 2 September, 1893, Division 2, v Royal Arsenal (a) D 2-2 – Ramsay; Jeffery, Miller; Crielly, Graham, McKane; Bowman, Crate (1), Thompson, Sorley (1), Wallace. Graham and not Crate scored according to some reports.

Record League Victory: 13–0 v Newport Co, Division 2, 5 October 1946 – Garbutt; Cowell, Graham; Harvey, Brennan, Wright; Milburn (2), Bentley (1), Wayman (4), Shackleton (6), Pearson.

Record Cup Victory: 9–0 v Southport (at Hillsborough) FA Cup, 4th rd, 1 February 1932 – McInroy; Nelson, Fairhurst; McKenzie, Davidson, Weaver (1); Boyd (1), Jimmy Richardson (3), Cape (2), McMenemy (1), Lang (1).

Record Defeat: 0–9 v Burton Wanderers, Division 2, 15 April 1895.

Most League Points (2 for a win): 57, Division 2, 1964–65.

Most League Points (3 for a win): 96, Division 1, 1992–93.

Most League Goals: 98, Division 1, 1951–52.

Highest League Scorer in Season: Hughie Gallacher, 36, Division 1, 1926–27.

Most League Goals in Total Aggregate: Jackie Milburn, 178, 1946–57.

Most Capped Player: Alf McMichael, 40, Northern Ireland.

Most League Appearances: Jim Lawrence, 432, 1904–22.

Record Transfer Fee Received: £6,250,000 from Manchester U for Andy Cole, January 1995.

Record Transfer Fee Paid: £6,000,000 to QPR for Les Ferdinand, June 1995.

Football League Record: 1893 Elected to Division 2; 1898–1934 Division 1; 1934–48 Division 2; 1948–61 Division 1; 1961–65 Division 2; 1965–78 Division 1; 1978–84 Division 2; 1984–89 Division 1; 1989–92 Division 2; 1992–93 Division 1; 1993– FA Premier League.

Honours: *Football League:* Division 1 – Champions 1904–05, 1906–07, 1908–09, 1926–27, 1992–93; Division 2 – Champions 1964–65; Runners-up 1897–98, 1947–48. *FA Cup:* Winners 1910, 1924, 1932, 1951, 1952, 1955; Runners-up 1905, 1906, 1908, 1911, 1974. *Football League Cup:* Runners-up 1976. *Texaco Cup:* Winners 1974, 1975. **European Competitions:** *European Fairs Cup:* 1968–69 (winners), 1969–70, 1970–71 *UEFA Cup:* 1977–78, 1994–95. *Anglo-Italian Cup:* Winners 1972–73.

Colours: Black and white striped shirts, black shorts, black stockings. **Change colours:** Maroon and navy hooped shirts, cream shorts, maroon stockings.

NEWCASTLE UNITED 1994–95 LEAGUE RECORD

Match No.	Date	Venue	Opponents	Result	H/T Score	Lg. Pos.	Goalscorers	Attendance
1	Aug 21	A	Leicester C	W 3-1	0-0	—	Cole, Beardsley, Elliott	20,048
2	24	H	Coventry C	W 4-0	3-0	—	Lee 2, Watson, Cole	34,163
3	27	H	Southampton	W 5-1	3-0	1	Watson 2, Cole 2, Lee	34,182
4	31	A	West Ham U	W 3-1	2-0	—	Potts (og), Lee, Mathie	17,375
5	Sept 10	H	Chelsea	W 4-2	2-2	1	Cole 2, Fox, Lee	34,435
6	18	A	Arsenal	W 3-2	2-1	1	Keown (og), Beardsley (pen), Fox	36,819
7	24	H	Liverpool	D 1-1	0-0	1	Lee	34,435
8	Oct 1	A	Aston Villa	W 2-0	0-0	1	Lee, Cole	29,960
9	9	H	Blackburn R	D 1-1	0-0	1	Flowers (og)	34,344
10	15	A	Crystal Palace	W 1-0	0-0	1	Beardsley	17,739
11	22	H	Sheffield W	W 2-1	2-0	1	Watson, Cole	34,369
12	29	A	Manchester U	L 0-2	0-1	1		43,795
13	Nov 5	H	QPR	W 2-1	0-1	1	Kitson, Beardsley	34,278
14	7	A	Nottingham F	D 0-0	0-0	—		22,102
15	19	A	Wimbledon	L 2-3	2-3	3	Beardsley, Kitson	14,203
16	26	H	Ipswich T	D 1-1	0-0	3	Cole	34,459
17	Dec 3	A	Tottenham H	L 2-4	2-2	3	Fox 2	28,002
18	10	H	Leicester C	W 3-1	1-0	3	Albert 2, Howey	34,400
19	17	A	Coventry C	D 0-0	0-0	3		17,237
20	26	A	Leeds U	D 0-0	0-0	3		39,337
21	31	A	Norwich C	L 1-2	1-2	4	Fox (pen)	21,172
22	Jan 2	H	Manchester C	D 0-0	0-0	5		34,437
23	15	H	Manchester U	D 1-1	0-1	5	Kitson	34,471
24	21	A	Sheffield W	D 0-0	0-0	4		31,215
25	25	H	Wimbledon	W 2-1	1-0	—	Fox, Kitson	34,374
26	Feb 1	H	Everton	W 2-0	0-0	—	Fox, Beardsley (pen)	34,465
27	4	A	QPR	L 0-3	0-3	3		16,576
28	11	H	Nottingham F	W 2-1	0-0	3	Fox, Lee	34,471
29	25	H	Aston Villa	W 3-1	1-1	3	Venison, Beardsley 2	34,637
30	28	A	Ipswich T	W 2-0	2-0	—	Fox, Kitson	18,639
31	Mar 4	A	Liverpool	L 0-2	0-0	3		39,300
32	8	H	West Ham U	W 2-0	1-0	—	Clark, Kitson	34,595
33	19	H	Arsenal	W 1-0	0-0	3	Beardsley	35,611
34	22	A	Southampton	L 1-3	1-0	—	Kitson	14,666
35	Apr 1	A	Chelsea	D 1-1	0-1	3	Hottiger	22,987
36	8	H	Norwich C	W 3-0	2-0	3	Beardsley 2 (1 pen), Kitson	35,518
37	14	A	Everton	L 0-2	0-1	—		34,628
38	17	H	Leeds U	L 1-2	1-2	5	Elliott	35,626
39	29	A	Manchester C	D 0-0	0-0	5		27,389
40	May 3	H	Tottenham H	D 3-3	2-3	—	Gillespie, Peacock, Beardsley	35,603
41	8	A	Blackburn R	L 0-1	0-1	—		30,545
42	14	H	Crystal Palace	W 3-2	3-0	6	Fox, Lee, Gillespie	35,626

Final League Position: 6

GOALSCORERS

League (67): Beardsley 12 (3 pens), Fox 10 (1 pen), Cole 9, Lee 9, Kitson 8, Watson 4, Albert 2, Elliott 2, Gillespie 2, Clark 1, Hottiger 1, Howey 1, Mathie 1, Peacock 1, Venison 1, own goals 3.
Coca-Cola Cup (6): Cole 2, Albert 1, Fox 1, Jeffrey 1, Kitson 1.
FA Cup (9): Kitson 3, Gillespie 2, Beresford 1, Clark 1, Hottiger 1, Lee 1.

Srnicek P. 38	Hottiger M. 38	Beresford J. 33	Venison B. 28	Peacock D. 35	Albert P. 17	Lee R.M. 35	Beardsley P.A. 34	Cole A. 18	Fox R.A. 40	Sellars S. 12	Elliott R.J. 10 + 4	Mathie A. 3 + 6	Hooper M.D. 4 + 2	Watson S.C. 22 + 5	Howey S.N. 29 + 1	Kitson P. 24 + 2	Neilson A.B. 5 + 1	Clark L.R. 9 + 10	Bracewell P.W. 13 + 3	Gillespie K.R. 15 + 2	Allen M. — + 1	Match No.
1	2	3	4	5	6	7	*8*	9	10	11	12	*14*	15									1
1	2	3	4	5	6	7		9	10	11	12	14		*8*								2
1	2	3	4	5	6	7		9	*10*	11	12	14		8								3
1	2	3	4	5	6	7		9		11	12	10		8								4
	2	3	4	5	6	7		9	10	11			1	8								5
1	2	3		5	6	7	8	9	10	11					4							6
1	2	3	*4*	5	6	7	8	9	10	11				12	14							7
1	2	3		5	6	7	8	9	10	11					4	12						8
1	2	3		5		7	8	9	10	11				6	4	12						9
1		3			6		8	9	10	11				5	4	7	2					10
1	2	3		5	6		8	9	10	11				4		7		12				11
1	2	3		5	6	9	8		*10*	11		12		7	4			14				12
1	2	3		5	6	9	8		10					7	4	11						13
1	2	3		5	6	9	8		10					7		11		4				14
1	2	3	7	*5*	6	9	8		10					12	4	11		14				15
1	2	3	4		*6*	7	8	9	10			12		11			5	14				16
1	2	3	4				8	9	10			7		6			5	11				17
1	2	11	4	5	3		8	9	10					7	6							18
1	2	3	4	5			8	9	10					7	6	11		12				19
1		3	2		6	7		9	10					4	5	11			8			20
1		3	2	5		7		9	10					6	4	11		12	8			21
1		3	2	5		7	8	9	10						6	11			4			22
1	2	3	4	5		7			10		11				6	9		8				23
1	2	3	4	5		7	8		10						6	9		11		12		24
1	2		4	5			8		10		3				6	9			7	11		25
	2		4			7	8		10		3	9	1				5	12	6	11		26
	2					7	8				3	12	1	4		9	5	10	6	11		27
1	2	3	4	5		7	8		10						6	9			12	11		28
1	2	3	4	5		7	8		10						6	9				11		29
1	2	3	4	5		7	8		10						6	9				11		30
1	2	3	4	5		7	8		*10*					12	6	9			14	11		31
1	2	3	4	5		7			10					12	*6*	9		8	14	11		32
1	2		4	5		7	8		10		3					9		12	6	11		33
1	2		4	5		7	8		10		3				6	9				11		34
1	2		4	5		7	8		10		3			14	6	*9*		12	11			35
1	2		4	5		7	8		10		3				6	9			11			36
	2		4	5		7	8		*10*		3		1		6	9		12	11	14		37
1	2					7	8		10		3			5	6	9	12		4	11		38
1	2	3		5			8		10					4	6			11	7	9		39
1	2	3		5		7	8		*10*				15	11	6				4	9	12	40
1	2	3		5		7	8		10					4	6			11		9		41
1	2	3		5		7	8		10					4	6			11		9		42

Coca-Cola Cup

Second Round	Barnsley (h)	2-1
	(a)	1-0
Third Round	Manchester U (h)	2-0
Fourth Round	Manchester C (a)	1-1
	(h)	0-2

FA Cup

Third Round	Blackburn R (h)	1-1
	(a)	2-1
Fourth Round	Swansea C (h)	3-0
Fifth Round	Manchester C (h)	3-1
Sixth Round	Everton (a)	0-1

NORTHAMPTON TOWN 1994–95 *Back row (left to right):* Lee Colkin, Jason Pascoe, Kevin Wilkin, Robbie Curtis, Scott Stackman, Richard Skelly.
Centre row: Dennis Casey (Physio), Ray Byrne, Mark Turner, Dean Trott, Billy Stewart, Ian Sampson, Scott Middlemass, Richard Preston, Paul Curtis (Youth Coach).
Front row: Peter Morris (Assistant Manager), Gary Harrison, Neil Grayson, Ray Warburton, Mickey Bell, Darren Harmon, John Barnwell (Manager).
(Photograph: Pete Norton)

Division 3 NORTHAMPTON TOWN

Sixfields Stadium, Upton Way, Northampton NN1 4PS. Telephone: (01604) 757773. Fax: (01604) 751613/754960. Ticket Office: (01604) 588338. Soccer Line: 0839 664477.

Ground capacity: 7650.

Record attendance (at County Ground): 24,523 v Fulham, Division 1, 23 April 1966.

Record receipts (at County Ground): £47,292.40 v Coventry C, FA Cup 3rd rd, 6 January 1990.

Pitch measurements: 116yd × 72yd.

Chairman: B. J. Ward.

Directors: B. Stonhill, B. Hancock, M. Church, B. Church, D. Kerr, B. Collins, B. Lomax.

Secretary: Barry Collins.

Manager: Ian Atkins. ***Assistant Manager:*** Peter Morris. ***Coach:*** Danny O'Shea.

Physio: Dennis Casey. ***Commercial Manager:*** Bob Gorrill.

Year Formed: 1897. ***Turned Professional:*** 1901. ***Ltd Co.:*** 1901.

Previous Ground: County Ground.

Club Nickname: 'The Cobblers'.

Foundation: Formed in 1897 by school teachers connected with the Northampton and District Elementary Schools' Association, they survived a financial crisis at the end of their first year when they were £675 in the red and became members of the Midland League – a fast move indeed for a new club. They achieved Southern League membership in 1901.

First Football League game: 28 August, 1920, Division 3, v Grimsby T (a) L 0-2 – Thorpe; Sproston, Hewison; Jobey, Tomkins, Pease; Whitworth, Lockett, Thomas, Freeman, MacKechnie.

Record League Victory: 10–0 v Walsall, Division 3 (S), 5 November 1927 – Hammond; Watson, Jeffs; Allen, Brett, Odell; Daley, Smith (3), Loasby (3), Hoten (1), Wells (3).

Record Cup Victory: 10–0 v Sutton T FA Cup pr rd, 7 December 1907 – Cooch; Drennan, Lloyd Davies, Tirrell (1), McCartney, Hickleton, Badenock (3), Platt (3), Lowe (1), Chapman (2), McDiarmid.

Record Defeat: 0–11 v Southampton, Southern League, 28 December 1901.

Most League Points (2 for a win): 68, Division 4, 1975–76.

Most League Points (3 for a win): 99, Division 4, 1986–87.

Most League Goals: 109, Division 3, 1962–63 and Division 3 (S), 1952–53.

Highest League Scorer in Season: Cliff Holton, 36, Division 3, 1961–62.

Most League Goals in Total Aggregate: Jack English, 135, 1947–60.

Most Capped Player: E. Lloyd Davies, 12 (16), Wales.

Most League Appearances: Tommy Fowler, 521, 1946–61.

Record Transfer Fee Received: £265,000 from Watford for Richard Hill, July 1987.

Record Transfer Fee Paid: £85,000 to Manchester C for Tony Adcock, January 1988.

Football League Record: 1920 Original Member of Division 3; 1921 Division 3 (S); 1958–61 Division 4; 1961–63 Division 3; 1963–65 Division 2; 1965–66 Division 1; 1966–67 Division 2; 1967–69 Division 3; 1969–76 Division 4; 1976–77 Division 3; 1977–87 Division 4; 1987–90 Division 3; 1990–92 Division 4; 1992– Division 3.

Honours: *Football League:* Division 1 best season: 21st, 1965–66; Division 2 – Runners-up 1964–65; Division 3 – Champions 1962–63; Division 3 (S) – Runners-up 1927–28, 1949–50; Division 4 – Champions 1986–87; Runners-up 1975–76. *FA Cup:* best season: 5th rd, 1934, 1950, 1970. *Football League Cup:* best season: 5th rd, 1965, 1967.

Colours: Claret with white shirts, yellow shoulder panel (Lotto logo), white shorts, claret stockings. **Change colours:** Reverse of (home) first choice.

NORTHAMPTON TOWN 1994–95 LEAGUE RECORD

Match No.	Date	Venue	Opponents	Result	H/T Score	Lg. Pos.	Goalscorers	Attendance
1	Aug 20	A	Doncaster R	L 0-1	0-1	20		2194
2	27	A	Scunthorpe U	D 1-1	1-1	17	Trott	2499
3	30	A	Torquay U	L 1-2	0-2	—	Sampson	3619
4	Sept 3	A	Walsall	D 1-1	1-1	21	Trott	4249
5	10	H	Rochdale	L 1-2	1-0	22	Trott	3052
6	13	H	Hartlepool U	D 1-1	0-0	—	Aldridge	2466
7	17	A	Mansfield T	D 1-1	0-0	21	Aldridge	2557
8	24	H	Carlisle U	W 2-1	1-0	20	Aldridge, Bell	3508
9	Oct 1	A	Lincoln C	D 2-2	2-1	19	Harmon, Warburton	3248
10	8	A	Exeter C	D 0-0	0-0	20		3015
11	11	H	Mansfield T	L 0-1	0-1	—		4993
12	15	H	Barnet	D 1-1	0-0	21	Aldridge	7461
13	22	H	Wigan Ath	W 1-0	1-0	18	Grayson	6379
14	29	A	Scarborough	D 0-0	0-0	18		1468
15	Nov 5	H	Fulham	L 0-1	0-1	18		7366
16	19	A	Preston NE	L 0-2	0-1	18		7297
17	26	H	Hereford U	L 1-3	0-0	21	Cahill	5148
18	Dec 10	H	Doncaster R	D 0-0	0-0	21		4538
19	16	H	Scunthorpe U	L 0-1	0-1	—		3845
20	26	A	Colchester U	W 1-0	1-0	20	Harmon (pen)	5064
21	27	H	Chesterfield	L 2-3	1-2	21	Brown, Harmon (pen)	6329
22	31	A	Darlington	L 1-4	0-1	21	Grayson	2250
23	Jan 7	A	Wigan Ath	L 1-2	0-1	21	Colkin	1911
24	14	H	Gillingham	W 2-0	0-0	20	Harmon (pen), Trott	5529
25	28	H	Scarborough	L 0-3	0-0	20		5737
26	Feb 4	A	Hereford U	L 1-2	1-1	21	Grayson	2365
27	11	H	Preston NE	W 2-1	0-0	20	Burns, Smith	5195
28	14	A	Fulham	D 4-4	1-2	—	Aldridge 2, Brown, Grayson	3423
29	18	A	Gillingham	L 1-3	0-1	20	Thompson	4075
30	25	H	Lincoln C	W 3-1	1-0	19	Brown (og), Grayson, Aldridge	4821
31	Mar 4	A	Carlisle U	L 1-2	0-2	19	Martin	6755
32	7	H	Bury	L 0-5	0-1	—		4208
33	11	A	Rochdale	D 0-0	0-0	19		1894
34	18	H	Torquay U	W 2-0	0-0	18	Grayson, Brown	3832
35	25	H	Walsall	D 2-2	1-1	18	Grayson, Warburton	6282
36	Apr 1	A	Hartlepool U	D 1-1	0-1	18	Thompson	2113
37	8	H	Darlington	W 2-1	1-0	17	Thompson, Grayson	4496
38	15	A	Chesterfield	L 0-3	0-1	19		4884
39	17	H	Colchester U	D 1-1	1-0	17	Brown	5011
40	22	A	Bury	L 0-5	0-1	20		2921
41	29	A	Barnet	W 3-2	2-1	18	Burns, Thompson, Warburton	2796
42	May 6	H	Exeter C	W 2-1	1-0	17	O'Shea, Sampson	6734

Final League Position: 17

GOALSCORERS

League (45): Grayson 8, Aldridge 7, Brown 4, Harmon 4 (3 pens), Thompson 4, Trott 4, Warburton 3, Burns 2, Sampson 2, Bell 1, Cahill 1, Colkin 1, Martin 1, O'Shea 1, Smith 1, own goal 1.
Coca-Cola Cup (0).
FA Cup (0).

Stewart W.I. 26 + 1	Pascoe J. 11 + 4	Curtis R. 13	Norton D.W. 36 + 2	Warburton R. 39	Sampson I. 42	Harmon D.J. 26 + 7	Byrne R. 2	Trott D. 20 + 2	Grayson N. 34 + 4	Bell M. 12	Colkin L. 28 + 5	Wilkin K. 2 + 2	Aldridge M.J. 18 + 9	Robinson P.J. 14	McNamara B. — + 1	Williams G.J. 13 + 2	Cahill O.F. 5 + 3	Skelly R.B. 3	Ovendale M.J. 6	Harrison G.M. 5	Sedgemore B.R. 1	Brown I.O. 23	Flounders A.J. 2	Patmore W.J. 1 + 3	Hughes D.J. 12 + 1	Burns C. 16 + 1	Smith N. 6	Daniels S. 5 + 3	Thompson G.L. 15	Martin D. 7	Turner G.M. 2 + 2	Woodman A.J. 10	O'Shea D.E. 7	*Match No.*
1	2	3	4	5	6	7	*8*	9	10	11	12	14																						1
1	2		4	5	6	7	8	9	12	11	3	10																						2
1	2	6	8	5	4	7		9	10	11	3		12																					3
1		6	2	5	4	7		9	10	11	3		12	8																				4
1			2	5	4	7		9	10	11	3	8		6	12																			5
1	6		2	5	4	7		9	10	11	3		12	8																				6
1		6	2	5	4	7		9		11	3		10	8																				7
1		6	2	5	4	7		9		11	3		10	8																				8
1		6	2	5	4	7		9		11	3		10	8																				9
1		6	2	5	4	7		9		11	3			8		10																		10
1		*6*	2	5	4	7		9	14	11	3		12	8		10																		11
1	2			5	4	7		9	12	11	3		10	6		8																		12
1	2	6		5	4	7			9		3		10	11		8	12																	13
1	2			5	4	7		9	8		11		12	10		6		3																14
1	2		12	5	4	7			8		3		9	10		6	11																	15
	12		2	5	4	7		9	11		3		8	10		6	14		1															16
1			2	5	4	7		9	12				8	10		6	11	3																17
1	3		2	5	4	7		9	8				12			6	11			10														18
1	12		2	5	4	7		*9*	3			14	8			6	11			10														19
1	12	5	2		4	7			9		3					11					6	8	*10*	14										20
1	2	5	6		4	7			9		3					*11*	12					8	10	14										21
1		6	2	5	4				10		3		12			11				7		8		9										22
1	12	6	2	5	4				11		10		9					3		7		8												23
1			2	5	4	7		12	11		6		9									8			3	10								24
1			2	5	4	7		9	11													8		12	3	10	6							25
			2	5	6	12		9	10										1	11		8			14	7	4	*3*						26
			2	5	4	6			11				7						1			8				10	3		9					27
			2	5	4	12			11				7						1			8				10	3		9	6				28
1			2	5	4	12			11				7									8					3		9	6	10			29
			2	5	4	10			11				7						1			8					3		9	6	12			30
15			2	5	4	12			11		3		7			14			*1*			*8*				10			9	6				31
1			2	5	4	12			11		3		*7*									8				10			9	6	14			32
			2	5	4				11		12		14									8			3	10			9	6	*7*	1		33
			2	5	4				11		12		7									8			3	10			9	6		1		34
			2	5	4	12			11		6					14						*8*			3	10		7	9			1		35
			2	5	4				11		12											8			3	10		7	9			1	6	36
			2	5	4				11		7											8			3	10		12	9			1	6	37
	5		2		4	12		14	11		7											8			*3*	10			9			1	6	38
			12	5	4				11		7											8			3	10		2	9			1	6	39
				5	4	10		9	11		7											8			3	12		2				1	6	40
			2	5	4				11		7		12									*8*			3	10		14	9			1	6	41
			2	5	4				*11*		12						7					8			3	10		14	9			1	6	42

Coca-Cola Cup

First Round	Bournemouth	(a)	0-2
		(h)	0-1

FA Cup

First Round	Peterborough U	(a)	0-4

NORWICH CITY 1994–95 *Back row (left to right):* Efan Ekoku, Keith O'Neill, Andy Johnson, Spencer Prior, Jon Newsome, Rob Newman, Ian Butterworth, Daryl Sutch, Ade Akinbiyi.
Centre row: Tim Sheppard (Physio), Stacey Kreft, Johnny Wright, Shaun Carey, Mark Robins, Jeremy Goss, John Faulkner, Andy Marshall, Gary Megson, (Assistant Manager), Carl Bradshaw, Mark Bowen, Robert Ullathorne, Alistair Gibb, Justin Harrington, Keith Webb.
Front row: Marcus Oldbury, Darren Eadie, Neil Adams, John Polston, Bryan Gunn, John Deehan (Manager), Scott Howie, Ian Crook, Mike Milligan, Jamie Cureton, Jimmy Simpson.

Division 1 NORWICH CITY

Carrow Road, Norwich NR1 1JE. Telephone: (01603) 760760. Fax: (01603) 665510. Box Office: (01603) 761661. Canary Call: 0891 424212.

Ground capacity: 21,994.

Record attendance: 43,984 v Leicester C, FA Cup 6th rd, 30 March 1963.

Record receipts: £261,918 v Internazionale, UEFA Cup 3rd rd 1st leg, 24 November 1993.

Pitch measurements: 114yd × 74yd.

President: G. C. Watling.

Chairman: Robert T. Chase JP. ***Vice-Chairman:*** J. A. Jones.

Directors: B. W. Lockwood, G. A. Paterson.

Manager: Martin O'Neill. ***Assistant Manager:*** Paul Franklin.

Youth Team Coach: Steve Walford.

Commercial Manager: Ray Cossey.

Physio: Tim Sheppard MCSP, SRP.

Secretary: A. R. W. Neville.

Year Formed: 1902. ***Turned Professional:*** 1905. ***Ltd Co.:*** 1905.

Club Nickname: 'The Canaries'.

Previous Grounds: 1902, Newmarket Road; 1908–35, The Nest, Rosary Road.

Foundation: Formed in 1902, largely through the initiative of two local schoolmasters who called a meeting at the Criterion Cafe, they were shocked by an FA Commission which in 1904 declared the club professional and ejected them from the FA Amateur Cup. However, this only served to strengthen their determination. New officials were appointed and a professional club established at a meeting in the Agricultural Hall in March 1905.

First Football League game: 28 August, 1920, Division 3, v Plymouth A (a) D 1-1 – Skermer; Gray, Gadsden; Wilkinson, Addy, Martin; Laxton, Kidger, Parker, Whitham (1), Dobson.

Record League Victory: 10–2 v Coventry C, Division 3 (S), 15 March 1930 – Jarvie; Hannah, Graham; Brown, O'Brien, Lochhead (1); Porter (1), Anderson, Hunt (5), Scott (2), Slicer (1).

Record Cup Victory: 8–0 v Sutton U, FA Cup, 4th rd, 28 January 1989 – Gunn; Culverhouse, Bowen, Butterworth, Linighan, Townsend (Crook), Gordon, Fleck (3), Allen (4), Phelan, Putney (1).

Record Defeat: 2–10 v Swindon T, Southern League, 5 September 1908.

Most League Points (2 for a win): 64, Division 3 (S), 1950–51.

Most League Points (3 for a win): 84, Division 2, 1985–86.

Most League Goals: 99, Division 3 (S), 1952–53.

Highest League Scorer in Season: Ralph Hunt, 31. Division 3 (S), 1955–56.

Most League Goals in Total Aggregate: Johnny Gavin, 122, 1945–54, 1955–58.

Most Capped Player: Mark Bowen, 30 (32), Wales.

Most League Appearances: Ron Ashman, 592, 1947–64.

Record Transfer Fee Received: £5,000,000 from Blackburn R for Chris Sutton, July 1994.

Record Transfer Fee Paid: £1,000,000 to Leeds U for Jon Newsome, June 1994.

Football League Record: 1920 Original Member of Division 3; 1921 Division 3 (S): 1934–39 Division 2; 1946–58 Division 3 (S); 1958–60 Division 3; 1960–72 Division 2; 1972–74 Division 1; 1974–75 Division 2; 1975–81 Division 1; 1981–82 Division 2; 1982–85 Division 1; 1985–86 Division 2; 1986–92 Division 1; 1992–95 FA Premier League; 1995– Division 1.

Honours: *FA Premier League* best season: 3rd 1992–93. *Football League:* Division 2 – Champions 1971–72, 1985–86. Division 3 (S) – Champions 1933–34; Division 3 – Runners-up 1959–60. *FA Cup:* Semi-finals 1959, 1989, 1992. *Football League Cup:* Winners 1962, 1985; Runners-up 1973, 1975. **European Competitions:** *UEFA Cup:* 1993–94.

Colours: Yellow shirts, green shorts, yellow stockings. **Change colours:** All blue.

NORWICH CITY FC

NORWICH CITY 1994–95 LEAGUE RECORD

Match No.	Date	Venue	Opponents	Result		H/T Score	Lg. Pos.	Goalscorers	Attendance
1	Aug 20	A	Chelsea	L	0-2	0-1	—		23,098
2	24	H	Crystal Palace	D	0-0	0-0	—		19,015
3	27	H	West Ham U	W	1-0	0-0	11	Robins	19,110
4	31	A	Sheffield W	D	0-0	0-0	—		25,072
5	Sept 10	H	Arsenal	D	0-0	0-0	11		17,768
6	19	A	Ipswich T	W	2-1	1-1	—	Newman, Bradshaw	17,405
7	24	A	Manchester C	L	0-2	0-0	11		21,031
8	Oct 1	H	Blackburn R	W	2-1	1-1	9	Bowen, Newsome	18,146
9	8	H	Leeds U	W	2-1	0-0	8	Robins, Adams	17,390
10	15	A	Aston Villa	D	1-1	0-0	6	Milligan	22,468
11	22	H	QPR	W	4-2	0-1	6	Robins, Bowen, Sheron, White (og)	19,431
12	30	A	Wimbledon	L	0-1	0-0	8		8242
13	Nov 2	A	Southampton	D	1-1	0-0	—	Robins	12,876
14	5	H	Everton	D	0-0	0-0	7		18,377
15	19	A	Coventry C	L	0-1	0-0	9		11,891
16	26	H	Leicester C	W	2-1	0-1	9	Newsome, Sutch	20,657
17	Dec 3	A	Manchester U	L	0-1	0-1	9		43,789
18	10	H	Chelsea	W	3-0	2-0	9	Ward 2, Cureton	18,246
19	17	A	Crystal Palace	W	1-0	0-0	7	Ward	12,473
20	26	H	Tottenham H	L	0-2	0-1	7		21,814
21	27	A	Nottingham F	L	0-1	0-0	—		21,010
22	31	H	Newcastle U	W	2-1	2-1	7	Adams, Ward	21,172
23	Jan 2	A	Liverpool	L	0-4	0-2	8		34,709
24	14	H	Wimbledon	L	1-2	1-1	9	Goss	18,261
25	25	H	Coventry C	D	2-2	1-1	—	Adams (pen), Ward	14,024
26	Feb 4	A	Everton	L	1-2	0-1	10	Milligan	23,295
27	11	H	Southampton	D	2-2	1-2	10	Newsome, Ward	18,361
28	22	H	Manchester U	L	0-2	0-2	—		21,824
29	25	A	Blackburn R	D	0-0	0-0	14		25,579
30	Mar 4	H	Manchester C	D	1-1	0-0	14	Cureton	16,266
31	8	H	Sheffield W	D	0-0	0-0	—		13,530
32	11	A	West Ham U	D	2-2	1-0	14	Eadie, Ullathorne	21,464
33	15	A	QPR	L	0-2	0-0	—		10,519
34	20	H	Ipswich T	W	3-0	0-0	—	Cureton, Ward, Eadie	17,510
35	Apr 1	A	Arsenal	L	1-5	1-3	14	Cureton	36,942
36	5	A	Leicester C	L	0-1	0-0	—		15,992
37	8	A	Newcastle U	L	0-3	0-2	14		35,518
38	12	H	Nottingham F	L	0-1	0-0	—		19,005
39	17	A	Tottenham H	L	0-1	0-1	20		32,304
40	29	H	Liverpool	L	1-2	1-1	20	Ullathorne	21,843
41	May 6	A	Leeds U	L	1-2	1-0	20	Ward	31,981
42	14	H	Aston Villa	D	1-1	0-1	20	Goss	19,374

Final League Position: 20

GOALSCORERS

League (37): Ward 8, Robins 4, Cureton 4, Adams 3 (1 pen), Newsome 3, Bowen 2, Eadie 2, Goss 2, Milligan 2, Ullathorne 2, Bradshaw 1, Newman 1, Sheron 1, Sutch 1, own goal 1.
Coca-Cola Cup (9): Polston 2, Adams 1, Bradshaw 1 (pen), Eadie 1, Newman 1, Prior 1, Sheron 1, own goal 1.
FA Cup (4): Sheron 2, Crook 1, Eadie 1.

Gunn B. 21	Bradshaw C. 25 + 1	Bowen M.R. 34 + 2	Newsome J. 35	Polston J.D. 38	Newman R.N. 23 + 9	Crook I.S. 33 + 1	Ullathorne R. 27	Robins M.G. 14 + 3	Ekoku E. 5 + 1	Goss J. 19 + 6	Adams N.J. 23 + 10	Sutch D. 20 + 10	Eadie D.M. 22 + 4	Akinbiyi A.P. 6 + 7	Sheron M.N. 17 + 4	Milligan M.J. 25 + 1	Prior S. 12 + 5	Wright J. 1 + 1	O'Neill K.P. — + 1	Cureton J. 9 + 8	Ward A.S. 25	Marshall A.J. 20 + 1	Tracey S.P. 1	Johnson A.J. 6 + 1	Megson G.J. 1	*Match No.*
1	2	3	4	5	6	7	8	9	*10*	11	12	14														1
1	2	3	4	5		7	8	9	10	6	11		12													2
1	2	3	4	5	12	7	8	9	*10*	6	11			14												3
1	2	3	4	5	12	7	8	9		6	11			*10*	14											4
1	2	3	4	5	9	7	8	12	10	6	*11*	14														5
1	2	3	4	5	9	7			12	6	11		14		10	8										6
1	2	3	4	5	9	7	8	12		6	*11*				10	14										7
1	2	3	4	5	9	6		14	*10*	12	11		7			8										8
1	2	3	*4*		5	6		9		12	11		7		10	8	14									9
1	*2*	3			4	6		9			11		7	12	10	8	5	14								10
1		3	4	5	12	6		9		14	*11*		7		10	8		2								11
1		3		5	8	12	6			11	14	2		*9*	10	7	4									12
1		3		5	*2*	7		9		4	11	12		10		8	6		14							13
1		3		5	8	7		9		6	11	2				10	4			12						14
1		3	5	2	8	4		9		12	*11*	14	7			10	6									15
1		3	4	5	9	6				12	11	2	7		*10*	8				14						16
1	2	3	4	5	8	10	6	9		11		7								12						17
1	2		4	5	12	6	3	*9*				7	11			8				14	10					18
1	2	12	4	5	14	*6*	3	9				7	11			8					10					19
1		2	4	5	12	6	3	9		11	14	*7*	8								10					20
1			4	5	8	6	3			11	12	2			9					7	10	15				21
			4	5	12	7	3			6	11	2			*9*	8				14	10	1				22
				5	*4*	7	3			11	12	2	14		9	8	6				10	1				23
		3	4	5		7	8			6	*11*	2		12	9		14				10	1				24
		3	4	5	8						11	2	12		9	7	6				10		1			25
		3	4	5		7	6			12	14	*2*	11		9	8					10	1				26
	2	3	4			7	6			11	14	12	8		9		*5*				10	1				27
	2	3	4	5							7		11		9	8					10	1		6		28
	2	3	4	5							7	12	11		9	*8*				14	10	1		6		29
	2	3		5	4						7		11		12	8	14			*9*	10	1		6		30
	2	3	4	5	12	7	6					8	11							9	10	1		14		31
			4	5	8		3				12	2	*11*	14			6			9	10	1		7		32
				5	4		3				12	2	11	14		8	6			*9*	10	1		7		33
		3	4	5	12	2	6				7	14	11			8				9	10	1				34
	2	3	4		5		6				7	12	11							9	10	1		8		35
	2	12	4	5	8		3					7	11				14			9	10	1			*6*	36
	2	3	4	*5*		7	8					12	11			10	6			14	9	1				37
	2	3	4	5		6					7		11	14		8	12			*9*	10	1				38
	2	3	4	5	11	7						12		14	*9*	8	6				10	1				39
	2	3	4	5		11	6				12	7		9		8				14	10	1				40
	12	3	4	5	2	11	8			6		7		*9*	14						10	1				41
	2	3	4	5		7	8			6		11		9	12						10	1				42

Coca-Cola Cup

Second Round	Swansea C (h)	3-0
	(a)	0-1
Third Round	Tranmere R (a)	1-1
	(h)	4-2
Fourth Round	Notts Co (h)	1-0
Fifth Round	Bolton W (a)	0-1

FA Cup

Third Round	Grimsby T (a)	1-0
Fourth Round	Coventry C (a)	0-0
	(h)	3-1
Fifth Round	Everton (a)	0-5

NOTTINGHAM FOREST 1994–95 *Back row (left to right):* Des Lyttle, Gary Crosby, Steven Stone, Vance Warner, Neil Webb, Gary Bull, Kingsley Black, Steven Howe.
Centre row: Liam O'Kane (Coach), Richard Money (Reserve Coach), Alf Haaland, Carl Tiler, Mark Crossley, Jason Lee, Robert Rosario, Tommy Wright, Lars Bohinen, Steven Chettle, John Haselden (Physio), Peter Edwards (Fitness Coach).
Front row: Scot Gemmill, Brian Laws, Stan Collymore, Brian Roy, Frank Clark (Manager), Alan Hill (Assistant Manager), Stuart Pearce, Ian Woan, David Philips, Colin Cooper.

FA Premiership **NOTTINGHAM FOREST**

City Ground, Nottingham NG2 5FJ. Telephone: (0115) 9526000. Fax: (0115) 9526003. Information Desk: (0115) 9526016. Commercial Office: (0115) 9526006. Commercial Office Fax: (0115) 9526007. Ticket Office: (0115) 9526002. Souvenir Shop: (0115) 9526026. Junior Reds: (0115) 9526001. Lottery Office: (0115) 9526005.

Ground capacity: 30,539.

Record attendance: 49,946 v Manchester U, Division 1, 28 October 1967.

Record receipts: £272,735 v Sheffield W, FA Cup 3rd rd replay, 19 January 1994.

Pitch measurements: 115yd × 78yd.

Chairman: Fred Reacher. ***Vice-Chairman:*** I. I. Korn.

Directors: G. E. Macpherson, J. M. Smith, C. Wootton, K. Gibson, R. A. Fairhall.

Manager: Frank Clark. ***Assistant Manager:*** Alan Hill.

Secretary: Paul White. ***Commercial Manager:*** David Pullan.

Coach: Liam O'Kane. ***Physio:*** John Haselden.

Year Formed: 1865. ***Turned Professional:*** 1889. ***Ltd Co.:*** 1982.

Club Nickname: 'Reds'.

Previous Grounds: 1865, Forest Racecourse; 1879, The Meadows; 1880, Trent Bridge Cricket Ground; 1882, Parkside, Lenton; 1885, Gregory, Lenton; 1890, Town Ground; 1898, City Ground.

Foundation: One of the oldest football clubs in the world, Nottingham Forest was formed at a meeting in the Clinton Arms in 1865. Known originally as the Forest Football Club, the game which first drew the founders together was "shinney" a form of hockey. When they determined to change to football in 1865, one of their first moves was to buy a set of red caps to wear on the field.

First Football League game: 3 September, 1892, Division 1, v Everton (a) D 2-2 – Brown; Earp, Scott; Hamilton, A. Smith, McCracken; McCallum, W. Smith, Higgins (2), Pike, McInnes.

Record League Victory: 12–0 v Leicester Fosse, Division 1, 12 April 1909 – Iremonger; Dudley, Maltby; Hughes (1), Needham, Armstrong; Hooper (3), Marrison, West (3), Morris (2), Spouncer (3 incl. 1p).

Record Cup Victory: 14–0 v Clapton (away), FA Cup, 1st rd, 17 January 1891 – Brown; Earp, Scott; A. Smith, Russell, Jeacock; McCallum (2), 'Tich' Smith (1), Higgins (5), Lindley (4), Shaw (2).

Record Defeat: 1–9 v Blackburn R, Division 2, 10 April 1937.

Most League Points (2 for a win): 70, Division 3 (S), 1950–51.

Most League Points (3 for a win): 83, Division 1, 1993–94.

Most League Goals: 110, Division 3 (S), 1950–51.

Highest League Scorer in Season: Wally Ardron, 36, Division 3 (S), 1950–51.

Most League Goals in Total Aggregate: Grenville Morris, 199, 1898–1913.

Most Capped Player: Stuart Pearce, 59, England.

Most League Appearances: Bob McKinlay, 614, 1951–70.

Record Transfer Fee Received: £8,500,000 from Liverpool for Stan Collymore, June 1995.

Record Transfer Fee Paid: £2,900,000 to Foggia for Bryan Roy, August 1994.

Football League Record: 1892 Elected to Division 1; 1906–07 Division 2; 1907–11 Division 1; 1911–22 Division 2; 1922–25 Division 1; 1925–49 Division 2; 1949–51 Division 3 (S); 1951–57 Division 2; 1957–72 Division 1; 1972–77 Division 2; 1977–92 Division 1; 1992–93 FA Premier League; 1993–94 Division 1; 1994– FA Premier League.

Honours: *Football League:* Division 1 – Champions 1977–78; Runners-up 1966–67, 1978–79; Division 2 – Champions 1906–07, 1921–22; Runners-up 1956–57; Division 3 (S) – Champions 1950–51. *FA Cup:* Winners 1898, 1959; Runners-up 1991. *Anglo-Scottish Cup:* Winners 1977; *Football League Cup:* Winners 1978, 1979, 1989, 1990; Runners-up 1980. *Simod Cup:* Winners 1989. *Zenith Data Systems Cup:* Winners: 1992. **European Competitions:** *Fairs Cup:* 1961–62, 1967–68. *European Cup:* 1978–79 (winners), 1979–80 (winners), 1980–81. *Super Cup:* 1979–80 (winners), 1980–81 (runners-up). *World Club Championship:* 1980. *UEFA Cup:* 1983–84, 1984–85.

Colours: Red shirts with black shoulders, white shorts, red stockings. **Change colours:** All blue/green.

NOTTINGHAM FOREST 1994–95 LEAGUE RECORD

Match No.	Date	Venue	Opponents	Result	H/T Score	Lg. Pos.	Goalscorers	Attendance
1	Aug 20	A	Ipswich T	W 1-0	1-0	—	Roy	18,763
2	22	H	Manchester U	D 1-1	1-1	—	Collymore	22,072
3	27	H	Leicester C	W 1-0	1-0	4	Collymore	21,601
4	30	A	Everton	W 2-1	1-0	—	Hinchcliffe (og), Cooper	26,689
5	Sept 10	H	Sheffield W	W 4-1	1-0	2	Black, Bohinen, Pearce (pen), Roy	22,022
6	17	A	Southampton	D 1-1	1-0	3	Collymore	14,185
7	24	A	Tottenham H	W 4-1	1-1	3	Stone, Roy 2, Bohinen	24,558
8	Oct 2	H	QPR	W 3-2	0-0	2	Black, Roy, Collymore	21,449
9	8	A	Manchester C	D 3-3	1-1	2	Collymore, Dibble (og), Woan	23,150
10	17	H	Wimbledon	W 3-1	1-0	—	Bohinen, Collymore, Woan	20,287
11	22	A	Aston Villa	W 2-0	1-0	2	Pearce (pen), Stone	29,217
12	29	H	Blackburn R	L 0-2	0-1	2		22,131
13	Nov 5	A	Liverpool	L 0-1	0-1	4		33,329
14	7	H	Newcastle U	D 0-0	0-0	—		22,102
15	19	H	Chelsea	L 0-1	0-1	5		22,092
16	26	A	Leeds U	L 0-1	0-0	5		37,709
17	Dec 3	H	Arsenal	D 2-2	1-0	5	Pearce (pen), Roy	21,662
18	10	H	Ipswich T	W 4-1	4-1	5	Collymore, Gemmill, Haaland, Pearce	21,340
19	17	A	Manchester U	W 2-1	1-0	4	Collymore, Pearce	43,744
20	26	A	Coventry C	D 0-0	0-0	5		19,116
21	27	H	Norwich C	W 1-0	0-0	—	Bohinen	21,010
22	31	A	West Ham U	L 1-3	0-3	5	McGregor	20,644
23	Jan 2	H	Crystal Palace	W 1-0	0-0	4	Bull	21,326
24	14	A	Blackburn R	L 0-3	0-0	4		27,510
25	21	H	Aston Villa	L 1-2	0-1	5	Collymore (pen)	24,598
26	25	A	Chelsea	W 2-0	1-0	—	Collymore 2	17,890
27	Feb 4	H	Liverpool	D 1-1	1-0	5	Collymore	25,418
28	11	A	Newcastle U	L 1-2	0-0	5	Lee	34,471
29	21	A	Arsenal	L 0-1	0-0	—		35,441
30	26	A	QPR	D 1-1	0-0	5	Stone	13,363
31	Mar 4	H	Tottenham H	D 2-2	0-0	5	Bohinen, Lee	28,711
32	8	H	Everton	W 2-1	1-1	—	Collymore, Pearce	24,526
33	11	A	Leicester C	W 4-2	1-1	5	Pearce (pen), Collymore, Woan, Lee	20,423
34	18	H	Southampton	W 3-0	1-0	5	Roy 2, Collymore	24,146
35	22	H	Leeds U	W 3-0	3-0	—	Roy 2, Collymore	26,299
36	Apr 1	A	Sheffield W	W 7-1	2-0	4	Pearce, Woan, Roy 2, Collymore 2, Bohinen	30,060
37	8	H	West Ham U	D 1-1	0-0	4	Collymore	28,361
38	12	A	Norwich C	W 1-0	0-0	—	Stone	19,005
39	17	H	Coventry C	W 2-0	2-0	3	Woan, Collymore	26,253
40	29	A	Crystal Palace	W 2-1	1-0	3	Roy, Collymore	16,335
41	May 6	H	Manchester C	W 1-0	1-0	3	Collymore	28,882
42	13	A	Wimbledon	D 2-2	1-2	3	Phillips, Stone	15,341

Final League Position: 3

GOALSCORERS

League (72): Collymore 22 (1 pen), Roy 13, Pearce 8 (4 pens), Bohinen 6, Stone 5, Woan 5, Lee 3, Black 2, Bull 1, Cooper 1, Gemmill 1, Haaland 1, McGregor 1, Phillips 1, own goals 2.
Coca-Cola Cup (5): Collymore 2, Roy 2, Pearce 1.
FA Cup (3): Bohinen 1, Collymore 1, Gemmill 1.

Crossley M.G. 42	Lyttle D. 38	Pearce S. 36	Cooper C.T. 35	Chettle S. 41	Stone S.B. 41	Phillips D.O. 38	Gemmill S. 19	Lee J.B. 5 + 17	Woan I.S. 35 + 2	Roy B. 37	Bohinen L. 30 + 4	Rosario R.M. — + 1	Collymore S.V. 37	Black K. 5 + 5	Haaland A-I.R. 18 + 2	McGregor P.A. — + 11	Warner V. 1	Bull G.W. 1	Tiler C. 3	*Match No.*
1	2	3	4	5	6	7	8	9	10	*11*	12	14								1
1	2	3	4	5	6	7	8		11	9	12		10							2
1	2	3	4	5	6	7	8		11	9			10							3
1	2	3	4	5	6	7	8		11	9	12		10							4
1	2	3	4	5	6	7				8	9		10	11						5
1	2	3	4		6	7				8	9		10	11	5					6
1	2	3	4	5	6	7				8	9		10	11	12					7
1	2	3	4	5	6	7				8	9		10	11						8
1		3	4	5	6	7	8	12	14		9		10	*11*	2					9
1		3	4	5	6	7			11	8	9		10		2					10
1		3	4	5	6	7		12	11	8	9		10		2					11
1	2	3	4	5	6	7		10	11	8	9			12						12
1	2	3	4	5	6	7		10	11	8	9									13
1	2	3	4	5	6	7			11	8	9		10	12						14
1	2	3	4	5	6	7		12	11	8	9		10							15
1	2	3	4	5	6	7		12	11	8	9		10							16
1	2	3		5		4	7		11	8	9		10	12	6					17
1	2	3		5	6		7	12	11	8	*9*		10		4	14				18
1	2	3		5	6	7	8		11	9	12		10		4					19
1	2	3	4	5	6	7	*8*		11		9		10		12	14				20
1	2	3	4	5	6				11	8	9		10	12	7					21
1	2	3	*4*	5	6				11	8	9		10	12	7	14				22
1	2	3		5	6		8		11	10					7	12	4	9		23
1	2			5	6	7	8		11	9			10		3	12			4	24
1	2			5	6	7			11	8	9		10		3				4	25
1	2			5	6	7	8			11	9		10		4	12			3	26
1	2		4	5	6	3	8	12	11	9			10		7					27
1	2	3	4	5	6	7	8	12	11				10		9					28
1	2	3	4	5	6	7	8	10	11		9					12				29
1	2		4	5	6	3	8		12	11	9		10		7					30
1	2		4	5	6	3		12	11	8	9		10		7					31
1	2	3	4	5	6	7		12	11	8	9		10							32
1	2	3	4	5	6	7		12	11	8	9		10							33
1		3	4	5	6	7		12	11	8	9		10		2					34
1	*2*	3	4	5	6	7		12	11	8	9		10			14				35
1	2	3	4	5	6	7			11	8	9		10			12				36
1	2	3	4	5	6	7		12	11	8	*9*		10			14				37
1	2	3	4	5	6	7		12	11	8	9		10							38
1	2	3	4	5	6	7		12	*11*	8	9		10			14				39
1	2	3	4	5	6	7	8	12	11	9			10							40
1	2	3	4	5	6	7	8	12	11	9			10							41
1	2	3	4	5	6	7	8	9	11				10							42

Coca-Cola Cup

Second Round	Hereford U (h)	2-1
	(a)	0-0
Third Round	Wolverhampton W (a)	3-2
Fourth Round	Millwall (h)	0-2

FA Cup

Third Round	Plymouth Arg (h)	2-0
Fourth Round	Crystal Palace (h)	1-2

NOTTS COUNTY 1994–95 *Back row (left to right):* Tony Agana, Shaun Murphy, Steve Cherry, Paul Reece, Steve Slawson, Gary McSwegan.
Centre row: Wayne Jones (Assistant Manager), Tommy Gallagher, Chris Short, Michael Simpson, Paul Cox, Paul Sherlock, Richard Walker, Gary Lund, Dean Yates, Gary Mills, Rob Matthews, Dennis Petitt (Physio), John Gaunt (Youth Coach).
Front row: Peter Butler, Michael Johnson, Michael Emenalo, Dean Thomas, Derek Pavis (Chairman), Russell Slade (Manager), Phil Turner, Paul Devlin, Nigel Jemson, Andy Legg.

Division 2 NOTTS COUNTY

County Ground, Meadow Lane, Nottingham NG2 3HJ. Telephone: (0115) 9529000. Fax: (0115) 9553994. Ticket office: (0115) 9557210. Clubline: 0891 888684. Football in the Community: (0115) 9863656. Supporters Club: (0115) 9557255.

Ground capacity: 20,300.

Record attendance: 47,310 v York C, FA Cup 6th rd, 12 March 1955.

Record receipts: £124,539.10 v Manchester C, FA Cup 6th rd, 16 February 1991.

Pitch measurements: 114yd × 74yd.

Chairman: D. C. Pavis. ***Vice-Chairman:*** J. Mounteney.

Directors: W. A. Hopcroft, D. Ward, F. Sherwood (President), Mrs V. Pavis.

Manager: Colin Murphy. ***Assistant Manager:*** Steve Thompson. ***Commerical Manager:*** Helen Marsh.

Coach: D. Thomas. ***Chief Executive:*** Neal Hook MCIM. AMLD.

Physio: Dennis Pettitt.

Year Formed: 1862 *(*see Foundation*).

Turned Professional: 1885. ***Ltd Co.:*** 1888.

Club Nickname: 'Magpies'.

Previous Grounds: 1862, The Park; 1864, The Meadows; 1877, Beeston Cricket Ground; 1880, Castle Ground; 1883, Trent Bridge; 1910, Meadow Lane.

Foundation: For many years the foundation date of the Football League's oldest club was given as 1862 and the club celebrated its centenary in 1962. However, the researches of Keith Warsop have since shown that the club was on a very haphazard basis at that time, playing little more than practice matches. The meeting which put it on a firm footing was held at the George IV Hotel in December 1864, when they became known as the Notts Football Club.

First Football League game: 15 September, 1888, Football League, v Everton (a) L 1-2 – Holland; Guttridge, McLean; Brown, Warburton, Shelton; Hodder, Harker, Jardine, Moore (1), Wardle.

Record League Victory: 11–1 v Newport C, Division 3 (S), 15 January 1949 – Smith; Southwell, Purvis; Gannon, Baxter, Adamson; Houghton (1), Sewell (4), Lawton (4), Pimbley, Johnston (2).

Record Cup Victory: 15–0 v Rotherham T (at Trent Bridge), FA Cup, 1st rd, 24 October 1885 – Sherwin; Snook, H. T. Moore; Dobson (1), Emmett (1), Chapman; Gunn (1), Albert Moore (2), Jackson (3), Daft (2), Cursham (4). (1 og).

Record Defeat: 1–9 v Blackburn R, Division 1, 16 November, 1889 and v Aston Villa, Division 1, 29 September, 1888 and v Portsmouth, Division 2, 9 April, 1927.

Most League Points (2 for a win): 69, Division 4, 1970–71.

Most League Points (3 for a win): 87, Division 3, 1989–90.

Most League Goals: 107, Division 4, 1959–60.

Highest League Scorer in Season: Tom Keetley, 39, Division 3 (S), 1930–31.

Most League Goals in Total Aggregate: Les Bradd, 124, 1967–78.

Most Capped Player: Kevin Wilson, 15 (42), Northern Ireland.

Most League Appearances: Albert Iremonger, 564, 1904–26.

Record Transfer Fee Received: £2,500,000 from Derby Co for Craig Short, September 1992.

Record Transfer Fee Paid: £685,000 to Sheffield U for Tony Agana, November 1991.

Football League Record: 1888 Founder Member of the Football League; 1893–97 Division 2; 1897–1913 Division 1; 1913–14 Division 2; 1914–20 Division 1; 1920–23 Division 2; 1923–26 Division 1; 1926–30 Division 2; 1930–31 Division 3 (S); 1931–35 Division 2; 1935–50 Division 3 (S); 1950–58 Division 2; 1958–59 Division 3; 1959–60 Division 4; 1960–64 Division 3; 1964–71 Division 4; 1971–73 Division 3; 1973–81 Division 2; 1981–84 Division 1; 1984–85 Division 2; 1985–90 Division 3; 1990–91 Division 2; 1991–95 Division 1; 1995– Division 2.

Honours: *Football League:* Division 1 best season: 3rd, 1890–91, 1900–01; Division 2 – Champions 1896–97, 1913–14, 1922–23; Runners-up 1894–95, 1980–81; Division 3 (S) – Champions 1930–31, 1949–50; Runners-up 1936–37; Division 3 – Runners-up 1972-73; Division 4 – Champions 1970–71; Runners-up 1959–60. *FA Cup:* Winners 1894; Runners-up 1891. *Football League Cup:* best season: 5th rd, 1964, 1973, 1976. *Anglo-Italian Cup:* Winners; 1995; Runners-up 1994.

Colours: Black and white striped shirts, white shorts, black stockings. **Change colours:** Tartan shirts, black shorts, tartan stockings.

NOTTS COUNTY 1994–95 LEAGUE RECORD

Match No.	Date	Venue	Opponents	Result	H/T Score	Lg. Pos.	Goalscorers	Attendance
1	Aug 13	A	Portsmouth	L 1-2	0-1	—	Sherlock	10,487
2	21	H	Wolverhampton W	D 1-1	1-0	—	Simpson	8569
3	27	A	Sheffield U	W 3-1	2-0	10	McSwegan 2, Lund	15,301
4	30	H	Oldham Ath	L 1-3	1-1	—	McSwegan	6603
5	Sept 3	H	Swindon T	L 0-1	0-1	19		6537
6	10	A	Bristol C	L 1-2	1-1	22	Jemson	6670
7	13	A	Barnsley	D 1-1	0-0	—	Lund	3928
8	17	H	Stoke C	L 0-2	0-1	23		8281
9	24	H	Charlton Ath	D 3-3	2-1	24	Agana, Lund, Sturgess (og)	5726
10	Oct 1	A	Reading	L 0-2	0-1	24		7465
11	8	H	Port Vale	D 2-2	1-0	23	Williams, Agana	6903
12	15	A	Watford	L 1-3	0-2	23	Williams	7008
13	23	H	Derby Co	D 0-0	0-0	24		6389
14	29	A	Burnley	L 1-2	0-1	24	Davis (og)	12,876
15	Nov 1	A	Southend U	L 0-1	0-1	—		4302
16	5	H	Sunderland	W 3-2	2-0	24	Devlin 2, Legg	8890
17	19	A	Bolton W	L 0-2	0-1	24		11,698
18	26	H	WBA	W 2-0	1-0	24	Turner, Lund	10,088
19	Dec 3	A	Derby Co	D 0-0	0-0	24		14,278
20	6	H	Tranmere R	W 1-0	0-0	—	Devlin	4703
21	10	A	Wolverhampton W	L 0-1	0-0	24		25,786
22	17	H	Portsmouth	L 0-1	0-0	24		6382
23	26	H	Millwall	L 0-1	0-0	24		6758
24	28	A	Middlesbrough	L 1-2	1-2	—	McSwegan	21,558
25	31	H	Luton T	L 0-1	0-0	24		6249
26	Jan 14	H	Burnley	W 3-0	0-0	24	White, Devlin, McSwegan	8702
27	21	A	Sunderland	W 2-1	1-0	24	Matthews, Lund	14,334
28	28	A	Grimsby T	L 1-2	0-1	24	White	5161
29	Feb 4	A	Tranmere R	L 2-3	0-1	24	Legg, Devlin (pen)	6105
30	7	H	Bolton W	D 1-1	0-0	—	Matthews	7553
31	11	H	Southend U	D 2-2	1-1	24	Legg, Matthews	6768
32	18	A	WBA	L 2-3	0-1	24	Devlin 2	13,748
33	25	H	Reading	W 1-0	0-0	23	Agana	7183
34	Mar 4	A	Charlton Ath	L 0-1	0-1	23		13,638
35	11	H	Sheffield U	W 2-1	1-0	23	White, Simpson	11,102
36	14	A	Oldham Ath	D 1-1	0-1	—	Devlin	5465
37	21	H	Bristol C	D 1-1	0-0	—	White	5692
38	25	A	Stoke C	L 1-2	0-1	24	White	10,204
39	Apr 1	H	Barnsley	L 1-3	1-1	24	Devlin	6834
40	8	A	Luton T	L 0-2	0-1	24		6482
41	15	H	Middlesbrough	D 1-1	0-0	24	White	9377
42	19	A	Millwall	D 0-0	0-0	—		5471
43	22	H	Grimsby T	L 0-2	0-1	24		5286
44	29	H	Watford	W 1-0	1-0	24	White	5083
45	May 3	A	Swindon T	L 0-3	0-1	—		6553
46	7	A	Port Vale	D 1-1	0-1	24	McSwegan	9452

Final League Position: 24

GOALSCORERS

League (45): Devlin 9 (1 pen), White 7, McSwegan 6, Lund 5, Agana 3, Legg 3, Matthews 3, Simpson 2, Williams 2, Jemson 1, Sherlock 1, Turner 1, own goals 2.
Coca-Cola Cup (7): Lund 2, McSwegan 2, Agana 1, Devlin 1, Jemson 1.
FA Cup (4): Matthews 2, McSwegan 1, White 1.

Cherry S.R. 25	Hoyle C.R. 3	Johnson M.O. 27 + 4	Turner P. 37 + 1	Murphy S.P. 31 + 4	Yates D.R. 21	Agana P.A.O. 25 + 6	Legg A. 32 + 2	Lund G.J. 17 + 6	McSwegan G.J. 19 + 3	Simpson M. 15 + 4	Sherlock P.G. 2 + 3	Cox P.R. 3	Emenalo M. 7	Devlin P.J. 37 + 3	Matthews R. 11 + 7	Gallagher T.D. 7	Jemson N.B. 5 + 6	Kuhl M. 2	Walker R.N. 6 + 1	Mills G.R. 33 + 1	Williams J.N. 3 + 2	Butler P.J.F. 20	Reece P.J. 11	Daniel R.C. 5	Marsden C. 7	White D.W. 16 + 4	Kearton J.B. 10	Nicol S. 19	Hogg G.J. 17	Forsyth M.E. 7	Russell K.J. 9 + 2	Short C.M. 11 + 2	Slawson S.M. — + 1	Galloway M.A. 6 + 1	Ridgeway I.D. — + 1	Match No.
1	2	3	4	5	6	7	8	9	10	11	12																									1
1	2		4	5	6	7	8	9	10	11			3		12																					2
1			4	5	6	7	8	9	10	12		2	3	11																						3
1			4	5		7	8	9	10		2	6	3	11	12																					4
1			4	5	6	12	8	9	10			2	3	7	11																					5
1		5	3		6		8	12	10				4		9	2	7	11																		6
1		5	4		6		8	12	10					9		2	7	11	3																	7
1		5	4		6		8	12	10	11			3	9		2	7																			8
1		5	4	3	6	11	8	9	12		2			7			10																			9
1		3	4	6	5	11	8	9						7	12		10			2																10
1		3	4	6	5	11		9						7	12				8	2	10															11
1		3		6	5	11		*9*		4				7			12		14	2	10	8														12
		6	4		5	11		9						7			12		3	2	10	8	1													13
			4		5	11	9		10					7		2			3		12	8	1	6												14
			4		5	11			10		14			7	9	2			*6*		12	8	1	3												15
		6	4		5	11	10				12			7	9	2						8	1	3												16
		6	4	5		11		12						7	9					2		8	1	3	10											17
1		6	4		5	11		9						7		10				2		8		3												18
1		6	4	12	5	11	3	9	10					7						2		8														19
1		6		12	5	11	3	9	10					7						2		8			4											20
1		6	*4*	14	5	11	3	9						7			12			2		8			10											21
1		6	4	12	5	11	3	9						7			14			2		8			*10*											22
1		6	4		5	11	3		10					7						2		8				9										23
1		6	4	*5*		11	3		10						14		12			2		8			7	9										24
1		6	4	5			*3*		11					7	14		12			2		8			10	9										25
1		6	4	5		12	3		10					7	11					2		8				9										26
		6	4	5			3	9						7	11					2		8				12	1	10								27
		6	4	5			3	9						7	11					2		8				12	1	10								28
		11	4	5		9	3			12				7						*2*					8	14	1	10	6							29
		11	4	5		9	3			8				7	12					2							1	10	6							30
		11	4	5		9	3	12		14				7	8					2							1	*10*	6							31
		11	4	5			3	14	*9*	12				7	8					2							1	10	6							32
		12	4	5		14	11		10					7	*8*					2							1		6	3	9					33
		12	4	5		*11*								7						2						14	1	10	6	3	9	8				34
				5		12	11			4				7						2						8	1	10	6	3	*9*	14				35
				5		12	11			4				7						2						8	1	10	6	3	*9*	14				36
1		12	14			9	11							7						2						8		10	6	5	*4*	3				37
1			4	5			*11*						9	7						12						8		10	6	3	14	2				38
1		12	4				11		*9*					7						3						8		10	6	5		2	14			39
1	6	11	4	5						7				12						3						8		10			9	*2*		14		40
			4	5		12				7										3			1			8		10	6		9	2		11		41
			4	5			14			7				12						3			1			8		10	6		9	2		11		42
				5			14			7				12						3		4	1			8		10	6		9	*2*		11		43
				5					12	7				9						3		4	1			8		10	6		14	2		*11*		44
				5					12	7				9						3		4	1			8		10	6			2		*11*	14	45
				5					9	7									4	3			1			8		10	6			2		11		46

Coca-Cola Cup

Second Round	Bristol C (a)	1-0
	(h)	3-0
Third Round	Tottenham H (h)	3-0
Fourth Round	Norwich C (a)	0-1

FA Cup

Third Round	Manchester C (h)	2-2
	(a)	2-5

OLDHAM ATHLETIC 1994–95 *Back row (left to right):* Paul Rickers, John Eyre, Richard Jobson, Jon Hallworth, Ian Olney, Paul Gerrard, Gunnar Halle, Chris Makin, Neil Pointon. *Centre row:* Bill Urmson (Youth Team Coach), Mark Brennan, Richard Graham, Paul Bernard, Ronnie Evans (Kit Manager), Andy Holden (Reserve Team Coach), Jim Cassell (Chief Scout), Darren Beckford, Nicky Banger, Billy Kenny, Colin Harvey (Coach).
Front row: Lee Richardson, Rick Holden, Sean McCarthy, Nick Henry, Graeme Sharp (Manager), Steve Redmond, Craig Fleming, Andy Ritchie, Andy Barlow.

Division 1 **OLDHAM ATHLETIC**

Boundary Park, Oldham OL1 2PA. Telephone: (0161) 624 4972. Fax: (0161) 652 6501. Ticket Call: 0891 121582. Commercial Office: (0161) 627 1802. Clubcall: 0891 121142.

Ground capacity: 13,544 (all seated).

Record attendance: 47,671 v Sheffield W, FA Cup 4th rd. 25 January 1930.

Record receipts: £138,680 v Manchester U, FA Premier League, 29 December 1993.

Pitch measurements: 110yd × 74yd.

President: R. Schofield.

Chairman & Chief Executive: I. H. Stott, ***Vice-Chairman:*** D. A. Brierley.

Directors: G. T. Butterworth, R. Adams, D. R. Taylor, P. Chadwick, J. Slevin, N. Holden.

Manager: Graeme Sharp. ***Assistant Manager:*** Colin Harvey.

Secretary: Terry Cale. ***Commercial Manager:*** Alan Hardy. ***Public Relations Office:*** Gordon A. Lawton.

Coaches: Billy Urmson, Andy Holden. ***Physio:*** Alex Moreno MCSP.

Year Formed: 1895. ***Turned Professional:*** 1899. ***Ltd Co.:*** 1906.

Previous Name: 1895, Pine Villa; 1899, Oldham Athletic.

Club Nickname: 'The Latics'.

Previous Ground: Sheepfoot Lane; 1905, Boundary Park.

Foundation: It was in 1895 that John Garland, the landlord of the Featherstall and Junction Hotel, decided to form a football club. As Pine Villa they played in the Oldham Junior League. In 1899 the local professional club Oldham County, went out of existence and one of the liquidators persuaded Pine Villa to take over their ground at Sheepfoot Lane and change their name to Oldham Athletic.

First Football League game: 9 September, 1907, Division 2, v Stoke (a) W 3-1 – Hewitson; Hodson, Hamilton; Fay, Walders, Wilson; Ward, W. Dodds (1), Newton (1), Hancock, Swarbrick (1).

Record League Victory: 11–0 v Southport, Division 4, 26 December 1962 – Hollands; Branagan, Marshall; McCall, Williams, Scott; Ledger (1), Johnstone, Lister (6), Colquhoun (1), Whitaker (3).

Record Cup Victory: 10–1 v Lytham, FA Cup, 1st rd, 28 November 1925 – Gray; Wynne, Grundy; Adlam, Heaton, Naylor (1), Douglas, Pynegar (2), Ormston (2), Barnes (3), Watson (2).

Record Defeat: 4–13 v Tranmere R, Division 3 (N), 26 December 1935.

Most League Points (2 for a win): 62, Division 3, 1973–74.

Most League Points (3 for a win): 88, Division 2, 1990–91.

Most League Goals: 95, Division 4, 1962–63.

Highest League Scorer in Season: Tom Davis, 33, Division 3 (N), 1936–37.

Most League Goals in Total Aggregate: Roger Palmer, 141, 1980–94.

Most Capped Player: Gunnar Halle, (46), Norway.

Most League Appearances: Ian Wood, 525, 1966–80.

Record Transfer Fee Received: £1,700,000 from Aston Villa for Earl Barrett, February 1992.

Record Transfer Fee Paid: £700,000 to Aston Villa for Ian Olney, June 1992.

Football League Record: 1907 Elected to Division 2; 1910–23 Division 1; 1923–35 Division 2; 1935–53 Division 3 (N); 1953–54 Division 2; 1954–58 Division 3 (N); 1958–63 Division 4; 1963–69 Division 3; 1969–71 Division 4; 1971–74 Division 3; 1974–91 Division 2; 1991–92 Division 1; 1992–94 FA Premier League; 1994– Division 1.

Honours: *Football League:* Division 1 – Runners-up 1914–15; Division 2 – Champions 1990–91; Runners-up 1909–10; Division 3 (N) – Champions 1952–53; Division 3 – Champions 1973–74; Division 4 – Runners-up 1962–63. *FA Cup:* Semi-final 1913, 1990. *Football League Cup:* Runners-up 1990.

Colours: All blue with red and white trim. **Change colours:** Tangerine and blue shirts, blue shorts, tangerine stockings.

OLDHAM ATHLETIC 1994–95 LEAGUE RECORD

Match No.	Date	Venue	Opponents	Result		H/T Score	Lg. Pos.	Goalscorers	Attendance
1	Aug 13	H	Charlton Ath	W	5-2	2-2	—	McCarthy 2, Richardson 2, Sharp	8924
2	20	A	Port Vale	L	1-3	0-0	7	Sharp	10,051
3	27	H	Burnley	W	3-0	0-0	4	Ritchie, McCarthy 2 (1 pen)	11,310
4	30	A	Notts Co	W	3-1	1-1	—	McCarthy 3	6603
5	Sept 3	A	Southend U	L	0-1	0-0	3		4435
6	10	H	Reading	L	1-3	1-1	6	Richardson	8412
7	13	H	Watford	L	0-2	0-1	—		7243
8	17	A	Derby Co	L	1-2	0-1	14	McCarthy (pen)	13,746
9	24	H	Barnsley	W	1-0	0-0	10	Halle	7941
10	Oct 1	A	Sheffield U	L	0-2	0-1	15		14,223
11	8	H	Portsmouth	W	3-2	1-0	8	Holden R 2 (2 pens), Graham	7683
12	16	A	Bolton W	D	2-2	0-2	9	Bernard, McCarthy	11,106
13	22	H	Stoke C	D	0-0	0-0	13		8954
14	29	A	Sunderland	D	0-0	0-0	14		17,252
15	Nov 1	A	Middlesbrough	L	1-2	1-0	—	Graham	15,929
16	6	H	Tranmere R	D	0-0	0-0	19		6475
17	12	H	Luton T	D	0-0	0-0	15		7907
18	19	A	WBA	L	1-3	0-2	18	Halle (pen)	14,616
19	26	H	Bristol C	W	2-0	0-0	17	Richardson, McCarthy	7277
20	Dec 4	A	Stoke C	W	1-0	0-0	14	McCarthy	12,558
21	10	H	Port Vale	W	3-2	1-1	12	Ritchie 3	7712
22	17	A	Charlton Ath	L	0-2	0-0	14		8970
23	26	H	Wolverhampton W	W	4-1	1-0	11	Ritchie 3, McCarthy	11,962
24	27	A	Grimsby T	W	3-1	2-0	8	Ritchie, Henry, McCarthy	6958
25	31	H	Swindon T	D	1-1	1-1	9	Halle	8917
26	Jan 3	A	Millwall	D	1-1	1-0	—	Richardson (pen)	7438
27	14	H	Sunderland	D	0-0	0-0	8		9742
28	22	A	Tranmere R	L	1-3	1-1	10	Makin	5581
29	Feb 4	A	Luton T	L	1-2	0-1	13	Holden R	6903
30	18	A	Bristol C	D	2-2	1-2	13	Halle, Ritchie	7851
31	21	H	WBA	W	1-0	1-0	—	Richardson	7690
32	25	H	Sheffield U	D	3-3	2-2	11	Banger 2, Ritchie	9640
33	Mar 7	H	Southend U	L	0-2	0-1	—		7168
34	11	A	Burnley	L	1-2	0-1	14	McCarthy	11,620
35	14	H	Notts Co	D	1-1	1-0	—	Henry	5465
36	21	A	Reading	L	1-2	1-0	—	Halle	6921
37	25	H	Derby Co	W	1-0	1-0	15	Graham	7696
38	Apr 1	A	Watford	W	2-1	2-1	14	Banger, Brennan	8090
39	5	H	Middlesbrough	W	1-0	0-0	—	Ritchie	11,024
40	8	A	Swindon T	L	1-3	1-2	13	Ritchie	7488
41	15	H	Grimsby T	W	1-0	1-0	13	McCarthy	6757
42	17	A	Wolverhampton W	L	1-2	1-1	13	Bernard	25,840
43	22	H	Millwall	L	0-1	0-0	15		6319
44	29	H	Bolton W	W	3-1	2-1	12	McCarthy 2, Rickers	11,901
45	May 2	A	Barnsley	D	1-1	1-1	—	Eyre	9838
46	7	A	Portsmouth	D	1-1	1-0	14	McCarthy (pen)	11,002

Final League Position: 14

GOALSCORERS

League (60): McCarthy 18 (3 pens), Ritchie 12, Halle 5 (1 pen), Richardson 6 (1 pen), Banger 3, Graham 3, Holden R 3 (2 pens), Henry 2, Sharp 2, Bernard 2, Brennan 1, Eyre 1, Makin 1, Rickers 1.
Coca-Cola Cup (2): Richardson 1, Ritchie 1.
FA Cup (5): Halle 2, Richardson 1, Sharp 1, own goal 1.

Hallworth J.G. 4 + 2	Makin C. 28	Barlow A.J. 2	Kenny W. 4	Jobson R.I. 20	Fleming C. 5	Halle G. 40	Richardson L.J. 28 + 2	Sharp G.M. 10 + 2	McCarthy S.C. 35 + 4	Holden R.W. 18 + 13	Henry N.I. 33 + 1	Ritchie A.T. 25 + 8	Gerrard P.W. 42	Brennan M.R. 34 + 6	Redmond S. 43	Graham R.E. 29 + 3	Banger N.L. 20 + 8	Pointon N.G. 32	Rickers P.S. 4	Bernard P.R.J. 16 + 1	Eyre J.R. 3 + 5	Holden A.I. 1	Beckford D.R. — + 3	Snodin I. 17	Moore N. 5	Webster S.P. 7	McNiven S.A. 1	Beresford D. — + 2	Match No.
1	2	3	4	5	6	7	8	9	10	11																			1
1	2	3	4	5	6	7	*8*	9	10	11	12	14																	2
	3			5	6	2	7	9	10	11	4	12	1	8															3
	3			5	6	2	7	9	10	11			1	8	4														4
15	3			5	6	2	7	9	10	11		12	1	8	*4*														5
	3		4	5		2	7	9	10	11		12	1	8	6														6
15	3		4			2	7	9	10	11		12	1	*8*	6	5													7
1	3			5		2	7		10	12	4	11		8	6	9													8
	3			5		2	7	14	10	12	4	*11*	1	8	6	9													9
1	3			5		2	12	*9*	10	14	4	11		8	6	7													10
	3			5		2	7	12	10	11	*4*		1	14	6	9	8												11
				5		2	7		10	11	4		1		6	9	8	3		12									12
				5		2			10	11	4		1		6	9	8	3	7										13
				5		2			10	11	4		1		6	9	8	3		7	12								14
				5		2			10	11	4	*8*	1	12	6	9		3		7	14								15
	3			5		2			10	11	4		1		6	9	8			7									16
	2			5		7				11	4	10	1	12	6	9	8	3											17
	2			5		7			9		4	10	1	11	6	8	12	3											18
	2			5			7		9	*11*	4	8	1	14	6	10	12	3											19
	2			5			7		9	*11*	4	8	1	14	6	10	12	3											20
	2			5			7		9	11	4	8	1	14	6	10	12	*3*											21
	3					2			9	14	4	8	1	11	6	10	12			7		5							22
	2					7	10		9		4	8	1	11	6	5		3					12						23
	2					7	10		9		4	8	1	11	6	5		3					12						24
	2					7	10		*9*	14	4	8	1	11	6	5	12	3											25
	2					7	10	9			4		1	11	6	5	8	3					12						26
	2					7	10	9		14		*8*	1	11	6	5	12	3						4					27
	2					7	10			12		8	1	11	6	5	9	3						4					28
						7	10		12	14	*4*	8	1	11	6	5	9	3						2					29
						7	10		12	14	4	8	1	*11*	6		9	3						2	5				30
						7	*10*		12	14	4	8	1	11	6		9	3						2	5				31
						7	10			12	4	8	1	11	6		9	3						2	5				32
						7	10			4		8	1	11	6		9	3			12			2	5				33
						7	10		12	14		8	1	11	6			3		4	9			2	5				34
						7			9	12	4		1	11	6	5	10	3		8				2					35
						7			9		4	12	1	11	6	5	10	3		8				2					36
						7			9			12	1	11	6	4	10	3		8				2		5			37
						7			9		4		1	11	6	12	10	3		8				2		5			38
						7			9		4	12	1	11	6		10	3		8				2		5			39
						7					4	9	1	11	6	12	10	3		8				2		5			40
						7			9		4	10	1	11	6			3		8				2		5			41
						7			9		4	10	1	11	6	12	14	*3*		8				2		5			42
	2					7			9		4	8	1	11	6	10		3			12					5			43
	2						12		9		4		1	11	6	5	*10*	3	7	8	14								44
	3						4		9				1	11	6	5			7	8	10						2	12	45
	2						4		9				1	11	6			3	7	8	10			5				12	46

Coca-Cola Cup

Second Round	Oxford U (a)		1-1
		(h)	1-0
Third Round	Arsenal (h)		0-0
		(a)	0-2

FA Cup

Third Round	Reading (a)	3-1
Fourth Round	Leeds U (a)	2-3

OXFORD UNITED 1994–95 *Back row (left to right):* Paul Wanless, David Collins, John Byrne, Nick Cusack, Mike Ford, Alex Dyer.
Centre row: Maurice Evans (General Manager), Malcolm Crosby (Assistant Manager), Anton Rogan, Paul Moody, Paul Reece, Phil Whitehead, Matt Elliott, Steve Wood, John Clinkard (Physio), Steve McClaren (Reserve/Youth Team Coach).
Front row: Chris Allen, Les Robinson, Stuart Massey, Bobby Ford, Denis Smith (Manager), Dave Smith, Mickey Lewis, Matt Murphy, Mark Druce.

Division 2 **OXFORD UNITED**

Manor Ground, Headington, Oxford, OX3 7RS. Telephone: (01865) 61503. Fax: (01865) 741820. Supporters Club: (01865) 63063. Clubline: 0891 440055.

Ground capacity: 9572.

Record attendance: 22,750 v Preston NE, FA Cup 6th rd, 29 February 1964.

Record receipts: £103,411 v Leeds U, FA Cup 4th rd, 29 January 1994.

Pitch measurements: 110yd × 75yd.

President: The Duke of Marlborough.

Directors: K. A. Cox (Managing), D. M. Clitheroe, G. E. Coppock, N. J. W. Harris, P. L. Lowe.

Manager: Denis Smith. ***Assistant Manager:*** Malcolm Crosby. ***Physio:*** John Clinkard.

Secretary: Mick Brown. ***Commercial Manager:*** Tony Watson.

Year Formed: 1893. ***Turned Professional:*** 1949. ***Ltd Co.:*** 1949.

Club Nickname: 'The U's'.

Previous Names: 1893, Headington; 1894, Headington United; 1960, Oxford United.

Previous Grounds: 1893–94 Headington Quarry; 1894–98 Wootten's Field; 1898–1902 Sandy Lane Ground; 1902–09 Britannia Field; 1909–10 Sandy Lane; 1910–14 Quarry Recreation Ground; 1914–22 Sandy Lane; 1922–25 The Paddock Manor Road; 1925– Manor Ground.

Foundation: There had been an Oxford United club around the time of World War I but only in the Oxfordshire Thursday League and there is no connection with the modern club which began as Headington in 1893, adding "United" a year later. Playing first on Quarry Fields and subsequently Wooton's Fields, they owe much to a Dr. Hitchings for their early development.

First Football League game: 18 August, 1962, Division 4, v Barrow (a) L 2-3 – Medlock; Beavon, Quartermain; R. Atkinson, Kyle, Jones; Knight, G. Atkinson (1), Houghton (1), Cornwell, Colfar.

Record League Victory: 7–0 v Barrow, Division 4, 19 December 1964 – Fearnley; Beavon, Quartermann; Ron Atkinson (1), Kyle, Jones; Morris, Booth (3), Willey (1), Graham Atkinson (1), Harrington (1).

Record Cup Victory: 6–0 v Gillingham, League Cup, 2nd rd (1st leg), 24 September 1986 – Judge; Langan, Trewick, Phillips (Brock), Briggs, Shotton, Houghton (1), Aldridge (4 incl. 1p), Charles (Leworthy), Hebberd, Slatter. (1 og).

Record Defeat: 0–6 v Liverpool, Division 1, 22 March 1986.

Most League Points (2 for a win): 61, Division 4, 1964–65.

Most League Points (3 for a win): 95, Division 3, 1983–84.

Most League Goals: 91, Division 3, 1983–84.

Highest League Scorer in Season: John Aldridge, 30, Division 2, 1984–85.

Most League Goals in Total Aggregate: Graham Atkinson, 77, 1962–73.

Most Capped Player: Jim Magilton, 18 (29), Northern Ireland.

Most League Appearances: John Shuker, 478, 1962–77.

Record Transfer Fee Received: £1,190,000 from Derby Co for Dean Saunders, October 1988.

Record Transfer Fee Paid: £285,000 to Gillingham for Colin Greenall, February 1988.

Football League Record: 1962 Elected to Division 4; 1965–68 Division 3; 1968–76 Division 2; 1976–84 Division 3; 1984–85 Division 2; 1985–88 Division 1; 1988–92 Division 2; 1992–94 Division 1; 1994– Division 2.

Honours: *Football League:* Division 1 best season: 18th, 1985–86, 1986–87; Division 2 – Champions 1984–85; Division 3 – Champions 1967–68, 1983–84; Division 4 – Promoted 1964–65 (4th). *FA Cup:* best season: 6th rd, 1964 (record for 4th Division club). *Football League Cup:* Winners 1986.

Colours: Gold shirts with blue sleeves, blue shorts, blue stockings. **Change colours:** Red and black striped shirts, black shorts, black stockings.

OXFORD UNITED F.C.

OXFORD UNITED 1994–95 LEAGUE RECORD

Match No.	Date		Venue	Opponents	Result		H/T Score	Lg. Pos.	Goalscorers	Attendance
1	Aug	13	H	Hull C	W	4-0	4-0	—	Byrne 3, Moody	5485
2		20	A	Cardiff C	W	3-1	2-1	2	Moody 3	7281
3		27	H	Cambridge U	W	1-0	1-0	3	Moody (pen)	5513
4		30	A	Bradford C	W	2-0	1-0	—	Moody, Jacobs (og)	9005
5	Sept	3	A	Huddersfield T	D	3-3	2-1	2	Moody (pen), Druce, Rogan	10,122
6		10	H	Birmingham C	D	1-1	0-0	2	Moody (pen)	8077
7		13	H	Crewe Alex	W	2-1	2-0	—	Byrne 2	6499
8		17	A	Brighton & HA	D	1-1	0-1	1	Moody	9970
9		24	H	Leyton Orient	W	3-2	0-0	1	Moody, Elliott, Rush	5814
10	Oct	1	A	Chester C	L	0-2	0-1	2		2324
11		8	H	Plymouth Arg	W	1-0	1-0	2	Byrne	6550
12		15	A	Swansea C	W	3-1	3-1	2	Byrne 2, Moody	3724
13		22	A	Wrexham	L	2-3	2-2	2	Humes (og), Hunter (og)	3925
14		29	H	Shrewsbury T	D	0-0	0-0	3		6094
15	Nov	1	H	Blackpool	W	3-2	1-1	—	Elliott, Byrne, Rush	5610
16		5	A	Stockport Co	W	2-0	1-0	2	Moody 2 (1 pen)	5132
17		19	H	Rotherham U	W	2-1	2-1	2	Moody 2	5801
18		26	A	Bournemouth	W	2-0	1-0	1	Byrne, Butters	4277
19	Dec	10	H	Cardiff C	W	1-0	1-0	1	Murphy	6181
20		17	A	Hull C	L	1-3	1-2	1	Elliott	4884
21		26	A	Peterborough U	W	4-1	2-1	1	Ford R, Rush 2, Murphy	5803
22		27	H	Wycombe W	L	0-2	0-1	1		9540
23		31	A	Brentford	L	0-2	0-1	2		7125
24	Jan	2	H	York C	L	0-2	0-1	3		6386
25		14	A	Bristol R	L	2-3	2-0	4	Druce 2	5875
26		28	A	Shrewsbury T	D	1-1	1-1	4	Byrne	3768
27	Feb	4	H	Bournemouth	L	0-3	0-2	6		5473
28		11	A	Blackpool	L	1-2	0-0	7	Rush	5206
29		18	H	Bristol R	D	0-0	0-0	7		6349
30		21	A	Rotherham U	D	1-1	1-0	—	Murphy	2833
31		25	H	Chester C	W	1-0	0-0	7	Gilchrist	4930
32		28	H	Stockport Co	W	4-0	1-0	—	Murphy, Lewis, Rush (pen), Allen	4594
33	Mar	4	A	Leyton Orient	D	1-1	0-1	6	Moody	4052
34		7	H	Huddersfield T	W	3-1	0-0	—	Elliott, Murphy, Moody	7160
35		11	A	Cambridge U	W	2-1	1-0	3	Rush 2	3558
36		18	H	Bradford C	W	1-0	0-0	3	Moody	5363
37		21	A	Birmingham C	L	0-3	0-1	—		19,781
38		25	H	Brighton & HA	D	0-0	0-0	4		6725
39	Apr	1	A	Crewe Alex	L	2-3	2-1	5	Moody, Allen	3928
40		4	H	Wrexham	D	0-0	0-0	—		4729
41		8	H	Brentford	D	1-1	1-1	5	Dyer	7800
42		15	A	Wycombe W	L	0-1	0-1	7		7683
43		17	H	Peterborough U	W	1-0	1-0	6	Moody	5163
44		22	A	York C	W	2-0	1-0	6	Murphy 2	3732
45		30	H	Swansea C	L	1-2	1-1	7	Rush	5244
46	May	6	A	Plymouth Arg	D	1-1	0-1	7	Ford R	4953

Final League Position: 7

GOALSCORERS

League (66): Moody 20 (4 pens), Byrne 11, Rush 9 (1 pen), Murphy 7, Elliott 4, Druce 3, Allen 2, Ford R 2, Butters 1, Dyer 1, Gilchrist 1, Lewis 1, Rogan 1, own goals 3.
Coca-Cola Cup (5): Dyer 1, Ford M 1, Massey 1, Moody 1 (pen), Robinson 1.
FA Cup (0).

Whitehead P.M. 38	Robinson L. 46	Ford M.P. 15 + 3	Dyer A.C. 32 + 6	Elliott M.S. 45	Rogan A.G.P. 27 + 2	Massey S.A. 20 + 2	Smith D. 41 + 1	Moody P. 34 + 7	Byrne J.F. 25	Allen C.A. 32 + 4	Lewis M. 30 + 9	Cusack N.J. — + 2	Druce M.A. 9 + 10	Ford R.J. 20 + 3	Murphy M.S. 17 + 5	Deegan M. 2	Marsh S.T. 8	Rush D. 22 + 12	Collins D.D. 3	Butters G. 3	Wanless P.S. 3 + 7	Dobson A.J. 5	Carter J.W.C. 3 + 1	Key L.W. 6	Wood S.A. 2	Gilchrist P.A. 18	Match No.
1	2	3	4	5	6	7	8	9	*10*	11	12	14															1
1	2	3	4	5	6	7	8	9	10	11	12																2
1	2	3	4	5	6	7	8	9	10	11			12														3
1	2	3	4	5	6	7	8	9		11			10														4
1	2	3	4	5	6	7	8	9		11			10	12													5
1	2	3	4	5	6	7	8	9		11			10		12												6
1	2	3	4	5	6	7	8	*9*	10	11	12		14														7
	2	3		5		7	8	9	10	11	4					1	6										8
1	2	3		5		7	8	9	10	11	4						6	12									9
1	2	3	6	5		7	8	9	10	11	4							12									10
1	2	3	4	5	6	7	8	*9*	10	11	12							14									11
1	2	3	4	5	6	7	8	9	10	*11*	12							14									12
1	2	3	4	5	6	7	8	9	*10*		12	14		11													13
1	2	3	4	5	6	7	*8*	9	10		12			11				14									14
1	2		4	5		7	8	9	10					11			6	12	3								15
1	2		4	5		7	8	9	*10*		12			11			6	14		3							16
1	2		4	5			8	9	10	7	6			11				12		3							17
1	2		4	5			8	9	10		6		12	11				14		3	*7*						18
1	2		4	5			8	9	*10*		3		12	11	7			14			6						19
1	2		4	5			8	9	10		3		12	*11*	7			14				6					20
1	2		4	5	12		8		10		3			11	14			9				6	7				21
1	2		4	5	12		8	14	10		3			*11*				9				6	7				22
1	2		4	5			8	9	10		*3*			11	12						14	6	7				23
1	2		4	5			8	9		12	3				*7*		11	10				6	14				24
	2		4	5	6		8			*11*			9	7	12	1	3	10			14						25
	2		4	5	6		8	*9*	10	11	12		14	7					3					1			26
	2		4	5	6		8	9	10	11			14	7				12						1	*3*		27
	2		12	5	6		8	14	*10*	11	4			7				9						1	3		28
	2		11	5			8		10	12	4		14		7		3	*9*						1		6	29
	2		11	5			8	12	10	14	4				7		*3*	9						1		6	30
	2		3	5			8	9		11	4				7			10						1		6	31
1	*2*		3	5		12	8			11	4		9		7			10			14					6	32
1	2	3		5			8	12		11	4		9		7			10								6	33
1	2			5	3		8	12		11	4		9		7			10								6	34
1	2		12	5	3		8	*9*		11	4		14		7			10								6	35
1	2		12	5	3		8	14		11	4		*9*		7			10								6	36
1	2		12	5	3		8	14		11	4		*9*		7			10								6	37
1	2		11	5	3		8	9		12	4		14		*7*			10								6	38
1	2		12	5	3	7	*8*	9		11	4				14			10								6	39
1	2		12	5	3	7	*8*	9		11	4			14				10								6	40
1	2		10	5	3	7	*8*	9		11	4			12							14					6	41
1	2	12	10	5	3			9		11	*4*			7				8			14					6	42
1	2	12		5	3			9		11	4			7	8			*10*			14					6	43
1	2			5	3			9		11	4			7	8			10								6	44
1	2	12			3	14		9		11	4			7	*8*			10			5					6	45
1	2			5		9	12			11	4			7	8			10	3		14					*6*	46

Coca-Cola Cup

First Round	Peterborough U (h)	3-1
	(a)	1-0
Second Round	Oldham Ath (h)	1-1
	(a)	0-1

FA Cup

First Round	Marlow (a)	0-2

PETERBOROUGH UNITED 1994–95 *Back row (left to right):* Tony Lormor, Nick Dunphy, David Morrison, Sean Farrell, Gary Breen, Greg Heald, Ashley Warner, Kenny Webster, Liburd Henry.

Centre row: Simon Clark, Kenny Charlery, Fred Barber, Brian McGorry, Scott Cooksey, Jason Brissett, Paul Moran

Front row: Keith Oakes (Physio), Lee Williams, Tony Spearing, Mark Peters, John Still (Manager), Steve Welsh, Marcus Ebdon, Andy Curtis, Michael Halsall (Assistant Manager).

Division 2 PETERBOROUGH UNITED

London Road Ground, Peterborough PE2 8AL. Telephone: (01733) 63947. Fax: (01733) 577210.

Ground capacity: 14,300 (rising to 16,300 when completed).

Record attendance: 30,096 v Swansea T, FA Cup 5th rd, 20 February 1965.

Record receipts: £51,315 v Brighton & HA, 5th rd, 15 February 1986.

Pitch measurements: 112yd × 75yd.

Chairman: A. H. Hand. ***Vice-Chairman:*** N. Hards.

Directors: R. Terrell, P. Sagar. ***Company Secretary:*** Miss Caroline Hand.

Chief Executive: Chris Turner.

Manager: John Still. ***Assistant Manager/Coach:*** Mick Halsall.

Physio: Keith Oakes.

Commercial Manager: Michael Vincent.

Year Formed: 1934. ***Turned Professional:*** 1934. ***Ltd Co.:*** 1934.

Club Nickname: 'The Posh'.

Foundation: The old Peterborough & Fletton club, founded in 1923, was suspended by the FA during season 1932–33 and disbanded. Local enthusiasts determined to carry on and in 1934 a new professional club Peterborough United was formed and entered the Midland League the following year.

First Football League game: 20 August, 1960, Division 4, v Wrexham (h) W 3-0 – Walls; Stafford, Walker; Rayner, Rigby, Norris; Halls, Emery (1), Bly (1), Smith, McNamee (1).

Record League Victory: 8–1 v Oldham Ath, Division 4, 26 November 1969 – Drewery; Potts, Noble; Conmy, Wile, Wright; Moss (1), Price (3), Hall (4), Halliday, Robson.

Record Cup Victory: 6–0 v Redditch, FA Cup, 1st rd (replay), 22 November 1971 – Drewery; Carmichael, Brookes; Oakes, Turner, Wright; Conmy, Price (1), Hall (2), Barker (2), Robson (1).

Record Defeat: 1–8 v Northampton T, FA Cup 2nd rd (2nd replay), 18 December, 1946.

Most League Points (2 for a win): 66, Division 4, 1960–61.

Most League Points (3 for a win): 82, Division 4, 1981–82.

Most League Goals: 134, Division 4, 1960–61.

Highest League Scorer in Season: Terry Bly, 52, Division 4, 1960–61.

Most League Goals in Total Aggregate: Jim Hall, 122, 1967–75.

Most Capped Player: Tony Millington, 8 (21), Wales.

Most League Appearances: Tommy Robson, 482, 1968–81.

Record Transfer Fee Received: £400,000 from Notts Co for David Robinson, October 1992.

Record Transfer Fee Paid: £176,000 to Watford for Ken Charlery, December 1993.

Football League Record: 1960 Elected to Division 4; 1961–68 Division 3, when they were demoted for financial irregularities; 1968–74 Division 4; 1974–79 Division 3; 1979–91 Division 4; 1991–92 Division 3; 1992–94 Division 1; 1994– Division 2.

Honours: *Football League:* Division 1 best season: 10th Division 1 1992–93; Division 4 – Champions 1960–61, 1973–74. *FA Cup:* best season: 6th rd, 1965. *Football League Cup:* Semi-final 1966.

Colours: Royal blue shirts, white shorts, white stockings. **Change colours:** All red.

PETERBOROUGH UNITED 1994–95 LEAGUE RECORD

Match No.	Date	Venue	Opponents	Result	H/T Score	Lg. Pos.	Goalscorers	Attendance
1	Aug 13	H	Bristol R	D 0-0	0-0	—		5695
2	20	A	Brentford	W 1-0	1-0	10	Charlery	5516
3	27	H	Crewe Alex	L 1-5	0-3	15	Morrison	4579
4	30	A	Bournemouth	W 3-0	2-0	—	Farrell, Morrison, Charlery	2649
5	Sept 3	A	Shrewsbury T	D 2-2	2-0	9	Henry 2	3879
6	10	H	Hull C	W 2-1	1-1	7	Morrison, Charlery	5044
7	13	H	Huddersfield T	D 2-2	2-1	—	Farrell, Charlery	5316
8	18	A	Birmingham C	L 0-4	0-3	12		10,600
9	24	H	Rotherham U	D 2-2	1-2	13	Henry 2	4894
10	Oct 1	A	Cardiff C	W 2-1	1-1	10	McGorry, Charlery	4225
11	8	A	York C	D 1-1	0-0	11	Williams	3601
12	15	H	Stockport Co	L 0-1	0-0	12		5369
13	22	H	Wycombe W	L 1-3	1-1	13	Henry	5924
14	29	A	Swansea C	L 0-2	0-1	14		2733
15	Nov 1	A	Plymouth Arg	W 1-0	1-0	—	Henry	4145
16	5	H	Chester C	W 2-0	1-0	13	Charlery, Farrell	4610
17	19	A	Brighton & HA	W 2-1	2-1	12	Charlery, Ebdon	6445
18	26	H	Leyton Orient	D 0-0	0-0	13		5114
19	Dec 10	H	Brentford	D 2-2	2-1	14	Henry, Kelly	4102
20	17	A	Bristol R	L 1-3	1-0	14	Farrell	4635
21	26	H	Oxford U	L 1-4	1-2	15	Charlery	5803
22	27	A	Wrexham	D 3-3	2-0	14	Morrison 2, Ebdon	4689
23	31	H	Cambridge U	D 2-2	1-1	14	Charlery 2	7412
24	Jan 2	A	Blackpool	L 0-4	0-1	16		3692
25	14	H	Bradford C	D 0-0	0-0	16		4400
26	28	A	Chester C	D 1-1	0-0	16	Morrison	1501
27	Feb 4	A	Leyton Orient	L 1-4	0-2	16	Ebdon	3447
28	11	H	Plymouth Arg	L 1-2	0-1	18	Farrell	4318
29	18	A	Bradford C	L 2-4	0-2	18	Farrell, Ebdon	4806
30	21	H	Brighton & HA	W 2-1	1-0	—	Charlery, Farrell	3870
31	25	H	Cardiff C	W 2-1	1-1	16	Charlery 2	4226
32	Mar 4	A	Rotherham U	D 0-0	0-0	16		3123
33	7	H	Shrewsbury T	D 1-1	0-0	—	Charlery	3554
34	11	A	Crewe Alex	W 3-1	2-0	16	Ebdon, Morrison, Breen	3983
35	18	H	Bournemouth	D 0-0	0-0	16		4495
36	21	A	Hull C	D 1-1	1-1	—	McGorry	4609
37	25	H	Birmingham C	D 1-1	0-0	16	Charlery	8796
38	28	A	Wycombe W	L 1-3	0-1	—	Gordon	4590
39	Apr 1	A	Huddersfield T	W 2-1	1-0	16	Ebdon, McGorry	11,324
40	4	H	Swansea C	W 1-0	1-0	—	Kelly (pen)	3764
41	8	A	Cambridge U	L 0-2	0-1	16		5828
42	15	H	Wrexham	W 1-0	1-0	15	Manuel	4309
43	17	A	Oxford U	L 0-1	0-1	15		5163
44	22	H	Blackpool	W 1-0	0-0	15	Farrell	5716
45	29	A	Stockport Co	D 1-1	0-1	15	Morrison	4387
46	May 6	H	York C	D 1-1	0-0	15	Charlery (pen)	4983

Final League Position: 15

GOALSCORERS

League (54): Charlery 16 (1 pen), Farrell 8, Morrison 8, Henry 7, Ebdon 6, McGorry 3, Kelly 2 (1 pen), Breen 1, Gordon 1, Manuel 1, Williams 1.
Coca-Cola Cup (1): Morrison 1.
FA Cup (4): Charlery 2 (1 pen), Henry 1, Williams 1.

Cooksey S.A. 12	Ashley K.M. 27	Clark S. 32	Ebdon M. 35	Heald G. 27 + 2	Welsh S. 14	Morrison D.E. 34 + 8	Breen G. 43 + 1	Farrell S.P. 25 + 8	Charlery K. 44	Moran P. 5 + 2	Williams L. 35 + 5	Henry L.A. 22 + 10	McGorry B.P. 30 + 4	Dunphy N. — + 2	Spearing A. 31 + 2	Furnell A.P. 4 + 4	Tyler M.R. 4 + 1	Brissett J.C. 4 + 1	Prudhoe M. 6	Lormor A. 2 + 3	Thomas G.A. 6 + 2	Kelly A.G. 12 + 1	Barber F. 5	Soloman J.R. 4	Keeley J.H. 3	Feuer A.I. 16	Manuel W.A.J. 14	Gordon D.A. 6	Le Bihan N.E.R. 3 + 1	Semple R.E.J. 1 + 1	*Match No.*
1	2	3	4	5	6	7	8	9	10	11	12																				1
1	2	3	4		6	7	5	9	10	11	8	12																			2
1	2	3	4		6	7	5	9	10		*8*	11	12	14																	3
1	2	3		5	6	7		9	*10*			11	4	12	8	14															4
1	2	3		5	6	7	12	9	10		4	11			8																5
1	2	3		5	6	7	8	9	10		4	11	12																		6
1	2	3		5	6	7	8	9	10			11	4		12																7
	2	3		5	6	7	8	*9*	10		12	11	4				1	14													8
	2	3	4	5	6	7	8	12	10		9	11	14				1														9
	2	3	4		6	7	5		10			11	8					9	1												10
	2	3	4		6	7	5		10		12	11	8					9	1	14											11
	2	3	4		6	7	5	12	10		14	11	8					9	1												12
	2	3	4		6	7	5	9	10		12	11	8						1												13
	2	3	4		6	7	5	12	10		9	11	8		14				1												14
	2	6	4				5	7	10		9	11	8		3				1												15
1	2	6	4			12	5	7	10		9	11	8		3																16
1	2	6	4			7	5		10		9	11	8		3					12											17
1	2	6	4			12	5		10		9		*8*		3			7		11	14										18
1	*2*	6	4			7	5	12			9	10			3					11	14	8									19
1	2	6	4			7	5	11			9	10			3					12		8									20
	2		4	12		7	5		10		9	*11*			3	14					6	8	1								21
	2		4	7		9	5		10			12			3	11					6	8	1								22
	2	6	4			7	5	12	10			11			3	9						8	1								23
	2	6		4		7		12	10				11		3	9					5	8	1								24
		6		2		7	5	9	10		11		4			12	15				3		*1*	8							25
		6		2		7	5		10	12	11		4			9	1				3			8							26
	2		9			11	5		10	12	7				3						6	4		8	1						27
	2	6	4			12	5	9	10	11	7				3									8	1						28
		6	4	2		12	5	9	10	11	7		8		3										1						29
		6	4	2		12	5	9	10		7	11	8		3											1					30
		6	4	2		12	5	9	10		7	*11*	8		3							14				1					31
	2	6	4	12			5	9	10		7		8		3											1	11				32
		6	4			7	5	9	10	11	2		12		3											1	8				33
			4	6		7	5	*9*	10		2	12	11		3	14										1	8				34
			4	6		7	5	9	10		2	12	11		3											1	8				35
			4	6		7	5	9	10		2	12	11		3											1	8				36
			4	6		7	5		10		2		11		3											1	8	9			37
			4	6		7	5		10		2	12	11		3											1	8	9			38
			4	6			5		10		2		11		3							7				1	8	9			39
			4	6			5		10		2		11		3							7				1	8	9			40
			4	6		12	5		10		2	14	*11*		3							7				1	8	9			41
			4	6		11	5	12	10		2	9			3							7				1	8				42
				6		11	5	9	10		2	12			3							7				1	8		4		43
		7		6		11	5	12	10		2		8		3		1											9	4	14	44
			8	6		12	5	9	10		2	14	7		3											1	11		*4*		45
		3		6		11	5	9	10		2	12	*4*													1	8		14	7	46

Coca-Cola Cup

First Round	Oxford U (a)	1-3	
	(h)	0-1	

FA Cup

First Round	Northampton T (h)	4-0
Second Round	Cambridge U (h)	0-2

PLYMOUTH ARGYLE 1994–95 *Back row (left to right):* Craig Skinner, Wayne Burnett, Kevin Nugent, Alan Nicholls, Richard Landon, Michael Evans, Daniel O'Hagan.
Centre row: Paul Sumner (Physio), Marc Edworthy, Chris Twiddy, Marcus Crocker, Jamie Morgan, Dominic Naylor, Martin Barlow.
Front row: Keith Hill, Paul Dalton, Steve Castle, John McGovern (Assistant Manager), Peter Shilton (Team Manager), Ian Bowyer (Youth Team Manager), Andy Comyn, Steve McCall, Mark Patterson.

Division 3 **PLYMOUTH ARGYLE**

Home Park, Plymouth, Devon PL2 3DQ. Telephone: (01752) 562561. Fax: (01752) 606167. Marketing Department: (01752) 569597. Lottery Shop: (01752) 561041. Pilgrim Shop: (01752) 558292.

Ground capacity: 19,630.

Record attendance: 43,596 v Aston Villa, Division 2, 10 October1936.

Record receipts: £128,000 v Burnley, Division 2 play-off, 18 May 1994.

Pitch measurements: 110yd × 72yd.

President: S. J. Rendell.

Chairman: D. McCauley. ***Vice-Chairman:*** P. Bloom.

Directors: D. Angilley, G. Jasper, I. Jones.

Manager: Neil Warnock. ***Assistant Manager:*** Ian Bowyer. ***Physio:*** Paul Sumner.

Secretary: Michael Holladay.

Year Formed: 1886. ***Turned Professional:*** 1903. ***Ltd Co.:*** 1903.

Club Nickname: 'The Pilgrims'.

Previous Name: 1886–1903, Argyle Athletic Club.

Foundation: The club was formed in September 1886 as the Argyle Football Club by former public and private school pupils who wanted to continue playing the game. The meeting was held in a room above the Borough Arms (a Coffee House), Bedford Street, Plymouth. It was common then to choose a local street/terrace as a club name and Argyle or Argyll was a fashionable name throughout the land due to Queen Victoria'great interest in Scotland.

First Football League game: 28 August, 1920, Division 3, v Norwich C (h) D 1-1 – Craig; Russell, Atterbury; Logan, Dickinson, Forbes; Kirkpatrick, Jack, Bowler, Heeps (1), Dixon.

Record League Victory: 8–1 v Millwall, Division 2, 16 January 1932 – Harper; Roberts, Titmuss; Mackay, Pullan, Reed; Grozier, Bowden (2), Vidler (3), Leslie (1), Black (1). (1 og). 8–1 v Hartlepool U (a), Division 2, 7 May 1994 – Nicholls; Patterson (Naylor), Hill, Burrows, Comyn, McCall, Barlow, Castle, Landon, Marshall, Dalton.

Record Cup Victory: 6–0 v Corby T, FA Cup, 3rd rd, 22 January 1966 – Leiper; Book, Baird; Williams, Nelson, Newman; Jones (1), Jackson (1), Bickle (3), Piper (1), Jennings.

Record Defeat: 0–9 v Stoke C, Division 2, 17 December 1960.

Most League Points (2 for a win): 68, Division 3 (S), 1929–30.

Most League Points (3 for a win): 87, Division 3, 1985–86.

Most League Goals: 107, Division 3 (S), 1925–26 and 1951–52.

Highest League Scorer in Season: Jack Cock, 32, Division 3 (S), 1925–26.

Most League Goals in Total Aggregate: Sammy Black, 180, 1924–38.

Most Capped Player: Moses Russell, 20 (23), Wales.

Most League Appearances: Kevin Hodges, 530, 1978–92.

Record Transfer Fee Received: £350,000 from Southend U for Gary Poole, July 1993.

Record Transfer Fee Paid: £250,000 to Hartlepool U for Paul Dalton, June 1992.

Football League Record: 1920 Original Member of Division 3; 1921–30 Division 3 (S); 1930–50 Division 2; 1950–52 Division 3 (S); 1952–56 Division 2; 1956–58 Division 3 (S); 1958–59 Division 3; 1959–68 Division 2; 1968–75 Division 3; 1975–77 Division 2; 1977–86 Division 3; 1986–95 Division 2; 1995– Division 3.

Honours: *Football League:* Division 2 best season: 4th, 1931–32, 1952–53; Division 3 (S) – Champions 1929–30, 1951–52; Runners-up 1921–22, 1922–23, 1923–24, 1924–25, 1925–26, 1926–27 (record of six consecutive years); Division 3 – Champions 1958–59; Runners-up 1974–75, 1985–86. *FA Cup:* best season: Semi-final 1984. *Football League Cup:* Semi-final 1965, 1974.

Colours: Green and black striped shirts, black shorts, black stockings. **Change colours:** All white.

PLYMOUTH ARGYLE 1994–95 LEAGUE RECORD

Match No.	*Date*		*Venue*	*Opponents*	*Result*		*H/T Score*	*Lg. Pos.*	*Goalscorers*	*Attendance*
1	Aug	13	H	Brentford	L	1-5	1-3	—	Swan	7976
2		20	A	Brighton & HA	D	1-1	0-0	17	Bradshaw	8309
3		27	H	Bradford C	L	1-5	0-4	20	Dalton	6469
4		30	A	Hull C	L	0-2	0-0	—		3384
5	Sept	3	A	Birmingham C	L	2-4	0-2	22	Castle, Nugent	13,202
6		10	H	Huddersfield T	L	0-3	0-2	22		5464
7		13	H	Cambridge U	D	0-0	0-0	—		3824
8		17	A	Cardiff C	W	1-0	0-0	22	Castle	5674
9		24	H	Chester C	W	1-0	1-0	21	Twiddy	5329
10	Oct	1	A	Leyton Orient	W	2-0	2-0	19	Landon 2	4140
11		8	A	Oxford U	L	0-1	0-1	19		6550
12		15	H	Wycombe W	D	2-2	2-1	18	Skinner (pen), Barlow	6864
13		22	A	Stockport Co	W	4-2	2-1	17	Edworthy, O'Hagan, Landon 2	5652
14		29	H	Blackpool	L	0-2	0-1	19		6285
15	Nov	1	H	Peterborough U	L	0-1	0-1	—		4145
16		5	A	Rotherham U	L	1-3	0-1	20	Skinner	2848
17		19	H	Wrexham	W	4-1	2-1	17	Hughes (og), Burnett, Phillips (og), Barlow	6936
18		26	A	York C	L	0-1	0-0	17		3185
19	Dec	10	H	Brighton & HA	L	0-3	0-0	19		6091
20		17	A	Brentford	L	0-7	0-2	19		4492
21		26	A	Swansea C	L	0-3	0-3	21		4859
22	Jan	2	H	Crewe Alex	W	3-2	1-2	20	Patterson, Evans 2	6802
23		14	A	Bournemouth	D	0-0	0-0	20		4913
24		21	H	Rotherham U	D	0-0	0-0	20		5484
25		28	A	Blackpool	L	2-5	1-0	20	Patterson, Dalton	3599
26	Feb	4	H	York C	L	1-2	1-0	20	Skinner	5572
27		7	A	Shrewsbury T	L	2-3	1-0	—	Nugent, Evans	3029
28		11	A	Peterborough U	W	2-1	1-0	20	McCall, Nugent	4318
29		18	H	Bournemouth	L	0-1	0-1	20		5435
30		21	A	Wrexham	L	1-3	1-0	—	Castle	3030
31		25	H	Leyton Orient	W	1-0	0-0	20	Landon	5173
32	Mar	4	A	Chester C	L	0-1	0-1	21		1823
33		11	A	Bradford C	L	0-2	0-0	21		5399
34		18	H	Hull C	W	2-1	2-1	20	Nugent, Evans	4839
35		21	A	Huddersfield T	L	0-2	0-1	—		12,099
36		25	H	Cardiff C	D	0-0	0-0	21		5611
37		28	H	Stockport Co	L	0-2	0-1	—		4618
38	Apr	1	A	Cambridge U	D	1-1	0-0	21	Landon	3913
39		4	H	Bristol R	D	1-1	1-0	—	Nugent	6743
40		8	H	Shrewsbury T	W	1-0	1-0	21	Patterson	5089
41		15	A	Bristol R	L	0-2	0-1	21		7068
42		17	H	Swansea C	W	2-1	1-1	21	Swan, Nugent	5890
43		19	H	Birmingham C	L	1-3	0-0	—	Dalton	8550
44		22	A	Crewe Alex	D	2-2	1-2	21	Gardiner (og), Dalton (pen)	3786
45		29	A	Wycombe W	W	2-1	1-0	21	Hill, Landon	6850
46	May	6	H	Oxford U	D	1-1	1-0	21	Nugent	4953

Final League Position: 21

GOALSCORERS

League (45): Landon 7, Nugent 7, Dalton 4 (1 pen), Evans 4, Castle 3, Patterson 3, Skinner 3 (1 pen), Barlow 2, Swan 2, Bradshaw 1, Burnett 1, Edworthy 1, Hill 1, McCall 1, O'Hagan 1, Twiddy 1, own goals 3.
Coca-Cola Cup (2): Castle 1, Swan 1.
FA Cup (3): Ross 2, Skinner 1.

Hodge M.J. 17	Patterson M. 37 + 1	Hill K.J. 32 + 2	Comyn A.J. 30	Swan P.H. 24 + 3	Payne I.N. 1	Barlow M.D. 40 + 2	Burnett W. 25 + 7	Nugent K.P. 34 + 3	Evans M.J. 12 + 11	Skinner C.R. 21 + 3	Edworthy M. 24 + 3	Landon R.J. 18 + 6	Naylor D.J. 42	Bradshaw D. 5 + 1	Dalton P. 23 + 3	Castle S.C. 23 + 3	Shaw G.P. 6	Twiddy C. 13 + 2	Nicholls A. 26 + 1	Morgan J.A. 6 + 2	O'Hagan D.A.N. 1 + 2	Dungey J.A. 3 + 1	Crocker M.A. 3 + 2	Quinn M. 3	Ross M.P. 11 + 6	Dawe S. 3 + 1	Shilton S. 1 + 1	Barber P.A. 4	Gee P. 6	McCall S.H. 7	Wotton P.A. 5 + 2	*Match No.*
1	2	3	4	5	*6*	7	8	9	10	11	12	14																				1
1		6	4	5		7	12	9	10		2		3	8	11																	2
1			4	5		7		9			2		3	6	11	8	10	12														3
1	2	4		5			7	9					3	6	11	8	10	12														4
1	2	6	4	5		7		9					3	12		8	10	11														5
1		12	4	5		7	6	9					3	2		8	10	11	15													6
		4	5			7	6	9					3	2		8	10	11	1													7
	2	4	5	12		7	6	9				14	3			8	*10*	11	1													8
1	2	4	5	12		7	6	9	14			*10*	3					11		8												9
	2	4	5			7	6			9	12	10	3					11	1	8												10
	2	4	5			7	6	12		9	14	10	3					11	1	8												11
		2	5	4		7	6			9		10	3					11	1	8	12											12
	2	4	5			7	6			9	8	10	3					*11*	1		12	15										13
	2		5			7	6			9	4	10	3					11	1		8		12									14
	2		5			7	6	12			4	10	3					11	1	8			9									15
1	2		5			7	*6*	9	12	11	4	14	3							8			10									16
	2		5			7	6	9	11	8	4		3						1	12				10								17
	2		5	12		7	6	9		8	4		3					*11*	1					10	14							18
	2		5	4		7	6		12				3						1					9	10	8	11					19
1	2		5	4		7	6	8	9														11		10	3	12					20
	2	3	5	4		7	6	12	*9*										1				14		10	8		11				21
	2	5		4		7		9	12	8	6		3						1						10			11				22
	2	4	5			7	6	9	10	8		12	3						1							14		11				23
		4	5			8	6		10	7	2	9	3		12				1									11				24
	2	4	5			8	12			7	6	*10*	3		14				1										9	11		25
	2	4	5			8	11	10	12	7			3		14				1										9	*6*		26
	2	4	5			7		10	12				3		11	14			1										9	*6*	8	27
	2	4		5		7		10	9	12			3		11	14			1											*6*	8	28
	2	4		5		7		10	12				3		11	8			1										9	*6*	14	29
1	2	4		5		7				12		9	3		11	8													10	6		30
1	2	4	5			7	12			14		9	3		11	8													10		*6*	31
1	2	4	5			7		9	12			10	3		11	8		*6*													14	32
1			5	4			6	9	10		2		3		11	8				12					14						*7*	33
1			5	4			6	9	7		2		3		11	8									10							34
1	14		5	4		12	6	9	7		2		3		11	8									*10*							35
1	2	12		4		6		9	7		5		3		11	8									10							36
1	2			4		7		9	12		5		3		11	8									10						6	37
	2	6		4		7	12	9			5	*10*	3		11	8			1						14							38
	2	6		4		7	12	9			5	*10*	3		11	8			1						14							39
	2	6				8		9		7	5	*10*	3		11	12			1						14					4		40
	2	6				8	4	9		7	5	10			11	3			1						12							41
	2	6		4		12		9		7	5		3		11	8			1						10							42
	2	6		4				9		7	5	12	3		11	8			1						10							43
	2	6		4		5	12	9		7		14	3		11	8						1			*10*							44
	2	4				6		9	12	7	5	10	3		11	8						1										45
	2	4				6	12	9	14	7	5	*10*	3		11	8						1										46

Coca-Cola Cup		
First Round	Walsall (a)	0-4
	(h)	2-1

FA Cup		
First Round	Kettering T (a)	1-0
Second Round	Bournemouth (h)	2-1
Third Round	Nottingham F (a)	0-2

PORTSMOUTH 1994–95 *Back row (left to right):* Neil Sillett (Physio), Gorden Neave (Kit Manager), Martin Hinshelwood (Youth Team Manager), Mike Bailey (Reserve Team Manager), Graham Paddon (Assistant Manager).
Third row: Jason Rees, Stuart Doling, Deon Burton, Sam Igoe.
Second row: Darryl Powell, Lee Russell, Tony Dobson, Aaron Flahavan, Mart Poom, Alan Knight, Guy Butters, Robbie Pethick, Ray Daniel.
Front row: Paul Hall, Andy Awford, Pedrag Radosavljevic, Mark Stimson, Gerry Creaney, Bjorn Kristensen, Jim Smith (Manager), Kit Symons, Warren Neill, Alan McLoughlin, Paul Wood, John Durnin, Jon Gittens.

Division 1 PORTSMOUTH

Fratton Park, Frogmore Rd, Portsmouth PO4 8RA. Telephone: (01705) 731204. Fax: (01705) 734129. Commercial Dept: (01705) 827111. Ticket Office: (01705) 750825. Lottery Office: (01705) 825016. Clubcall: 0891 338383.

Ground capacity: 26,452.

Record attendance: 51,385 v Derby Co, FA Cup 6th rd, 26 February 1949.

Record receipts: £214,000 v Manchester U, Coca-Cola Cup 5th rd replay, 26 January 1994.

Pitch measurements: 114yd × 72yd.

Chairman: J. A. Gregory.

Directors: M. H. Gregory, D. K. Deacon, B. A. V. Henson, J. S. Hutchison, R. E. Smith.

Manager: Terry Fenwick. ***First Team Coach:*** Keith Waldon.

Secretary: Paul Weld. ***Marketing Manager:*** Julie Baker.

Physio: Neil Sillett. ***Youth Team Coach:*** K. Todd.

Year Formed: 1898. ***Turned Professional:*** 1898. ***Ltd Co.:*** 1898.

Club Nickname: 'Pompey'.

Foundation: At a meeting held in his High Street, Portsmouth offices in 1898, solicitor Alderman J. E. Pink and five other business and professional men agreed to buy some ground close to Goldsmith Avenue for £4,950 which they developed into Fratton Park in record breaking time. A team of professionals was signed up by manager Frank Brettell and entry to the Southern League obtained for the new club's September 1899 kick-off.

First Football League game: 28 August, 1920, Division 3, v Swansea T (h) W 3-0 – Robson; Probert, Potts; Abbott, Harwood, Turner; Thompson, Stringfellow (1), Reid (1), James (1), Beedie.

Record League Victory: 9–1 v Notts Co, Division 2, 9 April 1927 – McPhail; Clifford, Ted Smith; Reg Davies (1), Foxall, Moffat; Forward (1), Mackie (2), Haines (3), Watson, Cook (2).

Record Cup Victory: 7–0 v Stockport Co, FA Cup, 3rd rd, 8 January 1949 – Butler; Rookes, Ferrier; Scoular, Flewin, Dickinson; Harris (3), Barlow, Clarke (2), Phillips (2), Froggatt.

Record Defeat: 0–10 v Leicester C, Division 1, 20 October 1928.

Most League Points (2 for a win): 65, Division 3, 1961–62.

Most League Points (3 for a win): 91, Division 3, 1982–83.

Most League Goals: 91, Division 4, 1979–80.

Highest League Scorer in Season: Guy Whittingham, 42, Division 1, 1992–93.

Most League Goals in Total Aggregate: Peter Harris, 194, 1946–60.

Most Capped Player: Jimmy Dickinson, 48, England.

Most League Appearances: Jimmy Dickinson, 764, 1946–65.

Record Transfer Fee Received: £2,000,000 from Tottenham H for Darren Anderton, May 1992.

Record Transfer Fee Paid: £650,000 to Celtic for Gerry Creaney, January 1994.

Football League Record: 1920 Original Member of Division 3; 1921 Division 3 (S); 1924–27 Division 2; 1927–59 Division 1; 1959–61 Division 2; 1961–62 Division 3; 1962–76 Division 2; 1976–78 Division 3; 1978–80 Division 4; 1980–83 Division 3; 1983–87 Division 2; 1987–88 Division 1; 1988–92 Division 2; 1992– Division 1.

Honours: *Football League:* Division 1 – Champions 1948–49, 1949–50; Division 2 – Runners-up 1926–27, 1986–87; Division 3 (S) – Champions 1923–24; Division 3 – Champions 1961–62, 1982–83. *FA Cup:* Winners 1939; Runners-up 1929, 1934. *Football League Cup:* best season: 5th rd, 1961, 1986.

Colours: Blue shirts, white shorts, red stockings. **Change colours:** Red and black shirts, black shorts, red stockings.

PORTSMOUTH 1994–95 LEAGUE RECORD

Match No.	Date	Venue	Opponents	Result	H/T Score	Lg. Pos.	Goalscorers	Attendance
1	Aug 13	H	Notts Co	W 2-1	1-0	—	Powell, Symons	10,487
2	20	A	Reading	D 0-0	0-0	5		9106
3	27	H	Charlton Ath	D 1-1	1-1	7	Symons	10,566
4	30	A	Southend U	W 2-1	1-1	—	Creaney, Powell	4333
5	Sept 10	H	Port Vale	L 0-2	0-1	13		8989
6	14	H	Tranmere R	D 1-1	0-0	—	Hall	6383
7	17	A	Bolton W	D 1-1	0-1	13	Creaney	11,284
8	24	H	Wolverhampton W	L 1-2	1-1	19	Creaney (pen)	13,466
9	28	A	WBA	W 2-0	1-0	—	Pethick, Hall	13,545
10	Oct 1	A	Grimsby T	L 0-2	0-1	14		4172
11	8	A	Oldham Ath	L 2-3	0-1	17	Creaney, Hall	7683
12	15	H	Swindon T	W 4-3	2-1	12	McLoughlin 2, Powell, Creaney (pen)	10,610
13	23	H	Middlesbrough	D 0-0	0-0	14		7281
14	29	A	Bristol C	D 1-1	0-1	15	Powell	7238
15	Nov 2	A	Millwall	D 2-2	1-2	—	Rees, McLoughlin (pen)	7108
16	6	H	Derby Co	L 0-1	0-0	20		5507
17	19	A	Luton T	L 0-2	0-1	21		8214
18	26	H	Sunderland	L 1-4	0-3	21	Powell	7527
19	30	H	Stoke C	L 0-1	0-0	—		5272
20	Dec 3	A	Middlesbrough	L 0-4	0-2	22		17,185
21	10	H	Reading	D 1-1	1-0	22	Creaney	8578
22	17	A	Notts Co	W 1-0	0-0	22	Wood	6382
23	26	A	Watford	L 0-2	0-0	22		9953
24	27	H	Barnsley	W 3-0	3-0	19	Newhouse, Creaney 2	6751
25	31	A	Sheffield U	L 1-3	1-0	21	Creaney	13,467
26	Jan 2	H	Burnley	W 2-0	1-0	19	Radosavljevic, Creaney	9097
27	14	H	Bristol C	D 0-0	0-0	19		8803
28	22	A	Derby Co	L 0-3	0-0	19		11,143
29	Feb 4	A	Stoke C	W 2-0	0-0	18	Radosavljevic, Creaney	9704
30	18	A	Sunderland	D 2-2	1-2	19	McLoughlin, Doling	12,372
31	21	H	Luton T	W 3-2	0-1	—	McLoughlin, Radosavljevic, Creaney (pen)	7363
32	25	H	Grimsby T	W 2-1	1-1	14	Creaney, Symons	8274
33	Mar 5	A	Wolverhampton W	L 0-1	0-0	16		23,284
34	8	H	WBA	L 1-2	1-1	—	Creaney	7160
35	11	A	Charlton Ath	L 0-1	0-1	20		9443
36	15	H	Millwall	W 3-2	1-1	—	Creaney 2, Hall	6032
37	18	H	Southend U	D 1-1	1-1	15	McLoughlin	6667
38	21	A	Port Vale	L 0-1	0-1	—		7388
39	25	H	Bolton W	D 1-1	0-1	18	Creaney	7765
40	Apr 1	A	Tranmere R	L 2-4	1-3	19	Radosavljevic, Irons (og)	8722
41	8	H	Sheffield U	W 1-0	0-0	19	Creaney	8216
42	15	A	Barnsley	L 0-1	0-0	20		6825
43	17	H	Watford	W 2-1	1-0	18	Durnin (pen), Burton	8396
44	22	A	Burnley	W 2-1	1-0	18	Durnin (pen), Symons	10,666
45	29	A	Swindon T	W 2-0	1-0	18	Radosavljevic, Burton	9220
46	May 7	H	Oldham Ath	D 1-1	0-1	18	Hall	11,002

Final League Position: 18

GOALSCORERS

League (53): Creaney 18 (3 pens), McLoughlin 6 (1 pen), Hall 5, Powell 5, Radosavljevic 5, Symons 4, Burton 2, Durnin 2 (2 pens), Doling 1, Newhouse 1, Pethick 1, Rees 1, Wood 1, own goal 1.
Coca-Cola Cup (9): Creaney 3, Powell 3, Hall 1, Kristensen 1, Stimson 1.
FA Cup (3): Radosavljevic 2, Creaney 1.

Knight A.E. 43	Gittens J. 37 + 1	Stimson M. 15	McLoughlin A.F. 36 + 2	Symons C.J. 40	Dobson A.J. 14	Neill W.A. 7	Pethick R.J. 39 + 5	Powell D.A. 34	Creaney G. 39	Hall P.A. 30 + 13	Daniel R.C. 17 + 5	Lee D.J. 4 + 1	Awford A.T. 3 + 1	Kristensen B. 15 + 10	Radosavljevic P. 30 + 10	Burton D.J. 5 + 2	Rees J.M. 14 + 5	McGrath L.A. 15 + 3	Russell L. 18 + 1	Totten A.R. 3 + 1	Durnin J. 8 + 8	Butters G. 24	Newhouse A.R. 6	Wood P.A. 5	Glass J.R. 3	Doling S.J. 2 + 3	Igoe S.G. — + 1	*Match No.*
1	2	3	4	5	6	7	8	9	*10*	11	12	14																1
1	2	3	4	5	6	7	14	9	10	11	12	*8*																2
1	2	3	4	5	6	7	14	9	10	11	12	*8*																3
1	2	3	4	5	6	7		9	10	11		8																4
1	2	3	*4*	5	6	7	14	9	10	11	12	8																5
1	2	3	4	5		7		9	10	11	12		6	8														6
1	2	3	4	5	6		12		10	*11*	9		7	8	14													7
1	2	3	4	5			12	9	10	11	7		6	*8*	14													8
1	2	3	4	5	6		9		10	12	*7*		14	11	8													9
1	2	3	4	5	*6*		9		10	11	7				8	12	14											10
1	*2*	3	4	5			6	9	10	11	7			8	12		14											11
1	2	3	4	5			7	9	10	11				12	8			6										12
1	2	3	4	5			7	9	10	11					8			6										13
1	2	3		5	11		7	9	10	12				4	*8*		14	6										14
1	2		4	5	11		7	9		12				3	8		10	*6*	14									15
1		3	4	5			7	9	10					*8*	12		11		6	2	14							16
1	2		4		3		7	9	10					8	5	*11*	12		6	14								17
1	2		4		3	6	7	9	10	8					12	11				5								18
1	2		4	5	6		7	9	10	11	3			8	12													19
1	2			5	6		7	9	10	14				*8*	12				4			3	11					20
1	2		12				7	9	10	14					8			4		3		5	*11*	6				21
1	2		12	5			7	9		14	10				*8*			4				3	11	6				22
1	2			5			*7*	9	10	14	8				12			4				3	11	6				23
1	2			5			7	9	10		3				8			4				6	11					24
1	2			5			7	9	10	12	3				8			4				6	11					25
1	2			5			7	9	10	12	3				8			4				6		11				26
1				5			7	9	10	12	3				8			4	2			6		11				27
1			4				7	9	10	12	3			11	8			5	2			6						28
1	2		4	5			7	9	10	12	3				8		11					6						29
			4	5			2		10	9	3			*7*	8		11				12	6			1	14		30
1			4	5			2		10	9	3				8		11	7				6				12		31
1	2		4	5			7		10	9	3				8		*11*	14			12	6						32
1	2		4	5			7		10	9				12	*8*			11	3		14	6						33
1	2		4	5			7	11	10	9					8			12	3			6						34
1	2		4	5			7	9	10	12					8			11	*3*		14	6						35
1	2		4	5			7	9	10	11					8			*12*	3		14	6						36
1	2		4	5			7	9	10	11				12	8		*6*		3		14							37
	2		4	5			7	9	10	11				12	*8*		3				14	6			1			38
	2						7	9	10	11				5	8		3		6		4				1	12		39
1			4				7	9	10	11				5	8				6		3	2						40
1			4	5			7	*9*	10	11				12	8		14		6		3	2						41
1	12		4	5			7			11				14	8		*9*		6		10	3				2		42
1	3		4	5			7			11				12	*8*	14	9		6		10					2		43
1	3		4	5			7			11				14	12	8	9		6		*10*	2						44
1	3		4	5			7			*11*				12	14	8	9		6		10	2						45
1			4	5			2			11				12	*7*	8	9		6		10	3					14	46

Coca-Cola Cup

First Round	Cambridge U (h)	2-0
	(a)	3-2
Second Round	Everton (a)	3-2
	(h)	1-1
Third Round	Derby Co (h)	0-1

FA Cup

Third Round	Bolton W (h)	3-1
Fourth Round	Leicester C (h)	0-1

PORT VALE 1994–95 *Back row (left to right):* Joe Allon, Dean Glover, Peter Billing, Stuart Talbot, Paul Musselwhite, Gareth Griffiths, Arjen van Heusden, Robin van der Laan, Neil Aspin, John Morris, Martin Foyle.

Centre row: Bill Dearden (First Team Coach), Stan Nicholls (Kit Man), Lee Glover, Wayne Corden, Oliver Heald, Paul Kerr, John Jeffers, Allen Tankard, Jim Joyce (Physio), Ian Miller (Youth Team Coach).

Front row: Kevin Kent, Ray Walker, Bradley Sandeman, John Rudge (Manager), Andy Porter, Dean Stokes, Tony Naylor.

Division 1 PORT VALE

Vale Park, Burslem, Stoke-on-Trent ST6 1AW. Telephone: (01782) 814134. Fax: (01782) 834981. Commercial Dept: (01782) 835524. Clubcall: 0891 121636. Commercial Fax: (01782) 836875. Valiant Leisure Shop: (01782) 818718.

Ground capacity: 22,359.

Record attendance: 50,000 v Aston Villa, FA Cup 5th rd, 20 February 1960.

Record receipts: £170,022 v Liverpool, Rumbelows Cup 3rd rd replay, 20 November 1991.

Pitch measurements: 116yd × 76yd.

President: J. Burgess.

Chairman: W. T. Bell TECH. ENG, MIMI.

Directors: A. Belfield, I. McPherson, D. Bundy (vice-chairman).

Manager: John Rudge. ***Secretary:*** R. A. Allan. ***Commercial Executive:*** Keith Dale.
Commercial Manager: Mrs Margaret Moran-Smith.

Coach: Bill Dearden. ***Physio:*** Rick Carter. ***Medical Officer:*** Dr. D. Phillips. ***Stadium Manager:*** F. W. Lodey. ***Groundsman:*** R. Fairbanks. ***Community Scheme Officer:*** Jim Cooper (0782 575594).

Year Formed: 1876. ***Turned Professional:*** 1885. ***Ltd Co.:*** 1911.

Club Nickname: 'Valiants'.

Previous Name: Burslem Port Vale; became Port Vale, 1911.

Previous Grounds: 1876, Limekin Lane, Longport; 1881, Westport; 1884, Moorland Road, Burslem; 1886, Athletic Ground, Cobridge; 1913, Recreation Ground, Hanley; 1950, Vale Park.

Foundation: Formed in 1876 as Port Vale, adopting the prefix 'Burslem' in 1884 upon moving to that part of the city. It was dropped in 1911.

First Football League game: 3 September, 1892, Division 2, v Small Heath (a) L 1-5 – Frail; Clutton, Elson; Farrington, McCrindle, Delves; Walker, Scarratt, Bliss (1), Jones. (Only 10 men).

Record League Victory: 9–1 v Chesterfield, Division 2, 24 September 1932 – Leckie; Shenton, Poyser; Sherlock, Round, Jones; McGrath, Mills, Littlewood (6), Kirkham (2), Morton (1).

Record Cup Victory: 7–1 v Irthlingborough (away), FA Cup, 1st rd, 12 January 1907 – Matthews; Dunn, Hamilton; Eardley, Baddeley, Holyhead; Carter, Dodds (2), Beats, Mountford (2), Coxon (3).

Record Defeat: 0–10 v Sheffield U, Division 2, 10 December 1892 and v Notts Co, Division 2, 26 February 1895.

Most League Points (2 for a win): 69, Division 3 (N), 1953–54.

Most League Points (3 for a win): 89, Division 2, 1992–93.

Most League Goals: 110, Division 4, 1958–59.

Highest League Scorer in Season: Wilf Kirkham 38, Division 2, 1926–27.

Most League Goals in Total Aggregate: Wilf Kirkham, 154, 1923–29, 1931–33.

Most Capped Player: Sammy Morgan, 7 (18), Northern Ireland.

Most League Appearances: Roy Sproson, 761, 1950–72.

Record Transfer Fee Received: £925,000 from Norwich C for Darren Beckford, June 1991.

Record Transfer Fee Paid: £375,000 from Oxford U for Martin Foyle, June 1991.

Football League Record: 1892 Original Member of Division 2, Failed re-election in 1896; Re-elected 1898; Resigned 1907; Returned in Oct, 1919, when they took over the fixtures of Leeds City; 1929–30 Division 3 (N); 1930–36 Division 2; 1936–38 Division 3 (N); 1938–52 Division 3 (S); 1952–54 Division 3 (N); 1954–57 Division 2; 1957–58 Division 3 (S); 1958–59 Division 4; 1959–65 Division 3; 1965–70 Division 4; 1970–78 Division 3; 1978–83 Division 4; 1983–84 Division 3; 1984–86 Division 4; 1986–89 Division 3; 1989–94 Division 2; 1994– Division 1.

Honours: *Football League:* Division 2 – Runners-up 1993–94; Division 3 (N) – Champions 1929–30, 1953–54; Runners-up 1952–53; Division 4 – Champions 1958–59; Promoted 1969–70 (4th). *FA Cup:* Semi-final 1954, when in Division 3. *Football League Cup:* never past 2nd rd. *Autoglass Trophy:* Winners: 1993.

Colours: White shirts, black shorts, black and white stockings. **Change colours:** All yellow.

PORT VALE 1994–95 LEAGUE RECORD

Match No.	Date	Venue	Opponents	Result		H/T Score	Lg. Pos.	Goalscorers	Attendance
1	Aug 14	A	Swindon T	L	0-2	0-1	—		10,431
2	20	H	Oldham Ath	W	3-1	0-0	10	Kenny (og), Foyle, Naylor	10,051
3	27	A	Bristol C	D	0-0	0-0	12		8588
4	30	H	Barnsley	W	2-1	1-0	—	Glover L, Burke	7228
5	Sept 3	H	Luton T	L	0-1	0-0	12		8541
6	10	A	Portsmouth	W	2-0	1-0	5	Glover L, Naylor	8989
7	13	A	Grimsby T	L	1-4	0-1	—	Foyle	3216
8	17	H	Middlesbrough	W	2-1	0-1	7	Naylor, Glover L	10,313
9	24	H	Sheffield U	L	0-2	0-0	9		9324
10	Oct 1	A	Wolverhampton W	L	1-2	0-0	12	Allon	27,469
11	8	A	Notts Co	D	2-2	0-1	15	Kelly, Foyle	6903
12	15	H	Charlton Ath	L	0-2	0-0	19		7707
13	22	H	Bolton W	D	1-1	0-0	19	Allon	10,003
14	29	A	Tranmere R	D	1-1	0-0	20	Jeffers	6972
15	Nov 2	A	WBA	D	0-0	0-0	—		14,513
16	5	H	Southend U	W	5-0	2-0	14	Van Der Laan, Allon, Foyle, Walker, Porter	7141
17	19	A	Derby Co	L	0-2	0-1	19		13,357
18	26	H	Millwall	W	2-1	0-0	18	Allon, Burke	8016
19	29	H	Sunderland	D	0-0	0-0	—		8121
20	Dec 6	A	Bolton W	L	0-1	0-0	—		10,324
21	10	A	Oldham Ath	L	2-3	1-1	17	Van Der Laan, Guppy	7712
22	17	H	Swindon T	D	2-2	1-1	18	Foyle 2	7747
23	28	H	Reading	L	0-2	0-1	—		7891
24	31	A	Watford	L	2-3	1-1	22	Foyle 2	7794
25	Jan 15	H	Tranmere R	W	2-0	1-0	21	Tankard, Foyle	7944
26	28	A	Southend U	W	2-1	1-1	18	Foyle, Van Der Laan	3619
27	Feb 4	A	Sunderland	D	1-1	1-1	20	Naylor	13,377
28	11	H	WBA	W	1-0	0-0	17	Guppy	10,751
29	21	H	Derby Co	W	1-0	0-0	—	Kent	9387
30	25	H	Wolverhampton W	L	2-4	1-3	18	Naylor, Kent	13,676
31	Mar 4	A	Sheffield U	D	1-1	0-0	17	Glover L	13,647
32	7	A	Luton T	L	1-2	0-0	—	Porter	5947
33	11	H	Bristol C	W	2-1	1-1	15	Scott, Naylor	7646
34	14	H	Stoke C	D	1-1	1-1	—	Naylor	19,510
35	18	A	Barnsley	L	1-3	0-2	17	Allon	6878
36	21	H	Portsmouth	W	1-0	1-0	—	Allon	7388
37	26	A	Middlesbrough	L	0-3	0-2	17		17,401
38	28	A	Burnley	L	3-4	1-1	—	Foyle 2, Allon	10,058
39	Apr 1	H	Grimsby T	L	1-2	0-2	17	Naylor	7150
40	5	A	Millwall	W	3-1	2-0	—	Van Der Laan, Foyle, Bogie	5260
41	8	H	Watford	L	0-1	0-0	17		7276
42	15	A	Reading	D	3-3	0-3	17	Porter, Bogie (pen), Naylor	8635
43	17	H	Burnley	W	1-0	1-0	16	Van Der Laan	9663
44	22	A	Stoke C	W	1-0	0-0	14	Foyle	20,429
45	29	A	Charlton Ath	D	1-1	1-1	17	Foyle	12,596
46	May 7	H	Notts Co	D	1-1	1-0	17	Foyle	9452

Final League Position: 17

GOALSCORERS

League (58): Foyle 16, Naylor 9, Allon 7, Van Der Laan 5, Glover L 4, Porter 3, Bogie 2 (1 pen), Burke 2, Guppy 2, Kent 2, Jeffers 1, Kelly 1, Scott 1, Tankard 1, Walker 1, own goal 1.
Coca-Cola Cup (5): Glover L 3, Foyle 1, Naylor 1.
FA Cup (6): Foyle 3, Allon 1, Glover D 1, Griffiths 1.

Musselwhite P.S. 44	Sandeman B.R. 37	Tankard A.J. 39	Porter A.M. 43 + 1	Griffiths G.J. 20	Glover D.V. 28 + 1	Kent K.J. 19 + 4	Van Der Laan R.P. 43 + 1	Foyle M.J. 40 + 2	Glover E.L. 21 + 7	Jeffers J.J. 6 + 4	Walker R. 20 + 3	Naylor A.J. 29 + 4	Burke M. 4 + 11	Allon J.B. 10 + 9	Kelly A.G. 3 + 1	Billing P.G. 6	Aspin N. 37	Guppy S.A. 25 + 2	Lawton C.T. — + 1	Scott K.W. 17	Stokes D.A. 3	Bogie I. 7 + 2	Van Heusden A. 2	Talbot S. 2	Burndred J.N. 1	Corden S.W. — + 1	Match No.
1	2	3	4	5	6	7	8	9	10	11	12																1
1	2	3	4	5	6	7	8	9	10			11															2
1	2	3	4	5	6	7	8	9	10			11	12														3
1	2	3	4	5	6	7	8	9	10			11	12														4
1	2	3	*4*	5	6	7	8	9	10		14	11	12														5
1	2	3	4	5	6	7	8	9	10		12	11															6
1	2	3	4	5	6	7	8	9	10			11	12	14													7
1	2	3	4	5	6	7	8	9	10			11															8
1	2	3	4	5	6	7	8	9	10				11		12												9
1	2	3	4		6		14		10			9	11	12	7	*5*	8										10
1	2	3	4				8	9	10			11			7	6	5										11
1	2	3	4				*8*	9	10	12		11	14		7	6	5										12
1		3	4	5		7	8		10	11		*9*	12	14		6	2										13
1		3	4	5	6	7	8	10		12	11			9			2										14
1		3	4	5	6		8	10		7	11			9			2										15
1		3	4	5	6		8	10		7	11			9			2										16
1		3	4	5	6		8	10	12	7	11		14	9			2										17
1		3	4	5	6		*8*	10	12		11		14	9			2	7									18
1		3	4	5	6		8	10			11		12	9			2	7									19
1		3	12	5	6	*11*	8	9	10		4		14				2	7									20
1			4	5	6	7	*8*	9	10	3		12	14				2	11									21
1	3		4	5	6		8	9	10			12	7				2	11									22
1	3		4	5	6		8	9	10			12	7				2	11									23
1	3		4		6	7	8	9	10		11					5	2		12								24
1	2	3	4				8	9			11	10					5	7		6							25
1	2	3	4			12	8	9			11	*10*		14			5	7		6							26
1	2	3	4		12	11	8	9				10					5	7		6							27
1	2	3	4			11	8	9				10					5	7		6							28
1	2	3				11	8	9			4	10		12			5	7		6							29
1	2	3				11	8	9	12		*4*	10		14			5	7		6							30
1	2	3	4				8	9	12		11	10					5	7		6							31
1	2	3	4				8	9	12		11	*10*		14			5	7		6							32
1	2	3	4				8	9	12		11	10					5	7		6							33
1	2	3	4			12	8		*9*		11	10		14		6	5	7									34
1	2	3	4			12	8		*9*		11	10		14			5	7		6							35
1	2		4				8	12		14	11	10		*9*			5	7		6	3						36
1	2		4				8	12			11	10		9			5	7		6	3						37
1	2	3	4				8	10			11			9			5	7		6		12					38
1	2	3	4			11	8	10				12		9			5	*7*		6		14					39
1	2	3	4		11		8	9				10					5			6		7					40
1	2	*3*	4		11		8	9	12			10					5	14		6		7					41
1	2	3	4		11		8	9				10					5	12		6		7					42
1	2	3	4		6	12	8	9				10					5	11				7					43
1	2	3	4		6		8	9				10					5	11				7					44
	2	3	4		6			9	10								5	11				7	1	8			45
	2		4		6			9		12							5	11			3	7	1	8	*10*	14	46

Coca-Cola Cup

First Round	Bristol R (a)	3-1
	(h)	1-1
Second Round	Manchester U (h)	1-2
	(a)	0-2

FA Cup

First Round	Hartlepool U (h)	6-0
Second Round	Scarborough (a)	0-1

PRESTON NORTH END 1994–95 *Back row (left to right):* Stuart Hicks, Ryan Kidd, Jamie Squires, Neil Trebble, Mark Sale, Steve Holmes, David Moyes, Mike Conroy, Gavin Nebbeling.
Centre row: Glenn Bonnell, Ian Bryson, Greg Challender, Farrell Kilbane, John Vaughan, Barry Richardson, Kelham O'Hanlon, Neil Whalley, Mickey Norbury, Paul Raynor, Geoff McDougall (Youth Team Scout).
Front row: Alexis Moreno (Physio), Chris Sulley (Youth Development Officer), Terry Fleming, Kevin Magee, Gary Peters (Manager), John Beck, Gareth Ainsworth, Lee Cartwright, Andy Fensome, Brian Hickson (Kit Man).
(Photograph: Karen Pearson)

Division 3 — PRESTON NORTH END

Deepdale, Preston PR1 6RU. Telephone: (01772) 795919. Fax: (01772) 653266. Commercial/Shop: (01772) 795465. Community Office: (01772) 704275.

Ground capacity: 14,659.

Record attendance: 42,684 v Arsenal, Division 1, 23 April 1938.

Record receipts: £68,650 v Sheffield W, FA Cup 3rd rd, 4 January 1992.

Pitch measurements: 110yd × 75yd.

President: Tom Finney OBE, JP.

Vice President: T. C. Nicholson JP, FCIOB.

Chairman: Bryan M. Gray.

Directors: K. W. Leeming, (vice-chairman), M. J. Woodhouse (snr) (vice-chairman), D. Shaw (managing), L. King (company secretary), M. J. Woodhouse (jnr).

Manager: Gary Peters. ***Coach:*** Joe Jakub.

Secretary: Mrs Audrey Shaw.

General Manager: Phil Critchley.

Year Formed: 1881. ***Turned Professional:*** 1885. ***Ltd Co.:*** 1893.

Club Nicknames: 'The Lilywhites' or 'North End'.

Foundation: North End Cricket and Rugby Club which was formed in 1863, indulged in most sports before taking up soccer in about 1879. In 1881 they decided to stick to football to the exclusion of other sports and even a 16–0 drubbing by Blackburn Rovers in an invitation game at Deepdale, a few weeks after taking this decision, did not deter them for they immediately became affiliated to the Lancashire FA.

First Football League game: 8 September, 1888, Football League, v Burnley (h) W 5-2 – Trainer; Haworth, Holmes; Robertson, W. Graham, J. Graham; Gordon (1), Ross (2), Goodall, Dewhurst (2), Drummond.

Record League Victory: 10–0 v Stoke, Division 1, 14 September 1889 – Trainer; Howarth, Holmes; Kelso, Russell (1), Graham; Gordon, Jimmy Ross (2), Nick Ross (3), Thomson (2), Drummond (2).

Record Cup Victory: 26–0 v Hyde, FA Cup, 1st rd, 15 October 1887 – Addision; Howarth, Nick Ross; Russell (1), Thomson (5), Graham (1); Gordon (5), Jimmy Ross (8), John Goodall (1), Dewhurst (3), Drummond (2).

Record Defeat: 0–7 v Blackool, Division 1, 1 May 1948.

Most League Points (2 for a win): 61, Division 3, 1970–71.

Most League Points (3 for a win): 90, Division 4, 1986–87.

Most League Goals: 100, Division 2, 1927–28 and Division 1, 1957–58.

Highest League Scorer in Season: Ted Harper, 37, Division 2, 1932–33.

Most League Goals in Total Aggregate: Tom Finney, 187, 1946–60.

Most Capped Player: Tom Finney, 76, England.

Most League Appearances: Alan Kelly, 447, 1961–75.

Record Transfer Fee Received: £765,000 from Manchester C for Michael Robinson, June 1979.

Record Transfer Fee Paid: £125,000 to Norwich C for Mike Flynn, December 1989.

Football League Record: 1888 Founder Member of League; 1901–04 Division 2; 1904–12 Division 1; 1912–13 Division 2; 1913–14 Division 1; 1914–15 Division 2; 1919–25 Division 1; 1925–34 Division 2; 1934–49 Division 1; 1949–51 Division 2; 1951–61 Division 1; 1961–70 Division 2; 1970–71 Division 3; 1971–74 Division 2; 1974–78 Division 3; 1978–81 Division 2; 1981–85 Division 3; 1985–87 Division 4; 1987–92 Division 3; 1992–93 Division 2; 1993– Division 3.

Honours: *Football League:* Division 1 – Champions 1888–89 (first champions), 1889–90; Runners-up 1890–91, 1891–92, 1892–93, 1905–06, 1952–53, 1957–58; Division 2 – Champions 1903–04, 1912–13, 1950–51; Runners-up 1914–15, 1933–34; Division 3 – Champions 1970–71; Division 4 – Runners-up 1986–87. *FA Cup:* Winners 1889, 1938; Runners-up 1888, 1922, 1937, 1954, 1964. *Double Performed:* 1888–89. *Football League Cup:* best season: 4th rd, 1963, 1966, 1972, 1981.

Colours: White and navy shirts, navy shorts, navy stockings. **Change colours:** Red/navy.

PRESTON NORTH END FC

PRESTON NORTH END 1994–95 LEAGUE RECORD

Match No.	Date	Venue	Opponents	Result	H/T Score	Lg. Pos.	Goalscorers	Attendance
1	Aug 13	A	Darlington	D 0-0	0-0	—		3800
2	20	A	Hereford U	W 2-0	0-0	8	Conroy, Sale	3039
3	27	A	Barnet	L 1-2	0-0	12	Sale	2441
4	30	A	Bury	D 0-0	0-0	—		3623
5	Sept 3	H	Lincoln C	W 4-0	0-0	7	Moyes, Sale 2, Ainsworth	8337
6	10	A	Fulham	W 1-0	0-0	7	Trebble	5001
7	13	A	Gillingham	W 3-2	2-2	—	Sale 2, Fleming	2555
8	17	H	Darlington	L 1-3	0-1	6	Trebble	8884
9	24	A	Doncaster R	L 1-2	0-0	8	Fleming	3321
10	Oct 1	H	Walsall	L 1-2	1-0	11	Whalley	7852
11	8	H	Scunthorpe U	L 0-1	0-0	11		6895
12	15	A	Hartlepool U	L 1-3	1-2	14	Atkinson	2002
13	22	A	Colchester U	L 1-3	0-1	16	Trebble	3015
14	29	H	Exeter C	L 0-1	0-1	16		6808
15	Nov 5	A	Mansfield T	W 2-1	2-1	16	Conroy 2	2602
16	19	H	Northampton T	W 2-0	1-0	14	Moyes, Raynor	7297
17	26	A	Chesterfield	L 0-1	0-0	15		3191
18	Dec 10	H	Hereford U	W 4-2	3-0	10	Magee, Conroy, Bryson 2 (2 pens)	6581
19	17	H	Barnet	W 1-0	0-0	9	Kidd	6429
20	26	H	Rochdale	W 3-0	3-0	9	Smart, Kidd, Conroy	10,491
21	31	H	Scarborough	W 1-0	0-0	10	Smart	8407
22	Jan 2	A	Torquay U	L 0-1	0-1	11		3770
23	10	H	Colchester U	W 2-1	1-0	—	Smart, Trebble	6377
24	14	A	Carlisle U	D 0-0	0-0	10		10,684
25	21	H	Mansfield T	W 2-1	1-1	6	Bryson, Smart	8448
26	24	A	Wigan Ath	D 1-1	0-1	—	Cartwright	3618
27	Feb 4	H	Chesterfield	D 0-0	0-0	7		8544
28	11	A	Northampton T	L 1-2	0-0	8	Smart	5195
29	18	H	Carlisle U	W 1-0	1-0	6	Conroy	11,867
30	28	A	Walsall	D 2-2	1-1	—	Conroy, Raynor	4492
31	Mar 4	H	Doncaster R	D 2-2	0-1	9	Davey, Beckham	9624
32	11	H	Fulham	W 3-2	1-1	6	Conroy, Raynor, Beckham	8601
33	18	H	Bury	W 5-0	2-0	6	Carmichael 2, Conroy 2, Moyes	9626
34	21	A	Exeter C	W 1-0	0-0	—	Bryson	2057
35	25	A	Lincoln C	D 1-1	0-1	6	Kidd	5487
36	Apr 1	H	Gillingham	D 1-1	1-0	6	Carmichael	9100
37	8	A	Scarborough	D 1-1	1-1	6	Bryson	4266
38	15	H	Wigan Ath	W 1-0	1-0	6	Smart	10,238
39	17	A	Rochdale	W 1-0	1-0	5	Davey	4012
40	22	H	Torquay U	L 0-1	0-0	6		9173
41	29	H	Hartlepool U	W 3-0	2-0	5	Moyes, Holmes, Davey	9129
42	May 6	A	Scunthorpe U	L 1-2	1-2	5	Sale	3691

Final League Position: 5

GOALSCORERS

League (58): Conroy 10, Sale 7, Smart 6, Bryson 5 (2 pens), Moyes 4, Trebble 4, Carmichael 3, Davey 3, Kidd 3, Raynor 3, Beckham 2, Fleming 2, Ainsworth 1, Atkinson 1, Cartwright 1, Holmes 1, Magee 1, Whalley 1.
Coca-Cola Cup (2): Fensome 1 (pen), Moyes 1.
FA Cup (2): Conroy 1, Smart 1.

Richardson B. 17	Fensome A.B. 42	Fleming T.M. 20 + 7	Whalley D.N. 14 + 1	Hicks S.J. 8	Moyes D.W. 38	Ainsworth G. 16	Cartwright L. 25 + 11	Raynor P.J. 34 + 4	Trebble N.D. 8 + 11	Bryson J.I.C. 41	Kidd R.A. 32	Sale M.D. 10 + 3	Conroy M.K. 22 + 3	Squires J.A. 11	Vaughan J. 25 + 1	Sharp R. 21	Atkinson G. 8 + 7	Holmes S.P. 5	Emerson D. 1 + 1	Smart A. 17 + 2	Magee K. 14	Rimmer S.A. — + 2	Lancashire G. 9 + 8	Davey S. 13	Beckham D.R.J. 4 + 1	Carmichael M. 7 + 3	*Match No.*
1	2	3	4	5	6	7	8	9	10	11																	1
1	2	11	4	5	6	7	8	9			3	10	12														2
1	2	3	4	5		7	8	12	*9*	11	6	14	10														3
1	2		4		6	7		11		8	3	10	9	5													4
1	2	14	4		6	7	12	9		8	3	10	*11*	5													5
1	2	*11*	4	5	6	7	12	9	14	8	3	10															6
1	2	11	4	5	6	7	12	*9*	14	8	3	10															7
1	2	11	4		6	7	12	9	14	8	*3*	*10*		5													8
1	2	9	4		6	7		11	10	8	3			5													9
1	2	14	4		6	7	12	*11*	10	8	3	9		5													10
1	2	10	4	5	6	7		11	12	8	3	9															11
	2	12	*4*	5		7	14		10	8	6	9			1	3	11										12
	2	14	4	5	6		7		9	8		12	10		1	3	11										13
	2	7	*4*		6		14	9		8		12	10		1	3	11	5									14
	2	7	12		6		4	9		8			10	5	1	3	11										15
1	2	12			6	7	4	9	11	*8*			10			3		5	14								16
1	2				6		4	12	7	8	11		10			3		5		9							17
1	2	12			6		4	11		8			10			3		5		*9*	7	14					18
1	2				6		7	11		8	5		10			3			4	9		12					19
1	2				6		4	11		8	5		10			3	12			*9*	7		14				20
1	2				6		4	11		8	5		*10*		15	3	12			9	7		14				21
	2	3			6	7	4		12	8	5		14		1		11			*9*			10				22
	2	3			6		4	11	12	8	5				1		14			9	7		10				23
	2	3			6		4	11	12	8	5				1		14			9	7		10				24
	2	3			6		4	11	12	8	5				1		14			9	7		10				25
	2	12			6	7	4	11	14	8	5				1	*3*				9			10				26
	2				6		4	11	12	8	5				1	3	14			9	7		10				27
	2				6	7	4	11	12	8	5				1	3	10			9							28
	2				6		4	11		8	5		10		1	3	12			*9*	7		14				29
	2				6		4	11		8	5		10		1	3				9			12	7			30
	2				6		4	*11*		8	5		10		1	3				12			9	7	14		31
	2				6		12	9		8	5		10		1	3					11			7	4		32
	2				6					8	5		10		1	3					11			7	4	9	33
	2				6			12		8			10	5	1	3					11			7	4	9	34
	2				6		12	14		8	5		10		1	3					11			7	4	*9*	35
	2				6		12	4		8				5	1	*3*	10			14	11			7		9	36
	2	3			6		11	4		8			10	5	1								12	7		9	37
	2	3			*6*		4	11		8	5		10		1					9			12	7		14	38
	2	3					4	11		8	5		12	6	1					*9*			14	7		10	39
	2	3					4	11		8	*5*		10	6	1					9			12	7		14	40
	2	3			6			4		8					1			5			11		9	7		10	41
	2	3			6		12	4		8	5	*10*			1		11						9	7		14	42

Coca-Cola Cup

First Round	Stockport Co (h)	1-1
	(a)	1-4

FA Cup

First Round	Blackpool (h)	1-0
Second Round	Walsall (h)	1-1
	(a)	0-4

QUEENS PARK RANGERS 1994–95 *Back row (left to right):* Brian Croft, Trevor Chellis, Steve Yates, Daniele Dichio, Alan McCarthy, Tony Witter, Kevin Gallen, Karl Ready, Chris Plummer, Marvin Bryan, Matthre Brazier.
Centre row: Phil Parkes (Goalkeeping Coach), Des Bulpin (Youth Team Manager), Les Boyle (Kit Manager), Dennis Bailey, John Cross, Michael Meaker, Peter Caldwell, Tony Roberts, Sieb Dykstra, Devon White, Danny Maddix, Andrew Impey, Roger Cross (Reserve Team Manager), John Nolan (Assistant Kit Manager), Brian Morris (Physio).
Front row: Bradley Allen, Ian Holloway, David Bardsley, Rufus Brevett, Les Ferdinand, Gerry Francis, Alan McDonald, Frank Sibley (Assistant Manager), Gary Penrice, Mark Graham, Clive Wilson, Maurice Doyle, Trevor Sinclair.
(Photograph: Action Images)

FA Premiership **QUEENS PARK RANGERS**

South Africa Road, W12 7PA. Telephone: (0181) 743 0262. Fax: (0181) 749 0994. Box Office: (0181) 749 5744 (24 hour information service 0181 749 7798). Supporters Club: (0181) 749 6771. Club Shop: (0181) 749 6862. Marketing: (0181) 740 8737.

Ground capacity: 18,919.

Record attendance: 35,353 v Leeds U, Division 1, 27 April 1974.

Record receipts: £218,475 v Manchester U, FA Premier League, 5 February 1994.

Pitch measurements: 112yd × 72yd.

Chairman: P. D. Ellis.

Directors: R. B. Copus ACA, A. Ellis, A. Ingham, R. C. Thompson.

Manager: Ray Wilkins MBE. ***Assistant Manager/Coach:*** Frank Sibley.

Secretary: Miss S. F. Marson. ***Commercial Controller:*** Leon Gold.

Reserve Team Coach: Roger Cross.

Physio: Brian Morris.

Year Formed: 1885 *(*see Foundation*). ***Turned Professional:*** 1898. ***Ltd Co.:*** 1899.

Club Nicknames: 'Rangers' or 'Rs'. ***Previous Name:*** 1885–87, St Jude's.

Previous Grounds: 1885 *(*see Foundation*), Welford's Fields; 1888–99; London Scottish Ground, Brondesbury, Home Farm, Kensal Rise Green, Gun Club Wormwood Scrubs, Kilburn Cricket Ground; 1899, Kensal Rise Athletic Ground; 1901, Latimer Road, Notting Hill; 1904, Agricultural Society, Park Royal; 1907, Park Royal Ground; 1917, Loftus Road; 1931, White City; 1933, Loftus Road; 1962, White City; 1963, Loftus Road.

Foundation: There is an element of doubt about the date of the foundation of this club, but it is believed that in either 1885 or 1886 it was formed through the amalgamation of Christchurch Rangers and St. Jude's Institute FC. The leading light was George Wodehouse, whose family maintained a connection with the club until comparatively recent times. Most of the players came from the Queen's Park district so this name was adopted after a year as St. Jude's Institute.

First Football League game: 28 August, 1920, Division 3, v Watford (h) L 1-2 – Price; Blackman, Wingrove; McGovern, Grant, O'Brien; Faulkner, Birch (1), Smith, Gregory, Middlemiss.

Record League Victory: 9–2 v Tranmere R, Division 3, 3 December 1960 – Drinkwater; Woods, Ingham; Keen, Rutter, Angell; Lazarus (2), Bedford (2), Evans (2), Andrews (1), Clark (2).

Record Cup Victory: 8–1 v Bristol R (away), FA Cup, 1st rd, 27 November 1937 – Gilfillan; Smith, Jefferson; Lowe, James, March; Cape, Mallett, Cheetham (3), Fitzgerald (3) Bott (2). 8–1 v Crewe Alex, Milk Cup, 1st rd, 3 October 1983 – Hucker; Neill, Dawes, Waddock (1), McDonald (1), Fenwick, Micklewhite (1), Stewart (1), Allen (1), Stainrod (3), Gregory.

Record Defeat: 1–8 v Mansfield T, Division 3, 15 March 1965 and v Manchester U, Division 1, 19 March 1969.

Most League Points (2 for a win): 67, Division 3, 1966–67.

Most League Points (3 for a win): 85, Division 2, 1982–83.

Most League Goals: 111, Division 3, 1961–62.

Highest League Scorer in Season: George Goddard, 37, Division 3 (S), 1929–30.

Most League Goals in Total Aggregate: George Goddard, 172, 1926–34.

Most Capped Player: Alan McDonald, 50, Northern Ireland.

Most League Appearances: Tony Ingham, 519, 1950–63.

Record Transfer Fee Received: £6,000,000 from Newcastle U for Les Ferdinand, June 1995.

Record Transfer Fee Paid: £1,000,000 to Luton T for Roy Wegerle, December 1989.

Football League Record: 1920 Original Members of Division 3; 1921–48 Division 3 (S); 1948–52 Division 2; 1952–58 Division 3 (S); 1958–67 Division 3; 1967–68 Division 2; 1968–69 Division 1; 1969–73 Division 2; 1973–79 Division 1; 1979–83 Division 2; 1983–92 Division 1; 1992– FA Premier League.

Honours: *Football League:* Division 1 – Runners-up 1975–76; Division 2 – Champions 1982–83; Runners-up 1967–68, 1972–73; Division 3 (S) – Champions 1947–48; Runners-up 1946–47; Division 3 – Champions 1966–67. *FA Cup:* Runners-up 1982. *Football League Cup:* Winners 1967; Runners-up 1986. (In 1966–67 won Division 3 and Football League Cup). **European Competition:** *UEFA Cup:* 1976–77, 1984–85.

Colours: Blue and white hooped shirts, white shorts, white stockings. **Change colours:** All red with black trim.

QUEENS PARK RANGERS 1994–95 LEAGUE RECORD

Match No.	*Date*	*Venue*	*Opponents*	*Result*	*H/T Score*	*Lg. Pos.*	*Goalscorers*	*Attendance*
1	Aug 20	A	Manchester U	L 0-2	0-0	—		43,214
2	24	H	Sheffield W	W 3-2	1-1	—	Ferdinand, Sinclair, Gallen	12,788
3	27	H	Ipswich T	L 1-2	0-1	15	Ferdinand	12,456
4	31	A	Leicester C	D 1-1	1-0	—	Willis (og)	18,695
5	Sept 10	H	Coventry C	D 2-2	2-1	13	Penrice 2	11,398
6	17	A	Everton	D 2-2	1-2	12	Ferdinand 2	27,291
7	24	H	Wimbledon	L 0-1	0-0	16		11,061
8	Oct 2	A	Nottingham F	L 2-3	0-0	18	Ferdinand, Allen	21,449
9	8	A	Tottenham H	D 1-1	1-0	17	Impey	25,799
10	15	H	Manchester C	L 1-2	0-0	19	Wilson	13,631
11	22	A	Norwich C	L 2-4	1-0	20	Barker, Gallen	19,431
12	29	H	Aston Villa	W 2-0	1-0	18	Dichio, Penrice	16,073
13	31	H	Liverpool	W 2-1	1-0	—	Sinclair, Ferdinand	18,295
14	Nov 5	A	Newcastle U	L 1-2	1-0	17	Dichio	34,278
15	19	H	Leeds U	W 3-2	2-0	18	Ferdinand 2, Gallen	17,416
16	26	A	Blackburn R	L 0-4	0-1	18		21,302
17	Dec 4	H	West Ham U	W 2-1	2-0	16	Ferdinand, Sinclair	12,780
18	10	H	Manchester U	L 2-3	1-2	17	Ferdinand 2	18,948
19	17	A	Sheffield W	W 2-0	0-0	13	Maddix, Ferdinand	23,288
20	26	A	Crystal Palace	D 0-0	0-0	16		16,699
21	28	H	Southampton	D 2-2	1-1	16	Barker, Gallen	16,078
22	31	A	Arsenal	W 3-1	1-0	14	Gallen, Allen, Impey	32,393
23	Jan 14	A	Aston Villa	L 1-2	0-1	15	Yates	26,578
24	24	A	Leeds U	L 0-4	0-2	—		28,750
25	Feb 4	H	Newcastle U	W 3-0	3-0	17	Ferdinand 2, Barker	16,576
26	11	A	Liverpool	D 1-1	1-0	16	Gallen	35,996
27	26	H	Nottingham F	D 1-1	0-0	17	Barker	13,363
28	Mar 4	A	Wimbledon	W 3-1	1-1	16	Ferdinand 2, Holloway	9176
29	8	H	Leicester C	W 2-0	0-0	—	McDonald, Wilson	10,189
30	15	H	Norwich C	W 2-0	0-0	—	Ferdinand, Gallen	10,519
31	18	H	Everton	L 2-3	1-0	11	Ferdinand, Gallen	14,488
32	22	H	Chelsea	W 1-0	0-0	—	Gallen	15,103
33	Apr 1	A	Coventry C	W 1-0	0-0	9	Sinclair	15,751
34	4	H	Blackburn R	L 0-1	0-0	—		16,508
35	8	H	Arsenal	W 3-1	1-0	9	Impey, Gallen, Ready	16,341
36	11	A	Ipswich T	W 1-0	0-0	—	Ferdinand	11,736
37	15	A	Southampton	L 1-2	0-0	8	Ferdinand	15,210
38	17	H	Crystal Palace	L 0-1	0-0	8		14,227
39	29	A	Chelsea	L 0-1	0-0	8		21,704
40	May 3	A	West Ham U	D 0-0	0-0	—		22,923
41	6	H	Tottenham H	W 2-1	0-1	8	Ferdinand 2	18,637
42	14	A	Manchester C	W 3-2	1-1	8	Ferdinand 2, Dichio	27,850

Final League Position: 8

GOALSCORERS

League (61): Ferdinand 24, Gallen 10, Barker 4, Sinclair 4, Dichio 3, Impey 3, Penrice 3, Allen 2, Wilson 2, Holloway 1, McDonald 1, Maddix 1, Ready 1, Yates 1, own goal 1.
Coca-Cola Cup (6): Allen 1, Ferdinand 1, Gallen 1, Penrice 1, Sinclair 1, Wilson 1 (pen).
FA Cup (6): Ferdinand 1, Gallen 1, Impey 1, Maddix 1, Meaker 1, Wilson 1 (pen).

Roberts A.M. 31	Bardsley D.J. 30	Wilson C. 36	Barker S. 37	Yates S. 22 + 1	McDonald A. 39	Impey A.R. 40	Holloway I.S. 28 + 3	Ferdinand L. 37	Gallen K.A. 31 + 6	Sinclair T. 32 + 1	Maddix D.S. 21 + 6	Penrice G.K. 9 + 10	Brevett R.E. 17 + 2	Ready K. 11 + 2	Meaker M.J. 7 + 1	Allen B.J. 2 + 3	Dykstra S. 11	White D.W. 1	Dichio D.S.E. 4 + 5	Hodge S.B. 15	McCarthy A.J. — + 2	Wilkins R.C. 1 + 1	*Match No.*
1	2	3	4	5	6	7	8	*9*	10	11	12	14											1
1	2	3	4	5	6	7	8	9	10	11	12												2
1	2	3	4	5	6	7	8	9	10	11		12											3
1	2	3	4	5	6	7	8	9	12	11		10											4
1	2		4	5	6	7	8	9	12	11		10	3										5
1	2	11	4	5	6	7	8	9				10	3	12									6
1	2	11	4	5	6	7		9	12			10	3		8								7
1	2		10	5	6	7	8	9		11	4		3			12							8
1	2	3	4	5	6	7	8	9		11	12					10							9
1	2	3	4	5	6	7	8	9	12	11						10							10
	2	3	4	5	6		8		10	11					7	12	1	9					11
	2	3	8	5	6		7		10	11	14	12					1		9	4			12
	2	3	8	5	6	7		9	10	11							1			4			13
	2	3	8	5	6	7		9	10	11							1		12	4			14
		3	8	2	6	7	12	9	10	11				5			1			4			15
		3	8	2	6	7		9	10	11				5			1			4			16
		3	8	5	6	7	12	9	10	11	2						1			4			17
	2	3	8		6	7		9	10	11	5						1			4			18
	2	3	8		6	7	12	9	10	11	5						1			4			19
		3	8	2	6	7		9	10	11	5				12		1			4			20
		3	8	2	6	7		9	10		5		12		11		1			4			21
1	2	3	8		6	7		9	10		5				11	12				4			22
1	2	3		5		7	8	9	10		6				11					4	12		23
1	2			5		7	8	9	*10*	12	6		3		11					4	14		24
1	2		4		6	7	8	9	10	11	5		3						12				25
1	2	3	4		6	7	8	9	10		5		11										26
1		3	4	2	6	7	8	9	10		5	12		14	*11*								27
1		3	4		6	7	8	9	10		5	12	11	2									28
1		3	4		6	7	8		10	11	5	12		2					9				29
1	2	3	4		6	7	8	9	10	11	5												30
1	2	3	4		6	7	8	9	10	11	5	12											31
1	2	3	4		6	7	8		10	11				5					9				32
1		3	4		6	7	8		10	11			2	5					9				33
1		3	4		6	7	8	9	10	11			2	5					12				34
1		3	4		6	7	8	9	10	11		12	2	5									35
1		3	*4*		6	7	8	9	10	11	14	12	2	5									36
1	2	11				7		9	10	8	6	12	3	5						4		14	37
1	2	4			6	7	8	9		11	12	10	*3*	5					14				38
1	2	11			6	7		9	12		5	10	3							4		8	39
1	2	*3*	4		6	7	8	9	12	11	5	10	14										40
1	2		4		6	7	8	9		11	5	10	3										41
1	2		4	12	6	7		9	*10*	11	5	8	3						14				42

Coca-Cola Cup

Second Round	Carlisle U (a)	1-0
	(h)	2-0
Third Round	Manchester C (h)	3-4

FA Cup

Third Round	Aylesbury (a) (at QPR)	4-0
Fourth Round	West Ham U (h)	1-0
Fifth Round	Millwall (h)	1-0
Sixth Round	Manchester U (a)	0-2

READING 1994–95 *Back row (left to right):* Alan Carey, Ray Ranson, James Lambert, Shaka Hislop, Micky Gooding, Scott Taylor, Michael Gilkes.
Centre row: Colin Lee (Assistant Manager), Phil Parkinson, Jeff Hopkins, Andy Bernal, Dariusz Wdowczyk, David Bass, Keith McPherson, Uwe Hartenberger, Jimmy Quinn, Mark McGhee (Manager).
Front row: Lea Barkus, Tom Jones, Dylan Kerr, Adrian Williams, Simon Osborn, Stuart Lovell, Paul Holsgrove.

Division 1 **READING**

Elm Park, Norfolk Road, Reading RG3 2EF. Telephone: (01734) 507878. Fax: (01734) 566628. Community Office: (01734) 560898. Promotions Office: (01734) 464008.

Ground capacity: 14,058.

Record attendance: 33,042 v Brentford, FA Cup 5th rd, 19 February 1927.

Record receipts: £83,671 v Manchester C, FA Cup 3rd rd, 13 January 1993.

Pitch measurements: 112yd × 77yd.

Life President: J. H. Brooks.

Chairman: John Madejski. ***Managing Director:*** M. J. Lewis.

Directors: G. Denton, I. Wood-Smith.

Joint Managers: Jimmy Quinn/Mick Gooding.

Coach: Phil Holder. ***Youth Development Officer:*** Mike Hickman.

Physio: Paul Turner.

Commercial Manager: Kevin Girdler.

Secretary: Ms Andrea Barker.

Year Formed: 1871. ***Turned Professional:*** 1895. ***Ltd Co.:*** 1895.

Club Nickname: 'The Royals'.

Previous Grounds: 1871, Reading Recreation; Reading Cricket Ground; 1882, Coley Park; 1889, Caversham Cricket Ground; 1896, Elm Park.

Foundation: Reading was formed as far back as 1871 at a public meeting held at the Bridge Street Rooms. They first entered the FA Cup as early as 1877 when they amalgamated with the Reading Hornets. The club was further strengthened in 1889 when Earley FC joined them. They were the first winners of the Berks and Bucks Cup in 1878–79.

First Football League game: 28 August, 1920, Division 3, v Newport C (a) W 1-0 – Crawford; Smith, Horler; Christie, Mavin, Getgood; Spence, Weston, Yarnell, Bailey (1), Andrews.

Record League Victory: 10–2 v Crystal Palace, Division 3 (S), 4 September 1946 – Groves; Glidden, Gulliver; McKenna, Ratcliffe, Young; Chitty, Maurice Edelston (3), McPhee (4), Barney (1), Deverell (2).

Record Cup Victory: 6–0 v Leyton, FA Cup, 2nd rd, 12 December 1925 – Duckworth; Eggo, McConnell; Wilson, Messer, Evans; Smith (2), Braithwaite (1), Davey (1), Tinsley, Robson (2).

Record Defeat: 0–18 v Preston NE, FA Cup 1st rd, 1893–94.

Most League Points (2 for a win): 65, Division 4, 1978–79.

Most League Points (3 for a win): 94, Division 3, 1985–86.

Most League Goals: 112, Division 3 (S), 1951–52.

Highest League Scorer in Season: Ronnie Blackman, 39, Division 3 (S), 1951–52.

Most League Goals in Total Aggregate: Ronnie Blackman, 158, 1947–54.

Most Capped Player: Jimmy Quinn, 15 (44), Northern Ireland.

Most League Appearances: Martin Hicks, 500, 1978–91.

Record Transfer Fee Received: £500,000 from Wimbledon for Keith Curle, October 1988.

Record Transfer Fee Paid: £250,000 to Leicester C for Steve Moran, November 1987, £250,000 to Huddersfield T for Craig Maskell, August 1990 and £250,000 to Watford for Lee Nogan, December 1994.

Football League Record: 1920 Original Member of Division 3; 1921–26 Division 3 (S); 1926–31 Division 2; 1931–58 Division 3 (S); 1958–71 Division 3; 1971–76 Division 4; 1976–77 Division 3; 1977–79 Division 4; 1979–83 Division 3; 1983–84 Division 4; 1984–86 Division 3; 1986–88 Division 2; 1988–92 Division 3; 1992–94 Division 2; 1994– Division 1.

Honours: *Football League:* Division 1 – Runners-up 1994–95; Division 2 – Champions 1993–94; Division 3 – Champions 1985–86. Division 3 (S) – Champions 1925–26; Runners-up 1931–32, 1934–35, 1948–49, 1951–52; Division 4 – Champions 1978–79. *FA Cup:* Semi-final 1927. *Football League Cup:* best season: 4th rd, 1965, 1966, 1978. *Simod Cup:* Winners 1988.

Colours: Navy and white hooped shirts, white shorts, white stockings. **Change colours:** All red.

READING 1994–95 LEAGUE RECORD

Match No.	Date	Venue	Opponents	Result		H/T Score	Lg. Pos.	Goalscorers	Attendance
1	Aug 13	A	Wolverhampton W	L	0-1	0-1	—		27,012
2	20	H	Portsmouth	D	0-0	0-0	21		9106
3	27	A	Barnsley	W	2-0	1-0	13	Osborn, Taylor	4771
4	30	H	Stoke C	W	4-0	0-0	—	Lovell, Kerr, Gilkes, Taylor	7103
5	Sept 3	H	Millwall	D	0-0	0-0	6		8715
6	10	A	Oldham Ath	W	3-1	1-1	2	Lovell 2, Osborn	8412
7	14	A	Swindon T	L	0-1	0-0	—		11,551
8	17	H	Sheffield U	W	1-0	0-0	3	Quinn	9036
9	24	A	Watford	D	2-2	0-2	5	Osborn, Lovell	8015
10	Oct 1	H	Notts Co	W	2-0	1-0	3	Lovell, Hartenberger	7465
11	8	A	Charlton Ath	W	2-1	1-0	3	Osborn, Gilkes	10,544
12	15	H	Bristol C	W	1-0	0-0	2	Gilkes	9389
13	22	H	Sunderland	L	0-2	0-1	2		10,757
14	29	A	WBA	L	0-2	0-0	4		14,313
15	Nov 2	A	Derby Co	W	2-1	1-0	—	Taylor, Gilkes	10,585
16	5	H	Burnley	D	0-0	0-0	4		8150
17	19	A	Southend U	L	1-4	1-1	5	Quinn	5511
18	26	H	Tranmere R	L	1-3	0-2	8	Jones	7887
19	Dec 3	A	Sunderland	W	1-0	0-0	5	Taylor	14,021
20	6	H	Middlesbrough	D	1-1	0-0	—	Taylor	10,301
21	10	A	Portsmouth	D	1-1	0-1	6	Quinn (pen)	8578
22	18	H	Wolverhampton W	W	4-2	2-1	5	Osborn, Quinn, Gilkes 2	10,136
23	26	H	Luton T	D	0-0	0-0	6		11,623
24	28	A	Port Vale	W	2-0	1-0	—	Quinn (pen), Taylor	7891
25	31	H	Grimsby T	D	1-1	0-1	4	Lambert	8526
26	Jan 2	A	Bolton W	L	0-1	0-1	6		14,705
27	14	H	WBA	L	0-2	0-0	7		9390
28	21	A	Burnley	W	2-1	2-0	5	Nogan, Taylor	9841
29	Feb 4	A	Middlesbrough	W	1-0	0-0	5	Holsgrove	17,982
30	11	H	Derby Co	W	1-0	1-0	4	Kavanagh (og)	8834
31	18	A	Tranmere R	L	0-1	0-0	5		8744
32	21	H	Southend U	W	2-0	0-0	—	Holsgrove, Nogan	7895
33	25	A	Notts Co	L	0-1	0-0	6		7183
34	Mar 4	H	Watford	W	4-1	1-0	5	Gilkes 2, Holsgrove, Hartenberger	9705
35	8	A	Millwall	L	0-2	0-1	—		7546
36	11	H	Barnsley	L	0-3	0-1	6		7556
37	18	A	Stoke C	W	1-0	1-0	6	Taylor	10,006
38	21	H	Oldham Ath	W	2-1	0-1	—	Nogan, Lovell	6921
39	25	A	Sheffield U	D	1-1	0-0	5	Nogan	19,241
40	Apr 1	H	Swindon T	W	3-0	2-0	4	Lovell 3 (1 pen)	12,565
41	8	A	Grimsby T	L	0-1	0-0	5		4519
42	15	H	Port Vale	D	3-3	3-0	6	Nogan 3	8635
43	17	A	Luton T	W	1-0	1-0	5	Taylor (og)	8717
44	21	H	Bolton W	W	2-1	1-0	—	Lovell, Nogan	13,223
45	29	A	Bristol C	W	2-1	1-0	2	Lovell, Nogan	9474
46	May 7	H	Charlton Ath	W	2-1	1-0	2	Nogan, Williams	12,137

Final League Position: 2

GOALSCORERS

League (58): Lovell 11 (1 pen), Nogan 10, Gilkes 8, Taylor 8, Osborn 5, Quinn 5 (2 pens), Holsgrove 3, Hartenberger 2, Jones 1, Kerr 1, Lambert 1, Williams 1, own goals 2.
Coca-Cola Cup (7): Quinn 4, Holsgrove 1, Lovell 1, Williams 1.
FA Cup (1): Taylor 1.

Hislop N.S. 46	Bernal A. 33	Kerr D. 35 + 1	Wdowczyk D. 37 + 1	Williams A. 20 + 2	Parkinson P.J. 25 + 6	Taylor S.D. 31 + 13	Gooding M.C. 37 + 2	Quinn J.M. 31 + 4	Lovell S.A. 25 + 5	Osborn S.E. 31 + 1	Hopkins J. 20 + 1	Gilkes E.G.M. 37 + 3	Holsgrove P. 23 + 1	Jones T. 18 + 2	Hartenberger U. 8 + 7	Murphy M. — + 1	Lambert C.J.P. 3 + 8	McPherson K.A. 19 + 4	Barnard D.S. 3 + 1	Carey A.W. — + 2	Nogan L.M. 18 + 2	Viveash A.L. 6	Match No.
1	2	3	4	5	6	7	8	9	10	11	12	14											1
1	2	3	4	5	6	7	8	9	10	11		12											2
1		3	4	5	6	12	8	9	10	11	2	7											3
1		3	4	5	6	12	8	9	10	11	2	7	14										4
1		3	4		6	12	8	9	10	11	2	7	5	14									5
1		3	4	5			8	9	10	11	2	7	6										6
1	2	3	4	5		12	8	9	10	11		7	6										7
1	2	3	4	5	12	14	8	9	10	11		7	6										8
1		12	4	5	3	10	8	9	14	11	2	7	6										9
1		3	4	5	8	12		9	10	11	2	7	6		14								10
1	2	3	4	5	12	14	8	9		11		7	6		10								11
1	2	3	4	5	12		8	9		11		7	6		10	14							12
1	2	3	4	5	6	10	8	9		11		7					12	14					13
1		3	4	5	6	12	8			11	2	7		10	9			14					14
1	2	3	4		6	9	8			11	5	7		10									15
1	2	3	4		6	9	8			11	5	7		10				12					16
1		3	4			7	8	9		11	2			6				5	10	12			17
1	2	3	4			7	8	9		11	5			6			12	14	10				18
1	2	3	4			12	8	9	10	11				6			14	5	7				19
1	2	3	4			12	8	9	10	11		7		6				5					20
1	2	3			6	4	8	9	10	11		7						5	12				21
1	2	3			6	4	8	9	10	11		7			12			5					22
1	2		5		6	4	8	9	10	11		7		3			12						23
1	2		4		6	12	8	9	10	11		7		3				5					24
1	2		4		6	12	8	9	10	11		7		3			14	5					25
1			4		6	3	8	9	10			7		2	12		11	5					26
1	5				6	3	8	9	12		4	7	11	2							10		27
1	2					11	8	10	12		5	7	4	3							9	6	28
1	2		3			12	8	10	14		5	7	4	11							9	6	29
1		3	4		12	8		10			2	7	6	11			14				9	5	30
1		3	4		7	8		10			2		6	11	14		12				9	5	31
1		3			8	11		12			4		6	2	10		7			14	9	5	32
1		3		14	8	7		12			5		4	2	10		11				9	6	33
1	2	3		5	12	11	8				4	7	6		10						9		34
1	2	3	12	5		11	8	14			6	7	4		10						9		35
1	2	3	4			11	8	9	12			7	6				14	5			10		36
1	2	3	4		10	11	8	9				7	6					5			12		37
1	2	3	4		8	11	12	9	10			7	6					5			14		38
1	2	3	4		8	11			10			7	6		12			5			9		39
1	2	3	4		8	11			10	12		7	6		14			5			9		40
1	2	3	4	12		11	14			8		7	6		10			5			9		41
1	2	3		5		11	8		10	6		7			12			4			9		42
1	2	3	4	5		11	8		10	7		12						6			9		43
1	2		4	5		11	8		10	3		7						6			9		44
1	2		4	5	12	11	8		10	3		7						6			9		45
1	2		4	5		11	8	12	10	3		7		14				6			9		46

Coca-Cola Cup

First Round	Gillingham (a)	1-0
	(h)	3-0
Second Round	Derby Co (h)	3-1
	(a)	0-2

FA Cup

Third Round	Oldham Ath (h)	1-3

ROCHDALE 1994–95 *Back row (left to right):* Kevin Formby, Neil Matthews, Paul Butler, Paul Williams, Alan Reeves, Mark Stuart, Steve Doyle.
Centre row: Darren Ryan, Trevor Jones (Youth Coach), Keith Hicks (Youth Coach), Chris Clarke, John Dawson (Physio), Jimmy Robson (Youth Team Manager), Steve Whitehall.
Front row: Jason Peake, Dave Thompson, Andy Thackeray, Mick Docherty (Assistant Manager), Dave Sutton (Manager), Darren Oliver, Shaun Reid, Alex Russell.

Division 3 ROCHDALE

Spotland, Sandy Lane, Rochdale OL11 5DS. Telephone: (01706) 44648. Fax: (01706) 48466. Commercial: (01706) 47521.

Ground capacity: 6655.

Record attendance: 24,231 v Notts Co, FA Cup 2nd rd, 10 December 1949.

Record receipts: £46,000 v Burnley, Division 4, 5 May 1992.

Pitch measurements: 114yd × 76yd.

President: Mrs L. Stoney.

Chairman: D. F. Kilpatrick.

Directors: G. R. Brierley, T. Butterworth, C. Dunphy, M. Mace, J. Marsh, G. Morris.

Manager: Mick Docherty.

Secretary: Keith Clegg. ***Coach:*** Jimmy Robson. ***Commercial Manager:*** S. Walmsley.
Advertising & Sponsorship Manager: L. Duckworth.

Physio: J. Dawson.

Year Formed: 1907. ***Turned Professional:*** 1907. ***Ltd Co.:*** 1910.

Club Nickname: 'The Dale'.

Foundation: Considering the love of rugby in their area, it is not surprising that Rochdale had difficulty in establishing an Association Football club. The earlier Rochdale Town club formed in 1900 went out of existence in 1907 when the present club was immediately established and joined the Manchester League, before graduating to the Lancashire Combination in 1908.

First Football League game: 27 August, 1921, Division 3(N), v Accrington Stanley (h) W 6-3 – Crabtree; Nuttall, Sheehan; Hill, Farrer, Yarwood; Hoad, Sandiford, Dennison (2), Owens (3), Carney (1).

Record League Victory: 8–1 v Chesterfield, Division 3 (N), 18 December 1926 – Hill; Brown, Ward; Hillhouse, Parkes, Braidwood; Hughes, Bertram, Whitehurst (5), Schofield (2), Martin (1).

Record Cup Victory: 8–2 v Crook T, FA Cup, 1st rd, 26 November 1927 – Moody; Hopkins, Ward; Braidwood, Parkes, Barker; Tompkinson, Clennell (3) Whitehurst (4), Hall, Martin (1).

Record Defeat: 0–8 v Wrexham, Division 3 (N), 28 December 1929, 0–8 v Leyton Orient, Division 4, 20 October 1987, and 1–9 v Tranmere R, Division 3 (N), 25 December 1931.

Most League Points (2 for a win): 62, Division 3 (N), 1923–24.

Most League Points (3 for a win): 67, Division 4, 1991–92.

Most League Goals: 105, Division 3 (N), 1926–27.

Highest League Scorer in Season: Albert Whitehurst, 44, Division 3 (N), 1926–27.

Most League Goals in Total Aggregate: Reg Jenkins, 119, 1964–73.

Most Capped Player: None.

Most League Appearances: Graham Smith, 317, 1966–74.

Record Transfer Fee Received: £300,000 from Wimbledon for Alan Reeves, September 1994.

Record Transfer Fee Paid: £80,000 to Scunthorpe U for Andy Flounders, August 1991.

Football League Record: 1921 Elected to Division 3 (N); 1958–59 Division 3; 1959–69 Division 4; 1969–74 Division 3; 1974–92 Division 4; 1992– Division 3.

Football League: Division 3 best season: 9th, 1969–70; Division 3 (N) – Runners-up 1923–24, 1926–27. *FA Cup:* best season: 5th rd, 1990. *Football League Cup:* Runners-up 1962 (record for 4th Division club).

Colours: Blue with red and white chevrons. **Change colours:** White shirts, white shorts, blue stockings.

ROCHDALE 1994–95 LEAGUE RECORD

Match No.	*Date*	*Venue*	*Opponents*	*Result*	*H/T Score*	*Lg. Pos.*	*Goalscorers*	*Attendance*
1	Aug 13	A	Bury	W 1-0	0-0	—	Thompson	3230
2	20	H	Chesterfield	W 4-1	1-0	1	Reid, Thompson, Thackeray, Whitehall	2122
3	27	A	Gillingham	D 1-1	1-0	2	Hall	3015
4	30	H	Lincoln C	W 1-0	1-0	—	Whitehall	1974
5	Sept 3	H	Hereford U	L 1-3	0-1	6	Williams	2258
6	10	A	Northampton T	W 2-1	0-1	4	Reid, Thompson	3052
7	13	A	Barnet	L 2-6	1-4	—	Reid (pen), Williams	1688
8	17	H	Bury	L 0-3	0-0	9		3748
9	24	A	Scarborough	W 4-2	1-1	6	Williams 2, Whitehall, Butler	1200
10	Oct 1	H	Doncaster R	W 2-0	0-0	4	Williams, Peake	2445
11	8	H	Fulham	L 1-2	1-0	6	Whitehall	2573
12	15	A	Wigan Ath	L 0-4	0-4	7		2118
13	22	A	Torquay U	L 1-4	0-1	10	Thackeray	2547
14	29	H	Mansfield T	D 3-3	1-2	10	Butler, Whitehall 2	1968
15	Nov 5	A	Carlisle U	L 1-4	0-1	10	Stuart	5984
16	19	H	Colchester U	D 0-0	0-0	10		1903
17	26	A	Hartlepool U	L 0-1	0-1	12		1387
18	Dec 10	A	Chesterfield	D 2-2	1-2	13	Russell, Whitehall (pen)	2457
19	17	H	Gillingham	W 2-1	2-0	12	Stuart, Valentine	1665
20	26	A	Preston NE	L 0-3	0-3	13		10,491
21	27	H	Walsall	L 0-2	0-1	14		2438
22	31	A	Scunthorpe U	L 1-4	0-2	15	Butler	2653
23	Jan 7	H	Torquay U	W 2-0	0-0	14	Sharpe, Thompson	1636
24	14	A	Exeter C	D 0-0	0-0	14		2316
25	21	H	Carlisle U	D 1-1	0-0	13	Peake	3289
26	Feb 4	H	Hartlepool U	W 1-0	1-0	13	Deary	1848
27	11	A	Colchester U	D 0-0	0-0	13		3080
28	18	H	Exeter C	L 0-1	0-1	13		1945
29	25	A	Doncaster R	W 1-0	1-0	14	Sharpe	2246
30	Mar 7	A	Mansfield T	D 1-1	1-0	—	Whitehall	2931
31	11	H	Northampton T	D 0-0	0-0	15		1894
32	18	A	Lincoln C	D 2-2	0-2	15	Thompson, Valentine	2939
33	21	H	Darlington	W 2-0	0-0	—	Thompson, Whitehall	1471
34	25	A	Hereford U	D 0-0	0-0	13		1954
35	Apr 1	H	Barnet	D 2-2	1-1	14	McDonald (og), Thackeray	1834
36	8	H	Scunthorpe U	L 1-2	1-0	15	Ryan	1720
37	15	A	Walsall	D 0-0	0-0	15		3766
38	17	H	Preston NE	L 0-1	0-1	15		4012
39	22	A	Darlington	L 0-4	0-2	15		1886
40	25	H	Scarborough	D 1-1	0-1	—	Ryan	1170
41	29	H	Wigan Ath	W 1-0	1-0	14	Whitehall (pen)	1949
42	May 6	A	Fulham	L 0-5	0-3	15		4342

Final League Position: 15

GOALSCORERS

League (44): Whitehall 10 (2 pens), Thompson 6, Williams 5, Butler 3, Reid 3 (1 pen), Thackeray 3, Peake 2, Ryan 2, Sharpe 2, Stuart 2, Valentine 2, Deary 1, Hall 1, Russell 1, own goal 1.
Coca-Cola Cup (1): Whitehall 1.
FA Cup (0).

Clarke C.J. 24	Thackeray A.J. 41	Formby K. 27 + 1	Reid S. 27 + 1	Reeves A. 5	Matthews N.P. 10 + 3	Thompson D.S. 38 + 2	Peake J.W. 36 + 3	Bowden J.L. 6 + 5	Whitehall S.C. 41 + 1	Stuart M.R. 26 + 5	Ryan D.T. 15 + 10	Williams P.A. 12 + 2	Doyle S.C. 7 + 4	Butler P.J. 39	Hall D.R. 5 + 4	Rimmer S.A. 3	Russell A. 2 + 5	Dunford N. 2	Dickins M.J. 4	Taylor J.L. 1 + 8	Sharpe R. 9 + 7	Oliver D. 8 + 1	Gray I.J. 12	Valentine P. 27	Whitington C. 1	Martin D. 12 + 3	Deary J.S. 17	Shaw G.P. 4	Bayliss D.A. 1	Match No.
1	2	3	4	5	6	7	8	9	10	11	12																			1
1	2	3	4	5	6	7	*8*		10	11	12	9	14																	2
1	2	3	4	5		7	12		10	11		9		6	8															3
1	2	3	4	5		7	12		10	11		9	14	6	*8*															4
1	2	3	4	5		7	8		10		14	9	12	6		*11*														5
1	2	3	4		5	7	8		12			9	10	6		11														6
1	2	3	4		5	7	8		10			14	11	6	12	*9*														7
1	2	3	4		5	7			10	11		9		6	8															8
1	2	3	4		5	7	12		10	11		9		6	*8*		14													9
	2	3	12			7	8		10	11	14	9	5	6			4	1												10
	2	3	4			12	8		10	*11*	7	9	5	6			14	1												11
	2	3	4			7	8		10	11	12	9	5	6			14		1											12
	2	3	4			7			10		11	9	*5*	6	8				1	12	14									13
	2		4		5	7	8		10	11				6					1	12	9	3								14
	2	3	4		5	12	8		10	9	11			6					1		14	7								15
	2	3	4		5				10	11		9	7	6						12			1	8						16
	2		4		5		7		10	*11*			12	6							14	3	1	8	9					17
	2					7	*8*	9	10		11	12		6	14		4					3	1	5						18
	2					7	8	9	10	*4*	11			6	12					14		3	1	5						19
	2	*3*				7	8	9	10	4	11			6			12					14	1	5						20
	2		4			7	8	9	*10*	11				6			12				14	3	1	5						21
	2		4			7	8	12	*10*	11	14			6							9	3	1	5						22
	2		4			7	8	9	10					6							11	3	1	5						23
	2	3	4		14	7	8		10	12				6							*11*		1	5		9				24
	2	3	4			7	8		10	11				6									1	5		9				25
	2	3	4			7	8		10	*11*				6							14		1	5		12	9			26
	2	*3*	4			7	8		10	12				6							11		1	5		14	9			27
1	2	3	4		14	7	8		10	11				6						12				5			9			28
1	2	3	4		12	7	*8*		10					6	14						11			5			9			29
1	2	3	4			7	8		10	12	14			6							11			5			*9*			30
1	2	3	4			7	8		10	14	12			6							*11*			5			9			31
1	2	3				7	8		10	12	14			6							*9*			5		4	11			32
1	2					7	8		10	3	9			6							12			5		4	11			33
1	2					7	3		10		11			6							12			5		4	8	9		34
1	2					7	3	12	10		11													5		4	8	9	6	35
1	2					7	*3*	12	10		11			6						14				5		4	8	9		36
1	2					7	3	12	10		11			6										5		4	8	9		37
1	2	12				7	3		10	9	11			6										5		4	8			38
1	2	3				7	4	12	10	9	*11*			6										5		14	8			39
1	2					7	3		10	9	11			6						12				5		4	8			40
1	2					7	3		10	9	11			6						12				5		4	8			41
1		2				7	3		10	9	12			6						11				5		4	8			42

Coca-Cola Cup
First Round Mansfield T (h) 1-2
(a) 0-1

FA Cup
First Round Walsall (a) 0-3

ROTHERHAM UNITED 1994–95 *Back row (left to right):* Andy Williams, Tony Brien, Carey Williams, Neil Richardson, Ian Helliwell, Billy Mercer, Matthew Clarke, Nigel Johnson, Ian Breckin, Shaun Goater, Mark Barnard, Martin Pike.
Centre row: Chris Hutchings, Billy Russell, Jonathan Howard, Paul Green, Karl Marginson, Chris Wilder, Martin James, Des Hazel, John Breckin, Ian Bailey.
Front row: Scott Smith, Glynn Roberts, Mark Todd, Imri Varadi, Phil Henson, Chris Dolby, Shaun Goodwin, Paul Hurst, Chris Hilton.

Division 2 ROTHERHAM UNITED

Millmoor Ground, Rotherham S60 1HR. Telephone: (01709) 562434. Fax: (01709) 563336.

Ground Capacity: 11,533.

Record attendance: 25,000 v Sheffield U, Division 2, 13 December 1952 and v Sheffield W, Division 2, 26 January 1952.

Record receipts: £79,155 v Newcastle U, FA Cup 4th rd, 23 January 1993.

Pitch measurements. 115yd × 75yd.

President: Sir J. Layden.

Chairman: K. F. Booth.

Directors: R. Hull (vice-chairman), C. A. Luckock, J. A. Webb. ***Chief Executive:*** Phil Henson.

Joint Managers: Archie Gemmill/John McGovern. ***Assistant Manager/Coach:*** John Breckin. ***Physio:*** Ian Bailey.

Secretary: N. Darnill.

Commercial Manager: D. Nicholls.

Year Formed: 1884. ***Turned Professional:*** 1905. ***Ltd Co.:*** 1920.

Club Nickname: 'The Merry Millers'.

Previous Names: 1884, Thornhill United; 1905, Rotherham County; 1925, amalgamated with Rotherham Town under Rotherham United.

Previous Ground: Red House Ground; 1907, Millmoor.

Foundation: This club traces its history back to the formation of Thornhill United in 1878 (reformed 1884). They changed their name to Rotherham County in 1905. Confusion exists because of the existence of the Rotherham Town club (founded c. 1885) and in the Football League as early as 1893 but this club was not the one previously mentioned. The Town amalgamated with Rotherham County to form Rotherham United in 1925.

First Football League game: 2 September, 1893, Division 2, Rotherham T v Lincoln C (a) D 1-1 – McKay; Thickett, Watson; Barr, Brown, Broadhead; Longden, Cutts, Leatherbarrow, McCormick, Pickering. 1 o.g. 30 August, 1919, Division 2, Rotherham C v Nottingham F (h) W 2-0 – Branston; Alton, Baines; Bailey, Coe, Stanton; Lee (1), Cawley (1), Glennon, Lees, Lamb.

Record League Victory: 8–0 v Oldham Ath, Division 3 (N), 26 May 1947 – Warnes; Selkirk, Ibbotson; Edwards, Horace Williams, Danny Williams; Wilson (2), Shaw (1), Ardron (3), Guest (1), Hainsworth (1).

Record Cup Victory: 6–0 v Spennymoor U, FA Cup, 2nd rd, 17 December 1977 – McAlister; Forrest, Breckin, Womble, Stancliffe, Green, Finney, Phillips (3), Gwyther (2) (Smith), Goodfellow, Crawford (1). 6–0 v Wolverhampton W, FA Cup, 1st rd, 16 November 1985 – O'Hanlon; Forrest, Dungworth, Gooding (1), Smith (1), Pickering, Birch (2), Emerson, Tynan (1), Simmons (1), Pugh.

Record Defeat: 1–11 v Bradford C, Division 3 (N), 25 August 1928.

Most League Points (2 for a win): 71, Division 3 (N), 1950–51.

Most League Points (3 for a win): 82, Division 4, 1988–89.

Most League Goals: 114, Division 3 (N), 1946–47.

Highest League Scorer in Season: Wally Ardron, 38, Division 3 (N), 1946–47.

Most League Goals in Total Aggregate: Gladstone Guest, 130, 1946–56.

Most Capped Player: Harold Millership, 6, Wales.

Most League Appearances: Danny Williams, 459, 1946–62.

Record Transfer Fee Received: £200,000 from Bristol C for Martin Scott, December 1990.

Record Transfer Fee Paid: £110,000 to Wolverhampton W for Paul Blades, July 1995.

Football League Record: 1893 Rotherham Town elected to Division 2; 1896 Failed re-election; 1919 Rotherham County elected to Division 2; 1923–51 Division 3 (N); 1951–68 Division 2; 1968–73 Division 3; 1973–75 Division 4; 1975–81 Division 3; 1981–83 Division 2; 1983–88 Division 3; 1988–89 Division 4; 1989–91 Division 3; 1991–92 Division 4; 1992– Division 2.

Honours: *Football League:* Division 2 best season: 3rd, 1954–55 (equal points with champions and runners-up); Division 3 – Champions 1980–81; Division 3 (N) – Champions 1950–51; Runners-up 1946–47, 1947–48, 1948–49; Division 4 – Champions 1988–89; Runners-up 1991–92. *FA Cup:* best season: 5th rd, 1953, 1968. *Football League Cup:* Runners-up 1961.

Colours: Red and white. **Change colours:** White shirts with black sleeves, black shorts, black stockings.

ROTHERHAM UNITED 1994–95 LEAGUE RECORD

Match No.	Date	Venue	Opponents	Result	H/T Score	Lg. Pos.	Goalscorers	Attendance
1	Aug 13	H	Shrewsbury T	L 0-4	0-3	—		3762
2	20	A	Crewe Alex	L 1-3	0-2	23	Varadi	3505
3	27	H	Bournemouth	W 4-0	0-0	16	Goater 2, Hayward, Morris (og)	2306
4	30	A	Brentford	L 0-2	0-1	—		4031
5	Sept 3	A	Cambridge U	L 1-2	0-1	20	Goater	2885
6	10	H	Bristol R	L 0-3	0-3	20		2596
7	13	H	Birmingham C	D 1-1	1-0	—	Hazel	3799
8	17	A	Hull C	W 2-0	2-0	20	Goodwin, Goater	4431
9	24	A	Peterborough U	D 2-2	2-1	18	Goodwin, Goater	4894
10	Oct 1	H	Blackpool	L 0-2	0-2	20		3517
11	8	A	Stockport Co	L 0-1	0-0	21		4991
12	15	H	York C	W 2-1	2-0	21	Goater, Goodwin	3380
13	22	H	Leyton Orient	W 2-0	1-0	18	Marginson (pen), Goater	2700
14	29	A	Brighton & HA	D 1-1	1-0	18	Davison	6734
15	Nov 1	A	Swansea C	L 0-1	0-0	—		2511
16	5	H	Plymouth Arg	W 3-1	1-0	16	Goater 2, Varadi	2848
17	19	A	Oxford U	L 1-2	1-2	16	Helliwell	5801
18	26	H	Chester C	W 2-0	0-0	16	Goater 2 (1 pen)	2947
19	Dec 10	H	Crewe Alex	D 2-2	0-2	16	McGlashan, Hayward	2907
20	16	A	Shrewsbury T	L 0-1	0-1	—		3243
21	26	H	Bradford C	W 3-1	3-0	16	Roscoe, Goater (pen), Davison	5400
22	27	A	Huddersfield T	L 0-1	0-1	17		15,557
23	31	H	Cardiff C	W 2-0	1-0	16	Monington, Breckin	3064
24	Jan 7	A	Leyton Orient	D 0-0	0-0	17		2796
25	14	H	Wycombe W	W 2-0	1-0	15	Brown (og), Hayward	3537
26	21	A	Plymouth Arg	D 0-0	0-0	15		5484
27	Feb 4	A	Chester C	D 4-4	2-3	15	Monington, McGlashan 2, Wilder	1794
28	11	H	Swansea C	D 3-3	3-2	15	Roscoe, Hayward, Davison	2858
29	18	A	Wycombe W	L 0-2	0-0	16		5153
30	21	H	Oxford U	D 1-1	0-1	—	Goater	2833
31	25	A	Blackpool	D 2-2	1-1	17	Davison, Goater	5043
32	Mar 4	H	Peterborough U	D 0-0	0-0	17		3123
33	7	H	Cambridge U	W 1-0	1-0	—	Goater	2208
34	11	A	Bournemouth	D 1-1	0-0	17	Goater	5666
35	14	A	Wrexham	L 1-3	1-1	—	Goater	1823
36	18	H	Brentford	L 0-2	0-2	18		2968
37	22	A	Bristol R	L 0-2	0-0	—		4420
38	25	H	Hull C	W 2-0	1-0	18	Peel, Roscoe	3692
39	28	H	Brighton & HA	W 4-3	3-1	—	Breckin, Peel, Roscoe, Goater	2316
40	Apr 1	A	Birmingham C	L 1-2	1-0	17	Goater (pen)	16,077
41	8	A	Cardiff C	D 1-1	0-1	17	Peel	6412
42	15	H	Huddersfield T	D 1-1	0-0	17	Hayward	6687
43	17	A	Bradford C	W 3-0	2-0	17	Farrelly, Hayward, Peel	3535
44	22	H	Wrexham	L 0-1	0-0	17		2628
45	29	A	York C	L 0-2	0-0	17		3183
46	May 6	H	Stockport Co	W 1-0	0-0	17	Farrelly	3469

Final League Position: 17

GOALSCORERS

League (57): Goater 19 (3 pens), Hayward 6, Davison 4, Peel 4, Roscoe 4, Goodwin 3, McGlashan 3, Breckin 2, Farrelly 2, Monington 2, Varadi 2, Hazel 1, Helliwell 1, Marginson 1 (pen), Wilder 1, own goals 2.
Coca-Cola Cup (2): Hayward 1, Varadi 1.
FA Cup (8): Davison 3, Goater 3, Helliwell 1, Hurst 1.

Clarke M.J. 45	Smith S.D. 3 + 1	Hurst P.M. 8 + 5	Wilder C.J. 45	Breckin I. 41	Richardson N.T. 23 + 2	Hazel D.L. 16 + 5	Goodwin S.L. 10	Goater L.S. 45	Varadi I. 6 + 11	James M.J. 40	Brien A.J. 16 + 1	Mercer W. 1	Williams A. 17	Helliwell I. 10 + 2	Hayward A. 33 + 4	Williams C. — + 2	Pike M.R. 7	Foran M.J. 3	Todd M.K. 12 + 2	Dolby C.J. — + 2	Roberts G.S. — + 2	Marginson K.K. 5 + 3	Davison R. 19 + 2	Roscoe A.R. 31	McGlashan J. 27	Monington M.D. 25	Farrelly G. 9 + 1	Peel N.J. 9	*Match No.*
1	2	3	4	5	6	7	8	9	10	11	12																		1
			2		6	7	8	*11*	10	3	5	1	4	9	12	14													2
1			2			7		8		11			4	10	9		3	5	6	12									3
1			2			7		8		11			4	10	9		3	5	6	12									4
1			2			7		8	12	11			4	10	*9*		3	5	6		14								5
1			2	5		7		8		11			4	10	9		3		6										6
1			2	5		7	8	10			6		4	9			3		11		12								7
1			2	5		7	8	10		3	6		4	9					11										8
1			2	5		7	8	10		3	6		4	9					11										9
1			2	5		7	8	10	12	3	6		4	9					11										10
1			2	5			8	10		7	6		4			12	3		11			9							11
1			2	5		7	8	10		11	6		4		12		3						9						12
1			2	5			8	10	12	3	6		4		7							11	9						13
1			2	5			*8*	10	12	3	6		4		7							14	9	11					14
1			2	5				10	9	3	6		4		7							8		11					15
1		12	2	5				10	9	3	6		4		7							8		11					16
1	7		2	5	12			10	9	3	6		4	*8*	14									11					17
1		14	2	5	8			10	12	3	6		*4*		7								9	11					18
1		11	2		4			10		3	6				7								9		8	5			19
1		11	2	6	4			10		3					7								9		8	5			20
1		12	2	6	4			10		3				14	7								*9*	11	8	5			21
1			2	6	4	12		10		3					7								9	11	8	5			22
1		12	2	6	4	14		10		3					7								*9*	11	8	5			23
1			2	6	*4*	10				3				12	7							14	9	11	8	5			24
1			2	6	4	12		10		3					7								9	11	8	5			25
1			2	6	4			10	12	3					7								9	11	8	5			26
1			2	6	4	12		10		3					7								9	11	8	5			27
1			2	6	4	12		10		3					7								9	11	8	5			28
1			2	6	4			10	12	3					7							14	9	11	*8*	5			29
1			2	6	4	7		10		3													9	11	8	5			30
1			2	6	4	7		10		3													9	11	8	5			31
1		12	2	6	4	7		*10*	14	3													9	11	8	5			32
1		3	2	6	4			10	12						7								9	11	8	5			33
1		3	2	6	4			10							7				9					11	8	5			34
1		3	2	6	4			10	12						7				9			8		11		5			35
1	2	3		6	4	7		10	*9*						12				14					11	8	5			36
1		3	2	6	4			10	12						*7*				9					11	8	5	14		37
1			2	6				10		3					7									11	8	5	4	9	38
1			2	6				10		3	5				7									11	8		4	9	39
1			2	6				10		3					7				12					11	8	5	4	9	40
1			2	6				10		3	5				7									11	8		4	9	41
1			2	6				10		3					7									11	8	5	4	9	42
1			2	6	12			*10*		3					7								14	11	8	5	4	9	43
1			2	6				10		3					7								12	11	8	5	4	9	44
1	12		2	6	5			10		3					7									11	8		4	9	45
1			2	6				10		3					7									11	8	5	4	9	46

Coca-Cola Cup

First Round	Carlisle U (h)		1-0
	(a)		1-3

FA Cup

First Round	York C (a)		3-3
	(h)		3-0
Second Round	Wrexham (a)		2-5

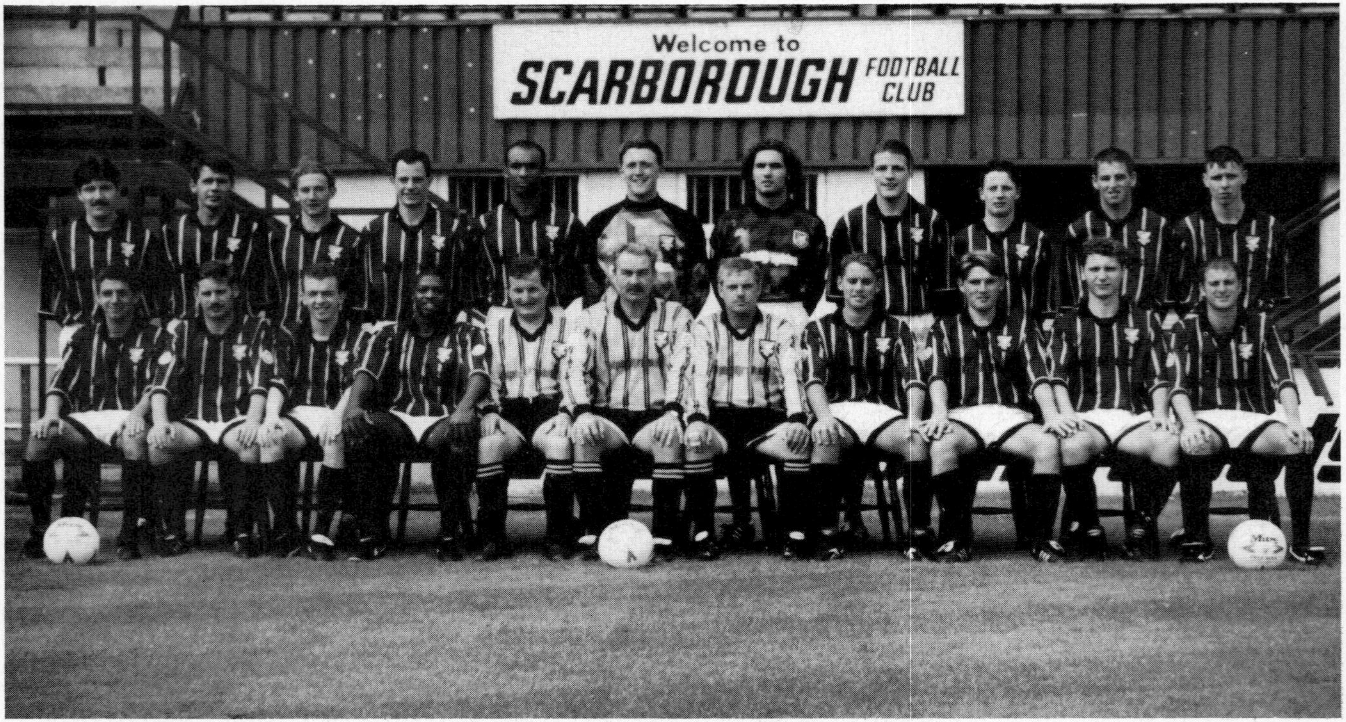

SCARBOROUGH 1994–95 *Back row (left to right):* Gary Swann, Andy Toman, Stephen Swales, Steve Charles, Jason Rockett, Gavin Kelly, Stuart Ford, Adrian Meyer, Alex Willgrass, Lee Harper, Andrew Hudson.
Front row: Mark Wells, Darren Knowles, Michael McHugh, Jason White, John Murray (Physio), Billy Ayre (Manager), Phil Chambers (Assistant Manager), Mark Calvert, Simon Thompson, Stuart Young, Darren Foreman.

Division 3 SCARBOROUGH

The McCain Stadium, Seamer Road, Scarborough YO12 4HF. Telephone: (01723) 375094. Fax: (01723) 378733.

Ground capacity: 6899.

Record Attendance: 11,130 v Luton T, FA Cup 3rd rd, 8 January 1938. Football League: 7314 v Wolverhampton W, Division 4, 15 August 1987.

Record receipts: £37,609.50 v Arsenal, Coca-Cola Cup 4th rd, 6 January 1993.

Pitch measurements: 114yd × 74yd.

President and Chief Executive: John Birley.

Chairman: J. Russell.

Directors: Mrs G. Russell.

Manager: Ray McHale. ***Assistant Manager:*** Phil Chambers.

Secretary: Eric V. Hall. ***Physio:*** J. Murray.

Year Formed: 1879. ***Turned Professional:*** 1926. ***Ltd Co.:*** 1933.

Club Nickname: 'The Boro'.

Previous Grounds: 1879–87, Scarborough Cricket Ground; 1887–98, Recreation Ground; 1898– Athletic Ground.

Foundation: Scarborough came into being as early as 1879 when they were formed by members of the town's cricket club and went under the name of Scarborough Cricketers' FC with home games played on the North Marine Road Cricket Ground.

First Football League game: 15 August, 1987, Division 4, v Wolverhampton W (h) D 2-2 – Blackwell; McJannet, Thompson, Bennyworth, Richards, Kendall, Hamill, Moss, McHale (1), Mell (1), Graham.

Record League Victory: 4–0 v Bolton W, Division 4, 29 August 1987 – Blackwell; McJannet, Thompson, Bennyworth (Walker), Richards (1) (Cook), Kendall, Hamill (1), Moss, McHale, Mell (1), Graham. (1 og). 4–0 v Newport Co (away), Division 4, 12 April 1988 – Ironside; McJannet, Thompson, Kamara, Richards (1), Short (1), Adams (Cook 1), Brook, Outhart (1), Russell, Graham.

Record Cup Victory: 6–0 v Rhyl Ath, FA Cup, 1st rd, 29 November 1930 – Turner; Severn, Belton; Maskell, Robinson, Wallis; Small (1), Rand (2), Palfreman (2), A. D. Hill (1), Mickman.

Record Defeat: 1–16 v Southbank, Northern League, 15 November 1919.

Most League Points (3 for a win): 77, Division 4, 1988–89.

Most League Goals: 69, Division 4, 1990–91.

Highest League Scorer in Season: Darren Foreman, 27, Division 4, 1992–93.

Most League Goals in Total Aggregate: Darren Foreman, 35, 1991–95.

Most Capped Player: None.

Most League Appearances: Steve Richards, 119, 1987–90.

Record Transfer Fee Received: £240,000 from Notts Co for Chris Short, September 1990.

Record Transfer Fee Paid: £102,000 to Leicester C for Martin Russell, March 1989.

Football League Record: Promoted to Division 4 1987; 1992– Division 3.

Honours: *Football League:* Division 4 best season: 5th, 1988–89. *FA Cup:* best seasons: 3rd rd, 1931, 1938, 1976, 1978, 1995. *Football League Cup:* best season: 4th rd 1993. *FA Trophy:* Winners 1973, 1976, 1977. *GM Vauxhall Conference:* Winners 1986–87.

Colours: Red and white. **Change colours:** Yellow and black.

SCARBOROUGH 1994–95 LEAGUE RECORD

Match No.	Date		Venue	Opponents	Result		H/T Score	Lg. Pos.	Goalscorers	Attendance
1	Aug	13	A	Chesterfield	W	1-0	1-0	—	Charles (pen)	3099
2		20	H	Barnet	L	0-1	0-0	15		1471
3		27	A	Carlisle U	L	0-2	0-2	16		5720
4		30	H	Hereford U	W	3-1	1-0	—	Foreman, Rowe, White	1490
5	Sept	3	H	Colchester U	L	0-1	0-0	13		1494
6		10	A	Gillingham	L	1-3	0-1	16	Calvert	2414
7		13	A	Fulham	W	2-1	2-1	—	Swann, D'Auria	2729
8		17	H	Chesterfield	L	0-1	0-1	14		1475
9		24	H	Rochdale	L	2-4	1-1	16	Charles (pen), White	1200
10	Oct	1	A	Wigan Ath	D	1-1	1-1	16	Charles (pen)	1403
11		8	A	Walsall	L	1-4	1-1	19	White	3601
12		15	H	Doncaster R	D	2-2	2-0	18	Rutherford, Swann	1641
13		22	A	Lincoln C	L	0-2	0-1	21		2396
14		29	H	Northampton T	D	0-0	0-0	21		1468
15	Nov	5	A	Bury	L	0-1	0-0	21		3016
16		19	H	Torquay U	D	1-1	1-0	20	White	1241
17		26	A	Exeter C	L	2-5	1-2	22	Young, D'Auria	2179
18	Dec	10	A	Barnet	L	1-3	0-0	22	White	1988
19		17	H	Carlisle U	L	1-2	1-1	22	Rodwell	1910
20		26	A	Darlington	L	0-1	0-1	22		2958
21		27	H	Mansfield T	L	2-5	1-2	22	Griffiths, Thompson	1926
22		31	A	Preston NE	L	0-0	0-0	22		8407
23	Jan	14	A	Hartlepool U	D	3-3	1-0	22	Norris 2 (1 pen), D'Auria	1784
24		28	A	Northampton T	W	3-0	0-0	22	Swann, Norris, D'Auria	5737
25	Feb	4	H	Exeter C	L	0-2	0-1	22		1512
26		7	H	Lincoln C	D	1-1	0-1	—	D'Auria	1217
27		18	H	Hartlepool U	D	2-2	1-1	22	Norris, Wells	1517
28		25	H	Wigan Ath	L	0-1	0-1	22		1416
29		28	H	Scunthorpe U	W	3-0	0-0	—	Trebble, Swales, D'Auria	1179
30	Mar	7	A	Torquay U	L	1-2	1-1	—	White	1492
31		11	H	Gillingham	D	0-0	0-0	22		1949
32		18	A	Hereford U	L	1-2	0-0	22	White	1479
33		21	H	Bury	L	1-2	1-1	—	White	1744
34		25	A	Colchester U	W	2-0	0-0	22	Charles, Trebble	3025
35	Apr	1	H	Fulham	W	3-1	0-0	22	White, D'Auria, Scott	2050
36		8	H	Preston NE	D	1-1	1-1	22	Charles	4266
37		15	A	Mansfield T	L	2-3	2-2	22	White 2	2931
38		18	H	Darlington	W	3-1	1-0	—	Davis, Scott 2	2182
39		22	A	Scunthorpe U	L	1-3	0-1	22	Trebble	2079
40		25	A	Rochdale	D	1-1	1-0	—	Davis	1170
41		29	A	Doncaster R	L	0-1	0-0	21		1710
42	May	2	H	Walsall	L	1-2	0-0	—	Calvert	2841

Final League Position: 21

GOALSCORERS

League (49): White 11, D'Auria 7, Charles 5 (3 pens), Norris 4 (1 pen), Scott 3, Swann 3, Trebble 3, Calvert 2, Davis 2, Foreman 1, Griffiths 1, Rodwell 1, Rowe 1, Rutherford 1, Swales 1, Thompson 1, Wells 1, Young 1.
Coca-Cola Cup (5): Blackstone 2, Charles 1 (pen), Rowe 1, Young 1.
FA Cup (3): Swann 1, Toman 1, White 1.

Kelly G.J. 24	Knowles D.T. 39	Charles S. 40	Calvert M.R. 26 + 4	Meyer A.M. 13	Rockett J. 27	Rowe R.C. 10 + 4	Swann G. 24 + 3	Young S.R. 7 + 6	White J.G. 36 + 3	Blackstone I.K. 11 + 2	Thompson S.L. 14 + 2	Foreman D. 10 + 4	Dunphy S. 10	D'Auria D. 31 + 3	Rutherford P. 6 + 2	Toman J.A. 9 + 7	Davis D.J. 22 + 1	Swales S.C. 21	Ford S.T. 6	Wells M.A. 16 + 2	Martin K. 3	Rodwell A. 6 + 2	Griffiths B.K. 5	Norris S.M. 8	Mardenborough S.A. — + 1	Hicks S.J. 6	Trebble N.D. 15	Scott R. 8	Ironside I. 9	Match No.
1	2	3	4	5	6	7	8	9	10	11																				1
1	2	3	4	5	6	7	8	9		11	10	12																		2
1	2	3	4		6	7	8	12	10	11		9	5	14																3
1	2	3	7		6	12	8	14	10	11		*9*	5	4																4
1	2	3	12		6	7	8	14	10	11		*9*	5	4																5
1		3	7		6	12	8		10	11	2		5	4	9															6
1		3	7		6	9	8		10	11	2		5	4		12														7
1		3	7		*6*	9	8	12	10	11	2		5	4		14														8
1	2	9	4	6		7		11	8		3	10	5																	9
1	2	8	4			7	12			*9*	3	10	5	11	14		6													10
1	*2*		4			12	8	7	9		3			11	10	14	6	5												11
1	2	8				12	4	7	9		3			11	10		6	5												12
	2	8	12				4	7	9	14	3			11			6	*5*	1	10										13
	2	8				7	4		12	9			5		10		6	3	1	11										14
	2	8			4	9	7	12	14				5		10		6	*3*		11	1									15
	2	8	*11*		6		7	12	9					14	10	4	5	3			1									16
	2	8			6		7	10	9					12	14	*4*	5	3		11	1									17
	2	8		5			7		9	12				11			6		1	3		4	10							18
	2	8		5	6		7		9		14			11		12			1	3		4	*10*							19
	2	3	*4*	5	6		10		9		12					14			1			*7*	11	8						20
	2	3		5	6		10		9		7					4			1				11	8						21
1	2	3		5	6		10		9		7					4	12						11	8						22
1	2	3		5			10		9		7			4			6			11				8						23
1	2	3		5			10		9		*7*	12		4		14	6			11				8						24
1	2	3	12	5			10		9			*7*		4		14	6			11				8						25
1	2	3	4	5					9					10		7	6			11				8	12					26
1	2	3	4		6		12		14	*9*				7		10	5			11				8						27
1	2	3	4		6		12		9		*7*	14		8						11						5	10			28
1	2				6		4		9			7		8				3		11						5	10			29
1	2	3			6				9			*7*		8				4		11						5	10			30
1	2	3	12		6				9			*7*		8				4		11		14				5	10			31
1	2	3	11		6				9					8				4				7				5	10			32
1	2	3	11		6				9			12		8				4		14		7				*5*	10			33
	2	4	11	5	6				9					8				3		12							10	7	1	34
	2	4	11		6				9					8			5	3									10	7	1	35
	2	4	11		6				9					8			5	3									10	7	1	36
	2	4	11						9					8		6	5	3									10	7	1	37
	2	4	11						9					8		6	5	3									10	7	1	38
	2	4	11						9					8		6	5	3									10	7	1	39
	2	4	11		6				9					8			5	3									10	7	1	40
	2	4	11		6				9					8			5	3				12					10	7	1	41
	2	4	11									9		8			5	3		6		7					10		1	42

Coca-Cola Cup

First Round	Hull C (a)	1-2
	(h)	2-0
Second Round	Middlesbrough (h)	1-4
	(a)	1-4

FA Cup

First Round	Chesterfield (a)	0-0
	(h)	2-0
Second Round	Port Vale (h)	1-0
Third Round	Watford (h)	0-0
	(a)	0-2

SCUNTHORPE UNITED 1994–95 *Back row (left to right):* Ian Juryeff, Damian Henderson, Christian Sansam, Timothy Ryan, Wayne Bullimore, Steven Housham.
Centre row: Ian Whyte (Youth Development Officer), Christopher Hope, Russell Bradley, Mark Samways, Alan Knill, Michael Heath, Ian Thompstone, Matthew Carmichael.
Front row (left to right): Dean Martin, Paul Mudd, Graham Alexander, David Moore (Manager), Tony Ford, Stephen Thornber, Mark Smith, Samuel Goodacre.

Division 3 SCUNTHORPE UNITED

Glanford Park, Scunthorpe, South Humberside DN15 8TD. Telephone: (01724) 848077. Fax: (01724) 857986.

Ground capacity: 9183.

Record attendance: Old Showground: 23,935 v Portsmouth, FA Cup 4th rd, 30 January 1954. Glanford Park: 8775 v Rotherham U, Division 4, 1 May 1989.

Record receipts: £44,481.50 v Leeds U, Rumbelows Cup 2nd rd lst leg, 24 September 1991.

Pitch measurements: 110yd × 71yd.

Vice-Presidents: I. T. Botham, G. Johnson, A. Harvey, G. J. Alston, R. Ashman.

Chairman: K. Wagstaff.

Vice-Chairman: R. Garton.

Directors: J. B. Borrill, C. Plumtree, S. Wharton, B. Collen, J. A. C. Godfrey.

Team Manager: David Moore. ***Physio:*** D. Moore.

Chief Executive/Secretary: A. D. Rowing. ***Commercial Manager:*** A. D. Rowing.

Year Formed:1899. ***Turned Professional:*** 1912. ***Ltd Co.:*** 1912.

Club Nickname: 'The Iron'.

Previous Names: Amalgamated with Brumby Hall: North Lindsey United to become Scunthorpe & Lindsey United, 1910; dropped '& Lindsey' in 1958.

Previous ground: Old Showground to 1988.

Foundation: The year of foundation for Scunthorpe United has often been quoted as 1910, but the club can trace its history back to 1899 when Brumby Hall FC, who played on the Old Showground, consolidated their position by amalgamating with some other clubs and changing their name to Scunthorpe United. The year 1910 was when that club amalgamated with North Lindsey United as Scunthorpe and Lindsey United. The link is Mr. W. T. Lockwood whose chairmanship covers both years.

First Football League game: 19 August, 1950, Division 3(N), v Shrewsbury T (h) D 0-0 – Thompson; Barker, Brownsword; Allen, Taylor, McCormick; Mosby, Payne, Gorin, Rees, Boyes.

Record League Victory: 8–1 v Luton T, Division 3, 24 April 1965 – Sidebottom; Horstead, Hemstead; Smith, Neale, Lindsey; Bramley (1), Scott, Thomas (5), Mahy (1), Wilson (1).

Record Cup Victory: 9–0 v Boston U, FA Cup, 1st rd, 21 November 1953 – Malan; Hubbard, Brownsword; Sharpe, White, Bushby; Mosby (1), Haigh (3), Whitfield (2), Gregory (1), Mervyn Jones (2).

Record Defeat: 0–8 v Carlisle U, Division 3 (N), 25 December 1952.

Most League Points (2 for a win): 66, Division 3 (N), 1956–57, 1957–58.

Most League Points (3 for a win): 83, Division 4, 1982–83.

Most League Goals: 88, Division 3 (N), 1957–58.

Highest League Scorer in Season: Barrie Thomas, 31, Division 2, 1961–62.

Most League Goals in Total Aggregate: Steve Cammack, 110, 1979–81, 1981–86.

Most Capped Player: None.

Most League Appearances: Jack Brownsword, 595, 1950–65.

Record Transfer Fee Received: £350,000 from Aston Villa for Neil Cox, February 1991.

Record Transfer Fee Paid: £80,000 to York City for Ian Helliwell, August 1991.

Football League Record: 1950 Elected to Division 3 (N); 1958–64 Division 2; 1964–68 Division 3; 1968–72 Division 4; 1972–73 Division 3; 1973–83 Division 4; 1983–84 Division 3; 1984–92 Division 4; 1992– Division 3.

Honours: *Football League:* Division 2 best season: 4th, 1961–62; Division 3 (N) – Champions 1957–58. *FA Cup:* best season: 5th rd, 1958, 1970. *Football League Cup:* never past 3rd rd.

Colours: White shirts, claret and blue trim collar and sleeves, sky blue shorts, claret and white trim, sky blue stockings with claret and white trim. **Change colours:** Red with green, yellow and claret flashes.

SCUNTHORPE UNITED 1994–95 LEAGUE RECORD

Match No.	Date	Venue	Opponents	Result	H/T Score	Lg. Pos.	Goalscorers	Attendance
1	Aug 13	A	Barnet	W 2-1	2-0	—	Henderson, Juryeff	2208
2	20	H	Fulham	L 1-2	1-1	12	Juryeff	3165
3	27	H	Northampton T	D 1-1	1-1	11	Bradley	2499
4	30	H	Gillingham	W 3-0	0-0	—	Thornber, Henderson, Smith	2098
5	Sept 3	H	Carlisle U	L 2-3	2-0	10	Juryeff, Thornber	3217
6	10	A	Bury	L 0-2	0-1	11		2540
7	13	A	Darlington	W 3-1	2-1	—	Bullimore, Ford, Alexander	2181
8	17	H	Barnet	W 1-0	0-0	8	Juryeff	2481
9	24	H	Wigan Ath	W 3-1	1-0	5	Thornber, Alexander, Bullimore (pen)	2602
10	Oct 1	A	Hereford U	L 1-2	1-1	6	Bradley	2267
11	8	A	Preston NE	W 1-0	0-0	7	Alexander	6895
12	15	H	Walsall	L 0-1	0-1	8		3609
13	22	A	Exeter C	D 2-2	1-1	8	Henderson, Juryeff	2511
14	29	H	Hartlepool U	D 0-0	0-0	8		2624
15	Nov 5	A	Torquay U	D 1-1	0-1	9	Juryeff	3036
16	19	H	Mansfield T	L 3-4	1-0	9	Bullimore, Nicholson, Juryeff	2975
17	26	A	Colchester U	L 2-4	0-2	9	Thornber, Knill	2904
18	Dec 10	A	Fulham	L 0-1	0-1	12		3358
19	16	A	Northampton T	W 1-0	1-0	—	Knill	3845
20	26	H	Lincoln C	W 2-0	0-0	11	Juryeff, Eyre	4785
21	27	A	Doncaster R	D 1-1	0-1	10	Carmichael	3852
22	31	H	Rochdale	W 4-1	2-0	9	Mudd, Bullimore (pen), Eyre, Thompstone	2653
23	Jan 7	H	Exeter C	W 3-0	2-0	8	Eyre 2, Alexander	2463
24	14	A	Chesterfield	L 1-3	0-3	11	Bullimore (pen)	3245
25	21	H	Torquay U	W 3-2	2-2	8	Smith, Eyre, Carmichael	2229
26	28	A	Hartlepool U	W 4-1	1-0	5	Knill, Young, Thornber, Eyre	1660
27	Feb 4	H	Colchester U	L 3-4	3-2	6	Eyre 2, Bullimore	2748
28	18	H	Chesterfield	L 0-1	0-0	10		3566
29	21	A	Mansfield T	L 0-1	0-0	—		3079
30	25	H	Hereford U	W 1-0	1-0	8	Nicholson	2193
31	28	A	Scarborough	L 0-3	0-0	—		1179
32	Mar 11	H	Bury	W 3-2	1-1	8	Gregory 2, Hughes (og)	2767
33	18	A	Gillingham	D 2-2	1-0	9	Young, Turnbull	2459
34	25	A	Carlisle U	L 1-2	0-0	10	Kiwomya	6704
35	Apr 1	H	Darlington	W 2-1	1-1	8	Gregory 2	2449
36	4	A	Wigan Ath	D 0-0	0-0	—		1307
37	8	A	Rochdale	W 2-1	0-1	7	Turnbull, Kiwomya	1720
38	15	H	Doncaster R	L 0-5	0-3	9		4366
39	17	A	Lincoln C	D 3-3	2-2	9	Turnbull, Gregory, Nicholson	3330
40	22	H	Scarborough	W 3-1	1-0	7	Gregory, Nicholson, Kiwomya	2079
41	29	A	Walsall	L 1-2	0-0	8	Gregory	4539
42	May 6	H	Preston NE	W 2-1	2-1	7	Ford, Knill	3691

Final League Position: 7

GOALSCORERS

League (68): Eyre 8, Juryeff 8, Gregory 7, Bullimore 6 (3 pens), Thornber 5, Alexander 4, Knill 4, Nicholson 4, Henderson 3, Kiwomya 3, Turnbull 3, Bradley 2, Carmichael 2, Ford 2, Smith 2, Young 2, Mudd 1, Thompstone 1, own goal 1.
Coca-Cola Cup (2): Bullimore 1, Henderson 1.
FA Cup (5): Alexander 1, Bullimore 1, Carmichael 1, Hope 1, Thompstone 1.

Samways M. 42	Ford T. 38	Mudd P.A. 35	Thornber S.J. 36 + 1	Knill A.R. 39	Bradley R. 24 + 1	Alexander G. 38 + 2	Bullimore W.A. 34 + 1	Juryeff I.M. 21	Henderson D.M. 16 + 1	Smith M.C. 24 + 8	Carmichael M. 9 + 11	Goodacre S.D. 1 + 4	Hope C.J. 22 + 2	Martin D.S. — + 5	Thompstone I.P. 8 + 11	Nicholson M. 14 + 1	Sansam C. 4 + 2	Eyre J.R. 9	Young S.R. 12 + 2	Eli R. — + 2	Turnbull L.M. 10	Gregory N.R. 10	Kiwomya A.D. 9	Housham S.J. 4	Walsh M.S. 3	*Match No.*
1	2	3	4	5	6	7	8	9	10	11																1
1	2	3	4	5	6	7	8	9	*10*	11	12	14														2
1	2	3	4		6	7	*8*	9	10	11	12		5	14												3
1	2	3	4	5	6	7	8		10	11		9		12												4
1	2	3	4	5	6	7	8	*9*	10	11		14		12												5
1	4	3		5	6	7	8	9	10	11	2															6
1	4	3		5	6	7	8	9	10	11	2			12												7
1	2	3	4	5	6	7	8	9	10	11																8
1	2	3	4	5	6	7	8	9	10	11																9
1	2	3	*4*	5	6	7	8	9	10	11			12	14												10
1	2	3	4	5	6	7	8	9	10				11													11
1	2	3	4	5	6	7	8	9	*10*	12			11		14											12
1	2	3	4	*5*	6	7		9	10	11		12	8		14											13
1	2	3	4	5	6	7		*9*	10	11	12	14	8													14
1	2	3	4	5	6	7		9	10	11	12		8													15
1	4	3		5	6	7	8	9					2			11	10									16
1	2	3	4	5		7	8	9			6		12		14	11	*10*									17
1	2	3	4	5	6	7	8	9	*10*	11	12				14											18
1	2	3	4	5	6	7	8	*9*		11	12						14	10								19
1	2	3	4	5	6	7	8	*9*		11	12				14			10								20
1	2	3	4	5	6	7	8	*9*		11	12				14			10								21
1	2	3	4		6	7	8			11	5				12			10	9							22
1	2	3	4		6	7	8			11	5							10	9							23
1	2	3	4	5	6	7	8			11	12				14			10	*9*							24
1	2	3	4	5	6	7	8			11	12							10	9							25
1	2	3	4	5		7	8			*11*	6				12	14		10	9							26
1	2	3	4	5		7	8			12	6				14	11		*10*	9							27
1	2		4	5		7		10			6		3		8	11			9	12						28
1	2		4	5		7				12	6		3		8	11	*10*		9	14						29
1	2	3	4	5		7	8				12		6		10	11			9							30
1	2	3	4	5		7	11		12	14			6		9	10			*8*							31
1	2	3	4	5						12			6		7	11			9		8	10				32
1	2	3	4	5		7	12			14			6			11			*9*		8	10				33
1	2	3	4	5		7	9						6								8	10	11			34
1	2	3	4	5		7	9						6		12						8	10	11			35
1		3	4	5		7	9						6		2						8	10	11			36
1		3	4	5		7				12			6		2	*9*			14		8	10	11			37
1			4	5	14	7	9			3			6		*2*				12		8	10	11			38
1				5		7	4			3			6			9					8	10	11	2		39
1	7		4	5			8			12			6			9						10	11	2	3	40
1	7			5		12	8						6			9	14				4	10	11	*2*	3	41
1	7		12	5		14	8						6			9	*10*				4		11	2	3	42

Coca-Cola Cup

First Round	Huddersfield T	(h)	2-1
		(a)	0-3

FA Cup

First Round	Bradford C	(a)	1-1
		(h)	3-2
Second Round	Birmingham C	(a)	0-0
		(h)	1-2

SHEFFIELD UNITED 1994–95 *Back row (left to right):* Rob Scott, David Tuttle, Doug Hodgson, Jostein Flo, Alan Kelly, Billy Mercer, Mark Foran, Brian Gayle, Paul Beesley, Paul Rogers.
Centre row: Derek French (Physio), Tony Battersby, Roger Nilsen, Ash Fickling, Carl Veart, Simon Tracey, Glyn Hodges, Charlie Hartfield, Nathan Blake, Andy Scott, Geoff Taylor (Assistant Manager).
Front row: John Gannon, Kevin Gage, Mitch Ward, Dave Bassett (Manager), Dane Whitehouse, John Reed, Adrian Littlejohn.

Division 1 **SHEFFIELD UNITED**

Bramall Lane Ground, Sheffield S2 4SU. Telephone: (0114) 2738955. Fax: (0114) 2723030. Ticket Office: (0114) 2766771. Pools Office: (0114) 2727901. Club Shop: (0114) 2750596. Community Scheme: (0114) 2769314. Executive Suite: (0114) 2755277. Ticket info line: 0891 332950.

Ground capacity: 23,459.

Record attendance: 68,287 v Leeds U, FA Cup 5th rd, 15 February 1936.

Record receipts: £261,758 v Manchester U, FA Cup 5th rd, 14 February 1993.

Pitch measurements: 112yd × 72yd.

Chairman: R. L. Brealey.

Directors: A. H. Laver, D. Dooley, B. Proctor, J. A. Plant JP.

Team Manager: Dave Bassett. ***Assistant Manager:*** Geoff Taylor. ***Coaches:*** Brian Eastick, Wally Downes. ***Youth Coach:*** Keith Mincher.

Physios: Derek French, Denis Circuit.

Secretary: D. Capper AFA. ***Commercial Manager:*** Andy R. Daykin.

Youth Development Officer: John Dungworth.

Community Programme Organiser: Tony Currie, Tel: (0114) 2769314.

Year Formed: 1889. ***Turned Professional:*** 1889. ***Ltd Co.:*** 1899.

Club Nickname: 'The Blades'.

Foundation: In March 1889, Yorkshire County Cricket Club formed Sheffield United six days after an FA Cup semi-final between Preston North End and West Bromwich Albion had finally convinced Charles Stokes, a member of the cricket club, that the formation of a professional football club would prove successful at Bramall Lane. The United's first secretary, Mr. J. B. Wostinholm was also secretary of the cricket club.

First Football League game: 3 September, 1892, Division 2, v Lincoln C (h) W 4-2 – Lilley; Witham, Cain; Howell, Hendry, Needham (1); Wallace, Dobson, Hammond (3), Davies, Drummond.

Record League Victory: 10–0 v Burslem Port Vale (away), Division 2, 10 December 1892 – Howlett; Witham, Lilley; Howell, Hendry, Needham; Drummond (1), Wallace (1), Hammond (4), Davies (2), Watson (2).

Record Cup Victory: 5–0 v Newcastle U (away), FA Cup, 1st rd, 10 January 1914 – Gough; Cook, English; Brelsford, Howley, Sturgess; Simmons (2), Gillespie (1), Kitchen (1), Fazackerley, Revill (1). 5–0 v Corinthians, FA Cup, 1st rd, 10 January 1925 – Sutcliffe; Cook, Milton; Longworth, King, Green; Partridge, Boyle (1), Johnson 4), Gillespie, Tunstall. 5–0 v Barrow, FA Cup, 3rd rd, 7 January 1956 – Burgin; Coldwell, Mason; Fountain, Johnson, Iley; Hawksworth (1), Hoyland (2), Howitt, Wragg (1), Grainger (1).

Record Defeat: 0–13 v Bolton W, FA Cup 2nd rd, 1 February 1890.

Most League Points (2 for a win): 60, Division 2, 1952–53.

Most League Points (3 for a win): 96, Division 4, 1981–82.

Most League Goals: 102, Division 1, 1925–26.

Highest League Scorer in Season: Jimmy Dunne, 41, Division 1, 1930–31.

Most League Goals in Total Aggregate: Harry Johnson, 205, 1919–30.

Most Capped Player: Billy Gillespie, 25, Northern Ireland.

Most League Appearances: Joe Shaw, 629, 1948–66.

Record Transfer Fee Received: £2,700,000 from Leeds U for Brian Deane, July 1993.

Record Transfer Fee Paid: £700,000 to Ipswich T for Brian Gayle, September 1991.

Football League Record: 1892 Elected to Division 2; 1893–1934 Division 1; 1934–39 Division 2; 1946–49 Division 1; 1949–53 Division 2; 1953–56 Division 1; 1956–61 Division 2; 1961–68 Division 1; 1968–71 Division 2; 1971–76 Division 1; 1976–79 Division 2; 1979–81 Division 3; 1981–82 Division 4; 1982–84 Division 3; 1984–88 Division 2; 1988–89 Division 3; 1989–90 Division 2; 1990–92 Division 1; 1992–94 FA Premier League; 1994– Division 1.

Honours: *Football League:* Division 1 – Champions 1897–98; Runners-up 1896–97, 1899–1900; Division 2 – Champions 1952–53; Runners-up 1892–93, 1938–39, 1960–61, 1970–71, 1989–90; Division 4 – Champions 1981–82. *FA Cup:* Winners 1899, 1902, 1915, 1925; Runners-up 1901, 1936. *Football League Cup:* best season: 5th rd, 1962, 1967, 1972.

Colours: Broad red, thin white striped shirts with large white diamond overlay, black shorts with red/white trim, black stockings with red/white trim. **Change colours:** Purple and yellow halved shirts with matching trim, yellow shorts with purple trim, yellow stockings with purple trim.

SHEFFIELD UNITED 1994–95 LEAGUE RECORD

Match No.	Date		Venue	Opponents	Result		H/T Score	Lg. Pos.	Goalscorers	Attendance
1	Aug	13	H	Watford	W	3-0	2-0	—	Flo, Ward 2	16,820
2		27	H	Notts Co	L	1-3	0-2	15	Whitehouse (pen)	15,301
3		30	A	Charlton Ath	D	1-1	1-1	—	Rogers	8678
4	Sept	3	A	Tranmere R	L	1-2	0-2	18	Hodges (pen)	7253
5		10	H	Bolton W	W	3-1	1-0	14	Veart 2, Davison	14,116
6		13	H	Sunderland	D	0-0	0-0	—		15,239
7		17	A	Reading	L	0-1	0-0	20		9036
8		24	A	Port Vale	W	2-0	0-0	13	Blake, Whitehouse (pen)	9324
9	Oct	1	H	Oldham Ath	W	2-0	1-0	9	Reed, Flo	14,223
10		8	A	Grimsby T	D	0-0	0-0	10		8930
11		16	H	Barnsley	D	0-0	0-0	13		12,317
12		18	A	WBA	L	0-1	0-0	—		12,713
13		22	H	Luton T	L	1-3	1-1	17	Blake	13,317
14		29	A	Millwall	L	1-2	0-0	19	Blake	8445
15	Nov	2	A	Stoke C	D	1-1	1-0	—	Gage	11,556
16		5	H	Bristol C	W	3-0	2-0	15	Hartfield, Gage, Whitehouse	11,568
17		12	H	Derby Co	W	2-1	0-0	9	Blake, Whitehouse	15,001
18		20	A	Burnley	L	2-4	1-1	12	Winstanley (og), Scott A	11,475
19		26	H	Southend U	W	2-0	1-0	10	Whitehouse (pen), Veart	13,405
20	Dec	3	A	Luton T	W	6-3	2-0	6	Gage 2, Veart 2, Hodges, Scott A	8516
21		10	H	WBA	W	2-0	1-0	7	Veart, Scott A	13,891
22		17	A	Watford	D	0-0	0-0	7		8919
23		26	H	Middlesbrough	D	1-1	0-0	7	Hodges	20,693
24		27	A	Swindon T	W	3-1	1-0	6	Reed, Bodin (og), Littlejohn	11,007
25		31	H	Portsmouth	W	3-1	0-1	5	Blake 2, Scott A	13,467
26	Jan	2	A	Wolverhampton W	D	2-2	0-0	5	Blake 2	27,809
27		14	H	Millwall	D	1-1	0-1	5	Gage	12,650
28		21	A	Bristol C	L	1-2	0-0	6	Gayle	10,211
29	Feb	4	A	Derby Co	W	3-2	1-1	6	Veart 2, Whitehouse	15,882
30		11	H	Stoke C	D	1-1	1-1	7	Starbuck	13,900
31		18	A	Southend U	W	3-1	1-1	6	Blake 2, Veart	4700
32		21	H	Burnley	W	2-0	1-0	—	Blake 2	13,349
33		25	A	Oldham Ath	D	3-3	2-2	4	Rogers, Blake, Flo	9640
34	Mar	4	H	Port Vale	D	1-1	0-0	6	Veart	13,647
35		7	H	Tranmere R	W	2-0	1-0	—	Black, Blake	14,127
36		11	A	Notts Co	L	1-2	0-1	5	Beesley	11,102
37		18	H	Charlton Ath	W	2-1	0-0	4	Flo, Beesley	11,862
38		22	A	Bolton W	D	1-1	1-1	—	Blake	16,756
39		25	H	Reading	D	1-1	0-0	6	Blake	19,241
40	Apr	1	A	Sunderland	L	0-1	0-0	6		17,259
41		8	A	Portsmouth	L	0-1	0-0	7		8216
42		15	H	Swindon T	D	2-2	0-1	7	Rogers, Hodges	12,217
43		17	A	Middlesbrough	D	1-1	1-1	8	Blake	23,225
44		22	H	Wolverhampton W	D	3-3	1-0	8	Whitehouse (pen), Foran, Flo	16,714
45		29	A	Barnsley	L	1-2	1-1	8	Rogers	10,844
46	May	6	H	Grimsby T	W	3-1	2-1	8	Whitehouse, Black, Flo	14,323

Final League Position: 8

GOALSCORERS

League (74): Blake 17, Veart 10, Whitehouse 8 (4 pens), Flo 6, Gage 5, Hodges 4 (1 pen), Rogers 4, Scott A 4, Beesley 2, Black 2, Reed 2, Ward 2, Davison 1, Foran 1, Gayle 1, Hartfield 1, Littlejohn 1, Starbuck 1, own goals 2.
Coca-Cola Cup (7): Whitehouse 3 (1 pen), Flo 2, Blake 1, Scott A 1.
FA Cup (0).

Kelly A.T. 38	Gage K.W. 40	Nilsen R. 33	Rogers P.A. 44	Gayle B.W. 35	Beesley P. 26 + 1	Ward M.D. 10 + 4	Flo J. 25 + 7	Blake N.A. 28 + 7	Hodges G.P. 20 + 5	Whitehouse D.L. 35 + 4	Littlejohn A.S. 9 + 7	Hartfield C.J. 23 + 2	Tracey S.P. 5	Marshall S.R. 17	Veart C. 30 + 9	Davison R. 1 + 2	Reed J.P. 11 + 1	Scott A. 18 + 19	Gannon J.S. 12	Hoyland J.W. — + 2	Hodgson D.J.H. — + 1	Starbuck P.M. 20 + 3	Mercer W. 3	Scott R. — + 1	Blount M. 4 + 1	Foran M.J. 4	Anthony G.J. — + 1	Black K. 8 + 3	Tuttle D.P. 6	Davidson R. 1	Match No.
1	2	3	4	5	6	7	8	9	*10*	11	12	14																			1
	2	3	4	5		7	8	9	10	11	12		1	6	14																2
	2	3	4	5		7	8	9	10	11			1	6	12																3
	2	3	4	5			12		10		11	*8*	1	6	7	9	14														4
	2	3	6	4				9	10	*11*			1	5	8	12	7	14													5
	2	3	4	5				9	10	11			1	6	8	14	*7*	12													6
1	2	3	4	5				9		*11*				6	8		7	12	10	14											7
1	2	3	4	5			10	12		11	*9*			6			7		8	14											8
1	2		4	5		12	10	14		11	*9*			6			7	3	8												9
1	2		4	5			10	12		11	9			6	14		7	3	8												10
1	2		4	5			10	9		11		12		6	14		7	3	8												11
1	2		4	5		7	*10*	12		11	9			6	14			3	8												12
1	2		4	5			*10*	9		11	12			6			7	3	8		14										13
1	2	3		5				9		11	10	4		6	8		7					12									14
1	2	3	7		5			10		11		4		6	8			12				9									15
1	2	3	7	5				*10*	14	11		4		6	8			12				9									16
	2	3	7	5				10	14	*11*		4		6	8			12				9	1								17
1	2	3	7	5			10		12	11		4		6	*8*			14				9									18
1	2	3	7	5	6		14		*10*	11		4			8			12				9									19
1	2	3	7	5	6	12	14		10			4			8			*11*				9									20
1	2	3	7	5	6			12	10	14		*4*			8			11				9									21
1	2	3	7	5	6			12	*10*	14		4			8			11				9									22
1	2	3	7	5	6				10	9		4			8			11				12									23
1	2		7	5	6		9				10	4					11	3				8		12							24
1	2	3	7	5				11	10	12		4			8			6				9									25
1	2	6	7	5				12	10	3		4			8			11				9									26
1	2	3	7	5	6				10	12	14	4			8			11				*9*									27
	2	3	7	5	12		14		10	6		4			8			*11*				9	1								28
		3	7	5	6	2	10			11	12				8			14	4			*9*	1								29
1		*3*	7	5	6	2	10			11	12				8			14	4			9									30
1			7		6	2	10	11							8			12	4			9			3	5					31
1	2		7		6	9	10	11							8			5	*4*			12			3		14				32
1	2		7	5	6	12	10	11		*9*					8			14	4						3						33
1	2		7	5	6	12	14	11		3		4			*8*							9						10			34
1	2		7	5	6	8	9	11		3		4													12			10			35
1	2		7	5	6	8	9	11		3		4			12													10			36
1	2	3	7	5	6		9	11		4					12		8	14										*10*			37
1	2	3	7	5	6		12	10		9	14	4			*8*			11													38
1	2		7		6		*9*	10		3		4			12			14				8						11	5		39
1	2	3	7		6			10	12	*9*		4			8			14										11	5		40
1	2	3			6		10		12		9	4			8			14				*7*						11	5		41
1	2	3	7		6		9	11	10	5								12				*8*			4			14			42
1	2	3	7				9	11	10	4					8			12								6			5		43
1		3	7		2		12	11	10	*4*					8			9								6		14	5		44
1		3	7		6		4	11	10		9				8			2								5		12			45
1		3	4		6		8	9	10	*11*					12			14										7	5	2	46

Coca-Cola Cup

Second Round	Stockport Co (a)	5-1
	(h)	1-0
Third Round	Bolton W (h)	1-2

FA Cup

Third Round	Manchester U (h)	0-2

SHEFFIELD WEDNESDAY 1994–95 *Back row (left to right):* Ryan Jones, Brian Linighan, Chris Woods, Simon Coleman, Andy Pearce, Kevin Pressman, Julian Watts, Mark Bright.
Centre row: Richie Barker (Assistant Manager), Chris Waddle, Gordon Watson, John Sheridan, Lee Briscoe, Chris Bart-Williams, Adem Poric, Michael Williams, Ian Taylor, Dave Galley (Physio).
Front row: Ian Nolan, Dan Petrescu, Graham Hyde, Des Walker, Trevor Francis (Manager), David Hirst, Andy Sinton, Peter Atherton, Nigel Jemson.

FA Premiership **SHEFFIELD WEDNESDAY**

Hillsborough, Sheffield, S6 1SW. Telephone: (0114) 2343122. Fax: (0114) 2337145. Ticket Office: (0114) 2337233. Clubcall: 0891 121186.

Ground capacity: 36,020.

Record attendance: 72,841 v Manchester C, FA Cup 5th rd, 17 February 1934.

Record receipts: £533,918 Sunderland v Norwich C, FA Cup semi-final, 5 April 1992.

Pitch measurements: 115yd × 77yd.

Chairman: D. G. Richards. ***Vice-Chairman:*** K. T. Addy.

Directors: G. K. Hulley, R. M. Grierson FCA, J. Ashton MP, G. A. Thorpe.

Manager: David Pleat. ***Assistant Manager:*** Danny Bergara.

Physio: David Galley.

Secretary: Graham Mackrell FCCA. ***Commercial Manager:*** Sean O'Toole.

Year Formed: 1867 (fifth oldest League club).

Turned Professional: 1887. ***Ltd Co.:*** 1899.

Former Names: The Wednesday until 1929.

Club Nickname: 'The Owls'.

Previous Grounds: 1867, Highfield; 1869, Myrtle Road; 1877, Sheaf House; 1887, Olive Grove; 1899, Owlerton (since 1912 known as Hillsborough). Some games were played at Endcliffe in the 1880s. Until 1895 Bramall Lane was used for some games.

Foundation: Sheffield, being one of the principal centres of early Association Football, this club was formed as long ago as 1867 by the Sheffield Wednesday Cricket Club (formed 1825) and their colours from the start were blue and white. The inaugural meeting was held at the Adelphi Hotel and the original committee included Charles Stokes who was subsequently a founder member of Sheffield United.

First Football League game: 3 September, 1892, Division 1, v Notts C (a) W 1-0 – Allan; T. Brandon (1), Mumford; Hall, Betts, H. Brandon; Spiksley, Brady, Davis, R.N. Brown, Dunlop.

Record League Victory: 9–1 v Birmingham, Division 1, 13 December 1930 – Brown; Walker, Blenkinsop; Strange, Leach, Wilson; Hooper (3), Seed (2), Ball (2), Burgess (1), Rimmer (1).

Record Cup Victory: 12–0 v Halliwell, FA Cup, 1st rd, 17 January 1891 – Smith; Thompson, Brayshaw; Harry Brandon (1), Betts, Cawley (2); Winterbottom, Mumford (2), Bob Brandon (1), Woolhouse (5), Ingram (1).

Record Defeat: 0–10 v Aston Villa, Division 1, 5 October 1912.

Most League Points (2 for a win): 62, Division 2, 1958–59.

Most League Points (3 for a win): 88, Division 2, 1983–84.

Most League Goals: 106, Division 2, 1958–59.

Highest League Scorer in Season: Derek Dooley, 46, Division 2, 1951–52.

Most League Goals in Total Aggregate: Andy Wilson, 199, 1900–20.

Most Capped Player: Nigel Worthington, 50 (58), Northern Ireland.

Most League Appearances: Andy Wilson, 502, 1900–20.

Record Transfer Fee Received: £2,650,000 from Blackburn R for Paul Warhurst, September 1993.

Record Transfer Fee Paid: £2,750,000 to Sampdoria for Des Walker, July 1993 and £2,750,000 to QPR for Andy Sinton, August 1993.

Football League Record: 1892 Elected to Division 1; 1899–1900 Division 2; 1900–20 Division 1; 1920–26 Division 2; 1926–37 Division 1; 1937–50 Division 2; 1950–51 Division 1; 1951–52 Division 2; 1952–55 Division 1; 1955–56 Division 2; 1956–58 Division 1; 1958–59 Division 2; 1959–70 Division 1; 1970–75 Division 2; 1975–80 Division 3; 1980–84 Division 2; 1984–90 Division 1; 1990–91 Division 2; 1991–92 Division 1; 1992– FA Premier League.

Honours: *Football League:* Division 1 – Champions 1902–03, 1903–04, 1928–29, 1929–30; Runners-up 1960–61; Division 2 – Champions 1899–1900, 1925–26, 1951–52, 1955–56, 1958–59; Runners-up 1949–50, 1983–84. *FA Cup:* Winners 1896, 1907, 1935; Runners-up 1890, 1966, 1993. *Football League Cup:* Winners 1991; Runners-up 1993. **European Competitions:** *Fairs Cup:* 1961–62, 1963–64, 1992–93.

Colours: Blue and white striped shirts, blue shorts, blue stockings. **Change colours:** All black with yellow and grey trim.

SHEFFIELD WEDNESDAY 1994–95 LEAGUE RECORD

Match No.	Date	Venue	Opponents	Result	H/T Score	Lg. Pos.	Goalscorers	Attendance
1	Aug 20	H	Tottenham H	L 3-4	0-2	—	Petrescu, Calderwood (og), Hirst	34,051
2	24	A	QPR	L 2-3	1-1	—	Sheridan, Hyde	12,788
3	27	A	Wimbledon	W 1-0	0-0	13	Watson	7453
4	31	H	Norwich C	D 0-0	0-0	—		25,072
5	Sept 10	A	Nottingham F	L 1-4	0-1	15	Hyde	22,022
6	17	H	Manchester C	D 1-1	0-1	16	Watson	26,585
7	26	H	Leeds U	D 1-1	1-1	—	Bright	23,227
8	Oct 1	A	Liverpool	L 1-4	1-0	19	Nolan	31,493
9	8	H	Manchester U	W 1-0	1-0	16	Hirst	32,616
10	16	A	Ipswich T	W 2-1	1-0	13	Bright, Hirst	12,825
11	22	A	Newcastle U	L 1-2	0-2	14	Taylor	34,369
12	29	H	Chelsea	D 1-1	0-1	15	Bright	25,356
13	Nov 2	H	Blackburn R	L 0-1	0-0	—		24,207
14	6	A	Arsenal	D 0-0	0-0	16		33,705
15	19	H	West Ham U	W 1-0	1-0	16	Petrescu	25,300
16	27	A	Aston Villa	D 1-1	0-1	15	Atherton	25,082
17	Dec 3	H	Crystal Palace	W 1-0	1-0	14	Bart-Williams	21,930
18	10	A	Tottenham H	L 1-3	1-0	15	Nolan	25,912
19	17	H	QPR	L 0-2	0-0	18		23,288
20	26	A	Everton	W 4-1	2-1	15	Bright, Ingesson, Whittingham 2	37,089
21	28	H	Coventry C	W 5-1	3-1	13	Bright 2, Waddle, Whittingham 2	26,056
22	31	A	Leicester C	W 1-0	1-0	9	Hyde	20,624
23	Jan 2	H	Southampton	D 1-1	1-0	10	Hyde	28,424
24	14	A	Chelsea	D 1-1	0-1	10	Nolan	17,285
25	21	H	Newcastle U	D 0-0	0-0	9		31,215
26	23	A	West Ham U	W 2-0	1-0	—	Waddle, Bright	14,554
27	Feb 4	H	Arsenal	W 3-1	2-1	8	Petrescu, Ingesson, Bright	23,468
28	12	A	Blackburn R	L 1-3	1-2	8	Waddle	22,223
29	18	H	Aston Villa	L 1-2	0-2	8	Bright	24,063
30	25	H	Liverpool	L 1-2	1-1	9	Bart-Williams	31,964
31	Mar 4	A	Leeds U	W 1-0	1-0	8	Waddle	33,774
32	8	A	Norwich C	D 0-0	0-0	—		13,530
33	11	H	Wimbledon	L 0-1	0-0	8		20,395
34	14	A	Crystal Palace	L 1-2	1-0	—	Whittingham	10,964
35	18	A	Manchester C	L 2-3	2-1	9	Whittingham, Hyde	23,355
36	Apr 1	H	Nottingham F	L 1-7	0-2	11	Bright (pen)	30,060
37	8	H	Leicester C	W 1-0	1-0	10	Whittingham	22,551
38	15	A	Coventry C	L 0-2	0-1	11		15,733
39	17	H	Everton	D 0-0	0-0	13		27,880
40	29	A	Southampton	D 0-0	0-0	14		15,189
41	May 7	A	Manchester U	L 0-1	0-1	14		43,868
42	14	H	Ipswich T	W 4-1	1-0	13	Whittingham 2, Williams, Bright	30,307

Final League Position: 13

GOALSCORERS

League (49): Bright 11 (1 pen), Whittingham 9, Hyde 5, Waddle 4, Hirst 3, Nolan 3, Petrescu 3, Bart-Williams 2, Ingesson 2, Watson 2, Atherton 1, Sheridan 1, Taylor 1, Williams 1, own goal 1.
Coca-Cola Cup (4): Bart-Williams 2, Hyde 1, Taylor 1.
FA Cup (3): Bright 2, Waddle 1.

Pressman K.P. 34	Petrescu D. 20 + 9	Nolan I.R. 42	Taylor I.K. 9 + 5	Atherton P. 41	Walker D.S. 38	Sheridan J.J. 34 + 2	Bart-Williams C.G. 32 + 6	Hirst D.E. 13 + 2	Bright M.A. 33 + 4	Sinton A. 22 + 3	Watson G.W.G. 5 + 18	Hyde G. 33 + 2	Jones R.A. 3 + 2	Pearce A.J. 34	Coleman S. 1	Ingesson K. 9 + 4	Briscoe L.S. 6	Waddle C.R. 20 + 5	Whittingham G. 16 + 5	Poric A. 1 + 3	Woods C.C. 8 + 1	Williams M.A. 8 + 2	Donaldson O'.M. — + 1	Match No.
1	2	3	4	5	6	7	8	9	10	11	12													1
1	2	3	4	5	6	7	12	9		*11*	10	8	14											2
1	*8*	3	4	2	6	11	10	9			12	14	7	5										3
1	8	3	*4*	2	6	7	14	9	10	11	12			5										4
1	4	3		2		7	14	9		11	12	8		5	6	10								5
1	2	3		4		7	6	9	10	*11*	12	8		5		14								6
1	2	3	14	5	6	7	4	12	10	*11*	9	8												7
1	2	3		5	6	7	4	12	10	11	9	8												8
1		3	14	2	6	7	*4*	9	10		12	8		5			11							9
1		3	14	2	6	7	*4*	9	10	12		8		5			11							10
1	12	3	4	2	6	7	14	*9*	10	11		8		5										11
1	12	3	4	2	6	7	10		9	11	14	8		5										12
1	12	3	4	2	6	7	*10*		9	11	14	8		5										13
1	12	3	4	2	6	7	10		9	*11*	14	8		5										14
1	4	3	12	2	6	7	*10*		9	11	14	8		5										15
1	4	3	12	2	6	7	10			11	9	8		5										16
1	4	3	6	2		7	10		9	11		8		5				12						17
1		2		4		7	6		9	11		10		5			3	8						18
1	12	3		2	6	7	4		*9*			10	11	5		14		8						19
1		3		2	6	7	4		9			8		5		11			10	12				20
1		3		2	6	7	4		9		12	8		5		*11*		14	10					21
1	14	3		2	6	7	4		9		12	10		5				*8*	11					22
1	14	3		2	6	7	4		9		12	10		5				*8*	11					23
1	14	2		5	6	7	4		9		12					11	*3*	8	10					24
	2	3		5	6	7	4		12		9					11		8	10		1			25
1	14	3		2	6		4		9		12	7		5		11		*8*	10					26
1	4	3		2	6	12	*10*		9			7		5		11		8	14					27
1	*4*	3		2	6	7	10		9	*11*				5				8	12		15	14		28
1	4	2		5	6	7	12		9	11		10					*3*	8	14					29
1	2	3		5	6	14	4		9	11	12	7						*8*	10					30
	4	3		2	6		7		9	12		10		5				8			1	11		31
		3		2	6		4		9		12	10		5			11	8			1	7		32
1	*4*	3		2	6				9	11		10		5				8	12	14		7		33
1		3		2	6				9	11	14	8	*7*	5				12	10			4		34
1		*3*		2	6	7	4		9			10		5				8	11			12	14	35
1	2	3			6	7	4		9	11		10		5				8	12					36
		3		2	6	7		9	12	14				5		*4*		8	10		1	11		37
	4	3		2	6	7	12	9				8		5		11		14	10		1			38
1		3		2	6	7	4	9	12			*10*		5		14		8	11					39
		3		2	6		4		9				12	5		14		*8*	10	7	1	11		40
		3		2	6	7	4		9			8		5				12	*10*	14	1	11		41
		3		2	6	7		*9*	14	11		12		5				8	10		1	4		42

Coca-Cola Cup

Second Round	Bradford C (h)	2-1
	(a)	1-1
Third Round	Southampton (h)	1-0
Fourth Round	Arsenal (a)	0-2

FA Cup

Third Round	Gillingham (a)	2-1
Fourth Round	Wolverhampton W (h)	0-0
	(a)	1-1

SHREWSBURY TOWN 1994–95 *Back row (left to right):* Fred Davies (Manager), Paul Edwards, Kevin Summerfield, Wayne Clarke, Tommy Lynch, Dean Spink, Mark Hughes, Gary Patterson, Mark Williams, David Walton, Tim Clarke, Malcolm Musgrove (Physio).
Front row: David Hockaday, Kevin Seabury, Nathan King, Paul Evans, Michael Brown, Mark Smith, Mark Taylor, Ian Reed, Joe Gallen, Chris Withe, Ray Woods.

Division 2 SHREWSBURY TOWN

Gay Meadow, Shrewsbury SY2 6AB. Telephone: (01743) 360111. Commercial Dept: (01743) 56316. Clubcall: 0891 121194.

Ground capacity: 7500.

Record attendance: 18,917 v Walsall, Division 3, 26 April 1961.

Record receipts: £36,240 v Ipswich T, FA Cup 5th rd, 13 February 1982.

Pitch measurements: 116yd × 76yd.

Vice-President: Dr J. Millard Bryson.

Chairman: R. Bailey.

Directors: F. C. G. Fry, M. J. Starkey, G. W. Nelson, W. H. Richards, K. R. Woodhouse.

Manager: Fred Davies. ***Commercial Manager:*** M. Thomas.

Physio: Malcolm Musgrove.

Secretary: M. J. Starkey.

Club Nickname: 'Town' or 'Shrews'.

Year Formed: 1886. ***Turned Professional:*** 1905 (approx). ***Ltd Co.:*** 1936.

Previous Ground: Old Shrewsbury Racecourse.

Foundation: Shrewsbury School having provided a number of the early England and Wales internationals it is not surprising that there was a Town club as early as 1876 which won the Birmingham Senior Cup in 1879. However, the present Shrewsbury Town club was formed in 1886 and won the Welsh FA Cup as early as 1891.

First Football League game: 19 August, 1950, Division 3(N), v Scunthorpe U (a) D 0-0 – Eggleston; Fisher, Lewis; Wheatley, Depear, Robinson; Griffin, Hope, Jackson, Brown, Barker.

Record League Victory: 7–0 v Swindon T, Division 3 (S), 6 May 1955 – McBride; Bannister, Keech; Wallace, Maloney, Candlin; Price, O'Donnell (1), Weigh (4), Russell, McCue (2).

Record Cup Victory: 7–1 v Banbury Spencer, FA Cup, 1st rd, 4 November 1961 – Gibson; Walters, Skeech; Wallace, Pountney, Harley; Kenning (2), Pragg, Starkey (1), Rowley (2), McLaughlin (2).

Record Defeat: 1–8 v Norwich C, Division 3 (S), 1952–53 and v Coventry C, Division 3, 22 October 1963.

Most League Points (2 for a win): 62, Division 4, 1974–75.

Most League Points (3 for a win): 79, Division 3, 1993–94.

Most League Goals: 101, Division 4, 1958–59.

Highest League Scorer in Season: Arthur Rowley, 38, Division 4, 1958–59.

Most League Goals in Total Aggregate: Arthur Rowley, 152, 1958–65 (thus completing his League record of 434 goals).

Most Capped Player: Jimmy McLaughlin, 5 (12), Northern Ireland and Bernard McNally, 5, Northern Ireland.

Most League Appearances: Colin Griffin, 406, 1975–89.

Record Transfer Fee Received: £385,000 from WBA for Bernard McNally, July 1989.

Record Transfer Fee Paid: £100,000 to Aldershot for John Dungworth, November 1979 and £100,000 to Southampton for Mark Blake, August 1990.

Football League Record: 1950 Elected to Division 3 (N); 1951–58 Division 3 (S); 1958–59 Division 4; 1959–74 Division 3; 1974–75 Division 4; 1975–79 Division 3; 1979–89 Division 2; 1989–94 Division 3; 1994– Division 2.

Honours: *Football League:* Division 2 best season: 8th, 1983–84, 1984–85; Division 3 – Champions 1978–79, 1993–94; Division 4 – Runners-up 1974–5. *FA Cup:* best season: 6th rd, 1979, 1982. *Football League Cup:* Semi-final 1961. *Welsh Cup:* Winners 1891, 1938, 1977, 1979, 1984, 1985; Runners-up 1931, 1948, 1980.

Colours: Blue shirts, white trim, blue shorts, blue stockings, white trim. **Change colours:** Red shirts, white shorts, red stockings.

SHREWSBURY TOWN 1994–95 LEAGUE RECORD

Match No.	*Date*	*Venue*	*Opponents*	*Result*	*H/T Score*	*Lg. Pos.*	*Goalscorers*	*Attendance*
1	Aug 13	A	Rotherham U	W 4-0	3-0	—	Taylor, Spink 2, Clarke W	3762
2	20	H	Wrexham	D 2-2	1-2	6	Clarke W, Brown	5748
3	27	A	Blackpool	L 1-2	1-0	12	Clarke W (pen)	4428
4	Sept 3	H	Peterborough U	D 2-2	0-2	16	Spink, Clarke W	3879
5	6	H	Swansea C	D 3-3	1-0	—	Clarke W, Currie, Stevens	3534
6	10	A	York C	L 0-3	0-1	18		3196
7	13	A	Stockport Co	L 1-2	0-0	—	Patterson	3473
8	17	H	Leyton Orient	W 3-0	3-0	17	Brown, Clarke W, Currie	3560
9	24	H	Bristol R	W 1-0	1-0	14	Stevens	4596
10	Oct 1	A	Brentford	L 0-1	0-1	15		4556
11	8	H	Bournemouth	W 3-0	1-0	14	Brown, Clarke W 2	3684
12	15	A	Crewe Alex	L 0-1	0-1	15		4296
13	22	H	Hull C	L 2-3	0-2	16	Clarke W, Stevens	3685
14	29	A	Oxford U	D 0-0	0-0	16		6094
15	Nov 1	A	Wycombe W	L 0-1	0-1	—		4620
16	5	H	Birmingham C	L 0-2	0-1	18		5942
17	19	A	Cambridge U	L 1-3	1-1	19	Stevens	2748
18	26	H	Bradford C	L 1-2	0-1	19	Stevens	3776
19	Dec 10	A	Wrexham	W 1-0	0-0	18	Evans	5859
20	16	H	Rotherham U	W 1-0	1-0	—	Walton	3243
21	26	H	Cardiff C	L 0-1	0-0	18		4933
22	27	A	Brighton & HA	L 1-2	1-0	18	Clarke W	7290
23	Jan 2	A	Huddersfield T	L 1-2	1-1	19	Withe	12,748
24	7	A	Hull C	D 2-2	2-0	19	Clarke W, Jeffers	4369
25	14	H	Chester C	W 1-0	0-0	19	Evans	3879
26	28	H	Oxford U	D 1-1	1-1	19	Stevens	3768
27	Feb 4	A	Bradford C	D 1-1	0-1	19	Spink	4817
28	7	H	Plymouth Arg	W 3-2	0-1	—	Spink 2, Withe	3029
29	11	H	Wycombe W	D 2-2	1-0	17	Spink, Taylor	3945
30	18	A	Chester C	W 3-1	1-0	15	Evans (pen), Spink, Walton	2720
31	21	H	Cambridge U	D 1-1	0-1	—	Evans	3200
32	25	H	Brentford	W 2-1	1-1	15	Spink, Lynch	4570
33	Mar 4	A	Bristol R	L 0-4	0-1	15		4338
34	7	A	Peterborough U	D 1-1	0-0	—	Spink	3554
35	11	H	Blackpool	D 0-0	0-0	18		4261
36	17	A	Swansea C	D 0-0	0-0	—		4130
37	21	H	York C	W 1-0	1-0	—	Evans	2849
38	25	A	Leyton Orient	L 1-2	1-1	17	Williams	2724
39	Apr 1	H	Stockport Co	D 1-1	0-1	18	Stevens	3655
40	8	A	Plymouth Arg	L 0-1	0-1	18		5089
41	11	A	Birmingham C	L 0-2	0-1	—		18,366
42	15	H	Brighton & HA	D 1-1	1-1	18	Scott	3597
43	17	A	Cardiff C	W 2-1	1-0	18	Smith, Spink	4677
44	22	H	Huddersfield T	W 2-1	2-0	18	Walton, Stevens	4758
45	29	H	Crewe Alex	L 1-2	1-2	18	Smith	4381
46	May 2	A	Bournemouth	L 0-3	0-3	—		10,737

Final League Position: 18

GOALSCORERS

League (54): Clarke W 11 (1 pen), Spink 11, Stevens 8, Evans 5 (1 pen), Brown 3, Walton 3, Currie 2, Smith 2, Taylor 2, Withe 2, Jeffers 1, Lynch 1, Patterson 1, Scott 1, Williams 1.
Coca-Cola Cup (2): Clarke W 1, Spink 1.
FA Cup (1): Spink 1.

Edwards P. 31	Hockaday D. 16	Lynch T.M. 34	Taylor R.M. 44	Williams M.S. 33 + 2	Patterson G. 17 + 1	Brown M.A. 9	Clarke W. 26 + 5	Spink D.P. 36 + 3	Walton D.L. 36	Woods R.G. 15 + 4	Summerfield K. 14 + 4	Withe C. 27 + 4	Hughes M. 18 + 2	Stevens I.D. 26 + 12	Currie D. 15 + 2	Clarke T.J. 15 + 1	Seabury K. 27 + 3	Evans P.S. 27 + 5	Smith M.A. 10 + 7	Slawson S.M. 6	Harford P. 3 + 3	Simkin D.S. 10 + 2	Jeffers J.J. 3	Scott R.P. 7 + 1	Reed I.P. 1 + 3	*Match No.*
1	2	3	4	5	6	7	8	9	10	11	12															1
1	2	3	4	5	10	7	8	9	6			11														2
1	2	3	4	5	6	7	8	9	10		12	*11*	14													3
1	2	3	4		6		8	9	10	11	7		5	12												4
1	*2*	3	4	14	6		8	9	10	11			5	12	7											5
		3	4	5	6		8	9		*11*		12	10		7	1	2	14								6
		3	4	5	8	*7*		9	10				6	12	11	1	2	14								7
1		3	*4*	5	6	7	8	9	10			2		12	11			14								8
1	2	3	4	5	6	7	8		10					9	11			12								9
1	2	3	4	5	6	7	8		10			12		9	*11*				14							10
1	2	3	4	5	6	7	8		10					9	11				12							11
1		3	4	5	6		8		10					9	11		2	7	12							12
1		3	4	5	6		8	12	10	7				9	11		2									13
1			4	5	6		8		10	7	11	3		9	12		2									14
1		9	4	5	6				10	7	8	3			12		2			11						15
1		3	4	5	6	7		12		14	10		8		*11*		2			9						16
1	2	3	4	5	12			9		7	8		6	10						11						17
1		3	4	5	8			9		7			6	10			2		12	11						18
1	2	*3*	4	5			12	9	10				6	7			14	8		11						19
1	2		8				12	9	4			5	3	10		15	6	7		*11*	14					20
1	2		6				8	9		11		5	3	12			4	10			7					21
1		6	*4*	5			8	9		12	10	3		7				11			14	2				22
1	2		4	5			8	9	10		6	3		7				11			12					23
1	2		4	5			8	9	10	7	6	3		12									11			24
1	2		4	5			8	9	10	7	*6*	3		12				14					11			25
1	2	6		5			8	12		7		3		9				4			10		11			26
1		6	4					9	10			3		7	11		12	8			5	2				27
1		6	4					9	10			3		7	11		12	8	5			2				28
1		6	4					9	10			3		7	11		5	8				2				29
1		6	4				12	9	10			3	14	7	11		5	8				*2*				30
1		6	4					9	10			3		7	11		5	8				2				31
1		6	4					9	10			3	11	7			5	8				2				32
1		6	4	12				9	10		14	3	*11*	7			5	8				2				33
		6	4	5			8	9			11	3		12		1	2	10	7							34
		6	4	5			8	9			11	3	7	12		1	2	10								35
		3	4	5			8	9	10		11		6			1	2	7	12							36
		3	4	5			8		10				7	9		1	2	6	11			12				37
		3	4	5			8	9	10				7	12		1		6	11			*2*		14		38
		3	4	5			8	9	10			12		14		1	2	6	*11*					7		39
		3	4	5			*8*	9	10			12		14		1	2	6	11					7		40
			4	5				9	10	7	12	3	*6*	11		1	2	8	14							41
			4	5				9	10	7		3		8		1	2	*6*	12					11	14	42
			4					9	10		5	3		8		1	2	6	11			12		7	14	43
			4	5				9	10	12		3		7		1	2	6	11					8		44
			4	5			12	9	10			3		8		1	2	6	7					11	14	45
							12	9		14	*10*	3	5			1	2	4	7			6		8	11	46

Coca-Cola Cup
First Round Birmingham C (h) 2-1
(a) 0-2

FA Cup
First Round Burnley (a) 1-2

SOUTHAMPTON 1994–95 *Back row (left to right):* Nicky Banger, Kevin Doherty, Paul McDonald, Derek Allan, Colin Cramb, Matthew Bound, David Hughes, Frankie Bennett, Neal Bartlett, Matthew Robinson, Paul Tisdale, Paul Sheerin.
Centre row: Dave Merrington (Reserve Team Manager), Jason Dodd, Tommy Widdrington, Craig Maskell, Ian Andrews, Richard Hall, Dave Beasant, Ken Monkou, Neil Hopper, Iain Dowie,, Perry Groves, Neil Heaney, Don Taylor (Physio).
Front row: Lew Chatterley (Assistant Manager), Simon Charlton, Jeff Kenna, Neil Maddison, Lawrie McMenemy (Director of Football), Matthew Le Tissier, Alan Ball (Manager), Francis Benali, Jim Magilton, Paul Allen, John Mortimore (Assistant Manager).

FA Premiership **SOUTHAMPTON**

The Dell, Milton Road, Southampton SO9 4XX. Telephone: (01703) 220505. Fax: (01703) 330360. Recorded Ticket Information: (01703) 228575.

Ground capacity: 15,000.

Record attendance: 31,044 v Manchester U, Division 1, 8 October 1969.

Record receipts: £193,229 v Tottenham H, FA Cup 5th rd replay, 1 March 1995.

Pitch measurements: 110yd × 72yd.

Chairman: F. G. L. Askham FCA.

Vice-Chairman: K. St. J. Wiseman.

Directors: I. L. Gordon, B. H. D. Hunt, L. McMenemy, M. R. Richards FCA.

President: J. Corbett. ***Vice-President:*** E. T. Bates. ***Manager:*** Dave Merrington.

Joint Assistant Managers: John Mortimore, Lew Chatterley.

Coach: Lew Chatterley. ***Physio:*** Don Taylor.

Secretary: Brian Truscott.

Year Formed: 1885. ***Turned Professional:*** 1894. ***Ltd Co.:*** 1897.

Club Nickname: 'The Saints'.

Previous Name: Southampton St Mary's until 1885.

Previous Grounds: 1885, Antelope Ground; 1897, County Cricket Ground; 1898, The Dell.

Foundation: Formed largely by players from the Deanery FC, which had been established by school teachers in 1880. Most of the founders were connected with the young men's association of St. Mary's Church. At the inaugural meeting held in November 1885 the club was named Southampton St. Mary's and the church's curate was elected president.

First Football League game: 28 August, 1920, Division 3, v Gillingham (a) D 1-1 – Allen; Parker, Titmuss; Shelley, Campbell, Turner; Barratt, Dominy (1), Rawlings, Moore, Foxall.

Record League Victory: 9–3 v Wolverhampton W, Division 2, 18 September 1965 – Godfrey; Jones, Williams; Walker, Knapp, Huxford; Paine (2), O'Brien (1), Melia, Chivers (4), Sydenham (2).

Record Cup Victory: 7–1 v Ipswich T, FA Cup, 3rd rd, 7 January 1961 – Reynolds; Davies, Traynor; Conner, Page, Huxford; Paine (1), O'Brien (3 incl. 1p), Reeves, Mulgrew (2), Penk (1).

Record Defeat: 0–8 v Tottenham H, Division 2, 28 March 1936 and v Everton, Division 1, 20 November 1971.

Most League Points (2 for a win): 61, Division 3 (S), 1921–22 and Division 3, 1959–60.

Most League Points (3 for a win): 77, Division 1, 1983–84.

Most League Goals: 112, Division 3 (S), 1957–58.

Highest League Scorer in Season: Derek Reeves, 39, Division 3, 1959–60.

Most League Goals in Total Aggregate: Mike Channon, 185, 1966–77, 1979–82.

Most Capped Player: Peter Shilton, 49 (125), England.

Most League Appearances: Terry Paine, 713, 1956–74.

Record Transfer Fee Received: £3,300,000 from Blackburn R for Alan Shearer, July 1992.

Record Transfer Fee Paid: £1,200,000 to Chelsea for Neil Shipperley, January 1995 and to Sheffield W for Gordon Watson, March 1995.

Football League Record: 1920 Original Member of Division 3; 1921–22 Division 3 (S); 1922–53 Division 2; 1953–58 Division 3 (S); 1958–60 Division 3; 1960–66 Division 2; 1966–74 Division 1; 1974–78 Division 2; 1978–92 Division 1; 1992– FA Premier League.

Honours: *Football League:* Division 1 – Runners-up 1983–84; Division 2 – Runners-up 1965–66, 1977–78; Division 3 (S) – Champions 1921–22; Runners-up 1920–21; Division 3 – Champions 1959–60. *FA Cup:* Winners 1976; Runners-up 1900, 1902. *Football League Cup:* Runners-up 1979. *Zenith Data Systems Cup:* Runners-up 1992. **European Competitions:** *European Fairs Cup:* 1969–70. *UEFA Cup:* 1971–72, 1981–82, 1982–83, 1984–85. *European Cup-Winners' Cup:* 1976–77.

Colours: Red and white striped shirts, black shorts, red and white hooped stockings. **Change colours:** Blue and yellow striped shirts, blue shorts, blue and yellow hooped stockings.

SOUTHAMPTON 1994–95 LEAGUE RECORD

Match No.	Date	Venue	Opponents	Result	H/T Score	Lg. Pos.	Goalscorers	Attendance
1	Aug 20	H	Blackburn R	D 1-1	1-0	—	Banger	14,209
2	24	A	Aston Villa	D 1-1	0-1	—	Le Tissier	24,179
3	27	A	Newcastle U	L 1-5	0-3	17	Banger	34,182
4	31	H	Liverpool	L 0-2	0-1	—		15,190
5	Sept 12	A	Tottenham H	W 2-1	0-1	—	Le Tissier 2 (1 pen)	22,387
6	17	H	Nottingham F	D 1-1	0-1	14	Le Tissier (pen)	14,185
7	24	A	Coventry C	W 3-1	1-1	13	Dowie 2, Ekelund	11,798
8	Oct 1	H	Ipswich T	W 3-1	0-0	8	Maddison, Ekelund, Dowie	13,266
9	8	H	Everton	W 2-0	1-0	7	Ekelund, Le Tissier	15,163
10	15	A	Leicester C	L 3-4	0-2	10	Dowie 2, Le Tissier	20,020
11	22	A	West Ham U	L 0-2	0-0	11		18,853
12	29	H	Leeds U	L 1-3	1-0	12	Maddison	15,202
13	Nov 2	H	Norwich C	D 1-1	0-0	—	Le Tissier (pen)	12,876
14	5	A	Manchester C	D 3-3	1-0	12	Hall, Ekelund 2	21,589
15	19	H	Arsenal	W 1-0	0-0	10	Magilton	15,201
16	26	A	Crystal Palace	D 0-0	0-0	11		14,186
17	Dec 3	H	Chelsea	L 0-1	0-0	13		14,404
18	10	A	Blackburn R	L 2-3	0-2	14	Le Tissier 2	23,372
19	19	H	Aston Villa	W 2-1	1-0	—	Hall, Le Tissier	13,874
20	26	H	Wimbledon	L 2-3	2-2	14	Dodd, Le Tissier	14,603
21	28	A	QPR	D 2-2	1-1	14	Dodd, Hughes	16,078
22	31	H	Manchester U	D 2-2	1-0	15	Magilton, Hughes	15,204
23	Jan 2	A	Sheffield W	D 1-1	0-1	15	Le Tissier (pen)	28,424
24	14	A	Leeds U	D 0-0	0-0	14		28,869
25	24	A	Arsenal	D 1-1	0-1	—	Magilton	27,213
26	Feb 4	H	Manchester C	D 2-2	1-1	15	Coton (og), Le Tissier	14,902
27	11	A	Norwich C	D 2-2	2-1	15	Hall, Magilton	18,361
28	25	A	Ipswich T	L 1-2	1-0	18	Maddison	15,788
29	Mar 4	H	Coventry C	D 0-0	0-0	18		14,505
30	15	H	West Ham U	D 1-1	0-1	—	Shipperley	15,178
31	18	A	Nottingham F	L 0-3	0-1	20		24,146
32	22	H	Newcastle U	W 3-1	0-1	—	Heaney, Watson, Shipperley	14,666
33	Apr 2	H	Tottenham H	W 4-3	2-2	17	Heaney, Le Tissier 2, Magilton	15,105
34	5	A	Liverpool	L 1-3	1-1	—	Hall	29,881
35	12	A	Chelsea	W 2-0	2-0	—	Shipperley, Le Tissier	16,739
36	15	H	QPR	W 2-1	0-0	13	Shipperley, Watson	15,210
37	17	A	Wimbledon	W 2-0	2-0	11	Le Tissier, Magilton	10,521
38	29	H	Sheffield W	D 0-0	0-0	11		15,189
39	May 3	H	Crystal Palace	W 3-1	2-1	—	Wilmot (og), Watson, Le Tissier	15,151
40	6	A	Everton	D 0-0	0-0	10		36,851
41	10	A	Manchester U	L 1-2	1-1	—	Charlton	43,479
42	14	H	Leicester C	D 2-2	1-0	10	Monkou, Le Tissier	15,101

Final League Position: 10

GOALSCORERS

League (61): Le Tissier 19 (4 pens), Magilton 6, Dowie 5, Ekelund 5, Hall 4, Shipperley 4, Maddison 3, Watson 3, Banger 2, Dodd 2, Heaney 2, Hughes 2, Charlton 1, Monkou 1, own goals 2.
Coca-Cola Cup (5): Le Tissier 5 (1 pen).
FA Cup (12): Le Tissier 5 (3 pens), Heaney 2, Shipperley 2, Hughes 1, Magilton 1, Monkou 1.

Grobbelaar B.D. 30	Kenna J.J. 28	Benali F.V. 32 + 3	Charlton S.T. 25	Hall R.A. 36 + 1	Widdrington T. 23 + 5	Le Tissier M.P. 41	Magilton J. 42	Banger N.L. 4	Maddison N.S. 35	Allen P.K. 11	Heaney N. 21 + 13	Whiston P. — + 1	Monkou K.J. 31	Dowie I. 17	Ekelund R. 15 + 2	Dodd J.R. 24 + 2	Beasant D. 12 + 1	Hughes D.R. 2 + 10	McDonald P. — + 2	Maskell C.D. 2 + 4	Tisdale P.R. — + 7	Shipperley N.J. 19	Watson G.W.G. 12	Robinson M.R. — + 1	Oakley M. — + 1	Match No.
1	2	3	4	5	6	7	8	9	10	11	12															1
1	2	3	4	5	6	7	8	9	10	11	12															2
1	2	3	4	*5*	6	7	8	9	10	11	12	14														3
1	2	4	3	12		7	8	9	10	11	6		5													4
1	2	4	3	5		7	8		10	11	6			9												5
1	2	4	3	5		7	8		10	11	6			9	12											6
1	2	4	3			7	6		10	11			5	9	8											7
1			3	5		7	4		10	11	12		6	9	8	2										8
1	2	5	3			7	4		10		11		6	9	8		15									9
	2	5	3			7	4		10	11	*12*		6	9	8	14	1									10
	2	12	3	5		7	4		*10*	11			6	9	8		1	14								11
1	2	12	3	5		7	*4*		10	11	14		6	9	8											12
1	2	3		5		7	4		10		11		6	9	8				12							13
1	2	3		5	11	7	4		10		12		*6*	9	8	14										14
1	2	3		5	6	7	4		10		11			9	8											15
1	2	3		5	6	7	4		10		11			9	8											16
1	2	3		5	6	7	4		10		11			9	8											17
1	2	3	4	5	9	7	11		10				6		*8*			12		14						18
1	2	3		5	10	7	4				11		6		8			12		9						19
1	2			5	10	7	4				11		6	9		3		*8*	14	12						20
1	2			5	10	7	4				3		6	9	*8*	11		14		12						21
1	2	3			6	7	4				12		5	9	8	11		10								22
1	*2*	3		5	10	7	4				12		6	9		11				8	14					23
1	2	3		5	4	7	8		10				6			11		12				9				24
1	2	3		*5*	14	7	4		10		11		6			8		12				9				25
1	2	3	4	5		7	8		10		6					11						9				26
1	2			5	4	7	8		10		11		6			3		12				9				27
1	2	5			4	7	8		10		*11*		6			3		12			14	9				28
1	2	3		5		7	8		10		11		6			4				12		9				29
		3		5	4	7	8		*10*		11		6		12	2	1	14				9				30
		3		5	*4*	7	8		10		12		6			2	1	14				9	11			31
1		3	4	5		7	8		10		12		6			2						9	11			32
1			3	5	12	7	4		10		11		6			2						9	8			33
1			3	5	6	7	4		10		11					2					12	9	8			34
			3	5	11	7	4		10				6			2	1				12	9	8			35
		12	3	5	4	7	8				11		6			2	1					9	10			36
		6	4	5	11	7	8				3					2	1				12	9	10			37
		3	*4*	5		7	8		10				6			2	1				12	9	11	14		38
		3	4	5	12	7	8		10				6			2	1				14	*9*	11			39
		3	4	5	11		8		10				6			2	1					9	7		12	40
		3	4	5	14	7	8		10		12		6			2	1					9	11			41
		3	4	5	14	7	8		10		12		6			2	1					*9*	11			42

Coca-Cola Cup

Second Round	Huddersfield T (a)	1-0
	(h)	4-0
Third Round	Sheffield W (a)	0-1

FA Cup

Third Round	Southend U (h)	2-0
Fourth Round	Luton T (a)	1-1
	(h)	6-0
Fifth Round	Tottenham H (a)	1-1
	(h)	2-6

SOUTHEND UNITED 1994–95 *Back row (left to right):* Daniel Foot, Andy Sussex, Andy Edwards, Keith Dublin, Paul Sansome, John Cornwell, Simon Royce, Dominic Iorfa, Mark Hone, Graham Bressington, Phil Gridelet.
Centre row: Danny Greaves, Ijah Anderson, Gary Poole, Steve Tilson, Mick Bodley, Chris Powell, Declan Perkins, Gary Jones, Craig Davidson, Mark Hall, John Gowens.
Front row: Andy Ansah, Andy Thomson, Keith Jones, Theo Foley, Vic Jobson, Peter Taylor, Ricky Otto, Jon Hunt, Jae Martin.

Division 1 SOUTHEND UNITED

Roots Hall Football Ground, Victoria Avenue, Southend-on-Sea SS2 6NQ. Telephone: (01702) 340707. Fax: (01702) 330164. Commercial Dept: (01702) 437154/6. Soccerline: 0839 664444. Ticket Office: (01702) 435602. Infoline: 0839 664443.

Ground capacity: 10,350.

Record attendance: 31,090 v Liverpool FA Cup 3rd rd, 10 January 1979.

Record receipts: £83,999 v West Ham U, Division 1, 7 April 1993.

Pitch measurements: 110yd × 74yd.

President: N. J. Woodcock.

Chairman and Managing Director: V. T. Jobson. ***Vice-Chairman and Chief Executive:*** J. W. Adams.

Secretary: J. W. Adams.

Directors: J. A. Bridge, B. R. Gunner, W. R. Kelleway, C. Wooldridge. ***Associate Directors:*** A. W. Jobson, R. J. Osborne, W. E. Parsons.

Manager: Ronnie Whelan. ***Assistant Manager:*** Theo Foley. ***Youth Team Coach:*** Danny Greaves.

Physio: John Cowens. ***Commercial Manager:*** C. Wooldridge. ***Stadium Manager:*** David Jobson.

Club Nickname: 'The Blues or The Shrimpers'.

Year Formed: 1906. ***Turned Professional:*** 1906. ***Ltd Co.:*** 1919.

Previous Grounds: 1906, Roots Hall, Prittlewell; 1920, Kursaal; 1934, Southend Stadium; 1955, Roots Hall Football Ground.

Foundation: The leading club in Southend around the turn of the century was Southend Athletic, but they were an amateur concern. Southend United was a more ambitious professional club when they were founded in 1906, employing Bob Jack as secretary-manager and immediately joining the Second Division of the Southern League.

First Football League game: 28 August, 1920, Division 3, v Brighton & HA (a) W 2-0 – Capper; Reid, Newton; Wileman, Henderson, Martin; Nicholls, Nuttall, Fairclough (2), Myers, Dorsett.

Record League Victory: 9–2 v Newport Co, Division 3 (S), 5 September 1936 – McKenzie; Nelson, Everest (1); Deacon, Turner, Carr; Bolan, Lane (1), Goddard (4), Dickinson (2), Oswald (1).

Record Cup Victory: 10–1 v Golders Green, FA Cup, 1st rd, 24 November 1934 – Moore; Morfitt, Kelly; Mackay, Joe Wilson, Carr (1); Lane (1), Johnson (5), Cheesmuir (2), Deacon (1), Oswald. 10–1 v Brentwood, FA Cup, 2nd rd, 7 December 1968 – Roberts; Bentley, Birks; McMillan (1) Beesley, Kurila; Clayton, Chisnall, Moore (4), Best (5), Hamilton. 10–1 v Aldershot, Leyland Daf Cup, Pr rd, 6 November 1990 – Sansome; Austin, Powell, Cornwell, Prior (1), Tilson (3), Cawley, Butler, Ansah (1), Benjamin (1), Angell (4).

Record Defeat: 1–9 v Brighton & HA, Division 3, 27 November 1965.

Most League Points (2 for a win): 67, Division 4, 1980–81.

Most League Points (3 for a win): 85, Division 3, 1990–91.

Most League Goals: 92, Division 3 (S), 1950–51.

Highest League Scorer in Season: Jim Shankly, 31, 1928–29 and Sammy McCrory, 1957–58, both in Division 3 (S).

Most League Goals in Total Aggregate: Roy Hollis, 122, 1953–60.

Most Capped Player: George Mackenzie, 9, Eire.

Most League Appearances: Sandy Anderson, 451, 1950–63.

Record Transfer Fee Received: £2,000,000 from Nottingham F for Stan Collymore, June 1993.

Record Transfer Fee Paid: £350,000 to Plymouth Arg for Gary Poole, June 1993.

Football League Record: 1920 Original Member of Division 3; 1921–58 Division 3 (S); 1958–66 Division 3; 1966–72 Division 4; 1972–76 Division 3; 1976–78 Division 4; 1978–80 Division 3; 1980–81 Division 4; 1981–84 Division 3; 1984–87 Division 4; 1987–89 Division 3; 1989–90 Division 4; 1990–91 Division 3; 1991–92 Division 2; 1992– Division 1.

Honours: *Football League:* Best season: 15th, Division 1, 1993–94. Division 3 – Runners-up 1990–91; Division 4 – Champions 1980–81; Runners-up 1971–72, 1977–78. *FA Cup:* best season: old 3rd rd, 1921, 5th rd, 1926, 1952, 1976, 1993. *Football League Cup:* never past 3rd rd.

Colours: All royal blue. **Change colours:** All red.

SOUTHEND UNITED 1994–95 LEAGUE RECORD

Match No.	Date	Venue	Opponents	Result	H/T Score	Lg. Pos.	Goalscorers	Attendance
1	Aug 13	A	Millwall	L 1-3	0-1	—	Iorfa	8283
2	20	H	Middlesbrough	L 0-2	0-1	24		5722
3	27	A	Luton T	D 2-2	0-1	20	Dublin, Otto	5918
4	30	H	Portsmouth	L 1-2	1-1	—	Thomson	4333
5	Sept 3	H	Oldham Ath	W 1-0	0-0	20	Otto	4435
6	10	A	Stoke C	L 1-4	0-2	23	Butler (og)	11,808
7	13	A	Wolverhampton W	L 0-5	0-3	—		23,608
8	17	H	Bristol C	W 2-1	1-0	22	Thomson, Whelan	3663
9	24	H	Bolton W	W 2-1	0-1	17	Otto, Thomson	4507
10	Oct 1	A	Sunderland	W 1-0	1-0	13	Thomson	15,520
11	8	A	Barnsley	D 0-0	0-0	16		3659
12	16	H	Derby Co	W 1-0	0-0	8	Regis	4218
13	22	A	Swindon T	D 2-2	2-1	10	Thomson, Otto	9909
14	29	H	Grimsby T	D 0-0	0-0	12		5086
15	Nov 1	H	Notts Co	W 1-0	1-0	—	Thomson	4302
16	5	A	Port Vale	L 0-5	0-2	9		7141
17	12	A	Watford	L 0-1	0-0	12		8551
18	19	H	Reading	W 4-1	1-1	10	Bressington (pen), Jones G 2, Thomson	5511
19	26	A	Sheffield U	L 0-2	0-1	12		13,405
20	Dec 3	H	Swindon T	W 2-0	1-0	11	Willis, Edwards	5803
21	10	A	Middlesbrough	W 2-1	1-0	9	Hails, Gridelet	16,843
22	17	H	Millwall	L 0-1	0-1	11		5833
23	26	A	Charlton Ath	L 1-3	1-0	15	Bressington (pen)	9525
24	27	H	WBA	W 2-1	1-1	12	Gridelet 2	6856
25	31	A	Burnley	L 1-5	0-2	14	Willis	10,561
26	Jan 2	H	Tranmere R	D 0-0	0-0	13		5195
27	14	A	Grimsby T	L 1-4	1-1	15	Chapman	3915
28	28	H	Port Vale	L 1-2	1-1	14	Thomson	3619
29	Feb 4	H	Watford	L 0-4	0-3	15		4914
30	11	A	Notts Co	D 2-2	1-1	15	Edwards, Willis	6768
31	18	H	Sheffield U	L 1-3	1-1	16	Willis	4700
32	21	A	Reading	L 0-2	0-0	—		7895
33	25	H	Sunderland	L 0-1	0-1	20		4686
34	Mar 4	A	Bolton W	L 0-3	0-1	20		10,766
35	7	A	Oldham Ath	W 2-0	1-0	—	Jones G, Thomson	7168
36	11	H	Luton T	W 3-0	1-0	16	Jones G, Thomson, Dublin	4558
37	18	A	Portsmouth	D 1-1	1-1	18	Jones G	6667
38	21	H	Stoke C	W 4-2	2-0	—	Jones G, Tilson, Edwards, Sussex (pen)	4240
39	25	A	Bristol C	D 0-0	0-0	16		6159
40	Apr 1	H	Wolverhampton W	L 0-1	0-0	16		8522
41	8	H	Burnley	W 3-1	2-0	15	Jones G, Hails, Battersby	5027
42	15	A	WBA	L 0-2	0-1	18		14,393
43	18	H	Charlton Ath	W 2-1	0-0	—	Jones G, Tilson	6397
44	21	A	Tranmere R	W 2-0	2-0	—	McGreal (og), Jones G	9971
45	29	A	Derby Co	W 2-1	2-0	14	Gridelet, Jones G	12,528
46	May 7	H	Barnsley	W 3-1	1-0	13	Gridelet, Thomson, Jones G	6425

Final League Position: 13

GOALSCORERS

League (54): Jones G 11, Thomson 11, Gridelet 5, Otto 4, Willis 4, Edwards 3, Bressington 2 (2 pens), Dublin 2, Hails 2, Tilson 2, Battersby 1, Chapman 1, Iorfa 1, Regis 1, Sussex 1 (pen), Whelan 1, own goals 2.
Coca-Cola Cup (0).
FA Cup (0).

Sansome P.E. 33	Poole G.J. 5 + 1	Powell C.G.R. 44	Jones K.A. 7	Edwards A.D. 42 + 2	Dublin K.B.L. 40	Hunt J.R. 5 + 2	Tilson S.B. 17 + 9	Iorfa D. 4 + 4	Otto R. 19	Thomson A. 35 + 4	Hone M. 39 + 1	Royce S. 13	Bressington G. 19 + 1	Martin J.A. — + 4	Sussex A.R. 14 + 1	Forrester J. 3 + 2	Whelan R.A. 33	Gridelet P.R. 26 + 3	Willis R.C. 21	Regis D. 9	Jones G. 19 + 6	Hails J. 20 + 6	Ansah A. 7 + 2	Chapman L.R. 1	Foot D.F. 2 + 1	Westley S.L.M. 4 + 1	Harkness S. 6	Perkins D.O. 1 + 5	Bodley M.J. 12	Battersby T. 6 + 2	Roche D. — + 4	*Match No.*
1	2	3	4	5	6	7	8	9	10	11	12																					1
	2	3	4	11	6	7		9	10		8	1	5	12																		2
1	2	3	4	5	6	12		*9*	10	11	7			14	8																	3
1	2	3	4	5		7			10	9	8		6	12	11																	4
1	2	3	4	5		12			10	9	8		6		11	7																5
1		3	4	5		7			10	9	2		6			11	8															6
1	14	3	4	12	5	7			10	9	2		6			*11*	8															7
1		3		5	6		14		10	9	2					12	8	*4*	7	11												8
1		3		5	6				10	11	2					12	8	4	7	9												9
1		3		5	6				10	11	2						8	4	7	9												10
1		3		5	6		12		10	11	2						8	4	7	9												11
1		3		5	6				10	11	2						8	4	7	9												12
1		3		5	6		12		10	11	2		4				8		7		9											13
1		3		5	6		12		10	11	2		14				8	*4*	7	9												14
1		3		5	6		12		10	11	2		7				8	4		9												15
1		3		5	6		12		10	11	2						8	4	7	*9*	14											16
1		3		5	6				10	11	2		8					4	7	9	12											17
1		3		5	6		12		10	11	2		8					4	7		9											18
1		3		5	6		12		10		2		8				7	4	9		11											19
1		3		5	6		10			11	2						8	4	7		9	12										20
1		3		5	6					11	2		7				8	4			9	10										21
1		3		5	6		12	14		11	2		7				8	4			*9*	10										22
1		3		5	6			14		12	2		7				8	4	9			*11*	10									23
1		3		5	6					11	2						8	4	9			7	10									24
1		3		5						11	2		6		12		8	4	9			7	10									25
1		3			6		11			9	2		5				8	4	10		12	7										26
1		3		5	6					11	2						*8*		10		12	4	7	9	14							27
1		3		5	6		8	12		9	2		4						7		10	*11*	14									28
1		3		5	6			*10*		9	2								7			11	12			4	8	14				29
1				5	6					*9*	2		3					4	7			11	10			14	8	12				30
1		3		5	6			12		9	2		*11*					4	7			14	10				8					31
1				12	6					*9*	2		7					4				11	10		3	5	8	14				32
1		3		6						*9*	2			12	8						14	7			4	5	10	11				33
1		3		6			8			9	2				10		4				12	7				5	11					34
		3		6	11		10			9	2	1			8		4				7								5			35
		3		6	11		*10*			9	2	1			8		4				7	12						14	5			36
		3		6	11		10			9	2	1			8		4				7	12							5			37
		3		6	11		10				2	1			8		4	12			9	7							5			38
		3		6	11		10				2	1			8		4				7	9							5	12		39
		3		6	11		10				*2*	1			8		4	12			7	9							5	14		40
		3			6		10					1			*8*		4	2			7	9						12	5	11	14	41
		3		6	2		10			12		1			*8*		4	14			7	9							5	11		42
		3		6	2		10			9		1					4	8			7	12							5	11		43
		3		6	2		10					1			9		4	8			7	12							5	*11*	14	44
		3		6	2		10			12		1					4	8			7	9							5	*11*	14	45
		3		5	2		10			12		1					4	*8*			7	9							6	11	14	46

Coca-Cola Cup
First Round — Watford (h) 0-0
(a) 0-1

FA Cup
Third Round — Southampton (a) 0-2

STOCKPORT COUNTY 1994–95 *Back row (left to right):* Alun Armstrong, Tony Dinning, Jeff Eckhardt, Michael Flynn, Michael Olliver, Kevin Slinn, Dean Emerson. *Centre row:* Dave Philpotts, Dean Connelly, Sean Connelly, Neil Edwards, Ian Ironside, John Keeley, Chris Beaumont, David Miller, John Sainty (Assistant Manager). *Front row:* Dave Jones, Deiniol Graham, Kevin Francis, David Frain, Danny Bergara (Manager), Peter Ward, Martyn Chalk, Lee Todd, Rodger Wylde (Physio).

Division 2 STOCKPORT COUNTY

Edgeley Park, Hardcastle Road, Stockport, Cheshire SK3 9DD. Telephone: (0161) 480 8888. Fax: (0161) 480 0230. Club Shop: (0161) 480 8117. Clubcall: 0891 121638.

Ground capacity: 12,500 (approx).

Record attendance: 27,833 v Liverpool, FA Cup 5th rd, 11 February 1950.

Record receipts: £66,807 v Bristol C, FA Cup 4th rd, 9 February 1994.

Pitch measurements: 111yd × 72yd.

Hon. Vice-Presidents: Mike Yarwood OBE, Freddie Pye, Andrew Barlow.

Chairman: Brendan Elwood. ***Vice-Chairman:*** Grahame White.

Directors: Mike Baker, Michael Rains, Brian Taylor, David Jolley.

Secretary: Gary Glendenning BAACA.

Manager: Dave Jones. ***Assistant Manager:*** John Sainty.

Physio: Rodger Wylde.

Assistant Secretary: Andrea Welborn. ***Commercial Manager:*** John Rutter.
Marketing Manager and Programme Editor: Steve Bellis.

Year Formed: 1883. ***Turned Professional:*** 1891. ***Ltd Co.:*** 1908.

Club Nicknames: 'County' or 'Hatters'.

Previous Names: Heaton Norris Rovers, 1883–88; Heaton Norris, 1888–90.

Previous Grounds: 1883 Heaton Norris Recreation Ground; 1884 Heaton Norris Wanderers Cricket Ground; 1885 Chorlton's Farm, Chorlton's Lane; 1886 Heaton Norris Cricket Ground; 1887 Wilkes' Field, Belmont Street; 1889 Nursery Inn, Green Lane; 1902 Edgeley Park.

Foundation: Formed at a meeting held at Wellington Road South by members of Wycliffe Congregational Chapel in 1883, they called themselves Heaton Norris Rovers until changing to Stockport County in 1890, a year before joining the Football Combination.

First Football League game: 1 September, 1900, Division 2, v Leicester Fosse (a) D 2-2 – Moores; Earp, Wainwright; Pickford, Limond, Harvey; Stansfield, Smith (1), Patterson, Foster, Betteley (1).

Record League Victory: 13–0 v Halifax T, Division 3 (N), 6 January 1934 – McGann; Vincent (1p), Jenkinson; Robinson, Stevens, Len Jones; Foulkes (1), Hill (3), Lythgoe (2), Stevenson (2), Downes (4).

Record Cup Victory: 6–2 v West Auckland T (away), FA Cup, 1st rd, 14 November 1959 – Lea; Betts (1), Webb; Murray, Hodder, Porteous; Wilson (1), Holland, Guy (2), Ritchie (1), Davock (1).

Record Defeat: 1–8 v Chesterfield, Division 2, 19 April 1902.

Most League Points (2 for a win): 64, Division 4, 1966–67.

Most League Points (3 for a win): 85, Division 2, 1993–94.

Most League Goals: 115, Division 3 (N), 1933–34.

Highest League Scorer in Season: Alf Lythgoe, 46, Division 3 (N), 1933–34.

Most League Goals in Total Aggregate: Jack Connor, 132, 1951–56.

Most Capped Player: Harry Hardy, 1, England.

Most League Appearances: Andy Thorpe, 489, 1978–86, 1988–92.

Record Transfer Fee Received: £250,000 from WBA for Paul A. Williams, March 1991.

Record Transfer Fee Paid: £125,000 to Preston NE for Mike Flynn, March 1993.

Football League Record: 1900 Elected to Division 2; 1904 Failed re-election; 1905–21 Division 2; 1921–22 Division 3 (N); 1922–26 Division 2; 1926–37 Division 3 (N); 1937–38 Division 2; 1938–58 Division 3 (N); 1958–59 Division 3; 1959–67 Division 4; 1967–70 Division 3; 1970–91 Division 4; 1991–92 Division 3; 1992– Division 2.

Honours: *Football League:* Division 2 best season: 10th, 1905–06; Division 3 (N) – Champions 1921–22, 1936–37; Runners-up 1928–29, 1929-30; Division 4 – Champions 1966–67; Runners-up 1990–91. *FA Cup:* best season: 5th rd, 1935, 1950. *Football League Cup:* best season: 4th rd, 1973. *Autoglass Trophy:* Runners-up 1992, 1993.

Colours: White shirts with double royal pinstripe, white shorts with double royal pinstripe, white stockings. **Change colours:** Red and black striped shirts, black shorts, red and black stockings.

STOCKPORT COUNTY 1994–95 LEAGUE RECORD

Match No.	Date	Venue	Opponents	Result	H/T Score	Lg. Pos.	Goalscorers	Attendance
1	Aug 13	H	Cardiff C	W 4-1	1-1	—	Ward, Francis 2, Armstrong	5139
2	20	A	Cambridge U	W 4-3	2-1	1	Francis 2, Armstrong, Gannon	3163
3	27	H	Brentford	L 0-1	0-1	6		4399
4	30	A	Crewe Alex	L 1-2	0-0	—	Armstrong	5050
5	Sept 3	A	Bristol R	D 2-2	1-2	11	Sterling (og), Eckhardt	4263
6	10	H	Bournemouth	W 1-0	0-0	9	Francis	4054
7	13	H	Shrewsbury T	W 2-1	0-0	—	Flynn, Armstrong	3473
8	17	A	Huddersfield T	L 1-2	1-1	9	Chalk	9526
9	24	H	Wycombe W	W 4-1	3-0	4	Francis 2, Armstrong, Chalk	4607
10	Oct 1	A	York C	W 4-2	2-2	3	Tutill (og), Slinn, Francis, Ward	3790
11	8	H	Rotherham U	W 1-0	0-0	3	Francis	4991
12	15	A	Peterborough U	W 1-0	0-0	3	Armstrong	5369
13	22	H	Plymouth Arg	L 2-4	1-2	4	Chalk, Francis	5652
14	29	A	Leyton Orient	W 1-0	0-0	2	Francis	3267
15	Nov 2	A	Chester C	L 0-1	0-0	—		2400
16	5	H	Oxford U	L 0-2	0-1	7		5132
17	19	A	Swansea C	L 0-2	0-0	7		3019
18	26	H	Birmingham C	L 0-1	0-0	10		5577
19	Dec 10	H	Cambridge U	W 2-1	0-0	7	Gannon 2	3903
20	17	A	Cardiff C	D 1-1	0-0	11	Gannon	3448
21	26	H	Wrexham	D 1-1	1-0	10	Todd	5636
22	27	A	Blackpool	W 2-1	1-0	9	Wallace, Gannon	5745
23	31	H	Bradford C	L 1-2	0-1	10	Francis	4613
24	Jan 2	A	Brighton & HA	L 0-2	0-0	11		8842
25	14	H	Hull C	W 4-0	1-0	10	Beaumont, Helliwell 2, Armstrong	4516
26	28	H	Leyton Orient	W 2-1	1-0	10	Ware, Armstrong	4250
27	Feb 4	A	Birmingham C	L 0-1	0-0	10		17,160
28	11	H	Chester C	D 2-2	0-2	10	Wallace, Beaumont	4405
29	18	A	Hull C	D 0-0	0-0	11		4576
30	21	H	Swansea C	L 0-1	0-1	—		3088
31	25	H	York C	L 2-3	1-2	13	Armstrong, Gannon	3570
32	28	A	Oxford U	L 0-4	0-1	—		4594
33	Mar 4	A	Wycombe W	D 1-1	1-0	14	Gannon	5275
34	7	H	Bristol R	W 2-1	1-1	—	Flynn, Armstrong	3580
35	11	A	Brentford	L 0-1	0-1	13		6513
36	18	H	Crewe Alex	W 3-1	1-0	13	Chalk 2, Armstrong	4946
37	21	A	Bournemouth	L 0-2	0-1	—		2892
38	25	H	Huddersfield T	L 1-2	0-1	14	Armstrong	5383
39	28	A	Plymouth Arg	W 2-0	1-0	—	Graham, Dinning	4618
40	Apr 1	A	Shrewsbury T	D 1-1	1-0	14	Graham	3655
41	8	A	Bradford C	W 2-1	0-1	13	Armstrong, Ward	3927
42	15	H	Blackpool	W 3-2	2-0	12	Helliwell 2, Todd	5021
43	17	A	Wrexham	L 0-1	0-0	12		3041
44	22	H	Brighton & HA	W 2-0	1-0	11	Chalk, Davenport	3789
45	29	H	Peterborough U	D 1-1	1-0	11	Armstrong	4387
46	May 6	A	Rotherham U	L 0-1	0-0	11		3469

Final League Position: 11

GOALSCORERS

League (63): Armstrong 14, Francis 12, Gannon 7, Chalk 6, Helliwell 4, Ward 3, Beaumont 2, Flynn 2, Graham 2, Todd 2, Wallace 2, Davenport 1, Dinning 1, Eckhardt 1, Slinn 1, Ware 1, own goals 2.
Coca-Cola Cup (6): Armstrong 1, Beaumont 1, Chalk 1, Emerson 1, Francis 1, Ward 1.
FA Cup (0).

Keeley J.H. 10	Connelly S.P. 37 + 2	Todd L. 37	Eckhardt J.E. 26 + 1	Flynn M.A. 43	Gannon J.P. 43 + 2	Emerson D. 1 + 2	Ward P. 27 + 1	Francis K.D.M. 16 + 1	Armstrong A. 40 + 5	Chalk M.P.G. 24 + 9	Miller D.B. — + 3	Graham D.W. 5 + 6	Frain D. 2	Slinn K.P. 2 + 2	Ironside I. 7 + 1	Beaumont C.P. 33 + 5	Wallace M. 24 + 1	Dinning T. 38 + 2	Ware P.D. 16 + 3	Edwards N.R. 18 + 1	Bound M.T. 14	Helliwell I. 17	Dickins M.J. 11 + 1	Oliver M. 10 + 3	Brown R.A. 1	Davenport P. 3 + 3	Marshall L.A. 1	Williams M. — + 1	*Match No.*
1	2	3	4	5	6	7	8	9	*10*	11	12	14																	1
1	2	3	4	5	6		8	9	*10*	11	12		7	14	15														2
1	5		*4*		6		8	9	10	11		12	7			2	3	14											3
1	2		4		6		8	9	10	11		7					3	5											4
1	2		4		6	14	8	9	10	*11*	12	7					3	5											5
1	2	3	4	5	7		8	9	10	11								6											6
1	2	3	4	5	7		8	9	10	11								6											7
1	2	3	4	5	7	12	8	9	10	11								6											8
1	2	3	4	5	7		8	9	10	11								6	12										9
1	2	3	4	5	7		8	*9*	10					11		12		6	14										10
	2	3	4	5	7		8	9	10	11					1	12		6											11
		3	4	5	7		8	9	10						1	11		6	2										12
	2	*3*	4	5	7		8	9	10	11					*1*	12		6	14	15									13
	2		4	5	7		8	9	10						1	11	3				6								14
	2		4	5	7		*8*	9	10	12					1	11	3	14			6								15
	2		4	5	7				9	11					1	10	3		8		6								16
	2	3	4	5	7				9	11					1	10		8			6								17
	2	3	4	5	7			9	10					12		11		8		1	6								18
	2	3	9	5	7				12	11						10	8	4		1	6								19
	2	3	9	5	7				12	11						10	8	4		1	6								20
	2	3	8	5	7		12		*9*	14						10	11	4		1	6								21
	2	3	9	5	7		8			11						10	12	4		1	6								22
	2	3	9	5	7			12	14	11						10	8	4		1	6								23
		2		5	7				9	12		11				10	3	4	8	1	6								24
	2	3		5	7				10							11	8	6	4	1		9							25
	2	3		5	7				10							11	8	6	4	1		9							26
	2	3	12	5	7				10	14						11	8	6	4	1		9							27
	2	3	7	5	12				*10*	14						11	8	6	4	1		9							28
	2	3	9	5	7				12					10		11	8	6	4	1									29
	2	3	9	5	7				12	11						10	8	6	4	1									30
	2	3		5	7				10	12						11	8	6	4	*1*		9	15						31
				5	7				10	8		12				11	3	2	4		6	9	1	14					32
				5	7				10	12						11	3	6	4			9	1	8	2				33
		2		5	7				10	12						11	3	6	4	1		9		8					34
		2		5	7		8		10							11	3	6	4			9	1	12					35
	2			5	7		8		10	11		12				9	3	6	4				1						36
	6	2		5	7		8		10	11						9	3		4				1	12					37
	2	3		5	7				10			12				9		6			4		1	8		11			38
	2	3		5	7		8		10			11				12		6				9	1	4					39
	2	3		5	7		8		10			11				12		6				9	1	4					40
	2	3		5			8		10			12				7		6				9	1	4		11			41
	2	3		5	12		8		10							7		6				9	1	4		11			42
	2	3		5	7		8		10	12						11		*6*				9	1	4		14			43
	12	3		5	7		8		*10*	11						2		6		1		9		4		14			44
	12	3		5	7		8		10	*11*						2		6		1		9		4		14			45
		3		5	7		8		10	11						2				1	6	9					4	12	46

Coca-Cola Cup

First Round	Preston NE (a)	1-1
	(h)	4-1
Second Round	Sheffield U (h)	1-5
	(a)	0-1

FA Cup

First Round	Wrexham (a)	0-1

STOKE CITY 1994–95 *Back row (left to right):* John Clark, Carl Beeston, Ian Cranson, Graham Potter, John Dreyer, Vince Overson, Nigel Cleghorn, Lee Sandford.
Centre row: Brian Caswell (Youth Coach), Ian Clarkson, Toddy Orlygsson, Mark Prudhoe, Ron Sinclair, Carl Muggleton, Wayne Biggins, John Butler, Richard Gray.
Front row: Graham Shaw, Simon Sturridge, Mick Gynn, Asa Hartford (Coach), Joe Jordan, Dennis Rofe, Martin Carruthers, Paul Peschisolido, Paul Ware.

Division 1 **STOKE CITY**

Victoria Ground, Stoke-on-Trent ST4 4EG. Telephone: (01782) 413511. Fax: (01782) 745340. Commercial Dept: (01782) 45840. Soccerline Information: 0891 700278. Football in the Community: (01782) 744347.

Ground capacity: 24,071.

Record attendance: 51,380 v Arsenal, Division 1, 29 March 1937.

Record receipts: £97,000 v Liverpool, FA Cup 3rd rd, 9 January 1988.

Pitch measurements: 116yd × 75yd.

Vice-President: J. A. M. Humphries.

Chairman: P. Coates. ***Vice-Chairman:*** K. A. Humphreys.

Directors: D. J. Edwards, M. E. Moors.

Manager: Lou Macari. ***Assistant Manager:*** Asa Hartford.

Physio: David Looms.

Secretary: M. J. Potts.

Chief Executive: Jez Moxey F. INST SMM.

Year Formed: 1863 *(*see Foundation*).

Turned Professional: 1885. ***Ltd Co.:*** 1908.

Club Nickname: 'The Potters'.

Previous Name: Stoke.

Previous Grounds: 1875, Sweeting's Field; 1878, Victoria Ground (previously known as the Athletic Club Ground).

Foundation: The date of the formation of this club has long been in doubt. The year 1863 was claimed, but more recent research by Wade Martin has uncovered nothing earlier than 1868, when a couple of Old Carthusians, who were apprentices at the local works of the old North Staffordshire Railway Company, met with some others from that works, to form Stoke Ramblers. It should also be noted that the old Stoke club went bankrupt in 1908 when a new club was formed.

First Football League game: 8 September, 1888, Football League, v WBA (h) L 0-2 – Rowley; Clare, Underwood; Ramsey, Shutt, Smith; Sayer, McSkimming, Staton, Edge, Tunnicliffe.

Record League Victory: 10–3 v WBA, Division 1, 4 February 1937 – Doug Westland; Brigham, Harbot; Tutin, Turner (1p), Kirton; Matthews, Antonio (2), Freddie Steele (5), Jimmy Westland, Johnson (2).

Record Cup Victory: 7–1 v Burnley, FA Cup, 2nd rd (replay), 20 February 1896 – Clawley; Clare, Eccles; Turner, Grewe, Robertson; Willie Maxwell, Dickson, A. Maxwell (3), Hyslop (4), Schofield.

Record Defeat: 0–10 v Preston NE, Division 1, 14 September 1889.

Most League Points (2 for a win): 63, Division 3 (N), 1926–27.

Most League Points (3 for a win): 93, Division 2, 1992–93.

Most League Goals: 92, Division 3 (N), 1926–27.

Highest League Scorer in Season: Freddie Steele, 33, Division 1, 1936–37.

Most League Goals in Total Aggregate: Freddie Steele, 142, 1934–49.

Most Capped Player: Gordon Banks, 36 (73), England.

Most League Appearances: Eric Skeels, 506, 1958–76.

Record Transfer Fee Received: £1,500,000 from Chelsea for Mark Stein, October 1993.

Record Transfer Fee Paid: £480,000 to Sheffield W for Ian Cranson, July 1989.

Football League Record: 1888 Founder Member of Football League; 1890 Not re-elected; 1891 Re-elected; relegated in 1907, and after one year in Division 2, resigned for financial reasons; 1919 re-elected to Division 2; 1922–23 Division 1; 1923–26 Division 2; 1926–27 Division 3 (N); 1927–33 Division 2; 1933–53 Division 1; 1953–63 Division 2; 1963–77 Division 1; 1977–79 Division 2; 1979–85 Division 1; 1985–90 Division 2; 1990–92 Division 3; 1992–93 Division 2; 1993– Division 1.

Honours: *Football League:* Division 1 best season: 4th, 1935–36, 1946–47; Division 2 – Champions 1932–33, 1962–63, 1992–93; Runners-up 1921–22; Promoted 1978–79 (3rd); Division 3 (N) – Champions 1926–27. *FA Cup:* Semi-finals 1899, 1971, 1972. *Football League Cup:* Winners 1972. *Autoglass Trophy:* Winners: 1992. **European Competitions:** *UEFA Cup:* 1972–73, 1974–75.

Colours: Red and white striped shirts, white shorts, red stockings. **Change colours:** Green and black striped shirts, black shorts, black stockings.

STOKE CITY 1994–95 LEAGUE RECORD

Match No.	Date	Venue	Opponents	Result	H/T Score	Lg. Pos.	Goalscorers	Attendance
1	Aug 13	H	Tranmere R	W 1-0	0-0	—	Gleghorn	15,915
2	20	A	Burnley	D 1-1	0-1	6	Dreyer	15,331
3	27	H	Sunderland	L 0-1	0-1	14		15,159
4	30	A	Reading	L 0-4	0-0	—		7103
5	Sept 3	A	Bolton W	L 0-4	0-1	22		11,515
6	10	H	Southend U	W 4-1	2-0	16	Orlygsson, Edwards (og), Dreyer, Biggins	11,808
7	14	H	Charlton Ath	W 3-2	2-0	—	Gleghorn, Orlygsson, Peschisolido	10,643
8	17	A	Notts Co	W 2-0	1-0	6	Peschisolido 2	8281
9	25	A	Derby Co	L 0-3	0-2	8		11,782
10	Oct 2	H	WBA	W 4-1	2-1	7	Carruthers 2, Wallace, Peschisolido	14,203
11	9	H	Luton T	L 1-2	0-1	7	Carruthers	11,712
12	15	A	Millwall	D 1-1	0-1	7	Peschisolido	7856
13	22	A	Oldham Ath	D 0-0	0-0	9		8954
14	30	H	Wolverhampton W	D 1-1	1-1	11	Keen	15,928
15	Nov 2	H	Sheffield U	D 1-1	0-1	—	Gleghorn	11,556
16	5	A	Barnsley	L 0-2	0-1	16		5117
17	19	H	Grimsby T	W 3-0	2-0	13	Peschisolido 2, Carruthers	12,055
18	26	A	Watford	D 0-0	0-0	14		9126
19	30	A	Portsmouth	W 1-0	0-0	—	Beeston	5272
20	Dec 4	H	Oldham Ath	L 0-1	0-0	12		12,558
21	10	H	Burnley	W 2-0	0-0	11	Orlygsson 2 (1 pen)	13,040
22	17	A	Tranmere R	W 1-0	0-0	9	Carruthers	7601
23	26	H	Swindon T	D 0-0	0-0	8		17,662
24	27	A	Bristol C	L 1-3	0-0	11	Cranson	8500
25	31	H	Middlesbrough	D 1-1	1-1	12	Gleghorn	15,914
26	Jan 14	A	Wolverhampton W	L 0-2	0-1	14		28,298
27	Feb 4	H	Portsmouth	L 0-2	0-0	16		9704
28	11	A	Sheffield U	D 1-1	1-1	16	Peschisolido	13,900
29	21	A	Grimsby T	D 0-0	0-0	—		6384
30	25	A	WBA	W 3-1	1-1	15	Scott, Peschisolido 2	16,591
31	Mar 4	H	Derby Co	D 0-0	0-0	15		13,462
32	11	A	Sunderland	L 0-1	0-0	18		12,282
33	14	A	Port Vale	D 1-1	1-1	—	Sandford	19,510
34	18	H	Reading	L 0-1	0-1	20		10,006
35	21	A	Southend U	L 2-4	0-2	—	Allen, Biggins (pen)	4240
36	25	H	Notts Co	W 2-1	1-0	19	Gleghorn, Sturridge	10,204
37	Apr 1	A	Charlton Ath	D 0-0	0-0	18		10,008
38	4	H	Watford	W 1-0	1-0	—	Sigurdsson	9576
39	8	A	Middlesbrough	L 1-2	1-1	18	Peschisolido	20,867
40	12	H	Barnsley	D 0-0	0-0	—		10,752
41	15	H	Bristol C	W 2-1	1-1	16	Andrade, Peschisolido	10,172
42	17	A	Swindon T	W 1-0	1-0	14	Orlygsson	10,549
43	22	H	Port Vale	L 0-1	0-0	17		20,429
44	29	H	Millwall	W 4-3	2-2	15	Scott, Gleghorn 2, Keen	9111
45	May 3	H	Bolton W	D 1-1	1-1	—	Orlygsson (pen)	15,557
46	7	A	Luton T	W 3-2	0-1	11	Orlygsson, Peschisolido, Scott	8252

Final League Position: 11

GOALSCORERS

League (50): Peschisolido 13, Gleghorn 7, Orlygsson 7 (2 pens), Carruthers 5, Scott 3, Biggins 2 (1 pen), Dreyer 2, Keen 2, Allen 1, Andrade 1, Beeston 1, Cranson 1, Sandford 1, Sigurdsson 1, Sturridge 1, Wallace 1, own goal 1.
Coca-Cola Cup (4): Peschisolido 2, Gleghorn 1, Orlygsson 1 (pen).
FA Cup (1): Scott 1.

Muggleton C. 24	Clark J.B. 5	Sandford L.R. 34 + 1	Dreyer J.B. 16 + 2	Overson V.D. 33 + 2	Orlygsson T. 38	Carruthers M.G. 26 + 6	Wallace R.G. 16 + 4	Biggins W. 8 + 9	Peschisolido P.P. 39 + 1	Gleghorn N.W. 44 + 2	Beckford J.N. 2 + 2	Sturridge S.A. 2 + 6	Butler J.E. 38 + 3	Shaw G.P. 1 + 2	Cranson I. 37	Downing K.G. 16	Keen K.I. 15 + 6	Potter G.S. 1	Beeston C.F. 15 + 1	Wade S.P. — + 1	Clarkson I.S. 15 + 3	Sigurdsson L. 22 + 1	Sinclair R.M. 22 + 2	Williams J.N. 1 + 3	Scott K. 16 + 2	Allen P.K. 17	Leslie S. — + 1	Gayle J. 1 + 3	Andrade J. 2 + 2	Match No.
1	2	3	4	5	6	7	8	9	10	11	12																			1
1	2	3	4	5	6	7	8	9		11		10	12	14																2
1	2	3	4			12	8	9	7	11		10			5	6														3
1	2	3	4	5		12	8	9	7	11			10			6														4
1	2	3	4	5			8	9	7	11	10		12			6														5
1		3	4	5	6	12	14	9	10	11	7		2			8														6
1		3	4		6	9	7		10	11			2		5	8														7
1		3	4		6	9	7		10	11			2		5	8														8
1		3	4		6	9	7	12	10	11			2		5	8														9
1		3	4	14	6	9	2	12	10	11			7		5	8														10
1		3	4	12	6	9	*2*		10	11	14		7		5	8														11
1		3	4	2	6	9	12		10	11			7		5	8														12
1		3		5	6	9		12	10	11			2		4		7	*8*	14											13
1		3		5	6	9		12	10	11			2		4		7		8											14
1		3		5	6	9			10	11			2		4		7		8	12										15
1		3		5	6	9			10	11		12			4		7		8		2									16
1		3		5	6	9			10	11			2		4		7		8											17
1		3		5	6	9		12	10	11			2		4		7				8									18
1		3		5	6	9			10	11			2		4				8			7								19
1		3		5	6	9		12	10	11					4		7		8		2									20
1		3		5	6	*9*		12	10	11				7	4				8		2	14								21
1		3	12	5	6	*9*		14	10	11			2		4				8		7		15							22
1		3	5		6	9			10	11			2		4		8				7			12						23
		3	*5*		6			9	12	11			2	14	4						8	7	1	10						24
1		3		5	6	9			10	11			2		4						7		15	12	8					25
		3	*8*	5	6			12	10	11			7		4						2		1	14	9					26
			3		7				8	11			12		4	10					*2*	5	1		9	6	14			27
			12		7				8	11			3		4	10					2	5	1		*9*	6		14		28
		3		5	6		12		8	11			10		4							2	1		9	7				29
		3		5	6				*9*	11		14	7		4		12					2	1		10	8				30
		3		5	6				*9*	12			7		4		14		11			2	1		10	8				31
		3		5		9				11		14	7		4		12		6			2	1		*10*	8				32
		3		5	6	*9*				11			2		4		12		8			7	1		14	10				33
		3		5	6	9				12		14	2		4				8			7	1		*11*	10				34
		3		5	6			9		11		12	2		4				*10*			8	1			7		14		35
				5	6				9	11		12	2		4		14		8			3	1		10	7				36
				5		12			10	11			2		4		6		*8*		14	3	1		9	7				37
				5					9	11			2		4	8	6				12	3	1		10	7				38
						8	4		9	11			2			6					5	3	1			7		10	12	39
					6				9	11			2		4	7					3	5	1		10	8			12	40
					6	12	4		9	11			2			8	14				5	3	1			*7*			10	41
				5	6	9	12			11			2				8				4	3	1		14	7			*10*	42
				5		10	3		9	11			2		4		8					6	1			7		12		43
				5	6		7		9	11			2		4		8					3	1		10					44
		12		5	6	14	7		9	11			2		4		8					3	1		*10*					45
		3		5	6		7		9	11			2				8				12	4	1		10					46

Coca-Cola Cup

Second Round	Fulham (a)	2-3
	(h)	1-0
Third Round	Liverpool (a)	1-2

FA Cup

Third Round	Bristol C (a)	0-0
	(h)	1-3

SUNDERLAND 1994–95 *Back row (left to right):* Martin Smith, Gary Bennett, Gordon Armstrong, Ian Sampson, Richard Ord, Andy Melville, Lee Howey, Gary Owers.
Centre row: Jimmy Montgomery, Ian Ross, Derek Ferguson, Don Goodman, John Kay, Anthony Smith, Sean Musgrave, Alec Chamberlain, Tony Norman, David Preece, Sean Cunnington, Michael Gray, David Rush, Phil Gray, Mick Buxton (Manager), Steve Smelt.
Front row: George Herd, Gudni Helgason, Mark Angel, Chris Lawless, Ian Rodgerson, Dariusz Kubicki, Kevin Ball, Craig Russell, Brian Atkinson, Martin Gray, Phillip Brumwell, John Waldock, Stephen Brodie, Trevor Hartley.

Division 1 SUNDERLAND

Roker Park Ground, Sunderland SR6 9SW. Telephone: (0191) 514 0332. Fax: (0191) 514 5854.

Ground capacity: 22,657.

Record attendance: 75,118 v Derby Co, FA Cup 6th rd replay, 8 March 1933.

Record receipts: £186,000 v Tottenham H, Division 1, 28 August 1990.

Pitch measurements: 113yd × 74yd.

Chairman: J. R. Featherstone.

Deputy chairman: G. S. Wood.

Directors: R. S. Murray, G. S. Wood, J. G. Wood, Alec King.

Manager: Peter Reid.

General Manager/Secretary: P. Fiddaman BA (HONS) ACA.

Chief Coach: Paul Bracewell. ***Youth Team Coach:*** Ricky Sbragia.

Physio: Steve Smelt. ***Director of Youth:*** Jimmy Montgomery. ***Commercial Manager:*** Alec King.

Year Formed: 1879. ***Turned Professional:*** 1886. ***Ltd Co.:*** 1906.

Club Nickname: 'Rokermen'.

Previous Name: 1879–80, Sunderland and District Teacher's AFC.

Previous Grounds: 1879, Blue House Field, Hendon; 1882, Groves Field, Ashbrooke; 1883, Horatio Street; 1884, Abbs Field, Fulwell; 1886, Newcastle Road; 1898, Roker Park.

Foundation: A Scottish schoolmaster named James Allan, working at Hendon Boarding School, took the initiative in the foundation of Sunderland in 1879 when they were formed as The Sunderland and District Teachers' Association FC at a meeting in the Adults School, Norfolk Street. Because of financial difficulties, they quickly allowed members from outside the teaching profession and so became Sunderland AFC in October 1880.

First Football League game: 13 September, 1890, Football League, v Burnley (h) L 2-3 – Kirtley; Porteous, Oliver; Wilson, Auld, Gibson; Spence (1), Miller, Campbell (1), Scott, D. Hannah.

Record League Victory: 9–1 v Newcastle U (away), Division 1, 5 December 1908 – Roose; Forster, Melton; Daykin, Thomson, Low; Mordue, Hogg (4), Brown, Holley (3), Bridgett (2).

Record Cup Victory: 11–1 v Fairfield, FA Cup, 1st rd, 2 February 1895 – Doig; McNeill, Johnston; Dunlop, McCreadie (1), Wilson; Gillespie (1), Millar (5), Campbell, Hannah (3), Scott (1).

Record Defeat: 0–8 v West Ham U, Division 1, 19 October 1968 and v Watford, Division 1, 25 September 1982.

Most League Points (2 for a win): 61, Division 2, 1963–64.

Most League Points (3 for a win): 93, Division 3, 1987–88.

Most League Goals: 109, Division 1, 1935–36.

Highest League Scorer in Season: Dave Halliday, 43, Division 1, 1928–29.

Most League Goals in Total Aggregate: Charlie Buchan, 209, 1911–25.

Most Capped Player: Martin Harvey, 34, Northern Ireland.

Most League Appearances: Jim Montgomery, 537, 1962–77.

Record Transfer Fee Received: £1,500,000 from Crystal Palace for Marco Gabbiadini, September 1991.

Record Transfer Fee Paid: £900,000 to WBA for Don Goodman, December 1991.

Football League Record: 1890 Elected to Division 1; 1958–64 Division 2; 1964–70 Division 1; 1970–76 Division 2; 1976–77 Division 1; 1977–80 Division 2; 1980–85 Division 1; 1985–87 Division 2; 1987–88 Division 3; 1988–90 Division 2; 1990–91 Division 1; 1991–92 Division 2; 1992– Division 1.

Honours: *Football League:* Division 1 – Champions 1891–92, 1892–93, 1894–95, 1901–02, 1912–13, 1935–36; Runners-up 1893–94; 1897–98, 1900–01, 1922–23, 1934–35; Division 2 – Champions 1975–76; Runners-up 1963–64, 1979–80; Division 3 – Champions 1987–88. *FA Cup:* Winners 1937, 1973; Runners-up 1913, 1992. *Football League Cup:* Runners-up 1985. **European Competitions:** *Cup-Winners' Cup:* 1973–74.

Colours: Red and white striped shirts, black shorts, red stockings, white turnover. **Change colours:** White shirts, blue and green sleeves, navy blue shorts, white stockings, navy blue trim.

SUNDERLAND 1994–95 LEAGUE RECORD

Match No.	*Date*	*Venue*	*Opponents*	*Result*	*H/T Score*	*Lg. Pos.*	*Goalscorers*	*Attendance*
1	Aug 13	A	Bristol C	D 0-0	0-0	—		11,127
2	20	H	Millwall	D 1-1	0-1	15	Goodman	17,296
3	27	A	Stoke C	W 1-0	1-0	9	Gray P	15,159
4	30	H	Grimsby T	D 2-2	1-1	—	Goodman (pen), Gray P	15,788
5	Sept 3	H	Wolverhampton W	D 1-1	1-1	11	Gray P	15,111
6	11	A	Middlesbrough	D 2-2	1-0	11	Russell 2	19,578
7	13	A	Sheffield U	D 0-0	0-0	—		15,239
8	17	H	Barnsley	W 2-0	0-0	9	Gray P, Goodman	16,145
9	24	A	Tranmere R	L 0-1	0-0	11		7500
10	Oct 1	H	Southend U	L 0-1	0-1	16		15,520
11	8	A	WBA	W 3-1	2-0	12	Smith M, Gray P 2	13,717
12	15	H	Burnley	D 0-0	0-0	14		17,700
13	22	A	Reading	W 2-0	1-0	8	Melville, Gray P	10,757
14	29	H	Oldham Ath	D 0-0	0-0	8		17,252
15	Nov 1	H	Charlton Ath	D 1-1	1-0	—	Smith M	14,085
16	5	A	Notts Co	L 2-3	0-2	12	Gray P, Owers	8890
17	19	H	Watford	L 1-3	0-2	17	Smith M	15,063
18	26	A	Portsmouth	W 4-1	3-0	13	Russell, Melville, Gray P (pen), Smith M	7527
19	29	A	Port Vale	D 0-0	0-0	—		8121
20	Dec 3	H	Reading	L 0-1	0-0	15		14,021
21	10	A	Millwall	L 0-2	0-0	16		7698
22	17	H	Bristol C	W 2-0	0-0	16	Howey 2	11,661
23	26	H	Bolton W	D 1-1	0-0	17	Smith M	19,758
24	27	A	Luton T	L 0-3	0-2	17		8953
25	31	H	Derby Co	D 1-1	0-0	17	Gray P	13,979
26	Jan 14	A	Oldham Ath	D 0-0	0-0	18		9742
27	21	H	Notts Co	L 1-2	0-1	18	Armstrong	14,334
28	Feb 4	H	Port Vale	D 1-1	1-1	21	Ball	13,377
29	11	A	Charlton Ath	L 0-1	0-0	21		12,380
30	18	H	Portsmouth	D 2-2	2-1	21	Smith M 2	12,372
31	21	A	Watford	W 1-0	1-0	—	Russell	8189
32	25	A	Southend U	W 1-0	1-0	17	Agnew	4686
33	Mar 5	H	Tranmere R	L 0-1	0-0	18		12,043
34	8	A	Wolverhampton W	L 0-1	0-0	—		25,926
35	11	H	Stoke C	W 1-0	0-0	17	Melville	12,282
36	15	A	Swindon T	L 0-1	0-1	—		8233
37	19	A	Grimsby T	L 1-3	0-1	19	Agnew	5697
38	21	H	Middlesbrough	L 0-1	0-0	—		16,501
39	24	A	Barnsley	L 0-2	0-0	—		7803
40	Apr 1	H	Sheffield U	W 1-0	0-0	20	Russell	17,259
41	8	A	Derby Co	W 1-0	1-0	20	Ball	15,442
42	15	H	Luton T	D 1-1	0-1	19	Gray P	17,292
43	17	A	Bolton W	L 0-1	0-0	20		15,030
44	22	H	Swindon T	W 1-0	1-0	20	Smith M	16,874
45	29	A	Burnley	D 1-1	1-1	20	Smith M	15,121
46	May 7	H	WBA	D 2-2	1-0	20	Smith M, Gray P	18,232

Final League Position: 20

GOALSCORERS

League (41): Gray P 12 (1 pen), Smith M 10, Russell 5, Goodman 3 (1 pen), Melville 3, Agnew 2, Ball 2, Howey 2, Armstrong 1, Owers 1.
Coca-Cola Cup (2): Gray P 1, Russell 1.
FA Cup (5): Armstrong 2, Gray P 2, Russell 1.

Norman A.J. 29	Kubicki D. 46	Martin D Gray 17 + 5	Bennett G.E. 19 + 1	Ferguson D. 23	Melville A.R. 36	Owers G. 18 + 1	Goodman D.R. 17 + 1	Gray P. 41 + 1	Michael Gray 10 + 6	Ball K.A. 42	Atkinson B. 16 + 1	Cunnington S.G. 3 + 5	Ord R.J. 33	Russell C.S. 28 + 10	Smith M. 33 + 2	Rodgerson I. 3 + 3	Chamberlain A.F.R. 17 + 1	Snodin I. 6	Howey L.M. 6 + 9	Armstrong G.I. 10 + 5	Scott M. 24	Agnew S.M. 16	Williams P.A. 3	Brodie S.E. 1 + 7	Matteo D. 1	Angell B.A.M. 8	Smith A. — + 1	Match No.
1	2	3	4	5	6	7	8	9	10	11	12																	1
1	3		4	5	6	2	8	9	10	11	7	12																2
1	3		4	5	6	2	8	9	10	11	7	12																3
1	3		4	5	6	2	8	9	10	11	7	12																4
1	3			5		2	8	9	10	6	7		4	11														5
1	2			5	6	7	8	9	12	4	*11*	14	3	10														6
1	2		12	5	6	7	8	9		4		11	3	10														7
1	2		4	5	6	7	8	9		11			3	10	12													8
1	2	5			6	7	8	9		4			3	10		11												9
1	2	5			6	7	8	9		4			3	11	10	12	15											10
	2	5	4		6		8	9		7			3	11	10	12	1											11
	2	5			6		8	9		7			3	11	10		1	4	12									12
	2	5			6		8	9		7			3	11	10	12	1	4										13
	2	5			6	12	8	9		7			3	11	10		1	*4*	14									14
	2	12			6	7	8	9		5			3	14	10	11	1	*4*										15
	2				6	7	8	9		5			3	12	10	11	1	4										16
	2				6	7	8	9		5	11		*3*	12	10		1	4		14								17
	2	5			6	7		9		4	11		3	8	10		1											18
	2	5			6	7	12	9		4	11		3	8	10		1											19
	2	5			6	7		9		4	*11*		3	8	10		1		14	12								20
	2	5	4			7		9		6			3	8	10		1		12	11								21
	3		4	7	6	2			12	5				8	10		1		9	11								22
	2	12	4	7	6			9		5				8	10		1		11		3							23
	2	5			6			9		4	7	11		8	10		1		12		3							24
	2		4		6			9	12	5	7			8	10		1			11	3							25
	2			5	6			9	12	4				8	10		1			11	3	7						26
	2		4	5	6			9							10		1		12	11	3	7	8					27
1	2			5	6			9		4				12	10					11	3	7	8					28
1	2		6	5				9	12	11			4	8					14		3	7	*10*					29
1	2			5				9	8	4			6	12	10				11		3	7						30
1	2			5	6			9		4			7	8	*10*					12	3	11		14				31
1	2		4	5				9		11			6	8	*10*					12	3	7		14				32
1	2		4	5				9		6			11	8	10				12		3	7						33
1	2		4	5						6			11	8	10				9		3	7		12				34
1	2			5	6					4				8	10				9	11	3	7		12				35
1	2		4	5	6			9		11					*10*				8	12	3	7		14				36
1	2			5	6			9		4		12	*11*	8						10	3	7		14				37
1	2				6			9		4		*5*	11	8					12	10	3	7		14				38
1	2	*12*			6			9					4	14	10					11	3	7			5	8		39
1	2	12	4	5				9			11		6	14	10						3	7				*8*		40
1	2	12	4							5	11		6	8	10						3	7				9		41
1	2	7	*4*					9	14	5	11		6	12	10						3					8		42
1	2	10			6			9	5	7	11		4	14	12						3					*8*		43
1	2	7			6			9	5		11		4		10						3					8	12	44
1	2	7			6			9	5	11			4	12	10						3					8		45
1	2	5			6			12	4	7			11		10						3			9		8		46

Coca-Cola Cup

Second Round	Millwall (a)		1-2
	(h)		1-1

FA Cup

Third Round	Carlisle U (h)		1-1
	(a)		3-1
Fourth Round	Tottenham H (h)		1-4

SWANSEA CITY 1994–95 *Back row (left to right):* David Barnhouse, Martin Hayes, Roger Freestone, Andy McFarlane, Lee Jones, David Penney, Darren Perrett.
Centre row: Jimmy Rimmer (Youth Team Coach), Bobby Smith (Assistant Manager), Michael Basham, Mark Harris, John Ford, Steve Torpey, Steve Jenkins, Shaun Chapple, Ron Walton (Youth Development Officer).
Front row: Mark Clode, Kwame Ampadu, John Hodge, Frank Burrows (Manager), John Cornforth, Colin Pascoe, Jason Bowen.

Division 2 — SWANSEA CITY

Vetch Field, Swansea SA1 3SU. Telephone: (01792) 474114. Fax: (01792) 646120. Club Shop: 33 William St, Swansea SA1 3QS. Telephone: (01792) 462584.

Ground capacity: 16,540.

Record attendance: 32,796 v Arsenal, FA Cup 4th rd, 17 February 1968.

Record receipts: £36,477.42 v Liverpool, Division 1, 18 September 1982.

Pitch measurements: 112yd × 74yd.

President: I. C. Pursey MBE.

Chairman: D. J. Sharpe.

Directors: D. G. Hammond FCA, MBIM (vice-chairman), M. Griffiths.

Chief Executive: Robin Sharpe.

Team Manager: Frank Burrows. ***Assistant Manager:*** Bobby Smith.

Youth Team Manager: Jimmy Rimmer. ***Physio:*** Mike Davenport.

Programme Editor: Major Reg Pike.

Year Formed: 1912. ***Turned Professional:*** 1912. ***Ltd Co.:*** 1912.

Secretary: George Taylor.

Previous Name: Swansea Town until February 1970.

Club Nickname: 'The Swans'.

Foundation: The earliest Association Football in Wales was played in the Northern part of the country and no international took place in the South until 1894, when a local paper still thought it necessary to publish an outline of the rules and an illustration of the pitch markings. There had been an earlier Swansea club, but this has no connection with Swansea Town (now City) formed at a public meeting in June 1912.

First Football League game: 28 August, 1920, Division 3, v Portsmouth (a) L 0-3 – Crumley; Robson, Evans; Smith, Holdsworth, Williams; Hole, I. Jones, Edmundson, Rigsby, Spottiswood.

Record League Victory: 8–0 v Hartlepool U, Division 4, 1 April 1978 – Barber; Evans, Bartley, Lally (1) (Morris), May, Bruton, Kevin Moore, Robbie James (3 incl. 1p), Curtis (3), Toshack (1), Chappell.

Record Cup Victory: 12–0 v Sliema W (Malta), ECWC 1st rd 1st leg, 15 September 1982 – Davies; Marustik, Hadziabdic (1), Irwin (1), Kennedy, Rajkovic (1), Loveridge (2) (Leighton James), Robbie James, Charles (2), Stevenson (1), Latchford (1) (Walsh (3)).

Record Defeat: 0–8 v Liverpool, FA Cup 3rd rd, 9 January 1990.

Most League Points (2 for a win): 62, Division 3 (S), 1948–49.

Most League Points (3 for a win): 73, Division 2, 1992–93.

Most League Goals: 90, Division 2, 1956–57.

Highest League Scorer in Season: Cyril Pearce, 35, Division 2, 1931–32.

Most League Goals in Total Aggregate: Ivor Allchurch, 166, 1949–58, 1965–68.

Most Capped Player: Ivor Allchurch, 42 (68), Wales.

Most League Appearances: Wilfred Milne, 585, 1919–37.

Record Transfer Fee Received: £375,000 from Nottingham F for Des Lyttle, July 1993.

Record Transfer Fee Paid: £340,000 to Liverpool for Colin Irwin, August 1981.

Football League Record: 1920 Original Member of Division 3; 1921–25 Division 3 (S); 1925–47 Division 2; 1947–49 Division 3 (S); 1949–65 Division 2; 1965–67 Division 3; 1967–70 Division 4; 1970–73 Division 3; 1973–78 Division 4; 1978–79 Division 3; 1979–81 Division 2; 1981–83 Division 1; 1983–84 Division 2; 1984–86 Division 3; 1986–88 Division 4; 1988–92 Division 3; 1992– Division 2.

Honours: *Football League:* Division 1 best season: 6th, 1981–82; Division 2 – Promoted 1980–81 (3rd); Division 3 (S) – Champions 1924–25, 1948–49; Division 3 – Promoted 1978–79 (3rd); Division 4 – Promoted 1969–70 (3rd), 1977–78 (3rd). *FA Cup:* Semi-finals 1926, 1964. *Football League Cup:* best season: 4th rd, 1965, 1977. *Welsh Cup:* Winners 9 times; Runners-up 8 times. *Autoglass Trophy:* Winners 1994. **European Competitions:** *European Cup-Winners' Cup:* 1961–62, 1966–67, 1981–82, 1982–83, 1983–84, 1989–90, 1991–92.

Colours: White shirts with black double pin stripes, black sleeve with red, white shorts with red trim, white stockings with black top. **Change colours:** Black shirts with red stripes, black shorts with red trim, red stockings with black/white hooped tops.

SWANSEA CITY 1994–95 LEAGUE RECORD

Match No.	Date		Venue	Opponents	Result		H/T Score	Lg. Pos.	Goalscorers	Attendance
1	Aug	13	H	Brighton & HA	D	1-1	1-0	—	Penney (pen)	4640
2		20	A	Hull C	W	2-0	0-0	9	Cornforth, Ampadu	3797
3		27	H	Birmingham C	L	0-2	0-0	13		5797
4	Sept	3	A	Cardiff C	D	1-1	1-0	17	Hayes	5523
5		6	A	Shrewsbury T	D	3-3	0-1	—	Hodge, Pascoe, Ford	3534
6		10	H	Bradford C	D	0-0	0-0	16		3445
7		13	H	Bristol R	D	0-0	0-0	—		3226
8		17	A	Cambridge U	W	3-1	2-1	15	Penney 2, Torpey	2795
9		24	H	York C	D	0-0	0-0	16		2875
10	Oct	1	A	Wycombe W	L	0-1	0-1	17		4150
11		8	A	Chester C	D	2-2	1-1	17	Ampadu, Ford	2186
12		15	H	Oxford U	L	1-3	1-3	17	Hendry	3724
13		22	A	Blackpool	L	1-2	0-2	19	Ampadu	4911
14		29	H	Peterborough U	W	2-0	1-0	17	Hendry, Bowen	2733
15	Nov	1	H	Rotherham U	W	1-0	0-0	—	Pascoe	2511
16		5	A	Crewe Alex	W	2-1	1-0	14	Bowen 2	3242
17		19	H	Stockport Co	W	2-0	0-0	14	Ampadu, Cornforth	3019
18		26	A	Wrexham	L	1-4	0-2	15	Ford	3598
19	Dec	10	H	Hull C	W	2-0	1-0	13	Torpey 2	4903
20		17	A	Brighton & HA	D	1-1	1-0	13	Torpey	6817
21		26	H	Plymouth Arg	W	3-0	3-0	12	Hodge, Hayes 2	4859
22		27	A	Leyton Orient	W	1-0	1-0	10	Hayes	3259
23		31	H	Huddersfield T	D	1-1	0-0	11	Torpey	5438
24	Jan	2	A	Bournemouth	L	2-3	1-2	10	Hodge, Penney	3816
25		14	A	Brentford	D	0-0	0-0	14		7211
26	Feb	4	H	Wrexham	D	0-0	0-0	14		4563
27		11	A	Rotherham U	D	3-3	2-3	14	Williams, Pascoe, Hodge	2858
28		17	H	Brentford	L	0-2	0-1	—		3935
29		21	A	Stockport Co	W	1-0	1-0	—	Torpey	3088
30		25	H	Wycombe W	D	1-1	0-0	14	Torpey	3699
31		28	H	Blackpool	W	1-0	0-0	—	Torpey	2308
32	Mar	4	A	York C	W	4-2	1-1	11	Bowen 2, Torpey, Hodge (pen)	2920
33		7	H	Cardiff C	W	4-1	3-0	—	Williams, Penney, Pascoe, Chapple	3943
34		11	A	Birmingham C	W	1-0	1-0	8	Hodge (pen)	16,191
35		17	H	Shrewsbury T	D	0-0	0-0	—		4130
36		21	A	Bradford C	W	3-1	1-0	—	Cornforth, Ampadu 2	4417
37		24	H	Cambridge U	W	1-0	1-0	—	Torpey	4007
38	Apr	1	A	Bristol R	L	0-1	0-0	7		7062
39		4	A	Peterborough U	L	0-1	0-1	—		3764
40		8	A	Huddersfield T	L	0-2	0-1	9		10,105
41		15	H	Leyton Orient	W	2-0	2-0	9	Torpey, Pascoe	3277
42		17	A	Plymouth Arg	L	1-2	1-1	10	Hodge	5890
43		22	H	Bournemouth	W	1-0	0-0	10	Clode	2664
44		25	H	Crewe Alex	L	0-1	0-1	—		2600
45		30	A	Oxford U	W	2-1	2-1	10	Freestone (pen), Chapple	5244
46	May	6	H	Chester C	L	0-1	0-1	10		2065

Final League Position: 10

GOALSCORERS

League (57): Torpey 11, Hodge 7 (2 pens), Ampadu 6, Bowen 5, Pascoe 5, Penney 5 (1 pen), Hayes 4, Cornforth 3, Ford 3, Chapple 2, Hendry 2, Williams 2, Clode 1, Freestone 1 (pen).
Coca-Cola Cup (5): Penney 2 (1 pen), Harris 1, Hodge 1, Pascoe 1.
FA Cup (6): Ford 2, Torpey 2, Ampadu 1, Penney 1.

Freestone R. 44 + 1	Jenkins S.R. 42	Clode M.J. 33	Ford J.S. 46	Harris M.A. 14	Ampadu P.K. 36 + 8	Bowen J.P. 25 + 6	Penney D.M. 29 + 6	Hayes M. 14 + 10	Cornforth J.M. 32 + 1	Hodge J. 38 + 6	Pascoe C.J. 32 + 3	Torpey S.D.J. 37 + 4	Perrett D.J. 3 + 12	Hendry J. 8	Jones L. 2	Basham M. 13	Chapple S.R. 4 + 5	Burns C. 3 + 2	Walker K.C. 28	Barnhouse D.J. 4	McFarlane A.A. 1 + 2	Williams J.N. 6 + 1	Edwards C. 9	Coates J.S. — + 5	Cook A.C. 1	Thomas D.J. 2 + 2	*Match No.*
1	2	3	4	5	6	7	8	9	10	11	12																1
1	2	3	4	5	6	7	8	9	10	11		12															2
1	2	3	4	5	6		8	7	10	11	12	9	14														3
1	2	3	4	5	6		8	7	10	11	12	9	14														4
1	2	3	4	5			8	7	10	11	6	9	12														5
1	2	3	4	5	14	12	8	7	10	*11*	6	9															6
1	2	3	4	5	14	12	8		10	11	6	9	7														7
1	2	3	4	5	14	7	8		10	12	6	9	11														8
1	2	3	4	5	12	7	8		10	*11*	6	9	14														9
1	2	3	4	5	12	7	8		10	11	*6*	9	14														10
1	2	3	4	5	7	14	8		10	12	6	*9*		11													11
1	2	3	4	5	7	12	8	14		11	6	*9*		10													12
15	2		3	5	10	7	8			11	6			9	*1*	4	12										13
1	2		3	*5*	14	7	8	12	10	11	6			9		4											14
1	2	3	5		14	7	*8*	12	10	11	6			9		4											15
1	2	3	5		6	7	*8*	12	10	11				9		4	14										16
1	2	3	5		6	7	8		10	*11*		12	14	9		4											17
1	2	3	5		6	7	*8*	12	10	11		14		9		4											18
1	2		5		10	7	8			11		9				4	6	12	3								19
1	*2*		5		10	7	8			11		9	12			4	6	14	3								20
1			5		10		12	7		*11*		9	14			4	6	8	3	2							21
1			5		10		8	7	6	11		9	12			4			3	2							22
1			5		8		12	*7*	10	11		9	14			4		6	3	2							23
1			5		8		12	7	10	11		9	14			4		*6*	3	2							24
1	2		5		6		8	7	10	11		9				4			3		12						25
1	2		5		3	12	8	7	10		6	9							4			11					26
1	2		5		3		8	7	10	12	6	*9*							4		14	11					27
1	2	3	5				8	7	10	12	6	14							4		*9*	11					28
1	2	3	5		10	7				12	6	9							4			11	8				29
1	2	*3*	5		10	7				12	6	9					14		4			11	8				30
1	2	3	5		10	7	8			11	6	9							4								31
1	2	3	5		10	7	12			11	6	9							4			14	8				32
1	2	3	5		10		8			11	6	9					12		4			7					33
1	2	3	5		10	7	12			11	6	9							4				8	14			34
1	2	3	5		10	7	8		12	11	6	9							4					14			35
1	2	3	5		7		12		10	11	6	9							4				8				36
1	2	3	5		7		8		10	11	6	9							4					12			37
1	2		5		7				10	11	*6*	9	8				12		4				3	14			38
1	2	3	5		7				10	11	6	9	12						4				8				39
1	2		5		7	12		14	10	*11*	6	9							4				8		3		40
1	2	3	5		8	7		12	10	11	6	9							4								41
1	2	3	5		*8*	7		12	10	11	6	9							4							14	42
1	2	3	5		8	7		12		11	6	9							4							10	43
	2	3	5		10	7		12		*11*	6	9			1				4				8			14	44
1	2	3	5		11	7			10		6	9					8		4								45
1	2	3	5		12	7			10	11	6	*9*							4					14		8	46

Coca-Cola Cup

First Round	Exeter C (a)	2-2
	(h)	2-0
Second Round	Norwich C (a)	0-3
	(h)	1-0

FA Cup

First Round	Walton & Hersham (a)	2-0
Second Round	Bashley (a)	1-0
Third Round	Middlesbrough (h)	1-1
	(a)	2-1
Fourth Round	Newcastle U (a)	0-3

SWINDON TOWN 1994–95 *Back row (left to right):* Paul Bodin, Luc Nijholt, Brian Kilcline, Fraser Digby, Keith Scott, Nicky Hammond, Shaun Taylor, Andrew Thomson, Edwin Murray. *Third row:* Jonathan Trigg (Physio), Ross MacLaren, Mark Robinson, Austin Berkley, Adrian Viveash, Jan Aage Fjortoft, Chris Hamon, Andy Mutch, Marcus Phillips, Ty Gooden, Eddie Buckley (Kit Manager).
Second row: Joey Beauchamp, Martin Ling, Andy Rowland (First Team Coach), Steve McMahon (Player/Manager), John Trollope (Youth Team Manager), Kevin Horlock, Wayne O'Sullivan.
Front row: Ben Worrall, Jamie Pitman, Stuart James, David Elsey.

Division 2 **SWINDON TOWN**

County Ground, Swindon, Wiltshire SN1 2ED. Telephone: (01793) 430430. Fax: (01793) 536170. Marketing: (01793) 532121. Marketing Fax: (01793) 423771. Superstore: (01793) 423030. Community Office: (01793) 421303. Clubcall: 0891 121640.

Ground capacity: 15,341.

Record attendance: 32,000 v Arsenal, FA Cup 3rd rd, 15 January 1972.

Record receipts: £149,371 v Bolton W, Coca-Cola Cup semi-final 1st leg, 12 February 1995.

Pitch measurements: 114yd × 74yd.

President: C. J. Green.

Chairman: R. V. Hardman. ***Vice-Chairman:*** J. M. Spearman.

Directors: P. T. Archer, Sir Seton Willis Bt, C. J. Puffett, J. R. Hunt (Associate), P. R. Godwin CBE. ***Chief Executive:*** Steve Jones.

Manager: Steve McMahon. ***Assistant Manager:*** Andy Rowland.

Coach: Ross MacLaren. ***Physio:*** Jonathan Trigg.

Secretary: Jon Pollard. ***Youth Team Manager:*** John Trollope.

Marketing Manager: Phil Alexander. ***Community Officer:*** Shane Cook.

Year Formed: 1881 *(*see Foundation*). ***Turned Professional:*** 1894. ***Ltd Co.:*** 1894.

Club Nickname: 'Robins'.

Previous Ground: 1881–96, The Croft.

Foundation: It is generally accepted that Swindon Town came into being in 1881, although there is no firm evidence that the club's founder, Rev. William Pitt, captain of the Spartans (an offshoot of a cricket club) changed his club's name to Swindon Town before 1883, when the Spartans amalgamated with St. Mark's Young Men's Friendly Society.

First Football League game: 28 August, 1920, Division 3, v Luton T (h) W 9-1 – Nash; Kay, Macconachie; Langford, Hawley, Wareing; Jefferson (1), Fleming (4), Rogers, Batty (2), Davies (1). 1 o.g.

Record League Victory: 9–1 v Luton T, Division 3 (S), 28 August 1920 – Nash; Kay, Macconachie; Langford, Hawley, Wareing; Jefferson (1), Fleming (4), Rogers, Batty (2), Davies (1). (1 og).

Record Cup Victory: 10–1 v Farnham U Breweries (away), FA Cup, 1st rd (replay), 28 November 1925 – Nash; Dickenson, Weston, Archer, Bew, Adey; Denyer (2), Wall (1), Richardson (4), Johnson (3), Davies.

Record Defeat: 1–10 v Manchester C, FA Cup 4th rd (replay), 25 January 1930.

Most League Points (2 for a win): 64, Division 3, 1968–69.

Most League Points (3 for a win): 102, Division 4, 1985–86 (League record).

Most League Goals: 100, Division 3 (S), 1926–27.

Highest League Scorer in Season: Harry Morris, 47, Division 3 (S), 1926–27.

Most League Goals in Total Aggregate: Harry Morris, 216, 1926–33.

Most Capped Player: Rod Thomas, 30 (50), Wales.

Most League Appearances: John Trollope, 770, 1960–80.

Record Transfer Fee Received: £1,300,000 from Middlesbrough for Jan-Aage Fjortoft, March 1995.

Record Transfer Fee Paid: £800,000 to West Ham U for Joey Beauchamp, August 1994.

Football League Record: 1920 Original Member of Division 3; 1921–58 Division 3 (S); 1958–63 Division 3; 1963–65 Division 2; 1965–69 Division 3; 1969–74 Division 2; 1974–82 Division 3; 1982–86 Division 4; 1986–87 Division 3; 1987–92 Division 2; 1992–93 Division 1; 1993–94 FA Premier League; 1994–95 Division 1; 1995– Division 2.

Honours: *FA Premier League:* best season: 22nd 1993–94; *Football League* : Division 3 – Runners-up 1962–63, 1968–69; Division 4 – Champions 1985–86 (with record 102 points). *FA Cup:* Semi-finals 1910, 1912. *Football League Cup:* Winners 1969. *Anglo-Italian Cup:* Winners 1970.

Colours: All red. **Change colours:** Black/blue shirts, blue shorts, blue stockings.

SWINDON TOWN FC

SWINDON TOWN 1994–95 LEAGUE RECORD

Match No.	Date		Venue	Opponents	Result		H/T Score	Lg. Pos.	Goalscorers	Attendance
1	Aug	14	H	Port Vale	W	2-0	1-0	—	Fjortoft, Scott	10,431
2		20	A	Tranmere R	L	2-3	2-1	8	Fjortoft 2	8482
3		27	H	Watford	W	1-0	1-0	5	Ling	9781
4		31	H	WBA	D	0-0	0-0	—		11,188
5	Sept	3	A	Notts Co	W	1-0	1-0	2	Fjortoft	6537
6		11	H	Derby Co	D	1-1	1-1	4	Fjortoft	9054
7		14	H	Reading	W	1-0	0-0	—	Scott	11,551
8		17	A	Charlton Ath	L	0-1	0-1	4		9794
9		24	H	Grimsby T	W	3-2	1-1	3	Bodin 2 (1 pen), Scott	8219
10	Oct	1	A	Barnsley	L	1-2	0-1	5	Taylor	3911
11		8	H	Wolverhampton W	W	3-2	2-2	5	Bodin, Scott, Beauchamp	14,036
12		15	A	Portsmouth	L	3-4	1-2	5	Bodin (pen), Fjortoft 2	10,610
13		22	H	Southend U	D	2-2	1-2	5	Fjortoft 2	9909
14		29	A	Middlesbrough	L	1-3	0-1	5	Fjortoft	17,328
15	Nov	1	A	Bolton W	L	0-3	0-1	—		10,046
16		5	H	Millwall	L	1-2	0-0	11	Bodin (pen)	9311
17		20	A	Bristol C	L	2-3	0-0	16	Scott 2	9086
18		23	H	Burnley	D	1-1	1-0	—	Scott	7654
19		26	H	Luton T	L	1-2	1-1	19	Scott	9455
20	Dec	3	A	Southend U	L	0-2	0-1	19		5803
21		10	H	Tranmere R	D	2-2	2-1	20	Bodin, Fjortoft	8608
22		17	A	Port Vale	D	2-2	1-1	19	Taylor, Fjortoft	7747
23		26	A	Stoke C	D	0-0	0-0	19		17,662
24		27	H	Sheffield U	L	1-3	0-1	20	Fjortoft	11,007
25		31	A	Oldham Ath	D	1-1	1-1	20	Ling	8917
26	Jan	15	H	Middlesbrough	W	2-1	1-1	20	Fjortoft, Horlock	8888
27	Feb	4	A	Burnley	W	2-1	1-0	19	Thorne 2	10,960
28		15	H	Bristol C	L	0-3	0-1	—		9881
29		18	A	Luton T	L	0-3	0-1	22		6595
30		25	H	Barnsley	D	0-0	0-0	22		8158
31	Mar	1	A	Millwall	L	1-3	0-0	—	Beauchamp	5950
32		4	A	Grimsby T	D	1-1	0-1	22	Taylor	4934
33		11	A	Watford	L	0-2	0-0	22		7123
34		15	H	Sunderland	W	1-0	1-0	—	Thorne	8233
35		19	A	WBA	W	5-2	0-0	21	Thorne 3, Fjortoft, Gooden	12,960
36		22	A	Derby Co	L	1-3	1-1	—	Fjortoft	16,839
37		25	H	Charlton Ath	L	0-1	0-0	22		9106
38	Apr	1	A	Reading	L	0-3	0-2	22		12,565
39		5	H	Bolton W	L	0-1	0-0	—		8100
40		8	H	Oldham Ath	W	3-1	2-1	21	Viveash, Beauchamp, Taylor	7488
41		15	A	Sheffield U	D	2-2	1-0	21	Gooden, Ling	12,217
42		17	H	Stoke C	L	0-1	0-1	21		10,549
43		22	A	Sunderland	L	0-1	0-1	21		16,874
44		29	H	Portsmouth	L	0-2	0-1	22		9220
45	May	3	H	Notts Co	W	3-0	1-0	—	Hamon, Thorne 2	6553
46		7	A	Wolverhampton W	D	1-1	1-1	21	Thorne	26,245

Final League Position: 21

GOALSCORERS

League (54): Fjortoft 16, Thorne 9, Scott 8, Bodin 6 (3 pens), Taylor 4, Beauchamp 3, Ling 3, Gooden 2, Hamon 1, Horlock 1, Viveash 1.
Coca-Cola Cup (18): Fjortoft 9, Scott 3, Mutch 2, Thorne 2, Thomson 1, own goal 1.
FA Cup (2): Fjortoft 1, Nijholt 1.

Digby F.C. 39	Robinson M. 40	Bodin P. 25	Nijholt L. 35	Whitbread A.R. 1	Taylor S. 37	Ling M. 31 + 5	Fenwick T.W. 2	Fjortoft J.A. 36	Mutch A. 7 + 13	Horlock K. 34 + 4	O'Sullivan W.S. 22 + 8	Scott K. 21 + 3	Kilcline B. 6 + 1	Beauchamp J.D. 38 + 4	Thomson A. 20 + 1	Berkley A.J. — + 1	Webb N.J. 5 + 1	Tiler C. 2	MacLaren R. 3	Murray E.J. 4 + 2	Hamon C. 2 + 3	McMahon S. 16 + 1	Culverhouse I.B. 9	Hammond N.D. 7	Thorne P.L. 20	Gooden T.M. 13 + 3	Todd A.J.J. 13	Viveash A.L. 14	Hooper D. — + 4	Drysdale J. 1	Worrall B.J. 1 + 2	Pitman J.R. 2 + 1	*Match No.*
1	2	3	4	5	6	7	8	9	*10*	11	12	14																					1
1	2	3	5		6	7	8	9	10	11		14	*4*	12																			2
1	2	3	5		6	7		9			11	10		8	4																		3
1	2	3	5		6	7		9	12	14	*11*	10		8	4																		4
1	2		5		6	7		9	12	3	11	10		8	4																		5
1	2	3	5		6	7		9	12	*11*	14	10		8	4																		6
1	2	3	5		6	10		9		11	7	12		8	4																		7
1	2	3	5		6	10		9		11	7	8	12		4	14																	8
1	2	3	5		6	7		9	12	*11*	14	10		8	4																		9
1	2	3	5		6	7		9		11		10		8	4																		10
1	2	3	5		6	10		9	12			11		8	4		7																11
1	2	3	4		6	10		9	12	14		11	5	8			*7*																12
1	2	3	5		6	10		9	12	14		11		*8*	4		7																13
1	2	3	5		*6*	10		9	12	7		11		8	4		14																14
1	2	3	5			12		9	14	7		11	6	*8*	4		10																15
1	2	3	5			12		9	14	*7*		11	6	8	4		10																16
1	2	3						9	10	7	12	11	*6*	8				5	4	14													17
1	2	3						9	10	12	7	11		8	5			6	4														18
1	2	3						9	10	8	7	11	6	12	5				4		14												19
1	2	3	5			10		9		7		11		8	4							6											20
1	2	3	5					9		7		11		8	4							10	6										21
1		3	5		6	10		9	12	7		11		8	4								2										22
1	2	3	5		6	10		9		7		11		8									4										23
1	2	3	*5*		6	10		9	12	7	14	11		8									4										24
	2	3	5		6	11		9	8	7				12								10	4	1									25
	2	3	5		6	11		9	10	7				8									4	1									26
	2		5		6	11		9		7	8									3			4	1	10	12							27
	2		5			11		9		7	4			8	6					3		12		1	10								28
	2					11		9	12	5	4			8						3		6		1	10	7							29
	2		5		6			9		3	7			8								11	4	1	10								30
					6	12		9		3	7			8						*5*		11	2	1	10	14	4						31
1					6			9		3	2			8								11			10	7	4	5	12				32
1			5		6			9		7	2			12								11			10	*8*	3	4	14				33
1					6			9		5	3			8								11			10	7	2	4					34
1	5				6			9		7	2			8								11			10	12	3	4					35
1	11		5		6	12		9			3			8											10	7	2	4					36
1	5				6	9					12			8								11			10	7	2	4		3			37
1	5				6	7				3				8							12	11			10	9	2	4					38
1	5				6					3	7			8								11			10	9	2	4					39
1	2		5		6	3					7			8								11			10	9		4	12				40
1	3		5		6	7								8								11			10	9	2	4					41
1	3		5		6	7					14			8	12							11			10	9	2	4					42
1	2		5		6	11				8	7										12				10	9	3	4	14				43
1			5		6	11					7			8	3										10	*9*	2	4			12	14	44
1	2		5		6	11				3	12			8							10				9			4			14	7	45
1	4		5		6	12				3	2			11						14	*10*				9						8	7	46

Coca-Cola Cup

Second Round	Charlton Ath (h)	1-3
	(a)	4-1
Third Round	Brighton & HA (a)	1-1
	(h)	4-1
Fourth Round	Derby Co (h)	2-1
Fifth Round	Millwall (h)	3-1
Semi-final	Bolton W (h)	2-1
	(a)	1-3

FA Cup

Third Round	Marlow (h)	2-0
Fourth Round	Watford (a)	0-1

TORQUAY UNITED 1994–95 *Back row (left to right):* Ellis Laight, Kevin Hodges, Nick Burton, Lee Barrow, Scott Stamps, Duane Darby, Richard Hancox, Paul Buckle.
Centre row: John James, Paul Trollope, Darren Moore, Tim Thornley, Ashley Bayes, Adrian Tucker, Chima Okorie, Adrian Foster, Bruce Stuckey.
Front row: Norman Medhurst, Tom Kelly, Gregory Goodridge, Don O'Riordan, Mike Bateson, Chris Curran, Ian Hathaway, Paul Compton.

Division 3 **TORQUAY UNITED**

Plainmoor Ground, Torquay, Devon TQ1 3PS. Telephone: (01803) 328666. Fax: (01803) 323976. Clubcall: 0891 121641.

Ground capacity: 6000.

Record attendance: 21,908 v Huddersfield T, FA Cup 4th rd, 29 January 1955.

Record receipts: £26,205 v Exeter C, Division 3, 1 January 1992.

Pitch measurements: 112yd × 74yd.

President: A. J. Boyce.

Chairman/Managing Director: M. Bateson. ***Directors:*** Mrs S. Bateson, M. Beer, M. Benney, I. Hayman, Miss H. Kindeleit, T. Lilley, B. Palk, W. Rogers, D. Turner.

Player-Manager: Don O'Riordan. ***Physio:*** Norman Medhurst.

Company Secretary: Miss H. Kindeleit.

Secretary General Manager: D. F. Turner. ***Lottery Administrators:*** C. Munslow and A. Sandford. ***Commercial Manager:*** D. Turner.

Year Formed: 1898. ***Turned Professional:*** 1921. ***Ltd Co.:*** 1921.

Previous Name: 1910, Torquay Town; 1921, Torquay United.

Nickname: 'The Gulls'.

Previous Grounds: 1898, Teignmouth Road; 1901, Torquay Recreation Ground; 1905, Cricket Field Road; 1907–10, Torquay Cricket Ground.

Foundation: The idea of establishing a Torquay club was agreed by old boys of Torquay College and Torbay College, while sitting in Princess Gardens listening to the band. A proper meeting was subsequently held at Tor Abbey Hotel at which officers were elected. This was in 1898 and the club's first competition was the Eastern League (later known as the East Devon League).

First Football League game: 27 August, 1927, Division 3(S), v Exeter C (h) D 1-1 – Millsom; Cook, Smith; Wellock, Wragg, Connor, Mackey, Turner (1), Jones, McGovern, Thomson.

Record League Victory: 9–0 v Swindon T, Division 3 (S), 8 March 1952 – George Webber; Topping, Ralph Calland; Brown, Eric Webber, Towers; Shaw (1), Marchant (1), Northcott (2), Collins (3), Edds (2).

Record Cup Victory: 7–1 v Northampton T, FA Cup, 1st rd, 14 November 1959 – Gill; Penford, Downs; Bettany, George Northcott, Rawson; Baxter, Cox, Tommy Northcott (1), Bond (3), Pym (3).

Record Defeat: 2–10 v Fulham, Division 3 (S), 7 September 1931 and v Luton T, Division 3 (S), 2 September 1933.

Most League Points (2 for a win): 60, Division 4, 1959–60.

Most League Points (3 for a win): 77, Division 4, 1987–88.

Most League Goals: 89, Division 3 (S), 1956–57.

Highest League Scorer in Season: Sammy Collins, 40, Division 3 (S), 1955–56.

Most League Goals in Total Aggregate: Sammy Collins, 204, 1948–58.

Most Capped Player: None.

Most League Appearances: Dennis Lewis, 443, 1947–59.

Record Transfer Fee Received: £180,000 from Manchester U for Lee Sharpe, May 1988.

Record Transfer Fee Paid: £60,000 to Dundee for Wes Saunders, July 1990.

Football League Record: 1927 Elected to Division 3 (S); 1958–60 Division 4; 1960–62 Division 3; 1962–66 Division 4; 1966–72 Division 3; 1972–91 Division 4; 1991– Division 3.

Honours: *Football League:* Division 3 best season: 4th, 1967–68; Division 3 (S) – Runners-up 1956–57; Division 4 – Promoted 1959–60 (3rd), 1965–66 (3rd), 1990–91 (Play-offs). *FA Cup:* best season: 4th rd, 1949, 1955, 1971, 1983, 1990. *Football League Cup:* never past 3rd rd. *Sherpa Van Trophy:* Runners-up 1989.

Colours: Yellow and navy striped shirts, navy shorts, yellow stockings. **Change colours:** Blue and white striped shirts, white shorts, blue stockings.

TORQUAY UNITED 1994–95 LEAGUE RECORD

Match No.	Date	Venue	Opponents	Result	H/T Score	Lg. Pos.	Goalscorers	Attendance
1	Aug 13	A	Colchester U	W 3-1	2-1	—	Okorie, Buckle, Trollope	3175
2	20	H	Carlisle U	D 1-1	0-0	3	Hancox	3506
3	27	A	Lincoln C	W 2-1	1-1	3	Hancox 2	3154
4	30	H	Northampton T	W 2-1	2-0	—	Okorie 2	3619
5	Sept 3	H	Fulham	W 2-1	2-1	2	Stamps, Okorie	4739
6	10	A	Darlington	L 1-2	1-1	2	Trollope	2161
7	13	A	Hereford U	D 1-1	0-1	—	Goodridge	2153
8	17	H	Colchester U	D 3-3	1-0	4	Trollope, Hancox, Darby	3390
9	24	H	Barnet	L 1-2	0-2	7	Newson (og)	3280
10	Oct 1	A	Chesterfield	L 0-1	0-0	10		2465
11	8	A	Gillingham	L 0-1	0-1	10		2439
12	15	H	Mansfield T	W 2-1	1-1	9	Trollope, Moore	2800
13	22	H	Rochdale	W 4-1	1-0	6	Goodridge 2, Hodges, Hathaway	2547
14	29	A	Doncaster R	L 0-3	0-0	7		2697
15	Nov 5	H	Scunthorpe U	D 1-1	1-0	8	Barrow	3036
16	19	A	Scarborough	D 1-1	0-1	8	Buckle	1241
17	26	H	Wigan Ath	D 0-0	0-0	8		2509
18	Dec 10	A	Carlisle U	L 0-1	0-1	9		5141
19	17	H	Lincoln C	W 2-1	1-0	8	Hancox, Sturridge	2004
20	26	A	Exeter C	W 2-1	0-1	8	Moore, O'Riordan	5538
21	27	H	Hartlepool U	D 2-2	1-1	9	Sturridge, Kelly	3172
22	Jan 2	H	Preston NE	W 1-0	1-0	9	Sturridge	3770
23	7	A	Rochdale	L 0-2	0-0	10		1636
24	14	H	Walsall	W 3-2	0-1	7	Okorie, Hathaway, Sturridge	2976
25	21	A	Scunthorpe U	L 2-3	2-2	9	Curran, Hancox	2229
26	28	H	Doncaster R	L 0-1	0-0	10		2852
27	Feb 4	A	Wigan Ath	D 1-1	1-0	11	Sturridge	1609
28	18	A	Walsall	L 0-1	0-0	12		3708
29	25	H	Chesterfield	D 3-3	1-1	11	Hathaway 2, Darby	3236
30	28	A	Bury	L 1-3	0-1	—	Darby	2241
31	Mar 4	A	Barnet	L 0-2	0-1	14		1816
32	7	H	Scarborough	W 2-1	1-1	—	Barrow, Byng	1492
33	11	H	Darlington	W 1-0	0-0	11	Kelly	2332
34	18	A	Northampton T	L 0-2	0-0	12		3832
35	25	A	Fulham	L 1-2	1-0	12	Hathaway	4941
36	Apr 1	H	Hereford U	L 0-1	0-1	12		2410
37	8	H	Bury	D 2-2	1-1	13	Curran, Moore	1969
38	15	A	Hartlepool U	D 1-1	0-0	14	Hancox	1770
39	18	H	Exeter C	D 0-0	0-0	—		4155
40	22	A	Preston NE	W 1-0	0-0	13	Hancox	9173
41	29	A	Mansfield T	D 2-2	1-1	13	Darby, Barrow	3216
42	May 6	H	Gillingham	W 3-1	1-0	13	Hancox, Kelly, Buckle	2638

Final League Position: 13

GOALSCORERS

League (54): Hancox 9, Hathaway 5, Okorie 5, Sturridge 5, Darby 4, Trollope 4, Barrow 3, Buckle 3, Goodridge 3, Kelly 3, Moore 3, Curran 2, Byng 1, Hodges 1, O'Riordan 1, Stamps 1, own goal 1.
Coca-Cola Cup (4): Hancox 3, Goodridge 1.
FA Cup (3): Hancox 1, Hathaway 1, Okorie 1.

Bayes A.J. 37	Hodges K. 15 + 13	Stamps S. 23 + 2	O'Riordan D.J. 23 + 1	Barrow L.A. 40	Curran C. 27	Trollope P.J. 18	Buckle P.J. 30 + 2	Hancox R. 29 + 7	Okorie C. 26 + 1	Goodridge G.R.S. 27 + 3	Hathaway I.A. 33 + 5	Darby D.A. 13 + 11	Moore D.M. 30	Kelly T.J. 32 + 1	Burton N.J. 7 + 1	Nicholson M. 1	Byng D.G. 6 + 1	Thornley T.J. — + 1	Davis K.G. 2	Winstone S.J. 1 + 1	Laight E.S. 4 + 6	Brass C.P. 7	Sturridge D.C. 10	Pettinger P.A. 3	Povey N.A. 5 + 3	Colcombe S. 10	Morah O. 2	Hawthorne M.D. 1 + 1	*Match No.*
1	2	3	4	5	6	7	8	*9*	10	11	12	14																	1
1	2	3	4	5	6	7	8	9	10	11	12																		2
1		3	4	5	6	7	8	9	10	11		12	2																3
1	2	3		5	6	7	*8*	9	10	11	4	12		14															4
1		3	*4*	5	6	7	8	9	10	11	14	12	2																5
1	12	3		2	6	7	8		10	11		9	5		4														6
1		3		2	6	7	8	*9*	10	11	12		5			4	14	15											7
	2	*3*		6		7	8	9	10	11	4	12	5		14				1										8
	14			2	6	7	8	9	10	11		12	5	3	*4*				1										9
1				2		7	12	8	10	11			5	3	6		*9*			4	14								10
1	12				6	7	8	9	10	*11*	4		5	3	2					14									11
1					6	7		9	10	11	12	8	5	3	4							2							12
1	8	3		6		7		12		11	10		5	4			9					2							13
1	8	3		6		7		12		11	10		5	4			9					2							14
1	12	3	14	6		7		9	8	*11*	10		5	4								2							15
1	9		4	6		7	8		11		10		5	3								2							16
1	9		*4*	6		7	8	11	12	14	10		5	3								2							17
1	12		4	6		7	8	11	9		10		5	3								2							18
1	12		4	6	2			7	8	11	10		5	3									9						19
1	12		4	6	2			7	8	11	10		5	3									9						20
	12		4	6	2			7	8	11	10		5	3									9	1					21
			4	6	2			7	8	11	10		5	3									9	1					22
	12		4	6	2			7	8	11	10		5	3									9	1					23
1	12		4	6	2			7	8	11	10			3									9		5				24
1	12	5		6	2		14	7		11	*10*	8		3									9			4			25
1	5			6	2		4	7		11	*10*	8									12		9		14	3			26
1	5		4	6			11		7	12	10	8		3									9			2			27
1		7	4	6			8		11	12	10			3	5								9			2			28
1	12	7	4	6			5	*9*	8	11	10	14		3												2			29
1		5	4	6			8	12	7		10	9		3	11											2			30
1	*7*		4	6			8	12		11	10	9	5	3							14					2			31
1			*4*	6			8	12			10	9	5	3			11				14				7	2			32
1		12	4	6			8	14			10	*9*	5	3			11								7	2			33
1		12	4	6	5		8	14			10	9		3			*11*								7	2			34
1		2	4	*6*	5		8				10	12	*7*	3							11						9	14	35
1		7	4	6	2		8	11			10	12	5	3							14						*9*		36
1	*7*	2		6	4		8		11		10	12	5	3							9				14				37
1	7	3		6	4		8	11			10		5								9							2	38
1	7	2		6	4		8	5		11	10	12		3							9								39
1		2		6	4		8	7		11	10	9	5	3															40
1	11	2		6	4		8	7			*10*	9	5	3							12				14				41
1	12	2		6	4		8	7			10	9	5	3											11				42

Coca-Cola Cup

First Round	Cardiff C (a)	0-1
	(h)	4-2
Second Round	Wimbledon (a)	0-2
	(h)	0-1

FA Cup

First Round	Kidderminster H (a)	1-1
	(h)	1-0
Second Round	Enfield (a)	1-1
	(h)	0-1

TOTTENHAM HOTSPUR 1994–95 *Back row (left to right):* Darren Anderton, Jason Dozzell, Kevin Scott, Ian Walker, Erik Thorstvedt, Chris Day, Sol Campbell, Jason Cundy, Stuart Nethercott.
Centre row: Pat Jennings (Goalkeeping Coach), Danny Hill, Colin Calderwood, Justin Edinburgh, Jurgen Klinsmann, David Howells, Ilie Dumitrescu, Paul Mahorn, Tony Lenaghan (Physio), Roy Reyland (Kit Manager).
Front row: Steve Perryman (Assistant Manager), Micky Hazard, David Kerslake, Nick Barmby, Gary Mabbutt, Ossie Ardiles, Teddy Sheringham, Dean Austin, Steve Carr, Darren Caskey, Chris Hughton (Reserve Team Manager).
(Photograph: Action Images)

FA Premiership **TOTTENHAM HOTSPUR**

748 High Rd, Tottenham, London N17 0AP. Telephone: (0181) 365 5000. Fax: (0181) 365 5005. Commercial Dept: (0181) 365 5010. Ticketline: 0891 100515. Telephone Bookings: (0171) 396 4567. Ticket Office: (0181) 365 5050. Spurs Line: 0891 100500. Members Ticketline: (0181) 365 5100. Additional Recorded Information: (0181) 880 3377.

Ground capacity: 33,147.

Record attendance: 75,038 v Sunderland, FA Cup 6th rd, 5 March 1938.

Record receipts: £336,702 v Manchester U, Division 1, 28 September 1991.

Pitch measurements: 110yd × 73yd.

Directors: A. M. Sugar (Chairman), C. Littner (Chief Executive), C. T. Sandy (Finance). ***Non-Executive:*** A. G. Berry (Deputy Chairman), D. A. Alexiou, I. Yawetz.

President: W. E. Nicholson OBE. ***Vice-President:*** N. Soloman.

Manager: Gerry Francis. ***Assistant Manager:*** Roger Cross. ***Coach:*** Chris Hughton. ***Physio:*** Tony Lenaghan. ***Secretary:*** Peter Barnes. ***Commercial Manager:*** Mike Rollo. ***PRO:*** John Fennelly.

Year Formed: 1882. ***Turned Professional:*** 1895. ***Ltd Co.:*** 1898.

Club Nickname: 'Spurs'.

Previous Name: 1882–85, Hotspur Football Club.

Previous Grounds: 1882, Tottenham Marshes; 1885, Northumberland Park; 1898, White Hart Lane.

Foundation: The Hotspur Football Club was formed from an older cricket club in 1882. Most of the founders were old boys St. John's Presbyterian School and Tottenham Grammar School. The Casey brothers were well to the fore as the family provided the club's first goalposts (painted blue and white) and their first ball. They soon adopted the local YMCA as their meeing place, but after a couple of moves settled at the Red House, which is still their headquarters, although now known simply as 748 High Road.

First Football League game: 1 September, 1908, Division 2, v Wolverhampton W (h) W 3-0 – Hewitson; Coquet, Burton; Morris (1), Steel (D), Darnell; Walton, Woodward (2), Macfarlane, R. Steel, Middlemiss.

Record League Victory: 9–0 v Bristol R, Division 2, 22 October 1977 – Davies; Naylor, Holmes, Hoddle (1), McAllister, Perryman, Pratt, McNab, Morris (3), Lee (4), Taylor (1).

Record Cup Victory: 13–2 v Crewe Alex, FA Cup, 4th rd (replay), 3 February 1960 – Brown; Hills, Henry; Blanchflower, Norman, Mackay; White, Harmer (1), Smith (4), Allen (5), Jones (3 incl. 1p).

Record Defeat: 0–7 v Liverpool, Division 1, 2 September 1978.

Most League Points (2 for a win): 70, Division 2, 1919–20.

Most League Points (3 for a win): 77, Division 1, 1984–85.

Most League Goals: 115, Division 1, 1960–61.

Highest League Scorer in Season: Jimmy Greaves, 37, Division 1, 1962–63.

Most League Goals in Total Aggregate: Jimmy Greaves, 220, 1961–70.

Most Capped Player: Pat Jennings, 74 (119), Northern Ireland.

Most League Appearances: Steve Perryman, 655, 1969–86.

Record Transfer Fee Received: £5,500,000 from Lazio for Paul Gascoigne, May 1992.

Record Transfer Fee Paid: £4,500,000 to Crystal Palace for Chris Armstrong, June 1995.

Football League Record: 1908 Elected to Division 2; 1909–15 Division 1; 1919–20 Division 2; 1920–28 Division 1; 1928–33 Division 2; 1933–35 Division 1; 1935–50 Division 2; 1950–77 Division 1; 1977–78 Division 2; 1978–92 Division 1; 1992– FA Premier League.

Honours: *Football League:* Division 1 – Champions 1950–51, 1960–61; Runners-up 1921–22, 1951–52, 1956–57, 1962–63; Division 2 – Champions 1919–20, 1949–50; Runners-up 1908–09, 1932–33; Promoted 1977–78 (3rd). *FA Cup:* Winners 1901 (as non-League club), 1921, 1961, 1962, 1967, 1981, 1982, 1991 (8 wins stands as the record); Runners-up 1987. *Football League Cup:* Winners 1971, 1973; Runners-up 1982. **European Competitions:** *European Cup:* 1961–62. *European Cup-Winners' Cup:* 1962–63 (winners), 1963–64, 1967–68, 1981–82 (runners-up), 1982–83, 1991–92. *UEFA Cup:* 1971–72 (winners), 1972–73, 1973–74 (runners-up), 1983–84 (winners), 1984–85.

Colours: White shirts, navy blue shorts, white stockings. **Change colours:** Navy/purple.

TOTTENHAM HOTSPUR 1994–95 LEAGUE RECORD

Match No.	*Date*	*Venue*	*Opponents*	*Result*	*H/T Score*	*Lg. Pos.*	*Goalscorers*	*Atten-dance*
1	Aug 20	A	Sheffield W	W 4-3	2-0	—	Sheringham, Anderton, Barmby, Klinsmann	34,051
2	24	H	Everton	W 2-1	2-0	—	Klinsmann 2	24,553
3	27	H	Manchester U	L 0-1	0-0	8		24,502
4	30	A	Ipswich T	W 3-1	3-0	—	Klinsmann 2, Dumitrescu	22,430
5	Sept 12	H	Southampton	L 1-2	1-0	—	Klinsmann	22,387
6	17	A	Leicester C	L 1-3	0-1	9	Klinsmann	21,300
7	24	H	Nottingham F	L 1-4	1-1	12	Dumitrescu	24,558
8	Oct 1	A	Wimbledon	W 2-1	1-1	10	Sheringham, Popescu	16,802
9	8	H	QPR	D 1-1	0-1	10	Barmby	25,799
10	15	A	Leeds U	D 1-1	1-0	12	Sheringham	39,362
11	22	A	Manchester C	L 2-5	1-3	13	Dumitrescu 2 (1 pen)	25,473
12	29	H	West Ham U	W 3-1	1-1	11	Klinsmann, Sheringham, Barmby	26,271
13	Nov 5	A	Blackburn R	L 0-2	0-1	13		26,933
14	19	H	Aston Villa	L 3-4	1-3	15	Sheringham, Klinsmann (pen), Bosnich (og)	26,899
15	23	H	Chelsea	D 0-0	0-0	—		27,037
16	26	A	Liverpool	D 1-1	0-1	14	Ruddock (og)	35,007
17	Dec 3	H	Newcastle U	W 4-2	2-2	11	Sheringham 3, Popescu	28,002
18	10	H	Sheffield W	W 3-1	0-1	10	Barmby, Klinsmann, Calderwood	25,912
19	17	A	Everton	D 0-0	0-0	10		32,813
20	26	A	Norwich C	W 2-0	1-0	8	Barmby, Sheringham	21,814
21	27	H	Crystal Palace	D 0-0	0-0	—		27,730
22	31	A	Coventry C	W 4-0	1-0	6	Darby (og), Barmby, Anderton, Sheringham	19,965
23	Jan 2	H	Arsenal	W 1-0	1-0	6	Popescu	28,747
24	14	A	West Ham U	W 2-1	0-1	6	Sheringham, Klinsmann	24,578
25	25	A	Aston Villa	L 0-1	0-1	—		40,017
26	Feb 5	H	Blackburn R	W 3-1	1-0	6	Klinsmann, Anderton, Barmby	28,124
27	11	A	Chelsea	D 1-1	1-0	6	Sheringham	30,812
28	25	H	Wimbledon	L 1-2	0-1	7	Klinsmann	27,258
29	Mar 4	A	Nottingham F	D 2-2	0-0	6	Sheringham, Calderwood	28,711
30	8	H	Ipswich T	W 3-0	2-0	—	Klinsmann, Barmby, Youds (og)	24,930
31	15	A	Manchester U	D 0-0	0-0	—		43,802
32	18	H	Leicester C	W 1-0	0-0	7	Klinsmann	30,851
33	22	H	Liverpool	D 0-0	0-0	—		31,988
34	Apr 2	A	Southampton	L 3-4	2-2	7	Sheringham 2, Klinsmann	15,105
35	11	H	Manchester C	W 2-1	0-0	—	Howells, Klinsmann	27,410
36	14	A	Crystal Palace	D 1-1	0-1	—	Klinsmann	18,068
37	17	H	Norwich C	W 1-0	1-0	7	Sheringham	32,304
38	29	A	Arsenal	D 1-1	0-0	7	Klinsmann	38,377
39	May 3	A	Newcastle U	D 3-3	3-2	—	Barmby, Klinsmann, Anderton	35,603
40	6	A	QPR	L 1-2	1-0	7	Sheringham	18,637
41	9	H	Coventry C	L 1-3	0-1	—	Anderton	24,930
42	14	H	Leeds U	D 1-1	1-0	7	Sheringham	33,040

Final League Position: 7

GOALSCORERS

League (66): Klinsmann 20 (1 pen), Sheringham 18, Barmby 9, Anderton 5, Dumitrescu 4 (1 pen), Popescu 3, Calderwood 2, Howells 1, own goals 4.
Coca-Cola Cup (8): Klinsmann 4, Anderton 1, Barmby 1, Dumitrescu 1, Sheringham 1.
FA Cup (17): Klinsmann 5 (2 pens), Rosenthal 4, Sheringham 4, Anderton 1, Barmby 1, Nethercott 1, own goal 1.

Walker I.M. 41	Kerslake D. 16 + 2	Edinburgh J.C. 29 + 2	Nethercott S. 8 + 9	Calderwood C. 35 + 1	Campbell S. 29 + 1	Anderton D.R. 37	Barmby N.J. 37 + 1	Klinsmann J. 41	Sheringham E.P. 41 + 1	Dumitrescu I. 11 + 2	Hazard M. 2 + 9	Mabbutt G.V. 33 + 3	Popescu G. 23	Hill D.R.L. 1 + 2	Scott K.W. 4	Dozzell J.A.W. 6 + 1	Austin D.B. 23 + 1	Rosenthal R. 14 + 6	Thorstvedt E. 1	Howells D. 26	Caskey D.M. 1 + 3	McMahon G.J. 2	Turner A.P. 1	*Match No.*
1	2	3	4	5	*6*	7	8	9	10	11	12	14												1
1	2	3	*4*	5	6	7	8	9	10	11	12	14												2
1	2	3	4	5	6	7	8	9	10	11	12													3
1	2	3	4	5	6	7	8	9	10	11		12												4
1	2	3	4	5	6	7	8	9	10	11	12													5
1	2	3	4	5	6	7	8	9	10	11	12													6
1	2	3			5	7		9	10	11	8	6	4	12										7
1	2					7		9	10	11	12	6	4		5	8	3							8
1	2	3		4	6		8	9	10		12			11	5	*7*		14						9
1	2	3		12	6		8	9	10	11			4		5	7								10
1	2	3			6		8	9	10	11	12		4		5	7								11
	2	3			5		8	9	12	11	*7*	6	4	14		10			1					12
1	2	3			5		8	9	10		12	6	4			*11*		14		7				13
1	*2*		14	5	3	7	12	9	10			6	4							11	8			14
1				5	3	7	8	9	10	12		6	4				2			11				15
1				5	3	7	8	9	10	12		6	4				2			11				16
1		12		5	3	7	8	9	10			6	4				2			11				17
1				5	3	7	8	9	10			6					2	11		4				18
1				5	3	7	8		10			6	4				2	9		11				19
1			12	5	3	7	8	9	10			6	4				2			11				20
1			12	5	3	7	*8*	9	10			6	4				2	14		11				21
1			14	5	3	7	8	9	10			6	*4*				2	12		11				22
1			12	5	3	7		9	10			6	4				2	11		8				23
1		12		5	3	7	8	9	10			6	4				2			11				24
1		3		5	11	7	8	9	10			6	4				2				12			25
1		3	12	5	2	7	8	9	10			6	4							11				26
1		3		5	2	7	8	9	10			6	4							11				27
1		3		5	2	7	8	9	10			6	*4*				12	14		11				28
1		3		5		7	8	9	10			6					2	11		4				29
1		3		5		7	8	9	10			6					2	11		4	12			30
1		3		5		7	8	9	10			6					2	11		4				31
1		3		5		7	8	9	10			6					2	11		4				32
1	12	3	4			7	8	9	10			6					2	11		5				33
1	3			5		7	8	9	10			6					2	11		4				34
1		3	12	5		7	8	9	10			6	4				2	14		*11*				35
1		3		5		7	8	9	10			6	4				2	11						36
1		3		5		7	8	9	10			6	4				2	11			12			37
1		3		5		7	8	9	10			6					2	11		4				38
1		3		5	12	7	8	9	10			6					2	11		4				39
1	12	3	14	5	2	7	*8*	9	10			6						11		4				40
1		3	12	5	2	7	8	9	10			6								11		4		41
1	2	3	4	5		7		9	10			6				12						11	8	42

Coca-Cola Cup

Second Round	Watford (a)	6-3
	(h)	2-3
Third Round	Notts Co (a)	0-3

FA Cup

Third Round	Altrincham (h)	3-0
Fourth Round	Sunderland (a)	4-1
Fifth Round	Southampton (h)	1-1
	(a)	6-2
Sixth Round	Liverpool (a)	2-1
Semi-final	Everton at Elland Road	1-4

TRANMERE ROVERS 1994–95 *Back row (left to right):* Kenny Jones (Trainer), Warwick Rimmer (Youth Development Officer), Alan Morgan, Dave Higgins, Dave Rogers, Dave Challinor, Gary Jones, Graham Branch, John McGreal, Ged Brannan, Shaun Garnett, Kenny Irons, John Morrissey, Les Parry (Physio), Ray Mathias (Reserve Team Coach).
Centre row: Harry McNally (Chief Scout), Norman Wilson (Secretary), Ian Moore, Gavin Allen, Chris Malkin, Martin Jones, Eric Nixon, Danny Coyne, Mick Edwards, Jonathan Kenworthy, Ian Nolan, Ronnie Moore (Coach), F. D. Corfe (Chairman).
Front row: Mark Proctor, Tony Thomas, Ian Muir, Steve Mungall, John King (Manager), John Aldridge, Phil Johnson, Liam O'Brien, Pat Nevin.

Division 1 — TRANMERE ROVERS

Prenton Park, Prenton Road West, Birkenhead L42 9PN. Telephone: (0151) 608 3677. Fax: (0151) 608 4385. Commercial: (0151) 608 0371. Valley Road Training Centre: (0151) 652 2578. Shop: (0151) 608 0438. Ticket Office: (0151) 609 0137.

Ground capacity: 16,789 (all seated).

Record attendance: 24,424 v Stoke C, FA Cup 4th rd, 5 February 1972.

Record receipts: £114,150 v Aston Villa, Coca-Cola Cup semi-final 16 February 1994.

Pitch measurements: 110yd × 70yd.

President: H. B. Thomas.

Chairman and Chief Executive: F. D. Corfe.

Directors: Norman Wilson FAAI, A. J. Adams BDS, G. E. H. Jones LLB, F. J. Williams, J. J. Holsgrove FCA.

Secretary: Norman Wilson FAAI. ***Commercial Manager:*** Janet Ratcliffe.

Manager: John King. ***Trainer:*** Kenny Jones.

Youth Development Officer: Warwick Rimmer.

Coach: Ronnie Moore. ***Physio:*** Les Parry.

Year Formed: 1884. ***Turned Professional:*** 1912. ***Ltd Co.:*** 1920.

Previous Name: Belmont AFC, 1884–85.

Club Nickname: 'The Rovers'.

Previous Grounds: 1884, Steeles Field; 1887, Ravenshaws Field/Old Prenton Park; 1912, Prenton Park.

Foundation: Formed in 1884 as Belmont they adopted their present title the following year and eventually joined their first league, the West Lancashire League in 1889–90, the same year as their first success in the Wirral Challenge Cup. The club almost folded in 1899–1900 when all the players left en bloc to join a rival club, but they survived the crisis and went from strength to strength winning the 'Combination' title in 1907–08 and the Lancashire Combination in 1913–14. They joined the Football League in 1921 from the Central League.

First Football League game: 27 August 1921, Division 3(N), v Crewe Alex (h) W 4-1 – Bradshaw; Grainger, Stuart (1); Campbell, Milnes (1), Heslop; Moreton, Groves (1), Hyam, Ford (1), Hughes.

Record League Victory: 13–4 v Oldham Ath, Division 3 (N), 26 December 1935 – Gray; Platt, Fairhurst; McLaren, Newton, Spencer; Eden, MacDonald (1), Bell (9), Woodward (2), Urmson (1).

Record Cup Victory: 13–0 v Oswestry U, FA Cup 2nd pr rd, 10 October 1914 – Ashcroft; Stevenson, Bullough, Hancock, Taylor, Holden (1), Moreton (1), Cunningham (2), Smith (5), Leck (3), Gould (1).

Record Defeat: 1–9 v Tottenham H, FA Cup 3rd rd (replay), 14 January 1953.

Most League Points (2 for a win): 60, Division 4, 1964–65.

Most League Points (3 for a win): 80, Division 4, 1988–89 and Division 3, 1989–90.

Most League Goals: 111, Division 3 (N), 1930–31.

Highest League Scorer in Season: Bunny Bell, 35, Division 3 (N), 1933–34.

Most League Goals in Total Aggregate: Ian Muir, 141, 1985–95.

Most Capped Player: John Aldridge, 25 (64), Republic of Ireland.

Most League Appearances: Harold Bell, 595, 1946–64 (incl. League record 401 consecutive appearances).

Record Transfer Fee Received: £1,500,000 from Sheffield W for Ian Nolan, August 1994.

Record Transfer Fee Paid: £350,000 to Celtic for Tommy Coyne, March 1993 and £350,000 to Rangers for Gary Stevens, October 1994.

Football League Record: 1921 Original Member of Division 3 (N): 1938–39 Division 2; 1946–58 Division 3 (N); 1958–61 Division 3; 1961–67 Division 4; 1967–75 Division 3; 1975–76 Division 4; 1976–79 Division 3; 1979–89 Division 4; 1989–91 Division 3; 1991–92 Division 2; 1992– Division 1.

Honours: *Football League* Division 1 best season: 4th, 1992–93; Division 3 (N) – Champions 1937–38; Promotion to 3rd Division: 1966–67, 1975–76; Division 4 – Runners-up 1988–89. *FA Cup:* best season: 5th rd, 1968. *Football League Cup:* best season: semi-final 1994. *Welsh Cup:* Winners 1935; Runners-up 1934. *Leyland Daf Cup:* Winners 1990; Runners-up 1991.

Colours: All white. **Change colours:** Yellow and black striped shirts, black shorts, black stockings.

TRANMERE ROVERS 1994–95 LEAGUE RECORD

Match No.	Date	Venue	Opponents	Result	H/T Score	Lg. Pos.	Goalscorers	Attendance
1	Aug 13	A	Stoke C	L 0-1	0-0	—		15,915
2	20	H	Swindon T	W 3-2	1-2	11	Aldridge 2, Nevin	8482
3	27	A	Grimsby T	L 1-3	0-2	16	Aldridge (pen)	4087
4	30	H	Luton T	W 4-2	0-0	—	Aldridge 3 (1 pen), Malkin	5480
5	Sept 3	H	Sheffield U	W 2-1	2-0	4	Malkin, Aldridge	7253
6	10	A	Wolverhampton W	L 0-2	0-1	9		27,030
7	14	A	Portsmouth	D 1-1	0-0	—	O'Brien	6383
8	17	H	Millwall	W 3-1	1-1	5	Malkin 2, Aldridge	6243
9	24	H	Sunderland	W 1-0	0-0	4	Malkin	7500
10	Oct 1	A	Burnley	D 1-1	1-0	4	Aldridge	12,427
11	8	A	Middlesbrough	W 1-0	0-0	4	Aldridge	18,497
12	15	H	WBA	W 3-1	2-1	3	Aldridge 3	7397
13	22	A	Watford	L 0-2	0-1	4		6987
14	29	H	Port Vale	D 1-1	0-0	3	Morrissey	6972
15	Nov 1	H	Barnsley	W 6-1	2-0	—	Aldridge 4, Malkin 2	5592
16	6	A	Oldham Ath	D 0-0	0-0	3		6475
17	19	H	Charlton Ath	D 1-1	0-1	4	Malkin	7567
18	26	A	Reading	W 3-1	2-0	3	Brannan, Muir 2	7887
19	Dec 3	H	Watford	W 2-1	0-0	2	Irons, Malkin	7301
20	6	A	Notts Co	L 0-1	0-0	—		4703
21	10	A	Swindon T	D 2-2	1-2	3	Mungall, Stevens	8608
22	17	H	Stoke C	L 0-1	0-0	4		7601
23	26	H	Derby Co	W 3-1	1-0	2	Malkin 2, Jones	11,581
24	27	A	Bolton W	L 0-1	0-1	3		16,782
25	31	H	Bristol C	W 2-0	2-0	3	Jones, Irons	7439
26	Jan 2	A	Southend U	D 0-0	0-0	3		5195
27	15	A	Port Vale	L 0-2	0-1	4		7944
28	22	H	Oldham Ath	W 3-1	1-1	4	Malkin, Muir, Brannan	5581
29	Feb 4	H	Notts Co	W 3-2	1-0	2	Malkin 2, Morrissey	6105
30	11	A	Barnsley	D 2-2	1-1	3	Jones, Muir	5506
31	18	H	Reading	W 1-0	0-0	2	Muir	8744
32	21	A	Charlton Ath	W 1-0	0-0	—	Nevin	11,860
33	25	H	Burnley	W 4-1	1-0	1	Muir 2, Nevin, Aldridge	9909
34	Mar 5	A	Sunderland	W 1-0	0-0	1	Garnett	12,043
35	7	A	Sheffield U	L 0-2	0-1	—		14,127
36	11	H	Grimsby T	W 2-0	2-0	1	Morrissey, Aldridge (pen)	15,810
37	18	A	Luton T	L 0-2	0-1	1		6660
38	25	A	Millwall	L 1-2	0-0	3	Malkin	7470
39	Apr 1	H	Portsmouth	W 4-2	3-1	2	Malkin, Aldridge 2, Irons	8722
40	8	A	Bristol C	W 1-0	1-0	2	Aldridge (pen)	6723
41	14	H	Bolton W	W 1-0	1-0	—	Nevin	14,959
42	17	A	Derby Co	L 0-5	0-2	3		13,957
43	21	H	Southend U	L 0-2	0-2	—		9971
44	30	A	WBA	L 1-5	0-1	5	Aldridge (pen)	17,486
45	May 3	H	Wolverhampton W	D 1-1	1-0	—	Aldridge	12,306
46	7	H	Middlesbrough	D 1-1	1-0	5	Irons	16,377

Final League Position: 5

GOALSCORERS

League (67): Aldridge 24 (5 pens), Malkin 16, Muir 7, Irons 4, Nevin 4, Jones 3, Morrissey 3, Brannan 2, Garnett 1, Mungall 1, O'Brien 1, Stevens 1.
Coca-Cola Cup (4): Aldridge 1, Brannan 1, Irons 1, Nevin 1.
FA Cup (5): Muir 3, Malkin 1, O'Brien 1.

Coyne D. 5	Higgins D.A. 16	Mungall S.H. 19 + 7	Brannan G.D. 37 + 4	Garnett S.M. 34	O'Brien L.F. 38	Morrissey J.J. 34 + 2	Aldridge J.W. 31 + 2	Irons K. 37 + 1	Nevin P.K.F. 44	Thomas T. 26	Muir I.J. 12 + 7	Malkin C.G. 42 + 1	McGreal J. 42 + 1	Kenworthy J.R. 3 + 3	Jones G.S. 6 + 13	Nixon E.W. 41	Edwards M. 2 + 1	Stevens M.G. 37	Branch G. — + 1	Moore I.R. — + 1	*Match No.*
1	2	3	4	5	6	7	8	9	10	11	12										1
1	2	14	3	5	6	7	8	4	10	*11*	12	9									2
1	2	11	3	*5*	6	7	8	4	10		12	9	14								3
1	2		3		6	7	8	4	10	11		9	5								4
1		12	3	5	6	7	8	4		11		9	2	10	14						5
			3	5	6	7	8	4	10	11	12	9	2			1					6
		12	3	5	6		8	4	10	11		9	2			1	7				7
		12	3	5	*6*	7	8	4	10	11		9	2		14	1					8
		3	10	5	6	7	8		11			9	4			1		2			9
		3	10	5	6	7	8		11			9	4			1		2			10
		3	10	5	6	7	8		11			9	4			1		2			11
		3	10	5	6	7	8		11			9	4			1		2			12
		3	10	5	6	12	8		11			9	4			1	7	2			13
		3	10	5		7	8	6	11			9	4			1		2			14
	5	3	10			7	8	6	11			9	4			1		2			15
		3	10	5		7		6	11		8	9	4		12	1		2			16
		3	10	5		7		6	11		8	9	4			1		2			17
		3	10	5		7		6	11		8	9	4			1		2			18
		3	10	5		7	8	6	11			9	4			1		2			19
	7	*3*	10	5			8	6	11		12	9	4			1	14	2			20
	4	3	10	5		7	8	6	11		12	9				1		2			21
	5		3		10	7	8	6		11		9	4			1		2	12		22
	5	12			6	7		3	10	11		9	4		8	1		2			23
		5			6	7		3	10	11		9	4		8	1		2			24
	5				6	7		3	10	11		9	4		8	1		2			25
	5	12	3		6	7		10	11			9	4		8	1		2			26
	5		12		6	7		10	11	3	8	9	4			1		2			27
	2	12	5		6	7		10	11	3	8	9	4			1					28
			10	5	6	7			11	3	8	9	4			1		2			29
			10	5	6			7	11	3	8	9	4		12	1		2			30
			10	5	6	7			11	3	8	9	4			1		2			31
			10	5	6	12		7	11	3	8	*9*	4		14	1		2			32
			10	5	6	7	12		11	3	8	9	4			1		2			33
			10	5	6	7	12	14	11	3	8	9	4			1		2			34
			3	5	6	7	8	9	*11*		10	12	4		14	1		2			35
			3	5	6	7	8	10	11		12	9	4			1		2			36
			10	5	6		8	7	11	3		9	4	14	12	1		2			37
	5	3			6		8	10	11			9	4	7	12	1		2			38
	5	3			6	7	8	10	11			*9*	4	12	14	1		2			39
		3	7	5	6		8	10	11				4		9	1		2			40
			12	5	6	7	8	10	11	3		9	4		14	1		2			41
			7	5	6		8	10	11	3		9	4		12	1		2			42
			12	5	6	7	8	10	11	3		*9*	4		14	1		2			43
	5		12		6		8	10	*11*	3			4	7	9	1		2		14	44
			7	5	6		8	10	11	3		9	4			1		2			45
			7	*5*	6		8	10	11	3		9	4	12	14	1		2			46

Coca-Cola Cup

Second Round	Brentford (h)	1-0
	(a)	0-0
Third Round	Norwich C (h)	1-1
	(a)	2-4

FA Cup

Third Round	Bury (a)	2-2
	(h)	3-0
Fourth Round	Wimbledon (h)	0-2

WALSALL 1994–95 *Back row (left to right):* Stuart Watkiss, Dean Peer, Charlie Ntamark, Charlie Palmer, James Walker, Trevor Wood, John Keister, David Mehew, Scott Houghton, Colin Gibson.
Front row: Wayne Evans, Stuart Ryder, Richard Knight, Chris Marsh, Kevin Wilson, Chris Nicholl (Manager), Martin O'Connor, James Rollo, Martin Butler, Kyle Lightbourne, Darren Rogers.

Division 2 WALSALL

Bescot Stadium, Bescot Cresent, Walsall WS1 4SA. Telephone: (01922) 22791. Fax: (01922) 613202. Commercial Dept: (01922) 30696. Saddlers Hotline: 0891 555800.

Ground capacity: 9000.

Record attendance: 10,628 B International, England v Switzerland, 20 May 1991.

Record receipts: £98,828 v Leeds U, FA Cup 3rd rd, 7th January 1995.

Pitch measurements: 110yd × 73yd.

Chairman: J. W. Bonsor.

Directors: M. N. Lloyd, K. R. Whalley, C. Welch, R. M. Tisdale.

Manager: Chris Nicholl. ***General Manager:*** Paul Taylor. ***Physio:*** Tom Bradley. ***Coach:*** Kevin Wilson.

Secretary/Commercial Manager: Roy Whalley.

Year Formed: 1888. ***Turned Professional:*** 1888. ***Ltd Co.:*** 1921.

Club Nickname: 'The Saddlers'.

Previous Names: Walsall Swifts (founded 1877) and Walsall Town (founded 1879) amalgamated in 1888 and were known as Walsall Town Swifts until 1895.

Previous Grounds: Fellows Park to 1990.

Foundation: Two of the leading clubs around Walsall in the 1880s were Walsall Swifts (formed 1877) and Walsall Town (formed 1879). The Swifts were winners of the Birmingham Senior Cup in 1881, while the Town reached the 4th round (5th round modern equivalent) of the FA Cup in 1883. These clubs amalgamated as Walsall Town Swifts in 1888, becoming simply Walsall in 1895.

First Football League game: 3 September, 1892, Division 2, v Darwen (h) L 1-2 – Hawkins; Withington, Pinches; Robinson, Whitrick, Forsyth; Marshall, Holmes, Turner, Gray (1), Pangbourn.

Record League Victory: 10–0 v Darwen, Division 2, 4 March 1899 – Tennent; E. Peers (1), Davies; Hickinbotham, Jenkyns, Taggart; Dean (3), Vail (2), Aston (4), Martin, Griffin.

Record Cup Victory: 6–1 v Leytonstone (away), FA Cup, 1st rd, 30 November 1946 – Lewis; Netley, Skidmore; Crutchley, Foulkes, Newman; Maund (1), Talbot, Darby (1), Wilshaw (2), Davies (2). 6–1 v Margate, FA Cup, 1st rd (replay), 24 November 1955 – Davies; Haddington, Vinall; Dorman, McPherson, Crook; Morris, Walsh (3), Richards (2), McLaren (1), Moore.

Record Defeat: 0–12 v Small Heath, 17 December 1892 and v Darwen, 26 December 1896, both Division 2.

Most League Points (2 for a win): 65, Division 4, 1959–60.

Most League Points (3 for a win): 82, Division 3, 1987–88.

Most League Goals: 102, Division 4, 1959–60.

Highest League Scorer in Season: Gilbert Alsop, 40, Division 3 (N), 1933–34 and 1934–35.

Most League Goals in Total Aggregate: Tony Richards, 184, 1954–63, and Colin Taylor, 184, 1958–63, 1964–68, 1969–73.

Most Capped Player: Mick Kearns, 15 (18), Republic of Ireland.

Most League Appearances: Colin Harrison, 467, 1964–82.

Record Transfer Fee Received: £600,000 from West Ham U for David Kelly, July 1988.

Record Transfer Fee Paid: £175,000 to Birmingham C for Alan Buckley, June 1979.

Football League Record: 1892 Elected to Division 2; 1895 Failed re-election; 1896–1901 Division 2; 1901 Failed re-election; 1921 Original Member of Division 3 (N); 1927–31 Division 3 (S); 1931–36 Division 3 (N); 1936–58 Division 3 (S); 1958–60 Division 4; 1960–61 Division 3; 1961–63 Division 2; 1963–79 Division 3; 1979–80 Division 4; 1980–88 Division 3; 1988–89 Division 2; 1989–90 Division 3; 1990–92 Division 4; 1992–95 Division 3; 1995– Division 2.

Honours: *Football League:* Division 2 best season: 6th, 1898–99; Division 3 – Runners-up 1960–61, 1994–95; Division 4 – Champions 1959–60; Runners-up 1979–80. *FA Cup:* best season: 5th rd, 1939, 1975, 1978, and last 16 1889. *Football League Cup:* Semi-final 1984.

Colours: Red shirts, black shorts, red stockings. **Change colours:** Claret and blue shirts, blue shorts, blue stockings.

WALSALL 1994–95 LEAGUE RECORD

Match No.	Date	Venue	Opponents	Result	H/T Score	Lg. Pos.	Goalscorers	Attendance
1	Aug 13	A	Fulham	D 1-1	1-0	—	Lightbourne	5308
2	20	H	Lincoln C	W 2-1	1-0	7	O'Connor (pen), Marsh	3813
3	27	A	Hereford U	D 0-0	0-0	10		3004
4	30	H	Carlisle U	L 1-2	1-1	—	Marsh	3610
5	Sept 3	H	Northampton T	D 1-1	1-1	12	Lightbourne	4249
6	10	A	Chesterfield	D 0-0	0-0	13		3027
7	13	A	Colchester U	L 2-3	1-0	—	Lightbourne, Houghton	2239
8	17	H	Fulham	W 5-1	3-0	11	Marsh 2, Lightbourne 3	3378
9	24	H	Gillingham	W 2-1	1-0	10	Wilson, Ryder	3654
10	Oct 1	A	Preston NE	W 2-1	0-1	7	O'Connor, Marsh	7852
11	8	H	Scarborough	W 4-1	1-1	5	O'Connor 2 (2 pens), Ryder, Houghton	3601
12	15	A	Scunthorpe U	W 1-0	1-0	3	Wilson	3609
13	22	A	Hartlepool U	D 1-1	1-1	4	Lightbourne	1704
14	29	H	Bury	L 0-1	0-0	5		5255
15	Nov 5	A	Darlington	D 2-2	0-1	5	Gregan (og), Marsh	2186
16	19	H	Exeter C	W 1-0	1-0	5	O'Connor	3629
17	26	A	Mansfield T	W 3-1	2-0	5	Wilson, O'Connor, Ntamark	2733
18	Dec 10	A	Lincoln	D 1-1	1-1	5	Wilson	2717
19	17	H	Hereford U	W 4-3	1-2	5	Houghton, Lightbourne 2, Ryder	3652
20	26	H	Barnet	W 4-0	2-0	3	Palmer, Wilson, Lightbourne 2	5392
21	27	A	Rochdale	W 2-0	1-0	3	Wilson (pen), Lightbourne	2438
22	31	H	Doncaster R	W 1-0	0-0	2	Marsh	4561
23	Jan 14	A	Torquay U	L 2-3	1-0	2	Houghton, Marsh	2976
24	Feb 4	H	Mansfield T	W 1-0	0-0	2	Wilson	4369
25	18	H	Torquay U	W 1-0	0-0	3	Ryder	3708
26	28	H	Preston NE	D 2-2	1-1	—	Marsh, Wilson	4492
27	Mar 4	A	Gillingham	W 3-1	0-0	3	Lightbourne 2, Houghton	3669
28	7	H	Hartlepool U	W 4-1	1-1	—	O'Connor, Houghton 2, Wilson	3314
29	11	H	Chesterfield	L 1-3	0-1	4	Lightbourne	6219
30	14	H	Darlington	W 2-0	1-0	—	Lightbourne, Wilson	3154
31	18	A	Carlisle U	L 1-2	1-0	3	Wilson	7769
32	25	A	Northampton T	D 2-2	1-1	3	Lightbourne, Wilson	6282
33	Apr 1	H	Colchester U	W 2-0	0-0	3	Lightbourne, O'Connor (pen)	3622
34	4	A	Exeter C	W 3-1	1-0	—	O'Connor, Lightbourne 2	1551
35	8	A	Doncaster R	W 2-0	1-0	3	Wilson 2	2368
36	11	A	Wigan Ath	L 0-1	0-1	—		2176
37	15	H	Rochdale	D 0-0	0-0	3		3766
38	17	A	Barnet	W 3-1	2-1	3	Ryder, Wilson, Lightbourne	2078
39	22	H	Wigan Ath	W 2-0	0-0	3	O'Connor, Lightbourne	3508
40	29	H	Scunthorpe U	W 2-1	0-0	3	Palmer, Lightbourne	4539
41	May 2	A	Scarborough	W 2-1	0-0	—	Houghton, Wilson	2841
42	4	A	Bury	D 0-0	0-0	—		6790

Final League Position: 2

GOALSCORERS

League (75): Lightbourne 23, Wilson 16 (1 pen), O'Connor 10 (4 pens), Marsh 9, Houghton 8, Ryder 5, Palmer 2, Ntamark 1, own goal 1.
Coca-Cola Cup (7): Wilson 3, Lightbourne 1, O'Connor 1, Watkiss 1, own goal 1.
FA Cup (11): Lightbourne 3, Butler 2, Wilson 2, Houghton 1, Marsh 1, O'Connor 1 (pen), own goal 1.

Wood T.J. 39	Evans D.W. 36	Rogers D.J. 20 + 7	Watkiss S.P. 8	Marsh C.J. 36 + 2	Palmer C.A. 39	O'Connor M.J. 39	Ntamark C.B. 31 + 4	Lightbourne K.L. 42	Wilson K.J. 42	Mehew D.S. 6 + 7	Keister J.E.S. 9 + 2	Lillis J.W. — + 1	Butler M.N. 1 + 7	Peer D. 8 + 4	Embleton D.C. — + 1	Houghton S.A. 38	Walker J.B. 3 + 1	Gibson C.J. 31 + 2	Ryder S.H. 34 + 2	Match No.
1	2	3	4	5	6	7	8	9	10	11	12									1
1	2	3	4	5	6	7	8	9	10	*11*	14	12								2
1	2	3		5	6	7	8	9	10	*11*			4	12	15					3
1	2	3	4	5	6	7	8	9	10	11			12							4
1	2	3	4	5	6	7	8	9	10							11				5
	2	3		5	6	7	8	9	10							11	1	4	12	6
		3		5	6		8	9	10					7		11	1	4	2	7
1	2	3		5	6	7	12	9	10					8		11		4		8
1	2	3	4	5		7		9	10					8		11		6	12	9
1		3	4	5		7		9	10					8		11		6	2	10
1	*5*	12	4		6	7		9	10	8			14			11		3	2	11
1		4			6	7	5	9	10	8				12		11		3	2	12
1		4		5	6	7	8	9	10				12			11		3	2	13
1		4		5	6	7	8	9	10	12						11		3	2	14
1		4		5	6	7	8	9	10							11		3	2	15
1	2			5	6	7	8	9	10				12			11		3	4	16
1	2			5	6	7	8	9	10	12				14		11		3	4	17
1	2			5	6	7	8	9	10				12			11		3	4	18
1	2			5	6	7	8	9	10				12			11		3	4	19
1	2	12		5	6	7	8	9	*10*	14						11		3	4	20
1	2	12		5	6		8	9	10		7			14		*11*		3	4	21
1	2			5	6	7	8	9	10							11		3	4	22
1	2			5	6	7	8	9	10							11		3	4	23
1	2	3		5	6	7	8	9	10							11			4	24
1	2	3		5	6	7	8	9	10							11			4	25
1	2			5	6	7	8	9	10							11		3	4	26
1	2			5	6	7	8	9	10							11		3	4	27
1	2			5	6	7	8	9	10	12						11		3	4	28
1	2			5	6	7	8	9	10							11		3	4	29
1	2	12		5	6		8	9	*10*	14	7					11		3	4	30
1	2	3		5	6	7		9	10		8					11			4	31
1	2		6	5		7		9	10	12	8					11		3	4	32
1	2			5	6	7	12	9	10		8					11		3	4	33
1	2			5	6	7		9	10	12	8					11		3	4	34
1	2	12		5	6	7		9	10		8					11		3	4	35
1	2			5	6	7	12	9	10		8					11		3	4	36
1	2			5	6	7	12	9	10		8					11		3	4	37
1	2	12			6	7	8	9	*10*				14	5		11		3	4	38
1	2	12			6	7	8	9	10					5		11		3	4	39
1	2	3		12	6	7	8	9	10					5		11			4	40
1	2	3		12	6	7	8	9	10					5		*11*	15	14	4	41
	2	3		5	6	7	8	9	10							11	1	12	4	42

Coca-Cola Cup

First Round	Plymouth Arg (h)		4-0
	(a)		1-2
Second Round	West Ham U (h)		2-1
	(a)		0-2

FA Cup

First Round	Rochdale (h)	3-0
Second Round	Preston NE (a)	1-1
	(h)	4-0
Third Round	Leeds U (h)	1-1
	(a)	2-5

WATFORD 1994–95 *Back row (left to right):* Ken Brooks (Kit Manager), Alex Inglethorpe, Tommy Mooney, David Holdsworth, Robert Page, Colin Foster, Keith Millen, Jason Soloman, David Barnes, Colin Simpson, Darren Bazeley, Billy Hails (Physio).
Centre row: Stuart Murdoch (Reserve Team Manager), Craig Ramage, Jamie Moralee, Mark Watson, Paul Wilkerson, Perry Digweed, Simon Sheppard, Richard Johnson, Jason Drysdale, Lee Nogan, John McDermott (Youth Development Officer).
Front row: Kenny Jackett (Youth Team Manager), Geoffrey Pitcher, Gerard Lavin, John White, Gary Porter, Glenn Roeder (Manager), Andy Hessenthaler, Matthew Vier, Nigel Gibbs, Derek Payne, Kenny Sansom (Player/Coach).

Division 1 **WATFORD**

Vicarage Road Stadium, Watford WD1 8ER. Telephone: (01923) 230933. Fax: (01923) 239759. Hornet Hotline: 0891 121030. Ticket Office: (01923) 220393. Club Shop: (01923) 220847. Catering: (01923) 221457. Junior Hornets Club/Marketing: (01923) 230933.

Ground capacity: 22,000.

Record attendance: 34,099 v Manchester U, FA Cup 4th rd (replay), 3 February 1969.

Record receipts: £115,000 v Leeds U, Coca Cola Cup 3rd rd, 10 November 1992.

Pitch measurements: 115yd × 75yd.

Life President: Elton John.

Chairman: Dr. S. R. Timperley PHD.

Directors: G. S. Lawson Rogers, C. D. Lissack, J. Petchey, E. Plumley FAAI, M. Winwood.

Chief Executive: Eddie Plumley FAAI. ***Secretary:*** John Alexander.

Team Manager: Glenn Roeder. ***Player-Coach:*** Kenny Sansom.

Reserve Team Coach: Stuart Murdoch. ***Youth Team Coach:*** Kenny Jackett. ***Physio:*** Billy Hails.

Director of Marketing: Brian Blower. ***Public Relations Manager:*** Ed Coan.
Commercial Manager: Paul Biffen.

Year Formed: 1891*(*see Foundation*). ***Turned Professional:*** 1897. ***Ltd Co.:*** 1909.

Club Nickname: 'The Hornets'.

Previous Name: West Herts.

Previous Ground: 1899, Cassio Road; 1922, Vicarage Road.

Foundation: Tracing this club's foundation proves difficult. Nowadays it is suggested that Watford was formed as Watford Rovers in 1891. Another version is that Watford Rovers were not forerunners of the present club whose history began in 1898 with the amalgamation of West Herts and Watford St. Mary's.

First Football League game: 28 August, 1920, Division 3, v QPR (a) W 2-1 – Williams; Horseman, F. Gregory; Bacon, Toone, Wilkinson; Bassett, Ronald (1), Hoddinott, White (1), Waterall.

Record League Victory: 8–0 v Sunderland, Division 1, 25 September 1982 – Sherwood; Rice, Rostron, Taylor, Terry, Bolton, Callaghan (2), Blissett (4), Jenkins (2), Jackett, Barnes.

Record Cup Victory: 10–1 v Lowestoft T, FA Cup, 1st rd, 27 November 1926 – Yates; Prior, Fletcher (1); F. Smith, 'Bert' Smith, Strain; Stephenson, Warner (3), Edmonds (2), Swan (2), Daniels (1). (1 og).

Record Defeat: 0–10 v Wolverhampton W, FA Cup 1st rd (replay), 13 January 1912.

Most League Points (2 for a win): 71, Division 4, 1977–78.

Most League Points (3 for a win): 80, Division 2, 1981–82.

Most League Goals: 92, Division 4, 1959–60.

Highest League Scorer in Season: Cliff Holton, 42, Division 4, 1959–60.

Most League Goals in Total Aggregate: Luther Blissett, 158, 1976–83, 1984–88, 1991–92.

Most Capped Player: John Barnes, 31 (78), England and Kenny Jackett, 31, Wales.

Most League Appearances: Luther Blissett, 415, 1976–83, 1984–88, 1991–92.

Record Transfer Fee Received: £2,300,000 from Chelsea for Paul Furlong, May 1994.

Record Transfer Fee Paid: £550,000 to AC Milan for Luther Blissett, August 1984.

Football League Record: 1920 Original Member of Division 3; 1921–58 Division 3 (S); 1958–60 Division 4; 1960–69 Division 3; 1969–72 Division 2; 1972–75 Division 3; 1975–78 Division 4; 1978–79 Division 3; 1979–82 Division 2; 1982–88 Division 1; 1988–92 Division 2; 1992– Division 1.

Honours: *Football League:* Division 1 – Runners-up 1982–83; Division 2 – Runners-up 1981–82; Division 3 – Champions 1968–69; Runners-up 1978–79; Division 4 – Champions 1977–78; Promoted 1959–60 (4th). *FA Cup:* Runners-up 1984. *Football League Cup:* Semi-final 1979. **European Competitions:** *UEFA Cup:* 1983–84.

Colours: Yellow shirts, black shorts, black stockings. **Change colours:** Burgundy/jade shirts, burgundy shorts, burgundy stockings.

Watford

WATFORD 1994–95 LEAGUE RECORD

Match No.	Date	Venue	Opponents	Result	H/T Score	Lg. Pos.	Goalscorers	Attendance
1	Aug 13	A	Sheffield U	L 0-3	0-2	—		16,820
2	20	H	Grimsby T	D 0-0	0-0	22		6324
3	27	A	Swindon T	L 0-1	0-1	24		9781
4	30	H	Wolverhampton W	W 2-1	1-0	—	Foster, Johnson	10,108
5	Sept 3	H	Middlesbrough	D 1-1	0-1	17	Johnson	9478
6	10	A	Barnsley	D 0-0	0-0	19		4251
7	13	A	Oldham Ath	W 2-0	1-0	—	Holdsworth, Porter (pen)	7243
8	17	H	Luton T	L 2-4	2-3	19	Moralee, Mooney	8880
9	24	H	Reading	D 2-2	2-0	18	Johnson, Moralee	8015
10	Oct 1	A	Charlton Ath	L 0-3	0-0	21		8169
11	8	A	Derby Co	D 1-1	1-0	20	Nogan	13,413
12	15	H	Notts Co	W 3-1	2-0	18	Nogan, Moralee, Ramage	7008
13	22	H	Tranmere R	W 2-0	1-0	15	Nogan 2	6987
14	29	A	Bolton W	L 0-3	0-1	17		10,483
15	Nov 1	A	Burnley	D 1-1	1-0	—	Nogan	11,739
16	5	H	WBA	W 1-0	1-0	13	Mooney	8419
17	12	H	Southend U	W 1-0	0-0	7	Nogan	8551
18	19	A	Sunderland	W 3-1	2-0	7	Hessenthaler, Nogan, Mooney (pen)	15,063
19	26	H	Stoke C	D 0-0	0-0	9		9126
20	Dec 3	A	Tranmere R	L 1-2	0-0	10	Moralee	7301
21	10	A	Grimsby T	D 0-0	0-0	13		6288
22	17	H	Sheffield U	D 0-0	0-0	13		8919
23	26	H	Portsmouth	W 2-0	0-0	10	Ramage, Shipperley	9953
24	27	A	Millwall	L 1-2	0-0	14	Ramage	12,289
25	31	H	Port Vale	W 3-2	1-1	10	Foster, Musslewhite (og), Ramage	7794
26	Jan 2	A	Bristol C	D 0-0	0-0	9		9423
27	14	H	Bolton W	D 0-0	0-0	9		9113
28	Feb 1	A	WBA	W 1-0	0-0	—	Ramage (pen)	15,754
29	4	A	Southend U	W 4-0	3-0	7	Bazeley 3, Ramage (pen)	4914
30	11	H	Burnley	W 2-0	0-0	6	Ramage, Bazeley	9297
31	21	H	Sunderland	L 0-1	0-1	—		8189
32	Mar 4	A	Reading	L 1-4	0-1	8	Phillips	9705
33	7	A	Middlesbrough	L 0-2	0-1	—		16,630
34	11	H	Swindon T	W 2-0	0-0	8	Hessenthaler, Phillips	7123
35	18	A	Wolverhampton W	D 1-1	0-1	11	Phillips	24,380
36	21	H	Barnsley	W 3-2	1-0	—	Millen, Porter, Phillips	6883
37	26	A	Luton T	D 1-1	0-1	9	Phillips	7984
38	Apr 1	H	Oldham Ath	L 1-2	1-2	10	Ramage	8090
39	4	A	Stoke C	L 0-1	0-1	—		9576
40	8	A	Port Vale	W 1-0	0-0	10	Porter	7276
41	14	H	Millwall	W 1-0	1-0	—	Pitcher	6907
42	17	A	Portsmouth	L 1-2	0-1	10	Phillips	8396
43	22	H	Bristol C	W 1-0	0-0	10	Phillips	7190
44	29	A	Notts Co	L 0-1	0-1	10		5083
45	May 2	H	Charlton Ath	W 2-0	0-0	—	Beadle, Phillips	6024
46	7	H	Derby Co	W 2-1	1-0	7	Phillips, Ramage (pen)	8492

Final League Position: 7

GOALSCORERS

League (52): Phillips 9, Ramage 9 (3 pens), Nogan 7, Bazeley 4, Moralee 4, Johnson 3, Mooney 3 (1 pen), Porter 3 (1 pen), Foster 2, Hessenthaler 2, Beadle 1, Holdsworth 1, Millen 1, Pitcher 1, Shipperley 1, own goal 1.
Coca-Cola Cup (7): Nogan 2, Ramage 2, Foster 1, Mooney 1, own goal 1.
FA Cup (3): Hessenthaler 2, Holdsworth 1.

Miller K. 44	Bazeley D.S. 22 + 6	Watson M.S. 1	Foster C.J. 34	Holdsworth D.G. 38 + 1	Ramage C.D. 44	Hessenthaler A. 43	Payne D.R. 24	Moralee J.D. 23 + 1	Porter G. 41	Mooney T.J. 29	Soloman J.R. — + 2	Johnson R.M. 27 + 8	Ludden D.J.R. 1	Digweed P.M. 2 + 1	Millen K.D. 31	Sansom K.G. 1	Nogan L.M. 13 + 1	Fitzgerald G.M. 1	Lavin G. 35	Beadle P.C. 9 + 11	Shipperley N.J. 5 + 1	Gibbs N.J. 9 + 2	Jemson N.B. 3 + 1	Connolly D.J. — + 2	Phillips K. 15 + 1	Barnes D. 1	Page R.J. 4 + 1	Quinn M. 4 + 1	Pitcher G. 2 + 2	*Match No.*
1	2	3	4	5	6	7	8	9	10	11	12																		1
1	2		4	5	6	7	8	9	10	11		3																	2
1	2		4	5	6	7	8	9	10	11		3																	3
1	2		4	5	6	7	8	9	10	11		3																	4
1	2		4	5	6	7		9	10	11		3	*8*	15															5
1	2		4	5	6	7		9		11		3			8	10													6
1	2		4	5	6	7	8	9	10	11		3					12												7
	2			5	6	7	8	9	10	11	12	3		1				4											8
	2		4	5	6	7	8	9				3		1			11		10	12									9
1	3		4	5	6	7		9	10	11		8							2										10
1			4		6	7		9	10	11		3			5		8		2										11
1			4		6	7		9	10	11		3			5		8		2	12									12
1			4		6	7		9	10	11		3			5		8		2										13
1	12		4		6	7			10	11		3			5		8		2	9									14
1	12			4	6	7		9	10	11		3			5		*8*		2	14									15
1				4	6	7		9	10	11		3			5		8		2										16
1			4	5	6	7		9	10	11		3					8		2										17
1			4	5	6	7			10	11		3			9		8		2										18
1			4	5	6	7		12	10	11		3			9		8		2										19
1				5	6	7		9	10	11		3			4		8		2										20
1				5	6	7		9	10	11		3			4		8		2		12								21
1			4	5	6	7			10	11		3					8		2		9								22
1			4	5	6	7		8	10	11		3							2	12	9								23
1	12		4	5	6	7		*8*	10	11		3							2	14	9								24
1	3		4	5	6	7		8	10	11									2	*12*	9	14							25
1	8		4	5	6	7			10	11									2		9	3							26
1	3		4	5	6	7		8	10						11				2				9						27
1	3		4	12	6	7	8		10						5				2			11	*9*	14					28
1	3		4		6	7	8		10						5				2			11	9						29
1	3		4	7	6		8	9	10						5				2			11	12						30
1	3		4	7	6		8		10			12			5				2			11			9				31
1	3		4	8	6	7			*10*	9		12			5							2			14	11				32
1	2			4	6	7	8		10	11		3			*5*							12			9		14			33
1	2			4	6	7	8		10	*11*		12			5					14		3			9					34
1				4	6	7	8		10			12			5				2	14		3			11			*9*		35
1			7	4	6				10	11		3			5				2	12					8			9		36
1			4		6	7	8		10			3			5				2	12					11			9		37
1				4	6	7	8		10			3			5				2	12					11			9		38
1			3	4	6	7	8					12			5				2	9		10			11					39
1			4		6	7	8		10						5				2	9					11		3		12	40
1				4		7	8		10			12			5				2	*9*					11		3	14	6	41
1	12			4		7	8		10			14			5				2	9					11		3		*6*	42
1	12			4	6	7	8		10						5				2	9					11		3			43
1	12		3	4	6	7	8		*10*						5				2	9					11				14	44
1	10		3	4	6	7	8								5				2	9				12	11					45
1	10		3	4	6	7	8					12			5				2	9					11					46

Coca-Cola Cup

First Round	Southend U (a)	0-0
	(h)	1-0
Second Round	Tottenham H (h)	3-6
	(a)	3-2

FA Cup

Third Round	Scarborough (a)	0-0
	(h)	2-0
Fourth Round	Swindon T (h)	1-0
Fifth Round	Crystal Palace (h)	0-0
	(a)	0-1

WEST BROMWICH ALBION 1994–95 *Back row (left to right):* Daryl Burgess, Carl Heggs, Stuart Naylor, Tony Lange, Bob Taylor, Mike Phelan, Steve Lilwall.
Centre row: Danny Thomas (Physio), Michael Mellon, Ian Hamilton, Paul Raven, Paul Mardon, Darren Bradley, Kieran O'Regan, John Trewick (Reserve Coach).
Front row: Neil Parsley, Stacy Coldicott, Lee Ashcroft, Alan Buckley (Manager), Arthur Mann (Assistant Manager), Paul Edwards, Bernard McNally, David Smith.
(Photograph: Action Images)

Division 1 WEST BROMWICH ALBION

The Hawthorns, West Bromwich B71 4LF. Telephone: (0121) 525 8888 (all Depts). Fax: (0121) 553 6634.

Ground capacity: 25,100.

Record attendance: 64,815 v Arsenal, FA Cup 6th rd, 6 March 1937.

Record receipts: £174,235.95 v Stoke C, Div 2, 23 January 1993.

Pitch measurements: 115yd × 74yd.

President: Sir F. A. Millichip. ***Vice-President:*** John G. Silk LL.B (Lond).

Chairman: A. B. Hale.

Directors: C. M. Stapleton, T. J. Summers, J. W. Brandrick, T. K. Guy, B. Hurst.

Manager: Alan Buckley. ***Assistant Manager:*** Arthur Mann. ***Coach:*** John Trewick. ***Physio:*** Danny Thomas.

Secretary: Dr. John J. Evans BA, PHD. (Wales).

Club Statistician: Tony Matthews. ***Commercial Manager:*** Tom Cardall.

Year Formed: 1879. ***Turned Professional:*** 1885. ***Ltd Co.:*** 1892.

Previous Name: 1879–81, West Bromwich Strollers.

Club Nicknames: 'Throstles', 'Baggies', 'Albion'.

Previous Grounds: 1879, Coopers Hill; 1879, Dartmouth Park; 1881, Bunns Field, Walsall Street; 1882, Four Acres (Dartmouth Cricket Club); 1885, Stoney Lane; 1900, The Hawthorns.

Foundation: There is a well known story that when employees of Salter's Spring Works in West Bromwich decided to form a football club in 1879, they had to send someone to the nearby Association Football stronghold of Wednesbury to purchase a football. A weekly subscription of 2d (less than 1p) was imposed and the name of the new club was West Bromwich Strollers.

First Football League game: 8 September, 1888, Football League, v Stoke (a) W 2-0 – Roberts; J. Horton, Green; E. Horton, Perry, Bayliss; Bassett, Woodhall (1), Hendry, Pearson, Wilson (1).

Record League Victory: 12–0 v Darwen, Division 1, 4 April 1892 – Reader; Horton, McCulloch; Reynolds (2), Perry, Groves; Bassett (3), McLeod, Nicholls (1), Pearson (4), Geddes (1). (1 og).

Record Cup Victory: 10–1 v Chatham (away), FA Cup, 3rd rd, 2 March 1889 – Roberts; Horton, Green; Timmins (1), Charles Perry, Horton; Bassett (2), Perry (1), Bayliss (2), Pearson, Wilson (3). (1 og).

Record Defeat: 3–10 v Stoke C, Division 1, 4 February 1937.

Most League Points (2 for a win): 60, Division 1, 1919–20.

Most League Points (3 for a win): 85, Division 2, 1992–93.

Most League Goals: 105, Division 2, 1929–30.

Highest League Scorer in Season: William 'Ginger' Richardson, 39, Division 1, 1935–36.

Most League Goals in Total Aggregate: Tony Brown, 218, 1963–79.

Most Capped Player: Stuart Williams, 33 (43), Wales.

Most League Appearances: Tony Brown, 574, 1963–80.

Record Transfer Fee Received: £1,500,000 from Manchester U for Bryan Robson, October 1981.

Record Transfer Fee Paid: £748,000 to Manchester C for Peter Barnes, July 1979.

Football League Record: 1888 Founder Member of Football League; 1901–02 Division 2; 1902–04 Division 1; 1904–11 Division 2; 1911–27 Division 1; 1927–31 Division 2; 1931–38 Division 1; 1938–49 Division 2; 1949–73 Division 1; 1973–76 Division 2; 1976–86 Division 1; 1986–91 Division 2; 1991–92 Division 3; 1992–93 Division 2; 1933– Division 1.

Honours: *Football League:* Division 1 – Champions 1919–20; Runners-up 1924–25, 1953–54; Division 2 – Champions 1901–02, 1910–11; Runners-up 1930–31, 1948–49; Promoted to Division 1 1975–76 (3rd). *FA Cup:* Winners 1888, 1892, 1931, 1954, 1968; Runners-up 1886, 1887, 1895, 1912, 1935. *Football League Cup:* Winners 1966; Runners-up 1967, 1970. **European Competitions:** *European Cup-Winners' Cup:* 1968–69; *European Fairs Cup:* 1966–67; *UEFA Cup:* 1978–79, 1979–80, 1981–82.

Colours: Navy blue and white striped shirts, white shorts, blue and white stockings. **Change colours:** Yellow shirts with sky blue sleeves, sky blue shorts, yellow stockings.

WEST BROMWICH ALBION 1994–95 LEAGUE RECORD

Match No.	Date	Venue	Opponents	Result	H/T Score	Lg. Pos.	Goalscorers	Attendance
1	Aug 13	A	Luton T	D 1-1	1-0	—	Taylor	8640
2	28	A	Wolverhampton W	L 0-2	0-1	22		27,764
3	31	A	Swindon T	D 0-0	0-0	—		11,188
4	Sept 10	A	Millwall	D 2-2	1-1	24	Taylor 2	8378
5	14	A	Middlesbrough	L 1-2	1-1	—	Ashcroft	14,878
6	17	H	Grimsby T	D 1-1	1-0	24	Ashcroft	14,496
7	24	H	Burnley	W 1-0	0-0	23	Taylor	13,539
8	28	H	Portsmouth	L 0-2	0-1	—		13,545
9	Oct 2	A	Stoke C	L 1-4	1-2	23	Taylor	14,203
10	8	H	Sunderland	L 1-3	0-2	24	Ashcroft	13,717
11	15	A	Tranmere R	L 1-3	1-2	24	Hunt	7397
12	18	H	Sheffield U	W 1-0	0-0	—	Mellon	12,713
13	22	A	Barnsley	L 0-2	0-1	23		5082
14	29	H	Reading	W 2-0	0-0	23	Hunt, Ashcroft	14,313
15	Nov 2	H	Port Vale	D 0-0	0-0	—		14,513
16	5	A	Watford	L 0-1	0-1	23		8419
17	13	A	Charlton Ath	D 1-1	0-1	23	Taylor	10,876
18	19	H	Oldham Ath	W 3-1	2-0	23	Donovan, Ashcroft, Taylor	14,616
19	26	A	Notts Co	L 0-2	0-1	23		10,088
20	Dec 3	H	Barnsley	W 2-1	1-0	21	Heggs, Hamilton	13,921
21	10	A	Sheffield U	L 0-2	0-1	21		13,891
22	18	H	Luton T	W 1-0	1-0	21	Donovan	14,392
23	26	H	Bristol C	W 1-0	0-0	18	Munro (og)	21,071
24	27	A	Southend U	L 1-2	1-1	18	Ashcroft	6856
25	31	H	Bolton W	W 1-0	1-0	18	Hunt	18,184
26	Jan 2	A	Derby Co	D 1-1	1-0	17	Hamilton	16,035
27	14	A	Reading	W 2-0	0-0	16	Hunt, Donovan	9390
28	Feb 1	H	Watford	L 0-1	0-0	—		15,754
29	5	H	Charlton Ath	L 0-1	0-0	17		12,084
30	11	A	Port Vale	L 0-1	0-0	18		10,751
31	18	H	Notts Co	W 3-2	1-0	15	Mardon, Hunt 2	13,748
32	21	A	Oldham Ath	L 0-1	0-1	—		7690
33	25	H	Stoke C	L 1-3	1-1	19	Hamilton	16,591
34	Mar 4	A	Burnley	D 1-1	0-0	19	Hunt	11,885
35	8	A	Portsmouth	W 2-1	1-1	—	Taylor 2	7160
36	15	H	Wolverhampton W	W 2-0	1-0	—	Ashcroft, Taylor	20,661
37	19	H	Swindon T	L 2-5	0-0	16	Hunt, Rees	12,960
38	22	H	Millwall	W 3-0	1-0	—	Hunt 3 (1 pen)	11,782
39	25	A	Grimsby T	W 2-0	1-0	14	Hunt, Donovan	7393
40	Apr 1	H	Middlesbrough	L 1-3	1-0	15	Rees	20,256
41	8	A	Bolton W	L 0-1	0-0	16		16,207
42	15	H	Southend U	W 2-0	1-0	15	Hamilton, Strodder	14,393
43	17	A	Bristol C	L 0-1	0-0	17		8777
44	22	H	Derby Co	D 0-0	0-0	19		15,265
45	30	H	Tranmere R	W 5-1	1-0	19	Donovan, Ashcroft 3 (1 pen), Taylor	17,486
46	May 7	A	Sunderland	D 2-2	0-1	19	Hunt, Agnew	18,232

Final League Position: 19

GOALSCORERS

League (51): Hunt 13 (1 pen), Taylor 11, Ashcroft 10 (1 pen), Donovan 5, Hamilton 4, Rees 2, Agnew 1, Heggs 1, Mardon 1, Mellon 1, Strodder 1, own goal 1.
Coca-Cola Cup (0).
FA Cup (2): Ashcroft 1 (pen), Raven 1.

Naylor S.W. 42	Parsley N. 19 + 4	Edwards P.R. 20	Phelan M.C. 17 + 3	Herbert C.J. 8	Burgess D. 22	Ashcroft L. 36 + 2	Hamilton I.R. 35	Taylor R. 38 + 4	Heggs C.S. 7 + 7	McNally B.A. 16 + 5	Donovan K. 31 + 2	Darton S.R. 7	Mellon M.J. 5 + 2	Strodder G.J. 19	Lilwall S. 14 + 2	Boere J.W.J. 5	Smith D. 16 + 6	Coldicott S. 9 + 2	Mardon P.J. 27 + 1	Hunt A. 33 + 6	O'Regan K. 12 + 8	Raven P.D. 31	Bradley D.M. 11 + 5	Rees A.A. 8 + 6	Lange A.S. 4 + 1	Agnew P. 14	*Match No.*
1	2	3	4	5	6	7	8	9	10	11	12																1
1	2		4	5	6	12	8	9	10	7	11	3	14														2
1	2		4		6		8	9	10		7	3	11	5													3
1			4	6	2	*8*		9		12		3		5	7	10	11	14									4
1				6	2	8		9				3		5	7	10	11	4	12								5
1	12			6		8		9				3		5	7	10	*11*	4	2	14							6
1	2		4	6		*8*		9		12	11	3		5	14	10				7							7
1	2		4	6		8		9		12	11	*3*		5	14	10				7							8
1	2		4	6		8		9		10				5	3		11	12		7							9
1	2		4			8		9	12				11	5	3		10	6		7							10
1	2	6				8		9	12				11	5	3		10		4	7							11
1	2	6				8		9					11		3		10	4	5	7	12						12
1	2	6	12			8		9	14				10	5	3		*11*	4		7							13
1	2	3	4			8	11	9		7									5	10		6					14
1	2	3	4			8	11	9		7			12						5	10		6					15
1	2	3	4			8	11	9	12	*7*									5	10		6	14				16
1	2	3	*4*			8	11	9	12	7									5	10	14	6					17
1		3				8	11	9	10	7	4								5	12	2	6					18
1	12	3				8	11	9	14	7	4								5		2	6		*10*			19
1		3				8	11	9	10	*7*	4								5	12	2	6	14				20
1						8	11	9	*10*	7	4				3				5	14	2	6	12				21
1	12					8	11	*9*	14		7				3				5	10	2	6	4				22
1		6				8	11	12	9		7				3				5	10	2		4				23
1	12	6				8	11	9			7				3		14		5	10	*2*		4				24
1	2	3				8	11	9			7						12		5	10		6	4				25
1	2	3				8	11	*9*			7						12		5	10		6	4	14			26
1	2	3				8	11				7						12		5	10	14	6	*4*	9			27
1	*2*	3	12				11	9		14	7						8		5	10	4	6					28
1						14	11	12			7				3		*8*		5	10	2	6	4	9	15		29
		3	11		2	8		9			7								5	10		6	4	12	1		30
		3	12		2	8	11	9			*7*								5	10		6	4		1		31
		3	4		2	*8*	11	9			12						7		5	10		6		14	1		32
	2				5	8	11	9			*7*									10	12	6	4	14	1	3	33
1			4		2		11							5			8			10	7	6		9		3	34
1			4		2		11	9		12	8								5	10	7	6				3	35
1			4		2	8	11	9			7								5	10	12	6				3	36
1					2	8	11	9		4	7								*5*	10	14	6		12		3	37
1					2	8	11			4	7								5	10		6		9		3	38
1					2		11			4	7			8					5	10	12	6		9		3	39
1					2	8	11	12		*4*	7			5						10	14	6		9		3	40
1					2		11	12		*4*	7			5	8		14			10		6		9		3	41
1					2		11	9			7			5			8			10		6	4			3	42
1					2		11	9			7			5			*12*	3		10	4	6		14		8	43
1					2	8	11	9			7			5			10	4				6				3	44
1					2	8	11	9			*7*			5			*10*	4		14		6	12			3	45
1					2	8	11	9			7			5			*10*	4		14		6	12			3	46

Coca-Cola Cup

First Round	Hereford U (a)	0-0
	(h)	0-1

FA Cup

Third Round	Coventry C (a)	1-1
	(h)	1-2

WEST HAM UNITED 1994–95 *Back row (left to right):* Tim Breacker, Simon Webster, Ludek Miklosko, Jeroen Boere, Ian Feuer, Lee Chapman, Alvin Martin.
Centre row: Joey Beauchamp, Danny Williamson, Steve Jones, Mike Marsh, Dale Gordon, Trevor Morley, Matthew Rush, Kenny Brown, Martin Allen.
Front row: Keith Rowland, Peter Butler, Ian Bishop, Steve Potts, David Burrows, John Moncur, Matty Holmes.

FA Premiership **WEST HAM UNITED**

Boleyn Ground, Green Street, Upton Park, London E13 9AZ. Telephone General Office: (0181) 548 2748. Fax: (0181) 548 2758. Membership Office: (0181) 552 7640. Promotions: (0181) 472 5656. Dial-a-seat: (0181) 472 3322. Football in the Community: (0181) 472 2422. Clubcall: 0891 121165.

Ground capacity: 26,014.

Record attendance: 42,322 v Tottenham H, Division 1, 17 October 1970.

Record receipts: £146,074 v Tottenham H, League Cup 5th rd, 27 January 1987.

Pitch measurements: 112yd × 72yd.

Chairman: T. W. Brown FCIS, ATH, FCCA. ***Vice-Chairman:*** M. W. Cearns ACIB.

Directors: C. J. Warner, P. J. Storrie (managing).

Manager: Harry Redknapp. ***Assistant Manager:*** Frank Lampard. ***Coaches:*** Paul Hilton, Tony Carr. ***Physio:*** John Green BSC (hons) MCSP, SRP.

Secretary: Richard Skirrow.

Year Formed: 1895. ***Turned Professional:*** 1900. ***Ltd Co.:*** 1900.

Previous Name: Thames Ironworks FC, 1895–1900.

Club Nickname: 'The Hammers'.

Previous Ground: Memorial Recreation Ground, Canning Town: 1904 Boleyn Ground.

Foundation: Thames Ironworks FC was formed by employees of this shipbuilding yard in 1895 and entered the FA Cup in their initial season at Chatham and the London League in their second. Short of funds, the club was wound up in June 1900 and relaunched a month later as West Ham United. Connection with the Ironworks was not finally broken until four years later.

First Football League game: 30 August, 1919, Division 2, v Lincoln City (h) D 1-1 – Hufton; Cope, Lee; Lane, Fenwick, McCrae; D. Smith, Moyes (1), Puddefoot, Morris, Bradshaw.

Record League Victory: 8–0 v Rotherham U, Division 2, 8 March 1958 – Gregory; Bond, Wright; Malcolm, Brown, Lansdowne; Grice, Smith (2), Keeble (2), Dick (4), Musgrove. 8–0 v Sunderland, Division 1, 19 October 1968 – Ferguson; Bonds, Charles; Peters, Stephenson, Moore (1); Redknapp, Boyce, Brooking (1), Hurst (6), Sissons.

Record Cup Victory: 10–0 v Bury, League Cup, 2nd rd (2nd leg), 25 October 1983 – Parkes; Stewart (1), Walford, Bonds (Orr), Martin (1), Devonshire (2), Allen, Cottee (4), Swindlehurst, Brooking (2), Pike.

Record Defeat: 2–8 v Blackburn R, Division 1, 26 December 1963.

Most League Points (2 for a win): 66, Division 2, 1980–81.

Most League Points (3 for a win): 88, Division 1, 1992–93.

Most League Goals: 101, Division 2, 1957–58.

Highest League Scorer in Season: Vic Watson, 41, Division 1, 1929–30.

Most League Goals in Total Aggregate: Vic Watson, 298, 1920–35.

Most Capped Player: Bobby Moore, 108, England.

Most League Appearances: Billy Bonds, 663, 1967–88.

Record Transfer Fee Received: £2,000,000 from Everton for Tony Cottee, July 1988.

Record Transfer Fee Paid: £1,500,000 to Liverpool for Don Hutchison, August 1994.

Football League Record: 1919 Elected to Division 2; 1923–32 Division 1; 1932–58 Division 2; 1958–78 Division 1; 1978–81 Division 2; 1981–89 Division 1; 1989–91 Division 2; 1991–93 Division 1; 1993– FA Premier League.

Honours: *Football League:* Division 1 best season: 3rd, 1985–86; Division 2 – Champions 1957–58, 1980–81; Runners-up 1922–23, 1990–91. *FA Cup:* Winners 1964, 1975, 1980; Runners-up 1923. *Football League Cup:* Runners-up 1966, 1981. **European Competitions:** *European Cup-Winners' Cup:* 1964–65 (winners), 1965–66, 1975–76 (runners-up), 1980–81.

Colours: Claret shirts, white shorts, white stockings. **Change colours:** All blue.

WEST HAM UNITED 1994–95 LEAGUE RECORD

Match No.	Date	Venue	Opponents	Result	H/T Score	Lg. Pos.	Goalscorers	Attendance
1	Aug 20	H	Leeds U	D 0-0	0-0	—		18,610
2	24	A	Manchester C	L 0-3	0-2	—		19,150
3	27	A	Norwich C	L 0-1	0-0	19		19,110
4	31	H	Newcastle U	L 1-3	0-2	—	Hutchison (pen)	17,375
5	Sept 10	A	Liverpool	D 0-0	0-0	19		30,907
6	17	H	Aston Villa	W 1-0	0-0	17	Cottee	18,326
7	25	H	Arsenal	L 0-2	0-1	19		18,495
8	Oct 2	A	Chelsea	W 2-1	0-0	15	Allen, Moncur	18,696
9	8	H	Crystal Palace	W 1-0	0-0	13	Hutchison	16,959
10	15	A	Manchester U	L 0-1	0-1	15		43,795
11	22	H	Southampton	W 2-0	0-0	12	Allen, Rush	18,853
12	29	A	Tottenham H	L 1-3	1-1	14	Rush	26,271
13	Nov 1	A	Everton	L 0-1	0-0	—		28,353
14	5	H	Leicester C	W 1-0	0-0	14	Dicks (pen)	18,780
15	19	A	Sheffield W	L 0-1	0-1	17		25,300
16	26	H	Coventry C	L 0-1	0-0	17		17,251
17	Dec 4	A	QPR	L 1-2	0-2	18	Boere	12,780
18	10	A	Leeds U	D 2-2	1-2	19	Boere 2	28,987
19	17	H	Manchester C	W 3-0	2-0	17	Cottee 3	17,286
20	26	H	Ipswich T	D 1-1	1-0	18	Cottee	20,562
21	28	A	Wimbledon	L 0-1	0-0	18		11,212
22	31	H	Nottingham F	W 3-1	3-0	16	Cottee, Bishop, Hughes	20,644
23	Jan 2	A	Blackburn R	L 2-4	1-1	16	Cottee, Dicks	25,503
24	14	H	Tottenham H	L 1-2	1-0	19	Boere	24,578
25	23	H	Sheffield W	L 0-2	0-1	—		14,554
26	Feb 4	A	Leicester C	W 2-1	2-1	19	Cottee, Dicks (pen)	20,375
27	13	H	Everton	D 2-2	1-1	—	Cottee 2	21,081
28	18	A	Coventry C	L 0-2	0-1	20		17,563
29	25	H	Chelsea	L 1-2	1-0	20	Hutchison	21,500
30	Mar 5	A	Arsenal	W 1-0	1-0	19	Hutchison	36,295
31	8	A	Newcastle U	L 0-2	0-1	—		34,595
32	11	H	Norwich C	D 2-2	0-1	18	Cottee 2	21,464
33	15	A	Southampton	D 1-1	1-0	—	Hutchison	15,178
34	18	A	Aston Villa	W 2-0	1-0	18	Moncur, Hutchison	28,682
35	Apr 8	A	Nottingham F	D 1-1	0-0	20	Dicks	28,361
36	13	H	Wimbledon	W 3-0	1-0	—	Dicks (pen), Boere, Cottee	21,804
37	17	A	Ipswich T	D 1-1	0-1	18	Boere	18,882
38	30	H	Blackburn R	W 2-0	0-0	16	Reiper, Hutchison	24,202
39	May 3	H	QPR	D 0-0	0-0	—		22,923
40	6	A	Crystal Palace	L 0-1	0-0	16		18,224
41	10	H	Liverpool	W 3-0	1-0	—	Holmes, Hutchison 2	22,446
42	14	H	Manchester U	D 1-1	1-0	14	Hughes	24,783

Final League Position: 14

GOALSCORERS

League (44): Cottee 13, Hutchison 9 (1 pen), Boere 6, Dicks 5 (3 pens), Allen 2, Hughes 2, Moncur 2, Rush 2, Bishop 1, Holmes 1, Rieper 1.
Coca-Cola Cup (5): Hutchison 2, Cottee 1, Moncur 1, own goal 1.
FA Cup (2): Brown 1, Cottee 1.

Miklosko L. 42	Breacker T.S. 33	Burrows D. 4	Potts S.J. 42	Martin A.E. 24	Allen M.J. 26 + 3	Bishop I.W. 31	Butler P.J.F. 5	Morley T.W. 10 + 4	Chapman L.R. 7 + 3	Holmes M.J.E. 24	Whitbread A.R. 3 + 5	Marsh M.A. 13 + 3	Moncur J.F. 30	Jones S.G. 1 + 1	Rowland K. 11 + 1	Hutchison D. 22 + 1	Cottee A.R. 31	Rush M.J. 15 + 8	Dicks J.A. 29	Brown K.J. 8 + 1	Hughes M. 15 + 2	Boere J.W.J. 15 + 5	Reiper M. 17 + 4	Williamson D.A. 4	Webster S.P. — + 5	*Match No.*
1	2	3	4	5	6	7	8	9	10	*11*	12	14														1
1	2	3	4	5	6	7	8	9	*10*	11	12	14														2
1	2	3	4	5	6	7			14		12	10	8	9	*11*											3
1	2	3	4	5	6		8			11		10	7	12		9										4
1	2		4	5	6		8					10	7		3		9	11								5
1	2		4	5	6		8		12			10	7		3		9	11								6
1	2		4	5	6				8	11		10	7		3	9		12								7
1	2		4	5	6				8			10	7		3	9		11								8
1	2		4	5	6				8			10	7		3	11	9	12								9
1	2		4	5	6							10	7		3	8	9	11								10
1	2		4	5	6	7			8			10					9	11	3							11
1			4	5	*6*	7			12		14	10			2	8	9	11	3							12
1			4	5		6			8		2	10				7	9	11	3							13
1			4	5		6		8			2		7			10	9	11	3	12						14
1			4	5	6	8		10				12	7				9	11	3	2						15
1			4			6		8		11	5	10	7				9	12	3	2						16
1			4									6	7		5		9	8	3	2	11	10				17
1			4			6				11					7		9	8	3	2	12	10	5			18
1	2		4	5		6				7							9	10	3		11	8				19
1	2		4	5		6				7							9	8	3		11	10	12			20
1	2		4	5		8				7							9	12	3		11	10	6			21
1	2		4	5		6				7			*8*				9	12	3		11	10	14			22
1	2		4			6				7			8				9	12	3		11	10	5			23
1	2		4	5	12	6		14		*7*			8				9			3	11	10				24
1	2		4	5	12	6				*7*			8				9			3	*11*	10	14			25
1	2		4	5	6								7			8	9		3		11	12		10		26
1			4	5	6								7			10	9		3	2	11	12		8		27
1	2		4	*5*	6					11			7			10	9		3			12	14	8		28
1	2		4		6	11		8					7			10	9		3				5			29
1	2		4		6	11		8					7			10	9	12	3				5			30
1	2		4		6	7		12								8	9	10	3		11		5			31
1	2		4			6		8					7			10	9		3		12		5	11		32
1	2		4			6				11			7			10	9	8	3			12	5			33
1	2		4		6	8				11			7		12	*10*	9		3			14	5			34
1			4		6	8				7	12						9		3	2	11	10	5			35
1	2		4		6	8				7							9		3		11	10	5			36
1	2		4		6	8				11			7			12	9		3			10	5			37
1	2		4		6	8				11			7			*9*		12	3			10	5		14	38
1	2		4		6	8		12		11			7			9			3			*10*	5		14	39
1	2		4		*6*	8		12		11			7			9			3			10	5		14	40
1	2		4			6		9		7			8			10			3		11		5		12	41
1	2		4		12	6		9		7			8		3	10					*11*		5		14	42

Coca-Cola Cup

Second Round	Walsall (a)	1-2
	(h)	2-0
Third Round	Chelsea (h)	1-0
Fourth Round	Bolton W (h)	1-3

FA Cup

Third Round	Wycombe W (a)	2-0
Fourth Round	QPR (a)	0-1

WIGAN ATHLETIC 1994–95 *Back row (left to right):* Mark Wright, David Adekola, Chris Duffy, Paul Tait, Neil Ogden.
Centre row: Joe Hinnigan (Coach), Mark Leonard, Ian Patterson, John Robertson, Mark Statham, Simon Farnworth, Greg Strong, David Millar, Ian Kilford, Alex Cribley (Coach/Physio).
Front row: David McKearney, Andy Lyons, Neil Rimmer, John Doolan, Graham Barrow (Manager), Stephen Gage (Chairman), David Crompton (Youth Development Officer), Paul Rennie, Andy Farrell, Matthew Carragher, Joe Jakub.
(Photograph: Derek Davies)

Division 3 **WIGAN ATHLETIC**

Springfield Park, Wigan WN6 7BA. Telephone: (01942) 244433. Fax: (01942) 494654. Commercial Dept: (01942) 243067. Latics Clubcall: 0891 121655. Football in the Community: (01942) 824599.

Ground capacity: 6674.

Record attendance: 27,500 v Hereford U, 12 December 1953.

Record receipts: £40,577 v Leeds U, FA Cup 6th rd, 15 March 1987.

Pitch measurements: 114yd × 72yd.

President: T. Hitchen.

Chairman: S. Gage

Directors: N. Bitel, S. Jackson, J. Bennett, E. Fryer, C. Ronnie, D. Sharpe, D. Whelan.

Secretary: Mrs Brenda Spencer. ***Assistant Secretary:*** Gordon Allan. ***Marketing Manager:*** B. Eccles. ***Commercial Manager:*** Rod Barry.

Manager: Graham Barrow. ***Coach:*** Joe Hinnigan. ***Physio/Coach:*** Alex Cribley. ***Safety Officer:*** David Johnson. ***Groundsman:*** John Parr.

Year Formed: 1932.

Club Nickname: 'The Latics'.

Foundation: Following the demise of Wigan Borough and their resignation from the Football League in 1931, a public meeting was called in Wigan at the Queen's Hall in May 1932 at which a new club Wigan Athletic, was founded in the hope of carrying on in the Football League. With this in mind, they bought Springfield Park for £2,250, but failed to gain admission to the Football League until 46 years later.

First Football League game: 19 August, 1978, Division 4, v Hereford U (a) D 0-0 – Brown; Hinnigan, Gore, Gillibrand, Ward, Davids, Corrigan, Purdie, Houghton, Wilkie, Wright.

Record League Victory: 7–2 v Scunthorpe U (away), Division 4, 12 March 1982 – Tunks; McMahon, Glenn, Wignall, Cribley, Methven (1), O'Keefe, Barrow (1), Bradd (3), Houghton (2), Evans.

Record Cup Victory: 6–0 v Carlisle U (away), FA Cup, 1st rd, 24 November 1934 – Caunce; Robinson, Talbot; Paterson, Watson, Tufnell; Armes (2), Robson (1), Roberts (2), Felton, Scott (1).

Record Defeat: 1–6 v Bristol R, Division 3, 3 March 1990.

Most League Points (2 for a win): 55, Division 4, 1978–79 and 1979–80.

Most League Points (3 for a win): 91, Division 4, 1981–82.

Most League Goals: 80, Division 4, 1981–82.

Highest League Scorer in Season: Warren Aspinall, 21, Division 3, 1985–86.

Most League Goals in Total Aggregate: Peter Houghton, 62, 1978–84.

Most Capped Player: None.

Most League Appearances: Kevin Langley, 317, 1981–86, 1990–94.

Record Transfer Fee Received: £329,000 from Coventry C for Peter Atherton, August 1991.

Record Transfer Fee Paid: £87,500 to Chester C for Chris Lightfoot, July 1995.

Football League Record: 1978 Elected to Division 4; 1982 –92 Division 3; 1992–93 Division 2; 1993– Division 3.

Honours: *Football League:* Best season in Division 3: 4th, 1985–86, 1986–87; Division 4 – Promoted (3rd) 1981–82. *FA Cup:* 6th rd 1987. *Football League Cup:* best season: 4th rd, 1982. *Freight Rover Trophy:* Winners 1985.

Colours: Blue and white striped shirts, black shorts blue stockings. **Change colours:** Burgundy with gold trim.

WIGAN ATHLETIC 1994–95 LEAGUE RECORD

Match No.	Date		Venue	Opponents	Result		H/T Score	Lg. Pos.	Goalscorers	Attendance
1	Aug	13	A	Carlisle U	L	1-2	0-1	—	Walling (og)	6231
2		20	H	Gillingham	L	0-3	0-1	19		1514
3		27	A	Fulham	L	0-2	0-1	20		4241
4		30	H	Chesterfield	L	2-3	1-2	—	Morton, Gavin	1231
5	Sept	3	H	Barnet	L	1-2	1-1	22	Gavin	1438
6		10	A	Hereford U	W	2-1	0-1	21	Rennie (pen), Rimmer	2771
7		13	A	Lincoln C	L	0-1	0-0	—		2030
8		17	H	Carlisle U	L	0-2	0-0	22		3003
9		24	A	Scunthorpe U	L	1-3	0-1	22	McKearney	2602
10	Oct	1	H	Scarborough	D	1-1	1-1	22	Kilford	1403
11		8	A	Doncaster R	L	3-5	1-3	22	Leonard 2 (1 pen), Benjamin	2060
12		15	H	Rochdale	W	4-0	4-0	22	Kilford 2, Strong, Benjamin	2118
13		22	A	Northampton T	L	0-1	0-1	22		6379
14		29	H	Colchester U	L	1-2	0-2	22	Robertson	1621
15	Nov	5	A	Hartlepool U	W	1-0	1-0	22	McKearney	1683
16		19	H	Darlington	W	4-1	2-1	19	Strong, Lyons 3 (1 pen)	1785
17		26	A	Torquay U	D	0-0	0-0	20		2509
18	Dec	10	A	Gillingham	W	1-0	0-0	18	Leonard	2257
19		17	H	Fulham	D	1-1	1-0	18	Leonard	1791
20		26	A	Bury	D	3-3	2-2	19	Lyons 2, Leonard	3616
21	Jan	7	H	Northampton T	W	2-1	1-0	17	Rimmer, Kilford	1911
22		14	A	Mansfield T	L	3-4	0-1	18	Kilford, Rimmer, Lyons	2618
23		24	H	Preston NE	D	1-1	1-0	—	Lyons	3618
24		28	A	Colchester U	W	1-0	0-0	16	Doolan	3067
25	Feb	4	H	Torquay U	D	1-1	0-1	16	Miller	1609
26		11	A	Darlington	W	3-1	1-0	16	Rodwell, Benjamin, Lyons	1780
27		18	H	Mansfield T	L	0-4	0-2	16		1884
28		21	A	Exeter C	W	4-2	2-1	—	Lyons, McKearney (pen), Benjamin 2	2370
29		25	A	Scarborough	W	1-0	1-0	15	Lyons	1416
30		28	H	Hartlepool U	W	2-0	1-0	—	McKearney, Lyons	1452
31	Mar	18	A	Chesterfield	D	0-0	0-0	14		3808
32		25	A	Barnet	D	1-1	1-1	15	McKearney	2362
33		29	H	Hereford U	D	1-1	0-0	—	Benjamin	1492
34	Apr	1	H	Lincoln C	L	0-1	0-1	15		1696
35		4	H	Scunthorpe U	D	0-0	0-0	—		1307
36		8	H	Exeter C	W	3-1	2-0	12	Miller, Lyons, Rimmer	1417
37		11	H	Walsall	W	1-0	1-0	—	Lyons	2176
38		15	A	Preston NE	L	0-1	0-1	12		10,238
39		18	H	Bury	L	0-3	0-1	—		2531
40		22	A	Walsall	L	0-2	0-0	14		3508
41		29	A	Rochdale	L	0-1	0-1	15		1949
42	May	6	H	Doncaster R	W	3-2	0-0	14	Lyons 2 (1 pen), Miller	1576

Final League Position: 14

GOALSCORERS

League (53): Lyons 15 (2 pens), Benjamin 6, Kilford 5, Leonard 5 (1 pen), McKearney 5 (1 pen), Rimmer 4, Miller 3, Gavin 2, Strong 2, Doolan 1, Morton 1, Rennie 1 (pen), Robertson 1, Rodwell 1, own goal 1.
Coca-Cola Cup (4): Gavin 2, Carragher 1, Rennie 1.
FA Cup (4): Carragher 2, Kilford 1, Leonard 1.

Farnworth S. 41	Rennie P.A. 11 + 3	Wright M.A. 14 + 2	West P.D. 1	Robertson J.N. 39 + 1	Kilford I.A. 35	Campbell D.A. 7	Morton N. 9	Gavin P.J. 9 + 3	Rimmer N. 33	Lyons A. 32	Duffy C.J. — + 4	Strong G. 12 + 5	Carragher M. 41	Ormsby B.T. 2	Harford P. 3	Tait P. 1 + 4	McKearney D.J. 17 + 4	Jakub Y. 16	Leonard M. 28 + 1	Farrell A.J. 30 + 1	Benjamin I.T. 12 + 5	Miller D.B. 31	Adekola D. 1 + 3	Doolan J. 9 + 7	Rodwell A. 5	Furlong C.D. — + 1	Whitney J.D. 12	Black A. 9	Ogden N. — + 1	Statham M. 1 + 1	Millett M.P. 1 + 2	Match No.
1	2	3	*4*	5	6	7	8	9	10	11	12	14																				1
1	4	3		5	6	7	8	9	10	11		12	2																			2
1	2	3		5	6	7	8	9		11	12	4	10																			3
1	2	*3*		5	6	7	8	9		11	12	14	10	4																		4
1	2			5	6		8	9			12	3	10	4	7	11																5
1	2	3		5	6		8	9	10			4	11		7	12																6
1	2	3		5	6		8	9	10			4	11		7		12															7
1	2			5	6		8	9	10			4	11				12	3	7													8
1	2			5	6	7	8	9	10			4	11			14	*12*			3												9
1				5	8	7		12	10			4	2					3	9	6	11											10
1	14				8	*7*		12		11		4	2					3	9	6	10	5										11
1					7				10	11		4	2			12		3	9	6	8	5										12
1				12	7				10	11		4	*2*					3	9	6	8	5	14									13
1	12			5	7					11		4	2					*3*	9	6	8	10	14									14
1	2			5	7					11			8				10	3	9	6		4										15
1	2			5	7					11		12	8				10	3	9	6		4										16
1				5	7				4	11		2	8				10	3	9	6												17
1				5	7				10	11			2				8	3	9	6		4										18
1				5	7				10	11		12	2				*8*	3	9	6		4	14									19
1		12		5					10	11			2			14		3	9	7		6	*8*	4								20
1				5	7				10	11			8					3	9	6		4		2								21
1	12	3		5	7				10	11			8						9	6	14	4		*2*								22
1		3		5					10	11			2				8		9	6	12	4			7							23
1		3		5						11			2				8		9	6		4		10	7							24
1		3		5					10	11			2				8		9	6	12	4			7							25
1				5					10	11			2				8	3		6	9	4			7							26
1				5					10	11			2				*8*	3		6	9	4		12	7	14						27
1		12		5	7				10	11			2				8	3			9	4		6								28
1		3		5	7				10	11			2				8				9	4		6								29
1		3		5	7				10	11			2				8		12	14	9	4		*6*								30
1		11		5					10				2				8		9	7		4		6			3					31
1		11		5	7				10				2				8		9	6		4		12			3					32
1				5	8				10				2				11		9	6	12	4					3	7				33
1				5	8				10				2						9	6	11	4		12			3	7				34
1				5	8				10	11			2						9	6		4					3	7	12			35
1				5	8				10	11			2				12		9	6		4					3	7				36
1				5	8				10	11			2						9	6		4					3	7				37
1				5	8				10	11			2						9	6		4		12			3	7				38
1				5	8				10	11			2						9	6		4		12			3	7				39
1				5	8				10	11			2				7		9	6		4		12			3			15	14	40
				5	8				10	11			2						9		14	4		12			3	7		1	*6*	41
1				5	8			12		11			2							6	10	4		9			3	7			14	42

Coca-Cola Cup

First Round	Crewe Alex (a)	1-2
	(h)	3-0
Second Round	Aston Villa (a)	0-5
	(h)	0-3

FA Cup

First Round	Spennymoor U (h)	4-0
Second Round	Altrincham (a)	0-1

WIMBLEDON 1994–95 *Back row (left to right):* Joe Dillon (Kit Man), Grant Payne, Neal Ardley, Dean Blackwell, Stewart Castledine, Steve Anthrobus, Aidan Newhouse, Brian McAllister, Steve Talboys, Ron Suart (Chief Scout).
Centre row: Syd Neal (Kit Manager), Gavin Fell, John Scales, Gary Blissett, Marcus Gayle, Neil Sullivan, Dean Holdsworth, Hans Segers, Robbie Earle, Vinnie Jones, Scott Fitzgerald, Roger Smith (Youth Development Officer).
Front row: Brian Sparrow (Reserve Team Manager), Gary Elkins, Gerald Dobbs, Chris Perry, Roger Joseph, Warren Barton, Terry Burton (Assistant Manager), Joe Kinnear (Manager), Peter Fear, Andy Clarke, Alan Kimble, Mark Thomas, Paul McGee, Ernie Tippett (Youth Team Manager).

FA Premiership **WIMBLEDON**

Selhurst Park, South Norwood, London SE25 6PY. Telephone: (0181) 771 2233. Fax: (0181) 768 0640. Box Office: (0181) 771 8841.

Ground capacity: 26,500.

Record attendance: 30,115 v Manchester U, FA Premier League, 9 May 1993.

Record receipts: £312,024 v Manchester U, FA Premier League, 16 April 1994.

Pitch measurements: 110yd × 74yd.

Chairman: S. G. Reed. ***Vice-Chairman:*** J. Lelliott.

Managing Director: S. Hammam.

Directors: P. Cork, P. R. Cooper, N. N. Hammam, P. Miller.

Chief Executive: David Barnard.

Manager: Joe Kinnear. ***Assistant Manager:*** Terry Burton. ***Physio:*** Steve Allen.

Secretary: Steve Rooke. ***Marketing Manager:*** Sharon Sillitoe. ***Press Manager:*** Reg Davis.

Year Formed: 1889. ***Turned Professional:*** 1964. ***Ltd Co.:*** 1964.

Previous Name: Wimbledon Old Centrals, 1899–1905.

Previous Ground: Plough Lane.

Club Nickname: 'The Dons'.

Foundation: Old boys from Central School formed this club as Wimbledon Old Centrals in 1889. Their earliest successes were in the Clapham League before switching to the Southern Suburban League in 1902.

First Football League game: 20 August, 1978, Division 4, v Halifax T (h) D 3-3 – Guy; Bryant (1), Galvin, Donaldson, Aitken, Davies, Galliers, Smith, Connell (1), Holmes, Leslie (1).

Record League Victory: 6–0 v Newport C, Division 3, 3 September 1983 – Beasant; Peters, Winterburn, Galliers, Morris, Hatter, Evans (2), Ketteridge (1), Cork (3 incl. 1p), Downes, Hodges (Driver).

Record Cup Victory: 7–2 v Windsor & Eton, FA Cup, 1st rd, 22 November 1980 – Beasant; Jones, Armstrong, Galliers, Mick Smith (2), Cunningham (1), Ketteridge, Hodges, Leslie, Cork (1), Hubbick (3).

Record Defeat: 0–8 v Everton, League Cup 2nd rd, 29 August 1978.

Most League Points (2 for a win): 61, Division 4, 1978–79.

Most League Points (3 for a win): 98, Division 4, 1982–83.

Most League Goals: 97, Division 3, 1983–84.

Highest League Scorer in Season: Alan Cork, 29, 1983–84.

Most League Goals in Total Aggregate: Alan Cork, 145, 1977–92.

Most Capped Player: Terry Phelan, 8 (26), Republic of Ireland.

Most League Appearances: Alan Cork, 430, 1977–92.

Record Transfer Fee Received: £4,000,000 from Newcastle U for Warren Barton, June 1995.

Record Transfer Fee Paid: £920,000 to Norwich C for Efan Ekoku, October 1994.

Football League Record: 1977 Elected to Division 4; 1979–80 Division 3; 1980–81 Division 4; 1981–82 Division 3; 1982–83 Division 4; 1983–84 Division 3; 1984–86 Division 2; 1986–92 Division 1; 1992– FA Premier League.

Honours: *FA Premier League* : best season: 6th, 1993–94; *Football League:* Division 3 – Runners-up 1983–84; Division 4 – Champions 1982–83. *FA Cup:* Winners 1988. *Football League Cup:* best season: 4th rd, 1980, 1984, 1989. *League Group Cup:* Runners-up 1982. *Amateur Cup:* Winners 1963; Runners-up 1935, 1947.

Colours: All navy blue with gold trim. **Change colours:** Red shirts, red shorts, black stockings.

WIMBLEDON 1994–95 LEAGUE RECORD

Match No.	Date	Venue	Opponents	Result	H/T Score	Lg. Pos.	Goalscorers	Attendance
1	Aug 20	A	Coventry C	D 1-1	0-0	—	Castledine	11,005
2	23	H	Ipswich T	D 1-1	1-0	—	Holdsworth	6341
3	27	H	Sheffield W	L 0-1	0-0	16		7453
4	31	A	Manchester U	L 0-3	0-1	—		43,440
5	Sept 10	H	Leicester C	W 2-1	2-1	14	Harford, Willis (og)	7683
6	17	A	Crystal Palace	D 0-0	0-0	13		12,366
7	24	A	QPR	W 1-0	0-0	10	Reeves	11,061
8	Oct 1	H	Tottenham H	L 1-2	1-1	13	Talboys	16,802
9	8	H	Arsenal	L 1-3	0-1	15	Jones	10,842
10	17	A	Nottingham F	L 1-3	0-1	—	Gayle	20,287
11	22	A	Liverpool	L 0-3	0-2	19		31,139
12	30	H	Norwich C	W 1-0	0-0	17	Ekoku	8242
13	Nov 5	A	Leeds U	L 1-3	1-3	18	Ekoku	27,246
14	9	H	Aston Villa	W 4-3	1-2	—	Barton (pen), Ardley, Jones, Leonhardsen	6221
15	19	H	Newcastle U	W 3-2	3-2	14	Clarke, Ekoku, Harford	14,203
16	26	A	Manchester C	L 0-2	0-1	16		21,131
17	Dec 3	H	Blackburn R	L 0-3	0-0	17		12,341
18	10	H	Coventry C	W 2-0	2-0	16	Leonhardsen, Harford	7349
19	16	A	Ipswich T	D 2-2	1-1	—	Holdsworth, Goodman	11,282
20	26	A	Southampton	W 3-2	2-2	13	Holdsworth 2 (1 pen), Harford	14,603
21	28	H	West Ham U	W 1-0	0-0	12	Fear	11,212
22	31	A	Chelsea	D 1-1	0-0	12	Ekoku	16,009
23	Jan 2	H	Everton	W 2-1	2-1	9	Harford 2	9506
24	14	A	Norwich C	W 2-1	1-1	7	Reeves, Ekoku	18,261
25	25	A	Newcastle U	L 1-2	0-1	—	Ekoku	34,374
26	Feb 4	H	Leeds U	D 0-0	0-0	9		10,211
27	11	A	Aston Villa	L 1-7	1-4	9	Barton	23,982
28	22	A	Blackburn R	L 1-2	1-2	—	Ekoku	20,586
29	25	A	Tottenham H	W 2-1	1-0	10	Ekoku 2	27,258
30	Mar 4	H	QPR	L 1-3	1-1	10	Holdsworth	9176
31	7	H	Manchester U	L 0-1	0-0	—		18,224
32	11	A	Sheffield W	W 1-0	0-0	9	Reeves	20,395
33	18	H	Crystal Palace	W 2-0	1-0	8	Jones, Gayle	8835
34	21	H	Manchester C	W 2-0	0-0	—	Thorn, Elkins	5268
35	Apr 1	A	Leicester C	W 4-3	0-1	8	Goodman 2, Leonhardsen 2	15,489
36	10	H	Chelsea	D 1-1	0-1	—	Goodman	7022
37	13	A	West Ham U	L 0-3	0-1	—		21,804
38	17	H	Southampton	L 0-2	0-2	9		10,521
39	29	A	Everton	D 0-0	0-0	9		31,567
40	May 2	H	Liverpool	D 0-0	0-0	—		12,041
41	4	A	Arsenal	D 0-0	0-0	—		32,822
42	13	H	Nottingham F	D 2-2	2-1	9	Holdsworth 2 (1 pen)	15,341

Final League Position: 9

GOALSCORERS

League (48): Ekoku 9, Holdsworth 7 (2 pens), Harford 6, Goodman 4, Leonhardsen 4, Jones 3, Reeves 3, Barton 2 (1 pen), Gayle 2, Ardley 1, Castledine 1, Clarke 1, Elkins 1, Fear 1, Talboys 1, Thorn 1, own goal 1.
Coca-Cola Cup (3): Gayle 1, Harford 1, Holdsworth 1.
FA Cup (4): Clarke 1, Earle 1, Harford 1, Leonhardsen 1.

Segers H. 31 + 1	Barton W.D. 39	Elkins G. 33 + 3	Jones V.P. 33	Scales J.R. 3	Fitzgerald S.B. 14 + 3	Gayle M.A. 22 + 1	Castledine S.M. 5 + 1	Harford M.G. 17 + 10	Holdsworth D.C. 27 + 1	Talboys S. 7	Ardley N.C. 9 + 5	Blissett G.P. 4 + 5	Clarke A.W. 8 + 17	Kimble A.F. 26	Reeves A. 31	Fear P. 8 + 6	Perry C.J. 17 + 5	Thorn A.C. 22 + 1	Ekoku E. 24	Joseph R. 3	Leonhardsen O. 18 + 2	Cunningham K.E. 28	Goodman J. 13 + 6	Earle R.G. 9	Sullivan N. 11	*Match No.*
1	2	3	4	5	6	7	8	9	10	*11*	12	14														1
1	2	3	4	5	6	7	8		10		11	9	12													2
1	2	3	4	5	6	7	8	9			11	10	12													3
1	2	5	4		6	10	8	9		11	7		12	3												4
1	2	*11*	4		6	8		9	10		7		12	3	5	14										5
1	2	11	4		6	8		9	10		7			3	5											6
1	2	11			6	8		9		4		12	10	3	5	7	14									7
1	2	11			6			9	10	4	7		12	3	*5*	8	14									8
1	2	11	4		6	*8*		9	10		12			3	5	7		14								9
1	2	11	4		6	8	10				12				5	7		3	9							10
1	2	11			6	*8*	14				7	12			5	10	4		9	3						11
1	7	3	4			8				11		10	12		5			6	9	2						12
1	7	3	4			8				11		10	12		5			6	9	2						13
1	2	3	4		14			12		11	7		*9*		5			6	10		8					14
1	2	11	4		12			14					7		5			6	9		10	3	*8*			15
1	7	3	4		12				10				11		5			6	9		8	2				16
1	4	3			5			12	10				11			7		6	9		8	2				17
1	4	11			5			*9*	10				12	3				6	7		8	2	14			18
1	7	12	4		5			14	*10*					3				6	9		11	2	8			19
1	4	11						9	10		12			3			5	6	7			2		8		20
1	7	11	*4*					9	10				12	3		14	5	6	8			2				21
1	7		4					9	10				12	3			5	6	11			2		8		22
1	7		4					9					10	3	5	12	6		11			2		8		23
1	7	12	4						*10*				14	3	5		6		11			2	9	8		24
1	7	12	4									14	*11*	3			5	6	9			2	10	8		25
1	7	3	4					*9*				12			5			6	11		10	2	14	8		26
1	7	3	4					9	*10*						5		12	6	11		8	2	14			27
1	4							12	14		7		*9*	3	5		6		11		10	2		8		28
1	7					10								3	5	11	4	6	9			2		8		29
1	7		4					9	10				12	3	5		6				*11*	2	14	8		30
1	7	11	4			9			10		12			3	5		6					2	8			31
	7	11	4			9		12	*10*					3	5		6				14	2	8		1	32
	7	11	4			*9*		12	10					3	5		6				14	2	8		1	33
		3	4			*9*		12	10						5	14	7	6			11	2	8		1	34
	4	11				9		12	10					3	5		14	6			7	2	8		1	35
	7	11	4			14		12	10					3	5			6			8	2	*9*		1	36
	7	3	4			11		9	10				12		5			6			8	2			1	37
	2		4			9			10				12		5			6	11		8	3	7		1	38
		11	4						10					3	5	7	12	6	*9*		8	2	14		1	39
	7	11	4			*10*							12	3	5	14	6		9			2	8		1	40
	7	11	4						10				12	3	5	14	6				*8*	2	9		1	41
15		*11*	4			7			10				12	3	5		6		9		8	2	14		*1*	42

Coca-Cola Cup

Second Round	Torquay U (h)	2-0
	(a)	1-0
Third Round	Crystal Palace (h)	0-1

FA Cup

Third Round	Colchester U (h)	1-0
Fourth Round	Tranmere R (a)	2-0
Fifth Round	Liverpool (a)	1-1
	(h)	0-2

WOLVERHAMPTON WANDERERS 1994–95 *Back row (left to right):* Andy Thompson, Tony Daley, James Smith, Robbie Dennison, Andy Debont, Tom Bennett, Steven Piearce, Michael Innes, Kevin Keen, James Kelly, Mark Rankine, Paul Birch.

Centre row: Barry Holmes (Physio), Darren Shaw, Chris Marsden, Steve Froggatt, David Kelly, Neil Masters, Mick Stowell, Paul Jones, Neil Emblem, Lee Mills, Paul Cook, Darren Ferguson, Scott Voice, Rob Kelly (Youth Development Officer).

Front row: Andrew Macbeth, Bobby Downes (Assistant Manager), Stuart Gray (Reserve Team Coach), Paul Blades, Steve Bull, Peter Shirtliff, Graham Taylor (Manager), Geoff Thomas, Mark Venus, Darren Simkin, Chris Evans (Youth Team Coach), Steve Harrison (First Team Coach), Jason Barnett.

(Photograph: Action Images)

Division 1 **WOLVERHAMPTON WANDERERS**

Molineux Grounds, Wolverhampton WV1 4QR. Telephone: (01902) 655000; Fax: (01902) 687006.

Ground capacity: 28,525.

Record attendance: 61,315 v Liverpool, FA Cup 5th rd, 11 February 1939.

Record receipts: £236,972 v Leicester C, FA Cup 5th rd, 18 February 1995.

Pitch measurements: 116yd × 74yd.

President: Sir Jack Hayward.

Chairman: Jonathan Hayward.

Directors: Jack Harris, John Harris, Nic Stones, John Richards.

Team Manager: Graham Taylor. ***Assistant Manager:*** Bobby Downes.

Coach: Steve Harrison. ***Physio:*** Barry Holmes.

Secretary: Tom Finn. ***Commercial Director:*** D. Clayton.

Year Formed: 1877*(*see Foundation*). ***Turned Professional:*** 1888. ***Ltd Co.:*** 1982.

Club Nickname: 'Wolves'.

Previous Grounds: 1877, Goldthorn Hill; 1879, John Harper's Field; 1881, Dudley Road; 1889, Molineux.

Previous Names: 1880, St Luke's, Blakenhall combined with Blakenhall Wanderers to become Wolverhampton Wanderers (1923) Ltd until 1982.

Foundation: Another club where precise details of information are confused, due in part to the existence of an earlier Wolverhampton club which played rugby. However, it is now considered likely that it came into being in 1879 when players from St. Luke's (founded 1877) and Goldthorn (founded 1876) broke away to form Wolverhampton Wanderers Association FC.

First Football League game: 8 September, 1888, Football League, v Aston Villa (h) D 1-1 – Baynton; Baugh, Mason; Fletcher, Allen, Lowder; Hunter, Cooper, Anderson, White, Cannon. Scorer – Cox o.g.

Record League Victory: 10–1 v Leicester C, Division 1, 15 April 1938 – Sidlow; Morris, Dowen; Galley, Cullis, Gardiner; Maguire (1), Horace Wright, Westcott (4), Jones (1), Dorsett (4).

Record Cup Victory: 14–0 v Cresswell's Brewery, FA Cup, 2nd rd, 13 November 1886 – I. Griffiths; Baugh, Mason; Pearson, Allen (1), Lowder; Hunter (4), Knight (2), Brodie (4), B. Griffiths (2), Wood. Plus one goal 'scrambled through'.

Record Defeat: 1–10 v Newton Heath, Division 1, 15 October 1892.

Most League Points (2 for a win): 64, Division 1, 1957–58.

Most League Points (3 for a win): 92, Division 4, 1988–89.

Most League Goals: 115, Division 2, 1931–32.

Highest League Scorer in Season: Dennis Westcott, 38, Division 1, 1946–47.

Most League Goals in Total Aggregate: Steve Bull, 202, 1986–95.

Most Capped Player: Billy Wright, 105, England (70 consecutive).

Most League Appearances: Derek Parkin, 501, 1967–82.

Record Transfer Fee Received: £1,150,000 from Manchester C for Steve Daley, September 1979.

Record Transfer Fee Paid: £1,300,000 to Bradford C for Dean Richards, May 1995.

Football League Record: 1888 Founder Member of Football League: 1906–23 Division 2; 1923–24 Division 3 (N); 1924–32 Division 2; 1932–65 Division 1; 1965–67 Division 2; 1967–76 Division 1; 1976–77 Division 2; 1977–82 Division 1; 1982–83 Division 2; 1983–84 Division 1; 1984–85 Division 2; 1985–86 Division 3; 1986–88 Division 4; 1988–89 Division 3; 1989–92 Division 2; 1992– Division 1.

Honours: *Football League:* Division 1 – Champions 1953–54, 1957–58, 1958–59; Runners-up 1937–38, 1938–39, 1949–50, 1954–55, 1959–60; Division 2 – Champions 1931–32, 1976–77; Runners-up 1966–67, 1982–83; Division 3 (N) – Champions 1923–24; Division 3 – Champions 1988–89; Division 4 – Champions 1987–88. *FA Cup:* Winners 1893, 1908, 1949, 1960; Runners-up 1889, 1896, 1921, 1939. *Football League Cup:* Winners 1974, 1980. *Texaco Cup:* 1971. *Sherpa Van Trophy:* Winners 1988. **European Competitions:** *European Cup:* 1958–59, 1959–60. *European Cup-Winners' Cup:* 1960–61. *UEFA Cup:* 1971–72 (runners-up), 1973–74, 1974–75, 1980–81.

Colours: Gold shirts, black shorts, gold stockings. **Change colours:** White shirts, white shorts, white stockings.

WOLVERHAMPTON WANDERERS 1994–95 LEAGUE RECORD

Match No.	Date		Venue	Opponents	Result		H/T Score	Lg. Pos.	Goalscorers	Attendance
1	Aug	13	H	Reading	W	1-0	1-0	—	Froggatt	27,012
2		21	A	Notts Co	D	1-1	0-1	—	Thompson (pen)	8569
3		28	H	WBA	W	2-0	1-0	3	Thompson (pen), Kelly	27,764
4		30	A	Watford	L	1-2	0-1	—	Emblen	10,108
5	Sept	3	A	Sunderland	D	1-1	1-1	7	Venus	15,111
6		10	H	Tranmere R	W	2-0	1-0	3	Stewart, Emblen	27,030
7		13	H	Southend U	W	5-0	3-0	—	Emblen, Kelly, Froggatt, Walters, Bull	23,608
8		17	A	Burnley	W	1-0	0-0	1	Bull	17,766
9		24	A	Portsmouth	W	2-1	1-1	1	Walters, Kelly	13,466
10	Oct	1	H	Port Vale	W	2-1	0-0	1	Thompson 2 (2 pens)	27,469
11		8	A	Swindon T	L	2-3	2-2	1	Kelly 2	14,036
12		15	H	Grimsby T	W	2-1	1-1	1	Thompson (pen), Venus	24,447
13		22	H	Millwall	D	3-3	1-1	1	Bull 2, Venus	25,059
14		30	A	Stoke C	D	1-1	1-1	1	Bull	15,928
15	Nov	1	A	Bristol C	W	5-1	2-1	—	Walters, Thompson (pen), Kelly 3	10,401
16		5	H	Luton T	L	2-3	0-1	1	Stewart, Johnson (og)	26,749
17		20	A	Middlesbrough	L	0-1	0-0	2		19,953
18		23	H	Bolton W	W	3-1	0-1	—	Thompson (pen), Coleman (og), Birch	25,903
19		27	H	Derby Co	L	0-2	0-1	2		22,768
20	Dec	4	A	Millwall	L	0-1	0-0	3		8025
21		10	H	Notts Co	W	1-0	0-0	2	Bull	25,786
22		18	A	Reading	L	2-4	1-2	2	Bull, Quinn (og)	10,136
23		26	A	Oldham Ath	L	1-4	0-1	4	Dennison	11,962
24		28	H	Charlton Ath	W	2-0	2-0	—	Bull, Chapple (og)	26,738
25		31	A	Barnsley	W	3-1	2-1	2	Dennison, Mills, Emblen	9207
26	Jan	2	H	Sheffield U	D	2-2	0-0	2	De Wolf (pen), Emblen	27,809
27		14	H	Stoke C	W	2-0	1-0	2	Kelly, Dennison	28,298
28	Feb	4	A	Bolton W	L	1-5	1-2	4	Goodman	16,964
29		11	H	Bristol C	W	2-0	1-0	2	Dennison, Kelly	25,451
30		21	H	Middlesbrough	L	0-2	0-0	—		27,611
31		25	A	Port Vale	W	4-2	3-1	5	De Wolf 3 (1 pen), Bull	13,676
32	Mar	5	H	Portsmouth	W	1-0	0-0	4	Bull	23,284
33		8	H	Sunderland	W	1-0	0-0	—	Thompson (pen)	25,926
34		15	A	WBA	L	0-2	0-1	—		20,661
35		18	H	Watford	D	1-1	1-0	5	Thomas	24,380
36		24	H	Burnley	W	2-0	1-0	—	Bull, Emblen	25,703
37	Apr	1	A	Southend U	W	1-0	0-0	3	Bull	8522
38		4	A	Luton T	D	3-3	0-2	—	Kelly 2, Emblen	9651
39		8	H	Barnsley	D	0-0	0-0	4		26,385
40		12	A	Derby Co	D	3-3	1-1	—	Goodman, Richards 2	16,040
41		15	A	Charlton Ath	L	2-3	1-1	4	Bull 2	10,922
42		17	H	Oldham Ath	W	2-1	1-1	4	Kelly 2	25,840
43		22	A	Sheffield U	D	3-3	0-1	4	Goodman, Bull, Kelly	16,714
44		29	A	Grimsby T	D	0-0	0-0	4		10,112
45	May	3	A	Tranmere R	D	1-1	0-1	—	Bull	12,306
46		7	H	Swindon T	D	1-1	1-1	4	Thompson (pen)	26,245

Final League Position: 4

GOALSCORERS

League (77): Bull 16, Kelly D 15, Thompson 9 (9 pens), Emblen 7, Dennison 4, De Wolf 4 (2 pens), Goodman 3, Venus 3, Walters 3, Froggatt 2, Richards 2, Stewart 2, Birch 1, Mills 1, Thomas 1, own goals 4.
Coca-Cola Cup (6): Bull 2, Kelly D 2, Birch 1, Froggatt 1.
FA Cup (7): Kelly D 4, Cowans 1, Dennison 1, Mills 1.

Stowell M. 37	Smith J.J.A. 24 + 1	Thompson A.R. 30 + 1	Ferguson D. 22 + 2	Emblen N.R. 23 + 4	Shirtliff P.A. 26 + 2	Keen K.I. 1	Thomas G.R. 13 + 1	Bull S.G. 31	Kelly D.T. 38 + 4	Froggatt S.J. 20	Mills R.L. 6 + 5	Blades P.A. 30 + 2	Venus M. 35 + 4	Rankine S.M. 24 + 3	Birch P. 8 + 2	Stewart P.A. 5 + 3	Walters M.E. 11	Daley A.M. — + 1	Bennett T.M. 4 + 4	De Wolf J. 13	Goodman D.R. 24	Jones P.S. 9	Law B.J. 17	Cowans G.S. 21	Dennison R. 21 + 1	Masters N.B. 3 + 2	Wright J.H. — + 6	Richards D.I. 10	Match No.
1	2	3	4	5	6	7	8	9	10	11	12																		1
1	2	3	4		6		8		10	11		5	7	9															2
1	2	3	4	7	6		8		10	11		5	12		9														3
1	2	3	4	7	6		8		*10*	11		5	12	14	9														4
1	2	3	11	4	6				10			5	8	12	7	9													5
1	2	3	8	4	6			9	12	11			5			10	7												6
1	2	3	8	4	6			9	10	11			5				7												7
1	2	3	8	4	6			9	10	11			5				7												8
1	2	3	8		6			9	10	11		5	4				7												9
1	2	3	8		6			9		11		5	4	10			7												10
1	2	3	8		6			9	10			5	4		7		11												11
1	2	3	8		6			9	10	11		5	4	12			7												12
1	2	3	8		6			9	10	11		5	4				7	12											13
1	*2*	3	12	4			8	9	10	11		5	6			14	7												14
1	2	3	4				8	9	10	11		5	6			12	7												15
1	2	3	4	12			8	9	10	11		5	6			14	*7*												16
1		3	4	7			8		10	11		5	6	2	12	9													17
1		3	4	12			8		10	11		5	6	2	7	9													18
1	12	3	4	14			8		10	11		5	6	2	7	*9*													19
1	2		4	7			8	9	10	11	12	5	6						3										20
1	2		4	6				9	12	11		14	3	7					*10*	5	8								21
1	2		10	4				9		11	14	6	3	7	*12*					5	8								22
	2		10	4							9		3	7						5		1	6	8	11	12			23
				4				9			8	2	3						12	5	*7*	1	6	10	11	14			24
				4					12		9	2	3						8	5	7	1	6	10	11				25
				4					8		9	3	2							5	7	1	6	10	11				26
				4					8		9	2	3		7					5		1	6	10	11				27
		3		*4*			12		8		9	2							14	5	7	1	6	10	11				28
		3		*4*					8		12	2		7					14	5	9	1	6	10	11				29
		3			12		4		8		14		*2*	7						5	9	1	6	10	11				30
		3			6			9	8			2	12	4						5	7	1		10	11				31
1		3			6			9	8			2		4						5	7			10	11				32
1	2	3			6			*9*	8					4					12	5	7			10	11		14		33
1	2	3		12	6			*9*	8					4							7		5	10	11		14		34
1		3			6		8		9			2	12	*7*					4		10		5		11		14		35
1				10	6			9	8			2	3	4							7		5		11				36
1				4				9	8			2	10								7		5		11	3		6	37
1				4				9	12			2	11		7						8		5	10	14	*3*		6	38
1			14	4	12			9	8					2							7		5	10	*11*	3		6	39
1	3				6			9	8				11	4							7		5	10			12	2	40
1	3				*6*			9	8			12	11	4							7		5	10			14	2	41
1					6			9	8				3	4							7		5	10	11			2	42
1		12			6			9	8			2	3	4							7			10	11			5	43
1		2			6			9	8				3	4							7			10	11			5	44
1		2			6			9	8				3	4							7			10	11			5	45
1		2			6			9	8				3	4							7			10	11		12	5	46

Coca-Cola Cup

Second Round	Chesterfield (a)	3-1
	(h)	1-1
Third Round	Nottingham F (h)	2-3

FA Cup

Third Round	Mansfield T (a)	3-2
Fourth Round	Sheffield W (a)	0-0
	(h)	1-1
Fifth Round	Leicester C (h)	1-0
Sixth Round	Crystal Palace (a)	1-1
	(h)	1-4

WREXHAM 1994–95 *Back row (left to right):* Barry Jones, Barry Hunter, Mike Lake, Scott Williams, Karl Connolly, Mark Taylor, Jonathan Cross.
Third row: Kevin Reeves (Assistant Manager), Cliff Sear (Youth Development Officer), Gary Bennett, Mark Cartwright, Bryan Hughes, Andy Marriott, Gareth Owen, Ken Dixon, Phil Hardy, Dudley Hall (Reserve Physio), Steve Wade (Physio).
Second row: Mike Rigg (Community Scheme Organiser), Stephen Pugh, Mel Pejic, David Brammer, Tony Humes, Mr W. P. Griffiths (Chairman), Brian Flynn (Manager), Steve Watkin, Wayne Phillips, Deryn Brace, Mike Buxton (Schoolboy Development Officer).
Front row: Steve Morgan, Tony Merola, Richard Barnes, Kieron Durkan.

Division 2 **WREXHAM**

Racecourse Ground, Mold Road, Wrexham LL11 2AN. Telephone: (01978) 262129. Fax: (01978) 357821. Commercial Dept: (01978) 352536. Community Office: (01978) 358545. Clubcall: 0891 121642.

Ground capacity: 11,881.

Record attendance: 34,445 v Manchester U, FA Cup 4th rd, 26 January 1957.

Record receipts: £126,012 v West Ham U, FA Cup 4th rd, 4 February 1992.

Pitch measurements: 111yd × 71yd.

Chairman: W. P. Griffiths.

Managing Director: D. L. Rhodes.

Directors: C. Griffiths, S. Mackreth, G. Paletta, B. Williams (vice-chairman), P. Griffiths.

Manager: Brian Flynn. ***Assistant Manager:*** Kevin Reeves.

Secretary: D. L. Rhodes. ***Player-Coach:*** Joey Jones.

Commercial Manager: P. Stokes. ***Physio:*** Steve Wade.

Year Formed: 1873 (oldest club in Wales).

Turned Professional: 1912. ***Ltd Co.:*** 1912.

Previous Ground: Acton Park.

Club Nickname: 'Robins'.

Foundation: The oldest club still in existence in Wales, Wrexham was founded in 1873 by a group of local businessmen initially to play a 17-a-side game against the Provincial Insurance team. By 1875 their team formation was reduced to 11 men and a year later they were among the founders of the Welsh FA.

First Football League game: 27 August, 1921, Division 3(N), v Hartlepools U (h) L 0-2 – Godding; Ellis, Simpson; Matthias, Foster, Griffiths; Burton, Goode, Cotton, Edwards, Lloyd.

Record League Victory: 10–1 v Hartlepools, Division 4, 3 March 1962 – Keelan; Peter Jones, McGavan; Tecwyn Jones, Fox, Ken Barnes; Ron Barnes (3), Bennion (1), Davies (3), Ambler (3), Ron Roberts.

Record Cup Victory: 6–0 v Gateshead, FA Cup, 1st rd, 20 November 1976 – Lloyd; Evans, Whittle, Davis, Roberts, Thomas (Hill), Shinton (3 incl. 1p), Sutton, Ashcroft (2), Lee (1), Griffiths. 6–0 v Charlton Ath, FA Cup, 3rd rd, 5 January 1980 – Davies; Darracott, Kenworthy, Davis, Jones (Hill), Fox, Vinter (3), Sutton, Edwards (1), McNeil (2), Carrodus.

Record Defeat: 0–9 v Brentford, Division 3, 15 October 1963.

Most League Points (2 for a win): 61, Division 4, 1969–70 and Division 3, 1977–78.

Most League Points (3 for a win): 80, Division 3, 1992–93.

Most League Goals: 106, Division 3 (N), 1932–33.

Highest League Scorer in Season: Tom Bamford, 44, Division 3 (N), 1933–34.

Most League Goals in Total Aggregate: Tom Bamford, 175, 1928–34.

Most Capped Player: Dai Davies, 28 (51), Wales.

Most League Appearances: Arfon Griffiths, 592, 1959–61, 1962–79.

Record Transfer Fee Received: £300,000 from Manchester U for Mickey Thomas, November 1978, from Manchester C for Bobby Shinton, July 1979 and from Liverpool for Lee Jones, March 1992.

Record Transfer Fee Paid: £210,000 to Liverpool for Joey Jones, October 1978.

Football League Record: 1921 Original Member of Division 3 (N); 1958–60 Division 3; 1960–62 Division 4; 1962–64 Division 3; 1964–70 Division 4; 1970–78 Division 3; 1978–82 Division 2; 1982–83 Division 3; 1983–92 Division 4; 1992–93 Division 3; 1993– Division 2.

Honours: *Football League:* Division 2 best season: 15th, 1978–79; Division 3 – Champions 1977–78; Division 3 (N) – Runners-up 1932–33; Division 4 – Runners-up 1969–70. *FA Cup:* best season: 6th rd, 1974, 1978. *Football League Cup:* best season: 5th rd, 1961, 1978. *Welsh Cup:* Winners 23 times. Runners-up 22 times. Victories equal record, but record number of final appearances. **European Competition:** *European Cup-Winners' Cup:* 1972–73, 1975–76, 1978–79, 1979–80, 1984–85, 1986–87, 1990–91.

Colours: Red shirts, white shorts, red stockings. **Change colours:** Gold shirts, black shorts, black stockings.

WREXHAM 1994–95 LEAGUE RECORD

Match No.	Date	Venue	Opponents	Result	H/T Score	Lg. Pos.	Goalscorers	Attendance
1	Aug 13	H	Bournemouth	W 2-0	2-0	—	Pejic, Bennett (pen)	3580
2	20	A	Shrewsbury T	D 2-2	2-1	7	Bennett 2 (1 pen)	5748
3	27	H	Brighton & HA	W 2-1	1-0	4	Bennett 2 (1 pen)	3339
4	30	A	Cardiff C	D 0-0	0-0	—		4903
5	Sept 3	A	Brentford	W 2-0	2-0	4	Watkin, Phillips	5820
6	10	H	Crewe Alex	W 1-0	0-0	3	Owen	6399
7	13	H	Bradford C	L 0-1	0-1	—		4179
8	17	A	Bristol R	L 2-4	0-1	8	Brammer, Connolly	4441
9	24	A	Blackpool	L 1-2	0-0	12	Cross	5015
10	Oct 1	H	Birmingham C	D 1-1	1-0	13	Connolly	6002
11	8	A	Cambridge U	W 2-1	0-0	8	Bennett 2 (1 pen)	3221
12	15	H	Hull C	D 2-2	0-1	10	Bennett (pen), Hughes	3418
13	22	H	Oxford U	W 3-2	2-2	10	Richardson 2, Connolly	3925
14	30	A	Chester C	D 1-1	0-1	11	Owen	4974
15	Nov 1	A	Huddersfield T	L 1-2	0-1	—	Connolly	9639
16	5	H	Wycombe W	W 4-1	2-0	8	Bennett 3, Connolly	3747
17	19	A	Plymouth Arg	L 1-4	1-2	9	Durkan	6936
18	26	H	Swansea C	W 4-1	2-0	7	Hughes, Watkin 2, Owen	3598
19	Dec 10	H	Shrewsbury T	L 0-1	0-0	11		5859
20	16	A	Bournemouth	W 3-1	1-1	—	Hughes, Watkin, Bennett	2505
21	26	A	Stockport Co	D 1-1	0-1	9	Bennett (pen)	5636
22	27	H	Peterborough U	D 3-3	0-2	11	Bennett 2 (2 pens), Morris	4689
23	Jan 14	H	Leyton Orient	W 4-1	1-0	13	Bennett 3, Connolly	6616
24	Feb 4	A	Swansea C	D 0-0	0-0	13		4563
25	7	A	York C	W 1-0	1-0	—	Bennett	3140
26	11	H	Huddersfield T	L 1-2	1-0	12	Bennett	5894
27	14	H	Chester C	D 2-2	2-1	—	Connolly, Bennett	5698
28	18	A	Leyton Orient	D 1-1	0-1	12	Hughes	3135
29	21	H	Plymouth Arg	W 3-1	0-1	—	Bennett 2, Hughes	3030
30	25	A	Birmingham C	L 2-5	2-1	12	Bennett 2	18,884
31	Mar 4	H	Blackpool	L 0-1	0-0	13		4251
32	7	H	Brentford	D 0-0	0-0	—		2834
33	11	A	Brighton & HA	L 0-4	0-0	14		7514
34	14	H	Rotherham U	W 3-1	1-1	—	Hughes, Durkan, Bennett	1823
35	18	H	Cardiff C	L 0-3	0-1	14		3023
36	21	A	Crewe Alex	W 3-1	0-0	—	Morris, Connolly, Bennett	3632
37	25	H	Bristol R	D 1-1	0-1	13	Hughes	3170
38	Apr 1	A	Bradford C	D 1-1	1-1	13	Bennett	4461
39	4	A	Oxford U	D 0-0	0-0	—		4729
40	8	H	York C	D 1-1	0-0	14	Connolly	2558
41	11	A	Wycombe W	L 0-3	0-3	—		5115
42	15	A	Peterborough U	L 0-1	0-1	14		4309
43	17	H	Stockport Co	W 1-0	0-0	13	Hughes	3041
44	22	A	Rotherham U	W 1-0	0-0	12	Bennett	2628
45	29	A	Hull C	L 2-3	1-2	13	Connolly, Hughes	3683
46	May 6	H	Cambridge U	L 0-1	0-1	13		3172

Final League Position: 13

GOALSCORERS

League (65): Bennett 29 (8 pens), Connolly 10, Hughes 9, Watkin 4, Owen 3, Durkan 2, Morris 2, Richardson 2, Brammer 1, Cross 1, Pejic 1, Phillips 1.
Coca-Cola Cup (8): Bennett 2 (1 pen), Watkin 2, Connolly 1, Cross 1, Humes 1, Jones 1.
FA Cup (10): Bennett 2 (1 pen), Connolly 2, Durkan 2, Watkin 2, Cross 1, Hughes 1.

Marriott A. 46	Jones B. 44	Hardy P. 44	Lake M.C. 2	Humes A. 28 + 1	Pejic M. 18 + 2	Bennett G.M. 45	Owen G. 24 + 4	Connolly K. 45	Watkin S. 24 + 8	Cross J.N. 18 + 6	Phillips W. 13 + 5	Brammer D. 13 + 1	Taylor P.M.R. 3	Hunter B.V. 35 + 2	Hughes B. 37 + 1	Brace D. 10 + 4	Durkan K.J. 28 + 2	Williams S.J. 8 + 2	Richardson N.J. 4	Morris S. 10 + 2	Pugh S. — + 1	Quigley M.A. 4	Coady L. 2	Barnes R.I. — + 1	McGregor M.D.T. 1	Match No.
1	2	3	4	5	6	7	8	9	10	11	12															1
1	2	3	4	5	*6*	7		9	10		12	8	11	14												2
1	2	3		5		*7*		9	10		4	8	11	6												3
1	2	3		5		*7*		9	10		4	8	11	6	12	14										4
1	2	3		5				9	10	7	4	8		6		12	11									5
1	2	3		5		7	8	9	10	12	*4*			6		14	11									6
1	2	3		5		7	8	9		10		4		6			11									7
1	2	3		5		7	8	9	12	10		4		6			11									8
1	*2*	3			6	7	8	9	10	12		4		5		14	11									9
1	2	3			6	7	8	9		10				5	4		11									10
1	2	3		6		7	8	9		10				5	4		11									11
1	2			3	6	7	8	9		10				5	4		11	12								12
1	2	3		6		7	8	9		10				5	11				4							13
1	2	3		6		7	8	9		10				5	11				4							14
1	2	3		6		7	8	9	12	10				5	11				4							15
1	2	3		6		7	8	9	12	10				5	11				4							16
1	2	3		6		7	8	9	10	14	12			5	4		11									17
1	5	3			6	7	8	9	10						4	2	11									18
1	5	3			6	7	8	9	10	12		11			4	2										19
1	2	3		5	6	7	8	9	10	12					4		11									20
1	2	3		5	6	7	8	9							4		11			10						21
1	2	3		5	6	7	8	9						12	4		*11*			10	14					22
1	2	3		6	12	7	8	9		*10*				5	4		11			14						23
1	2	3		6		7		9	10	11	8			5	4											24
1	2	3		6	12	7		9	10					5	4		11	8								25
1	2	3			6	7	12	9	10					5	4		11	8								26
1	2	3			6	7	8	9	10	12				5	4		11									27
1	2	3			6	7		9	10	11				5	4							8				28
1	2	3			6	7		9	10	11				5	4							8				29
1	2	3			6	7		9	10	11				5	4		12					8				30
1	2	3		6		7	12	9	10					5	4		11					8				31
1	2	3		5	6	7	8	9	10		11				4											32
1	2	3		5	6	7	*8*		10	9	11	12			4			14								33
1	6	3		5		7	8	9			4				10	2	11									34
1	2	3		6		7	8	9	10		4			5	11					12						35
1	6	3				7		9						5	4	2	11	8		10						36
1	6	3				7		9	12	10				5	4	2	11	8								37
1	5	3				7		8			12			6	11	2	4	10		9						38
1	6	3				7		9	12					5	4	2	11	8		10						39
1	6	3				7		9	12		2			5	4		11	8		10						40
1	6	3				7		9	12		14			5	4	2	11	*8*		10						41
1	6	3				7	12	9	10		2	8		5	4		11									42
1	6	3		12		7		9	*10*			8		5	4	2	14						11			43
1		3		6		7		9				8		5	4	2				10			11			44
1				3	6	7		9			2	8		5	4		11			10				12		45
1	6	3				7	12	9	14		2	8			4		11			10					5	46

Coca-Cola Cup

First Round	Doncaster R (a)	4-2
	(h)	1-1
Second Round	Coventry C (h)	1-2
	(a)	2-3

FA Cup

First Round	Stockport Co (h)	1-0
Second Round	Rotherham U (h)	5-2
Third Round	Ipswich T (h)	2-1
Fourth Round	Manchester U (a)	2-5

WYCOMBE WANDERERS 1994–95 *Back row (left to right):* Steve Guppy, Simon Stapleton, Glyn Creaser, Terry Evans, Dave Carroll, Simon Garner, Duncan Hocton.
Centre row: Clive Jones, Nicky Smith, Shaun Stevens, Matt Crossley, Keith Ryan, Paul Hyde, Chuck Moussaddik, Lee Turnbull, David Titterton, Jason Cousins, Steve Walford (Youth Team Coach).
Front row: Steve Thompson, Simon Hutchinson, Tony Hemmings, Martin O'Neill (Manager), Paul Franklin (Coach), Steve Brown, Tim Langford, Nicky Reid.

Division 2 WYCOMBE WANDERERS

Adams Park, Hillbottom Road, Sands, High Wycombe HP12 4HJ. Telephone (01494) 472100. Fax: (01494) 527633. Credit Card Hotline: (01494) 441118. Information Line 0891 446855.

Ground Capacity: 9650.

Record attendance: 9002 v West Ham U, FA Cup 3rd rd, 7 January 1995.

Record receipts: £61,221 (net of VAT) v West Ham U, FA Cup 3rd rd, 7 January 1995.

Pitch measurements: 115 × 75yd.

Patron: J. Adams.

President: M. E. Seymour.

Chairman: I. L. Beeks.

Directors: G. Peart (Financial), G. Richards, B. R. Lee, A. Parry, A. Thibault, G. Cox.

Manager: Alan Smith. ***Assistant Manager:*** –. ***Secretary:*** John Reardon. ***Coach:***– . ***Physio:*** David Jones. ***Marketing Manager:*** Mark Austin. ***Promotions Manager:*** Mike Phillips.

Year Formed: 1884. ***Turned professional:*** 1974. ***Club Nicknames:*** 'Chairboys' (after High Wycombe's tradition of furniture making), 'The Blues'.

Previous Ground: 1887 The Rye; 1893 Spring Meadow; 1895 Loakes Park, 1899 Daws Hill Park; 1901 Loakes Park; 1990 Adams Park.

Foundation: In 1884 a group of young furniture trade workers started playing together informally under the name of North Town Wanderers, the area of the town where they lived. They decided to better themselves by entering junior football and in 1887 Jim Ray, secretary, and Datchett Webb, captain, called a meeting at the Steam Engine public house. Wycombe Wanderers FC was formed and probably named after the famous FA Cup winners, The Wanderers, who had visited the town in 1877 for a tie with the original High Wycombe club.

First Football League game: 14 August 1993, Division 3 v Carlisle U (a), D 2-2: Hyde; Cousins, Horton (Langford), Kerr, Crossley, Ryan, Carroll, Stapleton, Thompson, Scott, Guppy (1) (Hutchinson). Wycombe's first goal was an own goal by Chris Curran.

Record League Victory: 4–0 v Scarborough (h), Division 3, 2 November 1993: Hyde; Cousins, Horton, Crossley (1), Evans T, Ryan, Carroll (1), Hayrettin, Thompson (Hemmings), Scott (2), Guppy.

Record Cup Victory: 4–0 v Boston U (h), FA Cup 1st rd replay, 21 November 1990: Granville; Crossley, Walford, Kerr, Creaser (1), Carroll, Blackler, Stapleton (Smith), West (2), Evans N (Ryan (1)), Hutchinson.

Most League points: 70, Division 3, 1993–94.

Most League goals: 66, Division 3, 1993–94.

Highest League goalscorer in season: Keith Scott, 10, 1993–94.

Most League appearances: Paul Hyde 88, 1993–95.

Record Transfer Fee Received: £375,000 from Swindon T for Keith Scott, November 1993.

Record Transfer Fee Paid: £140,000 to Birmingham C for Steve McGavin, March 1995.

Football League Record: Promoted to Division 3 from GMVC in 1993; 1993–94 Division 3; 1994– Division 2.

Honours: *Football League:* Division 2 best season: 6th, 1994–95; *FA Amateur Cup:* Winners 1931; *FA Trophy:* Winners 1991, 1993; *GM Vauxhall Conference:*Winners 1992–93; *FA Cup:* best season: 3rd rd 1975, 1986, 1994, 1995; *Football League Cup:* best season: 2nd rd 1994.

Colours: Light & dark blue quartered shirts, dark blue shorts, dark blue stockings. **Change colours:** First: all yellow. Second: black and red striped shirts.

Founded 1884

WYCOMBE WANDERERS 1994–95 LEAGUE RECORD

Match No.	*Date*	*Venue*	*Opponents*	*Result*	*H/T Score*	*Lg. Pos.*	*Goalscorers*	*Attendance*
1	Aug 13	H	Cambridge U	W 3-0	1-0	—	Garner, Hemmings, Cousins (pen)	5782
2	20	A	Huddersfield T	W 1-0	1-0	5	Garner	13,334
3	27	H	Bristol R	D 0-0	0-0	5		5895
4	30	A	Birmingham C	W 1-0	0-0	—	Regis	14,305
5	Sept 3	A	Bradford C	L 1-2	0-1	6	Cousins (pen)	8010
6	10	H	Brentford	W 4-3	1-1	6	Evans, Garner 2, Regis	6847
7	13	H	Hull C	L 1-2	0-1	—	Evans	4626
8	17	A	Crewe Alex	W 2-1	2-0	4	Regis, Carroll	4466
9	24	A	Stockport Co	L 1-4	0-3	5	Turnbull	4607
10	Oct 1	H	Swansea C	W 1-0	1-0	4	Carroll	4150
11	8	H	Leyton Orient	W 2-1	1-0	4	Regis, Thompson	5668
12	15	A	Plymouth Arg	D 2-2	1-2	5	Regis 2	6864
13	22	A	Peterborough U	W 3-1	1-1	3	Regis, Garner, Thompson	5924
14	29	H	York C	D 0-0	0-0	4		7140
15	Nov 1	H	Shrewsbury T	W 1-0	1-0	—	Regis	4620
16	5	A	Wrexham	L 1-4	0-2	5	Ryan	3747
17	19	H	Cardiff C	W 3-1	1-0	4	Ryan 2, Hemmings	5391
18	26	A	Blackpool	W 1-0	0-0	4	Kerr	4846
19	Dec 10	H	Huddersfield T	W 2-1	0-1	3	Booth (og), Garner	6790
20	16	A	Cambridge U	D 2-2	1-1	—	Patterson, Evans	3713
21	26	H	Brighton & HA	D 0-0	0-0	3		7085
22	27	A	Oxford U	W 2-0	1-0	2	Ryan, Garner	9540
23	31	H	Bournemouth	D 1-1	0-1	3	Carroll	5990
24	Jan 14	A	Rotherham U	L 0-2	0-1	6		3537
25	31	A	Chester C	W 2-0	2-0	—	De Souza 2	1524
26	Feb 4	H	Blackpool	D 1-1	1-0	5	De Souza	6380
27	11	A	Shrewsbury T	D 2-2	0-1	5	Stapleton, De Souza (pen)	3945
28	18	H	Rotherham U	W 2-0	0-0	5	De Souza, Stapleton	5153
29	21	A	Cardiff C	L 0-2	0-0	—		3024
30	25	A	Swansea C	D 1-1	0-0	6	De Souza	3699
31	Mar 4	H	Stockport Co	D 1-1	0-1	7	Evans	5275
32	11	A	Bristol R	L 0-1	0-1	9		5118
33	14	A	York C	D 0-0	0-0	—		2800
34	18	H	Birmingham C	L 0-3	0-2	11		7289
35	21	A	Brentford	D 0-0	0-0	—		9530
36	25	H	Crewe Alex	D 0-0	0-0	10		6288
37	28	H	Peterborough U	W 3-1	1-0	—	Garner 2, Brown	4590
38	Apr 1	A	Hull C	D 0-0	0-0	8		5054
39	4	H	Bradford C	W 3-1	3-0	—	Soloman, Hemmings, Carroll	4522
40	8	A	Bournemouth	L 0-2	0-1	7		8615
41	11	H	Wrexham	W 3-0	3-0	—	McGavin, Bell 2	5115
42	15	H	Oxford U	W 1-0	1-0	5	Carroll	7683
43	19	A	Brighton & HA	D 1-1	0-1	—	Carroll	8094
44	22	H	Chester C	W 3-1	2-1	5	Hemmings 2, McGavin	5284
45	29	H	Plymouth Arg	L 1-2	0-1	6	Bell	6850
46	May 6	A	Leyton Orient	W 1-0	0-0	6	Regis	4698

Final League Position: 6

GOALSCORERS

League (60): Garner 9, Regis 9, Carroll 6, De Souza 6 (1 pen), Hemmings 5, Evans 4, Ryan 4, Bell 3, Cousins 2 (2 pens), McGavin 2, Stapleton 2, Thompson 2, Brown 1, Kerr 1, Patterson 1, Soloman 1, Turnbull 1, own goal 1.
Coca-Cola Cup (2): Regis 1, Turnbull 1.
FA Cup (9): Garner 3, Bell 2, Ryan 2, Stapleton 2.

Hyde P.D. 46	Cousins J.M. 41	Titterton D.S.J. 1	Crossley M.J.W. 35 + 1	Evans T.W. 44	Ryan K.J. 24	Carroll D.F. 41	Thompson S. 25 + 10	Regis C. 30 + 5	Garner S. 35 + 6	Stapleton S.J. 24 + 2	Hemmings A.G. 10 + 10	Creaser G.R. 2 + 2	Brown S. 38 + 2	Turner A.P. 3 + 1	Skinner J.J. 4 + 1	Hutchinson S. — + 4	Langford T. 1 + 5	Turnbull L.M. 2 + 3	Bell M. 31	Kerr P.A. — + 1	Patterson G. 9 + 4	De Souza J.M. 6 + 1	Howard T. 20	Skiverton T.J. 8 + 2	Reid N.S. 3	Garland P.J. 5	Soloman J.R. 5 + 1	McGavin S.J. 12	Wallace D.L. — + 1	Clark A.J. 1	*Match No.*
1	2	3	4	5	6	7	8	9	10	*11*	12	14																			1
1	2			5	6	7	8	9	10	11	12	4	3																		2
1	2			5	6	7	8	9	*10*	11	12		3	4	14																3
1	2			5	6	7	8	9	10	11			3	4		12															4
1	2		12	5	6	7	8	9	10	11			*4*		3	14															5
1	2		4	5	6	7	8	9	10	11				12	3																6
1	2		4	5	6	7	8	9	10					11	3		12														7
1	2		4	5	6	7	8	9	10	11					3																8
1	2		4	5	6	7		9	10	11			3				8	12													9
1	2		4	5	6	7	8	9	10	14	12		3					*11*													10
1	2		4	5	6	7	8	9		10	12		3					11													11
1	2		4	5	6	7	8	9	*10*	11			3			12	14														12
1	2			5	6	7	11	9	10	4			3						8												13
1	2			5	6	7	11	9	10	4			3				12		8												14
1	2		4	5	6	7	*12*	9	10	11			3					14	8												15
1	2		4	5	6	7	12	9	10	11			3						8												16
1	2		4	5	6	7	9		10	11	12		3						8												17
1	2		4	5	6	7	9			11	10		3						8	12											18
1	2		4	5	6	7	9		10		11		3					12			8										19
1	2		4	5	6	7	9		10		11		3				12				8										20
1	2		4	5	6	7	8	9	10	11	12		3																		21
1	2		4	5	6	7	12	*9*	10	11			3						8		14										22
1	2		4	5	6	7	12	9	*10*	11			3						8		14										23
1	2		4	5	6	7	11	*9*	10	12			3				14		8												24
1	2		4	5		7	12	9	*10*	11			3						8		14	6									25
1	2		4	5		7	12	9	10	11			3						8			6									26
1	2		4	5				9	10	11		12							8		7	6	3								27
1			4	5			12	9	10	11									8		7	6	3	2							28
1			4	5			12	*9*	10	11			14						8		7	6	3	2							29
1				5			7	9	10				3						8			6	4	2	11						30
1	2			5		7	10	9			12		3						8				4	6	11						31
1	2			5		7	11	9	10				6						8		12		3	4							32
1	2			5		7	12	9	10				4						8		11		3		6						33
1	2			5			7	9	10				*4*			12			8				3	14		6	11				34
1	2		3	5		7		12	10				14						8				4			*6*	11	9			35
1	2		3	5		7		12	10				8						11				4			*6*		9	14		36
1	*2*		3	5		7			10		12		6						8		11		4	14				9			37
1			3	5		7			10		12		6						8		11		4	2				9			38
1	2		3	5		7	12		14		*10*		6						8				4				11	9			39
1	2		3	5		7		12	14		10		6						8				4				*11*	9			40
1	2		4	5		7					10		6						8				3			11		9			41
1	2		4	5		7			12		10		6						8				3			11		9			42
1	2		4			7		12	14		10		6						8				3	5			11	*9*			43
1			4			7	11		12		10	*5*	6						8				3	2			14	9			44
1	2		4	5		7	11		12		10		6						8				3					9			45
1	2		3	5		7		12					6						8		11	14	4					9		*10*	46

Coca-Cola Cup

First Round	Brighton & HA (a)	1-2
	(h)	1-3

FA Cup

First Round	Chelmsford C (h)	4-0
Second Round	Hitchin (a)	5-0
Third Round	West Ham U (h)	0-2

YORK CITY 1994–95 *Back row (left to right):* Paul Mockler, Andy McMillan, Paul Atkin, Paul Stancliffe, Steve Tutill, Tony Barras, Dean Kiely, Andy Warrington, Steve Cooper, Ian Blackstone, Elliott Simpson, Jeff Miller (Physio).

Front row: Scott Jordan, Glenn Naylor, Nigel Pepper, Paul Barnes, Jon McCarthy, Alan Little (Manager), Graeme Murty, Steve Bushell, Tony Canham, Wayne Hall, Tony Barratt.

Division 2 **YORK CITY**

Bootham Crescent, York YO3 7AQ. Telephone: (01904) 624447. Fax: (01904) 631457.

Ground capacity: 9459.

Record attendance: 28,123 v Huddersfield T, FA Cup 6th rd, 5 March 1938.

Record receipts: £38,054 v Liverpool, FA Cup 5th rd, 15 February 1986.

Pitch measurements: 115yd × 74yd.

Chairman: D. M. Craig OBE, JP, BSC, FICE, FI, MUN E, FCI ARB, M CONS E

Directors: B. A. Houghton, C. Webb, E. B. Swallow, J. E. H. Quickfall FCA.

Manager: Alan Little.

Secretary: Keith Usher. ***Commercial Manager:*** Mrs Maureen Leslie.

Physio: Jeff Miller.

Hon. Orthopaedic Surgeon: Mr Peter De Boer MA, FRCS. ***Medical Officer:*** Dr R. Porter.

Year Formed: 1922. ***Turned Professional:*** 1922. ***Ltd Co.:*** 1922.

Club Nickname: 'Minstermen'.

Previous Ground: 1922, Fulfordgate; 1932, Bootham Crescent.

Foundation: Although there was a York City club formed in 1903 by a soccer enthusiast from Darlington, this has no connection with the modern club because it went out of existence during World War I. Unlike many others of that period who restarted in 1919, York City did not re-form until 1922 and the tendency now is to ignore the modern club's pre-1922 existence.

First Football League game: 31 August, 1929, Division 3(N), v Wigan Borough (a) W 2-0 – Farmery; Archibald, Johnson; Beck, Davis, Thompson; Evans, Gardner, Cowie (1), Smailes, Stockhill (1).

Record League Victory: 9–1 v Southport, Division 3 (N), 2 February 1957 – Forgan; Phillips, Howe; Brown (1), Cairney, Mollatt; Hill, Bottom (4 incl. 1p), Wilkinson (2), Wragg (1), Fenton (1).

Record Cup Victory: 6–0 v South Shields (away), FA Cup, 1st rd, 16 November 1968 – Widdowson; Baker (1p), Richardson; Carr, Jackson, Burrows; Taylor, Ross (3), MacDougall (2), Hodgson, Boyer.

Record Defeat: 0–12 v Chester, Division 3 (N), 1 February 1936.

Most League Points (2 for a win): 62, Division 4, 1964–65.

Most League Points (3 for a win): 101, Division 4, 1983–84.

Most League Goals: 96, Division 4, 1983–84.

Highest League Scorer in Season: Bill Fenton, 31, Division 3 (N), 1951–52; Arthur Bottom, 31, Division 3 (N), 1954–55 and 1955–56.

Most League Goals in Total Aggregate: Norman Wilkinson, 125, 1954–66.

Most Capped Player: Peter Scott, 7 (10), Northern Ireland.

Most League Appearances: Barry Jackson, 481, 1958–70.

Record Transfer Fee Received: £100,000 from Carlisle U for Gordon Staniforth, October 1979, and from QPR for John Byrne, October 1985.

Record Transfer Fee Paid: £50,000 to Aldershot for Dale Banton, November 1984 and £50,000 to Stoke C for Paul Barnes, July 1992.

Football League Record: 1929 Elected to Division 3 (N); 1958–59 Division 4; 1959–60 Division 3; 1960–65 Division 4; 1965–66 Division 3; 1966–71 Division 4; 1971–74 Division 3; 1974–76 Division 2; 1976–77 Division 3; 1977–84 Division 4; 1984–88 Division 3; 1988–92 Division 4; 1992–93 Division 3; 1993– Division 2.

Honours: *Football League:* Division 2 best season: 15th, 1974–75; Division 3 – Promoted 1973–74 (3rd); Division 4 – Champions 1983–84. *FA Cup:* Semi-finals 1955, when in Division 3. *Football League Cup:* best season: 5th rd, 1962.

Colours: Red shirts, blue shorts, red stockings. **Change colours:** All blue.

YORK CITY 1994–95 LEAGUE RECORD

Match No.	Date		Venue	Opponents	Result		H/T Score	Lg. Pos.	Goalscorers	Attendance
1	Aug	13	H	Crewe Alex	L	1-2	0-0	—	Cooper	4420
2		20	A	Bristol R	L	1-3	1-1	19	McCarthy	3957
3		27	H	Cardiff C	D	1-1	0-0	18	Barnes	2861
4		31	A	Brighton & HA	L	0-1	0-0	—		6996
5	Sept	3	A	Bournemouth	W	4-1	3-0	18	Barnes 3, McCarthy	3181
6		10	H	Shrewsbury T	W	3-0	1-0	14	Barnes, Pepper, Naylor	3196
7		13	H	Brentford	W	2-1	1-1	—	Pepper, Jordan	2836
8		17	A	Bradford C	D	0-0	0-0	14		8670
9		24	A	Swansea C	D	0-0	0-0	15		2875
10	Oct	1	H	Stockport Co	L	2-4	2-2	16	Barnes (pen), Naylor	3790
11		8	H	Peterborough U	D	1-1	0-0	16	McCarthy	3601
12		15	A	Rotherham U	L	1-2	0-2	16	Pepper	3380
13		22	H	Chester C	W	2-0	1-0	14	McCarthy, Barnes	2820
14		29	A	Wycombe W	D	0-0	0-0	13		7140
15	Nov	1	A	Hull C	L	0-3	0-3	—		6551
16		5	H	Huddersfield T	W	3-0	2-0	15	Baker, Naylor, Barnes	6345
17		19	A	Leyton Orient	W	1-0	0-0	15	Barnes	3532
18		26	H	Plymouth Arg	W	1-0	0-0	14	McCarthy	3185
19	Dec	10	H	Bristol R	L	0-3	0-1	15		3094
20		16	A	Crewe Alex	L	1-2	0-2	—	Barnes (pen)	3432
21		26	H	Blackpool	W	4-0	2-0	14	Barnes 3, Naylor	4542
22		28	A	Cambridge U	L	0-1	0-0	—		3285
23	Jan	2	A	Oxford U	W	2-0	1-0	14	Naylor, Marsh (og)	6386
24		7	A	Chester C	W	4-0	0-0	13	Barnes, Jordan, McCarthy, Alsford (og)	1844
25		14	H	Birmingham C	W	2-0	1-0	12	McCarthy, Canham	6828
26	Feb	4	A	Plymouth Arg	W	2-1	0-1	11	Baker, Naylor	5572
27		7	H	Wrexham	L	0-1	0-1	—		3140
28		18	A	Birmingham C	L	2-4	0-2	13	Baker, McCarthy	14,846
29		21	H	Leyton Orient	W	4-1	2-1	—	Bellamy (og), Baker 2, Naylor	2926
30		25	A	Stockport Co	W	3-2	2-1	10	Baker, Pepper, Dinning (og)	3570
31		28	A	Huddersfield T	L	0-3	0-1	—		10,468
32	Mar	4	H	Swansea C	L	2-4	1-1	12	Canham, Barnes	2920
33		7	H	Bournemouth	W	1-0	0-0	—	Jordan	2301
34		11	A	Cardiff C	W	2-1	2-1	12	Naylor 2	2689
35		14	H	Wycombe W	D	0-0	0-0	—		2800
36		18	H	Brighton & HA	W	1-0	1-0	8	Barnes	2915
37		21	A	Shrewsbury T	L	0-1	0-1	—		2849
38		25	H	Bradford C	D	0-0	0-0	9		5431
39	Apr	1	A	Brentford	L	0-3	0-1	12		6474
40		4	H	Hull C	W	3-1	1-0	—	Baker 2, Murty	4612
41		8	A	Wrexham	D	1-1	0-0	8	Peverell	2558
42		15	H	Cambridge U	W	2-0	1-0	8	Barras, McMillan	3278
43		18	A	Blackpool	W	5-0	3-0	—	Baker 2 (1 pen), Bushell, McCarthy, Murty	3517
44		22	H	Oxford U	L	0-2	0-1	8		3732
45		29	H	Rotherham U	W	2-0	0-0	8	Baker 2 (1 pen)	3183
46	May	6	A	Peterborough U	D	1-1	0-0	9	Baker	4983

Final League Position: 9

GOALSCORERS

League (67): Barnes 16 (2 pens), Baker 13 (2 pens), McCarthy 9, Naylor 9, Pepper 4, Jordan 3, Canham 2, Murty 2, Barras 1, Bushell 1, Cooper 1, McMillan 1, Peverell 1, own goals 4.
Coca-Cola Cup (2): Cooper 1, Pepper 1.
FA Cup (3): Naylor 2, McCarthy 1.

Kiely D.L. 46	McMillan L.A. 39 + 4	Hall W. 33 + 4	Pepper C.N. 35	Tutill S.A. 37 + 2	Stancliffe P.I. 4	McCarthy J.D. 44	Cooper S.B. 9	Barnes P.L. 35 + 1	Bushell S. 10	Canham A. 30 + 5	Naylor G. 21 + 8	Barras A. 27 + 4	Atkin P.A. 30 + 4	Jordan S.D. 33 + 4	Simpson E. 1	Wilson P.A. 21 + 1	Baker D.P. 25 + 5	Murty G.S. 17 + 3	Williams D. — + 1	Peverell N.J. 2 + 7	Barratt A. 7 + 3	Scaife N. — + 1	Match No.
1	2	3	4	5	6	7	8	9	10	11	12												1
1	2	3	4	5		7	8	9	10	11		6	12										2
1	2	3	4	5		7	8	9	10	11		6											3
1	2	3	4	5		7	8	9	10	11		6	12										4
1	2	12	4	5		7	8	9		11		6	3	10									5
1	2	12	4	5		7	*8*	9		11	14	6	3	10									6
1	2		4	5		7	8	9		11		12	6	10	3								7
1	2	3	4	5		7	8	9			12	6	11	10									8
1	2	3	4	5		7	8	9				6	11	10									9
1	2	3	4	5		7		9		12	8	6	11	10									10
1	2		4	5		7		9		11	8	6		10		3							11
1	2		4	5		7		9		11	8	6		10		3	12						12
1	2		4	5		7		9		11	8	6		10		3							13
1	2	12	4	5		7		9		11	8	6		10		3							14
1	2	3	4		5	7		9		11	8	6		10			12						15
1	2	3	4		5	7		9		11	8	6		12			10						16
1	2				5	7		9		11	8	6	4	12		3	10						17
1	2		4			7		9		11	8	6	5	12		3	10						18
1	2	3	4	12		7		9		11	14	6	5	*8*			10						19
1	2	3	4	12		7		9		11		*6*	5	8			10	14					20
1	2	3	4	5		7		9		11	8		6	*10*				12	14				21
1	2	3	4	5		7		9		11	8		6	10									22
1	2	3	4	5		7		9			8		6	10		11							23
1	2	11	4	5		7		*9*			8		6	10		3	12	14					24
1	2	11	4	5		7				12			6	10		3	9	8					25
1	2	11	4	*5*		7				12	14		6	10		3	9	8					26
1	2	11	4	5		7		14		12	8		6	10		3	*9*						27
1	2	12	4	5		7		*9*		11	8		6	10		3	14						28
1	2		4	5		7				11	8		6			3	9	10					29
1	2	10	4	5						11			6	8		3	9			7	12		30
1	2	10	4	5		7		*8*		11		12	6			3	9			14			31
1	2		4	5		7		8		11			6	10		3	9				12		32
1		3		5		7		8		11	12	14	6	10			9	4			2		33
1		3		5		7		8			11	12	6	10			9	4			2		34
1	12	11		5				8			10		6	7		3	9	4			2		35
1	12	11		5		7		9			14		6	4		3	*10*	8			2		36
1	12	11		5		7		9					6	4		3	10	8			2		37
1	12	11	4	5		7		9			*10*	6				3	14	8			2		38
1	2		*4*	5		7		9	8			6	12			3	10	11			14		39
1	2	3		5		7			8		9	6		4			10	11		12			40
1	2	3				7			4	12	*10*	6	5	8			9	11		14			41
1	2	3		5		7			4	11		6		*8*			9	10		12		14	42
1	2	3		5		7			4	11		6		8			9	10		12			43
1		3		*5*		7				11	12	6	14	4			9	10		8	2		44
1	2	3	4			7		*8*		11		6	5	12			9	10		14			45
1	2	3	4			7			8	11		6	5			12	*9*	10		14			46

Coca-Cola Cup
First Round — Burnley (a) 0-1
(h) 2-2

FA Cup
First Round — Rotherham U (h) 3-3
(a) 0-3

THE COMMUNITY PROGRAMME IN PROFESSIONAL FOOTBALL

The first Football and Community Capital Schemes established in 1978 attempted to bridge the gap between Professional Football Clubs and their communities and, whilst facilities were successfully established in some areas, it has become clear that there was no attempt made to extend these projects in the long term to help promote football or to cater for local people's needs. During the early 1980's, football experienced a number of difficulties not least of which was the continuing fall in average attendances. The Professional Footballers' Association took the lead in investigating the reasons why football was perceived to be ailing on many fronts. It was evident that supporters had become disenchanted with high admission costs, increased hooliganism and an underlying feeling that their Clubs had lost contact with their community and, particularly, their supporters.

The Professional Footballers' Association decided to bridge the gap that had developed and, with the support of The Football League, launched an experimental "Football and Community Programme Scheme" in 1985. Initially launched on a pilot scheme basis at 6 Clubs in the North West, the project soon expanded further afield with the addition of more Clubs in Lancashire and Cheshire. These early projects, originally funded through the Government's Community Programme Scheme, were so successful that by the end of 1990 a total of 50 Clubs had become involved in locally-based projects.

Club Project	*Telephone Number*	*Club Officer*
AFC Bournemouth	—	—
Arsenal	0171 226 2150	To Be Appointed
Aston Villa	0121 327 2299 ext 256	Ron Wylie
Barnet	0181 441 6932 (Club)	To Be Appointed
Barnsley	01226 731994	Steve Lister
Birmingham City	0121 766 6180	Jason Withe
Blackburn Rovers	01254 698888 ext. 2256	Pete Devine
Blackpool	01253 403268	Craig Madden
Bolton Wanderers	01204 364555	Geoff Lomax
Bradford City	01274 307564	Richard Angus
Brentford	0181 758 9430	Lee Doyle
Brighton & Hove Albion	01273 778855 (Club)	Steve Ford
Bristol City	0117 966 4685	Shaun Parker
Bristol Rovers	0117 986 0809	Terry Connor
Burnley	01282 831456	Bob Oates
Bury	0161 797 5423	Brian Taylor
Cambridge United	01223 416238	Mike Cook
Cardiff City	01222 668325	Glyn Jones
Carlisle United	01228 512266	John Halpin
Charlton Athletic	0181 850 2866	Jason Morgan
Chelsea	0171 385 0710	Shaun Gore
Chester City	01244 377408	John Kerr
Chesterfield	01246 550930	Adrian Shaw
Colchester United	01206 572378	Steve Bradshaw
Coventry City	01203 224093	Barry Powell
Crewe Alexandra	01270 216682	Chris Walters
Crystal Palace	0181 771 5886	Nicky Johns
Darlington	01325 381972	Iain Leckie
Derby County	—	—
Doncaster Rovers	01302 370250	Eric Randerson
Durham County FA	0191 384 8653	Keith Longstaff
Everton	0151 252 0104	Ted Sutton
Exeter City	01395 232784	Steve Neville
Farnborough Town	01252 372640	Geoff Noonan
Fulham	0171 736 6561	Gary Mulcahey
Gillingham	01634 582303	Philip Attfield
Grimsby Town	01472 291776	Ian Knight
Halifax Town	01422 368470	Paddy Roche
Hartlepool United	01429 862595	Terry Bainbridge
Hereford United	01432 341065	Brian Williams
Huddersfield Town	01484 435087	Mark Lillis
Hull City	01482 568088	John Davies
Ipswich Town	—	—
Kent County FA	01634 812032	Darren Hare
Kettering Town	01536 83028 (Club)	Domenico Genovese
Kidderminster Harriers	01562 863821	Nick Griffiths
Leeds United	0113 277 9851	Ces Podd
Leicester City	0116 255 3195	Neville Hamilton
Leyton Orient	0181 556 5973	Neil Watson
Lincoln City	01522 539671	Dean Wheatley
Liverpool	0151 263 2361 (Club)	Brian Hall
Luton Town	01582 411622 (Club)	Colwyn Rowe
Manchester City	0161 226 1782	Alex Williams
Manchester United	0161 930 2903	Dave Ryan
Mansfield Town	01623 25197	Dave Bentley
Merthyr Tydfil	01443 485888	Tommy Hutchison

Middlesbrough	01642 824605	Lawrie Pearson
Millwall	0171 231 0379	Jim Hicks
Newcastle United	0191 261 9715	Ray Hankin
Northampton Town	01604 232101	Russell Lewis
Norwich City	01603 761122	Peter Mendham
Norfolk County FA	01603 761122	Jamie Houchen
Notts County	0115 986 3656	Alan Young
Nottingham Forest	0115 981 0089	Gordon Coleman
Oldham Athletic	0161 678 8464	John Platt
Oxford United	01865 64853	Peter Rhoades-Brown
Peterborough United	—	—
Plymouth Argyle	01752 606710	Steve Rogers
Portsmouth	01705 737391	Gary Holland
Port Vale	01782 575594	Jim Cooper
Preston North End	01772 704275	Ian Johnstone
Queens Park Rangers	0181 743 0262 (Club)	Emlyn Brown
Reading	01734 560898	Chris Whalley
Rochdale	01706 43836	Keith Hicks
Rotherham United	01709 740846	Fraser Foster
Scarborough	01723 367884	Ian Kerr
Scunthorpe United	01724 280716	Richard Passmoor
Sheffield and Hallamshire CFA	0114 267 0068	Jack Detchon
Sheffield United	0114 276 9314	Tony Currie
Sheffield Wednesday	0114 231 3262	Charlie Williamson
Shrewsbury Town	01743 356623	Dick Pratley
Southampton	01703 334172	Alan Smith
Southend United	01702 341351	Frank Banks
Stockport County	0161 477 7560	Neil Mather
Stoke City	01782 744347	To Be Appointed
Sunderland	0191 510 9111	Mick Ferguson
Swansea City	01792 459363	Alan Curtis
Swindon Town	01793 421303	Shane Cook
Torquay United	01803 322551	Frank Prince
Tottenham Hotspur	—	—
Tranmere Rovers	0151 608 2354	Steve Williams
Walsall	01922 644742	Mick Kearns
Watford	01923 440449	Jimmy Gilligan
West Bromwich Albion	0121 525 0226	Mark Ashton
West Ham United	0181 548 2707	Roger Morgan
Wigan Athletic	01942 824599	Frankie Bunn
Wimbledon	0181 771 1772	Jim Lowther
Wolverhampton Wanderers	01902 716348	Tony Evans
Wrexham	01978 358545	Steve Weaver
Wycombe Wanderers	—	—
York City	01904 613017	Gordon Staniforth

Tommy Hutchinson demonstrates to a group of girls at the Llantrisant Leisure Centre.

ENGLISH LEAGUE PLAYERS DIRECTORY

Player	Ht	Wt	Pos	Birth Date	Birth Place	Source	Clubs	League App	League Gls
ABBOTT Greg	5 9	10 07	M	14 12 63	Coventry	Apprentice	Coventry C	—	—
							Bradford C	281	38
							Halifax T	28	1
						Guiseley	**Hull C**	93	10
ABLETT Gary	6 2	12 07	D	19 11 65	Liverpool	Apprentice	Liverpool	109	1
							Derby Co (loan)	6	—
							Hull C (loan)	5	—
							Everton	115	5
ABRAHAMS Paul	5 9	11 03	F	31 10 73	Colchester	Trainee	Colchester U	55	8
							Brentford	10	3
ADAMS Darren	5 7	10 07	F	12 1 74	Newham	Danson Furnace	**Cardiff C**	20	1
ADAMS Derek	5 8	11 06	M	25 6 75	Aberdeen	Aberdeen	**Burnley**	—	—
ADAMS Kieran §	5 10	11 06	M	20 10 77	St Ives	Trainee	**Barnet**	4	—
ADAMS Micky	5 8	11 03	M	8 11 61	Sheffield	Apprentice	Gillingham	92	5
							Coventry C	90	9
							Leeds U	73	2
							Southampton	144	7
							Stoke C	10	3
							Fulham	21	7
ADAMS Neil	5 8	10 08	M	23 11 65	Stoke	Local	Stoke C	32	4
							Everton	20	—
							Oldham Ath (loan)	9	—
							Oldham Ath	129	23
							Norwich C	47	3
ADAMS Tony	6 3	13 11	D	10 10 66	London	Apprentice	**Arsenal**	346	23
ADCOCK Tony *	5 10	11 09	F	27 2 63	Bethnal Green	Apprentice	Colchester U	210	98
							Manchester C	15	5
							Northampton T	72	30
							Bradford C	38	6
							Northampton T	35	10
							Peterborough U	111	35
							Luton T	2	—
ADEBOLA Dele	6 3	12 08	F	23 6 75	Lagos	Trainee	**Crewe Alex**	36	8
ADEKOLA David ‡	5 11	12 02	F	19 5 68	Lagos		Bury	35	12
							Exeter C (loan)	3	1
							Bournemouth	—	—
							Wigan Ath	4	—
							Hereford U	—	—
AFFOR Louis ‡	5 4	11 07	F	29 8 72	London	Southend U	**Barnet**	3	—
AGANA Tony	6 0	12 02	F	2 10 63	London	Weymouth	Watford	15	1
							Sheffield U	118	42
							Notts C	13	1
							Leeds U (loan)	2	—
							Notts Co	80	9
AGIADIS Charlie ‡	5 8	10 05	F	18 11 75	Middlesbrough	Trainee	**Middlesbrough**	—	—
AGNEW Paul	5 9	10 07	D	15 8 65	Lisburn	Cliftonville	Grimsby T	241	3
							WBA	14	1
AGNEW Steve	5 10	11 09	M	9 11 65	Shipley	Apprentice	Barnsley	194	29
							Blackburn R	2	—
							Portsmouth (loan)	5	—
							Leicester C	56	4
							Sunderland	16	2
AINSCOUGH Paul ‡	5 11	10 08	M	22 8 75	Blackburn	Trainee	**Blackburn R**	—	—
AINSLEY Jason	6 0	13 01	M	30 7 70	Stockton	Spennymoor	**Hartlepool U**	15	1
AINSWORTH Gareth	5 10	12 05	M	10 5 73	Blackburn	Blackburn R	Preston NE	5	—
							Cambridge U	4	1
							Preston NE	80	12

Player	Ht	Wt	Pos	Birth Date	Birth Place	Source	Clubs	League App	League Gls
AIZLEWOOD Mark *	6 1	13 12	D	1 10 59	Newport	Apprentice	Newport Co	38	1
							Luton T	98	3
							Charlton Ath	152	9
							Leeds U	70	3
							Bradford C	39	1
							Bristol C	101	3
							Cardiff C	39	3
AKINBIYI Adeola	6 1	12 08	F	10 10 74	Hackney	Trainee	**Norwich C**	15	—
							Hereford U (loan)	4	2
							Brighton (loan)	7	4
ALBERT Philippe	6 3	13 00	D	10 8 67	Bouillon	Anderlecht	**Newcastle U**	17	2
ALDOUS Richard	6 0	11 07	G	2 9 76	Sheffield	Trainee	**Sheffield W**	—	—
ALDRIDGE John	5 11	11 04	F	18 9 58	Liverpool	South Liverpool	Newport Co	170	69
							Oxford U	114	72
							Liverpool	83	50
							Real Sociedad	63	33
							Tranmere R	140	88
ALDRIDGE Martin	5 11	12 02	F	6 12 74	Northampton	Trainee	**Northampton T**	70	17
ALEXANDER Graham	5 10	12 07	M	10 10 71	Coventry	Trainee	**Scunthorpe U**	159	18
ALEXANDER Ian ‡	5 8	10 07	D	26 1 63	Glasgow	Leicester J	Rotherham U	11	—
							Motherwell	24	2
							Morton	7	1
						Pezoporikos	**Bristol R**	291	6
ALEXANDER Keith ‡	6 4	13 06	F	14 11 58	Nottingham	Barnet	Grimsby T	83	26
							Stockport Co	11	—
							Lincoln C	45	4
							Mansfield T	2	—
ALEXANDER Tim ‡	6 0	12 00	D	29 3 74	Chertsey	Wimbledon	**Barnet**	36	—
ALLAN Derek	6 0	12 01	D	24 12 74	Irving	Ayr U BC	Ayr U	5	—
							Southampton	1	—
ALLARDYCE Craig	6 3	13 07	D	9 6 75	Bolton	Trainee	Preston NE	1	—
							Blackpool	—	—
ALLEN Bradley	5 7	10 00	F	13 9 71	Harold Wood	School	**QPR**	73	26
ALLEN Chris	5 11	12 02	F	18 11 72	Oxford	Trainee	**Oxford U**	126	9
ALLEN Clive *	5 10	12 03	F	20 5 61	London	Apprentice	QPR	49	32
							Arsenal	—	—
							Crystal Palace	25	9
							QPR	87	40
							Tottenham H	105	60
						Bordeaux	Manchester C	53	16
							Chelsea	16	7
							West Ham U	38	17
							Millwall	12	—
ALLEN Gavin *	5 8	10 05	F	17 6 76	Bangor	Trainee	**Tranmere R**	—	—
ALLEN Graham	6 1	12 00	D	8 4 77	Bolton	Trainee	**Everton**	—	—
ALLEN Leighton ‡	6 0	11 02	F	22 11 73	Brighton	Trainee	Wimbledon	—	—
							Colchester U	2	—
							Gillingham	—	—
ALLEN Malcolm	5 8	11 08	F	21 3 67	Dioniolen	Apprentice	Watford	39	5
							Aston Villa (loan)	4	—
							Norwich C	35	8
							Millwall	81	24
							Newcastle U	10	5
ALLEN Martin	5 10	11 00	M	14 8 65	Reading	School	QPR	136	16
							West Ham U	187	24
ALLEN Paul	5 7	11 03	M	28 8 62	Aveley	Apprentice	West Ham U	152	6
							Tottenham H	292	23
							Southampton	43	1
							Luton T (loan)	4	—
							Stoke C (loan)	17	1
ALLISON Neil	6 2	11 10	D	20 10 73	Hull	Trainee	**Hull C**	60	1

Player	Ht	Wt	Pos	Birth Date	Birth Place	Source	Clubs	League App	League Gls
ALLISON Wayne	6 1	12 06	F	16 10 68	Huddersfield		Halifax T	84	23
							Watford	7	—
							Bristol C	195	48
ALLON Joe	5 11	12 02	F	12 11 66	Gateshead	England Youth	Newcastle U	9	2
							Swansea C	34	11
							Hartlepool U	112	50
							Chelsea	14	2
							Port Vale (loan)	6	—
							Brentford	45	19
							Southend U (loan)	3	—
							Port Vale	23	9
ALLPRESS Tim ‡	6 0	12 10	D	27 1 71	Hitchin	Trainee	Luton T	1	—
							Preston NE (loan)	9	—
						Bayer Uerdingen	**Colchester U**	34	—
ALSFORD Julian	6 2	13 07	D	24 12 72	Poole	Trainee	Watford	13	1
							Chester C	35	—
AMMANN Mike	6 2	14 04	G	8 2 71	California	Cal State Univ	**Charlton Ath**	19	—
AMOKACHI Daniel	5 10	13 00	F	30 12 72	Nigeria	FC Brugge	**Everton**	18	4
AMPADU Kwame	5 10	11 10	F	20 12 70	Bradford	Trainee	Arsenal	2	—
							Plymouth Arg (loan)	6	1
							WBA (loan)	7	1
							WBA	42	3
							Swansea C	57	6
ANDERSON Colin	5 8	10 06	M	26 4 62	Newcastle	Apprentice	Burnley	6	—
							Torquay U	109	11
							QPR (loan)	—	—
							WBA	140	10
							Walsall	26	2
							Hereford U	70	1
							Exeter C	21	1
ANDERSON Ijah			D	30 12 75	Hackney	Tottenham H	**Southend U**	—	—
ANDERSON Lee *	5 7	10 08	D	4 10 73	Manchester	Trainee	**Bury**	29	—
ANDERSON Viv	6 1	13 00	D	29 8 56	Nottingham	Apprentice	Nottingham F	328	15
							Arsenal	120	9
							Manchester U	54	2
							Sheffield W	70	8
							Barnsley	20	3
							Middlesbrough	2	—
ANDERTON Darren	6 1	12 00	F	3 3 72	Southampton	Trainee	Portsmouth	62	7
							Tottenham H	108	17
ANDRADE Jose ‡	5 11	11 07	F	1 6 70	Gaboverde	Academico	**Stoke C**	4	1
ANDREWS Ian	6 2	12 13	G	1 12 64	Nottingham	Apprentice	Leicester C	126	—
							Swindon T (loan)	1	—
							Celtic	5	—
							Leeds U (loan)	1	—
							Southampton	10	—
							Bournemouth	38	—
ANDREWS Nicky ‡	5 10	11 02	D	10 10 75	London	Trainee	**Fulham**	—	—
ANDREWS Philip §	5 11	11 00	F	14 9 76	Andover	Trainee	**Brighton**	10	—
ANGEL Mark *	5 8	11 01	F	23 8 75	Newcastle	Trainee	**Sunderland**	—	—
ANGELL Brett	6 2	13 11	F	20 8 68	Marlborough	Cheltenham T	Derby Co	—	—
							Stockport Co	70	28
							Southend U	115	47
							Everton (loan)	1	—
							Everton	19	1
							Sunderland	8	—
ANGUS Terry	6 0	13 09	D	14 1 66	Coventry	VS Rugby	Northampton T	116	6
							Fulham	59	2
ANNAN Richard ‡	5 8	10 00	D	4 12 68	Leeds	Guiseley	**Crewe Alex**	19	1
ANNON Darren	5 5	10 11	M	17 2 72	London	Carshalton Ath	**Brentford**	19	2
ANSAH Andy	5 9	11 01	F	19 3 69	Lewisham	Crystal Palace	Brentford	8	2
							Southend U	153	33
							Brentford (loan)	3	1

Player	Ht	Wt	Pos	Birth Date	Birth Place	Source	Clubs	League App	League Gls
ANTHONY Graham	5 10	10 08	M	9 8 75	Jarrow	Trainee	**Sheffield U**	1	—
ANTHROBUS Steve	6 0	12 02	F	10 11 68	Lewisham		Millwall	21	4
							Southend U (loan)	—	—
							Wimbledon	28	—
							Peterborough U (loan)	2	—
							Chester C (loan)	7	—
APPLEBY Matty	5 10	11 05	D	16 4 72	Middlesbrough	Trainee	Newcastle U	20	—
							Darlington (loan)	10	1
							Darlington	36	1
APPLEBY Richie	5 8	10 06	M	18 9 75	Middlesbrough	Trainee	**Newcastle U**	—	—
							Darlington (loan)	—	—
APPLETON Michael	5 9	11 13	M	4 12 75	Salford	Trainee	**Manchester U**	—	—
ARCHDEACON Owen	5 7	10 09	M	4 3 66	Glasgow	Gourock U	Celtic	76	7
							Barnsley	195	20
ARCHER Lee	5 6	9 06	M	6 11 72	Bristol	Trainee	**Bristol R**	86	12
ARCHER Paul	5 7	9 04	M	25 4 78	Leicester	Trainee	**Nottingham F**	—	—
ARDLEY Neil	5 9	11 08	M	1 9 72	Epsom	Trainee	**Wimbledon**	65	6
ARMSTRONG Alun	6 0	12 00	F	22 2 75	Gateshead	School	Newcastle U	—	—
							Stockport Co	45	14
ARMSTRONG Chris	6 0	13 03	F	19 6 71	Newcastle	Llay Welfare	Wrexham	60	13
							Millwall	28	5
							Crystal Palace	118	45
ARMSTRONG Craig	5 11	12 04	D	23 5 75	South Shields	Trainee	**Nottingham F**	—	—
							Burnley (loan)	4	—
ARMSTRONG Gordon	6 0	12 11	M	15 7 67	Newcastle	Apprentice	**Sunderland**	348	50
ARNOLD Ian ‡	5 9	11 09	F	4 7 72	Durham City	Trainee	Middlesbrough	3	—
							Carlisle U	47	11
ARNOTT Andy	6 1	12 00	F	18 10 73	Chatham	Trainee	**Gillingham**	72	12
							Manchester U (loan)	—	—
ASABA Carl	6 1	12 12	F	28 1 73	London	Dulwich Hamlet	**Brentford**	—	—
							Colchester U (loan)	12	2
ASHBEE Ian	6 1	12 10	D	6 9 76	Birmingham	Trainee	**Derby Co**	1	—
ASHBY Barry	6 2	12 03	D	21 11 70	London	Trainee	Watford	114	3
							Brentford	48	2
ASHCROFT Lee	5 10	11 00	F	7 9 72	Preston	Trainee	Preston NE	91	13
							WBA	59	13
ASHLEY Kevin	5 7	11 10	D	31 12 68	Birmingham	Apprentice	Birmingham C	57	1
							Wolverhampton W	88	1
							Peterborough U	27	—
ASPIN Neil	6 0	12 06	D	12 4 65	Gateshead	Apprentice	Leeds U	207	5
							Port Vale	237	2
ASPINALL Brendan *	6 0	11 13	D	22 7 75	South Africa	Huddersfield T	**Mansfield T**	20	—
ASPINALL Warren	5 8	10 06	F	13 9 67	Wigan	Apprentice	Wigan Ath	10	1
							Everton	7	—
							Wigan Ath (loan)	41	21
							Aston Villa	44	14
							Portsmouth	132	21
							Swansea C (loan)	5	—
							Bournemouth	33	9
							Carlisle U (loan)	7	1
ATHERTON Peter	5 10	13 12	D	6 4 70	Wigan	Trainee	Wigan Ath	149	1
							Coventry C	114	—
							Sheffield W	41	1
ATKIN Paul	6 0	12 11	D	3 9 69	Nottingham	Trainee	Notts Co	—	—
							Bury	21	1
							York C	112	3

				Birth				League	
Player	*Ht*	*Wt*	*Pos*	*Date*	*Place*	*Source*	*Clubs*	*App*	*Gls*
ATKINS Ian †	6 0	12 03	M	16 1 57	Birmingham	Apprentice	Shrewsbury T	278	58
							Sunderland	77	6
							Everton	7	1
							Ipswich T	77	4
							Birmingham C	93	6
							Colchester U	—	—
							Birmingham C	8	—
							Cambridge U	2	—
							Sunderland	—	—
							Doncaster R	7	—
							Northampton T	—	—
ATKINS Mark	6 1	12 00	D	14 8 68	Doncaster		Scunthorpe U	48	2
							Blackburn R	253	35
ATKINSON Brian	5 9	12 05	M	19 1 71	Darlington	Trainee	**Sunderland**	134	4
ATKINSON Craig	6 0	11 02	M	29 9 77	Rotherham	Trainee	**Nottingham F**	—	—
ATKINSON Dalian	6 0	13 10	F	21 3 68	Shrewsbury		Ipswich T	60	18
							Sheffield W	38	10
							Real Sociedad	26	12
							Aston Villa	87	23
ATKINSON Graeme	5 8	11 07	M	11 11 71	Hull	Trainee	Hull C	149	23
							Preston NE	15	1
AUNGER Geoff ‡	5 8	11 10	F	4 2 68	Red Deer	Vancouver 86ers	Luton T	5	1
							Chester C	5	—
AUSTIN Dean	6 0	11 06	D	26 4 70	Hemel Hempstead	St. Albans C	Southend U	96	2
							Tottenham H	81	—
AUSTIN Kevin	6 1	14 00	D	12 2 73	Hackney	Saffron Walden	**Leyton Orient**	69	2
AWFORD Andy	5 9	11 07	D	14 7 72	Worcester	Worcester C	**Portsmouth**	146	—
BAAH Peter ‡	5 9	10 04	F	1 5 73	Littleborough	Trainee	Blackburn R	1	—
							Fulham	49	4
							Bury	—	—
BABB Phil	6 0	12 03	D	30 11 70	Lambeth	Trainee	Millwall	—	—
							Bradford C	80	14
							Coventry C	77	3
							Liverpool	34	—
BADDELEY Lee	6 1	12 07	D	12 7 74	Cardiff	Trainee	**Cardiff C**	94	1
BAGNALL John ‡	6 0	12 00	G	23 11 73	Southport	Preston NE	Chester C	—	—
							Wigan Ath	—	—
BAILEY Danny *	5 9	12 07	M	21 5 64	Leyton	Apprentice	Bournemouth	2	—
						Local	Torquay U	1	—
						Wealdstone	Exeter C	64	2
							Reading	50	2
							Fulham (loan)	3	—
							Exeter C	75	1
BAILEY Dennis	5 10	11 06	F	13 11 65	Lambeth	Farnborough T	Crystal Palace	5	1
							Bristol R (loan)	17	9
							Birmingham C	75	23
							Bristol R (loan)	6	1
							QPR	39	10
							Charlton Ath (loan)	4	—
							Watford (loan)	8	4
							Brentford (loan)	6	3
BAILEY Gavin	5 8	10 07	F	10 10 76	Chesterfield	Trainee	**Sheffield W**	—	—
BAILEY Mark	5 8	10 12	M	12 8 76	Stoke	Trainee	**Stoke C**	—	—
BAILEY Neil †	5 6	11 04	D	26 9 58	Wigan	Apprentice	Burnley	—	—
							Newport Co	134	7
							Wigan Ath	41	2
							Stockport Co	51	—
							Newport Co (loan)	9	1
						Retired	**Blackpool**	9	—

Player	Ht	Wt	Pos	Birth Date	Birth Place	Source	Clubs	League App	League Gls
BAIRD Ian	6 2	12 12	F	1 4 64	Rotherham	Apprentice	Southampton	22	5
							Cardiff C (loan)	12	6
							Newcastle U (loan)	5	1
							Leeds U	85	33
							Portsmouth	20	1
							Leeds U	77	17
							Middlesbrough	63	19
							Hearts	64	15
							Bristol C	56	11
BAKER Clive	5 9	11 00	G	14 3 59	North Walsham	Amateur	Norwich C	4	—
							Barnsley	291	—
							Coventry C	—	—
							Ipswich T	48	—
BAKER Desmond	5 9	10 12	F	25 8 77	Dublin	Trainee	**Manchester U**	—	—
BAKER Jospeh			M	19 4 77	London	Charlton Ath	**Leyton Orient**	—	—
BAKER Paul	6 1	13 02	F	5 1 63	Newcastle	Bishop Auckland	Southampton	—	—
							Carlisle U	71	11
							Hartlepool U	197	67
							Motherwell	9	1
							Gillingham	62	16
							York C	30	13
BALDRY Simon	5 11	11 00	F	12 2 76	Huddersfield	Trainee	**Huddersfield T**	21	2
BALL Kevin	5 9	12 06	D	12 11 64	Hastings	Apprentice	Portsmouth	105	4
							Sunderland	187	9
BALL Steve	5 11	13 00	M	2 9 69	Colchester	Trainee	Arsenal	—	—
							Colchester U	4	—
							Norwich C	2	—
							Colchester U	56	6
BALMER Stuart	6 1	12 04	D	20 9 69	Falkirk	Celtic BC	Celtic	—	—
							Charlton Ath	147	5
BAMBER Dave *	6 3	13 10	F	1 2 59	St. Helens	Manchester Univ	Blackpool	86	29
							Coventry C	19	3
							Walsall	20	7
							Portsmouth	4	1
							Swindon T	106	31
							Watford	18	3
							Stoke C	43	8
							Hull C	28	5
							Blackpool	113	60
BANGER Nicky	5 9	11 05	F	25 2 71	Southampton	Trainee	Southampton	55	8
							Oldham Ath	28	3
BANKS Ian *	5 10	12 04	M	9 1 61	Mexborough	Apprentice	Barnsley	164	37
							Leicester C	93	14
							Huddersfield T	78	17
							Bradford C	30	3
							WBA	4	—
							Barnsley	96	7
							Rotherham U	76	8
							Darlington	39	1
BANKS Steven	6 0	13 02	G	9 2 72	Hillingdon	Trainee	West Ham U	—	—
							Gillingham	67	—
BANNISTER Andrew *	5 11	11 13	F	23 7 76	Burnley	Trainee	**Burnley**	—	—
BANNISTER Gary *	5 8	11 10	F	22 7 60	Warrington	Apprentice	Coventry C	22	3
							Sheffield W	118	55
							QPR	136	56
							Coventry C	43	11
							WBA	72	18
							Oxford U (loan)	10	2
							Nottingham F	31	8
							Stoke C	15	2
						Hong Kong	**Lincoln C**	29	7
BARACLOUGH Ian	6 1	11 10	M	4 12 70	Leicester	Trainee	Leicester C	—	—
							Wigan Ath (loan)	9	2
							Grimsby T (loan)	4	—
							Grimsby T	1	—
							Lincoln C	73	10
							Mansfield T	36	3

				Birth				League	
Player	*Ht*	*Wt*	*Pos*	*Date*	*Place*	*Source*	*Clubs*	*App*	*Gls*
BARBER Fred	5 10	12 00	G	26 8 63	Ferryhill	Apprentice	Darlington	135	—
							Everton	—	—
							Walsall	153	—
							Peterborough U (loan)	6	—
							Chester (loan)	8	—
							Blackpool (loan)	2	—
							Peterborough U	68	—
							Colchester U (loan)	10	—
							Chesterfield (loan)	—	—
							Luton T (loan)	—	—
BARBER Phil	5 11	12 12	M	10 6 65	Tring	Aylesbury	Crystal Palace	234	35
							Millwall	110	12
							Plymouth Arg (loan)	4	—
BARCLAY Dominic §			F	5 9 76	Bristol	Trainee	**Bristol C**	2	—
BARDSLEY David	5 10	11 00	D	11 9 64	Manchester	Apprentice	Blackpool	45	—
							Watford	100	7
							Oxford U	74	7
							QPR	212	4
BARFOOT Stuart †	5 11	11 00	D	10 12 75	Southampton	Trainee	Bournemouth	2	—
							Torquay U	—	—
BARKER Richard	6 0	11 06	F	30 5 75	Sheffield	Trainee	**Sheffield W**	—	—
BARKER Simon	5 9	11 00	M	4 11 64	Farnworth	Apprentice	Blackburn R	182	35
							QPR	221	21
BARKUS Lea	5 6	9 13	F	7 12 74	Reading	Trainee	**Reading**	15	1
BARLOW Andy *	5 9	11 01	D	24 11 65	Oldham		**Oldham Ath**	261	5
							Bradford C (loan)	2	—
BARLOW Martin	5 7	10 01	M	25 6 71	Barnstable	Trainee	**Plymouth Arg**	152	9
BARLOW Stuart	5 10	11 02	F	16 7 68	Liverpool		**Everton**	68	10
							Rotherham U (loan)	—	—
BARMBY Nick	5 7	11 04	F	11 2 74	Hull	Trainee	**Tottenham H**	87	20
BARNARD Darren	5 10	12 00	D	30 11 71	Rinteln	Wokingham	**Chelsea**	29	2
							Reading (loan)	4	—
BARNARD Mark *	6 0	11 10	D	27 11 75	Sheffield	Trainee	**Rotherham U**	—	—
BARNES David	5 10	11 01	D	16 11 61	London	Apprentice	Coventry C	9	—
							Ipswich T	17	—
							Wolves	88	4
							Aldershot	69	1
							Sheffield U	82	1
							Watford	6	—
BARNES John	5 11	12 07	M	7 11 63	Jamaica	Sudbury Court	Watford	233	65
							Liverpool	243	77
BARNES Paul	5 10	12 09	F	16 11 67	Leicester	Apprentice	Notts Co	53	14
							Stoke C	24	3
							Chesterfield (loan)	1	—
							York C	118	61
BARNES Richard †	5 8	10 00	F	6 9 75	Wrexham	Trainee	**Wrexham**	1	—
BARNESS Anthony	5 10	13 01	D	25 3 72	London	Trainee	Charlton Ath	27	1
							Chelsea	14	—
							Middlesbrough (loan)	—	—
BARNETT Dave	6 0	13 00	D	16 4 67	London	Windsor & Eton	Colchester U	20	—
							WBA	—	—
							Walsall	5	—
						Kidderminster H	Barnet	59	3
							Birmingham C	40	—
BARNETT Gary *	5 6	9 13	M	11 3 63	Stratford upon Avon	Apprentice	Coventry C	—	—
							Huddersfield T	22	1
							Oxford U	45	9
							Wimbledon (loan)	5	1
							Fulham (loan)	2	1
							Fulham	180	30
							Huddersfield T	100	11
							Leyton Orient	63	7
BARNETT Jason	5 9	10 10	F	21 4 76	Shrewsbury	Trainee	**Wolverhampton W**	—	—

Player	Ht	Wt	Pos	Birth Date	Birth Place	Source	Clubs	League App	League Gls
BARNHOUSE David	5 8	10 09	D	19 3 75	Swansea	Trainee	**Swansea C**	8	—
BARNWELL-EDINBORO Jamie	5 10	11 06	F	26 12 75	Hull	Trainee	**Coventry C**	—	—
BARR Billy	5 11	10 08	M	21 1 69	Halifax	Trainee	Halifax T	196	13
						Halifax T	**Crewe Alex**	34	2
BARRAS Tony	6 0	12 09	D	29 3 71	Stockton	Trainee	Hartlepool U	12	—
							Stockport Co	99	5
							Rotherham U (loan)	5	1
							York C	31	1
BARRATT Tony *	5 8	11 00	D	18 10 65	Salford	Billingham T	Grimsby T	22	—
						Billingham T	Hartlepool U	98	4
							York C	147	10
BARRETT Earl	5 11	11 00	D	28 4 67	Rochdale	Apprentice	Manchester C	3	—
							Chester C (loan)	12	—
							Oldham Ath	183	7
							Aston Villa	119	1
							Everton	17	—
BARRETT Michael ‡			G	20 10 63	Exeter	Liskeard	**Exeter C**	4	—
BARRETT Richard	5 0	9 08	D	1 11 77	Sutton Coldfield	Trainee	**Nottingham F**	—	—
BARRETT Scott *	5 11	13 08	G	2 4 63	Derby	Ilkeston T	Wolverhampton W	30	—
							Stoke C	51	—
							Colchester U (loan)	13	—
							Stockport Co (loan)	10	—
							Colchester U	—	—
							Gillingham	51	—
BARRICK Dean	5 7	11 07	D	30 9 69	Hemsworth	Trainee	Sheffield W	11	2
							Rotherham U	99	7
							Cambridge U	88	2
BARRON Michael	5 11	11 09	D	22 12 74	Chester le Street	Trainee	**Middlesbrough**	2	—
BARROW Graham †	6 2	13 07	M	13 6 54	Chorley	Altrincham	Wigan Ath	179	36
							Chester C	248	17
							Wigan Ath	—	—
BARROW Lee	5 11	13 00	D	1 5 73	Worksworth	Trainee	Notts Co	—	—
							Scarborough	11	—
							Torquay U	75	5
BARRY George ‡			D	19 9 67	London		**Leyton Orient**	6	—
BARTLETT Kevin ‡	5 8	11 01	F	12 10 62	Portsmouth	Apprentice	Portsmouth	3	—
						Fareham	Cardiff C	82	25
							WBA	37	10
							Notts Co	99	33
							Port Vale (loan)	5	1
							Cambridge U	8	1
BARTLETT Neal ‡	5 8	12 00	M	7 4 75	Southampton	Trainee	**Southampton**	8	—
BARTLEY Carl §			F	6 10 76	Lambeth	Trainee	**Fulham**	1	—
BARTON Warren	5 11	11 00	D	19 3 69	London	Leytonstone/ Ilford	Maidstone U	42	—
							Wimbledon	180	10
BARTRAM Vince	6 2	13 07	G	7 8 68	Birmingham	Local	Wolverhampton W	5	—
							Blackpool (loan)	9	—
							WBA (loan)	—	—
							Bournemouth	132	—
							Arsenal	11	—
BART-WILLIAMS Chris	5 10	11 11	M	16 6 74	Freetown	Trainee	Leyton Orient	36	2
							Sheffield W	124	16
BASHAM Mike	6 2	12 08	M	27 9 73	Barking	Trainee	West Ham U	—	—
							Colchester U (loan)	1	—
							Swansea C	18	—
BASS David	5 11	12 07	M	29 11 74	Frimley	Trainee	**Reading**	9	—
BASS Jonathan	6 0	12 02	D	1 7 76	Weston Super Mare	Trainee	**Birmingham C**	—	—

Player	Ht	Wt	Pos	Birth Date	Birth Place	Source	Clubs	League App	League Gls
BATES Jamie	6 1	12 12	D	24 2 68	London	Trainee	**Brentford**	279	10
BATTERSBY Tony	6 0	12 09	F	30 8 75	Doncaster	Trainee	**Sheffield U**	—	—
							Southend U (loan)	8	1
BATTY David	5 8	12 00	M	2 12 68	Leeds	Trainee	Leeds U	211	4
							Blackburn R	31	—
BAYES Ashley	6 1	13 05	G	19 4 72	Lincoln	Trainee	Brentford	4	—
							Torquay U	69	—
BAYLISS David §			D	8 6 76	Liverpool	Trainee	**Rochdale**	1	—
BAZELEY Darren	5 10	11 02	F	5 10 72	Northampton	Trainee	**Watford**	102	12
BEADLE Peter	6 0	11 12	F	13 5 72	London	Trainee	Gillingham	67	14
							Tottenham H	—	—
							Bournemouth (loan)	9	2
							Southend U (loan)	8	1
							Watford	20	1
BEAGRIE Peter	5 8	9 10	M	28 11 65	Middlesbrough	Local	Middlesbrough	33	2
							Sheffield U	84	11
							Stoke C	54	7
							Everton	114	11
							Sunderland (loan)	5	1
							Manchester C	46	3
BEARD Mark	5 10	10 12	D	8 10 74	Roehampton	Trainee	**Millwall**	45	2
BEARDSLEY Peter	5 8	11 07	F	18 1 61	Newcastle	Wallsend BC	Carlisle U	102	22
						Vancouver Whitecaps	Manchester U	—	—
						Vancouver Whitecaps	Newcastle U	147	61
							Liverpool	131	46
							Everton	81	25
							Newcastle U	69	33
BEARDSMORE Russell	5 6	8 10	M	28 9 68	Wigan	Apprentice	Manchester U	56	4
							Blackburn R (loan)	2	—
							Bournemouth	67	3
BEASANT Dave	6 4	14 03	G	20 3 59	Ealing	Edgware T	Wimbledon	340	—
							Newcastle U	20	—
							Chelsea	133	—
							Grimsby T (loan)	6	—
							Wolverhampton W (loan)	4	—
							Southampton	38	—
BEASLEY Andy	6 0	13 08	G	5 2 64	Sedgley	Apprentice	Luton T.	—	—
							Mansfield T (loan)	—	—
							Gillingham (loan)	—	—
							Mansfield T	94	—
							Peterborough U (loan)	7	—
							Scarborough (loan)	4	—
							Bristol R (loan)	1	—
							Doncaster R	37	—
							Chesterfield	21	—
BEATTIE James	6 1	12 00	F	27 2 78	Lancaster	Trainee	**Blackburn R**	—	—
BEAUCHAMP Joey	5 10	11 10	M	13 3 71	Oxford	Trainee	Oxford U	124	20
							Swansea C (loan)	5	2
							West Ham U	—	—
							Swindon T	42	3
BEAUMONT Chris	5 11	11 07	F	5 12 65	Sheffield	Denaby	Rochdale	34	7
							Stockport Co	215	39
BECKETT Nathan ‡	6 2	13 00	D	31 5 75	Hertford	Trainee	**Leyton Orient**	—	—
BECKFORD Darren	6 1	11 01	F	12 5 67	Manchester	Apprentice	Manchester C	11	—
							Bury (loan)	12	5
							Port Vale (loan)	11	4
							Port Vale	167	68
							Norwich C	38	8
							Oldham Ath	32	9

				Birth				League	
Player	*Ht*	*Wt*	*Pos*	*Date*	*Place*	*Source*	*Clubs*	*App*	*Gls*
BECKFORD Jason	5 9	12 04	F	14 2 70	Manchester	Trainee	Manchester C	20	1
							Blackburn R (loan)	4	—
							Port Vale (loan)	5	1
							Birmingham C	7	2
							Bury (loan)	3	—
							Stoke C	4	—
							Millwall	9	—
							Northampton T	—	—
BECKHAM David	6 0	11 02	M	2 5 75	Leytonstone	Trainee	**Manchester U**	4	—
							Preston NE (loan)	5	2
BEDROSSIAN Ara ‡	5 9	10 10	M	2 6 67	Cyprus	AP Limassol	**Fulham**	42	1
BEECH Chris	5 10	11 00	M	16 9 74	Blackpool	Trainee	**Blackpool**	64	4
BEECH Chris	5 9	11 00	F	5 11 75	Congleton	Trainee	**Manchester C**	—	—
BEENEY Mark	6 4	14 07	G	30 12 67	Pembury		Gillingham	2	—
							Maidstone U	50	—
							Aldershot (loan)	7	—
							Brighton & HA	69	—
							Leeds U	23	—
BEESLEY Paul	6 1	12 06	D	21 7 65	Liverpool	Marine	Wigan Ath	155	3
							Leyton Orient	32	1
							Sheffield U	168	7
BEESTON Carl	5 10	12 04	M	30 6 67	Stoke	Apprentice	**Stoke C**	202	13
BEINLICH Stefan (To Hansa Rostock)	5 11	11 02	F	13 1 72	Berlin	Bergmann Borsig	**Aston Villa**	16	1
BELL Mike	5 10	11 04	F	15 11 71	Newcastle	Trainee	Northampton T	153	10
							Wycombe W	31	3
BELLAMY Gary	6 2	11 05	D	4 7 62	Worksop	Apprentice	Chesterfield	184	7
							Wolverhampton W	136	9
							Cardiff C (loan)	9	—
							Leyton Orient	100	5
BELLOTTI Ross §			G	15 5 78	Pembury	Trainee	**Exeter C**	2	—
BENALI Francis	5 10	11 01	D	30 12 68	Southampton	Apprentice	**Southampton**	173	—
BENJAMIN Ian	5 11	13 01	F	11 12 61	Nottingham	Apprentice	Sheffield U	5	3
							WBA	2	—
							Notts Co	—	—
							Peterborough U	80	14
							Northampton T	150	59
							Cambridge U	25	2
							Chester C	22	2
							Exeter C	32	4
							Southend U	122	33
							Luton T	13	2
							Brentford	15	2
							Wigan Ath	17	6
BENN Wayne	5 9	11 12	D	7 8 76	Pontefract	Trainee	**Bradford C**	10	—
BENNETT Frankie	5 7	11 12	F	3 1 69	Birmingham	Halesowen T	**Southampton**	8	1
BENNETT Gary	6 0	13 00	D	4 12 61	Manchester	Amateur	Manchester C	—	—
							Cardiff C	87	11
							Sunderland	369	23
BENNETT Gary	5 11	11 00	F	20 9 63	Kirby	Kirby T	Wigan Ath	20	3
							Chester C	126	36
							Southend U	42	6
							Chester C	80	15
							Wrexham	121	77
BENNETT Ian	6 0	12 00	G	10 10 71	Worksop	Newcastle U	Peterborough U	72	—
							Birmingham C	68	—
BENNETT Mickey	5 10	11 11	M	27 7 69	Camberwell	Apprentice	Charlton Ath	35	2
							Wimbledon	18	2
							Brentford	46	4
							Charlton Ath	24	1
							Millwall	—	—
BENNETT Tom	5 11	11 08	D	12 12 69	Falkirk	Trainee	Aston Villa	—	—
							Wolverhampton W	115	2

				Birth				League	
Player	*Ht*	*Wt*	*Pos*	*Date*	*Place*	*Source*	*Clubs*	*App*	*Gls*
BENNETT Troy	5 9	11 13	M	25 12 75	Barnsley	Trainee	**Barnsley**	2	—
BENT Junior	5 5	10 06	F	1 3 70	Huddersfield	Trainee	Huddersfield T	36	6
							Burnley (loan)	9	3
							Bristol C	119	15
							Stoke C (loan)	1	—
BENTLEY Jim	6 1	13 00	D	11 6 76	Liverpool	Trainee	**Manchester C**	—	—
BERESFORD David	5 8	10 09	F	11 11 76	Middlesbrough	Trainee	**Oldham Ath**	3	—
BERESFORD John	5 6	10 12	M	4 9 66	Sheffield	Apprentice	Manchester C	—	—
							Barnsley	88	5
							Portsmouth	107	8
							Newcastle U	109	1
BERESFORD Marlon	6 1	13 01	G	2 9 69	Lincoln	Trainee	Sheffield W	—	—
							Bury (loan)	1	—
							Ipswich T (loan)	—	—
							Northampton T (loan)	13	—
							Crewe Alex (loan)	3	—
							Northampton T (loan)	15	—
							Burnley	130	—
BERG Henning	6 0	12 07	D	1 9 69	Eidsvell	Lillestrom	**Blackburn R**	85	2
BERGKAMP Dennis	6 0	12 05	F	18 5 69	Amsterdam		Ajax	185	103
							Internazionale	52	11
							Arsenal	—	—
BERGSSON Gudni	6 1	12 03	D	21 7 65	Iceland	Valur	Tottenham H	71	2
							Bolton W	8	—
BERKLEY Austin	5 9	10 10	M	28 1 73	Gravesend	Trainee	Gillingham	3	—
							Swindon T	1	—
BERNAL Andy	5 10	12 05	D	16 7 66	Canberra	Sporting Gijon	Ipswich T	9	—
						Sydney Olympic	**Reading**	33	—
BERNARD Paul	5 11	11 08	M	30 12 72	Edinburgh	Trainee	**Oldham Ath**	105	17
BERRY Greg	5 10	12 00	F	5 3 71	Essex	East Thurrock	Leyton Orient	80	14
							Wimbledon	7	1
							Millwall	19	1
BERRY Trevor	5 7	10 08	F	1 8 74	Haslemere	Bournemouth	**Aston Villa**	—	—
BETTS Simon	5 7	11 05	D	3 3 73	Middlesbrough	Trainee	Ipswich T	—	—
							Scarborough	—	—
							Colchester U	91	3
BIBBO Sal	6 2	13 05	G	24 8 74	Basingstoke	Bournemouth	**Sheffield U**	—	—
							Chesterfield (loan)	1	—
BIGGINS Wayne *	5 10	13 00	F	20 11 61	Sheffield	Apprentice	Lincoln C	8	1
						Matlock Town and King's Lynn	Burnley	78	29
							Norwich C	79	16
							Manchester C	32	9
							Stoke C	122	46
							Barnsley	47	16
							Celtic	9	—
							Stoke C	27	6
							Luton T (loan)	7	1
BILLING Peter *	6 2	13 00	D	24 10 64	Liverpool	South Liverpool	Everton	1	—
							Crewe Alex	88	1
							Coventry C	58	1
							Port Vale (loan)	12	—
							Port Vale	14	—
BILLY Chris	6 0	10 09	D	2 1 73	Huddersfield	Trainee	**Huddersfield T**	94	4
BIMSON Stuart	5 11	11 07	D	29 9 69	Liverpool	Macclesfield	**Bury**	19	—
BIRCH Paul	5 6	10 04	M	20 11 62	West Bromwich	Apprentice	Aston Villa	173	16
							Wolverhampton W	135	15
BIRD Anthony	5 10	10 07	F	1 9 74	Cardiff	Trainee	**Cardiff C**	63	10
BISHOP Charlie	5 11	13 07	D	16 2 68	Nottingham	Stoke C	Watford	—	—
							Bury	114	6
							Barnsley	117	1

Player	Ht	Wt	Pos	Birth Date	Birth Place	Source	Clubs	League App	League Gls
BISHOP Eddie *	5 10	12 06	M	28 11 62	Liverpool	Runcorn	Tranmere R	76	19
							Chester C	106	23
							Crewe Alex (loan)	3	—
BISHOP Ian	5 9	10 12	M	29 5 65	Liverpool	Apprentice	Everton	1	—
							Crewe Alex (loan)	4	—
							Carlisle U	132	14
							Bournemouth	44	2
							Manchester C	19	2
							West Ham U	187	10
BISSETT Nicky *	6 2	12 10	D	5 4 64	Fulham	Barnet	**Brighton**	97	9
BJORNEBYE Stig Inge	5 10	11 09	D	11 12 69	Norway	Rosenborg	**Liverpool**	51	—
BLACK Kingsley	5 8	10 11	M	22 6 68	Luton	School	Luton T	127	26
							Nottingham F	96	14
							Sheffield U (loan)	11	2
BLACK Simon	6 1	12 00	F	9 11 75	Marston Green	Trainee	**Birmingham C**	2	—
BLACK Tony	5 8	11 00	F	15 7 69	Barrow	Bamber Bridge	**Wigan Ath**	9	—
BLACKMORE Clayton	5 8	11 12	M	23 9 64	Neath	Apprentice	Manchester U	186	19
							Middlesbrough	30	2
BLACKSTONE Ian	6 0	13 00	F	7 8 64	Harrogate	Harrogate T	York C	129	37
							Scarborough	13	—
BLACKWELL Dean	6 1	12 07	D	5 12 69	London	Trainee	**Wimbledon**	84	1
							Plymouth Arg (loan)	7	—
BLACKWELL Kevin *	5 11	12 10	G	21 12 58	Luton	Barnet	Scarborough	44	—
							Notts Co	—	—
							Torquay U	18	—
							Huddersfield T	5	—
BLADES Paul	6 0	10 12	D	5 1 65	Peterborough	Apprentice	Derby Co	166	1
							Norwich C	47	—
							Wolverhampton W	107	2
BLAIR Scott *	5 10	11 00	D	24 11 75	Nuneaton	Trainee	**Stoke C**	—	—
BLAKE Mark	6 0	12 09	D	17 12 67	Portsmouth	Apprentice	Southampton	18	2
							Colchester U (loan)	4	1
							Shrewsbury T (loan)	10	—
							Shrewsbury T	132	3
							Fulham	35	3
BLAKE Mark	5 11	12 06	M	16 12 70	Nottingham	Trainee	Aston Villa	31	2
							Wolverhampton W (loan)	2	—
							Portsmouth	15	—
							Leicester C	41	4
BLAKE Nathan	5 11	13 12	F	27 1 72	Cardiff	Chelsea	Cardiff C	131	35
							Sheffield U	47	22
BLAKE Robert	5 8	11 00	F	4 3 76	Middlesbrough	Trainee	**Darlington**	9	—
BLAKE Timothy	6 2	13 00	D	25 9 75	Merthyr	Trainee	**Coventry C**	—	—
BLATHERWICK Steve	6 1	12 12	D	20 9 73	Nottingham	Notts Co	**Nottingham F**	3	—
							Wycombe W (loan)	2	—
BLISSETT Gary	6 1	12 02	F	29 6 64	Manchester	Altrincham	Crewe Alex	122	39
							Brentford	233	79
							Wimbledon	27	3
BLOUNT Mark	5 10	12 04	M	5 1 74	Derby	Gresley R	**Sheffield U**	5	—
BLUNT Jason	5 8	10 10	M	16 8 77	Penzance	Trainee	**Leeds U**	—	—
BLYTH Ian ‡	5 10	11 04	D	21 10 74	Coventry	Trainee	**Leicester C**	—	—
BOCHENSKI Simon	5 8	11 13	F	6 12 75	Worksop	Trainee	**Barnsley**	—	—
BODEN Chris	5 9	11 00	D	13 10 73	Wolverhampton	Trainee	Aston Villa	1	—
							Barnsley (loan)	4	—
							Derby Co	6	—

Player	Ht	Wt	Pos	Birth Date	Birth Place	Source	Clubs	League App	League Gls
BODIN Paul	6 0	13 01	D	13 9 64	Cardiff	Chelsea	Newport Co	—	—
							Cardiff C	57	3
						Bath C	Newport Co	6	1
							Swindon T	93	9
							Crystal Palace	9	—
							Newcastle U (loan)	6	—
							Swindon T	113	26
BODLEY Mike	6 1	13 02	D	14 9 67	Hayes	Apprentice	Chelsea	6	1
							Northampton T	20	—
							Barnet	69	3
							Southend U	28	1
							Gillingham (loan)	7	—
							Birmingham C (loan)	3	—
BOERE Jeroen	6 3	13 05	F	18 11 67	Arnheim	Go Ahead	**West Ham U**	24	6
							Portsmouth (loan)	5	—
							WBA (loan)	5	—
BOGIE Ian	5 7	12 00	M	6 12 67	Newcastle	Apprentice	Newcastle U	14	—
							Preston NE	79	12
							Millwall	51	1
							Leyton Orient	65	5
							Port Vale	9	2
BOHINEN Lars	5 11	12 02	M	8 9 66	Vadso	Young Boys	**Nottingham F**	57	7
BOLAND Willie	5 9	11 02	M	6 8 75	Ennis	Trainee	**Coventry C**	40	—
BOLT Danny	5 7	11 08	M	5 2 76	Wandsworth	Trainee	**Fulham**	2	—
BOLTON Nigel *			F	14 1 75	Bishop Auckland	Shildon	**Darlington**	2	—
BONNER Mark	5 10	11 00	M	7 6 74	Ormskirk	Trainee	**Blackpool**	75	7
BOOTH Andy	6 0	11 00	F	17 3 73	Huddersfield	Trainee	**Huddersfield T**	80	38
BOOTHROYD Adrian	5 10	11 04	D	8 2 71	Bradford	Trainee	Huddersfield T	10	—
							Bristol R	16	—
							Hearts	4	—
							Mansfield T	59	1
BOOTY Justin *	5 11	13 12	F	2 6 76	Colchester	Trainee	**Colchester U**	1	—
BOOTY Martyn	5 8	11 02	D	30 5 71	Kirby Muxloe	Trainee	Coventry C	5	—
							Crewe Alex	75	3
BORROWS Brian	5 10	10 12	D	20 12 60	Liverpool	Amateur	Everton	27	—
							Bolton W	95	—
							Coventry C	365	11
							Bristol C (loan)	6	—
BOSNICH Mark	6 1	13 07	G	13 1 72	Fairfield	Croatia Sydney	Manchester U	3	—
							Aston Villa	76	—
BOULD Steve	6 4	14 02	D	16 11 62	Stoke	Apprentice	Stoke C	183	6
							Torquay U (loan)	9	—
							Arsenal	192	5
BOUND Matthew	6 2	14 06	D	9 11 72	Trowbridge	Trainee	Southampton	5	—
							Hull C (loan)	7	1
							Stockport Co	14	—
BOWDEN Jon *	5 10	11 07	F	21 1 63	Stockport	Local	Oldham Ath	82	5
							Port Vale	70	7
							Wrexham	147	20
							Rochdale	106	17
BOWEN Jason	5 6	8 10	M	24 8 72	Merthyr	Trainee	**Swansea C**	124	26
BOWEN Mark	5 8	11 11	D	7 12 63	Neath	Apprentice	Tottenham H	17	2
							Norwich C	289	22
BOWLING Ian *	6 3	13 11	G	27 7 65	Sheffield	Gainsborough T	Lincoln C	59	—
							Hartlepool U (loan)	1	—
							Bradford C (loan)	7	—
							Bradford C	29	—
BOWMAN Robert	6 1	11 12	D	21 11 75	Durham	Trainee	**Leeds U**	4	—
BOWRY Bobby	5 8	10 08	M	19 5 71	Croydon		**Crystal Palace**	50	1
BOWYER Gary *	6 0	12 13	D	26 6 71	Manchester		Hereford U	14	2
							Nottingham F	—	—

Player	Ht	Wt	Pos	Birth Date	Birth Place	Source	Clubs	League App	League Gls
BOWYER Lee	5 9	9 09	M	3 1 77	London	Trainee	**Charlton Ath**	5	—
BOXALL Danny	5 8	10 05	D	24 8 77	Croydon	Trainee	**Crystal Palace**	—	—
BRABIN Gary	5 11	12 00	M	9 12 70	Liverpool	Trainee	Stockport Co	2	—
						Runcorn	**Doncaster R**	28	8
BRACE Deryn	5 9	10 00	D	15 3 75	Haverfordwest	Trainee	Norwich C	—	—
							Wrexham	15	—
BRACEWELL Paul	5 8	10 09	M	19 7 62	Stoke	Apprentice	Stoke C	129	5
							Sunderland	38	4
							Everton	95	7
							Sunderland	113	2
							Newcastle U	73	3
BRACEY Lee	6 0	13 05	G	11 9 68	Ashford	Trainee	West Ham U	—	—
							Swansea C	99	—
							Halifax T	73	—
							Bury	46	—
BRADBURY Shaun ‡	5 10	11 00	F	11 2 74	Birmingham	Trainee	Wolverhampton W	2	2
							Hereford U	—	—
BRADLEY Darren *	5 7	11 12	D	24 11 65	Birmingham	Apprentice	Aston Villa	20	—
							WBA	254	9
BRADLEY Russell	6 2	13 00	D	28 3 66	Birmingham	Dudley T	Nottingham F	—	—
							Hereford U (loan)	12	1
							Hereford U	77	3
							Halifax T	56	3
							Scunthorpe U	59	3
BRADSHAW Carl	5 10	11 06	D	2 10 68	Sheffield	Apprentice	Sheffield W	32	4
							Barnsley (loan)	6	1
							Manchester C	5	—
							Sheffield U	147	8
							Norwich C	26	1
BRADSHAW Darren	5 11	11 04	M	19 3 67	Sheffield	Matlock T	Chesterfield	18	—
							York C	59	3
							Newcastle U	38	—
							Peterborough U	73	1
							Plymouth Arg (loan)	6	1
							Blackpool	26	1
BRADY Gary	5 10	10 02	M	7 9 76	Glasgow	Trainee	**Tottenham H**	—	—
BRADY Matthew §	6 0	10 04	M	27 10 77	London	Trainee	**Barnet**	1	—
BRAMMER David	5 10	11 05	M	28 2 75	Bromborough	Trainee	**Wrexham**	38	3
BRANAGAN Keith	6 0	13 02	G	10 7 66	Fulham		Cambridge U	110	—
							Millwall	46	—
							Brentford (loan)	2	—
							Gillingham (loan)	1	—
							Fulham (loan)	—	—
							Bolton W	99	—
BRANCH Graham	6 2	12 02	F	12 2 72	Liverpool	Heswall Ath	**Tranmere R**	21	—
							Bury (loan)	4	1
BRANNAN Ged	6 0	12 03	D	15 1 72	Liverpool	Trainee	**Tranmere R**	160	14
BRASS Chris	5 9	11 08	D	24 7 75	Easington	Trainee	**Burnley**	5	—
							Torquay U (loan)	7	—
BRAZIER Matthew	5 8	10 07	D	2 7 76	Whipps Cross	Trainee	**QPR**	—	—
BRAZIL Derek	5 11	10 05	D	14 12 68	Dublin	Rivermount BC	Manchester U	2	—
							Oldham Ath (loan)	1	—
							Swansea C (loan)	12	1
							Cardiff C	95	1
BRAZIL Gary	5 11	11 03	F	19 9 62	Tunbridge Wells	Crystal Palace	Sheffield U	62	9
							Port Vale (loan)	6	3
							Preston NE	166	58
							Newcastle U	23	2
							Fulham	195	46
BREACKER Tim	5 11	13 00	D	2 7 65	Bicester		Luton T	210	3
							West Ham U	170	8
BREBNER Grant			M	6 12 77	Edinburgh		**Manchester U**	—	—

				Birth				League	
Player	Ht	Wt	Pos	Date	Place	Source	Clubs	App	Gls
BRECKIN Ian	6 0	11 06	D	24 7 75	Rotherham	Trainee	**Rotherham U**	51	2
BREEN Gary	6 1	12 00	D	12 12 73	London	Charlton Ath	Maidstone U	19	—
							Gillingham	51	—
							Peterborough U	44	1
BREITKREUTZ Matthias (To Hertha Berlin)	5 9	11 03	M	12 5 71	Crivitz	Bergmann Borsig	**Aston Villa**	13	—
BRENNAN Jim	5 9	11 06	M	8 5 77		Sora Lazio	**Bristol C**	—	—
BRENNAN Mark	5 10	10 13	M	4 10 65	Rossendale	Apprentice	Ipswich T	168	19
							Middlesbrough	65	6
							Manchester C	29	6
							Oldham Ath	65	4
BRESSINGTON Graham *	6 0	13 10	D	8 7 66	Eton	Wycombe W	Lincoln C	141	7
							Southend U	48	5
BREVETT Rufus	5 8	11 00	D	24 9 69	Derby	Trainee	Doncaster R	109	3
							QPR	58	—
BRIEN Tony *	6 0	13 00	D	10 2 69	Dublin	Apprentice	Leicester C	16	1
							Chesterfield	204	8
							Rotherham U	43	2
BRIGGS Gary *	6 3	12 10	D	8 5 58	Leeds	Apprentice	Middlesbrough	—	—
							Oxford U	420	18
							Blackpool	137	4
BRIGHT Mark	6 0	12 13	F	6 6 62	Stoke	Leek T	Port Vale	29	10
							Leicester C	42	6
							Crystal Palace	227	92
							Sheffield W	107	41
BRIGHTWELL David	6 1	13 05	D	7 1 71	Lutterworth	Trainee	**Manchester C**	43	1
							Chester C (loan)	6	—
BRIGHTWELL Ian	5 10	11 07	M	9 4 68	Lutterworth	Congleton T	**Manchester C**	234	16
BRISCOE Lee	5 7	10 09	F	30 9 75	Pontefract	Trainee	**Sheffield W**	7	—
BRISSETT Jason	5 11	11 10	M	7 9 74	Redbridge	Arsenal	Peterborough U	35	—
							Bournemouth	25	—
BROCK Kevin ‡	5 9	10 12	M	9 9 62	Middleton Stoney	Apprentice	Oxford U	246	26
							QPR	40	2
							Newcastle U	145	15
							Cardiff C (loan)	14	2
							Stockport Co	—	—
BROCK Stuart			G	26 9 76	Birmingham	Trainee	**Aston Villa**	—	—
BRODIE Stephen	5 6	10 06	F	14 1 73	Sunderland	Trainee	**Sunderland**	12	—
BROOKE David	5 11	11 03	M	23 11 75	Barnsley	Trainee	**Barnsley**	—	—
BROOKES Mark	5 9	10 06	M	19 9 75	Nottingham	Trainee	**Grimsby T**	—	—
BROOKS Matthew ‡	5 11	12 06	M	23 4 75	Warrington	Trainee	**Wigan Ath**	—	—
BROOKS Shaun	5 8	11 00	M	9 10 62	London	Apprentice	Crystal Palace	54	4
							Orient	148	26
							Bournemouth	129	13
							Stockport Co (loan)	—	—
							Leyton Orient	9	—
BROOMES Marlon	6 0	12 07	D	28 11 77	Birmingham	Trainee	**Blackburn R**	—	—
BROUGH John	6 0	12 10	D	8 1 73	Heanor	Trainee	Notts Co	—	—
							Shrewsbury T	16	1
						Telford U	**Hereford U**	18	1
BROWN Andrew	6 3	13 00	F	11 10 76	Edinburgh	Trainee	**Leeds U**	—	—
BROWN Grant	6 0	11 12	D	19 11 69	Sunderland	Trainee	Leicester C	14	—
							Lincoln C	220	11
BROWN Ian *	5 10	13 04	D	2 9 75	Wolverhampton	Trainee	**Aston Villa**	—	—
BROWN Ian *	5 10	11 05	F	11 9 65	Ipswich	Chelmsford C	Bristol C	12	1
							Colchester U (loan)	4	1
							Northampton T	23	4
BROWN Jon *	5 10	11 03	D	8 9 66	Barnsley	Denaby U	**Exeter C**	164	3

Player	Ht	Wt	Pos	Birth Date	Birth Place	Source	Clubs	League App	League Gls
BROWN Kenny	5 8	11 06	D	11 7 67	Barking	Apprentice	Norwich C	25	—
							Plymouth Arg	126	4
							West Ham U	60	5
BROWN Linton	5 9	11 00	F	12 4 68	Driffield	Guiseley	Halifax T	3	—
							Hull C	98	22
BROWN Michael	5 7	10 06	M	25 1 77	Hartlepool	Trainee	**Manchester C**	—	—
BROWN Mickey	5 9	10 12	F	8 2 68	Birmingham	Apprentice	Shrewsbury T	190	9
							Bolton W	33	3
							Shrewsbury T	67	11
							Preston NE	—	—
BROWN Phil	5 11	11 08	D	30 5 59	South Shields	Local	Hartlepool U	217	8
							Halifax T	135	19
							Bolton W	256	14
							Blackpool	31	5
BROWN Richard ‡	5 10	11 02	D	13 1 67	Nottingham	Ilkeston T	Sheffield W	—	—
						Kettering T	Blackburn R	28	—
							Maidstone U (loan)	3	—
							Stockport Co	1	—
BROWN Steve	6 1	13 10	D	13 5 72	Brighton	Trainee	**Charlton Ath**	62	3
BROWN Steve	5 11	12 07	F	6 12 73	Southend	Trainee	Southend U	10	2
							Scunthorpe U	—	—
							Colchester U	62	17
							Gillingham	8	2
BROWN Steve	6 1	10 11	D	6 7 66	Northampton		Northampton T	—	—
						Irthlingborough D	Northampton T	158	19
							Wycombe W	49	3
BROWN Steven ‡	5 9	10 04	M	15 10 74	Sheffield	Trainee	**Sheffield W**	—	—
BROWN Wayne §			G	14 1 77	Southampton	Trainee	**Bristol C**	1	—
BROWNE Paul	6 1	12 00	D	17 2 75	Glasgow	Trainee	**Aston Villa**	—	—
BROWNING Marcus	5 11	13 00	F	22 4 71	Bristol	Trainee	**Bristol R**	103	7
							Hereford U (loan)	7	5
BROWNRIGG Andrew	6 0	11 13	D	2 8 76	Sheffield	Trainee	Hereford U	8	—
							Norwich C	—	—
BRUCE Steve	6 0	13 00	D	31 12 60	Newcastle	Apprentice	Gillingham	205	29
							Norwich C	141	14
							Manchester U	279	35
BRUMWELL Philip *	5 7	11 02	M	8 8 75	Darlington	Trainee	**Sunderland**	—	—
BRUNSKILL Iain	5 10	12 05	D	5 11 76	Ormskirk	Trainee	**Liverpool**	—	—
BRYAN Marvin	6 0	12 02	F	2 8 75	Paddington	Trainee	**QPR**	—	—
							Doncaster R (loan)	5	1
BRYANT Matthew	6 1	12 11	D	21 9 70	Bristol	Trainee	**Bristol C**	171	7
							Walsall (loan)	13	—
BRYDEN Lee	5 11	11 00	D	15 11 74	Stockton	Trainee	**Liverpool**	—	—
BRYSON Ian	5 11	11 11	M	26 11 62	Kilmarnock		Kilmarnock	215	40
							Sheffield U	155	36
							Barnsley	16	3
							Preston NE	66	7
BUCKLE Paul	5 7	10 10	M	16 12 70	Hatfield	Trainee	Brentford	57	1
							Torquay U	48	5
BUCKLEY Simon	5 10	11 02	M	29 2 76	Stafford	Trainee	**Grimsby T**	—	—
BULL Gary	5 9	11 07	F	12 6 66	West Bromwich		Southampton	—	—
							Cambridge U	19	4
						Barnet	Barnet	83	37
							Nottingham F	12	1
							Birmingham C (loan)	10	6
BULL Steve	5 11	11 04	F	28 3 65	Tipton	Apprentice	WBA	4	2
							Wolverhampton W	341	202

				Birth				League	
Player	*Ht*	*Wt*	*Pos*	*Date*	*Place*	*Source*	*Clubs*	*App*	*Gls*
BULLIMORE Wayne	5 10	11 07	M	12 9 70	Mansfield	Trainee	Manchester U	—	—
							Barnsley	35	1
							Stockport Co	—	—
							Scunthorpe U	53	9
BULLOCK Darren	5 8	12 06	M	12 2 69	Worcester	Nuneaton	**Huddersfield T**	59	9
BULLOCK Martin	5 4	10 09	M	5 3 75	Derby	Eastwood T	**Barnsley**	29	—
BURCHELL Lee	5 7	10 06	M	12 11 76	Birmingham	Trainee	**Aston Villa**	—	—
BURGESS Daryl	5 11	12 03	D	20 4 71	Birmingham	Trainee	**WBA**	178	5
BURGESS Dave *	5 10	11 02	D	20 1 60	Liverpool.	Local	Tranmere R	218	1
							Grimsby T	69	—
							Blackpool	101	1
							Carlisle U (loan)	6	—
							Carlisle U	40	1
							Hartlepool U (loan)	11	—
BURKE David	5 10	11 06	D	6 8 60	Liverpool	Apprentice	Bolton W	69	1
							Huddersfield T	189	3
							Crystal Palace	81	—
							Bolton W	106	—
							Blackpool	23	—
BURKE Mark *	5 10	11 08	F	12 2 69	Solihull	Apprentice	Aston Villa	7	—
							Middlesbrough	57	6
							Darlington (loan)	5	1
							Ipswich T (loan)	—	—
							Wolverhampton W	68	11
							Luton T (loan)	3	—
							Port Vale	15	2
BURKE Robert ‡	5 11	11 06	M	19 11 75	Burton	Trainee	**Stoke C**	—	—
BURKILL Matthew *	5 10	10 00	F	9 3 76	Doncaster	Trainee	**Sheffield W**	—	—
BURLEY Craig	6 1	11 07	M	24 9 71	Ayr	Trainee	**Chelsea**	60	5
BURLEY George	5 10	11 00	D	3 6 56	Cumnock		Ipswich T	394	5
							Sunderland	54	—
							Gillingham	46	2
							Motherwell	54	—
							Ayr U	67	—
							Falkirk	1	—
							Motherwell	5	—
							Colchester U	7	—
BURNDRED John ‡	5 7	10 00	F	23 3 68	Stoke	Knypersley Vic	**Port Vale**	1	—
BURNETT Wayne	5 11	12 01	M	4 9 71	London	Trainee	Leyton Orient	40	—
							Blackburn R	—	—
							Plymouth Arg	64	3
BURNHAM Jason	5 10	13 03	D	8 5 73	Mansfield	Notts County	Northampton T	88	2
							Chester C	24	—
BURNS Chris	6 0	12 00	M	9 11 67	Manchester	Cheltenham T	Portsmouth	90	9
							Swansea C (loan)	4	—
							Bournemouth (loan)	14	1
							Swansea C	5	—
							Northampton T	17	2
BURNS John	5 8	10 08	M	4 12 77	Dublin	Trainee	**Nottingham F**	—	—

Player	Ht	Wt	Pos	Birth Date	Birth Place	Source	Clubs	League App	League Gls
BURRIDGE John *	5 11	13 03	G	3 12 51	Workington	Apprentice	Workington	27	—
							Blackpool	134	—
							Aston Villa	65	—
							Southend U (loan)	6	—
							Crystal Palace	88	—
							QPR	39	—
							Wolverhampton W	74	—
							Derby Co (loan)	6	—
							Sheffield U	109	—
							Southampton	62	—
							Newcastle U	67	—
							Hibernian	65	—
							Newcastle U	—	—
							Scarborough	3	—
							Lincoln C	4	—
							Aberdeen	3	—
							Newcastle U	—	—
							Dumbarton	3	—
							Falkirk	3	—
							Manchester C	4	—
BURROWS David	5 10	11 08	D	25 10 68	Dudley	Apprentice	WBA	46	1
							Liverpool	146	3
							West Ham U	29	1
							Everton	19	—
							Coventry C	11	—
BURROWS Marc	5 9	10 05	D	20 12 75	Sheffield	Trainee	**Sheffield W**	—	—
BURTON Deon	5 8	10 10	F	25 10 76	Ashford	Trainee	**Portsmouth**	9	2
BURTON Mark	5 7	11 11	M	7 5 73	Barnsley	Trainee	**Barnsley**	5	—
BURTON Nick ‡	5 11	11 12	D	10 2 75	Bury St Edmunds	Portsmouth	**Torquay U**	16	2
BUSHELL Steve	5 9	11 06	M	28 12 72	Manchester	Trainee	**York C**	80	5
BUSST Dave	6 1	12 10	D	30 6 67	Birmingham	Moor Green	**Coventry C**	33	2
BUTLER John	5 11	11 07	D	7 2 62	Liverpool	Prescot Cables	Wigan Ath	245	15
							Stoke C	262	7
BUTLER Lee	6 1	14 04	G	30 5 66	Sheffield	Haworth Colliery	Lincoln C	30	—
							Aston Villa	8	—
							Hull C (loan)	4	—
							Barnsley	117	—
BUTLER Martin	5 11	11 07	F	15 9 74	Dudley	Trainee	**Walsall**	23	3
BUTLER Neal ‡			M	11 9 75	Newport Pagnall	Luton T	**Colchester U**	—	—
BUTLER Paul	6 2	13 00	D	2 11 72	Manchester	Trainee	**Rochdale**	120	7
BUTLER Peter	5 9	11 02	M	27 8 66	Halifax	Apprentice	Huddersfield T	5	—
							Cambridge U (loan)	14	1
							Bury	11	—
							Cambridge U	55	9
							Southend U	142	9
							Huddersfield T (loan)	7	—
							West Ham U	70	3
							Notts Co	20	—
BUTLER Steve	6 2	13 00	F	27 1 62	Birmingham	Wokingham	Brentford	97	44
						Maidstone U (1986)	Watford	62	9
							Bournemouth (loan)	1	—
							Cambridge U	93	41
BUTLER Tony	6 2	11 12	D	28 9 72	Stockport	Trainee	**Gillingham**	112	3
BUTT Nicky	5 10	10 10	M	21 1 75	Manchester	Trainee	**Manchester U**	24	1
BUTTERFIELD Tim *	5 11	11 12	M	18 10 74	Sheffield	Trainee	**Sheffield U**	—	—
BUTTERS Guy	6 3	13 00	D	30 10 69	Hillingdon	Trainee	Tottenham H	35	1
							Southend U (loan)	16	3
							Portsmouth	110	4
							Oxford U (loan)	3	1
BUTTERWORTH Ian ‡	6 1	12 12	D	25 1 64	Crewe	Apprentice	Coventry C	90	—
							Nottingham F	27	—
							Norwich C	235	4

Player	Ht	Wt	Pos	Birth Date	Birth Place	Source	Clubs	League App	League Gls
BYFIELD Darren	5 10	11 00	F	29 9 76	Birmingham	Trainee	**Aston Villa**	—	—
BYNG David §	6 1	13 00	F	9 7 77	Coventry	Trainee	**Torquay U**	10	3
BYRNE John	6 0	12 13	F	1 2 61	Manchester	Apprentice	York C	175	55
							QPR	126	30
						Le Havre	Brighton	51	14
							Sunderland	33	8
							Millwall	17	1
							Brighton (loan)	7	2
							Oxford U	55	18
							Brighton	14	4
BYRNE Paul (on loan from Celtic)	5 11	13 00	M	30 6 72	Dublin		**Brighton**	8	1
BYRNE Ray ‡	6 1	11 02	D	4 7 72	Newry	Newry	Nottingham F	—	—
							Northampton T	2	—
BYRNE Wesley	5 9	11 03	D	9 2 77	Dublin	Trainee	**Middlesbrough**	—	—
CADETTE Richard	5 7	12 00	F	21 3 65	Hammersmith	Wembley	Orient	21	4
							Southend U	90	48
							Sheffield U	28	7
							Brentford	87	20
							Bournemouth (loan)	8	1
							Falkirk	92	32
							Millwall	16	4
CAESAR Gus	6 0	12 09	D	5 3 66	London	Apprentice	Arsenal	44	—
							QPR (loan)	5	—
							Cambridge U	—	—
							Bristol C	10	—
							Airdrieonians	57	1
							Colchester U	39	1
CAHILL Ollie	5 10	11 02	F	29 9 75	Clonmel	Clonmel	**Northampton T**	8	1
CAIG Tony	6 0	13 04	G	11 4 74	Whitehaven	Trainee	**Carlisle U**	61	—
CALDERWOOD Colin	6 0	12 12	D	20 1 65	Stranraer	Amateur	Mansfield T	100	1
							Swindon T	330	20
							Tottenham H	62	2
CALDWELL Peter *	6 1	13 00	G	5 6 72	Dorchester	Trainee	**QPR**	—	—
CALVERT Mark	5 9	11 08	M	11 9 70	Consett	Trainee	Hull C	30	1
							Scarborough	72	5
CAME Mark	6 1	13 00	D	14 9 61	Exeter	Winsford U	Bolton W	195	7
							Chester C	47	1
							Exeter C	32	1
CAMPBELL Corey	5 11	11 06	D	6 3 76	London	Trainee	**Brentford**	—	—
CAMPBELL Dave ‡	5 10	11 02	M	2 6 65	Eglinton	Oxford BC	Nottingham F	41	3
							Notts Co (loan)	18	2
							Charlton Ath	30	1
							Plymouth Arg (loan)	1	—
							Bradford C	35	4
							Shamrock R (loan)	31	5
							WBA	—	—
							Rotherham U	1	—
							Burnley	8	—
							Lincoln C (loan)	4	1
							Wigan Ath	7	—
							Cambridge U	1	—
CAMPBELL Jamie *	6 1	11 03	F	21 10 72	Birmingham	Trainee	**Luton T**	36	1
							Mansfield U (loan)	3	1
							Cambridge U (loan)	12	—
CAMPBELL Kevin	6 1	13 08	F	4 2 70	Lambeth	Trainee	**Arsenal**	166	46
							Leyton Orient (loan)	16	9
							Leicester C (loan)	11	5
CAMPBELL Sol	6 2	14 01	M	18 9 74	Newham	Trainee	**Tottenham H**	65	1
CANHAM Scott	5 7	11 07	M	5 11 74	London	Trainee	**West Ham U**	—	—
CANHAM Tony *	5 8	11 04	M	8 6 60	Leeds	Harrogate Railway	**York C**	347	57

Player	Ht	Wt	Pos	Birth Date	Birth Place	Source	Clubs	League App	League Gls
CANTONA Eric	6 2	14 00	F	24 5 66	Paris		Auxerre	13	2
							Martigues	—	—
							Auxerre	68	21
							Marseille	22	5
							Bordeaux	11	6
							Montpellier	33	10
							Marseille	18	8
							Nimes	17	2
							Leeds U	28	9
							Manchester U	77	39
CAPLETON Mel	5 11	12 00	G	24 10 73	London	Trainee	Southend U	—	—
							Blackpool	10	—
CARBON Matthew	6 2	11 13	D	8 6 75	Nottingham	Trainee	**Lincoln C**	43	7
CARBONE Anthony	5 10	11 06	M	13 10 74	Perth	Perth Italia	**Nottingham F**	—	—
CAREY Alan	5 7	10 10	D	21 8 75	Greenwich	Trainee	**Reading**	3	—
CAREY Brian	6 2	14 04	D	31 5 68	Cork	Cork C	Manchester U	—	—
							Wrexham (loan)	3	—
							Wrexham (loan)	13	1
							Leicester C	39	—
CAREY Shaun	5 9	10 06	M	13 5 76	Kettering	Trainee	**Norwich C**	—	—
CARMICHAEL Matt *	6 0	12 04	F	13 5 64	Singapore	Army	Lincoln C	133	18
							Scunthorpe U	62	20
							Barnet (loan)	3	—
							Preston NE	10	3
CARPENTER Richard	5 10	13 00	M	30 9 72	Sheppey	Trainee	**Gillingham**	109	4
CARR Darren	6 2	13 02	D	4 9 68	Bristol	Trainee	Bristol R	30	—
							Newport Co	9	—
							Sheffield U	13	1
							Crewe Alex	104	5
							Chesterfield	63	3
CARR Franz	5 7	10 12	M	24 9 66	Preston	Apprentice	Blackburn R	—	—
							Nottingham F	131	17
							Sheffield W (loan)	12	—
							West Ham U (loan)	3	—
							Newcastle U	25	3
							Sheffield U	18	4
							Leicester C (loan)	13	1
							Aston Villa	2	—
CARR Steve	5 9	12 02	D	29 8 76	Dublin	Trainee	**Tottenham H**	1	—
CARRAGHER Matthew	5 9	10 07	D	14 1 76	Liverpool	Trainee	**Wigan Ath**	73	—
CARROLL Dave	6 0	11 09	F	20 9 66	Paisley	Ruislip Manor	**Wycombe W**	82	12
CARRUTHERS Martin	5 11	11 10	F	7 8 72	Nottingham	Trainee	Aston Villa	4	—
							Hull C (loan)	13	6
							Stoke C	66	10
CARSLEY Lee	5 11	11 12	D	28 2 74	Birmingham	Trainee	**Derby Co**	23	2
CARSS Anthony *	5 11	12 00	M	31 3 76	Alnwick	Bradford C	**Blackburn R**	—	—
CARTER Danny	5 11	11 12	M	29 6 69	Hackney	Billericay	**Leyton Orient**	188	22
CARTER Jimmy *	5 10	11 01	M	9 11 65	London	Apprentice	Crystal Palace	—	—
							QPR	—	—
							Millwall	110	10
							Liverpool	5	—
							Arsenal	25	2
							Oxford U (loan)	5	—
							Oxford U (loan)	4	—
CARTER Mark	5 10	12 06	F	17 12 60	Liverpool	Runcorn	Barnet	82	30
							Bury	62	34
CARTER Simon *	6 0	11 04	D	8 3 76	Kidderminster	Trainee	**Sheffield W**	—	—

Player	Ht	Wt	Pos	Birth Date	Birth Place	Source	Clubs	League App	League Gls
CARTER Tim *	6 2	13 11	G	5 10 67	Bristol	Apprentice	Bristol R	47	—
							Newport Co (loan)	1	—
							Carlisle U (loan)	4	—
							Sunderland	37	—
							Bristol C (loan)	3	—
							Birmingham C (loan)	2	—
							Hartlepool U	18	—
							Millwall	4	—
CARTWRIGHT Lee	5 10	11 00	M	19 9 72	Rossendale	Trainee	**Preston NE**	156	10
CARTWRIGHT Mark	6 1	12 05	G	13 1 73	Chester	York C	**Wrexham**	—	—
CASE Jimmy *	5 9	12 12	M	18 5 54	Liverpool	South Liverpool	Liverpool	186	23
							Brighton	127	10
							Southampton	215	10
							Bournemouth	40	1
							Halifax T	21	2
							Wrexham	4	—
							Darlington	1	—
						Sittingbourne	**Brighton**	30	—
CASH Stuart ‡	5 10	11 11	D	5 9 65	Tipton	Halesowen	Nottingham F	—	—
							Rotherham U (loan)	8	1
							Brentford (loan)	11	—
							Shrewsbury T (loan)	8	1
							Chesterfield	29	—
							Wycombe W	—	—
CASKEY Darren	5 8	11 09	M	21 8 74	Basildon	Trainee	**Tottenham H**	29	4
CASPER Chris	6 0	11 02	D	28 4 75	Burnley	Trainee	**Manchester U**	—	—
CASS Jamie *	5 4	9 03	M	24 1 76	Hull	Trainee	**Hull C**	—	—
CASSIDY Jamie	5 9	10 07	M	21 11 77	Liverpool	Trainee	**Liverpool**	—	—
CASSIN Graham	5 8	10 07	F	24 3 78	Dublin	Trainee	**Blackburn R**	—	—
CASTLE Steve	5 11	12 10	M	17 5 66	Barkingside	Apprentice	Orient	243	55
							Plymouth Arg	101	35
CASTLEDINE Gary ‡	5 8	11 12	F	27 3 70	Dumfries	Shirebrook	**Mansfield T**	66	3
CASTLEDINE Stewart	6 0	12 00	M	22 1 73	London	Trainee	**Wimbledon**	11	2
CAWLEY Peter	6 3	14 06	D	15 9 65	London	Chertsey	Wimbledon	1	—
							Bristol R (loan)	10	—
							Fulham (loan)	5	—
							Bristol R	3	—
							Southend U	7	1
							Exeter C	7	—
							Barnet	3	—
							Colchester U	83	6
CECERE Michele	6 0	11 04	F	4 1 68	Chester	Apprentice	Oldham Ath	52	8
							Huddersfield T	54	8
							Stockport Co (loan)	1	—
							Walsall	112	32
							Exeter C	30	10
CERAOLO Mark *			F	10 11 75	Birkenhead		**Crewe Alex**	—	—
CHALK Martyn	5 6	10 00	F	30 8 69	Louth	Louth U	Derby Co	7	1
							Stockport Co	33	6
CHALLENDER Greg ‡	6 0	12 08	D	5 2 73	Rochdale	Mossley	**Preston NE**	10	2
CHALLINER Dave	6 1	12 00	D	2 10 75	Chester	Brombrough Pool	**Tranmere R**	—	—
CHALLINOR Paul	6 1	12 02	D	6 4 76	Newcastle under Lyne	Trainee	**Birmingham C**	—	—
CHALLIS Trevor	5 7	10 00	D	23 10 75	Paddington	Trainee	**QPR**	—	—
CHAMBERLAIN Alec	6 2	13 09	G	20 6 64	March	Ramsey T	Ipswich T	—	—
							Colchester U	184	—
							Everton	—	—
							Tranmere R (loan)	15	—
							Luton T	138	—
							Chelsea (loan)	—	—
							Sunderland	61	—
							Liverpool (loan)	—	—

				Birth				League	
Player	*Ht*	*Wt*	*Pos*	*Date*	*Place*	*Source*	*Clubs*	*App*	*Gls*
CHAMBERLAIN Mark *	5 9	10 07	M	19 11 61	Stoke	Apprentice	Port Vale	96	17
							Stoke C	112	17
							Sheffield W	66	8
							Portsmouth	167	20
							Brighton	19	2
CHAMBERS Leroy	5 11	12 00	F	25 10 72	Sheffield	Trainee	Sheffield W	—	—
							Chester C	13	—
CHAMP Paul *	5 10	12 12	D	18 12 75	Colchester	Trainee	**Colchester U**	—	—
CHANDLER Dean	6 1	11 02	D	6 5 76	Ilford	Trainee	**Charlton Ath**	1	1
CHANNING Justin	5 11	11 07	D	19 11 68	Reading	Apprentice	QPR	55	5
							Bristol R	94	10
CHAPMAN Danny *	5 10	11 06	M	21 11 74	Peckham	Trainee	**Millwall**	12	—
CHAPMAN Gary *	5 8	11 07	F	1 5 64	Bradford	Frickley Ath	Bradford C	5	—
							Notts Co	25	4
							Mansfield T (loan)	6	—
							Exeter C	24	5
							Torquay U	8	—
							Darlington	74	9
CHAPMAN Ian	5 9	12 08	M	31 5 70	Brighton	Trainee	**Brighton**	245	11
CHAPMAN Lee	6 2	13 00	F	5 12 59	Lincoln	Amateur	Stoke C	99	34
							Plymouth Arg (loan)	4	—
							Arsenal	23	4
							Sunderland	15	3
							Sheffield W	149	63
						Niort	Nottingham F	48	15
							Leeds U	137	62
							Portsmouth	5	2
							West Ham U	40	7
							Southend U (loan)	1	1
							Ipswich T	16	1
CHAPPLE Phil	6 2	12 07	D	26 11 66	Norwich	Apprentice	Norwich C	—	—
							Cambridge U	187	19
							Charlton Ath	65	7
CHAPPLE Shaun	5 11	12 03	M	14 2 73	Swansea	Trainee	**Swansea C**	63	7
CHARLERY Ken	6 1	13 03	F	28 11 64	Stepney	Beckton U	Maidstone U	59	11
							Peterborough U	51	19
							Watford	48	13
							Peterborough U	70	24
CHARLES Gary	5 9	10 13	D	13 4 70	London	Trainee	Nottingham F	56	1
							Leicester C (loan)	8	—
							Derby Co	61	3
							Aston Villa	16	—
CHARLES Steve *	5 11	11 12	M	10 5 60	Sheffield	Sheffield Univ	Sheffield U	123	10
							Wrexham	113	37
							Mansfield T	237	39
							Scunthorpe U (loan)	4	—
							Scarborough	93	15
CHARLTON Simon	5 8	11 04	D	25 10 71	Huddersfield	Trainee	Huddersfield T	124	1
							Southampton	58	2
CHARNOCK Phil	5 11	11 02	M	14 2 75	Southport	Trainee	**Liverpool**	—	—
CHEESEWRIGHT John *	6 0	13 11	G	12 1 73	Hornchurch	Tottenham H	Southend U	—	—
							Birmingham C	1	—
						Braintree T	**Colchester U**	40	—
CHEETHAM Michael	5 9	12 03	M	30 6 67	Amsterdam	Army	Ipswich T	4	—
							Cambridge U	132	22
							Chesterfield	5	—
							Colchester U	9	1
CHENERY Ben	6 0	12 00	D	28 1 77	Ipswich	Trainee	**Luton T**	—	—
CHERRY Steve *	6 1	13 00	G	5 8 60	Nottingham	Apprentice	Derby Co	77	—
							Port Vale (loan)	4	—
							Walsall	71	—
							Plymouth Arg	73	—
							Chesterfield (loan)	10	—
							Notts Co	266	—

Player	Ht	Wt	Pos	Birth Date	Birth Place	Source	Clubs	League App	League Gls
CHETTLE Steve	6 1	13 03	D	27 9 68	Nottingham	Apprentice	**Nottingham F**	256	7
CHILDS Gary	5 7	10 08	M	19 4 64	Birmingham	Apprentice	WBA	3	—
							Walsall	131	17
							Birmingham C	55	2
							Grimsby T	171	22
CHISHOLM Craig	5 10	10 04	M	21 9 77	Glasgow	Trainee	**Blackburn R**	—	—
CHIVERS Gary ‡	5 11	11 05	D	15 5 60	Stockwell	Apprentice	Chelsea	133	4
							Swansea C	10	—
							QPR	60	—
							Watford	14	—
							Brighton	217	13
							Bournemouth	31	2
CHRISTIE Iyseden			F	14 11 76	Coventry	Trainee	**Coventry C**	—	—
CLAPHAM Jamie	5 9	10 08	M	7 12 75	Lincoln	Trainee	**Tottenham H**	—	—
CLARIDGE Steve	5 11	11 08	F	10 4 66	Portsmouth	Fareham	Bournemouth	7	1
						Weymouth	Crystal Palace	—	—
							Aldershot	62	19
							Cambridge U	79	28
							Luton T	16	2
							Cambridge U	53	18
							Birmingham C	60	27
CLARK Billy	6 0	12 03	D	19 5 67	Christchurch	Trainee	Bournemouth	4	—
							Bristol R	182	11
CLARK Howard *	6 0	12 07	D	19 9 68	Coventry	Apprentice	Coventry C	20	1
							Darlington (loan)	5	—
							Shrewsbury T	56	—
							Hereford U	55	7
CLARK John (To Falkirk)	6 0	13 01	D	22 9 64	Edinburgh	S Form	Dundee U	242	19
							Stoke C	17	—
CLARK Lee	5 7	11 07	M	27 10 72	Wallsend	Trainee	**Newcastle U**	142	19
CLARK Richard	5 11	12 04	G	6 4 77	Nuneaton	Trainee	**Nottingham F**	—	—
CLARK Simon	6 1	12 06	D	12 3 67	London	Stevenage Bor	**Peterborough U**	33	—
CLARK Tony §			F	7 4 77	London		**Wycombe W**	1	—
CLARKE Adrian	5 10	11 00	F	28 9 74	Suffolk	Trainee	**Arsenal**	1	—
CLARKE Andy	5 10	11 07	F	22 7 67	London	Barnet	**Wimbledon**	127	14
CLARKE Chris	6 1	12 10	G	1 5 74	Barnsley	Trainee	Bolton W	—	—
							Rochdale	24	—
CLARKE Dean §	5 9	10 05	F	28 7 77	Hereford	Trainee	**Hereford U**	6	—
CLARKE Matthew	6 3	11 04	G	3 11 73	Sheffield	Trainee	**Rotherham U**	84	—
CLARKE Steve	5 10	10 02	D	29 8 63	Saltcoats	Beith J	St Mirren	151	6
							Chelsea	251	6
CLARKE Tim	6 3	13 07	G	19 9 68	Stourbridge	Halesowen	Coventry C	—	—
							Huddersfield T	70	—
							Rochdale (loan)	2	—
						Halesowen	**Shrewsbury T**	16	—
CLARKE Wayne *	6 0	11 08	F	28 2 61	Wolverhampton	Apprentice	Wolverhampton W	148	30
							Birmingham C	92	38
							Everton	57	18
							Leicester C	11	1
							Manchester C	21	2
							Shrewsbury T (loan)	7	6
							Stoke C (loan)	9	3
							Wolverhampton W (loan)	1	—
							Walsall	39	21
							Shrewsbury T	59	22
CLARKSON Ian	5 10	12 00	D	4 12 70	Birmingham	Trainee	Birmingham C	136	—
							Stoke C	32	—
CLARKSON Phil	5 8	11 02	M	13 11 68	Hambleton	Fleetwood	**Crewe Alex**	93	27

Player	Ht	Wt	Pos	Birth Date	Birth Place	Source	Clubs	League App	League Gls
CLAYTON Gary	5 10	12 03	M	2 2 63	Sheffield	Burton Alb	Doncaster R	35	5
							Cambridge U	179	17
							Peterborough U (loan)	4	—
							Huddersfield T	19	1
CLEGG David			M	23 10 76	Liverpool	Trainee	**Liverpool**	—	—
CLEMENCE Stephen			M	31 3 78	Liverpool	Trainee	**Tottenham H**	—	—
CLIFFORD Mark §			D	11 9 77	Nottingham	Trainee	**Mansfield T**	1	—
CLODE Mark	5 10	10 10	D	24 2 73	Plymouth	Trainee	Plymouth Arg	—	—
							Swansea C	61	2
CLOUGH Nigel	5 9	11 04	M	19 3 66	Sunderland	AC Hunters	Nottingham F	311	101
							Liverpool	37	7
CLYDE Darran	6 4	13 00	D	26 3 76	N Ireland	Trainee	**Barnsley**	—	—
COADY Lewis §	6 1	11 05	F	20 9 76	Liverpool	Trainee	**Wrexham**	2	—
COATES Jonathan	5 8	10 04	F	27 6 75	Swansea	Trainee	**Swansea C**	9	1
COATSWORTH Gary ‡	6 0	13 01	D	7 10 68	Sunderland		Barnsley	6	—
							Darlington	22	2
							Leicester C	32	4
COCKERILL Glenn	5 10	12 06	M	25 8 59	Grimsby	Louth U	Lincoln C	71	10
							Swindon T	26	1
							Lincoln C	115	25
							Sheffield U	62	10
							Southampton	287	32
							Leyton Orient	52	6
CODNER Robert *	5 11	11 08	M	23 1 65	Walthamstow	Barnet	**Brighton**	266	39
COLCOMBE Scott *	5 6	9 13	F	15 12 71	West Bromwich	Trainee	WBA	—	—
							Torquay U	89	1
COLDICOTT Stacy	5 11	11 02	D	29 4 74	Worcester	Trainee	**WBA**	30	—
COLE Andy	5 11	11 02	F	15 10 71	Nottingham	Trainee	Arsenal	1	—
							Fulham (loan)	13	3
							Bristol C (loan)	12	8
							Bristol C	29	12
							Newcastle U	70	55
							Manchester U	18	12
COLEMAN Chris	6 2	14 06	D	10 6 70	Swansea	Apprentice	Swansea C	160	2
							Crystal Palace	137	13
COLEMAN Simon	6 0	10 09	D	13 3 68	Worksop		Mansfield T	96	7
							Middlesbrough	55	2
							Derby Co	70	2
							Sheffield W	16	1
							Bolton W	22	4
COLGAN Nick	6 1	12 00	G	19 9 73	Eire	Drogheda	**Chelsea**	—	—
							Crewe Alex (loan)	—	—
							Grimsby T (loan)	—	—
COLKIN Lee	5 11	12 00	D	15 7 74	Nuneaton	Trainee	**Northampton T**	69	2
COLL Owen	6 1	11 07	D	9 4 76	Donegal	Amateur	**Tottenham H**	—	—
COLLETT Andy	6 0	13 02	G	28 10 73	Middlesbrough	Trainee	Middlesbrough	2	—
							Bristol R	4	—
COLLIER Danny	6 3	12 08	D	15 1 74	Eccles	Trainee	Wolverhampton W	—	—
							Crewe Alex	5	—
COLLIER Darren *	5 11	12 00	G	1 12 67	Stockton	Middlesbrough	Blackburn R	27	—
							Darlington	44	—
COLLINS David *	6 1	12 10	D	30 10 71	Dublin	Trainee	Liverpool	—	—
							Wigan Ath (loan)	9	—
							Oxford U	42	—
COLLINS Sam	6 2	13 05	D	5 6 77	Pontefract	Trainee	**Huddersfield T**	—	—
COLLINS Simon	5 11	13 00	M	16 12 73	Pontefract	Trainee	**Huddersfield T**	6	—
COLLINS Wayne	6 0	12 00	M	4 3 69	Manchester	Winsford U	**Crewe Alex**	75	13

Player	Ht	Wt	Pos	Birth Date	Birth Place	Source	Clubs	League App	League Gls
COLLYMORE Stan	6 2	13 11	F	22 1 71	Stone	Stafford R	Crystal Palace	20	1
							Southend U	30	15
							Nottingham F	65	41
COMYN Andy	6 1	11 13	D	2 6 68	Manchester	Alvechurch	Aston Villa	15	—
							Derby Co	63	1
							Plymouth Arg	76	5
CONNELL Graham *	5 10	11 05	M	31 10 74	Glasgow	Trainee	**Ipswich T**	—	—
CONNELLY Dino ‡	5 9	10 08	M	6 1 70	St. Helier	Celtic BC	Arsenal	—	—
							Barnsley	13	—
							Wigan Ath (loan)	12	2
							Carlisle U (loan)	3	—
							Wigan Ath	20	1
							Stockport Co	—	—
CONNELLY Sean	5 10	11 10	D	26 6 70	Sheffield	Hallam	**Stockport Co**	78	—
CONNOLLY David	5 8	10 09	F	6 6 77	Willesden	Trainee	**Watford**	2	—
CONNOLLY Karl	5 9	11 00	F	9 2 70	Prescot	Napoli (Liverpool Sunday League)	**Wrexham**	162	29
CONNOR James	6 0	13 00	M	22 8 74	Middlesbrough	Trainee	**Millwall**	1	—
CONROY Mike	6 0	12 07	F	31 12 65	Glasgow	Apprentice	Coventry C	—	—
							Clydebank	114	38
							St Mirren	10	1
							Reading	80	7
							Burnley	77	30
							Preston NE	57	22
CONWAY Paul	6 1	12 07	M	17 4 70	London	Oldham Ath	**Carlisle U**	42	10
COOK Andy	5 9	12 00	D	10 8 69	Romsey	Apprentice	Southampton	16	1
							Exeter C	70	1
							Swansea C	29	—
COOK Anthony §			M	17 9 76	Hemel Hempstead	Trainee	**Colchester U**	2	—
COOK Mitch *	6 0	12 00	M	15 10 61	Scarborough	Scarborough	Darlington	34	4
							Middlesbrough	6	—
							Scarborough	81	10
							Halifax T	54	2
							Scarborough (loan)	9	1
							Darlington (loan)	9	—
							Darlington	27	3
							Blackpool	68	—
							Hartlepool U	24	—
COOK Paul	5 11	10 10	M	22 2 67	Liverpool	Marine	Wigan Ath	83	14
							Norwich C	6	—
							Wolverhampton W	193	19
							Coventry C	34	3
COOKE Andrew	6 0	12 00	F	2 1 74	Shrewsbury	Newtown	**Burnley**	—	—
COOKE Terry	5 7	9 09	F	5 8 76	Marston Green	Trainee	**Manchester U**	—	—
COOKSEY Scott	6 3	13 10	G	24 6 72	Birmingham	Bromsgrove R	**Peterborough U**	15	—
COOPER Colin	5 9	11 02	D	28 2 67	Durham		Middlesbrough	188	6
							Millwall	77	6
							Nottingham F	72	8
COOPER David *	6 0	12 00	D	7 3 73	Welwyn	Luton T	**Exeter C**	48	—
COOPER Gary	5 8	11 03	D	20 11 65	Edgware	Fisher Ath	Maidstone U	60	7
							Peterborough U	88	10
							Birmingham C	44	2
COOPER Geoff ‡	5 10	11 00	M	27 12 60	Kingston	Bognor Regis	Brighton	7	—
						Barnet	Barnet	31	1
							Wycombe W	—	—
							Barnet	37	3
COOPER Kevin	5 6	10 07	M	8 2 75	Derby	Trainee	**Derby Co**	1	—

Player	Ht	Wt	Pos	Birth Date	Birth Place	Source	Clubs	League App	League Gls
COOPER Mark	6 2	13 04	F	5 4 67	Cambridge	Apprentice	Cambridge U	71	17
							Tottenham H	—	—
							Shrewsbury T	6	2
							Gillingham	49	11
							Leyton Orient	150	45
							Barnet	34	11
COOPER Mark	5 8	11 04	M	18 12 68	Wakefield	Trainee	Bristol C	—	—
							Exeter C	50	12
							Southend U (loan)	5	—
							Birmingham C	39	4
							Fulham	14	—
							Huddersfield T (loan)	10	4
							Wycombe W	2	1
							Exeter C	61	14
COOPER Steve (To Airdrie)	5 11	10 12	F	22 6 64	Birmingham	Moor Green	Birmingham C	—	—
							Halifax T (loan)	7	1
							Mansfield T (loan)	—	—
							Newport Co	38	11
							Plymouth Arg	73	15
							Barnsley	77	13
							Tranmere R	32	3
							Peterborough U (loan)	9	—
							Wigan Ath (loan)	4	—
							York C	38	6
CORAZZIN Carlo	5 9	12 04	F	25 12 71	Canada	Vancouver 86ers	**Cambridge U**	74	29
CORDEN Wayne			M	1 11 75	Leek	Trainee	**Port Vale**	1	—
CORK Alan ‡	6 0	14 01	F	4 3 59	Derby	Amateur	Derby C	—	—
							Lincoln C (loan)	5	—
							Wimbledon	430	145
							Sheffield U	54	7
							Fulham	15	3
CORNFORTH John	6 1	12 11	M	7 10 67	Whitley Bay	Apprentice	Sunderland	32	2
							Doncaster R (loan)	7	3
							Shrewsbury T (loan)	3	—
							Lincoln C (loan)	9	1
							Swansea C	132	14
CORNWELL John ‡	6 4	13 00	M	13 10 64	Bethnal Green	Apprentice	Orient	202	35
							Newcastle U	33	1
							Swindon T	25	—
							Southend U	101	5
							Cardiff C (loan)	5	2
							Brentford (loan)	4	—
							Northampton T (loan)	13	1
COSTELLO Lorcan	5 9	11 02	D	11 11 76	Dublin	Trainee	**Coventry C**	—	—
COTON Tony	6 2	13 07	G	19 5 61	Tamworth	Mile Oak	Birmingham C	94	—
							Hereford U (loan)	—	—
							Watford	233	—
							Manchester C	164	—
COTTEE Tony	5 7	11 03	F	11 7 65	West Ham	Apprentice	West Ham U	212	92
							Everton	184	72
							West Ham U	31	13
COTTERELL Leo	5 9	10 00	D	2 9 74	Cambridge	Trainee	**Ipswich T**	2	—
COTTERILL Steve	6 1	12 05	F	20 7 64	Cheltenham	Burton A	Wimbledon	17	6
							Brighton (loan)	11	4
							Bournemouth	45	15
COUGHLIN Russell *	5 8	11 12	M	15 2 60	Swansea	Apprentice	Manchester C	—	—
							Blackburn R	24	—
							Carlisle U	130	13
							Plymouth Arg	131	18
							Blackpool	102	8
							Shrewsbury T (loan)	5	—
							Swansea C	101	2
							Exeter C	60	—
COUSIN Scott ‡			G	31 1 75	Leeds	Trainee	**Leeds U**	—	—
COUSINS Jason	5 11	12 06	D	14 10 70	Hayes	Trainee	Brentford	21	—
						Wycombe W	**Wycombe W**	78	3
COUZENS Andrew	5 9	11 06	D	4 6 75	Shipley	Trainee	**Leeds U**	4	—

Player	Ht	Wt	Pos	Birth Date	Birth Place	Source	Clubs	League App	League Gls
COWAN Tom	5 8	10 08	D	28 8 69	Bellshill	Netherdale BC	Clyde	16	2
							Rangers	12	—
							Sheffield U	45	—
							Stoke C (loan)	14	—
							Huddersfield T (loan)	10	—
							Huddersfield T	37	2
COWANS Gordon	5 7	9 08	M	27 10 58	Durham	Apprentice	Aston Villa	286	42
							Bari	94	3
							Aston Villa	117	7
							Blackburn R	50	2
							Aston Villa	11	—
							Derby Co	36	—
							Wolverhampton W	21	—
COWE Steven	5 7	10 02	M	29 9 74	Gloucester	Trainee	**Aston Villa**	—	—
COWLING Lee	5 8	9 04	M	22 9 77	Doncaster	Trainee	**Nottingham F**	—	—
COX Ian	6 0	12 00	M	25 3 71	Croydon	Carshalton Ath	**Crystal Palace**	11	—
COX Neil	6 0	13 02	D	8 10 71	Scunthorpe	Trainee	Scunthorpe U	17	1
							Aston Villa	42	3
							Middlesbrough	40	1
COX Paul *	5 11	11 12	D	1 1 72	Nottingham	Trainee	**Notts Co**	44	1
							Hull C (loan)	5	1
COYLE Owen	5 11	10 05	F	14 7 66	Glasgow	Renfrew YM	Dumbarton	103	36
							Clydebank	63	33
							Airdrieonians	123	50
							Bolton W	49	12
COYNE Danny	6 0	12 07	G	27 8 73	Prestatyn	Trainee	**Tranmere R**	11	—
CRADDOCK Jody	6 0	12 04	D	25 7 75	Redditch	Christchurch	**Cambridge U**	58	—
CRAGGS Graham	6 1	13 06	D	5 6 76	Ashington	Trainee	**Blackpool**	—	—
CRANSON Ian	6 0	13 04	D	2 7 64	Easington	Apprentice	Ipswich T	131	5
							Sheffield W	30	—
							Stoke C	193	8
CRAWFORD James	5 11	11 06	M	1 5 73	USA	Bohemians	**Newcastle U**	—	—
CRAWLEY David ‡	6 0	12 00	F	10 6 77	Dundalk	Dundalk	**Manchester C**	—	—
CREANEY Gerry	5 10	10 10	F	13 4 70	Coatbridge	Celtic BC	Celtic	113	36
							Portsmouth	57	29
CREASER Glyn	6 4	14 10	D	1 9 59	London	Barnet	**Wycombe W**	19	2
CRICHTON Paul	6 1	12 05	G	3 10 68	Pontefract	Apprentice	Nottingham F	—	—
							Notts Co (loan)	5	—
							Darlington (loan)	5	—
							Peterborough U (loan)	4	—
							Darlington (loan)	3	—
							Swindon T (loan)	4	—
							Rotherham U (loan)	6	—
							Torquay U (loan)	13	—
							Peterborough U	47	—
							Doncaster R	77	—
							Grimsby T	89	—
CROCKER Marcus *	5 10	12 03	F	8 10 74	Plymouth	Trainee	**Plymouth Arg**	10	—
CROFT Brian *	5 9	10 10	M	27 9 67	Chester	Trainee	Chester C	59	3
							Cambridge U	17	2
							Chester C	114	3
							QPR	—	—
							Shrewsbury T (loan)	4	—
CROFT Gary	5 9	10 08	D	17 2 74	Burton-on-Trent	Trainee	**Grimsby T**	113	2
CROOK Ian	5 8	10 06	M	18 1 63	Romford	Apprentice	Tottenham H	20	1
							Norwich C	276	14
CROOKS Lee	6 1	11 01	M	14 1 78	Wakefield	Trainee	**Manchester C**	—	—
CROSBY Andy	6 2	13 00	D	3 3 73	Rotherham	Leeds U	Doncaster R	51	—
							Darlington	60	—

Player	Ht	Wt	Pos	Birth Date	Birth Place	Source	Clubs	League App	League Gls
CROSBY Gary	5 7	9 11	F	8 5 64	Sleaford	Lincoln U	Lincoln C	7	—
						Grantham	Nottingham F	152	12
							Grimsby T (loan)	3	—
							Huddersfield T	19	4
CROSS John	5 8	10 10	M	6 4 76	Barking	Trainee	**QPR**	—	—
CROSS Jonathan	5 10	11 05	M	2 3 75	Wallasey	Trainee	**Wrexham**	92	10
CROSS Mark ‡			F	6 5 76	Abergavenny	Trainee	**Hereford U**	1	—
CROSS Nicky	5 9	11 12	F	7 2 61	Birmingham	Apprentice	WBA	105	15
							Walsall	109	45
							Leicester C	58	15
							Port Vale	144	39
							Hereford U	28	6
CROSS Paul *	5 7	10 00	M	31 10 65	Barnsley	Apprentice	Barnsley	118	—
							Preston NE (loan)	5	—
							Hartlepool U	74	1
							Darlington	39	2
CROSS Ryan	6 0	13 10	D	11 10 72	Plymouth	Trainee	Plymouth Arg	19	—
							Hartlepool U	50	2
							Bury	29	—
CROSSLEY Mark	6 0	13 09	G	16 6 69	Barnsley	Trainee	**Nottingham F**	200	—
							Manchester U (loan)	—	—
CROSSLEY Matt	6 2	13 04	D	18 3 68	Basingstoke	Overton U	**Wycombe W**	75	2
CRUMPLIN John ‡	5 8	11 10	M	26 5 67	Bath	Bognor Regis	**Brighton**	207	7
CULLING Gary ‡	5 9	11 00	D	6 4 72	Braintree	Braintree	**Colchester U**	2	—
CULVERHOUSE Ian	5 10	11 02	D	22 9 64	Bishop's Stortford	Apprentice	Tottenham H	2	—
							Norwich C	296	1
							Swindon T	9	—
CUNDY Jason	6 0	13 13	D	12 11 69	Wimbledon	Trainee	Chelsea	41	1
							Tottenham H (loan)	10	—
							Tottenham H	15	1
CUNNINGHAM Aaron *			F	11 11 73	New Jersey	Trainee	**Portsmouth**	—	—
CUNNINGHAM Ken	6 0	11 08	D	28 6 71	Dublin	Tolka R	Millwall	136	1
							Wimbledon	28	—
CUNNINGTON Shaun	5 10	11 12	M	4 1 66	Bourne	Bourne T	Wrexham	199	12
							Grimsby T	182	13
							Sunderland	58	8
CURBISHLEY Alan	5 10	11 07	M	8 11 57	Forest Gate	Apprentice	West Ham U	85	5
							Birmingham C	130	11
							Aston Villa	36	1
							Charlton Ath	63	6
							Brighton	116	13
							Charlton Ath	28	—
CURETON Jamie	5 8	10 07	F	28 8 75	Bristol	Trainee	**Norwich C**	17	4
CURLE Keith	6 0	12 07	D	14 11 63	Bristol	Apprentice	Bristol R	32	4
							Torquay U	16	5
							Bristol C	121	1
							Reading	40	—
							Wimbledon	93	3
							Manchester C	139	11
CURRAN Chris	5 11	12 04	D	17 9 71	Birmingham	Trainee	**Torquay U**	133	3
CURRIE Darren	5 9	11 07	M	29 11 74	Hampstead	Trainee	**West Ham U**	—	—
							Shrewsbury T (loan)	17	2
CURRIE David	5 11	12 09	F	27 11 62	Stockton	Local	Middlesbrough	113	31
							Darlington	76	33
							Barnsley	80	30
							Nottingham F	8	1
							Oldham Ath	31	3
							Barnsley	75	12
							Rotherham U (loan)	5	2
							Huddersfield T (loan)	7	1
							Carlisle U	38	4

Player	Ht	Wt	Pos	Birth Date	Birth Place	Source	Clubs	League App	League Gls
CURTIS Andy ‡	5 8	12 00	F	2 12 72	Doncaster	Trainee	York C	12	—
							Peterborough U	11	1
CURTIS Robbie *	6 0	13 00	D	21 5 72	Mansfield	Boston U	**Northampton T**	13	—
CURTIS Tommy	5 8	11 05	M	1 3 73	Exeter	School	Derby Co	—	—
							Chesterfield	76	5
CUSACK Nick	6 0	11 13	F	24 12 65	Rotherham	Alvechurch	Leicester C	16	1
							Peterborough U	44	10
							Motherwell	77	17
							Darlington	21	6
							Oxford U	61	10
							Wycombe W (loan)	4	—
							Fulham	27	7
CUTLER Neil	6 4	14 00	G	3 9 76	Birmingham	Trainee	**WBA**	—	—
DAISH Liam	6 2	13 05	D	23 9 68	Portsmouth	Apprentice	Portsmouth	1	—
							Cambridge U	139	4
							Birmingham C	56	3
DAKIN Simon	5 9	11 02	D	30 11 74	Nottingham	Derby Co	**Hull C**	30	1
DALE Carl	6 0	12 00	F	29 4 66	Colwyn Bay	Bangor C	Chester C	116	41
							Cardiff C	111	38
DALEY Philip	6 2	12 09	F	12 4 67	Walton	Newton	Wigan Ath	161	39
							Lincoln C	20	4
DALEY Tony	5 8	10 08	F	18 10 67	Birmingham	Apprentice	Aston Villa	233	31
							Wolverhampton W	1	—
DALLI Jean †			D	13 8 76	Enfield		**Colchester U**	1	—
DALTON Paul	5 11	12 07	M	25 4 67	Middlesbrough	Brandon	Manchester U	—	—
							Hartlepool U	151	37
							Plymouth Arg	98	25
DANIEL Ray *	5 8	11 09	D	10 12 64	Luton	Apprentice	Luton T	22	4
							Gillingham (loan)	5	—
							Hull C	58	3
							Cardiff C	56	1
							Portsmouth	100	4
							Notts Co (loan)	5	—
DANIELS Scott *	6 1	11 09	D	22 11 69	Benfleet	Trainee	Colchester U	73	—
							Exeter C	117	7
							Northampton T	8	—
DANZEY Michael †	6 1	12 00	F	8 2 71	Widnes	Trainee	Nottingham F	—	—
							Chester C (loan)	2	—
							Peterborough U	1	—
						St Albans	**Cambridge U**	27	3
							Scunthorpe U (loan)	3	1
DARBY Duane	5 11	12 13	F	17 10 73	Birmingham	Trainee	**Torquay U**	108	26
DARBY Julian	6 0	11 04	D	3 10 67	Bolton	Trainee	Bolton W	270	36
							Coventry C	55	5
DARNBOROUGH Lee			G	15 9 77	Ashton	Trainee	**Oldham Ath**	—	—
DARTON Scott	5 11	11 02	D	27 3 75	Ipswich	Trainee	WBA	15	—
							Blackpool	18	—
DAUGHTRY Paul ‡	5 8	10 07	F	14 2 73	Oldham	Winsford	Stockport Co	—	—
							Hartlepool U	15	—
D'AURIA David	5 9	11 00	M	26 3 70	Swansea	Trainee	Swansea C	45	6
						Barry T	**Scarborough**	34	7
DAVENPORT Peter	5 10	11 06	F	24 3 61	Birkenhead	Everton	Nottingham F	118	54
							Manchester U	92	22
							Middlesbrough	59	7
							Sunderland	99	15
							Airdrie	38	9
							St Johnstone	22	4
							Stockport Co	6	1
DAVEY Simon	5 10	10 05	M	1 10 70	Swansea	Trainee	Swansea C	49	4
							Carlisle U	105	18
							Preston NE	13	3
DAVIDSON Craig *	6 0	12 02	D	2 5 74	Harold Wood	Trainee	**Southend U**	—	—

Player	Ht	Wt	Pos	Birth Date	Birth Place	Source	Clubs	League App	League Gls
DAVIDSON Ross	5 10	12 04	D	13 11 73	Chertsey	Walton & Hersham	**Sheffield U**	1	—
DAVIES Gareth	6 1	11 12	D	11 12 73	Hereford	Trainee	**Hereford U**	95	1
DAVIES Glen	6 1	12 10	D	20 2 76	Brighton	Trainee	**Burnley**	—	—
DAVIES Kevin	6 0	12 12	F	26 3 77	Sheffield	Trainee	**Chesterfield**	65	15
DAVIES Martin ‡	6 2	13 07	G	28 6 74	Swansea	Trainee	**Coventry C**	—	—
DAVIES Michael *	5 8	10 07	D	19 1 66	Stretford	Apprentice	**Blackpool**	310	16
DAVIES Simon	6 0	11 07	M	23 4 74	Middlewich	Trainee	**Manchester U**	5	—
							Exeter C (loan)	6	1
DAVIES Will	6 2	13 04	F	27 9 75	Derby	Trainee	**Derby Co**	2	—
DAVIS Aaron ‡	5 8	11 00	D	11 2 72	London		Torquay U	24	—
							Colchester U	4	—
DAVIS Darren *	6 0	11 00	D	5 2 67	Sutton-in-Ashfield	Apprentice	Notts Co	92	1
							Lincoln C	102	4
							Maidstone U	31	2
						Frickley Ath	**Scarborough**	48	3
DAVIS Kelvin	6 1	13 06	G	29 9 76	Bedford	Trainee	**Luton T**	10	—
							Torquay U (loan)	2	—
DAVIS Mike	6 0	12 00	F	19 10 74	Bristol	Yate T	**Bristol R**	13	1
							Hereford U (loan)	1	1
DAVIS Neil	5 8	11 00	F	15 8 73	Bloxwich	Redditch U	**Aston Villa**	—	—
DAVIS Paul *	5 10	10 13	M	9 12 61	London	Apprentice	**Arsenal**	351	30
DAVIS Steve	5 11	12 12	D	26 7 65	Birmingham	Stoke C	Crewe Alex	145	1
							Burnley	147	11
							Barnsley	56	2
DAVIS Steve	6 2	14 07	D	30 10 68	Hexham	Trainee	Southampton	7	—
							Burnley (loan)	9	—
							Notts Co (loan)	2	—
							Burnley	162	22
DAVISON Aidan	6 1	13 12	G	11 5 68	Sedgefield	Billingham Syn	Notts Co	1	—
							Leyton Orient (loan)	—	—
							Bury	—	—
							Chester C (loan)	—	—
							Blackpool (loan)	—	—
							Millwall	34	—
							Bolton W	35	—
DAVISON Bobby	5 8	11 09	F	17 7 59	South Shields	Seaham CW	Huddersfield T	2	—
							Halifax T	63	29
							Derby Co	206	83
							Leeds U	91	31
							Derby Co (loan)	10	8
							Sheffield U (loan)	11	4
							Leicester C	25	6
							Sheffield U	12	1
							Rotherham U	21	4
DAWE Simon §			M	16 3 77	Plymouth	Trainee	**Plymouth Arg**	4	—
DAWES Ian	5 7	11 10	D	22 2 63	Croydon	Apprentice	QPR	229	3
							Millwall	225	5
DAWS Nick	5 11	13 06	D	15 3 70	Manchester	Altrincham	**Bury**	107	4
DAWS Tony	5 8	11 10	F	10 9 66	Sheffield	Apprentice	Notts Co	8	1
							Sheffield U	11	3
							Scunthorpe U	183	63
							Grimsby T	16	1
							Lincoln C	40	10
DAY Chris	6 3	13 06	G	28 7 75	Whipps Cross	Trainee	**Tottenham H**	—	—

Player	Ht	Wt	Pos	Birth Date	Birth Place	Source	Clubs	League App	League Gls
DAY Mervyn	6 2	14 13	G	26 6 55	Chelmsford	Apprentice	West Ham U	194	—
							Orient	170	—
							Aston Villa	30	—
							Leeds U	227	—
							Coventry C (loan)	—	—
							Luton T (loan)	4	—
							Sheffield U (loan)	1	—
							Carlisle U	16	—
DE FREITAS Fabian	6 1	12 09	F	28 7 72	Paramaribo	Volendam	**Bolton W**	13	2
DE SOUZA Juan	6 1	12 06	F	11 2 70	Newham	Dagenham	Birmingham C	15	—
							Bury (loan)	3	—
							Wycombe W	7	6
DE WOLF John	6 2	14 03	D	10 12 62	Schiedam	Feyenoord	**Wolverhampton W**	13	4
DEAN Craig *	5 10	11 04	M	1 7 75	Nuneaton	Trainee	**Manchester U**	—	—
DEANE Brian	6 3	12 07	F	7 2 68	Leeds	Apprentice	Doncaster R	66	12
							Sheffield U	197	82
							Leeds U	76	20
DEARDEN Kevin	5 11	12 08	G	8 3 70	Luton	Trainee	Tottenham H	1	—
							Cambridge U (loan)	15	—
							Hartlepool U (loan)	10	—
							Oxford U (loan)	—	—
							Swindon T (loan)	1	—
							Peterborough U (loan)	7	—
							Hull C (loan)	3	—
							Rochdale (loan)	2	—
							Birmingham C (loan)	12	—
							Portsmouth (loan)	—	—
							Brentford	78	—
DEARY John	5 9	12 07	M	18 10 62	Ormskirk	Apprentice	Blackpool	303	43
							Burnley	215	23
							Rochdale	17	1
DEBONT Andy	6 2	15 06	G	7 2 74	Wolverhampton	Trainee	**Wolverhampton W**	—	—
DEEGAN Mark *	6 1	11 02	G	12 11 71	Liverpool	Holywell T	**Oxford U**	2	—
DELAP Rory	6 0	11 11	M	6 7 76	Coldfield	Trainee	**Carlisle U**	5	—
DEMPSEY Mark	5 7	11 10	M	10 12 72	Dublin	Trainee	Gillingham	48	2
							Leyton Orient	43	1
DENNIS Tony	5 7	10 02	M	1 12 63	Eton	Slough	Cambridge U	111	10
							Chesterfield	10	—
							Colchester U	33	2
DENNISON Robert	5 7	11 00	F	30 4 63	Banbridge	Glenavon	WBA	16	1
							Wolverhampton W	279	39
DEVLIN Mark	5 10	11 01	M	18 1 73	Irvine	Trainee	**Stoke C**	24	2
DEVLIN Paul	5 8	10 05	F	14 4 72	Birmingham	Stafford R	**Notts Co**	115	19
DEWHURST Rob	6 3	12 00	D	10 9 71	Keighley	Trainee	Blackburn R	13	—
							Darlington R (loan)	11	1
							Huddersfield T (loan)	7	—
							Hull C	68	10
DIBBLE Andy	6 2	13 07	G	8 5 65	Cwmbran	Apprentice	Cardiff C	62	—
							Luton T	30	—
							Sunderland (loan)	12	—
							Huddersfield T (loan)	5	—
							Manchester C	102	—
							Aberdeen (loan)	5	—
							Middlesbrough (loan)	19	—
							Bolton W (loan)	13	—
							WBA (loan)	9	—
							Oldham Ath (loan)	—	—
DICHIO Daniele	6 3	11 00	F	19 10 74	London	Trainee	**QPR**	9	3
							Barnet (loan)	9	2

Player	Ht	Wt	Pos	Birth Date	Birth Place	Source	Clubs	League App	League Gls
DICKINS Matt	6 4	14 00	G	3 9 70	Sheffield	Trainee	Sheffield U	—	—
							Leyton Orient (loan)	—	—
							Lincoln C	27	—
							Blackburn R	1	—
							Blackpool (loan)	19	—
							Lincoln C (loan)	—	—
							Grimsby T (loan)	—	—
							Rochdale (loan)	4	—
							Stockport Co	12	—
DICKOV Paul	5 5	11 09	F	1 11 72	Glasgow	Trainee	**Arsenal**	13	2
							Luton T (loan)	15	1
							Brighton (loan)	8	5
DICKS Julian	5 10	13 00	D	8 8 68	Bristol	Apprentice	Birmingham C	89	1
							West Ham U	159	29
							Liverpool	24	3
							West Ham U	29	5
DIGBY Fraser	6 1	12 12	G	23 4 67	Sheffield	Apprentice	Manchester U	—	—
							Oldham Ath (loan)	—	—
							Swindon T (loan)	—	—
							Swindon T	323	—
							Manchester U (loan)	—	—
DIGWEED Perry *	6 0	11 04	G	26 10 59	London	Apprentice	Fulham	15	—
							Brighton	179	—
							WBA (loan)	—	—
							Charlton Ath (loan)	—	—
							Newcastle U (loan)	—	—
							Chelsea (loan)	3	—
							Wimbledon (loan)	—	—
							Wimbledon	—	—
							Watford	29	—
DINEEN Jack ‡	5 7	10 10	M	29 9 70	Brighton	Torsby	**Scarborough**	2	—
DINNING Tony	5 11	12 00	D	12 4 75	Wallsend	Trainee	Newcastle U	—	—
							Stockport Co	40	1
DIXON Ben	6 1	11 00	F	16 9 74	Lincoln	Trainee	**Lincoln C**	31	—
DIXON Edward ‡	5 9	11 00	M	12 12 75	Gateshead	Trainee	**Crystal Palace**	—	—
DIXON Ken	5 11	11 00	G	24 2 76	Knowsley	Trainee	**Wrexham**	—	—
DIXON Kerry	6 0	13 10	F	24 7 61	Luton	Dunstable	Reading	116	51
							Chelsea	335	147
							Southampton	9	2
							Luton T (loan)	17	3
							Luton T	58	16
							Millwall	9	4
DIXON Lee	5 8	11 08	D	17 3 64	Manchester	Local	Burnley	4	—
							Chester	57	1
							Bury	45	5
							Stoke C	71	5
							Arsenal	254	16
DOBBIN Jim	5 9	10 07	M	17 9 63	Dunfermline	Whitburn BC	Celtic	2	—
							Motherwell (loan)	2	—
							Doncaster R	64	13
							Barnsley	129	12
							Grimsby T	138	18
DOBBS Gerald	5 8	11 07	D	24 1 71	London	Trainee	**Wimbledon**	33	1
DOBSON Tony	6 1	12 10	D	5 2 69	Coventry	Apprentice	Coventry C	54	1
							Blackburn R	41	—
							Portsmouth	38	2
							Oxford U (loan)	5	—
DODD Jason	5 11	12 00	D	2 11 70	Bath	Bath C	**Southampton**	135	3
DOHERTY Kevin ‡	5 9	11 00	F	2 9 75	Londonderry	Trainee	**Southampton**	—	—
DOHERTY Neil	5 8	10 09	M	21 2 69	Barrow	Trainee	Watford	—	—
						Barrow	**Birmingham C**	21	1
DOLAN Paul ‡	6 4	13 05	G	16 4 66	Ottawa	Vancouver W	**Notts Co**	—	—
DOLBY Chris *	5 8	9 12	F	4 9 74	Dewsbury	Trainee	**Rotherham U**	3	—
DOLBY Gavin *	5 9	11 10	F	26 1 76	Peterborough	Trainee	**Ipswich T**	—	—

Player	Ht	Wt	Pos	Birth Date	Birth Place	Source	Clubs	League App	League Gls
DOLBY Tony	5 10	13 00	F	16 4 74	Greenwich	Trainee	**Millwall**	35	1
							Barnet (loan)	16	2
DOLING Stuart	5 6	10 06	M	28 10 72	Newport, IOW	Trainee	**Portsmouth**	37	4
DOMINGUEZ Jose	5 3	10 00	F	16 2 74	Lisbon	Benfica	**Birmingham C**	35	3
DONALDSON O'Neill	6 1	11 08	F	24 11 69	Birmingham	Hinckley	Shrewsbury T	28	4
							Doncaster R	9	2
							Mansfield T (loan)	4	6
							Sheffield W	1	—
DONOVAN Kevin	5 7	10 10	F	17 12 71	Halifax	Trainee	Huddersfield T	20	1
							Halifax T (loan)	6	—
							WBA	102	19
DONOWA Lou	5 9	11 00	F	24 9 64	Ipswich	Apprentice	Norwich C	62	11
							Stoke C (loan)	4	1
						Coruna, Willem II	Ipswich T	23	1
							Bristol C	24	3
							Birmingham C	99	18
							Crystal Palace (loan)	—	—
							Burnley (loan)	4	—
							Shrewsbury T (loan)	4	—
DOOLAN John ‡	6 1	12 10	D	7 5 74	Liverpool	Trainee	Everton	—	—
							Mansfield T	24	1
DOOLAN John	5 10	10 12	M	10 11 68	South Liverpool	Knowsley U	**Wigan Ath**	35	1
DORIGO Tony	5 9	10 10	D	31 12 65	Australia	Apprentice	Aston Villa	111	1
							Chelsea	146	11
							Leeds U	136	4
DOW Andrew	5 9	10 07	M	7 2 73	Dundee	Sporting Club 85	Dundee	18	1
							Chelsea	14	—
							Bradford C (loan)	5	—
DOWELL Wayne	5 10	11 02	D	28 12 73	Co Durham	Trainee	**Burnley**	5	—
DOWIE Iain	6 1	13 11	F	9 1 65	Hatfield	Hendon	Luton T	66	16
							Fulham (loan)	5	1
							West Ham U	12	4
							Southampton	122	30
							Crystal Palace	15	4
DOWNING Keith *	5 8	11 00	M	23 7 65	Oldbury	Mile Oak R	Notts Co	23	1
							Wolverhampton W	191	8
							Birmingham C	1	—
							Stoke C	16	—
DOWNS Greg ‡	5 9	10 07	D	13 12 58	Carlton	Apprentice	Norwich C	169	7
							Torquay U (loan)	1	1
							Coventry C	146	4
							Birmingham C	17	—
							Hereford U	108	2
DOYLE Maurice	5 8	10 07	F	17 10 69	Ellesmere Port	Trainee	Crewe Alex	8	2
							QPR	6	—
							Crewe Alex (loan)	7	2
							Wolverhampton W (loan)	—	—
							Millwall	—	—
DOYLE Steve ‡	5 9	11 01	M	2 6 58	Neath	Apprentice	Preston NE	197	8
							Huddersfield T	161	6
							Sunderland	100	2
							Hull C	47	2
							Rochdale	121	1
DOZZELL Jason	6 1	13 08	M	9 12 67	Ipswich	School	Ipswich T	332	52
							Tottenham H	39	8
DRAPER Mark	5 10	12 00	M	11 11 70	Long Eaton	Trainee	Notts Co	222	40
							Leicester C	39	5
DREYER John	6 1	13 02	D	11 6 63	Alnwick	Wallingford T	Oxford U	60	2
							Torquay U (loan)	5	—
							Fulham (loan)	12	2
							Luton T	214	13
							Stoke C	18	2
							Bolton W (loan)	2	—
DRUCE Mark	6 0	11 11	F	3 3 74	Oxford	Trainee	**Oxford U**	44	4

Player	Ht	Wt	Pos	Birth Date	Birth Place	Source	Clubs	League App	League Gls
DRURY Nathan ‡	6 0	11 02	D	15 1 76	Leeds	Trainee	**Nottingham F**	—	—
DRYDEN Richard	6 0	11 02	D	14 6 69	Stroud	Trainee	Bristol R	13	—
							Exeter C	51	7
							Manchester C (loan)	—	—
							Notts Co	31	1
							Plymouth Arg (loan)	5	—
							Birmingham C	48	—
							Bristol C	19	1
DRYSDALE Jason	5 10	12 00	D	17 11 70	Bristol	Trainee	Watford	145	11
							Swindon T	1	—
DUBERRY Michael	6 1	12 13	D	14 10 75	Enfield	Trainee	**Chelsea**	1	—
DUBLIN Dion	6 0	12 04	F	22 4 69	Leicester		Norwich C	—	—
							Cambridge U	156	52
							Manchester U	12	2
							Coventry C	31	13
DUBLIN Keith	6 0	12 10	D	29 1 66	Wycombe	Apprentice	Chelsea	51	—
							Brighton	132	5
							Watford	168	2
							Southend U	40	2
DUCROS Andrew	5 4	9 08	F	16 9 77	Evesham	Trainee	**Coventry C**	—	—
DUDLEY Derek ‡	6 4	14 00	G	2 2 70	Birmingham	VS Rugby	**WBA**	—	—
DUFFIN Stuart ‡	5 9	11 07	F	27 6 75	Glasgow		**Bristol C**	—	—
DUFFY Chris ‡	5 10	11 11	M	31 10 73	Manchester	Trainee	Crewe Alex	—	—
							Wigan Ath	31	1
DUMITRESCU Ilie ‡	5 9	10 07	M	6 1 69	Bucharest	Steaua	**Tottenham H**	13	4
DUNFORD Neil ‡			G	18 7 67	Rochdale		**Rochdale**	2	—
DUNGEY James §			G	7 2 78	Plymouth	Trainee	**Plymouth Arg**	4	—
DUNN Iain	5 10	11 07	F	1 4 70	Derwent	School	York C	77	11
							Chesterfield	13	1
						Goole T	**Huddersfield T**	101	14
DUNNE Joe	5 8	11 06	D	25 5 73	Dublin	Trainee	**Gillingham**	113	1
DUNPHY Nick	6 0	12 00	D	3 8 74	Birmingham	Hednesford	**Peterborough U**	2	—
DUNPHY Sean ‡	6 3	13 05	D	5 11 70	Rotherham	Trainee	Barnsley	6	—
							Lincoln C	53	2
							Doncaster R (loan)	1	—
							Scarborough (loan)	10	—
DURKAN Kieron	5 10	10 05	M	1 12 73	Chester	Trainee	**Wrexham**	42	3
DURNIN John	5 10	11 04	F	18 8 65	Bootle	Waterloo Dock	Liverpool	—	—
							WBA (loan)	5	2
							Oxford U	161	44
							Portsmouth	44	8
DURRANT Iain (On loan from Rangers)	5 8	9 07	M	29 10 66	Glasgow	Glasgow U	**Rangers**	217	26
							Everton (loan)	5	—
DURRANT Lee	5 10	11 07	M	18 12 73	Gt Yarmouth	Trainee	**Ipswich T**	7	—
DUXBURY Lee	5 8	11 13	M	7 10 69	Keighley	Trainee	Bradford C	209	25
							Rochdale (loan)	10	—
							Huddersfield T	26	2
DYCHE Sean	6 0	13 02	D	28 6 71	Kettering	Trainee	Nottingham F	—	—
							Chesterfield	154	8
DYER Alex	5 11	11 12	M	14 11 65	West Ham	Watford	Blackpool	108	19
							Hull C	60	14
							Crystal Palace	17	2
							Charlton Ath	78	13
							Oxford U	76	6
DYER Bruce	5 11	11 03	F	13 4 75	Ilford	Trainee	Watford	31	6
							Crystal Palace	27	1
DYKSTRA Sieb	6 5	14 07	G	20 10 66	Kerkrade	Roda JC	Motherwell	80	—
							QPR	11	—
DYSON Jon	6 1	12 00	D	18 12 71	Mirfield	School	**Huddersfield T**	65	2

Player	Ht	Wt	Pos	Birth Date	Birth Place	Source	Clubs	League App	League Gls
EADEN Nicky	5 10	11 09	D	12 12 72	Sheffield	Trainee	**Barnsley**	84	3
EADIE Darren	5 7	11 05	F	10 6 75	Chippenham	Trainee	**Norwich C**	41	5
EARLE Robbie	5 9	10 10	F	27 1 65	Newcastle, Staffs.	Stoke C	Port Vale	294	77
							Wimbledon	133	30
EBBRELL John	5 7	9 12	M	1 10 69	Bromborough		**Everton**	185	9
EBDON Marcus	5 8	12 04	M	17 10 70	Pontypool	Trainee	Everton	—	—
							Peterborough U	88	12
ECKHARDT Jeff	6 0	11 07	D	7 10 65	Sheffield		Sheffield U	74	2
							Fulham	249	25
							Stockport Co	27	1
ECKSTEIN Dieter ‡	5 11	11 06	F	12 3 64	Germany	Schalke 04	**West Ham U**	—	—
EDESON Matt *	5 10	11 00	F	11 8 76	Beverley	Trainee	**Hull C**	5	—
EDGHILL Richard	5 9	10 01	D	23 9 74	Oldham	Trainee	**Manchester C**	36	—
EDINBURGH Justin	5 10	11 08	D	18 12 69	Brentwood	Trainee	Southend U	37	—
							Tottenham H (loan)	—	—
							Tottenham H	127	1
EDMONDSON Darren	6 0	12 01	M	4 11 71	Coniston	Trainee	**Carlisle U**	152	7
EDWARDS Alistair	6 1	12 06	F	21 6 68	Wyalla	Selangor	**Millwall**	4	—
EDWARDS Andy	6 3	13 07	D	17 9 71	Epping	Trainee	**Southend U**	147	5
EDWARDS Christian	6 2	11 09	D	23 11 75	Caerphilly	Trainee	**Swansea C**	9	—
EDWARDS David ‡	5 10	10 08	M	13 1 74	Bridgnorth	Trainee	**Walsall**	27	1
EDWARDS Mike	5 11	11 05	M	10 9 74	Bebbington	Trainee	**Tranmere R**	3	—
EDWARDS Neil	5 8	11 02	G	5 12 70	Aberdare	Trainee	Leeds U	—	—
							Huddersfield T (loan)	—	—
							Stockport Co	119	—
EDWARDS Paul	5 11	11 05	G	22 2 65	Liverpool	St. Helens T	Crewe Alex	29	—
							Shrewsbury T	115	—
EDWARDS Paul R	5 11	11 00	D	25 12 63	Birkenhead	Altrincham	Crewe Alex	86	6
							Coventry C	36	—
							Wolverhampton W	46	—
							WBA	35	—
EDWARDS Robert	6 0	11 06	D	1 7 73	Kendal	Trainee	Carlisle U	48	5
							Bristol C	106	3
EDWARDS Robert	5 8	11 07	F	23 2 70	Manchester	Trainee	**Crewe Alex**	123	29
EDWORTHY Mark	5 8	11 10	D	24 12 72	Barnstaple	Trainee	**Plymouth Arg**	69	1
EHIOGU Ugo	6 2	13 03	D	3 11 72	London	Trainee	WBA	2	—
							Aston Villa	68	3
EKELUND Ronnie ‡	5 10	12 06	M	21 8 72	Denmark	Barcelona	**Southampton**	17	5
EKOKU Efan	6 1	12 00	F	8 6 67	Manchester	Sutton U	Bournemouth	62	21
							Norwich C	37	15
							Wimbledon	24	9
ELAD Efon ‡	5 10	12 00	F	5 9 70	Hillingdon	Cologne	Northampton T	10	—
							Cambridge U	3	—
							Mansfield T	2	—
ELI Roger ‡	5 11	11 03	D	11 9 65	Bradford	Apprentice	Leeds U	2	—
							Wolverhampton W	18	—
							Cambridge U	—	—
							Crewe Alex	27	1
							York C	4	1
							Bury	2	—
						Northwich Vic	Burnley	99	11
							Partick T	2	—
							Scunthorpe U	2	—
ELKINS Gary	5 09	11 12	M	4 5 66	Wallingford	Apprentice	Fulham	104	2
							Exeter C (loan)	5	—
							Wimbledon	100	3

Player	Ht	Wt	Pos	Birth Date	Birth Place	Source	Clubs	League App	League Gls
ELLIOTT Matthew	6 3	14 05	D	1 11 68	Epsom	Epsom & Ewell	Charlton Ath	—	—
							Torquay U	124	15
							Scunthorpe U (loan)	8	1
							Scunthorpe U	53	7
							Oxford U	77	9
ELLIOTT Robbie	5 10	10 13	D	25 12 73	Newcastle	Trainee	**Newcastle U**	44	2
ELLIOTT Tony	6 0	13 07	G	30 11 69	Nuneaton		Birmingham C	—	—
							Hereford U	75	—
							Huddersfield T	15	—
							Carlisle U	9	—
ELLIS Kevin §			D	12 5 77	Gt Yarmouth	Trainee	**Ipswich T**	1	—
ELLIS Tony	5 11	11 00	F	20 10 64	Salford	Northwich Vic	Oldham Ath	8	—
							Preston NE	86	26
							Stoke C	77	19
							Preston NE	72	48
							Blackpool	40	17
ELLISON Tony *	5 11	12 03	F	13 1 73	Bishop Auckland	Trainee	Darlington	72	17
							Hartlepool U (loan)	4	1
							Leicester C	—	—
ELSEY David *			D	19 11 75	Swindon	Trainee	**Swindon T**	—	—
EMBERSON Carl	6 1	13 11	G	13 7 73	Epsom	Trainee	Millwall	—	—
							Colchester U (loan)	13	—
							Colchester U	20	—
EMBLEN Neil	6 1	12 07	D	19 6 71	Bromley	Sittingbourne	Millwall	12	—
							Wolverhampton W	27	7
EMBLETON Daniel †	5 11	11 04	G	27 3 75	Liverpool	Trainee	Liverpool	—	—
							Bury	—	—
							Walsall	1	—
EMENALO Michael	5 11	11 04	D	14 7 65	Nigeria	Eintracht Trier	**Notts Co**	7	—
EMERSON Dean ‡	5 11	12 06	M	27 12 62	Salford	Local	Stockport Co	156	7
							Rotherham U	55	8
							Coventry C	114	—
							Hartlepool U	45	1
							Stockport Co	11	—
							Preston NE	2	—
ENGLISH Tony	6 1	12 09	D	19 10 66	Luton	Coventry C	**Colchester U**	330	42
ENQVIST Bjorn	5 10	10 09	M	12 10 77	Lund	Malmo	**Crystal Palace**	—	—
ESTEVES Rui ‡			F	30 1 67	Lisbon	Benfica	**Birmingham C**	—	—
EUSTACE Scott *	6 0	13 12	D	13 6 75	Leicester	Trainee	**Leicester C**	1	—
EVANS Andy	6 1	12 01	F	25 11 75	Aberystwyth	Trainee	**Cardiff C**	13	—
EVANS Darren *	5 10	11 00	D	30 9 74	Wolverhampton	Trainee	**Aston Villa**	—	—
EVANS John ‡	5 10	11 00	M	8 9 74	Liverpool	Trainee	**Tranmere R**	—	—
EVANS Mark ‡	6 0	11 08	G	24 8 70	Leeds	Trainee	Bradford C	12	—
							Scarborough	46	—
EVANS Mike	6 0	13 04	F	1 1 73	Plymouth	Trainee	**Plymouth Arg**	85	14
							Blackburn R (loan)	—	—
EVANS Paul	5 6	10 08	M	1 9 74	Oswestry	Trainee	**Shrewsbury T**	51	5
EVANS Terry	5 8	10 07	D	8 1 76	Pontypridd	Trainee	**Cardiff C**	12	—
EVANS Terry	6 4	15 08	D	12 4 65	Hammersmith	Hillingdon B	Brentford	229	23
							Wycombe W	66	10
EVANS Wayne	5 10	12 02	D	25 8 71	Abermule	Welshpool	**Walsall**	77	—
EVERSHAM Paul *	5 10	11 08	M	28 1 75	Hereford	Trainee	**Hereford U**	13	1
EYRE John	6 1	11 03	F	9 10 74	Humberside	Trainee	**Oldham Ath**	10	1
							Scunthorpe U (loan)	9	8
EYRES David	5 9	11 08	F	26 2 64	Liverpool	Rhyl	Blackpool	158	38
							Burnley	84	27

Player	Ht	Wt	Pos	Birth Date	Birth Place	Source	Clubs	League App	League Gls
FAIRCLOUGH Chris	5 11	11 07	D	12 4 64	Nottingham	Apprentice	Nottingham F	107	1
							Tottenham H	60	5
							Leeds U	193	21
FAIRCLOUGH Wayne	5 10	12 00	D	27 4 68	Nottingham	Apprentice	Notts Co	71	—
							Mansfield T	141	12
							Chesterfield	13	—
FARNWORTH Simon	6 0	11 13	G	28 10 63	Chorley	Apprentice	Bolton W	113	—
							Stockport Co (loan)	10	—
							Tranmere R (loan)	7	—
							Bury	105	—
							Preston NE	81	—
							Wigan Ath	83	—
FARRELL Andy	6 0	11 00	D	7 10 65	Colchester	School	Colchester U	105	5
							Burnley	257	19
							Wigan Ath	31	—
FARRELL David	5 11	11 02	F	11 11 71	Birmingham	Redditch U	**Aston Villa**	6	—
							Scunthorpe U (loan)	5	1
FARRELL Sean	6 0	13 07	F	28 2 69	Watford	Apprentice	Luton T	25	1
							Colchester U (loan)	9	1
							Northampton T (loan)	4	1
							Fulham	94	31
							Peterborough U	33	8
FARRELLY Gareth	6 0	12 07	M	28 8 75	Dublin	Home Farm	**Aston Villa**	—	—
							Rotherham U (loan)	10	2
FARRINGTON Mark ‡	5 10	11 12	F	15 6 65	Liverpool	Everton	Norwich C	14	2
							Cambridge U	10	1
							Cardiff C	31	3
						Feyenoord	Brighton	28	4
							Hereford U	1	—
FASHANU John	6 2	13 07	F	18 9 63	Kensington	Cambridge U	Norwich C	7	1
							Crystal Palace (loan)	1	—
							Lincoln C	36	10
							Millwall	50	12
							Wimbledon	276	107
							Aston Villa	13	3
FAULKNER David	6 0	11 12	D	8 10 75	Sheffield	Trainee	**Sheffield W**	—	—
FEAR Peter	5 10	11 05	D	10 9 73	London	Trainee	**Wimbledon**	41	2
FEARON Dean	6 1	13 12	D	9 1 76	Barnsley	Schoolboy	**Barnsley**	—	—
FEENEY Mark	5 7	11 00	M	26 7 74	Derry	Trainee	**Barnsley**	2	—
FELGATE David	6 1	15 00	G	4 3 60	Blaenau Ffestiniog	Blaenau Ffestiniog	Bolton W	—	—
							Rochdale (loan)	35	—
							Bradford C (loan)	—	—
							Crewe Alex (loan)	14	—
							Rochdale (loan)	12	—
							Lincoln C	198	—
							Cardiff C (loan)	4	—
							Grimsby T (loan)	12	—
							Grimsby T	12	—
							Bolton W	238	—
							Rotherham U (loan)	—	—
							Bury	—	—
							Wolverhampton W	—	—
							Chester C	72	—
FELL Gavin *	5 10	11 10	M	6 6 76	Newcastle	Trainee	**Wimbledon**	—	—
FENSOME Andy	5 8	11 02	D	18 2 69	Northampton	Trainee	Norwich C	—	—
							Newcastle U (loan)	—	—
							Cambridge U	126	1
							Preston NE	73	1
FENTON Graham	5 10	11 03	F	22 5 74	Wallsend	Trainee	**Aston Villa**	29	3
							WBA (loan)	7	3
FENWICK Paul ‡	6 1	12 01	D	25 8 69	London	Winnipeg Fury	**Birmingham C**	19	—

Player	Ht	Wt	Pos	Birth Date	Birth Place	Source	Clubs	League App	League Gls
FENWICK Terry ‡	5 10	11 12	D	17 11 59	Camden, Co. Durham	Apprentice	Crystal Palace	70	—
							QPR	256	33
							Tottenham H	93	8
							Leicester C (loan)	8	1
							Swindon T	28	—
FERDINAND Les	5 11	13 05	F	18 12 66	London	Hayes	**QPR**	163	80
							Brentford (loan)	3	—
							Besiktas (loan)	—	—
FEREDAY Wayne *	5 9	11 08	M	16 6 63	Warley	Apprentice	QPR	197	21
							Newcastle U	33	—
							Bournemouth	23	—
							WBA	48	3
							Cardiff C	44	2
FERGUSON Darren	5 10	10 04	M	9 2 72	Glasgow	Trainee	Manchester U	27	—
							Wolverhampton W	38	—
FERGUSON Derek	5 8	11 12	M	31 7 67	Glasgow	Gartcosh U	Rangers	111	7
							Dundee (loan)	4	—
							Hearts	103	4
							Sunderland	64	—
FERGUSON Duncan	6 3	13 05	F	27 12 71	Stirling	Carse T	Dundee U	77	28
							Rangers	14	2
							Everton	23	7
FERNANDES Tamer	6 3	13 07	G	7 12 74	London	Trainee	**Brentford**	5	—
FERNEY Martin *	5 11	12 10	M	8 11 71	Lambeth	Trainee	**Fulham**	60	1
FERRETT Chris §			M	10 2 77	Poole	Trainee	**Bournemouth**	1	—
FETTIS Alan	6 1	11 04	G	1 2 71	Belfast	Ards	**Hull C**	128	2
FEUER Tony	6 7	14 00	G	20 5 71	Las Vegas	Los Angeles Salsa	**West Ham U**	—	—
							Peterborough U (loan)	16	—
FEWINGS Paul §			F	18 2 78	Hull	Trainee	**Hull C**	2	—
FICKLING Ashley	5 10	11 06	D	15 11 72	Sheffield	Trainee	Sheffield U	—	—
							Darlington (loan)	15	—
							Grimsby T	1	—
FIELD Darren *	5 8	11 00	M	8 3 73	Barnsley	Local	**Barnsley**	—	—
FILAN John	5 11	13 02	G	8 2 70	Sydney	Budapest St George	Cambridge U	68	—
							Nottingham F (loan)	—	—
							Coventry C	2	—
FINLAY Darren ‡	5 4	10 00	F	19 12 73	Belfast	Trainee	QPR	—	—
							Doncaster R	8	1
FINNEY Stephen *	5 10	12 00	F	31 10 73	Hexham	Trainee	Preston NE	6	1
							Manchester C	—	—
FINNIGAN John	5 8	10 05	M	29 3 76	Wakefield	Trainee	**Nottingham F**	—	—
FINNIGAN Tony ‡	5 10	11 09	M	17 10 62	Wimbledon	Crystal Palace	Fulham	—	—
							Crystal Palace	105	10
							Blackburn R	36	—
							Hull C	18	1
							Swindon T	3	—
							Brentford	3	—
							Barnet	6	1
							Fulham	11	—
FISHER Neil *	5 10	10 09	M	7 11 70	St Helens	Trainee	**Bolton W**	24	1
FISHLOCK Murray	5 7	11 00	D	23 9 73	Marlborough	Trowbridge T	**Hereford U**	14	—
FITZGERALD Gary	6 1	11 07	D	27 10 76	Hampstead	Trainee	**Watford**	1	—
FITZGERALD Scott	6 0	12 02	D	13 8 69	London	Trainee	**Wimbledon**	102	1
FJORTOFT Jan-Aage	6 3	13 04	F	10 1 67	Aalesund	Rapid Vienna	Swindon T	72	28
							Middlesbrough	8	3
FLAHAVAN Aaron	6 1	12 10	G	15 12 75	Southampton	Trainee	**Portsmouth**	—	—
FLASH Richard *	5 9	11 08	M	8 4 76	Birmingham	Trainee	**Manchester U**	—	—

Player	Ht	Wt	Pos	Birth Date	Birth Place	Source	Clubs	League App	League Gls
FLATTS Mark	5 6	9 08	M	14 10 72	Haringey	Trainee	**Arsenal**	16	—
							Cambridge U (loan)	5	1
							Brighton (loan)	10	1
							Bristol C (loan)	6	—
FLECK Robert	5 10	10 03	F	11 8 65	Glasgow	Possil YM	Partick T	2	1
							Rangers	85	29
							Norwich C	143	40
							Chelsea	40	3
							Bolton W (loan)	7	1
							Bristol C (loan)	10	1
FLEMING Craig	6 0	11 07	D	6 10 71	Calder	Trainee	Halifax T	57	—
							Oldham Ath	98	1
FLEMING Curtis	5 10	12 09	D	8 10 68	Manchester	St Patrick's Ath	Swindon T	—	—
						St Patrick's Ath	**Middlesbrough**	113	—
FLEMING Gary	5 9	11 09	D	17 2 67	Derry	Apprentice	Nottingham F	74	—
							Manchester C	14	—
							Notts Co (loan)	3	—
							Barnsley	236	—
FLEMING Paul ‡	5 7	11 08	D	6 9 67	Halifax		Halifax T	139	1
							Mansfield T	68	—
FLEMING Terry	5 9	10 09	D	5 1 73	Marston Green	Trainee	Coventry C	13	—
							Northampton T	31	1
							Preston NE	27	2
FLETCHER Steve	6 2	14 00	F	26 6 72	Hartlepool	Trainee	Hartlepool U	32	4
							Bournemouth	107	16
FLITCROFT David	5 11	13 05	M	14 1 74	Bolton	Trainee	Preston NE	8	2
							Lincoln C (loan)	2	—
							Chester C	40	1
FLITCROFT Garry	6 0	11 08	M	6 11 72	Bolton	Trainee	**Manchester C**	90	13
							Bury (loan)	12	—
FLO Jostein	6 4	13 08	F	3 10 64	Norway	Sogndal	**Sheffield U**	65	15
FLOUNDERS Andy *	5 11	11 06	F	13 12 63	Hull	Apprentice	Hull C	159	54
							Scunthorpe U	196	87
							Rochdale	85	31
							Rotherham U (loan)	6	2
							Carlisle U (loan)	8	1
						Halifax T	**Northampton T**	2	—
FLOWERS Tim	6 2	14 04	G	3 2 67	Kenilworth	Apprentice	Wolverhampton W	63	—
							Southampton (loan)	—	—
							Southampton	192	—
							Swindon T (loan)	2	—
							Swindon T (loan)	5	—
							Blackburn R	68	—
FLYNN Mike	6 0	11 00	D	23 2 69	Oldham	Trainee	Oldham Ath	40	1
							Norwich C	—	—
							Preston NE	136	7
							Stockport Co	99	3
FLYNN Sean	5 8	11 08	M	13 3 68	Birmingham	Halesowen T	**Coventry C**	97	9
FOLEY Steve ‡	5 7	11 03	M	4 10 62	Liverpool	Apprentice	Liverpool	—	—
							Fulham (loan)	3	—
							Grimsby T	31	2
							Sheffield U	66	14
							Swindon T	151	23
							Stoke C	107	10
							Lincoln C	16	—
FOOT Daniel	6 0	11 00	D	6 9 75	Edmonton	Tottenham H	**Southend U**	3	—
FORAN Mark	6 4	13 12	D	30 10 73	Aldershot	Trainee	Millwall	—	—
							Sheffield U	4	1
							Rotherham U (loan)	3	—
FORBES Steven	6 2	12 06	M	24 12 75	London	Sittingbourne	**Millwall**	1	—
FORD Bobby	5 8	10 06	M	22 9 74	Bristol	Trainee	**Oxford U**	37	2
FORD John	6 0	12 00	M	12 4 68	Birmingham	Cradley T	**Swansea C**	160	7
FORD Mark	5 8	10 08	M	10 10 75	Pontefract	Trainee	**Leeds U**	1	—

Player	Ht	Wt	Pos	Birth Date	Birth Place	Source	Clubs	League App	League Gls
FORD Mike	6 0	11 02	D	9 2 66	Bristol	Apprentice	Leicester C	—	—
						Devizes	Cardiff C	145	13
							Oxford U	181	10
FORD Stuart *	5 11	11 13	G	20 7 71	Sheffield	Trainee	Rotherham U	5	—
							Scarborough (loan)	6	—
							Scarborough	22	—
							Bury	—	—
							Doncaster R	6	—
							Scarborough	6	—
FORD Tony	5 9	12 07	D	14 5 59	Grimsby	Apprentice	Grimsby T	354	54
							Sunderland (loan)	9	1
							Stoke C	112	13
							WBA	114	14
							Grimsby T	68	3
							Bradford C (loan)	5	—
							Scunthorpe U	38	2
FOREMAN Darren ‡	5 10	10 08	F	12 2 68	Southampton	Fareham	Barnsley	47	8
							Crewe Alex	23	4
							Scarborough	97	35
FOREMAN Matt ‡	6 0	12 04	D	15 2 75	Gateshead	Trainee	**Sheffield U**	—	—
FORMBY Kevin	5 9	11 04	D	22 7 71	Ormskirk	Burscough	**Rochdale**	33	—
FORREST Craig	6 5	14 00	G	20 9 67	Vancouver	Apprentice	**Ipswich T**	236	—
							Colchester U (loan)	11	—
FORRESTER Jamie	5 7	10 00	F	1 11 74	Bradford	Auxerre	**Leeds U**	9	—
							Southend U (loan)	5	—
							Grimsby T (loan)	9	1
FORSTER Nick	5 9	10 11	F	8 9 73	Oxted	Horley T	Gillingham	67	24
							Brentford	46	24
FORSYTH Mike	5 11	12 05	D	20 3 66	Liverpool	Apprentice	WBA	29	—
							Northampton T (loan)	—	—
							Derby Co	325	8
							Notts Co	7	—
FOSTER Adrian	5 9	11 00	F	19 3 71	Kidderminster	Trainee	WBA	27	2
							Torquay U	75	24
							Gillingham	29	8
FOSTER Colin	6 4	14 01	D	16 7 64	Chislehurst	Apprentice	Orient	174	10
							Nottingham F	72	5
							West Ham U	93	5
							Notts Co (loan)	9	—
							Watford	40	3
FOSTER John	5 10	11 01	D	19 9 73	Manchester	Trainee	**Manchester C**	12	—
FOSTER Martin	5 5	9 10	M	29 10 77	Sheffield	Trainee	**Leeds U**	—	—
FOSTER Steve	6 1	14 00	D	24 9 57	Portsmouth	Apprentice	Portsmouth	109	6
							Brighton	172	6
							Aston Villa	15	3
							Luton T	163	11
							Oxford U	95	9
							Brighton	107	6
FOSTER Wayne (on loan from Partick T)	5 8	11 00	F	11 9 63	Leigh		**Hartlepool U**	4	1
FOWLER Jason	6 1	11 06	M	20 8 74	Bristol	Trainee	**Bristol C**	15	—
FOWLER John	5 10	11 07	M	27 10 74	Preston	Trainee	**Cambridge U**	39	—
							Preston NE (loan)	6	—
FOWLER Robbie	5 11	11 10	F	9 4 75	Liverpool	Trainee	**Liverpool**	70	37
FOX Mark	5 11	10 11	M	17 11 75	Basingstoke	Trainee	**Brighton**	21	1
FOX Peter *	5 10	12 04	G	5 7 57	Scunthorpe	Apprentice	Sheffield W	49	—
							West Ham U (loan)	—	—
							Barnsley (loan)	1	—
							Stoke C	409	—
							Wrexham (loan)	—	—
							Exeter C	57	—

				Birth				League	
Player	*Ht*	*Wt*	*Pos*	*Date*	*Place*	*Source*	*Clubs*	*App*	*Gls*
FOX Ruel	5 6	10 00	M	14 1 68	Ipswich	Apprentice	Norwich C	172	22
							Newcastle U	54	12
FOX Simon §	5 10	10 02	F	28 8 77	Basingstoke	Trainee	**Brighton**	3	—
FOYLE Martin	5 10	11 02	F	2 5 63	Salisbury	Amateur	Southampton	12	1
							Blackburn R (loan)	—	—
							Aldershot	98	35
							Oxford U	126	36
							Port Vale	138	49
FRAIN David ‡	5 8	10 05	F	11 10 62	Sheffield	Rowlinson YC	Sheffield U	44	5
							Rochdale	42	12
							Stockport Co	187	12
							Mansfield T (loan)	6	—
FRAIN John	5 7	11 10	M	8 10 68	Birmingham	Apprentice	**Birmingham C**	250	23
FRANCIS John	5 8	12 13	F	21 11 63	Dewsbury	Emley	Halifax T	4	—
							Sheffield U	42	6
							Burnley	101	26
							Cambridge U	29	3
							Burnley	54	8
FRANCIS Kevin	6 7	15 08	F	6 12 67	Moseley	Mile Oak R	Derby Co	10	—
							Stockport Co	152	88
							Birmingham C	15	8
FRANCIS Steve	6 0	11 05	G	29 5 64	Billericay	Apprentice	Chelsea	71	—
							Reading	216	—
							Huddersfield T	89	—
FREEDMAN Doug	5 9	11 00	F	21 1 74	Glasgow	Trainee	QPR	—	—
							Barnet	42	24
FREEMAN Darren	5 11	13 00	F	22 8 73	Brighton	Horsham T	**Gillingham**	2	—
FREESTONE Chris			F	4 9 71	Nottingham	Arnold T	**Middlesbrough**	1	—
FREESTONE Roger	6 3	14 06	G	19 8 68	Newport	Trainee	Newport Co	13	—
							Chelsea	42	—
							Swansea C (loan)	14	—
							Hereford U (loan)	8	—
							Swansea C	179	1
FROGGATT Steve	5 10	11 00	M	9 3 73	Lincoln	Trainee	Aston Villa	35	2
							Wolverhampton W	20	2
FRY Chris	5 8	10 05	F	23 10 69	Cardiff	Trainee	Cardiff C	55	1
							Hereford U	90	10
							Colchester U	50	8
FUCHS Uwe *	6 0	13 08	F	23 7 66	Germany	Kaiserslautern	**Middlesbrough**	15	9
FUNNELL Simon ‡	6 0	12 08	F	8 8 74	Shoreham	Trainee	**Brighton**	28	2
FURLONG Carl §	5 11	12 06	F	18 10 76	Liverpool	Trainee	**Wigan Ath**	3	1
FURLONG Paul	6 0	12 11	F	1 10 68	London	Enfield	Coventry C	37	4
							Watford	79	37
							Chelsea	36	10
FURNELL Andy	5 10	13 07	F	13 2 77	Peterborough	Trainee	**Peterborough U**	18	1
FUTCHER Andy	5 7	10 07	D	10 2 78	Enfield	Trainee	**Wimbledon**	—	—
FUTCHER Paul ‡	6 0	12 03	D	25 9 56	Chester	Apprentice	Chester	20	—
							Luton T	131	1
							Manchester C	37	—
							Oldham Ath	98	1
							Derby Co	35	—
							Barnsley	230	—
							Halifax T	15	—
							Grimsby T	132	—
GABBIADINI Marco	5 10	13 04	F	20 1 68	Nottingham	Apprentice	York C	60	14
							Sunderland	157	74
							Crystal Palace	15	5
							Derby Co	135	39
GAGE Kevin	5 10	11 02	D	21 4 64	Chiswick	Apprentice	Wimbledon	168	15
							Aston Villa	115	8
							Sheffield U	110	7

				Birth				League	
Player	*Ht*	*Wt*	*Pos*	*Date*	*Place*	*Source*	*Clubs*	*App*	*Gls*
GALE Shaun	6 0	11 06	D	8 10 69	Reading	Trainee	Portsmouth	3	—
							Barnet	27	2
GALE Tony *	6 1	13 07	D	19 11 59	London	Apprentice	Fulham	277	19
							West Ham U	300	5
							Blackburn R	15	—
GALLACHER Kevin	5 8	11 00	F	23 11 66	Clydebank	Duntocher BC	Dundee U	131	27
							Coventry C	100	28
							Blackburn R	40	13
GALLAGHER Tommy	5 10	10 08	D	25 8 74	Nottingham	Trainee	**Notts Co**	20	—
GALLEN Joe *	5 11	11 08	F	2 9 72	Hammersmith	Trainee	Watford	—	—
							Exeter C (loan)	6	—
							Shrewsbury T	6	1
GALLEN Kevin	5 11	12 03	F	21 9 75	Hammersmith	Trainee	**QPR**	37	10
GALLEN Stephen	6 2	13 00	D	21 11 73	Acton	Trainee	QPR	—	—
							Doncaster R	—	—
GALLIMORE Tony	5 10	11 10	D	21 2 72	Crewe	Trainee	Stoke C	11	—
							Carlisle U (loan)	16	—
							Carlisle U (loan)	8	1
							Carlisle U	80	6
GALLOWAY Mick (on loan from Celtic)	5 11	11 07	D	30 5 65	Oswestry		**Leicester C**	5	—
GALLOWAY Mick	5 11	11 05	M	13 10 74	Nottingham	Trainee	**Notts Co**	7	—
GANNON Jim	6 2	13 00	D	7 9 68	London	Dundalk	Sheffield U	—	—
							Halifax T (loan)	2	—
							Stockport Co	217	46
							Notts Co (loan)	2	—
GANNON John	5 9	10 10	M	18 12 66	Wimbledon	Apprentice	Wimbledon	16	2
							Crewe Alex (loan)	15	—
							Sheffield U (loan)	16	1
							Sheffield U	146	5
							Middlesbrough (loan)	7	—
GARDINER Mark *	5 10	10 07	F	25 12 66	Cirencester	Apprentice	Swindon T	10	—
							Torquay U	49	4
							Crewe Alex	193	33
							Chester C (loan)	3	—
GARLAND Peter	5 10	12 00	M	20 1 71	Croydon	Trainee	Tottenham H	1	—
							Newcastle U	2	—
							Charlton Ath	50	2
							Wycombe W (loan)	5	—
GARNER Simon *	5 8	12 07	F	23 11 59	Boston	Apprentice	Blackburn R	484	168
							WBA	33	8
							Wycombe W	53	12
GARNETT Shaun	6 2	13 04	D	22 11 69	Wallasey	Trainee	**Tranmere R**	94	5
							Chester C (loan)	9	—
							Preston NE (loan)	10	2
							Wigan Ath (loan)	13	1
GARRETT Scott ‡	5 10	13 07	D	9 1 74	Gateshead	Trainee	**Hartlepool U**	15	—
GARVEY Steve	5 9	11 01	F	22 11 73	Tameside	Trainee	**Crewe Alex**	50	4
GAUDINO Maurizio	5 11	12 02	M	12 12 66	Brule	Eintracht Frankfurt	**Manchester C**	20	3
GAUGHAN Kevin			D	6 3 78	Glasgow		**Ipswich T**	—	—
GAUGHAN Steve	5 11	11 02	M	14 4 70	Doncaster	Hatfield Main	Doncaster R	67	3
							Sunderland	—	—
							Darlington	130	12

Player	Ht	Wt	Pos	Birth Date	Birth Place	Source	Clubs	League App	League Gls
GAVIN Mark	5 8	10 07	M	10 12 63	Bailleston	Apprentice	Leeds U	30	3
							Hartlepool U (loan)	7	—
							Carlisle U	13	1
							Bolton W	49	3
							Rochdale	23	6
							Hearts	9	—
							Bristol C	69	6
							Watford	13	—
							Bristol C	41	2
							Exeter C	49	2
GAVIN Pat *	6 0	12 00	F	5 6 67	Hammersmith	Hanwell T	Gillingham	13	7
							Leicester C	3	—
							Gillingham (loan)	34	1
							Peterborough U	23	5
							Barnet	—	—
							Northampton T	14	4
							Wigan Ath	42	8
GAYLE Brian	6 2	12 07	D	6 3 65	Kingston		Wimbledon	83	3
							Manchester C	55	3
							Ipswich T	58	4
							Sheffield U	112	9
GAYLE John	6 2	15 04	F	30 7 64	Birmingham	Burton Alb	Wimbledon	20	2
							Birmingham C	44	10
							Walsall (loan)	4	1
							Coventry C	3	—
							Burnley	14	3
							Stoke C	4	—
GAYLE Marcus	6 2	12 13	M	27 9 70	Hammersmith	Trainee	Brentford	156	22
							Wimbledon	33	2
GAYLE Mark	6 0	12 00	G	21 10 69	Bromsgrove	Trainee	Leicester C	—	—
							Blackpool	—	—
						Worcester C	Walsall	75	—
							Crewe Alex	33	—
							Liverpool (loan)	—	—
GEE Phil	5 10	12 03	F	19 12 64	Pelsall	Gresley R	Derby Co	124	26
							Leicester C	51	9
							Plymouth Arg (loan)	6	—
GEMMILL Scot	5 10	10 01	M	2 1 71	Paisley	School	**Nottingham F**	126	18
GENTLE Justin ‡	5 7	10 09	F	6 6 74	Enfield	Trainee	Luton T	—	—
							Colchester U	2	—
GERMAINE Gary	6 2	14 00	G	2 8 76	Birmingham	Trainee	**WBA**	—	—
GERRARD Paul	6 1	12 06	G	22 1 73	Heywood	Trainee	**Oldham Ath**	83	—
GIBB Alistair	5 9	10 08	M	17 2 76	Salisbury	Trainee	**Norwich C**	—	—
GIBBS Nigel	5 7	11 01	D	20 11 65	St Albans	Apprentice	**Watford**	282	3
GIBBS Paul	5 9	11 04	D	26 10 72	Gorleston	Diss T	**Colchester U**	9	—
GIBSON Colin	5 9	11 03	D	6 4 60	Bridport	Apprentice	Aston Villa	185	10
							Manchester U	79	9
							Port Vale (loan)	6	2
							Leicester C	59	4
							Blackpool	2	—
							Walsall	33	—
GIBSON Terry *	5 5	10 00	F	23 12 62	Walthamstow	Apprentice	Tottenham H	18	4
							Coventry C	98	43
							Manchester U	23	1
							Wimbledon	86	22
							Swindon T (loan)	9	1
							Peterborough U	1	—
							Barnet	32	5
GIGGS Ryan	5 11	10 06	F	29 11 73	Cardiff	School	**Manchester U**	148	28
GILBERT David	5 4	10 04	M	22 6 63	Lincoln	Apprentice	Lincoln C	30	1
							Scunthorpe U	1	—
						Boston U	Northampton T	120	21
							Grimsby T	259	41

Player	Ht	Wt	Pos	Birth Date	Place	Source	Clubs	League App	Gls
GILCHRIST Phil	6 0	12 10	D	25 8 73	Stockton	Trainee	Nottingham F	—	—
							Middlesbrough	—	—
							Hartlepool U	82	—
							Oxford U	18	1
GILKES Michael	5 8	10 10	F	20 7 65	Hackney	Leicester C	**Reading**	317	42
							Chelsea (loan)	1	—
							Southampton (loan)	6	—
GILL Wayne	5 10	11 03	M	28 11 75	Chorley	Trainee	**Blackburn R**	—	—
GILLESPIE Gary	6 2	12 07	D	5 7 60	Stirling	School	Falkirk	22	—
							Coventry C	172	6
							Liverpool	156	14
							Celtic	69	2
							Coventry C	3	—
GILLESPIE Keith	5 10	11 03	F	18 2 75	Larne	Trainee	Manchester U	9	1
							Wigan Ath (loan)	8	4
							Newcastle U	17	2
GILMORE Craig *	5 10	11 00	D	8 12 76	Leeds	Trainee	**Nottingham F**	—	—
GINOLA David	6 0	13 00	F	25 1 67	Gossin		Toulon	81	4
							Racing Paris	61	8
							Brest	50	10
							Paris St Germain	115	32
							Newcastle U	—	—
GINTY Rory	5 9	10 02	F	23 1 77	Galway	Trainee	**Crystal Palace**	—	—
GITTENS Jon	6 0	12 06	D	22 1 64	Moseley	Paget R	Southampton	18	—
							Swindon T	126	6
							Southampton	19	—
							Middlesbrough (loan)	12	1
							Middlesbrough	13	—
							Portsmouth	68	1
GIVEN Shay	6 2	13 04	G	20 4 76	Lifford	Celtic	**Blackburn R**	—	—
							Swindon T (loan)	—	—
GLASS Jimmy	6 1	13 04	G	1 8 73	Epsom	Trainee	**Crystal Palace**	—	—
							Portsmouth (loan)	3	—
GLEGHORN Nigel	6 0	13 02	M	12 8 62	Seaham	Seaham Red Star	Ipswich T	66	11
							Manchester C	34	7
							Birmingham C	142	33
							Stoke C	120	17
GLOVER Dean	5 10	11 13	D	29 12 63	West Bromwich	Apprentice	Aston Villa	23	—
							Sheffield U (loan)	10	—
							Middlesbrough	50	5
							Port Vale	267	12
GLOVER Lee	5 10	12 01	F	24 4 70	Kettering	Trainee	Nottingham F	76	9
							Leicester C (loan)	5	1
							Barnsley (loan)	8	—
							Luton T (loan)	1	—
							Port Vale	28	4
GOATER Shaun	6 1	11 10	F	25 2 70	Bermuda		Manchester U	—	—
							Rotherham U	165	52
							Notts Co (loan)	1	—
GODDARD Paul *	5 7	12 00	F	12 10 59	Harlington	Apprentice	QPR	70	23
							West Ham U	170	54
							Newcastle U	61	19
							Derby Co	49	15
							Millwall	20	1
							Ipswich T	72	13
GONZAQUE Michael ‡	6 1	12 00	D	27 3 75	Canning Town	Trainee	Southend U	—	—
							Hereford U	3	—
GOODACRE Sam *	5 9	10 10	F	1 12 70	Sheffield	School	Sheffield W	—	—
							Scunthorpe U	44	12
GOODALL Danny	5 8	10 04	D	3 9 75	Bury	Trainee	**Blackburn R**	—	—
GOODEN Ty	5 8	12 06	M	23 10 72	Canvey Island	Wycombe W	**Swindon T**	20	2

Player	Ht	Wt	Pos	Birth Date	Birth Place	Source	Clubs	League App	League Gls
GOODING Mick	5 9	10 07	M	12 4 59	Newcastle	Bishop Auckland	Rotherham U	102	10
							Chesterfield	12	—
							Rotherham U	156	33
							Peterborough U	47	21
							Wolverhampton W	44	4
							Reading	231	23
GOODMAN Don	5 10	11 10	F	9 5 66	Leeds	School	Bradford C	70	14
							WBA	158	60
							Sunderland	116	40
							Wolverhampton W	24	3
GOODMAN Jon	5 11	12 11	F	2 6 71	Walthamstow	Bromley	Millwall	109	35
							Wimbledon	19	4
GOODRIDGE Greg	5 6	10 00	F	10 7 71	Barbados	Lambada	**Torquay U**	38	4
GOODWIN Shaun	5 9	10 09	M	14 6 69	Rotherham	Trainee	**Rotherham U**	233	30
GORDON Dale	5 10	11 08	F	9 1 67	Gt Yarmouth	Apprentice	Norwich C	206	31
							Rangers	45	6
							West Ham U	8	1
							Peterborough U (loan)	6	1
GORDON Dean	6 0	13 04	D	10 2 73	Thornton Heath	Trainee	**Crystal Palace**	100	7
GORDON Neville *			F	15 11 75	Greenwich	Trainee	**Millwall**	—	—
GORE Ian *	5 11	12 04	M	10 1 68	Liverpool		Birmingham C	—	—
						Southport	**Blackpool**	200	—
GOSS Jeremy	5 9	11 04	M	11 5 65	Oekolia	Amateur	**Norwich C**	172	13
GOUCK Andy	5 9	11 02	M	8 6 72	Blackpool	Trainee	**Blackpool**	132	11
GOULD Jonathan	6 1	12 07	G	18 7 68	Paddington	Clevedon T	Halifax T	32	—
							WBA	—	—
							Coventry C	25	—
GOURLAY Archie ‡	5 8	10 00	M	29 6 69	Greenock		Morton	2	—
							Newcastle U	3	—
							Morton (loan)	4	—
							Motherwell	3	—
							Hartlepool U	1	—
GOWSHALL Joby	6 1	13 00	D	7 8 75	Louth	Trainee	**Grimsby T**	—	—
GRAHAM Benjamin *			D	23 9 75	Pontypool	Trainee	**Cardiff C**	1	—
GRAHAM Deniol *	5 10	10 05	F	4 10 69	Cannock	Trainee	Manchester U	2	—
							Barnsley	38	2
							Preston NE (loan)	8	—
							Carlisle U (loan)	2	1
							Stockport Co	11	2
GRAHAM Jimmy	6 0	11 08	D	15 11 69	Glasgow	Trainee	Bradford C	7	—
							Rochdale (loan)	11	—
							Rochdale	126	1
							Hull C	39	—
GRAHAM Mark	5 6	10 00	F	24 10 74	Newry	Trainee	**QPR**	—	—
GRAHAM Richard	6 2	12 01	M	28 11 74	Dewsbury	Trainee	**Oldham Ath**	37	3
GRAINGER Martin	5 11	12 00	D	23 8 72	Enfield	Trainee	Colchester U	46	7
							Brentford	68	9
GRANT Kim	5 10	10 12	F	25 9 72	Ghana	Trainee	**Charlton Ath**	93	11
GRANT Tony	5 9	10 00	M	14 11 74	Liverpool	Trainee	**Everton**	5	—
GRANT Tony	5 10	11 08	D	20 8 76	Louth	Trainee	**Leeds U**	—	—
GRANVILLE Danny	6 0	12 00	M	19 1 75	Islington	Trainee	**Cambridge U**	27	7
GRAY Andy	5 6	10 10	F	25 10 73	Southampton	Trainee	Reading	17	3
							Leyton Orient	25	3
GRAY Ian	6 2	12 00	G	25 2 75	Manchester	Trainee	**Oldham Ath**	—	—
							Rochdale (loan)	12	—
GRAY Kevin	6 0	13 00	D	7 1 72	Sheffield	Trainee	Mansfield T	141	3
							Huddersfield T	5	—

Player	Ht	Wt	Pos	Birth Date	Birth Place	Source	Clubs	League App	League Gls
GRAY Martin	5 9	11 04	M	17 8 71	Stockton	Trainee	**Sunderland**	57	1
							Aldershot (loan)	5	—
GRAY Michael	5 8	10 07	D	3 8 74	Sunderland	Trainee	**Sunderland**	65	3
GRAY Phil	5 9	12 05	F	2 10 68	Belfast	Apprentice	Tottenham H	9	—
							Barnsley (loan)	3	—
							Fulham (loan)	3	—
							Luton T	59	22
							Sunderland	83	26
GRAYSON Neil	5 10	12 04	F	1 11 64	York	Rowntree Mackintosh	Doncaster R	29	6
							York C	1	—
							Chesterfield	15	—
						Boston U	**Northampton T**	38	8
GRAYSON Simon	5 11	12 07	D	16 12 69	Ripon	Trainee	Leeds U	2	—
							Leicester C	111	2
GRAYSTON Neil	5 7	10 11	D	25 11 75	Keighley	Trainee	**Bradford C**	5	—
GREEN Matt	5 8	11 04	M	22 10 75	Northampton	Trainee	**Derby Co**	—	—
GREEN Paul *	5 10	10 10	D	25 5 76	Carlisle	Trainee	**Rotherham U**	—	—
GREEN Richard	6 1	13 11	D	22 11 67	Wolverhampton	Apprentice	Shrewsbury T	125	5
							Swindon T	—	—
							Gillingham	127	12
GREEN Scott	5 10	12 05	M	15 1 70	Walsall	Trainee	Derby Co	—	—
							Bolton W	177	21
GREENALL Colin	5 10	11 06	D	30 12 63	Billinge	Apprentice	Blackpool	183	9
							Gillingham	62	4
							Oxford U	67	2
							Bury (loan)	3	—
							Bury	68	5
							Preston NE	29	1
							Chester C	42	1
							Lincoln C	39	3
GREENE David	6 2	13 05	D	26 10 73	Luton	Trainee	**Luton T**	19	—
GREGAN Sean	6 2	13 07	D	29 3 74	Cleveland	Trainee	**Darlington**	82	4
GREGORY David	5 11	11 10	M	23 1 70	Colchester	Trainee	**Ipswich T**	32	2
							Hereford U (loan)	2	—
GREGORY John §			G	16 5 77	Hounslow	Trainee	**Fulham**	1	—
GREGORY Neil	5 11	11 10	F	7 10 72	Zambia	Trainee	**Ipswich T**	3	—
							Chesterfield (loan)	3	1
							Scunthorpe U (loan)	10	7
GRIDELET Phil	5 11	13 00	M	30 4 67	Edgware	Barnet	Barnsley	6	—
							Rotherham U (loan)	9	—
							Southend U	58	5
GRIFFITH Cohen *	5 10	11 07	F	26 12 62	Georgetown	Kettering T	**Cardiff C**	234	39
GRIFFITHS Brian ‡	5 9	11 00	F	26 1 65	Prescot	St Helens T	Wigan Ath	189	44
							Blackpool	57	17
							Scarborough (loan)	5	1
GRIFFITHS Carl	5 9	10 06	F	15 7 71	Oswestry	Trainee	Shrewsbury T	143	54
							Manchester C	18	4
GRIFFITHS Gareth	6 4	14 00	D	10 4 70	Winsford	Rhyl	**Port Vale**	24	2
GRITT Steve	5 9	10 10	D	31 10 57	Bournemouth	Apprentice	Bournemouth	6	3
							Charlton Ath	347	24
							Walsall	20	1
							Charlton Ath	33	1
GROBBELAAR Bruce	6 1	14 02	G	6 10 57	Durban	Vancouver Whitecaps	Crewe Alex	24	1
						Vancouver Whitecaps	Liverpool	440	—
							Stoke C (loan)	4	—
							Southampton	30	—
GROGAN Darren ‡	5 7	10 00	M	16 12 74	Dublin	Trainee	**Tottenham H**	—	—

Player	Ht	Wt	Pos	Birth Date	Birth Place	Source	Clubs	League App	League Gls
GROVES Paul	5 11	11 05	M	28 2 66	Derby	Burton Alb	Leicester C	16	1
							Lincoln C (loan)	8	1
							Blackpool	107	21
							Grimsby T	138	28
GRUGEL Mark	5 8	10 00	M	9 3 76	Liverpool	Local	**Everton**	—	—
GUENTCHEV Bontcho *	5 10	11 07	F	7 7 64	Bulgaria	Sporting Lisbon	**Ipswich T**	61	6
GUEST Mark	5 7	10 00	F	21 1 76	Mexborough	Trainee	**Sheffield W**	—	—
GUINAN Stephen ‡	6 1	12 12	F	24 12 75	Birmingham	Trainee	**Nottingham F**	—	—
GULLIT Ruud	6 0	13 00	F	1 9 62	Surinam	DWS Amsterdam	Haarlem	91	32
							Feyenoord	85	30
							PSV Eindhoven	68	46
							AC Milan	117	35
							Sampdoria	31	15
							AC Milan	8	3
							Sampdoria	22	9
							Chelsea	—	—
GUNN Bryan	6 2	13 13	G	22 12 63	Thurso	Invergordon BC	Aberdeen	15	—
							Norwich C	304	—
GUPPY Steve	5 11	12 00	M	29 3 69	Winchester	Southampton	Wycombe W	41	8
							Newcastle U	—	—
							Port Vale	27	2
GURNEY Andrew	5 7	10 08	D	25 1 74	Bristol	Trainee	**Bristol R**	41	1
GYNN Mick ‡	5 5	11 06	M	19 8 61	Peterborough	Apprentice	Peterborough U	156	33
							Coventry C	241	32
							Stoke C	21	—
							Mansfield T	—	—
HAALAND Alf-Inge	5 10	12 12	M	23 11 72	Stavanger	Bryne	**Nottingham F**	23	1
HACKETT Gary *	5 8	11 06	M	11 10 62	Stourbridge	Bromsgrove R	Shrewsbury T	150	17
							Aberdeen	15	—
							Stoke C	73	7
							WBA	44	3
							Peterborough U	22	1
							Chester C	35	5
HACKETT Warren	6 0	12 05	D	16 12 71	Newham	Tottenham H	Leyton Orient	72	3
							Doncaster R	39	2
HADLEY Stewart	6 1	13 05	F	30 12 73	Dudley	Halesowen	Derby Co	—	—
							Mansfield T	53	19
HAGUE Paul	6 3	13 03	D	16 9 72	Consett	Trainee	Gillingham	9	—
							Leyton Orient	18	1
HAILS Julian	5 10	11 01	F	20 11 67	Lincoln	Hemel Hempstead	Fulham	109	12
							Southend U	26	2
HALL Derek	5 8	11 12	M	5 1 65	Manchester	Apprentice	Coventry C	1	—
							Torquay U (loan)	10	2
							Torquay U	45	4
							Swindon T	10	—
							Southend U	123	15
							Halifax T	49	4
							Hereford U	103	18
							Rochdale	9	1
HALL Gareth	5 8	10 07	D	20 3 69	Croydon	Apprentice	**Chelsea**	133	3
HALL Graeme *			D	22 11 75	Stockton	Trainee	**Arsenal**	—	—
HALL Kevin ‡	5 10	11 00	M	7 2 76	Edinburgh	Trainee	**Crystal Palace**	—	—
HALL Leigh †			F	10 6 75	Hereford		**Hereford U**	1	—
HALL Marcus	6 1	12 02	D	24 3 76	Coventry	Trainee	**Coventry C**	5	—
HALL Mark *	5 6	10 12	M	13 1 73	London	Tottenham H	**Southend U**	12	—
							Barnet (loan)	3	—
HALL Paul	5 9	10 04	F	3 7 72	Manchester	Trainee	Torquay U	93	1
							Portsmouth	71	9

Player	Ht	Wt	Pos	Birth Date	Birth Place	Source	Clubs	League App	League Gls
HALL Richard	6 2	13 11	D	14 3 72	Ipswich	Trainee	Scunthorpe U	22	3
							Southampton	96	11
HALL Wayne	5 9	10 06	D	25 10 68	Rotherham	Darlington	**York C**	236	8
HALLE Gunnar	5 11	11 02	D	11 8 65	Oslo	Lillestrom	**Oldham Ath**	131	11
HALLIDAY Stephen	5 10	11 11	F	3 5 76	Sunderland	Charlton Ath	**Hartlepool U**	39	5
HALLWORTH Jon	6 1	14 03	G	26 10 65	Stockport	School	Ipswich T	45	—
							Swindon T (loan)	—	—
							Fulham (loan)	—	—
							Bristol R (loan)	2	—
							Oldham Ath	159	—
HAMILL Rory	5 8	12 03	F	4 5 76	Coleraine	Portstewart	**Fulham**	23	5
HAMILTON Derrick	5 11	12 09	M	15 8 76	Bradford	Trainee	**Bradford C**	32	2
HAMILTON Ian	5 9	11 03	F	14 12 67	Stevenage	Apprentice	Southampton	—	—
							Cambridge U	24	1
							Scunthorpe U	145	18
							WBA	123	14
HAMLET Alan §	6 0	11 03	D	30 9 77	Watford	Trainee	**Barnet**	3	—
HAMMOND Nicky	6 0	11 13	G	7 9 67	Hornchurch	Apprentice	Arsenal	—	—
							Bristol R (loan)	3	—
							Peterborough U (loan)	—	—
							Aberdeen (loan)	—	—
							Swindon T	67	—
HAMON Chris	6 1	13 07	F	27 4 70	Jersey	St Peter	**Swindon T**	8	1
HANBY Robert	5 10	11 09	D	24 12 74	Pontefract	Trainee	**Barnsley**	—	—
HANCOX Richard	5 10	13 00	F	4 10 70	Stourbridge	Stourbridge S	**Torquay U**	46	9
HANDYSIDE Peter	6 1	12 03	D	31 7 74	Dumfries	Trainee	**Grimsby T**	59	—
HANSEN Vergard	6 2	13 00	D	8 8 69	Drammen	Stromsgodset	**Bristol C**	29	—
HARDING Paul	5 9	12 05	M	6 3 64	Mitcham	Barnet	Notts Co	54	1
							Southend U (loan)	5	—
							Watford (loan)	2	—
							Birmingham C	22	—
HARDWICK Matthew ‡	5 10	11 04	F	12 9 74	Rotherham	School	**Sheffield W**	—	—
HARDY Paul ‡	5 8	10 05	M	29 8 75	Plymouth	Trainee	**Torquay U**	1	—
HARDY Phil	5 8	11 00	D	9 4 73	Chester	Trainee	**Wrexham**	176	—
HARDYMAN Paul *	5 8	11 07	D	11 3 64	Portsmouth	Waterford	Portsmouth	117	3
							Sunderland	106	9
							Bristol R	67	5
HARFORD Mick	6 3	14 05	F	12 2 59	Sunderland	Lambton St BC	Lincoln C	115	41
							Newcastle U	19	4
							Bristol C	30	11
							Birmingham C	92	25
							Luton T	139	57
							Derby Co	58	15
							Luton T	29	12
							Chelsea	28	9
							Sunderland	11	2
							Coventry C	1	1
							Wimbledon	27	6
HARFORD Paul	6 4	13 12	F	21 10 74	Kent	Trainee	**Blackburn R**	—	—
							Wigan Ath (loan)	3	—
							Shrewsbury T (loan)	6	—
HARGREAVES Chris *	5 11	11 00	F	12 5 72	Cleethorpes	Trainee	Grimsby T	51	5
							Scarborough (loan)	3	—
							Hull C	49	—
HARKES John	5 10	11 12	M	8 3 67	New Jersey	USSF	Sheffield W	81	7
							Derby Co	66	2
HARKIN Joe	5 10	11 04	D	9 12 75	Derry	Trainee	**Manchester C**	—	—

Player	Ht	Wt	Pos	Birth Date	Birth Place	Source	Clubs	League App	League Gls
HARKNESS Steve	5 10	11 02	M	27 8 71	Carlisle	Trainee	Carlisle U	13	—
							Liverpool	40	1
							Huddersfield T (loan)	5	—
							Southend U (loan)	6	—
HARLE Mike	5 10	11 12	D	31 10 72	Lewisham	Sittingbourne	**Millwall**	—	—
HARMON Darren	5 5	9 12	M	30 1 73	Northampton	Trainee	Notts Co	—	—
							Shrewsbury T	6	2
							Northampton T	89	12
HARPER Alan	5 9	11 09	M	1 11 60	Liverpool	Apprentice	Liverpool	—	—
							Everton	127	4
							Sheffield W	35	—
							Manchester C	50	1
							Everton	51	—
							Luton T	41	1
							Burnley	27	—
HARPER Lee	6 1	13 00	G	30 10 71	London	Sittingbourne	**Arsenal**	—	—
HARPER Lee	5 11	12 05	D	24 3 75	Bridlington	York C	**Scarborough**	2	—
HARPER Steve	5 10	11 12	F	3 2 69	Stoke	Trainee	Port Vale	28	2
							Preston NE	77	10
							Burnley	69	8
							Doncaster R	64	11
HARPER Steve	6 2	13 00	G	3 2 70	Easington	Seaham Red Star	**Newcastle U**	—	—
HARRINGTON Justin	5 9	10 09	F	18 6 75	Truro	Trainee	**Norwich C**	—	—
HARRIOTT Marvin	5 8	11 06	D	20 4 74	Dulwich	West Ham U	Oldham Ath	—	—
							Barnsley	—	—
							Leyton Orient (loan)	8	—
							Bristol C	36	—
HARRIS Andrew	5 10	11 11	D	26 2 77	Springs	Trainee	**Liverpool**	—	—
HARRIS Mark	6 3	13 11	M	15 7 63	Reading	Wokingham	Crystal Palace	2	—
							Burnley (loan)	4	—
							Swansea C	228	14
HARRISON Gary †	5 9	11 05	F	12 3 75	Northampton	Aston Villa	**Northampton T**	7	—
HARRISON Gerry	5 10	12 12	M	15 4 72	Lambeth	Trainee	Watford	9	—
							Bristol C	38	1
							Cardiff C (loan)	10	1
							Hereford U (loan)	6	—
							Huddersfield T	—	—
							Burnley	19	2
HARRISON Lee	6 2	11 13	G	12 9 71	Billericay	Trainee	Charlton Ath	—	—
							Fulham (loan)	—	—
							Gillingham (loan)	2	—
							Fulham (loan)	—	—
							Fulham	7	—
HART Andy ‡			D	11 3 76	Pontefract		**Carlisle U**	—	—
HARTENBERGER Uwe *	6 1	13 00	F	1 2 68	Lauterecken	Bayer Uerdingen	**Reading**	24	4
HARTFIELD Charles	6 0	12 02	D	4 9 71	London	Trainee	Arsenal	—	—
							Sheffield U	54	1
HARTSON John	5 11	11 13	F	5 4 75	Swansea	Trainee	Luton T	54	11
							Arsenal	15	7
HARVEY Lee	5 11	11 07	M	21 12 66	Harlow	Harrow	Leyton Orient	184	23
							Nottingham F	2	—
							Brentford	51	6
HARVEY Richard	5 10	11 10	D	17 4 69	Letchworth	Apprentice	**Luton T**	117	3
							Blackpool (loan)	5	—
HATHAWAY Ian	5 6	11 00	M	22 8 68	Wordsley	Bedworth U	Mansfield T	44	2
							Rotherham U	13	1
							Torquay U	79	12
HAWORTH Robert *	6 2	13 04	F	21 11 75	Edgware	Trainee	**Fulham**	21	1

				Birth				League	
Player	*Ht*	*Wt*	*Pos*	*Date*	*Place*	*Source*	*Clubs*	*App*	*Gls*
HAWTHORNE Mark ‡	5 9	10 12	M	31 10 73	Glasgow	Trainee	Crystal Palace	—	—
							Sheffield U	—	—
							Walsall	—	—
							Torquay U	2	—
HAY Darran ‡	6 0	13 08	F	17 12 69	Hitchin	Biggleswade	**Cambridge U**	29	3
HAYES Martin *	6 0	12 04	F	21 3 66	Walthamstow	Apprentice	Arsenal	102	26
							Celtic	7	—
							Wimbledon (loan)	2	—
							Swansea C	61	8
HAYNES Junior ‡			M	16 4 76	Croydon		**Barnet**	6	—
HAYRETTIN Hakan *	5 9	11 02	M	4 2 70	London	Trainee	Leyton Orient	—	—
						Barnet	Barnet	6	—
							Torquay U (loan)	4	—
							Wycombe W	19	1
							Cambridge U	17	—
HAYWARD Andy	6 0	11 02	F	21 6 70	Barnsley	Frickley Ath	**Rotherham U**	37	6
HAYWARD Steve	5 10	12 05	M	8 9 71	Walsall	Trainee	Derby Co	26	1
							Carlisle U	9	2
HAYWOOD Paul ‡	5 11	10 02	D	4 10 75	Barnsley	Trainee	**Nottingham F**	—	—
HAZARD Mickey	5 8	11 08	M	5 2 60	Sunderland	Apprentice	Tottenham H	91	13
							Chelsea	81	9
							Portsmouth	8	1
							Swindon T	119	17
							Tottenham H	28	2
HAZEL Des	5 10	11 05	M	15 7 67	Bradford	Apprentice	Sheffield W	6	—
							Grimsby T (loan)	9	2
							Rotherham U	238	30
							Chesterfield	—	—
HEALD Greg	6 1	12 08	D	26 9 71	London	Enfield	**Peterborough U**	29	—
HEALD Oliver *	6 0	12 00	F	13 3 75	Vancouver		**Port Vale**	—	—
HEALD Paul	6 2	14 00	G	20 9 68	Wath-on-Dearne	Trainee	Sheffield U	—	—
							Leyton Orient	176	—
							Coventry C (loan)	2	—
							Crystal Palace (loan)	—	—
							Swindon T (loan)	2	—
HEALY Brett	5 8	10 08	M	6 10 77	Coventry	Trainee	**Coventry C**	—	—
HEANEY Neil	5 9	11 13	F	3 11 71	Middlesbrough	Trainee	Arsenal	7	—
							Hartlepool U (loan)	3	—
							Cambridge U (loan)	13	2
							Southampton	36	2
HEATH Adrian	5 6	11 00	F	11 1 61	Newcastle under Lyne	Apprentice	Stoke C	95	16
							Everton	226	71
						Espanol	Aston Villa	9	—
							Manchester C	75	4
							Stoke C	6	—
							Burnley	111	29
HEATH Michael ‡	5 9	11 00	G	7 2 74	Hull	Trainee	Tottenham H	—	—
							Scunthorpe U	2	—
HEATH Stephen			D	15 11 77	Hull	Trainee	**Leeds U**	—	—
HEATHCOTE Mike	6 2	12 06	D	10 9 65	Durham	Spennymoor U	Sunderland	9	—
							Halifax T (loan)	7	1
							York C (loan)	3	—
							Shrewsbury T	44	6
							Cambridge U	128	13
HEBBERD Trevor *	6 0	11 04	M	19 6 58	Winchester	Apprentice	Southampton	97	7
							Bolton W (loan)	6	—
							Leicester C (loan)	4	1
							Oxford U	260	37
							Derby Co	81	10
							Portsmouth	4	—
							Chesterfield	74	1
							Lincoln C	25	—
HEGGS Carl	6 0	11 08	F	11 10 70	Leicester	Paget R	**WBA**	40	3
							Bristol R (loan)	5	1

Player	Ht	Wt	Pos	Birth Date	Birth Place	Source	Clubs	League App	League Gls
HELDER Glenn	5 11	11 07	F	28 10 68	Leiden		Sparta	93	9
							Vitesse	52	12
							Arsenal	13	—
HELGASON Gudni ‡	5 10	11 10	F	16 7 76	Iceland	Volsungur	**Sunderland**	—	—
HELLIWELL Ian	6 3	14 00	F	7 11 62	Rotherham	Matlock T	York C	160	40
							Scunthorpe U	80	22
							Rotherham U	52	4
							Stockport Co	17	4
HEMMINGS Tony	5 10	12 09	F	21 9 67	Burton	Northwich Vic	**Wycombe W**	46	12
HENDERSON Damian *	6 2	13 10	F	12 5 73	Leeds	Trainee	Leeds U	—	—
							Scarborough	17	5
							Scunthorpe U	37	4
							Hereford U (loan)	5	—
							Hartlepool U (loan)	12	3
HENDERSON Nicky ‡	5 10	11 08	D	11 2 76	Newcastle	Trainee	**Brighton & HA**	—	—
HENDON Ian	6 0	12 10	D	5 12 71	Ilford	Trainee	Tottenham H	4	—
							Portsmouth (loan)	4	—
							Leyton Orient (loan)	6	—
							Barnsley (loan)	6	—
							Leyton Orient	65	2
							Birmingham C (loan)	4	—
HENDRIE John	5 8	12 05	F	24 10 63	Lennoxtown	Apprentice	Coventry C	21	2
							Hereford U (loan)	6	—
							Bradford C	173	46
							Newcastle U	34	4
							Leeds U	27	5
							Middlesbrough	179	43
HENDRIE Lee	5 7	9 00	F	18 5 77	Birmingham	Trainee	**Aston Villa**	—	—
HENDRY Colin	6 1	12 00	D	7 12 65	Keith	Islavale	Dundee	41	2
							Blackburn R	102	22
							Manchester C	63	5
							Blackburn R	132	9
HENDRY John	5 11	10 12	F	6 1 70	Glasgow	Hillington YC	Dundee	2	—
							Forfar Ath (loan)	10	6
							Tottenham H	17	5
							Charlton Ath (loan)	5	1
							Swansea C (loan)	8	2
HENRY Liburd *	5 11	12 12	F	29 8 67	London	Leytonstone/ Ilford	Watford	10	1
							Halifax T (loan)	5	—
							Maidstone U	67	9
							Gillingham	42	2
							Peterborough U	32	7
HENRY Nick	5 6	9 08	M	21 2 69	Liverpool	Trainee	**Oldham Ath**	237	18
HERBERT Craig	6 0	12 00	D	9 11 75	Coventry	Torquay U	**WBA**	8	—
HERRERA Robbie	5 6	10 02	D	12 6 70	Torbay	Trainee	QPR	6	—
							Torquay U (loan)	11	—
							Torquay U (loan)	5	—
							Fulham	50	1
HESKEY Emile §			M	11 1 78	Leicester	Trainee	**Leicester C**	1	—
HESSENTHALER Andy	5 7	11 05	M	17 8 65	Gravesend	Redbridge Forest	**Watford**	165	11
HEWITT Jamie	5 10	11 09	M	17 5 68	Chesterfield	School	Chesterfield	249	14
							Doncaster R	33	—
							Chesterfield	67	6
HEWLETT Matthew	6 2	10 11	M	25 2 76	Bristol	Trainee	**Bristol C**	13	—
HICKS Stuart	6 1	13 00	D	30 5 67	Peterborough	Wisbech	Colchester U	64	—
							Scunthorpe U	67	1
							Doncaster R	36	—
							Huddersfield T	22	1
							Preston NE	12	—
							Scarborough	6	—
HIGGINS Dave	6 0	11 00	D	19 8 61	Liverpool	Eagle	Tranmere R	28	—
						S. Liverpool, Caernarfon	**Tranmere R**	280	10

Player	Ht	Wt	Pos	Birth Date	Birth Place	Source	Clubs	League App	League Gls
HIGGS Shane §	6 2	12 12	G	13 5 77	Oxford	Trainee	**Bristol R**	—	—
HIGNETT Craig	5 9	11 10	M	12 1 70	Whiston	Liverpool	Crewe Alex	121	42
							Middlesbrough	76	17
HILEY Scott	5 9	10 07	M	27 9 68	Plymouth	Trainee	Exeter C	210	12
							Birmingham C	44	—
HILL Andy	5 11	12 00	D	20 1 65	Maltby	Apprentice	Manchester U	—	—
							Bury	264	10
							Manchester C	98	6
HILL Colin	6 0	12 05	D	12 11 63	Hillingdon	Apprentice	Arsenal	46	1
							Brighton (loan)	—	—
						Maritimo	Colchester U	69	—
							Sheffield U	82	1
							Leicester C (loan)	10	—
							Leicester C	101	—
HILL Danny	5 9	11 03	M	1 10 74	Edmonton	Trainee	**Tottenham H**	10	—
HILL David *	5 11	12 04	M	6 6 66	Nottingham	Local	Scunthorpe U	140	10
							Ipswich T	61	—
							Scunthorpe U	65	6
							Lincoln C	58	6
							Chesterfield (loan)	3	—
HILL Keith	6 0	12 06	D	17 5 69	Bolton	Apprentice	Blackburn R	96	3
							Plymouth Arg	99	2
HILLIER David	5 10	12 05	M	19 12 69	Blackheath	Trainee	**Arsenal**	97	2
HILTON Chris ‡	5 9	10 06	D	8 12 75	Barnsley	Trainee	**Rotherham U**	—	—
HILTON David			D	10 11 77	Barnsley	Trainee	**Manchester U**	—	—
HILTON Robert *			D	5 11 75	Warrington	Trainee	**Oldham Ath**	—	—
HIMSWORTH Gary	5 7	9 10	D	19 12 69	Appleton	Trainee	York C	88	8
							Scarborough	92	6
							Darlington	66	5
HINCHCLIFFE Andy	5 10	12 10	D	5 2 69	Manchester	Apprentice	Manchester C	112	8
							Everton	119	4
HINES Leslie			D	7 1 77	Germany	Trainee	**Aston Villa**	—	—
HINSHELWOOD Danny	5 9	10 11	D	4 12 75	Bromley	Trainee	**Nottingham F**	—	—
HIRST David	5 11	13 10	F	7 12 67	Barnsley	Apprentice	Barnsley	28	9
							Sheffield W	233	87
HISLOP Shaka	6 6	12 02	G	22 2 69	London	Howard Univ.	**Reading**	104	—
HITCHCOCK Kevin	6 1	12 02	G	5 10 62	Custom House	Barking	Nottingham F	—	—
							Mansfield T (loan)	14	—
							Mansfield T	168	—
							Chelsea	69	—
							Northampton T (loan)	17	—
							West Ham U (loan)	—	—
HOBSON Gary	6 1	12 10	D	12 11 71	North Ferriby	Trainee	**Hull C**	113	—
HOCKADAY David *	5 9	11 02	D	9 11 57	Billingham	Amateur	Blackpool	147	24
							Swindon T	245	6
							Hull C	72	2
							Stoke C (loan)	7	—
							Shrewsbury T	48	—
HODDLE Carl *	6 4	11 00	M	8 3 67	Harlow	Bishop's Stortford	Leyton Orient	28	2
							Barnet	92	3
HODDLE Glenn	6 0	11 06	M	27 10 57	Hayes	Apprentice	Tottenham	377	88
						Monaco	Chelsea	—	—
							Swindon T	64	1
							Chelsea	31	1
HODGE John	5 7	11 03	F	1 4 69	Ormskirk	Exmouth	Exeter C	65	10
							Swansea C	71	9

Player	Ht	Wt	Pos	Birth Date	Birth Place	Source	Clubs	League App	League Gls
HODGE Martin	6 2	15 03	G	4 2 59	Southport	Apprentice	Plymouth Arg	43	—
							Everton	25	—
							Preston NE (loan)	28	—
							Oldham Ath (loan)	4	—
							Gillingham (loan)	4	—
							Preston NE (loan)	16	—
							Sheffield W	197	—
							Leicester C	75	—
							Hartlepool U	69	—
							Rochdale	42	—
							Plymouth Arg	17	—
HODGE Steve	5 8	9 11	M	25 10 62	Nottingham	Apprentice	Nottingham F	123	30
							Aston Villa	53	12
							Tottenham H	45	7
							Nottingham F	82	20
							Leeds U	54	10
							Derby Co (loan)	10	2
							QPR	15	—
HODGES Glyn	6 1	12 03	M	30 4 63	Streatham	Apprentice	Wimbledon	232	49
							Newcastle U	7	—
							Watford	86	15
							Crystal Palace	7	—
							Sheffield U	125	16
HODGES Kevin *	5 8	10 11	M	12 6 60	Bridport	Apprentice	Plymouth Arg	530	81
							Torquay U (loan)	3	—
							Torquay U	65	4
HODGES Lee	5 9	11 06	F	4 9 73	Epping	Trainee	Tottenham H	4	—
							Plymouth Arg (loan)	7	2
							Wycombe W (loan)	4	—
							Barnet	34	4
HODGES Lee	5 4	9 06	F	2 3 78	Newham	Trainee	**West Ham U**	—	—
HODGSON Doug	6 1	12 05	M	27 2 69	Frankston	Heidelberg	**Sheffield U**	1	—
HOGG Graeme	6 1	13 01	D	17 6 64	Aberdeen	Apprentice	Manchester U	83	1
							WBA (loan)	7	—
							Portsmouth	100	2
							Hearts	58	3
							Notts Co	17	—
HOLCROFT Peter	5 8	10 00	M	3 1 76	Liverpool	Trainee	**Everton**	—	—
HOLDEN Andy	6 1	13 10	D	14 9 62	Flint	Rhyl	Chester C	100	17
							Wigan Ath	49	4
							Oldham Ath	22	4
HOLDEN Mark	5 8	11 00	D	2 4 76	Tamworth	Trainee	**Stoke C**	—	—
HOLDEN Rick	5 11	12 07	M	9 9 64	Skipton		Burnley	1	—
							Halifax T	67	12
							Watford	42	8
							Oldham Ath	129	19
							Manchester C	50	3
							Oldham Ath	60	9
HOLDSWORTH David	6 1	12 04	D	8 11 68	Walthamstow	Trainee	**Watford**	231	9
HOLDSWORTH Dean	5 11	11 13	F	8 11 68	Walthamstow	Trainee	Watford	16	3
							Carlisle U (loan)	4	1
							Port Vale (loan)	6	2
							Swansea C (loan)	5	1
							Brentford (loan)	7	1
							Brentford	110	53
							Wimbledon	106	43
HOLLAND Chris	5 9	11 05	M	11 9 75	Whalley	Trainee	Preston NE	1	—
							Newcastle U	3	—
HOLLAND Matthew	5 9	11 00	M	11 4 74	Bury	Trainee	West Ham U	—	—
							Bournemouth	16	1
HOLLAND Paul	5 11	12 10	M	8 7 73	Lincoln	School	**Mansfield T**	149	25
HOLLIS Steve ‡	6 0	11 00	D	22 8 72	Liverpool	Liverpool	**Wigan Ath**	1	—

Player	Ht	Wt	Pos	Birth Date	Birth Place	Source	Clubs	League App	League Gls
HOLLOWAY Ian	5 8	10 10	M	12 3 63	Kingswood	Apprentice	Bristol R	111	14
							Wimbledon	19	2
							Brentford (loan)	13	2
							Brentford	16	—
							Torquay U (loan)	6	—
							Bristol R	179	26
							QPR	120	3
HOLMES Darren	5 8	11 02	M	30 1 75	Sheffield	Trainee	**Sheffield W**	—	—
HOLMES Matt	5 7	10 07	F	1 8 69	Luton	Trainee	Bournemouth	114	8
							Cardiff C (loan)	1	—
							West Ham U	76	4
HOLMES Paul	5 10	11 03	D	18 2 68	Wortley	Apprentice	Doncaster R	47	1
							Torquay U	138	4
							Birmingham C	12	—
							Everton	20	—
HOLMES Steve	6 2	13 00	D	13 1 72	Middlesbrough	Guisborough T	**Preston NE**	5	1
							Hartlepool U (loan)	5	2
HOLSGROVE Paul	6 1	11 10	F	26 8 69	Wellington	Trainee	Aldershot	3	—
							Wimbledon (loan)	—	—
							WBA (loan)	—	—
						Wokingham	Luton T	2	—
						Heracles	Millwall	11	—
							Reading	24	3
HOLT Gary	6 1	11 11	M	9 3 73	Irvine	Celtic	**Stoke C**	—	—
HOMER Chris §	5 9	11 05	M	16 4 77	Stockton	Trainee	**Hartlepool U**	1	—
HONE Mark	6 1	12 05	D	31 3 68	Croydon	Trainee	Crystal Palace	4	—
						Welling	**Southend U**	40	—
HONOR Chris (on loan from Airdrieonians)	5 9	10 09	D	5 6 68	Bristol		**Cardiff C**	10	—
HONOUR Brian ‡	5 7	12 05	M	16 2 64	Horden	Apprentice	Darlington	74	4
						Peterlee	**Hartlepool U**	319	25
HOOKER Jon	5 7	11 00	M	31 3 72	London	Hertford T	Gillingham	—	—
							Brentford	1	—
HOOPER Dean	5 10	11 06	M	13 4 71	Harefield	Hayes	**Swindon T**	4	—
HOOPER Lyndon ‡	5 4	10 00	M	30 5 66	Guyana	Toronto Blizzard	**Birmingham C**	5	—
HOOPER Michael	6 2	13 05	G	10 2 64	Bristol	Mangotsfield	Bristol C	1	—
							Wrexham (loan)	20	—
							Wrexham	14	—
							Liverpool	51	—
							Leicester C (loan)	14	—
							Newcastle U	25	—
HOPE Chris	6 1	12 07	D	14 11 72	Sheffield	Darlington	Nottingham F	—	—
							Scunthorpe U	65	—
HOPKIN David	5 9	10 03	M	21 8 70	Greenock	Pt Glasgow R BC	Morton	18	—
							Chelsea	40	1
HOPKINS Jeff	6 0	12 11	D	14 4 64	Swansea	Apprentice	Fulham	219	4
							Crystal Palace	70	2
							Plymouth Arg (loan)	8	—
							Bristol R	6	—
							Reading	99	3
HOPPER Neil ‡	6 1	12 08	G	27 1 76	Southampton	Trainee	**Southampton**	—	—
HOPPER Tony	5 11	11 07	M	31 5 76	Carlisle	Trainee	**Carlisle U**	6	—
HORLOCK Kevin	6 0	12 00	D	1 11 72	Plumstead	Trainee	West Ham U	—	—
							Swindon T	90	2
HORNE Barry	5 10	12 02	M	18 5 62	St Asaph	Rhyl	Wrexham	136	17
							Portsmouth	70	7
							Southampton	112	6
							Everton	97	2

Player	Ht	Wt	Pos	Birth Date	Birth Place	Source	Clubs	League App	League Gls
HORNE Brian	5 9	14 06	G	5 10 67	Billericay	Apprentice	Millwall	163	—
							Watford (loan)	—	—
							Middlesbrough (loan)	4	—
							Stoke C (loan)	1	—
							Portsmouth	3	—
							Hartlepool U	41	—
HORNER Philip	6 1	12 07	F	10 11 66	Leeds	Lincoln C	Leicester C	10	—
							Rotherham U (loan)	4	—
							Halifax T	72	4
							Blackpool	187	22
HOTTIGER Marc	5 10	12 09	D	7 11 67	Lausanne	Sion	**Newcastle U**	38	1
HOUCHEN Keith	6 1	13 07	F	25 7 60	Middlesbrough	Chesterfield	Hartlepool U	170	65
							Orient	76	20
							York C	67	19
							Scunthorpe U	9	3
							Coventry C	54	7
							Hibernian	57	11
							Port Vale	49	10
							Hartlepool U	66	21
HOUGHTON Ray	5 7	10 10	M	9 1 62	Glasgow	Amateur	West Ham U	1	—
							Fulham	129	16
							Oxford U	83	10
							Liverpool	153	28
							Aston Villa	95	6
							Crystal Palace	10	2
HOUGHTON Scott	5 7	12 04	F	22 10 71	Hitchin	Trainee	Tottenham H	10	2
							Ipswich T (loan)	8	1
							Cambridge U (loan)	—	—
							Gillingham (loan)	3	—
							Charlton Ath (loan)	6	—
							Luton T	16	1
							Walsall	38	8
HOULT Russell	6 4	14 09	G	22 11 72	Leicester	Trainee	**Leicester C**	10	—
							Lincoln C (loan)	2	—
							Blackpool (loan)	—	—
							Bolton W (loan)	4	—
							Lincoln C (loan)	15	—
							Derby Co (loan)	15	—
HOUSHAM Steven	5 10	11 07	D	24 2 76	Gainsborough T	Trainee	**Scunthorpe U**	4	—
HOVI Tom ‡			D	5 1 72	Norway	Hamkam	**Charlton Ath**	2	—
HOWARD John ‡	6 2	13 02	D	2 4 74	Stafford	Trainee	Wolverhampton W	—	—
							Stockport Co	—	—
HOWARD Jonathan	5 11	12 06	F	7 10 71	Sheffield	Trainee	Rotherham U	36	5
							Chesterfield	12	1
HOWARD Terry	6 1	11 07	D	26 2 66	Stepney	Apprentice	Chelsea	6	—
							C Palace (loan)	4	—
							Chester C (loan)	2	—
							Leyton Orient	328	31
							Wycombe W	20	—
HOWARTH Lee	6 1	13 06	D	3 1 68	Bolton	Chorley	Peterborough U	62	—
							Mansfield T	40	2
HOWE Stephen	5 7	10 04	M	6 11 73	Annitsford	Trainee	**Nottingham F**	4	—
HOWELL David †	6 0	12 00	D	10 10 58	London	Enfield	Barnet	57	3
							Southend U	6	—
							Birmingham C	2	—
HOWELLS David	6 0	12 04	M	15 12 67	Guildford	Trainee	**Tottenham H**	196	17
HOWEY Lee	6 2	13 09	F	1 4 69	Sunderland	AC Hemptinne	**Sunderland**	30	5
HOWEY Steve	6 1	10 05	M	26 10 71	Sunderland	Trainee	**Newcastle U**	118	4
HOY Kristian †			F	27 4 76	Doncaster		**Doncaster R**	1	—
HOYLAND Jamie	6 0	12 08	M	23 1 66	Sheffield	Apprentice	Manchester C	2	—
							Bury	172	35
							Sheffield U	89	6
							Bristol C (loan)	6	—
							Burnley	30	2

				Birth				League	
Player	Ht	Wt	Pos	Date	Place	Source	Clubs	App	Gls
HOYLE Colin	5 11	12 03	F	15 1 72	Derby	Trainee	Arsenal	—	—
							Chesterfield (loan)	3	—
							Barnsley	—	—
							Bradford C	62	1
							Notts Co	3	—
							Mansfield T (loan)	5	—
HUCKERBY Darren	5 9	11 00	M	23 4 76	Nottingham	Trainee	**Lincoln C**	12	3
HUGHES Anthony	6 0	12 05	D	3 10 73	Liverpool	Trainee	**Crewe Alex**	23	1
HUGHES Bryan	5 9	10 00	M	19 6 76	Liverpool	Trainee	**Wrexham**	49	9
HUGHES Ceri	5 10	11 05	M	26 2 71	Pontypridd	Trainee	**Luton T**	116	12
HUGHES Darren ‡	5 11	10 11	D	6 10 65	Prescot	Apprentice	Everton	3	—
							Shrewsbury T	37	1
							Brighton	26	2
							Port Vale	184	4
							Northampton T	13	—
HUGHES David	5 10	11 08	M	30 12 72	St Albans	Trainee	**Southampton**	14	2
HUGHES Ian	5 11	12 00	M	2 8 74	Bangor	Trainee	**Bury**	108	1
HUGHES Luke ‡	5 10	10 04	F	17 9 75	Sunderland	Trainee	**Nottingham F**	—	—
HUGHES Mark	5 10	13 05	F	1 11 63	Wrexham	Apprentice	Manchester U	89	37
							Barcelona	28	4
							Bayern Munich (loan)	18	6
							Manchester U	256	82
HUGHES Mark	6 0	13 00	D	3 2 62	Port Talbot	Apprentice	Bristol R	74	3
							Torquay U (loan)	9	1
							Swansea C	12	—
							Bristol C	22	—
							Tranmere R	266	9
							Shrewsbury T	20	—
HUGHES Michael (on loan from Strasbourg)	5 6	10 08	F	2 8 71	Larne		**West Ham U**	17	2
HUGHES Paul	6 0	11 05	M	19 4 76	Hammersmith	Trainee	**Chelsea**	—	—
HUGHES Steve §			M	18 9 76	Wokingham	Trainee	**Arsenal**	1	—
HULME Kevin	5 10	13 02	F	7 12 67	Farnworth	Radcliffe Borough	Bury	110	21
							Chester C (loan)	4	—
							Doncaster R	34	8
							Bury	28	—
HUMES Tony	5 11	11 05	D	19 3 66	Blyth	Apprentice	Ipswich T	120	10
							Wrexham	102	1
HUMPHREY John *	5 10	11 04	D	31 1 61	Paddington	Apprentice	Wolverhampton W	149	3
							Charlton Ath	194	3
							Crystal Palace	160	2
							Reading (loan)	8	—
HUMPHRIES Mark	5 10	12 12	D	23 12 71	Glasgow	Cove R	Aberdeen	2	—
							Leeds U	—	—
							Bristol C	4	—
HUNT Andy	6 0	11 07	F	9 6 70	Thurrock	Kettering T	Newcastle U	43	11
							WBA (loan)	10	9
							WBA	74	25
HUNT James			M	17 12 76	Derby	Trainee	**Notts Co**	—	—
HUNT Jonathan	5 11	11 10	M	2 11 71	London		Barnet	33	—
							Southend U	49	6
							Birmingham C	20	5
HUNT Kevin	5 10	11 00	M	4 7 75	Chatham		**Gillingham**	—	—
HUNTER Barry	6 4	12 00	D	18 11 68	Coleraine	Crusaders	**Wrexham**	60	1
HUNTER Junior *	5 8	11 00	F	1 2 75	Lambeth	Trainee	**Cambridge U**	40	—
HUNTER Roy *	5 9	11 00	M	29 10 73	Cleveland	Trainee	**WBA**	9	1
HURDLE Gus	5 9	11 01	D	14 10 73	London	Fulham	**Brentford**	9	—

Player	Ht	Wt	Pos	Birth Date	Birth Place	Source	Clubs	League App	League Gls
HURLOCK Terry	5 9	14 01	M	22 9 58	Hackney	Leytonstone/ Ilford	Brentford	220	18
							Reading	29	—
							Millwall	104	8
							Rangers	29	2
							Southampton	61	—
							Millwall	13	—
							Fulham	27	1
HURST Glynn	5 10	11 06	D	17 1 76	Barnsley	Tottenham H	**Barnsley**	2	—
HURST Lee	6 0	11 09	M	21 9 70	Nuneaton	Trainee	**Coventry C**	49	2
HURST Matthew	5 7	10 03	F	3 11 77	Farnborough	Trainee	**Nottingham F**	—	—
HURST Paul	5 7	10 04	D	25 9 74	Sheffield	Trainee	**Rotherham U**	17	—
HURST Richard	6 0	12 00	G	23 12 76	Hammersmith	Trainee	**QPR**	—	—
HUTCHINGS Carl	5 11	11 00	M	24 9 74	London	Trainee	**Brentford**	68	—
HUTCHINSON Simon *	5 10	12 12	F	24 9 69	Sheffield	Eastwood T	**Wycombe W**	12	—
HUTCHISON Don	6 2	11 08	F	9 5 71	Gateshead	Trainee	Hartlepool U	24	2
							Liverpool	45	7
							West Ham U	23	9
HUTCHISON Ian ‡			F	7 11 72	Teeside		**Gillingham**	5	—
HUXFORD Richard	5 10	11 06	D	25 7 69	Scunthorpe	Kettering T	Barnet	33	1
							Millwall	32	—
							Birmingham C (loan)	5	—
							Bradford C	33	1
HYDE Graham	5 7	11 06	M	10 11 70	Doncaster	Trainee	**Sheffield W**	104	7
HYDE Micah	5 10	11 02	M	10 11 74	Newham	Trainee	**Cambridge U**	45	2
HYDE Paul	6 1	15 07	G	7 4 63	Hayes	Hayes	**Wycombe W**	88	—
HYSLOP Christian ‡	5 11	11 13	D	14 6 72	Watford	Trainee	Southend U	19	—
							Northampton T (loan)	8	—
							Colchester U	8	—
HYSON Matty ‡	6 2	12 12	F	2 5 76	Stockton	Trainee	**Hartlepool U**	5	—
IGOE Sammy	5 6	10 08	M	30 9 75	Spelthorne	Trainee	**Portsmouth**	1	—
IMPEY Andrew	5 8	10 06	F	13 9 71	Hammersmith	Yeading	**QPR**	126	8
IMPEY James			M	28 7 77	Bournemouth	Trainee	**Aston Villa**	—	—
INCE Paul	5 10	12 02	M	21 10 67	Ilford	Trainee	West Ham U	72	7
							Manchester U	206	24
INGEBRIGTSEN Kare	5 7	10 03	D	11 11 65	Rosenborg	Rosenborg	**Manchester C**	15	—
INGESSON Klas	6 3	14 00	M	20 8 68	Odeshog	PSV Eindhoven	**Sheffield W**	13	2
INGLETHORPE Alex	5 11	11 04	F	14 11 71	Epsom	School	Watford	12	2
							Barnet (loan)	6	3
							Leyton Orient	—	—
INGRAM Denny	5 10	11 06	D	27 6 76	Sunderland	Trainee	**Hartlepool U**	48	—
INGRAM Rae	5 11	12 02	D	6 12 74	Manchester	Trainee	**Manchester C**	—	—
INNES Lee ‡	6 2	11 10	F	28 2 76	Co Durham	Trainee	**Sheffield U**	—	—
INNES Michael *	6 0	11 00	G	5 11 75	Bangor	Trainee	**Wolverhampton W**	—	—
IORFA Dominic	6 0	12 12	F	1 10 68	Lagos	Antwerp	QPR	8	—
							Peterborough U	60	9
							Southend U	8	1
IRELAND Simon	5 11	10 05	M	23 11 71	Barnstaple	School	Huddersfield T	19	—
							Wrexham (loan)	5	—
							Blackburn R	1	—
							Mansfield T (loan)	9	1
							Mansfield T	40	5
IRONS Kenny	5 9	11 00	M	4 11 70	Liverpool	Trainee	**Tranmere R**	192	27

Player	Ht	Wt	Pos	Birth Date	Birth Place	Source	Clubs	League App	League Gls
IRONSIDE Ian	6 2	13 00	G	8 3 64	Sheffield	N. Ferriby U	Scarborough	88	—
							Middlesbrough	13	—
							Scarborough (loan)	7	—
							Stockport Co	19	—
							Scarborough	9	—
IRVING Richard	5 7	10 06	F	10 9 75	Halifax	Trainee	**Manchester U**	—	—
IRWIN Denis	5 8	10 11	D	31 10 65	Cork	Apprentice	Leeds U	72	1
							Oldham Ath	167	4
							Manchester U	194	13
IZZET Mustafa	5 10	10 03	M	31 10 74	Mile End	Trainee	**Chelsea**	—	—
JACKS Danny *	5 6	9 12	M	21 8 76	Worksop	Trainee	**Sheffield W**	—	—
JACKSON Chris	6 0	11 06	F	16 1 76	Barnsley	Trainee	**Barnsley**	15	2
JACKSON Kirk			F	16 10 76	Barnsley	Trainee	**Sheffield W**	—	—
JACKSON Matthew	6 1	12 09	D	19 10 71	Leeds	School	Luton T	9	—
							Preston NE (loan)	4	—
							Everton	124	4
JACKSON Michael	6 0	13 08	D	4 12 73	West Cheshire	Trainee	Crewe Alex	5	—
							Bury	63	2
JACKSON Peter	6 0	13 06	D	6 4 61	Bradford	Apprentice	Bradford C	278	24
							Newcastle U	60	3
							Bradford C	58	5
							Huddersfield T	155	3
							Chester C	32	1
JACOBS Wayne	5 8	11 02	D	3 2 69	Sheffield	Apprentice	Sheffield W	6	—
							Hull C	129	4
							Rotherham U	42	2
							Bradford C	38	1
JAKUB Joe *	5 6	9 06	M	7 12 56	Falkirk	Apprentice	Burnley	42	—
							Bury	265	27
						AZ Alkmaar	Chester C	42	1
							Burnley	163	8
							Chester C	36	—
							Wigan Ath	16	—
JAMES David	6 5	14 02	G	1 8 70	Welwyn	Trainee	Watford	89	—
							Liverpool	85	—
JAMES Julian	5 10	11 10	M	22 3 70	Tring	Trainee	**Luton T**	187	12
							Preston NE (loan)	6	—
JAMES Martin	5 10	11 10	M	18 5 71	Formby	Trainee	Preston NE	98	11
							Stockport Co	32	—
							Rotherham U	40	—
JAMES Stuart *			D	12 9 75	Bristol	Trainee	**Swindon T**	—	—
JAMES Tony	6 3	14 07	D	27 6 67	Sheffield	Gainsborough T	Lincoln C	29	—
							Leicester C	107	11
							Hereford U	18	2
JAQUES Daniel			M	18 1 78	North Ormesby	Trainee	**Leeds U**	—	—
JEFFERS John	5 10	11 10	F	5 10 68	Liverpool	Trainee	Liverpool	—	—
							Port Vale	180	10
							Shrewsbury T (loan)	3	1
JEFFREY Andrew	5 10	12 02	D	15 1 72	Bellshill	Cambridge C	**Cambridge U**	68	2
JEFFREY Mike	5 11	11 06	F	11 8 71	Liverpool	Trainee	Bolton W	15	—
							Doncaster R (loan)	11	6
							Doncaster R	38	13
							Newcastle U	2	—
JEMSON Nigel	5 10	11 10	F	10 8 69	Hutton	Trainee	Preston NE	32	8
							Nottingham F	47	13
							Bolton W (loan)	5	—
							Preston NE (loan)	9	2
							Sheffield W	51	9
							Grimsby T (loan)	6	2
							Notts Co	11	1
							Watford (loan)	4	—
							Coventry C (loan)	—	—

Player	Ht	Wt	Pos	Birth Date	Birth Place	Source	Clubs	League App	League Gls
JENKINS Iain	5 9	11 10	D	24 11 72	Whiston	Trainee	Everton	5	—
							Bradford C (loan)	6	—
							Chester C	74	—
JENKINS Steve	5 10	10 09	D	16 7 72	Merthyr	Trainee	**Swansea C**	150	1
JENKINSON Leigh	6 0	12 02	F	9 7 69	Thorne	Trainee	Hull C	130	13
							Rotherham U (loan)	7	—
							Coventry C	32	1
							Birmingham C (loan)	3	—
JENSEN John	5 10	12 06	M	3 5 65	Denmark	Brondby	**Arsenal**	83	1
JEPSON Ronnie	6 1	13 00	F	12 5 63	Stoke	Nantwich	Port Vale	22	—
							Peterborough U (loan)	18	5
							Preston NE	38	8
							Exeter C	54	21
							Huddersfield T	64	24
JEWELL Paul	5 8	12 01	F	28 9 64	Liverpool	Apprentice	Liverpool	—	—
							Wigan Ath	137	35
							Bradford C	251	53
JOACHIM Julian	5 6	11 11	F	20 9 74	Peterborough	Trainee	**Leicester C**	77	24
JOBLING Kevin	5 9	10 11	M	1 1 68	Sunderland	Apprentice	Leicester C	9	—
							Grimsby T	224	9
							Scunthorpe U (loan)	—	—
JOBSON Richard	6 1	13 05	D	9 5 63	Hull	Burton Alb	Watford	28	4
							Hull C	221	17
							Oldham Ath	177	10
JOHNROSE Lenny	5 11	12 06	F	29 11 69	Preston	Trainee	Blackburn R	42	11
							Preston NE (loan)	3	1
							Hartlepool U	66	11
							Bury	40	4
JOHNSEN Erland	6 0	12 10	D	5 4 67	Fredrikstad (Norway)	Bayern Munich	**Chelsea**	105	1
JOHNSON Alan	5 11	11 12	D	19 2 71	Ince	Trainee	Wigan Ath	180	13
							Lincoln C	41	—
JOHNSON Andy	6 1	12 00	M	2 5 74	Bristol	Trainee	**Norwich C**	13	1
JOHNSON David	6 2	14 03	F	29 10 70	Rother Valley	Trainee	Sheffield W	6	—
							Hartlepool U (loan)	7	2
							Hartlepool U (loan)	3	—
							Lincoln C	65	12
JOHNSON David *	5 6	12 03	F	15 8 76	Kingston	Trainee	**Manchester U**	—	—
JOHNSON Gavin *	5 11	11 12	D	10 10 70	Stowmarket	Trainee	**Ipswich T**	132	11
JOHNSON Ian ‡	5 9	11 08	F	1 9 75	Sunderland	Trainee	Middlesbrough	2	—
							Bradford C	2	—
JOHNSON Marvin	6 0	12 03	D	29 10 68	Wembley	Apprentice	**Luton T**	166	4
JOHNSON Michael	5 11	11 00	D	4 7 73	Nottingham	Trainee	**Notts Co**	107	—
JOHNSON Phil *	5 8	10 06	D	7 4 75	Liverpool	Trainee	**Tranmere R**	—	—
JOHNSON Richard	5 10	11 13	M	27 4 74	Kurri, Kurri	Trainee	**Watford**	65	3
JOHNSON Ross	6 0	12 04	D	2 1 76	Brighton	Trainee	**Brighton**	2	—
JOHNSON Tommy	5 10	11 02	F	15 1 71	Newcastle	Trainee	Notts Co	118	47
							Derby Co	98	30
							Aston Villa	14	4
JONES Barry	6 0	11 07	D	20 6 70	Prescot	Prescot T	Liverpool	—	—
							Wrexham	119	4
JONES Cobi *	5 7	11 04	M	16 6 70	Detroit	USSF	**Coventry C**	21	2
JONES Gary	6 0	12 08	F	6 4 69	Huddersfield	Rossington Main	Doncaster R	20	2
						Boston U	**Southend U**	47	14
							Lincoln C (loan)	4	2
JONES Gary	6 3	14 00	F	10 5 75	Chester	Trainee	**Tranmere R**	25	5
JONES Graeme	6 0	12 12	F	13 3 70	Gateshead	Bridlington T	**Doncaster R**	60	16

				Birth				League	
Player	*Ht*	*Wt*	*Pos*	*Date*	*Place*	*Source*	*Clubs*	*App*	*Gls*
JONES Ian §			D	26 8 76	Germany	Trainee	**Cardiff C**	2	—
JONES Keith	5 9	10 11	M	14 10 65	Dulwich	Apprentice	Chelsea	52	7
							Brentford	169	13
							Southend U	90	11
							Charlton Ath	31	1
JONES Lee	5 8	10 08	F	29 5 73	Wrexham	Trainee	Wrexham	39	10
							Liverpool	1	—
							Crewe Alex (loan)	8	1
JONES Lee	6 3	14 04	G	9 8 70	Pontypridd	Porth	**Swansea C**	2	—
JONES Martin	6 1	12 00	G	27 3 75	Liverpool	Trainee	**Tranmere R**	—	—
JONES Paul	6 3	14 00	G	18 4 67	Chirk	Kidderminster H	**Wolverhampton W**	25	—
JONES Rob	5 8	11 00	D	5 11 71	Wrexham	Trainee	Crewe Alex	75	2
							Liverpool	127	—
JONES Ryan	6 1	12 12	M	23 7 73	Sheffield	Trainee	**Sheffield W**	41	6
JONES Scott	5 10	11 06	D	1 5 75	Sheffield	Trainee	**Barnsley**	—	—
JONES Steve	5 11	12 00	F	17 3 70	Cambridge	Billericay	West Ham U	16	4
							Bournemouth	30	9
JONES Steve	5 11	13 07	G	31 1 74	Teeside	Trainee	**Hartlepool U**	39	—
JONES Tom	5 10	11 07	M	7 10 64	Aldershot	Weymouth	Aberdeen	28	3
							Swindon T	168	12
							Reading	58	2
JONES Vinny	5 11	11 10	M	5 1 65	Watford	Wealdstone	Wimbledon	77	9
							Leeds U	46	5
							Sheffield U	35	2
							Chelsea	42	4
							Wimbledon	93	6
JORDAN Scott	5 10	11 04	M	19 7 75	Newcastle	Trainee	**York C**	38	3
JOSEPH Matthew	5 7	10 00	D	30 9 72	Bethnal Green	Trainee	Arsenal	—	—
							Gillingham	—	—
							Cambridge U	66	4
JOSEPH Roger	5 11	11 10	D	24 12 65	Paddington	Juniors	Brentford	104	2
							Wimbledon	162	—
							Millwall (loan)	5	—
JOYCE Joe	5 10	11 05	D	18 3 61	Consett	School	Barnsley	334	4
							Scunthorpe U	91	2
							Carlisle U	50	—
							Darlington (loan)	4	—
JOYCE Warren	5 8	11 13	M	20 1 65	Oldham	Local	Bolton W	184	17
							Preston NE	177	34
							Plymouth Arg	30	3
							Burnley	27	4
							Hull C (loan)	9	3
JUDGE Alan ‡	5 11	11 06	G	14 5 60	Kingsbury	Amateur	Luton T	11	—
							Reading (loan)	33	—
							Reading	44	—
							Oxford U	80	—
							Lincoln C (loan)	2	—
							Cardiff C (loan)	8	—
							Hereford U	105	—
							Chelsea	—	—
JULES Mark	5 7	11 00	F	5 9 71	Bradford	Trainee	Bradford C	—	—
							Scarborough	77	16
							Chesterfield	56	1
JUPP Duncan	6 0	12 12	D	25 1 75	Guildford	Trainee	**Fulham**	69	2

Player	Ht	Wt	Pos	Birth Date	Birth Place	Source	Clubs	League App	League Gls
JURYEFF Ian ‡	5 11	12 07	F	24 11 62	Gosport	Apprentice	Southampton	—	—
						Sweden	Southampton	2	—
							Mansfield T (loan)	12	5
							Reading (loan)	7	1
							Orient	111	44
							Ipswich T (loan)	2	—
							Halifax T	17	7
							Hereford U	28	4
							Halifax T	72	13
							Darlington	34	6
							Scunthorpe U	44	13
KALOGERACOS Vasili ‡	5 7	10 06	F	21 3 75	Perth	Floreat Athena	**Birmingham C**	—	—
KAMARA Abdul ‡	5 9	11 00	M	10 2 74	Southampton	Southampton	Bristol C	1	—
							Gillingham	—	—
KAMARA Chris †	6 1	12 10	M	25 12 57	Middlesbrough	Apprentice	Portsmouth	63	7
							Swindon T	147	21
							Portsmouth	11	—
							Brentford	152	28
							Swindon T	87	6
							Stoke C	60	5
							Leeds U	20	1
							Luton T	49	—
							Sheffield U (loan)	8	—
							Middlesbrough (loan)	5	—
							Sheffield U	16	—
							Bradford C	23	3
KANCHELSKIS Andrei	5 10	13 03	F	23 1 69	Kirovograd	Donezts	**Manchester U**	123	28
KARL Stefan ‡	5 11	11 12	M	3 2 70	Hohenm-Oelsen	Dortmund	**Manchester C**	6	1
KAVANAGH Graham	5 10	12 08	M	2 12 73	Dublin	Home Farm	**Middlesbrough**	28	2
							Darlington (loan)	5	—
KAVANAGH Jason	5 9	12 04	D	23 11 71	Birmingham	Birmingham C	**Derby Co**	90	1
KAY John	5 9	11 06	D	29 1 64	Sunderland	Apprentice	Arsenal	14	—
							Wimbledon	63	2
							Middlesbrough (loan)	8	—
							Sunderland	199	—
KEANE Roy	5 10	12 05	M	10 8 71	Cork	Cobh Ramblers	Nottingham F	114	22
							Manchester U	62	7
KEARN Stewart *			G	1 12 75	Salisbury		**Sheffield W**	—	—
KEARTON Jason	5 11	12 00	G	9 7 69	Ipswich (Australia)	Brisbane Lions	**Everton**	6	—
							Stoke C (loan)	16	—
							Blackpool (loan)	14	—
							Notts Co (loan)	10	—
KEELEY John ‡	6 1	14 02	G	27 7 61	Plaistow	Apprentice	Southend U	54	—
						Chelmsford C	Brighton	138	—
							Oldham Ath	2	—
							Oxford U (loan)	6	—
							Reading (loan)	6	—
							Chester C (loan)	4	—
							Colchester U	15	—
							Stockport Co	20	—
							Peterborough U	3	—
KEEN Kevin	5 7	10 10	M	25 2 67	Amersham	Apprentice	West Ham U	219	21
							Wolverhampton W	42	7
							Stoke C	21	2
KEISTER John	5 7	10 12	M	11 11 70	Manchester	Fawah FC	**Walsall**	33	1
KELLER Kasey	6 1	13 07	G	27 11 69	Washington	Portland Univ	**Millwall**	134	—
KELLY Alan	6 2	12 05	G	11 8 68	Preston	Trainee	Preston NE	142	—
							Sheffield U	101	—
KELLY David	5 11	11 03	F	25 11 65	Birmingham	Alvechurch	Walsall	147	63
							West Ham U	41	7
							Leicester C	66	22
							Newcastle U	70	35
							Wolverhampton W	78	26

Player	Ht	Wt	Pos	Birth Date	Birth Place	Source	Clubs	League App	League Gls
KELLY Gary	5 11	13 06	G	3 8 66	Fulwood	Apprentice	Newcastle U	53	—
							Blackpool (loan)	5	—
							Bury	211	—
							West Ham U (loan)	—	—
KELLY Gary	5 8	10 12	D	9 7 74	Drogheda	Home Farm	**Leeds U**	86	—
KELLY Gavin	6 0	12 13	G	29 9 68	Beverley	Trainee	Hull C	11	—
							Bristol R (loan)	—	—
							Bristol R	30	—
							Scarborough	24	—
KELLY Jimmy	5 7	11 10	M	14 2 73	Liverpool	Trainee	Wrexham	21	—
							Wolverhampton W	7	—
							Walsall (loan)	10	2
							Wrexham (loan)	9	—
KELLY Ray			F	29 12 76	Athlone	Athlone T	**Manchester C**	—	—
KELLY Tom	5 9	12 07	D	28 3 64	Bellshill	Hibs	Hartlepool U	15	—
							Torquay U	120	—
							York C	35	2
							Exeter C	88	9
							Torquay U	86	8
KELLY Tony	5 11	11 08	F	14 2 66	Meridan		Bristol C	6	1
						St Albans C	Stoke C	58	5
							Hull C (loan)	6	1
							Cardiff C (loan)	5	1
							Bury	57	10
KELLY Tony	5 10	13 10	M	1 10 64	Prescot	Liverpool	Derby Co	—	—
							Wigan Ath	101	15
							Stoke C	36	4
							WBA	26	1
							Chester C (loan)	5	—
							Colchester U (loan)	13	2
							Shrewsbury T	101	15
							Bolton W	106	5
							Port Vale	4	1
							Millwall	2	—
							Wigan Ath	—	—
							Peterborough U	13	2
KENNA Jeff	5 11	12 02	D	27 8 70	Dublin	Trainee	Southampton	114	4
							Blackburn R	9	1
KENNEDY Andy ‡	6 2	13 00	F	8 10 64	Stirling	Sauchie Ath	Rangers	15	3
							Birmingham C	76	18
							Sheffield U (loan)	9	1
							Blackburn R	59	23
							Watford	25	4
							Bolton W (loan)	1	—
							Brighton	42	10
							Gillingham	2	—
KENNEDY Mark	5 11	11 09	F	15 5 76	Dublin	Trainee	Millwall	43	9
							Liverpool	6	—
KENNY Billy	5 07	10 10	M	19 9 73	Liverpool	Trainee	Everton	17	1
							Oldham Ath	4	—
KENT Kevin	5 11	11 00	F	19 3 65	Stoke	Apprentice	WBA	2	—
							Newport Co	33	1
							Mansfield T	229	36
							Port Vale	114	7
KENWORTHY Jon	5 7	10 06	F	18 8 74	St Asaph	Trainee	**Tranmere R**	22	2
KEOWN Martin	6 1	12 04	D	24 7 66	Oxford	Apprentice	Arsenal	22	—
							Brighton (loan)	16	—
							Brighton (loan)	7	1
							Aston Villa	112	3
							Everton	96	—
							Arsenal	80	1
KERNAGHAN Alan	6 2	13 00	D	25 4 67	Otley	Apprentice	Middlesbrough	212	16
							Charlton Ath (loan)	13	—
							Manchester C	46	1
							Bolton W (loan)	11	—
KERR David	5 11	11 00	M	6 9 74	Dumfries	Trainee	**Manchester C**	5	—

Player	Ht	Wt	Pos	Birth Date	Birth Place	Source	Clubs	League App	League Gls
KERR Dylan	5 9	11 04	D	14 1 67	Valetta	Arcadia Shepherds	Leeds U	13	—
							Doncaster R (loan)	7	1
							Blackpool (loan)	12	1
							Reading	81	3
KERR John *	5 8	11 05	F	6 3 65	Toronto	Harrow Borough	Portsmouth	4	—
							Peterborough U (loan)	10	1
						San Diego Sockers	**Millwall**	43	8
KERR Paul ‡	5 8	11 03	F	9 6 64	Portsmouth	Apprentice	Aston Villa	24	3
							Middlesbrough	125	13
							Millwall	44	14
							Port Vale	63	15
							Leicester C (loan)	7	2
							Wycombe W	1	1
KERR Stuart (on loan from Celtic)	6 2	13 00	G	13 11 74	Bellshill		**Brighton**	2	—
KERRY Chris ‡	5 7	10 04	F	15 4 76	Chesterfield	Trainee	**Mansfield T**	2	—
KERSLAKE David	5 9	12 03	D	19 6 66	Stepney	Apprentice	QPR	58	6
							Swindon T	135	1
							Leeds U	8	—
							Tottenham H	35	—
KEY Lance	6 2	14 00	G	13 5 68	Kettering	Histon	**Sheffield W**	—	—
							York C (loan)	—	—
							Oldham Ath (loan)	2	—
							Portsmouth (loan)	—	—
							Oxford U (loan)	6	—
KHARINE Dmitri	6 2	12 04	G	16 8 68	Moscow	CSKA Moscow	**Chelsea**	76	—
KIDD Ryan	6 1	13 00	D	6 10 71	Radcliffe	Trainee	Port Vale	1	—
							Preston NE	83	4
KIELY Dean	6 0	12 13	G	10 10 70	Salford	WBA	Coventry C	—	—
							Ipswich T (loan)	—	—
							York C (loan)	—	—
							York C	170	—
KILBANE Farrell ‡	6 0	13 00	D	21 10 74	Preston	Cambridge U	**Preston NE**	1	—
KILCLINE Brian	6 2	12 00	D	7 5 62	Nottingham	Apprentice	Notts Co	158	9
							Coventry C	173	28
							Oldham Ath	8	—
							Newcastle U	32	—
							Swindon T	17	—
KILFORD Ian	5 10	10 05	M	6 10 73	Bristol	Trainee	Nottingham F	1	—
							Wigan Ath (loan)	8	3
							Wigan Ath	35	5
KIMBLE Alan	5 8	11 00	D	6 8 66	Poole		Charlton Ath	6	—
							Exeter C (loan)	1	—
							Cambridge U	299	24
							Wimbledon	40	—
KING Nathan	6 0	12 06	D	1 8 75	West Bromwich	Trainee	**Shrewsbury T**	—	—
KING Phil	5 8	12 07	D	28 12 67	Bristol	Apprentice	Exeter C	27	—
							Torquay U	24	3
							Swindon T	116	4
							Sheffield W	129	2
							Notts Co (loan)	6	—
							Aston Villa	16	—
KINSELLA Mark	5 9	10 09	M	12 8 72	Dublin	Home Farm	**Colchester U**	128	20
KIRBY Alan			M	8 9 77	Waterford	Johnville	**Aston Villa**	—	—
KIRBY Ryan	6 0	12 00	D	6 9 74	Chingford	Trainee	Arsenal	—	—
							Doncaster R	42	—
KIRKHAM Peter	6 0	11 04	M	28 10 74	Newcastle	Newcastle U	**Darlington**	13	—
KITCHEN Sam ‡	6 0	13 02	D	11 6 67	Rinteln	Frickley Ath	Leyton Orient	43	1
							Doncaster R	22	1

				Birth				League	
Player	Ht	Wt	Pos	Date	Place	Source	Clubs	App	Gls
KITE Phil	6 1	14 07	G	26 10 62	Bristol	Apprentice	Bristol R	96	—
							Tottenham H (loan)	—	—
							Southampton	4	—
							Middlesbrough (loan)	2	—
							Gillingham	70	—
							Bournemouth	7	—
							Sheffield U	11	—
							Mansfield T (loan)	11	—
							Plymouth Arg (loan)	2	—
							Rotherham U (loan)	1	—
							Crewe Alex (loan)	5	—
							Stockport Co (loan)	5	—
							Cardiff C	18	—
							Bristol C	2	—
KITSON Paul	5 11	10 12	F	9 1 71	Co Durham	Trainee	Leicester C	50	6
							Derby Co	105	36
							Newcastle U	26	8
KIWOMYA Andrew †	5 9	10 10	F	1 10 67	Huddersfield	Trainee	Barnsley	1	—
							Sheffield W	—	—
						Retired injury	Dundee	21	1
							Rotherham U	7	—
						Halifax T	**Scunthorpe U**	9	3
KIWOMYA Chris	5 10	10 12	F	2 12 69	Huddersfield	Trainee	Ipswich T	225	51
							Arsenal	14	3
KJELDBJERG Jakob	6 2	13 08	D	21 10 69	Denmark	Silkeborg	**Chelsea**	52	2
KLINSMANN Jurgen	6 2	12 13	F	30 7 64	Goppingen	Gingen	Stuttgart Kickers	61	22
							Stuttgart	156	79
							Internazionale	95	34
							Monaco	65	29
							Tottenham H	41	20
KNIGHT Alan	6 0	13 00	G	3 6 61	Balham	Apprentice	**Portsmouth**	578	—
KNIGHT Richard *	5 9	11 10	D	21 8 74	Burton	Trainee	**Walsall**	29	1
KNILL Alan	6 4	13 00	D	8 10 64	Slough	Apprentice	Southampton	—	—
							Halifax T	118	6
							Swansea C	89	3
							Bury	144	8
							Cardiff C (loan)	4	—
							Scunthorpe U	64	5
KNOTT Gareth	5 11	11 04	F	19 1 76	Blackwood	Trainee	**Tottenham H**	—	—
							Gillingham (loan)	5	—
KNOWLES Darren	5 6	10 06	D	8 10 70	Sheffield	Trainee	Sheffield U	—	—
							Stockport Co	63	—
							Scarborough	81	1
KREFT Stacey	5 9	11 00	D	2 2 76	Southampton	Trainee	**Norwich C**	—	—
KRISTENSEN Bjorn *	6 1	12 05	M	10 10 63	Malling	Aarhus	Newcastle U	80	4
							Bristol C (loan)	4	—
							Portsmouth	71	1
KUBICKI Dariusz	5 11	11 02	D	6 6 63	Warsaw	Legia Warsaw	Aston Villa	25	—
							Sunderland (loan)	15	—
							Sunderland	46	—
KUHL Martin	5 11	11 13	M	10 1 65	Frimley	Apprentice	Birmingham C	111	5
							Sheffield U	38	4
							Watford	4	—
							Portsmouth	157	27
							Derby Co	68	1
							Notts Co (loan)	2	—
							Bristol C	17	1
KYD Michael	5 8	12 00	M	21 5 77	Hackney	Trainee	**Cambridge U**	19	1
KYDD Peter §	5 8	10 00	M	20 1 78	Bournemouth	Trainee	**West Ham U**	—	—
KYTE Jamie	5 7	10 00	M	17 9 77	Erith	Charlton Ath	**Charlton Ath**	—	—
LAIGHT Ellis	5 10	11 02	F	30 6 76	Birmingham	Trainee	**Torquay U**	11	—
LAKE Mike *	6 0	12 05	M	16 11 66	Manchester	Macclesfield T	Sheffield U	35	4
							Wrexham	58	6
LAKE Paul	6 0	12 02	M	28 10 68	Manchester	Trainee	**Manchester C**	110	7

Player	Ht	Wt	Pos	Birth Date	Birth Place	Source	Clubs	League App	League Gls
LAKIN Barry	5 9	12 02	M	19 9 73	Dartford	Trainee	**Leyton Orient**	46	2
LAMBERT Darren *	5 8	10 10	F	15 9 75	Grimsby	Trainee	**Grimsby T**	—	—
LAMBERT James	5 7	10 04	F	14 9 73	Henley	School	**Reading**	44	4
LAMPARD Frank §	5 10	12 04	M	21 6 78	Romford	Trainee	**West Ham U**	—	—
LAMPKIN Kevin	5 10	12 00	M	20 12 72	Liverpool	Trainee	Liverpool	—	—
							Huddersfield T	13	—
							Mansfield T	36	3
LAMPTEY Nii ‡	5 6	10 03	F	10 12 74	Accra	Anderlecht	**Aston Villa**	6	—
LANCASHIRE Graham	5 10	11 12	F	19 10 72	Blackpool	Trainee	Burnley	31	8
							Halifax T (loan)	2	—
							Chester C (loan)	11	7
							Preston NE	17	—
LANCASTER Dave	6 3	14 00	F	8 9 61	Preston	Colne Dynamoes	Blackpool	8	1
							Chesterfield (loan)	12	4
							Chesterfield	69	16
							Rochdale	40	14
						Halifax T	**Bury**	5	1
LANDON Richard	6 3	13 05	F	22 3 70	Barnsley	Bedworth U	**Plymouth Arg**	30	12
LANGE Tony *	6 0	12 09	G	10 12 64	London	Apprentice	Charlton Ath	12	—
							Aldershot (loan)	7	—
							Aldershot	125	—
							Wolverhampton W	8	—
							Aldershot (loan)	2	—
							Torquay U (loan)	1	—
							Portsmouth (loan)	—	—
							WBA	48	—
LANGFORD Tim *	5 6	12 00	F	12 9 65	Kingswinford	Telford U	**Wycombe W**	35	8
LARKIN Andy	6 1	11 09	D	24 9 77	Kent	Trainee	**Charlton Ath**	—	—
LAUNDERS Brian	5 8	11 00	M	8 6 76	Dublin	Trainee	**Crystal Palace**	2	—
LAVIN Gerard	5 9	10 07	M	5 2 74	Corby	Trainee	**Watford**	110	3
LAW Brian	6 2	11 12	D	1 1 70	Merthyr	Apprentice	QPR	20	—
							Wolverhampton W	17	—
LAW Marcus ‡	5 11	11 07	G	28 9 75	Coventry	Trainee	**Bristol R**	2	—
LAW Nicky	6 0	13 07	D	8 9 61	London	Apprentice	Arsenal	—	—
							Barnsley	114	1
							Blackpool	66	1
							Plymouth Arg	38	5
							Notts Co	47	4
							Scarborough (loan)	12	—
							Rotherham U	128	4
							Chesterfield	66	3
LAWFORD Craig	5 10	11 00	M	25 11 72	Dewsbury	Trainee	Bradford C	20	1
							Hull C	31	3
LAWLESS Chris	5 8	10 13	M	4 10 74	Dublin	Home Farm	**Sunderland**	—	—
LAWRENCE Jamie	5 10	12 03	F	8 3 70	Balham	Cowes	Sunderland	4	—
							Doncaster R	25	3
							Leicester C	17	1
LAWS Brian †	5 10	11 05	D	14 10 61	Wallsend	Apprentice	Burnley	125	12
							Huddersfield T	56	1
							Middlesbrough	107	12
							Nottingham F	147	4
							Grimsby T	16	1
LAWSON Ian	5 11	10 05	F	4 11 77	Huddersfield	Trainee	**Huddersfield T**	—	—
LAWTON Craig	5 7	10 03	M	5 1 72	Mancot	Trainee	Manchester U	—	—
							Port Vale	1	—
LE BIHAN Neil	5 11	12 13	M	14 3 76	London	Tottenham H	**Peterborough U**	4	—
LE SAUX Graeme	5 10	11 04	D	17 10 68	Jersey	St Pauls	Chelsea	90	8
							Blackburn R	89	5
LE TISSIER Matthew	6 1	13 08	F	14 10 68	Guernsey	Trainee	**Southampton**	292	119

Player	Ht	Wt	Pos	Birth Date	Birth Place	Source	Clubs	League App	League Gls
LEABURN Carl	6 3	13 00	F	30 3 69	Lewisham	Apprentice	**Charlton Ath**	224	33
							Northampton T (loan)	9	—
LEADBITTER Chris *	5 9	10 07	F	17 10 67	Middlesbrough	Apprentice	Grimsby T	—	—
							Hereford U	36	1
							Cambridge U	176	18
							Bournemouth	54	3
LEANING Andy	6 1	14 07	G	18 5 63	York	Rowntree Mackintosh	York C	69	—
							Sheffield U	21	—
							Bristol C	75	—
							Lincoln C	29	—
LEE Chris	5 10	11 07	M	18 6 71	Halifax	Trainee	Bradford C	—	—
							Rochdale	26	2
							Scarborough	78	3
							Hull C	88	4
LEE Dave	5 7	11 00	M	5 11 67	Whitefield	Schools	Bury	208	35
							Southampton	20	—
							Bolton W	112	14
LEE David	6 3	13 12	D	26 11 69	Kingswood	Trainee	**Chelsea**	118	9
							Reading (loan)	5	5
							Plymouth Arg (loan)	9	1
							Portsmouth (loan)	5	—
LEE Jason	6 3	13 08	F	9 5 71	Newham	Trainee	Charlton Ath	1	—
							Stockport Co (loan)	2	—
							Lincoln C	93	21
							Southend U	24	3
							Nottingham F	35	5
LEE Robert	5 10	11 13	F	1 2 66	West Ham	Hornchurch	Charlton Ath	298	59
							Newcastle U	112	26
LEGG Andy	5 8	10 07	M	28 7 66	Neath	Briton Ferry	Swansea C	163	29
							Notts Co	64	5
LENNON Neil	5 9	11 06	D	25 6 71	Lurgan	Trainee	Manchester C	1	—
							Crewe Alex	122	13
LEONARD Mark	5 11	11 10	F	27 9 62	St Helens	Witton Albion	Everton	—	—
							Tranmere R (loan)	7	—
							Crewe Alex	54	15
							Stockport Co	73	24
							Bradford C	157	29
							Rochdale	9	1
							Preston NE	22	1
							Chester C	32	8
							Wigan Ath	29	5
LEONHARDSEN Oyvind	5 10	11 02	M	17 8 70	Norway	Rosenborg	**Wimbledon**	20	4
LESLIE Steven	5 6	10 00	M	6 2 76	Dumfries	Trainee	**Stoke C**	1	—
LESTER Jack	5 9	11 00	F	8 10 75	Sheffield	Trainee	**Grimsby T**	7	—
LETTS Simon *	5 8	10 10	M	26 2 76	Sheffield	Trainee	**Sheffield U**	—	—
LEVER Mark	6 3	12 08	D	29 3 70	Beverley	Trainee	**Grimsby T**	219	7
LEWIS Mickey	5 8	10 10	M	15 2 65	Birmingham	School	WBA	24	—
							Derby Co	43	1
							Oxford U	281	7
LEWIS Neil	5 7	11 01	M	28 6 74	Wolverhampton	Trainee	**Leicester C**	47	—
LIBURD Richard	5 10	10 12	D	26 9 73	Nottingham	Forest Ath	Middlesbrough	41	1
							Bradford C	9	1
LIDDELL Andrew	5 8	10 09	F	28 6 73	Leeds	Trainee	**Barnsley**	83	16
LIDDLE Craig	5 11	12 03	M	21 10 71	Chester-le-Street	Blythe Spartans	**Middlesbrough**	1	—
LIGHTBOURNE Kyle	6 2	12 02	F	29 9 68	Bermuda		Scarborough	19	3
							Walsall	77	30
LIGHTFOOT Chris	6 2	13 06	M	1 4 70	Penketh	Trainee	**Chester C**	277	32

Player	Ht	Wt	Pos	Birth Date	Birth Place	Source	Clubs	League App	League Gls
LILLIS Jason †	5 11	11 10	M	1 10 69	Chatham	Trainee	Gillingham	29	3
							Maidstone U	75	18
							Carlisle U (loan)	4	1
						Sittingbourne	Walsall	25	6
							Cambridge U	19	4
LILWALL Steve *	5 11	12 00	D	5 2 70	Solihull	Kidderminster H	**WBA**	73	—
LIMBER Nick ‡	5 10	11 12	D	23 1 74	Doncaster	Trainee	Doncaster R	13	1
							Manchester C	—	—
							Peterborough U (loan)	2	—
							Doncaster R	4	—
LIMPAR Anders	5 8	11 07	F	24 9 65	Solna	Cremonese	Arsenal	96	17
							Everton	36	2
LINDSEY Scott	5 9	11 10	D	4 5 72	Walsall	Bridlington T	**Gillingham**	12	—
LING Martin	5 7	10 02	M	15 7 66	West Ham	Apprentice	Exeter C	116	14
							Swindon T	2	—
							Southend U	138	31
							Mansfield T (loan)	3	—
							Swindon T (loan)	1	—
							Swindon T	133	10
LINGER Paul	5 6	10 03	M	20 12 74	Stepney	Trainee	**Charlton Ath**	15	—
LINIGHAN Andy	6 4	13 10	D	18 6 62	Hartlepool	Smiths BC	Hartlepool U	110	4
							Leeds U	66	3
							Oldham Ath	87	6
							Norwich C	86	8
							Arsenal	89	4
LINIGHAN Brian	6 1	11 04	D	2 11 73	Hartlepool	Trainee	**Sheffield W**	1	—
LINIGHAN David	6 2	13 00	D	9 1 65	Hartlepool	Local	Hartlepool U	91	5
							Leeds U (loan)	—	—
							Derby Co	—	—
							Shrewsbury T	65	1
							Ipswich T	275	12
LINTON Des	6 1	13 02	D	5 9 71	Birmingham	Trainee	Leicester C	11	—
							Luton T	66	1
LINYARD Paul §	6 1	12 00	G	18 7 77	Keighley	Trainee	**Hartlepool U**	—	—
LITTLE Glen ‡	6 3	13 00	M	15 10 75	Wimbledon	Trainee	**Crystal Palace**	—	—
LITTLEJOHN Adrian	5 9	10 04	F	26 9 70	Wolverhampton	WBA	Walsall	44	1
							Sheffield U	69	12
LIVETT Simon *	5 10	12 07	M	8 1 69	Newham	Trainee	West Ham U	1	—
							Leyton Orient	24	—
							Cambridge U	12	—
LIVINGSTONE Richard *	5 10	11 06	F	10 4 74	Aberdeen	Trainee	**Burnley**	—	—
LIVINGSTONE Steve	6 1	11 04	F	8 9 69	Middlesbrough	Trainee	Coventry C	31	5
							Blackburn R	30	10
							Chelsea	1	—
							Port Vale (loan)	5	—
							Grimsby T	61	11
LLEWELLYN Andy ‡	5 7	11 00	D	26 2 66	Bristol	Apprentice	Bristol C	301	3
							Exeter C (loan)	15	—
							Hereford U	4	—
LLOYD Kevin	6 0	12 01	D	26 9 70	Llanidloes	Caersws	**Hereford U**	24	3
LOCK Anthony			M	3 9 76	Harlow	Trainee	**Colchester U**	3	1
LOCKE Adam	5 10	12 02	M	20 8 70	Croydon	Trainee	Crystal Palace	—	—
							Southend U	73	4
							Colchester U (loan)	4	—
							Colchester U	22	1
LOCKWOOD Matthew	5 9	10 07	M	17 10 76	Rochford	Trainee	**QPR**	—	—
LOGAN Richard	6 0	13 03	M	24 5 69	Barnsley	Gainsborough T	**Huddersfield T**	43	1
LOMAS Andrew (on loan from Stevenage)			G	26 4 65	Hartlepool		**Cambridge U**	2	—

Player	Ht	Wt	Pos	Birth Date	Birth Place	Source	Clubs	League App	League Gls
LOMAS Steve	6 0	12 08	M	18 1 74	Hanover	Trainee	**Manchester C**	43	2
LONERGAN Darren			D	28 1 74	Cork	Waterford	**Oldham Ath**	—	—
LORMOR Tony	6 0	13 06	F	29 10 70	Ashington	Trainee	Newcastle U	8	3
							Norwich C (loan)	—	—
							Lincoln C	100	30
							Peterborough U	5	—
							Chesterfield	23	10
LOSS Colin *	5 11	11 04	M	15 8 73	Brentwood	Trainee	Norwich C	—	—
							Derby Co	—	—
						Gresley R	**Bristol C**	5	—
LOVELL Stuart	5 10	11 00	M	9 1 72	Sydney	Trainee	**Reading**	151	45
LOVELOCK Andrew	5 9	10 12	F	20 12 76	Swindon	Trainee	**Coventry C**	—	—
LOWE David	5 10	11 06	F	30 8 65	Liverpool	Apprentice	Wigan Ath	188	40
							Ipswich T	134	37
							Port Vale (loan)	9	2
							Leicester C	66	19
							Port Vale (loan)	19	5
LOWE Kenny	6 1	11 04	M	6 11 64	Sedgefield	Apprentice	Hartlepool U	54	3
						Barrow	Scarborough	4	—
						Barrow	Barnet	72	5
							Stoke C	9	—
							Birmingham C	19	3
							Carlisle U (loan)	2	—
LOWNDES Nathan	5 11	10 04	F	2 6 77	Salford	Trainee	**Leeds U**	—	—
LOWTHORPE Adam	5 7	10 06	D	7 8 75	Hull	Trainee	**Hull C**	25	—
LUCAS David			G	23 11 77	Preston	Trainee	**Preston NE**	—	—
LUCAS Richard ‡	5 10	11 04	M	22 9 70	Sheffield	Trainee	Sheffield U	10	—
							Preston NE	50	—
							Lincoln C (loan)	4	—
LUCKETTI Chris	6 0	13 06	D	28 9 71	Littleborough	Trainee	Rochdale	1	—
							Stockport Co	—	—
							Halifax T	78	2
							Bury	66	4
LUDDEN Dominic	5 7	10 09	D	30 3 74	Basildon	Trainee	Leyton Orient	58	1
							Watford	1	—
LUDLAM Craig	5 10	10 04	M	8 11 76	Sheffield	Trainee	**Sheffield W**	—	—
LUDLOW Lee ‡	6 0	11 00	F	14 3 76	Newcastle	Trainee	**Notts Co**	—	—
LUKIC John	6 4	13 12	G	11 12 60	Chesterfield	Apprentice	Leeds U	146	—
							Arsenal	223	—
							Leeds U	181	—
LUND Gary	6 0	11 00	F	13 9 64	Grimsby	School	Grimsby T	60	24
							Lincoln C	44	13
							Notts Co	248	62
							Hull C (loan)	11	3
							Hull C (loan)	11	3
LYDERSEN Pal ‡	6 0	14 01	D	10 9 65	Odense	IK Start.	**Arsenal**	15	—
LYDIATE Jason	5 11	12 04	D	29 10 71	Manchester	Trainee	Manchester U	—	—
							Bolton W	30	—
							Blackpool	11	—
LYNCH Chris	5 10	11 04	F	18 11 74	Middlesbrough	Halifax T	**Hartlepool U**	31	1
LYNCH Tommy	6 0	12 06	D	10 10 64	Limerick	Limerick	Sunderland	4	—
							Shrewsbury T	209	11
LYNE Neil	6 1	12 04	F	4 4 70	Leicester	Leicester U	Nottingham F	—	—
							Walsall (loan)	7	—
							Shrewsbury T (loan)	16	6
							Shrewsbury T	64	11
							Cambridge U	17	—
							Chesterfield (loan)	6	1
							Hereford U	31	1
LYONS Andy	5 10	11 00	M	19 10 66	Blackpool	Fleetwood	Crewe Alex	11	2
							Wigan Ath	65	26

Player	Ht	Wt	Pos	Birth Date	Place	Source	Clubs	League App	Gls
LYTTLE Des	5 9	12 00	D	24 9 71	Wolverhampton	Worcester C	Swansea C	46	1
							Nottingham F	75	1
MABBUTT Gary	5 10	12 09	D	23 8 61	Bristol	Apprentice	Bristol R	131	10
							Tottenham H	433	27
McALLISTER Brian	5 11	12 05	D	30 11 70	Glasgow	Trainee	**Wimbledon**	53	—
							Plymouth Arg (loan)	8	—
McALLISTER Gary	6 1	10 11	M	25 12 64	Motherwell	Fir Park BC	Motherwell	59	6
							Leicester C	201	47
							Leeds U	195	26
McAREE Rod	5 7	10 02	D	19 8 74	Dungannon	Trainee	Liverpool	—	—
							Bristol C	6	—
MACARI Michael	5 5	10 13	F	4 2 73	Kilwinning	Trainee	West Ham U	—	—
							Stoke C	—	—
MACARI Paul	5 8	11 00	F	23 8 76	Manchester	Trainee	**Stoke C**	—	—
McATEER Jason	5 9	11 05	M	18 6 71	Birkenhead	Marine	**Bolton W**	110	8
MACAULAY Lee ‡	5 9	10 12	D	9 11 75	Harthill	Trainee	**Brighton & HA**	—	—
McAULEY Sean (on loan from St Johnstone)	6 0	11 9	D	23 6 72	Sheffield		**Chesterfield**	1	1
MACAULEY Steve	6 1	12 00	D	4 3 69	Lytham	Fleetwood	**Crewe Alex**	94	11
MACBETH Andy ‡	5 10	10 11	F	9 1 76	Bangor	Trainee	**Wolverhampton W**	—	—
McCALL Steve	5 10	12 06	M	15 10 60	Carlisle	Apprentice	Ipswich T	257	7
							Sheffield W	29	2
							Carlisle U (loan)	6	—
							Plymouth Arg	96	5
McCARTHY Alan	5 11	12 10	D	11 1 72	London	Trainee	**QPR**	11	—
							Watford (loan)	9	—
							Plymouth Arg (loan)	2	—
McCARTHY Jamie ‡	5 10	11 07	M	14 8 73	London	Trainee	**Wimbledon**	—	—
McCARTHY Jon	5 10	11 00	M	18 8 70	Middlesbrough		Hartlepool U	1	—
						Shepshed	**York C**	199	31
McCARTHY Mick	6 2	13 12	D	7 2 59	Barnsley	Apprentice	Barnsley	272	7
							Manchester C	140	2
							Celtic	48	—
						Lyon	**Millwall**	35	2
McCARTHY Paul	6 0	13 06	D	4 8 71	Cork	Trainee	**Brighton**	148	5
McCARTHY Sean	6 0	12 05	F	12 9 67	Bridgend	Bridgend	Swansea C	91	25
							Plymouth Arg	70	19
							Bradford C	131	60
							Oldham Ath	59	22
McCARTHY Tony	6 1	12 03	D	9 11 69	Dublin	Shelbourne	Millwall	21	1
							Crewe Alex (loan)	2	—
							Colchester U	10	1
McCLAIR Brian	5 10	12 09	F	8 12 63	Bellshill	Apprentice	Aston Villa	—	—
							Motherwell	39	15
							Celtic	145	99
							Manchester U	301	85
McCLUSKEY Anthony *	6 0	21 02	M	29 10 75	Hartlepool	Trainee	**Burnley**	—	—
McCREERY David *	5 6	10 07	M	16 9 57	Belfast	Apprentice	Manchester U	87	7
							QPR	57	4
						Tulsa R	Newcastle U	243	2
							Hearts	29	—
							Hartlepool U	30	—
							Carlisle U	35	—
							Hartlepool U	9	—
McCUE James	5 8	10 00	F	29 6 75	Glasgow	Trainee	**WBA**	—	—
McDERMOTT John	5 7	10 00	D	3 2 69	Middlesbrough	Trainee	**Grimsby T**	276	4
McDONALD Alan	6 2	12 07	D	12 10 63	Belfast	Apprentice	**QPR**	337	10
							Charlton Ath (loan)	9	—

Player	Ht	Wt	Pos	Birth Date	Birth Place	Source	Clubs	League App	League Gls
McDONALD Chris *			M	14 10 75	Edinburgh	Trainee	**Arsenal**	—	—
McDONALD David	5 11	11 07	D	2 1 71	Dublin	Trainee	Tottenham H	2	—
							Gillingham (loan)	10	—
							Bradford C (loan)	7	—
							Reading (loan)	11	—
							Peterborough U	29	—
							Barnet	45	—
McDONALD Neil	5 11	11 04	D	2 11 65	Wallsend	Wallsend BC	Newcastle U	180	24
							Everton	90	4
							Oldham Ath	24	1
							Bolton W	4	—
McDONALD Paul	5 6	10 00	F	20 4 68	Motherwell	Merry Street BC	Hamilton Acad	215	26
							Southampton	2	—
McDOUGALD Junior	5 11	12 06	F	12 1 75	Big Spring	Trainee	Tottenham H	—	—
							Brighton	41	10
McELHATTON Michael	6 1	12 11	D	16 4 75	Co.Kerry	Trainee	**Bournemouth**	38	2
McFARLANE Andy	6 3	13 08	F	30 11 66	Wolverhampton	Cradley T	Portsmouth	2	—
							Swansea C	55	8
McGARGLE Stephen			F	24 10 75	Gateshead	Trainee	**Middlesbrough**	—	—
McGARRIGLE Kevin	5 11	11 05	D	9 4 77	Newcastle	Trainee	**Brighton**	18	—
McGAVIN Steve	5 8	11 00	F	24 1 69	North Walsham	Sudbury	Colchester U	58	17
							Birmingham C	23	2
							Wycombe W	12	2
McGEE Paul ‡	5 6	9 10	F	17 5 68	Dublin	Bohemians	Colchester U	3	—
							Wimbledon	60	9
							Peterborough U (loan)	6	—
McGHEE David	5 10	11 04	F	19 6 76	Sussex	Trainee	**Brentford**	7	1
McGIBBON Patrick	6 2	12 11	D	6 9 73	Lurgan	Portadown	**Manchester U**	—	—
McGINLAY John	5 9	11 04	F	8 4 64	Inverness	Elgin C	Shrewsbury T	60	27
							Bury	25	9
							Millwall	34	10
							Bolton W	110	57
McGLASHAN John	6 1	12 00	F	3 6 67	Dundee	Dundee Violet	Montrose	68	11
							Millwall	16	—
							Cambridge U (loan)	1	—
							Fulham (loan)	5	1
							Peterborough U	46	3
							Rotherham U	27	3
McGLEISH Scott *	5 9	10 08	F	10 2 74	London	Edgware T	**Charlton Ath**	6	—
							Leyton Orient (loan)	6	1
McGOLDRICK Eddie	5 10	11 07	F	30 4 65	London	Kettering T	Northampton T	107	9
							Crystal Palace	147	11
							Arsenal	37	—
McGORRY Brian	5 10	12 08	M	16 4 70	Liverpool	Weymouth	Bournemouth	61	11
							Peterborough U	52	6
McGOWAN Gavin	5 11	12 03	M	16 1 76	Blackheath	Trainee	**Arsenal**	3	—
McGRATH Lloyd	5 5	11 06	M	24 2 65	Birmingham	Apprentice	Coventry C	214	4
							Portsmouth	18	—
McGRATH Paul	6 2	14 00	D	4 12 59	Greenford	St Patrick's Ath	Manchester U	163	12
							Aston Villa	223	7
McGREAL John	5 11	10 11	D	2 6 72	Birkenhead	Trainee	**Tranmere R**	61	1
McGREGOR Mark §	5 10	10 05	D	16 2 77	Chester	Trainee	**Wrexham**	1	—
McGREGOR Paul	5 10	10 04	F	17 12 74	Liverpool	Trainee	**Nottingham F**	11	1
McGUCKIN Ian	6 2	14 02	D	24 4 73	Middlesbrough	Trainee	**Hartlepool U**	90	6
McHUGH Michael *	5 9	11 07	F	3 4 71	Donegal		Bradford C	31	4
							Scarborough	3	—
McKAY Andrew	5 10	11 10	D	16 1 75	Bolton	Trainee	**Bolton W**	—	—

Player	Ht	Wt	Pos	Birth Date	Birth Place	Source	Clubs	League App	League Gls
McKEARNEY Dave *	5 10	11 02	M	20 6 68	Crosby	Prescot Cables	Bolton W	—	—
							Crewe Alex	108	12
							Wigan Ath	49	9
MacKENZIE Chris	6 0	12 06	G	14 5 72	Northampton	Corby T	**Hereford U**	22	—
McKINLAY David ‡	6 3	13 11	D	20 11 75	Kinross	Trainee	Middlesbrough	—	—
							Bradford C	—	—
McKOP Henry	5 11	12 00	D	8 7 67	Zimbabwe	Bonner SC	**Bristol C**	5	—
McLAREN Paul	6 0	12 06	D	17 11 76	Wycombe	Trainee	**Luton T**	1	—
MacLAREN Ross	5 10	12 12	M	14 4 62	Edinburgh	Glasgow Rangers	Shrewsbury T	161	18
							Derby Co	122	4
							Swindon T	197	9
McLEAN Ian	6 2	13 02	D	13 8 66	Paisley	Metroford	**Bristol R**	28	2
							Cardiff C (loan)	4	—
McLEARY Alan *	5 10	10 09	D	6 10 64	Lambeth	Apprentice	Millwall	307	5
							Sheffield U (loan)	3	—
							Wimbledon (loan)	4	—
							Charlton Ath	66	3
McLOUGHLIN Alan	5 8	10 02	M	20 4 67	Manchester	Local	Manchester U	—	—
							Swindon T	9	—
							Torquay U	24	4
							Swindon T	97	19
							Southampton	24	1
							Aston Villa (loan)	—	—
							Portsmouth	136	23
McMAHON Gerard	5 11	11 00	F	29 12 73	Belfast	Glenavon	**Tottenham H**	2	—
							Barnet (loan)	10	2
McMAHON Sam	5 9	11 02	M	10 2 76	Newark	Trainee	**Leicester C**	1	—
McMAHON Steve	5 9	11 08	M	20 8 61	Liverpool	Apprentice	Everton	100	11
							Aston Villa	75	7
							Liverpool	204	29
							Manchester C	87	1
							Swindon T	17	—
McMANAMAN Steve	6 0	10 06	F	11 2 72	Liverpool	School	**Liverpool**	133	18
McMILLAN Andy	5 11	11 09	D	22 6 68	Bloemfontein		**York C**	266	3
McMINN Ted	6 0	13 08	F	28 9 62	Castle Douglas	Glenafton Athletic	Queen of the S	62	5
							Rangers	63	4
						Seville	Derby Co	123	9
							Birmingham C	22	—
							Burnley	36	3
McNALLY Bernard *	5 7	10 12	M	17 2 63	Shrewsbury	Apprentice	Shrewsbury T	282	23
							WBA	156	10
McNAMARA Brett *			F	8 7 72	Newark	Stamford	**Northampton T**	1	—
McNIVEN Scott §			D	27 5 78	Leeds	Trainee	**Oldham Ath**	1	—
MacPHAIL John ‡	6 0	12 03	D	7 12 55	Dundee	St. Columba's	Dundee	68	—
							Sheffield U	135	7
							York C	142	24
							Bristol C	26	1
							Sunderland	130	22
							Hartlepool U	163	4
McPHERSON Keith	5 11	11 00	D	11 9 63	Greenwich	Apprentice	West Ham U	1	—
							Cambridge U (loan)	11	1
							Northampton T	182	8
							Reading	177	6
McPHERSON Malcolm	5 10	12 00	F	9 12 74	Glasgow	Yeovil	**West Ham U**	—	—
McROBERT Lee	5 8	10 12	M	4 10 72	Bromley	Sittingbourne	**Millwall**	7	1
McSWEGAN Gary	5 7	10 09	F	24 9 70	Glasgow	Amateur BC	Rangers	18	4
							Notts Co	59	21

Player	Ht	Wt	Pos	Birth Date	Birth Place	Source	Clubs	League App	League Gls
MADDEN Lawrie	5 10	13 00	D	28 9 55	Hackney	Arsenal	Mansfield T	10	—
						Manchester Univ	Charlton Ath	113	7
							Millwall	47	2
							Sheffield W	212	2
							Leicester C (loan)	3	—
							Wolverhampton W	67	1
							Darlington	5	—
							Chesterfield	36	1
MADDISON Lee	5 11	11 00	D	5 10 72	Bristol	Trainee	**Bristol R**	73	—
MADDISON Neil	5 10	11 02	M	2 10 69	Darlington	Trainee	**Southampton**	130	16
MADDIX Danny	5 10	11 07	D	11 10 67	Ashford	Apprentice	Tottenham H	—	—
							Southend U (loan)	2	—
							QPR	166	7
MAGEE Kevin *	5 10	11 03	F	10 4 71	Edinburgh	Armadale Th	Partick T	11	—
							Preston NE	21	1
MAGILTON Jim	6 1	13 12	M	6 5 69	Belfast	Apprentice	Liverpool	—	—
							Oxford U	150	34
							Southampton	57	6
MAGUIRE Gavin	5 10	11 08	M	24 11 67	Hammersmith	Apprentice	QPR	40	—
							Portsmouth	91	—
							Newcastle U (loan)	3	—
							Millwall	12	—
							Scarborough (loan)	2	—
MAHON Alan	5 7	10 00	M	4 4 78	Dublin	Tranmere R	**Tranmere R**	—	—
MAHONEY-JOHNSON Michael	5 10	11 00	F	6 11 76	Paddington	Trainee	**QPR**	—	—
MAHORN Paul	5 10	11 06	F	13 8 73	Whipps Cross	Trainee	**Tottenham H**	1	—
							Fulham (loan)	3	—
MAIL David *	5 11	11 11	D	12 9 62	Bristol	Apprentice	Aston Villa	—	—
							Blackburn R	206	4
							Hull C	150	2
MAKEL Lee	5 11	11 07	M	11 1 73	Sunderland	Trainee	Newcastle U	12	1
							Blackburn R	3	—
MAKIN Chris	5 11	11 00	D	8 5 73	Manchester	Trainee	**Oldham Ath**	55	2
							Wigan Ath (loan)	15	2
MALKIN Chris	6 3	12 00	F	4 6 67	Bebington	Overpool	**Tranmere R**	232	60
MALONE Chris	5 8	10 07	F	29 12 75	Drogheda		**Blackburn R**	—	—
MANN Neil	5 10	12 01	M	19 11 72	Nottingham	Grantham T	**Hull C**	36	2
MANUEL Billy †	5 5	10 00	D	28 6 69	Hackney	Apprentice	Tottenham H	—	—
							Gillingham	87	5
							Brentford	94	1
							Cambridge U	10	—
							Peterborough U	14	1
MARDENBOROUGH Steve ‡	5 8	11 09	F	11 9 64	Birmingham	Apprentice	Coventry C	—	—
							Wolverhampton W	9	1
							Cambridge U (loan)	6	—
							Swansea C	36	7
							Newport Co	64	11
							Cardiff C	32	1
							Hereford U	27	—
							Darlington	106	18
							Lincoln C	21	2
							Scarborough	1	—
MARDON Paul	6 0	11 10	D	14 9 69	Bristol	Trainee	Bristol C	42	—
							Doncaster R (loan)	3	—
							Birmingham C	64	—
							WBA	50	2
MARGETSON Martyn	6 0	13 10	G	8 9 71	West Neath	Trainee	**Manchester C**	6	—
							Bristol R (loan)	3	—
							Bolton W (loan)	—	—
							Luton T (loan)	—	—
MARGINSON Karl *	6 0	11 11	M	11 11 70	Manchester	Ashton U	**Rotherham U**	15	1

Player	Ht	Wt	Pos	Birth Date	Birth Place	Source	Clubs	League App	League Gls
MARKER Nick	6 1	13 00	D	3 5 65	Exeter	Apprentice	Exeter C	202	3
							Plymouth Arg	202	13
							Blackburn R	38	—
MARKS Jamie	5 9	10 13	D	18 3 77	Belfast	Trainee	**Leeds U**	—	—
MARPLES Chris *	5 11	13 06	G	3 8 64	Chesterfield	Goole	Chesterfield	84	—
							Stockport Co	57	—
							York C	138	—
							Scunthorpe U (loan)	1	—
							Chesterfield	57	—
MARQUIS Paul	6 2	14 04	D	29 8 72	Enfield	Trainee	West Ham U	1	—
							Doncaster R	11	—
MARRIOTT Andy	6 0	12 05	G	11 10 70	Nottingham	Trainee	Arsenal	—	—
							Nottingham F	11	—
							WBA (loan)	3	—
							Blackburn R (loan)	2	—
							Colchester U (loan)	10	—
							Burnley (loan)	15	—
							Wrexham	82	—
MARSDEN Chris	5 11	10 12	M	3 1 69	Sheffield	Trainee	Sheffield U	16	1
							Huddersfield T	121	9
							Coventry C (loan)	7	—
							Wolverhampton W	8	—
							Notts Co	7	—
MARSH Chris	6 0	13 02	M	14 1 70	Dudley	Trainee	**Walsall**	195	19
MARSH Mike	5 8	11 00	F	21 7 69	Liverpool	Kirkby T	Liverpool	69	2
							West Ham U	49	1
							Coventry C	15	2
MARSH Simon			D	29 1 77	Ealing	Trainee	**Oxford U**	8	—
MARSHALL Andy	6 2	13 07	G	14 4 75	Bury	Trainee	**Norwich C**	21	—
MARSHALL Daniel *	5 10	11 05	D	18 12 75	Newark	Notts Co	**Chesterfield**	1	—
MARSHALL Dwight	5 7	10 10	F	3 10 65	Jamaica	Grays Ath	Plymouth Arg	99	27
							Middlesbrough (loan)	3	—
							Luton T	45	11
MARSHALL Ian	6 1	12 12	F	20 3 66	Liverpool	Apprentice	Everton	15	1
							Oldham Ath	170	36
							Ipswich T	47	13
MARSHALL John	5 10	12 06	M	18 8 64	Surrey	Apprentice	**Fulham**	395	28
MARSHALL Lee	5 9	9 12	F	1 8 75	Nottingham	Trainee	Nottingham F	—	—
						Grantham	**Stockport Co**	1	—
MARSHALL Scott	6 1	12 05	D	1 5 73	Edinburgh	Trainee	**Arsenal**	2	—
							Rotherham U (loan)	10	1
							Oxford U (loan)	—	—
							Sheffield U (loan)	17	—
MARSTON Marvin	6 5	14 00	D	27 8 76	London	Notts Co	**Sheffield U**	—	—
MARTIN Alvin	6 1	13 07	D	29 7 58	Bootle	Apprentice	**West Ham U**	455	27
MARTIN David	6 1	13 01	M	25 4 63	East Ham	Apprentice	Millwall	140	6
							Wimbledon	35	3
							Southend U	221	19
							Bristol C	38	1
							Northampton T (loan)	7	1
MARTIN Dean ‡	5 11	11 09	M	9 9 67	Halifax	Apprentice	Halifax T	153	7
							Scunthorpe U	106	7
							Rochdale	15	—
MARTIN Eliot	5 6	10 00	D	27 9 72	Plumstead	Trainee	**Gillingham**	60	1
MARTIN Jae *	5 9	11 00	F	5 2 76	London	Trainee	**Southend U**	8	—
							Leyton Orient (loan)	4	—
MARTIN Kevin §			G	22 6 76	Bromsgrove	Trainee	**Scarborough**	3	—
MARTIN Lee	6 0	13 00	G	9 9 68	Huddersfield	Trainee	Huddersfield T	54	—
							Blackpool	98	—
MARTINDALE Dave ‡	5 11	11 10	M	9 4 64	Liverpool	Caernarfon	Tranmere R	166	9
							Doncaster R	—	—

				Birth				League	
Player	Ht	Wt	Pos	Date	Place	Source	Clubs	App	Gls
MARTINDALE Gary *	5 11	11 09	F	24 6 71	Liverpool	Burscough	**Bolton W**	—	—
MARTYN Nigel	6 2	14 07	G	11 8 66	St Austell	St Blazey	Bristol R	101	—
							Crystal Palace	226	—
MASINGA Phil	6 1	12 07	F	28 6 69	South Africa	Mamelodi Sundowns	**Leeds U**	22	5
MASKELL Craig	5 10	11 11	F	10 4 68	Aldershot	Apprentice	Southampton	6	1
							Swindon T (loan)	—	—
							Huddersfield T	87	43
							Reading	72	26
							Swindon T	47	22
							Southampton	16	1
MASON Andrew *	5 11	11 08	F	22 11 74	Bolton	Trainee	**Bolton W**	—	—
MASON Paul	5 9	12 01	M	3 9 63	Liverpool	Groningen	Aberdeen	158	27
							Ipswich T	43	6
MASON Richard	5 9	10 02	D	5 6 77	Sheffield	Trainee	**Sheffield W**	—	—
MASSEY Stuart	5 10	10 10	M	17 11 64	Crawley	Sutton U	Crystal Palace	2	—
							Oxford U	22	—
MASTERS Neil	6 1	10 12	D	25 5 72	Lisburn	Trainee	Bournemouth	38	2
							Wolverhampton W	9	—
MATHIE Alex	5 10	10 07	F	20 12 68	Bathgate	Celtic BC	Celtic	11	—
							Morton	74	31
							Port Vale (loan)	3	—
							Newcastle U	25	4
							Ipswich T	13	2
MATTEO Dominic	6 1	11 10	D	24 4 74	Dumfries	Trainee	**Liverpool**	18	—
							Sunderland (loan)	1	—
MATTHEW Damian	5 11	10 10	M	23 9 70	Islington	Trainee	Chelsea	21	—
							Luton T (loan)	5	—
							Crystal Palace	16	1
MATTHEWS Martin *	5 10	11 03	D	22 12 75	Peterborough	Trainee	**Derby Co**	—	—
MATTHEWS Neil *	6 0	12 12	F	19 9 66	Grimsby	Apprentice	Grimsby T	11	1
							Scunthorpe U (loan)	1	—
							Halifax T (loan)	9	2
							Bolton W (loan)	1	—
							Halifax T	105	29
							Stockport Co	43	15
							Halifax T (loan)	3	—
							Lincoln C	83	20
							Bury (loan)	2	1
MATTHEWS Neil ‡	6 0	11 07	D	3 12 67	Manchester	Apprentice	Blackpool	76	1
							Cardiff C	66	2
							Rochdale	19	—
MATTHEWS Rob	6 0	12 05	F	14 10 70	Slough	Loughborough Univ	Notts Co	43	11
							Luton T	11	—
MATTHEWSON Trevor	6 4	13 06	D	12 2 63	Sheffield	Apprentice	Sheffield W	3	—
							Newport Co	75	—
							Stockport Co	80	—
							Lincoln C	83	8
							Birmingham C	168	12
							Preston NE	12	1
							Bury	18	—
MATTISON Paul	5 8	11 04	M	24 4 73	Wakefield	North Ferriby U	**Darlington**	10	—
MAUGE Ron	5 10	11 10	M	10 3 69	Islington	Trainee	Charlton Ath	—	—
							Fulham	50	2
							Bury	108	10
							Manchester C (loan)	—	—
MAXFIELD Scott	5 8	10 07	D	13 7 76	Doncaster	Trainee	**Doncaster R**	10	—
MAY Andy *	5 8	11 10	M	26 2 64	Bury	Apprentice	Manchester C	150	8
							Huddersfield T	114	5
							Bolton W (loan)	10	2
							Bristol C	90	4
							Millwall	54	1

Player	Ht	Wt	Pos	Birth Date	Birth Place	Source	Clubs	League App	League Gls
MAY David	6 0	12 06	D	24 6 70	Oldham	Trainee	Blackburn R	123	3
							Manchester U	19	2
MEADE Raphael ‡	5 10	11 09	F	22 11 62	Islington	Apprentice	Arsenal	41	14
						Sporting Lisbon	Dundee U	11	4
							Luton T	4	—
							Ipswich T	1	—
						Odense	Plymouth Arg	5	—
							Brighton & HA	40	9
						Dover Ath	**Brighton & HA**	3	—
MEAKER Michael	5 11	11 05	M	18 8 71	Greenford	Trainee	**QPR**	34	1
							Plymouth Arg (loan)	4	—
MEAN Scott	5 11	11 11	M	13 12 73	Crawley	Trainee	**Bournemouth**	60	7
MEARA Jim	5 9	11 02	M	7 10 72	London	Trainee	Watford	2	—
							Doncaster R	15	1
MEASHAM Ian	5 11	11 09	D	14 12 64	Barnsley	Apprentice	Huddersfield T	17	—
							Lincoln C (loan)	6	—
							Rochdale (loan)	12	—
							Cambridge U	46	—
							Burnley	182	2
							Doncaster R	22	—
MEGSON Gary *	5 10	12 00	M	2 5 59	Manchester	Apprentice	Plymouth Arg	78	10
							Everton	22	2
							Sheffield W	123	13
							Nottingham F	—	—
							Newcastle U	24	1
							Sheffield W	110	12
							Manchester C	82	2
							Norwich C	46	1
MEHEW David *	5 10	12 06	M	29 10 67	Camberley	Trainee	Leeds U	—	—
							Bristol R	222	63
							Exeter C (loan)	7	—
							Walsall	13	—
MELLON Michael	5 9	11 03	M	18 3 72	Paisley	Trainee	Bristol C	35	1
							WBA	45	6
							Blackpool	26	4
MELVILLE Andy	6 0	13 03	D	29 11 68	Swansea	School	Swansea C	175	22
							Oxford U	135	13
							Sunderland	80	5
MENDONCA Clive	5 10	10 07	F	9 9 68	Tullington	Apprentice	Sheffield U	13	4
							Doncaster R (loan)	2	—
							Rotherham U	84	27
							Sheffield U	10	1
							Grimsby T (loan)	10	3
							Grimsby T	103	35
MENDUM Craig ‡	5 9	10 08	F	13 4 77	Saltburn	Trainee	**Nottingham F**	—	—
MERCER Billy	6 1	13 07	G	22 5 69	Liverpool	Trainee	Liverpool	—	—
							Rotherham U	104	—
							Sheffield U	3	—
							Nottingham F (loan)	—	—
MEROLA Tony *	5 7	10 07	F	5 10 75	Wrexham	Trainee	**Wrexham**	—	—
MERSON Paul	6 0	13 02	F	20 3 68	London	Apprentice	**Arsenal**	257	67
							Brentford (loan)	7	—
MEYER Adrian	6 0	14 00	D	22 9 70	Bristol	Trainee	**Scarborough**	114	9
MICKLEWHITE Gary	5 7	10 04	M	21 3 61	Southwark	Apprentice	Manchester U	—	—
							QPR	106	11
							Derby Co	240	31
							Gillingham	64	3
MIDDLEMASS Scott *	6 3	12 04	D	17 5 72	Worksop	Morecambe	**Northampton T**	—	—
MIDDLETON Craig	5 9	11 00	M	10 9 70	Nuneaton	Trainee	Coventry C	3	—
							Cambridge U	19	2
MIDDLETON Lee	5 9	11 09	M	10 9 70	Nuneaton	Trainee	Coventry C	2	—
							Swindon T	—	—
MIDDLETON Matthew ‡			D	22 1 75	Lambeth	Trainee	**Millwall**	—	—

Player	Ht	Wt	Pos	Birth Date	Birth Place	Source	Clubs	League App	League Gls
MIDGLEY Craig §			F	24 5 76	Bradford	Trainee	**Bradford C**	3	—
MIDWOOD Michael *			F	19 4 76	Huddersfield	Trainee	**Huddersfield T**	—	—
MIKE Adie	6 0	11 06	F	16 11 73	Manchester	Trainee	**Manchester C**	16	2
							Bury (loan)	7	1
MIKLOSKO Ludek	6 5	14 00	G	9 12 61	Ostrava	Banik Ostrava	**West Ham U**	230	—
MILES Ben	6 1	11 07	G	13 4 76	Middlesex	Trainee	**Swansea C**	—	—
MILLAR Paul	6 2	12 07	F	16 11 66	Belfast	Portadown	Port Vale	40	5
							Hereford U (loan)	5	2
							Cardiff C	120	17
MILLEN Keith	6 2	12 04	D	26 9 66	Croydon	Juniors	Brentford	305	17
							Watford	41	1
MILLER Allan	6 3	14 08	G	29 3 70	Epping	Trainee	Arsenal	8	—
							Plymouth Arg (loan)	13	—
							WBA (loan)	3	—
							Birmingham C (loan)	15	—
							Middlesbrough	41	—
MILLER David	5 11	11 12	M	8 1 64	Burnley	Apprentice	Burnley	32	3
							Crewe Alex (loan)	3	—
							Tranmere R	29	1
							Preston NE	58	2
							Burnley (loan)	4	—
							Carlisle U	109	7
							Stockport Co	81	1
							Wigan Ath	31	3
MILLER Kevin	6 1	13 00	G	15 3 69	Falmouth	Newquay	Exeter C	163	—
							Birmingham C	24	—
							Watford	44	—
MILLER Paul	6 0	11 00	F	31 1 68	Bisley	Trainee	Wimbledon	80	10
							Newport Co (loan)	6	2
							Bristol C (loan)	3	—
							Bristol R	42	16
MILLETT Michael			D	22 9 77	Wigan	Trainee	**Wigan Ath**	3	—
MILLIGAN Mike	5 8	11 00	M	20 2 67	Manchester	Trainee	Oldham Ath	162	17
							Everton	17	1
							Oldham Ath	117	6
							Norwich C	26	2
MILLS Danny ‡	6 0	10 05	M	13 2 75	Sidcup	Trainee	**Charlton Ath**	—	—
MILLS Danny	5 11	11 09	D	18 5 77	Norwich	Trainee	**Norwich C**	—	—
MILLS Gary	5 10	11 10	M	11 11 61	Northampton	Apprentice	Nottingham F	58	8
						Seattle S	Derby Co	18	1
						Seattle S	Nottingham F	79	4
							Notts Co	75	8
							Leicester C	200	15
							Notts Co	34	—
MILLS Lee	6 1	12 11	F	10 7 70	Mexborough	Stocksbridge	Wolverhampton W	25	2
							Derby Co	16	7
MILNER Andy	6 0	11 00	F	10 2 67	Kendal	Netherfield	Manchester C	—	—
							Rochdale	127	25
							Chester C	36	8
MILSOM Paul ‡	6 1	13 03	F	5 10 74	Bristol	Trainee	Bristol C	3	—
							Cardiff C	3	—
MILTON Simon	5 10	11 05	M	23 8 63	Fulham	Bury St Edmunds	**Ipswich T**	201	39
							Exeter C (loan)	2	3
							Torquay U (loan)	4	1
MIMMS Bobby	6 2	12 13	G	12 10 63	York	Halifax T	Rotherham U	83	—
							Everton	29	—
							Notts Co (loan)	2	—
							Sunderland (loan)	4	—
							Blackburn R (loan)	6	—
							Manchester C (loan)	3	—
							Tottenham H	37	—
							Aberdeen (loan)	6	—
							Blackburn R	126	—

Player	Ht	Wt	Pos	Birth Date	Birth Place	Source	Clubs	League App	League Gls
MINETT Jason *	5 10	10 02	M	12 8 71	Peterborough	Trainee	Norwich C	3	—
							Exeter C (loan)	12	—
							Exeter C	76	3
MINTO Scott	5 10	10 00	D	6 8 71	Cheshire	Trainee	Charlton Ath	180	7
							Chelsea	19	—
MINTON Jeffrey	5 6	11 10	M	28 12 73	Hackney	Trainee	Tottenham H	2	1
							Brighton	39	5
MIOTTO Simon ‡			G	5 9 69	Australia	Riverside Olympic	**Blackpool**	—	—
MISON Michael	6 3	13 09	M	8 11 75	London	Trainee	**Fulham**	28	1
MITCHELL Andrew	5 10	11 06	D	12 9 76	Rotherham	Trainee	**Aston Villa**	—	—
MITCHELL Brian *	6 1	13 01	D	30 7 63	Stonehaven	King St	Aberdeen	65	1
							Bradford C	178	9
							Bristol C	16	—
							Hull C	9	—
MITCHELL David ‡	6 1	12 07	F	13 6 62	Glasgow		Rangers	26	6
						Feyenoord	Chelsea	7	—
							Newcastle U (loan)	2	1
							Swindon T	68	16
						Altay Izmir	**Millwall**	55	15
MITCHELL Graham	6 0	11 05	D	16 2 68	Shipley	Apprentice	Huddersfield T	244	2
							Bradford C	26	—
MITCHELL Neil	5 6	10 00	M	7 11 74	Lytham	Trainee	**Blackpool**	67	8
MITCHELL Paul	5 10	12 00	D	20 10 71	Bournemouth	Trainee	Bournemouth	16	—
							West Ham U	1	—
MOCKLER Paul *	6 0	12 13	M	13 2 76	Stockton	Trainee	**York C**	—	—
MOHAN Nicky	6 1	13 01	D	6 10 70	Middlesbrough	Trainee	Middlesbrough	99	4
							Hull C (loan)	5	1
							Leicester C	23	—
MOLBY Jan	6 1	14 07	M	4 7 63	Kolding	Ajax	**Liverpool**	218	44
MONCUR John	5 7	9 10	M	22 9 66	Stepney	Apprentice	Tottenham H	21	1
							Cambridge U (loan)	4	—
							Doncaster R (loan)	4	—
							Portsmouth (loan)	7	—
							Brentford (loan)	5	1
							Ipswich T (loan)	6	—
							Nottingham F (loan)	—	—
							Swindon T	58	5
							West Ham U	30	2
MONINGTON Mark	6 1	14 00	D	21 10 70	Bilsthorpe	Schoolboy	Burnley	84	5
							Rotherham U	25	2
MONKOU Kenneth	6 3	14 04	D	29 11 64	Surinam	Feyenoord	Chelsea	94	2
							Southampton	99	6
MOODY Jimmy	5 10	11 02	D	16 11 77	Hull	Trainee	**Leeds U**	—	—
MOODY Paul	6 3	14 03	F	13 6 67	Portsmouth	Waterlooville	Southampton	12	—
							Reading (loan)	5	1
							Oxford U	56	28
MOONEY Tommy	5 11	12 06	F	11 8 71	Teesside North	Trainee	Aston Villa	—	—
							Scarborough	107	30
							Southend U	14	5
							Watford (loan)	10	2
							Watford	29	3
MOORE Alan	5 9	10 08	F	25 11 74	Dublin	Rivermount	**Middlesbrough**	81	14
MOORE Darren	6 2	15 06	D	22 4 74	Birmingham	Trainee	**Torquay U**	103	8
MOORE David			M	23 11 76	Birmingham	Trainee	**Aston Villa**	—	—
MOORE Ian	5 11	12 00	F	26 8 76	Birkenhead	Trainee	**Tranmere R**	1	—

Player	Ht	Wt	Pos	Birth Date	Birth Place	Source	Clubs	League App	League Gls
MOORE Kevin	5 11	13 02	D	29 4 58	Grimsby	Local	Grimsby T	400	27
							Oldham Ath	13	1
							Southampton	148	10
							Bristol R (loan)	7	—
							Bristol R (loan)	4	1
							Fulham	31	3
MOORE Mike ‡	5 10	11 01	F	7 10 73	Derby	Derby Co	**Swansea C**	1	—
MOORE Neil	6 0	12 00	D	21 9 72	Liverpool	Trainee	**Everton**	5	—
							Blackpool (loan)	7	—
							Oldham Ath (loan)	5	—
MOORE Richard	6 1	12 07	G	2 9 77	Scunthorpe	Trainee	**Everton**	—	—
MORAH Ollie	5 11	13 02	F	3 9 72	Islington	Trainee	Tottenham H	—	—
							Hereford U (loan)	2	—
							Swindon T	—	—
						Sutton U	**Cambridge U**	14	2
							Torquay U (loan)	2	—
MORALEE Jamie	5 11	11 00	F	2 12 71	Wandsworth	Trainee	Crystal Palace	6	—
							Millwall	67	19
							Watford	24	4
MORAN Paul	5 8	11 12	F	22 5 68	Enfield	Trainee	Tottenham H	36	2
							Portsmouth (loan)	3	—
							Leicester C (loan)	10	1
							Newcastle U (loan)	1	—
							Southend U (loan)	1	—
							Cambridge U (loan)	—	—
							Peterborough U	7	—
MORAN Steve *	5 8	11 00	F	10 1 61	Croydon	Amateur	Southampton	180	78
							Leicester C	43	14
							Reading	116	30
							Exeter C	57	27
							Hull C	17	5
MORENO Jaime	5 9	11 09	F	19 1 74	Bolivia	Blooming	**Middlesbrough**	14	1
MORGAN Alan	5 9	10 12	D	2 11 73	Aberystwyth	Trainee	**Tranmere R**	—	—
MORGAN Ian	6 2	12 10	D	11 10 77	Birmingham	Trainee	**Nottingham F**	—	—
MORGAN Jamie *	5 11	11 09	M	1 10 75	Plymouth	Trainee	**Plymouth Arg**	11	—
MORGAN Philip *	6 1	13 00	G	18 12 74	Stoke	Trainee	**Ipswich T**	1	—
MORGAN Simon	5 10	11 13	M	5 9 66	Birmingham	Trainee	Leicester C	160	3
							Fulham	186	28
MORGAN Steve	5 11	13 00	D	19 9 68	Oldham	Apprentice	Blackpool	144	10
							Plymouth Arg	121	6
							Coventry C	68	2
MORGAN Steve ‡	5 8	10 05	F	27 7 76	Wrexham	Trainee	**Wrexham**	—	—
MORGAN Thomas			M	30 3 77	Dublin	Trainee	**Blackburn R**	—	—
MORGAN Trevor ‡	6 2	13 04	F	30 9 56	Forest Gate	Leytonstone	Bournemouth	53	13
							Mansfield T	12	6
							Bournemouth	88	33
							Bristol C	32	8
							Exeter C	30	9
							Bristol R	55	24
							Bristol C	19	8
							Bolton W	77	17
							Colchester U	32	12
							Exeter C	17	3
						Hong Kong	Birmingham C	1	—
							Exeter C	9	1
MORLEY Trevor ‡	5 11	12 01	F	20 3 61	Nottingham	Nuneaton	Northampton T	107	39
							Manchester C	72	18
							West Ham U	178	57
MORRIS Andy	6 5	15 05	F	17 11 67	Sheffield		Rotherham U	7	—
							Chesterfield	218	46
							Exeter C (loan)	7	2
MORRIS Chris	5 11	11 11	D	24 12 63	Newquay		Sheffield W	74	1
							Celtic	163	8
							Middlesbrough	55	1

Player	Ht	Wt	Pos	Birth Date	Birth Place	Source	Clubs	League App	League Gls
MORRIS John *			D	12 12 75	Stone	Trainee	**Port Vale**	—	—
MORRIS Mark	6 1	13 08	D	26 9 62	Morden	Apprentice	Wimbledon	168	9
							Aldershot (loan)	14	—
							Watford	41	1
							Sheffield U	56	3
							Bournemouth	162	7
MORRIS Steve	5 10	11 01	F	13 5 76	Liverpool	Liverpool	**Wrexham**	12	2
MORRISON Andy	5 11	13 10	D	30 7 70	Inverness	Trainee	Plymouth Arg	113	6
							Blackburn R	5	—
							Blackpool	18	—
MORRISON David	5 11	12 05	F	30 11 74	Waltham Forest	Chelmsford C	**Peterborough U**	42	8
MORRISSEY John	5 8	11 09	F	8 3 65	Liverpool	Apprentice	Everton	1	—
							Wolverhampton W	10	1
							Tranmere R	362	47
MORROW Steve	5 11	12 02	D	2 7 70	Belfast	Trainee	**Arsenal**	44	1
							Reading (loan)	10	—
							Watford (loan)	8	—
							Reading (loan)	3	—
							Barnet (loan)	1	—
MORTIMER Paul	5 11	11 03	M	8 5 68	Kensington	Fulham	Charlton Ath	113	17
							Aston Villa	12	1
							Crystal Palace	22	2
							Brentford (loan)	6	—
							Charlton Ath	26	4
MORTLEY Peter ‡	6 0	12 00	D	17 10 75	Gravesend	Trainee	**Ipswich T**	—	—
MORTON Neil ‡	5 9	10 07	F	21 12 68	Congleton	Trainee	Crewe Alex	31	1
						Northwich Vic	Chester C	95	13
							Wigan Ath	48	5
MOSES Adrian	6 1	12 08	D	4 5 75	Doncaster	School	**Barnsley**	4	—
MOSS David	6 0	13 07	F	15 11 68	Doncaster	Boston U	Doncaster R	18	5
							Chesterfield	58	16
MOSS Neil	6 1	12 11	G	10 5 75	New Milton	Trainee	**Bournemouth**	15	—
MOULDEN Paul *	5 8	11 03	F	6 9 67	Farnworth	Apprentice	Manchester C	64	18
							Bournemouth	32	13
							Oldham Ath	38	4
							Brighton (loan)	11	5
							Birmingham C	20	6
							Huddersfield T	2	—
MOUNTFIELD Derek	6 1	13 04	D	2 11 62	Liverpool	Apprentice	Tranmere R	26	1
							Everton	106	19
							Aston Villa	90	9
							Wolverhampton W	83	4
							Carlisle U	31	3
MOUSSADDIK Chuck †	5 11	13 01	G	23 2 70	Morocco	Wimbledon	**Wycombe W**	—	—
MOYES David	6 1	12 10	D	25 4 63	Glasgow	Drumchapel A	Celtic	24	—
							Cambridge U	79	1
							Bristol C	83	6
							Shrewsbury T	96	11
							Dunfermline Ath	105	13
							Hamilton A	5	—
							Preston NE	67	8
MUDD Paul *	5 9	11 04	D	13 11 70	Hull	Trainee	Hull C	1	—
							Scarborough	98	2
							Scunthorpe U	68	4
MUGGLETON Carl	6 2	13 04	G	13 9 68	Leicester	Apprentice	Leicester C	46	—
							Chesterfield (loan)	17	—
							Blackpool (loan)	2	—
							Hartlepool U (loan)	8	—
							Stockport Co (loan)	4	—
							Liverpool (loan)	—	—
							Stoke C (loan)	6	—
							Sheffield U (loan)	—	—
							Celtic	12	—
							Stoke C	24	—

Player	Ht	Wt	Pos	Birth Date	Birth Place	Source	Clubs	League App	League Gls
MUIR Ian	5 8	11 00	F	5 5 63	Coventry	Apprentice	QPR	2	2
							Burnley (loan)	2	1
							Birmingham C	1	—
							Brighton	4	—
							Swindon T (loan)	2	—
							Tranmere R	314	141
MULLIGAN James	5 6	11 07	F	21 4 74	Dublin	Trainee	Stoke C	—	—
							Bury (loan)	3	1
							Bury	15	2
MULLIN John	6 0	11 08	F	11 8 75	Bury	School	**Burnley**	18	2
MULRYNE Philip			M	1 1 78	Belfast	Trainee	**Manchester U**	—	—
MUNDAY Stuart	5 11	10 09	D	28 9 72	Newham	Trainee	**Brighton**	86	4
MUNDEE Denny	5 10	11 07	F	10 10 68	Swindon	Apprentice	QPR	—	—
							Swindon T	—	—
							Bournemouth	100	6
							Torquay U (loan)	9	—
							Brentford	78	16
MUNGALL Steve	5 8	11 05	D	22 5 58	Bellshill		Motherwell	20	—
							Tranmere R	506	13
MUNRO Stuart	5 8	10 05	D	15 9 62	Falkirk	Bo'ness U	St Mirren	1	—
							Alloa	60	6
							Rangers	179	3
							Blackburn R	1	—
							Bristol C	91	—
MURDOCK Colin	6 3	12 09	D	2 7 75	Ballymena	Trainee	**Manchester U**	—	—
MURPHY Brendan	5 11	11 12	G	19 8 75	Wexford	Bradford C	**Wimbledon**	—	—
MURPHY Danny	5 9	10 03	M	18 3 77	Chester	Trainee	**Crewe Alex**	47	7
MURPHY Jamie	6 1	13 00	D	25 2 73	Manchester	Trainee	**Blackpool**	55	1
MURPHY John *	5 9	11 11	D	9 9 75	Cork	Trainee	**Aston Villa**	—	—
MURPHY John §	6 1	14 00	F	18 10 76	Whiston	Trainee	**Chester C**	5	—
MURPHY Matthew	5 10	11 00	F	20 8 71	Northampton	Corby	**Oxford U**	24	7
MURPHY Michael	5 10	11 09	F	5 5 77	Slough	Slough	**Reading**	1	—
MURPHY Shaun	6 0	12 00	D	5 11 70	Sydney	Perth Italia	**Notts Co**	54	2
MURPHY Stephen			M	5 4 78	Dublin	Belvedere	**Huddersfield T**	—	—
MURRAY Edwin	5 11	12 00	D	31 8 73	Redbridge	Trainee	**Swindon T**	7	—
MURRAY Nathan *	6 1	12 07	D	10 9 75	South Shields	Trainee	**Newcastle U**	—	—
MURRAY Paul	5 8	10 00	M	31 8 76	Carlisle	Trainee	**Carlisle U**	13	—
MURRAY Robert	5 11	11 07	F	31 10 74	Hammersmith	Trainee	**Bournemouth**	76	8
MURRAY Scott	5 10	11 00	F	26 5 74	Aberdeen	Fraserburgh	**Aston Villa**	—	—
MURRAY Shaun	5 7	10 10	M	7 2 70	Newcastle	Trainee	Tottenham H	—	—
							Portsmouth	34	1
							Millwall (loan)	—	—
							Scarborough	29	5
							Bradford C	41	5
MURTY Graeme	5 10	11 10	M	13 11 74	Middlesbrough	Trainee	**York C**	21	2
MUSGRAVE Sean *	5 10	12 04	G	27 10 74	Penshaw	Trainee	**Sunderland**	—	—
MUSSELWHITE Paul	6 2	12 07	G	22 12 68	Portsmouth		Portsmouth	—	—
							Scunthorpe U	132	—
							Port Vale	131	—
MUSTOE Robbie	5 10	11 10	M	28 8 68	Oxford		Oxford U	91	10
							Middlesbrough	159	12
MUTCH Andy	5 10	11 00	F	28 12 63	Liverpool	Southport	Wolverhampton W	289	96
							Swindon T	50	6
MUTCHELL Robert ‡	5 10	11 02	D	2 1 74	Solihull	Trainee	Oxford U	—	—
							Barnet	22	—
MYALL Stuart	5 10	12 13	M	12 11 74	Eastbourne	Trainee	**Brighton**	47	2

Player	Ht	Wt	Pos	Birth Date	Place	Source	Clubs	League App	Gls
MYERS Andy	5 8	9 10	M	3 11 73	Hounslow	Trainee	**Chelsea**	33	1
NARBETT Jon	5 10	10 08	M	21 11 68	Birmingham	Apprentice	Shrewsbury T	26	3
							Hereford U	149	31
							Leicester C (loan)	—	—
							Oxford U	15	—
							Chesterfield	3	—
NAYLOR Dominic	5 9	13 03	D	12 8 70	Watford	Trainee	Watford	—	—
							Halifax T	6	1
						Barnet	Barnet	51	—
							Plymouth Arg	85	—
NAYLOR Glenn	5 11	11 01	F	11 8 72	York	Trainee	**York C**	85	23
NAYLOR Stuart	6 4	12 02	G	6 12 62	Wetherby	Yorkshire A	Lincoln C	49	—
							Peterborough U (loan)	8	—
							Crewe Alex (loan)	38	—
							Crewe Alex (loan)	17	—
							WBA	328	—
NAYLOR Tony	5 8	10 08	F	29 3 67	Manchester	Droylsden	Crewe Alex	122	45
							Port Vale	33	9
NDAH George	6 1	11 04	M	23 12 74	Camberwell	Trainee	**Crystal Palace**	26	1
NDLOVU Peter	5 8	10 02	F	25 2 73	Zimbabwe	Highlanders	**Coventry C**	125	31
NEAL Ashley	6 0	11 10	M	16 12 74	Liverpool	Trainee	**Liverpool**	—	—
NEBBELING Gavin ‡	6 0	12 10	D	15 5 63	Johannesburg	Arcadia Shepherds	Crystal Palace	151	8
							Northampton T (loan)	11	—
							Fulham	88	2
							Hereford U (loan)	3	—
							Preston NE	22	4
NEEDHAM Ben *	5 11	11 00	M	23 10 75	Leicester	Trainee	**Notts Co**	—	—
NEIL James	5 8	10 05	D	28 2 76	Bury St Edmunds	Trainee	**Grimsby T**	—	—
NEILL Warren *	5 9	11 05	M	21 11 62	Acton	Apprentice	QPR	181	3
							Portsmouth	218	2
NEILSON Alan	5 11	11 07	D	26 9 72	Wegburg	Trainee	**Newcastle U**	42	1
NELSON Garry	5 10	11 10	F	16 1 61	Braintree	Amateur	Southend U	129	17
							Swindon T	79	7
							Plymouth Arg	74	20
							Brighton	144	46
							Notts Co (loan)	2	—
							Charlton Ath	155	34
NETHERCOTT Stuart	6 1	13 08	D	21 3 73	Chadwell Heath	Trainee	**Tottenham H**	32	—
							Maidstone U (loan)	13	1
							Barnet (loan)	3	—
NEVILLE Gary	5 11	11 10	D	18 2 75	Bury	Trainee	**Manchester U**	19	—
NEVILLE Philip	5 11	12 00	D	21 1 77	Bury	Trainee	**Manchester U**	2	—
NEVIN Pat	5 6	11 05	F	6 9 63	Glasgow	Gartcosh U	Clyde	73	17
							Chelsea	193	36
							Everton	109	16
							Tranmere R (loan)	8	—
							Tranmere R	132	25
NEWELL Mike	6 1	11 00	F	27 1 65	Liverpool	Liverpool	Crewe Alex	3	—
							Wigan Ath	72	25
							Luton T	63	18
							Leicester C	81	21
							Everton	68	15
							Blackburn R	100	25
NEWELL Paul	6 1	11 05	G	23 2 69	Greenwich	Trainee	Southend U	15	—
							Leyton Orient	61	—
							Colchester U (loan)	14	—
							Barnet	15	—

				Birth				League	
Player	*Ht*	*Wt*	*Pos*	*Date*	*Place*	*Source*	*Clubs*	*App*	*Gls*
NEWHOUSE Aidan	6 2	13 05	M	23 5 72	Wallasey	Trainee	Chester C	44	6
							Wimbledon	23	2
							Tranmere R (loan)	—	—
							Port Vale (loan)	2	—
							Portsmouth (loan)	6	1
NEWLAND Ray	6 3	13 10	G	19 7 71	Liverpool	Everton	Plymouth Arg	26	—
							Chester C	10	—
NEWMAN Ricky	5 10	12 06	M	5 8 70	Guildford	Trainee	**Crystal Palace**	48	3
							Maidstone U (loan)	10	1
NEWMAN Rob	6 2	13 04	D	13 12 63	Bradford-on-Avon	Apprentice	Bristol C	394	52
							Norwich C	123	12
NEWSOME Jon	6 2	13 09	D	6 9 70	Sheffield	Trainee	Sheffield W	7	—
							Leeds U	76	3
							Norwich C	35	3
NEWSON Mark *	5 10	12 06	D	7 12 60	Stepney	Apprentice	Charlton Ath	—	—
						Maidstone U	Bournemouth	177	23
							Fulham	102	4
							Barnet	59	4
NEWTON Eddie	5 11	11 02	F	13 12 71	Hammersmith	Trainee	**Chelsea**	101	7
							Cardiff C (loan)	18	4
NEWTON Shaun	5 8	11 00	M	20 8 75	Camberwell	Trainee	**Charlton Ath**	47	2
NICHOLLS Alan	5 11	14 07	G	28 8 73	Birmingham	Cheltenham T	**Plymouth Arg**	65	—
NICHOLLS Ryan ‡	5 9	12 00	F	10 5 73	Cardiff	Trainee	Leeds U	—	—
							Cardiff C	12	1
NICHOLSON Max †	5 10	12 03	F	3 10 71	Leeds	Trainee	Doncaster R	27	2
							Hereford U	63	7
							Torquay U	1	—
							Scunthorpe U	15	4
NICHOLSON Shane	5 10	12 02	D	3 6 70	Newark	Trainee	Lincoln C	133	6
							Derby Co	54	1
NICOL Steve	5 10	12 00	D	11 12 61	Irvine	Ayr U BC	Ayr U	70	7
							Liverpool	343	36
							Notts Co	19	—
NIELSEN Jimmi	6 2	12 11	G	6 8 77	Aalborg	Aalborg	**Millwall**	—	—
NIJHOLT Luc	5 11	12 01	D	29 7 61	Zaandam	BSC Old Boys Basel	Motherwell	96	5
							Swindon T	67	1
NILSEN Roger	5 9	11 08	D	8 8 69	Norway	Viking St	**Sheffield U**	55	—
NIXON Eric	6 4	15 07	G	4 10 62	Manchester	Curzon Ashton	Manchester C	58	—
							Wolverhampton W (loan)	16	—
							Bradford C (loan)	3	—
							Southampton (loan)	4	—
							Carlisle U (loan)	16	—
							Tranmere R (loan)	8	—
							Tranmere R	308	—
NOGAN Kurt	5 11	12 07	F	9 9 70	Cardiff	Trainee	Luton T	33	3
							Peterborough U	—	—
							Brighton	97	49
							Burnley	15	3
NOGAN Lee	5 10	10 08	F	21 5 69	Cardiff	Apprentice	Oxford U	64	10
							Brentford (loan)	11	2
							Southend U (loan)	6	1
							Watford	105	26
							Southend U (loan)	5	—
							Reading	20	10
NOLAN Ian	6 0	12 01	D	9 7 70	Liverpool	Marine	Tranmere R	88	1
							Sheffield W	42	3
NORBURY Mike	6 1	11 10	F	22 1 69	Hemsworth	Bridlington	Cambridge U	26	3
							Preston NE	42	13
							Doncaster R	22	5
NORFOLK Lee	5 10	11 03	M	17 10 75	Dunedin NZ	Trainee	**Ipswich T**	3	—

Player	Ht	Wt	Pos	Birth Date	Birth Place	Source	Clubs	League App	League Gls
NORMAN Craig	5 10	11 09	D	21 3 75	Perivale	Trainee	**Chelsea**	—	—
NORMAN Tony *	6 2	14 05	G	24 2 58	Mancot	Amateur	Burnley	—	—
							Hull C	372	—
							Sunderland	198	—
NORRIS Steve ‡	5 10	11 00	F	22 9 61	Coventry	Telford	Scarborough	45	13
							Notts Co (loan)	1	—
							Carlisle U	29	5
							Halifax T	56	35
							Chesterfield	97	43
							Scarborough (loan)	8	4
NORTON David	5 7	11 03	M	3 3 65	Cannock	Apprentice	Aston Villa	44	2
							Notts Co	27	1
							Rochdale (loan)	9	—
							Hull C (loan)	15	—
							Hull C	134	5
							Northampton T	38	—
NORTON Paul ‡	5 6	10 08	M	15 10 75	Middlesbrough	Trainee	**Middlesbrough**	—	—
NOTEMAN Kevin *	5 10	12 02	F	15 10 69	Preston	Trainee	Leeds U	1	—
							Doncaster R	106	20
							Mansfield T	95	15
NTAMARK Charlie	5 10	11 10	M	22 7 64	Paddington	Boreham Wood	**Walsall**	196	11
NUGENT Kevin	6 1	13 03	F	10 4 69	Edmonton	Trainee	Leyton Orient	94	20
							Cork C (loan)	—	—
							Plymouth Arg	125	32
NYAMAH Kofi *	5 8	10 07	F	20 6 75	Islington	Trainee	**Cambridge U**	23	2
OAKES Michael	6 1	12 07	G	30 10 73	Northwich	Trainee	**Aston Villa**	—	—
							Scarborough (loan)	1	—
							Tranmere R (loan)	—	—
OAKES Scott	5 11	11 04	F	5 8 72	Leicester	Trainee	Leicester C	3	—
							Luton T	144	24
OAKLEY Matthew §	5 10	11 00	F	17 8 77	Peterborough	Trainee	**Southampton**	1	—
OATWAY Charlie	5 7	10 10	M	28 11 73	Hammersmith	Yeading	**Cardiff C**	30	—
O'BRIEN Liam	6 1	11 10	M	5 9 64	Dublin	Shamrock R	Manchester U	31	2
							Newcastle U	151	19
							Tranmere R	55	2
O'BRIEN Roy	6 1	12 00	D	27 11 74	Cork	Trainee	**Arsenal**	—	—
O'CONNELL Brendan	5 11	12 01	F	12 11 66	London		Portsmouth	—	—
							Exeter C	81	19
							Burnley	64	17
							Huddersfield T (loan)	11	1
							Barnsley	215	34
O'CONNOR Derek			G	9 3 78	Dublin	Crumplin U	**Huddersfield T**	—	—
O'CONNOR Jonathan	5 10	11 03	M	29 10 76	Darlington	Trainee	**Everton**	—	—
O'CONNOR Mark *	5 7	10 02	M	10 3 63	Rochdale	Apprentice	QPR	3	—
							Exeter C (loan)	38	1
							Bristol R	80	10
							Bournemouth	128	12
							Gillingham	116	8
							Bournemouth	58	3
O'CONNOR Martyn	5 9	12 08	M	10 12 67	Walsall	Bromsgrove R	Crystal Palace	2	—
							Walsall (loan)	10	1
							Walsall	53	12
O'DONNELL Paul *	5 10	11 03	M	6 10 75	Limerick	Trainee	**Liverpool**	—	—
O'DRISCOLL Sean *	5 8	11 03	M	1 7 57	Wolverhampton	Alvechurch	Fulham	148	13
							Bournemouth (loan)	19	1
							Bournemouth	404	18
OGDEN Neil	5 10	10 04	M	29 11 75	Billinge	Trainee	**Wigan Ath**	5	—
OGRIZOVIC Steve	6 5	15 00	G	12 9 57	Mansfield	ONRYC	Chesterfield	16	—
							Liverpool	4	—
							Shrewsbury T	84	—
							Coventry C	415	1

Player	Ht	Wt	Pos	Birth Date	Place	Source	Clubs	League App	Gls
O'HAGAN Danny	6 1	13 08	F	24 4 76	Padstow	Trainee	**Plymouth Arg**	3	1
O'HALLORAN Keith			D	10 11 75	Ireland	Cherry Orchard	**Middlesbrough**	1	—
O'HARA Gary ‡			D	13 12 73	Belfast	Trainee	**Leeds U**	—	—
O'KANE John	5 10	11 09	D	15 11 74	Nottingham	Trainee	**Manchester U**	—	—
OKORIE Chima *	5 10	12 08	F	8 10 68	Izomber		Peterborough U	—	—
							Grimsby T	5	—
							Torquay U	36	6
OLDBURY Marcus *	5 7	10 02	M	29 3 76	Bournemouth	Trainee	**Norwich C**	—	—
OLDFIELD David	6 0	13 04	M	30 5 68	Perth, Australia	Apprentice	Luton T	29	4
							Manchester C	26	6
							Leicester C	188	26
							Millwall (loan)	17	6
O'LEARY David	6 1	13 09	D	2 5 58	London	Apprentice	Arsenal	558	10
							Leeds U	10	—
OLIVER Darren *	5 8	10 05	D	1 11 71	Liverpool	Trainee	Bolton W	3	—
							Peterborough U (loan)	—	—
							Rochdale	28	—
OLIVER Gavin *	5 11	13 10	D	6 9 62	Felling	Apprentice	Sheffield W	20	—
							Tranmere R (loan)	17	1
							Brighton (loan)	16	—
							Bradford C	313	9
OLIVER Keith	5 8	10 09	M	15 1 76	South Shields	Trainee	**Hartlepool U**	19	—
OLIVER Michael	5 10	12 04	M	2 8 75	Cleveland	Trainee	Middlesbrough	—	—
							Stockport Co	13	—
OLNEY Ian	6 1	11 00	F	17 12 69	Luton	Trainee	Aston Villa	88	16
							Oldham Ath	44	13
OLSSON Paul	5 8	10 11	M	24 12 65	Hull	Apprentice	Hull C	—	—
							Exeter C (loan)	8	—
							Exeter C	35	2
							Scarborough	48	5
							Hartlepool U	171	13
							Darlington	42	4
OMIGIE Joe	6 2	13 00	F	13 6 72	Hammersmith	Donna	**Brentford**	—	—
OMOYIMNI Emmanuel ‡	5 8	10 00	M	28 12 77	Nigeria	Trainee	**West Ham U**	—	—
O'NEIL Phil	5 9	11 10	M	22 10 77	Sidcup	Trainee	**Millwall**	—	—
O'NEILL Keith	6 1	11 00	M	16 2 76	Dublin	Trainee	**Norwich C**	1	—
O'NEILL Shane §	5 10	12 00	M	20 6 78	Limavady	Trainee	**Nottingham F**	—	—
ONUORA Iffy	6 2	13 13	F	28 7 67	Glasgow	British Universities	Huddersfield T	165	30
							Mansfield T	14	7
ONWERE Udo	6 0	11 07	M	9 11 71	Hammersmith	Trainee	Fulham	85	7
							Lincoln C	8	—
ORD Richard	6 2	13 05	D	3 3 70	Easington	Trainee	**Sunderland**	154	4
							York C (loan)	3	—
O'REGAN Kieran *	5 8	10 12	M	9 11 63	Cork	Tramore Ath	Brighton	86	2
							Swindon T	26	1
							Huddersfield T	199	25
							WBA	45	2
O'RIORDAN Don	6 0	12 07	D	14 5 57	Dublin	Apprentice	Derby Co	6	1
							Doncaster R (loan)	2	—
						Tulsa	Preston NE	158	8
							Carlisle U	84	18
							Middlesbrough	41	2
							Grimsby T	86	14
							Notts Co	109	5
							Mansfield T (loan)	6	—
							Torquay U	71	3
ORLYGSSON Thorvaldur	5 11	11 03	M	2 8 66	Odense	FC Akureyri	Nottingham F	37	2
							Stoke C	83	16

Player	Ht	Wt	Pos	Birth Date	Birth Place	Source	Clubs	League App	League Gls
ORMEROD Mark	6 0	11 05	G	5 2 76	Bournemouth	Trainee	**Brighton & HA**	—	—
ORMONDROYD Ian	6 5	13 08	F	22 9 64	Bradford	Thackley	Bradford C	87	20
							Oldham Ath (loan)	10	1
							Aston Villa	56	6
							Derby Co	25	8
							Leicester C	77	7
							Hull C (loan)	10	6
ORMSBY Brendan ‡	5 11	11 12	D	1 10 60	Birmingham	Apprentice	Aston Villa	117	4
							Leeds U	46	5
							Shrewsbury T (loan)	1	—
							Doncaster R	78	7
							Scarborough	16	1
						Waterford	**Wigan Ath**	2	—
ORR Stephen	5 7	10 00	F	19 1 78	Belper	Trainee	**Nottingham F**	—	—
OSBORN Simon	5 10	11 04	M	19 1 72	New Addington	Apprentice	Crystal Palace	55	5
							Reading	32	5
O'SHEA Alan	5 10	10 12	D	21 7 77	Dublin	Trainee	**Leeds U**	—	—
O'SHEA Danny	6 0	13 00	D	26 3 63	Kennington	Apprentice	Arsenal	6	—
							Charlton Ath (loan)	9	—
							Exeter C	45	2
							Southend U	118	12
							Cambridge U	203	1
							Northampton T	7	1
OSMAN Russell †	5 11	12 01	D	14 2 59	Repton	Apprentice	Ipswich	294	17
							Leicester C	108	8
							Southampton	96	6
							Bristol C	70	3
							Plymouth Arg	—	—
O'SULLIVAN Wayne	5 8	10 06	D	25 2 74	Akrotiri	Trainee	**Swindon T**	30	—
O'TOOLE Gavin	5 9	11 01	M	19 9 75	Dublin	Trainee	**Coventry C**	—	—
OTTO Ricky	5 10	12 10	M	9 11 67	Hackney	Dartford	Leyton Orient	56	13
							Southend U	64	17
							Birmingham C	24	4
OVENDALE Mark *	6 2	13 02	G	22 11 73	Leicester	Wisbech T	**Northampton T**	6	—
OVERSON Vince	6 2	14 02	D	15 5 62	Kettering	Apprentice	Burnley	211	6
							Birmingham C	182	3
							Stoke C	152	6
OWEN Gareth	5 8	11 08	M	21 10 71	Chester	Trainee	**Wrexham**	172	18
OWEN Philip ‡			M	11 1 75	Bangor	Manchester C	Stockport Co	—	—
							Bradford C	—	—
OWERS Gary	5 10	11 10	M	3 10 68	Newcastle	Apprentice	Sunderland	268	25
							Bristol C	21	2
PAATELAINEN Mixu	6 0	13 11	F	3 2 67	Helsinki	Valkeakosken Haka	Dundee U	133	33
							Aberdeen	75	23
							Bolton W	44	12
PACK Lenny	5 10	12 01	M	27 9 76	Salisbury	Trainee	**Cambridge U**	3	—
PAGE Don *	5 10	11 02	F	18 1 64	Manchester	Runcorn	Wigan Ath	74	15
							Rotherham U	55	13
							Rochdale (loan)	4	1
							Doncaster R	22	4
							Chester C	30	5
PAGE Robert	6 0	11 08	D	3 9 74	Llwynypia	Trainee	**Watford**	9	—
PAINTER Robert	5 11	11 00	M	26 1 71	Ince	Trainee	Chester C	84	8
							Maidstone U	30	5
							Burnley	26	2
							Darlington	74	20
PALLISTER Gary	6 4	14 08	D	30 6 65	Ramsgate	Billingham	Middlesbrough	156	5
							Darlington (loan)	7	—
							Manchester U	236	8

Player	Ht	Wt	Pos	Birth Date	Birth Place	Source	Clubs	League App	League Gls
PALMER Carlton	6 2	12 04	D	5 12 65	West Bromwich	Trainee	WBA	121	4
							Sheffield W	205	14
							Leeds U	39	3
PALMER Charlie	6 0	13 02	D	10 7 63	Aylesbury	Apprentice	Watford	10	1
							Derby Co	51	2
							Hull C	70	1
							Notts Co	182	7
							Walsall	39	2
PALMER Lee *	5 11	13 00	D	19 9 70	Gillingham	Trainee	**Gillingham**	120	5
PALMER Steve	6 1	12 13	M	31 3 68	Brighton	Cambridge University	**Ipswich T**	106	2
PAPAVASILIOU Nicos ‡	5 8	10 02	M	31 8 70	Limassol	Ofi Crete	**Newcastle U**	7	—
PARDEW Alan *	5 11	11 00	M	18 7 61	Wimbledon	Yeovil	Crystal Palace	128	8
							Charlton Ath	104	24
PARKER Garry	5 11	12 05	M	7 9 65	Oxford	Apprentice	Luton T	42	3
							Hull C	84	8
							Nottingham F	103	17
							Aston Villa	95	13
							Leicester C	14	2
PARKER Justin			D	11 11 76	Stoke	Trainee	**Crewe Alex**	—	—
PARKER Paul	5 7	11 11	D	4 4 64	West Ham	Apprentice	Fulham	153	2
							QPR	125	1
							Manchester U	99	1
PARKIN Brian	6 1	12 00	G	12 10 65	Birkenhead	Local	Oldham Ath	6	—
							Crewe Alex (loan)	12	—
							Crewe Alex	86	—
							Crystal Palace (loan)	—	—
							Crystal Palace	20	—
							Bristol R	221	—
PARKIN Steve	5 6	11 03	M	7 11 65	Mansfield	Apprentice	Stoke C	113	5
							WBA	48	2
							Mansfield T	61	2
PARKINSON Gary	5 11	12 08	D	10 1 68	Thornaby	Everton	Middlesbrough	202	5
							Southend U (loan)	6	—
							Bolton W	3	—
							Burnley	63	3
PARKINSON Joe	6 0	13 00	D	11 6 71	Eccles	Trainee	Wigan Ath	119	6
							Bournemouth	30	1
							Everton	34	—
PARKINSON Phil	6 0	11 06	M	1 12 67	Chorley	Apprentice	Southampton	—	—
							Bury	145	5
							Reading	112	7
PARKINSON Steve ‡	5 11	11 11	M	27 8 74	Lincoln	Trainee	**Lincoln C**	5	—
PARKINSON Stuart	5 8	10 12	F	18 2 76	Blackpool	Trainee	**Blackpool**	1	—
PARLOUR Ray	5 10	11 12	M	7 3 73	Romford	Trainee	**Arsenal**	84	4
PARMENTER Steven	5 9	10 07	M	22 1 77	Chelmsford	Trainee	**QPR**	—	—
PARRIS George *	5 9	13 00	D	11 9 64	Ilford	Apprentice	West Ham U	239	12
							Birmingham C	39	1
							Brentford (loan)	5	—
							Bristol C (loan)	6	—
							Brighton (loan)	18	2
PARRISH Sean	5 9	10 00	M	14 3 72	Wrexham	Trainee Telford U	Shrewsbury T	3	—
							Doncaster R	25	3
PARSLEY Neil *	5 10	10 11	D	25 4 66	Liverpool	Witton Alb	Leeds U	—	—
							Chester C (loan)	6	—
							Huddersfield T	57	—
							Doncaster R (loan)	3	—
							WBA	43	—
PARTNER Andy	6 3	13 00	D	21 10 74	Colchester	Trainee	**Colchester U**	2	—
PARTRIDGE Scott	5 9	10 09	F	13 10 74	Leicester	Trainee	Bradford C	5	—
							Bristol C	42	6

Player	Ht	Wt	Pos	Birth Date	Birth Place	Source	Clubs	League App	League Gls
PASCOE Colin	5 10	12 00	F	9 4 65	Port Talbot	Apprentice	Swansea C	174	39
							Sunderland	126	22
							Swansea C (loan)	15	4
							Swansea C	68	10
PASCOE Jason *	5 11	11 11	D	15 2 70	Jarrow	Boston U	**Northampton T**	15	—
PASKIN John	6 1	13 06	F	1 2 62	Capetown	Seiko	WBA	25	5
							Wolverhampton W	34	3
							Stockport Co (loan)	5	1
							Birmingham C (loan)	10	3
							Shrewsbury T (loan)	1	—
							Wrexham	51	11
							Bury	26	8
PASS Steven	5 8	10 10	F	15 9 76	Leigh	Trainee	**Sheffield W**	—	—
PATERSON Scott	5 11	12 00	M	13 5 72	Aberdeen	Cove Rangers	Liverpool	—	—
							Bristol C	3	—
PATES Colin ‡	6 0	13 00	D	10 8 61	Mitcham	Apprentice	Chelsea	281	10
							Charlton Ath	38	—
							Arsenal	21	—
							Brighton (loan)	17	—
							Brighton	50	—
PATMORE Warren ‡			M	14 8 71	Kingsbury		Cambridge U	1	—
							Millwall	1	—
							Northampton T	21	2
PATTERSON Darren	6 2	12 07	D	15 10 69	Belfast	Trainee	WBA	—	—
							Wigan Ath	97	6
							Crystal Palace	22	1
PATTERSON Gary	6 0	12 07	M	27 11 72	Newcastle	Trainee	Notts Co	—	—
							Shrewsbury T	57	2
							Wycombe W	13	1
PATTERSON Ian ‡	6 2	13 00	D	4 4 73	Chatham	Trainee	Sunderland	—	—
							Burnley	1	—
							Wigan Ath	4	—
PATTERSON Mark	5 6	11 04	M	24 5 65	Darwen	Apprentice	Blackburn R	101	20
							Preston NE	55	19
							Bury	42	10
							Bolton W	153	10
PATTERSON Mark	5 10	12 04	D	13 9 68	Leeds	Trainee	Carlisle U	22	—
							Derby Co	51	3
							Plymouth Arg	79	3
PAUL Martin	5 8	9 07	F	2 2 75	Whalley	Trainee	**Bristol R**	9	—
PAYNE Derek	5 6	10 08	M	26 4 67	Edgware	Hayes	Barnet	51	6
							Southend U	35	—
							Watford	24	—
PAYNE Grant	5 9	11 04	F	25 12 75	Woking	Trainee	**Wimbledon**	—	—
PAYNE Ian §			M	19 1 77	Crawley	Trainee	**Plymouth Arg**	1	—
PAYNE Stephen ‡	5 11	12 00	D	1 8 75	Pontefract	Trainee	**Huddersfield T**	—	—
PAYTON Andy	5 9	11 13	F	23 10 67	Burnley	Apprentice	Hull C	144	55
							Middlesbrough	19	3
							Celtic	36	15
							Barnsley	68	24
PAZ Adrian	5 10	11 10	F	9 9 68	Uruguay	Penarol	**Ipswich T**	17	1
PEACOCK Darren	6 2	12 06	D	3 2 68	Bristol	Apprentice	Newport Co	28	—
							Hereford U	59	4
							QPR	126	6
							Newcastle U	44	1
PEACOCK Gavin	5 8	11 08	M	18 11 67	Kent	Apprentice	QPR	17	1
							Gillingham	70	11
							Bournemouth	56	8
							Newcastle U	105	35
							Chelsea	75	12
PEACOCK Lee	6 0	12 05	F	9 10 76	Paisley	Trainee	**Carlisle U**	8	—
PEACOCK Richard	5 10	10 09	F	29 10 72	Sheffield	Sheffield FC	**Hull C**	48	6

Player	Ht	Wt	Pos	Birth Date	Birth Place	Source	Clubs	League App	League Gls
PEAKE Jason	5 11	12 10	M	29 9 71	Leicester	Trainee	Leicester C	8	1
							Hartlepool U (loan)	6	1
							Halifax T	33	1
							Rochdale	49	2
PEAKE Trevor	6 0	12 10	D	10 2 57	Nuneaton	Nuneaton Bor	Lincoln C	171	7
							Coventry C	278	6
							Luton T	160	—
PEARCE Andy	6 4	13 09	D	20 4 66	Bradford on Avon	Halesowen	Coventry C	71	4
							Sheffield W	66	3
PEARCE Dennis *	5 9	11 00	F	10 9 74	Wolverhampton	Trainee	**Aston Villa**	—	—
PEARCE Ian	6 1	12 04	D	7 5 74	Bury St Edmunds	School	Chelsea	4	—
							Blackburn R	33	1
PEARCE Stuart	5 10	12 09	D	24 4 62	London	Wealdstone	Coventry C	51	4
							Nottingham F	337	55
PEARCEY Jason	6 1	13 12	G	23 7 71	Leamington Spa	Trainee	Mansfield T	77	—
							Grimsby T	3	—
PEARS Richard	5 10	11 07	F	16 7 76	Exeter	Trainee	**Exeter C**	30	2
PEARS Steve *	6 0	13 01	G	22 1 62	Brandon	Apprentice	Manchester U	4	—
							Middlesbrough (loan)	12	—
							Middlesbrough	327	—
PEARSON Chris	5 6	10 06	F	5 1 76	Leicester	Trainee	**Notts Co**	—	—
PEARSON John *	6 2	13 05	F	1 9 63	Sheffield	Apprentice	Sheffield W	105	24
							Charlton Ath	61	15
							Leeds U	99	12
							Rotherham U (loan)	11	5
							Barnsley	32	4
							Hull C (loan)	15	—
							Carlisle U	8	—
							Mansfield T	2	—
							Cardiff C	12	—
PEARSON Nigel	6 1	14 03	D	21 8 63	Nottingham	Heanor T	Shrewsbury T	153	5
							Sheffield W	180	14
							Middlesbrough	33	3
PEEL Nathan	6 1	13 03	F	17 5 72	Blackburn	Trainee	Preston NE	10	1
							Sheffield U	1	—
							Halifax T (loan)	3	—
							Burnley	16	2
							Rotherham U (loan)	9	4
PEER Dean *	6 1	12 04	M	8 8 69	Dudley	Trainee	Birmingham C	120	8
							Mansfield T (loan)	10	—
							Walsall	45	8
PEJIC Mel	5 9	11 05	D	27 4 59	Chesterton	Local	Stoke C	1	—
							Hereford U	412	14
							Wrexham	106	3
PEMBERTON John	5 11	12 12	D	18 11 64	Oldham	Chadderton	Rochdale	1	—
							Crewe Alex	121	1
							Crystal Palace	78	2
							Sheffield U	68	—
							Leeds U	36	—
PEMBERTON Martin			M	1 2 76	Bradford	Trainee	**Oldham Ath**	—	—
PEMBRIDGE Mark	5 8	11 12	M	29 11 70	Merthyr Tydfil	Trainee	Luton T	60	6
							Derby Co	110	28
PENDER John	6 0	13 12	D	19 11 63	Luton	Apprentice	Wolverhampton W	117	3
							Charlton Ath	41	—
							Bristol C	83	3
							Burnley	170	8
PENNEY David	5 10	12 00	M	17 8 64	Wakefield	Pontefract	Derby Co	19	—
							Oxford U	110	15
							Swansea C (loan)	12	3
							Swansea C (loan)	11	2
							Swansea C	35	5
PENNOCK Adrian	5 11	12 01	D	27 3 71	Ipswich	Trainee	Norwich C	1	—
							Bournemouth	114	9

Player	Ht	Wt	Pos	Birth Date	Birth Place	Source	Clubs	League App	League Gls
PENNOCK Tony *	6 0	12 06	G	10 4 71	Swansea	School	Stockport Co	—	—
							Wigan Ath (loan)	2	—
							Wigan Ath	8	—
							Hereford U	15	—
PENRICE Gary	5 8	10 06	F	23 3 64	Bristol	Bristol C	Bristol R	188	54
							Watford	43	18
							Aston Villa	20	1
							QPR	79	20
PEPPER Nigel	5 10	11 13	M	25 4 68	Rotherham	Apprentice	Rotherham U	45	1
							York C	166	19
PERIFIMOU Chris §			M	27 11 75	Enfield	Trainee	**Leyton Orient**	4	—
PERKINS Chris	5 11	11 00	M	9 1 74	Nottingham	Trainee	Mansfield T	8	—
							Chesterfield	18	—
PERKINS Declan	5 11	12 04	F	17 10 75	Ilford	Trainee	**Southend U**	6	—
PERRETT Darren	5 8	11 06	F	29 12 69	Cardiff	Cheltenham T	**Swansea C**	26	1
PERRY Chris	5 9	11 01	D	26 4 73	London	Trainee	**Wimbledon**	24	—
PERRY Jason	5 11	10 04	D	2 4 70	Newport	Trainee	**Cardiff C**	232	5
PESCHISOLIDO Paul	5 7	10 12	F	25 5 71	Canada	Toronto Blizzard	Birmingham C	43	16
							Stoke C	40	13
PETERS Mark	6 0	11 03	D	6 7 72	St Asaph	Trainee	Manchester C	—	—
							Norwich C	—	—
							Peterborough U	19	—
							Mansfield T	26	4
PETERS Rob †	5 8	11 02	D	18 5 71	Kensington	Trainee	Brentford	30	1
							Carlisle U	8	—
PETHICK Robbie	5 10	11 07	M	8 9 70	Tavistock	Weymouth	**Portsmouth**	62	1
PETRESCU Dan	5 9	11 09	M	22 12 67	Bucharest	Genoa	**Sheffield W**	29	3
PETTERSON Andy	6 2	14 12	G	26 9 69	Fremantle		Luton T	19	—
							Swindon T (loan)	—	—
							Ipswich T (loan)	—	—
							Ipswich T (loan)	1	—
							Charlton Ath	9	—
							Bradford C (loan)	3	—
PETTINGER Paul	6 0	13 07	G	1 10 75	Sheffield	Barnsley	**Leeds U**	—	—
							Torquay U (loan)	3	—
PETTY Ben			D	22 3 77	Solihull	Trainee	**Aston Villa**	—	—
PEVERELL Nick	5 11	11 10	F	28 4 73	Middlesbrough	Trainee	Middlesbrough	—	—
							Hartlepool U	36	3
							York C	9	1
PEYTON Gerry ‡	6 2	13 09	G	20 5 56	Birmingham	Atherstone T	Burnley	30	—
							Fulham	345	—
							Southend U (loan)	10	—
							Bournemouth	202	—
							Everton	—	—
							Bolton W (loan)	1	—
							Norwich C (loan)	—	—
							Chelsea (loan)	1	—
							Brentford	19	—
							West Ham U	—	—
PHELAN Mike	5 11	11 01	D	24 9 62	Nelson	Apprentice	Burnley	168	9
							Norwich C	156	9
							Manchester U	102	2
							WBA	20	—
PHELAN Terry	5 8	10 00	D	16 3 67	Manchester	Trainee	Leeds U	14	—
							Swansea C	45	—
							Wimbledon	159	1
							Manchester C	94	1
PHILIP Richard ‡	5 11	11 07	D	20 10 74	Surrey	Trainee	**Luton T**	—	—

Player	Ht	Wt	Pos	Birth Date	Birth Place	Source	Clubs	League App	League Gls
PHILLIPS David	5 10	11 02	M	29 7 63	Wegberg	Apprentice	Plymouth Arg	73	15
							Manchester C	81	13
							Coventry C	100	8
							Norwich C	152	18
							Nottingham F	81	5
PHILLIPS Gary	6 0	14 00	G	20 9 61	St Albans		WBA	—	—
						Barnet	Brentford	143	—
							Reading	24	—
							Hereford U	6	—
							Barnet	117	—
PHILLIPS Jimmy	6 0	12 07	D	8 2 66	Bolton	Apprentice	Bolton W	108	2
							Rangers	25	—
							Oxford U	79	8
							Middlesbrough	139	6
							Bolton W	88	1
PHILLIPS Kevin	5 7	11 00	F	25 7 73	Hitchin	Baldock T	**Watford**	16	9
PHILLIPS Marcus ‡	5 11	11 07	M	17 10 73	Bradford on Avon	Trainee	**Swindon T**	—	—
PHILLIPS Martin	5 11	12 08	F	13 3 76	Exeter	Trainee	**Exeter C**	39	2
PHILLIPS Wayne	5 10	10 09	M	15 12 70	Bangor	Trainee	**Wrexham**	117	5
PHILLISKIRK Tony	6 1	13 03	F	10 2 65	Sunderland	Amateur	Sheffield U	80	20
							Rotherham U (loan)	6	1
							Oldham Ath	10	1
							Preston NE	14	6
							Bolton W	141	51
							Peterborough U	43	15
							Burnley	32	8
PHILPOTT Lee	5 10	12 09	F	21 2 70	Hackney	Trainee	Peterborough U	4	—
							Cambridge U	134	17
							Leicester C	69	3
PICK Gary	5 9	11 10	M	9 7 71	Leicester	Leicester U	Stoke C	—	—
							Hereford U	29	2
PICKARD Owen ‡	5 10	11 03	F	18 11 69	Barnstaple	Trainee	Plymouth Arg	16	1
							Hereford U	73	14
							Rochdale	—	—
PICKERING Ally	5 11	11 01	D	22 6 67	Manchester	Buxton	Rotherham U	88	2
							Coventry C	35	—
PIEARCE Stephen	5 11	10 10	F	29 9 74	Sutton Coldfield	Trainee	**Wolverhampton W**	—	—
PIKE Chris	6 2	13 07	F	19 10 61	Cardiff	Barry T	Fulham	42	4
							Cardiff C (loan)	6	2
							Cardiff C	148	65
							Hereford U	38	18
							Gillingham	27	13
PIKE Martin	5 11	12 09	D	21 10 64	South Shields	Apprentice	WBA	—	—
							Peterborough U	126	8
							Sheffield U	129	5
							Tranmere R (loan)	2	—
							Bolton W (loan)	5	1
							Fulham	190	14
							Rotherham U	7	—
PILKINGTON Kevin	6 2	12 10	G	8 3 74	Hitchin	Trainee	**Manchester U**	1	—
PIRIE David *	5 9	11 05	F	15 4 75	Glasgow	Trainee	**Ipswich T**	—	—
PITCHER Darren	5 9	12 02	M	12 10 69	London	Trainee	Charlton Ath	173	8
							Galway (loan)	—	—
							Crystal Palace	25	—
PITCHER Geoffrey	5 6	10 13	M	15 8 75	Sutton	Trainee	Millwall	—	—
							Watford	4	1
PITMAN Jamie	5 9	10 09	M	6 1 76	Warminster	Trainee	**Swindon T**	3	—

Player	Ht	Wt	Pos	Birth Date	Birth Place	Source	Clubs	League App	League Gls
PLATNAUER Nicky *	5 11	12 10	D	10 6 61	Leicester	Bedford T	Bristol R	24	7
							Coventry C	44	6
							Birmingham C	28	2
							Reading (loan)	7	—
							Cardiff C	115	6
							Notts Co	57	1
							Port Vale (loan)	14	—
							Leicester C	35	—
							Scunthorpe U	14	2
							Mansfield T	25	—
							Lincoln C	26	—
PLATT David	5 10	11 12	F	10 6 66	Chadderton	Chadderton	Manchester U	—	—
							Crewe Alex	134	55
							Aston Villa	121	50
							Bari	29	11
							Juventus	16	3
							Sampdoria	55	17
							Arsenal	—	—
PLUMMER Chris	6 3	11 06	D	12 10 76	Isleworth	Trainee	**QPR**	—	—
POINTON Neil	5 10	11 00	D	28 11 64	Church Warsop	Apprentice	Scunthorpe U	159	2
							Everton	102	5
							Manchester C	74	2
							Oldham Ath	90	3
POLLITT Michael	6 4	14 00	G	29 2 72	Bolton	Trainee	Manchester U	—	—
							Oldham Ath (loan)	—	—
							Bury	—	—
							Lincoln C	57	—
							Darlington	40	—
POLLOCK Jamie	5 10	14 01	M	16 2 74	Stockton	Trainee	**Middlesbrough**	124	16
POLSTON John	5 11	11 12	D	10 6 68	Walthamstow	Apprentice	Tottenham H	24	1
							Norwich C	142	6
POOLE Darren	5 8	10 03	F	9 11 77	Northampton	Trainee	**Nottingham F**	—	—
POOLE Gary	6 0	12 04	D	11 9 67	Stratford	Arsenal	Tottenham H	—	—
							Cambridge U	43	—
						Barnet	Barnet	40	2
							Plymouth Arg	39	5
							Southend U	44	2
							Birmingham C	34	—
POOLE Kevin	5 11	12 06	G	21 7 63	Bromsgrove	Apprentice	Aston Villa	28	—
							Northampton T (loan)	3	—
							Middlesbrough	34	—
							Hartlepool U (loan)	12	—
							Leicester C	111	—
POOM Mart	6 4	13 07	G	3 2 72	Tallinn	FC Wil	**Portsmouth**	—	—
POPESCU Gica			M	9 10 67	Calafat	PSV Eindhoven	**Tottenham H**	23	3
PORIC Adem	5 9	11 11	M	22 4 73	London	St George's	**Sheffield W**	10	—
PORTER Andy	5 9	11 02	M	17 9 68	Manchester	Trainee	**Port Vale**	227	7
PORTER Gary	5 6	11 00	M	6 3 66	Sunderland	Apprentice	**Watford**	365	46
POTTER Graham	6 1	11 12	D	20 5 75	Solihull	Trainee	Birmingham C	25	2
							Wycombe W (loan)	3	—
							Stoke C	4	—
POTTS Steve	5 7	10 11	D	7 5 67	Hartford (USA)	Apprentice	**West Ham U**	278	1
POUNDER Tony *	5 10	11 02	M	11 3 66	Yeovil	Weymouth	Bristol R	113	10
						Weymouth	**Hereford U**	28	2
POVEY Neil §	5 8	10 00	M	26 6 77	Birmingham	Trainee	**Torquay U**	8	—
POWELL Chris	5 10	11 07	D	8 9 69	Lambeth	Trainee	Crystal Palace	3	—
							Aldershot (loan)	11	—
							Southend U	221	3
POWELL Darryl	6 0	12 03	F	15 1 71	Lambeth	Trainee	**Portsmouth**	132	16
POWELL Stephen	5 9	11 05	M	14 12 76	Derby	Trainee	**Derby Co**	—	—
POWER Graeme	5 9	12 00	D	7 3 77	Harrow	Trainee	**QPR**	—	—

Player	Ht	Wt	Pos	Birth Date	Birth Place	Source	Clubs	League App	League Gls
POWER Lee	6 0	11 10	F	30 6 72	Lewisham	Trainee	Norwich C	44	10
							Charlton Ath (loan)	5	—
							Sunderland (loan)	3	—
							Portsmouth (loan)	2	—
							Bradford C	30	5
							Millwall (loan)	—	—
PRATT David *	5 8	11 00	F	17 12 74	London		**West Ham U**	—	—
PREECE Andy	6 1	12 00	M	27 3 67	Evesham	Evesham	Northampton T	1	—
						Worcester C.	Wrexham	51	7
							Stockport Co	97	42
							Crystal Palace	20	4
PREECE David	5 6	11 05	M	28 5 63	Bridgnorth	Apprentice	Walsall	111	5
							Luton T	336	21
PREECE David	6 2	11 11	G	28 8 76	Sunderland	Trainee	**Sunderland**	—	—
PREECE Roger	5 8	10 13	M	9 6 69	Much Wenlock	Coventry C	Wrexham	110	12
							Chester C	169	4
PREEDY Phil	5 10	10 07	M	20 11 75	Hereford	Trainee	**Hereford U**	29	1
PRENDERVILLE Barry	6 0	12 08	D	16 10 76	Dublin	Trainee	**Coventry C**	—	—
PRESSLEY Steven	6 0	11 00	D	11 10 73	Elgin	Inverkeithling BC	Rangers	34	1
							Coventry C	19	1
PRESSMAN Kevin	6 1	14 02	G	6 11 67	Fareham	Apprentice	**Sheffield W**	128	—
							Stoke C (loan)	4	—
PRESTON Richard *	5 11	11 02	D	7 5 76	Basildon	Trainee	**Northampton T**	1	—
PRICE Chris	5 9	11 09	M	24 10 75	Liverpool	Trainee	**Everton**	—	—
PRICE Ryan	6 4	14 00	G	13 3 70	Stafford	Stafford R	**Birmingham C**	—	—
PRIEST Chris	5 9	10 10	M	18 10 73	Leigh	Trainee	Everton	—	—
							Chester C	24	1
PRIMUS Linvoy	5 10	12 04	D	14 9 73	Stratford	Trainee	Charlton Ath	4	—
							Barnet	39	—
PRIOR Spencer	6 3	13 00	D	22 4 71	Rochford	Trainee	Southend U	135	3
							Norwich C	30	—
PRITCHARD David	5 7	11 04	D	27 5 72	Wolverhampton	Telford	**Bristol R**	54	—
PROCTOR Mark *	5 10	11 09	M	30 1 61	Middlesbrough	Apprentice	Middlesbrough	109	12
							Nottingham F	64	5
							Sunderland (loan)	5	—
							Sunderland	112	19
							Sheffield W	59	4
							Middlesbrough	120	6
							Tranmere R (loan)	13	1
							Tranmere R	18	—
PROKAS Richard	5 9	11 00	M	22 1 76	Penrith	Trainee	**Carlisle U**	39	1
PRUDHOE Mark	6 0	13 00	G	8 11 63	Washington	Apprentice	Sunderland	7	—
							Hartlepool U (loan)	3	—
							Birmingham C	1	—
							Walsall	26	—
							Doncaster R (loan)	5	—
							Sheffield W (loan)	—	—
							Grimsby T (loan)	8	—
							Hartlepool U (loan)	13	—
							Bristol C (loan)	3	—
							Carlisle U	34	—
							Darlington	146	—
							Stoke C	30	—
							Peterborough U (loan)	6	—
							Liverpool (loan)	—	—
PUGH David	6 2	13 00	F	19 9 64	Liverpool	Runcorn	Chester C	179	23
							Bury	42	16
PUGH Stephen *	5 9	11 00	F	27 11 73	Bangor	Trainee	**Wrexham**	11	—
PURSE Darren	6 2	12 08	D	14 2 77	London	Trainee	**Leyton Orient**	43	3

Player	Ht	Wt	Pos	Birth Date	Birth Place	Source	Clubs	League App	League Gls
PUTNEY Trevor *	5 9	11 08	M	11 2 61	Harold Hill	Brentwood & W	Ipswich T	103	8
							Norwich C	82	9
							Middlesbrough	48	1
							Watford	52	2
							Leyton Orient	22	2
							Colchester U	28	2
PUTTNAM David	5 10	11 09	M	3 2 67	Leicester	Leicester U	Leicester C	7	—
							Lincoln C	172	20
QUIGLEY Jim ‡	5 8	11 02	M	21 9 76	Derry	Trainee	**Everton**	—	—
QUIGLEY Mike *	5 6	9 04	M	2 10 70	Manchester	Trainee	**Manchester C**	12	—
							Wrexham (loan)	4	—
QUINN James	6 1	12 10	F	15 12 74	Coventry	Trainee	Birmingham C	4	—
							Blackpool	55	11
							Stockport Co (loan)	1	—
QUINN Jimmy	6 0	11 06	F	18 11 59	Belfast	Oswestry T	Swindon T	49	10
							Blackburn R	71	17
							Swindon T	64	30
							Leicester C	31	6
							Bradford C	35	14
							West Ham U	47	18
							Bournemouth	43	19
							Reading	123	57
QUINN Mick ‡	5 9	13 00	F	2 5 62	Liverpool	Derby Co	Wigan Ath	69	19
							Stockport Co	63	39
							Oldham Ath	80	34
							Portsmouth	121	54
							Newcastle U	115	59
							Coventry C	64	25
							Plymouth Arg (loan)	3	—
							Portsmouth (loan)	—	—
							Watford (loan)	5	—
QUINN Niall	6 4	13 10	F	6 10 66	Dublin		Arsenal	67	14
							Manchester C	171	58
QUINN Robert	5 11	11 02	D	8 11 76	Sidcup	Trainee	**Crystal Palace**	—	—
QUINN Wayne	5 10	11 07	M	19 11 76	Cornwall		**Sheffield U**	—	—
QUY Andy	6 0	13 01	G	4 7 76	Harlow	Tottenham H	**Derby Co**	—	—
RACHEL Adam			G	10 12 76	Birmingham	Trainee	**Aston Villa**	—	—
RADEBE Lucas	5 11	11 09	M	12 4 69	South Africa	Kaiser Chiefs	**Leeds U**	12	—
RADOSAVLJEVIC Predrag	5 11	12 10	M	24 6 63	Belgrade	St Louis Storms	Everton	46	4
							Portsmouth	40	5
RAE Alex	5 9	11 05	M	30 9 69	Glasgow	Bishopbriggs	Falkirk	83	20
							Millwall	181	50
RAMAGE Andrew *	5 11	12 02	M	3 10 74	Hornchurch	Dagenham	**Gillingham**	13	1
RAMAGE Craig	5 9	11 08	M	30 3 70	Derby	Trainee	Derby Co	42	4
							Wigan Ath (loan)	10	2
							Watford	57	9
RAMMELL Andy	6 0	13 05	F	10 2 67	Nuneaton	Atherstone U	Manchester U	—	—
							Barnsley	165	40
RAMSEY Paul (on loan from St Johnstone)	5 11	13 00	D	3 9 62	Londonderry		**Cardiff C**	11	—
RANDALL Adrian	5 11	12 04	M	10 11 68	Amesbury	Apprentice	Bournemouth	3	—
							Aldershot	107	12
							Burnley	110	8
RANKINE Mark	5 10	11 01	M	30 9 69	Doncaster	Trainee	Doncaster R	164	20
							Wolverhampton W	100	1
RANSON Ray ‡	5 9	11 12	D	12 6 60	St. Helens	Apprentice	Manchester C	183	1
							Birmingham C	137	—
							Newcastle U	83	1
							Manchester C	17	—
							Reading	24	—

Player	Ht	Wt	Pos	Birth Date	Birth Place	Source	Clubs	League App	League Gls
RATCLIFFE Kevin	6 1	13 06	D	12 11 60	Mancot	Apprentice	Everton	359	2
							Dundee	4	—
							Everton	—	—
							Cardiff C	25	1
							Nottingham F	—	—
							Derby Co	6	—
							Chester C	23	—
RATCLIFFE Simon	5 11	11 09	M	8 2 67	Davyhulme	Apprentice	Manchester U	—	—
							Norwich C	9	—
							Brentford	214	14
RATTLE Jon ‡	5 9	11 13	D	22 7 76	Melton	Trainee	**Cambridge U**	6	—
RAVEN Paul	6 0	12 03	D	28 7 70	Salisbury	School	Doncaster R	52	4
							WBA	139	9
							Doncaster R (loan)	7	—
RAVENSCROFT Craig	5 6	9 07	F	20 12 74	London	Trainee	**Brentford**	8	1
RAWLINS Matthew *			F	12 9 75	Bristol	Trainee	**Arsenal**	—	—
RAWLINSON Mark *	5 10	11 00	M	9 6 75	Bolton	Trainee	**Manchester U**	—	—
RAYNOR Paul	6 0	12 11	M	29 4 66	Nottingham	Apprentice	Nottingham F	3	—
							Bristol R (loan)	8	—
							Huddersfield T	50	9
							Swansea C	191	27
							Wrexham (loan)	6	—
							Cambridge U	49	2
							Preston NE	77	9
REA Simon	6 1	13 00	D	20 9 76	Coventry	Trainee	**Birmingham C**	—	—
READ Paul	5 11	12 06	F	25 9 73	Harlow	Trainee	**Arsenal**	—	—
							Leyton Orient (loan)	11	—
READY Karl	6 1	12 00	D	14 8 72	Neath	Trainee	**QPR**	39	2
REDDISH Shane	5 10	11 10	M	5 5 71	Bolsover	Trainee	Doncaster R	60	3
							Carlisle U	37	1
							Chesterfield (loan)	3	—
							Hartlepool	23	—
REDFEARN Neil	5 10	12 08	M	20 6 65	Dewsbury	Nottingham F	Bolton W	35	1
							Lincoln C (loan)	10	1
							Lincoln C	90	12
							Doncaster R	46	14
							Crystal Palace	57	10
							Watford	24	3
							Oldham Ath	62	16
							Barnsley	167	30
REDKNAPP Jamie	6 0	12 00	M	25 6 73	Barton on Sea	Trainee	Bournemouth	13	—
							Liverpool	111	10
REDMOND Steven	5 11	12 13	D	2 11 67	Liverpool	Apprentice	Manchester C	235	7
							Oldham Ath	107	1
REECE Andy	5 10	12 02	M	5 9 62	Shrewsbury	Willenhall	Bristol R	239	17
							Walsall (loan)	9	1
							Walsall (loan)	6	—
							Hereford U	65	5
REECE Paul	5 11	12 07	G	16 7 68	Nottingham	Kettering T	Grimsby T	54	—
							Doncaster R	1	—
							Oxford U	39	—
							Notts Co	11	—
REED Adam	6 0	12 00	D	18 2 75	Bishop Auckland	Trainee	**Darlington**	52	1
REED Ian	5 8	10 09	M	4 9 75	Lichfield	Trainee	**Shrewsbury T**	4	—
REED John	5 6	10 11	F	27 8 72	Rotherham	Trainee	**Sheffield U**	13	2
							Scarborough (loan)	14	6
							Scarborough (loan)	6	—
							Darlington (loan)	10	2
							Mansfield T (loan)	13	2
REES Jason	5 5	9 10	F	22 12 69	Pontypridd	Trainee	Luton T	82	—
							Mansfield T (loan)	15	1
							Portsmouth	19	1

Player	Ht	Wt	Pos	Birth Date	Birth Place	Source	Clubs	League App	League Gls
REES Tony	5 9	11 13	F	1 8 64	Merthyr Tydfil	Apprentice	Aston Villa	—	—
							Birmingham C	95	12
							Peterborough U (loan)	5	2
							Shrewsbury T (loan)	2	—
							Barnsley	31	3
							Grimsby T	141	33
							WBA	14	2
REEVE James *	6 1	11 07	F	26 11 75	Weymouth	Trainee	Bournemouth	7	—
							Hereford U	5	—
REEVES Alan	6 0	12 00	D	19 11 67	Birkenhead	Heswall	Norwich C	—	—
							Gillingham (loan)	18	—
							Chester C	40	2
							Rochdale	121	9
							Wimbledon	31	3
REEVES David	6 0	11 05	F	19 11 67	Birkenhead	Heswall	Sheffield W	17	2
							Scunthorpe U (loan)	4	2
							Scunthorpe U (loan)	6	4
							Burnley (loan)	16	8
							Bolton W	134	29
							Notts Co	13	2
							Carlisle U	76	32
REEVES Steve *	5 11	13 00	G	24 9 74	Dagenham	Trainee	**Everton**	—	—
REGIS Cyrille *	6 0	13 06	F	9 2 58	French Guyana	Hayes	WBA	237	82
							Coventry C	238	47
							Aston Villa	52	12
							Wolverhampton W	19	2
							Wycombe W	35	9
REGIS Dave	6 1	13 08	F	3 3 64	Paddington	Barnet	Notts Co	46	15
							Plymouth Arg	31	4
							Bournemouth (loan)	6	2
							Stoke C	63	15
							Birmingham C	6	2
							Southend U	9	1
REID Nicky *	5 10	12 04	D	30 10 60	Ormston	Apprentice	Manchester C	217	2
							Blackburn R	174	9
							Bristol C (loan)	4	—
							WBA	20	—
							Wycombe W	8	—
REID Paul	5 9	10 08	M	19 1 68	Oldbury	Apprentice	Leicester C	162	21
							Bradford C (loan)	7	—
							Bradford C	82	15
							Huddersfield T	42	6
REID Peter ‡	5 8	12 02	M	20 6 56	Huyton	Apprentice	Bolton W	225	23
							Everton	159	8
							QPR	29	1
							Manchester C	103	1
							Southampton	7	—
							Notts Co	5	—
							Bury	1	—
REID Shaun	5 8	11 10	M	13 10 65	Huyton	Local	Rochdale	133	4
							Preston NE (loan)	3	—
							York C	106	7
							Rochdale	107	10
REINELT Robert	5 10	11 13	M	11 3 74	Epping	Trainee	Aldershot	5	—
							Gillingham	52	5
							Colchester U	5	—
RENNIE David	6 0	12 00	D	29 8 64	Edinburgh	Apprentice	Leicester C	21	1
							Leeds U	101	5
							Bristol C	104	8
							Birmingham C	35	4
							Coventry C	71	1
RENNIE Paul *	5 9	11 04	D	26 10 71	Nantwich	Trainee	Crewe Alex	2	—
							Stoke C	4	—
							Wigan Ath	40	3
RHODES Andy (on loan from St Johnstone)	6 1	13 06	G	23 8 64	Doncaster		**Bolton W**	—	—
RICE Gary *			D	29 9 75	Zambia	Trainee	**Exeter C**	10	—

				Birth				League	
Player	Ht	Wt	Pos	Date	Place	Source	Clubs	App	Gls
RICHARDS Dave			M	31 12 76	Birmingham	Trainee	**Walsall**	—	—
RICHARDS Dean	6 2	13 01	D	9 6 74	Bradford	Trainee	**Bradford C**	86	4
							Wolverhampton W (loan)	10	2
RICHARDSON Barry	6 1	12 01	G	5 8 69	Wallsend	Trainee	Sunderland	—	—
							Scunthorpe U	—	—
							Scarborough	30	—
							Northampton T	96	—
							Preston NE	17	—
RICHARDSON Jon	5 11	12 00	M	29 8 75	Nottingham	Trainee	**Exeter C**	45	1
RICHARDSON Kevin	5 7	11 07	M	4 12 62	Newcastle	Apprentice	Everton	109	16
							Watford	39	2
							Arsenal	96	5
						Real Sociedad	Aston Villa	143	13
							Coventry C	14	—
RICHARDSON Lee	5 11	11 00	M	12 3 69	Halifax		Halifax T	56	2
							Watford	41	1
							Blackburn R	62	3
							Aberdeen	64	6
							Oldham Ath	30	6
RICHARDSON Lloyd			M	7 10 77	Dewsbury	Trainee	**Oldham Ath**	—	—
RICHARDSON Neil	6 0	13 09	D	3 3 68	Sunderland	Brandon U	**Rotherham U**	102	4
RICHARDSON Nick	6 0	12 07	M	11 4 67	Halifax	Local	Halifax T	101	17
							Cardiff C	111	13
							Wrexham (loan)	4	2
							Chester C (loan)	6	1
RICKERS Paul	5 10	11 00	M	9 5 75	Pontefract	Trainee	**Oldham Ath**	4	1
RIDEOUT Paul	5 11	12 01	F	14 8 64	Bournemouth	Apprentice	Swindon T	95	38
							Aston Villa	54	19
							Bari	99	23
							Southampton	75	19
							Swindon T (loan)	9	1
							Notts Co	11	3
							Rangers	12	1
							Everton	77	23
RIDGEWAY Ian	5 8	10 06	M	28 12 75	Nottingham	Trainee	**Notts Co**	1	—
RIEPER Marc	6 4	13 10	D	5 6 68	Denmark	Brondby	**West Ham U**	21	1
RIGBY Malcolm	6 1	12 00	G	13 3 76	Nottingham	Notts Co	**Nottingham F**	—	—
RIGBY Tony	5 10	12 12	M	10 8 72	Ormskirk	Barrow	**Bury**	84	11
RIMMER Neill	5 6	10 03	M	13 11 67	Liverpool	Apprentice	Everton	1	—
							Ipswich T	22	3
							Wigan Ath	160	10
RIMMER Stuart	5 7	11 00	F	12 10 64	Southport	Apprentice	Everton	3	—
							Chester C	114	67
							Watford	10	1
							Notts Co	4	2
							Walsall	88	31
							Barnsley	15	1
							Chester C	147	43
							Rochdale (loan)	3	—
							Preston NE (loan)	2	—
RIOCH Greg *	5 11	10 09	D	24 6 75	Sutton Coldfield	Trainee	**Luton T**	—	—
							Barnet (loan)	3	—
RIPLEY Andrew *	5 8	11 10	M	10 12 75	Middlesbrough	Trainee	**Darlington**	2	—
RIPLEY Stuart	5 11	12 06	F	20 11 67	Middlesbrough	Apprentice	Middlesbrough	249	26
							Bolton W (loan)	5	1
							Blackburn R	117	11
RITCHIE Andy *	5 10	11 11	F	28 11 60	Manchester	Apprentice	Manchester U	33	13
							Brighton	89	23
							Leeds U	136	40
							Oldham Ath	217	82
RITCHIE Paul (on loan from Dundee)	5 11	12 00	F	25 1 69	St Andrews		**Gillingham**	5	1

Player	Ht	Wt	Pos	Birth		Source	Clubs	League	
				Date	Place			App	Gls
RIVERS Mark			D	26 11 75	Crewe	Trainee	**Crewe Alex**	—	—
RIX Graham †	5 9	11 00	F	23 10 57	Doncaster	Apprentice	Arsenal	351	41
							Brentford (loan)	6	—
						Caen, Le Havre	Dundee	14	2
							Chelsea	1	—
ROBERTS Andy	5 10	13 00	M	20 3 74	Dartford	Trainee	**Millwall**	138	5
ROBERTS Ben	6 1	12 11	G	22 6 75	Bishop Auckland	Trainee	**Middlesbrough**	—	—
ROBERTS Danny *	5 8	10 08	D	12 11 75	Chelmsford	Trainee	**Colchester U**	—	—
ROBERTS Darren	5 10	12 01	F	12 10 69	Birmingham	Burton Alb	Wolverhampton W	21	5
							Hereford U (loan)	6	5
							Doncaster R	—	—
							Chesterfield	11	1
ROBERTS Glyn	5 11	12 02	M	19 10 74	Ipswich	Norwich C	**Rotherham U**	16	1
ROBERTS Iwan	6 2	14 02	F	26 6 68	Bangor	Trainee	Watford	63	9
							Huddersfield T	142	50
							Leicester C	63	22
ROBERTS Tony	6 0	12 00	G	4 8 69	Bangor	Trainee	**QPR**	94	—
ROBERTSON John	6 2	13 02	D	8 1 74	Liverpool	Trainee	**Wigan Ath**	98	3
ROBERTSON Sandy	5 9	10 07	M	26 4 71	Edinburgh	S Form	Rangers	26	1
							Coventry C	4	—
ROBINS Mark	5 7	10 06	F	22 12 69	Ashton-under-Lyme	Apprentice	Manchester U	48	11
							Norwich C	67	20
							Leicester C	17	5
ROBINSON David *			D	30 10 74	Wrekin	Liverpool	**Stockport Co**	—	—
ROBINSON Jamie	6 0	12 03	D	22 2 72	Liverpool	Trainee	Liverpool	—	—
							Barnsley	9	—
							Carlisle U	30	2
ROBINSON John	5 10	11 02	M	29 8 71	Bulawayo, Rhodesia	Apprentice	Brighton	62	6
							Charlton Ath	63	6
ROBINSON Les	5 8	11 01	D	1 3 67	Shirerook	Local	Mansfield T	15	—
							Stockport Co	67	3
							Doncaster R	82	12
							Oxford U	169	2
ROBINSON Liam	5 7	12 07	F	29 12 65	Bradford	Nottingham F	Huddersfield T	21	2
							Tranmere R (loan)	4	3
							Bury	262	89
							Bristol C	41	4
							Burnley	39	7
ROBINSON Mark	5 9	11 08	D	21 11 68	Rochdale	Trainee	WBA	2	—
							Barnsley	137	6
							Newcastle U	25	—
							Swindon T	40	—
ROBINSON Matthew	5 10	11 02	M	23 12 74	Exeter	Trainee	**Southampton**	1	—
ROBINSON Phil	5 10	11 07	M	6 1 67	Stafford	Apprentice	Aston Villa	3	1
							Wolverhampton W	71	8
							Notts Co	66	5
							Birmingham C (loan)	9	—
							Huddersfield T	75	5
							Northampton T (loan)	14	—
							Chesterfield	22	8
ROBINSON Ronnie *	5 9	11 05	D	22 10 66	Sunderland	SC Vaux	Ipswich T	—	—
						Vaux Breweries	Leeds U	27	—
							Doncaster R	78	5
							WBA	1	—
							Rotherham U	86	2
							Peterborough U	47	—
							Exeter C	39	1
							Huddersfield T (loan)	2	—
ROBINSON Steve	5 8	10 07	F	10 12 74	Lisburn	Trainee	Tottenham H	2	—
							Leyton Orient (loan)	—	—
							Bournemouth	32	5

Player	Ht	Wt	Pos	Birth Date	Birth Place	Source	Clubs	League App	League Gls
ROBINSON Steven	5 4	10 11	M	17 1 75	Nottingham	Trainee	**Birmingham C**	6	—
ROBSON Bryan	5 9	12 05	M	11 1 57	Witton Gilbert	Apprentice	WBA	197	39
							Manchester U	345	74
							Middlesbrough	22	1
ROBSON Gary	5 8	11 06	M	6 7 65	Durham	Apprentice	WBA	218	28
							Bradford C	69	3
ROBSON Mark	5 7	10 02	M	22 5 69	Newham	Trainee	Exeter C	26	7
							Tottenham H	8	—
							Reading (loan)	7	—
							Watford (loan)	1	—
							Plymouth Arg (loan)	7	—
							Exeter C (loan)	8	1
							West Ham U	47	8
							Charlton Ath	63	5
ROBSON Stewart *	5 11	12 04	M	6 11 64	Billericay	Apprentice	Arsenal	151	16
							West Ham U	69	4
							Coventry C (loan)	4	—
							Coventry C	53	3
ROCASTLE David	5 9	11 12	F	2 5 67	Lewisham	Apprentice	Arsenal	218	24
							Leeds U	25	2
							Manchester C	21	2
							Chelsea	28	—
ROCHE David	6 0	13 02	M	13 12 70	Newcastle	Trainee	Newcastle U	36	—
							Peterborough U (loan)	4	—
							Doncaster R	50	8
							Southend U	4	—
ROCKETT Jason	6 1	13 00	D	26 9 69	London		Rotherham U	—	—
							Scarborough	61	—
RODEN Damien ‡	5 9	11 00	D	17 9 74	Wrexham	Trainee	**Wrexham**	—	—
RODGER Graham	6 2	11 13	D	1 4 67	Glasgow	Apprentice	Wolverhampton W	1	—
							Coventry C	36	2
							Luton T	28	2
							Grimsby T	91	9
RODGER Simon	5 9	11 09	M	3 10 71	Shoreham	Trainee	**Crystal Palace**	91	5
RODGERSON Ian *	5 8	11 06	M	9 4 66	Hereford	Pegasus Juniors	Hereford U	100	6
							Cardiff C	99	4
							Birmingham C	95	13
							Sunderland	10	—
RODWELL Tony	5 11	11 02	F	26 8 62	Southport	Colne Dynamoes	Blackpool	142	17
							Scarborough	8	1
							Wigan Ath (loan)	5	1
ROGAN Anton *	5 11	12 06	D	25 3 66	Belfast	Distillery	Celtic	127	4
							Sunderland	46	1
							Oxford U	58	3
ROGERS Darren	6 0	13 00	D	9 4 70	Birmingham	Trainee	WBA	14	1
							Birmingham C	18	—
							Wycombe W (loan)	1	—
							Walsall	27	—
ROGERS Dave *	6 0	11 01	M	25 8 75	Liverpool	Trainee	**Tranmere R**	—	—
ROGERS Lee	5 11	12 02	D	28 10 66	Doncaster	Doncaster R	**Chesterfield**	293	1
ROGERS Paul	6 0	12 05	M	21 3 65	Portsmouth	Sutton U	**Sheffield U**	109	10
ROOKYARD Carl ‡	5 9	10 05	F	3 9 75	Burton on Trent	Trainee	Nottingham F	—	—
							Walsall	—	—
ROPER Ian	6 4	14 00	D	20 6 77	Nuneaton	Trainee	**Walsall**	—	—
ROSARIO Robert	6 3	12 01	F	4 3 66	Hammersmith	Hillingdon Bor	Norwich C	126	18
							Wolverhampton W (loan)	2	1
							Coventry C	59	8
							Nottingham F	27	3
ROSCOE Andrew	5 9	10 12	M	4 6 73	Liverpool	Trainee	Liverpool	—	—
							Bolton W	3	—
							Rotherham U	31	4

Player	Ht	Wt	Pos	Birth Date	Birth Place	Source	Clubs	League App	League Gls
ROSE Matthew			M	24 9 75	Dartford	Trainee	**Arsenal**	—	—
ROSENIOR Leroy *	6 1	11 10	F	24 3 64	London	School	Fulham	54	16
							QPR	38	7
							Fulham	34	20
							West Ham U	53	15
							Fulham (loan)	11	3
							Charlton Ath (loan)	3	—
							Bristol C	51	12
ROSENTHAL Ronny	5 11	12 13	F	11 10 63	Haifa	Standard Liege	Luton T (loan)	—	—
							Liverpool (loan)	8	7
							Liverpool	66	14
							Tottenham H	35	2
ROSLER Uwe	6 1	12 04	F	15 11 68	Attenburg	Dynamo Dresden	**Manchester C**	43	20
ROSS Mike	5 6	9 13	F	2 9 71	Southampton	Trainee	Portsmouth	4	—
							Exeter C	28	9
							Plymouth Arg	17	—
ROUND Steve	5 10	11 03	D	9 11 70	Buxton	Trainee	**Derby Co**	9	—
ROWBOTHAM Darren *	5 10	11 05	M	22 10 66	Cardiff	Trainee	Plymouth Arg	46	2
							Exeter C	118	47
							Torquay U	14	3
							Birmingham C	36	6
							Hereford U (loan)	8	2
							Mansfield T (loan)	4	—
							Crewe Alex	61	21
ROWE Richard *			M	12 5 76	Plymouth	Southampton	**Bristol C**	—	—
ROWE Rodney	5 8	12 08	F	30 7 75	Huddersfield	Trainee	**Huddersfield T**	13	1
							Scarborough (loan)	14	1
							Bury (loan)	3	—
ROWE Zeke	5 6	9 08	M	30 10 73	Stoke Newington	Trainee	**Chelsea**	—	—
							Barnet (loan)	10	2
ROWETT Gary	6 0	12 10	F	6 3 74	Bromsgrove	Trainee	Cambridge U	63	9
							Everton	4	—
							Blackpool (loan)	17	—
ROWLAND Keith	5 10	10 00	M	1 9 71	Portadown	Trainee	Bournemouth	72	2
							Coventry C (loan)	2	—
							West Ham U	35	—
ROY Bryan	5 10	10 08	M	12 2 69	Amsterdam	Foggia	**Nottingham F**	37	13
ROYCE Simon	6 2	12 08	G	9 9 71	Forest Gate	Heybridge Swifts	**Southend U**	23	—
RUDDOCK Neil	6 2	12 12	D	9 5 68	London	Apprentice	Millwall	—	—
							Tottenham H	9	—
							Millwall	2	1
							Southampton	107	9
							Tottenham H	38	3
							Liverpool	76	5
RUFUS Marvin §			M	11 9 76	Lewisham	Charlton Ath	**Leyton Orient**	7	—
RUFUS Richard	6 1	10 05	D	12 1 75	Lewisham	Trainee	**Charlton Ath**	28	—
RUSH David	5 11	10 10	F	15 5 71	Sunderland	Trainee	Sunderland	59	12
							Hartlepool U (loan)	8	2
							Peterborough U (loan)	4	1
							Cambridge U (loan)	2	—
							Oxford U	34	9
RUSH Ian	6 0	12 06	F	20 10 61	St. Asaph	Apprentice	Chester	34	14
							Liverpool	224	139
							Juventus	29	7
							Liverpool	225	85
RUSH Matthew	5 11	12 10	M	6 8 71	Dalston	Trainee	**West Ham U**	48	5
							Cambridge U (loan)	10	—
							Swansea C (loan)	13	—
RUSSELL Alex	5 8	11 07	M	17 3 73	Crosby	Burscough	**Rochdale**	7	1
RUSSELL Craig	5 10	12 06	F	4 2 74	South Shields	Trainee	**Sunderland**	77	14

				Birth				League	
Player	*Ht*	*Wt*	*Pos*	*Date*	*Place*	*Source*	*Clubs*	*App*	*Gls*
RUSSELL Kevin	5 8	10 12	F	6 12 66	Portsmouth	Brighton	Portsmouth	4	1
							Wrexham	84	43
							Leicester C	43	10
							Peterborough U (loan)	7	3
							Cardiff C (loan)	3	—
							Hereford U (loan)	3	1
							Stoke C (loan)	5	1
							Stoke C	40	5
							Burnley	28	6
							Bournemouth	30	1
							Notts Co	11	—
RUSSELL Lee	5 11	11 04	D	3 9 69	Southampton	Trainee	**Portsmouth**	76	1
							Bournemouth (loan)	3	—
RUSSELL Wayne	6 2	12 13	G	29 11 67	Cardiff	Ebbw Vale	**Burnley**	8	—
RUST Nicky	6 0	13 01	G	25 9 74	Ely	Arsenal	**Brighton**	90	—
RUTHERFORD Paul (To Berwick Rangers)	5 11	12 07	F	23 2 67	Sunderland	Meadowbank T	**Scarborough**	8	1
RYAN Darren	5 9	11 00	M	3 7 72	Oswestry	Trainee	Shrewsbury T	4	—
							Chester C	17	2
							Stockport Co	36	6
							Rochdale	25	2
RYAN John	5 8	11 06	F	7 12 75	Cork	Cork C	**Brighton**	—	—
RYAN Keith	5 11	12 07	M	25 6 70	Northampton	Berkhamsted T	**Wycombe W**	66	5
RYAN Robbie	5 11	11 05	D	11 8 76	Dublin	Belvedere	**Huddersfield T**	—	—
RYAN Tim ‡	5 10	11 00	D	10 12 74	Stockport	Trainee	**Scunthorpe U**	2	—
RYAN Vaughan *	5 9	12 00	M	2 9 68	Westminster		Wimbledon	82	3
							Sheffield U (loan)	3	—
							Leyton Orient	44	—
RYDER Stuart	6 1	12 02	D	6 11 73	Sutton Coldfield	Trainee	**Walsall**	84	5
SADDINGTON James ‡	6 0	11 13	D	12 9 72	Cambridge	Cambridge C	**Millwall**	—	—
SALAKO John	5 9	12 03	F	11 2 69	Nigeria	Trainee	**Crystal Palace**	215	22
							Swansea C (loan)	13	3
SALE Mark	6 5	13 08	F	27 2 72	Burton-on-Trent	Trainee	Stoke C	2	—
							Cambridge U	—	—
							Birmingham C	21	—
							Torquay U	44	8
							Preston NE	13	7
SALMON Mike	6 2	12 12	G	14 7 64	Leyland	Local	Blackburn R	1	—
							Chester C (loan)	16	—
							Stockport Co	118	—
							Bolton W	26	—
							Wrexham (loan)	17	—
							Wrexham	83	—
							Charlton Ath	87	—
SAMPSON Ian	6 2	12 08	D	14 11 68	Wakefield	Goole T	Sunderland	17	1
							Northampton T (loan)	8	—
							Northampton T	42	2
SAMWAYS Mark	6 2	14 00	G	11 11 68	Doncaster	Trainee	Doncaster R	121	—
							Scunthorpe U (loan)	8	—
							Scunthorpe U	114	—
SAMWAYS Vinny	5 8	11 00	M	27 10 68	Bethnal Green	Apprentice	Tottenham H	193	11
							Everton	19	1
SANDEMAN Bradley	5 10	10 08	M	24 2 70	Northampton	Trainee	Northampton T	58	3
							Maidstone U	57	8
							Port Vale	68	1
SANDFORD Lee	6 0	12 12	D	22 4 68	Basingstoke	Apprentice	Portsmouth	72	1
							Stoke C	212	8
SANSAM Christian	6 0	11 07	F	26 12 75	Hull	Trainee	**Scunthorpe U**	16	—

Player	Ht	Wt	Pos	Birth Date	Birth Place	Source	Clubs	League App	League Gls
SANSOM Kenny ‡	5 7	10 04	D	26 9 58	Camberwell	Apprentice	Crystal Palace	172	3
							Arsenal	314	6
							Newcastle U	20	—
							QPR	64	—
							Coventry C	51	—
							Everton	7	1
							Brentford	8	—
						Chertsey	**Watford**	1	—
SANSOME Paul	6 0	13 10	G	6 10 61	N. Addington	Crystal Palace	Millwall	156	—
							Southend U	305	—
SARGENT David			D	22 12 77	Wembley	Watford	**Wycombe W**	—	—
SAUNDERS Dean	5 8	10 06	F	21 6 64	Swansea	Apprentice	Swansea C	49	12
							Cardiff C (loan)	4	—
							Brighton	72	21
							Oxford U	59	22
							Derby Co	106	42
							Liverpool	42	11
							Aston Villa	112	37
SAUNDERS Lee			D	23 3 77	Nuneaton	Trainee	**Doncaster R**	—	—
SAVAGE Dave	6 1	12 07	M	30 7 73	Dublin	Longford T	**Millwall**	37	2
SAVAGE Rob	6 0	10 01	F	18 10 74	Wrexham	Trainee	Manchester U	—	—
							Crewe Alex	6	2
SAVILLE Andrew	6 0	12 06	F	12 12 64	Hull	Local	Hull C	100	18
							Walsall	38	5
							Barnsley	82	21
							Hartlepool U	37	13
							Birmingham C	59	17
							Burnley (loan)	4	1
SCAIFE Nicky	6 0	11 13	M	14 5 75	Middlesbrough	Whitby	**York C**	1	—
SCALES John	6 2	13 05	D	4 7 66	Harrogate		Leeds U	—	—
							Bristol R	72	2
							Wimbledon	240	11
							Liverpool	35	2
SCARGILL Jonathan	6 0	13 10	G	9 4 77	Dewsbury	Trainee	**Sheffield W**	—	—
SCARGILL Wayne ‡	5 11	11 10	D	30 4 68	Barnsley	Frickley Ath	**Bradford C**	1	—
SCHMEICHEL Peter	6 4	16 01	G	18 11 63	Gladsaxe	Brondby	**Manchester U**	154	—
SCHOFIELD Jon	5 11	11 03	M	16 5 65	Barnsley	Gainsborough T	Lincoln C	231	11
							Doncaster R	27	1
SCHOLES Paul	5 7	10 11	F	16 11 74	Salford	Trainee	**Manchester U**	17	5
SCHWARZ Stefan	5 10	12 06	M	18 4 69	Malmo		Malmo	29	—
							Benfica	77	7
							Arsenal	34	2
SCIMECA Riccardo	6 1	12 09	D	13 6 75	Leamington Spa	Trainee	**Aston Villa**	—	—
SCOTT Andrew	6 0	12 11	D	27 6 75	Manchester	Trainee	Blackburn R	—	—
							Cardiff C	13	1
SCOTT Andy	6 1	11 05	F	2 8 72	Epsom	Sutton U	**Sheffield U**	54	5
SCOTT Keith	6 3	14 03	F	9 6 67	London	Leicester U	Lincoln C	16	2
						Wycombe W	Wycombe W	15	10
							Swindon T	51	12
							Stoke C	18	3
SCOTT Kevin	6 4	14 03	D	17 12 66	Easington	Middlesbrough	Newcastle U	227	8
							Tottenham H	16	1
							Port Vale (loan)	17	1
SCOTT Mark *	5 10	11 07	D	21 2 76	Darlington	Trainee	**Norwich C**	—	—
SCOTT Martin	5 10	11 07	M	7 1 68	Sheffield	Apprentice	Rotherham U	94	3
							Nottingham F (loan)	—	—
							Bristol C	171	14
							Sunderland	24	—
SCOTT Peter	5 9	11 12	M	1 10 63	London	Apprentice	Fulham	277	27
							Bournemouth	10	—
							Barnet	58	2

Player	Ht	Wt	Pos	Birth Date	Birth Place	Source	Clubs	League App	League Gls
SCOTT Richard	5 9	10 10	D	29 9 74	Dudley	Trainee	Birmingham C	12	—
							Shrewsbury T	8	1
SCOTT Rob	6 1	11 10	F	15 8 73	Epsom	Sutton U	**Sheffield U**	1	—
							Scarborough (loan)	8	3
SCOTT Ryan *	5 9	11 00	D	20 3 76	Saltburn	Trainee	**Darlington**	1	—
SCOTT Steve ‡	5 7	10 03	M	29 1 76	Edinburgh	Trainee	**Brighton & HA**	—	—
SCOWCROFT James	6 1	12 02	F	15 11 75	Bury St Edmunds	Trainee	**Ipswich T**	—	—
SCULLY Anthony	5 7	11 12	F	12 6 76	Dublin	Trainee	**Crystal Palace**	—	—
							Bournemouth (loan)	10	—
SCULLY Pat	6 1	12 07	D	23 6 70	Dublin	Trainee	Arsenal	—	—
							Preston NE (loan)	13	1
							Northampton T (loan)	15	—
							Southend U	115	6
							Huddersfield T	49	1
SEABURY Kevin	5 9	11 06	D	24 11 73	Shrewsbury	Trainee	**Shrewsbury T**	31	—
SEAGRAVES Mark	6 0	13 04	D	22 10 66	Bootle	Apprentice	Liverpool	—	—
							Norwich C (loan)	3	—
							Manchester C	42	—
							Bolton W	157	7
SEAL David	5 11	12 00	F	26 1 72	Penrith NSW	Aalst	**Bristol C**	9	—
SEALEY Les	6 1	13 06	G	29 9 57	Bethnal Green	Apprentice	Coventry C	158	—
							Luton T	207	—
							Plymouth Arg (loan)	6	—
							Manchester U (loan)	2	—
							Manchester U	31	—
							Aston Villa	18	—
							Coventry C (loan)	2	—
							Birmingham C (loan)	12	—
							Manchester U	—	—
							Blackpool	7	—
							West Ham U	—	—
SEAMAN David	6 4	14 10	G	19 9 63	Rotherham	Apprentice	Leeds U	—	—
							Peterborough U	91	—
							Birmingham C	75	—
							QPR	141	—
							Arsenal	189	—
SEARLE Damon	5 11	10 04	D	26 10 71	Cardiff	Trainee	**Cardiff C**	193	2
SEDGEMORE Ben	5 10	13 11	M	5 8 75	Wolverhampton	Trainee	**Birmingham C**	—	—
							Northampton T (loan)	1	—
SEDGLEY Steve	6 1	13 13	M	26 5 68	Enfield	Apprentice	Coventry C	84	3
							Tottenham H	164	8
							Ipswich T	26	4
SEGERS Hans	5 11	12 12	G	30 10 61	Eindhoven	PSV Eindhoven	Nottingham F	58	—
							Stoke C (loan)	1	—
							Sheffield U (loan)	10	—
							Dunfermline Ath (loan)	4	—
							Wimbledon	263	—
SELLARS Scott	5 7	9 10	M	27 11 65	Sheffield	Apprentice	Leeds U	76	12
							Blackburn R	202	35
							Leeds U	7	—
							Newcastle U	55	5
SELLEY Ian	5 9	10 01	M	14 6 74	Chertsey	Trainee	**Arsenal**	40	—
SEMPLE Ryan §			M	2 7 77	Derry	Trainee	**Peterborough U**	2	—
SERRANT Carl			D	12 9 75	Bradford	Trainee	**Oldham Ath**	—	—
SERTORI Mark	6 2	14 02	M	1 9 67	Manchester		Stockport Co	4	—
							Lincoln C	50	9
							Wrexham	110	3
							Bury	2	—
SHAIL Mark	6 1	13 03	D	15 10 66	Sweden	Yeovil	**Bristol C**	78	4

Player	Ht	Wt	Pos	Birth Date	Birth Place	Source	Clubs	League App	League Gls
SHAKESPEARE Craig	5 10	12 05	M	26 10 63	Birmingham	Apprentice	Walsall	284	45
							Sheffield W	17	—
							WBA	112	12
							Grimsby T	52	6
SHARP Graeme	6 1	11 09	F	16 10 60	Glasgow	Eastercraigs	Dumbarton	40	17
							Everton	322	111
							Oldham Ath	109	30
SHARP Kevin	5 9	11 11	M	19 9 74	Ontario	Auxerre	**Leeds U**	16	—
SHARP Raymond	5 11	12 06	D	16 11 69	Stirling	Gairdoch U	Dunfermline Ath	151	1
							Stenhousemuir (loan)	5	—
							Preston NE	21	—
SHARPE John	5 11	11 06	M	9 8 75	Birmingham	Trainee	**Manchester C**	—	—
SHARPE Lee	6 0	12 07	F	25 7 71	Halesowen	Trainee	Torquay U	14	3
							Manchester U	162	17
SHARPE Richard ‡			F	14 1 67	Wokingham	Coca Expos	**Rochdale**	16	2
SHAW Darren *	6 0	12 02	D	20 12 74	Telford	Trainee	Wolverhampton W	—	—
							Northampton T	—	—
SHAW Graham	5 9	11 05	F	7 6 67	Newcastle under Lyne	Apprentice	Stoke C	99	18
							Preston NE	121	29
							Stoke C	36	5
							Plymouth Arg (loan)	6	—
							Rochdale	4	—
SHAW Paul	5 11	12 02	F	4 9 73	Burnham	Trainee	**Arsenal**	1	—
							Burnley (loan)	9	4
SHAW Richard	5 9	12 08	D	11 9 68	Brentford	Apprentice	**Crystal Palace**	192	3
							Hull C (loan)	4	—
SHAW Simon	6 0	12 00	M	21 9 73	Teeside	Trainee	**Darlington**	66	6
SHEARER Alan	6 0	12 01	F	13 8 70	Newcastle	Trainee	Southampton	118	23
							Blackburn R	103	81
SHEARER Lee §			D	23 10 77	Southend	Trainee	**Leyton Orient**	2	—
SHEARER Peter	6 0	11 06	F	4 2 67	Birmingham	Apprentice	Birmingham C	4	—
							Rochdale	1	—
						Cheltenham T	Bournemouth	85	10
							Birmingham C	25	7
SHEEDY Kevin *	5 9	10 11	M	21 10 59	Builth Wells	Apprentice	Hereford U	51	4
							Liverpool	3	—
							Everton	274	67
							Newcastle U	37	4
							Blackpool	26	1
SHEERIN Paul	5 10	11 10	M	28 8 74	Edinburgh	Whitehill Welfare	Alloa	9	—
							Southampton	—	—
SHEFFIELD Jon	5 11	12 12	G	1 2 69	Bedworth		Norwich C	1	—
							Aldershot (loan)	11	—
							Ipswich T (loan)	—	—
							Aldershot (loan)	15	—
							Cambridge U (loan)	2	—
							Cambridge U	54	—
							Colchester U (loan)	6	—
							Swindon T (loan)	2	—
							Hereford U (loan)	8	—
SHELTON Gary	5 7	11 00	M	21 3 58	Nottingham	Apprentice	Walsall	24	—
							Aston Villa	24	7
							Notts Co (loan)	8	—
							Sheffield W	198	18
							Oxford U	65	1
							Bristol C	150	24
							Rochdale (loan)	3	—
							Chester C	33	2
SHEPPARD James	5 8	10 10	M	18 9 75	Preston	Trainee	**Blackpool**	—	—
SHEPPARD Simon	6 4	14 03	G	7 8 73	Clevedon	Trainee	Watford	23	—
							Scarborough (loan)	9	—
							Reading	—	—
SHERIDAN Darren	5 6	10 12	M	8 12 67	Manchester	Winsford	**Barnsley**	38	2

Player	Ht	Wt	Pos	Birth Date	Place	Source	Clubs	League App	Gls
SHERIDAN John	5 9	12 00	M	1 10 64	Stretford	Local	Leeds U	230	47
							Nottingham F	—	—
							Sheffield W	178	25
SHERIDAN Tony *	6 0	11 08	F	21 10 74	Dublin		**Coventry C**	9	—
SHERINGHAM Teddy	6 0	12 05	F	2 4 66	Highams Park	Apprentice	Millwall	220	93
							Aldershot (loan)	5	—
							Nottingham F	42	14
							Tottenham H	99	53
SHERLOCK Paul	5 11	11 05	D	17 11 73	Wigan	Trainee	Notts Co	12	1
							Mansfield T	2	—
SHERON Mike	5 9	11 07	F	11 1 72	Liverpool	Trainee	Manchester C	100	24
							Bury (loan)	5	1
							Norwich C	21	1
SHERWOOD Steve ‡	6 4	14 07	G	10 12 53	Selby	Apprentice	Chelsea	16	—
							Brighton (loan)	—	—
							Millwall (loan)	1	—
							Brentford (loan)	16	—
							Brentford (loan)	46	—
							Watford	211	1
							Grimsby T	183	—
							Northampton T	16	—
							Grimsby T	—	—
							Lincoln C	7	—
SHERWOOD Tim	6 0	11 06	M	6 2 69	St Albans	Trainee	Watford	32	2
							Norwich C	71	10
							Blackburn R	126	11
SHILTON Peter	6 1	14 00	G	18 9 49	Leicester	Apprentice	Leicester C	286	1
							Stoke C	110	—
							Nottingham F	202	—
							Southampton	188	—
							Derby Co	175	—
							Plymouth Arg	34	—
							Wimbledon	—	—
							Bolton W	1	—
SHILTON Sam §			M	21 7 78	Nottingham	Schoolboy	**Plymouth Arg**	2	—
SHIPPERLEY Neil	6 1	13 12	F	30 10 74	Chatham	Trainee	Chelsea	37	7
							Watford (loan)	6	1
							Southampton	19	4
SHIRTLIFF Peter	6 0	13 03	D	6 4 61	Barnsley	Apprentice	Sheffield W	188	4
							Charlton Ath	103	7
							Sheffield W	104	4
							Wolverhampton W	67	—
SHORE Jamie	5 9	10 09	M	1 9 77	Bristol	Trainee	**Norwich C**	—	—
SHORT Chris	5 10	12 02	D	9 5 70	Munster	Pickering T	Scarborough	43	1
							Manchester U (loan)	—	—
							Notts Co	92	2
							Huddersfield T (loan)	6	—
SHORT Craig	6 3	13 12	D	25 6 68	Bridlington	Pickering T	Scarborough	63	7
							Notts Co	128	6
							Derby Co	118	9
SHOTTON Malcolm †	6 3	13 12	D	16 2 57	Newcastle	Apprentice	Leicester C	—	—
						Nuneaton	Oxford U	263	12
							Portsmouth	10	—
							Huddersfield T	16	1
							Barnsley	66	6
							Hull C	59	2
							Ayr U	73	3
							Barnsley	8	1
SHOWLER Paul	5 11	11 02	M	10 10 66	Doncaster	Altrincham	Barnet	71	12
							Bradford C	55	7
SHUTT Carl	5 11	10 10	F	10 10 61	Sheffield	Spalding U	Sheffield W	40	16
							Bristol C	46	10
							Leeds U	79	17
							Birmingham C	26	4
							Manchester C (loan)	6	—
							Bradford C	32	4
SIBSON Andrew ‡	5 7	9 06	M	22 11 75	Leeds	Trainee	**Doncaster R**	—	—

Player	Ht	Wt	Pos	Birth Date	Birth Place	Source	Clubs	League App	League Gls
SIDDALL Barry ‡	6 1	14 02	G	12 9 54	Ellesmere Port	Apprentice	Bolton W	137	—
							Sunderland	167	—
							Darlington (loan)	8	—
							Port Vale	81	—
							Blackpool (loan)	7	—
							Stoke C	20	—
							Tranmere R (loan)	12	—
							Manchester C (loan)	6	—
							Blackpool	110	—
							Stockport Co	21	—
							Hartlepool U	11	—
							WBA	—	—
							Carlisle U	24	—
							Chester C	9	—
							Preston NE	1	—
							Bury	—	—
							Burnley	—	—
							Lincoln C	—	—
							Birmingham C	—	—
SIGURDSSON Larus	6 0	12 08	D	4 6 73	Akuveyni	Thor	**Stoke C**	23	1
SIMKIN Darren	6 0	12 00	D	24 3 70	Walsall	Blakenhall	Wolverhampton W	15	—
							Shrewsbury T	12	—
SIMMONDS Danny *	5 11	11 05	M	17 12 74	Eastbourne	Trainee	**Brighton**	18	—
SIMPSON Colin	6 1	11 05	F	30 4 76	Oxford	Trainee	**Watford**	—	—
SIMPSON Elliott *	5 11	11 11	M	1 7 76	York	Trainee	**York C**	1	—
SIMPSON Fitzroy	5 8	10 07	M	26 2 70	Trowbridge	Trainee	Swindon T	105	9
							Manchester C	71	4
							Bristol C (loan)	4	—
SIMPSON Gary	6 2	14 00	D	14 2 76	Ashford	Trainee	**Luton T**	—	—
SIMPSON Jimmy *	5 7	10 12	M	18 9 75	Portsmouth	Trainee	**Norwich C**	—	—
SIMPSON Michael	5 9	10 08	M	28 2 74	Nottingham	Trainee	**Notts Co**	25	3
SIMPSON Paul	5 7	11 12	F	26 7 66	Carlisle	Apprentice	Manchester C	121	18
							Oxford U	144	43
							Derby Co	127	36
SIMPSON Robert	5 10	10 07	F	3 3 76	Luton	Trainee	**Tottenham H**	—	—
SINCLAIR Frank	5 8	11 02	D	3 12 71	Lambeth	Trainee	**Chelsea**	114	4
							WBA (loan)	6	1
SINCLAIR Ron	5 11	12 03	G	19 11 64	Stirling	Apprentice	Nottingham F	—	—
							Wrexham (loan)	11	—
							Derby Co (loan)	—	—
							Sheffield U (loan)	—	—
							Leeds U (loan)	—	—
							Leeds U	8	—
							Halifax T (loan)	4	—
							Halifax T (loan)	10	—
							Bristol C	44	—
							Walsall (loan)	10	—
							Stoke C	79	—
							Bradford C (loan)	—	—
SINCLAIR Trevor	5 10	11 02	M	2 3 73	Dulwich	Trainee	Blackpool	112	15
							QPR	65	8
SINNOTT Lee	6 2	12 13	D	12 7 65	Pelsall	Apprentice	Walsall	40	2
							Watford	78	2
							Bradford C	173	6
							Crystal Palace	55	—
							Bradford C	34	1
							Huddersfield T	25	1
SINTON Andy	5 8	11 00	M	19 3 66	Newcastle	Apprentice	Cambridge U	93	13
							Brentford	149	28
							QPR	160	22
							Sheffield W	50	3
SKEDD Anthony *	5 5	10 01	M	19 5 75	Hartlepool	Trainee	**Hartlepool U**	46	—
SKELLY Richard	5 9	10 06	M	24 3 72	Norwich		Cambridge U	2	—
						Newmarket T	**Northampton T**	3	—

Player	Ht	Wt	Pos	Birth Date	Birth Place	Source	Clubs	League App	League Gls
SKELTON Aaron	5 10	11 05	M	22 11 74	Welwyn Garden	Trainee	**Luton T**	5	—
SKINNER Craig	5 9	11 06	F	21 10 70	Bury	Trainee	Blackburn R	16	—
							Plymouth Arg	53	4
SKINNER Justin	6 0	11 03	M	30 1 69	London	Apprentice	Fulham	135	23
							Bristol R	121	10
SKINNER Justin	5 7	11 00	D	17 9 72	London	Trainee	**Wimbledon**	1	—
							Bournemouth (loan)	16	—
							Wycombe W (loan)	5	—
SKIVERTON Terry	6 0	12 04	D	20 6 75	Mile End	Trainee	**Chelsea**	—	—
							Wycombe W (loan)	10	—
SLADE Steve	5 11	10 10	F	6 10 75	Romford	Trainee	**Tottenham H**	—	—
SLATER Robbie	5 11	13 00	M	26 11 64	Ormskirk	Lens	**Blackburn R**	18	—
SLATER Stuart	5 9	11 06	M	27 3 69	Sudbury	Apprentice	West Ham U	141	11
							Celtic	43	3
							Ipswich T	55	2
SLAVEN Bernie *	5 11	12 00	F	13 11 60	Paisley		Morton	22	1
							Airdrie	2	—
							Queen of the South	2	—
							Albion R	42	27
							Middlesbrough	307	118
							Port Vale	33	9
							Darlington	37	7
SLAWSON Stephen *	6 0	12 06	F	13 11 72	Nottingham	Trainee	**Notts Co**	38	4
							Burnley (loan)	5	2
							Shrewsbury T (loan)	6	—
SLINN Kevin ‡	5 11	11 00	F	2 9 74	Northampton	Trainee	Watford	—	—
							Stockport Co	4	1
SLOAN Scott	5 10	11 13	F	14 12 67	Wallsend	Ponteland	Berwick R	61	20
							Newcastle U	16	1
							Falkirk	64	11
							Cambridge U (loan)	4	1
							Hartlepool U	29	2
SMALL Bryan	5 9	11 09	D	15 11 71	Birmingham	Trainee	**Aston Villa**	36	—
							Birmingham C (loan)	3	—
SMART Allan	6 2	12 07	F	8 7 74	Perth	Caledonian Th	Caledonian Th	4	—
							Preston NE	19	6
SMILLIE Neil	5 6	10 07	F	19 7 58	Barnsley	Apprentice	Crystal Palace	83	7
							Brentford (loan)	3	—
							Brighton	75	2
							Watford	16	3
							Reading	39	—
							Brentford	172	18
							Gillingham	53	3
SMITH Alan	6 3	12 13	F	21 11 62	Birmingham	Alvechurch	Leicester C	191	73
							Leicester C (loan)	9	3
							Arsenal	264	86
SMITH Alex	5 7	9 00	D	15 2 76	Liverpool	Trainee	**Everton**	—	—
SMITH Chris			F	3 1 77	Birmingham	Trainee	**Walsall**	—	—
SMITH David	5 10	11 12	M	26 12 70	Liverpool	Trainee	Norwich C	18	—
							Oxford U	42	—
SMITH David	5 8	10 02	M	29 3 68	Gloucester		Coventry C	154	19
							Bournemouth (loan)	1	—
							Birmingham C	38	3
							WBA	40	—
SMITH Dean	6 1	12 10	D	19 3 71	West Bromwich	Trainee	Walsall	142	2
							Hereford U	35	3
SMITH Eric ‡	6 2	12 08	D	20 10 75	Dublin	Trainee	**Crystal Palace**	—	—

Player	Ht	Wt	Pos	Birth Date	Birth Place	Source	Clubs	League App	League Gls
SMITH Gary *	5 10	12 09	M	3 12 68	Harlow	Apprentice	Fulham	1	—
							Colchester U	11	—
						Enfield, Wycombe W, Welling U	**Barnet**	13	—
SMITH Gavin			F	24 9 77	Sheffield	Trainee	**Sheffield W**	—	—
SMITH Ian			D	28 11 76	Bury	Trainee	**Manchester C**	—	—
SMITH James	5 6	10 08	F	17 9 74	Birmingham	Trainee	**Wolverhampton W**	25	—
SMITH Jason *	6 2	12 04	D	6 9 74	Bromsgrove	Tiverton	**Coventry C**	—	—
SMITH Mark	6 1	13 09	G	2 1 73	Birmingham	Trainee	Nottingham F	—	—
							Crewe Alex	63	—
SMITH Mark *	6 2	13 11	D	21 3 60	Sheffield	Apprentice	Sheffield W	282	16
							Plymouth Arg	82	6
							Barnsley	104	10
							Notts Co	5	—
							Chesterfield (loan)	6	1
							Huddersfield T (loan)	5	—
							Port Vale (loan)	6	—
							Lincoln C	20	1
SMITH Mark *	5 10	12 07	M	19 12 61	Sheffield		Sheffield U	—	—
						Worksop, Gainsborough T	Scunthorpe U	1	—
						Kettering	Rochdale	27	7
							Huddersfield T	96	11
							Grimsby T	77	4
							Scunthorpe U	62	8
SMITH Mark *	5 9	10 04	M	16 12 64	Bellshill	St Mirren BC	Queen's Park	82	7
							Celtic	6	—
							Dunfermline Ath	53	6
							Stoke C (loan)	2	—
							Nottingham F	—	—
							Reading (loan)	3	—
							Shrewsbury T	56	3
SMITH Martin	5 11	12 06	F	13 11 74	Sunderland	Trainee	**Sunderland**	64	18
SMITH Neil	5 9	12 00	M	30 9 71	London	Trainee	Tottenham H	—	—
							Gillingham	133	8
SMITH Nicky ‡	5 7	10 00	M	28 1 69	Berkley		Southend U	60	6
							Colchester U	81	4
							Wycombe W	—	—
						Sudbury	**Northampton T**	6	1
SMITH Paul			M	2 11 71	Lewisham	Horsham	**Barnet**	—	—
SMITH Paul	5 11	13 08	M	18 9 71	Lenham	Trainee	Southend U	20	1
							Brentford	67	6
SMITH Paul	6 0	12 08	F	22 1 76	Easington	Trainee	**Burnley**	1	—
SMITH Paul *	5 10	10 09	F	9 11 64	Rotherham	Apprentice	Sheffield U	36	1
							Stockport Co (loan)	7	5
							Port Vale	44	7
							Lincoln C	232	27
SMITH Paul	5 11	11 03	M	25 1 76	Hastings	Hastings	**Nottingham F**	—	—
SMITH Peter	6 0	12 01	D	12 7 69	Stone	Alma Swanley	**Brighton & HA**	38	1
SMITH Richard	6 0	12 10	D	3 10 70	Leicester	Trainee	**Leicester C**	97	1
							Cambridge U (loan)	4	—
SMITH Richard ‡	5 11	11 10	D	24 1 74	Lichfield	Trainee	**Nottingham F**	—	—
SMITH Scott	5 8	11 06	D	6 3 75	Christchurch	Trainee	**Rotherham U**	11	—
SMITH Shaun	5 10	11 00	D	9 4 71	Leeds	Trainee	Halifax T	7	—
							Crewe Alex	128	19
SMITH Tom			M	25 11 77	Northampton	Trainee	**Manchester U**	—	—
SMITH Tony *	5 11	11 09	D	21 9 71	Sunderland	Trainee	**Sunderland**	20	—
							Hartlepool U (loan)	5	—
SMITHARD Matthew	5 9	10 09	F	13 6 76	Leeds	Trainee	**Leeds U**	—	—
SNEEKES Richard	5 11	12 02	M	30 10 68	Amsterdam	Fortuna Sittard	**Bolton W**	38	6

Player	Ht	Wt	Pos	Birth Date	Birth Place	Source	Clubs	League App	League Gls
SNODIN Glynn *	5 6	11 00	D	14 2 60	Rotherham	Apprentice	Doncaster R	309	61
							Sheffield W	59	1
							Leeds U	94	10
							Oldham Ath (loan)	8	1
							Rotherham U	3	—
							Hearts	34	—
							Barnsley	25	—
SNODIN Ian	5 7	9 01	M	15 8 63	Rotherham	Apprentice	Doncaster R	188	25
							Leeds U	51	6
							Everton	148	3
							Sunderland (loan)	6	—
							Oldham Ath	17	—
SNOOK Eddie ‡	5 7	10 01	M	18 10 68	Washington	Apprentice	**Notts Co**	—	—
SOLOMAN Jason	6 0	12 02	M	6 10 70	Welwyn	Trainee	Watford	100	5
							Peterborough U (loan)	4	—
							Wycombe W	6	1
SOMMER Jurgen	6 4	15 12	G	27 2 64	New York		**Luton T**	80	—
							Brighton (loan)	1	—
							Torquay U (loan)	10	—
SOUTHALL Neville	6 1	12 01	G	16 9 58	Llandudno	Winsford	Bury	39	—
							Everton	494	—
							Port Vale (loan)	9	—
SOUTHALL Nicky	5 10	12 12	F	28 1 72	Teeside	Trainee	**Hartlepool U**	138	24
SOUTHGATE Gareth	5 10	12 03	M	3 9 70	Watford	Trainee	**Crystal Palace**	152	15
SOUTHON Jamie *	5 9	11 09	M	13 10 74	Hornchurch	Trainee	**Southend U**	1	—
SPACKMAN Nigel	6 1	13 02	M	2 12 60	Romsey	Andover	Bournemouth	119	10
							Chelsea	141	12
							Liverpool	51	—
							QPR	29	1
							Rangers	100	1
							Chelsea	51	—
SPARROW Paul	6 0	11 04	D	24 3 75	London	Trainee	**Crystal Palace**	—	—
SPEARING Tony	5 6	11 10	D	7 10 64	Romford	Apprentice	Norwich C	69	—
							Stoke C (loan)	9	—
							Oxford U (loan)	5	—
							Leicester C	73	1
							Plymouth Arg	35	—
							Peterborough U	89	1
SPEED Gary	5 9	12 10	M	8 9 69	Hawarden	Trainee	**Leeds U**	219	37
SPEEDIE David ‡	5 6	11 02	F	20 2 60	Glenrothes	Amateur	Barnsley	23	—
							Darlington	88	21
							Chelsea	162	47
							Coventry C	122	31
							Liverpool	12	6
							Blackburn R	36	23
							Southampton	11	—
							Birmingham C (loan)	10	2
							WBA (loan)	7	2
							West Ham U (loan)	11	4
							Leicester C	37	12
SPENCER John	5 6	10 00	F	11 9 70	Glasgow	Rangers Am BC	Rangers	—	—
							Morton (loan)	4	1
						Lisbung, HK	Rangers	13	2
							Chelsea	71	23
SPINK Dean	5 11	13 08	F	22 1 67	Birmingham	Halesowen	Aston Villa	—	—
							Scarborough (loan)	3	2
							Bury (loan)	6	1
							Shrewsbury T	198	42
SPINK Nigel	6 2	14 08	G	8 8 58	Chelmsford	Chelmsford C	**Aston Villa**	359	—
SPOONER Nicky	5 10	11 09	D	5 6 71	Manchester	Trainee	**Bolton W**	23	2

				Birth				League	
Player	Ht	Wt	Pos	Date	Place	Source	Clubs	App	Gls
SPOONER Steve ‡	5 10	12 00	M	25 1 61	London	Apprentice	Derby Co	8	—
							Halifax T	72	13
							Chesterfield	93	14
							Hereford U	84	19
							York C	72	11
							Rotherham U	19	1
							Mansfield T	58	3
							Blackpool	2	—
							Chesterfield	12	—
SQUIRES Jamie	6 1	12 00	D	15 11 75	Preston	Trainee	**Preston NE**	15	—
SRNICEK Pavel	6 2	14 09	G	10 3 68	Ostrava	Banik Ostrava	**Newcastle U**	111	—
STABB Chris §			D	12 10 76	Bradford	Trainee	**Bradford C**	1	—
STACKMAN Scott ‡	5 11	12 06	D	16 11 75	Arizona	Trainee	**Northampton T**	1	—
STALLARD Mark	6 0	12 04	F	24 10 74	Derby	Trainee	**Derby Co**	24	2
							Fulham (loan)	4	3
STAMP Philip	5 10	12 05	M	12 12 75	Middlesbrough	Trainee	**Middlesbrough**	13	—
STAMPS Scott	5 10	11 02	D	20 3 75	Edgbaston	Trainee	**Torquay U**	33	1
STANCLIFFE Paul *	6 2	13 04	D	5 5 58	Sheffield	Apprentice	Rotherham U	285	8
							Sheffield U	278	12
							Rotherham U (loan)	5	—
							Wolverhampton W	17	—
							York C	91	3
STANISLAUS Roger	5 11	13 02	D	2 11 68	Hammersmith	Trainee	Arsenal	—	—
							Brentford	111	4
							Bury	176	5
STANNARD Jim	6 2	16 06	G	6 10 62	London	Local	Fulham	41	—
							Charlton Ath (loan)	1	—
							Southend U (loan)	17	—
							Southend U	92	—
							Fulham	348	1
STANT Phil	6 1	12 07	F	13 10 62	Bolton	Camberley	Reading	4	2
						Army	Hereford U	89	38
							Notts Co	22	6
							Blackpool (loan)	12	5
							Lincoln C (loan)	4	—
							Huddersfield T (loan)	5	1
							Fulham	19	5
							Mansfield T	57	32
							Cardiff C	79	34
							Mansfield T (loan)	4	1
							Bury	20	13
STAPLETON Frank †	6 0	13 01	F	10 7 56	Dublin	Apprentice	Arsenal	225	75
							Manchester U	223	60
							Ajax	4	—
							Derby Co	10	1
						Le Havre	Blackburn R	81	13
							Aldershot	—	—
							Huddersfield T	5	—
							Bradford C	68	2
							Brighton	2	—
STAPLETON Simon	6 0	13 02	M	10 12 68	Oxford	Portsmouth	Bristol R	5	—
						Wycombe W	**Wycombe W**	48	3
STARBUCK Philip	5 10	10 13	F	24 11 68	Nottingham	Apprentice	Nottingham F	36	2
							Birmingham C (loan)	3	—
							Hereford U (loan)	6	—
							Blackburn R (loan)	6	1
							Huddersfield T	137	36
							Sheffield U	23	1
STARK Wayne §			M	14 10 76	Derby	Trainee	**Mansfield T**	1	—
STATHAM Brian	5 11	11 00	D	21 5 69	Zimbabwe	Apprentice	Tottenham H	24	—
							Reading (loan)	8	—
							Bournemouth (loan)	2	—
							Brentford (loan)	18	—
							Brentford	112	1
STATHAM Mark	6 2	12 02	G	11 11 75	Barnsley	Trainee	Nottingham F	—	—
							Wigan Ath	2	—

Player	Ht	Wt	Pos	Birth Date	Birth Place	Source	Clubs	League App	League Gls
STAUNTON Steve	6 0	12 04	D	19 1 69	Drogheda	Dundalk	Liverpool	65	—
							Bradford C (loan)	8	—
							Aston Villa	138	13
STEAD Carl			D	3 9 71	Hull	Doncaster R	**Scarborough**	—	—
STEADMAN Richard *			G	21 10 75	Birmingham	Trainee	**Birmingham C**	—	—
STEELE Tim	5 9	11 07	F	1 12 67	Coventry	Apprentice	Shrewsbury T	61	5
							Wolverhampton W	75	7
							Stoke C (loan)	7	1
							Bradford C	11	—
							Hereford U	25	2
STEIN Mark	5 6	11 02	F	28 1 66	S. Africa		Luton T	54	19
							Aldershot (loan)	2	1
							QPR	33	4
							Oxford U	82	18
							Stoke C	94	50
							Chelsea	42	21
STENSGAARD Michael	6 2	13 04	G	1 9 74	Denmark	Hvidovre	**Liverpool**	—	—
STEPHENSON Paul	5 10	12 02	M	2 1 68	Wallsend	Apprentice	Newcastle U	61	1
							Millwall	98	6
							Gillingham (loan)	12	2
							Brentford	70	2
STERLING Worrell	5 7	10 11	M	8 6 65	Bethnal Green	Apprentice	Watford	94	14
							Peterborough U	193	29
							Bristol R	89	6
STEVENS Gary	5 11	10 11	D	27 3 63	Barrow	Apprentice	Everton	208	8
							Rangers	187	8
							Tranmere R	37	1
STEVENS Ian	5 10	11 07	F	21 10 66	Malta	Trainee	Preston NE	11	2
							Stockport Co	2	—
						Lancaster C	Bolton W	47	7
							Bury	110	38
							Shrewsbury T	38	8
STEVENS Keith	6 0	12 12	D	21 6 64	Merton	Apprentice	**Millwall**	410	7
STEVENS Shaun	5 10	11 05	D	8 3 76	Chertsey		**Wycombe W**	—	—
STEWART Billy *	5 11	11 07	G	1 1 65	Liverpool	Apprentice	Liverpool	—	—
							Wigan Ath	14	—
							Chester C	272	—
							Northampton T	27	—
							Chesterfield (loan)	1	—
STEWART Marcus	5 10	10 06	F	7 11 72	Bristol	Trainee	**Bristol R**	127	36
STEWART Paul	5 11	12 04	M	7 10 64	Manchester	Apprentice	Blackpool	201	56
							Manchester C	51	26
							Tottenham H	131	28
							Liverpool	32	1
							Crystal Palace (loan)	18	3
							Wolverhampton W (loan)	8	2
							Burnley (loan)	6	—
STEWART Simon	6 1	12 08	D	1 11 73	Leeds	Trainee	**Sheffield W**	6	—
STIMSON Mark	5 11	11 00	D	27 12 67	Plaistow	Trainee	Tottenham H	2	—
							Leyton Orient (loan)	10	—
							Gillingham (loan)	18	—
							Newcastle U	86	2
							Portsmouth (loan)	4	—
							Portsmouth	44	1
STOCKWELL Mick	5 9	11 04	M	14 2 65	Chelmsford	Apprentice	**Ipswich T**	315	20
STOKER Gareth	5 9	10 03	M	22 2 73	Bishop Auckland	Leeds U	Hull C	30	2
							Hereford U	10	—
STOKES Dean	5 7	10 07	D	23 5 70	Birmingham	Halesowen	**Port Vale**	24	—
STOKOE Graham †	6 0	11 11	M	17 12 75	Newcastle	Birmingham C	**Stoke C**	—	—
STONE Steven	5 9	11 03	M	20 8 71	Gateshead	Trainee	**Nottingham F**	99	11

Player	Ht	Wt	Pos	Birth Date	Birth Place	Source	Clubs	League App	League Gls
STONEMAN Paul *	6 1	13 06	D	26 2 73	Whitley Bay	Trainee	**Blackpool**	43	—
							Colchester U (loan)	3	1
STORER Stuart	5 11	12 13	F	16 1 67	Harborough	Local	Mansfield T	1	—
							Birmingham C	8	—
							Everton	—	—
							Wigan Ath (loan)	12	—
							Bolton W	123	12
							Exeter C	77	8
							Brighton	2	1
STOWELL Mike	6 2	11 10	G	19 4 65	Preston	Leyland Motors	Preston NE	—	—
							Everton	—	—
							Chester C (loan)	14	—
							York C (loan)	6	—
							Manchester C (loan)	14	—
							Port Vale (loan)	7	—
							Wolverhampton W (loan)	7	—
							Preston NE (loan)	2	—
							Wolverhampton W	194	—
STRACHAN Gordon	5 6	10 06	M	9 2 57	Edinburgh		Dundee	60	13
							Aberdeen	183	55
							Manchester U	160	33
							Leeds U	197	37
							Coventry C	5	—
STRANDLI Frank ‡	5 10	12 07	F	16 5 72	Norway	IK Start	**Leeds U**	14	2
STRANEY Paul ‡	5 11	12 04	G	7 10 75	Downpatrick	Trainee	**Stoke C**	—	—
STRATFORD Lee	5 10	10 08	M	11 11 75	Barnsley	Trainee	**Nottingham F**	—	—
STREET Danny *			D	20 3 76	Cardiff	Trainee	**Cardiff C**	—	—
STRODDER Gary	6 1	12 06	D	1 4 65	Leeds	Apprentice	Lincoln C	132	6
							West Ham U	65	2
							WBA	140	8
STRONG Greg	6 2	11 12	D	5 9 75	Bolton	Trainee	**Wigan Ath**	35	3
STRONG Steve §			F	15 3 78	Watford	Trainee	**Bournemouth**	1	—
STUART Graham	5 9	11 06	F	24 10 70	Tooting, London	Trainee	Chelsea	87	14
							Everton	58	6
STUART Jamie	5 10	11 00	D	15 10 76	Southwark	Trainee	**Charlton Ath**	12	—
STUART Mark	5 10	11 03	D	15 12 66	Hammersmith	QPR	Charlton Ath	107	28
							Plymouth Arg	57	11
							Ipswich T (loan)	5	2
							Bradford C	29	5
							Huddersfield T	15	3
							Rochdale	73	15
STUBBS Alan	6 2	13 10	D	6 10 71	Kirkby	Trainee	**Bolton W**	177	5
STURGESS Paul	5 11	12 05	D	4 8 75	Dartford	Trainee	**Charlton Ath**	35	—
STURRIDGE Dean	5 8	12 01	F	27 7 73	Birmingham	Trainee	**Derby Co**	23	1
							Torquay U (loan)	10	5
STURRIDGE Simon	5 5	10 13	F	9 12 69	Birmingham	Trainee	Birmingham C	150	30
							Stoke C	21	1
SUCKLING Perry	6 2	13 02	G	12 10 65	Leyton	Apprentice	Coventry C	27	—
							Manchester C	39	—
							Crystal Palace	59	—
							West Ham U (loan)	6	—
							Brentford (loan)	8	—
							Watford	39	—
							Doncaster R	9	—
SULLEY Chris *	5 8	10 00	D	3 12 59	Camberwell	Apprentice	Chelsea	—	—
							Bournemouth	206	3
							Dundee U	7	—
							Blackburn R	134	3
							Port Vale	40	1
							Preston NE	21	1
SULLIVAN Neil	6 0	12 01	G	24 2 70	Sutton	Trainee	**Wimbledon**	16	—
							Crystal Palace (loan)	1	—

				Birth				League	
Player	Ht	Wt	Pos	Date	Place	Source	Clubs	App	Gls
SUMMERBEE Nicky	5 11	11 08	F	26 8 71	Altrincham	Trainee	Swindon T	112	6
							Manchester C	41	1
SUMMERFIELD Kevin	5 11	11 00	M	7 1 59	Walsall	Apprentice	WBA	9	4
							Birmingham C	5	1
							Walsall	54	17
							Cardiff C	10	1
							Plymouth Arg	139	26
							Exeter C (loan)	4	—
							Shrewsbury T	162	22
SUNDERLAND Jonathan			M	2 11 75	Newcastle	Trainee	**Blackpool**	2	—
SUNLEY Mark ‡	6 1	12 07	D	13 10 71	Stockton		Middlesbrough	—	—
							Darlington	35	—
							Hartlepool U	2	—
SUSSEX Andy	6 3	13 08	M	23 11 64	Islington	Apprentice	Orient	144	17
							Crewe Alex	102	24
							Southend U	74	14
SUTCH Daryl	6 0	12 00	M	11 9 71	Lowestoft	Trainee	**Norwich C**	68	3
SUTTON Chris	6 3	13 05	F	10 3 73	Nottingham	Trainee	Norwich C	102	35
							Blackburn R	40	15
SUTTON Steve	6 1	14 11	G	16 4 61	Hartington	Apprentice	Nottingham F	199	—
							Mansfield T (loan)	8	—
							Derby Co (loan)	14	—
							Coventry C (loan)	1	—
							Luton T (loan)	14	—
							Derby Co	55	—
SUTTON Wayne	6 0	13 02	D	1 10 75	Derby	Trainee	**Derby Co**	6	—
SWAILES Chris	6 2	12 07	D	19 10 70	Gateshead	Bridlington T	Doncaster R	49	—
							Ipswich T	4	—
SWALES Steve	5 8	10 03	D	26 12 73	Whitby	Trainee	**Scarborough**	54	1
SWAN Peter	6 2	14 12	D	28 9 66	Leeds	Local	Leeds U	49	11
							Hull C	80	24
							Port Vale	111	5
							Plymouth Arg	27	2
SWANN Gary ‡	5 11	11 13	M	11 4 62	York	Apprentice	Hull C	186	9
							Preston NE	199	37
							York C	82	4
							Scarborough	27	3
SWEENEY Paul ‡	5 8	11 5	M	10 1 65	Glasgow	St Kentigern's Acad	Raith R	205	8
							Newcastle U	36	—
							St Johnstone	10	—
							Hartlepool U	1	—
SWEETMAN Nicky ‡	5 8	11 00	M	21 10 74	Herts	Trainee	**Leyton Orient**	—	—
SYKES Paul	6 0	10 05	D	13 1 77	Pontefract	Trainee	**Sheffield W**	—	—
SYMONS Kit	6 1	11 00	D	8 3 71	Basingstoke	Trainee	**Portsmouth**	160	10
SYMONS Paul	5 11	12 00	F	20 4 76	North Shields	Trainee	**Blackpool**	1	—
TAGGART Gerry	6 1	13 12	D	18 10 70	Belfast	Trainee	Manchester C	12	1
							Barnsley	212	16
TAIT Mick	5 11	12 05	M	30 9 56	Wallsend	Apprentice	Oxford U	64	23
							Carlisle U	106	20
							Hull C	33	3
							Portsmouth	240	30
							Reading	99	9
							Darlington	79	2
							Hartlepool U	81	1
TAIT Paul	6 1	10 00	M	31 1 71	Sutton Coldfield	Trainee	**Birmingham C**	117	11
							Millwall (loan)	—	—
TAIT Paul *	5 8	10 10	F	24 10 74	Newcastle	Trainee	Everton	—	—
							Wigan Ath	5	—
TALBOT Stuart			F	14 6 73	Birmingham	Moor Green	**Port Vale**	2	—
TALBOYS Steve	5 11	11 10	M	18 9 66	Bristol	Gloucester C	**Wimbledon**	21	1

Player	Ht	Wt	Pos	Birth Date	Birth Place	Source	Clubs	League App	League Gls
TALIA Frank	6 1	13 06	G	20 7 72	Melbourne	Sunshine George Cross	**Blackburn R**	—	—
							Hartlepool U (loan)	14	—
TALLON Gary	5 11	11 07	F	5 9 73	Drogheda	Trainee	**Blackburn R**	—	—
TANKARD Allen	5 10	11 07	D	21 5 69	Fleet	Trainee	Southampton	5	—
							Wigan Ath	209	4
							Port Vale	65	1
TANNER Adam	6 0	12 01	M	25 10 73	Maldon	Trainee	**Ipswich T**	10	2
TARICCO Mauricio	5 8	11 05	D	10 3 73	Buenos Aires	Argentinos J	**Ipswich T**	—	—
TAYLOR Bob	5 10	11 09	F	3 2 67	Horden	Horden CW	Leeds U	42	9
							Bristol C	106	50
							WBA	149	67
TAYLOR Gareth	6 2	12 05	F	25 2 73	Weston-Super-Mare	Southampton	**Bristol R**	40	12
TAYLOR Ian	6 2	11 06	M	4 6 68	Birmingham	Moor Green	Port Vale	83	28
							Sheffield W	14	1
							Aston Villa	22	1
TAYLOR Jamie	5 6	9 12	F	11 1 77	Bury	Trainee	**Rochdale**	19	1
TAYLOR John	6 3	13 06	F	24 10 64	Norwich	Local	Colchester U	—	—
						Sudbury	Cambridge U	160	46
							Bristol R	95	44
							Bradford C	36	11
							Luton T	9	3
TAYLOR Mark ‡	6 2	13 10	D	8 11 74	Saltburn	Trainee	**Middlesbrough**	—	—
							Darlington (loan)	8	—
TAYLOR Mark	5 8	11 08	M	22 2 66	Walsall	Local	Walsall	113	4
							Sheffield W	9	—
							Shrewsbury T (loan)	19	2
							Shrewsbury T	156	11
TAYLOR Mark ‡	5 7	11 08	M	20 11 64	Hartlepool	Local	Hartlepool U	47	4
							Crewe Alex (loan)	3	—
							Blackpool	100	40
							Cardiff C (loan)	6	3
							Wrexham	61	9
TAYLOR Martin	6 0	13 06	G	9 12 66	Tamworth	Mile Oak R	**Derby Co**	94	—
							Carlisle U (loan)	10	—
							Scunthorpe U (loan)	8	—
TAYLOR Matthew	5 7	11 12	D	6 3 76	Maidstone	Trainee	**Burnley**	—	—
TAYLOR Robert	6 1	13 08	F	30 4 71	Norwich	Trainee	Norwich C	—	—
							Leyton Orient (loan)	3	1
							Birmingham C	—	—
							Leyton Orient	73	20
							Brentford	48	25
TAYLOR Scott	5 10	11 04	F	5 5 76	Chertsey	Staines	**Millwall**	6	—
TAYLOR Scott	5 10	10 00	M	28 11 70	Portsmouth	Trainee	**Reading**	207	24
TAYLOR Shaun	6 1	13 00	D	26 2 63	Plymouth	Bideford	Exeter C	200	16
							Swindon T	167	23
TEALE Shaun	6 0	13 10	D	10 3 64	Southport	Weymouth	Bournemouth	100	4
							Aston Villa	147	2
TEATHER Paul			M	26 12 77	Rotherham	Trainee	**Manchester U**	—	—
TEE Jason *	5 8	11 05	F	28 9 75	Sheffield	Trainee	**Sheffield U**	—	—
TELFER Paul	5 9	11 06	M	21 10 71	Edinburgh	Trainee	**Luton T**	144	19
THACKERAY Andy	5 9	11 00	M	13 2 68	Huddersfield		Manchester C	—	—
							Huddersfield T	2	—
							Newport Co	54	4
							Wrexham	152	14
							Rochdale	119	13
THATCHER Ben	5 10	12 07	D	30 11 75	Swindon	Trainee	**Millwall**	48	1
THEW Lee ‡	5 10	11 05	M	23 10 74	Sunderland	Trainee	**Doncaster R**	32	2

Player	Ht	Wt	Pos	Birth Date	Place	Source	Clubs	League App	Gls
THIRLBY Anthony	5 9	11 00	M	4 3 76	Germany	Trainee	**Exeter C**	37	2
THOM Stuart	6 2	11 08	D	27 12 76	Dewsbury	Trainee	**Nottingham F**	—	—
THOMAS Brian ‡	5 10	12 00	G	7 6 76	Neath	Trainee	**Hereford U**	3	—
THOMAS David †	5 10	11 07	F	26 9 75	Caerphilly	Trainee	**Swansea C**	4	—
THOMAS Dean *	5 10	11 08	D	19 12 61	Bedworth	Nuneaton Borough	Wimbledon	57	8
						Fortuna Dusseldorf	Northampton T	74	11
							Notts Co	134	8
THOMAS Geoff	5 10	10 07	M	5 8 64	Manchester	Local	Rochdale	11	1
							Crewe Alex	125	20
							Crystal Palace	195	26
							Wolverhampton W	22	5
THOMAS Glen	6 1	12 07	D	6 10 67	Hackney	Apprentice	Fulham	251	6
							Peterborough U	8	—
							Barnet	7	—
THOMAS Mark	5 9	10 10	M	22 11 74	Tooting	Trainee	**Wimbledon**	—	—
THOMAS Martin	5 8	10 08	F	12 9 73	Lyndhurst	Trainee	Southampton	—	—
							Leyton Orient	5	2
							Fulham	23	3
THOMAS Michael	5 9	12 06	M	24 8 67	Lambeth	Apprentice	Arsenal	163	24
							Portsmouth (loan)	3	—
							Liverpool	55	4
THOMAS Mitchell	6 2	12 00	D	2 10 64	Luton	Apprentice	Luton T	107	1
							Tottenham H	157	6
							West Ham U	38	3
							Luton T	56	1
THOMAS Rod	5 7	11 00	F	10 10 70	London	Trainee	Watford	84	9
							Gillingham (loan)	8	1
							Carlisle U	74	15
THOMAS Scott	5 9	10 08	M	30 10 74	Bury	Trainee	**Manchester C**	2	—
THOMAS Tony	5 11	12 05	D	12 7 71	Liverpool	Trainee	**Tranmere R**	196	12
THOMPSON Adrian			G	13 3 77	Sydney		**Walsall**	—	—
THOMPSON Alan	6 0	12 08	M	22 12 73	Newcastle	Trainee	Newcastle U	16	—
							Bolton W	64	13
THOMPSON Andy	5 4	10 06	D	9 11 67	Cannock	Apprentice	WBA	24	1
							Wolverhampton W	299	35
THOMPSON David	6 1	12 07	D	20 11 68	Ashington	Trainee	Millwall	92	6
							Bristol C	17	—
							Brentford	10	1
							Blackpool	17	—
							Cambridge U	7	—
THOMPSON David	5 7	10 00	M	12 9 77	Berkenhead	Trainee	**Liverpool**	—	—
THOMPSON David	5 7	11 12	D	27 5 62	Manchester	Local	Rochdale	155	13
							Manchester U (loan)	—	—
							Notts Co	55	8
							Wigan Ath	108	14
							Preston NE	46	4
							Chester C	80	9
							Rochdale	40	6
THOMPSON Garry	6 1	14 00	F	7 10 59	Birmingham	Apprentice	Coventry C	134	38
							WBA	91	39
							Sheffield W	36	7
							Aston Villa	60	17
							Watford	34	8
							Crystal Palace	20	3
							QPR	19	1
							Cardiff C	43	5
							Northampton T	15	4
THOMPSON Gary ‡	6 0	11 10	F	7 9 72	Ipswich		**Ipswich T**	—	—
THOMPSON Ian *	5 11	12 04	M	17 2 75	Leicester	Trainee	**Leicester C**	—	—

Player	Ht	Wt	Pos	Birth Date	Birth Place	Source	Clubs	League App	League Gls
THOMPSON Neil	5 11	13 08	D	2 10 63	Beverley	Nottingham F	Hull C	31	—
						Scarborough	Scarborough	87	15
							Ipswich T	201	18
THOMPSON Niall *	5 11	11 00	F	16 4 74	Birmingham	Trainee	Crystal Palace	—	—
							Colchester U	13	5
THOMPSON Paul *	5 11	11 13	F	17 4 73	Newcastle	Trainee	**Hartlepool U**	56	9
THOMPSON Simon *	5 9	10 06	D	7 1 68	Sheffield	Trainee	Rotherham U	28	—
							Scarborough	108	6
THOMPSON Steve	5 11	13 00	M	2 11 64	Oldham	Apprentice	Bolton W	335	49
							Luton T	5	—
							Leicester C	127	18
							Burnley	12	—
THOMPSON Steve	5 7	11 09	M	12 1 63	Plymouth	Slough	**Wycombe W**	62	3
THOMPSTONE Ian *	6 0	13 00	F	17 1 71	Manchester	Trainee	Manchester C	1	1
							Oldham Ath	—	—
							Exeter C	15	3
							Halifax T	31	9
							Scunthorpe U	60	8
THOMSEN Claus	6 3	13 06	M	31 5 70	Aarhus	Aarhus	**Ipswich T**	33	5
THOMSON Andrew	6 3	14 12	D	28 3 74	Swindon	Trainee	**Swindon T**	22	—
THOMSON Andy	5 10	10 07	F	1 4 71	Motherwell	Jerviston BC	Q of S	175	93
							Southend U	39	11
THOMSON Martin ‡	5 10	11 08	D	3 10 74	Bradford	Trainee	**Sheffield U**	—	—
THORN Andy	6 0	11 05	D	12 11 66	Carshalton	Apprentice	Wimbledon	107	2
							Newcastle U	36	2
							Crystal Palace	128	3
							Wimbledon	23	1
THORNBER Stephen	5 9	11 08	M	11 10 65	Dewsbury	Local	Halifax T	104	4
							Swansea C	117	6
							Blackpool	24	—
							Scunthorpe U	61	7
THORNE Peter	6 0	12 10	F	21 6 73	Manchester	Trainee	Blackburn R	—	—
							Wigan Ath (loan)	11	—
							Swindon T	20	9
THORNLEY Ben	5 8	11 04	F	21 4 75	Bury	Trainee	**Manchester U**	1	—
THORNLEY Timothy §			G	3 3 77	Leicester	Trainee	**Torquay U**	1	—
THORP Michael			D	5 12 75	Wallington	Trainee	**Reading**	—	—
THORPE Jeff	5 10	12 09	M	17 11 72	Whitehaven	Trainee	**Carlisle U**	97	5
THORPE Lee	6 0	11 06	F	14 12 75	Wolverhampton	Trainee	**Blackpool**	2	—
THORPE Tony	5 9	12 00	F	10 4 74	Leicester	Leicester C	**Luton T**	18	1
THORSTVEDT Erik	6 4	14 03	G	28 10 62	Stavanger	IFK Gothenburg	**Tottenham H**	173	—
TIERNEY Francis	5 10	10 12	M	10 9 75	Liverpool	Trainee	**Crewe Alex**	29	5
TILER Carl	6 2	13 00	D	11 2 70	Sheffield	Trainee	Barnsley	71	3
							Nottingham F	69	1
							Swindon T (loan)	2	—
TILLSON Andy	6 2	12 07	D	30 6 66	Huntingdon	Kettering T	Grimsby T	105	5
							QPR	29	2
							Grimsby T (loan)	4	—
							Bristol R	82	2
TILSON Steve	5 11	12 06	M	27 7 66	Wickford	Burnham	**Southend U**	183	22
							Brentford (loan)	2	—
TIMONS Chris	6 0	12 04	D	8 12 74	Longworth	Clipstone W	**Mansfield T**	22	1
TINKLER Mark	5 11	13 03	M	24 10 74	Bishop Auckland	Trainee	**Leeds U**	13	—
TINNION Brian	5 11	11 05	D	23 2 68	Stanley	Apprentice	Newcastle U	32	2
							Bradford C	145	22
							Bristol C	87	9

Player	Ht	Wt	Pos	Birth Date	Birth Place	Source	Clubs	League App	League Gls
TISDALE Paul	5 9	11 09	M	14 1 73	Malta	School	**Southampton**	7	—
							Northampton T (loan)	5	—
TITTERTON David *	5 11	13 08	D	25 9 71	Hatton	Trainee	Coventry C	2	—
							Hereford U	51	1
							Wycombe W	19	1
TODD Andy	5 10	11 12	D	21 9 74	Derby	Trainee	**Middlesbrough**	8	—
							Swindon T (loan)	13	—
TODD Lee	5 5	10 03	D	7 3 72	Hartlepool	Hartlepool U	**Stockport Co**	142	2
TODD Mark	5 9	10 04	M	4 12 67	Belfast	Trainee	Manchester U	—	—
							Sheffield U	70	5
							Wolverhampton W (loan)	7	—
							Rotherham U	64	7
TOLSON Neil	6 3	11 05	F	25 10 73	Wordley	Trainee	Walsall	9	1
							Oldham Ath	3	—
							Bradford C	32	4
							Chester C (loan)	4	—
TOMAN Andy	5 10	11 07	M	7 3 62	Northallerton	Bishop Auckland	Lincoln C	24	4
							Hartlepool U	112	28
							Darlington	115	10
							Scarborough (loan)	6	—
							Scunthorpe U	15	5
							Scarborough	29	1
TOMLINSON Graeme	5 9	11 05	F	10 12 75	Watford	Trainee	Bradford C	17	6
							Manchester U	—	—
TOMLINSON Michael	5 9	11 00	M	15 9 72	Lambeth	Trainee	Leyton Orient	14	1
							Barnet	38	1
TOMLINSON Paul	6 2	14 04	G	22 2 64	Brierley Hill	Middlewood R	Sheffield U	37	—
							Birmingham C (loan)	11	—
							Bradford C	293	—
TORFASON Gudmundor ‡	6 1	13 02	F	13 12 61	Westann Isles	RSC Genk	St Mirren	76	24
							St Johnstone	39	9
							Doncaster R	4	—
TORPEY Steve	6 3	14 13	F	8 12 70	Islington	Trainee	Millwall	7	—
							Bradford C	96	22
							Swansea C	81	20
TOTTEN Alex	5 8	10 07	M	1 10 76	Southampton	Trainee	**Portsmouth**	4	—
TOVEY Paul	5 8	11 07	M	5 12 73	Wokingham	Trainee	**Bristol R**	1	—
TOWN David			F	9 12 76	Bournemouth	Trainee	**Bournemouth**	6	—
TOWNLEY Leon	6 2	12 09	D	16 2 76	Loughton	Trainee	**Tottenham H**	—	—
TOWNSEND Andy	5 11	12 07	M	23 7 63	Maidstone	Weymouth	Southampton	83	5
							Norwich C	71	8
							Chelsea	110	12
							Aston Villa	64	4
TRACEY Simon	6 0	12 00	G	9 12 67	Woolwich	Apprentice	Wimbledon	1	—
							Sheffield U	143	—
							Manchester C (loan)	3	—
							Norwich C (loan)	1	—
TREBBLE Neil	6 3	13 10	F	16 2 69	Hitchin	Stevenage Bor	Scunthorpe U	14	2
							Preston NE	19	4
							Scarborough	15	3
TRETTON Andrew	6 1	12 07	D	9 10 76	Derby	Trainee	**Derby Co**	—	—
TREVITT Simon	5 11	11 10	D	20 12 67	Dewsbury	Apprentice	**Huddersfield T**	225	3
TRINDER Jason	5 11	14 00	G	3 3 70	Leicester	Grimsby T	**Mansfield T**	7	—
TROLLOPE Paul	6 0	12 05	M	3 6 72	Swindon	Trainee	Swindon T	—	—
							Torquay U (loan)	10	—
							Torquay U	96	16
							Derby Co	24	4
TROTT Dean *	6 2	14 00	F	13 5 67	Barnsley	Boston U	**Northampton T**	22	4
TROTT Robin *	6 1	13 04	D	17 8 74	Orpington	Trainee	**Gillingham**	10	—

Player	Ht	Wt	Pos	Birth Date	Birth Place	Source	Clubs	League App	League Gls
TUCK Stuart	5 11	11 07	D	1 10 74	Brighton	Trainee	**Brighton**	34	—
TURNBULL Lee	6 0	12 08	M	27 9 67	Stockton	Local	Middlesbrough	16	4
							Aston Villa	—	—
							Doncaster R	123	21
							Chesterfield	87	26
							Doncaster R	11	1
							Wycombe W	11	1
							Scunthorpe U (loan)	10	3
TURNER Andy	5 10	11 07	M	23 5 75	Woolwich	Trainee	**Tottenham H**	20	3
							Wycombe W (loan)	4	—
							Doncaster R (loan)	4	1
TURNER Chris *	5 11	11 12	G	15 9 58	Sheffield	Apprentice	Sheffield W	91	—
							Lincoln C (loan)	5	—
							Sunderland	195	—
							Manchester U	64	—
							Sheffield W	75	—
							Leeds U (loan)	2	—
							Leyton Orient	58	—
TURNER Darren	5 3	8 00	M	23 12 77	Derby	Trainee	**Nottingham F**	—	—
TURNER Mark	6 0	11 01	M	4 10 72	Bebbington	Trainee	Wolverhampton W	1	—
							Northampton T	4	—
TURNER Phil	5 9	10 13	M	12 2 62	Sheffield	Apprentice	Lincoln C	241	19
							Grimsby T	62	8
							Leicester C	24	2
							Notts Co	225	15
TURNER Robert	6 3	14 01	M	18 9 66	Durham	Apprentice	Huddersfield T	1	—
							Cardiff C	39	8
							Hartlepool U (loan)	7	1
							Bristol R	26	2
							Wimbledon	10	—
							Bristol C	52	12
							Plymouth Arg	66	17
							Notts Co	8	1
							Shrewsbury T (loan)	9	—
							Exeter C	33	4
TURPIN Simon			D	11 8 75	Blackburn		**Crewe Alex**	—	—
TUTILL Steve	6 1	12 06	D	1 10 69	Derwent	Trainee	**York C**	259	6
TUTTLE David	6 2	12 10	D	6 2 72	Reading	Trainee	Tottenham H	13	—
							Peterborough U (loan)	7	—
							Sheffield U	37	—
TWIDDY Chris	5 11	11 06	M	19 1 76	Pontyridd	Trainee	**Plymouth Arg**	15	1
TWYNHAM Gary ‡	6 0	12 01	M	8 2 76	Manchester	Trainee	**Manchester U**	—	—
TYLER Mark	6 0	12 09	G	2 4 77	Norwich	Trainee	**Peterborough U**	5	—
ULLATHORNE Robert	5 8	10 10	M	11 10 71	Wakefield	Trainee	**Norwich C**	65	7
UNSWORTH David	6 0	14 07	F	16 10 73	Preston	Trainee	**Everton**	51	4
UNSWORTH Lee			D	25 2 73	Eccles	Ashton U	**Crewe Alex**	—	—
VALENTINE Peter	5 10	12 00	D	16 6 63	Huddersfield	Apprentice	Huddersfield T	19	1
							Bolton W	68	1
							Bury	319	16
							Carlisle U	29	2
							Rochdale	27	2
VAN BLERK Jason	6 0	13 00	M	16 3 68	Sydney	Go Ahead Eagles	**Millwall**	27	1
VAN DEN HAUWE Pat ‡	5 11	11 10	D	16 12 60	Dendermonde	Apprentice	Birmingham C	123	1
							Everton	135	2
							Tottenham H	116	—
							Millwall	27	—
VAN DER LAAN Robin	5 11	12 05	F	5 9 68	Schiedam	Wageningen	**Port Vale**	176	24
VAN HEUSDEN Arjan	6 0	12 00	G	11 12 72	Alphen	Noordwijk	**Port Vale**	2	—

Player	Ht	Wt	Pos	Birth Date	Birth Place	Source	Clubs	League App	League Gls
VARADI Imre ‡	5 9	12 03	F	8 7 59	Paddington	Letchworth GC	Sheffield U	10	4
							Everton	26	6
							Newcastle U	81	39
							Sheffield W	76	33
							WBA	32	9
							Manchester C	65	26
							Sheffield W	22	3
							Leeds U	26	5
							Luton T (loan)	6	1
							Oxford U (loan)	5	—
							Rotherham U	67	25
VAUGHAN John	5 10	13 01	G	26 6 64	Isleworth	Apprentice	West Ham U	—	—
							Charlton Ath (loan)	6	—
							Bristol R (loan)	6	—
							Wrexham (loan)	4	—
							Bristol C (loan)	2	—
							Fulham	44	—
							Bristol C (loan)	3	—
							Cambridge U	178	—
							Charlton Ath	6	—
							Preston NE	26	—
VAUGHAN Tony	6 1	11 02	D	11 10 75	Manchester	Trainee	**Ipswich T**	10	—
VEART Carl	5 10	11 05	F	21 5 70	Whyalla	Adelaide C	**Sheffield U**	39	10
VENISON Barry	5 10	11 09	D	16 8 64	Consett	Apprentice	Sunderland	173	2
							Liverpool	110	1
							Newcastle U	109	1
VENUS Mark	6 0	11 08	D	6 4 67	Hartlepool		Hartlepool U	4	—
							Leicester C	61	1
							Wolverhampton W	225	7
VERVEER Etienne ‡	5 11	11 12	M	22 9 67	Surinam	Chur	**Millwall**	56	7
							Bradford C (loan)	9	1
VICK Leigh §			M	8 1 78	Cardiff	Trainee	**Cardiff C**	2	—
VICKERS Steve	6 1	12 12	D	13 10 67	Bishop Auckland	Spennymoor U	Tranmere R	311	11
							Middlesbrough	70	6
VICTORY Jamie *	5 10	12 00	D	14 11 75	London	Trainee	**West Ham U**	—	—
VIER Matthew *	5 10	12 00	M	6 6 76	Welwyn	Trainee	**Watford**	—	—
VINCENT Jamie	5 10	11 09	D	18 6 75	London	Trainee	**Crystal Palace**	—	—
							Bournemouth (loan)	8	—
VINNICOMBE Chris	5 9	10 04	M	20 10 70	Exeter		Exeter C	39	1
							Rangers	23	1
							Burnley	29	1
VIVEASH Adrian	6 1	11 02	D	30 9 69	Swindon	Trainee	**Swindon T**	54	2
							Reading (loan)	5	—
							Reading (loan)	6	—
VOICE Scott *	6 0	11 10	F	12 8 74	Wolverhampton	Trainee	**Wolverhampton W**	—	—
VONK Michael	6 3	13 03	D	28 10 68	Alkmaar	SVV/Dordrecht	**Manchester C**	91	3
VOWDEN Colin	6 0	13 00	D	13 9 71	Newmarket	Cambridge C	**Cambridge U**	—	—
WADDLE Chris	6 2	12 13	F	14 12 60	Hedworth	Tow Law T	Newcastle U	170	46
							Tottenham H	138	33
							Marseille	107	22
							Sheffield W	77	8
WADDOCK Gary	5 10	11 12	M	17 3 62	Alperton	Apprentice	QPR	203	8
						Charleroi	Millwall	58	2
							QPR	—	—
							Swindon T (loan)	6	—
							Bristol R	71	1
							Luton T	40	1
WADE Shaun ‡			F	22 9 69	Stoke	Newcastle T	**Stoke C**	1	—
WALDOCK John *	5 10	11 01	D	27 11 75	North Shields	Trainee	**Sunderland**	—	—

Player	Ht	Wt	Pos	Birth Date	Birth Place	Source	Clubs	League App	League Gls
WALKER Alan ‡	6 2	12 11	D	17 12 59	Mossley	Telford U	Lincoln C	75	4
							Millwall	92	8
							Gillingham	151	7
							Plymouth Arg	2	1
							Mansfield T	22	1
							Barnet	59	2
WALKER Des	5 11	11 09	D	26 11 65	Hackney	Apprentice	Nottingham F	264	1
							Sampdoria	30	—
							Sheffield W	80	—
WALKER Ian	6 2	12 09	G	31 10 71	Watford	Trainee	**Tottenham H**	88	—
							Oxford U (loan)	2	—
							Ipswich T (loan)	—	—
WALKER James	5 11	13 00	G	9 7 73	Sutton-in-Ashfield	Trainee	Notts Co	—	—
							Walsall	35	—
WALKER Justin	5 10	11 08	M	6 9 75	Nottingham	Trainee	**Nottingham F**	—	—
WALKER Keith	6 0	12 08	M	17 4 66	Edinburgh	ICI Juveniles	Stirling Albion	91	17
							St Mirren	43	6
							Swansea C	166	5
WALKER Ray	5 10	11 12	M	28 9 63	North Shields	Apprentice	Aston Villa	23	—
							Port Vale (loan)	15	1
							Port Vale	299	33
WALKER Richard §			M	14 3 77	Cambridge	Trainee	**Cambridge U**	5	—
WALKER Richard	6 0	12 00	D	9 11 71	Derby	Trainee	**Notts Co**	40	4
							Mansfield T (loan)	4	—
WALLACE Danny *	5 4	10 04	F	21 1 64	London	Apprentice	Southampton	255	64
							Manchester U	47	6
							Millwall (loan)	3	—
							Birmingham C	16	2
							Wycombe W	1	—
WALLACE Michael *	5 8	10 02	M	5 10 70	Farnworth	Trainee	Manchester C	—	—
							Stockport Co	70	5
WALLACE Ray	5 6	10 02	D	2 10 69	Lewisham	Trainee	Southampton	35	—
							Leeds U	7	—
							Swansea C (loan)	2	—
							Reading (loan)	3	—
							Stoke C	20	1
							Hull C (loan)	7	—
WALLACE Rodney	5 7	11 03	F	2 10 69	Lewisham	Trainee	Southampton	128	45
							Leeds U	135	39
WALLEY Mark	5 10	10 06	F	17 9 76	Barnsley	Trainee	**Nottingham F**	—	—
WALLING Dean	5 11	11 04	D	17 4 69	Leeds		Leeds U	—	—
							Rochdale	65	8
						Guiseley	**Carlisle U**	141	17
WALLWORK Ronald			D	10 9 77	Manchester	Trainee	**Manchester U**	—	—
WALSH Alan ‡	6 0	12 08	D	9 12 56	Darlington	Horden CW	Middlesbrough	3	—
							Darlington	251	87
							Bristol C	218	77
						Besiktas	Walsall	4	—
						Glenavon	Huddersfield T	4	—
							Shrewsbury T	2	—
							Cardiff C	1	—
							Southampton	—	—
						Taunton	**Hartlepool U**	4	1
WALSH Colin	5 9	11 00	M	22 7 62	Hamilton	Apprentice	Nottingham F	139	32
							Charlton Ath	236	21
							Peterborough U (loan)	5	1
							Middlesbrough (loan)	13	1
WALSH Gary	6 3	15 10	G	21 3 68	Wigan	Apprentice	**Manchester U**	50	—
							Airdrie (loan)	3	—
							Oldham Ath (loan)	6	—
WALSH Michael §			D	5 8 77	Rotherham	Trainee	**Scunthorpe U**	3	—

Player	Ht	Wt	Pos	Birth Date	Birth Place	Source	Clubs	League App	League Gls
WALSH Paul	5 7	10 08	F	1 10 62	Plumstead	Apprentice	Charlton Ath	87	24
							Luton T	80	24
							Liverpool	77	25
							Tottenham H	128	19
							QPR (loan)	2	—
							Portsmouth	73	14
							Manchester C	50	16
WALSH Steve	6 3	14 05	D	3 11 64	Fulwood	Local	Wigan Ath	126	4
							Leicester C	250	41
WALTERS Mark	5 9	11 08	M	2 6 64	Birmingham	Apprentice	Aston Villa	181	39
							Rangers	106	32
							Liverpool	94	14
							Stoke C (loan)	9	2
							Wolverhampton W (loan)	11	3
WALTERS Scott ‡	5 10	11 06	F	23 9 75	Hemel Hempstead	Watford	**Colchester U**	—	—
WALTERS Steve ‡	5 10	11 08	F	9 1 72	Plymouth	Trainee	**Crewe Alex**	146	10
WALTON David	6 2	13 04	D	10 4 73	Bedlingham	Trainee	Sheffield U	—	—
							Shrewsbury T	63	8
WANLESS Paul *	6 0	13 04	M	14 12 73	Banbury	Trainee	**Oxford U**	32	—
WARBURTON Ray	6 0	12 09	D	7 10 67	Rotherham	Apprentice	Rotherham U	4	—
							York C	90	9
							Northampton T (loan)	17	1
							Northampton T	39	3
WARD Ashley	6 1	11 07	F	24 11 70	Manchester	Trainee	Manchester C	1	—
							Wrexham (loan)	4	2
							Leicester C	10	—
							Blackpool (loan)	2	1
							Crewe Alex	61	25
							Norwich C	25	8
WARD Darren	5 11	13 00	G	11 5 74	Worksop	Trainee	**Mansfield T**	81	—
WARD Gavin	6 3	14 12	G	30 6 70	Sutton Coldfield	Aston Villa	Shrewsbury T	—	—
							WBA	—	—
							Cardiff C	59	—
							Leicester C	38	—
WARD Mark	5 6	9 12	M	10 10 62	Prescot	Northwich Vic	Oldham Ath	84	12
							West Ham U	165	12
							Manchester C	55	14
							Everton	83	6
							Birmingham C (loan)	9	1
							Birmingham C	41	3
WARD Mitch	5 8	10 12	M	19 6 71	Sheffield	Trainee	**Sheffield U**	72	5
							Crewe Alex (loan)	4	1
WARD Peter	6 0	11 10	F	15 10 64	Durham	Chester-le-Street	Huddersfield T	37	2
							Rochdale	84	10
							Stockport Co	142	10
WARD Richard ‡	5 8	11 00	M	17 11 73	Scarborough	Trainee	Notts Co	—	—
							Scarborough	—	—
							Huddersfield T	—	—
WARD Richard			M	6 1 77	Middlesbrough	Trainee	**Middlesbrough**	—	—
WARE Paul	5 9	11 05	M	7 11 70	Congleton	Trainee	Stoke C	115	10
							Stockport Co	19	1
WARHURST Paul	6 0	13 00	D	26 9 69	Stockport	Trainee	Manchester C	—	—
							Oldham Ath	67	2
							Sheffield W	66	6
							Blackburn R	36	2
WARK John	5 11	12 12	D	4 8 57	Glasgow	Apprentice	Ipswich T	296	94
							Liverpool	70	28
							Ipswich T	89	23
							Middlesbrough	32	2
							Ipswich T	138	16
WARNER Anthony	6 4	13 09	G	11 5 74	Liverpool	School	**Liverpool**	—	—
WARNER Ashley *	5 10	12 00	F	15 9 71	Leicester	VS Rugby	**Peterborough U**	—	—

				Birth				League	
Player	Ht	Wt	Pos	Date	Place	Source	Clubs	App	Gls
WARNER Robert	5 9	11 07	D	20 4 77	Stratford	Trainee	**Hereford U**	16	—
WARNER Vance	5 11	11 05	D	3 9 74	Leeds	Trainee	**Nottingham F**	2	—
WARREN Christer	5 10	11 03	M	10 10 74	Bournemouth	Cheltenham T	**Southampton**	—	—
WARREN Lee	6 0	12 00	M	28 2 69	Manchester	Trainee	Leeds U	—	—
							Rochdale	31	1
							Hull C	153	1
							Lincoln C (loan)	3	1
							Doncaster R	14	2
WARREN Mark	5 9	10 05	D	12 11 74	Clapton	Trainee	**Leyton Orient**	52	3
							West Ham U (loan)	—	—
WARREN Matt ‡	6 0	12 11	D	14 2 76	Derby	Trainee	**Derby Co**	—	—
WARRINGTON Andrew	6 3	12 13	G	10 6 76	Sheffield	Trainee	**York C**	—	—
WASSALL Darren	5 11	12 10	D	27 6 68	Edgbaston		Nottingham F	27	—
							Hereford U (loan)	5	—
							Bury (loan)	7	1
							Derby Co	81	—
WATKIN Steve	5 10	11 10	F	16 6 71	Wrexham	School	**Wrexham**	142	40
WATKINS Darren ‡	5 11	11 02	D	17 3 77	Middlesbrough	Trainee	**Nottingham F**	—	—
WATKISS Stuart	6 2	13 04	D	8 5 66	Wolverhampton	Apprentice	Wolverhampton W	2	—
						Rushall Olympic	**Walsall**	47	2
WATSON Alex	6 0	11 09	D	5 4 68	Liverpool	Apprentice	Liverpool	4	—
							Derby Co (loan)	5	—
							Bournemouth	151	5
WATSON Andy	5 9	11 02	D	1 4 67	Huddersfield	Harrogate T	Halifax T	83	15
							Swansea C	14	1
							Carlisle U	56	22
							Blackpool	88	37
WATSON Dave	6 0	13 07	D	20 11 61	Liverpool	Amateur	Liverpool	—	—
							Norwich C	212	11
							Everton	306	21
WATSON David	5 11	12 03	G	10 11 73	Barnsley	Trainee	**Barnsley**	51	—
WATSON Gordon	5 10	12 08	F	20 3 71	Sidcup	Trainee	Charlton Ath	31	7
							Sheffield W	66	15
							Southampton	12	3
WATSON Kevin	6 0	12 06	M	3 1 74	Hackney	Trainee	**Tottenham H**	5	—
							Brentford (loan)	3	—
							Bristol C (loan)	2	—
							Barnet (loan)	13	—
WATSON Mark *	6 0	12 06	D	8 9 70	Vancouver		**Watford**	18	—
WATSON Mark			F	28 12 73	Birmingham	Sutton U	**West Ham U**	—	—
WATSON Paul	5 8	10 10	D	4 1 75	Hastings	Trainee	**Gillingham**	54	2
WATSON Steve	6 0	12 07	D	1 4 74	North Shields	Trainee	**Newcastle U**	113	7
WATSON Tommy	5 8	10 10	M	29 9 69	Liverpool	Trainee	**Grimsby T**	170	24
WATTS Grant ‡	6 0	11 02	F	5 11 73	Croydon	Trainee	Crystal Palace	4	—
							Colchester U (loan)	12	2
							Gillingham	3	—
							Sheffield U	—	—
WATTS Julian	6 3	12 08	D	17 3 71	Sheffield	Trainee	Rotherham U	20	1
							Sheffield W	5	—
							Shrewsbury T (loan)	9	—
WDOWCZYK Dariusz	5 11	11 11	D	21 9 62	Warsaw	Legia Warsaw	Celtic	116	4
							Reading	38	—
WEBB Matthew §			M	24 9 76	Bristol	Trainee	**Birmingham C**	1	—
WEBB Neil	6 0	13 07	M	30 7 63	Reading	Apprentice	Reading	72	22
							Portsmouth	123	34
							Nottingham F	146	47
							Manchester U	75	8
							Nottingham F	30	3
							Swindon T (loan)	6	—

Player	Ht	Wt	Pos	Birth Date	Birth Place	Source	Clubs	League App	League Gls
WEBB Simon			M	19 1 78	Castle Bar	Trainee	**Tottenham H**	—	—
WEBBER Damien	6 4	14 00	D	8 10 68	Rustington	Bognor Regis T	**Millwall**	22	2
WEBSTER Kenny ‡	5 7	12 08	D	2 3 73	Hammersmith	Trainee	Arsenal	—	—
							Peterborough U	—	—
WEBSTER Simon	6 0	11 07	D	20 1 64	Earl Shilton	Apprentice	Tottenham H	3	—
							Exeter C (loan)	26	—
							Norwich C (loan)	—	—
							Huddersfield T	118	4
							Sheffield U	37	3
							Charlton Ath	127	7
							West Ham U	5	—
							Oldham Ath (loan)	7	—
WEGERLE Roy	5 11	11 00	F	19 3 64	South Africa	Tampa Bay R	Chelsea	23	3
							Swindon T (loan)	7	1
							Luton T	45	10
							QPR	75	29
							Blackburn R	34	6
							Coventry C	53	9
WELCH Keith	6 0	12 0	G	3 10 68	Bolton	Trainee	Bolton W	—	—
							Rochdale	205	—
							Bristol C	160	—
WELLER Paul	5 8	10 13	F	6 3 75	Brighton	Trainee	**Burnley**	—	—
WELLS David §			G	29 12 77	Portsmouth	Trainee	**Bournemouth**	1	—
WELLS Mark	5 8	10 08	M	17 10 71	Leicester	Trainee	Notts Co	2	—
							Huddersfield T	23	4
							Scarborough	18	1
WELSH Steve (To Partick T)	6 1	12 03	D	19 4 68	Glasgow	Army	Cambridge U	1	—
							Peterborough U	146	2
							Preston NE (loan)	—	—
WEST Colin	6 0	13 11	F	13 11 62	Wallsend	Apprentice	Sunderland	102	21
							Watford	45	20
							Rangers	10	2
							Sheffield W	45	8
							WBA	73	22
							Port Vale (loan)	5	1
							Swansea C	33	12
							Leyton Orient	73	23
WEST Daniel *	5 11	12 07	D	17 4 75	Poole	Christchurch	**Aston Villa**	—	—
WEST Dean	5 10	11 07	D	5 12 72	Wakefield	Leeds U	**Lincoln C**	111	19
WEST Paul *	5 11	11 00	D	22 6 70	Birmingham	Alcester T	Port Vale	—	—
							Bradford C	—	—
							Wigan Ath	3	—
WESTLEY Shane *	6 2	13 08	D	16 6 65	Canterbury	Apprentice	Charlton Ath	8	—
							Southend U	144	10
							Norwich C (loan)	—	—
							Wolverhampton W	50	2
							Brentford	64	1
							Southend U (loan)	5	—
WESTON Kenneth ‡	5 10	11 07	F	5 11 75	Manchester	Trainee	**Ipswich T**	—	—
WESTON Matthew ‡	5 10	11 07	F	5 11 75	Manchester	Trainee	**Ipswich T**	—	—
WESTWOOD Ashley	6 0	11 03	D	31 8 76	Bridgnorth	Trainee	**Manchester U**	—	—
WETHERALL David	6 3	13 12	D	14 3 71	Sheffield	School	Sheffield W	—	—
							Leeds U	84	5
WHALLEY Gareth	5 10	11 00	M	19 12 73	Manchester	Trainee	**Crewe Alex**	80	3
WHALLEY Neil ‡	5 10	11 02	M	29 10 65	Liverpool	Warrington T	**Preston NE**	50	1
WHARTON Paul	5 4	9 09	M	26 6 77	Newcastle	Trainee	**Leeds U**	—	—
WHELAN Noel	6 2	12 03	F	30 12 74	Leeds	Trainee	**Leeds U**	40	7
WHELAN Phil	6 4	14 01	D	7 8 72	Stockport		Ipswich T	82	2
							Middlesbrough	—	—
WHELAN Ronnie	5 9	10 13	M	25 9 61	Dublin	Home Farm	Liverpool	362	46
							Southend U	33	1

Player	Ht	Wt	Pos	Birth Date	Birth Place	Source	Clubs	League App	League Gls
WHELAN Spencer	6 2	13 00	D	17 9 71	Liverpool	Liverpool	**Chester C**	116	1
WHISTON Peter	6 1	12 04	D	4 1 68	Widnes		Plymouth Arg	10	—
							Torquay U (loan)	8	1
							Torquay U	32	—
							Exeter C	85	7
							Southampton	1	—
WHITBREAD Adrian	6 2	11 13	D	22 10 71	Epping	Trainee	Leyton Orient	125	2
							Swindon T	36	1
							West Ham U	8	—
WHITE Alan			D	22 3 76	Darlington		**Middlesbrough**	—	—
WHITE David	6 1	12 09	F	30 10 67	Manchester		Manchester C	285	79
							Leeds U	38	8
WHITE Devon	6 3	14 00	F	2 3 64	Nottingham	Arnold T	Lincoln C	29	4
						Boston U	Bristol R	202	53
							Cambridge U	22	4
							QPR	46	16
WHITE Jason	6 0	12 10	F	19 10 71	Meriden	Derby Co	Scunthorpe U	68	16
							Darlington (loan)	4	1
							Scarborough	63	20
WHITE John	5 8	11 03	M	9 9 74	Honiton	Trainee	**Watford**	—	—
WHITE Steve	5 11	12 02	F	2 1 59	Chipping Sodbury	Mangotsfield U	Bristol R	50	20
							Luton T	72	25
							Charlton Ath	29	12
							Lincoln C (loan)	3	—
							Luton T (loan)	4	—
							Bristol R	101	24
							Swindon T	244	83
							Hereford U	36	15
WHITE Tom	5 11	12 02	D	26 1 76	Bristol	Trainee	**Bristol R**	4	—
WHITEHALL Steve	5 9	11 00	F	8 12 66	Bromborough	Southport	**Rochdale**	157	46
WHITEHEAD Phil	6 3	13 07	G	17 12 69	Halifax	Trainee	Halifax T	42	—
							Barnsley	16	—
							Halifax T (loan)	9	—
							Scunthorpe U (loan)	8	—
							Scunthorpe U (loan)	8	—
							Bradford C (loan)	6	—
							Oxford U	77	—
WHITEHEAD Scot ‡	5 8	11 09	D	13 8 75	Doncaster	Trainee	**Huddersfield T**	—	—
WHITEHOUSE Dane	5 10	10 13	M	14 10 70	Sheffield	Trainee	**Sheffield U**	146	26
WHITINGTON Craig	5 11	12 04	F	3 9 70	Brighton	Crawley T	Scarborough	27	10
							Huddersfield T	1	—
							Rochdale (loan)	1	—
WHITLEY Jim	5 9	11 00	M	14 4 75	Zambia	Trainee	**Manchester C**	—	—
WHITLOW Mike	6 0	12 13	D	13 1 68	Northwich	Witton Alb	Leeds U	77	4
							Leicester C	88	5
WHITNEY Jonathan	5 10	12 00	D	23 12 70	Nantwich	Winsford	**Huddersfield T**	14	—
							Wigan Ath (loan)	12	—
WHITTAKER Stuart	5 7	9 03	M	2 1 75	Liverpool	Liverpool	**Bolton W**	3	—
WHITTAM Philip	5 8	9 08	D	12 8 76	Bolton	Trainee	**Manchester U**	—	—
WHITTINGHAM Guy	5 10	11 12	F	10 11 64	Evesham	Yeovil	Portsmouth	160	88
							Aston Villa	25	5
							Wolverhampton W (loan)	13	8
							Sheffield W	21	9
WHITTLE Justin	6 1	12 12	D	18 3 71	Derby	Celtic	**Stoke C**	—	—
WHITTON Steve	6 0	13 07	M	4 12 60	East Ham	Apprentice	Coventry C	74	21
							West Ham U	39	6
							Birmingham C (loan)	8	2
							Birmingham C	95	28
							Sheffield W	32	4
							Ipswich T	88	15
							Colchester U	44	12

Player	Ht	Wt	Pos	Birth Date	Birth Place	Source	Clubs	League App	League Gls
WHYTE Chris	6 1	11 10	D	2 9 61	London	Amateur	Arsenal	90	8
							Crystal Palace (loan)	13	—
						Los Angeles R	WBA	84	7
							Leeds U	113	5
							Birmingham C	64	1
WHYTE David	5 8	10 07	F	20 4 71	Greenwich	Greenwich Borough	Crystal Palace	27	4
							Charlton Ath (loan)	8	2
							Charlton Ath	38	19
WHYTE Derek	5 11	12 11	D	31 8 68	Glasgow	Celtic BC	Celtic	216	7
							Middlesbrough	113	2
WIDDRINGTON Tommy	5 10	11 12	D	1 10 71	Newcastle	Trainee	**Southampton**	54	1
							Wigan Ath (loan)	6	—
WIETECHA David	6 4	15 00	G	1 11 74	Colchester		**Millwall**	—	—
							Crewe Alex (loan)	—	—
							Rotherham U (loan)	—	—
WIGG Nathan	5 9	10 05	M	27 9 74	Cardiff	Trainee	**Cardiff C**	38	1
WILCOX Jason	5 11	11 10	F	15 7 71	Bolton	Trainee	**Blackburn R**	150	19
WILCOX Russell	6 0	11 10	D	25 3 64	Hemsworth	Apprentice	Doncaster R	1	—
						Cambridge U, Frickley Ath.	Northampton T	138	9
							Hull C	100	7
							Doncaster R	77	6
WILDER Chris	5 11	12 08	D	23 9 67	Wortley	Apprentice	Southampton	—	—
							Sheffield U	93	1
							Walsall (loan)	4	—
							Charlton Ath (loan)	1	—
							Charlton Ath (loan)	2	—
							Leyton Orient (loan)	16	1
							Rotherham U	114	11
WILKERSON Paul	6 3	13 11	G	11 12 74	Hertford		**Watford**	—	—
WILKIE Glen			D	22 1 77	Stepney	Trainee	**Leyton Orient**	11	—
WILKIN Kevin *	5 11	11 07	F	1 10 67	Cambridge	Cambridge C	**Northampton T**	78	11
WILKINS Dean	5 10	12 08	M	12 7 62	Hillingdon	Apprentice	QPR	6	—
							Brighton	2	—
							Orient (loan)	10	—
						PEC Zwolle	**Brighton**	275	22
WILKINS Ray †	5 8	11 02	M	14 9 56	Hillingdon	Apprentice	Chelsea	179	30
							Manchester U	160	7
							AC Milan	73	2
						Paris St Germain	Rangers	70	2
							QPR	154	7
							Crystal Palace	1	—
							QPR	2	—
WILKINS Richard	6 0	12 03	M	28 5 65	Streatham	Haverhill R	Colchester U	152	22
							Cambridge U	81	7
							Hereford U	35	2
WILKINSON Ian	5 11	12 00	G	2 7 73	Warrington	Trainee	Manchester U	—	—
							Stockport Co	—	—
							Crewe Alex	3	—
							Doncaster R (loan)	—	—
WILKINSON Paul	6 1	12 04	F	30 10 64	Louth	Apprentice	Grimsby T	71	27
							Everton	31	7
							Nottingham F	34	5
							Watford	134	52
							Middlesbrough	163	49
WILKINSON Steve	6 0	11 06	F	1 9 68	Lincoln	Apprentice	Leicester C	9	1
							Rochdale (loan)	—	—
							Crewe Alex (loan)	5	2
							Mansfield T	232	83
WILLGRASS Alexandre			M	8 4 76	Scarborough		**Scarborough**	—	—
WILLIAMS Adrian	6 2	12 06	D	16 8 71	Reading	Trainee	**Reading**	165	11

Player	Ht	Wt	Pos	Birth Date	Birth Place	Source	Clubs	League App	League Gls
WILLIAMS Andy *	6 2	12 00	M	29 7 62	Birmingham	Solihull B	Coventry C	9	—
							Rotherham U	87	13
							Leeds U	46	3
							Port Vale (loan)	5	—
							Notts Co	39	2
							Huddersfield T (loan)	6	—
							Rotherham U	51	2
WILLIAMS Chris *	5 9	11 07	F	21 9 76	Neath	Trainee	**Hereford U**	4	—
WILLIAMS Corey *	6 2	12 00	F	22 2 72	Sheffield	Denaby U	**Rotherham U**	2	—
WILLIAMS Darren §			M	28 4 77	Middlesbrough	Trainee	**York C**	1	—
WILLIAMS David	6 0	12 00	G	18 9 68	Liverpool	Trainee	Oldham Ath	—	—
							Burnley	24	—
							Rochdale (loan)	6	—
							Crewe Alex (loan)	—	—
							Cardiff C	40	—
WILLIAMS Dean A ‡	6 1	13 00	F	14 11 70	Hemel	Trainee	Cambridge U	1	—
					Hempstead	St Albans	Brentford	3	1
							Doncaster R	1	—
WILLIAMS Dean P	6 1	12 09	G	5 1 72	Lichfield	Tamworth	Brentford	7	—
							Doncaster R	35	—
WILLIAMS Gareth	5 10	11 08	F	12 3 67	Isle of Wight	Gosport Borough	Aston Villa	12	—
							Barnsley	34	6
							Hull C (loan)	4	—
							Hull C (loan)	16	2
							Bournemouth	1	—
							Northampton T	15	—
WILLIAMS Geraint	5 7	12 06	M	5 1 62	Cwmpare	Apprentice	Bristol R	141	8
							Derby Co	277	9
							Ipswich T	109	1
WILLIAMS John *	6 1	13 12	D	3 10 60	Liverpool	Amateur	Tranmere R	173	13
							Port Vale	50	2
							Bournemouth	117	9
							Wigan Ath (loan)	4	—
							Cardiff C	6	—
							Bournemouth	—	—
WILLIAMS John	6 2	12 04	M	11 5 68	Birmingham	Cradley T	Swansea C	39	11
							Coventry C	80	11
							Notts Co (loan)	5	2
							Stoke C (loan)	4	—
							Swansea C (loan)	7	2
WILLIAMS Lee	5 6	11 09	M	3 2 73	Birmingham	Trainee	Aston Villa	—	—
							Shrewsbury T (loan)	3	—
							Peterborough U	58	1
WILLIAMS Mark	6 0	13 00	D	28 9 70	Stalybridge	Newtown	**Shrewsbury T**	102	3
WILLIAMS Mark	5 11	12 00	F	8 2 73	Bangor	Bangor C	**Stockport Co**	1	—
WILLIAMS Martin *	5 9	11 12	F	12 7 73	Luton	Leicester C	**Luton T**	40	2
							Colchester U (loan)	3	—
WILLIAMS Mike ‡			F	3 11 76	Mansfield	Trainee	**Mansfield T**	1	—
WILLIAMS Mike	5 11	11 04	M	21 11 69	Bradford	Maltby	**Sheffield W**	17	1
							Halifax T (loan)	9	1
WILLIAMS Paul	5 7	10 00	F	11 9 69	Leicester	Trainee	Leicester C	—	—
							Stockport Co	70	4
							Coventry C	14	—
							WBA (loan)	5	—
							Huddersfield T (loan)	9	—
WILLIAMS Paul	5 7	10 09	F	16 8 65	London	Woodford T	Charlton Ath	82	23
							Brentford (loan)	7	3
							Sheffield W	93	25
							Crystal Palace	46	7
							Sunderland (loan)	3	—
							Birmingham C (loan)	11	—
WILLIAMS Paul	6 0	14 03	D	26 3 71	Burton	Trainee	**Derby Co**	160	26
							Lincoln C (loan)	3	—

Player	Ht	Wt	Pos	Birth Date	Birth Place	Source	Clubs	League App	League Gls
WILLIAMS Paul	5 11	12 02	D	25 9 70	Liverpool	Trainee	Sunderland	9	—
							Swansea C (loan)	12	1
							Doncaster R	8	—
WILLIAMS Paul A	6 3	14 08	F	8 9 63	Sheffield	Nuneaton	Preston NE	1	—
							Newport Co	26	3
							Sheffield U	8	—
							Hartlepool U	8	—
							Stockport Co	24	14
							WBA	44	5
							Coventry C (loan)	2	—
							Stockport Co	16	3
							Rochdale	25	7
WILLIAMS Scott	6 0	11 00	D	7 8 74	Bangor	Trainee	**Wrexham**	25	—
WILLIAMS Steven	6 3	12 12	G	16 10 74	Aberystwyth	Coventry C	**Cardiff C**	24	—
WILLIAMS Steven	5 11	12 00	F	3 11 75	Sheffield	Trainee	**Lincoln C**	14	2
WILLIAMSON Danny	5 10	11 06	M	5 12 73	London	Trainee	**West Ham U**	7	1
							Doncaster R (loan)	13	1
WILLIS Jimmy	6 0	12 03	D	12 7 68	Liverpool	Blackburn R	Halifax T	—	—
							Stockport Co	10	—
							Darlington	90	6
							Leicester C	48	3
							Bradford C (loan)	9	1
WILLIS Roger	6 1	11 06	D	17 6 67	Sheffield		Grimsby T	9	—
						Barnet	Barnet	44	13
							Watford	36	2
							Birmingham C	19	5
							Southend U	21	4
WILMOT Rhys	6 1	12 00	G	21 2 62	Newport	Apprentice	Arsenal	8	—
							Hereford U (loan)	9	—
							Orient (loan)	46	—
							Swansea C (loan)	16	—
							Plymouth Arg (loan)	17	—
							Plymouth Arg	116	—
							Grimsby T	33	—
							Crystal Palace	6	—
WILSON Clive	5 7	10 00	M	13 11 61	Manchester	Local	Manchester C	98	9
							Chester (loan)	21	2
							Chelsea	81	5
							Manchester C (loan)	11	—
							QPR	172	12
WILSON Danny	5 6	11 00	M	1 1 60	Wigan	Wigan Ath	Bury	90	8
							Chesterfield	100	13
							Nottingham F	10	1
							Scunthorpe U (loan)	6	3
							Brighton	135	33
							Luton T	110	24
							Sheffield W	98	11
							Barnsley	77	2
WILSON Gus *	5 11	12 00	D	11 4 63	Manchester	Runcorn	**Crewe Alex**	115	—
WILSON Kevin	5 7	11 04	F	18 4 61	Banbury	Banbury U	Derby Co	122	30
							Ipswich T	98	34
							Chelsea	152	42
							Notts Co	69	3
							Bradford C (loan)	5	—
							Walsall	42	16
WILSON Paul	5 9	11 04	D	26 9 64	London	Barking	**Barnet**	104	7
WILSON Paul			F	22 2 77	Maidstone	Trainee	**Gillingham**	2	—
WILSON Paul	5 10	11 08	D	2 8 68	Bradford	Trainee	Huddersfield T	15	—
							Norwich C	—	—
							Northampton T	141	6
							Halifax T	45	7
							Burnley	31	—
							York C	22	—
WILSON Ross ‡	5 8	10 00	M	29 9 76	Chatham	Trainee	**Nottingham F**	—	—
WILSON Steve	5 10	10 07	G	24 4 74	Hull	Trainee	**Hull C**	60	—
WINDASS Dean	5 10	12 03	F	1 4 69	Hull	N. Ferriby	**Hull C**	160	53

Player	Ht	Wt	Pos	Birth Date	Birth Place	Source	Clubs	League App	League Gls
WINSTANLEY Mark	6 1	12 07	D	22 1 68	St. Helens	Trainee	Bolton W	220	3
							Burnley	44	2
WINSTONE Simon ‡	5 7	10 00	D	4 10 74	Bristol	Trainee	Stoke C	—	—
							Torquay U	2	—
WINTERBURN Nigel	5 8	11 04	D	11 12 63	Coventry	Local	Birmingham C	—	—
							Oxford U	—	—
							Wimbledon	165	8
							Arsenal	272	5
WISE Dennis	5 6	9 05	F	15 12 66	Kensington	Southampton	Wimbledon	135	27
							Chelsea	152	33
WITHE Chris	5 10	11 12	D	25 9 62	Liverpool	Apprentice	Newcastle U	2	—
							Bradford C	143	2
							Notts Co	80	3
							Bury	31	1
							Chester C (loan)	2	—
							Mansfield T (loan)	11	—
							Mansfield T	65	5
							Shrewsbury T	57	2
WITSCHGE Richard *			F	20 9 69	Amsterdam	Bordeaux	**Blackburn R**	1	—
WITTER Tony	6 1	13 02	D	12 8 65	London	Grays Ath	Crystal Palace	—	—
							QPR	1	—
							Millwall (loan)	—	—
							Plymouth Arg (loan)	3	1
							Reading (loan)	4	—
							Millwall	27	1
WOAN Ian	5 10	11 09	M	14 12 67	Wirrall	Runcorn	**Nottingham F**	122	21
WOOD Paul	5 9	10 05	F	1 11 64	Middlesbrough	Apprentice	Portsmouth	47	6
							Brighton	92	8
							Sheffield U	28	3
							Bournemouth (loan)	21	—
							Bournemouth	78	18
							Portsmouth	17	2
WOOD Simon	5 9	11 08	M	24 9 76	Hull	Trainee	**Coventry C**	—	—
WOOD Steve	6 0	12 04	D	2 2 63	Bracknell	Apprentice	Reading	219	9
							Millwall	110	—
							Southampton	46	—
							Oxford U	2	—
WOOD Trevor	6 0	13 07	G	3 11 68	Jersey	Apprentice	Brighton	—	—
							Port Vale	42	—
							Walsall	39	—
WOODMAN Andy	6 1	12 04	G	11 8 71	Denmark Hill	Apprentice	Crystal Palace	—	—
							Exeter C	6	—
							Northampton T	10	—
WOODS Andrew *			G	15 1 76	Colchester	Trainee	**Oldham Ath**	—	—
WOODS Chris	6 2	14 05	G	14 11 59	Boston	Apprentice	Nottingham F	—	—
							QPR	63	—
							Norwich C (loan)	10	—
							Norwich C	206	—
							Rangers	173	—
							Sheffield W	99	—
WOODS Neil	6 0	12 11	F	30 7 66	York	Apprentice	Doncaster R	65	16
							Rangers	3	—
							Ipswich T	27	5
							Bradford C	14	2
							Grimsby T	159	38
WOODS Ray	5 10	11 09	F	7 6 65	Birkenhead	Apprentice	Tranmere R	7	2
						Colne D.	Wigan Ath	28	3
							Coventry C	21	1
							Wigan Ath (loan)	13	—
							Shrewsbury T (loan)	9	1
							Shrewsbury T	19	—
WOODSFORD Jamie	5 9	11 00	F	9 11 76	Ipswich	Trainee	**Luton T**	7	—
WOODWARD Andy	5 10	10 12	D	23 9 73	Stockport	Trainee	Crewe Alex	20	—
							Bury	8	—
WOOLFORD Stephen ‡	5 10	11 00	F	24 11 76	Leeds	Trainee	**Nottingham F**	—	—

				Birth				League	
Player	Ht	Wt	Pos	Date	Place	Source	Clubs	App	Gls
WOOLGAR Matthew	5 10	11 10	M	5 1 76	Bedford	Trainee	**Luton T**	—	—
WORBOYS Gavin	6 0	11 00	F	14 7 74	Doncaster	Trainee	Doncaster R	7	2
							Notts Co	—	—
							Exeter C (loan)	4	1
							Darlington	27	6
WORRALL Ben	5 8	10 06	M	7 12 75	Swindon	Trainee	**Swindon T**	3	—
WORRELL David	5 9	11 00	D	12 1 78	Dublin	Trainee	**Blackburn R**	—	—
WORTHINGTON Nigel	5 11	12 08	D	4 11 61	Ballymena	Ballymena U	Notts Co	67	4
							Sheffield W	338	12
							Leeds U	27	1
WOTTON Paul §			M	17 8 77	Plymouth	Trainee	**Plymouth Arg**	7	—
WRACK Darren	5 9	11 10	F	5 5 76	Cleethorpes	Trainee	**Derby Co**	16	1
WRATTEN Adam *	6 0	12 00	D	30 11 74	Coventry	Trainee	**Birmingham C**	—	—
WRATTEN Paul ‡	5 7	10 00	M	29 11 70	Middlesbrough	Trainee	Manchester U	2	—
							Hartlepool U	57	1
							York C	—	—
WRIGHT Alan	5 4	9 04	M	28 9 71	Ashton-under-Lyme	Trainee	Blackpool	98	—
							Blackburn R	74	1
							Aston Villa	8	—
WRIGHT Dale	6 00	12 05	D	21 12 74	Middlesbrough	Trainee	**Nottingham F**	—	—
WRIGHT Ian	5 9	11 08	F	3 11 63	Woolwich	Greenwich Borough	Crystal Palace	225	89
							Arsenal	131	80
WRIGHT Ian	6 1	12 08	D	10 3 72	Lichfield	Trainee	Stoke C	6	—
							Bristol R	36	1
WRIGHT Jermaine	5 9	10 03	F	21 10 75	Greenwich	Trainee	Millwall	—	—
							Wolverhampton W	6	—
WRIGHT Johnny	5 8	11 04	D	24 11 75	Belfast	Trainee	**Norwich C**	2	—
WRIGHT Mark	6 2	13 03	D	1 8 63	Dorchester	Amateur	Oxford U	10	—
							Southampton	170	7
							Derby Co	144	10
							Liverpool	91	3
WRIGHT Mark *	5 11	10 12	D	29 1 70	Manchester	Trainee	Everton	1	—
							Blackpool (loan)	3	—
							Huddersfield T (loan)	10	1
							Huddersfield T	22	—
							Wigan Ath	30	1
WRIGHT Nick	5 11	11 02	F	15 10 75	Derby	Trainee	**Derby Co**	—	—
WRIGHT Richard	6 2	13 00	G	5 11 77	Ipswich	Trainee	**Ipswich T**	3	—
WRIGHT Tommy *	5 7	11 05	F	10 1 66	Dunfermline	Apprentice	Leeds U	81	24
							Oldham Ath	112	23
							Leicester C	129	22
							Middlesbrough	53	5
WRIGHT Tommy	6 1	13 05	G	29 8 63	Belfast	Linfield	Newcastle U	73	—
							Hull C (loan)	6	—
							Nottingham F	10	—
WYATT Michael *	5 11	11 03	F	12 9 74	Bristol	Trainee	**Bristol C**	13	—
YALLOP Frank	5 11	12 00	D	4 4 64	Watford	Apprentice	**Ipswich T**	309	7
YATES Dean	6 1	12 00	D	26 10 67	Leicester	Apprentice	Notts Co	314	33
							Derby Co	11	1
YATES Steve	5 11	11 00	D	29 1 70	Bristol	Trainee	Bristol R	197	—
							QPR	52	1
YEBOAH Tony	5 10	13 13	F	6 6 66	Ghana	Okwawu U	Saarbrucken	65	26
							Eintracht Frankfurt	123	68
							Leeds U	18	12
YORKE Dwight	5 11	11 13	F	3 11 71	Tobago	Tobago	**Aston Villa**	128	27

Player	Ht	Wt	Pos	Birth Date	Birth Place	Source	Clubs	League App	League Gls
YOUDS Eddie	6 1	13 03	D	3 5 70	Liverpool	Trainee	Everton	8	—
							Cardiff C (loan)	1	—
							Wrexham (loan)	20	2
							Ipswich T	50	1
							Bradford C (loan)	17	3
YOUNG Eric	6 2	13 05	D	25 3 60	Singapore	Slough T	Brighton	126	10
							Wimbledon	99	9
							Crystal Palace	161	15
YOUNG Neil	5 8	11 03	D	31 8 73	Harlow	Trainee	Tottenham H	—	—
							Bournemouth	32	—
YOUNG Scott			F	14 1 76	Pontypridd	Trainee	**Cardiff C**	28	—
YOUNG Stuart †	5 11	13 00	F	16 12 72	Hull	Arsenal	Hull C	19	2
							Northampton T	8	2
							Scarborough	41	10
							Scunthorpe U	14	2
ZIVKOVIC Lee *	5 11	12 10	M	27 11 75	Doncaster	Trainee	**Sheffield U**	—	—
ZUMRUTEL Soner *	5 6	11 00	F	6 10 74	Islington	Trainee	**Arsenal**	—	—

FA CHARITY SHIELD WINNERS 1908–94

1908	Manchester U v QPR	4-0 after 1-1 draw
1909	Newcastle U v Northampton T	2-0
1910	Brighton v Aston Villa	1-0
1911	Manchester U v Swindon T	8-4
1912	Blackburn R v QPR	2-1
1913	Professionals v Amateurs	7-2
1920	WBA v Tottenham H	2-0
1921	Tottenham H v Burnley	2-0
1922	Huddersfield T v Liverpool	1-0
1923	Professionals v Amateurs	2-0
1924	Professionals v Amateurs	3-1
1925	Amateurs v Professionals	6-1
1926	Amateurs v Professionals	6-3
1927	Cardiff C v Corinthians	2-1
1928	Everton v Blackburn R	2-1
1929	Professionals v Amateurs	3-0
1930	Arsenal v Sheffield W	2-1
1931	Arsenal v WBA	1-0
1932	Everton v Newcastle U	5-3
1933	Arsenal v Everton	3-0
1934	Arsenal v Manchester C	4-0
1935	Sheffield W v Arsenal	1-0
1936	Sunderland v Arsenal	2-1
1937	Manchester C v Sunderland	2-0
1938	Arsenal v Preston NE	2-1
1948	Arsenal v Manchester U	4-3
1949	Portsmouth v Wolverhampton W	1-1*
1950	World Cup Team v Canadian Touring Team	4-2
1951	Tottenham H v Newcastle U	2-1
1952	Manchester U v Newcastle U	4-2
1953	Arsenal v Blackpool	3-1
1954	Wolverhampton W v WBA	4-4*
1955	Chelsea v Newcastle U	3-0
1956	Manchester U v Manchester C	1-0
1957	Manchester U v Aston Villa	4-0
1958	Bolton W v Wolverhampton W	4-1
1959	Wolverhampton W v Nottingham F	3-1
1960	Burnley v Wolverhampton W	2-2*
1961	Tottenham H v FA XI	3-2
1962	Tottenham H v Ipswich T	5-1
1963	Everton v Manchester U	4-0
1964	Liverpool v West Ham U	2-2*
1965	Manchester U v Liverpool	2-2*
1966	Liverpool v Everton	1-0
1967	Manchester U v Tottenham H	3-3*
1968	Manchester C v WBA	6-1
1969	Leeds U v Manchester C	2-1
1970	Everton v Chelsea	2-1
1971	Leicester C v Liverpool	1-0
1972	Manchester C v Aston Villa	1-0
1973	Burnley v Manchester C	1-0
1974	Liverpool† v Leeds U	1-1
1975	Derby Co v West Ham U	2-0
1976	Liverpool v Southampton	1-0
1977	Liverpool v Manchester U	0-0*
1978	Nottingham F v Ipswich T	5-0
1979	Liverpool v Arsenal	3-1
1980	Liverpool v West Ham U	1-0
1981	Aston Villa v Tottenham H	2-2*
1982	Liverpool v Tottenham H	1-0
1983	Manchester U v Liverpool	2-0
1984	Everton v Liverpool	1-0
1985	Everton v Manchester U	2-0
1986	Everton v Liverpool	1-1*
1987	Everton v Coventry C	1-0
1988	Liverpool v Wimbledon	2-1
1989	Liverpool v Arsenal	1-0
1990	Liverpool v Manchester U	1-1*
1991	Arsenal v Tottenham H	0-0*
1992	Leeds U v Liverpool	4-3
1993	Manchester U† v Arsenal	1-1

* *Each club retained shield for six months.* † *Won on penalties.*

FA CHARITY SHIELD 1994

Manchester U (1) 2, Blackburn R (0) 0

At Wembley, 14 August 1994, attendance 60,402

Manchester U: Schmeichel; May, Sharpe, Bruce, Kanchelskis, Pallister, Cantona, Ince, McClair, Hughes, Giggs.

Scorers: Cantona (pen), Ince.

Blackburn R: Flowers; Berg, Le Saux, Atkins (Thorne), Hendry, Gale, Ripley, Sherwood, Pearce, Slater, Wilcox.

LEADING GOALSCORERS 1994–95

	League	*FA Cup*	*Coca-Cola Cup*	*Other Cups*	*Total*
FA CARLING PREMIERSHIP					
Alan Shearer (*Blackburn R*)	34	0	2	1	37
Robbie Fowler (*Liverpool*)	25	2	4	0	31
Les Ferdinand (*QPR*)	24	1	1	0	26
Stan Collymore (*Nottingham F*)	22	1	2	0	25
Andy Cole (*Manchester U*)	21	0	2	0	23
(Includes nine League, two Coca-Cola Cup goals for Newcastle U.)					
Jurgen Klinsmann (*Tottenham H*)	20	5	4	0	29
Matt Le Tissier (*Southampton*)	19	5	5	0	29
Ian Wright (*Arsenal*)	18	0	3	9	30
Teddy Sheringham (*Tottenham H*)	18	4	1	0	23
Ashley Ward (*Norwich C*)	16	4	1	0	21
(Includes eight League, four FA Cup and one Coca-Cola Cup goal for Crewe Alex.)					
Uwe Rosler (*Manchester C*)	15	5	2	0	22
Chris Sutton (*Blackburn R*)	15	2	3	1	21
Dean Saunders (*Aston Villa*)	15	1	1	0	17
Paul Rideout (*Everton*)	14	2	0	0	16
Andrei Kanchelskis (*Manchester U*)	14	0	0	0	14
ENDSLEIGH INSURANCE DIVISION 1					
John Aldridge (*Tranmere R*)	24	0	1	1	26
Jan-Aage Fjortoft (*Middlesbrough*)	19	1	9	0	29
(Includes 16 League, one FA Cup and nine Coca-Cola Cup goals for Swindon T.)					
David Whyte (*Charlton Ath*)	19	0	2	0	21
Gerry Creaney (*Portsmouth*)	18	1	3	0	22
Sean McCarthy (*Oldham Ath*)	18	0	0	0	18
Nathan Blake (*Sheffield U*)	17	0	1	0	18
John McGinlay (*Bolton W*)	16	0	4	2	22
Martin Foyle (*Port Vale*)	16	3	1	0	20
Chris Malkin (*Tranmere R*)	16	1	0	2	19
Steve Bull (*Wolverhampton W*)	16	0	2	1	19
David Kelly (*Wolverhampton W*)	15	4	2	1	22
John Hendrie (*Middlesbrough*)	15	1	1	0	17
Neil Woods (*Grimsby T*)	14	0	0	0	14
DIVISION 2					
Gary Bennett (*Wrexham*)	29	2	2	6	39
Andy Booth (*Huddersfield T*)	26	1	0	3	30
Nicky Forster (*Brentford*)	24	0	0	2	26
Robert Taylor (*Brentford*)	23	1	1	0	25
Steve Claridge (*Birmingham C*)	20	0	1	4	25
Paul Moody (*Oxford U*)	20	0	1	2	23
Kevin Francis (*Birmingham C*)	20	0	1	1	22
(Includes 12 League and one Coca-Cola Cup goal for Stockport Co.)					
Shaun Goater (*Rotherham U*)	19	3	0	3	25
Ronnie Jepson (*Huddersfield T*)	19	1	2	1	23
Carlo Corazzin (*Cambridge U*)	19	0	0	2	21
Tony Ellis (*Blackpool*)	17	0	1	0	18
Paul Miller (*Bristol R*)	16	4	0	2	22
Dean Windass (*Hull C*)	16	2	0	0	18
Ken Charlery (*Peterborough U*)	16	2	0	0	18
Paul Barnes (*York C*)	16	0	0	1	17
DIVISION 3					
Phil Stant (*Bury*)	26	0	2	0	28
(Includes 13 League and two Coca-Cola Cup goals for Cardiff C.)					
Doug Freedman (*Barnet*)	24	0	5	0	29
Kyle Lightbourne (*Walsall*)	23	3	1	0	27
Steve Wilkinson (*Mansfield T*)	22	0	3	1	26
David Reeves (*Carlisle U*)	21	2	2	0	25
Kevin Wilson (*Walsall*)	16	2	3	0	21
David Pugh (*Bury*)	16	0	0	1	17
Steve White (*Hereford U*)	15	1	2	1	19
Andy Lyons (*Wigan Ath*)	15	0	0	0	15
Mark Carter (*Bury*)	14	0	1	0	15
Chris Pike (*Gillingham*)	13	4	0	1	18
Keith Houchen (*Hartlepool U*)	13	0	1	0	14
Graeme Jones (*Doncaster R*)	12	1	1	1	15

NB. Players are listed in order of League goals scored. Other cup goals refer to European matches, Auto Windscreens Shield and Anglo-Italian Cup plus play-offs.

Did You Know?

I'm all Wright, Jack
On 23 October 1994, Ian Wright completed 12 goals in 10 successive League and Cup matches, to establish a new **Arsenal** club record. In the 1931-32 season, David Jack had scored in nine consecutive games for 14 goals.

Viva Villa
On 11 February 1995, **Aston Villa** beat Wimbledon 7-1. It was their biggest win for 33 years. Previously they had defeated Leicester City 8-3 on 21 April 1962.

International take-off
Centre-forward George Sparrow was the first **Barnet** player to receive an Amateur International cap when he was chosen for England against Wales in 1925.

Beau legs
At 37 years 3 months, Beau Asquith became the oldest player to appear for **Barnsley** on 19 November 1947. But he still completed two further seasons with Bradford City.

Beau Brummies
In 1994-95, **Birmingham City** completed 20 League matches unbeaten between 3 September 1994 and 2 January 1995 to set a new club record. Previously they had remained undefeated for the last 18 games in 1971-72.

Rovers return
Blackburn Rovers still hold the record for the longest unbeaten run in the FA Cup: 24 matches from November 1883 to November 1886, including one walkover win against Halliwell and two drawn games.

Turn of the century
In 1899-1900, **Blackpool** won the Lancashire Combination. It was their only season out of the Football League after failing to gain re-election.

Red faced army
Bolton Wanderers held their second floodlight friendly match in November 1957 when they beat Soviet Army team CSKA Moscow 3-1 before a crowd of 34,139.

Court's No. 1
Goalkeeper Tom Godwin missed only one match in his first four seasons with **Bournemouth**. He made a then club record 358 League appearances between 1952 and 1962 and won four of his 13 Republic of Ireland caps while at Dean Court.

PT exercises
On 2 November 1994, **Bradford City** goalkeeper Paul Tomlinson set a club record with his 71st clean sheet in eight seasons. His first had been on his debut on 15 August 1987.

Candle power
In the 1973-74 season, **Brentford** general manager Denis Piggott, team manager Mike Everitt and trainer Jess Willard all celebrated their birthdays on 16 January.

Foster's saga
On 24 September 1994, Steve Foster celebrated his 37th birthday and his 250th League game for **Brighton & Hove Albion** in a 2-0 win against Cambridge United.

Seal of approval
In the close season of 1994, **Bristol City** signed Australian-born David Seal from the Belgian club Aalst after he had scored six goals in two trial matches.

Dai is cast
On 14 January 1995, Marcus Stewart's 80th minute goal equalled Dai Ward's 38-year-old record of scoring in eight consecutive League and Cup matches for **Bristol Rovers**.

Vale of nears
When **Burnley** defeated Port Vale 4-3 on 28 March 1995, four of the goals came during an eight minute spell in the second half. Burnley scored in the 60th, 64th and 66th minutes, Port Vale replying in the 68th.

One over the eight
On 15 October 1994, **Bury** had won 9 of their 12 matches, more than any other club in the four English divisions and the three goals they had conceded also represented the best defensive record

Home alone
In 1982-83, **Cambridge United** completed 12 successive home League games without conceding a goal. This is a Football League record.

Not Knighton's day
Cardiff City defeated Knighton Town of the Mid-Wales League 16-0 in a fifth round Welsh Cup tie on 28 January 1961.

Barnet fare
On 24 January 1995, **Carlisle United** completed their 16th successive League game by winning 2-0 at Barnet. Their previous club record had been established in 1950-51 and equalled in 1983-84.

Screen gems
On 5 February 1995, **Charlton Athletic** recorded their first win on live television since their 1-0 FA Cup Final victory over Burnley in 1947. Their victims were West Bromwich Albion in a 1-0 win.

International bridge club
Chelsea had eight internationals in a 5-0 win against Sunderland on 13 December 1930: Tommy Law, Alec Jackson, Alex Cheyne, Hughie Gallacher, Andy Wilson (Scotland), Jack Townrow, Sid Bishop (England), Sam Irving (Ireland).

Thirties something
When still known as **Chester**, the club completed 18 League games without defeat between 27 October 1934 and 16 February 1935 for a club record.

Playing pontoons only
On 18 March 1995, **Chesterfield** set a new club record with their 14th League game without defeat. They went on to increase this sequence to 21 matches.

Only one United?
On 4 February 1995, **Colchester United** were three goals down in eighteen minutes at Scunthorpe United, before eventually winning 4-3. Two of their goals came in the last ten minutes.

Peter the Great
Peter Ndlovu scored in the 21st, 35th (with a penalty) and 85th minutes for **Coventry City** at Liverpool on 14 March 1995 in a 3-2 win. It was the first hat-trick by a visiting player at Anfield for 33 years.

No change at Crewe
In 1938 **Crewe Alexandra** completed 16 home wins in succession. They comprised the last ten in 1937-38, including five in a row in 14 days, and the first six in 1938-39.

Palace gates
In 1969-70, the last season when as many as 29 million spectators attended Football League matches, the opening First Division programme attracted 367,157. The highest was 48,610 at **Crystal Palace** for the 2-2 draw with Manchester United.

Quaker routs
On 23 April 1927, Tom Ruddy scored five goals for **Darlington** in an 8-2 win against South Shields. That season he scored 26 League and Cup goals.

Status Quy
When **Derby County** goalkeeper Steve Sutton was injured in the 86th minute of a third round Coca-Cola Cup tie at Portsmouth on 26 October 1994, substitute goalkeeper Andrew Quy made a four-minute debut as Derby held on to win 1-0.

Workers playtime?
The previous ground record for **Doncaster Rovers** was established at 23,238 against Tranmere Rovers on 11 April 1935 -a Thursday afternoon.

Toffeemen stuck on seven
Everton set a club record of seven League games without conceding a goal in 1994-95. The total time involved was 12 hours 15 minutes.

City slicker
Henry Bartholomew scored for **Exeter City** against Barnet in a first round FA Cup tie at Underhill on 4 December 1948 after just 10 seconds. Exeter won 6-2.

Every second counts
Former Southampton trainee Rory Hamill scored for **Fulham** against Mansfield Town on 2 January 1995 after eight seconds at the beginning of a 4-2 win.

Spring collection
Gillingham assembled a run of unbeaten games at home consisting of 52 League and Cup games from 6 April 1963 to 10 April 1965. During this period, they reached the fourth round of the League Cup in 1963-64.

Watertight Mariners
Grimsby Town had 25 clean sheets in 1955-56 when winning the championship of Division 3 (North). These included the last eight successive matches.

Trading places
On 26 November 1994, **Hartlepool United** player/manager David McCreery, who had taken over from John MacPhail, dropped himself and put in MacPhail against Rochdale. United won 1-0 to move off the bottom.

Fast Eddie
The first Football League victims of a giant-killing act by **Hereford United** were Exeter City beaten 2-0 in a first round replay on 26 November 1953 following a 1-1 draw. Eddie O'Hara scored all three United goals.

Star(buck) struck
Phil Starbuck was a 54th minute substitute for **Huddersfield Town** against Wigan Athletic on Easter Monday 1993. He came on as a corner was about to be taken and scored with a header.

Fettis fetish
Hull City put on reserve goalkeeper Alan Fettis as an 80th minute outfield substitute and he scored after 88 minutes against Oxford United. On 6 May 1995, he played the entire game at Blackpool as a striker scoring in injury time.

Better late than...
On 14 January 1995, **Ipswich Town** won 1-0 at Liverpool. It was the first time they had achieved this feat in 28 visits to Anfield.

Blue was the colour
When **Leeds United** entered the Football League in 1920, their club colours were blue and white vertical stripes and white shorts. In 1934 they changed to blue and gold halved shirts.

Six of the best
In 1956-57 **Leicester City** set up six club records: most wins (35), most away wins (11), fewest defeats (6), most points (61), most goals (109) and the highest individual scorer was Arthur Rowley with 44 goals.

Dutch treat out East
Leyton Orient beat Racing Club Haarlem from Holland 3-1 in their 1951 Festival of Britain match. Jimmy Blair scored one of their goals.

Lincoln's in
The highest attendance recorded in a Vauxhall Conference match was 9432 for **Lincoln City** against Wycombe Wanderers at Sincil Bank on 2 May 1988.

First day clever
When **Liverpool** won 6-1 at Crystal Palace on 20 August 1994, they extended their record having opened a season with more wins than any other first class club -54 out of 92 seasons.

Town twinning
In successive years, **Luton Town** enjoyed runs of 19 matches unbeaten: January to April 1968 and April to October 1969, but in Divisions 3 and 4 respectively.

Under two flags
Manchester City fielded goalkeeper John Burridge against Newcastle United on 29 April 1995. At the time he was employed as part-time goalkeeping coach with Newcastle.

Home alone II
Manchester United conceded their first goal in League matches at Old Trafford on 17 December 1994 after 1135 minutes, when losing 2-1 to Nottingham Forest.

A positive Iffy
On 11 March 1995, **Mansfield Town** beat Lincoln City 6-2. Iffy Onuora scored a seven-minute second-half hat-trick between the 78th and 85th minutes. Mansfield's total of 71 League goals at the time was the highest in the four English Leagues.

Overseas Tees
In 1994-95 **Middlesbrough** fielded Uwe Fuchs (German) and Jaime Moreno (Bolivian), their first foreign duo since Rolando Ugolini (Italian) and Lindy Delapenha (Jamaican), on 28 April 1956.

Forest chopped down
On 30 November 1994, **Millwall** became the first team to win a League Cup tie at Nottingham Forest for 18 years, when they recorded a 2-0 victory.

Geordies' pet plan
Newcastle United equalled their best start to a season in 1994-95 when they remained unbeaten in the opening 11 matches. They had previously set the record in 1950-51.

All Cobblers
Northampton Town had three marksmen with 20 or more goals in 1952-53: Jack English 26, Willie O'Donnell 26 and Freddie Ramscar 22.

Super stiffs
In three successive seasons 1932-33 to 1934-35, Norwich City were Southern League (East) champions, a competition for the club's reserve team at the time.

More shinned against...
Sam Weller Widdowson, inventor of the shin pad, played in 23 FA Cup matches for **Nottingham Forest** between 1878 and 1885 scoring 19 goals. These included four against Sheffield Heeley on 2 December 1882.

Metre made
In August 1994 **Notts County** player Andy Legg, 28, entered the Guiness Book of Records with the longest recorded throw-in with a football: 41 metres.

Borderline case
Centre-forward Tommy Davis is the only **Oldham Athletic** player to have been capped for two different countries at full international level. In 1936-37 he played twice for the Republic of Ireland and once for Northern Ireland.

One over the eight II
In 1994-95, **Oxford United** equalled their best start to a season by remaining unbeaten for nine League games. They were the last English League team to remain undefeated. The club had set their record in 1983-84.

Fast Eddie II
On New Year's Day 1948, Eddie Friedmanis a Latvian International, scored a hat-trick on his debut for **Peterborough United** in a 3-0 Midland League victory over Mansfield Town reserves.

Pilgrim father's son
Sam Shilton was an 89th minute substitute for **Plymouth Argyle** against Bournemouth in a second round FA Cup tie on 3 December 1994, becoming at 16 years 4 months and 12 days, the club's youngest debutant.

Dan, Dan, the very first man
The first **Portsmouth** player to receive full international honours was inside-right Daniel Cunliffe, who was capped for England on 17 March 1900 against Ireland.

Only two can play
When **Port Vale** defeated Fulham 7-1 in a Division 2 match on 2 April 1927, Wilf Kirkham scored four goals and Harry Anstiss the other three.

Your number's up
Jimmy Ross scored 37 FA Cup goals for **Preston North End** between January 1887 and January 1894. These included one 8, two 6's and one 4.

A Royal occasion
The record attendance for any Southern League match is 29,786 for **Queens Park Rangers** v Plymouth Argyle at Park Royal on 25 December 1907. The match ended in a goalless draw.

Graduation Day
A 16th minute substitute for **Reading** against Bristol City on 15 October 1994 was Michael Murphy, 17, just a week after he had been a school student.

Neil downs Rovers
On 1 October 1994, debutant **Rochdale** goalkeeper Neil Dunford, a brickie and pub player, saved a 72nd minute penalty against Doncaster Rovers with the score at 0-0. Rochdale won 2-0.

Bobby's dazzler
On 22 November 1994, Bobby Davison scored a 10 second goal for **Rotherham United** in an FA Cup first round replay against York City. It equalled the second fastest goal in the Cup's history.

Species of eight
Scarborough scored a 1-0 win at Chesterfield on 13 August 1994. This continued their run of not losing the opening match of the season during their eight years in the Football League.

Seventeenth year hitch
Scunthorpe United completed 18 hours unbeaten in 26 home FA Cup matches dating back to 1977, when they lost 2-1 to Birmingham City in a second round replay in 1994-95.

Jock's away
When **Sheffield United** drew 2-2 with Tottenham Hotspur at White Hart Lane on 12 September 1938, Jock Dodds scored his 100th League goal for the club. The player was shortly afterwards transferred to Blackpool for £10,000.

Tied up in Notts
Tom Brandon, captain of **Sheffield Wednesday**, scored their first League goal on 3 September 1892 in a 1-0 win over Notts County. His only other goal that season was in the return match against Notts.

Jack-in-the-box
When **Shrewsbury Town** beat Walsall 5-0 in an FA Cup first round, first leg tie on 17 November 1945, Jackie Maund scored a hat-trick. He joined Walsall a year later.

On the spot
On 1 March 1995, Matt Le Tissier converted a 39th minute penalty in an FA Cup fifth round replay against Tottenham Hotspur. It was his 35th successful spot kick out of 36 attempts in his **Southampton** career.

Paul: on the overhaul
On 2 January 1995, Paul Sansome made his 344th appearance for **Southend United** beating fellow goalkeeper Harry Threadgold's appearances between 1953 and 1963.

Return to victory
A record Edgeley Park crowd of 7000 witnessed Chelsea's first competititve fixture on 2 September 1905. **Stockport County** had just regained their Football League status and won with a George Dodd goal.

The famous five
In the close season of 1895, **Stoke City** signed William Maxwell from Dundee. In six seasons he scored 85 goals in 173 League and Cup games and was leading League scorer for five successive seasons.

Drawn level
Sunderland drew 18 Division Two matches in 1994-95 to equal a club record set up 40 years earlier when they finished fourth in Division Two.

Pembroke(n)!
On 13 March 1995, two days after ending Birmingham City's home run of 22 matches unbeaten, **Swansea City** beat Pembroke Borough 16-0 in the semi-final of the West Wales Senior Cup.

Double with Harry
The career of Harry Cousins began as a 16 year old Chesterfield trialist against Notts County and ended on the same Meadow Lane ground after 24 years with **Swindon Town** in 1947.

Having a Rollerball
On 27 December 1994, 19 year old goalkeeper Paul Pettinger was Rolls-Royce chauffeur driven 300 miles on loan from Leeds United to make his **Torquay United** debut in a 2-2 draw with Hartlepool United.

Teutonic tradition
Jurgen Klinsmann was not the first German player to sign for **Tottenham Hotspur**. Max Seeburg was not only the first German with the club, but also the first foreigner in the Football League in 1907.

Milestone man
Steve Mungall made his 600th League and Cup appearance for **Tranmere Rovers** on 29 October 1994 in a 1-1 draw with Port Vale.

Blazing Saddlers
Walsall recorded their highest FA Cup score outside the competition proper when they beat Warmley 12-0 away in a first qualifying round tie on 27 September 1890.

Clean sheets
On 11 February 1995, **Watford** equalled a 46 year old club record with their eighth successive game without conceding a goal. They beat it the following week in an FA Cup tie against Crystal Palace.

Brave Bob
Bob Taylor, the **West Bromwich Albion** centre-forward was hospitalized on 10 September 1994 for tests on a kidney problem, but left his sick-bed to score twice in the 2-2 draw at Millwall.

Victor Bravo
Vic Watson scored 16 goals in four games for **West Ham United** against Leeds United: six on 9 February 1929, three on 16 November, four in an FA Cup tie on 25 January 1930 and three on 21 March 1931.

Magpies flutter
In the 1953-54 season, **Wigan Athletic**, top of the Lancashire Combination, forced a 2-2 third round FA Cup draw with First Division Newcastle United at St James' Park on 9 January 1954, watched by 52,222. United won the replay 2-2.

Swiftly flowed the Dons
Wimbledon were 3-1 down to Aston Villa on 9 November 1994, before scoring three goals in the last 25 minutes including a last minute winner to edge home 4-3.

Unload of Bull
Steve Bull completed 200 League goals for **Wolverhampton Wanderers** with headed efforts on either side of half-time on 15 April 1995 against Charlton Athletic. He also finished the game as captain.

What it's all about
Right-back Alfie Jones made 503 League and 72 FA Cup appearances between 1923-24 and 1935-36 for **Wrexham**, his only League club.

Barefoot on the park
In August 1956, **Wycombe Wanderers** became the first British team to play a Ugandan touring side, defeating their barefoot visitors 10-1 in front of a 7450 midweek crowd.

Lester's nap
When **York City** beat Horsforth 7-1 in a preliminary round FA Cup tie on 20 September 1924, centre-forward Lester Marshall scored five goals.

ENGLISH LEAGUE MANAGERS

ARSENAL

Managers (and Secretary-Managers)
Sam Hollis 1894–97, Tom Mitchell 1897–98, George Elcoat 1898–99, Harry Bradshaw 1899–1904, Phil Kelso 1904–08, George Morrell 1908–15, Leslie Knighton 1919–25, Herbert Chapman 1925–34, George Allison 1934–47, Tom Whittaker 1947–56, Jack Crayston 1956–58, George Swindin 1958–62, Billy Wright 1962–66, Bertie Mee 1966–76, Terry Neill 1976–83, Don Howe 1984–86, George Graham 1986–95, Bruce Rioch June 1995– .

ASTON VILLA

Managers (and Secretary-Managers)
George Ramsay 1884–1926*, W. J. Smith 1926–34*, Jimmy McMullan 1934–35, Jimmy Hogan 1936–44, Alex Massie 1945–50, George Martin 1950–53, Eric Houghton 1953–58, Joe Mercer 1958–64, Dick Taylor 1965–67, Tommy Cummings 1967–68, Tommy Docherty 1968–70, Vic Crowe 1970–74, Ron Saunders 1974–82, Tony Barton 1982–84, Graham Turner 1984–86, Billy McNeill 1986–87, Graham Taylor 1987–90, Dr. Jozef Venglos 1990–91, Ron Atkinson 1991–94, Brian Little November 1994– .

BARNET

Managers: (since 1946) Lester Finch, George Wheeler, Dexter Adams, Tommy Coleman, Gerry Ward, Gordon Ferry, Brian Kelly, Bill Meadows, Barry Fry, Roger Thompson, Don McAllister, Barry Fry, Edwin Stein, Gary Phillips (player-manager) 1993–94, Ray Clemence January 1994– .

BARNSLEY

Managers (and Secretary-Managers)
Arthur Fairclough 1898–1901*, John McCartney 1901–04*, Arthur Fairclough 1904–12, John Hastie 1912–14, Percy Lewis 1914–19, Peter Sant 1919–26, John Commins 1926–29, Arthur Fairclough 1929–30, Brough Fletcher 1930–37, Angus Seed 1937–53, Tim Ward 1953–60, Johnny Steele 1960–71 (continued as GM), John McSeveney 1971–72, Johnny Steele (GM) 1972–73, Jim Iley 1973–78, Allan Clarke 1978–80, Norman Hunter 1980–84, Bobby Collins 1984–85, Allan Clarke 1985–89, Mel Machin 1989–93, Viv Anderson 1993–94, Danny Wilson June 1994– .

BIRMINGHAM CITY

Managers (and Secretary-Managers)
Alfred Jones 1892–1908*, Alec Watson 1908–1910, Bob McRoberts 1910–15, Frank Richards 1915–23, Billy Beer 1923–27, Leslie Knighton 1928–33, George Liddell 1933–39, Harry Storer 1945–48, Bob Brocklebank 1949–54, Arthur Turner 1954–58, Pat Beasley 1959–60, Gil Merrick 1960–64, Joe Mallett 1965, Stan Cullis 1965–70, Fred Goodwin 1970–75, Willie Bell 1975–77, Jim Smith 1978–82, Ron Saunders 1982–86, John Bond 1986–87, Garry Pendrey 1987–89, Dave Mackay 1989–1991, Lou Macari 1991, Terry Cooper 1991–93, Barry Fry December 1993– .

BLACKBURN ROVERS

Managers (and Secretary-Managers)
Thomas Mitchell 1884–96*, J. Walmsley 1896–1903*, R. B. Middleton 1903–25, Jack Carr 1922–26 (TM under Middleton to 1925), Bob Crompton 1926–30 (Hon. TM), Arthur Barritt 1931–36 (had been Sec. from 1927), Reg Taylor 1936–38, Bob Crompton 1938–41, Eddie Hapgood 1944–47, Will Scott 1947, Jack Bruton 1947–49, Jackie Bestall 1949–53, Johnny Carey 1953–58, Dally Duncan 1958–60, Jack Marshall 1960–67, Eddie Quigley 1967–70, Johnny Carey 1970–71, Ken Furphy 1971–73, Gordon Lee 1974–75, Jim Smith 1975–78, Jim Iley 1978, John Pickering 1978–79, Howard Kendall 1979–81, Bobby Saxton 1981–86, Don Mackay 1987–91, Kenny Dalglish 1991–95, Ray Harford June 1995– .

BLACKPOOL

Managers (and Secretary-Managers)
Tom Barcroft 1903–33* (Hon. Sec.), John Cox 1909–11, Bill Norman 1919–23, Maj. Frank Buckley 1923–27, Sid Beaumont 1927–28, Harry Evans 1928–33 (Hon. TM), Alex "Sandy" Macfarlane 1933–35, Joe Smith 1935–58, Ronnie Suart 1958–67, Stan Mortensen 1967–69, Les Shannon 1969–70, Bob Stokoe 1970–72, Harry Potts 1972–76, Allan Brown 1976–78, Bob Stokoe 1978–79, Stan Ternent 1979–80, Alan Ball 1980–81, Allan Brown 1981–82, Sam Ellis 1982–89, Jimmy Mullen 1989–90, Graham Carr 1990, Bill Ayre 1990–94, Sam Allardyce July 1994– .

BOLTON WANDERERS

Managers (and Secretary-Managers)
Tom Rawthorne 1874–85*, J. J. Bentley 1885–86*, W. G. Struthers 1886–87*, Fitzroy Norris 1887*, J. J. Bentley 1887–95*, Harry Downs 1895–96*, Frank Brettell 1896–98*, John Somerville 1898–1910, Will Settle 1910–15, Tom Mather 1915–19, Charles Foweraker 1919–44, Walter Rowley 1944–50, Bill Ridding 1951–68, Nat Lofthouse 1968–70, Jimmy McIlroy 1970, Jimmy Meadows 1971, Nat Lofthouse 1971 (then admin. man. to 1972), Jimmy Armfield 1971–74, Ian Greaves 1974–80, Stan Anderson 1980–81, George Mulhall 1981–82, John McGovern 1982–85, Charlie Wright 1985, Phil Neal 1985–92, Bruce Rioch 1992–95, Roy McFarland June 1995– .

AFC BOURNEMOUTH

Managers (and Secretary-Managers)
Vincent Kitcher 1914–23*, Harry Kinghorn 1923–25, Leslie Knighton 1925–28, Frank Richards 1928–30, Billy Birrell 1930–35, Bob Crompton 1935–36, Charlie Bell 1936–39, Harry Kinghorn 1939–47, Harry Lowe 1947–50, Jack Bruton 1950–56, Fred Cox 1956–58, Don Welsh 1958–61, Bill McGarry 1961–63, Reg Flewin 1963–65, Fred Cox 1965–70, John Bond 1970–73, Trevor Hartley 1974–78, John Benson 1975–78, Alec Stock 1979–80, David Webb 1980–82, Don Megson 1983, Harry Redknapp 1983–92, Tony Pulis 1992–94, Mel Machin August 1994– .

BRADFORD CITY

Managers (and Secretary-Managers)
Robert Campbell 1903–05, Peter O'Rourke 1905–21, David Menzies 1921–26, Colin Veitch 1926–28, Peter O'Rourke 1928–30, Jack Peart 1930–35, Dick Ray 1935–37, Fred Westgarth 1938–43, Bob Sharp 1943–46, Jack Barker 1946–47, John Milburn 1947–48, David Steele 1948–52, Albert Harris 1952, Ivor Powell 1952–55, Peter Jackson 1955–61, Bob Brocklebank 1961–64, Bill Harris 1965–66, Willie Watson 1966–69, Grenville Hair 1967–68, Jimmy Wheeler 1968–71, Bryan Edwards 1971–75, Bobby Kennedy 1975–78, John Napier 1978, George Mulhall 1978–81, Roy McFarland 1981–82, Trevor Cherry 1982–87, Terry Dolan 1987–89, Terry Yorath 1989–90, John Docherty 1990–91, Frank Stapleton 1991–94, Lennie Lawrence May 1994– .

BRENTFORD

Managers (and Secretary-Managers)
Will Lewis 1900–03*, Dick Molyneux 1903–06, W. G. Brown 1906–08, Fred Halliday 1908–26 (only secretary to 1922), Ephraim Rhodes 1912–15, Archie Mitchell 1921–22, Harry Curtis 1926–49, Jackie Gibbons 1949–52, Jimmy Blain 1952–53, Tommy Lawton 1953, Bill Dodgin Snr 1953–57, Malcolm Macdonald 1957–65, Tommy Cavanagh 1965–66, Billy Gray 1966–67, Jimmy Sirrel 1967–69, Frank Blunstone 1969–73, Mike Everitt 1973–75, John Docherty 1975–76, Bill Dodgin Jnr 1976–80, Fred Callaghan 1980–84, Frank McLintock 1984–87, Steve Perryman 1987–90, Phil Holder 1990–93, David Webb May 1993– .

BRIGHTON & HOVE ALBION

Managers (and Secretary-Managers)
John Jackson 1901–05, Frank Scott-Walford 1905–08, John Robson 1908–14, Charles Webb 1919–47, Tommy Cook 1947, Don Welsh 1947–51, Billy Lane 1951–61, George Curtis 1961–63, Archie Macaulay 1963–68, Fred Goodwin 1968–70, Pat Saward 1970–73, Brian Clough 1973–74, Peter Taylor 1974–76, Alan Mullery 1976–81, Mike Bailey 1981–82, Jimmy Melia 1982–83, Chris Cattlin 1983–86, Alan Mullery 1986–87, Barry Lloyd 1987–93, Liam Brady 1993– .

BRISTOL CITY

Managers (and Secretary-Managers)
Sam Hollis 1897–99, Bob Campbell 1899–1901, Sam Hollis 1901–05, Harry Thickett 1905–10, Sam Hollis 1911–13, George Hedley 1913–15, Jack Hamilton 1915–19, Joe Palmer 1919–21, Alex Raisbeck 1921–29, Joe Bradshaw 1929–32, Bob Hewison 1932–49 (under suspension 1938–39), Bob Wright 1949–50, Pat Beasley 1950–58, Peter Doherty 1958–60, Fred Ford 1960–67, Alan Dicks 1967–80, Bobby Houghton 1980–82, Roy Hodgson 1982, Terry Cooper 1982–88 (Director from 1983), Joe Jordan 1988–90, Jimmy Lumsden 1990–92, Denis Smith 1992–93, Russell Osman 1993–94, Joe Jordan November 1994– .

BRISTOL ROVERS

Managers (and Secretary-Managers)
Alfred Homer 1899–1920 (continued as secretary to 1928), Ben Hall 1920–21, Andy Wilson 1921–26, Joe Palmer 1926–29, Dave McLean 1929–30, Albert Prince-Cox 1930–36, Percy Smith 1936–37, Brough Fletcher 1938–49, Bert Tann 1950–68 (continued as GM to 1972), Fred Ford 1968–69, Bill Dodgin Snr 1969–72, Don Megson 1972–77, Bobby Campbell 1978–79, Harold Jarman 1979–80, Terry Cooper 1980–81, Bobby Gould 1981–83, David Williams 1983–85, Bobby Gould 1985–87, Gerry Francis 1987–91, Martin Dobson 1991, Dennis Rofe 1992, Malcolm Allison 1992–93, John Ward March 1993– .

BURNLEY

Managers (and Secretary-Managers)
Arthur F. Sutcliffe 1893–96*, Harry Bradshaw 1896–99*, Ernest Magnall 1899–1903*, Spen Whittaker 1903–10, R. H. Wadge 1910–11*, John Haworth 1911–25, Albert Pickles 1925–32, Tom Bromilow 1932–35, Alf Boland 1935–39*, Cliff Britton 1945–48, Frank Hill 1948–54, Alan Brown 1954–57, Billy Dougall 1957–58, Harry Potts 1958–70 (GM to 1972), Jimmy Adamson 1970–76, Joe Brown 1976–77, Harry Potts 1977–79, Brian Miller 1979–83, John Bond 1983–84, John Benson 1984–85, Martin Buchan 1985, Tommy Cavanagh 1985–86, Brian Miller 1986–89, Frank Casper 1989–91, Jimmy Mullen October 1991– .

BURY

Managers (and Secretary-Managers)
T. Hargreaves 1887*, H. S. Hamer 1887–1907*, Archie Montgomery 1907–15, William Cameron 1919–23, James Hunter Thompson 1923–27, Percy Smith 1927–30, Arthur Paine 1930–34, Norman Bullock 1934–38, Jim Porter 1944–45, Norman Bullock 1945–49, John McNeil 1950–53, Dave Russell 1953–61, Bob Stokoe 1961–65, Bert Head 1965–66, Les Shannon 1966–69, Jack Marshall 1969, Les Hart 1970, Tommy McAnearney 1970–72, Alan Brown 1972–73, Bobby Smith 1973–77, Bob Stokoe 1977–78, David Hatton 1978–79, Dave Connor 1979–80, Jim Iley 1980–84, Martin Dobson 1984–89, Sam Ellis 1989–90, Mike Walsh December 1990– .

CAMBRIDGE UNITED

Managers (and Secretary-Managers)
Bill Whittaker 1949–55, Gerald Williams 1955, Bert Johnson 1955–59, Bill Craig 1959–60, Alan Moore 1960–63, Roy Kirk 1964–66, Bill Leivers 1967–74, Ron Atkinson 1974–78, John Docherty 1978–83, John Ryan 1984–85, Ken Shellito 1985, Chris Turner 1985–90, John Beck 1990–1992, Ian Atkins 1992–93, Gary Johnson 1993–95, Tommy Taylor May 1995– .

CARDIFF CITY
Managers (and Secretary-Managers)
Davy McDougall 1910–11, Fred Stewart 1911–33, Bartley Wilson 1933–34, B. Watts-Jones 1934–37, Bill Jennings 1937–39, Cyril Spiers 1939–46, Billy McCandless 1946–48, Cyril Spiers 1948–54, Trevor Morris 1954–58, Bill Jones 1958–62, George Swindin 1962–64, Jimmy Scoular 1964–73, Frank O'Farrell 1973–74, Jimmy Andrews 1974–78, Richie Morgan 1978–82, Len Ashurst 1982–84, Jimmy Goodfellow 1984, Alan Durban 1984–86, Frank Burrows 1986–89, Len Ashurst 1989–91, Eddie May 1991–94, Terry Yorath 1994–95, Eddie May March 1995– .

CARLISLE UNITED
Managers (and Secretary-Managers)
H. Kirkbride 1904–05*, McCumiskey 1905–06*, J. Houston 1906–08*, Bert Stansfield 1908–10, J. Houston 1910–12, D. Graham 1912–13, George Bristow 1913–30, Billy Hampson 1930–33, Bill Clarke 1933–35, Robert Kelly 1935–36, Fred Westgarth 1936–38, David Taylor 1938–40, Howard Harkness 1940–45, Bill Clark 1945–46*, Ivor Broadis 1946–49, Bill Shankly 1949–51, Fred Emery 1951–58, Andy Beattie 1958–60, Ivor Powell 1960–63, Alan Ashman 1963–67, Tim Ward 1967–68, Bob Stokoe 1968–70, Ian MacFarlane 1970–72, Alan Ashman 1972–75, Dick Young 1975–76, Bobby Moncur 1976–80, Martin Harvey 1980, Bob Stokoe 1980–85, Bryan "Pop" Robson 1985, Bob Stokoe 1985–86, Harry Gregg 1986–87, Cliff Middlemass 1987–91, Aidan McCaffery 1991–92, David McCreery 1992–93, Mick Wadsworth (Director of Coaching) July 1993– .

CHARLTON ATHLETIC
Managers (and Secretary-Managers)
Bill Rayner 1920–25, Alex McFarlane 1925–27, Albert Lindon 1928, Alex McFarlane 1928–32, Jimmy Seed 1933–56, Jimmy Trotter 1956–61, Frank Hill 1961–65, Bob Stokoe 1965–67, Eddie Firmani 1967–70, Theo Foley 1970–74, Andy Nelson 1974–79, Mike Bailey 1979–81, Alan Mullery 1981–82, Ken Craggs 1982, Lennie Lawrence 1982–91, Steve Gritt/Alan Curbishley 1991–95, Alan Curbishley June 1995– .

CHELSEA
Managers (and Secretary-Managers)
John Tait Robertson 1905–07, David Calderhead 1907–33, A. Leslie Knighton 1933–39, Billy Birrell 1939–52, Ted Drake 1952–61, Tommy Docherty 1962–67, Dave Sexton 1967–74, Ron Suart 1974–75, Eddie McCreadie 1975–77, Ken Shellito 1977–78, Danny Blanchflower 1978–79, Geoff Hurst 1979–81, John Neal 1981–85 (Director to 1986), John Hollins 1985–88, Bobby Campbell 1988–91, Ian Porterfield 1991–93, David Webb 1993, Glenn Hoddle June 1993– .

CHESTER CITY
Managers (and Secretary-Managers)
Charlie Hewitt 1930–36, Alex Raisbeck 1936–38, Frank Brown 1938–53, Louis Page 1953–56, John Harris 1956–59, Stan Pearson 1959–61, Bill Lambton 1962–63, Peter Hauser 1963–68, Ken Roberts 1968–76, Alan Oakes 1976–82, Cliff Sear 1982, John Sainty 1982–83, John McGrath 1984, Harry McNally 1985–92, Graham Barrow 1992–94, Mike Pejic 1994–95, Derek Mann 1995, Kevin Ratcliffe April 1995– .

CHESTERFIELD
Managers (and Secretary-Managers)
E. Russell Timmeus 1891–95*, Gilbert Gillies 1895–1901, E. F. Hind 1901–1902, Jack Hoskin 1902–1906, W. Furness 1906–07, George Swift 1907–10, G. H. Jones 1911–13, R. L. Weston 1913–17, T. Callaghan 1919, J. J. Caffrey 1920–22, Harry Hadley 1922, Harry Parkes 1922–27, Alec Campbell 1927, Ted Davison 1927–32, Bill Harvey 1932–38, Norman Bullock 1938–45, Bob Brocklebank 1945–48, Bobby Marshall 1948–52, Ted Davison 1952–58, Duggie Livingstone 1958–62, Tony McShane 1962–67, Jimmy McGuigan 1967–73, Joe Shaw 1973–76, Arthur Cox 1976–80, Frank Barlow 1980–83, John Duncan 1983–87, Kevin Randall 1987–88, Paul Hart 1988–91, Chris McMenemy 1991–93, John Duncan February 1993– .

COLCHESTER UNITED
Managers (and Secretary-Managers)
Ted Fenton 1946–48, Jimmy Allen 1948–53, Jack Butler 1953–55, Benny Fenton 1955–63, Neil Franklin 1963–68, Dick Graham 1968–72, Jim Smith 1972–75, Bobby Roberts 1975–82, Allan Hunter 1982–83, Cyril Lea 1983–86, Mike Walker 1986–87, Roger Brown 1987–88, Jock Wallace 1989, Mick Mills 1990. Ian Atkins 1990–91, Roy McDonough 1991–94, George Burley 1994, Steve Wignall January 1995– .

COVENTRY CITY
Managers (and Secretary-Managers)
H. R. Buckle 1909–10, Robert Wallace 1910–13*, Frank Scott-Walford 1913–15, William Clayton 1917–19, H. Pollitt 1919–20, Albert Evans 1920–24, Jimmy Kerr 1924–28, James McIntyre 1928–31, Harry Storer 1931–45, Dick Bayliss 1945–47, Billy Frith 1947–48, Harry Storer 1948–53, Jack Fairbrother 1953–54, Charlie Elliott 1954–55, Jesse Carver 1955–56, Harry Warren 1956–57, Billy Frith 1957–61, Jimmy Hill 1961–67, Noel Cantwell 1967–72, Bob Dennison 1972, Joe Mercer 1972–75, Gordon Milne 1972–81, Dave Sexton 1981–83, Bobby Gould 1983–84, Don Mackay 1985–86, George Curtis 1986–87 (became MD), John Sillett 1987–90, Terry Butcher 1990–92, Don Howe 1992, Bobby Gould 1992–93, Phil Neal 1993–95, Ron Atkinson February 1995– .

CREWE ALEXANDRA

Managers (and Secretary-Managers)
W. C. McNeill 1892–94*, J. G. Hall 1895–96*, 1897 R. Roberts* (1st team sec.), J. B. Bromerley 1898–1911* (continued as Hon. Sec. to 1925), Tom Bailey 1925–38, George Lillicrop 1938–44, Frank Hill 1944–48, Arthur Turner 1948–51, Harry Catterick 1951–53, Ralph Ward 1953–55, Maurice Lindley 1955–58, Harry Ware 1958–60, Jimmy McGuigan 1960–64, Ernie Tagg 1964–71 (continued as secretary to 1972), Dennis Viollet 1971, Jimmy Melia 1972–73, Ernie Tagg 1974, Harry Gregg 1975–78, Warwick Rimmer 1978–79, Tony Waddington 1979–81, Arfon Griffiths 1981–82, Peter Morris 1982–83, Dario Gradi June 1983– .

CRYSTAL PALACE

Managers (and Secretary-Managers)
John T. Robson 1905–07, Edmund Goodman 1907–25 (had been secretary since 1905 and afterwards continued in this position to 1933). Alec Maley 1925–27, Fred Maven 1927–30, Jack Tresadern 1930–35, Tom Bromilow 1935–36, R. S. Moyes 1936, Tom Bromilow 1936–39, George Irwin 1939–47, Jack Butler 1947–49, Ronnie Rooke 1949–50, Charlie Slade and Fred Dawes (joint managers) 1950–51, Laurie Scott 1951–54, Cyril Spiers 1954–58, George Smith 1958–60, Arthur Rowe 1960–62, Dick Graham 1962–66, Bert Head 1966–72 (continued as GM to 1973), Malcolm Allison 1973–76, Terry Venables 1976–80, Ernie Walley 1980, Malcolm Allison 1980–81, Dario Gradi 1981, Steve Kember 1981–82, Alan Mullery 1982–84, Steve Coppell 1984–93, Alan Smith 1993–95, Steve Coppell (TD) June 1995– .

DARLINGTON

Managers (and Secretary-Managers)
Tom McIntosh 1902–11, W. L. Lane 1911–12*, Dick Jackson 1912–19, Jack English 1919–28, Jack Fairless 1928–33, George Collins 1933–36, George Brown 1936–38, Jackie Carr 1938–42, Jack Surtees 1942, Jack English 1945–46, Bill Forrest 1946–50, George Irwin 1950–52, Bob Gurney 1952–57, Dick Duckworth 1957–60, Eddie Carr 1960–64, Lol Morgan 1964–66, Jimmy Greenhalgh 1966–68, Ray Yeoman 1968–70, Len Richley 1970–71, Frank Brennan 1971, Ken Hale 1971–72, Allan Jones 1972, Ralph Brand 1972–73, Dick Conner 1973–74, Billy Horner 1974–76, Peter Madden 1976–78, Len Walker 1978–79, Billy Elliott 1979–83, Cyril Knowles 1983–87, Dave Booth 1987–89, Brian Little 1989–91, Frank Gray 1991–92, Ray Hankin 1992, Billy McEwan 1992–93, Alan Murray 1993–95, Paul Futcher 1995, David Hodgson/ Jim Platt (Directors of Coaching) May 1995– .

DERBY COUNTY

Managers (and Secretary-Managers)
Harry Newbould 1896–1906, Jimmy Methven 1906–22, Cecil Potter 1922–25, George Jobey 1925–41, Ted Magner 1944–46, Stuart McMillan 1946–53, Jack Barker 1953–55, Harry Storer 1955–62, Tim Ward 1962–67, Brian Clough 1967–73, Dave Mackay 1973–76, Colin Murphy 1977, Tommy Docherty 1977–79, Colin Addison 1979–82, Johnny Newman 1982, Peter Taylor 1982–84, Roy McFarland 1984, Arthur Cox 1984–93, Roy McFarland 1993–95, Jim Smith June 1995– .

DONCASTER ROVERS

Managers (and Secretary-Managers)
Arthur Porter 1920–21*, Harry Tufnell 1921–22, Arthur Porter 1922–23, Dick Ray 1923–27, David Menzies 1928–36, Fred Emery 1936–40, Bill Marsden 1944–46, Jackie Bestall 1946–49, Peter Doherty 1949–58, Jack Hodgson and Sid Bycroft (joint managers) 1958, Jack Crayston 1958–59 (continued as Sec-Man to 1961), Jackie Bestall (TM) 1959–60, Norman Curtis 1960–61, Danny Malloy 1961–62, Oscar Hold 1962–64, Bill Leivers 1964–66, Keith Kettleborough 1966–67, George Raynor 1967–68, Lawrie McMenemy 1968–71, Maurice Setters 1971–74, Stan Anderson 1975–78, Billy Bremner 1978–85, Dave Cusack 1985–87, Dave Mackay 1987–89, Billy Bremner 1989–91, Steve Beaglehole 1991–93, Ian Atkins 1994, Sammy Chung July 1994– .

EVERTON

Managers (and Secretary-Managers)
W. E. Barclay 1888–89*, Dick Molyneux 1889–1901*, William C. Cuff 1901–18*, W. J. Sawyer 1918–19*, Thomas H. McIntosh 1919–35*, Theo Kelly 1936–48, Cliff Britton 1948–56, Ian Buchan 1956–58, Johnny Carey 1958–61, Harry Catterick 1961–73, Billy Bingham 1973–77, Gordon Lee 1977–81, Howard Kendall 1981–87, Colin Harvey 1987–90, Howard Kendall 1990–93, Mike Walker 1994, Joe Royle November 1994– .

EXETER CITY

Managers (and Secretary-Managers)
Arthur Chadwick 1910–22, Fred Mavin 1923–27, Dave Wilson 1928–29, Billy McDevitt 1929–35, Jack English 1935–39, George Roughton 1945–52, Norman Kirkman 1952–53, Norman Dodgin 1953–57, Bill Thompson 1957–58, Frank Broome 1958–60, Glen Wilson 1960–62, Cyril Spiers 1962–63, Jack Edwards 1963–65, Ellis Stuttard 1965–66, Jock Basford 1966–67, Frank Broome 1967–69, Johnny Newman 1969–76, Bobby Saxton 1977–79, Brian Godfrey 1979–83, Gerry Francis 1983–84, Jim Iley 1984–85, Colin Appleton 1985–87, Terry Cooper 1988–91, Alan Ball 1991–94, Terry Cooper 1994–95, Peter Fox June 1995– .

FULHAM

Managers (and Secretary-Managers)
Harry Bradshaw 1904–09, Phil Kelso 1909–24, Andy Ducat 1924–26, Joe Bradshaw 1926–29, Ned Liddell 1929–31, Jim MacIntyre 1931–34, Jim Hogan 1934–35, Jack Peart 1935–48, Frank Osborne 1948–64 (was secretary-manager or GM for most of this period), Bill Dodgin Snr 1949–53, Duggie Livingstone 1956–58, Bedford Jezzard 1958–64 (GM for last two months), Vic Buckingham 1965–68, Bobby Robson 1968, Bill Dodgin Jnr 1969–72, Alec Stock 1972–76, Bobby Campbell 1976–80, Malcolm Macdonald 1980–84, Ray Harford 1984–86, Ray Lewington 1986–90, Alan Dicks 1990–91, Don Mackay 1991–94, Ian Branfoot June 1994– .

GILLINGHAM

Managers (and Secretary-Managers)
W. Ironside Groombridge 1896–1906* (previously financial secretary), Steve Smith 1906–08, W. I. Groombridge 1908–19*, George Collins 1919–20, John McMillan 1920–23, Harry Curtis 1923–26, Albert Hoskins 1926–29, Dick Hendrie 1929–31, Fred Maven 1932–37, Alan Ure 1937–38, Bill Harvey 1938–39, Archie Clark 1939–58, Harry Barratt 1958–62, Freddie Cox 1962–65, Basil Hayward 1966–71, Andy Nelson 1971–74, Len Ashurst 1974–75, Gerry Summers 1975–81, Keith Peacock 1981–87, Paul Taylor 1988, Keith Burkinshaw 1988–89, Damien Richardson 1989–93, Mike Flanagan 1993–95, Neil Smillie 1995, Tony Pulis June 1995– .

GRIMSBY TOWN

Managers (and Secretary-Managers)
H. N. Hickson 1902–20*, Haydn Price 1920, George Fraser 1921–24, Wilf Gillow 1924–32, Frank Womack 1932–36, Charles Spencer 1937–51, Bill Shankly 1951–53, Billy Walsh 1954–55, Allenby Chilton 1955–59, Tim Ward 1960–62, Tom Johnston 1962–64, Jimmy McGuigan 1964–67, Don McEvoy 1967–68, Bill Harvey 1968–69, Bobby Kennedy 1969–71, Lawrie McMenemy 1971–73, Ron Ashman 1973–75, Tom Casey 1975–76, Johnny Newman 1976–79, George Kerr 1979–82, David Booth 1982–85, Mike Lyons 1985–87, Bobby Roberts 1987–88, Alan Buckley 1988–94, Brian Laws November 1994–

HARTLEPOOL UNITED

Managers (and Secretary-Managers)
Alfred Priest 1908–12, Percy Humphreys 1912–13, Jack Manners 1913–20, Cecil Potter 1920–22, David Gordon 1922–24, Jack Manners 1924–27, Bill Norman 1927–31, Jack Carr 1932–35 (had been player-coach since 1931), Jimmy Hamilton 1935–43, Fred Westgarth 1943–57, Ray Middleton 1957–59, Bill Robinson 1959–62, Allenby Chilton 1962–63, Bob Gurney 1963–64, Alvan Williams 1964–65, Geoff Twentyman 1965, Brian Clough 1965–67, Angus McLean 1967–70, John Simpson 1970–71, Len Ashurst 1971–74, Ken Hale 1974–76, Billy Horner 1976–83, Johnny Duncan 1983, Mike Docherty 1983, Billy Horner 1984–86, John Bird 1986–88, Bobby Moncur 1988–89, Cyril Knowles 1989–91, Alan Murray 1991–93, Viv Busby 1993, John MacPhail 1993–94, David McCreery 1994–95, Keith Houchen April 1995– .

HEREFORD UNITED

Managers (and Secretary-Managers)
Eric Keen 1939, George Tranter 1948–49, Alex Massie 1952, George Tranter 1953–55, Joe Wade 1956–62, Ray Daniels 1962–63, Bob Dennison 1963–67, John Charles 1967–71, Colin Addison 1971–74, John Sillett 1974–78, Mike Bailey 1978–79, Frank Lord 1979–82, Tommy Hughes 1982–83, Johnny Newman 1983–87, Ian Bowyer 1987–90, Colin Addison 1990–91, John Sillett 1991–92, Greg Downs 1992–94, John Layton November 1994– .

HUDDERSFIELD TOWN

Managers (and Secretary-Managers)
Fred Walker 1908–10, Richard Pudan 1910–12, Arthur Fairclough 1912–19, Ambrose Langley 1919–21, Herbert Chapman 1921–25, Cecil Potter 1925–26, Jack Chaplin 1926–29, Clem Stephenson 1929–42, David Steele 1943–47, George Stephenson 1947–52, Andy Beattie 1952–56, Bill Shankly 1956–59, Eddie Boot 1960–64, Tom Johnston 1964–68, Ian Greaves 1968–74, Bobby Collins 1974, Tom Johnston 1975–78 (had been GM since 1975), Mike Buxton 1978–86, Steve Smith 1986–87, Malcolm Macdonald 1987–88, Eoin Hand 1988–92, Ian Ross 1992–93, Neil Warnock 1993–95, Brian Horton June 1995– .

HULL CITY

Managers (and Secretary-Managers)
James Ramster 1904–05*, Ambrose Langley 1905–13, Harry Chapman 1913–14, Fred Stringer 1914–16, David Menzies 1916–21, Percy Lewis 1921–23, Bill McCracken 1923–31, Haydn Green 1931–34, John Hill 1934–36, David Menzies 1936, Ernest Blackburn 1936–46, Major Frank Buckley 1946–48, Raich Carter 1948–51, Bob Jackson 1952–55, Bob Brocklebank 1955–61, Cliff Britton 1961–70 (continued as GM to 1971), Terry Neill 1970–74, John Kaye 1974–77, Bobby Collins 1977–78, Ken Houghton 1978–79, Mike Smith 1979–82, Bobby Brown 1982, Colin Appleton 1982–84, Brian Horton 1984–88, Eddie Gray 1988–89, Colin Appleton 1989, Stan Ternent 1989–91, Terry Dolan February 1991– .

IPSWICH TOWN

Managers (and Secretary-Managers)
Mick O'Brien 1936–37, Scott Duncan 1937–55 (continued as secretary), Alf Ramsey 1955–63, Jackie Milburn 1963–64, Bill McGarry 1964–68, Bobby Robson 1969–82, Bobby Ferguson 1982–87, Johnny Duncan 1987–90, John Lyall 1990–94, George Burley December 1994– .

LEEDS UNITED

Managers (and Secretary-Managers)
Dick Ray 1919–20, Arthur Fairclough 1920–27, Dick Ray 1927–35, Bill Hampson 1935–47, Willis Edwards 1947–48, Major Frank Buckley 1948–53, Raich Carter 1953–58, Bill Lambton 1958–59, Jack Taylor 1959–61, Don Revie 1961–74, Brian Clough 1974, Jimmy Armfield 1974–78, Jock Stein 1978, Jimmy Adamson 1978–80, Allan Clarke 1980–82, Eddie Gray 1982–85, Billy Bremner 1985–88, Howard Wilkinson October 1988– .

LEICESTER CITY

Managers (and Secretary-Managers)
William Clark 1896–97, George Johnson 1898–1907*, James Blessington 1907–09, Andy Aitken 1909–11, J. W. Bartlett 1912–14, Peter Hodge 1919–26, William Orr 1926–32, Peter Hodge 1932–34, Andy Lochhead 1934–36, Frank Womack 1936–39, Tom Bromilow 1939–45, Tom Mather 1945–46, Johnny Duncan 1946–49, Norman Bullock 1949–55, David Halliday 1955–58, Matt Gillies 1959–68, Frank O'Farrell 1968–71, Jimmy Bloomfield 1971–77, Frank McLintock 1977–78, Jock Wallace 1978–82, Gordon Milne 1982–86, Bryan Hamilton 1986–87, David Pleat 1987–91, Brian Little May 1991–94, Mark McGhee December 1994– .

LEYTON ORIENT

Managers (and Secretary-Managers)

Sam Omerod 1905–06, Ike Ivenson 1906, Billy Holmes 1907–22, Peter Proudfoot 1922–29, Arthur Grimsdell 1929–30, Peter Proudfoot 1930–31, Jimmy Seed 1931–33, David Pratt 1933–34, Peter Proudfoot 1935–39, Tom Halsey 1939–39, Billy Wright 1939–45, Billy Hall 1945, Billy Wright 1945–46, Charlie Hewitt 1946–48, Neil McBain 1948–49, Alec Stock 1949–56, 1956–58, 1958–59, Johnny Carey 1961–63, Benny Fenton 1963–64, Dave Sexton 1965, Dick Graham 1966–68, Jimmy Bloomfield 1968–71, George Petchey 1971–77, Jimmy Bloomfield 1977–81, Paul Went 1981, Ken Knighton 1981, Frank Clark 1982–-91 (MD), Peter Eustace 1991–94, Chris Turner/John Sitton 1994–95, Pat Holland May 1995– .

LINCOLN CITY

Managers (and Secretary-Managers)

David Calderhead 1900–07, John Henry Strawson 1907–14 (had been secretary), George Fraser 1919–21, David Calderhead Jnr. 1921–24, Horace Henshall 1924–27, Harry Parkes 1927–36, Joe McClelland 1936–46, Bill Anderson 1946–65 (GM to 1966), Roy Chapman 1965–66, Ron Gray 1966–70, Bert Loxley 1970–71, David Herd 1971–72, Graham Taylor 1972–77, George Kerr 1977–78, Willie Bell 1977–78, Colin Murphy 1978–85, John Pickering 1985, George Kerr 1985–87, Peter Daniel 1987, Colin Murphy 1987–90, Allan Clarke 1990, Steve Thompson 1990–93, Keith Alexander 1993–94, Sam Ellis May 1994– .

LIVERPOOL

Managers (and Secretary-Managers)

W. E. Barclay 1892–96, Tom Watson 1896–1915, David Ashworth 1920–22, Matt McQueen 1923–28, George Patterson 1928–36 (continued as secretary), George Kay 1936–51, Don Welsh 1951–56, Phil Taylor 1956–59, Bill Shankly 1959–74, Bob Paisley 1974–83, Joe Fagan 1983–85, Kenny Dalglish 1985–91, Graeme Souness 1991–94, Roy Evans January 1994–

LUTON TOWN

Managers (and Secretary-Managers)

Charlie Green 1901–28*, George Thomson 1925, John McCartney 1927–29, George Kay 1929–31, Harold Wightman 1931–35, Ted Liddell 1936–38, Neil McBain 1938–39, George Martin 1939–47, Dally Duncan 1947–58, Syd Owen 1959–60, Sam Bartram 1960–62, Bill Harvey 1962–64, George Martin 1965–66, Allan Brown 1966–68, Alec Stock 1968–72, Harry Haslam 1972–78, David Pleat 1978–86, John Moore 1986–87, Ray Harford 1987–89, Jim Ryan 1900–91, David Pleat 1991–95, Terry Westley July 1995– .

MANCHESTER CITY

Managers (and Secretary-Managers)

Joshua Parlby 1893–95*, Sam Omerod 1895–1902, Tom Maley 1902–06, Harry Newbould 1906–12, Ernest Magnall 1912–24, David Ashworth 1924–25, Peter Hodge 1926–32, Wilf Wild 1932–46 (continued as secretary to 1950), Sam Cowan 1946–47, John "Jock" Thomson 1947–50, Leslie McDowall 1950–63, George Poyser 1963–65, Joe Mercer 1965–71 (continued as GM to 1972), Malcolm Allison 1972–73, Johnny Hart 1973, Ron Saunders 1973–74, Tony Book 1974–79, Malcolm Allison 1979–80, John Bond 1980–83, John Benson 1983, Billy McNeill 1983–86, Jimmy Frizzell 1986–87 (continued as GM), Mel Machin 1987–89, Howard Kendall 1990, Peter Reid 1990–93, Brian Horton 1993–95, Alan Ball July 1995– .

MANCHESTER UNITED

Managers (and Secretary-Managers)

Ernest Magnall 1900–12, John Robson 1914–21, John Chapman 1921–26, Clarence Hildrith 1926–27, Herbert Bamlett 1927–31, Walter Crickmer 1931–32, Scott Duncan 1932–37, Jimmy Porter 1938–44, Walter Crickmer 1944–45*, Matt Busby 1945–69 (continued as GM then Director), Wilf McGuinness 1969–70, Frank O'Farrell 1971–72, Tommy Docherty 1972–77, Dave Sexton 1977–81, Ron Atkinson 1981–86, Alex Ferguson November 1986– .

MANSFIELD TOWN

Managers (and Secretary-Managers)

John Baynes 1922–25, Ted Davison 1926–28, Jack Hickling 1928–33, Henry Martin 1933–35, Charlie Bell 1935, Harold Wightman 1936, Harold Parkes 1936–38, Jack Poole 1938–44, Lloyd Barke 1944–45, Roy Goodall 1945–49, Freddie Steele 1949–51, George Jobey 1952–53, Stan Mercer 1953–55, Charlie Mitten 1956–58, Sam Weaver 1958–60, Raich Carter 1960–63, Tommy Cummings 1963–67, Tommy Eggleston 1967–70, Jock Basford 1970–71, Danny Williams 1971–74, Dave Smith 1974–76, Peter Morris 1976–78, Billy Bingham 1978–79, Mick Jones 1979–81, Stuart Boam 1981–83, Ian Greaves 1983–89, George Foster 1989–93, Andy King November 1993– .

MIDDLESBROUGH

Managers (and Secretary-Managers)

John Robson 1899–1905, Alex Massie 1905–06, Andy Aitken 1906–09, J. Gunter 1908–10*, Andy Walker 1910–11, Tom McIntosh 1911–19, James Howie 1920–23, Herbert Bamlett 1923–26, Peter McWilliam 1927–34, Wilf Gillow 1934–44, David Jack 1944–52, Walter Rowley 1952–54, Bob Dennison 1954–63, Raich Carter 1963–66, Stan Anderson 1966–73, Jack Charlton 1973–77, John Neal 1977–81, Bobby Murdoch 1981–82, Malcolm Allison 1982–84, Willie Maddren 1984–86, Bruce Rioch 1986–90, Colin Todd 1990–91, Lennie Lawrence 1991–94, Bryan Robson May 1994– .

MILLWALL

Managers (and Secretary-Managers)

William Henderson 1894–99*, E. R. Stopher 1899–1900, George Saunders 1900–11, Herbert Lipsham 1911–19, Robert Hunter 1919–33, Bill McCracken 1933–36, Charlie Hewitt 1936–40, Bill Voisey 1940–44, Jack Cock 1944–48, Charlie Hewitt 1948–56, Ron Gray 1956–57, Jimmy Seed 1958–59, Reg Smith 1959–61, Ron Gray 1961–63, Billy Gray 1963–66, Benny Fenton 1966–74, Gordon Jago 1974–77, George Petchey 1978–80, Peter Anderson 1980–82, George Graham 1982–86, John Docherty 1986–90, Bob Pearson 1990, Bruce Rioch 1990–92, Mick McCarthy March 1992– .

NEWCASTLE UNITED

Managers (and Secretary-Managers)

Frank Watt 1895–32 (continued as secretary to 1932), Andy Cunningham 1930–35, Tom Mather 1935–39, Stan Seymour 1939–47 (Hon-manager), George Martin 1947–50, Stan Seymour 1950–54 (Hon-manager), Duggie Livingstone 1954–56, Stan Seymour (Hon-manager 1956–58), Charlie Mitten 1958–61, Norman Smith 1961–62, Joe Harvey 1962–75, Gordon Lee 1975–77, Richard Dinnis 1977, Bill McGarry 1977–80, Arthur Cox 1980–84, Jack Charlton 1984, Willie McFaul 1985–88, Jim Smith 1988–91, Ossie Ardiles 1991–92, Kevin Keegan February 1992– .

NORTHAMPTON TOWN

Managers (and Secretary-Managers)

Arthur Jones 1897–1907*, Herbert Chapman 1907–12, Walter Bull 1912–13, Fred Lessons 1913–19, Bob Hewison 1920–25, Jack Tresadern 1925–30, Jack English 1931–35, Syd Puddefoot 1935–37, Warney Cresswell 1937–39, Tom Smith 1939–49, Bob Dennison 1949–54, Dave Smith 1954–59, David Bowen 1959–67, Tony Marchi 1967–68, Ron Flowers 1968–69, Dave Bowen 1969–72 (continued as GM and secretary to 1985 when joined the board), Billy Baxter 1972–73, Bill Dodgin Jnr 1973–76, Pat Crerand 1976–77, Bill Dodgin Jnr 1977, John Petts 1977–78, Mike Keen 1978–79, Clive Walker 1979–80, Bill Dodgin Jnr 1980–82, Clive Walker 1982–84, Tony Barton 1984–85, Graham Carr 1985–90, Theo Foley 1990–92, Phil Chard 1992–93, John Barnwell 1993–95, Ian Atkins January 1995– .

NORWICH CITY

Managers (and Secretary-Managers)

John Bowman 1905–07, James McEwen 1907–08, Arthur Turner 1909–10, Bert Stansfield 1910–15, Major Frank Buckley 1919–20, Charles O'Hagan 1920–21, Albert Gosnell 1921–26, Bert Stansfield 1926, Cecil Potter 1926–29, James Kerr 1929–33, Tom Parker 1933–37, Bob Young 1937–39, Jimmy Jewell 1939, Bob Young 1939–45, Cyril Spiers 1946–47, Duggie Lochhead 1947–50, Norman Low 1950–55, Tom Parker 1955–57, Archie Macaulay 1957–61, Willie Reid 1961–62, George Swindin 1962, Ron Ashman 1962–66, Lol Morgan 1966–69, Ron Saunders 1969–73, John Bond 1973–80, Ken Brown 1980–87, Dave Stringer 1987–92, Mike Walker 1992–94, John Deehan 1994–95, Martin O'Neill June 1995– .

NOTTINGHAM FOREST

Managers (and Secretary-Managers)

Harry Radford 1889–97*, Harry Haslam 1897–1909*, Fred Earp 1909–12, Bob Masters 1912–25, John Baynes 1925–29, Stan Hardy 1930–31, Noel Watson 1931–36, Harold Wightman 1936–39, Billy Walker 1939–60, Andy Beattie 1960–63, John Carey 1963–68, Matt Gillies 1969–72, Dave Mackay 1972, Allan Brown 1973–75, Brian Clough 1975–93, Frank Clark May 1993– .

NOTTS COUNTY

Managers (and Secretary-Managers)

Edwin Browne 1883–93*, Tom Featherstone 1893*, Tom Harris 1893–13*, Albert Fisher 1913–27, Horace Henshall 1927–34, Charlie Jones 1934–35, David Pratt 1935, Percy Smith 1935–36, Jimmy McMullan 1936–37, Harry Parkes 1938–39, Tony Towers 1939–42, Frank Womack 1942–43, Major Frank Buckley 1944–46, Arthur Stollery 1946–49, Eric Houghton 1949–53, George Poyser 1953–57, Tommy Lawton 1957–58, Frank Hill 1958–61, Tim Coleman 1961–63, Eddie Lowe 1963–65, Tim Coleman 1965–66, Jack Burkitt 1966–67, Andy Beattie (GM 1967), Billy Gray 1967–68, Jimmy Sirrel 1969–75, Ron Fenton 1975–77, Jimmy Sirrel 1978–82 (continues as GM to 1984), Howard Wilkinson 1982–83, Larry Lloyd 1983–84, Richie Barker 1984–85, Jimmy Sirrel 1985–87, John Barnwell 1987–88, Neil Warnock 1989–93, Mick Walker 1993–94, Russell Slade 1994–95, Howard Kendall 1995, Colin Murphy June 1995– .

OLDHAM ATHLETIC

Managers (and Secretary-Managers)

David Ashworth 1906–14, Herbert Bamlett 1914–21, Charlie Roberts 1921–22, David Ashworth 1923–24, Bob Mellor 1924–27, Andy Wilson 1927–32, Jimmy McMullan 1933–34, Bob Mellor 1934–45 (continued as secretary to 1953), Frank Womack 1945–47, Billy Wootton 1947–50, George Hardwick 1950–56, Ted Goodier 1956–58, Norman Dodgin 1958–60, Jack Rowley 1960–63, Les McDowall 1963–65, Gordon Hurst 1965–66, Jimmy McIlroy 1966–68, Jack Rowley 1968–69, Jimmy Frizzell 1970–82, Joe Royle 1982–94, Graeme Sharp November 1994– .

OXFORD UNITED

Managers (and Secretary-Managers)

Harry Thompson 1949–58 (Player Manager 1949-51), Arthur Turner 1959–69 (continued as GM to 1972), Ron Saunders 1969, George Summers 1969–75, Mike Brown 1975–79, Bill Asprey 1979–80, Ian Greaves 1980–82, Jim Smith 1982–85, Maurice Evans 1985–88, Mark Lawrenson 1988, Brian Horton 1988–93, Denis Smith September 1993– .

PETERBOROUGH UNITED

Managers (and Secretary-Managers)

Jock Porter 1934–36, Fred Taylor 1936–37, Vic Poulter 1937–38, Sam Madden 1938–48, Jack Blood 1948–50, Bob Gurney 1950–52, Jack Fairbrother 1952–54, George Swindin 1954–58, Jimmy Hagan 1958–62, Jack Fairbrother 1962–64, Gordon Clark 1964–67, Norman Rigby 1967–69, Jim Iley 1969–72, Noel Cantwell 1972–77, John Barnwell 1977–78, Billy Hails 1978–79, Peter Morris 1979–82, Martin Wilkinson 1982–83, John Wile 1983–86, Noel Cantwell 1986–88 (continued as GM), Mick Jones 1988–89, Mark Lawrenson 1989–90, Chris Turner 1991–92, Lil Fuccillo 1992–93, John Still June 1994–

PLYMOUTH ARGYLE

Managers (and Secretary-Managers)

Frank Brettell 1903–05, Bob Jack 1905–06, Bill Fullerton 1906–07, Bob Jack 1910–38, Jack Tresadern 1938–47, Jimmy Rae 1948–55, Jack Rowley 1955–60, Neil Dougall 1961, Ellis Stuttard 1961–63, Andy Beattie 1963–64, Malcolm Allison 1964–65, Derek Ufton 1965–68, Billy Bingham 1968–70, Ellis Stuttard 1970–72, Tony Waiters 1972–77, Mike Kelly 1977–78, Malcolm Allison 1978–79, Bobby Saxton 1979–81, Bobby Moncur 1981–83, Johnny Hore 1983–84, Dave Smith 1984–88, Ken Brown 1988–90, David Kemp 1990–92, Peter Shilton 1992–95, Steve McCall 1995, Neil Warnock June 1995– .

PORTSMOUTH

Managers (and Secretary-Managers)

Frank Brettell 1898–1901, Bob Blyth 1901–04, Richard Bonney 1905–08, Bob Brown 1911–20, John McCartney 1920–27, Jack Tinn 1927–47, Bob Jackson 1947–52, Eddie Lever 1952–58, Freddie Cox 1958–61, George Smith 1961–70, Ron Tindall 1970–73 (GM to 1974), John Mortimore 1973–74, Ian St. John 1974–77, Jimmy Dickinson 1977–79, Frank Burrows 1979–82, Bobby Campbell 1982–84, Alan Ball 1984–89, John Gregory 1989–90, Frank Burrows 1990–1991, Jim Smith 1991–95, Terry Fenwick February 1995– .

PORT VALE

Managers (and Secretary-Managers)

Sam Gleaves 1896–1905*, Tom Clare 1905–11, A. S. Walker 1911–12, H. Myatt 1912–14, Tom Holford 1919–24 (continued as trainer), Joe Schofield 1924–30, Tom Morgan 1930–32, Tom Holford 1932–35, Warney Cresswell 1936–37, Tom Morgan 1937–38, Billy Frith 1945–46, Gordon Hodgson 1946–51, Ivor Powell 1951, Freddie Steele 1951–57, Norman Low 1957–62, Freddie Steele 1962–65, Jackie Mudie 1965–67, Sir Stanley Matthews (GM) 1965–68, Gordon Lee 1968–74, Roy Sproson 1974–77, Colin Harper 1977, Bobby Smith 1977–78, Dennis Butler 1978–79, Alan Bloor 1979, John McGrath 1980–83, John Rudge March 1984– .

PRESTON NORTH END

Managers (and Secretary-Managers)

Charlie Parker 1906–15, Vincent Hayes 1919–23, Jim Lawrence 1923–25, Frank Richards 1925–27, Alex Gibson 1927–31, Lincoln Hayes 1931–1932 (run by committee 1932–36), Tommy Muirhead 1936–37, (run by committee 1937–49), Will Scott 1949–53, Scot Symon 1953–54, Frank Hill 1954–56, Cliff Britton 1956–61, Jimmy Milne 1961–68, Bobby Seith 1968–70, Alan Ball Sr 1970–73, Bobby Charlton 1973–75, Harry Catterick 1975–77, Nobby Stiles 1977–81, Tommy Docherty 1981, Gordon Lee 1981–83, Alan Kelly 1983–85, Tommy Booth 1985–86, Brian Kidd 1986, John McGrath 1986–90, Les Chapman 1990–92, John Beck 1992–94, Gary Peters December 1994– .

QUEENS PARK RANGERS

Managers (and Secretary-Managers)

James Cowan 1906–13, James Howie 1913–20, Ted Liddell 1920–24, Will Wood 1924–25 (had been secretary since 1903), Bob Hewison 1925–30, John Bowman 1930–31, Archie Mitchell 1931–33, Mick O'Brien 1933–35, Billy Birrell 1935–39, Ted Vizard 1939–44, Dave Mangnall 1944–52, Jack Taylor 1952–59, Alec Stock 1959–65 (GM to 1968), Jimmy Andrews 1965, Bill Dodgin Jnr 1968, Tommy Docherty 1968, Les Allen 1969–70, Gordon Jago 1971–74, Dave Sexton 1974–77, Frank Sibley 1977–78, Steve Burtenshaw 1978–79, Tommy Docherty 1979–80, Terry Venables 1980–84, Gordon Jago 1984, Alan Mullery 1984, Frank Sibley 1984–85, Jim Smith 1985–88, Trevor Francis 1988–90, Don Howe 1990–91, Gerry Francis 1991–94, Ray Wilkins November 1994– .

READING

Managers (and Secretary-Managers)

Thomas Sefton 1897–1901*, James Sharp 1901–02, Harry Matthews 1902–20, Harry Marshall 1920–22, Arthur Chadwick 1923–25, H. S. Bray 1925–26 (secretary only since 1922 and 26–35), Andrew Wylie 1926–31, Joe Smith 1931–35, Billy Butler 1935–39, John Cochrane 1939, Joe Edelston 1939–47, Ted Drake 1947–52, Jack Smith 1952–55, Harry Johnston 1955–63, Roy Bentley 1963–69, Jack Mansell 1969–71, Charlie Hurley 1972–77, Maurice Evans 1977–84, Ian Branfoot 1984–89, Ian Porterfield 1989–91, Mark McGhee 1991–94, Jimmy Quinn, Mick Gooding December 1994– .

ROCHDALE

Managers (and Secretary-Managers)

Billy Bradshaw 1920, (run by committee 1920–22), Tom Wilson 1922–23, Jack Peart 1923–30, Will Cameron 1930–31, Herbert Hopkinson 1932–34, Billy Smith 1934–35, Ernest Nixon 1935–37, Sam Jennings 1937–38, Ted Goodier 1938–52, Jack Warner 1952–53, Harry Catterick 1953–58, Jack Marshall 1958–60, Tony Collins 1960–68, Bob Stokoe 1967–68, Len Richley 1968–70, Dick Conner 1970–73, Walter Joyce 1973–76, Brian Green 1976–77, Mike Ferguson 1977–78, Doug Collins 1979, Bob Stokoe 1979–80, Peter Madden 1980–83, Jimmy Greenhoff 1983–84, Vic Halom 1984–86, Eddie Gray 1986–88, Danny Bergara 1988–89, Terry Dolan 1989–91, Dave Sutton 1991–94, Mick Docherty January 1995– .

ROTHERHAM UNITED

Managers (and Secretary-Managers)

Billy Heald 1925–29 (secretary only for long spell), Stanley Davies 1929–30, Billy Heald 1930–33, Reg Freeman 1934–52, Andy Smailes 1952–58, Tom Johnston 1958–62, Danny Williams 1962–65, Jack Mansell 1965–67, Tommy Docherty 1967–68, Jimmy McAnearney 1968–73, Jimmy McGuigan 1973–79, Ian Porterfield 1979–81, Emlyn Hughes 1981–83, George Kerr 1983–85, Norman Hunter 1985–87, Dave Cusack 1987–88, Billy McEwan 1988–91, Phil Henson 1991–94, Archie Gemmill/ John McGovern September 1994– .

SCARBOROUGH

Managers (and Secretary-Managers)
B. Chapman 1945–47*, George Hall 1946–47, Harold Taylor 1947–48, Frank Taylor 1948–50, A. C. Bell (Director & Hon. TM) 1950–53, Reg Halton 1953–54, Charles Robson (Hon. TM) 1954–57, George Higgins 1957–58, Andy Smailes 1959–61, Eddie Brown 1961–64, Albert Franks 1964–65, Stuart Myers 1965–66, Graham Shaw 1968–69, Colin Appleton 1969–73, Ken Houghton 1974–75, Colin Appleton 1975–81, Jimmy McAnearney 1981–82, John Cottam 1982–84, Harry Dunn 1984–86, Neil Warnock 1986–88, Colin Morris 1989, Ray McHale 1989–93, Phil Chambers 1993, Steve Wicks 1993–94, Billy Ayre 1994, Ray McHale December 1994– .

SCUNTHORPE UNITED

Managers (and Secretary-Managers)
Harry Allcock 1915–53*, Tom Crilly 1936–37, Bernard Harper 1946–48, Leslie Jones 1950–51, Bill Corkhill 1952–56, Ron Suart 1956–58, Tony McShane 1959, Bill Lambton 1959, Frank Soo 1959–60, Dick Duckworth 1960–64, Fred Goodwin 1964–66, Ron Ashman 1967–73, Ron Bradley 1973–74, Dick Rooks 1974–76, Ron Ashman 1976–81, John Duncan 1981–83, Allan Clarke 1983–84, Frank Barlow 1984–87, Mick Buxton 1987–91, Bill Green 1991–93, Richard Money 1993–94, David Moore June 1994– .

SHEFFIELD UNITED

Managers (and Secretary-Managers)
J. B. Wostinholm 1889–1899*, John Nicholson 1899–1932, Ted Davison 1932–52, Reg Freeman 1952–55, Joe Mercer 1955–58, Johnny Harris 1959–68 (continued as GM to 1970), Arthur Rowley 1968–69, Johnny Harris (GM resumed TM duties) 1969–73, Ken Furphy 1973–75, Jimmy Sirrel 1975–77, Harry Haslam 1978–81, Martin Peters 1981, Ian Porterfield 1981–86, Billy McEwan 1986–88, Dave Bassett January 1988– .

SHEFFIELD WEDNESDAY

Managers (and Secretary-Managers)
Arthur Dickinson 1891–1920*, Robert Brown 1920–33, Billy Walker 1933–37, Jimmy McMullan 1937–42, Eric Taylor 1942–58 (continued as GM to 1974), Harry Catterick 1958–61, Vic Buckingham 1961–64, Alan Brown 1964–68, Jack Marshall 1968–69, Danny Williams 1969–71, Derek Dooley 1971–73, Steve Burtenshaw 1974–75, Len Ashurst 1975–77, Jackie Charlton 1977–83, Howard Wilkinson 1983–88, Peter Eustace 1988–89, Ron Atkinson 1989–91, Trevor Francis 1991–95, David Pleat June 1995– .

SHREWSBURY TOWN

Managers (and Secretary-Managers)
W. Adams 1905–12*, A. Weston 1912–34*, Jack Roscamp 1934–35, Sam Ramsey 1935–36, Ted Bousted 1936–40, Leslie Knighton 1945–49, Harry Chapman 1949–50, Sammy Crooks 1950–54, Walter Rowley 1955–57, Harry Potts 1957–58, Johnny Spuhler 1958, Arthur Rowley 1958–68, Harry Gregg 1968–72, Maurice Evans 1972–73, Alan Durban 1974–78, Richie Barker 1978, Graham Turner 1978–84, Chic Bates 1984–87, Ian McNeill 1987–90, Asa Hartford 1990–91, John Bond 1991–93, Fred Davies February 1994 (previously caretaker-manager from May 1993)– .

SOUTHAMPTON

Managers (and Secretary-Managers)
Cecil Knight 1894–95*, Charles Robson 1895–97, E. Arnfield 1897–1911* (continued as secretary), George Swift 1911–12, E. Arnfield 1912–19, Jimmy McIntyre 1919–24, Arthur Chadwick 1925–31, George Kay 1931–36, George Gross 1936–37, Tom Parker 1937–43, J. R. Sarjantson stepped down from the board to act as secretary-manager 1943–47 with the next two listed being team managers during this period), Arthur Dominy 1943–46, Bill Dodgin Snr 1946–49, Sid Cann 1949–51, George Roughton 1952–55, Ted Bates 1955–73, Lawrie McMenemy 1973–85, Chris Nicholl 1985–91, Ian Branfoot 1991–94, Alan Ball 1994–95, Dave Merrington July 1995–.

SOUTHEND UNITED

Managers (and Secretary-Managers)
Bob Jack 1906–10, George Molyneux 1910–11, O. M. Howard 1911–12, Joe Bradshaw 1912–19, Ned Liddell 1919–20, Tom Mather 1920–21, Ted Birnie 1921–34, David Jack 1934–40, Harry Warren 1946–56, Eddie Perry 1956–60, Frank Broome 1960, Ted Fenton 1961–65, Alvan Williams 1965–67, Ernie Shepherd 1967–69, Geoff Hudson 1969–70, Arthur Rowley 1970–76, Dave Smith 1976–83, Peter Morris 1983–84, Bobby Moore 1984–86, Dave Webb 1986–87, Dick Bate 1987, Paul Clark 1987–88, Dave Webb (GM) 1988–92, Colin Murphy 1992–93, Barry Fry 1993, Peter Taylor 1993–95, Steve Thompson 1995, Ronnie Whelan July 1995– .

STOCKPORT COUNTY

Managers (and Secretary-Managers)
Fred Stewart 1894–1911, Harry Lewis 1911–14, David Ashworth 1914–19, Albert Williams 1919–24, Fred Scotchbrook 1924–26, Lincoln Hyde 1926–31, Andrew Wilson 1932–33, Fred Westgarth 1934–36, Bob Kelly 1936–38, George Hunt 1938–39, Bob Marshall 1939–49, Andy Beattie 1949–52, Dick Duckworth 1952–56, Billy Moir 1956–60, Reg Flewin 1960–63, Trevor Porteous 1963–65, Bert Trautmann (GM) 1965–66, Eddie Quigley (TM) 1965–66, Jimmy Meadows 1966–69, Wally Galbraith 1969–70, Matt Woods 1970–71, Brian Doyle 1972–74, Jimmy Meadows 1974–75, Roy Chapman 1975–76, Eddie Quigley 1976–77, Alan Thompson 1977–78, Mike Summerbee 1978–79, Jimmy McGuigan 1979–82, Eric Webster 1982–85, Colin Murphy 1985, Les Chapman 1985–86, Jimmy Melia 1986, Colin Murphy 1986–87, Asa Hartford 1987–89, Danny Bergara 1989–95, Dave Jones March 1995– .

STOKE CITY

Managers (and Secretary-Managers)
Tom Slaney 1874–83*, Walter Cox 1883–84*, Harry Lockett 1884–90, Joseph Bradshaw 1890–92, Arthur Reeves 1892–95, William Rowley 1895–97, H. D. Austerberry 1897–1908, A. J. Barker 1908–14, Peter Hodge 1914–15, Joe Schofield 1915–19, Arthur Shallcross 1919–23, John "Jock" Rutherford 1923, Tom Mather 1923–35, Bob McGrory 1935–52, Frank Taylor 1952–60, Tony Waddington 1960–77, George Eastham 1977–78, Alan A'Court 1978, Alan Durban 1978–81, Richie Barker 1981–83, Bill Asprey 1984–85, Mick Mills 1985–89, Alan Ball 1989–91, Lou Macari 1991–93, Joe Jordan 1993–94, Lou Macari September 1994– .

SUNDERLAND

Managers (and Secretary-Managers)
Tom Watson 1888–96, Bob Campbell 1896–99, Alex Mackie 1899–1905, Bob Kyle 1905–28, Johnny Cochrane 1928–39, Bill Murray 1939–57, Alan Brown 1957–64, George Hardwick 1964–65, Ian McColl 1965–68, Alan Brown 1968–72, Bob Stokoe 1972–76, Jimmy Adamson 1976–78, Ken Knighton 1979–81, Alan Durban 1981–84, Len Ashurst 1984–85, Lawrie McMenemy 1985–87, Denis Smith 1987–91, Malcolm Crosby 1992–93, Terry Butcher 1993, Mick Buxton 1993–95, Peter Reid March 1995– .

SWANSEA CITY

Managers (and Secretary-Managers)
Walter Whittaker 1912–14, William Bartlett 1914–15, Joe Bradshaw 1919–26, Jimmy Thomson 1927–31, Neil Harris 1934–39, Haydn Green 1939–47, Bill McCandless 1947–55, Ron Burgess 1955–58, Trevor Morris 1958–65, Glyn Davies 1965–66, Billy Lucas 1967–69, Roy Bentley 1969–72, Harry Gregg 1972–75, Harry Griffiths 1975–77, John Toshack 1978–83 (resigned October re-appointed in December) 1983–84, Colin Appleton 1984, John Bond 1984–85, Tommy Hutchison 1985–86, Terry Yorath 1986–89, Ian Evans 1989–90, Terry Yorath 1990–91, Frank Burrows March 1991– .

SWINDON TOWN

Managers (and Secretary-Managers)
Sam Allen 1902–33, Ted Vizard 1933–39, Neil Harris 1939–41, Louis Page 1945–53, Maurice Lindley 1953–55, Bert Head 1956–65, Danny Williams 1965–69, Fred Ford 1969–71, Dave Mackay 1971–72, Les Allen 1972–74, Danny Williams 1974–78, Bobby Smith 1978–80, John Trollope 1980–83, Ken Beamish 1983–84, Lou Macari 1984–89, Ossie Ardiles 1989–91, Glenn Hoddle 1991–93, John Gorman 1993–94, Steve McMahon November 1994– .

TORQUAY UNITED

Managers (and Secretary-Managers)
Percy Mackrill 1927–29, A. H. Hoskins 1929*, Frank Womack 1929–32, Frank Brown 1932–38, Alf Steward 1938–40, Billy Butler 1945–46, Jack Butler 1946–47, John McNeil 1947–50, Bob John 1950, Alex Massie 1950–51, Eric Webber 1951–65, Frank O'Farrell 1965–68, Alan Brown 1969–71, Jack Edwards 1971–73, Malcolm Musgrove 1973–76, Mike Green 1977–81, Frank O'Farrell 1981–82 (continued as GM to 1983), Bruch Rioch 1982–84, Dave Webb 1984–85, John Sims 1985, Stuart Morgan 1985–87, Cyril Knowles 1987–89, Dave Smith 1989–91, John Impey 1991–92, Ivan Golac 1992, Paul Compton 1992–93, Don O'Riordan March 1993– .

TOTTENHAM HOTSPUR

Managers (and Secretary-Managers)
Frank Brettell 1898–99, John Cameron 1899–1906, Fred Kirkham 1907–08, Peter McWilliam 1912–27, Billy Minter 1927–29, Percy Smith 1930–35, Jack Tresadern 1935–38, Peter McWilliam 1938–42, Arthur Turner 1942–46, Joe Hulme 1946–49, Arthur Rowe 1949–55, Jimmy Anderson 1955–58, Bill Nicholson 1958–74, Terry Neill 1974–76, Keith Burkinshaw 1976–84, Peter Shreeves 1984–86, David Pleat 1986–87, Terry Venables 1987–91, Peter Shreeves 1991–92, Ossie Ardiles 1993–94, Gerry Francis November 1994– .

TRANMERE ROVERS

Managers (and Secretary-Managers)
Bert Cooke 1912–35, Jackie Carr 1935–36, Jim Knowles 1936–39, Bill Ridding 1939–45, Ernie Blackburn 1946–55, Noel Kelly 1955–57, Peter Farrell 1957–60, Walter Galbraith 1961, Dave Russell 1961–69, Jackie Wright 1969–72, Ron Yeats 1972–75, John King 1975–80, Bryan Hamilton 1980–85, Frank Worthington 1985–87, Ronnie Moore 1987, John King April 1987– .

WALSALL

Managers (and Secretary-Managers)
H. Smallwood 1888–91*, A. G. Burton 1891–93, J. H. Robinson 1893–95, C. H. Ailso 1895–96*, A. E. Parsloe 1896–97*, L. Ford 1897–98*, G. Hughes 1898–99*, L. Ford 1899–1901*, J. E. Shutt 1908–13*, Haydn Price 1914–20, Joe Burchell 1920–26, David Ashworth 1926–27, Jack Torrance 1927–28, James Kerr 1928–29, S. Scholey 1929–30, Peter O'Rourke 1930–32, G. W. Slade 1932–34, Andy Wilson 1934–37, Tommy Lowes 1937–44, Harry Hibbs 1944–51, Tony McPhee 1951, Brough Fletcher 1952–53, Major Frank Buckley 1953–55, John Love 1955–57, Billy Moore 1957–64, Alf Wood 1964, Reg Shaw 1964–68, Dick Graham 1968, Ron Lewin 1968–69, Billy Moore 1969–72, John Smith 1972–73, Doug Fraser 1973–77, Dave Mackay 1977–78, Alan Ashman 1978, Frank Sibley 1979, Alan Buckley 1979–86, Neil Martin (joint manager with Buckley) 1981–82, Tommy Coakley 1986–88, John Barnwell 1989–90, Kenny Hibbitt 1990–94, Chris Nicholl September 1994– .

WATFORD

Managers (and Secretary-Managers)
John Goodall 1903–10, Harry Kent 1910–26, Fred Pagnam 1926–29, Neil McBain 1929–37, Bill Findlay 1938–47, Jack Bray 1947–48, Eddie Hapgood 1948–50, Ron Gray 1950–51, Haydn Green 1951–52, Len Goulden 1952–55 (GM to 1956), Johnny Paton 1955–56, Neil McBain 1956–59, Ron Burgess 1959–63, Bill McGarry 1963–64, Ken Furphy 1964–71, George Kirby 1971–73, Mike Keen 1973–77, Graham Taylor 1977–87, Dave Bassett 1987–88, Steve Harrison 1988–90, Colin Lee 1990, Steve Perryman 1990–93, Glenn Roeder July 1993– .

WEST BROMWICH ALBION

Managers (and Secretary-Managers)
Louis Ford 1890–92*, Henry Jackson 1892–94*, Edward Stephenson 1894–95*, Clement Keys 1895–96*, Frank Heaven 1896–1902*, Fred Everiss 1902–48, Jack Smith 1948–52, Jesse Carver 1952, Vic Buckingham 1953–59, Gordon Clark 1959–61, Archie Macaulay 1961–63, Jimmy Hagan 1963–67, Alan Ashman 1967–71, Don Howe 1971–75, Johnny Giles 1975–77, Ronnie Allen 1977, Ron Atkinson 1978–81, Ronnie Allen 1981–82, Ron Wylie 1982–84, Johnny Giles 1984–85, Ron Saunders 1986–87, Ron Atkinson 1987–88, Brian Talbot 1988–91, Bobby Gould 1991–92, Ossie Ardiles 1992–93, Keith Burkinshaw 1993–94, Alan Buckley October 1994– .

WEST HAM UNITED

Managers (and Secretary-Managers)
Syd King 1902–32, Charlie Paynter 1932–50, Ted Fenton 1950–61, Ron Greenwood 1961–74 (continued as GM to 1977), John Lyall 1974–89, Lou Macari 1989–90, Billy Bonds 1990–94, Harry Redknapp August 1994– .

WIGAN ATHLETIC

Managers (and Secretary-Managers)
Charlie Spencer 1932–37, Jimmy Milne 1946–47, Bob Pryde 1949–52, Ted Goodier 1952–54, Walter Crook 1954–55, Ron Suart 1955–56, Billy Cooke 1956, Sam Barkas 1957, Trevor Hitchen 1957–58, Malcolm Barrass 1958–59, Jimmy Shirley 1959, Pat Murphy 1959–60, Allenby Chilton 1960, Johnny Ball 1961–63, Allan Brown 1963–66, Alf Craig 1966–67, Harry Leyland 1967–68, Alan Saunders 1968, Ian McNeill 1968–70, Gordon Milne 1970–72, Les Rigby 1972–74, Brian Tiler 1974–76, Ian McNeill 1976–81, Larry Lloyd 1981–83, Harry McNally 1983–85, Bryan Hamilton 1985–86, Ray Mathias 1986–89, Bryan Hamilton 1989–93, Dave Philpotts 1993, Kenny Swain 1993–94, Graham Barrow September 1994– .

WIMBLEDON

Managers (and Secretary-Managers)
Les Henley 1955–71, Mike Everitt 1971–73, Dick Graham 1973–74, Allen Batsford 1974–78, Dario Gradi 1978–81, Dave Bassett 1981–87, Bobby Gould 1987–90, Ray Harford 1990–91, Peter Withe 1991, Joe Kinnear January 1992– .

WOLVERHAMPTON WANDERERS

Managers (and Secretary-Managers)
George Worrall 1877–85*, John Addenbrooke 1885–1922, George Jobey 1922–24, Albert Hoskins 1924–26 (had been secretary since 1922), Fred Scotchbrook 1926–27, Major Frank Buckley 1927–44, Ted Vizard 1944–48, Stan Cullis 1948–64, Andy Beattie 1964–65, Ronnie Allen 1966–68, Bill McGarry 1968–76, Sammy Chung 1976–78, John Barnwell 1978–81, Ian Greaves 1982, Graham Hawkins 1982–84, Tommy Docherty 1984–85, Bill McGarry 1985, Sammy Chapman 1985–86, Brian Little 1986, Graham Turner 1986–94, Graham Taylor March 1994– .

WREXHAM

Managers (and Secretary-Managers)
Ted Robinson 1912–25* (continued as secretary to 1930), Charlie Hewitt 1925–29, Jack Baynes 1929–31, Ernest Blackburn 1932–36, Jimmy Logan 1937–38, Arthur Cowell 1938, Tom Morgan 1938–40, Tom Williams 1940–49, Les McDowall 1949–50, Peter Jackson 1951–54, Cliff Lloyd 1954–57, John Love 1957–59, Billy Morris 1960–61, Ken Barnes 1961–65, Billy Morris 1965, Jack Rowley 1966–67, Alvan Williams 1967–68, John Neal 1968–77, Arfon Griffiths 1977–81, Mel Sutton 1981–82, Bobby Roberts 1982–85, Dixie McNeil 1985–89, Brian Flynn November 1989– .

WYCOMBE WANDERERS

Managers (and Secretary-Managers)
First coach appointed 1951. Prior to Brian Lee's appointment in 1969, the team was selected by a Match Committee which met every Monday evening. James McCormack 1951–52, Sid Cann 1952–61, Graham Adams 1961–62, Don Welsh 1962–64, Barry Darvill 1964–68, Brian Lee 1969–76, Ted Powell 1976–77, John Reardon 1977–78, Andy Williams 1978–80, Mike Keen 1980–84, Paul Bence 1984–86, Alan Gane 1986–87, Peter Suddaby 1987–88, Jim Kelman 1988–90, Martin O'Neill 1990–95, Alan Smith June 1995– .

YORK CITY

Managers (and Secretary-Managers)
Bill Sherrington 1924–60 (was secretary for most of this time but virtually secretary-manager for a long pre-war spell), John Collier 1929–36, Tom Mitchell 1936–50, Dick Duckworth 1950–52, Charlie Spencer 1952–53, Jimmy McCormick 1953–54, Sam Bartram 1956–60, Tom Lockie 1960–67, Joe Shaw 1967–68, Tom Johnston 1968–75, Wilf McGuinness 1975–77, Charlie Wright 1977–80, Barry Lyons 1980–81, Denis Smith 1982–87, Bobby Saxton 1987–88, John Bird 1988–91, John Ward 1991–93, Alan Little March 1993– .

The things they said. . .

FIFA spokesman Guido Tognoni:
"*FIFA encourage players to drink, but they can't do it in the middle of the field.*"

Spurs chairman Alan Sugar, after the FA announced their swingeing punishments:
"*How tempting it will be for other club chairmen or chief executives to say that honesty is not, necessarily, the best policy.*"

Ireland manager Jack Charlton, commenting on Italy, their first World Cup opponents:
"*I've seen them on television on a Sunday morning most days of the week.*"

Spurs chairman Alan Sugar, after arranging the £2.6m transfer of Romanian star Ilie Dumitrescu while manager Ossie Ardiles was away:
"*I don't remember him from the World Cup, but I'm sure he impressed me and will do a great job at Spurs.*"

Spurs new signing Jürgen Klinsmann, pre-empting his reputation at his first press conference on arrival at Tottenham:
"*Is there a diving school in London?*"

Man Utd manager Alex Ferguson on his wayward star Eric Cantona, who got himself sent off against Rangers in the wooden-spoon match of the pre-season Ibrox international tournament:
"*When he feels he has been done an injustice, he's got to prove to the world that he's going to correct it. But he can't control his temper. Love him or hate him, we have to live with it.*"

Eric Cantona, suspended for the start of the Premiership season:
"*It's in my nature to react the way I do. It's an instinct, and to hell with people who are not happy about it.*"

Initial reactions to the trial kick-in law in the Diadora League:
"*Because there's no offside, the opposition can just crowd the 6-yard box and you can't push up. . . If the rule continues, everyone will have a team of giraffes and no midfield.*"

Slough Town manager Graham Roberts:
"*It's an absolute farce, a joke. It will take all the enjoyment out of football and ensure long-ball teams win everything. You need three huge defenders and a 7-ft goalkeeper.*"

PFA chief Gordon Taylor, warning about cheap foreign imports:
"*I think we should bear in mind what happened to English cricket. Not enough attention was given to our own talent. I'm worried that fees like Sutton's [£5m] are forcing clubs to look abroad.*"

Newcastle chairman Sir John Hall, on Gordon Taylor's outburst:
"*The man is an inward-looking islander, and it's his sort of attitude that has led to English football now being in the backwaters.*"

Man Utd chairman Martin Edwards, on the same subject:
"*The more transfer fees and players' wages rise here, the more our clubs are going to look abroad.*"

Wendy Toms, the Football League's first female linesman, on being asked how she found the crowd at Torquay after her first match:
"*No problem at all—abusive as usual.*"

Wimbledon manager Joe Kinnear, bemoaning the new law changes:
"*If football is simply going to be about going forward, then they'll ruin the game.*"

Leicester PRO Alan Birchenall, over the PA system at half-time in the match against Coventry, of the referee Keith Cooper who had sent off a player from each side:
"*The first lad deserved a yellow card and, as for the second, well, I've seen it on the box. It's a bloody joke. We'll end up with four players on each side. It's about contact, for Christ's sake.*"

Sacked Aston Villa manager Ron Atkinson, on remarks made by Tommy Docherty criticising his record:
"*All I do know is that I'll never be able to achieve what Tommy did, and that is take Aston Villa into the Third Division, and better than that, take Manchester United into the Second Division.*"

Opposition leader Tony Blair, speaking at the Scottish Press Fund lunch:
"*Walter Smith [Rangers manager] has done more than the Tory backbenchers to keep Britain out of Europe.*"

FIFA spokesman Guido Tognoni, in an open letter to new Bayern Munich chairman Franz Beckenbauer:
"*Go back to the golf course, breed horses, sail around the world, book a trip to the moon, but leave the rule book of our sport to us.*"

Steve McMahon, after being appointed Swindon player-manager:
"*No more nicey-nicey stuff. . . I don't mind if we pick up a few yellow cards. . . . I'm looking for a team which fights.*" [McMahon picks up two yellow cards himself in his first match, and is sent off.]

Forest manager Frank Clark, after Man Utd boss Alec Ferguson accused Forest of time wasting and fouling following their 2-1 victory over the champions:
"*You get the feeling you are supposed to go to Old Trafford and let them walk all over you.*"

Sheff Utd manager Dave Bassett on Charlie Hartfield's dismissal in the FA Cup against Man Utd:
"*It didn't matter whether Eric Cantona or Mickey Mouse kicked him, he should not have reacted. It cost us the game and will cost him three matches, a week's money and maybe his place in the team. He will look back on that mad moment for the rest of his life.*"

Teenage striker John Hartson, on signing for Arsenal:
"*People think I'm like Alan Smith, but I like the ball played on the floor and Arsenal play that way.*"

Arsenal manager George Graham, hastily intervening:
"*A lot of people, especially those in the media, would disagree.*"

Merthyr chairman John Reddy on the imminent departure of Welsh FA chief executive Alun Evans:
"*Now there could be a six-figure bill over an official who would have cost nothing had he got the sack he deserved. Yes, it's still pantomime time in Wales. . . .*"

Spurs manager Gerry Francis in a radio interview after they came from behind to win at West Ham:
"*What I said to them at half-time would be unprintable on the radio.*"

Beleaguered manager George Graham:
"*I know I have the backing of the Arsenal board.*"

Man Utd manager Alec Ferguson's first reactions to the Eric Cantona affair:
"*I'm devastated. This is a nightmare of the worst kind.*"

A member of the Man Utd Megastore staff the day after Cantona's assault at Selhurst Park, after the player came in to buy a replica United shirt for his 7-year-old son:
"*It was just the normal Eric. He was cool as a cucumber—you would have thought nothing had happened. He walked round as if he did not have a care in the world.*"

Everton chairman Peter Johnson, after referee David Ellery sends two of their players off and books another five at Newcastle:
"*I'm sorry to have to say it, but we do now have a major refereeing problem in this country. I don't believe I'm alone in thinking this way—it's just that many people within the game are scared to speak out and voice an opinion. No one in their right mind is going to hand over hard-earned cash to watch 11 men play against nine men, as happened on Wednesday. This is a physical sport, a man's game.*"

Selhurst Park safety officer George Crawford, quoting a saying of his trade:
"*You can take the supporter out of the terrace, but you can't take the terraces out of the supporter.*"

David Mellor, MP, speaking on BBC 2's *Westminster On-Line*, about the police approach at the Bruges-Chelsea Cup-Winners Cup tie:
"*I think this is what happens when we invite relatively ramshackle countries like Belgium to take part in European competition with a silly little football ground that wasn't really fit. It was an 18,000 maximum for the stadium, with a pitch that Farmer Brown wouldn't let his cows loose on, and mounted police behaved quite outrageously towards perfectly respectable supporters.*"

Wimbledon manager Joe Kinnear's view of Robbie Hart, who refereed their game with Man Utd:
"*He ordered me off the pitch in his normal Hitler fashion. He was a dreadful referee and I know I've got myself into trouble again. He was up for it all night and also threatened to send off [club owner] Sam Hammam. . . . With these refs it depends on what shirt you're wearing.*"

Pseudo philosopher Eric Cantona, at a press conference after his jail sentence was commuted to community service:
"*When seagulls follow the trawler, it is because they think that sardines will be thrown into the sea.*"

The half-time announcement—referring to the dismissal of player-manager Steve McMahon—at the Swindon v Bolton League match that earned PA announcer Pete Lewis the sack:
"*I've seen some crap refereeing decisions, but that's the worst.*"

Gordon Strachan, speaking at the PFA awards:
"*If a Frenchman goes on about seagulls, sardines and trawlers, he's called a philosopher. I'd just be called a short Scottish bum talking crap.*"

Man Utd manager Alex Ferguson, after Eric Cantona decides to stay at the club:
"*I don't think any player in the history of football will get the sentence he got unless they had killed Bert Millichip's dog. . . . When someone is doing well we have to knock him down. We don't do it with horses. Red Rum is more loved than anyone I know. . . . But he must have lost one race.*"

Former Leeds star John Giles, writing in the *Daily Express*:
"*I will always be proud of being part of a Leeds team that was as good as any post-war British club team. But as the years have rolled by, and after talking with Don Revie shortly before his death, I have come to a painful conclusion. It is that at Leeds we got it wrong, as Alex Ferguson is in danger of getting it wrong. . . . We didn't look beyond the business of winning. We didn't grasp that for all our achievements we would always be remembered as a negative influence on football. . . . Ferguson has done wonderfully well in playing terms. . . . But he must still accept that, at some future time, unless the trend is reversed, he will be remembered for giving English football the anarchy of Cantona, Keane and Ince.*"

Graham Souness, rejecting claims in a libel case he brought against a newspaper that he sought to dominate his ex-wife Danielle:
"*A Bengal tiger could not do that.*"

END OF SEASON PLAY-OFFS 1994–95

Semi-finals, First Leg

14 MAY

DIVISION 1

Tranmere R (1) 1 *(Malkin)*

Reading (1) 3 *(Lovell 2, Nogan)* 12,207

Tranmere R: Nixon; Stevens, Thomas (Brannan), McGreal, Garnett, O'Brien, Morrissey, Aldridge, Malkin, Irons, Nevin.
Reading: Hislop; Bernal, Osborn, Wdowczyk, Williams, McPherson, Gilkes, Gooding, Nogan, Lovell, Taylor.

Wolverhampton W (1) 2 *(Bull, Venus)*

Bolton W (0) 1 *(McAteer)* 26,153

Wolverhampton W: Stowell; Thompson, Venus, Rankine, Richards, Shirtliff, Goodman, Kelly D, Bull, Cowans, Dennison.
Bolton W: Shilton; Green, Phillips, McAteer, Bergsson, Stubbs, Dreyer, McDonald, Paatelainen, McGinlay (Coyle), Thompson.

DIVISION 2

Bristol R (0) 0

Crewe Alex (0) 0 8538

Bristol R: Parkin; Pritchard, Gurney, Stewart (Channing), Clark, Tillson, Sterling, Miller, Taylor, Skinner, Archer.
Crewe Alex: Gayle; Booty, Smith S (Wilson), Barr, Macauley, Whalley, Tierney, Collins, Adebola (Clarkson), Lennon, Murphy.

Huddersfield T (1) 1 *(Billy)*

Brentford (1) 1 *(Forster)* 14,160

Huddersfield T: Francis; Trevitt, Cowan, Bullock, Scully, Sinnott, Billy, Duxbury, Booth, Jepson, Crosby (Dunn).
Brentford: Dearden; Statham (Hutchings), Grainger, Bates, Ashby, Smith, Ratcliffe, Mundee, Taylor, Forster, Stephenson.

DIVISION 3

Mansfield T (0) 1 *(Hadley)*

Chesterfield (0) 1 *(Robinson)* 6582

Mansfield T: Ward; Boothroyd, Baraclough, Holland, Howarth, Peters, Ireland, Parkin, Wilkinson, Onuora (Lampkin), Hadley.
Chesterfield: Beasley; Hewitt, Rogers, Curtis, Carr, Law, Robinson, Davies (Howard), Lormor, Moss, Perkins.

Preston NE (0) 0

Bury (1) 1 *(Pugh)* 13,297

Preston NE: Vaughan; Fensome, Fleming, Raynor (Cartwright), Kidd, Moyes, Davey, Bryson, Lancashire, Sale (Conroy), Magee.
Bury: Kelly G; Woodward, Bimson (Hughes), Dawes, Jackson, Lucketti, Kelly T, Carter (Paskin), Stant, Rigby, Pugh.

Semi-finals, Second Leg

17 MAY

DIVISION 1

Bolton W (0) 2 *(McGinlay 2)*

Wolverhampton W (0) 0 *aet* 20,041

Bolton W: Branagan; Green, Phillips, McAteer, Bergsson, Stubbs (Dreyer), Lee (De Freitas), Coyle, Paatelainen, McGinlay, Thompson.
Wolverhampton W: Stowell; Thompson, Venus, Rankine, Richards, Shirtliff, Goodman, Kelly D, Bull, Cowans, Dennison (Wright).

Reading (0) 0

Tranmere R (0) 0 13,245

Reading: Hislop; Bernal, Osborn, Wdowczyk, Williams (Hopkins), McPherson, Gilkes, Gooding, Nogan, Lovell (Quinn), Taylor.
Tranmere R: Coyne; Stevens, Thomas, McGreal, Mungall, Brannan, Morrissey, Aldridge, Malkin (Jones), Irons, Nevin (O'Brien).

Mixu Paatelainen (second left) heads Bolton's third goal past Reading goalkeeper Shaka Hislop. (Colorsport)

Chris Billy dives to head the ball in for Huddersfield Town's final win over Bristol Rovers at 2-1. (Colorsport)

DIVISION 2

Brentford (1) 1 *(Grainger (pen))*
Huddersfield T (1) 1 *(Booth)* 11,161

Brentford: Dearden; Statham, Grainger, Bates, Ashby, Smith, Stephenson, Ratcliffe, Taylor, Forster, Abrahams (Mundee).
Huddersfield T: Francis; Trevitt, Cowan, Bullock, Scully, Sinnott, Billy, Duxbury, Booth, Jepson, Crosby (Dunn).
aet; Huddersfield T won 4-3 on penalties.

Crewe Alex (0) 1 *(Rowbotham)*
Bristol R (0) 1 *(Miller)* 6578

Crewe Alex: Gayle; Booty, Wilson, Barr, Macauley, Whalley, Tierney, Collins (Edwards), Adebola (Rowbotham), Lennon, Murphy.
Bristol R: Parkin; Pritchard, Gurney, Stewart, Clark, Tillson, Sterling, Miller, Taylor, Skinner (Browning), Channing (Archer).
aet; Bristol R won on away goals.

DIVISION 3

Bury (0) 1 *(Rigby)*
Preston NE (0) 0 9094

Bury: Kelly G; Woodward, Stanislaus, Dawes, Lucketti, Jackson, Kelly T, Carter (Paskin), Stant, Rigby, Pugh.
Preston NE: Vaughan; Fensome (Ainsworth), Fleming, Raynor, Kidd, Moyes, Davey, Bryson, Smart, Sale (Conroy), Cartwright.

Chesterfield (1) 5 *(Lormor, Robinson, Law 2 (1 pen), Howard)*
Mansfield T (2) 2 *(Holland, Wilkinson) aet* 8165

Chesterfield: Beasley (Stewart); Hewitt, Rogers, Curtis, Carr, Law, Robinson, Hazel (Perkins), Lormor, Morris, Howard.
Mansfield T: Ward; Boothroyd (Doolan), Baraclough, Holland, Howarth, Peters, Ireland, Parkin, Wilkinson, Hadley (Sherlock), Lampkin.

Finals (at Wembley)

27 MAY
DIVISION 3

Bury (0) 0
Chesterfield (2) 2 *(Lormor, Robinson)* 22,814

Bury: Kelly G; Woodward, Stanislaus, Daws, Lucketti, Jackson, Mulligan (Hughes), Carter (Paskin), Stant, Rigby, Pugh.
Chesterfield: Stewart; Hewitt, Rogers, Curtis, Carr, Law, Robinson, Hazel, Lormor (Davies), Morris, Howard (Perkins).

28 MAY
DIVISION 2

Bristol R (1) 1 *(Stewart)*
Huddersfield T (1) 2 *(Booth, Billy)* 59,175

Bristol R: Parkin; Pritchard, Gurney, Stewart, Clark, Tillson, Sterling, Miller, Taylor (Browning), Skinner, Channing (Archer).
Huddersfield T: Francis; Trevitt (Dyson), Cowan, Bullock, Scully, Sinnott, Billy, Duxbury, Booth, Jepson, Crosby (Dunn).

29 MAY
DIVISION 1

Bolton W (0) 4 *(Coyle, De Freitas 2, Paatelainen)*
Reading (2) 3 *(Nogan, Williams, Quinn) aet* 64,107

Bolton W: Branagan; Green, Phillips, McAteer, Bergsson, Stubbs, McDonald (De Freitas), Coyle, Paatelainen, McGinlay, Thompson.
Reading: Hislop; Bernal (Hopkins), Osborn, Wdowczyk, Williams, McPherson, Gilkes, Goodwin, Nogan (Quinn), Lovell, Taylor.

F.A. Carling Premiership

			Home			Goals		Away			Goals			
		P	W	D	L	F	A	W	D	L	F	A	Pts	GD
1	Blackburn R	42	17	2	2	54	21	10	6	5	26	18	89	+41
2	Manchester U	42	16	4	1	42	4	10	6	5	35	24	88	+49
3	Nottingham F	42	12	6	3	36	18	10	5	6	36	25	77	+29
4	Liverpool	42	13	5	3	38	13	8	6	7	27	24	74	+28
5	Leeds U	42	13	5	3	35	15	7	8	6	24	23	73	+21
6	Newcastle U	42	14	6	1	46	20	6	6	9	21	27	72	+20
7	Tottenham H	42	10	5	6	32	25	6	9	6	34	33	62	+8
8	QPR	42	11	3	7	36	26	6	6	9	25	33	60	+2
9	Wimbledon	42	9	5	7	26	26	6	6	9	22	39	56	-17
10	Southampton	42	8	9	4	33	27	4	9	8	28	36	54	-2
11	Chelsea	42	7	7	7	25	22	6	8	7	25	33	54	-5
12	Arsenal	42	6	9	6	27	21	7	3	11	25	28	51	+3
13	Sheffield W	42	7	7	7	26	26	6	5	10	23	31	51	-8
14	West Ham U	42	9	6	6	28	19	4	5	12	16	29	50	-4
15	Everton	42	8	9	4	31	23	3	8	10	13	28	50	-7
16	Coventry C	42	7	7	7	23	25	5	7	9	21	37	50	-18
17	Manchester C	42	8	7	6	37	28	4	6	11	16	36	49	-11
18	Aston Villa	42	6	9	6	27	24	5	6	10	24	32	48	-5
19	Crystal Palace	42	6	6	9	16	23	5	6	10	18	26	45	-15
20	Norwich C	42	8	8	5	27	21	2	5	14	10	33	43	-17
21	Leicester C	42	5	6	10	28	37	1	5	15	17	43	29	-35
22	Ipswich T	42	5	3	13	24	34	2	3	16	12	59	27	-57

Endsleigh Insurance League Division 1

			Home			Goals		Away			Goals			
		P	W	D	L	F	A	W	D	L	F	A	Pts	GD
1	Middlesbrough	46	15	4	4	41	19	8	9	6	26	21	82	+27
2	Reading	46	12	7	4	34	21	11	3	9	24	23	79	+14
3	Bolton W	46	16	6	1	43	13	5	8	10	24	32	77	+22
4	Wolverhampton W	46	15	5	3	39	18	6	8	9	38	43	76	+16
5	Tranmere R	46	17	4	2	51	23	5	6	12	16	35	76	+9
6	Barnsley	46	15	6	2	42	19	5	6	12	21	33	72	+11
7	Watford	46	14	6	3	33	17	5	7	11	19	29	70	+6
8	Sheffield U	46	12	9	2	41	21	5	8	10	33	34	68	+19
9	Derby Co	46	12	6	5	44	23	6	6	11	22	28	66	+15
10	Grimsby T	46	12	7	4	36	19	5	7	11	26	37	65	+6
11	Stoke C	46	10	7	6	31	21	6	8	9	19	32	63	-3
12	Millwall	46	11	8	4	36	22	5	6	12	24	38	62	+0
13	Southend U	46	13	2	8	33	25	5	6	12	21	48	62	-19
14	Oldham Ath	46	12	7	4	34	21	4	6	13	26	39	61	+0
15	Charlton Ath	46	11	6	6	33	25	5	5	13	25	41	59	-8
16	Luton T	46	8	6	9	35	30	7	7	9	26	34	58	-3
17	Port Vale	46	11	5	7	30	24	4	8	11	28	40	58	-6
18	Portsmouth	46	9	8	6	31	28	6	5	12	22	35	58	-10
19	WBA	46	13	3	7	33	24	3	7	13	18	33	58	-6
20	Sunderland	46	5	12	6	22	22	7	6	10	19	23	54	-4
21	Swindon T	46	9	6	8	28	27	3	6	14	26	46	48	-19
22	Burnley	46	8	7	8	36	33	3	6	14	13	41	46	-25
23	Bristol C	46	8	8	7	26	28	3	4	16	16	35	45	-21
24	Notts Co	46	7	8	8	26	28	2	5	16	19	38	40	-21

Endsleigh Insurance League Division 2

			Home			Goals		Away			Goals			
		P	W	D	L	F	A	W	D	L	F	A	Pts	GD
1	Birmingham C	46	15	6	2	53	18	10	8	5	31	19	89	+47
2	Brentford	46	14	4	5	44	15	11	6	6	37	24	85	+42
3	Crewe Alex	46	14	3	6	46	33	11	5	7	34	35	83	+12
4	Bristol R	46	15	7	1	48	20	7	9	7	22	20	82	+30
5	Huddersfield T	46	14	5	4	45	21	8	10	5	34	28	81	+30
6	Wycombe W	46	13	7	3	36	19	8	8	7	24	27	78	+14
7	Oxford U	46	13	6	4	30	18	8	6	9	36	34	75	+14
8	Hull C	46	13	6	4	40	18	8	5	10	30	39	74	+13
9	York C	46	13	4	6	37	21	8	5	10	30	30	72	+16
10	Swansea C	46	10	8	5	23	13	9	6	8	34	32	71	+12
11	Stockport Co	46	12	3	8	40	29	7	5	11	23	31	65	+3
12	Blackpool	46	11	4	8	40	36	7	6	10	24	34	64	-6
13	Wrexham	46	10	7	6	38	27	6	8	9	27	37	63	+1
14	Bradford C	46	8	6	9	29	32	8	6	9	28	32	60	-7
15	Peterborough U	46	7	11	5	26	29	7	7	9	28	40	60	-15
16	Brighton & H A	46	9	10	4	25	15	5	7	11	29	38	59	+1
17	Rotherham U	46	12	6	5	36	26	2	8	13	21	35	56	-4
18	Shrewsbury T	46	9	9	5	34	27	4	5	14	20	35	53	-8
19	AFC Bournemouth	46	9	4	10	30	34	4	7	12	19	35	50	-20
20	Cambridge U	46	8	9	6	33	28	3	6	14	19	41	48	-17
21	Plymouth Arg	46	7	6	10	22	36	5	4	14	23	47	46	-38
22	Cardiff C	46	5	6	12	25	31	4	5	14	21	43	38	-28
23	Chester C	46	5	6	12	23	42	1	5	17	14	42	29	-47
24	Leyton Orient	46	6	6	11	21	29	0	2	21	9	46	26	-45

Endsleigh Insurance League Division 3

			Home			Goals		Away			Goals			
		P	W	D	L	F	A	W	D	L	F	A	Pts	GD
1	Carlisle U	42	14	5	2	34	14	13	5	3	33	17	91	+36
2	Walsall	42	15	3	3	42	18	9	8	4	33	22	83	+35
3	Chesterfield	42	11	7	3	26	10	12	5	4	36	27	81	+25
4	Bury	42	13	7	1	39	13	10	4	7	34	23	80	+37
5	Preston NE	42	13	3	5	37	17	6	7	8	21	24	67	+17
6	Mansfield T	42	10	5	6	45	27	8	6	7	39	32	65	+25
7	Scunthorpe U	42	12	2	7	40	30	6	6	9	28	33	62	+5
8	Fulham	42	11	5	5	39	22	5	9	7	21	32	62	+6
9	Doncaster R	42	9	5	7	28	20	8	5	8	30	23	61	+15
10	Colchester U	42	8	5	8	29	30	8	5	8	27	34	58	-8
11	Barnet	42	8	7	6	37	27	7	4	10	19	36	56	-7
12	Lincoln C	42	10	7	4	34	22	5	4	12	20	33	56	-1
13	Torquay U	42	10	8	3	35	25	4	5	12	19	32	55	-3
14	Wigan Ath	42	7	6	8	28	30	7	4	10	25	30	52	-7
15	Rochdale	42	8	6	7	25	23	4	8	9	19	44	50	-23
16	Hereford U	42	9	6	6	22	19	3	7	11	23	43	49	-17
17	Northampton T	42	8	5	8	25	29	2	9	10	20	38	44	-22
18	Hartlepool U	42	9	5	7	33	32	2	5	14	10	37	43	-26
19	Gillingham	42	8	7	6	31	25	2	4	15	15	39	41	-18
20	Darlington	42	7	5	9	25	24	4	3	14	18	33	41	-14
21	Scarborough	42	4	7	10	26	31	4	3	14	23	39	34	-21
22	Exeter C	42	5	5	11	25	36	3	5	13	11	34	34	-34

In the Endsleigh Insurance League, goals scored determine League positions where clubs are level on points. If teams still cannot be separated, the team that has conceded fewer goals is placed higher.

FOOTBALL LEAGUE 1888–89 to 1994–95

FA PREMIER LEAGUE

Maximum points: 126

	First	*Pts*	*Second*	*Pts*	*Third*	*Pts*
1992–93	Manchester U	84	Aston Villa	74	Norwich C	72
1993–94	Manchester U	92	Blackburn R	84	Newcastle U	77
1994–95	Blackburn R	89	Manchester U	88	Nottingham F	77

FIRST DIVISION

Maximum points: 138

1992–93	Newcastle U	96	West Ham U	88	Portsmouth††	88
1993–94	Crystal Palace	90	Nottingham F	83	Millwall††	74
1994–95	Middlesbrough	82	Reading††	79	Bolton W	77

SECOND DIVISION

Maximum points: 138

1992–93	Stoke C	93	Bolton W	90	Port Vale††	89
1993–94	Reading	89	Port Vale	88	Plymouth Arg*††	85
1994–95	Birmingham C	89	Brentford††	85	Crewe Alex††	83

THIRD DIVISION

Maximum points: 126

1992–93	Cardiff C	83	Wrexham	80	Barnet	79
1993–94	Shrewsbury T	79	Chester C	74	Crewe Alex	73
1994–95	Carlisle U	91	Walsall	83	Chesterfield	81

††*Not promoted after play-offs.*

FOOTBALL LEAGUE

	First	*Pts*	*Second*	*Pts*	*Third*	*Pts*
1888–89*a*	Preston NE	40	Aston Villa	29	Wolverhampton W	28
1889–90*a*	Preston NE	33	Everton	31	Blackburn R	27
1890–91*a*	Everton	29	Preston NE	27	Notts Co	26
1891–92*b*	Sunderland	42	Preston NE	37	Bolton W	36

FIRST DIVISION to 1991–92

Maximum points: a 44; *b* 52; *c* 60; *d* 68; *e* 76; *f* 84; *g* 126; *h* 120; *k* 114.

1892–93*c*	Sunderland	48	Preston NE	37	Everton	36
1893–94*c*	Aston Villa	44	Sunderland	38	Derby Co	36
1894–95*c*	Sunderland	47	Everton	42	Aston Villa	39
1895–96*c*	Aston Villa	45	Derby Co	41	Everton	39
1896–97*c*	Aston Villa	47	Sheffield U*	36	Derby Co	36
1897–98*c*	Sheffield U	42	Sunderland	37	Wolverhampton W*	35
1898–99*d*	Aston Villa	45	Liverpool	43	Burnley	39
1899–1900*d*	Aston Villa	50	Sheffield U	48	Sunderland	41
1900–01*d*	Liverpool	45	Sunderland	43	Notts Co	40
1901–02*d*	Sunderland	44	Everton	41	Newcastle U	37
1902–03*d*	The Wednesday	42	Aston Villa*	41	Sunderland	41
1903–04*d*	The Wednesday	47	Manchester C	44	Everton	43
1904–05*d*	Newcastle U	48	Everton	47	Manchester C	46
1905–06*e*	Liverpool	51	Preston NE	47	The Wednesday	44
1906–07*e*	Newcastle U	51	Bristol C	48	Everton*	45
1907–08*e*	Manchester U	52	Aston Villa*	43	Manchester C	43
1908–09*e*	Newcastle U	53	Everton	46	Sunderland	44
1909–10*e*	Aston Villa	53	Liverpool	48	Blackburn R*	45
1910–11*e*	Manchester U	52	Aston Villa	51	Sunderland*	45
1911–12*e*	Blackburn R	49	Everton	46	Newcastle U	44
1912–13*e*	Sunderland	54	Aston Villa	50	Sheffield W	49
1913–14*e*	Blackburn R	51	Aston Villa	44	Middlesbrough*	43
1914–15*e*	Everton	46	Oldham Ath	45	Blackburn R*	43
1919–20*f*	WBA	60	Burnley	51	Chelsea	49
1920–21*f*	Burnley	59	Manchester C	54	Bolton W	52
1921–22*f*	Liverpool	57	Tottenham H	51	Burnley	49
1922–23*f*	Liverpool	60	Sunderland	54	Huddersfield T	53
1923–24*f*	Huddersfield T*	57	Cardiff C	57	Sunderland	53
1924–25*f*	Huddersfield T	58	WBA	56	Bolton W	55
1925–26*f*	Huddersfield T	57	Arsenal	52	Sunderland	48
1926–27*f*	Newcastle U	56	Huddersfield T	51	Sunderland	49
1927–28*f*	Everton	53	Huddersfield T	51	Leicester C	48
1928–29*f*	Sheffield W	52	Leicester C	51	Aston Villa	50
1929–30*f*	Sheffield W	60	Derby Co	50	Manchester C*	47
1930–31*f*	Arsenal	66	Aston Villa	59	Sheffield W	52
1931–32*f*	Everton	56	Arsenal	54	Sheffield W	50
1932–33*f*	Arsenal	58	Aston Villa	54	Sheffield W	51
1933–34*f*	Arsenal	59	Huddersfield T	56	Tottenham H	49
1934–35*f*	Arsenal	58	Sunderland	54	Sheffield W	49
1935–36*f*	Sunderland	56	Derby Co*	48	Huddersfield T	48
1936–37*f*	Manchester C	57	Charlton Ath	54	Arsenal	52
1937–38*f*	Arsenal	52	Wolverhampton W	51	Preston NE	49

**Won or placed on goal average, goal difference or most goals scored.*

	First	Pts	Second	Pts	Third	Pts
1938–39*f*	Everton	59	Wolverhampton W	55	Charlton Ath	50
1946–47*f*	Liverpool	57	Manchester U*	56	Wolverhampton W	56
1947–48*f*	Arsenal	59	Manchester U*	52	Burnley	52
1948–49*f*	Portsmouth	58	Manchester U*	53	Derby Co	53
1949–50*f*	Portsmouth*	53	Wolverhampton W	53	Sunderland	52
1950–51*f*	Tottenham H	60	Manchester U	56	Blackpool	50
1951–52*f*	Manchester U	57	Tottenham H*	53	Arsenal	53
1952–53*f*	Arsenal*	54	Preston NE	54	Wolverhampton W	51
1953–54*f*	Wolverhampton W	57	WBA	53	Huddersfield T	51
1954–55*f*	Chelsea	52	Wolverhampton W*	48	Portsmouth*	48
1955–56*f*	Manchester U	60	Blackpool*	49	Wolverhampton W	49
1956–57*f*	Manchester U	64	Tottenham H*	56	Preston NE	56
1957–58*f*	Wolverhampton W	64	Preston NE	59	Tottenham H	51
1958–59*f*	Wolverhampton W	61	Manchester U	55	Arsenal*	50
1959–60*f*	Burnley	55	Wolverhampton W	54	Tottenham H	53
1960–61*f*	Tottenham H	66	Sheffield W	58	Wolverhampton W	57
1961–62*f*	Ipswich T	56	Burnley	53	Tottenham H	52
1962–63*f*	Everton	61	Tottenham H	55	Burnley	54
1963–64*f*	Liverpool	57	Manchester U	53	Everton	52
1964–65*f*	Manchester U*	61	Leeds U	61	Chelsea	56
1965–66*f*	Liverpool	61	Leeds U*	55	Burnley	55
1966–67*f*	Manchester U	60	Nottingham F*	56	Tottenham H	56
1967–68*f*	Manchester C	58	Manchester U	56	Liverpool	55
1968–69*f*	Leeds U	67	Liverpool	61	Everton	57
1969–70*f*	Everton	66	Leeds U	57	Chelsea	55
1970–71*f*	Arsenal	65	Leeds U	64	Tottenham H*	52
1971–72*f*	Derby Co	58	Leeds U*	57	Liverpool*	57
1972–73*f*	Liverpool	60	Arsenal	57	Leeds U	53
1973–74*f*	Leeds U	62	Liverpool	57	Derby Co	48
1974–75*f*	Derby Co	53	Liverpool*	51	Ipswich T	57
1975–76*f*	Liverpool	60	QPR	59	Manchester U	56
1976–77*f*	Liverpool	57	Manchester C	56	Ipswich T	52
1977–78*f*	Nottingham F	64	Liverpool	57	Everton	55
1978–79*f*	Liverpool	68	Nottingham F	60	WBA	59
1979–80*f*	Liverpool	60	Manchester U	58	Ipswich T	53
1980–81*f*	Aston Villa	60	Ipswich T	56	Arsenal	53
1981–82*g*	Liverpool	87	Ipswich T	83	Manchester U	78
1982–83*g*	Liverpool	82	Watford	71	Manchester U	70
1983–84*g*	Liverpool	80	Southampton	77	Nottingham F*	74
1984–85*g*	Everton	90	Liverpool*	77	Tottenham H	77
1985–86g	Liverpool	88	Everton	86	West Ham U	84
1986–87*g*	Everton	86	Liverpool	77	Tottenham H	71
1987–88*h*	Liverpool	90	Manchester U	81	Nottingham F	73
1988–89*k*	Arsenal*	76	Liverpool	76	Nottingham F	64
1989–90*k*	Liverpool	79	Aston Villa	70	Tottenham H	63
1990–91*k*	Arsenal†	83	Liverpool	76	Crystal Palace	69
1991–92*g*	Leeds U	82	Manchester U	78	Sheffield W	75

No official competition during 1915–19 and 1939–46.
†2 pts deducted

SECOND DIVISION to 1991–92

Maximum points: a 44; *b* 56; *c* 60; *d* 68; *e* 76; *f* 84; *g* 126; *h* 132; *k* 138.

	First	Pts	Second	Pts	Third	Pts
1892–93*a*	Small Heath	36	Sheffield U	35	Darwen	30
1893–94*b*	Liverpool	50	Small Heath	42	Notts Co	39
1894–95*c*	Bury	48	Notts Co	39	Newton Heath*	38
1895–96*c*	Liverpool*	46	Manchester C	46	Grimsby T*	42
1896–97*c*	Notts Co	42	Newton Heath	39	Grimsby T	38
1897–98*c*	Burnley	48	Newcastle U	45	Manchester C	39
1898–99*d*	Manchester C	52	Glossop NE	46	Leicester Fosse	45
1899–1900*d*	The Wednesday	54	Bolton W	52	Small Heath	46
1900–01*d*	Grimsby T	49	Small Heath	48	Burnley	44
1901–02*d*	WBA	55	Middlesbrough	51	Preston NE*	42
1902–03*d*	Manchester C	54	Small Heath	51	Woolwich A	48
1903–04*d*	Preston NE	50	Woolwich A	49	Manchester U	48
1904–05*d*	Liverpool	58	Bolton W	56	Manchester U	53
1905–06*e*	Bristol C	66	Manchester U	62	Chelsea	53
1906–07*e*	Nottingham F	60	Chelsea	57	Leicester Fosse	48
1907–08*e*	Bradford C	54	Leicester Fosse	52	Oldham Ath	50
1908–09*e*	Bolton W	52	Tottenham H*	51	WBA	51
1909–10*e*	Manchester C	54	Oldham Ath*	53	Hull C*	53
1910–11*e*	WBA	53	Bolton W	51	Chelsea	49
1911–12*e*	Derby Co*	54	Chelsea	54	Burnley	52
1912–13*e*	Preston NE	53	Burnley	50	Birmingham	46
1913–14*e*	Notts Co	53	Bradford PA*	49	Woolwich A	49
1914–15*e*	Derby Co	53	Preston NE	50	Barnsley	47
1919–20*f*	Tottenham H	70	Huddersfield T	64	Birmingham	56
1920–21*f*	Birmingham*	58	Cardiff C	58	Bristol C	51
1921–22*f*	Nottingham F	56	Stoke C*	52	Barnsley	52
1922–23*f*	Notts Co	53	West Ham U*	51	Leicester C	51
1923–24*f*	Leeds U	54	Bury*	51	Derby Co	51
1924–25*f*	Leicester C	59	Manchester U	57	Derby Co	55

**Won or placed on goal average/goal difference.*

	First	Pts	Second	Pts	Third	Pts
1925–26*f*	Sheffield W	60	Derby Co	57	Chelsea	52
1926–27*f*	Middlesbrough	62	Portsmouth*	54	Manchester C	54
1927–28*f*	Manchester C	59	Leeds U	57	Chelsea	54
1928–29*f*	Middlesbrough	55	Grimsby T	53	Bradford*	48
1929–30*f*	Blackpool	58	Chelsea	55	Oldham Ath	53
1930–31*f*	Everton	61	WBA	54	Tottenham H	51
1931–32*f*	Wolverhampton W	56	Leeds U	54	Stoke C	52
1932–33*f*	Stoke C	56	Tottenham H	55	Fulham	50
1933–34*f*	Grimsby T	59	Preston NE	52	Bolton W*	51
1934–35*f*	Brentford	61	Bolton W*	56	West Ham U	56
1935–36*f*	Manchester U	56	Charlton Ath	55	Sheffield U*	52
1936–37*f*	Leicester C	56	Blackpool	55	Bury	52
1937–38*f*	Aston Villa	57	Manchester U*	53	Sheffield U	53
1938–39*f*	Blackburn R	55	Sheffield U	54	Sheffield W	53
1946–47*f*	Manchester C	62	Burnley	58	Birmingham C	55
1947–48*f*	Birmingham C	59	Newcastle U	56	Southampton	52
1948–49*f*	Fulham	57	WBA	56	Southampton	55
1949–50*f*	Tottenham H	61	Sheffield W*	52	Sheffield U*	52
1950–51*f*	Preston NE	57	Manchester C	52	Cardiff C	50
1951–52*f*	Sheffield W	53	Cardiff C*	51	Birmingham C	51
1952–53*f*	Sheffield U	60	Huddersfield T	58	Luton T	52
1953–54*f*	Leicester C*	56	Everton	56	Blackburn R	55
1954–55*f*	Birmingham C*	54	Luton T*	54	Rotherham U	54
1955–56*f*	Sheffield W	55	Leeds U	52	Liverpool*	48
1956–57*f*	Leicester C	61	Nottingham F	54	Liverpool	53
1957–58*f*	West Ham U	57	Blackburn R	56	Charlton Ath	55
1958–59*f*	Sheffield W	62	Fulham	60	Sheffield U*	53
1959–60*f*	Aston Villa	59	Cardiff C	58	Liverpool*	50
1960–61*f*	Ipswich T	59	Sheffield U	58	Liverpool	52
1961–62*f*	Liverpool	62	Leyton O	54	Sunderland	53
1962–63*f*	Stoke C	53	Chelsea*	52	Sunderland	52
1963–64*f*	Leeds U	63	Sunderland	61	Preston NE	56
1964–65*f*	Newcastle U	57	Northampton T	56	Bolton W	50
1965–66*f*	Manchester C	59	Southampton	54	Coventry C	53
1966–67*f*	Coventry C	59	Wolverhampton W	58	Carlisle U	52
1967–68*f*	Ipswich T	59	QPR*	58	Blackpool	58
1968–69*f*	Derby Co	63	Crystal Palace	56	Charlton Ath	50
1969–70*f*	Huddersfield T	60	Blackpool	53	Leicester C	51
1970–71*f*	Leicester C	59	Sheffield U	56	Cardiff C*	53
1971–72*f*	Norwich C	57	Birmingham C	56	Millwall	55
1972–73*f*	Burnley	62	QPR	61	Aston Villa	50
1973–74*f*	Middlesbrough	65	Luton T	50	Carlisle U	49
1974–75*f*	Manchester U	61	Aston Villa	58	Norwich C	53
1975–76*f*	Sunderland	56	Bristol C*	53	WBA	53
1976–77*f*	Wolverhampton W	57	Chelsea	55	Nottingham F	52
1977–78*f*	Bolton W	58	Southampton	57	Tottenham H*	56
1978–79*f*	Crystal Palace	57	Brighton*	56	Stoke C	56
1979–80*f*	Leicester C	55	Sunderland	54	Birmingham C*	53
1980–81*f*	West Ham U	66	Notts Co	53	Swansea C*	50
1981–82*g*	Luton T	88	Watford	80	Norwich C	71
1982–83*g*	QPR	85	Wolverhampton W	75	Leicester C	70
1983–84*g*	Chelsea*	88	Sheffield W	88	Newcastle U	80
1984–85*g*	Oxford U	84	Birmingham C	82	Manchester C	74
1985–86*g*	Norwich C	84	Charlton Ath	77	Wimbledon	76
1986–87*g*	Derby Co	84	Portsmouth	78	Oldham Ath††	75
1987–88*h*	Millwall	82	Aston Villa*	78	Middlesbrough	78
1988–89*k*	Chelsea	99	Manchester C	82	Crystal Palace	81
1989–90*k*	Leeds U*	85	Sheffield U	85	Newcastle U††	80
1990–91*k*	Oldham Ath	88	West Ham U	87	Sheffield W	82
1991–92*k*	Ipswich T	84	Middlesbrough	80	Derby Co	78

No competition during 1915–19 and 1939–46.
††*Not promoted after play-offs.*

THIRD DIVISION to 1991–92

Maximum points: 92; 138 from 1981–82.

	First	Pts	Second	Pts	Third	Pts
1958–59	Plymouth Arg	62	Hull C	61	Brentford*	57
1959–60	Southampton	61	Norwich C	59	Shrewsbury T*	52
1960–61	Bury	68	Walsall	62	QPR	60
1961–62	Portsmouth	65	Grimsby T	62	Bournemouth*	59
1962–63	Northampton T	62	Swindon T	58	Port Vale	54
1963–64	Coventry C*	60	Crystal Palace	60	Watford	58
1964–65	Carlisle U	60	Bristol C*	59	Mansfield T	59
1965–66	Hull C	69	Millwall	65	QPR	57
1966–67	QPR	67	Middlesbrough	55	Watford	54
1967–68	Oxford U	57	Bury	56	Shrewsbury T	55
1968–69	Watford*	64	Swindon T	64	Luton T	61
1969–70	Orient	62	Luton T	60	Bristol R	56
1970–71	Preston NE	61	Fulham	60	Halifax T	56
1971–72	Aston Villa	70	Brighton	65	Bournemouth*	62
1972–73	Bolton W	61	Notts Co	57	Blackburn R	55
1973–74	Oldham Ath	62	Bristol R*	61	York C	61
1974–75	Blackburn R	60	Plymouth Arg	59	Charlton Ath	55

**Won or placed on goal average/goal difference.*

	First	Pts	Second	Pts	Third	Pts
1975–76	Hereford U	63	Cardiff C	57	Millwall	56
1976–77	Mansfield T	64	Brighton & HA	61	Crystal Palace*	59
1977–78	Wrexham	61	Cambridge U	58	Preston NE*	56
1978–79	Shrewsbury T	61	Watford*	60	Swansea C	60
1979–80	Grimsby T	62	Blackburn R	59	Sheffield W	58
1980–81	Rotherham U	61	Barnsley*	59	Charlton Ath	59
1981–82	Burnley*	80	Carlisle U	80	Fulham	78
1982–83	Portsmouth	91	Cardiff C	86	Huddersfield T	82
1983–84	Oxford U	95	Wimbledon	87	Sheffield U*	83
1984–85	Bradford C	94	Millwall	90	Hull C	87
1985–86	Reading	94	Plymouth Arg	87	Derby Co	84
1986–87	Bournemouth	97	Middlesbrough	94	Swindon T	87
1987–88	Sunderland	93	Brighton & HA	84	Walsall	82
1988–89	Wolverhampton W	92	Sheffield U	84	Port Vale	84
1989–90	Bristol R	93	Bristol C	91	Notts Co	87
1990–91	Cambridge U	86	Southend U	85	Grimsby T*	83
1991–92	Brentford	82	Birmingham C	81	Huddersfield T	78

FOURTH DIVISION (1958–1992)

Maximum points: 92; 138 from 1981–82.

	First	Pts	Second	Pts	Third	Pts	Fourth	Pts
1958–59	Port Vale	64	Coventry C*	60	York C	60	Shrewsbury T	58
1959–60	Walsall	65	Notts Co*	60	Torquay U	60	Watford	57
1960–61	Peterborough U	66	Crystal Palace	64	Northampton T*	60	Bradford PA	60
1961–62†	Millwall	56	Colchester U	55	Wrexham	53	Carlisle U	52
1962–63	Brentford	62	Oldham Ath*	59	Crewe Alex	59	Mansfield T*	57
1963–64	Gillingham*	60	Carlisle U	60	Workington T	59	Exeter C	58
1964–65	Brighton	63	Millwall*	62	York C	62	Oxford U	61
1965–66	Doncaster R*	59	Darlington	59	Torquay U	58	Colchester U*	56
1966–67	Stockport Co	64	Southport*	59	Barrow	59	Tranmere R	58
1967–68	Luton T	66	Barnsley	61	Hartlepools U	60	Crewe Alex	58
1968–69	Doncaster R	59	Halifax T	57	Rochdale*	56	Bradford C	56
1969–70	Chesterfield	64	Wrexham	61	Swansea C	60	Port Vale	59
1970–71	Notts Co	69	Bournemouth	60	Oldham Ath	59	York C	56
1971–72	Grimsby T	63	Southend U	60	Brentford	59	Scunthorpe U	57
1972–73	Southport	62	Hereford U	58	Cambridge U	57	Aldershot*	56
1973–74	Peterborough U	65	Gillingham	62	Colchester U	60	Bury	59
1974–75	Mansfield T	68	Shrewsbury T	62	Rotherham U	59	Chester*	57
1975–76	Lincoln C	74	Northampton T	68	Reading	60	Tranmere R	58
1976–77	Cambridge U	65	Exeter C	62	Colchester U*	59	Bradford C	59
1977–78	Watford	71	Southend U	60	Swansea C*	56	Brentford	56
1978–79	Reading	65	Grimsby T*	61	Wimbledon*	61	Barnsley	61
1979–80	Huddersfield T	66	Walsall	64	Newport Co	61	Portsmouth*	60
1980–81	Southend U	67	Lincoln C	65	Doncaster R	56	Wimbledon	55
1981–82	Sheffield U	96	Bradford C*	91	Wigan Ath	91	AFC Bournemouth	88
1982–83	Wimbledon	98	Hull C	90	Port Vale	88	Scunthorpe U	83
1983–84	York C	101	Doncaster R	85	Reading*	82	Bristol C	82
1984–85	Chesterfield	91	Blackpool	86	Darlington	85	Bury	84
1985–86	Swindon T	102	Chester C	84	Mansfield T	81	Port Vale	79
1986–87	Northampton T	99	Preston NE	90	Southend U	80	Wolverhampton W††	79
1987–88	Wolverhampton W	90	Cardiff C	85	Bolton W	78	Scunthorpe U††	77
1988–89	Rotherham U	82	Tranmere R	80	Crewe Alex	78	Scunthorpe U††	77
1989–90	Exeter C	89	Grimsby T	79	Southend U	75	Stockport Co††	74
1990–91	Darlington	83	Stockport Co*	82	Hartlepool U	82	Peterborough U	80
1991–92†*	Burnley	80	Rotherham U*	77	Mansfield T	77	Blackpool	76

†*Maximum points:* 88 owing to Accrington Stanley's resignation. ††*Not promoted after play-offs.*
†**Maximum points:* 126 owing to Aldershot being expelled.

THIRD DIVISION—SOUTH (1920–1958)

Maximum points: a 84; *b* 92.

	First	Pts	Second	Pts	Third	Pts
1920–21*a*	Crystal Palace	59	Southampton	54	QPR	53
1921–22*a*	Southampton*	61	Plymouth Arg	61	Portsmouth	53
1922–23*a*	Bristol C	59	Plymouth Arg*	53	Swansea T	53
1923–24*a*	Portsmouth	59	Plymouth Arg	55	Millwall	54
1924–25*a*	Swansea T	57	Plymouth Arg	56	Bristol C	53
1925–26*a*	Reading	57	Plymouth Arg	56	Millwall	53
1926–27*a*	Bristol C	62	Plymouth Arg	60	Millwall	56
1927–28*a*	Millwall	65	Northampton T	55	Plymouth Arg	53
1928–29*a*	Charlton Ath*	54	Crystal Palace	54	Northampton T*	52
1929–30*a*	Plymouth Arg	68	Brentford	61	QPR	51
1930–31*a*	Notts Co	59	Crystal Palace	51	Brentford	50
1931–32*a*	Fulham	57	Reading	55	Southend U	53
1932–33*a*	Brentford	62	Exeter C	58	Norwich C	57
1933–34*a*	Norwich C	61	Coventry C*	54	Reading*	54
1934–35*a*	Charlton Ath	61	Reading	53	Coventry C	51
1935–36*a*	Coventry C	57	Luton T	56	Reading	54
1936–37*a*	Luton T	58	Notts Co	56	Brighton	53
1937–38*a*	Millwall	56	Bristol C	55	QPR*	53
1938–39*a*	Newport Co	55	Crystal Palace	52	Brighton	49
1939–46	Competition cancelled owing to war.					

**Won or placed on goal average/goal difference.*

	First	Pts	Second	Pts	Third	Pts
1946–47*a*	Cardiff C	66	QPR	57	Bristol C	51
1947–48*a*	QPR	61	Bournemouth	57	Walsall	51
1948–49*a*	Swansea T	62	Reading	55	Bournemouth	52
1949–50*a*	Notts Co	58	Northampton T*	51	Southend U	51
1950–51*b*	Nottingham F	70	Norwich C	64	Reading*	57
1951–52*b*	Plymouth Arg	66	Reading*	61	Norwich C	61
1952–53*b*	Bristol R	64	Millwall*	62	Northampton T	62
1953–54*b*	Ipswich T	64	Brighton	61	Bristol C	56
1954–55*b*	Bristol C	70	Leyton O	61	Southampton	59
1955–56*b*	Leyton O	66	Brighton	65	Ipswich T	64
1956–57*b*	Ipswich T*	59	Torquay U	59	Colchester U	58
1957–58*b*	Brighton	60	Brentford*	58	Plymouth Arg	58

THIRD DIVISION—NORTH (1921–1958)

Maximum points: a 76; *b* 84; *c* 80; *d* 92.

	First	Pts	Second	Pts	Third	Pts
1921–22*a*	Stockport Co	56	Darlington*	50	Grimsby T	50
1922–23*a*	Nelson	51	Bradford PA	47	Walsall	46
1923–24*b*	Wolverhampton W	63	Rochdale	62	Chesterfield	54
1924–25*b*	Darlington	58	Nelson*	53	New Brighton	53
1925–26*b*	Grimsby T	61	Bradford PA	60	Rochdale	59
1926–27*b*	Stoke C	63	Rochdale	58	Bradford PA	55
1927–28*b*	Bradford PA	63	Lincoln C	55	Stockport Co	54
1928–29*g*	Bradford C	63	Stockport Co	62	Wrexham	52
1929–30*b*	Port Vale	67	Stockport Co	63	Darlington*	50
1930–31*b*	Chesterfield	58	Lincoln C	57	Wrexham*	54
1931–32*c*	Lincoln C*	57	Gateshead	57	Chester	50
1932–33*b*	Hull C	59	Wrexham	57	Stockport Co	54
1933–34*b*	Barnsley	62	Chesterfield	61	Stockport Co	59
1934–35*b*	Doncaster R	57	Halifax T	55	Chester	54
1935–36*b*	Chesterfield	60	Chester*	55	Tranmere R	55
1936–37*b*	Stockport Co	60	Lincoln C	57	Chester	53
1937–38*b*	Tranmere R	56	Doncaster R	54	Hull C	53
1938–39*b*	Barnsley	67	Doncaster R	56	Bradford C	52
1939–46	Competition cancelled owing to war.					
1946–47*b*	Doncaster R	72	Rotherham U	60	Chester	56
1947–48*b*	Lincoln C	60	Rotherham U	59	Wrexham	50
1948–49*b*	Hull C	65	Rotherham U	62	Doncaster R	50
1949–50*b*	Doncaster R	55	Gateshead	53	Rochdale*	51
1950–51*d*	Rotherham U	71	Mansfield T	64	Carlisle U	62
1951–52*d*	Lincoln C	69	Grimsby T	66	Stockport Co	59
1952–53*d*	Oldham Ath	59	Port Vale	58	Wrexham	56
1953–54*d*	Port Vale	69	Barnsley	58	Scunthorpe U	57
1954–55*d*	Barnsley	65	Accrington S	61	Scunthorpe U*	58
1955–56*d*	Grimsby T	68	Derby Co	63	Accrington S	59
1956–57*d*	Derby Co	63	Hartlepools U	59	Accrington S*	58
1957–58*d*	Scunthorpe U	66	Accrington S	59	Bradford C	57

**Won or placed on goal average.*

PROMOTED AFTER PLAY-OFFS
(Not accounted for in previous section)

1986–87 Aldershot to Division 3.
1987–88 Swansea C to Division 3.
1988–89 Leyton O to Division 3.
1989–90 Cambridge U to Division 3; Notts Co to Division 2; Sunderland to Division 1.
1990–91 Notts Co to Division 1; Tranmere R to Division 2; Torquay U to Division 3.
1991–92 Blackburn R to Premier League; Peterborough U to Division 1.
1992–93 Swindon T to Premier League; WBA to Division 1; York C to Division 2.
1993–94 Leicester C to Premier League; Burnley to Division 1; Wycombe W to Division 2.
1994–95 Huddersfield T to Division 1.

LEAGUE TITLE WINS

FA PREMIER LEAGUE – Manchester U 2, Blackburn R 1.

LEAGUE DIVISION 1 – Liverpool 18, Arsenal 10, Everton 9, Manchester U 7, Aston Villa 7, Sunderland 6, Newcastle U 5, Sheffield W 4, Huddersfield T 3, Leeds U 3, Wolverhampton W 3, Blackburn R 2, Portsmouth 2, Preston NE 2, Burnley 2, Manchester C 2, Tottenham H 2, Derby Co 2, Chelsea 1, Crystal Palace 1, Sheffield U 1, WBA 1, Ipswich T 1, Nottingham F 1, Middlesbrough 1 each.

LEAGUE DIVISION 2 – Leicester C 6, Manchester C 6, Sheffield W 5, Birmingham C (one as Small Heath) 5, Derby Co 4, Liverpool 4, Ipswich T 3, Leeds U 3, Notts Co 3, Preston NE 3, Middlesbrough 3, Stoke C 3, Grimsby T 2, Norwich C 2, Nottingham F 2, Tottenham H 2, WBA 2, Aston Villa 2, Burnley 2, Chelsea 2, Manchester U 2, West Ham U 2, Wolverhampton W 2, Bolton W 2, Huddersfield T, Bristol C, Brentford, Bury, Bradford C, Everton, Fulham, Sheffield U, Newcastle U, Coventry C, Blackpool, Blackburn R, Sunderland, Crystal Palace, Luton T, QPR, Oxford U, Millwall, Oldham Ath, Reading 1 each.

LEAGUE DIVISION 3 – Portsmouth 2, Oxford U 2, Shrewsbury T 2, Carlisle U 2, Plymouth Arg, Southampton, Bury, Northampton T, Coventry C, Hull C, QPR, Watford, Leyton O, Preston NE, Aston Villa, Bolton W, Oldham Ath, Blackburn R, Hereford U, Mansfield T, Wrexham, Grimsby T, Rotherham U, Burnley, Bradford C, Bournemouth, Reading, Sunderland, Wolverhampton W, Bristol R, Cambridge U, Brentford, Cardiff C 1 each.

LEAGUE DIVISION 4 – Chesterfield 2, Doncaster R 2, Peterborough U 2, Port Vale, Walsall, Millwall, Brentford, Gillingham, Brighton, Stockport Co, Luton T, Notts Co, Grimsby T, Southport, Mansfield T, Lincoln C, Cambridge U, Watford, Reading, Huddersfield T, Southend U, Sheffield U, Wimbledon, York C, Swindon T, Northampton T, Wolverhampton W, Rotherham U, Exeter C, Darlington, Burnley 1 each.

To 1957–58

DIVISION 3 (South) – Bristol C 3; Charlton Ath, Ipswich T, Millwall, Notts Co, Plymouth Arg, Swansea T 2 each; Brentford, Bristol R, Cardiff C, Crystal Palace, Coventry C, Fulham, Leyton O, Luton T, Newport Co, Nottingham F, Norwich C, Portsmouth, QPR, Reading, Southampton, Brighton 1 each.

DIVISION 3 (North) – Barnsley, Doncaster R, Lincoln C 3 each; Chesterfield, Grimsby T, Hull C, Port Vale, Stockport Co 2 each; Bradford PA, Bradford C, Darlington, Derby Co, Nelson, Oldham Ath, Rotherham U, Stoke C, Tranmere R, Wolverhampton W, Scunthorpe U 1 each.

RELEGATED CLUBS

1891–92 League extended. Newton Heath, Sheffield W and Nottingham F admitted. *Second Division formed* including Darwen.

1892–93 In Test matches, Sheffield U and Darwen won promotion in place of Notts Co and Accrington S.

1893–94 In Tests, Liverpool and Small Heath won promotion. Newton Heath and Darwen relegated.

1894–95 After Tests, Bury promoted, Liverpool relegated.

1895–96 After Tests, Liverpool promoted, Small Heath relegated.

1896–97 After Tests, Notts Co promoted, Burnley relegated.

1897–98 Test system abolished after success of Stoke C and Burnley. League extended. Blackburn R and Newcastle U elected to First Division. *Automatic promotion and relegation introduced.*

FA PREMIER LEAGUE TO DIVISION 1

1992–93 Crystal Palace, Middlesbrough, Nottingham Forest
1993–94 Sheffield U, Oldham Ath, Swindon T
1994–95 Crystal Palace, Norwich C, Leicester C, Ipswich T

DIVISION 1 TO DIVISION 2

1898–99 Bolton W and Sheffield W
1899–1900 Burnley and Glossop
1900–01 Preston NE and WBA
1901–02 Small Heath and Manchester C
1902–03 Grimsby T and Bolton W
1903–04 Liverpool and WBA
1904–05 League extended. Bury and Notts Co, two bottom clubs in First Division, re-elected.
1905–06 Nottingham F and Wolverhampton W
1906–07 Derby Co and Stoke C
1907–08 Bolton W and Birmingham C
1908–09 Manchester C and Leicester Fosse
1909–10 Bolton W and Chelsea
1910–11 Bristol C and Nottingham F
1911–12 Preston NE and Bury
1912–13 Notts Co and Woolwich Arsenal
1913–14 Preston NE and Derby Co
1914–15 Tottenham H and Chelsea*
1919–20 Notts Co and Sheffield W
1920–21 Derby Co and Bradford PA
1921–22 Bradford C and Manchester U
1922–23 Stoke C and Oldham Ath
1923–24 Chelsea and Middlesbrough
1924–25 Preston NE and Nottingham F
1925–26 Manchester C and Notts Co
1926–27 Leeds U and WBA
1927–28 Tottenham H and Middlesbrough
1928–29 Bury and Cardiff C
1929–30 Burnley and Everton
1930–31 Leeds U and Manchester U
1931–32 Grimsby T and West Ham U
1932–33 Bolton W and Blackpool
1933–34 Newcastle U and Sheffield U
1934–35 Leicester C and Tottenham H
1935–36 Aston Villa and Blackburn R
1936–37 Manchester U and Sheffield W
1937–38 Manchester C and WBA
1938–39 Birmingham C and Leicester C
1946–47 Brentford and Leeds U
1947–48 Blackburn R and Grimsby T
1948–49 Preston NE and Sheffield U
1949–50 Manchester C and Birmingham C
1950–51 Sheffield W and Everton
1951–52 Huddersfield and Fulham
1952–53 Stoke C and Derby Co
1953–54 Middlesbrough and Liverpool
1954–55 Leicester C and Sheffield W
1955–56 Huddersfield and Sheffield U
1956–57 Charlton Ath and Cardiff C
1957–58 Sheffield W and Sunderland
1958–59 Portsmouth and Aston Villa
1959–60 Luton T and Leeds U
1960–61 Preston NE and Newcastle U
1961–62 Chelsea and Cardiff C
1962–63 Majchester C and Leyton O
1963–64 Bolton W and Ipswich T
1964–65 Wolverhampton W and Birmingham C
1965–66 Northampton T and Blackburn R
1966–67 Aston Villa and Blackpool
1967–68 Fulham and Sheffield U
1968–69 Leicester C and QPR
1969–70 Sunderland and Sheffield W
1970–71 Burnley and Blackpool
1971–72 Huddersfield T and Nottingham F
1972–73 Crystal Palace and WBA
1973–74 Southampton, Manchester U, Norwich C
1974–75 Luton T, Chelsea, Carlisle U
1975–76 Wolverhampton W, Burnley, Sheffield U
1976–77 Sunderland, Stoke C, Tottenham H
1977–78 West Ham U, Newcastle U, Leicester C
1978–79 QPR, Birmingham C, Chelsea
1979–80 Bristol C, Derby Co, Bolton W
1980–81 Norwich C, Leicester C, Crystal Palace
1981–82 Leeds U, Wolverhampton W, Middlesbrough
1982–83 Manchester C, Swansea C, Brighton & HA
1983–84 Birmingham C, Notts Co, Wolverhampton W
1984–85 Norwich C, Sunderland, Stoke C
1985–86 Ipswich T, Birmingham C, WBA
1986–87 Leicester C, Manchester C, Aston Villa
1987–88 Chelsea**, Portsmouth, Watford, Oxford U
1988–89 Middlesbrough, West Ham U, Newcastle U
1989–90 Sheffield W, Charlton Ath, Millwall
1990–91 Sunderland and Derby Co
1991–92 Luton T, Notts Co, West Ham U
1992–93 Brentford, Cambridge U, Bristol R
1993–94 Birmingham C, Oxford U, Peterborough U
1994–95 Swindon T, Burnley, Bristol C, Notts Co

***Relegated after play-offs.*

**Subsequently re-elected to Division 1 when League was extended after the War.*

DIVISION 2 TO DIVISION 3

1920–21 Stockport Co
1921–22 Bradford and Bristol C
1922–23 Rotherham C and Wolverhampton W
1923–24 Nelson and Bristol C
1924–25 Crystal Palace and Coventry C
1925–26 Stoke C and Stockport Co
1926–27 Darlington and Bradford C
1927–28 Fulham and South Shields
1928–29 Port Vale and Clapton O
1929–30 Hull C and Notts Co
1930–31 Reading and Cardiff C
1931–32 Barnsley and Bristol C
1932–33 Chesterfield and Charlton Ath
1933–34 Millwall and Lincoln C
1934–35 Oldham Ath and Notts Co
1935–36 Port Vale and Hull C
1936–37 Doncaster R and Bradford C
1937–38 Barnsley and Stockport Co
1938–39 Norwich C and Tranmere R
1946–47 Swansea T and Newport Co
1947–48 Doncaster R and Millwall
1948–49 Nottingham F and Lincoln C
1949–50 Plymouth Arg and Bradford
1950–51 Grimsby T and Chesterfield
1951–52 Coventry C and QPR
1952–53 Southampton and Barnsley
1953–54 Brentford and Oldham Ath
1954–55 Ipswich T and Derby Co

1955–56 Plymouth Arg and Hull C
1956–57 Port Vale and Bury
1957–58 Doncaster R and Notts Co
1958–59 Barnsley and Grimsby T
1959–60 Bristol C and Hull C
1960–61 Lincoln C and Portsmouth
1961–62 Brighton & HA and Bristol R
1962–63 Walsall and Luton T
1963–64 Grimsby T and Scunthorpe U
1964–65 Swindon T and Swansea T
1965–66 Middlesbrough and Leyton O
1966–67 Northampton T and Bury
1967–68 Plymouth Arg and Rotherham U
1968–69 Fulham and Bury
1969–70 Preston NE and Aston Villa
1970–71 Blackburn R and Bolton W
1971–72 Charlton Ath and Watford
1972–73 Huddersfield T and Brighton & HA
1973–74 Crystal Palace, Preston NE, Swindon T
1974–75 Millwall, Cardiff C, Sheffield W
1975–76 Oxford U, York C, Portsmouth
1976–77 Carlisle U, Plymouth Arg, Hereford U
1977–78 Blackpool, Mansfield T, Hull C
1978–79 Sheffield U, Millwall, Blackburn R
1979–80 Fulham, Burnley, Charlton Ath
1980–81 Preston NE, Bristol C, Bristol R
1981–82 Cardiff C, Wrexham, Orient
1982–83 Rotherham U, Burnley, Bolton W
1983–84 Derby Co, Swansea C, Cambridge U
1984–85 Notts Co, Cardiff C, Wolverhampton W
1985–86 Carlisle U, Middlesbrough, Fulham
1986–87 Sunderland**, Grimsby T, Brighton & HA
1987–88 Huddersfield T, Reading, Sheffield U**
1988–89 Shrewsbury T, Birmingham C, Walsall
1989–90 Bournemouth, Bradford, Stoke C
1990–91 WBA and Hull C
1991–92 Plymouth Arg, Brighton & HA, Port Vale
1992–93 Preston NE, Mansfield T, Wigan Ath, Chester C
1993–94 Fulham, Exeter C, Hartlepool U, Barnet
1994–95 Cambridge U, Plymouth Arg, Cardiff C, Chester C, Leyton Orient

DIVISION 3 TO DIVISION 4

1958–59 Rochdale, Notts Co, Doncaster R, Stockport
1959–60 Accrington S, Wrexham, Mansfield T, York C
1960–61 Chesterfield, Colchester U, Bradford C, Tranmere R
1961–62 Newport Co, Brentford, Lincoln C, Torquay U
1962–63 Bradford PA, Brighton, Carlisle U, Halifax T
1963–64 Millwall, Crewe Alex, Wrexham, Notts Co
1964–65 Luton T, Port Vale, Colchester U, Barnsley
1965–66 Southend U, Exeter C, Brentford, York C
1966–67 Doncaster R, Workington, Darlington, Swansea T
1967–68 Scunthorpe U, Colchester U, Grimsby T, Peterborough U (demoted)
1968–69 Oldham Ath, Crewe Alex, Hartlepool, Northampton T
1969–70 Bournemouth, Southport, Barrow, Stockport Co
1970–71 Reading, Bury, Doncaster R, Gillingham
1971–72 Mansfield T, Barnsley, Torquay U, Bradford C
1972–73 Rotherham U, Brentford, Swansea C, Scunthorpe U
1973–74 Cambridge U, Shrewsbury T, Southport, Rochdale
1974–75 AFC Bournemouth, Tranmere R, Watford, Huddersfield T
1975–76 Aldershot, Colchester U, Southend U, Halifax T
1976–77 Reading, Northampton T, Grimsby T, York C
1977–78 Port Vale, Bradford C, Hereford U, Portsmouth
1978–79 Peterborough U, Walsall, Tranmere R, Lincoln C
1979–80 Bury, Southend U, Mansfield T, Wimbledon
1980–81 Sheffield U, Colchester U, Blackpool, Hull C
1981–82 Wimbledon, Swindon T, Bristol C, Chester
1982–83 Reading, Wrexham, Doncaster R, Chesterfield
1983–84 Scunthorpe U, Southend U, Port Vale, Exeter C
1984–85 Burnley, Orient, Preston NE, Cambridge U
1985–86 Lincoln C, Cardiff C, Wolverhampton W, Swansea C
1986–87 Bolton W**, Carlisle U, Darlington, Newport Co
1987–88 Doncaster R, York C, Grimsby T, Rotherham U**
1988–89 Southend U, Chesterfield, Gillingham, Aldershot
1989–90 Cardiff C, Northampton T, Blackpool, Walsall
1990–91 Crewe Alex, Rotherham U, Mansfield T
1991–92 Bury, Shrewsbury T, Torquay U, Darlington

***Relegated after play-offs.*

APPLICATIONS FOR RE-ELECTION

FOURTH DIVISION

Eleven: Hartlepool U.
Seven: Crewe Alex.
Six: Barrow (lost League place to Hereford U 1972), Halifax T, Rochdale, Southport (lost League place to Wigan Ath 1978), York C.
Five: Chester C, Darlington, Lincoln C, Stockport Co, Workington (lost League place to Wimbledon 1977).
Four: Bradford PA (lost League place to Cambridge U 1970), Newport Co, Northampton T.
Three: Doncaster R, Hereford U.
Two: Bradford C, Exeter C, Oldham Ath, Scunthorpe U, Torquay U.
One: Aldershot, Colchester U, Gateshead (lost League place to Peterborough U 1960), Grimsby T, Swansea C, Tranmere R, Wrexham, Blackpool, Cambridge U, Preston NE.
Accrington S resigned and Oxford U were elected 1962.
Port Vale were forced to re-apply following expulsion in 1968.

THIRD DIVISIONS NORTH & SOUTH

Seven: Walsall.
Six: Exeter C, Halifax T, Newport Co.
Five: Accrington S, Barrow, Gillingham, New Brighton, Southport.
Four: Rochdale, Norwich C.
Three: Crystal Palace, Crewe Alex, Darlington, Hartlepool U, Merthyr T, Swindon T.
Two: Aberdare Ath, Aldershot, Ashington, Bournemouth, Brentford, Chester, Colchester U, Durham C, Millwall, Nelson, QPR, Rotherham U, Southend U, Tranmere R, Watford, Workington.
One: Bradford C, Bradford PA, Brighton, Bristol R, Cardiff C, Carlisle U, Charlton Ath, Gateshead, Grimsby T, Mansfield T, Shrewsbury T, Torquay U, York C.

LEAGUE STATUS FROM 1986–87

	RELEGATED FROM LEAGUE	PROMOTED TO LEAGUE
1986–87	Lincoln C	Scarborough
1987–88	Newport Co	Lincoln C
1988–89	Darlington	Maidstone U
1989–90	Colchester U	Darlington
1990–91	—	Barnet
1991–92	—	Colchester U
1992–93	Halifax T	Wycombe W
1993–94	—	—
1994–95	—	—

TRANSFERS 1994–95

	From	To	Fee in £s
June 1994			
21 Abbott, Gary	Welling United	Enfield	undisclosed
16 Appleby, Matthew W.	Newcastle United	Darlington	Free
19 Armstrong, Alun	Newcastle United	Stockport County	35,000
1 Atherton, Peter	Coventry City	Sheffield Wednesday	800,000
21 Beauchamp, Joseph D.	Oxford United	West Ham United	1,000,000
20 Chalk, Martyn P. G.	Derby County	Stockport County	40,000
16 Collier, Daniel	Wolverhampton Wanderers	Crewe Alexandra	Free
3 Daley, Anthony M.	Aston Villa	Wolverhampton Wanderers	1,250,000
17 Forster, Nicholas	Gillingham	Brentford	100,000
30 Frampton, Mark R.	Aldershot Town	Fleet Town	400
6 Gillett, Craig	Kidderminster Harriers	Solihull Borough	undisclosed
27 Milligan, Michael J.	Oldham Athletic	Norwich City	850,000
21 Moncur, John F.	Swindon Town	West Ham United	1,000,000
8 Morah, Olisa H.	Woking	Cambridge United	50,000
30 Newsome, Jon	Leeds United	Norwich City	1,000,000
18 Pape, Andrew M.	Barnet	Enfield	undisclosed
23 Preece, Andrew P.	Stockport County	Crystal Palace	350,000
15 Sedgley, Stephen P.	Tottenham Hotspur	Ipswich Town	1,000,000
14 Smith, Dean	Walsall	Hereford United	80,000
21 Summerbee, Nicholas J.	Swindon Town	Manchester City	1,150,000
24 Warburton, Raymond	York City	Northampton Town	35,000
July 1994			
21 Alford, Carl P.	Macclesfield Town	Kettering Town	25,000
28 Archer, Graeme	Corby Town	Nuneaton Borough	undisclosed
2 Barras, Anthony	Stockport County	York City	25,000
30 Bown, Matthew R.	Poole Town	Trowbridge Town	undisclosed
13 Brabin, Gary	Runcorn	Doncaster Rovers	40,000
13 Collins, Darren	Enfield	Rushden & Diamonds	undisclosed
13 Cowan, Thomas	Sheffield United	Huddersfield Town	150,000
19 Cox, Neil J.	Aston Villa	Middlesbrough	1,000,000
28 Dawber, Mark	Chesham United	Sutton United	undisclosed
20 Diaz, Antonio	Dorchester Town	Clevedon Town	undisclosed
26 Draper, Mark A.	Notts County	Leicester City	1,250,000
22 Dublin, Keith B. L.	Watford	Southend United	exch.
12 Dykstra, Sieb	Motherwell	Queens Park Rangers	250,000
21 Ellis, Anthony	Preston North End	Blackpool	165,000
8 Emberson, Carl W.	Millwall	Colchester United	Free
14 Emblen, Neil R.	Millwall	Wolverhampton Wanderers	600,000 + 400,000
21 Evans, Keith	Curzon Ashton	Ashton United	undisclosed
9 Forbes, Steven D.	Sittingbourne	Millwall	50,000
26 Freedman, Douglas A.	Queens Park Rangers	Barnet	Free
8 Froggatt, Stephen J.	Aston Villa	Wolverhampton Wanderers	1,500,000
19 Gray, Andrew	Reading	Leyton Orient	Free
18 Gray, Kevin J.	Mansfield Town	Huddersfield Town	20,000
9 Heald, Greg J.	Enfield	Peterborough United	35,000
14 Kubicki, Dariusz	Aston Villa	Sunderland	100,000
20 Lancaster, David	Rochdale	Halifax Town	10,000
22 Liburd, Richard	Middlesbrough	Bradford City	200,000
27 Lyne, Neil G. F.	Cambridge United	Hereford United	Free
15 Marshall, Dwight W.	Plymouth Argyle	Luton Town	150,000
1 May, David	Blackburn Rovers	Manchester United	1,400,000
7 Mohan, Nicholas	Middlesbrough	Leicester City	330,000
21 Mooney, Thomas J.	Southend United	Watford	exch. + 95,000
15 Moralee, Jamie D.	Millwall	Watford	450,000 (combined)
21 Muggleton, Carl D.	Celtic	Stoke City	200,000
13 Mulligan, James	Stoke City	Bury	15,000
18 Naylor, Anthony	Crewe Alexandra	Port Vale	150,000
29 Newell, Paul C.	Leyton Orient	Barnet	Free
7 Oliver, Michael	Middlesbrough	Stockport County	15,000
20 Onuora, Ifem	Huddersfield Town	Mansfield Town	undisclosed
21 Payne, Derek R.	Southend United	Watford	exch. + 95,000
19 Pearson, Nigel G.	Sheffield Wednesday	Middlesbrough	500,000 + 250,000
15 Petterson, Andrew K.	Luton Town	Charlton Athletic	35,000
15 Pitcher, Geoffrey	Millwall	Watford	450,000 (combined)
7 Randall, Martin	Northwood	Hayes	undisclosed
26 Redgate, Gary P.	Burton Albion	VS Rugby	undisclosed
25 Richardson, Barry	Northampton Town	Preston North End	20,000
19 Richardson, Lee	Aberdeen	Oldham Athletic	300,000
22 Robinson, Mark	Newcastle United	Swindon Town	600,000
26 Robinson, Spencer L.	Bristol City	Burnley	250,000
26 Sale, Mark D.	Torquay United	Preston North End	20,000
5 Smith, David C.	Norwich City	Oxford United	100,000
13 Sutton, Christopher R.	Norwich City	Blackburn Rovers	5,000,000
23 Swan, Peter H.	Port Vale	Plymouth Argyle	300,000
1 Taylor, Ian K.	Port Vale	Sheffield Wednesday	1,000,000
5 Taylor, John P.	Bristol Rovers	Bradford City	300,000
4 Thomson, Andrew	Queen of the South	Southend United	250,000
1 Walker, Andrew F.	Bolton Wanderers	Celtic	undisclosed
9 Wardle, Paul G.	Bromsgrove Rovers	Gresley Rovers	undisclosed
8 Whyte, David A.	Crystal Palace	Charlton Athletic	exch.
21 Woods, Stephen G.	Preston North End	Motherwell	75,000
4 Worthington, Nigel	Sheffield Wednesday	Leeds United	325,000
Temporary transfers			
26 Kenny, William	Everton	Oldham Athletic	
August 1994			
4 Adcock, Anthony C.	Peterborough United	Luton Town	20,000
11 Alsford, Julian	Watford	Chester City	Free
12 Barber, Frederick	Peterborough United	Luton Town	25,000
10 Bartram, Vincent L.	AFC Bournemouth	Arsenal	250,000 + 150,000
1 Batty, Paul W.	Bath City	Salisbury City	undisclosed
12 Beasley, Andrew	Doncaster Rovers	Chesterfield	nominal
18 Beauchamp, Joseph D.	West Ham United	Swindon Town	800,000
11 Bermingham, Michael J.	Dorchester Town	Bognor Regis Town	undisclosed

	From	*To*	*Fee*
12 Blackstone, Ian K.	York City	Scarborough	15,000
4 Bradder, Gary V.	Nuneaton Borough	Hinckley Town	undisclosed
1 Bradshaw, Carl	Sheffield United	Norwich City	500,000
5 Breen, Gary	Gillingham	Peterborough United	50,000
18 Brown, Steven M.	Cheltenham Town	Burton Albion	undisclosed
18 Cook, Paul A.	Wolverhampton Wanderers	Coventry City	600,000
1 Daley, Phillip	Wigan Athletic	Lincoln City	40,000
11 Deighan, Ben	Bognor Regis Town	Basingstoke Town	undisclosed
10 Dennis, John A.	Chesterfield	Colchester United	Free
3 Drysdale, Jason	Watford	Newcastle United	425,000
5 Farrell, Sean P.	Fulham	Peterborough United	80,000
4 Fashanu, John.	Wimbledon	Aston Villa	1,350,000
11 Foster, Adrian M.	Torquay United	Gillingham	60,000
12 Fulton, Stephen	Bolton Wanderers	Falkirk	undisclosed
26 Gayle, John	Coventry City	Burnley	undisclosed
2 Glover, Edward L.	Nottingham Forest	Port Vale	200,000
1 Grainger, Phillip J.	Sutton United	Staines Town	undisclosed
1 Gray, Kevin J.	Mansfield Town	Huddersfield Town	20,000
3 Guppy, Stephen A.	Wycombe Wanderers	Newcastle United	150,000
5 Hall, Derek R.	Hereford United	Rochdale	Free
18 Harford, Michael G.	Coventry City	Wimbledon	70,000
10 Hodge, Martin	Rochdale	Plymouth Argyle	10,000
11 Hone, Mark J.	Welling United	Southend United	50,000
5 Howarth, Lee	Peterborough United	Mansfield Town	15,000
11 Hulme, Kevin	Doncaster Rovers	Bury	42,500
30 Hutchison, Donald	Liverpool	West Ham United	1,500,000
3 Iorfa, Dominic	Peterborough United	Southend United	15,000
12 Ireland, Simon P.	Blackburn Rovers	Mansfield Town	60,000
3 James, Martin J.	Stockport County	Rotherham United	50,000
26 Kenny, William	Everton	Oldham Athletic	Free
3 Kilford, Ian A.	Nottingham Forest	Wigan Athletic	Free
12 Kite, Philip D.	Cardiff City	Bristol City	Free
1 Lovell, Jason P.	Wimborne Town	Salisbury City	undisclosed
7 Ludden, Dominic J.	Leyton Orient	Watford	100,000
12 Miller, Alan J.	Arsenal	Middlesbrough	500,000
7 Miller, Kevin	Birmingham City	Watford	250,000
16 Miller, Paul A.	Wimbledon	Bristol Rovers	100,000
9 Mitchell, Stewart	Marlow	Aldershot Town	Free
11 Murray, Shaun	Scarborough	Bradford City	nominal
17 Nolan, Ian R.	Tranmere Rovers	Sheffield Wednesday	1,500,000
10 O'Neill, Darren S.	Aldershot Town	Kingstonian	2000
12 Osborn, Simon E.	Crystal Palace	Reading	90,000
1 Paatelainen, Mika	Aberdeen	Bolton Wanderers	300,000
1 Peschisolido, Paul P.	Birmingham City	Stoke City	200,000 + exch.
5 Pitcher, Darren E.J.	Charlton Athletic	Crystal Palace	40,000
11 Pollitt, Michael F.	Lincoln City	Darlington	nominal
3 Pugh, David	Chester City	Bury	22,500
2 Reece, Paul J.	Oxford United	Notts County	Free
1 Regis, David	Stoke City	Birmingham City	exch.
1 Richardson, Barry	Northampton Town	Preston North End	20,000
5 Richardson, Stephen J.	Poole Town	Dorchester Town	undisclosed
3 Robinson, Mark J.	Newcastle United	Swindon Town	600,000
12 Rocastle, David C.	Manchester City	Chelsea	1,250,000
13 Russell, Andrew	Kingstonian	Aldershot Town	undisclosed
1 Sale, Mark D.	Torquay United	Preston North End	20,000
5 Sampson, Ian	Sunderland	Northampton Town	30,000
2 Samways, Vincent	Tottenham Hotspur	Everton	2,200,000
9 Scott, Andrew M.	Blackburn Rovers	Cardiff City	Free
26 Sheron, Michael N.	Manchester City	Norwich City	800,000
16 Smith, Malcolm A.	Margate	Ashford Town	undisclosed
11 Stevens, Ian D.	Bury	Shrewsbury Town	20,000
8 Thompson, David S.	Chester City	Rochdale	6000
22 Ullathorne, Simon	Gravesend & Northfleet	Sittingbourne	undisclosed
4 Ward, Mark W.	Everton	Birmingham City	200,000
10 Whiston, Peter M.	Exeter City	Southampton	30,000
17 Whitbread, Adrian R.	Swindon Town	West Ham United	500,000 + exch.
12 Whitington, Craig	Scarborough	Huddersfield Town	nominal
5 Whyte, David A.	Crystal Palace	Charlton Athletic	exch.
3 Williams, Darren P.	Welling United	Dover Athletic	undisclosed
9 Wilmot, Rhys	Grimsby Town	Crystal Palace	80,000
8 Winstanley, Mark A.	Bolton Wanderers	Burnley	150,000

Temporary transfers

	From	To
26 Anthrobus, Stephen A.	Wimbledon	Chester City
23 Ashdjian, John A.	Kettering Town	Corby Town
11 Bass, David	Reading	Aldershot Town
26 Beckett, Nathan J.	Leyton Orient	Leyton
18 Bradshaw, Darren S.	Peterborough United	Plymouth Argyle
20 Cook, Anthony C.	Gloucester City	Dorchester Town
19 Davis, Michael V.	Bristol Rovers	Hereford United
26 Dunphy, Sean	Lincoln City	Scarborough
20 Flemming, David	Enfield	Sittingbourne
26 Foran, Mark J.	Sheffield United	Rotherham United
17 Gayle, John	Coventry City	Burnley
19 Hay, Darren A.	Cambridge United	Woking
22 Hill, David M.	Lincoln City	Chesterfield
30 Hodge, Stephen B.	Leeds United	Derby County
12 Hoult, Russell	Leicester City	Lincoln City
18 Kernaghan, Alan N.	Manchester City	Bolton Wanderers
10 Kilbane, Farrell N.	Preston North End	Barrow
12 Lee, David J.	Chelsea	Portsmouth
25 Marshall, Scott R.	Arsenal	Sheffield United
20 Mitchell, Richard D.	Southport	Hyde United
15 Norton, David W.	Hull City	Northampton Town
8 Parris, George M.	Birmingham City	Brentford
20 Pettinger, Paul A.	Leeds United	Dagenham & Redbridge
25 Powell, Richard	Welling United	Gravesend & Northfleet
26 Putney, Trevor A.	Leyton Orient	Colchester United
11 Rowe, Rodney C.	Huddersfield Town	Scarborough
26 Shaw, Graham P.	Stoke City	Plymouth Argyle
11 Shutt, Carl S.	Birmingham City	Bradford City
26 Sinclair, Ronald M.	Stoke City	Bradford City

	From	To	Fee
26 Skinner, Justin J.	Wimbledon	Wycombe Wanderers	
19 Smith, Andrew	Havant Town	Fareham Town	
26 Turner, Andrew P.	Tottenham Hotspur	Wycombe Wanderers	
24 Voice, Scott	Wolverhampton Wanderers	Shelbourne	
19 Williams, Wayne	Kidderminster Harriers	Bridgnorth Town	
13 Worrall, Rodger	Molesey	Whyteleafe	
September 1994			
5 Andrews, Ian E.	Southampton	AFC Bournemouth	20,000
1 Babb, Philip A.	Coventry City	Liverpool	3,600,000
12 Beadle, Peter C.	Tottenham Hotspur	Watford	undisclosed
6 Burrows, David	West Ham United	Everton	exch.
16 Clark, John B.	Stoke City	Falkirk	100,000
30 Cooper, Stephen	York City	Airdrieonians	undisclosed
7 Cottee, Antony R.	Everton	West Ham United	exch.
27 Crosby, Gary	Nottingham Forest	Huddersfield Town	Free
9 Diaz, Antonio	Clevedon Town	Poole Town	undisclosed
9 Dublin, Dion	Manchester United	Coventry City	1,950,000
22 Farrell, Andrew J.	Burnley	Wigan Athletic	20,000
9 Hague, Paul	Gillingham	Leyton Orient	undisclosed
9 Houghton, Scott A.	Luton Town	Walsall	15,000
16 Hunt, Jonathan R.	Southend United	Birmingham City	exch.
8 Jemson, Nigel B.	Sheffield Wednesday	Notts County	350,000
16 Jones, Keith A.	Southend United	Charlton Athletic	150,000
26 Kitson, Paul	Derby County	Newcastle United	2,250,000
23 McDonald, Rodney	Walsall	Partick Thistle	undisclosed
2 Matthewson, Trevor	Preston North End	Bury	10,000
26 Mills, Gary R.	Leicester City	Notts County	undisclosed
14 O'Hanlon, Kelham	Preston North End	Dundee United	undisclosed
9 Pearson, Neil	Molesey	Crawley Town	undisclosed
30 Peters, Mark	Peterborough United	Mansfield Town	Free
30 Pike, Christopher	Hereford United	Gillingham	15,000
16 Poole, Gary J.	Southend United	Birmingham City	exch.
9 Quail, Simon I.	Sutton United	Wealdstone	undisclosed
7 Reeves, Alan	Rochdale	Wimbledon	300,000
16 Regis, David	Birmingham City	Southend United	exch.
23 Rush, David	Sunderland	Oxford United	100,000
9 Rutherford, Jonathan P.	Meadowbank Thistle	Scarborough	15,000
2 Scales, John R.	Wimbledon	Liverpool	3,500,000
2 Sheppard, Simon	Watford	Reading	undisclosed
28 Shildrick, Andrew	Peppard	Thame United	undisclosed
9 Shutt, Carl S.	Birmingham City	Bradford City	75,000
8 Smith, Adrian	Willenhall Town	Bromsgrove Rovers	undisclosed
8 Teggart, Darren	Witney Town	Salisbury City	undisclosed
8 Ware, Paul D.	Stoke City	Stockport County	15,000
16 Willis, Roger C.	Birmingham City	Southend United	exch.
Temporary transfers			
2 Appleby, Richard D.	Newcastle United	Darlington	
24 Ashdjian, John A.	Kettering Town	Corby Town	
26 Beckett, Nathan J.	Leyton Orient	Leyton	
8 Boere, Jeroen W.J.	West Ham United	West Bromwich Albion	
12 Bull, Gary W.	Nottingham Forest	Birmingham City	
15 Burgess, David J.	Carlisle United	Hartlepool United	
23 Carmichael, Matthew	Scunthorpe United	Barnet	
8 Carr, Franz A.	Sheffield United	Leicester City	
2 Costello, Peter	Dover Athletic	Telford United	
16 Croxford, Stephen	Walton & Hersham	Staines Town	
5 Currie, Darren	West Ham United	Shrewsbury Town	
16 Davis, Kelvin G.	Luton Town	Torquay United	
9 Dickins, Matthew J.	Blackburn Rovers	Grimsby Town	
30 Dunphy, Sean	Lincoln City	Scarborough	
27 Flemming, David	Enfield	Leyton	
1 Forrester, Jamie	Leeds United	Southend United	
2 Frain, David	Stockport County	Mansfield Town	
24 Gallagher, Philip	Hendon	Hampton	
2 Harford, Paul	Blackburn Rovers	Wigan Athletic	
20 Hay, Darren A.	Cambridge United	Woking	
28 Hodge, Stephen B.	Leeds United	Derby County	
2 Houghton, Scott A.	Luton Town	Walsall	
14 Hoult, Russell	Leicester City	Lincoln City	
6 Iddles, Daniel M.	Clevedon Town	Trowbridge Town	
29 Jackson, Peter A.	Huddersfield Town	Chester City	
20 Kalogeracos, Vasili	Birmingham City	Stevenage Borough	
19 Kernaghan, Alan N.	Manchester City	Bolton Wanderers	
8 Kirkham, Paul	Stalybridge Celtic	Witton Albion	
9 Kuhl, Martin	Derby County	Notts County	
23 Le Bihan, Neil R.	Peterborough United	Bishops Stortford	
15 Leonard, Mark A.	Chester City	Wigan Athletic	
22 Lowe, Kenneth	Birmingham City	Carlisle United	
25 Marshall, Scott R.	Arsenal	Sheffield United	
9 McLean, Ian	Bristol Rovers	Cardiff City	
9 Martin, Jae A.	Southend United	Leyton Orient	
30 Mee, Andrew	Stafford Rangers	Bedworth United	
27 Milsom, Paul J.	Bristol City	Clevedon Town	
9 Moore, Neil	Everton	Blackpool	
16 Norton, David W.	Hull City	Northampton Town	
19 Parsons, Mark C.	Kettering Town	Racing Club Warwick	
16 Payne, Stephen J.	Huddersfield Town	Macclesfield Town	
9 Priest, Christopher	Everton	Chester City	
30 Prudhoe, Mark	Stoke City	Peterborough United	
30 Reddish, Shane	Carlisle United	Chesterfield	
2 Rimmer, Stuart A.	Chester City	Rochdale	
9 Ritchie, Paul M.	Dundee	Gillingham	
2 Robinson, Philip J.	Huddersfield Town	Northampton Town	
11 Rowe, Rodney C.	Huddersfield Town	Scarborough	
9 Russell, Lee E.	Portsmouth	AFC Bournemouth	
16 Saddington, James	Millwall	Shelbourne	
21 Shaw, Christopher	Witton Albion	Ashton United	
15 Sheffield, Jonathan	Cambridge United	Hereford United	
16 Simpson, Fitzroy	Manchester City	Bristol City	
8 Skinner, Justin J.	Wimbledon	Wycombe Wanderers	

	From	*To*	*Fee*
9 Small, Bryan	Aston Villa	Birmingham City	
23 Stallard, Mark	Derby County	Fulham	
22 Stevens, Michael G.	Rangers	Tranmere Rovers	
2 Stewart, Paul A.	Liverpool	Wolverhampton Wanderers	
30 Sweetman, Nicholas E.	Leyton Orient	Hendon	
12 Symons, Paul	Blackpool	Southport	
9 Thompson, David	Brentford	Blackpool	
9 Waddock, Gary P.	Bristol Rovers	Luton Town	
23 Walker, Raymond	Port Vale	Cambridge United	
9 Walters, Mark E.	Liverpool	Wolverhampton Wanderers	
23 Ward, Richard	Huddersfield Town	Goole Town	
2 Warner, Ashley S.	Peterborough United	Corby Town	
17 Warner, Steven P.	Billericay Town	Collier Row	
16 Whitehead, Scot	Huddersfield Town	Frickley Athletic	
2 Wietecha, David	Millwall	Chesham United	
2 Wilkinson, Ian M.	Crewe Alexandra	Doncaster Rovers	
19 Williams, Wayne	Kidderminster Harriers	Bridgnorth Town	
22 Woodward, Andrew	Crewe Alexandra	Stafford Rangers	
October 1994			
7 Atkinson, Graeme	Hull City	Preston North End	undisclosed
3 Baker, David P.	Gillingham	York City	undisclosed
21 Bell, Michael	Northampton Town	Wycombe Wanderers	nominal
26 Bound, Matthew T.	Southampton	Stockport County	125,000
20 Bradshaw, Darren S.	Peterborough United	Blackpool	undisclosed
4 Butler, Peter J.	West Ham United	Notts County	350,000
11 Carr, Franz A.	Sheffield United	Leicester City	100,000
13 Carty, Paul	Tamworth	Hednesford Town	undisclosed
5 Coleman, Simon	Sheffield Wednesday	Bolton Wanderers	350,000
14 Davison, Robert	Sheffield United	Rotherham United	Free
20 Dicks, Julian A.	Liverpool	West Ham United	2,500,000
14 Ekoku, Efangwu	Norwich City	Wimbledon	920,000
28 Foy, David L.	Stafford Rangers	Tamworth	undisclosed
28 Hodge, Stephen B.	Leeds United	Queens Park Rangers	300,000
5 Humphries, Mark	Leeds United	Bristol City	undisclosed
19 Keen, Kevin I.	Wolverhampton Wanderers	Stoke City	300,000
14 Leonard, Mark A.	Chester City	Wigan Athletic	undisclosed
12 Mercer, William	Rotherham United	Sheffield United	75,000
10 Roberts, Graham P.	Slough Town	Stevenage Borough	undisclosed
20 Robinson, Stephen	Tottenham Hotspur	AFC Bournemouth	Free
4 Sharp, Raymond	Dunfermline Athletic	Preston North End	undisclosed
26 Shaw, Christopher	Witton Albion	Ashton United	undisclosed
14 Stevens, Michael G.	Rangers	Tranmere Rovers	350,000
5 Thorn, Andrew C.	Crystal Palace	Wimbledon	Free
28 Walker, Gary	Buxton	Stafford Rangers	undisclosed
20 Whittle, Justin P.	Celtic	Stoke City	Free
11 Young, Neil A.	Tottenham Hotspur	AFC Bournemouth	Free
Temporary transfers			
28 Alexander, Timothy M.	Barnet	Gravesend & Northfleet	
27 Ashdjian, John A.	Kettering Town	Corby Town	
4 Banger, Nicholas L.	Southampton	Oldham Athletic	
14 Brass, Christopher P.	Burnley	Torquay United	
11 Bull, Gary W.	Nottingham Forest	Birmingham City	
24 Burton, Christopher	Solihull Borough	Tamworth	
13 Cadette, Richard R.	Falkirk	Millwall	
8 Clark, Paul D.	Walton & Hersham	Molesey	
11 Colgan, Nicholas V.	Chelsea	Grimsby Town	
18 Collett, Andrew A.	Middlesbrough	Bristol Rovers	
11 Cooksey, Scott A.	Peterborough United	Welling United	
2 Costello, Peter	Dover Athletic	Telford United	
18 Croxford, Stephen	Walton & Hersham	Staines Town	
4 Currie, Darren	West Ham United	Shrewsbury Town	
28 Daniel, Raymond C.	Portsmouth	Notts County	
14 Dickins, Matthew J.	Blackburn Rovers	Rochdale	
14 Dow, Andrew	Chelsea	Bradford City	
28 Dunphy, Sean	Lincoln City	Scarborough	
3 Durrant, Ian	Rangers	Everton	
25 Eriemo, Soloman	Kingstonian	Hayes	
15 Evans, Richard J	Sutton United	Abingdon Town	
4 Ferguson, Duncan	Rangers	Everton	
1 Fleming, Mark J.	Aylesbury United	Staines Town	
28 Flemming, David	Enfield	Leyton	
14 Foster, Wayne P.	Heart of Midlothian	Hartlepool United	
22 Fowler, Lee	Dagenham & Redbridge	Barking	
24 Gallagher, Phillip	Hendon	Hampton	
28 Hall, Mark	Southend United	Dover Athletic	
7 Hendry, John	Tottenham Hotspur	Swansea City	
15 Hoult, Russell	Leicester City	Lincoln City	
14 Hoyland, Jamie W.	Sheffield United	Burnley	
3 Hoyle, Colin R.	Notts County	Mansfield Town	
7 Huxford, Richard J.	Millwall	Bradford City	
8 Iddles, Daniel M.	Clevedon Town	Trowbridge Town	
31 Jackson, Peter A.	Huddersfield Town	Chester City	
21 Jones, Stephen G.	West Ham United	AFC Bournemouth	
18 Jukes, Andrew	Luton Town	Wealdstone	
23 Le Bihan, Neil E.	Peterborough United	Bishops Stortford	
1 Livett, Simon	Cambridge United	Dagenham & Redbridge	
14 Lucas, Richard	Preston North End	Lincoln City	
7 McKenzie, Christopher	Hereford United	Rushden & Diamonds	
14 McKinlay, David	Middlesbrough	Cork City	
20 McMahon, Gerard J.	Tottenham Hotspur	Barnet	
31 Marshall, Scott R.	Arsenal	Sheffield United	
17 Martin, Dean S.	Scunthorpe United	Halifax Town	
6 Miller, David B.	Stockport County	Wigan Athletic	
12 Moore, Neil	Everton	Blackpool	
28 Morton, Neil	Wigan Athletic	Altrincham	
18 Page, Darrell	Rushden & Diamonds	Wealdstone	
24 Parsons, Mark C.	Kettering Town	Racing Club Warwick	
7 Patterson, Ian D.	Wigan Athletic	Stallybridge Celtic	
17 Payne, Stephen J.	Huddersfield Town	Macclesfield Town	
11 Priest, Christopher	Everton	Chester City	

	From	*To*	*Fee*
31 Prudhoe, Mark	Stoke City	Peterborough United	
3 Pugh, Stephen	Wrexham	Runcorn	
13 Putney, Trevor A.	Leyton Orient	Colchester United	
21 Richardson, Nicholas J.	Cardiff City	Wrexham	
4 Robinson, Phillip J.	Huddersfield Town	Northampton Town	
27 Roscoe, Andrew R.	Bolton Wanderers	Rotherham United	
12 Rowe, Rodney C.	Huddersfield Town	Scarborough	
31 Ryan, Tim J.	Scunthorpe United	Buxton	
14 Scully, Anthony D.T.	Crystal Palace	AFC Bournemouth	
15 Sheffield, Jonathon	Cambridge United	Hereford United	
25 Shirtliff, Paul R.	Gateshead	Farsley Celtic	
31 Slawson, Stephen M.	Notts County	Shrewsbury Town	
14 Smith, Paul M.	Lincoln City	Kettering Town	
13 Snodin, Ian	Everton	Sunderland	
1 Stacey, Phillip G.	Aylesbury United	Barton Rovers	
28 Starbuck, Phillip M.	Huddersfield Town	Sheffield United	
4 Stewart, Paul A.	Liverpool	Wolverhampton Wanderers	
5 Sweetman, Nicholas E.	Leyton Orient	Hendon	
28 Taylor, Mark S.	Middlesbrough	Darlington	
12 Thompson, David G.	Brentford	Blackpool	
28 Tracey, Simon P.	Sheffield United	Manchester City	
10 Turner, Andrew P.	Tottenham Hotspur	Doncaster Rovers	
9 Waddock, Gary P.	Bristol Rovers	Luton Town	
11 Walters, Mark E.	Liverpool	Wolverhampton Wanderers	
28 Warner, Ashley S.	Peterborough United	Telford United	
7 Webb, Neil J.	Nottingham Forest	Swindon Town	
7 Webster, Kenneth	Peterborough United	Rushden & Diamonds	
7 Williams, John N.	Coventry City	Notts County	
6 Wilson, Paul A.	Burnley	York City	
14 Witter, Anthony J.	Queens Park Rangers	Millwall	

November 1994

4 Banger, Nicholas L.	Southampton	Oldham Athletic	250,000
30 Brown, Michael A.	Shrewsbury Town	Preston North End	75,000
3 Cadette, Richard R.	Falkirk	Millwall	135,000
18 Cook, Mitchel C.	Blackpool	Hartlepool United	Free
9 Cunningham, Kenneth	Millwall	Wimbledon	1,300,000*
2 Emerson, Dean	Stockport County	Preston North End	Free
9 Goodman, Jonathan	Millwall	Wimbledon	1,300,000*
25 Guppy, Stephen	Newcastle United	Port Vale	225,000
4 Hoyland, Jamie W.	Sheffield United	Burnley	130,000
22 Jackson, Peter A.	Huddersfield Town	Chester City	Free
8 Jones, Stephen G.	West Ham United	Bournemouth AFC	150,000
15 Marsden, Christopher	Wolverhampton Wanderers	Notts County	250,000
23 Mellon, Michael J.	West Bromwich Albion	Blackpool	50,000
4 Miller, David B.	Stockport County	Wigan Athletic	undisclosed
28 Monington, Mark D.	Burnley	Rotherham United	undisclosed
28 Morton, Neil	Wigan Athletic	Altrincham	Free
21 Norbury, Michael S.	Preston North End	Doncaster Rovers	10,000
4 Norton, David W.	Hull City	Northampton Town	undisclosed
30 Portway, Steven	Gravesend & Northfleet	Gloucester City	undisclosed
18 Reddish, Shane	Carlisle United	Hartlepool United	Free
25 Rees, Anthony A.	Grimsby Town	West Bromwich Albion	50,000
22 Ross, Michael P.	Exeter City	Plymouth Argyle	undisclosed
28 Sealey, Leslie J.	Blackpool	West Ham United	Free
22 Smart, Allan A.C.	Caledonian Thistle	Preston North End	15,000
4 Smith, Brett R.	Chesham United	Slough Town	undisclosed
7 Thompson, David G.	Brentford	Blackpool	undisclosed
18 Valentine, Peter	Carlisle United	Rochdale	15,000
5 Watson, David G.	Thame United	Witney Town	undisclosed
4 Wilson, Paul A.	Burnley	York City	undisclosed
18 Worboys, Gavin A.	Notts County	Darlington	Free

Temporary transfers

24 Akinbiyi, Adeola P.	Norwich City	Brighton & Hove Albion	
4 Ansah, Andrew	Southend United	Brentford	
18 Barnard, Darren S.	Chelsea	Reading	
4 Benning, Paul M.	Sutton United	Walton & Hersham	
23 Bodley, Michael J.	Southend United	Gillingham	
16 Brass, Christopher P.	Burnley	Torquay United	
4 Butters, Guy	Portsmouth	Oxford United	
25 Campbell, Jamie	Luton Town	Mansfield Town	
18 Cormack, Lee D.	Newport (IW) FC	Fareham Town	
4 Cusack, Nicholas J.	Oxford United	Fulham	
16 Daly, Thomas	Worcester City	Solihull Borough	
25 De Souza, Miguel	Birmingham City	Bury	
29 Dudley, Derek A.	West Bromwich Albion	Halesowen Town	
18 Duffy, Christopher J.	Wigan Athletic	Northwich Victoria	
15 Dunphy, Nicholas O.	Peterborough United	Dagenham & Redbridge	
18 Evans, Richard J.	Sutton United	Abingdon Town	
26 Evans, Richard J.	Sutton United	Marlow	
28 Flemming, David	Enfield	Leyton	
18 Foot, Daniel F.	Southend United	Crawley Town	
29 Fox, Richard	Chelmsford City	Aveley	
4 Gill, Andrew	Chorley	Morecambe	
18 Gray, Ian J.	Oldham Athletic	Rochdale	
28 Hall, Mark A.	Southend United	Dover Athletic	
3 Hoyle, Colin	Notts County	Mansfield Town	
7 Huxford, Richard	Millwall	Bradford City	
9 Innes, Lee M.	Sheffield United	Boston United	
15 Jukes, Andrew	Luton Town	Wealdstone	
1 Kerr, James S.R.	Celtic	Brighton & Hove Albion	
23 Le Bihan, Neil E.	Peterborough United	Bishops Stortford	
4 McAuley, Sean	St. Johnstone	Chesterfield	
26 Magee, Jonathan P.	Kettering Town	Burton Albion	
18 Martin, Dean S.	Scunthorpe United	Halifax Town	
18 Midwood, Michael A.	Huddersfield Town	Macclesfield Town	
28 Milsom, Paul J.	Bristol City	Stafford Rangers	
29 Morrell, Darren	Chelmsford City	Aveley	
5 Morton, Neil	Wigan Athletic	Altrincham	
4 Munden, Maurice	Dover Athletic	Ashford Town	
25 Page, Darrell	Rushden & Diamonds	Wealdstone	

	From	To	Fee
7 Patterson, Ian D.	Wigan Athletic	Stalybridge Celtic	
21 Payne, Stephen J.	Huddersfield Town	Macclesfield Town	
15 Pearcey, Jason	Mansfield Town	Grimsby Town	
29 Prudhoe, Mark	Stoke City	Liverpool	
17 Quinn, Michael	Coventry City	Plymouth Argyle	
4 Ramsey, Paul	St. Johnstone	Cardiff City	
25 Ravenscroft, Craig A.	Brentford	Woking	
4 Robinson, Phillip J.	Huddersfield Town	Northampton Town	
4 Ryan, Tim J.	Scunthorpe United	Buxton	
14 Scully, Anthony D.T.	Crystal Palace	Bournemouth AFC	
3 Slawson, Stephen M.	Notts County	Shrewsbury Town	
28 Smith, Eric	Crystal Palace	Croydon	
13 Smith, Paul M.	Lincoln City	Kettering Town	
28 Starbuck, Philip M.	Huddersfield Town	Sheffield United	
3 Stewart, Paul A.	Liverpool	Wolverhampton Wanderers	
28 Sweetman, Nicholas E.	Leyton Orient	Hendon	
17 Taylor, Colin D.	Telford United	Atherstone United	
28 Taylor, Mark S.	Middlesbrough	Darlington	
18 Tiler, Carl	Nottingham Forest	Swindon Town	
27 Tracey, Simon P.	Sheffield United	Manchester City	
18 Vincent, Jamie R.	Crystal Palace	Bournemouth AFC	
10 Waddock, Gary P.	Bristol Rovers	Luton Town	
28 Warner, Ashley S.	Peterborough United	Telford United	
7 Welsh, Stephen	Peterborough United	Preston North End	
25 Whitington, Craig	Huddersfield Town	Rochdale	
16 Wilkin, Kevin	Northampton Town	Sudbury Town	
17 Williams, Paul R.	Coventry City	Huddersfield Town	
14 Witter, Anthony K.	Queens Park Rangers	Millwall	
1 Worboys, Gavin A.	Notts County	Darlington	

December 1994

	From	To	Fee
15 Arnold, Ian	Carlisle United	Kettering Town	10,000
30 Bailey, Shane M.	Sudbury Town	Braintree Town	undisclosed
23 Brissett, Jason C.	Peterborough United	Bournemouth AFC	Free
2 Brown, Michael A.	Shrewsbury Town	Preston North End	75,000
13 Burke, Brendon	Witton Albion	Stalybridge Celtic	undisclosed
19 Cowans, Gordon S.	Derby County	Wolverhampton Wanderers	25,000
30 Culverhouse, Ian B.	Norwich City	Swindon Town	250,000
16 Dryden, Richard A.	Birmingham City	Bristol City	200,000
23 Duxbury, Lee E.	Bradford City	Huddersfield Town	250,000
23 Evans, Richard J.	Sutton United	Marlow	undisclosed
13 Ferguson, Duncan	Glasgow Rangers	Everton	4,000,000
21 Flounders, Andrew J.	Halifax Town	Northampton Town	Free
6 Goodman, Donald	Sunderland	Wolverhampton Wanderers	1,100,000
15 Gunn, Brynley C.	Corby Town	Hednesford Town	undisclosed
22 Harlow, David S.	Kingstonian	Farnborough Town	undisclosed
30 Kuhl, Martin	Derby County	Bristol City	330,000
23 Lancashire, Graham	Burnley	Preston North End	55,000
23 Law, Brian J.	Queens Park Rangers	Wolverhampton Wanderers	undisclosed
1 Lay, David	Marlow	Slough Town	undisclosed
23 Lormor, Anthony	Peterborough United	Chesterfield	Free
1 McMahon, Stephen	Manchester City	Swindon Town	undisclosed
23 Mitchell, Graham L.	Huddersfield Town	Bradford City	undisclosed
9 Morrison, Andrew C.	Blackburn Rovers	Blackpool	undisclosed
19 Otto, Ricky	Southend United	Birmingham City	800,000
23 Owers, Gary	Sunderland	Bristol City	exch.
23 Page, Darrell	Rushden & Diamonds	Wealdstone	undisclosed
2 Parnell, Steven P.	Sudbury Town	Halstead Town	undisclosed
9 Patterson, Gary	Shrewsbury Town	Wycombe Wanderers	75,000
14 Pearcey, Jason	Mansfield Town	Grimsby Town	undisclosed
19 Phillips, Kevin	Baldock Town	Watford	undisclosed
9 Robinson, Philip J.	Huddersfield Town	Chesterfield	undisclosed
5 Rodwell, Anthony	Blackpool	Scarborough	10,000
23 Rutherford, Jonathan P.	Scarborough	Berwick Rangers	undisclosed
30 Scott, Keith	Swindon Town	Stoke City	300,000
23 Scott, Martin	Bristol City	Sunderland	450,000
20 Simkin, Darren S.	Wolverhampton Wanderers	Shrewsbury Town	36,000
23 Sinnott, Lee	Bradford City	Huddersfield Town	105,000
21 Taylor, Ian K.	Sheffield Wednesday	Aston Villa	1,000,000
30 Walters, Steven P.	Crewe Alexandra	Northwich Victoria	Free
8 Ward, Ashley S.	Crewe Alexandra	Norwich City	350,000
23 Welsh, Steven G.	Peterborough United	Partick Thistle	undisclosed
23 White, Devon W.	Queens Park Rangers	Notts County	100,000
8 White, Stuart	Welling United	Ashford Town	undisclosed
21 Whittingham, Guy	Aston Villa	Sheffield Wednesday	700,000
12 Witter, Anthony J.	Queens Park Rangers	Millwall	100,000
29 Wright, Jermaine M.	Millwall	Wolverhampton Wanderers	50,000

Temporary transfers

	From	To	Fee
6 Affor, Louis K.J.	Barnet	Wokingham Town	
23 Akinbiyi, Adeola P.	Norwich City	Brighton & Hove Albion	
23 Allen, Gavin	Tranmere Rovers	Macclesfield Town	
9 Allen, Paul K.	Southampton	Luton Town	
16 Alsop, Julian M.	Tamworth	Racing Club Warwick	
30 Armstrong, Craig	Nottingham Forest	Burnley	
30 Barber, Frederick	Luton Town	Peterborough United	
23 Barber, Philip A.	Millwall	Plymouth Argyle	
7 Barker, Dean E.	Sudbury Town	Braintree Town	
10 Barnett, Benjamin J.	Boreham Wood	Molesey	
13 Berry, Gwynne	Woking	Stafford Rangers	
23 Bodley, Michael J.	Southend United	Gillingham	
23 Brown, Ian	Bristol City	Northampton Town	
8 Bryan, Marvin L.	Queens Park Rangers	Doncaster Rovers	
23 Carter, James W.	Arsenal	Oxford United	
17 Casey, Kim T.	Solihull Borough	Kidderminster Harriers	
9 Chester, Martin G.	Enfield	Purfleet	
19 Conroy, Stephen	Stevenage Borough	Aylesbury United	
16 Cormack, Lee D.	Newport (IW)	Fareham Town	
16 Cox, Paul R.	Notts County	Hull City	
9 Croxford, Stephen	Walton & Hersham	Uxbridge	
9 Culverhouse, Ian B.	Norwich City	Swindon Town	
2 Cusack, Nicholas J.	Oxford United	Fulham	

	From	To	Fee
9 Cutler, Neil	West Bromwich Albion	Cheltenham Town	
15 Dobson, Anthony J.	Portsmouth	Oxford United	
16 Dolby, Tony C.	Millwall	Chesham United	
23 Donaldson, O'Neill M.	Doncaster Rovers	Mansfield Town	
17 Duffy, Christopher J.	Wigan Athletic	Northwich Victoria	
15 Eyre, John R.	Oldham Athletic	Scunthorpe United	
23 Filan, John R.	Cambridge United	Nottingham Forest	
2 Fleming, Mark J.	Aylesbury United	Staines Town	
20 Foot, Daniel F.	Southend United	Crawley Town	
31 Fowler, Lee	Dagenham & Redbridge	Barking	
18 Gray, Ian J.	Oldham Athletic	Rochdale	
5 Griffiths, Bryan K.	Blackpool	Scarborough	
15 Harford, Paul	Blackburn Rovers	Shrewsbury Town	
23 Harle, Michael J.L.	Millwall	Sittingbourne	
30 Hewlett, Matthew	Bristol City	Bath City	
16 Howe, Stephen R.	Nottingham Forest	Kettering Town	
8 Huxford, Richard	Millwall	Bradford City	
16 Innes, Lee M.	Sheffield United	Boston United	
24 Jones, Stuart J.	Hednesford Town	Bilston Town	
9 Joyce, Paul	Buckingham Town	Bedford Town	
13 Kalogeracos, Vasili	Birmingham City	Waterford United	
6 Kirkham, Paul	Stalybridge Celtic	Hyde United	
30 Loss, Colin P.	Bristol City	Bath City	
23 Lunn, Stephen	Sutton United	Dorking	
2 Lyons, Darren P.	Macclesfield Town	Fleetwood	
25 Magee, Jonathan P.	Kettering Town	Burton Albion	
23 Matthews, Neil	Lincoln City	Bury	
9 McCarthy, Anthony P.	Millwall	Crewe Alexandra	
21 McLean, Ian	Bristol Rovers	Cardiff City	
3 McMamara, Brett	Northampton Town	Corby Town	
2 Moore, Chris T.	Dagenham & Redbridge	Sudbury Town	
30 Morrell, Darren	Chelmsford City	Aveley	
8 Munden, Maurice	Dover Athletic	Ashford Town	
2 Murray, Mark	Macclesfield Town	Fleetwood	
2 Newhouse, Aidan R.	Wimbledon	Portsmouth	
23 Norris, Stephen M.	Chesterfield	Scarborough	
16 Nyamah, Kofi	Cambridge United	Stevenage Borough	
1 Parris, George M.	Birmingham City	Bristol City	
9 Patterson, Ian D.	Wigan Athletic	Stalybridge Celtic	
22 Perkins, Declan O.	Southend United	Chelmsford City	
8 Petterson, Andrew K.	Charlton Athletic	Bradford City	
23 Pettinger, Paul A.	Leeds United	Torquay United	
3 Preston, Richard J.	Northampton Town	Corby Town	
16 Rattle, Jonathan P.	Cambridge United	Stevenage Borough	
16 Richardson, Nicholas J.	Cardiff City	Chester City	
5 Rimmer, Stuart A.	Chester City	Preston North End	
30 Roberts, Darren A.	Chesterfield	Telford United	
16 Roberts, Glyn S.	Rotherham United	Buxton	
22 Roscoe, Andrew R.	Bolton Wanderers	Rotherham United	
30 Saville, Andrew V.	Birmingham City	Burnley	
22 Sedgemore, Benjamin R.	Birmingham City	Northampton Town	
8 Shipperley, Neil J.	Chelsea	Watford	
23 Short, Christian M.	Notts County	Huddersfield Town	
10 Stacey, Philip G.	Aylesbury United	Wokingham Town	
30 Starbuck, Philip M.	Huddersfield Town	Sheffield United	
23 Stoneman, Paul	Blackpool	Colchester United	
16 Sturridge, Dean	Derby County	Torquay United	
2 Taylor, Andrew	Morecambe	Bamber Bridge	
31 Tracey, Simon P.	Sheffield United	Norwich City	
16 Trollope, Paul J.	Torquay United	Derby County	
30 Turpin, Simon J.	Crewe Alexandra	Chorley	
19 Vincent, Jamie R.	Crystal Palace	AFC Bournemouth	
16 Wallace, Raymond G.	Stoke City	Hull City	
7 Wallis, Nigel	Sudbury Town	Braintree Town	
27 Warner, Ashley S.	Peterborough United	Telford United	
2 Watson, Kevin E.	Tottenham Hotspur	Bristol City	
22 Williams, Corey	Rotherham United	Boston United	
23 Williams, John N.	Coventry City	Stoke City	
January 1995			
11 Agnew, Stephen M.	Leicester City	Sunderland	250,000
30 Barrett, Earl D.	Aston Villa	Everton	1,700,000
13 Berry, Gwynne	Woking	Sutton United	undisclosed
19 Chapman, Lee R.	West Ham United	Ipswich Town	70,000
6 Charles, Gary A.	Derby County	Aston Villa	2,900,000**
12 Cole, Andrew	Newcastle United	Manchester United	6,250,000
12 Cormack, Lee D.	Newport (IW)	Fareham Town	undisclosed
6 Cusack, Nicholas J.	Oxford United	Fulham	Free
30 Daniels, Scott	Exeter City	Northampton Town	Free
30 Deary, John S.	Burnley	Rochdale	undisclosed
18 Dennis, Leonard C.	Woking	Sutton United	undisclosed
9 Donaldson, O'Neill M.	Doncaster Rovers	Sheffield Wednesday	50,000
13 Dowie, Iain	Southampton	Crystal Palace	400,000
20 Francis, Kevin M.	Stockport County	Birmingham City	800,000
23 Gayle, John	Burnley	Stoke City	70,000
10 Gillespie, Keith R.	Manchester United	Newcastle United	1,000,000
13 Hartson, John	Luton Town	Arsenal	2,500,000
27 Hogg, Graeme J.	Heart of Midlothian	Notts County	75,000
9 Huxford, Richard	Millwall	Bradford City	50,000
6 Johnson, Thomas	Derby County	Aston Villa	combined fee**
25 Kerton, Neil	Havant Town	Fareham Town	undisclosed
13 Kiwomya, Christopher	Ipswich Town	Arsenal	1,550,000
6 Lawrence, James H.	Doncaster Rovers	Leicester City	175,000
20 Nicol, Stephen	Liverpool	Notts County	Free
12 Nogan, Lee M.	Watford	Reading	250,000
11 Odey, Paul A.	Weymouth	Fareham Town	undisclosed
11 Priest, Christopher	Everton	Chester City	Free
16 Robins, Mark G.	Norwich City	Leicester City	1,000,000
6 Shipperley, Neil J.	Chelsea	Southampton	1,200,000
9 Snodin, Ian	Everton	Oldham Athletic	Free
26 Stant, Philip	Cardiff City	Bury	undisclosed
5 Starbuck, Philip M.	Huddersfield Town	Sheffield United	150,000

	From	To	Fee
27 Teggart, Darren	Salisbury City	Witney Town	undisclosed
18 Thorne, Peter L.	Blackburn Rovers	Swindon Town	200,000
17 Trollope, Paul J.	Torquay United	Derby County	100,000
26 Yates, Dean R.	Notts County	Derby County	350,000

Temporary transfers

20 Allen, Paul K.	Southampton	Stoke City
29 Armstrong, Craig	Nottingham Forest	Burnley
26 Bailey, Dennis L.	Queens Park Rangers	Brentford
12 Barnett, Benjamin J.	Boreham Wood	Molesey
25 Bayliss, Karl	Gloucester City	Forest Green Rovers
20 Biggins, Wayne	Stoke City	Luton Town
28 Black, Simon A.	Birmingham City	Sutton United
23 Bodley, Michael J.	Southend United	Birmingham City
24 Brown, Ian	Bristol City	Northampton Town
7 Brown, John C.	Leek Town	Ashton United
12 Challender, Gregory L.	Preston North End	Southport
13 Chapman, Lee R.	West Ham United	Southend United
14 Cherry, Richard W.	Enfield	Walton & Hersham
13 Chester, Martin G.	Enfield	Purfleet
9 Crawshaw, Gary	Stevenage Borough	Boreham Wood
13 Crocker, Marcus A.	Plymouth Argyle	Bath City
20 Darton, Scott R.	West Bromwich Albion	Blackpool
27 De Souza, Miguel	Birmingham City	Wycombe Wanderers
4 Dudley, Derek A.	West Bromwich Albion	Halesowen Town
22 Duffy, Christopher J.	Wigan Athletic	Northwich Victoria
16 Eyre, John R.	Oldham Athletic	Scunthorpe United
23 Filan, John R.	Cambridge United	Nottingham Forest
12 Fleck, Robert	Chelsea	Bristol City
13 Fleming, Mark J.	Aylesbury United	Wokingham Town
27 Gee, Philip J.	Leicester City	Plymouth Argyle
19 Given, Seamus J.J.	Blackburn Rovers	Swindon Town
15 Gray, Ian J.	Olham Athletic	Rochdale
9 Gregory, David S.	Ipswich Town	Hereford United
17 Harford, Paul	Blackburn Rovers	Shrewsbury Town
26 Haywood, Paul	Nottingham Forest	Grantham Town
27 Heggs, Carl S.	West Bromwich Albion	Bristol Rovers
12 Helliwell, Ian	Rotherham United	Stockport County
27 Henderson, Damien M.	Scunthorpe United	Hereford United
13 Hilton, Robert C.	Oldham Athletic	Northwich Victoria
27 Holland, Matthew R.	West Ham United	Bournemouth AFC
2 Hough, John A.	Sittingbourne	Ashford Town
16 Howe, Stephen R.	Nottingham Forest	Kettering Town
6 Jeffers, John J.	Port Vale	Shrewsbury Town
12 Jemson, Nigel B.	Notts County	Watford
27 Jones, Stuart J.	Hednesford Town	Bilston Town
20 Joyce, Warren G.	Burnley	Hull City
19 Kearton, Jason B.	Everton	Notts County
26 Key, Lance W.	Sheffield Wednesday	Oxford United
27 Livingstone, Richard	Burnley	Stalybridge Celtic
27 Marshall, Lee A.	Nottingham Forest	Grantham Town
13 Martin, Dean S.	Scunthorpe United	Rochdale
6 McNamara, Brett	Northampton Town	Corby Town
27 McPherson, Malcolm	West Ham United	Dagenham & Redbridge
1 Milsom, Paul J.	Bristol City	Stafford Rangers
14 Moore, Chris T.	Dagenham & Redbridge	Bishops Stortford
5 Norris, Stephen M.	Chesterfield	Scarborough
16 Nyamah, Kofi	Cambridge United	Stevenage Borough
27 Ormondroyd, Ian	Leicester City	Hull City
13 Payne, Grant	Wimbledon	Woking
9 Power, Lee M.	Bradford City	Millwall
6 Preston, Richard J.	Northampton Town	Corby Town
16 Rattle, Jonathan P.	Cambridge United	Stevenage Borough
20 Reeve, James M.	Bournemouth AFC	Weymouth
30 Roberts, Darren A.	Chesterfield	Telford United
20 Rodwell, Anthony	Scarborough	Wigan Athletic
23 Rowett, Gary	Everton	Blackpool
13 Scott, Kevin W.	Tottenham Hotspur	Port Vale
23 Short, Christian M.	Notts County	Huddersfield Town
27 Smith, Nicholas L.	Sudbury Town	Northampton Town
20 Smith, Richard	Nottingham Forest	Nuneaton Borough
13 Soloman, Jason R.	Watford	Peterborough United
16 Squires, James A.	Preston North End	Stafford Rangers
13 Stacey, Philip G.	Aylesbury United	Wokingham Town
24 Stoneman, Paul	Blackpool	Colchester United
18 Sturridge, Dean	Derby County	Torquay United
6 Taylor, Andrew	Morecambe	Fleetwood
6 Tolson, Neil	Bradford City	Chester City
31 Tracey, Simon P.	Sheffield United	Norwich City
31 Turpin, Simon J.	Crewe Alexandra	Chorley
20 Viveash, Adrian L.	Swindon Town	Reading
28 Wardle, Paul G.	Gresley Rovers	Tamworth
19 Williams, Paul A.	Crystal Palace	Sunderland
20 Youds, Edward P.	Ipswich Town	Bradford City
2 Young, Roy E.	Poole Town	Stockport County

February 1995

23 Agnew, Paul	Grimsby Town	West Bromwich Albion	65,000
6 Bimson, Stuart J.	Macclesfield Town	Bury	12,500
18 Bradshaw, Mark	Stafford Rangers	Macclesfield Town	undisclosed
13 Brown, Ian	Bristol City	Northampton Town	nominal
24 Byrne, John F.	Oxford United	Brighton & Hove Albion	Free
10 Carr, Franz A.	Leicester City	Aston Villa	250,000
22 Davey, Simon	Carlisle United	Preston North End	75,000
4 De Souza, Juan M.	Birmingham City	Wycombe Wanderers	100,000
23 Forsyth, Michael E.	Derby County	Notts County	undisclosed
22 Gilchrist, Philip A.	Hartlepool United	Oxford United	100,000
8 Helliwell, Ian	Rotherham United	Stockport County	undisclosed
22 Hicks, Stuart J.	Preston North End	Scarborough	undisclosed
10 Lovell, Stephen J.	Hastings Town	Sittingbourne	undisclosed
21 Manson, Gary	Dorchester Town	Salisbury City	undisclosed
24 Mathie, Alexander	Newcastle United	Ipswich Town	500,000

	From	To	Fee
17 McRobert, Lee P.	Sittingbourne	Millwall	35,000
13 Mortimore, Paul J.	Cheltenham Town	Clevedon Town	undisclosed
24 Nogan, Kurt	Brighton & Hove Albion	Burnley	250,000
10 Parker, Garry S.	Aston Villa	Leicester City	550,000
16 Richardson, Kevin	Aston Villa	Coventry City	300,000
2 Roscoe, Andrew R.	Bolton Wanderers	Rotherham United	undisclosed
24 Russell, Kevin J.	AFC Bournemouth	Notts County	60,000
28 Shearer, Michael K.	Gloucester City	Halesowen Town	undisclosed
8 Taylor, Scott	Staines Town	Millwall	15,000
10 Thompson, Garry L.	Cardiff City	Northampton Town	Free
24 Thompson, Steven J.	Leicester City	Burnley	200,000
11 Ullathorne, Simon	Sittingbourne	Gloucester City	undisclosed
21 Young, Roy E.	Poole Town	Aldershot Town	200,000

Temporary transfers

20 Allen, Paul K.	Southampton	Stoke City
16 Asaba, Carl	Brentford	Colchester United
8 Bannister, Andrew	Burnley	Bangor
11 Barnett, Benjamin J.	Boreham Wood	Molesey
25 Bayliss, Karl	Gloucester City	Forest Green Rovers
28 Beckham, David R.	Manchester United	Preston North End
10 Bibo, Salvatore	Sheffield United	Chesterfield
20 Biggins, Wayne	Stoke City	Luton Town
1 Black, Simon	Birmingham City	Sutton United
10 Blackhurst, James	Southport	Barrow
4 Brown, John C.	Leek Town	Ashton United
27 Burns, Philip M.	Aldershot Town	Chesham United
27 Carruthers, Matthew J.	Dover Athletic	Ashford Town
24 Clarke, Michael D.	Solihull Borough	Sutton Coldfield Town
2 Coll, Owen O.	Tottenham Hotspur	Yeovil Town
17 Cooksey, Scott A.	Peterborough United	Stalybridge Celtic
21 Cousins, Clifford M.	Buckingham Town	Chesham United
3 Currie, Darren	West Ham United	Shrewsbury Town
3 Cutler, Neil	West Bromwich Albion	Cheltenham Town
19 Darton, Scott R.	West Bromwich Albion	Blackpool
13 Dickins, Matthew J.	Blackburn Rovers	Stockport County
13 Donovan, Neil	Worcester City	Racing Club Warwick
2 Dudley, Derek A.	West Bromwich Albion	Halesowen Town
10 Dunphy, Nicholas O.	Peterborough United	Hednesford Town
20 Feuer, Anthony I.	West Ham United	Peterborough United
13 Fleck, Robert	Chelsea	Bristol City
11 Fleming, Mark J.	Aylesbury United	Wokingham Town
1 Fowler, Lee	Dagenham & Redbridge	Barking
3 Galloway, Michael	Celtic	Leicester City
17 Gilchrist, Philip A.	Hartlepool United	Oxford United
10 Glass, James R.	Crystal Palace	Portsmouth
3 Harkness, Steven	Liverpool	Southend United
2 Harle, Michael J.	Millwall	Sittingbourne
27 Holland, Matthew R.	West Ham United	AFC Bournemouth
3 Honor, Christian R.	Airdrieonians	Cardiff City
7 Hough, John A.	Sittingbourne	Ashford Town
17 Hoult, Russell	Leicester City	Derby County
20 Joyce, Warren G.	Burnley	Hull City
21 Kearton, Jason B.	Everton	Notts County
3 Knight, Richard	Walsall	Armitage
17 Knott, Gareth R.	Tottenham Hotspur	Gillingham
16 Livett, Simon R.	Cambridge United	Dover Athletic
1 Livingstone, Richard	Burnley	Stalybridge Celtic
1 Loss, Colin P.	Bristol City	Bath City
4 Lunn, Stephen	Sutton United	Dorking
13 Martin, David	Bristol City	Northampton Town
3 Middlemass, Scott L.	Northampton Town	Sudbury Town
24 Midwood, Michael A.	Huddersfield Town	Macclesfield Town
2 Millen, Andrew F.	Kilmarnock	Ipswich Town
24 Mills, Lee	Wolverhampton Wanderers	Derby County
11 Moore, Chris T.	Dagenham & Redbridge	Bishops Stortford
16 Moore, Neil	Everton	Oldham Athletic
1 Morrell, Darren	Chelmsford City	Aveley
3 Musgrave, Sean	Sunderland	Gateshead
16 Nyamah, Kofi	Cambridge United	Stevenage Borough
24 Oldfield, David C.	Leicester City	Millwall
28 Ormondroyd, Ian	Leicester City	Hull City
9 Parris, George M.	Birmingham City	Brighton & Hove Albion
14 Payne, Grant	Wimbledon	Woking
3 Pettinger, Paul A.	Leeds United	Halifax Town
16 Quigley, Michael A.	Manchester City	Wrexham
16 Rattle, Jonathan P.	Cambridge United	Stevenage Borough
18 Reeve, James M.	AFC Bournemouth	Weymouth
14 Rhodes, Andrew C.	St. Johnstone	Bolton Wanderers
4 Roberts, Barry J.&	Dagenham & Redbridge	Billericay Town
27 Roberts, Darren A.	Chesterfield	Telford United
17 Romasz, Anton	Bognor Regis Town	Worthing
19 Rowett, Gary	Everton	Blackpool
13 Scott, Kevin W.	Tottenham Hotspur	Port Vale
11 Sheppard, James	Blackpool	Horwich RMI
3 Skelly, Richard B.	Northampton Town	Sudbury Town
17 Skiverton, Terence J.	Chelsea	Wycombe Wanderers
16 Squires, James A.	Preston North End	Stafford Rangers
11 Stacey, Philip G.	Aylesbury United	Wokingham Town
8 Stewart, Paul A.	Liverpool	Burnley
3 Taylor, Raymond	Chelmsford City	Purfleet
11 Thorpe, Lee A.	Blackpool	Horwich RMI
27 Todd, Andrew	Middlesbrough	Swindon Town
20 Trebble, Neil D.	Preston North End	Scarborough
14 Verrall, Damon	Sittingbourne	Ashford Town
6 Verveer, Etienne	Millwall	Bradford City
20 Viveash, Adrian L.	Swindon Town	Reading
10 Watson, David G.	Witney Town	Marlow
16 Watson, Kevin E.	Tottenham Hotspur	Barnet
3 Westley, Shane L.M.	Brentford	Southend United
14 Wilkin, Kevin	Northampton Town	Rushden & Diamonds
3 Williams, John	Coventry City	Swansea City

	From	To	Fee
4 Wordsworth, Dean	Dagenham & Redbridge	Billericay Town	
22 Youds, Edward P.	Ipswich Town	Bradford City	
2 Young, Roy E.	Poole Town	Stockport County	

March 1995

9 Abrahams, Paul	Colchester United	Brentford	30,000
23 Angell, Brett A.M.	Everton	Sunderland	600,000
17 Bale, Kevin	Newport (IW)	Whitchurch United	undisclosed
18 Bayliss, Karl	Gloucester City	Forest Green Rovers	undisclosed
2 Blewden, Colin G.	Dover Athletic	Gravesend & Northfleet	undisclosed
24 Boden, Christopher D.	Aston Villa	Derby County	150,000
23 Bogie, Ian	Leyton Orient	Port Vale	50,000
24 Boyce, David J.	Gravesend & Northfleet	Havant Town	undisclosed
22 Brown, Steven R.	Colchester United	Gillingham	exch.
9 Brownrigg, Andrew D.	Hereford United	Norwich City	100,000
2 Burrows, David	Everton	Coventry City	1,100,000
26 Clarke, Kenneth R.	Abingdon Town	Marlow	undisclosed
23 Collett, Andrew A.	Middlesbrough	Bristol Rovers	10,000
22 Darton, Scott R.	West Bromwich Albion	Blackpool	nominal
17 Dickins, Matthew J.	Blackburn Rovers	Stockport County	undisclosed
23 Dickson, Kerry M.	Luton Town	Millwall	5000
23 Drysdale, Jason	Newcastle United	Swindon Town	340,000
23 Fickling, Ashley	Sheffield United	Grimsby Town	Free
17 Filan, John R.	Cambridge United	Coventry City	300,000
31 Fjortoft, Jan-Aage.	Swindon Town	Middlesbrough	1,300,000
30 Hay, Darren A.	Cambridge United	Woking	undisclosed
13 Hayward, Steve L.	Derby County	Carlisle United	100,000
23 Hazel, Desmond L.	Rotherham United	Chesterfield	undisclosed
28 Holmes, David J.	Gresley Rovers	Gloucester City	undisclosed
3 Hooper, Dean R.	Hayes	Swindon Town	undisclosed
23 Houghton, Raymond J.	Aston Villa	Crystal Palace	300,000
23 Ironside, Ian	Stockport County	Scarborough	Free
3 Isaac, Lee	Burgess Hill Town	Hastings Town	undisclosed
15 Kenna, Jeffrey J.	Southampton	Blackburn Rovers	1,500,000
21 Kennedy, Mark	Millwall	Liverpool	2,300,000
12 Lancaster, David	Halifax Town	Bury	Free
31 Lomas, Andrew J.	Stevenage Borough	Rushden & Diamonds	undisclosed
2 Lydiate, Jason L.	Bolton Wanderers	Blackpool	75,000
17 Matthews, Robert	Notts County	Luton Town	80,000
17 McCarthy, Anthony P.	Millwall	Colchester United	Free
20 McGavin, Steven J.	Birmingham City	Wycombe Wanderers	140,000
2 Mills, Lee	Wolverhampton Wanderers	Derby County	400,000
23 O'Shea, Daniel E.	Cambridge United	Northampton Town	Free
6 Rake, Barry D.	Chesham United	Slough Town	undisclosed
23 Reeve, James M.	Bournemouth AFC	Hereford United	undisclosed
10 Reeves, Neil	Clevedon Town	Gloucester City	undisclosed
22 Reinelt, Robert S.	Gillingham	Colchester United	exch.
23 Roche, David	Doncaster Rovers	Southend United	55,000
22 Scott, Richard P.	Birmingham City	Shrewsbury Town	undisclosed
22 Shaw, Darren R.	Wolverhampton Wanderers	Northampton Town	Free
23 Sherlock, Paul G.	Notts County	Mansfield Town	15,000
10 Simpson, Wayne W.	Stafford Rangers	Hednesford Town	undisclosed
17 Soloman, Jason R.	Watford	Wycombe Wanderers	Free
2 Storer, Stuart J.	Exeter City	Brighton & Hove Albion	15,000
22 Strachan, Gordon D.	Leeds United	Coventry City	Free
23 Swailes, Christopher W.	Doncaster Rovers	Ipswich Town	150,000
23 Taylor, John P.	Bradford City	Luton Town	200,000
23 Thompson, David G.	Blackpool	Cambridge United	Free
10 Trebble, Neil D.	Preston North End	Scarborough	undisclosed
17 Watson, Gordon W.	Sheffield Wednesday	Southampton	1,200,000
22 Williams, Richard J.	Atherstone United	Hednesford Town	undisclosed
23 Withers, Peter	Chorley	Morecambe	undisclosed
10 Woodman, Andrew J.	Exeter City	Northampton Town	Free
13 Woodward, Andrew	Crewe Alexandra	Bury	undisclosed
10 Wright, Alan	Blackburn Rovers	Aston Villa	900,000
17 Youds, Edward P.	Ipswich Town	Bradford City	150,000

Temporary transfers

26 Allen, Paul K.	Southampton	Stoke City
19 Asaba, Carl	Brentford	Colchester United
8 Aspinall, Warren	Bournemouth AFC	Carlisle United
31 Banton, Michael	Walton & Hersham	Chertsey Town
28 Barnett, Benjamin J.	Boreham Wood	Leyton
23 Battersby, Tony	Sheffield United	Southend United
10 Bibbo, Salvatore	Sheffield United	Chesterfield
2 Black, Kingsley	Nottingham Forest	Sheffield United
2 Black, Simon A.	Birmingham City	Yeovil Town
29 Bolton, James I.	Kingstonian	Carshalton Athletic
15 Booth, Kevin J.	Stalybridge Celtic	Ashton United
23 Booty, Justin	Colchester United	Wivenhoe Town
31 Brown, Dereck	Walton & Hersham	St Albans City
4 Brown, John C.	Leek Town	Ashton United
9 Byrne, Paul P.	Celtic	Brighton & Hove Albion
10 Campbell, Jamie	Luton Town	Cambridge United
6 Carey, Alan W.	Reading	Weymouth
25 Carruthers, Matthew J.	Dover Athletic	Ashford Town
7 Ceraolo, Mark	Crewe Alexandra	Congleton Town
22 Chamberlain, Alec F.	Sunderland	Liverpool
18 Cooksey, Scott A.	Peterborough United	Stalybridge Celtic
29 Crocker, Marcus A.	Plymouth Argyle	Dorchester Town
19 Darton, Scott R.	West Bromwich Albion	Blackpool
14 Donovan, Neil	Worcester City	Racing Club Warwick
23 Dreyer, John B.	Stoke City	Bolton Wanderers
21 Farrelly, Gareth	Aston Villa	Rotherham United
20 Feuer, Anthony I.	West Ham United	Peterborough United
2 Filan, John R.	Cambridge United	Coventry City
23 Flatts, Mark	Arsenal	Bristol City
16 Fleming, Mark J.	Aylesbury United	Wokingham Town
17 Ford, Stuart T.	Scarborough	Halifax Town
10 Forrester, Jamie	Leeds United	Grimsby Town
7 Galloway, Michael	Celtic	Leicester City
3 Gardiner, Mark C.	Crewe Alexandra	Chester City

	From	To	Fee
18 Garland, Peter J.	Charlton Athletic	Wycombe Wanderers	
10 Germaine, Gary	West Bromwich Albion	Halesowen Town	
28 Gittings, Martin A.	Stevenage Borough	Hendon	
13 Glass, James R.	Crystal Palace	Portsmouth	
23 Gordon, Dale A.	West Ham United	Peterborough United	
24 Gore, Ian G.	Blackpool	Chorley	
3 Gregory, Neil R.	Ipswich Town	Scunthorpe United	
5 Harle, Michael J.	Millwall	Sittingbourne	
4 Harper, Lee J.	Scarborough	Goole Town	
6 Henderson, Damien M.	Scunthorpe United	Hartlepool United	
23 Hendon, Ian M.	Leyton Orient	Birmingham City	
30 Holden, Mark C.	Stoke City	Telford United	
27 Holland, Matthew R.	West Ham United	Bournemouth AFC	
10 Holmes, Steven P.	Preston North End	Hartlepool United	
20 Hoult, Russell	Leicester City	Derby County	
23 Inglethorpe, Alex M.	Watford	Barnet	
23 Jemson, Nigel B.	Notts County	Coventry City	
2 Joseph, Roger A.	Wimbledon	Millwall	
31 Kempton, David H.	Kingstonian	Walton & Hersham	
18 Kirkham, Paul	Stalybridge Celtic	Hyde United	
6 Knight, Richard	Walsall	Armitage	
21 Knott, Gareth R.	Tottenham Hotspur	Gillingham	
10 Langford, Timothy	Wycombe Wanderers	Kidderminster Harriers	
10 Le Bihan, Neil E.	Peterborough United	Yeovil Town	
17 Lomas, Andrew J.	Stevenage Borough	Cambridge United	
23 Lund, Gary J.	Notts County	Hull City	
7 Lunn, Stephen	Sutton United	Dorking	
31 Lyons, Darren P.	Macclesfield Town	Ashton United	
23 Margetson, Martyn W.	Manchester City	Luton Town	
30 Marginson, Karl K.	Rotherham United	Macclesfield Town	
16 Martin, David	Bristol City	Northampton Town	
28 Matteo, Dominic	Liverpool	Sunderland	
10 McGleish, Scott	Charlton Athletic	Leyton Orient	
23 McNamara, Brett	Northampton Town	Kings Lynn	
7 McPherson, Malcolm	West Ham United	Dagenham & Redbridge	
20 Mercer, William	Sheffield United	Nottingham Forest	
27 Midwood, Michael A.	Huddersfield Town	Macclesfield Town	
3 Miles, Benjamin D.	Swansea City	Trowbridge Town	
11 Moore, Chris T.	Dagenham & Redbridge	Bishops Stortford	
23 Morah, Olisa H.	Cambridge United	Torquay United	
5 Musgrave, Sean	Sunderland	Gateshead	
24 Norman, John	Morecambe	Chorley	
28 Norris, Stephen M.	Chesterfield	VS Rugby	
26 Oldfield, David C.	Leicester City	Millwall	
23 O'Neill, Darren S.	Kingstonian	Wealdstone	
20 Owers, Adrian R.	Chelmsford City	Worthing	
29 Palmer, Lee J.	Gillingham	Sittingbourne	
13 Parris, George M.	Birmingham City	Brighton & Hove Albion	
17 Payne, Grant	Wimbledon	Woking	
23 Peel, Nathan J.	Burnley	Rotherham United	
3 Pettinger, Paul A.	Leeds United	Halifax Town	
17 Pettinger, Paul A.	Leeds United	Kettering Town	
9 Price, Gareth	Kettering Town	Gainsborough Trinity	
16 Quinn, Michael	Coventry City	Watford	
10 Read, Paul	Arsenal	Leyton Orient	
14 Rhodes, Andrew C.	Bolton Wanderers	Norwich City	
25 Richards, Dean I.	Bradford City	Wolverhampton Wanderers	
20 Rowe, Rodney C.	Huddersfield Town	Bury	
19 Rowett, Gary	Everton	Blackpool	
15 Scott, Kevin W.	Tottenham Hotspur	Port Vale	
22 Scott, Robert	Sheffield United	Scarborough	
23 Shaw, Paul	Arsenal	Burnley	
24 Shea, Peter	Collier Row	East Thurrock United	
19 Skiverton, Terence J.	Chelsea	Wycombe Wanderers	
17 Stewart, William I.	Northampton Town	Chesterfield	
17 Sugrue, James S.	Kingstonian	Aldershot Town	
3 Taylor, Raymond	Chelmsford City	Purfleet	
18 Timons, Christopher	Mansfield Town	Stafford Rangers	
27 Todd, Andrew	Middlesbrough	Swindon Town	
6 Turnbull, Lee M.	Wycombe Wanderers	Scunthorpe United	
10 Turpin, Simon J.	Crewe Alexandra	Northwich Victoria	
31 Verrall, Damon	Sittingbourne	Erith & Belvedere	
8 Verveer, Etienne	Millwall	Bradford City	
23 Walker, Richard N.	Notts County	Mansfield Town	
28 Warner, Ashley S.	Peterborough United	Bromsgrove Rovers	
31 Warren, Christer	Southampton	Cheltenham Town	
19 Watson, Kevin E.	Tottenham Hotspur	Barnet	
24 Webster, Simon P.	West Ham United	Oldham Athletic	
17 Whitney, John D.	Huddersfield Town	Wigan Athletic	
4 Wild, Robert P.	Aylesbury United	Walton & Hersham	
10 Wilkinson, Ian M.	Crewe Alexandra	Congleton Town	
1 Williams, Christopher	Hereford United	Worcester City	
6 Williams, Darren P.	Dover Athletic	Welling United	
9 Williams, Martin K.	Luton Town	Colchester United	
13 Williams, Paul A.	Crystal Palace	Birmingham City	
17 Williams, Paul R.C.	Coventry City	Huddersfield Town	
13 Wordsworth, Dean	Dagenham & Redbridge	Harlow Town	
2 Wratten, Adam P.	Birmingham City	Yeovil Town	
April 1995			
25 Holland, Matthew R.	West Ham United	AFC Bournemouth	undisclosed
7 Page, Darrell	Wealdstone	Raunds Town	undisclosed
12 Whelan, Philip J.	Ipswich Town	Middlesbrough	undisclosed
May 1995			
15 Beckford, Jason N.	Millwall	Northampton Town	undisclosed
23 Bracewell, Paul W.	Newcastle United	Sunderland	undisclosed
17 Doyle, Maurice	Queens Park Rangers	Millwall	undisclosed
18 Inglethorpe, Alex M.	Watford	Leyton Orient	undisclosed
19 Vowden, Colin D.	Cambridge City	Cambridge United	undisclosed
9 Watson, Mark L.	Sutton United	West Ham United	undisclosed

LEAGUE ATTENDANCES 1994–95

FA CARLING PREMIERSHIP STATISTICS

	Average Gate			*Season 1994/95*	
	1993/94	1994/95	+/–%	Highest	Lowest
Arsenal	30,563	35,330	+15.6	38,368	27,213
Aston Villa	29,015	29,756	+2.6	40,154	22,241
Blackburn Rovers	17,721	25,272	+42.6	30,545	20,586
Chelsea	19,416	21,057	+8.5	31,139	14,130
Coventry City	13,352	15,980	+19.7	21,858	9,509
Crystal Palace	15,656	14,992	–4.2	18,224	10,964
Everton	22,876	31,291	+36.8	40,011	23,295
Ipswich Town	16,382	16,818	+2.7	22,553	11,282
Leeds United	34,493	32,925	–4.5	39,426	27,246
Leicester City	16,005	19,532	+22.0	21,393	15,248
Liverpool	38,493	34,176	–11.2	40,014	27,183
Manchester City	26,709	22,725	–14.9	27,850	19,150
Manchester United	44,244	43,681	–1.3	43,868	43,120
Newcastle United	33,679	34,690	+3.0	35,626	34,163
Norwich City	18,164	18,625	+2.5	21,843	13,530
Nottingham Forest	23,051	23,633	+2.5	28,882	20,287
Queens Park Rangers	14,228	14,613	+2.7	18,948	10,189
Sheffield Wednesday	27,191	26,572	–2.3	34,051	20,395
Southampton	14,751	14,685	–0.4	15,202	12,876
Tottenham Hotspur	27,160	27,259	+0.4	33,040	22,387
West Ham United	20,572	20,118	–2.2	24,783	16,959
Wimbledon	10,474	10,230	–2.3	18,224	5,268

ENDSLEIGH INSURANCE LEAGUE: DIVISION ONE ATTENDANCES

	Average Gate			*Season 1994/95*	
	1993/94	1994/95	+/–%	Highest	Lowest
Barnsley	7,610	6,509	–14.5	11,782	3,659
Bolton Wanderers	10,498	13,029	+24.1	18,370	9,519
Bristol City	8,852	8,005	–9.6	11,127	6,030
Burnley	11,317	12,135	+7.2	17,808	9,551
Charlton Athletic	8,056	10,211	+26.8	13,863	8,167
Derby County	15,937	13,589	–14.7	16,839	10,585
Grimsby Town	5,989	5,921	–1.1	10,112	3,216
Luton Town	7,878	7,350	–6.7	9,651	5,764
Middlesbrough	10,400	18,807	+80.8	23,903	14,878
Millwall	9,821	7,685	–21.7	12,412	5,260
Notts County	8,314	7,195	–13.5	11,102	4,703
Oldham Athletic	12,563	8,444	–32.8	11,962	5,465
Port Vale	8,323	9,174	+10.2	19,510	7,141
Portsmouth	11,692	8,269	–29.3	13,466	5,272
Reading	6,932	9,350	+34.9	13,223	6,921
Sheffield United	19,562	14,462	–26.1	20,693	11,568
Southend United	6,105	5,146	–15.7	8,522	3,619
Stoke City	15,931	12,910	–18.9	20,408	9,105
Sunderland	16,934	15,344	–9.4	19,549	11,661
Swindon Town	15,274	9,744	–56.8	14,436	7,658
Tranmere Rovers	8,099	8,906	+10.0	16,377	5,480
Watford	7,907	8,125	+2.8	10,108	6,024
West Bromwich Albion	16,840	15,200	–9.7	21,071	11,782
Wolverhampton Wanderers	22,008	25,940	+17.9	28,298	22,768

ENDSLEIGH INSURANCE LEAGUE: DIVISION TWO ATTENDANCES

	Average Gate			*Season 1994/95*	
	1993/94	1994/95	+/–%	Highest	Lowest
AFC Bournemouth	4,355	4,391	+0.8	10,747	2,505
Birmingham City	14,506	16,983	+17.1	25,581	10,600
Blackpool	4,757	4,771	+0.3	8,333	3,438
Bradford City	6,395	6,152	–3.8	11,300	3,535
Brentford	5,611	6,536	+16.5	10,079	4,031
Brighton & Hove Albion	7,730	7,563	–2.2	11,004	5,316
Bristol Rovers	5,338	5,173	–3.1	8,256	3,694
Cambridge United	3,686	3,443	–6.6	5,828	2,328
Cardiff City	6,072	4,543	–25.2	7,420	2,560
Chester City	3,191	2,388	–25.2	4,974	1,191
Crewe Alexandra	3,991	4,239	+6.2	6,359	3,242
Huddersfield Town	6,372	11,665	+83.1	18,775	8,552
Hull City	5,943	4,721	–20.6	10,220	2,694
Leyton Orient	4,237	3,436	–18.9	7,578	2,338
Oxford United	6,877	6,148	–10.6	9,540	4,594
Peterborough United	7,412	5,055	–31.8	8,796	3,554
Plymouth Argyle	9,003	5,832	–35.2	8,550	3,824
Rotherham United	3,736	3,278	–12.3	6,687	2,208
Shrewsbury Town	4,402	4,013	–8.8	5,949	2,849
Stockport County	5,090	4,525	–11.1	5,652	3,040
Swansea City	3,534	3,582	+1.4	5,807	2,065
Wrexham	3,961	4,071	+2.8	6,472	1,823
Wycombe Wanderers	5,448	5,856	+7.5	7,683	4,388
York City	4,633	3,685	–20.5	6,828	2,301

ENDSLEIGH INSURANCE LEAGUE: DIVISION THREE ATTENDANCES

	Average Gate			*Season 1994/95*	
	1993/94	1994/95	+/–%	Highest	Lowest
Barnet	2,431	2,201	–9.5	3,579	1,325
Bury	2,597	3,223	+24.1	6,790	2,145
Carlisle United	5,524	7,422	+34.4	12,412	5,141
Chesterfield	3,188	3,528	+10.7	7,283	2,136
Colchester United	2,857	3,280	+14.8	6,055	2,231
Darlington	2,276	2,346	+3.1	3,992	1,548
Doncaster Rovers	2,478	2,585	+4.3	4,796	1,611
Exeter City	3,320	2,484	–25.2	5,538	1,551
Fulham	4,655	4,207	–9.6	6,195	2,729
Gillingham	3,148	3,206	+1.8	4,737	2,257
Hartlepool United	2,076	1,953	–5.9	3,854	1,354
Hereford United	2,262	2,367	+4.6	3,135	1,489
Lincoln City	3,179	3,276	+3.1	6,477	1,969
Mansfield Town	2,718	2,946	+8.4	5,197	2,247
Northampton Town	3,454	5,086	+47.2	7,461	2,466
Preston North End	7,377	8,469	+14.8	11,866	5,833
Rochdale	2,657	2,184	–17.8	4,012	1,170
Scarborough	1,681	1,771	+5.4	4,266	1,179
Scunthorpe United	3,182	2,917	–8.3	4,785	2,079
Torquay United	3,437	2,968	–13.7	4,739	1,492
Walsall	4,237	4,071	–3.9	6,219	3,154
Wigan Athletic	1,897	1,748	–7.9	3,618	1,231

LEAGUE ATTENDANCES SINCE 1946–47

Season	*Matches*	*Total*	*Div. 1*	*Div. 2*	*Div. 3 (S)*	*Div. 3 (N)*
1946–47	1848	35,604,606	15,005,316	11,071,572	5,664,004	3,863,714
1947–48	1848	40,259,130	16,732,341	12,286,350	6,653,610	4,586,829
1948–49	1848	41,271,414	17,914,667	11,353,237	6,998,429	5,005,081
1949–50	1848	40,517,865	17,278,625	11,694,158	7,104,155	4,440,927
1950–51	2028	39,584,967	16,679,454	10,780,580	7,367,884	4,757,109
1951–52	2028	39,015,866	16,110,322	11,066,189	6,958,927	4,880,428
1952–53	2028	37,149,966	16,050,278	9,686,654	6,704,299	4,708,735
1953–54	2028	36,174,590	16,154,915	9,510,053	6,311,508	4,198,114
1954–55	2028	34,133,103	15,087,221	8,988,794	5,996,017	4,051,071
1955–56	2028	33,150,809	14,108,961	9,080,002	5,692,479	4,269,367
1956–57	2028	32,744,405	13,803,037	8,718,162	5,622,189	4,601,017
1957–58	2028	33,562,208	14,468,652	8,663,712	6,097,183	4,332,661
					Div. 3	*Div. 4*
1958–59	2028	33,610,985	14,727,691	8,641,997	5,946,600	4,276,697
1959–60	2028	32,538,611	14,391,227	8,399,627	5,739,707	4,008,050
1960–61	2028	28,619,754	12,926,948	7,033,936	4,784,256	3,874,614
1961–62	2015	27,979,902	12,061,194	7,453,089	5,199,106	3,266,513
1962–63	2028	28,885,852	12,490,239	7,792,770	5,341,362	3,261,481
1963–64	2028	28,535,022	12,486,626	7,594,158	5,419,157	3,035,081
1964–65	2028	27,641,168	12,708,752	6,984,104	4,436,245	3,512,067
1965–66	2028	27,206,980	12,480,644	6,914,757	4,779,150	3,032,429
1966–67	2028	28,902,596	14,242,957	7,253,819	4,421,172	2,984,648
1967–68	2028	30,107,298	15,289,410	7,450,410	4,013,087	3,354,391
1968–69	2028	29,382,172	14,584,851	7,382,390	4,339,656	3,075,275
1969–70	2028	29,600,972	14,868,754	7,581,728	4,223,761	2,926,729
1970–71	2028	28,194,146	13,954,337	7,098,265	4,377,213	2,764,331
1971–72	2028	28,700,729	14,484,603	6,769,308	4,697,392	2,749,426
1972–73	2028	25,448,642	13,998,154	5,631,730	3,737,252	2,081,506
1973–74	2027	24,982,203	13,070,991	6,326,108	3,421,624	2,163,480
1974–75	2028	25,577,977	12,613,178	6,955,970	4,086,145	1,992,684
1975–76	2028	24,896,053	13,089,861	5,798,405	3,948,449	2,059,338
1976–77	2028	26,182,800	13,647,585	6,250,597	4,152,218	2,132,400
1977–78	2028	25,392,872	13,255,677	6,474,763	3,332,042	2,330,390
1978–79	2028	24,540,627	12,704,549	6,153,223	3,374,558	2,308,297
1979–80	2028	24,623,975	12,163,002	6,112,025	3,999,328	2,349,620
1980–81	2028	21,907,569	11,392,894	5,175,442	3,637,854	1,701,379
1981–82	2028	20,006,961	10,420,793	4,750,463	2,836,915	1,998,790
1982–83	2028	18,766,158	9,295,613	4,974,937	2,943,568	1,552,040
1983–84	2028	18,358,631	8,711,448	5,359,757	2,729,942	1,557,484
1984–85	2028	17,849,835	9,761,404	4,030,823	2,667,008	1,390,600
1985–86	2028	16,488,577	9,037,854	3,551,968	2,490,481	1,408,274
1986–87	2028	17,379,218	9,144,676	4,168,131	2,350,970	1,715,441
1987–88	2030	17,959,732	8,094,571	5,341,599	2,751,275	1,772,287
1988–89	2036	18,464,192	7,809,993	5,887,805	3,035,327	1,791,067
1989–90	2036	19,445,442	7,883,039	6,867,674	2,803,551	1,891,178
1990–91	2036	19,508,202	8,618,709	6,285,068	2,835,759	1,768,666
1991–92	2064*	20,487,273	9,989,160	5,809,787	2,993,352	1,694,974
			FA Premier	*Div. 1*	*Div. 2*	*Div. 3*
1992–93	2028	20,657,327	9,759,809	5,874,017	3,483,073	1,540,428
1993–94	2028	21,683,381	10,644,551	6,487,104	2,972,702	1,579,024
1994–95	2028	21,856,020	11,213,168	6,044,293	3,037,752	1,560,807

This is the first time since the war that attendances have risen for nine consecutive seasons.

**Figures include matches played by Aldershot.*

LEAGUE CUP FINALISTS 1961–95

Played as a two-leg final until 1966. All subsequent finals at Wembley.

Year	Winners	Runners-up	Score
1961	Aston Villa	Rotherham U	0-2, 3-0 (aet)
1962	Norwich C	Rochdale	3-0, 1-0
1963	Birmingham C	Aston Villa	3-1, 0-0
1964	Leicester C	Stoke C	1-1, 3-2
1965	Chelsea	Leicester C	3-2, 0-0
1966	WBA	West Ham U	1-2, 4-1
1967	QPR	WBA	3-2
1968	Leeds U	Arsenal	1-0
1969	Swindon T	Arsenal	3-1 (aet)
1970	Manchester C	WBA	2-1 (aet)
1971	Tottenham H	Aston Villa	2-0
1972	Stoke C	Chelsea	2-1
1973	Tottenham H	Norwich C	1-0
1974	Wolverhampton W	Manchester C	2-1
1975	Aston Villa	Norwich C	1-0
1976	Manchester C	Newcastle U	2-1
1977	Aston Villa	Everton	0-0, 1-1 (aet), 3-2 (aet)
1978	Nottingham F	Liverpool	0-0 (aet), 1-0
1979	Nottingham F	Southampton	3-2
1980	Wolverhampton W	Nottingham F	1-0
1981	Liverpool	West Ham U	1-1 (aet), 2-1
MILK CUP			
1982	Liverpool	Tottenham H	3-1 (aet)
1983	Liverpool	Manchester U	2-1 (aet)
1984	Liverpool	Everton	0-0 (aet), 1-0
1985	Norwich C	Sunderland	1-0
1986	Oxford U	QPR	3-0
LITTLEWOODS CUP			
1987	Arsenal	Liverpool	2-1
1988	Luton T	Arsenal	3-2
1989	Nottingham F	Luton T	3-1
1990	Nottingham F	Oldham Ath	1-0
RUMBELOWS LEAGUE CUP			
1991	Sheffield W	Manchester U	1-0
1992	Manchester U	Nottingham F	1-0
COCA COLA CUP			
1993	Arsenal	Sheffield W	2-1
1994	Aston Villa	Manchester U	3-1
1995	Liverpool	Bolton W	2-1

LEAGUE CUP WINS
Liverpool 5, Aston Villa 4, Nottingham F 4, Arsenal 2, Manchester C 2, Norwich C 2, Tottenham H 2, Wolverhampton W 2, Birmingham C 1, Chelsea 1, Leeds U 1, Leicester C 1, Luton T 1, Manchester U 1, Oxford U 1, QPR 1, Sheffield W 1, Stoke C 1, Swindon T 1, WBA 1.

APPEARANCES IN FINALS
Liverpool 7, Aston Villa 6, Nottingham F 6, Arsenal 5, Manchester U 4, Norwich C 4, Manchester C 3, Tottenham H 3, WBA 3, Chelsea 2, Everton 2, Leicester C 2, Luton T 2, QPR 2, Sheffield W 2, Stoke C 2, West Ham U 2, Wolverhampton W 2, Birmingham C 1, Bolton W 1, Leeds U 1, Newcastle U 1, Oldham Ath 1, Oxford U 1, Rochdale 1, Rotherham U 1, Southampton 1, Sunderland 1, Swindon T 1.

APPEARANCES IN SEMI-FINALS
Aston Villa 9, Liverpool 9, Tottenham H 8, Arsenal 7, Manchester U 7, West Ham U 7, Nottingham F 6, Chelsea 5, Manchester C 5, Norwich C 5, Leeds U 4, WBA 4, Burnley 3, Everton 3, QPR 3, Sheffield W 3, Swindon T 3, Wolverhampton W 3, Birmingham C 2, Blackburn R 2, Bolton W 2, Bristol C 2, Coventry C 2, Crystal Palace 2, Ipswich T 2, Leicester C 2, Luton T 2, Middlesbrough 2, Oxford U 2, Plymouth Arg 2, Southampton 2, Stoke C 2, Sunderland 2, Blackpool 1, Bury 1, Cardiff C 1, Carlisle U 1, Chester C 1, Derby Co 1, Huddersfield T 1, Newcastle U 1, Oldham Ath 1, Peterborough U 1, Rochdale 1, Rotherham U 1, Shrewsbury T 1, Tranmere R 1, Walsall 1, Watford 1.

COCA-COLA CUP 1994–95

FIRST ROUND FIRST LEG

15 AUG

Doncaster R (1) 2 *(Jones, Torfason)*
Wrexham (0) 4 *(Bennett, Connolly, Humes, Watkin)* 1925
Doncaster R: Suckling; Kitchen, Limber, Brabin, Hackett, Swailes, Lawrence, Thew, Jones (Torfason), Donaldson, Parrish (Finlay).
Wrexham: Marriott; Jones, Hardy, Blake, Humes, Pejic, Bennett, Brammer, Connolly, Watkin, Phillips (Taylor).

16 AUG

Barnet (0) 4 *(Freedman 2, Cooper 2)*
Leyton Orient (0) 0 2187
Barnet: Phillips; McDonald, Gale, Hoddle, Walker, Newson (Primus), Tomlinson (Scott), Freedman, Hodges, Cooper, Wilson.
Leyton Orient: Heald; Warren, Austin, Purse, Hendon, Lakin, Barnett (Gray), Cockerill, Bogie, West, Dempsey.

Blackpool (0) 1 *(Quinn)*
Chesterfield (2) 2 *(Perkins, Cheetham)* 2570
Blackpool: Sealey; Brown, Burke, Horner (Gouck), Briggs, Gore, Rodwell (Quinn), Gibson, Bamber, Ellis, Griffiths.
Chesterfield: Marples; Hewitt, Rogers, Fairclough, Carr, Perkins, Curtis, Norris, Davies, Moss, Cheetham.

Bournemouth (2) 2 *(Russell, Cotterill)*
Northampton T (0) 0 2587
Bournemouth: Moss; O'Driscoll, O'Connor, Morris, Watson, Leadbitter, Beardsmore, Aspinall (Mean), Fletcher, Cotterill, Russell.
Northampton T: Stewart; Pascoe (Wilkin), Curtis, Norton, Warburton, Sampson, Harmon, Byrne, Trott, Grayson, Bell.

Bradford C (0) 2 *(Taylor, Duxbury)*
Grimsby T (0) 1 *(Gilbert)* 5986
Bradford C: Tomlinson; Benn, Jacobs, Robson, Sinnott, Richards, Shutt, Kamara (Duxbury), Taylor, Jewell, Murray (Tolson).
Grimsby T: Crichton; Jobling, Croft, Futcher, Lever, Shakespeare, Watson, Gilbert, Livingstone (Woods), Mendonca, Groves.

Burnley (0) 1 *(Joyce)*
York C (0) 0 6390
Burnley: Beresford; Parkinson, Dowell, Davis, Winstanley, Joyce, Harper, Deary, Heath, Robinson, Lancashire.
York C: Kiely; McMillan, Hall, Pepper, Tutill, Barras, McCarthy, Cooper, Barnes, Bushell, Canham.

Bury (1) 2 *(Carter (pen), Lynch (og))*
Hartlepool U (0) 0 1515
Bury: Kelly G; Cross, Stanislaus, Mauge, Jackson, Lucketti, Mulligan, Carter, Hulme, Hughes (Johnrose), Pugh.
Hartlepool U: Jones; Ingram, Sweeney (Lynch), Gilchrist, McGuckin, Oliver, Ainsley, Sloan, Houchen, Honour (Thompson), Southall.

Cardiff C (0) 1 *(Oatway)*
Torquay U (0) 0 2690
Cardiff C: Williams D; Evans, Brazil, Aizlewood, Perry, Oatway, Griffith, Richardson, Stant, Bird (Dale), Fereday (Millar).
Torquay U: Bayes; Hodges, Stamps, Hathaway, Barrow, Curran, Trollope, Buckle, Hancox, Okorie, Goodridge.

Colchester U (0) 0
Brentford (1) 2 *(Stephenson, Taylor)* 2521
Colchester U: Cheesewright; Culling, English, Allpress, Caesar, Dennis, Fry (Roberts), Brown, Whitton, Kinsella, Abrahams.
Brentford: Dearden; Hurdle, Hutchings, Westley, Bates, Smith, Parris, Harvey, Taylor, Forster (Benjamin), Stephenson.

Crewe Alex (1) 2 *(Garvey, Ward)*
Wigan Ath (0) 1 *(Gavin)* 3054
Crewe Alex: Smith M; Booty, Annan, Wilson (Collier), Macauley, Barr, Tierney, Walters, Ward, Whalley, Garvey (Adebola).
Wigan Ath: Farnworth; Rennie, Wright, Strong, Robertson, Kilford, Campbell, Morton, Gavin (Duffy), Rimmer, Lyons.

Gillingham (0) 0
Reading (0) 1 *(Williams)* 2556
Gillingham: Barrett; Dunne, Palmer, Micklewhite, Green, Butler, Reinelt, Smith, Foster, Baker (Arnott), Watson.
Reading: Hislop; Bernal, Kerr, Hopkins, Williams, Parkinson (Holsgrove), Taylor, Gooding, Quinn, Lovell, Osborn.

Hereford U (0) 0
WBA (0) 0 5425
Hereford U: Pennock; Reece, Preedy (Pick), Davies, Smith, James, Wilkins, Downs, Cross, Williams (Clark), Steele.
WBA: Naylor; Parsley, Edwards, Phelan, Herbert, Raven, Donovan, Hamilton, Taylor, Heggs, McNally (Mellon).

Hull C (1) 2 *(Peacock, Lee)*
Scarborough (0) 1 *(Young)* 2546
Hull C: Fettis; Dakin, Graham, Hobson, Dewhurst, Abbott (Mann), Peacock, Lee, Brown, Windass, Lawford (Atkinson).
Scarborough: Kelly; Knowles, Charles, Calvert, Meyer, Rockett, Rowe, Swann, Young, Thompson, Blackstone.

Lincoln C (1) 2 *(Carbon, Schofield)*
Chester C (0) 0 2531
Lincoln C: Leaning; Schofield, Platnauer, Hebberd, Greenall, Brown, West, Onwere, Daley, Carbon, Johnson D.
Chester C: Felgate; Jenkins, Burnham, Ratcliffe, Whelan, Preece, Flitcroft, Bishop, Milner, Rimmer, Page.

Luton T (0) 1 *(Oakes)*
Fulham (0) 1 *(Moore)* 3287
Luton T: Sommer; James, Johnson, Hughes (Marshall), Greene, Peake, Telfer, Oakes, Dixon, Preece, Houghton (Linton).
Fulham: Stannard; Morgan, Herrera, Mison, Moore, Thomas, Marshall, Jupp, Cork, Brazil, Haworth.

Oxford U (1) 3 *(Moody (pen), Massey, Robinson)*
Peterborough U (1) 1 *(Morrison)* 4185
Oxford U: Whitehead; Robinson, Ford M, Dyer (Druce), Elliott, Rogan, Massey, Smith, Moody, Byrne, Allen.
Peterborough U: Cooksey; Ashley, Clark, Ebdon, Heald, Welsh, Morrison (Williams), Breen, Farrell (McGorry), Charlery, Moran.

Rochdale (1) 1 *(Whitehall)*
Mansfield T (0) 2 *(Wilkinson 2)* 1746
Rochdale: Clarke; Thackeray, Formby, Reid, Reeves, Matthews, Thompson (Ryan), Peake (Hall), Bowden, Whitehall, Stuart.
Mansfield T: Ward; Boothroyd, Baraclough, Holland, Howarth, Aspinall, Ireland, Parkin, Wilkinson, Hadley, Noteman (Castledine).

Rotherham U (0) 1 *(Varadi)*
Carlisle U (0) 0 2055
Rotherham U: Mercer; Wilder, James, Williams A, Brien (Williams C), Richardson, Hazel, Goodwin, Helliwell, Varadi, Goater (Hayward).
Carlisle U: Caig; Joyce, Gallimore, Walling, Mountfield, Edmonson, Thomas, Currie (Thorpe), Reeves, Davey, Reddish.

Scunthorpe U (1) 2 *(Henderson, Bullimore)*
Huddersfield T (0) 1 *(Scully)* 2841
Scunthorpe U: Samways; Ford, Mudd, Thornber, Knill, Bradley, Alexander, Bullimore, Juryeff, Henderson, Smith.
Huddersfield T: Francis; Billy, Cowan, Starbuck, Scully, Dyson, Baldry (Dunn), Bullock, Booth, Jepson, Reid.

Shrewsbury T (1) 2 *(Clarke W, Spink)*
Birmingham C (0) 1 *(Daish)* 5049
Shrewsbury T: Edwards; Hockaday, Lynch, Taylor, Williams, Patterson, Brown (Stevens), Clarke W, Spink, Walton, Woods (Withe).
Birmingham C: Bennett; Hiley, Scott, Shearer, Whyte, Daish, Donowa (Dominguez), Claridge, Regis, Harding, Doherty.

Southend U (0) 0
Watford (0) 0 2859
Southend U: Royce; Poole, Powell, Jones K, Bressington, Dublin, Hunt, Hone, Iorfa, Otto, Thomson (Martin).
Watford: Miller; Bazeley, Johnson, Foster, Holdsworth, Ramage, Hessenthaler, Payne, Moralee, Porter, Mooney.

Walsall (0) 4 *(Wilson 2, Lightbourne, O'Connor)*
Plymouth Arg (0) 0 2810
Walsall: Wood; Evans (Lillis), Rogers, Watkiss, Marsh, Palmer, O'Connor, Ntamark, Lightbourne, Wilson, Mehew.
Plymouth Arg: Hodge; Payne, Edworthy, Comyn, Swan, Hill, Barlow, Burnett, Nugent, Evans, Skinner (Morgan).

17 AUG

Brighton & HA (1) 2 *(McDougald, Nogan)*
Wycombe W (0) 1 *(Regis)* 6884
Brighton & HA: Rust; Munday, Pates, Chapman (Smith), Foster, McCarthy, Minton, McDougald, Nogan, Codner, Wilkins.
Wycombe W: Hyde; Cousins, Titterton (Brown), Creaser, Evans, Ryan, Carroll, Thompson, Regis, Garner (Hemmings), Stapleton.

Bristol R (1) 1 *(Tillson)*
Port Vale (0) 3 *(Foyle, Naylor, Glover L)* 3307
Bristol R: Parkin; Pritchard, Maddison, Channing, Clark, Tillson, Sterling, Miller, Stewart, Skinner, Archer.
Port Vale: Musselwhite; Sandeman, Tankard, Porter, Griffiths, Glover D, Kent, Van der Laan, Foyle, Glover L, Naylor.

Darlington (0) 2 *(Cross, Slaven)*
Barnsley (2) 2 *(Taggart, Redfearn)* 2207
Darlington: Pollitt; Appleby, Cross, Banks, Crosby, Gregan, Slaven, Painter, Gaughan, Olsson, Himsworth (Chapman).
Barnsley: Watson; Eaden, Fleming, Wilson, Taggart, Bishop, O'Connoll, Redfearn, Rammell, Payton, Snodin.

Exeter C (2) 2 *(Turner, Cecere)*
Swansea C (0) 2 *(Harris, Hodge)* 2050
Exeter C: Woodman; Daniels, Anderson (Brown), Bailey, Came, Richardson, Phillips, Thirlby, Turner, Cecere (Pears), Gavin.
Swansea C: Freestone; Jenkins, Clode, Ford, Harris, Ampadu, Bowen, Penney (Pascoe), Hayes, Cornforth, Hodge.

Portsmouth (2) 2 *(Stimson, Powell)*.
Cambridge U (0) 0 3854
Portsmouth: Poom; Gittens, Stimson, McLoughlin, Symons, Dobson, Neill, Pethick, Powell, Daniel, Hall (Rees).
Cambridge U: Filan; Hunter, Barrick, Craddock, Heathcote, O'Shea, Hyde, Rattle, Morah (Butler), Corazzin, Joseph.

Preston NE (0) 1 *(Fensome (pen))*
Stockport Co (1) 1 *(Chalk) (at Bury)* 2385
Preston NE: Richardson; Fensome, Fleming, Whalley, Hicks, Moyes, Cartwright, Kidd, Raynor, Trebble (Sale), Bryson (Conroy).
Stockport Co: Keeley; Miller, Todd, Connelly, Flynn, Gannon, Eckhardt, Ward, Francis, Armstrong, Chalk.

FIRST ROUND SECOND LEG

23 AUG

Barnsley (0) 0
Darlington (0) 0 3263
Barnsley: Watson; Eaden (Liddell), Fleming, Wilson, Taggart, Bishop, O'Connell (Bullock), Redfearn, Rammell, Payton, Snodin.
Darlington: Pollitt; Appleby, Cross, Banks, Crosby, Reed, Slaven, Painter, Gaughan, Olsson, Mattison (Himsworth).
aet; 2-2 on aggregate; Barnsley won on away goals.

Birmingham C (2) 2 *(Saville, Claridge (pen))*
Shrewsbury T (0) 0 9847
Birmingham C: Bennett; Hiley, Scott, Ward, Whyte, Daish, De Souza, Claridge, Saville, Harding, Donowa.
Shrewsbury T: Edwards; Hockaday, Lynch, Taylor, Williams, Patterson, Brown, Clarke W (Summerfield), Spink, Watson, Withe.
Birmingham C won 3-2 on aggregate.

Brentford (1) 2 *(Parris, Smith)*
Colchester U (0) 0 2315
Brentford: Dearden; Hurdle, Hutchings, Bates, Ashby, Smith, Parris, Harvey, Taylor (Mundee), Forster (Ratcliffe), Stephenson.
Colchester U: Emberson; English (Burley), Davis, Allpress, Caesar, Dennis, Roberts, Brown S, Whitton, Kinsella, Abrahams.
Brentford won 4-0 on aggregate.

Cambridge U (1) 2 *(Craddock, Barrick)*
Portsmouth (1) 3 *(Creaney, Powell 2)* 2571
Cambridge U: Filan; Hunter, Barrick, Craddock, Heathcote, O'Shea, Hyde, Granville (Morah), Butler, Corazzin (Elad), Joseph.
Portsmouth: Poom; Gittens, Stimson, McLoughlin, Symons, Dobson, Neill (Daniel), Pethick, Powell, Creaney, Hall (Burton).
Portsmouth won 5-2 on aggregate.

Carlisle U (0) 3 *(Reeves 2, Walling)*
Rotherham U (1) 1 *(Hayward)* 5004
Carlisle U: Caig; Joyce, Gallimore, Walling, Mountfield, Edmondson (Thorpe), Thomas, Currie, Reeves, Davey, Prokas.
Rotherham U: Mercer; Wilder, James, Williams A, Brien, Breckin, Hazel, Goodwin, Hayward, Varadi (Williams C), Todd.
Carlisle U won 3-2 on aggregate.

Chester C (0) 2 *(Whelan, Chambers)*
Lincoln C (3) 3 *(Schofield, West, Johnson D (pen))* 1568
Chester C: Felgate; Jenkins, Burnham, Ratcliffe, Whelan, Preece, Chambers, Bishop, Alsford, Rimmer (Milner), Page.
Lincoln C: Leaning; Schofield, Platnauer, Hebberd, Greenall, Brown, West, Johnson A, Daley, Carbon (Puttnam), Johnson D.
Lincoln C won 5-2 on aggregate.

Chesterfield (3) 4 *(Norris (pen), Davies, Morris, Curtis)*
Blackpool (2) 2 *(Ellis, Brown)* 2516
Chesterfield: Marples; Hewitt, Rogers, Fairclough, Carr, Cheetham, Curtis, Norris, Davies, Spooner, Morris (Jules).
Blackpool: Sealey; Brown, Burke, Horner, Beech, Gore (Gouck), Rodwell, Gibson, Quinn, Ellis, Griffiths (Bamber).
Chesterfield won 6-3 on aggregate.

Fulham (1) 1 *(Haworth)*
Luton T (0) 1 *(Marshall)* 5134
Fulham: Stannard; Morgan, Herrera, Mison, Moore, Thomas G, Marshall (Hails), Jupp, Cork, Brazil, Haworth (Hurlock).
Luton T: Sommer; James, Johnson, Linton (Skelton), Greene (Oakes), Peake, Telfer, Marshall, Dixon, Preece, Hughes.
aet; 2-2 on aggregate; Fulham won 4-3 on penalties.

Grimsby T (1) 1 *(Groves)*
Bradford C (2) 2 *(Murray, Richards)* 3498
Grimsby T: Crichton; Croft, Agnew, Futcher, Lever (Lester), Shakespeare, Childs (Woods), Gilbert, Livingstone, Mendonca, Groves.
Bradford C: Tomlinson; Liburd, Jacobs, Duxbury, Sinnott, Richards, Shutt, Robson (Tolson), Taylor, Jewell, Murray.
Bradford C won 4-2 on aggregate.

Hartlepool U (1) 5 *(Houchen, Southall 2, Jackson (og), Thompson)*
Bury (1) 1 *(Rigby)* 1505
Hartlepool U: Horne; Ingram, Skedd, Gilchrist, McGuckin, Oliver, Thompson, Sloan (Halliday), Houchen, Lynch, Southall.
Bury: Kelly G; Cross, Stanislaus, Mauge, Lucketti, Jackson, Mulligan, Carter, Paskin, Johnrose, Rigby.
aet; Hartlepool U won 5-3 on aggregate.

Huddersfield T (3) 3 *(Jepson 2, Reid)*
Scunthorpe U (0) 0 6455
Huddersfield T: Francis; Billy, Cowan, Logan, Scully, Dyson, Baldry, Bullock, Booth, Jepson, Reid.
Scunthorpe U: Samways; Ford, Mudd, Martin, Knill (Carmichael), Bradley, Alexander, Bullimore, Juryeff, Henderson, Smith (Goodacre).
Huddersfield T won 4-2 on aggregate.

Leyton Orient (0) 1 *(Cockerill)*
Barnet (1) 1 *(Freedman)* 2464
Leyton Orient: Heald; Howard, Austin, Purse, Hendon, Lakin, (Gray), Barnett (Carter), Cockerill, Bogie, West, Dempsey.
Barnet: Phillips; McDonald (Alexander), Gale, Hoddle, Walker, Primus, Tomlinson, Freedman (Scott), Hodges, Cooper, Wilson.
Barnet won 5-1 on aggregate.

Mansfield T (1) 1 *(Wilkinson)*
Rochdale (0) 0 2234
Mansfield T: Ward; Boothroyd, Baraclough (Fleming), Holland, Howarth, Aspinall, Ireland, Parkin, Wilkinson, Hadley, Noteman.
Rochdale: Clarke; Thackeray, Formby, Reid, Reeves, Butler, Thompson, Hall, Williams, Whitehall, Ryan (Stuart).
Mansfield T won 3-1 on aggregate.

Peterborough U (0) 0
Oxford U (1) 1 *(Dyer)* 3351
Peterborough U: Cooksey; Ashley, Clark, Ebdon, Breen, Welsh, Brissett (Henry), Williams, Farrell, Charlery, Moran (McGorry).
Oxford U: Whitehead; Robinson, Ford M, Dyer, Elliott, Rogan, Massey, Smith, Moody, Byrne, Allen (Lewis).
Oxford U won 4-1 on aggregate.

Plymouth Arg (1) 2 *(Swan, Castle)*
Walsall (0) 1 *(Wilson)* 2801
Plymouth Arg: Hodge; Bradshaw, Edworthy, Comyn, Swan, Hill, Barlow, Castle (Twiddy), Nugent, Evans (Landon), Dalton.
Walsall: Wood; Evans, Rogers, Watkiss, Marsh, Palmer, O'Connor, Ntamark, Lightbourne (Butler), Wilson, Mehew.
Walsall won 5-2 on aggregate.

Port Vale (1) 1 *(Glover L)*
Bristol R (0) 1 *(Stewart)* 4728
Port Vale: Musselwhite; Sandeman, Tankard, Porter (Walker), Griffiths, Glover D, Kent, Van der Laan, Foyle, Glover L, Naylor (Burke).
Bristol R: Parkin; Pritchard, Gurney, Channing (Browning), Clark, Tillson, Sterling, Miller, Stewart, Skinner, Archer.
Port Vale won 4-2 on aggregate.

Reading (0) 3 *(Quinn 2, Lovell)*
Gillingham (0) 0 3436
Reading: Hislop; Hopkins, Kerr, Wdowczyk, Williams, Parkinson (Holsgrove), Gilkes, Gooding, Quinn, Lovell, Osborn.
Gillingham: Barrett; Dunne, Palmer, Micklewhite, Green, Butler, Reinelt, Smith, Foster, Baker (Arnott), Watson.
Reading won 4-0 on aggregate.

Scarborough (1) 2 *(Blackstone 2)*
Hull C (0) 0 2287
Scarborough: Kelly; Knowles, Charles, Calvert, Meyer, Rockett, Rowe, Swann, Foreman (Young), White (D'Auria), Blackstone.
Hull C: Fettis; Lowthorpe, Graham, Hobson, Dewhurst, Mann, Peacock, Hargreaves (Dakin), Brown, Windass, Lawford (Atkinson).
Scarborough won 3-2 on aggregate.

Stockport Co (0) 4 *(Emerson, Armstrong, Ward, Beaumont)*
Preston NE (0) 1 *(Moyes)* 5450
Stockport Co: Keeley; Connelly (Wallace), Todd (Beaumont), Eckhardt, Flynn, Gannon, Emerson, Ward, Frain, Armstrong, Chalk.
Preston NE: Richardson; Fensome, Kidd, Whalley, Hicks, Moyes, Ainsworth (Bryson), Cartwright, Sale (Raynor), Conroy, Fleming.
Stockport Co won 5-2 on aggregate.

Swansea C (0) 2 *(Penney 2 (1 pen))*
Exeter C (0) 0 2523
Swansea C: Freestone; Jenkins, Clode, Ford, Harris, Ampadu, Bowen (Hayes), Pascoe, Torpey, Cornforth (Penney), Hodge.
Exeter C: Fox; Minett, Rice, Bailey, Came, Brown, Cooper M, Thirlby, Cecere, Pears, Gavin.
Swansea C won 4-2 on aggregate.

Torquay U (2) 4 *(Goodridge, Hancox 3)*
Cardiff C (2) 2 *(Stant 2)* 2719
Torquay U: Bayes; Hodges, Stamps, Hathaway, Barrow, Curran, Trollope, Buckle, Hancox, Okorie, Goodridge.
Cardiff C: Williams D; Evans, Street (Adams), Young, Brazil, Oatway, Bird, Richardson, Stant, Dale, Millar.
Torquay U won 4-3 on aggregate.

Watford (1) 1 *(Ramage)*
Southend U (0) 0 4582
Watford: Miller; Bazeley, Johnson, Foster, Holdsworth, Ramage, Hessenthaler, Payne, Moralee, Porter, Mooney.
Southend U: Royce; Poole, Powell, Jones K, Edwards, Dublin, Hone, Martin (Hunt), Iorfa (Davidson), Tilson, Sussex.
Watford won 1-0 on aggregate.

Wigan Ath (0) 3 *(Gavin, Rennie, Carragher)*
Crewe Alex (0) 0 1421
Wigan Ath: Farnworth; Rennie, Wright, Strong, Robertson, Kilford, Campbell, Morton, Gavin, Carragher, Lyons.
Crewe Alex: Smith M; Booty, Smith S, Collins, Macauley, Barr, Tierney, Murphy, Ward, Whalley, Rowbotham.
Wigan Ath won 4-2 on aggregate.

Wrexham (1) 1 *(Watkin)*
Doncaster R (0) 1 *(Swailes)* 2215
Wrexham: Marriott; Jones, Hardy, Phillips, Humes, Hunter, Bennett, Brammer, Connolly, Watkin (Cross), Taylor.
Doncaster R: Williams D; Limber (Parrish), Hackett, Brabin, Wilcox, Swailes, Lawrence, Meara, Torfason, Donaldson, Finlay (Kirby).
Wrexham won 5-3 on aggregate.

Wycombe W (0) 1 *(Turnbull)*
Brighton & HA (3) 3 *(Nogan 2, McDougald)* 5281
Wycombe W: Hyde; Cousins, Brown, Creaser (Hemmings), Evans, Ryan, Carroll, Thompson, Regis (Turnbull), Garner, Stapleton.
Brighton & HA: Rust; Bissett, Pates, Case, Foster, McCarthy, Chamberlain (Funnell), McDougald, Nogan, Codner, Wilkins (Simmonds).
Brighton & HA won 5-2 on aggregate.

York C (1) 2 *(Pepper, Cooper)*
Burnley (0) 2 *(Robinson, Gayle)* 3089
York C: Kiely; McMillan, Hall, Pepper, Tutill, Barras, McCarthy, Cooper, Barnes, Bushell, Canham.
Burnley: Beresford; Parkinson, Vinnicombe (Deary), Davis, Winstanley, Joyce (Lancashire), Harper, Gayle, Heath, Robinson, McMinn.
Burnley won 3-2 on aggregate.

6 SEPT

Northampton T (0) 0
Bournemouth (1) 1 *(Cotterill)* 3249
Northampton T: Stewart; Norton, Colkin, Sampson, Warburton, Curtis (Bell), Harmon, Robinson, Trott, Grayson, Aldridge.
Bournemouth: Andrews; O'Driscoll, O'Connor, McElhatton, Watson, Fletcher, Beardsmore, Aspinall (Murray), Russell K, Cotterill (Town), Leadbitter.
Bournemouth won 3-0 on aggregate.

7 SEPT

WBA (0) 0
Hereford U (0) 1 *(White)* 10,604
WBA: Naylor; Burgess, Darton, Phelan, Strodder, Herbert, Mellon, Ashcroft, Heggs, Donovan, Smith.
Hereford U: Pennock; Clark, Preedy (Davies), Pick, Smith, James, Wilkins, Pounder, Cross, White, Pike.
Hereford U won 1-0 on aggregate.

SECOND ROUND FIRST LEG

20 SEPT

Barnet (1) 1 *(Freedman)*
Manchester C (0) 0 3120
Barnet: Phillips; McDonald, Gale, Hoddle, Newson, Primus, Haynes, Freedman, Hodges, Scott, Wilson.
Manchester C: Coton; Edghill, Brightwell I, McMahon, Hill, Vonk (Foster), Summerbee, Walsh, Rosler (Quinn), Lomas, Beagrie.

Blackburn R (0) 2 *(Wilcox, Sutton)*
Birmingham C (0) 0 14,517
Blackburn R: Flowers; Berg, Le Saux, Sherwood, Hendry, Atkins, Ripley, Slater (Pearce), Warhurst, Sutton, Wilcox.
Birmingham C: Bennett; Scott, Frain, Ward, Dryden, Whyte, Harding, Claridge, Cooper (McGavin), Tait, Wallace (Dominguez).

Bristol C (0) 0
Notts Co (0) 1 *(Devlin)* 2546
Bristol C: Welch; Harriott, Scott, Shail, Bryant, Tinnion, McAree, Bent, Partridge, Loss (Brown), Edwards.
Notts Co: Cherry; Sherlock, Turner, Johnson, Murphy, Yates, Devlin, Legg, Lund (Agana), Simpson, McSwegan (Jemson).

Carlisle U (0) 0
QPR (1) 1 *(Ferdinand)* 9570
Carlisle U: Caig; Joyce, Gallimore, Walling, Valentine (Thorpe), Edmondson, Thomas, Currie, Reeves, Davey, Prokas (Mountfield).
QPR: Roberts; Bardsley, Wilson, Barker, Yates, McDonald, Impey, Holloway, Ferdinand, Penrice, Sinclair (Ready).

Chesterfield (1) 1 *(Moss)*
Wolverhampton W (0) 3 *(Bull 2, Kelly D)* 5895
Chesterfield: Marples; Hewitt, Rogers, Madden, Carr, Law, Curtis, Roberts (Jules), Davies (Norris), Moss, Spooner.
Wolverhampton W: Stowell; Smith, Thompson, Emblen (Blades), Venus, Shirtliff, Birch, Ferguson, Bull, Kelly D, Froggatt.

Everton (0) 2 *(Samways, Stuart (pen))*
Portsmouth (2) 3 *(Creaney 2, Kristensen)* 14,043
Everton: Southall; Jackson (Snodin), Burrows, Parkinson, Watson, Unsworth, Samways, Stuart, Amokachi, Rideout (Angell), Hinchcliffe.
Portsmouth: Knight; Gittens, Stimson (Radosavljevic), Symons, Awford, Daniel, Kristensen, McLoughlin, Powell, Creaney, Hall (Pethick).

Fulham (0) 3 *(Moore, Haworth, Blake)*
Stoke C (0) 2 *(Orlygsson (pen), Gleghorn)* 3721
Fulham: Stannard; Morgan, Herrera, Hurlock, Moore, Blake, Marshall, Jupp, Cork, Brazil, Haworth.
Stoke C: Muggleton; Butler, Sandford, Cranson, Dreyer, Orlygsson, Wallace, Downing, Carruthers, Peschisolido, Gleghorn.

Huddersfield T (0) 0
Southampton (0) 1 *(Le Tissier)* 13,814
Huddersfield: Francis; Billy (Jepson), Cowan, Logan, Scully, Dyson, Trevitt, Starbuck, Booth, Dunn, Reid.
Southampton: Grobbelaar; Kenna, Benali, Charlton, Hall, Heaney, Le Tissier, Magilton, Dowie, Maddison (Ekelund), Allen.

Lincoln C (0) 1 *(Johnson D)*
Crystal Palace (0) 0 4310
Lincoln C: Leaning; Schofield, Platnauer, Foley, Greenall, Brown, West, Onwere, Bannister, Puttnam, Johnson D.
Crystal Palace: Martyn; Patterson, Gordon, Southgate, Shaw, Coleman, Ndah, Newman, Armstrong, Dyer (Preece), Salako.

Oxford U (1) 1 *(Ford M)*
Oldham Ath (1) 1 *(Ritchie)* 5070
Oxford U: Whitehead; Robinson, Ford M, Lewis, Elliott, Marsh, Massey, Smith, Moody (Druce), Byrne, Allen.
Oldham Ath: Gerrard; Halle, Makin, Henry, Jobson, Redmond, Richardson, Brennan, Graham, McCarthy, Ritchie (Eyre).

Reading (1) 3 *(Quinn 2, Holsgrove)*
Derby Co (1) 1 *(Gabbiadini)* 6056
Reading: Hislop; Bernal (Hopkins), Kerr, Wdowczyk, Williams, Holsgrove, Gilkes, Gooding, Quinn, Lovell (Taylor), Osborn.
Derby Co: Taylor; Charles, Forsyth, Harkes, Short, Williams, Cowans, Gabbiadini, Johnson, Pembridge, Carsley.

Scarborough (1) 1 *(Rowe)* 4751
Middlesbrough (4) 4 *(Hendrie, Pollock, Moore, Mustoe)*
Scarborough: Kelly; Knowles, Thompson, D'Auria (Young), Dunphy, Meyer, Calvert, Rowe, Charles, Toman (White), Blackstone.
Middlesbrough: Pears; Cox, Fleming, Vickers, Whyte, Hignett, Mustoe, Pollock, Wilkinson, Hendrie, Moore (Wright).

Stockport Co (0) 1 *(Francis)*
Sheffield U (1) 5 *(Whitehouse 3 (1 pen), Flo 2)* 5109
Stockport Co: Keeley; Connelly, Todd, Eckhardt, Flynn, Dinning, Gannon, Ward, Francis, Emerson, Chalk (Ware).
Sheffield U: Kelly; Gage, Nilsen, Rogers, Gayle, Hodgson (Gannon), Ward, Hoyland, Flo, Davison (Blake), Whitehouse.

Tranmere R (1) 1 *(Brannan)*
Brentford (0) 0 3754
Tranmere R: Nixon; Higgins (Jones G), Brannan, Irons (Edwards), Garnett, O'Brien, Morrissey, Aldridge, Malkin, Nevin, Mungall.
Brentford: Dearden; Statham, Grainger, Westley, Ashby, Smith, Hutchings, Harvey, Taylor, Forster, Stephenson.

Walsall (1) 2 *(Watkiss, Potts (og))*
West Ham U (1) 1 *(Ntamark (og))* 5994
Walsall: Wood; Evans, Rogers, Watkiss, Marsh, Palmer (Ryder), O'Connor, Peer, Lightbourne, Wilson, Ntamark (Mehew).
West Ham U: Miklosko; Breacker, Rowland, Potts, Martin, Allen (Whitbread), Moncur, Hutchison, Cottee, Marsh, Rush (Chapman).

Wimbledon (2) 2 *(Gayle, Harford)*
Torquay U (0) 0 2451
Wimbledon: Segers; Barton, Kimble, Jones, Perry, Fitzgerald, Ardley (Fear), Gayle, Harford (Clarke), Holdsworth, Elkins.
Torquay U: Davis; Barrow, Kelly, Burton, Moore, Curran, Trollope, Buckle, Hancox, Okorie, Goodridge.

Wrexham (1) 1 *(Jones)*
Coventry C (0) 2 *(Darby, Flynn)* 5286
Wrexham: Marriott; Jones, Hardy, Brammer, Humes, Hunter, Bennett, Owen, Connolly, Watkin, Durkan.
Coventry C: Ogrizovic; Pickering, Morgan, Cook, Rennie, Busst, Darby, Jones, Dublin, Flynn, Boland.

21 SEPT

Aston Villa (2) 5 *(Yorke, Atkinson 2, Saunders, Lamptey)*
Wigan Ath (0) 0 12,433
Aston Villa: Bosnich; Barrett, King, Teale, Ehiogu, Parker, Lamptey, Townsend (Fenton), Saunders, Atkinson, Yorke.
Wigan Ath: Farnworth; Rennie, Jakub (McKearney), Strong, Robertson, Kilford, Campbell, Morton, Gavin, Rimmer, Carragher.

Brighton & HA (0) 1 *(Nogan)*
Leicester C (0) 0 11,481
Brighton & HA: Rust; Smith, Pates, Wilkins (Munday), Foster, Bissett, Minton, McDougald, Nogan, Codner, Chapman.
Leicester C: Poole; Grayson, Lewis, Mohan, Willis, Draper, Joachim, Blake, Agnew, Roberts (Lowe), Philpott.

Chelsea (1) 1 *(Rocastle)*
Bournemouth (0) 0 8974
Chelsea: Kharine; Clarke, Sinclair, Kjeldbjerg, Johnsen, Newton, Rocastle, Spencer (Shipperley), Furlong, Peacock, Wise.
Bournemouth: Andrews; O'Driscoll (Barfoot), O'Connor, McElhatton, Watson, Fletcher, Beardsmore, Mean, Aspinall (Reeve), Russell K, Leadbitter.

Hartlepool U (0) 0
Arsenal (2) 5 *(Adams, Smith, Wright 2, Merson)* 4421
Hartlepool U: Horne; Burgess, Walsh, Gilchrist, McGuckin, Oliver (Ingram), Thompson, Tait, Houchen, Halliday, Lynch (Hyson).
Arsenal: Seaman; Dixon, Keown, Davis, Linighan, Adams, Selley, Wright, Smith (McGoldrick), Merson, Parlour.

Ipswich T (0) 0
Bolton W (1) 3 *(McAteer, McGinlay, Thompson)* 7787
Ipswich T: Forrest; Yallop, Johnson, Taricco, Wark, Williams, Sedgley, Slater (Kiwomya), Milton, Guentchev, Thomsen (Linighan).
Bolton W: Branagan; Lydiate, Phillips, McAteer, Thompson, Stubbs, Lee, Sneekes, Paatelainen (De Freitas), McGinlay (Coyle), Fisher.

Leeds U (0) 0
Mansfield T (1) 1 *(Ireland)* 7844
Leeds U: Lukic; Kelly, Worthington, Palmer, Fairclough, Strachan (Radebe), Masinga (Deane), Wallace, Whelan, McAllister, Speed.
Mansfield T: Ward; Boothroyd, Baraclough, Holland, Aspinall, Howarth, Ireland, Frain, Wilkinson, Hadley, Noteman (Timons).

Liverpool (1) 2 *(Scales, Fowler)*
Burnley (0) 0 23,359
Liverpool: James, Jones R, Bjornebye, Scales, Molby, Ruddock, McManaman, Redknapp, Rush, Barnes, Fowler.
Burnley: Beresford; Parkinson, Vinnicombe, Davis, Winstanley, Eyres, Harper, Harrison (Deary), Heath, Robinson (Philliskirk), McMinn.

Millwall (2) 2 *(Goodman, Kennedy)*
Sunderland (0) 1 *(Russell)* 5095
Millwall: Keller; Cunningham, Thatcher, Van Den Hauwe, McCarthy, Roberts, Savage, Rae, Mitchell, Goodman, Kennedy (Carter).
Sunderland: Norman; Kubicki, Ord, Bennett, Ferguson (Smith), Melville, Owers, Goodman, Gray P, Russell, Ball.

Newcastle U (1) 2 *(Cole, Fox)*
Barnsley (1) 1 *(Redfearn)* 27,208
Newcastle U: Srnicek; Hottiger, Beresford, Howey, Peacock, Albert (Mathie), Lee, Beardsley, Cole, Fox, Sellars (Watson).
Barnsley: Watson; Snodin, Fleming, Wilson, Taggart, Bishop, O'Connell, Redfearn, Rammell (Liddell), Payton, Davis.

Norwich C (1) 3 *(Sheron, Bradshaw (pen), Adams)*
Swansea C (0) 0 8053
Norwich C: Gunn; Bradshaw, Johnson (Crook), Newsome, Polston (Newman), Goss, Eadie, Ullathorne, Robins, Sheron, Adams.
Swansea C: Freestone; Jenkins, Clode, Ford, Harris, Pascoe (Hodge), Bowen, Penney, Torpey, Cornforth, Perrett (Ampadu).

Nottingham F (0) 2 *(Collymore 2)*
Hereford U (1) 1 *(White)* 10,076
Nottingham F: Crossley; Lyttle, Pearce, Cooper, Chettle, Stone, Phillips, Roy (Woan), Bohinen, Collymore, Black.
Hereford U: Sheffield; Clark, Preedy, Reece, Smith, James, Wilkins, Pick, Cross (Pike), White, Steele (Davies).

Port Vale (1) 1 *(Glover L)*
Manchester U (1) 2 *(Scholes 2)* 18,605
Port Vale: Musselwhite; Sandeman, Tankard, Porter, Griffiths, Glover D, Kent, Van der Laan, Foyle, Glover L, Naylor (Burke).
Manchester U: Walsh; Neville G (O'Kane), Irwin, Butt (Sharpe), May, Keane, Gillespie, Beckham, McClair, Scholes, Davies.

Middlesbrough (1) 4 *(Wilkinson 3, Hignett)*
Scarborough (1) 1 *(Charles (pen))* 7739
Middlesbrough: Pears; Morris, Fleming, Vickers (Cox), Whyte, Hignett, Mustoe, Pollock, Wilkinson, Moreno, Wright.
Scarborough: Kelly; Knowles, Thompson (D'Auria), Calvert, Dunphy, Meyer (Davis), Rowe, Charles, White, Foreman, Blackstone.
Middlesbrough won 8-2 on aggregate

Sheffield W (0) 2 *(Taylor, Hyde)*
Bradford C (0) 1 *(Shutt)* 15,705
Sheffield W: Pressman; Petrescu, Nolan, Atherton, Pearce, Bart-Williams, Ingesson (Taylor), Hyde, Hirst, Bright (Watson), Sheridan.
Bradford C: Tomlinson; Liburd, Jacobs, Duxbury, Benn, Richards, Shutt, Kamara, Taylor, Jewell (Power), Murray.

Notts Co (1) 3 *(Jemson, Lund 2)*
Bristol C (0) 0 2721
Notts Co: Cherry; Mills, Johnson, Turner, Yates, Murphy, Devlin, Legg, Lund, Jemson (Matthews), Agana.
Bristol C: Welch; Munro, Scott, Shail, Bryant, Paterson, McAree (Fowler), Bent (Brown), Baird, Tinnion, Edwards.
Notts Co won 4-0 on aggregate

Swindon T (0) 1 *(Scott)*
Charlton Ath (0) 3 *(Nelson 2, Whyte)* 4932
Swindon T: Digby; Robinson, Bodin, Thomson, Nijholt (Berkley), Kilcline, Ling, Beauchamp, Fjortoft, Scott, O'Sullivan.
Charlton Ath: Petterson; Brown, Sturgess, Garland, Chapple, Balmer, Newton, Nelson, Walsh, Whyte, Robson.

Sheffield U (1) 1 *(Scott A)*
Stockport Co (0) 0 5065
Sheffield U: Kelly; Fickling, Scott A, Rogers, Foran, Hoyland, Ward, Gannon, Flo (Littlejohn), Blake, Whitehouse.
Stockport Co: Keeley; Connelly, Todd, Eckhardt (Slinn), Flynn, Dinning, Gannon, Ware, Francis, Armstrong, Brock (Wallace).
Sheffield U won 6-1 on aggregate

Watford (1) 3 *(Ramage, Mooney, Mabbutt (og))*
Tottenham H (4) 6 *(Anderton, Klinsmann 3, Sheringham, Dumitrescu)* 13,659
Watford: Digweed; Bazeley, Johnson, Millen, Holdsworth, Ramage, Hessenthaler, Payne, Moralee, Porter, Mooney.
Tottenham H: Walker, Kerslake, Edinburgh (Howells), Popescu, Campbell, Mabbutt, Anderton, Hazard (Hill), Klinsmann, Sheringham, Dumitrescu.

Wolverhampton W (1) 1 *(Froggatt)*
Chesterfield (0) 1 *(Jules)* 14,815
Wolverhampton W: Stowell; Smith, Thompson, Venus, Blades, Shirtliff, Birch, Ferguson, Bull (Rankine), Kelly D (Keen), Froggatt.
Chesterfield: Beasley; Hewitt, Rogers, Spooner, Carr, Law, Curtis, Roberts, Morris, Fairclough, Jules.
Wolverhampton W won 4-2 on aggregate

SECOND ROUND, SECOND LEG

27 SEPT

Brentford (0) 0
Tranmere R (0) 0 4076
Brentford: Dearden; Statham, Grainger, Westley, Ashby, Smith, Hutchings, Harvey, Taylor, Forster, Stephenson.
Tranmere R: Nixon; Stevens, Mungall, McGreal, Garnett, O'Brien, Morrissey, Aldridge, Malkin, Brannan, Nevin (Edwards).
Tranmere R won 1-0 on aggregate

Charlton Ath (0) 1 *(Whyte)*
Swindon T (2) 4 *(Fjortoft 3, Petterson (og))* 4932
Charlton Ath: Petterson; Brown, Sturgess, Garland (Bowyer), Chapple, Balmer, Newton (Grant), Nelson, Walsh, Whyte, Robson.
Swindon T: Digby; Robinson, Bodin, Thomson, Nijholt, Taylor, O'Sullivan, Beauchamp, Fjortoft, Ling, Scott (Mutch).
aet; Swindon T won 5-4 on aggregate

28 SEPT

Derby Co (1) 2 *(Gabbiadini, Williams)*
Reading (0) 0 9476
Derby Co: Taylor; Charles, Forsyth, Harkes (Carsley), Short, Williams, Cowans, Gabbiadini, Johnson (Simpson), Pembridge, Wassall.
Reading: Hislop; Bernal (McPherson), Kerr, Hopkins, Williams, Holsgrove, Parkinson (Taylor), Gooding, Quinn, Lovell, Osborn.
aet; 3-3 on aggregate, Derby Co won on away goals

Stoke C (1) 1 *(Peschisolido)*
Fulham (0) 0 7440
Stoke C: Muggleton; Butler, Sandford, Dreyer, Cranson, Orlygsson, Carruthers, Downing, Biggins, Peschisolido, Gleghorn.
Fulham: Stannard; Morgan, Adams, Mison, Moore (Bedrossian), Blake, Marshall, Jupp, Bartley (Haworth), Brazil, Thomas.
aet; 3-3 on aggregate, Stoke C won on away goals

4 OCT

Birmingham C (1) 1 *(McGavin)*
Blackburn R (0) 1 *(Sutton)* 16,275
Birmingham C: Bennett; Bass, Frain, Ward, Barnett, Daish, De Souza (Moulden), Shearer, McGavin, Dominguez, Donowa (Wallace).
Blackburn R: Flowers; Berg, Le Saux, Sherwood, Hendry, Warhurst, Ripley, Atkins, Shearer, Sutton, Wilcox.
Blackburn R won 3-1 on aggregate

Bournemouth (0) 0
Chelsea (0) 1 *(Peacock)* 9784
Bournemouth: Andrews; O'Driscoll (Murray), O'Connor (Adekola), McElhatton, Watson, Fletcher, Beardsmore, Mean, Aspinall, Reeve, Leadbitter.
Chelsea: Kharine; Clarke, Sinclair, Kjeldbjerg, Johnsen, Spackman (Newton), Rocastle, Shipperley, Furlong (Lee), Peacock, Wise.
Chelsea won 2-0 on aggregate

Bradford C (0) 1 *(Taylor)*
Sheffield W (1) 1 *(Bart-Williams)* 13,092
Bradford C: Tomlinson; Benn (Power), Jacobs, Duxbury, Oliver, Robson (Tolson), Shutt, Kamara, Taylor, Jewell, Hamilton.
Sheffield W: Pressman; Atherton, Nolan, Bart-Williams, Pearce, Walker, Sheridan, Hyde, Watson, Bright (Hirst), Sinton (Taylor).
Sheffield W won 3-2 on aggregate

Crystal Palace (0) 3 *(Gordon, Armstrong, Dyer)*
Lincoln C (0) 0 6870
Crystal Palace: Martyn; Patterson (Dyer), Gordon, Southgate, Shaw, Coleman, Bowry, Newman, Armstrong, Ndah (Launders), Salako.
Lincoln C: Leaning; Schofield, Platnauer, Hebberd (Smith), Greenall, Brown, West, Onwere, Bannister, Puttnam (Daley), Johnson D.
aet; Crystal Palace won 3-1 on aggregate

Hereford U (0) 0
Nottingham F (0) 0 8953
Hereford U: Sheffield; Clark, Fishlock, Reece, Smith, James, Wilkins, Pick, Cross, White, Preedy.
Nottingham F: Crossley; Lyttle, Pearce, Cooper, Chettle, Stone, Phillips, Roy, Bohinen, Collymore, Black.
Nottingham F won 2-1 on aggregate

Mansfield T (0) 0
Leeds U (0) 0 7227
Mansfield T: Ward; Boothroyd, Baraclough, Holland, Howarth, Peters, Ireland (Hadley), Hoyle, Wilkinson, Doolan, Noteman.
Leeds U: Lukic; Kelly, Worthington, Palmer, Fairclough (Dorigo), Wetherall, Whelan, Wallace (Pemberton), Deane, McAllister, Speed.
Mansfield T won 1-0 on aggregate

Oldham Ath (0) 1 *(Richardson)*
Oxford U (0) 0 4525
Oldham Ath: Hallworth; Halle, Makin, Henry, Jobson, Redmond, Richardson, Brennan (Holden R), Graham, McCarthy, Ritchie (Sharp).
Oxford U: Whitehead; Robinson, Ford M, Dyer, Elliott, Marsh (Rush), Massey, Smith, Moody, Byrne, Allen.
Oldham Ath won 2-1 on aggregate

Sunderland (0) 1 *(Gray P)*
Millwall (0) 1 *(Goodman)* 9698
Sunderland: Norman; Kubicki, Ord (Michael Gray), Ball, Martin Gray (Howey), Melville, Owers, Goodman, Gray P, Smith, Russell.
Millwall: Keller; Beard, Thatcher, Van Blerk (Chapman), McCarthy, Roberts, Savage, Rae, Kerr, Goodman, Kennedy.
Millwall 3-2 on aggregate

Swansea C (0) 1 *(Pascoe)*
Norwich C (0) 0 3568
Swansea C: Freestone; Jenkins, Clode, Ford, Harris, Pascoe, Ampadu, Penney, Torpey, Cornforth (Bowen), Hodge.
Norwich C: Gunn; Bradshaw, Bowen, Newsome, Prior, Goss, Eadie, Milligan (Crook), Newman, Ekoku (Robins), Adams.
Norwich C won 3-1 on aggregate

Tottenham H (1) 2 *(Barmby, Klinsmann)*
Watford (1) 3 *(Foster, Nogan 2)* 17,798
Tottenham H: Walker; Kerslake, Austin, Howells, Campbell, Mabbutt, Anderton (Hill), Barmby, Klinsmann, Dozzell, Rosenthal.
Watford: Miller; Lavin, Bazeley (Nogan), Foster, Holdsworth, Ramage, Hessenthaler, Johnson, Moralee, Porter, Mooney.
Tottenham H won 8-6 on aggregate

5 OCT

Arsenal (0) 2 *(Campbell, Dickov)*
Hartlepool U (0) 0 20,520
Arsenal: Seaman; Dixon, Winterburn, Hillier, Bould, Keown, McGoldrick, Davis, Campbell, Dickov, Parlour.
Hartlepool U: Horne; Burgess, Walsh, Gilchrist, McGuckin, Oliver, Thompson (Skedd), Ingram, Houchen, Halliday (Sloan), Ainsley.
Arsenal won 7-0 on aggregate

Barnsley (0) 0
Newcastle U (1) 1 *(Cole)* 10,992
Barnsley: Watson; Eaden, Fleming (Liddell), Wilson, Taggart, Davis, O'Connell, Redfearn, Jackson (Rammell), Payton, Bishop.
Newcastle U: Srnicek; Hottiger, Beresford, Howey, Peacock, Albert, Lee, Clark, Cole, Kitson (Mathie), Sellars.
Newcastle U won 3-1 on aggregate

Bolton W (0) 1 *(Sneekes)*
Ipswich T (0) 0 8212
Bolton W: Branagan; Lydiate, Phillips, McAteer (Patterson), Thompson, Spooner, Fisher, Sneekes, Paatelainen (De Freitas), McGinlay, Lee.
Ipswich T: Forrest; Yallop, Johnson, Linighan, Wark (Cotterell), Williams, Sedgley, Slater, Palmer, Guentchev, Thomsen.
Bolton W won 4-0 on aggregate

Burnley (0) 1 *(Robinson)*
Liverpool (1) 4 *(Redknapp 2, Fowler, Clough)* 19,032
Burnley: Beresford; Parkinson, Vinnicombe, Davis, Winstanley, Harper (Harrison), McMinn (Gayle), Philliskirk, Heath, Robinson, Eyres.
Liverpool: James; Jones R, Bjornebye, Nicol, Babb, Ruddock, McManaman (Jones L), Redknapp, Clough, Molby (Thomas), Fowler.
Liverpool won 6-1 on aggregate

Coventry C (1) 3 *(Dublin 2, Wegerle)*
Wrexham (1) 2 *(Cross, Bennett (pen))* 8561
Coventry C: Ogrizovic; Pickering, Morgan, Cook, Gillespie, Busst, Darby, Jones, Dublin, Wegerle, Flynn.
Wrexham: Marriott; Jones, Hardy, Hughes (Watkin), Hunter, Pejic, Bennett, Owen, Connolly, Cross, Durkan.
Coventry C won 5-3 on aggregate

Leicester C (0) 0
Brighton & HA (1) 2 *(Munday, Nogan)* 14,258
Leicester C: Poole; Grayson, Lewis, Mohan, Willis, Whitlow, Draper (Oldfield), Blake (Agnew), Joachim, Roberts, Philpott.
Brighton & HA: Rust; Smith, Tuck, Munday, Foster, Bissett, Case, Minton, Nogan, McDougald (Codner), Chapman.
Brighton & HA won 3-0 on aggregate

Manchester C (0) 4 *(Quinn 2, Walsh, Summerbee)*
Barnet (0) 1 *(Freedman)* 11,545
Manchester C: Dibble; Edghill, Phelan, Flitcroft, Hill, Brightwell I, Summerbee, Walsh (Griffiths), Quinn, Lomas, Beagrie.
Barnet: Phillips; McDonald, Gale (Newell), Hoddle, Newson, Primus, Tomlinson (Haynes), Freedman, Hodges, Scott, Wilson.
Manchester C won 4-2 on aggregate

Manchester U (1) 2 *(McClair, May)*
Port Vale (0) 0 31,615
Manchester U: Walsh; Casper, O'Kane, Butt, May, Pallister, Gillespie (Tomlinson), Beckham, McClair, Scholes, Davies (Neville G).
Port Vale: Musselwhite; Sandeman, Tankard, Porter, Aspin, Glover D, Kelly, Kent (Van der Laan), Foyle, Glover L, Burke (Allon).
Manchester U won 4-1 on aggregate

Portsmouth (0) 1 *(Hall)*
Everton (1) 1 *(Watson)* 13,605
Portsmouth: Knight; Gittens, Stimson, McLoughlin, Symons, Dobson, Radosavljevic (Hall), Kristensen, Powell, Creaney, Pethick.
Everton: Southall; Snodin, Burrows, Parkinson, Watson, Unsworth, Samways, Stuart, Amokachi, Ferguson, Hinchcliffe (Rideout).
Portsmouth won 4-3 on aggregate

QPR (2) 2 *(Allen, Wilson (pen))*
Carlisle U (0) 0 6561
QPR: Roberts; Bardsley, Wilson, Barker, Yates, McDonald, Impey, Holloway, Ferdinand (Gallen), Allen, Sinclair.
Carlisle U: Caig; Joyce (Currie), Gallimore, Walling, Valentine, Mountfield, Thomas (Arnold), Reeves, Davey, Edmondson, Conway.
QPR won 3-0 on aggregate

Southampton (1) 4 *(Le Tissier 4 (1 pen))*
Huddersfield T (0) 0 12,032
Southampton: Grobbelaar; Dodd, Charlton, Magilton, Benali, Monkou, Le Tissier, Ekelund, Dowie (Bennett), Widdrington (Tisdale), Heaney.
Huddersfield T: Francis (Blackwell); Trevitt, Cowan, Logan, Scully, Dyson, Crosby (Billy), Bullock, Booth (Dunn), Jepson, Starbuck.
Southampton won 5-0 on aggregate

Torquay U (0) 0
Wimbledon (1) 1 *(Holdsworth)* 4244
Torquay U: Bayes; Burton, Kelly, Hathaway, Moore, Curran, Trollope, Buckle, Hancox, Okorie, Goodridge.
Wimbledon: Segers; Barton, Kimble, Perry, Clarke (Joseph), Fitzgerald, Fear, Talboys (Ardley), Harford, Holdsworth, Elkins.
Wimbledon won 3-0 on aggregate

West Ham U (0) 2 *(Hutchison, Moncur)*
Walsall (0) 0 13,553
West Ham U: Miklosko; Breacker, Rowland, Potts, Whitbread, Allen, Moncur (Brown), Chapman, Hutchison, Marsh, Bishop.
Walsall: Wood; Ryder, Rogers, Watkiss, Palmer, Marsh (Ntamark), O'Connor (Evans), Peer, Lightbourne, Wilson, Mehew.
aet; West Ham U won 2-1 on aggregate

Wigan Ath (0) 0
Aston Villa (1) 3 *(Lamptey 2, Whittingham)* 2633
Wigan Ath: Farnworth; Carragher (Rennie), Jakub, Strong, Robertson, Farrell, Campbell, Kilford, Gavin, Rimmer, Lyons (Morton).
Aston Villa: Oakes; Staunton, King, Teale, McGrath, Parker, Yorke, Lamptey, Fenton, Whittingham, Farrell.
Aston Villa won 8-0 on aggregate

THIRD ROUND

25 OCT

Liverpool (1) 2 *(Rush 2)*
Stoke C (1) 1 *(Peschisolido)* 32,060
Liverpool: James; Jones R, Bjornebye, Scales, Babb, Ruddock, McManaman, Redknapp, Rush, Barnes, Fowler.
Stoke C: Muggleton; Butler, Sandford, Cranson, Overson, Orlygsson, Beeston, Clarkson, Carruthers (Biggins), Peschisolido, Gleghorn (Potter).

Mansfield T (0) 0
Millwall (1) 2 *(Cadette, Kennedy)* 5359
Mansfield T: Ward; Boothroyd, Baraclough, Holland, Howarth, Peters, Ireland (Hadley), Hoyle, Wilkinson, Doolan, Noteman.
Millwall: Keller; Cunningham, Thatcher, Van Den Hauwe (Beard), McCarthy, Roberts, Savage (Mitchell), Dawes, Cadette, Goodman, Kennedy.

QPR (2) 3 *(Gallen, Sinclair, Penrice)*
Manchester C (1) 4 *(Summerbee, Curle (pen), Beagrie, Lomas)* 11,701
QPR: Dykstra; Bardsley, Wilson, Barker (Penrice), Yates, McDonald, Meaker, Holloway, Dichio, Gallen, Sinclair.
Manchester C: Dibble; Edghill, Phelan, Flitcroft, Curle, Brightwell I, Summerbee, Walsh, Quinn, Lomas, Beagrie.

Sheffield U (0) 1 *(Blake)*
Bolton W (1) 2 *(Paatelainen, Scott A (og))* 6939
Sheffield U: Kelly; Gage, Scott A, Hartfield, Gayle, Beesley (Fickling), Reed, Veart, Blake, Littlejohn (Scott R), Whitehouse.
Bolton W: Branagan; Lydiate, Phillips, Patterson, Thompson, Coleman, Green, Sneekes, Paatelainen, McGinlay, Lee (De Freitas).

Wimbledon (0) 0
Crystal Palace (0) 1 *(Armstrong)* 9394
Wimbledon: Segers; Joseph, Elkins, Jones, Thorn, Fitzgerald (Harford), Barton, Gayle (Fear), Clarke, Blissett, Ardley.
Crystal Palace: Martyn; Humphrey, Gordon, Southgate, Shaw, Coleman, Bowry, Newman, Armstrong, Preece, Salako.

26 OCT

Aston Villa (1) 1 *(Townsend)*
Middlesbrough (0) 0 19,254
Aston Villa: Bosnich; Barrett, Staunton, Ehiogu, McGrath, Parker, Houghton, Townsend, Saunders, Whittingham (Lamptey), Yorke.
Middlesbrough: Miller; Cox, Fleming, Vickers, Whyte, Blackmore, Todd (Hignett), Pollock, Wilkinson, Hendrie, Moore.

Blackburn R (0) 2 *(Shearer 2)*
Coventry C (0) 0 14,538
Blackburn R: Flowers; Berg, Le Saux, Warhurst, Hendry, Gale, Ripley, Atkins, Shearer, Sutton, Wilcox.
Coventry C: Ogrizovic; Borrows, Pickering, Cook, Rennie, Busst, Darby, Ndlovu, Dublin, Wegerle, Flynn (Jones).

Brighton & HA (0) 1 *(McCarthy)*
Swindon T (1) 1 *(Thomson)* 11,382
Brighton & HA: Rust; Bissett, Pates, Smith, Foster, McCarthy, Chamberlain (Codner), McDougald, Nogan, Minton, Chapman.
Swindon T: Digby; Robinson, Bodin, Thomson, Nijholt, Taylor, Horlock, Beauchamp, Fjortoft, Ling, Scott.

Newcastle U (0) 2 *(Albert, Kitson)*
Manchester U (0) 0 34,178
Newcastle U: Srnicek; Hottiger, Beresford, Howey, Peacock, Albert, Watson, Beardsley, Cole (Guppy), Kitson, Sellars.
Manchester U: Walsh; Neville G, Irwin (Sharpe) (Tomlinson), Bruce, Pallister, Gillespie, Beckham, Scholes, McClair, Davies, Butt.

Notts Co (2) 3 *(Agana, McSwegan 2)*
Tottenham H (0) 0 16,952
Notts Co: Reece; Mills, Walker, Turner, Yates, Johnson (Murphy), Devlin, Butler, Legg, McSwegan (Matthews), Agana.
Tottenham H: Thorstvedt; Edinburgh, Austin, Popescu, Calderwood (Hazard), Campbell, Dozzell, Barmby, Klinsmann, Sheringham, Dumitrescu.

Oldham Ath (0) 0
Arsenal (0) 0 9303
Oldham Ath: Gerrard; Halle, Pointon, Henry, Jobson, Redmond, Bernard, Banger, Graham, McCarthy, Holden R.
Arsenal: Seaman, Dixon (Keown), Winterburn, Schwarz, Bould, Adams, Selley, Campbell (McGoldrick), Smith, Merson, Parlour.

Portsmouth (0) 0
Derby Co (0) 1 *(Simpson)* 8568
Portsmouth: Knight; Gittens (Durnin), Stimson, McLoughlin, Symons, McGrath (Kristensen), Pethick, Radosavljevic, Powell, Creaney, Hall.
Derby Co: Sutton (Quy); Charles, Forsyth, Wassall, Short, Williams, Cowans, Carsley, Johnson (Stallard), Gabbiadini, Simpson (Kavanagh).

Sheffield W (0) 1 *(Bart-Williams)*
Southampton (0) 0 16,715
Sheffield W: Pressman; Atherton, Nolan, Taylor, Pearce, Walker, Sheridan, Hyde, Wright, Bart-Williams, Sinton.
Southampton: Grobbelar; Kenna, Benali (Charlton), Magilton, Hall, Monkou, Le Tissier, Ekelund (Heaney), Dowie, Maddison, Allen.

Tranmere R (0) 1 *(Aldridge)*
Norwich C (1) 1 *(Polston)* 10,232
Tranmere R: Nixon; Stevens, Mungall, McGreal, Garnett, O'Brien (Irons), Morrissey, Aldridge, Malkin, Brannan, Nevin.
Norwich C: Gunn; Polston, Bowen, Crook, Prior, Newman, Adams (Sutch), Milligan, Robins, Sheron, Eadie (Goss).

West Ham U (1) 1 *(Hutchison)*
Chelsea (0) 0 18,815
West Ham U: Miklosko; Breacker, Dicks, Potts, Martin, Allen, Bishop, Hutchison, Cottee, Marsh, Rush.
Chelsea: Kharine; Hall (Lee), Barness, Kjeldbjerg, Johnsen, Spackman, Rocastle, Newton, Shipperley, Peacock (Hopkin), Wise.

Wolverhampton W (1) 2 *(Birch, Kelly D)*
Nottingham F (2) 3 *(Pearce, Roy 2)* 28,369
Wolverhampton W: Stowell; Smith, Thompson, Ferguson (Emblen), Blades, Venus, Birch, Thomas, Bull, Kelly D, Froggatt.
Nottingham F: Crossley; Lyttle, Pearce, Cooper, Chettle, Stone, Phillips, Roy, Bohinen, Collymore (Lee), Woan.

THIRD ROUND REPLAYS

9 NOV

Arsenal (2) 2 *(Dickov 2)*
Oldham Ath (0) 0 22,746
Arsenal: Seaman; Keown, Winterburn, Schwarz, Bould, Adams, Selley (Jensen), Campbell, Dickov, Parlour, McGoldrick.
Oldham Ath: Gerrard; Halle, Makin, Henry, Jobson, Redmond, Bernard, Banger, Graham, McCarthy (Ritchie), Brennan (Holden R).

Norwich C (0) 4 *(Prior, McGreal (og), Polston, Newman)*
Tranmere R (1) 2 *(Irons, Nevin)* 13,311
Norwich C: Gunn; Sutch, Bowen, Crook (Goss), Polston, Prior, Eadie, Newman, Robins, Milligan, Adams.
Tranmere R: Nixon; Stevens, Mungall, McGreal, Garnett, Irons, Morrissey, Aldridge, Malkin, Brannan, Nevin.

Swindon T (2) 4 *(Scott 2, Fjortoft 2)*
Brighton & HA (0) 1 *(Chamberlain)* 6482
Swindon T: Digby; Robinson, Bodin, Thomson, Nijholt, Kilcline, Ling, Beauchamp, Fjortoft, Mutch, Scott.
Brighton & HA: Rust; Smith, Tuck, Minton, Pates, McCarthy, Chamberlain, McDougald (Andrews), Nogan, Codner, Chapman.

Norwich C (1) 1 *(Eadie)*
Notts Co (0) 0 14,030
Norwich C: Gunn; Sutch, Bowen, Newsome, Polston, Crook, Milligan, Newman, Eadie (Goss), Sheron (Cureton), Adams.
Notts Co: Cherry; Mills, Legg, Turner, Yates, Johnson, Devlin, Butler, Lund, McSwegan, Agana.

Nottingham F (0) 0
Millwall (2) 2 *(Berry 2)* 12,393
Nottingham F: Crossley; Lyttle, Phillips, Cooper (Haaland), Chettle, Stone, Gemmill, Roy, Bohinen (Lee), Collymore, Woan.
Millwall: Keller; Beard, Thatcher, Roberts, Witter, Stevens, Savage (Dawes), Rae, Berry, Mitchell, Kennedy (Webber).

Swindon T (1) 2 *(Fjortoft 2)*
Derby Co (1) 1 *(Stallard)* 8920
Swindon T: Digby; Robinson, Bodin, Thomson, Nijholt, Kilcline (Ling), O'Sullivan, Horlock, Fjortoft, Mutch (Beauchamp), Scott.
Derby Co: Sutton; Kavanagh, Nicholson, Kuhl, Short, Williams, Harkes (Sturridge), Carsley, Johnson, Stallard, Simpson.

FOURTH ROUND

30 NOV

Arsenal (2) 2 *(Morrow, Wright)*
Sheffield W (0) 0 27,390
Arsenal: Seaman (Bartram); Dixon, Winterburn, Schwarz, Bould, Adams, Morrow (Keown), Wright, Smith, Campbell, McGoldrick (Dickov).
Sheffield W: Pressman; Atherton, Nolan, Petrescu, Pearce, Taylor, Sheridan, Hyde, Watson (Jones), Bart-Williams, Sinton.

Blackburn R (0) 1 *(Sutton)*
Liverpool (1) 3 *(Rush 3)* 30,115
Blackburn R: Flowers; Warhurst, Le Saux, Gale (Newell), Hendry, Berg, Ripley, Sherwood, Shearer, Sutton, Wilcox.
Liverpool: James; Jones R, Bjornebye, Scales, Babb, Ruddock, McManaman, Redknapp, Rush, Thomas, Fowler.

Crystal Palace (0) 4 *(Armstrong 2, Southgate 2)*
Aston Villa (1) 1 *(Atkinson)* 12,653
Crystal Palace: Martyn; Humphrey, Gordon, Southgate, Shaw, Coleman, Bowry, Newman, Armstrong, Preece, Salako.
Aston Villa: Bosnich; Barrett, King, Ehiogu, McGrath, Parker, Houghton, Farrell (Whittingham), Saunders, Atkinson (Fenton), Yorke.

Manchester C (0) 1 *(Rosler)*
Newcastle U (1) 1 *(Jeffrey)* 25,162
Manchester C: Dibble; Hill (Rosler), Brightwell D, Flitcroft, Curle, Brightwell I, Summerbee, Walsh, Quinn, Lomas, Beagrie.
Newcastle U: Srnicek; Hottiger, Beresford, Venison, Neilson, Watson, Mathie, Beardsley, Cole, Clark, Jeffrey.

West Ham U (0) 1 *(Cottee)*
Bolton W (1) 3 *(McGinlay 2, Lee)* 18,190
West Ham U: Miklosko; Brown, Dicks, Potts, Whitbread, Bishop, Moncur, Rush, Cottee, Boere, Holmes (Morley).
Bolton W: Branagan; Green, Phillips, McAteer, Thompson, Stubbs, Coleman, Sneekes, Paatelainen, McGinlay, Lee (Patterson).

FOURTH ROUND REPLAY

21 DEC

Newcastle U (0) 0
Manchester C (1) 2 *(Rosler, Walsh)* 30,156
Newcastle U: Srnicek; Hottiger (Bracewell), Beresford, Venison, Peacock, Albert, Watson, Clark, Cole, Fox, Kitson.
Manchester C: Dibble; Foster, Lomas, Flitcroft, Kernaghan (Vonk), Brightwell I, Summerbee, Walsh, Rosler, Gaudino (Quinn), Beagrie.

FIFTH ROUND

11 JAN

Bolton W (0) 1 *(Lee)*
Norwich C (0) 0 17,029
Bolton W: Branagan; Green, Phillips, McAteer, Coleman, Stubbs, Lee, Sneekes, Paatelainen, McGinlay, Thompson.
Norwich C: Marshall; Sutch, Bowen, Newsome, Polston, Goss, Crook, Newman, Sheron, Eadie (Ullathorne), Adams (Akinbiyi).

Crystal Palace (0) 4 *(Pitcher, Salako, Armstrong, Preece)*

Manchester C (0) 0 16,668

Crystal Palace: Martyn; Humphrey, Gordon, Southgate, Shaw, Coleman, Ndah (Preece), Newman, Armstrong, Pitcher, Salako.
Manchester C: Dibble; Summerbee, Phelan, Lomas (Brightwell D), Curle, Kernaghan, Rosler, Walsh, Quinn (Gaudino), Flitcroft, Beagrie.

Liverpool (0) 1 *(Rush)*

Arsenal (0) 0 35,026

Liverpool: James; Jones R, Bjornebye, Scales, Babb, Ruddock, McManaman, Redknapp, Rush, Barnes (Thomas), Fowler.
Arsenal: Seaman; Dixon, Winterburn, Schwarz, Bould (Morrow), Linighan, Jensen, Wright, Campbell, Hillier, Parlour (Dickov).

Swindon T (2) 3 *(Mutch 2, Fjortoft)*

Millwall (0) 1 *(Mitchell)* 11,772

Swindon T: Hammond; Robinson, Bodin, Culverhouse, Nijholt, Taylor, Horlock, Beauchamp, Fjortoft, Mutch, Ling.
Millwall: Keller; Dawes, Van Blerk, Roberts, Webber, Stevens, Savage, Rae, Cadette, Mitchell, Kennedy.

SEMI-FINALS FIRST LEG

12 FEB

Swindon T (1) 2 *(Thorne 2)*

Bolton W (1) 1 *(Stubbs)* 15,341

Swindon T: Hammond; O'Sullivan, Murray, Robinson, Nijholt, Taylor, Horlock, Beauchamp, Fjortoft, Thorne, Ling.
Bolton W: Branagan; Green, Phillips, McAteer, Coleman, Stubbs, Lee, Sneekes, Paatelainen, Coyle (McGinlay), Thompson.

15 FEB

Liverpool (0) 1 *(Fowler)*

Crystal Palace (0) 0 25,480

Liverpool: James; Jones R, Babb, Redknapp, Scales, Ruddock, McManaman, Walters, Rush, Barnes, Fowler.
Crystal Palace: Martyn; Patterson, Gordon, Southgate, Shaw, Coleman, Humphrey, Pitcher, Matthew, Preece, Salako.

SEMI-FINALS SECOND LEG

8 MAR

Bolton W (0) 3 *(McAteer, Paatelainen, McGinlay)*

Swindon T (0) 1 *(Fjortoft)* 19,851

Bolton W: Branagan; Green, Phillips, McAteer, Seagraves, Stubbs, Lee (Sneekes), Patterson, Coyle (Paatelainen), McGinlay, Thompson.
Swindon T: Digby; O'Sullivan (Hooper), Murray, Viveash, Nijholt, Taylor, Horlock, Beauchamp, Fjortoft, Thorne, Gooden.

Crystal Palace (0) 0

Liverpool (1) 1 *(Fowler)* 18,224

Crystal Palace: Martyn; Patterson, Gordon, Southgate, Shaw, Young, Ndah (Dyer), Pitcher, Coleman, Preece, Salako.
Liverpool: James; Jones R, Bjornebye, Scales, Babb, Ruddock, McManaman, Redknapp, Rush, Barnes, Fowler.

FINAL at Wembley

2 APR

Bolton W (0) 1 *(Thompson)*

Liverpool (1) 2 *(McManaman 2)* 75,595

Bolton W: Branagan; Green (Bergsson), Phillips, McAteer, Seagraves, Stubbs, Lee, Sneekes, Paatelainen, McGinlay, Thompson.
Liverpool: James; Jones R, Bjornebye, Scales, Babb, Ruddock, McManaman, Redknapp, Rush, Barnes, Fowler.
Referee: P. Don (Hanworth Park).

Liverpool's Ian Rush and Robbie Fowler celebrate on the way to Wembley and Coca-Cola Cup success. (Colorsport)

LEAGUE CUP ATTENDANCES

Totals	*Season*	*Attendances*	*Games*	*Average*
	1960/61	1,204,580	112	10,755
	1961/62	1,030,534	104	9,909
	1962/63	1,029,893	102	10,097
	1963/64	945,265	104	9,089
	1964/65	962,802	98	9,825
	1965/66	1,205,876	106	11,376
	1966/67	1,394,553	118	11,818
	1967/68	1,671,326	110	15,194
	1968/69	2,064,647	118	17,497
	1969/70	2,299,819	122	18,851
	1970/71	2,035,315	116	17,546
	1971/72	2,397,154	123	19,489
	1972/73	1,935,474	120	16,129
	1973/74	1,722,629	132	13,050
	1974/75	1,901,094	127	14,969
	1975/76	1,841,735	140	13,155
	1976/77	2,236,636	147	15,215
	1977/78	2,038,295	148	13,772
	1978/79	1,825,643	139	13,134
	1979/80	2,322,866	169	13,745
	1980/81	2,051,576	161	12,743
	1981/82	1,880,682	161	11,681
	1982/83	1,679,756	160	10,498
	1983/84	1,900,491	168	11,312
	1984/85	1,876,429	167	11,236
	1985/86	1,579,916	163	9,693
	1986/87	1,531,498	157	9,755
	1987/88	1,539,253	158	9,742
	1988/89	1,552,780	162	9,585
	1989/90	1,836,916	168	10,934
	1990/91	1,675,496	159	10,538
	1991/92	1,622,337	164	9,892
	1992/93	1,558,031	161	9,677
	1993/94	1,744,120	163	10,700
	1994/95	1,500,322	156	9,617

THE FOOTBALL TRUST
Helping the game

Middlesbrough made a return to the Premiership after a one-year break and moved to their new Riverside stadium, which was the chief beneficiary of some £30,000,000 of grants by the Football Trust to clubs.

Top grant for the 1995-96 season was £5,000,000 to Hampden Park in Glasgow for the refurbishment of the South Stand at the mecca of Scottish Football.

The Football Trust, which is jointly financed by the Littlewoods, Vernons and Zetters pools conpanies and the government, has – as its priority task – been helping professional soccer clubs implement the recommendation of the Taylor report. It gives grants for the new stadia, stands, cover and safety work and, since its inception in 1990, has helped fund projects costing a total of £420,000,000 with grants of some £132,000,000.

It also gives financial help to clubs putting in important safety and facility alterations, like facilities for the disabled, family enclosures, toilets and anti-hooligan measures such as closed-circuit television and better stewards' and transport set-ups. In short, better, safer and more comfortable watching of the game in Britain.

TREVOR WILLIAMSON

Schedule of Major Project Grants Offered During 1995-96

Club	Total Project Cost	Trust Grant	Major Project
Barnsley	2,400,000	1,000,000	South Stand
Barnsley	2,400,000	1,050,000	South Stand
Brentford	316,000	222,000	Ealing Road Stand
Bristol City	266,882	186,818	Dolman Stand
Burnley	5,700,000	2,000,000	Redevelopment of ground
Bury	782,570	306,000	East and West Stands
Carlisle United	2,138,000	750,000	East Stand
Celtic	14,900,000	2,000,000	North Stand
Coventry City	1,500,000	200,000	South Stand
Crewe Alexandra	797,042	568,870	West and East Stands
Hampden Park		5,000,000	South Stand
Hibernian	4,200,000	2,000,000	North and South Stands
Leeds United	1,100,000	400,000	North Stand
Lincoln City	1,200,000	692,016	Sincil Bank End
Luton Town	64,647	38,788	Kenilworth Road End
Meadowbank Thistle	6,000,000	500,000	New Stadium
Middlesbrough	10,000,000	2,225,000	Riverside Stadium
Peterborough United	1,400,000	905,000	Glebe Road Stand
Port Vale	1,070,000	663,000	Hamil Road Stand
Preston North End	4,750,000	750,000	West Stand
Queen of the South	523,056	371,228	East Stand
Ross County	92,709	66,000	Jubilee Terrace
Ross County	581,756	407,925	West Stand
Scarborough	474,718	354,484	East Stand
Sheffield Wednesday	4,750,000	756,897	South Stand
Shrewsbury Town	240,524	165,000	Centre Stand
Southend United	630,000	473,569	South Stand
Southend United	145,660	109,245	North Stand
Stockport County	1,200,000	700,000	Cheadle End Stand
Stranraer	43,758	32,819	West Terrace
Tranmere Rovers	2,670,000	2,000,000	Three Stands
Windsor Park	1,800,000	1,500,000	Spion Kop End
Wycombe Wanderers	1,800,000	1,000,000	South Stand
	75,667,322	31,238,733	

INTER-TOTO CUP

The five British teams who entered the UEFA Inter-Totc competition in June/July 1995 were all eliminated before the final stages. In Group 1, Sheffield Wednesday narrowly missed the draw for the Second Round after a spirited improvement. But Tottenham Hotspur fared less well in Group 2, fielding a mixture of young players and those on loan from other clubs. In fact they crashed 8-0 in their last match in Cologne, while the first team were touring Scandinavia. In Group 4, the Welsh League representatives Ton Pentre gave a plucky display considering they were almost out of their depth and improved noticeably towards the end of their matches, though they did not manage to score a goal. In Group 6, Partick Thistle fell away after a promising start, but Wimbledon managed just one goal in four attempts in Group 10, but again turned out a combination of youngsters and loaned players.

Second Round draw: Cologne v Tirol, Bordeaux v Eintracht Frankfurt, Bayer Leverkusen v Odense, Bursaspor v Ofi Crete, Aarau v Karlsruhe, Heerenveen v Farul Constanta, Ceahlaul v Metz, Strasbourg v Steyr.

Tottenham Hotspur, Group 2
v Lucerne, Lost 0-2. 2497 at Brighton.
Day; Newson, Coll, Sampson, Clapham, Byrne (Spencer), Pardew, Watson, McMahon, Slade, Hendry (Wormull).

v Rudar, Won 2-1 away. *Scorers:* Sampson, Hendry.
Day; Newson, Coll, Watson, Clapham, Byrne (Spencer), Pardew, Sampson, McMahon, Hendry, Slade.

v Oysters, Lost 1-2. *Scorer:* McMahon. 2143 at Brighton.
Day; Carr, Newson, Sampson, Clapham, Byrne (Simpson), Watson, Pardew, Hill, Slade, McMahon.

v Cologne, Lost 0-8 away.
Day; Carr, Coll, Newson, Clapham, Byrne (Wormull), Watson, Pardew, Spencer (Simpson), Slade (Mahorn), Turner.

Loan players: Newson (Barnet), Sampson (Northampton T), Byrne (St Mirren), Pardew (Charlton Ath).

Wimbledon, Group 10
v Bursaspor, Lost 0-4. 1879 at Brighton.
Cheesewright; O'Kane, Skinner, Newhouse, O'Shea, Laidlaw (Thomas), Byrne (Euell), Appleton, Dobbs, Piper, Tomlinson.

v Kosice, Drew 1-1 away. *Scorer:* Hodges.
Cheesewright (Murphy); O'Kane, Skinner, O'Shea, Hodges, Thomas, Appleton, Piper, Newhouse, Euell, Tomlinson.

v Beitar, Drew 0-0. 702 at Brighton.
Murphy; O'Kane, Skinner, O'Shea, Hodges, Thomas, Appleton, Piper, Newhouse, Euell (Payne), Tomlinson (Dobbs).

v Charleroi, Lost 0-3 away.
Cheesewright; Appleton, Skinner, O'Shea, Laidlaw, Thomas, Futcher, Piper, Payne (Dobbs), Newhouse (Euell), Tomlinson.

Loan players: Cheesewright (Colchester U), Appleton (Manchester U), O'Shea (Northampton T), Tomlinson (Manchester U), O'Kane (Manchester U).

Sheffield Wednesday, Group 1
v Basle, Lost 1-0.
Bowling; Brien, Williams A, Stewart, Briscoe, German (Faulkner), Williams M, Hyde, Holmes, Pearson, Barker (Bailey).

v Gornik Zabrze, Won 3-2. *Scorers:* Bright, Waddle, Krzetowski (og). 5592 at Rotherham.
Woods; Nolan, Briscoe, Atherton, Walker, Watts, Poric (Whittingham), Hyde, Bright (Barker), Waddle, Sinton.

v Karlsruhe, Drew 1-1 away. *Scorer:* Bright.
Woods; Atherton, Nolan, Walker, Watts, Hyde, Whittingham, Waddle, Hirst (Williams M.), Bright, Sinton.

v Aarhus, Won 3-1. *Scorers:* Bright 2, Petrescu. 6990 at Rotherham
Woods; Petrescu, Nolan (Briscoe), Atherton, Pearce, Walker, Bright, Hyde (Sinton), Hirst (Whittingham), Sheridan, Pembridge.

Ton Pentre, Group 4
v Heerenveen, Lost 7-0; v Bekescsaba, Lost 4-0 away; v Uniao Leiria, Lost 3-0; v Nasteved, Lost 2-0 away.

Loan players: Bowling (Bradford C), German (ex-Halifax) T), Williams A (Rotherham U), Pearson (Cardiff C), Brien (Rotherham U).

Partick Thistle, Group 6
v Linz, Drew 2-2 away; v Keflavik, Won 3-1; v Metz, Lost 1-0 away; v Zagreb, Lost 2-1.

FOOTBALL LEAGUE REPRESENTATIVE MATCH

Italian Serie B Under-21's (1) 2 (*Sala, Amaruso (pen)*) *in Andria*
Football League Under-21's (1) 3 (*Allen, Booth, Stallard*) 3000
Italy: De Sanctis; Nicola, Pierini, Sala, Sussi, Binotto, Cozza, Boscolo (Pavan), Macellari (Micelli), Lemme (Morfeo), Amaruso.
League: Watson (Barnsley); Smith (Wolverhampton W), Rufus (Charlton Ath), Richards (Bradford C), Thatcher (Millwall), Carsley (Derby Co), (Simpson (Notts Co)), Pollock (Middlesbrough), Roberts (Millwall), Allen (Oxford U), Forster (Brentford) (Stallard (Derby Co)), Booth (Huddersfield T).

ANGLO-ITALIAN CUP 1994–95

International Stage

24 AUG

Group A

Ascoli (1) 1 *(Incocciati)*
Notts Co (0) 1 *(Devlin)* 7000
Ascoli: Bizzarri; Fusco, Fiondella (Mancuso), Zanoncelli, Benetti, Zaini, Binotto, Galia, Bierhoff (Spinelli), Menolascina, Incocciati.
Notts Co: Cherry; Hoyle (Cox), Emenalo, Turner, Yates, Murphy, Devlin, Sherlock (Matthews), Lund, Agana, Simpson.

Lecce (0) 0
Wolverhampton W (1) 1 *(Kelly D)* 1795
Lecce: Torchia; Biondo, Fattizzo, Ceramicola, Ricci (Trinchero), Macellari, D'Onofrio (Cazzella), Olive, Monaco, Melchiori, Ayew.
Wolverhampton W: Jones; Smith, Thompson, Ferguson, Blades, Shirtliff, Venus (Emblen), Thomas, Rankine (Birch), Kelly D, Froggatt.

Swindon T (0) 0
Atalanta (0) 2 *(Saurini, Fortunato)* 5167
Swindon T: Digby; Robinson, Bodin, Kilcline, Nijholt, Thomson, Ling, Beauchamp, Fjortoft, Scott (White), Horlock (Gooden).
Atalanta: Ferron; Pavan, Tresoldi, Fortunato, Boselli, Montero, Magoni, Bonacina, Saurini, Scapolo (Zanchi), Vecchiola (Rodriguez).

Tranmere R (2) 2 *(Aldridge, Malkin)*
Venezia (0) 2 *(Cerbone (pen), Bonaldi)* 3012
Tranmere R: Coyne; Higgins, Brannan, Irons, Garnett, O'Brien, Morrissey, Aldridge, Malkin, Nevin, Mungall.
Venezia: Visi; Centurion, Vamoli, Rossi, Servidei, Mariani, Morello (Bonaldi), Fogli, Vieri, Bortolazzi, Cerbone.

Group B

Ancona (2) 2 *(Caccia 2)*
Derby Co (1) 1 *(Pembridge)* 748
Ancona: Pinna; Nicola, Sergio, Sgro, Baroni, Germoni (Cornacchia), Baglieri (Cangini), De Angelis, Caccia, Catanese, Centofanti.
Derby Co: Taylor; Charles (Kavanagh), Forsyth, Kuhl, Nicholson (Cowans), Wassall, Stallard, Hayward, Gabbiadini, Pembridge, Simpson.

Cesena (0) 0
Stoke C (2) 2 *(Carruthers, Clark)* 1065
Cesena: Santarelli; Scugugia, Medri, Romano, Sadotti (Calcaterra), Sussi, Teodorani, Ambrosini (Scarafoni), Zagati, Piangerelli, Hubner.
Stoke C: Muggleton; Clark, Sandford, Dreyer, Cranson, Downing (Clarkson), Butler, Wallace, Biggins (Carruthers), Sturridge, Gleghorn.

Middlesbrough (0) 0
Piacenza (0) 0 5348
Middlesbrough: Miller; Morris, Taylor, Vickers, Todd, Whyte, Stamp (Cox), Pollock (Wilkinson), Hignett, Mustoe, Wright.
Piacenza: Ramon; Polonia (Cesari), Rossini, Suppa, Di Cintio, Lucci, Turrini (Moretti), Brioschi, De Vitis, Iacobelli, Piovani.

Sheffield U (1) 1 *(Littlejohn)*
Udinese (1) 2 *(Marino, Scarchilli)* 7497
Sheffield U: Tracey; Gage, Davidson, Rogers, Hoyland, Hodgson, Veart, Hartfield, Blake, Hodges, Littlejohn.
Udinese: Caniato; Pellegrini, Bertotto, Ametrano, Calori, Pierini, Helveg, Scarchilli, Marino, Pizzi, Kozminski.

6 SEPT

Group A

Atalanta (2) 2 *(Montero, Saurini)*
Tranmere R (0) 0 4000
Atalanta: Ferron; Zanchi, Boselli, Fortunato, Montero, Bonacina, Rotella (Salvatori), Magoni, Saurini (Pavone), Rodriguez, Scapolo.
Tranmere R: Nixon; Higgins, Brannan, Irons, Garnett (Moore), Mungall, Edwards, McGreal, Jones, Branch, Thomas.

Notts Co (0) 1 *(Turner)*
Lecce (0) 0 2495
Notts Co: Reece; Galloway, Emenalo, Turner, Johnson, Yates, Devlin, Legg (Simpson), Agana, McSwegan, Matthews.
Lecce: Torchia; Ricci, Trinchera, Melchiori, Ceramicola, Macellari, Russo (Ayew), Gumprecht, Pittalis, Olive, Cazzella.

Venezia (1) 1 *(Mariani)*
Swindon T (0) 0 1325
Venezia: Visi; Filippini (Centurioni), Ballarin, Rossi, Servidei, Mariani, Morello, Nardini, Bonaldi, Bottazzi, Cerbone (Varriale).
Swindon T: Hammond; Robinson, Horlock, Kilcline, Nijholt, Thomson (Murray), Ling, Beauchamp, Mutch (Digby), Berkley, O'Sullivan (Hamon).

Wolverhampton W (0) 0
Ascoli (0) 1 *(Marcato)* 9599
Wolverhampton W: Jones; Smith, Thompson, Ferguson, Blades, Shirtliff, Emblen, Birch, Stewart, Keen, Venus.
Ascoli: Bizzarri; Fusco, Fiondella (Mancuso), Zanoncelli, Benetti, Marcato, Milana, Bosi, Bierhoff (Spinelli), Menolascina, Pasino.

Group B

Derby Co (5) 6 *(Hodge 2, Kitson 4)*
Cesena (0) 1 *(Ambrosini)* 2010
Derby Co: Taylor; Charles (Kavanagh), Nicholson, Hodge, Short, Wassall, Cowans, Carsley, Kitson, Gabbiadini (Sutton S), Simpson.
Cesena: Santarelli; Scugugia, Calcaterra, Ambrosini, Aloisi, Sussi, Teodorani, Del Bianco (Maenza), Zagati (Piangerelli), Piraccini, Hubner.

Piacenza (1) 2 *(Brioschi, Suppa)*
Sheffield U (1) 2 *(Carr, Gannon)* 4744
Piacenza: Ramon; Di Cintio, Rossini (Manganiello), Suppa (Moretti), Cesari, Lucci, Turrini, Brioschi, De Vitis, Iacobelli, Piovani.
Sheffield U: Tracey; Foreman, Scott A, Blount, Fickling, Hoyland, Scott R, Gannon, Davison, Carr (Battersby), Hawthorne.

Stoke C (0) 1 *(Biggins)*
Ancona (1) 1 *(Caccia)* 3330

Stoke C: Muggleton; Butler, Sandford, Dreyer, Overson, Downing (Leslie), Peschisolido, Wallace, Biggins (Carruthers), Beckford, Gleghorn.
Ancona: Pinna; Cornacchia, Centofanti (Pesaresi), Nicola, Baroni, Sergio, De Angelis, Catanese, Caccia (Cangini), Picasso, Baglieri.

4 OCT

Group A

Tranmere R (0) 0
Ascoli (1) 1 *(Bierhoff (pen)* 4546

Tramere R: Nixon; Stevens, Mungall, McGreal, Garnett, O'Brien, Morrissey, Aldridge, Malkin, Edwards, Nevin.
Ascoli: Bizzarri; Marcato, Mancuso, Zanoncelli, Fusco, Zaini, Milana, Galia, Bierhoff, Bosi, Menolascina.

5 OCT

Atalanta (1) 1 *(Rodriguez)*
Notts Co (0) 1 *(Agana)* 5000

Atalanta: Pinato; Zanchi, Valentini (Bigliardi), Fortunato, Pavan, Montero, Salvatori, Magoni (Rotella), Pisani, Rodriguez, Vecchiola.
Notts Co: Cherry; Mills, Emenalo (Legg), Turner, Yates, Murphy, Matthews, Walker, Lund, Jemson, Agana.

Swindon T (2) 3 *(Mutch 2, Scott)*
Lecce (0) 1 *(Ayew)* 2375

Swindon T: Digby; Robinson, Bodin, Kilcline, Nijholt, Taylor, Horlock, Beauchamp, Mutch, Berkley (Ling), Scott (Fjortoft).
Lecce: Torchia; Biondo, Fattizzo, Trinchera, Melchiori, Frisullo (Ceramicola), Russo (Olive), Gazzani, Ayew, Pittalis, Monaco.

Venezia (1) 2 *(Rankine (og), Vieri (pen))*
Wolverhampton W (1) 1 *(Venus)* 750

Venezia: Visi; Filippini, Vanoli, Nardini, Servidei, Ballarin, Morello (Bonaldi), Di Gia, Vieri, Bottazzi, Cerboni (Bortoluzzi).
Wolverhampton W: Jones; Rankine, Thompson, Venus, Blades, Bennett, Birch, Ferguson, Bull, Mills, Keen.

Group B

Middlesbrough (0) 1 *(Moreno)*
Cesena (0) 1 *(Hubner)* 3273

Middlesbrough: Pears; Morris, Taylor, Barron, Whyte, Todd, Stamp, Kavanagh, Moreno, Blackmore, Wright.
Cesena: Santarelli; Scugugia, Sussi, Ambrosini, Farabegoli (Confalone), Medri, Del Bianco, Leoni, Maenza (Bombardini), Piraccini, Hubner.

Piacenza (0) 1 *(De Vitis)*
Derby Co (0) 1 *(Williams)* 1710

Piacenza: Ramon; Di Cintio, Manganiello (Moretti), Suppa, Cesari, Lucci, Turrini, Brioschi, De Vitis, Iacobelli, Piovani.
Derby Co: Sutton S; Charles, Nicholson (Kavanagh), Carsley (Davies), Wassall, Williams, Cowans, Sturridge, Harkes, Pembridge, Simpson.

Sheffield U (2) 3 *(Ward, Battersby, Scott A)*
Ancona (1) 3 *(Baglieri, Catanese, De Angelis)* 1827

Sheffield U: Bibbo; Davidson (Scott R), Scott A, Hawthorne, Fickling, Hoyland, Veart, Ward (Foran), Battersby, Anthony, Davison.
Ancona: Berti; Cornacchia (Pesaresi), Cangini, Sgro, Baroni, Sergio, De Angelis, Catanese, Caccia (Arno), Centofanti, Baglieri.

Udinese (1) 1 *(Pizzi)*
Stoke C (0) 3 *(Downing, Biggins, Butler)* 1306

Udinese: Caniato; Bertotto, Compagnon, Pierini, Calori, Ripa, Helveg, Ametrano, Poggi, Pizzi (Zampieri), Bachini (Rossitto).
Stoke C: Muggleton; Wallace, Sandford, Dreyer (Butler), Cranson, Orlygsson, Overson, Downing, Carruthers (Peschisolido), Biggins, Gleghorn.

18 OCT

Udinese (0) 0
Middlesbrough (0) 0 300

Udinese: Camiato; Pellegrini, Bertotto (Compagnon), Ametrano, Calori, Pierini, Lasalandra, Helveg (Ripa), Poggi, Pizzi, Marino.
Middlesbrough: Miller; Fleming, Taylor, Cox (Barron), Vickers, Liddle, Stamp, Kavanagh, Moreno, Todd, Wright.

15 NOV

Group A

Notts Co (1) 3 *(Devlin, Marsden, Murphy)*
Venezia (0) 3 *(Ambrosetti, Barollo 2 (1 pen))* 2861

Notts Co: Reece; Gallagher, Daniel, Turner, Yates, Johnson, Devlin, Butler, Matthews (Murphy), Marsden, Agana.
Venezia: Visi; Accarni, Ballarin, Bortoluzzi, Vanoli, Mariani, Pellegrini, Fogli, Ambrosetti, Di Gia, Cerbone (Barollo).

Wolverhampton W (1) 1 *(Mills)*
Atalanta (1) 1 *(Bonacina)* 7285

Wolverhampton W: Stowell; Emblen, Thompson, Ferguson (Rankine), Blades, Venus, Birch, Thomas, Mills, Stewart, Froggatt.
Atalanta: Pinato; Pavone, Tresoldi, Bonacina, Pavan, Magoni, Rotella (Zauri), Morfeo (Gibellini), Pisani, Rodriguez, Locatelli.

Lecce (0) 0
Tranmere R (0) 0 286

Lecce: Torchia; Biondo, Macellari, Olive, Rossi (Gazzani), Ricci (Frisulio), Melchiori, Pittalis, Russo, Notaristefano, Baldieri.
Tranmere R: Nixon; Stevens, Mungall (Proctor), McGreal, Garnett, Higgins, Morrissey, Muir, Malkin, Irons (Kenworthy), Edwards.

Ascoli (1) 3 *(Bierhoff 3)*
Swindon T (0) 1 *(Hamon)* 3000

Ascoli: Bizzarri; Mancini, Fiondella, Bosi, Pascucci, Marcato, Cavaliere, Favo, Bierhoff, Menolascina (Mancuso), Mirabelli (Incocciati).
Swindon T: Hammond; Robinson, Horlock, MacLaren, Thomson, Kilcline, O'Sullivan (Berkley), Beauchamp, Mutch, Ling (Hamon), Scott.

Group B

Cesena (1) 1 *(Bombardini)*
Sheffield U (1) 4 *(Scott A 2, Hawthorne, Reed)* 3200

Cesena: Santarelli; Farabegoli, Sussi, Del Bianco (Tamburini), Sadotti (Baschetti), Piraccini, Teodorani, Piangerelli, Cagati, Maenza, Bombardini.
Sheffield U: Bibbo; Ward, Scott A, Hawthorne, Fickling, Blount, Scott R, Reed (Foreman), Battersby, Anthony, Gannon.

Derby Co (2) 3 *(Johnson 2, Stallard)*

Udinese (0) 1 *(Berlotto)* 1562

Derby Co: Sutton S; Charles (Kavanagh), Nicholson, Kuhl, Short, Williams, Harkes, Carsley, Johnson (Cooper), Stallard, Sturridge.
Udinese: Battistini; Compagnon, Berlotto, Pierini, Calori, Ripa, Lasalandra, Scarchilli, Banchelli (Prevedini), Pizzi, Poggi.

Stoke C (2) 4 *(Butler, Carruthers 2, Gleghorn)*

Piacenza (0) 0 7240

Stoke C: Muggleton; Butler, Sandford, Cranson, Overson, Clarkson (Shaw), Wallace, Beeston, Carruthers (Biggins), Peschisolido, Gleghorn.
Piacenza: Ramon; Cesari, Rossini, Suppa, Di Cintio, Lucci, Piovani, Brioschi (Colombotti), De Vitis, Moretti, Manganiello (Papais).

Ancona (0) 3 *(Caccia 2, Artistico)*

Middlesbrough (1) 1 *(Morris)* 1500

Ancona: Pinna; Nicola, Cangini (Pasaresi), Tangorra, Tomei, Sergio, Sesia, Catanese, Artistico, Centofanti (Baglieri), Caccia.
Middlesbrough: Roberts; Morris, Byrne, Liddle, Barron, White, Stamp, O'Halloran, Moreno (Richardson), Mustoe (Norton), Wright.

Semi-Final First Leg

8 DEC

Ancona (0) 1 *(Centofanti)*

Ascoli (0) 2 *(Incocciati 2)* 4311

Ancona: Berti; Nicola, Sergio, Tangorra (Centofanti), Cornacchia, Sgro, Cangini, Sesia, Artistico (Baglieri), Catanese, Caccia.
Ascoli: Bizzarri; Mancini, Mancuso (Binotto), Marcato, Pascucci, Zanoncelli, Menolascina, Cavaliere, Mirabelli (Benetti), Favo, Incocciati.

Semi-Final Second Leg

30 DEC

Ascoli (0) 0

Ancona (1) 1 *(Cornacchia)* 3705

Ascoli: Bizzarri; Mancini, Mancuso, Marcato (Spinelli), Fusco, Zanoncelli, Cavaliere, Bosi, Bierhoff, Favo, Mirabelli (Binotto).
Ancona: Berti; Cornacchia, Sergio, Tangorra, Baroni, Sgro, De Angelis, Sesia, Artistico, Cantanese (Cangini), Caccia.

Semi-Final First Leg

24 JAN

Notts Co (0) 0

Stoke C (0) 0 5135

Notts Co: Kearton; Mills, Legg, Turner, Murphy, Johnson (Matthews), Devlin, Butler, Lund (Slawson), Nicol, White.
Stoke C: Sinclair; Clarkson, Sandford, Cranson, Overson, Allen, Butler, Wallace, Carruthers, Gayle, Gleghorn (Downing).

Semi-Final Second Leg

31 JAN

Stoke C (0) 0

Notts Co (0) 0 10,741

Stoke C: Sinclair; Clarkson, Sandford, Cranson, Overson, Allen, Wallace, Peschisolido (Downing), Carruthers, Gayle (Sturridge), Gleghorn.
Notts Co: Kearton; Mills, Legg, Turner, Murphy, Hogg, Simpson, Butler (Johnson), Agana, Nicol, White (Devlin).
aet; Notts Co won 3-2 on penalties.

Final at Wembley

19 MAR

Notts Co (2) 2 *(Agana, White)*

Ascoli (1) 1 *(Mirabelli)* 11,704

Notts Co: Cherry (Reece); Mills, Legg, Turner, Murphy, Johnson (Emenalo), Devlin, Simpson, White, Short, Agana (Gallagher).
Ascoli: Bizzarri; Benetti, Mancuso (Milana), Marcato, Pascucci, Zanoncelli, Binotto (Menolascina), Bosi, Favo, Mirabelli, Bierhoff.
Referee: C. Agius (Malta).

AUTO WINDSCREENS SHIELD 1994–95

First Round

27 SEPT

Darlington (2) 2 *(Himsworth, Olsson)*
Carlisle U (2) 3 *(Currie 2, Gallimore (pen))* 1583
Darlington: Pollitt; Appleby, Cross, Banks, Crosby, Reed (Gregan), Himsworth (Slaven), Painter, Gaughan, Olsson, Chapman.
Carlisle U: Caig; Joyce, Gallimore, Walling, Valentine, Edmondson, Thomas, Currie (Thorpe), Reeves, Davey, Prokas.

Hull C (0) 0
Doncaster R (1) 2 *(Thew, Jones)* 890
Hull C: Wilson; Mail, Graham, Allison, Dewhurst, Abbott, Peacock, Lee, Hargreaves (Mann), Atkinson, Lawford.
Doncaster R: Williams D; Kirby, Hackett, Thew, Wilcox, Swailes, Lawrence, Roche, Jones, Harper, Parrish.

Scunthorpe U (0) 1 *(Alexander)*
Rotherham U (3) 3 *(Helliwell, Goater, Todd)* 1404
Scunthorpe U: Samways; Ford, Mudd, Thornber, Knill, Bradley, Alexander, Bullimore (Martin), Goodacre (Sansam), Henderson, Smith.
Rotherham U: Clarke; Wilder, James, Williams A, Breckin, Brien, Hazel, Goodwin, Helliwell, Goater (Varadi), Todd.

Crewe Alex (0) 0
Wrexham (0) 0 1573
Crewe Alex: Gayle; Booty, Smith S, Murphy, Whalley, Barr, Garvey, Collins, Ward, Gardiner, Rowbotham.
Wrexham: Marriott; Jones, Hardy, Hughes (Williams), Hunter, Pejic, Bennett, Owen, Connolly, Watkin (Cross), Durkan.

Blackpool (1) 1 *(Mitchell)*
Rochdale (0) 2 *(Stuart, Burke (og))* 1817
Blackpool: Martin; Brown, Burke, Horner, Thompson, Moore, Rodwell, Beech, Quinn, Ellis, Mitchell.
Rochdale: Clarke (Ryan); Thackeray, Formby, Russell, Matthews, Butler, Thompson, Peake, Williams, Whitehall, Stuart.

Preston NE (1) 1 *(Trebble)*
Chester C (0) 1 *(Page)* 3242
Preston NE: Richardson; Fensome, Kidd, Whalley (Cartwright), Squires, Moyes, Ainsworth, Bryson, Sale, Trebble (Fleming), Raynor.
Chester C: Newland; Jenkins, Burnham (Ratcliffe), Alsford, Preece, Shelton, Page, Priest, Lightfoot, Chambers (Murphy), Flitcroft.

Cardiff C (0) 2 *(Griffith, Dale)*
Plymouth Arg (0) 0 1299
Cardiff C: Williams D; Perry, Searle, Aizlewood, Baddeley, Oatway, Millar, Griffith, Bird, Dale, Adams (Richardson).
Plymouth Arg: Nicholls; Patterson, Naylor, Hill, Comyn, Burnett (Edworthy), Barlow, Morgan, Evans (Skinner), Landon, Twiddy.

Hereford U (2) 4 *(Smith, Preedy, White, Cross)*
Torquay U (0) 2 *(Laight, Darby)* 1046
Hereford U: Pennock; Clark, Preedy, Reece, Smith, James, Gonzague, Pick, Cross, White, Lyne.
Torquay U: Davis; Hodges (Hathaway), Kelly, Okorie, Moore, Barrow, Trollope, Buckle (Laight), Hancox, Darby, Goodridge.

Oxford U (1) 2 *(Moody 2)*
Bristol R (0) 2 *(Skinner (pen), Clark)* 1518
Oxford U: Deegan; Robinson, Ford M, Lewis, Elliott, Dyer, Massey, Smith, Moody, Byrne (Rush), Allen.
Bristol R: Parkin; Pritchard, Gurney, Browning, Clark, Wright, Paul, Miller, Taylor, Skinner, Archer.

Gillingham (1) 1 *(Carpenter)*
Brighton & HA (1) 1 *(McDougald)* 963
Gillingham: Banks; Dunne, Watson, Carpenter, Green, Butler, Micklewhite, Smith, Reinelt, Ritchie, Smillie (Watts).
Brighton & HA: Rust; Smith, Tuck, Simmonds, McCarthy, Bissett, Munday, McDougald (Andrews), Nogan, Minton, Chapman.

Colchester U (0) 1 *(Abrahams)*
Leyton Orient (0) 0 1486
Colchester U: Cheesewright; Betts, English, Cawley, Caesar, Dennis, Locke, Brown, Whitton, Kinsella, Abrahams.
Leyton Orient: Heald; Warren (Lakin), Austin, Purse, Howard, Hague, Putney, Cockerill, Carter, West, Martin (Barnett).

Barnet (0) 0
Cambridge U (2) 2 *(Lillis, Corazzin)* 995
Barnet: Phillips; McDonald, Gale, Hoddle, Newson, Primus (Alexander) (Tomlinson), Haynes, Freedman, Hodges, Scott, Wilson.
Cambridge U: Filan; Hunter, Barrick, Craddock, O'Shea, Hayrettin (Fowler), Lillis (Morah), Walker, Butler, Corazzin, Joseph.

Peterborough U (2) 3 *(Henry, Brissett, Charlery)*
Birmingham C (3) 5 *(Bull, Dominguez, Hunt 3)* 2044
Peterborough U: Tyler; Webster, Spearing, Ebdon, Heald, Breen, Morrison (Lormor), McGorry, Brissett, Charlery, Henry.
Birmingham C: Price; Scott, Frain, Ward, Barnett, Daish, Hunt, Claridge, Bull (McGavin), Poole, Dominguez (Wallace).

11 OCT

Bradford C (1) 1 *(Kamara)*
Huddersfield T (0) 2 *(Baldry, Booth)* 2772
Bradford C: Tomlinson; Huxford, Grayston, Duxbury, Oliver, Benn, Shutt, Kamara, Taylor, Power, Midgley.
Hudderfield T: Blackwell, Billy, Cowan, Logan, Gray, Mitchell, Crosby (Baldry), Clayton, Booth, Dunn, Starbuck (Collins).

17 OCT

Doncaster R (1) 1 *(Turner)*
Lincoln C (0) 0 1480
Doncaster R: Williams D; Kirby, Hackett, Brabin, Wilcox, Swailes, Lawrence, Roche, Turner (Finlay), Harper, Parrish.
Lincoln C: Hoult; West, Lucas, Foley, Greenall, Brown, Hebberd, Onwere (Daley), Bannister, Carbon, Puttnam (Johnson A).

18 OCT

Carlisle U (0) 2 *(Thomas, Arnold)*
Hartlepool U (0) 0 2563
Carlisle U: Elliott; Edmondson (Murray), Gallimore, Walling, Mountfield, Conway, Thomas (Thorpe), Arnold, Reeves, Davey, Prokas.
Hartlepool U: Horne; Ingram, Walsh, Gilchrist, McGuckin, Ainsley, Sloan, Oliver, Houchen (Thompson), Foster, Southall.

Hudderfield T (1) 3 *(Mitchell, Clayton, Starbuck (pen))*
York C (0) 0 4183
Huddersfield T: Blackwell; Trevitt, Billy, Mitchell, Scully (Dyson), Gray, Crosby, Clayton, Dunn (Baldry), Jepson, Starbuck.
York C: Kiely; McMillan, Wilson, Pepper, Tutill, Barras, McCarthy, Naylor (Baker), Barnes, Jordan (Atkin), Canham.

Rotherham U (0) 1 *(Goater)*
Chesterfield (0) 1 *(Roberts)* 1585
Rotherham U: Clarke; Wilder, James, Williams A, Breckin, Brien, Hayward, Marginson, Davison, Goater, Dolby.
Chesterfield: Beasley; Hewitt, Rogers, Perkins, Madden (Cheetham), Fairclough, Curtis, Davies, Morris (Roberts), Moss, Dyche.

Wrexham (1) 2 *(Bennett 2)*
Mansfield T (0) 0 1002
Wrexham: Marriott; Jones, Hardy, Brammer, Hunter, Humes, Bennett, Owen, Connolly, Cross, Hughes.
Mansfield T: Pearcey; Boothroyd, Aspinall (Marrows), Timons, Howarth, Peters, Ireland, Castledine, Hadley, Doolan, Noteman.

Rochdale (0) 1 *(Taylor)*
Wigan Ath (0) 0 1004
Rochdale: Dickins; Thackeray, Formby, Reid, Doyle, Butler, Thompson (Ryan), Hall, Williams, Whitehall, Sharpe (Taylor).
Wigan Ath: Farnworth; Carragher, Jakub, Strong, Rennie, Farrell, Kilford, Morton (Adekola), Leonard, Rimmer, Lyons.

Chester C (2) 3 *(Shelton 2, Page)*
Bury (0) 1 *(Rigby)* 841
Chester C: Felgate; Jenkins, Burnham, Ratcliffe, Lightfoot, Shelton, Chambers, Priest, Preece, Page, Hackett.
Bury: Kelly G; Jackson (Hughes), Stanislaus, Daws, Lucketti, Matthewson, Paskin (Mulligan), Carter, Rigby, Johnrose, Pugh.

Birmingham C (1) 3 *(Shearer 2, Donowa)*
Walsall (0) 0 10,089
Birmingham C: Bennett; Poole, Donowa, Ward, Barnett, Daish, Hunt, Claridge (Doherty), Bull, De Souza (McGavin), Shearer.
Walsall: Wood; Ryder, Gibson, Rogers, Ntamark, Palmer, Peer, Mehew (Keister), Lightbourne, Wilson, Houghton.

Cambridge U (1) 1 *(Lillis)*
Northampton T (0) 3 *(Warburton, Grayson, Aldridge)* 1497
Cambridge U: Filan; Nyamah (Granville), Barrick, Craddock, O'Shea, Danzey, Lillis (Hay), Walker, Butler, Corazzin, Joseph.
Northampton T: Ovendale; Pascoe (Cahill), Skelly, Sampson, Warburton, Curtis, Harmon, Williams, McNamara (Wilkin), Aldridge, Grayson.

Leyton Orient (4) 5 *(Purse, Dempsey, West 3 (1 pen))*
Fulham (1) 2 *(Mison, Haworth)* 1282
Leyton Orient: Heald; Howard (Warren), Austin, Bellamy, Hendon, Bogie, Lakin, Cockerill, Purse (Carter), West, Dempsey.
Fulham: Stannard; Jupp, Angus, Hurlock, Moore, Blake, Mison, Morgan, Hails (Haworth), Brazil, Thomas M (Bedrossian).

Plymouth Arg (0) 1 *(Naylor)*
Exeter C (1) 3 *(Cecere 2, Cooper)* 1847
Plymouth Arg: Nicholls; Edworthy, Naylor, Hill, Comyn, Burnett, Barlow, Skinner, O'Hagan, Landon (Nugent), Twiddy.
Exeter C: Fox; Minett, Rice, Cooper M, Hare, Brown, Storer, Thirlby (Phillips), Turner, Coughlin, Cecere.

Torquay U (1) 1 *(Moore)*
Swansea C (2) 3 *(Hendry 2, Bowen)* 885
Torquay U: Bayes; Brass, Kelly (Goodridge), Burton, Moore, Curran, Trollope, Darby (Laight), Hancox, Okorie, Hathaway.
Swansea C: Jones; Jenkins, Ford, Basham, Harris, Pascoe, Bowen, Penney, Hendry, Chapple, Hodge (Hayes).

19 OCT

Bristol R (0) 1 *(Stewart (pen))*
Bournemouth (0) 1 *(Murray)* 1725
Bristol R: Collett; Pritchard, Maddison, Channing, Clark, Tillson (Skinner), Sterling, Paul (McLean), Stewart, Browning, Gurney.
Bournemouth: Andrews; Young, Chivers, Morris, Watson (Murray), Pennock, Beardsmore, Mean, Aspinall (Reeve), Fletcher, Scully.

Brighton & HA (0) 0
Brentford (0) 1 *(Forster)* 1104
Brighton & HA: Rust; Munday, Tuck, Simmonds (Pates), McCarthy, Bissett, Chamberlain (Funnell), McDougald, Nogan, Codner, Fox M.
Brentford: Dearden; Statham, Grainger, Westley, Ashby, Ratcliffe, Harvey, Hutchings, Mundee, Forster, Stephenson.

1 NOV

Northampton T (1) 3 *(Aldridge, Harmon, Grayson)*
Barnet (0) 1 *(Cooper)* 2618
Northampton T: Ovendale; Pascoe, Colkin, Sampson, Warburton, Williams, Harmon, Grayson, Aldridge, Robinson, Turner (Cahill).
Barnet: Newell; McDonald (Tomlinson), Walker, Hoddle, Newson, Primus, McMahon, Freedman, Hodges (Wilson), Cooper, Scott.

8 NOV

Bury (0) 1 *(Sertori)*
Preston NE (0) 0 1756
Bury: Kelly G; Jackson, Stanislaus, Daws, Lucketti, Matthewson, Hughes, Sertori, Rigby, Johnrose, Mauge.
Preston NE: Vaughan; Fensome, Sharp, Cartwright, Holmes, Moyes, Trebble, Bryson, Raynor, Sale, Fleming (Whalley).

Chesterfield (0) 1 *(Davies)*
Scunthorpe U (0) 1 *(Bullimore (pen))* 1424
Chesterfield: Beasley; Hewitt, Jules, Perkins, Carr, Fairclough, McAuley, Norris, Roberts (Davies), Moss, Dyche.
Scunthorpe U: Samways; Hope, Bradley, Thompstone, Knill, Thornber (Housham), Alexander, Bullimore, Carmichael, Goodacre (Sansam), Smith.

Lincoln C (0) 1 *(West)*
Hull C (0) 0 1626
Lincoln C: Leaning; West, Johnson A, Schofield, Greenall, Brown, Lucas, Matthews, Daley, Johnson D (Carbon), Hill.
Hull C: Wilson; Dakin, Graham, Hobson, Dewhurst, Mann (Abbott), Peacock, Lee, Hargreaves, Windass, Lawford.

Mansfield T (0) 2 *(Alexander 2)*
Crewe Alex (1) 2 *(Collins, Ward)* 1250
Mansfield T: Ward; Timons, Baraclough, Holland (Alexander), Howarth, Peters, Aspinall, Hoyle, Wilkinson, Stark, Noteman.
Crewe Alex: Gayle; Booty, Smith S, Wilson, Barr, Whalley, Garvey (Collier), Collins, Ward, Lennon, Rowbotham.

Hartlepool U (0) 0
Darlington (0) 2 *(Worboys 2)* 1211
Hartlepool U: Horne; Ingram, Walsh, Gilchrist, McGuckin, Ainsley, Oliver, Halliday, Houchen, Foster, Southall.
Darlington: Pollitt; Appleby, Taylor, Banks, Crosby, Gregan, Worboys, Painter, Gaughan, Casson, Himsworth.

Wigan Ath (1) 1 *(Leonard)*
Blackpool (0) 0 1161
Wigan Ath: Farnworth (Statham); Rennie, Jakub, Miller (Strong), Robertson, Farrell, Kilford, Carragher, Leonard, McKearney, Lyons.
Blackpool: Martin; Brown, Burke, Bradshaw, Thompson, Horner, Mitchell, Gouck (Bonner), Watson, Quinn, Griffiths (Sunderland).

York C (1) 2 *(Barnes, Baker)*
Bradford C (0) 2 *(Murray, Tolson)* 2326
York C: Kiely; McMillan, Hall, Pepper, Atkin, Barras, McCarthy, Naylor, Barnes, Baker, Canham.
Bradford C: Tomlinson; Hamilton, Huxford, Duxbury, Sinnott, Oliver, Murray, Kamara, Taylor, Jewell (Tolson), Showler.

Bournemouth (0) 0
Oxford U (0) 0 1374
Bournemouth: Andrews; Young, Pennock, Morris, Watson (Chivers), Leadbitter, Beardsmore, Mean, Robinson, Jones, Scully (Murray).
Oxford U: Deegan; Robinson, Butters, Lewis, Collins, Marsh, Druce (Murphy), Smith, Wanless, Rush, Ford R.

Brentford (2) 3 *(Annon, Asaba, Ansah)*
Gillingham (0) 1 *(Pike)* 1795
Brentford: Dearden (Fernandes); Hurdle, Grainger, Bates, Ashby, Smith, Hutchings, Asaba (Forster), Taylor (Ravenscroft), Annon, Ansah.
Gillingham: Barrett; Arnott, Palmer, Carpenter, Trott, Butler, Hutchinson, Kamara (Ramage), Pike (Micklewhite), Reinelt, Hooker.

Fulham (1) 3 *(Haworth, Adams, Cusack)*
Colchester U (0) 2 *(Abrahams, Kinsella)* 1451
Fulham: Harrison; Finnigan (Jupp), Herrera, Marshall, Angus, Blake, Mison, Morgan, Cusack, Haworth (Williams), Adams.
Colchester U: Cheeswright; Betts, English, Cawley, Caesar, Dennis, Locke, Brown (Fry), Whitton, Kinsella, Abrahams (Burley).

Swansea C (0) 1 *(Torpey)*
Hereford U (1) 1 *(Reece)* 1215
Swansea C: Freestone; Jenkins, Clode (Torpey), Basham, Ford, Ampadu, Bowen, Penney (Hayes), Hendry, Cornforth, Hodge.
Hereford U: Pennock; Llewellyn, Lloyd, Reece, Davies, James, Steele (Smith), Wilkins, Cross (White), Lyne, Fishlock.

Walsall (1) 2 *(Gibson, Marsh)*
Peterborough U (0) 3 *(Heald, Breen, Henry)* 2104
Walsall: Wood; Evans, Gibson, Rogers, Marsh, Palmer, O'Connor, Ntamark, Butler, Wilson, Houghton.
Peterborough U: Cooksey; Heald, Spearing, Ebdon, Breen, Thomas, Farrell, McGorry, Williams, Morrison, Henry.

15 NOV

Exeter C (0) 1 *(Minett (pen))*
Cardiff C (0) 1 *(Young)* 1203
Exeter C: Fox; Minett, Robinson (Phillips), Cooper M, Came, Richardson, Storer, Bailey, Turner, Brown, Gavin (Ross).
Cardiff C: Williams D; Young, Searle, Aizlewood, Baddeley, Millar, Ramsey, Griffith, Stant, Thompson, Adams (Wigg).
Byes to Second Round: Stockport Co, Scarborough, Wycombe W, Shrewsbury T.

Second Round

28 NOV

Doncaster R (0) 0
Bury (1) 1 *(Pugh)* 2859
Doncaster R: Williams D; Kirby, Hackett, Brabin, Wilcox, Kitchen, Lawrence, Meara (Donaldson), Jones, Norbury, Thew (Warren).
Bury: Kelly G; Jackson, Stanislaus, Johnrose, Lucketti, Matthewson, Kelly T, Hulme (Sertori), Hughes, Reid (Daws), Pugh.

29 NOV

Carlisle U (0) 1 *(Currie)*
Chesterfield (0) 0 3531
Carlisle U: Beasley; Dyche, Rogers, Fairclough, Carr, Law, Hewitt, Davies, Morris, McAuley, Jules.
Chesterfield: Caig; Edmondson, Gallimore, Walling, Mountfield, Conway, Thomas, Currie, Reeves, Davey, Prokas.

Chester C (0) 0 1890
Crewe Alex (3) 6 *(Ward 3 (1 pen), Collins, Whalley, Adebola)*
Chester C: Felgate; Jenkins, Ratcliffe, Alsford, Jackson, Preece, Milner, Flitcroft, Murphy (Bishop), Page, Hackett (Rimmer).
Crewe Alex: Smith M; Booty, Smith S, Wilson, Macauley, Whalley (Gardiner), Garvey (Clarkson), Collins, Ward, Lennon, Adebola.

Rochdale (1) 2 *(Whitehall 2)*
Darlington (2) 2 *(Worboys, Appleby (pen)) aet* 1069
Rochdale: Gray; Thackeray, Formby, Reid, Matthews, Butler, Thompson (Taylor), Doyle (Stuart), Sharpe, Whitehall, Ryan.
Darlington: Pollitt; Appleby, Taylor, Banks, Reed, Gregan, Gaughan, Chapman, Worboys, Olsson, Himsworth (Kirkham).
Rochdale won 4-3 on penalties

Rotherham U (0) 1 *(Goater)*
Wigan Ath (2) 3 *(Rimmer, Leonard, Kilford)* 1587
Rotherham U: Clarke; Wilder, James, Ayrton (Smith), Breckin, Brien, Hayward, Richardson, Davison, Goater, Hurst (Varadi).
Wigan Ath: Farnworth; Strong, Jakub, Miller, Robertson, Farrell, Kilford, Carragher, Leonard, Rimmer, Lyons.

Stockport Co (0) 3 *(Dinning, Bound, Ward)*
Scarborough (0) 1 *(Charles)* 2310
Stockport Co: Edwards; Dinning, Todd, Eckhardt, Flynn, Bound, Gannon, Ward (Wallace), Armstrong, Beaumont, Slinn (Chalk).
Scarborough: Martin; Knowles, Wells, Toman (Thompson), Davis, Rockett, Swann (Calvert), Charles, White, Rutherford, D'Auria.

Wrexham (4) 6 *(Bennett 3, Watkin 2, Owen)*
Bradford C (0) 1 *(Power)* 1407
Wrexham: Marriott; Brace, Hardy, Hughes, Hunter, Jones (Phillips), Bennett, Owen, Connolly, Watkin, Durkan (Cross).
Bradford C: Tomlinson; Huxford, Jacobs, Duxbury, Sinnott, Richards (Power), Shutt (Showler), Oliver, Taylor, Jewell, Murray.

Birmingham C (2) 3 *(McGavin, Poole, Tait)*
Gillingham (0) 0 17,028
Birmingham C: Bennett; Poole, Whyte, Ward (Lowe), Barnett, Daish, Donowa (Cooper), Claridge, McGavin, Dominguez, Tait.
Gillingham: Barrett; Lindsey, Palmer, Carpenter, Arnott, Bodley, Hutchinson, Foster (Ramage), Pike, Reinelt, Watson.

Bristol R (2) 4 *(Skinner, Stewart 2 (1 pen), Miller)*
Cambridge U (2) 2 *(Corazzin, Hay)* 2373
Bristol R: Parkin; Pritchard, Gurney, Browning, Clark, Tillson, Sterling, Miller, Stewart, Skinner, Archer.
Cambridge U: Sheffield; Joseph, Barrick, Craddock, Jeffrey, Hyde, Fowler, Granville, Butler (Lillis), Corazzin (Hunter), Hay.

Exeter C (0) 1 *(Brown)*
Cardiff C (0) 0 1452
Exeter C: Woodman; Minett, Brown, Bailey, Daniels, Richardson, Storer, Coughlin, Cooper M, Cecere (Morgan), Gavin.
Cardiff C: Williams S; Evans (Griffith), Searle, Oatway, Baddeley, Brazil, Ramsey, Richardson, Stant, Thompson, Fereday (Dale).

Hereford U (1) 2 *(James, Reece)*
Peterborough U (0) 0 1301
Hereford U: Pennock; Reece, Lloyd, Smith, Fishlock, James, Pounder, Wilkins, White, Lyne, Pick.
Peterborough U: Tyler; Heald, Spearing, Ebdon (Brissett), Breen, Thomas, Moran, Webster (Clark), Williams, Charlery, Lormor.

Leyton Orient (1) 1 *(West)*
Fulham (0) 0 1575
Leyton Orient: Heald; Hendon, Austin, Bellamy, Howard, Brooks, Barnett, Cockerill, Purse (Bogie), West (Warren), Carter.
Fulham: Stannard; Jupp, Herrera, Hurlock, Moore, Blake, Marshall (Hamill), Morgan, Cusack, Brazil, Adams.

Northampton T (0) 0
Swansea C (1) 1 *(Hendry)* 2706
Northampton T: Stewart; Norton, Skelly, Sampson, Warburton (Curtis), Williams, Harmon, Grayson, Trott (Harrison), Robinson, Cahill.
Swansea C: Freestone; Jenkins, Barnhouse, Basham, Ford, Chapple, Bowen, Penney, Hendry, Cornforth, Hodge (Hayes).

Shrewsbury T (1) 2 *(Williams, Stevens)*
Wycombe W (0) 0 1785
Shrewsbury T: Edwards; Seabury, Lynch, Taylor, Williams, Patterson, Smith, Hughes, Spink (Slawson), Stevens, Evans.
Wycombe W: Hyde; Cousins, Brown, Crossley, Creaser, Ryan, Kerr (Langford), Bell, Turnbull (Hemmings), Reid, Stapleton.

30 NOV

Huddersfield T (0) 3 *(Crosby, Jepson (pen), Dunn)*
Lincoln C (2) 2 *(Daley, Johnson D) aet, sd* 5738
Huddersfield T: Blackwell; Trevitt, Williams, Logan, Gray, Mitchell, Billy, Clayton (Booth), Dunn, Jepson, Collins (Crosby).
Lincoln C: Leaning; West, Johnson A, Foley (Carbon), Dixon, Brown, Johnson D, Hebberd (Matthews), Daley, Daws, Hill.

3 DEC

Brentford (0) 1 *(Grainger (pen))*
Oxford U (0) 2 *(Murphy, Ashby (og))* 2410
Brentford: Dearden; Statham, Grainger, Ashby, Westley (Annon), Harvey, Forster (Hutchings), Taylor, Bates, Mundee, Ansah.
Oxford U: Whitehead; Robinson, Lewis, Dyer, Elliott, Wood (Wanless), Murphy, Smith, Rush, Byrne, Ford R.

Northern Section quarter-final

10 JAN

Carlisle U (1) 2 *(Thomas, Hunter (og))*
Wrexham (0) 1 *(Bennett)* 8771
Carlisle U: Caig; Edmondson, Gallimore, Walling, Robinson, Conway, Thomas (Thorpe), Currie, Reeves (Peters), Davey, Prokas.
Wrexham: Marriott; Jones, Hardy, Hughes, Hunter, Humes, Bennett, Owen, Connolly, Cross (Morris), Durkan.

Southern Section quarter-finals

Birmingham C (1) 3 *(Claridge, Ward (pen), Otto)*
Hereford U (1) 1 *(Lyne)* 22,352
Birmingham C: Bennett; Poole, Cooper, Ward, Barnett, Daish, Donowa, Claridge, Lowe (Dominguez), Otto, Shearer.
Hereford U: McKenzie; Davies, Lloyd, Reece, Smith, Brownrigg, Clark, Gregory (Brough), White, Lyne, Pick.

Leyton Orient (0) 0
Bristol R (0) 0 1381
Leyton Orient: Heald; Howard, Austin, Purse, Hague, Bogie, Carter, Hendon, Warren (Barnett), Brooks, Dempsey.
Bristol R: Parkin; Channing, Gurney, Hardyman, Clark, Tillson, Sterling, Miller, Taylor (Paul), Skinner (Maddison), Archer.
aet; Leyton Orient won 4-3 on penalties

Oxford U (0) 1 *(Ford R)*
Swansea C (1) 2 *(Torpey, Hayes)* 2321
Oxford U: Deegan; Robinson, Marsh, Dyer (Murphy), Elliott, Rogan, Ford R, Smith, Druce, Rush, Allen.
Swansea C: Freestone; Jenkins (Chapple), Walker, Basham, Ford, Ampadu, Hayes, Penney, Torpey, Cornforth, Hodge.

Shrewsbury T (1) 3 *(Spink, Stevens 2)*
Exeter C (0) 1 *(Richardson)* 1960
Shrewsbury T: Edwards; Hockaday, Withe, Taylor (Lynch), Williams, Summerfield, Woods, Clarke W (Stevens), Spink, Walton, Jeffers.
Exeter C: Woodman; Minett, Robinson, Bailey, Daniels, Richardson, Storer, Cooper M, Gavin, Anderson, Cecere.

Northern Section quarter-finals

11 JAN

Rochdale (1) 2 *(Whitehall 2)*
Stockport Co (1) 1 *(Wallace)* 2154
Rochdale: Gray; Thackeray, Formby, Reid (Hall), Matthews, Butler, Thompson, Peake, Sharpe (Russell), Whitehall, Stuart.
Stockport Co: Edwards; Connelly (Gannon), Todd, Dinning (Young), Flynn, Bound, Ware, Wallace, Armstrong, Beaumont, Chalk.

24 JAN

Bury (1) 2 *(Kelly T 2)*
Huddersfield T (0) 1 *(Clayton)* 3311
Bury: Kelly G; Cross, Stanislaus, Mauge (Daws), Lucketti, Hughes, Kelly T, Carter, Paskin, Johnrose, Pugh.
Huddersfield T: Francis; Short (Billy), Cowan, Logan, Scully, Dyson, Dunn, Clayton (Crosby), Booth, Jepson, Reid.

Southern Section semi-finals

31 JAN

Birmingham C (1) 3 *(Claridge, Francis, Tait)*
Swansea C (2) 2 *(Pascoe, Lowe (og)) aet, sd* 20,326
Birmingham C: Bennett; Scott, Cooper, Ward, Barnett, Whyte, Donowa (Dominguez), Claridge, Francis, Otto, Lowe (Tait).
Swansea C: Freestone; Jenkins, Walker, Basham, Ford, Pascoe (McFarlane), Hayes, Penney, Torpey, Cornforth, Hodge (Bowen).

Leyton Orient (1) 2 *(Warren, Brooks)*
Shrewsbury T (0) 1 *(Stevens)* 2913
Leyton Orient: Heald; Hendon, Howard, Bellamy, Purse, Brooks, Carter, Cockerill, Bogie (Gray), Warren, Dempsey.
Shrewsbury T: Edwards; Hockaday, Withe, Taylor, Williams, Lynch, Woods (Seabury), Evans, Spink, Stevens, Jeffers.

Northern Section quarter-final

7 FEB

Wigan Ath (0) 1 *(Farrell)*
Crewe Alex (2) 3 *(Whalley, Macauley, Adebola)* 2063
Wigan Ath: Farnworth; Carragher (Benjamin), Wright (Jakub), Miller, Robertson, Farrell, Doolan, McKearney, Leonard, Rimmer, Lyons.
Crewe Alex: Smith M; Booty, Smith S, Barr, Macauley, Whalley, Murphy, Collins (Collier), Adebola (Tierney), Lennon, Clarkson.

Northern Section semi-finals

Bury (1) 1 *(Paskin)*
Rochdale (2) 2 *(Sharpe, Reid)* 3341
Bury: Kelly G; Daws, Bimson, Mauge, Lucketti, Matthewson (Rigby), Kelly T, Hulme, Paskin (Carter), Johnrose, Pugh.
Rochdale: Gray; Thackeray (Russell), Formby, Reid, Matthews, Butler, Thompson, Peake, Sharpe (Stuart), Whitehall, Deary.

14 FEB

Crewe Alex (0) 0
Carlisle U (1) 1 *(Thomas)* 4046
Crewe Alex: Smith M; Booty, Smith S, Barr, Macauley, Whalley, Murphy, Tierney (Rowbotham), Clarkson, Lennon, Garvey.
Carlisle U: Caig; Edmondson, Gallimore, Walling, Mountfield, Conway, Thomas, Currie (Peters), Reeves, Davey, Murray (Robinson).

Northern Section final, first leg

28 FEB

Carlisle U (3) 4 *(Currie, Thomas 2, Conway)*
Rochdale (0) 1 *(Whitehall (pen))* 8647

Carlisle U: Caig; Edmondson, Gallimore, Walling, Mountfield, Peters, Thomas, Currie (Thorpe), Reeves (Robinson), Conway, Prokas.
Rochdale: Clarke; Thackeray, Formby, Reid, Matthews, Butler, Thompson, Peake, Deary (Hall), Whitehall, Sharpe (Ryan).

Southern Section final, first leg

Birmingham C (0) 1 *(Shearer)*
Leyton Orient (0) 0 24,002

Birmingham C: Bennett; Poole, Cooper, Tait (Whyte), Barnett, Daish, Donowa, Saville (McGavin), Francis, Otto, Shearer.
Leyton Orient: Heald; Hendon, Austin, Bellamy, Purse, Bogie, Carter, Cockerill, Barnett (Warren), West, Dempsey.

Northern Section final, second leg

14 MAR

Rochdale (2) 2 *(Whitehall, Reid)*
Carlisle U (1) 1 *(Mountfield)* 4082

Rochdale: Clarke; Thackeray, Formby (Stuart), Reid (Ryan), Matthews, Butler, Thompson, Peake, Sharpe, Whitehall, Deary.
Carlisle U: Caig; Edmondson, Gallimore, Walling, Mountfield, Hayward, Thorpe (Robinson), Currie, Reeves, Conway, Prokas.

Southern Section final, second leg

Leyton Orient (0) 2 *(Purse, McGleish)*
Birmingham C (1) 3 *(Claridge 2, Williams)* 10,830

Leyton Orient: Heald; Hendon, Austin, Bellamy, Purse, Bogie, McGleish, Cockerill, Read (Hague), West (Warren), Dempsey.
Birmingham C: Bennett; Poole, Whyte, Ward, Barnett, Daish, Esteves (Tait), Claridge, Robinson, Otto (Doherty), Williams.

Final at Wembley

23 APR

Birmingham C (0) 1 *(Tait)*
Carlisle U (0) 0 76,663

Birmingham C: Bennett; Poole, Cooper, Ward, Barnett, Daish, Hunt, Claridge, Francis (Donowa), Otto, Shearer (Tait).
Carlisle U: Caig; Edmondson, Gallimore, Walling, Mountfield (Robinson), Hayward, Thomas, Currie, Reeves, Conway, Prokas (Thorpe).
aet; Birmingham C won on sudden death.
Referee: P. Foakes (Clacton).

David Currie (centre) is carefully watched by two Birmingham defenders as Carlisle lose 1-0 in the Auto Windscreens Shield Final at Wembley. (Colorsport)

FOOTBALL LEAGUE COMPETITION ATTENDANCES

SEASON 1994–1995

ANGLO-ITALIAN CUP

(Games played in England only)

Round	*Aggregate*	*Matches*	*Average*
Inter	67,354	16	4,210
Semi-finals	15,876	2	7,938
Final	11,704	1	11,704
Total	94,934	19	4,997

COCA-COLA CUP

Round	*Aggregate*	*Matches*	*Average*
Round one	195,339	56	3,488
Round two	624,836	64	9,763
Round three	296,298	19	15,595
Round four	148,853	8	18,607
Round five	80,505	4	20,126
Semi-finals	78,896	4	19,724
Final	75,595	1	75,595
Total	1,500,322	156	9,617

AUTO WINDSCREENS SHIELD

Round	*Aggregate*	*Matches*	*Average*
Round one	77,233	42	1,839
Round two	51,203	16	3,200
Area quarter-finals	44,313	8	5,539
Area semi-finals	30,626	4	7,657
Area finals	47,561	4	11,890
Final	76,633	1	76,633
Total	327,569	75	4,368

FA CUP FINALS 1872–1995

1872 and 1874–92	Kennington Oval	1911	Replay at Old Trafford
1873	Lillie Bridge	1912	Replay at Bramall Lane
1886	Replay at Derby (Racecourse Ground)		
1893	Fallowfield, Manchester	1915	Old Trafford, Manchester
1894	Everton	1920–22	Stamford Bridge
1895–1914	Crystal Palace	1923 to date	Wembley
1901	Replay at Bolton	1970	Replay at Old Trafford
1910	Replay at Everton	1981	Replay at Wembley

Year	*Winners*	*Runners-up*	*Score*
1872	Wanderers	Royal Engineers	1-0
1873	Wanderers	Oxford University	2-0
1874	Oxford University	Royal Engineers	2-0
1875	Royal Engineers	Old Etonians	2-0 (after 1-1 draw aet)
1876	Wanderers	Old Etonians	3-0 (after 1-1 draw aet)
1877	Wanderers	Oxford University	2-1 (aet)
1878	Wanderers*	Royal Engineers	3-1
1879	Old Etonians	Clapham R	1-0
1880	Clapham R	Oxford University	1-0
1881	Old Carthusians	Old Etonians	3-0
1882	Old Etonians	Blackburn R	1-0
1883	Blackburn Olympic	Old Etonians	2-1 (aet)
1884	Blackburn R	Queen's Park, Glasgow	2-1
1885	Blackburn R	Queen's Park, Glasgow	2-0
1886	Blackburn R†	WBA	2-0 (after 0-0 draw)
1887	Aston Villa	WBA	2-0
1888	WBA	Preston NE	2-1
1889	Preston NE	Wolverhampton W	3-0
1890	Blackburn R	Sheffield W	6-1
1891	Blackburn R	Notts Co	3-1
1892	WBA	Aston Villa	3-0
1893	Wolverhampton W	Everton	1-0
1894	Notts Co	Bolton W	4-1
1895	Aston Villa	WBA	1-0
1896	Sheffield W	Wolverhampton W	2-1
1897	Aston Villa	Everton	3-2
1898	Nottingham F	Derby Co	3-1
1899	Sheffield U	Derby Co	4-1
1900	Bury	Southampton	4-0
1901	Tottenham H	Sheffield U	3-1 (after 2-2 draw)
1902	Sheffield U	Southampton	2-1 (after 1-1 draw)
1903	Bury	Derby Co	6-0
1904	Manchester C	Bolton W	1-0
1905	Aston Villa	Newcastle U	2-0
1906	Everton	Newcastle U	1-0
1907	Sheffield W	Everton	2-1
1908	Wolverhampton W	Newcastle U	3-1
1909	Manchester U	Bristol C	1-0
1910	Newcastle U	Barnsley	2-0 (after 1-1 draw)
1911	Bradford C	Newcastle U	1-0 (after 0-0 draw)
1912	Barnsley	WBA	1-0 (aet, after 0-0 draw)
1913	Aston Villa	Sunderland	1-0
1914	Burnley	Liverpool	1-0
1915	Sheffield U	Chelsea	3-0
1920	Aston Villa	Huddersfield T	1-0 (aet)
1921	Tottenham H	Wolverhampton W	1-0
1922	Huddersfield T	Preston NE	1-0
1923	Bolton W	West Ham U	2-0
1924	Newcastle U	Aston Villa	2-0
1925	Sheffield U	Cardiff C	1-0
1926	Bolton W	Manchester C	1-0
1927	Cardiff C	Arsenal	1-0
1928	Blackburn R	Huddersfield T	3-1
1929	Bolton W	Portsmouth	2-0
1930	Arsenal	Huddersfield T	2-0
1931	WBA	Birmingham	2-1
1932	Newcastle U	Arsenal	2-1
1933	Everton	Manchester C	3-0
1934	Manchester C	Portsmouth	2-1
1935	Sheffield W	WBA	4-2
1936	Arsenal	Sheffield U	1-0
1937	Sunderland	Preston NE	3-1
1938	Preston NE	Huddersfield T	1-0 (aet)
1939	Portsmouth	Wolverhampton W	4-1
1946	Derby Co	Charlton Ath	4-1 (aet)
1947	Charlton Ath	Burnley	1-0 (aet)
1948	Manchester U	Blackpool	4-2
1949	Wolverhampton W	Leicester C	3-1
1950	Arsenal	Liverpool	2-0
1951	Newcastle U	Blackpool	2-0
1952	Newcastle U	Arsenal	1-0

Year	Winners	Runners-up	Score
1953	Blackpool	Bolton W	4-3
1954	WBA	Preston NE	3-2
1955	Newcastle U	Manchester C	3-1
1956	Manchester C	Birmingham C	3-1
1957	Aston Villa	Manchester U	2-1
1958	Bolton W	Manchester U	2-0
1959	Nottingham F	Luton T	2-1
1960	Wolverhampton W	Blackburn R	3-0
1961	Tottenham H	Leicester C	2-0
1962	Tottenham H	Burnley	3-1
1963	Manchester U	Leicester C	3-1
1964	West Ham U	Preston NE	3-2
1965	Liverpool	Leeds U	2-1 (aet)
1966	Everton	Sheffield W	3-2
1967	Tottenham H	Chelsea	2-1
1968	WBA	Everton	1-0 (aet)
1969	Manchester C	Leicester C	1-0
1970	Chelsea	Leeds U	2-1 (aet)
	(after 2-2 draw, after extra time, at Wembley)		
1971	Arsenal	Liverpool	2-1 (aet)
1972	Leeds U	Arsenal	1-0
1973	Sunderland	Leeds U	1-0
1974	Liverpool	Newcastle U	3-0
1975	West Ham U	Fulham	2-0
1976	Southampton	Manchester U	1-0
1977	Manchester U	Liverpool	2-1
1978	Ipswich	Arsenal	1-0
1979	Arsenal	Manchester U	3-2
1980	West Ham U	Arsenal	1-0
1981	Tottenham H	Manchester C	3-2
	(after 1-1 draw, after extra time, at Wembley)		
1982	Tottenham H	QPR	1-0
	(after 1-1 draw, after extra time, at Wembley)		
1983	Manchester U	Brighton & HA	4-0
	(after 2-2 draw, after extra time, at Wembley)		
1984	Everton	Watford	2-0
1985	Manchester U	Everton	1-0 (aet)
1986	Liverpool	Everton	3-1
1987	Coventry C	Tottenham H	3-2 (aet)
1988	Wimbledon	Liverpool	1-0
1989	Liverpool	Everton	3-2 (aet)
1990	Manchester U	Crystal Palace	1-0
	(after 3-3 draw, after extra time, at Wembley)		
1991	Tottenham H	Nottingham F	2-1 (aet)
1992	Liverpool	Sunderland	2-0
1993	Arsenal	Sheffield W	2-1 (aet)
	(after 1-1 draw, after extra time, at Wembley)		
1994	Manchester U	Chelsea	4-0
1995	Everton	Manchester U	1-0

* *Won outright, but restored to the Football Association.*
† *A special trophy was awarded for third consecutive win.*

FA CUP WINS

Manchester U 8, Tottenham H 8, Aston Villa 7, Arsenal 6, Blackburn R 6, Newcastle U 6, Everton 5, Liverpool 5, The Wanderers 5, WBA 5, Bolton W 4, Manchester C 4, Sheffield U 4, Wolverhampton W 4, Sheffield W 3, West Ham U 3, Bury 2, Nottingham F 2, Old Etonians 2, Preston NE 2, Sunderland 2, Barnsley 1, Blackburn Olympic 1, Blackpool 1, Bradford C 1, Burnley 1, Cardiff C 1, Charlton Ath 1, Chelsea 1, Clapham R 1, Coventry C 1, Derby Co 1, Huddersfield T 1, Ipswich T 1, Leeds U 1, Notts Co 1, Old Carthusians 1, Oxford University 1, Portsmouth 1, Royal Engineers 1, Southampton 1, Wimbledon 1.

APPEARANCES IN FINALS

Manchester U 13, Arsenal 12, Everton 12, Newcastle U 11, WBA 10, Liverpool 10, Aston Villa 9, Tottenham H 9, Blackburn R 8, Manchester C 8, Wolverhampton W 8, Bolton W 7, Preston NE 7, Old Etonians 6, Sheffield U 6, Sheffield W 6, Huddersfield T 5, *The Wanderers 5, Chelsea 4, Derby Co 4, Leeds U 4, Leicester C 4, Oxford University 4, Royal Engineers 4, Sunderland 4, West Ham U 4, Blackpool 3, Burnley 3, Nottingham F 3, Portsmouth 3, Southampton 3, Barnsley 2, Birmingham C 2, *Bury 2, Cardiff C 2, Charlton Ath 2, Clapham R 2, Notts Co 2, Queen's Park (Glasgow) 2, *Blackburn Olympic 1, *Bradford C 1, Brighton & HA 1, Bristol C 1, *Coventry C 1, Crystal Palace 1, Fulham 1, *Ipswich T 1, Luton 4, *Old Carthusians 1, QPR 1, Watford 1, *Wimbledon 1.

* *Denotes undefeated.*

APPEARANCES IN SEMI-FINALS

Everton 23, Manchester U 20, Liverpool 19, WBA 19, Arsenal 18, Aston Villa 17, Blackburn R 16, Sheffield W 16, Tottenham H 15, Derby Co 13, Newcastle U 13, Wolverhampton W 13, Bolton W 12, Nottingham F 12, Chelsea 11, Sheffield U 11, Sunderland 11, Manchester C 10, Preston NE 10, Southampton 10, Birmingham C 9, Burnley 8, Leeds U 8, Huddersfield T 7, Leicester C 7, Old Etonians 6, Oxford University 6, West Ham U 6, Fulham 5, Notts Co 5, Portsmouth 5, The Wanderers 5, Luton T 4, Queen's Park (Glasgow) 4, Royal Engineers 4, Blackpool 3, Cardiff C 3, Clapham R 3, Crystal Palace (professional club) 3, Ipswich T 3, Millwall 3, Norwich C 3, Old Carthusians 3, Oldham Ath 3, Stoke C 3, The Swifts 3, Watford 3, Barnsley 2, Blackburn Olympic 2, Bristol C 2, Bury 2, Charlton Ath 2, Grimsby T 2, Swansea T 2, Swindon T 2, Bradford C 1, Brighton & HA 1, Cambridge University 1, Coventry C 1, Crewe Alex 1, Crystal Palace (amateur club) 1, Darwen 1, Derby Junction 1, Glasgow R 1, Hull C 1, Marlow 1, Old Harrovians 1, Orient 1, Plymouth Arg 1, Port Vale 1, QPR 1, Reading 1, Shropshire W 1, Wimbledon 1, York C 1.

FA CUP 1994–95

SPONSORED BY LITTLEWOODS

PRELIMINARY AND QUALIFYING ROUNDS

Preliminary Round

Dunston Federation Brewery v Darlington Cleveland Social 1-0
Seaham Red Star v Easington Colliery 3-1
Brandon United v Alnwick Town 5-2
Crook Town v Billingham Town 1-1, 2-1
Murton v Hebburn 3-2
Stockton v RTM Newcastle 2-2, 1-6
Guisborough Town v Eppleton CW 2-0
Harrogate Town v Esh Winning 7-0
Penrith v Tow Law Town 2-3
Evenwood Town v Consett 0-3
Ryhope CA v Pickering Town 1-5
South Shields v Prudhoe Town 7-1
Clitheroe v Bamber Bridge 1-0
Farsley Celtic v Great Harwood Town 3-1
Whickham v Willington 1-2
(at Willington)
West Auckland Town v Workington 1-1, 2-1
Yorkshire Amateur v Atherton LR 0-1
Atherton Collieries v Blidworth MW 1-1, 3-1
Belper Town v Blackpool (wren) Rovers 2-1
Alfreton Town v Ashton United 3-1
Chadderton v Armthorpe Welfare 3-2
Arnold Town v Castleton Gabriels 3-2
Caernarfon Town v Darwen 3-1
Congleton Town v Curzon Ashton 4-2
Bradford (Park Avenue) v Burscough 0-3
Hatfield Main v Brigg Town 1-2
Goole Town v Glossop North End 0-2
Denaby United v Hallam 1-1, 0-1
Fleetwood v Eastwood Town 0-3
Glasshoughton Welfare v Eccleshill United 1-0
Maine Road v Louth United 3-1
Bootle v Maltby MW 0-0, 0-1
Immingham Town v Heanor Town 1-2
(at Goole Town)
Liversedge v Ilkeston Town 2-2, 1-4
Prescot AFC v Pontefract Collieries 2-0
Thackley v Radcliffe Borough 0-2
Nantwich Town v Newcastle Town 2-1
Ossett Town v Mossley 0-0, 0-3
Winterton Rangers v Stocksbridge Park Steels 3-0
Ossett Albion v Rossendale United 1-4
Sheffield v Rossington Main 3-1
St Helens Town v Salford City 7-1
Armitage v Brierley Hill Town 1-1, 3-1
Long Buckby v Northampton Spencer 3-3, 1-2
Blakenall v Banbury United 3-2
Bolehall Swifts v Barwell 3-1
Stratford Town v Halesowen Harriers 0-2
Grantham Town v Leicester United 2-0
Hinckley Athletic v Hinckley Town 2-1
Cogenhoe United v Eastwood Hanley 1-1, 0-0, 2-4
Wednesfield v Desborough Town 1-1, 1-2
Lye Town v Racing Club Warwick 2-0
(at Halesowen Harriers)
Bridgnorth Town v Bilston Town 3-1
Oldbury United v Moor Green 1-3
Pelsall Villa v Newport Pagnell Town 2-0
Sutton Coldfield Town v Stourport Swifts 2-3
Dudley Town v Rothwell Town 2-1
Stapenhill v Rushall Olympic 2-1
Stourbridge v Sandwell Borough 1-1, 0-2
Redditch United v Bedworth United 7-0
Evesham United v Tamworth 1-3
Westfields v Wellingborough Town 1-1, 3-1
Hucknall Town v West Midlands Police 0-0, 1-1, 0-1
Cornard United v Chatteris Town 2-0
Lowestoft Town v Diss Town 2-2, 3-3, 0-1
Bourne Town v Billericay Town 1-4
Bury Town v Boston Town 0-4
Holbeach United v Heybridge Swifts 1-2
Burnham Ramblers v Kings Lynn 2-3
Eynesbury Rovers v Gorleston 2-3
Haverhill Rovers v Great Yarmouth Town 2-1
Mirrlees Blackstone v Stamford 2-2, 1-4
Spalding United v March Town United 1-0
Stowmarket Town v Tiptree United 2-2, 1-3
Newmarket Town v Soham Town Rangers 4-2
Hertford Town v Saffron Walden Town 2-5
Kingsbury Town v Kempston Rovers 1-4
Witham Town v Watton United 1-0
Wisbech Town v Fakenham Town 3-0
Brimsdown Rovers v Sudbury Wanderers 1-1, 0-1
Arlesey Town v Brook House 1-2
Aveley v Wootton Blue Cross 1-1, 3-1
Berkhamsted Town v Baldock Town 1-3
Bowers United v Barking 1-4
Chalfont St Peter w.o. v Dunstable removed from competition
Biggleswade Town v Feltham & Hounslow Borough 0-1
(at Feltham & Hounslow Borough)
Collier Row v Cheshunt 2-1
Burnham v Clapton 4-0
(at Flackwell Heath)
Ruislip Manor v Flackwell Heath 5-0
Thamesmead Town v Bedfont 0-3
Harringey Borough v Ford United 1-2
(at Ford United)
Hoddesdon Town v Harefield United 1-1, 0-1
Hillingdon Borough v Royston Town 2-2, 2-1
Romford v Wingate & Finchley 2-0
Southall v Langford 2-1
(at Langford)
Leighton Town v Leyton 2-2, 0-1
Leatherhead v Letchworth Garden City 8-0
Welwyn Garden City v Viking Sports 1-1, 1-0
Tring Town v Wealdstone 0-1
Walthamstow Pennant v Ware 2-2, 0-4
Stotfold v Tower Hamlets 2-1
Slade Green v Tilbury 0-3
Arundel v Burgess Hill Town 1-3
Hampton v Pagham 1-0
Banstead Athletic w.o. v Ash United withdrew
Bracknell Town v Ashford Town 1-3
Tonbridge v Chipstead 1-1, 3-0
Croydon v Three Bridges 7-0
Eastbourne Town v Egham Town 1-7
(at Langney Sports)
Corinthian v Crowborough Athletic 9-0
Uxbridge v Corinthian-Casuals 1-0
Worthing v Horsham 1-0
Herne Bay v Langney Sports 3-0
Horsham YMCA v Lancing 2-1
Folkestone Invicta v Hailsham Town 2-0
Northwood v Godalming & Guildford 2-1
Canterbury City v Newhaven 6-0
Lewes v Fisher 0-1
Oakwood v Peacehaven & Telscombe 0-3
Littlehampton Town v Merstham 2-7
(at Portfield)
Croydon Athletic v Malden Vale 5-2
Ramsgate v Redhill 4-0
Hanwell Town v Whyteleafe 1-2
Shoreham v Ringmer 1-0
Steyning Town v Sheppey United 0-2
Epsom & Ewell v Wembley 1-3
Selsey v Portfield 1-4
Whitstable Town v Tunbridge Wells 2-3

Windsor & Eton v Whitehawk 1-0
Buckingham Town v Brockenhurst 1-0
Abingdon Town v Cove 0-0, 0-1
Bemerton Heath Harlequins v Aldershot Town 0-4
Bournemouth v Basingstoke Town 0-0, 1-3
Fareham Town v Eastleigh 3-1
Fleet Town v Oxford City 3-1
Hungerford Town v Gosport Borough 3-2
Maidenhead United v Havant Town 0-1
Poole Town v Witney Town 3-0
Thame United v Devizes Town 2-0
Ryde v Thatcham Town 3-2
Salisbury City v Totton AFC 5-0
Bridport v Backwell United 1-2
Yate Town v Swanage Town & Herston 2-1
Elmore v Chippenham Town 4-0
Forest Green Rovers v Cinderford Town 0-0, 2-3
(at Gloucester City)
Odd Down v Newport AFC 0-6
Ilfracombe Town v Paulton Rovers 0-2
Melksham Town v Keynsham Town 4-1
Glastonbury v Frome Town 4-1
Bideford v Falmouth Town 2-1
Taunton Town v Clevedon Town 3-2
Welton Rovers v Saltash United 1-1, 0-4
Calne Town v Torrington 1-3

First Qualifying Round
Barrow v Chester-Le-Street Town 4-1
Seaham Red Star v Billingham Synthonia 2-2, 0-2
Dunston Fed Brewery v Brandon United 2-0
Crook Town v Blyth Spartans 0-2
Bishop Auckland v Harrogate Railway 2-0
RTM Newcastle v Gateshead 0-3
Murton v Guisborough Town 1-1, 4-3
Harrogate Town v Gretna 4-1
Spennymoor United v Shildon 4-1
Consett v Northallerton 1-1, 3-1
Tow Law Town v Pickering Town 4-0
South Shields v Netherfield 0-0, 1-0
Durham City v Peterlee Newtown 5-0
Farsley Celtic v Whitley Bay 3-0
Clitheroe v Willington 1-2
West Auckland Town v Whitby Town 0-2
Chadderton v Winsford United 1-1, 6-5
Atherton Collieries v Buxton 2-0
Atherton LR v Belper Town 1-1, 2-0
Alfreton Town v Guiseley 2-2, 2-4
Brigg Town v Morecambe 0-4
Caernarfon Town v Chorley 2-2, 1-2
Arnold Town v Congleton Town 1-2
Burscough v Horwich RMI 1-0
Colwyn Bay v Flixton 4-0
Hallam v Hyde United 0-3
Glossop North End v Eastwood Town 2-2, 1-1, 3-5
Glasshoughton Welfare v Worksop Town 0-5
Droylsden v Lincoln United 0-3
Maltby MW v Knowsley United 0-4
Maine Road v Heanor Town 1-0
Ilkeston Town v Lancaster City 2-2, 1-3
Emley v Oldham Town 4-1
Radcliffe Borough v North Ferriby United 1-0
Prescot AFC v Nantwich Town 1-3
Mossley v Northwich Victoria 2-4
Frickley Athletic v Skelmersdale United 1-1, 4-1
Rossendale United v Matlock Town 1-2
Winterton Rangers v Sheffield 0-1
St Helens Town v Warrington Town 0-4
Atherstone United v Boldmere St Michaels 1-1, 1-0
Northampton Spencer v Hednesford Town 1-4
Armitage v Blakenall 2-2, 0-2
Bolehall Swifts v Solihull Borough 2-3
Desborough Town v Chasetown 1-0
Grantham Town v Burton Albion 2-4
Halesowen Harriers v Hinckley Athletic 3-3, 1-2
Eastwood Hanley v Rushden & Diamonds 1-0
Corby Town v Paget Rangers 0-5
Bridgnorth Town v Pershore Town 1-1, 2-0
Lye Town v Moor Green 1-5
Pelsall Villa v Raunds Town 0-1
Rocester v Stewarts & Lloyds 1-0
Dudley Town v Leek Town 0-1
Stourport Swifts v Stapenhill 2-1
Sandwell Borough v Gresley Rovers 1-2
Halesowen Town v Willenhall Town 2-1
Tamworth v Telford United 1-1, 1-4
Redditch United v Westfields 1-1, 3-2
West Midlands Police v Gainsborough Trinity 0-0, 0-6
Bishop's Stortford v Braintree Town 1-1, 0-3
Diss Town v Sudbury Town 1-0
Cornard United v Billericay Town 0-4
Boston Town v Basildon United 1-0
Boston United v Harwich & Parkeston 2-0
Kings Lynn v Halstead Town 0-1
Heybridge Swifts v Gorleston 0-0, 2-0
Haverhill Rovers v Felixstowe Town 1-1, 0-2
Saffron Walden Town v Stevenage Borough 1-4
Spalding United v Cambridge City 0-3
Stamford AFC v Tiptree United 2-3
Newmarket Town v Hitchin Town 1-2
Chelmsford City v Barton Rovers 1-0
Witham Town v Wivenhoe Town 2-0
Kempston Rovers v Wisbech Town 2-4
Sudbury Wanderers v Hendon 0-1
Aylesbury United v Boreham Wood 3-1
Aveley v Edgware Town 1-2
Brook House v Baldock Town 0-7
Barking v Canvey Island 3-1
Chesham United v Concord Rangers 4-2
Feltham & Hounslow Boro v Dagenham & Redbridge 1-3
(at Dagenham & Redbridge)
Chalfont St Peter v Collier Row 2-2, 1-2
Burnham v East Thurrock United 2-0
(at East Thurrock United)
Enfield v Hemel Hempstead 5-2
Bedfont v Purfleet 0-3
Ruislip Manor v Ford United 2-1
Harefield United v Hornchurch 0-3
Leatherhead v Hayes 1-1, 0-4
Romford v Grays Athletic 4-3
Hillingdon Borough v Southall 2-1
Leyton v St Albans City 1-2
Tilbury v Staines Town 0-1
Wealdstone v Harrow Borough 0-1
Welwyn Garden City v Ware 1-2
Stotfold v Yeading 1-3
Bromley v Bognor Regis Town 3-2
Hampton v Gravesend & Northfleet 1-1, 0-1
Burgess Hill Town v Banstead Athletic 4-3
Ashford Town v Chatham Town 5-0
Uxbridge v Dorking 1-1, 1-3
Croydon v Carshalton Athletic 0-0, 0-5
Tonbridge v Egham Town 3-1
Corinthian v Hastings Town 1-2
Northwood v Erith & Belvedere 3-0
Herne Bay v Dulwich Hamlet 1-3
Worthing v Horsham YMCA 5-3
Folkestone Invicta v Sittingbourne 1-0
Croydon Athletic v Metropolitan Police 2-2, 1-0
Fisher 93 v Kingstonian 2-4
Canterbury City v Peacehaven & Telscombe 1-2
Merstham v Margate 0-2
Molesey v Southwick 1-1, 1-0
Whyteleafe v Dover Athletic 0-0, 0-3
Ramsgate v Shoreham 0-0, 0-2
Sheppey United v Chertsey Town 0-1
Walton & Hersham v Wick 3-0
Portfield v Tooting & Mitcham United 0-3
Wembley v Tunbridge Wells 4-1
Windsor & Eton v Welling United 0-1
Wokingham Town v Bicester Town 5-0
Cove v Andover 0-2
Buckingham Town v Aldershot Town 2-1
Basingstoke Town v Newport (IW) 2-4
Dorchester Town v Lymington AFC 3-1
Fleet Town v Newbury Town 0-1
Fareham Town v Hungerford Town 1-2
Havant Town v Bashley 1-1, 1-3

Waterlooville v Westbury United	1-0
Thame United v Wimborne Town	0-0, 3-3, 3-1
Poole Town v Ryde	5-1
Salisbury City v Worcester City	2-0
Gloucester City v Exmouth Town	3-0
Yate Town v Merthyr Tydfil	0-3
Backwell United v Elmore	0-6
Cinderford Town v Mangotsfield United	3-2
(at Gloucester City FC)	
Trowbridge Town v Minehead	7-0
Paulton Rovers v Moreton Town	2-0
Newport AFC v Melksham Town	4-1
Glastonbury v Barnstaple Town	0-3
Tiverton Town v St Blazey	7-1
Taunton Town v Weston-Super-Mare	2-2, 2-3
Bideford v Saltash United	4-0
Torrington v Weymouth	2-0

Second Qualifying Round

Blyth Spartans v Dunston Federation Brewery	3-2
Barrow v Billingham Synthonia	5-2
Harrogate Town v Murton	1-0
Bishop Auckland v Gateshead	3-1
South Shields v Tow Law Town	2-2, 1-2
Spennymoor United v Consett	3-2
Whitby Town v Willington	6-1
Durham City v Farsley Celtic	1-0
Guiseley v Atherton LR	3-1
Chadderton v Atherton Collieries	1-2
Burscough v Congleton Town	0-0, 3-3, 2-2, 2-5
Morecambe v Chorley	4-2
Worksop Town v Eastwood Town	2-0
Colwyn Bay v Hyde United	2-2, 0-8
Lancaster City v Maine Road	3-2
Lincoln United v Knowsley United	3-2
Northwich Victoria v Nantwich Town	10-0
Emley v Radcliffe Borough	2-0
Warrington Town v Sheffield	2-1
Frickley Athletic v Matlock Town	3-1
Solihull Borough v Blakenall	4-0
Atherstone United v Hednesford Town	3-4
Eastwood Hanley v Hinckley Athletic	2-2, 1-0
Desborough Town v Burton Albion	0-2
Raunds Town v Moor Green	1-2
Paget Rangers v Bridgnorth Town	2-1
Gresley Rovers v Stourport Swifts	4-0
Rocester v Leek Town	0-4
Gainsborough Trinity v Redditch United	3-1
Halesowen Town v Telford United	1-1, 1-3
Boston Town v Billericay Town	1-2
Braintree Town v Diss Town	2-1
Felixstowe Town v Heybridge Swifts	1-5
Boston United v Halstead Town	3-0
Hitchin Town v Tiptee United	3-3, 1-3
Stevenage Borough v Cambridge City	0-2
Hendon v Wisbech Town	2-1
Chelmsford City v Witham Town	1-0
Barking v Baldock Town	2-2, 2-3
Aylesbury United v Edgware Town	2-0
Burnham v Collier Row	0-1
Chesham United v Dagenham & Redbridge	2-0
Hornchurch v Ruislip Manor	0-1
Enfield v Purfleet	3-1
St Albans City v Hillingdon Borough	11-1
Hayes v Romford	1-2
Yeading v Ware	8-0
Staines Town v Harrow Borough	5-3
Ashford Town v Burgess Hill Town	3-2
Bromley v Gravesend & Northfleet	2-2, 1-1, 0-1
Hastings Town v Tonbridge	1-1, 1-0
Dorking v Carshalton Athletic	0-8
Folkestone Invicta v Worthing	1-2
Northwood v Dulwich Hamlet	1-4
Margate v Peacehaven & Telscombe	1-1, 5-3
Croydon Athletic v Kingstonian	1-2
Chertsey Town v Shoreham	1-0
Molesey v Dover Athletic	1-4
Welling United v Wembley	1-4
Walton & Hersham v Tooting & Mitcham United	3-0
Newport (IW) v Buckingham Town	1-0
Wokingham Town v Andover	3-0
Bashley v Hungerford Town	3-0
Dorchester Town v Newbury Town	4-2
Salisbury City v Poole Town	3-2
Waterlooville v Thame United	4-0
Cinderford Town v Elmore	5-4
(at Elmore)	
Gloucester City v Merthyr Tydfil	7-1
Barnstaple Town v Newport AFC	1-2
Trowbridge Town v Paulton Rovers	4-1
Torrington v Bideford	1-5
Tiverton Town v Weston-Super-Mare	4-2

Third Qualifying Round

Blyth Spartans v Barrow	3-1
Harrogate Town v Bishop Auckland	0-3
Tow Law Town v Spennymoor United	0-0, 1-2
Whitby Town v Durham City	1-1, 1-3
Guiseley v Atherton Collieries	3-1
Congleton Town v Morecambe	0-3
Eastwood Town v Hyde United	1-1, 0-3
Lancaster City v Lincoln United	5-1
Northwich Victoria v Emley	2-1
Warrington Town v Frickley Athletic	2-0
Solihull Borough v Hednesford Town	3-0
Eastwood Hanley v Burton Albion	0-1
Moor Green v Paget Rangers	4-1
Gresley Rovers v Leek Town	3-1
Gainsborough Trinity v Telford United	0-3
Billericay Town v Braintree Town	1-1, 3-3, 2-3
Heybridge Swifts v Boston United	3-0
Hitchin Town v Cambridge City	3-3, 3-2
Hendon v Chelmsford City	0-1
Baldock Town v Aylesbury United	0-2
Collier Row v Chesham United	0-1
Ruislip Manor v Enfield	0-3
St Albans City v Romford	1-0
Yeading v Staines Town	4-1
Ashford Town v Gravesend & Northfleet	2-1
Hastings Town v Carshalton Athletic	2-2, 2-1
Worthing v Dulwich Hamlet	2-1
Margate v Kingstonian	0-1
Chertsey Town v Dover Athletic	0-0, 0-1
Wembley v Walton & Hersham	0-1
Newport (IW) v Wokingham Town	3-0
Bashley v Dorchester Town	1-1, 2-0
Salisbury City v Waterlooville	3-3, 1-0
Cinderford Town v Gloucester City	0-2
Newport AFC v Trowbridge Town	2-2, 1-1, 1-3
Bideford v Tiverton Town	1-8

Fourth Qualifying Round

Accrington Stanley v Spennymoor United	0-1
Southport v Stalybridge Celtic	2-1
Altrincham v Marine	2-1
Guiseley v Durham City	6-0
Bishop Auckland v Macclesfield Town	2-2, 1-0
Morecambe v Witton Albion	0-1
Northwich Victoria v Blyth Spartans	2-0
Hyde United v Warrington Town	1-1, 2-0
Halifax Town v Lancaster City	3-1
Stafford Rangers v Slough Town	0-4
St Albans City v Enfield	0-0, 2-4
Chesham United v Bromsgrove Rovers	1-1, 1-0
Braintree Town v Gresley Rovers	0-2
Burton Albion v Hitchin Town	0-1
Nuneaton Borough v Heybridge Swifts	2-2, 2-3
VS Rugby v Chelmsford City	0-0, 1-2
Yeading v Telford United	1-0
Moor Green v Aylesbury United	1-1, 1-3
Solihull Borough v Kettering Town	2-4
Gloucester City v Worthing	1-1, 1-2
Marlow v Sutton United	1-0
Tiverton Town v Farnborough Town	4-4, 5-1
Dover Athletic v Kingstonian	1-2
Hastings Town v Crawley Town	1-1, 2-3
Walton & Hersham v Yeovil Town	3-2
Salisbury City v Ashford Town	2-3
Newport (IW) v Trowbridge Town	1-0
Cheltenham Town v Bashley	1-1, 1-2

FA CUP 1994–95

sponsored by Littlewoods Pools

COMPETITION PROPER

FIRST ROUND

11 NOV

Heybridge (0) 0

Gillingham (0) 2 *(Reinelt, Pike) (at Colchester)* 4614

Heybridge: McCutcheon; Bain, Adcock, May, Rolfe, Brush (Sach), Jenkins, Springett, Jones, Hull (Payne), Pollard.
Gillingham: Banks; Dunne, Watson, Carpenter, Green, Butler, Micklewhite, Arnott, Pike, Reinelt, Smillie.

12 NOV

Altrincham (2) 3 *(Green, Morton, France)*

Southport (1) 2 *(Cunningham, McDonald)* 2523

Altrincham: Collings; Cross, Heesom, France, Reid, Morton, Terry, Shaw, Green, Carmody, Sharratt.
Southport: McKenna; Ward, Fuller (Blackhurst), Simms, Goulding, Lodge, Clark (McDonald), Cunningham, Haw, Gamble, Thomas.

Ashford T (1) 2 *(Arter, Dent)*

Fulham (0) 2 *(Adams 2 (2 pens))* 3363

Ashford T: Munden; Morris, Lemoine, Pearson A, Pearson R, Smith, Wheeler, Dent, Arter, Stanton, Ross.
Fulham: Stannard; Finnigan (Jupp), Herrera, Marshall, Moore, Blake, Mison, Morgan, Cork, Haworth, Adams.

Barnet (0) 4 *(McMahon, Cooper 2, Hodges)*

Woking (3) 4 *(Fielder, Dennis, Walker, Steele)* 3114

Barnet: Phillips; McDonald, Walker, Hoddle, Newson (Wilson), Primus, McMahon, Freedman, Hodges (Tomlinson), Cooper, Scott.
Woking: Batty; Tucker, Wye L, Fielder, Brown K, Tierling (Rattray), Wye S, Ellis, Steele (Brown D), Dennis, Walker.

Bath C (0) 0

Bristol R (1) 5 *(Stewart, Miller 4)* 6751

Bath C: Mogg; Gill, Jones, Forbes, Birks, Brooks, Hedges, Mings (Vernon), Adcock, Smart, Dicks.
Bristol R: Parkin; Pritchard, Gurney, Channing (Archer), Clark, Tillson, Sterling, Miller, Stewart, Skinner, Browning.

Bishop Auckland (0) 0

Bury (0) 0 3135

Bishop Auckland: Bishop; West S, Logan (Butler), Waller, Lobb, Adams, Wratten (West C), Todd, Toone, Laws, Parkinson.
Bury: Kelly; Cross, Stanislaus, Daws, Lucketti, Matthewson, Rigby, Johnrose (Mulligan), Sertori, Mauge, Pugh.

Bournemouth (1) 3 *(Morris, Russell, McElhatton)*

Worthing (1) 1 *(Mintram)* 3922

Bournemouth: Andrews; Chivers, Young, Morris, Watson, Leadbitter, Beardsmore (McElhatton), Mean, Robinson (Murray), Pennock, Russell.
Worthing: Penhaligan; Ball, Mintram, Riley, Darnton, Moss (Benson), Quinn, Robson, Brown, Traylen (Dunford), Tiltman.

Bradford C (1) 1 *(Tolson)*

Scunthorpe U (1) 1 *(Hope)* 5481

Bradford C: Tomlinson; Hamilton, Huxford, Duxbury, Sinnott, Oliver, Murray (Shutt), Kamara, Taylor (Power), Tolson, Showler.
Scunthorpe U: Samways; Hope, Mudd, Bullimore, Knill, Bradley, Alexander, Ford, Juryeff, Sansam, Smith.

Burnley (1) 2 *(Heath, Deary)*

Shrewsbury T (1) 1 *(Spink)* 9269

Burnley: Beresford; Parkinson, Dowell, Davis, Winstanley, Randall, Harper, Heath, Deary, Robinson (Francis), Eyres.
Shrewsbury T: Edwards; Hockaday, Withe, Taylor, Williams, Patterson, Woods, Hughes, Spink, Summerfield, Stevens.

Cambridge U (1) 2 *(Lillis, Butler)*

Brentford (1) 2 *(Annon, Taylor)* 3353

Cambridge U: Sheffield; Joseph, Barrick, Craddock, O'Shea, Hyde, Manuel, Lillis (Hunter), Butler, Corazzin, Hay.
Brentford: Dearden; Statham, Grainger, Westley, Ashby, Smith, Annon (Hurdle), Harvey, Taylor, Forster, Hutchings.

Chesham (0) 0

Bashley (0) 1 *(Paskins)* 1302

Chesham: Granville; Cobb, Hyslop, Roberts, Coleman, Kelly, Attrell (Gentle), Rake, Stanley, Dickens (Morgan), Scott.
Bashley: Flower; Ingman, Lisk, Powell, Bye, Sheppard, Stagg, Wilkinson (Stone), Walker, Stickler, Paskins (Sales).

Chester C (2) 2 *(Page, Alsford)*

Witton Alb (0) 0 2666

Chester C: Felgate; Jenkins, Burnham, Alsford, Ratcliffe, Shelton (Rimmer), Milner (Murphy), Flitcroft, Preece, Page, Hackett.
Witton Alb: Mason; Mellor, Macauley, Edey, McNeilis, Brown, Rose, Quirk (O'Callaghan), Higginbotham, Burke, Newton (Quinlan).

Chesterfield (0) 0

Scarborough (0) 0 2902

Chesterfield: Marples; Hewitt, Rogers, Perkins (Jules), Carr, Fairclough, Curtis (Moss), Norris, Morris, McAuley, Dyche.
Scarborough: Martin; Knowles, Swales, Toman, Davis, Rockett, Swann, Charles, White, Rutherford (Young), Wells.

Crewe Alex (1) 7 *(Rowbotham 2, Smith S, Ward 3, Garvey)*

Gresley R (0) 1 *(Devaney)* 4539

Crewe Alex: Smith M; Booty, Smith S, Wilson, Macauley, Whalley, Garvey, Collins, Ward, Lennon, Rowbotham.
Gresley R: Aston; Dick, Harbey, Denby, Evans, Stanborough, Elliot (Wardle), Rigg, Holmes, Garner, Marsden (Devaney).

Doncaster R (0) 1 *(Jones)*
Huddersfield T (2) 4 *(Bullock, Booth, Jepson, Dunn)* 6626
Doncaster R: Williams; Kirby (Jones), Hackett, Brabin, Wilcox, Swailes, Lawrence, Roche, Meara (Thew), Harper, Parrish.
Huddersfield T: Francis; Trevitt, Cowan, Logan (Clayton), Scully, Mitchell, Billy, Bullock, Booth, Jepson (Dunn), Reid.

Enfield (0) 1 *(Abbott)*
Cardiff C (0) 0 2345
Enfield: Pape; Blackford, Carstairs, Turner, Hannigan, Pye, Bailey, Hobson, Abbott, Whale (St Hilaire), Ryan.
Cardiff C: Williams D; Evans, Scott, Oatway, Baddeley, Perry, Ramsey, Griffith (Thompson), Stant, Millar (Aizlewood), Dale.

Exeter C (1) 1 *(Cecere)*
Crawley T (0) 0 3214
Exeter C: Fox; Minett, Robinson, Cooper M, Came, Richardson, Brown, Coughlin, Turner (Storer), Cecere (Morgan), Gavin.
Crawley T: Chatfield; Shepherd, Turner, Smart (Pearson N), O'Shaughnessy, Jeffery, Payne (Pearson M), Lempriere, Fishenden, Vansittart, Dack.

Halifax T (0) 1 *(Kiwomya)*
Runcorn (0) 1 *(Thomas (pen))* 1286
Halifax T: Heyes; German, Prindiville, Jones, Boardman, Fowler, Paterson, Lambert, Lancaster, Worthington (Flounders), Kiwomya.
Runcorn: Morris; Bates, Robertson, Lee (Smith), Hill, Anderson, Thomas, Connor, Hughes, Rutter, McInerney.

Hereford U (0) 2 *(Lyne 2)*
Hitchin T (2) 2 *(Marshall 2)* 3078
Hereford U: Pennock; Llewellyn, Preedy, Smith, Reece, James (Pick), Steele (Pounder), Wilkins, Cross, White, Lyne.
Hitchin T: Sylvester; Bone, Covington, Burke, Price, Scott, Wilson (Ryan), Marshall, Williams, Thompson, Miller.

Hull C (0) 0
Lincoln C (0) 1 *(Bannister)* 5758
Hull C: Wilson; Dakin, Graham, Hobson, Dewhurst, Mann (Abbott), Peacock (Hargreaves), Lee, Brown, Windass, Lawford.
Lincoln C: Leaning; West, Johnson A, Foley, Greenall, Brown, Matthews, Hebberd, Bannister, Hill, Carbon.

Hyde U (1) 1 *(Kimmins)*
Darlington (1) 3 *(Slaven, Worboys 2)* 2315
Hyde U: Williams A; Megram, Switzer, O'Brian, Garton, Little, Kimmins, McMahon, Williams O (Camilleri), Chadwick, Nolan.
Darlington: Pollitt; Appleby, Himsworth, Banks, Crosby, Gregan, Slaven, Painter, Gaughan, Olsson, Worboys.

Kidderminster H (1) 1 *(Humphreys)*
Torquay U (0) 1 *(Hathaway)* 4144
Kidderminster H: Rose, Hodson, Bancroft, Weir, Brindley, Forsyth, Yates (Cartwright), Grainger, Humphreys, Palmer, Hughes.
Torquay U: Bayes; Curran, Stamps (Goodridge), O'Riordan, Moore, Barrow, Trollope, Okorie (Hodges), Hancox, Hathaway, Kelly.

Kingstonian (1) 2 *(Ndah J 2)*
Brighton & HA (1) 1 *(Codner)* 3815
Kingstonian: Root; O'Neill, Barton, Finch, Ndah M (Bird), Okenla (Wingfield), Harlow, Daly, Ndah J, Akuamoah, Kempton.
Brighton & HA: Rust; Smith, Tuck, Minton, Pates, McCarthy, Chamberlain (Munday), McDougald, Nogan, Codner, Chapman (Andrews).

Newport IOW (1) 2 *(Soares 2)*
Aylesbury (1) 3 *(Hercules 2, Pluckrose (pen))* 2217
Newport IOW: Simpkins; Woollen, Wickens, Savage, Phillips, Webb, Rodgers (Cormack), Ritchie, Baldwin, Soares, Fearon (Butler).
Aylesbury: Wild; Harvey, Bashir, Hayward, Barnes, Pluckrose, Hazel, Heard, Hercules, Brayshaw, Murray (Blencowe).

Peterborough U (0) 4 *(Charlery 2 (1 pen), Williams, Henry)*
Northampton T (0) 0 8739
Peterborough U: Cooksey; Ashley, Spearing, Ebdon, Breen, Clark, Farrell (Morrison), McGorry, Williams, Charlery, Henry.
Northampton T: Stewart; Pascoe, Colkin, Sampson, Warburton, Williams, Harmon, Grayson (Aldridge), Trott, Robinson, Norton.

Port Vale (3) 6 *(Griffiths, Allon, Foyle 3, Glover D)*
Hartlepool U (0) 0 6199
Port Vale: Musselwhite; Aspin, Tankard, Porter (Burke), Griffiths, Glover D, Jeffers, Van der Laan, Allon, Foyle (Glover L), Walker.
Hartlepool U: Horne; Ingram, Walsh, Gilchrist, McGuckin, Ainsley (Skedd), Thompson, McCreery (Sloan), Houchen, Halliday, Southall.

Slough (0) 0 13,394
Birmingham C (4) 4 *(Shearer 2, McGavin 2)(at Birmingham)*
Slough: Bunting; Clement, Lee, Richardson (Blackman), Baron, Dell, Catlin, Stone (Bateman), West, Sayer, Bushay.
Birmingham C: Bennett; Poole, Whyte, Ward, Barnett (De Souza), Daish, Hunt, Claridge, McGavin, Donowa, Shearer (Tait).

Tiverton (1) 1 *(Smith)*
Leyton Orient (3) 3 *(Gray, Carter, West)* 3000
Tiverton: Nott; Edwards, Saunders N, Saunders M, Leonard, Steele, Grimshaw, Smith, Everett, Daly, Hynds (Annunziata) (Tragedeon).
Leyton Orient: Heald; Hendon, Austin, Bellamy, Howard, Bogie, Barnett (Lakin), Cockerill, Gray (Dempsey), West, Carter.

Walsall (2) 3 *(Lightbourne, Butler 2)*
Rochdale (0) 0 3619
Walsall: Wood; Evans, Gibson, Rogers, Marsh, Palmer, O'Connor, Ntamark, Butler (Peer), Lightbourne (Mehew), Houghton.
Rochdale: Dunford; Thackeray, Formby (Sharpe), Reid, Matthews, Butler, Doyle, Peake (Ryan), Williams, Whitehall, Stuart.

Wigan Ath (3) 4 *(Leonard, Carragher 2, Kilford)*
Spennymoor (0) 0 2183
Wigan Ath: Farnworth; Rennie, Jakub, Miller, Robertson, Farrell, Kilford, Carragher, Leonard (Adekola), McKearney, Lyons.
Spennymoor: McNary; Tinkler, Petitjean, Watson, Saunders, Mason, Robson, Goodrick, Shaw, Gorman, Veart.

Wrexham (0) 1 *(Watkin)*

Stockport Co (0) 0 4740

Wrexham: Marriott; Jones, Hardy, Phillips (Durkan), Hunter, Humes, Bennett, Owen, Connolly, Cross (Watkin), Hughes.
Stockport Co: Ironside; Connelly, Wallace, Ware (Dinning), Flynn, Bound, Gannon, Ward (Armstrong), Eckhardt, Beaumont, Chalk.

Wycombe W (1) 4 *(Stapleton 2, Bell, Ryan)*

Chelmsford C (0) 0 5654

Wycombe W: Hyde; Cousins, Brown, Crossley, Evans, Ryan, Carroll, Bell, Turnbull (Thompson), Garner (Reid), Stapleton.
Chelmsford C: Shoemake; Hunter, Eliot Martin (Eddie Martin), Clark, Jacques, Keen, Hoddy, Garvey, Rogers, Restarick, Owers (Campbell).

Yeading (1) 2 *(Hippolyte, Graham)*

Colchester U (1) 2 *(Kinsella, Abrahams)* 1715

Yeading: Mackenzie; Dicker, Cuffie, Bunce, McGrath, Hoon-Park, Graham, Bowder, Hippolyte, McKinnon, Cordery.
Colchester U: Emberson; Betts, English, Cawley, Caesar, Dennis, Locke, Brown, Whitton, Kinsella, Abrahams.

York C (1) 3 *(Naylor 2, McCarthy)*

Rotherham U (1) 3 *(Goater 2, Helliwell)* 4020

York C: Kiely; McMillan, Wilson, Atkin, Stancliffe, Barras, McCarthy, Naylor, Barnes, Baker, Canham.
Rotherham U: Clarke; Wilder, James (Helliwell), Williams A, Breckin, Brien, Dolby, Smith, Varadi, Goater, Marginson.

13 NOV

Guiseley (0) 1 *(Brockie) (at Bradford)*

Carlisle U (2) 4 *(Reeves 2, Conway, Mountfield)* 6548

Guiseley: Dickinson; Atkinson, Hogarth, Brockie, Richards, Bottomley, Cawthorns (James), Allen, Colville (Flanagan), Horsfield, Roberts.
Carlisle U: Caig; Edmondson (Joyce), Gallimore, Walling, Mountfield, Conway (Thorpe), Thomas, Currie, Reeves, Davey, Prokas.

Kettering T (0) 0

Plymouth Arg (0) 1 *(Skinner)* 4602

Kettering T: Benstead; Smith, Ashby, Holden, Oxbrow, Taylor (Magee), Martin (Wright), Stringfellow, Alford, Thomas, Brown.
Plymouth Arg: Hodge; Patterson, Naylor, Edworthy, Comyn, Burnett, Barlow, Skinner, Nugent, Evans, Twiddy.

Marlow (0) 2 *(Caesar 2)*

Oxford U (0) 0 3000

Marlow: Mitchell; Nolan, Rhoades-Brown, Ferguson, Muckelberg, Muir, Lay, Phillips (Floyd), Rayson (Holmes), Caesar, McNamara.
Oxford U: Whitehead; Robinson, Collins, Dyer, Elliott, Marsh (Rush), Massey, Smith, Moody, Byrne, Ford R.

14 NOV

Preston NE (1) 1 *(Conroy)*

Blackpool (0) 0 14,036

Preston NE: Richardson; Fensome, Sharp, Cartwright, Holmes, Moyes, Ainsworth (Whalley), Bryson, Raynor, Conroy (Sale), Trebble.
Blackpool: Martin; Brown, Burke, Bradshaw, Thompson, Horner, Mitchell, Beech, Watson, Ellis, Griffiths (Quinn).

21 NOV

Walton & Hersham (0) 0

Swansea C (1) 2 *(Ford, Ampadu)* 2230

Walton & Hersham: McCann; Turner (Joseph), Warmington, Benning, Terry, Gasson, Adams, Wilson, Banton, Price (Davidson), Mitchell.
Swansea C: Freestone; Jenkins, Clode, Basham, Ford, Ampadu, Bowen, Penney, Torpey, Cornforth, Hodge (Hayes).

FIRST ROUND REPLAY

Runcorn (0) 1 *(Pugh)*

Halifax T (0) 3 *(Lancaster 2, Lambert) aet* 728

Runcorn: Morris; Bates, Robertson, Ruffer, Hill, Anderson, Thomas, Connor (Godfrey), Hughes (Pugh), McInerney, Smith.
Halifax T: Heyes; German, Prindiville, Jones, Boardman, Fowler, Paterson, Lambert, Lancaster, Worthington, Flounders.

22 NOV

FIRST ROUND

Mansfield T (1) 3 *(Hadley, Holland 2)*

Northwich V (1) 1 *(Oghani)* 2999

Mansfield T: Ward; Boothroyd, Baraclough, Holland, Howarth, Doolan, Ireland, Parkin, Wilkinson, Hadley, Noteman (Aspinall).
Northwich V: Greygoose; Tinson (Norman), Jones, Abel, Parker, Gallagher (O'Connor), Boyd, Butler, Oghani, Williams, Hardy.

FIRST ROUND REPLAYS

Brentford (1) 1 *(Grainger)*

Cambridge U (2) 2 *(Lillis, Butler (pen))* 4096

Brentford: Dearden; Statham, Grainger, Westley, Ashby, Smith, Bates, Harvey, Taylor, Forster (Hutchings), Mundee.
Cambridge U: Sheffield; Joseph, Barrick, Craddock, O'Shea, Hyde, Fowler, Lillis (Nyamah), Butler, Corazzin (Granville), Hay.

Bury (1) 1 *(Paskin)*

Bishop Auckland (1) 1 *(Todd) aet* 3517

Bury: Kelly G; Cross, Stanislaus, Daws (Hughes), Lucketti, Matthewson, Rigby (Mulligan), Johnrose, Paskin, Mauge, Pugh.
Bishop Auckland: Bishop; Elliott, Logan (Coverdale), Waller, Lobb, Toone, Wratten, Todd, Hyde, Laws, Parkinson.
Bury won 4-2 on penalties.

Colchester U (3) 7 *(Abrahams 2, Whitton 2, Brown 2, Kinsella)*

Yeading (1) 1 *(McKinnon (pen))* 4016

Colchester U: Cheesewright; Betts, English, Cawley, Caesar, Locke (Dennis), Fry, Brown, Whitton (Thompson), Kinsella, Abrahams.
Yeading: MacKenzie; Dicker, Cuffie, Woods, McGrath, Hoon-Park, Graham, Bowder, Hippolyte, McKinnon, Cordery.

Fulham (2) 5 *(Morgan, Adams 2, Blake, Cork)*
Ashford T (1) 3 *(Stanton 2, Dent) aet* 6539
Fulham: Stannard; Jupp, Herrera, Hurlock, Moore, Blake, Mison (Haworth), Morgan, Cork, Marshall, Adams.
Ashford T: Munden; Morris, Lemoine (Ager), Pearson A, Pearson R, Smith, Wheeler, Dent, Arter (Carlton), Stanton, Ross.

Hitchin (1) 4 *(Bone, Williams, Wilson, Marshall)*
Hereford U (2) 2 *(White, Pick)* 3098
Hitchin: Sylvester; Bone, Covington, Burke, Miller, Scott, Wilson, Marshall, Williams, Thompson, Ryan.
Hereford U: Pennock; Reece, Preedy, Smith, Davies, Pick, Pounder (Williams), Wilkins, Cross, White, Lyne.

Rotherham U (3) 3 *(Davison 2, Goater)*
York C (0) 0 4391
Rotherham U: Clarke; Wilder, James, Williams A, Breckin, Brien, Hayward, Richardson, Davison (Varadi), Goater, Hurst.
York C: Kiely; McMillan, Wilson, Atkin, Stancliffe, Barras, McCarthy, Naylor, Barnes, Baker, Canham.

Scarborough (1) 2 *(Toman, White)*
Chesterfield (0) 0 1564
Scarborough: Martin; Knowles, Swales, Toman, Davis, Rockett, Swann, Charles, White, Young (Rutherford), Wells (D'Auria).
Chesterfield: Marples; Dyche, Rogers, Perkins, Carr, Fairclough, Curtis (McAuley), Norris, Davies, Moss, Jules (Morris).

Scunthorpe U (0) 3 *(Carmichael, Alexander, Thompstone)*
Bradford C (0) 2 *(Power, Richards) aet* 4514
Scunthorpe U: Samways; Hope, Mudd, Ford, Knill, Bradley (Carmichael), Alexander, Bullimore, Juryeff, Sansam (Thompstone), Thornber.
Bradford C: Tomlinson; Huxford, Jacobs, Duxbury, Sinnott, Richards, Shutt (Bowling), Kamara, Taylor, Jewell (Power), Murray.

Woking (1) 1 *(Tucker)*
Barnet (0) 0 4859
Woking: Batty; Tucker, Wye L, Fielder, Brown K, Tierling (Rattray), Wye S, Ellis, Steele, Walker, Dennis.
Barnet: Phillips; McDonald, Walker, Hoddle, Newson (Mutchell), Primus, McMahon, Freedman, Wilson, Cooper (Tomlinson), Scott.

23 NOV

Torquay U (0) 1 *(Hancox)*
Kidderminster H (0) 0 3809
Torquay U: Bayes; Curran, Kelly, O'Riordan, Moore, Barrow, Trollope, Buckle, Hodges (Hancox), Hathaway, Okorie.
Kidderminster H: Rose; Hodson, Bancroft, Weir, Brindley, Forsyth, Webb, Grainger, Humphreys, Yates, Hughes.

SECOND ROUND

2 DEC

Birmingham C (0) 0
Scunthorpe U (0) 0 13,832
Birmingham C: Bennett; Poole, Whyte, Ward, Barnett, Daish, Donowa (Lowe), Claridge, McGavin (Cooper), Tait, Dominguez.
Scunthorpe U: Samways; Ford, Mudd, Thornber, Knill, Bradley, Alexander, Bullimore, Juryeff (Thompstone), Henderson, Smith.

3 DEC

Altrincham (1) 1 *(Sharratt)*
Wigan Ath (0) 0 3020
Altrincham: Collings; Cross, Heesom, France, Reid, Morton, Terry, Butler, Green (Shaw), Carmody, Sharratt.
Wigan Ath: Farnworth; Strong (Benjamin), Jakub, Miller, Robertson, Farrell, Kilford, Carragher, Leonard, Rimmer, Lyons.

Crewe Alex (1) 1 *(Ward)*
Bury (0) 2 *(Johnrose, Rigby)* 4875
Crewe Alex: Smith M; Booty, Smith S, Wilson, Macauley, Whalley, Garvey, Collins, Ward, Lennon, Adebola.
Bury: Bracey; Jackson, Stanislaus, Daws, Lucketti, Matthewson, Kelly T, Hughes, Sertori (Rigby), Johnrose, Pugh.

Enfield (1) 1 *(Abbott)*
Torquay U (1) 1 *(Okorie)* 2326
Enfield: Pape; Blackford, Carstairs, Kerr, Hannigan, Pye, Bailey, Hobson, Abbott (Cherry), St Hilaire, Ryan.
Torquay U: Bayes; Brass, Kelly (Hancox), O'Riordan, Moore, Barrow, Trollope, Buckle, Okorie, Hathaway, Goodridge.

Exeter C (1) 1 *(Morgan)*
Colchester U (0) 2 *(Whitton, English)* 3528
Exeter C: Woodman; Minett, Brown, Bailey, Daniels, Richardson, Storer, Coughlin (Robinson), Cooper M (Thirlby), Morgan (Bellotti), Gavin.
Colchester U: Cheesewright; Betts, English, Cawley, Caesar, Locke, Putney (Dennis), Brown (Fry), Whitton, Kinsella, Abrahams.

Gillingham (1) 1 *(Pike)*
Fulham (0) 1 *(Hamill)* 6253
Gillingham: Banks; Carpenter, Watson, Smith, Arnott, Green, Micklewhite, Reinelt, Foster, Pike, Smillie.
Fulham: Harrison; Jupp, Herrera, Hurlock, Moore, Blake, Marshall, Morgan, Cusack (Hamill), Brazil, Cork.

Halifax T (0) 0
Mansfield T (0) 0 2396
Halifax T: Heyes; German, Prindiville, Jones, Boardman, Fowler, Paterson, Lambert, Lancaster, Worthington (Flounders), Kiwomya.
Mansfield T: Ward; Boothroyd, Baraclough, Holland, Howarth, Aspinall, Ireland, Doolan, Wilkinson, Hadley, Campbell.

Hitchin (0) 0
Wycombe W (2) 5 *(Garner 3, Ryan, Bell)* 2765
Hitchin: Sylvester; Bone, Covington, Burke, Miller, Rutherford (McGonagle), Wilson, Marshall (Caines), Williams, Thompson, Ryan.
Wycombe W: Hyde; Cousins, Brown, Crossley, Evans, Ryan, Carroll, Bell, Thompson, Garner (Hemmings), Stapleton (Langford).

Kingstonian (0) 1 *(Akuamoah (pen))*
Aylesbury (2) 4 *(Hercules, Bashir, Pluckrose (pen), Blencowe)* 1891
Kingstonian: Root; O'Neill, Barton, Finch, Ndah M (Bird), Sugrue, Harlow, Daly, Ndah J, Akuamoah, Kempton (Okenla).
Aylesbury: Wild; Harvey, Bashir, Hayward, Brayshaw (Murray), Pluckrose, Hobbs, Heard, Hercules (Ketteridge), Danzey, Blencowe.

Leyton Orient (0) 0
Bristol R (1) 2 *(Stewart 2)* 5071
Leyton Orient: Heald; Howard, Austin, Bellamy (Lakin), Purse, Bogie, Barnett (Brooks), Cockerill, Carter, West, Dempsey.
Bristol R: Parkin; Pritchard, Gurney, Browning, Clark, Tillson, Sterling, Miller, Stewart, Skinner, Archer (Hardyman).

Lincoln C (0) 1 *(Johnson D)*
Huddersfield T (0) 0 4143
Lincoln C: Leaning; West, Johnson A, Carbon, Greenall, Brown, Matthews, Hebberd, Daley, Johnson D (Daws), Hill.
Huddersfield T: Blackwell; Trevitt, Cowan, Crosby, Scully, Mitchell, Billy (Dunn), Bullock, Booth, Jepson, Reid.

Peterborough U (0) 0
Cambridge U (2) 2 *(Barrick, Hay)* 9576
Peterborough U: Cooksey; Ashley, Spearing, Ebdon, Breen, Clark (Thomas), Moran (Brissett), McGorry, Williams, Henry, Lormor.
Cambridge U: Sheffield; Hunter, Barrick, Craddock, Jeffrey, Hyde, Manuel, Joseph, Butler (Fowler), Corazzin, Hay (Lillis).

Plymouth Arg (2) 2 *(Ross 2)*
Bournemouth (0) 1 *(Jones)* 6739
Plymouth Arg: Nicholls; Edworthy, Naylor, Swan, Comyn, Burnett, Barlow, Patterson, Nugent (Landon), Ross, Evans (Shilton S).
Bournemouth: Andrews; Young, Pennock (McElhatton), Morris, Watson, Leadbitter, Beardsmore (Murray), Mean, Robinson, Jones, Russell.

Preston NE (1) 1 *(Smart)*
Walsall (1) 1 *(Wilson)* 9767
Preston NE: Richardson; Fensome, Sharp, Cartwright, Holmes, Moyes, Trebble (Fleming), Bryson, Smart, Conroy, Raynor (Emerson).
Walsall: Wood; Evans, Gibson, Ryder, Marsh, Palmer, O'Connor, Ntamark, Lightbourne, Wilson, Houghton (Butler).

Scarborough (0) 1 *(Swann)*
Port Vale (0) 0 2382
Scarborough: Kelly; Knowles, Wells, Toman (Thompson), Meyer, Rockett, Swann, Charles, White, Rutherford (Blackstone), D'Auria.
Port Vale: Musselwhite; Aspin, Tankard, Porter (Burke), Griffiths, Glover D, Guppy, Van der Laan, Allon (Glover L), Foyle, Walker.

Wrexham (1) 5 *(Connolly 2, Bennett, Hughes, Watkin)*
Rotherham U (1) 2 *(Davison, Hurst)* 4521
Wrexham: Marriott; Brace, Hardy, Hughes, Jones, Pejic, Bennett, Owen, Connolly, Watkin, Cross (Phillips).
Rotherham U: Clarke; Wilder, James, Smith, Breckin, Brien, Hayward (Helliwell), Richardson, Davison, Goater, Hurst.

4 DEC

Bashley (0) 0
Swansea C (0) 1 *(Torpey)* 2047
Bashley: Flower; Ingma (Stone), Lisk, Powell, Bye, Sheppard, Stagg, Wilkinson, Walker, Stickler (Smith P), Paskins.
Swansea C: Freestone; Jenkins, Walker, Basham, Ford, Chapple (Burns), Bowen (Perrett), Penney, Torpey, Cornforth, Hodge.

Carlisle U (0) 2 *(Conway, Currie)*
Darlington (0) 0 8365
Carlisle U: Caig; Edmondson, Gallimore, Walling, Mountfield, Conway, Thomas (Thorpe), Currie (Arnold), Reeves, Davey, Prokas.
Darlington: Pollitt; Gaughan, Himsworth, Banks, Crosby, Reed, Slaven, Painter (Kirkham), Worboys, Olsson, Chapman.

Chester C (0) 1 *(Milner)*
Burnley (0) 2 *(Eyres (pen), Heath)* 4231
Chester C: Felgate; Jenkins, Lightfoot, Alsford, Jackson, Shelton, Flitcroft, Bishop (Milner), Preece, Page, Hackett.
Burnley: Beresford; Parkinson, Dowell (Gayle), Davis, Winstanley, Randall, Harper, Heath, Hoyland, Robinson, Eyres.

Marlow (0) 2 *(Evans R, Evans C)*
Woking (0) 1 *(Tucker)* 2845
Marlow: Mitchell; Regan, Puttnam, Ferguson, Evans C, Rhoades-Brown, Nolan, Phillips (Floyd), McNamara, Rayson (Walton), Evans R.
Woking: Batty; Berry (Brown D), Brown K, Fielder, Tucker, Tierling (Rattray), Wye S, Ellis, Steele, Walker, Dennis.

SECOND ROUND REPLAYS

13 DEC

Fulham (0) 1 *(Hamill)*
Gillingham (1) 2 *(Pike, Reinelt) aet* 6536
Fulham: Stannard; Jupp, Herrera, Mison, Moore, Blake, Marshall, Morgan, Cusack, Brazil, Cork (Hamill).
Gillingham: Banks; Carpenter, Watson, Smith, Arnott, Green, Micklewhite, Butler, Foster (Reinelt), Pike, Smillie.

Mansfield T (0) 2 *(Aspinall, Holland)*
Halifax T (1) 1 *(Lancaster)* 2648
Mansfield T: Ward; Boothroyd, Baraclough, Holland, Aspinall, Peters, Ireland, Campbell, Wilkinson, Pearson, Noteman.
Halifax T: Hayes; German, Prindiville, Jones, Boardman, Fowler (Hall), Martin, Lambert, Lancaster, Flounders, Kiwomya.

Torquay U (0) 0
Enfield (1) 1 *(Kerr)* 3174
Torquay U: Bayes; Brass, Kelly (Okorie), Hodges (Hancox), Moore, Barrow, Trollope, Buckle, Darby, Hathaway, Goodridge (Tucker). *Enfield:*Pape, Blackford, Carstairs, Kerr, Hannigan, Pye, St Hilaire, Hobson, Abbott, Whale (Cherry), Ryan.

Walsall (2) 4 *(Houghton, Wilson, Lightbourne 2)*
Preston NE (0) 0 6468
Walsall: Wood; Evans, Gibson, Ryder, Marsh, Palmer, O'Connor (Peer), Ntamark, Lightbourne, Wilson (Butler), Houghton.
Preston NE: Richardson; Fensome (Emerson), Sharp, Whalley, Holmes, Moyes, Cartwright, Bryson, Smart, Conroy, Raynor (Trebble).

14 DEC

Scunthorpe U (0) 1 *(Bullimore)*
Birmingham C (0) 2 *(McGavin, Cooper)* 6280
Scunthorpe U: Samways; Ford, Mudd (Sansam), Thornber, Knill, Bradley, Alexander, Bullimore, Juryeff, Thompstone (Carmichael), Smith.
Birmingham C: Bennett; Poole, Whyte, Cooper, Barnett, Daish, Donowa, Claridge, McGavin, Dominguez (Doherty), Tait.

THIRD ROUND

7 JAN

Aylesbury (0) 0
QPR (3) 4 *(Maddix, Ferdinand, Gallen, Meaker)* 15,417
Aylesbury: O'Reilly; Harvey, Bashir (Murray), Brayshaw, Barnes, Pluckrose, Hobbs, Heard, Hercules, Danzey (Blencowe), Hazel.
QPR: Roberts; Bardsley, Wilson, Hodge, Maddix, McDonald, Impey, Barker (Holloway), Ferdinand, Gallen (Allen), Meaker.

Barnsley (0) 0
Aston Villa (0) 2 *(Yorke, Saunders)* 11,469
Barnsley: Watson; Eaden, Fleming (Rammell), Wilson (Bullock), Moses, Davis, O'Connell, Redfearn, Payton, Liddell, Sheridan.
Aston Villa: Spink; Barrett, Staunton, Teale, McGrath, Ehiogu, Yorke, Fashanu, Saunders, Taylor, Townsend.

Birmingham C (0) 0
Liverpool (0) 0 25,326
Birmingham C: Bennett; Poole, Cooper, Ward, Barnett, Daish, Donowa, Claridge, Lowe, Otto, Shearer.
Liverpool: James; Jones R, Bjornebye, Scales, Babb, Ruddock, McManaman, Redknapp, Rush, Barnes, Fowler.

Bristol C (0) 0
Stoke C (0) 0 9683
Bristol C: Welch; Hansen, Munro, Shail, Bryant, Tinnion, Kuhl, Bent, Baird (Partridge), Allison, Owers.
Stoke C: Sinclair; Butler, Sandford, Cranson, Overson, Orlygsson, Clarkson, Downing (Sturridge), Scott, Peschisolido, Gleghorn.

Bury (2) 2 *(Lucketti, Stanislaus)*
Tranmere R (0) 2 *(Muir 2)* 5755
Bury: Kelly G; Cross, Stanislaus, Mauge, Lucketti, Matthewson, Hulme (Hughes), Paskin (Rigby), Carter, Johnrose, Pugh.
Tranmere R: Nixon; Stevens, Brannan, Mungall (Muir), Garnett, O'Brien, Morrissey, Jones, Malkin, Irons, Thomas.

Cambridge U (1) 2 *(Butler 2 (1 pen))*
Burnley (2) 4 *(Eyres (pen), Robinson, Randall, Gayle)* 6275
Cambridge U: Sheffield; Joseph, Barrick, Heathcote, Jeffrey, O'Shea, Hyde, Lillis, Butler, Corazzin, Hay (Hunter).
Burnley: Beresford; Parkinson, Eyres, Hoyland, Winstanley, Randall, Harper, Heath, Gayle, Robinson, McMinn (Deary).

Chelsea (2) 3 *(Peacock, Sinclair, Spencer)*
Charlton Ath (0) 0 24,485
Chelsea: Kharine; Clarke, Minto, Kjeldbjerg, Johnsen, Sinclair, Spencer, Furlong, Stein (Newton), Peacock, Spackman.
Charlton Ath: Salmon; Brown, Mortimer, Bennett (Nelson), Chapple, McLeary, Robson, Robinson (Pardew), Leaburn, Whyte, Walsh.

Coventry C (0) 1 *(Wegerle (pen))*
WBA (0) 1 *(Ashcroft (pen))* 16,555
Coventry C: Ogrizovic; Borrows, Morgan, Cook, Pressley, Williams, Flynn, Wegerle (Darby), Dublin, Marsh, Jenkinson.
WBA: Naylor; Parsley, Edwards, Bradley, Mardon, Raven, Donovan, Ashcroft, Hunt, Rees (Smith), Hamilton.

Everton (0) 1 *(Hinchcliffe)*
Derby Co (0) 0 29,406
Everton: Southall; Jackson, Burrows (Limpar), Ebbrell, Watson, Unsworth, Horne, Parkinson, Ferguson, Rideout, Hinchcliffe.
Derby Co: Sutton S; Kavanagh, Nicholson, Sutton W (Forsyth), Short, Williams, Wassall, Carsley, Stallard (Wrack), Gabbiadini, Simpson.

Gillingham (1) 1 *(Pike (pen))*
Sheffield W (2) 2 *(Waddle, Bright)* 10,425
Gillingham: Banks; Arnott, Watson, Carpenter, Butler, Green, Micklewhite, Smith, Foster, Pike, Reinelt.
Sheffield W: Pressman; Atherton, Nolan, Bart-Williams, Pearce, Walker, Hyde, Waddle (Petrescu), Bright, Whittingham (Key), Sheridan.

Grimsby T (0) 0
Norwich C (0) 1 *(Crook)* 11,198
Grimsby T: Crichton; McDermott, Croft, Handyside, Rodger, Groves, Childs (Jobling), Shakespeare, Woods, Mendonca, Gilbert (Lester)
Norwich C: Marshall; Sutch, Ullathorne, Newsome, Polston, Crook, Adams (Cureton), Milligan, Newman, Sheron (Goss), Eadie.

Leicester C (1) 2 *(Oldfield, Roberts)*
Enfield (0) 0 17,351
Leicester C: Poole; Grayson, Whitlow, Hill, Willis, Agnew (Lowe), Oldfield, Thompson, Lewis, Roberts, Philpott.
Enfield: Pape; Blackford, Carstairs, Turner, Hannigan, Pye, Kerr, Hobson, Whale (Bailey), St Hilaire, Ryan (Ridout).

Luton T (1) 1 *(Hartson)*
Bristol R (1) 1 *(Stewart)* 7571
Luton T: Sommer; James, Johnson, Waddock, Thomas, Peake, Telfer, Oakes, Hartson, Preece, Marshall (Adcock).
Bristol R: Parkin; Channing, Gurney, Hardyman, Clark, Tillson, Sterling, Miller (Taylor), Stewart, Skinner, Archer.

Mansfield T (2) 2 *(Donaldson, Ireland)*
Wolverhampton W (0) 3 *(Kelly D, Dennison, Mills)* 6701
Mansfield T: Ward; Boothroyd, Baraclough, Holland, Howarth, Peters, Ireland (Parkin), Donaldson, Wilkinson (Pearson), Hadley, Lampkin.
Wolverhampton W: Jones; Blades, Venus, Emblen, De Wolf (Rankine), Law, Goodman, Kelly D, Mills, Cowans, Dennison.

Millwall (0) 0
Arsenal (0) 0 17,715
Millwall: Keller; Dawes, Thatcher (Kennedy), Roberts, Witter, Stevens, Savage, Rae, Cadette, Mitchell, Van Blerk.
Arsenal: Seaman; Dixon, Winterburn, Schwarz, Bould, Linighan, Jensen (Keown), Wright, Smith (Campbell), Hillier, Parlour.

Nottingham F (2) 2 *(Collymore, Gemmill)*
Plymouth Arg (0) 0 19,821
Nottingham F: Crossley; Lyttle, Pearce, Haaland, Chettle, Stone, Phillips, Gemmill, Roy (Webb), Collymore, Woan.
Plymouth Arg: Nicholls; Patterson, Naylor, Swan, Hill, Edworthy, Barlow, Skinner, Nugent, Burnett, Barber (Evans).

Portsmouth (1) 3 *(Creaney, Radosavljevic 2)*
Bolton W (1) 1 *(Sneekes)* 9721

Portsmouth: Knight; Gittens, Daniel, McGrath, Symons, Butters, Pethick, Radosavljevic, Powell, Creaney, Wood.
Bolton W: Branagan; Green, Phillips, McAteer, Coleman, Stubbs, Paatelainen (Thompson), Sneekes, Coyle, McGinlay, Patterson (Lee).

Reading (1) 1 *(Taylor)*
Oldham Ath (2) 3 *(Sharp, Richardson, Halle)* 8886

Reading: Hislop; Jones, Taylor (Hopkins), Wdowczyk, Bernal, Parkinson, Gilkes, Gooding, Quinn, Lovell (Hartenberger), Holsgrove.
Oldham Ath: Gerrard; Makin, Pointon, Henry, Graham, Redmond, Halle, Sharp, McCarthy (Beckford), Richardson, Brennan.

Scarborough (0) 0
Watford (0) 0 3544

Scarborough: Kelly; Knowles, Charles, D'Auria, Meyer, Davis, Thompson, Rodwell, White, Swann, Swales.
Watford: Digweed; Lavin, Bazeley, Foster, Holdsworth, Ramage, Hessenthaler, Gibbs, Millen, Porter, Mooney.

Southampton (2) 2 *(Heaney, Le Tissier)*
Southend U (0) 0 13,003

Southampton: Grobbelaar; Kenna, Benali, Magilton, Hall, Monkou, Le Tissier, Dodd (Hughes), Maskell, Widdrington, Heaney.
Southend U: Sansome; Hone, Powell, Gridelet, Bressington, Dublin, Ansah, Whelan, Thomson, Willis, Tilson.

Sunderland (0) 1 *(Russell)*
Carlisle U (0) 1 *(Davey)* 15,523

Sunderland: Chamberlain; Kubicki, Scott, Bennett, Ferguson, Ball, Atkinson (Michael Gray), Russell, Gray P, Smith, Armstrong.
Carlisle U: Caig; Edmondson, Gallimore, Walling, Mountfield, Conway, Thomas, Currie, Reeves, Davey, Prokas.

Swansea C (1) 1 *(Ford)*
Middlesbrough (0) 1 *(Moore)* 8407

Swansea C: Freestone; Barnhouse, Walker, Basham, Ford, Ampadu, Hayes (McFarlane), Penney, Torpey, Cornforth, Hodge.
Middlesbrough: Miller; Morris, Fleming, Vickers, Pearson, Whyte (Moore), Mustoe, Pollock, Wilkinson, Hendrie, Hignett.

Swindon T (0) 2 *(Fjortoft, Nijholt)*
Marlow (0) 0 7007

Swindon T: Hammond; Robinson, Bodin, Culverhouse (O'Sullivan), Nijholt, Taylor, Horlock, Beauchamp (Hamon), Fjortoft, Mutch, Ling.
Marlow: Mitchell; Nolan, Rhoades-Brown, Ferguson (Muckelberg), Evans C, McNamara, Mikurenva, Phillips, Evans R (Regan), Caesar, Rayson.

Tottenham H (2) 3 *(Sheringham, Rosenthal, Nethercott)*
Altrincham (0) 0 25,057

Tottenham H: Walker; Austin, Campbell, Howells, Calderwood, Mabbutt, Anderton, Barmby, Klinsmann, Sheringham, Rosenthal (Nethercott).
Altrincham: Collings; Cross, Heesom, France, Reid, Morton (Shaw), Terry, Butler, Green, Carmody, Sharratt (Constable).

Walsall (1) 1 *(Marsh)*
Leeds U (0) 1 *(Wetherall)* 8619

Walsall: Wood; Evans, Gibson (Rogers), Ryder, Marsh, Palmer, O'Connor, Ntamark, Lightbourne, Wilson, Houghton.
Leeds U: Lukic; Kelly, Worthington, Palmer, Wetherall, Pemberton, White (Wallace), Radebe (Masinga), Deane, McAllister, Speed.

Wimbledon (1) 1 *(Harford)*
Colchester U (0) 0 6903

Wimbledon: Segers; Cunningham, Kimble, Jones, Reeves, Thorn, Clarke, Earle, Harford, Holdsworth, Fear.
Colchester U: Cheesewright; Betts, English, Cawley, Caesar, Locke, Putney, Brown, Whitton, Kinsella, Abrahams (Dennis).

Wrexham (0) 2 *(Durkan, Bennett (pen))*
Ipswich T (0) 1 *(Linighan)* 8324

Wrexham: Marriott; Jones, Hardy, Hughes, Hunter, Humes, Bennett, Owen, Connolly, Cross, Durkan.
Ipswich T: Baker; Yallop, Vaughan, Mason (Johnson), Whelan, Linighan, Sedgley, Slater (Paz), Kiwomya, Tanner, Thomsen.

Wycombe W (0) 0
West Ham U (0) 2 *(Cottee, Brown)* 9007

Wycombe W: Hyde; Cousins, Brown, Crossley, Evans, Ryan, Carroll, Bell, Regis (Hemmings), Garner, Thompson (Stapleton).
West Ham U: Miklosko; Breacker, Dicks, Potts, Martin, Bishop, Holmes (Brown), Moncur, Cottee, Boere (Morley), Hughes.

8 JAN

Crystal Palace (3) 5 *(Coleman, Armstrong, Gordon (pen), Salako 2)*
Lincoln C (0) 1 *(Greenall)* 6541

Crystal Palace: Martyn; Humphrey, Gordon, Southgate, Shaw, Coleman, Ndah (Preece), Newman, Armstrong, Pitcher, Salako.
Lincoln C: Leaning; West, Johnson A (Dixon), Hebberd, Greenall, Brown, Hill, Foley (Bannister), Carbon, Daws, Johnson D.

Newcastle U (0) 1 *(Lee)*
Blackburn R (1) 1 *(Sutton)* 31,721

Newcastle U: Srnicek; Venison, Beresford, Elliott (Kitson), Peacock, Howey, Lee, Beardsley, Cole, Fox, Bracewell.
Blackburn R: Flowers; Berg, Le Saux, Sherwood, Hendry, Warhurst, Ripley (Newell), Atkins, Shearer, Sutton, Wilcox.

Notts Co (2) 2 *(Matthews, White)*
Manchester C (1) 2 *(Beagrie, Brightwell D)* 12,376

Notts Co: Cherry; Mills, Legg, Turner, Murphy, Johnson, Devlin, Butler, White, McSwegan, Matthews.
Manchester C: Dibble; Foster (Quinn), Phelan, Lomas, Kernaghan, Brightwell I (Brightwell D), Summerbee, Walsh, Rosler, Flitcroft, Beagrie.

9 JAN

Sheffield U (0) 0
Manchester U (0) 2 *(Hughes, Cantona)* 22,322

Sheffield U: Kelly; Gage, Nilsen, Hartfield, Gayle, Whitehouse (Flo), Rogers, Veart, Blake, Hodges (Starbuck), Scott A.
Manchester U: Schmeichel; O'Kane (Sharpe), Irwin, Bruce, Keane, Pallister, Cantona, Butt, McClair (Scholes), Hughes, Giggs.

THIRD ROUND REPLAYS

17 JAN

Carlisle U (0) 1 *(Walling)*
Sunderland (2) 3 *(Armstrong 2, Gray P)* 12,201
Carlisle U: Caig; Edmondson, Gallimore, Walling, Mountfield, Thorpe (Peters), Thomas, Conway, Reeves, Davey, Robinson.
Sunderland: Chamberlain; Kubicki, Scott, Bennett, Ferguson, Melville, Ball, Russell (Howey), Gray P, Smith, Armstrong.

Leeds U (2) 5 *(Deane, Wetherall, Masinga 3)*
Walsall (1) 2 *(O'Connor (pen), Wetherall (og)) aet* 17,881
Leeds U: Lukic; Kelly, Worthington, Palmer (Radebe), Wetherall, Pemberton, Whelan, Wallace (Masinga), Deane, McAllister, Speed.
Walsall: Wood; Evans, Gibson, Watkiss, Marsh, Palmer, O'Connor (Rogers), Ntamark, Lightbourne, Wilson (Mehew), Houghton.

Middlesbrough (0) 1 *(Hendrie)*
Swansea C (1) 2 *(Torpey, Penney)* 13,940
Middlesbrough: Miller; Morris, Fleming, Vickers, Pearson, Mustoe, Hignett, Pollock, Wilkinson, Hendrie, Moore (Kavanagh).
Swansea C: Freestone; Jenkins, Walker, Basham, Ford, Ampadu, Hayes, Penney, Torpey, Cornforth, Hodge (Chapple).

Watford (0) 2 *(Hessenthaler, Holdsworth)*
Scarborough (0) 0 7047
Watford: Miller; Lavin, Bazeley, Foster, Holdsworth (Page), Ramage, Hessenthaler, Connolly (Watson), Gibbs, Porter, Millen.
Scarborough: Kelly; Knowles, Charles, D'Auria, Meyer, Davis, Thompson (Blackstone), Rodwell, White, Swann (Calvert), Wells.

18 JAN

Arsenal (0) 0
Millwall (1) 2 *(Beard, Kennedy)* 32,319
Arsenal: Seaman; Dixon, Winterburn, Morrow, Keown (Adams), Linighan, Jensen (Flatts), Wright, Campbell, Hillier, Parlour.
Millwall: Keller; Dawes, Van Blerk, Roberts, Witter, Stevens, Beard, Rae, Edwards (Savage), Mitchell (Webber), Kennedy.

Blackburn R (0) 1 *(Sutton)*
Newcastle U (0) 2 *(Hottiger, Clark)* 22,658
Blackburn R: Flowers; Berg, Le Saux, Warhurst, Hendry, Pearce, Slater (Wright), Atkins (Newell), Shearer, Sutton, Wilcox.
Newcastle U: Srnicek; Hottiger, Beresford, Elliott, Peacock, Howey, Lee, Venison, Kitson, Fox, Clark.

Bristol R (0) 0
Luton T (0) 1 *(Marshall)* 8218
Bristol R: Parkin; Pritchard (Hardyman), Clark, Tillson, Gurney, Sterling, Channing, Browning, Taylor, Miller, Archer.
Luton T: Sommer; Chenery, Johnson, Waddock, Thomas, Peake, Telfer, Oakes, Dixon, Preece, Marshall.

Liverpool (1) 1 *(Redknapp)*
Birmingham C (0) 1 *(Otto)* 36,275
Liverpool: James; Jones R, Bjornebye, Scales, Babb, Ruddock, McManaman, Redknapp, Rush, Thomas, Fowler.
Birmingham C: Bennett; Poole, Frain (Dominguez) (McGavin), Ward, Barnett, Daish, Donowa, Claridge, Lowe, Otto, Cooper.
aet; Liverpool won 2-0 on penalties.

Manchester C (3) 5 *(Rosler 4, Gaudino)*
Notts Co (1) 2 *(McSwegan, Matthews)* 14,261
Manchester C: Dibble; Summerbee, Brightwell D, Kernaghan, Curle, Brightwell I, Gaudino, Walsh, Rosler (Quinn), Flitcroft (Simpson), Beagrie.
Notts Co: Cherry; Mills, Legg, Turner, Murphy, Johnson, Devlin, Butler, White, McSwegan (Lund), Matthews.

Stoke C (1) 1 *(Scott)*
Bristol C (0) 3 *(Bent, Baird, Tinnion) aet* 11,579
Stoke C: Sinclair; Clarkson (Carruthers), Sandford, Cranson, Overson, Orlygsson, Butler, Wallace, Scott, Peschisolido, Gleghorn.
Bristol C: Welch; Hansen, Munro, Shail, Bryant, Tinnion, Kuhl (Edwards), Bent, Baird, Allison (Partridge), Owers.

Tranmere R (3) 3 *(O'Brien, Muir, Malkin)*
Bury (0) 0 7921
Tranmere R: Nixon; Stevens (Jones), Thomas, McGreal, Brannan, O'Brien, Morrissey, Muir, Malkin, Irons, Nevin.
Bury: Kelly G; Cross, Stanislaus, Daws, Lucketti, Hughes, Hulme, Carter, Paskin (Kelly T), Johnrose, Rigby.

WBA (0) 1 *(Raven)*
Coventry C (0) 2 *(Dublin, Ndlovu)* 23,230
WBA: Naylor; O'Regan, Edwards, Bradley, Mardon, Raven (Smith), Donovan, Ashcroft, Rees (Taylor), Hunt, Hamilton.
Coventry C: Ogrizovic; Borrows, Morgan, Cook, Rennie, Williams, Darby, Ndlovu, Dublin, Marsh, Jenkinson (Wegerle).

FOURTH ROUND

28 JAN

Burnley (0) 0
Liverpool (0) 0 20,551
Burnley: Russell; Parkinson, Eyres, Davis, Winstanley, Randall, Harper, Hoyland, Mullin, Robinson (McMinn), Saville.
Liverpool: James; Jones R, Matteo, Scales, Babb, Ruddock, McManaman, Redknapp, Rush, Barnes, Fowler.

Coventry C (0) 0
Norwich C (0) 0 15,101
Coventry C: Ogrizovic; Borrows, Morgan (Wegerle), Pickering, Rennie, Pressley, Cook, Ndlovu, Dublin, Marsh, Jenkinson.
Norwich C: Tracey (Marshall); Sutch, Bowen, Newsome, Polston, Ullathorne, Adams, Newman (Akinbiyi), Sheron (Cureton), Milligan, Eadie.

Leeds U (2) 3 *(White, Palmer, Masinga)*
Oldham Ath (0) 2 *(Halle, Palmer (og))* 25,010
Leeds U: Lukic; Kelly, Worthington, Palmer, Wetherall, Pemberton, White, Masinga (Yeboah), Deane, McAllister, Speed.
Oldham Ath: Gerrard; Makin (Holden R), Pointon, Henry, Graham, Redmond, Halle, Ritchie (Beckford), Banger, Richardson, Brennan.

Luton T (0) 1 *(Biggins)*
Southampton (0) 1 *(Shipperley)* 9938
Luton T: Sommer; Oakes, Johnson, Waddock, Thomas, Peake, Telfer, Biggins, Dixon (Williams), Preece, Marshall.
Southampton: Grobbelaar; Kenna, Benali, Charlton (Hughes), Hall, Widdrington, Le Tissier, Magilton, Shipperley, Maddison, Heaney.

Manchester C (1) 1 *(Walsh)*
Aston Villa (0) 0 21,177
Manchester C: Coton; Summerbee, Brightwell D, Brightwell I, Curle, Vonk, Gaudino, Walsh (Quinn), Rosler, Flitcroft, Beagrie.
Aston Villa: Bosnich; Barrett, Staunton, Teale, McGrath, Ehiogu, Yorke (Johnson), Fashanu, Saunders, Taylor, Townsend.

Manchester U (2) 5 *(Irwin 2 (1 pen), Giggs, McClair, Humes (og))*
Wrexham (1) 2 *(Durkan, Cross)* 43,222
Manchester U: Schmeichel; Neville P, Irwin, May, Sharpe, Pallister, Keane (Kanchelskis), Ince, McClair (Beckham), Scholes, Giggs.
Wrexham: Marriott; Jones, Hardy, Hughes (Phillips), Hunter, Humes, Bennett, Owen, Connolly (Cross), Watkin, Durkan.

Millwall (0) 0
Chelsea (0) 0 18,573
Millwall: Keller; Dawes, Van Blerk, Roberts, Witter, Thatcher, Beard, Rae, Edwards, Mitchell, Kennedy.
Chelsea: Kharine; Clarke, Minto, Kjeldbjerg (Burley), Johnsen, Sinclair, Spencer, Spackman, Stein, Peacock, Wise.

Newcastle U (1) 3 *(Kitson 3)*
Swansea C (0) 0 34,372
Newcastle U: Srnicek; Hottiger, Elliott, Venison, Peacock, Howey, Bracewell, Beardsley, Kitson, Fox, Gillespie.
Swansea C: Freestone; Jenkins, Walker, Basham, Ford, Chapple, Hayes (McFarlane), Penney, Torpey, Cornforth, Hodge.

Nottingham F (1) 1 *(Bohinen)*
Crystal Palace (1) 2 *(Armstrong, Dowie)* 16,790
Nottingham F: Crossley; Lyttle, Tiler, Cooper, Chettle, Stone, Phillips, Gemmill (Bull), Bohinen, Collymore, Roy.
Crystal Palace: Martyn; Patterson, Gordon, Southgate, Shaw, Coleman, Dowie, Newman, Armstrong (Preece), Pitcher, Salako.

Portsmouth (0) 0
Leicester C (1) 1 *(Roberts)* 14,928
Portsmouth: Knight; Gittens, Daniel, McGrath (McLoughlin), Russell, Butters, Pethick, Radosavljevic, Powell, Creaney (Flahavan), Kristensen (Rees).
Leicester C: Poole; Smith, Whitlow, Mohan, Hill, Draper, Grayson, Thompson, Robins, Roberts, Philpott.

QPR (1) 1 *(Impey)*
West Ham U (0) 0 17,694
QPR: Roberts; Bardsley, Maddix, Barker, Yates, McDonald, Impey, Holloway, Dichio, Gallen, Sinclair.
West Ham U: Miklosko; Breacker, Dicks, Potts, Martin, Allen, Bishop (Hutchison), Moncur, Cottee, Boere, Hughes.

Watford (1) 1 *(Hessenthaler)*
Swindon T (0) 0 11,202
Watford: Miller; Lavin, Bazeley, Foster, Millen, Ramage, Hessenthaler, Payne, Moralee (Connolly), Porter, Gibbs.
Swindon T: Hammond; Robinson, Murray, Culverhouse, Nijholt (Thorne), Taylor, Horlock, Beauchamp, Fjortoft, Mutch (O'Sullivan), Ling.

29 JAN

Bristol C (0) 0
Everton (0) 1 *(Jackson)* 19,816
Bristol C: Welch; Hansen, Munro, Shail, Bryant (Dryden), Tinnion, Edwards, Bent, Partridge (Seal), Allison, Owers.
Everton: Southall; Jackson, Burrows, Horne, Watson, Unsworth, Limpar, Parkinson, Barlow, Rideout, Hinchcliffe (Stuart).

Sunderland (0) 1 *(Gray P)*
Tottenham H (0) 4 *(Klinsmann 2 (1 pen), Sheringham, Melville (og))* 21,135
Sunderland: Chamberlain; Kubicki, Scott, Bennett, Ferguson, Melville, Howey, Russell, Gray P, Smith, Armstrong (Martin Gray).
Tottenham H: Walker; Campbell, Edinburgh, Popescu, Calderwood, Mabbutt, Anderton, Barmby, Klinsmann, Sheringham, Howells (Nethercott).

Tranmere R (0) 0
Wimbledon (1) 2 *(Leonhardsen, Earle)* 11,637
Tranmere R: Nixon; Stevens, Thomas, McGreal, Garnett, O'Brien (Brannan), Morrissey, Muir (Aldridge), Malkin, Irons, Nevin.
Wimbledon: Segers; Cunningham, Elkins, Jones, Perry, Thorn, Barton, Earle, Harford (Goodman), Leonhardsen, Ekoku (Blissett).

30 JAN

Sheffield W (0) 0
Wolverhampton W (0) 0 21,757
Sheffield W: Pressman; Atherton, Nolan, Bart-Williams, Pearce, Walker, Hyde, Waddle, Bright, Whittingham (Watson), Sheridan (Petrescu).
Wolverhampton W: Jones; Blades, Thompson, Emblen, De Wolf, Law, Birch (Venus), Kelly D, Mills (Goodman), Cowans, Dennison.

FOURTH ROUND REPLAYS

7 FEB

Liverpool (1) 1 *(Barnes)*
Burnley (0) 0 32,109
Liverpool: James; Jones R, Bjornebye (Walters), Scales, Babb, Ruddock, McManaman, Thomas, Rush, Barnes, Fowler.
Burnley: Beresford; Parkinson, Eyres, Davis, Winstanley, Randall, Harper, Hoyland (Peel), Mullin, Robinson, Harrison (McMinn).

8 FEB

Chelsea (0) 1 *(Stein)*
Millwall (0) 1 *(Savage)* 25,515
Chelsea: Kharine; Clarke, Minto, Burley, Lee, Sinclair, Spackman (Newton), Spencer, Stein, Peacock (Furlong), Wise.
Millwall: Keller; Dawes (Webber), Thatcher, Roberts, Witter, Stevens, Beard, Rae, Edwards (Savage), Mitchell, Van Blerk.
aet; Millwall won 5-4 on penalties.

Norwich C (1) 3 *(Sheron 2, Eadie)*
Coventry C (1) 1 *(Ndlovu) aet* 14,673
Norwich C: Marshall; Sutch, Bowen, Newsome, Polston, Ullathorne, Crook (Goss), Milligan, Sheron, Eadie, Adams (Akinbiyi).
Coventry C: Ogrizovic; Borrows, Morgan, Pressley, Rennie, Pickering, Flynn, Ndlovu, Dublin (Darby), Marsh, Wegerle (Jones).

Southampton (4) 6 *(Le Tissier 2 (1 pen), Magilton, Heaney, Monkou, Hughes)*
Luton T (0) 0 15,075
Southampton: Grobbelaar; Kenna, Dodd, Widdrington, Hall, Monkou, Le Tissier (Hughes), Magilton, Shipperley, Maddison (Tisdale), Heaney.
Luton T: Sommer; James (Dixon), Johnson, Waddock, Thomas, Peake, Telfer, Oakes, Biggins (Thorpe), Preece, Marshall.

Wolverhampton W (1) 1 *(Kelly D)*
Sheffield W (0) 1 *(Bright)* 28,136
Wolverhampton W: Jones; Blades (Mills), Thompson, Emblen, De Wolf, Law, Rankine (Bennett), Kelly D, Goodman, Cowans, Dennison.
Sheffield W: Pressman; Atherton, Nolan, Bart-Williams, Pearce, Walker, Hyde, Waddle, Bright, Ingesson (Sheridan), Sinton (Whittingham).
aet; Wolverhampton W won 4-3 on penalties.

FIFTH ROUND

18 FEB

Everton (2) 5 *(Limpar, Parkinson, Rideout, Ferguson, Stuart)*
Norwich C (0) 0 31,616
Everton: Southall; Jackson, Hinchcliffe, Ebbrell, Watson, Ablett, Stuart, Parkinson, Ferguson, Rideout (Barlow), Limpar.
Norwich C: Tracey; Bradshaw, Bowen, Newsome, Newman, Ullathorne (Prior), Sutch, Johnson, Sheron, Eadie, Goss.

QPR (0) 1 *(Wilson (pen))*
Millwall (0) 0 16,457
QPR: Roberts; Bardsley, Wilson, Barker, Maddix, McDonald, Impey, Holloway, Ferdinand, Gallen, Meaker.
Millwall: Keller; Beard, Thatcher, Roberts, Witter, Webber, Savage, May, Mitchell (Edwards), Van Blerk, Kennedy.

Tottenham H (1) 1 *(Klinsmann)*
Southampton (1) 1 *(Le Tissier (pen))* 28,091
Tottenham H: Walker; Campbell, Edinburgh, Popescu, Calderwood, Mabbutt, Anderton, Barmby, Klinsmann (Austin), Sheringham, Howells.
Southampton: Grobbelaar; Kenna, Benali, Widdrington, Hall, Monkou, Le Tissier, Magilton, Shipperley, Maddison, Heaney.

Watford (0) 0
Crystal Palace (0) 0 13,814
Watford: Miller; Lavin, Bazeley, Foster, Millen, Ramage, Holdsworth, Payne, Moralee (Watson), Porter, Gibbs.
Crystal Palace: Martyn; Patterson, Gordon, Southgate, Shaw, Coleman, Humphrey, Pitcher, Armstrong, Preece, Salako.

Wolverhampton W (1) 1 *(Kelly D)*
Leicester C (0) 0 28,544
Wolverhampton W: Jones; Venus, Thompson, Bennett, De Wolf, Law, Rankine, Kelly D, Goodman, Cowans, Dennison.
Leicester C: Poole (Ward); Grayson (Philpott), Whitlow, Hill, Willis, Draper, Galloway, Thompson, Robins, Roberts, Parker.

19 FEB

Liverpool (1) 1 *(Fowler)*
Wimbledon (1) 1 *(Clarke)* 25,124
Liverpool: James; Jones R, Bjornebye, Redknapp, Scales, Ruddock, McManaman, Walters, Rush, Barnes, Fowler.
Wimbledon: Segers; Cunningham, Kimble, Perry, Reeves, Barton, Ardley, Earle, Clarke (Holdsworth), Leonhardsen, Ekoku (Harford).

Manchester U (2) 3 *(Bruce, McClair, Hughes)*
Leeds U (0) 1 *(Yeboah)* 42,744
Manchester U: Schmeichel; Keane, Irwin, Bruce, Sharpe, Pallister, Kanchelskis, Ince, McClair, Hughes, Giggs.
Leeds U: Lukic; Kelly, Dorigo, Whelan, Wetherall, Pemberton, White, Wallace (Worthington), Masinga (Yeboah), McAllister, Speed.

Newcastle U (1) 3 *(Gillespie 2, Beresford)*
Manchester C (1) 1 *(Rosler)* 33,219
Newcastle U: Srnicek; Hottiger, Beresford, Venison, Peacock, Howey, Lee, Beardsley, Kitson, Fox, Gillespie.
Manchester C: Dibble; Summerbee, Brightwell D (Foster), Kernaghan, Curle, Brightwell I, Gaudino, Rosler, Quinn (Mike), Flitcroft, Beagrie.

FIFTH ROUND REPLAYS

28 FEB

Wimbledon (0) 0
Liverpool (2) 2 *(Barnes, Rush)* 12,553
Wimbledon: Segers; Cunningham, Kimble, Barton, Perry, Thorn (Harford), Ardley, Earle, Clarke, Leonhardsen, Ekoku (Holdsworth).
Liverpool: James; Jones R, Bjornebye, Scales, Babb, Ruddock, McManaman, Redknapp, Rush, Barnes, Fowler (Walters).

1 MAR

Crystal Palace (0) 1 *(Ndah)*
Watford (0) 0 aet 10,321
Crystal Palace: Martyn; Humphrey (Preece), Gordon, Southgate, Shaw, Patterson, Dyer (Ndah), Newman, Dowie, Pitcher, Salako.
Watford: Miller; Gibbs, Bazeley (Pitcher), Foster, Millen, Ramage, Holdsworth, Johnson, Moralee (Mooney), Porter, Barnes.

Southampton (2) 2 *(Shipperley, Le Tissier (pen))*
Tottenham H (0) 6 *(Rosenthal 3, Sheringham, Barmby, Anderton) aet* 15,172
Southampton: Grobbelaar; Kenna, Benali, Widdrington (Hughes), Monkou, Dodd, Le Tissier, Magilton, Shipperley, Maddison, Heaney.
Tottenham: Walker; Edinburgh, Austin, Nethercott (Rosenthal), Calderwood, Mabbutt, Anderton, Barmby, Klinsmann, Sheringham, Howells (Caskey).

SIXTH ROUND

11 MAR

Crystal Palace (0) 1 *(Dowie)*
Wolverhampton W (0) 1 *(Cowans)* 14,604
Crystal Palace: Martyn; Southgate, Coleman, Pitcher, Shaw, Young, Matthew (Humphrey), Newman, Dowie (Dyer), Preece, Salako.
Wolverhampton W: Stowell; Smith, Thompson, Law, Rankine, Shirtliff, Goodman, Kelly D, Bull, Cowans, Dennison (Emblen).

Liverpool (1) 1 *(Fowler)*

Tottenham H (1) 2 *(Sheringham, Klinsmann)* 39,592

Liverpool: James; Jones R, Babb, Redknapp, Scales, Ruddock, McManaman, Walters (Bjornebye), Rush, Barnes (Thomas), Fowler.
Tottenham H: Walker; Austin, Edinburgh, Howells, Calderwood, Mabbutt, Anderton, Barmby, Klinsmann, Sheringham, Rosenthal.

12 MAR

Everton (0) 1 *(Watson)*

Newcastle U (0) 0 35,203

Everton: Southall; Jackson, Unsworth, Ebbrell, Watson, Ablett, Horne, Parkinson, Ferguson, Barlow, Limpar (Stuart).
Newcastle: Srnicek; Hottiger (Watson), Beresford (Elliott), Venison, Peacock, Bracewell, Lee, Clark, Kitson, Fox, Gillespie.

Manchester U (1) 2 *(Irwin, Sharpe)*

QPR (0) 0 42,830

Manchester U: Schmeichel; Neville G, Irwin, Bruce, Sharpe, Pallister, Kanchelskis, Ince, McClair, Hughes, Giggs (Keane).
QPR: Roberts; Bardsley, Wilson, Barker, Maddix, McDonald, Impey, Holloway, Ferdinand, Gallen, Brevett (Penrice).

SIXTH ROUND REPLAY

22 MAR

Wolverhampton W (1) 1 *(Kelly D)*

Crystal Palace (3) 4 *(Armstrong 2, Dowie, Pitcher)* 27,548

Wolverhampton W: Stowell; Rankine, Thompson, Bennett (Emblen), Law, Shirtliff, Venus, Goodman, Bull, Kelly D, Dennison.
Crystal Palace: Martyn; Patterson, Coleman, Southgate, Shaw, Young, Dowie, Cox (Newman), Armstrong (Dyer), Pitcher, Salako.

SEMI-FINALS

9 APR

Crystal Palace (1) 2 *(Dowie, Armstrong)* 38,256

Manchester U (0) 2 *(Irwin, Pallister) aet* (at Villa Park)

Crystal Palace: Martyn; Patterson, Coleman (Gordon), Southgate, Shaw, Young, Dowie, Houghton, Armstrong, Pitcher, Salako.
Manchester U: Schmeichel; Neville G, Irwin, Keane, Sharpe, Pallister, Beckham (Butt), Ince, McClair, Hughes, Giggs.

Everton (1) 4 *(Jackson, Stuart, Amokachi 2)* 38,226

Tottenham H (0) 1 *(Klinsmann (pen))* (at Elland Road)

Everton: Southall; Jackson, Ablett, Parkinson, Watson, Unsworth, Limpar, Horne, Stuart, Rideout (Amokachi), Hinchcliffe.
Tottenham H: Walker; Austin, Nethercott (Rosenthal), Popescu, Calderwood, Mabbutt, Anderton, Barmby, Klinsmann, Sheringham, Howells.

SEMI-FINAL REPLAY

12 APR

Manchester U (2) 2 *(Bruce, Pallister)*

Crystal Palace (0) 0 (at Villa Park) 17,987

Manchester U: Schmeichel; Neville G, Irwin, Bruce, Sharpe, Pallister, Butt, Ince, Keane, Hughes, Giggs (McClair).
Crystal Palace: Wilmot; Patterson, Gordon, Southgate, Shaw, Young, Dowie (Cox), Houghton, Armstrong, Pitcher (Newman), Salako.

FINAL at Wembley

20 MAY

Everton (1) 1 *(Rideout)*

Manchester U (0) 0 79,592

Everton: Southall; Jackson, Ablett, Parkinson, Watson, Unsworth, Limpar (Amokachi), Horne, Stuart, Rideout (Ferguson), Hinchcliffe.
Manchester U: Schmeichel; Neville G, Irwin, Bruce (Giggs), Sharpe (Scholes), Pallister, Keane, Ince, McClair, Hughes, Butt.
Referee: G. Ashby (Worcester).

Paul Rideout heads the only goal in the 1995 FA Cup Final to give Everton a 1-0 win over Manchester United. (Colorsport)

FOOTBALL AND THE LAW

Sir Stanley Matthews' 80th birthday on the first day of February crystallised the true dimension of Football and the Law during the 1994-95 season. He was never booked or dismissed from the field and he surfaced as an 18-year-old winger during Stoke City's Football League Second Division Championship-winning team of 1932-33.

Four years later, in a replayed 5th round FA Cup tie at White Hart Lane – won 4-3 by Tottenham after being 3-1 down four minutes from time and described by the losing Everton captain, Joe Mercer, as the greatest game in which he played – his veteran centre-forward, Dixie Dean, was insulted by a fan as he entered the dressing-room tunnel. Retaliation with a punch is alleged in Dean's biography by a former Lord Chancellor's Department Official, Nick Walsh, to have been assisted by a police officer. Yet since no television existed, the occasion has been unrecorded until now, recalled by Cantona's Kung-Fu spectacular counter-attack upon his own abusive spectator.

Correspondingly, Duncan Ferguson's head-butt against a Raith Rovers opponent, which has landed him – subject to appeal – with a prison sentence, was missed by the referee but trapped on television, in the manner that Paul Davis' breakage of Glenn Cockerill's jaw, which resulted in a £3,000 fine and a nine-match suspension, surfaced by disciplinary action. Thus it is not possible to identify the number of criminal or civilly liable offences resulting from deliberately violent foul play which escape unknown and unpunished. In the Peterborough Crown Court, a criminal trial for an alleged assault by a defendant upon an attacker, resulting in a broken chest bone, is in the pipeline; and the ITN London Programme, during a Sunday examination of Park Football, uncovered significant occasions even more serious than the Cantona and Ferguson prosecutions.

Civil actions for damages surface in local county courts more frequently than the two high-profile High Court trials which resulted in Paul Elliott failing to win damages against Dean Saunders and Liverpool, and John O'Neill's settlement out of court against John Fashanu and Wimbledon.

Off the field, the law has been in and out of football's news with George Graham's Arsenal dispute, alleged match throwing and two governing bodies biting the dust. The FA's sanctions on Spurs of ejection from the FA Cup and deduction of Premier League points were overturned on appeal to arbitrators, and the FA of Wales' refusal to allow three Welsh clubs to play in England was twice held in London's High Court as acting in restraint of trade. Finally, yet to come are proceedings in the European Court of Justice by Jean Bosman for breaches of the Treaty of Rome equivalent to restraint of trade that could yet destroy the current transfer system that existed even before Stanley Matthews' day.

Throughout that period when Matthews' Stoke City and Arthur Rowe's Spurs were surviving on £8 per week wages with a £2 bonus for a win and £1 for a draw, British football reigned supreme, and apart from a hiccup when England beat Italy 3-2 in 1934 in what became known as the Battle of Highbury, foul play of the kind which has landed Ferguson in the courts and led to claims for damages in county courts was never prevalent to the degree which is now captured on television. Was the reason discipline in homes, schools and lack of significant financial rewards? Or is there a deeper reason which chroniclers of the future will unravel for those of us unable to do so today?

EDWARD GRAYSON,
Founder President, British Association for Sport and the Law.

THE SCOTTISH SEASON 1994-95

The new system of four divisions in the League caused many comments throughout the season, and a fairly generous slice of self-preservation was apparent in those from the clubs. It could not be said that there was a lack of interest: when it was possible to go from promotion contender to the relegation zone with one loss, there was little chance of boredom. Certainly there was much coming and going, and the only sure fact that established itself early on was that Rangers were going to win the Premier Division title yet again.

The two main contenders for the other honours in this division were Motherwell and Hibernian: two shrewd managers made the best from what they had, and in the end it was the new boy who slipped into the runners-up position. Celtic never quite settled, but promised for the future, whilst Falkirk surprised many with some sound performances. Hearts had a purple patch, but finished in some danger, whilst Kilmarnock had a charge to safety at the right moment; Partick Thistle certainly looked doomed until well into the new year, but they showed real grit and determination in forcing their way from the bottom of the table.

It was left to the unlikely pair of Aberdeen and Dundee United to face the drop: Aberdeen, with a new manager, won the showdown a fortnight from the end of the season, and United sank with hardly a murmur: it was a sad day for Jim McLean who had done so much to create the team and to lead it to a proud position in Europe. Aberdeen were left to play-off for the remaining place with Dunfermline, and they were successful with something to spare.

The First Division was most exciting right to the wire: for some weeks there had been a running battle for the promotion spot, and the lead changed several times. On the last afternoon, all options were still open for Raith Rovers, Dundee and Dunfermline; but Raith achieved the draw they required at Hamilton, whilst a frenzied burst of late goals nearly put Dundee into the play-off place; as it was, Dunfermline finished as runners-up and, as has been noted, they lost the play-off to Aberdeen. It was hugely frustrating for the Pars who thus missed out on promotion for the third time running; whilst Dundee could only look on in despair and regret some throwing away of points in the final weeks of the season. Airdrie never quite maintained the pace with the leaders in the last session, whilst at the foot of the table Stranraer, after enjoying their year in the upper echelons, struggled, and they were joined by Ayr United, who comfortably lost to St Mirren in the race for safety.

Likewise there was a storming finish in the Second Division: here there were four clubs seriously concerned with promotion: Greenock Morton, Dumbarton, Stenhousemuir and Stirling Albion: Stirling had a late run which brought them to the brink of success, whilst Stenhousemuir never quite recovered their form after a magnificent Cup run; Greenock Morton drew clear at the end, but on the last day Dumbarton played Stirling Albion -and won. It was as close as that. At the other end, Brechin and Meadowbank had lifted the relegation spots without much attention from other teams.

There was much interest in the new Third Division, with the two new teams. Ross County were challenging for the top position until very nearly the end of the season, and they quickly adapted to their status. They drew their crowds, too. Caledonian Thistle did not have quite such a comfortable year, but they finished in mid-table. Both these former Highland League teams should soon be looking for promotion.

It was the East coast sides who prospered: Forfar Athletic had a good season throughout, and a series of steady results put them well ahead of the others as they clinched promotion with weeks to go. Montrose were several games behind. and this is not always a healthy position to be in; however, they made no mistakes, and came away strongly in the end to finish as runners-up.

The first year of the Coca-Cola Cup saw the remarkable achievement of Raith Rovers in winning the first final of the year against Celtic at Ibrox. It was a rip-roaring match, with Celtic scoring a late goal which looked to have won them the trophy; but a couple of minutes later, Raith equalized, and extra time led to no further goals: so to the penalty shoot out, and Raith's youngsters kept cool heads, and it was all over. What a season for manager Jimmy Nicholl and the Kirkcaldy club, who went on to clinch promotion to the Premier Division later!

In the earlier stages there were some fine achievements to record: whatever may be the dislike of many for the penalty shoot-out, it certainly breeds excitement, and this form of ending with a result was often in evidence: Falkirk had a real nail-biter against Montrose, but went on to dispose of Rangers at Ibrox -no mean task; Hamilton Accies just failed to oust Dundee United; whilst Airdrie started a remarkable run of cup matches by taking Motherwell in the depths of extra time. Airdrie continued by dismissing Hibs, and then failed to hold Raith Rovers on penalties in the semi-final at McDiarmid Park: it was their only cup failure till the last day of the season.

The B&Q Cup went to Airdrie, who, incidentally, had another penalty duel with Raith, but won this one. The final, in early November, was closely contested, and Dundee lost by the odd goal in five.

The Scottish Cup was notable for two particular performances above all others: Stenhousemuir, who started their campaign in the first round on December 17, won convincing victories over East Stirling and Arbroath before coming against St Johnstone, where they held the home team; at Ochilview a week later they stunned the Perth team, and followed this by disposing of Aberdeen in the fourth round. In the Quarter-finals they took on Hibs (also at Ochilview) and finally met their match in the second half after a 0-0 half time score. Astute instructions to his players, and their whole-hearted enthusiasm meant that Terry Christie made a considerable impact on the competition. Then there was Airdrie -who again came against Raith, and this time defeated them roundly. In the semi-final they won a hard encounter against Hearts, who had themselves had a good run. The final was not a particularly good game, and Celtic beat Airdrie to take their first silverware home for some years: at last the Parkhead fans had something really to cheer, and it was a deserved victory which they had worked hard to achieve.

The club season in Europe was, to say the least, undistinguished, and there was little to give pleasure to Scottish fans. However, Motherwell did well in the two matches with Borussia Dortmund, although in the end lack of experience showed. There has not been much to cheer about in the last year or two, but perhaps next season is the one in which we may make some impact.

On the international front it was encouraging: with the European Championship looming, we still look to have a fair chance of qualifying. This has been done by some workmanlike performances and a good deal of hard graft both by management and players; there have been the usual times when everyone seemed to be injured, but qualification is now in our own hands, and good results in the later stages can ensure success. Craig Brown is to be congratulated, both at the senior level and with the Under 21s who have a batch of young players coming on well.

There was great sadness late in the season when Davie Cooper died suddenly; a very modest and even retiring person, he had not looked for the kind of rewards abroad which his talents could so easily have brought to him. A player of immense ability, he added light to every game he played; after years with Rangers and Motherwell, he had returned to his first club, Clydebank, and was still showing all his old skill, and the ability to beat men and cross to perfection. His death shocked the whole country: it showed the stature of the man that his club asked that his Number 7 jersey should not be used again for the rest of the season -a request willingly granted by the Scottish Football League.

ALAN ELLIOTT

Editor's note: In Match 1, Brechin City v Meadowbank Thistle on 13 August, Meadowbank had three points deducted for fielding an ineligible player. The goals from the game were not counted in the season's totals for either club. Also for Clydebank, the last six appearances by Lansdowne listed as No. 15, are full appearances (see above) and his total should be amended accordingly to 20 + 3.

ABERDEEN Premier Division

Year Formed: 1903. *Ground & Address:* Pittodrie Stadium, Pittodrie St, Aberdeen AB2 1QH. *Telephone:* 01224 632328.
Ground Capacity: 21,634 seated: All. *Size of Pitch:* 110yd × 72yd.
Chairman: Ian R. Donald. *Secretary:* Ian J. Taggart. *General Manager:* David Johnston.
Manager: Roy Aitken. *Assistant Managers:* Tommy Craig, Drew Jarvie, Neil Cooper. *Physios:* David Wylie, John Sharp.
Managers since 1975: Ally MacLeod; Billy McNeill; Alex Ferguson; Ian Porterfield; Alex Smith and Jocky Scott; Willie Miller. *Club Nicknames(s):* The Dons. *Previous Grounds:* None.
Record Attendance: 45,061 v Hearts, Scottish Cup 4th rd; 13 Mar, 1954.
Record Transfer Fee received: £970,000 for David Robertson to Rangers (July 1991).
Record Transfer Fee paid: £800,000 for Billy Dodds from St Johnstone, 1994.
Record Victory: 13-0 v Peterhead, Scottish Cup; 9 Feb, 1923.
Record Defeat: 0-8 v Celtic, Division 1; 30 Jan, 1965.
Most Capped Players: Alex McLeish, 77, Scotland.
Most League Appearances: 556: Willie Miller, 1973-90.
Most League Goals in Season (Individual): 38: Benny Yorston, Division I; 1929-30.
Most Goals Overall (Individual): 199: Joe Harper.

ABERDEEN 1994–95 LEAGUE RECORD

Match No.	*Date*	*Venue*	*Opponents*	*Result*		*H/T Score*	*Lg. Pos.*	*Goalscorers*	*Attendance*
1	Aug 13	H	Hearts	W	3-1	1-0	—	Robertson, Dodds, Booth	14,238
2	20	H	Falkirk	D	2-2	1-1	3	Robertson, Booth	11,143
3	27	A	Dundee U	L	1-2	0-0	5	Grant	9332
4	Sept 10	A	Hibernian	D	2-2	1-2	5	Dodds, Grant	9728
5	17	H	Partick T	D	1-1	0-0	4	Dodds	10,425
6	24	H	Rangers	D	2-2	1-1	4	Booth, Dodds	19,191
7	Oct 1	A	Kilmarnock	L	1-2	1-1	6	Booth	7445
8	8	A	Celtic	D	0-0	0-0	8		29,454
9	15	H	Motherwell	L	1-3	1-0	8	Dodds	12,489
10	22	A	Hearts	L	0-2	0-2	9		10,655
11	29	H	Dundee U	W	3-0	2-0	7	Kane 2, Booth	11,744
12	Nov 5	A	Falkirk	L	1-2	1-1	8	Booth	6185
13	9	H	Hibernian	D	0-0	0-0	—		10,882
14	19	A	Partick T	L	1-2	1-0	8	Dodds	3795
15	25	A	Rangers	L	0-1	0-0	—		45,072
16	Dec 3	H	Kilmarnock	L	0-1	0-1	10		10,345
17	10	A	Motherwell	W	1-0	1-0	9	McCart (og)	7020
18	26	H	Celtic	D	0-0	0-0	—		19,206
19	31	H	Hearts	W	3-1	2-0	9	Shearer 2, Inglis	11,392
20	Jan 2	A	Dundee U	D	0-0	0-0	—		10,560
21	7	H	Falkirk	D	0-0	0-0	7		14,141
22	14	H	Partick T	W	3-1	1-0	6	Dinnie (og), Jess, Shearer	9833
23	21	A	Hibernian	L	2-4	1-3	8	Dodds 2	8076
24	Feb 4	A	Kilmarnock	L	1-3	1-2	9	McKimmie	9384
25	12	H	Rangers	W	2-0	0-0	—	Dodds, Shearer	18,060
26	25	H	Motherwell	L	0-2	0-1	9		10,319
27	Mar 5	A	Celtic	L	0-2	0-1	—		20,621
28	11	A	Partick T	D	2-2	2-0	9	Wright, Dodds	6886
29	18	H	Hibernian	D	0-0	0-0	9		10,384
30	Apr 1	H	Kilmarnock	L	0-1	0-0	9		14,041
31	8	A	Rangers	L	2-3	2-2	10	Dodds, Shearer	44,460
32	15	H	Celtic	W	2-0	2-0	10	Shearer, Irvine	16,668
33	18	A	Motherwell	L	1-2	1-1	—	Dodds	7155
34	29	A	Hearts	W	2-1	0-0	10	Dodds 2	11,466
35	May 6	H	Dundee U	W	2-1	1-0	9	Dodds,Shearer	20,124
36	13	A	Falkirk	W	2-0	1-0	9	Thomson, Glass	12,835

Final League Position: 9

Honours

League Champions: Division I 1954-55. Premier Division 1979-80, 1983-84, 1984-85; *Runners-up:* Division I 1910-11, 1936-37, 1955-56, 1970-71, 1971-72. Premier Division 1977-78, 1980-81, 1981-82, 1988-89, 1989-90, 1990-91, 1992-93, 1993-94.
Scottish Cup Winners: 1947, 1970, 1982, 1983, 1984, 1986, 1990; *Runners-up:* 1937, 1953, 1954, 1959, 1967, 1978, 1993.
League Cup Winners: 1955-56, 1976-77, 1985-86, 1989-90; *Runners-up:* 1946-47, 1978-79, 1979-80, 1987-88, 1988-89, 1992-93.
Drybrough Cup Winners: 1971, 1980.

European: *European Cup* 12 matches (1980-81, 1984-85, 1985-86); *Cup Winners Cup Winners:* 1982-83. Semi-finals 1983-84. 37 matches (1967-68, 1970-71, 1978-79, 1982-83, 1983-84, 1986-87, 1990-91, 1993-94); *UEFA Cup* 36 matches (*Fairs Cup:* 1968-69. *UEFA Cup:* 1971-72, 1972-73, 1973-74, 1977-78, 1979-80, 1981-82, 1987-88, 1988-89, 1989-90, 1991-92, 1994-95).
Club colours: Shirt, Shorts, Stockings: Red with white trim.

Goalscorers: *League (43):* Dodds 15, Shearer 7, Booth 6, Grant 2, Kane 2, Robertson 2, Glass 1, Inglis 1, Irvine 1, Jess 1, McKimmie 1, Thomson 1, Wright 1, own goals 2. *Cup (1):* Jess 1. *League Cup (10):* Shearer 4 (1 pen), Booth 3, Dodds 1, Kane 1, own goal 1.

Snelders T 24	McKimmie S 34	Winnie D 6 + 2	Grant B 32	Irvine B 17	Wright S 33 + 1	Jess E 15 + 10	Shearer D 19 + 4	Kane P 27	Dodds W 35	Robertson H 2 + 1	Hetherston P 13 + 9	Booth S 11 + 1	Miller J 21 + 6	Woodthorpe C 14	McKinnon R 17 + 3	Smith G 31	Watt M 12 + 2	Glass S 11 + 8	Inglis J 16 + 1	Thomson S 6 + 4	Aitken R — + 2	Kpedekpo M — + 1	Match No.
1	2	3	4	5	6	7	*8*	9	10	11	12	14											1
1	2	3	4	*5*	6	14	8	9	10	11		7	12										2
1	2		4	5	6	7	*8*	9	10				14	3	11								3
1	2	11	4		6	7			10			9		3	8	5							4
	2		4	5	6	7			10			*9*	14	3	11	8	1						5
	2		4	5	6	7			*10*		12	9	14	3	11	8	1						6
	2	8	4	5	6				10		7	9	12	3	11		1						7
	2		4	5	6			8	10			9		3	11	7	1						8
	2		4	5	6			8	10		*11*	9	14	3		7	1						9
	2	12	4	5	6			8	10	14	*11*	9		3		7	1						10
1	2	5	4		6			8	10		12	9		3	*11*	7		14					11
1	2	5	4		6		12	8	10			9		*3*	11	7			14				12
1	2	14					*8*	4	10			9		3	11	6			5	7			13
1	2				14	8		4	*10*		12			3	11	6		9	5	7			14
1	*2*		8		6	11		4	10		12			3		7		14	5	9			15
1	2		8		6	7		4	10		12		9	*3*				11	5	14			16
1	2		8		3			4	10		6		9			7		11	5				17
1	2		8		3	14	12	4	10		6		*9*			7		11	5				18
1	2		11		3		8	4	10		7		9		12	6			5				19
1	2		7		3	14	*8*	4	10				9		11	6			5		12		20
1			7		3	14	8	4	10				9		*11*	6		2	5				21
1	2		11		*3*	7	8	4	10				9			6		14	5	12			22
1	2		11			7	8	4	10				*9*		14	6		3	5				23
1	2		8		3		14	4	10				9			6		11	5	7	12		24
1	*2*				3	7	8	4	10				9		11	6		14	5				25
1				5	2	7	*8*	4	10		12		9		*11*	6	15	3		14			26
	2		*4*	5	3	7	12		10		14		9		11	6	1	8					27
1	2		4	5	3	14			10		12		9		*11*	6		8		7			28
1	2		11		3	12	8	4	10		7		*9*			6	15		5	14			29
	2		*11*		3	14	8	4	10		7		9			6	1		5				30
	2		*11*		3	14	8	4	10		7		9			6	1		5				31
	2		11	5	3	12	8	4	10		7		*9*			6	1	14					32
	2		11	5	3	12	8	4	10		7		9			*6*	1	14					33
	2		4	5	3	11	8		10		7		9		12	*6*	1	14					34
1	2		4	5	3	*11*	8		10		7		9			6		14					35
1	2		4	5	3		8						9		10	6		11		*7*		14	36

AIRDRIEONIANS First Division

Year Formed: 1878. *Ground & Address:* Broadwood Stadium, Cumbernauld G68 9NE. Address for all correspondence: 32 Stirling Street, Airdrie, ML6 0AH *Telephone:* 01236 762067.
Ground Capacity: all seated: 6203. *Size of Pitch:* 112yd × 76yd.
Chairman and Secretary: George W. Peat CA. *Commercial Manager:* Dorothy Martin.
Manager: Alex MacDonald. *Assistant Manager:* John McVeigh. *Physio:* Dan Young. *Coach:* John Binnie.
Managers since 1975: I. McMillan; J. Stewart; R. Watson; W. Munro; A. MacLeod; D. Whiteford; G. McQueen; J. Bone.
Club Nickname(s): The Diamonds or The Waysiders. *Previous Grounds:* Mavisbank, Broomfield Park.
Record Attendance: 24,000 v Hearts, Scottish Cup; 8 Mar, 1952.
Record Transfer Fee received: £200,000 for Sandy Clark to West Ham U, May 1982.
Record Transfer Fee paid: £175,000 for Owen Coyle from Clydebank, February 1990.
Record Victory: 15-1 v Dundee Wanderers, Division II; 1 Dec, 1894.
Record Defeat: 1-11 v Hibernian, Division I; 24 Oct, 1959.
Most Capped Player: Jimmy Crapnell, 9, Scotland.
Most League Appearances: 523: Paul Jonquin, 1962-79.
Most League Goals in Season (Individual): 53, Hugh Baird, Division II, 1954-55. *Most Goals Overall (Individual):* —

AIRDRIEONIANS 1994–95 LEAGUE RECORD

Match No.	Date		Venue	Opponents	Result		H/T Score	Lg. Pos.	Goalscorers	Attendance
1	Aug	13	H	Dunfermline Ath	D	0-0	0-0	—		2964
2		20	H	St Johnstone	D	0-0	0-0	8		2161
3		27	A	Hamilton A	W	6-2	3-2	3	Harvey, Lawrence 3, Andrew Smith 2	1180
4	Sept	3	A	Dundee	D	1-1	1-0	3	Lawrence	4020
5		10	H	Ayr U	D	0-0	0-0	3		1620
6		24	H	Clydebank	W	2-0	1-0	2	Andrew Smith, Lawrence	1542
7	Oct	1	A	Stranraer	W	1-0	0-0	2	Lawrence	1001
8		8	H	Raith R	D	0-0	0-0	2		2096
9		15	A	St Mirren	W	1-0	1-0	2	Davies	2930
10		22	A	Dunfermline Ath	D	2-2	1-0	2	Cooper, Andrew Smith	5642
11		29	H	Hamilton A	W	1-0	0-0	2	Andrew Smith	1422
12	Nov	12	A	Ayr U	W	3-0	2-0	2	Cooper 2, Lawrence	2210
13		19	H	Dundee	W	2-1	0-0	2	Anthony Smith, Andrew Smith	2022
14		22	A	St Johnstone	L	0-4	0-1	—		3110
15		26	A	Clydebank	W	1-0	0-0	2	Andrew Smith	1197
16	Dec	3	H	Stranraer	W	8-1	2-1	1	Harvey, Boyle 2 (2 pens), Andrew Smith, Cooper 2, Davies 2	1207
17		26	A	Raith R	L	2-3	1-2	—	Cooper, Boyle	4338
18		31	H	Dunfermline Ath	D	0-0	0-0	3		3252
19	Jan	2	A	Hamilton A	L	0-3	0-2	—		2178
20		7	H	St Johnstone	L	0-2	0-2	3		1957
21		10	H	St Mirren	W	2-0	1-0	—	Cooper, Andrew Smith	1325
22		14	A	Dundee	W	1-0	0-0	2	Andrew Smith	4084
23		24	H	Ayr U	D	2-2	1-1	—	Boyle, Black	1320
24	Feb	4	A	Stranraer	W	4-1	2-0	3	Anthony Smith, Lawrence 2, Hay	945
25		14	H	Clydebank	L	1-2	0-2	—	Black (pen)	1033
26		25	A	St Mirren	W	1-0	0-0	4	Andrew Smith	2564
27	Mar	6	H	Raith R	L	1-2	0-0	—	Cooper	1726
28		18	A	Ayr U	W	2-0	0-0	4	Lawrence 2	1372
29		25	H	Dundee	L	0-3	0-0	4		2528
30	Apr	1	H	Stranraer	W	2-0	0-0	4	Cooper, Andrew Smith	851
31		11	A	Clydebank	D	1-1	0-1	—	Cooper	709
32		15	A	Raith R	W	1-0	1-0	4	Cooper	4494
33		22	H	St Mirren	W	1-0	0-0	4	McIntyre J	2245
34		29	A	Dunfermline Ath	D	0-0	0-0	4		6603
35	May	6	H	Hamilton A	L	0-1	0-0	4		1501
36		13	A	St Johnstone	L	1-2	1-1	4	Stewart	2868

Final League Position: 4

Honours
League Champions: Division II 1902-03, 1954-55, 1973-74; *Runners-up:* Division I 1922-23, 1923-24, 1924-25, 1925-26. First Division 1979-80, 1989-90, 1990-91. Division II 1900-01, 1946-47, 1949-50, 1965-66.
Scottish Cup Winners: 1924; *Runners-up:* 1975, 1992, 1995. *Scottish Spring Cup Winners:* 1976.
League Cup semi-finalists: 1991-92, 1994-95.
B&Q Cup Winners:R: 1994-95.

European: *UEFA Cup* 2 matches (1992-93).
Club colours: Shirt: White with Red diamond. Shorts: White. Stockings: Red.

Goalscorers: *League (50):* Andrew Smith 12, Cooper 11, Lawrence 11, Boyle 4 (2 pens), Davies 3, Black 2 (1 pen), Harvey 2, Tony Smith 2, Hay 1, McIntyre J 1, Stewart 1. *Scottish Cup (9):* Andrew Smith 3, Cooper 2, Harvey 2, Black 1, Davies 1. *League Cup (6):* Boyle 2, Andrew Smith 2, Cooper 1, Lawrence 1. *B&Q Cup (12):* Andrew Smith 3, Boyle 2 (1 pen), Cooper 2, Davies 2, Harvey 1, Lawrence 1, Stewart 1.

Martin J 35	Stewart A 32	Smith Ant 12 + 15	Sandison J 32 + 1	McIntyre T 15 + 1	Black K 31	Boyle J 33 + 1	Wilson M 12 + 3	Smith And 24 + 12	Harvey P 33	Lawrence A 24 + 8	McIntyre J 2 + 11	Hay G 25 + 1	Ferguson I — + 3	Jack P 28	Davies J 25	Honor C 1	Cooper S 26 + 3	McCulloch W 1 + 1	Connelly G 1 + 3	McLelland J 2	Tait S 1	McKenna G — + 1	Match No.
1	2	3	4	5	6	7	8	9	10	11	12												1
1		3	4	5	10	2	8	9	7	11	14	6	12										2
1	8	3	4	5	10	12		9	7	11		6		2									3
1	2	12	4	5	6	7	8	9	10	*11*			14	3									4
1	2		4	5	6	7		9	10	*11*			14	3	8								5
1	2				6	7	12	*9*	10	11	14	5		3	8	4							6
1	2		4			7	6	9	*10*	11	14	5		3	8		12						7
1	2		4	5	6	7		14	*10*	11				3	8		9						8
1	2		4	*5*	6	7		12	10	11		14		3	8		9						9
1	2		4		6	7	12	11	10		14	5		3	*8*		9						10
1	2	14	4		6	7	8	12		*11*		5		3	10		9						11
1	3	14	4		10	2		12	7	*11*		5		6	8		9						12
1	*2*	11	4		6	7	14	12	10	8		5		3			9	15					13
1		11	4	14	6	2		12	7	10		5		*3*	8		9						14
1	2	12	4		6	7		14	10	*11*		5		3	8		9						15
1	2	14	4		6	7		11	10	12		5		*3*	8		9						16
1	2	14	4		6	7	8	11	*10*	12		5		3			9						17
1	2	14	4		6	7		12	*10*	11		5		3	8		9						18
1	2	3	4		6	7		12	10	11		5			8		9						19
1	2	14	*4*		6	7	8	12		11		5		3	10		9						20
1	2	3	12	*5*	6	7		11	10					4	8		9		14				21
1	2		4	5	6	7		11	*10*	14		3			8		9						22
1	2	14	4	5	6	7		11	10	12		3			*8*		9						23
1	2	3	4		6	7	8	9	*10*	11	14	5					12						24
1	2	14	4		6	7	8	9	*10*	11		5		3			12						25
1	2		4	5	6	7		12	*10*	11	14			3	8		9						26
1	2	12	4	*5*	6	7		10		11	14			3	8		9						27
1	2	14	4	5	6	7		11	*10*	12				3	8		9						28
1		*2*	4		6	7		11	10	12	14	5		3	8		9						29
1		2	4		*6*	7	8	12	10	11		5		3			9		14				30
1	2	14	4		6	7		11	10	12		5		*3*	8		9						31
1	2	14	4		6	7		11	10	12		5		*3*	8		9						32
1	2	3	4			7		6	10	11	14	5			*8*		9						33
1	2		4			7		6	10	11	12	5		3	8		9						34
1	2	11		4			8	6	10		7			3			9		12	5			35
	2	14		4			6	9	10		11			*3*				1	7	8	5	12	36

ALBION ROVERS Third Division

Year Formed: 1882. *Ground & Address:* Cliftonhill Stadium, Main St, Coatbridge ML5 3RB. *Telephone:* 01236 432350.
Ground capacity: total: 1238, seated: 538. *Size of Pitch:* 110yd × 70yd.
Chairman: Robin W Marwick. *Secretary:* D. Forrester CA. *Commercial Manager:* Laurie Cameron. *Manager:* Jim Crease
Coach: Joe McBride. *Physio:* Michael McBride. *Managers since 1975:* G. Caldwell; S. Goodwin; H. Hood; J. Baker; D. Whiteford; M. Ferguson; W. Wilson; B. Rooney; A. Ritchie; T. Gemmell; D. Provan; M. Oliver; B. McLaren; T. Gemmell; T Spence. *Club Nickname(s):* The Wee Rovers. *Previous Grounds:* Cowheath Park, Meadow Park, Whifflet.
Record Attendance: 27,381 v Rangers, Scottish Cup 2nd rd; 8 Feb, 1936.
Record Transfer Fee received: £40,000 from Motherwell for Bruce Cleland.
Record Transfer Fee paid: £7000 for Gerry McTeague to Stirling Albion, September 1989.
Record Victory: 12-0 v Airdriehill, Scottish Cup; 3 Sept, 1887.
Record Defeat: 1-11 v Partick T, League Cup, 11 August 1993.
Most Capped Player: Jock White, 1 (2), Scotland.
Most League Appearances: 399, Murdy Walls, 1921-36.

ALBION ROVERS 1994–95 LEAGUE RECORD

Match No.	Date	Venue	Opponents	Result		H/T Score	Lg. Pos.	Goalscorers	Attendance
1	Aug 13	H	Alloa	L	0-4	0-3	—		310
2	20	H	Montrose	L	2-4	1-2	9	Scott, Seggie	274
3	27	A	Queen's Park	L	1-2	1-0	9	McBride J	443
4	Sept 3	H	Caledonian Th	L	0-1	0-0	10		539
5	10	A	East Stirling	L	0-4	0-2	10		377
6	24	H	Cowdenbeath	L	2-4	1-1	10	Conn, Quinn	314
7	Oct 1	A	Forfar Ath	D	1-1	0-0	10	Deeley	424
8	8	H	Arbroath	L	1-2	0-0	10	Conn	315
9	15	A	Ross C	L	0-3	0-0	10		1017
10	22	A	Alloa	L	0-1	0-0	10		440
11	29	H	Queen's Park	W	3-2	1-1	10	Kerr, McBride J 2	345
12	Nov 5	A	Montrose	L	1-4	0-2	10	McBride J	629
13	12	H	East Stirling	L	0-2	0-1	10		361
14	19	A	Caledonian Th	L	1-2	0-0	10	Scott	954
15	26	A	Cowdenbeath	D	2-2	2-1	10	Scott, Young	380
16	Dec 3	H	Forfar Ath	L	0-1	0-0	10		303
17	24	A	Arbroath	W	1-0	1-0	10	Ryan	467
18	31	H	Ross C	L	0-1	0-0	10		354
19	Jan 2	A	Queen's Park	D	0-0	0-0	—		705
20	14	H	Alloa	L	0-1	0-0	10		400
21	Feb 11	H	Caledonian Th	L	1-2	0-1	10	McBride J	274
22	18	H	Cowdenbeath	W	2-0	0-0	10	Ryan, Scott	273
23	25	A	Forfar Ath	L	0-4	0-3	10		510
24	Mar 4	A	Arbroath	L	0-2	0-0	10		436
25	7	A	East Stirling	L	0-3	0-1	—		312
26	22	H	Montrose	L	1-4	0-2	—	McEwan	187
27	29	A	Ross C	L	1-4	0-1	—	Seggie	967
28	Apr 1	H	Forfar Ath	L	0-3	0-2	10		270
29	5	H	East Stirling	W	3-1	1-0	—	Scott 2, Young	211
30	8	A	Cowdenbeath	L	0-2	0-0	10		186
31	11	A	Caledonian Th	W	2-0	1-0	—	Thompson, Scott	524
32	15	H	Arbroath	L	0-3	0-0	10		214
33	22	H	Ross C	L	1-2	1-1	10	Wilcox	334
34	29	A	Alloa	L	0-5	0-1	10		324
35	May 6	H	Queen's Park	L	0-2	0-1	10		337
36	13	A	Montrose	L	1-4	0-3	10	McEwan	893

Final League Position: 10

Most League Goals in Season (Individual): 41: Jim Renwick, Division II; 1932-33.
Most Goals Overall (Individual): 105: Bunty Weir, 1928-31.

Honours
League Champions: Division II 1933-34, Second Division 1988-89; *Runners-up:* Division II 1913-14, 1937-38, 1947-48.
Scottish Cup Runners-up: 1920. *League Cup:* —.
Club Colours: Shirt: Yellow with red trim. Shorts: Yellow. Stockings: Yellow.

Goalscorers: *League (27):* Scott 7, McBride J 5, Conn 2, McEwan 2, Ryan 2, Seggie 2, Young 2, Deeley 1, Kerr 1, Quinn 1, Thompson 1, Wilcox 1. *Scottish Cup (2):* Docherty 1, McBride J 1. *League Cup (0) B&Q Cup (0)*

Davidson A 21	McDonald D 18 + 1	Beattie J 10 + 1	Conn S 7	Malone P 4	Collins L 16 + 1	McBride M 22 + 4	Docherty A 7 + 3	Thompson D 18 + 2	Quinn K 7 + 4	Gallagher J 26	Seggie D 12 + 7	McBride J 31 + 4	Wight J 15 + 2	Philliben R 4	Riley D 6 + 1	Scott M 33 + 1	Tomnay D 1	Young G 12 + 7	Deeley B 20 + 2	Parry K 3 + 1	Kelly J 14	Ryan M 29	Miller D — + 2	Kerr J 12	Shah S 9	Dolan W 16 + 1	Miller S 1	McEwan A 10 + 2	Brown M 1	Arthur R 2	Wilcox D 9	*Match No.*
1	2	3	4	5	6	7	8	9	*10*	11	12	14	15																			1
1	5	*3*	4		8			11	10	6	12	14		2	7	9																2
1		3	10	4	6		8					11		2	7		5	9	14													3
1	4		5	6	8		7				12	11		2		9		10		3												4
					8		7				12	11	1	2		9		10	6	3	4	5	14									5
1	2		3		8	7			10		12	11				9			6		5			4								6
1			3		8	7			10		*11*	14				9			6		2	5		4								7
1			3		8	7			10		11					9		12	6		2	5		4								8
1	4					7		14	*10*	6	11	12			8	9			3		2	5										9
1				*8*		7	14	10	12	6		11				9			4	3	2	5										10
1						7	6	10				11				9			3		2	5		4	8							11
1					12	7	6	10				*11*				9		14	3		2	5		4	8							12
1					8	7		10				11				9			3		2	5		4	6							13
1					8	7	14	10				9				11		12	3		2	5		*4*	6							14
1	14				8					3		9				11		10			7	5		*4*	6	2						15
1	4					12				3		9	15			11		10	6		2	5			8	7						16
1	2				6	10				3		9				11						5		4	8	7						17
	2				6	11				3		9	1			12		10	14			5		4	*8*	7						18
	2				6					3	12	9	1			11		10				5		4		7	8					19
					6	7				3		9	1			11		12				5		4	8	2		10				20
1	4					7	14			3	11	8			*6*	9										2		10	5			21
1	4					7				3	11	8				9		12			6	5				2		10				22
1		4				7		14		3	11	8				9		12			6	5				2		*10*				23
1	4	*6*				12	10	7		3		8	15			*9*		11				5						14		2		24
	4				10			*7*		3		8	1		6	9						5				14		11		2		25
1	4	5				12		7		3	11	8				9			6							2		10				26
		4						7		3	11	8	1		*6*	9		12		14		5				2		10				27
		6				14		7		3	11	8	1			9						5				2		10			4	28
						11		7		3		8	1			9		10	6			5				2		12			4	29
						11		7		3		8	1			9		10	6			5				2					4	30
		11						7	12	3		8	1			9		10	6			5				2					4	31
		11						7		3	12	8	1			9		10	6			5				2					4	32
	2					11		7	10	3		8	1		12	9			6			5									4	33
	2	14				10		7	12	3	11	8	1			9			6			5									4	34
	2					7			12	3	11	8	1			9			6			5	14					10			4	35
	2					7				3	11	8	1			9			6			5						10			4	36

ALLOA Third Division

Year Formed: 1883. *Ground & Address:* Recreation Park, Clackmannan Rd, Alloa FK10 1RR. *Telephone:* 01259 722695.
Ground Capacity: total: 4100, seated: 424. *Size of Pitch:* 110yd × 75yd.
Chairman: Pat Lawlor. *Secretary:* E. G. Cameron. *Commercial Manager:* William McKie.
Manager: Pat Macaulay. *Assistant Manager:* Jim Dempsey. *Physio:* Alan Anderson.
Managers since 1975: H. Wilson; A. Totten; W. Garner; J. Thomson; D. Sullivan; G. Abel; B. Little; H. McCann; W. Lamont. *Club Nickname(s):* The Wasps. *Previous Grounds:* None.
Record Attendance: 13,000 v Dunfermline Athletic, Scottish Cup 3rd rd replay; 26 Feb, 1939.
Record Transfer Fee received: £60,000 for Paul Sheerin to Southampton (1992).
Record Transfer Fee paid: £10,000 for Douglas Lawrie from Stirling Albion.
Record Victory: 9-2 v Forfar Ath, Division II; 18 Mar, 1933.
Record Defeat: 0-10 v Dundee, Division II; 8 Mar, 1947: v Third Lanark, League Cup, 8 Aug, 1953.
Most Capped Player: Jock Hepburn, 1, Scotland.
Most League Appearances: —.

ALLOA 1994–95 LEAGUE RECORD

Match No.	Date	Venue	Opponents	Result		H/T Score	Lg. Pos.	Goalscorers	Attendance
1	Aug 13	A	Albion R	W	4-0	3-0	—	Nelson, McCormick S, McCulloch, Moffat	310
2	20	A	Forfar Ath	L	2-3	0-2	4	Newbigging, McCulloch	540
3	27	H	East Stirling	L	1-3	0-1	7	Newbigging	404
4	Sept 3	A	Ross C	D	3-3	2-3	7	McAnenay 3	1457
5	10	H	Arbroath	W	3-1	2-0	6	Lamont, McAnenay 2	473
6	24	H	Caledonian Th	D	1-1	1-0	6	Moffat	590
7	Oct 1	A	Cowdenbeath	W	3-1	1-0	5	Moffat, McAnenay, Black (og)	368
8	8	H	Montrose	D	1-1	1-0	6	Lamont	460
9	15	A	Queen's Park	W	1-0	1-0	5	Moffat	520
10	22	H	Albion R	W	1-0	0-0	4	Lamont	440
11	29	A	East Stirling	W	2-1	1-0	3	Moffat, Kemp	570
12	Nov 5	H	Forfar Ath	L	0-1	0-1	4		525
13	12	A	Arbroath	D	0-0	0-0	5		414
14	19	H	Ross C	D	1-1	0-0	6	Lawrie	479
15	26	A	Caledonian Th	D	2-2	0-1	6	Moffat, McAnenay	1039
16	Dec 3	H	Cowdenbeath	W	1-0	0-0	5	McAvoy	462
17	24	A	Montrose	W	2-1	2-0	4	McAvoy, Diver	641
18	31	H	Queen's Park	L	2-3	2-2	4	Lamont, Moffat	541
19	Jan 14	A	Albion R	W	1-0	0-0	5	McCulloch	400
20	24	H	Forfar Ath	L	0-2	0-2	—		498
21	Feb 4	H	Arbroath	W	3-2	1-1	3	Diver 3	384
22	7	H	East Stirling	L	0-1	0-0	—		395
23	11	A	Ross C	L	0-6	0-2	4		1686
24	18	H	Caledonian Th	W	1-0	1-0	4	Lamont	386
25	25	A	Cowdenbeath	W	3-1	2-1	3	Diver, Moffat, Bennett	260
26	Mar 11	A	Queen's Park	L	1-2	0-2	3	Moffat	506
27	18	A	Arbroath	L	1-2	0-1	4	Diver	464
28	25	H	Ross C	D	1-1	1-1	4	McCulloch	535
29	28	H	Montrose	L	0-1	0-0	—		416
30	Apr 1	H	Cowdenbeath	W	2-1	0-1	5	McCulloch, Cadden	367
31	8	A	Caledonian Th	W	1-0	1-0	5	Wylie	912
32	15	A	Montrose	D	0-0	0-0	5		649
33	22	H	Queen's Park	L	0-1	0-0	5		421
34	29	H	Albion R	W	5-0	1-0	5	Moffat 4, Conway	324
35	May 6	A	East Stirling	D	1-1	1-1	5	Diver	418
36	13	A	Forfar Ath	L	0-2	0-2	5		655

Final League Position: 5

Most League Goals in Season (Individual): 49: William 'Wee' Crilley, Division II; 1921-22.
Most Goals Overall (Individual): —.

Honours
League Champions: Division II 1921-22; *Runners-up:* Division II 1938-39. Second Division 1976-77, 1981-82, 1984-85, 1988-89.
Scottish Cup: —.
League Cup: —.
Club colours: Shirt: Gold with black trim. Shorts: Black. Stockings: Gold.

Goalscorers: *League (50):* Moffat 13, Diver 7, McAnenay 7, Lamont 5, McCulloch 5, McAvoy 2, Newbigging 2, Bennett 1, Cadden 1, Conway 1, Kemp 1, Lawrie 1, McCormick S 1, Nelson 1, Wylie 1, own goal 1. *Scottish Cup (2):* Diver 1, Lamont 1. *League Cup (1):* Morrison 1. *B&Q Cup (2):* McAnenay 1, Moffat 1.

Butter J 36	McMillan T 1	Kemp B 20 + 4	Campbell C 3	McCulloch K 28 + 1	Newbigging W 29	Nelson M 17 + 8	McCormack J 34	McCormick S 2	Bennett N 28 + 2	Morrison S 5	McNiven J 1 + 1	Moffat B 28 + 3	Lamont P 21 + 5	Diver D 19 + 8	McAnenay M 17 + 4	McAvoy N 6 + 1	Graham P — + 1	Lawrie D 21 + 2	Cadden S 22	Willock A 3 + 9	Hannah K 13 + 2	Wylie R 11	Whyte M 10 + 4	Conway V 6 + 1	Kirkham D 3 + 4	Cully D 1	Bell D 5	Rixon S 6	Match No.
1	2	3	4	5	6	7	8	9	*10*	11	12	14																	1
1		*3*	4	12	5	10	6	9	8	11	2	14	*7*																2
1		3	4	5	6	8	2		10	11		14	7	*9*	12														3
1		12		5	6	4	2		3	8			11	9	7	10													4
1		3			5	4	2		6	8		9	11	12	7	*10*	14												5
1		3		5	4	7	2		8			10	14	9	12	*11*		6											6
1		3		5	4	10	2					9	11		7			6	8										7
1		3		5	4	10	2					9	11		7			6	8										8
1		3		5	4	10	2					*9*	11	12	7			6	8	14									9
1		3		5	4	6	2		11			9	*12*	10	7				8	14									10
1		3		5	4	12	2		11			9		10	*7*			6	8	14									11
1		3		5	4	2			11			9	7	10	12			*6*	8	14									12
1		3		5	4	7	2					10	11	9	12			6	*8*	14									13
1		*3*		5	4	8	2		10			9	11	12	7	14		6											14
1		14		5	4		2		11			9	12	10	7			6	8		*3*								15
1					4	6	2		3			9	11	12	7	*10*		5	8		14								16
1		6					4		3				11	9		10		5	8	7	2								17
1		*3*		5			4		14			9	10			7		6	8	11	2								18
1		3		5	6		4		14			10	11	9	7				8	12	*2*								19
1		3		5	4	14	2		10			*9*	11	8	7			6		12									20
1		3		5	4		2		10			9	11	12						14	8	6	*7*						21
1		3		5	4		2		10			9	12	11							8	6	7						22
1		10		5	4	12	2		3			9	*11*	7				6	8	14									23
1		12		5		4	2					10	11	*9*					8		3	6	7	14					24
1		12		5		14	4		3			10	11	9					8		*2*	6	7						25
1				5		10	4		3			9						12	*8*	11	2	6	7		14				26
1				5		14	4		8			9		10				12			2	6	11		7	*3*			27
1				4		12	2		3			9	11	7	10			5				6					8		28
1				5	4		2		3				11	12	7			6			*8*		14				10	9	29
1				5	4		2		3			9			7			*6*	8		12		11		14		10		30
1					4	14	3								7			5	8		2	*6*	9	11	12		10		31
1				5	4		2		11			10	14		7			6				*8*	12	3				9	32
1				5	4		2		10					12				6	7				11	3			8	9	33
1					4	*5*			11			10		12				6	8		2		7	3	14			9	34
1					4		2		11			10		7					8			6	12	3	5			9	35
1					4	14	2		11			10		7					8			*6*	12	3	5			9	36

ARBROATH Third Division

Year Formed: 1878. *Ground & Address:* Gayfield Park, Arbroath DD11 1QB. *Telephone:* 01241 872157.
Ground Capacity: 6488. seated: 715. *Size of Pitch:* 115yd × 71yd.
President: John D. Christison. *Secretary:* Charles Kinnear. *Commercial Manager:* Sandy Watt.
Manager: John Brogan. *Physio:* William Shearer. *Coach:* Jim Kerr.
Managers since 1975: A. Henderson; I. J. Stewart; G. Fleming; J. Bone; J. Young; W. Borthwick; M. Lawson, D. McGrain MBE, J. Scott.
Club Nickname(s): The Red Lichties. *Previous Grounds:* None.
Record Attendance: 13,510 v Rangers, Scottish Cup 3rd rd; 23 Feb, 1952.
Record Transfer Fee received: £120,000 for Paul Tosh to Dundee (Aug 1993).
Record Transfer Fee paid: £20,000 for Douglas Robb from Montrose (1981).
Record Victory: 36-0 v Bon Accord, Scottish Cup 1st rd; 12 Sept, 1885.
Record Defeat: 1-9 v Celtic, League Cup 3rd rd; 25 Aug 1993.
Most Capped Player: Ned Doig, 2 (5), Scotland.
Most League Appearances: 445: Tom Cargill, 1966-81.

ARBROATH 1994–95 LEAGUE RECORD

Match No.	Date		Venue	Opponents	Result		H/T Score	Lg. Pos.	Goalscorers	Attendance
1	Aug	13	A	Caledonian Th	L	2-5	0-3	—	Farnan, Reilly	1855
2		20	A	Cowdenbeath	L	2-6	0-4	10	Reilly, Tosh	315
3		27	H	Forfar Ath	L	0-1	0-0	10		691
4	Sept	3	H	Queen's Park	D	1-1	1-0	9	Tosh	535
5		10	A	Alloa	L	1-3	0-2	9	Downie	473
6		24	A	Ross C	W	4-1	1-0	9	Reid (og), Tosh 3	1320
7	Oct	1	H	Montrose	L	0-3	0-1	9		802
8		8	A	Albion R	W	2-1	0-0	9	Craib, Florence	315
9		15	H	East Stirling	L	0-1	0-0	9		404
10		22	H	Caledonian Th	L	1-2	0-1	9	Elder	542
11		29	A	Forfar Ath	L	0-3	0-0	9		721
12	Nov	5	H	Cowdenbeath	L	0-3	0-3	9		426
13		12	H	Alloa	D	0-0	0-0	9		414
14		19	A	Queen's Park	W	4-0	2-0	9	Murray 2, Scott 2	407
15		26	H	Ross C	L	0-1	0-0	9		568
16	Dec	3	A	Montrose	L	1-3	0-1	9	Craib	1085
17		24	H	Albion R	L	0-1	0-1	9		467
18		31	A	East Stirling	L	0-1	0-0	9		436
19	Jan	14	A	Caledonian Th	D	1-1	0-0	9	Murray	1038
20		21	H	Cowdenbeath	L	0-3	0-1	9		388
21		28	H	Forfar Ath	D	1-1	1-1	9	Shanks	802
22	Feb	4	A	Alloa	L	2-3	1-1	9	Pew, Brock	384
23		15	H	Queen's Park	W	3-1	1-1	—	Porteous 2, Gardner	347
24		18	A	Ross C	W	1-0	1-0	9	Gardner	1648
25		25	H	Montrose	W	4-1	2-1	9	Tosh, Gardner, Scott 2	951
26	Mar	4	H	Albion R	W	2-0	0-0	8	Pew, Scott	436
27		11	H	East Stirling	W	5-2	3-0	8	Scott, Tosh 3, McMillan	596
28		18	H	Alloa	W	2-1	1-0	8	Porteous, Tosh	464
29		25	A	Queen's Park	W	3-2	1-1	8	Tosh, Pew, Gardner	616
30	Apr	1	A	Montrose	L	0-5	0-4	8		1179
31		8	H	Ross C	L	0-1	0-0	8		680
32		15	A	Albion R	W	3-0	0-0	8	McMillan, Pew, Lindsay	214
33		22	A	East Stirling	W	2-0	1-0	7	Porteous, Pew	414
34		29	H	Caledonian Th	W	2-0	0-0	6	Gardner 2	492
35	May	6	A	Forfar Ath	L	1-4	0-3	7	Florence	1069
36		13	A	Cowdenbeath	D	1-1	1-1	7	Farnan	200

Final League Position: 7

Most League Goals in Season (Individual): 45: Dave Easson, Division II; 1958-59.
Most Goals Overall (Individual): 120: Jimmy Jack; 1966-71.

Honours
League Champions Runners-up: Division II 1934-35, 1958-59, 1967-68, 1971-72.
Scottish Cup: Quarter-finals: 1993.
League Cup: —.
Club colours: Shirt: Maroon with sky blue trim. Shorts: White. Stockings: Maroon with sky blue hooped tops.

Goalscorers: *League (51):* Tosh 11, Gardner 6, Scott 6, Pew 5, Porteous 4, Murray 3, Craib 2, Farnan 2, Florence 2, McMillan 2, Reilly 2, Brock 1, Downie 1, Elder 1, Lindsay 1, Shanks 1, own goal 1. *Scottish Cup (0) League Cup (2):* McKinnon 1, Reilly 1. *B&Q Cup (0)*

Jackson D 8 + 1	Mitchell B 2	Dickson A 2	Elder S 18 + 7	Farnan C 31 + 3	Murray M 24	Downie I 6 + 5	Reilly J 3	Brock J 7 + 3	Tosh S 29 + 2	McGovern J 3 + 1	McKinnon C 1 + 2	Elliot D 9 + 10	Middleton A 16 + 4	Shanks D 22 + 1	Craib S 10 + 5	Duncan R 2	Spittal I 25	McGregor S 1 + 1	Florence S 18	Lindsay J 10 + 4	Dunn G 25	McMillan T 27	Benvie G 1	Scott B 14 + 8	Binnie G — + 1	Gardner R 22 + 1	Heggie A 3 + 1	Hendry M 1	Ward J 5	Scott L 1	Martin M 3	Pew D 14	Kerr J 10	Porteous I 14	Martin E 2	Crawford J 7	*Match No.*
1	2	3	4	5	6	7	*8*	9	10	11	12	14																									1
1	3	2	*4*	5	6	7	9	12	10	11	8	14																									2
1			5	2	6		9	12	10	8		7	3	4	11																							3
			8	2	6	7		9	10		12		3	4	11	1	5																					4
			8	2	4	7		9	10	14			3	6	11	1	5	12																				5
1			12	7	4			9	10				3	6	14		5	*11*	2	8																		6
1			14	8	4	12			10			*9*	3	6	11		5		2	7																		7
			11	8	6				*10*			14		4	12		5		3	7	1	2	9																8
			11	6	4	12									8	*10*		5		3	7	1	2		9	14														9
			11		4				7			12	6	8	14		5		3		1	2		*9*		10												10
			9	14	4	12			7				11	*6*	8		5		3		1	2				10												11
			8	4	6				7									5		3		1	2		12		10	9	11									12
15			6		8				7			14					5		3		*1*	2		*9*		11	10		4									13
			6	11	8							9					5		3		1	2		14		7	*10*		4									14
			6	*11*	8				10			9					5		3		1	2		14		7	12		4									15
			6	12	8				10			*11*	3		14		5				1	2				7			4	9								16
				8	6	11			10			7	3		9		4				1	2		12		5											17
				8	5	11			*9*			7	3	14	10		6				1	2				12			4									18
			4	8	6			9	10					7	11		5			12	1	2		14							3						19
			4	7	6			9				12	14	8	11		5			*10*	1	2									3						20
			6	7	4			*9*	11				3	8	14		5				1	2				10											21
1			10	7	4	14		12	11					*8*			5					2				6					3	9					22
				11					12			7		4			5		3		1			2		10						9	6	8			23
				4		14			12			*7*		5					3		1	2		11		10						9	6	8			24
				4					7			12	14	5					*3*		1	2		11		10						9	6	8			25
				4					*7*			12	3	5						14	1	2		11		10							9	6	8		26
				4					*7*			12	3	5						14	1	2		11		10						9	6	8			27
				4					7				3	5							1	2		11		10						9	6	8			28
			14	4	2				7			12	*3*	5										11		10						9	6	8	1		29
1			14	4	3				7					5								2		*11*								9	6	8		10	30
1			12	4					7					5						10		2		11								9	6	8		3	31
				12					7								5		3	4	1	2		14		10						*9*	6	8		11	32
				4					7								5		3	11	1	2		14		10						*9*		8		6	33
			14	4									12				5		3	11	1	2		*7*		10						9		8		6	34
			14	4									12				5		3	*11*	1	2		*7*		10						9		8		6	35
				4					7				*11*				5		3	12	1	2		14		10						9		8		6	36

AYR UNITED Second Division

Year Formed: 1910. *Ground & Address:* Somerset Park, Tryfield Place, Ayr KA8 9NB. *Telephone:* 01292 263435.
Ground Capacity: 13,918. seated: 1450. *Size of Pitch:* 110yd × 72yd.
Chairman: D. M. MacIntyre. *Secretary:* J. E. Eyley. *Commercial Manager:* Sandy Kerr.
Manager: Simon Stainrod. *Assistant Manager:* Malcolm Shotton.
Managers since 1975: Alex Stuart; Ally MacLeod; Willie McLean; George Caldwell; Ally MacLeod; George Burley. *Club Nickname(s):* The Honest Men. *Previous Grounds:* None.
Record Attendance: 25,225 v Rangers, Division I; 13 Sept, 1969.
eltic*Record Transfer Fee received:* £300,000 for Steven Nicol to Liverpool (Oct 1981).
Record Transfer Fee paid: £50,000 for Peter Weir from St Mirren, June 1990.
Record Victory: 11-1 v Dumbarton, League Cup; 13 Aug, 1952.
Record Defeat: 0-9 in Division I v Rangers (1929); v Hearts (1931); v Third Lanark (1954).
Most Capped Player: Jim Nisbet, 3, Scotland.
Most League Appearances: 371: Ian McAllister, 1977-90.

AYR UNITED 1994–95 LEAGUE RECORD

Match No.	Date		Venue	Opponents	Result		H/T Score	Lg. Pos.	Goalscorers	Attendance
1	Aug	13	H	Hamilton A	D	1-1	0-1	—	Traynor	2097
2		20	H	St Mirren	D	1-1	0-0	4	Bilsland	2787
3		27	A	Stranraer	L	1-2	1-0	7	McGivern	1653
4	Sept	3	H	St Johnstone	L	3-4	0-2	10	Stainrod, Traynor, Gilzean	2367
5		10	A	Airdrieonians	D	0-0	0-0	10		1620
6		24	H	Dundee	W	3-2	2-1	7	Jackson 2, George	1901
7	Oct	1	A	Raith R	L	0-3	0-1	9		2854
8		8	A	Clydebank	L	0-3	0-1	9		891
9		15	H	Dunfermline Ath	D	0-0	0-0	9		2302
10		22	A	Hamilton A	L	0-2	0-2	9		1066
11		29	H	Stranraer	W	2-1	1-1	8	Burns 2	2073
12	Nov	5	A	St Mirren	L	0-1	0-1	9		2482
13		12	H	Airdrieonians	L	0-3	0-2	9		2210
14		19	A	St Johnstone	L	0-1	0-1	9		2755
15		26	A	Dundee	D	1-1	0-1	9	Hood	2506
16	Dec	3	H	Raith R	D	1-1	1-0	9	Hood	2216
17		10	A	Dunfermline Ath	L	0-6	0-2	9		3197
18		26	H	Clydebank	D	1-1	1-0	—	Gorgues	1969
19		31	H	Hamilton A	L	1-2	1-2	9	Dowe	2079
20	Jan	2	A	Stranraer	L	0-2	0-1	—		1899
21		7	H	St Mirren	W	2-0	1-0	9=	Rolling, Bilsland	2237
22		14	H	St Johnstone	L	1-3	1-0	10	Jackson	1955
23		24	A	Airdrieonians	D	2-2	1-1	—	Gilzean, Rolling	1320
24	Feb	4	A	Raith R	L	1-2	0-1	9	Moore	2799
25		11	H	Dundee	W	1-0	1-0	8	Moore	2042
26		25	H	Dunfermline Ath	L	1-2	0-1	8	McCathie (og)	2183
27	Mar	11	A	Clydebank	D	1-1	0-0	9	Hood	720
28		18	H	Airdrieonians	L	0-2	0-0	9		1372
29		25	A	St Johnstone	D	1-1	0-1	9	Tannock	3551
30	Apr	1	H	Raith R	L	0-1	0-1	9		1995
31		8	A	Dundee	D	1-1	0-1	9	Burns	2765
32		15	H	Clydebank	W	1-0	1-0	9	Gilzean	1798
33		22	A	Dunfermline Ath	L	0-3	0-1	9		4808
34		29	A	Hamilton A	L	0-1	0-0	9		1073
35	May	6	H	Stranraer	W	3-0	1-0	9	Tannock, Jackson, Stainrod	1204
36		13	A	St Mirren	L	1-2	1-1	9	Bilsland	2179

Final League Position: 9

Most League Goals in Season (Individual): 66: Jimmy Smith, 1927-28.
Most Goals Overall (Individual): —.

Honours
League Champions: Division II 1911-12, 1912-13, 1927-28, 1936-37, 1958-59, 1965-66. Second Division 1987-88;
Runners-up: Division II 1910-11, 1955-56, 1968-69.
Scottish Cup: —. *League Cup:* —.
*B&Q Cup: Runners-up:*1990-91, 1991-92.
Club colours: Shirt: White with black sleeves. Shorts: Black. Stockings: White.

Goalscorers: *League (31):* Jackson 4, Bilsland 3, Burns 3, Gilzean 3, Hood 3, Moore 2, Rolling 2, Stainrod 2, Tannock 2, Traynor 2, Dowe 1, George 1, Gorgues 1, McGivern 1, own goal 1. *Scottish Cup (0) League Cup (0) B&Q Cup (5):* Burns 2, George 1, Jackson 1, Paterson 1.

Duncan C 29	Burns H 23	McVicar D 5	Paterson G 10 + 1	Rolling F 33	Sharples J 27	Moore V 13 + 4	McKilligan N 30 + 4	McGivern S 9 + 2	Gilzean I 21 + 2	Bilsland B 11 + 7	Traynor J 9 + 2	Woods T — + 3	Connie C 20 + 1	Stainrod S 15 + 4	McIntosh S 6 + 2	Biggart K 22 + 1	Tannock R 11 + 3	George D 29	Gorgues R 18 + 1	Jackson J 18 + 9	Hood G 15	Spence W 1	Lamont L 1	Nylen N 2	Valetta C 3 + 2	Murray B 1	Fortes J 1 + 1	Dowe J 4 + 3	Grierson G — + 1	Gribben K 4	McFarlane C 3	Agnew S 1 + 1	Okorie K — + 1	Connelly S 1 + 3	*Match No.*
1	2	3	4	5	6	7	8	9	10	*11*	12	14																							1
1	2	3	4	5	6		8	9	*10*	12	7		11	14																					2
1	2	3	4	5		14	6	*9*	10	*8*	7	12	11		15																				3
	2	3	12	5	4		*8*		9	14	6			10	1	7	11																		4
1	2	3	4	5				9	11	12	8			10				6	7																5
1	2		4	5		8					7		3	10				6	11	9															6
1	7		4	5		*8*	10				2	12	3			14		6	11	9															7
1	7		4	5		8	2	14						*10*		3		6	11	9															8
1	7			5		8	14	*9*			2			10		3		6	11	12	4														9
	7		6	5		8	14							10		2		11	3	12	4	1	*9*												10
1	7		9	5		8	2							14		3		6	11	*10*	4														11
1	7		9	5		8	14	12								3		6	11					2	*4*	10									12
1	7			5	4		12	9		14						3		6	11					2	8		*10*								13
1	7			5	6		11	9						*10*		2		8	3		4				12		14								14
1	7			5	6	14	11	9					3			*2*		8		10	4				12										15
1	7			5	6	11	2	*9*					3	14				8		10	4														16
	2			5	6		11		12				3	10	*1*			8		9					4			7	15						17
1	7			5	6		2		9				3					8	11	12	4							10							18
1				5	6		2		9				3			7	14	8	11	12	4							10							19
1				5	6	14	2		9				*3*					8	11	12	4							10		7					20
1				5	6	12	2		9	14			3					8	11	*10*	4									7					21
1				5	6		2		9	12			3						11	10	4							14		7	8				22
1				5	4	*8*	2		9	12			3				14		11	10										7	6				23
1				5	4	8	2		9	7			3	14			11			*10*											6				24
1				5	6	8	2		9	7				10		3		11		12	4														25
1				5	6		2		*9*	7			12	10		3	8	11		14	4														26
1				5	6		2		9	7				10		3		11		8	4														27
1				5	6		2		9	7	14			*10*		3	12	11		8	4														28
1	7				6		2		*9*	10	5		11			3	4	8		14												12			29
1	7				6		2		*9*	10	5					3	4	8		14												11	12		30
1	2			5	6		7		9						15	3	8	4	*11*	10															31
	2			5	6		7		9				11		1	3	8	4		10														12	32
	2				6		5		*9*				11		1	3	8	4	12	10								14						7	33
1				5	6		7						3	10		2	4	8	*11*	9								14							34
				5	6		7			11			3	*10*	1	2	8	4		9														14	35
				5	6	11	7		14	9			3	10	1	2	*8*	4																12	36

BERWICK RANGERS Second Division

Year Formed: 1881. *Ground & Address:* Shielfield Park, Tweedmouth, Berwick-upon-Tweed TD15 2EF. *Telephone:* 01289 307424. Club 24 hour hotline 01891 800697. *Ground Capacity:* 4131. seated: 1366. *Size of Pitch:* 112yd × 76yd.
Chairman: Roy McDowell. *Vice-chairman:* Tom Davidson. *Company Secretary:* Colin Walker. *Club Secretary:* Dennis McCleary.
Team Manager: Tom Hendrie. *Assistant Manager:* John Coughlin. *Physio/Coach:* Ian Oliver. *Youth Coaches:* Tom Smith, Warren Hawke
Managers since 1975: H. Melrose; G. Haig; W. Galbraith; D. Smith; F. Connor; J. McSherry; E. Tait; J. Thomson; J. Jefferies; J. Anderson, J. Crease.
Club Nickname(s): The Borderers. *Previous Grounds:* Bull Stob Close, Pier Field, Meadow Field, Union Park, Old Shielfield.
Record Attendance: 13,365 v Rangers, Scottish Cup 1st rd; 28 Jan, 1967.
Record Victory: 8-1 v Forfar Ath. Division II; 25 Dec, 1965: v Vale of Leithen, Scottish Cup; Dec, 1966.
Record Defeat: 1-9 v Hamilton A, First Division; 9 Aug, 1980.
Most Capped Player: —.

BERWICK RANGERS 1994–95 LEAGUE RECORD

Match No.	*Date*	*Venue*	*Opponents*	*Result*		*H/T Score*	*Lg. Pos.*	*Goalscorers*	*Atten-dance*
1	Aug 13	A	Morton	D	1-1	0-0	—	Irvine	1454
2	20	A	Brechin C	W	2-1	2-1	1	Irvine, Fraser	539
3	27	H	Queen of the S	W	1-0	0-0	1	Banks	610
4	Sept 3	A	Clyde	W	4-3	1-0	1	Banks, Forrester, Hawke, Irvine	1141
5	10	H	Dumbarton	W	1-0	0-0	1	Banks	533
6	24	A	Stenhousemuir	D	1-1	0-1	1	Irvine	373
7	Oct 1	H	East Fife	D	1-1	1-1	1	Irvine	573
8	8	H	Meadowbank T	W	2-1	2-1	1	Hawke, Neil	520
9	15	A	Stirling Albion	L	2-3	1-1	2	Hawke, Irvine	863
10	22	H	Morton	W	2-1	1-0	1	Hawke 2	738
11	29	A	Queen of the S	L	4-5	1-3	1	Irvine, Hawke 2, Neil	1298
12	Nov 5	H	Brechin C	W	2-1	1-1	1	Banks 2 (1 pen)	478
13	12	A	Dumbarton	L	2-3	1-0	1	Irvine, Hawke	733
14	19	H	Clyde	W	2-1	2-0	1	Hawke 2	611
15	26	H	Stenhousemuir	D	0-0	0-0	1		703
16	Dec 3	A	East Fife	L	0-3	0-2	1		756
17	10	A	Meadowbank T	L	1-2	1-1	1	Cowan	338
18	31	H	Stirling Albion	W	1-0	1-0	2	Banks (pen)	736
19	Jan 10	H	Queen of the S	W	3-1	1-1	—	Greenwood, Gallacher, Irvine (pen)	448
20	14	A	Morton	L	1-2	0-0	2	Gallacher	1951
21	21	A	Brechin C	L	0-1	0-0	2		387
22	Feb 4	H	Dumbarton	L	1-2	1-0	4	Neil	508
23	11	A	Clyde	W	3-1	2-0	4	Reid, Neil, Hawke	882
24	25	H	East Fife	D	0-0	0-0	4		503
25	Mar 4	H	Meadowbank T	W	1-0	1-0	4	Hawke	455
26	7	A	Stenhousemuir	D	2-2	1-1	—	Neil, Reid	534
27	11	A	Stirling Albion	D	2-2	0-1	3	Irvine, Hawke	582
28	21	A	Dumbarton	L	0-1	0-0	—		1012
29	25	H	Clyde	D	1-1	1-*1	4	Graham	581
30	Apr 1	A	East Fife	W	1-0	1-0	4	Irvine	628
31	8	H	Stenhousemuir	D	0-0	0-0	6		571
32	15	A	Meadowbank T	W	3-0	2-0	5	Fraser, Forrester 2	296
33	22	H	Stirling Albion	D	0-0	0-0	5		601
34	29	H	Morton	L	3-4	3-2	6	Hawke 3	992
35	May 6	A	Queen of the S	L	0-2	0-1	6		1061
36	13	H	Brechin C	W	2-0	1-0	5	Graham, Banks	439

Final League Position: 5

Most League Appearances: 435;: Eric Tait, 1970-87.
Most League Goals in Season (Individual): 38: Ken Bowron, Division II; 1963-64.
Most Goals Overall (Individual): 115: Eric Tait, 1970-87.

Honours
League Champions: Second Division 1978-79. *Runners-up* Second Division 1993-94.
Scottish Cup: —.
League Cup: Semi-final 1963-64.
Club colours: Shirt: Gold with Black seams, shoulders and collar. Shorts: Black, gold trim. Stockings: Black.

Goalscorers: *League (52):* Hawke 16, Irvine 11 (1 pen), Banks 7 (2 pens), Neil 5, Forrester 3, Fraser 2, Gallacher 2, Graham 2, Reid 2, Cowan 1, Greenwood 1. *Scottish Cup (8):* Clegg 1, Fraser 1, Graham 1, Hawke 1, Irvine 1, Neil 1, Valentine 1, own goal 1. *League Cup (0) B&Q Cup (1):* Fraser 1.

Young N 24	Valentine C 36	Banks A 32	Cole A 22	Cowan M 33	Bell D 1 + 1	Forrester P 23 + 9	Neil M 34	Hawke W 35	Irvine W 36	Wilson M 17 + 3	Kane K 15 + 4	Fraser G 20 + 11	Gallacher J 11 + 8	Graham T 23 + 7	Osborne M 12 + 1	Rutherford P 1	Greenwood P 2 + 1	King T 3 + 3	Reid A 14	Robinson A 2	Macaulay L — + 1	Match No.
1	2	*3*	4	5	6	7	8	9	10	11	12	14										1
1	2	3	*4*	5		7	8	9	10	6	11	14	12									2
1	2	3	4	5		7	8	9	10	6			11									3
1	2	3	4	*5*	12	7	8	9	10	6		14	11									4
1	2	3	4			7	6	9	10	8		5	*11*	14								5
1	2	3	4	5		7	8	9	10	6		12	14	11								6
1	2	3	4	5		7	8	9	10	6			14	*11*								7
1	2	3	4	5		7	8	9	10	6			14	*11*								8
1	2	3	4	5		7	8	9	10	6		12	14	11								9
1	2	3	4	5		7	8	*9*	10	6		12	14	11								10
1	2	3	4	5		7	8	9	10	6			14	*11*								11
	2	3	*4*	5		7	8	9	10	6		14	11	12	1							12
	2	3	4	5		8		9	10	6			7	11	1							13
	2	3	4	5		7	8	9	10	6		14	11	12	1							14
	2	3	4	5		*6*	8	9	10	11		14	7	12	1							15
	2	3	*4*	5		7	8	9	10	6		14	12	11	1							16
	2	3	4	5		12	*8*	9	10	6		14	7	11	1							17
	2	3	4	5			8	9	10			6	7		1	11						18
	3		4	5		12	8	9	10			6	7	11	1		2					19
	2	3	4	5			8	9	10		14	6	7	*11*	1		12					20
	3		4	5		*7*	8	9	10		12	6		11	1		2	14				21
	2	3	*4*	5		7	8	9	10		12	6		11	1			14				22
1	2	3		5		12	8	9	10		7	6		11					4			23
1	4	3				12	8	9	10		7	6		11					5	2		24
1	2	3		5			8	9	10		7	6		11					4			25
1	2	3		5		12	8	9	10		7	6		11					4			26
1	2	3		5		14	8	9	10		11	*7*		12					4	6		27
1	2	*3*		5		12	8	9	10		11	4		7				14	6			28
1	3			5		12	8	9	10		11	6		7				2	4			29
1	3			5		12	8	9	10		11	6		7				2	4			30
1	2	3		5			8	9	10		11	6		7					4			31
1	2	3		5		9	8		10		11	6		7					4			32
1	2	3		5		7	8	9	10		11	6							4			33
1	2	3		5		7	8	9	10	14	11	*6*		12	15				4			34
	2	3		*5*		7	8	9	10	14	11	6		12	1				4			35
1	5	3				*8*		9	10	12	11	6		7				2	4		14	36

BRECHIN CITY Third Division

Year Formed: 1906. *Ground & Address:* Glebe Park, Trinity Rd, Brechin, Angus DD9 6BJ. *Telephone:* 01356 622856.
Ground Capacity: total: 3980. seated: 1518. *Size of Pitch:* 110yd × 67yd.
Chairman: Hugh Campbell Adamson. *Secretary:* George C. Johnston. *Commercial Manager:* —.
Manager: John Young. *Assistant Manager:* Cammy Evans. *Physio:* Tom Gilmartin.
Managers since 1975: Charlie Dunn; Ian Stewart; Doug Houston; Ian Fleming; John Ritchie, Ian Redford. *Club Nickname(s):* The City. *Previous Grounds:* Nursery Park.
Record Attendance: 8122 v Aberdeen, Scottish Cup 3rd rd; 3 Feb, 1973.
Record Transfer Fee received: £100,000 for Scott Thomson to Aberdeen (1991).
Record Transfer Fee paid: £16,000 for Sandy Ross from Berwick Rangers (1991).
Record Victory: 12-1 v Thornhill, Scottish Cup 1st rd; 28 Jan, 1926.
Record Defeat: 0-10 v Airdrieonians, Albion R and Cowdenbeath, all in Division II; 1937-38.
Most Capped Player: —.
Most League Appearances: 459: David Watt, 1975-89.

BRECHIN CITY 1994–95 LEAGUE RECORD

Match No.	Date		Venue	Opponents	Result		H/T Score	Lg. Pos.	Goalscorers	Attendance
1	Aug	13	H	Meadowbank T	L	1-5	0-0	—	Millar	432
2		20	H	Berwick R	L	1-2	1-2	10	McNeill	539
3		27	A	East Fife	D	1-1	0-0	10	Millar	795
4	Sept	3	H	Stenhousemuir	D	1-1	1-1	10	Vannett	436
5		10	A	Morton	L	0-2	0-0	10		1093
6		24	A	Queen of the S	W	2-0	0-0	9	Smith 2	1032
7	Oct	1	H	Dumbarton	L	1-2	1-1	10	Smith	427
8		8	H	Stirling Albion	L	1-2	0-1	10	Brand	555
9		15	A	Clyde	L	0-4	0-1	10		762
10		22	A	Meadowbank T	L	0-1	0-1	10		149
11		29	H	East Fife	W	2-0	1-0	10	Price, Smith	613
12	Nov	5	A	Berwick R	L	1-2	1-1	10	Smith	478
13		12	H	Morton	L	1-3	0-3	10	Smith	623
14		19	A	Stenhousemuir	L	0-2	0-2	10		342
15		26	H	Queen of the S	L	0-1	0-0	10		406
16	Dec	3	A	Dumbarton	L	0-6	0-3	10		554
17		24	A	Stirling Albion	L	0-2	0-1	10		760
18		31	H	Clyde	L	0-2	0-2	10		484
19	Jan	2	A	East Fife	L	0-4	0-2	—		1155
20		14	H	Meadowbank T	W	3-1	2-0	10	McKellar, Price 2	356
21		21	H	Berwick R	W	1-0	0-0	10	Brand	387
22	Feb	4	A	Morton	L	0-1	0-1	10		1464
23		14	H	Stenhousemuir	L	0-2	0-1	—		345
24		18	A	Queen of the S	W	1-0	0-0	10	Price	1002
25		25	H	Dumbarton	D	0-0	0-0	10		480
26	Mar	4	H	Stirling Albion	W	2-1	1-0	10	Brand, Price	465
27		11	A	Clyde	L	0-1	0-0	10		907
28		18	H	Morton	D	1-1	0-0	10	Brand	481
29		25	A	Stenhousemuir	L	0-3	0-3	10		396
30	Apr	1	A	Dumbarton	L	1-4	0-3	10	McKellar	1103
31		8	H	Queen of the S	L	0-2	0-1	10		389
32		15	A	Stirling Albion	L	0-2	0-1	10		607
33		22	H	Clyde	D	0-0	0-0	10		413
34		29	A	Meadowbank T	L	1-2	0-1	10	McNeill	144
35	May	6	H	East Fife	D	1-1	1-1	10	Price	386
36		13	A	Berwick R	L	0-2	0-1	10		439

Final League Position: 10

Most League Goals in Season (Individual): 26: W. McIntosh, Division II; 1959-60.
Most Goals Overall (Individual): 131: Ian Campbell.

Honours
League Champions: Second Division 1982-83. C Division 1953-54. Second Division 1989-90. *Runners-up:* 1992-93.
Scottish Cup: —.
League Cup: —.
Club colours: Shirt, Shorts, Stockings: Red with white trimmings.

Goalscorers: *League (22):* Price 6, Smith 6, Brand 4, McKellar 2, McNeill 2, Millar 1, Vannett 1. *Scottish Cup (2):* Brand 1, McNeill 1. *League Cup (0) B&Q Cup (0)*

Balfour D 27 + 1	Cairney H 32	Christie G 15	Conway F 33	Nicolson K 9	Scott D 27	Kemlo S 11	Redford I 1	McNeill W 31 + 3	Millar M 8	Vannett R 24 + 3	McKellar J 20 + 7	Bell S 6 + 7	Brown R 21	Brand R 17 + 7	Marr S 14 + 2	Smith R 22 + 3	Mitchell B 27	Feroz C — + 1	Lawrie D 9	Price G 23	Buick G 5 + 2	Mearns G 8 + 1	Baillie R 4	Ferguson S 2	*Match No.*
1	2	*3*	4	5	6	7	8	9	10	11	12	14													1
1	4	3	2	5	6	11		9	10	8		7													2
1	4	8	2	5	6			11	10	7	12		3	9											3
1	4	3	2	5	6			9	10	8	7	12			11										4
1	4	3	2	5	6			9	10	8	7	12				11									5
1	4		2	5	6			8	10		7	12	3		11	9									6
1	4		2	5	6			8	10			7	3	12	11	9									7
1	4		2	5	6			11	10			7	3	12		9	8								8
1	4		2	5	6	8		11		7			3	9		10		12							9
	4		2		6	3		11			7	14	5	*10*		9	8		1						10
	4		2		6	3		7					5		11	10	8		1	9					11
1	4		2			3		6		12	7		5	14	11	10	8			9					12
			4		6	3		8		2	7		5	12	11	10			1	9					13
			5		6	3		8			14		4	7	11	10	2		1	*9*					14
			4		6			8		14	7		5	12	11	10	3		1	9	2				15
	4		5		6			8					3	12	11	10	2		1	9	7				16
	4		5			3		11		6			2	10		12	8		1	9	7				17
	4		5			3		11		6	14		2			10	8		1	9	*7*				18
15	4		5					14		6	7		3		*11*	10	8		1	9	*2*				19
1	4		5		6			11		8	7		3	10			2			9					20
1	4		5		6			11		8	7		3	10			2			9					21
1	4		5		6			11		8	7		3	10		9	2								22
1	5				6			*11*		2	12	*7*	3		14	10	4			9		8			23
1	4	5			6			11		8	7	14	*3*			10	2			9					24
1	4	5			6	3		11		8	7					10	2			9					25
1	4	3	5		6			11			7	14		10			2			9		8			26
1	4	3	5		6			*11*		14		7		10		12	2			9		8			27
1	4	3	5		6					8	*7*			10	11		2			9	14				28
1	4		5							6	7	8		10	*11*	12	2			9	14		3		29
1	5		4					7		6	12			10		11	2			9		8	3		30
1	4	3	5					7		6	12			10		11	2			9		8			31
1	4	3	5					12		11	7			9		10	2					8	6		32
1		5	4					10		11	7			9	14		2					8	*6*	3	33
1	4	3	5		6			10			7				11		2			9		8			34
1	4		5		6			10		8	7		3	12	11		2			9					35
1	4	3	5		6			12		*8*				10		7	2			9		14		11	36

CALEDONIAN THISTLE Third Division

Year Formed: 1994. *Ground & Address:* Telford Street Park, Inverness IV3 5LU. *Telephone:* 01463 230274.
Ground Capacity: 5498, seated 498. *Size of Pitch:* 110 × 70yd.
President: Dugald McGilvray. *Hon. Life President:* John S.McDonald. *Secretary:* Jim Falconer.
Manager: S.W.Paterson.
Record Attendance: 3062, v Ross County, Third Division, 6 May 1995.
Record Victory: 5-2, v Arbroath, Third Division, 13 August 1994.
Record Defeat: 0-4, v Queen's Park, Third Division, 20 August 1994 and v Montrose, Third Division, 14 February 1995.

CALEDONIAN THISTLE 1994–95 LEAGUE RECORD

Match No.	*Date*		*Venue*	*Opponents*	*Result*		*H/T Score*	*Lg. Pos.*	*Goalscorers*	*Atten-dance*
1	Aug	13	H	Arbroath	W	5-2	3-0	—	Hercher 3, MacKenzie, Robertson	1855
2		20	H	Queen's Park	L	0-4	0-2	7		1565
3		27	A	Ross C	W	3-1	1-0	4	Somerville (og), Andrew MacLeod (og), Robertson	3197
4	Sept	3	A	Albion R	W	1-0	0-0	3	MacMillan	539
5		10	H	Forfar Ath	W	3-1	1-1	1	Bennett 2, MacKenzie	1731
6		24	A	Alloa	D	1-1	0-1	1	Scott	590
7	Oct	1	H	East Stirling	D	3-3	1-2	1	Noble (pen), McAllister, Robertson	1229
8		8	H	Cowdenbeath	L	0-3	0-1	4		1273
9		15	A	Montrose	L	1-3	1-0	6	MacMillan	758
10		22	A	Arbroath	W	2-1	1-0	5	McCraw 2	542
11		29	H	Ross C	D	0-0	0-0	5		2866
12	Nov	5	A	Queen's Park	W	2-0	0-0	5	Robertson, MacKenzie (pen)	692
13		12	A	Forfar Ath	L	1-2	1-2	6	McAllister	647
14		19	H	Albion R	W	2-1	0-0	5	Christie 2	954
15		26	H	Alloa	D	2-2	1-0	4	Christie, Andrew (pen)	1039
16	Dec	3	A	East Stirling	L	0-2	0-1	6		508
17		26	A	Cowdenbeath	D	1-1	0-1	—	Andrew	464
18	Jan	2	A	Ross C	L	1-3	1-0	—	Andrew	2749
19		14	H	Arbroath	D	1-1	0-0	7	Brennan	1038
20		21	A	Queen's Park	L	1-4	0-2	7	MacDonald J	456
21	Feb	4	H	Forfar Ath	D	1-1	0-1	7	Scott	793
22		11	A	Albion R	W	2-1	1-0	7	MacMillan, Lisle	274
23		14	H	Montrose	L	0-4	0-0	—		851
24		18	A	Alloa	L	0-1	0-1	7		386
25		25	H	East Stirling	D	3-3	1-1	7	Christie 2, MacKenzie	886
26	Mar	4	H	Cowdenbeath	W	3-1	2-0	7	McAllister, MacMillan, Mitchell	659
27		11	A	Montrose	W	1-0	0-0	6	Robertson	781
28		18	A	Forfar Ath	L	1-4	0-2	6	Scott	538
29	Apr	1	A	East Stirling	L	0-1	0-1	6		391
30		8	H	Alloa	L	0-1	0-1	7		912
31		11	H	Albion R	L	0-2	0-1	—		524
32		15	A	Cowdenbeath	W	3-1	1-0	6	Bennett, Scott, Hercher	183
33		22	H	Montrose	L	0-3	0-2	6		942
34		29	A	Arbroath	L	0-2	0-0	7		492
35	May	6	H	Ross C	W	3-0	1-0	6	MacMillan, Hercher, Christie	3062
36		13	H	Queen's Park	D	1-1	0-1	6	Hercher	782

Final League Position: 6

Most League Appearances: 35, Mark McAllister, 1994-95.
Most League Goals in Season: 6, Charles Christie and Alan Hercher, 1994-95.
Club Colours: Shirts: Blue with White flashes; Shorts: White with Blue flashes; Stockings: Blue.

Goalscorers: *League (48):* Christie 6, Hercher 6, McMillan 5, Robertson 5, MacKenzie 4 (1 pen), Scott 4, Andrew 3 (1 pen), Bennett 3, McAllister 3, McCraw 2, Brennan 1, Lisle 1, MacDonald J 1, Mitchell 1, Noble 1 (pen), own goals 2. *Scottish Cup (1):* McAllister. *League Cup (2):* Robertson 1, own goal 1. *B&Q Cup (1):* MacDonald J 1.

McRitchie M 29	Brennan D 25 + 1	McAllister M 35	Hercher A 13 + 8	Scott J 21 + 2	Andrew M 19	Lisle M 22 + 6	MacKenzie P 20 + 2	Noble M 21	Bennett G 15 + 1	Robertson W 23 + 4	Smart A 2 + 2	MacDonald D 7 + 1	Hastings R 8 + 3	MacMillan N 23 + 4	Christie C 24 + 2	Mitchell C 26 + 2	Baltacha S 9	McCraw B 7 + 8	MacDonald S 10 + 1	Sinclair C 10	Watt G 1 + 1	Calder J 7	Sweeney K 6 + 1	MacDonald J 2	Buchanan D 5 + 1	Sanderson M 3 + 4	Urquhart W 2 + 1	Holmes M 1	Match No.
1	2	3	4	5	6	7	8	9	10	11	12	14																	1
1	2	3	*4*	5	6		8	9	10	11		7	12	14															2
1	2	3	4	5	6		8	9	10	11		7	12																3
1	2	3	4	5			8	9	10	11		7		12	6														4
1	2	3	14	5			8	9	6	11		7		*4*	10														5
1	2	3		5	6		8	9		11		7		4	10														6
1	2	3		14	6	4	8	9	*5*	11	7				10	12													7
1	2	3		5	6	12	8	9		*11*		7		4	10	14													8
1	2	3		12	6	7	8	9				5		11	10	4													9
1	2	3		5	6	8			10					11		7	4	9											10
1	2	3			5	8		6		11				12	10	7	4	*9*	14										11
1	2	3			6	12	8	5	10	11	14			*9*		7	4												12
1	2	3			5	8	11	6	*10*		9					7	4	14											13
1	2	3			5	8	*9*	6	10					11	12	7	4	14											14
1	12	3			6	8	14	*4*						9	10	7		11	2	5									15
1	2	3			5	8	6		12					9	10	7	4	11											16
1		3	4		5	12	9	*8*		11					10	7	6		2		14								17
1	2	3	4		5		9	*8*		11			14		10	7	6												18
	2	3	4			14	9			11			7		10		6	12		5	*8*	1							19
	2	3		8		12	7			11			6	14	10					5		1	4	*9*					20
	5	3		4	6	8				11					10	7		14	2			1		*9*					21
		3	12	4		8				11			5	9	10	7		14	*2*	6		1							22
		3	12	4		8				11			5	9	10	7		14	*2*	6		1							23
			12	4	6	8	14			*11*			3	9	10	7				5		1	2						24
		3		4		8	11			14			6	*9*	10	7				5		1	2						25
1	2	3	12	4		8	11							9	10	7							5		6	14			26
1	2	3		4		8	*11*			14				9	10	7							5		6				27
1	2	3	12	4		8				11				9	*10*	7							5		6	14			28
1	2	3	12	4		8		5		14			6	11	10	7											*9*		29
1		3	12	10	6	*8*		5		11				9		7			2						4	14			30
1		3	4	8				5						11	10	7		14	2				12			*6*	9		31
1		3	4	10				5	8				6	9		7		11	2							12			32
1		3	4			8		5	9	12				10		7		11	2							6			33
1		3	4			8			10	11				9		7			2	5					12	6			34
1	2	*3*	4			12			8	11				9	10	7		14		5					6				35
1	2	3	4			8			6	11					12	7		*9*		5							14	10	36

CELTIC Premier Division

Year Formed: 1888. *Ground & Address:* Celtic Park, 95 Kerrydale St, Glasgow G40 3RE. *Telephone:* 041 556 2611.
Ground Capacity: all seated: 34,000. *Size of Pitch:* 115yd × 75yd.
Managing Director Fergus McCann. *Secretary:* Dominic Keane. *Chief Scout* Davie Hay.
Manager: Tommy Burns. *Assistant Manager:* Billy Stark. *Physio:* Brian Scott. *Coaches:* Frank Connor, Tom McAdam, Willie McStay.
Managers since 1975: Jock Stein, Billy McNeill, David Hay, Billy McNeill, Liam Brady, Lou Macari. *Club Nickname(s):* The Bhoys. *Previous Grounds:* None.
Record Attendance: 92,000 v Rangers, Division I; 1 Jan, 1938.
Record Transfer Fee received: £1,400,000 for Paul Elliott to Chelsea, July 1991.
Record Transfer Fee paid: £1,750,000 for Phil O'Donnell from Motherwell, September 1994.
Record Victory: 11-0 Dundee, Division I; 26 Oct, 1895.
Record Defeat: 0-8 v Motherwell, Division I; 30 Apr, 1937.
Most Capped Player: Paul McStay, 72, Scotland.
Most League Appearances: 486: Billy McNeill 1957-75.
Most League Goals in Season (Individual): 50: James McGrory, Division I; 1935-36.
Most Goals Overall (Individual): 397: James McGrory; 1922-39.

Honours
League Champions: (35 times) Division I 1892-93, 1893-94, 1895-96, 1897-98, 1904-05, 1905-06, 1906-07, 1907-08, 1908-09,

CELTIC 1994–95 LEAGUE RECORD

Match No.	Date	Venue	Opponents	Result	H/T Score	Lg. Pos.	Goalscorers	Attendance
1	Aug 13	A	Falkirk	D 1-1	0-0	—	Walker	12,635
2	20	H	Dundee U	W 2-1	0-0	4	Walker, Mowbray	25,817
3	27	A	Rangers	W 2-0	1-0	2	Collins, McStay	44,607
4	Sept 10	A	Partick T	W 2-1	2-0	1	O'Donnell 2	14,439
5	17	H	Kilmarnock	D 1-1	0-0	2	McGinlay	28,457
6	24	H	Hibernian	W 2-0	1-0	1	O'Donnell, Collins	28,170
7	Oct 1	A	Motherwell	D 1-1	1-0	2	Walker	10,869
8	8	H	Aberdeen	D 0-0	0-0	2		29,454
9	15	A	Hearts	L 0-1	0-1	3		12,086
10	22	H	Falkirk	L 0-2	0-1	4		23,688
11	30	H	Rangers	L 1-3	1-2	—	Byrne	32,171
12	Nov 5	A	Dundee U	D 2-2	2-1	5	Collins 2	10,496
13	9	H	Partick T	D 0-0	0-0	—		21,462
14	19	A	Kilmarnock	D 0-0	0-0	5		13,932
15	30	A	Hibernian	D 1-1	1-0	—	Collins	12,295
16	Dec 3	H	Motherwell	D 2-2	2-1	5	Falconer, Philliben (og)	21,465
17	26	A	Aberdeen	D 0-0	0-0	—		19,206
18	31	H	Falkirk	W 2-0	0-0	4	Grant, Walker	21,294
19	Jan 4	A	Rangers	D 1-1	0-1	—	Byrne	45,794
20	7	H	Dundee U	D 1-1	1-1	4	Collins	21,436
21	11	H	Hearts	D 1-1	1-0	—	Van Hooijdonk	26,491
22	14	H	Kilmarnock	W 2-1	0-0	4	Falconer, Collins	25,342
23	21	A	Partick T	D 0-0	0-0	4		11,904
24	Feb 4	A	Motherwell	L 0-1	0-0	4		10,771
25	11	H	Hibernian	D 2-2	1-1	4	Collins, Falconer	24,284
26	25	A	Hearts	D 1-1	0-0	4	O'Donnell	11,185
27	Mar 5	H	Aberdeen	W 2-0	1-0	—	Van Hooijdonk 2	20,621
28	21	A	Kilmarnock	W 1-0	0-0	—	Walker	10,112
29	Apr 1	H	Motherwell	D 1-1	0-0	4	Walker	24,047
30	15	A	Aberdeen	L 0-2	0-2	6		16,668
31	19	H	Hearts	L 0-1	0-0	—		18,638
32	29	A	Falkirk	W 2-1	1-0	5	O'Donnell, Boyd	9714
33	May 2	H	Partick T	L 1-3	1-1	—	Grant	18,963
34	7	H	Rangers	W 3-0	0-0	—	Van Hooijdonk, Moore (og), Vata	31,025
35	9	A	Hibernian	D 1-1	0-1	—	Falconer	6019
36	13	A	Dundee U	W 1-0	0-0	4	O'Donnell	10,993

Final League Position: 4

1909-10, 1913-14, 1914-15, 1915-16, 1916-17, 1918-19, 1921-22, 1925-26, 1935-36, 1937-38, 1953-54, 1965-66, 1966-67, 1967-68, 1968-69, 1969-70, 1970-71, 1971-72, 1972-73, 1973-74. Premier Division 1976-77, 1978-79, 1980-81, 1981-82, 1985-86, 1987-88. *Runners-up:* 22 times.
Scottish Cup Winners: (30 times) 1892, 1899, 1900, 1904, 1907, 1908, 1911, 1912, 1914, 1923, 1925, 1927, 1931, 1933, 1937, 1951, 1954, 1965, 1967, 1969, 1971, 1972, 1974, 1975, 1977, 1980, 1985, 1988, 1989, 1995; *Runners-up:* 16 times.
League Cup Winners: (9 times) 1956-57, 1957-58, 1965-66, 1966-67, 1967-68, 1968-69, 1969-70, 1974-75, 1982-83; *Runners-up:* 10 times.

European: *European Cup Winners:* 1966-67. 78 matches (1966-67 winners, 1967-68, 1968-69, 1969-70 runners-up, 1970-71, 1971-72 semi-finals, 1972-73, 1973-74 semi-finals, 1974-75, 1977-78, 1979-80, 1981-82, 1982-83, 1986-87, 1988-89); *Cup Winners Cup:* 35 matches (1963-64 semi-finals, 1965-66 semi-finals, 1975-76, 1980-81, 1984-85, 1985-86, 1989-90); *UEFA Cup:* 28 matches (*Fairs Cup:* 1962-63, 1964-65. *UEFA Cup:* 1976-77, 1983-84, 1987-88, 1991-92, 1992-93, 1993-94).
Club colours: Shirt: Green and white hoops. Shorts: White. Stockings: White.

Goalscorers: *League (39):* Collins 8, O'Donnell 6, Walker 6, Falconer 4, Van Hooijdonk 4, Byrne 2, Grant 2, Boyd 1, McGinlay 1, McStay 1, Mowbray 1, Vata 1, own goals 2. *Scottish Cup (10):* Van Hooijdonk 4, Falconer 3, Collins 2, O'Donnell 1. *League Cup (7):* Collins 2, Walker 2, Grant 1, Nicholas 1, O'Neil B 1.

Marshall G 16	Martin L 4	Boyd T 35	McNally M 19 + 1	Mowbray A 15	Grant P 27 + 1	Galloway M 11	McStay P 28 + 1	Falconer W 19 + 7	Walker A 22 + 4	Collins J 33 + 1	Nicholas C 5 + 7	Donnelly S 7 + 10	McGinlay P 7 + 1	O'Neil B 24 + 2	O'Donnell P 25 + 2	McLaughlin B 19 + 2	Smith B 3	Byrne P 6	McKinlay T 17	O'Neill J — + 1	Gray S 8 + 3	Bonner P 20	Hay C 2 + 3	Slavin J 3	Van Hooijdonk P 13 + 1	Vata R 7	Mackay M 1	Match No.
1	2	3	4	5	6	7	8	9	10	11																		1
1	2	3	4	5	6		8	9	10	11	7	12	14															2
1		3	4	5	2	7	8		10	11	12	9	*6*	14														3
1		3	4	5	2	7			10	11	12	9	6		8	14												4
1	*2*	3	4	5	6		8		9	11		14	7		10													5
1		3	4	5	6	2			10	11	*9*	12	7	14	8													6
1		3	4		6	2	12	14	10	11	*9*		7	5	8													7
1		3	4			2	8	14	10	11	12	9	7	*5*	6													8
1		3	4		6	2	8	14	10	11	12	*9*			7		5											9
1	2	*3*	4		6			9	12	11	10	14	7	5	8													10
1		3	4				8	14	10	11	12	9		5	6		*2*	7										11
1		2	4		6		8	9	10	11	12	14		5				7	*3*									12
1		2	12	5	6		8			11	10	*9*		4				7	3	14								13
1		2	4		6		8	9	10	11		12		5	7				3									14
1		2	4			6	8	9	10	11				5		7			3		12							15
1		2			6	4	8	9	10			12		5		7			3		11							16
		2		5	6		8		10	11		14		4		9			3			1	7					17
		2			6		8		10	11				4		9	5		*3*		14	1	7					18
		2				5	8		10	11				4	6	9		7			3	1	12					19
		2					8	12	10	11				4	6	9		7			3	1	14	5				20
		2				4	8		12	11					6	10		7			3	1		5	9			21
		2	4				8	10		11					6	7					3	1	14	5	9			22
		2	5		6			10		11				4	8	7					3	1			9			23
		2	5		6		8	10		11				4	7	14					*3*	1			9			24
		2	5		6			10		11				4	8	7					3	1			9			25
			2	5	6			10	12	11				4	8	7			3			1			9			26
		2		5	6		8	10		12				4	11	7			3			1			9			27
		2		5	12		8	*10*	14	11					6	7			3			1			9	4		28
		2		5			8	12	10	11					6	7			3			1			9	4		29
		2			6		8	9	10	11		12		5	14	7			*3*			1				4		30
		3		5	6			9	10	11		12		4	8	7						1				2		31
		2		5	6		8	9	*10*	11				4	7				3			1			14			32
		2		5	6		8	9		11				4	7				3			1			10			33
		2			6		8	12		11		10		5	14	7			3			1			*9*	4		34
		2			6		8	10						5	11	7			3			1			9	4		35
		2			*6*		8			11	12				10	7			3		14	1			9	4	5	36

CLYDE Second Division

Year Formed: 1878. *Ground & Address:* Broadwood Stadium, Cumbernauld, G68 9NE. *Telephone:* 01236 451511.
Ground Capacity: total: 6103 all seated. *Size of Pitch:* 112yd × 76yd.
Chairman: John F. McBeth FRICS. *Secretary:* John D. Taylor. *Commercial Manager:* John Donnelly.
Manager: Alex Smith. *Assistant Manager:* John Brownlie. *Physio:* J. Watson: *Coach:* Gardner Speirs.
Managers since 1975: S. Anderson; C. Brown; J. Clark. *Club Nickname(s):* The Bully Wee. *Previous Grounds:* Barrowfield & Shawfield Stadium.
Record Attendance: 52,000 v Rangers, Division I; 21 Nov, 1908.
Record Transfer Fee received: £95,000 for Pat Nevin to Chelsea (July 1983).
Record Transfer Fee paid: £14,000 for Harry Hood from Sunderland (1966).
Record Victory: 11-1 v Cowdenbeath, Division II; 6 Oct, 1951.
Record Defeat: 0-11 v Dumbarton, Scottish Cup 4th rd, 22 Nov, 1879; v Rangers, Scottish Cup 4th rd, 13 Nov, 1880.
Most Capped Player: Tommy Ring, 12, Scotland.
Most League Appearances: 428: Brian Ahern.
Most League Goals in Season (Individual): 32: Bill Boyd, 1932-33.
Most Goals Overall (Individual): —.

CLYDE 1994–95 LEAGUE RECORD

Match No.	Date	Venue	Opponents	Result		H/T Score	Lg. Pos.	Goalscorers	Attendance
1	Aug 13	A	Stenhousemuir	L	0-1	0-1	—		680
2	20	A	Queen of the S	W	2-1	1-0	7	Dickson, McConnell	1435
3	27	H	Stirling Albion	L	1-2	0-2	9	Knox	1162
4	Sept 3	H	Berwick R	L	3-4	0-1	9	Parks, MacKenzie, Tennant	1141
5	10	A	East Fife	L	0-2	0-1	9		925
6	24	A	Dumbarton	L	1-2	1-1	10	McGill	776
7	Oct 1	H	Meadowbank T	W	2-1	1-1	8	Knox 2	865
8	8	A	Morton	W	1-0	0-0	7	Knox	1801
9	15	H	Brechin C	W	4-0	1-0	7	McCheyne, Knox, Angus (pen), MacKenzie	762
10	22	H	Stenhousemuir	D	0-0	0-0	6		1072
11	29	A	Stirling Albion	W	1-0	0-0	4	Knox	1118
12	Nov 5	H	Queen of the S	D	2-2	0-2	6	MacKenzie, McAulay	1112
13	12	H	East Fife	D	1-1	0-0	7	McCluskey	1212
14	19	A	Berwick R	L	1-2	0-2	7	Angus	611
15	26	H	Dumbarton	W	3-1	1-1	5	McAulay 2, McCluskey	1102
16	Dec 3	A	Meadowbank T	D	2-2	1-0	7	Dickson, Angus	382
17	26	H	Morton	D	0-0	0-0	—		2023
18	31	A	Brechin C	W	2-0	2-0	6	McCluskey, MacKenzie	484
19	Jan 14	A	Stenhousemuir	D	2-2	0-0	7	Dickson, Parks	669
20	17	H	Stirling Albion	W	2-0	0-0	—	Dickson 2	1345
21	21	H	Queen of the S	L	3-4	1-3	5	Dickson 2, Parks	998
22	Feb 4	A	East Fife	W	3-1	1-1	5	Angus, O'Neill, Parks	885
23	11	H	Berwick R	L	1-3	0-2	5	MacKenzie	882
24	18	A	Dumbarton	D	2-2	1-2	5	Angus, Parks	1183
25	25	H	Meadowbank T	W	4-1	1-0	5	Thomson, Nisbet, O'Neill, McCarron	825
26	Mar 11	H	Brechin C	W	1-0	0-0	5	Dickson	907
27	14	A	Morton	L	1-4	0-4	—	Dickson	1421
28	18	H	East Fife	D	1-1	0-0	5	Nisbet	602
29	25	A	Berwick R	D	1-1	1-1	5	McCluskey	581
30	Apr 1	A	Meadowbank T	W	1-0	1-0	5	Dickson	377
31	8	H	Dumbarton	W	1-0	1-0	4	McCluskey	1189
32	15	H	Morton	L	1-3	0-2	6	Brown	2163
33	22	A	Brechin C	D	0-0	0-0	6		413
34	29	H	Stenhousemuir	W	3-2	0-0	5	McCheyne 2, Muir	1043
35	May 6	A	Stirling Albion	L	0-2	0-0	5		1122
36	13	A	Queen of the S	L	0-1	0-1	6		1502

Final League Position: 6

Honours
League Champions: Division II 1904-05, 1951-52, 1956-57, 1961-62, 1972-73. Second Division 1977-78, 1981-82, 1992-93.
Runners-up: Division II 1903-04, 1905-06, 1925-26, 1963-64.
Scottish Cup Winners: 1939, 1955, 1958; *Runners-up:* 1910, 1912, 1949.
League Cup: —
Club colours: Shirt: White with red and black trim. Shorts: Black. Stockings: Black with red and white tops.

Goalscorers: *League (53):* Dickson 10, Knox 6, Angus 5 (1 pen), McCluskey 5, MacKenzie 5, Parks 5, McAulay 3, McCheyne 3, Nisbet 2, O'Neill 2, Brown 1, McCarron 1, McConnell 1, McGill 1, Muir 1, Tennant 1, Thomson 1. *Scottish Cup (3):* Angus 1, Dickson 1, O'Neill 1. *League Cup (0) B&Q Cup (1):* MacKenzie 1.

Fridge L 25 + 1	Clark M 18	Neill A 10	Knox K 30	Thomson J 30	Watson G 28 + 3	Dickson J 23 + 4	McCheyne G 13	McConnell I 7 + 5	McAulay J 8 + 8	MacKenzie A 22 + 7	Wright A 9	McFarlane R 2	Frater A 2	McCarron J 17 + 5	Wylde G 2	Nisbet I 18 + 7	Angus I 24	Tennant S 1	O'Neill M 20	Parks G 11 + 7	Hillcoat J 11	Brown J 23 + 2	McGill D 2 + 4	Prunty J 11 + 5	Strain B 3 + 3	Falconer M 6 + 4	McCluskey G 18 + 1	Muir J 1 + 1	Fay J 1	*Match No.*
1	2	3	4	5	6	7	8	9	10	11																				1
1	2		4	5	8	7		12			3	6	9	*10*	11	14														2
1	2		4	5	8	7		12				*6*	9	10	11	14	3													3
1		6	5		2	*11*		9	8	14	4						10	3	7	12										4
	2		4	5	*8*		3	9		11						14	10			7	1	6	12							5
12	2		4	5			8	14		7				10		6					1		9	3	11					6
1	2		4	5			8			11				10		6			*7*				9	3	14	12				7
1	2		4	5	14		8			11				10		7	3						12		*6*	9				8
1	2		4	5	*6*		8			11				10		7	3						12		14	9				9
1	2		4	5	*6*		8			11				10		7	3						12		14	9				10
1	2		4	5	6	12	8		14	11				*10*		7	3										9			11
1	2		4	5	6		8		14	12				10		*7*	3									11	9			12
1	2		4		6				8	11				*10*		7	3					12		5		14	9			13
1	2		*4*	5	6					12				10		*7*	3			11		14		8			9			14
1		*10*		5	2	7			8	11	4			14			3			12		6					9			15
1		10		5	2	7			*8*	11	4			14			3			12		6					9			16
1	2	10		5	8	7			4	11				12			3			14		6					*9*			17
1		10		5	8	7			12	11				4			3		2	14		6					*9*			18
1		10			8	7		14	12					4			3		2	11		6			5		*9*			19
1		10	5		8	7			14	9				4			3		2	*11*		6		12						20
1		10	5		8	7			11	14				*4*			3		2	9		6		12						21
1		11	10	5	8	7				12						*4*	3		2	9		6		14						22
1			10	5	8	7			14	12						*4*	3		2	11		6					9			23
1	11		10	5	8	7			12							4	3		2	9		6								24
1	11		10	5	12	7			*8*					14		4	3		2	9		6								25
1	11		10	5	12	7				14				*8*		4	3		2	9		6								26
1	11		10	*5*	8	7				9				12		4	3		2			6					14			27
			10	5		7				11	8					4			2	12	1	6		3			9			28
			10	5	4	7				*11*	8					14			2	12	1	6		3			9			29
			10	5	4	7				11	8					12			2		1	6		3		14	*9*			30
			10	5	8	7				11	*4*					14			2		1	6		3		12	9			31
			10	5	8	7		14		11	4					12			2		1	6		3			9			32
			5		4	14	3	8						10		7			*2*		1	6		12		11	9			33
			10	5		14	11	4		8									2		1	6		3			*9*	7		34
			10	5		7	11	4	12	8									2		1	6		3			*9*	14		35
				5	2	14	3	4								7	10			*8*	1	6		12		9			11	36

CLYDEBANK First Division

Year Formed: 1965. *Ground & Address:* Kilbowie Park, Arran Place, Clydebank G81 2PB. *Telephone:* 0141 952 2887.
Ground Capacity: total: 9950. seated: All. *Size of Pitch:* 110yd × 68yd.
Chairman: C.G.Steedman. *Secretary:* A.Steedman. *Commercial Manager:* David Curwood.
Managing Director: I.C.Steedman. *Physio:* Peter Saula. *Coach:* Brian Wright.
Managers since 1975: William Munro, J.S.Steedman. *Club Nickname(s):* The Bankies. *Previous Grounds:* None.
Record Attendance: 14,900 v Hibernian, Scottish Cup 1st rd; 10 Feb, 1965.
Record Transfer Fee received: £175,000 for Owen Coyle from Airdrieonians, (Feb 1990).
Record Transfer Fee paid: £50,000 for Gerry McCabe from Clyde.
Record Victory: 8-1 Arbroath, First Division; 3 Jan 1977.
Record Defeat: 1-9 v Gala Fairydean, Scottish Cup qual rd; 15 Sept, 1965.
Most Capped Player: —.
Most League Appearances: 620: Jim Fallon; 1968-86.
Most League Goals in Season (Individual): 29: Ken Eadie, First Division, 1990-91.
Most League Goals Overall (Individual): 138, Ken Eadie 1988-95.

CLYDEBANK 1994–95 LEAGUE RECORD

Match No.	Date		Venue	Opponents	Result		H/T Score	Lg. Pos.	Goalscorers	Attendance
1	Aug	13	H	Stranraer	W	2-0	0-0	—	Eadie, Cooper	908
2		20	H	Dunfermline Ath	L	0-1	0-1	3		1597
3		27	A	St Mirren	L	1-2	1-0	5	Currie	2414
4	Sept	3	A	Raith R	D	1-1	0-1	7	Currie	2861
5		10	H	Dundee	W	5-2	2-1	4	Jack, Flannigan 2, Sweeney, Grady	1437
6		24	A	Airdrieonians	L	0-2	0-1	4		1542
7	Oct	1	H	St Johnstone	D	0-0	0-0	5		1025
8		8	H	Ayr U	W	3-0	1-0	4	Grady, Eadie 2	891
9		15	A	Hamilton A	D	0-0	0-0	4		1042
10		22	A	Stranraer	W	1-0	0-0	4	Grady	781
11		29	H	St Mirren	D	1-1	1-0	4	Sweeney	1675
12	Nov	5	A	Dunfermline Ath	L	1-4	0-1	4	Jack	4611
13		12	A	Dundee	L	0-2	0-1	5		2240
14		19	H	Raith R	L	0-3	0-1	6		1002
15		26	H	Airdrieonians	L	0-1	0-0	7		1197
16	Dec	3	A	St Johnstone	D	1-1	0-1	7	Eadie	2724
17		26	A	Ayr U	D	1-1	0-1	—	Currie	1969
18		31	H	Stranraer	L	2-3	0-2	7	Murdoch, Flannigan	652
19	Jan	2	A	St Mirren	D	0-0	0-0	—		3217
20		7	H	Dunfermline Ath	L	1-2	1-0	7	Eadie	1468
21		10	H	Hamilton A	D	0-0	0-0	—		578
22		14	A	Raith R	L	0-1	0-0	7		3129
23		21	H	Dundee	L	0-3	0-2	7		900
24	Feb	4	H	St Johnstone	D	0-0	0-0	7		949
25		14	A	Airdrieonians	W	2-1	2-0	—	Eadie, Grady	1033
26		25	A	Hamilton A	W	1-0	0-0	7	Sherry (og)	1017
27	Mar	11	H	Ayr U	D	1-1	0-0	7	Grady	720
28		18	A	Dundee	L	2-3	1-1	7	Grady, Eadie	1788
29	Apr	1	A	St Johnstone	L	0-1	0-1	7		3337
30		4	H	Raith R	L	1-2	0-0	—	Robertson	1261
31		11	H	Airdrieonians	D	1-1	1-0	—	Grady	709
32		15	A	Ayr U	L	0-1	0-1	8		1798
33		22	H	Hamilton A	L	1-4	1-3	8	Eadie	716
34		29	A	Stranraer	W	1-0	1-0	8	Robertson	582
35	May	6	H	St Mirren	W	2-1	1-0	7	Murdoch, Bowman	1399
36		13	A	Dunfermline Ath	L	1-2	0-2	8	Eadie	7709

Final League Position: 8

Honours
League Champions: Second Division 1975-76; *Runners-up:* First Division 1976-77, 1984-85.
Scottish Cup: Semi-finalists 1990. *League Cup:* —.
Club colours: Shirt: White with Red shoulder band with Black trim. Shorts: White with Red trim. Stockings: White with Red trim.

Goalscorers: *League (33):* Eadie 9, Grady 7, Currie 3, Flannigan 3, Jack 2, Murdoch 2, Robertson 2, Sweeney 2, Bowman 1, Cooper 1, own goal 1. *Scottish Cup (2):* Eadie 2. *League Cup (1):* Grady 1. *B&Q Cup (11):* Grady 4, Cooper 3, Eadie 2, Flannigan 1, Harris 1.

Matthews G 36	Lansdowne A 14 + 9	Bowman G 29 + 2	Murdoch S 28	Sweeney S 27	Currie T 27	Cooper D 19 + 2	Harris C 7 + 1	Eadie K 26 + 3	Grady J 30 + 6	Ferguson G 9 + 3	Flannigan C 11 + 10	Jack S 33 + 2	Kerrigan S 8 + 6	Sutherland S 9	Crawford D 12 + 4	Walker J 14 + 7	Keane G 3	Butcher T 3	Tomlinson C 10	Agnew P 4 + 2	McStay J 19 + 1	Connelly D 1 + 4	Robertson J 6 + 1	Lovering P 3	Dunn R — + 1	*Match No.*
1	2	3	4	5	6	7	8	9	10	11	12															1
1	2	3	4	*5*	6	7	8	9	10	14		11	12													2
1	2	3	4		5	7	8		9	14	10	11	12	*6*												3
1	2		4		5	7			12	*8*	10	11	9	6	3	14										4
1	2		4	5	6	7			9		10	11		3	12	8										5
1	2	*3*	4	5	6	7		12	10		9	11			8	14										6
1	2		4	5	6	7		9	10		12	11			3	8										7
1		3	4	5	6	7	11	9	10		12	2				8										8
1		3	4	5		7	11	9	10		12	2			14	8	*6*									9
1	12	3	4	5		7		9	11		10	2				8	6									10
1	*11*	3	4	5	6	7		9	10		12	2			14	8										11
1	11	3	4		5	7	14	9	10		12	2				*8*		6								12
1		3	4		5	7		12	9		10	11				*8*		6	2	14						13
1		3			5	7	4	9	10			11	12			8		6	*2*	14						14
1		11			5	7		9	10		12	2			3		6		4	8						15
1		11		5	6	12		9	8			14	*10*		3				4	7	2					16
1		11	4	5	6	7		*9*	10		14	12			3					8	2					17
1		3	4	5	6	7	*8*	9	12		10	11				14					2					18
1		*3*	4	5	6	12			14		10	11	9			7				8	2					19
1	14	3	4	5	6			9	8			11	*10*			7					2					20
1		11	4	5	6			9	*10*		14	8			3	7					2					21
1		11	4	5	6	7		9	12		10	8			3	14					*2*					22
1	14	11	*4*	5		7		9	12		10	6			3	8					2					23
1	8	3	4	5	6			9	14		10	11									2	*7*				24
1	7	11	4	5	6			9	*10*	3		8	12								2	14				25
1	7	11		5	6			9	10	3		8				14			4		*2*					26
1	7	11		5	6			9	10	3		8							4		2					27
1	7	11		5	6			9	10	3		8	12	4							2					28
1	15	11		5	6				*10*			8	9	3		12			4		2		14			29
1	15	14	4	5					10			8	9	6	3	12					2		*11*			30
1	15	14	4	5				9	10			8		6	3						2		*11*			31
1	15		4	5				9	10			8	12	6	3						2		11			32
1	15	11	4	5				9	10	12	14	8		*3*		6					2					33
1	15	6			5			9	10	2		8							4			14	*11*	3		34
1		8	6						10	2		5	9						4		12	15	*11*	3	14	35
1			6					12	10	2		5	9		14				4		8	15	*11*	3		36

COWDENBEATH Third Division

Year Formed: 1881. *Ground & Address:* Central Park, Cowdenbeath KY4 9EY. *Telephone:* 01383 610166. *Fax:* 01383 512132.
Ground Capacity: total: 5268. seated: 1622. *Size of Pitch:* 107yd × 66yd.
Chairman: Gordon McDougall. *Secretary:* Tom Ogilvie. *Commercial Manager:* Joe McNamara.
Manager: Thomas Steven.
Managers since 1975: D. McLindon; F. Connor; P. Wilson; A. Rolland; H. Wilson; W. McCulloch; J. Clark; J. Craig; R. Campbell; J. Blackley; J. Brownlie, A. Harrow, J. Reilly, P Dolan. *Previous Grounds:* North End Park, Cowdenbeath.
Record Attendance: 25,586 v Rangers, League Cup quarter-final; 21 Sept, 1949.
Record Transfer Fee received: £30,000 for Nicky Henderson to Falkirk, (March 1994).
Record Transfer Fee paid: —
Record Victory: 12-0 v Johnstone, Scottish Cup 1st rd; 21 Jan, 1928.
Record Defeat: 1-11 v Clyde, Division II; 6 Oct, 1951.
Most Capped Player: Jim Paterson, 3, Scotland.
Most League and Cup Appearances: 491 Ray Allan 1972-75, 1979-89.
Most League Goals in Season (Individual): 53, Rab Walls, Division II, 1938-39.
Most Goals Overall (Individual): 120, Willie Devlin, 1922-26, 1929-30.

COWDENBEATH 1994–95 LEAGUE RECORD

Match No.	Date	Venue	Opponents	Result		H/T Score	Lg. Pos.	Goalscorers	Attendance
1	Aug 13	H	Ross C	L	0-2	0-0	—		678
2	20	H	Arbroath	W	6-2	4-0	6	Yardley 4, Malloy, Soutar	315
3	27	A	Montrose	L	0-2	0-2	8		584
4	Sept 3	H	East Stirling	D	1-1	0-0	8	Winter	258
5	10	A	Queen's Park	W	3-0	0-0	7	Yardley 3	509
6	24	A	Albion R	W	4-2	1-1	4	Malloy, Yardley, Callaghan 2	314
7	Oct 1	H	Alloa	L	1-3	0-1	7	Yardley	368
8	8	A	Caledonian Th	W	3-0	1-0	5	Winter, Yardley 2	1273
9	15	H	Forfar Ath	W	1-0	0-0	3	Callaghan	403
10	22	A	Ross C	L	0-4	0-0	6		1284
11	29	H	Montrose	D	1-1	1-1	6	Yardley	301
12	Nov 5	A	Arbroath	W	3-0	3-0	6	Conn, Yardley, Wardell	426
13	12	H	Queen's Park	W	2-0	0-0	4	Yardley 2	281
14	19	A	East Stirling	W	2-0	0-0	3	Black, Wardell	553
15	26	H	Albion R	D	2-2	1-2	3	Yardley 2	380
16	Dec 3	A	Alloa	L	0-1	0-0	4		462
17	26	H	Caledonian Th	D	1-1	1-0	—	Callaghan	464
18	31	A	Forfar Ath	D	1-1	1-0	5	Yardley	603
19	Jan 2	A	Montrose	W	2-1	2-1	—	Yardley 2	452
20	14	H	Ross C	L	0-3	0-1	6		361
21	21	A	Arbroath	W	3-0	1-0	3	Callaghan, Black, Wardell	388
22	Feb 4	A	Queen's Park	L	0-1	0-0	5		477
23	18	A	Albion R	L	0-2	0-0	6		273
24	25	H	Alloa	L	1-3	1-2	6	Winter	260
25	Mar 4	A	Caledonian Th	L	1-3	0-2	6	De Melo	659
26	11	H	Forfar Ath	L	1-3	1-1	7	Yardley	280
27	18	H	Queen's Park	L	1-3	1-1	7	De Melo	137
28	22	H	East Stirling	L	1-4	0-2	—	Wardell	172
29	25	A	East Stirling	L	0-1	0-1	7		338
30	Apr 1	A	Alloa	L	1-2	1-0	7	Conn	367
31	8	H	Albion R	W	2-0	0-0	6	Black, Yardley	186
32	15	H	Caledonian Th	L	1-3	0-1	7	Yardley	183
33	22	A	Forfar Ath	D	2-2	2-2	8	Black, Wardell	611
34	29	A	Ross C	L	0-2	0-1	8		1356
35	May 6	H	Montrose	L	0-4	0-1	9		379
36	13	H	Arbroath	D	1-1	1-1	9	Soutar	200

Final League Position: 9

Honours
League Champions: Division II 1913-14, 1914-15, 1938-39; *Runners-up:* Division II 1921-22, 1923-24, 1969-70. Second Division 1991-92.
Scottish Cup: Quarter-finals: 1931.
League Cup: Semi-finals: 1959-60, 1970-71.
Club colours: Shirt: Royal Blue 1" vertical stripe with Red piping on sleeve seam. Shorts: White with blue side stripe. Stockings: Royal blue.

Goalscorers: *League (48):* Yardley 23, Callaghan 5, Wardell 5, Black 4, Winter 3, Conn 2, De Melo 2, Malloy 2, Soutar 2. *Scottish Cup (1):* Conn 1. *League Cup (2):* Black 1, Soutar 1. *B&Q Cup (6):* Yardley 4, Soutar 1, Tait 1.

Russell N 31	Scott S 12 + 2	Hamill A 4 + 2	Malloy B 30	Humphreys M 21 + 1	Winter C 23 + 5	Petrie E 12	Black I 31 + 2	Soutar G 16 + 3	Thomson J 1 + 1	Stout D 4	Lynch J 2 + 14	Carr R — + 2	Tait G 22	Yardley M 32	McMahon B 17 + 5	Davidson I 1	Bowmaker K 2	Callaghan W 18 + 2	Murdoch S 17	Hamilton A — + 1	Barclay A 3 + 4	Fellenger D 23 + 1	Maloney J 3	Conn S 19	Wardell S 20 + 3	Weatherston P 8 + 7	Wood G 9	Maratea D 3 + 1	De Melo A 7 + 2	Watson D 2 + 2	Craib S 3	Stewart W — + 2	*Match No.*
1	2	3	4	5	6	7	*8*	9	10	11	12	14																					1
1		3	4	5	7	*2*	8	10	12	11			6	9	14																		2
1		3	4	5	12		8	*10*		11	14		7	9	6	2																	3
1			4	5	6		8	12		*11*	14		7	9	2		3	10															4
1		14	4	5	6	2	*8*	11			12		7	9				10	3														5
1		8	4	5	*6*	2	14	11					7	9	12			10	3														6
1				4	*6*	2	8	11			14		7	9	5			10	3	12													7
1	14		4	5	6	2	8	11					7	9				*10*	3		12												8
1			5	14	7	2	8	*11*						9	4			10	3			6											9
1	12		5	4	6	2	8	*11*			14			9				10	3			7											10
	2		5	4			8				12			9				10	3			6	1	7	11								11
1	2	14		4			*8*				12		6	9				10	3			7		5	11								12
1	2		4		10		8				12		7	9	14				3			*6*		5	11								13
1	2		4		*6*		11				12		7	9				14	3			8		5	10								14
1	2		4		14		8				12		7	9				10	3			6		5	*11*								15
1	2		4		12		8						*6*	9	14			10	3			7		5	11								16
1	2		5		6		12						8	9	4			10	3			7			11								17
1	2		4				8						7	9				10	3			6		5	11	12							18
1	2		4				8	10					7	9	5				3		12	14		*6*	11								19
			4	2			11	9										10	3			8	1	5		6	7	12					20
				4	14		8							9	5			10	3		12		1		11	6	7	*2*					21
1	2			4	14		8	12						9	5			10			*6*				11	3	7						22
1	*2*			7			11				12		3	9	4			10				8		5	6	14							23
1			4	2	7			10					8	9							*11*	6		5	12	3			14				24
1			4		7						14		8	9	2						12	*6*		5	11	3			10	15			25
1			4		7		6						8	9	2			12						5		3			10		11		26
1			5		6		8						7	9	4			10				2			12	3			11	15			27
			6		7		3						8	9								2		4	12		5		10	1	11		28
1			6				3						10	9	4							2		5	*7*	14	8		12		11		29
1				5		2	8	10						9	14							7		3		12	*6*	4	11				30
1			5	4	6	2	8							9								7			11	14	3		*10*				31
			5	3	6	2	8							9								7			11			4	10	1			32
1			4	*5*	8		9	11				12			3						6	7			10	2						14	33
1			5	2	8		9	11			7				4							6		3	10	12							34
1			5		8		10	12			6			9	3							7		4	11		*2*					14	35
1			5		7	2		11			14			9	6		3							4	*10*	12	8						36

DUMBARTON First Division

Year Formed: 1872. *Ground & Address:* Boghead Park, Miller St, Dumbarton G82 2JA. *Telephone:* 01389 62569/67864.
Ground Capacity: total: 10,700. seated: 303. *Size of Pitch:* 110yd × 68yd.
Chairman: D.Dalglish. *Secretary:* Alistair Paton.
Manager: Murdo MacLeod. *Assistant Manager:* Jim Fallon. *Physio:* D.Stobie. *Coach:* Alistair MacLeod.
Managers since 1975: A. Wright; D. Wilson; S. Fallon; W. Lamont; D. Wilson; D. Whiteford; A. Totten; M. Clougherty; R. Auld; J. George; W. Lamont. *Club Nickname(s):* The Sons. *Previous Grounds:* Broadmeadow, Ropework Lane.
Record Attendance: 18,000 v Raith Rovers, Scottish Cup; 2 Mar, 1957.
Record Transfer Fee received: £125,000 for Graeme Sharp to Everton (March 1982).
Record Transfer Fee paid: £50,000 for Charlie Gibson from Stirling Albion (1989).
Record Victory: 13-1 v Kirkintilloch Cl. 1st Rd; 1 Sept, 1888.
Record Defeat: 1-11 v Albion Rovers, Division II; 30 Jan, 1926: v Ayr United, League Cup; 13 Aug, 1952.
Most Capped Player: John Lindsay, 8, Scotland; James McAulay, 8, Scotland.
Most League Appearances: 297: Andy Jardine, 1957-67.

DUMBARTON 1994–95 LEAGUE RECORD

Match No.	Date	Venue	Opponents	Result		H/T Score	Lg. Pos.	Goalscorers	Attendance
1	Aug 13	A	Queen of the S	L	1-4	0-1	—	Mooney M	1389
2	20	A	Stirling Albion	D	1-1	0-0	9	Mooney M	715
3	27	H	Morton	W	2-1	0-1	6	Mooney M, Ward	1168
4	Sept 3	H	Meadowbank T	L	0-1	0-1	7		644
5	10	A	Berwick R	L	0-1	0-0	8		533
6	24	H	Clyde	W	2-1	1-1	6	Boyd 2	776
7	Oct 1	A	Brechin C	W	2-1	1-1	5	Martin, McGarvey	427
8	8	A	East Fife	W	3-2	1-1	4	Mooney M (pen), Gibson 2	795
9	15	H	Stenhousemuir	L	1-2	0-1	5	Mooney M	601
10	22	H	Queen of the S	D	0-0	0-0	5		725
11	29	A	Morton	L	0-1	0-0	8		1429
12	Nov 5	H	Stirling Albion	W	1-0	1-0	7	McKinnon	778
13	12	H	Berwick R	W	3-2	0-1	4	Mooney M, King, McGarvey	733
14	19	A	Meadowbank T	D	0-0	0-0	5		210
15	26	A	Clyde	L	1-3	1-1	6	Mooney M	1102
16	Dec 3	H	Brechin C	W	6-0	3-0	5	McGarvey 2, McKinnon, Mooney M, King, Campbell	554
17	26	H	East Fife	W	4-0	2-0	—	Mooney M, Ward, McGarvey, Meechan	862
18	31	A	Stenhousemuir	L	0-1	0-0	5		638
19	Jan 14	A	Queen of the S	D	0-0	0-0	6		1066
20	21	H	Stirling Albion	D	2-2	2-0	7	Mooney M, Ward	700
21	24	H	Morton	W	2-1	0-1	—	Ward, Gibson	1307
22	Feb 4	A	Berwick R	W	2-1	0-1	2	Gibson, Meechan	508
23	11	H	Meadowbank T	W	4-0	3-0	2	Mooney M, Ward, Gibson, McGarvey	749
24	18	H	Clyde	D	2-2	2-1	2	Martin, Mooney M	1183
25	25	A	Brechin C	D	0-0	0-0	3		480
26	Mar 4	A	East Fife	W	2-0	1-0	1	Ward 2	662
27	14	H	Stenhousemuir	W	5-1	2-1	—	Mooney M, Ward 3, McKinnon	1132
28	21	H	Berwick R	W	1-0	0-0	—	Ward	1012
29	25	A	Meadowbank T	L	0-1	0-1	1		389
30	Apr 1	H	Brechin C	W	4-1	3-0	1	Mooney M 2, Meechan, Fabiani	1103
31	8	A	Clyde	L	0-1	0-1	1		1189
32	15	H	East Fife	W	2-0	1-0	1	Mooney M, McKinnon	1253
33	22	A	Stenhousemuir	D	0-0	0-0	1		989
34	29	H	Queen of the S	D	2-2	1-1	2	Meechan, Mooney M	1369
35	May 6	A	Morton	L	0-2	0-0	3		6242
36	13	A	Stirling Albion	W	2-0	0-0	2	Ward, Gibson	3003

Final League Position: 2

Most Goals in Season (Individual): 38: Kenny Wilson, Division II; 1971-72.
Most Goals Overall (Individual): 169: Hughie Gallacher, 1954-62 (including C Division 1954-55).

Honours
League Champions: Division I 1890-91 (shared with Rangers), 1891-92. Division II 1910-11, 1971-72. Second Division 1991-92; *Runners-up:* First Division 1983-84. Division II 1907-08.
Scottish Cup Winners: 1883; *Runners-up:* 1881, 1882, 1887, 1891, 1897. *League Cup:* —.
Club colours: Shirt: Gold. Shorts: Gold. Stockings: Gold and black.

Goalscorers: *League (57):* Mooney M 17 (1 pen), Ward 12, Gibson 6, McGarvey 6, McKinnon 4, Meechan 4, Boyd 2, King 2, Martin 2, Campbell 1, Fabiani 1. *Scottish Cup (3):* Ward 2, McKinnon 1. *League Cup (0) B&Q Cup (2):* Campbell 2.

MacFarlane I 33	Marsland J 29	Fabiani R 27 + 1	Melvin M 16	Martin P 28	MacLeod M 24	Mooney M 33 + 3	Meechan J 25 + 3	Gibson C 21 + 5	McGarvey M 23 + 7	Foster A 5	Campbell C 4 + 10	Ward H 24 + 9	Boyd J 10 + 1	Gow S 30 + 1	McKinnon C 25 + 4	Hendry M 1 + 3	Burridge J 3	King T 25 + 1	Mooney S — + 2	McConville R — + 1	Farrell G 1	Hamilton J 9	Dallas S — + 1	Match No.
1	2	3	4	5	6	7	8	9	10	*11*	12	14												1
1	2	3	4		6	7	8	9	10		*11*	14	5											2
1	2	3	4		6	7	8	9	10		*11*	14	5											3
1	2	3	4		6	7	8	9	10		12	11	5											4
1		3	4		6	7	8	9	10		11	12	5	2										5
1		3	4	8	6	7		9	10		11		5	2										6
1	3		4	5	6	7	8	9	10			12		2	*11*	14								7
1	3	*6*	4	5		7	8	9	10			12		2	11	14								8
	3	*6*	4	5		7	8	9	10					2	11	12	1	14						9
	3		4	5	6	7		12					*10*	2	11	9	1	8	14					10
	3		4	5	6	7			8			12	*11*	2	9		1	10	14					11
1		3	4	5	6	14		*9*	12			7	11	2	10			8						12
1		3	4	5	6	12		9	11			7		2	10			8						13
1		3	4		6	7		12	10	5		11	14	2	*9*			8						14
1			4	5		7		*9*	8	3		14	6	2	11			10						15
1			4	5		7	12		8	3	14	11	6	2	9			10						16
1	6	3		5		7	4		10		12	11		2	9			*8*		14				17
1	6	3		5		7	4		10		12	11		2	9			8						18
1	6	3		5		7	4		10			11		2	9			8						19
1	2	3		5	6	7	4		10		14	11		12	*9*			8						20
1	4	3		5	*6*	7	10	9	14			11		2				8						21
1	6	3		5		12	4	9				11		2	10			8			7			22
1	6	3		5		7	4	9	10			11		2	12			8						23
1	6	3		5		7	4		10		12	11		2	9			8						24
1	3			5	6	7	4				12	11		2	9			8				10		25
1	3			5	6	*7*	4	9	10		14	11		2	12							8		26
1	3	14		5	6	7		9	*10*		12	11		2	8							4		27
1	6	3		5		7	12	9				11		2	10			8				4		28
1	6	3		5		7	12	9	14			*11*		2	10			8				4		29
1	5	3			6	7	10		14			11		2	9			*8*				4	12	30
1	5	3			6	7	10	14	12			11		2	*9*			8				4		31
1	5	3			6	7	10	9	14			11		2	12			8				*4*		32
1	4	3		5	6	7	10		14			*11*		2	9			8						33
1	4	3		5	6	7	10	12				11		2	9			8						34
1	4	3		5	6	7	10	14	11			12		2	*9*			8						35
1	4			5	6	7	10	9		3		11			12			8				2		36

DUNDEE First Division

Year Formed: 1893. *Ground & Address:* Dens Park, Sandeman St, Dundee DD3 7JY. *Telephone:* 01382 826104. *Fax:* 01382 832284.
Ground Capacity: 16,871. seated: 11,516. *Size of Pitch:* 110yd × 70yd.
Chairman: Ron Dixon. *Vice-chairman:* Malcolm Reid. *Secretary:* Andrew Drummond. *Managing Director:* Nigel Squire.
Manager: Jim Duffy. *Coach:* John McCormack.
Managers since 1975: David White; Tommy Gemmell; Donald Mackay; Archie Knox; Jocky Scott; Dave Smith; Gordon Wallace; Iain Munro, Simon Stainrod. *Club Nickname(s):* The Dark Blues or The Dee. *Previous Grounds:* Carolina Port 1893-98.
Record Attendance: 43,024 v Rangers, Scottish Cup; 1953.
Record Transfer Fee received: £500,000 for Tommy Coyne to Celtic (March 1989).
Record Transfer Fee paid: £200,000 for Jim Leighton (Feb 1992).
Record Victory: 10-0 Division II v Alloa; 9 Mar, 1947 and v Dunfermline Ath; 22 Mar, 1947.
Record Defeat: 0-11 v Celtic, Division I; 26 Oct, 1895.
Most Capped Player: Alex Hamilton, 24, Scotland.
Most League Appearances: 341: Doug Cowie 1945-61.
Most League Goals in Season (Individual): 38: Dave Halliday, Division I; 1923-24.
Most Goals Overall (Individual): 113: Alan Gilzean.

DUNDEE 1994–95 LEAGUE RECORD

Match No.	Date	Venue	Opponents	Result		H/T Score	Lg. Pos.	Goalscorers	Attendance
1	Aug 13	H	St Mirren	W	2-0	1-0	—	Shaw, Britton	4125
2	20	H	Stranraer	W	3-1	2-0	1	Britton 2, McCaffrey (og)	3186
3	27	A	St Johnstone	W	1-0	1-0	1	Pittman	6021
4	Sept 3	H	Airdrieonians	D	1-1	0-1	1	Farningham	4020
5	10	A	Clydebank	L	2-5	1-2	2	Britton 2	1437
6	24	A	Ayr U	L	2-3	1-2	3	Britton, Hamilton	1901
7	Oct 1	H	Dunfermline Ath	D	4-4	1-1	3	Shaw 2, Tosh, Britton	4784
8	8	H	Hamilton A	W	2-0	2-0	3	Hamilton, Britton	2370
9	15	A	Raith R	D	1-1	0-1	3	Anderson	3834
10	22	A	St Mirren	W	2-1	1-0	3	McCann 2	2758
11	29	H	St Johnstone	W	1-0	0-0	3	Shaw	4327
12	Nov 12	H	Clydebank	W	2-0	1-0	3	Bain, Shaw	2240
13	19	A	Airdrieonians	L	1-2	0-0	3	Britton	2022
14	23	A	Stranraer	W	2-0	1-0	—	Tosh, Cargill	765
15	26	H	Ayr U	D	1-1	1-0	3	Tosh	2506
16	Dec 3	A	Dunfermline Ath	W	1-0	0-0	2	Ritchie	6065
17	10	H	Raith R	W	2-1	0-0	1	Hamilton, Wieghorst	3493
18	26	A	Hamilton A	W	1-0	1-0	—	Hamilton	1552
19	31	H	St Mirren	W	4-0	1-0	1	Hamilton, Shaw 3	3715
20	Jan 7	H	Stranraer	W	2-0	1-*0	1	Duffy C, Ritchie	2615
21	11	A	St Johnstone	D	2-2	1-0	—	Hamilton, Britton	5636
22	14	H	Airdrieonians	L	0-1	0-0	1		4084
23	21	A	Clydebank	W	3-0	2-0	1	Jack (og), Duffy C, Hamilton	900
24	Feb 4	H	Dunfermline Ath	L	2-3	1-2	1	Tosh, Britton	5896
25	11	A	Ayr U	L	0-1	0-1	1		2042
26	25	A	Raith R	D	0-0	0-0	2		5885
27	Mar 4	H	Hamilton A	W	2-0	1-0	1	Britton, Teasdale	2342
28	18	H	Clydebank	W	3-2	1-1	1	Shaw 2, Farningham	1788
29	25	A	Airdrieonians	W	3-0	0-0	1	Farningham, Shaw 2	2528
30	Apr 1	A	Dunfermline Ath	D	1-1	1-0	1	Shaw	8341
31	8	H	Ayr U	D	1-1	1-0	3	Duffy C	2765
32	15	A	Hamilton A	W	4-1	4-0	1	Shaw, Hamilton 3	1471
33	22	H	Raith R	L	0-2	0-0	3		7849
34	29	A	St Mirren	L	0-1	0-0	3		2976
35	May 6	H	St Johnstone	W	2-1	0-0	3	Hamilton, Shaw	3906
36	13	A	Stranraer	W	5-0	1-0	3	Hamilton, Wieghorst 2, Shaw, Tosh	1589

Final League Position: 3

Honours
League Champions: Division I 1961-62. First Division 1978-79, 1991-92. Division II 1946-47; *Runners-up:* Division I 1902-03, 1906-07, 1908-09, 1948-49, 1980-81.
Scottish Cup Winners: 1910; *Runners-up:* 1925, 1952, 1964.
League Cup Winners: 1951-52, 1952-53, 1973-74; *Runners-up:* 1967-68, 1980-81.
B&Q (Centenary) Cup: Winners: 1990-91 *Runners-up:* 1994-95.

European: *European Cup:* 1962-63 (semi-final). *Cup Winners:* 1964-65.
UEFA Cup: (*Fairs Cup* 1967-68 semi-final), 1971-72, 1973-74, 1974-75.
Club colours: Shirt: Dark blue with red and white trim. Shorts: White. Stockings: Blue and White.

Goalscorers: *League (65):* Shaw 16, Britton 12, Hamilton 12, Tosh 5, Duffy C 5, Farningham 3, Wieghorst 3, McCann 2, Ritchie 2, Anderson 1, Bain 1, Cargill 1, Pittman 1, Teasdale 1, own goals 2. *Scottish Cup (3):* Shaw 2, Hamilton 1. *League Cup (4):* Tosh 2, Farningham 1, Shaw 1. *B&Q Cup (12):* Britton 6, Wieghorst 2, Bain 1 (pen), McCann 1, Shaw 1, own goal 1.

Pageaud M 35	McQuillan J 30 + 2	Pittman S 3	Duffy C 23 + 1	Blake N 29 + 2	Duffy J 16	Shaw G 33 + 1	Dinnie A 1	Wieghorst M 29	Britton G 23 + 3	McCann N 29 + 3	Tosh P 13 + 14	Farningham R 25 + 2	Anderson I 4 + 6	Vrto D 22	McKeown G — + 1	Teasdale M 13 + 4	Hutchison M 7	Hamilton J 23 + 5	Mathers P 1 + 1	Bain K 20	Cargill A 10 + 4	Dailly M 1	Ritchie P 6 + 9	Match No.
1	2	*3*	4	5	6	7	8	9	10	11	14													1
1	2		6	5		7		9	10	11	14	3	*4*	8	12									2
1	2	3	6	5		7		9	10	*11*	12	4		8		14								3
1	2	3	4	5	6	7		9	10	11	14	*8*												4
1	2		4	5		7		9	10	11	12	6	14	8			3							5
1	2		6	5		7		9	10		*11*	4		8			3	14						6
	3			5	6	7		8	10		9	2				12		11	1	4				7
1	2			5		7		6	10		9			8				11		3	4			8
1	2			5		7		6	10	12	9	4	14	*8*				11		3				9
1	2			14	5			*6*	10	11	12	4	7	8				9		3				10
1	2			12	5	7			*10*	11	9	4					3	14		6	8			11
1	2			5		7		*6*	10	11	12			8		14		9		3	4			12
1	2			5	6	7		9	10	11	12	4		8				14				*3*		13
1	2			5	6	7		8		11	9					3		10			4			14
1	2			5		7		8	10	11	9					3		12		6	4			15
1	2			5		7				*11*	9	4	12			3		10		6	8		14	16
1	2		14	5		7		8		*11*	9	4	12			3		10		6				17
1			2	5		7		6		11	*9*	4		8		3		10			12		14	18
1			2	5		7		*9*	12	11		4		8		3		10		6			14	19
1	14		2	5		7			12	11				8		3		10		6	*4*		9	20
1	14		2	5		7			12	11				8		*3*		10		6	4		9	21
1	2			5		7			10	11		3		8				9		6	4		12	22
1	2		*3*	5		7		4	10	11		12		8				9		6			14	23
1	2		*3*	5				*4*	10	11	7		14	8				9	15	6				24
1	2			5		7		4	10	11	12		*6*	8				9		3			14	25
1			2			7		*9*	10	11		4		8		3		12		6	5		14	26
1			2			14		9	*10*	12		4		8		5	3	11		6			7	27
1	2		5		3	7			10	11	12	4		8				9		6				28
1	2		4		5	7		6		11	14	*10*		8		3							9	29
1	2		4		3	7			10	11		6		8		12				5			9	30
1	2		4	5	6	7		9	11	12	14	8					*3*						10	31
1	2		4	5	6	7		8		11	*9*	12					3	10					14	32
1	2		6	5	4	7		9		11	12	8					3	10						33
1	2		4	5	6	7		9			11	8				*3*		10			14		12	34
1	2		*4*	5	6	7		9		11		8	14			3		10			12			35
1	2		4	5	3	7		9		11	12	*8*	6					10			14			36

DUNDEE UNITED First Division

Year Formed: 1909 (1923). *Ground & Address:* Tannadice Park, Tannadice St, Dundee DD3 7JW. *Telephone:* 01382 833166. *Fax:* 01382 882689. *Ground Capacity:* total: 12,616 all seated: stands: east 2868, west 2104, south 2201, George Fox 5151, executive boxes 292.
Size of Pitch: 110yd × 74yd.
Chairman: James Y. McLean. *Company Secretary:* Miss Priti Trivedi. *Commercial Manager:* Bobby Brown.
Manager: Billy Kirkwood. *Assistant Manager:* Maurice Malpas. *Physio:* David Rankin. *Coach:* Gordon Wallace.
Managers since 1975: J. McLean, I.Golac. *Club Nickname(s):* The Terrors. *Previous Grounds:* None.
Record Attendance: 28,000 v Barcelona, Fairs Cup; 16 Nov, 1966.
Record Transfer Fee received: £4,000,000 for Duncan Ferguson from Rangers (July 1993).
Record Transfer Fee paid: £600,000 for Gordon Petric from Partizan Belgrade (Nov 1993).
Record Victory: 14-0 v Nithsdale Wanderers, Scottish Cup 1st rd; 17 Jan, 1931.
Record Defeat: 1-12 v Motherwell, Division II; 23 Jan, 1954.
Most Capped Player: Maurice Malpas, 55, Scotland.
Most League Appearances: 612, Dave Narey; 1973-94.
Most Appearances in European Matches: 76, Dave Narey (record for Scottish player).
Most League Goals in Season (Individual): 41: John Coyle, Division II; 1955-56.
Most Goals Overall (Individual): 158: Peter McKay.

DUNDEE UNITED 1994–95 LEAGUE RECORD

Match No.	Date	Venue	Opponents	Result		H/T Score	Lg. Pos.	Goalscorers	Attendance
1	Aug 13	A	Hibernian	L	0-5	0-3	—		8838
2	20	A	Celtic	L	1-2	0-0	10	Nixon	25,817
3	27	H	Aberdeen	W	2-1	0-0	8	Welsh, Brewster	9332
4	Sept 10	H	Motherwell	D	1-1	1-0	7	Ristic	7440
5	17	A	Hearts	L	1-2	0-2	9	Nixon	7392
6	24	H	Falkirk	W	1-0	0-0	7	Petric	6899
7	Oct 1	A	Rangers	L	0-2	0-1	8		43,635
8	8	A	Kilmarnock	W	2-0	1-0	6	Welsh, Ristic	7127
9	15	H	Partick T	L	0-1	0-0	7		6687
10	22	H	Hibernian	D	0-0	0-0	7		7983
11	29	A	Aberdeen	L	0-3	0-2	8		11,744
12	Nov 5	H	Celtic	D	2-2	1-2	7	Brewster, Dailly	10,496
13	8	A	Motherwell	D	1-1	0-0	—	Brewster	6145
14	19	H	Hearts	W	5-2	4-1	7	Johnson, Brewster, McKinlay, Dailly 2	7719
15	26	A	Falkirk	W	3-1	0-1	6	Brewster, Nixon, McKinlay	5933
16	Dec 4	H	Rangers	L	0-3	0-1	—		11,187
17	26	H	Kilmarnock	D	2-2	0-1	—	Hannah, Winters	8468
18	31	A	Hibernian	L	0-4	0-3	8		7754
19	Jan 2	H	Aberdeen	D	0-0	0-0	—		10,560
20	7	A	Celtic	D	1-1	1-1	6	Cleland	21,436
21	14	A	Hearts	L	0-2	0-1	8		8656
22	21	H	Motherwell	W	6-1	2-1	7	McKinlay 2, Brewster, Nixon 2, Dailly	7062
23	Feb 4	A	Rangers	D	1-1	1-1	8	Nixon	44,197
24	21	H	Falkirk	W	1-0	0-0	—	Malpas	6457
25	25	H	Partick T	W	2-0	0-0	6	Brewster, Gomes	7227
26	Mar 4	A	Kilmarnock	L	0-2	0-2	7		7630
27	7	A	Partick T	L	0-2	0-0	—		2126
28	18	A	Motherwell	L	1-2	0-0	8	Malpas	4457
29	21	H	Hearts	D	1-1	0-1	—	Gomes	6862
30	Apr 1	H	Rangers	L	0-2	0-2	8		11,035
31	8	A	Falkirk	L	1-3	1-0	9	Gomes	5894
32	15	H	Kilmarnock	L	1-2	1-1	9	Petric	8223
33	18	A	Partick T	W	3-1	1-1	—	Hannah, Welsh 2	4962
34	29	H	Hibernian	L	0-1	0-0	9		8376
35	May 6	A	Aberdeen	L	1-2	0-1	10	Winters	20,124
36	13	H	Celtic	L	0-1	0-0	10		10,993

Final League Position: 10

Honours
League Champions: Premier Division 1982-83. Division II 1924-25, 1928-29; *Runners-up:* Division II 1930-31, 1959-60.
Scottish Cup Winners: 1994; *Runners-up:* 1974, 1981, 1985, 1987, 1988, 1991.
League Cup Winners: 1979-80, 1980-81;*Runners-up:* 1981-82, 1984-85.
Summer Cup Runners-up: 1964-65. *Scottish War Cup Runners-up:* 1939-40.

European: *European Cup:* 8 matches: 1983-84 (semi-finals), 1988-89; *Cup Winners Cup:* 4 matches: 1974-75; *UEFA Cup Runners-up:* 1986-87. *Fairs Cup:* 10 matches: 1966-67, 1969-70, 1970-71. *UEFA Cup:* 70 matches: 1971-72, 1975-76, 1977-78, 1978-79, 1979-80, 1980-81, 1981-82, 1982-83, 1984-85, 1985-86, 1986-87, 1987-88, 1989-90, 1990-91, 1993-94.
Club colours: Tangerine jersey, Black shorts. Change colours: White with two Black hoops with Mauve trim, Black and White with Mauve trim shorts.

Goalscorers: *League (40):* Brewster 7, Nixon 6, Dailly 4, McKinlay 4, Welsh 4, Gomes 3, Hannah 2, Malpas 2, Petric 2, Ristic 2, Winters 2, Cleland 1, Johnson 1. *Scottish Cup (9):* Hannah 2, Bowman 1, Brewster 1, Craig 1, Gomes 1, McKinlay 1, Malpas 1, Nixon 1. *League Cup (3):* Hannah 2, Ristic 1.

Jorgensen H 1 + 1	Cleland A 18	Perry M 9	Hannah D 31 + 1	Petric G 33	Welsh B 26 + 1	Bowman D 31	Connolly P 4 + 2	Ristic D 8 + 2	Brewster C 25 + 2	Nixon J 8 + 20	Bollan G 5 + 2	Main A 6	McInally J 22 + 2	McKinlay W 26 + 1	McLaren A 16 + 4	Dailly C 30 + 3	Malpas M 31	Myers C — + 1	Johnson G 12 + 1	O'Hanlon K 29	Moule A — + 1	Craig D 3 + 3	Winters R 6 + 7	Gomes S 11 + 3	Ferreri J — + 1	Crabbe S 5 + 4	Match No.
1	2	3	4	5	6	7	8	9	10	11	12																1
	2		4	5	6	7		9	10	12		1	3	8	11												2
	2		*4*	5	6	7		9	10	14		1	3	8	11	12											3
	2		4	5	6		*10*	9		14		1	3	8	11	7											4
	2		4	5		7		9	10	14		1	6		11	8	3	12									5
	2		4	5	6				10	11		1		8	9	7	3										6
15				5	6	7			10	14	2	*1*	4	8	*9*	11	3		12								7
	2		4	5	6	7		9		11	12		14	8	10		3			1							8
	2		4	5	6	7		*9*		11				8	10	14	3			1							9
	2		4	*5*	6	7		9		14				8		10	3		11	1	12						10
	2		4	5	6	7				14			12	8	9	10	3		*11*	1							11
	2			5	6	7			10	14				8	*9*	11	3		4	1		12					12
	2		14	5	6	7			10					8	*9*	11	3		4	1							13
	2		4	5	6	7			*10*					8	12	9	3		11	1			14				14
			4	5	6	7			10	12	2			8		*9*	3		11	1			14				15
	2		4		6	7			10		5			8		9	3		11	1			14				16
			4	5		7	12		10	14	2			8		6	3		11	1			*9*				17
	2		4	5		7			10	14					*8*	6	3		11	1			9				18
	2		4	5		7	9		*10*	14	6			8		11	3			1			12				19
	2		4	5	6	7	12		10	14			8			11	3			1			*9*				20
	2		4	5	6	7	*9*		10				8	12		11	3			1			14				21
			4	5	6	7			10	14			2	8		11	3			1				*9*	12		22
			4	5		7			10	11			2	8		6	3			1		12	14	*9*			23
			4	5	6	7		12	10	14			*2*	8		11	3			1				9			24
			4	5	6	7			10	14			2	*8*		11	3			1				9		12	25
			4	5	6	7		14	*10*	8			2			11	3			1				9		12	26
			4	5	6	7			14	10			2			11	3			1			8	*9*		12	27
			4	5	6	7			14	12			2	8		11	3			1				*9*		10	28
		4		5		7			10	14			2	8		11	3			1		*6*		9			29
		11	4	5	6	7			*10*				2	8	9	12	3			1				14			30
		4		5	6	7				12			2	8	10	11	3			1				9			31
		2	10	5	12	6				*11*			3	8	14	4				1				9		7	32
		2	10	4	*5*	7							6	8	12	11	3			1				14		9	33
		2	11	4						12			6		*10*	5	3		8	1		14	9			7	34
		2	11						*10*				8		12	4	3		6	1		5	14	9		7	35
		2	10						*9*				6		7	5	3		8	1		4	11	14		12	36

DUNFERMLINE ATHLETIC First Division

Year Formed: 1885. *Ground & Address:* East End Park, Halbeath Rd, Dunfermline KY12 7RB. *Telephone:* 01383 724295. *Fax:* 01383 723468.
Ground Capacity: total: 18,340. seated: 4020. *Size of Pitch:* 114yd × 72yd.
Chairman: C. R. Woodrow. *Secretary:* P. A. M. D'Mello. *Commercial Manager:* Audrey Kelly.
Manager: Bert Paton. *Assistant Manager:* Dick Campbell.
Physio: Philip Yeates, MCSP.
Managers since 1975: G. Miller; H. Melrose; P. Stanton; T. Forsyth; J. Leishman; I. Munro; J. Scott. *Club Nickname(s):* The Pars. *Previous Grounds:* None.
Record Attendance: 27,816 v Celtic, Division I, 30 April, 1968.
Record Transfer Fee received: £200,000 for Ian McCall to Rangers (Aug 1987).
Record Transfer Fee paid: £540,000 for Istvan Kozma from Bordeaux (Sept 1989).
Record Victory: 11-2 v Stenhousemuir, Division II, 27 Sept, 1930.
Record Defeat: 1-11 v Hibernian, Scottish Cup, 3rd rd replay, 26 Oct, 1889.
Most Capped Player: Andy Wilson, 6 (12), Scotland.
Most League Appearances: 360: Bobby Robertson; 1977-88.
Most League Goals in Season (Individual): 55: Bobby Skinner, Division II, 1925-26.
Most Goals Overall (Individual): 154: Charles Dickson.

DUNFERMLINE ATHLETIC 1994–95 LEAGUE RECORD

Match No.	Date	Venue	Opponents	Result		H/T Score	Lg. Pos.	Goalscorers	Attendance
1	Aug 13	A	Airdrieonians	D	0-0	0-0	—		2964
2	20	A	Clydebank	W	1-0	1-0	2	Petrie	1597
3	27	H	Raith R	W	1-0	0-0	2	French (pen)	7373
4	Sept 3	A	St Mirren	D	1-1	0-1	2	French	3895
5	10	H	Hamilton A	W	4-0	3-0	1	McCathie, Petrie 2, French	4029
6	24	H	Stranraer	W	1-0	1-0	1	Petrie	3893
7	Oct 1	A	Dundee	D	4-4	1-1	1	Petrie, Smith, French, McCathie	4784
8	8	H	St Johnstone	W	3-0	2-0	1	Tod, Smith, Petrie	6931
9	15	A	Ayr U	D	0-0	0-0	1		2302
10	22	H	Airdrieonians	D	2-2	0-1	1	French 2	5642
11	29	A	Raith R	W	5-2	2-2	1	Petrie 2, Ward 2, French	5965
12	Nov 5	H	Clydebank	W	4-1	1-0	1	Robertson, Petrie 2, Den Bieman	4611
13	12	A	Hamilton A	L	1-3	1-3	1	Petrie	2103
14	19	H	St Mirren	W	1-0	0-0	1	Smith	4660
15	26	A	Stranraer	D	0-0	0-0	1		1118
16	Dec 3	H	Dundee	L	0-1	0-0	3		6065
17	10	H	Ayr U	W	6-0	2-0	2	French 3 (1 pen), Den Bieman, McNamara, Tod	3197
18	26	A	St Johnstone	L	2-3	2-1	—	Den Bieman 2	6091
19	31	A	Airdrieonians	D	0-0	0-0	2		3252
20	Jan 7	A	Clydebank	W	2-1	0-1	2	Millar, Robertson	1468
21	11	H	Raith R	L	0-1	0-0	—		8457
22	14	A	St Mirren	D	2-2	2-1	3	Petrie 2	2736
23	21	H	Hamilton A	W	2-1	1-0	2	Tod, Petrie	3973
24	Feb 4	A	Dundee	W	3-2	2-1	2	Smith P 2 (1 pen), Fleming	5896
25	14	H	Stranraer	W	3-1	1-0	—	Tod, Ward, McNamara	3528
26	25	A	Ayr U	W	2-1	1-0	1	Ward, Smith P	2183
27	Mar 11	H	St Johnstone	D	1-1	0-0	1	Millar	6522
28	22	A	Hamilton A	W	3-1	1-0	—	Moore, French 2	1343
29	25	H	St Mirren	D	1-1	0-0	2	Tod	5055
30	Apr 1	H	Dundee	D	1-1	0-1	2	Den Bieman	8341
31	8	A	Stranraer	W	1-0	1-0	2	Robertson	988
32	15	A	St Johnstone	D	1-1	0-0	3	Robertson	5039
33	22	H	Ayr U	W	3-0	1-0	2	McCathie, Robertson, Tod	4808
34	29	H	Airdrieonians	D	0-0	0-0	2		6603
35	May 6	A	Raith R	D	0-0	0-0	2		6361
36	13	H	Clydebank	W	2-1	2-0	2	Robertson, McCathie	7709

Final League Position: 2

Honours
League Champions: First Division 1988-89. Division II 1925-26. Second Division 1985-86; *Runners-up:* First Division 1986-87, 1993-94, 1994-95. Division II 1912-13, 1933-34, 1954-55, 1957-58, 1972-73. Second Division 1978-79.
Scottish Cup Winners: 1961, 1968; *Runners-up:* 1965.
League Cup Runners-up: 1949-50, 1991-92.

European: *European Cup:* —. *Cup Winners Cup:* 1961-62, 1968-69 (semi-finals). *UEFA Cup:* 1962-63, 1964-65, 1965-66, 1966-67, 1969-70 (*Fairs Cup*).
Club colours: Shirt: Black and white vertical stripes, stippled with red dots. Shorts: Black with white side panel. Stockings: White with red chevrons.

Goalscorers: *League (63):* Petrie 14, French 12 (2 pens), Robertson 6, Smith 6 (1 pen), Tod 6, Den Bieman 5, McCathie 4, Ward 4, McNamara 2, Millar 2, Fleming 1, Moore 1. *Scottish Cup (4):* Petrie 2, Hawkins 1, Smith 1. *League Cup (4):* Den Bieman 1, McCathie 1, Petrie 1, Ward 1. *B&Q Cup (10):* Petrie 4, French 2 (1 pen), McCathie 1, Robertson 1, Smith 1, Tod 1.

Westwater I 17	Den Bieman I 19 + 12	Bowes M 7	McCathie N 32	Cooper N 14 + 1	Smith P 34	Moore A 11 + 1	Robertson C 35	Petrie S 31 + 2	Laing D 2 + 4	Tod A 30 + 5	McCulloch M 5 + 4	McNamara J 30	Ward K 19 + 4	French H 24 + 1	Will J 5 + 1	McQueen J 1	Sharp R 2	Sinclair C — + 1	Hawkins A 1 + 4	Fleming D 29	Millar M 22 + 2	Higgins G 1 + 1	Paterson G 5	Harrison T 1 + 1	Van De Kamp G 13	Shaw G 6	Fenwick P — + 2	Match No.
1	2	3	4	5	6	7	8	9	*10*	11	14																	1
1	2	3	4	5	6		8	9		11		7	10	12														2
1	2	3	4	5	6		8	10	12	11		7		9	15													3
	2	3	4	5	6		8	10	12	11			7	9	1													4
	7	2	4	5	6		8	10					11	9		1	3											5
1	7	2	4		6		8	10	12	5			*11*	9			3	14										6
1	7	*2*	4		6		8	10	12	5		3	11	9					14									7
1	7		4		6		8	10		5		2	11	9						3								8
1	7		4		6			10		5		2	11	9						3	8							9
1	14				6		8	10	7	5	*4*	2	12	9						3	11							10
1	12		4		6		8	10		5	2		7	*9*						3	11	14						11
1	12		4		6		8	10		5		2	7	9						3	11							12
1	12		4	14	6		8	10		5		2	7	*9*						3	11							13
1	12		4	*5*	6		8	10		14		2	7	9						3	11							14
1	12		4	5	6		8	10		7		2		9						3	11							15
1			4	5	6		8	10		14		2	7	9						3	11							16
1	7		4	5	6		8	*10*		14		2	11	9						3	12							17
1	7			5	6		8	14		*10*		2	11	9						3	12		4					18
	7			5	6		8	10		12		*2*	14	9	1					3	11		4					19
	7		4		6		8	14		12		2		9	1					3	11	*10*	5					20
	14		4		6		8	10		5		2	7	9	1					3	*11*							21
			4	5	6		8	10		9		2	7		1					3	11			14				22
	7			5	6		8	10		9		2	11							3				4	1			23
	7		4		6		8	10		11		2	14	9						3			5		1			24
	14		4		6		8	10		*9*		2	12	7					11	3			5		1			25
	12		4	5	6	7	8	10		2			11							3	9				1			26
			4			7	8			5	6	2	11	9					12	3	10				1			27
	7		4			11	8			5	6	2		9					12	3	10				1			28
1	12		4		6	7	8	10		5		2		9						3	11							29
	14		4		6	7	8	10		5		2								3	11				1	*9*		30
			4		6	7	8	10		5	12	2								3	11				1	9		31
			4		6	9	8	10		5	7	2							12	3	11				1		14	32
	12		4		6	7	8	10		5		2								3	11				1	9		33
	7		4		6	11	8	10		5	14	*2*								3					1	9	12	34
	10		4		6	7	8			5		2								3	11				1	9		35
	7		4		6	12	8	10		5	14	2								3	11				1	*9*		36

EAST FIFE

Second Division

Year Formed: 1903. *Ground & Address:* Bayview Park, Methil, Fife KY8 3AG. *Telephone:* 01333 426323. *Fax:* 01333 426376.
Ground Capacity: total: 5385. seated: 600. *Size of Pitch:* 110yd × 71yd.
Chairman: James Baxter. *General Manager:* David Gorman. *Secretary:* Leona Walker. *Commercial Manager:* James Bonthrone.
Manager: Steve Archibald. *Assistant Manager:* Alan Sneddon. *Physio:* Alex MacQueen. *Coach:* Gordon Rae.
Managers since 1975: Frank Christie; Roy Barry; David Clarke; Gavin Murray, Alex Totten. *Club Nickname(s):* The Fifers.
Previous Grounds: None.
Record Attendance: 22,515 v Raith Rovers, Division I; 2 Jan, 1950.
Record Transfer Fee received: £150,000 for Paul Hunter from Hull C (March 1990).
Record Transfer Fee paid: £70,000 for John Sludden from Kilmarnock (July 1991).
Record Victory: 13-2 v Edinburgh City, Division II; 11 Dec, 1937.
Record Defeat: 0-9 v Hearts, Division I; 5 Oct, 1957.
Most Capped Player: George Aitken, 5 (8), Scotland.
Most League Appearances: 517: David Clarke, 1968-86.

EAST FIFE 1994–95 LEAGUE RECORD

Match No.	Date		Venue	Opponents	Result		H/T Score	Lg. Pos.	Goalscorers	Attendance
1	Aug	13	A	Stirling Albion	W	1-0	0-0	—	Hildersley	808
2		20	A	Stenhousemuir	D	1-1	0-1	2	Hunter	544
3		27	H	Brechin C	D	1-1	0-0	3	Burns	795
4	Sept	3	A	Queen of the S	W	2-0	1-0	2	Andrew, Scott	1412
5		10	H	Clyde	W	2-0	1-0	2	Hunter, Dow	925
6		24	H	Morton	L	1-2	1-1	2	Sneddon	1173
7	Oct	1	A	Berwick R	D	1-1	1-1	4	Scott	573
8		8	H	Dumbarton	L	2-3	1-1	5	Beaton, Scott	795
9		15	A	Meadowbank T	W	1-0	0-0	3	Scott	314
10		22	H	Stirling Albion	W	4-3	1-1	3	Scott, Beaton, Hope, Burns	1039
11		29	A	Brechin C	L	0-2	0-1	3		613
12	Nov	5	H	Stenhousemuir	L	2-3	0-2	4	Hutcheon, Scott	719
13		12	A	Clyde	D	1-1	0-0	5	Archibald	1212
14		19	H	Queen of the S	W	3-1	2-1	3	Hutcheon 2, Scott	699
15		26	A	Morton	L	0-3	0-1	4		1884
16	Dec	3	H	Berwick R	W	3-0	2-0	4	Scott 3	756
17		26	A	Dumbarton	L	0-4	0-2	—		862
18		31	H	Meadowbank T	W	2-1	1-1	4	Scott, Hutcheon	686
19	Jan	2	H	Brechin C	W	4-0	2-0	—	Sneddon, Cusick, Donaghy, Hildersley	1155
20		14	A	Stirling Albion	L	0-3	0-2	4		810
21		21	H	Stenhousemuir	L	0-2	0-2	4		713
22	Feb	4	H	Clyde	L	1-3	1-1	7	Cusick	885
23		14	A	Queen of the S	D	3-3	1-1	—	Hunter 2, Donaghy	890
24		25	A	Berwick R	D	0-0	0-0	7		503
25		28	H	Morton	D	1-1	1-0	—	Hamill	558
26	Mar	4	H	Dumbarton	L	0-2	0-1	7		662
27		11	A	Meadowbank T	W	3-1	1-1	7	Beaton 2, Hope	222
28		18	A	Clyde	D	1-1	0-0	7	Cusick	602
29		25	H	Queen of the S	W	3-1	0-1	7	Scott 2, Hunter	594
30	Apr	1	H	Berwick R	L	0-1	0-1	7		628
31		8	A	Morton	L	1-4	0-1	7	Hamill	1789
32		15	A	Dumbarton	L	0-2	0-1	7		1253
33		22	H	Meadowbank T	D	1-1	0-1	7	Dwarika	355
34		29	H	Stirling Albion	L	1-2	1-0	7	Beaton	510
35	May	6	A	Brechin C	D	1-1	1-1	7	Scott	386
36		13	A	Stenhousemuir	L	1-2	1-2	8	Hutcheon	433

Final League Position: 8

Most League Goals in Season (Individual): 41: Jock Wood, Division II; 1926-27 and Henry Morris, Division II; 1947-48.
Most Goals Overall (Individual): 196: George Dewar (149 in League).

Honours
League Champions: Division II 1947-48; *Runners-up:* Division II 1929-30, 1970-71. Second Division 1983-84.
Scottish Cup Winners: 1938; *Runners-up:* 1927, 1950.
League Cup Winners: 1947-48, 1949-50, 1953-54.
Club colours: Shirt: Amber with black collar and cuffs. Shorts: Amber with black flashes. Stockings: Amber with 3 black stripes on top.

Goalscorers: *League (48):* Scott 14, Beaton 5, Hunter 5, Hutcheon 5, Cusick 3, Burns 2, Donaghy 2, Hamill 2, Hildersley 2, Hope 2, Sneddon 2, Andrew 1, Archibald 1, Dow 1, Dwarika 1. *Scottish Cup (7):* Hutcheon 3, Allan 2, Burns 1 (pen), Donaghy 1. *League Cup (2):* Allan 1, Hope 1. *B&Q Cup (2):* Hunter 1, Scott 1.

Wilson E 23	Bell G 12	Williamson A 1	Barron D 3	Sneddon A 34	Hildersley R 17 + 1	Cusick J 28 + 1	Hope D 31	Scott R 31 + 1	Hunter P 24 + 3	Gibb R 23 + 5	Allan G 18 + 6	Irvine A 1 + 13	Beaton D 29 + 1	Burns W 27 + 1	Andrew B 10 + 7	Dow C 5 + 3	Donaghy M 23 + 3	Hutcheon S 9 + 11	Archibald S 12 + 1	Robertson D 13 + 1	Hamill A 15 + 1	Struthers D 1 + 4	Dwarika A 5 + 1	Balmain K 1	Match No.
1	2	3	4	5	6	7	8	*9*	10	11	12	14													1
1	2		3	4	7	*6*	8	9	10	11	12		5	14											2
1	*2*		6	4	7		11	9	10	3	14		5	8	12										3
1	3			2	8			9	10	11	7	12	5	4	6	14									4
1	3			2	*8*			9	10	11	14	12	5	4	6	7									5
1				2	6	8	3	9	10	11	7	12	5	4		14									6
1	2			3			11	9	10		7	12	5	4	*8*	6	14								7
1				2		12	6	9	10	3	7		5	4		11	*8*	14							8
1	2			3			8	9	10	11			5	4		*6*	7	12	14						9
1	2			3	7		11	9	10				5	4			6		8						10
1				2	7		11	9	10	3			5	4	14		*6*	12	8						11
1				3	*6*	2	11	9					5	4	7	10		14	8						12
1				2		7	11	9		3		12	5	4	14		6	10	8						13
1	3			2		7	6	9		11		14	5	4	12		8	*10*							14
1	3			2	14	7	11	9				12	5	4	8		6	10							15
1				2	6	7	3	9			12	14	5	4			11	*10*	8						16
1				2	3	*7*	11	9			14	12	5	4			6	10	8						17
1				2	3	6	11	9			7		5	4			10	14	*8*						18
1				2	3	6	11	9		12	7		5	4			10	14	*8*						19
	2				8	6	11	9	12	*3*	7		5	4				10		1	14				20
				2		6	11	9	12	*3*	7		5			14	8	10		1	4				21
	2			4	6	5	*11*	9	10	3	7				12			14		1	8				22
				5		2	11		10	6	7			4	12		8	9		1	3				23
				5		2	11		10	6	7	9		4	*8*			14		1	3				24
1				2		5	11		10	3	7			4			6	12	8		9				25
1				2		5	11	9	10	*3*	7		12	4			8			15	6				26
				2		6	11	*9*	10	12	7	14	5	4			8			1	3				27
				2		3	11	*9*	10	12	7	14	5	4			8			1	6				28
				2		3	11	9	10				5	4	7		8			1	6	12			29
				2		3	11	9	10	14			5	4			8			1	6	*7*	12		30
				2		3		9	12	14	7		5	4			*8*			1	6		10	11	31
				2	*6*	4	11	12	10	7			5		14		8			1	3		9		32
				4	6	5		9	10	3					*2*		12		8	1	11	14	7		33
				2		4		9	10	11	7		5				14	12	8	1	3		*6*		34
1				2		4	11	9		3			5		7		6	14	*8*		10	12			35
1						4	11		7	3	*2*	12	5		10		6	9				14	8		36

EAST STIRLINGSHIRE Third Division

Year Formed: 1880. *Ground & Address:* Firs Park, Firs St, Falkirk FK2 7AY. *Telephone:* 01324 623583.
Ground Capacity: total: 1880. seated: 200. *Size of Pitch:* 112yd × 72yd.
Chairman: William C. White. *Secretary:* Alex Forsyth. *Commercial Manager:* Tom Kirk.
Manager: Billy Little. *Assistant Manager/Coach:* Lenny Reid. *Physio:* Sandra Lawler.
Managers since 1975: I. Ure; D. McLinden; W. P. Lamont; M. Ferguson; W. Little; D. Whiteford; D. Lawson; J. D. Connell; A. Mackin; Dom Sullivan, Bobby McCulley. *Club Nickname(s):* The Shire. *Previous Grounds:* Burnhouse, Randyford Park, Merchiston Park, New Kilbowie Park.
Record Attendance: 12,000 v Partick T, Scottish Cup 3rd rd; 19 Feb 1921.
Record Transfer Fee received: £35,000 for Jim Docherty to Chelsea (1978).
Record Transfer Fee paid: £6,000 for Colin McKinnon from Falkirk (March 1991).
Record Victory: 11-2 v Vale of Bannock, Scottish Cup 2nd rd; 22 Sept, 1888.
Record Defeat: 1-12 v Dundee United, Division II; 13 Apr, 1936.
Most Capped Player: Humphrey Jones, 5 (14), Wales.
Most League Appearances: 379: Gordon Simpson, 1968-80.

EAST STIRLINGSHIRE 1994–95 LEAGUE RECORD

Match No.	Date	Venue	Opponents	Result		H/T Score	Lg. Pos.	Goalscorers	Attendance
1	Aug 13	A	Montrose	L	0-2	0-1	—		537
2	20	H	Ross C	D	2-2	1-1	8	McCallum, Scott	632
3	27	A	Alloa	W	3-1	1-0	5	Millar, Geraghty, Loney	404
4	Sept 3	A	Cowdenbeath	D	1-1	0-0	6	McCallum	258
5	10	H	Albion R	W	4-0	2-0	4	Geraghty 2, Lee I 2	377
6	24	H	Forfar Ath	W	3-1	1-1	3	Russell, Lee I, Cuthbert	419
7	Oct 1	A	Caledonian Th	D	3-3	2-1	4	Sneddon 2, Lee I	1229
8	8	H	Queen's Park	W	3-2	1-1	2	Lee R, Geraghty, McCallum	464
9	15	A	Arbroath	W	1-0	0-0	1	Geraghty	404
10	22	H	Montrose	L	1-2	0-0	3	Russell	631
11	29	H	Alloa	L	1-2	0-1	4	Millar	570
12	Nov 5	A	Ross C	W	4-1	2-0	3	Conroy, Lee I, Yates, Geraghty	1194
13	12	A	Albion R	W	2-0	1-0	3	Lee R, Millar	361
14	19	H	Cowdenbeath	L	0-2	0-0	4		553
15	26	A	Forfar Ath	L	2-3	2-2	5	Dwyer,Lee I	527
16	Dec 3	H	Caledonian Th	W	2-0	1-0	3	Lee I, Geraghty	508
17	26	A	Queen's Park	W	3-2	2-0	—	Russell, Geraghty 2	502
18	31	H	Arbroath	W	1-0	0-0	3	Geraghty	436
19	Jan 21	H	Ross C	L	0-2	0-0	5		459
20	Feb 7	A	Alloa	W	1-0	0-0	—	Dwyer	395
21	18	H	Forfar Ath	L	1-2	0-0	5	McCallum	528
22	25	A	Caledonian Th	D	3-3	1-1	5	Dwyer, Lee R, Geraghty	886
23	Mar 7	H	Albion R	W	3-0	1-0	—	Geraghty, Lee I, Dwyer	312
24	11	A	Arbroath	L	2-5	0-3	4	Dwyer, Cuthbert	596
25	15	H	Montrose	W	1-0	0-0	—	Dwyer	297
26	22	A	Cowdenbeath	W	4-1	2-0	—	Geraghty 2, Lee I, Dwyer	172
27	25	H	Cowdenbeath	W	1-0	1-0	2	Hunter	338
28	Apr 1	H	Caledonian Th	W	1-0	1-0	2	Geraghty	391
29	5	A	Albion R	L	1-3	0-1	—	Dwyer	211
30	8	A	Forfar Ath	L	0-1	0-1	3		623
31	15	A	Queen's Park	L	0-1	0-1	4		480
32	18	H	Queen's Park	W	3-2	2-2	—	Sneddon, Hunter, Watt	382
33	22	H	Arbroath	L	0-2	0-1	4		414
34	29	A	Montrose	L	0-1	0-0	4		858
35	May 6	H	Alloa	D	1-1	1-1	4	Dwyer	418
36	13	A	Ross C	W	3-2	1-2	4	Geraghty, Lee I, Hunter	1005

Final League Position: 4

Most League Goals in Season (Individual): 36: Malcolm Morrison, Division II; 1938-39.
Most Goals Overall (Individual): —.

Honours
League Champions: Division II 1931-32; C Division 1947-48. *Runners-up:* Division II 1962-63. Second Division 1979-80. Division Three 1923-24.
Scottish Cup: —.
League Cup: —.
Club colours: Shirt: Black and white hoops. Shorts: Black. Stockings: Black.

Goalscorers: *League (61):* Garaghty 16, Lee I 10, Dwyer 9, McCallum 4, Hunter 3, Lee R 3, Millar 3, Russell 3, Sneddon 3, Cuthbert 2, Conroy 1, Loney 1, Scott 1, Watt 1, Yates 1. *Scottish Cup (0) League Cup (0) B&Q Cup (1):* Watt 1.

Moffat J 6	Watt D 28 + 3	Cuthbert L 17 + 5	Russell G 22	Yates D 12	Lee R 33	Lee I 36	Millar G 28 + 6	McCallum M 11 + 1	Scott C 16 + 2	Geraghty M 36	Dempsey S — + 1	Stirling D 16 + 5	Scott B 1	Loney J 5 + 5	Sneddon S 32	Ross B 25	Robertson A — + 1	Conroy J 5 + 9	McDougall G 30	Abercromby M 9 + 7	Dwyer P 20	Hunter M 7 + 3	McConville R — + 5	Gilogley W 1	Match No.
1	2	*3*	4	5	6	7	8	9	10	11	12	14													1
1	2		4	5	6	7	8	9	10	11			3	12											2
1	12		4		3	7	8	9	10	11		14		2	*5*	6									3
1	3		2	4		7	8	9	*6*	10		12		11	5		14								4
1	2	3	4			7	8		6	10		9		*11*	5			14							5
1	4	11	2	6	3	7	8	12		10		*9*			5			14							6
	2	11	6	4	3	7	8	9	12	10		14			*5*				1						7
		11	2	4	3	7	8	9	6	10					5			14	1						8
	2	12	11	4	3	7	8	*9*	6	10					5			14	1						9
	2	11	6	4	3	7	8		12	10		*9*		14	5				1						10
			2	4	3	7	8		6	10		9		12	5			11	1						11
		12	2	4	3	7	8		6	10		9		14	5			*11*	1						12
		12	2	4	3	7	8			10		9			5	6		*11*	1	14					13
	4		2		3	7	8			10		*9*			5	6		11	1	14					14
	4		2		3	7	8			10				11	5	6			1	14	9				15
	4		2		3	7	8			10		12			5	6		11	1		9				16
	4		2	5	3	7	8		*11*	10						6		14	1		9				17
	4		2		3	7	*8*		11	10					5	6		14	1		9				18
	2		4		3	7	12	9	10	8					5	6		14	1		11				19
	12		2		3	7	8	9	*4*	10				14	5	6			1		11				20
	14		2		3	7	4	9		8				*11*	5	6			1		10				21
	4	12	2		3	7			10	8					5	6		14	1	*9*	11				22
	2	10			3	7	12		4	8					5	6			1	9	11				23
	2	10			3	7	4			8					5	6		12	1	9	11				24
	2	10			3	7	14			9		*4*			5	6			1		11	8			25
	2	10			3	7	14			9		4			5	6			1	12	11	*8*			26
	2	10			3	7				9		4			5	6			1		11	8			27
	2	*10*			3	7	12			9		4			5	6			1	14	11	8			28
	2	10			3	7	12			9		4			5	6			1	14	11	*8*			29
	2	*10*			3	7	4	9		8					5	6			1	12	11	14			30
	2	*10*			3	7	4			9					5	6			1	8	11	12	14		31
	2				3	7	4			9		10			5	6			1	8		11	12		32
	2	12			3	7	4			*9*					5	6			1	8	11	10	14		33
	2				3	7	4			9		10			5	6			1	8	11		14		34
	2	3				7	4			9		10			5	6			1	8	11		12		35
		3			5	7	4		8	9		10				6			1	11		12		2	36

FALKIRK — Premier Division

Year Formed: 1876. *Ground & Address:* Brockville Park, Hope St, Falkirk FK1 5AX. *Telephone:* 01324 624121/632487. *Fax:* 01324 612418.
Ground Capacity: total: 12,800. seated: 2661. *Size of Pitch:* 110yd × 70yd.
Chairman: G. J. Fulston. *Secretary:* A. D. Moffat. *Commercial Executive:* George Miller.
Manager: Jim Jefferies. *Assistant Manager:* Billy Brown. *Physio:* Bob McCallum. *Coach:* Willie Wilson.
Managers since 1975: J. Prentice; G. Miller; W. Little; J. Hagart; A. Totten; G. Abel; W. Lamont; D. Clarke; J. Duffy. *Club Nickname(s):* The Bairns. *Previous Grounds:* Randyford; Blinkbonny Grounds; Hope Street.
Record Attendance: 23,100 v Celtic, Scottish Cup 3rd rd; 21 Feb, 1953.
Record Transfer Fee received: £270,000 for Gordon Marshall to Celtic (Aug 1991).
Record Transfer Fee paid: £225,000 to Chelsea for Kevin McAllister (Aug 1991).
Record Victory: 12-1 v Laurieston, Scottish Cup 2nd rd; 23 Mar, 1893.
Record Defeat: 1-11 v Airdrieonians, Division I; 28 Apr, 1951.
Most Capped Player: Alex Parker, 14 (15), Scotland.
Most League Appearances: (post-war): John Markie, 349.

FALKIRK 1994–95 LEAGUE RECORD

Match No.	Date	Venue	Opponents	Result		H/T Score	Lg. Pos.	Goalscorers	Attendance
1	Aug 13	H	Celtic	D	1-1	0-0	—	McCall	12,635
2	20	A	Aberdeen	D	2-2	1-1	6	Cadette, McDonald	11,143
3	27	H	Partick T	W	2-1	0-1	4	Fulton, Cadette	5402
4	Sept 10	A	Kilmarnock	D	1-1	0-1	3	Cadette	8021
5	17	H	Rangers	L	0-2	0-1	6		12,419
6	24	A	Dundee U	L	0-1	0-0	8		6899
7	Oct 1	H	Hearts	W	2-1	1-1	4	McLaughlin, McAvennie	7589
8	8	A	Motherwell	L	3-5	1-2	7	Clark 2, McAvennie	6239
9	15	H	Hibernian	D	0-0	0-0	6		7388
10	22	A	Celtic	W	2-0	1-0	6	Henderson, Clark	23,688
11	29	A	Partick T	W	2-1	2-1	5	Clark, May	4215
12	Nov 5	H	Aberdeen	W	2-1	1-1	4	Cramb, McGowan	6185
13	8	H	Kilmarnock	D	3-3	0-3	—	Clark 2, Henderson	6134
14	19	A	Rangers	D	1-1	0-1	4	Henderson	44,018
15	26	H	Dundee U	L	1-3	1-0	4	Henderson	5933
16	Dec 3	A	Hearts	D	1-1	1-1	4	McDonald	8960
17	10	A	Hibernian	D	2-2	1-0	4	McDonald, Rice (pen)	7725
18	26	H	Motherwell	L	0-1	0-0	—		7937
19	31	A	Celtic	L	0-2	0-0	5		21,294
20	Jan 7	A	Aberdeen	D	0-0	0-0	5		14,141
21	14	H	Rangers	L	2-3	0-1	7	McDonald, May	12,507
22	17	H	Partick T	L	1-3	0-1	—	MacKenzie	3958
23	21	A	Kilmarnock	L	1-2	1-1	9	Clark	7648
24	Feb 4	H	Hearts	W	2-0	1-0	7	Fulton, Henderson	6028
25	21	A	Dundee U	L	0-1	0-0	—		6457
26	25	H	Hibernian	W	1-0	0-0	7	Kirk	6501
27	Mar 7	A	Motherwell	D	2-2	1-1	—	McLaughlin, Kirk	6100
28	11	A	Rangers	D	2-2	1-1	7	McDonald 2	43,359
29	25	H	Kilmarnock	W	2-0	1-0	6	Kirk, McDonald	5714
30	Apr 1	A	Hearts	W	1-0	1-0	5	McGrillen	9003
31	8	H	Dundee U	W	3-1	0-1	5	Johnston M, Kirk, McDonald	5894
32	15	H	Motherwell	W	3-0	1-0	3	Kirk, Weir, Fulton	5756
33	19	A	Hibernian	W	2-0	1-0	—	Clark, McDonald	5450
34	29	H	Celtic	L	1-2	0-1	3	Rice	9714
35	May 6	A	Partick T	D	0-0	0-0	4		5927
36	13	H	Aberdeen	L	0-2	0-1	5		12,835

Final League Position: 5

Most League Goals in Season (Individual): 43: Evelyn Morrison, Division I; 1928-29.
Most Goals Overall (Individual): Dougie Moran, 86.

Honours
League Champions: Division II 1935-36, 1969-70, 1974-75. First Division 1990-91, 1993-94. Second Division 1979-80; *Runners-up:* Division I 1907-08, 1909-10. First Division 1985-86, 1988-89. Division II 1904-05, 1951-52, 1960-61.
Scottish Cup Winners: 1913, 1957. *League Cup Runners-up:* 1947-48. ***B&Q Cup Winners:*** 1993-94.
Club colours: Shirt: Dark blue with white flashings. Shorts: White. Stockings: Red.

Goalscorers: *League (48):* McDonald 9, Clark 8. Henderson 5, Kirk 5, Cadette 3, Fulton 3, McAvennie 2, McLaughlin 2, May 2, Rice 2 (1 pen), Cramb 1, Johnston 1, McCall 1, McGowan 1, McGrillen 1, MacKenzie 1, Weir 1. *Scottish Cup (0):* League Cup (4): Cadette 3, McDonald 1.

Parks A 28	Weir D 32	McGowan J 27 + 4	Hughes J 17 + 3	Oliver N 26 + 1	MacKenzie N 36	May E 24	Fulton S 25 + 3	Cadette R 8	McCall I 3 + 2	Johnston F 3	Hamilton G 2 + 1	McDonald C 26 + 5	McLaughlin J 28	Rice B 19 + 7	McStay J — + 1	Henderson N 14 + 7	Cramb C 6 + 2	Lamont W 5 + 3	Clark J 31	McAvennie F 1 + 2	James K 1	Shaw G — + 3	Burridge J 3	Paterson J 1 + 3	McQueen T 3 + 1	Kirk S 11	McGrillen P 6	Johnston M 10	Match No.
1	2	3	4	5	6	7	8	9	*10*	11	12	14																	1
1	2	3		4	6	7	8	9				11	5	*10*	14														2
1	2	3		4	6	7	8	9				11	5			10													3
1	2	3		4	6	7	8	9				11	5			*10*	12	15											4
	2	12		3	6	7	8	9				*11*	5	10				1	4	14									5
1	2			3	*6*	7	8	9				11	5	10		14			4										6
1	2	12		3	6	7	8	9					5	10		14			4	*11*									7
1	2			3	*6*	7	8	9				11		10					4	14	5								8
1	2	3		4	6	7			10				5	*11*		14	9		8			12							9
1	2	3		4	6	7			14			11	5			*10*	9		8										10
1	2	3		4	6	7						11	5			10	9		8										11
1	2	3		4	6	7						11	5			10	9	15	8										12
	2	3		4	6	7			14			11	5	12		10	*9*	1	8										13
	2	3		4	6	7	9					11	5			10			8				1						14
	2	3	12	4	6		9					7	5	11		10	14		*8*				1						15
	2	3	14	4	6	7	9		*10*			11	5						8				1						16
	2	3	14	4	6	7	*9*					11	5	12		10		1	8										17
	2	3	5	4	6	7	9					*11*		12		10		1	8					14					18
	2	14	3	4	*6*	7	9						5	12		10		1	8					11					19
1	2	12	3	4	6	7	10					9	5	*11*					8					14					20
1		3	5	4	11	7	10					9		6		8			2					12					21
1				4	11	7	10				2	8		6		12	9		5						3				22
1		2	5	4	11	7	8					9		12		*10*			6			14			3				23
1	2	8		4	11	7	10					9	5	6		12									3				24
1	2			4	11	7	10			3		*9*	5			8			6			14							25
1	2		4	3	11		10			8			5	12				15	6							7	9		26
1	2	3	4		11		8						5	12					6							7	9	10	27
1		3	4		11						2	9	5	*8*		12			6						14	7		10	28
1	2	3	4		11							8		6					5							7	9	10	29
1	2	3	4	14	11							12	5	*8*					6							7	9	10	30
1	2	3	4		11		14					12	5	*8*					6							7	9	10	31
1	2	3	4		11		12					9	5	8					6							7		10	32
1	2	3	4		11		12					14	5	8					6							7	*9*	10	33
1	2	3	4		11		8					*9*		6		14			5							7		10	34
1	2	3	4		11		8					9	5						6							7		10	35
1	2	3	4		11		9					12	5	8					6							7		10	36

FORFAR ATHLETIC Second Division

Year Formed: 1885. *Ground & Address:* Station Park, Carseview Road, Forfar. *Telephone:* 01307 463576.
Ground Capacity: total: 8372. seated: 719. *Size of Pitch:* 115yd × 69yd.
Chairman: George Enston. *Secretary:* David McGregor.
Manager: Tommy Campbell. *Assistant Manager:* Brian McLaughlin. *Physio:* Jim Peacock. *Coaches:* Gordon Arthur, Ian McPhee, Tom McCallum, Steven Jackson.
Managers since 1975: Jerry Kerr; Archie Knox; Alex Rae; Doug Houston; Henry Hall; Bobby Glennie; Paul Hegarty. *Club Nickname(s):* Loons. *Previous Grounds:* None.
Record Attendance: 10,780 v Rangers, Scottish Cup 2nd rd; 2 Feb, 1970.
Record Transfer Fee received: £57,000 for Craig Brewster to Raith R (July 1991).
Record Transfer Fee paid: £50,000 for Ian McPhee from Airdrieonians (1991).
Record Victory: 14-1 v Lindertis, Scottish Cup 1st rd; 1 Sept 1988.
Record Defeat: 2-12 v King's Park, Division II; 2 Jan, 1930.
Most Capped Player: —.

FORFAR ATHLETIC 1994–95 LEAGUE RECORD

Match No.	Date		Venue	Opponents	Result		H/T Score	Lg. Pos.	Goalscorers	Attendance
1	Aug	13	A	Queen's Park	W	2-1	1-1	—	Archibald, Lees	457
2		20	H	Alloa	W	3-2	2-0	2	Bingham 2, Kopel	540
3		27	A	Arbroath	W	1-0	0-0	2	McPhee	691
4	Sept	3	H	Montrose	W	1-0	0-0	1	Bingham	1077
5		10	A	Caledonian Th	L	1-3	1-1	2	Heddle	1731
6		24	A	East Stirling	L	1-3	1-1	2	McPhee	419
7	Oct	1	H	Albion R	D	1-1	0-0	3	Bingham	424
8		8	H	Ross C	W	1-0	0-0	1	McPhee	650
9		15	A	Cowdenbeath	L	0-1	0-0	4		403
10		22	H	Queen's Park	W	2-0	1-0	2	Bingham 2	534
11		29	H	Arbroath	W	3-0	0-0	1	Bingham, Ross, McCormick	721
12	Nov	5	A	Alloa	W	1-0	1-0	1	McCormick	525
13		12	H	Caledonian Th	W	2-1	2-1	1	McCormick, Ross	647
14		19	A	Montrose	L	0-2	0-1	2		1259
15		26	H	East Stirling	W	3-2	2-2	2	McCormick 3	527
16	Dec	3	A	Albion R	W	1-0	0-0	2	McCormick	303
17		31	H	Cowdenbeath	D	1-1	0-1	1	Hannigan	603
18	Jan	11	A	Ross C	L	1-2	0-1	—	Ross	1215
19		14	H	Queen's Park	W	3-0	0-0	1	Bingham, Hannigan, Morgan	501
20		24	A	Alloa	W	2-0	2-0	—	McCormick, Bingham	498
21		28	A	Arbroath	D	1-1	1-1	1	Bingham	802
22	Feb	4	A	Caledonian Th	D	1-1	1-0	1	Bingham	793
23		18	A	East Stirling	W	2-1	0-0	1	Morgan, Ross	528
24		25	H	Albion R	W	4-0	3-0	1	Bingham, Ross, Hannigan, Morgan	510
25	Mar	4	H	Ross C	W	4-2	3-2	1	Bingham 2, Hannigan, Ross	880
26		11	A	Cowdenbeath	W	3-1	1-1	1	Ross 3	280
27		18	H	Caledonian Th	W	4-1	2-0	1	Mann, Bingham 3	538
28		25	A	Montrose	W	2-1	1-0	1	McCormick, McPhee	1240
29	Apr	1	A	Albion R	W	3-0	2-0	1	Ross 2, McCormick	270
30		4	H	Montrose	L	1-3	1-2	—	Bingham	1176
31		8	H	East Stirling	W	1-0	1-0	1	Bingham	623
32		15	A	Ross C	W	1-0	1-0	1	Mann	2453
33		22	H	Cowdenbeath	D	2-2	2-2	1	Ross, McVicar	611
34		29	A	Queen's Park	W	2-0	1-0	1	Hannigan 2	557
35	May	6	H	Arbroath	W	4-1	3-0	1	Ross, Morgan, Bingham 2	1069
36		13	H	Alloa	W	2-0	2-0	1	Bingham, Morgan	655

Final League Position: 1

Most League Appearances: 376: Alex Brash, 1974-86.
Most League Goals in Season (Individual): 45: Dave Kilgour, Division II; 1929-30.
Most Goals Overall (Individual): 124, John Clark.

Honours
League Champions: Second Division 1983-84. Third Division 1994-95. C Division 1948-49.
Scottish Cup: Semi-finals 1982.
League Cup: Semi-finals 1977-78.
Club colours: Shirt: Sky Blue with narrow Navy vertical stripe. Shorts: Navy. Stockings: Navy.

Goalscorers: *League (67):* Bingham 22, Ross 13, McCormick 10, Hannigan 6, Morgan 5, McPhee 4, Mann 2, Archibald 1, Heddle 1, Kopel 1, Lees 1, McVicar 1. *Scottish Cup (0) League Cup (0) B&Q Cup (0)*

Arthur G 35	McLaren P 3 + 4	McPhee I 32 + 1	Mann R 26	Archibald E 16	McKillop A 33	O'Neill H 15 + 1	Irvine N 18	Lees G 7 + 7	Bingham D 36	Heddle I 25 + 5	Kopel S 7 + 3	Smith R — + 2	Mearns G 3 + 2	McCormick S 24 + 7	Ross A 28 + 1	Reilly J — + 1	Glennie S 19 + 1	Craig 17 + 5	Hannigan P 12 + 11	Stephen C 1 + 2	Morgan A 20	McVicar D 15 + 1	Loney J 2 + 2	Guthrie D 2	*Match No.*
1	2	3	4	5	6	7	8	*9*	10	11	12	14													1
1		3	4	5	6	7	8	*9*	10	11	2	14													2
1	12	3	4	5	6	*7*	8	9	10	11	2		14												3
1		3	4	5	6	2	*8*	14	10	11			12	7	9										4
1	2	3	4	5	*6*		8	9	10	11	14			7											5
1	2	3	4	5	6	11			10	8				7	9										6
1		10		5	6	4	7		11	3	2			8	9										7
1		3	4	5	6	11	8		10	12	2			*7*	9	14									8
1		3	4	5	6	11	8	14	10	12	*2*			7	9										9
1		3	4		5	*2*	8	7	11	6				10	9		14								10
1	14	3			5	2	8	*7*	11	6	12			10	9		4								11
1	14	3			5	2	8	12	11	6	7			*10*	9			4							12
1	12					2	8	7	11	6	3			10	9		5	4							13
1		3	4		5	*2*	8		11	6				*10*	9			7	14	15					14
		3	4	6	5		2	12	11	8			7	10					9	1					15
1			4	6	5		2	12	11	8			7	10				3	9						16
1		3	4	5			2		11	8			6	10					9		7				17
1		3		5	6		4		11	8				10	9		2		14		*7*				18
1		3	4		5		*2*		11	8				10	9		6	14	12		7				19
1		3	4		5	14			11	*8*				10	9		2	6	12		7				20
1		3	4		5	8			11					10	9			6	12		7	2			21
1		3			5	*8*		14	11					10	9		4	6	12		7	2			22
1				4	5				11	8				10	9		2	3	12		7	6			23
1		*3*			5			14	11	8				12	9		2	4	10		7	6			24
1		3		*4*	5				11	8					9		2	14	10		7	6			25
1		3			5				*11*	8				12	9		2	4	10		7	6	14		26
1		3	4		5				11	*8*				12	9		2	14	10		7	6			27
1		3	4		5				11	12				10	*9*		2	8	14		7	6			28
1		3	4		5				*11*	8				10	9		2	14	12		7	6			29
1		3	4		5				11	*8*				10	9		2	14	12		7	6			30
1		3	4		5				11	12				14	9		2	8	*10*		7	6			31
1		3	4		5				11					12	9		2	8	10		7	6			32
1		*3*	4		5				11	14				10	9			8	12		7	6	2		33
1		12	4		5				*11*					14	9		2	3	10		7	6		8	34
1		3	4		5				11					12	9		2	8	10	15	7	*6*	14		35
1		3	4	5					11						14		2	8	10		7	12	*9*	6	36

GREENOCK MORTON First Division

Year Formed: 1874. *Ground & Address:* Cappielow Park, Sinclair St, Greenock. *Telephone:* 01475 723511.
Ground Capacity: total: 14,250. seated: 5150. *Size of Pitch:* 110yd × 71yd.
Chairman: John Wilson. *Secretary:* Mrs Jane Rankin.
Manager: Allan McGraw. *Assistant Manager:* John McMaster. *Physio:* John Tierney. *Coach:* Billy Osborne.
Managers since 1975: Joe Gilroy; Benny Rooney; Alex Miller; Tommy McLean; Willie McLean. *Club Nickname(s):* The Ton. *Previous Grounds:* Grant Street 1874, Garvel Park 1875, Cappielow Park 1879, Ladyburn Park 1882, (Cappielow Park 1883).
Record Attendance: 23,000 v Celtic; 1922.
Record Transfer Fee received: £350,000 for Neil Orr to West Ham U.
Record Transfer Fee paid: £150,000 for Allan Mahood from Nottingham Forest.
Record Victory: 11-0 v Carfin Shamrock, Scottish Cup 1st rd; 13 Nov, 1886.
Record Defeat: 1-10 v Port Glasgow Ath, Division II; 5 May, 1894 and v St Bernards, Division II; 14 Oct, 1933.
Most Capped Player: Jimmy Cowan, 25, Scotland.
Most League Appearances: 358: David Hayes, 1969-84.

GREENOCK MORTON 1994–95 LEAGUE RECORD

Match No.	Date	Venue	Opponents	Result		H/T Score	Lg. Pos.	Goalscorers	Attendance
1	Aug 13	H	Berwick R	D	1-1	0-0	—	Alexander	1454
2	20	A	Meadowbank T	W	1-0	0-0	3	Lilley (pen)	398
3	27	A	Dumbarton	L	1-2	1-0	4	Lilley	1168
4	Sept 3	A	Stirling Albion	L	0-2	0-0	6		1026
5	10	H	Brechin C	W	2-0	0-0	4	McArthur, Alexander	1093
6	24	A	East Fife	W	2-1	1-1	3	Lilley, Alexander	1173
7	Oct 1	H	Stenhousemuir	W	3-2	0-0	3	Anderson, Alexander 2	1280
8	8	H	Clyde	L	0-1	0-0	3		1801
9	15	A	Queen of the S	L	0-3	0-3	6		1126
10	22	A	Berwick R	L	1-2	0-1	7	Lilley	738
11	29	H	Dumbarton	W	1-0	0-0	5	Alexander	1429
12	Nov 5	H	Meadowbank T	W	4-0	1-0	3	Rajamaki 2, Lilley 2	1453
13	12	A	Brechin C	W	3-1	3-0	2	Lindberg, Alexander, McCahill	623
14	22	H	Stirling Albion	D	1-1	0-0	—	Alexander	1941
15	26	H	East Fife	W	3-0	1-0	2	Anderson, Rajamaki 2	1884
16	Dec 3	A	Stenhousemuir	D	0-0	0-0	2		842
17	26	A	Clyde	D	0-0	0-0	—		2023
18	31	H	Queen of the S	D	1-1	0-0	3	Rajamaki	2112
19	Jan 14	H	Berwick R	W	2-1	0-0	3	Rajamaki, Lilley	1951
20	21	A	Meadowbank T	L	0-1	0-0	3		416
21	24	A	Dumbarton	L	1-2	1-0	—	Rajamaki	1307
22	Feb 4	H	Brechin C	W	1-0	1-0	3	Alexander	1464
23	11	A	Stirling Albion	W	3-0	1-0	3	Lilley, McInnes, Mahood	1069
24	25	H	Stenhousemuir	W	1-0	1-0	2	Rajamaki	2754
25	28	A	East Fife	D	1-1	0-1	—	Archibald (og)	558
26	Mar 11	A	Queen of the S	L	0-1	0-1	4		1505
27	14	H	Clyde	W	4-1	4-0	—	Lilley 2, McInnes, Rajamaki	1421
28	18	A	Brechin C	D	1-1	0-0	2	Rajamaki	481
29	25	H	Stirling Albion	D	2-2	1-1	2	Rajamaki 2	2025
30	Apr 1	A	Stenhousemuir	D	1-1	0-0	2	Lilley	1126
31	8	H	East Fife	W	4-1	1-0	2	Anderson, McCahill, Lilley, Laing	1789
32	15	A	Clyde	W	3-1	2-0	2	McArthur, McInnes, Laing	2163
33	22	H	Queen of the S	D	0-0	0-0	2		2395
34	29	A	Berwick R	W	4-3	2-3	1	Lilley 2, Collins, Rajamaki	992
35	May 6	H	Dumbarton	W	2-0	0-0	1	Lilley, Rajamaki	6242
36	13	H	Meadowbank T	W	1-0	1-0	1	Lilley	3165

Final League Position: 1

Most League Goals in Season (Individual): 58: Allan McGraw, Division II; 1963-64.
Most Goals Overall (Individual): —.

Honours
League Champions: First Division 1977-78, 1983-84, 1986-87. Division II 1949-50, 1963-64, 1966-67. Second Division 1994-95. *Runners-up:* Division 1 1916-17, Division II 1899-1900, 1928-29, 1936-37.
Scottish Cup Winners: 1922; *Runners-up:* 1948. *League Cup Runners-up:* 1963-64.
B&Q Cup: Runners-up: 1992-93.

European: *UEFA Cup (Fairs):* 1968-69.
Club colours: Shirt: Royal blue tartan. Shorts: Royal blue. Stockings: Royal blue.

Goalscorers: *League (55):* Lilley 16 (1 pen), Rajamaki 14, Alexander 9, Anderson 3, McInnes 3, Laing 2, McArthur 2, McCahill 2, Collins 1, Lindberg 1, Mahood 1, own goal 1. *Scottish Cup (5):* Anderson 2, Alexander 1, Lilley 1, Rajamaki 1. *League Cup (1):* Lilley 1. *B&Q Cup (5):* Lilley 2, Alexander 1, Anderson 1, Fowler 1.

Wylie D 36	Collins D 33	Cormack P 12	Hunter J 6 + 2	McCahill S 27	Johnstone D 22 + 2	Lilley D 34 + 1	Anderson J 28 + 2	Alexander R 26 + 6	McArthur S 30 + 3	Flannery P 2 + 1	Blair P 8 + 8	Fowler J 9 + 5	Mahood A 18 + 3	Pickering M 6 + 2	Gibson L 3 + 1	McPherson C 9 + 7	McCann M 2	Lindberg J 25	McInnes D 26	Rajamaki M 25	Laing D 9 + 3	Match No.
1	2	3	4	5	6	7	8	9	10	*11*	14											1
1	2	3	4	5	6	7		9	11		14	*8*	10									2
1	2	3	4	5	6	7		9	11		14	*8*	10	12								3
1	2	3	4	5	6	7	14	9	11			8	*10*	12								4
1	2		12	5	6	7		9	11			4	10	3	8							5
1	2	5	4		6	7		9	11			8	10	3								6
1	2	5			6	7	4	9	11	*12*		8	10	3	14							7
1	2	5			6	7	4						10	3	11	8	9					8
1	2	5	6				4		14	7		12	10	3	*11*	8	9					9
1	2	5				7	4	9					8	3				6	10	11		10
1	2	3		5		7	4	9								8		6	10	11		11
1	2	3	12	5	4	7		9	14							*8*		6	10	11		12
1	2			5	4	7		9	3			14				8		*6*	10	11		13
1	2			5	4	7	12	9	3		14	*8*						6	10	11		14
1	2			5		7	4	9	3		8	12						6	10	11		15
1	2			5		7	4	9	3		*8*		14					6	10	11		16
1	2			5		7	4	9	3		8		12					6	10	11		17
1	2			5		7	4	9	3		12		8					6	10	11		18
1	2	*3*		5		7	4	9	12		14		8					6	10	11		19
1	2			5		7	4	12	3		9		8					6	10	11		20
1	2			5		7	4	9	3				8			12		6	10	11		21
1	2			5	14	7	4	9	3		*8*	6				12			10	11		22
1	2				5	7	4	9	3			12	8			14		6	10	*11*		23
1	2				5	7	4	9	3				8					6	10	11	12	24
1	2				5	7	4	9	3				8			14		6	10	11	12	25
1	2				5	12	4	9	3			8				10		6		11	7	26
1	2			5	14	7	4	*9*	3		8					12		6	10	11		27
1	2			5		7	4	*9*	3		8					12		6	10	11	14	28
1	2			5		7	4	9	3		12							6	10	11	8	29
1				5	2	7	4		3				*8*			14		6	10	11	9	30
1				5	2	7	4	12	3			14				8		*6*	10	11	9	31
1	2			5	11	7	4	12	3							8		6	10		9	32
1	2			5	6	7	4	12	3		14					*8*			10	11	9	33
1	8			5	2	7	4		3									6	10	11	9	34
1				5	2	7	4	12	3				8					6	10	11	9	35
1	*8*			5	2	7	4	12	3		11		14					6	10		9	36

HAMILTON ACADEMICAL Division 1

Year Formed: 1874. *Ground:* Firhill Stadium, Glasgow G20 7AL *Telephone (match days only):* 0141 945 4811. *Club Address:* Douglas Park, Douglas Park Lane, Hamilton ML3 0DF. *Telephone:* 01698 286103. *Fax:* 01698 285422.
Ground Capacity: 20,676, seated: 9076. *Size of Pitch:* 110yd × 74yd.
Chairman: David Campbell. *Secretary:* Scott A. Struthers BA. *Commercial Manager:* Sandy Clark.
Manager: Iain Munro. *Physio:* Tom Williamson and Alistair Macfie.
Managers since 1975: J. Eric Smith; Dave McParland; John Blackley; Bertie Auld; John Lambie; Jim Dempsey; John Lambie; Billy McLaren. *Club Nickname(s):* The Accies. *Previous Grounds:* Bent Farm, South Avenue, South Haugh.
Record Attendance: 28,690 v Hearts, Scottish Cup 3rd rd; 3 Mar, 1937.
Record Transfer Fee received: £225,000 for James Weir to Hearts (Aug 1993).
Record Transfer Fee paid: £60,000 for Paul Martin from Kilmarnock (Oct 1988) and for John McQuade from Dumbarton (Aug 1993).
Record Victory: 11-1 v Chryston, Lanarkshire Cup; 28 Nov, 1885.
Record Defeat: 1-11 v Hibernian, Division I; 6 Nov, 1965.
Most Capped Player: Colin Miller, 29 (51), Canada, 1988-95.
Most League Appearances: 447: Rikki Ferguson, 1974-88.

HAMILTON ACADEMICAL 1994–95 LEAGUE RECORD

Match No.	*Date*	*Venue*	*Opponents*	*Result*		*H/T Score*	*Lg. Pos.*	*Goalscorers*	*Attendance*
1	Aug 13	A	Ayr U	D	1-1	1-0	—	Lorimer	2097
2	20	A	Raith R	D	1-1	1-1	5	Chalmers	2825
3	27	H	Airdrieonians	L	2-6	2-3	10	McIntosh, Duffield	1180
4	Sept 3	H	Stranraer	W	1-0	1-0	6	Duffield	1083
5	10	A	Dunfermline Ath	L	0-4	0-3	7		4029
6	24	A	St Johnstone	D	1-1	1-0	9	McGill	2790
7	Oct 1	H	St Mirren	D	2-2	1-0	8	Duffield, McQuade	1613
8	8	A	Dundee	L	0-2	0-2	8		2370
9	15	H	Clydebank	D	0-0	0-0	8		1042
10	22	H	Ayr U	W	2-0	2-0	7	Duffield, Renicks	1066
11	29	A	Airdrieonians	L	0-1	0-0	7		1422
12	Nov 5	H	Raith R	L	0-3	0-2	8		1112
13	12	H	Dunfermline Ath	W	3-1	3-1	7	Tighe, Duffield 2 (1 pen)	2103
14	19	A	Stranraer	L	0-2	0-1	7		784
15	26	H	St Johnstone	W	3-1	2-1	6	Duffield 2, McQuade	1445
16	Dec 3	A	St Mirren	W	1-0	0-0	6	Duffield	2273
17	26	H	Dundee	L	0-1	0-1	—		1552
18	31	A	Ayr U	W	2-1	2-1	6	Clark G, McInulty	2079
19	Jan 2	H	Airdrieonians	W	3-0	2-0	—	Duffield, McIntosh, Chalmers	2178
20	7	A	Raith R	L	0-2	0-1	6		3130
21	10	A	Clydebank	D	0-0	0-0	—		578
22	14	H	Stranraer	W	1-0	0-0	6	Duffield	1015
23	21	A	Dunfermline Ath	L	1-2	0-1	6	Clark G	3973
24	Feb 4	H	St Mirren	W	2-0	2-0	6	Clark G, Duffield	1534
25	18	A	St Johnstone	L	0-3	0-1	6		2589
26	25	H	Clydebank	L	0-1	0-0	6		1017
27	Mar 4	A	Dundee	L	0-2	0-1	6		2342
28	22	H	Dunfermline Ath	L	1-3	0-1	—	Duffield	1343
29	25	A	Stranraer	W	5-0	2-0	6	Duffield 2, McCall, McLean, McStay	655
30	Apr 1	A	St Mirren	L	2-3	1-0	6	McCulloch, McEntegart (pen)	2272
31	8	H	St Johnstone	W	1-0	0-0	6	Duffield	858
32	15	H	Dundee	L	1-4	0-4	6	Duffield	1471
33	22	A	Clydebank	W	4-1	3-1	6	McCormick, Duffield 3	716
34	29	H	Ayr U	W	1-0	0-0	6	Lorimer	1073
35	May 6	A	Airdrieonians	W	1-0	0-0	6	Clark G	1501
36	13	H	Raith R	D	0-0	0-0	6		5333

Final League Position: 6

Most League Goals in Season (Individual): 34: David Wilson, Division I; 1936-37.
Most Goals Overall (Individual): 246: David Wilson, 1928-39.

Honours
League Champions: First Division 1985-86, 1987-88. Division II 1903-04; *Runners-up:* Division II 1952-53, 1964-65.
Scottish Cup Runners-up: 1911, 1935. *League Cup:* Semi-finalists three times.
B&Q Cup Winners: 1991-92 and 1992-93.
Club colours: Shirt: Red and white hoops. Shorts: White. Stockings: White.

Goalscorers: *League (42):* Duffield 20 (1 pen), Clark G 4, Chalmers 2, Lorimer 2, McIntosh 2, McQuade 2, McCall 1, McCormick 1, McCulloch 1, McEntegart 1 (pen), McGill 1, McInulty 1, McLean 1, McStay 1, Renicks 1, Tighe 1. *Scottish Cup (1):* Lorimer 1. *League Cup (7):* Baptie 1, Campbell 1, Duffield 1, McEntegart 1, McLean 1, Sherry 1, own goal 1. *B&Q Cup (4):* Duffield 3 (1 pen), McIntosh 1.

Ferguson A 24	McKenzie P 29	McInulty S 29	McEntegart S 30 + 2	Baptie C 24 + 6	McIntosh M 30	McQuade J 27 + 3	Sherry J 12 + 2	Chalmers P 18 + 5	Duffield P 36	Lorimer D 15 + 12	Campbell D — + 2	McLean C 5 + 2	Hartley P 10 + 6	Nicholls D 3	Cormack D 12	Clark P 4	McGill D 4 + 3	McStay J 2	Renicks S 19	Clark G 12 + 5	Tighe M 7 + 3	McCormick S 5 + 3	Hillcoat C 15 + 2	McStay R 9 + 1	Waters M 2 + 1	McCall I 5 + 1	McCulloch S 8	Match No.
1	2	3	4	5	6	7	8	9	10	11	12																	1
1	2	3	4	5	6	7	8	*9*	10	11		14																2
1	2	3	4	5	6	7	8	*9*	10	11		12	14															3
1	2	*3*	4	5	6	12	8	9	10			*7*	14	11														4
1	2	3	4	5	6	11	8	9	10				7															5
	2	3	4	5	6	7			10					11	1	8	9											6
	2	3	4	5	6	7			10						1	11	9	8										7
	2	3	4	5	6	7	11		10		14				1		*9*	8										8
	2	3	4	5	6	7	14	12	10				11		1				*8*	9								9
	2	3	4	5	6	7		12	10	14			11		1				8	*9*								10
	2	3	4	5	6	7		12	10	9			14		1				*8*		11							11
	2	3	4	5	6	7		12	10	9					1				8		11							12
	5		4	12	6	7	2	9	10	*11*					1		14		3		8							13
	5		4	12	6	7	2	9	10	11					1				3		8							14
	5	3	4		6	8		9	10	11			*7*		1				2		14							15
	5	3	4		6	8		9	10	*11*					1		14		2		7							16
	5	3			6	8		9	10	*11*				4	1		14		2	12	7							17
1	5	3	4	12	6	*8*		9	10	11									2	7	14							18
1	5	3	4	8	6			9	*10*	11									2	7	12	14						19
1	5	3	*4*	8	6			9	10	11			12						2	7			14					20
1		3		8	6			9	10	11			14						2	*7*			5	4	12			21
1		3		12	6			*9*	10								8		2	14			5	4	7	11		22
1		3	14	9	6	*8*			10	12									2	7			5	4		11		23
1	5		4		6	*11*		9	10	14									2	7			3	8		12		24
1	9		4	5	6	8			10	11			14						*2*	7			3	12				25
1	5		4	6		*9*	2	14	10	12										7			3	8		11		26
1	5	*3*	4		6	8		9	10										2	7		14	12			*11*		27
1	5	3	4	12				9	10	14									2	*7*	8	11	6					28
1	5	3		6		12			*10*	14		9											2	4	7	8	11	29
1	5	3	14	6		8			10	12		9	7										2	4			*11*	30
1	5		4	12		8			10	14		9	*7*			2							3	6			11	31
1	5		4			8	14		10			9	7			2						12	3	*6*			11	32
1		3	4	5	6		8		10	14			*7*							12		9	2				11	33
1		3	4	5	6	12	8		10	14			*7*									9	2				*11*	34
1		3	4	5	6	8			10	14			*7*							12		*9*	2				11	35
1		3	4	5	6	8	7		10	14										12		*9*	2				11	36

HEART OF MIDLOTHIAN Premier Division

Year Formed: 1874. *Ground & Address:* Tynecastle Park, Gorgie Rd, Edinburgh EH11 2NL. *Telephone:* 0131 337 6132. *Fax:* 0131 346 0699.
Ground Capacity: variable due to reconstruction. *Size of Pitch:* 108yd × 72yd.
Chairman: Christopher P.Robinson. *Secretary:* L. W. Porteous. *Commercial Managers:* Brian Whittaker, Gary Mackay.
Manager: Tommy McLean. *General Manager:* Sally Robinson.
Physio: Alan Rae. *Coach:* Walter Kidd, Eamonn Bannon, Tom Forsyth.
Managers since 1975: J. Hagart; W. Ormond; R. Moncur; T. Ford; A. MacDonald; A. MacDonald & W. Jardine; A. MacDonald; J. Jordan, S. Clark.
Club Nickname(s): Hearts. *Previous Grounds:* The Meadows 1874, Powderhall 1878, Old Tynecastle 1881, (Tynecastle Park, 1886).
Record Attendance: 53,396 v Rangers, Scottish Cup 3rd rd; 13 Feb, 1932.
Record Transfer Fee received: £2,000,000 for Andy McLaren from Rangers (October 1994).
Record of Transfer paid: £750,000 for Derek Ferguson to Rangers (July 1990).
Record Victory: 21-0 v Anchor, EFA Cup 1880.
Record Defeat: 1-8 v Vale of Leithen, Scottish Cup, 1888.
Most Capped Player: Bobby Walker, 29, Scotland.
Most League Appearances: 482: Henry Smith, 1981-95.

HEART OF MIDLOTHIAN 1994–95 LEAGUE RECORD

Match No.	Date	Venue	Opponents	Result		H/T Score	Lg. Pos.	Goalscorers	Atten-dance
1	Aug 13	A	Aberdeen	L	1-3	0-1	—	Colquhoun	14,238
2	20	A	Motherwell	D	1-1	0-0	8	Johnston M	8249
3	27	H	Hibernian	L	0-1	0-0	9		12,371
4	Sept 11	A	Rangers	L	0-3	0-0	—		40,653
5	17	H	Dundee U	W	2-1	2-0	8	Thomas, Frail	7392
6	24	H	Kilmarnock	W	3-0	2-0	6	Millar J, McLaren, Mackay	9302
7	Oct 1	A	Falkirk	L	1-2	1-1	7	Robertson	7589
8	8	A	Partick T	W	1-0	1-0	5	Robertson	5076
9	15	H	Celtic	W	1-0	1-0	5	Robertson	12,086
10	22	H	Aberdeen	W	2-0	2-0	5	Frail, Robertson	10,655
11	29	A	Hibernian	L	1-2	0-2	6	Robertson	13,622
12	Nov 5	H	Motherwell	L	1-2	1-1	6	Robertson	8889
13	9	H	Rangers	D	1-1	0-0	—	Colquhoun	12,347
14	19	A	Dundee U	L	2-5	1-4	6	Thomas 2	7719
15	26	A	Kilmarnock	L	1-3	1-0	7	Robertson	8069
16	Dec 3	H	Falkirk	D	1-1	1-1	8	Thomas	8960
17	26	H	Partick T	W	3-0	0-0	—	Hagen, Robertson, Bett	8920
18	31	A	Aberdeen	L	1-3	0-2	6	Thomas	11,392
19	Jan 8	A	Motherwell	W	2-1	1-1	—	Hamilton, Miller C	5117
20	11	A	Celtic	D	1-1	0-1	—	Bett	26,491
21	14	H	Dundee U	W	2-0	1-0	5	Millar J, Jamieson	8656
22	18	H	Hibernian	W	2-0	1-0	—	McPherson, Millar J	12,630
23	21	A	Rangers	L	0-1	0-1	5		44,231
24	Feb 4	A	Falkirk	L	0-2	0-1	5		6028
25	11	H	Kilmarnock	D	2-2	2-2	5	Millar J, Mackay	8374
26	25	H	Celtic	D	1-1	0-0	5	Jamieson	11,185
27	Mar 18	H	Rangers	W	2-1	2-1	5	Robertson, Millar J	9806
28	21	A	Dundee U	D	1-1	1-0	—	Johnston A	6862
29	Apr 1	H	Falkirk	L	0-1	0-1	6		9003
30	4	A	Partick T	L	1-3	1-0	—	Millar J	4526
31	12	A	Kilmarnock	L	2-3	1-2	—	Cramb, Jamieson	7239
32	15	H	Partick T	L	0-1	0-0	7		9007
33	19	A	Celtic	W	1-0	0-0	—	Hagen	18,638
34	29	H	Aberdeen	L	1-2	0-	7	McPherson	11,466
35	May 6	A	Hibernian	L	1-3	1-0	8	Hagen	7122
36	13	H	Motherwell	W	2-0	0-0	6	Hamilton, Robertson (pen)	11,172

Final League Position: 6

Most League Goals in Season (Individual): 44: Barney Battles.
Most Goals Overall (Individual): 206: Jimmy Wardhaugh, 1946-59.

Honours
League Champions: Division I 1894-95, 1896-97, 1957-58, 1959-60. First Division 1979-80; *Runners-up:* Division I 1893-94, 1898-99, 1903-04, 1905-06, 1914-15, 1937-38, 1953-54, 1956-57, 1958-59, 1964-65. Premier Division 1985-86, 1987-88, 1991-92. First Division 1977-78, 1982-83.
Scottish Cup Winners: 1891, 1896, 1901, 1906, 1956; *Runners-up:* 1903, 1907, 1968, 1976, 1986.
League Cup Winners: 1954-55, 1958-59, 1959-60, 1962-63; *Runners-up:* 1961-62.

European: *European Cup* 4 matches (1958-59, 1960-61). *Cup Winners Cup:* 4 matches (1976-77). *UEFA Cup:* 34 matches (*Fairs Cup:* 1961-62, 1963-64, 1965-66. *UEFA Cup:* 1984-85, 1986-87, 1988-89, 1990-91, 1992-93, 1993-94).
Club colours: Shirt: Maroon. Shorts: White. Stockings: Maroon with white tops.

Goalscorers: *League (44):* Robertson 10 (1 pen), Millar J 6, Thomas 5, Hagen 3, Jamieson 3, Bett 2, Colquhoun 2, Frail 2, Hamilton 2, Mackay 2, McPherson 2, Cramb 1, Johnston A 1, Johnston M 1, McLaren 1, Miller C 1. *Scottish Cup (7):* Millar J 2, Robertson 2, McPherson 1, Miller C 1, Thomas 1. *League Cup (6):* Johnston A 2, Colquhoun 1, Locke 1, Millar J 1, Robertson 1.

Smith H 14 + 1	Frail S 25	McKinlay T 11	Locke G 3 + 6	Weir J 2	McLaren A 10	Colquhoun J 23 + 8	Mackay G 21 + 13	Robertson J 27 + 4	Leitch S 18 + 3	Millar J 25 + 3	Johnston A 9 + 12	Thomas K 11 + 7	Walker N 2	Levein C 24	Johnston M 3 + 1	Berry N 29	Hogg G — + 1	Bett J 26	McPherson D 23	Miller C 16	Kidd W 1	Nelson C 20	Jamieson W 13 + 2	Hagen D 16 + 4	Wright G — + 1	Hamilton B 13	Cramb C 3 + 3	Wishart F 8	Match No.
1	2	*3*	4	5	6	7	8	9	10	11	12	14																	1
	2	3		5	6	7	8	*9*	14	11	12		1	4	10														2
	2	*3*			6	7	8	9	11	14	12		1	4	10	5													3
1		3	*2*		6	7		11	8	10	12			4	9	5	14												4
.1	2	3			6	7		9	8	10	14	11		4	12	5													5
1	2	3			6	7	14	9	8	10	12	11		4		5													6
1	2	3			6	7	14	9	8	10	12	11		4		5													7
1	2	3			6	7	12	9		10	14	*11*		4		5		8											8
1	2	3			6	12	7	9	*10*	14		11		4		5		8											9
1	2	3			6	12	7	9	14	10	11			4		5		8											10
1	2	3				12	7	9	*10*	14	11			4		5		8	6										11
1	2					7	8	9	10	3	11	12				5		4	6										12
1	2					7	4	9	10	3	11	12				5		8	6										13
1			14			7	4	9	10	3		11				*5*		8	6	2									14
1			*2*			7	4	9	12	10	14	11						8	6	3	5								15
	2					7	12	9		10		*11*				5		8	6	3		1	4	14					16
	2					7	14	9		10		12				5		8	6	*3*		1	4	11					17
	2					7	10	9				12				5		8	6	3		1	*4*	11	14				18
	2						14	12	*10*			9				5		8	6	3		1	4	11		7			19
	2						14	12	*10*			9				5		8	6	3		1	4	11		7			20
	2						12	9		10						5		8	6	3		1	4	11		7			21
	2					14	12	9		10				5				*8*	6	3		1	4	11		7			22
	2					*9*	14	12		10				4				8	6	3		1	5	11		7			23
	2					12	*10*	9			14			4		5		8	6	3		1		11		7			24
	2					7	12	9		10		11		4		*3*		5	6			1		14		8			25
	2					12	8		*3*	10	9	14		4					6			1	5	11		7			26
	2					14	7	*9*	3	10	12					4		8	6			1	5	11					27
	2		14				7		3	10	9			4		6		8				1	5	11			12		28
15							7	9	*10*	3	11			4		5		8	6			*1*		12			14	2	29
1						7	14	9		10		12		4				5	6	*3*				11		8		2	30
			14			7	8			10	11			4		5			6	*3*		1	12				9	2	31
			14			7	8		*3*	10	11			4		6						1	5	12			9	2	32
			14			12	10							4		6		8		3		1	5	*11*		7	9	2	33
						9	10	12						4		5		8	6	3		1	14	11		7		*2*	34
						7	12	9			14			4		5		8	6	*3*		1		11		10		2	35
			14			7	2	9						4		5		*8*	6			1		11		10	12	3	36

HIBERNIAN Premier Division

Year Formed: 1875. *Ground & Address:* Easter Road Stadium, Albion Rd, Edinburgh EH7 5QG. *Telephone:* 0131 661 2159. *Fax:* 0131 659 6488.
Ground Capacity: total: 16,218. *Size of Pitch:* 112yd × 74yd.
Chairman: Douglas Cromb. *Secretary:* Cecil F. Graham, FIFA, MInst CM. *Commercial Manager:* Ian Erskine.
Manager: Alex Miller. *Assistant Manager and Coach:* John Scott.
Physio: Stewart Collie. *Coach Assistant:* Martin Ferguson.
Managers since 1975: Eddie Turnbull; Willie Ormond; Bertie Auld; Pat Stanton; John Blackley. *Club Nickname(s):* Hibees.
Previous Grounds: Meadows 1875-78, Powderhall 1878-79, Mayfield 1879-80, First Easter Road 1880-92, Second Easter Road 1892-.
Record Attendance: 65,860 v Hearts, Division I; 2 Jan, 1950.
Record Transfer Fee received: £1,000,000 for Andy Goram to Rangers (June 1991).
Record Transfer Fee paid: £420,000 for Keith Wright from Dundee.
Record Victory: 22-1 v 42nd Highlanders; 3 Sept, 1881.
Record Defeat: 0-10 v Rangers; 24 Dec, 1898.
Most Capped Player: Lawrie Reilly, 38, Scotland.
Most League Appearances: 446: Arthur Duncan.

HIBERNIAN 1994–95 LEAGUE RECORD

Match No.	Date	Venue	Opponents	Result		H/T Score	Lg. Pos.	Goalscorers	Attendance
1	Aug 13	H	Dundee U	W	5-0	3-0	—	Findlay, Jackson D 2, Harper, O'Neill	8838
2	20	H	Kilmarnock	D	0-0	0-0	2		9107
3	27	A	Hearts	W	1-0	0-0	1	Hunter	12,371
4	Sept 10	H	Aberdeen	D	2-2	2-1	2	Jackson D, O'Neill	9728
5	17	A	Motherwell	D	1-1	0-0	3	O'Neill	7005
6	24	A	Celtic	L	0-2	0-1	3		28,170
7	Oct 1	H	Partick T	W	3-0	2-0	3	Jackson D 2, McGraw	7083
8	8	H	Rangers	W	2-1	0-1	3	Hunter, Harper	12,088
9	15	A	Falkirk	D	0-0	0-0	2		7388
10	22	A	Dundee U	D	0-0	0-0	2		7983
11	29	H	Hearts	W	2-1	2-0	1	Jackson D, O'Neill	13,622
12	Nov 5	A	Kilmarnock	D	0-0	0-0	3		8319
13	9	A	Aberdeen	D	0-0	0-0	—		10,882
14	19	H	Motherwell	D	2-2	2-1	3	McAllister, O'Neill	9160
15	30	H	Celtic	D	1-1	0-1	—	Jackson D	12,295
16	Dec 3	A	Partick T	D	2-2	0-1	3	McGinlay, O'Neill	4667
17	10	H	Falkirk	D	2-2	0-1	3	Jackson D, O'Neill	7725
18	26	A	Rangers	L	0-2	0-2	—		44,892
19	31	H	Dundee U	W	4-0	3-0	3	Wright 3, O'Neill	7754
20	Jan 7	H	Kilmarnock	W	2-1	1-0	2	McGinlay, O'Neill	8918
21	13	A	Motherwell	D	0-0	0-0	—		6724
22	18	A	Hearts	L	0-2	0-1	—		12,630
23	21	H	Aberdeen	W	4-2	3-1	2	McGinlay, Jackson D 2 (1 pen), Wright	8076
24	Feb 4	H	Partick T	L	1-2	1-1	2	McGinlay	7760
25	11	A	Celtic	D	2-2	1-1	2	McGinlay, McGraw	24,284
26	25	A	Falkirk	L	0-1	0-0	3		6501
27	Mar 4	H	Rangers	D	1-1	0-0	3	Wright	11,939
28	18	A	Aberdeen	D	0-0	0-0	3		10,384
29	22	H	Motherwell	W	2-0	1-0	—	Wright 2	5395
30	Apr 1	A	Partick T	D	2-2	1-0	3	Wright, Harper	4041
31	16	A	Rangers	L	1-3	1-1	—	O'Neill	44,193
32	19	H	Falkirk	L	0-2	0-1	—		5450
33	29	A	Dundee U	W	1-0	0-0	4	McGinlay	8376
34	May 6	H	Hearts	W	3-1	0-1	3	Weir, Wright, Harper	7122
35	9	H	Celtic	D	1-1	1-0	—	Harper	6019
36	13	A	Kilmarnock	W	2-1	0-1	3	McGinlay, Wright	11,676

Final League Position: 3

Most League Goals in Season (Individual): 42: Joe Baker.
Most Goals Overall (Individual): 364: Gordon Smith.

Honours
League Champions: Division I 1902-03, 1947-48, 1950-51, 1951-52. First Division 1980-81. Division II 1893-94, 1894-95, 1932-33; *Runners-up:* Division I 1896-97, 1946-47, 1949-50, 1952-53, 1973-74, 1974-75.
Scottish Cup Winners: 1887, 1902; *Runners-up:* 1896, 1914, 1923, 1924, 1947, 1958, 1972, 1979.
League Cup Winners: 1972-73, 1991-92; *Runners-up:* 1950-51, 1968-69, 1974-75, 1993-94.

European: *European Cup:* 6 matches (1955-56 semi-finals). *Cup Winners Cup:* 6 matches (1972-73). *UEFA Cup:* 56 matches (*Fairs Cup:* 1960-61 semi-finals, 1961-62, 1962-63, 1965-66, 1967-68, 1968-69, 1970-71. *UEFA Cup:* 1973-74, 1974-75, 1975-76, 1976-77, 1978-79, 1992-93).
Club colours: Shirt: Green with white sleeves. Shorts: White. Stockings: Green with white trim.

Goalscorers: *League (49):* Jackson D 10 (1 pen), O'Neill 10, Wright 10, McGinlay 7, Harper 5, Hunter 2, McGraw 2, Findlay 1, McAllister 1, Weir 1. *Scottish Cup (9):* Harper 3, McGinlay 2, Jackson D 1, O'Neill 1, Tortolano 1, Wright 1.
League Cup (6): O'Neill 3, Evans 2, Tweed 1.

Leighton J 36	Miller W 34	Mitchell G 18	Findlay W 12 + 6	Tweed S 33	Hunter G 29	McAllister K 17 + 6	Hamilton B 17 + 1	Evans G 16 + 8	Jackson D 30 + 1	O'Neill M 33	Harper K 15 + 8	Tortolano J 11 + 7	Beaumont D 7	Farrell D 15 + 4	McGraw M 2 + 6	Love G 11 + 1	Weir M 8 + 11	McGinlay P 24	Wright K 19	Millen A 8	Dods D 1	Renwick M — + 1	Match No.
1	2	3	4	5	6	7	8	9	*10*	11	14												1
1	2	3	4	5	6	7	8	*9*	10	11	14	12											2
1	*2*		4	5	6	12	8	9	10	11	7	14	3										3
1			*4*	5		7	8	9	10	11		3	6	2	12	14							4
1	2		7	5	6	12	8	*9*	10	11			4	3			14						5
1	2		7	5	6	12	8	14	10	*11*	9			4		3							6
1	2			5	6		8	9	10	11	7			4	14	3	12						7
1	2			5	6		8	9	*10*	11	7			4	14	3	12						8
1	2			5	6		8	9		11	7			4	10	3	12						9
1	2		12	5	*6*		8	9		11	10	14		4		3	7						10
1	2		9	5			8	12	10	11	14	*6*	4			3	7						11
1	2		9	5	6		8	14	10	11	12					3	7	4					12
1	2			5	6	7	8	12	10	11	9					3		4					13
1	2			5	6	7	8		10	11	9					3	12	4					14
1	2		14	5	6	7	*8*		10	11	12					3	9	4					15
1	2		*8*	5	6		14		10	11	9	7	3				12	4					16
1	2		8		6	7		9	10	11			5			3	12	4					17
1	*2*		14	5	6	12	4	8	10	11	7							3	9				18
1		3	12	5	6	7	8	14	10	11				2				4	*9*				19
1	2	3	*8*	5	6	7		12	10	11				14				4	9				20
1	2	3		5	6	7			10	11				8				4	9				21
1	2	3	14	5	6	7			10	11				12			*8*	4	9				22
1	2	3	12	5		7		*8*	10			11		6			14	4	9				23
1	2	3	*11*	5	6	7		8	10		12	14						4	9				24
1	2	3			6				10		8	*11*	5		14		7	4	9				25
1	2	3		5	6				10	11				8	7			4	9				26
1	2	3		5	6	7			10	11		8		4	12				9				27
1	2	3		5	6				10	11	*7*	8		14			12	4	9				28
1	2			5	6				10	11	7	8			14		12	4	9	*3*			29
1	2			5	*6*				12	11	7	10		8			14	4	9	3			30
1	2	3		5		14		*7*	10	11		12		8				4	9	6			31
1	2	3		5		7			10	11		14		*8*				4	9	6			32
1	2	3			6	7		8		11	12	10		14				4	9	5			33
1	2	3		5		7		12		11	14	6					10	4	9	8			34
1	2	3		5	6			14		11	*10*	12					7	4	9	8			35
1	2	3		5		12		*7*	10	*11*								4	9	8	6	14	36

KILMARNOCK Premier Division

Year Formed: 1869. *Ground & Address:* Rugby Park, Kilmarnock KA1 2DP. *Telephone:* 01563 525184. *Fax:* 01563 522181.
Ground Capacity: total: 18,168 seated. *Size of Pitch:* 114yd × 72yd.
Chairman: Robert Fleeting. *Secretary:* Kevin Collins. *Commercial Manager:* Denny Martin. *Stadium Manager:* G. Hollas.
Manager: Alex Totten. *Assistant Manager:* Kenny Thomson. *Physio:* Hugh Allan.
Managers since 1975: W. Fernie; D. Sneddon; J. Clunie; E. Morrison; J. Fleeting; T Burns. *Club Nickname(s):* Killie.
Previous Grounds: Rugby Park (Dundonald Road); The Grange; Holm Quarry; Present ground since 1899.
Record Attendance: 35,995 v Rangers, Scottish Cup; 10 March, 1962.
Record Transfer Fee received: £300,000 for Shaun McSkimming to Motherwell,1995.
Record Transfer Fee paid: £300,000 for Paul Wright from St Johnstone, 1995.
Record Victory: 11-1 v Paisley Academical, Scottish Cup; 18 Jan, 1930 (15-0 v Lanemark, Ayrshire Cup; 15 Nov, 1890).
Record Defeat: 1-9 v Celtic, Division I; 13 Aug, 1938.
Most Capped Player: Joe Nibloe, 11, Scotland.
Most League Appearances: 481: Alan Robertson, 1972-88.

KILMARNOCK 1994–95 LEAGUE RECORD

Match No.	Date	Venue	Opponents	Result		H/T Score	Lg. Pos.	Goalscorers	Attendance
1	Aug 13	A	Partick T	L	0-2	0-2	—		6606
2	20	A	Hibernian	D	0-0	0-0	9		9107
3	27	H	Motherwell	L	0-1	0-1	10		7388
4	Sept 10	H	Falkirk	D	1-1	1-0	9	Williamson	8021
5	17	A	Celtic	D	1-1	0-0	10	Williamson	28,457
6	24	A	Hearts	L	0-3	0-2	10		9302
7	Oct 1	H	Aberdeen	W	2-1	1-1	9	Winnie (og), Brown	7445
8	8	H	Dundee U	L	0-2	0-1	9		7127
9	15	A	Rangers	L	0-2	0-0	10		44,099
10	22	H	Partick T	W	2-0	0-0	8	McKee, Brown	7023
11	29	A	Motherwell	L	2-3	2-1	9	Henry, McKee	7436
12	Nov 5	H	Hibernian	D	0-0	0-0	9		8319
13	8	A	Falkirk	D	3-3	3-0	—	Skilling, Black, Henry	6134
14	19	H	Celtic	D	0-0	0-0	9		13,932
15	26	H	Hearts	W	3-1	0-1	8	Mitchell, McKee, Skilling	8069
16	Dec 3	A	Aberdeen	W	1-0	1-0	7	Maskrey	10,345
17	10	H	Rangers	L	1-2	0-1	8	McKee	17,219
18	26	A	Dundee U	D	2-2	1-0	—	Bollan (og), Mitchell	8468
19	31	A	Partick T	D	2-2	1-2	7	Maskrey, MacPherson	5799
20	Jan 7	A	Hibernian	L	1-2	0-1	9	McKee	8918
21	14	A	Celtic	L	1-2	0-0	9	Black (pen)	25,342
22	17	H	Motherwell	W	2-0	2-0	—	Black 2 (1 pen)	7521
23	21	H	Falkirk	W	2-1	1-1	6	Black, McKee	7648
24	Feb 4	H	Aberdeen	W	3-1	2-1	6	Maskrey, Brown, Roberts	9384
25	11	A	Hearts	D	2-2	2-2	6	Maskrey, Brown	8374
26	25	A	Rangers	L	0-3	0-0	8		44,859
27	Mar 4	H	Dundee U	W	2-0	2-0	6	Mitchell 2	7630
28	21	H	Celtic	L	0-1	0-0	—		10,112
29	25	A	Falkirk	L	0-2	0-1	7		5714
30	Apr 1	A	Aberdeen	W	1-0	0-0	7	Skilling	14,041
31	12	H	Hearts	W	3-2	2-1	—	Whitworth 2, Henry	7239
32	15	A	Dundee U	W	2-1	1-1	5	Whitworth, Henry	8223
33	20	H	Rangers	L	0-1	0-1	—		16,532
34	29	H	Partick T	D	0-0	0-0	6		9201
35	May 6	A	Motherwell	L	0-2	0-1	6		7760
36	13	H	Hibernian	L	1-2	1-0	7	Wright	11,676

Final League Position: 7

Most League Goals in Season (Individual): 34: Harry 'Peerie' Cunningham 1927-28 and Andy Kerr 1960-61.
Most Goals Overall (Individual): 148: W. Culley; 1912-23.

Honours
League Champions: Division I 1964-65. Division II 1897-98, 1898-99; *Runners-up:* Division I 1959-60, 1960-61, 1962-63, 1963-64. First Division 1975-76, 1978-79, 1981-82, 1992-93. Division II 1953-54, 1973-74. Second Division 1989-90.
Scottish Cup Winners: 1920, 1929; *Runners-up:* 1898, 1932, 1938, 1957, 1960.
League Cup Runners-up: 1952-53, 1960-61, 1962-63.

European: *European Cup:* 1965-66. *UEFA Cup (Fairs):* 1964-65 (semi-finals), 1969-70, 1970-71.
Club colours: Shirt: Blue and white vertical stripes. Shorts: Blue. Stockings: Blue.

Goalscorers: *League (40):* McKee 6, Black 5 (2 pens), Brown 4, Henry 4, Maskrey 4, Mitchell 4, Skilling 3, Whitworth 3, Williamson 2, MacPherson 1, Roberts 1, Wright 1, own goals 2. *Scottish Cup (6):* Maskrey 4, Black 1, Reilly 1. *League Cup (6):* Maskrey 2, Henry 1, McCluskey 1, Montgomerie 1, Williamson 1.

Geddes R 12	MacPherson A 33	Black T 31 + 1	Montgomerie R 9 + 3	Reilly M 31 + 1	Millen A 13	Mitchell A 33 + 2	Napier C 2 + 1	Williamson R 7 + 8	Connor R 27 + 1	Maskrey S 19 + 11	McCluskey G 2 + 1	Henry J 28 + 2	McSkimming S 8	Brown T 18 + 9	Whitworth N 30	McKee C 22 + 3	Meldrum C 4	Skilling M 13 + 4	Anderson D 20	Ledovic D 20	Roberts M — + 4	Lauchlan J 2	McCarrison D — + 1	Findlay W 5 + 4	Wright P 7	Match No.
1	2	3	4	5	6	7	*8*	9	10	11	14															1
1	2	3	4	5	6	7		14	11	9	*10*	8														2
1	2	3	4	5	6	7		12	10	9	*8*		11	14												3
1	2	3		4	6	7		*9*	10			12	11	14	5	8										4
1	2		12	11	6	7		9	10			4	3		5	8										5
1		12	2	11	6	7		9	10			4	3	14	5	*8*										6
1		3	2	12	6			9	4	14		8	11	10	5	*7*										7
1	2	3	4	11	6	12		9		14		8		10	5	*7*										8
1	2	3		4	6	7		*9*				8	11	10	5	14										9
	2	3		4	6	7						8	11	10	5	9	1									10
	2	3		4	6	*7*		12		14		8	11	10	5	9	1									11
1	2	3		11	6	*7*		12		14		8		10	5	9		4								12
1	2	3		11	6	7		12		14		8		10	5	*9*		4								13
	2	3		11		7				12		8		10	5	9	1	4	6							14
	2	3		11		7			12	14		8		10	5	*9*		4	6	1						15
	2			4		7	3	12	10	*11*					5	9		8	6	1	14					16
	2	3		4		7		14	*10*	11		12			5	9		8	6	1						17
	2	3		4		7		14	10	*11*		8			5	9		12	6	1						18
	2	3		4		7			10	*11*		8		14		9		5	6	1						19
	2	3		4		7	12		10	11		*8*		14	5	9			6	1						20
	2	3		4		7			10	14		8		*11*		9		5	6	1						21
	2	3		4		7			10			8		9	5	11			6	1						22
	2	3	4	6		7			10	14		8		*9*		11				1		5				23
	2	3		4		7			10	11		8		*9*	5				6	1	14					24
	2	3		4		7			10	11		8		*9*	5				6	1	14					25
	2	3	12	4		7			10	*11*		8			5	9			6	1	14					26
	2	3		4		7			10	*11*		8			5	9		12	6	1			14			27
	2	3		4		7			10	*11*				9	5	14		8	6	1				12		28
	2	3		4		7			10	11		8		*9*	5	14			6	1				12		29
	2	3		4		7			11	14				10	5			8	6	1				12	*9*	30
	2	3	12			7			10	11		8			5				6	1				4	9	31
	2	3				7			10	11		8		14	5			4	6	1				12	*9*	32
	2	3				7			10	*11*				14	5			4	6	1				8	9	33
	2	3				7			10	11		8		14	5			12	6	1				4	*9*	34
1	2		4	3		7				14		8		12	5	*11*		10						6	9	35
			4	3		14			10	11		*6*		9	5		1	12				2		7	8	36

LIVINGSTON (MEADOWBANK THISTLE)
Third Division

Year Formed: 1974. *Ground:* (at start of season) Meadowbank Stadium, London Rd, Edinburgh EH7 6AE. *Telephone:* 0131 661 5351. Address for correspondence: Preston Farm, Preston Road, Prestonpans, EH32 9LB. *Fax:* 01875 811130.
Ground Capacity: total: 16,500. seated: 16,500. Main stand only used 7500. *Size of Pitch:* 105yd × 72yd.
Chairman: William P Hunter. *Secretary:* J.R.S.Renton. *Vice-chairman:* Hugh Cowan.
Manager: Jim Leishman. *Club Doctor:* Dr M. M. Morrison. *Physio:* Arthur Duncan. *Coach:* Murray McDermott.
Managers since 1975: John Bain; Alec Ness; Willie MacFarlane; Terry Christie; Michael Lawson. *Club Nickname(s):* Thistle; Wee Jags. *Previous Grounds:* None.
Record Attendance: 4000 v Albion Rovers, League Cup 1st rd; 9 Sept, 1974.
Record Transfer Fee received: £115,000 for John Inglis to St Johnstone (1990).
Record Transfer Fee paid: £28,000 for Victor Kasule from Albion Rovers (1987).
Record Victory: 6-0 v Raith R, Second Division; 9 Nov, 1985.
Record Defeat: 0-8 v Hamilton A. Division II; 14 Dec, 1974.
Most Capped Player (under 18): I. Little.

MEADOWBANK THISTLE 1994–95 LEAGUE RECORD

Match No.	Date	Venue	Opponents	Result		H/T Score	Lg. Pos.	Goalscorers	Attendance
1	Aug 13	A	Brechin C	W	5-1	0-0	—	Rutherford, Bailey 3, Sorbie	432
2	20	H	Morton	L	0-1	0-0	5		398
3	27	H	Stenhousemuir	W	3-0	0-0	2	Little, Bailey 2	239
4	Sept 3	A	Dumbarton	W	1-0	1-0	4	Wilson	644
5	10	H	Queen of the S	L	0-1	0-0	6		279
6	24	H	Stirling Albion	L	1-2	0-1	7	Fleming	247
7	Oct 1	A	Clyde	L	1-2	1-1	7	McLeod	865
8	8	A	Berwick R	L	1-2	1-2	9	Little	520
9	15	H	East Fife	L	0-1	0-0	9		314
10	22	H	Brechin C	W	1-0	1-0	9	Williamson S	149
11	29	A	Stenhousemuir	D	1-1	1-0	9	Little	473
12	Nov 5	A	Morton	L	0-4	0-1	9		1453
13	12	A	Queen of the S	D	0-0	0-0	9		1418
14	19	H	Dumbarton	D	0-0	0-0	9		210
15	26	A	Stirling Albion	W	3-2	0-0	9	Samuel 2, Sorbie	518
16	Dec 3	H	Clyde	D	2-2	0-1	9	Bailey, Little	382
17	10	H	Berwick R	W	2-1	1-1	8	Sinclair, Williamson S	338
18	31	A	East Fife	L	1-2	1-1	9	Sorbie	686
19	Jan 10	A	Stenhousemuir	L	1-2	1-0	—	Thorburn	371
20	14	A	Brechin C	L	1-3	0-2	9	Sorbie	356
21	21	H	Morton	W	1-0	0-0	9	Sorbie	416
22	Feb 4	H	Queen of the S	L	1-2	0-1	9	Harris	265
23	11	A	Dumbarton	L	0-4	0-3	9		749
24	25	A	Clyde	L	1-4	0-1	9	Young	825
25	Mar 4	A	Berwick R	L	0-1	0-1	9		455
26	8	H	Stirling Albion	L	0-3	0-0	—		165
27	11	H	East Fife	L	1-3	1-1	9	Bailey	222
28	18	A	Queen of the S	W	3-2	2-0	9	Bailey, Wilson, Williamson S	705
29	25	H	Dumbarton	W	1-0	1-0	9	Young	389
30	Apr 1	H	Clyde	L	0-1	0-1	9		377
31	8	A	Stirling Albion	L	1-2	0-0	9	Callaghan	478
32	15	H	Berwick R	L	0-3	0-2	9		296
33	22	A	East Fife	D	1-1	1-0	9	Sorbie	355
34	29	H	Brechin C	W	2-1	1-0	9	McCartney, Graham	144
35	May 5	H	Stenhousemuir	W	1-0	1-0	—	Bailey	463
36	13	A	Morton	L	0-1	0-1	9		3165

Final League Position: 9

Most League Appearances: 446: Walter Boyd, 1979-89.
Most League Goals in Season (Individual): 21: John McGachie, 1986-87. *(Team):* 69; Second Division, 1986-87.
Most Goals Overall (Individual): 64: David Roseburgh, 1986-93.

Honours
League Champions: Second Division 1986-87; *Runners-up:* Second Division 1982-83. First Division 1987-88.
Scottish Cup: —. *League Cup:* Semi-finals 1984-85. *B&Q Cup:* Semi-finals 1992-93, 1993-94.
Club colours: Shirt: Amber with black trim. Shorts: Black. Stockings: Amber.

Goalscorers: *League (32):* Bailey 6, Sorbie 5, Little 4, Williamson S 3, Samuel 2, Wilson 2, Young 2, Callaghan 1, Fleming 1, Graham 1, Harris 1, McCartney 1, McLeod 1, Sinclair 1, Thorburn 1. *Scottish Cup (5):* Bailey 1, Graham 1, Sinclair 1, Wilson 1, own goal 1. *League Cup (5):* Bailey 1, Hutchison 1, Little 1, McLeod 1, Sorbie 1. *B&Q Cup (1):* Graham 1.

Ellison S 25	Graham T 32	Fleming D 7	Wilson S 32 + 1	Williamson S 28	Hutchison M 2 + 1	Duthie M 13 + 5	McLeod G 31	Little I 27 + 1	Rutherford P 4	Bailey L 24 + 10	Thorburn S 17 + 5	Sorbie S 26 + 6	Coyle M 1 + 7	Price G 2 + 1	Davidson G 26 + 1	Ingram N — + 2	Martin C 16 + 1	Sinclair C 13 + 4	Dallas A 6 + 1	Douglas R 8	Coulston D — + 2	Samuel D 9 + 2	Thomson M 10	Harris C 5 + 1	Young J 10 + 4	Williamson R — + 1	McCartney C 9	Alleyne D 5	Callaghan W 5 + 2	Stoute H 3	Match No.
1	*2*	3	4	5	6	7	8	9	10	11	12	14																			1
1	2	3	4	5	7		8	*9*	6	11		10	12	14																	2
1	2	3	4	*5*	14	7	8	9	6	11		10	12																		3
1	2	3	4	5		7	8	9	6	11		10	12																		4
1	2	3	4	5		7	8	9		11	12	10		6	14																5
1	2	3	4	5			8	9		11	6	10			7																6
1	*2*	3	4	5			8			11	6	10		9	7	12	14														7
1	4		12	5			6	9		*10*	7	8			2		3	11	14												8
	4		7	5		2	6	9		12		8					3	11	*10*	1	14										9
	4		7	5		2	6	9		*10*		8	14				3	11		1	12										10
	4		7	5		14	6	9		12		10			2		3	11	*8*	1											11
	4		8	5		14	6	9		12	7	10			2		3	*11*		1											12
	4		8	5		7	6	9		10	11				2		3			1											13
			8	5		7	6	9		10	11		12		2	14	3	4		1											14
	4		8	5			6	9		*10*		12	14		2		3	11		1		7									15
	4		8	5				9		10		6			2		3	11		1		7									16
1	4		8	5		14		9		*10*	3	6	12		2			11				7									17
1	4		8			14	10			9	5	6			2		3	*11*				7									18
1	4		8			14	10	9		12	7	6			2		3	*11*					5								19
1	*4*			7			10	14			12	6			2		3	11				8	5	9							20
1			7	2			11	9		14		6			4		3					10	5	*8*							21
1	4			7			10	11		14	12	6			2		*3*					8	5	9							22
1	5						*10*			11	8	6	7		2		3		9			12	4		14						23
1			7	*5*			10			8	14	6			2		3					11	4	12	9						24
1	2		7	5			10			8	3	11							*6*			14	4	9	12						25
1	2		7	5			10	8		12	3	14							6				4	*9*	11						26
1	2		8	*5*			10	9		11	3	7										6	4		12	14					27
1	5		6	2			10	9		7					3				11						12		4	8			28
1	5		6	2		11		9		*7*		12			3										8		4	10	14		29
1	5		6	2		11		9		*7*		12			3										8		4	10	14		30
1	5		7	*2*				8		12		14			4			11							10		3	6	9		31
1	5		7			2	3	8		12					4			14							10		11	*6*	9		32
1	5		7			*11*	8			12	2	6			4			14							10		3		9		33
	5		7			11	10				2	6			4			12							8		3		9	1	34
	5		10				8			7	2	6			4										11		3		9	1	35
			8				6	9		7	2	10			4			12					5		11		3			1	36

MONTROSE Second Division

Year Formed: 1879. *Ground & Address:* Links Park, Wellington St, Montrose DD10 8QD. *Telephone:* 01674 673200.
Ground Capacity: total: 4338. seated: 1398. *Size of Pitch:* 113yd × 70yd.
Chairman: Bryan Keith. *Secretary:* Malcolm J. Watters.
Manager: Andy Dornan. *Physio:* Bill Ramsay.
Managers since 1975: A. Stuart; K. Cameron; R. Livingstone; S. Murray; D. D'Arcy; I. Stewart; C. McLelland; D. Rougvie; J. Leishman, J Holt.
Club Nickname(s): The Gable Endies. *Previous Grounds:* None.
Record Attendance: 8983 v Dundee, Scottish Cup 3rd rd; 17 Mar, 1973.
Record Transfer Fee received: £50,000 for Gary Murray to Hibernian (Dec 1980).
Record Transfer Fee paid: £17,500 for Jim Smith from Airdrieonians (Feb 1992).
Record Victory: 12-0 v Vale of Leithen, Scottish Cup 2nd rd; 4 Jan, 1975.
Record Defeat: 0-13 v Aberdeen; 17 Mar, 1951.
Most Capped Player: Alexander Keillor, 2 (6), Scotland.
Most League Appearances: 343: Martin Allan, 1983-93.
Most League Goals in Season (Individual): 28: Brian Third, Division II; 1972-73.

MONTROSE 1994–95 LEAGUE RECORD

Match No.	Date	Venue	Opponents	Result		H/T Score	Lg. Pos.	Goalscorers	Attendance
1	Aug 13	H	East Stirling	W	2-0	1-0	—	Grant, Craib	537
2	20	A	Albion R	W	4-2	2-1	1	Masson, Haro, Kennedy 2	274
3	27	H	Cowdenbeath	W	2-0	2-0	1	Robertson, McGlashan	584
4	Sept 3	A	Forfar Ath	L	0-1	0-0	2		1077
5	10	H	Ross C	L	0-2	0-1	3		918
6	24	H	Queen's Park	D	1-1	0-1	5	Grant	575
7	Oct 1	A	Arbroath	W	3-0	1-0	2	McGlashan, Kennedy, Stephen	802
8	8	A	Alloa	D	1-1	0-1	3	MacRonald	460
9	15	H	Caledonian Th	W	3-1	0-1	2	Grant, McGlashan, MacRonald	758
10	22	A	East Stirling	W	2-1	0-0	1	Kennedy 2 (1 pen)	631
11	29	A	Cowdenbeath	D	1-1	1-1	2	Kennedy	301
12	Nov 5	H	Albion R	W	4-1	2-0	2	Tindal, McGlashan 2, Kennedy	629
13	12	A	Ross C	W	1-0	0-0	2	Kennedy	1154
14	19	H	Forfar Ath	W	2-0	1-0	1	Kennedy 2	1259
15	26	A	Queen's Park	D	1-1	0-0	1	Haro	443
16	Dec 3	H	Arbroath	W	3-1	1-0	1	McGlashan 3	1085
17	24	H	Alloa	L	1-2	0-2	1	Haro	637
18	Jan 2	H	Cowdenbeath	L	1-2	1-2	—	Masson	452
19	Feb 4	H	Ross C	D	1-1	0-1	4	McGlashan	882
20	14	A	Caledonian Th	W	4-0	0-0	—	Beedie 2, Milne, Haro	851
21	18	H	Queen's Park	D	2-2	0-0	3	Grant, Kennedy	674
22	25	A	Arbroath	L	1-4	1-2	4	McAvoy	951
23	Mar 11	H	Caledonian Th	L	0-1	0-0	5		781
24	15	A	East Stirling	L	0-1	0-0	—		297
25	22	A	Albion R	W	4-1	2-0	—	McGlashan, Haro, Smith 2	187
26	25	H	Forfar Ath	L	1-2	0-1	5	Kennedy	1240
27	23	A	Alloa	W	1-0	0-0	—	McGlashan	416
28	Apr 1	H	Arbroath	W	5-0	4-0	4	McGlashan 2, McMillan (og), Smith, Cooper	1179
29	4	A	Forfar Ath	W	3-1	2-1	—	Smith, Craib, McGlashan	1176
30	11	A	Queen's Park	L	0-1	0-0	—		367
31	15	H	Alloa	D	0-0	0-0	3		649
32	19	A	Ross C	W	3-0	2-0	—	McAvoy, Cooper, Smith	1702
33	22	A	Caledonian Th	W	3-0	2-0	2	McAvoy, McGlashan (pen), Smith	942
34	29	H	East Stirling	W	1-0	0-0	2	McGlashan	858
35	May 6	A	Cowdenbeath	W	4-0	1-0	2	McGl;ashan, Kennedy 3	379
36	13	H	Albion R	W	4-1	3-0	2	Kennedy 2, McGlashan 2	893

Final League Position: 2

Most Goals Overall (Individual): —.

Honours
League Champions: Second Division 1984-85, *Runners-up:* 1990-91. Third Division, *Runners-up:* 1994-95.
Scottish Cup: Quarter-finals 1973, 1976.
League Cup: Semi-finals 1975-76.
B&Q Cup: Semi-finals: 1992-93.
Club colours: Shirt: Royal Blue with white sleeves. Shorts: White with royal blue and red trim. Stockings: White with royal blue and red tops.

Goalscorers: *League (69):* McGlashan 19 (1 pen), Kennedy 17 (1 pen), Smith 6, Haro 5, Grant 4, McAvoy 3, Beedie 2, Cooper 2, Craib 2, MacRonald 2, Masson 2, Milne 1, Robertson 1, Stephen 1, Tindal 1, own goal 1. *Scottish Cup (10):* Kennedy 3 (1 pen), McGlashan 2, MacRonald 2, Masson 1, Milne 1, Stephen 1. *League Cup (1):* Kennedy 1. *B&Q Cup (6):* McGlashan 3, Cooper 1, Kennedy 1 (pen), Stephen 1.

Larter D 36	Robertson I 32	Tindal K 21	Craib M 22	Grant D 28 + 1	Haro M 34	Garden M 7 + 7	Stephen L 6 + 6	McGlashan C 34	Kennedy A 23 + 10	Masson P 32 + 2	Cooper C 24 + 5	Milne C 2 + 11	Taylor D — + 4	MacDonald I 22 + 1	Brown M — + 3	Tosh J 9	MacRonald C 20 + 1	Beedie S 7	McAvoy N 13 + 4	Mailer C 14	Smith S 10 + 1	Match No.
1	2	3	4	5	6	7	8	9	*10*	11	12	14										1
1	2	3	4	5	6	7	8	*9*	10	11	12		14									2
1	2	3	4	5	6	8		9	*10*	11	7	12	14									3
1	2	3	4	5	6	8		9	10	11	7											4
1	2	3	4	5	6		12	9	*10*	11	7	14		8								5
1	2	3		5	6	8	12	9	*10*	11	7		14	4								6
1	3	2		5	6		11	9	*10*	4	7		12	8	14							7
1	2	3			6		11	9	10	4	7			8	14	*5*	12					8
1	2	3		5	*6*	14	8	9	10	4	12			7			11					9
1	2	3		5	6	12		9	10	4	7			8			11					10
1	2	3		5				9	10	4	7			8		6	11					11
1	2	3	8	5	6			9	10	4				7			11					12
1	2	3	8	5	6	12		9	*10*	4		14		7			11					13
1	2	3	8	5	6			9	10	4				7			11					14
1	2	3	8	5	6	12		9	10	4		14		7			11					15
1	2			5	6	12		9	10	4	*7*	14		8			11	3				16
1	2			5	6	8		9	10	3	*7*	12		4			11					17
1	2	3		5	6			9	10	4	*7*	12		8			11					18
1	2	3		5	6	4	12	9	*10*		14			7			11	8				19
1	2	3		5	6		12			14	7	9		8			*11*	4	10			20
1	2	3		5					14	6	7	9		8			*11*	4	10			21
1	2	3		5	6			9	10	14	7	12		*11*				4	8			22
1		2		5	6		3	9	14	4		12		*11*				8	10	7		23
1			2	5	6			9	*10*	4	7				14			3	11	8		24
1			3		6			9	12	4		14		7		5	11		8	2	*10*	25
1			3		6			9	12	4	14			7		5	11		*8*	2	10	26
1	2		8	5	6			9		*4*	7						11		14	3	10	27
1	2		8	5	6			9	12	*4*	7						11		14	3	10	28
1	2		8	5	6			9	12	4	7						*11*		14	3	10	29
1	2		8	5	6			9	12		7						11		4	3	10	30
1	2		8	5	*6*			9	12	4	7						11		14	3	10	31
1	2		8		6		14	*9*	10	4	7					5			11	3	12	32
1	2		8		6		14	*9*	12	4	7					5			11	3	10	33
1	2		8		6			9		4	*7*			14		5			11	3	10	34
1	2		8		6	12		9	14	4	7					5			11	3	*10*	35
1	2		*8*	12	6	14		9	10	4				7		5			11	3		36

MOTHERWELL Premier Division

Year Formed: 1886. *Ground & Address:* Fir Park, Motherwell ML1 2QN. *Telephone:* 01698 261437.
Ground Capacity: total: 13,741 all seated. *Size of Pitch:* 110yd × 75yd.
Chairman: John C. Chapman. *Secretary:* Alan C. Dick. *Commercial Manager:* John Swinburne.
Manager: Alex McLeish. *Assistant Manager:* Andy Watson. *Physio:* John Porteous. *Coach:* Jim Griffin.
Managers since 1975: Ian St. John; Willie McLean; Rodger Hynd; Ally MacLeod; David Hay; Jock Wallace; Bobby Watson, Tommy McLean.
Club Nickname(s): The Well. *Previous Grounds:* Roman Road, Dalziel Park.
Record Attendance: 35,632 v Rangers, Scottish Cup 4th rd replay; 12 Mar, 1952.
Record Transfer Fee received: £1,750,000 for Phil O'Donnell to Celtic, September 1994.
Record Transfer Fee paid: £400,000 for Mitchell Van Der Gaag from PSV Eindhoven, March 1995.
Record Victory: 12-1 v Dundee U, Division II; 23 Jan, 1954.
Record Defeat: 0-8 v Aberdeen, Premier Division; 26 Mar, 1979.
Most Capped Player: George Stevenson, 12, Scotland.
Most League Appearances: 626: Bobby Ferrier, 1918-37.

MOTHERWELL 1994–95 LEAGUE RECORD

Match No.	Date	Venue	Opponents	Result		H/T Score	Lg. Pos.	Goalscorers	Attendance
1	Aug 13	A	Rangers	L	1-2	0-1	—	Coyne (pen)	42,491
2	20	H	Hearts	D	1-1	0-0	7	Coyne	8249
3	27	A	Kilmarnock	W	1-0	1-0	6	Coyne	7388
4	Sept 10	A	Dundee U	D	1-1	0-1	6	Kirk	7440
5	17	H	Hibernian	D	1-1	0-0	5	Shannon	7005
6	24	A	Partick T	D	2-2	0-1	5	Davies, Coyne	4786
7	Oct 1	H	Celtic	D	1-1	0-1	5	Arnott	10,869
8	8	H	Falkirk	W	5-3	2-1	4	Coyne 2, Davies, Arnott 2	6239
9	15	A	Aberdeen	W	3-1	0-1	4	McKinnon, Kirk, Coyne	12,489
10	22	H	Rangers	W	2-1	1-0	3	Arnott 2	11,160
11	29	H	Kilmarnock	W	3-2	1-2	2	Coyne 2, Martin	7436
12	Nov 5	A	Hearts	W	2-1	1-1	2	Shannon, Coyne	8889
13	8	H	Dundee U	D	1-1	0-0	—	Martin	6145
14	19	A	Hibernian	D	2-2	1-2	2	Coyne, Davies	9160
15	26	H	Partick T	W	3-1	3-1	2	Coyne, Davies, Arnott	6893
16	Dec 3	A	Celtic	D	2-2	1-2	2	Coyne 2	21,465
17	10	H	Aberdeen	L	0-1	0-1	2		7020
18	26	A	Falkirk	W	1-0	0-0	—	Shannon	7937
19	31	H	Rangers	L	1-3	0-1	2	McGrillen	11,269
20	Jan 8	H	Hearts	L	1-2	1-1	—	McGrillen	5117
21	13	H	Hibernian	D	0-0	0-0	—		6724
22	17	A	Kilmarnock	L	0-2	0-2	—		7521
23	21	A	Dundee U	L	1-6	1-2	3	Coyne	7062
24	Feb 4	H	Celtic	W	1-0	0-0	3	McKinnon	10,771
25	25	A	Aberdeen	W	2-0	1-0	2	Burns, McKinnon (pen)	10,319
26	Mar 7	H	Falkirk	D	2-2	1-1	—	Lambert, May	6100
27	14	A	Partick T	D	0-0	0-0	—		3525
28	18	H	Dundee U	W	2-1	0-0	2	Burns, Arnott	4457
29	22	A	Hibernian	L	0-2	0-1	—		5395
30	Apr 1	A	Celtic	D	1-1	0-0	2	Coyne	24,047
31	8	H	Partick T	L	1-2	1-1	2	Burns	9631
32	15	A	Falkirk	L	0-3	0-1	2		5756
33	18	H	Aberdeen	W	2-1	1-1	—	McSkimming, Arnott	7155
34	29	A	Rangers	W	2-0	1-0	2	Arnott, McSkimming	43,576
35	May 6	H	Kilmarnock	W	2-0	1-0	2	Arnott, May	7760
36	13	A	Hearts	L	0-2	0-0	2		11,172

Final League Position: 2

Most League Goals in Season (Individual): 52: Willie McFadyen, Division I; 1931-32.
Most Goals Overall (Individual): 283: Hugh Ferguson, 1916-25.

Honours
League Champions: Division I 1931-32. First Division 1981-82, 1984-85. Division II 1953-54, 1968-69; *Runners-up:* Premier Division 1994-95. Division I 1926-27, 1929-30, 1932-33, 1933-34. Division II 1894-95, 1902-03. *Scottish Cup:* 1952, 1991; *Runners-up:* 1931, 1933, 1939, 1951.
League Cup: 1950-51. *Runners-up:* 1954-55 *Scottish Summer Cup:* 1944, 1965.
Club colours: Shirt: Amber with claret hoop and trimmings. Shorts: Claret. Stockings: Amber.

Goalscorers: *League (50):* Coyne 16 (1 pen), Arnott 10, Davies 4, Burns 3, McKinnon 3 (1 pen), Shannon 3, Kirk 2, McGrillen 2, McSkimming 2, Martin 2, May 2, Lambert 1. *Scottish Cup (2):* Burns 2. *League Cup (4):* Burns 1, Coyne 1 (pen), Kirk 1, McCart 1.

Woods S 33	Shannon R 23 + 2	McKinnon R 32	Philliben J 30 + 1	Martin B 32	McCart C 24	Lambert P 36	Davies W 31	Coyne T 30 + 1	O'Donnell P 3	Kirk S 6 + 12	Dolan J 31	Roddie A 4 + 15	Burns A 7 + 7	Arnott D 26 + 1	McGrillen P 2 + 5	McLeish A 2	McSkimming S 10 + 4	Krivokapic M 16	Howie S 3	McMillan S 2 + 1	May E 10	Van Der Gaag M 2	Ritchie I 1	Match No.
1	2	3	4	5	6	7	8	9	10	11														1
1	2		3	5	6	7		9	10	*8*	4	11	14											2
1	2		3	5	6	7	*8*	9	10	12	4	11	14											3
1		3	2	5	6	7	11	9		4	8			*10*	14									4
1	2	3	4	5	6	7	11	9		12	*8*			10	14									5
1	*2*	3	4	5	6	7	11	9		12	8	10		14										6
1	2	3	4	5	6	7	*11*	9		12	8	14		10										7
1	2	3	4	5		7	11	9			8	14		10		6								8
1	2	3	4	5	6	7	11	9		12	*8*	14		10										9
1	2	3	4	5	6	7	*11*	9			8	14		10										10
1	2	3	4	5		7	11	9		12	8			10		6								11
1	2	3	4	5	6	7	11	9		12	*8*	14		10										12
1	2	3	4	5	6	7	*11*	9		12	8	14		10										13
1	2	3	4	5	6	7	11	9		10	8						14							14
1	2	*3*	4	5	6	7	11	9		12	8	14		10										15
1	2	3	4	5	6	7	11	9			8			10										16
1	2	3	4	*5*	6	7	11	9		12	8	14		10										17
1	2	3	4		6	7	11	9						10			8	5						18
1	2	3	4		6	7	11	9		12				*10*	14		8	5						19
1	2	3	4		6	7	11	9				14			10		*8*	5						20
	2	3		5	6	7	10	9		12	8				11			4	1					21
	2	3		5	6	7	*11*	9		10	8						14	4	1					22
	2	3		5		7	11	9		10	8	14			12		6	4	1					23
1		3	2	5	6	7	11	9			8			*10*	12			4		14				24
1	12	3	5		6	7					8	14	*9*	10			11	4			2			25
1		3	*2*	5	6	7					8	14	9	10				4			11			26
1		3		5	6	7	11				8		9	10				4			2			27
1			6	5		7	11				8	12	9	10				4		3	2			28
1	14		6	5		7	11	12			8		9	*10*				4		3	2			29
1		3		5		7	11	9			8		12	10			14	4			*2*	6		30
1		3	14	5		7	11	9			8	2	10				12	4				*6*		31
1	2	3	6	5		7		9			8		12	10			11	4						32
1		3	6	5		7		9			8	14	12	10			11	*4*			2			33
1		3	4	5		7	11	9			8		14	*10*			6				2			34
1		3	4	5		7	11	9			8		14	*10*			6				2			35
1		3	4	5		7	11					12	9	10			6				2		8	36

PARTICK THISTLE Premier Division

Year Formed: 1876. *Ground & Address:* Firhill Park, 80 Firhill Rd, Glasgow G20 7BA. *Telephone:* 0141 945 4811.
Ground Capacity: total: 20,676. seated: 2906. *Size of Pitch:* 110yd × 74yd.
Chairman: James Oliver. *Secretary:* Robert Reid. *Commercial Manager:* Thomas Dickson.
Manager: John Lambie. *Assistant Manager:* Gerry Collins. *Physio:* Frank Ness.
Managers since 1975: R. Auld; P. Cormack; B. Rooney; R. Auld; D. Johnstone; W. Lamont; S. Clark. *Club Nickname(s):* The Jags. *Previous Grounds:* Jordanvale Park; Muirpark; Inchview; Meadowside Park.
Record Attendance: 49,838 v Rangers, Division I; 18 Feb, 1922.
Record Transfer Fee received: £200,000 for Mo Johnston to Watford.
Record Transfer Fee paid: £85,000 for Andy Murdoch from Celtic (Feb 1991).
Record Victory: 16-0 v Royal Albert, Scottish Cup 1st rd; 17 Jan, 1931.
Record Defeat: 0-10 v Queen's Park, Scottish Cup; 3 Dec, 1881.
Most Capped Player: Alan Rough, 51 (53), Scotland.
Most League Appearances: 410: Alan Rough, 1969-82.
Most League Goals in Season (Individual): 41: Alec Hair, Division I; 1926-27.
Most Goals Overall (Individual): —.

PARTICK THISTLE 1994–95 LEAGUE RECORD

Match No.	*Date*	*Venue*	*Opponents*	*Result*	*H/T Score*	*Lg. Pos.*	*Goalscorers*	*Attendance*
1	Aug 13	H	Kilmarnock	W 2-0	2-0	—	McWilliams, English	6606
2	20	H	Rangers	L 0-2	0-1	5		14,361
3	27	A	Falkirk	L 1-2	1-0	7	Grant	5402
4	Sept 10	H	Celtic	L 1-2	0-2	8	Grant	14,439
5	17	A	Aberdeen	D 1-1	0-0	7	Charnley	10,425
6	24	H	Motherwell	D 2-2	1-0	9	Grant, McDonald	4786
7	Oct 1	A	Hibernian	L 0-3	0-2	10		7083
8	8	H	Hearts	L 0-1	0-1	10		5076
9	15	A	Dundee U	W 1-0	0-0	9	Cameron	6687
10	22	A	Kilmarnock	L 0-2	0-0	10		7023
11	29	H	Falkirk	L 1-2	1-2	10	Grant	4215
12	Nov 5	A	Rangers	L 0-3	0-0	10		43,696
13	9	A	Celtic	D 0-0	0-0	—		21,462
14	19	H	Aberdeen	W 2-1	0-1	10	Craig, Gibson	3795
15	26	A	Motherwell	L 1-3	1-3	10	Cameron	6893
16	Dec 3	H	Hibernian	D 2-2	1-0	9	Foster, English	4667
17	26	A	Hearts	L 0-3	0-0	—		8920
18	31	H	Kilmarnock	D 2-2	2-1	10	McDonald 2	5799
19	Jan 7	H	Rangers	D 1-1	0-0	10	Taylor	17,298
20	14	A	Aberdeen	L 1-3	0-1	10	Pittman	9833
21	17	A	Falkirk	W 3-1	1-0	—	Dinnie, Foster, McWilliams	3958
22	21	H	Celtic	D 0-0	0-0	10		11,904
23	Feb 4	A	Hibernian	W 2-1	1-1	10	Turner, McDonald	7760
24	25	A	Dundee U	L 0-2	0-0	10		7227
25	Mar 7	H	Dundee U	W 2-0	0-0	—	Smith, Foster	2126
26	11	H	Aberdeen	D 2-2	0-2	10	Pittman, Turner	6886
27	14	H	Motherwell	D 0-0	0-0	—		3525
28	Apr 1	H	Hibernian	D 2-2	0-1	10	Foster 2 (1 pen)	4041
29	4	H	Hearts	W 3-1	0-1	—	Pittman, McDonald, McWilliams	4526
30	8	A	Motherwell	W 2-1	1-1	8	Cameron, Craig	9631
31	15	A	Hearts	W 1-0	0-0	8	Dinnie	9007
32	18	H	Dundee U	L 1-3	1-1	—	Pittman	4962
33	29	A	Kilmarnock	D 0-0	0-0	8		9201
34	May 2	A	Celtic	W 3-1	1-1	—	Grant, Foster 2	18,963
35	6	H	Falkirk	D 0-0	0-0	7		5927
36	13	A	Rangers	D 1-1	0-1	8	Taylor	45,280

Final League Position: 8

Honours
League Champions: First Division 1975-76. Division II 1896-97, 1899-1900, 1970-71; *Runners-up:* First Division 1991-92. Division II 1901-02.
Scottish Cup Winners: 1921; *Runners-up:* 1930.
League Cup Winners: 1971-72; *Runners-up:* 1953-54, 1956-57, 1958-59.

European: *UEFA Cup:* 10 matches (*Fairs Cup:* 1963-64. *UEFA Cup:* 1972-73, 1994-95).
Club colours: Shirt: Red and Yellow broad vertical stripes. Shorts: Black. Stockings: Yellow with Red turnover.

Goalscorers: *League (40):* Foster 7 (1 pen), Grant 5, McDonald 5, Pittman 4, Cameron 3, McWilliams 3, Craig 2, Dinnie 2, English 2, Taylor 2, Turner 2, Charnley 1, Gibson 1, Smith 1. *Scottish Cup (1):* Jamieson 1. *League Cup (5):* Charnley 3 (1 pen), Jamieson 1, Taylor 1.

Nelson C 13	Byrne D 11 + 1	Law R 2 + 3	Jamieson W 15	Tierney G 4 + 1	McWilliams D 27 + 2	Taylor A 17 + 6	Craig A 30	Grant R 14 + 9	English I 6 + 5	Charnley J 19 + 1	Cameron I 27 + 7	Smith T 8 + 6	Dinnie A 23 + 2	Docherty S — + 1	Pittman S 27	Watson G 29	Gibson A 9 + 2	McKee K 16 + 1	McDonald R 22 + 3	Murdoch A 2	Walker N 20	Milne C 3 + 1	Foster W 15	Welsh S 20	Turner T 15	Gray D 1 + 1	Cairns M 1	Eli R — + 2	Ayton S — + 1	*Match No.*
1	2	3	4	5	6	7	8	9	10	11																				1
1	2	3	4	5	6	7	*8*	9	10	11	12	14																		2
1	2		4	*5*	6	7		9	10	11	8	12	3	14																3
1	2		5		6	11	8	9				12	7		3	4	10													4
1	2		5		6		8	*9*		11	7	12	3			4	10	14												5
1			5		6		8	9		11	14	10	*2*		3	4	12		7											6
	2		5		6		8	12	*10*	11	14	9			3	4			7	1										7
	2		5		6	12		9		11	*10*	8			3	4	14		7	1										8
1	2		5		6	8		14	10		11		12		3	4	9		*7*											9
1	2	14	5					12	*10*		11	6	8		3	4	9		7											10
1		14	5		6	8		9	12		11		10		*3*	4	7	2												11
1			5		11		8		12	14	10		6		3	4	9	*2*	7											12
1			5		6		8	*9*	14	11	7				3	4	10	2												13
1			5		6		8			11	10		3			4	9	2	7											14
1	12		5		6		8		14	11	10		3			4	9	2	*7*											15
	4				6		8		12	11	10		3					2	7		1	5	9							16
		14					8	12		11	10		6			4		2	7		1	3	*9*	5						17
	2					14	8	12			11		6		3	4			7		1		*9*	5	10					18
					9	11	8			10	12		2		3	4			7		1			5	6					19
					9	11	8			*10*	12		2		3	4			7		1			5	6	14				20
					9	11	8			10	12		2		3	4					1		7	5	6					21
					9	11	8			10	12		2		3	4			14		1		7	5	6					22
					14	11	8				10		2		3	4			7		1	12	*9*	5	6					23
				14	12	11	8				*10*		2		3	4			7				9	5	6		1			24
					11		8				10	14			3	4		2	*7*		1		9	5	6					25
					11		8	14			10	12			3	4		2	*7*		1		9	5	6					26
					11		8	7			10				3	4		2	14		1			*9*	5	6				27
					11	12	8				10				3	4		2	7		1		9	5	6			14		28
					11	12	8				10				3	4		2	7		1		9	5	6			14		29
					11	12	8	14			10				3	4		2	7		1		9	5	6					30
					9	11	8	12			10		14		3	4		*2*	7		1			5	6					31
					9	11	8	7			10		2		3	4			12		1			5	6					32
						6	8	9		11	10	7	2		3			4			1			5						33
						14	8	9		11	10	6	4		3			*2*			1		7	5						34
						6	8	9		11	10	2	4		3						1		7	5						35
				5		11		14			10	8	3			4			7		1	*2*	9	6					12	36

QUEEN OF THE SOUTH Second Division

Year Formed: 1919. *Ground & Address:* Palmerston Park, Terregles St, Dumfries DG2 9BA. *Telephone and Fax:* 01387 254853.
Ground Capacity: total: 8352. seated: 3470. *Size of Pitch:* 112yd × 72yd.
Chairman: Norman Blount. *Secretary:* Mrs Doreen Alcorn. *Commercial Manager:* Robert McKinnel.
Manager: William McLaren. *Physio:* Derek Kelly.
Managers since 1975: M. Jackson; G. Herd; A. Busby; R. Clark; M. Jackson; D. Wilson; W. McLaren; F. McGarvey; A. MacLeod. *Club Nickname(s):* The Doonhamers. *Previous Grounds:* None.
Record Attendance: 24,500 v Hearts, Scottish Cup 3rd rd; 23 Feb, 1952.
Record Transfer Fee received: £100,000 for K. McMinn to Rangers (1985).
Record Transfer Fee paid: —.
Record Victory: 11-1 v Stranraer, Scottish Cup 1st rd; 16 Jan, 1932.
Record Defeat: 2-10 v Dundee, Division I; 1 Dec, 1962.
Most Capped Player: Billy Houliston, 3, Scotland.
Most League Appearances: 619: Allan Ball; 1962-83.
Most League Goals in Season (Individual): 33: Jimmy Gray, Division II; 1927-28.

QUEEN OF THE SOUTH 1994–95 LEAGUE RECORD

Match No.	*Date*		*Venue*	*Opponents*	*Result*		*H/T Score*	*Lg. Pos.*	*Goalscorers*	*Atten-dance*
1	Aug	13	H	Dumbarton	W	4-1	1-0	—	Bryce 2 (1 pen), McGuire, McLaren	1389
2		20	H	Clyde	L	1-2	0-1	6	Bryce	1435
3		27	A	Berwick R	L	0-1	0-0	8		610
4	Sept	3	H	East Fife	L	0-2	0-1	8		1412
5		10	A	Meadowbank T	W	1-0	0-0	7	McLaren	279
6		24	H	Brechin C	L	0-2	0-0	8		1032
7	Oct	1	A	Stirling Albion	L	0-3	0-0	9		697
8		8	A	Stenhousemuir	D	0-0	0-0	8		403
9		15	H	Morton	W	3-0	3-0	8	Mallan 2, Kennedy	1126
10		22	A	Dumbarton	D	0-0	0-0	8		725
11		29	H	Berwick R	W	5-4	3-1	7	Bryce, McFarlane 2, Mallan, Rowe	1298
12	Nov	5	A	Clyde	D	2-2	2-0	8	Mallan, McLaren	1112
13		12	H	Meadowbank T	D	0-0	0-0	8		1418
14		19	A	East Fife	L	1-3	1-2	8	Mallan	699
15		26	A	Brechin C	W	1-0	0-0	8	Bryce	406
16	Dec	3	H	Stirling Albion	L	0-1	0-1	8		1197
17		26	H	Stenhousemuir	L	1-2	0-1	—	McLaren	1437
18		31	A	Morton	D	1-1	0-0	8	Jackson	2112
19	Jan	10	A	Berwick R	L	1-3	1-1	—	Campbell D	448
20		14	H	Dumbarton	D	0-0	0-0	8		1066
21		21	A	Clyde	W	4-3	3-1	8	McFarlane, Mallan, Campbell D, Kennedy	998
22	Feb	4	A	Meadowbank T	W	2-1	1-0	8	Campbell D, Mallan	265
23		14	H	East Fife	D	3-3	1-1	—	Gibb (og), Campbell D, Bryce	890
24		18	H	Brechin C	L	0-1	0-	8		1002
25		25	A	Stirling Albion	D	1-1	1-0	8	Campbell D	528
26	Mar	11	H	Morton	W	1-0	1-0	8	Bryce	1505
27		18	H	Meadowbank T	L	2-3	0-2	8	Mallan, Campbell D	705
28		21	A	Stenhousemuir	D	2-2	1-1	—	Bryce, Hetherington	454
29		25	A	East Fife	L	1-3	1-0	8	Mallan	594
30	Apr	1	H	Stirling Albion	L	1-3	0-1	8	Telfer	1056
31		8	A	Brechin C	W	2-0	1-0	8	Campbell D 2	389
32		15	H	Stenhousemuir	L	1-2	0-2	8	Orr	1230
33		22	A	Morton	D	0-0	0-0	8		2395
34		29	A	Dumbarton	D	2-2	1-*1	8	Marsland (og), McKeown D	1369
35	May	6	H	Berwick R	W	2-0	1-0	8	Ramsay, Campbell D	1061
36		13	H	Clyde	W	1-0	1-0	7	McFarlane	1502

Final League Position: 7

Most Goals Overall (Individual): 109, Andrew Thomson, 1989-94.

Honours
League Champions: Division II 1950-51; *Runners-up:* Division II 1932-33, 1961-62, 1974-75. Second Division 1980-81, 1985-86.
Scottish Cup: —.
League Cup: —.
Club colours: Shirt: Royal blue. Shorts: White. Stockings: Royal blue with white tops.

Goalscorers: *League (46):* Campbell D 9, Mallan 9, Bryce 8 (1 pen), McFarlane 4, McLaren 4, Kennedy 2, Hetherington 1, Jackson 1, McGuire 1, McKeown D 1, Orr 1, Ramsay 1, Rowe 1, Telfer 1, own goals 2. *Scottish Cup (2):* Bell 1, Bryce 1. League Cup (2): Bryce 1, McLaren 1. *B&Q Cup (0)*

Purdie D 24 + 1	Mills D 3	Hetherington K 18 + 3	McKeown D 34	Kennedy D 31 + 1	McFarlane A 28 + 1	McGuire D 5 + 2	Cochrane G 2	McLaren J 15 + 8	Bryce T 32 + 1	Mallan S 34 + 1	Sermanni P 1 + 2	Brown J 16 + 5	McKeown B 30 + 1	Ramsay S 22 + 4	Jackson D 18 + 7	Adams M 1	Leslie S 4 + 2	Campbell C 24	Rowe G 4	McQueen J 12 + 1	Bell A 3 + 6	Campbell D 19	Cook A — + 1	Telfer G 3 + 1	Kane M 1	Orr N 7	Cody S 5 + 1	*Match No.*
1	2	3	4	5	6	7	8	9	10	11	12																	1
1			2	5	6	7	8	9	10	11	12	3	4															2
1	5	2	3	8	6			9	7	11		12	4	*10*	14													3
1	2	3	4	5	6			7	10	12		14		8		9	11											4
1		2	3	5				9	7	11	8		4	6			10											5
1		2	5	7	6	14		*9*	8	11		3	12	10				4										6
1			3	5	6	14		*10*	8	9		12	2	11	7			4										7
1			3	5	8	*11*		14	9	10		12	2	6	7			4										8
1			3	5	6			9	7	10			4	8	11				2									9
1			3	5	8			7	9	10			6		11			4	2									10
1			3	5	8	*11*		14	7	10			6	12	9			4	2									11
1			3	5	6			*10*	7	11			8	12	9		14	4	2									12
1			2	5	8	11		12	7	10		3	4	6	9													13
1		14	2	5	8			10	7	11		3	4	6	9		*12*											14
1		2	3	5	6			10	7	11			4		9		8											15
1		2	3	5	6			11		10		14	8		*9*		7	4		15								16
1		5	3	8	11			7	10				2	14	12			4			*6*	9						17
		5	3	8	6			*10*		11			2	12	7			4		1	14	9						18
			3	6	10					11		5	2	8	7			4		1		9						19
			3	5	8				7	11		2		6	10			4		1	12	9						20
			3	8	7				12	10		5	2	6	11			4		1		9						21
			3	6				12	10	11		5	2		7			4		1	8	9						22
			3	8					7	11		5	*2*	6	10			4		1	12	9	14					23
			3	8				14	7	11		5	2	6	*10*			4		1	12	9						24
1			3	8					7	11		5	2	6				4			12	9		10				25
1		12	3	8					7	11		5	2	6				4				9		10				26
1		12	3	8					7	11		5	2	6	14			4				9		*10*				27
		5	2	*7*	14				9	11		3	8	6	12			4		1		10						28
		2		5	8				7	11		3			9			4		1	12	10			6			29
		5	3		6			14	9	*11*								4		1	7	10		12		2	8	30
		5	3		6			14	9	11			2					4		1		7				8	*10*	31
15		5	3		10				7	11			2		12			4		*1*		9				8	6	32
1		5	3		4				10	11			2	6								9				8	7	33
1		2	3	12	6				10	11			*7*	5	14							9				4	8	34
1		2	3	8	6				11	9			5	10								7				4	12	35
1		2		5	10			14	9	*11*		3	7	8	12			6								4		36

QUEEN'S PARK Third Division

Year Formed: 1867. *Ground & Address:* Hampden Park, Mount Florida, Glasgow G42 9BA. *Telephone:* 0141 632 1275.
Ground Capacity: total: 38,335 all seated. *Size of Pitch:* 115yd × 75yd.
President: Malcolm D.Mackay. *Secretary:* Alistair Mackay. *Physio:* R.C.Findlay. *Coach:* Hugh McCann.
Coaches since 1975: D.McParland, J.Gilroy, E Hunter. *Club Nickname(s):* The Spiders. *Previous Grounds:* 1st Hampden (Recreation Ground); (Titwood Park was used as an interim measure between 1st & 2nd Hampdens); 2nd Hampden (Cathkin); 3rd Hampden.
Record Attendance: 95,772 v Rangers, Scottish Cup, 18 Jan, 1930.
Record for Ground: 149,547 Scotland v England, 1937.
Record Transfer Fee received: Not applicable due to amateur status.
Record Transfer Fee paid: Not applicable due to amateur status.
Record Victory: 16-0 v St. Peters, Scottish Cup 1st rd; 29 Aug, 1885.
Record Defeat: 0-9 v Motherwell, Division I; 26 Apr, 1930.
Most Capped Player: Walter Arnott, 15, Scotland.
Most League Appearances: 473: J. B. McAlpine.

QUEEN'S PARK 1994–95 LEAGUE RECORD

Match No.	Date		Venue	Opponents	Result		H/T Score	Lg. Pos.	Goalscorers	Attendance
1	Aug	13	H	Forfar Ath	L	1-2	1-1	—	Orr G	457
2		20	A	Caledonian Th	W	4-0	2-0	5	Orr G, Maxwell 2, Graham	1565
3		27	H	Albion R	W	2-1	0-1	3	Rodden, Graham	443
4	Sept	3	A	Arbroath	D	1-1	0-1	4	Orr G	535
5		10	H	Cowdenbeath	L	0-3	0-0	8		509
6		24	A	Montrose	D	1-1	1-0	7	McPhee	575
7	Oct	1	H	Ross C	W	3-1	2-1	6	McCormick, Orr G, Fitzpatrick	729
8		8	A	East Stirling	L	2-3	1-1	7	Maxwell, McPhee	464
9		15	H	Alloa	L	0-1	0-1	7		520
10		22	A	Forfar Ath	L	0-2	0-1	8		534
11		29	A	Albion R	L	2-3	1-1	8	McGoldrick, Brodie	345
12	Nov	5	H	Caledonian Th	L	0-2	0-0	8		692
13		12	A	Cowdenbeath	L	0-2	0-0	8		281
14		19	H	Arbroath	L	0-4	0-2	8		407
15		26	H	Montrose.	D	1-1	0-0	8	Caven	443
16	Dec	3	A	Ross C	L	0-2	0-1	8		1322
17		26	H	East Stirling	L	2-3	0-2	—	McGoldrick 2	502
18		31	A	Alloa	W	3-2	2-2	8	Callan, Edgar, Maxwell	541
19	Jan	2	H	Albion R	D	0-0	0-0	—		705
20		14	A	Forfar Ath	L	0-3	0-0	8		501
21		21	H	Caledonian Th	W	4-1	2-0	8	Maxwell, Orr G, McPhee, Rodden	456
22	Feb	4	H	Cowdenbeath	W	1-0	0-0	8	Caven	477
23		15	A	Arbroath	L	1-3	1-1	—	Orr G	347
24		18	A	Montrose	D	2-2	0-0	8	Callan, Graham	674
25		25	H	Ross C	L	1-2	1-0	8	McCormick	753
26	Mar	11	H	Alloa	W	2-1	2-0	9	McCormick, McPhee	506
27		18	A	Cowdenbeath	W	3-1	1-1	9	McPhee, McCormick 2	137
28		25	H	Arbroath	L	2-3	1-1	9	McPhee, McCormick	616
29	Apr	1	A	Ross C	L	0-1	0-1	9		1469
30		11	H	Montrose	W	1-0	0-0	—	Kerr	367
31		15	H	East Stirling	W	1-0	1-0	9	Sneddon (og)	480
32		18	A	East Stirling	L	2-3	2-2	—	McCormick, Maxwell	382
33		22	A	Alloa	W	1-0	0-0	9	Kerr	421
34		29	H	Forfar Ath	L	0-2	0-1	9		557
35	May	6	A	Albion R	W	2-0	1-0	8	Orr G, McPhee	337
36		13	A	Caledonian Th	D	1-1	1-0	8	McCormick	782

Final League Position: 8

Most League Goals in Season (Individual): 30: William Martin, Division I; 1937-38.
Most Goals Overall (Individual): 163: J. B. McAlpine.

Honours
League Champions: Division II 1922-23. B Division 1955-56. Second Division 1980-81.
Scottish Cup Winners: 1874, 1875, 1876, 1880, 1881, 1882, 1884, 1886, 1890, 1893; *Runners-up:* 1892, 1900.
League Cup: —.
FA Cup runners-up: 1884, 1885.
Club colours: Shirt: White and black hoops. Shorts: White. Stockings: White with black hoops.

Goalscorers: *League (46):* McCormick 8, McPhee 7, Orr G 7, Maxwell 6, Graham 3, McGoldrick 3, Callan 2, Caven 2, Kerr 2, Rodden 2, Brodie 1, Edgar 1, Fitzpatrick 1, own goal 1. *Scottish Cup (3):* Caven 1, Orr G 1, Rodden 1. *League Cup (2):* Maxwell 1, Orr G 1. *B&Q Cup (0)*

Moonie D 15 + 1	Kavanagh J 9	Stevenson C 1	Kerr G 27 + 2	Maxwell I 34	Orr G 28	Brodie D 8 + 3	Fitzpatrick S 15	Edgar S 8 + 7	Rodden J 10 + 7	Graham D 29	Bradley R 4 + 3	McPhee B 22 + 11	Orr J 34	McCormick S 18 + 4	Elder G 19	Lynch M 6 + 1	Caven R 22 + 3	McGoldrick K 16 + 5	Chalmers J 21	Callan D 12 + 3	Ferguson P 10 + 3	Matchett J 7	Campbell S 1	Smith C 2 + 3	McFarlane R 1	Wilson D 10 + 1	Fraser R 7	Match No.
1	2	3	4	5	6	7	8	9	*10*	11	12	14																1
1	3		4	5	6		7	9	10	8	11	12	2															2
1	3		4	5	6	7	8		11	10			2	9														3
1	3		7	5	6		*8*	14	10	9			2	11	4	12												4
1	3		8	5	6	7		14	*10*	11		12	2	9	4													5
1	3		4	5	6	7	8					10	2	9		11												6
1	3		4	5	6	7	8	12		11		10	2	9			14											7
1	3		4	5		7	6		12	11		10	2	9			8											8
1	2			5	8	9	*6*			3		11	4	10			7	14										9
1				5		12	2		9	3	8	10	4			6	7	11										10
				5		14	2		*10*	3	8	9	4			6	7	11	1									11
				3			5		14	*10*		9	2	7	4	6	8	11	1	12								12
				3			5	7				12	2	9	4	8	10	11	1	6								13
				3			5	7	14			9	2	12	4	*8*	10	11	1	6								14
15			4	3			6	*8*		10		9	2	14	5		7	11	*1*	12								15
			4	3			6	8		10		9	2	14	5		7	11	1									16
			14	3	7	*11*		12	9	6	4		2		5		8	10	1									17
			4	3	*7*			11		6		14	2		5		10	9	1	8								18
			4	3	6	12		10	9			11	2		5		8		1	7								19
			4	5	7				12		14	*9*	2				10		1	8	3	6	11					20
			4	5	9				14	6		12	2				10	11	1	7	3			*8*				21
			4	5	7				14	6		12	2				10	*9*	1	8	3			11				22
			4	5	11				12	*8*		9	2	14			10		1	7	3	6						23
			12	5	9				11	6		14	2				8	*10*	1	7	3				4			24
			4	5	9					8	14	12	2	*11*				10	1	7	3	6						25
			3	5	9					6		11	2	10	4		8		1							7		26
			11	6	7					3		10	4	9	5		8	14	1					12		2		27
			11	6	7					3		*10*	4	9	5		8	14	1					12		2		28
			4	6	7			14		3		10			5			*9*	1	2		11				12	8	29
1			8	6	9			12		3		10	4		5						14	11				2	*7*	30
1			8	6	9			12		3		10	4		5						14	*11*				2	7	31
1			11	6	7					3		10	4	9	5						14					2	*8*	32
1			11	6	7							10	4	9	5		14	12			3					2	*8*	33
1			*11*	6	7							10	4	9	5		14	12			3					2	8	34
			5		10					3		14	4	9			8	11	1	12	6					2	*7*	35
					10					3		12	4	9			8	11	1	7	6	*5*		14		2		36

RAITH ROVERS Premier Division

Year Formed: 1883. *Ground & Address:* Stark's Park, Pratt St, Kirkcaldy KY1 1SA. *Telephone & Fax:* 01592 263514.
Ground Capacity: total: 9200. seated: 3040. *Size of Pitch:* 113yd × 67yd.
Chairman: Alex Penman. *Company Secretary:* C.Cant. *General Manager:* W.McPhee.
Manager: Jimmy Nicholl. *Assistant Manager and Coach:* Martin Harvey. *Physio:* Gerry Docherty. *Reserve Coach:* Derek Smith and Jimmy Thomson.
Managers since 1975: R. Paton; A. Matthew; W. McLean; G. Wallace; R. Wilson; F. Connor. *Club Nickname(s):* Rovers.
Previous Grounds: Robbie's Park.
Record Attendance: 31,306 v Hearts, Scottish Cup 2nd rd; 7 Feb, 1953.
Record Transfer Fee received: £250,000 for Craig Brewster to Dundee U (Aug 1993).
Record Transfer Fee paid: £100,000 for Alastair Graham from Motherwell (Sept 1993).
Record Victory: 10-1 v Coldstream, Scottish Cup 2nd rd; 13 Feb, 1954.
Record Defeat: 2-11 v Morton, Division II; 18 Mar, 1936.
Most Capped Player: David Morris, 6, Scotland.
Most League Appearances: 430: Willie McNaught.

RAITH ROVERS 1994–95 LEAGUE RECORD

Match No.	Date	Venue	Opponents	Result		H/T Score	Lg. Pos.	Goalscorers	Attendance
1	Aug 13	H	St Johnstone	D	1-1	0-1	—	Cameron	4374
2	20	H	Hamilton A	D	1-1	1-1	6	Graham	2825
3	27	A	Dunfermline Ath	L	0-1	0-0	8		7373
4	Sept 3	H	Clydebank	D	1-1	1-0	8	Cameron	2861
5	10	A	Stranraer	D	0-0	0-0	8		1078
6	24	A	St Mirren	W	2-1	1-1	6	Crawford, Graham	2967
7	Oct 1	H	Ayr U	W	3-0	1-0	4	Crawford, Dalziel 2 (1 pen)	2854
8	8	A	Airdrieonians	D	0-0	0-0	5		2096
9	15	H	Dundee	D	1-1	1-0	5	Cameron	3834
10	22	A	St Johnstone	L	1-3	0-1	6	Dalziel	3926
11	29	H	Dunfermline Ath	L	2-5	2-2	5	Wilson 2	5965
12	Nov 5	A	Hamilton A	W	3-0	0-0	5	Dalziel, Crawford 2	1112
13	12	H	Stranraer	W	4-2	2-0	4	Dalziel 3, Graham	2556
14	19	A	Clydebank	W	3-0	1-0	4	Dalziel, Graham, Narey	1002
15	Dec 3	A	Ayr U	D	1-1	0-1	4	Dalziel	2216
16	6	H	St Mirren	D	1-1	1-1	—	Dalziel	4084
17	10	A	Dundee	L	1-2	0-0	4	Dalziel	3493
18	26	H	Airdrieonians	W	3-2	2-1	—	Cameron, Dalziel, Sinclair	4338
19	31	H	St Johnstone	W	2-0	1-0	4	Broddle, Dalziel	4973
20	Jan 7	H	Hamilton A	W	2-0	1-0	4	Sinclair, Cameron	3130
21	11	A	Dunfermline Ath	W	1-0	0-0	—	Graham	8457
22	14	H	Clydebank	W	1-0	0-0	4	Dennis	3129
23	24	A	Stranraer	W	4-2	1-1	—	Wilson 2, Crawford, Dalziel	769
24	Feb 4	H	Ayr U	W	2-1	1-0	4	Sinclair, Crawford	2799
25	11	A	St Mirren	W	2-1	2-0	2	Crawford 2	2516
26	25	H	Dundee	D	0-0	0-0	3		5885
27	Mar 6	A	Airdrieonians	W	2-1	0-0	—	Dair, Graham	1726
28	18	H	Stranraer	D	1-1	1-0	2	Dalziel	2197
29	Apr 1	A	Ayr U	W	1-0	1-0	3	Kirkwood	1995
30	4	A	Clydebank	W	2-1	0-0	—	Murdoch (og), Crawford	1261
31	8	H	St Mirren	W	2-1	2-1	1	Cameron 2	3669
32	15	H	Airdrieonians	L	0-1	0-1	2		4494
33	22	A	Dundee	W	2-0	0-0	1	Wilson, Crawford	7849
34	29	A	St Johnstone	W	2-1	0-0	1	Preston (og), Crawford	5124
35	May 6	H	Dunfermline Ath	D	0-0	0-0	1		6361
36	13	A	Hamilton A	D	0-0	0-0	1		5333

Final League Position: 1

Most League Goals in Season (Individual): 38: Norman Haywood, Division II; 1937-38.
Most Goals Overall (Individual): 154: Gordon Dalziel (League), 1987-94.

Honours
League Champions: First Division: 1992-93, 1994-95. Division II 1907-08, 1909-10 (shared), 1937-38, 1948-49; *Runners-up:* Division II 1908-09, 1926-27, 1966-67. Second Division 1975-76, 1977-78, 1986-87.
Scottish Cup Runners-up: 1913. *League Cup Winners: (Coca-Cola Cup):* 1994-95.*Runners-up:* 1948-49.
Club colours: Shirt: Navy blue, white trim. Shorts: White. Stockings: White.

Goalscorers: *League (54):* Dalziel 15 (1 pen), Crawford 11, Cameron 7, Graham 6, Wilson 5, Sinclair 3, Broddle 1, Dair 1, Dennis 1, Kirkwood 1, Narey 1, own goals 2. *Scottish Cup (4):* Cameron 1, Crawford 1, Graham 1, Rowbotham 1. *League Cup (14):* Graham 5, Cameron 4, Dalziel 2, Crawford 1, Dennis 1, Lennon 1. *B&Q Cup (3):* Cameron 1, Crawford 1, Dalziel 1.

Thomson S 35	Rowbotham J 14 + 6	Kirkwood D 9 + 10	Coyle R 9	Dennis S 26	Sinclair D 31 + 1	Lennon D 19 + 1	Dalziel G 25 + 6	Graham A 25 + 2	Cameron C 33 + 2	Dair J 12 + 6	Crawford S 27 + 4	Raeside R 9 + 1	Broddle J 26 + 2	McAnespie S 33 + 1	Redford I 11 + 1	Narey D 21	Wilson B 14 + 12	Nicholl J 13	Allan R 1	McMillan I — + 1	Rougier A 3 + 1	Match No.
1	2	3	4	*5*	6	7	8	9	10	11	12	14										1
1	2		4		6	7	8	9	10	*11*	12	5	3	14								2
1			4		5	7	12	9	8	10	11		3	2	6							3
1	4				6	7	8	9	10		12		3	2	11	5						4
1	*4*	12			6	7	8	9	10				3	2	11	5	14					5
1	4			5		7	12	9	10	*11*	8		3	2	6		14					6
1				5	6	4	12	9	10	11	8		3	2				7				7
1		12		5	6	*4*	8	9	10		11		3	2			14	7				8
1	14			5	6	7	*8*	9	10	12	11		3	2		4						9
1		7		5	4		8	9	10	*11*	12		3	2		6	14					10
		14		5	4	7	12	9	10		8		3	2	*6*		11		1			11
1		12		5	4		*8*	9	10	14	11		3	2		6	7					12
1	14			5		4	8	*9*	10	12	11		3	2		6	7					13
1	4			*5*			8	9	10	12	11		3	2	7	6				14		14
1	12	14		5	4		8		10		9		3	2	7	6	*11*					15
1	12	14		5	4		*8*		10		9		3	2	7	6	11					16
1	4				6		8		10		9		3	2	11	5	12	7				17
1				5	12		8	9	10		11		3	2	6	4		7				18
1		12		5	4		8	9	10		*11*		3	2	7	6	14					19
1		11		5	4		8	9	10				*3*	2		6	14	7				20
1	3	11		5	6		*8*	9	10					2		4	14	7				21
1	3			5		4	*8*		10	14	9			2		6	11	7				22
1		12			4	10	8				9	5	3	2		6	11	7				23
1	14		*4*	5	7	10	8	12	9			6	3	2			11					24
1			4	5	8	11		9	14		10	6	3	2			*7*					25
1	3		4	5	6		12	9	*8*	11	10		14	2			7					26
1	3			5	6	4		9	8	11	10			2			7					27
1	3	2			5		8	9	6		*10*					4	14	7			11	28
1	3	10	4	5	11			14	12	*7*	9	6		2							8	29
1	3	*7*	4	5	6	10		8	11		9			2			14					30
1		3	4	5	6	11		9	7		*10*		14	2			12				8	31
1		3		5	6	4	12	9	8	*11*	10			2	14			7				32
1		12			4		8		10	14	9	5	3	2		6	*11*	7				33
1	12				6		8		10		9	*5*	3	2		4	11	7			14	34
1		14			6	12	*8*		10	11	9	5	3	2		4	*7*					35
1				5	11		8		10	*9*		6	3	2		4	14	7				36

RANGERS — Premier Division

Year Formed: 1873. *Ground & Address:* Ibrox Stadium, Edminston Drive, Glasgow G51 2XD. *Telephone:* 0141 427 8500. *Fax:* 0141 427 2676.
Ground Capacity: total: 44,500. seated: 36,500. *Size of Pitch:* 115yd × 75yd.
Chairman: David Murray. *Secretary:* R. C. Ogilvie. *Commercial Manager:* Bob Reilly.
Manager: Walter Smith. *Assistant Manager:* Archie Knox. *Physio:* Bill Collins. *Coach:* Davie Dodds. *Reserve team coaches:* John McGregor, Billy Kirkwood.
Managers since 1975: Jock Wallace; John Greig; Jock Wallace; Graeme Souness. *Club Nickname(s):* The Gers. *Previous Grounds:* Burnbank, Kinning Park.
Record Attendance: 118,567 v Celtic, Division I; 2 Jan, 1939.
Record Transfer Fee received: £5,580,000 for Trevor Steven to Marseille (Aug 1991).
Record Transfer Fee paid: £2,500,000 for Alexei Mikhailichenko from Sampdoria (June 1991).
Record Victory: 14-2 v Blairgowrie, Scottish Cup 1st rd; 20 Jan, 1934.
Record Defeat: 2-10 v Airdrieonians; 1886.
Most Capped Player: George Young, 53, Scotland.
Most League Appearances: 496: John Greig, 1962-78.
Most League Goals in Season (Individual): 44: Sam English, Division I; 1931-32.
Most Goals Overall (Individual): 233: Bob McPhail; 1927-39.

Honours
League Champions: (45 times) Division I 1890-91 (shared), 1898-99, 1899-1900, 1900-01, 1901-02, 1910-11, 1911-12, 1912-13, 1917-18, 1919-20, 1920-21, 1922-23, 1923-24, 1924-25, 1926-27, 1927-28, 1928-29, 1929-30, 1930-31, 1932-33, 1933-34, 1934-35, 1936-37, 1938-39, 1946-47, 1948-49, 1949-50, 1952-53, 1955-56, 1956-57, 1958-59, 1960-61, 1962-63,

RANGERS 1994–95 LEAGUE RECORD

Match No.	Date	Venue	Opponents	Result		H/T Score	Lg. Pos.	Goalscorers	Attendance
1	Aug 13	H	Motherwell	W	2-1	1-0	—	Hateley, Ferguson D	42,491
2	20	A	Partick T	W	2-0	1-0	1	Byrne (og), Hateley	14,361
3	27	H	Celtic	L	0-2	0-1	3		44,607
4	Sept 11	H	Hearts	W	3-0	0-0	—	Hateley 2 (1 pen), Durie	40,653
5	17	A	Falkirk	W	2-0	1-0	1	Boli, Laudrup	12,419
6	24	A	Aberdeen	D	2-2	1-1	2	Hateley, Moore	19,191
7	Oct 1	H	Dundee U	W	2-0	1-0	1	Hateley, Laudrup	43,635
8	8	A	Hibernian	L	1-2	1-0	1	Boli	12,088
9	15	H	Kilmarnock	W	2-0	0-0	1	Miller, Robertson D	44,099
10	22	A	Motherwell	L	1-2	0-1	1	Philliben (og)	11,160
11	30	A	Celtic	W	3-1	2-1	—	Hateley 2, Laudrup	32,171
12	Nov 5	H	Partick T	W	3-0	0-0	1	Laudrup, Miller, Hateley	43,696
13	9	A	Hearts	D	1-1	0-0	—	Hateley	12,347
14	19	H	Falkirk	D	1-1	1-0	1	Hateley	44,018
15	25	H	Aberdeen	W	1-0	0-0	—	McCoist	45,072
16	Dec 4	A	Dundee U	W	3-0	1-0	—	Laudrup, Huistra, Durrant	11,187
17	10	A	Kilmarnock	W	2-1	1-0	1	McLaren, Laudrup	17,219
18	26	H	Hibernian	W	2-0	2-0	—	Hateley, Gough	44,892
19	31	A	Motherwell	W	3-1	1-0	1	McCall, Laudrup, Durie	11,269
20	Jan 4	H	Celtic	D	1-1	1-0	—	Ferguson I	45,794
21	7	A	Partick T	D	1-1	0-0	1	Robertson D	17,298
22	14	A	Falkirk	W	3-2	1-0	1	Huistra 2 (1 pen), McCall	12,507
23	21	H	Hearts	W	1-0	1-0	1	Miller	44,231
24	Feb 4	H	Dundee U	D	1-1	1-1	1	Robertson D	44,197
25	12	A	Aberdeen	L	0-2	0-0	—		18,060
26	25	H	Kilmarnock	W	3-0	0-0	1	Durie, Laudrup, Durrant	44,859
27	Mar 4	A	Hibernian	D	1-1	0-0	1	Durie	11,939
28	11	H	Falkirk	D	2-2	1-1	1	Laudrup, Brown	43,359
29	18	A	Hearts	L	1-2	1-2	1	Laudrup	9806
30	Apr 1	A	Dundee U	W	2-0	2-0	1	McLaren, Durie	11,035
31	8	H	Aberdeen	W	3-2	2-2	1	Durrant, Murray, Hateley	44,460
32	16	H	Hibernian	W	3-1	1-1	—	Durie, Durrant, Mikhailichenko	44,193
33	20	A	Kilmarnock	W	1-0	1-0	—	Mikhailichenko	16,532
34	29	H	Motherwell	L	0-2	0-1	1		43,576
35	May 7	A	Celtic	W	0-3	0-0	—		31,025
36	13	H	Partick T	D	1-1	1-0	1	Moore	45,280

Final League Position: 1

1963-64, 1974-75. Premier Division: 1975-76, 1977-78, 1986-87, 1988-89, 1989-90, 1990-91, 1991-92, 1992-93, 1993-94, 1994-95; *Runners-up:* 23 times.
Scottish Cup Winners: (26 times) 1894, 1897, 1898, 1903, 1928, 1930, 1932, 1934, 1935, 1936, 1948, 1949, 1950, 1953, 1960, 1962, 1963, 1964, 1966, 1973, 1976, 1978, 1979, 1981, 1992, 1993; *Runners-up:* 16 times.
League Cup Winners: (19 times) 1946-47, 1948-49, 1960-61, 1961-62, 1963-64, 1964-65, 1970-71, 1975-76, 1977-78, 1978-79, 1981-82, 1983-84, 1984-85, 1986-87, 1987-88, 1988-89, 1990-91, 1992-93, 1993-94; *Runners-up:* 7 times.

European: *European Cup:* 73 matches (1956-57, 1957-58, 1959-60 semi-finals, 1961-62, 1963-64, 1964-65, 1975-76, 1976-77, 1978-79, 1987-88, 1989-90, 1990-91, 1991-92, 1992-93 final pool, 1993-94, 1994-95).
Cup Winners Cup Winners: 1971-72. 50 matches (1960-61 runners-up, 1962-63, 1966-67 runners-up, 1969-70, 1971-72 winners, 1973-74, 1977-78, 1979-80, 1981-82, 1983-84). *UEFA Cup:* 38 matches (*Fairs Cup:* 1967-68, 1968-69 semi-finals, 1970-71 *UEFA Cup*; 1982-83, 1984-85, 1985-86, 1986-87, 1988-89).
Club colours: Shirt: Royal blue with red and white trim. Shorts: White. Stockings: Red.

Goalscorers: *League (60):* Hateley 13 (1 pen), Laudrup 10, Durie 6, Durrant 4, Huistra 3 (1 pen), Miller 3, Robertson D 3, Boli 2, McCall 2, McLaren 2, Mikhailichenko 2, Moore 2, Brown 1, Ferguson D 1, Ferguson I 1, Gough 1, McCoist 1, Murray 1, own goals 2. *Cup (5):* Laudrup 2, Boli 1, Durie 1, Steven 1. *League Cup (7):* Ferguson D 3, Hateley 2, Laudrup 1, McCall 1.

Goram A 18 + 1	Murray N 14 + 6	Robertson D 23	Gough R 25	Boli B 28	McPherson D 9	Durrant I 15 + 10	McCall S 30	McCoist A 4 + 5	Hateley M 23	Laudrup B 33	Ferguson D 1 + 3	Brown J 10 + 3	Moore C 19 + 2	Ferguson I 13 + 3	Pressley S 2	Durie G 17 + 4	Mikhailichenko A 4 + 5	Miller C 21	Huistra P 15	Hagan D — + 2	Wishart F 3 + 1	McLaren A 24	Scott C 3 + 1	McGinty B 1	Maxwell A 10 + 1	Steven T 10 + 1	Bollan G 5 + 1	Cleland A 10	Thomson W 5	Robertson L — + 1	Caldwell N 1	McKnight P — + 1	Match No.
1	2	3	4	5	6	7	8	*9*	10	11	14																						1
1			4	5	6		2		10	11	9	3	7	8																			2
1			4	5	6	7	2		10	11	12			8	3	9																	3
1	7	3	4		5	9	2		10	*11*	14		6	8		12																	4
1		3	4	5		7	2		10	11			6	8		9																	5
1	7	3	4	6	5	12	8		10	11			2			9																	6
1	12	3	4	6	5		7	14	10	11			2				8	*9*															7
1	12	3	4	6	*5*		7	14	10	11			2					9	8														8
1	7	3			5		4		10	11			2		6			9	8														9
1	*7*	3		6	5		4		10	11			2					9	8	14													10
1	8	3		6			4	14	10	*11*								9	7	12	2	5											11
1	8	3		6		12	4		10	11								9	7		2	5											12
1	*8*	3		6		9	4	14	10	11			2						7			5											13
1		3		6		12	4	*9*	10	11			2			14		8	7			5											14
1		3		6			4	9	*10*	11						14		8	7		2	5											15
1		3	4	6		12	2	9		11						10		8	7			5											16
1	6	3	4			10	2			11				14		9		*8*	7			5											17
		3	4	6			2		10	11			12			9		8	7			5	1										18
		3	4	6			2			11			10	12		9		8	7			5	1										19
		3	4	6		14	2			11		12		8		9		*10*	7			5	1										20
1	11	3				9	4					6	2	8					7			5	15	10									21
	10	3				11	4					6	*2*	8				9	7		14	5			1	12							22
	10		4	6		12	2			11		3	14	8				9				5			1	*7*							23
		3	4	5			6	14	10	11		12	2			*9*		8							1	7							24
		3	4	5		12	8		10	11			2			14		9							1		*6*	7					25
		3	4	6		14	2			11		12				10		9				5			1	*7*		8					26
	8		4	6		12	10					11	*2*	14		9						5			1	7	3						27
			4	6		7	2			11		10		8		9	14					5			1		*3*						28
	14		4	6		12	10			11				8		9						5			1	7	*3*	2					29
			4	*6*		10	7			11		3				9	12	8				5					14	2	1				30
	12		4	6					10	*11*		3				9	14	8				5				7		2	1				31
	12		4			6			10	11		3				*9*	14	8				5				7		2	1				32
	6		4			9				11			2	*8*			10					5			1		3	7		14			33
			4	6		9			10	11				8			3					5				7		2	1				34
	14			4		9			10	*11*		*6*	2	8			12					5			15	7		3	1				35
15						9			10	11			4			*8*	6					5			*1*	7		3			2	14	36

ROSS COUNTY Third Division

Year Formed: 1929. *Ground & Address:* Victoria Park, Dingwall IV15 9QW. *Telephone:* 01349 862253. *Fax:* 01349 866277.
Ground Capacity: total 6500, seated 319. *Size of Ground:* 110 × 75yd.
Chairman: Hector Maclennan. *Vice-chairman & Secretary:* Donald MacBean. *Office Secretary:* Mrs Cathie Caird. *Commercial Manager:* Brian Campbell.
Manager: Robert Wilson. *Assistant Manager:* Graeme McKenzie. *Physio:* Douglas Sim. *Record Attendance:* 8000, v Rangers, Scottish Cup, 28 February 1966.
Record Transfer Fee Received: £40,000 for Barry Wilson to Raith R, Sept.1994.
Record Transfer Fee Paid: £25,000 for Barry Wilson from Southampton, Oct.1992.
Record Victory: 11-0 v St Cuthbert Wanderers, Scottish Cup, Dec.1993.

ROSS COUNTY 1994–95 LEAGUE RECORD

Match No.	*Date*	*Venue*	*Opponents*	*Result*		*H/T Score*	*Lg. Pos.*	*Goalscorers*	*Atten-dance*
1	Aug 13	A	Cowdenbeath	W	2-0	0-0	—	MacPherson, Herd	678
2	20	A	East Stirling	D	2-2	1-1	3	MacPherson, Wilson	632
3	27	H	Caledonian Th	L	1-3	0-1	6	Andrew MacLeod	3197
4	Sept 3	H	Alloa	D	3-3	3-2	5	Williamson, Grant, MacPherson	1457
5	10	A	Montrose	W	2-0	1-0	5	Robertson, Duff	918
6	24	H	Arbroath	L	1-4	0-1	8	MacPherson	1320
7	Oct 1	A	Queen's Park	L	1-3	1-2	8	MacPherson	729
8	8	A	Forfar Ath	L	0-1	0-0	8		650
9	15	H	Albion R	W	3-0	0-0	8	Williamson 2, Connelly	1017
10	22	H	Cowdenbeath	W	4-0	0-0	7	Andrew MacLeod 2, Grant 2	1284
11	29	A	Caledonian Th	D	0-0	0-0	7		2866
12	Nov 5	H	East Stirling	L	1-4	0-2	7	Andrew MacLeod	1194
13	12	H	Montrose	L	0-1	0-0	7		1154
14	19	A	Alloa	D	1-1	0-0	7	McKay	479
15	26	A	Arbroath	W	1-0	0-0	7	Bellshaw	568
16	Dec 3	H	Queen's Park	W	2-0	1-0	7	Chalmers (og), Connelly	1322
17	31	A	Albion R	W	1-0	0-0	7	Williamson	354
18	Jan 2	H	Caledonian Th	W	3-1	0-1	—	MacPherson, Grant 2	2749
19	11	H	Forfar Ath	W	2-1	1-0	—	Connelly, MacPherson	1215
20	14	A	Cowdenbeath	W	3-0	1-0	3	Ferries 2, Grant (pen)	361
21	21	A	East Stirling	W	2-0	0-0	2	Connelly, Williamson	459
22	Feb 4	A	Montrose	D	1-1	1-0	2	Grant (pen)	882
23	11	H	Alloa	W	6-0	2-0	2	Andrew MacLeod 2, Grant 2, Connelly, Duff	1686
24	18	H	Arbroath	L	0-1	0-1	2		1648
25	25	A	Queen's Park	W	2-1	0-1	2	Grant, Williamson	753
26	Mar 4	A	Forfar Ath	L	2-4	2-3	2	Grant, Andrew MacLeod	880
27	25	A	Alloa	D	1-1	1-1	3	Wylie (og)	535
28	29	H	Albion R	W	4-1	1-0	—	Duff, Furphy, Connelly, Ferries	967
29	Apr 1	H	Queen's Park	W	1-0	1-0	3	Duff	1469
30	8	A	Arbroath	W	1-0	0-0	2	Duff	680
31	15	H	Forfar Ath	L	0-1	0-1	2		2453
32	19	H	Montrose	L	0-3	0-2	—		1702
33	22	A	Albion R	W	2-1	1-1	3	Andrew MacLeod, Williamson	334
34	29	H	Cowdenbeath	W	2-0	1-0	3	Grant, Andrew MacLeod	1356
35	May 6	A	Caledonian Th	L	0-3	0-1	3		3062
36	13	H	East Stirling	L	2-3	2-1	3	MacPherson, Alex MacLeod	1005

Final League Position: 3

Record Defeat: 1-10 v Inverness Thistle, Highland League.
Most League Appearances: 35, Robbie Williamson, 1994-95.
Most League Goals in Season: 12, Brian Grant, 1994-95.

Goalscorers: *League (59):* Grant 12 (2 pens), Andrew MacLeod 9, MacPherson 8, Williamson 7, Connelly 6, Duff 5, Ferries 3, Bellshaw 1, Furphy 1, Herd 1, McKay 1, Alexander MacLeod 1, Robertson 1, Wilson 1, own goals 2. *Scottish Cup (3):* Connelly 2, MacPherson 1. *League Cup (3):* Grant 2, MacPherson 1. *B&Q Cup (1):* Andrew Macleod 1 (pen).

Hutchison S 29	Somerville C 28	Campbell G 11	Williamson R 35	MacLeod Alex 15 + 3	MacLeod Andy 27 + 3	Ferries K 30 + 2	Grant B 32 + 3	MacPherson J 13 + 4	Herd W 28 + 2	Wilson B 3	Connelly G 28 + 3	Robertson C 6 + 3	Duff A 11 + 14	Reid C 31 + 1	McMillan D 7 + 2	Furphy W 28	McKay D 9 + 6	McFee R 1 + 7	Bellshaw J 24	Stewart R — + 1	Match No.
1	2	3	4	5	6	7	*8*	9	10	11	12	14									1
1	2	3	4	5	6	7	*8*	9	10	11	12		14								2
1	2	3	4	5	6	7	8	9	10	11	12										3
1	2		4	5		7	8	9	6		10	11	12	3							4
	2	6	4	5		7		8	10			11	9	3	1						5
1	2	6	4		11	7	14	10	5				*9*	3		8					6
1	2	6	4	5	7	12	8	*9*	11				14	3	15	10					7
	2	6	4	5	10	7	8					11	9	*3*	1		12	14			8
	2	3	4	5	11		*8*				10		9	7	1	6		14			9
	2	*3*	4	5	11		8				10		*9*	7	1	6	12	14			10
	2	3	4		11		8				10	5	9	7	1	6		14			11
		3	4		11	14	8				10	5	9	7	1	6		2			12
			4		9	7	8		*11*		10			3	1	6	2	14	5		13
1	2		4		*9*	7	8		12		10			3		6	11	14	5		14
1	2		4		9	7	*8*		12		10		14	3		6	11		5		15
1	2		4		*9*	7	8		6		10		14	3			11	12	5		16
1	2		4			7	8	*9*	6		10	12	14	3			11		5		17
1	2		4			7	8	9	11		10			3		6			5		18
1	2		*4*		14	7	8	9	11		10			3		6			5		19
1	2			14	11	7	8	9	4		10			*3*		6	12		5		20
1	2		4		*9*	7	8		11		10		14	3		6	12		5		21
1			4		14	7	8	*9*	11		10			3		6	2		5		22
1	2		4		11	7	8		9		10		14	*3*		6	12		5		23
1	2		*4*		11	7	8	14	9		10			3		6			5		24
1	2		4		*11*	7	8	14	9		10			3		6			5		25
1	2		4		11	7	8		9		10			3		6			5		26
1			4		*11*	7	8		9		10	12	14	3		6	2		5		27
1			4	12		7	8		11		10		9	3		6	*2*		5	14	28
1			4	3	14	7	*8*		11		10		9	2		6	12		5		29
1	2		4	12	11	7	14		8		10		*9*	3		6			5		30
1	2		4		11	7	14		8		10		*9*	3		6			5		31
1	2		4	3	11	7	8	12	*9*		10		14			6			5		32
1	2		4	3	11	7	*8*		9		10		14	12		6			5		33
1			4	3	11	7	*8*		9		10		14	2		6			5		34
1			4	*3*	11	7	8	12	9		*10*		14	2		6			5		35
1	2		4	10			8	9				11	12	3	15	6	7		5		36

ST JOHNSTONE First Division

Year Formed: 1884. *Ground & Address:* McDiarmid Park, Crieff Road, Perth PH1 2SJ. *Telephone:* 01738 626961. *Clubcall:* 0898 121559.
Ground Capacity: total: 10,721. seated: 10,721. *Size of Pitch:* 115yd × 75yd.
Chairman: G.S.Brown. *Secretary and Managing Director:* Stewart Duff.
Manager: Paul Sturrock. *Sales Executive:* Stuart Turnbull. *Physio:* David Henderson. *Coach:* John Blackley. *Youth Development Coach:* Alistair Stevenson.
Managers since 1975: J. Stewart; J. Storrie; A. Stuart; A. Rennie; I. Gibson; A. Totten, J. McClelland. *Club Nickname(s):* Saints. *Previous Grounds:* Recreation Grounds, Muirton Park.
Record Attendance: (McDiarmid Park): 10,504 v Rangers, Premier Division; 20 Oct, 1990.
Record Transfer Fee received: £750,000 for Billy Dodds to Aberdeen, 1994.
Record Transfer Fee paid: £300,000 for Billy Dodds from Dundee, 1994.
Record Victory: 9-0 v Albion R, League Cup; 9 March, 1946.
Record Defeat: 1-10 v Third Lanark, Scottish Cup; 24 January, 1903.
Most Capped Player: Sandy McLaren, 5, Scotland.
Most League Appearances: 298: Drew Rutherford.
Most League Goals in Season (Individual): 36: Jimmy Benson, Division II; 1931-32.

St JOHNSTONE 1994–95 LEAGUE RECORD

Match No.	Date	Venue	Opponents	Result		H/T Score	Lg. Pos.	Goalscorers	Attendance
1	Aug 13	A	Raith R	D	1-1	1-0	—	Irons	4374
2	20	A	Airdrieonians	D	0-0	0-0	7		2161
3	27	H	Dundee	L	0-1	0-1	9		6021
4	Sept 3	A	Ayr U	W	4-3	2-0	4	O'Boyle 3, Irons	2367
5	10	H	St Mirren	D	1-1	0-1	5	O'Boyle	3957
6	24	H	Hamilton A	D	1-1	0-1	5	O'Boyle	2790
7	Oct 1	A	Clydebank	D	0-0	0-0	6		1025
8	8	A	Dunfermline Ath	L	0-3	0-2	7		6931
9	15	H	Stranraer	W	3-0	0-0	6	Noren, O'Boyle 2	2678
10	22	H	Raith R	W	3-1	1-0	5	Curran, O'Boyle 2 (1 pen)	3926
11	29	A	Dundee	L	0-1	0-0	5		4327
12	Nov 12	A	St Mirren	D	2-2	1-2	6	Deas, Davenport	2970
13	19	H	Ayr U	W	1-0	1-0	5	Davidson	2755
14	22	H	Airdrieonians	W	4-0	1-0	—	Cherry, O'Boyle, Farquhar, Preston	3110
15	26	A	Hamilton A	L	1-3	1-2	5	McGowne	1445
16	Dec 3	H	Clydebank	D	1-1	1-0	5	Curran	2724
17	10	A	Stranraer	D	2-2	1-1	5	Twaddle, Davenport	780
18	26	H	Dunfermline Ath	W	3-2	1-2	—	McMartin, Davenport, O'Neil	6091
19	31	A	Raith R	L	0-2	0-1	5		4973
20	Jan 7	A	Airdrieonians	W	2-0	2-0	5	Twaddle, Cherry	1957
21	11	H	Dundee	D	2-2	0-1	—	O'Neil, Curran	5636
22	14	A	Ayr U	W	3-1	0-1	5	Curran, Davenport, McMartin	1955
23	21	H	St Mirren	W	5-1	3-0	5	O'Boyle, Dick 2 (2 og), Preston, Cherry	3321
24	Feb 4	A	Clydebank	D	0-0	0-0	5		949
25	18	H	Hamilton A	W	3-0	1-0	5	O'Boyle 2, Cherry	2589
26	25	H	Stranraer	W	3-0	1-0	5	Twaddle, O'Boyle, Wright	2725
27	Mar 11	A	Dunfermline Ath	D	1-1	0-0	5	Twaddle	6522
28	21	A	St Mirren	D	0-0	0-0	—		2169
29	25	H	Ayr U	D	1-1	1-0	5	McKilligan (og)	3551
30	Apr 1	H	Clydebank	W	1-0	1-0	5	O'Boyle	3337
31	8	A	Hamilton A	L	0-1	0-0	5		858
32	15	H	Dunfermline Ath	D	1-1	0-0	5	Farquhar	5039
33	22	A	Stranraer	W	6-2	2-0	5	Cherry, O'Neil, O'Boyle 3, Twaddle	702
34	29	H	Raith R	L	1-2	0-0	5	McMartin	5124
35	May 6	A	Dundee	L	1-2	0-0	5	O'Boyle	3906
36	13	H	Airdrieonians	W	2-1	1-1	5	Scott, Twaddle	2868

Final League Position: 5

Most Goals Overall (Individual): 114: John Brogan, 1977-83.

Honours
League Champions: First Division 1982-83, 1989-90. Division II 1923-24, 1959-60, 1962-63; *Runners-up:* Division II 1931-32. Second Division 1987-88.
Scottish Cup: Semi-finals 1934, 1968, 1989, 1991.
League Cup Runners-up: 1969.

European: *UEFA Cup:* 1971-72.
Club colours: Shirt: Royal blue with white trim. Shorts: White. Stockings: Royal blue, white trim.

Goalscorers: *League (59):* O'Boyle 19 (1 pen), Twaddle 6, Cherry 5, Curran 4, Davenport 4, McMartin 3, O'Neil 3, Farquhar 2, Irons 2, Preston 2, Davidson 1, Deas 1, McGowne 1, Noren 1, Scott 1, Wright 1, own goals 3. *Scottish Cup (1):* own goal 1. *League Cup (7):* O'Boyle 2, O'Neil 2, Irons 1, Miller 1, Scott 1. *B&Q Cup (7):* O'Boyle 5, Davenport 1, Ramsey 1.

Rhodes A 19	Miller C 12	Davidson C 4 + 3	Turner T 10 + 1	McGinnis G 10	McGowne K 30	O'Neil J 26 + 1	Davies J 1 + 2	Davenport P 12 + 10	O'Boyle G 32	Irons D 34	Ramsey P 9 + 2	Scott P 9 + 2	Inglis J 5	Cherry P 27	Preston A 24 + 2	McAuley S 7 + 1	McMartin G 13 + 10	Morgan A — + 2	Curran H 22 + 4	Twaddle K 21 + 4	Farquhar G 10 + 7	Noren P 1	Deas P 7	Walemark J 2	Wright P 5 + 7	Weir J 17	English I 4 + 5	Main A 17	McCluskey S 2	Griffin D 3	Young S 1 + 1	*Match No.*
1	2	3	4	5	6	7	8	*9*	10	11	12	14																				1
1	3		4	*2*		7	12	9	10	11	8	14	5	6																		2
1	3	*11*	8		6	7	12	9	10	4	14		5	2																		3
1	3		8	6		7		9	10	11	4		5	2	12																	4
1	3		8	6		7		9	10	2	4		5		*11*	12	14															5
1	3		8		2	7		*9*	10	6			5		11	4	12	14														6
1	3			8	5	7		*9*	10	6	4			2	11		12	14														7
1	3				5	7		9	10	6	4			*2*	11		12		8	14												8
1	3	12			6	7		14	10	4				5			2		11		*8*	9										9
1	3				6	7		14	10	4							2		11		8		5	*9*								10
1	*3*				6	7			10	4					12		2		11		8		5	*9*	14							11
1	3	12	4		6	7		*9*							8		2		11	10	14		5									12
1		7	8		6			*9*	10					5	3		2		11	14						4						13
1			8		6	7			10	4				2	3				11	*9*	12				14	5						14
1			8		6				10	4				2	*3*		12		11	9	7				14	5						15
1			12		6				10	4				2	3		8		11	14	7				*9*	5						16
1					6	7		14		4				2	3		8		11	*10*	12				9	5						17
1					6	7		14		4				2	3		8		11	*10*	12				9	5						18
1					6	7		14		4				2	3		8		11		12				9	5	*10*					19
					6	7			10	4				2	3				8	9			11			5	12	1				20
					6	7		14	*10*	4				2	3				8	9			11			5	12	1				21
					6	7		14	10	4				2	3		12		8	9			*11*			5		1				22
					6	7		14	*10*	4				2	3		12		8	9			11			5		1				23
					6	7		12	*10*	4				2	3	11			8	14					9	5		1				24
					6			14	10	4	8	7		2		3			12	9						5	11	1				25
					6			*11*	10	4	8	7		2		3			12	9					14	5		1				26
					6			*11*	10	4	8	7		2		3			12	9					14	5		1				27
									10	4	8	7		2		3	12		6	9					14	5	*11*	1				28
				6		*11*			10	4		7		2		3			12	9					14	5		1	8			29
					6	11			10	4		7			3		2			9	8							1		5		30
		12				*11*			10	4		8			3		2			9	7						14	1	6	5		31
				5	6				10	4		7		2	3		12		8	9	14						11	1				32
				5	6	7			10	4				2	3				11	9	12						14	1			8	33
				5	6	12			10	4				2	3		7		11	9	8							1				34
				5	6	7			10	4				2	3		12		11	9	8							1			14	35
		11			6				10	4		7			3		2			9	8						14	1		*5*		36

ST MIRREN First Division

Year Formed: 1877. *Ground & Address:* St Mirren Park, Love St, Paisley PA3 2EJ. *Telephone:* 0141 889 2558/0141 840 1337. *Fax:* 0141 848 6444.
Ground Capacity: total: 15,410. seated 9395. *Size of Pitch:* 112yd × 73yd.
Chairman/Chief Executive: Bob Earlie. *Secretary and General Manager:* Jack Copland.
Manager: Jimmy Bone. *Physio:* Andrew Binning. *Coaches* Campbell Money and Kenny McDowall.
Managers since 1975: Alex Ferguson; Jim Clunie; Rikki MacFarlane; Alex Miller; Alex Smith; Tony Fitzpatrick; David Hay.
Club Nickname(s): The Buddies. *Previous Grounds:* Short Roods 1877-79, Thistle Park Greenhill 1879-83, Westmarch 1883-94.
Record Attendance: 47,438 v Celtic, League Cup, 20 Aug, 1949.
Record Transfer Fee received: £850,000 for Ian Ferguson to Rangers (1988).
Record Transfer Fee paid: £400,000 for Thomas Stickroth from Bayer Uerdingen (1990).
Record Victory: 15-0 v Glasgow University, Scottish Cup 1st rd; 30 Jan, 1960.
Record Defeat: 0-9 v Rangers, Division I; 4 Dec, 1897.
Most Capped Player: Godmundor Torfason, 29, Iceland.
Most League Appearances: 351: Tony Fitzpatrick, 1973-88.

St MIRREN 1994–95 LEAGUE RECORD

Match No.	Date		Venue	Opponents	Result		H/T Score	Lg. Pos.	Goalscorers	Attendance
1	Aug	13	A	Dundee	L	0-2	0-1	—		4125
2		20	A	Ayr U	D	1-1	0-0	9	Lavety	2787
3		27	H	Clydebank	W	2-1	0-1	4	Gillies R, Lavety	2414
4	Sept	3	H	Dunfermline Ath	D	1-1	1-0	5	Lavety	3895
5		10	A	St Johnstone	D	1-1	1-0	6	Gillies K	3957
6		24	H	Raith R	L	1-2	1-1	8	Lavety	2967
7	Oct	1	A	Hamilton A	D	2-2	0-1	7	Dick, Elliot	1613
8		8	A	Stranraer	D	1-1	0-0	6	Baker	1157
9		15	H	Airdrieonians	L	0-1	0-1	7		2930
10		22	H	Dundee	L	1-2	0-1	8	Elliot	2758
11		29	A	Clydebank	D	1-1	0-1	9	Watson	1675
12	Nov	5	H	Ayr U	W	1-0	1-0	7	Dawson (pen)	2482
13		12	H	St Johnstone	D	2-2	2-1	8	Gillies R, Fullarton	2970
14		19	A	Dunfermline Ath	L	0-1	0-0	8		4660
15	Dec	3	H	Hamilton A	L	0-1	0-0	8		2273
16		6	A	Raith R	D	1-1	1-1	—	Hewitt	4084
17		26	H	Stranraer	W	1-0	0-0	—	Elliot	2505
18		31	A	Dundee	L	0-4	0-1	8		3715
19	Jan	2	H	Clydebank	D	0-0	0-0	—		3217
20		7	A	Ayr U	L	0-2	0-1	8		2237
21		10	A	Airdrieonians	L	0-2	0-1	—		1325
22		14	H	Dunfermline Ath	D	2-2	1-2	8	Taylor, Inglis	2736
23		21	A	St Johnstone	L	1-5	0-3	8	Bone	3321
24	Feb	4	A	Hamilton A	L	0-2	0-2	8		1534
25		11	H	Raith R	L	1-2	0-2	9	McWhirter	2516
26		25	H	Airdrieonians	L	0-1	0-0	9		2564
27	Mar	11	A	Stranraer	W	3-1	1-1	8	Dawson, Watson, Bone	935
28		21	H	St Johnstone	D	0-0	0-0	—		2169
29		25	A	Dunfermline Ath	D	1-1	0-0	8	Lavety	5055
30	Apr	1	H	Hamilton A	W	3-2	0-1	8	Lavety, Baker, Inglis	2272
31		8	A	Raith R	L	1-2	1-2	8	Lavety	3669
32		15	H	Stranraer	W	2-0	2-0	7	Inglis, Dick	2315
33		22	A	Airdrieonians	L	0-1	0-0	7		2245
34		29	H	Dundee	W	1-0	0-0	7	Hewitt	2976
35	May	6	A	Clydebank	L	1-2	0-1	8	Watson	1399
36		13	H	Ayr U	W	2-1	1-1	7	Gillies R, McGrotty	2179

Final League Position: 7

Most League Goals in Season (Individual): 45: Dunky Walker, Division I; 1921-22.
Most Goals Overall (Individual): 221: David McCrae, 1923-24.

Honours
League Champions: First Division 1976-77. Division II 1967-68; *Runners-up:* 1935-36.
Scottish Cup Winners: 1926, 1959, 1987. *Runners-up* 1908, 1934, 1962.
League Cup: Runners-up 1955-56.
B&Q Cup: Runners-up 1993-94 *Victory Cup:* 1919-20. *Summer Cup:* 1943-44. *Anglo-Scottish Cup:* 1979-80.

European: *Cup Winners Cup:* 1987-88. *UEFA Cup:* 1980-81, 1983-84, 1985-86.
Club colours: Shirt: Black and white vertical stripes. Shorts: Black. Stockings: Black with White trim. Change colours: Predominantly red.

Goalscorers: *League (34):* Lavety 7, Elliot 3, Gillies R 3, Inglis 3, Watson 3, Baker 2, Bone 2, Dawson 2 (1 pen), Dick 2, Hewitt 2, Fullarton 1, Gillies K 1, McGrotty 1, McWhirter 1, Taylor 1. *Scottish Cup (0) League Cup (0) B&Q Cup (1):* Watson 1 (pen).

Combe A 20 + 1	Dawson R 29	Watson S 25 + 4	McLaughlin B 31	Taylor S 10 + 3	Archdeacon P 1 + 1	McIntyre P 19 + 1	Bone A 19 + 6	Lavety B 29 + 2	Gardner J 17 + 3	Elliot D 26 + 2	Hick M 2 + 1	Gillies R 13 + 11	Gillies K 5 + 4	Baker M 23 + 3	Dick J 24 + 1	Money C 15	Fullarton J 13 + 4	McWhirter N 23	Scott B — + 1	Orr N 4 + 1	McGrotty G — + 2	McAvennie F 7	Hewitt J 9 + 7	Okorie K 2	Smith B 4 + 1	Boyd J 10 + 2	Hetherston B 1 + 2	Inglis G 7 + 8	Byrne D 6	Galloway G 1	Scrimgeour D 1	Match No.
1	2	3	4	5	*6*	7	8	9	10	11	12	14																				1
1		3	4	5		6	8	9	10	11	*2*	14	7	12																		2
1	2	3	4			5	*8*	9	10	11		14	7	12	6																	3
	2	3	4		14	5		9	10	11		8	7		6	1	12															4
	2	3	4			5		9	10	11		8	7	12	6	1	14															5
	2	3	5			6	7	9	10	11		14	12		8	1		4														6
	2	3	5			12	7	9	10	11				8	6	1		4	14													7
	2		5	12		4	7	9	10	11				3	8	1				6	14											8
1	2	12	5			4		9	*10*	11		14		3	7					6		8										9
1	*2*	3	5			8	14		12	11		10			7			4		6		9										10
1		6	5			8		9	14	11	2	12		3	7			4				*10*										11
1	2	6	5			8	14	9		11				3	7		12	4				*10*										12
1	2	*6*	5				14		9	11		7		3			8	4				10	12									13
1	2	6	5					14	*9*	11		7		3			8			4		10	12									14
1		6	5				9	14	7	11		12		3			8					*10*		2	4							15
1	2			5				9		11		*8*	14	3	7					12			10	6	4							16
1	2	12	5					9		11		8		3	7			4					*10*			6	14					17
1	2	8	*5*	12				9		11		14		3	7			4					10			6						18
1	2	5						9		11		8		3	7			4					10			6	12					19
1	2	5						9		11		8	10	3	7			4					14			*6*		12				20
1	2	5	8				14	9		11				3	7			4					12			*6*		10				21
1		5		6			8	9						3	7		11	4					10		*2*	12		14				22
1		5		6			8	9		11		12			2		10	4					14			*3*		7				23
1	2		5	12		*3*	8	9					14		7		6	4					10					11				24
	2	6	5	8		7		9						3	12	1	11	4					*10*					14				25
	2		4			5	14	9	*11*			10		3	8	1	6											12	7			26
	2	6	5	8		9	14			11		*10*		3		1	12	4											7			27
	2		6	5		7	*9*	10	14	11				3		1	8	4										12				28
	2	12	6	5		7	*9*	10	11					3		1	8	4										14				29
	2		6	5		*7*	9	10	11	14				3		1	8	4										12				30
	2	12	6				9	10	*11*	7			14		5	1		4										8	3			31
	2		6				9	*10*	11	7		14			5	1		4								12		8	3			32
15	2	3	6				*9*	10				14			5	*1*		4					11			8		7				33
	2	5	6			7	9	*10*		14						1		4					11			8		12	3			34
1		6	5				9					10		3			4						14		12	8		7	2	*11*		35
		6	5				*9*					10		3	11		4				12		14		2	8	7				1	36

STENHOUSEMUIR Second Division

Year Formed: 1884. *Ground & Address:* Ochilview Park, Gladstone Rd, Stenhousemuir FK5 5QL. *Telephone:* 01324 562992.
Ground Capacity: total: 3480. seated: 340. *Size of Pitch:* 113yd × 78yd.
Chairman: A Terry Bulloch. *Secretary:* David O.Reid. *Commercial Manager:* John Sharp.
Manager: Terry Christie. *Assistant Manager:* Graeme Armstrong. *Physio:* Lee Campbell. *Coach:* Gordon Buchanan.
Managers since 1975: H. Glasgow; J. Black; A. Rose; W. Henderson; A. Rennie; J. Meakin; D. Lawson. *Club Nickname(s):* The Warriors. *Previous Grounds:* Tryst Ground 1884-86, Goschen Park 1886-90.
Record Attendance: 12,500 v East Fife, Scottish Cup 4th rd; 11 Mar, 1950.
Record Transfer Fee received: £30,000 for David Beaton to Falkirk (June 1989).
Record Transfer Fee paid: £7000 to Meadowbank T for Lee Bullen (Nov 1990).
Record Victory: 9-2 v Dundee U, Division II; 19 Apr, 1937.
Record Defeat: 2-11 v Dunfermline Ath. Division II; 27 Sept, 1930.
Most Capped Player: —.

STENHOUSEMUIR 1994–95 LEAGUE RECORD

Match No.	Date	Venue	Opponents	Result		H/T Score	Lg. Pos.	Goalscorers	Attendance
1	Aug 13	H	Clyde	W	1-0	1-0	—	Hutchison	680
2	20	H	East Fife	D	1-1	1-0	4	Sludden	544
3	27	A	Meadowbank T	L	0-3	0-0	7		239
4	Sept 3	A	Brechin C	D	1-1	1-1	5	Steel	436
5	10	H	Stirling Albion	W	3-0	2-0	3	Hutchison, Steel, Christie	555
6	24	H	Berwick R	D	1-1	1-0	5	Hutchison	373
7	Oct 1	A	Morton	L	2-3	0-0	6	Sprott, Hutchison	1280
8	8	H	Queen of the S	D	0-0	0-0	6		403
9	15	A	Dumbarton	W	2-1	1-0	4	Steel, Fisher	601
10	22	A	Clyde	D	0-0	0-0	4		1072
11	29	H	Meadowbank T	D	1-1	0-1	6	Mathieson	473
12	Nov 5	A	East Fife	W	3-2	2-0	5	Mathieson 2, Hutchison	719
13	12	A	Stirling Albion	W	2-0	1-0	3	Steel, Hutchison	696
14	19	H	Brechin C	W	2-0	2-0	2	Steel, Christie	342
15	26	A	Berwick R	D	0-0	0-0	3		703
16	Dec 3	H	Morton	D	0-0	0-0	3		842
17	26	A	Queen of the S	W	2-1	1-0	—	Steel 2	1437
18	31	H	Dumbarton	W	1-0	0-0	1	Steel	638
19	Jan 10	H	Meadowbank T	W	2-1	0-1	—	Donaldson, Mathieson	371
20	14	H	Clyde	D	2-2	0-0	1	Hutchison, Sprott	669
21	21	A	East Fife	W	2-0	2-0	1	Sprott, Mathieson	713
22	Feb 4	H	Stirling Albion	L	0-2	0-1	1		797
23	14	A	Brechin C	W	2-0	1-0	—	Sprott, Hutchison	345
24	25	A	Morton	L	0-1	0-1	1		2754
25	Mar 7	H	Berwick R	D	2-2	1-1	—	Hutchison, Sprott	534
26	14	A	Dumbarton	L	1-5	1-2	—	Donaldson	1132
27	18	A	Stirling Albion	L	1-3	0-1	4	Sprott	431
28	21	H	Queen of the S	D	2-2	1-1	—	Clarke, Christie	454
29	25	H	Brechin C	W	3-0	3-0	3	Fisher, Mathieson 2	396
30	Apr 1	H	Morton	D	1-1	0-0	3	Sprott	1126
31	8	A	Berwick R	D	0-0	0-0	3		571
32	15	A	Queen of the S	W	2-1	2-0	3	Clarke, Steel	1230
33	22	H	Dumbarton	D	0-0	0-00	3		989
34	29	A	Clyde	L	2-3	0-0	4	Haddow, Hutchison	1043
35	May 5	A	Meadowbank T	L	0-1	0-1	—		463
36	13	H	East Fife	W	2-1	2-1	4	Fisher, Mathieson	433

Final League Position: 4

Most League Appearances: 360: Archie Rose.
Most League Goals in Season (Individual): 32: Robert Taylor, Division II; 1925-26.
Most Goals Overall (Individual): —.

Honours
League Champions: —. *Scottish Cup:* Semi-finals 1902-03. Quarter-finals 1994-95 *League Cup:* Quarter-finals 1947-48, 1960-61, 1975-76.
Club colours: Shirt: Maroon with silver stripe. Shorts: White with maroon insert. Stockings: White.

Goalscorers: *League (46):* Hutchison 10, Steel 9, Mathieson 8, Sprott 7, Christie 3, Fisher 3, Clarke 2, Donaldson 2, Haddow 1, Sludden 1. *Scottish Cup (14):* Sprott 4 (1 pen), Mathieson 3, Steel 3, Christie 1, Clarke 1, Donaldson 1, Fisher 1. *League Cup (0) B&Q Cup (0)*

Harkness M 36	Aitken N 2 + 2	Haddow L 18 + 2	Salton K 4	McGeachie G 21 + 1	Christie M 28	Steel T 34 + 1	Swanson D 3	Hutchison G 34	Sludden J 4 + 1	Sprott A 28 + 1	Mathieson M 35	Fisher J 32 + 1	Henderson J 1 + 4	Clarke J 14 + 4	Godfrey P 17 + 3	Irvine J — + 6	Armstrong G 33	McNiven J 19	Roseburgh D 8 + 5	Donaldson E 16 + 1	Russell G 9 + 1	Match No.
1	2	3	4	5	6	7	8	9	10	11												1
1	2	3	4	*5*	6	7	8		10	11	9	12	14									2
1		3	4		6	*7*	8		10	11	9		12	2	5	14						3
1		3			6	7		10		11	9	8		2	5	12	4					4
1		3			6	7		10		11	9	8		2	5	12	4					5
1		3		6	8	7		*10*	14		9	11		2	5		4					6
1		3		5	6	7		10		11	9	8		2		12	4					7
1		3	2	5	6			10	7	11	9	8				12	4					8
1		3		5	6	7		10		11	9	8			12		4	2				9
1		3			6	7		10		11	9	8		2	5		4					10
1		3		5	6	7		10			9	8			12	14	4	*2*	11			11
1		3			6	7		10			9	8			5		4	2	11			12
1		3			6	7		10		12	9	8			5		4	2	11			13
1		3			6	7		10		11	9	8			5		4	2				14
1		3			6	7		10		11	9	8			5		4	2	12			15
1					6	7		10		11	9	8			5		4	2	3			16
1					6	7		10		11	9	8			5		4	2	3			17
1				12	6	7		10		11	9	*8*		2	5		4		3	14		18
1				6		7		10		11	9	8		12	5		4	2		3		19
1				6		7		10		11	9	8			5		4	2		3		20
1				5	6	7		10		11	9	8		14			4	2		3		21
1				5	6	7		10		11	9	*8*					4	2	14	3		22
1				5	6	7		10		11	*9*	8		14			4	2	12	3		23
1				5	6	7		10		11	9	8					4	2	12	3		24
1				5	6	7		10		11	9	8		12			4		3		2	25
1	14				*6*	12		10		11	9	8			5		4		7	3	2	26
1	14				6	7		10		11	9	8			5		4		*12*	3	2	27
1				5	6	7		10		11	9			8	12		4	2		3		28
1					6	7		10			9	8		11	5		4	2		3		29
1				5	6	7		10		11	9	8					4	2		3	12	30
1				5		7		10		11	9	8					4	2		3	6	31
1		14		5		7		10		11	9	8		*6*			4			3	2	32
1		14		5		7		10		*11*	9	8		6			4			3	2	33
1		11		5		7		10			9	8	14	*6*			4			3	2	34
1		11		5		7		10			9	8	14	6			4			3	*2*	35
1		11				7		10			9	8	6	5			4	2			3	36

STIRLING ALBION Second Division

Year Formed: 1945. *Ground & Address:* Forthbank Stadium, Springkerse Industrial Estate, Stirling FK7 7UJ. *Telephone:* 01786 450399.
Chairman: Peter McKenzie. *Secretary:* Marlyn Hallam. *Commercial Manager:* —.
Manager: Kevin Drinkell. *Assistant Manager:* Ray Stewart. *Physio:* George Cameron.
Managers since 1975: A.Smith; G.Peebles; J.Fleeting, J.Brogan. *Club Nickname(s):* The Binos. *Previous Grounds:* Annfield.
Record Attendance: 26,400 v Celtic, Scottish Cup 4th rd; 14 Mar, 1959.
Record Transfer Fee received: £70,000 for John Philliben to Doncaster R (Mar 1984).
Record Transfer Fee paid: £17,000 for Douglas Lawrie from Airdrieonians (Dec 1989).
Record Victory: 20-0 v Selkirk, Scottish Cup 1st rd; 8 Dec, 1984.
Record Defeat: 0-9 v Dundee U, Division I; 30 Dec, 1967.
Most Capped Player: —.
Most League Appearances: 504: Matt McPhee, 1967-81.

STIRLING ALBION 1994–95 LEAGUE RECORD

Match No.	Date	Venue	Opponents	Result		H/T Score	Lg. Pos.	Goalscorers	Attendance
1	Aug 13	H	East Fife	L	0-1	0-0	—		808
2	20	H	Dumbarton	D	1-1	0-0	8	McLeod	715
3	27	A	Clyde	W	2-1	2-0	5	Tait, Watters	1162
4	Sept 3	H	Morton	W	2-0	0-0	3	Gibson, Watters	1026
5	10	A	Stenhousemuir	L	0-3	0-2	5		555
6	24	A	Meadowbank T	W	2-1	1-0	4	Watters, Roberts	247
7	Oct 1	H	Queen of the S	W	3-0	0-0	2	Watters, McLeod, Campbell (og)	697
8	8	A	Brechin C	W	2-1	1-0	2	Watters, Taggart	555
9	15	H	Berwick R	W	3-2	1-1	1	Mitchell, McQuilter, Drinkell	863
10	22	A	East Fife	L	3-4	1-1	2	McInnes, Taggart, Tait	1039
11	29	H	Clyde	L	0-1	0-0	2		1118
12	Nov 5	A	Dumbarton	L	0-1	0-1	2		778
13	12	H	Stenhousemuir	L	0-2	0-1	6		696
14	22	A	Morton	D	1-1	0-0	—	Taggart	1941
15	26	H	Meadowbank T	L	2-3	0-0	7	Taggart, Watters	518
16	Dec 3	A	Queen of the S	W	1-0	1-0	6	Mitchell	1197
17	24	H	Brechin C	W	2-0	1-0	6	Armstrong, McLeod	760
18	31	A	Berwick R	L	0-1	0-1	7		736
19	Jan 14	H	East Fife	W	3-0	2-0	—	McInnes 3	810
20	17	A	Clyde	L	0-2	0-0	5		1345
21	21	A	Dumbarton	D	2-2	0-2	6	Tait, Drinkell	700
22	Feb 4	A	Stenhousemuir	W	2-0	1-0	6	McInnes, Watters	797
23	11	H	Morton	L	0-3	0-1	6		1069
24	25	H	Queen of the S	D	1-1	0-1	6	McInnes	528
25	Mar 4	A	Brechin C	L	1-2	0-1	6	Watters	465
26	8	A	Meadowbank T	W	3-0	0-0	—	Paterson G, Taggart, McInnes	165
27	11	H	Berwick R	D	2-2	1-0	6	McLeod, Farquhar	582
28	18	H	Stenhousemuir	W	3-1	1-0	6	McLeod, Watters 2	431
29	25	A	Morton	D	2-2	1-1	6	Watters, Lilley (og)	2025
30	Apr 1	A	Queen of the S	W	3-1	1-0	6	Watters, Gibson, McLeod	1056
31	8	H	Meadowbank T	W	2-1	0-0	5	Gibson, Watters	478
32	15	H	Brechin C	W	2-0	1-0	4	Watters 2	607
33	22	A	Berwick R	D	0-0	0-0	4		601
34	29	A	East Fife	W	2-1	0-1	3	McLeod, Mitchell	510
35	May 6	H	Clyde	W	2-0	0-0	2	Gibson, McLeod	1122
36	13	H	Dumbarton	L	0-2	0-0	3		3003

Final League Position: 3

Most League Goals in Season (Individual): 27: Joe Hughes, Division II; 1969-70.
Most Goals Overall (Individual): 129: Billy Steele, 1971-83.

Honours
League Champions: Division II 1952-53, 1957-58, 1960-61, 1964-65. Second Division 1976-77, 1990-91; *Runners-up:* Division II 1948-49, 1950-51.
Scottish Cup: —. *League Cup:* —.
Club colours: Shirt: Red with white sleeves. Shorts: White. Stockings: White.

Goalscorers: *League (54):* Watters 15, McLeod 8, McInnes 7, Taggart 5, Gibson 4, Mitchell 3, Tait 3, Drinkell 2, Armstrong 1, Farquhar 1, McQuilter 1, Paterson G 1, Roberts 1, own goals 2. *Scottish Cup (10):* McInnes 3, Taggart 3, McQuilter 1, Mitchell 1 (pen), Tait 1, Watters 1. *League Cup (0) B&Q Cup (4):* Taggart 2, McInnes 1, Watters 1.

McGeown M 29	Hamilton J 3	Tait T 34	Mitchell C 31 + 1	McQuilter R 29 + 1	Reid W 5	McInnes I 34 + 1	Roberts P 3 + 9	Watters W 31 + 3	Taggart C 32 + 2	McLeod J 36	Gibson J 32 + 2	Callaghan T 1 + 3	Armstrong P 18 + 5	Paterson A 28 + 2	Stewart R 1 + 1	Farquhar A 2 + 10	Drinkell K 8 + 2	McAneny P 3 + 1	Kerr R 5 + 3	Monaghan M 7	Watson P 4 + 2	Paterson G 11	Deas P 9 + 1	*Match No.*
1	2	3	4	5	6	7	*8*	9	10	11	12	14												1
1	*2*	6	4	5	7	12	8	9	10	11	14		3											2
1		6	4	5	8	7	12	*9*	10	11	2	14	3											3
1			4	5	8	7		9	10	11	2	6	*3*	12	14									4
1		6	4	5	8	7		9	10	11	2	14	3	12										5
1		6	4	5		7	14	9	10	11	3			2		*8*								6
1		6	4	5		7	14	9	10	11	3		12	2			*8*							7
1		6	4	5		7	14	*9*	10	11	3			2			8							8
1		6	4	5		7		9	10	11	3		12	2			8							9
1		6	4	5		7	14	*9*	10	11	3		12	2			8							10
1		6		5		7		14	10	11	3		9	2			*8*	4						11
1		6		5		7	14		10	11	3		9	*2*			8	4						12
1	2	6	12	5		7		9	10	11	3		8			14		4						13
1		6	4	5		7	12	9	10	*11*	3		8	2					14					14
1		6	4	5		7	12	9	10	*11*	3		8	2					14					15
1		6	4	5		7	14	*9*	10	11	3		12	2	8									16
		6	4			7		*9*	10	11	3		8	2		14				1	5			17
		6	4			7	9		10	11	3		*8*	2		14				1	5			18
			4	5		7		9	10	11	3		8	2					6	1				19
		8	4	5		7		9	10	11	3			2			12		6	1				20
		8	4	5		7		9	10	11	3		14	2			12		*6*	1				21
		6	4	5		7		14	10	11	3		8	2			*9*		12	1				22
		6	4	5		7		14	10	11			3	2			9		*8*	1	12			23
1		6	4	5		7		9	10	11			3	2		14			*8*					24
1		6	*4*	5		7		9	10	11	3		8	2		14								25
1		6	4			7		9	10	*11*	3		8			14		12			2	5		26
1		6	4			7		9	10	11	2		*8*			14					3	5	12	27
1		6		5		7		9	10	11	3			2								4	8	28
1		6		5				9	*10*	11	3			2		7					14	4	8	29
1		6	10	5		7		9		*11*	3			2		14						4	8	30
1		6	5			7		9	*10*	11	3			2		14						4	8	31
1		6	5			7		9	10	11	3			2								4	8	32
1		6	5	12		7		9	10	11	3			2								4	8	33
1		6	5	10		7		9		11	3			2								4	8	34
1		6	5	10		7		9	12	11	3			2								4	8	35
1		6	5	10		7		9	12	11	*3*			2		14						4	8	36

STRANRAER Second Division

Year Formed: 1870. *Ground & Address:* Stair Park, London Rd, Stranraer DG9 8BS. *Telephone:* 01776 703271.
Ground Capacity: total: 5000. seated: 700. *Size of Pitch:* 110yd × 70yd.
Chairman: G. F. Compton. *Secretary:* Graham Rodgers. *Commercial Manager: T. L. Sutherland.*
Manager: Alex McAnespie. *Coach:* Derek McHarg.
Managers since 1975: J. Hughes; N. Hood; G. Hamilton; D. Sneddon; J. Clark; R. Clark; A. McAnespie. *Club Nickname(s):* The Blues. *Previous Grounds:* None.
Record Attendance: 6500 v Rangers, Scottish Cup 1st rd; 24 Jan, 1948.
Record Transfer Fee received: £30,000 for Duncan George to Ayr Utd.
Record Transfer Fee paid: £15,000 for Colin Harkness from Kilmarnock (Aug 1989).
Record Victory: 7-0 v Brechin C, Division II; 6 Feb, 1965.
Record Defeat: 1-11 v Queen of the South, Scottish Cup 1st rd; 16 Jan, 1932.
Most Capped Player: —.
Most League Appearances: 256: Ian McDonald.

STRANRAER 1994–95 LEAGUE RECORD

Match No.	Date	Venue	Opponents	Result		H/T Score	Lg. Pos.	Goalscorers	Attendance
1	Aug 13	A	Clydebank	L	0-2	0-0	—		908
2	20	A	Dundee	L	1-3	0-2	10	Walker	3186
3	27	H	Ayr U	W	2-1	0-1	6	McCaffrey, Hughes (pen)	1653
4	Sept 3	A	Hamilton A	L	0-1	0-1	9		1083
5	10	H	Raith R	D	0-0	0-0	9		1078
6	24	A	Dunfermline Ath	L	0-1	0-1	10		3893
7	Oct 1	H	Airdrieonians	L	0-1	0-0	10		1001
8	8	H	St Mirren	D	1-1	0-0	10	Walker	1157
9	15	A	St Johnstone	L	0-3	0-0	10		2678
10	22	H	Clydebank	L	0-1	0-0	10		781
11	29	A	Ayr U	L	1-2	1-1	10	Sloan	2073
12	Nov 12	A	Raith R	L	2-4	0-2	10	Ferguson, Walker	2556
13	19	H	Hamilton A	W	2-0	1-0	10	Brannigan, Millar	784
14	23	H	Dundee	L	0-2	0-1	—		765
15	26	H	Dunfermline Ath	D	0-0	0-0	10		1118
16	Dec 3	A	Airdrieonians	L	1-8	1-2	10	Gallagher	1207
17	10	H	St Johnstone	D	2-2	1-1	10	Sloan, Farrell	780
18	26	A	St Mirren	L	0-1	0-0	—		2505
19	31	A	Clydebank	W	3-2	2-0	9=	Grant, Henderson, Ferguson	652
20	Jan 2	H	Ayr U	W	2-0	1-0	—	Gallagher, Grant	1899
21	7	A	Dundee	L	0-2	0-1	9=		2615
22	14	A	Hamilton A	L	0-1	0-0	9		1015
23	24	H	Raith R	L	2-4	1-1	—	Gallagher, Sinclair (og)	769
24	Feb 4	H	Airdrieonians	L	1-4	0-2	10	Sloan	945
25	14	A	Dunfermline Ath	L	1-3	0-1	—	Sloan	3528
26	25	A	St Johnstone	L	0-3	0-1	10		2725
27	Mar 11	H	St Mirren	L	1-3	1-1	10	Henderson	935
28	18	A	Raith R	D	1-1	0-1	10	Reilly	2197
29	25	H	Hamilton A	L	0-5	0-2	10		655
30	Apr 1	A	Airdrieonians	L	0-2	0-0	10		851
31	8	H	Dunfermline Ath	L	0-1	0-1	10		988
32	15	A	St Mirren	L	0-2	0-2	10		2315
33	22	H	St Johnstone	L	2-6	0-2	10	Henderson 2	702
34	29	H	Clydebank	L	0-1	0-1	10		582
35	May 6	A	Ayr U	L	0-3	0-1	10		1204
36	13	H	Dundee	L	0-5	0-1	10		1589

Final League Position: 10

Most League Goals in Season (Individual): 27: Derek Frye, Second Division; 1977-78.
Most Goals Overall (Individual): —.

Honours
League Champions: Second Division 1993-94.
Scottish Cup: —.
League Cup: —.
Qualifying Cup Winners: 1937.
Club colours: Shirt: Royal blue with geometrical design. Shorts: White. Stockings: Royal blue.

Goalscorers: *League (25):* Henderson 4, Sloan 4, Gallagher 3, Walker 3, Ferguson 2, Grant 2, Brannigan 1, Farrell 1, Hughes 1 (pen), McCaffrey 1, Millar 1, Reilly 1, own goal 1. *Scottish Cup (0) League Cup (2):* Cody 1, Ferguson 1. *B&Q Cup (3):* Ferguson 1, Henderson 1, Walker 1.

Ross S 28	Treanor M 4	Hughes J 33	Millar G 28 + 1	Brannigan K 31	McCaffrey J 14 + 3	Reilly R 16 + 9	Cody S 16	Walker T 28 + 3	Duncan G 30 + 1	Henderson D 22	Ferguson W 1 + 13	Gallagher A 23 + 1	McLean P 14 + 12	Grant A 21 + 5	Sloan T 29 + 3	Howard N 16 + 1	McCann J 15 + 1	Farrell S 1 + 3	McAuley I 1	Callaghan T 14 + 2	Duffy B 8 + 1	Robertson J 2 + 1	Fulton B — + 1	McGuire D 1 + 5	Match No.
1	*2*	3	4	5	6	7	8	9	10	11	12	14													1
1	2	3	6	5	4		10	9	8	11	12		7	14											2
1		3	2	5	4		6	*8*	9	11	12	10		14	7										3
1	10	3	2	*5*	4		6	8		11	12	9	14		7										4
1	4	3	2		5		10	8	9	11		6	12		7	14									5
1		3	2		*6*		10	14	9	11		5	12	8	7		4								6
1		3	2	5	4		10			*11*		6	9	8	7			14							7
1		3	2	5	4		10	11	9			6	12	8	*7*			14							8
1		3	2	5	4	7		8	9	11		6		12			10								9
1		3		5	*6*	12	10	9	14	11		8		7			4	2							10
1		3	2	5		12		9	6	11			10	8	7		4								11
1		3	2	5		14		9	6		12		10	8	7	4			*11*						12
1		3	2	5		14	*10*	9	11		12				7	6	4			8					13
1		3	*2*	5			10	9	11		12	6	14		7		4			8					14
1		3	2	5		11	*10*	9			12	6	14		7		4			8					15
1		3	2	5		11	10	9				6	14	7	12		*4*			8					16
		3	2	5		*10*			9	11	12	6	8		7	4		14			1				17
1		3	2	5		14			9	11	12	6	10	8	*7*		4								18
1		3	2	5		10			9	11	12	*4*	14	8	7	6									19
1		3		5		10		14	9	*11*	12	4		8	7	6	2								20
1		3		5		10		12	*9*	11		4	14	8	7		2			6					21
1		3		5		2		11	9				12	8	7	4	6			10					22
1		3	2	5	14	11		*10*	9			4	12		7	6				8					23
1		3	2			14	*10*	7				6	11	8	12	5	4			9	15				24
1		3		5	14	*2*		11	9			4	12	8	7	6				10					25
1		2		5	14	12		9	3			4	11	8	7	6				*10*					26
1		3	2	5				10	9	11			7	8	12		4			6					27
1		2	3			11	10	9	6			5		8	7		4			12					28
1			2	5		3	10	8	9	11		*6*			7	4						12	14		29
			4	5		3		8	10	11			7		9	6					1	2		12	30
			4	5		3		7	10				11	8	9	6	14				1	*2*		12	31
		3	2	5		12		9	6	11			*10*	8	7	4					1			14	32
		3	14	5	6			9	2	11				12	8	4				10	1			7	33
		2	*3*	5	4	14			6	11			8	9	7					10	1			12	34
		3	*2*	5	4	8		10	6	11	9			12	7					14	1				35
		2			6			9	11		12	*5*	3	8	7	4				10	1			14	36

Scottish League 1994–95

Premier Division

		Home			Goals		Away			Goals		
	P	W	D	L	F	A	W	D	L	F	A	Pts
Rangers	36	11	5	2	31	14	9	4	5	29	21	69
Motherwell	36	8	6	4	29	23	6	6	6	21	27	54
Hibernian	36	9	7	2	37	19	3	10	5	12	18	53
Celtic	36	6	8	4	23	19	5	10	3	16	14	51
Falkirk	36	8	3	7	26	24	4	9	5	22	23	48
Hearts	36	9	4	5	26	14	3	3	12	18	37	43
Kilmarnock	36	8	4	6	22	16	3	6	9	18	32	43
Partick T	36	4	9	5	23	23	6	4	8	17	27	43
Aberdeen	36	7	7	4	24	16	3	4	11	19	30	41
Dundee U	36	6	6	6	24	20	3	3	12	16	36	36–1

First Division

		Home			Goals		Away			Goals		
	P	W	D	L	F	A	W	D	L	F	A	Pts
Raith R	36	8	8	2	27	18	11	4	3	27	14	69
Dunfermline Ath	36	11	5	2	35	11	7	9	2	28	21	68
Dundee	36	11	4	3	34	18	9	4	5	31	18	68
Airdrieonians	36	7	6	5	22	14	10	4	4	28	19	61
St Johnstone	36	10	6	2	36	15	4	8	6	23	24	56
Hamilton A	36	9	3	6	23	22	5	4	9	19	26	49
St Mirren	36	7	5	6	20	18	1	7	10	14	32	36
Clydebank	36	4	6	8	20	25	4	5	9	13	22	35
Ayr U	36	6	5	7	22	24	0	6	12	9	34	29
Stranraer	36	3	4	11	15	37	1	1	16	10	44	17

Second Division

		Home			Goals		Away			Goals		
	P	W	D	L	F	A	W	D	L	F	A	Pts
Greenock Morton	36	12	5	1	33	11	6	5	7	22	22	64
Dumbarton	36	12	4	2	43	16	5	5	8	14	19	60
Stirling Albion	36	9	3	6	28	20	8	4	6	26	23	58
Stenhousemuir	36	7	10	1	24	14	7	4	7	22	25	56
Berwick R	36	10	6	2	23	13	5	4	9	29	33	55
Clyde	36	8	5	5	33	25	6	5	7	20	23	52
Queen of the S	36	6	3	9	25	26	5	8	5	21	25	44
East Fife	36	7	3	8	31	27	4	7	7	17	29	43
Meadowbank T*	36	7	2	9	16	21	4	3	11	16	33	35
Brechin C	36	4	5	9	15	26	2	1	15	7	34	24

*Meadowbank T had 3 points deducted for fielding an ineligible player

Third Division

		Home			Goals		Away			Goals		
	P	W	D	L	F	A	W	D	L	F	A	Pts
Forfar Ath	36	14	3	1	42	16	11	2	5	25	17	80
Montrose	36	9	4	5	33	17	11	3	4	36	15	67
Ross County	36	9	1	8	35	26	9	5	4	24	18	60
East Stirling	36	10	2	6	28	20	8	3	7	33	30	59
Alloa	36	7	4	7	23	20	8	5	5	27	25	54
Caledonian T	36	5	7	6	27	33	7	2	9	21	28	45
Arbroath	36	6	3	9	21	23	7	2	9	30	39	44
Queen's Park	36	7	2	9	21	27	5	4	9	25	30	42
Cowdenbeath	36	4	5	9	23	36	7	2	9	25	24	40
Albion R	36	3	0	15	16	39	2	3	13	11	43	18

PLAY-OFF: Aberdeen (9th place, Premier Division) v Dunfermline Ath (runners-up, First Division)

21 MAY at Pittodrie
Aberdeen (1) 3 *(Glass, Shearer 2)*
Dunfermline Ath (0) 1 *(Robertson)* 21,000
Aberdeen: Snelders; McKimmie, Wright, Grant, Irvine, Smith, Hetherston, Shearer, Miller, Thomson, Glass.
Dunfermline Ath: Van De Kamp; McNamara, Fleming, McCathie, Tod, Smith, Den Bieman, Robertson, Moore (Shaw), Petrie, McCulloch (Hawkins).

25 MAY at East End Park
Dunfermline Ath (0) 1 *(Smith)*
Aberdeen (0) 3 *(Dodds, Miller, Glass)* 16,000
Dunfermline Ath: Van De Kamp; McNamara, Fleming, McCathie, Tod, Smith, Den Bieman, Robertson, Moore, Petrie, McCulloch (Shaw).
Aberdeen: Snelders; McKimmie, Wright, Grant, Irvine (Inglis), Smith, Hetherston, Shearer, Miller (Kane), Dodds, Glass.

SCOTTISH LEAGUE 1890–91 to 1994–95

*On goal average/difference. †Held jointly after indecisive play-off. ‡Won on deciding match.
††Held jointly. ¶Two points deducted for fielding ineligible player.
Competition suspended 1940–45 during war. ‡‡Two points deducted for registration irregularities.

PREMIER DIVISION

	First	*Pts*	*Second*	*Pts*	*Third*	*Pts*
			Maximum points: 72			
1975–76	Rangers	54	Celtic	48	Hibernian	43
1976–77	Celtic	55	Rangers	46	Aberdeen	43
1977–78	Rangers	55	Aberdeen	53	Dundee U	40
1978–79	Celtic	48	Rangers	45	Dundee U	44
1979–80	Aberdeen	48	Celtic	47	St Mirren	42
1980–81	Celtic	56	Aberdeen	49	Rangers*	44
1981–82	Celtic	55	Aberdeen	53	Rangers	43
1982–83	Dundee U	56	Celtic*	55	Aberdeen	55
1983–84	Aberdeen	57	Celtic	50	Dundee U	47
1984–85	Aberdeen	59	Celtic	52	Dundee U	47
1985–86	Celtic*	50	Hearts	50	Dundee U	47
			Maximum points: 88			
1986–87	Rangers	69	Celtic	63	Dundee U	60
1987–88	Celtic	72	Hearts	62	Rangers	60
			Maximum points: 72			
1988–89	Rangers	56	Aberdeen	50	Celtic	46
1989–90	Rangers	51	Aberdeen*	44	Hearts	44
1990–91	Rangers	55	Aberdeen	53	Celtic*	41
			Maximum points: 88			
1991–92	Rangers	72	Hearts	63	Celtic	62
1992–93	Rangers	73	Aberdeen	64	Celtic	60
1993–94	Rangers	58	Aberdeen	55	Motherwell	54
			Maximum points: 108			
1994–95	Rangers	69	Motherwell	54	Hibernian	53

FIRST DIVISION

			Maximum points: 52			
1975–76	Partick T	41	Kilmarnock	35	Montrose	30
			Maximum points: 78			
1976–77	St Mirren	62	Clydebank	58	Dundee	51
1977–78	Morton*	58	Hearts	58	Dundee	57
1978–79	Dundee	55	Kilmarnock*	54	Clydebank	54
1979–80	Hearts	53	Airdrieonians	51	Ayr U	44
1980–81	Hibernian	57	Dundee	52	St Johnstone	51
1981–82	Motherwell	61	Kilmarnock	51	Hearts	50
1982–83	St Johnstone	55	Hearts	54	Clydebank	50
1983–84	Morton	54	Dumbarton	51	Partick T	46
1984–85	Motherwell	50	Clydebank	48	Falkirk	45
1985–86	Hamilton A	56	Falkirk	45	Kilmarnock	44
			Maximum points: 88			
1986–87	Morton	57	Dunfermline Ath	56	Dumbarton	53
1987–88	Hamilton A	56	Meadowbank T	52	Clydebank	49
			Maximum points: 78			
1988–89	Dunfermline Ath	54	Falkirk	52	Clydebank	48
1989–90	St Johnstone	58	Airdrieonians	54	Clydebank	44
1990–91	Falkirk	54	Airdrieonians	53	Dundee	52
			Maximum points: 88			
1991–92	Dundee	58	Partick T*	57	Hamilton A	57
1992–93	Raith R	65	Kilmarnock	54	Dunfermline Ath	52
1993–94	Falkirk	66	Dunfermline Ath	65	Airdrieonians	54
			Maximum points: 108			
1994–95	Raith R	69	Dunfermline Ath*	68	Dundee	68

SECOND DIVISION

			Maximum points: 52			
1975–77	Clydebank*	40	Raith R	40	Alloa	35
			Maximum points: 78			
1976–77	Stirling A	55	Alloa	51	Dunfermline Ath	50
1977–78	Clyde*	53	Raith R	53	Dunfermline Ath	48
1978–79	Berwick R	54	Dunfermline Ath	52	Falkirk	50
1979–80	Falkirk	50	East Stirling	49	Forfar Ath	46
1980–81	Queen's Park	50	Queen of the S	46	Cowdenbeath	45
1981–82	Clyde	59	Alloa*	50	Arbroath	50
1982–83	Brechin C	55	Meadowbank T	54	Arbroath	49

1983–84	Forfar Ath	63	East Fife	47	Berwick R	43
1984–85	Montrose	53	Alloa	50	Dunfermline Ath	49
1985–86	Dunfermline Ath	57	Queen of the S	55	Meadowbank T	49
1986–87	Meadowbank T	55	Raith R*	52	Stirling A	52
1987–88	Ayr U	61	St Johnstone	59	Queen's Park	51
1988–89	Albion R	50	Alloa	45	Brechin C	43
1989–90	Brechin C	49	Kilmarnock	48	Stirling A	47
1990–91	Stirling A	54	Montrose	46	Cowdenbeath	45
			Maximum points: 78			
1991–92	Dumbarton	52	Cowdenbeath	51	Alloa	50
1992–93	Clyde	54	Brechin C*	53	Stranraer	53
1993–94	Stranraer	56	Berwick R	48	Stenhousemuir*	47
			Maximum points: 108			
1994–95	Morton	64	Dumbarton	60	Stirling A	58

THIRD DIVISION

Maximum points: 108

1994–95	Forfar Ath	80	Montrose	67	Ross Co	60

FIRST DIVISION to 1974–75

Maximum points: a 36; *b* 44; *c* 40; *d* 52; *e* 60; *f* 68; g 76; *h* 84.

	First	*Pts*	*Second*	*Pts*	*Third*	*Pts*
1890–91*a*††	Dumbarton	29	Rangers	29	Celtic	24
1891–92*b*	Dumbarton	37	Celtic	35	Hearts	30
1892–93*a*	Celtic	29	Rangers	28	St Mirren	23
1893–94*a*	Celtic	29	Hearts	26	St Bernard's	22
1894–95*a*	Hearts	31	Celtic	26	Rangers	21
1895–96*a*	Celtic	30	Rangers	26	Hibernian	24
1896–97*a*	Hearts	28	Hibernian	26	Rangers	25
1897–98*a*	Celtic	33	Rangers	29	Hibernian	22
1898–99*a*	Rangers	36	Hearts	26	Celtic	24
1899–1900*a*	Rangers	32	Celtic	25	Hibernian	24
1900–01*c*	Rangers	35	Celtic	29	Hibernian	25
1901–02*a*	Rangers	28	Celtic	26	Hearts	22
1902–03*b*	Hibernian	37	Dundee	31	Rangers	29
1903–04*d*	Third Lanark	43	Hearts	39	Rangers*	38
1904–05*d*	Celtic‡	41	Rangers	41	Third Lanark	35
1905–06*e*	Celtic	49	Hearts	43	Airdrieonians	38
1906–07*f*	Celtic	55	Dundee	48	Rangers	45
1907–08*f*	Celtic	55	Falkirk	51	Rangers	50
1908–09*f*	Celtic	51	Dundee	50	Clyde	48
1909–10*f*	Celtic	54	Falkirk	52	Rangers	46
1910–11*f*	Rangers	52	Aberdeen	48	Falkirk	44
1911–12*f*	Rangers	51	Celtic	45	Clyde	42
1912–13*f*	Rangers	53	Celtic	49	Hearts*	41
1913–14*g*	Celtic	65	Rangers	59	Hearts*	54
1914–15*g*	Celtic	65	Hearts	61	Rangers	50
1915–16*g*	Celtic	67	Rangers	56	Morton	51
1916–17*g*	Celtic	64	Morton	54	Rangers	53
1917–18*f*	Rangers	56	Celtic	55	Kilmarnock	43
1918–19*f*	Celtic	58	Rangers	57	Morton	47
1919–20*h*	Rangers	71	Celtic	68	Motherwell	57
1920–21*h*	Rangers	76	Celtic	66	Hearts	56
1921–22*h*	Celtic	67	Rangers	66	Raith R	56
1922–23*g*	Rangers	55	Airdrieonians	50	Celtic	46
1923–24*g*	Rangers	59	Airdrieonians	50	Celtic	41
1924–25*g*	Rangers	60	Airdrieonians	57	Hibernian	52
1925–26*g*	Celtic	58	Airdrieonians*	50	Hearts	50
1926–27*g*	Rangers	56	Motherwell	51	Celtic	49
1927–28*g*	Rangers	60	Celtic*	55	Motherwell	55
1928–29*g*	Rangers	67	Celtic	51	Motherwell	50
1929–30*g*	Rangers	60	Motherwell	55	Aberdeen	53
1930–31*g*	Rangers	60	Celtic	58	Motherwell	56
1931–32*g*	Motherwell	66	Rangers	61	Celtic	48
1932–33*g*	Rangers	62	Motherwell	59	Hearts	50
1933–34*g*	Rangers	66	Motherwell	62	Celtic	47
1934–35*g*	Rangers	55	Celtic	52	Hearts	50
1935–36*g*	Celtic	66	Rangers*	61	Aberdeen	61
1936–37*g*	Rangers	61	Aberdeen	54	Celtic	52
1937–38*g*	Celtic	61	Hearts	58	Rangers	49
1938–39*g*	Rangers	59	Celtic	48	Aberdeen	46
1946–47*e*	Rangers	46	Hibernian	44	Aberdeen	39
1947–48*e*	Hibernian	48	Rangers	46	Partick T	36
1948–49*e*	Rangers	46	Dundee	45	Hibernian	39

1949–50*e*	Rangers	50	Hibernian	49	Hearts	43
1950–51*e*	Hibernian	48	Rangers*	38	Dundee	38
1951–52*e*	Hibernian	45	Rangers	41	East Fife	37
1952–53*e*	Rangers*	43	Hibernian	43	East Fife	39
1953–54*e*	Celtic	43	Hearts	38	Partick T	35
1954–55*e*	Aberdeen	49	Celtic	46	Rangers	41
1955–56*f*	Rangers	52	Aberdeen	46	Hearts*	45
1956–57*f*	Rangers	55	Hearts	53	Kilmarnock	42
1957–58*f*	Hearts	62	Rangers	49	Celtic	46
1958–59*f*	Rangers	50	Hearts	48	Motherwell	44
1959–60*f*	Hearts	54	Kilmarnock	50	Rangers*	42
1960–61*f*	Rangers	51	Kilmarnock	50	Third Lanark	42
1961–62*f*	Dundee	54	Rangers	51	Celtic	46
1962–63*f*	Rangers	57	Kilmarnock	48	Partick T	46
1963–64*f*	Rangers	55	Kilmarnock	49	Celtic*	47
1964–65*f*	Kilmarnock*	50	Hearts	50	Dunfermline Ath	49
1965–66*f*	Celtic	57	Rangers	55	Kilmarnock	45
1966–67*f*	Celtic	58	Rangers	55	Clyde	46
1967–68*f*	Celtic	63	Rangers	61	Hibernian	45
1968–69*f*	Celtic	54	Rangers	49	Dunfermline Ath	45
1969–70*f*	Celtic	57	Rangers	45	Hibernian	44
1970–71*f*	Celtic	56	Aberdeen	54	St Johnstone	44
1971–72*f*	Celtic	60	Aberdeen	50	Rangers	44
1972–73*f*	Celtic	57	Rangers	56	Hibernian	45
1973–74*f*	Celtic	53	Hibernian	49	Rangers	48
1974–75*f*	Rangers	56	Hibernian	49	Celtic	45

SECOND DIVISION to 1974–75

Maximum points: a 76; *b* 72; *c* 68; *d* 52; *e* 60; *f* 36; *g* 44; *h* 52.

1893–94*f*	Hibernian	29	Cowlairs	27	Clyde	24
1894–95*f*	Hibernian	30	Motherwell	22	Port Glasgow	20
1895–96*f*	Abercorn	27	Leith Ath	23	Renton	21
1896–97*f*	Partick T	31	Leith Ath	27	Kilmarnock	21
1897–98*f*	Kilmarnock	29	Port Glasgow	25	Morton	22
1898–99*f*	Kilmarnock	32	Leith Ath	27	Port Glasgow	25
1899–1900*f*	Partick T	29	Morton	26	Port Glasgow	20
1900–01*f*	St Bernard's	26	Airdrieonians	23	Abercorn	21
1901–02*g*	Port Glasgow	32	Partick T	31	Motherwell	26
1902–03*g*	Airdrieonians	35	Motherwell	28	Ayr U	27
1903–04*g*	Hamilton A	37	Clyde	29	Ayr U	28
1904–05*g*	Clyde	32	Falkirk	28	Hamilton A	27
1905–06*g*	Leith Ath	34	Clyde	31	Albion R	27
1906–07*g*	St Bernard's	32	Vale of Leven*	27	Arthurlie	27
1907–08*g*	Raith R	30	Dumbarton	‡‡27	Ayr U	27
1908–09*g*	Abercorn	31	Raith R*	28	Vale of Leven	28
1909–10*g*‡	Leith Ath	33	Raith R	33	St Bernard's	27
1910–11*g*	Dumbarton	31	Ayr U	27	Albion R	25
1911–12*g*	Ayr U	35	Abercorn	30	Dumbarton	27
1912–13*h*	Ayr U	34	Dunfarmline Ath	33	East Stirling	32
1913–14*g*	Cowdenbeath	31	Albion R	27	Dunfermline Ath	26
1914–15*h*	Cowdenbeath*	37	St Bernard's*	37	Leith Ath	37
1921–22*a*	Alloa	60	Cowdenbeath	47	Armadale	45
1922–23*a*	Queen's Park	57	Clydebank	¶50	St Johnstone	¶45
1923–24*a*	St Johnstone	56	Cowdenbeath	55	Bathgate	44
1924–25*a*	Dundee U	50	Clydebank	48	Clyde	47
1925–26*a*	Dunfermline Ath	59	Clyde	53	Ayr U	52
1926–27*a*	Bo'ness	56	Raith R	49	Clydebank	45
1927–28*a*	Ayr U	54	Third Lanark	45	King's Park	44
1928–29*b*	Dundee U	51	Morton	50	Arbroath	47
1929–30*a*	Leith Ath*	57	East Fife	57	Albion R	54
1930–31*a*	Third Lanark	61	Dundee U	50	Dunfermline Ath	47
1931–32*a*	East Stirling*	55	St Johnstone	55	Raith Rovers*	46
1932–33*c*	Hibernian	54	Queen of the S	49	Dunfermline Ath	47
1933–34*c*	Albion R	45	Dunfermline Ath*	44	Arbroath	44
1934–35*c*	Third Lanark	52	Arbroath	50	St Bernard's	47
1935–36*c*	Falkirk	59	St Mirren	52	Morton	48
1936–37*c*	Ayr U	54	Morton	51	St Bernard's	48
1937–38*c*	Raith R	59	Albion R	48	Airdrieonians	47
1938–39*c*	Cowdenbeath	60	Alloa*	48	East Fife	48
1946–47*d*	Dundee	45	Airdrieonians	42	East Fife	31
1947–48*e*	East Fife	53	Albion R	42	Hamilton A	40
1948–49*e*	Raith R*	42	Stirling Albion	42	Airdrieonians*	41
1949–50*e*	Morton	47	Airdrieonians	44	St Johnstone*	36
1950–51*e*	Queen of the S*	45	Stirling Albion	45	Ayr U	36

1951–52*e*	Clyde	44	Falkirk	43	Ayr U	39
1952–53*e*	Stirling Albion	44	Hamilton A	43	Queen's Park	37
1953–54*e*	Motherwell	45	Kilmarnock	42	Third Lanark*	36
1954–55*e*	Airdrieonians	46	Dunfermline Ath	42	Hamilton A	39
1955–56*b*	Queen's Park	54	Ayr U	51	St Johnstone	49
1956–57*b*	Clyde	64	Third Lanark	51	Cowdenbeath	45
1957–58*b*	Stirling Albion	55	Dunfermline Ath	53	Arbroath	47
1958–59*b*	Ayr U	60	Arbroath	51	Stenhousemuir	40
1959–60*b*	St Johnstone	53	Dundee U	50	Queen of the S	49
1960–61*b*	Stirling Albion	55	Falkirk	54	Stenhousemuir	50
1961–62*b*	Clyde	54	Queen of the S	53	Morton	44
1962–63*b*	St Johnstone	55	East Stirling	49	Morton	48
1963–64*b*	Morton	67	Clyde	53	Arbroath	46
1964–65*b*	Stirling Albion	59	Hamilton A	50	Queen of the S	45
1965–66*b*	Ayr U	53	Airdrieonians	50	Queen of the S	49
1966–67*b*	Morton	69	Raith R	58	Arbroath	57
1967–68*b*	St Mirren	62	Arbroath	53	East Fife	40
1968–69*b*	Motherwell	64	Ayr U	53	East Fife*	47
1969–70*b*	Falkirk	56	Cowdenbeath	55	Queen of the S	50
1970–71*b*	Partick T	56	East Fife	51	Arbroath	46
1971–72*b*	Dumbarton*	52	Arbroath	52	Stirling Albion	50
1972–73*b*	Clyde	56	Dumfermline Ath	52	Raith R*	47
1973–74*b*	Airdrieonians	60	Kilmarnock	59	Hamilton A	55
1974–75*a*	Falkirk	54	Queen of the S	53	Montrose	53

Elected to First Division: 1894 Clyde; 1897 Partick T; 1899 Kilmarnock; 1900 Partick T; 1902 Partick T; 1903 Airdrieonians; 1905 Falkirk, Aberdeen and Hamilton A; 1906 Clyde; 1910 Raith R; 1913 Ayr U.

RELEGATED FROM PREMIER DIVISION

1975–76 Dundee, St Johnstone
1976–77 Hearts, Kilmarnock
1977–78 Ayr U, Clydebank
1978–79 Hearts, Motherwell
1979–80 Dundee, Hibernian
1980–81 Kilmarnock, Hearts
1981–82 Partick T, Airdrieonians
1982–83 Morton, Kilmarnock
1983–84 St Johnstone, Motherwell
1984–85 Dumbarton, Morton
1985–86 *No relegation due to League reorganization*
1986–87 Clydebank, Hamilton A
1987–88 Falkirk, Dunfermline Ath, Morton
1988–89 Hamilton A
1989–90 Dundee
1990–91 None
1991–92 St Mirren, Dunfermline Ath
1992–93 Falkirk, Airdrieonians
1993–94 *See footnote*
1994–95 Dundee U

RELEGATED FROM DIVISION 1

1975–76 Dunfermline Ath, Clyde
1976–77 Raith R, Falkirk
1977–78 Alloa Ath, East Fife
1978–79 Montrose, Queen of the S
1979–80 Arbroath, Clyde
1980–81 Stirling A, Berwick R
1981–82 East Stirling, Queen of the S
1982–83 Dunfermline Ath, Queen's Park
1983–84 Raith R, Alloa
1984–85 Meadowbank T, St Johnstone
1985–86 Ayr U, Alloa
1986–87 Brechin C, Montrose
1987–88 East Fife, Dumbarton
1988–89 Kilmarnock, Queen of the S
1989–90 Albion R, Alloa
1990–91 Clyde, Brechin C
1991–92 Montrose, Forfar Ath
1992–93 Meadowbank T, Cowdenbeath
1993–94 *See footnote*
1994–95 Ayr U, Stranraer

RELEGATED FROM DIVISION 2

1994–95 Meadowbank T, Brechin C

RELEGATED FROM DIVISION 1 (TO 1973–74)

1921–22 *Queen's Park, Dumbarton, Clydebank
1922–23 Albion R, Alloa Ath
1923–24 Clyde, Clydebank
1924–25 Third Lanark, Ayr U
1925–26 Raith R, Clydebank
1926–27 Morton, Dundee U
1927–28 Dunfermline Ath, Bo'ness
1928–29 Third Lanark, Raith R
1929–30 St Johnstone, Dundee U
1930–31 Hibernian, East Fife
1931–32 Dundee U, Leith Ath
1932–33 Morton, East Stirling
1933–34 Third Lanark, Cowdenbeath
1934–35 St Mirren, Falkirk
1935–36 Airdrieonians, Ayr U
1936–37 Dunfermline Ath, Albion R
1937–38 Dundee, Morton
1938–39 Queen's Park, Raith R
1946–47 Kilmarnock, Hamilton A
1947–48 Airdrieonians, Queen's Park
1948–49 Morton, Albion R
1949–50 Queen of the S, Stirling Albion
1950–51 Clyde, Falkirk
1951–52 Morton, Stirling Albion
1952–53 Motherwell, Third Lanark
1953–54 Airdrieonians, Hamilton A
1954–55 *No clubs relegated*
1955–56 Stirling Albion, Clyde
1956–57 Dunfermline Ath, Ayr U
1957–58 East Fife, Queen's Park
1958–59 Queen of the S, Falkirk
1959–60 Arbroath, Stirling Albion
1960–61 Ayr U, Clyde
1961–62 St Johnstone, Stirling Albion
1962–63 Clyde, Raith R
1963–64 Queen of the S, East Stirling
1964–65 Airdrieonians, Third Lanark
1965–66 Morton, Hamilton A

1966–67 St Mirren, Ayr U
1967–68 Motherwell, Stirling Albion
1968–69 Falkirk, Arbroath
1969–70 Raith R, Partick T
1970–71 St Mirren, Cowdenbeath
1971–72 Clyde, Dunfermline Ath
1972–73 Kilmarnock, Airdrieonians
1973–74 East Fife, Falkirk

*Season 1921–22 – only 1 club promoted, 3 clubs relegated.

Scottish League championship wins: Rangers 45, Celtic 35, Aberdeen 4, Hearts 4, Hibernian 4, Dumbarton 2, Dundee 1, Dundee United 1, Kilmarnock 1, Motherwell 1, Third Lanark 1.

At the end of the 1993–94 season four divisions were created assisted by the admission of two new clubs Ross County and Caledonian Thistle. Only one club was promoted from Division 1 and Division 2. Three relegated from the Premier joined with teams finishing second to seventh in Division 1 to form the new Division 1. Five relegated from Division 1 combined with those who finished second to sixth to form a new Division 2 and the bottom eight in Division 2 linked with the two newcomers to form a new Division 3.

Rangers Brian Laudrup is tackled by Mick Galloway of Celtic. (Action Images)

SCOTTISH LEAGUE CUP FINALS 1946–95

Season	*Winners*	*Runners-up*	*Score*
1946–47	Rangers	Aberdeen	4-0
1947–48	East Fife	Falkirk	4-1 after 0-0 draw
1948–49	Rangers	Raith R	2-0
1949–50	East Fife	Dunfermline Ath	3-0
1950–51	Motherwell	Hibernian	3-0
1951–52	Dundee	Rangers	3-2
1952–53	Dundee	Kilmarnock	2-0
1953–54	East Fife	Partick T	3-2
1954–55	Hearts	Motherwell	4-2
1955–56	Aberdeen	St Mirren	2-1
1956–57	Celtic	Partick T	3-0 after 0-0 draw
1957–58	Celtic	Rangers	7-1
1958–59	Hearts	Partick T	5-1
1959–60	Hearts	Third Lanark	2-1
1960–61	Rangers	Kilmarnock	2-0
1961–62	Rangers	Hearts	3-1 after 1-1 draw
1962–63	Hearts	Kilmarnock	1-0
1963–64	Rangers	Morton	5-0
1964–65	Rangers	Celtic	2-1
1965–66	Celtic	Rangers	2-1
1966–67	Celtic	Rangers	1-0
1967–68	Celtic	Dundee	5-3
1968–69	Celtic	Hibernian	6-2
1969–70	Celtic	St Johnstone	1-0
1970–71	Rangers	Celtic	1-0
1971–72	Partick T	Celtic	4-1
1972–73	Hibernian	Celtic	2-1
1973–74	Dundee	Celtic	1-0
1974–75	Celtic	Hibernian	6-3
1975–76	Rangers	Celtic	1-0
1976–77	Aberdeen	Celtic	2-1
1977–78	Rangers	Celtic	2-1
1978–79	Rangers	Aberdeen	2-1
1979–80	Dundee U	Aberdeen	3-0 after 0-0 draw
1980–81	Dundee U	Dundee	3-0
1981–82	Rangers	Dundee U	2-1
1982–83	Celtic	Rangers	2-1
1983–84	Rangers	Celtic	3-2
1984–85	Rangers	Dundee U	1-0
1985–86	Aberdeen	Hibernian	3-0
1986–87	Rangers	Celtic	2-1
1987–88	Rangers	Aberdeen	3-3
		(Rangers won 5-3 on penalties)	
1988–89	Rangers	Aberdeen	3-2
1989–90	Aberdeen	Rangers	2-1
1990–91	Rangers	Celtic	2-1
1991–92	Hibernian	Dunfermline Ath	2-0
1992–93	Rangers	Aberdeen	2-1
1993–94	Rangers	Hibernian	2-1
1994–95	Raith R	Celtic	2-2
		(Raith R won 6-5 on penalties)	

SCOTTISH LEAGUE CUP WINS

Rangers 19, Celtic 9, Hearts 4, Aberdeen 4, Dundee 3, East Fife 3, Dundee U 2, Hibernian 2, Motherwell 1, Partick T 1, Raith R 1.

APPEARANCES IN FINALS

Rangers 25, Celtic 21, Aberdeen 10, Hibernian 7, Dundee 5, Hearts 5, Dundee U 4, Partick T 4, East Fife 3, Kilmarnock 3, Dunfermline Ath 2, Motherwell 2, Raith R 2, Falkirk 1, Morton 1, St Johnstone 1, St Mirren 1, Third Lanark 1.

COCA-COLA CUP 1994–95

FIRST ROUND

9 AUG

Berwick R (0) 0
Montrose (0) 0 *aet* 515

Berwick R: Young N; Bell, Banks, Valentine, Cole (Fraser), Wilson, Forrester, Neil, Hawke, Irvine, Kane.
Montrose: Larter; Robertson, Tindal, Craib, Grant, Haro, Garden, Stephen, McGlashan, Kennedy, Masson.
(Montrose won 3-2 on penalties)

East Fife (0) 1 *(Allan)*
Forfar Ath (0) 0 797

East Fife: Wilson; Bell, Williamson, Barron, Sneddon, Hildersley, Cusick (Allan), Hope, Scott (Irvine), Hunter, Gibb.
Forfar Ath: Arthur; McLaren, McPhee, Mann, Archibald, McKillop, O'Neill, Irvine, Lees, Bingham, Heddle.

East Stirling (0) 0
Caledonian T (2) 2 *(Robertson, Lee I (og))* 899

East Stirling: Moffat; Watt, Cuthbert, Russell, Yates, Lee R, Lee I, Millar, McCallum, Scott (Stirling), Geraghty.
Caledonian T: McRitchie; Brennan, McAllister, Hercher, Scott, Andrew, MacDonald, MacKenzie (Smart), Noble, Bennett, Robertson.

Stenhousemuir (0) 0 396
Meadowbank T (1) 4 *(Bailey, McLeod, Hutchison, Little)*

Stenhousemuir: Harkness; Aitken, Hallford, Clarke (Hutchison), McGeachie, Christie, Steel, Haddow, Mathieson, Sludden (Henderson), Sprott.
Meadowbank T: Ellison; Graham, Fleming, Wilson, Williamson, Hutchison, Duthie, McLeod, Little, Rutherford (Price), Bailey (Thorburn).

10 AUG

Arbroath (0) 1 *(Reilly)*
Alloa (1) 1 *(Morrison) aet* 750

Arbroath: Jackson; Mitchell, McKinnon, Murray, Elder, McGovern, Downie, Reilly (Elliot), Brock, Tosh, Finlay.
Alloa: Butter; McNiven (Nelson), Kemp, Campbell, McCulloch, McCormack J, Morrison, Cadden, McCormick S, Bennett, Willock (McAvoy).
(Arbroath won 5-4 on penalties)

Queen of the S (0) 2 *(McLaren, Bryce)*
Albion R (0) 0 1304

Queen of the S: Purdie; Hetherington, Rowe (Sermanni), McKeown D, Mills, Kennedy, McGuire, Bryce, McLaren, McFarlane, Mallan.
Albion R: Davidson; Riley, Conn, McDonald, Malone, Collins, Walker (McBride M), Docherty, Thompson, Quinn, Gallagher.

Ross Co (1) 3 *(Grant 2, MacPherson)*
Queen's Park (0) 2 *(Orr G, Maxwell)* 1924

Ross Co: Hutchison; Somerville, Campbell, Williamson, Alex MacLeod, Andrew MacLeod, Ferries, Grant, MacPherson, Herd, Wilson (Robertson).
Queen's Park: Moonie; Fitzpatrick, Kavanagh, Kerr, Maxwell, Orr G, Campbell (Bradley), Graham, Brodie, McCormick (Edgar), Rodden.

Stranraer (1) 2 *(Cody, Ferguson)*
Cowdenbeath (1) 2 *(Black, Soutar) aet* 776

Stranraer: Ross; Millar, Hughes, Cody, Brannigan, Howard (McLean), Reilly, Grant, Walker (Ferguson), Duncan, Henderson.
Cowdenbeath: Russell; Scott, Hamill, Malloy, Humphreys, Davidson, Carr (Winter), Black, Soutar (Lynch), Thomson, Stout.
(Stranraer won 4-2 on penalties)

SECOND ROUND

16 AUG

Ayr U (0) 0
Celtic (1) 1 *(Grant)* 8182

Ayr U: Duncan; Burns, McVicar, Paterson, Rolling, Sharples, Traynor (Moore), McKilligan, McGivern, Gilzean (Woods), Connie.
Celtic: Marshall; Martin, Boyd, McNally, Mowbray, Grant, Galloway, McStay, Falconer, Walker (Donnelly), Collins.

Dumbarton (0) 0
Hearts (2) 4 *(Millar, Robertson, Johnston A 2)* 1412

Dumbarton: MacFarlane; Marsland, Boyd, Melvin, Martin, MacLeod, Mooney M, Meechan, Gibson, McGarvey, Ward (Campbell).
Hearts: Walker; Frail, McKinlay (Leitch), Levein, MacKay (Weir), McLaren, Colquhoun, Johnston A, Robertson, Johnston M, Millar.

Falkirk (0) 1 *(Cadette)*
Montrose (0) 1 *(Kennedy) aet* 2467

Falkirk: Parks; Hamilton, Weir (James), Oliver, McLaughlin, McKenzie, May, Fulton, Cadette, McCall, Johnston (McDonald).
Montrose: Larter; Robertson, Tindal, Craib, Grant, Haro, Garden (Cooper), Stephen, McGlashan, Kennedy, Masson.
(Falkirk won 5-4 on penalties)

Greenock Morton (1) 1 *(Lilley)*
Airdrieonians (1) 1 *(Andrew Smith) aet* 1417

Greenock Morton: Wylie; Collins, Pickering (Anderson), Hunter, McCahill, Johnstone, Lilley, Fowler, Alexander, McArthur, Cormack.
Airdrieonians: Martin; Stewart, Tony Smith, Sandison, McIntyre T, Hay (Boyle), Harvey (Ferguson), Wilson, Andrew Smith, Black, Lawrence.
(Airdrieonians won 5-3 on penalties)

Motherwell (1) 3 *(Burns, Coyne (pen), Kirk)*
Clydebank (0) 1 *(Grady)* 4172

Motherwell: Woods; Philliben, McKinnon, Davies (Ritchie), McLeish, Martin, Lambert, Burns, Coyne, O'Donnell, Arnott (Kirk).
Clydebank: Matthews; Lansdowne (Kerrigan), Bowman, Murdoch, Sweeney, Currie, Cooper, Harris, Eadie (Sutherland), Grady, Jack.

Partick T (3) 5 *(Taylor, Jamieson, Charnley 3 (1 pen))*
Brechin C (0) 0 1970

Partick T: Nelson; Byrne, Law, Jamieson, Tierney, McWilliams (Cameron), Taylor, Smith, Grant, English, Charnley.
Brechin C: Balfour; Conway, Christie, Cairney, Nicolson, Scott, Bell, Vannett, McNeill (McKellar), Millar, Kemlo.

St Mirren (0) 0

Dundee U (0) 1 *(Ristic) aet* 3002

St Mirren: Combe; Hick (Gillies R), Watson, McLaughlin, Taylor, McIntyre, Gillies K (Hetherston), Bone, Lavety, Gardner, Elliot.
Dundee U: Jorgensen; McInally (Craig), Bollan, Hannah, Petric, Welsh, Bowman, Perry, Ristic, Brewster, Nixon (Connolly).

17 AUG

Aberdeen (0) 1 *(Shearer)*

Stranraer (0) 0 8158

Aberdeen: Snelders; McKimmie, Winnie, Grant, Irvine, Wright, Jess (Miller), Shearer (Booth), Kane, Dodds, Robertson.
Stranraer: Ross; Treanor, Hughes, McCaffrey (Ferguson), Brannigan, Millar, McLean, Duncan (Brown), Walker, Cody, Henderson.

Arbroath (1) 1 *(McKinnon)*

Rangers (3) 6 *(Hateley 2, Ferguson D 3, McCall)* 4556

Arbroath: Jackson; Mitchell, Rae, Farnan, Elder, Murray, Downie (Finlay), McKinnon, Reilly (Brock), Tosh, McGovern.
Rangers: Maxwell; McCall, Brown, Gough, Boli, McPherson, Moore, Ferguson I, Ferguson D, Hateley, Durrant (Murray).

Dundee (1) 3 *(Shaw, Tosh 2)*

Caledonian T (0) 0 3112

Dundee: Pageaud; McQuillan, Pittman, McKeown, Blake, Dinnie, Shaw, Anderson (Tosh), Duffy C, Britton (Farningham), McCann.
Caledonian T: McRitchie; Brennan, McAllister, Hercher, Scott, Andrew, Smart, MacKenzie (MacDonald), Noble, Bennett, Robertson.

Dunfermline Ath (2) 4 *(McCathie, Den Bieman, Petrie, Ward)*

Meadowbank T (0) 1 *(Sorbie)* 3230

Dunfermline Ath: Westwater; Den Bieman, Bowes, McCathie, Cooper, Smith, McNamara, Robertson, Tod (Laing), Petrie, Moore (Ward).
Meadowbank T: Ellison; Graham, Fleming, Wilson, Williamson, Hutchison (Thorburn), Duthie, McLeod, Little (Coyle), Sorbie, Bailey.

Hamilton A (1) 5 *(McEntegart, Baptie, McLean, Campbell, Sherry)*

Clyde (0) 0 942

Hamilton A: Ferguson; McKenzie, McInulty, McEntegart, Baptie, McIntosh, McQuade, Sherry, Chalmers (McLean), Duffield, Lorimer (Campbell).
Clyde: Fridge; Clark (O'Neill), Neil (Frater), Knox, Thomson, Strain, Watson, Wright, McConnell, McAulay, Parks.

Kilmarnock (2) 4 *(Henry, McCluskey, Maskrey 2)*

East Fife (0) 1 *(Hope)* 4243

Kilmarnock: Geddes; MacPherson, Black, Montgomerie, Reilly, Millen, Mitchell, Henry, Maskrey, McCluskey (Williamson), Connor (McSkimming).
East Fife: Wilson; Bell, Williamson, Barron, Sneddon, Hildersley (Cusick), Allan, Hope, Scott (Irvine), Hunter, Gibb.

Queen of the S (0) 0

Hibernian (2) 3 *(Evans, Tweed, O'Neill)* 5022

Queen of the S: Purdie; Hetherington, McKeown D, McKeown B (Adams), Mills, McFarlane, McGuire, Kennedy, McLaren (Sermanni), Bryce, Mallan.
Hibernian: Leighton; Miller, Mitchell, Findlay, Tweed, Hunter (Beaumont), McAllister, Hamilton, Evans, Jackson D, O'Neill (Harper).

Ross Co (0) 0

Raith R (0) 5 *(Cameron, Graham 3, Dalziel)* 2288

Ross Co: Hutchison; Somerville, Campbell, Williamson, Alex MacLeod, Andrew MacLeod, Ferries, Grant (Duff), MacPherson, Herd, Wilson.
Raith R: Thomson; Rowbotham, Kirkwood (Broddle), Coyle, Raeside, Sinclair, Lennon, Dalziel, Graham, Cameron (Crawford), Dair.

Stirling Albion (0) 0

St Johnstone (1) 2 *(O'Boyle, Scott)* 1512

Stirling Albion: McGeown; Hamilton, Armstrong, Mitchell, McQuilter, Tait, Reid (McInnes), Roberts, Watters, Taggart, McLeod.
St Johnstone: Rhodes; McGinnis, Miller, Turner, Inglis, McGowne (Scott), O'Neil, Ramsey, Davenport, O'Boyle, Irons.

THIRD ROUND

30 AUG

Hibernian (1) 2 *(O'Neill 2)*

Dunfermline Ath (0) 0 9305

Hibernian: Leighton; Beaumont, Tortolano, Findlay (Farrell), Tweed, Hunter (Harper), McAllister, Hamilton, Evans, Jackson D, O'Neill.
Dunfermline Ath: Will; Den Bieman, Bowes, McCathie, Cooper, Smith, Ward, Robertson, French, Petrie, Tod (Laing).

Partick T (0) 0

Aberdeen (2) 5 *(Shearer 3 (1 pen), Kane, Dodds)* 5046

Partick T: Nelson; Byrne, Law, Jamieson, Tierney, McWilliams, Taylor, Cameron, Grant (Smith), English, Charnley.
Aberdeen: Snelders; McKimmie, Woodthorpe, Grant, Irvine (Winnie), Wright, Jess, Shearer, Kane, Dodds, McKinnon (Booth).

31 AUG

Dundee (1) 1 *(Farningham)*

Celtic (1) 2 *(Collins, Walker)* 11,431

Dundee: Pageaud; McQuillan, Duffy J, Duffy C, Blake (Teasdale), Farningham, Shaw, Vrto, Wieghorst (Tosh), Britton, McCann.
Celtic: Marshall; Grant, Boyd, McNally, Mowbray, McGinlay, Galloway, McStay, Donnelly (Nicholas), Walker, Collins.

Hamilton A (0) 2 *(Cleland (og), Duffield)*

Dundee U (1) 2 *(Hannah 2) aet* 2180

Hamilton A: Ferguson; McKenzie, McInulty, McEntegart, Baptie, McIntosh, McLean (McQuade), Sherry, Chalmers (Hartley), Duffield, Nicholls.
Dundee U: Main; Cleland, McInally, Hannah, Petric, Dailly, Bowman, McKinlay, Ristic (Myers), Brewster (Nixon), McLaren.
(Dundee U won 5-3 on penalties)

Hearts (2) 2 *(Locke, Colquhoun)*

St Johnstone (0) 4 *(O'Neil, Miller, O'Boyle, Irons)* 8467

Hearts: Walker; Frail, Weir, Levein, Berry, McLaren, Colquhoun, Locke, Robertson, Johnston A (Foster) (Harrison), Millar.
St Johnstone: Rhodes; Cherry, Miller, Ramsey, McGinnis, Deas (Preston), O'Neil, Davies, Davenport, O'Boyle, Irons.

Motherwell (0) 1 *(McCart)*
Airdrieonians (1) 2 *(Boyle 2) aet* 6010
Motherwell: Woods; Shannon, Philliben, Dolan (Davies), Martin, McCart, Lambert, Burns (Kirk), Coyne, O'Donnell, Roddie.
Airdrieonians: Martin; Boyle, Stewart, Sandison, McIntyre T, Black, Lawrence (McIntyre J), Harvey, Smith (Ferguson), Wilson, Jack.

Raith R (2) 3 *(Cameron 3)*
Kilmarnock (1) 2 *(Montgomerie, Williamson)* 4181
Raith R: Thomson; McAnespie, Broddle, Rowbotham, Narey, Sinclair, Lennon, Dalziel (Crawford), Graham, Cameron, Redford (Coyle).
Kilmarnock: Geddes; MacPherson, Black, Montgomerie, Reilly, Millen, Mitchell, Napier (Williamson), Brown, Connor, Maskrey.

Rangers (0) 1 *(Laudrup)*
Falkirk (1) 2 *(Cadette 2)* 40,741
Rangers: Goram; McCall, Robertson, Gough, McPherson (Ferguson D), Moore, Durrant, Ferguson I, Durie, Hateley, Laudrup.
Falkirk: Parks; Weir, McGowan, Oliver, McLaughlin, McKenzie, May, Fulton, Cadette, Henderson (Cramb), McDonald.

QUARTER-FINALS

20 SEPT

St Johnstone (0) 1 *(O'Neil)*
Raith R (2) 3 *(Dennis, Graham, Lennon)* 6287
St Johnstone: Rhodes; Cherry, Miller, Ramsey (Preston), McGinnis, McGowne, O'Neil, Turner (McMartin), Davenport, O'Boyle, Irons.
Raith R: Thomson; McAnespie, Broddle, Rowbotham, Dennis, Sinclair, Nicholl, Crawford (Dair), Graham, Cameron, Lennon.

21 SEPT

Celtic (0) 1 *(Collins)*
Dundee U (0) 0 28,859
Celtic: Marshall; Galloway, Boyd, McNally, Mowbray, Grant, McGinlay, McStay (O'Neil B), Donnelly (Nicholas), Walker, Collins.
Dundee U: Main; Cleland, Malpas, Hannah, Petric, Welsh, McInally (Myers), McKinlay, Ristic, Connolly (Brewster), Nixon.

Falkirk (1) 1 *(McDonald)*
Aberdeen (2) 4 *(Booth 3, Rice (og))* 9450
Falkirk: Parks; McGowan, McQueen, Clark, McLaughlin, McKenzie, May, Henderson (McAvennie), Cadette, Rice, McDonald.
Aberdeen: Watt; McKimmie, Woodthorpe, Grant, Winnie, Wright, Jess, Smith, Booth, Dodds (Miller), McKinnon.

Hibernian (0) 1 *(Evans)*
Airdrieonians (2) 2 *(Andrew Smith, Lawrence)* 9578
Hibernian: Leighton; Miller, Farrell, Jackson C (Harper), Tweed, Hunter, McAllister, Hamilton, Evans, Jackson D, O'Neill.
Airdrieonians: Martin; Boyle, Jack, Sandison, McIntyre T, Stewart, Harvey (Hay), Wilson, Andrew Smith, Black, Lawrence (McIntyre J).

SEMI-FINALS

25 OCT at McDiarmid Park

Airdrieonians (0) 1 *(Cooper)*
Raith R (1) 1 *(Graham) aet* 7260
Airdrieonians: Martin; Stewart, Jack, Sandison, Hay, Black, Boyle, Wilson (McIntyre T), Cooper, Harvey (Andrew Smith), Lawrence.
Raith R: Thomson; McAnespie, Broddle (Rowbotham), Sinclair, Dennis, Narey, Lennon, Dalziel (Crawford), Graham, Cameron, Kirkwood (Potter).
(Raith R won 5-4 on penalties)

26 OCT at Ibrox Stadium

Celtic (0) 1 *(O'Neil B)*
Aberdeen (0) 0 44,000
Celtic: Marshall; Smith, Boyd, McNally, O'Neil B, Grant, Byrne (McGinlay), McStay, Donnelly, Walker (Nicholas), Collins.
Aberdeen: Snelders; McKimmie, Woodthorpe, Grant, Winnie, Wright, Smith, Kane (Robertson), Booth, Dodds, McKinnon (Hetherston).

FINAL at Ibrox Stadium

27 NOV

Raith R (1) 2 *(Crawford, Dalziel)*
Celtic (1) 2 *(Walker, Nicholas) aet* 45,384
Raith R: Thomson; McAnespie, Broddle (Rowbotham), Narey, Dennis, Sinclair, Crawford, Dalziel (Redford), Graham, Cameron, Dair.
Celtic: Marshall; Galloway, Boyd, McNally, Mowbray, O'Neil B, Donnelly (Falconer), McStay, Nicholas (Byrne), Walker, Collins.
(Raith R won 6-5 on penalties)
Referee: J McCluskey (Stewarton).

SCOTTISH CUP FINALS 1874–1995

Year	*Winners*	*Runners-up*	*Score*
1874	Queen's Park	Clydesdale	2-0
1875	Queen's Park	Renton	3-0
1876	Queen's Park	Third Lanark	2-0 after 1-1 draw
1877	Vale of Leven	Rangers	3-2 after 0-0 and 1-1 draws
1878	Vale of Leven	Third Lanark	1-0
1879	Vale of Leven*	Rangers	
1880	Queen's Park	Thornlibank	3-0
1881	Queen's Park†	Dumbarton	3-1
1882	Queen's Park	Dumbarton	4-1 after 2-2 draw
1883	Dumbarton	Vale of Leven	2-1 after 2-2 draw
1884	Queen's Park‡	Vale of Leven	
1885	Renton	Vale of Leven	3-1 after 0-0 draw
1886	Queen's Park	Renton	3-1
1887	Hibernian	Dumbarton	2-1
1888	Renton	Cambuslang	6-1
1889	Third Lanark§	Celtic	2-1
1890	Queen's Park	Vale of Leven	2-1 after 1-1 draw
1891	Hearts	Dumbarton	1-0
1892	Celtic¶	Queen's Park	5-1
1893	Queen's Park	Celtic	2-1
1894	Rangers	Celtic	3-1
1895	St Bernard's	Renton	2-1
1896	Hearts	Hibernian	3-1
1897	Rangers	Dumbarton	5-1
1898	Rangers	Kilmarnock	2-0
1899	Celtic	Rangers	2-0
1900	Celtic	Queen's Park	4-3
1901	Hearts	Celtic	4-3
1902	Hibernian	Celtic	1-0
1903	Rangers	Hearts	2-0 after 1-1 and 0-0 draws
1904	Celtic	Rangers	3-2
1905	Third Lanark	Rangers	3-1 after 0-0 draw
1906	Hearts	Third Lanark	1-0
1907	Celtic	Hearts	3-0
1908	Celtic	St Mirren	5-1
1909	●●		
1910	Dundee	Clyde	2-1 after 2-2 and 0-0 draws
1911	Celtic	Hamilton A	2-0 after 0-0 draw
1912	Celtic	Clyde	2-0
1913	Falkirk	Raith R	2-0
1914	Celtic	Hibernian	4-1 after 0-0 draw
1920	Kilmarnock	Albion R	3-2
1921	Partick T	Rangers	1-0
1922	Morton	Rangers	1-0
1923	Celtic	Hibernian	1-0
1924	Airdrieonians	Hibernian	2-0
1925	Celtic	Dundee	2-1
1926	St Mirren	Celtic	2-0
1927	Celtic	East Fife	3-1
1928	Rangers	Celtic	4-0
1929	Kilmarnock	Rangers	2-0
1930	Rangers	Partick T	2-1 after 0-0 draw
1931	Celtic	Motherwell	4-2 after 2-2 draw
1932	Rangers	Kilmarnock	3-0 after 1-1 draw
1933	Celtic	Motherwell	1-0
1934	Rangers	St Mirren	5-0
1935	Rangers	Hamilton A	2-1
1936	Rangers	Third Lanark	1-0
1937	Celtic	Aberdeen	2-1
1938	East Fife	Kilmarnock	4-2 after 1-1 draw
1939	Clyde	Motherwell	4-0
1947	Aberdeen	Hibernian	2-1
1948	Rangers	Morton	1-0 after 1-1 draw
1949	Rangers	Clyde	4-1
1950	Rangers	East Fife	3-0
1951	Celtic	Motherwell	1-0
1952	Motherwell	Dundee	4-0
1953	Rangers	Aberdeen	1-0 after 1-1 draw
1954	Celtic	Aberdeen	2-1
1955	Clyde	Celtic	1-0 after 1-1 draw
1956	Hearts	Celtic	3-1
1957	Falkirk	Kilmarnock	2-1 after 1-1 draw
1958	Clyde	Hibernian	1-0
1959	St Mirren	Aberdeen	3-1
1960	Rangers	Kilmarnock	2-0
1961	Dunfermline Ath	Celtic	2-0 after 0-0 draw
1962	Rangers	St Mirren	2-0
1963	Rangers	Celtic	3-0 after 1-1 draw
1964	Rangers	Dundee	3-1

Year	*Winners*	*Runners-up*	*Score*
1965	Celtic	Dunfermline Ath	3-2
1966	Rangers	Celtic	1-0 after 0-0 draw
1967	Celtic	Aberdeen	2-0
1968	Dunfermline Ath	Hearts	3-1
1969	Celtic	Rangers	4-0
1970	Aberdeen	Celtic	3-1
1971	Celtic	Rangers	2-1 after 1-1 draw
1972	Celtic	Hibernian	6-1
1973	Rangers	Celtic	3-2
1974	Celtic	Dundee U	3-0
1975	Celtic	Airdrieonians	3-1
1976	Rangers	Hearts	3-1
1977	Celtic	Rangers	1-0
1978	Rangers	Aberdeen	2-1
1979	Rangers	Hibernian	3-2 after 0-0 and 0-0 draws
1980	Celtic	Rangers	1-0
1981	Rangers	Dundee U	4-1 after 0-0 draw
1982	Aberdeen	Rangers	4-1 (aet)
1983	Aberdeen	Rangers	1-0 (aet)
1984	Aberdeen	Celtic	2-1 (aet)
1985	Celtic	Dundee U	2-1
1986	Aberdeen	Hearts	3-0
1987	St Mirren	Dundee U	1-0 (aet)
1988	Celtic	Dundee U	2-1
1989	Celtic	Rangers	1-0
1990	Aberdeen	Celtic	0-0 (aet)
		(Aberdeen won 9-8 on penalties)	
1991	Motherwell	Dundee U	4-3 (aet)
1992	Rangers	Airdrieonians	2-1
1993	Rangers	Aberdeen	2-1
1994	Dundee U	Rangers	1-0
1995	Celtic	Airdrieonians	1-0

*Vale of Leven awarded cup, Rangers failing to appear for replay after 1-1 draw.
†After Dumbarton protested the first game, which Queen's Park won 2-1.
‡Queen's Park awarded cup, Vale of Leven failing to appear.
§Replay by order of Scottish FA because of playing conditions in first match, won 3-0 by Third Lanark.
¶After mutually protested game which Celtic won 1-0.
●●Owing to riot, the cup was withheld after two drawn games – Celtic 2-1, Rangers 2-1.

SCOTTISH CUP WINS

Celtic 30, Rangers 26, Queen's Park 10, Aberdeen 7, Hearts 5, Clyde 3, St Mirren 3, Vale of Leven 3, Dunfermline Ath 2, Falkirk 2, Hibernian 2, Kilmarnock 2, Motherwell 2, Renton 2, Third Lanark 2, Airdrieonians 1, Dumbarton 1, Dundee 1, Dundee U 1, East Fife 1, Morton 1, Partick Th 1, St Bernard's 1.

APPEARANCES IN FINAL

Celtic 47, Rangers 43, Aberdeen 14, Queen's Park 12, Hearts 10, Hibernian 10, Kilmarnock 7, Vale of Leven 7, Clyde 6, Dumbarton 6, St Mirren 6, Third Lanark 6, Dundee U 7, Motherwell 6, Renton 5, Airdrieonians 4, Dundee 4, Dunfermline Ath 3, East Fife 3, Falkirk 2, Hamilton A 2, Morton 2, Partick Th 2, Albion R 1, Cambuslang 1, Clydesdale 1, Raith R 1, St Bernard's 1, Thornlibank 1.

SCOTTISH CUP 1995

FIRST ROUND

17 DEC

Caledonian T (0) 1 *(McAllister)*
Queen of the S (0) 2 *(Bell, Bryce)* 1112
Caledonian T: McRitchie; Brennan, McAllister, Hercher, Andrew, Baltacha, MacDonald, Noble, MacMillan (MacKenzie), Christie, Robertson.
Queen of the S: Purdie; McKeown B, McKeown D, Campbell C, Hetherington, McFarlane, Bryce, Bell, McLaren (Brown), Kennedy, Jackson.

Dumbarton (1) 3 *(Ward 2, McKinnon)*
Stirling Albion (1) 3 *(Watters, Mitchell (pen), Tait)* 794
Dumbarton: MacFarlane; Gow, Foster, Melvin, Fabiani, MacLeod (Meechan), Mooney M (Campbell), King, McKinnon, McGarvey, Ward.
Stirling Albion: Monaghan; Paterson, Gibson, Mitchell, Watson, Tait, McInnes, Stewart (Armstrong), Watters (Farquhar), Taggart, McLeod.

Stenhousemuir (1) 3 *(Mathieson, Sprott (pen), Christie)*
East Stirling (0) 0 745
Stenhousemuir: Harkness; McNiven, Donaldson, Armstrong, Godfrey, Christie, Steel, Fisher, Mathieson, Hutchison, Sprott.
East Stirling: McDougall; Russell, Lee R, Watt (Stirling), Millar, Ross, Lee I, Scott, Dwyer, Geraghty, Conroy.

26 DEC

Albion R (1) 2 *(McBride J, Docherty)*
Montrose (2) 5 *(MacRonald 2, Milne, Kennedy (pen), McGlashan)* 356
Albion R: Davidson; McDonald, Gallagher, Kerr, Ryan, Collins, Dolan, Shah (Docherty), McBride J, McBride M (Quinn), Scott.
Montrose: Larter; Robertson, Tindal, Garden, Masson, Haro, Cooper (Milne), Stephen, McGlashan, Kennedy, MacRonald.

FIRST ROUND REPLAYS

19 DEC

Stirling Albion (1) 3 *(Taggart 2, McInnes)*
Dumbarton (0) 0 727
Stirling Albion: Monaghan; Paterson (Kerr), Gibson, Mitchell, Watson, Tait, McInnes, Armstrong, Watters, Taggart, McLeod.
Dumbarton: MacFarlane; Gow, Fabiani, Melvin, Marsland, Campbell, Mooney (Gibson), King, McKinnon, McGarvey, Ward.

SECOND ROUND

7 JAN

Alloa (1) 2 *(Lamont, Diver)*
Ross Co (2) 3 *(Connelly 2, McPherson)* 1364
Alloa: Butter; Hannah (Willock), Bennett (McAnenay), Kemp, McCulloch, Lawrie, McAvoy, Cadden, Diver, Moffat, Lamont.
Ross Co: Hutchison; Somerville, Reid, Williamson, Bellshaw, Furphy, Ferries (McKay), Grant, McPherson (Duff), Connelly, Herd.

Brechin C (0) 2 *(McNeill, Brand)*
Stirling Albion (2) 3 *(McInnes 2, Taggart)* 503
Brechin C: Balfour; Buick, Marr, Cairney, Conway, Vannett (Bell), McKellar, Mitchell, Price, Smith (Brand), McNeill.
Stirling Albion: Monaghan; Paterson, Gibson, Mitchell, McQuilter, Kerr, McInnes, Armstrong, Watters (Drinkell), Taggart, McLeod.

Buckie T (1) 1 *(Robertson)*
Berwick R (2) 4 *(Hawke, Graham, Mann (og), Valentine)* 907
Buckie T: Innes; Girling, Bruce I, Mathieson, Henderson, Mann, Gibson, Robertson, Begg (Galbraith), McPherson, Smith.
Berwick R: Osborne; Fraser, Valentine, Cole, Cowan, Irvine, Gallagher, Forrester (Kane), Hawke, Rutherford, Graham (Clegg).

Burntisland Shipyards (5) 6 *(Matthew 3, Taylor, Paton, Drummond)*
St Cuthbert W (0) 2 *(Tweedie, Baker)* 654
Burntisland Shipyards: Shanahan; Parnell, Taylor (Lewis), Lawrie, Bray, McIlvean, Matthew, Horsburgh (Murray), Campbell, Paton, Drummond.
St Cuthbert W: McHenry; Johnston, Kirkpatrick, Christie, McCulloch, Crosbie (Murray), Niven, Durham (Maxwell), Tweedie, Simpson, Baker.

Cove R (1) 2 *(Caldwell 2)*
Cowdenbeath (1) 1 *(Conn)* 490
Cove R: MacLean; Morrison, Whyte, Morland, Paterson, Baxter, Megginson, Park (Walker), Caldwell, Lorimer, Beattie (Buchan).
Cowdenbeath: Russell; Scott (Barclay), Murdoch, Humphreys, Conn, Tait (Callaghan), Fellenger, Black, Yardley, Soutar (Maloney), Wardell.

Forfar Ath (0) 0
Meadowbank T (0) 1 *(Sinclair)* 656
Forfar Ath: Arthur; Irvine, McPhee, Mann, Archibald, Glennie, Mearns (Hannigan), Heddle, Ross, McCormick, Bingham.
Meadowbank T: Ellison; Davidson, Martin, Graham (Thorburn), Thomson, Sorbie, Samuel, Wilson, Little, McLeod, Bailey (Sinclair).

Gala Fairydean (1) 2 *(Cockburn, Hunter)*
East Fife (3) 6 *(Burns (pen), Hutcheon 3, Allan, Donaghy)* 789
Gala Fairydean: Brown; Catterson, Henry, Potts (Dixon), Rae, Wilson (Campbell), Hunter, Sinclair, De Melo, Cockburn, Ritchie.
East Fife: Wilson; Sneddon (Gibb), Hildersley, Burns, Beaton, Cusick, Allan, Donaghy, Scott, Hutcheon (Hunter), Hope.

Keith (0) 2 *(Rougvie (og), Thomson)*
Huntly (2) 2 *(Whyte, Thomson)* 1370
Keith: Thain (Marr); Thow, Tosh, Allan, Collie, Gibson, Maver, Thomson, Lavelle, Will, Wilson (McPherson).
Huntly: Gardiner; Murphy, Dunsire, Mone, Rougvie, De Barros, Gray, Stewart (Grant), Thomson (Yeats), Whyte, Lennox.

Queen of the S (0) 0
Clyde (0) 2 *(Dickson, O'Neill)* 1803
Queen of the S: McQueen; McKeown B, McKeown D, Campbell C, Hetherington, Bell (McLaren), Kennedy (Jackson), Ramsay, Campbell D, Bryce, Mallan.

Clyde: Fridge; O'Neill, Angus, McCarron (McAulay), Thomson, Brown, Dickson, Watson, McCluskey (McConnell), Neill, Parks.

Stenhousemuir (3) 4 *(Fisher, Mathieson 2, Steel)*
Arbroath (0) 0 685
Stenhousemuir: Harkness; McNiven, Roseburgh (McGeachie), Armstrong, Godfrey, Christie, Steel, Fisher (Donaldson), Mathieson, Hutchison, Sprott.
Arbroath: Dunn; McMillan (Shanks), Elder, Ward, Murray, Spittal, Elliot, Farnan, Gardner, Tosh (Craib), Downie.

Whitehill Welfare (0) 0
Montrose (0) 0 853
Whitehill Welfare: Elen; Richford, Gowrie, Hunter, Steel, Millar, O'Rourke (Smith R), Bird (Blackie), Sneddon, Purves, Smith D.
Montrose: Larter; Robertson, Tindal, Stephen, Masson, Haro, Cooper, MacDonald (Milne), McGlashan, Kennedy, MacRonald.

9 JAN

Queen's Park (0) 2 *(Orr G, Rodden)*
Greenock Morton (2) 2 *(Alexander, Anderson)* 1516
Queen's Park: Chalmers; Orr J (Campbell), Maxwell, Kerr, Elder, Graham, Callan, Orr G, McPhee, Caven, Edgar (Rodden).
Greenock Morton: Wylie; Collins, Cormack, Anderson, McCahill, Lindberg, McArthur, Mahood, Alexander, McInnes, Rajamaki.

SECOND ROUND REPLAYS

14 JAN

Huntly (1) 3 *(Rougvie, Stewart, Whyte)*
Keith (1) 1 *(Lavelle)* 1777
Huntly: Gardiner; Grant, Dunsire, Mone, Rougvie, De Barros, Gray, Stewart (Yeats), Thomson, Whyte (Copland), Lennox.
Keith: Cathcart; Thow (Leddie), Tosh, Allan, Collie, Gibson, Maver, Thomson, Lavelle, Will, Wilson (McPherson).

Montrose (2) 5 *(Kennedy 2, Masson, McGlashan, Stephen)*
Whitehill Welfare (1) 2 *(Millar, Steel)* 807
Montrose: Larter; Robertson, Tindal, Masson, Grant, Haro, MacDonald (Cooper), Stephen, McGlashan, Kennedy, MacRonald.
Whitehill Welfare: Elen; Purves, Gowrie, Hunter, Steel, Millar, O'Rourke (McCulloch), Smith R, Sneddon, Brown, Smith D (Bird).

17 JAN

Greenock Morton (0) 2 *(Rajamaki, Lilley)*
Queen's Park (1) 1 *(Caven) aet* 2127
Greenock Morton: Wylie; Collins, McArthur, Anderson, McCahill, Lindberg, Lilley, Mahood, Alexander, Blair (McPherson), Rajamaki.
Queen's Park: Chalmers; Orr J, Ferguson, Kerr, Maxwell, Matchett, Callan, Smith (Bradley), Orr G, Caven, McGoldrick (Rodden).

THIRD ROUND

28 JAN

Aberdeen (1) 1 *(Jess)*
Stranraer (0) 0 9183
Aberdeen: Snelders; Wright, Glass, Kane, Inglis, Smith, Jess, Shearer (Thomson), Miller, Dodds, Grant.
Stranraer: Ross; McLean, Hughes, Gallagher, Howard, Millar, Sloan, Walker, Duncan, Callaghan (Cody), Reilly.

Celtic (0) 2 *(Falconer, Van Hooijdonk)*
St Mirren (0) 0 28,449
Celtic: Bonner; Boyd, Gray, O'Neil B, McNally, Grant, McLaughlin, O'Donnell, Van Hooijdonk (Walker), Falconer, Collins.
St Mirren: Money; Dawson, McIntyre, McWhirter, McLaughlin, Fullarton, Dick, Bone (Inglis), Lavety, Gillies R (Hewitt), Elliot.

Cove R (0) 0
Dunfermline Ath (4) 4 *(Petrie 2, Smith, Hawkins)* 2200
Cove R: Charles; Morrison, Whyte, Walker, Paterson, Buchan, Megginson (Gibson), Park, Caldwell (Leslie), Lorimer, Beattie.
Dunfermline Ath: Van De Kamp; McNamara, Fleming, McCathie, Cooper, Smith, French, Robertson, Tod, Petrie, Hawkins (Ward).

Dundee U (0) 0
Clyde (0) 0 7413
Dundee U: O'Hanlon; Perry, Malpas, Hannah, Petric, Welsh, Bowman, McInally, Nixon, Brewster, Dailly.
Clyde: Fridge; O'Neill, Angus, Nisbet, Knox, Brown, Dickson, Watson, McCluskey (MacKenzie), Neill, Parks.

Huntly (4) 7 *(Stewart 3, Whyte, Lawrie (og), Thornton, De Barros)*
Burntisland Shipyards (0) 0 1420
Huntly: Gardiner; Yeats, Dunsire (Copland), Mone, Grant, De Barros, Gray, Stewart, Thomson, Whyte, Lennox (Robertson).
Burntisland Shipyards: Shanahan (Kelly); Parnell, Taylor, Lawrie (Lewis), Bray, McIlvean, Matthew, Horsburgh, Campbell, Paton (Murray), Drummond.

Kilmarnock (0) 0
Greenock Morton (0) 0 8271
Kilmarnock: Lekovic; MacPherson, Black, Montgomerie, Anderson, Reilly, Mitchell (Maskrey), Henry, Brown, Connor, McKee (Williamson).
Greenock Morton: Wylie; Collins, McArthur, Anderson, McCahill, Lindberg, Lilley, Blair (Fowler), Alexander, McInnes, Rajamaki.

Montrose (0) 0
Hibernian (0) 2 *(McGinlay, Jackson D)* 3812
Montrose: Larter; Robertson, Tindal, Masson (Cooper), Grant, Haro (Stephen), Garden, Beedie, McGlashan, Kennedy, MacRonald.
Hibernian: Leighton; Miller, Mitchell, McGinlay, Tweed, Farrell, McAllister (Findlay), Evans, Wright, Jackson D, Tortolano.

Raith R (1) 1 *(Crawford)*
Ayr U (0) 0 4156
Raith R: Thomson; McAnespie, Broddle, Coyle, Raeside, Sinclair, Nicoll, Dalziel, Crawford (Graham), Lennon, Wilson.
Ayr U: Duncan; McKilligan, Connie, Sharples, Rolling, MacFarlane, Gribben (Bilsland), Moore, Gilzean, Jackson, Gorgues (Tannock).

29 JAN

Dundee (1) 2 *(Shaw, Hamilton)*
Partick T (0) 1 *(Craig)* 6320
Dundee: Pageaud; McQuillan, Duffy C, Wieghorst (Ritchie), Duffy J, Bain, Shaw, Vrto, Hanilton, Britton, McCann.

Partick T: Walker; Dinnie, Pittman, Watson, Welsh, Turner, McDonald (Gibson), Craig, Foster, McWilliams, Taylor.

31 JAN

St Johnstone (1) 1 *(McNiven (og))*
Stenhousemuir (0) 1 *(Sprott)* 3173
St Johnstone: Main; Cherry, Preston, Irons, Weir, McGowne, O'Neil, Curran, Twaddle (Davenport), O'Boyle, Deas.
Stenhousemuir: Harkness; McNiven, Donaldson, Armstrong, McGeachie, Christie, Steel, Fisher, Mathieson, Hutchison, Sprott.

1 FEB

Clydebank (1) 1 *(Eadie)*
Hearts (1) 1 *(Robertson)* 3427
Clydebank: Matthews; McStay, Crawford, Murdoch, Sweeney, Currie, Cooper, Lansdowne, Eadie, Flannigan, Jack.
Hearts: Nelson; Frail, Miller C, Levein, Mackay, McPherson, Hamilton, Bett (Colquhoun), Thomas (Jamieson), Robertson, Hagen.

East Fife (0) 1 *(Allan)*
Ross Co (0) 0 2106
East Fife: Robertson; Bell, Hamill, Sneddon, Cusick, Donaghy, Allan, Hildersley, Scott, Hunter (Hutcheon), Hope.
Ross CO: Hutchison; Somerville, Reid, Williamson, Bellshaw, Furphy, Ferries, Grant, Herd, Connelly, Andrew MacLeod (MacPherson).

Stirling Albion (1) 1 *(McQuilter)*
Airdrieonians (2) 2 *(Andrew Smith 2)* 1699
Stirling Albion: Monaghan; Paterson, Gibson, Mitchell, McQuilter, Kerr (Drinkell), McInnes, Tait, Watters, Taggart, McLeod.
Airdrieonians: Martin; Stewart, Tony Smith, Sandison, Hay, Black, Boyle, Lawrence, Cooper (McIntyre J), Harvey (Wilson), Andrew Smith.

6 FEB

Falkirk (0) 0
Motherwell (1) 2 *(Burns 2)* 7552
Falkirk: Parks; Weir, McQueen (James), Oliver, McLaughlin, Rice, May, McGowan, McDonald (Henderson), Fulton, MacKenzie.
Motherwell: Woods; Philliben, McKinnon, Krivokapic (McMillan), Martin, McCart, Lambert, Dolan, Burns, McGrillen (Roddie), Davies.

Hamilton A (0) 1 *(Lorimer)*
Rangers (2) 3 *(Steven, Boli, Laudrup)* 18,379
Hamilton A: Ferguson; Renicks, Hillcoat, McEntegart, McCall, McIntosh, Clark, McStay (Lorimer), Chalmers, Duffield, McQuade (Baptie).
Rangers: Maxwell; Moore, Robertson, Gough, Boli, McCall, Steven, Miller, Durie (Brown), Hateley, Laudrup.

Meadowbank T (0) 1 *(Cowan (og))*
Berwick R (0) 1 *(Fraser)* 858
Meadowbank T: Ellison; Davidson, Martin, Williamson, Thomson, Sorbie (Little), Wilson, Bailey, Harris, McLeod, Sinclair (Samuel).
Berwick R: Osborne; Greenwood, Banks, Valentine, Cowan, Fraser, Forrester (Kane), Neil, Hawke, Irvine, Graham.

THIRD ROUND REPLAYS

31 JAN

Greenock Morton (1) 1 *(Anderson)*
Kilmarnock (0) 2 *(Maskrey 2) aet* 6533
Greenock Morton: Wylie; Collins, McArthur, Anderson, McCahill, Lindberg, Lilley (Fowler), Mahood, Alexander (McPherson), McInnes, Rajamaki.
Kilmarnock: Lekovic; MacPherson, Black, Montgomerie, Whitworth, Anderson (Maskrey), Mitchell, Henry, Brown, Reilly, Williamson (Napier).

7 FEB

Berwick R (0) 3 *(Irvine, Neil, Clegg)*
Meadowbank T (1) 3 *(Graham, Bailey, Wilson) aet* 991
Berwick R: Osborne; Greenwood, Banks, Valentine, Cowan (Clegg), Fraser, Forrester (Graham), Neil, Hawke, Irvine, Kane.
Meadowbank T: Ellison; Davidson, Martin, Williamson, Graham, Samuel, Wilson, Little, Harris (Bailey), McLeod, Sinclair (Sorbie).
(Meadowbank T won 7-6 on penalties)

Clyde (1) 1 *(Angus)*
Dundee U (3) 5 *(McKinlay, Craig, Hannah, Bowman, Nixon)* 5387
Clyde: Fridge; O'Neill, Angus, Nisbet (Neill), Thomson, Brown, Dickson, Watson, Parks, Knox, MacKenzie (Prunty).
Dundee U: O'Hanlon; McInally (Welsh), Malpas, Hannah, Petric, Dailly, Bowman, McKinlay (Nixon), Brewster, Ristic, Craig.

Hearts (1) 2 *(Robertson, Thomas)*
Clydebank (0) 1 *(Eadie)* 8503
Hearts: Nelson; Frail, Berry, Levein, Bett, McPherson, Colquhoun (Mackay), Hamilton, Thomas (Miller C), Robertson, Hagen.
Clydebank: Matthews; McStay, Crawford (Bowman), Murdoch, Sweeney, Currie, Cooper, Lansdowne, Eadie, Flannigan (Grady), Jack.

Stenhousemuir (2) 4 *(Sprott 2, Clarke, Donaldson)*
St Johnstone (0) 0 2340
Stenhousemuir: Harkness; McNiven, Donaldson, Armstrong, McGeachie, Christie, Steel (Clarke), Fisher, Mathieson, Hutchison (Roseburgh), Sprott.
St Johnstone: Main; Cherry, Preston (O'Boyle), Irons, Weir, McGowne, O'Neil, Curran, Wright, Twaddle (English), Farquhar.

FOURTH ROUND

18 FEB

Airdrieonians (1) 2 *(Cooper, Andrew Smith)*
Dunfermline Ath (0) 0 4397
Airdrieonians: Martin; Stewart, Jack, Sandison, McIntyre T, Black, Boyle, Davies, Cooper, Harvey (Andrew Smith), Lawrence.
Dunfermline Ath: Van De Kamp; Den Bieman, Fleming, McCathie, Paterson, Smith, French, Robertson, Tod (Moore), Petrie, Ward.

Celtic (3) 3 *(Van Hooijdonk 2, Falconer)*
Meadowbank T (0) 0 23,710
Celtic: Marshall; McNally, McKinlay, O'Neil, Mowbray, Grant, McLaughlin (Walker), O'Donnell (Craig), Van Hooijdonk, Falconer, Collins.
Meadowbank T: Ellison; Davidson, Martin, Graham, Williamson, Sorbie, Wilson, Bailey (Thorburn), Harris (Little), McLeod, Samuel.

Dundee (1) 1 *(Shaw)*

Raith R (0) 2 *(Graham, Rowbotham)* 7622

Dundee: Pageaud; Farningham, Duffy J (Hamilton), Duffy C, Blake (Tosh), Bain, Shaw, Vrto, Wieghorst, Britton, McCann.
Raith R: Thomson; McAnespie, Broddle (Rowbotham), Coyle, Dennis, Raeside (Wilson), Sinclair, Cameron, Graham, Lennon, Crawford.

Hibernian (1) 2 *(Harper, McGinlay)*

Motherwell (0) 0 10,639

Hibernian: Leighton; Miller, Mitchell, McGinlay, Tweed, Hunter (Tortolano), Weir, Harper, Wright, Jackson D (McGraw), Jackson C.
Motherwell: Woods; Shannon, McKinnon, Krivokapic, Martin, Philliben, Lambert (McGrillen), Dolan (Kirk), Burns, Arnott, Davies.

Huntly (0) 1 *(Stewart)*

Dundee U (2) 3 *(Brewster, Malpas, Hannah)* 4524

Huntly: Gardiner; Murphy, Dunsire, Mone, Rougvie, De Barros, Gray (Copland), Stewart, Thomson, Whyte (Yeats), Lennox.
Dundee U: O'Hanlon; McInally, Malpas, Hannah, Petric, Welsh, Bowman, McKinlay, Gomes (Nixon), Brewster (Ristic), Dailly.

Kilmarnock (2) 4 *(Maskrey 2, Reilly, Black)*

East Fife (0) 0 7003

Kilmarnock: Lekovic; MacPherson (McKee), Black, Reilly, Whitworth, Anderson, Mitchell, Henry, Brown, Connor, Maskrey.
East Fife: Robertson; Bell, Hamill, Burns, Sneddon, Gibb, Allan, Archibald, Andrews, Hunter, Hope (Hutcheon).

Stenhousemuir (0) 2 *(Steel 2)*

Aberdeen (0) 0 3452

Stenhousemuir: Harkness; Clarke, Donaldson, Armstrong, McGeachie, Christie, Steel, Fisher, Mathieson, Hutchison, Sprott.
Aberdeen: Snelders; Wright, Glass, Kane, Inglis (Irvine), Smith, Jess, Shearer, Miller (Hetherston), Dodds, McKinnon.

20 FEB

Hearts (2) 4 *(Miller C, McPherson, Robertson, Thomas)*

Rangers (0) 2 *(Laudrup, Durie)* 12,375

Hearts: Nelson; Frail, Miller C (Colquhoun), Levein, Bett, McPherson, Hamilton, Mackay, Robertson (Thomas), Millar J, Hagen.
Rangers: Maxwell; Moore, Robertson (Durrant), Gough, McLaren, Cleland (Brown), Steven, McCall, Miller, Durie, Laudrup.

QUARTER-FINALS

10 MAR

Celtic (1) 1 *(Collins)*

Kilmarnock (0) 0 30,881

Celtic: Bonner; Boyd, McKinlay, O'Neil, Mowbray, O'Donnell (Grant), McLaughlin, McStay, Van Hooijdonk, Falconer, Collins.
Kilmarnock: Lekovic; MacPherson, Black, Reilly, Whitworth, Anderson, Mitchell, Henry, McKee (Skilling), Connor (McCarrison), Maskrey.

11 MAR

Raith R (0) 1 *(Cameron)*

Airdrieonians (2) 4 *(Harvey 2, Davies, Black)* 7130

Raith R: Thomson; McAnespie, Rowbotham, Cameron, Dennis, Sinclair, Wilson (Dalziel), Crawford, Graham, Lennon (Broddle), Dair.
Airdrieonians: Martin; Stewart, Jack, Sandison, Hay, Black, Boyle, Davies, Cooper, Harvey (Lawrence), Andrew Smith.

Stenhousemuir (0) 0

Hibernian (0) 4 *(Harper 2, Tortolano, O'Neill)* 3520

Stenhousemuir: Harkness; Clarke (Roseburgh), Donaldson, Armstrong, McGeachie (McNiven), Christie, Steel, Fisher, Mathieson, Hutchison, Sprott.
Hibernian: Leighton; Miller, Mitchell, Farrell, Tweed, Hunter, Harper, Tortolano, Wright, Jackson D, O'Neill.

12 MAR

Hearts (2) 2 *(Millar J 2)*

Dundee U (1) 1 *(Gomes)* 12,515

Hearts: Nelson; Frail, Millar J, Berry, Jamieson, McPherson, Colquhoun (Thomas), Hamilton, Robertson, Mackay, Hagen (Leitch).
Dundee U: O'Hanlon; McInally, Malpas, Hannah (Brewster), Petric, Welsh, Bowman, McKinlay, Gomes, Crabbe (Nixon), Dailly.

SEMI-FINALS

7 APR at Ibrox Stadium

Celtic (0) 0

Hibernian (0) 0 40,950

Celtic: Bonner; Boyd, McKinlay, Vata, O'Neil, Grant, McLaughlin, McStay, Van Hooijdonk (Falconer), Walker, Collins
Hibernian: Leighton; Miller, Mitchell, McGinlay, Tweed, Millen, Harper, Farrell, Wright, Jackson D, O'Neill.

8 APR at Hampden Park

Airdrieonians (1) 1 *(Cooper)*

Hearts (0) 0 22,538

Airdrieonians: Martin; Stewart, Jack, Sandison, Andrew Smith (Hay), Black, Boyle, Davies, Cooper, Harvey (Tony Smith), Lawrence.
Hearts: Nelson; Mackay, Miller C, Levein, Jamieson (Thomas), McPherson, Hamilton (Colquhoun), Bett, Robertson, Millar J, Hagen.

SEMI-FINAL REPLAY at Ibrox Stadium

11 APR

Celtic (2) 3 *(Falconer, Collins, O'Donnell)*

Hibernian (0) 1 *(Wright)* 32,410

Celtic: Bonner; Boyd, McKinlay, Vata, O'Neil, Grant (O'Donnell), McLaughlin, McStay, Falconer, Walker (Donnelly), Collins.
Hibernian: Leighton; Miller, Mitchell, McGinlay, Tweed, Millen, Harper (Tortolano), McGraw (Evans), Wright, Jackson D, O'Neill.

FINAL at Hampden Park

27 MAY

Celtic (1) 1 *(Van Hooijdonk)*

Airdrieonians (0) 0 36,915

Celtic: Bonner; Boyd, McKinlay, Vata, McNally, Grant, McLaughlin, McStay, Van Hooijdonk (Falconer), Donnelly (O'Donnell), Collins.
Airdrieonians: Martin; Stewart, Jack, Sandison, Hay (McIntyre J), Black, Boyle, Andrew Smith, Cooper, Harvey (Tony Smith), Lawrence.

B & Q CUP 1994–95

FIRST ROUND

17 SEPT

Airdrieonians (2) 3 *(Davies, Andrew Smith 2)*
Berwick R (0) 1 *(Fraser)* 985
Airdrieonians: Martin; Boyle, Stewart, Sandison, McIntyre T, Jack, Harvey, Davies, Andrew Smith, Black (Honor), Lawrence.
Berwick R: Young N; Valentine, Banks, Cole, Fraser, Wilson (King), Forrester, Neil, Hawke, Irvine, Gallacher (Graham).

Brechin C (0) 0
Dunfermline Ath (2) 2 *(Petrie, McCathie)* 857
Brechin C: Balfour; Conway, Brown, Cairney, Nicolson, Scott, Bell, McNeill, Smith (Feroz), Millar, Christie.
Dunfermline Ath: McQueen; Bowes, Sharp, McCathie, Tod, Smith, Den Bieman, Robertson, French (Laing), Petrie, Ward (Sinclair).

Cowdenbeath (0) 2 *(Soutar, Tait)*
Clyde (0) 1 *(MacKenzie)* 454
Cowdenbeath: Russell; Petrie, Murdoch, Malloy, Humphreys, Winter, Tait, Hamill, Yardley, Callaghan, Black (Soutar).
Clyde: Hillcoat; Prunty, McCheyne, Knox, Thomson, Watson (O'Neill), Dickson, McAulay, MacKenzie, McCarron, Nisbet.

Dumbarton (0) 2 *(Campbell 2)*
St Johnstone (2) 4 *(Ramsey, O'Boyle 2, Davenport)* 961
Dumbarton: MacFarlane (Dennison); Marsland (Farrell), Fabiani, Melvin, Boyd, MacLeod, Mooney M, Meechan (Campbell), Gibson, McGarvey, Ward.
St Johnstone: Rhodes; Cherry, Miller, Ramsey (McGinnis), Inglis, McGowne, O'Neil, Irons, Davenport, O'Boyle, Davidson (McMartin).

Dundee (2) 5 *(Britton 4, Shaw)*
Arbroath (0) 0 2205
Dundee: Pageaud; McQuillan, Hutchison, Teasdale, Blake, Duffy J, Shaw, Farningham, Tosh, Britton (Hamilton), Anderson (Vrto).
Arbroath: Jackson; Mitchell, Middleton, Murray, Spittal, Shanks, McGovern, Elder, McGregor, Tosh, Downie (Finlay).

East Fife (0) 2 *(Hunter, Scott)*
Ross Co (0) 1 *(Andrew MacLeod (pen))* 1031
East Fife: Wilson; Bell (Irvine), Sneddon, Burns, Beaton, Dow, Allan, Hildersley (Cusick), Scott, Hunter, Gibb.
Ross Co: McMillan; Somerville, Reid, Williamson, Herd, Campbell, Ferries, Grant, Duff, McPherson, Andrew MacLeod.

Forfar Ath (0) 0
Alloa (0) 1 *(Moffat)* 516
Forfar Ath: Arthur; Mearns, McPhee, Mann, Archibald, McKillop (Heddle), O'Neill, Irvine (Kopel), McCormick, Bingham, Lees.
Alloa: Graham; McCormack J, Kemp, Nelson, McCulloch, Lawrie, McAnenay, Moffat, Diver, Bennett, Lamont.

Hamilton A (2) 2 *(Duffield 2 (1 pen))*
Stenhousemuir (0) 0 738
Hamilton A: Cormack; McKenzie, McInulty, McEntegart, Baptie, Nicholls, McQuade (Hartley), Sherry, Campbell, Duffield, Lorimer.
Stenhousemuir: Harkness; Clarke, Roseburgh (Hallford), Armstrong, Godfrey, Christie, Steel, Fisher, Irvine (Sludden), Hutchison, Sprott.

Meadowbank T (1) 1 *(Graham)*
Montrose (1) 2 *(McGlashan, Cooper) aet* 171
Meadowbank T: Ellison; Graham, Fleming, Wilson, Williamson, Martin (Duthie), Davidson (Price), McLeod, Little, Sorbie, Bailey.
Montrose: Larter; Robertson, Craib (Garden), Beedie, Grant, Haro, MacDonald, Stephen (Cooper), McGlashan, Milne, Masson.

Queen of the S (0) 0
Raith R (2) 2 *(Cameron, Crawford)* 1376
Queen of the S: Purdie; Kennedy, McKeown D, McKeown B, McFarlane, Ramsay, Sermanni, Bryce, McLaren (Cochrane), Leslie (McGuire), Mallan.
Raith R: Thomson; McAnespie, Rowbotham, Lennon, Narey, Sinclair, Nicholl, Crawford, Graham, Cameron, Wilson (Dair).

Queen's Park (0) 0
Clydebank (3) 5 *(Grady 3, Cooper, Eadie)* 894
Queen's Park: Moonie; Orr J, Kavanagh, Kerr, Maxwell, Orr G, Fitzpatrick, Lynch, McCormick (Edgar), McPhee, Graham (Williamson).
Clydebank: Matthews; Lansdowne, Crawford, Murdoch, Sweeney, Currie, Walker (Agnew), Jack, Eadie, Grady (Kerrigan), Cooper.

Stirling Albion (3) 4 *(McInnes, Taggart 2, Watters)*
Albion R (0) 0 517
Stirling Albion: McGeown; Paterson, Gibson, Mitchell (Kerr), McQuilter, Tait, McInnes, Farquhar, Watters, Taggart, McLeod.
Albion R: Davidson; Philliben, Parry, McDonald, Conn, Kelly, Scott, Docherty (Seggie), Young, Quinn (McBride), Deeley.

Stranraer (0) 1 *(Ferguson)*
St Mirren (0) 1 *(Watson (pen)) aet* 1220
Stranraer: Ross; Millar, Hughes, McCann (Grant), McCaffrey, Gallagher, Sloan, McLean (Ferguson), Duncan, Cody, Henderson.
St Mirren: Money; Dawson, Watson, McLaughlin, McIntyre, Dick, Gillies K (Gillies R), Baker, Lavety, Gardner (Fullarton), Elliot.
(Stranraer won 5-4 on penalties)

18 SEPT

East Stirling (1) 1 *(Watt)*
Ayr U (0) 1 *(Burns) aet* 768
East Stirling: Moffat; Russell, Cuthbert, Yates, Sneddon, Watt, Lee I, Millar, Geraghty (Conroy), Scott, Stirling (McCallum).
Ayr U: Duncan; Burns, Connie, Paterson, Rolling, George, Gorgues, Moore, McGivern (Sharples), Stainrod, Bilsland (Gilzean).
(Ayr U won 4-2 on penalties)

SECOND ROUND

27 SEPT

Airdrieonians (1) 1 *(Lawrence)*
Raith R (1) 1 *(Dalziel) aet* 1360
Airdrieonians: Martin; Stewart, Jack (Wilson), Sandison, Hay, Black, Boyle, Davies, Andrew Smith, Harvey, Lawrence.
Raith R: Thomson; McAnespie, Redford (Broddle), Lennon, Dennis, Narey, Wilson, Dalziel (Sinclair), Crawford, Cameron, Dair.
(Airdrieonians won 5-3 on penalties)

Alloa (1) 1 *(McAnenay)*
Clydebank (2) 3 *(Grady, Eadie, Harris)* 452

Alloa: Graham; McCormack J, Kemp (Bennett), Newbigging, McCulloch, Lawrie, McAvoy (Diver), Nelson, Moffat, McAnenay, Lamont.
Clydebank: Matthews; Lansdowne, Crawford, Murdoch, Currie, Harris (Flannigan), Cooper, Agnew, Eadie (Walker), Grady, Jack.

Ayr U (2) 4 *(Burns, Jackson, Paterson, George)*
Stranraer (2) 2 *(Walker, Henderson)* 2489

Ayr U: Duncan; Burns, Connie, Paterson, Rolling, George, Traynor, Moore, Jackson, Stainrod (Gilzean) (McKilligan), Gorgues.
Stranraer: Ross; Millar, Hughes, McLean, Gallagher, McCaffrey, Sloan, Walker (Grant), Duncan, Cody (McCann), Henderson.

Dunfermline Ath (2) 4 *(French (pen), Robertson, Petrie 2)*
Hamilton A (1) 2 *(McIntosh, Duffield)* 2884

Dunfermline Ath: Westwater; Bowes, McNamara, McCathie, Tod, Smith, Den Bieman, Robertson, French, Petrie, Ward.
Hamilton A: Cormack; McKenzie, McNulty, McEntegart, Baptie, McIntosh, McQuade, Sherry (Clark), McGill, Duffield, Nicholls.

East Fife (0) 0
Cowdenbeath (1) 3 *(Yardley 3)* 949

East Fife: Wilson; Sneddon, Hope, Burns, Beaton, Hildersley, Allan (Dow), Irvine, Scott, Hunter, Gibb.
Cowdenbeath: Russell; Petrie, Murdoch, Malloy, McMahon, Winter, Tait, Hamill (Black), Yardley, Callaghan, Soutar (Humphreys).

Greenock Morton (2) 4 *(Lilley 2, Alexander, Fowler)*
St Johnstone (2) 3 *(O'Boyle 3) aet* 1446

Greenock Morton: Wylie; Collins, Pickering, Anderson, Cormack, Johnstone, Lilley, Fowler, Alexander, Mahood, McArthur (Gibson).
St Johnstone: Rhodes; Cherry (Turner), McAuley, McGinnis, Inglis, McGowne, O'Neil, McMartin (Ramsey), Davenport, O'Boyle, Irons.

Montrose (1) 3 *(Stephen, McGlashan 2)*
Stirling Albion (0) 0 561

Montrose: Larter; Robertson, Tindal, Masson, Grant, Haro, Cooper (Brown), MacDonald, McGlashan, Kennedy (Milne), Stephen.
Stirling Albion: McGeown; Paterson, Gibson, Mitchell, McQuilter, Tait, McInnes, Farquhar (Roberts), Watters, Taggart, McLeod.

28 SEPT

Caledonian T (1) 1 *(MacDonald)*
Dundee (0) 1 *(Wieghorst) aet* 1336

Caledonian T: McRitchie; Brennan, McAllister, Sinclair, Scott (Lisle), Andrew, MacDonald (Smart), MacKenzie, MacMillan, Christie, Robertson.
Dundee: Mathers; Farningham, Hutchison, Duffy C, Blake, Duffy J, Shaw, Dailly (Hamilton), Wieghorst (Teasdale), Britton, Bain.
(Dundee won 4-3 on penalties)

QUARTER-FINALS

4 OCT

Airdrieonians (1) 2 *(Cooper, Davies)*
Ayr U (0) 0 1500

Airdrieonians: Martin; Stewart, Jack, Sandison, McIntyre T, Black, Boyle, Davies, Cooper, Harvey (Honor), Lawrence.
Ayr U: Duncan; Biggart, McVicar (Bilsland), Sharples, Rolling, McKilligan, Burns, Moore (Connie), Paterson, Jackson, Gorgues.

Cowdenbeath (0) 1 *(Yardley)*
Dunfermline Ath (2) 3 *(Smith, French, Petrie)* 3163

Cowdenbeath: Russell; Petrie, Murdoch, Malloy, McMahon, Winter, Lynch (Humphreys), Black, Yardley, Callaghan, Soutar (Barclay).
Dunfermline Ath: Westwater; McNamara, Hawkins, McCathie, Tod, Smith, Den Bieman, Robertson, French, Petrie (Laing), Ward.

Dundee (1) 2 *(Britton, Wieghorst)*
Greenock Morton (0) 1 *(Anderson)* 2199

Dundee: Pageaud; McQuillan, Bain, Farningham, Blake, Duffy J (Hutchison), Shaw, Wieghorst, Tosh, Britton, Hamilton.
Greenock Morton: Wylie; Collins, Pickering, Anderson, Cormack, Johnstone, McCann, Fowler (Hunter), Alexander (Gibson), Mahood, McArthur.

5 OCT

Montrose (0) 1 *(Kennedy (pen))*
Clydebank (0) 2 *(Flannigan, Cooper) aet* 825

Montrose: Larter; Robertson, Tindal, Masson, Tosh, Haro, Cooper (Brown), MacDonald, McGlashan, Kennedy, Stephen (MacRonald).
Clydebank: Matthews; Lansdowne, Crawford, Murdoch, Currie, Bowman, Cooper, Walker, Eadie, Grady (Flannigan), Jack (Harris).

SEMI-FINALS

18 OCT

Airdrieonians (0) 3 *(Boyle, Stewart, Cooper)*
Clydebank (0) 1 *(Cooper)* 1737

Airdrieonians: Martin; Stewart, Jack, Sandison, Hay, Black, Boyle, Davies, Cooper, Harvey (Wilson), Andrew Smith (McIntyre J).
Clydebank: Matthews; Jack, Crawford, Murdoch, Sweeney, Bowman (Grady), Cooper, Walker, Eadie, Flannigan, Harris (Lansdowne).

Dunfermline Ath (0) 1 *(Tod)*
Dundee (1) 2 *(Bain (pen), McCann)* 7154

Dunfermline Ath: Westwater; McNamara, Bowes, McCathie, Tod, Smith, Den Bieman, Robertson, French, Petrie, Ward (Hawkins).
Dundee: Pageaud; McQuillan, Bain, Farningham, Duffy J, Wieghorst, Shaw, Vrto, Tosh, Britton, McCann.

FINAL

6 NOV at McDiarmid Park, Perth

Airdrieonians (1) 3 *(Harvey, Boyle (pen), Andrew Smith)*
Dundee (1) 2 *(Hay (og), Britton) aet* 8844

Airdrieonians: Martin; Stewart (Tony Smith), Jack, Sandison, Hay, Black, Boyle, Davies, Cooper, Harvey, Lawrence (Andrew Smith).
Dundee: Pageaud; McQuillan, Bain, Farningham, Duffy J, Wieghorst, Shaw, Vrto, Tosh (Hamilton), Britton, McCann.
Referee: H F Williamson (Renfrew).

KONICA LEAGUE OF WALES 1994–95

		Home			Goals		Away			Goals		
	P	*W*	*D*	*L*	*F*	*A*	*W*	*D*	*L*	*F*	*A*	*Pts*
Bangor City	38	14	4	1	58	17	13	3	3	38	9	88
Afan Lido	38	12	4	3	31	19	12	3	4	29	17	79
Ton Pentre	38	12	4	3	34	19	11	4	4	50	31	77
Newtown	38	12	4	3	50	20	8	4	7	28	27	68
Cwmbran Town	38	10	3	6	37	26	10	4	5	32	23	67
Flint Town United	38	10	3	6	44	23	10	0	9	33	37	63
Barry Town	38	10	5	4	38	25	6	6	7	33	32	59
Holywell United	38	10	3	6	35	27	6	7	6	27	28	58
Llansantffraid	38	7	7	5	33	27	8	3	8	24	30	55
Inter Cardiff	38	8	2	9	34	20	6	9	4	24	23	53
Rhyl	38	8	3	8	40	36	8	2	9	34	33	53
Conwy United	38	9	3	7	36	30	5	4	10	24	35	49
Ebbw Vale	38	8	4	7	30	27	4	5	10	21	30	45
Caersws	38	6	5	8	27	31	5	6	8	30	33	44
Connah's Quay Nomads	38	7	3	9	24	37	5	4	10	33	42	43
Porthmadog	38	3	5	11	25	33	8	2	9	32	40	40
Aberystwyth Town	38	5	8	6	31	29	4	4	11	26	46	39
Llanelli	38	6	2	11	37	52	4	4	11	27	52	36
Mold Alexandra	38	6	2	11	29	36	4	2	13	28	54	34
Maesteg Park Athletic	38	2	4	13	15	47	0	2	17	8	66	12

KONICA LEAGUE OF WALES

	Aberystwyth Town	Afan Lido	Bangor City	Barry Town	Caersws	Connah's Quay	Conwy Utd	Cwmbran Town	Ebbw Vale	Flint Town U	Holywell Town	Inter Cardiff	Llanelli	Llansantffraid	Maesteg Park Ath	Mold Alexandra	Newtown	Porthmadog	Rhyl	Ton Pentre
Aberystwyth Town	—	1-1	1-2	2-2	1-1	1-2	1-1	0-2	4-1	1-3	1-1	1-1	2-2	1-2	2-0	1-0	2-2	5-1	1-4	3-1
Afan Lido	2-2	—	0-1	2-0	1-0	2-0	3-2	2-1	1-1	0-2	3-2	2-1	2-1	2-1	2-2	3-1	1-0	0-1	2-0	1-1
Bangor City	7-2	2-3	—	2-0	3-1	2-2	4-1	3-2	2-0	6-3	1-1	1-1	3-0	2-1	7-0	4-0	3-0	4-0	2-0	0-0
Barry Town	3-1	0-2	1-0	—	1-1	1-1	2-1	2-3	1-1	3-0	2-1	2-2	6-3	2-2	3-0	3-0	3-0	2-3	2-1	0-3
Caersws	2-1	0-1	0-5	0-1	—	2-2	4-1	2-2	2-4	2-3	1-1	0-0	0-2	0-1	2-0	5-2	0-0	0-1	3-1	2-1
Connah's Quay Nomads	3-2	1-2	0-8	2-2	2-1	—	0-0	0-1	1-0	2-1	2-2	0-1	1-2	1-2	1-0	1-3	1-4	4-1	0-4	2-1
Conwy United	3-2	1-0	1-4	3-1	0-3	4-5	—	0-1	3-0	4-1	0-1	1-1	0-0	2-0	3-0	3-3	4-2	2-0	1-2	2-4
Cwmbran Town	2-2	2-0	0-2	2-3	1-1	3-0	1-1	—	1-0	2-0	2-0	4-0	3-1	5-2	2-0	4-3	1-2	1-4	1-4	0-1
Ebbw Vale	2-2	0-3	2-2	2-2	0-3	2-0	3-2	0-0	—	1-2	1-0	1-0	1-2	2-0	3-0	6-1	0-2	1-0	1-3	2-3
Flint Town United	3-0	1-2	1-0	1-3	4-1	1-0	1-3	0-1	2-2	—	1-1	0-0	8-0	4-0	5-1	3-1	5-0	3-2	0-3	1-3
Holywell Town	1-2	1-2	0-2	1-0	2-0	2-0	2-0	1-4	1-0	2-3	—	1-1	4-2	0-2	2-0	3-1	1-0	5-2	3-3	3-3
Inter Cardiff	1-2	0-2	0-0	2-3	3-0	5-0	4-0	0-1	1-1	3-1	1-2	—	3-0	1-2	5-0	3-2	0-1	0-1	1-0	1-2
Llanelli	0-2	1-3	1-0	3-2	2-2	0-9	2-4	2-3	1-3	4-1	2-3	0-3	—	3-3	6-0	2-1	2-4	1-4	5-2	0-2
Llansantffraid	3-0	0-0	1-1	1-1	2-3	4-3	3-0	0-2	0-0	0-3	2-0	1-3	4-2	—	1-1	5-3	0-0	1-2	3-1	2-2
Maesteg Park Athletic	0-1	2-1	0-2	2-1	1-1	1-1	0-4	0-4	1-5	0-4	0-1	0-1	2-6	0-3	—	1-2	1-1	2-2	1-2	1-5
Mold Alexandra	4-2	1-2	1-2	0-2	2-1	1-3	0-2	3-1	2-1	0-2	2-3	1-2	5-1	0-0	2-0	—	0-2	1-1	1-2	3-7
Newtown	1-1	1-1	0-2	2-2	3-3	3-0	2-0	2-1	1-0	2-1	4-1	3-4	4-0	0-1	9-0	4-0	—	3-1	3-0	3-2
Porthmadog	4-0	1-2	0-1	1-4	1-3	2-0	0-1	2-2	0-1	1-4	1-1	1-1	1-1	0-1	5-0	1-2	0-4	—	2-2	2-3
Rhyl	3-2	0-1	0-1	3-1	4-3	2-3	1-1	1-1	3-0	1-2	1-2	3-1	2-2	3-1	3-1	1-2	3-2	3-4	—	3-6
Ton Pentre	2-0	2-1	0-3	1-1	0-2	4-2	2-0	3-0	3-1	3-0	1-1	1-1	2-0	2-0	3-2	1-1	0-2	3-2	1-0	—

ALLBRIGHT BITTER WELSH CUP 1994–95

Preliminary Round

Abercynon Athletic v Chepstow Town	1-2
Albion Rovers v Fields Park/Pontllanfraith	3-2
Bala Town v Llay Welfare	2-3
British Steel v BP Llandarcy	0-2
Cardiff Corinthians v Cardiff Institute	3-1
Felinheli v Llanrwst United	0-0, 4-3
Goytre United v Seven Sisters	6-1
Newport YMCA v Pontlottyn Blast Furnace	4-4, 0-7
Panteg v Trelewis Welfare	2-1
Pontyclun v Risca United	2-2, 3-4
Porthcawl Town v Newcastle Emlyn	6-0
Presteigne St Andrews v Penparcau	7-2
Rhyl Delta v British Aerospace	2-1
Skewen Athletic v Pontardawe Athletic	1-2
Tondu Robins v South Wales Constabulary	4-0

First Round

Abergavenny Thursdays v Panteg	1-1, 2-1
AFC Porth v Pontardawe Athletic	3-0
Albion Rovers v Tondu Robins	0-3
BP Llandarcy v Morrison Town	2-0
Brecon Corinthians v Goytre United	1-1, 1-2
Briton Ferry Athletic v Carmarthen Town	0-0, 1-2
Brymbo v Llanfairfech	2-2, 2-2, 2-0
Buckley Town v Penycae	3-5
Cardiff Corinthians v Caerau	2-1
Cardiff Civil Services v Caldicot Town	3-1
Carno v Llanidloes Town	7-1
Chepstow Town v Bridgend Town	3-0
Ferndale Athletic v Ammanford Town	0-1
Lex XI v Camaesbay AFC	1-2
Llandrindod Wells v Welshpool Town	0-3
Llandudno v Llay Welfare	7-1
Locomotive Llanberis v Gresford Athletic	0-2
Mostyn v Llanfairpwll	2-2, 1-6
Nantlle Vale v Llangefni Town	2-6
Nefyn United v Knighton Town	3-0
New Broughton v Cefn Druids	0-2
Oswestry Town v New Brighton	1-0
Pembroke Borough v Haverfordwest County	0-5
Pontlottyn Blast Furnace v Caerleon	2-0
Pontypridd Town v Porthcawl Town	3-1
Port Talbot Athletic v Aberaman Athletic	0-1
Presteigne St Andrews v Penrhyncoch	2-1
Rhos Aelwyd v Chirk AAA	2-2, 3-1
Rhyl Delta v Rhayader Town	1-2
Risca United v Llanwern	2-2, 4-1
Ruthin Town v Llandyrnog United	0-3
Treowen Stars v Taffs Well	1-3
Felinheli v Prestatyn Town	0-5

Second Round

Ebbw Vale v Aberaman Athletic	3-0
Cardiff Corinthians v Llanelli	2-0
Cardiff Civil Services v Cwmbran Town	0-3
Carmarthen Town v Haverfordwest County	3-0
Cefn Druids v Llansantffraid	1-0
Connah's Quay Nomads v Mold Alexandra	3-2
Flint Town United v Brymbo	2-2, 1-3
Gresford Athletic v Aberystwyth Town	1-2
Llandyrnog United v Rhos Aelwyd	0-3
Llangefni Town v Welshpool Town	3-0
Maesteg Park Athletic v BP Llandarcy	2-1
Merthyr Tydfil v Goytre United	5-0
Nefyn United v Llandudno	1-2
Newtown v Penycae	6-0
Oswestry Town v Caersws	1-1, 1-3
Pontlottyn Blast Furnace v Afan Lido	1-1, 0-5
Pontypridd Town v AFC Porth	3-2
Porthmadog v Conwy United	3-0
Prestatyn Town v Cemaes Bay	0-4
Presteigne St Andrews v Carno	3-3, 1-6
Rhayader Town v Holywell Town	0-2
Rhyl v Llanfairpwll	3-0
Risca United v Ammanford Town	3-0
Taffs Well v Chepstow Town	2-0
Tondu Robins v Abergavenny Thursdays	0-2

Third Round

Taffs Well v Swansea City	0-7
Bangor City v Carno	2-0
Brymbo v Aberystwyth Town	1-3
Caersws v Rhos Aelwyd	4-0
Cardiff Corinthians v Afan Lido	0-1
Carmarthen Town v Barry Town	2-3
Cefn Druids v Connah's Quay Nomads	0-2
Holywell Town v Porthmadog	1-3
Llandudno v Llangefni Town	3-0
Maesteg Park Athletic v Inter Cardiff	1-0
Merthyr Tydfil v Cwmbran Town	5-0
Rhyl v Cemaes Bay	3-0
Risca United v Pontypridd Town	2-0
Ton Pentre v Abergavenny Thursdays	2-1
Ebbw Vale v Cardiff City	1-1, 0-7
Newtown v Wrexham	1-1, 0-2

Fourth Round

Swansea City v Rhyl	5-1
Afan Lido v Ton Pentre	0-3
Bangor City v Maesteg Park Athletic	12-1
Barry Town v Llandudno	1-1, 1-3
Merthyr Tydfil v Aberystwyth Town	1-0
Porthmadog v Caersws	0-0, 2-1
Wrexham v Connah's Quay Nomads	4-0
Cardiff City v Risca United	4-0

Fifth Round

Bangor City v Wrexham	2-2, 0-1
Merthyr Tydfil v Ton Pentre	2-0
Swansea City v Porthmadog	8-0
Llandudno v Cardiff City	0-1

Semi-finals (two legs)

Wrexham v Merthyr Tydfil	3-1
Merthyr Tydfil v Wrexham	0-1
Swansea City v Cardiff City	0-1
Cardiff City v Swansea City	0-0

Final: Cardiff City 1, Wrexham 2

(At National Stadium, Cardiff, 21 May 1995) Att: 12,810

Cardiff City: Williams S; Brazil, Searle, Richardson, Baddeley, Perry, Wigg, Bird (Young), Millar (Oatway), Dale, Griffith. *Scorer:* Dale.

Wrexham: Marriott; Brace, Hardy, Hunter, Jones, Hughes, Bennett, Owen, Connolly, Morris (Watkin), Durkan. *Scorer:* Bennett 2 (1 pen).

Referee: V. Reed.

NORTHERN IRISH FOOTBALL 1994–95

"Northern Ireland soccer is at the crossroads" was the message hammered out by Jim Boyce following his election as President of the Irish FA in succession to Sammy Walker (Coleraine). He is the first Cliftonville delegate to occupy the office.

His sentiments aptly summed up the situation at both international and domestic level after a season of dramatic change – a season of frenzy and fear.

The introduction of promotion and relegation from this new campaign generated an astonishing battle between clubs attempting to finish in the top eight.

Huge sums were spent on English, Scottish and South of Ireland players in an attempt to prevent the dreaded drop into a lower division. Some succeeded but others failed and now wonder just what fate will befall them in the financially stringent days ahead.

P and R was generally accepted with the consensus that eight was too small a number. This and other aspects of the system, however, will be examined over the next few months and a report issued before next April's annual general meeting.

This is how the new set-up is composed based on accumulated placings over two seasons: Premier Division—Glenavon, Crusaders, Portadown, Linfield, Ards, Cliftonville, Glentoran, Bangor; First Division—Coleraine, Distillery, Ballymena United, Omagh Town, Ballyclare Comrades, Carrick Rangers, Newry Town, Larne.

There was a spread of the trophies with Crusaders, always the pacemakers, winning the Irish League Championship for the first time in 19 years and Linfield, who had an indifferent season, ensuring qualification for Europe by winning the Irish Cup.

Glenavon, as runners-up, took the second UEFA Cup representation but, unless there is an improvement in the Irish League clubs co-efficient over the next two years, this place could be in jeopardy.

Sponsorship continues with virtually every tournament commercially backed although there were several changes in companies involved. "We are happy with the outcome of all our discussions. Football is generally well supported by the Ulster business community but it is an on-going process and we must be continually searching for new outlets" said League president Morton McKnight.

Internationally it was a peculiar nine months. Manager Bryan Hamilton, who has worked prodigiously in the development of the game from schoolboys to the senior squad, had a sweet and sour experience.

There were excellent European Championship results against Austria in Vienna (2-1), Latvia in Rigo (1-0) and the Republic in Dublin (1-1). Then came a disastrous 2-0 defeat by Canada in Edmonton, then 2-1 by Chile but with a much improved performance before the 2-1 humiliation by Latvia at Windsor Park.

What a catastrophe that proved to be in view of the Republic being held to a scoreless draw in Liechtenstein and then losing 2-1 to Austria at Lansdowne Road. Those three points would have put Northern Ireland back into qualification reckoning for next summer's finals in England. All hope has gone and now the build-up must be for the France 98 World Cup preliminary series.

There is a long hard road ahead but the Irish FA general secretary David Bowen in his annual report stresed there was a "feel good" climate in the game with the advent of a youth development programme, appointment of special staff to deal with this and the introduction of mini-soccer.

The basis of long-term strategy has been laid but it is essential to have teams competing in every category especially under-21 to bridge that all important gap between under-18 and the senior side.

And, as Hamilton stressed, young players with English clubs must figure regularly in the first eleven. "The more we have in the Premier Division the better it will be for us. Languishing in the reserves or on the substitutes bench is not the preparation for international football" he said. Nobody would disagree.

MALCOLM BRODIE

BUDWEISER CUP 1994-95

First Round

Glentoran v Distillery	2-3
Glenavon v Cliftonville	1-2
Omagh Town v Linfield	0-2
Ards v Bangor	1-2
Crusaders v Newry Town	0-0
(Newry won 3-2 on penalties)	
Ballymena United v Ballyclare Comrades	0-1
Portadown v Carrick Rangers	3-1
Larne v Coleraine	1-2

Quarter-finals

Linfield v Distillery	1-2
Ballyclare Comrades v Newry Town	1-0
Bangor v Coleraine	3-2
Portadown v Cliftonville	1-0

Semi-finals

Distillery v Ballyclare Comrades	
Bangor v Portadown	1-3

Final

Portadown 4 Distillery 2 *(at Windsor Park, 6 December 1994)*

Portadown: Hamilton; Major, Murray, Casey, Strain, Tlemo, Cunningham, Shepherd, Ferguson (Doolin), Candlish (Fraser), Russell.

Distillery: O'Neill; Drake, Kennedy B, Kennedy J, Brady, Allen, Totten, Armstrong (Trainor), Hall (Small), Mitchell, Dykes.

Scorers: Portadown–Strain, Cunningham, Russell, Doolin; Distillery–Totten, Dykes.

Referee: L. Irvine (Limavady).

Previous Winners: 1988: Glentoran, 1989: Glenavon, 1990: Glentoran, 1991: Portadown, 1992: Omagh Town, 1993: Portadown, 1994: Linfield.

WILKINSON SWORD LEAGUE CUP FINAL 1994-95

Ards 0 Cliftonville 0 *(at Windsor Park, Belfast, 25 April 1995)*

(Aet; Ards won 2-0 on penalties)

Ards: Kee; McBride, Murphy, Brady, Mooney, O'Sullivan, Cullen C, McCann M, Patmore (Erskine), Cullen P, Morrison (Heaney).

Cliftonville: Rice; Hill, Loughran (Gill), McDonald, Kerr, Strang, McCann T, Sliney (O'Neill), Manley, McAllister, Donnelly.

Referee: N. Cowie (Belfast).

Attendance: 4500

Previous Winners: 1992: Linfoeld, 1993: Bangor, 1994: Linfield.

SMIRNOFF IRISH LEAGUE CHAMPIONSHIP FINAL TABLE

	P	*W*	*D*	*L*	*F*	*A*	*Pts*
Crusaders	30	20	7	3	58	25	67
Glenavon	30	18	6	6	76	40	60
Portadown	30	15	5	10	59	41	50
Ards	30	15	5	10	55	42	50
Glentoran	30	14	8	8	53	41	50
Cliftonville	30	13	11	6	44	32	50
Coleraine	30	12	13	5	52	39	49
Linfield	30	11	11	8	48	34	44
Omagh Town	30	10	12	8	42	38	42
Distillery	30	12	6	12	45	47	42
Bangor	30	8	14	8	42	38	38
Ballymena United	30	7	8	15	43	53	29
Carrick Rangers	30	7	7	16	46	75	28
Ballyclare Comrades	30	5	6	19	39	66	21
Newry Town	30	4	9	17	34	74	21
Larne	30	3	4	23	18	69	13

IRISH LEAGUE CHAMPIONSHIP WINNERS

1891	Linfield	1910	Cliftonville	1934	Linfield	1961	Linfield	1981	Glentoran
1892	Linfield	1911	Linfield	1935	Linfield	1962	Linfield	1982	Linfield
1893	Linfield	1912	Glentoran	1936	Belfast Celtic	1963	Distillery	1983	Linfield
1894	Glentoran	1913	Glentoran	1937	Belfast Celtic	1964	Glentoran	1984	Linfield
1895	Linfield	1914	Linfield	1938	Belfast Celtic	1965	Derry City	1985	Linfield
1896	Distillery	1915	Belfast Celtic	1939	Belfast Celtic	1966	Linfield	1986	Linfield
1897	Glentoran	1920	Belfast Celtic	1940	Belfast Celtic	1967	Glentoran	1987	Linfield
1898	Linfield	1921	Glentoran	1948	Belfast Celtic	1968	Glentoran	1988	Glentoran
1899	Distillery	1922	Linfield	1949	Linfield	1969	Linfield	1989	Linfield
1900	Belfast Celtic	1923	Linfield	1950	Linfield	1970	Glentoran	1990	Portadown
1901	Distillery	1924	Queen's Island	1951	Glentoran	1971	Linfield	1991	Portadown
1902	Linfield	1925	Glentoran	1952	Glenavon	1972	Glentoran	1992	Glentoran
1903	Distillery	1926	Belfast Celtic	1953	Glentoran	1973	Crusaders	1993	Linfield
1904	Linfield	1927	Belfast Celtic	1954	Linfield	1974	Coleraine	1994	Linfield
1905	Glentoran	1928	Belfast Celtic	1955	Linfield	1975	Linfield	1995	Crusaders
1906	Cliftonville/ Distillery	1929	Belfast Celtic	1956	Linfield	1976	Crusaders		
		1930	Linfield	1957	Glentoran	1977	Glentoran		
1907	Linfield	1931	Glentoran	1958	Ards	1978	Linfield		
1908	Linfield	1932	Linfield	1959	Linfield	1979	Linfield		
1909	Linfield	1933	Belfast Celtic	1960	Glenavon	1980	Linfield		

ULSTER CUP

SECTIONAL TABLES

Section A	*P*	*W*	*D*	*L*	*F*	*A*	*Pts*
Bangor	3	2	1	0	6	2	7
Linfield	3	2	0	1	4	3	6
Carrick Rangers	3	1	0	2	7	7	3
Glentoran	3	0	1	2	2	7	1
Section B	*P*	*W*	*D*	*L*	*F*	*A*	*Pts*
Portadown	3	2	1	0	9	4	7
Newry Town	3	2	0	1	5	6	6
Coleraine	3	1	1	1	4	4	4
Ards	3	0	0	3	2	6	0
Section C	*P*	*W*	*D*	*L*	*F*	*A*	*Pts*
Glenavon	3	3	0	0	10	1	9
Distillery	3	2	0	1	4	3	6
Ballymena United	3	0	1	1	1	7	1
Larne	3	0	1	2	2	6	1
Section D	*P*	*W*	*D*	*L*	*F*	*A*	*Pts*
Ballyclare Comrades	3	3	0	0	7	3	9
Crusaders	3	2	0	1	8	3	6
Cliftonville	3	0	1	2	2	4	1
Omagh Town	3	0	1	2	1	8	1

ULSTER CUP FINAL 1994–95

Quarter-finals

Glenavon v Crusaders	4-1
Ballyclare Comrades v Distillery	1-2
Portadown v Linfield	0-3
Bangor v Newry Town	1-0

Semi-finals

Bangor v Glenavon *(New Grosvesnor Stadium)*	3-2 (aet)
Linfield v Distillery *(The Oval)*	3-1

Final

Bangor 2 Linfield 1 *(at The Oval, Belfast 4 October 1994)*
Bangor: Currie; Dornan R, Glendenning, McCaffrey, Brown, Melly, Surgeon, Kenny, Collins, Hill, Batey.
Linfield: Lamont; Dornan A, Easton, Peebles, McConnell, Beatty, Campbell, Gorman, Haylock, Fenlon, Bailie.
Scorers: Bangor–Brown, Kenny; Linfield–Campbell.
Referee: A. Snoddy (Carryduff).
Attendance: 4200

Winners

1949	Linfield	1959	Glenavon	1969	Coleraine	1979	Linfield	1989	Glentoran
1950	Larne	1960	Linfield	1970	Linfield	1980	Ballymena U	1990	Portadown
1951	Glentoran	1961	Ballymena U	1971	Linfield	1981	Glentoran	1991	Bangor
1952		1962	Linfield	1972	Coleraine	1982	Glentoran	1992	Linfield
1953	Glentoran	1963	Crusaders	1973	Ards	1983	Glentoran	1993	Crusaders
1954	Crusaders	1964	Linfield	1974	Linfield	1984	Linfield	1994	Bangor
1955	Glenavon	1965	Coleraine	1975	Coleraine	1985	Coleraine		
1956	Linfield	1966	Glentoran	1976	Glentoran	1986	Coleraine		
1957	Linfield	1967	Linfield	1977	Linfield	1987	Larne		
1958	Distillery	1968	Coleraine	1978	Linfield	1988	Glentoran		

TNT GOLD CUP

SECTIONAL TABLES

Section A	*P*	*W*	*D*	*L*	*F*	*A*	*Pts*
Linfield	3	3	0	0	9	1	9
Coleraine	3	2	0	1	5	4	6
Distillery	3	1	0	2	5	8	3
Larne	3	0	0	3	2	8	0
Section B	*P*	*W*	*D*	*L*	*F*	*A*	*Pts*
Ballymena United	3	2	0	1	5	3	6
Portadown	3	2	0	1	3	2	6
Bangor	3	2	0	1	3	3	6
Omagh Town	3	0	0	3	2	5	0
Section C	*P*	*W*	*D*	*L*	*F*	*A*	*Pts*
Glenavon	3	2	1	0	12	2	7
Cliftonville	3	2	0	1	6	7	6
Ballyclare Comrades	3	1	0	2	4	7	3
Newry Town	3	0	1	2	5	11	1
Section D	*P*	*W*	*D*	*L*	*F*	*A*	*Pts*
Glentoran	3	3	0	0	10	3	9
Crusaders	3	1	1	1	6	7	4
Carrick Rangers	3	1	1	1	3	5	4
Ards	3	1	1	3	2	6	1

TNT GOLD CUP FINAL 1994-95

Quarter-finals

Linfield v Portadown	2-2 (aet)
(Linfield won 4-2 on penalties)	
Ballymena United v Coleraine	0-1
Glentoran v Cliftonville	2-1 (aet)
Glenavon v Crusaders	0-1

Semi-finals

Linfield v Crusaders *(The Oval)*	1-2
Coleraine v Glentoran *(Windsor Park)*	2-0

Final

Crusaders 1 Glentoran 1 *(at Windsor Park, Belfast, 25 October 1994)*
(aet; 90 mins 1-1; Glentoran won 3-0 on penalties)
Crusaders: McKeown; Lawlor, Stewart, Dunlop, Callaghan, Hunter K, McCartney, Murray (Carroll), Baxter (Livingstone), Hunter G, Burrows.
Glentoran: Armstrong; Neill, Smyth M, Parker, Smyth G, Mathieson (Kelly) D), Kelly N, Martindale (Nixon), Campbell, Cunnington, McBride.
Scorers: Crusaders–Murray; Glentoran–Campbell.
Referee: D. Magill (Belfast).
Attendance: 2000

Club Records: Linfield 30, Glentoran 11, Belfast Celtic 10, Portadown 6, Coleraine 4, Distillery 5, Cliftonville 3, Glenavon 3, Ards 2, Ballymena United 1, Crusaders 1, Derry City 1, Shelbourne 1.

IRISH CUP FINALS (from 1946–47)

1946–47	Belfast Celtic 1, Glentoran 0
1947–48	Linfield 3, Coleraine 0
1948–49	Derry City 3, Glentoran 1
1949–50	Linfield 2, Distillery 1
1950–51	Glentoran 3, Ballymena U 1
1951–52	Ards 1, Glentoran 0
1952–53	Linfield 5, Coleraine 0
1953–54	Derry City 1, Glentoran 0
1954–55	Dundela 3, Glenavon 0
1955–56	Distillery 1, Glentoran 0
1956–57	Glenavon 2, Derry City 0
1957–58	Ballymena U 2, Linfield 0
1958–59	Glenavon 2, Ballymena U 0
1959–60	Linfield 5, Ards 1
1960–61	Glenavon 5, Linfield 1
1961–62	Linfield 4, Portadown 0
1962–63	Linfield 2, Distillery 1
1963–64	Derry City 2, Glentoran 0
1964–65	Coleraine 2, Glenavon 1
1965–66	Glentoran 2, Linfield 0
1966–67	Crusaders 3, Glentoran 1
1967–68	Crusaders 2, Linfield 0
1968–69	Ards 4, Distillery 2
1969–70	Linfield 2, Ballymena U 1
1970–71	Distillery 3, Derry City 0
1971–72	Coleraine 2, Portadown 1
1972–73	Glentoran 3, Linfield 2
1973–74	Ards 2, Ballymena U 1
1974–75	Coleraine 1 : 0 : 1, Linfield 1 : 0 : 0
1975–76	Carrick Rangers 2, Linfield 1
1976–77	Coleraine 4, Linfield 1
1977–78	Linfield 3, Ballymena U 1
1978–79	Cliftonville 3, Portadown 2
1979–80	Linfield 2, Crusaders 0
1980–81	Ballymena U 1, Glenavon 0
1981–82	Linfield 2, Coleraine 1
1982–83	Glentoran 1 : 2, Linfield 1 : 1
1983–84	Ballymena U 4, Carrick Rangers 1
1984–85	Glentoran 1 : 1, Linfield 1 : 0
1985–86	Glentoran 2, Coleraine 1
1986–87	Glentoran 1, Larne 0
1987–88	Glentoran 1, Glenavon 0
1988–89	Ballymena U 1, Larne 0
1989–90	Glentoran 3, Portadown 0
1990–91	Portadown 2, Glenavon 1
1991–92	Glenavon 2, Linfield 1
1992–93	Bangor 1:1:1, Ards 1:1:0
1993–94	Linfield 2, Bangor 0
1994-95	Linfield 3, Carrick Rangers 1

WHERE THE TROPHIES WENT

	Winners	*Runners-up*
Smirnoff Irish League	Crusaders	Glenavon
Bass Irish Cup	Linfield	Carrick Rangers
TNT Gold Cup	Glentoran	Crusaders
Budweiser Cup	Portadown	Distillery
Wilkinson Sword League Cup	Ards	Cliftonville
Ulster Cup	Bangor	Linfield
Cawoods Co Antrim Shield	Linfield	Glenavon

Wilkinson Sword B Division

Section One	Loughall	Dungannon Swifts
Section Two	Bangor Res	Glentoran II
Coca Cola Irish Youth Cup	Glentoran Colts	Lurgan Town Boys
Intermediate Cup	Ballinamallard Utd	Park
Cawood Co Antrim Junior Shield	Immaculata	
Wilkinson Sword George Wilson Cup	Bangor Res	Crusaders Res
Ted Clark Mid Ulster Cup	Portadown	Newry Town
Mid Ulster Shield	Oxford Utd	Sparta
Cawoods Steel and Sons Cup	Bangor Res	Linfield Swifts
North West Senior Cup	Coleraine	Limavady Utd
North West Junior Cup	Ardmore	Tullyally Colts
McEwans Sixes	Cliftonville	Ballyclare Comrades
Bob Radcliffe Memorial Cup	Dungannon Swifts	Loughgall
McEwans Charity Shield	Linfield	Bangor
Ormo Irish Junior Cup	Oxford Utd	Dergview
Smirnoff Knock Out Cup	Dundela	Loughgall
Irish Youth League	Linfield Rangers	Glentoran Colts
Irish Youth League Cup	Ballyclare Colts	Linfield Rangers

BASS IRISH CUP 1994–95

Fifth Round (First Round Proper)

Ards v Chimney Corner	3-1
Newry Town v Larne	3-0
Omagh Town v Ballymena United	0-0, 1-0
Ballyclare Comrades v Glenavon	2-3
Dundela v Crumlin United	3-1
Linfield v Crusaders	2-0
Glentoran v Coleraine	1-1, 1-2
Portadown v Donegall Celtic	4-0
Brantwood v Moyola Park	2-2, 3-2
Distillery v Bangor	1-5
Carrick Rangers v Ballinamallard United	2-0
Crewe United v Cliftonville	0-2
Limavady United v Dungiven	1-2
Dungannon Swifts v Cookstown United	1-0
Loughgall v Kilmore Rec	2-1
Banbridge Town v Dunmurry Rec	7-0

(For the first time in the history of the competition, all matches were postponed on Saturday, January 22 because of flooded pitches. They were staged throughout the following week).

Sixth Round

Ards v Brantwood	4-1
Carrick Rangers v Dundela	2-1
Cliftonville v Banbridge	4-0
Coleraine v Portadown	0-0, 1-3
Loughgall v Dungiven	2-1
Newry Town v Bangor	1-1, 1-2
Omagh Town v Glenavon	1-1, 1-3
Dungannon Swifts v Linfield	3-5

Quarter-finals

Ards v Glenavon	3-2
Carrick Rangers v Bangor	2-1
Linfield v Loughgall	1-1, 1-0
Portadown v Cliftonville	0-1

Semi-finals

Ards v Linfield *(The Oval)*	0-0, 1-2
Carrick Rangers v Portadown *(Windsor Park)*	1-0

Final

Carrick Rangers 1 Linfield 3 *(at The Oval, Belfast, 7 May 1995)*

Carrick Rangers: Miskelly; Wilson, Gilmore, Muldoon, Gordon, Coulter, Kirk, McDermott, Donaghy (Doherty), Ferris, McAuley (Crawford).

Linfield: Lamont; Dornan, Easton, Peebles (McCoosh), Spiers, Beatty, Campbell, Gorman, Haylock, Fenlon, Bailie.

Scorers: Carrick Rangers–Gilmore; Linfield–Haylock (2), McCoosh.

Referee: G. Keatley (Bangor).

Attendance: 6000.

INTERNATIONAL DIRECTORY

The latest available information has been given regarding numbers of clubs and players registered with FIFA, the world governing body. Where known, official colours are listed. With European countries, League tables show a number of signs. * indicates relegated teams, + play-offs, *+ relegated after play-offs, + + promoted.
When provisional members are added there will be 190 FIFA countries. The four home countries, England, Scotland, Northern Ireland and Wales, are dealt with elsewhere in the Yearbook; but basic details appear in this directory.

EUROPE

ALBANIA

Federation Albanaise De Football, Rruga Dervish Hima Nr. 31, Tirana.
Founded: 1930; *Number of Clubs:* 49; *Number of Players:* 5,192; *National Colours:* Red shirts, black shorts, red stockings.
Telephone: 00–355–42 27 877; *Cable:* ALBSPORT TIRANA; *Telex:* 2228 bfssh ab. *Fax:* 00 355–42 27 877.

International matches 1994
Macedonia (a) 1-5, Wales (a) 0-2, Germany (h) 1-2, Georgia (h) 0-1, Germany (a) 1-2.

League Championship wins (1945–95)
Dinamo Tirana 15; Partizani Tirana 15; 17 Nentori 8; Vllaznia 7; Flamurtari 1; Labinoti 1; Teuta 1, SK Tirana 1.

Cup wins (1948–95)
Partizani Tirana 13; Dinamo Tirana 12; 17 Nentori 6; Vllaznia 5; Flamurtari 2; Labinoti 1; Elbasan 1; SK Tirana 1, Teuta 1.

Final League Table 1994–95

	P	*W*	*D*	*L*	*F*	*A*	Pts
SK Tirana	30	19	6	5	57	27	44
Teuta	30	13	6	11	37	27	32
Partizani	30	12	8	10	36	30	32
Flamurtari	30	11	10	9	34	29	32
Shqiponia	30	11	9	10	38	33	31
Albpetrol	30	13	5	12	37	43	31
Shkumbini	30	11	8	11	32	20	30
Dinamo	30	10	10	10	37	27	30
Tomori	30	12	6	12	21	25	30
Apolonia	30	12	6	12	33	38	30
Vllaznia	30	12	5	13	31	29	29
Elbasan	30	10	9	11	22	20	29
Beselidhja	30	11	7	12	29	34	29
Laci*	30	13	3	14	30	40	29
Beca*	30	12	2	16	30	40	26
Iliria*	30	7	2	21	22	64	16

Top scorer: Shehu (Shqiponia) 21.
Cup Final: Teuta 0, SK Tirana 0.
Teuta won 4-3 on penalties.

ARMENIA

Football Federation of Armenia, 9, Abovian Str. 375001 Erevan, Armenia.
Number of Clubs: 956; *Number of Players:* 12,055.
Telephone: 007 8852 52 98 62; *Telex:* 885–52 3376. *Fax:* 007 8852 15 15 73.

International matches 1994
USA (a) 0-1, Belgium (1) 0-2, Cyprus (h) 0-0, Cyprus (a) 0-2.

League Championship wins 1992–94
Shirak Gyumri 2; Ararat Erevan 1.

Cup winners 1992–94
Ararat Erevan 2.

Final League Table 1994

	P	*W*	*D*	*L*	*F*	*A*	Pts
Shirak Gyumri	28	24	4	0	83	19	52
Homenetmen	28	23	1	4	113	24	47
Ararat Erevan	28	21	5	2	109	21	47
Homenmen	28	15	6	7	65	45	36
Banants	28	17	1	10	95	56	35
Tsement	28	11	6	11	54	49	28
Kotaik	28	12	3	13	73	53	27
Aznavour	28	11	3	14	43	72	25
Yerazank	28	9	5	14	29	50	23
Van	28	9	4	15	34	72	22
Zankezour	28	9	4	15	25	77	22
Nayrit*	28	7	6	15	22	43	18
Armee Arayi*	28	6	5	17	39	79	17
Lori*	28	5	6	17	22	65	16
Kanaz*	28	1	3	24	15	89	5

Top scorers: Avetissian A (Homenetmen) 39.
Cup Final: Ararat Erevan 4, Kotaik 2.

AUSTRIA

Oesterreichischer Fussball-Bund, Wiener Stadion, Sektor A/F, Meierestrasse, A-1020 Wien.
Founded: 1904; *Number of Clubs:* 2,081; *Number of Players:* 253,576; *National Colours:* White shirts, black shorts, black stockings.
Telephone: 0043 1 727 18; *Cable:* FOOTBALL WIEN; *Telex:* 111919 oefb a; *Fax:* 0043 1 728 1632.

International matches 1994
Hungary (h) 1-1, Scotland (h) 1-2, Poland (a) 4-3, Germany (h) 1-5, Russia (h) 0-3, Liechtenstein (a) 4-0, Northern Ireland (h) 1-2, Portugal (a) 0-1.

League Championship wins (1912–95)
Rapid Vienna 29; FK Austria 22; Admira-Energie-Wacker (prev. Sportklub Admira & Admira-Energie) 8; First Vienna 6; Tirol-Svarowski-Innsbruck (prev. Wacker Innsbruck) 7; Wiener Sportklub 3; Austria Salzburg 2; FAC 1; Hakoah 1; Linz ASK 1; Wacker Vienna 1; WAF 1; Voest Linz 1.

Cup wins (1919–95)
FK Austria 25; Rapid Vienna 14; TS Innsbruck (prev. Wacker Innsbruck) 7; Admira-Energie-Wacker (prev. Sportklub Admira & Admira-Energie) 5; First Vienna 3; Linz ASK 1; Wacker Vienna 1; WAF 1; Wiener Sportklub 1; Graz 1; Stockerau 1.

Final table 1994–95

	P	*W*	*D*	*L*	*F*	*A*	Pts
Austria Salzburg	36	15	17	4	48	24	47
Sturm Graz	36	18	11	7	58	41	47
Rapid	36	18	9	9	61	50	44
FK Austria	36	16	11	9	58	38	43
Innsbruck	36	15	10	11	61	44	40
Linz ASK	36	14	11	11	51	44	39
Admira Wacker	36	11	12	13	48	53	34
Vorwaerts	36	9	11	16	40	49	29
Linz*+	36	5	10	21	33	81	20
Modling*	36	4	8	24	28	62	16

Top scorer: Sane (Innsbruck) 20.
Cup Final: Rapid 1, Leoben 0.

AZERBAIJAN

Azerbaijan Football Association, G.Gadjiev Street 42, 370009 Baku, Azerbaijan.
Number of Clubs: 2,200. *Number of Players:* 131,000.
Telephone: 00994 12 94 05 42; *Fax:* 00994 12 98 93 93; *Telex:* 142349 affa su.

International matches 1994
Malta (a) 0-5, Moldovo (a) 1-2, Romania (a) 0-3, Poland (a) 0-1, Israel (h) 0-2, France (h) 0-2.

BELARUS

Football Federation of Belarus, 8–2 Kyrov Str. 220600 Minsk, Belarus.
Founded: 1992; Number of Players: 120,000.
Telephone: 007 0172 27 29 20; *Telex:*252175 athlet su; *Fax:* 007 0172 27 29 20.

International matches 1994
Ukraine (a) 1-3, Poland (a) 1-1, Norway (a) 0-1, Luxembourg (h) 2-0, Norway (h) 0-4.

League Championship wins 1992–95
Dynamo Minsk 4.

Cup wins 1992–94
Dynamo Minsk 2; Neman 1.

Final League Table 1994–95

	P	*W*	*D*	*L*	*F*	*A*	Pts
Dynamo Minsk	30	20	8	2	83	24	48
Dvina	30	17	12	1	46	13	46
Dynamo 93	30	16	10	4	52	22	42
Molodechno	30	12	11	7	48	30	35
Dnepr	30	12	9	9	43	33	33
Torpedo Minsk	30	11	10	9	36	29	32
Neman	30	10	10	10	24	27	30
Obuvshchik	30	10	10	10	32	36	30
Dynamo Brest	30	9	10	11	33	33	28
Torpedo Mogilev	30	8	12	10	28	32	28
Traktor	30	8	12	10	31	36	28
Vedrich	30	10	8	12	22	33	28
Shnnik	30	7	9	14	31	50	23
Shakhtjor	30	6	9	15	24	41	21
Gomselmash	30	6	6	18	26	59	18
Lokomotiv	30	3	4	23	14	75	10

BELGIUM

Union Royale Belge Des Societes De Football; Eturl, Association, Rue De La Loi 43, Boite 1, B-1040 Bruxelles.
Founded: 1895; *Number of Clubs:* 2,120; *Number of Players:* 390,468; *National Colours:* Red shirts with tri-coloured trim, red shorts, red stockings with trim.
Telephone: 0032 2 477 12 11; *Cable:* UBSFA BRUXELLES; *Telex:* 23257 bvbfbf b; *Fax:* 0032 2 478 23 91.

International matches 1994
Malta (a) 0-1, Zambia (h) 9-0, Hungary (h) 3-1, Morocco (n) 1-0, Holland (n) 1-0, Saudi Arabia (n) 0-1, Germany (n) 2-3, Armenia (h) 2-0,.Denmark (a) 1-3, Macedonia (h) 1-1, Spain (h) 1-4.

League Championship wins (1896–1995)
Anderlecht 24; Union St Gilloise 11; FC Brugge 9; Standard Liege 8; Beerschot 7; RC Brussels 6; FC Liège 5; Daring Brussels 5; Antwerp 4; Mechelen 4; Lierse SK 3; SV Brugge 3; Beveren 2; RWD Molenbeek 1.

Cup wins (1954–95)
Anderlecht 8; FC Brugge 6; Standard Liege 5; Beerschot 2; Waterschei 2; Beveren 2; Gent 2; Antwerp 2; Lierse SK 1; Racing Doornik 1; Waregem 1; SV Brugge 1; Mechelen 1; FC Liège 1.

Final League Table 1994–95

	P	*W*	*D*	*L*	*F*	*A*	Pts
Anderlecht	34	23	6	5	80	31	52
Standard Liege	34	21	9	4	53	23	51
FC Brugge	34	21	7	6	68	32	49
Aalst	34	14	11	9	58	56	39
Ekeren	34	12	13	9	57	39	37
Lierse	34	14	9	11	52	52	37
Lommel	34	13	9	12	44	40	35
St Truiden	34	11	13	10	34	35	35
Seraing	34	12	10	12	53	45	34
Beveren	34	10	12	12	40	46	32
RWD Molenbeek	34	10	11	13	34	41	31
Charleroi	34	10	11	13	33	43	31
Gent	34	11	8	15	41	53	30
Mechelen	34	10	9	15	40	47	29
CS Brugge	34	9	10	15	43	52	28
Antwerp	34	8	8	18	40	56	24
Liege*	34	6	7	21	36	71	19
Ostend*	34	5	9	20	32	76	19

Top scorer: Vidmar (Standard) 22.
Cup Final: FC Brugge 3, Ekeren 1.

BULGARIA

Bulgarian Football Union, Gotcho Gopin 19, 1000 Sofia.
Founded: 1923; *Number of Clubs:* 376; *Number of Players:* 48,240; *National Colours:* White shirts, green shorts, red stockings.
Telephone: 00359 2 87 74 90; *Cable:* BULFUTBOL; *Telex:* 23145 bfs bg; *Fax:* 00359 2 80 32 37.

International matches 1994
Mexico (h) 1-1, Oman (a) 1-1, Kuwait (a) 2-2, Ukraine (h) 1-1, Nigeria (n) 0-3, Greece (n) 4-0, Argentina (n) 2-0, Mexico (n) 1-1, Germany (n) 2-1, Italy (n) 1-2, Sweden (n) 0-4, Georgia (h) 2-0, Moldovo (h) 4-1, Wales (a) 3-0.

League Championship wins (1925–95)
CSKA Sofia 27; Levski Sofia 19; Slavia Sofia 6; Vladislav Varna 3; Lokomotiv Sofia 3; Trakia Plovdiv 2; AS 23 Sofia 1; Botev Plovdiv 1; SC Sofia 1; Sokol Varna 1; Spartak Plovdiv 1; Tichka Varna 1; ZSZ Sofia 1; Beroe Stara Zagora 1; Etur 1.

Cup wins (1946–95)
Levski Sofia 18; CSKA Sofia 14; Slavia Sofia 6; Lokomotiv Sofia 4; Botev Plovdiv 1; Spartak Plovdiv 1; Spartak Sofia 1; Marek Stanke 1; Trakia Plovdiv 1; Spartak Varna 1; Sliven 1.

Final League Table 1994–95

	P	*W*	*D*	*L*	*F*	*A*	Pts
Levski Sofia	30	26	1	3	84	15	79
Lokomotiv Sofia	30	21	5	4	59	30	68
Botev Plovdiv	30	18	6	6	66	31	60
Slavia Sofia	30	16	5	9	63	35	53
CSKA Sofia	30	13	7	10	51	46	46
Spartak Plovdiv	30	12	7	11	33	34	43
Lokomotiv Plovdiv	30	13	3	14	48	38	42
Neftochimik	30	12	3	15	41	50	39
Chumen	30	10	6	14	33	50	36
Lovetch Lex	30	10	6	14	25	46	36
Etur	30	10	6	14	31	54	36
Dobroudja	30	10	5	15	32	43	35
Montana	30	9	7	14	31	41	34
Lokomotiv Gorna*	30	10	3	17	35	53	33
Pirin*	30	9	3	18	30	46	30
Beroe*	30	3	3	24	27	77	12

Top scorer: Mihtarski (CSKA Sofia) 23.
Cup Final: Lokomotiv Sofia 4, Botev Plovdiv 2.

CROATIA

Croatian Football Federation, Illica 21/11, CRO-41000 Zagreb, Croatia.
Telephone: 00385 41 45 41 00. *Fax:* 00385 41 42 46 39.

International matches 1994
Spain (a) 2-0, Slovakia (a) 1-4, Hungary (a) 2-2, Argentina (h) 0-0, Israel (a) 4-0, Estonia (a) 2-0, Lithuania (h) 2-0, Italy (a) 2-1.

League Championship wins 1993–95
Hajduk Split 2; Croatia Zagreb 1.

Cup wins 1993–95
Hajduk Split 2, Croatia Zagreb 1.

Final League Table 1994–95

	P	*W*	*D*	*L*	*F*	*A*	Pts
Hajduk Split	30	19	8	3	68	25	65
Croatia Zagreb	30	19	7	4	53	26	64
Osijek	30	16	11	3	65	30	59
Zagreb	30	14	11	5	41	26	53
Marsonia	30	13	8	9	42	32	47
Varteks	30	11	10	9	35	27	43
Inker	30	11	6	13	41	41	39
Segesta	30	10	7	13	32	31	37
Sibenik	30	9	10	11	44	46	37
Vinkovci	30	9	10	11	20	31	37
Rijeka	30	8	10	12	28	34	34
Istra Pola	30	8	8	14	30	46	32
Zadar*	30	7	10	13	33	47	31
Promarac*	30	7	10	13	27	49	31
Neretva*	30	4	11	15	20	44	23
Belisce*	30	4	4	22	26	69	16

Top scorer: Spehar (Osijek) 23.
Cup Final: Hajduk Split 3, 1, Croatia Zagreb 2, 0.

CYPRUS

Cyprus Football Association, Stasinos Str. 1, Engomi 152, P.O. Box 5071, Nicosia.
Founded: 1934; *Number of Clubs:* 85; *Number of Players:* 6,000; *National Colours:* Sky blue shirts, white shorts, blue and white stockings.
Telephone: 00357 2 44 53 41; *Cable:* FOOTBALL NICOSIA; *Telex:* 3880 football cy; *Fax:* 00357 2 47 25 44.

International matches 1994
Estonia (h) 2-0, Slovenia (a) 0-3, Spain (h) 1-2, Armenia (a) 0-0, Armenia (h) 2-0, Macedonia (a) 0-3.

League Championship wins (1935–95)
Omonia 17; Apoel 15; Anorthosis 7; AEL 5; EPA 3; Olympiakos 3; Apollon 2; Pezoporikos 2; Chetin Kayal 1; Trast 1.

Cup wins (1935–95)
Apoel 14; Omonia 10; AEL 6; EPA 5; Anorthosis 4; Apollon 4; Trast 3; Chetin Kayal 2; Olympiakos 1; Pezoporikos 1; Salamina 1.

Final League Table 1993–95

	P	*W*	*D*	*L*	*F*	*A*	Pts
Anorthosis	33	22	7	4	71	25	73
Omonia	33	20	7	6	82	32	67
Salamina	33	17	6	10	59	50	57
Ethnikos	33	14	5	14	52	59	47
Apoel	33	13	7	13	43	43	46
Apollon	33	13	6	14	50	46	45
Paralimni	33	12	9	12	44	49	45
Olympiakos	33	13	5	15	41	65	44
AEK	33	12	6	15	50	48	42
AEL	33	12	5	16	44	57	41
Aris*	33	10	7	16	44	49	37
Aradippu*	33	3	4	26	37	94	13

Top scorer: Androu (Salmina) 25.
Cup Final: Apoel 4, Apollon 2.

CZECH REPUBLIC

Football Association of Czech Republic, Diskarska 100, 169 00 Prague 6, Czech Republic.
Number of Clubs: 3,562; *Number of Players:* 237,200; *National Colours:* Red shirts, white shorts, blue stockings.
Telephone: 0042 2 35 69 13; *Fax:* 0042 2 35 27 84.

International matches 1994
Turkey (a) 4-1, Switzerland (a) 0-3, Lithuania (h) 5-3, Republic of Ireland (a) 3-1, France (a) 2-2, Malta (h) 6-1, Malta (a) 0-0, Holland (a) 0-0.

League Championship wins (1926–93)
Sparta Prague 20; Slavia Prague 12; Dukla Prague (prev. UDA) 11; Slovan Bratislava 7; Spartak Trnava 5; Banik Ostrava 3; Inter-Bratislava 1; Spartak Hradec Kralove 1; Viktoria Zizkov 1; Zbrojovka Brno 1; Bohemians 1; Vitkovice 1.

Cup wins (1961–93)
Dukla Prague 8; Sparta Prague 8; Slovan Bratislava 5; Spartak Trnava 4; Banik Ostrava 3; Lokomotiv Kosice 3; TJ Gottwaldov 1; Dunajska Streda 1.
From 1993–94, there were two separate countries: the Czech Republic and Slovakia.

League Championship wins (1994–95)
Sparta Prague 2.

Cup wins (1994–95)
Viktoria Zizkov 1; Spartak Hradec Kralove 1.

Final League Table 1994–95

	P	*W*	*D*	*L*	*F*	*A*	Pts
Sparta Prague	30	22	4	4	67	17	70
Slavia Prague	30	19	7	4	52	20	64
Boby Brno	30	15	9	6	52	27	54
Slovan Liberec	30	16	3	11	49	46	51
Viktoria Zizkov	30	15	4	11	61	38	49
Petra Drnovice	30	15	3	12	46	44	48
Ceske Budejovice	30	12	10	8	29	28	46
Sigma Olomouc	30	12	7	11	31	31	43
Viktoria Plzen	30	12	4	14	32	37	40
Jablonek	30	11	6	13	37	33	39
Banik Ostrava	30	10	8	12	36	41	38
Hradec Kralove	30	10	6	14	35	45	36
Union Cheb	30	8	7	15	29	45	31
Svit Zlin	30	8	6	16	21	40	30
Bohemians*	30	6	5	19	35	62	23
Svarc Benesov*	30	3	3	24	23	78	12

Top scorer: Drulak (Petra Drnovice) 15.
Cup Final: Hradec Kralove 0, Viktoria Zizkov 0.
Hradec Kralove won 3-1 on penalties.

DENMARK

Dansk Boldspil Union, Ved Amagerbanen 15, DK-2300, Copenhagen S.
Founded: 1889; *Number of Clubs:* 1,555; *Number of Players:* 268,517; *National Colours:* Red shirts, white shorts, red stockings.
Telephone: 0045 31 95 05 11; *Cable:* DANSKBOLDSPIL COPENHAGEN; *Telex:* 15545 dbu dk; *Fax:* 0045 31 95 05 88.

International matches 1994
England (a) 0-1, Hungary (h) 3-1, Sweden (h) 1-0, Norway (a) 1-2, Finland (h) 2-1, Macedonia (a) 1-1, Belgium (h) 3-1, Spain (a) 0-3.

League Championship wins (1913–95)
KB Copenhagen 15; B 93 Copenhagen 9; AB (Akademisk) 9; B 1903 Copenhagen 7; Frem 6; Esbjerg BK 5; Vejle BK 5; AGF Aarhus 5; Brondby 4; Hvidovre 3; Odense BK 3; B 1909 Odense 2; Koge BK 2; Lyngby 2; FC Copenhagen 1; Silkeborg 1, AaB Aalborg 1.

Cup wins (1955–95)
Aarhus GF 8; Vejle BK 6; Randers Freja 3; Lyngby 3; OB Odense 3; B1909 Odense 2; Aalborg BK 2; Esbjerg BK 2; Frem 2; B 1903 Copenhagen 2; Brondby 2; B 93 Copenhagen 1; KB Copenhagen 1; Vanlose 1; Hvidovre 1; B1913 Odense 1, FC Copenhagen 1.

Qualifying Table 1994

	P	*W*	*D*	*L*	*F*	*A*	Pts
Brondby	18	12	3	3	41	19	27
Aalborg	18	12	2	4	44	25	26
Odense	18	10	4	4	31	21	24
Lynby	18	6	7	5	34	27	19
Silkeborg	18	5	7	6	21	23	17
Naestved	18	5	7		26	31	17
FC Copenhagen	18	6	4	8	30	34	16
Aarhus	18	5	5	8	21	35	15
Ikast	18	3	5	10	22	29	11
Fremad	18	4	0	14	21	47	8

Final League Table 1994–95

	P	*W*	*D*	*L*	*F*	*A*	Pts
Aalborg	14	7	4	3	30	13	31
Brondby	14	6	3	5	21	18	29
Silkeborg	14	6	3	5	23	16	24
Aarhus	14	7	2	5	21	23	24
Naestved	14	5	4	5	21	22	23
FC Copenhagen	14	5	4	5	21	28	22
Lyngby	14	5	1	8	20	28	21
Odense	14	3	3	8	17	26	21

Top scorer: Andersen (Aalborg) 24.
Cup Final: FC Copenhagen 5, AB Copenhagen 0.

ENGLAND

The Football Association, 16 Lancaster Gate, London W2 3LW*Founded:* 1863; *Number of Clubs:* 42,000; *Number of Players:* 2,250,000; *National Colours:* White shirts, navy blue shorts, white stockings.
Telephone: 0171 262 4542; *Cable:* FOOTBALL ASSOCIATION LONDON W2; *Telex:* 261110; *Fax:* 0171 402 0486.

ESTONIA

Estonian Football Association, Refati PST 1-376, 20 0103 Tallinn.
Number of Clubs: 40; *Number of Players:* 12,000.
Telephone: 00372 2 23 77 58; *Telex:* 173236 sport su; *Fax:* 00372 2 23 77 58.

International matches 1994
Cyprus (a) 0-2, USA (a) 0-4, Wales (h) 1-2, Macedonia (a) 0-2, Lithuania (a) 0-3, Latvia (a) 0-2, Iceland (a) 0-4, Croatia (h) 0-2, Italy (h) 0-2, Finland (h) 0-7, Latvia (a) 0-0, Ukraine (a) 0-3

League Championship wins (1992–95)
Norma Tallinn 2; Flora Tallinn 2.

Cup Wins (1992–95)
VMV Tallinn 1; Nikol Tallinn 1; Norma Tallinn 1; Lantana 1.

Final Pool Table 1994–95

	P	*W*	*D*	*L*	*F*	*A*	Pts
Flora	10	7	3	0	27	6	41
Lantana	10	7	2	1	26	9	40
Trans	10	4	1	5	9	15	26
Sadam	10	4	0	6	11	14	25
Johvi	10	4	0	6	17	24	21
Norma	10	1	0	9	6	28	8

Top Scorer: Morozov (Lantana) 25.
Cup Final: Lantana 5, Trans Narva 3 aet.

FAEROE ISLANDS

Fotboltssamband Foroya, The Faeroes' Football Assn., Gundalur, P.O. Box 1028, FR-110, Torshavn.
Founded: 1979; *Number of Clubs:* 16; *Number of Players:* 1,014.
Telephone: 00298 16 707; *Telex:* 81332 itrott FA; *Fax:* 00298 19 079.

International matches 1994
Greece (h) 1-5, Scotland (a) 1-5, Finland (a) 0-5.

League Championship wins 1942–94
KI Klaksvik 15; HB Torshavn 14; TB Tvoroyri 7; B36 Torshavn 5; GI Gotu 5; B68 Toftir 3; SI Sorvag 1; IF Fuglafjordur 1; B71 Sandur 1.

Cup wins 1955–94
HB Torshavn 23; TB Tvoroyri 5; KI Klaksvik 4; B36 Torshavn 2; GI Gotu 2; B71 Sandur 1, VB Vagur 1; NSI Runavik 1.

Final League Table 1994

	P	*W*	*D*	*L*	*F*	*A*	Pts
GI	18	14	2	2	59	16	30
HB	18	14	2	2	47	14	30
B71	18	10	4	4	31	12	24
KI	18	8	4	6	40	26	20
B68	18	5	7	6	22	30	17
NSI	18	6	3	9	28	29	16
B36	18	5	5	8	24	34	15
TB	18	6	2	10	32	49	14
IF*	18	3	2	13	17	44	8
EB*	18	2	3	13	15	61	7

Cup Final: KI 2, B71 1.

FINLAND

Suomen Palloliitto Finlands Bollfoerbund, Kuparitie 1, P.O. Box 29, SF-00441 Helsinki.
Founded: 1907; *Number of Clubs:* 1,135; *Number of Players:* 66,100; *National Colours:* White shirts, blue shorts, white stockings.
Telephone: 00358 0 701 01 01; *Cable:* SUOMIFOTBOLL HELSINKI; *Telex :* 126033 spl sf; *Fax:* 00358 0 701 01 099.

International matches 1994
Qatar (a) 0-1, Oman (a) 2-0, Oman (a) 1-1, Morocco (a) 0-0, Italy (a) 0-2, Spain (h) 1-2, Denmark (a) 1-2, Scotland (h) 0-2, Greece (a) 0-4, Estonia (a) 7-0, Faeroes (h) 5-0, San Marino (h) 4-1.

League Championship wins (1949–94)
Helsinki JK 9; Turun Palloseura 5; Kuopion Palloseura 5; Valkeakosken Haka 4; Kuusysi 4; Lahden Reipas 3; Ilves-Kissat 2; IF Kamraterna 2; Kotkan TP 2; OPS Oulu 2; Torun Pyrkivä 1; IF Kronohagens 1; Helsinki PS 1; Kokkolan PV 1; IF Kamraterna 1; Vasa 1; Jazz Pori 1; TPV Tampere 1.

Cup wins (1955–94)
Valkeakosken Haka 9; Lahden Reipas 7; Kotkan TP 4; Helsinki JK 4; Mikkelin 2; Kuusysi 2; Kuopion Palloseura 2; Ilves Tampere 2; TPS Turku 2; IFK Abo 1; Drott 1; Helsinki PS 1; Pallo-Peikot 1; Rovaniemi PS 1; MyPa 1.

Final League Table 1994

	P	*W*	*D*	*L*	*F*	*A*	Pts
TPV Tampere	26	16	4	6	46	27	52
MyPa	26	15	5	6	49	21	50
HJK Helsinki	26	12	7	7	40	29	43
Jazz Pori	26	13	3	10	49	36	42
Haka	26	12	4	10	38	29	40
RoPS Rovaniemi	26	10	8	8	32	32	38
Jaro	26	10	7	9	35	39	37
TPS Turku	26	9	7	10	38	34	34
Finn Pa	26	8	9	9	25	35	33
Kuusysi	26	9	4	13	41	50	31
Mikkeli	26	7	8	11	25	31	29
Ilves	26	7	7	12	35	45	28
Oulu*	26	6	9	11	32	42	27
KuPS Kuopio*	26	6	2	18	24	59	20

Top scorer: Dionisio (TPV Tampere) 17.
Cup Final: HJK Helsinki 2, Jazz Pori 0.

FRANCE

Federation Francaise De Football, 60 Bis A venue D'Iena, F-75783 Paris, Cedex 16.
Founded: 1919; *Number of Clubs:* 21,629; *Number of Players:* 1,692,205; *National Colours:* Blue shirts, white shorts, red stockings.
Telephone: 0033 1 44 31 73 00; *Cable:* CEFI PARIS 034; *Telex:* 640000 fedfoot f; *Fax:* 0033 1 47 20 82 96.

International matches 1994
Italy (a) 1-0, Chile (h) 3-1, Australia (h) 1-0, Japan (a) 4-1, Czech Republic (h) 2-2, Slovakia (a) 0-0, Romania (h) 0-0, Poland (a) 0-0, Azerbaijan (a) 2-0.

League Championship wins (1933–95)
Saint Etienne 10; Olympique Marseille 8; Nantes 7; Stade de Reims 6; AS Monaco 5; OGC Nice 4; Girondins Bordeaux 4; Lille OSC 3; Paris St Germain 2; FC Sete 2; Sochaux 2; Racing Club Paris 1 Roubaix-Tourcoing 1; Strasbourg 1.

Cup wins (1918–95)
Olympique Marseille 10; Saint Etienne 6; Lille OSC 5; Racing Club Paris 5; Red Star 5; AS Monaco 5; Olympique Lyon 4; Girondins Bordeaux 3; Paris St Germain 3; CAS Genereaux 2; Nancy 2; OGC Nice 2; Racing Club Strasbourg 2; Sedan 2; FC Sete 2; Stade de Reims 2; SO Montpellier 2; Stade Rennes 2; AS Cannes 1; Club Français 1; Excelsior Roubaix 1; Le Havre 1; Olympique de Pantin 1; CA Paris 1; Sochaux 1; Toulouse 1; Bastia 1; Nantes 1; Metz 1; Auxerre 1.

Final League Table 1994–95

	P	*W*	*D*	*L*	*F*	*A*	Pts
Nantes	38	21	16	1	71	34	79
Lyon	38	19	12	7	56	38	69
Paris St Germain	38	20	7	11	58	41	67
Auxerre	38	15	17	6	59	34	62
Lens	38	15	14	9	48	44	59
Monaco	38	15	12	11	60	39	57
Bordeaux	38	16	9	13	52	47	57
Metz	38	16	8	14	50	44	56
Cannes	38	15	8	15	56	48	53
Strasbourg	38	13	12	13	43	43	51
Martigues	38	13	12	13	37	49	51
Le Havre	38	12	13	13	46	49	49
Rennes	38	12	12	14	53	55	48
Lille	38	13	9	16	29	44	48
Bastia	38	11	11	16	44	56	44
Nice	38	11	10	17	39	52	43
Montpellier	38	9	14	15	38	53	41
St Etienne	38	9	11	18	45	55	38
Caen*	38	10	6	22	38	58	36
Sochaux*	38	6	5	27	29	68	23

Top scorer: Loko (Nantes) 22.
Cup Final: Paris St Germain 1, Strasbourg 0.

GEORGIA

Football Federation of Georgia, 5 Shota Iamanidze Str, Tbillisi 380012, Georgia.
Founded: 1992; Number of Clubs: 4050. *Number of Players:* 115,000.
Telephone: 007 8832 96 07 10; *Telex:* 340744. *Fax:* 0049 5151 86 33 (satellite-fax).

International matches 1994
Slovenia (h) 0-1, Malta (a) 1-0, Tunisia (a) 2-0, Israel (a) 0-2, Nigeria (a) 1-5, Latvia (a) 3-1, Moldovo (h) 0-1, Bulgaria (a) 0-2, Wales (h) 5-0, Albania (a) 1-0.

League Championship wins (1991–95)
Dynamo Tbilisi 5.

Cup wins (1991–95)
Dynamo Tbilisi 5.
Although Dynamo Tbilisi won the championship with 78 points from 30 matches four teams were deducted points on the last day of the season. After Kolcheti had beaten Samgurali 10-5 and Torpedo had defeated Sapovnela 11-4, the teams involved were accused of arranging for both winners to have their top scorers credited with 9 goals each!
Cup Final: Dynamo Tbilisi 1, Batumi 0.

GERMANY

Deutsche Fussball-Bund, Otto-Fleck-Schneise 6, Postfach 710265, D-6000, Frankfurt (Main) 71.
Founded: 1900; *Number of Clubs:* 26,760; *Number of Players:* 5,260,320; *National Colours:* White shirts, black shorts, white stockings.
Telephone: 0049 69 678 80; *Cable:* FUSSBALL FRANKFURT; *Telex:* 416815 dfb d; *Fax:* 0049 69 678 82 66.

International matches 1994
Italy (h) 2-1, UAR (a) 2-0, Republic of Ireland (h) 0-2, Austria (a) 5-1, Canada (a) 2-0, Bolivia (n) 1-0, Spain (n) 1-1, South Korea (n) 3-2, Belgium (n) 3-2, Bulgaria (n) 1-2, Russia (a) 1-0,.Hungary (a) 0-0, Albania (a) 2-1, Moldovo (a) 3-0, Albania (h) 2-1.

League Championship wins (1903–95)
Bayern Munich 13; IFC Nuremberg 9; Schalke 04 7; SV Hamburg 6; Borussia Moenchengladbach 5; VfB Stuttgart 4; Borussia Dortmund 4; VfB Leipzig 3; Sp Vgg Furth 3; IFC Cologne 3; IFC Kaiserslautern 3; Werder Bremen 3; Viktoria Berlin 2; Hertha Berlin 2; Hanover 96 2; Dresden SC 2; Munich 1860 1; Union Berlin 1; FC Freiburg 1; Phoenix Karlsruhe 1; Karlsruher FV 1; Holsten Kiel 1; Fortuna Dusseldorf 1; Rapid Vienna 1; VfB Mannheim 1; Rot-Weiss Essen 1; Eintracht Frankfurt 1; Eintracht Brunswick 1.

Cup wins (1935–95)
Bayern Munich 8; IFC Cologne 4; Eintracht Frankfurt 4; IFC Nuremberg 3; SV Hamburg 3; Werder Bremen 3; Moenchengladbach 3; Dresden SC 2; Fortuna Dusseldorf 2; Karlsruhe SC 2; Munich 1860 2; Schalke 04 2; VfB Stuttgart 2; Borussia Borussia Dortmund 2; First Vienna 1; VfB Leipzig 1; Kickers Offenbach 1; Rapid Vienna 1; Rot-Weiss Essen 1; SW Essen 1; Bayer Uerdingen 1; IFC Kaiserslautern 1; Hannover 96 1; Leverkusen 1.

Final League Table 1994–95

	P	*W*	*D*	*L*	*F*	*A*	Pts
Borussia Dortmund	34	20	9	5	67	33	49
Werder Bremen	34	20	8	6	70	39	48
Freiburg	34	20	6	8	66	44	46
Kaiserslautern	34	17	12	5	58	41	46
Moenchengladbach	34	17	9	8	66	41	43
Bayern Munich	34	15	13	6	55	41	43
Leverkusen	34	13	10	11	62	51	36
Karlsruhe	34	11	14	9	51	47	36
Eintracht Frankfurt	34	12	9	13	41	49	33
Cologne	34	11	10	13	54	54	32
Schalke	34	10	11	13	48	54	31
Stuttgart	34	10	10	14	52	66	30
Hamburg	34	10	9	15	43	50	29
Munich 1860	34	8	11	15	41	57	27
Uerdingen	34	7	11	16	37	52	25
Bochum*	34	9	4	21	43	67	22
Duisburg*	34	6	8	20	31	64	20
Dynamo Dresden*	34	4	8	22	33	68	16

Top scorers: Basler (Werder Bremen), Herrlich (Moenchengladbach) 20.
Cup Final: Moenchengladbach 3, Wolfsburg 0.

GREECE

Federation Hellenique De Football, Singrou Avenue 137, Athens.
Founded: 1926; *Number of Clubs:* 4,050; *Number of Players:* 180,000; *National Colours:* White shirts, blue shorts, white stockings.
Telephone: 0030 1 933 88 50; *Cable:* FOOTBALL ATHENES; *Telex:* 215328 epo gr; *Fax:* 0030 1 935 96 66.

International matches 1994
Poland (h) 0-0, Saudi Arabia (h) 5-1, Cameroon (h) 0-3, Bolivia (h) 0-0, England (a) 0-5, USA (a) 1-1, Colombia (a) 0-2,.Argentina (n) 0-4, Bulgaria (n) 0-4, Nigeria (n) 0-2, Faeroes (a) 5-1, Finland (h) 4-0, San Marino (h) 2-0, Scotland (h) 1-0.

League Championship wins (1928–95)
Olympiakos 25; Panathinaikos 17; AEK Athens 11; Aris Salonika 3; PAOK Salonika 2; Larissa 1.

Cup wins (1932–95)
Olympiakos 20; Panathinaikos 16; AEK Athens 9; PAOK Salonika 2; Aris Salonika 1; Ethnikos 1; Iraklis 1; Panionios 1; Kastoria 1; Larissa 1; Ofi Crete 1.

Final League Table 1994–95

	P	*W*	*D*	*L*	*F*	*A*	Pts
Panathinaikos	34	26	5	3	83	21	83
Olympiakos	34	20	7	7	69	31	67
PAOK Salonika	34	20	5	9	55	29	65
Apollon	34	20	3	11	61	37	63
AEK Athens	34	17	11	6	61	33	62
Aris Salonika	34	19	5	10	46	34	62
Iraklis	34	17	8	9	62	40	59
Xanthi	34	14	8	12	52	54	50
Ofi Crete	34	15	4	15	40	38	49
Ethnikos	34	11	9	14	40	48	42
Edessiakos	34	13	3	18	45	54	42
Larissa	34	11	7	16	41	46	40
Athinaikos	34	10	10	14	29	35	40
Panionios	34	10	6	18	36	58	36
Ionikos	34	9	7	18	27	53	34
Doxa Drama*	34	8	5	21	27	71	29
Levadiakos*	34	5	5	24	23	67	20
Kavala*	34	5	4	25	27	75	19

Top scorers: R. Warzycha (Panathinaikos) 29.
Cup Final: Panathinaikos 1, AEK Athens 0 aet.

HOLLAND

Koninklijke Nederlandsche Voetbalbond, Woudenbergseweg 56, Postbus 515, NL-3700 AM, Zeist.
Founded: 1889; *Number of Clubs:* 3,097; *Number of Players:* 962,397; *National Colours:* Orange shirts, white shorts, orange stockings.
Telephone: 0031 3439 92 11; *Cable:* VOETBAL ZEIST; *Telex:* 40497 knvb nl; *Fax:* 0031 3439 1397.

International matches 1994
Tunisia (a) 2-2, Scotland (a) 1-0, Republic of Ireland (h) 0-1, Scotland (h) 3-1, Hungary (h) 7-1, Canada (a) 3-0, Saudi Arabia (n) 2-1,.Belgium (n) 0-1, Morocco (n) 2-1, Republic of Ireland (n) 2-0, Brazil (n) 2-3, Luxembourg (a) 4-0, Norway (a) 1-1, Czech Republic (h) 0-0, Luxembourg (h) 5-0.

League Championship wins (1898–95)
Ajax Amsterdam 25; Feyenoord 14; PSV Eindhoven 13; HVV The Hague 8; Sparta Rotterdam 6; Go Ahead Deventer 4; HBS The Hague 3; Willem II Tilburg 3; RCH Haarlem 2; RAP 2; Heracles 2; ADO The Hague 2; Quick The Hague 1; BVV Schiedam 1; NAC Breda 1; Eindhoven 1; Enschede 1; Volewijckers Amsterdam 1; Limburgia 1; Rapid JC Haarlem 1; DOS Utrecht 1; DWS Amsterdam 1; Haarlem 1; Be Quick Groningen 1; SVV Schiedam 1; AZ 67 Alkmaar 1.

Cup wins (1899–95)
Ajax Amsterdam 12; Feyenoord 10; PSV Eindhoven 7; Quick The Hague 4; AZ 67 Alkemaar 3; Rotterdam 3; DFC 2; Fortuna Geleen 2; Haarlem 2; HBS The Hague 2; RCH 2; VOC 2; Wageningen 2; Willem II Tilburg 2; FC Den Haag 2; Concordia Rotterdam 1; CVV 1; Eindhoven 1; HVV The Hague 1; Longa 1; Quick Nijmegen 1; RAP 1; Roermond 1; Schoten 1; Velocitas Breda 1; Velocitas Gr oningen 1; VSV 1; VUC 1; VVV Groningen 1; ZFC 1; NAC Breda 1; Twente Enschede 1; Utrecht 1.

Final League Table 1994–95

	P	W	D	L	F	A	Pts
Ajax	34	27	7	0	106	28	61
Roda	34	22	10	2	70	28	54
PSV Eindhoven	34	20	7	7	85	46	47
Feyenoord	34	19	5	10	66	56	43
Twente	34	17	8	9	66	50	42
Vitesse	34	14	12	8	53	44	40
Willem II	34	13	8	13	44	48	34
RKC Waalwijk	34	11	11	12	46	49	33
Heerenveen	34	12	6	16	48	60	30
NAC Breda	34	11	7	16	54	60	29
Volendam	34	8	13	13	37	55	29
Utrecht	34	8	11	15	43	60	27
Groningen	34	8	10	16	47	63	26
Sparta	34	8	10	16	42	58	26
NEC Nijmegen	34	9	7	18	48	60	25
Maastricht* +	34	7	9	18	41	71	23
Go Ahead +	34	7	9	18	41	74	23
Dordrecht*	34	5	10	19	40	67	20

Top scorer: Ronaldo (PSV Eindhoven) 30.
Cup Final: Feyenoord 2, Volendam 1.

HUNGARY

Magyar Labdarugo Szovetseg, Hungarian Football Federation, Nepkoztarsasag Utja 47, H-1061 Budapest VI.
Founded: 1901; *Number of Clubs:* 1944; *Number of Players* 95,986; *National Colours:* Red shirts, white shorts, green stockings.
Telephone: 0036 1 252 92 96; *Cable:* MLSZ BUDAPEST; *Telex:* 225782 misz h; *Fax:* 0036 1 252 99 86.

International matches 1994
Switzerland (h) 1-2, Austria (a) 1-1, Slovenia (h) 0-1, Denmark (a) 1-3, Poland (a) 2-3, Croatia (h) 2-2, Holland (a) 1-7, Belgium (a) 1-3, Turkey (h) 2-2, Germany (h) 0-0, Sweden (a) 0-2, Mexico (a) 1-5.

League Championship wins (1901–95)
Ferencvaros (prev. FRC) 25; MTK-VM Budapest (prev. Hungaria, Bastay and Vörös Lobogo) 19; Ujpest Dozsa 19; Honved 13; Vasas Budapest 6; Csepel 3; Raba Györ (prev. Vasas Györ) 3; BTC 2; Nagyvarad 1; Vac 1.

Cup wins (1910–95)
Ferencvaros (prev. FRC)17; MTK-VM Budapest (prev. Hungaria, Bastay and Vörös Lobogo) 9; Ujpest Dozsa 8; Raba Györ (prev. Vasas Györ) 4; Vasas Budapest 3; Honved 3; Diösgyör 2; Bocskai 1; III Ker 1; Kispesti AC 1; Soroksar 1; Szolnoki MAV 1; Siofok Banyasz 1; Bekescsaba 1; Pecs 1.
Cup not regularly held until 1964

Final League Table 1994–95

	P	W	D	L	F	A	Pts
Ferencvaros	30	17	8	5	62	41	59
Ujpest	30	15	7	8	57	34	52
Debrecen	30	14	7	9	45	37	49
Kispest Honved	30	14	6	10	60	42	48
Bekescsaba	30	11	15	4	48	33	48
BVSC	30	14	4	12	51	46	46
Zalaegerszeg	30	12	6	12	49	55	42
PMSC	30	12	6	12	37	43	42
Stadler	30	9	10	11	31	35	37
Vasas	30	10	7	13	38	45	37
Gyori	30	11	5	14	42	40	35
Csepel	30	8	11	11	23	26	35
Vac +	30	8	11	11	39	46	35
Parmalat +	30	9	7	14	44	50	34
Nagykanizsa*	30	7	6	17	24	57	27
Sopron*	30	6	10	14	36	56	25

Top scorer: Preisinger (Zalaegerszeg) 21.
Cup Final: Ferencvaros 2, 4, Vac 0, 3.

ICELAND

Knattspyrnusamband Island, P.O. Box 8511, 128 Reykjavik.
Founded: 1929; *Number of Clubs:* 73; *Number of Players:* 23,673; *National Colours;* Blue shirts, white shorts, blue stockings.
Telephone: 00354 1 81 44 44; *Cable* KSI REYKJAVIK; *Telex:* 2314 isi is; *Fax:* 00354 1 68 97 93.

International matches 1994
Saudia Arabia (a) 0-2, USA (a) 2-1, Brazil (a) 0-3, Bolivia (h) 1-0, Estonia (h) 4-0, Sweden (h) 0-1, Turkey (a) 0-5, Kuwait (a) 1-0, Switzerland (a) 0-1.

League Championship wins (1912–94)
KR 20; Valur 19; Fram 18; IA Akranes 15; Vikingur 5; IBK Keflavik 3; IBV Vestmann 2; KA Akureyri 1.

Cup wins (1960–94)
Valur 8; KR 7; Fram 7; IA Akranes 5; IBV Vestmann 3; IBA Akureyri 1; Vikingur 1; IBK Keflavik 1, KR Reykjavik 1.

Final League Table 1994

	P	W	D	L	F	A	Pts
IA Akranes	18	12	3	3	35	11	39
FH	18	10	3	5	25	17	33
IBK	18	8	7	3	36	24	31
KR	18	8	6	4	29	19	30
Valur	18	8	4	6	25	25	28
Fram	18	4	8	6	27	30	20
UBK	18	6	2	10	23	35	20
IBV	18	4	7	7	22	29	19
Thor*	18	3	5	10	27	38	14
Starjnan*	18	2	5	11	18	39	11

Top scorer: Bibercic (IA Akranes) 14.
Cup Final: KR Reykjavik 2, UMF Grindavik 0.

REPUBLIC OF IRELAND

The Football Association of Ireland, (Cumann Peile Na H-Eireann), 80 Merrion Square, South Dublin 2.
Founded: 1921; *Number of Clubs:* 3,190; *Number of Players:* 124,615; *National Colours:* Green shirts, white shorts, green stockings.
Telephone: 00353 1 676 68 64; *Cable:* SOCCER DUBLIN; *Telex:* 91397 fai ei; *Fax:* 00353 1 661 09 31.

League Championship wins (1922–95)
Shamrock Rovers 15; Dundalk 9; Shelbourne 8; Bohemians 7; Waterford 6; Cork United 5; Drumcondra 5; St Patrick's Athletic 4; St James's Gate 2; Cork Athletic 2; Sligo Rovers 2; Limerick 2; Athlone Town 2; Dolphin 1; Cork Hibernians 1; Cork Celtic 1; Derry City 1, Cork City 1.

Cup wins (1922–95)
Shamrock Rovers 24; Dundalk 8; Drumcondra 5; Bohemians 5; Shelbourne 3; Cork Athletic 2; Cork United 2; St James's Gate 2; St Patrick's Athletic 2; Cork Hibernians 2; Limerick 2; Waterford 2; Derry City 2; Alton United 1; Athlone Town 2; Sligo 2; Cork 1; Fordsons 1; Transport 1; Finn Harps 1; Home Farm 1; UCD 1; Bray Wanderers 1; Galway United 1.

Final League Table 1994–95

	P	W	D	L	F	A	Pts
Dundalk	33	17	8	8	41	25	51
Shelbourne	33	16	9	8	45	32	49
Derry City	33	16	10	7	45	30	46
Bohemians	33	14	11	8	48	31	45
St Patricks Ath	33	13	14	6	53	36	41
Cork City	33	15	4	14	54	42	39
Shamrock Rovers	33	14	9	10	46	36	39
Sligo Rovers	33	12	7	14	43	41	35
Galway U	33	10	9	14	39	53	31
Athlone T +	33	6	14	13	31	44	30
Cobh Ramblers*	33	5	11	17	29	51	26
Monaghan U*	33	5	4	24	22	75	25

Top scorer: Caufield (Cork City) 16. *Cup Final:* Derry City 2, Shelbourne 1.

ISRAEL

Israel Football Association, 12 Carlibach Street, P.O. Box 20188, Tel Aviv 61201.
Founded: 1928; *Number of Clubs:* 544; *Number of Players:* 30,449; *National Colours:* White shirts, blue shorts, white stockings.
Telephone: 00972 3 570 90 59; *Cable:* CADUREGEL TEL AVIV; *Fax:* 00972 3 570 20 44.

International matches 1994
Georgia (h) 2-0, Ukraine (h) 1-0, Lithuania (a) 1-1, Croatia (h) 0-4, Poland (h) 2-1, Slovakia (h) 2-2, Azerbaijan (a) 2-0, Romania (h) 1-1.

League Championship wins (1932–95)
Maccabi Tel Aviv 17; Hapoel Tel Aviv 12; Hapoel Petah Tikva 6; Maccabi Haifa 5; Maccabi Netanya 5; Beitar Jerusalem 2; Hakoah Ramat Gan 2; Hapoel Beersheba 2; Bnei Yehouda 1; British Police 1; Hapoel Kfar Sava 1; Hapoel Ramat Gan 1.

Cup wins (1928–95)
Maccabi Tel Aviv 18; Hapoel Tel Aviv 9; Beitar Jerusalem 5; Maccabi Haifa 4; Hapoel Haifa 3; Hapoel Kfar Sava 3; Beitar Tel Aviv 2; Bnei Yehouda 2; Hakoah Ramat Gan 2; Hapoel Petah Tikva 2; Maccabi Petah Tikva 2; British Police 1; Hapoel Jerusalem 1; Hapoel Lod 1; Maccabi Netanya 1.

Final League Table 1994–95

	P	*W*	*D*	*L*	*F*	*A*	Pts
Maccabi Tel Aviv	30	19	6	5	59	27	63
Maccabi Haifa	30	17	7	6	68	34	58
Hapoel Beersheba	30	14	8	8	53	35	50
Hapoel Tel Aviv	30	10	15	5	40	32	45
Hapoel Petah Tikva	30	12	8	10	42	36	44
Beitar Jerusalem	30	12	8	10	42	36	44
Zafirim Holon	30	13	5	12	56	56	44
Maccabi Petah Tikva	30	7	14	9	40	41	35
Ironi Rishon	30	7	13	10	39	44	34
Bnei Yehuda	30	8	10	12	43	49	34
Beitar Tel Aviv	30	10	4	16	43	60	34
Hapoel Beit Shean	30	8	10	12	30	50	34
Hapoel Haifa	30	8	9	13	45	51	33
Maccabi Herzliya	30	8	9	13	30	49	33
Ironi Ashdod*	30	7	11	12	42	52	32
Maccabi Netanya*	30	7	9	14	33	50	30

Top scorers: Revivo (Maccabi Haifa), Turjeman (Ironi) 17.
Cup Final: Maccabi Haifa 2, Hapoel Haifa 0.

ITALY

Federazione Italiana Giuoco Calcio, Via Gregorio Allegri 14, C.P. 2450, 1-00198, Roma.
Founded: 1898; *Number of Clubs:* 20,961; *Number of Players:* 1,420,160; *National Colours:* Blue shirts, white shorts, blue stockings, white trim.
Telephone: 0039 6 849 11 11; *Cable:* FEDERCALCIO ROMA; *Telex:* 611483 calcio i; *Fax:* 0039 6 849 12 239.

International matches 1994
France (h) 0-1, Germany (a) 1-2, Finland (h) 2-0, Switzerland (h) 1-0, Costa Rica (h) 1-0, Republic of Ireland (n) 0-1, Norway (n) 1-0, Mexico (n) 1-1, Nigeria (n) 2-1, Spain (n) 2-1, Bulgaria (n) 2-1, Brazil (n) 0-0, Slovenia (a) 1-1, Estonia (a) 2-0, Croatia (h) 1-2, Turkey (h) 3-1.

League Championship wins (1898–1995)
Juventus 23; AC Milan 14; Inter-Milan 13; Genoa 9; Torino 8; Pro Vercelli 7; Bologna 7; Fiorentina 2; Napoli 2; AS Roma 2; Casale 1; Novese 1; Cagliari 1; Lazio 1; Verona 1; Sampdoria 1.

Cup wins (1922–95)
Juventus 9; AS Roma 8; Torino 4; Fiorentina 4; AC Milan 4; Sampdoria 4; Inter-Milan 3; Napoli 3; Bologna 2; Atalanta 1; Genoa 1; Lazio 1; Vado 1; Venezia 1; Parma 1.

Final League Table 1994–95

	P	*W*	*D*	*L*	*F*	*A*	Pts
Juventus	34	23	4	7	59	32	73
Lazio	34	19	6	9	69	34	63
Parma	34	18	9	7	51	30	63
AC Milan	34	17	9	8	53	32	60
Roma	34	16	11	7	46	25	59
Internazionale	34	14	10	10	39	34	52
Napoli	34	13	12	9	40	45	51
Sampdoria	34	13	11	10	51	37	50
Cagliari	34	13	10	11	40	39	49
Fiorentina	34	12	11	11	61	57	47
Torino	34	12	9	13	44	48	45
Bari	34	12	8	14	40	43	44
Cremonese	34	11	8	15	35	38	41
Genoa	34	10	10	14	34	49	40
Padova +	34	12	4	18	37	58	40
Foggia*	34	8	10	16	32	50	34
Reggiana*	34	4	6	24	23	56	18
Brescia*	34	2	6	26	18	65	12

Top scorer: Batistuta (Fiorentina) 26.
Cup Final: Juventus 1, 2, Parma 0, 0.

LATVIA

Latvian Football Federation, Augsiela, 1, LV-1009, Riga.
Founded: 1921; *Number of Clubs:* 50; *Number of Players:* 12,000.
National Colours: Carmine red shirts, white shorts, carmine red stockings.
Telephone: 00371 2 29 29 88; *Telex:* 161183 ritm su; *Fax:* 00371 8 82 83 31.
Cable: Augsiela 1, LV–1009, Riga.

International matches 1994
Malta (h) 2-0, Georgia (h) 1-3, Estonia (h) 2-0, Lithuania (a) 0-1, Republic of Ireland (h) 0-3, Portugal (h) 1-3, Estonia (h) 0-0, Liechtenstein (a) 1-0.

League Championship wins (1922–94)
ASK Riga 9; RFK Riga 8; Olympia Liepaya 7; Sarkanais Metalurgs Liepaya 7; VEF Riga 6; Energija Riga 4; Skonto Riga 4; Elektrons Riga 3; Torpedo Riga 3; Daugava Liepaya 2; ODO Riga 2; Khimikis Daugavpils 2; RAF Yelgava 2; Keisermezhs Riga 2; Dinamo Riga 1; Zhmilyeva Team 1; Darba Rezervi 1; REZ Riga 1; Start Brotseni 1; Venta Ventspils 1; Yurnieks Riga 1; Alfa Riga 1; Gauya Valmiera 1.

Cup wins (1937–94)
Elektrons Riga 7; Sarkanais Metalurgs Liepaya 5; ODO Riga 3; VEF Riga 3; ASK Riga 3; Tseltnieks Riga 3; RFK Riga 2; Daugava Liepaya 2; Start Brotseni 2; Selmash Liepaya 2; Yurnieks Riga 2; Khimikis Daugavpils 2; RAF Yelgava 2; Rigas Vilki 1; Dinamo Liepaya 1; Dinamo Riga 1; REZ Riga 1; Voulkan Kouldiga 1; Baltija Liepaya 1; Venta Ventspils 1; Pilot Riga 1; Lielupe Yurmala 1; Energija Riga 1; Torpedo Riga 1; Daugava SKIF Riga 1; Tseltnieks Daugavpils 1; Skonto Riga 1, Olympia Riga 1.

Final League Table 1994

	P	*W*	*D*	*L*	*F*	*A*	Pts
Skonto Riga	22	20	2	0	65	9	42
RAF Yelgava	22	13	7	2	38	11	33
DAG Riga	22	11	7	4	35	17	29
Olympia Riga	22	10	8	4	32	19	28
Vairogs Rezekne	22	9	6	7	29	28	24
Pardaugava Riga	22	6	10	6	24	24	22
Vidus Riga	22	8	5	9	22	31	21
Auseklis Daugavplis	22	5	7	10	26	29	16
Interskonto Riga	22	5	7	10	17	27	16
Gemma Riga	22	4	6	12	17	46	14
FK Liepaja*	22	2	5	15	16	46	9
Kimikis Daugavplis*	22	1	6	15	10	44	8

Top scorer: Zuyev (RAF Yelgava) 13.
Cup Final: Olympia 2, DAG 0.

LIECHTENSTEIN

Liechtensteiner Fussball-Verband, Am schragen Weg 17, Postfach 165, 9490 Vaduz.
Founded: 1933; *Number of Clubs:* 7; *Number of Players:* 1,247; *National Colours:* Blue & red shirts, red shorts, blue stockings.
Telephone: 004175 233 24 28; *Cable:* FUSSBALLVERBAND VADUZ; *Fax:* 004175 233 24 30.

International matches 1994
Northern Ireland (a) 1-4, Switzerland (a) 0-2, Austria (h) 0-4, Republic of Ireland (a) 0-4, Latvia (h) 0-1, Portugal (a) 0-8.
Liechtenstein has no national league. Teams compete in Swiss regional leagues.
Cup wins (1946–94)
Vaduz 25; Balzers 10; Triesen 8; Eschen/Mauren 4; Schaan 2.

LITHUANIA

Lithuanian Football Federation, 6, Zemaites Street, 232675 Vilnius. Championship of 14 teams.
Number of Clubs: 20; *Number of Players:* 16,600.
Telephone: 00370 2 35 36 54; *Telex:* 261118 lsk su; *Fax:* 00370 2 35 36 51.
International matches 1994
Israel (h) 1-1, Czech Republic (a) 3-5, Estonia (h) 3-0, Latvia (h) 1-0, Sweden (a) 2-4, Ukraine (a) 2-0, Croatia (a) 0-2, Slovenia (a) 2-1.
League Championship wins (1922–95)
Kovas Kaunas 6; KSS Klaipeda 6; LFLS Kaunas 4; Zalgiris Vilnius 3; LGSF Kaunas 2; MSK Kaunas 1; Ekranas Panevezys 1; Romar Mazeikiai 1.
Cup wins 1992–95

Zalgiris Vilnius 3; Inkaras 1.

Final League Table 1994–95

	P	*W*	*D*	*L*	*F*	*A*	Pts
Zalgiris	22	17	2	3	61	14	36
Inkaras	22	16	4	2	50	12	36
Romar	22	15	4	3	49	12	34
Panerys	22	11	6	5	35	25	28
Aras	22	13	1	8	41	28	27
FBK	22	8	8	6	23	20	24
Siauliai	22	9	4	9	37	23	22
Ekranas	22	7	8	7	21	18	22
Banga	22	3	6	13	19	56	12
Musa*	22	3	5	14	12	58	11
Sirius*	22	2	3	17	12	39	7
Interas*	22	1	3	18	8	63	5

Top scorer; Poderis (Inkaras) 24.
Cup Final: Inkaras 2, Zalgiris 1.

LUXEMBOURG

Federation Luxembourgeoise De Football, (F.L.F.), 50, Rue De Strasbourg, L-2560, Luxembourg.
Founded: 1908; *Number of Clubs:* 126; *Number of Players:* 21,684; *National Colours:* Red shirts, white shorts, blue stockings.
Telephone: 00352 48 86 65; *Cable:* FOOTBALL LUXEMBOURG; *Telex:* 2426 flf lu; *Fax:* 00352 40 02 01.
International matches 1994
Morocco (h) 1-2, Holland (h) 0-4, Belarus (a) 0-2,.Holland (a) 0-5.
League Championship wins (1910–95)
Jeunesse Esch 22; Spora Luxembourg 11; Stade Dudelange 10; Avenir Beggen 7; Red Boys Differdange 6; US Hollerich-Bonnevoie 5; Fola Esch 5; US Luxembourg 5; Aris Bonnevoie 3; Progres Niedercor 3.
Cup wins (1922–95)
Red Boys Differdange 16; Jeunesse Esch 9; US Luxembourg 9; Spora Luxembourg 8; Avenir Beggen 6; Stade Dudelange 4; Progres Niedercorn 4; Fola Esch 3; Alliance Dudelange 2; US Rumelange 2; Aris Bonnevoie 1; US Dudelange 1; Jeunesse Hautchar age 1; National Schiffige 1; Racing Luxembourg 1; SC Tetange 1; Hesperange 1, Grevenmacher 1.
Final Table 1994–95

	P	*W*	*D*	*L*	*F*	*A*	Pts
Jeunesse Esch	22	15	5	2	63	17	35
Grevenmacher	22	15	5	2	35	12	35
Avenir Beggen	22	13	4	5	64	31	30
F91 Dudelange	22	10	3	9	41	37	23
Union	22	8	6	8	40	30	22
FC Wiltz 71	22	7	8	7	36	40	22
Spora	22	7	6	9	38	36	20
Aris	22	7	5	10	39	45	19
Petange	22	7	5	10	30	43	19
Red Boys	22	6	5	11	44	60	17
Swift*	22	6	4	12	33	58	16
Wormeldange*	22	1	4	17	13	68	6

Top scorer: Heinen (Red Boys) 22.
Cup Final: Grevenmacher 3, Jeunesse Esch 2.
After a 1-1 draw.

MACEDONIA

Football Association of the Former Yugoslav Republic of Macedonia, VIII-ma Udarna Brigada 31A, MAC-91000Skopje.
Telephone: 00389 1 22 90 42; *Fax:* 00389 1 23 54 48.

International matches 1994
Slovenia (h) 2-0, Albania (h) 5-1, Estonia (h) 2-0, Turkey (h) 0-2, Denmark (h) 1-1, Spain (h) 0-2, Belgium (a) 1-1, Cyprus (h) 3-0.

League Championship wins (1994–95)
Vardar 2.

Cup wins (1994)
Sileks 1.

Final League Table 1994–95

	P	*W*	*D*	*L*	*F*	*A*	Pts
Vardar	30	23	7	0	79	17	76
Sileks	30	18	6	6	66	28	60
Sloga	30	17	7	6	43	26	58
Pobeda	30	16	5	9	55	35	53
Pelister	30	15	6	9	57	40	51
Osogovo	30	11	9	10	53	34	42
Sasa	30	11	8	11	39	30	41
FK Ohrid	30	11	5	14	45	43	38
Balkan Bisi	30	11	5	14	48	51	38
Belasica	30	11	4	15	48	62	37
Tikves	30	11	4	15	35	53	37
Rudar	30	10	4	16	32	45	34
Ljuboten	30	10	4	16	37	54	34
FCU 55	30	9	6	15	31	40	33
Borec*	30	9	6	15	28	57	33
Kozuv*	30	2	4	24	18	99	7

Kozuv had three points deducted.
Cup Final: Vardar 2, Sileks 1.

MALTA

Malta Football Association, 280 St. Paul Street, Valletta.
Founded: 1900; *Number of Clubs:* 252; *Number of Players:* 5,544; *National Colours:* Red shirts, white shorts, red stockings.
Telephone: 00356 22 26 97; *Cable:* FOOTBALL MALTA VALLETTA; *Telex:* 1752 malfa mw; *Fax:* 00356 24 51 36.

International matches 1994
Tunisia (h) 1-1, Georgia (h) 0-1, Slovenia (h) 0-1, Belgium (h) 1-0, Slovakia (h) 1-2, Azerbaijan (h) 5-0, Latvia (a) 0-2, Slovakia (a) 1-1, Czech Republic (a) 1-6, Czech Republic (h) 0-0, Norway (h) 0-1.

League Championship wins (1910–95)
Floriana 25; Sliema Wanderers 22; Valletta 15; Hibernians 8; Hamrun Spartans 6; Rabat Ajax 2; St George's 1; KOMR 1.

Cup wins (1935–95)
Floriana 18; Sliema Wanderers 17; Valletta 7; Hamrun Spartans 6; Hibernians 5; Gzira United 1; Melita 1; Zurrieq 1; Rabat Ajax 1.

Final League Table 1994–95

	P	*W*	*D*	*L*	*F*	*A*	Pts
Hibernians	18	13	4	1	42	10	43
Sliema Wanderers	18	12	3	3	55	22	39
Valletta	18	11	4	3	45	12	37
Floriana	18	10	5	3	33	13	35
Hamrun Spartans	18	10	2	6	33	23	32
Birkirkara	18	5	6	7	17	24	21
Zurrieq	18	6	2	10	18	36	20
Naxxar Lions	18	4	3	11	15	37	15
Pieta Hotspurs*	18	2	3	13	11	40	9
St George's*	18	0	2	16	4	56	2

Top scorer: Saunders (Sliema) 18.
Cup Final: Valletta 1, Hamrun Spartans 0.

MOLDOVA

Moldavian Football Federation, Bd Stefan cel Mare 73, 277001 Chisinau, Moldavia.
Number of Clubs: 143; *Number of Players:* 75,000.
Telephone: 00373 2 22 12 95. *Fax:* 00373 2 22 22 44. *Telex:* 64163218.

International matches 1994
USA (a) 0-3, Azerbaijan (h) 2-1, Georgia (a) 1-0, Wales (h) 3-2, Bulgaria (a) 1-4, Germany (h) 0-3.

League Championship wins (1994–95)
Zimbru Chisinau 2.

Cup wins (1994–95)
Tiligul Tiraspol 2.

Final League Table 1994–95

	P	*W*	*D*	*L*	*F*	*A*	Pts
Zimbru Chisinau	26	21	4	1	71	10	67
Tiligul Tiraspol	26	21	3	2	78	18	66
Balti	26	17	6	3	54	24	57
Bender	26	18	2	6	43	18	56
Otaci	26	15	4	7	55	25	49
MHM 93	26	10	6	10	28	30	36
Comrat	26	10	1	15	29	56	31
Agro	26	8	6	12	24	37	30
Calarasi	26	8	5	13	28	38	29
Torentul	26	6	5	15	24	46	23
Sportul	26	7	2	17	23	46	23
Briceni	26	7	2	17	22	56	23
Cioburciu	26	5	5	16	27	46	20
Falesti	26	2	3	21	15	71	9

Top scorer: Gavriliuc (Zimbru Chisinau) 20.
Cup Final: Tiligul Tiraspol 1, Zimbru Chisinau 0.

NORTHERN IRELAND

Irish Football Association Ltd, 20 Windsor Avenue, Belfast BT9 6EG.
Founded: 1880; *Number of Clubs:* 1,555; *Number of Players:* 24,558; *National Colours:* Green shirts, white shorts, green stockings.
Telephone: 01232 66 94 58/59; *Cable:* FOOTBALL BELFAST; *Telex:* 747317 ifa ni g; *Fax:* 01232 66 76 20.

NORWAY

Norges Fotballforbund Ullevaal Stadion, Postboks 3823, Ulleval Hageby, 0805 Oslo 8.
Founded: 1902; *Number of Clubs:* 1,810; *Number of Players:* 300,000; *National Colours:* Red shirts, white shorts, blue & white stockings.
Telephone: 0047 22 95 10 00; *Cable* FOTBALLFORBUND OSLO; *Telex:* 71722 nff n; *Fax:* 0047 22 95 10 10.

International matches 1994
USA (a) 1-2, Costa Rica (a) 0-0, Wales (a) 3-1, Portugal (h) 0-0, England (a) 0-0, Denmark (h) 2-1, Sweden (a) 0-2, Mexico(n)1-0,.Italy(n)0-1,RepublicofIreland(n)0-0,Belarus (h) 1-0, Holland (h) 1-1, Belarus (a) 4-0, Malta (a) 1-0.

League Championship wins (1938–94)
Fredrikstad 9; Viking Stavanger 8; Rosenborg Trondheim 8; Lillestroem 6; Valerengen 4; Larvik Turn 3; Brann Bergen 2; Lyn Oslo 2; IK Start 2; Friedig 1; Fram 1; Skeid Oslo 1; Strömsgodset Drammen 1; Moss 1.

Cup wins (1902–94)
Odds Bk, Skien 11; Fredrikstad 10; Lyn Oslo 8; Skeid Oslo 8; Sarpsborg FK 6; Brann Bergen 5; Rosenborg Trondheim 5; Orn F Horten 4; Lillestroem 4; Viking Stavanger 4; Strömsgodset Drammen 4; Frigg 3; Mjondalens F 3; Bodo Glimt 2; Mercantile 2; Grane Nordstrand 1; Kvik Halden 1; Sparta 1; Gjovik 1; Valerengen 1; Moss 1; Tromso 1; Byrne 1, Molde 1.
(Until 1937 the cup-winners were regarded as champions.)

Final League Table 1994

	P	*W*	*D*	*L*	*F*	*A*	Pts
Rosenborg	22	15	4	3	70	23	49
Lillestrom	22	12	5	5	42	23	41
Viking	22	11	6	5	41	26	39
Start	22	9	8	5	42	22	35
Kongsvinger	22	11	2	9	38	35	35
Brann	22	9	4	9	38	46	31
Tromso	22	7	7	8	22	28	28
Hamark	22	7	5	10	34	46	26
Valerengen	22	5	7	10	32	40	22
Bodo-Glimt	22	5	7	10	30	46	22
Sogndal*	22	6	4	12	19	40	22
Stromsgodset*	22	4	3	15	22	55	15

Top scorer: Brattbakk (Rosenborg) 17.
Cup Final: Molde 3, Lyn 2.

POLAND

Federation Polonaise De Foot-Ball, Al. Ujazdowskie 22, 00-478 Warszawa.
Founded: 1923; *Number of Clubs:* 5,881; *Number of Players:* 317,442; *National Colours:* White shirts, red shorts, white & red stockings.
Telephone: 0048 2 621 91 75; *Cable:* PEZETPEEN WARSZAWA; *Telex:* 815320 pzpn pl; *Fax:* 0048 2 229 24 89.

International matches 1994
Spain (a) 1-1, Greece (a) 0-0,.Saudi Arabia (h) 1-0, Hungary (h) 3-2, Austria (h) 3-4, Belarus (h) 1-1, Israel (a) 1-2, Azerbaijan (h) 1-0, France (h) 0-0, Saudi Arabia (a) 2-0,.Saudi Arabia (a) 2-1.

League Championship wins (1921–95)
Gornik Zabrze 14; Ruch Chorzow 13; Wisla Krakow 6; Legia Warsaw 6; Lech Poznan 5; Pogon Lwow 4; Cracovia 3; Warta Poznan 2; Polonia Bytom 2; Stal Mielec 2; Widzew Lodz 2; Garbarnia Krakow 1; Polonia Warsaw 1; LKS Lodz 1; Slask Wroclaw 1; Szombierki Bytom 1; Zaglebie Lubin 1.

Cup wins (1951–95)
Legia Warsaw 11; Gornik Zabrze 6; Zaglebie Sosnowiec 4; Lech Poznan 3; GKS Katowice 3: Ruch Chorzow 2; Slask Wroclaw 2; Gwardia Warsaw 1; LKS Lodz 1; Polonia Warsaw 1; Wisla Krakow 1; Stal Rzeszow 1; Arka Gdynia 1; Lechia Gdansk 1; Widzew Lodz 1; Miedz Legnica 1.

Final League Table 1994–95

	P	*W*	*D*	*L*	*F*	*A*	Pts
Legia	34	23	5	6	58	20	51
Widzew	34	17	11	6	47	25	45
Katowice	34	16	10	8	45	27	42
Zaglebie Lubin	34	16	10	8	48	41	42
Gornik Zabrze	34	12	13	9	48	39	37
Lech	34	13	8	13	46	40	34
LKS Lodz	34	10	14	10	39	41	34
Pogon	34	10	13	11	33	34	33
Sokol	34	9	14	11	33	43	32
Olimpia	34	9	13	12	46	41	31
Hutnik	33	9	13	11	36	38	31
Rakow	34	9	13	12	31	43	31
Stomil	34	7	16	11	35	40	30
Stal	33	8	14	11	43	49	30
Petrochemia*	34	8	14	12	35	42	30
Ruch*	34	7	15	12	39	46	29
Wola*	34	10	9	15	34	47	29
Warta*	34	7	5	22	35	75	19

Top scorers: Cygan (Stal) 16.
Cup Final: Legia 2, Katowice 0.

PORTUGAL

Federacao Portuguesa De Futebol, Praca De Alegria N.25, Apartado 21.100, P-1128, Lisboa Codex.
Founded: 1914; *Number of Clubs:* 204; *Number of Players:* 79,235; *National Colours:* Red shirts, white shorts, red stockings.
Telephone: 00351 1 347 59 34; *Cable:* FUTEBOL LISBOA; *Telex:* 13489 fpf p; *Fax:* 00351 1 346 72 31.

International matches 1994
Spain (a) 2-2, Norway (a) 0-0, Northern Ireland (a) 2-1, Latvia (a) 3-1, Austria (h) 1-0, Liechtenstein (h) 8-0.

League Championship wins (1935–95)
Benfica 30; Sporting Lisbon 16; FC Porto 14; Belenenses 1.

Cup wins (1939–95)
Benfica 22; Sporting Lisbon 12; FC Porto 8; Boavista 4; Belenenses 3; Vitoria Setubal 2; Academica Coimbra 1; Leixoes Porto 1; Sporting Braga 1; Amadora 1.

Final League Table 1994–95

	P	*W*	*D*	*L*	*F*	*A*	Pts
Porto	34	29	4	1	73	15	62
Sporting Lisbon	34	22	9	3	57	22	53
Benfica	34	22	5	7	61	28	49
Guimaraes	34	16	10	8	54	43	42
Farense	34	16	5	13	44	38	37
Leiria	34	13	10	11	41	44	36
Maritimo	34	12	11	11	41	45	35
Tirsense	34	14	6	14	35	34	34
Braga	34	11	10	13	34	42	32
Boavista	34	12	8	14	40	49	32
Salgueiros	34	11	7	16	43	50	29
Belenenses	34	10	7	17	30	39	27
Gil Vicente	34	7	13	14	30	40	27
Chaves	34	10	7	17	33	49	27
Amadora	34	6	14	14	27	40	26
Madeira*	34	7	10	17	30	54	24
Beira Mar*	34	8	5	21	33	54	21
Setubal*	34	3	13	18	25	45	19

Top scorer: Hassan Nader (Farense) 21.
Cup Final: Sporting Lisbon 2, Maritimo 0.

ROMANIA

Federatia Romana De Fotbal, Vasile Conta 16, Bucharest 70130.
Founded: 1908; *Number of Clubs:* 414; *Number of Players:* 22,920; *National Colours:* Yellow shirts, blue shorts, red stockings.
Telephone: 0040 1 617 33 43; *Cable:* SPORTROM BUCURESTI-FOTBAL; *Telex:* 10097 frf r; *Fax:* 0040 1 312 83 24

International matches 1994
Hong Kong (a) 1-1, USA (h) 2-1, South Korea (a) 2-1, Northern Ireland (a) 0-2, Bolivia (h) 3-0,.Nigeria (h) 2-0, Slovenia (h) 0-0, Sweden (h) 1-1, Colombia (n) 3-1, Switzerland (n) 1-4, USA (n) 1-0, Argentina (n) 3-2, Sweden (n) 2-2, Azerbaijan (h) 3-0, France (a) 0-0, England (a) 1-1, Slovakia (h) 3-2, Israel (a) 1-1.

League Championship wins (1910–95)
Steaua Bucharest (prev. CCA) 17; Dinamo Bucharest 14; Venus Bucharest 8, Chinezul Timisoara 6; UT Arad 6; Ripensia Temesvar 4; Uni Craiova 4; Petrolul Ploesti 3; Olimpia Bucharest 2; Colentina Bucharest 2; Arges Pitesti 2; ICO Oradea 2; Soc RA Bucharest 1; Prahova Ploesti 1; Coltea Brasov 1; Juventus Bucharest 1; Metalochimia Resita1; Ploesti United 1; Unirea Tricolor 1; Rapid Bucharest 1.

Cup wins (1934–95)
Steaua Bucharest (prev. CCA) 17; Rapid Bucharest 9; Dinamo Bucharest 7; Uni Craiova 6; UT Arad 2; Ripensia Temesvar 2; Politehnica Timisoara 2; Petrolul Ploesti 2; ICO Oradeo 1; Metalochimia Resita 1; Stinta Cluj 1; CFR Turnu Severin 1; Chimia Rannicu Vilcea 1; Jiul Petroseni 1; Progresul Bucharest 1; Progresul Oradea 1; Gloria Bistrita 1.

Final League Table 1994–95

	P	*W*	*D*	*L*	*F*	*A*	Pts
Steaua	34	23	8	3	72	25	77
Uni Craiova	34	21	5	8	84	41	68
Dinamo	34	20	5	9	61	35	65
Rapid Bucharest	34	16	6	12	55	42	54
Ceahlaul	34	16	5	13	56	54	53
Gloria	34	16	4	14	66	59	52
National	34	16	4	14	66	60	52
Arges	34	16	4	14	47	54	52
Inter Sibiu	34	16	3	15	53	52	51
Petrolul	34	14	7	13	44	41	49
Farul	34	13	6	15	43	50	45
Uni Cluj	34	13	4	17	39	42	43
Otelul	34	11	9	14	47	51	42
Brasov	34	10	9	15	40	54	39
Elect. Craiova	34	11	5	18	42	53	38
Sportul	34	8	10	16	26	44	34
Maramures*	34	6	9	19	34	69	27
UT Arad*	34	4	9	21	28	77	21

Top scorer: Craioveanu (Uni Craiova) 25.
Cup Final: Rapid Bucharest 1, Petrolul 1.
Petrolul won 5-3 on penalties.

RUSSIA

Football Union of Russia; Luzhnetskaya Naberezyhnaja, 8. SU-119270 Moscow. Telephone: 0070 95 248 08 34; *Telex:* 411287 priz su; *Fax:* 0070 502 220 20 37;
Founded: 1992; *Number of Clubs:* 43,700; *Number of Players:* 2,170,000.

International matches 1994
USA (a) 1-1, Mexico (a) 4-1, Republic of Ireland (a) 0-0, Turkey (a) 1-0, Slovakia (h) 2-1, Brazil (h) 0-2, Sweden (h) 1-3, Cameroon (h) 6-1, Austria (a) 3-0, Germany (h) 0-1, San Marino (h) 4-0, Scotland (a) 1-1.

League Championship wins (1945–95)
Spartak Moscow 14; Dynamo Kiev 13; Dynamo Moscow 11; CSKA Moscow 7; Torpedo Moscow 3; Dynamo Tbilisi 2; Dnepr Dnepropetrovsk 2; Saria Voroshilovgrad 1; Ararat Erevan 1; Dynamo Minsk 1; Zenit Leningrad 1.

Cup wins (1936–95)
Spartak Moscow 11; Dynamo Kiev 10; Torpedo Moscow 7; Dynamo Moscow 7; CSKA Moscow 5; Donetsk Shaktyor 4; Lokomotiv Moscow 2; Dynamo Tbilisi 2; Ararat Erevan 2; Karpaty Lvov 1; SKA Rostov 1; Zenit Leningrad 1; Metallist Kharkov 1; Dnepr 1.

Final League Table 1994–95

	P	*W*	*D*	*L*	*F*	*A*	Pts
Spartak Moscow	30	21	8	1	73	21	50
Dynamo Moscow	30	13	13	4	55	35	39
Lokomotiv Moscow	30	12	12	6	49	28	36
Volgograd	30	10	16	4	39	23	36
Vladikavkaz	30	11	11	8	32	34	33
Novgorod	30	11	9	10	36	34	31
Kamaz	30	11	9	10	38	37	31
Tekstilchik Kamychin	30	11	7	12	30	37	29
Sotchi	30	8	11	11	44	48	27
CSKA Moscow	30	8	10	12	30	32	25
Torpedo Moscow	30	7	12	11	28	37	25
Krylia Sovekov	30	6	12	12	30	51	24
Toumen	30	7	10	13	24	49	24
Ekaterinbourg	30	7	9	14	33	49	23
Stavropol*	30	6	11	13	25	34	23
Lada*	30	6	10	14	24	41	22

Top scorer: Simoutenkov (Dynamo Moscow) 21.
Cup Final: Dynamo Moscow 0, Volgograd 0.
Dynamo Moscow won 8-7 on penalties.

SAN MARINO

Federazione Sammarinese Giuoco Calcio, Viale Campo dei Giudei, 14; 47031-Rep. San Marino.
Founded: 1931; *Number of Clubs:* 17; *Number of Players:* 1,033; *Colours:* Blue and white.
Telephone: 0039549 99 05 15; *Cable:*FEDERCALCIO SAN MARINO; *Telex:* 0505284 cogmar;*Fax:* 0039549 99 23 48.

International matches 1994
Russia (a) 0-4, Greece (a) 0-2, Finland (a) 1-4.

League Championship wins (1986–95)
Tre Fiori 4; Fiorita 2; Faetano 2; Domagnano 1; Montevito 1.

Cup wins (1986–94)
Domagnano 3; Libertas 3; Faetano 1, Fiorita 1, Tre Fiori 1.

Final League Table 1994–95

	P	*W*	*D*	*L*	*F*	*A*	Pts
Tre Fiori +*	18	12	2	4	36	15	26
Cosmos +*	18	9	6	3	29	20	24
Domagnano +*	18	9	5	4	29	7	23
La Fiorita +*	18	10	3	5	24	25	23
Murata	18	8	6	4	22	16	22
Cailungo	18	4	6	8	18	26	14
Virtus	18	3	8	7	12	20	14
Faetano	18	5	3	10	26	24	13
Libertas*	18	4	5	9	25	32	13
Juvenes*	18	2	4	12	18	34	8

Play-Offs
San Giovanni 0, Domagnano 3; Cosmos 2, La Fiorita 3; San Giovanni 0, Cosmos 1; Domagnano 0, La Fiorita 2; Domagnano 2, Cosmos 4; Tre Fiori 0, La Fiorita 0 (Tre Fiori won 6-5 on penalties); La Fiorita 1, Cosmos 0.

Final
Tre Fiori 1, La Fiorita 0.
Top scorer: Ugolini (Tre Fiori) 16.

SCOTLAND

The Scottish Football Association Ltd, 6 Park Gardens, Glasgow G3 7YF.
Founded: 1873; *Number of Clubs:* 6,148; *Number of Players:* 135,474; *National Colours:* Dark blue shirts, white shorts, red stockings.
Telephone: 0141 332 6372; *Cable:* EXECUTIVE GLASGOW; *Telex:* 778904 sfa g; *Fax:* 0141 332 7559.

SLOVAKIA

Slovak Football Association, Junacka 6, 83280 Bratislava, Slovakia.
Number of Clubs: 2,140; *Number of Players:* 141,000.
Telephone: 0042 7 279 01 51; *Fax:* 0042 7 279 05 54.

International matches 1994
UAR (a) 1-0, Egypt (a) 0-1, Morocco (a) 1-2, Malta (a) 2-1, Croatia (h) 4-1, Russia (a) 1-2, Malta (h) 1-1, France (h) 0-0, Israel (a) 2-2, Romania (a) 2-3.

League Championship wins (1994–95)
Slovan Bratislava 2.

Cup wins (1994–95)
Tatran Presov 1, Inter 1.

Final League Table 1994–95

	P	*W*	*D*	*L*	*F*	*A*	Pts
Slovan Bratislava	32	21	9	2	63	25	72
Kosice	32	15	7	10	54	42	52
Inter	32	14	8	10	47	45	50
Dunajska Streda	32	13	7	12	41	42	46
Dukla Bystrica	32	12	8	12	53	44	44
Spartak Trnava	32	12	8	12	43	35	44

Promotion/Relegation Table 1994–95

	P	*W*	*D*	*L*	*F*	*A*	Pts
Bardejov + +	32	12	7	13	46	46	43
Prievidza + +	32	12	6	14	35	50	42
Lokomotiv Kosice + +	32	13	3	16	55	60	39
Tatran Presov + +	32	9	10	13	42	49	37
Humenne*	32	8	8	16	32	57	32
Zilina*	32	9	3	20	37	53	30

Top scorer: Semenik (Dukla Bystrica) 18.
Cup Final: Inter 1, Dunajska Streda 1.
Inter won 3-1 on penalties.

SLOVENIA

Nogometna Zveza Slovenije, dunajska 47/V, P.P. 90, 61109 Ljubljana, Slovenia.
Founded: 1992; *Number of Clubs:* 232; *Number of Players:* 15,048.
Telephone: 00386 61 133 40 63; *Fax:* 00386 61 30 23 37.

International matches 1994
Georgia (a) 1-0, Tunisia (h) 2-2, Malta (a) 1-0, Macedonia (a) 0-2, Hungary (a) 1-0, Cyprus (h) 3-0, Romania (a) 0-0, Italy (h) 1-1, Ukraine (a) 0-0, Lithuania (h) 1-2.

League Championship wins 1992–95
SCT Olimpija 4.

Cup wins 1992–95
Branik Maribor 2; SCT Olimpija 1; Mura 1.

Final League Table 1994–95

	P	*W*	*D*	*L*	*F*	*A*	Pts
Olimpija	30	20	4	6	78	30	44
Branik Maribor	30	17	8	5	60	24	42
Gorica	30	18	5	7	66	30	41
Mura	30	17	6	7	46	24	40
Beltinci	30	15	8	7	74	32	38
Publikum	30	16	6	8	50	27	38
Rudar	30	16	6	8	55	33	38
Korotan	30	14	4	12	53	36	32
Primorje +	30	12	8	10	50	45	32
Oscar +	30	13	4	13	49	43	30
Istrabenz +	30	9	8	18	24	34	26
Donit +	30	8	4	18	36	58	20
Isola*	30	7	6	17	30	73	20
Zivila*	30	5	9	16	34	48	19
Kocevje*	30	4	9	17	24	91	16
Jadran*	30	0	3	27	12	113	3

Top scorer: Skaper (Beltinci) 25.
Cup Final: Mura 1, 1, Publikum 1, 0.

SPAIN

Real Federacion Espanola De Futbol, Calle Alberto Bosch 13, Apartado Postal 347, E-28014 Madrid.
Founded: 1913; *Number of Clubs:* 10,240; *Number of Players:* 408,135; *National Colours:* Red shirts, dark blue shorts, black stockings, yellow trim.
Telephone: 0034 1 420 13 62; *Cable:* FUTBOL MADRID; *Telex:* 42420 rfef e; *Fax:* 0034 1 420 20 94.

International matches 1994
Portugal (h) 2-2, Poland (h) 1-1, Croatia (h) 0-2, Finland (a) 2-1, Canada (a) 2-0, South Korea (n) 2-2, Germany (n) 1-1, Bolivia (n) 3-1, Switzerland (n) 3-0, Italy (n) 1-2, Cyprus (a) 2-1, Macedonia (a) 2-0, Denmark (h) 3-0, Belgium (a) 4-1.

League Championship wins (1945–95)
Real Madrid 26; Barcelona 14; Atletico Madrid 8; Athletic Bilbao 8; Valencia 4; Real Sociedad 2; Real Betis 1; Seville 1.

Cup wins (1902–95)
Athletic Bilbao 23; Barcelona 22; Real Madrid 17; Atletico Madrid 8; Valencia 5; Real Zaragoza 4; Real Union de Irun 3; Seville 3; Espanol 2; Arenas 1; Ciclista Sebastian 1; Racing de Irun 1; Vizcaya Bilbao 1; Real Betis 1; Real Sociedad 1, La Coruna 1.

Final League Table 1994–95

	P	*W*	*D*	*L*	*F*	*A*	Pts
Real Madrid	38	23	9	6	76	29	55
La Coruna	38	20	11	7	68	32	51
Betis	38	15	16	7	46	25	46
Barcelona	38	18	10	10	60	45	46
Espanol	38	14	15	9	51	35	43
Sevilla	38	16	11	11	55	41	43
Zaragoza	38	18	7	13	56	51	43
Athletic Bilbao	38	16	10	12	39	42	42
Oviedo	38	13	13	12	45	42	39
Real Sociedad	38	12	14	12	56	44	38
Valencia	38	13	12	13	53	48	38
Santander	38	13	10	15	42	47	36
Celta	38	11	14	13	36	48	36
Atletico Madrid	38	13	9	16	56	54	35
Tenerife	38	13	9	16	57	57	35
Compostela	38	11	12	15	44	56	34
Albacete* +	38	10	14	14	44	61	34
Sporting Gijon +	38	8	12	18	42	67	28
Valladolid*	38	8	9	21	25	63	25
Logrones*	38	2	9	27	15	79	13

Top scorer: Zamorano (Real Madrid) 28.
Cup Final: La Coruna 2, Valencia 1.
Match abandoned 79 minutes waterlogged pitch, score at 1-1. Last 11 minutes replayed.

SWEDEN

Svenska Fotbollfoerbundet, Box 1216, S-17123 Solna.
Founded: 1904; *Number of Clubs:* 3,250; *Number of Players:* 485,000; *National Colours:* Yellow shirts, blue shorts, yellow and blue stockings.
Telephone: 0046 8 735 09 00; *Cable:* FOOTBALL-S; *Telex:* 17711 fotboll s; *Fax:* 0046 8 27 51 47.

International matches 1994
Colombia (a) 0-0, USA (a) 3-1, Mexico (a) 1-2, Wales (a) 2-0, Nigeria (h) 3-1, Denmark (a) 0-1, Norway (h) 2-0, Romania (a) 1-1, Cameroon (n) 2-2, Russia (n) 3-1, Brazil (n) 1-1, Saudi Arabia (n) 3-1, Romania (n) 2-2, Brazil (n) 0-1, Bulgaria (n) 4-0, Lithuania (h) 4-2, Iceland (a) 1-0, Switzerland (a) 2-4, Hungary (h) 2-0.

League Championship wins (1896–1994)
IFK Gothenburg 15; Oergryte IS Gothenburg 14; Malmo FF 14; IFK Norrköping 12; AIK Stockholm 9; Djurgaarden 8; GAIS Gothenburg 6; IF Helsingborg 5; Boras IF Elfsborg 4; Oster Vaxjo 4; Halmstad 2; Atvidaberg 2; IFK Ekilstune 1; IF Gavic Brynas 1; IF Gothenburg 1; Fassbergs 1; Norrköping IK Sleipner 1.

Cup wins (1941–94)
Malmo FF 13; IFK Norrköping 6; AIK Stockholm 4; IFK Gothenburg 4; Atvidaberg 2; Kalmar 2; GAIS Gothenburg 1; IF Helsingborg 1; Raa 1; Landskrona 1; Oster Vaxjo 1; Djurgaarden 1; Degerfors 1, Halmstad 1.

Final League Table 1994

	P	W	D	L	F	A	Pts
IFK Gothenburg	26	16	6	4	54	28	54
Orebro	26	15	7	4	61	30	52
Malmo	26	14	7	5	51	33	49
Norrkoping	26	13	8	5	52	21	47
Osters	26	13	6	7	48	30	45
AIK	26	11	6	9	42	41	39
Halmstad	26	10	8	8	41	39	38
Degerfors	26	8	8	10	28	37	32
Helsingborg	26	9	5	12	30	46	32
Trelleborg	26	7	9	10	25	40	30
Frolunda	26	7	6	13	30	33	27
Hammarby	26	4	8	14	25	44	20
Landskrona*	26	4	6	16	22	56	18
Hacken*	26	2	8	16	27	58	14

Top scorer: Kindvall (Norrkoping) 23.
Cup Final: Halmstad 3, AIK 1.

SWITZERLAND

Schweizerisher Fussballverband. Haus des Schweizer Fussballs, Worbstrasse 48, 3074 Muri/BE. Mailing Address: PO Box 3000 Bern 15.
Founded: 1895; *Number of Clubs:* 1,473; *Number of Players:* 185,286; *National Colours:* Red shirts, white shorts, red stockings.
Telephone: 0041 31 950 81 11; *Cable:* SWISSFOOT BERNE; *Telex:* 912910 sfv ch; *Fax:* 0041 31 950 81 81.

International matches 1994
USA (a) 1-1, Mexico (a) 5-1, Hungary (a) 2-1, Czech Republic (h) 3-0, Liechtenstein (h) 2-0, Italy (a) 0-1, Bolivia (a) 0-0, USA (n) 1-1, Romania (n) 4-1, Colombia (n) 0-2, Spain (n) 0-3, UAR (h) 1-0, Sweden (h) 4-2, Iceland (h) 1-0, Turkey (a) 2-1.

League Championship wins (1898–1995)
Grasshoppers 23; Servette 16; Young Boys Berne 11; FC Zurich 9; FC Basle 8; Lausanne 7; La Chaux-de-Fonds 3; FC Lugano 3; Winterthur 3; FX Aarau 3; Neuchatel Xamax 2; FC Anglo-American 1; St Gallen 1; FC Brühl 1; Cantonal-Neuchatel 1; Biel 1; Bellinzona 1; FC Etoile Le Chaux-de-Fonds 1; Lucerne 1; Sion 1.

Cup wins (1926–95)
Grasshoppers 18; Lausanne 7; FC Sion 7; La Chaux-de-Fonds 6; Young Boys Berne 6; Servette 6; FC Basle 5; FC Zurich 5; Lucerne 2; FC Lugano 2; FC Granges 1; St Gallen 1; Urania Geneva 1; Young Fellows Zurich 1; Aarau.

Qualifying Table 1994–95

	P	W	D	L	F	A	Pts
Grasshoppers	22	13	5	4	36	21	31
Lugano	22	8	9	5	30	17	25
Aarau	22	8	9	5	34	22	25
Neuchatel Xamax	22	9	6	7	33	31	24
Lausanne	22	8	8	6	34	34	24
Sion	22	10	3	9	32	37	23
Basle	22	6	8	8	18	15	20
Lucerne	22	7	6	9	22	31	20
Zurich	22	4	11	7	23	27	19
Servette	22	6	6	10	26	31	18
St Gallen	22	4	10	8	20	28	18
Young Boys Berne	22	6	5	11	23	37	17

Final Table 1995

	P	W	D	L	F	A	Pts
Grasshoppers	14	9	3	2	25	13	37
Lugano	14	6	5	3	25	17	30
Neuchatel Xamax	14	6	4	4	27	20	28
Aarau	14	5	4	5	17	16	27
Lucerne	14	5	5	4	14	18	25
Basle	14	7	0	7	20	19	24
Sion	14	5	2	7	24	25	24
Lausanne	14	1	1	12	11	35	15

Promotion/Relegation 1995

	P	W	D	L	F	A	Pts
Young Boys Berne + +	14	7	3	4	22	14	17
St Gallen + +	14	5	6	3	20	13	16
Zurich + +	14	5	6	3	19	16	16
Servette + +	14	5	6	3	15	13	16
Kriens*	14	4	7	3	18	14	15
Yverdon*	14	6	3	5	18	15	15
Winterthur*	14	3	7	4	13	13	13
Soleure*	14	0	4	10	4	31	4

Top scorer: Aleksandrov (Neuchatel Xamax) 24.
Cup Final: Sion 4, Grasshoppers 2.

TURKEY

Federation Turque De Football, Konur Sokak No. 10, Ankara Kizilay.
Founded: 1923; *Number of Clubs:* 230; *Number of Players:* 64,521; *National Colours:* White shirts, white shorts, red and white stockings.
Telephone: 0090 212 282 70 10; *Cable:* FUTBOLSPOR ANKARA; *Fax:* 0090 212 282 70 15.

International matches 1994
Czech Republic (h) 1-4, Russia (h) 0-1, Macedonia (a) 2-0, Hungary (a) 2-2, Iceland (h) 5-0, Switzerland (h) 1-2, Italy (a) 1-3.

League Championship wins (1960–95)
Fenerbahce 12; Galatasaray 10; Besiktas 10; Trabzonspor 6.

Cup wins (1963–95)
Galatasaray 10; Besiktas 5; Trabzonspor 5; Fenerbahce 4; Goztepe Izmir 2; Atay Ismir 2; Ankaragucu 2; Eskisehirspor 1; Bursapor 1; Genclerbirligi 1; Sakaryaspor 1.

Final League Table 1994–95

	P	W	D	L	F	A	Pts
Besiktas	34	24	7	3	80	26	79
Trabzonspor	34	23	7	4	79	28	76
Galatasaray	34	21	6	7	76	38	69
Fenerbahce	34	20	7	7	78	35	67
Genclerbirligi	34	17	8	9	61	45	59
Bursa	34	13	12	9	47	39	51
Gaziantep	34	14	6	14	50	51	48
Samsun	34	12	9	13	54	60	45
Kocaeli	34	12	8	14	57	60	44
Altay	34	11	11	12	42	55	44
Kayseri	34	12	6	16	62	69	42
Van	34	11	6	17	36	48	39
Antalya	34	10	8	16	39	46	38
Ankaragucu	34	10	8	16	39	57	38
Denizli	34	8	11	15	42	55	35
Zeytinburnu*	34	7	9	18	35	74	30
Petrolofisi*	34	8	5	21	38	73	29
Adanademir*	34	3	6	25	25	81	15

Top scorer: Aykut (Fenerbahce) 27.
Cup Final: Galatasaray 2, 0, Trabzonspor 3, 1.

UKRAINE

Football Federation of Ukraine, 42, Kuybysheva Street, 252023 Kiev 23, Ukraine.
Founded: 1992; *Number of Teams:* 30,460; *Number of Players:* 757,758.
Telephone: 0070 44 264 72 98; *Fax:* 0070 44 264 75 64.

International matches 1994
Israel (a) 0-1, Belarus (h) 3-1, Bulgaria (a) 1-1, Lithuania (h) 0-2, Slovenia (h) 0-0, Estonia (h) 3-0.

League Championship wins (1992–95)
Dynamo Kiev 3, Tavria Simferopol 1.

Cup wins (1992–95)
Chernomorets 2, Dynamo Kiev 1, Shakhtjor Donetsk 1.

Final League Table 1994–95

	P	W	D	L	F	A	Pts
Dynamo Kiev	34	25	8	1	87	25	83
Dnepr	34	21	8	5	62	29	71
Chernomorets	34	21	7	6	60	31	70
Donetsk	34	18	8	8	54	29	62
Tavria	34	17	8	9	61	37	59
Krivbass	34	13	9	12	36	31	48
Torpedo	34	14	3	17	47	49	45
Karpaty	34	12	9	13	32	36	45
Kremen	34	12	6	16	42	54	42
Ternopol	34	12	5	17	40	39	41
Prekarpate	34	11	8	15	40	52	41
Metallurg	34	10	10	14	41	42	40
Nikolaev	34	11	5	18	33	59	38
Vinnitsa	34	10	7	17	38	52	37
Volyn	34	11	3	20	29	58	36
Zarja	34	10	5	19	36	70	35
Temp	34	10	4	20	31	41	34
Veres	34	8	7	19	28	63	31

Cup Final: Donetsk 1, Dnepr 1.
Donetsk won 8-7 on penalties.

WALES

The Football Association of Wales Limited, Plymouth Chambers, 3 Westgate Street, Cardiff.
Founded: 1876; *Number of Clubs:* 2,326; *Number of Players:* 53,926; *National Colours:* All red. *Telephone:* 01222 372325; *Telex:* 497 363 faw g; *Fax:* 01222 343961.

YUGOSLAVIA

Yugoslav Football Association, P.O. Box 263, Terazije 35, 11000 Beograd.
Founded: 1919; *Number of Clubs:* 6,532; *Number of Players:* 229,024; *National Colours:* Blue shirts, white shorts, red stockings.
*Telephone:*00381 11 33 34 47; *Cable:* JUGOFUDBAL BEOGRAD; *Telex:* 11666 sfj yu; *Fax:* 00381 11 33 34 33.

International matches 1994
Brazil (a) 0-2, Argentina (a) 0-1.

League Championship wins (1923–95)
Red Star Belgrade 20; Partizan Belgrade 13; Hajduk Split 9; Gradjanski Zagreb; BSK Belgrade 5; Dynamo Zagreb 4; Jugoslavija Belgrade 2; Concordia Zagreb 2; FC Sarajevo 2; Vojvodina Novi Sad 2; HASK Zagreb 1; Zeljeznicar 1.

Cup wins (1947–95)
Red Star Belgrade 14; Hajduk Split 9; Dynamo Zagreb 8; Partizan Belgrade 7; BSK Belgrade 2; OFK Belgrade 2; Rejeka 2; Velez Mostar 2; Vardar Skopje 1; Borac Banjaluka 1.

Final League Table 1994–95
Group A

	P	*W*	*D*	*L*	*F*	*A*	Pts
Red Star Belgrade	18	14	3	1	63	17	42
Partizan Belgrade	18	13	2	3	43	20	38
Vojvodina	18	10	4	4	37	26	37
Becej	18	7	4	7	17	27	26
Zemun	18	7	4	7	25	25	25
OFK Belgrade	18	7	3	8	21	26	24
Rad*	18	4	6	8	24	38	20
Borac*	18	3	5	10	15	29	18
Radnicki Belgrade*	18	3	3	12	21	39	17
Hajduk Kula*	18	4	2	12	15	32	15

Group B

	P	*W*	*D*	*L*	*F*	*A*	Pts
Buducnost + +	18	9	4	5	31	23	30
Radnicki Nis + +	18	8	5	5	27	13	29
Proleter + +	18	8	4	6	30	27	24
Napredak + +	18	8	2	8	19	21	23
Obilic	18	7	3	8	25	27	22
Sloboda	18	7	5	6	16	18	21
Loznica	18	7	3	8	26	29	21
Spartak +	18	7	3	8	15	18	20
Sutjeska*	18	7	2	9	23	25	17
Rudar*	18	5	3	10	17	28	16

Top scorer: Milosevic (Partizan Belgrade) 30.
Cup Final: Red Star Belgrade 4, 0, Obilic 0, 0.

SOUTH AMERICA

ARGENTINA

Asociacion Del Futbol Argentina, Viamonte 1366/76, 1053 Buenos Aires.
Founded: 1893; *Number of Clubs:* 3,035; *Number of Players:* 306,365; *National Colours:* Blue & white shirts, black shorts, white stockings.
Telephone: 00541 404 276; *Cable:* FUTBOL BUENOS AIRES; *Telex:* 17848 AFA AR; *Fax:* 54-1 3754410.
League Champions 1994: Independiente.

BOLIVIA

Edificio Federacion Boliviana De Futbol, Av. Libertador Bolivar No. 1148, Casilla de Correo 484, Cochabamba, Bolivia.
Founded: 1925; *Number of Clubs:* 305; *Number of Players:* 15,290; *National Colours:* Green shirts, white shorts, green stockings.
Telephone: 0059142 45889; *Cable:* FEDFUTBOL COCHABAMBA; *Telex:* 6239 FEDBOL; *Fax:* 0059142 82132.
League Champions 1994: Bolivar.

BRAZIL

Confederacao Brasileira De Futebol, Rua Da Alfandega, 70, P.O. Box 1078, 20.070 Rio De Janeiro.
Founded: 1914; *Number of Clubs:* 12,987; *Number of Players:* 551,358; *National Colours:* Yellow shirts, blue shorts, white stockings, green trim.
Telephone: 005521 221 5937; *Cable:* DESPORTOS RIO DE JANEIRO; *Telex:* 2121509 CBDS BR; *Fax:* 005521 252 9294.
League Champions 1994: Palmeiras.

CHILE

Federacion De Futbol De Chile, Avda. Quillin No. 5635, Casilla postal 3733, Correo Central, Santiago de Chile.
Founded: 1895; *Number of Clubs:* 4,598; *Number of Players:* 609,724; *National Colours:* Red shirts, blue shorts, white stockings.
Telephone: 00562 2849000; *Cable:* FEDFUTBOL SANTIAGO DE CHILE; *Telex:* 440474 FEBOL CZ; *Fax:* 00562 2843510.
League Champions 1994: Uni de Chile.

COLOMBIA

Presidencia: Federacion Colombiana De Futbol, Avenida 32, No. 16-22 Apartado Aereo No. 17.602, Bogota D.E.
Founded: 1925; *Number of Clubs:* 3,685; *Number of Players:* 188,050; *National Colours:* Red shirts, blue shorts, tricolour stockings.
Telephone: 00571 2455370; *Telex:* 45598 COLFU CO; *Fax:* 00571 2854340.
League Champions 1994: Atletico Nacional.

ECUADOR

Federacion Ecuatoriana De Futbol, Calle Jose Mascote 1.103 (Piso 2), Luque, Casilla 7447, Guayaquil.
Founded: 1925; *Number of Clubs:* 170; *Number of Players:* 15,700; *National Colours:* Yellow shirts, blue shorts, red stockings.
Telephone: 005934 371674; *Cable:* ECUAFUTBOL GUAYAQUIL; *Telex:* 42970 FEECFU ED; *Fax:* 005934 373320.
League Champions 1994: Emelec.

PARAGUAY

Liga Paraguaya De Futbol, Estadio De Sajonia, Calles Mayor Martinez Y Alejo Garcia, Asuncion.
Founded: 1906; *Number of Clubs:* 1,500; *Number of Players:* 140,000; *National Colours:* Red & white shirts, blue shorts, blue stockings.
Telephone: 0059521 81743; *Telex:* 627 PY FUTBOL; *Fax:* 0059521 81743.
League Champions 1994: Cerro Porteno.

PERU

Federacion Peruana De Futbol, Estadio Nacional, Puerto No. 4, Calle Jose Diaz, Lima.
Founded: 1922; *Number of Clubs:* 10,000; *Number of Players:* 325,650; *National Colours:* White shirts, red trim, white shorts, white stockings.
Telephone: 005114 337070; *Cable* FEPEFUTBOL LIMA; *Fax:* 005114 335552; *Telex:* 20066 FEPEFUT PE.
League Champions 1994: Sporting Cristal.

URUGUAY

Asociacion Uruguaya De Futbol, Guayabo 1531, Montevideo.
Founded: 1900; *Number of Clubs:* 1,091; *Number of Players:* 134,310; *National Colours:* Light blue shirts, black shorts, black stockings.
Telephone: 00598442 407101; *Cable:* FUTBOL MONTEVIDEO; *Fax:* 00598442 407873; *Telex:* AUF UY 22607.
League Champions 1994: Penarol.

VENEZUELA

Federacion Venezolana De Futbol, Avda Este Estadio Nacional, El Paraiso Apdo. Postal 14160, Candelaria, Caracas.
Founded: 1926; *Number of Clubs:* 1,753; *Number of Players:* 63,175; *National Colours:* Magenta shirts, white shorts, white stockings.
Telephone/Fax: 00582 4618010; *Cable:* FEVEFUTBOL CARACAS; *Telex:* 26140 FVFCS VC.
League Champions 1994: Caracas.

ASIA

AFGHANISTAN

The Football Federation of National Olympic Committee, Kabul.
Founded: 1922; *Number of Clubs:* 30; *Number of Players:* 3,300; *National Colours:* White shirts, white shorts, white stockings.
Telephone: 0093 20579; *Cable:* OLYMPIC KABUL.

BAHRAIN

Bahrain Football Association, P.O. Box 5464, Bahrain.
Founded: 1951; *Number of Clubs:* 25; *Number of Players:* 2,030; *National Colours:* White shirts, red shorts, white stockings.
Telephone: 00973 728218; *Cable:* BAHKORA BAHRAIN; *Telex:* 9040 FAB BN; *Fax:* 00973 729361.

BANGLADESH

Bangladesh Football Federation, Stadium, Dhaka 2.
Founded: 1972; *Number of Clubs:* 1,265; *Number of Players:* 30,385; *National Colours:* Orange shirts, white shorts, green stockings.
Telephone: 008802 236072; *Cable:* FOOTBALFED DHAKA; *Telex:* 642460 BHL BJ. *Fax:* 00880–2 863191.

BRUNEI

Brunei Amateur Football Association, P.O. Box 2010, Bandar Seri Begawan 1920, Brunei Darussalam.
Founded: 1959; *Number of Clubs:* 22; *Number of Players:* 830; *National Colours:* Gold shirts, black shorts, gold stockings.
Telephone: 006732 242283; *Cable:* BAFA BRUNEI; *Telex:* BU 2575 Attn: BAFA; *Fax:* 006732 242300.

BURMA (now Myanmar)

Myanmar Football Federation, Aung San Memorial Stadium, Kandawgalay Post Office, Yangon.
Founded: 1947; *Number of Clubs:* 600; *Number of Players:* 21,000; *National Colours:* Red shirts, white shorts, red stockings.
Telephone: 00951 75249; *Cable:* YANGON MYANMAR; *Telex:* 21218 BRCROS BRN.

CAMBODIA

Federation Khmere De Football Association, C.P. 101, Complex Sportif National, Phnom-Penh.
Founded: 1933; *Number of Clubs:* 30; *Number of Players:* 650; *National Colours:* Red shirts, white shorts, red stockings.
Telephone: 0085523 22469; *Cable:* FKFA PHNOMPENH.

CHINA PR

Football Association of The People's Republic of China, 9 Tiyuguan Road, Beijing.
Founded: 1924; *Number of Clubs:* 1,045; *Number of Players:* 2,250,000; *National Colours:* Red shirts, white shorts, red stockings.
Telephone: 00861 7017018; *Cable:* SPORTSCHINE BEIJING; *Telex:* 22034 ACSF CN; *Fax:* 00861 5112533.

HONG KONG

The Hong Kong Football Association Ltd, 55 Fat Kwong Street, Homantin, Kowloon, Hong Kong.
Founded: 1914; *Number of Clubs:* 69; *Number of Players:* 3,274; *National Colours:* Red shirts, white shorts, red stockings.
Telephone: 00852 7129122; *Cable:* FOOTBALL HONG KONG; *Telex:* 40518 FAHKG HX; *Fax:* 00852 7604303.

INDIA

All India Football Federation Green Lawns, Talap, P.O. Box 429, Cannanore 670 002/ Kerala.
Founded: 1937; *Number of Clubs:* 2,000; *Number of Players:* 56,000; *National Colours:* Light blue shirts, white shorts, dark blue stockings.
Telephone: 0091497 500199; *Cable:* SOCCER CALCUTTA; *Telex:* 212216 MCPL IN; *Fax:* 0091 497500923.

INDONESIA

All Indonesia Football Federation, Main Stadium Senayan, Gate VII, P.O. Box 2305, Jakarta.
Founded: 1930; *Number of Clubs:* 2,880; *Number of Players:* 97,000; *National Colours:* Red shirts, white shorts, red stockings.
Telephone: 006221 581541; *Cable:* PSSI JAKARTA; *Telex:* 65739 as; *Fax:* 006221 584386.

IRAN

Football Federation of The Islamic Republic of Iran, Ave Varzandeh No. 10, P.O. Box 11/1642, Tehran.
Founded: 1920; *Number of Clubs:* 6,326; *Number of Players:* 306,000; *National Colours:* Green shirts, white shorts, red stockings.
Telephone: 009821 825534; *Cable:* FOOTBALL IRAN TEHRAN; *Fax:* 009821 8835672; *Telex:* 212691 VARZ IR.

IRAQ

Iraqi Football Association, Olympic Committee Building, Palestine Street, Baghdad.
Founded: 1948; *Number of Clubs:* 155; *Number of Players:* 4,400; *National Colours:* White shirts, white shorts, white stockings.
Telephone: 009641 774 8261; *Cable:* BALL BAGHDAD; *Telex:* 214074 IRFA IK; *Fax:* 009641 7728424.

JAPAN

The Football Association of Japan, 2nd Floor, Gotoh Ikueikai Bldg, 1-10-7 Dogenzaka, Shibuya-Ku, Tokyo 150, Japan.
Founded: 1921; *Number of Clubs:* 13,047; *Number of Players:* 358,989; *National Colours:* Blue shirts, white shorts, blue stockings.
Telephone: 00813 3476211; *Cable:* SOCCERJAPAN TOKYO; *Telex:* 2422975 FOTJPN J; *Fax:* 00813 34762291.

JORDAN

Jordan Football Association, P.O. Box 1054, Amman.
Founded: 1949; *Number of Clubs:* 98; *Number of Players:* 4,305; *National Colours:* White shirts, white shorts, white stockings.
Telephone: 009626 624481; *Cable:* JORDAN FOOTBALL ASSOCIATION AM; *Telex:* 22415 FOBALL JO. *Fax:* 009626 624454.

KAZAKHSTAN

Football Association of the Republic of Kazakhstan, 44 Abai Street, 480072 Almaty, Kazakhstan.
Number of Clubs: 5,793; *Number of Players:* 260,000.
Telephone: 0073272 674492; *Fax:* 0073272 671885; *Telex:* 251347 TREK SU.

KOREA, NORTH

Football Association of The Democratic People's Rep. of Korea, Munsin-Dong 2, Dongdaewon Distr, Pyongyang.
Founded: 1928; *Number of Clubs:* 90; *Number of Players:* 3,420; *National Colours:* Red shirts, white shorts, red stockings.
Telephone: 008502 3998; *Cable:* DPR KOREA FOOTBALL PYONGYANG; *Telex:* 5472 KP; *Fax:* 008502 814403.

KOREA, SOUTH

Korea Football Association, 110-39, Kyeonji-Dong, Chongro-Ku, Seoul.
Founded: 1928; *Number of Clubs:* 476; *Number of Players:* 2,047; *National Colours:* Red shirts, red shorts, red stockings.
Telephone: 00822 7336764; *Cable:* FOOTBALLKOREA SEOUL; *Telex:* KFASEL K 25373; *Fax:* 00822 7352755.

KUWAIT

Kuwait Football Association, Udailiyya, BL. 4, Al-Ittihad St, P.O. Box 2029 (Safat), 13021 Safat.
Founded: 1952; *Number of Clubs:* 14 (senior); *Number of Players:* 1,526; *National Colours:* Blue shirts, white shorts, blue stockings.
Telephone: 00965 2555851; *Cable:* FOOTKUWAIT; *Telex:* FOOTKUW 22600 KT; *Fax:* 00965 2563737.

KYRGYZSTAN

Football Association of Kyrgyzstan, 17 Togolok Moldo Street, 720033 Bishkek, Kyrgyzstan.
Number of Players: 20,000.
Telephone: 0073312 225492; *Fax:* 0073312 267004; *Telex:* 251239 SALAM SU.

LAOS

Federation De Foot-Ball Lao, c/o Dir. Des Sports, Education, Physique Et Artistique, Vientiane.
Founded: 1951; *Number of Clubs:* 76; *Number of Players:* 2,060; *National Colours:* Red shirts, white shorts, blue stockings.
Telephone: 0085621 2741; *Cable:* FOOTBALL VIENTIANE.

LEBANON

Federation Libanaise De Football Association, P.O. Box 4732, Verdun Street, Bristol, Radwan Centre Building, Beirut.
Founded: 1933; *Number of Clubs:* 105; *Number of Players:* 8,125; *National Colours:* Red shirts, white shorts, red stockings.
Telephone/Fax: 009611 868099; *Cable:* FOOTBALL BEIRUT; *Telex:* 21404 LIBALL.

MACAO

Associacao De Futebol De Macau (AFM), P.O. Box 920, Macau.
Founded: 1939; *Number of Clubs:* 52; *Number of Players:* 800; *National Colours:* Green shirts, white shorts, green and white stockings.
Telephone: 00853 71996; *Fax:* 00853 260148; *Cable:* FOOTBALL MACAU.

MALDIVES REPUBLIC

Football Association of Maldives, Attn. Mr. Bandhu Ahamed Saleem, Sports Division, G. Banafsa Magu 20-04, Male.
Founded: 1986; *Number of Clubs: Number of Players: National Colours:* Green shirts, white shorts, green and white stockings.
Telephone: 0096032 5758; *Telex:* 77039 MINHOM MF; *Fax:* 0096032 4739.

MALAYSIA

Football Association of Malaysia, Wisma Fam, Tingkat 4, Jalan SS5A/9, Kelana Jaya, 47301 Petaling, Jaya Selangor.
Founded: 1933; *Number of Clubs:* 450; *Number of Players:* 11,250; *National Colours:* Black and gold shirts, white shorts, black and gold stockings.
Telephone: 00603 7763766; *Cable:* FOOTBALL PETALING JAYA SELANGO; *Telex:* FAM PJ MA 35701; *Fax:* 00603 7757984.

NEPAL

All-Nepal Football Association, Dasharath Rangashala, Tripureshwor, Kathmandu.
Founded: 1951; *Number of Clubs:* 85; *Number of Players:* 2,550; *National Colours:* Red shirts, blue shorts, blue and white stockings.
Telephone: 009771 15703; *Cable:* ANFA KATHMANDU; *Telex:* 2390 NSC NP.

OMAN

Oman Football Association, P.O. Box 6462, Ruwi-Muscat.
Founded: 1978; *Number of Clubs:* 47; *Number of Players:* 2,340; *National Colours:* White shirts, red shorts, white stockings.
Telephone: 00968 593840; *Cable:* FOOTBALL MUSCAT; *Telex:* 5320 FOOTBALL ON; *Fax:* 00968 593736.

PAKISTAN

Pakistan Football Federation, Mr. Hafiz Salman Butt, General Secretary, Punjab University Ground, Lahore 54000, Pakistan.
Founded: 1948; *Number of Clubs:* 882; *Number of Players:* 21,000; *National Colours:* Green shirts, white shorts, green stockings.
Telephone: 009242 5832786; *Cable:* FOOTBALL QUETTA; *Telex:* 47643 PFF PK; *Fax:* 009242 7281541.

PHILIPPINES

Philippine Football Federation, Room 207, Administration Building, Rizal Memorial Sports Complex, Vito Cruz, Metro Manila.
Founded: 1907; *Number of Clubs:* 650; *Number of Players:* 45,000; *National Colours:* Blue shirts, white shorts, blue stockings.
Telephone: 00632 594655; *Cable:* FOOTBALL MANILA; *Telex:* 65014 POC PACA PN; *Fax:* 00632 588317.

QATAR

Qatar Football Association, P.O. Box 5333, Doha.
Founded: 1960; *Number of Clubs:* 8 (senior); *Number of Players:* 1,380; *National Colours:* White shirts, maroon shorts, white stockings.
Telephone: 00974 351641, 454444; *Cable:* FOOTQATAR DOHA; *Telex:* 4749 QATFOT DH; *Fax:* 00974 411660.

SAUDI ARABIA

Saudi Arabian Football Federation, Al Mather Quarter (Olympic Complex), P.O. Box 5844, Riyadh 11432.
Founded: 1959; *Number of Clubs:* 120; *Number of Players:* 9,600; *National Colours:* White shirts, white shorts, white stockings.
Telephone: 009661 4022699; *Cable:* KORA RIYADH; *Telex:* 404300 SAFOTB SJ; *Fax:* 009661 4921276.

SINGAPORE

Football Association of Singapore, Jalan Besar Stadium, Tyrwhitt Road, Singapore 0820.
Founded: 1892; *Number of Clubs:* 250; *Number of Players:* 8,000; *National Colours:* Sky blue shirts, sky blue shorts, sky blue stockings.
Telephone: 0065 2931477; *Cable:* SOCCER SINGAPORE; *Fax:* 0065 2933728; *Telex:* SINFA RS 37683.

SRI LANKA

Football Federation of Sri Lanka, No. 2, Old Grand Stand, Race Course, Reid Avenue, Colombo 7.
Founded: 1939; *Number of Clubs:* 600; *Number of Players:* 18,825; *National Colours:* Maroon shirts, white shorts, white stockings.
Telephone: 00941 696179; *Cable:* SOCCER COLOMBO; *Telex:* 21537 METALIX CE; *Fax:* 00941 580721.

SYRIA

Association Arabe Syrienne De Football, General Sport Fed. Building, October Stadium, Damascus _ Baremke.
Founded: 1936; *Number of Clubs:* 102; *Number of Players:* 30,600; *National Colours:* White shirts, white shorts, white stockings.
Telephone: 0096311 335866; *Cable:* FOOTBALL DAMASCUS; *Telex:* HOTECH 411935.

TAJIKISTAN

Football Federation of Tajikistan, 44, Rudaki Ave., PB 26, 734012 Dushanbe, Tajikistan.
Number of Clubs: 1,804; *Number of Players:* 71,400.
Telephone: 0073772 223603; *Fax:* 0073772 230996; *Telex:* 116119 SAWDO SU.

THAILAND

The Football Association of Thailand, c/o National Stadium, Rama I Road, Bangkok.
Founded: 1916; *Number of Clubs:* 168; *Number of Players:* 15,000; *National Colours:* Crimson shirts, white shorts, crimson stockings.
Telephone: 00662 2141058; *Cable:* FOOTBALL BANGKOK; *Telex:* 20211 FAT TH; *Fax:* 00662 2154494.

TURKMENISTAN

Football Federation of Turkmenistan, 44 Engels Street, 744000 Ashkabad, Turkmenistan.
Number of Players: 75,000.
Telephone: 0073632 253844; *Fax:* 0073632 290646; *Telex:* 116175 TINTO SU.

UNITED ARAB EMIRATES

United Arab Emirates Football Association, P.O. Box 5458, Dubai.
Founded: 1971; *Number of Clubs:* 23 (senior); *Number of Players:* 1,787; *National Colours:* White shirts, white shorts, white stockings.
Telephone: 009714 245636; *Cable:* FOOTBALL EMIRATES DUBAI; *Telex:* 47623 UAEFA EM; *Fax:* 009714 245559.

UZBEKISTAN

Football Federation of Uzbekistan, Karl Marx Street 32, 700047 Tashkent, Uzbekistan.
Number of Clubs: 15,000; *Number of Players:* 217,000.
Telephone: 0073712 322854; *Fax:* 0073712 443183; *Telex:* 116108 PTB SU.

VIETNAM

Association De Football De La Republique Du Viet-Nam, No. 36, Boulevard Tran-Phu, Hanoi. *Founded:* 1962; *Number of Clubs:* 55 (senior); *Number of Players:* 16,000; *National Colours:* Red shirts, white shorts, red stockings.
Telephone: 00844 4867; *Cable:* AFBVN, 36, TRAN-PHU-HANOI.

YEMEN

Yemen Football Association, P.O. Box 908, Sana'a.
Founded: 1962; *Number of Clubs:* 26; *Number of Players:* 1750; *National Colours:* Green.
Telephone: 009672 215720. *Telex:* 2710 YOUTH YE

CONCACAF

ANTIGUA

The Antigua Football Association, P.O. Box 773, St. Johns.
Founded: 1928; *Number of Clubs:* 60; *Number of Players:* 1,008; *National Colours:* Gold shirts, black shorts, black stockings.
Telephone: 001809 4623945; *Cable:* AFA ANTIGUA; *Telex:* 2177 SIDAN AK; *Fax:* 001809 4622649.

ARUBA

Arubaanse Voetbal Bond, Schoenerstraat 2, PO Box 376, Oranjestad, Aruba.
Founded: 1932; *Number of Clubs:* 50; *Number of Players:* 1,000; *National Colours:* Yellow shirts, blue shorts, yellow stockings.
Telephone: 00297 828016; *Fax:* 00297 838438.

BAHAMAS

Bahamas Football Association, P.O. Box N 8434, Nassau, N.P.
Founded: 1967; *Number of Clubs:* 14; *Number of Players:* 700; *National Colours:* Yellow shirts, black shorts, yellow stockings.
Telephone: 001809 3247099; *Cable:* BAHSOCA NASSAU; *Fax:* 001809 3246484.

BARBADOS

Barbados Football Association, P.O. Box 833E, Bridgetown.
Founded: 1910; *Number of Clubs:* 92; *Number of Players:* 1,100; *National Colours;* Royal blue shirts, gold shorts, royal blue stockings.
Telphone: 001809 426 1170; *Cable:* FOOTBALL BRIDGETOWN; *Telex:* 2306 SHAMROCK WB; *Fax:* 001809 4360363.

BELIZE

Belize National Football Association, P.O. Box 1742, Belize City.
Founded: 1986; *National Colours:* Blue shirts, red & white trim, white shorts, blue stockings.
Telephone: 005012 82609 or 82637; *Telex:* 102 FOREIGN BZ.

BERMUDA

The Bermuda Football Association, P.O. Box HM 745, Hamilton 5 HM CX.
Founded: 1928; *Number of Clubs:* 30; *Number of Players:* 1,947; *National Colours:* Blue shirts, white shorts, white stockings.
Telephone: 001809 2952199; *Cable:* FOOTBALL BERMUDA; *Telex:* 3441 BFA BA; *Fax:* 001809 2959773.

CANADA

The Canadian Soccer Association, 1600 James Naismith Drive, Gloucester, Ont. K1B 5N4.
Founded: 1912; *Number of Clubs:* 1,600; *Number of Players:* 224,290; *National Colours:* R ed shirts, red shorts, red stockings.
Telephone: 001613 7485667; *Cable:* SOCCANADA OTTAWA; *Telex:* 0533350; *Fax:* 001613 7451938.

CAYMAN ISLANDS

Cayman Islands Football Association, PO Box 178, George-town, Grand Cayman, Cayman Islands W1.
Number of Clubs: 25; *Number of Players:* 875.
Telephone: 001809 9494733, 809–949 8228. *Fax:* 001809 9498738.

COSTA RICA

Federacion Costarricense De Futbol, Apartado 670-1000, Calle 40, Avda CTL I, San Jose.
Founded: 1921; *Number of Clubs:* 431; *Number of Players:* 12,429; *National Colours:* Red shirts, blue shorts, white stockings.
Telephone: 00506 2221544; *Cable:* FEDEFUTBOL SAN JOSE; *Telex:* 3394 DIDER CR; *Fax:* 00506 2552674.

CUBA

Asociacion De Futbol De Cuba, c/o Comite Olimpico Cubano, Calle 13 No. 601, Esq. C. Vedado, La Habana, ZP4.
Founded: 1924; *Number of Clubs:* 70; *Number of Players:* 12,900; *National Colours:* White shirts, blue shorts, white stockings.
Telephone: 00537 403581; *Cable:* FOOTBALL HABANA; *Telex:* 511332 INDER CU.

DOMINICA

Dominica Football Association, P.O. Box 372, Roseau, Commonwealth of Dominica.
Number of Clubs: 30; *Number of Players:* 500.
Telephone: 00180944 87545; *Fax:* 00180944 81111.

DOMINICAN REPUBLIC

Federacion Dominicana de Futbol, Apartado De Correos No. 1953, Santo Domingo.
Founded: 1953; *Number of Clubs:* 128; *Number of Players:* 10,706; *National Colours:* Blue shirts, white shorts, red stockings.
Telephone: 001809542 6923. *Cable:* FEDOFUTBOL SANTO DOMINGO.

EL SALVADOR

Federacion Salvadorena De Futbol, Av. J.M. Delgado, Col. Escalon, Centro Espanol, Apartado 1029, San Salvador.
Founded: 1936; *Number of Clubs:* 944; *Number of Players:* 21,294; *National Colours:* Blue shirts, blue shorts, blue stockings.
Telephone: 00503 237362; *Cable:* FESFUT SAN SALVADOR; *Fax:* 00503 235893; *Telex:* 20484 FESFUT SAL.

GRENADA

Grenada Football Association, St. Juilles Street, P.O. Box 326, Grenada, West Indies.
Founded: 1924; *Number of Clubs:* 15; *Number of Players:* 200; *National Colours:* Green & yellow shirts, red shorts, green & yellow stockings.
Telephone: 001809 4401986; *Cable:* GRENBALL GRENADA; *Telex:* 3431 CW BUR; *Fax:* 001809 4401986.

GUATEMALA

Federacion Nacional De Futbol De Guatemala C.A., Palacio de los Deportes, Segundo Nivel, Zona 4, Ciudad de Guatemala.
Founded: 1933; *Number of Clubs:* 1,611; *Number of Players:* 43,516; *National Colours:* White/blue diagonal striped shirts, blue shorts, white stockings.
Telephone: 005022 362211; *Fax:* 005022 367268; *Cable:* FEDFUTBOL GUATEMALA.

GUYANA

Guyana Football Association, P.O. Box 10727 Georgetown.
Founded: 1902; *Number of Clubs:* 103; *Number of Players:* 1,665; *National Colours:* Green & yellow shirts, black shorts, white & green stockings.
Telephone: 005922 59458/9; *Cable:* FOOTBALL GUYANA; *Telex:* 2266 RICEBRD GY; *Fax:* 005922 52169.

HAITI

Federation Haitienne De Football, B.P. 2258, Stade Sylvio-Cator, Port-Au-Prince.
Founded: 1904; *Number of Clubs:* 40; *Number of Players:* 4,000; *National Colours:* Red shirts, black shorts, red stockings.
Telephone: 00509 223237; *Cable:* FEDHAFOOB PORT-AU-PRINCE.

HONDURAS

Federacion Nacional Autonoma De Futbol De Honduras, Apartado Postal 827, Costa Oeste Del Est. Nac, Tegucigalpa, De. C.
Founded: 1951; *Number of Clubs:* 1,050; *Number of Players:* 15,300; *National Colours:* Blue shirts, blue shorts, blue stockings.
Telephone: 00504 321897; *Cable* FENAFUTH TEGUCIGALPA; *Telex:* 1209 FENEFUTH; *Fax:* 00504 311428.

JAMAICA

Jamaica Football Federation, Attn. Anthony James, President, Room 8 INSPORTS, Independence Park, Kingston 6.
Founded: 1910; *Number of Clubs:* 266; *Number of Players:* 45,200; *National Colours:* Green shirts, black shorts, green & gold stockings.
Telephone: 001809 9290483; *Fax:* 001809 9622858; *Telex:* 2224 FEDLASCO JA; *Cable:* FOOTBALL JAMAICA KINGSTON.

MEXICO

Federacion Mexicana De Futbol Asociacion, A.C., Abraham Gonzales 74, C.P. 06600, Col. Juarez, Mexico 6, D.F.
Founded: 1927; *Number of Clubs:* 77 (senior); *Number of Players:* 1,402,270; *National Colours:* Green shirts, white shorts, green stockings.
Telephone: 00525 5662155; *Cable:* MEXFUTBOL MEXICO; *Telex:* 1771678 MSUTME; *Fax:* 00525 5667580.

NETHERLANDS ANTILLES

Nederlands Antiliaanse Voetbal Unie, P.O. Box 341, Curacao, N.A.
Founded: 1921; *Number of Clubs:* 85; *Number of Players:* 4,500; *National Colours:* white shirts, white shorts, red stockings.
Telephone:Cable: NAVU CURACAO; *Telex:* 1046 ENNIA NA; *Fax:* 005999 611173.

NICARAGUA

Federacion Nicaraguense De Futbol, Inst. Nicaraguense De Deportes, Apartado Postal 976 6 383, Managua.
Founded: 1968; *Number of Clubs:* 31; *Number of Players:* 160 (senior); *National Colours:* Blue shirts, blue shorts, blue stockings.
Telephone/Fax: 005052 664134; *Cable:* FEDEFOOT MANAGUA; *Telex:* 2156 IND NK.

PANAMA

Federacion Nacional De Futbol De Panama, Estadio Revolucion, Apartado Postal 1523, Panama 1.
Founded: 1937; *Number of Clubs:* 65; *Number of Players:* 4,225; *National Colours:* Red & white shirts, blue shorts, red stockings.
Telephone: 00507 335726; *Cable:* PANAOLIMPIC PANAMA; *Telex:* 2534 INDE PG; *Fax:* 00507 620289.

PUERTO RICO

Federacion Puertorriquena De Futbol, Coliseo Roberto Clemente, P.O. Box 4355, Hato Rey, 00919-4355.
Founded: 1940; *Number of Clubs:* 175; *Number of Players:* 4,200; *National Colurs:* White & red shirts, blue shorts, white & blue stockings.
Telephone/Fax: 001809 7642025; *Cable:* BORIKENFPF; *Telex:* 3450296.

SAINT LUCIA

St Lucia National Football Union, PO Box 255, Castries, St Lucia.
Number of Clubs: 100; *Number of Players:* 4,000; *National Colours:* Blue and white striped shirts, black shorts, blue stockings.
Telephone: 001809 31519; *Fax:* 001809 4524127; *Telex:* 6394 FOR AFF LC.

SAINT KITTS AND NEVIS

St Kitts and Nevis Football Association, P.O. Box 465, Basseterre, St Kitts, West Indies.
Number of Clubs: 36; *Number of Players:* 600.
Telephone: 001809 4652521/ 4654086; *Fax:* 001809 4655501/ 4651042.

SAINT VINCENT & THE GRENADINES

St Vincent & The Grenadines Football Federation, PO Box 1278, Kingstown, St Vincent.
Number of Clubs: 500; *Number of Players:* 5,000.
Telephone: 001809 4561525; *Fax:* 001809 4572970.

SURINAM

Surinaamse Voetbal Bond, Cultuuruinlaan 7, P.O. Box 1223, Paramaribo.
Founded: 1920; *Number of Clubs:* 168; *Number of Players:* 4,430; *National Colours:* Red shirts, white shorts, white stockings.
Telephone: 00597 473112; *Fax:* 00597 479718; *Cable:* SVB Paramaribo.

TRINIDAD AND TOBAGO

Trinidad & Tobago Football Association, Cor. Duke & Scott-Bushe Street, Port of Spain, Trinidad, P.O. Box 400.
Founded: 1906; *Number of Clubs:* 124; *Number of Players:* 5,050; *National Colours:* Red shirts, black shorts, red stockings.
Telephone: 001809 6245183. *Cable:* TRAFA PORT OF SPAIN; *Telex:* 22652 TRAFA WG; *Fax:* 001809 6277661.

USA

United States Soccer Federation, U.S. Soccer House, 1801-1811 S. Prairie Avenue, Chicago, Illinois 60616.
Founded: 1913; *Number of Clubs:* 7,000; *Number of Players:* 1,411,500; *National Colours:* White shirts, blue shorts, red stockings.
Telephone: 001312 5784678; *Telex:* 450024 US SOCCER FED; *Fax:* 001312 5784636.

OCEANIA

AUSTRALIA

Australian Soccer Federation, First Floor, 23-25 Frederick Street, Rockdale, NSW 2216.
Founded: 1961; *Number of Clubs:* 6,816; *Number of Players:* 433,957; *National Colours:* Gold shirts, green shorts, white stockings.
Telephone: 00612 5976611; *Cable:* FOOTBALL SYDNEY; *Telex:* AA 170512; *Fax:* 00612 5993593.

COOK ISLANDS

Cook Islands Football Federation, PO Box 473, Rarotonga, Cook Islands.
Number of Clubs: 9; *Number of Players:* -.
Telephone: 00682 29363; *Fax:* 00682 22095.

FIJI

Fiji Football Association, Mr. J.D. Maharaj, Hon. Secretary, Government Bldgs, P.O.Box 2514, Suva.
Founded: 1946; *Number of Clubs;* 140: *Number of Players:* 21,300; *National Colours:* White shirts, black shorts, black stockings.
Telephone: 00679 300453; *Cable:* FOOTSOCCER SUVA; *Telex:* 2366 FJ; *Fax:* 00679 304642.

NEW ZEALAND

New Zealand Football Association, Inc., P.O. Box 62-532, Central Park, Green Lane, Auckland 6.
Founded: 1891; *Number of Clubs:* 312; *Number of Players:* 52,969; *National Colours:* White shirts, black shorts, white stockings.
Telephone: 00649 5256120; *Fax:* 00649 5256123; *Telex:* NZ 63007 NZFAOFC.

PAPUA NEW GUINEA

Papua New Guinea Football (Soccer) Association Inc., c/o National Sports Institute, P.O. Box 337, Goroka, EHP.
Founded: 1962; *Number of Clubs:* 350; *Number of Players:* 8,250; *National Colours:* Red shirts, black shorts, red stockings.
Telephone: 00675 722391; *Telex:* TOTOTRA NE 23436; *Fax:* 00675 721941.

SOLOMAN ISLANDS

Soloman Islands Football Federation, PO Box 532, Honiara, Soloman Islands.
Number of Players: 4,000; *National Colours:* Blue shirts, white shorts, white stockings.
Telephone: 00677 23553; *Fax:* 00677 20391; *Telex:* HQ 66349.

TAHITI

Federation Tahitienne de Football, Attn. Napoleon Spitz, B.P. 650, Papeete, Tahiti, French Polynesia.
Founded: 1938; *National Colours:* Red shirts, white shorts, white stockings.
Telephone: 00689 420410; *Fax:* 00689 421479; *Telex:* 454 FP.

TONGA

Tonga Football Association, PO Box 36, Nuku'alofa, Kingdom of Tonga.
Number of Clubs: 23; *Number of Players:* 350.
Telephone: 00676 24417; *Fax:* 00676 23555.

VANUATU

Vanuatu Football Federation, P.O. Box 226, Port Vila, Vanuatu.
Founded: 1934; *National Colours:* Gold shirts, black shorts, gold stockings.
Telephone: 00678 22009; *Fax:* 00678 23579.

WESTERN SAMOA

Western Samoa Football (Soccer) Association, Min. of Youth, Sports Culture, Private Bag, Apia.
Founded: 1986; *National Colours:* Blue shirts, white shorts, blue and white stockings.
Telephone: 00685 21420; *Fax:* 00685 24166; *Telex:* 230 SAMGAMES SX.

AFRICA

ALGERIA

Federation Algerienne De Futbol, Route Ahmed Ouaked, Boite Postale No. 39, Alger _ Dely Ibrahim.
Founded: 1962; *Number of Clubs:* 780; *Number of Players:* 58,567; *National Colours:* Green shirts, white shorts, red stockings.
Telephone: 00213 799943; *Cable:* FAFOOT ALGER; *Telex:* 61378. *Fax:* 00213 366181.

ANGOLA

Federation Angolaise De Football, B.P. 3449, Luanda.
Founded: 1977; *Number of Clubs:* 276; *Number of Players:* 4,269; *National Colours:* Red shirts, black shorts, red stockings.
Telephone: 002442 338635/338233; *Cable:* FUTANGOLA; *Telex:* 4072 CIAM AN.

BENIN

Federation Beninoise De Football, B.P. 965, Cotonou.
Founded: 1968; *Number of Clubs:* 117; *Number of Players:* 6,700; *National Colours:* Green shirts, green shorts, green stockings.
Telephone: 00229 330537; *Cable:* FEBEFOOT COTONOU K; *Telex:* 5033 BIMEX COTONOU; *Fax:* 00229 312485.

BOTSWANA

Botswana Football Association, P.O. Box 1396, Gabarone.
Founded: 1976; *National Colours:* Sky blue shirts, white shorts, sky blue stockings.
Telephone: 00267 300279; *Cable:* BOTSBALL GABARONE; *Telex:* 2977 BD; *Fax:* 00267 372911.

BURKINA FASO

Federation Burkinabe De Foot-Ball, B.P. 57, Ouagadougou.

Founded: 1960; *Number of Clubs:* 57; *Number of Players:* 4,672; *National Colours:* Black shirts, white shorts, red stockings.
Telephone: 00226 302850; *Cable:* FEDEFOOT OUAGADOUGOU.

BURUNDI

Federation De Football Du Burundi, B.P. 3426, Bujumbura.
Founded: 1948; *Number of Clubs:* 132; *Number of Players:* 3,930; *National Colours:* Red shirts, white shorts, green stockings.
Telephone: 00257 225160; *Fax:* 00257 228283; *Cable:* FFB BUJA.

CAMEROON

Federation Camerounaise De Football, B.P. 1116, Yaounde.
Founded: 1960; *Number of Clubs:* 200; *Number of Players:* 9,328; *National Colours:* Green shirts, red shorts, yellow stockings.
Telephone: 00237 202538; *Cable:* FECAFOOT YAOUNDE; *Telex:* 8568 JEUNESPO KN.

CAPE VERDE ISLANDS

Federacao Cabo-Verdiana De Futebol, P.O. Box 234, Praia.
Founded: 1986; *National Colours:* Green shirts, green shorts, green stockings.
Telephone: 00238 611362; *Cable:* FCF-CV; *Telex:* 6030 MICDE CV.

CENTRAL AFRICAN REPUBLIC

Federation Centrafricaine De Football, B.P. 344, Bangui.
Founded: 1937; *Number of Clubs:* 256; *Number of Players:* 7,200; *National Colours:* Grey & blue shirts, white shorts, red stockings.
Telephone: 00236 2141; *Cable:* FOOTBANGUI BANGUI.

CONGO

Federation Congolaise De Football, B.P. 4041, Brazzaville.
Founded: 1962; *Number of Clubs:* 250; *Number of Players:* 5,940; *National Colours:* Red shirts, red shorts, white stockings.
Telephone: 00242 815101; *Cable:* FECOFOOT BRAZZAVILLE; *Telex:* 5210 KG.

DJIBOUTI

Federation Djiboutienne de Football, B.P. 1916, Djibouti.
Number of Players: 2,000.
Fax: 00253 356830.

EGYPT

Egyptian Football Association, 5, Shareh Gabalaya, Guezira, Al Borg Post Office, Cairo.
Founded: 1921; *Number of Clubs:* 247; *Number of Players:* 19,735; *National Colours:* Red shirts, white shorts, black stockings.
Telephone: 00202 3401793; *Cable:* KORA CAIRO; *Fax:* 00202 3417817; *Telex:* 23504 KORA.

ETHIOPIA

Ethiopia Football Federation, Addis Ababa Stadium, P.O. Box 1080, Addis Ababa.
Founded: 1943; *Number of Clubs:* 767; *Number of Players:* 20,594; *National Colours:* Green shirts, yellow shorts, red stockings.
Telephone: 002511 514453/514321. *Cable:* FOOTBALL ADDIS ABABA; *Fax:* 002511 513345; *Telex:* 21377 NESCO ET.

GABON

Federation Gabonaise De Football, B.P. 181, Libreville.
Founded: 1962; *Number of Clubs:* 320; *Number of Players:* 10,000; *National Colours:* Blue shirts, white shorts, white stockings.
Telephone: 00241 744747; *Cable:* FEGAFOOT LIBREVILLE; *Telex:* 5642 GO.

GAMBIA

Gambia Football Association, Independence Stadium, Bakau, P.O. Box 523, Banjul.
Founded: 1952; *Number of Clubs:* 30; *Number of Players:* 860; *National Colours:* White & red shirts, white shorts, white stockings.
Telephone: 00220 95834; *Cable:* SPORTS GAMBIA BANJUL; *Fax:* 00220 29837; *Telex:* 2262 FISCO GV.

GHANA

Ghana Football Association, P.O. Box 1272, Accra.
Founded: 1957; *Number of Clubs:* 347; *Number of Players:* 11,275; *National Colours:* White shirts, white shorts, white stockings.
Telephone: 0023321 663924; *Cable:* GFA, ACCRA; *Fax:* 0023321 21662; *Telex:* 2519 SPORTS GH.

GUINEA

Federation Guineenne De Football, P.O. Box 3645, Conakry.
Founded: 1959; *Number of Clubs:* 351; *Number of Players:* 10,000; *National Colours:* Red shirts, yellow shorts, green stockings.
Telephone: 00224 445041; *Cable:* GUINEFOOT CONAKRY; *Telex:* 22302 MJ GE; Fax: 00224 442781.

GUINEA-BISSAU

Federacao De Football Da Guinea-Bissau, Rua4 No. 10-C, Apartado 375, 1035 Bissau Codex.
Founded: 1986; *National Colours: Green shirts, green shorts, green stockings.*
Telephone: 00245 201918; *Cable:* FUTEBOL BISSAU; *Telex:* 205 PUBLICO BI.

GUINEA, EQUATORIAL

Federacion Ecuatoguineana De Futbol, Malabo.
Founded: 1986; *National Colours:* All red.
Telephone: 00240 26523; *Telex:* 9991111 EG; *Cable:* FEGUIFUT/MALABO.

IVORY COAST

Federation Ivoirienne De Football, Stade Felix Houphouet Boigny, B.P. 1202, Abidjan.
Founded: 1960; *Number of Clubs:* 84 (senior); *Number of Players:* 3,655; *National Colours:* Orange shirts, white shorts, green stockings.
Telephone: 00225 240027; *Cable:* FIF ABIDJAN; *Telex:* 42344 FIF CI.

KENYA

Kenya Football Federation, Nyayo National Stadium, P.O. Box 40234, Nairobi.
Founded: 1960; *Number of Clubs:* 351; *Number of Players:* 8,880; *National Colours:* Red shirts, red shorts, red stockings.
Telephone: 002542 501853; *Cable:* KEFF NAIROBI; *Fax:* 002542 501120; *Telex:* 25784 KFF.

LESOTHO

Lesotho Sports Council, P.O. Box 138, Maseru 100, Lesotho.
Founded: 1932; *Number of Clubs:* 88; *Number of Players:* 2,076; *National Colours:* Blue shirts, green shorts, white stockings.
Telephone: 00266 311291; *Cable:* LIPAPALI MASERU; *Fax:* 00266 310914; *Telex:* 4493.

LIBERIA

The Liberia Football Association, P.O. Box 1066, Monrovia 10.
Founded: 1962; *National Colours:* Blue & white shirts, white shorts, blue & white stockings.
Telephone: 00231 222177; *Cable:* LIBFOTASS MONROVIA; *Telex:* 44508 IFA LI. *Fax:* 00231 735003.

LIBYA

Libyan Arab Jamahiriya Football Federation, P.O. Box 5137, Tripoli.
Founded: 1963; *Number of Clubs:* 89; *Number of Players:* 2,941; *National Colours:* Green shirts, white shorts, green stockings.
Telephone: 0021821 46610; *Telex:* 20896 KURATP LY. *Fax:* 0021821 607016.

MADAGASCAR

Federation Malagasy De Football, c/o Comite Nat. De Coordination De Football, B.P. 4409, Antananarivo 101.
Founded: 1961; *Number of Clubs:* 775; *Number of Players:* 23,536; *National Colours:* Red shirts, white shorts, green stockings.
Telephone: 002612 28051; *Telex:* 22393 MOTEL MG.

MALAWI

Football Association of Malawi, P.O. Box 865, Blantyre.
Founded: 1966; *Number of Clubs:* 465; *Number of Players:* 12,500; *National Colours:* Red shirts, red shorts, red stockings.
Telephone: 00265 636686; *Cable:* FOOTBALL BLANTYRE; *Telex:* 4526 SPORTS MI. *Fax:* 00265 636941.

MALI

Federation Malienne De Football, Stade Mamdou Konate, B.P. 1020, Bamako.
Founded: 1960; *Number of Clubs:* 128; *Number of Players:* 5,480; *National Colours:* Green shirts, yellow shorts, red stockings.
Telephone: 00223 224152; *Cable:* MALIFOOT BAMAKO; Telex: 1200/1202.

MAURITANIA

Federation De Foot-Ball De La Rep. Isl. De Mauritanie, B.P. 566, Nouakshott.
Founded: 1961; *Number of Clubs:* 59; *Number of Players:* 1,930; *National Colours:* Green and yellow shirts, blue shorts, green stockings.
Telephone/Fax: 00222 259057; *Telex:* 577 MTN NKTT RIM; *Cable:* FOOTRIM NOUAKSHOTT.

MAURITIUS

Mauritius Football Association, Chancery House, 14 Lislet Geoffroy Street, (2nd Floor, Nos. 303.305), Port Louis.
Founded: 1952; *Number of Clubs:* 397; *Number of Players:* 29,375; *National Colours:* Red shirts, white shorts, red stockings.
Telephone: 00230 2121418, 2125771; *Cable:* MFA PORT LOUIS; *Telex:* 4427 MSA IW; *Fax:* 00230 2084100.

MOROCCO

Federation Royale Marocaine De Football, Av. Ibn Sina, C.N.S. Bellevue, B.P. 51, Rabat.
Founded: 1955; *Number of Clubs:* 350; *Number of Players:* 19,768; *National Colours:* Red shirts, green shorts, red stockings.
Telephone: 002127 672706/08 or 67 26 07; *Cable:* FERMAFOOT RABAT; *Telex:* 32940 FERMFOOT M. *Fax:* 002127 671070

MOZAMBIQUE

Federacao Mocambicana De Futebol, Av. Samora Machel, 11-2, Caixa Postal 1467, Maputo.
Founded: 1978; *Number of Clubs:* 144; *National Colours:* Red shirts, red shorts, red stockings.
Telephone: 002581 26475; *Cable:* MOCAMBOLA MAPUTO; *Telex:* 6575 PERCO MO.

NAMIBIA

Namibia Football Federation, 18 Curt von Francois Str. PO Box 1345, Windhoek 2000; Namibia.
Number of Clubs: 244; *Number of Players:* 7320.
Fax: 0026461 224454.

NIGER

Federation Nigerienne De Football, Stade du 29 Juillet, B.P. 10299, Niamey.
Founded: 1967; *Number of Clubs:* 64; *Number of Players:* 1,525; *National Colours:* Orange shirts, white shorts, green stockings.
Telephone: 00227 734705; *Fax:* 00227 735512; *Telex:* 5527 or 5349; *Cable:* FEDERFOOT NIGER NIAMEY.

NIGERIA

Nigeria Football Association National Sports Commission, National Stadium, P.O. Box 466, Lagos.
Founded: 1945; *Number of Clubs:* 326; *Number of Players:* 80,190; *National Colours:* Green shirts, white shorts, green stockings.
Telephone: 002341 835265; *Cable:* FOOTBALL LAGOS; *Telex:* 26570 NFA NG; *Fax:* 002341 2630810.

RWANDA

Federation Rwandaise De Foot-Ball Amateur, B.P. 2000, Kigali.
Founded: 1972; *Number of Clubs:* 167; *National Colours:* Red shirts, red shorts, red stockings.
Telephone: 00250 82605; *Cable:* MIJENCOOP KIGALI; *Telex:* 22504 PUBLIC RW; *Fax:* 00250 76574.

SENEGAL

Federation Senegalaise De Football, Stade De L'Amitie, Route De L'Aeroport De Yoff, B.P. 130 21, Dakar.
Founded: 1960; *Number of Clubs:* 75 (senior); *Number of Players:* 3,977; *National Colours:* Green shirts, yellow shorts, red stockings.
Telephone: 00221 243524; *Fax:* 00221 220241; *Telex:* 21741; *Cable:* SENEFOOT DAKAR.

SEYCHELLES

Seychelles Football Federation, P.O. Box 580, Mont Fleuri, Victoria.
Founded: 1986; *National Colours:* Green shirts, yellow shorts, red stockings.
Telephone: 00248 24126; *Telex:* 2240 CULSPT SZ; *Fax:* 00248 23518.

ST. THOMAS AND PRINCIPE

Federation Santomense De Fut., P.O. Box 42, Sao Tome.
Founded: 1986; *National Colours:* Green shirts, green shorts, green stockings.
Telephone: 0023912 22311; *Telex:* 213 PUBLICO STP.

SIERRA LEONE

Sierra Leone Amateur Football Association, Siaka Stevens Stadium, Brookfields, P.O. Box 672, Freetown.
Founded: 1967; *Number of Clubs:* 104; *Number of Players:* 8,120; *National Colours:* Green shirts, white shorts, blue stockings.
Telephone: 0023222 41872; *Cable:* SLAFA FREETOWN; *Telex:* 3210 BOOTH SL.

SOMALIA

Somali Football Federation, Ministry of Sports, P.O. Box 247, Mogadishu.
Founded: 1951; *Number of Clubs:* 46 (senior); *Number of Players:* 1,150; *National Colours:* Sky blue shirts, white shorts, white stockings.
Telephone: 002521 20501; *Cable:* SOMALIA FOOTBALL MOGADISHU; *Telex:* 3061 SONOC SM.

SOUTH AFRICA

South African Football Association, First National Bank Stadium, Nasrec; PO Box 910, Johannesburg 2000; South Africa.
Number of Teams: 51,944; *Number of Players:* 1,039,880.
Telephone: 002711 4943522; Fax: 002711 4943447.

SUDAN

Sudan Football Association, P.O. Box 437, Khartoum.
Founded: 1936; *Number of Clubs:* 750; *Number of Players:* 42,200; *National Colours:* White shirts, white shorts, white stockings.
Telephone: 0024911 76633; *Cable:* ALKOURA, KHARTOUM; *Telex:* 23007 KORA SD.

SWAZILAND

National Football Association of Swaziland, P.O. Box 641, Mbabane.
Founded: 1976; *Number of Clubs:* 136; *National Colours:* Blue and gold shirts, white shorts, blue and gold stockings.
Telephone: 00268 46852; *Telex:* 2245 EXP WD.

TANZANIA

Football Association of Tanzania, P.O. Box 1574, Dar Es Salaam.
Founded: 1930; *Number of Clubs:* 51; *National Colours:* Yellow shirts, yellow shorts, yellow stockings.
Telephone: 0025551 32334; *Telex:* 41873 TZ; *Cable:* FAT DAR ES SALAAM.

TOGO

Federation Togolaise De Football, C.P. 5, Lome.
Founded: 1960; *Number of Clubs:* 144; *Number of Players:* 4,346; *National Colours:* Red shirts, white shorts, red stockings.
Telephone: 00228 212698; *Cable:* TOGOFOOT LOME; *Telex:* 5015 CNOT TG. *Fax:* 00228 221314.

TUNISIA

Federation Tunisienne De Football, 2 rue Hamza Abderlmottaleb, El-Menzah VI, Tunis 1004.
Founded: 1957; *Number of Clubs:* 215; *Number of Players:* 18,300; *National Colours:* Red shirts, white shorts, red stockings.
Telephone: 002161 233303, 233544; *Cable:* FOOTBALL TUNIS; *Fax:* 002161 767929; *Telex:* 14783 FTFOOT TN.

UGANDA

Federation of Uganda Football Associations, P.O. Box 20077, Kampala, Uganda.
Founded: 1924; *Number of Clubs:* 400; *Number of Players:* 1,518; *National Colours:* Yellow shirts, black shorts, yellow stockings.
Telephone: 0025641 254477; *Cable:* FUFA KAMPALA; *Telex:* 61272; *Fax:* 0025641 245580; *Telegrams:* fufa lugogo stadium.

ZAIRE

Federation Zairoise De Football-Association, P.O. Box 1284, rue Dima No. 10, Kinshasa 1.
Founded: 1919; *Number of Clubs:* 3,800; *Number of Players:* 64,627; *National Colours:* Green shirts, yellow shorts, yellow stockings. *Cable:* FEZAFA KINSHASA; *Telex:* 63915. *Fax:* 0024312 506555.

ZAMBIA

Football Association of Zambia, P.O. Box 347 51, Lusaka.
Founded: 1929; *Number of Clubs:* 20 (senior); *Number of Players:* 4,100; *National Colours:* Green shirts, white shorts, black stockings.
Telephone: 002601 221145; *Cable:* FOOTBALL LUSAKA; *Telex:* 40204 FAZ ZA; *Fax:* 002601 225046.

ZIMBABWE

Zimbabwe Football Association, P.O. Box 8343, Causeway, Harare.
Founded: 1965; *National Colours:* White shirts, black shorts, black stockings.
Telephone: 002634 791275; *Cable:* SOCCER HARARE; *Telex:* 22299 SOCCER ZW; *Fax:* 002634 793320.
Other addition: CHAD (readmitted).

OTHER INTERNATIONAL TOURNAMENTS

BALTIC CUP

Latvia 2, Estonia 0
Lithuania 7, Estonia 0
Latvia 2, Lithuania 0

	P	*W*	*D*	*L*	*F*	*A*	Pts
Latvia	2	2	0	0	4	0	4
Lithuania	2	1	0	1	7	2	2
Estonia	2	0	0	2	0	9	0

US CUP

USA 3, Nigeria 2
Colombia 1, Nigeria 0
USA 4, Mexico 0
Mexico 0, Colombia 0
Mexico 2, Nigeria 1
USA 0, Colombia 0

	P	*W*	*D*	*L*	*F*	*A*	Pts
USA	3	2	1	0	7	2	7
Colombia	3	1	2	0	1	0	5
Mexico	3	1	1	1	2	5	4
Nigeria	3	0	0	3	3	6	0

COPA CENTENARIO (in Chile)

Paraguay 0, Turkey 0
Chile 3, New Zealand 1
Chile 0, Paraguay 1
Chile 0, Turkey 0
Paraguay 3, New Zealand 2
Turkey 2, New Zealand 1

	P	*W*	*D*	*L*	*F*	*A*	Pts
Paraguay	3	2	1	0	4	2	7
Turkey	3	1	2	0	2	1	5
Chile	3	1	1	1	3	2	4
New Zealand	3	0	0	3	4	8	0

CENTENARY TOURNAMENT (in Switzerland)

Switzerland 0, Italy 1
Italy 0, Germany 2
Switzerland 1, Germany 2

	P	*W*	*D*	*L*	*F*	*A*	Pts
Germany	2	2	0	0	4	1	6
Italy	2	1	0	1	1	2	3
Switzerland	2	0	0	2	1	3	0

EUROPEAN FOOTBALL CHAMPIONSHIP

(formerly EUROPEAN NATIONS' CUP)

Year	*Winners*		*Runners-up*		*Venue*	*Attendance*
1960	USSR	2	Yugoslavia	1	Paris	17,966
1964	Spain	2	USSR	1	Madrid	120,000
1968	Italy	2	Yugoslavia	0	Rome	60,000
	After 1-1 draw					75,000
1972	West Germany	3	USSR	0	Brussels	43,437
1976	Czechoslovakia	2	West Germany	2	Belgrade	45,000
	(Czechoslovakia won on penalties)					
1980	West Germany	2	Belgium	1	Rome	47,864
1984	France	2	Spain	0	Paris	48,000
1988	Holland	2	USSR	0	Munich	72,308
1992	Denmark	2	Germany	0	Gothenburg	37,800

EUROPEAN CHAMPIONSHIP 1994–96

Qualifying Tournament

Qualifying tournament

Group 1

Tel Aviv, 4 September 1994, 3500

Israel (1) 2 *(Harazi R 43, 58)*
Poland (0) 1 *(Kosecki 80)*

Israel: Ginzburg; Harazi A, Klinger, Balbul, Glam, Hazan, Berkovitch (Levi 86), Banin, Revivo, Rosenthal (Atar 89), Harazi R.
Poland: Wandzik; Bak, Szewczyk, Waldoch, Maciejewski, Lapinski, Jalocha (Chenik 46), Mielcarski (Gesior 58), Brzeczek, Kosecki, Kowalczyk.
Referee: Van den Wijngaert (Belgium).

Bratislava, 7 September 1994, 14,238

Slovakia (0) 0
France (0) 0

Slovakia: Molnar; Glonek, Stupala, Zeman, Tittel, Kinder, Tomaschek, Kristofik, Zvara (Penska 63), Rusnak (Weiss 80), Moravcik.
France: Lama; Angloma, Blanc, Roche, Di Meco, Deschamps, Le Guen, Ginola, Djorkaeff (Lizarazu 82), Cantona, Pedros (Dugarry 63).
Referee: Mikkelsen (Denmark).

Bucharest, 7 September 1994, 10,000

Romania (1) 3 *(Belodedici 43, Petrescu 58, Raducioiu 88)*
Azerbaijan (0) 0

Romania: Stelea (Stangaciu 85); Petrescu, Prodan, Belodedici, Selymes (Carstea 82), Lupescu (Timofte D 75), Popescu, Munteanu, Lacatus, Raducioiu, Dumitrescu.
Azerbaijan: Jidkov; Alazerdiev, Asadov, Achmedov T, Drozdov, Abusev, Diniev, Guseynov (Agalev 80), Alekperov, Suleimanov (Ryzalev 59), Kasumov.
Referee: Sedlacek (Austria).

St Etienne, 8 October 1994, 31,744

France (0) 0
Romania (0) 0

France: Lama; Blanc, Angloma, Roche, Lizarazu, Karembeu, Desailly, Loko (Dugarry 83), Pedros, Cantona, Ouedec (Zidane 71).
Romania: Stelea; Belodedici, Prodan, Petrescu, Lupescu, Timofte (Lacatus 71), Popescu, Hagi, Selymes, Dumitrescu, Raducioiu (Panduru 80).
Referee: Sundell (Sweden).

Tel Aviv, 12 October 1994, 10,000

Israel (2) 2 *(Harazi R 23, Banin 32 (pen))*
Slovakia (2) 2 *(Rusnak 5, Moravcik 14)*

Israel: Ginzburg; Balbul, Glam, Klinger (Shelach 67), Harazi A, Hazan, Berkovitch, Banin (Nimni 60), Revivo, Harazi R, Rosenthal.
Slovakia: Molnar; Stupala, Tittel, Glonek, Kinder, Zeman, Kristofik, Dubovsky, Weiss (Kozak 75), Moravcik, Rusnak (Zvara 76).
Referee: Blankenstein (Holland).

Mielec, 12 October 1994, 10,000

Poland (1) 1 *(Juskowiak 44)*
Azerbaijan (0) 0

Poland: Wandzik; Waldoch, Jaskulski, Lapinski (Maciejewski 79), Kozminski (Fedoruk 70), Swierczewski P, Czereszewski, Brzeczek, Kosecki, Warzycha, Juskowiak.
Azerbaijan: Jidkov; Alazerdiev, Kerimov, Achmedov T, Asadov, Abusev (Kurbanov 89), Guseynov, Diniev, Mardanov, Kasumov, Alekperov.
Referee: Koho (Finland).

Bucharest, 12 November 1994, 15,000

Romania (1) 3 *(Popescu 7, Hagi 46, Prodan 80)*
Slovakia (0) 2 *(Dubovsky 56, Chvila 78)*

Romania: Stelea; Petrescu, Belodedici, Prodan, Munteanu, Lacatus (Timofte 75), Popescu, Lupescu, Hagi, Raducioiu (Vladoiu 83), Dumitrescu.
Slovakia: Molnar; Stupala, Chvila, Tittel, Glonek, Kinder, Tomaschek, Kristofik, Moravcik, Penska (Timko 46), Dubovsky.
Referee: Zhuk (Russia).

Zabrze, 16 November 1994, 20,000

Poland (0) 0
France (0) 0

Poland: Wandzik; Jakulski, Czereszewski, Swierczewski M, Waldoch, Swierczewski P, Baluszynski (Gesior 80), Kozminski (Bak 28), Juskowiak, Kosecki, Warzycha.

France: Lama; Angloma, Blanc, Roche, Di Meco, Karembeu, Desailly, Le Guen, Ouedec (Dugarry 76), Cantona, Pedros (Djorkaeff 25).
Referee: Amendolia (Italy).

Trabzon, 16 November 1994, 3000

Azerbaijan (0) 0

Israel (1) 2 *(Harazi R 30, Rosenthal 51)*

Azerbaijan: Jidkov; Alazerdiev, Achmedov T, Mayorov (Adjaiev 46), Gadirov, Asadov, Guseynov (Ryzalev 77), Diniev, Kasumov, Suleimanov, Alekperov.
Israel: Ginzburg; Balbul, Harazi A, Klinger, Glam, Hazan, Banin, Berkovitch (Nimni 66), Revivo, Harazi R (Shelah 83), Rosenthal.
Referee: Vagner (Hungary).

Tel Aviv, 14 December 1994, 40,000

Israel (0) 1 *(Rosenthal 84)*

Romania (0) 1 *(Lacatus 70)*

Israel: Ginzburg; Balbul, Klinger, Harazi A, Glam, Hazan, Berkovitch, Levi R (Zohar 75), Revivo, Harazi R (Shelach 90), Rosenthal.
Romania: Stelea; Petrescu, Belodedici, Prodan, Selymes, Hagi, Popescu, Lupescu, Munteanu (Vladoiu 52), Lacatus, Dumitrescu (Galca 74).
Referee: Navarrete (Spain).

Trabzon, 14 December 1994, 4000

Azerbaijan (0) 0

France (1) 2 *(Papin 25, Loko 56)*

Azerbaijan: Jidkov (Gasanov 41); Alazerdiev, Varapzade, Abusev, Agalev, Jabarov, Asadov (Kerinov 78), Kasumov, Diniev (Ryzalev 78), Guseynov, Alekperov.
France: Lama; Angloma, Roche, Blanc, Di Meco, Desailly (Ferri 71), Le Guen, Cantona, Loko, Papin, Pedros (Martins 76).
Referee: Pedersen (Norway).

Bucharest, 29 March 1995, 22,000

Romania (1) 2 *(Raducioiu 45, Wandzik 55 (og))*

Poland (1) 1 *(Juskowiak 43 (pen))*

Romania: Stelea; Petrescu, Prodan, Belodedici, Selymes, Hagi (Vladoiu 88), Dumitrescu, Popescu, Munteanu, Lacatus (Lupu 46), Raducioiu.
Poland: Wandzik; Jaskulski, Swierczewski M, Waldoch, Swierczewski P, Novak (Wieszczycki 58), Czereszewski (Sokolowski 73), Baluszynski, Warzycha K, Juskowiak, Kosecki.
Referee: Rothlisberger (Switzerland).

Kosice, 29 March 1995, 12,400

Slovakia (3) 4 *(Tittel 35, Timko 40, 50, Dubovsky 45 (pen))*

Azerbaijan (0) 1 *(Suleimanov 80 (pen))*

Slovakia: Molnar; Stupala, Glonek, Zeman, Kinder, Kristofik, Tittel, Moravcik (Prazenica 73), Dubovsky, Timko, Penska.
Azerbaijan: Gasanov; Aliev (Kapirov 65), Varapzade, Abusev, Jabarov, Asadov, Guseynov, Agalev, Diniev, Suleimanov, Kasumov (Alekperov 56).
Referee: Nikakis (Greece).

Tel Aviv, 29 March 1995, 45,000

Israel (0) 0

France (0) 0

Israel: Ginzburg; Halfon, Klinger, Harazi A, Glam, Hazan, Banin, Revivo, Berkovitch (Zohar 64), Rosenthal, Harazi R.

France: Lama; Angloma, Roche, Blanc, Di Meco, Desailly, Le Guen, Martins (Djorkaeff 78), Pedros, Loko, Ouedec (Ginola 66).
Referee: McCluskey (Scotland).

Zabrze, 25 April 1995, 5500

Poland (1) 4 *(Nowak 1, Juskowiak 50, Kowalczyk 55, Kosecki 62)*

Israel (2) 3 *(Rosenthal 37, Revivo 42, Zohar 77)*

Poland: Wandzik; Lapinski, Swierczewski M, Waldoch, Swierczewski P, Nowak (Bukalski 46), Kozminski, Baluszynski (Wieszczycki 46), Juskowiak, Kowalczyk, Kosecki.
Israel: Ginzburg; Halfon, Harazi A, Klinger, Glam, Hazan, Banin, Revivo, Berkovitch, Mizrahi (Zohar 73), Rosenthal.
Referee: Anders (Sweden).

Trabzon, 26 April 1995, 500

Azerbaijan (1) 1 *(Suleimanov 4)*

Romania (2) 4 *(Raducioiu 1 (pen), 68, 76, Dumitrescu 38)*

Azerbaijan: Gasanov; Asadov, Ghesmam, Akhmedov (Varapzade 21), Jabarov (Kapirov 75), Abusev, Guseynov, Diniev, Lukin, Suleimanov, Alekperov.
Romania: Stelea; Petrescu, Prodan, Belodedici, Selymes, Popescu (Timofte D 81), Munteanu, Lupescu, Dumitrescu, Lacatus (Lupu 69), Raducioiu.
Referee: Momirov (Bulgaria).

Nantes, 26 April 1995, 26,000

France (2) 4 *(Kristofik 27 (og), Ginola 42, Blanc 57, Guerin 62)*

Slovakia (0) 0

France: Lama; Angloma, Blanc, Roche, Di Meco, Deschamps, Desailly, Guerin, Zidane (Djorkaeff 73), Loko, Ginola.
Slovakia: Molnar; Stupala, Zeman, Glonek, Kinder, Kristofik, Tittel, Tomaschek (Timko 46), Moravcik, Penska (Maixner 73), Dubovsky.
Referee: Heynemann (Germany).

Zabrze, 7 June 1995, 20,000

Poland (1) 5 *(Juskowiak 10, 70, Wieszczycki 58, Kosecki 63, Nowak 70)*

Slovakia (0) 0

Poland: Szczesny; Jaskulski (Czereszewski 76), Zielinski, Bukalski, Waldoch, Kozminski, Swierczewski P, Nowak, Kosecki, Juskowiak, Kowalczyk, (Wieszczycki 46).
Slovakia: Vencel; Kozak (Penska 60), Zeman, Glonek, Prazenica, Tomaschek, Solar, Kristofik (Weiss 71), Timko, Dubovsky, Moravcik.
Referee: Sedlacek (Austria).

Bucharest, 7 June 1995, 20,000

Romania (1) 2 *(Lacatus 16, Munteanu 65)*

Israel (0) 1 *(Berkovitch 50)*

Romania: Stelea; Petrescu, Prodan, Belodedici, Selymes, Munteanu, Lupescu, Lupu (Panduru 87), Dumitrescu (Vladoiu 63), Lacatus, Raducioiu.

Israel: Cohen; Halfon, Shelah (Balbul 65) (Zohar 74), Bruner, Amsalem, Hazan, Klinger, Mizrahi, Banin, Berkovitch, Dricks.
Referee: Pedersen (Norway).

	P	*W*	*D*	*L*	*F*	*A*	*Pts*
Romania	7	5	2	0	15	6	17
France	6	2	4	0	6	0	10
Poland	6	3	1	2	12	7	10
Israel	7	2	3	2	11	10	9
Slovakia	6	1	2	3	8	15	5
Azerbaijan	6	0	0	6	2	16	0

Group 2

Brussels, 7 September 1994, 11,000

Belgium (1) 2 *(Oliveira 3, Degryse 73)*

Armenia (0) 0

Belgium: Preud'homme; Genaux, De Wolf, Albert, Smidts, Staelens (Emmers 75), Van der Elst F, Van der Heyden (Boffin 67), Degryse, Oliveira, Weber.
Armenia: Arm. Petrossian; Art. Petrossian, Kerpasian, Tonoian, Ovsepian, Khatchatrian, Soukiassian, Oganesian, Shakhgeldian (Avetissian 46), Grigorian (Mikhitarian 75), Michitarian.
Referee: Ferry (Northern Ireland).

Limassol, 7 September 1994, 12,000

Cyprus (1) 1 *(Sotiriou 35)*

Spain (2) 2 *(Higuera 18, 26)*

Cyprus: Panayiotou; Costa, Constandinou, Christophi M, Charalambous M, Pittas, Ioannou D, Phasouliotis (Malekos 62), Savvides (Andreou 77), Gogic, Sotiriou.
Spain: Zubizarreta; Voro, Nadal, Camarasa, Sergi, Goicoechea, Hierro, Guerrero, Guardiola (Caminero 63), Higuera, Amavisca (Ciganda 78).
Referee: Batta (France).

Skopje, 7 September 1994, 22,000

Macedonia (1) 1 *(Stojkovski 4)*

Denmark (0) 1 *(Povlsen 87)*

Macedonia: Traciev; Stanojkovic, Najdoski, Markovski, Jovanovski, Stojkovski, Boskovski (Serafimovski 82), Djurovski B, Babunski (Kanatlarovski 65), Pancev, Micevski.
Denmark: Schmeichel; Helveg, Rieper, Olsen, Friis-Hansen, Steen-Nielsen, Jensen J (Larsen 65), Vilfort (Povlsen 50), Christensen B, Laudrup M, Laudrup B.
Referee: Van der Ende (Holland).

Erevan, 8 October 1994, 6000

Armenia (0) 0

Cyprus (0) 0

Armenia: Abramian; Soukissian, Hatslatian (Kerpasian 46), Donodjian, Ovsepian, Vardanian, Bedrossian, Grigorian, Adamian, Abedasian A, Mikhitarian (Abedasian B 79).
Cyprus: Christophi M; Kalotheou, Pittas, Ioannou D, Stephani, Zembashis, Charalambous, Sotiriou, Gogic, Phasouliotis (Malekos 70), Savvides.
Referee: Bremisla (Poland).

Copenhagen, 12 October 1994, 40,000

Denmark (1) 3 *(Vilfort 35, Jensen J 72, Strudal 86)*

Belgium (1) 1 *(Degryse 31)*

Denmark: Schmeichel; Helveg, Olsen, Rieper, Friis-Hansen, Risager (Kjeldbjerg 78), Vilfort (Jensen J 72), Laudrup M, Steen-Nielsen, Laudrup B, Strudal.
Belgium: Bodart; Genaux, Van Meir, Albert, Smidts, Borkelmans (Oliveira 77), Verheyen, Van der Elst, Staelens, Degryse, Weber.
Referee: Pairetto (Italy).

Skopje, 12 October 1994, 30,000

Macedonia (0) 0

Spain (2) 2 *(Julio Salinas 16, 25)*

Macedonia: Traciev (Micevski 50); Stanojkovic, Stojkovski, Djurovski B, Najdoski, Jovanovski, Boskovski, Savevski, Babunski (Markovski 39), Djurovski M (Serafimovski 70), Micevski.
Spain: Zubizarreta; Ferrer, Abelardo, Alkorta, Caminero, Nadal, Hierro (Amavisca 76), Sergi, Luis Enrique, Higuera, Julio Salinas (Loggi 65).
Referee: Grabner (Austria).

Brussels, 16 November 1994, 17,000

Belgium (1) 1 *(Verheyen 31)*

Macedonia (0) 1 *(Boskovski 54)*

Belgium: Preud'homme; Genaux, Crasson, Smidts, Boffin, Staelens, Van der Elst, Walem (De Bilde 72), Verheyen, Degryse, Nilis.
Macedonia: Celeski; Stanojkovic, Djurovski B, Najdoski, Janevski, Jovanovski, Boskovski (Kanatlarovski 87), Markovski, Djurovski M (Serafimovski 80), Stojkovski, Micevski T.
Referee: Kusainov (Russia).

Limassol, 16 November 1994, 8000

Cyprus (1) 2 *(Sotiriou 7, Phasouliotis 87)*

Armenia (0) 0

Cyprus: Christophi M; Andreou, Ioannou, Evagoras, Stephani, Zembashis (Elia 89), Malekos (Phasouliotis 68), Savvides, Pittas, Gogic, Sotiriou.
Armenia: Abramian; Tonoian, Oganesian, Vardanian, Kerpasian, Petrossian Art, Grigorian, Mikhitarian (Abedasian B 85), Obsenpian, Soukiassian, Egspegian (Abedasian A 69).
Referee: Ashby (England).

Seville, 16 November 1994, 38,000

Spain (1) 3 *(Nadal 41, Donato 57, Luis Enrique 87)*

Denmark (0) 0

Spain: Zubizarreta; Ferrer, Belsue, Alkorta, Abelardo, Nadal, Luis Enrique, Caminero (Bakero 72), Sergi, Donato, Julio Salinas (Higuera 57).
Denmark: Schmeichel; Helveg, Rieper, Olsen, Risager, Friis Hansen (Christensen B 65), Steen-Nielsen (Jensen J 46), Vilfort, Strudal, Laudrup B, Laudrup M.
Referee: McCluskey (Scotland).

Skopje, 17 December 1994, 12,000

Macedonia (2) 3 *(Djurovski B 15, 36, 89)*

Cyprus (0) 0

Macedonia: Celeski; Stanojkovic, Janevski, Najdoski, Stojkovski, Markovski, Babunski (Jovanovski 72), Djurovski B, Boskovski (Serafimovski 86), Djurovski M, Micevski.
Cyprus: Christophi M; Kalotheou, Charalambous M, Ioannou, Christophi E, Stephani, Charalambous C, Phasouliotis, Savvides (Malekos 67), Gogic, Sotiriou (Andreou 78).
Referee: Strampe (Germany).

Brussels, 17 December 1994, 25,000

Belgium (1) 1 *(Degryse 6)*

Spain (1) 4 *(Hierro 28, Donato 55 (pen), Julio Salinas 68, Luis Enrique 89)*

Belgium: Preud'homme; Genaux, Crasson, Albert, Smidts, Bettagno, Van der Elst F, Staelens, Boffin, Degryse, De Bilde.
Spain: Zubizaretta; Belsue, Abelardo, Nadal, Alkorta, Hierro, Sergi, Donato, Guerrero (Voro 57), Luis Enrique, Julio Salinas (Goicoechea 70).
Referee: Cakar (Turkey).

Seville, 29 March 1995, 27,000

Spain (1) 1 *(Guerrero 24)*
Belgium (1) 1 *(Degryse 25)*

Spain: Zubizaretta; Belsue, Abelardo, Nadal, Sergi, Hierro, Luis Enrique, Guerrero (Higuera 37), Donato, Julio Salinas (Pizzi 63), Amavisca.
Belgium: Bodart; Genaux, Medved, Renier, Smidts, Walem (Verheyen 68), Karagiannis (Crasson 83), Staelens, Degryse, De Bilde, Schepens.
Referee: Harrel (France).

Limassol, 29 March 1995, 15,000

Cyprus (1) 1 *(Agathocleous 45)*
Denmark (1) 1 *(Schjonberg 2)*

Cyprus: Panayiotou; Costa, Pittas, Ioannou D, Charalambous, Christodolou, Engomitis, Andreou A, Hadjilukas (Constandinou C 89), Gogic, Agathocleous.
Denmark: Schmeichel; Laursen, Rieper, Friis-Hansen (Helveg 46), Hogh, Schjonberg, Steen-Nielsen, Nielsen P, Laudrup M, Rasmussen, Laudrup B.
Referee: Shorte (Eire).

Erevan, 26 April 1995, 40,000

Armenia (0) 0
Spain (0) 2 *(Amavisca 49, Goicoechea 63)*

Armenia: Abramian; Soukissian, Hovsepian, Tonoian, Hovanesian, Vardanian, Petrossian, Grigorian (Takhmazian 65), Mikhitarian, Shakhgeldian, Adamian (Avetissian 55).
Spain: Zubizarreta; Belsue, Alkorta, Karanka, Otero, Nadal, Donato (Camarasa 69), Luis Enrique, Goicoechea, Pizzi (Julio Salinas 58), Amavisca.
Referee: Porumboiu (Romania).

Copenhagen, 26 April 1995, 38,888

Denmark (0) 1 *(Nielsen P 70)*
Macedonia (0) 0

Denmark: Schmeichel; Laursen, Rieper, Hogh, Schjonberg, Thomsen, Steen-Nielsen, Rasmussen (Andersen 46), Laudrup M, Nielsen P (Helveg 78), Laudrup B.
Macedonia: Celeski; Stanojkovic, Stojkovski, Najdoski, Markovski (Nedzmedine 26), Jovanovski, Boskovski, Djurovski, Micevski, Pancev, Serafimovski (Stojkoski 77).
Referee: Ihring (Slovakia).

Brussels, 26 April 1995, 13,000

Belgium (1) 2 *(Karagiannis 20, Schepens 47)*
Cyprus (0) 0

Belgium: Bodart; Renier, Medved, Grun, Smidts, Staelens, Karagiannis, Degryse, Schepens, Nilis, De Bilde (Goossens 81).
Cyprus: Panayiotou; Kalotheou, Charalambous M, Ioannou D, Pittas, Christodolou, Larkou, Andreou A, Engomitis, Agathocleous (Larkou 62), Papavassiliou (Sotiriou 85).
Referee: Elleray (England).

Erevan, 10 May 1995, 12,500

Armenia (1) 2 *(Grigorian 21, 51)*
Macedonia (0) 2 *(Hristov 59, Markovski 70)*

Armenia: Abramian; Soukissian, Hovsepian, Tonoian, Hovanesian, Vardanian, Petrossian, Grigorian, Mikhitarian (Gspeyan), Shakhgeldian, Avetissian (Takhmazian).
Macedonia: Celeski; Stanojkovic, Stojkovski, Najdoski, Markovski, Jovanovski (Kanatlarovski), Hristov, Babunski, Micevski (Nedzmedine), Pancev, Serafimovski.
Referee: Fajilstrom (Sweden).

Copenhagen, 7 June 1995, 40,199

Denmark (1) 4 *(Vilfort 45, 50, Laudrup B 58, Laudrup M 75)*
Cyprus (0) 0

Denmark: Schmeichel; Laursen, Rieper, Hogh, Schjonberg, Steen-Nielsen (Rasmussen P 46), Jensen, Vilfort (Andersen E 87), Beck, Laudrup M, Laudrup B.
Cyprus: Petrides; Costa, Pittas, Christodolou, Charalambous, Andreou A, Engomitis, Larkou, Hadjilucas (Phasouliotis 60), Gogic, Sotiriou (Andreou P 68).
Referee: Muller (Switzerland).

Seville, 7 June 1995, 20,000

Spain (0) 1 *(Hierro 64 (pen))*
Armenia (0) 0

Spain: Zubizarreta; Belsue, Aranzabal, Alkorta, Abelardo, Hierro, Goicoechea (Julio Salinas 46), Guerrero (Caminero 78), Nadal, Luis Enrique, Amavisca.
Armenia: Abrahamian; Sosoukiassian, Haousepian, Tonoyan, Nighoyan (Ter-petrossian 71), Valdanian, Petrossian (Avetissian V 76), Tahmazian, Mekhitarian, Shahgheldian, Avetissian A.
Referee: Philippi (Luxembourg).

Skopje, 7 June 1995, *

Macedonia (0) 0
Belgium (4) 5 *(Grun 15, Scifo 18, 60, Schepens 28, Versavel 43)*

Macedonia: Celeski; Stanojkovic, Najdovski, Stojkoviski, Boskovski, Djurovski (Hristov 61), Janevski, Bubunski, Micevski, Pancev, Serafimovski.
Belgium: Bodart; Genaux, Renier, Grun, Smidts, Staelens, Karagiannis, Schepens (Leonard 83), Scifo, Versavel, De Bilde.
Referee: Wojciki (Poland).
**Match played behind closed doors as disciplinary punishment.*

	P	*W*	*D*	*L*	*F*	*A*	*Pts*
Spain	7	6	1	0	15	3	19
Belgium	7	3	2	2	13	9	11
Denmark	6	3	2	1	10	6	11
Macedonia	7	1	3	3	7	12	6
Cyprus	7	1	2	4	4	12	5
Armenia	6	0	2	4	2	9	2

Group 3

Reykjavik, 7 September 1994, 15,000

Iceland (0) 0
Sweden (1) 1 *(Ingesson 37)*

Iceland: Kristinsson B; Kristinsson R, Jonsson K, Bergsson, Gislason, Gudjohnsen, Orlygsson (Gunnlaugsson B 60), Jonsson S, Stefansson, Gunnlaugsson A, Sverrisson.
Sweden: Ravelli; Nilsson, Andersson P, Bjorklund, Ljung, Brolin, Mild, Schwarz, Ingesson, Dahlin (Larsson 67), Andersson K.
Referee: Mottram (Scotland).

Budapest, 7 September 1994, 10,000

Hungary (2) 2 *(Kiprich 4, Halmai 45)*
Turkey (0) 2 *(Hakan 66, Bulent 70)*

Hungary: Petry; Telek, Meszoly, Lipcsei, Kozma, Halmai, Detari, Urban, Duro (Banfi 62), Kiprich (Wukovics 67), Kovacs.
Turkey: Engin; Gokhan (Arif 46), Recep, Bulent, Ilker, Ogun, Oguz, Tugay, Orhan, Ertugrul (Abdullah 87), Hakan.
Referee: Pairetto (Italy).

Istanbul, 12 October 1994, 20,000

Turkey (3) 5 *(Saffet 11, 28, Hakan 30, 62, Yalcin 65)*

Iceland (0) 0

Turkey: Engin; Gokhan, Recep, Bulent, Orhan (Mutlu 3), Arif, Oguz, Ogun, Abdullah, Saffet, Hakan (Yalcin 64).
Iceland: Kristinsson B (Finnbogasen 5), Jonsson S, Kristinsson R, Bergsson, Gislason, Gudjohnsen, Orlygsson, Jonsson K, Stefansson, Sverisson, Gunnlaugsson A.
Referee: Levnikov (Russia).

Berne, 12 October 1994, 24,000

Switzerland (1) 4 *(Ohrel 36, Blomqvist 64 (og), Sforza 79, Turkyilmaz 81)*

Sweden (1) 2 *(Andersson K 6, Dahlin 61)*

Switzerland: Pascolo; Hottiger, Herr, Geiger, Thuler, Ohrel, Yakin (Henchoz 83), Sforza, Sutter, Grassi (Turkyilmaz 69), Chapuisat.
Sweden: Ravelli; Nilsson, Andersson P, Bjorklund, Kamark, Brolin, Thern (Mild 49), Schwarz, Blomqvist (Larsson 82), Dahlin, Andersson K.
Referee: Elleray (England).

Stockholm, 16 November 1994, 27,571

Sweden (1) 2 *(Brolin 44, Dahlin 70)*

Hungary (0) 0

Sweden: Ravelli; Nilsson, Andersson P, Bjorklund, Kamark, Brolin (Rehn 70), Schwarz, Thern, Andersson K, Dahlin, Larsson.
Hungary: Petry; Banfi, Meszoly, Lorincz, Kozma, Lipcsei (Halmai 58), Urban, Detari, Duro (Kovacs 75), Kiprich, Klausz.
Referee: Van der Ende (Holland).

Lausanne, 16 November 1994, 15,800

Switzerland (1) 1 *(Bickel 45)*

Iceland (0) 0

Switzerland: Pascolo; Hottiger, Henchoz, Geiger, Thuler, Ohrel, Sforza, Bickel, Sutter, Grassi (Turkyilmaz 68), Chapuisat.
Iceland: Kristinsson B; Kristinsson R, Bergsson, Gislason (Ingolfsson 84), Jonsson K, Dervic, Gretarsson A (Gunnlaugsson B 64), Orlygsson, Stefansson, Sverrisson, Gunnlaugsson A.
Referee: Kelly (Northern Ireland).

Istanbul, 14 December 1994, 25,000

Turkey (1) 1 *(Recep 39)*

Switzerland (2) 2 *(Koller 7, Bickel 16)*

Turkey: Rustu; Recep, Bulent, Gokhan K, Abdullah, Ogun, Oguz, Cengiz (Ilker 46), Arif (Sergen 75), Hakan, Saffet.
Switzerland: Pascolo; Hottiger, Herr, Geiger, Thuler, Ohrel, Sforza, Koller, Sutter A, Bickel (Bonvin 65), Subiat (Grassi 80).
Referee: Craciunescu (Romania).

Budapest, 29 March 1995, 13,000

Hungary (0) 2 *(Kiprich 50, Illes 72)*

Switzerland (0) 2 *(Subiat 73, 85)*

Hungary: Petry; Mracsko, Lorincz, Meszoly, Kovacs, Kozma, Halmai, Salloi, Illes, Kiprich (Marton 69), Vincze (Klausz 82).
Switzerland: Pascolo; Hottiger, Herr, Geiger, Fernandez, Koller, Ohrel, Sforza, Bickel (Grassi 65), Sutter A, Subiat (Henchoz 89).
Referee: Wieser (Austria).

Istanbul, 29 March 1995, 20,000

Turkey (0) 2 *(Emre 64, Sergen 75)*

Sweden (1) 1 *(Andersson K 23 (pen))*

Turkey: Engin; Recep, Bulent, Emre, Alpay, Abdullah, Metin, Tolunay, Sergen (Mutlu 77), Hakan, Ertugrul (Oguz 46).
Sweden: Ravelli; Nilsson, Andersson P, Bjorklund, Ljung, Schwarz, Zetterberg (Rehn 81), Thern, Larsson (Blomqvist 75), Dahlin, Andersson K.
Referee: Trentalange (Italy).

Budapest, 26 April 1995, 10,000

Hungary (1) 1 *(Halmai 2)*

Sweden (0) 0

Hungary: Vegh; Csabi, Meszoly, Mracsko, Kozma, Halmai, Lipcsei, Illes, Salloi, Csertoi (Szlezak 86), Vincze (Urban 68).
Sweden: Ravelli; Nilsson, Andersson P, Kamark, Ljung, Schwarz, Zetterberg, Mild (Andersson R 62), Ingesson, Alexandersson (Gudmundsson 82), Andersson K.
Referee: Lopez Nieto (Spain).

Berne, 26 April 1995, 24,000

Switzerland (1) 1 *(Hottiger 38)*

Turkey (1) 2 *(Hakan 17, Ogun 56)*

Switzerland: Pascolo; Hottiger, Herr, Geiger, Fernandez (Walker 75), Ohrel, Sforza, Bickel, Sutter A, Grassi, Bonvin (Zuffi 70).
Turkey: Engin; Emre, Bulent, Alpay, Recep, Ogun, Oguz (Ertugrul 83), Tolunay, Sergen (Suat 79), Abdullah, Hakan.
Referee: Van den Wijngaert (Belgium).

Stockholm, 1 June 1995, 25,676

Sweden (1) 1 *(Brolin 16 (pen))*

Iceland (1) 1 *(Gunnlaugsson A 2)*

Sweden: Ravelli; Sundgren, Andersson P, Mattsson, Kamark, Brolin, Schwarz, Thern, Limpar (Larsson 51), Dahlin, Andersson K.
Iceland: Kristinsson B; Orlygsson, Bergsson, Adolfsson, Jonsson K, Gudjohnsen (Thordarsson 90), Stefansson, Jonsson S, Kristinsson R, Sverrisson, Gunnlaugsson A (Gunnlaugsson B 78).
Referee: Ouzounov (Bulgaria).

Reykjavik, 11 June 1995, 4500

Iceland (0) 2 *(Bergsson 63, Jonsson S 69)*

Hungary (1) 1 *(Vincze 20)*

Iceland: Kristinsson B; Bergsson, Adolfsson, Jonsson K, Jonsson S, Kristinsson R, Gretarsson, Gunnlaugsson A, Thordarsson (Gunnlaugsson B 68), Gudjohnsen, Sverrisson.
Hungary: Petry; Csabi, Meszoly, Lipcsei, Mracsko, Halmai, Illes (Marton 68), Salloi, Kozma, Csertoi, Vincze (Hamar 70).
Referee: Sars (France).

	P	*W*	*D*	*L*	*F*	*A*	*Pts*
Turkey	5	3	1	1	12	6	10
Switzerland	5	3	1	1	10	7	10
Sweden	6	2	1	3	7	8	7
Hungary	5	1	2	2	6	8	5
Iceland	5	1	1	3	3	9	4

Group 4

Tallinn, 4 September 1994, 1500

Estonia (0) 0

Croatia (1) 2 *(Suker 45, 72)*

Estonia: Poom; Lemsalu, Prins, Kaljend, Kallaste T, Alonen, Olumets (Reim 46), Klavan, Kristal, Kirs (Krom 75), Linnumae.

Croatia: Ladic; Turkovic, Bilic, Stimac, Jarni, Jerkan, Asanovic (Cvitanovic 90), Prosinecki, Boban, Suker, Boksic.
Referee: Krondl (Czech Republic).

Maribor, 7 September 1994, 18,000

Slovenia (1) 1 *(Udovic 13)*

Italy (1) 1 *(Costacurta 15)*

Slovenia: Simeunovic; Jermanis, Novak, Milanic, Galic, Englaro, Katanec (Binkovski 58), Zidan (Krizan 90), Ceh, Udovic, Gliha.
Italy: Pagliuca; Mussi, Baresi, Costacurta, Panucci, Donadoni, Dino Baggio (Evani 55), Albertini, Signori, Casiraghi, Zola (Berti 55).
Referee: Heynemann (Germany).

Kiev, 7 September 1994, 25,000

Ukraine (0) 0

Lithuania (0) 2 *(Ivanauskas 55, Skarbelius 61)*

Ukraine: Tiapushkin; Skripnik, Sak (Kovalets 8), Yevtushok, Popov, Petrov I, Pokhlebaev (Nagornyak 59), Maksimov, Finkel, Protassov, Konovalov.
Lithuania: Stauce; Ziukas, Sukristovas, Tereskinas, Vainoras, Vaineikas (Stonkas 81), Gudaitis, Stumbrys, Suika (Zuta 54), Ivanauskas, Skarbelius.
Referee: Karlsson (Sweden).

Tallinn, 8 October 1994, 4000

Estonia (0) 0

Italy (1) 2 *(Panucci 19, Casiraghi 77)*

Estonia: Poom; Lemsalu, Kallaste T, Alonen, Klavan (Kallaste R 75), Kaljend, Kristal, Reim, Krom (Olumets 67), Linnumae, Kirs.
Italy: Pagliuca; Panucci, Favalli (Apolloni 87), Evani (Albertini 83), Costacurta, Maldini, Rambaudi, Dino Baggio, Casiraghi, Zola, Signori.
Referee: Muller (Switzerland).

Zagreb, 9 October 1994, 12,000

Croatia (0) 2 *(Jerkan 56, Kozniku 61)*

Lithuania (0) 0

Croatia: Ladic; Mladenovic, Jarni, Bilic, Jerkan, Stimac (Brajkovic 88), Jurcevic, Asanovic, Suker, Boban, Boksic (Kozniku 78).
Lithuania: Stauce; Ziukas, Mazeikis, Gudaitis, Tereskinas, Vainoras, Sukristovas, Stumbrys, Suika (Poderis 76), Skarbelius, Vaineikas (Korsakovas 59).
Referee: Wieser (Austria).

Kiev, 12 October 1994, 12,000

Ukraine (0) 0

Slovenia (0) 0

Ukraine: Tiapushkin; Loujni, Dyriavka, Kuznetsov O, Shmatovalenko, Lezhentsev, Mikhailichenko (Petrov I 70), Mikhailenko, Konovalov (Guseynov 61), Kovalets, Leonenko.
Slovenia: Boskovic, Galic, Krizan, Milanic, Jermanis, Ceh, Novak (Kokol 75), Zidan, Benedejcic, Udovic (Gliha 65), Florjancic.
Referee: Oezenov (Bulgaria).

Kiev, 13 November 1994, 500

Ukraine (2) 3 *(Konovalov 31, Kirs 45 (og), Guseynov 76)*

Estonia (0) 0

Ukraine: Chovkovski (Suslov 83); Loujni, Kuznetsov O, Lezhentsev, Popov, Bezhenar, Kovalets (Petrov 75), Litovtchenko, Orbu, Skachenko (Guseynov 46), Konovalov.
Estonia: Vessenberg; Lemsalu, Kirs, Linnumae, Kallaste R, Alonen, Olumets, Lindmaa, Pari, Kristal, Zelinski.
Referee: Schellings (Belgium).

Palermo, 16 November 1994, 33,570

Italy (0) 1 *(Dino Baggio 90)*

Croatia (1) 2 *(Suker 32, 60)*

Italy: Pagliuca; Negro, Costacurta, Maldini, Panucci, Lombardo, Albertini (Di Matteo 65), Dino Baggio, Rambaudi (Donadoni 46), Casiraghi, Roberto Baggio.
Croatia: Ladic; Brajkovic, Jarni, Bilic, Stimac, Asanovic, Jerkan, Prosinecki (Mladenovic 57), Boban, Suker, Jurcevic (Kozniku 90).
Referee: Quiniou (France).

Maribor, 16 November 1994, 2500

Slovenia (0) 1 *(Zahovic 55)*

Lithuania (0) 2 *(Sukristovas 64, Zuta 87)*

Slovenia: Boskovic; Galic, Krizan, Englaro (Polisak 46), Jermanis, Ceh, Zidan, Benedejcic (Binkovski 46), Zahovic, Florjancic, Gliha.
Lithuania: Stauce; Suika (Zuta 76), Sukristovas, Mazeikis, Tereskinas, Vainoras, Gudaitis, Stumbrys, Narbekovas, Ivanauskas, Apanavicius.
Referee: Ihring (Slovakia).

Zagreb, 25 March 1995, 30,000

Croatia (2) 4 *(Boban 13, Suker 21, 79, Prosinecki 71)*

Ukraine (0) 0

Croatia: Ladic; Jerkan, Bilic, Pavlicic, Jarni, Prosinecki, Boban, Asanovic, Jurcevic (Vlaovic 79), Boksic (Turkovic 75), Suker.
Ukraine: Tiapushkin; Loujni, Shmatovalenko, Mizine, Telesnenko, Martynov (Orbu 46), Boukel, Kalitvintsev, Shevchenko, Leonenko, Konovalov.
Referee: Weber (Germany).

Salerno, 25 March 1995, 35,000

Italy (1) 4 *(Zola 45, 65, Albertini 58, Ravanelli 82)*

Estonia (0) 1 *(Reim 74)*

Italy: Peruzzi; Negro, Maldini, Minotti, Carboni, Albertini, Eranio (Lombardo 57), Dino Baggio, Del Piero (Berti 69), Zola, Ravanelli.
Estonia: Poom; Lemsalu, Kallaste T, Kirs, Kallaste R, Olumets, Lindmaa, Linnumae, Kristal, Lelle (Pari 76), Krom (Reim 72).
Referee: Philippi (Luxembourg).

Vilnus, 29 March 1995, 9500

Lithuania (0) 0

Croatia (0) 0

Lithuania: Stauce; Ziukas, Sukristovas, Stonkas, Vainoras, Suika, Gudaitis, Zdancius (Zuta 70), Narbekovas (Pocius 69), Ivanauskas, Skarbelius.
Croatia: Ladic; Pavlicic (Mladenovic 46), Stimac, Bilic, Jarni, Soldo, Prosinecki, Brajkovic, Asanovic, Suker, Boksic.
Referee: Burge (Wales).

Kiev, 29 March 1995, 10,000

Ukraine (0) 0

Italy (2) 2 *(Lombardo 11, Zola 37)*

Ukraine: Tiapushkin; Loujni (Boukel 60), Telesnenko, Khomin, Yevtushok, Orbu, Mizine, Kalitvintsev, Leonenko, Shevchenko, Konovalov (Pokhlebaev 76).
Italy: Peruzzi; Benarrivo, Apolloni, Minotti, Maldini, Albertini, Di Matteo, Zola, Berti, Lombardo (Conte 73), Casiraghi (Ravanelli 65).
Referee: Puhl (Hungary).

Maribor, 29 March 1995, 6000

Slovenia (1) 3 *(Zahovic 40, Gliha 53, Kokol 90)*

Estonia (0) 0

Slovenia: Boskovic; Galic, Milanic, Jermanis (Skaper 70), Englaro, Ceh, Novak, Zahovic (Kokol 68), Zidan, Florjancic, Gliha.

Estonia: Poom; Kallaste R, Kallaste T, Olesk, Arbeiter (Lelle 77), Olumets, Linnumae, Lindmaa, Lepik, Reim, Kirs.
Referee: Mendes (Portugal).

Tallinn, 26 April 1995, 500

Estonia (0) 0

Ukraine (1) 1 *(Guseynov 17)*

Estonia: Poom; Lemsalu, Kirs, Kallaste T, Kallaste R, Alonen, Olumets, Reim (Pari 68), Krom (Lepa 46), Lelle, Kristal.
Ukraine: Suslov; Loujni, Shmatovalenko, Dyriavka, Golovko, Orbu, Jabchenko, Maksimov, Nadouda (Yevtushok 85), Nagornyak (Konovalov 46), Guseynov.
Referee: Hollung (Norway).

Vilnius, 26 April 1995, 15,000

Lithuania (0) 0

Italy (1) 1 *(Zola 12)*

Lithuania: Stauce; Ziukas, Sukristovas, Vainoras, Tereskinas, Suika, Gudaitis (Poderis 70), Skarbelius, Apanavicius (Preiksaitis 46), Ivanauskas, Slekys.
Italy: Pagliuca; Benarrivo, Costacurta, Minotti, Maldini, Conte (Dino Baggio 24), Di Matteo, Crippa (Berti 85), Lombardo, Casiraghi, Zola.
Referee: McCluskey (Scotland).

Zagreb, 26 April 1995, 25,000

Croatia (1) 2 *(Prosinecki 17, Suker 90)*

Slovenia (0) 0

Croatia: Ladic; Jerkan, Bilic, Stimac, Jarni, Prosinecki, Boban, Asanovic, Jurcevic (Gabric 13), Suker, Boksic.
Slovenia: Boskovic; Galic, Englaro, Milanic (Skaper 89), Binkovski, Jermanis, Novak, Zidan, Zahovic (Kokol 71), Florjancic, Gliha.
Referee: Saravan (Turkey).

Vilnius, 7 June 1995, 6000

Lithuania (0) 2 *(Stonkas 47, Suika 69)*

Slovenia (0) 1 *(Gliha 82)*

Lithuania: Stauce; Ziukas, Sukristovas, Tereskinas, Vainoras, Stonkas, Maciulevicius (Baltusniskas 75), Preiksaitis (Suika 68), Skarbelius, Slekys, Ivanauskas.
Slovenia: Boskovic; Galic (Krizan 78), Englaro, Milanic, Jermanis, Ceh, Novak (Skaper 58), Kokol, Zahovic, Florjancic, Gliha.
Referee: Vagner (Hungary).

Tallinn, 11 June 1995, 2000

Estonia (1) 1 *(Reim 27)*

Slovenia (1) 3 *(Novak 37, 68, Zahovic 78)*

Estonia: Poom; Lepa (Klavan 46), Kirs, Kallaste T, Olumets, Alonen, Pari, Linnumae, Kristal, Reim, Arbeiter (Rajala 59).
Slovenia: Boskovic; Galic, Englaro, Milanic, Novak, Jermanis (Cviki 64), Kokol (Krizan 46), Ceh, Zahovic, Florjancic, Gliha.
Referee: Durkin (England).

Kiev, 11 June 1995, 8500

Ukraine (1) 1 *(Kalitvintsev 13)*

Croatia (0) 0

Ukraine: Suslov; Jabchenko, Skripnik, Golovko, Maksimov, Orbu, Pokhlebaev, Kalitvintsev, Palyanitsa (Nagornyak 77), Gorily, Guseynov (Chkapenko 46).
Croatia: Gabric; Pavlicic (Mrlic 28), Jarni, Soldo, Jerkan, Bilic, Asanovic (Pralija 48), Mladenovic, Suker, Boban (Butorovic 38), Boksic.
Referee: Rothlisberger (Switzerland).

	P	*W*	*D*	*L*	*F*	*A*	*Pts*
Croatia	7	5	1	1	12	2	16
Italy	6	4	1	1	11	4	13
Lithuania	6	3	1	2	6	5	10
Ukraine	7	3	1	3	5	8	10
Slovenia	7	2	2	3	9	8	8
Estonia	7	0	0	7	2	18	0

Group 5

Prague, 6 September 1994, 10,226

Czech Republic (3) 6 *(Smejkal 6 (pen), Kubik 33, Siegl 35, 49, 81, Berger P 89)*

Malta (0) 1 *(Laferla 75)*

Czech Republic: Kouba; Suchoparek, Kubik, Novotny J, Latal (Vesely 87), Nemecek, Frydek (Berger P 83), Nemec, Smejkal, Kuka, Siegl.
Malta: Cluett; Vella S, Galea, Buttigieg, Buhagiar, Camilleri J, Gregory (Camilleri E 83), Brincat, Saliba, Laferla, Busuttil.
Referee: Loizou (Cyprus).

Luxembourg, 7 September 1994, 8200

Luxembourg (0) 0

Holland (1) 4 *(Roy 22, Ronald de Boer 62, 64, Jonk 90)*

Luxembourg: Koch; Ferron, Weis, Strasser, Birsens, Wolf, Holtz, Saibene, Groff, Cardoni (Morocutti 80), Langers (Theis 89).
Holland: De Goey; Valckx, Blind, Frank de Boer, Winter, Jonk, Witschge, Overmars, Bosman, Ronald de Boer, Roy (Van Vossen 75).
Referee: Snoddy (Northern Ireland).

Oslo, 7 September 1994, 16,739

Norway (0) 1 *(Frigaard 88)*

Belarus (0) 0

Norway: Grodaas; Lydersen, Pedersen T, Berg H, Bjornebye, Flo (Frigaard 70), Mykland, Rekdal, Bohinen (Leonhardsen 46), Jakobsen, Fjortoft.
Belarus: Shantolosov; Gurenko, Sosnitski, Zygmantovich, Khatskevich, Yakhimovich, Gerasimets, Metlitsky, Kulanin (Kachuro 46), Antonovitch, Markhel.
Referee: Goethals (Belgium).

Valletta, 12 October 1994, 4000

Malta (0) 0

Czech Republic (0) 0

Malta: Cluett; Buttigieg, Galea, Vella S, Camilleri J, Saliba (Sant-fournier 77), Brincat, Carabott (Camilleri E 90), Gregory, Busuttil, Laferla.
Czech Republic: Srnicek; Suchoparek, Kubik, Novotny J, Latal, Nemecek (Kadlec 44), Hasek, Nemec, Smejkal (Frydek 70), Skuhravy, Kuka.
Referee: Coroado (Portugal).

Oslo, 12 October 1994, 22,293

Norway (0) 1 *(Rekdal 52 (pen))*

Holland (1) 1 *(Roy 22)*

Norway: Thorstvedt; Lydersen, Berg, Pedersen, Bjornebye, Rushfeldt (Flo 63), Bohinen, Rekdal, Mykland, Leonhardsen, Fjortoft (Frigaard 77).
Holland: De Goey; Blind, Reiziger (Van Gobbel 77), Valckx, Frank de Boer, Winter, Jonk, Witschge, Overmars, Bergkamp (Ronald de Boer 71), Roy.
Referee: McCluskey (Scotland).

Minsk, 12 October 1994, 5000

Belarus (0) 2 *(Romashchenko 67, Gerasimets 76)*

Luxembourg (0) 0

Belarus: Shantolosov; Gurenko, Rodnionok (Sosnitski 80), Jakhimovic, Zygmantovich, Gerasimets, Markhel (Antonovitch 65), Aleinikov, Romashchenko, Shukanov, Metlitsky.
Luxembourg: Koch; Ferron (Vanek 83), Strasser, Birsens, Wolf, Cardoni, Hellers, Weis, Holtz (Morocutti 58), Saibene, Fanelli.
Referee: O'Hanlon (Republic of Ireland).

Minsk, 16 November 1994, 8000

Belarus (0) 0

Norway (2) 4 *(Berg 34, Leonhardsen 39, Bohinen 52, Rekdal 83)*

Belarus: Shantalosov; Yaskovich, Zygmantovich, Rodnionok, Yakhimovich, Metlitsky, Markhel (Youssipets 82), Antonovitch, Romashchenko (Gurinovich 82), Gerasimets, Shukanov.
Norway: Grodaas; Halle, Berg, Johnsen (Jakobsen 80), Bjornebye (Lydersen 42), Mykland, Leonhardsen, Bohinen, Rekdal, Rushfeldt, Fjortoft.
Referee: Spassov (Bulgaria).

Rotterdam, 16 November 1994, 40,000

Holland (0) 0

Czech Republic (0) 0

Holland: De Goey; Valckx, Blind, Frank de Boer, Witschge (Numan 78), Winter, Roy, Jonk, Van Vossen, Mulder (Kluivert 70), Taument.
Czech Republic: Srnieck; Latal, Kadlec, Suchoparek, Hapal, Kubik, Nemec, Bilek, Kuka (Samec 90), Siegl, Poborsky (Berger 75).
Referee: Puhl (Hungary).

Rotterdam, 14 December 1994, 26,000

Holland (3) 5 *(Mulder 6, Roy 17, Jonk 40, Ronald de Boer 52, Seedorf 90)*

Luxembourg (0) 0

Holland: De Goey; Valckx, Blind, Frank de Boer, Winter (Van Hooydonk 75), Jonk, Numan, Overmars, Ronald de Boer, Mulder (Seedorf 46), Roy.
Luxembourg: Koch; Ferron, Weis, Wolf, Birsens, Strasser, Holtz, Hellers, Cardoni, Groff, Langers (Theis 61).
Referee: Roduit (Switzerland).

Ta Qali, 14 December 1994, 9000

Malta (0) 0

Norway (1) 1 *(Fjortoft 10)*

Malta: Cluett; Vella S, Woods, Buttigieg, Camilleri J, Brincat, Busuttil, Saliba (Scerri 82), Carabott (Buhagiar 60), Gregory, Laferla.
Norway: Grodaas; Halle, Berg, Johnsen, Bjornebye, Mykland, Rekdal, Ruschfeldt (Jakobsen 82), Flo, Bohinen, Fjortoft.
Referee: Beschin (Italy).

Valletta, 22 February 1995, 6000

Malta (0) 0

Luxembourg (0) 1 *(Cardoni 54)*

Malta: Cluett; Vella S, Brincat, Buttigieg, Buhagiar, Camilleri J, Busuttil, Suda (Sciberras 60), Carabott (Saliba 78), Gregory, Laferla.
Luxembourg: Koch; Vanek, Weis, Wolf, Deville, Saibene, Hellers, Birsens, Groff, Langers (Schneider 89), Cardoni (Holtz 87).
Referee: Berusan (Croatia).

Luxembourg, 29 March 1995, 3000

Luxembourg (0) 0

Norway (1) 2 *(Leonhardsen 35, Aase 80)*

Luxembourg: Rohmann; Ferron, Vanek, Birsens (Schneider 85), Strasser, Deville, Saibene (Feyder 78), Weis, Groff, Langers, Cardoni.
Norway: Thorstvedt; Haaland, Johnsen, Berg, Bjornebye, Flo (Aase 46), Leonhardsen, Rekdal, Bohinen, Fjortoft (Mykland 25), Jakobsen.
Referee: Levnikov (Russia).

Rotterdam, 29 March 1995, 34,000

Holland (1) 4 *(Seedorf 39, Bergkamp 77 (pen), Winter 80, Kluivert 85)*

Malta (0) 0

Holland: De Goey; Valckx, Blind, Frank de Boer, Jonk, Winter, Seedorf, Overmars, Ronald de Boer (Kluivert 76), Bergkamp, Roy (Van de Luer 58).
Malta: Cluett; Vella S (Gregory 90), Buhigiar, Galea, Woods, Camilleri J, Busuttil (Agius 88), Saliba, Sant Fournier, Camilleri E, Laferla.
Referee: Orrason (Iceland).

Ostrava, 29 March 1995, 5549

Czech Republic (2) 4 *(Kadlec 5, Berger 18, 63, Kuka 69)*

Belarus (1) 2 *(Gerasimets 44 (pen), Gurinovich 88)*

Czech Republic: Srnicek; Repka, Kadlec, Latal, Frydek (Bilek 86), Nemecek, Berger, Hapal, Smejkal, Kuka, Siegl (Samec 89).
Belarus: Shantolosov; Yakhimovich (Rodnionok 77), Gurenko, Zygmantovich, Sosnitski, Juravel (Kachentsev 81), Taikov, Metlitsky, Youssipets, Gerasimets, Gurinovich.
Referee: Veissiere (France).

Minsk, 26 April 1995, 13,000

Belarus (0) 1 *(Taikov 53)*

Malta (0) 1 *(Carabott 72)*

Belarus: Marchoukel; Gurenko, Zygmantovich, Taikov, Juravel, Metlitsky (Rodiokov 70), Youssipets (Romashchenko 75), Shukanov, Gerasimets, Gurinovich, Antonovitch.
Malta: Cluett; Vella S, Buttigieg, Camilleri E, Woods, Saliba, Gregory (Agius 24), Laferla, Sant Fournier, Carabott, Busuttil (Attard 88).
Referee: Gadosi (Slovakia).

Prague, 26 April 1995, 20,000

Czech Republic (0) 3 *(Skuhravy 49, Nemecek 57, Berger 62)*

Holland (1) 1 *(Jonk 7)*

Czech Republic: Kouba; Repka, Kadlec, Suchoparek, Berger, Hapal, Nemecek, Nemec, Frydek (Latal 46), Kuka (Siegl 89), Skuhravy.
Holland: De Goey; Valckx, Blind, Frank de Boer, Winter (Kluivert 65), Jonk, Seedorf, Numan, Overmars, Ronald de Boer, Van Vossen (Bosz 46).
Referee: Krug (Germany).

Oslo, 26 April 1995, 15,124

Norway (3) 5 *(Jakobsen 11, Fjortoft 12, Brattbakk 24, Berg 46, Rekdal 49)*

Luxembourg (0) 0

Norway: Grodaas; Berg (Haaland 76), Johnsen, Nielsen, Halle, Bohinen (Solbakken 35), Rekdal, Leonhardsen, Jakobsen, Brattbakk, Fjortoft.
Luxembourg: Koch; Feyder, Vanek, Holtz (Theis 34), Strasser, Deville, Hellers, Saibene (Lambourelle 75), Langers, Cardoni, Groff.
Referee: Ferry (Northern Ireland).

Luxembourg, 7 June 1995, 1500

Luxembourg (0) 1 *(Hellers 90)*

Czech Republic (0) 0

Luxembourg: Koch; Vanek, Strasser, Weis, Birsens, Ganser (Cardoni 87), Hellers, Groff, Deville, Langers, Theis (Saibene 75).
Czech Republic: Kouba; Suchoparek, Repka (Frydek 69), Kadlec, Hapal, Latal, Nemec, Nemecek, Berger, Kuka, Skuhravy (Drulak 60).
Referee: Ashman (Wales).

Oslo, 7 June 1995, 15,000

Norway (1) 2 *(Fjortoft 43, Flo 88)*

Malta (0) 0

Norway: Thorstvedt; Haaland (Brattbakk 69), Johnsen, Berg, Nilsen, Flo, Mykland, Solbakken, Rekdal (Ingebrigtsen 83), Fjortoft, Jakobsen.
Malta: Cluett; Vella S, Buhagiar (Saliba 76), Attard, Woods, Buttigieg (Camilleri E 28), Busuttil, Agius, Laferla, Sant Fournier, Carabott.
Referee: Przesmycki (Poland).

Minsk, 7 June 1995, 12,000

Belarus (1) 1 *(Gerasimets 27)*

Holland (0) 0

Belarus: Shantolosov; Dovnar (Kachentsev 86), Taikov, Gurenko, Rodnionok, Zygmantovitch, Juravel, Youssipets, Romashchenko (Antonovitch 54), Kachuro, Gerasimets.
Holland: Van der Sar; De Kock, Blind (Winter 69), Valckx (Numan 64), Seedorf, Jonk, Van't Schip, Davids, Ronald de Boer, Kluivert, Overmars.
Referee: Porumboiu (Romania).

	P	*W*	*D*	*L*	*F*	*A*	*Pts*
Norway	7	6	1	0	16	1	19
Holland	7	3	2	2	15	5	11
Czech Republic	6	3	2	1	13	5	11
Belarus	6	2	1	3	6	10	7
Luxembourg	7	2	0	5	2	18	6
Malta	7	0	2	5	2	15	2

Group 6

Windsor Park, 20 April 1994, 7000

Northern Ireland (3) 4 *(Quinn 5, 33, Lomas 25, Dowie 48)*

Liechtenstein (0) 1 *(Hasler 84)*

Northern Ireland: Wright; Fleming, Taggart, Donaghy, Worthington, Magilton (O'Neill 81), Wilson, Lomas, Hughes, Quinn, Dowie (Gray 78).
Liechtenstein: Oehry; Stocker, Frick C, Ospelt J, Moser, Quaderer, Ritter, Zech, Telser, Matt (Hasler 70), Frick M.
Referee: Luinge (Holland).

Riga, 7 September 1994, 2200

Latvia (0) 0

Republic of Ireland (2) 3 *(Aldridge 16, 75 (pen), Sheridan 29)*

Latvia: Karavayev; Troicki, Sevliakovs, Lobanev, Zemlinsky, Astafyev, Mikutsky (Yeliseyev 62), Milevskis (Stepanov 46), Sharando, Bulders, Babichev.
Republic of Ireland: Kelly A; Kelly G, Babb, McGrath, Irwin, McAteer (McGoldrick 80), Sheridan, Townsend, Staunton, Aldridge, Quinn (Cascarino 70).
Referee: Frisk (Sweden).

Eschen, 7 September 1994, 5800

Liechtenstein (0) 0

Austria (3) 4 *(Polster 18, 45, 79, Aigner 22)*

Liechtenstein: Heeb; Moser, Hefti, Ospelt J, Quaderer, Telser, Zech (Matt 68), Klaunzer, Ospelt W (Hanselmann 28), Frick M, Hasler.
Austria: Wohlfahrt; Schottel, Werner, Kogler, Prosenik, Stoger, Pfeifenberger (Flogel 74), Feiersinger, Aigner, Ogris (Cerny 63), Polster.
Referee: Ziller (Germany).

Windsor Park, 7 September 1994, 6000

Northern Ireland (0) 1 *(Quinn 58 (pen))*

Portugal (1) 2 *(Rui Costa 8, Oliveira 81)*

Northern Ireland: Fettis; Fleming, Morrow (Taggart 81), McDonald, Worthington, Gillespie (O'Boyle 81), Magilton, Lomas, Hughes, Quinn, Gray.
Portugal: Vitor Baia; Joao Pinto I, Paulo Madeira, Paulinho Santos, Helder, Tavares, Paulo Sousa, Vitor Paneira (Folha 63), Figo, Rui Costa, Sa Pinto (Oliveira 80).
Referee: Pedersen (Norway).

Riga, 9 October 1994, 2000

Latvia (0) 1 *(Monyak 88)*

Portugal (1) 3 *(Joao Pinto II 33, 72, Vigo 73)*

Latvia: Karavayev; Troicki, Astafyev, Zemlinsky, Sevliakovs, Sprogis (Monyak 69), Stepanov, Ivanov, Babichev, Glazov (Milevskis 46), Semenov.
Portugal: Vitor Baia; Joao Pinto I, Cristovao, Paulo Madeira, Nelo, Paulo Sousa, Vitor Paneira (Alves 60), Joao Pinto II, Figo (Tavares 81), Rui Costa, Domingos.
Referee: Blareau (Belgium).

Vienna, 12 October 1994, 20,000

Austria (1) 1 *(Polster 24 (pen))*

Northern Ireland (2) 2 *(Gillespie 3, Gray 36)*

Austria: Wohlfahrt; Kogler, Schottel, Werner, Artner, Prosenik (Pfeifenberger 65), Stoger, Feiersinger, Hutter, Ogris (Hasenhuttl 45), Polster.
Northern Ireland: Kee; Fleming, Worthington, Taggart, McDonald, Lomas, Gillespie (O'Neill 66), Magilton, Dowie (Quinn 74), Gray, Hughes.
Referee: Nieto (Spain).

Dublin, 12 October 1994, 32,980

Republic of Ireland (3) 4 *(Coyne 2, 4, Quinn 30, 82)*

Liechtenstein (0) 0

Republic of Ireland: Bonner; Kelly G, Irwin (McLoughlin 46), McAteer, Kernaghan, Babb, McGoldrick, Coyne, Quinn, Sheridan, Staunton.
Liechtenstein: Heeb; Hefti, Telser, Ritter, Moser, Ospelt J, Hanselmann, Zech, Modestus (Klaunzer 77), Frick M, Heidegger (Matt 71).
Referee: Bergmann (Iceland).

Lisbon, 13 November 1994, 50,000

Portugal (1) 1 *(Figo 36)*

Austria (0) 0

Portugal: Vitor Baia; Joao Pinto I, Paulo Madeira, Helder, Paulinho Santos, Paulo Sousa, Figo, Oceano, Rui Costa (Domingos 84), Joao Pinto II, Sa Pinto (Paneira 70).
Austria: Konrad; Schottel, Furstaller, Kogler, Feiersinger, Artner, Stoger, Winklhofer, Kuhbauer (Prosenik 46), Cerny (Hutter 70), Polster.
Referee: Mikkelsen (Denmark).

Eschen-Mauren, 15 November 1994, 1300

Liechtenstein (0) 0

Latvia (1) 1 *(Babichev 14)*

Liechtenstein: Heeb; Moser, Telser, Hefti, Ritter, Hilti, Zech (Klaunzer 60), Ospelt J, Frick M, Heidegger (Oehri 59), Hasler.
Latvia: Karavayev; Troicki, Astafyev, Zemlinsky, Sevliakovs, Sprogis, Blagonadiejny (Mikutsky 46), Ivanov, Semenov, Milevskis, Babichev (Sharando 71).
Referee: Werner (Poland).

Windsor Park, 16 November 1994, 10,336

Northern Ireland (0) 0

Republic of Ireland (3) 4 *(Aldridge 6, Keane 11, Sheridan 38, Townsend 54)*

Northern Ireland: Kee; Fleming, Worthington, Morrow, Taggart, O'Neill (Patterson 46), Gillespie (Wilson 62), Magilton, Dowie, Gray, Hughes.
Republic of Ireland: Kelly A; Kelly G, Irwin, Keane (McAteer 44), McGrath, Babb, Sheridan, Aldridge (Coyne 46), Quinn, Townsend, Staunton.
Referee: Muhmenthaler (Switzerland).

Lisbon, 18 December 1994, 30,000

Portugal (3) 8 *(Domingos 2, 11, Oceano 45, Joao Pinto II 56, Fernando Couto 72, Folha 74, Paulo Alves 75, 79)*

Liechtenstein (0) 0

Portugal: Vitor Baia; Joao Pinto I, Fernando Couto, Oceano, Paulinho Santos, Figo, Vitor Paneira (Paulo Alves 57), Rui Costa, Joao Pinto II (Secretario 70), Domingos, Folha.
Liechtenstein: Heeb; Telser, Hefti, Ospelt W (Oehri R 44), Moser, Hilti, Ritter, Zech, Hasler (Matt 58), Frick M, Heidegger.
Referee: Pucek (Czech Republic).

Dublin, 29 March 1995, 32,200

Republic of Ireland (0) 1 *(Quinn 47)*

Northern Ireland (0) 1 *(Dowie 72)*

Republic of Ireland: Kelly A; Kelly G, Irwin, Keane, McGrath, Babb, Sheridan, Kelly D (McAteer 75), Quinn (Cascarino 82), Townsend, Staunton.
Northern Ireland: Fettis; Patterson, Worthington, Hill, Taggart, McDonald, Morrow, Magilton, Dowie, Hughes, Gillespie.
Referee: Van der Ende (Holland).

Salzburg, 29 March 1995, 5500

Austria (2) 5 *(Herzog 18, 58, Pfeifenberger 41, Polster 69 (pen), 90)*

Latvia (0) 0

Austria: Konrad; Furstaller, Kogler, Feiersinger, Pfeifenberger, Marasek, Artner (Hutter 76), Kuhbauer, Herzog, Ogris (Ramusch 46), Polster.
Latvia: Laizan; Sevliakovs, Sprogis, Lobanev, Troicki, Astafyev, Zemlinsky (Mikutsky 66), Blagonadezhdin, Teplov, Monyak, Babichev (Shtolcers 74).
Referee: Agius (Malta).

Riga, 26 April 1995, 1560

Latvia (0) 0

Northern Ireland (0) 1 *(Dowie 69 (pen))*

Latvia: Laizan; Troicki, Astafyev, Zemlinsky, Sevliakovs, Sprogis, Stepanov, Blagonadezhdin (Butkus 30), Teplov, Babichev, Yeliseyev.
Northern Ireland: Fettis; Patterson, Worthington, Hunter, McDonald, Hill, Gillespie (O'Boyle 78), Wilson K, Dowie (Quinn 80), Horlock, Hughes.
Referee: Lambek (Denmark).

Salzburg, 26 April 1995, 5700

Austria (3) 7 *(Kuhbauer 8, Polster 11, 53, Sabitzer 17, Purk 84, Hutter 87, 90)*

Liechtenstein (0) 0

Austria: Konrad; Feiersinger, Kogler, Furstaller (Hutter A 71), Ramusch, Artner, Herzog, Kuhbauer, Marasek, Sabitzer (Purk 69), Polster.
Liechtenstein: Oehry; Moser, Stocker, Ospelt J, Ritter (Matt 66), Hilti, Telser, Zech H, Hasler, Oehri (Marxer 46), Burgmaier.
Referee: Melnitschuk (Ukraine).

Dublin, 26 April 1995, 33,000

Republic of Ireland (1) 1 *(Vitor Baia 45 (og))*

Portugal (0) 0

Republic of Ireland: Kelly A; Kelly G, Irwin, Townsend, McGrath, Babb, Sheridan, Houghton (Kenna 84), Aldridge (Cascarino 84), Quinn, Staunton.
Portugal: Vitor Baia; Joao Pinto I, Fernando Couto, Helder (Folha 64), Paulinho Santos, Jorge Costa, Paulo Sousa, Figo (Pedro Barbosa 76), Rui Costa, Joao Pinto II, Domingos.
Referee: Amendolia (Italy).

Porto, 3 June, 1995, 40,000

Portugal (3) 3 *(Figo 5, Secretario 19, Domingos 21)*

Latvia (0) 2 *(Rimkus 49, 83)*

Portugal: Vitor Baia; Nelson (Pedro Barbosa 79), Fernando Couto, Jorge Costa, Paulinho Santos, Figo, Secretario, Domingos, Folha, Paulo Sousa (Futre 46), Rui Costa.
Latvia: Laizan; Troicki, Sevliakovs, Teplov (Sprogis 59), Astafyev, Zemlinsky, Monyak, Valeriy, Zeiberlins, Rimkus, Bleidelis (Babichev 37).
Referee: Petrovic (Yugoslavia).

Eschen, 3 June 1995, 4500

Liechtenstein (0) 0

Republic of Ireland (0) 0

Liechtenstein: Heeb; Hasler, Hanselmann, Ospelt J (Zech J 32), Ritter, Zech H, Hilti, Telser, Ospelt W (Marxer 64), Burgmaier, Frick M.
Republic of Ireland: Kelly A; Kelly G, Irwin, McAteer (Kenna 73), McGrath, Babb, Sheridan, Aldridge, Quinn (Cascarino 60), Whelan, Staunton.
Referee: Agius (Malta).

Windsor Park, 7 June 1995, 6000

Northern Ireland (1) 1 *(Dowie 44)*

Latvia (0) 2 *(Zeiberlins 58, Astafyev 62)*

Northern Ireland: Fettis; McGibbon (Patterson 46), Worthington, Morrow, Taggart, McDonald, McMahon, Magilton, Dowie, Hughes, Rowland (Gillespie 64).
Latvia: Laizan; Monyak, Sprogis, Zakresevskis, Bleidelis, Troicki, Astafyev, Zeiberlins, Ivanov, Rimkus (Yeliseyev 69), Babichev (Teplov 82).
Referee: Roca (Spain).

Dublin, 11 June 1995, 33,000

Republic of Ireland (0) 1 *(Houghton 65)*

Austria (0) 3 *(Polster 69, 78, Ogris 72)*

Republic of Ireland: Kelly A; Kelly G, Irwin, Houghton, McGrath, Babb, Sheridan, Coyne, Quinn (Cascarino 57), Whelan, Staunton (Kenna 46).
Austria: Konsel; Pfeffer, Schottel, Furstaller, Kogler, Prosenik, Kuhbauer, Pfeifenberger (Hutter 83), Masarek, Ramusch (Ogris 71), Polster.
Referee: Merk (Germany).

	P	*W*	*D*	*L*	*F*	*A*	*Pts*
Portugal	6	5	0	1	17	5	15
Republic of Ireland	7	4	2	1	14	4	14
Austria	6	4	0	2	20	4	12
Northern Ireland	7	3	1	3	10	11	10
Latvia	7	2	0	5	6	16	6
Liechtenstein	7	0	1	6	1	28	1

Group 7

Tbilisi, 7 September 1994, 40,000

Georgia (0) 0

Moldova (1) 1 *(Oprea 40)*

Georgia: Zidze; Nemsadze, Tskhadadze, Shelia, Kavelashvili, Arveladze R (Revishvili 70), Arveladze A, Camarauli, Arveladze S, Guruli (Inalishvili 46), Kinkladze.

Moldova: Coshelev; Secu, Belous, Pogorelov, Stroenco A, Stroenco S (Rebeja 55), Curtianu, Nani, Clescenko, Oprea, Spiridon (Kosse 82).
Referee: Sakari (Turkey).

Cardiff Arms Park, 7 September 1994, 15,791

Wales (1) 2 *(Coleman 9, Giggs 67)*

Albania (0) 0

Wales: Southall; Williams, Melville, Coleman, Bodin, Goss (Pembridge 74), Phillips, Speed, Giggs, Rush, Blake (Roberts I 80).
Albania: Strakosha; Shulku, Xhumba, Vata, Kacaj, Kola A (Fortuzi 53), Bellai, Kola B, Demollari, Bano, Shehu (Dosti 81).
Referee: Beschin (Italy).

Kishinev, 12 October 1994, 12,000

Moldova (2) 3 *(Belous 9, Secu 29, Pogorelov 79)*

Wales (1) 2 *(Speed 6, Blake 70)*

Moldova: Coshelev; Secu, Stroenco S, Nani, Pogorelov, Rebeja, Belous, Oprea, Curtianu, Spiridon, Miterev (Kosse 46).
Wales: Southall; Bowen M, Coleman, Symons, Williams, Horne, Phillips, Blake (Melville 87), Roberts, Pembridge, Speed.
Referee: Vad (Hungary).

Sofia, 12 October 1994, 45,000

Bulgaria (0) 2 *(Kostadinov 55, 62)*

Georgia (0) 0

Bulgaria: Popov; Kiriakov, Ivanov, Houbchev, Tzvetanov, Yankov, Borimirov (Kostadinov 55), Lechkov, Balakov, Sirakov (Penev 70), Stoichkov.
Georgia: Devadze; Revishvili, Tskhadadze, Shelia, Chikhradze, Koudinov, Nemsadze (Inalishvili 71), Gogichaivshvili, Ketsbaia, Kinkladze, Arveladze S (Guruli 76).
Referee: Gadosi (Slovakia).

Tirana, 16 November 1994, 20,000

Albania (1) 1 *(Zmijani 32)*

Germany (1) 2 *(Klinsmann 18, Kirsten 46)*

Albania: Strakosha; Vata, Kacaj, Xhumba, Zmijani (Bano 65), Lekbello, Demollari (Kola 55), Millo, Bellai, Kushta, Rraklli.
Germany: Kopke; Matthaus, Kohler, Berthold, Reuter, Eilts, Sammer (Strunz 46), Weber (Schuster 83), Moller, Kirsten, Klinsmann.
Referee: Melnitschuk (Ukraine).

Sofia, 16 November 1994, 50,000

Bulgaria (1) 4 *(Stoichkov 45, 85, Balakov 65, Kostadinov 88)*

Moldova (0) 1 *(Clescenko 60)*

Bulgaria: Mikhailov; Houbchev, Kiriakov, Ivanov, Tsvetanov, Penev (Sirakov 80), Yordanov, Lechkov (Stoilov 86), Balakov, Stoichkov, Kostadinov.
Moldova: Coshelev; Stroenco S, Secu, Pogorelov, Nani, Rebeja, Belous, Curtianu (Kosse 86), Spiridon, Oprea, Clescenko.
Referee: McArdle (Northern Ireland).

Tbilisi, 16 November 1994, 45,000

Georgia (2) 5 *(Ketsbaia 31, 49, Kinkladze 41, Gogrichiani 59, Arveladze S 67)*

Wales (0) 0

Georgia: Devadze; Gogichaivshvili, Tskhadadze, Shelia, Chikhradze, Revishvili, Kinkladze, Nehsadze (Inalishvili 41), Ketsbaia (Kavelashvili 75), Gogrishiani, Arveladze S.
Wales: Southall; Neilson (Symons 46), Bowen, Horne, Melville, Coleman, Phillips, Saunders, Rush, Hughes, Speed.
Referee: Sars (France).

Chisinau, 14 December 1994, 20,000

Moldova (0) 0

Germany (2) 3 *(Kirsten 7, Klinnsman 38, Matthaus 73)*

Moldova: Coshelev; Secu, Stroenco S, Nani, Pogorelov, Rebeja (Testimitanu 81), Spiridon, Curtianu, Belous, Oprea (Gaidamasciuk 58), Clescenko.
Germany: Kopke; Berthold, Matthaus, Helmer, Reuter, Hassler, Sammer, Moller (Kuntz 79), Weber, Kirsten (Strunz 69), Klinsmann.
Referee: Van Vliet (Holland).

Cardiff, 14 December 1994, 20,000

Wales (0) 0

Bulgaria (2) 3 *(Ivanov 5, Kostadinov 15, Stoichkov 51)*

Wales: Southall; Phillips, Bowen, Aizlewood, Coleman, Melville, Jones, Saunders, Rush, Hughes, Speed.
Bulgaria: Mikhailov; Kremenliev, Ivanov, Tzvetanov, Yankov, Yordanov, Lechkov, Balakov, Kostadinov (Siriakov 73), Penev (Kiriakov 73), Stoichkov.
Referee: Sundell (Sweden).

Tirana, 14 December 1994, 15,000

Albania (0) 0

Georgia (1) 1 *(Arveladze S 17)*

Albania: Strakosha; Dema, Vata (Shulku 30), Xhumba, Kacaj, Lekbello (Malko 46), Bellai, Rraklli, Demollari, Fortuzi, Kola.
Georgia: Devadze; Revishvili, Shelia, Koudinov, Chikhradze, Gogichaivshvili (Djishkaran 62), Inalishvili, Gogrishiani, Ketsbaia, Kinkladze, Arveladze S (Djamarauli 30).
Referee: Molnar (Hungary).

Kaiserslautern, 18 December 1995, 20,310

Germany (2) 2 *(Matthaus 8 (pen), Klinsmann 17)*

Albania (0) 1 *(Rraklli 58)*

Germany: Kopke; Matthaus, Berthold, Helmer, Weber, Reuter, Sammer, Hassler (Strunz 77), Moller, Kirsten (Kuntz 59), Klinsmann.
Albania: Strakosha; Xhumba, Dema, Kajac, Shulka, Zmijani, Demollari, Malki, Bellai, Rraklli, Fortuzi (Zalla 62).
Referee: Christensen (Denmark).

Tbilisi, 29 March 1995, 75,000

Georgia (0) 0

Germany (2) 2 *(Klinsmann 24, 45)*

Georgia: Devadze; Revishvili, Tskhadadze, Shelia, Chikhradze, Gogichaivshvili, Koudinov, Kinkladze, Djamarauli (Gogrishiani 70), Arveladze R (Kavelashvili 75), Arveladze S.
Germany: Kopke; Reuter, Kohler, Helmer, Babbel, Weber (Freund 46), Eilts, Basler, Moller, Klinsmann, Herrlich.
Referee: Bodenham (England).

Sofia, 29 March 1995, 60,000

Bulgaria (1) 3 *(Balakov 37, Penev 70, 82)*

Wales (0) 1 *(Saunders 83)*

Bulgaria: Mikhailov; Ivanov, Houbchev, Tsvetanov (Kiriakov 85), Balakov, Yankov, Kremenliev, Lechkov, Stoichkov, Penev, Kostadinov.
Wales: Southall; Phillips, Bowen, Jones (Cornforth 78), Symons, Coleman, Speed, Horne, Saunders, Hartson, Giggs.
Referee: Piraux (Belgium).

Tirana, 29 March 1995, 20,000

Albania (2) 3 *(Kushta 32, 78, Kacaj 73)*

Moldova (0) 0

Albania: Strakosha (Nallbani 80); Malko, Xhumba (Fortuzi 66), Vata, Shulku, Kacaj, Bellai, Rraklli, Abazi, Kushta (Dalipi 88), Demollari.
Moldova: Coshelev; Secu, Pogorelov, Belous, Gaidamasciuk (Stroenco A 66), Stroenco S, Oprea, Curtianu (Caras 72), Spiridon, Nani, Clescenko.
Referee: Meier (Switzerland).

Tbilisi, 26 April 1995, 20,000

Georgia (2) 2 *(Arveladze S 3, Ketsbaia 43)*

Albania (0) 0

Georgia: Devadze; Revishvili, Tskhadadze, Koudinov, Shelia, Ketsbaia, Gogichaivshvili, Djamaramauli, Kinkladze, Arveladze S, Gogrishiani.
Albania: Strakosha; Nema, Vata, Xhumba, Kacaj, Fortuzi (Prenga 46), Malko, Dalipi, Demollari, Rraklli, Kushta (Dosti 87).
Referee: Luinge (Holland).

Chisinau, 26 April 1995, 17,000

Moldova (0) 0

Bulgaria (1) 3 *(Balakov 29, Stoichkov 54, 68)*

Moldova: Coshelev; Secu, Fistican, Nani, Pogorelov, Caras (Gaidamasciuk 65), Rebeja, Oprea (Cibotaru 72), Belous, Curtianu, Clescenko.
Bulgaria: Mikhailov; Kremenliev (Kiriakov 82), Houbchev, Ivanov, Tsvetanov, Yankov, Lechkov, Balakov, Yordanov, Penev, Stoichkov (Mihtarski 79).
Referee: Ulrich (Czech Republic).

Dusseldorf, 26 April 1995, 45,000

Germany (1) 1 *(Herrlich 42)*

Wales (1) 1 *(Saunders 7)*

Germany: Kopke; Reuter, Freund, Babbel, Eilts, Basler (Scholl 76), Hassler, Weber (Kuntz 86), Ziege, Herrlich, Klinsmann.
Wales: Southall; Phillips, Bowen, Jones, Symons, Coleman (Williams 45), Horne, Hughes (Hartson 90), Rush, Saunders, Speed.
Referee: Encinar (Spain).

Sofia, 7 June 1995, 50,000

Bulgaria (1) 3 *(Stoichkov 45 (pen), 66 (pen), Kostadinov 69)*

Germany (2) 2 *(Klinsmann 18, Strunz 44)*

Bulgaria: Mikhailov; Kremenliev, Houbchev, Ivanov, Tsvetanov, Yankov, Lechkov (Sirakov 80), Balakov, Yordanov (Kostadinov 65), Penev, Stoichkov.
Germany: Kopke; Helmer, Sammer, Babbel, Reuter, Eilts, Basler (Moller 80), Hassler, Strunz (Kirsten 89), Klinsmann, Herrlich.
Referee: Pairetto (Italy).

Cardiff, 7 June 1995, 6500

Wales (0) 0

Georgia (0) 1 *(Kinkladze 73)*

Wales: Southall; Phillips, Bowen, Jones, Williams, Symons, Horne, Saunders (Pembridge 84), Rush, Cornforth, Hughes (Hartson 84).
Georgia: Devadze; Beradze, Tskhadadze, Shelia, Chikhradze, Inalishvili, Gogichaivsili, Kinkladze, Ketsbaia, Kavelashvili (Tskitishvili 74), Arveladze S (Kilasonia 88).
Referee: Koho (Finland).

Chisinau, 7 June 1995, 7000

Moldova (2) 2 *(Curtianu 10, Cleschenko 15)*

Albania (2) 3 *(Kushta 7, Bellai 25, Vata 71)*

Moldova: Ivanov; Secu, Fistican, Pogorelov, Rebeja (Kosse 74), Stroenko S, Stroenko A, Belous (Miterev 55), Nani, Curtianu, Clescenko.
Albania: Strakosha; Bano, Shulku, Malko, Vata, Kacaj, Kushta, Bellai, Kola, Rraklli (Prenga 87), Demollari (Bano 79).
Referee: Schelings (Belgium).

	P	*W*	*D*	*L*	*F*	*A*	*Pts*
Bulgaria	6	6	0	0	18	4	18
Germany	6	4	1	1	12	6	13
Georgia	7	4	0	3	9	5	12
Albania	7	2	0	5	8	11	6
Moldova	7	2	0	5	7	18	6
Wales	7	1	1	5	6	16	4

Group 8

Toftir, 7 September 1994, 2412

Faeroes (0) 1 *(Apostolakis (og) 89)*

Greece (2) 5 *(Saravakos 12, Tsalouhidis 18, 85, Alexandris 54, 60)*

Faeroes: Knudsen; Hansen T, Hansen A, Johannesen O, Jarnskor M, Hansen J, Morkore A (Rasmussen 85), Dam J, Muller, Jonsson, Hansen O (Jarnskor H 56).
Greece: Karkamanis; Apostolakis, Pavlopoulos, Kallitzakis, Karataidis, Hantzidis (Zagorakis 82), Tsalouhidis, Tsartas, Kostis (Markos 77), Alexandris, Saravakos.
Referee: Piraux (Belgium).

Helsinki, 7 September 1994, 12,845

Finland (0) 0

Scotland (1) 2 *(Shearer 29, Collins 66)*

Finland: Jakonen; Makela, Hyrylainen, Kanerva, Heinola (Holmgren 28), Suominen, Litmanen, Lindberg, Rantanen (Jarvinen 41), Paatelainen, Hjelm.
Scotland: Goram; McKimmie, Hendry, Levein (McCall 78), Boyd, McLaren, McStay, McAllister, Collins, Walker (Jess 65), Shearer.
Referee: Wocjik (Poland).

Hampden Park, 12 October 1994, 20,885

Scotland (3) 5 *(McGinlay 4, Booth 34, Collins 40, 72, McKinlay 61)*

Faeroes (0) 1 *(Muller 75)*

Scotland: Goram; McLaren, McKimmie, Levein, Hendry (McKinlay 58), McStay, Boyd, Nevin, Booth (Walker 69), McGinlay, Collins.
Faeroes: Knudsen; Dam J (Joensen 53), Hansen T, Johannesen O, Hansen J, Hansen O (Rasmussen 73), Jarnskor H, Morkore K, Jarnskor M, Muller, Jonsson.
Referee: Hauge (Norway).

Salonika, 12 October 1994, 30,000

Greece (1) 4 *(Markos 23, Batista 70, Mahlas 76, 90)*

Finland (0) 0

Greece: Atmatzidis; Apostolakis, Kassapis, Dabizas, Kallitzakis, Tsalouhidis, Zagorakis, Markos (Toursounidis 65), Mahlas, Tsartas, Vrizas (Batista 43).
Finland: Jakonen; Makela, Kanerva, Hyrylainen, Heinola (Holmgren 30), Suominen, Jarvinen, Lindberg, Hjelm, Litmanen, Paatelainen.
Referee: Leduc (France).

Moscow, 12 October 1994, 20,000

Russia (1) 4 *(Karpin 43, Kolyvanov 64, Nikiforov 65, Radchenko 67)*

San Marino (0) 0

Russia: Cherchesov; Kulkov (Tetradze 65), Nikiforov, Tsymbalar (Kolyvanov 55), Shalimov, Karpin, Onopko, Kanchelskis, Pyatnitski, Radchenko, Kiryakov.
San Marino: Benedettini; Gobbi, Gennari, Mazza M, Valentini, Guerra (Della Valle 23), Manzaroli, Matteoni, Bacciocchi, Bonini, Francini (Canti 67).
Referee: Hamer (Luxembourg).

Helsinki, 16 November 1994, 2240

Finland (1) 5 *(Sumiala 37, Litmanen 51 (pen), 71, Paatelainen 75, 85)*

Faeroes (0) 0

Finland: Laukkanen; Makela, Kanerva, Eriksson, Helin, Litmanen, Ukkonen, Lindberg (Rajamaki 78), Sumiala (Ruhanen 90), Hjelm, Paatelainen.
Faeroes: Knudsen; Johannesen, Rasmussen, Hansen O (Rasmussen J E 80), Hansen T, Morkore K, Jarnskor M, Jarnskor H, Joensen, Muller, Jonsson.
Referee: Orrason (Iceland).

Athens, 16 November 1994, 15,000

Greece (1) 2 *(Mahlas 21, Frantzeskos 84)*

San Marino (0) 0

Greece: Atmatzidis; Apostolakis, Dabizas, Kallitzakis, Kassapis, Maragos (Frantzeskos 46), Zagorakis, Toursounidis, Tsartas, Mahlas, Vrizas (Batista 70).
San Marino: Benedettini; Gobbi, Valentini, Guerra, Gennari (Canti 46), Manzaroli, Della Valle (Gasperoni 75), Francini, Bonini, Bacciocchi, Gualtieri.
Referee: Lipkovitch (Israel).

Hampden Park, 16 November 1994, 31,254

Scotland (1) 1 *(Booth 19)*

Russia (1) 1 *(Radchenko 25)*

Scotland: Goram; McKimmie, Boyd, McCall, Levein, McLaren, McKinlay (Nevin 83), McAllister, Booth, McGinlay (Spencer 63), Collins.
Russia: Cherchesov; Gorlukovich, Nikiforov, Kulkov, Shalimov, Kanchelskis, Karpin, Pyatniski (Tetradze), Onopko, Radimov, Radchenko.
Referee: Karlsson (Sweden).

Helsinki, 14 December 1994, 3140

Finland (2) 4 *(Paatelainen 24, 30, 85, 90)*

San Marino (1) 1 *(Della Valle 34)*

Finland: Laukkanen; Makela, Kanerva, Eriksson, Lindberg, Helin (Myyry 74), Ukkonen, Sumiala, Litmanen, Hjelm, Paatelainen.
San Marino: Benedettini; Canti, Gasperoni, Gobbi, Gennari, Bonini, Guerra, Manzaroli, Della Valle, Bacciocchi (Peverani 15), Mularoni (Gualtieri 60).
Referee: Albrecht (Germany).

Athens, 18 December 1994, 20,310

Greece (1) 1 *(Apostolakis 18 (pen))*

Scotland (0) 0

Greece: Atmatzidis; Apostolakis, Vlahos, Kallitzakis, Kassapis, Tsalouhidis, Zagorakis, Nioblias (Karassavidis 88), Toursounidis, Mahlas, Alexandris (Maragos 72).
Scotland: Goram (Leighton 78); McKimmie, Hendry, McLaren, Boyd, McCall, McAllister, Collins, McGinlay, McKinlay (Spencer 46), Ferguson.
Referee: Blankenstein (Holland).

Moscow, 29 March 1995, 25,000

Russia (0) 0

Scotland (0) 0

Russia: Kharine; Khlestov, Nikiforov, Kovtoun, Karpin, Onopko, Dobrovolski, Shalimov (Radimov 69), Kanchelskis, Kiryakov, Radchenko (Pisarev 57).
Scotland: Leighton; McKimmie, Calderwood, Hendry, McLaren, McStay, Boyd, Collins, McAllister, McGinlay (McKinlay 84), Jackson (Shearer 78).
Referee: Strampe (Germany).

San Marino, 29 March 1995, 1000

San Marino (0) 0

Finland (1) 2 *(Litmanen 45, Sumiala 65)*

San Marino: Benedettini; Gobbi, Valentini, Guerra, Gennari, Mazza (Matteoni 70), Manzaroli, Francini, Bonini, Montagna (Gualtieri 75), Mularoni.
Finland: Laukkanen; Makela (Hyypia 74), Ukkonen, Helin, Lindberg, Eriksson, Sumiala, Myyry, Litmanen, Hjelm, Jarvinen (Rajamaki 69).
Referee: Suheli (Israel).

Serrevalle, 26 April 1995, 2738

San Marino (0) 0

Scotland (1) 2 *(Collins 19, Calderwood 85)*

San Marino: Benedettini; Manzaroli, Canti, Guerra, Gobbi, Gennari, Mazza M, Delia, Bonini (Matteoni 46), Mularoni (Gualtieri 72), Bacciocchi.
Scotland: Leighton; McLaren, Boyd, Calderwood, Hendry, Jackson, Collins, McGinlay, Shearer (Spencer 67), McAllister, Nevin (McKinlay 78).
Referee: Loizou (Cyprus).

Salonika, 26 April 1995, 30,000

Greece (0) 0

Russia (1) 3 *(Nikiforov 36, Zagorakis 78 (og), Bestchastnikh 79)*

Greece: Atmatzidis; Apostolakis, Kallitzakis, Dabizas, Zagorakis, Tsalouhidis, Kassapis, Nioplias (Tsartas 46), Toursounidis, Mahlas (Nikolaidis 60), Donis.
Russia: Kharine; Kovtoun, Nikiforov, Kulkov, Khlestov, Karpin, Onopko, Dobrovolski, Piatnitski (Kiryakov 46), Radchenko (Mostovoi 77), Bestchastnikh.
Referee: Stafoggia (Italy).

Toftir, 26 April 1995, 1000

Faeroes (0) 0

Finland (0) 4 *(Hjelm 55, Paatelainen 75, Lindberg 78, Helin 83)*

Faeroes: Knudsen; Morkore A, Rasmussen J, Johannesen O, Hansen J, Hansen O, Johnsson, Morkore K, Jonsen A, Jarnskor M (Jarnskor H 80), Jonsson.
Finland: Laukkanen; Makela, Ukkonen, Eriksson, Helin, Hyypia, Litmanen, Lindberg (Suominen 82), Sumiala (Kolkka 61), Hjelm, Paatelainen.
Referee: Howells (Wales).

Moscow, 6 May 1995, 9500

Russia (0) 3 *(Ketschinov 52, Pisarev 73, Moukhamadiev 80)*

Faeroes (0) 0

Russia: Cherchesov; Khlestov, Nikiforov, Kovtoun, Tetradze, Ketschinov, Onopko, Cherichev, Piatnitski (Lebed 22), Pisarev, Moukhamadiev.
Faeroes: Knudsen; Johannesen O, Hansen J, Rasmussen J, Morkore K, Jonsen A, Jarnskor M, Hansen E, Jarnskor H (Jonsen D 69), Jonsson, Rasmussen J E.
Referee: Kvartskelia (Georgia).

Toftir, 25 May 1995, 3452

Faeroes (2) 3 *(Hansen J 7, Rasmussen J E 9, Johnsson 62)*

San Marino (0) 0

Faeroes: Knudsen; Jarnskor H, Hansen J, Johannesen O, Rasmussen J, Hansen O, Johnsson, Morkore K, Jarnskor M, Jonsson, Rasmussen J E.
San Marino: Benedettini; Gasperoni, Gobbi, Valentini, Gennari, Canti, Manzaroli, Bonini (Ugolini 57), Francini, Bacciocchi, Mularoni.

Serravalle, 7 June 1995, 1400

San Marino (0) 0

Russia (2) 7 *(Dobrovolski 30 (pen), Gobbi 35 (og), Kiryakov 49, Shalimov 50, Bestchastnikh 59, Kolyvanov 65, Tcherychev 88)*

San Marino: Benedettini; Gobbi, Gennari, Mazza, Valentini, Guerra, Manzaroli, Della Valle (Canti 64), Francini, Montagna (Bonini 78), Bacciocchi.

Russia: Cherchesov; Kulkov, Tetradze, Kovtoun, Karpin, Onopko, Shalimov, Dobrovolski (Radchenko 60), Kiryakov, Kolyvanov, Bestchastnikh (Cherichev 84).
Referee: Bohunek (Czech Republic).

Toftir, 7 June 1995, 3881

Faeroes (0) 0

Scotland (2) 2 *(McKinlay 25, McGinlay 29)*

Faeroes: Knudsen; Jarnskor H, Hansen T, Johannesen O, Rasmussen J, Hansen J, Johnsson, Jarnskor M (Jonsen A 56), Hansen O, Rasmussen J E (Muller 75), Jonsson.
Scotland: Leighton; McKimmie, McLaren, Burley, Calderwood, McKinnon, McKinlay, Jackson, Shearer (Robertson 86), McGinlay (Gemmill 75), Collins.
Referee: Hrinak (Slovakia).

Helsinki, 11 June 1995, 7000

Finland (1) 2 *(Litmanen 45 (pen), Hjelm 55)*

Greece (1) 1 *(Nikolaidis 6)*

Finland: Laukkanen; Makela, Tuomela, Holmgren, Helin, Lindberg, Sumiala (Jarvinen 63), Myyry, Hjelm, Litmanen, Paatelainen (Tiainen 85).
Greece: Michopoulos; Apostolakis, Kassapis, Dabizas, Alexiou, Tsalouhidis, Nikolaidis, Markos (Batista 57), Zagorakis, Tsartas (Mahlas 70), Donis.
Referee: Krug (Germany).

	P	*W*	*D*	*L*	*F*	*A*	*Pts*
Finland	7	5	0	2	17	8	15
Russia	6	4	2	0	18	1	14
Scotland	7	4	2	1	12	3	14
Greece	6	4	0	2	13	6	12
Faeroes	7	1	0	6	5	24	3
San Marino	7	0	0	7	1	24	0

EUROPEAN CHAMPIONSHIP 1996

Remaining fixtures

Group 1
(France, Romania, Poland, Israel, Slovakia, Azerbaijan)
16. 8.95 France–Poland
16. 8.95 Azerbaijan–Slovakia
6. 9.95 France–Azerbaijan
6. 9.95 Slovakia–Israel
6. 9.95 Poland–Romania
11.10.95 Romania–France
11.10.95 Israel–Azerbaijan
11.10.95 Slovakia–Poland
15.11.95 Slovakia–Romania
15.11.95 Azerbaijan–Poland
15.11.95 France–Israel

Group 2
(Denmark, Spain, Belgium, F.Y.R. Macedonia, Cyprus, Armenia)
16. 8.95 Armenia–Denmark
6. 9.95 Belgium–Denmark
6. 9.95 Spain–Cyprus
6. 9.95 F.Y.R. Macedonia–Armenia
7.10.95 Armenia–Belgium
11.10.95 Denmark–Spain
11.10.95 Cyprus–F.Y.R. Macedonia
15.11.95 Spain–F.Y.R. Macedonia
15.11.95 Cyprus–Belgium
15.11.95 Denmark–Armenia

Group 3
(Sweden, Switzerland, Hungary, Iceland, Turkey)
16. 8.95 Iceland–Switzerland
6. 9.95 Sweden–Switzerland
6. 9.95 Turkey–Hungary
11.10.95 Switzerland–Hungary
11.10.95 Iceland–Turkey
11.11.95 Hungary–Iceland
15.11.95 Sweden–YTurkey

Group 4
(Italy, Ukraine, Croatia, Lithuania, Estonia, Slovenia)
16. 8.95 Estonia–Lithuania
3. 9.95 Croatia–Estonia
6. 9.95 Italy–Slovenia
6. 9.95 Lithuania–Ukraine
8.10.95 Croatia–Italy
11.10.95 Slovenia–Ukraine
11.10.95 Lithuania–Estonia
11.11.95 Italy–Ukraine
15.11.95 Slovenia–Croatia
15.11.95 Italy–Lithuania

Group 5
(Netherlands, Norway, Czech Republic, Belarus, Malta, Luxembourg)
16. 8.95 Norway–Czech Republic
6. 9.95 Czech Republic–Norway
6. 9.95 Luxembourg–Malta
6. 9.95 Netherlands–Belarus
7.10.95 Belarus–Czech Republic
8.10.95 Malta–Netherlands
11.10.95 Luxembourg–Belarus
12.11.95 Malta–Belarus
15.11.95 Czech Republic–Luxembourg
15.11.95 Netherlands–Norway

Group 6
(Rep. of Ireland, Portugal, Northern Ireland, Austria, Latvia, Liechtenstein)
15. 8.95 Liechtenstein–Portugal
16. 8.95 Latvia–Austria
3. 9.95 Portugal–Northern Ireland
6. 9.95 Austria–Rep. of Ireland
6. 9.95 Latvia–Liechtenstein
11.10.95 Rep. of Ireland–Latvia
11.10.95 Austria–Portugal
11.10.95 Liechtenstein–Northern Ireland
15.11.95 Portugal–Rep. of Ireland
15.11.95 Northern Ireland–Austria

Group 7
(Germany, Wales, Bulgaria, Georgia, Albania, Moldova)
6. 9.95 Germany–Georgia
6. 9.95 Wales–Moldova
6. 9.95 Albania–Bulgaria
7.10.95 Bulgaria–Albania
8.10.95 Germany–Moldova
11.10.95 Wales–Germany
11.10.95 Georgia–Bulgaria
15.11.95 Germany–Bulgaria
15.11.95 Albania–Wales
15.11.95 Moldova–Georgia

Group 8
(Russia, Greece, Scotland, Finland, Faroe Islands, San Marino)
16. 8.95 Scotland–Greece
16. 8.95 Finland–Russia
16. 8.95 Faroe Islands–San Marino
6. 9.95 Scotland–Finland
6. 9.95 Faroe Islands–Russia
6. 9.95 San Marino–Greece
11.10.95 Russia–Greece
11.10.95 Scotland–Faroe Islands
15.11.95 Scotland–San Marino
15.11.95 Russia–Finland
15.11.95 Greece–Faroe Islands

THE WORLD CUP 1930–94

Year	Winners	Runners-up	Venue	Attendance	Referee
1930	Uruguay 4	Argentina 2	Montevideo	90,000	Langenus (B)
1934	Italy 2 *(after extra time)*	Czechoslovakia 1	Rome	50,000	Eklind (Se)
1938	Italy 4	Hungary 2	Paris	45,000	Capdeville (F)
1950	Uruguay 2	Brazil 1	Rio de Janeiro	199,854	Reader (E)
1954	West Germany 3	Hungary 2	Berne	60,000	Ling (E)
1958	Brazil 5	Sweden 2	Stockholm	49,737	Guigue (F)
1962	Brazil 3	Czechoslovakia 1	Santiago	68,679	Latychev (USSR)
1966	England 4 *(after extra time)*	West Germany 2	Wembley	93,802	Dienst (Sw)
1970	Brazil 4	Italy 1	Mexico City	107,412	Glockner (EG)
1974	West Germany 2	Holland 1	Munich	77,833	Taylor (E)
1978	Argentina 3 *(after extra time)*	Holland 1	Buenos Aires	77,000	Gonella (1)
1982	Italy 3	West Germany 1	Madrid	90,080	Coelho (Br)
1986	Argentina 3	West Germany 2	Mexico City	114,580	Filho (Br)
1990	West Germany 1	Argentina 0	Rome	73,603	Codesal (Mex)
1994	Brazil 0 *(Brazil won 3-2 on penalties act)*	Italy 0	Los Angeles	94,194	Puhl (Hungary)

GOALSCORING AND ATTENDANCES IN WORLD CUP FINAL ROUNDS

Venue	*Matches*	*Goals (avge)*	*Attendance (avge)*
1930, Uruguay	18	70 (3.9)	434,500 (24,138)
1934, Italy	17	70 (4.1)	395,000 (23,235)
1938, France	18	84 (4.6)	483,000 (26,833)
1950, Brazil	22	88 (4.0)	1,337,000 (60,772)
1954, Switzerland	26	140 (5.4)	943,000 (36,270)
1958, Sweden	35	126 (3.6)	868,000 (24,800)
1962, Chile	32	89 (2.8)	776,000 (24,250)
1966, England	32	89 (2.8)	1,614,677 (50,458)
1970, Mexico	32	95 (2.9)	1,673,975 (52,311)
1974, West Germany	38	97 (2.5)	1,774,022 (46,684)
1978, Argentina	38	102 (2.7)	1,610,215 (42,374)
1982, Spain	52	146 (2.8)	2,064,364 (38,816)
1986, Mexico	52	132 (2.5)	2,441,731 (46,956)
1990, Italy	52	115 (2.2)	2,515,168 (48,368)
1994, USA	52	141 (2.71)	3,567,415 (68,604)

LEADING GOALSCORERS

Year	*Player*	*Goals*
1930	Guillermo Stabile (Argentina)	8
1934	Angelo Schiavio (Italy)	
	Oldrich Nejedly (Czechoslovakia)	
	Edmund Conen (Germany)	4
1938	Leonidas da Silva (Brazil)	8
1950	Ademir (Brazil)	9
1954	Sandor Kocsis (Hungary)	11
1958	Just Fontaine (France)	13
1962	Drazen Jerkovic (Yugoslavia)	5
1966	Eusebio (Portugal)	9
1970	Gerd Muller (West Germany)	10
1974	Grzegorz Lato (Poland)	7
1978	Mario Kempes (Argentina)	6
1982	Paolo Rossi (Italy)	6
1986	Gary Lineker (England)	6
1990	Salvatore Schillaci (Italy)	6
1994	Oleg Salenko (Russia)	
	Hristo Stoichkov (Bulgaria)	6

BRITISH AND IRISH INTERNATIONAL RESULTS 1872–1995

Note: In the results that follow, WC = World Cup, EC = European Championship, UI = Umbro International Trophy. For Ireland, read Northern Ireland from 1921.

ENGLAND v SCOTLAND

Played: 107; England won 43, Scotland won 40, Drawn 24. *Goals:* England 188, Scotland 168.

			E	*S*
1872	30 Nov	Glasgow	0	0
1873	8 Mar	Kennington Oval	4	2
1874	7 Mar	Glasgow	1	2
1875	6 Mar	Kennington Oval	2	2
1876	4 Mar	Glasgow	0	3
1877	3 Mar	Kennington Oval	1	3
1878	2 Mar	Glasgow	2	7
1879	5 Apr	Kennington Oval	5	4
1880	13 Mar	Glasgow	4	5
1881	12 Mar	Kennington Oval	1	6
1882	11 Mar	Glasgow	1	5
1883	10 Mar	Sheffield	2	3
1884	15 Mar	Glasgow	0	1
1885	21 Mar	Kennington Oval	1	1
1886	31 Mar	Glasgow	1	1
1887	19 Mar	Blackburn	2	3
1888	17 Mar	Glasgow	5	0
1889	13 Apr	Kennington Oval	2	3
1890	5 Apr	Glasgow	1	1
1891	6 Apr	Blackburn	2	1
1892	2 Apr	Glasgow	4	1
1893	1 Apr	Richmond	5	2
1894	7 Apr	Glasgow	2	2
1895	6 Apr	Everton	3	0
1896	4 Apr	Glasgow	1	2
1897	3 Apr	Crystal Palace	1	2
1898	2 Apr	Glasgow	3	1
1899	8 Apr	Birmingham	2	1
1900	7 Apr	Glasgow	1	4
1901	30 Mar	Crystal Palace	2	2
1902	3 Mar	Birmingham	2	2
1903	4 Apr	Sheffield	1	2
1904	9 Apr	Glasgow	1	0
1905	1 Apr	Crystal Palace	1	0
1906	7 Apr	Glasgow	1	2
1907	6 Apr	Newcastle	1	1
1908	4 Apr	Glasgow	1	1
1909	3 Apr	Crystal Palace	2	0
1910	2 Apr	Glasgow	0	2
1911	1 Apr	Everton	1	1
1912	23 Mar	Glasgow	1	1
1913	5 Apr	Chelsea	1	0
1914	14 Apr	Glasgow	1	3
1920	10 Apr	Sheffield	5	4
1921	9 Apr	Glasgow	0	3
1922	8 Apr	Aston Villa	0	1
1923	14 Apr	Glasgow	2	2
1924	12 Apr	Wembley	1	1
1925	4 Apr	Glasgow	0	2
1926	17 Apr	Manchester	0	1
1927	2 Apr	Glasgow	2	1
1928	31 Mar	Wembley	1	5
1929	13 Apr	Glasgow	0	1
1930	5 Apr	Wembley	5	2

			E	*S*
1931	28 Mar	Glasgow	0	2
1932	9 Apr	Wembley	3	0
1933	1 Apr	Glasgow	1	2
1934	14 Apr	Wembley	3	0
1935	6 Apr	Glasgow	0	2
1936	4 Apr	Wembley	1	1
1937	17 Apr	Glasgow	1	3
1938	9 Apr	Wembley	0	1
1939	15 Apr	Glasgow	2	1
1947	12 Apr	Wembley	1	1
1948	10 Apr	Glasgow	2	0
1949	9 Apr	Wembley	1	3
WC1950	15 Apr	Glasgow	1	0
1951	14 Apr	Wembley	2	3
1952	5 Apr	Glasgow	2	1
1953	18 Apr	Wembley	2	2
WC1954	3 Apr	Glasgow	4	2
1955	2 Apr	Wembley	7	2
1956	14 Apr	Glasgow	1	1
1957	6 Apr	Wembley	2	1
1958	19 Apr	Glasgow	4	0
1959	11 Apr	Wembley	1	0
1960	19 Apr	Glasgow	1	1
1961	15 Apr	Wembley	9	3
1962	14 Apr	Glasgow	0	2
1963	6 Apr	Wembley	1	2
1964	11 Apr	Glasgow	0	1
1965	10 Apr	Wembley	2	2
1966	2 Apr	Glasgow	4	3
EC1967	15 Apr	Wembley	2	3
EC1968	24 Jan	Glasgow	1	1
1969	10 May	Wembley	4	1
1970	25 Apr	Glasgow	0	0
1971	22 May	Wembley	3	1
1972	27 May	Glasgow	1	0
1973	14 Feb	Glasgow	5	0
1973	19 May	Wembley	1	0
1974	18 May	Wembley	0	2
1975	24 May	Wembley	5	1
1976	15 May	Glasgow	1	2
1977	4 June	Wembley	1	2
1978	20 May	Glasgow	1	0
1979	26 May	Wembley	3	1
1980	24 May	Glasgow	2	0
1981	23 May	Wembley	0	1
1982	29 May	Glasgow	1	0
1983	1 June	Wembley	2	0
1984	26 May	Glasgow	1	1
1985	25 May	Glasgow	0	1
1986	23 Apr	Wembley	2	1
1987	23 May	Glasgow	0	0
1988	21 May	Wembley	1	0
1989	27 May	Glasgow	2	0

ENGLAND v WALES

Played: 97; England won 62, Wales won 14, Drawn 21. *Goals:* England 239, Scotland 90.

			E	*W*
1879	18 Jan	Kennington Oval	2	1
1880	15 Mar	Wrexham	3	2
1881	26 Feb	Blackburn	0	1

			E	*W*
1882	13 Mar	Wrexham	3	5
1883	3 Feb	Kennington Oval	5	0
1884	17 Mar	Wrexham	4	0

			E	W				E	W
1885	14 Mar	Blackburn	1	1	1934	29 Sept	Cardiff	4	0
1886	29 Mar	Wrexham	3	1	1936	5 Feb	Wolverhampton	1	2
1887	26 Feb	Kennington Oval	4	0	1936	17 Oct	Cardiff	1	2
1888	4 Feb	Crewe	5	1	1937	17 Nov	Middlesbrough	2	1
1889	23 Feb	Stoke	4	1	1938	22 Oct	Cardiff	2	4
1890	15 Mar	Wrexham	3	1	1946	13 Nov	Manchester	3	0
1891	7 May	Sunderland	4	1	1947	18 Oct	Cardiff	3	0
1892	5 Mar	Wrexham	2	0	1948	10 Nov	Aston Villa	1	0
1893	13 Mar	Stoke	6	0	WC1949	15 Oct	Cardiff	4	1
1894	12 Mar	Wrexham	5	1	1950	15 Nov	Sunderland	4	2
1895	18 Mar	Queen's Club, Kensington	1	1	1951	20 Oct	Cardiff	1	1
					1952	12 Nov	Wembley	5	2
1896	16 Mar	Cardiff	9	1	WC1953	10 Oct	Cardiff	4	1
1897	29 Mar	Sheffield	4	0	1954	10 Nov	Wembley	3	2
1898	28 Mar	Wrexham	3	0	1955	27 Oct	Cardiff	1	2
1899	20 Mar	Bristol	4	0	1956	14 Nov	Wembley	3	1
1900	26 Mar	Cardiff	1	1	1957	19 Oct	Cardiff	4	0
1901	18 Mar	Newcastle	6	0	1958	26 Nov	Aston Villa	2	2
1902	3 Mar	Wrexham	0	0	1959	17 Oct	Cardiff	1	1
1903	2 Mar	Portsmouth	2	1	1960	23 Nov	Wembley	5	1
1904	29 Mar	Wrexham	2	2	1961	14 Oct	Cardiff	1	1
1905	27 Mar	Liverpool	3	1	1962	21 Oct	Wembley	4	0
1906	19 Mar	Cardiff	1	0	1963	12 Oct	Cardiff	4	0
1907	18 Mar	Fulham	1	1	1964	18 Nov	Wembley	2	1
1908	16 Mar	Wrexham	7	1	1965	2 Oct	Cardiff	0	0
1909	15 Mar	Nottingham	2	0	EC1966	16 Nov	Wembley	5	1
1910	14 Mar	Cardiff	1	0	EC1967	21 Oct	Cardiff	3	0
1911	13 Mar	Millwall	3	0	1969	7 May	Wembley	2	1
1912	11 Mar	Wrexham	2	0	1970	18 Apr	Cardiff	1	1
1913	17 Mar	Bristol	4	3	1971	19 May	Wembley	0	0
1914	16 Mar	Cardiff	2	0	1972	20 May	Cardiff	3	0
1920	15 Mar	Highbury	1	2	WC1972	15 Nov	Cardiff	1	0
1921	14 Mar	Cardiff	0	0	WC1973	24 Jan	Wembley	1	1
1922	13 Mar	Liverpool	1	0	1973	15 May	Wembley	3	0
1923	5 Mar	Cardiff	2	2	1974	11 May	Cardiff	2	0
1924	3 Mar	Blackburn	1	2	1975	21 May	Wembley	2	2
1925	28 Feb	Swansea	2	1	1976	24 Mar	Wrexham	2	1
1926	1 Mar	Crystal Palace	1	3	1976	8 May	Cardiff	1	0
1927	12 Feb	Wrexham	3	3	1977	31 May	Wembley	0	1
1927	28 Nov	Burnley	1	2	1978	3 May	Cardiff	3	1
1928	17 Nov	Swansea	3	2	1979	23 May	Wembley	0	0
1929	20 Nov	Chelsea	6	0	1980	17 May	Wrexham	1	4
1930	22 Nov	Wrexham	4	0	1981	20 May	Wembley	0	0
1931	18 Nov	Liverpool	3	1	1982	27 Apr	Cardiff	1	0
1932	16 Nov	Wrexham	0	0	1983	23 Feb	Wembley	2	1
1933	15 Nov	Newcastle	1	2	1984	2 May	Wrexham	0	1

ENGLAND v IRELAND

Played: 96; England won 74, Ireland won 6, Drawn 16. *Goals:* England 319, Ireland 80.

			E	I				E	I
1882	18 Feb	Belfast	13	0	1903	14 Feb	Wolverhampton	4	0
1883	24 Feb	Liverpool	7	0	1904	12 Mar	Belfast	3	1
1884	23 Feb	Belfast	8	1	1905	25 Feb	Middlesbrough	1	1
1885	28 Feb	Manchester	4	0	1906	17 Feb	Belfast	5	0
1886	13 Mar	Belfast	6	1	1907	16 Feb	Everton	1	0
1887	5 Feb	Sheffield	7	0	1908	15 Feb	Belfast	3	1
1888	31 Mar	Belfast	5	1	1909	13 Feb	Bradford	4	0
1889	2 Mar	Everton	6	1	1910	12 Feb	Belfast	1	1
1890	15 Mar	Belfast	9	1	1911	11 Feb	Derby	2	1
1891	7 Mar	Wolverhampton	6	1	1912	10 Feb	Dublin	6	1
1892	5 Mar	Belfast	2	0	1913	15 Feb	Belfast	1	2
1893	25 Feb	Birmingham	6	1	1914	14 Feb	Middlesbrough	0	3
1894	3 Mar	Belfast	2	2	1919	25 Oct	Belfast	1	1
1895	9 Mar	Derby	9	0	1920	23 Oct	Sunderland	2	0
1896	7 Mar	Belfast	2	0	1921	22 Oct	Belfast	1	1
1897	20 Feb	Nottingham	6	0	1922	21 Oct	West Bromwich	2	0
1898	5 Mar	Belfast	3	2	1923	20 Oct	Belfast	1	2
1899	18 Feb	Sunderland	13	2	1924	22 Oct	Everton	3	1
1900	17 Mar	Dublin	2	0	1925	24 Oct	Belfast	0	0
1901	9 Mar	Southampton	3	0	1926	20 Oct	Liverpool	3	3
1902	22 Mar	Belfast	1	0	1927	22 Oct	Belfast	0	2

			E	I				E	I
1928	22 Oct	Everton	2	1	1962	20 Oct	Belfast	3	1
1929	19 Oct	Belfast	3	0	1963	20 Nov	Wembley	8	3
1930	20 Oct	Sheffield	5	1	1964	3 Oct	Belfast	4	3
1931	17 Oct	Belfast	6	2	1965	10 Nov	Wembley	2	1
1932	17 Oct	Blackpool	1	0	EC1966	20 Oct	Belfast	2	0
1933	14 Oct	Belfast	3	0	EC1967	22 Nov	Wembley	2	0
1935	6 Feb	Everton	2	1	1969	3 May	Belfast	3	1
1935	19 Oct	Belfast	3	1	1970	21 Apr	Wembley	3	1
1936	18 Nov	Stoke	3	1	1971	15 May	Belfast	1	0
1937	23 Oct	Belfast	5	1	1972	23 May	Wembley	0	1
1938	16 Nov	Manchester	7	0	1973	12 May	Everton	2	1
1946	28 Sept	Belfast	7	2	1974	15 May	Wembley	1	0
1947	5 Nov	Everton	2	2	1975	17 May	Belfast	0	0
1948	9 Oct	Belfast	6	2	1976	11 May	Wembley	4	0
WC1949	16 Nov	Manchester	9	2	1977	28 May	Belfast	2	1
1950	7 Oct	Belfast	4	1	1978	16 May	Wembley	1	0
1951	14 Nov	Aston Villa	2	0	EC1979	7 Feb	Wembley	4	0
1952	4 Oct	Belfast	2	2	1979	19 May	Belfast	2	0
WC1953	11 Nov	Everton	3	1	EC1979	17 Oct	Belfast	5	1
1954	2 Oct	Belfast	2	0	1980	20 May	Wembley	1	1
1955	2 Nov	Wembley	3	0	1982	23 Feb	Wembley	4	0
1956	10 Oct	Belfast	1	1	1983	28 May	Belfast	0	0
1957	6 Nov	Wembley	2	3	1984	24 Apr	Wembley	1	0
1958	4 Oct	Belfast	3	3	WC1985	27 Feb	Belfast	1	0
1959	18 Nov	Wembley	2	1	WC1985	13 Nov	Wembley	0	0
1960	8 Oct	Belfast	5	2	EC1986	15 Oct	Wembley	3	0
1961	22 Nov	Wembley	1	1	EC1987	1 Apr	Belfast	2	0

SCOTLAND v WALES

Played: 101; Scotland won 60, Wales won 18, Drawn 23. *Goals:* Scotland 238, Wales 111.

			S	W				S	W
1876	25 Mar	Glasgow	4	0	1921	12 Feb	Aberdeen	2	1
1877	5 Mar	Wrexham	2	0	1922	4 Feb	Wrexham	1	2
1878	23 Mar	Glasgow	9	0	1923	17 Mar	Paisley	2	0
1879	7 Apr	Wrexham	3	0	1924	16 Feb	Cardiff	0	2
1880	3 Apr	Glasgow	5	1	1925	14 Feb	Tynecastle	3	1
1881	14 Mar	Wrexham	5	1	1925	31 Oct	Cardiff	3	0
1882	25 Mar	Glasgow	5	0	1926	30 Oct	Glasgow	3	0
1883	12 Mar	Wrexham	4	1	1927	29 Oct	Wrexham	2	2
1884	29 Mar	Glasgow	4	1	1928	27 Oct	Glasgow	4	2
1885	23 Mar	Wrexham	8	1	1929	26 Oct	Cardiff	4	2
1886	10 Apr	Glasgow	4	1	1930	25 Oct	Glasgow	1	1
1887	21 Mar	Wrexham	2	0	1931	31 Oct	Wrexham	3	2
1888	10 Mar	Edinburgh	5	1	1932	26 Oct	Edinburgh	2	5
1889	15 Apr	Wrexham	0	0	1933	4 Oct	Cardiff	2	3
1890	22 Mar	Paisley	5	0	1934	21 Nov	Aberdeen	3	2
1891	21 Mar	Wrexham	4	3	1935	5 Oct	Cardiff	1	1
1892	26 Mar	Edinburgh	6	1	1936	2 Dec	Dundee	1	2
1893	18 Mar	Wrexham	8	0	1937	30 Oct	Cardiff	1	2
1894	24 Mar	Kilmarnock	5	2	1938	9 Nov	Edinburgh	3	2
1895	23 Mar	Wrexham	2	2	1946	19 Oct	Wrexham	1	3
1896	21 Mar	Dundee	4	0	1947	12 Nov	Glasgow	1	2
1897	20 Mar	Wrexham	2	2	WC1948	23 Oct	Cardiff	3	1
1898	19 Mar	Motherwell	5	2	1949	9 Nov	Glasgow	2	0
1899	18 Mar	Wrexham	6	0	1950	21 Oct	Cardiff	3	1
1900	3 Feb	Aberdeen	5	2	1951	14 Nov	Glasgow	0	1
1901	2 Mar	Wrexham	1	1	WC1952	18 Oct	Cardiff	2	1
1902	15 Mar	Greenock	5	1	1953	4 Nov	Glasgow	3	3
1903	9 Mar	Cardiff	1	0	1954	16 Oct	Cardiff	1	0
1904	12 Mar	Dundee	1	1	1955	9 Nov	Glasgow	2	0
1905	6 Mar	Wrexham	1	3	1956	20 Oct	Cardiff	2	2
1906	3 Mar	Edinburgh	0	2	1957	13 Nov	Glasgow	1	1
1907	4 Mar	Wrexham	0	1	1958	18 Oct	Cardiff	3	0
1908	7 Mar	Dundee	2	1	1959	4 Nov	Glasgow	1	1
1909	1 Mar	Wrexham	2	3	1960	20 Oct	Cardiff	0	2
1910	5 Mar	Kilmarnock	1	0	1961	8 Nov	Glasgow	2	0
1911	6 Mar	Cardiff	2	2	1962	20 Oct	Cardiff	3	2
1912	2 Mar	Tynecastle	1	0	1963	20 Nov	Glasgow	2	1
1913	3 Mar	Wrexham	0	0	1964	3 Oct	Cardiff	2	3
1914	28 Feb	Glasgow	0	0	EC1965	24 Nov	Glasgow	4	1
1920	26 Feb	Cardiff	1	1	EC1966	22 Oct	Cardiff	1	1

			S	W				S	W
1967	22 Nov	Glasgow	3	2	wc1977	12 Oct	Liverpool	2	0
1969	3 May	Wrexham	5	3	1978	17 May	Glasgow	1	1
1970	22 Apr	Glasgow	0	0	1979	19 May	Cardiff	0	3
1971	15 May	Cardiff	0	0	1980	21 May	Glasgow	1	0
1972	24 May	Glasgow	1	0	1981	16 May	Swansea	0	2
1973	12 May	Wrexham	2	0	1982	24 May	Glasgow	1	0
1974	14 May	Glasgow	2	0	1983	28 May	Cardiff	2	0
1975	17 May	Cardiff	2	2	1984	28 Feb	Glasgow	2	1
1976	6 May	Glasgow	3	1	wc1985	27 Mar	Glasgow	0	1
wc1976	17 Nov	Glasgow	1	0	wc1985	10 Sept	Cardiff	1	1
1977	28 May	Wrexham	0	0					

SCOTLAND v IRELAND

Played: 91; Scotland won 60, Ireland won 15, Drawn 16. *Goals:* Scotland 253, Ireland 81.

			S	I				S	I
1884	26 Jan	Belfast	5	0	1934	20 Oct	Belfast	1	2
1885	14 Mar	Glasgow	8	2	1935	13 Nov	Edinburgh	2	1
1886	20 Mar	Belfast	7	2	1936	31 Oct	Belfast	3	1
1887	19 Feb	Glasgow	4	1	1937	10 Nov	Aberdeen	1	1
1888	24 Mar	Belfast	10	2	1938	8 Oct	Belfast	2	0
1889	9 Mar	Glasgow	7	0	1946	27 Nov	Glasgow	0	0
1890	29 Mar	Belfast	4	1	1947	4 Oct	Belfast	0	2
1891	28 Mar	Glasgow	2	1	1948	17 Nov	Glasgow	3	2
1892	19 Mar	Belfast	3	2	1949	1 Oct	Belfast	8	2
1893	25 Mar	Glasgow	6	1	1950	1 Nov	Glasgow	6	1
1894	31 Mar	Belfast	2	1	1951	6 Oct	Belfast	3	0
1895	30 Mar	Glasgow	3	1	1952	5 Nov	Glasgow	1	1
1896	28 Mar	Belfast	3	3	1953	3 Oct	Belfast	3	1
1897	27 Mar	Glasgow	5	1	1954	3 Nov	Glasgow	2	2
1898	26 Mar	Belfast	3	0	1955	8 Oct	Belfast	1	2
1899	25 Mar	Glasgow	9	1	1956	7 Nov	Glasgow	1	0
1900	3 Mar	Belfast	3	0	1957	5 Oct	Belfast	1	1
1901	23 Feb	Glasgow	11	0	1958	5 Nov	Glasgow	2	2
1902	1 Mar	Belfast	5	1	1959	3 Oct	Belfast	4	0
1903	21 Mar	Glasgow	0	2	1960	9 Nov	Glasgow	5	2
1904	26 Mar	Dublin	1	1	1961	7 Oct	Belfast	6	1
1905	18 Mar	Glasgow	4	0	1962	7 Nov	Glasgow	5	1
1906	17 Mar	Dublin	1	0	1963	12 Oct	Belfast	1	2
1907	16 Mar	Glasgow	3	0	1964	25 Nov	Glasgow	3	2
1908	14 Mar	Dublin	5	0	1965	2 Oct	Belfast	2	3
1909	15 Mar	Glasgow	5	0	1966	16 Nov	Glasgow	2	1
1910	19 Mar	Belfast	0	1	1967	21 Oct	Belfast	0	1
1911	18 Mar	Glasgow	2	0	1969	6 May	Glasgow	1	1
1912	16 Mar	Belfast	4	1	1970	18 Apr	Belfast	1	0
1913	15 Mar	Dublin	2	1	1971	18 May	Glasgow	0	1
1914	14 Mar	Belfast	1	1	1972	20 May	Glasgow	2	0
1920	13 Mar	Glasgow	3	0	1973	16 May	Glasgow	1	2
1921	26 Feb	Belfast	2	0	1974	11 May	Glasgow	0	1
1922	4 Mar	Glasgow	2	1	1975	20 May	Glasgow	3	0
1923	3 Mar	Belfast	1	0	1976	8 May	Glasgow	3	0
1924	1 Mar	Glasgow	2	0	1977	1 June	Glasgow	3	0
1925	28 Feb	Belfast	3	0	1978	13 May	Glasgow	1	1
1926	27 Feb	Glasgow	4	0	1979	22 May	Glasgow	1	0
1927	26 Feb	Belfast	2	0	1980	17 May	Belfast	0	1
1928	25 Feb	Glasgow	0	1	wc1981	25 Mar	Glasgow	1	1
1929	23 Feb	Belfast	7	3	1981	19 May	Glasgow	2	0
1930	22 Feb	Glasgow	3	1	wc1981	14 Oct	Belfast	0	0
1931	21 Feb	Belfast	0	0	1982	28 Apr	Belfast	1	1
1931	19 Sept	Glasgow	3	1	1983	24 May	Glasgow	0	0
1932	12 Sept	Belfast	4	0	1983	13 Dec	Belfast	0	2
1933	16 Sept	Glasgow	1	2	1992	19 Feb	Glasgow	1	0

WALES v IRELAND

Played: 90; Wales won 42, Ireland won 27, Drawn 21. *Goals:* Wales 181, Ireland 126.

			W	I				W	I
1882	25 Feb	Wrexham	7	1	1886	27 Feb	Wrexham	5	0
1883	17 Mar	Belfast	1	1	1887	12 Mar	Belfast	1	4
1884	9 Feb	Wrexham	6	0	1888	3 Mar	Wrexham	11	0
1885	11 Apr	Belfast	8	2	1889	27 Apr	Belfast	3	1

			W	I
1890	8 Feb	Shrewsbury	5	2
1891	7 Feb	Belfast	2	7
1892	27 Feb	Bangor	1	1
1893	8 Apr	Belfast	3	4
1894	24 Feb	Swansea	4	1
1895	16 Mar	Belfast	2	2
1896	29 Feb	Wrexham	6	1
1897	6 Mar	Belfast	3	4
1898	19 Feb	Llandudno	0	1
1899	4 Mar	Belfast	0	1
1900	24 Feb	Llandudno	2	0
1901	23 Mar	Belfast	1	0
1902	22 Mar	Cardiff	0	3
1903	28 Mar	Belfast	0	2
1904	21 Mar	Bangor	0	1
1905	18 Apr	Belfast	2	2
1906	2 Apr	Wrexham	4	4
1907	23 Feb	Belfast	3	2
1908	11 Apr	Aberdare	0	1
1909	20 Mar	Belfast	3	2
1910	11 Apr	Wrexham	4	1
1911	28 Jan	Belfast	2	1
1912	13 Apr	Cardiff	2	3
1913	18 Jan	Belfast	1	0
1914	19 Jan	Wrexham	1	2
1920	14 Feb	Belfast	2	2
1921	9 Apr	Swansea	2	1
1922	4 Apr	Belfast	1	1
1923	14 Apr	Wrexham	0	3
1924	15 Mar	Belfast	1	0
1925	18 Apr	Wrexham	0	0
1926	13 Feb	Belfast	0	3
1927	9 Apr	Cardiff	2	2
1928	4 Feb	Belfast	2	1
1929	2 Feb	Wrexham	2	2
1930	1 Feb	Belfast	0	7
1931	22 Apr	Wrexham	3	2
1931	5 Dec	Belfast	0	4
1932	7 Dec	Wrexham	4	1
1933	4 Nov	Belfast	1	1
1935	27 Mar	Wrexham	3	1
1936	11 Mar	Belfast	2	3
1937	17 Mar	Wrexham	4	1
1938	16 Mar	Belfast	0	1
1939	15 Mar	Wrexham	3	1
1947	16 Apr	Belfast	1	2
1948	10 Mar	Wrexham	2	0
1949	9 Mar	Belfast	2	0
WC1950	8 Mar	Wrexham	0	0
1951	7 Mar	Belfast	2	1
1952	19 Mar	Swansea	3	0
1953	15 Apr	Belfast	3	2
WC1954	31 Mar	Wrexham	1	2
1955	20 Apr	Belfast	3	2
1956	11 Apr	Cardiff	1	1
1957	10 Apr	Belfast	0	0
1958	16 Apr	Cardiff	1	1
1959	22 Apr	Belfast	1	4
1960	6 Apr	Wrexham	3	2
1961	12 Apr	Belfast	5	1
1962	11 Apr	Cardiff	4	0
1963	3 Apr	Belfast	4	1
1964	15 Apr	Cardiff	2	3
1965	31 Mar	Belfast	5	0
1966	30 Mar	Cardiff	1	4
EC1967	12 Apr	Belfast	0	0
EC1968	28 Feb	Wrexham	2	0
1969	10 May	Belfast	0	0
1970	25 Apr	Swansea	1	0
1971	22 May	Belfast	0	1
1972	27 May	Wrexham	0	0
1973	19 May	Everton	0	1
1974	18 May	Wrexham	1	0
1975	23 May	Belfast	0	1
1976	14 May	Swansea	1	0
1977	3 June	Belfast	1	1
1978	19 May	Wrexham	1	0
1979	25 May	Belfast	1	1
1980	23 May	Cardiff	0	1
1982	27 May	Wrexham	3	0
1983	31 May	Belfast	1	0
1984	22 May	Swansea	1	1

OTHER BRITISH INTERNATIONAL RESULTS 1908–1995

ENGLAND

		v ALBANIA	E	A
WC1989	8 Mar	Tirana	2	0
WC1989	26 Apr	Wembley	5	0

		v ARGENTINA	E	A
1951	9 May	Wembley	2	1
1953	17 May	Buenos Aires	0	0
(*abandoned after 21 mins*)				
WC1962	2 June	Rancagua	3	1
1964	6 June	Rio de Janeiro	0	1
WC1966	23 July	Wembley	1	0
1974	22 May	Wembley	2	2
1977	12 June	Buenos Aires	1	1
1980	13 May	Wembley	3	1
WC1986	22 June	Mexico City	1	2
1991	25 May	Wembley	2	2

		v AUSTRALIA	E	A
1980	31 May	Sydney	2	1
1983	11 June	Sydney	0	0
1983	15 June	Brisbane	1	0
1983	18 June	Melbourne	1	1
1991	1 June	Sydney	1	0

		v AUSTRIA	E	A
1908	6 June	Vienna	6	1
1908	8 June	Vienna	11	1
1909	1 June	Vienna	8	1
1930	14 May	Vienna	0	0
1932	7 Dec	Chelsea	4	3
1936	6 May	Vienna	1	2
1951	28 Nov	Wembley	2	2
1952	25 May	Vienna	3	2
WC1958	15 June	Boras	2	2
1961	27 May	Vienna	1	3
1962	4 Apr	Wembley	3	1
1965	20 Oct	Wembley	2	3
1967	27 May	Vienna	1	0
1973	26 Sept	Wembley	7	0
1979	13 June	Vienna	3	4

		v BELGIUM	E	B
1921	21 May	Brussels	2	0
1923	19 Mar	Highbury	6	1
1923	1 Nov	Antwerp	2	2
1924	8 Dec	West Bromwich	4	0
1926	24 May	Antwerp	5	3
1927	11 May	Brussels	9	1
1928	19 May	Antwerp	3	1
1929	11 May	Brussels	5	1
1931	16 May	Brussels	4	1
1936	9 May	Brussels	2	3

			E	*B*
1947	21 Sept	Brussels	5	2
1950	18 May	Brussels	4	1
1952	26 Nov	Wembley	5	0
WC1954	17 June	Basle	4	4*
1964	21 Oct	Wembley	2	2
1970	25 Feb	Brussels	3	1
EC1980	12 June	Turin	1	1
WC1990	27 June	Bologna	1	0*

**After extra time*

		v BOHEMIA	*E*	*B*
1908	13 June	Prague	4	0

		v BRAZIL	*E*	*B*
1956	9 May	Wembley	4	2
WC1958	11 June	Gothenburg	0	0
1959	13 May	Rio de Janeiro	0	2
WC1962	10 June	Vina del Mar	1	3
1963	8 May	Wembley	1	1
1964	30 May	Rio de Janeiro	1	5
1969	12 June	Rio de Janeiro	1	2
WC1970	7 June	Guadalajara	0	1
1976	23 May	Los Angeles	0	1
1977	8 June	Rio de Janeiro	0	0
1978	19 Apr	Wembley	1	1
1981	12 May	Wembley	0	1
1984	10 June	Rio de Janeiro	2	0
1987	19 May	Wembley	1	1
1990	28 Mar	Wembley	1	0
1992	17 May	Wembley	1	1
1993	13 June	Washington	1	1
UI1995	11 June	Wembley	1	3

		v BULGARIA	*E*	*B*
WC1962	7 June	Rancagua	0	0
1968	11 Dec	Wembley	1	1
1974	1 June	Sofia	1	0
EC1979	6 June	Sofia	3	0
EC1979	22 Nov	Wembley	2	0

		v CAMEROON	*E*	*C*
WC1990	1 July	Naples	3	2*
1991	6 Feb	Wembley	2	0

		v CANADA	*E*	*C*
1986	24 May	Burnaby	1	0

		v CHILE	*E*	*C*
WC1950	25 June	Rio de Janeiro	2	0
1953	24 May	Santiago	2	1
1984	17 June	Santiago	0	0
1989	23 May	Wembley	0	0

		v CIS	*E*	*C*
1992	29 Apr	Moscow	2	2

		v COLOMBIA	*E*	*C*
1970	20 May	Bogota	4	0
1988	24 May	Wembley	1	1

		v CYPRUS	*E*	*C*
EC1975	16 Apr	Wembley	5	0
EC1975	11 May	Limassol	1	0

		v CZECHOSLOVAKIA	*E*	*C*
1934	16 May	Prague	1	2
1937	1 Dec	Tottenham	5	4
1963	29 May	Bratislava	4	2
1966	2 Nov	Wembley	0	0
WC1970	11 June	Guadalajara	1	0
1973	27 May	Prague	1	1
EC1974	30 Oct	Wembley	3	0
EC1975	30 Oct	Bratislava	1	2
1978	29 Nov	Wembley	1	0
WC1982	20 June	Bilbao	2	0
1990	25 Apr	Wembley	4	2
1992	25 Mar	Prague	2	2

		v DENMARK	*E*	*D*
1948	26 Sept	Copenhagen	0	0
1955	2 Oct	Copenhagen	5	1
WC1956	5 Dec	Wolverhampton	5	2
WC1957	15 May	Copenhagen	4	1
1966	3 July	Copenhagen	2	0
EC1978	20 Sept	Copenhagen	4	3
EC1979	12 Sept	Wembley	1	0
EC1982	22 Sept	Copenhagen	2	2
EC1983	21 Sept	Wembley	0	1
1988	14 Sept	Wembley	1	0
1989	7 June	Copenhagen	1	1
1990	15 May	Wembley	1	0
EC1992	11 June	Malmo	0	0
1994	9 Mar	Wembley	1	0

		v ECUADOR	*E*	*Ec*
1970	24 May	Quito	2	0

		v EGYPT	*E*	*Eg*
1986	29 Jan	Cairo	4	0
WC1990	21 June	Cagliari	1	0

		v FIFA	*E*	*FIFA*
1938	26 Oct	Highbury	3	0
1953	21 Oct	Wembley	4	4
1963	23 Oct	Wembley	2	1

		v FINLAND	*E*	*F*
1937	20 May	Helsinki	8	0
1956	20 May	Helsinki	5	1
1966	26 June	Helsinki	3	0
WC1976	13 Juje	Helsinki	4	1
WC1976	13 Oct	Wembley	2	1
1982	3 June	Helsinki	4	1
WC1984	17 Oct	Wembley	5	0
WC1985	22 May	Helsinki	1	1
1992	3 June	Helsinki	2	1

		v FRANCE	*E*	*F*
1923	10 May	Paris	4	1
1924	17 May	Paris	3	1
1925	21 May	Paris	3	2
1927	26 May	Paris	6	0
1928	17 May	Paris	5	1
1929	9 May	Paris	4	1
1931	14 May	Paris	2	5
1933	6 Dec	Tottenham	4	1
1938	26 May	Paris	4	2
1947	3 May	Highbury	3	0
1949	22 May	Paris	3	1
1951	3 Oct	Highbury	2	2
1955	15 May	Paris	0	1
1957	27 Nov	Wembley	4	0
EC1962	3 Oct	Sheffield	1	1
EC1963	27 Feb	Paris	2	5
WC1966	20 July	Wembley	2	0
1969	12 Mar	Wembley	5	0
WC1982	16 June	Bilbao	3	1
1984	29 Feb	Paris	0	2
1992	19 Feb	Wembley	2	0
EC1992	14 June	Malmo	0	0

		v GERMANY	*E*	*G*
1930	10 May	Berlin	3	3
1935	4 Dec	Tottenham	3	0

			E	G
1938	14 May	Berlin	6	3
1991	11 Sept	Wembley	0	1
1993	19 June	Detroit	1	2

v EAST GERMANY

			E	EG
1963	2 June	Leipzig	2	1
1970	25 Nov	Wembley	3	1
1974	29 May	Leipzig	1	1
1984	12 Sept	Wembley	1	0

v WEST GERMANY

			E	WG
1954	1 Dec	Wembley	3	1
1956	26 May	Berlin	3	1
1965	12 May	Nuremberg	1	0
1966	23 Feb	Wembley	1	0
WC1966	30 July	Wembley	4	2*
1968	1 June	Hanover	0	1
WC1970	14 June	Leon	2	3*
EC1972	29 Apr	Wembley	1	3
EC1972	13 May	Berlin	0	0
1975	12 Mar	Wembley	2	0
1978	22 Feb	Munich	1	2
WC1982	29 June	Madrid	0	0
1982	13 Oct	Wembley	1	2
1985	12 June	Mexico City	3	0
1987	9 Sept	Dusseldorf	1	3
WC1990	4 July	Turin	1	1*

**After extra time*

v GREECE

			E	G
EC1971	21 Apr	Wembley	3	0
EC1971	1 Dec	Athens	2	0
EC1982	17 Nov	Athens	3	0
EC1983	30 Mar	Wembley	0	0
1989	8 Feb	Athens	2	1
1994	17 May	Wembley	5	0

v HOLLAND

			E	H
1935	18 May	Amsterdam	1	0
1946	27 Nov	Huddersfield	8	2
1964	9 Dec	Amsterdam	1	1
1969	5 Nov	Amsterdam	1	0
1970	14 Jun	Wembley	0	0
1977	9 Feb	Wembley	0	2
1982	25 May	Wembley	2	0
1988	23 Mar	Wembley	2	2
EC1988	15 June	Dusseldorf	1	3
WC1990	16 June	Cagliari	0	0
WC1993	28 Apr	Wembley	2	2
WC1993	13 Oct	Rotterdam	0	2

v HUNGARY

			E	H
1908	10 June	Budapest	7	0
1909	29 May	Budapest	4	2
1909	31 May	Budapest	8	2
1934	10 May	Budapest	1	2
1936	2 Dec	Highbury	6	2
1953	25 Nov	Wembley	3	6
1954	23 May	Budapest	1	7
1960	22 May	Budapest	0	2
WC1962	31 May	Rancagua	1	2
1965	5 May	Wembley	1	0
1978	24 May	Wembley	4	1
WC1981	6 June	Budapest	3	1
WC1982	18 Nov	Wembley	1	0
EC1983	27 Apr	Wembley	2	0
EC1983	12 Oct	Budapest	3	0
1988	27 Apr	Budapest	0	0
1990	12 Sept	Wembley	1	0
1992	12 May	Budapest	1	0

v ICELAND

			E	I
1982	2 June	Reykjavik	1	1

v REPUBLIC OF IRELAND

			E	RI
1946	30 Sept	Dublin	1	0
1949	21 Sept	Everton	0	2
WC1957	8 May	Wembley	5	1
WC1957	19 May	Dublin	1	1
1964	24 May	Dublin	3	1
1976	8 Sept	Wembley	1	1
EC1978	25 Oct	Dublin	1	1
EC1980	6 Feb	Wembley	2	0
1985	26 Mar	Wembley	2	1
EC1988	12 June	Stuttgart	0	1
WC1990	11 June	Cagliari	1	1
EC1990	14 Nov	Dublin	1	1
EC1991	27 Mar	Wembley	1	1
1995	15 Feb	Dublin	0	1

(abandoned after 27 mins)

v ISRAEL

			E	I
1986	26 Feb	Ramat Gan	2	1
1988	17 Feb	Tel Aviv	0	0

v ITALY

			E	I
1933	13 May	Rome	1	1
1934	14 Nov	Highbury	3	2
1939	13 May	Milan	2	2
1948	16 May	Turin	4	0
1949	30 Nov	Tottenham	2	0
1952	18 May	Florence	1	1
1959	6 May	Wembley	2	2
1961	24 May	Rome	3	2
1973	14 June	Turin	0	2
1973	14 Nov	Wembley	0	1
1976	28 May	New York	3	2
WC1976	17 Nov	Rome	0	2
WC1977	16 Nov	Wembley	2	0
EC1980	15 June	Turin	0	1
1985	6 June	Mexico City	1	2
1989	15 Nov	Wembley	0	0
WC1990	7 July	Bari	1	2

v JAPAN

			E	J
UI1995	3 June	Wembley	2	1

v KUWAIT

			E	K
WC1982	25 June	Bilbao	1	0

v LUXEMBOURG

			E	L
1927	21 May	Luxembourg	5	2
WC1960	19 Oct	Luxembourg	9	0
WC1961	28 Sept	Highbury	4	1
WC1977	30 Mar	Wembley	5	0
WC1977	12 Oct	Luxembourg	2	0
EC1982	15 Dec	Wembley	9	0
EC1983	16 Nov	Luxembourg	4	0

v MALAYSIA

			E	M
1991	12 June	Kuala Lumpur	4	2

v MALTA

			E	M
EC1971	3 Feb	Valletta	1	0
EC1971	12 May	Wembley	5	0

v MEXICO

			E	M
1959	24 May	Mexico City	1	2
1961	10 May	Wembley	8	0
WC1966	16 July	Wembley	2	0
1969	1 June	Mexico City	0	0
1985	9 June	Mexico City	0	1
1986	17 May	Los Angeles	3	0

v MOROCCO

			E	M
WC1986	6 June	Monterrey	0	0

		v NEW ZEALAND	E	NZ
1991	3 June	Auckland	1	0
1991	8 June	Wellington	2	0

		v NIGERIA	E	N
1994	16 Nov	Wembley	1	0

		v NORWAY	E	N
1937	14 May	Oslo	6	0
1938	9 Nov	Newcastle	4	0
1949	18 May	Oslo	4	1
1966	29 June	Oslo	6	1
WC1980	10 Sept	Wembley	4	0
WC1981	9 Sept	Oslo	1	2
WC1992	14 Oct	Wembley	1	1
WC1993	2 June	Oslo	0	2
1994	22 May	Wembley	0	0

		v PARAGUAY	E	P
WC1986	18 June	Mexico City	3	0

		v PERU	E	P
1959	17 May	Lima	1	4
1962	20 May	Lima	4	0

		v POLAND	E	P
1966	5 Jan	Everton	1	1
1966	5 July	Chorzow	1	0
WC1973	6 June	Chorzow	0	2
WC1973	17 Oct	Wembley	1	1
WC1986	11 June	Monterrey	3	0
WC1989	3 June	Wembley	3	0
WC1989	11 Oct	Katowice	0	0
EC1990	17 Oct	Wembley	2	0
EC1991	13 Nov	Poznan	1	1
WC1993	29 May	Katowice	1	1
WC1993	8 Sept	Wembley	3	0

		v PORTUGAL	E	P
1947	25 May	Lisbon	10	0
1950	14 May	Lisbon	5	3
1951	19 May	Everton	5	2
1955	22 May	Oporto	1	3
1958	7 May	Wembley	2	1
WC1961	21 May	Lisbon	1	1
WC1961	25 Oct	Wembley	2	0
1964	17 May	Lisbon	4	3
1964	4 June	São Paulo	1	1
WC1966	26 July	Wembley	2	1
1969	10 Dec	Wembley	1	0
1974	3 Apr	Lisbon	0	0
EC1974	20 Nov	Wembley	0	0
EC1975	19 Nov	Lisbon	1	1
WC1986	3 June	Monterrey	0	1

		v ROMANIA	E	R
1939	24 May	Bucharest	2	0
1968	6 Nov	Bucharest	0	0
1969	15 Jan	Wembley	1	1
WC1970	2 June	Guadalajara	1	0
WC1980	15 Oct	Bucharest	1	2
WC1981	29 April	Wembley	0	0
WC1985	1 May	Bucharest	0	0
WC1985	11 Sept	Wembley	1	1
1994	12 Oct	Wembley	1	1

		v SAN MARINO	E	SM
WC1992	17 Feb	Wembley	6	0
WC1993	17 Nov	Bologna	7	1

		v SAUDI ARABIA	E	SA
1988	16 Nov	Riyadh	1	1

		v SPAIN	E	S
1929	15 May	Madrid	3	4
1931	9 Dec	Highbury	7	1
WC1950	2 July	Rio de Janeiro	0	1
1955	18 May	Madrid	1	1
1955	30 Nov	Wembley	4	1
1960	15 May	Madrid	0	3
1960	26 Oct	Wembley	4	2
1965	8 Dec	Madrid	2	0
1967	24 May	Wembley	2	0
EC1968	3 Apr	Wembley	1	0
EC1968	8 May	Madrid	2	1
1980	26 Mar	Barcelona	2	0
EC1980	18 June	Naples	2	1
1981	25 Mar	Wembley	1	2
WC1982	5 July	Madrid	0	0
1987	18 Feb	Madrid	4	2
1992	9 Sept	Santander	0	1

		v SWEDEN	E	S
1923	21 May	Stockholm	4	2
1923	24 May	Stockholm	3	1
1937	17 May	Stockholm	4	0
1947	19 Nov	Highbury	4	2
1949	13 May	Stockholm	1	3
1956	16 May	Stockholm	0	0
1959	28 Oct	Wembley	2	3
1965	16 May	Gothenburg	2	1
1968	22 May	Wembley	3	1
1979	10 June	Stockholm	0	0
1986	10 Sept	Stockholm	0	1
WC1988	19 Oct	Wembley	0	0
WC1989	6 Sept	Stockholm	0	0
EC1992	17 June	Stockholm	1	2
UI1995	8 June	Leeds	3	3

		v SWITZERLAND	E	S
1933	20 May	Berne	4	0
1938	21 May	Zurich	1	2
1947	18 May	Zurich	0	1
1948	2 Dec	Highbury	6	0
1952	28 May	Zurich	3	0
WC1954	20 June	Berne	2	0
1962	9 May	Wembley	3	1
1963	5 June	Basle	8	1
EC1971	13 Oct	Basle	3	2
EC1971	10 Nov	Wembley	1	1
1975	3 Sept	Basle	2	1
1977	7 Sept	Wembley	0	0
WC1980	19 Nov	Wembley	2	1
WC1981	30 May	Basle	1	2
1988	28 May	Lausanne	1	0

		v TUNISIA	E	T
1990	2 June	Tunis	1	1

		v TURKEY	E	T
WC1984	14 Nov	Istanbul	8	0
WC1985	16 Oct	Wembley	5	0
EC1987	29 Apr	Izmir	0	0
EC1987	14 Oct	Wembley	8	0
EC1991	1 May	Izmir	1	0
EC1991	16 Oct	Wembley	1	0
WC1992	18 Nov	Wembley	4	0
WC1993	31 Mar	Izmir	2	0

		v URUGUAY	E	U
1953	31 May	Montevideo	1	2
WC1954	26 June	Basle	2	4
1964	6 May	Wembley	2	1
WC1966	11 July	Wembley	0	0
1969	8 June	Montevideo	2	1
1977	15 June	Montevideo	0	0

			E	U
1984	13 June	Montevideo	0	2
1990	22 May	Wembley	1	2
1995	29 Mar	Wembley	0	0

		v USA	E	USA
wc1950	29 June	Belo Horizonte	0	1
1953	8 June	New York	6	3
1959	28 May	Los Angeles	8	1
1964	27 May	New York	10	0
1985	16 June	Los Angeles	5	0
1993	9 June	Foxboro	0	2
1994	7 Sept	Wembley	2	0

		v USSR	E	USSR
1958	18 May	Moscow	1	1
wc1958	8 June	Gothenburg	2	2
wc1958	17 June	Gothenburg	0	1
1958	22 Oct	Wembley	5	0
1967	6 Dec	Wembley	2	2
EC1968	8 June	Rome	2	0
1973	10 June	Moscow	2	1
1984	2 June	Wembley	0	2
1986	26 Mar	Tbilisi	1	0
EC1988	18 June	Frankfurt	1	3
1991	21 May	Wembley	3	1

		v YUGOSLAVIA	E	Y
1939	18 May	Belgrade	1	2
1950	22 Nov	Highbury	2	2
1954	16 May	Belgrade	0	1
1956	28 Nov	Wembley	3	0
1958	11 May	Belgrade	0	5
1960	11 May	Wembley	3	3
1965	9 May	Belgrade	1	1
1966	4 May	Wembley	2	0
EC1968	5 June	Florence	0	1
1972	11 Oct	Wembley	1	1
1974	5 June	Belgrade	2	2
EC1986	12 Nov	Wembley	2	0
EC1987	11 Nov	Belgrade	4	1
1989	13 Dec	Wembley	2	1

SCOTLAND

		v ARGENTINA	S	A
1977	18 June	Buenos Aires	1	1
1979	2 June	Glasgow	1	3
1990	28 Mar	Glasgow	1	0

		v AUSTRALIA	S	A
wc1985	20 Nov	Glasgow	2	0
wc1985	4 Dec	Melbourne	0	0

		v AUSTRIA	S	A
1931	16 May	Vienna	0	5
1933	29 Nov	Glasgow	2	2
1937	9 May	Vienna	1	1
1950	13 Dec	Glasgow	0	1
1951	27 May	Vienna	0	4
wc1954	16 June	Zurich	0	1
1955	19 May	Vienna	4	1
1956	2 May	Glasgow	1	1
1960	29 May	Vienna	1	4
1963	8 May	Glasgow	4	1
(*abandoned after 79 mins*)				
wc1968	6 Nov	Glasgow	2	1
wc1969	5 Nov	Vienna	0	2
EC1978	20 Sept	Vienna	2	3
EC1979	17 Oct	Glasgow	1	1
1994	20 Apr	Vienna	2	1

		v BELGIUM	S	B
1947	18 May	Brussels	1	2
1948	28 Apr	Glasgow	2	0
1951	20 May	Brussels	5	0
EC1971	3 Feb	Liège	0	3
EC1971	10 Nov	Aberdeen	1	0
1974	2 June	Brussels	1	2
EC1979	21 Nov	Brussels	0	2
EC1979	19 Dec	Glasgow	1	3
EC1982	15 Dec	Brussels	2	3
EC1983	12 Oct	Glasgow	1	1
EC1987	1 Apr	Brussels	1	4
EC1987	14 Oct	Glasgow	2	0

		v BRAZIL	S	B
1966	25 June	Glasgow	1	1
1972	5 July	Rio de Janeiro	0	1
1973	30 June	Glasgow	0	1
wc1974	18 June	Frankfurt	0	0
1977	23 June	Rio de Janeiro	0	2
wc1982	18 June	Seville	1	4
1987	26 May	Glasgow	0	2
wc1990	20 June	Turin	0	1

		v BULGARIA	S	B
1978	22 Feb	Glasgow	2	1
EC1986	10 Sept	Glasgow	0	0
EC1987	11 Nov	Sofia	1	0
EC1990	14 Nov	Sofia	1	1
EC1991	27 Mar	Glasgow	1	1

		v CANADA	S	C
1983	12 June	Vancouver	2	0
1983	16 June	Edmonton	3	0
1983	20 June	Toronto	2	0
1992	21 May	Toronto	3	1

		v CHILE	S	C
1977	15 June	Santiago	4	2
1989	30 May	Glasgow	2	0

		v CIS	S	C
EC1992	18 June	Norrkoping	3	0

		v COLOMBIA	S	C
1988	17 May	Glasgow	0	0

		v COSTA RICA	S	CR
wc1990	11 June	Genoa	0	1

		v CYPRUS	S	C
wc1968	17 Dec	Nicosia	5	0
wc1969	11 May	Glasgow	8	0
wc1989	8 Feb	Limassol	3	2
wc1989	26 Apr	Glasgow	2	1

		v CZECHOSLOVAKIA	S	C
1937	22 May	Prague	3	1
1937	8 Dec	Glasgow	5	0
wc1961	14 May	Bratislava	0	4
wc1961	26 Sept	Glasgow	3	2
wc1961	29 Nov	Brussels	2	4*
1972	2 July	Porto Alegre	0	0
wc1973	26 Sept	Glasgow	2	1
wc1973	17 Oct	Prague	0	1
wc1976	13 Oct	Prague	0	2
wc1977	21 Sept	Glasgow	3	1

*After extra time

		v DENMARK	S	D
1951	12 May	Glasgow	3	1
1952	25 May	Copenhagen	2	1
1968	16 Oct	Copenhagen	1	0
EC1970	11 Nov	Glasgow	1	0
EC1971	9 June	Copenhagen	0	1
WC1972	18 Oct	Copenhagen	4	1
WC1972	15 Nov	Glasgow	2	0
EC1975	3 Sept	Copenhagen	1	0
EC1975	29 Oct	Glasgow	3	1
WC1986	4 June	Nezahualcayotl	0	1

		v ECUADOR	S	E
1995	24 May	Toyama	2	1

		v EGYPT	S	E
1990	16 May	Aberdeen	1	3

		v ESTONIA	S	E
WC1993	19 May	Tallinn	3	0
WC1993	2 June	Aberdeen	3	1

		v FAEROES	S	F
EC1994	12 Oct	Glasgow	5	1
EC1995	7 June	Toftir	2	0

		v FINLAND	S	F
1954	25 May	Helsinki	2	1
WC1964	21 Oct	Glasgow	3	1
WC1965	27 May	Helsinki	2	1
1976	8 Sept	Glasgow	6	0
1992	25 Mar	Glasgow	1	1
EC1994	7 Sept	Helsinki	2	0

		v FRANCE	S	F
1930	18 May	Paris	2	0
1932	8 May	Paris	3	1
1948	23 May	Paris	0	3
1949	27 Apr	Glasgow	2	0
1950	27 May	Paris	1	0
1951	16 May	Glasgow	1	0
WC1958	15 June	Orebro	1	2
1984	1 June	Marseilles	0	2
WC1989	8 Mar	Glasgow	2	0
WC1989	11 Oct	Paris	0	3

		v GERMANY	S	G
1929	1 June	Berlin	1	1
1936	14 Oct	Glasgow	2	0
EC1992	15 June	Norrkoping	0	2
1993	24 Mar	Glasgow	0	1

		v EAST GERMANY	S	EG
1974	30 Oct	Glasgow	3	0
1977	7 Sept	East Berlin	0	1
EC1982	13 Oct	Glasgow	2	0
EC1983	16 Nov	Halle	1	2
1985	16 Oct	Glasgow	0	0
1990	25 Apr	Glasgow	0	1

		v WEST GERMANY	S	WG
1957	22 May	Stuttgart	3	1
1959	6 May	Glasgow	3	2
1964	12 May	Hanover	2	2
WC1969	16 Apr	Glasgow	1	1
WC1969	22 Oct	Hamburg	2	3
1973	14 Nov	Glasgow	1	1
1974	27 Mar	Frankfurt	1	2
WC1986	8 June	Queretaro	1	2

		v GREECE	S	G
EC1994	18 Dec	Athens	0	1

		v HOLLAND	S	H
1929	4 June	Amsterdam	2	0
1938	21 May	Amsterdam	3	1
1959	27 May	Amsterdam	2	1
1966	11 May	Glasgow	0	3
1968	30 May	Amsterdam	0	0
1971	1 Dec	Rotterdam	1	2
WC1978	11 June	Mendoza	3	2
1982	23 Mar	Glasgow	2	1
1986	29 Apr	Eindhoven	0	0
EC1992	12 June	Gothenburg	0	1
1994	23 Mar	Glasgow	0	1
1994	27 May	Utrecht	1	3

		v HUNGARY	S	H
1938	7 Dec	Glasgow	3	1
1954	8 Dec	Glasgow	2	4
1955	29 May	Budapest	1	3
1958	7 May	Glasgow	1	1
1960	5 June	Budapest	3	3
1980	31 May	Budapest	1	3
1987	9 Sept	Glasgow	2	0

		v ICELAND	S	I
WC1984	17 Oct	Glasgow	3	0
WC1985	28 May	Reykjavik	1	0

		v IRAN	S	I
WC1978	7 June	Cordoba	1	1

		v REPUBLIC OF IRELAND	S	RI
WC1961	3 May	Glasgow	4	1
WC1961	7 May	Dublin	3	0
1963	9 June	Dublin	0	1
1969	21 Sept	Dublin	1	1
EC1986	15 Oct	Dublin	0	0
EC1987	18 Feb	Glasgow	0	1

		v ISRAEL	S	I
WC1981	25 Feb	Tel Aviv	1	0
WC1981	28 Apr	Glasgow	3	1
1986	28 Jan	Tel Aviv	1	0

		v ITALY	S	I
1931	20 May	Rome	0	3
WC1965	9 Nov	Glasgow	1	0
WC1965	7 Dec	Naples	0	3
1988	22 Dec	Perugia	0	2
WC1992	18 Nov	Glasgow	0	0
WC1993	13 Oct	Rome	1	3

		v JAPAN	S	J
1995	21 May	Hiroshima	0	0

		v LUXEMBOURG	S	L
1947	24 May	Luxembourg	6	0
EC1986	12 Nov	Glasgow	3	0
EC1987	2 Dec	Esch	0	0

		v MALTA	S	M
1988	22 Mar	Valletta	1	1
1990	28 May	Valletta	2	1
WC1993	17 Feb	Glasgow	3	0
WC1993	17 Nov	Valletta	2	0

		NEW ZEALAND	S	NZ
WC1982	15 June	Malaga	5	2

		v NORWAY	S	N
1929	28 May	Oslo	7	3
1954	5 May	Glasgow	1	0
1954	19 May	Oslo	1	1
1963	4 June	Bergen	3	4
1963	7 Nov	Glasgow	6	1

			S	N
1974	6 June	Oslo	2	1
EC1978	25 Oct	Glasgow	3	2
EC1979	7 June	Oslo	4	0
WC1988	14 Sept	Oslo	2	1
WC1989	15 Nov	Glasgow	1	1
1992	3 June	Oslo	0	0

		v PARAGUAY	S	P
WC1958	11 June	Norrkoping	2	3

		v PERU	S	P
1972	26 Apr	Glasgow	2	0
WC1978	3 June	Cordoba	1	3
1979	12 Sept	Glasgow	1	1

		v POLAND	S	P
1958	1 June	Warsaw	2	1
1960	4 June	Glasgow	2	3
WC1965	23 May	Chorzow	1	1
WC1965	13 Oct	Glasgow	1	2
1980	28 May	Poznan	0	1
1990	19 May	Glasgow	1	1

		v PORTUGAL	S	P
1950	21 May	Lisbon	2	2
1955	4 May	Glasgow	3	0
1959	3 June	Lisbon	0	1
1966	18 June	Glasgow	0	1
EC1971	21 Apr	Lisbon	0	2
EC1971	13 Oct	Glasgow	2	1
1975	13 May	Glasgow	1	0
EC1978	29 Nov	Lisbon	0	1
EC1980	26 Mar	Glasgow	4	1
WC1980	15 Oct	Glasgow	0	0
WC1981	18 Nov	Lisbon	1	2
WC1992	14 Oct	Glasgow	0	0
WC1993	28 Apr	Lisbon	0	5

		v ROMANIA	S	R
EC1975	1 June	Bucharest	1	1
EC1975	17 Dec	Glasgow	1	1
1986	26 Mar	Glasgow	3	0
EC1990	12 Sept	Glasgow	2	1
EC1991	16 Oct	Bucharest	0	1

		v RUSSIA	S	R
EC1994	16 Nov	Glasgow	1	1
EC1995	29 Mar	Moscow	0	0

		v SAN MARINO	S	SM
EC1991	1 May	Serravalle	2	0
EC1991	13 Nov	Glasgow	4	0
EC1995	26 Apr	Serravalle	2	0

		v SAUDI ARABIA	S	SA
1988	17 Feb	Riyadh	2	2

		v SPAIN	S	Sp
WC1957	8 May	Glasgow	4	2
WC1957	26 May	Madrid	1	4
1963	13 June	Madrid	6	2
1965	8 May	Glasgow	0	0
EC1974	20 Nov	Glasgow	1	2
EC1975	5 Feb	Valencia	1	1
1982	24 Feb	Valencia	0	3
WC1984	14 Nov	Glasgow	3	1
WC1985	27 Feb	Seville	0	1
1988	27 Apr	Madrid	0	0

		v SWEDEN	S	Sw
1952	30 May	Stockholm	1	3
1953	6 May	Glasgow	1	2
1975	16 Apr	Gothenburg	1	1
1977	27 Apr	Glasgow	3	1
WC1980	10 Sept	Stockholm	1	0
WC1981	9 Sept	Glasgow	2	0
WC1990	16 June	Genoa	2	1

		v SWITZERLAND	S	Sw
1931	24 May	Geneva	3	2
1948	17 May	Berne	1	2
1950	26 Apr	Glasgow	3	1
WC1957	19 May	Basle	2	1
WC1957	6 Nov	Glasgow	3	2
1973	22 June	Berne	0	1
1976	7 Apr	Glasgow	1	0
EC1982	17 Nov	Berne	0	2
EC1983	30 May	Glasgow	2	2
EC1990	17 Oct	Glasgow	2	1
EC1991	11 Sept	Berne	2	2
WC1992	9 Sept	Berne	1	3
WC1993	8 Sept	Aberdeen	1	1

		v TURKEY	S	T
1960	8 June	Ankara	2	4

		v URUGUAY	S	U
WC1954	19 June	Basle	0	7
1962	2 May	Glasgow	2	3
1983	21 Sept	Glasgow	2	0
WC1986	13 June	Nezahualcoyotl	0	0

		v USA	S	USA
1952	30 Apr	Glasgow	6	0
1992	17 May	Denver	1	0

		v USSR	S	USSR
1967	10 May	Glasgow	0	2
1971	14 June	Moscow	0	1
WC1982	22 June	Malaga	2	2
1991	6 Feb	Glasgow	0	1

		v YUGOSLAVIA	S	Y
1955	15 May	Belgrade	2	2
1956	21 Nov	Glasgow	2	0
WC1958	8 June	Vasteras	1	1
1972	29 June	Belo Horizonte	2	2
WC1974	22 June	Frankfurt	1	1
1984	12 Sept	Glasgow	6	1
WC1988	19 Oct	Glasgow	1	1
WC1989	6 Sept	Zagreb	1	3

		v ZAIRE	S	Z
WC1974	14 June	Dortmund	2	0

WALES

		v ALBANIA	W	A
EC1994	7 Sept	Cardiff	2	0

		v ARGENTINA	W	A
1992	3 June	Tokyo	0	1

		v AUSTRIA	W	A
1954	9 May	Vienna	0	2
EC1955	23 Nov	Wrexham	1	2
EC1974	4 Sept	Vienna	1	2
1975	19 Nov	Wrexham	1	0
1992	29 Apr	Vienna	1	1

		v BELGIUM	W	B
1949	22 May	Liège	1	3
1949	23 Nov	Cardiff	5	1
EC1990	17 Oct	Cardiff	3	1
EC1991	27 Mar	Brussels	1	1
WC1992	18 Nov	Brussels	0	2
WC1993	31 Mar	Cardiff	2	0

		v BRAZIL	W	B
WC1958	19 June	Gothenburg	0	1
1962	12 May	Rio de Janeiro	1	3
1962	16 May	São Paulo	1	3
1966	14 May	Rio de Janeiro	1	3
1966	18 May	Belo Horizonte	0	1
1983	12 June	Cardiff	1	1
1991	11 Sept	Cardiff	1	0

		v BULGARIA	W	B
EC1983	27 Apr	Wrexham	1	0
EC1983	16 Nov	Sofia	0	1
EC1994	14 Dec	Cardiff	0	3
EC1995	29 Mar	Sofia	1	3

		v CANADA	W	C
1986	10 May	Toronto	0	2
1986	20 May	Vancouver	3	0

		v CHILE	W	C
1966	22 May	Santiago	0	2

		v COSTA RICA	W	CR
1990	20 May	Cardiff	1	0

		v CYPRUS	W	C
WC1992	14 Oct	Limassol	1	0
WC1993	13 Oct	Cardiff	2	0

		v CZECHOSLOVAKIA	W	C
WC1957	1 May	Cardiff	1	0
WC1957	26 May	Prague	0	2
EC1971	21 Apr	Swansea	1	3
EC1971	27 Oct	Prague	0	1
WC1977	30 Mar	Wrexham	3	0
WC1977	16 Nov	Prague	0	1
WC1980	19 Nov	Cardiff	1	0
WC1981	9 Sept	Prague	0	2
EC1987	29 Apr	Wrexham	1	1
EC1987	11 Nov	Prague	0	2
WC1993	28 Apr	Ostrava†	1	1
WC1993	8 Sept	Cardiff†	2	2

		v DENMARK	W	D
WC1964	21 Oct	Copenhagen	0	1
WC1965	1 Dec	Wrexham	4	2
EC1987	9 Sept	Cardiff	1	0
EC1987	14 Oct	Copenhagen	0	1
1990	11 Sept	Copenhagen	0	1

		v ESTONIA	W	E
1994	23 May	Tallinn	2	1

		v FINLAND	W	F
EC1971	26 May	Helsinki	1	0
EC1971	13 Oct	Swansea	3	0
EC1987	10 Sept	Helsinki	1	1
EC1987	1 Apr	Wrexham	4	0
WC1988	19 Oct	Swansea	2	2
WC1989	6 Sept	Helsinki	0	1

		v FAEROES	W	F
WC1992	9 Sept	Cardiff	6	0
WC1993	6 June	Toftir	3	0

		v FRANCE	W	F
1933	25 May	Paris	1	1
1939	20 May	Paris	1	2
1953	14 May	Paris	1	6
1982	2 June	Toulouse	1	0

		v GEORGIA	W	G
EC1994	16 Nov	Tbilisi	0	5
EC1995	7 June	Cardiff	0	1

		v GERMANY	W	G
EC1995	26 Apr	Dusseldorf	1	1

		v EAST GERMANY	W	EG
WC1957	19 May	Leipzig	1	2
WC1957	25 Sept	Cardiff	4	1
WC1969	16 Apr	Dresden	1	2
WC1969	22 Oct	Cardiff	1	3

		v WEST GERMANY	W	WG
1968	8 May	Cardiff	1	1
1969	26 Mar	Frankfurt	1	1
1976	6 Oct	Cardiff	0	2
1977	14 Dec	Dortmund	1	1
EC1979	2 May	Wrexham	0	2
EC1979	17 Oct	Cologne	1	5
WC1989	31 May	Cardiff	0	0
WC1989	15 Nov	Cologne	1	2
EC1991	5 June	Cardiff	1	0
EC1991	16 Oct	Nuremberg	1	4

		v GREECE	W	G
WC1964	9 Dec	Athens	0	2
WC1965	17 Mar	Cardiff	4	1

		v HOLLAND	W	H
WC1988	14 Sept	Amsterdam	0	1
WC1989	11 Oct	Wrexham	1	2
1992	30 May	Utrecht	0	4

		v HUNGARY	W	H
WC1958	8 June	Sanviken	1	1
WC1958	17 June	Stockholm	2	1
1961	28 May	Budapest	2	3
EC1962	7 Nov	Budapest	1	3
EC1963	20 Mar	Cardiff	1	1
EC1974	30 Oct	Cardiff	2	0
EC1975	16 Apr	Budapest	2	1
1985	16 Oct	Cardiff	0	3

		v ICELAND	W	I
WC1980	2 June	Reykjavik	4	0
WC1981	14 Oct	Swansea	2	2
WC1984	12 Sept	Reykjavik	0	1
WC1984	14 Nov	Cardiff	2	1
1991	1 May	Cardiff	1	0

		v IRAN	W	I
1978	18 Apr	Teheran	1	0

		v REPUBLIC OF IRELAND	W	RI
1960	28 Sept	Dublin	3	2
1979	11 Sept	Swansea	2	1
1981	24 Feb	Dublin	3	1
1986	26 Mar	Dublin	1	0
1990	28 Mar	Dublin	0	1
1991	6 Feb	Wrexham	0	3
1992	19 Feb	Dublin	1	0
1993	17 Feb	Dublin	1	2

		v ISRAEL	W	I
WC1958	15 Jan	Tel Aviv	2	0
WC1958	5 Feb	Cardiff	2	0

			W	I
1984	10 June	Tel Aviv	0	0
1989	8 Feb	Tel Aviv	3	3

v ITALY

			W	I
1965	1 May	Florence	1	4
WC1968	23 Oct	Cardiff	0	1
WC1969	4 Nov	Rome	1	4
1988	4 June	Brescia	1	0

v JAPAN

			W	J
1992	7 June	Matsuyama	1	0

v KUWAIT

			W	K
1977	6 Sept	Wrexham	0	0
1977	20 Sept	Kuwait	0	0

v LUXEMBOURG

			W	L
EC1974	20 Nov	Swansea	5	0
EC1975	1 May	Luxembourg	3	1
EC1990	14 Nov	Luxembourg	1	0
EC1991	13 Nov	Cardiff	1	0

v MALTA

			W	M
EC1978	25 Oct	Wrexham	7	0
EC1979	2 June	Valletta	2	0
1988	1 June	Valletta	3	2

v MEXICO

			W	M
WC1958	11 June	Stockholm	1	1
1962	22 May	Mexico City	1	2

v MOLDOVA

			W	M
EC1994	12 Oct	Kishinev	2	3

v NORWAY

			W	N
EC1982	22 Sept	Swansea	1	0
EC1983	21 Sept	Oslo	0	0
1984	6 June	Trondheim	0	1
1985	26 Feb	Wrexham	1	1
1985	5 June	Bergen	2	4
1994	9 Mar	Cardiff	1	3

v POLAND

			W	P
WC1973	28 Mar	Cardiff	2	0
WC1973	26 Sept	Katowice	0	3
1991	29 May	Radom	0	0

v PORTUGAL

			W	P
1949	15 May	Lisbon	2	3
1951	12 May	Cardiff	2	1

v ROMANIA

			W	R
EC1970	11 Nov	Cardiff	0	0
EC1971	24 Nov	Bucharest	0	2
1983	12 Oct	Wrexham	5	0
WC1992	20 May	Bucharest	1	5
WC1993	17 Nov	Cardiff	1	2

v SAUDI ARABIA

			W	SA
1986	25 Feb	Dahran	2	1

v SPAIN

			W	S
WC1961	19 Apr	Cardiff	1	2
WC1961	18 May	Madrid	1	1
1982	24 Mar	Valencia	1	1
WC1984	17 Oct	Seville	0	3
WC1985	30 Apr	Wrexham	3	0

v SWEDEN

			W	S
WC1958	15 June	Stockholm	0	0
1988	27 Apr	Stockholm	1	4
1989	26 Apr	Wrexham	0	2
1990	25 Apr	Stockholm	2	4
1994	20 Apr	Wrexham	0	2

v SWITZERLAND

			W	S
1949	26 May	Berne	0	4
1951	16 May	Wrexham	3	2

v TURKEY

			W	T
EC1978	29 Nov	Wrexham	1	0
EC1979	21 Nov	Izmir	0	1
WC1980	15 Oct	Cardiff	4	0
WC1981	25 Mar	Ankara	1	0

v REST OF UNITED KINGDOM

			W	UK
1951	5 Dec	Cardiff	3	2
1969	28 July	Cardiff	0	1

v URUGUAY

			W	U
1986	21 Apr	Wrexham	0	0

v USSR

			W	USSR
WC1965	30 May	Moscow	1	2
WC1965	27 Oct	Cardiff	2	1
WC1981	30 May	Wrexham	0	0
WC1981	18 Nov	Tbilisi	0	3
1987	18 Feb	Swansea	0	0

v YUGOSLAVIA

			W	Y
1953	21 May	Belgrade	2	5
1954	22 Nov	Cardiff	1	3
EC1976	24 Apr	Zagreb	0	2
EC1976	22 May	Cardiff	1	1
EC1982	15 Dec	Titograd	4	4
EC1983	14 Dec	Cardiff	1	1
1988	23 Mar	Swansea	1	2

NORTHERN IRELAND

v ALBANIA

			NI	A
WC1965	7 May	Belfast	4	1
WC1965	24 Nov	Tirana	1	1
EC1982	15 Dec	Tirana	0	0
EC1983	27 Apr	Belfast	1	0
WC1992	9 Sept	Belfast	3	0
WC1993	17 Feb	Tirana	2	1

v ALGERIA

			NI	A
WC1986	3 June	Guadalajara	1	1

v ARGENTINA

			NI	A
WC1958	11 June	Halmstad	1	3

v AUSTRALIA

			NI	A
1980	11 June	Sydney	2	1
1980	15 June	Melbourne	1	1
1980	18 June	Adelaide	2	1

v AUSTRIA

			NI	A
WC1982	1 July	Madrid	2	2
EC1982	13 Oct	Vienna	0	2
EC1983	21 Sept	Belfast	3	1
EC1990	14 Nov	Vienna	0	0
EC1991	16 Oct	Belfast	2	1
EC1994	12 Oct	Vienna	2	1

		v BELGIUM	NI	B
WC1976	10 Nov	Liège	0	2
WC1977	16 Nov	Belfast	3	0

		v BRAZIL	NI	B
WC1986	12 June	Guadalajara	0	3

		v BULGARIA	NI	B
WC1972	18 Oct	Sofia	0	3
WC1973	26 Sept	Sheffield	0	0
EC1978	29 Nov	Sofia	2	0
EC1979	2 May	Belfast	2	0

		v CANADA	NI	C
1995	22 May	Edmonton	0	2

		v CHILE	NI	C
1989	26 May	Belfast	0	1
1995	25 May	Edmonton	1	2

		v COLOMBIA	NI	C
1994	4 June	Boston	0	2

		v CYPRUS	NI	C
EC1971	3 Feb	Nicosia	3	0
EC1971	21 Apr	Belfast	5	0
WC1973	14 Feb	Nicosia	0	1
WC1973	8 May	London	3	0

		v CZECHOSLOVAKIA	NI	C
WC1958	8 June	Halmstad	1	0
WC1958	17 June	Malmo	2	1*

**After extra time*

		v DENMARK	NI	D
EC1978	25 Oct	Belfast	2	1
EC1979	6 June	Copenhagen	0	4
1986	26 Mar	Belfast	1	1
EC1990	17 Oct	Belfast	1	1
EC1991	13 Nov	Odense	1	2
WC1992	18 Nov	Belfast	0	1
WC1993	13 Oct	Copenhagen	0	1

		v FAEROES	NI	F
EC1991	1 May	Belfast	1	1
EC1991	11 Sept	Landskrona	5	0

		v FINLAND	NI	F
WC1984	27 May	Pori	0	1
WC1984	14 Nov	Belfast	2	1

		v FRANCE	NI	F
1951	12 May	Belfast	2	2
1952	11 Nov	Paris	1	3
WC1958	19 June	Norrkoping	0	4
1982	24 Mar	Paris	0	4
WC1982	4 July	Madrid	1	4
1986	26 Feb	Paris	0	0
1988	27 Apr	Belfast	0	0

		v GERMANY	NI	G
1992	2 June	Bremen	1	1

		v WEST GERMANY	NI	WG
WC1918	15 June	Malmo	2	2
WC1960	26 Oct	Belfast	3	4
WC1961	10 May	Hamburg	1	2
1966	7 May	Belfast	0	2
1977	27 Apr	Cologne	0	5
EC1982	17 Nov	Belfast	1	0
EC1983	16 Nov	Hamburg	1	0

		v GREECE	NI	G
WC1961	3 May	Athens	1	2
WC1961	17 Oct	Belfast	2	0
1988	17 Feb	Athens	2	3

		v HOLLAND	NI	H
1962	9 May	Rotterdam	0	4
WC1965	17 Mar	Belfast	2	1
WC1965	7 Apr	Rotterdam	0	0
WC1976	13 Oct	Rotterdam	2	2
WC1977	12 Oct	Belfast	0	1

		v HONDURAS	NI	H
WC1982	21 June	Zaragoza	1	1

		v HUNGARY	NI	H
WC1988	19 Oct	Budapest	0	1
WC1989	6 Sept	Belfast	1	2

		v ICELAND	NI	I
WC1977	11 June	Reykjavik	0	1
WC1977	21 Sept	Belfast	2	0

		v REPUBLIC OF IRELAND	NI	RI
EC1978	20 Sept	Dublin	0	0
EC1979	21 Nov	Belfast	1	0
WC1988	14 Sept	Belfast	0	0
WC1989	11 Oct	Dublin	0	3
WC1993	31 Mar	Dublin	0	3
WC1993	17 Nov	Belfast	1	1
EC1994	16 Nov	Belfast	0	4
EC1995	29 Mar	Dublin	1	1

		v ISRAEL	NI	I
1968	10 Sept	Jaffa	3	2
1976	3 Mar	Tel Aviv	1	1
WC1980	26 Mar	Tel Aviv	0	0
WC1981	18 Nov	Belfast	1	0
1984	16 Oct	Belfast	3	0
1987	18 Feb	Tel Aviv	1	1

		v ITALY	NI	I
WC1957	25 Apr	Rome	0	1
1957	4 Dec	Belfast	2	2
WC1958	15 Jan	Belfast	2	1
1961	25 Apr	Bologna	2	3

		v LATVIA	NI	L
WC1993	2 June	Riga	2	1
WC1993	8 Sept	Belfast	2	0
EC1995	26 Apr	Riga	1	0
EC1995	7 June	Belfast	1	2

		v LIECHTENSTEIN	NI	L
EC1994	20 Apr	Belfast	4	1

		v LITHUANIA	NI	L
WC1992	28 Apr	Belfast	2	2
WC1993	25 May	Vilnius	1	0

		v MALTA	NI	M
1988	21 May	Belfast	3	0
WC1989	26 Apr	Valletta	2	0

		v MEXICO	NI	M
1966	22 June	Belfast	4	1
1994	11 June	Miami	0	3

		v MOROCCO	NI	M
1986	23 Apr	Belfast	2	1

		v NORWAY	NI	N
EC1974	4 Sept	Oslo	1	2
EC1975	29 Oct	Belfast	3	0
1990	27 Mar	Belfast	2	3

		v POLAND	NI	P
EC1962	10 Oct	Katowice	2	0
EC1962	28 Nov	Belfast	2	0
1988	23 Mar	Belfast	1	1
1991	5 Feb	Belfast	3	1

		v PORTUGAL	NI	P
WC1957	16 Jan	Lisbon	1	1
WC1957	1 May	Belfast	3	0
WC1973	28 Mar	Coventry	1	1
WC1973	14 Nov	Lisbon	1	1
WC1980	19 Nov	Lisbon	0	1
WC1981	29 Apr	Belfast	1	0
EC1994	7 Sept	Belfast	1	2

		v ROMANIA	NI	R
WC1984	12 Sept	Belfast	3	2
WC1985	16 Oct	Bucharest	1	0
1994	23 Mar	Belfast	2	0

		v SPAIN	NI	S
1958	15 Oct	Madrid	2	6
1963	30 May	Bilbao	1	1
1963	30 Oct	Belfast	0	1
EC1970	11 Nov	Seville	0	3
EC1972	16 Feb	Hull	1	1
WC1982	25 June	Valencia	1	0
1985	27 Mar	Palma	0	0
WC1986	7 June	Guadalajara	1	2
WC1988	21 Dec	Seville	0	4
WC1989	8 Feb	Belfast	0	2
WC1992	14 Oct	Belfast	0	0
WC1993	28 Apr	Seville	1	3

		v SWEDEN	NI	S
EC1974	30 Oct	Solna	2	0
EC1975	3 Sept	Belfast	1	2
WC1980	15 Oct	Belfast	3	0
WC1981	3 June	Solna	0	1

		v SWITZERLAND	NI	S
WC1964	14 Oct	Belfast	1	0
WC1964	14 Nov	Lausanne	1	2

		v TURKEY	NI	T
WC1968	23 Oct	Belfast	4	1
WC1968	11 Dec	Istanbul	3	0
EC1983	30 Mar	Belfast	2	1
EC1983	12 Oct	Ankara	0	1
WC1985	1 May	Belfast	2	0
WC1985	11 Sept	Izmir	0	0
EC1986	12 Nov	Izmir	0	0
EC1987	11 Nov	Belfast	1	0

		v URUGUAY	NI	U
1964	29 Apr	Belfast	3	0
1990	18 May	Belfast	1	0

		v USSR	NI	USSR
WC1969	19 Sept	Belfast	0	0
WC1969	22 Oct	Moscow	0	2
EC1971	22 Sept	Moscow	0	1
EC1971	13 Oct	Belfast	1	1

		v YUGOSLAVIA	NI	Y
EC1975	16 Mar	Belfast	1	0
EC1975	19 Nov	Belgrade	0	1
WC1982	17 June	Zaragoza	0	0
EC1987	29 Apr	Belfast	1	2
EC1987	14 Oct	Sarajevo	0	3
EC1990	12 Sept	Belfast	0	2
EC1991	27 Mar	Belgrade	1	4

REPUBLIC OF IRELAND

		v ALBANIA	RI	A
WC1992	26 May	Dublin	2	0
WC1993	26 May	Tirana	2	1

		v ALGERIA	RI	A
1982	28 Apr	Algiers	0	2

		v ARGENTINA	RI	A
1951	13 May	Dublin	0	1
1979	29 May	Dublin	0	0*
1980	16 May	Dublin	0	1

* Not considered a full international

		v AUSTRIA	RI	A
1952	7 May	Vienna	0	6
1953	25 Mar	Dublin	4	0
1958	14 Mar	Vienna	1	3
1962	8 Apr	Dublin	2	3
EC1963	25 Sept	Vienna	0	0
EC1963	13 Oct	Dublin	3	2
1966	22 May	Vienna	0	1
1968	10 Nov	Dublin	2	2
EC1971	30 May	Dublin	1	4
EC1971	10 Oct	Linz	0	6
EC1995	11 June	Dublin	1	3

		v BELGIUM	RI	B
1928	12 Feb	Liège	4	2
1929	30 Apr	Dublin	4	0
1930	11 May	Brussels	3	1
WC1934	25 Feb	Dublin	4	4
1949	24 Apr	Dublin	0	2
1950	10 May	Brussels	1	5
1965	24 Mar	Dublin	0	2
1966	25 May	Liège	3	2
WC1980	15 Oct	Dublin	1	1
WC1981	25 Mar	Brussels	0	1
EC1986	10 Sept	Brussels	2	2
EC1987	29 Apr	Dublin	0	0

		v BOLIVIA	RI	B
1994	24 May	Dublin	1	0

		v BRAZIL	RI	B
1974	5 May	Rio de Janeiro	1	2
1982	27 May	Uberlandia	0	7
1987	23 May	Dublin	1	0

		v BULGARIA	RI	B
WC1977	1 June	Sofia	1	2
WC1977	12 Oct	Dublin	0	0
EC1979	19 May	Sofia	0	1
EC1979	17 Oct	Dublin	3	0
WC1987	1 Apr	Sofia	1	2
WC1987	14 Oct	Dublin	2	0

		v CHILE	RI	C
1960	30 Mar	Dublin	2	0
1972	21 June	Recife	1	2
1974	12 May	Santiago	2	1
1982	22 May	Santiago	0	1
1991	22 May	Dublin	1	1

		v CHINA	RI	C
1984	3 June	Sapporo	1	0

		v CYPRUS	RI	C
WC1980	26 Mar	Nicosia	3	2
WC1980	19 Nov	Dublin	6	0

		v CZECHOSLOVAKIA	RI	C
1938	18 May	Prague	2	2
EC1959	5 Apr	Dublin	2	0
EC1959	10 May	Bratislava	0	4
WC1961	8 Oct	Dublin	1	3
WC1961	29 Oct	Prague	1	7
EC1967	21 May	Dublin	0	2
EC1967	22 Nov	Prague	2	1
WC1969	4 May	Dublin	1	2
WC1969	7 Oct	Prague	0	3
1979	26 Sept	Prague	1	4
1981	29 Apr	Dublin	3	1
1986	27 May	Reykjavik	1	0

		v CZECH REPUBLIC	RI	C
1994	5 June	Dublin	1	3

		v DENMARK	RI	D
WC1956	3 Oct	Dublin	2	1
WC1957	2 Oct	Copenhagen	2	0
WC1968	4 Dec	Dublin	1	1
(*abandoned after 51 mins*)				
WC1969	27 May	Copenhagen	0	2
WC1969	15 Oct	Dublin	1	1
EC1978	24 May	Copenhagen	3	3
EC1979	2 May	Dublin	2	0
WC1984	14 Nov	Copenhagen	0	3
WC1985	13 Nov	Dublin	1	4
WC1992	14 Oct	Copenhagen	0	0
WC1993	28 Apr	Dublin	1	1

		v ECUADOR	RI	E
1972	19 June	Natal	3	2

		v EGYPT	RI	E
WC1990	17 June	Palermo	0	0

		v ENGLAND	RI	E
1946	30 Sept	Dublin	0	1
1949	21 Sept	Everton	2	0
WC1957	8 May	Wembley	1	5
WC1957	19 May	Dublin	1	1
1964	24 May	Dublin	1	3
1976	8 Sept	Wembley	1	1
EC1978	25 Oct	Dublin	1	1
EC1980	6 Feb	Wembley	0	2
1985	26 Mar	Wembley	1	2
EC1988	12 June	Stuttgart	1	0
WC1990	11 June	Cagliari	1	1
EC1990	14 Nov	Dublin	1	1
EC1991	27 Mar	Wembley	1	1
1995	15 Feb	Dublin	1	0
(*abandoned after 27 mins*)				

		v FINLAND	RI	F
WC1949	8 Sept	Dublin	3	0
WC1949	9 Oct	Helsinki	1	1
1990	16 May	Dublin	1	1

		v FRANCE	RI	F
1937	23 May	Paris	2	0
1952	16 Nov	Dublin	1	1
WC1953	4 Oct	Dublin	3	5
WC1953	25 Nov	Paris	0	1
WC1972	15 Nov	Dublin	2	1
WC1973	19 May	Paris	1	1
WC1976	17 Nov	Paris	0	2
WC1977	30 Mar	Dublin	1	0
WC1980	28 Oct	Paris	0	2
WC1981	14 Oct	Dublin	3	2
1989	7 Feb	Dublin	0	0

		v GERMANY	RI	G
1935	8 May	Dortmund	1	3
1936	17 Oct	Dublin	5	2
1939	23 May	Bremen	1	1
1994	29 May	Hanover	2	0

		v WEST GERMANY	RI	WG
1951	17 Oct	Dublin	3	2
1952	4 May	Cologne	0	3
1955	28 May	Hamburg	1	2
1956	25 Nov	Dublin	3	0
1960	11 May	Dusseldorf	1	0
1966	4 May	Dublin	0	4
1970	9 May	Berlin	1	2
1975	1 Mar	Dublin	1	0†
1979	22 May	Dublin	1	3
1981	21 May	Bremen	0	3†
1989	6 Sept	Dublin	1	1

†v West Germany 'B'

		v HOLLAND	RI	H
1932	8 May	Amsterdam	2	0
1934	8 Apr	Amsterdam	2	5
1935	8 Dec	Dublin	3	5
1955	1 May	Dublin	1	0
1956	10 May	Rotterdam	4	1
WC1980	10 Sept	Dublin	2	1
WC1981	9 Sept	Rotterdam	2	2
EC1982	22 Sept	Rotterdam	1	2
EC1983	12 Oct	Dublin	2	3
EC1988	18 June	Gelsenkirchen	0	1
WC1990	21 June	Palermo	1	1
1994	20 Apr	Tilburg	1	0
WC1994	4 July	Orlando	0	2

		v HUNGARY	RI	H
1934	15 Dec	Dublin	2	4
1936	3 May	Budapest	3	3
1936	6 Dec	Dublin	2	3
1939	19 Mar	Cork	2	2
1939	18 May	Budapest	2	2
WC1969	8 June	Dublin	1	2
WC1969	5 Nov	Budapest	0	4
WC1989	8 Mar	Budapest	0	2
WC1989	4 June	Dublin	2	0
1991	11 Sept	Gyor	2	1

		v ICELAND	RI	I
EC1962	12 Aug	Dublin	4	2
EC1962	2 Sept	Reykjavik	1	1
EC1982	13 Oct	Dublin	2	0
EC1983	21 Sept	Reykjavik	3	0
1986	25 May	Reykjavik	2	1

		v IRAN	RI	I
1972	18 June	Recife	2	1

		v N. IRELAND	RI	NI
EC1978	20 Sept	Dublin	0	0
EC1979	21 Nov	Belfast	0	1

			RI	NI
WC1988	14 Sept	Belfast	0	0
WC1989	11 Oct	Dublin	3	0
WC1993	31 Mar	Dublin	3	0
WC1993	17 Nov	Belfast	1	1
EC1994	16 Nov	Belfast	4	0
EC1995	29 Mar	Dublin	1	1

		v ISRAEL	*RI*	*I*
1984	4 Apr	Tel Aviv	0	3
1985	27 May	Tel Aviv	0	0
1987	10 Nov	Dublin	5	0

		v ITALY	*RI*	*I*
1926	21 Mar	Turin	0	3
1927	23 Apr	Dublin	1	2
EC1970	8 Dec	Rome	0	3
EC1971	10 May	Dublin	1	2
1985	5 Feb	Dublin	1	2
WC1990	30 June	Rome	0	1
1992	4 June	Foxboro	0	2
WC1994	18 June	New York	1	0

		v LATVIA	*RI*	*L*
WC1992	9 Sept	Dublin	4	0
WC1993	2 June	Riga	2	1
EC1994	7 Sept	Riga	3	0

		v LIECHTENSTEIN	*RI*	*L*
EC1994	12 Oct	Dublin	4	0
EC1995	3 June	Eschen	0	0

		v LITHUANIA	*RI*	*L*
WC1993	16 June	Vilnius	1	0
WC1993	8 Sept	Dublin	2	0

		v LUXEMBOURG	*RI*	*L*
1936	9 May	Luxembourg	5	1
WC1953	28 Oct	Dublin	4	0
WC1954	7 Mar	Luxembourg	1	0
EC1987	28 May	Luxembourg	2	0
EC1987	9 Sept	Dublin	2	1

		v MALTA	*RI*	*M*
EC1983	30 Mar	Valletta	1	0
EC1983	16 Nov	Dublin	8	0
WC1989	28 May	Dublin	2	0
WC1989	15 Nov	Valletta	2	0
1990	2 June	Valletta	3	0

		v MEXICO	*RI*	*M*
1984	8 Aug	Dublin	0	0
WC1994	24 June	Orlando	1	2

		v MOROCCO	*RI*	*M*
1990	12 Sept	Dublin	1	0

		v NORWAY	*RI*	*N*
WC1937	10 Oct	Oslo	2	3
WC1937	7 Nov	Dublin	3	3
1950	26 Nov	Dublin	2	2
1951	30 May	Oslo	3	2
1954	8 Nov	Dublin	2	1
1955	25 May	Oslo	3	1
1960	6 Nov	Dublin	3	1
1964	13 May	Oslo	4	1
1973	6 June	Oslo	1	1
1976	24 Mar	Dublin	3	0
1978	21 May	Oslo	0	0
WC1984	17 Oct	Oslo	0	1
WC1985	1 May	Dublin	0	0
1988	1 June	Oslo	0	0
WC1994	28 June	New York	0	0

		v POLAND	*RI*	*P*
1938	22 May	Warsaw	0	6
1938	13 Nov	Dublin	3	2
1958	11 May	Katowice	2	2
1958	5 Oct	Dublin	2	2
1964	10 May	Cracow	1	3
1964	25 Oct	Dublin	3	2
1968	15 May	Dublin	2	2
1968	30 Oct	Katowice	0	1
1970	6 May	Dublin	1	2
1970	23 Sept	Dublin	0	2
1973	16 May	Wroclaw	0	2
1973	21 Oct	Dublin	1	0
1976	26 May	Poznan	2	0
1977	24 Apr	Dublin	0	0
1978	12 Apr	Lodz	0	3
1981	23 May	Bydgoszcz	0	3
1984	23 May	Dublin	0	0
1986	12 Nov	Warsaw	0	1
1988	22 May	Dublin	3	1
EC1991	1 May	Dublin	0	0
EC1991	16 Oct	Poznan	3	3

		v PORTUGAL	*RI*	*P*
1946	16 June	Lisbon	1	3
1947	4 May	Dublin	0	2
1948	23 May	Lisbon	0	2
1949	22 May	Dublin	1	0
1972	25 June	Recife	1	2
1992	7 June	Boston	2	0
EC1995	26 Apr	Dublin	1	0

		v ROMANIA	*RI*	*R*
1988	23 Mar	Dublin	2	0
WC1990	25 June	Genoa	0	0*

**After extra time*

		v RUSSIA	*RI*	*R*
1994	23 Mar	Dublin	0	0

		v SCOTLAND	*RI*	*S*
WC1961	3 May	Glasgow	1	4
WC1961	7 May	Dublin	0	3
1963	9 June	Dublin	1	0
1969	21 Sept	Dublin	1	1
EC1986	15 Oct	Dublin	0	0
EC1987	18 Feb	Glasgow	1	0

		v SPAIN	*RI*	*S*
1931	26 Apr	Barcelona	1	1
1931	13 Dec	Dublin	0	5
1946	23 June	Madrid	1	0
1947	2 Mar	Dublin	3	2
1948	30 May	Barcelona	1	2
1949	12 June	Dublin	1	4
1952	1 June	Madrid	0	6
1955	27 Nov	Dublin	2	2
EC1964	11 Mar	Seville	1	5
EC1964	8 Apr	Dublin	0	2
WC1965	5 May	Dublin	1	0
WC1965	27 Oct	Seville	1	4
WC1965	10 Nov	Paris	0	1
EC1966	23 Oct	Dublin	0	0
EC1966	7 Dec	Valencia	0	2
1977	9 Feb	Dublin	0	1
EC1982	17 Nov	Dublin	3	3
EC1983	27 Apr	Zaragoza	0	2
1985	26 May	Cork	0	0
WC1988	16 Nov	Seville	0	2
WC1989	26 Apr	Dublin	1	0
WC1992	18 Nov	Seville	0	0
WC1993	13 Oct	Dublin	1	3

v SWEDEN			RI	S
WC1949	2 June	Stockholm	1	3
WC1949	13 Nov	Dublin	1	3
1959	1 Nov	Dublin	3	2
1960	18 May	Malmo	1	4
EC1970	14 Oct	Dublin	1	1
EC1970	28 Oct	Malmo	0	1

v SWITZERLAND			RI	S
1935	5 May	Basle	0	1
1936	17 Mar	Dublin	1	0
1937	17 May	Berne	1	0
1938	18 Sept	Dublin	4	0
1948	5 Dec	Dublin	0	1
EC1975	11 May	Dublin	2	1
EC1975	21 May	Berne	0	1
1980	30 Apr	Dublin	2	0
WC1985	2 June	Dublin	3	0
WC1985	11 Sept	Berne	0	0
1992	25 Mar	Dublin	2	1

v TRINIDAD & TOBAGO			RI	TT
1982	30 May	Port of Spain	1	2

v TUNISIA			RI	T
1988	19 Oct	Dublin	4	0

v TURKEY			RI	T
EC1966	16 Nov	Dublin	2	1
EC1967	22 Feb	Ankara	1	2
EC1974	20 Nov	Izmir	1	1
EC1975	29 Oct	Dublin	4	0
1976	13 Oct	Ankara	3	3
1978	5 Apr	Dublin	4	2
1990	26 May	Izmir	0	0
EC1990	17 Oct	Dublin	5	0
EC1991	13 Nov	Istanbul	3	1

v URUGUAY			RI	U
1974	8 May	Montevideo	0	2
1986	23 Apr	Dublin	1	1

v USA			RI	USA
1979	29 Oct	Dublin	3	2
1991	1 June	Boston	1	1
1992	29 Apr	Dublin	4	1
1992	30 May	Washington	1	3

v USSR			RI	USSR
WC1972	18 Oct	Dublin	1	2
WC1973	13 May	Moscow	0	1
EC1974	30 Oct	Dublin	3	0
EC1975	18 May	Kiev	1	2
WC1984	12 Sept	Dublin	1	0
WC1985	16 Oct	Moscow	0	2
EC1988	15 June	Hanover	1	1
1990	25 Apr	Dublin	1	0

v WALES			RI	W
1960	28 Sept	Dublin	2	3
1979	11 Sept	Swansea	1	2
1981	24 Feb	Dublin	1	3
1986	26 Mar	Dublin	0	1
1990	28 Mar	Dublin	1	0
1991	6 Feb	Wrexham	3	0
1992	19 Feb	Dublin	0	1
1993	17 Feb	Dublin	2	1

v YUGOSLAVIA			RI	Y
1955	19 Sept	Dublin	1	4
1988	27 Apr	Dublin	2	0

OTHER BRITISH AND IRISH INTERNATIONAL MATCHES 1994–95

Wembley, 7 September 1994, 38,629

England (2) 2 *(Shearer 2)*

USA (0) 0

England: Seaman; Jones, Le Saux, Venison, Adams, Pallister, Anderton, Platt, Shearer (Wright), Sheringham (Ferdinand), Barnes.
USA: Friedel (Sommer); Caligiuri, Lalas, Balboa, Agoos (Lapper), Perez (Wynalda), Dooley, Reyna (Moore), Sorber, Jones, Stewart (Klopas).

Wembley, 12 October 1994, 48,754

England (1) 1 *(Lee)*

Romania (1) 1 *(Dumitrescu)*

England: Seaman; Jones (Pearce), Le Saux, Lee (Wise), Adams, Pallister, Le Tissier, Wright (Sheringham), Shearer, Ince, Barnes.
Romania: Stelea (Prunea); Belodedico, Petrescu, Prodan, Munteanu, Popescu, Lupescu, Dumitrescu, Hagi (Selymes), Lacatus (Cirstea), Raducioiu (Timofte).

Wembley, 16 November 1994, 37,196

England (1) 1 *(Platt)*

Nigeria (0) 0

England: Flowers; Jones, Le Saux, Lee (McManaman), Howey, Ruddock, Platt, Beardsley (Le Tissier), Shearer (Sheringham), Barnes, Wise.
Nigeria: Rufai; Okafor, Eguavon, Okechukwu, Iroha, George, Adepoju (Kanu), Okocha, Amunike, Amokachi (Ikpeba), Yekini (Ekoku).

Dublin, 15 February 1995, 46,000

Republic of Ireland (1) 1 *(Kelly D)*

England (0) 0

Republic of Ireland: Kelly A; Irwin, Phelan, Kernaghan, McGrath, Staunton, Sheridan, Kelly D, Quinn, Townsend, McGoldrick.
England: Seaman; Barton, Le Saux, Platt, Adams, Pallister, Beardsley, Ince, Shearer, Le Tissier, Anderton.
Match abandoned after 27 minutes.

Wembley, 29 March 1994, 34,849

England (0) 0

Uruguay (0) 0

England: Flowers; Jones, Le Saux (McManaman), Venison, Adams, Pallister, Anderton, Beardsley (Barmby), Sheringham (Cole), Platt, Barnes.
Uruguay: Ferro; Lopez, Aguirregaray, Gutierrez, Montero, Cedras, Dorta, Bengoechea, Francescoli (Debray), Poyet, Fonseca.

INTERNATIONAL APPEARANCES

This is a list of full international appearances by Englishmen, Irishmen, Scotsmen and Welshmen in matches against the Home Countries and against foreign nations. It does not include unofficial matches against Commonwealth and Empire countries. The year indicated refers to the season; ie 1994 is the 1993-94 season. Explanatory code for matches played by all five countries: A represents Austria; Alb, Albania; Alg, Algeria; Arg, Argentina; Aus, Australia; B, Bohemia; Bel, Belgium; Bol, Bolivia; Br, Brazil; Bul, Bulgaria; C, CIS; Ca, Canada; Cam, Cameroon; Ch, Chile; Chn, China; Co, Colombia; Cr, Costa Rica; Cy, Cyprus; Cz, Czechoslovakia; CzR, Czech Republic; D, Denmark; E, England; Ec, Ecuador; Ei, Republic of Ireland; EG, East Germany; Eg, Egypt; Es, Estonia; F, France; Fa, Faeroes; Fi, Finland; G, Germany; Ge, Georgia; Gr, Greece; H, Hungary; Ho, Holland; Hon, Honduras; I, Italy; Ic, Iceland; Ir, Iran; Is, Israel; J,Japan; K, Kuwait; L, Luxembourg; La, Latvia; Li, Lithuania; Lie, Liechtenstein; M, Mexico; Ma, Malta; Mal, Malaysia; Mol, Moldova; Mor, Morocco; N, Norway; Ni, Ng, Nigeria; Northern Ireland; Nz, New Zealand; P, Portugal; Para, Paraguay; Pe, Peru; Pol, Poland; R, Romania; RCS, Republic of Czechs and Slovaks; R of E, Rest of Europe; R of UK, Rest of United Kingdom; R of W, Rest of World; Ru, Russia; S.Ar, Saudi Arabia; S, Scotland; Se, Sweden; Sm, San Marino; Sp, Spain; Sw, Switzerland; T, Turkey; Tr, Trinidad & Tobago; Tun, Tunisia; U, Uruguay; US, United States of America; USSR, Soviet Union; W, Wales; WG, West Germany; Y, Yugoslavia; Z, Zaire.

As at June 1995.

ENGLAND

Abbott, W. (Everton), 1902 v W (1)
A'Court, A. (Liverpool), 1958 v Ni, Br, A, USSR; 1959 v W (5)
Adams, T. A. (Arsenal), 1987 v Sp, T, Br; 1988 v WG, T, Y, Ho, H, S, Co, Sw, Ei, Ho, USSR; 1989 v D, Se, S.Ar.; 1991 v Ei (2); 1993 v N, T, Sm, T, Ho, Pol, N; 1994 v Pol, Ho, D, Gr, N; 1995 v US, R, Ei, U (35)
Adcock, H. (Leicester C), 1929 v F, Bel, Sp; 1930 v Ni, W (5)
Alcock, C. W. (Wanderers), 1875 v S (1)
Alderson, J. T. (C Palace), 1923 v F (1)
Aldridge, A. (WBA), 1888 v Ni; (with Walsall Town Swifts), 1889 v Ni (2)
Allen, A. (Stoke C) 1960 v Se, W, Ni (3)
Allen, A. (Aston Villa), 1888 v Ni (1)
Allen, C. (QPR), 1984 v Br (sub), U, Ch; (with Tottenham H), 1987 v T; 1988 v Is (5)
Allen, H. (Wolverhampton W), 1888 v S, W, Ni; 1889 v S; 1890 v S (5)
Allen, J. P. (Portsmouth), 1934 v Ni, W (2)
Allen, R. (WBA), 1952 v Sw; 1954 v Y, S; 1955 v WG, W (5)
Alsford, W. J. (Tottenham H), 1935 v S (1)
Amos, A. (Old Carthusians), 1885 v S; 1886 v W (2)
Anderson, R. D. (Old Etonians), 1879 v W (1)
Anderson, S. (Sunderland), 1962 v A, S (2)
Anderson, V. (Nottingham F), 1979 v Cz, Se; 1980 v Bul, Sp; 1981 v N, R, W, S; 1982 v Ni, Ic; 1984 v Ni; (with Arsenal), 1985 v T, Ni, Ei, R, Fi, S, M, US; 1986 v USSR, M; 1987 v Se, Ni (2), Y, Sp, T; (with Manchester U), 1988 v WG, H, Co (30)
Anderton, D. R. (Tottenham H), 1994 v D, Gr, N; 1995 v US, Ei, U, J, Se, Br (9)
Angus, J. (Burnley), 1961 v A (1)
Armfield, J. C. (Blackpool), 1959 v Br, Pe, M, US; 1960 v Y, Sp, H, S; 1961 v L, P, Sp, M, I, A, W, Ni, S; 1962 v A, Sw, Pe, W, Ni, S, L, P, H, Arg, Bul, Br; 1963 v F (2), Br, EG, Sw, Ni, W, S; 1964 v R of W, W, Ni, S; 1966 v Y, Fi (43)
Armitage, G. H. (Charlton Ath), 1926 v Ni (1)
Armstrong, D. (Middlesbrough), 1980 v Aus; (with Southampton), 1983 v WG; 1984 v W (3)
Armstrong, K. (Chelsea), 1955 v S (1)
Arnold, J. (Fulham), 1933 v S (1)
Arthur, J. W. H. (Blackburn R), 1885 v S, W, Ni; 1886 v S, W; 1887 v W, Ni (7)
Ashcroft, J. (Woolwich Arsenal), 1906 v Ni, W, S (3)
Ashmore, G. S. (WBA), 1926 v Bel (1)
Ashton, C. T. (Corinthians), 1926 v Ni (1)
Ashurst, W. (Notts Co), 1923 v Se (2); 1925 v S, W, Bel (5)
Astall, G. (Birmingham C), 1956 v Fi, WG (2)
Astle, J. (WBA), 1969 v W; 1970 v S, P, Br (sub), Cz (5)
Aston, J. (Manchester U), 1949 v S, W, D, Sw, Se, N, F; 1950 v S, W, Ni, Ei, I, P, Bel, Ch, US; 1951 v Ni (17)
Athersmith, W. C. (Aston Villa), 1892 v Ni, 1897 v S, W, Ni; 1898 v S, W, Ni; 1899 v S, W, Ni; 1900 v S, W (12)
Atyeo, P. J. W. (Bristol C), 1956 v Br, Se, Sp; 1957 v D, Ei (2) (6)
Austin, S. W. (Manchester C), 1926 v Ni (1)

Bach, P. (Sunderland), 1899 v Ni (1)
Bache, J. W. (Aston Villa), 1903 v W; 1904 v W, Ni; 1905 v S; 1907 v Ni; 1910 v Ni; 1911 v S (7)
Baddeley, T. (Wolverhampton W), 1903 v S, Ni; 1904 v S, W, Ni (5)
Bagshaw, J. J. (Derby Co), 1920 v Ni (1)
Bailey, G. R. (Manchester U), 1985 v Ei, M (2)
Bailey, H. P. (Leicester Fosse), 1908 v W, A (2), H, B (5)
Bailey, M. A. (Charlton Ath), 1964 v US; 1965 v W (2)
Bailey, N. C. (Clapham Rovers), 1878 v S; 1879 v S, W; 1880 v S; 1881 v S; 1882 v S, W; 1883 v S, W; 1884 v S, W, Ni; 1885 v S, W, Ni; 1886 v S, W; 1887 v S, W (19)
Baily, E. F. (Tottenham H), 1950 v Sp; 1951 v Y, Ni, W; 1952 v A (2), Sw, W; 1953 v Ni (9)
Bain, J. (Oxford University), 1887 v S (1)
Baker, A. (Arsenal), 1928 v W (1)
Baker, B. H. (Everton), 1921 v Bel; (with Chelsea), 1926 v Ni (2)
Baker, J. H. (Hibernian), 1960 v Y, Sp, H, Ni, S; (with Arsenal) 1966 v Sp, Pol, Ni (8)
Ball, A. J. (Blackpool), 1965 v Y, WG, Se; 1966 v S, Sp, Fi, D, U, Arg, P, WG (2), Pol (2); (with Everton), 1967 v W, S, Ni, A, Cz, Sp; 1968 v W, S, USSR, Sp (2), Y, WG; 1969 v Ni, W, S, R (2), M, Br, U; 1970 v P, Co, Ec, R, Br, Cz (sub), WG, W, S, Bel; 1971 v Ma, EG, Gr, Ma (sub), Ni, S; 1972 v Sw, Gr; (with Arsenal) WG (2), S; 1973 v W (3), Y, S (2), Cz, Ni, Pol; 1974 v P (sub); 1975 v WG, Cy (2), Ni, W, S (72)
Ball, J. (Bury), 1928 v Ni (1)
Balmer, W. (Everton), 1905 v Ni (1)
Bamber, J. (Liverpool), 1921 v W (1)
Bambridge, A. L. (Swifts), 1881 v W; 1883 v W; 1884 v Ni (3)
Bambridge, E. C. (Swifts), 1879 v S; 1880 v S; 1881 v S; 1882 v S, W, Ni; 1883 v W; 1884 v S, W, Ni; 1885 v S, W, Ni; 1886 v S, W; 1887 v S, W, Ni (18)
Bambridge, E. H. (Swifts), 1876 v S (1)
Banks, G. (Leicester C), 1963 v S, Br, Cz, EG; 1964 v W, Ni, S, R of W, U, P (2), US, Arg; 1965 v Ni, S, H, Y, WG, Se; 1966 v Ni, S, Sp, Pol (2), WG (2), Y, Fi, U, M, F, Arg, P; 1967 v Ni, W, S, Cz; (with Stoke C), 1968 v W, Ni, S, USSR (2), Sp, WG, Y; 1969 v Ni, S, R (2), F, U, Br; 1970 v W, Ni, S, Ho, Bel, Co, Ec, R, Br, Cz; 1971 v Gr, Ma (2), Ni, S; 1972 v Sw, Gr, WG (2), W, S (73)
Banks, H. E. (Millwall), 1901 v Ni (1)

Banks, T. (Bolton W), 1958 v USSR (3), Br, A; 1959 v Ni (6)
Bannister, W. (Burnley), 1901 v W; (with Bolton W), 1902 v Ni (2)
Barclay, R. (Sheffield U), 1932 v S; 1933 v Ni; 1936 v S (3)
Bardsley, D. J. (QPR), 1993 v Sp (sub), Pol (2)
Barham, M. (Norwich C), 1983 v Aus (2) (2)
Barkas, S. (Manchester C), 1936 v Bel; 1937 v S; 1938 v W, Ni, Cz (5)
Barker, J. (Derby Co), 1935 v I, Ho, S, W, Ni; 1936 v G, A, S, W, Ni; 1937 v W (11)
Barker, R. (Herts Rangers), 1872 v S (1)
Barker, R. R. (Casuals), 1895 v W (1)
Barlow, R. J. (WBA), 1955 v Ni (1)
Barmby, N.J. (Tottenham H), 1995 v U (sub), Se (sub) (2)
Barnes, J. (Watford), 1983 v Ni (sub), Aus (sub), Aus (2); 1984 v D, L (sub), F (sub), S, USSR, Br, U, Ch; 1985 v EG, Fi, T, Ni, R, Fi, S, I (sub), M, WG (sub), US (sub); 1986 v R (sub), Is (sub), M (sub), Ca (sub), Arg (sub); 1987 v Se, T (sub), Br; (with Liverpool), 1988 v WG, T, Y, Is, Ho, S, Co, Sw, Ei, Ho, USSR; 1989 v Se, Gr, Alb, Pol, D; 1990 v Se, I, Br, D, U, Tun, Ei, Ho, Eg, Bel, Cam; 1991 v H, Pol, Cam, Ei, T, USSR, Arg; 1992 v Cz, Fi; 1993 v Sm, T, Ho, Pol, US, G; 1995 v US, R, Ng, U, Se (78)
Barnes, P. S. (Manchester C), 1978 v I, WG, Br, W, S, H; 1979 v D, Ei, Cz, Ni (2), S, Bul, A; (with WBA), 1980 v D, W; 1981 v Sp (sub), Br, W, Sw (sub); (with Leeds U), 1982 v N (sub), Ho (sub) (22)
Barnet, H. H. (Royal Engineers), 1882 v Ni (1)
Barrass, M. W. (Bolton W), 1952 v W, Ni; 1953 v S (3)
Barrett, A. F. (Fulham), 1930 v Ni (1)
Barrett, E. D. (Oldham Ath), 1991 v Nz; 1993 v Br, G (3)
Barrett, J. W. (West Ham U), 1929 v Ni (1)
Barry, L. (Leicester C), 1928 v F, Bel; 1929 v F, Bel, Sp (5)
Barson, F. (Aston Villa), 1920 v W (1)
Barton, J. (Blackburn R), 1890 v Ni (1)
Barton, P. H. (Birmingham), 1921 v Bel; 1922 v Ni; 1923 v F; 1924 v Bel, S, W; 1925 v Ni (7)
Barton, W. D. (Wimbledon), 1995 v Ei; (with Newcastle U), Se, Br (sub) (3)
Bassett, W. I. (WBA), 1888 v Ni, 1889 v S, W; 1890 v S, W; 1891 v S, Ni; 1892 v S; 1893 v S, W; 1894 v S; 1895 v S, Ni; 1896 v S, W, Ni (16)
Bastard, S. R. (Upton Park), 1880 v S (1)
Bastin, C. S. (Arsenal), 1932 v W; 1933 v I, Sw; 1934 v S, Ni, W, H, Cz; 1935 v S, Ni, I; 1936 v S, W, G, A; 1937 v W, Ni; 1938 v S, G, Sw, F (21)
Batty, D. (Leeds U), 1991 v USSR (sub), Arg, Aus, Nz, Mal; 1992 v G, T, H (sub), F, Se; 1993 v N, Sm, US, Br; (with Blackburn R), 1994 v D (sub); 1995 v J, Br (17)
Baugh, R. (Stafford Road), 1886 v Ni; (with Wolverhampton W) 1890 v Ni (2)
Bayliss, A. E. J. M. (WBA), 1891 v Ni (1)
Baynham, R. L. (Luton T), 1956 v Ni, D, Sp (3)
Beardsley, P. A. (Newcastle U), 1986 v Eg (sub), Is, USSR, M, Ca (sub), P (sub), Pol, Para, Arg; 1987 v Ni (2), Y, Sp, Br, S; (with Liverpool), 1988 v WG, T, Y, Is, Ho, H, S, Co, Sw, Ei, Ho; 1989 v D, Se, S.Ar, Gr (sub), Alb (sub + 1), Pol, D; 1990 v Se, Pol, I, Br, U (sub), Tun (sub), Ei, Eg (sub), Cam (sub), WG, I; 1991 v Pol (sub), Ei (2), USSR (sub); (with Newcastle U), 1994 v D, Gr, N; 1995 v Ng, Ei, U, J, Se (57)
Beasant, D. J. (Chelsea), 1990 v I (sub), Y (sub) (2)
Beasley, A. (Huddersfield T), 1939 v S (1)
Beats, W. E. (Wolverhampton W), 1901 v W; 1902 v S (2)
Beattie, T. K. (Ipswich T), 1975 v Cy (2), S; 1976 v Sw, P; 1977 v Fi, I (sub), Ho; 1978 v L (sub) (9)
Becton, F. (Preston NE), 1895 v Ni; (with Liverpool), 1897 v W (2)
Bedford, H. (Blackpool), 1923 v Se; 1925 v Ni (2)
Bell, C. (Manchester C), 1968 v Se, WG; 1969 v W, Bul, F, U, Br; 1970 v Ni (sub), Ho (2), P, Br (sub), Cz, WG (sub); 1972 v Gr, WG (2), W, Ni, S; 1973 v W (3), Y, S (2), Ni, Cz, Pol; 1974 v A, Pol, I, W, Ni, S, Arg, EG, Bul, Y; 1975 v Cz, P, WG, Cy (2), Ni, S; 1976 v Sw, Cy (48)
Bennett, W. (Sheffield U), 1901 v S, W (2)
Benson, R. W. (Sheffield U), 1913 v Ni (1)
Bentley, R. T. F. (Chelsea), 1949 v Se; 1950 v S, P, Bel, Ch, USA; 1953 v W, Bel; 1955 v W, WG, Sp, P (12)
Beresford, J. (Aston Villa), 1934 v Cz (1)
Berry, A. (Oxford University), 190 [illegible] Ni (1)
Berry, J. J. (Manchester U), 1953 v Arg, Ch, U; 1956 v Se (4)
Bestall, J. G. (Grimsby T), 1935 v Ni (1)
Betmead, H. A. (Grimsby T), 1937 v Fi (1)
Betts, M. P. (Old Harrovians), 1877 v S (1)
Betts, W. (Sheffield W), 1889 v W (1)
Beverley, J. (Blackburn R), 1884 v S, W, Ni (3)
Birkett, R. H. (Clapham Rovers), 1879 v S (1)
Birkett, R. J. E. (Middlesbrough), 1936 v Ni (1)
Birley, F. H. (Oxford University), 1874 v S; (with Wanderers), 1875 v S (2)
Birtles, G. (Nottingham F), 1980 v Arg (sub), I; 1981 v R (3)
Bishop, S. M. (Leicester C), 1927 v S, Bel, L, F (4)
Blackburn, F. (Blackburn R), 1901 v S; 1902 v Ni; 1904 v S (3)
Blackburn, G. F. (Aston Villa), 1924 v F (1)
Blenkinsop, E. (Sheffield W), 1928 v F, Bel; 1929 v S, W, Ni, F, Bel, Sp; 1930 v S, W, Ni, G, A; 1931 v S, W, Ni, F, Bel; 1932 v S, W, Ni, Sp; 1933 v S, W, Ni, A (26)
Bliss, H. (Tottenham H), 1921 v S (1)
Blissett, L. (Watford), 1983 v WG (sub), L, W, Gr (sub), H, Ni, S (sub), Aus (1 + 1 sub); (with AC Milan), 1984 v D (sub), H, W (sub), S, USSR (14)
Blockley, J. P. (Arsenal), 1973 v Y (1)
Bloomer, S. (Derby Co), 1895 v S, Ni; 1896 v W, Ni; 1897 v S, W, Ni; 1898 v S; 1899 v S, W, Ni; 1900 v S; 1901 v S, W; 1902 v S, W, Ni; 1904 v S; 1905 v S, W, Ni; (with Middlesbrough), 1907 v S, W (23)
Blunstone, F. (Chelsea), 1955 v W, S, F, P; 1957 v Y (5)
Bond, R. (Preston NE), 1905 v Ni, W; 1906 v S, W, Ni; (with Bradford C), 1910 v S, W, Ni (8)
Bonetti, P. P. (Chelsea), 1966 v D; 1967 v Sp, A; 1968 v Sp; 1970 v Ho, P, WG (7)
Bonsor, A. G. (Wanderers), 1873 v S; 1875 v S (2)
Booth, F. (Manchester C), 1905 v Ni (1)
Booth, T. (Blackburn R), 1898 v W; (with Everton), 1903 v S (2)
Bould, S. A. (Arsenal), 1994 v Gr, N (2)
Bowden, E. R. (Arsenal), 1935 v W, I; 1936 v W, Ni, A; 1937 v H (6)
Bower, A. G. (Corinthians), 1924 v Ni, Bel; 1925 v W, Bel; 1927 v W (5)
Bowers, J. W. (Derby Co), 1934 v S, Ni, W (3)
Bowles, S. (QPR), 1974 v P, W, Ni; 1977 v I, Ho (5)
Bowser, S. (WBA), 1920 v Ni (1)
Boyer, P. J. (Norwich C), 1976 v W (1)
Boyes, W. (WBA), 1935 v Ho; (with Everton), 1939 v W, R of E (3)
Boyle, T. W. (Burnley), 1913 v Ni (1)
Brabrook, P. (Chelsea), 1958 v USSR; 1959 v Ni; 1960 v Sp (3)
Bracewell, P. W. (Everton), 1985 v WG (sub), US; 1986 v Ni (3)
Bradford, G. R. W. (Bristol R), 1956 v D (1)
Bradford, J. (Birmingham), 1924 v Ni; 1925 v Bel; 1928 v S; 1929 v Ni, W, F, Sp; 1930 v S, Ni, G, A; 1931 v W (12)
Bradley, W. (Manchester U), 1959 v I, US, M (sub) (3)

Bradshaw, F. (Sheffield W), 1908 v A (1)
Bradshaw, T. H. (Liverpool), 1897 v Ni (1)
Bradshaw, W. (Blackburn R), 1910 v W, Ni; 1912 v Ni; 1913 v W (4)
Brann, G. (Swifts), 1886 v S, W; 1891 v W (3)
Brawn, W. F. (Aston Villa), 1904 v W, Ni (2)
Bray, J. (Manchester C), 1935 v W; 1936 v S, W, Ni, G; 1937 v S (6)
Brayshaw, E. (Sheffield W), 1887 v Ni (1)
Bridges, B. J. (Chelsea), 1965 v S, H, Y; 1966 v A (4)
Bridgett, A. (Sunderland), 1905 v S; 1908 v S, A (2), H, B; 1909 v Ni, W, H (2), A (11)
Brindle, T. (Darwen), 1880 v S, W (2)
Brittleton, J. T. (Sheffield W), 1912 v S, W, Ni; 1913 v S; 1914 v W (5)
Britton, C. S. (Everton), 1935 v S, W, Ni, I; 1937 v S, Ni, H, N, Se (9)
Broadbent, P. F. (Wolverhampton W), 1958 v USSR; 1959 v S, W, Ni, I, Br; 1960 v S (7)
Broadis, I. A. (Manchester C), 1952 v S, A, I; 1953 v S, Arg, Ch, U, US; (with Newcastle U), 1954 v S, H, Y, Bel, Sw, U (14)
Brockbank, J. (Cambridge University), 1872 v S (1)
Brodie, J. B. (Wolverhampton W), 1889 v S, Ni; 1891 v Ni (3)
Bromilow, T. G. (Liverpool), 1921 v W; 1922 v S, W; 1923 v Bel; 1926 v Ni (5)
Bromley-Davenport, W. E. (Oxford University), 1884 v S, W (2)
Brook, E. F. (Manchester C), 1930 v Ni; 1933 v Sw: 1934 v S, W, Ni, F, H, Cz; 1935 v S, W, Ni, I; 1936 v S, W, Ni; 1937 v H; 1938 v W, Ni (18)
Brooking, T. D. (West Ham U), 1974 v P, Arg, EG, Bul, Y; 1975 v Cz (sub), P; 1976 v P, W, Br, I, Fi; 1977 v Ei, Fi, I, Ho, Ni, W; 1978 v I, WG, W, S (sub), H; 1979 v D, Ei, Ni, W (sub), S, Bul, Se (sub), A; 1980 v D, Ni, Arg (sub), W, Ni, S, Bel, Sp; 1981 v Sw, Sp, R, H; 1982 v H, S, Fi, Sp (sub) (47)
Brooks, J. (Tottenham H), 1957 v W, Y, D (3)
Broome, F. H. (Aston Villa), 1938 v G, Sw, F; 1939 v N, I, R, Y (7)
Brown, A. (Aston Villa), 1882 v S, W, Ni (3)
Brown, A. S. (Sheffield U), 1904 v W; 1906 v Ni (2)
Brown, A. (WBA), 1971 v W (1)
Brown, G. (Huddersfield T), 1927 v S, W, Ni, Bel, L, F; 1928 v W; 1929 v S; (with Aston Villa), 1933 v W (9)
Brown, J. (Blackburn R), 1881 v W; 1882 v Ni; 1885 v S, W, Ni (5)
Brown, J. H. (Sheffield W), 1927 v S, W, Bel, L, F; 1930 v Ni (6)
Brown, K. (West Ham U), 1960 v Ni (1)
Brown, W. (West Ham U), 1924 v Bel (1)
Bruton, J. (Burnley), 1928 v F, Bel; 1929 v S (3)
Bryant, W. I. (Clapton), 1925 v F (1)
Buchan, C. M. (Sunderland), 1913 v Ni; 1920 v W; 1921 v W, Bel; 1923 v F; 1924 v S (6)
Buchanan, W. S. (Clapham R), 1876 v S (1)
Buckley, F. C. (Derby Co), 1914 v Ni (1)
Bull, S. G. (Wolverhampton W), 1989 v S (sub), D (sub); 1990 v Y, Cz, D (sub), U (sub), Tun (sub), Ei (sub), Ho (sub), Eg, Bel (sub); 1991 v H, Pol (13)
Bullock, F. E. (Huddersfield T), 1921 v Ni (1)
Bullock, N. (Bury), 1923 v Bel; 1926 v W; 1927 v Ni (3)
Burgess, H. (Manchester C), 1904 v S, W, Ni; 1906 v S (4)
Burgess, H. (Sheffield W), 1931 v S, Ni, F, Bel (4)
Burnup, C. J. (Cambridge University), 1896 v S (1)
Burrows, H. (Sheffield W), 1934 v H, Cz; 1935 v Ho (3)
Burton, F. E. (Nottingham F), 1889 v Ni (1)
Bury, L. (Cambridge University), 1877 v S; (with Old Etonians), 1879 v W (2)
Butcher, T. (Ipswich T), 1980 v Aus; 1981 v Sp; 1982 v W, S, F, Cz, WG, Sp; 1983 v D, WG, L, W, Gr, H, Ni, S, Aus (3); 1984 v D, H, L, F, Ni; 1985 v EG, Fi, T, Ni, Ei, R, Fi, S, I, WG, US; 1986 v Is, USSR, S, M, Ca, P, Mor, Pol, Para, Arg; (with Rangers), 1987 v Se, Ni (2), Y, Sp, Br, S; 1988 v T, Y; 1989 v D, Se, Gr, Alb (2), Ch, S, Pol, D; 1990 v Se, Pol, I, Y, Br, Cz, D, U, Tun, Ei, Ho, Bel, Cam, WG (77)
Butler, J. D. (Arsenal), 1925 v Bel (1)
Butler, W. (Bolton W), 1924 v S (1)
Byrne, G. (Liverpool), 1963 v S; 1966 v N (2)
Byrne, J. J. (C Palace), 1962 v Ni; (with West Ham U), 1963 v Sw; 1964 v S, U, P (2), Ei, Br, Arg; 1965 v W, S (11)
Byrne, R. W. (Manchester U), 1954 v S, H, Y, Bel, Sw, U; 1955 v S, W, Ni, WG, F, Sp, P; 1956 v S, W, Ni, Br, Se, Fi, WG, D, Sp; 1957 v S, W, Ni, Y, D (2), Ei (2); 1958 v W, Ni, F (33)

Callaghan, I. R. (Liverpool), 1966 v Fi, F; 1978 v Sw, L (4)
Calvey, J. (Nottingham F), 1902 v Ni (1)
Campbell, A. F. (Blackburn R), 1929 v W, Ni; (with Huddersfield T), 1931 v W, S, Ni; 1932 v W, Ni, Sp (8)
Camsell, G. H. (Middlesbrough), 1929 v F, Bel; 1930 v Ni, W; 1934 v F; 1936 v S, G, A, Bel (9)
Capes, A. J. (Stoke C), 1903 v S (1)
Carr, J. (Middlesbrough), 1920 v Ni; 1923 v W (2)
Carr, J. (Newcastle U), 1905 v Ni; 1907 v Ni (2)
Carr, W. H. (Owlerton, Sheffield), 1875 v S (1)
Carter, H. S. (Sunderland), 1934 v S, H; 1936 v G; 1937 v S, Ni, H; (with Derby Co), 1947 v S, W, Ni, Ei, Ho, F, Sw (13)
Carter, J. H. (WBA), 1926 v Bel; 1929 v Bel, Sp (3)
Catlin, A. E. (Sheffield W), 1937 v W, Ni, H, N, Se (5)
Chadwick, A. (Southampton), 1900 v S, W (2)
Chadwick, E. (Everton), 1891 v S, W; 1892 v S; 1893 v S; 1894 v S; 1896 v Ni; 1897 v S (7)
Chamberlain, M (Stoke C), 1983 v L (sub); 1984 v D (sub), S, USSR, Br, U, Ch; 1985 v Fi (sub) (8)
Chambers, H. (Liverpool), 1921 v S, W, Bel; 1923 v S, W, Ni, Bel; 1924 v Ni (8)
Channon, M. R. (Southampton), 1973 v Y, S (2), Ni, W, Cz, USSR, I; 1974 v A, Pol, I, P, W, Ni, S, Arg, EG, Bul, Y; 1975 v Cz, P, WG, Cy (2), Ni (sub), W, S; 1976 v Sw, Cz, P, W, Ni, S, Br, I, Fi; 1977 v Fi, I, L, Ni, W, S, Br (sub), Arg, U; (with Manchester C), 1978 v Sw (46)
Charles, G. A. (Nottingham F), 1991 v Nz, Mal (2)
Charlton, J. (Leeds U), 1965 v S, H, Y, WG, Se; 1966 v W, Ni, S, A, Sp, Pol (2), WG (2), Y, Fi, D, U, M, F, Arg, P; 1967 v W, S, Ni, Cz; 1968 v W, Sp; 1969 v W, R, F; 1970 v Ho (2), P, Cz (35)
Charlton, R. (Manchester U), 1958 v S, P, Y; 1959 v S, W, Ni, USSR, I, Br, Pe, M, US; 1960 v W, S, Se, Y, Sp, H; 1961 v Ni, W, S, L, P, Sp, M, I, A; 1962 v W, Ni, S, A, Sw, Pe, L, P, H, Arg, Bul, Br; 1963 v S, F, Br, Cz, EG, Sw; 1964 v S, W, Ni, R of W, U, P, Ei, Br, Arg, US (sub); 1965 v Ni, S, Ho; 1966 v W, Ni, S, A, Sp, WG (2), Y, Fi, N, Pol, U, M, F, Arg, P; 1967 v Ni, W, S, Cz; 1968 v W, Ni, S, USSR (2), Sp (2), Se, Y; 1969 v S, W, Ni, R (2), Bul, M, Br; 1970 v W, Ni, Ho (2), P, Co, Ec, Cz, R, Br, WG (106)
Charnley, R. O. (Blackpool), 1963 v F (1)
Charsley, C. C. (Small Heath), 1893 v Ni (1)
Chedgzoy, S. (Everton), 1920 v W; 1921 v W, S, Ni; 1922 v Ni; 1923 v S; 1924 v W; 1925 v Ni (8)
Chenery, C. J. (C Palace), 1872 v S; 1873 v S; 1874 v S (3)
Cherry, T. J. (Leeds U), 1976 v W, S (sub), Br, Fi; 1977 v Ei, I, L, Ni, S (sub), Br, Arg, U; 1978 v Sw, L, I, Br, W; 1979 v Cz, W, Se; 1980 v Ei, Arg (sub), W, Ni, S, Aus, Sp (sub) (27)
Chilton, A. (Manchester U), 1951 v Ni; 1952 v F (2)
Chippendale, H. (Blackburn R), 1894 v Ni (1)

Chivers, M. (Tottenham H), 1971 v Ma (2), Gr, Ni, S; 1972 v Sw (1 + 1 sub), Gr, WG (2), Ni (sub), S; 1973 v W (3), S (2), Ni, Cz, Pol, USSR, I; 1974 v A, Pol (24)
Christian, E. (Old Etonians), 1879 v S (1)
Clamp, E. (Wolverhampton W), 1958 v USSR (2), Br, A (4)
Clapton, D. R. (Arsenal), 1959 v W (1)
Clare, T. (Stoke C), 1889 v Ni; 1892 v Ni; 1893 v W; 1894 v S (4)
Clarke, A. J. (Leeds U), 1970 v Cz; 1971 v EG, Ma, Ni, W (sub), S (sub); 1973 v S (2), W, Cz, Pol, USSR, I; 1974 v A, Pol, I; 1975 v P; 1976 v Cz, P (sub) (19)
Clarke, H. A. (Tottenham H), 1954 v S (1)
Clay, T. (Tottenham H), 1920 v W; 1922 v W, S, Ni (4)
Clayton, R. (Blackburn R), 1956 v Ni, Br, Se, Fi, WG, Sp; 1957 v S, W, Ni, Y, D (2), Ei (2); 1958 v S, W, Ni, F, P, Y, USSR; 1959 v S, W, Ni, USSR, I, Br, Pe, M, US; 1960 v W, Ni, S, Se, Y (35)
Clegg, J. C. (Sheffield W), 1872 v S (1)
Clegg, W. E. (Sheffield W), 1873 v S; (with Sheffield Albion), 1879 v W (2)
Clemence, R. N. (Liverpool), 1973 v W (2); 1974 v EG, Bul, Y; 1975 v Cz, P, WG, Cy, Ni, W, S; 1976 v Sw, Cz, P, W (2), Ni, S, Br, Fi; 1977 v Ei, Fi, I, Ho, L, S, Br, Arg, U; 1978 v Sw, L, I, WG, Ni, S; 1979 v D, Ei, Ni (2), S, Bul, A (sub); 1980 v D, Bul, Ei, Arg, W, S, Bel, Sp; 1981 v R, Sp, Br, Sw, H; (with Tottenham H), 1982 v N, Ni, Fi; 1983 v L; 1984 v L (61)
Clement, D. T. (QPR), 1976 v W (sub + 1), I; 1977 v I, Ho (5)
Clough, B. H. (Middlesbrough), 1960 v W, Se (2)
Clough, N. H. (Nottingham F), 1989 v Ch; 1991 v Arg (sub), Aus, Mal; 1992 v F, Cz, C; 1993 v Sp, T (sub), Pol (sub), N (sub), US, Br, G (14)
Coates, R. (Burnley), 1970 v Ni; 1971 v Gr (sub); (with Tottenham H), Ma, W (4)
Cobbold, W. N. (Cambridge University), 1883 v S, Ni; 1885 v S, Ni; 1886 v S, W; (with Old Carthusians), 1887 v S, W, Ni (9)
Cock, J. G. (Huddersfield T), 1920 v Ni; (with Chelsea), v S (2)
Cockburn, H. (Manchester U), 1947 v W, Ni, Ei; 1948 v S, I; 1949 v S, Ni, D, Sw, Se; 1951 v Arg, P; 1952 v F (13)
Cohen, G. R. (Fulham), 1964 v U, P, Ei, US, Br; 1965 v W, S, Ni, Bel, H, Ho, Y, WG, Se; 1966 v W, S, Ni, A, Sp, Pol (2), WG (2), N, D, U, M, F, Arg, P; 1967 v W, S, Ni, Cz, Sp; 1968 v W, Ni (37)
Cole, A. (Manchester U), 1995 v U (sub) (1)
Coleclough, H. (C Palace), 1914 v W (1)
Coleman, E. H. (Dulwich Hamlet), 1921 v W (1)
Coleman, J. (Woolwich Arsenal), 1907 v Ni (1)
Collymore, S. V. (Nottingham F), 1995 v J, Br (sub) (2)
Common, A. (Sheffield U), 1904 v W, Ni; (with Middlesbrough), 1906 v W (3)
Compton, L. H. (Arsenal), 1951 v W, Y (2)
Conlin, J. (Bradford C), 1906 v S (1)
Connelly, J. M. (Burnley), 1960 v W, N, S, Se; 1962 v W, A, Sw, P; 1963 v W, F; (with Manchester U), 1965 v H, Y, Se; 1966 v W, Ni, S, A, N, D, U (20)
Cook, T. E. R. (Brighton), 1925 v W (1)
Cooper, C. T. (Nottingham F), 1995 v Se, Br (2)
Cooper, N. C. (Cambridge University), 1893 v Ni (1)
Cooper, T. (Derby Co), 1928 v Ni; 1929 v W, Ni, S, F, Bel, Sp; 1931 v F; 1932 v W, Sp; 1933 v S; 1934 v S, H, Cz; 1935 v W (15)
Cooper, T. (Leeds U), 1969 v W, S, F, M; 1970 v Ho, Bel, Co, Ec, R, Cz, Br, WG; 1971 v EG, Ma, Ni, W, S; 1972 v Sw (2); 1975 v P (20)
Coppell, S. J. (Manchester U), 1978 v I, WG, Br, W, Ni, S, H; 1979 v D, Ei, Cz, Ni (2), W (sub), S, Bul, A; 1980 v D, Ni, Ei (sub), Sp, Arg, W, S, Bel, I; 1981 v R (sub), Sw, R, Br, W, S, Sw, H; 1982 v H, S, Fi, F, Cz, K, WG; 1983 v L, Gr (42)
Copping, W. (Leeds U), 1933 v I, Sw; 1934 v S, Ni, W, F; (with Arsenal), 1935 v Ni, I; 1936 v A, Bel; 1937 v N, Se, Fi; 1938 v S, W, Ni, Cz; 1939 v W, R of E; (with Leeds U), R (20)
Corbett, B. O. (Corinthians), 1901 v W (1)
Corbett, R. (Old Malvernians), 1903 v W (1)
Corbett, W. S. (Birmingham), 1908 v A, H, B (3)
Corrigan, J. T. (Manchester C), 1978 v I (sub), Br; 1979 v W; 1980 v Ni, Aus; 1981 v W, S; 1982 v W, Ic (9)
Cottee, A. R. (West Ham U), 1987 v Se (sub), Ni (sub); 1988 v H (sub); (with Everton) 1989 v D (sub), Se (sub), Ch (sub), S (7)
Cotterill, G. H. (Cambridge University), 1891 v Ni; (with Old Brightonians), 1892 v W; 1893 v S, Ni (4)
Cottle, J. R. (Bristol C), 1909 v Ni (1)
Cowan, S. (Manchester C), 1926 v Bel; 1930 v A; 1931 v Bel (3)
Cowans, G. (Aston Villa), 1983 v W, H, Ni, S, Aus (3); (with Bari), 1986 v Eg, USSR; (with Aston Villa), 1991 v Ei (10)
Cowell, A. (Blackburn R), 1910 v Ni (1)
Cox, J. (Liverpool), 1901 v Ni; 1902 v S; 1903 v S (3)
Cox, J. D. (Derby Co), 1892 v Ni (1)
Crabtree, J. W. (Burnley), 1894 v Ni; 1895 v Ni, S; (with Aston Villa), 1896 v W, S, Ni; 1899 v S, W, Ni; 1900 v S, W, Ni; 1901 v W; 1902 v W (14)
Crawford, J. F. (Chelsea), 1931 v S (1)
Crawford, R. (Ipswich T), 1962 v Ni, A (2)
Crawshaw, T. H. (Sheffield W), 1895 v Ni; 1896 v S, W, Ni; 1897 v S, W, Ni; 1901 v Ni; 1904 v W, Ni (10)
Crayston, W. J. (Arsenal), 1936 v S, W, G, A, Bel; 1938 v W, Ni, Cz (8)
Creek, F. N. S. (Corinthians), 1923 v F (1)
Cresswell, W. (South Shields), 1921 v W; (with Sunderland), 1923 v F; 1924 v Bel; 1925 v Ni; 1926 v W; 1927 v Ni; (with Everton), 1930 v Ni (7)
Crompton, R. (Blackburn R), 1902 v S, W, Ni; 1903 v S, W; 1904 v S, W, Ni; 1906 v S, W, Ni; 1907 v S, W, Ni; 1908 v S, W, Ni, A (2), H, B; 1909 v S, W, Ni, H (2), A; 1910 v S, W; 1911 v S, W, Ni; 1912 v S, W, Ni; 1913 v S, W, Ni; 1914 v S, W, Ni (41)
Crooks, S. D. (Derby Co), 1930 v S, G, A; 1931 v S, W, Ni, F, Bel; 1932 v S, W, Ni, Sp; 1933 v Ni, W, A; 1934 v S, Ni, W, F, H, Cz; 1935 v Ni; 1936 v S, W; 1937 v W, H (26)
Crowe, C. (Wolverhampton W), 1963 v F (1)
Cuggy, F. (Sunderland), 1913 v Ni; 1914 v Ni (2)
Cullis, S. (Wolverhampton W), 1938 v S, W, Ni, F, Cz; 1939 v S, Ni, R of E, N, I, R, Y (12)
Cunliffe, A. (Blackburn R), 1933 v Ni, W (2)
Cunliffe, D. (Portsmouth), 1900 v Ni (1)
Cunliffe, J. N. (Everton), 1936 v Bel (1)
Cunningham, L. (WBA), 1979 v W, Se, A (sub); (with Real Madrid), 1980 v Ei, Sp (sub); 1981 v R (sub) (6)
Curle, K. (Manchester C), 1992 v C (sub), H, D (3)
Currey, E. S. (Oxford University), 1890 v S, W (2)
Currie, A. W. (Sheffield U), 1972 v Ni; 1973 v USSR, I; 1974 v A, Pol, I; 1976 v Sw; (with Leeds U), 1978 v Br, W (sub), Ni, S, H (sub); 1979 v Cz, Ni (2), W, Se (17)
Cursham, A. W. (Notts Co), 1876 v S; 1877 v S; 1878 v S; 1879 v W; 1883 v S, W (6)
Cursham, H. A. (Notts Co), 1880 v W; 1882 v S, W, Ni; 1883 v S, W, Ni; 1884 v Ni (8)

Daft, H. B. (Notts Co), 1889 v Ni; 1890 v S, W; 1891 v Ni; 1892 v Ni (5)
Daley, A. M. (Aston Villa), 1992 v Pol (sub), C, H, Br, Fi (sub), D (sub), Se (7)
Danks, T. (Nottingham F), 1885 v S (1)
Davenport, P. (Nottingham F), 1985 v Ei (sub) (1)
Davenport, J. K. (Bolton W), 1885 v W; 1890 v Ni (2)
Davis, G. (Derby Co), 1904 v W, Ni (2)

Davis, H. (Sheffield W), 1903 v S, W, Ni (3)
Davison, J. E. (Sheffield W), 1922 v W (1)
Dawson, J. (Burnley), 1922 v S, Ni (2)
Day, S. H. (Old Malvernians), 1906 v Ni, W, S (3)
Dean, W. R. (Everton), 1927 v S, W, F, Bel, L; 1928 v S, W, Ni, F, Bel; 1929 v S, W, Ni; 1931 v S; 1932 v Sp; 1933 v Ni (16)
Deane, B. C. (Sheffield U), 1991 v Nz (sub + 1); 1993 v Sp (sub) (3)
Deeley, N. V. (Wolverhampton W), 1959 v Br, Pe (2)
Devey, J. H. G. (Aston Villa), 1892 v Ni; 1894 v Ni (2)
Devonshire, A. (West Ham U), 1980 v Aus (sub), Ni; 1982 v Ho, Ic; 1983 v WG, W, Gr; 1984 v L (8)
Dewhurst, F. (Preston NE), 1886 v W, Ni; 1887 v S, W, Ni; 1888 v S, W, Ni; 1889 v W (9)
Dewhurst, G. P. (Liverpool Ramblers), 1895 v W (1)
Dickinson, J. W. (Portsmouth), 1949 v N, F; 1950 v S, W, Ei, P, Bel, Ch, US, Sp; 1951 v Ni, W, Y; 1952 v W, Ni, S, A (2), I, Sw; 1953 v W, Ni, S, Bel, Arg, Ch, U, US; 1954 v W, Ni, S, R of E, H (2), Y, Bel, Sw, U; 1955 v Sp, P; 1956 v W, Ni, S, D, Sp; 1957 v W, Y, D (48)
Dimmock, J. H. (Tottenham H), 1921 v S; 1926 v W, Bel (3)
Ditchburn, E. G. (Tottenham H), 1949 v Sw, Se; 1953 v US; 1957 v W, Y, D (6)
Dix, R. W. (Derby Co), 1939 v N (1)
Dixon, J. A. (Notts Co), 1885 v W (1)
Dixon, K. M. (Chelsea), 1985 v M (sub), WG, US; 1986 v Ni, Is, M (sub), Pol (sub); 1987 v Se (8)
Dixon, L. M. (Arsenal), 1990 v Cz; 1991 v H, Pol, Ei (2), Cam, T, Arg; 1992 v G, T, Pol, Cz (sub); 1993 v Sp, N, T, Sm, T, Ho, N, US; 1994 v Sm (21)
Dobson, A. T. C. (Notts Co), 1882 v Ni; 1884 v S, W, Ni (4)
Dobson, C. F. (Notts Co), 1886 v Ni (1)
Dobson, J. M. (Burnley), 1974 v P, EG, Bul, Y; (with Everton), 1975 v Cz (5)
Doggart, A. G. (Corinthians), 1924 v Bel (1)
Dorigo, A. R. (Chelsea), 1990 v Y (sub), Cz (sub), D (sub), I; 1991 v H (sub), USSR; (with Leeds U), 1992 v G, Cz (sub), H, Br; 1993 v Sm, Pol, US, Br; 1994 v H (15)
Dorrell, A. R. (Aston Villa), 1925 v W, Bel, F; 1926 v Ni (4)
Douglas, B. (Blackburn R), 1958 v S, W, Ni, F, P, Y, USSR (2), Br, A; 1959 v S, USSR; 1960 v Y, H; 1961 v Ni, W, S, L, P, Sp, M, I, A; 1962 v W, Ni, S, Pe, L, P, H, Arg, Bul, Br; 1963 v S, Br, Sw (36)
Downs, R. W. (Everton), 1921 v Ni (1)
Doyle, M. (Manchester C), 1976 v W, S (sub), Br, I; 1977 v Ho (5)
Drake, E. J. (Arsenal), 1935 v Ni, I; 1936 v W; 1937 v H; 1938 v F (5)
Ducat, A. (Woolwich Arsenal), 1910 v S, W, Ni; (with Aston Villa), 1920 v S, W; 1921 v Ni (6)
Dunn, A. T. B. (Cambridge University), 1883 v Ni; 1884 v Ni; (with Old Etonians), 1892 v S, W (4)
Duxbury, M. (Manchester U), 1984 v L, F, W, S, USSR, Br, U, Ch; 1985 v EG, Fi (10)

Earle, S. G. J. (Clapton), 1924 v F; (with West Ham U), 1928 v Ni (2)
Eastham, G. (Arsenal), 1963 v Br, Cz, EG; 1964 v W, Ni, S, R of W, U, P, Ei, US, Br, Arg; 1965 v H, WG, Se; 1966 v Sp, Pol, D (19)
Eastham, G. R. (Bolton W), 1935 v Ho (1)
Eckersley, W. (Blackburn R), 1950 v Sp; 1951 v S, Y, Arg, P; 1952 v A (2), Sw; 1953 v Ni, Arg, Ch, U, US; 1954 v W, Ni, R of E, H (17)
Edwards, D. (Manchester U), 1955 v S, F, Sp, P; 1956 v S, Br, Se, Fi, WG; 1957 v S, Ni, Ei (2), D (2); 1958 v W, Ni, F (18)
Edwards, J. H. (Shropshire Wanderers), 1874 v S (1)
Edwards, W. (Leeds U), 1926 v S, W; 1927 v W, Ni, S, F, Bel, L; 1928 v S, F, Bel; 1929 v S, W, Ni; 1930 v W, Ni (16)
Ellerington, W. (Southampton), 1949 v N, F (2)
Elliott, G. W. (Middlesbrough), 1913 v Ni; 1914 v Ni; 1920 v W (3)
Elliott, W. H. (Burnley), 1952 v I, A; 1953 v Ni, W, Bel (5)
Evans, R. E. (Sheffield U), 1911 v S, W, Ni; 1912 v W (4)
Ewer, F. H. (Casuals), 1924 v F; 1925 v Bel (2)

Fairclough, P. (Old Foresters), 1878 v S (1)
Fairhurst, D. (Newcastle U), 1934 v F (1)
Fantham, J. (Sheffield W), 1962 v L (1)
Fashanu, J. (Wimbledon), 1989 v Ch, S (2)
Felton, W. (Sheffield W), 1925 v F (1)
Fenton, M. (Middlesbrough), 1938 v S (1)
Fenwick, T. (QPR), 1984 v W (sub), S, USSR, Br, U, Ch; 1985 v Fi, S, M, US; 1986 v R, T, Ni, Eg, M, P, Mor, Pol, Arg; (with Tottenham H), 1988 v Is (sub) (20)
Ferdinand, L. (QPR), 1993 v Sm, Ho, N, US; 1994 v Pol, Sm; 1995 v US (sub) (7)
Field, E. (Clapham Rovers), 1876 v S; 1881 v S (2)
Finney, T. (Preston NE), 1947 v W, Ni, Ei, Ho, F, P; 1948 v S, W, Ni, Bel, Se, I; 1949 v S, W, Ni, Se, N, F; 1950 v S, W, Ni, Ei, I, P, Bel, Ch, US, Sp; 1951 v W, S, Arg, P; 1952 v W, Ni, S, F, I, Sw, A; 1953 v W, Ni, S, Bel, Arg, Ch, U, US; 1954 v W, S, Bel, Sw, U, H, Y; 1955 v WG; 1956 v S, W, Ni, D, Sp; 1957 v S, W, Y, D (2), Ei (2); 1958 v W, S, F, P, Y, USSR (2); 1959 v Ni, USSR (76)
Fleming, H. J. (Swindon T), 1909 v S, H (2); 1910 v W, Ni; 1911 v W, Ni; 1912 v Ni; 1913 v S, W; 1914 v S (11)
Fletcher, A. (Wolverhampton W), 1889 v W; 1890 v W (2)
Flowers, R. (Wolverhampton W), 1955 v F; 1959 v S, W, I, Br, Pe, US, M (sub); 1960 v W, Ni, S, Se, Y, Sp, H; 1961 v Ni, W, S, L, P, Sp, M, I, A; 1962 v W, Ni, S, A, Sw, Pe, L, P, H, Arg, Bul, Br; 1963 v Ni, W, S, F (2), Sw; 1964 v Ei, US, P; 1965 v W, Ho, WG; 1966 v N (49)
Flowers, T. D. (Southampton), 1993 v Br; (with Blackburn R), 1994 v Gr; 1995 v Ng, U, J, Se, Br (7)
Forman, Frank (Nottingham F), 1898 v S, Ni; 1899 v S, W, Ni; 1901 v S; 1902 v S, Ni; 1903 v W (9)
Forman, F. R. (Nottingham F), 1899 v S, W, Ni (3)
Forrest, J. H. (Blackburn R), 1884 v W; 1885 v S, W, Ni; 1886 v S, W; 1887 v S, W, Ni; 1889 v S; 1890 v Ni (11)
Fort, J. (Millwall), 1921 v Bel (1)
Foster, R. E. (Oxford University), 1900 v W; (with Corinthians), 1901 v W, Ni, S; 1902 v W (5)
Foster, S. (Brighton & HA), 1982 v Ni, Ho, K (3)
Foulke, W. J. (Sheffield U), 1897 v W (1)
Foulkes, W. A. (Manchester U), 1955 v Ni (1)
Fox, F. S. (Millwall), 1925 v F (1)
Francis, G. C. J. (QPR), 1975 v Cz, P, W, S; 1976 v Sw, Cz, P, W, Ni, S, Br, Fi (12)
Francis, T. (Birmingham C), 1977 v Ho, L, S, Br; 1978 v Sw, L, I (sub), WG (sub), Br, W, S, H; (with Nottingham F), 1979 v Bul (sub), Se, A (sub); 1980 v Ni, Bul, Sp; 1981 v Sp, R, S (sub), Sw; (with Manchester C), 1982 v N, Ni, W, S (sub), Fi (sub), F, Cz, K, WG, Sp; (with Sampdoria), 1983 v D, Gr, H, Ni, S, Aus (3); 1984 v D, Ni, USSR; 1985 v EG (sub), T (sub), Ni (sub), R, Fi, S, I, M; 1986 v S (52)
Franklin, C. F. (Stoke C), 1947 v S, W, Ni, Ei, Ho, F, Sw, P; 1948 v S, W, Ni, Bel, Se, I; 1949 v S, W, Ni, D, Sw, N, F, Se; 1950 v W, S, Ni, Ei, I (27)
Freeman, B. C. (Everton), 1909 v S, W; (with Burnley), 1912 v S, W, Ni (5)
Froggatt, J. (Portsmouth), 1950 v Ni, I; 1951 v S; 1952 v S, A (2), I, Sw; 1953 v Ni, W, S, Bel, US (13)
Froggatt, R. (Sheffield W), 1953 v W, S, Bel, US (4)
Fry, C. B. (Corinthians), 1901 v Ni (1)
Furness, W. I. (Leeds U), 1933 v I (1)

Galley, T. (Wolverhampton W), 1937 v N, Se (2)
Gardner, T. (Aston Villa), 1934 v Cz; 1935 v Ho (2)
Garfield, B. (WBA), 1898 v Ni (1)
Garratty, W. (Aston Villa), 1903 v W (1)
Garrett, T. (Blackpool), 1952 v S, I; 1954 v W (3)
Gascoigne, P. J. (Tottenham H), 1989 v D (sub), S.Ar (sub), Alb (sub), Ch, S (sub); 1990 v Se (sub), Br (sub), Cz, D, U, Tun, Ei, Ho, Eg, Bel, Cam, WG; 1991 v H, Pol, Cam; (with Lazio), 1993 v N, T, Sm, T, Ho, Pol, N; 1994 v Pol, D; 1995 v J (sub), Se (sub), Br (sub) (32)
Gates, E. (Ipswich T), 1981 v N, R (2)
Gay, L. H. (Cambridge University), 1893 v S; (with Old Brightonians), 1894 v S, W (3)
Geary, F. (Everton), 1890 v Ni; 1891 v S (2)
Geaves, R. L. (Clapham Rovers), 1875 v S (1)
Gee, C. W. (Everton), 1932 v W, Sp; 1937 v Ni (3)
Geldard, A. (Everton), 1933 v I, Sw; 1935 v S; 1938 v Ni (4)
George, C. (Derby Co), 1977 v Ei (1)
George, W. (Aston Villa), 1902 v S, W, Ni (3)
Gibbins, W. V. T. (Clapton), 1924 v F; 1925 v F (2)
Gidman, J. (Aston Villa), 1977 v L (1)
Gillard, I. T. (QPR), 1975 v WG, W; 1976 v Cz (3)
Gilliat, W. E. (Old Carthusians), 1893 v Ni (1)
Goddard, P. (West Ham U), 1982 v Ic (sub) (1)
Goodall, F. R. (Huddersfield T), 1926 v S; 1927 v S, F, Bel, L; 1928 v S, W, F, Bel; 1930 v S, G, A; 1931 v S, W, Ni, Bel; 1932 v Ni; 1933 v W, Ni, A, I, Sw; 1934 v W, Ni, F (25)
Goodall, J. (Preston NE), 1888 v S, W; 1889 v S, W; (with Derby Co), 1891 v S, W; 1892 v S; 1893 v W; 1894 v S; 1895 v S, Ni; 1896 v S, W; 1898 v W (14)
Goodhart, H. C. (Old Etonians), 1883 v S, W, Ni (3)
Goodwyn, A. G. (Royal Engineers), 1873 v S (1)
Goodyer, A. C. (Nottingham F), 1879 v S (1)
Gosling, R. C. (Old Etonians), 1892 v W; 1893 v S; 1894 v W; 1895 v W, S (5)
Gosnell, A. A. (Newcastle U), 1906 v Ni (1)
Gough, H. C. (Sheffield U), 1921 v S (1)
Goulden, L. A. (West Ham U), 1937 v Se, N; 1938 v W, Ni, Cz, G, Sw, F; 1939 v S, W, R of E, I, R, Y (14)
Graham, L. (Millwall), 1925 v S, W (2)
Graham, T. (Nottingham F), 1931 v F; 1932 v Ni (2)
Grainger, C. (Sheffield U), 1956 v Br, Se, Fi, WG; 1957 v W, Ni; (with Sunderland), 1957 v S (7)
Gray, A. A. (C Palace), 1992 v Pol (1)
Greaves, J. (Chelsea), 1959 v Pe, M, US; 1960 v W, Se, Y, Sp; 1961 v Ni, W, S, L, P, Sp, I, A; (with Tottenham H), 1962 v S, Sw, Pe, H, Arg, Bul, Br; 1963 v Ni, W, S, F (2), Br, Cz, Sw; 1964 v W, Ni, R of W, P (2), Ei, Br, U, Arg; 1965 v Ni, S, Bel, Ho, H, Y; 1966 v W, A, Y, N, D, Pol, U, M, F; 1967 v S, Sp, A (57)
Green, F. T. (Wanderers), 1876 v S (1)
Green, G. H. (Sheffield U), 1925 v F; 1926 v S, Bel, W; 1927 v W, Ni; 1928 v F, Bel (8)
Greenhalgh, E. H. (Notts Co), 1872 v S; 1873 v S (2)
Greenhoff, B. (Manchester U), 1976 v W, Ni; 1977 v Ei, Fi, I, Ho, Ni, W, S, Br, Arg, U; 1978 v Br, W, Ni, S (sub), H (sub); (with Leeds U), 1980 v Aus (sub) (18)
Greenwood, D. H. (Blackburn R), 1882 v S, Ni (2)
Gregory, J. (QPR), 1983 v Aus (3); 1984 v D, H, W (6)
Grimsdell, A. (Tottenham H), 1920 v S, W; 1921 v S, Ni; 1923 v W, Ni (6)
Grosvenor, A. T. (Birmingham), 1934 v Ni, W, F (3)
Gunn, W. (Notts Co), 1884 v S, W (2)
Gurney, R. (Sunderland), 1935 v S (1)

Hacking, J. (Oldham Ath), 1929 v S, W, Ni (3)
Hadley, N. (WBA), 1903 v Ni (1)
Hagan, J. (Sheffield U), 1949 v D (1)
Haines, J. T. W. (WBA), 1949 v Sw (1)
Hall, A. E. (Aston Villa), 1910 v Ni (1)
Hall, G. W. (Tottenham H), 1934 v F; 1938 v S, W, Ni, Cz; 1939 v S, Ni, R of E, I, Y (10)
Hall, J. (Birmingham C), 1956 v S, W, Ni, Br, Se, Fi, WG, D, Sp; 1957 v S, W, Ni, Y, D (2), Ei (2) (17)
Halse, H. J. (Manchester U), 1909 v A (1)
Hammond, H. E. D. (Oxford University), 1889 v S (1)
Hampson, J. (Blackpool), 1931 v Ni, W; 1933 v A (3)
Hampton, H. (Aston Villa), 1913 v S, W; 1914 v S, W (4)
Hancocks, J. (Wolverhampton W), 1949 v Sw; 1950 v W; 1951 v Y (3)
Hapgood, E. (Arsenal), 1933 v I, Sw; 1934 v S, Ni, W, H, Cz; 1935 v S, Ni, W, I, Ho; 1936 v S, Ni, W, G, A, Bel; 1937 v Fi; 1938 v S, G, Sw, F; 1939 v S, W, Ni, R of E, N, I, Y (30)
Hardinge, H. T. W. (Sheffield U), 1910 v S (1)
Hardman, H. P. (Everton), 1905 v W; 1907 v S, Ni; 1908 v W (4)
Hardwick, G. F. M. (Middlesbrough), 1947 v S, W, Ni, Ei, Ho, F, Sw, P; 1948 v S, W, Ni, Bel, Se (13)
Hardy, H. (Stockport Co), 1925 v Bel (1)
Hardy, S. (Liverpool), 1907 v S, W, Ni; 1908 v S; 1909 v S, W, Ni, H (2), A; 1910 v S, W, Ni; 1912 v Ni; (with Aston Villa), 1913 v S; 1914 v Ni, W, S; 1920 v S, W, Ni (21)
Harford, M. G. (Luton T), 1988 v Is (sub); 1989 v D (2)
Hargreaves, F. W. (Blackburn R), 1880 v W; 1881 v W; 1882 v Ni (3)
Hargreaves, J. (Blackburn R), 1881 v S, W (2)
Harper, E. C. (Blackburn R), 1926 v S (1)
Harris, G. (Burnley), 1966 v Pol (1)
Harris, P. P. (Portsmouth), 1950 v Ei; 1954 v H (2)
Harris, S. S. (Cambridge University), 1904 v S; (with Old Westminsters), 1905 v Ni, W; 1906 v S, W, Ni (6)
Harrison, A. H. (Old Westminsters), 1893 v S, Ni (2)
Harrison, G. (Everton), 1921 v Bel; 1922 v Ni (2)
Harrow, J. H. (Chelsea), 1923 v Ni, Se (2)
Hart, E. (Leeds U), 1929 v W; 1930 v W, Ni; 1933 v S, A; 1934 v S, H, Cz (8)
Hartley, F. (Oxford C), 1923 v F (1)
Harvey, A. (Wednesbury Strollers), 1881 v W (1)
Harvey, J. C. (Everton), 1971 v Ma (1)
Hassall, H. W. (Huddersfield T), 1951 v S, Arg, P; 1952 v F; (with Bolton W), 1954 v Ni (5)
Hateley, M. (Portsmouth), 1984 v USSR (sub), Br, U, Ch; (with AC Milan), 1985 v EG (sub), Fi, Ni, Ei, Fi, S, I, M; 1986 v R, T, Eg, S, M, Ca, P, Mor, Para (sub); 1987 v T (sub), Br (sub), S; (with Monaco), 1988 v WG (sub), Ho (sub), H (sub), Co (sub), Ei (sub), Ho (sub), USSR (sub); (with Rangers), 1992 v Cz (32)
Haworth, G. (Accrington), 1887 v Ni, W, S; 1888 v S; 1890 v S (5)
Hawtrey, J. P. (Old Etonians), 1881 v S, W (2)
Hawkes, R. M. (Luton T), 1907 v Ni; 1908 v A (2), H, B (5)
Haygarth, E. B. (Swifts), 1875 v S (1)
Haynes, J. N. (Fulham), 1955 v Ni; 1956 v S, Ni, Br, Se, Fi, WG, Sp; 1957 v W, Y, D, Ei (2); 1958 v W, Ni, S, F, P, Y, USSR (3), Br, A; 1959 v S, Ni, USSR, I, Br, Pe, M, US; 1960 v Ni, Y, Sp, H; 1961 v Ni, W, S, L, P, Sp, M, I, A; 1962 v W, Ni, S, A, Sw, Pe, P, H, Arg, Bul, Br (56)
Healless, H. (Blackburn R), 1925 v Ni; 1928 v S (2)
Hector, K. J. (Derby Co), 1974 v Pol (sub), I (sub) (2)
Hedley, G. A. (Sheffield U), 1901 v Ni (1)
Hegan, K. E. (Corinthians), 1923 v Bel, F; 1924 v Ni, Bel (4)
Hellawell, M. S. (Birmingham C), 1963 v Ni, F (2)
Henfrey, A. G. (Cambridge University), 1891 v Ni; (with Corinthians), 1892 v W; 1895 v W; 1896 v S, W (5)
Henry, R. P. (Tottenham H), 1963 v F (1)
Heron, F. (Wanderers), 1876 v S (1)
Heron, G. H. H. (Uxbridge), 1873 v S; 1874 v S; (with Wanderers), 1875 v S; 1876 v S; 1878 v S (5)
Hibbert, W. (Bury), 1910 v S (1)

Hibbs, H. E. (Birmingham), 1930 v S, W, A, G; 1931 v S, W, Ni; 1932 v W, Ni, Sp; 1933 v S, W, Ni, A, I, Sw; 1934 v Ni, W, F; 1935 v S, W, Ni, Ho; 1936 v G, W (25)
Hill, F. (Bolton W), 1963 v Ni, W (2)
Hill, G. A. (Manchester U), 1976 v I; 1977 v Ei (sub), Fi (sub), L; 1978 v Sw (sub), L (6)
Hill, J. H. (Burnley), 1925 v W; 1926 v S; 1927 v S, Ni, Bel, F; 1928 v Ni, W; (with Newcastle U), 1929 v F, Bel, Sp (11)
Hill, R. (Luton T), 1983 v D (sub), WG; 1986 v Eg (sub) (3)
Hill, R. H. (Millwall), 1926 v Bel (1)
Hillman, J. (Burnley), 1899 v Ni (1)
Hills, A. F. (Old Harrovians), 1879 v S (1)
Hilsdon, G. R. (Chelsea), 1907 v Ni; 1908 v S, W, Ni, A, H, B; 1909 v Ni (8)
Hine, E. W. (Leicester C), 1929 v W, Ni; 1930 v W, Ni; 1932 v W, Ni (6)
Hinton, A. T. (Wolverhampton W), 1963 v F; (with Nottingham F), 1965 v W, Bel (3)
Hirst, D. E. (Sheffield W), 1991 v Aus, Nz (sub); 1992 v F (3)
Hitchens, G. A. (Aston Villa), 1961 v M, I, A; (with Inter-Milan), 1962 v Sw, Pe, H, Br (7)
Hobbis, H. H. F. (Charlton Ath), 1936 v A, Bel (2)
Hoddle, G. (Tottenham H), 1980 v Bul, W, Aus, Sp; 1981 v Sp, W, S; 1982 v N, Ni, W, Ic, Cz (sub), K; 1983 v L (sub), Ni, S; 1984 v H, L, F; 1985 v Ei (sub), S, I (sub), M, WG, US; 1986 v R, T, Ni, Is, USSR, S, M, Ca, P, Mor, Pol, Para, Arg; 1987 v Se, Ni, Y, Sp, T, S; (with Monaco), 1988 v WG, T (sub), Y (sub), Ho (sub), H (sub), Co (sub), Ei (sub), Ho, USSR (53)
Hodge, S. B. (Aston Villa), 1986 v USSR (sub), S, Ca, P (sub), Mor (sub), Pol, Para, Arg; 1987 v Se, Ni, Y; (with Tottenham H), Sp. Ni, T, S; (with Nottingham F), 1989 v D; 1990 v I (sub), Y (sub), Cz, D, U, Tun; 1991 v Cam (sub), T (sub) (24)
Hodgetts, D. (Aston Villa), 1888 v S, W, Ni; 1892 v S, Ni; 1894 v Ni (6)
Hodgkinson, A. (Sheffield U), 1957 v S, Ei (2), D; 1961 v W (5)
Hodgson, G. (Liverpool), 1931 v S, Ni, W (3)
Hodkinson, J. (Blackburn R), 1913 v W, S; 1920 v Ni (3)
Hogg, W. (Sunderland), 1902 v S, W, Ni (3)
Holdcroft, G. H. (Preston NE), 1937 v W, Ni (2)
Holden, A. D. (Bolton W), 1959 v S, I, Br, Pe, M (5)
Holden, G. H. (Wednesbury OA), 1881 v S; 1884 v S, W, Ni (4)
Holden-White, C. (Corinthians), 1888 v W, S (2)
Holford, T. (Stoke), 1903 v Ni (1)
Holley, G. H. (Sunderland), 1909 v S, W, H (2), A; 1910 v W; 1912 v S, W, NI; 1913 v S (10)
Holliday, E. (Middlesbrough), 1960 v W, Ni, Se (3)
Hollins, J. W. (Chelsea), 1967 v Sp (1)
Holmes, R. (Preston NE), 1888 v Ni; 1891 v S; 1892 v S; 1893 v S, W; 1894 v Ni; 1895 v Ni (7)
Holt, J. (Everton), 1890 v W; 1891 v S, W; 1892 v S, Ni; 1893 v S; 1894 v S, Ni; 1895 v S; (with Reading), 1900 v Ni (10)
Hopkinson, E. (Bolton W), 1958 v W, Ni, S, F, P, Y; 1959 v S, I, Br, Pe, M, US; 1960 v W, Se (14)
Hossack, A. H. (Corinthians), 1892 v W; 1894 v W (2)
Houghton, W. E. (Aston Villa), 1931 v Ni, W, F, Bel; 1932 v S, Ni; 1933 v A (7)
Houlker, A. E. (Blackburn R), 1902 v S; (with Portsmouth), 1903 v S, W; (with Southampton), 1906 v W, Ni (5)
Howarth, R. H. (Preston NE), 1887 v Ni; 1888 v S, W; 1891 v S; (with Everton), 1894 v Ni (5)
Howe, D. (WBA), 1958 v S, W, Ni, F, P, Y, USSR (3), Br, A; 1959 v S, W, Ni, USSR, I, Br, Pe, M, US; 1960 v W, Ni, Se (23)
Howe, J. R. (Derby Co), 1948 v I; 1949 v S, Ni (3)
Howell, L. S. (Wanderers), 1873 v S (1)
Howell, R. (Sheffield U), 1895 v Ni; (with Liverpool) 1899 v S (2)
Howey, S. N. (Newcastle U), 1995 v Ng (1)
Hudson, A. A. (Stoke C), 1975 v WG, Cy (2)
Hudson, J. (Sheffield), 1883 v Ni (1)
Hudspeth, F. C. (Newcastle U), 1926 v Ni (1)
Hufton, A. E. (West Ham U), 1924 v Bel; 1928 v S, Ni; 1929 v F, Bel, Sp (6)
Hughes, E. W. (Liverpool), 1970 v W, Ni, S, Ho, P, Bel; 1971 v EG, Ma (2), Gr, W; 1972 v Sw, Gr, WG (2), W, Ni, S; 1973 v W (3), S (2), Pol, USSR, I; 1974 v A, Pol, I, W, Ni, S, Arg, EG, Bul, Y; 1975 v Cz, P, Cy (sub), Ni; 1977 v I, L, W, S, Br, Arg, U; 1978 v Sw, L, I, WG, Ni, S, H; 1979 v D, Ei, Ni, W, Se; (with Wolverhampton W), 1980 v Sp (sub), Ni, S (sub) (62)
Hughes, L. (Liverpool), 1950 v Ch, US, Sp (3)
Hulme, J. H. A. (Arsenal), 1927 v S, Bel, F; 1928 v S, Ni, W; 1929 v Ni, W; 1933 v S (9)
Humphreys, P. (Notts Co), 1903 v S (1)
Hunt, G. S. (Tottenham H), 1933 v I, Sw, S (3)
Hunt, Rev K. R. G. (Leyton), 1911 v S, W (2)
Hunt, R. (Liverpool), 1962 v A; 1963 v EG; 1964 v S, US, P; 1965 v W; 1966 v S, Sp, Pol (2), WG (2), Fi, N, U, M, F, Arg, P; 1967 v Ni, W, Cz, Sp, A; 1968 v W, Ni, USSR (2), Sp (2), Se, Y; 1969 v R (2) (34)
Hunt, S. (WBA), 1984 v S (sub), USSR (sub) (2)
Hunter, J. (Sheffield Heeley), 1878 v S; 1880 v S, W; 1881 v S, W; 1882 v S, W (7)
Hunter, N. (Leeds U), 1966 v WG, Y, Fi, Sp (sub); 1967 v A; 1968 v Sp, Se, Y, WG, USSR; 1969 v R, W; 1970 v Ho, WG (sub); 1971 v Ma; 1972 v WG (2), W, Ni, S; 1973 v W (2) USSR (sub); 1974 v A, Pol, Ni (sub), S; 1975 v Cz (28)
Hurst, G. C. (West Ham U), 1966 v S, WG (2), Y, Fi, D, Arg, P; 1967 v Ni, W, S, Cz, Sp, A; 1968 v W, Ni, S, Se (sub), WG, USSR (2); 1969 v Ni, S, R (2), Bul, F, M, U, Br; 1970 v W, Ni, S, Ho (1+1 sub), Bel, Co, Ec, R, Br, WG; 1971 v EG, Gr, W, S; 1972 v Sw (2), Gr, WG (49)

Ince, P. E. C. (Manchester U), 1993 v Sp, N, T (2), Ho, Pol, US, Br, G; 1994 v Pol, Ho, Sm, D, N; 1995 v R, Ei (16)
Iremonger, J. (Nottingham F), 1901 v S; 1902 v Ni (2)

Jack, D. N. B. (Bolton W), 1924 v S, W; 1928 v F, Bel; (with Arsenal), 1930 v S, G, A; 1933 v W, A (9)
Jackson, E. (Oxford University), 1891 v W (1)
Jarrett, B. G. (Cambridge University), 1876 v S; 1877 v S; 1878 v S (3)
Jefferis, F. (Everton), 1912 v S, W (2)
Jezzard, B. A. G. (Fulham), 1954 v H; 1956 v Ni (2)
Johnson, D. E. (Ipswich T), 1975 v W, S; 1976 v Sw; (with Liverpool), 1980 v Ei, Arg, Ni, S, Bel (8)
Johnson, E. (Saltley College), 1880 v W; (with Stoke C), 1884 v Ni (2)
Johnson, J. A. (Stoke C), 1937 v N, Se, Fi, S, Ni (5)
Johnson, T. C. F. (Manchester C), 1926 v Bel; 1930 v W; (with Everton), 1932 v S, Sp; 1933 v Ni (5)
Johnson, W. H. (Sheffield U), 1900 v S, W, Ni; 1903 v S, W, Ni (6)
Johnston, H. (Blackpool), 1947 v S, Ho; 1951 v S; 1953 v Arg, Ch, U, US; 1954 v W, Ni, H (10)
Jones, A. (Walsall Swifts), 1882 v S, W; (with Great Lever), 1883 v S (3)
Jones, H. (Blackburn R), 1927 v S, Bel, L, F; 1928 v S, Ni (6)
Jones, H. (Nottingham F), 1923 v F (1)
Jones, M. D. (Sheffield U), 1965 v WG, Se; (with Leeds U), 1970 v Ho (3)
Jones, R. (Liverpool), 1992 v F; 1994 v Pol, Gr, N; 1995 v US, R, Ng, U (8)

Jones, W. (Bristol C), 1901 v Ni (1)
Jones, W. H. (Liverpool), 1950 v P, Bel (2)
Joy, B. (Casuals), 1936 v Bel (1)

Kail, E. I. L. (Dulwich Hamlet), 1929 v F, Bel, Sp (3)
Kay, A. H. (Everton), 1963 v Sw (1)
Kean, F. W. (Sheffield W), 1923 v S, Bel; 1924 v W; 1925 v Ni; 1926 v Ni, Bel; 1927 v L; (with Bolton W), 1929 v F, Sp (9)
Keegan, J. K. (Liverpool), 1973 v W (2); 1974 v W, Ni, Arg, EG, Bul, Y; 1975 v Cz, WG, Cy (2), Ni, S; 1976 v Sw, Cz, P, W (2), Ni, S, Br, Fi; 1977 v Ei, Fi, I, Ho, L; (with SV Hamburg), W, Br, Arg, U; 1978 v Sw, I, WG, Br, H; 1979 v D, Ei, Cz, Ni, W, S, Bul, Se, A; 1980 v D, Ni, Ei, Sp (2), Arg, Bel, I; (with Southampton), 1981 v Sp, Sw, H; 1982 v N, H, Ni, S, Fi, Sp (sub) (63)
Keen, E. R. L. (Derby Co), 1933 v A; 1937 v W, Ni, H (4)
Kelly, R. (Burnley), 1920 v S; 1921 v S, W, Ni; 1922 v S, W; 1923 v S; 1924 v Ni; 1925 v W, Ni, S; (with Sunderland), 1926 v W; (with Huddersfield T), 1927 v L; 1928 v S (14)
Kennedy, A. (Liverpool), 1984 v Ni, W (2)
Kennedy, R. (Liverpool), 1976 v W (2), Ni, S; 1977 v L, W, S, Br (sub), Arg (sub); 1978 v Sw, L; 1980 v Bul, Sp, Arg, W, Bel (sub), I (17)
Kenyon-Slaney, W. S. (Wanderers), 1873 v S (1)
Keown, M. R. (Everton), 1992 v F, Cz, C, H, Br, Fi, D, Fe, Se; (with Arsenal), 1993 v Ho, G (sub) (11)
Kevan, D. T. (WBA), 1957 v S; 1958 v W, Ni, S, P. Y, USSR (3), Br, A; 1959 v M, US; 1961 v M (14)
Kidd, B. (Manchester U), 1970 v Ni, Ec (sub) (2)
King, R. S. (Oxford University), 1882 v Ni (1)
Kingsford, R. K. (Wanderers), 1874 v S (1)
Kingsley, M. (Newcastle U), 1901 v W (1)
Kinsey, G. (Wolverhampton W), 1892 v W; 1893 v S; (with Derby Co), 1896 v W, Ni (4)
Kirchen, A. J. (Arsenal), 1937 v N, Se, Fi (3)
Kirton, W. J. (Aston Villa), 1922 v Ni (1)
Knight, A. E. (Portsmouth), 1920 v Ni (1)
Knowles, C. (Tottenham H), 1968 v USSR, Sp, Se, WG (4)

Labone, B. L. (Everton), 1963 v Ni, W, F; 1967 v Sp, A; 1968 v S, Sp, Se, Y, USSR, WG; 1969 v Ni, S, R, Bul, M, U, Br; 1970 v S, W, Bel, Co, Ec, R, Br, WG (26)
Lampard, F. R. G. (West Ham U), 1973 v Y; 1980 v Aus (2)
Langley, E. J. (Fulham), 1958 v S, P, Y (3)
Langton, R. (Blackburn R), 1947 v W, Ni, Ei, Ho, F, Sw; 1948 v Se; (with Preston NE), 1949 v D, Se; (with Bolton W), 1950 v S; 1951 v Ni (11)
Latchford, R. D. (Everton), 1978 v I, Br, W; 1979 v D, Ei, Cz (sub), Ni (2), W, S, Bul, A (12)
Latheron, E. G. (Blackburn R), 1913 v W; 1914 v Ni (2)
Lawler, C. (Liverpool), 1971 v Ma, W, S; 1972 v Sw (4)
Lawton, T. (Everton), 1939 v S, W, Ni, R of E, N, I, R, Y; (with Chelsea), 1947 v S, W, Ni, Ei, Ho, F, Sw, P; 1948 v W, Ni, Bel; (with Notts Co), 1948 v S, Se, I; 1949 v D (23)
Leach, T. (Sheffield W), 1931 v W, Ni (2)
Leake, A. (Aston Villa), 1904 v S, Ni; 1905 v S, W, Ni (5)
Lee, E. A. (Southampton), 1904 v W (1)
Lee, F. H. (Manchester C), 1969 v Ni, W, S, Bul, F, M, U; 1970 v W, Ho (2), P, Bel, Co, Ec, R, Br, WG; 1971 v EG, Gr, Ma, Ni, W, S; 1972 v Sw (2), Gr, WG (27)
Lee, J. (Derby Co), 1951 v Ni (1)
Lee, R. M. (Newcastle U), 1995 v R, Ng (2)
Lee, S. (Liverpool), 1983 v Gr, L, W, Gr, H, S, Aus; 1984 v D, H, L, F, Ni, W, Ch (sub) (14)
Leighton, J. E. (Nottingham F), 1886 v Ni (1)
Le Saux, G. P. (Blackburn R), 1994 v D, Gr, N; 1995 v US, R, Ng, Ei, U, Se, Br (10)
Le Tissier, M. P. (Southampton), 1994 v D (sub), Gr (sub), N (sub); 1995 v R, Ng (sub), Ei (6)
Lilley, H. E. (Sheffield U), 1892 v W (1)
Linacre, H. J. (Nottingham F), 1905 v W, S (2)
Lindley, T. (Cambridge University), 1886 v S, W, Ni; 1887 v S, W, Ni; 1888 v S, W, Ni; (with Nottingham F), 1889 v S; 1890 v S, W; 1891 v Ni (13)
Lindsay, A. (Liverpool), 1974 v Arg, EG, Bul, Y (4)
Lindsay, W. (Wanderers), 1877 v S (1)
Lineker, G. (Leicester C), 1984 v S (sub); 1985 v Ei, R (sub), S (sub), I (sub), WG, US; (with Everton), 1986 v R, T, Ni, Eg, USSR, Ca, P, Mor, Pol, Para, Arg; (with Barcelona), 1987 v Ni (2), Y, Sp, T, Br; 1988 v WG, T, Y, Ho, H, S, Co, Sw, Ei, Ho, USSR; 1989 v Se, S.Ar, Gr, Alb (2), Pol, D; (with Tottenham H) 1990 v Se, Pol, I, Y, Br, Cz, D, U, Tun, Ei, Ho, Eg, Bel, Cam, WG, I; 1991 v H, Pol, Ei (2), Cam, T, Arg, Aus, Nz, Mal; 1992 v G, T, Pol, F (sub), Cz (sub), C, H, Br, Fi, D, F, Se (80)
Lintott, E. H. (QPR), 1908 v S, W, Ni; (with Bradford C), 1909 v S, Ni, H (2) (7)
Lipsham, H. B. (Sheffield U), 1902 v W (1)
Little, B. (Aston Villa), 1975 v W (sub) (1)
Lloyd, L. V. (Liverpool), 1971 v W; 1972 v Sw, Ni; (with Nottingham F), 1980 v W (4)
Lockett, A. (Stoke C), 1903 v Ni (1)
Lodge, L. V. (Cambridge University), 1894 v W; 1895 v S, W; (with Corinthians), 1896 v S, Ni (5)
Lofthouse, J. M. (Blackburn R), 1885 v S, W, Ni; 1887 v S, W; (with Accrington), 1889 v Ni; (with Blackburn R), 1890 v Ni (7)
Lofthouse, N. (Bolton W), 1951 v Y; 1952 v W, Ni, S, A (2), I, Sw; 1953 v W, Ni, S, Bel, Arg, Ch, U, US; 1954 v W, Ni, R of E, Bel, U; 1955 v Ni, S, F, Sp, P; 1956 v W, S, Sp, D, Fi (sub); 1959 v W, USSR (33)
Longworth, E. (Liverpool), 1920 v S; 1921 v Bel; 1923 v S, W, Bel (5)
Lowder, A. (Wolverhampton W), 1889 v W (1)
Lowe, E. (Aston Villa), 1947 v F, Sw, P (3)
Lucas, T. (Liverpool), 1922 v Ni; 1924 v F; 1926 v Bel (3)
Luntley, E. (Nottingham F), 1880 v S, W (2)
Lyttelton, Hon. A. (Cambridge University), 1877 v S (1)
Lyttelton, Hon. E. (Cambridge University), 1878 v S (1)

McCall, J. (Preston NE), 1913 v S, W; 1914 v S; 1920 v S; 1921 v Ni (5)
McDermott, T. (Liverpool), 1978 v Sw, L; 1979 v Ni, W, Se; 1980 v D, Ni (sub), Ei, Ni, S, Bel (sub), Sp; 1981 v N, R, Sw, R (sub), Br, Sw (sub), H; 1982 v N, H, W (sub), Ho, S (sub), Ic (25)
McDonald, C. A. (Burnley), 1958 v USSR (3), Br, A; 1959 v W, Ni, USSR (8)
McFarland, R. L. (Derby Co), 1971 v Gr, Ma (2), Ni, S; 1972 v Sw, Gr, WG, W, S; 1973 v W (3), Ni, S, Cz, Pol, USSR, I; 1974 v A, Pol, I, W, Ni; 1976 v Cz, S; 1977 v Ei, I (28)
McGarry, W. H. (Huddersfield T), 1954 v Sw, U; 1956 v W, D (4)
McGuinness, W. (Manchester U), 1959 v Ni, M (2)
McInroy, A. (Sunderland), 1927 v Ni (1)
McMahon, S. (Liverpool), 1988 v Is, H, Co, USSR; 1989 v D (sub); 1990 v Se, Pol, I, Y (sub), Br, Cz (sub), D, Ei (sub), Eg, Bel, I; 1991 v Ei (17)
McManaman, S. (Liverpool), 1995 v Ng (sub), U (sub), J (sub) (3)
McNab, R. (Arsenal), 1969 v Ni, Bul, R (1 + 1 sub) (4)
McNeal, R. (WBA), 1914 v S, W (2)
McNeil, M. (Middlesbrough), 1961 v W, Ni, S, L, P, Sp, M, I; 1962 v L (9)
Mabbutt, G. (Tottenham H), 1983 v WG, Gr, L, W, Gr, H, Ni, S (sub); 1984 v H; 1987 v Y, Ni, T; 1988 v WG; 1992 v T, Pol, Cz (16)
Macaulay, R. H. (Cambridge University), 1881 v S (1)

Macdonald, M. (Newcastle U), 1972 v W, Ni, S (sub); 1973 v USSR (sub); 1974 v P, S (sub), Y (sub); 1975 v WG, Cy (2), Ni; 1976 v Sw (sub), Cz, P (14)
Macrae, S. (Notts Co), 1883 v S, W, Ni; 1884 v S, W, Ni (6)
Maddison, F. B. (Oxford University), 1872 v S (1)
Madeley, P. E. (Leeds U), 1971 v Ni; 1972 v Sw (2), Gr, WG (2), W, S; 1973 v S, Cz, Pol, USSR, I; 1974 v A, Pol, I; 1975 v Cz, P, Cy; 1976 v Cz, P, Fi; 1977 v Ei, Ho (24)
Magee, T. P. (WBA), 1923 v W, Se; 1925 v S, Bel, F (5)
Makepeace, H. (Everton), 1906 v S; 1910 v S; 1912 v S, W (4)
Male, C. G. (Arsenal), 1935 v S, Ni, I, Ho; 1936 v S, W, Ni, G, A, Bel; 1937 v S, Ni, H, N, Se, Fi; 1939 v I, R, Y (19)
Mannion, W. J. (Middlesbrough), 1947 v S, W, Ni, Ei, Ho, F, Sw, P; 1948 v W, Ni, Bel, Se, I; 1949 v N, F; 1950 v S, Ei, P, Bel, Ch, US; 1951 v Ni, W, S, Y; 1952 v F (26)
Mariner, P. (Ipswich T), 1977 v L (sub), Ni; 1978 v L, W (sub), S; 1980 v W, Ni (sub), S, Aus, I (sub), Sp (sub); 1981 v N, Sw, Sp, Sw, H; 1982 v N, H, Ho, S, Fi, F, Cz, K, WG, Sp; 1983 v D, WG, Gr, W; 1984 v D, H, L; (with Arsenal), 1985 v EG, R (35)
Marsden, J. T. (Darwen), 1891 v Ni (1)
Marsden, W. (Sheffield W), 1930 v W, S, G (3)
Marsh, R. W. (QPR), 1972 v Sw (sub); (with Manchester C), WG (sub+1), W, Ni, S; 1973 v W (2), Y (9)
Marshall, T. (Darwen), 1880 v W; 1881 v W (2)
Martin, A. (West Ham U), 1981 v Br, S (sub); 1982 v H, Fi; 1983 v Gr, L, W, Gr, H; 1984 v H, L, W; 1985 v Ni; 1986 v Is, Ca, Para; 1987 v Se (17)
Martin, H. (Sunderland), 1914 v Ni (1)
Martyn, A. N. (C Palace), 1992 v C (sub), H; 1993 v G (3)
Marwood, B. (Arsenal), 1989 v S.Ar (sub) (1)
Maskrey, H. M. (Derby Co), 1908 v Ni (1)
Mason, C. (Wolverhampton W), 1887 v Ni; 1888 v W; 1890 v Ni (3)
Matthews, R. D. (Coventry C), 1956 v S, Br, Se, WG; 1957 v Ni (5)
Matthews, S. (Stoke C), 1935 v W, I; 1936 v G; 1937 v S; 1938 v S, W, Cz, G, Sw, F; 1939 v S, W, Ni, R of E, N, I, Y; 1947 v S; (with Blackpool), 1947 v Sw, P; 1948 v S, W, Ni, Bel, I; 1949 v S, W, Ni, D, Sw; 1950 v Sp; 1951 v Ni, S; 1954 v Ni, R of E, H, Bel, U; 1955 v Ni, W, S, F, WG, Sp, P; 1956 v W, Br; 1957 v S, W, Ni, Y, D (2), Ei (54)
Matthews, V. (Sheffield U), 1928 v F, Bel (2)
Maynard, W. J. (1st Surrey Rifles), 1872 v S; 1876 v S (2)
Meadows, J. (Manchester C), 1955 v S (1)
Medley, L. D. (Tottenham H), 1951 v Y, W; 1952 v F, A, W, Ni (6)
Meehan, T. (Chelsea), 1924 v Ni (1)
Melia, J. (Liverpool), 1963 v S, Sw (2)
Mercer, D. W. (Sheffield U), 1923 v Ni, Bel (2)
Mercer, J. (Everton), 1939 v S, Ni, I, R, Y (5)
Merrick, G. H. (Birmingham C), 1952 v Ni, S, A (2), I, Sw; 1953 v Ni, W, S, Bel, Arg, Ch, U; 1954 v W, Ni, S, R of E, H (2), Y, Bel, Sw, U (23)
Merson, P. C. (Arsenal), 1992 v G (sub), Cz, H, Br (sub), Fi (sub), D, Se (sub); 1993 v Sp (sub), N (sub), Ho (sub), Br (sub), G; 1994 v Ho, Gr (14)
Metcalfe, V. (Huddersfield T), 1951 v Arg, P (2)
Mew, J. W. (Manchester U), 1921 v Ni (1)
Middleditch, B. (Corinthians), 1897 v Ni (1)
Milburn, J. E. T. (Newcastle U), 1949 v S, W, Ni, Sw; 1950 v W, P, Bel, Sp; 1951 v W, Arg, P; 1952 v F; 1956 v D (13)
Miller, B. G. (Burnley), 1961 v A (1)
Miller, H. S. (Charlton Ath), 1923 v Se (1)
Mills, G. R. (Chelsea), 1938 v W, Ni, Cz (3)
Mills, M. D. (Ipswich T), 1973 v Y; 1976 v W (2), Ni, S, Br, I (sub), Fi; 1977 v Fi (sub), I, Ni, W, S; 1978 v WG, Br, W, Ni, S, H; 1979 v D, Ei, Ni (2), S, Bul, A; 1980 v D, Ni, Sp (2); 1981 v Sw (2), H; 1982 v N, H, S, Fi, F, Cz, K, WG, Sp (42)
Milne, G. (Liverpool), 1963 v Br, Cz, EG; 1964 v W, Ni, S, R of W, U, P, Ei, Br, Arg; 1965 v Ni, Bel (14)
Milton, C. A. (Arsenal), 1952 v A (1)
Milward, A. (Everton), 1891 v S, W; 1897 v S, W (4)
Mitchell, C. (Upton Park), 1880 v W; 1881 v S; 1883 v S, W; 1885 v W (5)
Mitchell, J. F. (Manchester C), 1925 v Ni (1)
Moffat, H. (Oldham Ath), 1913 v W (1)
Molyneux, G. (Southampton), 1902 v S; 1903 v S, W, Ni (4)
Moon, W. R. (Old Westminsters), 1888 v S, W; 1889 v S, W; 1890 v S, W; 1891 v S (7)
Moore, H. T. (Notts Co), 1883 v Ni; 1885 v W (2)
Moore, J. (Derby Co), 1923 v Se (1)
Moore, R. F. (West Ham U), 1962 v Pe, H, Arg, Bul, Br; 1963 v W, Ni, S, F (2), Br, Cz, EG, Sw; 1964 v W, Ni, S, R of W, U, P (2), Ei, Br, Arg; 1965 v Ni, S, Bel, H, Y, WG, Se; 1966 v W, Ni, S, A, Sp, Pol (2), WG (2), N, D, U, M, F, Arg, P; 1967 v W, Ni, S, Cz, Sp, A; 1968 v W, Ni, S, USSR (2), Sp (2), Se, Y, WG; 1969 v Ni, W, S, R, Bul, F, M, U, Br; 1970 v W, Ni, S, Ho, P, Bel, Co, Ec, R, Br, Cz, WG; 1971 v EG, Gr, Ma, Ni, S; 1972 v Sw (2), Gr, WG (2), W, S; 1973 v W (3), Y, S (2), Ni, Cz, Pol, USSR, I; 1974 v I (108)
Moore, W. G. B. (West Ham U), 1923 v Se (1)
Mordue, J. (Sunderland), 1912 v Ni; 1913 v Ni (2)
Morice, C. J. (Barnes), 1872 v S (1)
Morley, A. (Aston Villa), 1982 v H (sub), Ni, W, Ic; 1983 v D, Gr (6)
Morley, H. (Notts Co), 1910 v Ni (1)
Morren, T. (Sheffield U), 1898 v Ni (1)
Morris, F. (WBA), 1920 v S; 1921 v Ni (2)
Morris, J. (Derby Co), 1949 v N, F; 1950 v Ei (3)
Morris, W. W. (Wolverhampton W), 1939 v S, Ni, R (3)
Morse, H. (Notts Co), 1879 v S (1)
Mort, T. (Aston Villa), 1924 v W, F; 1926 v S (3)
Morten, A. (C Palace), 1873 v S (1)
Mortensen, S. H. (Blackpool), 1947 v P; 1948 v W, S, Ni, Bel, Se, I; 1949 v S, W, Ni, Se, N; 1950 v S, W, Ni, I, P, Bel, Ch, US, Sp; 1951 v S, Arg; 1954 v R of E, H (25)
Morton, J. R. (West Ham U), 1938 v Cz (1)
Mosforth, W. (Sheffield W), 1877 v S; (with Sheffield Albion), 1878 v S; 1879 v S, W; 1880 v S, W; (with Sheffield W), 1881 v W; 1882 v S, W (9)
Moss, F. (Arsenal), 1934 v S, H, Cz; 1935 v I (4)
Moss, F. (Aston Villa), 1922 v S, Ni; 1923 v Ni; 1924 v S, Bel (5)
Mosscrop, E. (Burnley), 1914 v S, W (2)
Mozley, B. (Derby Co), 1950 v W, Ni, Ei (3)
Mullen, J. (Wolverhampton W), 1947 v S; 1949 v N, F; 1950 v Bel (sub), Ch, US; 1954 v W, Ni, S, R of E, Y, Sw (12)
Mullery, A. P. (Tottenham H), 1965 v Ho; 1967 v Sp, A; 1968 v W, Ni, S, USSR, Sp (2), Se, Y; 1969 v Ni, S, R, Bul, F, M, U, Br; 1970 v W, Ni, S (sub), Ho (sub), Bel, P, Co, Ec, R, Cz, WG, Br; 1971 v Ma, EG, Gr; 1972 v Sw (35)

Neal, P. G. (Liverpool), 1976 v W, I; 1977 v W, S, Br, Arg, U; 1978 v Sw, I, WG, Ni, S, H; 1979 v D, Ei, Ni (2), S, Bul, A; 1980 v D, Ni, Sp, Arg, W, Bel, I; 1981 v R, Sw, Sp, Br, H; 1982 v N, H, W, Ho, Ic, F (sub), K; 1983 v D, Gr, L, W, Gr, H, Ni, S, Aus (2); 1984 v D (50)
Needham, E. (Sheffield U), 1894 v S; 1895 v S; 1897 v S, W, Ni; 1898 v S, W; 1899 v S, W, Ni; 1900 v S, Ni; 1901 v S, W, Ni; 1902 v W (16)
Neville, G. A. (Manchester U), 1995 v J, Br (2)
Newton, K. R. (Blackburn R), 1966 v S, WG; 1967 v Sp, A; 1968 v W, S, Sp, Se, Y, WG; 1969 v Ni, W, S, R, Bul, M, U, Br, F; (with Everton), 1970 v Ni, S, Ho, Co, Ec, R, Cz, WG (27)

Nicholls, J. (WBA), 1954 v S, Y (2)
Nicholson, W. E. (Tottenham H), 1951 v P (1)
Nish, D. J. (Derby Co), 1973 v Ni; 1974 v P, W, Ni, S (5)
Norman, M. (Tottenham H), 1962 v Pe, H, Arg, Bul, Br; 1963 v S, F, Br, Cz, EG; 1964 v W, Ni, S, R of W, U, P (2), US, Br, Arg; 1965 v Ni, Bel, Ho (23)
Nuttall, H. (Bolton W), 1928 v W, Ni; 1929 v S (3)

Oakley, W. J. (Oxford University), 1895 v W; 1896 v S, W, Ni; (with Corinthians), 1897 v S, W, Ni; 1898 v S, W, Ni; 1900 v S, W, Ni; 1901 v S, W, Ni (16)
O'Dowd, J. P. (Chelsea), 1932 v S; 1933 v Ni, Sw (3)
O'Grady, M. (Huddersfield T), 1963 v Ni; (with Leeds U), 1969 v F (2)
Ogilvie, R. A. M. M. (Clapham R), 1874 v S (1)
Oliver, L. F. (Fulham), 1929 v Bel (1)
Olney, B. A. (Aston Villa), 1928 v F, Bel (2)
Osborne, F. R. (Fulham), 1923 v Ni, F; (with Tottenham H), 1925 v Bel; 1926 v Bel (4)
Osborne, R. (Leicester C), 1928 v W (1)
Osgood, P. L. (Chelsea), 1970 v Bel, R (sub), Cz (sub); 1974 v I (4)
Osman, R. (Ipswich T), 1980 v Aus; 1981 v Sp, R, Sw; 1982 v N, Ic; 1983 v D, Aus (3); 1984 v D (11)
Ottaway, C. J. (Oxford University), 1872 v S; 1874 v S (2)
Owen, J. R. B. (Sheffield), 1874 v S (1)
Owen, S. W. (Luton T), 1954 v H, Y, Bel (3)

Page, L. A. (Burnley), 1927 v S, W, Bel, L, F; 1928 v W, Ni (7)
Paine, T. L. (Southampton), 1963 v Cz, EG; 1964 v W, Ni, S, R of W, U, US, P; 1965 v Ni, H, Y, WG, Se; 1966 v W, A, Y, N, M (19)
Pallister, G. A. (Middlesbrough), 1988 v H; 1989 v S.Ar; (with Manchester U), 1991 v Cam (sub), T; 1992 v G; 1993 v N, US, Br, G; 1994 v Pol, Ho, Sm, D; 1995 v US, R, Ei, U, Se (18)
Palmer, C. L. (Sheffield W), 1992 v C, H, Br, Fi (sub), D, F, Se; 1993 v Sp (sub), N (sub), T, Sm, T, Ho, Pol, N, US, Br (sub); 1994 v Ho (18)
Pantling, H. H. (Sheffield U), 1924 v Ni (1)
Paravacini, P. J. de (Cambridge University), 1883 v S, W, Ni (3)
Parker, P. A. (QPR), 1989 v Alb (sub), Ch, D; 1990 v Y, U, Ho, Eg, Bel, Cam, WG, I; 1991 v H, Pol, USSR, Aus, Nz; (with Manchester U), 1992 v G; 1994 v Ho, D (19)
Parker, T. R. (Southampton), 1925 v F (1)
Parkes, P. B. (QPR), 1974 v P (1)
Parkinson, J. (Liverpool), 1910 v S, W (2)
Parr, P. C. (Oxford University), 1882 v W (1)
Parry, E. H. (Old Carthusians), 1879 v W; 1882 v W, S (3)
Parry, R. A. (Bolton W), 1960 v Ni, S (2)
Patchitt, B. C. A. (Corinthians), 1923 v Se (2) (2)
Pawson, F. W. (Cambridge University), 1883 v Ni; (with Swifts), 1885 v Ni (2)
Payne, J. (Luton T), 1937 v Fi (1)
Peacock, A. (Middlesbrough), 1962 v Arg, Bul; 1963 v Ni, W; (with Leeds U), 1966 v W, Ni (6)
Peacock, J. (Middlesbrough), 1929 v F, Bel, Sp (3)
Pearce, S. (Nottingham F), 1987 v Br, S; 1988 v WG (sub), Is, H; 1989 v D, Se, S.Ar, Gr, Alb (2), Ch, S, Pol, D; 1990 v Pol, I, Y, Br, Cz, D, U, Tun, Ei, Ho, Eg, Bel, Cam, WG; 1991 v H, Pol, Ei (2), Cam, T, Arg, Aus, Nz (2), Mal; 1992 v T, Pol, F, Cz, Br (sub), Fi, D, F, Se; 1993 v Sp, N, T; 1994 v Pol, Sm, Gr (sub); 1995 v R (sub), J, Br (59)
Pearson, H. F. (WBA), 1932 v S (1)
Pearson, J. H. (Crewe Alex), 1892 v Ni (1)
Pearson, J. S. (Manchester U), 1976 v W, Ni, S, Br, Fi; 1977 v Ei, Ho (sub), W, S, Br, Arg, U; 1978 v I (sub), WG, Ni (15)
Pearson, S. C. (Manchester U), 1948 v S; 1949 v S, Ni; 1950 v Ni, I; 1951 v P; 1952 v S, I (8)
Pease, W. H. (Middlesbrough), 1927 v W (1)
Pegg, D. (Manchester U), 1957 v Ei (1)
Pejic, M. (Stoke C), 1974 v P, W, Ni, S (4)
Pelly, F. R. (Old Foresters), 1893 v Ni; 1894 v S, W (3)
Pennington, J. (WBA), 1907 v S, W; 1908 v S, W, Ni, A; 1909 v S, W, H (2), A; 1910 v S, W; 1911 v S, W, Ni; 1912 v S, W, Ni; 1913 v S, W; 1914 v S, Ni; 1920 v S, W (25)
Pentland, F. B. (Middlesbrough), 1909 v S, W, H (2), A (5)
Perry, C. (WBA), 1890 v Ni; 1891 v Ni; 1893 v W (3)
Perry, T. (WBA), 1898 v W (1)
Perry, W. (Blackpool), 1956 v Ni, S, Sp (3)
Perryman, S. (Tottenham H), 1982 v Ic (sub) (1)
Peters, M. (West Ham U), 1966 v Y, Fi, Pol, M, F, Arg, P, WG; 1967 v Ni, W, S, Cz; 1968 v W, Ni, S, USSR (2), Sp (2), Se, Y; 1969 v Ni, S, R, Bul, F, M, U, Br; 1970 v Ho (2), P (sub), Bel; (with Tottenham H), W, Ni, S, Co, Ec, R, Br, Cz, WG; 1971 v EG, Gr, Ma (2), Ni, W, S; 1972 v Sw, Gr, WG (1 + 1 sub), Ni (sub); 1973 v S (2), Ni, W, Cz, Pol, USSR, I; 1974 v A, Pol, I, P, S (67)
Phelan, M. C. (Manchester U), 1990 v I (sub) (1)
Phillips, L. H. (Portsmouth), 1952 v Ni; 1955 v W, WG (3)
Pickering, F. (Everton), 1964 v US; 1965 v Ni, Bel (3)
Pickering, J. (Sheffield U), 1933 v S (1)
Pickering, N. (Sunderland), 1983 v Aus (1)
Pike, T. M. (Cambridge University), 1886 v Ni (1)
Pilkington, B. (Burnley), 1955 v Ni (1)
Plant, J. (Bury), 1900 v S (1)
Platt, D. (Aston Villa), 1990 v I (sub), Y (sub), Br, D (sub), Tun (sub), Ho (sub), Eg (sub), Bel (sub), Cam, WG, I; 1991 v H, Pol, Ei (2), T, USSR, Arg, Aus, Nz (2), Mal; (with Bari), 1992 v G, T, Pol, Cz, C, Br, Fi, D, F, Se; (with Juventus), 1993 v Sp, N, T, Sm, T, Ho, Pol, N, Br (sub), G; (with Sampdoria), 1994 v Pol, Ho, Sm, D, Gr, N; 1995 v US, Ng, Ei, U, J, Se, Br (55)
Plum, S. L. (Charlton Ath), 1923 v F (1)
Pointer, R. (Burnley), 1962 v W, L, P (3)
Porteous, T. S. (Sunderland), 1891 v W (1)
Priest, A. E. (Sheffield U), 1900 v Ni (1)
Prinsep, J. F. M. (Clapham Rovers), 1879 v S (1)
Puddefoot, S. C. (Blackburn R), 1926 v S, Ni (2)
Pye, J. (Wolverhampton W), 1950 v Ei (1)
Pym, R. H. (Bolton W), 1925 v S, W; 1926 v W (3)

Quantrill, A. (Derby Co), 1920 v S, W; 1921 v W, Ni (4)
Quixall, A. (Sheffield W), 1954 v W, Ni, R of E; 1955 v Sp, P (sub) (5)

Radford, J. (Arsenal), 1969 v R; 1972 v Sw (sub) (2)
Raikes, G. B. (Oxford University), 1895 v W; 1896 v W, Ni, S (4)
Ramsey, A. E. (Southampton), 1949 v Sw; (with Tottenham H), 1950 v S, I, P, Bel, Ch, US, Sp; 1951 v S, Ni, W, Y, Arg, P; 1952 v S, W, Ni, F, A (2), I, Sw; 1953 v Ni, W, S, Bel, Arg, Ch, U, US; 1954 v R of E, H (32)
Rawlings, A. (Preston NE), 1921 v Bel (1)
Rawlings, W. E. (Southampton), 1922 v S, W (2)
Rawlinson, J. F. P. (Cambridge University), 1882 v Ni (1)
Rawson, H. E. (Royal Engineers), 1875 v S (1)
Rawson, W. S. (Oxford University), 1875 v S; 1877 v S (2)
Read, A. (Tufnell Park), 1921 v Bel (1)
Reader, J. (WBA), 1894 v Ni (1)
Reaney, P. (Leeds U), 1969 v Bul (sub); 1970 v P; 1971 v Ma (3)
Reeves, K. (Norwich C), 1980 v Bul; (with Manchester C), Ni (2)
Regis, C. (WBA), 1982 v Ni (sub), W (sub), Ic; 1983 v WG; (with Coventry C), 1988 v T (sub) (5)

Reid, P. (Everton), 1985 v M (sub), WG, US (sub); 1986 v R, S (sub), Ca (sub), Pol, Para, Arg; 1987 v Br; 1988 v WG, Y (sub), Sw (sub) (13)
Revie, D. G. (Manchester C), 1955 v Ni, S, F; 1956 v W, D; 1957 v Ni (6)
Reynolds, J. (WBA), 1892 v S; 1893 v S, W; (with Aston Villa), 1894 v S, Ni; 1895 v S; 1897 v S, W (8)
Richards, C. H. (Nottingham F), 1898 v Ni (1)
Richards, G. H. (Derby Co), 1909 v A (1)
Richards, J. P. (Wolverhampton W), 1973 v Ni (1)
Richardson, J. R. (Newcastle U), 1933 v I, Sw (2)
Richardson, K. (Aston Villa), 1994 v Gr (1)
Richardson, W. G. (WBA), 1935 v Ho (1)
Rickaby, S. (WBA), 1954 v Ni (1)
Rigby, A. (Blackburn R), 1927 v S, Bel, L, F; 1928 v W (5)
Rimmer, E. J. (Sheffield W), 1930 v S, G, A; 1932 v Sp (4)
Rimmer, J. J. (Arsenal), 1976 v I (1)
Ripley, S. E. (Blackburn R), 1994 v Sm (1)
Rix, G. (Arsenal), 1981 v N, R, Sw (sub), Br, W, S; 1982 v Ho (sub), Fi (sub), F, Cz, K, WG, Sp; 1983 v D, WG (sub), Gr (sub); 1984 v Ni (17)
Robb, G. (Tottenham H), 1954 v H (1)
Roberts, C. (Manchester U), 1905 v Ni, W, S (3)
Roberts, F. (Manchester C), 1925 v S, W, Bel, F (4)
Roberts, G. (Tottenham H), 1983 v Ni, S; 1984 v F, Ni, S, USSR (6)
Roberts, H. (Arsenal), 1931 v S (1)
Roberts, H. (Millwall), 1931 v Bel (1)
Roberts, R. (WBA), 1887 v S; 1888 v Ni; 1890 v Ni (3)
Roberts, W. T. (Preston NE), 1924 v W, Bel (2)
Robinson, J. (Sheffield W), 1937 v Fi; 1938 v G, Sw; 1939 v W (4)
Robinson, J. W. (Derby Co), 1897 v S, Ni; (with New Brighton Tower), 1898 v S, W, Ni; (with Southampton), 1899 v W, S; 1900 v S, W, Ni; 1901 v Ni (11)
Robson, B. (WBA), 1980 v Ei, Aus; 1981 v N, R, Sw, Sp, R, Br, W, S, Sw, H; 1982 v N; (with Manchester U), H, Ni, W, Ho, S, Fi, F, Cz, WG, Sp; 1983 v D, Gr, L, S; 1984 v H, L, F, Ni, S, USSR, Br, U, Ch; 1985 v EG, Fi, T, Ei, R, Fi, S, M, I, WG, US; 1986 v R, T, Is, M, P, Mor; 1987 v Ni (2), Sp, T, Br, S; 1988 v T, Y, Ho, H, S, Co, Sw, Ei, Ho, USSR; 1989 v S, Se, S.Ar, Gr, Alb (2), Ch, S, Pol, D; 1990 v Pol, I, Y, Cz, U, Tun, Ei, Ho; 1991 v Cam, Ei; 1992 v T (90)
Robson, R. (WBA), 1958 v F, USSR (2), Br, A; 1960 v Sp, H; 1961 v Ni, W, S, L, P, Sp, M, I; 1962 v W, Ni, Sw, L, P (20)
Rocastle, D. (Arsenal), 1989 v D, S.Ar, Gr, Alb (2), Pol (sub), D; 1990 v Se (sub), Pol, Y, D (sub); 1992 v Pol, Cz, Br (sub) (14)
Rose, W. C. (Wolverhampton W), 1884 v S, W, Ni; (with Preston NE), 1886 v Ni; (with Wolverhampton W), 1891 v Ni (5)
Rostron, T. (Darwen), 1881 v S, W (2)
Rowe, A. (Tottenham H), 1934 v F (1)
Rowley, J. F. (Manchester U), 1949 v Sw, Se, F; 1950 v Ni, I; 1952 v S (6)
Rowley, W. (Stoke C), 1889 v Ni; 1892 v Ni (2)
Royle, J. (Everton), 1971 v Ma; 1973 v Y; (with Manchester C), 1976 v Ni (sub), I; 1977 v Fi, L (6)
Ruddlesdin, H. (Sheffield W), 1904 v W, Ni; 1905 v S (3)
Ruddock, N. (Liverpool), 1995 v Ng (1)
Ruffell, J. W. (West Ham U), 1926 v S; 1927 v Ni; 1929 v S, W, Ni; 1930 v W (6)
Russell, B. B. (Royal Engineers), 1883 v W (1)
Rutherford, J. (Newcastle U), 1904 v S; 1907 v S, Ni, W; 1908 v S, Ni, W, A (2), H, B (11)

Sadler, D. (Manchester U), 1968 v Ni, USSR; 1970 v Ec (sub); 1971 v EG (4)
Sagar, C. (Bury), 1900 v Ni; 1902 v W (2)
Sagar, E. (Everton), 1936 v S, Ni, A, Bel (4)
Salako, J. A. (C Palace), 1991 v Aus (sub), Nz (sub + 1), Mal; 1992 v G (5)
Sandford, E. A. (WBA), 1933 v W (1)
Sandilands, R. R. (Old Westminsters), 1892 v W; 1893 v Ni; 1894 v W; 1895 v W; 1896 v W (5)
Sands, J. (Nottingham F), 1880 v W (1)
Sansom, K. (C Palace), 1979 v W; 1980 v Bul, Ei, Arg, W (sub), Ni, S, Bel, I; (with Arsenal), 1981 v N, R, Sw, Sp, R, Br, W, S, Sw; 1982 v Ni, W, Ho, S, Fi, F, Cz, WG, Sp; 1983 v D, WG, Gr, L, Gr, H, Ni, S; 1984 v D, H, L, F, S, USSR, Br, U, Ch; 1985 v EG, Fi, T, Ni, Ei, R, Fi, S, I, M, WG, US; 1986 v R, T, Ni, Eg, Is, USSR, S, M, Ca, P, Mor, Pol, Para, Arg; 1987 v Se, Ni (2), Y, Sp, T; 1988 v WG, T, Y, Ho, S, Co, Sw, Ei, Ho, USSR (86)
Saunders, F. E. (Swifts), 1888 v W (1)
Savage, A. H. (C Palace), 1876 v S (1)
Sayer, J. (Stoke C), 1887 v Ni (1)
Scales, J. R. (Liverpool), 1995 v J, Se (sub), Br (3)
Scattergood, E. (Derby Co), 1913 v W (1)
Schofield, J. (Stoke C), 1892 v W; 1893 v W; 1895 v Ni (3)
Scott, L. (Arsenal), 1947 v S, W, Ni, Ei, Ho, F, Sw, P; 1948 v S, W, Ni, Bel, Se, I; 1949 v W, Ni, D (17)
Scott, W. R. (Brentford), 1937 v W (1)
Seaman, D. A. (QPR), 1989 v S.Ar, D (sub); 1990 v Cz (sub); (with Arsenal), 1991 v Cam, Ei, T, Arg; 1992 v Cz, H (sub); 1994 v Pol, Ho, Sm, D, N; 1995 v US, R, Ei (17)
Seddon, J. (Bolton W), 1923 v F, Se (2); 1924 v Bel; 1927 v W; 1929 v S (6)
Seed, J. M. (Tottenham H), 1921 v Bel: 1923 v W, Ni, Bel; 1925 v S (5)
Settle, J. (Bury), 1899 v S, W, Ni; (with Everton), 1902 v S, Ni; 1903 v Ni (6)
Sewell, J. (Sheffield W), 1952 v Ni, A, Sw; 1953 v Ni; 1954 v H (2) (6)
Sewell, W. R. (Blackburn R), 1924 v W (1)
Shackleton, L. F. (Sunderland), 1949 v W, D; 1950 v W; 1955 v W, WG (5)
Sharp, J. (Everton), 1903 v Ni; 1905 v S (2)
Sharpe, L. S. (Manchester U), 1991 v Ei (sub); 1993 v T (sub), N, US, Br, G; 1994 v Pol, Ho (8)
Shaw, G. E. (WBA), 1932 v S (1)
Shaw, G. L. (Sheffield U), 1959 v S, W, USSR, I; 1963 v W (5)
Shea, D. (Blackburn R), 1914 v W, Ni (2)
Shearer, A. (Southampton), 1992 v F, C, F; (with Blackburn R), 1993 v Sp, N, T; 1994 v Ho, D, Gr, N; 1995 v US, R, Ng, Ei, J, Se, Br (17)
Shellito, K. J. (Chelsea), 1963 v Cz (1)
Shelton A. (Notts Co), 1889 v Ni; 1890 v S, W; 1891 v S, W; 1892 v S (6)
Shelton, C. (Notts Rangers), 1888 v Ni (1)
Shepherd, A. (Bolton W), 1906 v S; (with Newcastle U), 1911 v Ni (2)
Sheringham, E. P. (Tottenham H), 1993 v Pol, N; 1995 v US, R (sub), Ng (sub), U, J (sub), Se, Br (9)
Shilton, P. L. (Leicester C), 1971 v EG, W; 1972 v Sw, Ni; 1973 v Y, S (2), Ni, W, Cz, Pol, USSR, I; 1974 v A, Pol, I, W, Ni, S, Arg; (with Stoke C), 1975 v Cy; 1977 v Ni, W; (with Nottingham F), 1978 v W, H; 1979 v Cz, Se, A; 1980 v Ni, Sp, I; 1981 v N, Sw, R; 1982 v H, Ho, S, F, Cz, K, WG, Sp; (with Southampton), 1983 v D, WG, Gr, W, Gr, H, Ni, S, Aus (3); 1984 v D, H, F, Ni, W, S, USSR, Br, U, Ch; 1985 v EG, Fi, T, Ni, R, Fi, S, I, WG; 1986 v R, T, Ni, Eg, Is, USSR, S, M, Ca, P, Mor, Pol, Para, Arg; 1987 v Se, Ni (2), Sp, Br; (with Derby Co), 1988 v WG, T, Y, Ho, S, Co, Sw, Ei, Ho; 1989 v D, Se, Gr, Alb (2), Ch, S, Pol, D; 1990 v Se, Pol, I, Y, Br, Cz, D, U, Tun, Ei, Ho, Eg, Bel, Cam, WG, I (125)
Shimwell, E. (Blackpool), 1949 v Se (1)
Shutt, G. (Stoke C), 1886 v Ni (1)

Silcock, J. (Manchester U), 1921 v S, W; 1923 v Se (3)
Sillett, R. P. (Chelsea), 1955 v F, Sp, P (3)
Simms, E. (Luton T), 1922 v Ni (1)
Simpson, J. (Blackburn R), 1911 v S, W, Ni; 1912 v S, W, Ni; 1913 v S; 1914 v W (8)
Sinton, A. (QPR), 1992 v Pol, C, H (sub), Br, F, Se; 1993 v Sp, T, Br, G; (with Sheffield W), 1994 v Ho (sub), Sm (12)
Slater, W. J. (Wolverhampton W), 1955 v W, WG; 1958 v S, P, Y, USSR (3), Br, A; 1959 v USSR; 1960 v S (12)
Smalley, T. (Wolverhampton W), 1937 v W (1)
Smart, T. (Aston Villa), 1921 v S; 1924 v S, W; 1926 v Ni; 1930 v W (5)
Smith, A. (Nottingham F), 1891 v S, W; 1893 v Ni (3)
Smith, A. K. (Oxford University), 1872 v S (1)
Smith, A. M. (Arsenal), 1989 v S.Ar (sub), Gr, Alb (sub), Pol (sub); 1991 v T, USSR, Arg; 1992 v G, T, Pol (sub), H (sub), D, Se (sub) (13)
Smith, B. (Tottenham H), 1921 v S; 1922 v W (2)
Smith, C. E. (C Palace), 1876 v S (1)
Smith, G. O. (Oxford University), 1893 v Ni; 1894 v W, S; 1895 v W; 1896 v Ni, W, S; (with Old Carthusians), 1897 v Ni, W, S; 1898 v Ni, W, S; (with Corinthians), 1899 v Ni, W, S; 1899 v Ni, W, S; 1901 v S (20)
Smith, H. (Reading), 1905 v W, S; 1906 v W, Ni (4)
Smith, J. (WBA), 1920 v Ni; 1923 v Ni (2)
Smith, Joe (Bolton W), 1913 v Ni; 1914 v S, W; 1920 v W, Ni (5)
Smith, J. C. R. (Millwall), 1939 v Ni, N (2)
Smith, J. W. (Portsmouth), 1932 v Ni, W, Sp (3)
Smith, Leslie (Brentford), 1939 v R (1)
Smith, Lionel (Arsenal), 1951 v W; 1952 v W, Ni; 1953 v W, S, Bel (6)
Smith, R. A. (Tottenham H), 1961 v Ni, W, S, L, P, Sp; 1962 v S; 1963 v S, F, Br, Cz, EG; 1964 v W, Ni, R of W (15)
Smith, S. (Aston Villa), 1895 v S (1)
Smith, S. C. (Leicester C), 1936 v Ni (1)
Smith, T. (Birmingham C), 1960 v W, Se (2)
Smith, T. (Liverpool), 1971 v W (1)
Smith, W. H. (Huddersfield T), 1922 v W, S; 1928 v S (3)
Sorby, T. H. (Thursday Wanderers, Sheffield), 1879 v W (1)
Southworth, J. (Blackburn R), 1889 v W; 1891 v W; 1892 v S (3)
Sparks, F. J. (Herts Rangers), 1879 v S; (with Clapham Rovers), 1880 v S, W (3)
Spence, J. W. (Manchester U), 1926 v Bel; 1927 v Ni (2)
Spence, R. (Chelsea), 1936 v A, Bel (2)
Spencer, C. W. (Newcastle U), 1924 v S; 1925 v W (2)
Spencer, H. (Aston Villa), 1897 v S, W; 1900 v W; 1903 v Ni; 1905 v W, S (6)
Spiksley, F. (Sheffield W), 1893 v S, W; 1894 v S, Ni; 1896 v Ni; 1898 v S, W (7)
Spilsbury, B. W. (Cambridge University), 1885 v Ni; 1886 v Ni, S (3)
Spink, N. (Aston Villa), 1983 v Aus (sub) (1)
Spouncer, W. A. (Nottingham F), 1900 v W (1)
Springett, R. D. G. (Sheffield W), 1960 v Ni, S, Y, Sp, H; 1961 v Ni, S, L, P, Sp, M, I, A; 1962 v W, Ni, S, A, Sw, Pe, L, P, H, Arg, Bul, Br; 1963 v Ni, W, F (2), Sw; 1966 v W, A, N (33)
Sproston, B. (Leeds U), 1937 v W; 1938 v S, W, Ni, Cz, G, Sw, F; (with Tottenham H), 1939 v W, R of E; (with Manchester C), N (11)
Squire, R. T. (Cambridge University), 1886 v S, W, Ni (3)
Stanbrough, M. H. (Old Carthusians), 1895 v W (1)
Staniforth, R. (Huddersfield T), 1954 v S, H, Y, Bel, Sw, U; 1955 v W, WG (8)
Starling, R. W. (Sheffield W), 1933 v S; (with Aston Villa), 1937 v S (2)
Statham, D. (WBA), 1983 v W, Aus (2) (3)
Steele, F. C. (Stoke C), 1937 v S, W, Ni, N, Se, Fi (6)
Stein, B. (Luton T), 1984 v F (1)
Stephenson, C. (Huddersfield T), 1924 v W (1)
Stephenson, G. T. (Derby Co), 1928 v F, Bel; (with Sheffield W), 1931 v F (3)
Stephenson, J. E. (Leeds U), 1938 v S; 1939 v Ni (2)
Stepney, A. C. (Manchester U), 1968 v Se (1)
Sterland, M. (Sheffield W), 1989 v S.Ar (1)
Steven, T. M. (Everton), 1985 v Ni, Ei, R, Fi, I, US (sub); 1986 v T (sub), Eg, USSR (sub), M (sub), Pol, Para, Arg; 1987 v Se, Y (sub), Sp (sub); 1988 v T, Y, Ho, H, S, Sw, Ho, USSR; 1989 v S; (with Rangers), 1990 v Cz, Cam (sub), WG (sub), I; 1991 v Cam; (with Marseille), 1992 v G, C, Br, Fi, D, F (36)
Stevens, G. A. (Tottenham H), 1985 v Fi (sub), T (sub), Ni; 1986 v S (sub), M (sub), Mor (sub), Para (sub) (7)
Stevens, M. G. (Everton), 1985 v I, WG; 1986 v R, T, Ni, Eg, Is, S, Ca, P, Mor, Pol, Para, Arg; 1987 v Br, S; 1988 v T, Y, Is, Ho, H (sub), S, Sw, Ei, Ho, USSR; (with Rangers), 1989 v D, Se, Gr, Alb (2), S, Pol; 1990 v Se, Pol, I, Br, D, Tun, Ei, I; 1991 v USSR; 1992 v C, H, Br, Fi (46)
Stewart, J. (Sheffield W), 1907 v S, W; (with Newcastle U), 1911 v S (3)
Stewart, P. A. (Tottenham H), 1992 v G (sub), Cz (sub), C (sub) (3)
Stiles, N. P. (Manchester U), 1965 v S, H, Y, Se; 1966 v W, Ni, S, A, Sp, Pol (2), WG (2), N, D, U, M, F, Arg, P; 1967 v Ni, W, S, Cz; 1968 v USSR; 1969 v R; 1970 v Ni, S (28)
Stoker, J. (Birmingham), 1933 v W; 1934 v S, H (3)
Storer, H. (Derby Co), 1924 v F; 1928 v Ni (2)
Storey, P. E. (Arsenal), 1971 v Gr, Ni, S; 1972 v Sw, WG, W, Ni, S; 1973 v W (3), Y, S (2), Ni, Cz, Pol, USSR, I (19)
Storey-Moore, I. (Nottingham F), 1970 v Ho (1)
Strange, A. H. (Sheffield W), 1930 v S, A, G; 1931 v S, W, Ni, F, Bel; 1932 v S, W, Ni, Sp; 1933 v S, Ni, A, I, Sw; 1934 v Ni, W, F (20)
Stratford, A. H. (Wanderers), 1874 v S (1)
Streten, B. (Luton T), 1950 v Ni (1)
Sturgess, A. (Sheffield U), 1911 v Ni; 1914 v S (2)
Summerbee, M. G. (Manchester C), 1968 v S, Sp, WG; 1972 v Sw, WG (sub), W, Ni; 1973 v USSR (sub) (8)
Sunderland, A. (Arsenal), 1980 v Aus (1)
Sutcliffe, J. W. (Bolton W), 1893 v W; 1895 v S, Ni; 1901 v S; (with Millwall), 1903 v W (5)
Swan, P. (Sheffield W), 1960 v Y, Sp, H; 1961 v Ni, W, S, L, P, Sp, M, I, A; 1962 v W, Ni, S, A, Sw, L, P (19)
Swepstone, H. A. (Pilgrims), 1880 v S; 1882 v S, W; 1883 v S, W, Ni (6)
Swift, F. V. (Manchester C), 1947 v S, W, Ni, Ei, Ho, F, Sw, P; 1948 v S, W, Ni, Bel, Se, I; 1949 v S, W, Ni, D, N (19)

Tait, G. (Birmingham Excelsior), 1881 v W (1)
Talbot, B. (Ipswich T), 1977 v Ni (sub), S, Br, Arg, U; (with Arsenal), 1980 v Aus (6)
Tambling, R. V. (Chelsea), 1963 v W, F; 1966 v Y (3)
Tate, J. T. (Aston Villa), 1931 v F, Bel; 1933 v W (3)
Taylor, E. (Blackpool), 1954 v H (1)
Taylor, E. H. (Huddersfield T), 1923 v S, W, Ni, Bel; 1924 v S, Ni, F; 1926 v S (8)
Taylor, J. G. (Fulham), 1951 v Arg, P (2)
Taylor, P. H. (Liverpool), 1948 v W, Ni, Se (3)
Taylor, P. J. (C Palace), 1976 v W (sub + 1), Ni, S (4)
Taylor, T. (Manchester U), 1953 v Arg, Ch, U; 1954 v Bel, Sw; 1956 v S, Br, Se, Fi, WG; 1957 v Ni, Y (sub), D (2), Ei (2); 1958 v W, Ni, F (19)
Temple, D. W. (Everton), 1965 v WG (1)
Thickett, H. (Sheffield U), 1899 v S, W (2)
Thomas, D. (Coventry C), 1983 v Aus (1 + 1 sub) (2)
Thomas, D. (QPR), 1975 v Cz (sub), P, Cy (sub + 1), W, S (sub); 1976 v Cz (sub), P (sub) (8)

Thomas, G. R. (C Palace), 1991 v T, USSR, Arg, Aus, Nz (2), Mal; 1992 v Pol, F (9)
Thomas, M. L. (Arsenal), 1989 v S.Ar; 1990 v Y (2)
Thompson, P. (Liverpool), 1964 v P (2), Ei, US, Br, Arg; 1965 v Ni, W, S, Bel, Ho; 1966 v Ni; 1968 v Ni, WG; 1970 v S, Ho (sub) (16)
Thompson, P. B. (Liverpool), 1976 v W (2), Ni, S, Br, I, Fi; 1977 v Fi; 1979 v Ei (sub), Cz, Ni, S, Bul, Se (sub), A; 1980 v D, Ni, Bul, Ei, Sp (2), Arg, W, S, Bel, I; 1981 v N, R, H; 1982 v N, H, W, Ho, S, Fi, F, Cz, K, WG, Sp; 1983 v WG, Gr (42)
Thompson T. (Aston Villa), 1952 v W; (with Preston NE), 1957 v S (2)
Thomson, R. A. (Wolverhampton W), 1964 v Ni, US, P, Arg; 1965 v Bel, Ho, Ni, W (8)
Thornewell, G. (Derby Co), 1923 v Se (2); 1924 v F; 1925 v F (4)
Thornley, I. (Manchester C), 1907 v W (1)
Tilson, S. F. (Manchester C), 1934 v H, Cz; 1935 v W; 1936 v Ni (4)
Titmuss, F. (Southampton), 1922 v W; 1923 v W (2)
Todd, C. (Derby Co), 1972 v Ni; 1974 v P, W, Ni, S, Arg, EG, Bul, Y; 1975 v P (sub), WG, Cy (2), Ni, W, S; 1976 v Sw, Cz, P, Ni, S, Br, Fi; 1977 v Ei, Fi, Ho (sub), Ni (27)
Toone, G. (Notts Co), 1892 v S, W (2)
Topham, A. G. (Casuals), 1894 v W (1)
Topham, R. (Wolverhampton W), 1893 v Ni; (with Casuals) 1894 v W (2)
Towers, M. A. (Sunderland), 1976 v W, Ni (sub), I (3)
Townley, W. J. (Blackburn R), 1889 v W; 1890 v Ni (2)
Townrow, J. E. (Clapton Orient), 1925 v S; 1926 v W (2)
Tremelling, D. R. (Birmingham), 1928 v W (1)
Tresadern, J. (West Ham U), 1923 v S, Se (2)
Tueart, D. (Manchester C), 1975 v Cy (sub), Ni; 1977 v Fi, Ni, W (sub), S (sub) (6)
Tunstall, F. E. (Sheffield U), 1923 v S; 1924 v S, W, Ni, F; 1925 v Ni, S (7)
Turnbull, R. J. (Bradford), 1920 v Ni (1)
Turner, A. (Southampton), 1900 v Ni; 1901 v Ni (2)
Turner, H. (Huddersfield T), 1931 v F, Bel (2)
Turner, J. A. (Bolton W), 1893 v W; (with Stoke C) 1895 v Ni; (with Derby Co) 1898 v Ni (3)
Tweedy, G. J. (Grimsby T), 1937 v H (1)

Ufton, D. G. (Charlton Ath), 1954 v R of E (1)
Underwood A. (Stoke C), 1891 v Ni; 1892 v Ni (2)
Unsworth, D. G. (Everton), 1995 v J (1)
Urwin, T. (Middlesbrough), 1923 v Se (2); 1924 v Bel; (with Newcastle U), 1926 v W (4)
Utley, G. (Barnsley), 1913 v Ni (1)

Vaughton, O. H. (Aston Villa), 1882 v S, W, Ni; 1884 v S, W (5)
Veitch, C. C. M. (Newcastle U), 1906 v S, W, Ni; 1907 v S, W; 1909 v W (6)
Veitch, J. G. (Old Westminsters), 1894 v W (1)
Venables, T. F. (Chelsea), 1965 v Ho, Bel (2)
Venison, B. (Newcastle U), 1995 v US, U (2)
Vidal, R. W. S. (Oxford University), 1873 v S (1)
Viljoen, C. (Ipswich T), 1975 v Ni, W (2)
Viollet, D. S. (Manchester U), 1960 v H; 1962 v L (2)
Von Donop (Royal Engineers), 1873 v S; 1875 v S (2)

Wace, H. (Wanderers), 1878 v S; 1879 v S, W (3)
Waddle, C. R. (Newcastle U), 1985 v Ei, R (sub), Fi (sub), S (sub), I, M (sub), WG, US; (with Tottenham H), 1986 v R, T, Ni, Is, USSR, S, M, Ca, P, Mor, Pol (sub), Arg (sub); 1987 v Se (sub), Ni (2), Y, Sp, T, Br, S; 1988 v WG, Is, H, S (sub), Co, Sw (sub), Ei, Ho (sub); 1989 v Se, S.Ar, Alb (2), Ch, S, Pol, D (sub); (with Marseille), 1990 v Se, Pol, I, Y, Br, D, U, Tun, Ei, Ho, Eg, Bel, Cam, WG, I (sub); 1991 v H (sub), Pol (sub); 1992 v T (62)
Wadsworth, S. J. (Huddersfield T), 1922 v S; 1923 v S, Bel; 1924 v S, Ni; 1925 v S, Ni; 1926 v W; 1927 v Ni (9)
Wainscoat, W. R. (Leeds U), 1929 v S (1)
Waiters, A. K. (Blackpool), 1964 v Ei, Br; 1965 v W, Bel, Ho (5)
Walker, D. S. (Nottingham F), 1989 v D (sub), Se (sub), Gr, Alb (2), Ch, S, Pol, D; 1990 v Se, Pol, I, Y, Br, Cz, D, U, Tun, Ei, Ho, Eg, Bel, Cam, WG, I; 1991 v H, Pol, Ei (2), Cam, T, Arg, Aus, Nz (2), Mal; 1992 v T, Pol, F, Cz, C, H, Br, Fi, D, F, Se; (with Sampdoria), 1993 v Sp, N, T, Sm, T, Ho, Pol, N, US (sub), Br, G; (with Sheffield W), 1994 v Sm (59)
Walden, F. I. (Tottenham H), 1914 v S; 1922 v W (2)
Walker, W. H. (Aston Villa), 1921 v Ni; 1922 v Ni, W, S; 1923 v Se (2); 1924 v S; 1925 v Ni, W, S, Bel, F; 1926 v Ni, W, S; 1927 v Ni, W; 1933 v A (18)
Wall, G. (Manchester U), 1907 v W; 1908 v Ni; 1909 v S; 1910 v W, S; 1912 v S; 1913 v Ni (7)
Wallace, C. W. (Aston Villa), 1913 v W; 1914 v Ni; 1920 v S (3)
Wallace, D. L. (Southampton), 1986 v Eg (1)
Walsh, P. (Luton T), 1983 v Aus (2 + 1 sub); 1984 v F, W (5)
Walters, A. M. (Cambridge University), 1885 v S, N; 1886 v S; 1887 v S, W; (with Old Carthusians), 1889 v S, W; 1890 v S, W (9)
Walters, K. M. (Rangers), 1991 v Nz (1)
Walters, P. M. (Oxford University), 1885 v S, Ni; (with Old Carthusians), 1886 v S, W, Ni; 1887 v S, W; 1888 v S, Ni; 1889 v S, W; 1890 v S, W (13)
Walton, N. (Blackburn R), 1890 v Ni (1)
Ward, J. T. (Blackburn Olympic), 1885 v W (1)
Ward, P. (Brighton & HA), 1980 v Aus (sub) (1)
Ward, T. V. (Derby Co), 1948 v Bel; 1949 v W (2)
Waring, T. (Aston Villa), 1931 v F, Bel; 1932 v S, W, Ni (5)
Warner, C. (Upton Park), 1878 v S (1)
Warren, B. (Derby Co), 1906 v S, W, Ni; 1907 v S, W, Ni; 1908 v S, W, Ni, A (2), H, B; (with Chelsea), 1909 v S, Ni, W, H (2), A; 1911 v S, Ni, W (22)
Waterfield, G. S. (Burnley), 1927 v W (1)
Watson, D. (Norwich C), 1984 v Br, U, Ch; 1985 v M, US (sub); 1986 v S; (with Everton), 1987 v Ni; 1988 v Is, Ho, S, Sw (sub), USSR (12)
Watson, D. V. (Sunderland), 1974 v P, S (sub), Arg, EG, Bul, Y; 1975 v Cz, P, WG, Cy (2), Ni, W, S; (with Manchester C), 1976 v Sw, Cz (sub), P; 1977 v Ho, L, Ni, W, S, Br, Arg, U; 1978 v Sw, L, I, WG, Br, W, Ni, S, H; 1979 v D, Ei, Cz, Ni (2), W, S, Bul, Se, A; (with Werder Bremen), 1980 v D; (with Southampton), Ni, Bul, Ei, Sp (2), Arg, Ni, S, Bel, I; 1981 v N, R, Sw, R, W, S, Sw, H; (with Stoke C), 1982 v Ni, Ic (65)
Watson, V. M. (West Ham U), 1923 v W, S; 1930 v S, G, A (5)
Watson, W. (Burnley), 1913 v S; 1914 v Ni; 1920 v Ni (3)
Watson, W. (Sunderland), 1950 v Ni, I; 1951 v W, Y (4)
Weaver, S. (Newcastle U), 1932 v S, 1933 v S, Ni (3)
Webb, G. W. (West Ham U), 1911 v S, W (2)
Webb, N. J. (Nottingham F), 1988 v WG (sub), T, Y, Is, Ho, S, Sw, Ei, USSR (sub); 1989 v D, Se, Gr, Alb (2), Ch, S, Pol, D; (with Manchester U), 1990 v Se, I (sub); 1992 v F, H, Br (sub), Fi, D (sub), Se (26)
Webster, M. (Middlesbrough), 1930 v S, A, G (3)
Wedlock, W. J. (Bristol C), 1907 v S, Ni, W; 1908 v S, Ni, W, A (2), H, B; 1909 v S, W, Ni, H (2), A; 1910 v S, W, Ni; 1911 v S, W, Ni; 1912 v S, W, Ni; 1914 v W (26)
Weir, D. (Bolton W), 1889 v S, Ni (2)
Welch, R. de C. (Wanderers), 1872 v S; (with Harrow Chequers), 1874 v S (2)
Weller, K. (Leicester C), 1974 v W, Ni, S, Arg (4)
Welsh, D. (Charlton Ath), 1938 v G, Sw; 1939 v R (3)

West, G. (Everton), 1969 v W, Bul, M (3)
Westwood, R. W. (Bolton W), 1935 v S, W, Ho; 1936 v Ni, G; 1937 v W (6)
Whateley, O. (Aston Villa), 1883 v S, Ni (2)
Wheeler, J. E. (Bolton W), 1955 v Ni (1)
Wheldon, G. F. (Aston Villa), 1897 v Ni; 1898 v S, W, Ni (4)
White, D. (Manchester C), 1993 v Sp (1)
White, T. A. (Everton), 1933 v I (1)
Whitehead, J. (Accrington), 1893 v W; (with Blackburn R), 1894 v Ni (2)
Whitfeld, H. (Old Etonians), 1879 v W (1)
Whitham, M. (Sheffield U), 1892 v Ni (1)
Whitworth, S. (Leicester C), 1975 v WG, Cy, Ni, W, S; 1976 v Sw, P (7)
Whymark, T. J. (Ipswich T), 1978 v L (sub) (1)
Widdowson, S. W. (Nottingham F), 1880 v S (1)
Wignall, F. (Nottingham F), 1965 v W, Ho (2)
Wilkes, A. (Aston Villa), 1901 v S, W; 1902 v S, W, Ni (5)
Wilkins, R. G. (Chelsea), 1976 v I; 1977 v Ei, Fi, Ni, Br, Arg, U; 1978 v Sw (sub), L, I, WG, W, Ni, S, H; 1979 v D, Ei, Cz, Ni, W, S, Bul, Se (sub), A; (with Manchester U), 1980 v D, Ni, Bul, Sp (2), Arg, W (sub), Ni, S, Bel, I; 1981 v Sp (sub), R, Br, W, S, Sw, H (sub); 1982 v Ni, W, Ho, S, Fi, F, Cz, K, WG, Sp; 1983 v D, WG; 1984 v D, Ni, W, S, USSR, Br, U, Ch; (with AC Milan), 1985 v EG, Fi, T, Ni, Ei, R, Fi, S, I, M; 1986 v T, Ni, Is, Eg, USSR, S, M, Ca, P, Mor; 1987 v Se, Y (sub) (84)
Wilkinson, B. (Sheffield U), 1904 v S (1)
Wilkinson, L. R. (Oxford University), 1891 v W (1)
Williams, B. F. (Wolverhampton W), 1949 v F; 1950 v S, W, Ei, I, P, Bel, Ch, US, Sp; 1951 v Ni, W, S, Y, Arg, P; 1952 v W, F; 1955 v S, WG, F, Sp, P; 1956 v W (24)
Williams, O. (Clapton Orient), 1923 v W, Ni (2)
Williams, S. (Southampton), 1983 v Aus (1 + 1 sub); 1984 v F; 1985 v EG, Fi, T (6)
Williams, W. (WBA), 1897 v Ni; 1898 v W, Ni, S; 1899 v W, Ni (6)
Williamson, E. C. (Arsenal), 1923 v Se (2) (2)
Williamson, R. G. (Middlesbrough), 1905 v Ni; 1911 v Ni, S, W; 1912 v S, W; 1913 v Ni (7)
Willingham, C. K. (Huddersfield T), 1937 v Fi; 1938 v S, G, Sw, F; 1939 v S, W, Ni, R of E, N, I, Y (12)
Willis, A. (Tottenham H), 1952 v F (1)
Wilshaw, D. J. (Wolverhampton W), 1954 v W, Sw, U; 1955 v S, F, Sp, P; 1956 v W, Ni, Fi, WG; 1957 v Ni (12)
Wilson, C. P. (Hendon), 1884 v S, W (2)
Wilson, C. W. (Oxford University), 1879 v W; 1881 v S (2)
Wilson, G. (Sheffield W), 1921 v S, W, Bel; 1922 v S, Ni; 1923 v S, W, Ni, Bel; 1924 v W, Ni, F (12)
Wilson, G. P. (Corinthians), 1900 v S, W (2)
Wilson, R. (Huddersfield T), 1960 v S, Y, Sp, H; 1962 v W, Ni, S, A, Sw, Pe, P, H, Arg, Bul, Br; 1963 v Ni, F, Br, Cz, EG, Sw; 1964 v W, S, R of W, U, P (2), Ei, Br, Arg; (with Everton), 1965 v S, H, Y, WG, Se; 1966 v WG (sub), W, Ni, A, Sp, Pol (2), Y, Fi, D, U, M, F, Arg, P, WG; 1967 v Ni, W, S, Cz, A; 1968 v Ni, S, USSR (2), Sp (2), Y (63)
Wilson, T. (Huddersfield T), 1928 v S (1)
Winckworth, W. N. (Old Westminsters), 1892 v W; 1893 v Ni (2)
Windridge, J. E. (Chelsea), 1908 v S, W, Ni, A (2), H, B; 1909 v Ni (8)
Wingfield-Stratford, C. V. (Royal Engineers), 1877 v S (1)
Winterburn, N. (Arsenal), 1990 v I (sub); 1993 v G (sub) (2)
Wise, D. F. (Chelsea), 1991 v T, USSR, Aus (sub), Nz (2); 1994 v N; 1995 v R (sub), Ng (8)
Withe, P. (Aston Villa), 1981 v Br, W, S; 1982 v N (sub), W, Ic; 1983 v H, Ni, S; 1984 v H (sub); 1985 v T (11)
Wollaston, C. H. R. (Wanderers), 1874 v S; 1875 v S; 1877 v S; 1880 v S (4)
Wolstenholme, S. (Everton), 1904 v S; (with Blackburn R), 1905 v W, Ni (3)
Wood, H. (Wolverhampton W), 1890 v S, W; 1896 v S (3)
Wood, R. E. (Manchester U), 1955 v Ni, W; 1956 v Fi (3)
Woodcock, A. S. (Nottingham F), 1978 v Ni; 1979 v Ei (sub), Cz, Bul (sub), Se; 1980 v Ni; (with Cologne), Bul, Ei, Sp (2), Arg, Bel, I; 1981 v N, R, Sw, R, W (sub), S; 1982 v Ni (sub), Ho, Fi (sub), WG (sub), Sp; (with Arsenal), 1983 v WG (sub), Gr, L, Gr; 1984 v L, F (sub), Ni, W, S, Br, U (sub); 1985 v EG, Fi, T, Ni; 1986 v R (sub), T (sub), Is (sub) (42)
Woodger, G. (Oldham Ath), 1911 v Ni (1)
Woodhall, G. (WBA), 1888 v S, W (2)
Woodley, V. R. (Chelsea), 1937 v S, N, Se, Fi; 1938 v S, W, Ni, Cz, G, Sw, F; 1939 v S, W, Ni, R of E, N, I, R, Y (19)
Woods, C. C. E. (Norwich C), 1985 v US; 1986 v Eg (sub), Is (sub), Ca (sub); (with Rangers), 1987 v Y, Sp (sub), Ni (sub), T, S; 1988 v Is, H, Sw (sub), USSR; 1989 v D (sub); 1990 v Br (sub), D (sub); 1991 v H, Pol, Ei, USSR, Aus, Nz (2), Mal; (with Sheffield W), 1992 v G, T, Pol, F, C, Br, Fi, D, F, Se; 1993 v Sp, N, T, Sm, T, Ho, Pol, N, US (43)
Woodward, V. J. (Tottenham H), 1903 v S, W, Ni; 1904 v S, Ni; 1905 v S, W, Ni; 1907 v S; 1908 v S, W, Ni, A (2), H, B; 1909 v W, Ni, H (2), A; (with Chelsea), 1910 v Ni; 1911 v W (23)
Woosnam, M. (Manchester C), 1922 v W (1)
Worrall, F. (Portsmouth), 1935 v Ho; 1937 v Ni (2)
Worthington, F. S. (Leicester C), 1974 v Ni (sub), S, Arg, EG, Bul, Y; 1975 v Cz, P (sub) (8)
Wreford-Brown, C. (Oxford University), 1889 v Ni; (with Old Carthusians), 1894 v W; 1895 v W; 1898 v S (4)
Wright, E, G. D. (Cambridge University), 1906 v W (1)
Wright, I. E. (C Palace), 1991 v Cam, Ei (sub), USSR, Nz; (with Arsenal), 1992 v H (sub); 1993 v N, T (2), Pol (sub), N (sub), US (sub), Br, G (sub); 1994 v Pol, Ho (sub), Sm, Gr (sub), N (sub); 1995 v US (sub), R (20)
Wright, J. D. (Newcastle U), 1939 v N (1)
Wright, M. (Southampton), 1984 v W; 1985 v EG, Fi, T, Ei, R, I, WG; 1986 v R, T, Ni, Eg, USSR; 1987 v Y, Ni, S; (with Derby Co), 1988 v Is, Ho (sub), Co, Sw, Ei, Ho; 1990 v Cz (sub), Tun (sub), Ho, Eg, Bel, Cam, WG, I; 1991 v H, Pol, Ei (2), Cam, USSR, Arg, Aus, Nz, Mal; (with Liverpool), 1992 v F, Fi; 1993 v Sp (43)
Wright, T. J. (Everton), 1968 v USSR; 1969 v R (2), M (sub), U, Br; 1970 v W, Ho, Bel, R (sub), Br (11)
Wright, W. A. (Wolverhampton W), 1947 v S, W, Ni, Ei, Ho, F, Sw, P; 1948 v S, W, Ni, Bel, Se, I; 1949 v S, W, Ni, D, Sw, Se, N, F; 1950 v S, W, Ni, Ei, I, P, Bel, Ch, US, Sp; 1951 v Ni, S, Arg; 1952 v W, Ni, S, F, A (2), I, Sw; 1953 v Ni, W, S, Bel, Arg, Ch, U, US; 1954 v W, Ni, S, R of E, H (2), Y, Bel, Sw, U; 1955 v W, Ni, S, WG, F, Sp, P; 1956 v Ni, W, S, Br, Se, Fi, WG, D, Sp; 1957 v S, W, Ni, Y, D (2), Ei (2); 1958 v W, Ni, S, P, Y, USSR (3), Br, A, F; 1959 v W, Ni, S, USSR, I, Br, Pe, M, US (105)
Wylie, J. G. (Wanderers), 1878 v S (1)

Yates, J. (Burnley), 1889 v Ni (1)
York, R. E. (Aston Villa), 1922 v S; 1926 v S (2)
Young, A. (Huddersfield T), 1933 v W; 1937 v S, H, N, Se; 1938 v G, Sw, F; 1939 v W (9)
Young, G. M. (Sheffield W), 1965 v W (1)

R. E. Evans also played for Wales against E, Ni, S; J. Reynolds also played for Ireland against E, W, S.

NORTHERN IRELAND

Aherne, T. (Belfast C), 1947 v E; 1948 v S; 1949 v W; (with Luton T), 1950 v W (4)
Alexander, A. (Cliftonville), 1895 v S (1)
Allen, C. A. (Cliftonville), 1936 v E (1)
Allen, J. (Limavady), 1887 v E (1)
Anderson, T. (Manchester U), 1973 v Cy, E, S, W; 1974 v Bul, P; (with Swindon T), 1975 v S (sub); 1976 v Is; 1977 v Ho, Bel, WG, E, S, W, Ic; 1978 v Ic, Ho, Bel; (with Peterborough U), S, E, W; 1979 v D (sub) (22)
Anderson, W. (Linfield), 1898 v W, E, S; 1899 v S (4)
Andrews, W. (Glentoran), 1908 v S; (with Grimsby T), 1913 v E, S (3)
Armstrong, G. (Tottenham H), 1977 v WG, E, W (sub), Ic (sub); 1978 v Bel, S, E, W; 1979 v Ei, D, Bul, E, Bul, E, S, W, D; 1980 v E, Ei, Is, S, E, W, Aus (3); 1981 v Se; (with Watford), P, S, P, S, Se; 1982 v S, Is, E, F, W, Y, Hon, Sp, A, F; 1983 v A, T, Alb, S, E, W; (with Real Mallorca), 1984 v A, WG, E, W, Fi; 1985 v R, Fi, E, Sp; (with WBA), 1986 v T, R (sub), E (sub), F (sub); (with Chesterfield), D (sub), Br (sub) (63)

Baird, G. (Distillery), 1896 v S, E, W (3)
Baird, H. (Huddersfield T), 1939 v E (1)
Balfe, J. (Shelbourne), 1909 v E; 1910 v W (2)
Bambrick, J. (Linfield), 1929 v W, S, E; 1930 v W, S, E; 1932 v W; (with Chelsea), 1935 v W; 1936 v E, S; 1938 v W (11)
Banks, S. J. (Cliftonville), 1937 v W (1)
Barr, H. H. (Linfield), 1962 v E; (with Coventry C), 1963 v E, Pol (3)
Barron, H. (Cliftonville), 1894 v E, W, S; 1895 v S; 1896 v S; 1897 v E, W (7)
Barry, H. (Bohemians), 1900 v S (1)
Baxter, R. A. (Cliftonville), 1887 v S, W (2)
Bennett, L. V. (Dublin University), 1889 v W (1)
Berry, J. (Cliftonville), 1888 v S, W; 1889 v E (3)
Best, G. (Manchester U), 1964 v W, U; 1965 v E, Ho (2), S, Sw (2), Alb; 1966 v S, E, Alb; 1967 v E; 1968 v S; 1969 v E, S, W, T; 1970 v S, E, W, USSR; 1971 v Cy (2), Sp, E, S, W; 1972 v USSR, Sp; 1973 v Bul; 1974 v P; (with Fulham), 1977 v Ho, Bel, WG; 1978 v Ic, Ho (37)
Bingham, W. L. (Sunderland), 1951 v F; 1952 v E, S, W; 1953 v E, S, F, W; 1954 v E, S, W; 1955 v E, S, W; 1956 v E, S, W; 1957 v E, S, W, P (2), I; 1958 v S, E, W, I (2), Arg, Cz (2), WG, F; (with Luton T), 1959 v E, S, W, Sp; 1960 v S, E, W; (with Everton), 1961 v E, S, WG (2), Gr, I; 1962 v E, Gr; 1963 v E, S, Pol (2), Sp; (with Port Vale), 1964 v S, E, Sp (56)
Black, J. (Glentoran), 1901 v E (1)
Black, K. (Luton T), 1988 v Fr (sub), Ma (sub); 1989 v Ei, H, Sp (2), Ch (sub); 1990 v H, N, U; 1991 v Y (2), D, A, Pol, Fa; (with Nottingham F), 1992 v Fa, A, D, S, Li, G; 1993 v Sp, D (sub), Alb, Ei (sub), Sp; 1994 v D (sub), Ei (sub), R (sub) (30)
Blair, H. (Portadown), 1931 v S; 1932 v S; (with Swansea), 1934 v S (3)
Blair, J. (Cliftonville), 1907 v W, E, S; 1908 v E, S (5)
Blair, R. V. (Oldham Ath), 1975 v Se (sub), S (sub), W; 1976 v Se, Is (5)
Blanchflower, R. D. (Barnsley), 1950 v S, W; 1951 v E, S; (with Aston Villa), F; 1952 v W; 1953 v E, S, W, F; 1954 v E, S, W; 1955 v E, S (with Tottenham H), W; 1956 v E, S, W; 1957 v E, S, W, I, P (2); 1958 v E, S, W, I (2), Cz (2), Arg, F, WG; 1959 v E, S, W, Sp; 1960 v E, S, W; 1961 v E, S, W, WG (2); 1962 v E, S, W, Gr, Ho; 1963 v E, S, Pol (2) (56)
Blanchflower, J. (Manchester U), 1954 v W; 1955 v E, S; 1956 v S, W; 1957 v S, E, P; 1958 v S, E, I (2) (12)
Bookman, L. O. (Bradford C), 1914 v W; (with Luton T), 1921 v S, W; 1922 v E (4)
Bothwell, A. W. (Ards), 1926 v S, E, W; 1927 v E, W (5)
Bowler, G. C. (Hull C), 1950 v E, S, W (3)
Boyle, P. (Sheffield U), 1901 v E; 1902 v E; 1903 v S, W; 1904 v E (5)
Braithwaite, R. S. (Linfield), 1962 v W; 1963 v P, Sp; (with Middlesbrough), 1964 v W, U; 1965 v E, S, Sw (2), Ho (10)
Breen, T. (Belfast C), 1935 v E, W; 1937 v E, S; (with Manchester U), 1937 v W; 1938 v E, S; 1939 v W, S (9)
Brennan, B. (Bohemians), 1912 v W (1)
Brennan, R. A. (Luton T), 1949 v W; (with Birmingham C), 1950 v E, S, W; (with Fulham), 1951 v E (5)
Briggs, W. R. (Manchester U), 1962 v W; (with Swansea T), 1965 v Ho (2)
Brisby, D. (Distillery), 1891 v S (1)
Brolly, T. (Millwall), 1937 v W; 1938 v W; 1939 v E, W (4)
Brookes, E. A. (Shelbourne), 1920 v S (1)
Brotherston, N. (Blackburn R), 1980 v S, E, W, Aus (3); 1981 v Se, P; 1982 v S, Is, E, F, S, W, Hon (sub), A (sub); 1983 v A (sub), WG, Alb, T, Alb, S (sub), E (sub), W; 1984 v T; 1985 v Is (sub), T (27)
Brown, J. (Glenavon), 1921 v W; (with Tranmere R), 1924 v E, W (3)
Brown, J. (Wolverhampton W), 1935 v E, W; 1936 v E; (with Coventry C), 1937 v E, W; 1938 v S, W; (with Birmingham C), 1939 v E, S, W (10)
Brown, W. G. (Glenavon), 1926 v W (1)
Brown, W. M. (Limavady), 1887 v E (1)
Browne, F. (Cliftonville), 1887 v E, S, W; 1888 v E, S (5)
Browne, R. J. (Leeds U), 1936 v E, W; 1938 v E, W; 1939 v E, S (6)
Bruce, W. (Glentoran), 1961 v S; 1967 v W (2)
Buckle, H. (Cliftonville), 1882 v E (1)
Buckle, H. R. (Sunderland), 1904 v E; (with Bristol R), 1908 v W (2)
Burnett, J. (Distillery), 1894 v E, W, S; (with Glentoran), 1895 v E, W (5)
Burnison, J. (Distillery), 1901 v E, W (2)
Burnison, S. (Distillery), 1908 v E; 1910 v E, S; (with Bradford), 1911 v E, S, W; (with Distillery), 1912 v E; 1913 v W (8)
Burns, J. (Glenavon), 1923 v E (1)
Butler, M. P. (Blackpool), 1939 v W (1)

Campbell, A. C. (Crusaders), 1963 v W; 1965 v Sw (2)
Campbell, D. A. (Nottingham F), 1986 v Mor (sub), Br; 1987 v E (2), T, Y; (with Charlton Ath), 1988 v Y, T (sub), Gr (sub), Pol (sub) (10)
Campbell, J. (Cliftonville), 1896 v W; 1897 v E, S, W; (with Distillery), 1898 v E, S, W; (with Cliftonville), 1899 v E; 1900 v E, S; 1901 v S, W; 1902 v S; 1903 v E; 1904 v S (15)
Campbell, J. P. (Fulham), 1951 v E, S (2)
Campbell, R. (Bradford C), 1982 v S, W (sub) (2)
Campbell, W. G. (Dundee), 1968 v S, E; 1969 v T; 1970 v S, W, USSR (6)
Carey, J. J. (Manchester U), 1947 v E, S, W; 1948 v E; 1949 v E, S, W (7)
Carroll, E. (Glenavon), 1925 v S (1)
Casey, T. (Newcastle U), 1955 v W; 1956 v W; 1957 v E, S, W, I, P (2); 1958 v WG, F; (with Portsmouth), 1959 v E, Sp (12)
Cashin, M. (Cliftonville), 1898 v S (1)
Caskey, W. (Derby Co), 1979 v Bul, E, Bul, E, D (sub); 1980 v E (sub); (with Tulsa R), 1982 v F (sub) (7)
Cassidy, T. (Newcastle U), 1971 v E (sub); 1972 v USSR (sub); 1974 v Bul (sub), S, E, W; 1975 v N; 1976 v S, E, W; 1977 v WG (sub); 1980 v E, Ei (sub), Is, S, E, W, Aus

(3); (with Burnley), 1981 v Se, P; 1982 v Is, Sp (sub) (24)
Caughey, M. (Linfield), 1986 v F (sub), D (sub) (2)
Chambers, J. (Distillery), 1921 v W; (with Bury), 1928 v E, S, W; 1929 v E, S, W; 1930 v S, W; (with Nottingham F), 1932 v E, S, W (12)
Chatton, H. A. (Partick T), 1925 v E, S; 1926 v E (3)
Christian, J. (Linfield), 1889 v S (1)
Clarke, C. J. (Bournemouth), 1986 v F, D, Mor, Alg (sub), Sp, Br; (with Southampton), 1987 v E, T, Y; 1988 v Y, T, Gr, Pol, F, Ma; 1989 v Ei, H, Sp (1 + 1 sub); (with QPR), Ma, Ch; 1990 v H, Ei, N; (with Portsmouth), 1991 v Y (sub), D, A, Pol, Y (sub), Fa; 1992 v Fa, D, S, G; 1993 v Alb, Sp, D (38)
Clarke, R. (Belfast C), 1901 v E, S (2)
Cleary, J. (Glentoran), 1982 v S, W; 1983 v W (sub); 1984 v T (sub); 1985 v Is (5)
Clements, D. (Coventry C), 1965 v W, Ho; 1966 v M; 1967 v S, W; 1968 v S, E; 1969 v T (2), S, W; 1970 v S, E, W, USSR (2); 1971 v Sp, E, S, W, Cy; (with Sheffield W), 1972 v USSR (2), Sp, E, S, W; 1973 v Bul, Cy (2), P, E, S, W; (with Everton), 1974 v Bul, P, S, E, W; 1975 v N, Y, E, S, W; 1976 v Se, Y; (with New York Cosmos), E, W (48)
Clugston, J. (Cliftonville), 1888 v W; 1889 v W, S, E; 1890 v E, S; 1891 v E, W; 1892 v E, S, W; 1893 v E, S, W (14)
Cochrane, D. (Leeds U), 1939 v E, W; 1947 v E, S, W; 1948 v E, S, W; 1949 v S, W; 1950 v S, E (12)
Cochrane, M. (Distillery), 1898 v S, W, E; 1899 v E; 1900 v E, S, W; (with Leicester Fosse), 1901 v S (8)
Cochrane, T. (Coleraine), 1976 v N (sub); (with Burnley), 1978 v S (sub), E (sub), W (sub); 1979 v Ei (sub); (with Middlesbrough), D, Bul, E, Bul, E; 1980 v Is, E (sub), W (sub), Aus (1 + 2 sub); 1981 v Se (sub), P (sub), S, P, S, Se; 1982 v E (sub), F; (with Gillingham), 1984 v S, Fi (sub) (26)
Collins, F. (Celtic), 1922 v S (1)
Condy, J. (Distillery), 1882 v W; 1886 v E, S (3)
Connell, T. (Coleraine), 1978 v W (sub) (1)
Connor, J. (Glentoran), 1901 v S, E; (with Belfast C), 1905 v E, S, W; 1907 v E, S; 1908 v E, S; 1909 v W; 1911 v S, E, W (13)
Connor, M. J. (Brentford), 1903 v S, W; (with Fulham), 1904 v E (3)
Cook, W. (Celtic), 1933 v E, W, S; (with Everton), 1935 v E; 1936 v S, W; 1937 v E, S, W; 1938 v E, S, W; 1939 v E, S, W (15)
Cooke, S. (Belfast YMCA), 1889 v E; (with Cliftonville), 1890 v E, S (3)
Coulter, J. (Belfast C), 1934 v E, S, W; (with Everton), 1935 v E, S, W; 1937 v S, W; (with Grimsby T), 1938 v S, W; (with Chelmsford C), 1939 v S (11)
Cowan, J. (Newcastle U), 1970 v E (sub) (1)
Cowan, T. S. (Queen's Island), 1925 v W (1)
Coyle, F. (Coleraine), 1956 v E, S; 1957 v P; (with Nottingham F), 1958 v Arg (4)
Coyle, L. (Derry C), 1989 v Ch (sub) (1)
Coyle, R. I. (Sheffield W), 1973 v P, Cy (sub), W (sub); 1974 v Bul (sub), P (sub) (5)
Craig, A. B. (Rangers), 1908 v E, S, W; 1909 v S; (with Morton), 1912 v S, W; 1914 v E, S, W (9)
Craig, D. J. (Newcastle U), 1967 v W; 1968 v W; 1969 v T (2), E, S, W; 1970 v E, S, W, USSR; 1971 v Cy (2), Sp, S (sub); 1972 v USSR, S (sub); 1973 v Cy (2), E, S, W; 1974 v Bul, P; 1975 v N (25)
Crawford, S. (Distillery), 1889 v E, W; (with Cliftonville), 1891 v E, S, W; 1893 v E, W (7)
Croft, T. (Queen's Island), 1924 v E (1)
Crone, R. (Distillery), 1889 v S; 1890 v E, S, W (4)
Crone, W. (Distillery), 1882 v W; 1884 v E, S, W; 1886 v E, S, W; 1887 v E; 1888 v E, W; 1889 v S; 1890 v W (12)
Crooks, W. (Manchester U), 1922 v W (1)
Crossan, E. (Blackburn R), 1950 v S; 1951 v E; 1955 v W (3)
Crossan, J. A. (Sparta-Rotterdam), 1960 v E; (with Sunderland), 1963 v W, P, Sp; 1964 v E, S, W, U, Sp; 1965 v E, S, Sw (2); (with Manchester C), W, Ho (2), Alb; 1966 v S, E, Alb, WG; 1967 v E, S; (with Middlesbrough), 1968 v S (24)
Crothers, C. (Distillery), 1907 v W (1)
Cumming, L. (Huddersfield T), 1929 v W, S; (with Oldham Ath), 1930 v E (3)
Cunningham, R. (Ulster), 1892 v S, E, W; 1893 v E (4)
Cunningham, W. E. (St Mirren), 1951 v W; 1953 v E; 1954 v S; 1955 v S; (with Leicester C), 1956 v E, S, W; 1957 v E, S, W, I, P (2); 1958 v S, W, I, Cz (2), Arg, WG, F; 1959 v E, S, W; 1960 v E, S, W; (with Dunfermline Ath), 1961 v W; 1962 v W, Ho (30)
Curran, S. (Belfast C), 1926 v S, W; 1928 v S (3)
Curran, J. J. (Glenavon), 1922 v W; (with Pontypridd), 1923 v E, S; (with Glenavon), 1924 v E (4)
Cush, W. W. (Glenavon), 1951 v E, S; 1954 v S, E; 1957 v W, I, P (2); (with Leeds U), 1958 v I (2), W, Cz (2), Arg, WG, F; 1959 v E, S, W, Sp; 1960 v E, S, W; (with Portadown), 1961 v WG, Gr; 1962 v Gr (26)

Dalton, W. (YMCA), 1888 v S; (with Linfield), 1890 v S, W; 1891 v S, W; 1892 v E, S, W; 1894 v E, S, W (11)
D'Arcy, S. D. (Chelsea), 1952 v W; 1953 v E; (with Brentford), 1953 v S, W, F (5)
Darling, J. (Linfield), 1897 v E, S; 1900 v S; 1902 v E, S, W; 1903 v E, S, W; 1905 v E, S, W; 1906 v E, S, W; 1908 v W; 1909 v E; 1910 v E, S, W; 1912 v S (21)
Davey, H. H. (Reading), 1926 v E; 1927 v E, S; 1928 v E; (with Portsmouth), 1928 v W (5)
Davis, T. L. (Oldham Ath), 1937 v E (1)
Davison, J. R. (Cliftonville), 1882 v E, W; 1883 v E, W; 1884 v E, W, S; 1885 v E (8)
Dennison, R. (Wolverhampton W), 1988 v F, Ma; 1989 v H, Sp Ch (sub); 1990 v Ei, U; 1991 v Y (2), A. Pol, Fa (sub); 1992 v Fa, A, D (sub); 1993 v Sp (sub); 1994 v Co (sub) (17)
Devine, J. (Glentoran), 1990 v U (sub) (1)
Devine, W. (Limavady), 1886 v E, W; 1887 v W; 1888 v W (4)
Dickson, D. (Coleraine), 1970 v S (sub), W; 1973 v Cy, P (4)
Dickson, T. A. (Linfield), 1957 v S (1)
Dickson, W. (Chelsea), 1951 v W, F; 1952 v E, S, W; 1953 v E, S, W, F; (with Arsenal), 1954 v E, W; 1955 v E (12)
Diffin, W. (Belfast C), 1931 v W (1)
Dill, A. H. (Knock and Down Ath), 1882 v E, W; (with Cliftonville), 1883 v W; 1884 v E, S, W; 1885 v E, S, W (9)
Doherty, I. (Belfast C), 1901 v E (1)
Doherty, J. (Cliftonville), 1933 v E, W (2)
Doherty, L. (Linfield), 1985 v Is; 1988 v T (sub) (2)
Doherty, M. (Derry C), 1938 v S (1)
Doherty, P. D. (Blackpool), 1935 v E, W; 1936 v E, S; (with Manchester C), 1937 v E, W; 1938 v E, S; 1939 v E, W; (with Derby Co), 1947 v E; (with Huddersfield T), 1947 v W; 1948 v E, W; 1949 v S; (with Doncaster R), 1951 v S (16)
Donaghy, M. (Luton T), 1980 v S, E, W; 1981 v Se, P, S (sub); 1982 v S, Is, E, F, S, W, Y, Hon, Sp, F; 1983 v A, WG, Alb, T, Alb, S, E, W; 1984 v A, T, WG, S, E, W, Fi; 1985 v R, Fi, E, Sp, T; 1986 v T, R, E, F, D, Mor, Alg, Sp, Br; 1987 v E (2), T, Is, Y; 1988 v Y, T, Gr, Pol, F, Ma; 1989 v Ei, H; (with Manchester U), Sp (2), Ma, Ch; 1990 v Ei, N; 1991 v Y (2), D, A, Pol, Fa; 1992 v Fa, A, D, S, Li, G; (with Chelsea), 1993 v Alb, Sp, D, Alb, Ei, Sp, Li, La; 1994 v La, D, Ei, R, Lie, Co, M (91)
Donnelly, L. (Distillery), 1913 v W (1)
Doran, J. F. (Brighton), 1921 v E; 1922 v E, W (3)

Dougan, A. D. (Portsmouth), 1958 v Cz; (with Blackburn R), 1960 v S; 1961 v E, W, I, Gr; (with Aston Villa), 1963 v S, Pol (2); (with Leicester C), 1966 v S, E, W, M, Alb, WG; 1967 v E, S; (with Wolverhampton W), 1967 v W; 1968 v S, W, Is; 1969 v T (2), E, S, W; 1970 v S, E, USSR (2); 1971 v Cy (2), Sp, E, S, W; 1972 v USSR (2), E, S, W; 1973 v Bul, Cy (43)
Douglas, J. P. (Belfast C), 1947 v E (1)
Dowd, H. O. (Glenavon), 1974 v W; (with Sheffield W), 1975 v N (sub), Se (3)
Dowie, I. (Luton T), 1990 v N (sub), U; 1991 v Y, D, A (sub), (with West Ham U), Y, Fa; (with Southampton) 1992 v Fa, A, D (sub), S (sub), Li; 1993 v Alb (2), Ei, Sp (sub), Li, La; La, D, Ei (sub), R (sub), Lie, Co, M (sub); 1995 v A, Ei; (with C Palace) Ei, La, Ca, Ch, La (32)
Duggan, H. A. (Leeds U), 1930 v E; 1931 v E, W; 1933 v E; 1934 v E; 1935 v S, W; 1936 v S (8)
Dunlop, G. (Linfield), 1985 v Is; 1987 v E, Y; 1990 v Ei (4)
Dunne, J. (Sheffield U), 1928 v W; 1931 v W, E; 1932 v E, S; 1933 v E, W (7)

Eames, W. L. E. (Dublin U), 1885 v E, S, W (3)
Eglington, T. J. (Everton), 1947 v S, W; 1948 v E, S, W; 1949 v E (6)
Elder, A. R. (Burnley), 1960 v W; 1961 v S, E, W, WG (2), Gr; 1962 v E, S, Gr; 1963 v E, S, W, P (2), Sp; 1964 v W, U; 1965 v E, S, W, Sw (2), Ho (2), Alb; 1966 v E, S, W, M, Alb; 1967 v E, S, W; (with Stoke C), 1968 v E, W; 1969 v E (sub), S, W; 1970 v USSR (40)
Elleman, A. R. (Cliftonville), 1889 v W; 1890 v E (2)
Elwood, J. H. (Bradford), 1929 v W; 1930 v E (2)
Emerson, W. (Glentoran), 1920 v E, S, W; 1921 v E; 1922 v E, S; (with Burnley), 1922 v W; 1923 v E, S, W; 1924 v E (11)
English, S. (Rangers), 1933 v W, S (2)
Enright, J. (Leeds C), 1912 v S (1)

Falloon, E. (Aberdeen), 1931 v S; 1933 v S (2)
Farquharson, T. G. (Cardiff C), 1923 v S, W; 1924 v E, S, W; 1925 v E, S (7)
Farrell, P. (Distillery), 1901 v S, W (2)
Farrell, P. (Hibernian), 1938 v W (1)
Farrell, P. D. (Everton), 1947 v S, W; 1948 v E, S, W; 1949 v E, W (7)
Feeney, J. M. (Linfield), 1947 v S; (with Swansea T), 1950 v E (2)
Feeney, W. (Glentoran), 1976 v Is (1)
Ferguson, W. (Linfield), 1966 v M; 1967 v E (2)
Ferris, J. (Belfast C), 1920 v E, W; (with Chelsea), 1921 v S, E; (with Belfast C), 1928 v S (5)
Ferris, R. O. (Birmingham C), 1950 v S; 1951 v F; 1952 v S (3)
Fettis, A. (Hull C), 1992 v D, Li; 1993 v D; 1994 v M; 1995 v P, Ei, La, Ca, Ch, La (10)
Finney, T. (Sunderland), 1975 v N, E (sub), S, W; 1976 v N, Y, S; (with Cambridge U), 1980 v E, Is, S, E, W, Aus (2) (14)
Fitzpatrick, J. C. (Bohemians), 1896 v E, S (2)
Flack, H. (Burnley), 1929 v S (1)
Fleming, J. G. (Nottingham F), 1987 v E (2), Is, Y; 1988 v T, Gr, Pol; 1989 v Ma, Ch; (with Manchester C), 1990 v H, Ei; (with Barnsley), 1991 v Y; 1992 v Li (sub), G; 1993 v Alb, Sp, D, Alb, Sp, Li, La; 1994 v La, D, Ei, R, Lie, Co, M; 1995 v P, A, Ei (31)
Forbes, G. (Limavady), 1888 v W; (with Distillery), 1891 v E, S (3)
Forde, J. T. (Ards), 1959 v Sp; 1961 v E, S, WG (4)
Foreman, T. A. (Cliftonville), 1899 v S (1)
Forsyth, J. (YMCA), 1888 v E, S (2)
Fox, W. (Ulster), 1887 v E, S (2)

Fulton, R. P. (Belfast C), 1930 v W; 1931 v E, S, W; 1932 v W, E; 1933 v E, S; 1934 v E, W, S; 1935 v E, W, S; 1936 v S, W; 1937 v E, S, W; 1938 v W (20)

Gaffikin, J. (Linfield Ath), 1890 v S, W; 1891 v S, W; 1892 v E, S, W; 1893 v E, S, W; 1894 v E, S, W; 1895 v E, W (15)
Galbraith, W. (Distillery), 1890 v W (1)
Gallagher, P. (Celtic), 1920 v E, S; 1922 v S; 1923 v S, W; 1924 v S, W; 1925 v S, W, E; (with Falkirk), 1927 v S (11)
Gallogly, C. (Huddersfield T), 1951 v E, S (2)
Gara, A. (Preston NE), 1902 v E, S, W (3)
Gardiner, A. (Cliftonville), 1930 v S, W; 1931 v S; 1932 v E, S (5)
Garrett, J. (Distillery), 1925 v W (1)
Gaston, R. (Oxford U), 1969 v Is (sub) (1)
Gaukrodger, G. (Linfield), 1895 v W (1)
Gaussen, A. W. (Moyola Park), 1884 v E, S; 1888 v E, W; 1889 v E, W (6)
Geary, J. (Glentoran), 1931 v S; 1932 v S (2)
Gibb, J. T. (Wellington Park) 1884 v S, W; 1885 v S, E, W; 1886 v S; 1887 v S, E, W; 1889 v S (10)
Gibb, T. J. (Cliftonville), 1936 v W (1)
Gibson W. K. (Cliftonville), 1894 v S, W, E; 1895 v S; 1897 v W; 1898 v S, W, E; 1901 v S, W, E; 1902 v S, W (13)
Gillespie, K.R. (Manchester U), 1995 v P, A, Ei; (with Newcastle U) Ei, La, Ca, Ch (sub), La (sub) (8)
Gillespie, R. (Hertford), 1886 v E, S, W; 1887 v E, S, W (6)
Gillespie, W. (Sheffield U), 1913 v E, S; 1914 v E, W; 1920 v S, W; 1921 v E; 1922 v E, S, W; 1923 v E, S, W; 1924 v E, S, W; 1925 v E, S; 1926 v S, W; 1927 v E, W; 1928 v E; 1929 v E; 1931 v E (25)
Gillespie, W. (West Down), 1889 v W (1)
Goodall, A. L. (Derby Co), 1899 v S, W; 1900 v E, W; 1901 v E; 1902 v S; 1903 v E, W; (with Glossop), 1904 v E, W (10)
Goodbody, M. F. (Dublin University), 1889 v E; 1891 v W (2)
Gordon, H. (Linfield), 1891 v S; 1892 v E, S, W; 1893 v E, S, W; 1895 v E, W; 1896 v E, S (11)
Gordon, T. (Linfield), 1894 v W; 1895 v E (2)
Gorman, W. C. (Brentford), 1947 v E, S, W; 1948 v W (4)
Gowdy, J. (Glentoran), 1920 v E; (with Queen's Island), 1924 v W; (with Falkirk), 1926 v E, S; 1927 v E, S (6)
Gowdy, W. A. (Hull C), 1932 v S; (with Sheffield W), 1933 v S; (with Linfield), 1935 v E, S, W; (with Hibernian), 1936 v W (6)
Graham, W. G. L. (Doncaster R), 1951 v W, F; 1952 v E, S, W; 1953 v S, F; 1954 v E, W; 1955 v S, W; 1956 v E, S; 1959 v E (14)
Gray, P. (Luton T), 1993 v D (sub), Alb, Ei, Sp; (with Sunderland), 1994 v La, D, Ei, R, Lie (sub); 1995 v P, A, Ei, Ca, Ch (sub) (14)
Greer, W. (QPR), 1909 v E, S, W (3)
Gregg, H. (Doncaster R), 1954 v W; 1957 v E, S, W, I, P (2); 1958 v E, I; (with Manchester U), 1958 v Cz, Arg, WG, F, W; 1959 v E, W; 1960 v S, E, W; 1961 v E, S; 1962 v S, Gr; 1964 v S, E (25)

Hall, G. (Distillery), 1897 v E (1)
Halligan, W. (Derby Co), 1911 v W; (with Wolverhampton W), 1912 v E (2)
Hamill, M. (Manchester U), 1912 v E; 1914 v E, S; (with Belfast C), 1920 v E, S, W; (with Manchester C), 1921 v S (7)
Hamilton, B. (Linfield), 1969 v T; 1971 v Cy (2), E, S, W; (with Ipswich T), 1972 v USSR (1+1 sub), Sp; 1973 v Bul, Cy (2), P, E, S, W; 1974 v Bul, S, E, W; 1975 v N, Se, Y, E; 1976 v Se, N, Y; (with Everton), Is, S, E, W; 1977 v

Ho, Bel, WG, E, S, W, Ic; (with Millwall), 1978 v S, E, W; 1979 v Ei (sub); (with Swindon T), Bul (2), E, S, W, D; 1980 v Aus (2 sub) (50)
Hamilton, J. (Knock), 1882 v E, W (2)
Hamilton, R. (Distillery), 1908 v W (1)
Hamilton, R. (Rangers), 1928 v S; 1929 v E; 1930 v S, E; 1932 v S (5)
Hamilton, W. (QPR), 1978 v S (sub); (with Burnley), 1980 v S, E, W, Aus (2); 1981 v Se, P, S, P, S, Se; 1982 v S, Is, E, W, Y, Hon, Sp, A, F; 1983 v A, WG, Alb (2), S, E, W; 1984 v A, T, WG, S, E, W, Fi; (with Oxford U), 1985 v R, Sp; 1986 v Mor (sub), Alg, Sp (sub), Br (sub) (41)
Hamilton, W. D. (Dublin Association), 1885 v W (1)
Hamilton, W. J. (Dublin Association), 1885 v W (1)
Hampton, H. (Bradford C), 1911 v E, S, W; 1912 v E, W; 1913 v E, S, W; 1914 v E (9)
Hanna, D. R. A. (Portsmouth), 1899 v W (1)
Hanna, J. (Nottingham F), 1912 v S, W (2)
Hannon, D. J. (Bohemians), 1908 v E, S; 1911 v E, S; 1912 v W; 1913 v E (6)
Harkin, J. T. (Southport), 1968 v W; 1969 v T; (with Shrewsbury T), W (sub); 1970 v USSR; 1971 v Sp (5)
Harland, A. I. (Linfield), 1923 v E (1)
Harris, J. (Cliftonville), 1921 v W (1)
Harris, V. (Shelbourne), 1906 v E; 1907 v E, W; 1908 v E, W, S; (with Everton), 1909 v E, W, S; 1910 v E, S, W; 1911 v E, S, W; 1912 v E; 1913 v E, S; 1914 v S, W (20)
Harvey, M. (Sunderland), 1961 v I; 1962 v Ho; 1963 v W, Sp; 1964 v S, E, W, U, Sp; 1965 v E, S, W, Sw (2), Ho (2), Alb; 1966 v S, E, W, M, Alb, WG; 1967 v E, S; 1968 v E, W; 1969 v Is, T (2), E; 1970 v USSR; 1971 v Cy, W (sub) (34)
Hastings, J. (Knock), 1882 v E, W; (with Ulster), 1883 v W; 1884 v E, S; 1886 v E, S (7)
Hatton, S. (Linfield), 1963 v S, Pol (2)
Hayes, W. E. (Huddersfield T), 1938 v E, S; 1939 v E, S (4)
Healy, F. (Coleraine), 1982 v S, W, Hon (sub); (with Glentoran), 1983 v A (sub) (4)
Hegan, D. (WBA), 1970 v USSR; (with Wolverhampton W), 1972 v USSR, E, S, W; 1973 v Bul, Cy (7)
Hehir, J. C. (Bohemians), 1910 v W (1)
Henderson, A. W. (Ulster), 1885 v E, S, W (3)
Hewison, G. (Moyola Park), 1885 v E, S (2)
Hill, C. F. (Sheffield U), 1990 v N, U; 1991 v Pol, Y; 1992 v A, D; (with Leicester C) 1995 v Ei, La (8)
Hill, M. J. (Norwich C), 1959 v W; 1960 v W; 1961 v WG; 1962 v S; (with Everton), 1964 v S, E, Sp (7)
Hinton, E. (Fulham), 1947 v S, W; 1948 v S, E, W; (with Millwall), 1951 v W, F (7)
Hopkins, J. (Brighton), 1926 v E (1)
Horlock, K. (Swindon T), 1995 v La, Ca (2)
Houston, J. (Linfield), 1912 v S, W; 1913 v W; (with Everton), 1913 v E, S; 1914 v S (6)
Houston, W. (Linfield), 1933 v W (1)
Houston, W. G. (Moyola Park), 1885 v E, S (2)
Hughes, M. E. (Manchester C), 1992 v D, S, Li, G; (with Strasbourg), 1993 v Alb, Sp, D, Ei, Sp, Li, La; 1994 v La, D, Ei, R, Lie, Co, M; 1995 v P, A, Ei (2) La, Ca, Ch, La (26)
Hughes, P. (Bury), 1987 v E, T, Is (3)
Hughes, W. (Bolton W), 1951 v W (1)
Humphries, W. (Ards), 1962 v W; (with Coventry C), 1962 v Ho; 1963 v E, S, W, Pol, Sp; 1964 v S, E, Sp; 1965 v S; (with Swansea T), 1965 v W, Ho, Alb (14)
Hunter, A. (Distillery), 1905 v W; 1906 v W, E, S; (with Belfast C), 1908 v W; 1909 v W, E, S (8)
Hunter, A. (Blackburn R), 1970 v USSR; 1971 v Cy (2), E, S, W; (with Ipswich T), 1972 v USSR (2), Sp, E, S, W; 1973 v Bul, Cy (2), P, E, S, W; 1974 v Bul, S, E, W; 1975 v N, Se, Y, E, S, W; 1976 v Se, N, Y, Is, S, E, W; 1977 v Ho, Bel, WG, E, S, W, Ic; 1978 v Ic, Ho, Bel; 1979 v Ei, D, S, W, D; 1980 v E, Ei (53)
Hunter, B. V. (Wrexham), 1995 v La (1)
Hunter, R. J. (Cliftonville), 1884 v E, S, W (3)
Hunter, V. (Coleraine), 1962 v E; 1964 v Sp (2)

Irvine, R. J. (Linfield), 1962 v Ho; 1963 v E, S, W, Pol (2), Sp; (with Stoke C), 1965 v W (8)
Irvine, R. W. (Everton), 1922 v S; 1923 v E, W; 1924 v E, S; 1925 v E; 1926 v E; 1927 v E, W; 1928 v E, S; (with Portsmouth), 1929 v E; 1930 v S; (with Connah's Quay), 1931 v E; (with Derry C), 1932 v W (15)
Irvine, W. J. (Burnley), 1963 v W, Sp; 1965 v S, W, Sw, Ho (2), Alb; 1966 v S, E, W, M, Alb; 1967 v E, S; 1968 v E, W; (with Preston NE), 1969 v Is, T, E; (with Brighton), 1972 v E, S, W (23)
Irving, S. J. (Dundee), 1923 v S, W; 1924 v S, E, W; 1925 v S, E, W; 1926 v S, W; (with Cardiff C), 1927 v S, E, W; 1928 v S, E, W; (with Chelsea), 1929 v E; 1931 v W (18)

Jackson, T. (Everton), 1969 v Is, E, S, W; 1970 v USSR (1 + 1 sub); (with Nottingham F), 1971 v Sp; 1972 v E, S, W; 1973 v Cy, E, S, W; 1974 v Bul, P, S (sub), E (sub), W (sub); 1975 v N (sub), Se, Y, E, S, W; (with Manchester U); 1976 v Se, N, Y; 1977 v Ho, Bel, WG, E, S, W, Ic (35)
Jamison, J. (Glentoran), 1976 v N (1)
Jennings, P. A. (Watford), 1964 v W, U; (with Tottenham H), 1965 v E, S, Sw (2), Ho, Alb; 1966 v S, E, W, Alb, WG; 1967 v E, S; 1968 v S, E, W; 1969 v Is, T (2), E, S, W; 1970 v S, E, USSR (2); 1971 v Cy (2), E, S, W; 1972 v USSR, Sp, S, E, W; 1973 v Bul, Cy, P, E, S, W; 1974 v P, S, E, W; 1975 v N, Se, Y, E, S, W; 1976 v Se, N, Y, Is, S, E, W; 1977 v Ho, Bel, WG, E, S, W, Ic; (with Arsenal), 1978 v Ic, Ho, Bel; 1979 v Ei, D, Bul, E, Bul, E, S, W, D; 1980 v E, Ei, Is; 1981 v S, P, S, Se; 1982 v S, Is, E, W, Y, Hon, Sp, F; 1983 v Alb, S, E, W; 1984 v A, T, WG, S, W, Fi; 1985 v R, Fi, E, Sp, T; (with Tottenham H), 1986 v T, R, E, F, D, Mor; (with Tottenham H), Alg, Sp, Br (119)
Johnston, H. (Portadown), 1927 v W (1)
Johnston, R. (Old Park), 1885 v S, W (2)
Johnston, S. (Distillery), 1882 v W; 1884 v E; 1886 v E, S (4)
Johnston, S. (Linfield), 1890 v W; 1893 v S, W; 1894 v E (4)
Johnston, S. (Distillery), 1905 v W (1)
Johnston, W. C. (Glenavon), 1962 v W; (with Oldham Ath), 1966 v M (sub) (2)
Jones, J. (Linfield), 1930 v S, W; 1931 v S, W, E; 1932 v S, E; 1933 v S, E, W; 1934 v S, E, W; 1935 v S, E, W; 1936 v E, S; (with Hibernian), 1936 v W; 1937 v E, W, S; (with Glenavon), 1938 v E (23)
Jones, J. (Glenavon), 1956 v W; 1957 v E, W (3)
Jones, S. (Distillery), 1934 v E; (with Blackpool), 1934 v W (2)
Jordan, T. (Linfield), 1895 v E, W (2)

Kavanagh, P. J. (Celtic), 1930 v E (1)
Keane, T. R. (Swansea T), 1949 v S (1)
Kearns, A. (Distillery), 1900 v E, S, W; 1902 v E, S, W (6)
Kee, P. V. (Oxford U), 1990 v N; 1991 v Y (2), D, A, Pol, Fa; (with Ards), 1995 v A, Ei (9)
Keith, R. M. (Newcastle U), 1958 v E, W, Cz (2), Arg, I, WG, F; 1959 v E, S, W, Sp; 1960 v S, E; 1961 v S, E, W, I, WG (2), Gr; 1962 v W, Ho (23)
Kelly, H. R. (Fulham), 1950 v E, W; (with Southampton), 1951 v E, S (4)
Kelly, J. (Glentoran), 1896 v E (1)

Kelly, J. (Derry C), 1932 v E, W; 1933 v E, W, S; 1934 v W; 1936 v E, S, W; 1937 v S, E (11)
Kelly, P. (Manchester C), 1921 v E (1)
Kelly, P. M. (Barnsley), 1950 v S (1)
Kennedy, A. L. (Arsenal), 1923 v W; 1925 v E (2)
Kernaghan, N. (Belfast C), 1936 v W; 1937 v S; 1938 v E (3)
Kirkwood, H. (Cliftonville), 1904 v W (1)
Kirwan, J. (Tottenham H), 1900 v W; 1902 v E, W; 1903 v E, S, W; 1904 v E, S, W; 1905 v E, S, W; (with Chelsea), 1906 v E, S, W; 1907 v W; (with Clyde), 1909 v S (17)

Lacey, W. (Everton), 1909 v E, S, W; 1910 v E, S, W; 1911 v E, S, W; 1912 v E; (with Liverpool), 1913 v W; 1914 v E, S, W; 1920 v E, S, W; 1921 v E, S, W; 1922 v E, S; (with New Brighton), 1925 v E (23)
Lawther, W. I. (Sunderland), 1960 v W; 1961 v I; (with Blackburn R), 1962 v S, Ho (4)
Leatham, J. (Belfast C), 1939 v W (1)
Ledwidge, J. J. (Shelbourne), 1906 v S, W (2)
Lemon, J. (Glentoran), 1886 v W; 1888 v S; (with Belfast YMCA), 1889 v W (3)
Lennon, N. F. (Crewe Alex), 1994 v M (sub); 1995 v Ch (2)
Leslie, W. (YMCA), 1887 v E (1)
Lewis, J. (Glentoran), 1899 v S, E, W; (with Distillery), 1900 v S (4)
Little, J. (Glentoran), 1898 v W (1)
Lockhart, H. (Rossall School), 1884 v W (1)
Lockhart, N. (Linfield), 1947 v E; (with Coventry C), 1950 v W; 1951 v W; 1952 v W; (with Aston Villa), 1954 v S, E; 1955 v W; 1956 v W (8)
Lomas, S. M. (Manchester C), 1994 v R, Lie, Co (sub), M (sub); 1995 v P, A (6)
Lowther, R. (Glentoran), 1888 v E, S (2)
Loyal, J. (Clarence), 1891 v S (1)
Lutton, R. J. (Wolverhampton W), 1970 v S, E; (with West Ham U), 1973 v Cy (sub), S (sub), W (sub); 1974 v P (6)
Lyner, D. (Glentoran), 1920 v E, W; 1922 v S, W; (with Manchester U), 1923 v E; (with Kilmarnock), 1923 v W (6)

McAdams, W. J. (Manchester C), 1954 v W; 1955 v S; 1957 v E; 1958 v S, I; (with Bolton W), 1961 v E, S, W, I, WG (2), Gr; 1962 v E, Gr; (with Leeds U), Ho (15)
McAlery, J. M. (Cliftonville), 1882 v E, W (2)
McAlinden, J. (Belfast C), 1938 v S; 1939 v S; (with Portsmouth), 1947 v E; (with Southend U), 1949 v E (4)
McAllen, J. (Linfield), 1898 v E; 1899 v E, S, W; 1900 v E, S, W; 1901 v W; 1902 v S (9)
McAlpine, W. J. (Cliftonville), 1901 v S (1)
McArthur, A. (Distillery), 1886 v W (1)
McAuley, J. L. (Huddersfield T), 1911 v E, W; 1912 v E, S; 1913 v E, S (6)
McAuley, P. (Belfast C), 1900 v S (1)
McBride, S. (Glenavon), 1991 v D (sub), Pol (sub); 1992 v Fa (sub), D (4)
McCabe, J. J. (Leeds U), 1949 v S, W; 1950 v E; 1951 v W; 1953 v W; 1954 v S (6)
McCabe, W. (Ulster), 1891 v E (1)
McCambridge, J. (Ballymena), 1930 v S, W; (with Cardiff C), 1931 v W; 1932 v E (4)
McCandless, J. (Bradford), 1912 v W; 1913 v W; 1920 v W, S; 1921 v E (5)
McCandless, W. (Linfield), 1920 v E, W; 1921 v E; (with Rangers), 1921 v W; 1922 v S; 1924 v W, S; 1925 v S; 1929 v W (9)
McCann, P. (Belfast C), 1910 v E, S, W; 1911 v E; (with Glentoran), 1911 v S; 1912 v E; 1913 v W (7)
McCashin, J. (Cliftonville), 1896 v W; 1898 v S, W; 1899 v S (4)
McCavana, W. T. (Coleraine), 1955 v S; 1956 v E, S (3)
McCaw, D. (Distillery), 1882 v E (1)
McCaw, J. H. (Linfield), 1927 v W; 1930 v S; 1931 v E, S, W (5)
McClatchey, J. (Distillery), 1886 v E, S, W (3)
McClatchey, R. (Distillery), 1895 v S (1)
McCleary, J. W. (Cliftonville), 1955 v W (1)
McCleery, W. (Linfield), 1930 v E, W; 1931 v E, S, W; 1932 v S, W; 1933 v E, W (9)
McClelland, J. (Arsenal), 1961 v W, I, WG (2), Gr; (with Fulham), 1966 v M (6)
McClelland, J. (Mansfield T), 1980 v S (sub), Aus (3); 1981 v Se, S; (with Rangers), S, Se (sub); 1982 v S, W, Y, Hon, Sp, A, F; 1983 v A, WG, Alb, T, Alb, S, E, W; 1984 v A, T, WG, S, E, W, Fi; 1985 v R, Is; (with Watford), Fi, E, Sp, T; 1986 v T, F (sub); 1987 v E (2), T, Is, Y; 1988 v T, Gr, F, Ma; 1989 v Ei, H, Sp (2), Ma; (with Leeds U), 1990 v N (53)
McCluggage, A. (Bradford), 1924 v E; (with Burnley), 1927 v S, W; 1928 v S, E, W; 1929 v S, E, W; 1930 v W; 1931 v E, W (12)
McClure, G. (Cliftonville), 1907 v S, W; 1908 v E; (with Distillery), 1909 v E (4)
McConnell, E. (Cliftonville), 1904 v S, W; (with Glentoran), 1905 v S; (with Sunderland), 1906 v E; 1907 v E; 1908 v S, W; (with Sheffield W), 1909 v S, W; 1910 v S, W, E (12)
McConnell, P. (Doncaster R), 1928 v W; (with Southport), 1932 v E (2)
McConnell, W. G. (Bohemians), 1912 v W; 1913 v E, S; 1914 v E, S, W (6)
McConnell, W. H. (Reading), 1925 v W; 1926 v E, W; 1927 v E, S, W; 1928 v E, W (8)
McCourt, F. J. (Manchester C), 1952 v E, W; 1953 v E, S, W, F (6)
McCoy, J. (Distillery), 1896 v W (1)
McCoy, R. (Coleraine), 1987 v Y (sub) (1)
McCracken, R. (C Palace), 1921 v E; 1922 v E, S, W (4)
McCracken, W. (Distillery), 1902 v E, W; 1903 v E; 1904 v E, S, W; (with Newcastle U), 1905 v E, S, W; 1907 v E; 1920 v E; 1922 v E, S, W; (with Hull C), 1923 v S (15)
McCreery, D. (Manchester U), 1976 v S (sub), E, W; 1977 v Ho, Bel, WG, E, S, W, Ic; 1978 v Ic, Ho, Bel, S, E, W; 1979 v Ei, D, Bul, E, Bul, W, D; (with QPR), 1980 v E, Ei, S (sub), E (sub), W (sub), Aus (1 + 1 sub); 1981 v Se (sub), P (sub); (with Tulsa R), S, P, Se; 1982 v S, Is, E (sub), F, Y, Hon, Sp, A, F; (with Newcastle U), 1983 v A; 1984 v T (sub); 1985 v R, Sp (sub); 1986 v T (sub), R, E, F, D, Alg, Sp, Br; 1987 v T, E, Y; 1988 v Y; 1989 v Sp, Ma, Ch; (with Hearts), 1990 v H, Ei, N, U (sub) (67)
McCrory, S. (Southend U), 1958 v E (1)
McCullough, K. (Belfast C), 1935 v W; 1936 v E; (with Manchester C), 1936 v S; 1937 v E, S (5)
McCullough, W. J. (Arsenal), 1961 v I; 1963 v Sp; 1964 v S, E, W, U, Sp; 1965 v E, Sw; (with Millwall), 1967 v E (10)
McCurdy, C. (Linfield), 1980 v Aus (sub) (1)
McDonald, A. (QPR), 1986 v R, E, F, D, Mor, Alg, Sp, Br; 1987 v E (2), T, Is, Y; 1988 v Y, T, Pol, F, Ma; 1989 v Ei, H, Sp, Ch; 1990 v H, Ei, U; 1991 v Y, D, A, Fa; 1992 v Fa, S, Li, G; 1993 v Alb, Sp, D, Alb, Ei, Sp, Li, La; 1994 v D, Ei; 1995 v P, A, Ei, La, Ca, Ch, La (50)
McDonald, R. (Rangers), 1930 v S; 1932 v E (2)
McDonnell, J. (Bohemians), 1911 v E, S; 1912 v W; 1913 v W (4)
McElhinney, G. (Bolton W), 1984 v WG, S, E, W, Fi; 1985 v R (6)
McFaul, W. S. (Linfield), 1967 v E (sub); (with Newcastle U), 1970 v W; 1971 v Sp; 1972 v USSR; 1973 v Cy; 1974 v Bul (6)
McGarry, J. K. (Cliftonville), 1951 v W, F, S (3)
McGaughey, M. (Linfield), 1985 v Is (sub) (1)
McGee, G. (Wellington Park), 1885 v E, S, W (3)

McGibbon, P. C. G. (Manchester U), 1995 v Ca (sub), Ch, La (3)
McGrath, R. C. (Tottenham H), 1974 v S, E, W; 1975 v N; 1976 v Is (sub); 1977 v Ho; (with Manchester U), Bel, WG, E, S, W, Ic; 1978 v Ic, Ho, Bel, S, E, W; 1979 v Bul (sub), E (2 sub) (21)
McGregor, S. (Glentoran), 1921 v S (1)
McGrillen, J. (Clyde), 1924 v S; (with Belfast C), 1927 v S (2)
McGuire, E. (Distillery), 1907 v S (1)
McIlroy, H. (Cliftonville), 1906 v E (1)
McIlroy, J. (Burnley), 1952 v E, S, W; 1953 v E, S, W; 1954 v E, S, W; 1955 v E, S, W; 1956 v E, S, W; 1957 v E, S, W, I, P (2); 1958 v E, S, W, I (2), Cz (2), Arg, WG, F; 1959 v E, S, W, Sp; 1960 v E, S, W; 1961 v E, W, WG (2), Gr; 1962 v E, S, Gr, Ho; 1963 v E, S, Pol (2); (with Stoke C), 1963 v W; 1966 v S, E, Alb (55)
McIlroy, S. B. (Manchester U), 1972 v Sp, S (sub); 1974 v S, E, W; 1975 v N, Se, Y, E, S, W; 1976 v Se, N, Y, S, E, W; 1977 v Ho, Bel, E, S, W, Ic; 1978 v Ic, Ho, Bel, S, E, W; 1979 v Ei, D, Bul, E, Bul, E, S, W, D; 1980 v E, Ei, Is, S, E, W; 1981 v Se, P, S, P, S, Se; 1982 v S, Is; (with Stoke C), E, F, S, W, Y, Hon, Sp, A, F; 1983 v A, WG, Alb, T, Alb, S, E, W; 1984 v A, T, S, E, W, Fi; 1985 v Fi, E, T; (with Manchester C), 1986 v T, R, E, F, D, Mor, Alg, Sp, Br; 1987 v E (sub) (88)
McIlvenny, J. (Distillery), 1890 v E; 1891 v E (2)
McIlvenny, P. (Distillery), 1924 v W (1)
McKeag, W. (Glentoran), 1968 v S, W (2)
McKee, F. W. (Cliftonville), 1906 v S, W; (with Belfast C), 1914 v E, S, W (5)
McKelvie, H. (Glentoran), 1901 v W (1)
McKenna, J. (Huddersfield), 1950 v E, S, W; 1951 v E, S, F; 1952 v E (7)
McKenzie, H. (Distillery), 1923 v S (1)
McKenzie, R. (Airdrie), 1967 v W (1)
McKeown, H. (Linfield), 1892 v E, S, W; 1893 v S, W; 1894 v S, W (7)
McKie, H. (Cliftonville), 1895 v E, S, W (3)
McKinney, D. (Hull C), 1921 v S; (with Bradford C), 1924 v S (2)
McKinney, V. J. (Falkirk), 1966 v WG (1)
McKnight, A. (Celtic), 1988 v Y, T, Gr, Pol, F, Ma; (with West Ham U) 1989 v Ei, H, Sp (2) (10)
McKnight, J. (Preston NE), 1912 v S; (with Glentoran), 1913 v S (2)
McLaughlin, J. C. (Shrewsbury T), 1962 v E, S, W, Gr; 1963 v W; (with Swansea T), 1964 v W, U; 1965 v E, W, Sw (2); 1966 v W (12)
McLean, T. (Limavady), 1885 v S (1)
McMahon, G. J. (Tottenham H), 1995 v Ca (sub), Ch, La (3)
McMahon, J. (Bohemians), 1934 v S (1)
McMaster, G. (Glentoran), 1897 v E, S, W (3)
McMichael, A. (Newcastle U), 1950 v E, S; 1951 v E, S, F; 1952 v E, S, W; 1953 v E, S, W, F; 1954 v E, S, W; 1955 v E, W; 1956 v W; 1957 v E, S, W, I, P (2); 1958 v E, S, W, I (2), Cz (2), Arg, WG, F; 1959 v S, W, Sp; 1960 v E, S, W (40)
McMillan, G. (Distillery), 1903 v E; 1905 v W (2)
McMillan, S. (Manchester U), 1963 v E, S (2)
McMillen, W. S. (Manchester U), 1934 v E; 1935 v S; 1937 v S; (with Chesterfield), 1938 v S, W; 1939 v E, S (7)
McMordie, A. S. (Middlesbrough), 1969 v Is, T (2), E, S, W; 1970 v E, S, W, USSR; 1971 v Cy (2), E, S, W; 1972 v USSR, Sp, E, S, W; 1973 v Bul (21)
McMorran, E. J. (Belfast C), 1947 v E; (with Barnsley), 1951 v E, S, W; 1952 v E, S, W; 1953 v E, S, F; (with Doncaster R), 1953 v W; 1954 v E; 1956 v W; 1957 v I, P (15)
McMullan, D. (Liverpool), 1926 v E, W; 1927 v S (3)
McNally, B. A. (Shrewsbury T), 1986 v Mor; 1987 v T (sub); 1988 v Y, Gr, Ma (sub) (5)
McNinch, J. (Ballymena), 1931 v S; 1932 v S, W (3)
McParland, P. J. (Aston Villa), 1954 v W; 1955 v E, S; 1956 v E, S; 1957 v E, S, W, P; 1958 v E, S, W, I (2), Cz (2), Arg, WG, F; 1959 v E, S, W, Sp; 1960 v E, S, W; 1961 v E, S, W, I, WG (2), Gr; (with Wolverhampton W), 1962 v Ho (34)
McShane, J. (Cliftonville), 1899 v S; 1900 v E, S, W (4)
McVickers, J. (Glentoran), 1888 v E; 1889 v S (2)
McWha, W. B. R. (Knock), 1882 v E, W; (with Cliftonville), 1883 v E, W; 1884 v E; 1885 v E, W (7)
Macartney, A. (Ulster), 1903 v S, W; (with Linfield), 1904 v S, W; (with Everton), 1905 v E, S; (with Belfast C), 1907 v E, S, W; 1908 v E, S, W; (with Glentoran), 1909 v E, S, W (15)
Mackie, J. (Arsenal), 1923 v W; (with Portsmouth), 1935 v S, W (3)
Madden, O. (Norwich C), 1938 v E (1)
Magill, E. J. (Arsenal), 1962 v E, S, Gr; 1963 v E, S, W, Pol (2), Sp; 1964 v E, S, W, U, Sp; 1965 v E, S, Sw (2), Ho, Alb; 1966 v S, (with Brighton), E, Alb, W, WG, M (26)
Magilton, J. (Oxford U), 1991 v Pol, Y, Fa; 1992 v Fa, A, D, S, Li, G; 1993 v Alb, D, Alb, Ei, Li, La; 1994 v La, D, Ei; (with Southampton), R, Lie, Co, M; 1995 v P, A, Ei (2), Ca, Ch, La (29)
Maginnis, H. (Linfield), 1900 v E, S, W; 1903 v S, W; 1904 v E, S, W (8)
Maguire, E. (Distillery), 1907 v S (1)
Mahood, J. (Belfast C), 1926 v S; 1928 v E, S, W; 1929 v E, S, W; 1930 v W; (with Ballymena), 1934 v S (9)
Manderson, R. (Rangers), 1920 v W, S; 1925 v S, E; 1926 v S (5)
Mansfield, J. (Dublin Freebooters), 1901 v E (1)
Martin, C. J. (Glentoran), 1947 v S; (with Leeds U), 1948 v E, S, W; (with Aston Villa), 1949 v E; 1950 v W (6)
Martin, D. (Bo'ness), 1925 v S (1)
Martin, D. C. (Cliftonville), 1882 v E, W; 1883 v E (3)
Martin, D. K. (Belfast C), 1934 v E, S, W; 1935 v S; (with Wolverhampton W), 1935 v E; 1936 v W; (with Nottingham F), 1937 v S; 1938 v E, S; 1939 v S (10)
Mathieson, A. (Luton T), 1921 v W; 1922 v E (2)
Maxwell, J. (Linfield), 1902 v W; 1903 v W, E; (with Glentoran), 1905 v W, S; (with Belfast C), 1906 v W; 1907 v S (7)
Meek, H. L. (Glentoran), 1925 v W (1)
Mehaffy, J. A. C. (Queen's Island), 1922 v W (1)
Meldon, P. A. (Dublin Freebooters), 1899 v S, W (2)
Mercer, H. V. A. (Linfield), 1908 v E (1)
Mercer, J. T. (Distillery), 1898 v E, S, W; 1899 v E; (with Linfield), 1902 v E, W; (with Distillery), 1903 v S, W; (with Derby Co), 1904 v E, W; 1905 v S (11)
Millar, W. (Barrow), 1932 v W; 1933 v S (2)
Miller, J. (Middlesbrough), 1929 v W, S; 1930 v E (3)
Milligan, D. (Chesterfield), 1939 v W (1)
Milne, R. G. (Linfield), 1894 v E, S, W; 1895 v E, W; 1896 v E, S, W; 1897 v E, S; 1898 v E, S, W; 1899 v E, W; 1901 v W; 1902 v E, S, W; 1903 v E, S; 1904 v E, S, W; 1906 v E, S, W (27)
Mitchell, E. J. (Cliftonville), 1933 v S; (with Glentoran), 1934 v W (2)
Mitchell, W. (Distillery), 1932 v E, W; 1933 v E, W; (with Chelsea), 1934 v W, S; 1935 v S, E; 1936 v S, E; 1937 v E, S, W; 1938 v E, S (15)
Molyneux, T. B. (Ligoniel), 1883 v E, W; (with Cliftonville), 1884 v E, W, S; 1885 v E, W; 1886 v E, W, S; 1888 v S (11)
Montgomery, F. J. (Coleraine), 1955 v E (1)
Moore, C. (Glentoran), 1949 v W (1)
Moore, J. (Linfield Ath), 1891 v E, S, W (3)
Moore, P. (Aberdeen), 1933 v E (1)
Moore, T. (Ulster), 1887 v S, W (2)
Moore, W. (Falkirk), 1923 v S (1)
Moorhead, F. W. (Dublin University), 1885 v E (1)
Moorhead, G. (Linfield), 1923 v S; 1928 v S; 1929 v S (3)

Moran, J. (Leeds C), 1912 v S (1)
Moreland, V. (Derby Co), 1979 v Bul (2 sub), E, S; 1980 v E, Ei (6)
Morgan, F. G. (Linfield), 1923 v E; (with Nottingham F), 1924 v S; 1927 v E; 1928 v E, S, W; 1929 v E (7)
Morgan, S. (Port Vale), 1972 v Sp; 1973 v Bul (sub), P, Cy, E, S, W; (with Aston Villa), 1974 v Bul, P, S, E; 1975 v Se; 1976 v Se (sub), N, Y; (with Brighton & HA), S, W (sub); (with Sparta Rotterdam), 1979 v D (18)
Morrison, J. (Linfield Ath), 1891 v E, W (2)
Morrison, T. (Glentoran), 1895 v E, S, W; (with Burnley), 1899 v W; 1900 v W; 1902 v E, S (7)
Morrogh, E. (Bohemians), 1896 v S (1)
Morrow, S. J. (Arsenal), 1990 v U (sub); 1991 v A (sub), Pol, Y; 1992 v Fa, S (sub), G (sub); 1993 v Sp (sub), Alb, Ei; 1994 v R, Co, M (sub); 1995 v P, Ei (2), La (17)
Morrow, W. J. (Moyola Park), 1883 v E, W; 1884 v S (3)
Muir, R. (Oldpark), 1885 v S, W (2)
Mullan, G. (Glentoran), 1983 v S, E, W, Alb (sub) (4)
Mulholland, S. (Celtic), 1906 v S, E (2)
Mulligan, J. (Manchester C), 1921 v S (1)
Murphy, J. (Bradford C), 1910 v E, S, W (3)
Murphy, N. (QPR), 1905 v E, S, W (3)
Murray, J. M. (Motherwell), 1910 v E, S; (with Sheffield W), 1910 v W (3)

Napier, R. J. (Bolton W), 1966 v WG (1)
Neill, W. J. T. (Arsenal), 1961 v I, Gr, WG; 1962 v E, S, W, Gr; 1963 v E, W, Pol, Sp; 1964 v S, E, W, U, Sp; 1965 v E, S, W, Sw, Ho (2), Alb; 1966 v S, E, W, Alb, WG, M; 1967 v S, W; 1968 v S, E; 1969 v E, S, W, Is, T (2); 1970 v S, E, W, USSR (2); (with Hull C), 1971 v Cy, Sp; 1972 v USSR (2), Sp, S, E, W; 1973 v Bul, Cy (2), P, E, S, W (59)
Nelis, P. (Nottingham F), 1923 v E (1)
Nelson, S. (Arsenal), 1970 v W, E (sub); 1971 v Cy, Sp, E, S, W; 1972 v USSR (2), Sp, E, S, W; 1973 v Bul, Cy, P; 1974 v S, E; 1975 v Se, Y; 1976 v Se, N, Is, E; 1977 v Bel (sub), WG, W, Ic; 1978 v Ic, Ho, Bel; 1979 v Ei, D, Bul, E, Bul, E, S, W, D; 1980 v E, Ei, Is; 1981 v S, P, S, Se; (with Brighton & HA), 1982 v E, S, Sp (sub), A (51)
Nicholl, C. J. (Aston Villa), 1975 v Se, Y, E, S, W; 1976 v Se, N, Y, S, E, W; 1977 v W; (with Southampton), 1978 v Bel (sub), S, E, W; 1979 v Ei, Bul, E, Bul, E, W; 1980 v Ei, Is, S, E, W, Aus (3); 1981 v Se, P, S, P, S, Se; 1982 v S, Is, E, F, W, Y, Hon, Sp, A, F; 1983 v S (sub), E, W; (with Grimsby T), 1984 v A, T (51)
Nicholl, H. (Belfast C), 1902 v E, W; 1905 v E (3)
Nicholl, J. M. (Manchester U), 1976 v Is, W (sub); 1977 v Ho, Bel, E, S, W, Ic; 1978 v Ic, Ho, Bel, S, E, W; 1979 v Ei, D, Bul, E, Bul, E, S, W, D; 1980 v E, Ei, Is, S, E, W, Aus (3); 1981 v Se, P, S, P, S, Se; 1982 v S, Is, E; (with Toronto B), F, W, Y, Hon, Sp, A, F; (with Sunderland), 1983 v A, WG, Alb, T, Alb; (with Toronto B), S, E, W; 1984 v T; (with Rangers), WG, S, E; (with Toronto B), Fi; 1985 v R; (with WBA), Fi, E, Sp, T; 1986 v T, R, E, F, Alg, Sp, Br (73)
Nicholson, J. J. (Manchester U), 1961 v S, W; 1962 v E, W, Gr, Ho; 1963 v E, S, Pol (2); (with Huddersfield T), 1965 v W, Ho (2), Alb; 1966 v S, E, W, Alb, M; 1967 v S, W; 1968 v S, E, W; 1969 v S, E, W, T (2); 1970 v S, E, W, USSR (2); 1971 v Cy (2), E, S, W; 1972 v USSR (2) (41)
Nixon, R. (Linfield), 1914 v S (1)
Nolan-Whelan, J. V. (Dublin Freebooters), 1901 v E, W; 1902 v S, W (4)

O'Boyle, G. (Dunfermline Ath), 1994 v Co (sub), M; (with St Johnstone), 1995 v P (sub), La (sub), Ca (sub), Ch (sub) (6)
O'Brien, M. T. (QPR), 1921 v S; (with Leicester C), 1922 v S, W; 1924 v S, W; (with Hull C), 1925 v S, E, W; 1926 v W; (with Derby Co), 1927 v W (10)
O'Connell, P. (Sheffield W), 1912 v E, S; (with Hull C), 1914 v E, S, W (5)
O'Doherty, A. (Coleraine), 1970 v E, W (sub) (2)
O'Driscoll, J. F. (Swansea T), 1949 v E, S, W (3)
O'Hagan, C. (Tottenham H), 1905 v S, W; 1906 v S, W, E; (with Aberdeen), 1907 v E, S, W; 1908 v S, W; 1909 v E (11)
O'Hagan, W. (St Mirren), 1920 v E, W (2)
O'Kane, W. J. (Nottingham F), 1970 v E, W, S (sub); 1971 v Sp, E, S, W; 1972 v USSR (2); 1973 v P, Cy; 1974 v Bul, P, S, E, W; 1975 v N, Se, E, S (20)
O'Mahoney, M. T. (Bristol R), 1939 v S (1)
O'Neill, C. (Motherwell), 1989 v Ch (sub); 1990 v Ei (sub); 1991 v D (3)
O'Neill, J. (Leicester C), 1980 v Is, S, E, W, Aus (3); 1981 v P, S, P, S, Se; 1982 v S, Is, E, F, S, F (sub); 1983 v A, WG, Alb, T, Alb, S; 1984 v S (sub); 1985 v Is, Fi, E, Sp, T; 1986 v T, R, E, F, D, Mor, Alg, Sp, Br (39)
O'Neill, J. (Sunderland), 1962 v W (1)
O'Neill, M. A. (Newcastle U), 1988 v Gr, Pol, F, Ma; 1989 v Ei, H, Sp (sub), Sp (sub), Ma (sub), Ch; (with Dundee U), 1990 v H (sub), Ei; 1991 v Pol; 1992 v Fa (sub), S (sub), G (sub); 1993 v Alb (sub + 1), Ei, Sp, Li, La; (with Hibernian), 1994 v Lie (sub); 1995 v A (sub), Ei (25)
O'Neill, M. H. (Distillery), 1972 v USSR (sub), (with Nottingham F), Sp (sub), W (sub); 1973 v P, Cy, E, S, W; 1974 v Bul, P, E (sub), W; 1975 v Se, Y, E, S; 1976 v Y (sub); 1977 v E (sub), S; 1978 v Ic, Ho, S, E, W; 1979 v Ei, D, Bul, E, Bul, D; 1980 v Ei, Is, Aus (3); 1981 v Se, P; (with Norwich C), P, S, Se; (with Manchester C), 1982 v S; (with Norwich C), E, F, S, Y, Hon, Sp, A, F; 1983 v A, WG, Alb, T, Alb, S, E; (with Notts Co), 1984 v A, T, WG, E, W, Fi; 1985 v R, Fi (64)
O'Reilly, H. (Dublin Freebooters), 1901 v S, W; 1904 v S (3)

Parke, J. (Linfield), 1964 v S; (with Hibernian), 1964 v E, Sp; (with Sunderland), 1965 v Sw, S, W, Ho (2), Alb; 1966 v WG; 1967 v E, S; 1968 v S, E (14)
Patterson, D. J. (C Palace), 1994 v Co (sub), M (sub); 1995 v Ei (sub+1), La, Ca, Ch (sub), La (sub) (8)
Peacock, R. (Celtic), 1952 v S; 1953 v F; 1954 v W; 1955 v E, S; 1956 v E, S; 1957 v W, I, P; 1958 v S, E, W, I (2), Arg, Cz (2), WG; 1959 v E, S, W; 1960 v S, E; 1961 v E, S, I, WG (2), Gr; (with Coleraine), 1962 v S (31)
Peden, J. (Linfield), 1887 v S, W; 1888 v W, E; 1889 v S, E; 1890 v W, S; 1891 v W, E; 1892 v W, E; 1893 v E, S, W; (with Distillery), 1896 v W, E, S; 1897 v W, S; 1898 v W, E, S; (with Linfield), 1899 v W (24)
Penney, S. (Brighton & HA), 1985 v Is; 1986 v T, R, E, F, D, Mor, Alg, Sp; 1987 v E, T, Is; 1988 v Pol, F, Ma; 1989 v Ei, Sp (17)
Percy, J. C. (Belfast YMCA), 1889 v W (1)
Platt, J. A. (Middlesbrough), 1976 v Is (sub); 1978 v S, E, W; 1980 v S, E, W, Aus (3); 1981 v Se, P; 1982 v F, S, W (sub), A; 1983 v A, WG, Alb, T; (with Ballymena U), 1984 v E, W (sub); (with Coleraine), 1986 v Mor (sub) (23)
Ponsonby, J. (Distillery), 1895 v S; 1896 v E, S, W; 1897 v E, S, W; 1899 v E (8)
Potts, R. M. C. (Cliftonville), 1883 v E, W (2)
Priestley, T. J. (Coleraine), 1933 v S; (with Chelsea), 1934 v E (2)
Pyper, Jas. (Cliftonville), 1897 v S, W; 1898 v S, E, W; 1899 v S; 1900 v E (7)
Pyper, John (Cliftonville), 1897 v E, S, W; 1899 v E, W; 1900 v E, W, S; 1902 v S (9)
Pyper, M. (Linfield), 1932 v W (1)

Quinn, J. M. (Blackburn R), 1985 v Is, Fi, E, Sp, T; 1986 v T, R, E, F, D (sub), Mor (sub); 1987 v E (sub), T; (with Swindon T), 1988 v Y (sub), T, Gr, Pol, F (sub), Ma;

(with Leicester C), 1989 v Ei, H (sub), Sp (sub + 1); (with Bradford C), Ma, Ch; 1990 v H, (with West Ham U), N; 1991 v Y (sub); (with Bournemouth), 1992 v Li; (with Reading), 1993 v Sp, D, Alb (sub), Ei (sub), La (sub); 1994 v La, D (sub), Ei, R, Lie, Co, M; 1995 v P, A (sub), La (sub) (44)

Rafferty, P. (Linfield), 1980 v E (sub) (1)
Ramsey, P. (Leicester C), 1984 v A, WG, S; 1985 v Is, E, Sp, T; 1986 v T, Mor; 1987 v Is, E, Y (sub); 1988 v Y; 1989 v Sp (14)
Rankine, J. (Alexander), 1883 v E, W (2)
Raper, E. O. (Dublin University), 1886 v W (1)
Rattray, D. (Avoniel), 1882 v E; 1883 v E, W (3)
Rea, B. (Glentoran), 1901 v E (1)
Redmond, J. (Cliftonville), 1884 v W (1)
Reid, G. H. (Cardiff C), 1923 v S (1)
Reid, J. (Ulster), 1883 v E; 1884 v W; 1887 v S; 1889 v W; 1890 v S, W (6)
Reid, S. E. (Derby Co), 1934 v E, W; 1936 v E (3)
Reid, W. (Hearts), 1931 v E (1)
Reilly, M. M. (Portsmouth), 1900 v E; 1902 v E (2)
Renneville, W. T. (Leyton), 1910 v S, E, W; (with Aston Villa), 1911 v W (4)
Reynolds, J. (Distillery), 1890 v E, W; (with Ulster), 1891 v E, S, W (5)
Reynolds, R. (Bohemians), 1905 v W (1)
Rice, P. J. (Arsenal), 1969 v Is; 1970 v USSR; 1971 v E, S, W; 1972 v USSR, Sp, E, S, W; 1973 v Bul, Cy, E, S, W; 1974 v Bul, P, S, E, W; 1975 v N, Y, E, S, W; 1976 v Se, N, Y, Is, S, E, W; 1977 v Ho, Bel, WG, E, S, Ic; 1978 v Ic, Ho, Bel; 1979 v Ei, D, E (2), S, W, D; 1980 v E (49)
Roberts, F. C. (Glentoran), 1931 v S (1)
Robinson, P. (Distillery), 1920 v S; (with Blackburn R), 1921 v W (2)
Rogan, A. (Celtic), 1988 v Y (sub), Gr, Pol (sub); 1989 v Ei (sub), H, Sp (2), Ma (sub), Ch; 1990 v H, N (sub), U; 1991 v Y (2), D, A; (with Sunderland), 1992 v Li (sub) (17)
Rollo, D. (Linfield), 1912 v W; 1913 v W; 1914 v W, E; (with Blackburn R), 1920 v S, W; 1921 v E, S, W; 1922 v E; 1923 v E; 1924 v S, W; 1925 v W; 1926 v E; 1927 v E (16)
Rosbotham, A. (Cliftonville), 1887 v E, S, W; 1888 v E, S, W; 1889 v E (7)
Ross, W. E. (Newcastle U), 1969 v Is (1)
Rowland, K. (West Ham U), 1995 v Ca, Ch, La (3)
Rowley, R. W. M. (Southampton), 1929 v S, W; 1930 v W, E; (with Tottenham H), 1931 v W; 1932 v S (6)
Russell, A. (Linfield), 1947 v E (1)
Russell, S. R. (Bradford C), 1930 v E, S; (with Derry C), 1932 v E (3)
Ryan, R. A. (WBA), 1950 v W (1)

Sanchez, L. P. (Wimbledon), 1987 v T (sub); 1989 v Sp, Ma (3)
Scott, E. (Liverpool), 1920 v S; 1921 v E, S, W; 1922 v E; 1925 v W; 1926 v E, S, W; 1927 v E, S, W; 1928 v E, S, W; 1929 v E, S, W; 1930 v E; 1931 v E; 1932 v W; 1933 v E, S, W; 1934 v E, S, W; (with Belfast C), 1935 v S; 1936 v E, S, W (31)
Scott, J. (Grimsby), 1958 v Cz, F (2)
Scott, J. E. (Cliftonville), 1901 v S (1)
Scott, L. J. (Dublin University), 1895 v S, W (2)
Scott, P. W. (Everton), 1975 v W; 1976 v Y; (with York C), Is, S, E (sub), W; 1978 v S, E, W; (with Aldershot), 1979 v S (sub) (10)
Scott, T. (Cliftonville), 1894 v E, S; 1895 v S, W; 1896 v S, E, W; 1897 v E, W; 1898 v E, S, W; 1900 v W (13)
Scott, W. (Linfield), 1903 v E, S, W; 1904 v E, S, W; (with Everton), 1905 v E, S; 1907 v E, S; 1908 v E, S, W; 1909 v E, S, W; 1910 v E, S; 1911 v E, S, W; 1912 v E; (with Leeds City), 1913 v E, S, W (25)
Scraggs, M. J. (Glentoran), 1921 v W; 1922 v E (2)
Seymour, H. C. (Bohemians), 1914 v W (1)
Seymour, J. (Cliftonville), 1907 v W; 1909 v W (2)
Shanks, T. (Woolwich Arsenal), 1903 v S; 1904 v W; (with Brentford), 1905 v E (3)
Sharkey, P. (Ipswich T), 1976 v S (1)
Sheehan, Dr G. (Bohemians), 1899 v S; 1900 v E, W (3)
Sheridan, J. (Everton), 1903 v W, E, S; 1904 v E, S; (with Stoke C), 1905 v E (6)
Sherrard, J. (Limavady), 1885 v S; 1887 v W; 1888 v W (3)
Sherrard, W. (Cliftonville), 1895 v E, W, S (3)
Sherry, J. J. (Bohemians), 1906 v E; 1907 v W (2)
Shields, J. (Southampton), 1957 v S (1)
Silo, M. (Belfast YMCA), 1888 v E (1)
Simpson, W. J. (Rangers), 1951 v W, F; 1954 v E, S; 1955 v E; 1957 v I, P; 1958 v S, E, W, I; 1959 v S (12)
Sinclair, J. (Knock), 1882 v E, W (2)
Slemin, J. C. (Bohemians), 1909 v W (1)
Sloan, A. S. (London Caledonians), 1925 v W (1)
Sloan, D. (Oxford U), 1969 v Is; 1971 v Sp (2)
Sloan, H. A. de B. (Bohemians), 1903 v E; 1904 v S; 1905 v E; 1906 v W; 1907 v E, W; 1908 v W; 1909 v S (8)
Sloan, J. W. (Arsenal), 1947 v W (1)
Sloan, T. (Cardiff C), 1926 v S, W, E; 1927 v W, S; 1928 v E, W; 1929 v E; (with Linfield), 1930 v W, S; 1931 v S (11)
Sloan, T. (Manchester U), 1979 v S, W (sub), D (sub) (3)
Small, J. (Clarence), 1887 v E (1)
Small, J. M. (Cliftonville), 1893 v E, S, W (3)
Smith, E. E. (Cardiff C), 1921 v S; 1923 v W, E; 1924 v E (4)
Smith, J. (Distillery), 1901 v S, W (2)
Smyth, R. H. (Dublin University), 1886 v W (1)
Smyth, S. (Wolverhampton W), 1948 v E, S, W; 1949 v S, W; 1950 v E, S, W; (with Stoke C), 1952 v E (9)
Smyth, W. (Distillery), 1949 v E, S; 1954 v S, E (4)
Snape, A. (Airdrie), 1920 v E (1)
Spence, D. W. (Bury), 1975 v Y, E, S, W; 1976 v Se, Is, E, W, S (sub); (with Blackpool), 1977 v Ho (sub), WG (sub), E (sub), S (sub), W (sub), Ic (sub); 1979 v Ei, D (sub), E (sub), Bul (sub), E (sub), S, W, D; 1980 v Ei; (with Southend U), Is (sub), Aus (sub); 1981 v S (sub), Se (sub); 1982 v F (sub) (29)
Spencer, S. (Distillery), 1890 v E, S; 1892 v E, S, W; 1893 v E (6)
Spiller, E. A. (Cliftonville), 1883 v E, W; 1884 v E, W, S (5)
Stanfield, O. M. (Distillery), 1887 v E, S, W; 1888 v E, S, W; 1889 v E, S, W; 1890 v E, S; 1891 v E, S, W; 1892 v E, S, W; 1893 v E, W; 1894 v E, S, W; 1895 v E, S; 1896 v E, S, W; 1897 v E, S, W (30)
Steele, A. (Charlton Ath), 1926 v W, S; (with Fulham), 1929 v W, S (4)
Stevenson, A. E. (Rangers), 1934 v E, S, W; (with Everton), 1935 v E, S; 1936 v S, W; 1937 v E, W; 1938 v E, W; 1939 v E, S, W; 1947 v S, W; 1948 v S (17)
Stewart, A. (Glentoran), 1967 v W; 1968 v S, E; (with Derby Co), 1968 v W; 1969 v Is, T (1 + 1 sub) (7)
Stewart, D. C. (Hull C), 1978 v Bel (1)
Stewart, I. (QPR), 1982 v F (sub); 1983 v A, WG, Alb, T, Alb, S, E, W; 1984 v A, T, WG, S, E, W, Fi; 1985 v R, Fi, Is, E, Sp, T; (with Newcastle U), 1986 v R, E, D, Mor, Alg (sub), Sp (sub), Br; 1987 v E, Is (sub) (31)
Stewart, R. H. (St Columb's Court), 1890 v E, S, W; (with Cliftonville), 1892 v E, S, W; 1893 v E, W; 1894 v E, S, W (11)
Stewart, T. C. (Linfield), 1961 v W (1)
Swan, S. (Linfield), 1899 v S (1)

Taggart, G. P. (Barnsley), 1990 v N, U; 1991 v Y, D, A, Pol, Fa; 1992 v Fa, A, D, S, Li, G; 1993 v Alb, Sp, D, Alb, Ei,

Sp, Li, La; 1994 v La, D, Ei, R, Lie, Co, M; 1995 v P (sub), A, Ei (2), Ca, Ch, La (35)
Taggart, J. (Walsall), 1899 v W (1)
Thompson, F. W. (Cliftonville), 1910 v E, S, W; (with Bradford C), 1911 v E; (with Linfield), v W; 1912 v E, W; 1913 v E, S, W; (with Clyde), 1914 v E, S (12)
Thompson, J. (Belfast Ath), 1889 v S (1)
Thompson, J. (Distillery), 1897 v S (1)
Thunder, P. J. (Bohemians), 1911 v W (1)
Todd, S. J. (Burnley), 1966 v M (sub); 1967 v E; 1968 v W; 1969 v E, S, W; 1970 v S, USSR; (with Sheffield W), 1971 v Cy (2), Sp (sub) (11)
Toner, J. (Arsenal), 1922 v W; 1923 v W; 1924 v W, E; 1925 v E, S; (with St Johnstone), 1927 v E, S (8)
Torrans, R. (Linfield), 1893 v S (1)
Torrans, S. (Linfield), 1889 v S; 1890 v S, W; 1891 v S, W; 1892 v E, S, W; 1893 v E, S; 1894 v E, S, W; 1895 v E; 1896 v E, S, W; 1897 v E, S, W; 1898 v E, S; 1899 v E, W; 1901 v S, W (26)
Trainor, D. (Crusaders), 1967 v W (1)
Tully, C. P. (Celtic), 1949 v E; 1950 v E; 1952 v S; 1953 v E, S, W, F; 1954 v S; 1956 v E; 1959 v Sp (10)
Turner, E. (Cliftonville), 1896 v E, W (2)
Turner, W. (Cliftonville), 1886 v E; 1886 v S; 1888 v S (3)
Twoomey, J. F. (Leeds U), 1938 v W; 1939 v E (2)

Uprichard, W. N. M. C. (Swindon T), 1952 v E, S, W; 1953 v E, S; (with Portsmouth), 1953 v W, F; 1955 v E, S, W; 1956 v E, S, W; 1958 v S, I, Cz; 1959 v S, Sp (18)

Vernon, J. (Belfast C), 1947 v E, S; (with WBA), 1947 v W; 1948 v E, S, W; 1949 v E, S, W; 1950 v E, S; 1951 v E, S, W, F; 1952 v S, E (17)

Waddell, T. M. R. (Cliftonville), 1906 v S (1)
Walker, J. (Doncaster R), 1955 v W (1)
Walker, T. (Bury), 1911 v S (1)
Walsh, D. J. (WBA), 1947 v S, W; 1948 v E, S, W; 1949 v E, S, W; 1950 v W (9)
Walsh, W. (Manchester C), 1948 v E, S, W; 1949 v E, S (5)
Waring, R. (Distillery), 1899 v E (1)
Warren, P. (Shelbourne), 1913 v E, S (2)
Watson, J. (Ulster), 1883 v E, W; 1886 v E, S, W; 1887 v S, W; 1889 v E, W (9)
Watson, P. (Distillery), 1971 v Cy (sub) (1)
Watson, T. (Cardiff C), 1926 v S (1)
Wattle, J. (Distillery), 1899 v E (1)
Webb, C. G. (Brighton), 1909 v S, W; 1911 v S (3)
Weir, E. (Clyde), 1939 v W (1)
Welsh, E. (Carlisle U), 1966 v W, WG, M; 1967 v W (4)
Whiteside, N. (Manchester U), 1982 v Y, Hon, Sp, A, F; 1983 v WG, Alb, T; 1984 v A, T, WG, S, E, W, Fi; 1985 v R, Fi, Is, E, Sp, T; 1986 v R, E, F, D, Mor, Alg, Sp, Br; 1987 v E (2), Is, Y; 1988 v T, Pol, F; (with Everton), 1990 v H, Ei (38)
Whiteside, T. (Distillery), 1891 v E (1)
Whitfield, E. R. (Dublin University), 1886 v W (1)
Williams, J. R. (Ulster), 1886 v E, S (2)
Williams, P. A. (WBA), 1991 v Fa (sub) (1)
Williamson, J. (Cliftonville), 1890 v E; 1892 v S; 1893 v S (3)
Willigham, T. (Burnley), 1933 v W; 1934 v S (2)
Willis, G. (Linfield), 1906 v S, W; 1907 v S; 1912 v S (4)
Wilson, D. J. (Brighton & HA), 1987 v T, Is, E (sub); (with Luton T), 1988 v Y, T, Gr, Pol, F, Ma; 1989 v Ei, H, Sp, Ma, Ch; 1990 v H, Ei, N, U; (with Sheffield W), 1991 v Y, D, A, Fa; 1992 v A (sub), S (24)
Wilson, H. (Linfield), 1925 v W (1)
Wilson, K. J. (Ipswich T), 1987 v Is, E, Y; (with Chelsea), 1988 v Y, T, Gr (sub), Pol (sub), F (sub); 1989 v H (sub), Sp (2), Ma, Ch; 1990 v Ei (sub), N, U; 1991 v Y (2), A, Pol, Fa; 1992 v Fa, A, D, S; (with Notts Co), Li, G; 1993 v Alb, Sp, D, Sp, Li, La; 1994 v La, D, Ei, R, Lie, Co, M; (with Walsall), 1995 v Ei (sub), La (42)
Wilson, M. (Distillery), 1884 v E, S, W (3)
Wilson, R. (Cliftonville), 1888 v S (1)
Wilson, S. J. (Glenavon), 1962 v S; 1964 v S; (with Falkirk), 1964 v E, W, U, Sp; 1965 v E, Sw; (with Dundee), 1966 v W, WG; 1967 v S; 1968 v E (12)
Wilton, J. M. (St Columb's Court), 1888 v E, W; 1889 v S, E; (with Cliftonville), 1890 v E; (with St Columb's Court), 1892 v W; 1893 v S (7)
Worthington, N. (Sheffield W), 1984 v W, Fi (sub); 1985 v Is, Sp (sub); 1986 v T, R (sub), E (sub), D, Alg, Sp; 1987 v E (2), T, Is, Y; 1988 v Y, T, Gr, Pol, F, Ma; 1989 v Ei, H, Sp, Ma; 1990 v H, Ei, U; 1991 v Y, D, A, Fa; 1992 v A, D, S, Li, G; 1993 v Alb, Sp, D, Ei, Sp, Li, La; 1994 v La, D, Ei, Lie, Co, M; (with Leeds U), 1995 v P, A, Ei (2), La, Ca (sub), Ch, La (58)
Wright, J. (Cliftonville), 1906 v E, S, W; 1907 v E, S, W (6)
Wright, T. J. (Newcastle U), 1989 v Ma, Ch; 1990 v H, U; 1992 v Fa, A, S, G; 1993 v Alb, Sp, Alb, Ei, Sp, Li, La; 1994 v La; (with Nottingham F), D, Ei, R, Lie, Co, M (sub) (22)
Young, S. (Linfield), 1907 v E, S; 1908 v E, S; (with Airdrie), 1909 v E; 1912 v S; (with Linfield), 1914 v E, S, W (9)

SCOTLAND

Adams, J. (Hearts), 1889 v Ni; 1892 v W; 1893 v Ni (3)
Agnew, W. B. (Kilmarnock), 1907 v Ni; 1908 v W, Ni (3)
Aird, J. (Burnley), 1954 v N (2), A, U (4)
Aitken, A. (Newcastle U), 1901 v E; 1902 v E; 1903 v E, W; 1904 v E; 1905 v E, W; 1906 v E; (with Middlesbrough), 1907 v E, W; 1908 v E; (with Leicester Fosse), 1910 v E; 1911 v E, Ni (14)
Aitken, G. G. (East Fife), 1949 v E, F; 1950 v W, Ni, Sw; (with Sunderland), 1953 v W, Ni; 1954 v E (8)
Aitken, R. (Dumbarton), 1886 v E; 1888 v Ni (2)
Aitken, R. (Celtic), 1980 v Pe (sub), Bel, W (sub), E, Pol; 1983 v Bel, Ca (1 + 1 sub); 1984 v Bel (sub), Ni, W (sub); 1985 v E, Ic; 1986 v W, EG, Aus (2), Is, R, E, D, WG, U; 1987 v Bul, Ei (2), L, Bel, E, Br; 1988 v H, Bel, Bul, L, S.Ar, Ma, Sp, Co, E; 1989 v N, Y, I, Cy, F, Cy, E, Ch; 1990 v Y, F, N; (with Newcastle U), Arg (sub), Pol, Ma, Cr, Se, Br; (with St Mirren), 1992 v R (sub) (57)
Aitkenhead, W. A. C. (Blackburn R), 1912 v Ni (1)
Albiston, A. (Manchester U), 1982 v Ni; 1984 v U, Bel, EG, W, E; 1985 v Y, Ic, Sp (2), W; 1986 v EG, Ho, U (14)
Alexander, D. (East Stirlingshire), 1894 v W, Ni (2)
Allan, D. S. (Queen's Park), 1885 v E, W; 1886 v W (3)
Allan, G. (Liverpool), 1897 v E (1)
Allan, H. (Hearts), 1902 v W (1)
Allan, J. (Queen's Park), 1887 v E, W (2)
Allan, T. (Dundee), 1974 v WG, N (2)
Ancell, R. F. D. (Newcastle U), 1937 v W, Ni (2)
Anderson, A. (Hearts), 1933 v E; 1934 v A, E, W, Ni; 1935 v E, W, Ni; 1936 v E, W, Ni; 1937 v G, E, W, Ni, A; 1938 v E, W, Ni, Cz, Ho; 1939 v W, H (23)
Anderson, F. (Clydesdale), 1874 v E (1)
Anderson, G. (Kilmarnock), 1901 v Ni (1)
Anderson, H. A. (Raith R), 1914 v W (1)
Anderson, J. (Leicester C), 1954 v Fi (1)

Anderson, K. (Queen's Park), 1896 v Ni; 1898 v E, Ni (3)
Anderson, W. (Queen's Park), 1882 v E; 1883 v E, W; 1884 v E; 1885 v E, W (6)
Andrews, P. (Eastern), 1875 v E (1)
Archibald, A. (Rangers), 1921 v W; 1922 v W, E; 1923 v Ni; 1924 v E, W; 1931 v E; 1932 v E (8)
Archibald, S. (Aberdeen), 1980 v P (sub); (with Tottenham H), Ni, Pol, H; 1981 v Se (sub), Is, Ni, Is, Ni, E; 1982 v Ni, P, Sp (sub), Ho, Nz (sub), Br, USSR; 1983 v EG, Sw (sub), Bel; 1984 v EG, E, F; (with Barcelona), 1985 v Sp, E, Ic (sub); 1986 v WG (27)
Armstrong, M. W. (Aberdeen), 1936 v W, Ni; 1937 v G (3)
Arnott, W. (Queen's Park), 1883 v W; 1884 v E, Ni; 1885 v E, W; 1886 v E; 1887 v E, W; 1888 v E; 1889 v E; 1890 v E; 1891 v E; 1892 v E; 1893 v E (14)
Auld, J. R. (Third Lanark), 1887 v E, W; 1889 v W (3)
Auld, R. (Celtic), 1959 v H, P; 1960 v W (3)

Baird, A. (Queen's Park), 1892 v Ni; 1894 v W (2)
Baird, D. (Hearts), 1890 v Ni; 1891 v E; 1892 v W (3)
Baird, H. (Airdrieonians), 1956 v A (1)
Baird, J. C. (Vale of Leven), 1876 v E; 1878 v W; 1880 v E (3)
Baird, S. (Rangers), 1957 v Y, Sp (2), Sw, WG; 1958 v F, Ni (7)
Baird, W. U. (St Bernard), 1897 v Ni (1)
Bannon, E. (Dundee U), 1980 v Bel; 1983 v Ni, W, E, Ca; 1984 v EG; 1986 v Is, R, E, D (sub), WG (11)
Barbour, A. (Renton), 1885 v Ni (1)
Barker, J. B. (Rangers), 1893 v W; 1894 v W (2)
Barrett, F. (Dundee), 1894 v Ni; 1895 v W (2)
Battles, B. (Celtic), 1901 v E, W, Ni (3)
Battles, B. jun. (Hearts), 1931 v W (1)
Bauld, W. (Hearts), 1950 v E, Sw, P (3)
Baxter, J. C. (Rangers), 1961 v Ni, Ei (2), Cz; 1962 v Ni, W, E, Cz (2), U; 1963 v W, Ni, E, A, N, Ei, Sp; 1964 v W, E, N, WG; 1965 v W, Ni, Fi; (with Sunderland), 1966 v P, Br, Ni, W, E, I; 1967 v W, E, USSR; 1968 v W (34)
Baxter, R. D. (Middlesbrough), 1939 v E, W, H (3)
Beattie, A. (Preston NE), 1937 v E, A, Cz; 1938 v E; 1939 v W, Ni, H (7)
Beattie, R. (Preston NE), 1939 v W (1)
Begbie, I. (Hearts), 1890 v Ni; 1891 v E; 1892 v W; 1894 v E (4)
Bell, A. (Manchester U), 1912 v Ni (1)
Bell, J. (Dumbarton), 1890 v Ni; 1892 v E; (with Everton), 1896 v E; 1897 v E; 1898 v E; (with Celtic), 1899 v E, W, Ni; 1900 v E, W (10)
Bell, M. (Hearts), 1901 v W (1)
Bell, W. J. (Leeds U), 1966 v P, Br (2)
Bennett, A. (Celtic), 1904 v W; 1907 v Ni; 1908 v W; (with Rangers), 1909 v W, Ni, E; 1910 v E, W; 1911 v E, W; 1913 v Ni (11)
Bennie, R. (Airdrieonians), 1925 v W, Ni; 1926 v Ni (3)
Bernard, P. R. J. (Oldham Ath), 1995 v J (sub), Ec (2)
Berry, D. (Queen's Park), 1894 v W; 1899 v W, Ni (3)
Berry, W. H. (Queen's Park), 1888 v E; 1889 v E; 1890 v E; 1891 v E (4)
Bett, J. (Rangers), 1982 v Ho; 1983 v Bel; (with Lokeren), 1984 v Bel, W, E, F; 1985 v Y, Ic, Sp (2), W, E, Ic; (with Aberdeen), 1986 v W, Is, Ho; 1987 v Bel; 1988 v H (sub); 1989 v Y; 1990 v F (sub), N, Arg, Eg, Ma, Cr (25)
Beveridge, W. W. (Glasgow University), 1879 v E, W; 1880 v W (3)
Black, A. (Hearts), 1938 v Cz, Ho; 1939 v H (3)
Black, D. (Hurlford), 1889 v Ni (1)
Black, E. (Metz), 1988 v H (sub), L (sub) (2)
Black, I. H. (Southampton), 1948 v E (1)
Blackburn, J. E. (Royal Engineers), 1873 v E (1)
Blacklaw, A. S. (Burnley), 1963 v N, Sp; 1966 v I (3)
Blackley, J. (Hibernian), 1974 v Cz, E, Bel, Z; 1976 v Sw; 1977 v W, Se (7)
Blair, D. (Clyde), 1929 v W, Ni; 1931 v E, A, I; 1932 v W, Ni; (with Aston Villa), 1933 v W (8)
Blair, J. (Sheffield W), 1920 v E, Ni; (with Cardiff C), 1921 v E; 1922 v E; 1923 v E, W, Ni; 1924 v W (8)
Blair, J. (Motherwell), 1934 v W (1)
Blair, J. A. (Blackpool), 1947 v W (1)
Blair, W. (Third Lanark), 1896 v W (1)
Blessington, J. (Celtic), 1894 v E, Ni; 1896 v E, Ni (4)
Blyth, J. A. (Coventry C), 1978 v Bul, W (2)
Bone, J. (Norwich C), 1972 v Y (sub); 1973 v D (2)
Booth, S. (Aberdeen), 1993 v G (sub), Es (2 subs); 1994 v Sw, Ma (sub); 1995 v Fa, Ru (7)
Bowie, J. (Rangers), 1920 v E, Ni (2)
Bowie, W. (Linthouse), 1891 v Ni (1)
Bowman, D. (Dundee U), 1992 v Fi, US (sub); 1993 v G, Es; 1994 v Sw, I (6)
Bowman, G. A. (Montrose), 1892 v Ni (1)
Boyd, J. M. (Newcastle U), 1934 v Ni (1)
Boyd, R. (Mossend Swifts), 1889 v Ni; 1891 v W (2)
Boyd, T. (Motherwell), 1991 v R (sub), Sw, Bul, USSR; (with Chelsea), 1992 v Sw, R; (with Celtic), Fi, Ca, N, C; 1993 v Sw, P, I, Ma, G, Es (2); 1994 v I, Ma (sub), Ho (sub), A; 1995 v Fi, Fa, Ru, Gr, Ru, Sm (27)
Boyd, W. G. (Clyde), 1931 v I, Sw (2)
Brackenbridge, T. (Hearts), 1888 v Ni (1)
Bradshaw, T. (Bury), 1928 v E (1)
Brand, R. (Rangers), 1961 v Ni, Cz, Ei (2); 1962 v Ni, W, Cz, U (8)
Branden, T. (Blackburn R), 1896 v E (1)
Brazil, A. (Ipswich T), 1980 v Pol (sub), H; 1982 v Sp, Ho (sub), Ni, W, E, Nz, USSR (sub); 1983 v EG, Sw (with Tottenham H), W, E (sub) (13)
Bremner, D. (Hibernian), 1976 v Sw (sub) (1)
Bremner, W. J. (Leeds U), 1965 v Sp; 1966 v E, Pol, P, Br, I (2); 1967 v W, Ni, E; 1968 v W, E; 1969 v W, E, Ni, D, A, WG, Cy (2); 1970 v Ei, WG, A; 1971 v W, E; 1972 v P, Bel, Ho, Ni, W, E, Y, Cz, Br; 1973 v D (2), E (2), Ni (sub), Sw, Br; 1974 v Cz, WG, Ni, W, E, Bel, N, Z, Br, Y; 1975 v Sp (2); 1976 v D (54)
Brennan, F. (Newcastle U), 1947 v W, Ni; 1953 v W, Ni, E; 1954 v Ni, E (7)
Breslin, B. (Hibernian), 1897 v W (1)
Brewster, G. (Everton), 1921 v E (1)
Brogan, J. (Celtic), 1971 v W, Ni, P, E (4)
Brown, A. (Middlesbrough), 1904 v E (1)
Brown, A. (St Mirren), 1890 v W; 1891 v W (2)
Brown, A. D. (East Fife), 1950 v Sw, P, F; (with Blackpool), 1952 v USA, D, Se; 1953 v W; 1954 v W, E, N (2), Fi, A, U (14)
Brown, G. C. P. (Rangers), 1931 v W; 1932 v E, W, Ni; 1933 v E; 1934 v A; 1935 v E, W; 1936 v E, W; 1937 v G, E, W, Ni, Cz; 1938 v E, W, Cz, Ho (19)
Brown, H. (Partick T), 1947 v W, Bel, L (3)
Brown, J. (Cambuslang), 1890 v W (1)
Brown, J. B. (Clyde), 1939 v W (1)
Brown, J. G. (Sheffield U), 1975 v R (1)
Brown, R. (Dumbarton), 1884 v W, Ni (2)
Brown, R. (Rangers), 1947 v Ni; 1949 v Ni; 1952 v E (3)
Brown, R. jun. (Dumbarton), 1885 v W (1)
Brown, W. D. F. (Dundee), 1958 v F; 1959 v E, W, Ni; (with Tottenham H), 1960 v W, Ni, Pol, A, H, T; 1962 v Ni, W, E, Cz; 1963 v W, Ni, E, A; 1964 v Ni, W, N; 1965 v E, Fi, Pol, Sp; 1966 v Ni, Pol, I (28)
Browning, J. (Celtic), 1914 v W (1)
Brownlie, J. (Hibernian), 1971 v USSR; 1972 v Pe, Ni, E; 1973 v D (2); 1976 v R (7)
Brownlie, J. (Third Lanark), 1909 v E, Ni; 1910 v E, W, Ni; 1911 v W, Ni; 1912 v W, Ni, E; 1913 v W, Ni, E; 1914 v W, Ni, E (16)
Bruce, D. (Vale of Leven), 1890 v W (1)
Bruce, R. F. (Middlesbrough), 1934 v A (1)

Buchan, M. M. (Aberdeen), 1972 v P (sub), Bel; (with Manchester U), W, Y, Cz, Br; 1973 v D (2), E; 1974 v WG, Ni, W, N, Br, Y; 1975 v EG, Sp, P; 1976 v D, R; 1977 v Fi, Cz, Ch, Arg, Br; 1978 v EG, W (sub), Ni, Pe, Ir, Ho; 1979 v A, N, P (34)
Buchanan, J. (Cambuslang), 1889 v Ni (1)
Buchanan, J. (Rangers), 1929 v E; 1930 v E (2)
Buchanan, P. S. (Chelsea), 1938 v Cz (1)
Buchanan, R. (Abercorn), 1891 v W (1)
Buckley, P. (Aberdeen), 1954 v N; 1955 v W, Ni (3)
Buick, A. (Hearts), 1902 v W, Ni (2)
Burley, C. W. (Chelsea), 1995 v J, Ec, Fa (3)
Burley, G. (Ipswich T), 1979 v W, Ni, E, Arg, N; 1980 v P, Ni, E (sub), Pol; 1982 v W (sub), E (11)
Burns, F. (Manchester U), 1970 v A (1)
Burns, K. (Birmingham C), 1974 v WG; 1975 v EG (sub), Sp (2); 1977 v Cz (sub), W, Se, W (sub); (with Nottingham F), 1978 v Ni (sub), W, E, Pe, Ir; 1979 v N; 1980 v Pe, A, Bel; 1981 v Is, Ni, W (20)
Burns, T. (Celtic), 1981 v Ni; 1982 v Ho (sub), W; 1983 v Bel (sub), Ni, Ca (1 + 1 sub); 1988 v E (sub) (8)
Busby, M. W. (Manchester C), 1934 v W (1)

Cairns, T. (Rangers), 1920 v W; 1922 v E; 1923 v E, W; 1924 v Ni; 1925 v W, E, Ni (8)
Calderhead, D. (Queen of the South), 1889 v Ni (1)
Calderwood, C. (Tottenham H), 1995 v Ru, Sm, J, Ec, Fa (5)
Calderwood, R. (Cartvale), 1885 v Ni, E, W (3)
Caldow, E. (Rangers), 1957 v Sp (2), Sw, WG, E; 1958 v Ni, W, Sw, Par, H, Pol, Y, F; 1959 v E, W, Ni, WG, Ho, P; 1960 v E, W, Ni, A, H, T; 1961 v E, W, Ni, Ei (2), Cz; 1962 v Ni, W, E, Cz (2), U; 1963 v W, Ni, E (40)
Callaghan, P. (Hibernian), 1900 v Ni (1)
Callaghan, W. (Dunfermline Ath), 1970 v Ei (sub), W (2)
Cameron, J. (Rangers), 1886 v Ni (1)
Cameron, J. (Queen's Park), 1896 v Ni (1)
Cameron, J. (St Mirren), 1904 v Ni; (with Chelsea), 1909 v E (2)
Campbell, C. (Queen's Park), 1874 v E; 1876 v W; 1877 v E, W; 1878 v E; 1879 v E; 1880 v E; 1881 v E; 1882 v E, W; 1884 v E; 1885 v E; 1886 v E (13)
Campbell, H. (Renton), 1889 v W (1)
Campbell, Jas (Sheffield W), 1913 v W (1)
Campbell, J. (South Western), 1880 v W (1)
Campbell, J. (Kilmarnock), 1891 v Ni; 1892 v W (2)
Campbell, John (Celtic), 1893 v E, Ni; 1898 v E, Ni; 1900 v E, Ni; 1901 v E, W, Ni; 1902 v W, Ni; 1903 v W (12)
Campbell, John (Rangers), 1899 v E, W, Ni; 1901 v Ni (4)
Campbell, K. (Liverpool), 1920 v E, W, Ni; (with Partick T), 1921 v W, Ni; 1922 v W, Ni, E (8)
Campbell, P. (Rangers), 1878 v W; 1879 v W (2)
Campbell, P. (Morton), 1898 v W (1)
Campbell, R. (Falkirk), 1947 v Bel, L; (with Chelsea), 1950 v Sw, P, F (5)
Campbell, W. (Morton), 1947 v Ni; 1948 v E, Bel, Sw, F (5)
Carabine, J. (Third Lanark), 1938 v Ho; 1939 v E, Ni (3)
Carr, W. M. (Coventry C), 1970 v Ni, W, E; 1971 v D; 1972 v Pe; 1973 v D (sub) (6)
Cassidy, J. (Celtic), 1921 v W, Ni; 1923 v Ni; 1924 v W (4)
Chalmers, S. (Celtic), 1965 v W, Fi; 1966 v P (sub), Br; 1967 v Ni (5)
Chalmers, W. (Rangers), 1885 v Ni (1)
Chalmers, W. S. (Queen's Park), 1929 v Ni (1)
Chambers, T. (Hearts), 1894 v W (1)
Chaplin, G. D. (Dundee), 1908 v W (1)
Cheyne, A. G. (Aberdeen), 1929 v E, N, G, Ho; 1930 v F (5)
Christie, A. J. (Queen's Park), 1898 v W; 1899 v E, Ni (3)
Christie, R. M. (Queen's Park), 1884 v E (1)
Clark, J. (Celtic), 1966 v Br; 1967 v W, Ni, USSR (4)
Clark, R. B. (Aberdeen), 1968 v W, Ho; 1970 v Ni; 1971 v W, Ni, E, D, P, USSR; 1972 v Bel, Ni, W, E, Cz, Br; 1973 v D, E (17)
Clarke, S. (Chelsea), 1988 v H, Bel, Bul, S.Ar, Ma; 1994 v Ho (6)
Cleland, J. (Royal Albert), 1891 v Ni (1)
Clements, R. (Leith Ath), 1891 v Ni (1)
Clunas, W. L. (Sunderland), 1924 v E; 1926 v W (2)
Collier, W. (Raith R), 1922 v W (1)
Collins, J. (Hibernian), 1988 v S.Ar; 1990 v EG, Pol (sub), Ma (sub); (with Celtic), 1991 v Sw (sub), Bul (sub); 1992 v Ni (sub), Fi; 1993 v P, Ma, G, P, Es (2); 1994 v Sw, Ho (sub), A, Ho; 1995 v Fi, Fa, Ru, Gr, Ru, Sm, Fa (25)
Collins, R. Y. (Celtic), 1951 v W, Ni, A; 1955 v Y, A, H; 1956 v Ni, W; 1957 v E, W, Sp (2), Sw, WG; 1958 v Ni, W, Sw, H, Pol, Y, F, Par; (with Everton), 1959 v E, W, Ni, WG, Ho, P; (with Leeds U), 1965 v E, Pol, Sp (31)
Collins, T. (Hearts), 1909 v W (1)
Colman, D. (Aberdeen), 1911 v E, W, Ni; 1913 v Ni (4)
Colquhoun, E. P. (Sheffield U), 1972 v P, Ho, Pe, Y, Cz, Br; 1973 v D (2), E (9)
Colquhoun, J. (Hearts), 1988 v S.Ar (sub) (1)
Combe, J. R. (Hibernian), 1948 v E, Bel, Sw (3)
Conn, A. (Hearts), 1956 v A (1)
Conn, A. (Tottenham H), 1975 v Ni (sub), E (2)
Connachan, E. D. (Dunfermline Ath), 1962 v Cz, U (2)
Connelly, G. (Celtic), 1974 v Cz, WG (2)
Connolly, J. (Everton), 1973 v Sw (1)
Connor, J. (Airdrieonians), 1886 v Ni (1)
Connor, J. (Sunderland), 1930 v F; 1932 v Ni; 1934 v E; 1935 v Ni (4)
Connor, R. (Dundee), 1986 v Ho; (with Aberdeen), 1988 v S.Ar (sub); 1989 v E; 1991 v R (4)
Cook, W. L. (Bolton W), 1934 v E; 1935 v W, Ni (3)
Cooke, C. (Dundee), 1966 v W, I; (with Chelsea), P, Br; 1968 v E, Ho; 1969 v W, Ni, A, WG (sub), Cy (2); 1970 v A; 1971 v Bel; 1975 v Sp, P (16)
Cooper, D. (Rangers), 1980 v Pe, A (sub); 1984 v W, E; 1985 v Y, Ic, Sp (2), W; 1986 v W (sub), EG, Aus (2), Ho, WG (sub), U (sub); 1987 v Bul, L, Ei, Br; (with Motherwell), 1990 v N, Eg (22)
Cormack, P. B. (Hibernian), 1966 v Br; 1969 v D (sub); 1970 v Ei, WG; (with Nottingham F), 1971 v D (sub), W, P, E; 1972 v Ho (sub) (9)
Cowan, J. (Aston Villa), 1896 v E; 1897 v E; 1898 v E (3)
Cowan, J. (Morton), 1948 v Bel, Sw; F; 1949 v E, W, F; 1950 v E, W, Ni, Sw, P, F; 1951 v E, W, Ni, A (2), D, F, Bel; 1952 v Ni, W, USA, D, Se (25)
Cowan, W. D. (Newcastle U), 1924 v E (1)
Cowie, D. (Dundee), 1953 v E, Se; 1954 v Ni, W, Fi, N, A, U; 1955 v W, Ni, A, H; 1956 v W, A; 1957 v Ni, W; 1958 v H, Pol, Y, Par (20)
Cox, C. J. (Hearts), 1948 v F (1)
Cox, S. (Rangers), 1949 v E, F; 1950 v E, F, W, Ni, Sw, P; 1951 v E, D, F, Bel, A; 1952 v Ni, W, USA, D, Se; 1953 v W, Ni, E; 1954 v W, Ni, E (24)
Craig, A. (Motherwell), 1929 v N, Ho; 1932 v E (3)
Craig, J. (Celtic), 1977 v Se (sub) (1)
Craig, J. P. (Celtic), 1968 v W (1)
Craig, T. (Rangers), 1927 v Ni; 1928 v Ni; 1929 v N, G, Ho; 1930 v Ni, E, W (8)
Craig, T. B. (Newcastle U), 1976 v Sw (1)
Crapnell, J. (Airdrieonians), 1929 v E, N, G; 1930 v F; 1931 v Ni, Sw; 1932 v E, F; 1933 v Ni (9)
Crawford, D. (St Mirren), 1894 v W, Ni; 1900 v W (3)
Crawford, J. (Queen's Park), 1932 v F, Ni; 1933 v E, W, Ni (5)
Crawford, S. (Raith R), 1995 v Ec (sub) (1)
Crerand, P. T. (Celtic), 1961 v Ei (2), Cz; 1962 v Ni, W, E, Cz (2), U; 1963 v W, Ni; (with Manchester U), 1964 v Ni; 1965 v E, Pol, Fi; 1966 v Pol (16)

Cringan, W. (Celtic), 1920 v W; 1922 v E, Ni; 1923 v W, E (5)
Crosbie, J. A. (Ayr U), 1920 v W; (with Birmingham), 1922 v E (2)
Croal, J. A. (Falkirk), 1913 v Ni; 1914 v E, W (3)
Cropley, A. J. (Hibernian), 1972 v P, Bel (2)
Cross, J. H. (Third Lanark), 1903 v Ni (1)
Cruickshank, J. (Hearts), 1964 v WG; 1970 v W, E; 1971 v D, Bel; 1976 v R (6)
Crum, J. (Celtic), 1936 v E; 1939 v Ni (2)
Cullen, M. J. (Luton T), 1956 v A (1)
Cumming, D. S. (Middlesbrough), 1938 v E (1)
Cumming, J. (Hearts), 1955 v E, H, P, Y; 1960 v E, Pol, A, H, T (9)
Cummings, G. (Partick T), 1935 v E; 1936 v W, Ni; (with Aston Villa), E; 1937 v G; 1938 v W, Ni, Cz; 1939 v E (9)
Cunningham, A. N. (Rangers), 1920 v Ni; 1921 v W, E; 1922 v Ni; 1923 v E, W; 1924 v E, Ni; 1926 v E, Ni; 1927 v E, W (12)
Cunningham, W. C. (Preston NE), 1954 v N (2), U, Fi, A; 1955 v W, E, H (8)
Curran, H. P. (Wolverhampton W), 1970 v A; 1971 v Ni, E, D, USSR (sub) (5)

Dalglish, K. (Celtic), 1972 v Bel (sub), Ho; 1973 v D (1 + 1 sub), E (2), W, Ni, Sw, Br; 1974 v Cz (2), WG (2), Ni, W, E, Bel, N (sub), Z, Br, Y; 1975 v EG, Sp (sub + 1), Se, P, W, Ni, E, R; 1976 v D (2), R, Sw, Ni, E; 1977 v Fi, Cz, W (2), Se, Ni, E, Ch, Arg, Br; (with Liverpool), 1978 v EG, Cz, W, Bul, Ni (sub), W, E, Pe, Ir, Ho; 1979 v A, N, P, W, Ni, E, Arg, N; 1980 v Pe, A, Bel (2), P, Ni, W, E, Pol, H; 1981 v Se, P, Is; 1982 v Se, Ni, P (sub), Sp, Ho, Ni, W, E, Nz, Br (sub); 1983 v Bel, Sw; 1984 v U, Bel, EG; 1985 v Y, Ic, Sp, W; 1986 v EG, Aus, R; 1987 v Bul (sub), L (102)
Davidson, D. (Queen's Park), 1878 v W; 1879 v W; 1880 v W; 1881 v E, W (5)
Davidson, J. A. (Partick T), 1954 v N (2), A, U; 1955 v W, Ni, E, H (8)
Davidson, S. (Middlesbrough), 1921 v E (1)
Dawson, A. (Rangers), 1980 v Pol (sub), H; 1983 v Ni, Ca (2) (5)
Dawson, J. (Rangers), 1935 v Ni; 1936 v E; 1937 v G, E, W, Ni, A, Cz; 1938 v W, Ho, Ni; 1939 v E, Ni, H (14)
Deans, J. (Celtic), 1975 v EG, Sp (2)
Delaney, J. (Celtic), 1936 v W, Ni; 1937 v G, E, A, Cz; 1938 v Ni; 1939 v W, Ni; (with Manchester U), 1947 v E; 1948 v E, W, Ni (13)
Devine, A. (Falkirk), 1910 v W (1)
Dewar, G. (Dumbarton), 1888 v Ni; 1889 v E (2)
Dewar, N. (Third Lanark), 1932 v E, F; 1933 v W (3)
Dick, J. (West Ham U), 1959 v E (1)
Dickie, M. (Rangers), 1897 v Ni; 1899 v Ni; 1900 v W (3)
Dickson, W. (Dumbarton), 1888 v Ni (1)
Dickson, W. (Kilmarnock), 1970 v Ni, W, E; 1971 v D, USSR (5)
Divers, J. (Celtic), 1895 v W (1)
Divers, J. (Celtic), 1939 v Ni (1)
Docherty, T. H, (Preston NE), 1952 v W; 1953 v E, Se; 1954 v N (2), A, U; 1955 v W, E, H (2), A; 1957 v E, Y, Sp (2), Sw, WG; 1958 v Ni, W, E, Sw; (with Arsenal), 1959 v W, E, Ni (25)
Dodds, D. (Dundee U), 1984 v U (sub), Ni (2)
Dodds, J. (Celtic), 1914 v E, W, Ni (3)
Doig, J. E. (Arbroath), 1887 v Ni; 1889 v Ni; (with Sunderland), 1896 v E; 1899 v E; 1903 v E (5)
Donachie, W. (Manchester C), 1972 v Pe, Ni, E, Y, Cz, Br; 1973 v D, E, W, Ni; 1974 v Ni; 1976 v R, Ni, W, E; 1977 v Fi, Cz, W (2), Se, Ni, E, Ch, Arg, Br; 1978 v EG, W, Bul, W, E, Ir, Ho; 1979 v A, N, P (sub) (35)
Donaldson, A. (Bolton W), 1914 v E, Ni, W; 1920 v E, Ni; 1922 v Ni (6)
Donnachie, J. (Oldham Ath), 1913 v E; 1914 v E, Ni (3)
Dougall, C. (Birmingham C), 1947 v W (1)
Dougall, J. (Preston NE), 1939 v E (1)
Dougan, R. (Hearts), 1950 v Sw (1)
Douglas, A. (Chelsea), 1911 v Ni (1)
Douglas, J. (Renfrew), 1880 v W (1)
Dowds, P. (Celtic), 1892 v Ni (1)
Downie, R. (Third Lanark), 1892 v W (1)
Doyle, D. (Celtic), 1892 v E; 1893 v W; 1894 v E; 1895 v E, Ni; 1897 v E; 1898 v E, Ni (8)
Doyle, J. (Ayr U), 1976 v R (1)
Drummond, J. (Falkirk), 1892 v Ni; (with Rangers), 1894 v Ni; 1895 v Ni, E; 1896 v E, Ni; 1897 v Ni; 1898 v E; 1900 v E; 1901 v E; 1902 v E, W, Ni; 1903 v Ni (14)
Dunbar, M. (Cartvale), 1886 v Ni (1)
Duncan, A. (Hibernian), 1975 v P (sub), W, Ni, E, R; 1976 v D (sub) (6)
Duncan, D. (Derby Co), 1933 v E, W; 1934 v A, W; 1935 v E, W; 1936 v E, W, Ni; 1937 v G, E, W, Ni; 1938 v W (14)
Duncan, D. M. (East Fife), 1948 v Bel, Sw, F (3)
Duncan, J. (Alexandra Ath), 1878 v W; 1882 v W (2)
Duncan, J. (Leicester C), 1926 v W (1)
Duncanson, J. (Rangers), 1947 v Ni (1)
Dunlop, J. (St Mirren), 1890 v W (1)
Dunlop, W. (Liverpool), 1906 v E (1)
Dunn, J. (Hibernian), 1925 v W, Ni; 1927 v Ni; 1928 v Ni, E; (with Everton), 1929 v W (6)
Durie, G. S. (Chelsea), 1988 v Bul (sub); 1989 v I (sub), Cy; 1990 v Y, EG, Eg, Se; 1991 v Sw (sub), Bul (2), USSR (sub), Sm; (with Tottenham H), 1992 v Sw, R, Sm, Ni (sub), Fi, Ca, N (sub), Ho, G; 1993 v Sw, I; 1994 v Sw, I; (with Rangers), Ho (2) (27)
Durrant, I. (Rangers), 1988 v H, Bel, Ma, Sp; 1989 v N (sub); 1993 v Sw (sub), P (sub), I, P (sub); 1994 v I (sub), Ma (11)
Dykes, J. (Hearts), 1938 v Ho; 1939 v Ni (2)

Easson, J. F. (Portsmouth), 1931 v A, Sw; 1934 v W (3)
Ellis, J. (Mossend Swifts), 1892 v Ni (1)
Evans, A. (Aston Villa), 1982 v Ho, Ni, E, Nz (4)
Evans, R. (Celtic), 1949 v E, W, Ni, F; 1950 v W, Ni, Sw, P; 1951 v E, A; 1952 v Ni; 1953 v Se; 1954 v Ni, W, E, N, Fi; 1955 v Ni, P, Y, A, H; 1956 v E, Ni, W, A; 1957 v WG, Sp; 1958 v Ni, W, E, Sw, H, Pol, Y, Par, F; 1959 v E, WG, Ho, P; 1960 v E, Ni, W, Pol; (with Chelsea), 1960 v A, H, T (48)
Ewart, J. (Bradford C), 1921 v E (1)
Ewing, T. (Partick T), 1958 v W, E (2)

Farm, G. N. (Blackpool), 1953 v W, Ni, E, Se; 1954 v Ni, W, E; 1959 v WG, Ho, P (10)
Ferguson, D. (Rangers), 1988 v Ma, Co (sub) (2)
Ferguson, D. (Dundee U), 1992 v US (sub), Ca, Ho (sub); 1993 v G; (with Rangers) 1995 v Gr (5)
Ferguson, I. (Rangers), 1989 v I, Cy (sub), F; 1993 v Ma (sub), Es; 1994 v Ma, A (sub), Ho (sub) (8)
Ferguson, J. (Vale of Leven), 1874 v E; 1876 v E, W; 1877 v E, W; 1878 v W (6)
Ferguson, R. (Kilmarnock), 1966 v W, E, Ho, P, Br; 1967 v W, Ni (7)
Fernie, W. (Celtic), 1954 v Fi, A, U; 1955 v W, Ni; 1957 v E, Ni, W, Y; 1958 v W, Sw, Par (12)
Findlay, R. (Kilmarnock), 1898 v W (1)
Fitchie, T. T. (Woolwich Arsenal), 1905 v W; 1906 v W, Ni; (with Queen's Park), 1907 v W (4)
Flavell, R. (Airdrieonians), 1947 v Bel, L (2)
Fleck, R. (Norwich C), 1990 v Arg, Se, Br (sub); 1991 v USSR (4)
Fleming, C. (East Fife), 1954 v Ni (1)

Fleming, J. W. (Rangers), 1929 v G, Ho; 1930 v E (3)
Fleming, R. (Morton), 1886 v Ni (1)
Forbes, A. R. (Sheffield U), 1947 v Bel, L, E; 1948 v W, Ni; (with Arsenal), 1950 v E, P, F; 1951 v W, Ni, A; 1952 v W, D, Se (14)
Forbes, J. (Vale of Leven), 1884 v E, W, Ni; 1887 v W, E (5)
Ford, D. (Hearts), 1974 v Cz (sub), WG (sub), W (3)
Forrest, J. (Rangers), 1966 v W, I; (with Aberdeen), 1971 v Bel (sub), D, USSR (5)
Forrest, J. (Motherwell), 1958 v E (1)
Forsyth, A. (Partick T), 1972 v Y, Cz, Br; 1973 v D; (with Manchester U), E; 1975 v Sp, Ni (sub), R, EG; 1976 v D (10)
Forsyth, C. (Kilmarnock), 1964 v E; 1965 v W, Ni, Fi (4)
Forsyth, T. (Motherwell), 1971 v D; (with Rangers), 1974 v Cz; 1976 v Sw, Ni, W, E; 1977 v Fi, Se, W, Ni, E, Ch, Arg, Br; 1978 v Cz, W, Ni, W (sub), E, Pe, Ir (sub), Ho (22)
Foyers, R. (St Bernards), 1893 v W; 1894 v W (2)
Fraser, D. M. (WBA), 1968 v Ho; 1969 v Cy (2)
Fraser, J. (Moffat), 1891 v Ni (1)
Fraser, M. J. E. (Queen's Park), 1880 v W; 1882 v W, E; 1883 v W, E (5)
Fraser, J. (Dundee), 1907 v Ni (1)
Fraser, W. (Sunderland), 1955 v W, Ni (2)
Fulton, W. (Abercorn), 1884 v Ni (1)
Fyfe, J. H. (Third Lanark), 1895 v W (1)

Gabriel, J. (Everton), 1961 v W; 1964 v N (sub) (2)
Gallacher, H. K. (Airdrieonians), 1924 v Ni; 1925 v E, W, Ni; 1926 v W; (with Newcastle U), 1926 v E, Ni; 1927 v E, W, Ni; 1928 v E, W; 1929 v E, W, Ni; 1930 v W, Ni, F; (with Chelsea), 1934 v E; (with Derby Co), 1935 v E (20)
Gallacher, K. W. (Dundee U), 1988 v Co, E (sub); 1989 v N, I; (with Coventry C), 1991 v Sm; 1992 v R (sub), Sm (sub), Ni (sub), N (sub), Ho (sub), G (sub), C; 1993 v Sw (sub), P; (with Blackburn R), P, Es (2); 1994 v I, Ma (19)
Gallacher, P. (Sunderland), 1935 v Ni (1)
Galloway, M. (Celtic), 1992 v R (1)
Galt, J. H. (Rangers), 1908 v W, Ni (2)
Gardiner, I. (Motherwell), 1958 v W (1)
Gardner, D. R. (Third Lanark), 1897 v W (1)
Gardner, R. (Queen's Park), 1872 v E; 1873 v E; (with Clydesdale), 1874 v E; 1875 v E; 1878 v E (5)
Gemmell, T. (St Mirren), 1955 v P, Y (2)
Gemmell, T. (Celtic), 1966 v E; 1967 v W, Ni, E, USSR; 1968 v Ni, E; 1969 v W, Ni, E, D, A, WG, Cy; 1970 v E, Ei, WG; 1971 v Bel (18)
Gemmill, A. (Derby Co), 1971 v Bel; 1972 v P, Ho, Pe, Ni, W, E; 1976 v D, R, Ni, W, E; 1977 v Fi, Cz, W (2), Ni (sub), E (sub), Ch (sub), Arg, Br; 1978 v EG (sub); (with Nottingham F), Bul, Ni, W, E (sub), Pe (sub), Ir, Ho; 1979 v A, N, P, N; (with Birmingham C), 1980 v A, P, Ni, W, E, H; 1981 v Se, P, Is, Ni (43)
Gemmill, S. (Nottingham F), 1995 v J, Ec, Fa (sub) (3)
Gibb, W. (Clydesdale), 1873 v E (1)
Gibson, D. W. (Leicester C), 1963 v A, N, Ei, Sp; 1964 v Ni; 1965 v W, Fi (7)
Gibson, J. D. (Partick T), 1926 v E; 1927 v E, W, Ni; (with Aston Villa), 1928 v E, W; 1930 v W, Ni (8)
Gibson, N. (Rangers), 1895 v E, Ni; 1896 v E, Ni; 1897 v E, Ni; 1898 v E; 1899 v E, W, Ni; 1900 v E, Ni; 1901 v W; (with Partick T), 1905 v Ni (14)
Gilchrist, J. E. (Celtic), 1922 v E (1)
Gilhooley, M. (Hull C), 1922 v W (1)
Gillespie, G. (Rangers), 1880 v W; 1881 v E, W; 1882 v E; (with Queen's Park), 1886 v W; 1890 v W; 1891 v Ni (7)
Gillespie, G. T. (Liverpool), 1988 v Bel, Bul, Sp; 1989 v N, F, Ch; 1990 v Y, EG, Eg, Pol, Ma, Br (sub); 1991 v Bul (13)
Gillespie, Jas (Third Lanark), 1898 v W (1)
Gillespie, John (Queen's Park), 1896 v W (1)
Gillespie, R. (Queen's Park), 1927 v W; 1931 v W; 1932 v F; 1933 v E (4)
Gillick, T. (Everton), 1937 v A, Cz; 1939 v W, Ni, H (5)
Gilmour, J. (Dundee), 1931 v W (1)
Gilzean, A. J. (Dundee), 1964 v W, E, N, WG; 1965 v Ni, (with Tottenham H), Sp; 1966 v Ni, W, Pol, I; 1968 v W; 1969 v W, E, WG, Cy (2), A (sub); 1970 v Ni, E (sub), WG, A; 1971 v P (22)
Glavin, R. (Celtic), 1977 v Se (1)
Glen, A. (Aberdeen), 1956 v E, Ni (2)
Glen, R. (Renton), 1895 v W; 1896 v W; (with Hibernian), 1900 v Ni (3)
Goram, A. L. (Oldham Ath), 1986 v EG (sub), R, Ho; 1987 v Br; (with Hibernian) 1989 v Y, I; 1990 v EG, Pol, Ma; 1991 v R, Sw, Bul (2), USSR, Sm; (with Rangers), 1992 v Sw, R, Sm, Fi, N, Ho, G, C; 1993 v Sw, P, I, Ma, P; 1994 v Ho; 1995 v Fi, Fa, Ru, Gr (33)
Gordon, J. E. (Rangers), 1912 v E, Ni; 1913 v E, Ni, W; 1914 v E, Ni; 1920 v W, E, Ni (10)
Gossland, J. (Rangers), 1884 v Ni (1)
Goudle, J. (Abercorn), 1884 v Ni (1)
Gough, C. R. (Dundee U), 1983 v Sw, Ni, W, E, Ca (3); 1984 v U, Bel, EG, Ni, W, E, F; 1985 v Sp, E, Ic; 1986 v W, EG, Aus, Is, R, E, D, WG, U; (with Tottenham H), 1987 v Bul, L, Ei (2), Bel, E, Br; 1988 v H; (with Rangers), S.Ar, Sp, Co, E; 1989 v Y, I, Cy, F, Cy; 1990 v F, Arg, EG, Eg, Pol, Ma, Cr; 1991 v USSR, Bul; 1992 v Sm, Ni, Ca, N, Ho, G, C; 1993 v Sw, P (61)
Gourlay, J. (Cambuslang), 1886 v Ni; 1888 v W (2)
Govan, J. (Hibernian), 1948 v E, W, Bel, Sw, F; 1949 v Ni (6)
Gow, D. R. (Rangers), 1888 v E (1)
Gow, J. J. (Queen's Park), 1885 v E (1)
Gow, J. R. (Rangers), 1888 v Ni (1)
Graham, A. (Leeds U), 1978 v EG (sub); 1979 v A (sub), N, W, Ni, E, Arg, N; 1980 v A; 1981 v W (10)
Graham, G. (Arsenal), 1972 v P, Ho, Ni, Y, Cz, Br; 1973 v D (2); (with Manchester U), E, W, Ni, Br (sub) (12)
Graham, J. (Annbank), 1884 v Ni (1)
Graham, J. A. (Arsenal), 1921 v Ni (1)
Grant, J. (Hibernian), 1959 v W, Ni (2)
Grant, P. (Celtic), 1989 v E (sub), Ch (2)
Gray, A. (Hibernian), 1903 v Ni (1)
Gray, A. M. (Aston Villa), 1976 v R, Sw; 1977 v Fi, Cz; 1979 v A, N; (with Wolverhampton W), 1980 v P, E (sub); 1981 v Se, P, Is (sub), Ni; 1982 v Se (sub), Ni (sub); 1983 v Ni, W, E, Ca (1 + 1 sub); (with Everton), 1985 v Ic (20)
Gray, D. (Rangers), 1929 v W, Ni, G, Ho; 1930 v W, E, Ni; 1931 v W; 1933 v W, Ni (10)
Gray, E. (Leeds U), 1969 v E, Cy; 1970 v WG, A; 1971 v W, Ni; 1972 v Bel, Ho; 1976 v W, E; 1977 v Fi, W (12)
Gray, F. T. (Leeds U), 1976 v Sw; 1979 v N, P, W, Ni, E, Arg (sub); (with Nottingham F), 1980 v Bel (sub); 1981 v Se, P, Is, Ni, Is, W; (with Leeds U), Ni, E; 1982 v Se, Ni, P, Sp, Ho, W, Nz, Br, USSR; 1983 v EG, Sw, Bel, Sw, W, E, Ca (32)
Gray, W. (Pollokshields Ath), 1886 v E (1)
Green, A. (Blackpool), 1971 v Bel (sub), P (sub), Ni, E; (with Newcastle U), 1972 v W, E (sub) (6)
Greig, J. (Rangers), 1964 v E, WG; 1965 v W, Ni, E, Fi (2), Sp, Pol; 1966 v Ni, W, E, Pol, I (2), P, Ho, Br; 1967 v W, Ni, E; 1968 v Ni, W, E, Ho; 1969 v W, Ni, E, D, A, WG, Cy (2); 1970 v W, E, Ei, WG, A; 1971 v D, Bel, W (sub), Ni, E; 1976 v D (44)
Groves, W. (Hibernian), 1888 v W; (with Celtic), 1889 v Ni; 1890 v E (3)
Guilliland, W. (Queen's Park), 1891 v W; 1892 v Ni; 1894 v E; 1895 v E (4)
Gunn, B. (Norwich C), 1990 v Eg; 1993 v Es (2); 1994 v Sw, I, Ho (sub) (6)

Haddock, H. (Clyde), 1955 v E, H (2), P, Y; 1958 v E (6)
Haddow, D. (Rangers), 1894 v E (1)
Haffey, F. (Celtic), 1960 v E; 1961 v E (2)
Hamilton, A. (Queen's Park), 1885 v E, W; 1886 v E; 1888 v E (4)
Hamilton, A. W. (Dundee), 1962 v Cz, U, W, E; 1963 v W, Ni, E, A, N, Ei; 1964 v Ni, W, E, N, WG; 1965 v Ni, W, E, Fi (2), Pol, Sp; 1966 v Pol, Ni (24)
Hamilton, G. (Aberdeen), 1947 v Ni; 1951 v Bel, A; 1954 v N (2) (5)
Hamilton, G. (Port Glasgow Ath), 1906 v Ni (1)
Hamilton, J. (Queen's Park), 1892 v W; 1893 v E, Ni (3)
Hamilton, J. (St Mirren), 1924 v Ni (1)
Hamilton, R. C. (Rangers), 1899 v E, W, Ni; 1900 v W; 1901 v E, Ni; 1902 v W, Ni; 1903 v E; 1904 v Ni; (with Dundee), 1911 v W (11)
Hamilton, T. (Hurlford), 1891 v Ni (1)
Hamilton, T. (Rangers), 1932 v E (1)
Hamilton, W. M. (Hibernian), 1965 v Fi (1)
Hannah, A. B. (Renton), 1888 v W (1)
Hannah, J. (Third Lanark), 1889 v W (1)
Hansen, A. D. (Liverpool), 1979 v W, Arg; 1980 v Bel, P; 1981 v Se, P, Is; 1982 v Se, Ni, P, Sp, Ni (sub), W, E, Nz, Br, USSR; 1983 v EG, Sw, Bel, Sw; 1985 v W (sub); 1986 v R (sub); 1987 v Ei (2), L (26)
Hansen, J. (Partick T), 1972 v Bel (sub), Y (sub) (2)
Harkness, J. D. (Queen's Park), 1927 v E, Ni; 1928 v E; (with Hearts), 1929 v W, E, Ni; 1930 v E, W; 1932 v W, F; 1934 v Ni, W (12)
Harper, J. M. (Aberdeen), 1973 v D (1+1 sub); (with Hibernian), 1976 v D; (with Aberdeen), 1978 v Ir (sub) (4)
Harper, W. (Hibernian), 1923 v E, Ni, W; 1924 v E, Ni, W; 1925 v E, Ni, W; (with Arsenal), 1926 v E, Ni (11)
Harris, J. (Partick T), 1921 v W, Ni (2)
Harris, N. (Newcastle U), 1924 v E (1)
Harrower, W. (Queen's Park), 1882 v E; 1884 v Ni; 1886 v W (3)
Hartford, R. A. (WBA), 1972 v Pe, W (sub), E, Y, Cz, Br; (with Manchester C), 1976 v D, R, Ni (sub); 1977 v Cz (sub), W (sub), Se, W, Ni, E, Ch, Arg, Br; 1978 v EG, Cz, W, Bul, W, E, Pe, Ir, Ho; 1979 v A, N, P, W, Ni, E, Arg, N; (with Everton), 1980 v Pe, Bel; 1981 v Ni (sub), Is, W, Ni, E; 1982 v Se; (with Manchester C), Ni, P, Sp, Ni, W, E, Br (50)
Harvey, D. (Leeds U), 1973 v D; 1974 v Cz, WG, Ni, W, E, Bel, Z, Br, Y; 1975 v EG, Sp (2); 1976 v D (2); 1977 v Fi (sub) (16)
Hastings, A. C. (Sunderland), 1936 v Ni; 1938 v Ni (2)
Haughney, M. (Celtic), 1954 v E (1)
Hay, D. (Celtic), 1970 v Ni, W, E; 1971 v D, Bel, W, P, Ni; 1972 v P, Bel, Ho; 1973 v W, Ni, E, Sw, Br; 1974 v Cz (2), WG, Ni, W, E, Bel, N, Z, Br, Y (27)
Hay, J. (Celtic), 1905 v Ni; 1909 v Ni; 1910 v W, Ni, E; 1911 v Ni, E; (with Newcastle U), 1912 v E, W; 1914 v E, Ni (11)
Hegarty, P. (Dundee U), 1979 v W, Ni, E, Arg, N (sub); 1980 v W, E; 1983 v Ni (8)
Heggie, C. (Rangers), 1886 v Ni (1)
Henderson, G. H. (Rangers), 1904 v Ni (1)
Henderson, J. G. (Portsmouth), 1953 v Se; 1954 v Ni, E, N; 1956 v W; (with Arsenal), 1959 v W, Ni (7)
Henderson, W. (Rangers), 1963 v W, Ni, E, A, N, Ei, Sp; 1964 v W, Ni, E, N, WG; 1965 v Fi, Pol, E, Sp; 1966 v Ni, W, Pol, I, Ho; 1967 v W, Ni; 1968 v Ho; 1969 v Ni, E, Cy; 1970 v Ei; 1971 v P (29)
Hendry, E. C. J. (Blackburn R), 1993 v Es (2); 1994 v Ma, Ho, A, Ho; 1995 v Fi, Fa, Gr, Ru, Sm (11)
Hepburn, J. (Alloa Ath), 1891 v W (1)
Hepburn, R. (Ayr U), 1932 v Ni (1)
Herd, A. C. (Hearts), 1935 v Ni (1)
Herd, D. G. (Arsenal), 1959 v E, W, Ni; 1961 v E, Cz (5)
Herd, G. (Clyde), 1958 v E; 1960 v H, T; 1961 v W, Ni (5)
Herriot, J. (Birmingham C), 1969 v Ni, E, D, Cy (2), W (sub); 1970 v Ei (sub), WG (8)
Hewie, J. D. (Charlton Ath), 1956 v E, A; 1957 v E, Ni, W, Y, Sp (2), Sw, WG; 1958 v H, Pol, Y, F; 1959 v Ho, P; 1960 v Ni, W, Pol (19)
Higgins, A. (Kilmarnock), 1885 v Ni (1)
Higgins, A. (Newcastle U), 1910 v E, Ni; 1911 v E, Ni (4)
Highet, T. C. (Queen's Park), 1875 v E; 1876 v E, W; 1878 v E (4)
Hill, D. (Rangers), 1881 v E, W; 1882 v W (3)
Hill, D. A. (Third Lanark), 1906 v Ni (1)
Hill, F. R. (Aberdeen), 1930 v F; 1931 v W, Ni (3)
Hill, J. (Hearts), 1891 v E; 1892 v W (2)
Hogg, G (Hearts), 1896 v E, Ni (2)
Hogg, J. (Ayr U), 1922 v Ni (1)
Hogg, R. M. (Celtic), 1937 v Cz (1)
Holm, A. H. (Queen's Park), 1882 v W; 1883 v E, W (3)
Holt, D. D. (Hearts), 1963 v A, N, Ei, Sp; 1964 v WG (sub) (5)
Holton, J. A. (Manchester U), 1973 v W, Ni, E, Sw, Br; 1974 v Cz, WG, Ni, W, E, N, Z, Br, Y; 1975 v EG (15)
Hope, R. (WBA), 1968 v Ho; 1969 v D (2)
Houliston, W. (Queen of the South), 1949 v E, Ni, F (3)
Houston, S. M. (Manchester U), 1976 v D (1)
Howden, W. (Partick T), 1905 v Ni (1)
Howe, R. (Hamilton A), 1929 v N, Ho (2)
Howie, J. (Newcastle U), 1905 v E; 1906 v E; 1908 v E (3)
Howie, H. (Hibernian), 1949 v W (1)
Howieson, J. (St Mirren), 1927 v Ni (1)
Hughes, J. (Celtic), 1965 v Pol, Sp; 1966 v Ni, I (2); 1968 v E; 1969 v A; 1970 v Ei (8)
Hughes, W. (Sunderland), 1975 v Se (sub) (1)
Humphries, W. (Motherwell), 1952 v Se (1)
Hunter, A. (Kilmarnock), 1972 v Pe, Y; (with Celtic), 1973 v E; 1974 v Cz (4)
Hunter, J. (Dundee), 1909 v W (1)
Hunter, J. (Third Lanark), 1874 v E; (with Eastern), 1875 v E; (with Third Lanark), 1876 v E; 1877 v W (4)
Hunter, R. (St Mirren), 1890 v Ni (1)
Hunter, W. (Motherwell), 1960 v H, T; 1961 v W (3)
Husband, J. (Partick T), 1947 v W (1)
Hutchison, T. (Coventry C), 1974 v Cz (2), WG (2), Ni, W, Bel (sub), N, Z (sub), Y (sub); 1975 v EG, Sp (2), P, E (sub), R (sub); 1976 v D (17)
Hutton, J. (Aberdeen), 1923 v E, W, Ni; 1924 v Ni; 1926 v W, E, Ni; (with Blackburn R), 1927 v Ni; 1928 v W, Ni (10)
Hutton, J. (St Bernards), 1887 v Ni (1)
Hyslop, T. (Stoke C), 1896 v E; (with Rangers), 1897 v E (2)

Imlach, J. J. S. (Nottingham F), 1958 v H, Pol, Y, F (4)
Imrie, W. N. (St Johnstone), 1929 v N, G (2)
Inglis, J. (Kilmarnock Ath), 1884 v Ni (1)
Inglis, J. (Rangers), 1883 v E, W (2)
Irons, J. H. (Queen's Park), 1900 v W (1)
Irvine, B. (Aberdeen), 1991 v R; 1993 v G, Es (2); 1994 v Sw, I, Ma, A, Ho (9)

Jackson, A. (Cambuslang), 1886 v W; 1888 v Ni (2)
Jackson, A. (Aberdeen), 1925 v E, W, Ni; (with Huddersfield T), 1926 v E, W, Ni; 1927 v W, Ni; 1928 v E, W; 1929 v E, W, Ni; 1930 v E, W, Ni, F (17)
Jackson, C. (Rangers), 1975 v Se, P (sub), W; 1976 v D, R, Ni, W, E (8)
Jackson, D. (Hibernian), 1995 v Ru, Sm, J, Ec, Fa (5)
Jackson, J. (Partick T), 1931 v A, I, Sw; 1933 v E; (with Chelsea), 1934 v E; 1935 v E; 1936 v W, Ni (8)

Jackson, T. A. (St Mirren), 1904 v W, E, Ni; 1905 v W; 1907 v W, Ni (6)
James, A. W. (Preston NE), 1926 v W; 1928 v E; 1929 v E, Ni; (with Arsenal), 1930 v E, W, Ni; 1933 v W (8)
Jardine, A. (Rangers), 1971 v D (sub); 1972 v P, Bel, Ho; 1973 v E, Sw, Br; 1974 v Cz (2), WG (2), Ni, W, E, Bel, N, Z, Br, Y; 1975 v EG, Sp (2), Se, P, W, Ni, E; 1977 v Se (sub), Ch (sub), Br (sub); 1978 v Cz, W, Ni, Ir; 1980 v Pe, A, Bel (2) (38)
Jarvie, A. (Airdrieonians), 1971 v P (sub), Ni (sub), E (sub) (3)
Jenkinson, T. (Hearts), 1887 v Ni (1)
Jess, E. (Aberdeen), 1993 v I (sub), Ma; 1994 v Sw (sub), I, Ho (sub), A, Ho (sub); 1995 v Fi (sub) (8)
Johnston, L. H. (Clyde), 1948 v Bel, Sw (2)
Johnston, M. (Watford), 1984 v W (sub), E (sub), F; 1985 v Y; (with Celtic), Ic, Sp (2), W; 1986 v EG; 1987 v Bul, Ei (2), L; (with Nantes), 1988 v H, Bel, L, S.Ar, Sp, Co, E; 1989 v N, Y, I, Cy, F, Cy, E, Ch (sub); (with Rangers), 1990 v F, N, EG, Pol, Ma, Cr, Se, Br; 1992 v Sw, Sm (sub) (38)
Johnston, R. (Sunderland), 1938 v Cz (1)
Johnston, W. (Rangers), 1966 v W, E, Pol, Ho; 1968 v W, E; 1969 v Ni (sub); 1970 v Ni; 1971 v D; (with WBA), 1977 v Se, W (sub), Ni, E, Ch, Arg, Br; 1978 v EG, Cz, W (2), E, Pe (22)
Johnstone, D. (Rangers), 1973 v W, Ni, E, Sw, Br; 1975 v EG (sub), Se (sub); 1976 v Sw, Ni (sub), E (sub); 1978 v Bul (sub), Ni, W; 1980 v Bel (14)
Johnstone, J. (Abercorn), 1888 v W (1)
Johnstone, J. (Celtic), 1965 v W, Fi; 1966 v E; 1967 v W, USSR; 1968 v W; 1969 v A, WG; 1970 v E, WG; 1971 v D, E; 1972 v P, Bel, Ho, Ni, E (sub); 1974 v W, E, Bel, N; 1975 v EG, Sp (23)
Johnstone, Jas (Kilmarnock), 1894 v W (1)
Johnstone, J. A. (Hearts), 1930 v W; 1933 v W, Ni (3)
Johnstone, R. (Hibernian), 1951 v E, D, F; 1952 v Ni, E; 1953 v E, Se; 1954 v W, E, N, Fi; 1955 v Ni, H; (with Manchester C), 1955 v E; 1956 v E, Ni, W (17)
Johnstone, W. (Third Lanark), 1887 v Ni; 1889 v W; 1890 v E (3)
Jordan, J. (Leeds U), 1973 v E (sub), Sw (sub), Br; 1974 v Cz (sub + 1), WG (sub), Ni (sub), W, E, Bel, N, Z, Br, Y; 1975 v EG, Sp (2); 1976 v Ni, W, E; 1977 v Cz, W, Ni, E; 1978 v EG, Cz, W; (with Manchester U), Bul, Ni, E, Pe, Ir, Ho; 1979 v A, P, W (sub), Ni, E, N; 1980 v Bel, Ni (sub), W, E, Pol; 1981 v Is, W, E; (with AC Milan), 1982 v Se, Ho, W, E, USSR (52)

Kay, J. L. (Queen's Park), 1880 v E; 1882 v E, W; 1883 v E, W; 1884 v W (6)
Keillor, A. (Montrose), 1891 v W; 1892 v Ni; (with Dundee), 1894 v Ni; 1895 v W; 1896 v W; 1897 v W (6)
Keir, L. (Dumbarton), 1885 v W; 1886 v Ni; 1887 v E, W; 1888 v E (5)
Kelly, H. T. (Blackpool), 1952 v USA (1)
Kelly, J. (Renton), 1888 v E; (with Celtic), 1889 v E; 1890 v E; 1892 v E; 1893 v E, Ni; 1894 v W; 1896 v Ni (8)
Kelly, J. C. (Barnsley), 1949 v W, Ni (2)
Kelso, R. (Renton), 1885 v W, Ni; 1886 v W; 1887 v E, W; 1888 v E, Ni; (with Dundee), 1898 v Ni (8)
Kelso, T. (Dundee), 1914 v W (1)
Kennaway, J. (Celtic), 1934 v A (1)
Kennedy, A. (Eastern), 1875 v E; 1876 v E, W; (with Third Lanark), 1878 v E; 1882 v W; 1884 v W (6)
Kennedy, J. (Celtic), 1964 v W, E, WG; 1965 v W, Ni, Fi (6)
Kennedy, J. (Hibernian), 1897 v W (1)
Kennedy, S. (Aberdeen), 1978 v Bul, W, E, Pe, Ho; 1979 v A, P; 1982 v P (sub) (8)
Kennedy, S. (Partick T), 1905 v W (1)
Kennedy, S. (Rangers), 1975 v Se, P, W, Ni, E (5)
Ker, G. (Queen's Park), 1880 v E; 1881 v E, W; 1882 v W, E (5)
Ker, W. (Granville), 1872 v E; (with Queen's Park), 1873 v E (2)
Kerr, A. (Partick T), 1955 v A, H (2)
Kerr, P. (Hibernian), 1924 v Ni (1)
Key, G. (Hearts), 1902 v Ni (1)
Key, W. (Queen's Park), 1907 v Ni (1)
King, A. (Hearts), 1896 v E, W; (with Celtic), 1897 v Ni; 1898 v Ni; 1899 v Ni, W (6)
King, J. (Hamilton A), 1933 v Ni; 1934 v Ni (2)
King, W. S. (Queen's Park), 1929 v W (1)
Kinloch, J. D. (Partick T), 1922 v Ni (1)
Kinnaird, A. F. (Wanderers), 1873 v E (1)
Kinnear, D. (Rangers), 1938 v Cz (1)

Lambert, P. (Motherwell), 1995 v J, Ec (sub) (2)
Lambie, J. A. (Queen's Park), 1886 v Ni; 1887 v Ni; 1888 v E (3)
Lambie, W. A. (Queen's Park), 1892 v Ni; 1893 v W; 1894 v E; 1895 v E, Ni; 1896 v E, Ni; 1897 v E, Ni (9)
Lamont, D. (Pilgrims), 1885 v Ni (1)
Lang, A. (Dumbarton), 1880 v W (1)
Lang, J. J. (Clydesdale), 1876 v W; (with Third Lanark), 1878 v W (2)
Latta, A. (Dumbarton), 1888 v W; 1889 v E (2)
Law, D. (Huddersfield T), 1959 v W, Ni, Ho, P; 1960 v Ni, W; (with Manchester C), 1960 v E, Pol, A; 1961 v E, Ni; (with Torino), 1962 v Cz (2), E; (with Manchester U), 1963 v W, Ni, E, A, N, Ei, Sp; 1964 v W, E, N, WG; 1965 v W, Ni, E, Fi (2), Pol, Sp; 1966 v Ni, E, Pol; 1967 v W, E, USSR; 1968 v Ni; 1969 v Ni, A, WG; 1972 v Pe, Ni, W, E, Y, Cz, Br; (with Manchester C), 1974 v Cz (2), WG (2), Ni, Z (55)
Law, G. (Rangers), 1910 v E, Ni, W (3)
Law, T. (Chelsea), 1928 v E; 1930 v E (2)
Lawrence, J. (Newcastle U), 1911 v E (1)
Lawrence, T. (Liverpool), 1963 v Ei; 1969 v W, WG (3)
Lawson, D. (St Mirren), 1923 v E (1)
Leckie, R. (Queen's Park), 1872 v E (1)
Leggat, G. (Aberdeen), 1956 v E; 1957 v W; 1958 v Ni, H, Pol, Y, Par; (with Fulham), 1959 v E, W, Ni, WG, Ho; 1960 v E, Ni, W, Pol, A, H (18)
Leighton, J. (Aberdeen), 1983 v EG, Sw, Bel, Sw, W, E, Ca (2); 1984 v U, Bel, Ni, W, E, F; 1985 v Y, Ic, Sp (2), W, E, Ic; 1986 v W, EG, Aus (2), Is, D, WG, U; 1987 v Bul, Ei (2), L, Bel, E; 1988 v H, Bel, Bul, L, S.Ar, Ma, Sp; (with Manchester U), Co, E; 1989 v N, Cy, F, Cy, E, Ch; 1990 v Y, F, N, Arg, Ma (sub, Cr, Se, Br; (with Hibernian), 1994 v Ma, A, Ho; 1995 v Gr (sub), Ru, Sm, J, Ec, Fa (67)
Lennie, W. (Aberdeen), 1908 v W, Ni (2)
Lennox, R. (Celtic), 1967 v Ni, E, USSR; 1968 v W, L; 1969 v D, A, WG, Cy (sub); 1970 v W (sub) (10)
Leslie, L. G. (Airdrieonians), 1961 v W, Ni, Ei (2), Cz (5)
Levein, C. (Hearts), 1990 v Arg, EG, Eg (sub), Pol, Ma (sub), Se; 1992 v R, Sm; 1993 v P, G, P; 1994 v Sw, Ho; 1995 v Fi, Fa, Ru (16)
Liddell, W. (Liverpool), 1947 v W, Ni; 1948 v E, W, Ni; 1950 v E, W, P, F; 1951 v W, Ni, E, A; 1952 v W, Ni, E, USA, D, Se; 1953 v W, Ni, E; 1954 v W; 1955 v P, Y, A, H; 1956 v Ni (28)
Liddle, D. (East Fife), 1931 v A, I, Sw (3)
Lindsay, D. (St Mirren), 1903 v Ni (1)
Lindsay, J. (Dumbarton), 1880 v W; 1881 v W, E; 1884 v W, E; 1885 v W, E; 1886 v E (8)
Lindsay, J. (Renton), 1888 v E; 1893 v E, Ni (3)
Linwood, A. B. (Clyde), 1950 v W (1)
Little, R. J. (Rangers), 1953 v Se (1)
Livingstone, G. T. (Manchester C), 1906 v E; (with Rangers), 1907 v W (2)
Lochhead, A. (Third Lanark), 1889 v W (1)
Logan, J. (Ayr U), 1891 v W (1)

Logan, T. (Falkirk), 1913 v Ni (1)
Logie, J. T. (Arsenal), 1953 v Ni (1)
Loney, W. (Celtic), 1910 v W, Ni (2)
Long, H. (Clyde), 1947 v Ni (1)
Longair, W. (Dundee), 1894 v Ni (1)
Lorimer, P. (Leeds U), 1970 v A (sub); 1971 v W, Ni; 1972 v Ni (sub), W, E; 1973 v D (2), E (2); 1974 v WG (sub), E, Bel, N, Z, Br, Y; 1975 v Sp (sub); 1976 v D (2), R (sub) (21)
Love, A. (Aberdeen), 1931 v A, I, Sw (3)
Low, A. (Falkirk), 1934 v Ni (1)
Low, T. P. (Rangers), 1897 v Ni (1)
Low, W. L. (Newcastle U), 1911 v E, W; 1912 v Ni; 1920 v E, Ni (5)
Lowe, J. (Cambuslang), 1891 v Ni (1)
Lowe, J. (St Bernards), 1887 v Ni (1)
Lundie, J. (Hibernian), 1886 v W (1)
Lyall, J. (Sheffield W), 1905 v E (1)

McAdam, J. (Third Lanark), 1880 v W (1)
McAllister, G. (Leicester C), 1990 v EG, Pol, Ma (sub); (with Leeds U), 1991 v R, Sw, Bul, USSR (sub), Sm; 1992 v Sw (sub), Sm, Ni, Fi (sub), US, Ca, N, Ho, G, C; 1993 v Sw, P, I, Ma; 1994 v Sw, I, Ma, Ho, A, Ho; 1995 v Fi, Ru, Gr, Ru, Sm (33)
McArthur, D. (Celtic), 1895 v E, Ni; 1899 v W (3)
McAtee, A. (Celtic), 1913 v W (1)
McAulay, J. (Dumbarton), 1882 v W; (with Arthurlie), 1884 v Ni (2)
McAulay, J. (Dumbarton), 1883 v E, W; 1884 v E; 1885 v E, W; 1886 v E; 1887 v E, W (8)
McAuley, R. (Rangers), 1932 v Ni, W (2)
McAvennie, F. (West Ham U), 1986 v Aus (2), D (sub), WG (sub); (with Celtic), 1988 v S.Ar (5)
McBain, E. (St Mirren), 1894 v W (1)
McBain, N. (Manchester U), 1922 v E; (with Everton), 1923 v Ni; 1924 v W (3)
McBride, J. (Celtic), 1967 v W, Ni (2)
McBride, P. (Preston NE), 1904 v E; 1906 v E; 1907 v E, W; 1908 v E; 1909 v W (6)
McCall, J. (Renton), 1886 v W; 1887 v E, W; 1888 v E; 1890 v E (5)
McCall, S. M. (Everton), 1990 v Arg, EG, Eg (sub), Pol, Ma, Cr, Se, Br; 1991 v Sw, USSR, Sm; (with Rangers), 1992 v Sw, R, Sm, US, Ca, N, Ho, G, C; 1993 v Sw, P (2); 1994 v I, Ho, A (sub), Ho; 1995 v Fi (sub), Ru, Gr (30)
McCalliog, J. (Sheffield W), 1967 v E, USSR; 1968 v Ni; 1969 v D; (with Wolverhampton W), 1971 v P (5)
McCallum, N. (Renton), 1888 v Ni (1)
McCann, R. J. (Motherwell), 1959 v WG; 1960 v E, Ni, W; 1961 v E (5)
McCartney, W. (Hibernian), 1902 v Ni (1)
McClair, B. (Celtic), 1987 v L, Ei, E, Br (sub); (with Manchester U), 1988 v Bul, Ma (sub), Sp (sub); 1989 v N, Y, I (sub), Cy, F (sub); 1990 v N (sub), Arg (sub); 1991 v Bul (2), Sm; 1992 v Sw (sub), R, Ni, US, Ca (sub), N, Ho, G, C; 1993 v Sw, P (sub), Es (2) (30)
McClory, A. (Motherwell), 1927 v W; 1928 v Ni; 1935 v W (3)
McCloy, P. (Ayr U), 1924 v E; 1925 v E (2)
McCloy, P. (Rangers), 1973 v W, Ni, Sw, Br (4)
McCoist, A. (Rangers), 1986 v Ho; 1987 v L (sub), Ei (sub), Bel, E, Br; 1988 v H, Bel, Ma, Sp, Co, E; 1989 v Y (sub), F, Cy, E; 1990 v Y, F, N, EG (sub), Eg, Pol, Ma (sub), Cr (sub), Se (sub), Br; 1991 v R, Sw, Bul (2), USSR; 1992 v Sw, Sm, Ni, Fi (sub), US, Ca, N, Ho, G, C; 1993 v Sw, P, I, Ma, P (46)
McColl, A. (Renton), 1888 v Ni (1)
McColl, I. M. (Rangers), 1950 v E, F; 1951 v W, Ni, Bel; 1957 v E, Ni, W, Y, Sp, Sw, WG; 1958 v Ni, E (14)
McColl, R. S. (Queen's Park), 1896 v W, Ni; 1897 v Ni; 1898 v Ni; 1899 v Ni, E, W; 1900 v E, W; 1901 v E, W; (with Newcastle U), 1902 v E; (with Queen's Park), 1908 v Ni (13)
McColl, W. (Renton), 1895 v W (1)
McCombie, A. (Sunderland), 1903 v E, W; (with Newcastle U), 1905 v E, W (4)
McCorkindale, J. (Partick T), 1891 v W (1)
McCormick, R. (Abercorn), 1886 v W (1)
McCrae, D. (St Mirren), 1929 v N, G (2)
McCreadie, A. (Rangers), 1893 v W; 1894 v E (2)
McCreadie, E. G. (Chelsea), 1965 v E, Sp, Fi, Pol; 1966 v P, Ni, W, Pol, I; 1967 v E, USSR; 1968 v Ni, W, E, Ho; 1969 v W, Ni, E, D, A, WG, Cy (2) (23)
McCulloch, D. (Hearts), 1935 v W; (with Brentford), 1936 v E; 1937 v W, Ni; 1938 v Cz; (with Derby Co), 1939 v H, W (7)
MacDonald, A. (Rangers), 1976 v Sw (1)
McDonald, J. (Edinburgh University), 1886 v E (1)
McDonald, J. (Sunderland), 1956 v W, Ni (2)
MacDougall, E. J. (Norwich C) 1975 v Se, P, W, Ni, E; 1976 v D, R (sub) (7)
McDougall, J. (Liverpool), 1931 v I, A (2)
McDougall, J. (Airdrieonians), 1926 v Ni (1)
McDougall, J. (Vale of Leven), 1877 v E, W; 1878 v E; 1879 v E, W (5)
McFadyen, W. (Motherwell), 1934 v A, W (2)
Macfarlane, A. (Dundee), 1904 v W; 1906 v W; 1908 v W; 1909 v Ni; 1911 v W (5)
McFarlane, R. (Greenock Morton), 1896 v W (1)
Macfarlane, W. (Hearts), 1947 v L (1)
McGarr, E. (Aberdeen), 1970 v Ei, A (2)
McGarvey, F. P. (Liverpool), 1979 v Ni (sub), Arg; (with Celtic), 1984 v U, Bel (sub), EG (sub), Ni, W (7)
McGeoch, A. (Dumbreck), 1876 v E, W; 1877 v E, W (4)
McGhee, J. (Hibernian), 1886 v W (1)
McGhee, M. (Aberdeen), 1983 v Ca (1 + 1 sub); 1984 v Ni (sub), E (4)
McGinlay, J. (Bolton W), 1994 v A, Ho; 1995 v Fa, Ru, Gr, Ru, Sm, Fa (8)
McGonagle, W. (Celtic), 1933 v E; 1934 v A, E, Ni; 1935 v Ni, W (6)
McGrain, D. (Celtic), 1973 v W, Ni, E, Sw, Br; 1974 v Cz (2), WG, W (sub), E, Bel, N, Z, Br, Y; 1975 v Sp, Se, P, W, Ni, E, R; 1976 v D (2), Sw, Ni, W, E; 1977 v Fi, Cz, W (2), Se, Ni, E, Ch, Arg, Br; 1978 v EG, Cz; 1980 v Bel, P, Ni, W, E, Pol, H; 1981 v Se, P, Is, Ni, Is, W (sub), Ni, E; 1982 v Se, Sp, Ho, Ni, E, Nz, USSR (sub) (62)
McGregor, J. C. (Vale of Leven), 1877 v E, W; 1878 v E; 1880 v E (4)
McGrory, J. E. (Kilmarnock), 1965 v Ni, Fi; 1966 v P (3)
McGrory, J. (Celtic), 1928 v Ni; 1931 v E; 1932 v Ni, W; 1933 v E, Ni; 1934 v Ni (7)
McGuire, W. (Beith), 1881 v E, W (2)
McGurk, F. (Birmingham), 1934 v W (1)
McHardy, H. (Rangers), 1885 v Ni (1)
McInally, A. (Aston Villa), 1989 v Cy (sub), Ch; (with Bayern Munich), 1990 v Y (sub), F (sub), Arg, Pol (sub), Ma, Cr (8)
McInally, J. (Dundee U), 1987 v Bel, Br; 1988 v Ma (sub); 1991 v Bul (2); 1992 v US (sub), N (sub), C (sub); 1993 v G, P (10)
McInally, T. B. (Celtic), 1926 v Ni; 1927 v W (2)
McInnes, T. (Cowlairs), 1889 v Ni (1)
McIntosh, W. (Third Lanark), 1905 v Ni (1)
McIntyre, A. (Vale of Leven), 1878 v E; 1882 v E (2)
McIntyre, H. (Rangers), 1880 v W (1)
McIntyre, J. (Rangers), 1884 v W (1)
McKay, D. (Celtic), 1959 v E, WG, Ho, P; 1960 v E, Pol, A, H, T; 1961 v W, Ni; 1962 v Ni, Cz, U (sub) (14)
Mackay, D. C. (Hearts), 1957 v Sp; 1958 v F; 1959 v W, Ni; (with Tottenham H), 1959 v WG, E; 1960 v W, Ni, A, Pol, H, T; 1961 v W, Ni, E; 1963 v E, A, N; 1964 v Ni, W, N; 1966 v Ni (22)

Mackay, G. (Hearts), 1988 v Bul (sub), L (sub), S.Ar (sub), Ma (4)
McKay, J. (Blackburn R), 1924 v W (1)
McKay, R. (Newcastle U), 1928 v W (1)
McKean, R. (Rangers), 1976 v Sw (sub) (1)
McKenzie, D. (Brentford), 1938 v Ni (1)
Mackenzie, J. A. (Partick T), 1954 v W, E, N, Fi, A, U; 1955 v E, H; 1956 v A (9)
McKeown, M. (Celtic), 1889 v Ni; 1890 v E (2)
McKie, J. (East Stirling), 1898 v W (1)
McKillop, T. R. (Rangers), 1938 v Ho (1)
McKimmie, S. (Aberdeen), 1989 v E, Ch; 1990 v Arg, Eg, Cr (sub), Br; 1991 v R, Sw, Bul, Sm; 1992 v Sw, R, Ni, Fi, US, Ca (sub), N (sub), Ho, G, C; 1993 v P, Es (sub); 1994 v Sw, I, Ho, A, Ho; 1995 v Fi, Fa, Ru, Gr, Ru, Fa (33)
McKinlay, D. (Liverpool), 1922 v W, Ni (2)
McKinlay, W. (Dundee U), 1994 v Ma, Ho (sub), A, Ho; 1995 v Fa (sub), Ru, Gr, Ru (sub), Sm (sub), J, Ec, Fa (12)
McKinnon, A. (Queen's Park), 1874 v E (1)
McKinnon, R. (Rangers), 1966 v W, E, I (2), Ho, Br; 1967 v W, Ni, E; 1968 v Ni, W, E, Ho; 1969 v D, A, WG, Cy; 1970 v Ni, W, E, Ei, WG, A; 1971 v D, Bel, P, USSR, D (28)
McKinnon, R. (Motherwell), 1994 v Ma; 1995 v J, Fa (3)
MacKinnon, W. (Dumbarton), 1883 v E, W; 1884 v E, W (4)
McKinnon, W. W. (Queen's Park), 1872 v E; 1873 v E; 1874 v E; 1875 v E; 1876 v E, W; 1877 v E; 1878 v E; 1879 v E (9)
McLaren, A. (St Johnstone), 1929 v N, G, Ho; 1933 v W, Ni (5)
McLaren, A. (Preston NE), 1947 v E, Bel, L; 1948 v W (4)
McLaren, A. (Hearts), 1992 v US, Ca, N; 1993 v I, Ma, G, Es (sub + 1); 1994 v I, Ma, Ho, A; 1995 v Fi, Fa; (with Rangers), Ru, Gr, Ru, Sm, J, Ec, Fa (21)
McLaren, J. (Hibernian), 1888 v W; (with Celtic), 1889 v E; 1890 v E (3)
McLean, A. (Celtic), 1926 v W, Ni; 1927 v W, E (4)
McLean, D. (St Bernards), 1896 v W; 1897 v Ni (2)
McLean, D. (Sheffield W), 1912 v E (1)
McLean, G. (Dundee), 1968 v Ho (1)
McLean, T. (Kilmarnock), 1969 v D, Cy, W; 1970 v Ni, W; 1971 v D (6)
McLeish, A. (Aberdeen), 1980 v F, Ni, W, E, Pol, H; 1981 v Se, Is, Ni, Is, Ni, E; 1982 v Se, Sp, Ni, Br (sub); 1983 v Bel, Sw (sub), W, E, Ca (3); 1984 v U, Bel, EG, Ni, W, E, F; 1985 v Y, Ic, Sp (2), W, E, Ic; 1986 v W, EG, Aus (2), E, Ho, D; 1987 v Bel, E, Br; 1988 v Bel, Bul, L, S.Ar (sub), Ma, Sp, Co, E; 1989 v N, Y, I, Cy, F, Cy, E, Ch; 1990 v Y, F, N, Arg, EG, Eg, Cr, Se, Br; 1991 v R, Sw, USSR, Bul; 1993 v Ma (77)
McLeod, D. (Celtic), 1905 v Ni; 1906 v E, W, Ni (4)
McLeod, J. (Dumbarton), 1888 v Ni; 1889 v W; 1890 v Ni; 1892 v E; 1893 v W (5)
MacLeod, J. M. (Hibernian), 1961 v E, Ei (2), Cz (4)
MacLeod, M. (Celtic), 1985 v E (sub); 1987 v Ei, L, E, Br; (with Borussia Dortmund), 1988 v Co, E; 1989 v I, Ch; 1990 v Y, F, N (sub), Arg, EG, Pol, Se Br; (with Hibernian), 1991 v R, Sw, USSR (sub) (20)
McLeod, W. (Cowlairs), 1886 v Ni (1)
McLintock, A. (Vale of Leven), 1875 v E; 1876 v E; 1880 v E (3)
McLintock, F. (Leicester C), 1963 v N (sub), Ei, Sp; (with Arsenal), 1965 v Ni; 1967 v USSR; 1970 v Ni; 1971 v W, Ni, E (9)
McLuckie, J. S. (Manchester C), 1934 v W (1)
McMahon, A. (Celtic), 1892 v E; 1893 v E, Ni; 1894 v E; 1901 v Ni; 1902 v W (6)
McMenemy, J. (Celtic), 1905 v Ni; 1909 v Ni; 1910 v E, W; 1911 v Ni, W, E; 1912 v W; 1914 v W, Ni, E; 1920 v Ni (12)
McMenemy, J. (Motherwell), 1934 v W (1)
McMillan, J. (St Bernards), 1897 v W (1)
McMillan, I. L. (Airdrieonians), 1952 v E, USA, D; 1955 v E; 1956 v E; (with Rangers), 1961 v Cz (6)
McMillan, T. (Dumbarton), 1887 v Ni (1)
McMullan, J. (Partick T), 1920 v W; 1921 v W, Ni, E; 1924 v E, Ni; 1925 v E; 1926 v W; (with Manchester C), 1926 v E; 1927 v E, W; 1928 v E, W; 1929 v W, E, Ni (16)
McNab, A. (Morton), 1921 v E, Ni (2)
McNab, A. (Sunderland), 1937 v A; (with WBA), 1939 v E (2)
McNab, C. D. (Dundee), 1931 v E, W, A, I, Sw; 1932 v E (6)
McNab, J. S. (Liverpool), 1923 v W (1)
McNair, A. (Celtic), 1906 v W; 1907 v Ni; 1908 v E, W; 1909 v E; 1910 v W; 1912 v E, W, Ni; 1913 v E; 1914 v E, Ni; 1920 v E, W, Ni (15)
McNaught, W. (Raith R), 1951 v A, W, Ni; 1952 v E; 1955 v Ni (5)
McNeil, H. (Queen's Park), 1874 v E; 1875 v E; 1876 v E, W; 1877 v W; 1878 v E; 1879 v E, W; 1881 v E, W (10)
McNeil, M. (Rangers), 1876 v W; 1880 v E (2)
McNeill, W. (Celtic), 1961 v E, Ei (2), Cz; 1962 v Ni, E, Cz, U; 1963 v Ei, Sp; 1964 v W, E, WG; 1965 v E, Fi, Pol, Sp; 1966 v Ni, Pol; 1967 v USSR; 1968 v E; 1969 v Cy, W, E, Cy (sub); 1970 v WG; 1972 v Ni, W, E (29)
McPhail, J. (Celtic), 1950 v W; 1951 v W, Ni, A; 1954 v Ni (5)
McPhail, R. (Airdrieonians), 1927 v E; (with Rangers), 1929 v W; 1931 v E, Ni; 1932 v W, Ni, F; 1933 v E, Ni; 1934 v A, Ni; 1935 v E; 1937 v G, E, Cz; 1938 v W, Ni (17)
McPherson, D. (Kilmarnock), 1892 v Ni (1)
McPherson, D. (Hearts), 1989 v Cy, E; 1990 v N, Ma, Cr, Se, Br; 1991 v Sw, Bul (2), USSR (sub), Sm; 1992 v Sw, R, Sm, Ni, Fi, US, Ca, N, Ho, G, C; (with Rangers), 1993 v Sw, I, Ma, P (27)
McPherson, J. (Clydesdale), 1875 v E (1)
McPherson, J. (Vale of Leven), 1879 v E, W; 1880 v E; 1881 v W; 1883 v E, W; 1884 v E; 1885 v Ni (8)
McPherson, J. (Kilmarnock), 1888 v W; (with Cowlairs), 1889 v E; 1890 v Ni, E; (with Rangers), 1892 v W; 1894 v E; 1895 v E, Ni; 1897 v Ni (9)
McPherson, J. (Hearts), 1891 v E (1)
McPherson, R. (Arthurlie), 1882 v E (1)
McQueen, G. (Leeds U), 1974 v Bel; 1975 v Sp (2), P, W, Ni, E, R; 1976 v D; 1977 v Cz, W (2), Ni, E; 1978 v EG, Cz, W; (with Manchester U), Bul, Ni, W; 1979 v A, N, P, Ni, E, N; 1980 v Pe, A, Bel; 1981 v W (30)
McQueen, M. (Leith Ath), 1890 v W; 1891 v W (2)
McRorie, D. M. (Morton), 1931 v W (1)
McSpadyen, A. (Partick T), 1939 v E, H (2)
McStay, P. (Celtic), 1984 v U, Bel, EG, Ni, W, E (sub); 1985 v Y, Ic, Sp (2), W; 1986 v EG (sub), Aus, Is, U; 1987 v Bul, Ei (1 + 1 sub), L (sub), Bel, E, Br; 1988 v H, Bel, Bul, L, S.Ar, Sp, Co, E; 1989 v N, Y, I, Cy, F, Cy, E, Ch; 1990 v Y, F, N, Arg, EG (sub), Eg, Pol (sub), Ma, Cr, Se (sub), Br; 1991 v R, USSR, Bul; 1992 v Sm, Fi, US, Ca, N, Ho, G, C; 1993 v Sw, P, I, Ma, P, Es (2); 1994 v I (sub), Ho; 1995 v Fi, Fa, Ru (72)
McStay, W. (Celtic), 1921 v W, Ni; 1925 v E, Ni, W; 1926 v E, Ni, W; 1927 v E, Ni, W; 1928 v W, Ni (13)
McTavish, J. (Falkirk), 1910 v Ni (1)
McWhattie, G. C. (Queen's Park), 1901 v W, Ni (2)
McWilliam, P. (Newcastle U), 1905 v E; 1906 v E; 1907 v E, W; 1909 v E, W; 1910 v E; 1911 v W (8)
Macari, L. (Celtic), 1972 v W (sub), E, Y, Cz, Br; 1973 v D; (with Manchester U), E (2), W (sub), Ni (sub); 1975 v Se, P (sub), W, E (sub), R; 1977 v Ni (sub), E (sub), Ch, Arg; 1978 v EG, W, Bul, Pe (sub), Ir (24)
Macauley, A. R. (Brentford), 1947 v E; (with Arsenal), 1948 v E, W, Ni, Bel, Sw, F (7)

Madden, J. (Celtic), 1893 v W; 1895 v W (2)
Main, F. R. (Rangers), 1938 v W (1)
Main, J. (Hibernian), 1909 v Ni (1)
Maley, W. (Celtic), 1893 v E, Ni (2)
Malpas, M. (Dundee U), 1984 v F; 1985 v E, Ic; 1986 v W, Aus (2), Is, R, E, Ho, D, WG; 1987 v Bul, Ei, Bel; 1988 v Bel, Bul, L, S.Ar, Ma; 1989 v N, Y, I, Cy, F, Cy, E, Ch; 1990 v Y, F, N, Eg, Pol, Ma, Cr, Se, Br; 1991 v R, Bul (2), USSR, Sm; 1992 v Sw, R, Sm, Ni, Fi, US, Ca (sub), N, Ho, G; 1993 v Sw, P, I (55)
Marshall, G. (Celtic), 1992 v US (1)
Marshall, H. (Celtic), 1899 v W; 1900 v Ni (2)
Marshall, J. (Middlesbrough), 1921 v E, W, Ni; 1922 v E, W, Ni; (with Llanelly), 1924 v W (7)
Marshall, J. (Third Lanark), 1885 v Ni; 1886 v W; 1887 v E, W (4)
Marshall, J. (Rangers), 1932 v E; 1933 v E; 1934 v E (3)
Marshall, R. W. (Rangers), 1892 v Ni; 1894 v Ni (2)
Martin, B. (Motherwell), 1995 v J, Ec (2)
Martin, F. (Aberdeen), 1954 v N (2), A, U; 1955 v E, H (6)
Martin, N. (Hibernian), 1965 v Fi, Pol; (with Sunderland), 1966 v I (3)
Martis, J. (Motherwell), 1961 v W (1)
Mason, J. (Third Lanark), 1949 v E, W, Ni; 1950 v Ni; 1951 v Ni, Bel, A (7)
Massie, A. (Hearts), 1932 v Ni, W, F; 1933 v Ni; 1934 v E, Ni; 1935 v E, Ni, W; 1936 v W, Ni; (with Aston Villa), 1936 v E; 1937 v G, E, W, Ni, A; 1938 v W (18)
Masson, D. S. (QPR), 1976 v Ni, W, E; 1977 v Fi, Cz, W, Ni, E, Ch, Arg, Br; 1978 v EG, Cz, W; (with Derby Co), Ni, E, Pe (17)
Mathers, D. (Partick T), 1954 v Fi (1)
Maxwell, W. S. (Stoke C), 1898 v E (1)
May, J. (Rangers), 1906 v W, Ni; 1908 v E, Ni; 1909 v W (5)
Meechan, P. (Celtic), 1896 v Ni (1)
Meiklejohn, D. D. (Rangers), 1922 v W; 1924 v W; 1925 v W, Ni, E; 1928 v W, Ni; 1929 v E, Ni; 1930 v E, Ni; 1931 v E; 1932 v W, Ni; 1934 v A (15)
Menzies, A. (Hearts), 1906 v E (1)
Mercer, R. (Hearts), 1912 v W; 1913 v Ni (2)
Middleton, R. (Cowdenbeath), 1930 v Ni (1)
Millar, A. (Hearts), 1939 v W (1)
Millar, J. (Rangers), 1897 v E; 1898 v E, W (3)
Millar, J. (Rangers), 1963 v A, Ei (2)
Miller, J. (St Mirren), 1931 v E, I, Sw; 1932 v F; 1934 v E (5)
Miller, P. (Dumbarton), 1882 v E; 1883 v E, W (3)
Miller, T. (Liverpool), 1920 v E; (with Manchester U), 1921 v E, Ni (3)
Miller, W. (Third Lanark), 1876 v E (1)
Miller, W. (Celtic), 1947 v E, W, Bel, L; 1948 v W, Ni (6)
Miller, W. (Aberdeen), 1975 v R; 1978 v Bul; 1980 v Bel, W, E, Pol, H; 1981 v Se, P, Is (sub), Ni, W, Ni, E; 1982 v Ni, P, Ho, Br, USSR; 1983 v EG, Sw (2), W, E, Ca (3); 1984 v U, Bel, EG, W, E, F; 1985 v Y, Ic, Sp (2), W, E, Ic; 1986 v W, EG, Aus (2), Is, R, E, Ho, D, WG, U; 1987 v Bul, E, Br; 1988 v H, L, S.Ar, Ma, Sp, Co, E; 1989 v N, Y; 1990 v Y, N (65)
Mills, W. (Aberdeen), 1936 v W, Ni; 1937 v W (3)
Milne, J. V. (Middlesbrough), 1938 v E; 1939 v E (2)
Mitchell, D. (Rangers), 1890 v Ni; 1892 v E; 1893 v E, Ni; 1894 v E (5)
Mitchell, J. (Kilmarnock), 1908 v Ni; 1910 v Ni, W (3)
Mitchell, R. C. (Newcastle U), 1951 v D, F (2)
Mochan, N. (Celtic), 1954 v N, A, U (3)
Moir, W. (Bolton W), 1950 v E (1)
Moncur, R. (Newcastle U), 1968 v Ho; 1970 v Ni, W, E, Ei; 1971 v D, Bel, W, P, Ni, E, D; 1972 v Pe, Ni, W, E (16)
Morgan, H. (St Mirren), 1898 v W; (with Liverpool), 1899 v E (2)
Morgan, W. (Burnley), 1968 v Ni; (with Manchester U), 1972 v Pe, Y, Cz, Br; 1973 v D (2), E (2), W, Ni, Sw, Br; 1974 v Cz (2), WG (2), Ni, Bel (sub), Br, Y (21)
Morris, D. (Raith R), 1923 v Ni; 1924 v E, Ni; 1925 v E, W, Ni (6)
Morris, H. (East Fife), 1950 v Ni (1)
Morrison, T. (St Mirren), 1927 v E (1)
Morton, A. L. (Queen's Park), 1920 v W, Ni; (with Rangers), 1921 v E; 1922 v E, W; 1923 v E, W, Ni; 1924 v E, W, Ni; 1925 v E, W, Ni; 1927 v E, Ni; 1928 v E, W, Ni; 1929 v E, W, Ni; 1930 v E, W, Ni; 1931 v E, W, Ni; 1932 v E, W, F (31)
Morton, H. A. (Kilmarnock), 1929 v G, Ho (2)
Mudie, J. K. (Blackpool), 1957 v W, Ni, E, Y, Sw, Sp (2), WG; 1958 v Ni, E, W, Sw, H, Pol, Y, Par, F (17)
Muir, W. (Dundee), 1907 v Ni (1)
Muirhead, T. A. (Rangers), 1922 v Ni; 1923 v E; 1924 v W; 1927 v Ni; 1928 v Ni; 1929 v W, Ni; 1930 v W (8)
Mulhall, G. (Aberdeen), 1960 v Ni; (with Sunderland), 1963 v Ni; 1964 v Ni (3)
Munro, A. D. (Hearts), 1937 v W, Ni; (with Blackpool), 1938 v Ho (3)
Munro, F. M. (Wolverhampton W), 1971 v Ni (sub), E (sub), D, USSR; 1975 v Se, W (sub), Ni, E, R (9)
Munro, I. (St Mirren), 1979 v Arg, N; 1980 v Pe, A, Bel, W, E (7)
Munro, N. (Abercorn), 1888 v W; 1889 v E (2)
Murdoch, J. (Motherwell), 1931 v Ni (1)
Murdoch, R. (Celtic), 1966 v W, E, I (2); 1967 v Ni; 1968 v Ni; 1969 v W, Ni, E, WG, Cy; 1970 v A (12)
Murphy, F. (Celtic), 1938 v Ho (1)
Murray, J. (Renton), 1895 v W (1)
Murray, J. (Hearts), 1958 v E, H, Pol, Y, F (5)
Murray, J. W. (Vale of Leven), 1890 v W (1)
Murray, P. (Hibernian), 1896 v Ni; 1897 v W (2)
Murray, S. (Aberdeen), 1972 v Bel (1)
Mutch, G. (Preston NE), 1938 v E (1)

Napier, C. E. (Celtic), 1932 v E; 1935 v E, W; (with Derby Co), 1937 v Ni, A (5)
Narey, D. (Dundee U), 1977 v Se (sub); 1979 v P, Ni (sub), Arg; 1980 v P, Ni, Pol, H; 1981 v W, E (sub); 1982 v Ho, W, E, Nz (sub), Br, USSR; 1983 v EG, Sw, Bel, Ni, W, E, Ca (3); 1986 v Is, R, Ho, WG, U; 1987 v Bul, E, Bel; 1989 v I, Cy (35)
Neil, R. G. (Hibernian), 1896 v W; (with Rangers), 1900 v W (2)
Neill, R. W. (Queen's Park), 1876 v W; 1877 v E, W; 1878 v W; 1880 v E (5)
Neilles, P. (Hearts), 1914 v W, Ni (2)
Nelson, J. (Cardiff C), 1925 v W, Ni; 1928 v E; 1930 v F (4)
Nevin, P. K. F. (Chelsea), 1986 v R (sub), E (sub); 1987 v L, Ei, Bel (sub); 1988 v L; (with Everton), 1989 v Cy, E; 1991 v R (sub), Bul (sub), Sm (sub); 1992 v US, G (sub), C (sub); (with Tranmere R), 1993 v Ma, P (sub), Es; 1994 v Sw, Ma, Ho, A (sub), Ho; 1995 v Fa, Ru (sub), Sm (25)
Niblo, T. D. (Aston Villa), 1904 v E (1)
Nibloe, J. (Kilmarnock), 1929 v E, N, Ho; 1930 v W; 1931 v E, Ni, A, I, Sw; 1932 v E, F (11)
Nicholas, C. (Celtic), 1983 v Sw, Ni, E, Ca (3); (with Arsenal), 1984 v Bel, F (sub); 1985 v Y (sub), Ic (sub), Sp (sub), W (sub); 1986 v Is, R (sub), E, D, U (sub); 1987 v Bul, E (sub); (with Aberdeen), 1989 v Cy (sub) (20)
Nicol, S. (Liverpool), 1985 v Y, Ic, Sp, W; 1986 v W, EG, Aus, E, D, WG, U; 1988 v H, Bul, S.Ar, Sp, Co, E; 1989 v N, Y, Cy, F; 1990 v Y, F; 1991 v Sw, USSR, Sm; 1992 v Sw (27)
Nisbet, J. (Ayr U), 1929 v N, G, Ho (3)
Niven, J. B. (Moffatt), 1885 v Ni (1)

O'Donnell, F. (Preston NE), 1937 v E, A, Cz; 1938 v W; (with Blackpool), E, Ho (6)
O'Donnell, P. (Motherwell), 1994 v Sw (sub) (1)
Ogilvie, D. H. (Motherwell), 1934 v A (1)
O'Hare, J. (Derby Co), 1970 v W, Ni, E; 1971 v D, Bel, W, Ni; 1972 v P, Bel, Ho (sub), Pe, Ni, W (13)
Ormond, W. E. (Hibernian), 1954 v E, N, Fi, A, U; 1959 v E (6)
O'Rourke, F. (Airdrieonians), 1907 v Ni (1)
Orr, J. (Kilmarnock), 1892 v W (1)
Orr, R. (Newcastle U), 1902 v E; 1904 v E (2)
Orr, T. (Morton), 1952 v Ni, W (2)
Orr, W. (Celtic), 1900 v Ni; 1903 v Ni; 1904 v W (3)
Orrock, R. (Falkirk), 1913 v W (1)
Oswald, J. (Third Lanark), 1889 v E; (with St Bernards), 1895 v E; (with Rangers), 1897 v W (3)

Parker, A. H. (Falkirk), 1955 v P, Y, A; 1956 v E, Ni, W, A; 1957 v Ni, W, Y; 1958 v Ni, W, E, Sw; (with Everton), Par (15)
Parlane, D. (Rangers), 1973 v W, Sw, Br; 1975 v Sp (sub), Se, P, W, Ni, E, R; 1976 v D (sub); 1977 v W (12)
Parlane, R. (Vale of Leven), 1878 v W; 1879 v E, W (3)
Paterson, G. D. (Celtic), 1939 v Ni (1)
Paterson, J. (Leicester C), 1920 v E (1)
Paterson, J. (Cowdenbeath), 1931 v A, I, Sw (3)
Paton, A. (Motherwell), 1952 v D, Se (2)
Paton, D. (St Bernards), 1896 v W (1)
Paton, M. (Dumbarton), 1883 v E; 1884 v W; 1885 v W, E; 1886 v E (5)
Paton, R. (Vale of Leven), 1879 v E, W (2)
Patrick, J. (St Mirren), 1897 v E, W (2)
Paul, H. McD. (Queen's Park), 1909 v E, W, Ni (3)
Paul, W. (Partick T), 1888 v W; 1889 v W; 1890 v W (3)
Paul, W. (Dykebar), 1891 v Ni (1)
Pearson, T. (Newcastle U), 1947 v E, Bel (2)
Penman, A. (Dundee), 1966 v Ho (1)
Pettigrew, W. (Motherwell), 1976 v Sw, Ni, W; 1977 v W (sub), Se (5)
Phillips, J. (Queen's Park), 1877 v E, W; 1878 v W (3)
Plenderleith, J. B. (Manchester C), 1961 v Ni (1)
Porteous, W. (Hearts), 1903 v Ni (1)
Pringle, C. (St Mirren), 1921 v W (1)
Provan, D. (Rangers), 1964 v Ni, N; 1966 v I (2), Ho (5)
Provan, D. (Celtic), 1980 v Bel (2 sub), P (sub), Ni (sub); 1981 v Is, W, E; 1982 v Se, P, Ni (10)
Pursell, P. (Queen's Park), 1914 v W (1)

Quinn, J. (Celtic), 1905 v Ni; 1906 v Ni, W; 1908 v Ni, E; 1909 v E; 1910 v E, Ni, W; 1912 v E, W (11)
Quinn, P. (Motherwell), 1961 v E, Ei (2); 1962 v U (4)

Rae, J. (Third Lanark), 1889 v W; 1890 v Ni (2)
Raeside, J. S. (Third Lanark), 1906 v W (1)
Raisbeck, A. G. (Liverpool), 1900 v E; 1901 v E; 1902 v E; 1903 v E, W; 1904 v E; 1906 v E; 1907 v E (8)
Rankin, G. (Vale of Leven), 1890 v Ni; 1891 v E (2)
Rankin, R. (St Mirren), 1929 v N, G, Ho (3)
Redpath, W. (Motherwell), 1949 v W, Ni; 1951 v E, D, F, Bel, A; 1952 v Ni, E (9)
Reid, J. G. (Airdrieonians), 1914 v W; 1920 v W; 1924 v Ni (3)
Reid, R. (Brentford), 1938 v E, Ni (2)
Reid, W. (Rangers), 1911 v E, W, Ni; 1912 v Ni; 1913 v E, W, Ni; 1914 v E, Ni (9)
Reilly, L. (Hibernian), 1949 v E, W, F; 1950 v W, Ni, Sw, F; 1951 v W, E, D, F, Bel, A; 1952 v Ni, W, E, USA, D, Se; 1953 v Ni, W, E, Se; 1954 v W; 1955 v H (2), P, Y, A, E; 1956 v E, W, Ni, A; 1957 v E, Ni, W, Y (38)
Rennie, H. G. (Hearts), 1900 v E, Ni; (with Hibernian), 1901 v E; 1902 v E, Ni, W; 1903 v Ni, W; 1904 v Ni; 1905 v W; 1906 v Ni; 1908 v Ni, W (13)
Renny-Tailyour, H. W. (Royal Engineers), 1873 v E (1)
Rhind, A. (Queen's Park), 1872 v E (1)
Richmond, A. (Queen's Park), 1906 v W (1)
Richmond, J. T. (Clydesdale), 1877 v E; (with Queen's Park), 1878 v E; 1882 v W (3)
Ring, T. (Clyde), 1953 v Se; 1955 v W, Ni, E, H; 1957 v E, Sp (2), Sw, WG; 1958 v Ni, Sw (12)
Rioch, B. D. (Derby Co), 1975 v P, W, Ni, E, R; 1976 v D (2), R, Ni, W, E; 1977 v Fi, Cz, W; (with Everton), W, Ni, E, Ch, Br; 1978 v Cz; (with Derby Co), Ni, E, Pe, Ho (24)
Ritchie, A. (East Stirlingshire), 1891 v W (1)
Ritchie, H. (Hibernian), 1923 v W; 1928 v Ni (2)
Ritchie, J. (Queen's Park), 1897 v W (1)
Ritchie, W. (Rangers), 1962 v U (sub) (1)
Robb, D. T. (Aberdeen), 1971 v W, E, P, D (sub), USSR (5)
Robb, W. (Rangers), 1926 v W; (with Hibernian), 1928 v W (2)
Robertson, A. (Clyde), 1955 v P, A, H; 1958 v Sw, Par (5)
Robertson, D. (Rangers), 1992 v Ni; 1994 v Sw, Ho (3)
Robertson, G. (Motherwell), 1910 v W; (with Sheffield W), 1912 v W; 1913 v E, Ni (4)
Robertson, G. (Kilmarnock), 1938 v Cz (1)
Robertson, H. (Dundee), 1962 v Cz (1)
Robertson, J. (Dundee), 1931 v A, I (2)
Robertson, J. (Hearts), 1991 v R, Sw, Bul (sub), Sm (sub); 1992 v Sm, Ni (sub), Fi; 1993 v I (sub), Ma (sub), G, Es; 1995 v J (sub), Ec, Fa (sub) (14)
Robertson, J. N. (Nottingham F), 1978 v Ni, W (sub), Ir; 1979 v P, N; 1980 v Pe, A, Bel (2), P; 1981 v Se, P, Is, Ni, Is, Ni, E; 1982 v Se, Ni (2), E (sub), Nz, Br, USSR; 1983 v EG, Sw; (with Derby Co), 1984 v U, Bel (28)
Robertson, J. G. (Tottenham H), 1965 v W (1)
Robertson, J. T. (Everton), 1898 v E; (with Southampton), 1899 v E; (with Rangers), 1900 v E, W; 1901 v W, Ni, E; 1902 v W, Ni, E; 1903 v E, W; 1904 v E, W, Ni; 1905 v W (16)
Robertson, P. (Dundee), 1903 v Ni (1)
Robertson, T. (Queen's Park), 1889 v Ni; 1890 v E; 1891 v W; 1892 v Ni (4)
Robertson, T. (Hearts), 1898 v Ni (1)
Robertson, W. (Dumbarton), 1887 v E, W (2)
Robinson, R. (Dundee), 1974 v WG (sub); 1975 v Se, Ni, R (sub) (4)
Rough, A. (Partick T), 1976 v Sw, Ni, W, E; 1977 v Fi, Cz, W (2), Se, Ni, E, Ch, Arg, Br; 1978 v Cz, W, Ni, E, Pe, Ir, Ho; 1979 v A, P, W, Arg, N; 1980 v Pe, A, Bel (2), P, W, E, Pol, H; 1981 v Se, P, Is, Ni, Is, W, E; 1982 v Se, Ni, Sp, Ho, W, E, Nz, Br, USSR; (with Hibernian), 1986 v W (sub), E (53)
Rougvie, D. (Aberdeen), 1984 v Ni (1)
Rowan, A. (Caledonian), 1880 v E; (with Queen's Park), 1882 v W (2)
Russell, D. (Hearts), 1895 v E, Ni; (with Celtic), 1897 v W; 1898 v Ni; 1901 v W, Ni (6)
Russell, J. (Cambuslang), 1890 v Ni (1)
Russell, W. F. (Airdrieonians), 1924 v W; 1925 v E (2)
Rutherford, E. (Rangers), 1948 v F (1)

St John, I. (Motherwell), 1959 v WG; 1960 v E, Ni, W, Pol, A; 1961 v E; (with Liverpool), 1962 v Ni, W, E, Cz (2), U; 1963 v W, Ni, E, N, Ei (sub), Sp; 1964 v Ni; 1965 v E (21)
Sawers, W. (Dundee), 1895 v W (1)
Scarff, P. (Celtic), 1931 v Ni (1)
Schaedler, E. (Hibernian), 1974 v WG (1)
Scott, A. S. (Rangers), 1957 v Ni, Y, WG; 1958 v W, Sw; 1959 v P; 1962 v Ni, W, E, Cz, U; (with Everton), 1964 v W, N; 1965 v Fi; 1966 v P, Br (16)
Scott, J. (Hibernian), 1966 v Ho (1)
Scott, J. (Dundee), 1971 v D (sub), USSR (2)

Scott, M. (Airdrieonians), 1898 v W (1)
Scott, R. (Airdrieonians), 1894 v Ni (1)
Scoular, J. (Portsmouth), 1951 v D, F, A; 1952 v E, USA, D, Se; 1953 v W, Ni (9)
Sellar, W. (Battlefield), 1885 v E; 1886 v E; 1887 v E, W; 1888 v E; (with Queen's Park), 1891 v E; 1892 v E; 1893 v E, Ni (9)
Semple, W. (Cambuslang), 1886 v W (1)
Shankly, W. (Preston NE), 1938 v E; 1939 v E, W, Ni, H (5)
Sharp, G. M. (Everton), 1985 v Ic; 1986 v W, Aus (2 sub), Is, R, U; 1987 v Ei; 1988 v Bel (sub), Bul, L, Ma (12)
Sharp, J. (Dundee), 1904 v W; (with Woolwich Arsenal), 1907 v W, E; 1908 v E; (with Fulham), 1909 v W (5)
Shaw, D. (Hibernian), 1947 v W, Ni; 1948 v E, Bel, Sw, F; 1949 v W, Ni (8)
Shaw, F. W. (Pollokshields Ath), 1884 v E, W (2)
Shaw, J. (Rangers), 1947 v E, Bel, L; 1948 v Ni (4)
Shearer, D. (Aberdeen), 1994 v A (sub), Ho (sub); 1995 v Fi, Ru (sub), Sm, Fa (6)
Shearer, R. (Rangers), 1961 v E, Ei (2), Cz (4)
Sillars, D. C. (Queen's Park), 1891 v Ni; 1892 v E; 1893 v W; 1894 v E; 1895 v W (5)
Simpson, J. (Third Lanark), 1895 v E, W, Ni (3)
Simpson, J. (Rangers), 1935 v E, W, Ni; 1936 v E, W, Ni; 1937 v G, E, W, Ni, A, Cz; 1938 v W, Ni (14)
Simpson, N. (Aberdeen), 1983 v Ni; 1984 v F (sub); 1987 v E; 1988 v E (4)
Simpson, R. C. (Celtic), 1967 v E, USSR; 1968 v Ni, E; 1969 v A (5)
Sinclair, G. L. (Hearts), 1910 v Ni; 1912 v W, Ni (3)
Sinclair, J. W. E. (Leicester C), 1966 v P (1)
Skene, L. H. (Queen's Park), 1904 v W (1)
Sloan, T. (Third Lanark), 1904 v W (1)
Smellie, R. (Queen's Park), 1887 v Ni; 1888 v W; 1889 v E; 1891 v E; 1893 v E, Ni (6)
Smith, A. (Rangers), 1898 v E; 1900 v E, Ni, W; 1901 v E, Ni, W; 1902 v E, Ni, W; 1903 v E, Ni, W; 1904 v Ni; 1905 v W; 1906 v E, Ni; 1907 v W; 1911 v E, Ni (20)
Smith, D. (Aberdeen), 1966 v Ho; (with Rangers), 1968 v Ho (2)
Smith, G. (Hibernian), 1947 v E, Ni; 1948 v W, Bel, Sw, F; 1952 v E, USA; 1955 v P, Y, A, H; 1956 v E, Ni, W; 1957 v Sp (2), Sw (18)
Smith, H. G. (Hearts), 1988 v S.Ar (sub); 1992 v Ni, Ca (3)
Smith, J. (Rangers), 1935 v Ni; 1938 v Ni (2)
Smith, J. (Ayr U), 1924 v E (1)
Smith, J. (Aberdeen), 1968 v Ho (sub); (with Newcastle U), 1974 v WG, Ni (sub), W (sub) (4)
Smith, J. E. (Celtic), 1959 v H, P (2)
Smith, Jas (Queen's Park), 1872 v E (1)
Smith, John (Mauchline), 1877 v E, W; 1879 v E, W; (with Edinburgh University), 1880 v E; (with Queen's Park), 1881 v W, E; 1883 v E, W; 1884 v E (10)
Smith, N. (Rangers), 1897 v E; 1898 v W; 1899 v E, W, Ni; 1900 v E, W, Ni; 1901 v Ni, W; 1902 v E, Ni (12)
Smith, R. (Queen's Park), 1872 v E; 1873 v E (2)
Smith, T. M. (Kilmarnock), 1934 v E; (with Preston NE), 1938 v E (2)
Somers, P. (Celtic), 1905 v E, Ni; 1907 v Ni; 1909 v W (4)
Somers, W. S. (Third Lanark), 1879 v E, W; (with Queen's Park), 1880 v W (3)
Somerville, G. (Queen's Park), 1886 v E (1)
Souness, G. J. (Middlesbrough), 1975 v EG, Sp, Se; (with Liverpool), 1978 v Bul, W, E (sub), Ho; 1979 v A, N, W, Ni, E; 1980 v Pe, A, Bel, P, Ni; 1981 v P, Is (2); 1982 v Ni, P, Sp, W, E, Nz, Br, USSR; 1983 v EG, Sw, Bel, Sw, W, E, Ca (2 + 1 sub); 1984 v U, Ni, W; (with Sampdoria), 1985 v Y, Ic, Sp (2), W, E, Ic; 1986 v EG, Aus (2), R, E, D, WG (54)
Speedie, D. R. (Chelsea), 1985 v E; 1986 v W, EG (sub), Aus, E; (with Coventry C), 1989 v Y (sub), I (sub), Cy (1 + 1 sub), Ch (10)
Speedie, F. (Rangers), 1903 v E, W, Ni (3)
Speirs, J. H. (Rangers), 1908 v W (1)
Spencer, J. (Chelsea), 1995 v Ru (sub), Gr (sub), Sm (sub), J (4)
Stanton, P. (Hibernian), 1966 v Ho; 1969 v Ni; 1970 v Ei, A; 1971 v D, Bel, P, USSR, D; 1972 v P, Bel, Ho, W; 1973 v W, Ni; 1974 v WG (16)
Stark, J. (Rangers), 1909 v E, Ni (2)
Steel, W. (Morton), 1947 v E, Bel, L; (with Derby Co), 1948 v F, E, W, Ni; 1949 v E, W, Ni, F; 1950 v E, W, Ni, Sw, P, F; (with Dundee), 1951 v W, Ni, E, A (2), D, F, Bel; 1952 v W; 1953 v W, E, Ni, Se (30)
Steele, D. M. (Huddersfield), 1923 v E, W, Ni (3)
Stein, C. (Rangers), 1969 v W, Ni, D, E, Cy (2); 1970 v A (sub), Ni (sub), W, E, Ei, WG; 1971 v D, USSR, Bel, D; 1972 v Cz (sub); (with Coventry C), 1973 v E (2 sub), W (sub), Ni (21)
Stephen, J. F. (Bradford), 1947 v W; 1948 v W (2)
Stevenson, G. (Motherwell), 1928 v W, Ni; 1930 v Ni, E, F; 1931 v E, W; 1932 v W, Ni; 1933 v Ni; 1934 v E; 1935 v Ni (12)
Stewart, A. (Queen's Park), 1888 v Ni; 1889 v W (2)
Stewart, A. (Third Lanark), 1894 v W (1)
Stewart, D. (Dumbarton), 1888 v Ni (1)
Stewart, D. (Queen's Park), 1893 v W; 1894 v Ni; 1897 v Ni (3)
Stewart, D. S. (Leeds U), 1978 v EG (1)
Stewart, G. (Hibernian), 1906 v W, E; (with Manchester C), 1907 v E, W (4)
Stewart, J. (Kilmarnock), 1977 v Ch (sub); (with Middlesbrough), 1979 v N (2)
Stewart, R. (West Ham U), 1981 v W, Ni, E; 1982 v Ni, P, W; 1984 v F; 1987 v Ei (2), L (10)
Stewart, W. E. (Queen's Park), 1898 v Ni; 1900 v Ni (2)
Storrier, D. (Celtic), 1899 v E, W, Ni (3)
Strachan, G. (Aberdeen), 1980 v Ni, W, E, Pol, H (sub); 1981 v Se, P; 1982 v Ni, P, Sp, Ho (sub), Nz, Br, USSR; 1983 v EG, Sw, Bel, Sw, Ni (sub), W, E, Ca (2 + 1 sub); 1984 v EG, Ni, E, F; (with Manchester U), 1985 v Sp (sub), E, Ic; 1986 v W, Aus, R, D, WG, U; 1987 v Bul, Ei (2); 1988 v H; 1989 v F (sub); (with Leeds U), 1990 v F; 1991 v USSR, Bul, Sm; 1992 v Sw, R, Ni, Fi (50)
Sturrock, P. (Dundee U), 1981 v W (sub), Ni, E (sub); 1982 v P, Ni (sub), W (sub), E (sub); 1983 v EG (sub), Sw, Bel (sub), Ca (3); 1984 v W; 1985 v Y (sub); 1986 v Is (sub), Ho, D, U; 1987 v Bel (20)
Summers, W. (St Mirren), 1926 v E (1)
Symon, J. S. (Rangers), 1939 v H (1)

Tait, T. S. (Sunderland), 1911 v W (1)
Taylor, J. (Queen's Park), 1872 v E; 1873 v E; 1874 v E; 1875 v E; 1876 v E, W (6)
Taylor, J. D. (Dumbarton), 1892 v W; 1893 v W; 1894 v Ni; (with St Mirren), 1895 v Ni (4)
Taylor, W. (Hearts), 1892 v E (1)
Telfer, W. (Motherwell), 1933 v Ni; 1934 v Ni (2)
Telfer, W. D. (St Mirren), 1954 v W (1)
Templeton, R. (Aston Villa), 1902 v E; (with Newcastle U), 1903 v E, W; 1904 v E; (with Woolwich Arsenal), 1905 v W; (with Kilmarnock), 1908 v Ni; 1910 v E, Ni; 1912 v E, Ni; 1913 v W (11)
Thomson, A. (Arthurlie), 1886 v Ni (1)
Thomson, A. (Third Lanark), 1889 v W (1)
Thomson, A. (Airdrieonians), 1909 v Ni (1)
Thomson, A. (Celtic), 1926 v E; 1932 v F; 1933 v W (3)
Thomson, C. (Hearts), 1904 v Ni; 1905 v E, Ni, W; 1906 v W, Ni; 1907 v E, W, Ni; 1908 v E, W, Ni; (with Sunderland), 1909 v W; 1910 v E; 1911 v Ni; 1912 v E, W; 1913 v E, W; 1914 v E, Ni (21)
Thomson, C. (Sunderland), 1937 v Cz (1)

Thomson, D. (Dundee), 1920 v W (1)
Thomson, J. (Celtic), 1930 v F; 1931 v E, W, Ni (4)
Thomson, J. J. (Queen's Park), 1872 v E; 1873 v E; 1874 v E (3)
Thomson, J. R. (Everton), 1933 v W (1)
Thomson, R. (Celtic), 1932 v W (1)
Thomson, R. W. (Falkirk), 1927 v E (1)
Thomson, S. (Rangers), 1884 v W, Ni (2)
Thomson, W. (Dumbarton), 1892 v W; 1893 v W; 1898 v Ni, W (4)
Thomson, W. (Dundee), 1896 v W (1)
Thornton, W. (Rangers), 1947 v W, Ni; 1948 v E, Ni; 1949 v F; 1952 v D, Se (7)
Thomson, W. (St Mirren), 1980 v Ni; 1981 v Ni (sub+1) 1982 v P; 1983 v Ni, Ca; 1984 v EG (7)
Toner, W. (Kilmarnock), 1959 v W, Ni (2)
Townsley, T. (Falkirk), 1926 v W (1)
Troup, A. (Dundee), 1920 v E; 1921 v W, Ni; 1922 v Ni; (with Everton), 1926 v E (5)
Turnbull, E. (Hibernian), 1948 v Bel, Sw; 1951 v A; 1958 v H, Pol, Y, Par, F (8)
Turner, T. (Arthurlie), 1884 v W (1)
Turner, W. (Pollokshields Ath), 1885 v Ni; 1886 v Ni (2)

Ure, J. F. (Dundee), 1962 v W, Cz; 1963 v W, Ni, E, A, N, Sp; (with Arsenal), 1964 v Ni, N; 1968 v Ni (11)
Urquhart, D. (Hibernian), 1934 v W (1)

Vallance, T. (Rangers), 1877 v E, W; 1878 v E; 1879 v E, W; 1881 v E, W (7)
Venters, A. (Cowdenbeath), 1934 v Ni; (with Rangers), 1936 v E; 1939 v E (3)

Waddell, T. S. (Queen's Park), 1891 v Ni; 1892 v E; 1893 v E, Ni; 1895 v E, Ni (6)
Waddell, W. (Rangers), 1947 v W; 1949 v E, W, Ni, F; 1950 v E, Ni; 1951 v E, D, F, Bel, A; 1952 v Ni, W; 1954 v Ni; 1955 v W, Ni (17)
Wales, H. M. (Motherwell), 1933 v W (1)
Walker, A. (Celtic), 1988 v Co (sub); 1995 v Fi, Fa (sub) (3)
Walker, F. (Third Lanark), 1922 v W (1)
Walker, G. (St Mirren), 1930 v F; 1931 v Ni, A, Sw (4)
Walker, J. (Hearts), 1895 v Ni; 1897 v W; 1898 v Ni; (with Rangers), 1904 v W, Ni (5)
Walker, J. (Swindon T), 1911 v E, W, Ni; 1912 v E, W, Ni; 1913 v E, W, Ni (9)
Walker, N. (Hearts), 1993 v G (1)
Walker, R. (Hearts), 1900 v E, Ni; 1901 v E, W; 1902 v E, W, Ni; 1903 v E, W, Ni; 1904 v E, W, Ni; 1905 v E, W, Ni; 1906 v Ni; 1907 v E, Ni; 1908 v E, W, Ni; 1909 v E, W; 1912 v E, W, Ni; 1913 v E, W (29)
Walker, T. (Hearts), 1935 v E, W; 1936 v E, W, Ni; 1937 v G, E, W, Ni, A, Cz; 1938 v E, W, Ni, Cz, Ho; 1939 v E, W, Ni, H (20)
Walker, W. (Clyde), 1909 v Ni; 1910 v Ni (2)
Wallace, I. A. (Coventry C), 1978 v Bul (sub); 1979 v P (sub), W (3)
Wallace, W. S. B. (Hearts), 1965 v Ni; 1966 v E, Ho; (with Celtic), 1967 v E, USSR (sub); 1968 v Ni; 1969 v E (sub) (7)
Wardhaugh, J. (Hearts), 1955 v H; 1957 v Ni (2)
Wark, J. (Ipswich T), 1979 v W, Ni, E, Arg, N (sub); 1980 v Pe, A, Bel (2); 1981 v Is, Ni; 1982 v Se, Sp, Ho, Ni, Nz, Br, USSR; 1983 v EG, Sw (2), Ni, E (sub); 1984 v U, Bel, EG; (with Liverpool), E, F; 1985 v Y (29)
Watson, A. (Queen's Park), 1881 v E, W; 1882 v E (3)
Watson, J. (Sunderland), 1903 v E, W; 1904 v E; 1905 v E; (with Middlesbrough), 1909 v E, Ni (6)
Watson, J. (Motherwell), 1948 v Ni; (with Huddersfield T), 1954 v Ni (2)
Watson, J. A. K. (Rangers), 1878 v W (1)
Watson, P. R. (Blackpool), 1934 v A (1)
Watson, R. (Motherwell), 1971 v USSR (1)
Watson, W. (Falkirk), 1898 v W (1)
Watt, F. (Kilbirnie), 1889 v W, Ni; 1890 v W; 1891 v E (4)
Watt, W. W. (Queen's Park), 1887 v Ni (1)
Waugh, W. (Hearts), 1938 v Cz (1)
Weir, A. (Motherwell), 1959 v WG; 1960 v E, P, A, H, T (6)
Weir, J. (Third Lanark), 1887 v Ni (1)
Weir, J. B. (Queen's Park), 1872 v E; 1874 v E; 1875 v E; 1878 v W (4)
Weir, P. (St Mirren), 1980 v Ni, W, Pol (sub), H; (with Aberdeen), 1983 v Sw; 1984 v Ni (6)
White, John (Albion R), 1922 v W; (with Hearts), 1923 v Ni (2)
White, J. A. (Falkirk), 1959 v WG, Ho, P; 1960 v Ni; (with Tottenham H), 1960 v W, Pol, A, T; 1961 v W; 1962 v Ni, W, E, Cz (2); 1963 v W, Ni, E; 1964 v Ni, W, E, N, WG (22)
White, W. (Bolton W), 1907 v E; 1908 v E (2)
Whitelaw, A. (Vale of Leven), 1887 v Ni; 1890 v W (2)
Whyte, D. (Celtic), 1988 v Bel (sub), L; 1989 v Ch (sub); 1992 v US (sub); (with Middlesbrough), 1993 v P, I; 1995 v J (sub), Ec (8)
Wilson, A. (Sheffield W), 1907 v E; 1908 v E; 1912 v E; 1913 v E, W; 1914 v Ni (6)
Wilson, A. (Portsmouth), 1954 v Fi (1)
Wilson, A. N. (Dunfermline), 1920 v E, W, Ni; 1921 v E, W, Ni; (with Middlesbrough), 1922 v E, W, Ni; 1923 v E, W, Ni (12)
Wilson, D. (Queen's Park), 1900 v W (1)
Wilson, D. (Oldham Ath), 1913 v E (1)
Wilson, D. (Rangers), 1961 v E, W, Ni, Ei (2), Cz; 1962 v Ni, W, E, Cz, U; 1963 v W, E, A, N, Ei, Sp; 1964 v E, WG; 1965 v Ni, E, Fi (22)
Wilson, G. W. (Hearts), 1904 v W; 1905 v E, Ni; 1906 v W; (with Everton), 1907 v E; (with Newcastle U), 1909 v E (6)
Wilson, Hugh, (Newmilns), 1890 v W; (with Sunderland), 1897 v E; (with Third Lanark), 1902 v W; 1904 v Ni (4)
Wilson, I. A. (Leicester C), 1987 v E, Br; (with Everton), 1988 v Bel, Bul, L (5)
Wilson, J. (Vale of Leven), 1888 v W; 1889 v E; 1890 v E; 1891 v E (4)
Wilson, P. (Celtic), 1926 v Ni; 1930 v F; 1931 v Ni; 1933 v E (4)
Wilson, P. (Celtic), 1975 v Sp (sub) (1)
Wilson, R. P. (Arsenal), 1972 v P, Ho (2)
Wiseman, W. (Queen's Park), 1927 v W; 1930 v Ni (2)
Wood, G. (Everton), 1979 v Ni, E, Arg (sub); (with Arsenal), 1982 v Ni (4)
Woodburn, W. A. (Rangers), 1947 v E, Bel, L; 1948 v W, Ni; 1949 v E, F; 1950 v E, W, Ni, P, F; 1951 v E, W, Ni, A (2), D, F, Bel; 1952 v E, W, Ni, USA (24)
Wotherspoon, D. N. (Queen's Park), 1872 v E; 1873 v E (2)
Wright, K. (Hibernian), 1992 v Ni (1)
Wright, S. (Aberdeen), 1993 v G, Es (2)
Wright, T. (Sunderland), 1953 v W, Ni, E (3)
Wylie, T. G. (Rangers), 1890 v Ni (1)

Yeats, R. (Liverpool), 1965 v W; 1966 v I (2)
Yorston, B. C. (Aberdeen), 1931 v Ni (1)
Yorston, H. (Aberdeen), 1955 v W (1)
Young, A. (Hearts), 1960 v E, A (sub), H, T; 1961 v W, Ni; (with Everton), Ei; 1966 v P (8)
Young, A. (Everton), 1905 v E; 1907 v W (2)
Young, G. L. (Rangers), 1947 v E, Ni, Bel, L; 1948 v E, Ni, Bel, Sw, F; 1949 v E, W, Ni, F; 1950 v E, W, Ni, Sw, P,

F; 1951 v E, W, Ni, A (2), D, F, Bel; 1952 v E, W, Ni, USA, D, Se; 1953 v W, E, Ni, Se; 1954 v Ni, W; 1955 v W, Ni, P, Y; 1956 v Ni, W, E, A; 1957 v E, Ni, W, Y, Sp, Sw (53)

Young, J. (Celtic), 1906 v Ni (1)

Younger, T. (Hibernian), 1955 v P, Y, A, H; 1956 v E, Ni, W, A; (with Liverpool), 1957 v E, Ni, W, Y, Sp (2), Sw, WG; 1958 v Ni, W, E, Sw, H, Pol, Y, Par (24)

WALES

Adams, H. (Berwyn R), 1882 v Ni, E; (with Druids), 1883 v Ni, E (4)

Aizlewood, M. (Charlton Ath), 1986 v S.Ar, Ca (2); 1987 v Fi; (with Leeds U), USSR, Fi (sub); 1988 v D (sub), Se, Ma, I; 1989 v Ho, Se (sub), WG; (with Bradford C), 1990 v Fi, WG, Ei, Cr; (with Bristol C), 1991 v D, Bel (2), L, Ei, Ic, Pol, WG; 1992 v Br, L, Ei, A, R, Ho, Arg, J; 1993 v Ei, Bel, Fa; 1994 v RCS, Cy; (with Cardiff C) 1995 v Bul (39)

Allchurch, I. J. (Swansea T), 1951 v E, Ni, P, Sw; 1952 v E, S, Ni, R of UK; 1953 v S, E, Ni, F, Y; 1954 v S, E, Ni, A; 1955 v S, E, Ni, Y; 1956 v E, S, Ni, A; 1957 v E, S; 1958 v Ni, Is (2), H (2), M, Sw, Br; (with Newcastle U), 1959 v E, S, Ni; 1960 v E, S; 1961 v Ni, H, Sp (2); 1962 v E, S, Br (2), M; (with Cardiff C), 1963 v S, E, Ni, H (2); 1964 v E; 1965 v S, E, Ni, Gr, I, USSR; (with Swansea T), 1966 v USSR, E, S, D, Br (2), Ch (68)

Allchurch, L. (Swansea T), 1955 v Ni; 1956 v A; 1958 v S, Ni, EG, Is; 1959 v S; (with Sheffield U), 1962 v S, Ni, Br; 1964 v E (11)

Allen, B. W. (Coventry C), 1951 v S, E (2)

Allen, M. (Watford), 1986 v S.Ar (sub), Ca (1 + 1 sub); (with Norwich C), 1989 v Is (sub); 1990 v Ho, WG; (with Millwall), Ei, Se, Cr (sub); 1991 v L (sub), Ei (sub); 1992 v A; 1993 v Ei (sub); (with Newcastle U), 1994 v R (sub) (14)

Arridge, S. (Bootle), 1892 v S, Ni; (with Everton), 1894 v Ni; 1895 v Ni; 1896 v E; (with New Brighton Tower), 1898 v E, Ni; 1899 v E (8)

Astley, D. J. (Charlton Ath), 1931 v Ni; (with Aston Villa), 1932 v E; 1933 v E, S, Ni; 1934 v E, S; 1935 v S; 1936 v E, Ni; (with Derby Co), 1939 v E, S; (with Blackpool), F (13)

Atherton, R. W. (Hibernian), 1899 v E, Ni; 1903 v E, S, Ni; (with Middlesbrough), 1904 v E, S, Ni; 1905 v Ni (9)

Bailiff, W. E. (Llanelly), 1913 v E, S, Ni; 1920 v Ni (4)

Baker, C. W. (Cardiff C), 1958 v M; 1960 v S, Ni; 1961 v S, E, Ei; 1962 v S (7)

Baker, W. G. (Cardiff C), 1948 v Ni (1)

Bamford, T. (Wrexham), 1931 v E, S, Ni; 1932 v Ni; 1933 v F (5)

Barnes, W. (Arsenal), 1948 v E, S, Ni; 1949 v E, S, Ni; 1950 v E, S, Ni, Bel; 1951 v E, S, Ni, P; 1952 v E, S, Ni, R of UK; 1954 v E, S; 1955 v S, Y (22)

Bartley, T. (Glossop NE), 1898 v E (1)

Bastock, A. M. (Shrewsbury), 1892 v Ni (1)

Beadles, G. H. (Cardiff C), 1925 v E, S (2)

Bell, W. S. (Shrewsbury Engineers), 1881 v E, S; (with Crewe Alex), 1886 v E, S, Ni (5)

Bennion, S. R. (Manchester U), 1926 v S; 1927 v S; 1928 v S, E, Ni; 1929 v S, E, Ni; 1930 v S; 1932 v Ni (10)

Berry, G. F. (Wolverhampton W), 1979 v WG; 1980 v Ei, WG (sub), T; (with Stoke C), 1983 v E (sub) (5)

Blackmore, C. G. (Manchester U), 1985 v N (sub); 1986 v S (sub), H (sub), S.Ar, Ei, U; 1987 v Fi (2), USSR, Cz; 1988 v D (2), Cz, Y, Se, Ma, I; 1989 v Ho, Fi, Is, WG; 1990 v F; Ho, WG, Cr; 1991 v Bel, L; 1992 v Ei (sub), A, R (sub), Ho, Arg, J; 1993 v Fa, Cy, Bel, RCS; 1994 v Se (sub) (38)

Blake, N. A. (Sheffield U), 1994 v N, Se (sub); 1995 v Alb, Mol (4)

Blew, H. (Wrexham), 1899 v E, S, Ni; 1902 v S, Ni; 1903 v E, S; 1904 v E, S, Ni; 1905 v S, Ni; 1906 v E, S, Ni; 1907 v S; 1908 v E, S, Ni; 1909 v E, S; 1910 v E (22)

Boden, T. (Wrexham), 1880 v E (1)

Bodin, P. J. (Swindon T), 1990 v Cr; 1991 v D, Bel, L, Ei; (with C Palace), Bel, Ic, Pol, WG; 1992 v Br, G, L (sub); (with Swindon T), Ei (sub), Ho, Arg; 1993 v Ei, Bel, RCS, Fa; 1994 v R, Se, Es (sub); 1995 v Alb (23)

Boulter, L. M. (Brentford), 1939 v Ni (1)

Bowdler, H. E. (Shrewsbury), 1893 v S (1)

Bowdler, J. C. H. (Shrewsbury), 1890 v Ni; (with Wolverhampton W), 1891 v S; 1892 v Ni; (with Shrewsbury), 1894 v E (4)

Bowen, D. L. (Arsenal), 1955 v S, Y; 1957 v Ni, Cz, EG; 1958 v E, S, Ni, EG, Is (2), H (2), M, Se, Br; 1959 v E, S, Ni (19)

Bowen, E. (Druids), 1880 v S; 1883 v S (2)

Bowen, J. P. (Swansea C), 1994 v Es (1)

Bowen, M. R. (Tottenham H), 1986 v Ca (2 sub); (with Norwich C), 1988 v Y (sub); 1989 v Fi (sub), Is, Se, WG (sub); 1990 v Fi (sub), Ho, WG, Se; 1992 v Br (sub), G, L, Ei, A, R, Ho (sub), J; 1993 v Fa, Cy, Bel (1 + sub), RCS (sub); 1994 v RCS, Se; 1995 v Mol, Ge, Bul (2), G, Ge (32)

Bowsher, S. J. (Burnley), 1929 v Ni (1)

Boyle, T. (C Palace), 1981 v Ei, S (sub) (2)

Britten, T. J. (Parkgrove), 1878 v S; (with Presteigne), 1880 v S (2)

Brookes, S. J. (Llandudno), 1900 v E, Ni (2)

Brown, A. I. (Aberdare Ath), 1926 v Ni (1)

Bryan, T. (Oswestry), 1886 v E, Ni (2)

Buckland, T. (Bangor), 1899 v E (1)

Burgess, W. A. R. (Tottenham H), 1947 v E, S, Ni; 1948 v E, S; 1949 v E, S, Ni, P, Bel, Sw; 1950 v E, S, Ni, Bel; 1951 v S, Ni, P, Sw; 1952 v E, S, Ni, R of UK; 1953 v S, E, Ni, F, Y; 1954 v S, E, Ni, A (32)

Burke, T. (Wrexham), 1883 v E; 1884 v S; 1885 v E, S, Ni; (with Newton Heath), 1887 v E, S; 1888 v S (8)

Burnett, T. B. (Ruabon), 1877 v S (1)

Burton, A. D. (Norwich C), 1963 v Ni, H; (with Newcastle U), 1964 v E; 1969 v S, E, Ni, I, EG; 1972 v Cz (9)

Butler, J. (Chirk), 1893 v E, S, Ni (3)

Butler, W. T. (Druids), 1900 v S, Ni (2)

Cartwright, L. (Coventry C), 1974 v E (sub), S, Ni; 1976 v S (sub); 1977 v WG (sub); (with Wrexham), 1978 v Ir (sub); 1979 v Ma (7)

Carty, T. – See McCarthy – (Wrexham).

Challen, J. B. (Corinthians), 1887 v E, S; 1888 v E; (with Wellingborough GS), 1890 v E (4)

Chapman, T. (Newtown), 1894 v E, S, Ni; 1895 v S, Ni; (with Manchester C), 1896 v E; 1897 v E (7)

Charles, J. M. (Swansea C), 1981 v Cz, T (sub), S (sub), USSR (sub); 1982 v Ic; 1983 v N (sub), Y (sub), Bul (sub), S, Ni, Br; 1984 v Bul (sub); (with QPR), Y (sub), S; (with Oxford U), 1985 v Ic (sub), Sp, Ic; 1986 v Ei; 1987 v Fi (19)

Charles, M. (Swansea T), 1955 v Ni; 1956 v E, S, A; 1957 v E, Ni, Cz (2), EG; 1958 v E, S, EG, Is (2), H (2), M, Se, Br; 1959 v E, S; (with Arsenal), 1961 v Ni, H, Sp (2); 1962 v E, S; (with Cardiff C), 1962 v Br, Ni; 1963 v S, H (31)

Charles, W. J. (Leeds U), 1950 v Ni; 1951 v Sw; 1953 v Ni, F, Y; 1954 v E, S, Ni, A; 1955 v S, E, Ni, Y; 1956 v E, S,

A, Ni; 1957 v E, S, Ni, Cz (2), EG; (with Juventus), 1958 v Is (2), H (2) M, Se; 1960 v S; 1962 v E, Br (2), M; (with Leeds U), 1963 v S; (with Cardiff C), 1964 v S; 1965 v S, USSR (38)
Clarke, R. J. (Manchester C), 1949 v E; 1950 v S, Ni, Bel; 1951 v E, S, Ni, P, Sw; 1952 v S, E, Ni, R of UK; 1953 v S, E; 1954 v E, S, Ni; 1955 v Y, S, E; 1956 v Ni (22)
Coleman, C. (C Palace), 1992 v A (sub); 1993 v Ei (sub); 1994 v N, Es; 1995 v Alb, Mol, Ge, Bul (2), G (10)
Collier, D. J. (Grimsby T), 1921 v S (1)
Collins, W. S. (Llanelly), 1931 v S (1)
Conde, C. (Chirk), 1884 v E, S, Ni (3)
Cook, F. C. (Newport Co), 1925 v E, S; (with Portsmouth), 1928 v E, S; 1930 v E, S, Ni; 1932 v E (8)
Cornforth, J.M. (Swansea C), 1995 v Bul (sub), Ge (2)
Crompton, W. (Wrexham), 1931 v E, S, Ni (3)
Cross, E. A. (Wrexham), 1876 v S; 1877 v S (2)
Cross, K. (Druids), 1879 v S; 1881 v E, S (3)
Crowe, V. H. (Aston Villa), 1959 v E, Ni; 1960 v E, Ni; 1961 v S, E, Ni, Ei, H, Sp (2); 1962 v E, S, Br, M; 1963 v H (16)
Cumner, R. H. (Arsenal), 1939 v E, S, Ni (3)
Curtis, A. (Swansea C), 1976 v E, Y (sub), S, Ni, Y (sub), E; 1977 v WG, S (sub), Ni (sub); 1978 v WG, E, S; 1979 v WG, S; (with Leeds U), E, Ni, Ma; 1980 v Ei, WG, T; (with Swansea C), 1982 v Cz, Ic, USSR, Sp, E, S, Ni; 1983 v N; 1984 v R (sub); (with Southampton), S; 1985 v Sp, N (1 + 1 sub); 1986 v H; (with Cardiff C), 1987 v USSR (35)
Curtis, E. R. (Cardiff C), 1928 v S; (with Birmingham), 1932 v S; 1934 v Ni (3)

Daniel, R. W. (Arsenal), 1951 v E, Ni, P; 1952 v E, S, Ni, R of UK; 1953 v S, E, Ni, F, Y; (with Sunderland), 1954 v E, S, Ni; 1955 v E, Ni; 1957 v S, E, Ni, Cz (21)
Darvell, S. (Oxford University), 1897 v S, Ni (2)
Davies, A. (Manchester U), 1983 v Ni, Br; 1984 v E, Ni; 1985 v Ic; (with Newcastle U), 1986 v H; (with Swansea C), 1988 v Ma, I; 1989 v Ho; (with Bradford C), 1990 v Fi, Ei (11)
Davies, A. (Wrexham), 1876 v S; 1877 v S (2)
Davies, A. (Druids), 1904 v S; (with Middlesbrough), 1905 v S (2)
Davies, A. O. (Barmouth), 1885 v Ni; 1886 v E, S; (with Swifts), 1887 v E, S; 1888 v E, Ni; (with Wrexham), 1889 v S; (with Crewe Alex), 1890 v E (9)
Davies, A. T. (Shrewsbury), 1891 v Ni (1)
Davies, C. (Brecon), 1899 v Ni; (with Hereford), 1900 v Ni (2)
Davies, C. (Charlton Ath), 1972 v R (sub) (1)
Davies, D. (Bolton W), 1904 v S, Ni; 1908 v E (sub) (3)
Davies, D. C. (Brecon), 1899 v Ni; (with Hereford); 1900 v Ni (2)
Davies, D. W. (Treharris), 1912 v Ni; (with Oldham Ath), 1913 v Ni (2)
Davies, E. Lloyd (Stoke C), 1904 v E; 1907 v E, S, Ni; (with Northampton T), 1908 v S; 1909 v Ni; 1910 v Ni; 1911 v E, S; 1912 v E, S; 1913 v E, S; 1914 v Ni, E, S (16)
Davies, E. R. (Newcastle U), 1953 v S, E; 1954 v E, S; 1958 v E, EG (6)
Davies, G. (Fulham), 1980 v T, Ic; 1982 v Sp (sub), F (sub); 1983 v E, Bul, S, Ni, Br; 1984 v R (sub), S (sub), E, Ni; 1985 v Ic; (with Manchester C), 1986 v S.Ar, Ei (16)
Davies, Rev. H. (Wrexham), 1928 v Ni (1)
Davies, Idwal (Liverpool Marine), 1923 v S (1)
Davies, J. E. (Oswestry), 1885 v E (1)
Davies, Jas (Wrexham), 1878 v S (1)
Davies, John (Wrexham), 1879 v S (1)
Davies, Jos (Newton Heath), 1888 v E, S, Ni; 1889 v S; 1890 v E; (with Wolverhampton W), 1892 v E; 1893 v E (7)
Davies, Jos (Everton), 1889 v S, Ni; (with Chirk), 1891 v Ni; (with Ardwick), v E, S; (with Sheffield U), 1895 v E, S, Ni; (with Manchester C), 1896 v E; (with Millwall), 1897 v E; (with Reading), 1900 v E (11)
Davies, J. P. (Druids), 1883 v E, Ni (2)
Davies, Ll. (Wrexham), 1907 v Ni; 1910 v Ni, S, E; (with Everton), 1911 v S, Ni; (with Wrexham), 1912 v Ni, S, E; 1913 v Ni, S, E; 1914 v Ni (13)
Davies, L. S. (Cardiff C), 1922 v E, S, Ni; 1923 v E, S, Ni; 1924 v E, S, Ni; 1925 v S, Ni; 1926 v E, Ni; 1927 v E, Ni; 1928 v S, Ni, E; 1929 v S, Ni, E; 1930 v E, S (23)
Davies, O. (Wrexham), 1890 v S (1)
Davies, R. (Wrexham), 1883 v Ni; 1884 v Ni; 1885 v Ni (3)
Davies, R. (Druids), 1885 v E (1)
Davies, R. O. (Wrexham), 1892 v Ni, E (2)
Davies, R. T. (Norwich C), 1964 v Ni; 1965 v E; 1966 v Br (2), Ch; (with Southampton), 1967 v S, E, Ni; 1968 v S, Ni, WG; 1969 v S, E, Ni, I, WG, R of UK; 1970 v E, S, Ni; 1971 v Cz, S, E, Ni; 1972 v R, E, S, N; (with Portsmouth), 1974 v E (29)
Davies, R. W. (Bolton W), 1964 v E; 1965 v E, S, Ni, D, Gr, USSR; 1966 v E, S, Ni, USSR, D, Br (2), Ch (sub); 1967 v S; (with Newcastle U), E; 1968 v S, Ni, WG; 1969 v S, E, Ni, I; 1970 v EG; 1971 v R, Cz; (with Manchester C), 1972 v E, S, Ni; (with Manchester U), 1973 v E, S (sub), Ni; (with Blackpool), 1974 v Pol (34)
Davies, Stanley (Preston NE), 1920 v E, S, Ni; (with Everton), 1921 v E, S, Ni; (with WBA), 1922 v E, S, Ni; 1923 v S; 1925 v S, Ni; 1926 v S, E, Ni; 1927 v S; 1928 v S; (with Rotherham U), 1930 v Ni (18)
Davies, T. (Oswestry), 1886 v E (1)
Davies, T. (Druids), 1903 v E, Ni, S; 1904 v S (4)
Davies, W. (Wrexham), 1884 v Ni (1)
Davies, W. (Swansea T), 1924 v E, S, Ni; (with Cardiff C), 1925 v E, S, Ni; 1926 v E, S, Ni; 1927 v S; 1928 v Ni; (with Notts Co), 1929 v E, S, Ni; 1930 v E, S, Ni (17)
Davies, William (Wrexham), 1903 v Ni; 1905 v Ni; (with Blackburn R), 1908 v E, S; 1909 v E, S, Ni; 1911 v E, S, Ni; 1912 v Ni (11)
Davies, W. C. (C Palace), 1908 v S; (with WBA), 1909 v E; 1910 v S; (with C Palace), 1914 v E (4)
Davies, W. D. (Everton), 1975 v H, L, S, E, Ni; 1976 v Y (2), E, Ni; 1977 v WG, S (2), Cz, E, Ni; 1978 v K; (with Wrexham), S, Cz, WG, Ir, E, S, Ni; 1979 v Ma, T, WG, S, E, Ni, Ma; 1980 v Ei, WG, T, E, S, Ni, Ic; 1981 v T, Cz, Ei, T, S, E, USSR; (with Swansea C), 1982 v Cz, Ic, USSR, Sp, E, S, F; 1983 v Y (52)
Davies, W. H. (Oswestry), 1876 v S; 1877 v S; 1879 v E; 1880 v E (4)
Davies, W. O. (Millwall Ath), 1913 v E, S, Ni; 1914 v S, Ni (5)
Davis, G. (Wrexham), 1978 v Ir, E (sub), Ni (3)
Day, A. (Tottenham H), 1934 v Ni (1)
Deacy, N. (PSV Eindhoven), 1977 v Cz, S, E, Ni; 1978 v K (sub), S (sub), Cz (sub), WG, Ir, S (sub), Ni; (with Beringen), 1979 v T (12)
Dearson, D. J. (Birmingham), 1939 v S, Ni, F (3)
Derrett, S. C. (Cardiff C), 1969 v S, WG; 1970 v I; 1971 v Fi (4)
Dewey, F. T. (Cardiff Corinthians), 1931 v E, S (2)
Dibble, A. (Luton T), 1986 v Ca (1+1 sub); (with Manchester C), 1989 v Is (3)
Doughty, J. (Druids), 1886 v S; (with Newton Heath), 1887 v S, Ni; 1888 v E, S, Ni; 1889 v S; 1890 v E (8)
Doughty, R. (Newton Heath and Druids), 1888 v S, Ni (2)
Durban, A. (Derby Co), 1966 v Br (sub); 1967 v Ni; 1968 v E, S, Ni, WG; 1969 v EG, S, E, Ni, WG; 1970 v E, S, Ni, EG, I; 1971 v R, S, E, Ni, Cz, Fi; 1972 v Fi, Cz, E, S, Ni (27)
Dwyer, P. (Cardiff C), 1978 v Ir, E, S, Ni; 1979 v T, S, E, Ni, Ma (sub); 1980 v WG (10)

Edwards, C. (Wrexham), 1878 v S (1)
Edwards, G. (Birmingham C), 1947 v E, S, Ni; 1948 v E, S, Ni; (with Cardiff C), 1949 v Ni, P, Bel, Sw; 1950 v E, S (12)
Edwards, H. (Wrexham Civil Service), 1878 v S; 1880 v E; 1882 v E, S; 1883 v S; 1884 v Ni; 1887 v Ni (7)
Edwards, J. H. (Wanderers), 1876 v S (1)
Edwards, J. H. (Oswestry), 1895 v Ni; 1897 v E, Ni (3)
Edwards, J. H. (Aberystwyth), 1898 v Ni (1)
Edwards, L. T. (Charlton Ath), 1957 v Ni, EG (2)
Edwards, R. I. (Chester), 1978 v K (sub); 1979 v Ma, WG; (with Wrexham), 1980 v T (sub) (4)
Edwards, T. (Linfield), 1932 v S (1)
Egan, W. (Chirk), 1892 v S (1)
Ellis, B. (Motherwell), 1932 v E; 1933 v E, S; 1934 v S; 1936 v E; 1937 v S (6)
Ellis, E. (Nunhead), 1931 v S; (with Oswestry), E; 1932 v Ni (3)
Emanuel, W. J. (Bristol C), 1973 v E (sub), Ni (sub) (2)
England, H. M. (Blackburn R), 1962 v Ni, Br, M; 1963 v Ni, H; 1964 v E, S, Ni; 1965 v E, D, Gr (2), USSR, Ni, I; 1966 v E, S, Ni, USSR, D; (with Tottenham H), 1967 v S, E; 1968 v E, Ni, WG; 1969 v EG; 1970 v R of UK, EG, E, S, Ni, I; 1971 v R; 1972 v Fi, E, S, Ni; 1973 v E (3), S; 1974 v Pol; 1975 v H, L (44)
Evans, B. C. (Swansea C), 1972 v Fi, Cz; 1973 v E (2), Pol, S; (with Hereford U), 1974 v Pol (7)
Evans, D. G. (Reading), 1926 v Ni; 1927 v Ni, E; (with Huddersfield T), 1929 v S (4)
Evans, H. P. (Cardiff C), 1922 v E, S, Ni; 1924 v E, S, Ni (6)
Evans, I. (C Palace), 1976 v A, E, Y (2), E, Ni; 1977 v WG, S (2), Cz, E, Ni; 1978 v K (13)
Evans, J. (Oswestry), 1893 v Ni; 1894 v E, Ni (3)
Evans, J. (Cardiff C), 1912 v Ni; 1913 v Ni; 1914 v S; 1920 v S, Ni; 1922 v Ni; 1923 v E, Ni (8)
Evans, J. H. (Southend U), 1922 v E, S, Ni; 1923 v S (4)
Evans, Len (Aberdare Ath), 1927 v Ni; (with Cardiff C), 1931 v E, S; (with Birmingham), 1934 v Ni (4)
Evans, M. (Oswestry), 1884 v E (1)
Evans, R. (Clapton), 1902 v Ni (1)
Evans, R. E. (Wrexham), 1906 v E, S; (with Aston Villa), Ni; 1907 v E; 1908 v E, S; (with Sheffield U), 1909 v S; 1910 v E, S, Ni (10)
Evans, R. O. (Wrexham), 1902 v Ni; 1903 v E, S, Ni; (with Blackburn R), 1908 v Ni; (with Coventry C), 1911 v E, Ni; 1912 v E, S, Ni (10)
Evans, R. S. (Swansea T), 1964 v Ni (1)
Evans, T. J. (Clapton Orient), 1927 v S; 1928 v E, S; (with Newcastle U), Ni (4)
Evans, W. (Tottenham H), 1933 v Ni; 1934 v E, S; 1935 v E; 1936 v E, Ni (6)
Evans, W. A. W. (Oxford University), 1876 v S; 1877 v S (2)
Evans, W. G. (Bootle), 1890 v E; 1891 v E; (with Aston Villa), 1892 v E (3)
Evelyn, E. C. (Crusaders), 1887 v E (1)
Eyton-Jones, J. A. (Wrexham), 1883 v Ni; 1884 v Ni, E, S (4)

Farmer, G. (Oswestry), 1885 v E, S (2)
Felgate, D. (Lincoln C), 1984 v R (sub) (1)
Finnigan, R. J. (Wrexham), 1930 v Ni (1)
Flynn, B. (Burnley), 1975 v L (2 sub), H (sub), S, E, Ni; 1976 v A, E, Y (2), E, Ni; 1977 v WG (sub), S (2), Cz, E, Ni; 1978 v K (2), S; (with Leeds U), Cz, WG, Ir (sub), E, S, Ni; 1979 v Ma, T, S, E, Ni, Ma; 1980 v Ei, WG, E, S, Ni, Ic; 1981 v T, Cz, Ei, T, S, E, USSR; 1982 v Cz, USSR, E, S, Ni, F; 1983 v N; (with Burnley), Y, E, Bul, S, Ni, Br; 1984 v N, R, Bul, Y, S, N, Is (66)
Ford, T. (Swansea T), 1947 v S; (with Aston Villa), 1947 v Ni; 1948 v S, Ni; 1949 v E, S, Ni, P, Bel, Sw; 1950 v E, S, Ni, Bel; 1951 v S; (with Sunderland), 1951 v E, Ni, P, Sw; 1952 v E, S, Ni, R of UK; 1953 v S, E, Ni, F, Y; (with Cardiff C), 1954 v A; 1955 v S, E, Ni, Y; 1956 v S, Ni, E, A; 1957 v S (38)
Foulkes, H. E. (WBA), 1932 v Ni (1)
Foulkes, W. I. (Newcastle U), 1952 v E, S, Ni, R of UK; 1953 v E, S, F, Y; 1954 v E, S, Ni (11)
Foulkes, W. T. (Oswestry), 1884 v Ni; 1885 v S (2)
Fowler, J. (Swansea T), 1925 v E; 1926 v E, Ni; 1927 v S; 1928 v S; 1929 v E (6)

Garner, J. (Aberystwyth), 1896 v S (1)
Giggs, R. J. (Manchester U), 1992 v G (sub), L (sub), R (sub); 1993 v Fa (sub), Bel (sub + 1), RCS, Fa; 1994 v RCS, Cy, R; 1995 v Alb, Bul (13)
Giles, D. (Swansea C), 1980 v E, S, Ni, Ic; 1981 v T, Cz, T (sub), E (sub), USSR (sub); (with C Palace), 1982 v Sp (sub); 1983 v Ni (sub), Br (12)
Gillam, S. G. (Wrexham), 1889 v S (sub), Ni; (with Shrewsbury), 1890 v E, Ni; (with Clapton), 1894 v S (5)
Glascodine, G. (Wrexham), 1879 v E (1)
Glover, E. M. (Grimsby T), 1932 v S; 1934 v Ni; 1936 v S; 1937 v E, S, Ni; 1939 v Ni (7)
Godding, G. (Wrexham), 1923 v S, Ni (2)
Godfrey, B. C. (Preston NE), 1964 v Ni; 1965 v D, I (3)
Goodwin, U. (Ruthin), 1881 v E (1)
Goss, J. (Norwich C), 1991 v Ic, Pol (sub); 1992 v A; 1994 v Cy (sub), R (sub), Se; 1995 v Alb (7)
Gough, R. T. (Oswestry White Star), 1883 v S (1)
Gray, A. (Oldham Ath), 1924 v E, S, Ni; 1925 v E, S, Ni; 1926 v E, S; 1927 v S; (with Manchester C), 1928 v E, S; 1929 v E, S, Ni; (with Manchester Central), 1930 v S; (with Tranmere R), 1932 v E, S, Ni; (with Chester), 1937 v E, S, Ni; 1938 v E, S, Ni (24)
Green, A. W. (Aston Villa), 1901 v Ni; (with Notts Co), 1903 v E; 1904 v S, Ni; 1906 v Ni, E; (with Nottingham F), 1907 v E; 1908 v S (8)
Green, C. R. (Birmingham C), 1965 v USSR, I; 1966 v E, S, USSR, Br (2); 1967 v E; 1968 v E, S, Ni, WG; 1969 v S, I, Ni (sub) (15)
Green, G. H. (Charlton Ath), 1938 v Ni; 1939 v E, Ni, F (4)
Grey, Dr W. (Druids), 1876 v S; 1878 v S (2)
Griffiths, A. T. (Wrexham), 1971 v Cz (sub); 1975 v A, H (2), L (2), E, Ni; 1976 v A, E, S, E (sub), Ni, Y (2); 1977 v WG, S (17)
Griffiths, F. J. (Blackpool), 1900 v E, S (2)
Griffiths, G. (Chirk), 1887 v Ni (1)
Griffiths, J. H. (Swansea T), 1953 v Ni (1)
Griffiths, L. (Wrexham), 1902 v S (1)
Griffiths, M. W. (Leicester C), 1947 v Ni; 1949 v P, Bel; 1950 v E, S, Bel; 1951 v E, Ni, P, Sw; 1954 v A (11)
Griffiths, P. (Chirk), 1884 v E, Ni; 1888 v E; 1890 v S, Ni; 1891 v Ni (6)
Griffiths, P. H. (Everton), 1932 v S (1)
Griffiths, S. (Wrexham), 1902 v S (1)
Griffiths, T. P. (Everton), 1927 v E, Ni; 1929 v E; 1930 v E; 1931 v Ni; 1932 v Ni, S, E; (with Bolton W), 1933 v E, S, Ni; (with Middlesbrough), F; 1934 v E, S; 1935 v E, Ni; 1936 v S; (with Aston Villa), Ni; 1937 v E, S, Ni (21)

Hall, G. D. (Chelsea), 1988 v Y (sub), Ma, I; 1989 v Ho, Fi, Is; 1990 v Ei; 1991 v Ei; 1992 v A (sub) (9)
Hallam, J. (Oswestry), 1889 v E (1)
Hanford, H. (Swansea T), 1934 v Ni; 1935 v S; 1936 v E; (with Sheffield W), 1936 v Ni; 1938 v E, S; 1939 v F (7)
Harrington, A. C. (Cardiff C), 1956 v Ni; 1957 v E, S; 1958 v S, Ni, Is (2); 1961 v S, E; 1962 v E, S (11)
Harris, C. S. (Leeds U), 1976 v E, S; 1978 v WG, Ir, E, S, Ni; 1979 v Ma, T, WG, E (sub), Ma; 1980 v Ni (sub), Ic (sub); 1981 v T, Cz (sub), Ei, T, S, E, USSR; 1982 v Cz, Ic, E (sub) (24)

Harris, W. C. (Middlesbrough), 1954 v A; 1957 v EG, Cz; 1958 v E, S, EG (6)
Harrison, W. C. (Wrexham), 1899 v E; 1900 v E, S, Ni; 1901 v Ni (5)
Hartson, J. (Arsenal), 1995 v Bul, G (sub), Ge (sub) (3)
Hayes, A. (Wrexham), 1890 v Ni; 1894 v Ni (2)
Hennessey, W. T. (Birmingham C), 1962 v Ni, Br (2); 1963 v S, E, H (2); 1964 v E, S; 1965 v S, E, D, Gr, USSR; 1966 v E, USSR; (with Nottingham F), 1966 v S, Ni, D, Br (2), Ch; 1967 v S, E; 1968 v E, S, Ni; 1969 v WG, EG, R of UK; 1970 v EG; (with Derby Co), E, S, Ni; 1972 v Fi, Cz, E, S; 1973 v E (39)
Hersee, A. M. (Bangor), 1886 v S, Ni (2)
Hersee, R. (Llandudno), 1886 v Ni (1)
Hewitt, R. (Cardiff C), 1958 v Ni, Is, Se, H, Br (5)
Hewitt, T. J. (Wrexham), 1911 v E, S, Ni; (with Chelsea), 1913 v E, S, Ni; (with South Liverpool), 1914 v E, S (8)
Heywood, D. (Druids), 1879 v E (1)
Hibbott, H. (Newtown Excelsior), 1880 v E, S; (with Newtown), 1885 v S (3)
Higham, G. G. (Oswestry), 1878 v S; 1879 v E (2)
Hill, M. R. (Ipswich T), 1972 v Cz, R (2)
Hockey, T. (Sheffield U), 1972 v Fi, R; 1973 v E (2); (with Norwich C), Pol, S, E, Ni; (with Aston Villa), 1974 v Pol (9)
Hoddinott, T. F. (Watford), 1921 v E, S (2)
Hodges, G. (Wimbledon), 1984 v N (sub), Is (sub); 1987 v USSR, Fi, Cz; (with Newcastle U), 1988 v D; (with Watford), D (sub), Cz (sub), Se, Ma (sub), I (sub); 1990 v Se, Cr; (with Sheffield U), 1992 v Br (sub), Ei (sub), A (16)
Hodgkinson, A. V. (Southampton), 1908 v Ni (1)
Holden, A. (Chester C), 1984 v Is (sub) (1)
Hole, B. G. (Cardiff C), 1963 v Ni; 1964 v Ni; 1965 v S, E, Ni, D, Gr (2), USSR, I; 1966 v E, S, Ni, USSR, D, Br (2), Ch; (with Blackburn R), 1967 v S, E, Ni; 1968 v E, S, Ni, WG; (with Aston Villa), 1969 v I, WG, EG; 1970 v I; (with Swansea C), 1971 v R (30)
Hole, W. J. (Swansea T), 1921 v Ni; 1922 v E; 1923 v E, Ni; 1928 v E, S, Ni; 1929 v E, S (9)
Hollins, D. M. (Newcastle U), 1962 v Br (sub), M; 1963 v Ni, H; 1964 v E; 1965 v Ni, Gr, I; 1966 v S, D, Br (11)
Hopkins, I. J. (Brentford), 1935 v S, Ni; 1936 v E, Ni; 1937 v E, S, Ni; 1938 v E, Ni; 1939 v E, S, Ni (12)
Hopkins, J. (Fulham), 1983 v Ni, Br; 1984 v N, R, Bul, Y, S, E, Ni, N, Is; 1985 v Ic (1 + 1 sub), N; (with C Palace), 1990 v Ho, Cr (16)
Hopkins, M. (Tottenham H), 1956 v Ni; 1957 v Ni, S, E, Cz (2), EG; 1958 v E, S, Ni, EG, Is (2), H (2), M, Se, Br; 1959 v E, S, Ni; 1960 v E, S; 1961 v Ni, H, Sp (2); 1962 v Ni, Br (2), M; 1963 v S, Ni, H (34)
Horne, B. (Portsmouth), 1988 v D (sub), Y, Se (sub), Ma, I; 1989 v Ho, Fi, Is; (with Southampton), Se, WG; 1990 v WG (sub), Ei, Se, Cr; 1991 v D, Bel (2), L, Ei, Ic, Pol, WG; 1992 v Br, G, L, Ei, A, R, Ho, Arg, J; (with Everton), 1993 v Fa, Cy, Bel, Ei, Bel, RCS, Fa; 1994 v RCS, Cy, R, N, Se, Es; 1995 v Mol, Ge, Bul, G, Ge (49)
Howell, E. G. (Builth), 1888 v Ni; 1890 v E; 1891 v E (3)
Howells, R. G. (Cardiff C), 1954 v E, S (2)
Hugh, A. R. (Newport Co), 1930 v Ni (1)
Hughes, A. (Rhos), 1894 v E, S (2)
Hughes, A. (Chirk), 1907 v Ni (1)
Hughes, C. M. (Luton T), 1992 v Ho (sub); 1994 v N (sub), Se (sub), Es (4)
Hughes, E. (Everton), 1899 v S, Ni; (with Tottenham H), 1901 v E, S; 1902 v Ni; 1904 v E, Ni, S; 1905 v E, Ni, S; 1906 v E, Ni; 1907 v E (14)
Hughes, E. (Wrexham), 1906 v S; (with Nottingham F), 1906 v Ni; 1908 v S, E; 1910 v Ni, E, S; 1911 v Ni, E, S; (with Wrexham), 1912 v Ni, E, S; (with Manchester C), 1913 v E, S; 1914 v N (16)
Hughes, F. W. (Northwich Victoria), 1882 v E, Ni; 1883 v E, Ni, S; 1884 v S (6)
Hughes, I. (Luton T), 1951 v E, Ni, P, Sw (4)
Hughes, J. (Cambridge University), 1877 v S; (with Aberystwyth), 1879 v S (2)
Hughes, J. (Liverpool), 1905 v E, S, Ni (3)
Hughes, J. I. (Blackburn R), 1935 v Ni (1)
Hughes, L. M. (Manchester U), 1984 v E, Ni; 1985 v Ic, Sp, Ic, N, S, Sp, N; 1986 v S, H, U; (with Barcelona), 1987 v USSR, Cz; 1988 v D (2), Cz, Se, Ma, I; (with Manchester U), 1989 v Ho, Fi, Is, Se, WG; 1990 v Fi, WG, Cr; 1991 v D, Bel (2), L, Ic, Pol, WG; 1992 v Br, G, L, Ei, R, Ho, Arg, J; 1993 v Fa, Cy, Bel, Ei, Bel, RCS, Fa; 1994 v RCS, Cy, N; 1995 v Ge, Bul, G, Ge (57)
Hughes, P. W. (Bangor), 1887 v Ni; 1889 v Ni, E (3)
Hughes, W. (Bootle), 1891 v E; 1892 v S, Ni (3)
Hughes, W. A. (Blackburn R), 1949 v E, Ni, P, Bel, Sw (5)
Hughes, W. M. (Birmingham), 1938 v E, Ni, S; 1939 v E, Ni, S, F; 1947 v E, S, Ni (10)
Humphreys, J. V. (Everton), 1947 v Ni (1)
Humphreys, R. (Druids), 1888 v Ni (1)
Hunter, A. H. (FA of Wales Secretary), 1887 v Ni (1)

Jackett, K. (Watford), 1983 v N, Y, E, Bul, S; 1984 v N, R, Y, S, Ni, N, Is; 1985 v Ic, Sp, Ic, N, S, Sp, N; 1986 v S, H, S.Ar, Ei, Ca (2); 1987 v Fi (2); 1988 v D, Cz, Y, Se (31)
Jackson, W. (St Helens Rec), 1899 v Ni (1)
James, E. (Chirk), 1893 v E, Ni; 1894 v E, S, Ni; 1898 v S, E; 1899 v Ni (8)
James, E. G. (Blackpool), 1966 v Br (2), Ch; 1967 v Ni; 1968 v S; 1971 v Cz, S, E, Ni (9)
James, L. (Burnley), 1972 v Cz, R, S (sub); 1973 v E (3), Pol, S, Ni; 1974 v Pol, E, S, Ni; 1975 v A, H (2), L (2), S, E, Ni; 1976 v A; (with Derby Co), S, E, Y (2), Ni; 1977 v WG, S (2), Cz, E, Ni; 1978 v K (2); (with QPR), WG; (with Burnley), 1979 v T; (with Swansea C), 1980 v E, S, Ni, Ic; 1981 v T, Ei, T, S, E; 1982 v Cz, Ic, USSR, E (sub), S, Ni, F; (with Sunderland), 1983 v E (sub) (54)
James, R. M. (Swansea C), 1979 v Ma, WG (sub), S, E, Ni, Ma; 1980 v WG; 1982 v Cz (sub), Ic, Sp, E, S, Ni, F; 1983 v N, Y, E, Bul; (with Stoke C), 1984 v N, R, Bul, Y, S, E, Ni, N, Is; 1985 v Ic, Sp, Ic; (with QPR), N, S, Sp, N; 1986 v S, S.Ar, Ei, U, Ca (2); 1987 v Fi (2), USSR, Cz; (with Leicester C), 1988 v D (2); (with Swansea C), Y (47)
James, W. (West Ham U), 1931 v Ni; 1932 v Ni (2)
Jarrett, R. H. (Ruthin), 1889 v Ni; 1890 v S (2)
Jarvis, A. L. (Hull C), 1967 v S, E, Ni (3)
Jenkins, E. (Lovell's Ath), 1925 v E (1)
Jenkins, J. (Brighton), 1924 v Ni, E, S; 1925 v S, Ni; 1926 v E, S; 1927 v S (8)
Jenkins, R. W. (Rhyl), 1902 v Ni (1)
Jenkyns, C. A. L. (Small Heath), 1892 v E, S, Ni; 1895 v E; (with Woolwich Arsenal), 1896 v S; (with Newton Heath), 1897 v Ni; (with Walsall), 1898 v S, E (8)
Jennings, W. (Bolton W), 1914 v E, S; 1920 v S; 1923 v Ni, E; 1924 v E, S, Ni; 1927 v S, Ni; 1929 v S (11)
John, R. F. (Arsenal), 1923 v S, Ni; 1925 v Ni; 1926 v E; 1927 v E; 1928 v E, Ni; 1930 v E, S; 1932 v E; 1933 v F, Ni; 1935 v Ni; 1936 v S; 1937 v E (15)
John, W. R. (Walsall), 1931 v Ni; (with Stoke C), 1933 v E, S, Ni, F; 1934 v E, S; (with Preston NE), 1935 v E, S; (with Sheffield U), 1936 v E, S, Ni; (with Swansea T), 1939 v E, S (14)
Johnson, M. G. (Swansea T), 1964 v Ni (1)
Jones, A. (Port Vale), 1987 v Fi, Cz (sub); 1988 v D, (with Charlton Ath), D (sub), Cz (sub); 1990 v Hol (sub) (6)
Jones, A. F. (Oxford University), 1877 v S (1)
Jones, A. T. (Nottingham F), 1905 v E; (with Notts Co), 1906 v E (2)

Jones, Bryn (Wolverhampton W), 1935 v Ni; 1936 v E, S, Ni; 1937 v E, S, Ni; 1938 v E, S, Ni; (with Arsenal), 1939 v E, S, Ni; 1947 v S, Ni; 1948 v E; 1949 v S (17)
Jones, B. S. (Swansea T), 1963 v S, E, Ni, H (2); 1964 v S, Ni; (with Plymouth Arg), 1965 v D; (with Cardiff C), 1969 v S, E, Ni, I (sub), WG, EG, R of UK (15)
Jones, Charlie (Nottingham F), 1926 v E; 1927 v S, Ni; 1928 v E; (with Arsenal), 1930 v E, S; 1932 v E; 1933 v F (8)
Jones, Cliff (Swansea T), 1954 v A; 1956 v E, Ni, S, A; 1957 v E, S, Ni, Cz (2), EG; 1958 v EG, E, S, Is (2); (with Tottenham H), 1958 v Ni, H (2), M, Se, Br; 1959 v Ni; 1960 v E, S, Ni; 1961 v S, E, Ni, Sp, H, Ei; 1962 v E, Ni, S, Br (2), M; 1963 v S, Ni, H; 1964 v E, S, Ni; 1965 v E, S, Ni, D, Gr (2), USSR, I; 1967 v S, E; 1968 v E, S, WG; (with Fulham), 1969 v I, R of UK (59)
Jones, C. W. (Birmingham), 1935 v Ni; 1939 v F (2)
Jones, D. (Chirk), 1888 v S, Ni; (with Bolton W), 1889 v E, S, Ni; 1890 v E; 1891 v S; 1892 v Ni; 1893 v E; 1894 v E; 1895 v E; 1898 v S; (with Manchester C), 1900 v E, Ni (14)
Jones, D. E. (Norwich C), 1976 v S, E (sub); 1978 v S, Cz, WG, Ir, E; 1980 v E (8)
Jones, D. O. (Leicester C), 1934 v E, Ni; 1935 v E, S; 1936 v E, Ni; 1937 v Ni (7)
Jones, Evan (Chelsea), 1910 v S, Ni; (with Oldham Ath), 1911 v E, S; 1912 v E, S; (with Bolton W), 1914 v Ni (7)
Jones, F. R. (Bangor), 1885 v E, Ni; 1886 v S (3)
Jones, F. W. (Small Heath), 1893 v S (1)
Jones, G. P. (Wrexham), 1907 v S, Ni (2)
Jones, H. (Aberaman), 1902 v Ni (1)
Jones, Humphrey (Bangor), 1885 v E, Ni, S; 1886 v E, Ni, S; (with Queen's Park), 1887 v E; (with East Stirlingshire), 1889 v E, Ni; 1890 v E, S, Ni; (with Queen's Park), 1891 v E, S (14)
Jones, Ivor (Swansea T), 1920 v S, Ni; 1921 v Ni, E; 1922 v S, Ni; (with WBA), 1923 v E, Ni; 1924 v S; 1926 v Ni (10)
Jones, Jeffrey (Llandrindod Wells), 1908 v Ni; 1909 v Ni; 1910 v S (3)
Jones, J. (Druids), 1876 v S (1)
Jones, J. (Berwyn Rangers), 1883 v S, Ni; 1884 v S (3)
Jones, J. (Wrexham), 1925 v Ni (1)
Jones, J. L. (Sheffield U), 1895 v E, S, Ni; 1896 v Ni, S, E; 1897 v Ni, S, E; (with Tottenham H), 1898 v Ni, E, S; 1899 v S, Ni; 1900 v S; 1902 v E, S, Ni; 1904 v E, S, Ni (21)
Jones, J. Love (Stoke C), 1906 v S; (with Middlesbrough), 1910 v Ni (2)
Jones, J. O. (Bangor), 1901 v S, Ni (2)
Jones, J. P. (Liverpool), 1976 v A, E, S; 1977 v WG, S (2), Cz, E, Ni; 1978 v K (2), S, Cz, WG, Ir, E, S, Ni; (with Wrexham), 1979 v Ma, T, WG, S, E, Ni, Ma; 1980 v Ei, WG, T, E, S, Ni, Ic; 1981 v T, Ei, T, S, E, USSR; 1982 v Cz, Ic, USSR, Sp, E, S, Ni, F; 1983 v N; (with Chelsea), Y, E, Bul, S, Ni, Br; 1984 v N, R, Bul, Y, S, E, Ni, N, Is; 1985 v Ic, N, S, N; (with Huddersfield T), 1986 v S, H, Ei, U, Ca (2) (72)
Jones, J. T. (Stoke C), 1912 v E, S, Ni; 1913 v E, Ni; 1914 v S, Ni; 1920 v E, S, Ni; (with C Palace), 1921 v E, S; 1922 v E, S, Ni (15)
Jones, K. (Aston Villa), 1950 v S (1)
Jones, Leslie J. (Cardiff C), 1933 v F; (with Coventry C), 1935 v Ni; 1936 v S; 1937 v E, S, Ni; (with Arsenal), 1938 v E, S, Ni; 1939 v E, S (11)
Jones, P. W. (Bristol R), 1971 v Fi (1)
Jones, R. (Bangor), 1887 v S; 1889 v E; (with Crewe Alex), 1890 v E (3)
Jones, R. (Leicester Fosse), 1898 v S (1)
Jones, R. (Druids), 1899 v S (1)
Jones, R. (Bangor), 1900 v S, Ni (2)
Jones, R. (Millwall), 1906 v S, Ni (2)
Jones, R. A. (Druids), 1884 v E, Ni, S; 1885 v S (4)
Jones, R. A. (Sheffield W), 1994 v Es (1)
Jones, R. S. (Everton), 1894 v Ni (1)
Jones, S. (Wrexham), 1887 v Ni; (with Chester), 1890 v S (2)
Jones, S. (Wrexham), 1893 v S, Ni; (with Burton Swifts), 1895 v S; 1896 v E, Ni; (with Druids), 1899 v E (6)
Jones, T. (Manchester U), 1926 v Ni; 1927 v E, Ni; 1930 v Ni (4)
Jones, T. D. (Aberdare), 1908 v Ni (1)
Jones, T. G. (Everton), 1938 v Ni; 1939 v E, S, Ni; 1947 v E, S; 1948 v E, S, Ni; 1949 v E, Ni, P, Bel, Sw; 1950 v E, S, Bel (17)
Jones, T. J. (Sheffield W), 1932 v Ni; 1933 v F (2)
Jones, V. P. (Wimbledon), 1995 v Bul (2), G, Ge (4)
Jones, W. E. A. (Swansea T), 1947 v E, S; (with Tottenham H), 1949 v E, S (4)
Jones, W. J. (Aberdare), 1901 v E, S; (with West Ham U), 1902 v E, S (4)
Jones, W. Lot (Manchester C), 1905 v E, Ni; 1906 v E, S, Ni; 1907 v E, S, Ni; 1908 v S; 1909 v E, S, Ni; 1910 v E; 1911 v E; 1913 v E, S; 1914 v S, Ni; (with Southend U), 1920 v E, Ni (20)
Jones, W. P. (Druids), 1889 v E, Ni; (with Wynstay), 1890 v S, Ni (4)
Jones, W. R. (Aberystwyth), 1897 v S (1)

Keenor, F. C. (Cardiff C), 1920 v E, Ni; 1921 v E, Ni, S; 1922 v Ni; 1923 v E, Ni, S; 1924 v E, Ni, S; 1925 v E, Ni, S; 1926 v S; 1927 v E, Ni, S; 1928 v E, Ni, S; 1929 v E, Ni, S; 1930 v E, Ni, S; 1931 v E, Ni, S; (with Crewe Alex), 1933 v S (32)
Kelly, F. C. (Wrexham), 1899 v S, Ni; (with Druids), 1902 v Ni (3)
Kelsey, A. J. (Arsenal), 1954 v Ni, A; 1955 v S, Ni, Y; 1956 v E, Ni, S, A; 1957 v E, Ni, S, Cz (2), EG; 1958 v E, S, Ni, Is (2), H (2), M, Se, Br; 1959 v E, S; 1960 v E, Ni, S; 1961 v E, Ni, S, H, Sp (2); 1962 v E, S, Ni, Br (2) (41)
Kenrick, S. L. (Druids), 1876 v S; 1877 v S; (with Oswestry), 1879 v E, S; (with Shropshire Wanderers), 1881 v E (5)
Ketley, C. F. (Druids), 1882 v Ni (1)
King, J. (Swansea T), 1955 v E (1)
Kinsey, N. (Norwich C), 1951 v Ni, P, Sw; 1952 v E; (with Birmingham C), 1954 v Ni; 1956 v E, S (7)
Knill, A. R. (Swansea C), 1989 v Ho (1)
Krzywicki, R. L. (WBA), 1970 v EG, I; (with Huddersfield T), Ni, E, S; 1971 v R, Fi; 1972 v Cz (sub) (8)

Lambert, R. (Liverpool), 1947 v S; 1948 v E; 1949 v P, Bel, Sw (5)
Latham, G. (Liverpool), 1905 v E, S; 1906 v S; 1907 v E, S, Ni; 1908 v E; 1909 v Ni; (with Southport Central), 1910 v E; (with Cardiff C), 1913 v Ni (10)
Law, B. J. (QPR), 1990 v Se (1)
Lawrence, E. (Clapton Orient), 1930 v Ni; (with Notts Co), 1932 v S (2)
Lawrence, S. (Swansea T), 1932 v Ni; 1933 v F; 1934 v S, E, Ni; 1935 v E, S; 1936 v S (8)
Lea, A. (Wrexham), 1889 v E; 1891 v S, Ni; 1893 v Ni (4)
Lea, C. (Ipswich T), 1965 v Ni, I (2)
Leary, P. (Bangor), 1889 v Ni (1)
Leek, K. (Leicester C), 1961 v S, E, Ni, H, Sp (2); (with Newcastle U), 1962 v S; (with Birmingham C), v Br (sub), M; 1963 v E; 1965 v S, Gr; (with Northampton T), 1965 v Gr (13)
Lever, A. R. (Leicester C), 1953 v S (1)
Lewis, B. (Chester), 1891 v Ni; (with Wrexham), 1892 v S, E, Ni; (with Middlesbrough), 1893 v S, E; (with Wrexham), 1894 v S, E, Ni; 1895 v S (10)
Lewis, D. (Arsenal), 1927 v E; 1928 v Ni; 1930 v E (3)

Lewis, D. (Swansea C), 1983 v Br (sub) (1)
Lewis, D. J. (Swansea T), 1933 v E, S (2)
Lewis, D. M. (Bangor), 1890 v Ni, S (2)
Lewis, J. (Bristol R), 1906 v E (1)
Lewis, J. (Cardiff C), 1926 v S (1)
Lewis, T. (Wrexham), 1881 v E, S (2)
Lewis, W. (Bangor), 1885 v E; 1886 v E, S; 1887 v E, S; 1888 v E; 1889 v E, Ni, S; (with Crewe Alex), 1890 v E; 1891 v E, S; 1892 v E, S, Ni; 1894 v E, S, Ni; (with Chester), 1895 v S, Ni, E; 1896 v E, S, Ni; (with Manchester C), 1897 v E, S; (with Chester), 1898 v Ni (27)
Lewis, W. L. (Swansea T), 1927 v E, Ni; 1928 v E, Ni; 1929 v S; (with Huddersfield T), 1930 v E (6)
Lloyd, B. W. (Wrexham), 1976 v A, E, S (3)
Lloyd, J. W. (Wrexham), 1879 v S; (with Newtown), 1885 v S (2)
Lloyd, R. A. (Ruthin), 1891 v Ni; 1895 v S (2)
Lockley, A. (Chirk), 1898 v Ni (1)
Lovell, S. (C Palace), 1982 v USSR (sub); (with Millwall), 1985 v N; 1986 v S (sub), H (sub), Ca (1 + 1 sub) (6)
Lowrie, G. (Coventry C), 1948 v E, S, Ni; (with Newcastle U), 1949 v P (4)
Lowndes, S. (Newport Co), 1983 v S (sub), Br (sub); (with Millwall), 1985 v N (sub); 1986 v S.Ar (sub), Ei, U, Ca (2); (with Barnsley), 1987 v Fi (sub); 1988 v Se (sub) (10)
Lucas, P. M. (Leyton Orient), 1962 v Ni, M; 1963 v S, E (4)
Lucas, W. H. (Swansea T), 1949 v S, Ni, P, Bel, Sw; 1950 v E; 1951 v E (7)
Lumberg, A. (Wrexham), 1929 v Ni; 1930 v E, S; (with Wolverhampton W), 1932 v S (4)

McCarthy, T. P. (Wrexham), 1899 v Ni (1)
McMillan, R. (Shrewsbury Engineers), 1881 v E, S (2)
Maguire, G. T. (Portsmouth), 1990 v Fi (sub), Ho, WG, Ei, Se; 1992 v Br (sub), G (7)
Mahoney, J. F. (Stoke C), 1968 v E; 1969 v EG; 1971 v Cz; 1973 v E (3), Pol, S, Ni; 1974 v Pol, E, S, Ni; 1975 v A, H (2), L (2), S, E, Ni; 1976 v A, Y (2), E, Ni; 1977 v WG, Cz, S, E, Ni; (with Middlesbrough), 1978 v K (2), S, Cz, Ir, E (sub), S, Ni; 1979 v WG, S, E, Ni, Ma; (with Swansea C), 1980 v Ei, WG, T (sub); 1982 v Ic, USSR; 1983 v Y, E (51)
Martin, T. J. (Newport Co), 1930 v Ni (1)
Marustik, C. (Swansea C), 1982 v Sp, E, S, Ni, F; 1983 v N (6)
Mates, J. (Chirk), 1891 v Ni; 1897 v E, S (3)
Mathews, R. W. (Liverpool), 1921 v Ni; (with Bristol C), 1923 v E; (with Bradford), 1926 v Ni (3)
Matthews, W. (Chester), 1905 v Ni; 1908 v E (2)
Matthias, J. S. (Brymbo), 1896 v S, Ni; (with Shrewsbury), 1897 v E, S; (with Wolverhampton W), 1899 v S (5)
Matthias, T. J. (Wrexham), 1914 v S, E; 1920 v Ni, S, E; 1921 v S, E, Ni; 1922 v S, E, Ni; 1923 v S (12)
Mays, A. W. (Wrexham), 1929 v Ni (1)
Medwin, T. C. (Swansea T), 1953 v Ni, F, Y; (with Tottenham H), 1957 v E, S, Ni, Cz (2), EG; 1958 v E, S, Ni, Is (2), H (2), M, Br; 1959 v E, S, Ni; 1960 v E, S, Ni; 1961 v S, Ei, E, Sp; 1963 v E, H (30)
Melville, A. K. (Swansea C), 1990 v WG, Ei, Se, Cr (sub); (with Oxford U), 1991 v Ic, Pol, WG; 1992 v Br, G, L, R, Ho, J (sub); 1993 v RCS, Fa (sub); (with Sunderland), 1994 v RCS (sub), R, N, Se, Es; 1995 v Alb, Mol (sub), Ge, Bul (24)
Meredith, S. (Chirk), 1900 v S; 1901 v S, E, Ni; (with Stoke C), 1902 v E; 1903 v Ni; 1904 v E; (with Leyton), 1907 v E (8)
Meredith, W. H. (Manchester C), 1895 v E, Ni; 1896 v E, Ni; 1897 v E, Ni, S; 1898 v E, Ni; 1899 v E; 1900 v E, Ni; 1901 v E, Ni; 1902 v E, S; 1903 v E, S, Ni; 1904 v E; 1905 v E, S; (with Manchester U), 1907 v E, S, Ni; 1908 v E, Ni; 1909 v E, S, Ni; 1910 v E, S, Ni; 1911 v E, S, Ni; 1912 v E, S, Ni; 1913 v E, S, Ni; 1914 v E, S, Ni; 1920 v E, S, Ni (48)
Mielczarek, R. (Rotherham U), 1971 v Fi (1)
Millership, H. (Rotherham Co), 1920 v E, S, Ni; 1921 v E, S, Ni (6)
Millington, A. H. (WBA), 1963 v S, E, H; (with C Palace), 1965 v E, USSR; (with Peterborough U), 1966 v Ch, Br; 1967 v E, Ni; 1968 v Ni, WG; 1969 v I, EG; (with Swansea T), 1970 v E, S, Ni; 1971 v Cz, Fi; 1972 v Fi (sub), Cz, R (21)
Mills, T. J. (Clapton Orient), 1934 v E, Ni; (with Leicester C), 1935 v E, S (4)
Mills-Roberts, R. H. (St Thomas' Hospital), 1885 v E, S, Ni; 1886 v E; 1887 v E; (with Preston NE), 1888 v E, Ni; (with Llanberis), 1892 v E (8)
Moore, G. (Cardiff C), 1960 v E, S, Ni; 1961 v Ei, Sp; (with Chelsea), 1962 v Br; 1963 v Ni, H; (with Manchester U), 1964 v S, Ni; (with Northampton T), 1966 v Ni, Ch; (with Charlton Ath), 1969 v S, E, Ni, R of UK; 1970 v E, S, Ni, I; 1971 v R (21)
Morgan, J. R. (Cambridge University), 1877 v S; (with Swansea T), 1879 v S; (with Derby School Staff), 1880 v E, S; 1881 v E, S; 1882 v E, S, Ni; (with Swansea T), 1883 v E (10)
Morgan, J. T. (Wrexham), 1905 v Ni (1)
Morgan-Owen, H. (Oxford University), 1901 v E; 1902 v S; 1906 v E, Ni; (with Welshpool), 1907 v S (5)
Morgan-Owen, M. M. (Oxford University), 1897 v S, Ni; 1898 v E, S; 1899 v S; 1900 v E, S; (with Corinthians), 1903 v S; 1906 v S, E, Ni; 1907 v E (12)
Morley, E. J. (Swansea T), 1925 v E; (with Clapton Orient), 1929 v E, S, Ni (4)
Morris, A. G. (Aberystwyth), 1896 v E, Ni, S; (with Swindon T), 1897 v E; 1898 v S; (with Nottingham F), 1899 v E, S; 1903 v E, S; 1905 v E, S; 1907 v E, S; 1908 v E; 1910 v E, S, Ni; 1911 v E, S, Ni; 1912 v E (21)
Morris, C. (Chirk), 1900 v E, S, Ni; (with Derby Co), 1901 v E, S, Ni; 1902 v E, S; 1903 v E, S, Ni; 1904 v Ni; 1905 v E, S, Ni; 1906 v S; 1907 v S; 1908 v E, S; 1909 v E, S, Ni; 1910 v E, S, Ni; (with Huddersfield T), 1911 v E, S, Ni (28)
Morris, E. (Chirk), 1893 v E, S, Ni (3)
Morris, H. (Sheffield U), 1894 v S; (with Manchester C), 1896 v E; (with Grimsby T), 1897 v E (3)
Morris, J. (Oswestry), 1887 v S (1)
Morris, J. (Chirk), 1898 v Ni (1)
Morris, R. (Chirk), 1900 v E, Ni; 1901 v Ni; 1902 v S; (with Shrewsbury T), 1903 v E, Ni (6)
Morris, R. (Druids), 1902 v E, S; (with Newtown), Ni; (with Liverpool), 1903 v S, Ni; 1904 v E, S, Ni; (with Leeds C), 1906 v S; (with Grimsby T), 1907 v Ni; (with Plymouth Arg), 1908 v Ni (11)
Morris, S. (Birmingham), 1937 v E, S; 1938 v E, S; 1939 v F (5)
Morris, W. (Burnley), 1947 v Ni; 1949 v E; 1952 v S, Ni, R of UK (5)
Moulsdale, J. R. B. (Corinthians), 1925 v Ni (1)
Murphy, J. P. (WBA), 1933 v F, E, Ni; 1934 v E, S; 1935 v E, S, Ni; 1936 v E, S, Ni; 1937 v S, Ni; 1938 v E, S (15)

Nardiello, D. (Coventry C), 1978 v Cz, WG (sub) (2)
Neal, J. E. (Colwyn Bay), 1931 v E, S (2)
Neilson, A. B. (Newcastle U), 1992 v Ei; 1994 v Se, Es; 1995 v Ge (4)
Newnes, J. (Nelson), 1926 v Ni (1)
Newton, L. F. (Cardiff Corinthians), 1912 v Ni (1)
Nicholas, D. S. (Stoke C), 1923 v S; (with Swansea T), 1927 v E, Ni (3)
Nicholas, P. (C Palace), 1979 v S (sub), Ni (sub), Ma; 1980 v Ei, WG, T, E, S, Ni, Ic; 1981 v T, Cz, E; (with Arsenal), T, S, E, USSR; 1982 v Cz, Ic, USSR, Sp, E, S, Ni, F; 1983 v Y, Bul, S, Ni; 1984 v N, Bul, N, Is; (with C Palace),

1985 v Sp; (with Luton T), N, S, Sp, N; 1986 v S, H, S.Ar, Ei, U, Ca (2); 1987 v Fi (2) USSR, Cz; (with Aberdeen), 1988 v D (2), Cz, Y, Se; (with Chelsea), 1989 v Ho, Fi, Is, Se, WG; 1990 v Fi, Ho, WG, Ei, Se, Cr; 1991 v D (sub), Bel, L, Ei; (with Watford), Bel, Pol, WG; 1992 v L (73)

Nicholls, J. (Newport Co), 1924 v E, Ni; (with Cardiff C), 1925 v E, S (4)

Niedzwiecki, E. A. (Chelsea), 1985 v N (sub); 1988 v D (2)

Nock, W. (Newtown), 1897 v Ni (1)

Nogan, L. M. (Watford), 1992 v A (sub) (1)

Norman, A. J. (Hull C), 1986 v Ei (sub), U, Ca; 1988 v Ma, I (5)

Nurse, M. T. G. (Swansea T), 1960 v E, Ni; 1961 v S, E, H, Ni, Ei, Sp (2); (with Middlesbrough), 1963 v E, H; 1964 v S (12)

O'Callaghan, E. (Tottenham H), 1929 v Ni; 1930 v S; 1932 v S, E; 1933 v Ni, S, E; 1934 v Ni, S, E; 1935 v E (11)

Oliver, A. (Blackburn R), 1905 v E; (with Bangor), S (2)

O'Sullivan, P. A. (Brighton), 1973 v S (sub); 1976 v S; 1979 v Ma (sub) (3)

Owen, D. (Oswestry), 1879 v E (1)

Owen, E. (Ruthin Grammar School), 1884 v E, Ni, S (3)

Owen, G. (Chirk), 1888 v S; (with Newton Heath), 1889 v S, Ni; 1893 v Ni (4)

Owen, J. (Newton Heath), 1892 v E (1)

Owen, Trevor (Crewe Alex), 1899 v E, S (2)

Owen, T. (Oswestry), 1879 v E (1)

Owen, W. (Chirk), 1884 v E; 1885 v Ni; 1887 v E; 1888 v E; 1889 v E, Ni, S; 1890 v S, Ni; 1891 v E, S, Ni; 1892 v E, S; 1893 v S, Ni (16)

Owen, W. P. (Ruthin), 1880 v E, S; 1881 v E, S; 1882 v E, S, Ni; 1883 v E, S; 1884 v E, S, Ni (12)

Owens, J. (Wrexham), 1902 v S (1)

Page, M. E. (Birmingham C), 1971 v Fi; 1972 v S, Ni; 1973 v E (1 + 1 sub), Ni; 1974 v S, Ni; 1975 v H, L, S, E, Ni; 1976 v E, Y (2), E, Ni; 1977 v WG, S; 1978 v K (sub + 1), WG, Ir, E, S; 1979 v Ma, WG (28)

Palmer, D. (Swansea T), 1957 v Cz; 1958 v E, EG (3)

Parris, J. E. (Bradford), 1932 v Ni (1)

Parry, B. J. (Swansea T), 1951 v S (1)

Parry, C. (Everton), 1891 v E, S; 1893 v E; 1894 v E; 1895 v E, S; (with Newtown), 1896 v E, S, Ni; 1897 v Ni; 1898 v E, S, Ni (13)

Parry, E. (Liverpool), 1922 v S; 1923 v E, Ni; 1925 v Ni; 1926 v Ni (5)

Parry, M. (Liverpool), 1901 v E, S, Ni; 1902 v E, S, Ni; 1903 v E, S; 1904 v E, Ni; 1906 v E; 1908 v E, S, Ni; 1909 v E, S (16)

Parry, T. D. (Oswestry), 1900 v E, S, Ni; 1901 v E, S, Ni; 1902 v E (7)

Parry, W. (Newtown), 1895 v Ni (1)

Pascoe, C. (Swansea C), 1984 v N, Is; (with Sunderland), 1989 v Fi, Is, WG (sub); 1990 v Ho (sub), WG (sub); 1991 v Ei, Ic (sub); 1992 v Br (10)

Paul, R. (Swansea T), 1949 v E, S, Ni, P, Sw; 1950 v E, S, Ni, Bel; (with Manchester C), 1951 v S, E, Ni, P, Sw; 1952 v E, S, Ni, R of UK; 1953 v S, E, Ni, F, Y; 1954 v E, S, Ni; 1955 v S, E, Y; 1956 v E, Ni, S, A (33)

Peake, E. (Aberystwyth), 1908 v Ni; (with Liverpool), 1909 v Ni, S, E; 1910 v S, Ni; 1911 v Ni; 1912 v E; 1913 v E, Ni; 1914 v Ni (11)

Peers, E. J. (Wolverhampton W), 1914 v Ni, S, E; 1920 v E, S; 1921 v S, Ni, E; (with Port Vale), 1922 v E, S, Ni; 1923 v E (12)

Pembridge, M. A. (Luton T), 1992 v Br, Ei, R (with Derby Co), Ho, J (sub); 1993 v Bel (sub), Ei; 1994 v N (sub); 1995 v Alb (sub), Mol, Ge (sub) (11)

Perry, E. (Doncaster R), 1938 v E, S, Ni (3)

Perry, J. (Cardiff C), 1994 v N (1)

Phennah, E. (Civil Service), 1878 v S (1)

Phillips, C. (Wolverhampton W), 1931 v Ni; 1932 v E; 1933 v S; 1934 v E, S, Ni; 1935 v E, S, Ni; 1936 v S; (with Aston Villa), 1936 v E, Ni; 1938 v S (13)

Phillips, D. (Plymouth Arg), 1984 v E, Ni, N; (with Manchester C), 1985 v Sp, Ic, S, Sp, N; 1986 v S, H, S.Ar, Ei, U; (with Coventry C), 1987 v Fi, Cz; 1988 v D (2), Cz, Y, Se; 1989 v Se, WG; (with Norwich C), 1990 v Fi, Ho, WG, Ei, Se; 1991 v D, Bel, Ic, Pol, WG; 1992 v L, Ei, A, R, Ho (sub), Arg, J; 1993 v Fa, Cy, Bel, Ei, Bel, RCS, Fa; (with Nottingham F), 1994 v RCS, Cy, R, N, Se, Es; 1995 v Alb, Mol, Ge, Bul (2), G, Ge (59)

Phillips, L. (Cardiff C), 1971 v Cz, S, E, Ni; 1972 v Cz, R, S, Ni; 1973 v E; 1974 v Pol (sub), Ni; 1975 v A; (with Aston Villa), H (2), L (2), S, E, Ni; 1976 v A, E, Y (2), E, Ni; 1977 v WG, S (2), Cz, E; 1978 v K (2), S, Cz, WG, E, S; 1979 v Ma; (with Swansea C), T, WG, S, E, Ni, Ma; 1980 v Ei, WG, T, S (sub), Ni, Ic; 1981 v T, Cz, T, S, E, USSR; (with Charlton Ath), 1982 v Cz, USSR (58)

Phillips, T. J. S. (Chelsea), 1973 v E; 1974 v E; 1975 v H (sub); 1978 v K (4)

Phoenix, H. (Wrexham), 1882 v S (1)

Poland, G. (Wrexham), 1939 v Ni, F (2)

Pontin, K. (Cardiff C), 1980 v E (sub), S (2)

Powell, A. (Leeds U), 1947 v E, S; 1948 v E, S, Ni; (with Everton), 1949 v E; 1950 v Bel; (with Birmingham C), 1951 v S (8)

Powell, D. (Wrexham), 1968 v WG; (with Sheffield U), 1969 v S, E, Ni, I, WG; 1970 v E, S, Ni, EG; 1971 v R (11)

Powell, I. V. (QPR), 1947 v E; 1948 v E, S, Ni; (with Aston Villa), 1949 v Bel; 1950 v S, Bel; 1951 v S (8)

Powell, J. (Druids), 1878 v S; 1880 v E, S; 1882 v E, S, Ni; 1883 v E, S, Ni; (with Bolton W), 1884 v E; (with Newton Heath), 1887 v E, S; 1888 v E, S, Ni (15)

Powell, Seth (WBA), 1885 v S; 1886 v E, Ni; 1891 v E, S; 1892 v E, S (7)

Price, H. (Aston Villa), 1907 v S; (with Burton U), 1908 v Ni; (with Wrexham), 1909 v S, E, Ni (5)

Price, J. (Wrexham), 1877 v S; 1878 v S; 1879 v E; 1880 v E, S; 1881 v E, S; (with Druids), 1882 v S, E, Ni; 1883 v S, Ni (12)

Price, P. (Luton T), 1980 v E, S, Ni, Ic; 1981 v T, Cz, Ei, T, S, E, USSR; (with Tottenham H), 1982 v USSR, Sp, F; 1983 v N, Y, E, Bul, S, Ni; 1984 v N, R, Bul, Y, S (sub) (25)

Pring, K. D. (Rotherham U), 1966 v Ch, D; 1967 v Ni (3)

Pritchard, H. K. (Bristol C), 1985 v N (sub) (1)

Pryce-Jones, A. W. (Newtown), 1895 v E (1)

Pryce-Jones, W. E. (Cambridge University), 1887 v S; 1888 v S, E, Ni; 1890 v Ni (5)

Pugh, A. (Rhostyllen), 1889 v S (1)

Pugh, D. H. (Wrexham), 1896 v S, Ni; 1897 v S, Ni; (with Lincoln C), 1900 v S; 1901 v S, E (7)

Pugsley, J. (Charlton Ath), 1930 v Ni (1)

Pullen, W. J. (Plymouth Arg), 1926 v E (1)

Rankmore, F. E. J. (Peterborough), 1966 v Ch (sub) (1)

Ratcliffe, K. (Everton), 1981 v Cz, Ei, T, S, E, USSR; 1982 v Cz, Ic, USSR, Sp, E; 1983 v Y, E, Bul, S, Ni, Br; 1984 v N, R, Bul, Y, S, E, Ni, N, Is; 1985 v Ic, Sp, Ic, N, S, Sp; 1986 v S, H, S.Ar, U; 1987 v Fi (2), USSR, Cz; 1988 v D (2), Cz; 1989 v Fi, Is, Se, WG; 1990 v Fi; 1991 v D, Bel (2), L, Ei, Ic, Pol, WG; 1992 v Br, G; (with Cardiff C), 1993 v Bel (59)

Rea, J. C. (Aberystwyth), 1894 v Ni, S, E; 1895 v S; 1896 v S, Ni; 1897 v S, Ni; 1898 v Ni (9)

Reece, G. I. (Sheffield U), 1966 v E, S, Ni, USSR; 1967 v S; 1969 v R of UK (sub); 1970 v I (sub); 1971 v S, E, Ni, Fi; 1972 v Fi, R, E (sub), S, Ni; (with Cardiff C), 1973 v E (sub), Ni; 1974 v Pol (sub), E, S, Ni; 1975 v A, H (2), L (2), S, Ni (29)

Reed, W. G. (Ipswich T), 1955 v S, Y (2)

Rees, A. (Birmingham C), 1984 v N (sub) (1)
Rees, J. M. (Luton T), 1992 v A (sub) (1)
Rees, R. R. (Coventry C), 1965 v S, E, Ni, D, Gr (2), I, R; 1966 v E, S, Ni, R, D, Br (2), Ch; 1967 v E, Ni; 1968 v E, S, Ni; (with WBA), WG; 1969 v I; (with Nottingham F), 1969 v WG, EG, S (sub), R of UK; 1970 v E, S, Ni, EG, I; 1971 v Cz, R, E (sub), Ni (sub), Fi; 1972 v Cz (sub), R (39)
Rees, W. (Cardiff C), 1949 v Ni, Bel, Sw; (with Tottenham H), 1950 v Ni (4)
Richards, A. (Barnsley), 1932 v S (1)
Richards, D. (Wolverhampton W), 1931 v Ni; 1933 v E, S, Ni; 1934 v E, S, Ni; 1935 v E, S, Ni; 1936 v S; (with Brentford), 1936 v E, Ni; 1937 v S, E; (with Birmingham), Ni; 1938 v E, S, Ni; 1939 v E, S (21)
Richards, G. (Druids), 1899 v E, S, Ni; (with Oswestry), 1903 v Ni; (with Shrewsbury), 1904 v S; 1905 v Ni (6)
Richards, R. W. (Wolverhampton W), 1920 v E, S; 1921 v Ni; 1922 v E, S; (with West Ham U), 1924 v E, S, Ni; (with Mold), 1926 v S (9)
Richards, S. V. (Cardiff C), 1947 v E (1)
Richards, W. E. (Fulham), 1933 v Ni (1)
Roach, J. (Oswestry), 1885 v Ni (1)
Robbins, W. W. (Cardiff C), 1931 v E, S; 1932 v Ni, E, S; (with WBA), 1933 v F, E, S, Ni; 1934 v S; 1936 v S (11)
Roberts, A. M. (QPR), 1993 v Ei (sub) (1)
Roberts, D. F. (Oxford U), 1973 v Pol, E (sub), Ni; 1974 v E, S; 1975 v A; (with Hull C), L, Ni; 1976 v S, Ni, Y; 1977 v E (sub), Ni; 1978 v K (1+1 sub), S, Ni (17)
Roberts, I. W. (Watford), 1990 v Ho; (with Huddersfield T), 1992 v A, Arg, J; (with Leicester C), 1994 v Se; 1995 v Alb (sub), Mol (7)
Roberts, Jas (Chirk), 1898 v S (1)
Roberts, Jas (Wrexham), 1913 v S, Ni (2)
Roberts, J. (Corwen), 1879 v S; 1880 v E, S; 1882 v E, S, Ni; (with Berwyn R), 1883 v E (7)
Roberts, J. (Ruthin), 1881 v S; 1882 v S (2)
Roberts, J. (Bradford C), 1906 v Ni; 1907 v Ni (2)
Roberts, J. G. (Arsenal), 1971 v S, E, Ni, Fi; 1972 v Fi, E, Ni; (with Birmingham C), 1973 v E (2), Pol, S, Ni; 1974 v Pol, E, S, Ni; 1975 v A, H, S, E; 1976 v E, S (22)
Roberts, J. H. (Bolton), 1949 v Bel (1)
Roberts, P. S. (Portsmouth), 1974 v E; 1975 v A, H, L (4)
Roberts, R. (Druids), 1884 v S; (with Bolton W), 1887 v S; 1888 v S, E; 1889 v S, E; 1890 v S; 1892 v Ni; (with Preston NE), S (9)
Roberts, R. (Wrexham), 1886 v Ni; 1887 v Ni (2)
Roberts, R. (Rhos), 1891 v Ni; (with Crewe Alex), 1893 v E (2)
Roberts, W. (Llangollen), 1879 v E, S; 1880 v E, S; (with Berwyn R), 1881 v S; 1883 v S (6)
Roberts, W. (Wrexham), 1886 v E, S, Ni; 1887 v Ni (4)
Roberts, W. H. (Ruthin), 1882 v E, S; 1883 v E, S, Ni; (with Rhyl), 1884 v S (6)
Rodrigues, P. J. (Cardiff C), 1965 v Ni, Gr (2); 1966 v USSR, E, S, D; (with Leicester C), Ni, Br (2), Ch; 1967 v S; 1968 v E, S, Ni; 1969 v E, Ni, EG, R of UK; 1970 v E, S, Ni, EG; (with Sheffield W), 1971 v R, E, S, Cz, Ni; 1972 v Fi, Cz, R, E, Ni (sub); 1973 v E (3), Pol, S, Ni; 1974 v Pol (40)
Rogers, J. P. (Wrexham), 1896 v E, S, Ni (3)
Rogers, W. (Wrexham), 1931 v E, S (2)
Roose, L. R. (Aberystwyth), 1900 v Ni; (with London Welsh), 1901 v E, S, Ni; (with Stoke C), 1902 v E, S; 1904 v E; (with Everton), 1905 v S, E; (with Stoke C), 1906 v E, S, Ni; 1907 v E, S, Ni; (with Sunderland), 1908 v E, S; 1909 v E, S, Ni; 1910 v E, S, Ni; 1911 v S (24)
Rouse, R. V. (C Palace), 1959 v Ni (1)
Rowlands, A. C. (Tranmere R), 1914 v E (1)
Rowley, T. (Tranmere R), 1959 v Ni (1)
Rush, I. (Liverpool), 1980 v S (sub), Ni; 1981 v E (sub); 1982 v Ic (sub), USSR, E, S, Ni, F; 1983 v N, Y, E, Bul; 1984 v N, R, Bul, Y, S, E, Ni; 1985 v Ic, N, S, Sp; 1986 v S, S.Ar, Ei, U; 1987 v Fi (2), USSR, Cz; (with Juventus), 1988 v D, Cz, Y, Se, Ma, I; (with Liverpool), 1989 v Ho, Fi, Se, WG; 1990 v Fi, Ei; 1991 v D, Bel (2), L, Ei, Pol, WG; 1992 v G, L, R; 1993 v Fa, Cy, Bel (2), RCS, Fa; 1994 v RCS, Cy, R, N, Se, Es; 1995 v Alb, Ge, Bul, G, Ge (71)
Russell, M. R. (Merthyr T), 1912 v S, Ni; 1914 v E; (with Plymouth Arg), 1920 v E, S, Ni; 1921 v E, S, Ni; 1922 v E, Ni; 1923 v E, S, Ni; 1924 v E, S, Ni; 1925 v E, S; 1926 v E, S; 1928 v S; 1929 v E (23)

Sabine, H. W. (Oswestry), 1887 v Ni (1)
Saunders, D. (Brighton & HA), 1986 v Ei (sub), Ca (2); 1987 v Fi, USSR (sub); (with Oxford U), 1988 v Y, Se, Ma, I (sub); 1989 v Ho (sub), Fi; (with Derby Co), Is, Se, WG; 1990 v Fi, Ho, WG, Se, Cr; 1991 v D, Bel (2), L, Ei, Ic, Pol, WG; (with Liverpool), 1992 v Br, G, Ei, R, Ho, Arg, J; 1993 v Fa; (with Aston Villa), Cy, Bel (2), RCS, Fa; 1994 v RCS, Cy, R, N (sub); 1995 v Ge, Bul (2), G, Ge (49)
Savin, G. (Oswestry), 1878 v S (1)
Sayer, P. (Cardiff C), 1977 v Cz, S, E, Ni; 1978 v K (2), S (7)
Scrine, F. H. (Swansea T), 1950 v E, Ni (2)
Sear, C. R. (Manchester C), 1963 v E (1)
Shaw, E. G. (Oswestry), 1882 v Ni; 1884 v S, Ni (3)
Sherwood, A. T. (Cardiff C), 1947 v E, Ni; 1948 v S, Ni; 1949 v E, S, Ni, P, Sw; 1950 v E, S, Ni, Bel; 1951 v E, S, Ni, P, Sw; 1952 v E, S, Ni, R of UK; 1953 v S, E, Ni, F, Y; 1954 v E, S, Ni, A; 1955 v S, E, Y, Ni; 1956 v E, S, Ni, A; (with Newport Co), 1957 v E, S (41)
Shone, W. W. (Oswestry), 1879 v E (1)
Shortt, W. W. (Plymouth Arg), 1947 v Ni; 1950 v Ni, Bel; 1952 v E, S, Ni, R of UK; 1953 v S, E, Ni, F, Y (12)
Showers, D. (Cardiff C), 1975 v E (sub), Ni (2)
Sidlow, C. (Liverpool), 1947 v E, S; 1948 v E, S, Ni; 1949 v S; 1950 v E (7)
Sisson, H. (Wrexham Olympic), 1885 v Ni; 1886 v S, Ni (3)
Slatter, N. (Bristol R), 1983 v S; 1984 v N (sub), Is; 1985 v Ic, Sp, Ic, N, S, Sp, N; (with Oxford U), 1986 v H (sub), S.Ar, Ca (2); 1987 v Fi (sub), Cz; 1988 v D (2), Cz, Ma, I; 1989 v Is (sub) (22)
Smallman, D. P. (Wrexham), 1974 v E (sub), S (sub), Ni; (with Everton), 1975 v H (sub), E, Ni (sub); 1976 v A (7)
Southall, N. (Everton), 1982 v Ni; 1983 v N, E, Bul, S, Ni, Br; 1984 v N, R, Bul, Y, S, E, Ni, N, Is; 1985 v Ic, Sp, Ic, N, S, Sp, N; 1986 v S, H, S.Ar, Ei; 1987 v USSR, Fi, Cz; 1988 v D, Cz, Y, Se; 1989 v Ho, Fi, Se, WG; 1990 v Fi, Ho, WG, Ei, Se, Cr; 1991 v D, Bel (2), L, Ei, Ic, Pol, WG; 1992 v Br, G, L, Ei, A, R, Ho, Arg, J; 1993 v Fa, Cy, Bel, Ei, Bel, RCS, Fa; 1994 v RCS, Cy, R, N, Se, Es; 1995 v Alb, Mol, Ge, Bul (2), G, Ge (81)
Speed, G. A. (Leeds U), 1990 v Cr (sub); 1991 v D, L (sub), Ei (sub), Ic, WG (sub); 1992 v Br, G (sub), L, Ei, R, Ho, Arg, J; 1993 v Fa, Cy, Bel, Ei, Bel, Fa (sub); 1994 v RCS (sub), Cy, R, N, Se; 1995 v Alb, Mol, Ge, Bul (2), G (31)
Sprake, G. (Leeds U), 1964 v S, Ni; 1965 v S, D, Gr; 1966 v E, Ni, USSR; 1967 v S; 1968 v E, S; 1969 v S, E, Ni, WG, R of UK; 1970 v EG, I; 1971 v R, S, E, Ni; 1972 v Fi, E, S, Ni; 1973 v E (2), Pol, S, Ni; 1974 v Pol; (with Birmingham C), S, Ni; 1975 v A, H, L (37)
Stansfield, F. (Cardiff C), 1949 v S (1)
Stevenson, B. (Leeds U), 1978 v Ni; 1979 v Ma, T, S, E, Ni, Ma; 1980 v WG, T, Ic (sub); 1982 v Cz; (with Birmingham C), Sp, S, Ni, F (15)
Stevenson, N. (Swansea C), 1982 v E, S, Ni; 1983 v N (4)
Stitfall, R. F. (Cardiff C), 1953 v E; 1957 v Cz (2)

Sullivan, D. (Cardiff C), 1953 v Ni, F, Y; 1954 v Ni; 1955 v E, Ni; 1957 v E, S; 1958 v Ni, H (2), Se, Br; 1959 v S, Ni; 1960 v E, S (17)

Symons, C. J. (Portsmouth), 1992 v Ei, Ho, Arg, J; 1993 v Fa, Cy, Bel, Ei, RCS, Fa; 1994 v RCS, Cy, R; 1995 v Mol, Ge (sub), Bul, G, Ge (18)

Tapscott, D. R. (Arsenal), 1954 v A; 1955 v S, E, Ni, Y; 1956 v E, Ni, S, A; 1957 v Ni, Cz, EG; (with Cardiff C), 1959 v E, Ni (14)

Taylor, J. (Wrexham), 1898 v E (1)

Taylor, O. D. S. (Newtown), 1893 v S, Ni; 1894 v S, Ni (4)

Thomas, C. (Druids), 1899 v Ni; 1900 v S (2)

Thomas, D. A. (Swansea T), 1957 v Cz; 1958 v EG (2)

Thomas, D. S. (Fulham), 1948 v E, S, Ni; 1949 v S (4)

Thomas, E. (Cardiff Corinthians), 1925 v E (1)

Thomas, G. (Wrexham), 1885 v E, S (2)

Thomas, H. (Manchester U), 1927 v E (1)

Thomas, M. (Wrexham), 1977 v WG, S (1+1 sub), Ni (sub); 1978 v K (sub), S, Cz, Ir, E, Ni (sub); 1979 v Ma; (with Manchester U), T, WG, Ma (sub); 1980 v Ei, WG (sub), T, E, S, Ni; 1981 v Cz, S, E, USSR; (with Everton), 1982 v Cz; (with Brighton & HA), USSR (sub), Sp, E, S (sub), Ni (sub); 1983 (with Stoke C), v N, Y, E, Bul, S, Ni, Br; 1984 v R, Bul, Y; (with Chelsea), S, E; 1985 v Ic, Sp, Ic, S, Sp, N; 1986 v S; (with WBA), H, S.Ar (sub) (51)

Thomas, M. R. (Newcastle U), 1987 v Fi (1)

Thomas, R. J. (Swindon T), 1967 v Ni; 1968 v WG; 1969 v E, Ni, I, WG, R of UK; 1970 v E, S, Ni, EG, I; 1971 v S, E, Ni, R, Cz; 1972 v Fi, Cz, R, E, S, Ni; 1973 v E (3), Pol, S, Ni; 1974 v Pol; (with Derby Co), E, S, Ni; 1975 v H (2), L (2), S, E, Ni; 1976 v A, Y, E; 1977 v Cz, S, E, Ni; 1978 v K, S; (with Cardiff C), Cz (50)

Thomas, T. (Bangor), 1898 v S, Ni (2)

Thomas, W. R. (Newport Co), 1931 v E, S (2)

Thomson, D. (Druids), 1876 v S (1)

Thomson, G. F. (Druids), 1876 v S; 1877 v S (2)

Toshack, J. B. (Cardiff C), 1969 v S, E, Ni, WG, EG, R of UK; 1970 v EG, I; (with Liverpool), 1971 v S, E, Ni, Fi; 1972 v Fi, E; 1973 v E (3), Pol, S; 1975 v A, H (2), L (2), S, E; 1976 v Y (2), E; 1977 v S; 1978 v K (2), S, Cz; (with Swansea C), 1979 v WG (sub), S, E, Ni, Ma; 1980 v WG (40)

Townsend, W. (Newtown), 1887 v Ni; 1893 v Ni (2)

Trainer, H. (Wrexham), 1895 v E, S, Ni (3)

Trainer, J. (Bolton W), 1887 v S; (with Preston NE), 1888 v S; 1889 v E; 1890 v S; 1891 v S; 1892 v Ni, S; 1893 v E; 1894 v Ni, E; 1895 v Ni, E; 1896 v S; 1897 v Ni, S, E; 1898 v S, E; 1899 v Ni, S (20)

Turner, H. G. (Charlton Ath), 1937 v E, S, Ni; 1938 v E, S, Ni; 1939 v Ni, F (8)

Turner, J. (Wrexham), 1892 v E (1)

Turner, R. E. (Wrexham), 1891 v E, Ni (2)

Turner, W. H. (Wrexham), 1887 v E, Ni; 1890 v S; 1891 v E, S (5)

Van Den Hauwe, P. W. R. (Everton), 1985 v Sp; 1986 v S, H; 1987 v USSR, Fi, Cz; 1988 v D (2), Cz, Y, I; 1989 v Fi, Se (13)

Vaughan, Jas (Druids), 1893 v E, S, Ni; 1899 v E (4)

Vaughan, John (Oswestry), 1879 v S; 1880 v S; 1881 v E, S; 1882 v E, S, Ni; 1883 v E, S, Ni; (with Bolton W), 1884 v E (11)

Vaughan, J. O. (Rhyl), 1885 v Ni; 1886 v Ni, E, S (4)

Vaughan, N. (Newport Co), 1983 v Y (sub), Br; 1984 v N; (with Cardiff C), R, Bul, Y, Ni (sub), N, Is; 1985 v Sp (sub) (10)

Vaughan, T. (Rhyl), 1885 v E (1)

Vearncombe, G. (Cardiff C), 1958 v EG; 1961 v Ei (2)

Vernon, T. R. (Blackburn R), 1957 v Ni, Cz (2), EG; 1958 v E, S, EG, Se; 1959 v S; (with Everton), 1960 v Ni; 1961 v S, E, Ei; 1962 v Ni, Br (2), M; 1963 v S, E, H; 1964 v E, S; (with Stoke C), 1965 v Ni, Gr, I; 1966 v E, S, Ni, USSR, D; 1967 v Ni; 1968 v E (32)

Villars, A. K. (Cardiff C), 1974 v E, S, Ni (sub) (3)

Vizard, E. T. (Bolton W), 1911 v E, S, Ni; 1912 v E, S; 1913 v S; 1914 v E, Ni; 1920 v E; 1921 v E, S, Ni; 1922 v E, S; 1923 v E, Ni; 1924 v E, S, Ni; 1926 v E, S; 1927 v S (22)

Walley, J. T. (Watford), 1971 v Cz (1)

Walsh, I. (C Palace), 1980 v Ei, T, E, S, Ic; 1981 v T, Cz, Ei, T, S, E, USSR; 1982 v Cz (sub), Ic; (with Swansea C), Sp, S (sub), Ni (sub), F (18)

Ward, D. (Bristol R), 1959 v E; (with Cardiff C), 1962 v E (2)

Warner, J. (Swansea T), 1937 v E; (with Manchester U), 1939 v F (2)

Warren, F. W. (Cardiff C), 1929 v Ni; (with Middlesbrough), 1931 v Ni; 1933 v F, E; (with Hearts), 1937 v Ni; 1938 v Ni (6)

Watkins, A. E. (Leicester Fosse), 1898 v E, S; (with Aston Villa), 1900 v E, S; (with Millwall), 1904 v Ni (5)

Watkins, W. M. (Stoke C), 1902 v E; 1903 v E, S; (with Aston Villa); 1904 v E, S, Ni; (with Sunderland), 1905 v E, S, Ni; (with Stoke C), 1908 v Ni (10)

Webster, C (Manchester U), 1957 v Cz; 1958 v H, M, Br (4)

Whatley, W. J. (Tottenham H), 1939 v E, S (2)

White, P. F. (London Welsh), 1896 v Ni (1)

Wilcocks, A. R. (Oswestry), 1890 v Ni (1)

Wilding, J. (Wrexham Olympians), 1885 v E, S, Ni; 1886 v E, Ni; (with Bootle), 1887 v E; 1888 v S, Ni; (with Wrexham), 1892 v S (9)

Williams, A. (Reading), 1994 v Es; 1995 v Alb, Mol, G (sub), Ge (5)

Williams, A. L. (Wrexham), 1931 v E (1)

Williams, B. (Bristol C), 1930 v Ni (1)

Williams, B. D. (Swansea T), 1928 v Ni, E; 1930 v E, S; (with Everton), 1931 v Ni; 1932 v E; 1933 v E, S, Ni; 1935 v Ni (10)

Williams, D. G. (Derby Co), 1988 v Cz, Y, Se, Ma, I; 1989 v Ho, Is, Se, WG; 1990 v Fi, Ho; (with Ipswich T), 1993 v Ei (12)

Williams, D. M. (Norwich C), 1986 v S.Ar (sub), U, Ca (2); 1987 v Fi (5)

Williams, D. R. (Merthyr T), 1921 v E, S; (with Sheffield W), 1923 v S; 1926 v S; 1927 v E, Ni; (with Manchester U), 1929 v E, S (8)

Williams, E. (Crewe Alex), 1893 v E, S (2)

Williams, E. (Druids), 1901 v E, Ni, S; 1902 v E, Ni (5)

Williams, G. (Chirk), 1893 v S; 1894 v S; 1895 v E, S, Ni; 1898 v Ni (6)

Williams, G. E. (WBA), 1960 v Ni; 1961 v S, E, Ei; 1963 v Ni, H; 1964 v E, S, Ni; 1965 v S, E, Ni, D, Gr (2), USSR, I; 1966 v Ni, Br (2), Ch; 1967 v S, E, Ni; 1968 v Ni; 1969 v I (26)

Williams, G. G. (Swansea T), 1961 v Ni, H, Sp (2); 1962 v E (5)

Williams, G. J. J. (Cardiff C), 1951 v Sw (1)

Williams, G. O. (Wrexham), 1907 v Ni (1)

Williams, H. J. (Swansea), 1965 v Gr (2); 1972 v R (3)

Williams, H. T. (Newport Co), 1949 v Ni, Sw; (with Leeds U), 1950 v Ni; 1951 v S (4)

Williams, J. H. (Oswestry), 1884 v E (1)

Williams, J. J. (Wrexham), 1939 v F (1)

Williams, J. T. (Middlesbrough), 1925 v Ni (1)

Williams, J. W. (C Palace), 1912 v S, Ni (2)

Williams, R. (Newcastle U), 1935 v S, E (2)

Williams, R. P. (Caernarvon), 1886 v S (1)

Williams, S. G. (WBA), 1954 v A; 1955 v E, Ni; 1956 v E, S, A; 1958 v E, S, Ni, Is (2), H (2), M, Se, Br; 1959 v E, S, Ni; 1960 v E, S, Ni; 1961 v Ni, Ei, H, Sp (2); 1962 v E,

S, Ni, Br (2), M; (with Southampton), 1963 v S, E, H (2); 1964 v E, S; 1965 v S, E, D; 1966 v D (43)

Williams, W. (Druids), 1876 v S; 1878 v S; (with Oswestry), 1879 v E, S; (with Druids), 1880 v E; 1881 v E, S; 1882 v E, S, Ni; 1883 v Ni (11)

Williams, W. (Northampton T), 1925 v S (1)

Witcomb, D. F. (WBA), 1947 v E, S; (with Sheffield W), 1947 v Ni (3)

Woosnam, A. P. (Leyton Orient), 1959 v S; (with West Ham U), E; 1960 v E, S, Ni; 1961 v S, E, Ni, Ei, Sp, H; 1962 v E, S, Ni, Br; (with Aston Villa), 1963 v Ni, H (17)

Woosnam, G. (Newton White Star), 1879 v S (1)

Worthington, T. (Newtown), 1894 v S (1)

Wynn, G. A. (Wrexham), 1909 v E, S, Ni; (with Manchester C), 1910 v E; 1911 v Ni; 1912 v E, S; 1913 v E, S; 1914 v E, S (11)

Wynn, W. (Chirk), 1903 v Ni (1)

Yorath, T. C. (Leeds U), 1970 v I; 1971 v S, E, Ni; 1972 v Cz, E, S, Ni; 1973 v E, Pol, S; 1974 v Pol, E, S, Ni; 1975 v A, H (2), L (2), S; 1976 v A, E, S, Y (2), E, Ni; (with Coventry C), 1977 v WG, S (2), Cz, E, Ni; 1978 v K (2), S, Cz, WG, Ir, E, S, Ni; 1979 v T, WG, S, E, Ni; (with Tottenham H), 1980 v Ei, T, E, S, Ni, Ic; 1981 v T, Cz; (with Vancouver W), Ei, T, USSR (59)

Young, E. (Wimbledon), 1990 v Cr; (with C Palace), 1991 v D, Bel (2), L, Ei; 1992 v G, L, Ei, A; 1993 v Fa, Cy, Bel, Ei, Bel, Fa; 1994 v RCS, Cy, R, N (20)

REPUBLIC OF IRELAND

Aherne, T. (Belfast C), 1946 v P, Sp; (with Luton T), 1950 v Fi, E, Fi, Se, Bel; 1951 v N, Arg, N; 1952 v WG (2), A, Sp; 1953 v F; 1954 v F (16)

Aldridge, J. W. (Oxford U), 1986 v W, U, Ic, Cz; 1987 v Bel, S, Pol; (with Liverpool), S, Bul, Bel, Br, L; 1988 v Bul, Pol, N, E, USSR, Ho; 1989 v Ni, Tun, Sp, F (sub), H, Ma (sub), H; 1990 v WG; (with Real Sociedad), Ni, Ma, Fi (sub), T. E, Eg, Ho, R, I; 1991 v T, E (2), Pol; (with Tranmere R), 1992 v H (sub), T, W (sub), Sw (sub), US (sub), Alb, I, P (sub); 1993 v La, D, Sp, D, Alb, La, Li; 1994 v Li, Ni, CzR, I (sub), M (sub), N; 1995 v La, Ni, P, Lie (64)

Ambrose, P. (Shamrock R), 1955 v N, Ho; 1964 v Pol, N, E (5)

Anderson, J. (Preston NE), 1980 v Cz (sub), US (sub); 1982 v Ch, Br, Tr; (with Newcastle U), 1984 v Chn; 1986 v W, Ic, Cz; 1987 v Bul, Bel, Br, L; 1988 v R (sub), Y (sub); 1989 v Tun (16)

Andrews, P. (Bohemians), 1936 v Ho (1)

Arrigan, T. (Waterford), 1938 v N (1)

Babb, P. A. (Coventry C), 1994 v Ru, Ho, Bol, G, CzR (sub), I, M, N, Ho; (with Liverpool), 1995 v La, Lie, Ni (2), P, Lie, A (16)

Bailham, E. (Shamrock R), 1964 v E (1)

Barber, E. (Shelbourne), 1966 v Sp; (with Birmingham C), 1966 v Bel (2)

Barry, P. (Fordsons), 1928 v Bel; 1929 v Bel (2)

Beglin, J. (Liverpool), 1984 v Chn; 1985 v M, D, I, Is, E, N, Sw; 1986 v Sw, USSR, D, W; 1987 v Bel (sub), S, Pol (15)

Bermingham, J. (Bohemians), 1929 v Bel (1)

Bermingham, P. (St James' Gate), 1935 v H (1)

Braddish, S. (Dundalk), 1978 v T (sub), Pol (2)

Bonner, P. (Celtic), 1981 v Pol; 1982 v Alg; 1984 v Ma, Is, Chn; 1985 v I, Is, E, N; 1986 v U, Ic; 1987 v Bel (2), S (2), Pol, Bul, Br, L; 1988 v Bul, R, Y, N, E, USSR, Ho; 1989 v Sp, F, H, Sp, Ma, H; 1990 v WG, Ni, Ma, W, Fi, T, E, Eg, Ho, R, I; 1991 v Mor, T, E (2), W, Pol, US; 1992 v H, Pol, T, W, Sw, Alb, I; 1993 v La, D, Sp, W, Ni, D, Alb, La, Li; 1994 v Li, Sp, Ni, Ru, Ho, Bol, CzR, I, M, N, Ho; 1995 v Lie (78)

Bradshaw, P. (St James' Gate), 1939 v Sw, Pol, H (2), G (5)

Brady, F. (Fordsons), 1926 v I; 1927 v I (2)

Brady, T. R. (QPR), 1964 v A (2), Sp (2), Pol, N (6)

Brady, W. L. (Arsenal), 1975 v USSR, T, Sw, USSR, Sw, WG; 1976 v T, N, Pol; 1977 v E, T, F (2), Sp, Bul; 1978 v Bul, N; 1979 v Ni, E, D, Bul, WG; 1980 v W, Bul, E, Cy; (with Juventus), 1981 v Ho, Bel, F, Cy, Bel; 1982 v Ho, F, Ch, Br, Tr; (with Sampdoria), 1983 v Ho, Sp, Ic, Ma; 1984 v Ic, Ho, Ma, Pol, Is; (with Internazionale), 1985 v USSR, N, D, I, E, N, Sp, Sw; 1986 v Sw, USSR, D, W; (with Ascoli), 1987 v Bel, S (2), Pol; (with West Ham U), Bul, Bel, Br, L; 1988 v L, Bul; 1989 v F, H (sub), H (sub); 1990 v WG, Fi (72)

Breen, T. (Manchester U), 1937 v Sw, F; (with Shamrock R), 1947 v E, Sp, P (5)

Brennan, F. (Drumcondra), 1965 v Bel (1)

Brennan, S. A. (Manchester U), 1965 v Sp; 1966 v Sp, A, Bel; 1967 v Sp, T, Sp; 1969 v Cz, D, H; 1970 v S, Cz, D, H, Pol (sub), WG; (with Waterford), 1971 v Pol, Se, I (19)

Brown, J. (Coventry C), 1937 v Sw, F (2)

Browne, W. (Bohemians), 1964 v A, Sp, E (3)

Buckley, L. (Shamrock R), 1984 v Pol (sub); (with Waregem), 1985 v M (2)

Burke, F. (Cork Ath), 1952 v WG (1)

Burke, J. (Cork), 1934 v Bel (1)

Burke, J. (Shamrock R), 1929 v Bel (1)

Byrne, A. B. (Southampton), 1970 v D, Pol, WG; 1971 v Pol, Se (2), I (2), A; 1973 v F, USSR (sub), F, N; 1974 v Pol (14)

Byrne, D. (Shelbourne), 1929 v Bel; (with Shamrock R), 1932 v Sp; (with Coleraine), 1934 v Bel (3)

Byrne, J. (Bray Unknowns), 1928 v Bel (1)

Byrne, J. (QPR), 1985 v I, Is (sub), E (sub), Sp (sub); 1987 v S (sub), Bel (sub), Br, L (sub); 1988 v L, Bul (sub), Is, R, Y (sub), Pol (sub); (with Le Havre), 1990 v WG (sub), W, Fi, T (sub), Ma; (with Brighton & HA), 1991 v W; (with Sunderland), 1992 v T, W; (with Millwall), 1993 v W (23)

Byrne, P. (Shamrock R), 1984 v Pol, Chn; 1985 v M; 1986 v D (sub), W (sub), U (sub), Ic (sub), Cz (8)

Byrne, P. (Dolphin), 1931 v Sp; 1932 v Ho; (with Drumcondra), 1934 v Ho (3)

Byrne, S. (Bohemians), 1931 v Sp (1)

Campbell, A. (Santander), 1985 v I (sub), Is, Sp (3)

Campbell, N. (St Patrick's Ath), 1971 v A (sub); (with Fortuna, Cologne), 1972 v Ir, Ec, Ch, P; 1973 v USSR, F (sub); 1975 v WG; 1976 v N; 1977 v Sp, Bul (sub) (11)

Cannon, H. (Bohemians), 1926 v I; 1928 v Bel (2)

Cantwell, N. (West Ham U), 1954 v L; 1956 v Sp, Ho; 1957 v D, WG, E (2); 1958 v D, Pol, A; 1959 v Pol, Cz (2); 1960 v Se, Ch, Se; 1961 v N; (with Manchester U), S (2); 1962 v Cz (2), A; 1963 v Ic (2), S; 1964 v A, Sp, E; 1965 v Pol, Sp; 1966 v Sp (2), A, Bel; 1967 v Sp, T (36)

Carey, B. P. (Manchester U), 1992 v US (sub); 1993 v W; (with Leicester C), 1994 v Ru (3)

Carey, J. J. (Manchester U), 1938 v N, Cz, Pol; 1939 v Sw, Pol, H (2), G; 1946 v P, Sp; 1947 v E, Sp, P; 1948 v P, Sp; 1949 v Sw, Bel, P, Se, Sp; 1950 v Fi, E, Fi, Se; 1951 v N, Arg, N; 1953 v F, A (29)

Carolan, J. (Manchester U), 1960 v Se, Ch (2)
Carroll, B. (Shelbourne), 1949 v Bel; 1950 v Fi (2)
Carroll, T. R. (Ipswich T), 1968 v Pol; 1969 v Pol, A, D; 1970 v Cz, Pol, WG; 1971 v Se; (with Birmingham C), 1972 v Ir, Ec, Ch, P; 1973 v USSR (2), Pol, F, N (17)
Cascarino, A. G. (Gillingham), 1986 v Sw, USSR, D; (with Millwall), 1988 v Pol, N (sub), USSR (sub), Ho (sub); 1989 v Ni, Tun, Sp, F, H, Sp, Ma, H; 1990 v WG (sub), Ni, Ma; (with Aston Villa), W, Fi, T, E, Eg, Ho (sub), R (sub), I (sub); 1991 v Mor (sub), T (sub), E (2 sub), Pol (sub), Ch (sub), US; (with Celtic), 1992 v Pol, T; (with Chelsea), W, Sw, US (sub); 1993 v W, Ni (sub), D (sub), Alb (sub), La (sub); 1994 v Li (sub), Sp (sub), Ni (sub), Ru, Bol (sub), G, CzR, Ho (sub); (with Marseille), 1995 v La (sub), Ni (sub), P (sub), Lie (sub), A (sub) (56)
Chandler, J. (Leeds U), 1980 v Cz (sub), US (2)
Chatton, H. A. (Shelbourne), 1931 v Sp; (with Dumbarton), 1932 v Sp; (with Cork), 1934 v Ho (3)
Clarke, J. (Drogheda U), 1978 v Pol (sub) (1)
Clarke, K. (Drumcondra), 1948 v P, Sp (2)
Clarke, M. (Shamrock R), 1950 v Bel (1)
Clinton, T. J. (Everton), 1951 v N; 1954 v F, L (3)
Coad, P. (Shamrock R), 1947 v E, Sp, P; 1948 v P, Sp; 1949 v Sw, Bel, P, Se; 1951 v N (sub); 1952 v Sp (11)
Coffey, T. (Drumcondra), 1950 v Fi (1)
Colfer, M. D. (Shelbourne), 1950 v Bel; 1951 v N (2)
Collins, F. (Jacobs), 1927 v I (1)
Conmy, O. M. (Peterborough U), 1965 v Bel; 1967 v Cz; 1968 v Cz, Pol; 1970 v Cz (5)
Connolly, H. (Cork), 1937 v G (1)
Connolly, J. (Fordsons), 1926 v I (1)
Conroy, G. A. (Stoke C), 1970 v Cz, D, H, Pol, WG; 1971 v Pol, Se (2), I; 1973 v USSR, F, USSR, N; 1974 v Pol, Br, U, Ch; 1975 v T, Sw, USSR, Sw, WG (sub); 1976 v T (sub), Pol; 1977 v E, T, Pol (27)
Conway, J. P. (Fulham), 1967 v Sp, T, Sp; 1968 v Cz; 1969 v A (sub), H; 1970 v S, Cz, D, H, Pol, WG; 1971 v I, A; 1974 v U, Ch; 1975 v WG (sub); 1976 v N, Pol; (with Manchester C), 1977 v Pol (20)
Corr, P. J. (Everton), 1949 v P, Sp; 1950 v E, Se (4)
Courtney, E. (Cork U), 1946 v P (1)
Coyle, O. C. (Bolton W), 1994 v Ho (sub) (1)
Coyne, T. (Celtic), 1992 v Sw, US, Alb (sub), US (sub), I (sub), P (sub); 1993 v W (sub), La (sub); (with Tranmere R), Ni; (with Motherwell), 1994 v Ru (sub), Ho, Bol, G (sub), CzR (sub), I, M, Ho; 1995 v Lie, Ni (sub), A (20)
Cummins, G. P. (Luton T), 1954 v L (2); 1955 v N (2), WG; 1956 v Y, Sp; 1958 v D, Pol, A; 1959 v Pol, Cz (2); 1960 v Se, Ch, WG, Se; 1961 v S (2) (19)
Cuneen, T. (Limerick), 1951 v N (1)
Curtis, D. P. (Shelbourne), 1957 v D, WG; (with Bristol C), 1957 v E (2); 1958 v D, Pol, A; (with Ipswich T), 1959 v Pol; 1960 v Se, Ch, WG, Se; 1961 v N, S; 1962 v A; 1963 v Ic; (with Exeter C), 1964 v A (17)
Cusack, S. (Limerick), 1953 v F (1)

Daish, L. S. (Cambridge U), 1992 v W, Sw (sub) (2)
Daly, G. A. (Manchester U), 1973 v Pol (sub), N; 1974 v Br (sub), U (sub); 1975 v Sw (sub), WG; 1977 v E, T, F; (with Derby Co), F, Bul; 1978 v Bul, T, D; 1979 v Ni, E, D, Bul; 1980 v Ni, E, Cy, Sw, Arg; (with Coventry C), 1981 v WG'B', Ho, Bel, Cy, W, Bel, Cz, Pol (sub); 1982 v Alg, Ch, Br, Tr; 1983 v Ho, Sp (sub), Ma (sub); 1984 v Is (sub), Ma; (with Birmingham C), 1985 v M (sub), N, Sp, Sw; 1986 v Sw; (with Shrewsbury T), U, Ic (sub), Cz (sub); 1987 v S (sub) (48)
Daly, J. (Shamrock R), 1932 v Ho; 1935 v Sw (2)
Daly, M. (Wolverhampton W), 1978 v T, Pol (2)
Daly, P. (Shamrock R), 1950 v Fi (sub) (1)
Davis, T. L. (Oldham Ath), 1937 v G, H; (with Tranmere R), 1938 v Cz, Pol (4)
Deacy, E. (Aston Villa), 1982 v Alg (sub), Ch, Br, Tr (4)
De Mange, K. J. P. P. (Liverpool), 1987 v Br (sub); (with Hull C), 1989 v Tun (sub) (2)
Dempsey, J. T. (Fulham), 1967 v Sp, Cz; 1968 v Cz, Pol; 1969 v Pol, A, D; (with Chelsea), 1969 v Cz, D; 1970 v H, WG; 1971 v Pol, Se (2), I; 1972 v Ir, Ec, Ch, P (19)
Dennehy, J. (Cork Hibernians), 1972 v Ec (sub), Ch; (with Nottingham F), 1973 v USSR (sub), Pol, F, N; 1974 v Pol (sub); 1975 v T (sub), WG (sub); (with Walsall), 1976 v Pol (sub); 1977 v Pol (sub) (11)
Desmond, P. (Middlesbrough), 1950 v Fi, E, Fi, Se (4)
Devine, J. (Arsenal), 1980 v Cz, Ni; 1981 v WG'B', Cz; 1982 v Ho, Alg; 1983 v Sp, Ma; (with Norwich C), 1984 v Ic, Ho, Is; 1985 v USSR, N (13)
Donnelly, J. (Dundalk), 1935 v H, Sw, G; 1936 v Ho, Sw, H, L; 1937 v G, H; 1938 v N (10)
Donnelly, T. (Drumcondra), 1938 v N; (Shamrock R), 1939 v Sw (2)
Donovan, D. C. (Everton), 1955 v N, Ho, N, WG; 1957 v E (5)
Donovan, T. (Aston Villa), 1980 v Cz; 1981 v WG'B'(sub) (2)
Dowdall, C. (Fordsons), 1928 v Bel; (with Barnsley), 1929 v Bel; (with Cork), 1931 v Sp (3)
Doyle, C. (Shelbourne), 1959 v Cz (1)
Doyle, D. (Shamrock R), 1926 v I (1)
Doyle, L. (Dolphin), 1932 v Sp (1)
Duffy, B. (Shamrock R), 1950 v Bel (1)
Duggan, H. A. (Leeds U), 1927 v I; 1930 v Bel; 1936 v H, L; (with Newport Co), 1938 v N (5)
Dunne, A. P. (Manchester U), 1962 v A; 1963 v Ic, S; 1964 v A, Sp, Pol, N, E; 1965 v Pol, Sp; 1966 v Sp (2), A, Bel; 1967 v Sp, T, Sp; 1969 v Pol, D, H; 1970 v H; 1971 v Se, I, A; (with Bolton W), 1974 v Br (sub), U, Ch; 1975 v T, Sw, USSR, Sw, WG; 1976 v T (33)
Dunne, J. (Sheffield U), 1930 v Bel; (with Arsenal), 1936 v Sw, H, L; (with Southampton), 1937 v Sw, F; (with Shamrock R), 1938 v N (2), Cz, Pol; 1939 v Sw, Pol, H (2), G (15)
Dunne, J. C. (Fulham), 1971 v A (1)
Dunne, L. (Manchester C), 1935 v Sw, G (2)
Dunne, P. A. J. (Manchester U), 1965 v Sp; 1966 v Sp (2), WG; 1967 v T (5)
Dunne, S. (Luton T), 1953 v F, A; 1954 v F, L; 1956 v Sp, Ho; 1957 v D, WG, E; 1958 v D, Pol, A; 1959 v Pol; 1960 v WG, Se (15)
Dunne, T. (St Patrick's Ath), 1956 v Ho; 1957 v D, WG (3)
Dunning, P. (Shelbourne), 1971 v Se, I (2)
Dunphy, E. M. (York C), 1966 v Sp; (with Millwall), 1966 v WG; 1967 v T, Sp, T, Cz; 1968 v Cz, Pol; 1969 v Pol, A, D (2), H; 1970 v D, H, Pol, WG (sub); 1971 v Pol, Se (2), I (2), A (23)
Dwyer, N. M. (West Ham U), 1960 v Se, Ch, WG, Se; (with Swansea T), 1961 v W, N, S (2); 1962 v Cz (2); 1964 v Pol (sub), N, E; 1965 v Pol (14)

Eccles, P. (Shamrock R), 1986 v U (sub) (1)
Egan, R. (Dundalk), 1929 v Bel (1)
Eglington, T. J. (Shamrock R), 1946 v P, Sp; (with Everton), 1947 v E, Sp, P; 1948 v P; 1949 v Sw, P, Se; 1951 v N, Arg; 1952 v WG (2), A, Sp; 1953 v F, A; 1954 v F, L, F; 1955 v N, Ho, WG; 1956 v Sp (24)
Ellis, P. (Bohemians), 1935 v Sw, G; 1936 v Ho, Sw, L; 1937 v G, H (7)

Fagan, E. (Shamrock R), 1973 v N (sub) (1)
Fagan, F. (Manchester C), 1955 v N; 1960 v Se; (with Derby Co), 1960 v Ch, WG, Se; 1961 v W, N, S (8)
Fagan, J. (Shamrock R), 1926 v I (1)
Fairclough, M. (Dundalk), 1982 v Ch (sub), Tr (sub) (2)
Fallon, S. (Celtic), 1951 v N; 1952 v WG (2), A, Sp; 1953 v F; 1955 v N, WG (8)

Fallon, W. J. (Notts Co), 1935 v H; 1936 v H; 1937 v H, Sw, F; 1939 v Sw, Pol; (with Sheffield W), 1939 v H, G (9)
Farquharson, T. G. (Cardiff C), 1929 v Bel; 1930 v Bel; 1931 v Sp; 1932 v Sp (4)
Farrell, P. (Hibernian), 1937 v Sw, F (2)
Farrell, P. D. (Shamrock R), 1946 v P, Sp; (with Everton), 1947 v Sp, P; 1948 v P, Sp; 1949 v Sw, P (sub), Sp; 1950 v E, Fi, Se; 1951 v Arg, N; 1952 v WG (2), A, Sp; 1953 v F, A; 1954 v F (2); 1955 v N, Ho, WG; 1956 v Y, Sp; 1957 v E (28)
Feenan, J. J. (Sunderland), 1937 v Sw, F (2)
Finucane, A. (Limerick), 1967 v T, Cz; 1969 v Cz, D, H; 1970 v S, Cz; 1971 v Se, I (1+1 sub); 1972 v A (11)
Fitzgerald, F. J. (Waterford), 1955 v Ho; 1956 v Ho (2)
Fitzgerald, P. J. (Leeds U), 1961 v W, N, S; (with Chester), 1962 v Cz (2) (5)
Fitzpatrick, K. (Limerick), 1970 v Cz (1)
Fitzsimons, A. G. (Middlesbrough), 1950 v Fi, Bel; 1952 v WG (2), A, Sp; 1953 v F, A; 1954 v F, L, F; 1955 v Ho, N, WG; 1956 v Y, Sp, Ho; 1957 v D, WG, E (2); 1958 v D, Pol, A; 1959 v Pol; (with Lincoln C), 1959 v Cz (26)
Flood, J. J. (Shamrock R), 1926 v I; 1929 v Bel; 1930 v Bel; 1931 v Sp; 1932 v Sp (5)
Fogarty, A. (Sunderland), 1960 v WG, Se; 1961 v S; 1962 v Cz (2); 1963 v Ic (2), S (sub); 1964 v A (2); (with Hartlepools U), Sp (11)
Foley, J. (Cork), 1934 v Bel, Ho; (with Celtic), 1935 v H, Sw, G; 1937 v G, H (7)
Foley, M. (Shelbourne), 1926 v I (1)
Foley, T. C. (Northampton T), 1964 v Sp, Pol, N; 1965 v Pol, Bel; 1966 v Sp (2), WG; 1967 v Cz (9)
Foy, T. (Shamrock R), 1938 v N; 1939 v H (2)
Fullam, J. (Preston NE), 1961 v N; (with Shamrock R), 1964 v Sp, Pol, N; 1966 v A, Bel; 1968 v Pol; 1969 v Pol, A, D; 1970 v Cz (sub) (11)
Fullam, R. (Shamrock R), 1926 v I; 1927 v I (2)

Gallagher, C. (Celtic), 1967 v T, Cz (2)
Gallagher, M. (Hibernian), 1954 v L (1)
Gallagher, P. (Falkirk), 1932 v Sp (1)
Galvin, A. (Tottenham H), 1983 v Ho, Ma; 1984 v Ho (sub), Is (sub); 1985 v M, USSR, N, D, I, N, Sp; 1986 v U, Ic, Cz; 1987 v Bel (2), S, Bul, L; (with Sheffield W), 1988 v L, Bul, R, Pol, N, E, USSR, Ho; 1989 v Sp; (with Swindon T), 1990 v WG (29)
Gannon, E. (Notts Co), 1949 v Sw; (with Sheffield W), 1949 v Bel, P, Se, Sp; 1950 v Fi; 1951 v N; 1952 v WG, A; 1954 v L, F; 1955 v N; (with Shelbourne), 1955 v N, WG (14)
Gannon, M. (Shelbourne), 1972 v A (1)
Gaskins, P. (Shamrock R), 1934 v Bel, Ho; 1935 v H, Sw, G; (with St James' Gate), 1938 v Cz, Pol (7)
Gavin, J. T. (Norwich C), 1950 v Fi (2); 1953 v F; 1954 v L; (with Tottenham H), 1955 v Ho, WG; (with Norwich C), 1957 v D (7)
Geoghegan, M. (St James' Gate), 1937 v G; 1938 v N (2)
Gibbons, A. (St Patrick's Ath), 1952 v WG; 1954 v L; 1956 v Y, Sp (4)
Gilbert, R. (Shamrock R), 1966 v WG (1)
Giles, C. (Doncaster R), 1951 v N (1)
Giles, M. J. (Manchester U), 1960 v Se, Ch; 1961 v W, N, S (2); 1962 v Cz (2), A; 1963 v Ic, S; (with Leeds U), 1964 v A (2), Sp (2), Pol, N, E; 1965 v Sp; 1966 v Sp (2), A, Bel; 1967 v Sp, T (2); 1969 v A, D, Cz; 1970 v S, Pol, WG; 1971 v I; 1973 v F, USSR; 1974 v Br, U, Ch; 1975 v USSR, T, Sw, USSR, Sw; (with WBA), 1976 v T; 1977 v E, T, F (2), Pol, Bul; (with Shamrock R), 1978 v Bul, T, Pol, N, D; 1979 v Ni, D, Bul, WG (59)
Givens, D. J. (Manchester U), 1969 v D, H; 1970 v S, Cz, D, H; (with Luton T), 1970 v Pol, WG; 1971 v Se, I (2), A; 1972 v Ir, Ec, P; (with QPR), 1973 v F, USSR, Pol, F, N; 1974 v Pol, Br, U, Ch; 1975 v USSR, T, Sw, USSR, Sw, WG; 1976 v T, N, Pol; 1977 v E, T, F (2), Sp, Bul; 1978 v Bul, N, D; (with Birmingham C), 1979 v Ni (sub), E, D, Bul, WG; 1980 v US (sub), Ni (sub), Sw, Arg; 1981 v Ho, Bel, Cy (sub), W; (with Neuchatel X), 1982 v F (sub) (56)
Glen, W. (Shamrock R), 1927 v I; 1929 v Bel; 1930 v Bel; 1932 v Sp; 1936 v Ho, Sw, H, L (8)
Glynn, D. (Drumcondra), 1952 v WG; 1955 v N (2)
Godwin, T. F. (Shamrock R), 1949 v P, Se, Sp; 1950 v Fi, E; (with Leicester C), 1950 v Fi, Se, Bel; 1951 v N; (with Bournemouth), 1956 v Ho; 1957 v E; 1958 v D, Pol (13)
Golding, J. (Shamrock R), 1928 v Bel; 1930 v Bel (2)
Gorman, W. C. (Bury), 1936 v Sw, H, L; 1937 v G, H; 1938 v N, Cz, Pol; 1939 v Sw, Pol (with Brentford) H; 1947 v E, P (13)
Grace, J. (Drumcondra), 1926 v I (1)
Grealish, A. (Orient), 1976 v N, Pol; 1978 v N, D; 1979 v Ni, E, WG; (with Luton T), 1980 v W, Cz, Bul, US, Ni, E, Cy, Sw, Arg; 1981 v WG'B', Ho, Bel, F, Cy, W, Bel, Pol; (with Brighton & HA), 1982 v Ho, Alg, Ch, Br, Tr; 1983 v Ho, Sp, Ic, Sp; 1984 v Ic, Ho; (with WBA), Pol, Chn; 1985 v M, USSR, N, D, Sp (sub), Sw; 1986 v USSR, D (45)
Gregg, E. (Bohemians), 1978 v Pol, D (sub); 1979 v E (sub), D, Bul, WG; 1980 v W, Cz (8)
Griffith, R. (Walsall), 1935 v H (1)
Grimes, A. A. (Manchester U), 1978 v T, Pol, N (sub); 1980 v Bul, US, Ni, E, Cy; 1981 v WG'B' (sub), Cz, Pol; 1982 v Alg; 1983 v Sp (2); (with Coventry C), 1984 v Pol, Is; (with Luton T), 1988 v L, R (18)

Hale, A. (Aston Villa), 1962 v A; (with Doncaster R), 1963 v Ic; 1964 v Sp (2); (with Waterford), 1967 v Sp; 1968 v Pol (sub); 1969 v Pol, A, D; 1970 v S, Cz; 1971 v Pol (sub); 1972 v A (sub) (13)
Hamilton, T. (Shamrock R), 1959 v Cz (2) (2)
Hand, E. K. (Portsmouth), 1969 v Cz (sub); 1970 v Pol, WG; 1971 v Pol, A; 1973 v USSR, F, USSR, Pol, F; 1974 v Pol, Br, U, Ch; 1975 v T, Sw, USSR, Sw, WG; 1976 v T (20)
Harrington, W. (Cork), 1936 v Ho, Sw, H, L; 1938 v Pol (sub) (5)
Hartnett, J. B. (Middlesbrough), 1949 v Sp; 1954 v L (2)
Haverty, J. (Arsenal), 1956 v Ho; 1957 v D, WG, E (2); 1958 v D, Pol, A; 1959 v Pol; 1960 v Se, Ch; 1961 v W, N, S (2); (with Blackburn R), 1962 v Cz (2); (with Millwall), 1963 v S; 1964 v A, Sp, Pol, N, E; (with Celtic), 1965 v Pol; (with Bristol R), 1965 v Sp; (with Shelbourne), 1966 v Sp (2), WG, A, Bel; 1967 v T, Sp (32)
Hayes, A. W. P. (Southampton), 1979 v D (1)
Hayes, W. E. (Huddersfield T), 1947 v E, P (2)
Hayes, W. J. (Limerick), 1949 v Bel (1)
Healey, R. (Cardiff C), 1977 v Pol; 1980 v E (sub) (2)
Heighway, S. D. (Liverpool), 1971 v Pol, Se (2), I, A; 1973 v USSR; 1975 v USSR, T, USSR, WG; 1976 v T, N; 1977 v E, F (2), Sp, Bul; 1978 v Bul, N, D; 1979 v Ni, Bul; 1980 v Bul, US, Ni, E, Cy, Arg; 1981 v Bel, F, Cy, W, Bel; (with Minnesota K), 1982 v Ho (34)
Henderson, B. (Drumcondra), 1948 v P, Sp (2)
Hennessy, J. (Shelbourne), 1965 v Pol, Bel, Sp; 1966 v WG; (with St Patrick's Ath), 1969 v A (5)
Herrick, J. (Cork Hibernians), 1972 v A, Ch (sub); (with Shamrock R), 1973 v F (sub) (3)
Higgins, J. (Birmingham C), 1951 v Arg (1)
Holmes, J. (Coventry C), 1971 v A (sub); 1973 v F, USSR, Pol, F, N; 1974 v Pol, Br; 1975 v USSR, Sw; 1976 v T, N, Pol; 1977 v E, T, F, Sp; (with Tottenham H), F, Pol, Bul; 1978 v Bul, T, Pol, N, D; 1979 v Ni, E, D, Bul; (with Vancouver W), 1981 v W (30)
Horlacher, A. F. (Bohemians), 1930 v Bel; 1932 v Sp, Ho; 1934 v Ho (sub); 1935 v H; 1936 v Ho, Sw (7)

Houghton, R. J. (Oxford U), 1986 v W, U, Ic, Cz; 1987 v Bel (2), S (2), Pol, L; 1988 v L, Bul; (with Liverpool), Is, Y, N, E, USSR, Ho; 1989 v Ni, Tun, Sp, F, H, Sp, Ma, H; 1990 v Ni, Ma, Fi, E, Eg, Ho, R, I; 1991 v Mor, T, E (2), Pol, Ch, US; 1992 v H, Alb, US, I, P; (with Aston Villa), 1993 v D, Sp, Ni, D, Alb, La, Li; 1994 v Li, Sp, Ni, Bol, G (sub), I, M, N, Ho; (with C Palace), 1995 v P, A (64)

Howlett, G. (Brighton & HA), 1984 v Chn (sub) (1)

Hoy, M. (Dundalk), 1938 v N; 1939 v Sw, Pol, H (2), G (6)

Hughton, C. (Tottenham H), 1980 v US, E, Sw, Arg; 1981 v Ho, Bel, F, Cy, W, Bel, Pol; 1982 v F; 1983 v Ho, Sp, Ma, Sp; 1984 v Ic, Ho, Ma; 1985 v M (sub), USSR, N, I, Is, E, Sp; 1986 v Sw, USSR, U, Ic; 1987 v Bel, Bul; 1988 v Is, Y, Pol, N, E, USSR, Ho; 1989 v Ni, F, H, Sp, Ma, H; 1990 v W (sub), USSR (sub), Fi, T (sub), Ma; 1991 v T; (with West Ham U), Ch; 1992 v T (53)

Hurley, C. J. (Millwall), 1957 v E; (with Sunderland), 1958 v D, Pol, A; 1959 v Cz (2); 1960 v Se, Ch, WG, Se; 1961 v W, N, S (2); 1962 v Cz (2), A; 1963 v Ic (2), S; 1964 v A (2), Sp (2), Pol, N; 1965 v Sp; 1966 v WG, A, Bel; 1967 v T, Sp, T, Cz; 1968 v Cz, Pol; 1969 v Pol, D, Cz, (with Bolton W), H (40)

Hutchinson, F. (Drumcondra), 1935 v Sw, G (2)

Irwin, D. J. (Manchester U), 1991 v Mor, T, W, E, Pol, US; 1992 v H, Pol, W, US, Alb, US (sub), I; 1993 v La, D, Sp, Ni, D, Alb, La, Li; 1994 v Li, Sp, Ni, Bol, G, I, M; 1995 v La, Lie, Ni, E, Ni, P, Lie, A (36)

Jordan, D. (Wolverhampton W), 1937 v Sw, F (2)

Jordan, W. (Bohemians), 1934 v Ho; 1938 v N (2)

Kavanagh, P. J. (Celtic), 1931 v Sp; 1932 v Sp (2)

Keane, R. M. (Nottingham F), 1991 v Ch; 1992 v H, Pol, W, Sw, Alb, US; 1993 v La, D, Sp, W, Ni, D, Alb, La, Li; (with Manchester U), 1994 v Li, Sp, Ni, Bol, G, CzR (sub), I, M, N, Ho; 1995 v Ni (2) (28)

Keane, T. R. (Swansea T), 1949 v Sw, P, Se, Sp (4)

Kearin, M. (Shamrock R), 1972 v A (1)

Kearns, F. T. (West Ham U), 1954 v L (1)

Kearns, M. (Oxford U), 1971 v Pol (sub); (with Walsall), 1974 v Pol (sub), U, Ch; 1976 v N, Pol; 1977 v E, T, F (2), Sp, Bul; 1978 v N, D; 1979 v Ni, E; (with Wolverhampton W), 1980 v US, Ni (18)

Kelly, A. T. (Sheffield U), 1993 v W (sub); 1994 v Ru (sub), G; 1995 v La, Ni, E, Ni, P, Lie, A (10)

Kelly, D. T. (Walsall), 1988 v Is, R, Y; (with West Ham U), 1989 v Tun (sub); (with Leicester C), 1990 v USSR, Ma; 1991 v Mor, W (sub), Ch, US; 1992 v H; (with Newcastle U), I (sub), P; 1993 v Sp (sub), Ni; (with Wolverhampton W), 1994 v Ru, N (sub); 1995 v E, Ni (19)

Kelly, G. (Leeds U), 1994 v Ru, Ho, Bol (sub), G (sub), CzR, N, Ho; 1995 v La, Lie, Ni (2), P, Lie, A (14)

Kelly, J. (Derry C), 1932 v Ho; 1934 v Bel; 1936 v Sw, L (4)

Kelly, J. A. (Drumcondra), 1957 v WG, E; (with Preston NE), 1962 v A; 1963 v Ic (2), S; 1964 v A (2), Sp (2), Pol; 1965 v Bel; 1966 v A, Bel; 1967 v Sp (2), T, Cz; 1968 v Pol, Cz; 1969 v Pol, A, D, Cz, D, H; 1970 v S, D, H, Pol, WG; 1971 v Pol, Se (2), I (2), A; 1972 v Ir, Ec, Ch, P; 1973 v USSR, F, USSR, Pol, F, N (47)

Kelly, J. P. V. (Wolverhampton W), 1961 v W, N, S; 1962 v Cz (2) (5)

Kelly, M. J. (Portsmouth), 1988 v Y, Pol (sub); 1989 v Tun; 1991 v Mor (4)

Kelly, N. (Nottingham F), 1954 v L (1)

Kendrick, J. (Everton), 1927 v I; (with Dolphin) 1934 v Bel, Ho; 1936 v Ho (4)

Kenna, J. J. (Blackburn R), 1995 v P (sub), Lie (sub), A (sub) (3)

Kennedy, M. F. (Portsmouth), 1986 v Ic, Cz (sub) (2)

Kennedy, W. (St James' Gate), 1932 v Ho; 1934 v Bel, Ho (3)

Keogh, J. (Shamrock R), 1966 v WG (sub) (1)

Keogh, S. (Shamrock R), 1959 v Pol (1)

Kernaghan, A. N. (Middlesbrough), 1993 v La, D (2), Alb, La, Li; 1994 v Li; (with Manchester C), Sp, Ni, Bol (sub), CzR; 1995 v Lie, E (13)

Kiernan, F. W. (Shamrock R), 1951 v Arg, N; (with Southampton), 1952 v WG (2), A (5)

Kinnear, J. P. (Tottenham H), 1967 v T; 1968 v Cz, Pol; 1969 v A; 1970 v Cz, D, H, Pol; 1971 v Se (sub), I; 1972 v Ir, Ec, Ch, P; 1973 v USSR, F; 1974 v Pol, Br, U, Ch; 1975 v USSR, T, Sw, USSR, WG; (with Brighton & HA), 1976 v T (sub) (26)

Kinsella, J. (Shelbourne), 1928 v Bel (1)

Kinsella, O. (Shamrock R), 1932 v Ho; 1938 v N (2)

Kirkland, A. (Shamrock R), 1927 v I (1)

Lacey, W. (Shelbourne), 1927 v I; 1928 v Bel; 1930 v Bel (3)

Langan, D. (Derby Co), 1978 v T, N; 1980 v Sw, Arg; (with Birmingham C), 1981 v WG'B', Ho, Bel, F, Cy, W, Bel, Cz, Pol; 1982 v Ho, F; (with Oxford U), 1985 v N, Sp, Sw; 1986 v W, U; 1987 v Bel, S, Pol, Br (sub), L (sub); 1988 v L (26)

Lawler, J. F. (Fulham), 1953 v A; 1954 v L, F; 1955 v N, H, N, WG; 1956 v Y (8)

Lawlor, J. C. (Drumcondra), 1949 v Bel; (with Doncaster R), 1951 v N, Arg (3)

Lawlor, M. (Shamrock R), 1971 v Pol, Se (2), I (sub); 1973 v Pol (5)

Lawrenson, M. (Preston NE), 1977 v Pol; (with Brighton), 1978 v Bul, Pol, N (sub); 1979 v Ni, E; 1980 v E, Cy, Sw; 1981 v Ho, Bel, F, Cy, Pol; (with Liverpool), 1982 v Ho, F; 1983 v Ho, Sp, Ic, Ma, Sp; 1984 v Ic, Ho, Ma, Is; 1985 v USSR, N, D, I, E, N; 1986 v Sw, USSR, D; 1987 v Bel, S; 1988 v Bul, Is (38)

Leech, M. (Shamrock R), 1969 v Cz, D, H; 1972 v A, Ir, Ec, P; 1973 v USSR (sub) (8)

Lennon, C. (St James' Gate), 1935 v H, Sw, G (3)

Lennox, G. (Dolphin), 1931 v Sp; 1932 v Sp (2)

Lowry, D. (St Patrick's Ath), 1962 v A (sub) (1)

Lunn, R. (Dundalk), 1939 v Sw, Pol (2)

Lynch, J. (Cork Bohemians), 1934 v Bel (1)

McAlinden, J. (Portsmouth), 1946 v P, Sp (2)

McAteer, J. W. (Bolton W), 1994 v Ru, Ho (sub), Bol (sub), G, CzR (sub), I (sub), M (sub), N, Ho (sub); 1995 v La, Lie, Ni (2 sub), Lie (14)

McCann, J. (Shamrock R), 1957 v WG (1)

McCarthy, J. (Bohemians), 1926 v I; 1928 v Bel; 1930 v Bel (3)

McCarthy, M. (Manchester C), 1984 v Pol, Chn; 1985 v M, D, I, Is, E, Sp, Sw; 1986 v Sw, USSR, W (sub), U, Ic, Cz; 1987 v S (2), Pol, Bul, Bel (with Celtic), Br, L; 1988 v Bul, Is, R, Y, N, E, USSR, Ho; 1989 v Ni, Tun, Sp, F, H, Sp; (with Lyon), 1990 v WG, Ni (with Millwall), W, USSR, Fi, T, E, Eg, Ho, R, I; 1991 v Mor, T, E, US; 1992 v H, T, Alb (sub), US, I, P (57)

McCarthy, M. (Shamrock R), 1932 v Ho (1)

McConville, T. (Dundalk), 1972 v A; (with Waterford), 1973 v USSR, F, USSR, Pol, F (6)

McDonagh, Joe (Shamrock R), 1984 v Pol (sub), Ma (sub); 1985 v M (sub) (3)

McDonagh, J. (Everton), 1981 v WG'B', W, Bel, Cz; (with Bolton W), 1982 v Ho, F, Ch, Br; 1983 v Ho, Sp, Ic, Ma, Sp; (with Notts Co), 1984 v Ic, Ho, Pol; 1985 v M, USSR, N, D, Sp, Sw; 1986 v Sw, USSR (with Wichita Wings) D (25)

McEvoy, M. A. (Blackburn R), 1961 v S (2); 1963 v S; 1964 v A, Sp (2), Pol, N, E; 1965 v Pol, Bel, Sp; 1966 v Sp (2); 1967 v Sp, T, Cz (17)

McGee, P. (QPR), 1978 v T, N (sub), D (sub); 1979 v Ni, E, D (sub), Bul (sub); 1980 v Cz, Bul; (with Preston NE), US, Ni, Cy, Sw, Arg; 1981 v Bel (sub) (15)
McGoldrick, E. J. (C Palace), 1992 v Sw, US, I, P (sub); 1993 v D, W, Ni (sub), D; (with Arsenal), 1994 v Ni, Ru, Ho, CzR; 1995 v La (sub), Lie, E (15)
McGowan, D. (West Ham U), 1949 v P, Se, Sp (3)
McGowan, J. (Cork U), 1947 v Sp (1)
McGrath, M. (Blackburn R), 1958 v A; 1959 v Pol, Cz (2); 1960 v Se, WG, Se; 1961 v W; 1962 v Cz (2); 1963 v S; 1964 v A (2), E; 1965 v Pol, Bel, Sp; 1966 v Sp; (with Bradford), 1966 v WG, A, Bel; 1967 v T (22)
McGrath, P. (Manchester U), 1985 v I (sub), Is, E, N (sub), Sw (sub); 1986 v Sw (sub), D, W, Ic, Cz; 1987 v Bel (2), S (2), Pol, Bul, Br, L; 1988 v L, Bul, Y, Pol, N, E, Ho; 1989 v Ni, F, H, Sp, Ma, H; (with Aston Villa), 1990 v WG, Ma, USSR, Fi, T, E, Eg, Ho, R, I; 1991 v E (2), W, Pol, Ch (sub), US; 1992 v Pol, T, Sw, US, Alb, US, I, P; 1993 v La, Sp, Ni, D, La, Li; 1994 v Sp, Ni, G, CzR, I, M, N, Ho; 1995 v La, Ni, E, Ni, P, Lie, A (76)
McGuire, W. (Bohemians), 1936 v Ho (1)
McKenzie, G. (Southend U), 1938 v N (2), Cz, Pol; 1939 v Sw, Pol, H (2), G (9)
Mackey, G. (Shamrock R), 1957 v D, WG, E (3)
McLoughlin, A. F. (Swindon T), 1990 v Ma, E (sub), Eg (sub); 1991 v Mor (sub), E (sub); (with Southampton), W, Ch (sub); 1992 v H (sub), W (sub); (with Portsmouth), US, I (sub), P; 1993 v W; 1994 v Ni (sub), Ru, Ho (sub); 1995 v Lie (sub) (17)
McLoughlin, F. (Fordsons), 1930 v Bel; (with Cork), 1932 v Sp (2)
McMillan, W. (Belfast Celtic), 1946 v P, Sp (2)
McNally, J. B. (Luton T), 1959 v Cz; 1961 v S; 1963 v Ic (3)
Macken, A. (Derby Co), 1977 v Sp (1)
Madden, O. (Cork), 1936 v H (1)
Maguire, J. (Shamrock R), 1929 v Bel (1)
Malone, G. (Shelbourne), 1949 v Bel (1)
Mancini, T. J. (QPR), 1974 v Pol, Br, U, Ch; (with Arsenal), 1975 v USSR (5)
Martin, C. (Bo'ness), 1927 v I (1)
Martin, C. J. (Glentoran), 1946 v P (sub), Sp; 1947 v E; (with Leeds U), 1947 v Sp; 1948 v P, Sp; (with Aston Villa), 1949 v Sw, Bel, P, Se, Sp; 1950 v Fi, E, Fi, Se, Bel; 1951 v Arg; 1952 v WG, A, Sp; 1954 v F (2), L; 1955 v N, Ho, N, WG; 1956 v Y, Sp, Ho (30)
Martin, M. P. (Bohemians), 1972 v A, Ir, Ec, Ch, P; 1973 v USSR; (with Manchester U), 1973 v USSR, Pol, F, N; 1974 v Pol, Br, U, Ch; 1975 v USSR, T, Sw, USSR, Sw, WG; (with WBA), 1976 v T, N, Pol; 1977 v E, T, F (2), Sp, Pol, Bul; (with Newcastle U), 1979 v D, Bul, WG; 1980 v W, Cz, Bul, US, Ni; 1981 v WG'B', F, Bel, Cz; 1982 v Ho, F, Alg, Ch, Br, Tr; 1983 v Ho, Sp, Ma, Sp (52)
Meagan, M. K. (Everton), 1961 v S; 1962 v A; 1963 v Ic; 1964 v Sp; (with Huddersfield T), 1965 v Bel; 1966 v Sp (2), A, Bel; 1967 v Sp, T, Sp, T, Cz; 1968 v Cz, Pol; (with Drogheda), 1970 v S (17)
Meehan, P. (Drumcondra), 1934 v Ho (1)
Milligan, M. J. (Oldham Ath), 1992 v US (sub) (1)
Monahan, P. (Sligo R), 1935 v Sw, G (2)
Mooney, J. (Shamrock R), 1965 v Pol, Bel (2)
Moore, P. (Shamrock R), 1931 v Sp; 1932 v Ho; (with Aberdeen), 1934 v Bel, Ho; 1935 v H, G; (with Shamrock R), 1936 v Ho; 1937 v G, H (9)
Moran, K. (Manchester U), 1980 v Sw, Arg; 1981 v WG'B', Bel, F, Cy, W (sub), Bel, Cz, Pol; 1982 v F, Alg; 1983 v Ic; 1984 v Ic, Ho, Ma, Is; 1985 v M; 1986 v D, Ic, Cz; 1987 v Bel (2), S (2), Pol, Bul, Br, L; 1988 v L, Bul, Is, R, Y, Pol, N, E, USSR, Ho; (with Sporting Gijon), 1989 v Ni, Sp, H, Sp, Ma, H; 1990 v Ni, Ma; (with Blackburn R), W, USSR (sub), Ma, E, Eg, Ho, R, I; 1991 v T (sub), W, E, Pol, Ch, US; 1992 v Pol, US; 1993 v D, Sp, Ni, Alb; 1994 v Li, Sp, Ho, Bol (71)
Moroney, T. (West Ham U), 1948 v Sp; 1949 v P, Se, Sp; 1950 v Fi, E, Fi, Bel; 1951 v N (2); 1952 v WG; (with Evergreen U), 1954 v F (12)
Morris, C. B. (Celtic), 1988 v Is, R, Y, Pol, N, E, USSR, Ho; 1989 v Ni, Tun, Sp, F, H (1 + 1 sub); 1990 v WG, Ni, Ma (sub), W, USSR, Fi (sub), T, E, Eg, Ho, R, I; 1991 v E; 1992 v H (sub), Pol, W, Sw, US (2), P; (with Middlesbrough), 1993 v W (35)
Moulson, C. (Lincoln C), 1936 v H, L; (with Notts Co), 1937 v H, Sw, F (5)
Moulson, G. B. (Lincoln C), 1948 v P, Sp; 1949 v Sw (3)
Mucklan, C. (Drogheda U), 1978 v Pol (1)
Muldoon, T. (Aston Villa), 1927 v I (1)
Mulligan, P. M. (Shamrock R), 1969 v Cz, D, H; 1970 v S, Cz, D; (with Chelsea), 1970 v H, Pol, WG; 1971 v Pol, Se, I; 1972 v A, Ir, Ec, Ch, P; (with C Palace), 1973 v F, USSR, Pol, F, N; 1974 v Pol, Br, U, Ch; 1975 v USSR, T, Sw, USSR, Sw; (with WBA), 1976 v T, Pol; 1977 v E, T, F (2), Pol, Bul; 1978 v Bul, N, D; 1979 v E, D, Bul (sub), WG; (with Shamrock R), 1980 v W, Cz, Bul, US (sub) (50)
Munroe, L. (Shamrock R), 1954 v L (1)
Murphy, A. (Clyde), 1956 v Y (1)
Murphy, B. (Bohemians), 1986 v U (1)
Murphy, J. (C Palace), 1980 v W, US, Cy (3)
Murray, T. (Dundalk), 1950 v Bel (1)

Newman, W. (Shelbourne), 1969 v D (1)
Nolan, R. (Shamrock R), 1957 v D, WG, E; 1958 v Pol; 1960 v Ch, WG, Se; 1962 v Cz (2); 1963 v Ic (10)

O'Brien, F. (Philadelphia F), 1980 v Cz, E, Cy (sub) (3)
O'Brien, L. (Shamrock R), 1986 v U; (with Manchester U), 1987 v Br; 1988 v Is (sub), R (sub), Y (sub), Pol (sub); 1989 v Tun; (with Newcastle U), Sp (sub); 1992 v Sw (sub); 1993 v W; (with Tranmere R), 1994 v Ru (11)
O'Brien, M. T. (Derby Co), 1927 v I; (with Walsall), 1929 v Bel; (with Norwich C), 1930 v Bel; (with Watford), 1932 v Ho (4)
O'Brien, R. (Notts Co), 1976 v N, Pol; 1977 v Sp, Pol; 1980 v Arg (sub) (5)
O'Byrne, L. B. (Shamrock R), 1949 v Bel (1)
O'Callaghan, B. R. (Stoke C), 1979 v WG (sub); 1980 v W, US; 1981 v W; 1982 v Br, Tr (6)
O'Callaghan, K. (Ipswich T), 1981 v WG'B', Cz, Pol; 1982 v Alg, Ch, Br, Tr (sub); 1983 v Sp, Ic (sub), Ma (sub), Sp (sub); 1984 v Ic, Ho, Ma; 1985 v M (sub), N (sub), D (sub), (with Portsmouth) E (sub); 1986 v Sw (sub), USSR (sub); 1987 v Br (21)
O'Connell, A. (Dundalk), 1967 v Sp; (with Bohemians), 1971 v Pol (sub) (2)
O'Connor, T. (Shamrock R), 1950 v Fi, E, Fi, Se (4)
O'Connor, T. (Fulham), 1968 v Cz; (with Dundalk), 1972 v A, Ir (sub), Ec (sub), Ch; (with Bohemians), 1973 v F (sub), Pol (sub) (7)
O'Driscoll, J. F. (Swansea T), 1949 v Sw, Bel, Se (3)
O'Driscoll, S. (Fulham), 1982 v Ch, Br, Tr (sub) (3)
O'Farrell, F. (West Ham U), 1952 v A; 1953 v A; 1954 v F; 1955 v Ho, N; 1956 v Y, Ho; (with Preston NE), 1958 v D; 1959 v Cz (9)
O'Flanagan, K. P. (Bohemians), 1938 v N, Cz, Pol; 1939 v Pol, H (2), G; (with Arsenal), 1947 v E, Sp, P (10)
O'Flanagan, M. (Bohemians), 1947 v E (1)
O'Hanlon, K. G. (Rotherham U), 1988 v Is (1)
O'Kane, P. (Bohemians), 1935 v H, Sw, G (3)
O'Keefe, E. (Everton), 1981 v W; (with Port Vale), 1984 v Chn; 1985 v M, USSR (sub), E (5)
O'Keefe, T. (Cork), 1934 v Bel; (with Waterford), 1938 v Cz, Pol (3)
O'Leary, D. (Arsenal), 1977 v E, F (2), Sp, Bul; 1978 v Bul, N, D; 1979 v E, Bul, WG; 1980 v W, Bul, Ni, E, Cy; 1981

v WG'B', Ho, Cz, Pol; 1982 v Ho, F; 1983 v Ho, Ic, Sp; 1984 v Pol, Is, Chn; 1985 v USSR, N, D, Is, E (sub), N, Sp, Sw; 1986 v Sw, USSR, D, W; 1989 v Sp, Ma, H; 1990 v WG, Ni (sub), Ma, W (sub), USSR, Fi, T, Ma, R (sub); 1991 v Mor, T, E (2), Pol, Ch; 1992 v H, Pol, T, W, Sw, US, Alb, I, P; 1993 v W (68)

O'Leary, P. (Shamrock R), 1980 v Bul, US, Ni, E (sub), Cz, Arg; 1981 v Ho (7)

O'Mahoney, M. T. (Bristol R), 1938 v Cz, Pol; 1939 v Sw, Pol, H, G (6)

O'Neill, F. S. (Shamrock R), 1962 v Cz (2); 1965 v Pol, Bel, Sp; 1966 v Sp (2), WG, A; 1967 v Sp, T, Sp, T; 1969 v Pol, A, D, Cz, D (sub), H (sub); 1972 v A (20)

O'Neill, J. (Everton), 1952 v Sp; 1953 v F, A; 1954 v F, L, F; 1955 v N, Ho, N, WG; 1956 v Y, Sp; 1957 v D; 1958 v A; 1959 v Pol, Cz (2) (17)

O'Neill, J. (Preston NE), 1961 v W (1)

O'Neill, W. (Dundalk), 1936 v Ho, Sw, H, L; 1937 v G, H, Sw, F; 1938 v N; 1939 v H, G (11)

O'Regan, K. (Brighton & HA), 1984 v Ma, Pol; 1985 v M, Sp (sub) (4)

O'Reilly, J. (Brideville), 1932 v Ho; (with Aberdeen), 1934 v Bel, Ho; (with Brideville), 1936 v Ho; Sw, H, L; (with St James' Gate), 1937 v G, H, Sw, F; 1938 v N (2), Cz, Pol; 1939 v Sw, Pol, H (2), G (20)

O'Reilly, J. (Cork U), 1946 v P, Sp (2)

Peyton, G. (Fulham), 1977 v Sp (sub); 1978 v Bul, T, Pol; 1979 v D, Bul, WG; 1980 v W, Cz, Bul, E, Cy, Sw, Arg; 1981 v Ho, Bel, F, Cy; 1982 v Tr; 1985 v M (sub); 1986 v W, Cz; (with Bournemouth), 1988 v L, Pol; 1989 v Ni, Tun; 1990 v USSR, Ma; 1991 v Ch; (with Everton) 1992 v US (2), I (sub), P (33)

Peyton, N. (Shamrock R), 1957 v WG; (with Leeds U), 1960 v WG, Se (sub); 1961 v W; 1963 v Ic, S (6)

Phelan, T. (Wimbledon), 1992 v H, Pol (sub), T, W, Sw, US, I (sub), P; (with Manchester C), 1993 v La (sub), D, Sp, Ni, Alb, La, Li; 1994 v Li, Sp, Ni, Ho, Bol, G, CzR, I, M, Ho; 1995 v E (26)

Quinn, N. J. (Arsenal), 1986 v Ic (sub), Cz; 1987 v Bul (sub), Br (sub); 1988 v L (sub), Bul (sub), Is, R (sub), Pol (sub), E (sub); 1989 v Tun (sub), Sp (sub), H (sub); (with Manchester C), 1990 v USSR, Ma, Eg (sub), Ho, R, I; 1991 v Mor, T, E (2) W, Pol; 1992 v H, W (sub), US, Alb, US, I (sub), P; 1993 v La, D, Sp, Ni, D, Alb, La, Li; 1994 v Li, Sp, Ni; 1995 v La, Lie, Ni, E, Ni, P, Lie, A (51)

Reid, C. (Brideville), 1931 v Sp (1)

Richardson, D. J. (Shamrock R), 1972 v A (sub); (with Gillingham), 1973 v N (sub); 1980 v Cz (3)

Rigby, A. (St James' Gate), 1935 v H, Sw, G (3)

Ringstead, A. (Sheffield U), 1951 v Arg, N; 1952 v WG (2), A, Sp; 1953 v A; 1954 v F; 1955 v N; 1956 v Y, Sp, Ho; 1957 v E (2); 1958 v D, Pol, A; 1959 v Pol, Cz (2) (20)

Robinson, J. (Bohemians), 1928 v Bel; (with Dolphin), 1931 v Sp (2)

Robinson, M. (Brighton & HA), 1981 v WG'B', F, Cy, Bel, Pol; 1982 v Ho, F, Alg, Ch; 1983 v Ho, Sp, Ic, Ma; (with Liverpool), 1984 v Ic, Ho, Is; 1985 v USSR, N; (with QPR), N, Sp, Sw; 1986 v D (sub), W, Cz (24)

Roche, P. J. (Shelbourne), 1972 v A; (with Manchester U), 1975 v USSR, T, Sw, USSR, Sw, WG; 1976 v T (8)

Rogers, E. (Blackburn R), 1968 v Cz, Pol; 1969 v Pol, A, D, Cz, D, H; 1970 v S, D, H; 1971 v I (2), A; (with Charlton Ath), 1972 v Ir, Ec, Ch, P; 1973 v USSR (19)

Ryan, G. (Derby Co), 1978 v T; (with Brighton & HA), 1979 v E, WG; 1980 v W, Cy (sub), Sw, Arg (sub); 1981 v WG'B', F (sub), Pol (sub); 1982 v Br (sub), Ho (sub), Alg (sub), Ch (sub), Tr; 1984 v Pol, Chn; 1985 v M (18)

Ryan, R. A. (WBA), 1950 v Se, Bel; 1951 v N, Arg, N; 1952 v WG (2), A, Sp; 1953 v F, A; 1954 v F, L, F; 1955 v N; (with Derby Co), 1956 v Sp (16)

Saward, P. (Millwall), 1954 v L; (with Aston Villa), 1957 v E (2); 1958 v D, Pol, A; 1959 v Pol, Cz; 1960 v Se, Ch, WG, Se; 1961 v W, N; (with Huddersfield T), 1961 v S; 1962 v A; 1963 v Ic (2) (18)

Scannell, T. (Southend U), 1954 v L (1)

Scully, P. J. (Arsenal), 1989 v Tun (sub) (1)

Sheedy, K. (Everton), 1984 v Ho (sub), Ma; 1985 v D, I, Is, Sw; 1986 v Sw, D; 1987 v S, Pol; 1988 v Is, R, Pol, E (sub), USSR; 1989 v Ni, Tun, H, Sp, Ma, H; 1990 v Ni, Ma, W (sub), USSR, Fi (sub), T, E, Eg, Ho, R, I; 1991 v W, E, Pol, Ch, US; 1992 v H, Pol, T, W; (with Newcastle U), Sw (sub), Alb; 1993 v La, W (sub) (45)

Sheridan, J. J. (Leeds U), 1988 v R, Y, Pol, N (sub); 1989 v Sp; (with Sheffield W), 1990 v W, T (sub), Ma, I (sub); 1991 v Mor (sub), T, Ch, US (sub); 1992 v H; 1993 v La; 1994 v Sp (sub), Ho, Bol, G, CzR, I, M, N, Ho; 1995 v La, Lie, Ni, E, Ni, P, Lie, A (32)

Slaven, B. (Middlesbrough), 1990 v W, Fi, T (sub), Ma; 1991 v W, Pol (sub); 1993 v W (7)

Sloan, J. W. (Arsenal), 1946 v P, Sp (2)

Smyth, M. (Shamrock R), 1969 v Pol (sub) (1)

Squires, J. (Shelbourne), 1934 v Ho (1)

Stapleton, F. (Arsenal), 1977 v T, F, Sp, Bul; 1978 v Bul, N, D; 1979 v Ni, E (sub), D, WG; 1980 v W, Bul, Ni, E, Cy; 1981 v WG'B', Ho, Bel, F, Cy, Bel, Cz, Pol; (with Manchester U), 1982 v Ho, F, Alg; 1983 v Ho, Sp, Ic, Ma, Sp; 1984 v Ic, Ho, Ma, Pol, Is, Chn; 1985 v N, D, I, Is, E, N, Sw; 1986 v Sw, USSR, D, U, Ic, Cz (sub); 1987 v Bel (2), S (2), Pol, Bul, L; (with Ajax), 1988 v L, Bul; (with Derby Co), R, Y, N, E, USSR, Ho; (with Le Havre), 1989 v F, Sp, Ma; (with Blackburn R), 1990 v WG, Ma (sub) (71)

Staunton, S. (Liverpool), 1989 v Tun, Sp (2), Ma, H; 1990 v WG, Ni, Ma, W, USSR, Fi, T, Ma, E, Eg, Ho, R, I; 1991 v Mor, T, E (2), W, Pol, Ch, US; (with Aston Villa), 1992 v Pol, T, Sw, US, Alb, US, I, P; 1993 v La, Sp, Ni, D, Alb, La, Li; 1994 v Li, Sp, Ho, Bol, G, CzR, I, M, N, Ho; 1995 v La, Lie, Ni, E, Ni, P, Lie, A (59)

Stevenson, A. E. (Dolphin), 1932 v Ho; (with Everton), 1947 v E, Sp, P; 1948 v P, Sp; 1949 v Sw (7)

Strahan, F. (Shelbourne), 1964 v Pol, N, E; 1965 v Pol; 1966 v WG (5)

Sullivan, J. (Fordsons), 1928 v Bel (1)

Swan, M. M. G. (Drumcondra), 1960 v Se (sub) (1)

Synnott, N. (Shamrock R), 1978 v T, Pol; 1979 v Ni (3)

Taylor, T. (Waterford), 1959 v Pol (sub) (1)

Thomas, P. (Waterford), 1974 v Pol, Br (2)

Townsend, A. D. (Norwich C), 1989 v F, Sp (sub), Ma (sub), H; 1990 v WG (sub), Ni, Ma, W, USSR, Fi (sub), T, Ma (sub), E, Eg, Ho, R, I; (with Chelsea), 1991 v Mor, T, E (2), W, Pol, Ch, US; 1992 v Pol, W, US, Alb, US, I; 1993 v La, D, Sp, Ni, D, Alb, La, Li; (with Aston Villa), 1994 v Li, Ni, Ho, Bol, G, CzR, I, M, N, Ho; 1995 v La, Ni, E, Ni, P (54)

Traynor, T. J. (Southampton), 1954 v L; 1962 v A; 1963 v Ic (2), S; 1964 v A (2), Sp (8)

Treacy, R. C. P. (WBA), 1966 v WG; 1967 v Sp, Cz; 1968 v Cz; (with Charlton Ath), 1968 v Pol; 1969 v Pol, Cz, D; 1970 v S, D, H (sub), Pol (sub), WG (sub); 1971 v Pol, Se (sub + 1), I, A; (with Swindon T), 1972 v Ir, Ec, Ch, P; 1973 v USSR, F, USSR, Pol, F, N; 1974 v Pol; (with Preston NE), Br; 1975 v USSR, Sw (2), WG; 1976 v T, N (sub), Pol (sub); (with WBA), 1977 v F, Pol; (with Shamrock R), 1978 v T, Pol; 1980 v Cz (sub) (42)

Tuohy, L. (Shamrock R), 1956 v Y; 1959 v Cz (2); (with Newcastle U), 1962 v A; 1963 v Ic (2); (with Shamrock R), 1964 v A; 1965 v Bel (8)

Turner, C. J. (Southend U), 1936 v Sw; 1937 v G, H, Sw, F; 1938 v N (2), (with West Ham U) Cz, Pol; 1939 v H (10)
Turner, P. (Celtic), 1963 v S; 1964 v Sp (2)

Vernon, J. (Belfast C), 1946 v P, Sp (2)

Waddock, G. (QPR), 1980 v Sw, Arg; 1981 v W, Pol (sub); 1982 v Alg; 1983 v Ic, Ma, Sp, Ho (sub); 1984 v Ma (sub), Ic, Ho, Is; 1985 v I, Is, E, N, Sp; 1986 v USSR; (with Millwall), 1990 v USSR, T (21)
Walsh, D. J. (Linfield), 1946 v P, Sp; (with WBA), 1947 v Sp, P; 1948 v P, Sp; 1949 v Sw, P, Se, Sp; 1950 v E, Fi, Se; 1951 v N; (with Aston Villa), Arg, N; 1952 v Sp; 1953 v A; 1954 v F (2) (20)
Walsh, J. (Limerick), 1982 v Tr (1)
Walsh, M. (Blackpool), 1976 v N, Pol; 1977 v F (sub), Pol; (with Everton), 1979 v Ni (sub); (with QPR), D (sub), Bul, WG (sub); (with Porto), 1981 v Bel (sub), Cz; 1982 v Alg (sub); 1983 v Sp, Ho (sub), Sp (sub); 1984 v Ic (sub), Ma, Pol, Chn; 1985 v USSR, N (sub), D (21)
Walsh, M. (Everton), 1982 v Ch, Br, Tr; 1983 v Ic (4)
Walsh, W. (Manchester C), 1947 v E, Sp, P; 1948 v P, Sp; 1949 v Bel; 1950 v E, Se, Bel (9)
Waters, J. (Grimsby T), 1977 v T; 1980 v Ni (sub) (2)
Watters, F. (Shelbourne), 1926 v I (1)
Weir, E. (Clyde), 1939 v H (2), G (3)
Whelan, R. (St Patrick's Ath), 1964 v A, E (sub) (2)
Whelan, R. (Liverpool), 1981 v Cz (sub); 1982 v Ho (sub), F; 1983 v Ic, Ma, Sp; 1984 v Is; 1985 v USSR, N, I (sub), Is, E, N (sub), Sw (sub); 1986 v USSR (sub), W; 1987 v Bel (sub), S, Bul, Bel, Br, L; 1988 v L, Bul, Pol, N, E, USSR, Ho; 1989 v Ni, F, H, Sp, Ma; 1990 v WG, Ni, Ma, W, Ho (sub); 1991 v Mor, E; 1992 v Sw; 1993 v La, W (sub), Li (sub); 1994 v Li (sub), Sp, Ru, Ho, G (sub), N (sub); (with Southend U), 1995 v Lie, A (53)
Whelan, W. (Manchester U), 1956 v Ho; 1957 v D, E (2) (4)
White, J. J. (Bohemians), 1928 v Bel (1)
Whittaker, R. (Chelsea), 1959 v Cz (1)
Williams, J. (Shamrock R), 1938 v N (1)

UMBRO INTERNATIONAL TROPHY

Wembley, 3 June 1995, 21,142

England (0) 2 *(Anderton, Platt (pen))*
Japan (0) 1 *(Ihara)*

England: Flowers; Neville G, Pearce, Batty (Gascoigne), Scales, Unsworth, Anderton, Beardsley (McManaman), Shearer, Collymore (Sheringham), Platt.
Japan: Maekawa; Tasaka, Hashiratani, Ihara, Narahashi, Morishama (Fukuda), Yamaguchi, Kitazawa, Soma (Yanagimoto), Miura, Nakayama (Kurosaki).

Villa Park, 4 June 1995, 20,131

Brazil (1) 1 *(Edmundo)*
Sweden (0) 0

Brazil: Zetti; Jorginho, Roberto Carlos, Ronaldao, Aldair, Cesar Sampaio (Cruz), Zinho, Dunga, Ronaldo, Edmundo, Juninho.
Sweden: Andersson B; Kamark, Ljung, Alexandersson, Lucic, Bjorklund, Mild, Erlingmark, Dahlin (Lidman), Andersson K (Larsson), Thern (Gudmundsson).

Goodison Park, 6 June 1995, 29,327

Japan (0) 0
Brazil (1) 3 *(Roberto Carlos, Zinho 2)*

Japan: Kojima; Ihara, Narahashi, Tasaka (Moriyasu), Omura, Souma, Morishima (Kurosaki), Kitazawa, Yamaguchi, Miura, Nakayama (Fukuda).
Brazil: Zetti; Jorginho, Roberto Carlos, Marcio Santos, Aldair, Doriva, Zinho (Rivaldo), Dunga, Ronaldo, Edmundo, Juninho (Leonardo).

Elland Road, 8 June 1995, 32,008

England (1) 3 *(Sheringham, Platt, Anderton)*
Sweden (2) 3 *(Mild 2, Andersson K)*

England: Flowers; Barton, Le Saux, Platt, Cooper, Pallister (Scales), Anderton, Beardsley (Barmby), Shearer, Barnes (Gascoigne), Sheringham.
Sweden: Ravelli; Sundgren, Kamark, Alexandersson, Lucic, Bjorklund, Mild, Erlingmark (Andersson O), Gudmundsson, Andersson K (Lidman), Larsson.

City Ground, 10 June 1995, 5591

Sweden (0) 2 *(Andersson K 2)*
Japan (1) 2 *(Fujita, Kurosaki)*

Sweden: Ravelli; Sundgren, Kamark, Alexandersson, Lucic, Bjorklund, Wibran, Andersson O, Gudmundsson (Nilsson), Andersson K, Larsson.
Japan: Shimokawa; Narahashi (Yangaimoto), Ihara, Hashiratani, Omura, Fujita (Moriyasu), Yamaguchi, Kitazawa (Fukuda), Soma, Miura, Kurosaki.

Wembley, 11 June 1995, 67,318

England (1) 1 *(Le Saux)*
Brazil (0) 3 *(Juninho, Ronaldo, Edmundo)*

England: Flowers; Neville G, Pearce, Batty (Gascoigne), Scales (Barton), Cooper, Anderton, Platt, Shearer (Collymore), Sheringham, Le Saux.
Brazil: Zetti; Jorginho, Roberto Carlos, Marcio Santos, Aldair (Ronaldao), Cesar Sampaio, Zinho, Dunga, Ronaldo (Giovanni), Edmundo, Juninho (Leonardo).

	P	*W*	*D*	*L*	*F*	*A*	*Pts*
Brazil	3	3	0	0	7	1	9
England	3	1	1	1	6	7	4
Sweden	3	0	2	1	5	6	2
Japan	3	0	1	2	3	7	1

BRITISH AND IRISH INTERNATIONAL GOALSCORERS SINCE 1872

Where two players with the same surname and initials have appeared for the same country, and one or both have scored, they have been distinguished by reference to the club which appears *first* against their name in the international appearances section (pages 780–830). Unfortunately, four of the scorers in Scotland's 10-2 victory v Ireland in 1888 are unknown, as is the scorer of one of their nine goals v Wales in March 1878.

ENGLAND

A'Court, A.	1
Adams, T. A.	4
Adcock, H.	1
Alcock, C. W.	1
Allen, A.	3
Allen, R.	2
Anderson, V.	2
Anderton, D. R.	3
Astall, G.	1
Athersmith, W. C.	3
Atyeo, P. J. W.	5
Bache, J. W.	4
Bailey, N. C.	2
Baily, E. F.	5
Baker, J. H.	3
Ball, A. J.	8
Bambridge, A. L.	1
Bambridge, E. C.	12
Barclay, R.	2
Barnes, J.	11
Barnes, P. S.	4
Barton, J.	1
Bassett, W. I.	7
Bastin, C. S.	12
Beardsley, P. A.	9
Beasley, A.	1
Beattie, T. K.	1
Becton, F.	2
Bedford, H.	1
Bell, C.	9
Bentley, R. T. F.	9
Bishop, S. M.	1
Blackburn, F.	1
Blissett, L.	3
Bloomer, S.	28
Bond, R.	2
Bonsor, A. G.	1
Bowden, E. R.	1
Bowers, J. W.	2
Bowles, S.	1
Bradford, G. R. W.	1
Bradford, J.	7
Bradley, W.	2
Bradshaw, F.	3
Bridges, B. J.	1
Bridgett, A.	3
Brindle, T.	1
Britton, C. S.	1
Broadbent, P. F.	2
Broadis, I. A.	8
Brodie, J. B.	1
Bromley-Davenport, W.	2
Brook, E. F.	10
Brooking, T. D.	5
Brooks, J.	2
Broome, F. H.	3
Brown, A.	4
Brown, A. S.	1
Brown, G.	5
Brown, J.	3
Brown, W.	1
Buchan, C. M.	4
Bull, S. G.	4
Bullock, N.	2
Burgess, H.	4
Butcher, T.	3
Byrne, J. J.	8
Camsell, G. H.	18
Carter, H. S.	7
Carter, J. H.	4
Chadwick, E.	3
Chamberlain, M.	1
Chambers, H.	5
Channon, M. R.	21
Charlton, J.	6
Charlton, R.	49
Chenery, C. J.	1
Chivers, M.	13
Clarke, A. J.	10
Cobbold, W. N.	7
Cock, J. G.	2
Common, A.	2
Connelly, J. M.	7
Coppell, S. J.	7
Cotterill, G. H.	2
Cowans, G.	2
Crawford, R.	1
Crawshaw, T. H.	1
Crayston, W. J.	1
Creek, F. N. S.	1
Crooks, S. D.	7
Currey, E. S.	2
Currie, A. W.	3
Cursham, A. W.	2
Cursham, H. A.	5
Daft, H. B.	3
Davenport, J. K.	2
Davis, G.	1
Davis, H.	1
Day, S. H.	2
Dean, W. R.	18
Devey, J. H. G.	1
Dewhurst, F.	11
Dix, W. R.	1
Dixon, K. M.	4
Dixon, L. M.	1
Douglas, B.	11
Drake, E. J.	6
Ducat, A.	1
Dunn, A. T. B.	2
Eastham, G.	2
Edwards, D.	5
Elliott, W. H.	3
Evans, R. E.	1
Ferdinand, L.	3
Finney, T.	30
Fleming, H. J.	9
Flowers, R.	10
Forman, Frank	1
Forman, Fred	3
Foster, R. E.	3
Francis, G. C. J.	3
Francis, T.	12
Freeman, B. C.	3
Froggatt, J.	2
Froggatt, R.	2
Galley, T.	1
Gascoigne, P. J.	6
Geary, F.	3
Gibbins, W. V. T.	3
Gilliatt, W. E.	3
Goddard, P.	1
Goodall, J.	12
Goodyer, A. C.	1
Gosling, R. C.	2
Goulden, L. A.	4
Grainger, C.	3
Greaves, J.	44
Grovesnor, A. T.	2
Gunn, W.	1
Haines, J. T. W.	2
Hall, G. W.	9
Halse, H. J.	2
Hampson, J.	5
Hampton, H.	2
Hancocks, J.	2
Hardman, H. P.	1
Harris, S. S.	2
Hassall, H. W.	4
Hateley, M.	9
Haynes, J. N.	18
Hegan, K. E.	4
Henfrey, A. G.	2
Hilsdon, G. R.	14
Hine, E. W.	4
Hirst, D. E.	1
Hitchens, G. A.	5
Hobbis, H. H. F.	1
Hoddle, G.	8
Hodgetts, D.	1
Hodgson, G.	1
Holley, G. H.	8
Houghton, W. E.	5
Howell, R.	1
Hughes, E. W.	1
Hulme, J. H. A.	4
Hunt, G. S.	1
Hunt, R.	18
Hunter, N.	2
Hurst, G. C.	24
Ince, P. E. C.	2
Jack, D. N. B.	3
Johnson, D. E.	6
Johnson, E.	2
Johnson, J. A.	2
Johnson, T. C. F.	5
Johnson, W. H.	1
Kail, E. I. L.	2
Kay, A. H.	1
Keegan, J. K.	21
Kelly, R.	8
Kennedy, R.	3
Kenyon-Slaney, W. S.	2
Keown, M. R.	3
Kevan, D. T.	8
Kidd, B.	1
Kingsford, R. K.	1
Kirchen, A. J.	2
Kirton, W. J.	1
Langton, R.	1
Latchford, R. D.	5
Latherton, E. G.	1
Lawler, C.	1
Lawton, T.	22
Lee, F.	10
Lee, J.	1
Lee, R. M.	1
Lee, S.	2
Le Saux, G. P.	1
Lindley, T.	15
Lineker, G.	48
Lofthouse, J. M.	3
Lofthouse, N.	30
Hon. A. Lyttelton	1
Mabbutt, G.	1
Macdonald, M.	6
Mannion, W. J.	11
Mariner, P.	13
Marsh, R. W.	1
Matthews, S.	11
Matthews, V.	1
McCall, J.	1
McDermott, T.	3
Medley, L. D.	1
Melia, J.	1
Mercer, D. W.	1
Metson, P. C.	1
Milburn, J. E. T.	10
Miller, H. S.	1
Mills, G. R.	3
Milward, A.	3
Mitchell, C.	5
Moore, J.	1
Moore, R. F.	2
Moore, W. G. B.	2
Morren, T.	1
Morris, F.	1
Morris, J.	3
Mortensen, S. H.	23
Morton, J. R.	1
Mosforth, W.	3
Mullen, J.	6
Mullery, A. P.	1
Neal, P. G.	5
Needham, E.	3
Nicholls, J.	1
Nicholson, W. E.	1
O'Grady, M.	3
Osborne, F. R.	3
Own goals	22
Page, L. A.	1
Paine, T. L.	7
Palmer, C. L.	1
Parry, E. H.	1
Parry, R. A.	1
Pawson, F. W.	1
Payne, J.	2
Peacock, A.	3
Pearce, S.	4
Pearson, J. S.	5
Pearson, S. C.	5
Perry, W.	2
Peters, M.	20
Pickering, F.	5
Platt, D.	26
Pointer, R.	2
Quantrill, A.	1
Ramsay, A. E.	3
Revie, D. G.	4
Reynolds, J.	3
Richardson, J. R.	2
Rigby, A.	3
Rimmer, E. J.	2
Roberts, H.	1
Roberts, W. T.	4
Robinson, J.	3

Robson, B. 26
Robson, R. 4
Rowley, J. F. 6
Royle, J. 2
Rutherford, J. 3

Sagar, C. 1
Sandilands, R. R. 2
Sansom, K. 1
Schofield, J. 1
Seed, J. M. 1
Settle, J. 6
Sewell, J. 3
Shackleton, L. F. 1
Sharp, J. 1
Shearer, A. 5
Shepherd, A. 2
Sheringham, E. P. 1
Simpson, J. 1
Smith, A. M. 2
Smith, G. O. 12
Smith, Joe 1
Smith, J. R. 2
Smith, J. W. 4
Smith, R. 13
Smith, S. 1
Sorby, T. H. 1
Southworth, J. 3
Sparks, F. J. 3
Spence, J. W. 1
Spiksley, F. 5
Spilsbury, B. W. 5
Steele, F. C. 8
Stephenson, G. T. 2
Steven, T. M. 4
Stewart, J. 2
Stiles, N. P. 1
Storer, H. 1
Summerbee, M. G. 1

Tambling, R. V. 1
Taylor, P. J. 2
Taylor, T. 16
Thompson, P. B. 1
Thornewell, G. 1
Tilson, S. F. 6
Townley, W. J. 2
Tueart, D. 2

Vaughton, O. H. 6
Veitch, J. G. 3
Violett, D. S. 1

Waddle, C. R. 6
Walker, W. H. 9
Wall, G. 2
Wallace, D. 1
Walsh, P. 1
Waring, T. 4
Warren, B. 2
Watson, D. V. 4
Watson, V. M. 4
Webb, G. W. 1
Webb, N. 4
Wedlock, W. J. 2
Weir, D. 2
Weller, K. 1
Welsh, D. 1
Whateley, O. 2
Wheldon, G. F. 6
Whitfield, H. 1
Wignall, F. 2
Wilkes, A. 1
Wilkins, R. G. 3
Willingham, C. K. 1
Wilshaw, D. J. 10
Wilson, D. 1
Wilson, G. P. 1
Winckworth, W. N. 1
Windridge, J. E. 7
Wise, D. F. 1
Withe, P. 1
Wollaston, C. H. R. 1
Wood, H. 1
Woodcock, T. 16
Woodhall, G. 1
Woodward, V. J. 29
Worrall, F. 2
Worthington, F. S. 2
Wright, I. E. 5
Wright, M. 1
Wright, W. A. 3
Wylie, J. G. 1

Yates, J. 3

NORTHERN IRELAND
Anderson, T. 4
Armstrong, G. 12

Bambrick, J. 12
Barr, H. H. 1
Barron, H. 3
Best, G. 9
Bingham, W. L. 10
Black, K. 1
Blanchflower, D. 2
Blanchflower, J. 1
Brennan, B. 1
Brennan, R. A. 1
Brotherston, N. 3
Brown, J. 1
Browne, F. 2

Campbell, J. 1
Campbell, W. G. 1
Casey, T. 2
Caskey, W. 1
Cassidy, T. 1
Chambers, J. 3
Clarke, C. J. 13
Clements, D. 2
Cochrane, T. 1
Condy, J. 1
Connor, M. J. 1
Coulter, J. 1
Croft, T. 1
Crone, W. 1
Crossan, E. 1
Crossan, J. A. 10
Curran, S. 2
Cush, W. W. 5

Dalton, W. 6
D'Arcy, S. D. 1
Darling, J. 1
Davey, H. H. 1
Davis, T. L. 1
Dill, A. H. 1
Doherty, L. 1
Doherty, P. D. 3
Dougan, A. D. 8
Dowie, I. 7
Dunne, J. 4

Elder, A. R. 1
Emerson, W. 1
English, S. 1

Ferguson, W. 1
Ferris, J. 1
Ferris, R. O. 1
Finney, T. 2

Gaffkin, J. 5
Gara, A. 3
Gawkrodger, G. 1
Gibb, J. T. 2
Gibb, T. J. 1
Gibson, W. K. 1
Gillespie, K. R. 1
Gillespie, W. 12
Goodall, A. L. 2
Gray, P. 3

Halligan, W. 1
Hamill, M. 1
Hamilton, B. 4
Hamilton, W. 5
Hannon, D. J. 1
Harkin, J. T. 2
Harvey, M. 3
Hill, C. F. 1
Hughes, M. 1
Humphries, W. 1
Hunter, A. (*Distillery*) 1
Hunter, A. (*Blackburn R*) 1

Irvine, R. W. 3
Irvine, W. J. 8

Johnston, H. 2
Johnston, S. 2
Johnston, W. C. 1
Jones, S. 1
Jones, J. 1

Kelly, J. 4
Kernaghan, N. 2
Kirwan, J. 2

Lacey, W. 3
Lemon, J. 2
Lockhart, N. 3
Lomas, S. M. 1

Magilton, J. 4
Mahood, J. 2
Martin, D. K. 3
Maxwell, J. 7
McAdams, W. J. 7
McAllen, J. 1
McAuley, J. L. 1
McCandless, J. 3
McCaw, J. H. 1
McClelland, J. 1
McCluggage, A. 2
McCracken, W. 1
McCrory, S. 1
McCurdy, C. 1
McDonald, A. 3
McGarry, J. K. 1
McGrath, R. C. 4
McIlroy, J. 10
McIlroy, S. B. 5
McKnight, J. 2
McLaughlin, J. C. 6
McMordie, A. S. 3
McMorran, E. J. 4
McParland, P. J. 10
McWha, W. B. R. 1
Meldon, J. 1
Mercar, J. 1
Mercer, J. T. 1
Millar, W. 1
Milligan, D. 1
Milne, R. G. 2
Molyneux, T. B. 1
Moreland, V. 1
Morgan, S. 3
Morrow, S. J. 1
Morrow, W. J. 1
Murphy, N. 1

Neill, W. J. T. 2
Nelson, S. 1
Nicholl, C. J. 3
Nicholl, J. M. 2
Nicholson, J. J. 6

O'Hagan, C. 2
O'Kane, W. J. 1
O'Neill, J. 1
O'Neill, M. A. 1
O'Neill, M. H. 8
Own goals 5

Peacock, R. 2
Peden, J. 7
Penney, S. 2
Pyper, James 2
Pyper, John 1

Quinn, J. M. 11

Reynolds, J. 1
Rowley, R. W. M. 2
Sheridan, J. 2
Sherrard, J. 1
Simpson, W. J. 5
Sloan, H. A. de B. 4
Smyth, S. 5
Spence, D. W. 3
Stanfield, O. M. 9
Stevenson, A. E. 5
Stewart, I. 2

Taggart, G. P. 5
Thompson, F. W. 2
Tully, C. P. 3
Turner, E. 1

Walker, J. 1
Walsh, D. J. 5
Welsh, E. 1
Whiteside, N. 9
Whiteside, T. 1
Williams, J. R. 1
Williamson, J. 1
Wilson, D. J. 1
Wilson, K. J. 6
Wilson, S. J. 7
Wilton, J. M. 2

Young, S. 2

SCOTLAND
Aitken, R. 1
Aitkenhead, W. A. C. 2
Alexander, D. 1
Allan, D. S. 4
Allan, J. 2
Anderson, F. 1
Anderson, W. 4
Andrews, P. 1
Archibald, A. 1
Archibald, S. 4

Baird, D. 2
Baird, J. C. 2
Baird, S. 2
Bannon, E. 1
Barbour, A. 1
Barker, J. B. 4
Battles, B. Jr 1
Bauld, W. 2
Baxter, J. C. 3
Bell, J. 5
Bennett, A. 2
Berry, D. 1
Bett, J. 1
Beveridge, W. W. 1
Black, A. 3
Black, D. 1
Bone, J. 1
Booth, S. 3
Boyd, R. 2
Boyd, W. G. 1
Brackenridge, T. 1
Brand, R. 8
Brazil, A. 1
Bremner, W. J. 3
Brown, A. D. 6
Buchanan, P. S. 1
Buchanan, R. 1
Buckley, P. 1
Buick, A. 2
Burns, K. 1

Cairns, T. 1
Calderwood, C. 1
Calderwood, R. 2
Caldow, E. 4
Campbell, C. 1
Campbell, John (*Celtic*) 5
Campbell, John (*Rangers*) 4
Campbell, P. 2
Campbell, R. 1
Cassidy, J. 1
Chalmers, S. 3
Chambers, T. 1

Cheyne, A. G. 4
Christie, A. J. 1
Clunas, W. L. 1
Collins, J. 8
Collins, R. Y. 10
Combe, J. R. 1
Conn, A. 1
Cooper, D. 6
Craig, J. 1
Craig, T. 1
Crawford, S. 1
Cunningham, A. N. 5
Curran, H. P. 1

Dalglish, K. 30
Davidson, D. 1
Davidson, J. A. 1
Delaney, J. 3
Devine, A. 1
Dewar, G. 1
Dewar, N. 4
Dickson, W. 4
Divers, J. 1
Docherty, T. H. 1
Dodds, D. 1
Donaldson, A. 1
Donnachie, J. 1
Dougall, J. 1
Drummond, J. 2
Dunbar, M. 1
Duncan, D. 7
Duncan, D. M. 1
Duncan, J. 1
Dunn, J. 2
Durie, G. S. 4

Easson, J. F. 1
Ellis, J. 1

Ferguson, J. 6
Fernie, W. 1
Fitchie, T. T. 1
Flavell, R. 2
Fleming, C. 2
Fleming, J. W. 3
Fraser, M. J. E. 4

Gallacher, H. K. 23
Gallacher, K. W. 2
Gallacher, P. 1
Galt, J. H. 1
Gemmell, T. (*St Mirren*) 1
Gemmell, T. (*Celtic*) 1
Gemmill, A. 8
Gibb, W. 1
Gibson, D. W. 3
Gibson, J. D. 2
Gibson, N. 1
Gillespie, Jas. 3
Gillick, T. 3
Gilzean, A. J. 12
Gossland, J. 2
Goudie, J. 1
Gough, C. R. 6
Gourlay, J. 1
Graham, A. 2
Graham, G. 3
Gray, A. 7
Gray, E. 3
Gray, F. 1
Greig, J. 3
Groves, W. 5

Hamilton, G. 4
Hamilton, J. (*Queen's Park*) 3
Hamilton, R. C. 14
Harper, J. M. 2
Harrower, W. 5
Hartford, R. A. 4
Heggie, C. 5
Henderson, J. G. 1
Henderson, W. 5
Hendry, E. C. J. 1
Herd, D. G. 4
Hewie, J. D. 2

Higgins, A. (*Newcastle U*) 1
Higgins, A. (*Kilmarnock*) 4
Highet, T. C. 1
Holton, J. A. 2
Houliston, W. 2
Howie, H. 1
Howie, J. 2
Hughes, J. 1
Hunter, W. 1
Hutchison, T. 1
Hutton, J. 1
Hyslop, T. 1

Imrie, W. N. 1

Jackson, A. 8
Jackson, C. 1
James, A. W. 3
Jardine, A. 1
Jenkinson, T. 1
Johnston, L. H. 1
Johnston, M. 14
Johnstone, D. 2
Johnstone, J. 4
Johnstone, Jas. 1
Johnstone, R. 9
Johnstone, W. 1
Jordan, J. 11

Kay, J. L. 5
Keillor, A. 3
Kelly, J. 1
Kelso, J. 1
Ker, G. 10
King, A. 1
King, J. 1
Kinnear, D. 1

Lambie, W. A. 5
Lang, J. J. 1
Law, D. 30
Leggat, G. 8
Lennie, W. 1
Lennox, R. 3
Liddell, W. 6
Lindsay, J. 6
Linwood, A. B. 1
Logan, J. 1
Lorimer, P. 4
Love, A. 1
Lowe, J. (*Cambuslang*) 1
Lowe, J. (*St Bernards*) 1

Macari, L. 5
MacDougall, E. J. 3
MacLeod, M. 1
Mackay, D. C. 4
Mackay, G. 1
MacKenzie, J. A. 1
Madden, J. 5
Marshall, H. 1
Marshall, J. 1
Mason, J. 4
Massie, A. 1
Masson, D. S. 5
McAdam, J. 1
McAllister, G. 4
McAulay, J. 1
McAvennie, F. 1
McCall, J. 1
McCall, S. M. 1
McCalliog, J. 1
McCallum, N. 1
McClair, B. J. 2
McCoist, A. 15
McColl, R. S. 13
McCulloch, D. 3
McDougall, J. 4
McFarlane, A. 1
McFadyen, W. 2
McGhee, M. 2
McGinlay, J. 3
McGregor, J. C. 1
McGrory, J. 6
McGuire, W. 1

McInally, A. 3
McInnes, T. 2
McKie, J. 2
McKimmie, S. 1
McKinlay, W. 4
McKinnon, A. 1
McKinnon, R. 1
McKinnon, W. W. 5
McLaren, A. 4
McLaren, J. 1
McLean, A. 1
McLean, T. 1
McLintock, F. 1
McMahon, A. 6
McMenemy, J. 5
McMillan, I. L. 2
McNeil, H. 5
McNeill, W. 3
McPhail, J. 3
McPhail, R. 7
McPherson, J. 8
McPherson, R. 1
McQueen, G. 5
McStay, P. 9
Meiklejohn, D. D. 3
Millar, J. 2
Miller, T. 2
Miller, W. 1
Mitchell, R. C. 1
Morgan, W. 1
Morris, D. 1
Morris, H. 3
Morton, A. L. 5
Mudie, J. K. 9
Mulhall, G. 1
Munro, A. D. 1
Munro, N. 1
Murdoch, R. 5
Murphy, F. 1
Murray, J. 1

Napier, C. E. 3
Narey, D. 1
Neil, R. G. 2
Nevin, P. K. F. 4
Nicholas, C. 5
Nisbet, J. 2

O'Donnell, F. 2
O'Hare, J. 5
Ormond, W. E. 1
O'Rourke, F. 1
Orr, R. 1
Orr, T. 1
Oswald, J. 1
Own goals 14

Parlane, D. 1
Paul, H. McD. 2
Paul, W. 6
Pettigrew, W. 2
Provan, D. 1

Quinn, J. 7
Quinn, P. 1

Rankin, G. 2
Rankin, R. 2
Reid, W. 4
Reilly, L. 22
Renny-Tailyour, H. W. 1
Richmond, J. T. 1
Ring, T. 2
Rioch, B. D. 6
Ritchie, J. 1
Robertson, A. 2
Robertson, J. 2
Robertson, J. N. 9
Robertson, J. T. 2
Robertson, T. 1
Robertson, W. 1
Russell, D. 1

Scott, A. S. 5
Sellar, W. 4
Sharp, G. 1

Shaw, F. W. 1
Shearer, D. 2
Simpson, J. 1
Smith, A. 5
Smith, G. 4
Smith, J. 1
Smith, John 12
Somerville, G. 1
Souness, G. J. 3
Speedie, F. 2
St John, I. 9
Steel, W. 12
Stein, C. 10
Stevenson, G. 4
Stewart, R. 1
Stewart, W. E. 1
Strachan, G. 5
Sturrock, P. 3

Taylor, J. D. 1
Templeton, R. 1
Thomson, A. 1
Thomson, C. 4
Thomson, R. 1
Thomson, W. 1
Thornton, W. 1

Waddell, T. S. 1
Waddell, W. 6
Walker, J. 2
Walker, R. 7
Walker, T. 9
Wallace, I. A. 1
Wark, J. 7
Watson, J. A. K. 1
Watt, F. 2
Watt, W. W. 1
Weir, A. 1
Weir, J. B. 2
White, J. A. 3
Wilson, A. 2
Wilson, A. N. 13
Wilson, D. (*Queen's Park*) 2
Wilson, D. (*Rangers*) 9
Wilson, H. 1
Wylie, T. G. 1

Young, A. 5

WALES

Allchurch, I. J. 23
Allen, M. 3
Astley, D. J. 12
Atherton, R. W. 2

Bamford, T. 1
Barnes, W. 1
Blackmore, C. G. 1
Blake, N. A. 1
Bodin, P. J. 3
Boulter, L. M. 1
Bowdler, J. C. H. 3
Bowen, D. L. 1
Bowen, M. 3
Boyle, T. 1
Bryan, T. 1
Burgess, W. A. R. 1
Burke, T. 1
Butler, A. 1

Chapman, T. 2
Charles, J. 1
Charles, M. 6
Charles, W. J. 15
Clarke, R. J. 5
Coleman, C. 3
Collier, D. J. 1
Cross, K. 1
Cumner, R. H. 1
Curtis, A. 6
Curtis, E. R. 3

Davies, D. W. 1
Davies, E. Lloyd 1

Davies, G. 2
Davies, L. S. 6
Davies, R. T. 8
Davies, R. W. 7
Davies, S. 5
Davies, W. 6
Davies, W. H. 1
Davies, William 5
Davies, W. O. 1
Deacy, N. 4
Doughty, J. 6
Doughty, R. 2
Durban, A. 2
Dwyer, P. 2

Edwards, G. 2
Edwards, R. I. 4
England, H. M. 3
Evans, I. 1
Evans, J. 1
Evans, R. E. 2
Evans, W. 1
Eyton-Jones, J. A. 1

Flynn, B. 7
Ford, T. 23
Foulkes, W. I. 1
Fowler, J. 3

Giles, D. 2
Giggs, R. J. 3
Glover, E. M. 7
Godfrey, B. C. 2
Green, A. W. 3
Griffiths, A. T. 6
Griffiths, M. W. 2
Griffiths, T. P. 3

Harris, C. S. 1
Hersee, R. 1
Hewitt, R. 1
Hockey, T. 1
Hodges, G. 2
Hole, W. J. 1
Hopkins, I. J. 2
Horne, B. 2
Howell, E. G. 3
Hughes, L. M. 12

James, E. 2
James, L. 10
James, R. 8
Jarrett, R. H. 3
Jenkyns, C. A. 1
Jones, A. 1
Jones, Bryn 6
Jones, B. S. 2
Jones, Cliff 15
Jones, C. W. 1
Jones, D. E. 1
Jones, Evan 1
Jones, H. 1
Jones, I. 1
Jones, J. O. 1
Jones, J. P. 1
Jones, Leslie J. 1
Jones, R. A. 2
Jones, W. L. 6

Keenor, F. C. 2
Krzywicki, R. L. 1

Leek, K. 5
Lewis, B. 3
Lewis, J. 1
Lewis, W. 10
Lewis, W. L. 2
Lovell, S. 1
Lowrie, G. 2

Mahoney, J. F. 1
Mays, A. W. 1
Medwin, T. C. 6
Meredith, W. H. 11
Mills, T. J. 1
Moore, G. 1
Morgan, J. R. 2
Morgan-Owen, H. 1
Morgan-Owen, M. M. 2
Morris, A. G. 9
Morris, H. 2
Morris, R. 1

Nicholas, P. 2

O'Callaghan, E. 3
O'Sullivan, P. A. 1
Owen, G. 2
Owen, W. 4
Owen, W. P. 6
Own goals 12

Palmer, D. 3
Parry, T. D. 3
Paul, R. 1
Peake, E. 1
Pembridge, M. 1
Perry, E. 1
Phillips, C. 5
Phillips, D. 2
Powell, A. 1
Powell, D. 1
Price, J. 4
Price, P. 1
Pryce-Jones, W. E. 3
Pugh, D. H. 2

Reece, G. I. 2
Rees, R. R. 3
Richards, R. W. 1
Roach, J. 2
Robbins, W. W. 4
Roberts, J. (*Corwen*) 1
Roberts, Jas. 1
Roberts, P. S. 1
Roberts, R. (*Druids*) 1
Roberts, W. (*Llangollen*) 2
Roberts, W. (*Wrexham*) 1
Roberts, W. H. 1
Rush, I. 28
Russell, M. R. 1

Sabine, H. W. 1
Saunders, D. 16
Shaw, E. G. 2
Sisson, H. 4
Slatter, N. 2
Smallman, D. P. 1
Speed, G. A. 1

Tapscott, D. R. 4
Thomas, M. 4
Thomas, T. 1
Toshack, J. B. 13
Trainer, H. 2

Vaughan, John 2
Vernon, T. R. 8
Vizard, E. T. 1

Walsh, I. 7
Warren, F. W. 3
Watkins, W. M. 4
Wilding, J. 4
Williams, G. E. 1
Williams, G. G. 1
Williams, W. 1
Woosnam, A. P. 4
Wynn, G. A. 1

Yorath, T. C. 2
Young, E. 1

EIRE

Aldridge, J. 17
Ambrose, P. 1
Anderson, J. 1

Bermingham, P. 1
Bradshaw, P. 4
Brady, L. 9
Brown, D. 1
Byrne, J. (*Bray*) 1
Byrne, J. (*QPR*) 4

Cantwell, J. 14
Carey, J. 3
Carroll, T. 1
Cascarino, A. 12
Coad, P. 3
Conroy, T. 2
Conway, J. 3
Coyne, T. 6
Cummings, G. 5
Curtis, D. 8

Daly, G. 13
Davis, T. 4
Dempsey, J. 1
Dennehy, M. 2
Donnelly, J. 3
Donnelly, T. 1
Duffy, B. 1
Duggan, H. 1
Dunne, J. 12
Dunne, L. 1

Eglington, T. 2
Ellis, P. 1

Fagan, F. 5
Fallon, S. 2
Fallon, W. 2
Farrell, P. 3
Fitzgerald, P. 2
Fitzgerald, J. 1
Fitzsimmons, A. 7
Flood, J. J. 4
Fogarty, A. 3
Fullam, J. 1
Fullam, R. 1

Galvin, A. 1
Gavin, J. 2
Geoghegan, M. 2
Giles, J. 5
Givens, D. 19
Glynn, D. 1
Grealish, T. 8
Grimes, A. A. 1

Hale, A. 2
Hand, E. 2
Haverty, J. 3
Holmes, J. 1
Horlacher, A. 2
Houghton, R. 5
Hughton, C. 1
Hurley, C. 2

Irwin, D. 1

Jordan, D. 1

Keane, R. M. 1
Kelly, D. 8
Kelly, G. 1
Kelly, J. 2
Kernaghan, A. N. 1

Lacey, W. 1
Lawrenson, M. 5
Leech, M. 2

McCann, J. 1
McCarthy, M. 2
McEvoy, A. 6
McGee, P. 4
McGrath, P. 7
McLoughlin, A. F. 1
Madden, O. 1
Mancini, T. 1
Martin, C. 6
Martin, M. 4
Mooney, J. 1
Moore, P. 7
Moran, K. 6
Moroney, T. 1
Mulligan, P. 1

O'Callaghan, K. 1
O'Connor, T. 2
O'Farrell, F. 2
O'Flanagan, K. 3
O'Keefe, E. 1
O'Leary, D. A. 1
O'Neill, F. 1
O'Reilly, J. 2
O'Reilly, J. 1
Own goals 7

Quinn, N. 13

Ringstead, A. 7
Robinson, M. 4
Rogers, E. 5
Ryan, G. 1
Ryan, R. 3

Sheedy, K. 9
Sheridan, J. 5
Slaven, B. 1
Sloan, W. 1
Squires, J. 1
Stapleton, F. 20
Staunton, S. 5
Strahan, J. 1
Sullivan, J. 1

Townsend, A. D. 6
Treacy, R. 5
Touhy, L. 4

Waddock, G. 3
Walsh, D. 5
Walsh, M. 3
Waters, J. 1
White, J. J. 2
Whelan, R. 3

KIRIN CUP AND CANADA CUP

Kirin Cup

Hiroshima, 21 May 1995, 24,566

Japan (0) 0

Scotland (0) 0

Japan: Maekawa, Hashiratanai, Ihara, Omura, Narahashi, Yanagimoto, Ramos (Fukuda), Yamagaguchi, Miura, Nakayama, Morishima (Kitazawa).
Scotland: Leighton; McLaren, McKinnon, Martin, Calderwood (Whyte), Lambert (Robertson), McKinlay, Spencer, Gemmill (Bernard), Jackson, Burley.

Kirin Cup

Toyama, 24 May 1995, 5669

Ecuador (0) 1 *(Hurtado I (pen))*

Scotland (0) 2 *(Robertson, Crawford)*

Ecuador: Cevallos; Capurro, Nonega, Hurtado I, Verduga, Guaman, Carcelen, Garay (Delgado), Zambrano, Herrera (Mora), Hurtado E.
Scotland: Leighton; McLaren, Martin, Calderwood, Bernard, McKinlay, Gemmill, Jackson (Crawford), Whyte (Lambert), Robertson, Burley.

Canada Cup

Edmonton, 22 May 1995, 12,112

Canada (2) 2 *(Peschisolido 2)*

Northern Ireland (0) 0

Canada: Dolan; Yallop, Fraser, Samuel, Watson, Dasovic (Rizi), Miller, Hooper, Aunger (Holness), Peschisolido, Corazzin.
Northern Ireland: Fettis; Patterson, Taggart, McDonald (McGibbon), Rowland, Horlock (Worthington), Gillespie (McMahon), Magilton, Hughes, Dowie (O'Boyle), Gray.

Canada Cup

Edmonton, 26 May 1995, 6124

Chile (1) 2 *(Valencia, Mardones)*

Northern Ireland (0) 1 *(Dowie)*

Chile: Cornez; Acuna, Fuentes, Ramirez, Mendoza, Mussri (Fabian), Mardones, Guevara, Perez (Valencia), Goldberg (Rozental), Salas.
Northern Ireland: Fettis; Worthington, Taggart, McDonald, McGibbon (Patterson), Hughes, Lennon, Rowland, McMahon (Gillespie), Magilton (O'Boyle), Dowie (Gray).

INTERNATIONAL MANAGERS

England

Walter Winterbottom 1946–1962 (after period as coach); Alf Ramsey 1963–1974; Joe Mercer (caretaker) 1974; Don Revie 1974–1977; Ron Greenwood 1977–1982; Bobby Robson 1982–1990; Graham Taylor 1990–1993; Terry Venables (coach) from January 1994.

Northern Ireland

Billy Bingham 1967–1971; Terry Neill 1971–1975; Dave Clements (player-manager)1975–76; Danny Blanchflower 1976–1979; Billy Bingham 1980–1993; Bryan Hamilton from February 1994.

Scotland

Bobby Brown 1967–1971; Tommy Docherty 1971–1972; Willie Ormond 1973–1977; Ally MacLeod 1977–1978; Jock Stein 1978–1985; Alex Ferguson (caretaker) 1985–1986; Andy Roxburgh (coach) 1986–1993; Craig Brown from September 1993.

Wales

Mike Smith 1974–1979; Mike England 1980–1988; David Williams (caretaker) 1988; Terry Yorath 1988–1993; John Toshack 1994 for one match; Mike Smith 1994–1995.

Republic of Ireland

Liam Tuohy 1971–1972; Johnny Giles 1973–1980 (after period as player-manager); Eoin Hand 1980–1985; Jack Charlton from February 1986.

OTHER FOREIGN INTERNATIONAL MATCHES 1994

(For European Matches—see International Directory)

January
Barbados 0, Grenada 0
Ghana 2, Egypt 1
Mali 1, Burkina Faso 1
Mauritania 1, Mali 3
Barbados 0, Puerto Rico 1
Guyana 0, Surinam 2
Mali 1, Senegal 0
Saudi Arabia 1, China 0
Puerto Rico 0, Grenada 1
Saudi Arabia 1, China 1
Barbados 3, Grenada 2
Burkina Faso 5, Guinea 4
Burkina Faso 0, Ivory Coast 1
Niger 3, Guinea 1
Senegal 0, Mali 0

February
Morocco 1, Egypt 1
Oman 1, Kenya 0
UEA 1, Morocco 1
Oman 2, Kenya 0
Saudi Arabia 1, Colombia 1
UEA 0, Egypt 1
Saudi Arabia 0, Colombia 1
Malawi 0, Zambia 3
Malawi 0, Zambia 2
USA 1, Bolivia 1
Colombia 2, Bolivia 0
Mali 0, Ghana 0
Colombia 2, South Korea 2
Zimbabwe 2, Zambia 2
Gabon 0, Senegal 0

March
Mexico 0, Colombia 0
USA 1, South Korea 0
Cayman Islands 3, Jamaica 2
Nigeria 0, Ghana 0
Dominican Republic 0, Haiti 1
USA 1, South Korea 1
Zambia 2, Zimbabwe 1
Egypt 0, Cameroon 0
Tunisia 4, Niger 2
Brazil 2, Argentina 0
Saudi Arabia 0, Chile 2
USA 2, Bolivia 2
Barbados 2, St Vincent/Grenadines 0
Saudi Arabia 2, Chile 2

April
Cayman Islands 2, Haiti 3
Colombia 0, Bolivia 1
Surinam 2, Cayman Islands 0
Surinam 1, Haiti 1
Trinidad & Tobago 2, Barbados 0
Trinidad & Tobago 3, Surinam 2
Colombia 1, Nigeria 0
Argentina 3, Morocco 1
Swaziland 0, Mozambique 1
South Africa 1, Zimbabwe 0
USA 0, Chile 2

May
South Korea 2, Cameroon 2
Colombia 1, Peru 0
Honduras 1, El Salvador 3
South Korea 2, Cameroon 1
Saudi Arabia 0, Bolivia 1
Colombia 3, El Salvador 0
Honduras 2, Peru 1
South Africa 1, Zambia 0
Cameroon 1, Bolivia 1
Chile 3, Argentina 3
Japan 1, Australia 1
Fiji 2, Tahiti 2
Chile 2, Peru 1
Fiji 2, Tahiti 0

June
Canada 1, Morocco 1
Trinidad & Tobago 2, Saudi Arabia 3
USA 1, Mexico 0
Canada 1, Brazil 1
Ivory Coast 4, Liberia 1
South Korea 1, Ecuador 2
Australia 1, South Africa 0
Bolivia 0, Peru 0
Brazil 8, Honduras 2
South Korea 3, Honduras 0
Australia 1, South Africa 0
Brazil 4, El Salvador 0

July
Botswana 0, Namibia 1
Japan 3, Ghana 2
Japan 2, Ghana 1

August
Ivory Coast 2, Mali 1
Niger 0, Togo 0
Niger 3, Togo 2
Peru 2, Ecuador 0
Egypt 2, Ghana 0

September
Liberia 1, Togo 1
India 4, Bangladesh 2
Oman 2, Qatar 0
Bangladesh 1, Yemen 0
Qatar 2, Sudan 0
India 0, Yemen 2
South Korea 0, UAE 0
Sudan 1, Oman 1
Chile 1, Bolivia 2
Ecuador 0, Peru 0
Oman 4, India 1
Yemen 0, Qatar 2
India 0, Yemen 2
Qatar 1, Oman 2
Kuwait 0, Australia 0
Zambia 3, Ghana 0
Japan 0, Australia 0

October
Senegal 3, Niger 1
Zambia 2, Malawi 1
Peru 0, Uruguay 1
Saudi Arabia 2, USA 1
Oman 0, Senegal 1
Oman 2, Senegal 1
UAE 3, Senegal 2

November
UAE 2, Qatar 0
Bahrain 2, Kuwait 1
Oman 1, Saudi Arabia 2
Bahrain 1, Oman 1
UAE 1, Saudi Arabia 1
Kuwait 1, Qatar 0
Morocco 1, Cameroon 1
Tunisia 2, Ivory Coast 0
Qatar 4, Oman 2
UAE 2, Kuwait 0
Saudi Arabia 3, Bahrain 1
Qatar 1, Saudi Arabia 2
UAE 0, Bahrain 0
Oman 0, Kuwait 0
Bahrain 1, Qatar 1
Chile 0, Argentina 3
Kuwait 0, Saudi Arabia 2
Oman 0, UAE 2
Trinidad & Tobago 1, USA 0
Jamaica 0, USA 3
Ivory Coast 2, Cameroon 1
Kenya 3, Somalia 1
South Africa 2, Ghana 1
Kenya 4, Djibouti 1
Tanzania 4, Somalia 0
Ghana 1, Cameroon 0
South Africa 0, Ivory Coast 0

December
Somalia 2, Djibouti 1
Tanzania 1, Kenya 0
Uganda 2, Seychelles 0
Tanzania 3, Djibouti 0
Ghana 1, Ivory Coast 1
South Africa 1, Cameroon 1
Togo 2, Burkina Faso 0
Namibia 2, Ivory Coast 1
USA 1, Honduras 1
Tunisia 1, Algeria 0
Saudi Arabia 3, Costa Rica 1
Cameroon 1, Togo 1
Saudi Arabia 0, South Korea 1
Mali 0, Mauritania 0
Saudi Arabia 1, Zambia 0
Mali 0, Mauritania 0

UEFA UNDER-21 CHAMPIONSHIP 1994–96

(Also used as qualification for Olympics)

Group 1
Israel 2, Poland 2
Romania 5, Azerbaijan 2
Slovakia 0, France 3
France 0, Romania 0
Israel 2, Slovakia 0
Poland 5, Azerbaijan 0
Romania 0, Slovakia 0
Poland 0, France 4
Azerbaijan 1, Israel 2
Israel 0, Romania 1
Azerbaijan 0, France 5
Israel 1, France 1
Romania 1, Poland 2
Slovakia 3, Azerbaijan 0
Poland 1, Israel 0
Azerbaijan 0, Romania 5
France 0, Slovakia 1
Poland 1, Slovakia 0
Romania 1, Israel 0

Group 2
Belgium 7, Armenia 0
Cyprus 0, Spain 6
Macedonia 5, Denmark 3
Armenia 1, Cyprus 2
Denmark 0, Belgium 1
Macedonia 0, Spain 1
Belgium 7, Macedonia 0
Spain 1, Denmark 0
Cyprus 2, Armenia 1
Belgium 3, Spain 3
Macedonia 1, Cyprus 0
Spain 1, Belgium 1
Cyprus 1, Denmark 5
Belgium 1, Cyprus 0
Denmark 5, Macedonia 2
Armenia 0, Spain 3
Armenia 2, Macedonia 0
Denmark 4, Cyprus 0
Spain 4, Armenia 0
Macedonia 3, Belgium 0

Group 3
Hungary 2, Turkey 1
Iceland 0, Sweden 1
Switzerland 0, Sweden 5
Turkey 3, Iceland 0
Sweden 0, Hungary 1
Switzerland 2, Iceland 1
Turkey 1, Switzerland 1
Hungary 1, Switzerland 0
Turkey 0, Sweden 0
Hungary 2, Sweden 1
Switzerland 0, Turkey 2
Sweden 1, Iceland 0
Iceland 1, Hungary 2

Group 4
Estonia 1, Croatia 2
Ukraine 3, Lithuania 2
Slovenia 1, Italy 1
Estonia 1, Italy 4
Croatia 2, Lithuania 0
Ukraine 1, Slovenia 0
Ukraine 3, Estonia 0
Slovenia 3, Lithuania 0
Italy 2, Croatia 1
Italy 7, Estonia 0
Croatia 1, Ukraine 0
Lithuania 0, Croatia 1
Slovenia 5, Estonia 0
Ukraine 2, Italy 1
Croatia 0, Slovenia 2
Estonia 2, Ukraine 5
Lithuania 0, Italy 2
Lithuania 1, Slovenia 2
Estonia 1, Slovenia 2
Ukraine 1, Croatia 1

Group 5
Czech Republic 1, Malta 0
Luxembourg 0, Holland 4
Norway 4, Belarus 0
Malta 0, Czech Republic 7
Norway 1, Holland 0
Belarus 3, Luxembourg 0
Holland 2, Czech Republic 2
Malta 2, Norway 3
Holland 3, Luxembourg 0
Malta 1, Luxembourg 0
Luxembourg 0, Norway 8
Holland 4, Malta 0
Czech Republic 2, Belarus 0
Norway 5, Luxembourg 0
Belarus 4, Malta 0
Czech Republic 2, Holland 2
Belarus 4, Norway 2
Luxembourg 0, Czech Republic 7
Norway 3, Malta 0
Belarus 3, Holland 1

Group 6
England 0, Portugal 0
Latvia 1, Republic of Ireland 1
Latvia 0, Portugal 1
Austria 1, England 3
Portugal 2, Austria 0
England 1, Republic of Ireland 0
Republic of Ireland 0, England 2
Austria 0, Latvia 0
Republic of Ireland 1, Portugal 1
Latvia 0, England 1
Portugal 4, Latvia 0
Republic of Ireland 3, Austria 0

Group 7
Georgia 3, Moldova 0
Bulgaria 1, Georgia 0
Moldova 1, Wales 0
Bulgaria 2, Moldova 0
Georgia 1, Wales 2
Wales 1, Bulgaria 1
Moldova 1, Germany 1
Bulgaria 3, Wales 1
Georgia 0, Germany 2
Germany 1, Wales 0
Moldova 0, Bulgaria 0
Bulgaria 2, Germany 0
Wales 5, Georgia 1

Group 8
Finland 1, Scotland 0
Greece 3, Finland 4
Russia 3, San Marino 0
Greece 4, San Marino 0
Scotland 2, Russia 1
Finland 4, San Marino 0
Greece 1, Scotland 2
San Marino 0, Finland 6
Russia 1, Scotland 2
Greece 0, Russia 1
San Marino 0, Scotland 1
San Marino 0, Russia 7
Finland 1, Greece 0

OLYMPIC FOOTBALL

Previous medallists

1896 Athens*	1 Denmark 2 Greece
1990 Paris*	1 Great Britain 2 France
1904 St Louis**	1 Canada 2 USA
1908 London	1 Great Britain 2 Denmark 3 Holland
1912 Stockholm	1 England 2 Denmark 3 Holland
1920 Antwerp	1 Belgium 2 Spain 3 Holland
1924 Paris	1 Uruguay 2 Switzerland 3 Sweden
1928 Amsterdam	1 Uruguay 2 Argentina 3 Italy
1932 Los Angeles	no tournament
1936 Berlin	1 Italy 2 Austria 3 Norway
1948 London	1 Sweden 2 Yugoslavia 3 Denmark
1952 Helsinki	1 Hungary 2 Yugoslavia 3 Sweden
1956 Melbourne	1 USSR 2 Yugoslavia 3 Bulgaria
1960 Rome	1 Yugoslavia 2 Denmark 3 Hungary
1964 Tokyo	1 Hungary 2 Czechoslovakia 3 East Germany
1968 Mexico City	1 Hungary 2 Bulgaria 3 Japan
1972 Munich	1 Poland 2 Hungary 3 E Germany/USSR
1976 Montreal	1 East Germany 2 Poland 3 USSR
1980 Moscow	1 Czechoslovakia 2 East Germany 3 USSR
1984 Los Angeles	1 France 2 Brazil 3 Yugoslavia
1988 Seoul	1 USSR 2 Brazil 3 West Germany
1992 Barcelona	1 Spain 2 Poland 3 Ghana

* No official tournament
** No official tournament but gold medal later awarded by IOC

10th UEFA UNDER-18 CHAMPIONSHIP 1993–94

Final tournament in Spain, July 1994

Group 1
France 1, Portugal 3
Holland 1, Sweden 1
France 2, Holland 3
Portugal 2, Sweden 0
Portugal 1, Holland 0
Sweden 1, France 3

Group 2
Spain 4, Russia 2
Belarus 0, Germany 3
Germany 1, Russia 2
Belarus 1, Spain 4
Germany 3, Spain 1
Russia 3, Belarus 2

Fifth place
France 0, Russia 2

Third place
Holland 2, Spain 5

Final
Portugal 1, Germany 1
(*Portugal won 5-2 on penalties*)
(*Portugal, Germany, Holland, Spain and Russia qualified for the FIFA Under-20 World Championship*)

8th WORLD YOUTH CHAMPIONSHIP

(in Qatar, April 1995)

Group A
Qatar 1, Russia 1
Syria 0, Brazil 6
Qatar 0, Syria 1
Russia 0, Brazil 0
Qatar 0, Brazil 2
Russia 2, Syria 0

Group B
Burundi 1, Spain 5
Chile 2, Japan 2
Burundi 1, Chile 1
Spain 2, Japan 1
Burundi 0, Japan 2
Spain 6, Chile 3

Group C
Holland 0, Argentina 1
Honduras 2, Portugal 3
Holland 7, Honduras 1*
Argentina 0, Portugal 1
Holland 0, Portugal 3
Argentina 4, Honduras 2
**match abandoned after 80 mins; Honduras reduced to six players.*

Group D
Australia 2, Costa Rica 0
Cameroon 1, Germany 1
Australia 2, Cameroon 3
Costa Rica 2, Germany 1
Australia 1, Germany 1
Costa Rica 1, Cameroon 3

Quarter-finals
Brazil 2, Japan 1
Spain 4, Russia 1
Portugal 2, Australia 1 *in sudden death*
Cameroon 0, Argentina 2

Semi-finals
Brazil 1, Portugal 0
Spain 0, Argentina 3

Third place
Portugal 3, Spain 2

Final
Brazil 0, Argentina 2

13th UEFA UNDER-16 CHAMPIONSHIP 1995

Group 1
Luxembourg 0, France 1
Northern Ireland 1, Luxembourg 0
France 4, Northern Ireland 0

Group 2
Sweden 2, Denmark 0
Republic of Ireland 0, Sweden 2
Denmark 2, Republic of Ireland 1

Group 3
Iceland 0, Finland 2
Finland 0, Scotland 1
Iceland 0, Scotland 0
Finland 1, Iceland 0
Scotland 3, Finland 2
Scotland 4, Iceland 0

Group 4
Latvia 0, Spain 2
Croatia 3, Latvia 0
Spain 1, Croatia 0

Group 5
Czech Republic 6, Malta 0
Malta 2, Estonia 0
Estonia 0, Czech Republic 10

Group 6
Poland 2, Switzerland 0
Switzerland 3, Poland 1

Group 7
Moldova 1, Austria 1
Albania 0, Moldova 3
Austria 4, Albania 0

Group 8
Slovakia, Cyprus, Azerbaijan

Group 9
Georgia 5, Armenia 2
Armenia 0, Slovenia 4
Slovenia 2, Georgia 1

Group 10
Israel 3, Ukraine 0
Germany 4, Ukraine 2
Israel 1, Germany 3

Group 11
Liechtenstein 0, Lithuania 1
Norway 6, Liechtenstein 0
Lithuania 0, Norway 1

Group 12
England, Greece, Romania

Group 13
Holland 8, Belarus 1
Turkey 3, Belarus 0
Belarus 0, Turkey 1
Belarus 0, Holland 2
Holland 4, Turkey 3
Turkey v Holland

Group 14
Wales, Bulgaria, Portugal

Group 15
Hungary 4, Russia 1
Russia 3, Hungary 1
Russia 0, Italy 1
Italy 2, Hungary 1
Italy v Russia
Hungary v Italy

Final tournament in Belgium, April 1995

Group A
Poland 1, Czech Republic 2
Sweden 1, Italy 1
Poland 0, Sweden 1
Czech Republic 1, Italy 0
Italy 0, Poland 0
Czech Republic 4, Sweden 1

Group B
Belgium 4, France 1
Norway 0, Austria 1
Belgium 3, Norway 0
France 1, Austria 0
Austria 0, Belgium 0
France 4, Norway 0

Group C
Germany 0, Spain 3
Slovenia 0, Turkey 2
Turkey 0, Spain 2
Slovenia 0, Germany 3
Spain 3, Slovenia 1
Turkey 1, Germany 4

Group D
Portugal 4, Slovakia 0
Scotland 1, England 1
England 2, Slovakia 1
Scotland 1, Portugal 3
England 3, Portugal 1
Slovakia 2, Scotland 1

Quarter-finals
Czech Republic 0, Germany 2
Spain 1, Sweden 0
Belgium 0, Portugal 1
England 0, France 1 *aet*

Semi-finals
France 0, Spain 2
Germany 1, Portugal 3

Third place
Germany 2, France 1 *in sudden death*

Final
Portugal 2, Spain 0

ENGLAND UNDER-21 RESULTS 1976–95

EC UEFA Competition for Under-21 Teams

v ALBANIA

Year	Date		Venue	Eng	Alb
EC1989	Mar	7	Shkroda	2	1
EC1989	April	25	Ipswich	2	0

v ANGOLA

				Eng	Ang
1995	June	10	Toulon	1	0

v AUSTRIA

				Eng	Aus
1994	Oct	11	Kapfenberg	3	1

v BELGIUM

				Eng	Bel
1994	June	5	Marseille	2	1

v BRAZIL

				Eng	B
1993	June	11	Toulon	0	0
1995	June	6	Toulon	0	2

v BULGARIA

				Eng	Bulg
EC1979	June	5	Pernik	3	1
EC1979	Nov	20	Leicester	5	0
1989	June	5	Toulon	2	3

v CZECHOSLOVAKIA

				Eng	Cz
1990	May	28	Toulon	2	1
1992	May	26	Toulon	1	2
1993	June	9	Toulon	1	1

v DENMARK

				Eng	Den
EC1978	Sept	19	Hvidovre	2	1
EC1979	Sept	11	Watford	1	0
EC1982	Sept	21	Hvidovre	4	1
EC1983	Sept	20	Norwich	4	1
EC1986	Mar	12	Copenhagen	1	0
EC1986	Mar	26	Manchester	1	1
1988	Sept	13	Watford	0	0
1994	Mar	8	Brentford	1	0

v EAST GERMANY

				Eng	EG
EC1980	April	16	Sheffield	1	2
EC1980	April	23	Jena	0	1

v FINLAND

				Eng	Fin
EC1977	May	26	Helsinki	1	0
EC1977	Oct	12	Hull	8	1
EC1984	Oct	16	Southampton	2	0
EC1985	May	21	Mikkeli	1	3

v FRANCE

				Eng	Fra
EC1984	Feb	28	Sheffield	6	1
EC1984	Mar	28	Rouen	1	0
1987	June	11	Toulon	0	2
EC1988	April	13	Besancon	2	4
EC1988	April	27	Highbury	2	2
1988	June	12	Toulon	2	4
1990	May	23	Toulon	7	3
1991	June	3	Toulon	1	0
1992	May	28	Toulon	0	0
1993	June	15	Toulon	1	0
1994	May	31	Aubagne	0	3
1994	Sept	6	Leicester	0	0
1995	June	10	Toulon	0	2

v GERMANY

				Eng	G
1991	Sept	10	Scunthorpe	2	1

v GREECE

				Eng	Gre
EC1982	Nov	16	Piraeus	0	1
EC1983	Mar	29	Portsmouth	2	1
1989	Feb	7	Patras	0	1

v HOLLAND

				Eng	H
EC1993	Apr	27	Portsmouth	3	0
EC1993	Oct	12	Utrecht	1	1

v HUNGARY

				Eng	Hun
EC1981	June	5	Keszthely	2	1
EC1981	Nov	17	Nottingham	2	0
EC1983	April	26	Newcastle	1	0
EC1983	Oct	11	Nyiregyhaza	2	0
1990	Sept	11	Southampton	3	1
1992	May	12	Budapest	2	2

v ITALY

				Eng	Italy
EC1978	Mar	8	Manchester	2	1
EC1978	April	5	Rome	0	0
EC1984	April	18	Manchester	3	1
EC1984	May	2	Florence	0	1
EC1986	April	9	Pisa	0	2
EC1986	April	23	Swindon	1	1

v ISRAEL

				Eng	Isr
1985	Feb	27	Tel Aviv	2	1

v LATVIA

				Eng	Lat
1995	April	25	Riga	1	0
1995	June	7	Burnley	4	0

v MALAYSIA

				Eng	Mal
1995	June	8	Toulon	2	0

v MEXICO

				Eng	Mex
1988	June	5	Toulon	2	1
1991	May	29	Toulon	6	0
1992	May	25	Toulon	1	1

v MOROCCO

				Eng	Mor
1987	June	7	Toulon	2	0
1988	June	9	Toulon	1	0

v NORWAY

				Eng	Nor
EC1977	June	1	Bergen	2	1
EC1977	Sept	6	Brighton	6	0
1980	Sept	9	Southampton	3	0
1981	Sept	8	Drammen	0	0
EC1992	Oct	13	Peterborough	0	2
EC1993	June	1	Stavanger	1	1

v POLAND

				Eng	Pol
EC1982	Mar	17	Warsaw	2	1
EC1982	April	7	West Ham	2	2
EC1989	June	2	Plymouth	2	1
EC1989	Oct	10	Jastrzebie	3	1
EC1990	Oct	16	Tottenham	0	1
EC1993	May	28	Zdroj	4	1
EC1993	Sept	7	Millwall	1	2

v PORTUGAL

				Eng	Por
1987	June	13	Toulon	0	0
1990	May	21	Toulon	0	1
1993	June	7	Toulon	2	0
1994	June	7	Toulon	2	0

v REPUBLIC OF IRELAND

				Eng	Rep Ire
1981	Feb	25	Liverpool	1	0
1985	Mar	25	Portsmouth	3	2
1989	June	9	Toulon	0	0
EC1990	Nov	13	Cork	3	0
EC1991	Mar	26	Brentford	3	0
1994	Nov	15	Newcastle	1	0
1995	Mar	27	Dublin	2	0

v ROMANIA

				Eng	Rom
EC1980	Oct	14	Ploesti	0	4
EC1981	April	28	Swindon	3	0
EC1985	April	30	Brasov	0	0
EC1985	Sept	10	Ipswich	3	0

v RUSSIA

				Eng	Rus
1994	May	30	Bandol	2	0

v SAN MARINO

				Eng	SM
EC1993	Feb	16	Luton	6	0
EC1993	Nov	17	San Marino	4	0

v SENEGAL

				Eng	Sen
1989	June	7	Toulon	6	1
1991	May	27	Toulon	2	1

v SCOTLAND

				Eng	Scot
1977	April	27	Sheffield	1	0
EC1980	Feb	12	Coventry	2	1
EC1980	Mar	4	Aberdeen	0	0
EC1982	April	19	Glasgow	1	0
EC1982	April	28	Manchester	1	1
EC1988	Feb	16	Aberdeen	1	0
EC1988	Mar	22	Nottingham	1	0
1993	June	13	Toulon	1	0

			v SPAIN	Eng	Spa
EC1984	May	17	Seville	1	0
EC1984	May	24	Sheffield	2	0
1987	Feb	18	Burgos	2	1
1992	Sept	8	Burgos	1	0

			v SWEDEN	Eng	Swe
1979	June	9	Vasteras	2	1
1986	Sept	9	Ostersund	1	1
EC1988	Oct	18	Coventry	1	1
EC1989	Sept	5	Uppsala	0	1

			v SWITZERLAND	Eng	Swit
EC1980	Nov	18	Ipswich	5	0
EC1981	May	31	Neuenburg	0	0
1988	May	28	Lausanne	1	1

			v USA	Eng	USA
1989	June	11	Toulon	0	2
1994	June	2	Toulon	3	0

			v TURKEY	Eng	Tur
EC1984	Nov	13	Bursa	0	0
EC1985	Oct	15	Bristol	3	0
EC1987	April	28	Izmir	0	0
EC1987	Oct	13	Sheffield	1	1
EC1991	April	30	Izmir	2	2
1991	Oct	15	Reading	2	0
EC1992	Nov	17	Orient	0	1
EC1993	Mar	30	Izmir	0	0

			v USSR	Eng	USSR
1987	June	9	Toulon	0	0
1988	June	7	Toulon	1	0
1990	May	25	Toulon	2	1
1991	May	31	Toulon	2	1

			v WALES	Eng	Wales
1976	Dec	15	Wolverhampton	0	0
1979	Feb	6	Swansea	1	0
1990	Dec	5	Tranmere	0	0

			v WEST GERMANY	Eng	WG
EC1982	Sept	21	Sheffield	3	1
EC1982	Oct	12	Bremen	2	3
1987	Sept	8	Ludenscheid	0	2

			v YUGOSLAVIA	Eng	Yugo
EC1978	April	19	Novi Sad	1	2
EC1978	May	2	Manchester	1	1
EC1986	Nov	11	Peterborough	1	1
EC1987	Nov	10	Zemun	5	1

ENGLAND B RESULTS 1949–95

Year	*Date*		*Venue* v ALGERIA	Eng	Alg
1990	Dec	11	Algiers	0	0

			v AUSTRALIA	Eng	Aust
1980	Nov	17	Birmingham	1	0

			v CIS	Eng	CIS
1992	April	28	Moscow	1	1

			v CZECHOSLOVAKIA	Eng	Cz
1978	Nov	28	Prague	1	0
1990	April	24	Sunderland	2	0
1992	Mar	24	Budejovice	1	0

			v FINLAND	Eng	Fin
1949	May	15	Helsinki	4	0

			v FRANCE	Eng	Fra
1952	May	22	Le Havre	1	7
1992	Feb	18	Loftus Road	3	0

			v WEST GERMANY	Eng	WG
1954	Mar	24	Gelsenkirchen	4	0
1955	Mar	23	Sheffield	1	1
1978	Feb	21	Augsburg	2	1

			v HOLLAND	Eng	Hol
1949	May	18	Amsterdam	4	0
1950	Feb	22	Newcastle	1	0
1952	Mar	26	Amsterdam	1	0

			v ICELAND	Eng	Ice
1989	may	19	reykjavik	2	0
1991	April	27	Watford	1	0

			v ITALY	Eng	It
1950	May	11	Milan	0	5
1989	Nov	14	Brighton	1	1

			v LUXEMBOURG	Eng	Lux
1950	May	21	Luxembourg	2	1

			v MALAYSIA	Eng	Mal
1978	May	30	Kuala Lumpur	1	1

			v MALTA	Eng	Mal
1987	Oct	14	Ta'Qali	2	0

			v NEW ZEALAND	Eng	NZ
1978	June	7	Christchurch	4	0
1978	June	11	WEllington	3	1
1978	June	14	Auckland	4	0
1979	Oct	15	Leyton	4	1
1984	Nov	13	Nottingham	2	0

			v NORTHERN IRELAND	Eng	NI
1994	May	10	Sheffield	4	2

			v NORWAY	Eng	Nor
1989	May	22	Stavanger	1	0

			v REPUBLIC OF IRELAND	Eng	RoI
1990	Mar	27	Cork	1	4
1994	Dec	13	Liverpool	2	0

			v SCOTLAND	Eng	Scot
1953	Mar	11	Edinburgh	2	2
1954	Mar	3	Sunderland	1	1
1956	Feb	29	Dundee	2	2
1957	Feb	6	Birmingham	4	1

			v SINGAPORE	Eng	Sin
1978	June	18	Singapore	8	0

			v SPAIN	Eng	Sp
1980	Mar	26	Sunderland	1	0
1981	Mar	25	Granada	2	3
1991*	Dec	18	Castellon	1	0

*Spanish Olympic IX

			v SWITZERLAND	Eng	SW
1950	Jan	18	Sheffield	5	0
1954	May	22	Basle	0	2
1956	Mar	21	Southampton	4	1
1989	May	16	Winterthur	2	0
1991	May	20	Walsall	2	1

			v USA	Eng	USA
1980	Oct	14	Manchester	1	0

			v WALES	Eng	Wal
1991	Feb	5	Swansea	1	0

			v YUGOSLAVIA	Eng	Yug
1954	May	16	Ljubljana	1	2
1955	Oct	19	Manchester	5	1
1989	Dec	12	Millwall	2	1

BRITISH AND IRISH UNDER-21 TEAMS 1994-95

England Under-21 internationals

6 Sept

England (0) 0

France (0) 0 6487

England: Gerrard; Watson S, Gordon, Sinclair, Campbell, Unsworth, Redknapp, Barmby (Dyer), Fowler, Bart-Williams, Joachim.

11 Oct

Austria (1) 1 *(Haas)*

England (2) 3 *(Redknapp 3)* 2800

England: Gerrard; Edghill, Gordon, Watson S, Campbell, Unsworth, Redknapp, Parlour, Fowler, Bart-Williams (Whelan), Joachim (Barmby).

15 Nov

England (1) 1 *(Whelan)*

Republic of Ireland (0) 0 25,863

England: Gerrard; Watson S, Gordon, Butt, Campbell, Unsworth, Fenton, Sinclair, Whelan (Pollock), Bart-Williams (Smith M), Joachim.

Republic of Ireland: Given; Carr, Woods, Greene, Breen, Boland, Kavanagh, Moore (Scully), Perkins (Launders), Kennedy, Turner.

27 Mar

Republic of Ireland (0) 0

England (0) 2 *(Sinclair, Shipperley)* 6000

Republic of Ireland: Given; Carr, Hardy, Greene, Breen, Woods, Boland (Farrelly), Savage, Durkan, Kennedy, Turner (Launders).

England: Gerrard; Watson S, Pearce, Gordon, Unsworth, Roberts, Butt, Gallen, Shipperley, Bart-Williams, Sinclair.

25 Apr

Latvia (0) 0

England (0) 1 *(Sinclair)* 300

England: Gerrard; Watson S, Gordon, Nethercott, Unsworth, Roberts, Butt, Gallen (Booth), Shipperley, Bart-Williams, Sinclair.

6 June

England (0) 0

Brazil (1) 2 *(Leonardo, Leandro)* 3000

England: Watson D; Neville P, Croft, Hill, Richards, Ryder, Beckham, Holland P, Joachim, Forster, Myers (Allen).

7 June

England (2) 4 *(Bart-Williams, Shipperley, Watson S, Booth)*

Latvia (0) 0 7288

England: Gerrard; Watson S, Gordon, Pearce, Nethercott, Roberts, Holland C, Gallen (Booth), Shipperley, Bart-Williams, Thompson.

8 June

England (2) 2 *(Joachim, Myers)*

Malaysia (0) 0 700

England: Marshall; Neville P, Croft, Hill (Couzens), Richards, Casper, Beckham, Holland P, Joachim, Forster, Myers.

10 June

England (1) 1 *(Forster)*

Angola (0) 0 250

England: Davis; Neville P, Croft, Hill, Richards, Ryder, Beckham, Holland P, Joachim, Forster, Couzens (Myers).

12 June

England (0) 0

France (0) 2 *(Corridon, Histilloles)* 650

England: Watson D; Neville P, Croft, Hill, Richards, Ryder (Allen), Beckham, Holland P (Couzens), Joachim, Forster, Myers.

Scotland Under-21 internationals

6 Sept

Finland (1) 1 *(Ristilla (pen))*

Scotland (0) 0 2321

Scotland: Kerr; Jupp, Robertson, Murray, Pressley, Dailly, Lock, Hannah, Crawford (Lavety), Donnelly (McDonald), McCann.

15 Nov

Scotland (0) 2 *(Crawford, Varlamov (og))*

Russia (0) 1 *(Simoutenkov)* 6350

Scotland: Stille; Jupp, Love, Handyside, Pressley, Marshall (Freedman), Johnston, Murray, Crawford, Dailly, McDonald (Hannah).

17 Dec

Greece (0) 1 *(Gianakopoulos)*

Scotland (0) 2 *(Crawford 2)* 1000

Scotland: Kerr; McNamara, Baker, Murray, Marshall, Dailly, Thomas (McCann), Hannah, Crawford, Miller (Donnelly), Bollan.

28 Mar

Russia (1) 1 *(Lebed)*

Scotland (1) 2 *(Miller, Freedman)* 2464

Scotland: Stille; Jupp, Bollan, Dailly, Pressley, Hannah (Harper), McNamara (O'Neill), Miller, Crawford, Freedman, McLaughlin.

25 Apr

San Marino (0) 0

Scotland (0) 1 *(Pressley)* 930

Scotland: Stille; Jupp, Murray, Dailly, McLaughlin, McNamara, Crawford, Freedman (Hamilton), McCann (Liddell).

5 June

Scotland (1) 1 *(Freedman)*

Mexico (1) 2 *(Luna 2)* 400

Scotland: Stille; Jupp, Dailly, Pressley, Baker, Hannah, Fullarton, Glass, McLaughlin (McDonald), Freedman (Liddell), Crawford.

7 June

France (1) 1 *(Histilloles)*

Scotland (1) 2 *(Glass, Gray)* 1500

Scotland: Stille; Jupp (Crawford), Pressley, Dailly, Gray, Hannah (Baker), Fullarton, Glass, O'Neill (McDonald), Liddell, Freedman.

9 June

South Korea (0) 0

Scotland (0) 1 *(Hannah)* 500
Scotland: Stille; Jupp (Crawford), Pressley, Dailly, Gray, O'Neill (Baker), Hannah, Fullarton, Glass (McLaughlin), Freedman, Liddell.

12 June

Brazil (2) 4 *(Caico, Juninho, Leonardo, Jupp (og))*

Scotland (0) 0 1100
Scotland: Stille; Jupp, Pressley, Dailly, Gray (Crawford), Hannah, Fullarton (McLaughlin), Glass, O'Neill, Freedman (McDonald), Hamilton.

Wales Under-21 internationals

11 Oct

Moldovo (1) 1 *(Khizilov)*

Wales (0) 0 5000
Wales: Coyne; Barnhouse, Williams, Twiddy, Page, Hughes, Bird, Morgan, Hartson, Jones L, Kenworthy (Davies).

15 Nov

Georgia (0) 1 *(Anchabadze)*

Wales (1) 2 *(Twiddy, Jones (pen))* 10,000

Wales: Coyne; Williams, Brace, Page, Edwards, Hughes, Jones L, Davies, Hartson, Taylor, Twiddy (Bird).

13 Dec

Wales (0) 1 *(Hartson)*

Bulgaria (0) 1 *(Ionkov)* 630
Wales: Coyne; Williams, Brace, Davies (Evans), Hughes, Chapple, Morgan, Bird, Hartson, Taylor, Jones R.

28 Mar

Bulgaria (2) 3 *(Ivanov, Pramatarov, Hristo)*

Wales (1) 1 *(Savage)* 25,000
Wales: Coyne; Williams, Brace, Davies, Page, Edwards, Savage, Chapple, Taylor, Jones R, Kenworthy.

Republic of Ireland Under-21 internationals

6 Sept

Latvia (1) 1 *(Bleidelis)*

Republic of Ireland (0) 1 *(Moore)* 500
Republic of Ireland: Given; Gallen, Hardy, Greene, Breen, Boland, Sheridan, Kavanagh, Moore, Launders (Perkins), Kennedy.

25 Apr

Republic of Ireland (0) 1 *(Kennedy)*

Portugal (0) 1 *(Kenedy)* 2300
Republic of Ireland: Colgan; Carr, Hardy (Woods), Greene, Breen, Savage, Scully, Kavanagh, Moore, Launders, Kennedy.

10 June

Republic of Ireland (2) 3 *(Durkan, Perkins 2)*

Austria (0) 0 1654
Republic of Ireland: Colgan; Carr, Hardy, Greene, Breen, Woods, Boland, Farrelly, Durkan, Perkins, Launders (Sherlock).

B INTERNATIONALS

13 Dec

England B (1) 2 *(Cole, Fowler)*

Republic of Ireland B (0) 0 7431
England B: Pressman (James); Barton, Beresford, Sherwood, Scales (Ehiogu), Ruddock, Campbell (Redknapp), Sutton (Barmby), Cole (Fowler), Fox, Wilcox.
Republic of Ireland B: Branagan; Cunningham, Kenna, McAteer, Babb, Daish, Whelan (Milligan), McLoughlin, Kelly D (Coyle), Coyne, Townsend.

21 Feb

Scotland B (1) 3 *(Tweed, Jackson, Wright)*

Northern Ireland B (0) 0 5067
Scotland B: Walker (Woods); Wright, McKinnon, Tweed, Martin, O'Neil, Lambert (Cameron), Rae, Brown (Dodds), Jackson, McGinlay
Northern Ireland B: Fettis; Wright, Rowland, Dunlop, McGibbon, Matthews, Morrow, Sonner, O'Boyle, Lennon, Finlay.

SEMI-PROFESSIONAL INTERNATIONALS

28 Feb

England (0) 1 *(Hine)*

Wales (0) 0 703
England: Batty (Woking); Webb (Kidderminster Harriers), Hogarth (Guiseley), Reid (Altrincham), Brown (Woking), Stott (Bromsgrove Rovers), Terry (Altrincham), Forsyth (Kidderminster Harriers) [Hine (Gateshead)], Ross (Marine), Humphreys (Kidderminster Harriers), Watson (Marine) [Arnold (Kettering Town)].

11 Apr

Holland (0) 0

England (0) 0 500
England: Batty (Woking) [Farrelly (Macclesfield Town)]; Webb (Kidderminster Harriers), Hogarth (Guiseley), Brown (Woking), Holden (Kettering Town) [Howarth (Macclesfield Town)], Forsyth (Kidderminster Harriers), Venables (Stevenage Borough), Hine (Gateshead) [Stott (Bromsgrove Rovers)], Ross (Marine), Arnold (Kettering Town) [Browne (Dover Athletic)], Humphreys (Kidderminster Harriers) [Watson (Marine)].

31 May

Gibraltar (1) 2

England (2) 3 *(Taylor, Bolton, Venables)* 800
England: Batty (Woking) [Farrelly (Macclesfield Town)]; Webb (Kidderminster Harriers), Ashby (Kettering Town), Brown (Woking), Holden (Kettering Town), Stott (Bromsgrove Rovers) [McDonald (Macclesfield Town)], Venables (Stevenage Borough), Forsyth (Kidderminster Harriers), Bolton (Kingstonian), Taylor (Bromsgrove Rovers), Richardson (Dagenham & Redbridge) [May (Stafford Rangers)].

UNDER-21 APPEARANCES 1976–1995

ENGLAND

Ablett, G. (Liverpool), 1988 v F (1)
Adams, A. (Arsenal). 1985 v Ei, Fi; 1986 v D; 1987 v Se, Y (5)
Adams, N. (Everton), 1987 v Se (1)
Allen, B. (QPR), 1992 v H, M, Cz, F; 1993 v N (sub), T, P, Cz (sub) (8)
Allen, C. A. (Oxford U), 1995 v Br (sub), F (sub) (2)
Allen, C. (QPR), 1980 v EG (sub); (with C Palace), 1981 v N, R (3)
Allen, M. (QPR), 1987 v Se (sub); 1988 v Y (sub) (2)
Allen, P. (West Ham U), 1985 v Ei, R; (with Tottenham H, 1986 v R (3)
Anderson, V. A. (Nottingham F), 1978 v I (1)
Anderton, D. R. (Tottenham H), 1993 v Sp, Sm, Ho, Pol, N, P, Cz, Br, S, F; 1994 v Pol, Sm (12)
Andrews, I. (Leicester C), 1987 v Se (1)
Ardley, N. C. (Wimbledon), 1993 v Pol, N, P, Cz, Br, S, F, 1994 v Pol (sub), Ho, Sm (10)
Ashcroft, L. (Preston NE), 1992 v H (sub) (1)
Atherton, P. (Coventry C), 1992 v T (1)
Atkinson, B. (Sunderland), 1991 v W (sub), Sen, M, USSR (sub), F; 1992 v Pol (sub) (6)
Awford, A. T. (Portsmouth), 1993 v Sp, N, T, P, Cz, Br, S, F; 1994 v Ho (9)

Bailey, G. R. (Manchester U), 1979 v W, Bul; 1980 v D, S (2), EG; 1982 v N; 1983 v D, Gr; 1984 v H, F (2), I, Sp (14)
Baker, G. E. (Southampton), 1981 v N, R (2)
Barker, S. (Blackburn R), 1985 v Is (sub), Ei, R; 1986 v I (4)
Barmby, N. J. (Tottenham H), 1994 v D; 1995 v P, A (sub) (3)
Bannister, G. (Sheffield W), 1982 v Pol (1)
Barnes, J. (Watford), 1983 v D, Gr (2)
Barnes, P. S. (Manchester C), 1977 v W (sub), S, Fi, N; 1978 v N, Fi, I (2), Y (9)
Barrett, E. D. (Oldham Ath), 1990 v P, F, USSR, Cz (4)
Bart-Williams, C. G. (Sheffield W), 1993 v Sp, N, T; 1994 v D, Ru, F, Bel, P; 1995 v P, A, Ei (2), La (2) (14)
Batty, D. (Leeds U), 1988 v Sw (sub); 1989 v Gr (sub), Bul, Sen, Ei, US; 1990 v Pol (7)
Bazeley, D. S. (Watford), 1992 v H (sub) (1)
Beagrie, P. (Sheffield U), 1988 v WG, T (2)
Beardsmore, R. (Manchester U), 1989 v Gr, Alb (sub), Pol, Bul, USA (5)
Beckham, D. R. J. (Manchester U), 1995 v Br, Mal, An, F (4)
Beeston, C (Stoke C), 1988 v USSR (1)
Bertschin, K. E. (Birmingham C), 1977 v S; 1978 v Y (2) (3)
Birtles, G. (Nottingham F), 1980 v Bul, EG (sub) (2)
Blackwell, D. R. (Wimbledon), 1991 v W, T, Sen (sub), M, USSR, F (6)
Blake, M. A. (Aston Villa), 1990 v F (sub), Cz (sub); 1991 v H, Pol, Ei (2), W; 1992 v Pol (8)
Blissett, L. L. (Watford), 1979 v W, Bul (sub), Se; 1980 v D (4)
Booth, A. D. (Huddersfield T), 1995 v La (2 subs) (2)
Bracewell, P. (Stoke C), 1983 v D, Gr (1 + 1 sub), H; 1984 v D, H, F (2), I (2), Sp (2); 1985 v T (13)
Bradshaw, P. W. (Wolverhampton W), 1977 v W, S; 1978 v Fi, Y (4)
Breacker, T. (Luton T), 1986 v I (2) (2)
Brennan, M. (Ipswich T), 1987 v Y, Sp, T, Mor, F (5)
Brightwell, I. (Manchester C), 1989 v D, Alb; 1990 v Se (sub), Pol (4)
Brock, K. (Oxford U), 1984 v I, Sp (2); 1986 v I (4)
Bull, S. G. (Wolverhampton W), 1989 v Alb (2) Pol; 1990 v Se, Pol (5)
Burrows, D. (WBA), 1989 v Se (sub); (with Liverpool), Gr, Alb (2), Pol; 1990 v Se, Pol (7)
Butcher, T. I. (Ipswich T), 1979 v Se; 1980 v D, Bul, S (2), EG (2) (7)
Butt, N. (Manchester U), 1995 v Ei (2), La (3)
Butters, G. (Tottenham H), 1989 v Bul, Sen (sub), Ei (sub) (3)
Butterworth, I. (Coventry C), 1985 v T, R; (with Nottingham F), 1986 v R, T, D (2), I (2) (8)

Caesar, G. (Arsenal), 1987 v Mor, USSR (sub), F (3)
Callaghan, N. (Watford), 1983 v D, Gr (sub), H (sub); 1984 v D, H, F (2), I, Sp (9)
Campbell, K. J. (Arsenal), 1991 v H, T (sub); 1992 v G, T (4)
Campbell, S. (Tottenham), 1994 v D, Ru, F, US, Bel, P; 1995 v P, A, Ei (9)
Carr, C. (Fulham), 1985 v Ei (sub) (1)
Carr, F. (Nottingham F), 1987 v Se, Y, Sp (sub), Mor, USSR; 1988 v WG (sub), T, Y, F (9)
Casper, C. M. (Manchester U), 1995 v Mal (1)
Caton, T. (Manchester C), 1982 v N, H (sub), Pol (2), S; 1983 v WG (2), Gr; 1984 v D, H, F (2), I (2) (14)
Chamberlain, M. (Stoke C), 1983 v Gr; 1984 v F (sub), I, Sp (4)
Chapman, L. (Stoke C), 1981 v Ei (1)
Charles, G. A. (Nottingham F), 1991 v H, W (sub), Ei; 1992 v T (4)
Chettle, S. (Nottingham F), 1988 v M, USSR, Mor, F; 1989 v D, Se, Gr, Alb (2), Bul; 1990 v Se, Pol (12)
Clark, L. R. (Newcastle U), 1992 v Cz, F; 1993 v Sp, N, T, Ho (sub), Pol (sub), Cz, Br, S; 1994 v Ho (11)
Clough, N. (Nottingham F), 1986 v D (sub); 1987 v Se, Y, T, USSR, F (sub), P; 1988 v WG, T, Y, S (2), M, Mor, F (15)
Cole, A. A. (Arsenal), 1992 v H, Cz (sub), F (sub); (with Bristol C), 1993 v Sm; (with Newcastle U), Pol, N; 1994 v Pol, Ho (8)
Coney, D. (Fulham), 1985 v T (sub); 1986 v R; 1988 v T, WG (4)
Connor, T. (Brighton & HA), 1987 v Y (1)
Cooke, R. (Tottenham H), 1986 v D (sub) (1)
Cooper, C. (Middlesbrough), 1988 v F (2), M, USSR, Mor; 1989 v D, Se, Gr (8)
Corrigan, J. T. (Manchester C), 1978 v I (2), Y (3)
Cottee, A. (West Ham U), 1985 v Fi (sub), Is (sub), Ei, R, Fi; 1987 v Sp, P; 1988 v WG (8)
Couzens, A. J. (Leeds U), 1995 v Mal (sub), An, F (sub) (3)
Cowans, G. S. (Aston Villa), 1979 v W, Se; 1980 v Bul, EG; 1981 v R (5)
Cox, N. J. (Aston Villa), 1993 v T, Ho, Pol, N; 1994 v Pol, Sm (6)
Cranson, I. (Ipswich T), 1985 v Fi, Is, R; 1986 v R, I (5)
Croft, G. (Grimsby T), 1995 v Br, Mal, An, F (4)
Crooks, G. (Stoke C), 1980 v Bul, S (2), EG (sub) (4)
Crossley, M. G. (Nottingham F), 1990 v P, USSR, Cz (3)
Cundy, J. V. (Chelsea), 1991 v Ei (2); 1992 v Pol (3)
Cunningham, L. (WBA), 1977 v S, Fi, N (sub); 1978 v N, Fi, I (6)
Curbishley, L. C. (Birmingham C), 1981 v Sw (1)

Daniel, P. W. (Hull C), 1977 v S, Fi, N; 1978 v Fi, I, Y (2) (7)
Davis, K. G. (Luton T), 1995 v An (1)
Davis, P. (Arsenal), 1982 v Pol, S; 1983 v D, Gr (1 + 1 sub), H (sub); 1987 v T; 1988 v WG, T, Y, Fr (11)
D'Avray, M. (Ipswich T), 1984 v I, Sp (sub) (2)

Deehan, J. M. (Aston Villa), 1977 v N; 1978 v N, Fi, I; 1979 v Bul, Se (sub); 1980 v D (7)
Dennis, M. E. (Birmingham C), 1980 v Bul; 1981 v N, R (3)
Dickens, A. (West Ham U), 1985 v Fi (sub) (1)
Dicks, J. (West Ham U), 1988 v Sw (sub), M, Mor, F (4)
Digby, F. (Swindon T), 1987 v Sp (sub), USSR, P; 1988 v T; 1990 v Pol (5)
Dillon, K. P. (Birmingham C), 1981 v R (1)
Dixon, K. (Chelsea), 1985 v Fi (1)
Dobson, A. (Coventry C), 1989 v Bul, Sen, Ei, US (4)
Dodd, J. R. (Southampton), 1991 v Pol, Ei, T, Sen, M, F; 1992 v G, Pol (8)
Donowa, L. (Norwich C), 1985 v Is, R (sub), Fi (sub) (3)
Dorigo, A. (Aston Villa), 1987 v Se, Sp, T, Mor, USSR, F, P; 1988 v WG, Y, S (2) (11)
Dozzell, J. (Ipswich T), 1987 v Se, Y (sub), Sp, USSR, F, P; 1989 v Se, Gr (sub); 1990 v Se (sub) (9)
Draper, M. A. (Notts Co), 1991 v Ei (sub); 1992 v G, Pol (3)
Duxbury, M. (Manchester U), 1981 v Sw (sub), Ei (sub), R (sub), Sw; 1982 v N; 1983 v WG (2) (7)
Dyer, B. A. (Crystal Palace), 1994 v Ru, F, US, Bel, P; 1995 v P (sub) (6)
Dyson, P. I. (Coventry C), 1981 v N, R, Sw, Ei (4)

Eadie, D. M. (Norwich C), 1994 v F (sub), US (2)
Ebbrell, J. (Everton), 1989 v Sen, Ei, US (sub); 1990 v P, F, USSR, Cz; 1991 v H, Pol, Ei, W, T; 1992 v G, T (14)
Edghill, R. A. (Manchester C), 1994 v D, Ru; 1995 v A (3)
Ehiogu, U. (Aston Villa), 1992 v H, M, Cz, F; 1993 v Sp, N, T, Sm, T, Ho, Pol, N; 1994 v Pol, Ho, Sm (15)
Elliott, P. (Luton T), 1985 v Fi; 1986 v T, D (3)

Fairclough, C. (Nottingham F), 1985 v T, Is, Ei; 1987 v Sp, T; (with Tottenham H), 1988 v Y, F (7)
Fairclough, D. (Liverpool), 1977 v W (1)
Fashanu, J. (Norwich C), 1980 v EG; 1981 v N (sub), R, Sw, Ei (sub), H; (with Nottingham F), 1982 v N, H, Pol, S; 1983 v WG (sub) (11)
Fear, P. (Wimbledon), 1994 v Ru, F, US (sub) (3)
Fenton, G. A. (Aston Villa), 1995 v Ei (1)
Fenwick, T. W. (C Palace), 1981 v N, R, Sw, Ei; (with QPR), R; 1982 v N, H, S (2); 1983 v WG (2) (11)
Fereday, W. (QPR), 1985 v T, Ei (sub). Fi; 1986 v T (sub), I (5)
Flitcroft, G. W. (Manchester C), 1993 v Sm, Hol, N, P, Cz, Br, S, F; 1994 v Pol, Ho (10)
Flowers, T. (Southampton), 1987 v Mor, F; 1988 v WG (sub) (3)
Forster, N. M. (Brentford), 1995 v Br, Mal, An, F (4)
Forsyth, M. (Derby Co), 1988 v Sw (1)
Foster, S. (Brighton & HA), 1980 v EG (sub) (1)
Fowler, R. B. (Liverpool), 1994 v Sm, Ru (sub), F, US; 1995 v P, A (6)
Froggatt, S. J. (Aston Villa), 1993 v Sp, Sm (sub) (2)
Futcher, P. (Luton T), 1977 v W, S, Fi, N; (with Manchester C), 1978 v N, Fi, I (2), Y (2); 1979 v D (11)

Gabbiadini, M. (Sunderland), 1989 v Bul, USA (2)
Gale, A. (Fulham), 1982 v Pol (1)
Gallen, K. A. (QPR), 1995 v Ei, La (2) (3)
Gascoigne, P. (Newcastle U), 1987 v Mo, USSR, P; 1988 v WG, Y, S (2), F (2), Sw, M, USSR (sub), Mor (13)
Gayle, H. (Birmingham C), 1984 v I, Sp (2) (3)
Gernon, T. (Ipswich T), 1983 v Gr (1)
Gerrard, P. W. (Oldham Ath), 1993 v T, Ho, Pol, N, P, Cz, Br, S, F; 1994 v D, Ru; 1995 v P, A, Ei (2), La (2) (17)
Gibbs, N. (Watford), 1987 v Mor, USSR, F, P; 1988 v T (5)
Gibson, C. (Aston Villa), 1982 v N (1)
Gilbert, W. A. (C Palace), 1979 v W, Bul; 1980 v Bul; 1981 v N, R, Sw, R, Sw, H; 1982 v N (sub), H (11)
Goddard, P. (West Ham U), 1981 v N, Sw, Ei (sub); 1982 v N (sub), Pol, S; 1983 v WG (2) (8)
Gordon, D. (Norwich C), 1987 v T (sub), Mor (sub), F, P (4)
Gordon, D. D. (Crystal Palace), 1994 v Ru, F, US, Bel, P; 1995 v P, A, Ei (2), La (2) (11)
Gray, A. (Aston Villa), 1988 v S, F (2)

Haigh, P. (Hull C), 1977 v N (sub) (1)
Hall, R. A. (Southampton), 1992 v H (sub), F; 1993 v Sm, T, Ho, Pol, P, Cz, Br, S, F (11)
Hardyman, P. (Portsmouth), 1985 v Ei; 1986 v D (2)
Hateley, M. (Coventry C), 1982 v Pol, S; 1983 v Gr (2), H; (with Portsmouth), 1984 v F (2), I, Sp (2) (10)
Hayes, M. (Arsenal), 1987 v Sp, T; 1988 v F (sub) (3)
Hazell, R. J. (Wolverhampton W), 1979 v D (1)
Heaney, N. A. (Arsenal), 1992 v H, M, Cz, F; 1993 v N, T (6)
Heath, A. (Stoke C), 1981 v R, Sw, H; 1982 v N, H; (with Everton), Pol, S; 1983 v WG (8)
Hendon, I. M. (Tottenham H), 1992 v H, M, Cz, F; 1993 v Sp, N, T (7)
Hesford, I. (Blackpool), 1981 v Ei (sub), Pol (2), S (2); 1983 v WG (2) (7)
Hilaire, V. (C Palace), 1980 v Bul, S (1+1 sub), EG (2); 1981 v N, R, Sw (sub); 1982 v Pol (sub) (9)
Hill, D. R. L. (Tottenham H), 1995 v Br, Mal, An, F (4)
Hillier, D. (Arsenal), 1991 v T (1)
Hinchcliffe, A. (Manchester C), 1989 v D (1)
Hinshelwood, P. A. (C Palace), 1978 v N; 1980 v EG (2)
Hirst, D. (Sheffield W), 1988 v USSR, F; 1989 v D, Bul (sub), Sen, Ei, US (7)
Hoddle, G. (Tottenham H), 1977 v W (sub); 1978 v Fi (sub), I (2), Y; 1979 v D, W, Bul; 1980 v S (2), EG (2) (12)
Hodge, S. (Nottingham F), 1983 v Gr (sub); 1984 v D, F, I, Sp (2); (with Aston Villa), 1986 v R, T (8)
Hodgson, D. J. (Middlesbrough), 1981 v N, R (sub), Sw, Ei; 1982 v Pol; 1983 v WG (6)
Holdsworth, D. (Watford), 1989 v Gr (sub) (1)
Holland, C. J. (Newcastle U), 1995 v La (1)
Holland, P. (Mansfield T), 1995 v Br, Mal, An, F (4)
Horne, B. (Millwall), 1989 v Gr (sub), Pol, Bul, Ei, US (5)
Hucker, P. (QPR), 1984 v I, Sp (2)

Impey, A. R. (QPR), 1993 v T (1)
Ince, P. (West Ham U), 1989 v Alb; 1990 v Se (2)

Jackson, M. A. (Everton), 1992 v H, M, Cz, F; 1993 v Sm (sub), T, Ho, Pol, N; 1994 v Pol (10)
James, D. (Watford), 1991 v Ei (2), T, Sen, M, USSR, F; 1992 v G, T, Pol (10)
James, J. C. (Luton T), 1990 v F, USSR (2)
Jemson, N. B. (Nottingham F), 1991 v W (1)
Joachim, J. K. (Leicester C), 1994 v D (sub); 1995 v P, A, Ei, Br, Mal, An, F (8)
Johnson, T. (Notts Co), 1991 v H (sub), Ei (sub); 1992 v G, T, Pol; (with Derby Co), M, Cz (sub) (7)
Johnston, C. P. (Middlesbrough), 1981 v N, Ei (2)
Jones, D. R. (Everton), 1977 v W (1)
Jones, C. H. (Tottenham H), 1978 v Y (sub) (1)
Jones, R. (Liverpool), 1993 v Sm, Ho (2)

Keegan, G. A. (Manchester C), 1977 v W (1)
Kenny, W. (Everton), 1993 v T (1)
Keown, M. (Aston Villa), 1987 v Sp, Mor, USSR, P; 1988 v T, S, F (2) (8)
Kerslake, D. (QPR), 1986 v T (1)
Kilcline, B. (Notts C), 1983 v D, Gr (2)
King, A. E. (Everton), 1977 v W; 1978 v Y (2)
Kitson, P. (Leicester C), 1991 v Sen (sub), M, F; 1992 v Pol; (with Derby Co), M, Cz, F (7)
Knight, A. (Portsmouth), 1983 v Gr, H (2)
Knight, I. (Sheffield W), 1987 v Se (sub), Y (2)

Lake, P. (Manchester C), 1989 v D, Alb (2), Pol; 1990 v Pol (5)
Langley, T. W. (Chelsea), 1978 v I (sub) (1)
Lee, D. J. (Chelsea), 1990 v F; 1991 v H, Pol, Ei (2), T, Sen, USSR, F; 1992 v Pol (10)
Lee, R. (Charlton Ath), 1986 v I (sub); 1987 v Se (sub) (2)
Lee, S. (Liverpool), 1981 v R, Sw, H; 1982 v S; 1983 v WG (2) (6)
Le Saux, G. (Chelsea), 1990 v P, F, USSR, Cz (4)
Lowe, D. (Ipswich T), 1988 v F, Sw (sub) (2)
Lukic, J. (Leeds U), 1981 v N, R, Ei, R, Sw, H; 1982 v H (7)
Lund, G. (Grimsby T), 1985 v T; 1986 v R, T (3)

McCall, S. H. (Ipswich T), 1981 v Sw, H; 1982 v H, S; 1983 v WG (2) (6)
McDonald, N. (Newcastle U), 1987 v Se (sub), Sp, T; 1988 v WG, Y (sub) (5)
McGrath, L. (Coventry C), 1986 v D (1)
MacKenzie, S. (WBA), 1982 v N, S (2) (3)
McLeary, A. (Millwall), 1988 v Sw (1)
McMahon, S. (Everton), 1981 v Ei; 1982 v Pol; 1983 v D, Gr (2); (with Aston Villa), 1984 v H (6)
McManaman, S. (Liverpool), 1991 v W, M (sub); 1993 v N, T, Sm, T; 1994 v Pol (7)
Mabbutt, G. (Bristol R), 1982 v Pol (2), S; (with Tottenham H), 1983 v D; 1984 v F; 1986 v D, I (7)
Makin, C. (Oldham Ath), 1994 v Ru (sub), F, US, Bel, P (5)
Marriott, A. (Nottingham F), 1992 v M (1)
Marshall, A. J. (Norwich C), 1995 v Mal (1)
Martin, L. (Manchester U), 1989 v Gr (sub), Alb (sub) (2)
Martyn, N. (Bristol R), 1988 v S (sub), M, USSR, Mor, F; 1989 v D, Se, Gr, Alb (2); 1990 v Se (11)
Matteo, D. (Liverpool), 1994 v F (sub), Bel, P (3)
Matthew, D. (Chelsea), 1990 v P, USSR (sub), Cz; 1991 v Ei, M, USSR, F; 1992 v G (sub), T (9)
May, A. (Manchester C), 1986 v I (sub) (1)
Merson, P. (Arsenal), 1989 v D, Gr, Pol (sub); 1990 v Pol (4)
Middleton, J. (Nottingham F), 1977 v Fi, N; (with Derby Co), 1978 v N (3)
Miller, A. (Arsenal), 1988 v Mor (sub); 1989 v Sen; 1991 v H, Pol (4)
Mills, G. R. (Nottingham F), 1981 v R; 1982 v N (2)
Mimms, R. (Rotherham U), 1985 v Is (sub), Ei (sub); (with Everton), 1986 v I (3)
Minto, S. C. (Charlton Ath), 1991 v W; 1992 v H, M, Cz; 1993 v T; 1994 v Ho (6)
Moran, S. (Southampton), 1982 v N (sub); 1984 v F (2)
Morgan, S. (Leicester C), 1987 v Se, Y (2)
Mortimer, P. (Charlton Ath), 1989 v Sen, Ei (2)
Moses, R. M. (WBA), 1981 v N (sub), Sw, Ei, R, Sw, H; 1982 v N (sub); (with Manchester U), H (8)
Mountfield, D. (Everton), 1984 v Sp (1)
Muggleton, C. D. (Leicester C), 1990 v F (1)
Mutch, A. (Wolverhampton W), 1989 v Pol (1)
Myers. A. (Chelsea), 1995 v Br, Mal, An (sub), F (4)

Nethercott, S. (Tottenham), 1994 v D, Ru, F, US, Bel, P; 1995 v La (2) (8)
Neville, P. J. (Manchester U), 1995 v Br, Mal, An, F (4)
Newell, M. (Luton T), 1986 v D (1 + 1 sub), I (1 + 1 sub) (4)
Newton, E. J. I. (Chelsea), 1993 v T (sub); 1994 v Sm (2)
Nicholls, A. (Plymouth Arg), 1994 v F (1)

Oakes, M. C. (Aston Villa), 1994 v D (sub), F (sub), US, Bel, P (5)
Oakes, S. J. (Luton T), 1993 v Br (sub) (1)
Oldfield, D. (Luton T), 1989 v Se (1)
Olney, I. A. (Aston Villa), 1990 v P, F, USSR, Cz; 1991 v H, Pol, Ei (2), T; 1992 v Pol (sub) (10)
Ord, R. J. (Sunderland), 1991 v W, M, USSR (3)
Osman, R. C. (Ipswich T), 1979 v W (sub), Se; 1980 v D, S (2), EG (2) (7)
Owen, G. A. (Manchester C), 1977 v S, Fi, N; 1978 v N, Fi, I (2), Y; 1979 v D, W; (with WBA), Bul, Se (sub); 1980 v D, S (2), EG; 1981 v Sw, R; 1982 v N (sub), H; 1983 v WG (2) (22)

Painter, I. (Stoke C), 1986 v I (1)
Palmer, C. (Sheffield W), 1989 v Bul, Sen, Ei, US (4)
Parker, G. (Hull C), 1986 v I (2); (with Nottingham F), F; 1987 v Se, Y (sub), Sp (6)
Parker, P. (Fulham), 1985 v Fi, T, Is (sub), Ei, R, Fi; 1986 v T, D (8)
Parkes, P. B. F. (QPR), 1979 v D (1)
Parkin, S. (Stoke C), 1987 v Sp (sub); 1988 v WG (sub), T, S (sub), F (5)
Parlour, R. (Arsenal), 1992 v H, M, Cz, F; 1993 v Sp, N, T; 1994 v D, Ru, Bel, P; 1995 v A (12)
Peach, D. S. (Southampton), 1977 v S, Fi, N; 1978 v N, I (2) (6)
Peake, A. (Leicester C), 1982 v Pol (1)
Pearce, I. A. (Blackburn R), 1995 v Ei, La (2)
Pearce, S. (Nottingham F), 1987 v Y (1)
Pickering N. (Sunderland), 1983 v D (sub), Gr, H; 1984 v F (sub + 1), I (2), Sp; 1985 v Is, R, Fi; 1986 v R, T; (with Coventry C), D, I (15)
Platt, D. (Aston Villa), 1988 v M, Mor, F (3)
Pollock, J. (Middlesbrough), 1995 v Ei (sub) (1)
Porter, G. (Watford), 1987 v Sp (sub), T, Mor, USSR, F, P (sub); 1988 v T (sub), Y, S (2), F, Sw (12)
Pressman, K. (Sheffield W), 1989 v D (sub) (1)
Proctor, M. (Middlesbrough), 1981 v Ei (sub), Sw; (with Nottingham F) 1982 v N, Pol (4)

Ramage, C. D. (Derby Co), 1991 v Pol (sub), W; 1992 v Fr (sub) (3)
Ranson, R. (Manchester C), 1980 v Bul, EG; 1981 v R (sub), R, Sw (1 + 1 sub), H, Pol (2), S (10)
Redknapp, J. F. (Liverpool), 1993 v Sm, Pol, N, P, Cz, Br, S, F; 1994 v Pol, Ho (sub), D, Ru, F, US, Bel, P; 1995 v P, A (18)
Redmond, S. (Manchester C), 1988 v F (2), M, USSR, Mor, F; 1989 v D, Se, Gr, Alb (2), Pol; 1990 v Se, Pol (14)
Reeves, K. P. (Norwich C), 1978 v I, Y (2); 1979 v N, W, Bul, Sw; 1980 v D, S; (with Manchester C), EG (10)
Regis, C. (WBA), 1979 v D, Bul, Se; 1980 v S, EG; 1983 v D (6)
Reid, N. S. (Manchester C), 1981 v H (sub); 1982 v H, Pol (2), S (2) (6)
Reid, P. (Bolton W), 1977 v S, Fi, N; 1978 v Fi, I, Y (6)
Richards, D. I. (Wolverhampton W), 1995 v Br, Mal, An, F (4)
Richards, J. P. (Wolverhampton W), 1977 v Fi, N (2)
Rideout, P. (Aston Villa), 1985 v Fi, Is, Ei (sub), R; (with Bari), 1986 v D (5)
Ripley, S. (Middlesbrough), 1988 v USSR, F (sub); 1989 v D (sub), Se, Gr, Alb (2); 1990 v Se (8)
Ritchie, A. (Brighton & HA), 1982 v Pol (1)
Rix, G. (Arsenal), 1978 v Fi (sub), Y; 1979 v D, Se; 1980 v D (sub), Bul, S (7)
Roberts, A. J. (Millwall), 1995 v Ei, La (2) (3)
Robins, M. G. (Manchester U), 1990 v P, F, USSR, Cz; 1991 v H (sub), Pol (6)
Robson, B. (WBA), 1979 v W, Bul (sub), Se; 1980 v D, Bul, S (2) (7)
Robson, S. (Arsenal), 1984 v I; 1985 v Fi, Is, Fi; 1986 v R, I (with West Ham U); 1988 v S, Sw (8)
Rocastle, D. (Arsenal), 1987 v Se, Y, Sp, T; 1988 v WG, T, Y, S (2), F (2 subs), M, USSR, Mor (14)
Rodger, G. (Coventry C), 1987 v USSR, F, P; 1988 v WG (4)
Rosario, R. (Norwich C), 1987 v T (sub), Mor, F, P (sub) (4)

Rowell, G. (Sunderland), 1977 v Fi (1)
Ruddock, N. (Southampton), 1989 v Bul (sub), Sen, Ei, US (4)
Ryan, J. (Oldham Ath), 1983 v H (1)
Ryder, S.H. (Walsall), 1995 v Br, An, F (3)

Samways, V. (Tottenham H), 1988 v Sw (sub), USSR, F; 1989 v D, Se (5)
Sansom, K. G. (C Palace), 1979 v D, W, Bul, Se; 1980 v S (2), EG (2) (8)
Seaman, D. (Birmingham C), 1985 v Fi, T, Is, Ei, R, Fi; 1986 v R, F, D, I (10)
Sedgley, S. (Coventry C), 1987 v USSR, F (sub), P; 1988 v F; 1989 v D (sub), Se, Gr, Alb (2), Pol; (with Tottenham H), 1990 v Se (11)
Sellars, S. (Blackburn R), 1988 v S (sub), F, Sw (3)
Selley, I. (Arsenal), 1994 v Ru (sub), F (sub), US (3)
Sharpe, L. (Manchester U), 1989 v Gr; 1990 v P (sub), F, USSR, Cz; 1991 v H, Pol (sub), Ei (8)
Shaw, G. R. (Aston Villa), 1981 v Ei, Sw, H; 1982 v H, S; 1983 v WG (2) (7)
Shearer, A. (Southampton), 1991 v Ei (2), W, T, Sen, M, USSR, F; 1992 v G, T, Pol (11)
Shelton, G. (Sheffield W), 1985 v Fi (1)
Sheringham, T. (Millwall), 1988 v Sw (1)
Sheron, M. N. (Manchester C), 1992 v H, F; 1993 v N (sub), T (sub), Sm, Ho, Pol, N, P, Cz, Br, S, F; 1994 v Pol (sub), Ho, Sm (16)
Sherwood, T. A. (Norwich C), 1990 v P, F, USSR, Cz (4)
Shipperley, N. J. (Chelsea), 1994 v Sm (sub); (with Southampton) 1995 v Ei, La (2) (4)
Simpson, P. (Manchester C), 1986 v D (sub); 1987 v Y, Mor, F, P (5)
Sims, S. (Leicester C), 1977 v W, S, Fi, N; 1978 v N, Fi, I (2), Y (2) (10)
Sinclair, F. M. (Chelsea), 1994 v Ho, Sm, D, Ru, F, US, Bel, P (8)
Sinclair, T. (QPR), 1995 v P, Ei (2), La (4)
Sinnott, L. (Watford), 1985 v Is (sub) (1)
Slater, S. I. (West Ham U), 1990 v P, USSR (sub), Cz (sub) (3)
Small, B. (Aston Villa), 1993 v Sm, T, Ho, Pol, N, P, Cz, Br, S, F; 1994 v Pol, Sm (12)
Smith, D. (Coventry C), 1988 v M, USSR (sub), Mor; 1989 v D, Se, Alb (2), Pol; 1990 v Se, Pol (10)
Smith, M. (Sheffield W), 1981 v Ei, R, Sw, H; 1982 v Pol (sub) (5)
Smith, M. (Sunderland), 1995 v Ei (sub) (1)
Snodin, I. (Doncaster R), 1985 v T, Is, R, Fi (4)
Statham, B. (Tottenham H), 1988 v Sw; 1989 v D (sub), Se (3)
Statham, D. J. (WBA), 1978 v Fi, 1979 v W, Bul, Se; 1980 v D; 1983 v D (6)
Stein, B. (Luton T), 1984 v D, H, I (3)
Sterland, M. (Sheffield W), 1984 v D, H, F (2), I, Sp (2) (7)
Steven, T. (Everton), 1985 v Fi, T (2)
Stevens, G. (Brighton & HA), 1983 v H; (with Tottenham H), 1984 v H, F (1 + 1 sub), I (sub), Sp (1 + 1 sub); 1986 v I (8)
Stewart, P. (Manchester C), 1988 v F (1)
Stuart, G. C. (Chelsea), 1990 v P (sub), F, USSR, Cz; 1991 v T (sub) (5)
Suckling, P. (Coventry C), 1986 v D; (with Manchester C), 1987 v Se (sub), Y, Sp, T; (with C Palace), 1988 v S (2), F (2), Sw (10)
Summerbee, N.J. (Swindon T), 1993 v P (sub), S (sub), F (3)
Sunderland, A. (Wolverhampton W), 1977 v W (1)
Sutton, C. R. (Norwich), 1993 v Sp (sub), T (sub + 1), Ho, P (sub), Cz, Br, S, F; 1994 v Pol, Ho, Sm, D (13)
Swindlehurst, D. (C Palace), 1977 v W (1)
Sutch, D. (Norwich C), 1992 v H, M, Cz; 1993 v T (4)

Talbot, B. (Ipswich T), 1977 v W (1)
Thomas, D. (Coventry C), 1981 v Ei; 1983 v WG (2), Gr, H; (with Tottenham H), I, Sp (7)
Thomas, M. (Luton T), 1986 v T, D, I (3)
Thomas, M. (Arsenal), 1988 v Y, S, F (2), M, USSR, Mor; 1989 v Gr, Alb (2), Pol; 1990 v Se (12)
Thomas, R. E. (Watford), 1990 v P (1)
Thompson, A. (Bolton W), 1995 v La (1)
Thompson, G. L. (Coventry C), 1981 v R, Sw, H; 1982 v N, H, S (6)
Thorn, A. (Wimbledon), 1988 v WG (sub). Y, S, F, Sw (5)
Tiler, C. (Barnsley), 1990 v P, USSR, Cz; 1991 v H, Pol, Ei (2), T, Sen, USSR, F; (with Nottingham F), 1992 v G, T (13)

Unsworth, D. G. (Everton), 1995 v A, Ei (2), La (4)

Venison, B. (Sunderland), 1983 v D, Gr; 1985 v Fi, T, Is, Fi; 1986 v R, T, D (2) (10)
Vinnicombe, C. (Rangers), 1991 v H (sub), Pol, Ei (2), T, Sen, M, USSR (sub), F; 1992 v G, T, Pol (12)

Waddle, C. (Newcastle U), 1985 v Fi (1)
Wallace, D. (Southampton), 1983 v Gr, H; 1984 v D, H, F (2), I, Sp (sub); 1985 v Fi, T, Is; 1986 v R, D, I (14)
Wallace, Ray (Southampton), 1989 v Bul, Sen (sub), Ei; 1990 v Se (4)
Wallace, Rod (Southampton), 1989 v Bul, Ei (sub), US; 1991 v H, Pol, Ei, T, Sen, M, USSR, F (11)
Walker, D. (Nottingham F), 1985 v Fi; 1987 v Se, T; 1988 v WG, T, S (2) (7)
Walker, I. M. (Tottenham H), 1991 v W; 1992 v H, Cz, F; 1993 v Sp, N, T, Sm; 1994 v Pol (9)
Walsh, G. (Manchester U), 1988 v WG, Y (2)
Walsh, P. M. (Luton T), 1983 v D (sub), Gr (2), H (4)
Walters, K. (Aston Villa), 1984 v D (sub), H (sub); 1985 v Is, Ei, R; 1986 v R, T, D, I (sub) (9)
Ward, P. D. (Brighton & HA), 1978 v N; 1980 v EG (2)
Warhurst, P. (Oldham Ath), 1991 v H, Pol, W, Sen, M (sub), USSR, F (sub); (with Sheffield W), 1992 v G (8)
Watson, D. (Norwich C), 1984 v D, F (2), I (2), Sp (2) (7)
Watson, D. N. (Barnsley), 1994 v Ho, Sm; 1995 v Br, F (4)
Watson, G. (Sheffield W), 1991 v Sen, USSR (2)
Watson, S. C. (Newcastle U), 1993 v Sp (sub), N; 1994 v Sm (sub), D; 1995 v P, A, Ei (2), La (2) (10)
Webb, N. (Portsmouth), 1985 v Ei; (with Nottingham F), 1986 v D (2) (3)
Whelan, P. J. (Ipswich T), 1993 v Sp, T (sub), P (3)
Whelan, N. (Leeds U), 1995 v A (sub), Ei (2)
White, D. (Manchester C), 1988 v S (2), F, USSR; 1989 v Se; 1990 v Pol (6)
Whyte, C. (Arsenal), 1982 v S (1 + 1 sub); 1983 v D, Gr (4)
Wicks, S. (QPR), 1982 v S (1)
Wilkins, R. C. (Chelsea), 1977 v W (1)
Wilkinson, P. (Grimsby T), 1985 v Ei, R (sub); (with Everton), 1986 v R (sub), I (4)
Williams, P. (Charlton Ath), 1989 v Bul, Sen, Ei, US (sub) (4)
Williams, P. D. (Derby Co), 1991 v Sen, M, USSR; 1992 v G, T, Pol (6)
Williams, S. C. (Southampton), 1977 v S, Fi, N; 1978 v N, I (1 + 1 sub), Y (2); 1979 v D, Bul, Se (sub); 1980 v D, EG (2) (14)
Winterburn, N. (Wimbledon), 1986 v I (1)
Wise, D. (Wimbledon), 1988 v Sw (1)
Woodcook, A. S. (Nottingham F), 1978 v Fi, I (2)
Woods, C. C. E. (Nottingham F), 1979 v W (sub), Se; (with QPR), 1980 v Bul, EG; 1981 v Sw; (with Norwich C), 1984 v D (6)
Wright, A. G. (Blackburn), 1993 v Sp, N (2)
Wright, M. (Southampton), 1983 v Gr, H; 1984 v D, H (4)

Wright, W. (Everton), 1979 v D, W, Bul; 1980 v D, S (2) (6)

Yates, D. (Notts Co), 1989 v D (sub), Bul, Sen, Ei, US (5)

SCOTLAND

Aitken, R. (Celtic), 1977 v Cz, W, Sw; 1978 v Cz, W; 1979 v P, N (2); 1980 v Bel, E; 1984 v EG, Y (2); 1985 v WG, Ic, Sp (16)
Albiston, A. (Manchester U), 1977 v Cz, W, Sw; 1978 v Sw, Cz (5)
Archdeacon, O. (Celtic), 1987 v WG (sub) (1)
Archibald, S. (Aberdeen), 1980 v B, E (2), WG; (with Tottenham H), 1981 v D (5)

Bain, K. (Dundee), 1993 v P, I, Ma, P (4)
Baker, M. (St. Mirren), 1993 v F, M, E; 1994 v Ma, A; 1995 v Gr, M, F (sub), Sk (sub) (9)
Bannon, E. J. P. (Hearts), 1979 v US; (with Chelsea), P, N (2); (with Dundee U), 1980 v Bel, WG, E (7)
Beattie, J. (St Mirren), 1992 v D, US, P, Y (4)
Beaumont, D. (Dundee U), 1985 v Ic (1)
Bell, D. (Aberdeen), 1981 v D; 1984 v Y (2)
Bernard, P. R. J. (Oldham Ath), 1992 v R (sub), D, Se (sub), US; 1993 v Sw, P, I, Ma, P, F, Bul, M, E; 1994 v I, Ma (15)
Bett, J. (Rangers), 1981 v Se, D; 1982 v Se, D, I, E (2) (7)
Black, E. (Aberdeen), 1983 v EG, Sw (2), Bel; 1985 v Ic, Sp (2), Ic (8)
Blair, A. (Coventry C), 1980 v E; 1981 v Se; (with Aston Villa), 1982 v Se, D, I (5)
Bollan, G. (Dundee U), 1992 v D, G (sub), US, P, Y; 1993 v Sw, P, I, P, F, Bul, M, E; 1994 v Sw; 1995 v Gr; (with Rangers) v Ru, Sm (17)
Booth, S. (Aberdeen), 1991 v R (sub), Bul (sub + 1), Pol, F (sub); 1992 v Sw, R, D, Se, US, P, Y; 1993 v Ma, P (14)
Bowes, M. J. (Dunfermline Ath), 1992 v D (sub) (1)
Bowman, D. (Hearts), 1985 v WG (sub) (1)
Boyd, T. (Motherwell), 1987 v WG, Ei (2), Bel; 1988 v Bel (5)
Brazil, A. (Hibernian), 1978 v W (1)
Brazil, A. (Ipswich T), 1979 v N; 1980 v Bel (2), E (2), WG; 1981 v Se; 1982 v Se (8)
Brough, J. (Hearts), 1981 v D (1)
Burley, G. E. (Ipswich T), 1977 v Cz, W, Sw; 1978 v Sw, Cz (5)
Burley, C. (Chelsea), 1992 v D; 1993 v Sw, P, I, P; 1994 v Sw, I (sub) (7)
Burns, H. (Rangers), 1985 v Sp, Ic (sub) (2)
Burns, T. (Celtic), 1977 v Cz, W, E; 1978 v Sw; 1982 v E (5)

Campbell, S. (Dundee), 1989 v N (sub), Y, F (3)
Casey, J. (Celtic), 1978 v W (1)
Christie, M. (Dundee), 1992 v D, P (sub), Y (3)
Clark, R. (Aberdeen), 1977 v Cz, W, Sw (3)
Clarke, S. (St Mirren), 1984 v Bel, EG, Y; 1985 v WG, Ic, Sp (2), Ic (8)
Cleland, A. (Dundee U), 1990 v F, N (2); 1991 v R, Sw, Bul; 1992 v Sw, R, G, Se (2) (11)
Collins, J. (Hibernian), 1988 v Bel, E; 1989 v N, Y, F; 1990 v Y, F, N (8)
Connolly, P. (Dundee U), 1991 v R (sub), Sw, Bul (3)
Connor, R. (Ayr U), 1981 v Se; 1982 v Se (2)
Cooper, D. (Clydebank), 1977 v Cz, W, Sw, E; (with Rangers), 1978 v Sw, Cz (6)
Cooper, N. (Aberdeen), 1982 v D, E (2); 1983 v Bel, EG, Sw (2); 1984 v Bel, EG, Y; 1985 v Ic, Sp, Ic (13)
Crabbe, S. (Hearts), 1990 v Y (sub), F (2)
Craig, T. (Newcastle U), 1977 v E (1)
Crainie, D. (Celtic), 1983 v Sw (sub) (1)
Crawford, S. (Raith R), 1994 v A, Eg, P, Bel; 1995 v Fi, Ru, Gr, Ru, Sm, M, F (sub), Sk (sub), Br (sub) (13)
Creaney, G. (Celtic), 1991 v Sw, Bul (2), Pol, F; 1992 v Sw, R, G (2), Se (2) (11)

Dailly, C. (Dundee U), 1991 v R; 1992 v US, R; 1993 v Sw, P, I, Ic, P, F, Bul, M, E; 1994 v Sw, I, Ma, A, Eg, P, Bel; 1995 v Fi, Ru, Gr, Ru, Sm, M, F, Sk, Br (28)
Dawson, A. (Rangers), 1979 v P, N (2); 1980 v B (2), E (2), WG (8)
Deas, P. A. (St Johnstone), 1992 v D (sub); 1993 v Ma (2)
Dennis, S. (Raith R), 1992 v Sw (1)
Dickov, P. (Arsenal), 1992 v Y; 1993 v F, M, E (4)
Dodds, D. (Dundee U), 1978 v W (1)
Donald, G. S. (Hibernian), 1992 v US (sub), P, Y (sub) (3)
Donnelly, S. (Celtic), 1994 v Eg, P, Bel; 1995 v Fi, Gr (sub) (5)
Dow, A. (Dundee), 1993 v Ma (sub), Ic; (with Chelsea) 1994 v I (3)
Duffy, J. (Dundee), 1987 v Ei (1)
Durie, G. S. (Chelsea), 1987 v WG, Ei, Bel; 1988 v Bel (4)
Durrant, I. (Rangers), 1987 v WG, Ei, Bel; 1988 v E (4)
Doyle, J. (Partick Th), 1981 v D, I (sub) (2)

Ferguson, D. (Rangers), 1987 v WG, Ei, Bel; 1988 v E; 1990 v Y (5)
Ferguson, D. (Dundee U), 1992 v D, G, Se (2); 1993 v Sw, I, Ma (7)
Ferguson, D. (Manchester U), 1992 v US, P (sub), Y; 1993 v Sw, Ma (5)
Ferguson, I. (Dundee), 1983 v EG (sub), Sw (sub); 1984 v Bel (sub), EG (4)
Ferguson, I. (Clyde), 1987 v WG (sub), Ei; (with St Mirren), Ei, Bel; 1988 v Bel; (with Rangers), E (sub) (6)
Ferguson, R. (Hamilton A), 1977 v E (1)
Findlay, W. (Hibernian), 1991 v R, Pol, Bul (2), Pol (5)
Fitzpatrick, A. (St Mirren), 1977 v W (sub), Sw (sub), E; 1978 v Sw, Cz (5)
Flannigan, C. (Clydebank), 1993 v Ic (sub) (1)
Fleck, R. (Rangers), 1987 v WG (sub), Ei, Bel; (with Norwich C), 1988 v E (2); 1989 v Y (6)
Freedman, D. A. (Barnet), 1995 v Ru (sub + 1), Sm, M, F, Sk, Br (7)
Fridge, L. (St Mirren), 1989 v F; 1990 v Y (2)
Fullarton, J. (St. Mirren), 1993 v F, Bul; 1994 v Ma, A, Eg, P, Bel; 1995 v M, F, Sk, Br (11)
Fulton, M. (St Mirren), 1980 v Bel, WG, E; 1981 v Se, D (sub) (5)
Fulton, S. (Celtic), 1991 v R, Sw, Bul, Pol, F; 1992 v G (2) (7)

Gallacher, K. (Dundee U), 1987 v WG, Ei (2), Bel (sub); 1988 v E (2); 1990 v Y (7)
Galloway, M. (Hearts), 1989 v F; (with Celtic), 1990 v N (2)
Gardiner, J. (Hibernian), 1993 v F (1)
Geddes, R. (Dundee), 1982 v Se, D, E (2); 1988 v E (5)
Gemmill, S. (Nottingham F), 1992 v Sw, R (sub), G (sub), Se (sub) (4)
Gillespie, G. (Coventry C), 1979 v US; 1980 v E; 1981 v D; 1982 v Se, D, I (2), E (8)
Glass, S. (Aberdeen), 1995 v M, F, Sk, Br (4)
Glover, L. (Nottingham F), 1988 v Bel (sub); 1989 v N; 1990 v Y (3)
Goram, A. (Oldham Ath), 1987 v Ei (1)
Gough, C. R. (Dundee U), 1983 v EG, Sw, Bel; 1984 v Y (2) (5)
Grant, P. (Celtic), 1985 v WG, Ic, Sp; 1987 v WG, Ei (2), Bel; 1988 v Bel, E (2) (10)
Gray S. (Celtic), 1995 v F, Sk, Br (3)
Gray, S. (Aberdeen), 1987 v WG (1)
Gunn, B. (Aberdeen), 1984 v EG, Y (2); 1985 v WG, Ic, Sp (2), Ic; 1990 v F (9)

Hagen, D. (Rangers), 1992 v D (sub), US (sub), P, Y; 1993 v Sw (sub), P, Ic, P (8)
Hamilton, B. (St Mirren), 1989 v Y, F (sub); 1990 v F, N (4)
Hamilton, J. (Dundee) 1995 v Sm (sub), Br (2)
Handyside, P. (Grimsby T), 1993 v Ic (sub), Bul, M, E; 1995 v Ru (5)
Hannah, D. (Dundee U), 1993 v F (sub), Bul, M; 1994 v A, Eg, P, Bel; 1995 v Fi, Ru (sub), Gr, Ru, M, F, Sk, Br (15)
Harper, K. (Hibernian), 1995 v Ru (sub) (1)
Hartford, R. A. (Manchester C), 1977 v Sw (1)
Hegarty, P. (Dundee U), 1987 v WG, Bel; 1988 v E (2); 1990 v F, N (6)
Hendry, J. (Tottenham H), 1992 v D (sub) (1)
Hewitt, J. (Aberdeen), 1982 v I; 1983 v EG, Sw (2); 1984 v Bel, Y (sub) (6)
Hogg, G. (Manchester U), 1984 v Y; 1985 v WG, Ic, Sp (4)
Hood, G. (Ayr U), 1993 v F, E (sub); 1994 v A (3)
Howie, S. (Cowdenbeath), 1993 v Ma, Ic, P; 1994 v Sw, I (5)
Hunter, G. (Hibernian), 1987 v Ei (sub); 1988 v Bel, E (3)
Hunter, P. (East Fife), 1989 v N (sub), F (sub); 1990 v F (sub) (3)

Jardine, I. (Kilmarnock), 1979 v US (1)
Jess, E. (Aberdeen), 1990 v F (sub), N (sub); 1991 v R, Sw, Bul (2), Pol, F; 1992 v Sw, R, G (2), Se (1 + 1 sub) (14)
Johnson, G. I. (Dundee U), 1992 v US, P, Y; 1993 v Sw, P, Ma (6)
Johnston, A. (Hearts), 1994 v Bel; 1995 v Ru (2)
Johnston, F. (Falkirk), 1993 v Ic (1)
Johnston, M. (Partick Th), 1984 v EG (sub); (with Watford), Y (2) (3)
Jupp, D. A. (Fulham), 1995 v Fi, Ru (2), Sm, M, F, Sk, Br (8)

Kirkwood, D. (Hearts), 1990 v Y (1)
Kerr, S. (Celtic), 1993 v Bul, M, E; 1994 v Ma, A, Eg, P, Bel; 1995 v Fi, Gr (10)

Lambert, P. (St Mirren), 1991 v R, Sw, Bul (2), Pol, F; 1992 v Sw, R, G (2), Se (11)
Lavety, B. (St. Mirren), 1993 v Ic, Bul (sub), M (sub), E; 1994 v Ma, A (sub), Eg (sub), Bel (sub); 1995 v Fi (sub) (9)
Lavin, G. (Watford), 1993 v F, Bul, M; 1994 v Ma, Eg, P, Bel (7)
Leighton, J. (Aberdeen), 1982 v I (1)
Levein, C. (Hearts), 1985 v Sp, Ic (2)
Liddell, A. M. (Barnsley), 1994 v Ma (sub); 1995 v Sm (sub), M (sub), F, Sk (5)
Lindsey, J. (Motherwell), 1979 v US (1)
Locke, G. (Hearts), 1994 v Ma, A, Eg, P; 1995 v Fi (5)
Love, G. (Hibernian), 1995 v Ru (1)

McAllister, G. (Leicester C), 1990 v N (1)
McAlpine, H. (Dundee U), 1983 v EG, Sw (2), Bel; 1984 v Bel (5)
McAuley, S. (St. Johnstone), 1993 v P (sub) (1)
McAvennie, F. (St Mirren), 1982 v I, E; 1985 v Is, Ei, R (5)
McBride, J. (Everton), 1981 v D (1)
McCall, S. (Bradford C), 1988 v E; (with Everton), 1990 v F (2)
McCann, N. (Dundee), 1994 v A, Eg, P, Bel; 1995 v Fi, Gr (sub), Sm, (7)
McClair, B. (Celtic), 1984 v Bel (sub), EG, Y (1 + 1 sub); 1985 v WG, Ic, Sp, Ic (8)
McCluskey, G. (Celtic), 1979 v US, P; 1980 v Bel (2); 1982 v D, I (6)
McCoist, A. (Rangers), 1984 v Bel (1)
McCulloch, A. (Kilmarnock); 1981 v Se (1)
McCulloch, I. (Notts Co), 1982 v E (2)
MacDonald, J. (Rangers), 1980 v WG (sub); 1981 v Se; 1982 v Se (sub), L, I (2), E (2 sub) (8)
McDonald, C. (Falkirk), 1995 v Fi (sub), Ru, M (sub), F (sub), Br (sub) (5)
McGarvey, F. (St Mirren), 1977 v E; 1978 v Cz; (with Celtic), 1982 v D (3)
McGarvey, S. (Manchester U), 1982 v E (sub); 1983 v Bel, Sw; 1984 v Bel (4)
McGhee, M. (Aberdeen), 1981 v D (1)
McGinnis, G. (Dundee U), 1985 v Sp (1)
McGrillen, P. (Motherwell), 1994 v Sw (sub), I (2)
McInally, J. (Dundee U), 1989 v F (1)
McKimmie, S. (Aberdeen), 1985 v WG, Ic (2) (3)
McKinlay, T. (Dundee), 1984 v EG (sub); 1985 v WG, Ic, Sp (2), Ic (6)
McKinlay, W. (Dundee U), 1989 v N, Y (sub), F; 1990 v Y, F, N (6)
McKinnon, R. (Dundee U), 1991 v R, Pol (sub); 1992 v G (2), Se (2) (6)
McLaren, A, (Hearts), 1989 v F; 1990 v Y, N; 1991 v Sw, Bul, Po1, F; 1992 v R, G, Se (2) (11)
McLaren, A. (Dundee U), 1993 v I, Ma (sub); 1994 v Sw, I (sub) (4)
McLaughlin, B. (Celtic), 1995 v Ru, Sm, M, Sk (sub), Br (sub) (5)
McLaughlin, J. (Morton), 1981 v D; 1982 v Se, D, I, E (2); 1983 v EG, Sw (2), Bel (10)
McLeish, A. (Aberdeen), 1978 v W; 1979 v US; 1980 v Bel, E (2); 1987 v Ei (6)
MacLeod, A. (Hibernian), 1979 v P, N (2) (3)
McLeod, J. (Dundee U), 1989 v N; 1990 v F (2)
MacLeod, M. (Dumbarton), 1979 v US; (with Celtic), P (sub), N (2); 1980 v Bel (5)
McNab, N. (Tottenham H), 1978 v W (1)
McNally, M. (Celtic), 1991 v Bul; 1993 v Ic (2)
McNamara, J. (Dunfermline Ath), 1994 v A, Bel; 1995 v Gr, Ru, Sm (5)
McNichol, J. (Brentford), 1979 v P, N (2); 1980 v Bel (2), WG, E (7)
McNiven, D. (Leeds U), 1977 v Cz, W (sub), Sw (sub) (3)
McPherson, D. (Rangers), 1984 v Bel; 1985 v Sp; (with Hearts), 1989 v N, Y (4)
McQuilken, J. (Celtic), 1993 v Bul, E (2)
McStay, P. (Celtic), 1983 v EG, Sw (2); 1984 v Y (2) (5)
McWhirter, N. (St Mirren), 1991 v Bul (sub) (1)
Main, A. (Dundee U), 1988 v E; 1989 v Y; 1990 v N (3)
Malpas, M. (Dundee U), 1983 v Bel, Sw (1 + 1 sub); 1984 v Bel, EG, Y (2); 1985 v Sp (8)
Marshall, S. R. (Arsenal), 1995 v Ru, Gr (2)
May, E. (Hibernian), 1989 v Y (sub), F (2)
Melrose, J. (Partick Th), 1977 v Sw; 1979 v US, P, N (2); 1980 v Bel (sub), WG, E (8)
Miller, C. (Rangers), 1995 v Gr, Ru (2)
Miller, J. (Aberdeen), 1987 v Ei (sub); 1988 v Bel; (with Celtic), E; 1989 v N, Y; 1990 v F, N (7)
Miller, W. (Aberdeen), 1978 v Sw, Cz (2)
Miller, W. (Hibernian), 1991 v R, Sw, Bul, Pol, F; 1992 v R, G (sub) (7)
Milne, R. (Dundee U), 1982 v Se (sub); 1984 v Bel, EG (3)
Money, I. C. (St Mirren), 1987 v Ei; 1988 v Bel; 1989 v N (3)
Muir, L. (Hibernian), 1977 v Cz (sub) (1)
Murray, N. (Rangers), 1993 v P (sub), Ma, Ic, P; 1994 v Sw, I; 1995 v Fi, Ru, Gr, Sm (10)
Murray, R. (Bournemouth), 1993 v Ic (sub) (1)

Narey, D. (Dundee U), 1977 v Cz, Sw; 1978 v Sw, Cz (4)
Nevin, P. (Chelsea), 1985 v WG, Ic, Sp (2), Ic (5)
Nicholas, C. (Celtic), 1981 v Se; 1982 v Se; 1983 v EG, Sw, **Bel; (with Arsenal), 1984 v Y (6)**

Nicol, S. (Ayr U), 1981 v Se; 1982 v Se, D; (with Liverpool), I (2), E (2); 1983 v EG, Sw (2), Bel; 1984 v Bel, EG, Y (14)
Nisbet, S. (Rangers), 1989 v N, Y, F; 1990 v Y, F (5)

O'Donnell, P. (Motherwell), 1992 v Sw (sub), R, D, G (2), Se (1 + 1 sub); 1993 v P (8)
O'Neil, B. (Celtic), 1992 v D, G, Se (2); 1993 v Sw, P, I (7)
O'Neil, J. (Dundee U), 1991 v Bul (sub) (1)
O'Neill, M. (Clyde), 1995 v Ru (sub), F, Sk, Br (4)
Orr, N. (Morton), 1978 v W (sub); 1979 v US, P, N (2); 1980 v Bel, E (7)

Parlane, D. (Rangers), 1977 v W (1)
Paterson, C. (Hibernian), 1981 v Se; 1982 v I (2)
Payne, G. (Dundee U), 1978 v Sw, Cz, W (3)
Pressley, S. (Rangers), 1993 v Ic, F, Bul, M, E; 1994 v Sw, I, M, A, Eg, P, Bel; 1995 v Fi; (with Coventry C), Ru (2), Sm, M, F, Sk, Br (20)
Provan, D. (Kilmarnock), 1977 v Cz (sub) (1)

Rae, A. (Millwall), 1991 v Bul (sub + 1), F (sub); 1992 v Sw, R, G (sub), Se (2) (8)
Redford, I. (Rangers), 1981 v Se (sub); 1982 v Se, D, I (2), E (6)
Reid, B. (Rangers), 1991 v F; 1992 v D, US, P (4)
Reid, C. (Hibernian), 1993 v Sw, P, I (3)
Reid, M. (Celtic), 1982 v E; 1984 v Y (2)
Reid, R. (St Mirren), 1977 v W, Sw, E (3)
Rice, B. (Hibernian), 1985 v WG (1)
Richardson, L. (St Mirren), 1980 v WG, E (sub) (2)
Ritchie, A. (Morton), 1980 v Bel (1)
Robertson, A. (Rangers) 1991 v F (1)
Robertson, C. (Rangers), 1977 v E (sub) (1)
Robertson, D. (Aberdeen), 1987 v Ei (sub); 1988 v E (2); 1989 v N, Y; 1990 v Y, N (7)
Robertson, H. (Aberdeen), 1994 v Eg; 1995 v Fi (2)
Robertson, J. (Hearts), 1985 v WG, Ic (sub) (2)
Robertson, L. (Rangers), 1993 v F, M (sub), E (sub) (3)
Roddie, A. (Aberdeen), 1992 v US, P; 1993 v Sw (sub), P, Ic (5)
Ross, T. W. (Arsenal), 1977 v W (1)
Russell, R. (Rangers), 1978 v W; 1980 v Bel; 1984 v Y (3)

Salton, D. B. (Luton T), 1992 v D, US, P, Y; 1993 v Sw, I (6)
Scott, P. (St Johnstone), 1994 v A (sub), Eg (sub), P, Bel (4)
Shannon, R. (Dundee), 1987 v WG, Ei (2), Bel; 1988 v Bel, E (2) (7)
Sharp, G. (Everton), 1982 v E (1)
Sharp, R. (Dunfermline Ath), 1990 v N (sub); 1991 v R, Sw, Bul (4)
Simpson, N. (Aberdeen), 1982 v I (2), E; 1983 v EG, Sw (2), Bel; 1984 v Bel, EG, Y; 1985 v Sp (11)
Sinclair, G. (Dumbarton), 1977 v E (1)
Skilling, M. (Kilmarnock), 1993 v Ic (sub); 1994 v I (2)
Smith, B. M. (Celtic), 1992 v G (2), US, P, Y (5)
Smith, G. (Rangers), 1978 v W (1)
Smith, H. G. (Hearts), 1987 v WG, Bel (2)
Sneddon, A. (Celtic), 1979 v US (1)
Speedie, D. (Chelsea), 1985 v Sp (1)
Spencer, J. (Rangers), 1991 v Sw (sub), F; 1992 v Sw (3)
Stanton, P. (Hibernian), 1977 v Cz (1)
Stark, W. (Aberdeen), 1985 v Ic (1)
Stephen, R. (Dundee), 1983 v Bel (sub) (1)
Stevens, G. (Motherwell), 1977 v E (1)
Stewart, J. (Kilmarnock), 1978 v Sw, Cz; (with Middlesbrough), 1979 v P (3)
Stewart, R. (Dundee U), 1979 v P, N (2); (with West Ham U), 1980 v Bel (2), E (2), WG; 1981 v D; 1982 v I (2), E (12)
Stille, D. (Aberdeen), 1995 v Ru (2), Sm, M, F, Sk, Br (7)
Strachan, G. (Aberdeen), 1980 v Bel (1)
Sturrock, P. (Dundee U), 1977 v Cz, W, Sw, E; 1978 v Sw, Cz; 1982 v Se, I, E (9)
Sweeney, S. (Clydebank), 1991 v R, Sw (sub), Bul (2), Pol; 1992 v Sw, R (7)

Telfer, P. (Luton T), 1993 v Ma, P; 1994 v Sw (3)
Thomas, K. (Hearts), 1993 v F (sub), Bul, M, E; 1994 v Sw, Ma; 1995 v Gr (7)
Thomson, W. (Partick Th), 1977 v E (sub); 1978 v W; (with St Mirren), 1979 v US, N (2); 1980 v Bel (2), E (2), WG (10)
Tolmie, J. (Morton), 1980 v Bel (sub) (1)
Tortolano, J. (Hibernian), 1987 v WG, Ei (2)
Tweed, S. (Hibernian), 1993 v Ic; 1994 v Sw, I (3)

Walker, A. (Celtic), 1988 v Bel (1)
Wallace, I. (Coventry C), 1978 v Sw (1)
Walsh, C. (Nottingham F), 1984 v EG, Sw (2), Bel; 1984 v EG (5)
Wark, J. (Ipswich T), 1977 v Cz, W, Sw; 1978 v W; 1979 v P; 1980 v E (2), WG (8)
Watson, A. (Aberdeen), 1981 v Se, D; 1982 v D, I (sub) (4)
Watson, K. (Rangers), 1977 v E; 1978 v Sw (sub) (2)
Watt, M. (Aberdeen), 1991 v R, Sw, Bul (2), Pol, F; 1992 v Sw, R, G (2), Se (2) (12)
Whyte, D. (Celtic), 1987 v Ei (2), Bel; 1988 v E (2); 1989 v N, Y; 1990 v Y, N (9)
Will, J. A. (Arsenal), 1992 v D (sub), Y; 1993 v Ic (sub) (3)
Wilson, T. (St Mirren), 1983 v Sw (sub) (1)
Wilson, T. (Nottingham F), 1988 v E; 1989 v N, Y; 1990 v F (4)
Winnie, D. (St Mirren), 1988 v Bel (1)
Wright, P. (Aberdeen), 1989 v Y, F; (with QPR), 1990 v Y (sub) (3)
Wright, S. (Aberdeen), 1991 v Bul, Pol, F; 1992 v Sw, G (2), Se (2); 1993 v Sw, P, I, Ma; 1994 v I, Ma (14)
Wright, T. (Oldham Ath), 1987 v Bel (sub) (1)

WALES

Aizlewood, M. (Luton T), 1979 v E; 1981 v Ho (2)

Balcombe, S. (Leeds U), 1982 v F (sub) (1)
Barnhouse, D. J. (Swansea), 1995 v Mol (1)
Bater, P. T. (Bristol R), 1977 v E, S (2)
Bird, A. (Cardiff C), 1993 v Cy (sub); 1994 v Cy (sub); 1995 v Mol, Ge (sub), Bul (5)
Blackmore, C. (Manchester U), 1984 v N, Bul, Y (3)
Blake, N. (Cardiff C), 1991 v Pol (sub); 1993 v Cy, Bel, RCS; 1994 v RCS (5)
Bodin, P. (Cardiff C), 1983 v Y (1)
Bowen, J. P. (Swansea C), 1993 v Cy, Bel (2); 1994 v RCS, R (sub) (5)
Bowen, M. (Tottenham H), 1983 v N; 1984 v Bul, Y (3)
Boyle, T. (C Palace), 1982 v F (1)
Brace, D. P. (Wrexham), 1995 v Ge, Bul (2) (3)

Cegielski, W. (Wrexham), 1977 v E (sub), S (2)
Chapple, S. R. (Swansea C), 1992 v R; 1993 v Cy, Bel (2), RCS; 1994 v RCS; Bul (2) (8)
Charles, J. M. (Swansea C), 1979 v E; 1981 v Ho (2)
Clark, J. (Manchester U), 1978 v S; (with Derby Co), 1979 v E (2)
Coleman, C. (Swansea C); 1990 v Pol; 1991 v E, Pol (3)
Coyne, D. (Tranmere R), 1992 v R; 1994 v Cy (sub), R; 1995 v Mol, Ge, Bul (2) (7)
Curtis, A. T. (Swansea C), 1977 v E (1)

Davies, A. (Manchester U), 1982 v F (2), Ho; 1983 v N, Y, Bul (6)
Davies, G. M. (Hereford U), 1993 v Bel, RCS; 1995 v Mol (sub), Ge, Bul (2) (6)
Davies, I. C. (Norwich C), 1978 v S (sub) (1)
Deacy, N. (PSV Eindhoven), 1977 v S (1)
Dibble, A. (Cardiff C), 1983 v Bul; 1984 v N, Bul (3)

Doyle, S. C. (Preston NE), 1979 v E (sub); (with Huddersfield T), 1984 v N (2)
Dwyer, P. J. (Cardiff C), 1979 v E (1)

Ebdon, M. (Everton), 1990 v Pol; 1991 v E (2)
Edwards, R. (Bristol C), 1991 v Pol; 1992 v R; 1995 v Ge, Bul (4)
Edwards, R. I. (Chester), 1977 v S; 1978 v W (2)
Edwards, R. W. (Bristol C), 1993 v Cy, Bel (2), RCS; 1994 v RCS, Cy, R (7)
Evans, A. (Bristol R), 1977 v E (1)
Evans, T. (Cardiff C), 1995 v Bul (sub) (1)

Foster, M. G. (Tranmere R), 1993 v RCS (1)
Freestone, R. (Chelsea), 1990 v Pol (1)

Gale, D. (Swansea C), 1983 v Bul; 1984 v N (sub) (2)
Giggs, R. (Manchester U), 1991 v Pol (1)
Giles, D. C. (Cardiff C), 1977 v S; 1978 v S; (with Swansea C), 1981 v Ho; (with C Palace), 1983 v Y (4)
Giles, P. (Cardiff C), 1982 v F (2), Ho (3)
Graham, D. (Manchester U), 1991 v E (1)
Griffith, C. (Cardiff C), 1990 v Pol (1)
Griffiths, C. (Shrewsbury T), 1991 v Pol (sub) (1)

Hall, G. D. (Chelsea), 1990 v Pol (1)
Hartson, J. (Luton T), 1994 v Cy, R; 1995 v Mol, Ge, Bul (5)
Hodges, G. (Wimbledon), 1983 v Y (sub), Bul (sub); 1984 v N, Bul, Y (5)
Holden, A. (Chester C), 1984 v Y (sub) (1)
Hopkins, J. (Fulham), 1982 v F (sub), Ho; 1983 v N, Y, Bul (5)
Hughes, D. R. (Southampton), 1994 v R (1)
Hughes, I. (Bury), 1992 v R; 1993 v Cy, Bel (sub), RCS; 1994 v Cy, R; 1995 v Mol, Ge, Bul (9)
Hughes, L. M. (Manchester U), 1983 v N, Y; 1984 v N, Bul, Y (5)
Hughes, W. (WBA), 1977 v E, S; 1978 v S (3)

Jackett, K. (Watford), 1981 v Ho; 1982 v F (2)
James, R. M. (Swansea C), 1977 v E, S; 1978 v S (3)
Jenkins, S. R. (Swansea C), 1993 v Cy (sub), Bel (2)
Jones, F. (Wrexham), 1981 v Ho (1)
Jones, L. (Cardiff C), 1982 v F (2), Ho (3)
Jones, P. L. (Liverpool), 1992 v R; 1993 v Cy, Bel (2), RCS; 1994 v RCS (sub), Cy, R; 1995 v Mol, Ge (10)
Jones, R. (Sheffield W), 1994 v R; 1995 v Bul (2) (3)
Jones, V. (Bristol R), 1979 v E; 1981 v Ho (2)

Kendall, M. (Tottenham H), 1978 v S (1)
Kenworthy, J. R. (Tranmere R), 1994 v Cy; 1995 v Mol, Bul (3)

Law, B. J. (QPR), 1990 v Pol; 1991 v E (2)
Letheran, G. (Leeds U), 1977 v E, S (2)
Lewis, D. (Swansea C), 1982 v F (2), Ho; 1983 v N, Y, Bul; 1984 v N, Bul, Y (9)
Lewis, J. (Cardiff C), 1983 v N (1)
Loveridge, J. (Swansea C), 1982 v Ho; 1983 v N, Bul (3)
Lowndes, S. R. (Newport Co), 1979 v E; 1981 v Ho; (with Millwall), 1984 v Bul, Y (4)

McCarthy, A. J. (QPR), 1994 v RCS, Cy, R (3)
Maddy, P. (Cardiff C), 1982 v Ho; 1983 v N (sub) (2)
Margetson, M. W. (Manchester C), 1992 v R; 1993 v Cy, Bel (2), RCS; 1994 v RCS, Cy (7)
Marustik, C. (Swansea C), 1982 v F (2); 1983 v Y, Bul; 1984 v N, Bul, Y (7)
Meaker, M. J. (QPR), 1994 v RCS (sub), R (sub) (2)
Melville, A. K. (Swansea C), 1990 v Pol; (with Oxford U), 1991 v E (2)
Micallef, C. (Cardiff C), 1982 v F, Ho; 1983 v N (3)
Morgan, A. M. (Tranmere R), 1995 v Mol, Bul (2)

Nardiello, D. (Coventry C), 1978 v S (1)
Neilson, A. B. (Newcastle U), 1993 v Cy, Bel (2), RCS; 1994 v RCS, Cy, R (7)
Nicholas, P. (C Palace), 1978 v S; 1979 v E; (with Arsenal), 1982 v F (3)
Nogan, K. (Luton T), 1990 v Pol; 1991 v E (2)
Nogan, L. (Oxford U) 1991 v E (1)

Owen, G. (Wrexham), 1991 v E (sub), Pol; 1992 v R; 1993 v Cy, Bel (2); 1994 v Cy, R (8)

Page, R. J. (Watford), 1995 v Mol, Ge, Bul (3)
Pascoe, C. (Swansea C), 1983 v Bul (sub); 1984 v N (sub), Bul, Y (4)
Pembridge, M. (Luton T), 1991 v Pol (1)
Perry, J. (Cardiff C), 1990 v Pol; 1991 v E, Pol (3)
Peters, M. (Manchester C), 1992 v R; (with Norwich C), 1993 v Cy, RCS (3)
Phillips, D. (Plymouth Arg), 1984 v N, Bul, Y (3)
Phillips, L. (Swansea C), 1979 v E; (with Charlton Ath), 1983 v N (2)
Pontin, K. (Cardiff C), 1978 v S (1)
Powell, L. (Southampton), 1991 v Pol (sub); 1992 v R (sub); 1993 v Bel (sub); 1994 v RCS (4)
Price, P. (Luton T), 1981 v Ho (1)
Pugh, D. (Doncaster R), 1982 v F (2) (2)
Pugh, S. (Wrexham), 1993 v Bel (2 subs) (2)

Ratcliffe, K. (Everton), 1981 v Ho; 1982 v F (2)
Ready, K. (QPR), 1992 v R; 1993 v Bel (2); 1994 v RCS, Cy (5)
Rees, A. (Birmingham C), 1984 v N (1)
Rees, J. (Luton T), 1990 v Pol; 1991 v E, Pol (3)
Roberts, A. (QPR), 1991 v E, Pol (2)
Roberts, G. (Hull C), 1983 v Bul (1)
Roberts, J. G. (Wrexham), 1977 v E (1)
Robinson, J. (Brighton & HA), 1992 v R; (with Charlton Ath), 1993 v Bel; 1994 v RCS, Cy, R (5)
Rush, I. (Liverpool), 1981 v Ho; 1982 v F (2)

Savage, R. W. (Crewe Alex), 1995 v Bul (1)
Sayer, P. A. (Cardiff C), 1977 v E, S (2)
Searle, D. (Cardiff C), 1991 v Pol (sub); 1992 v R; 1993 v Cy, Bel (2), RCS; 1994 v RCS (6)
Slatter, N. (Bristol R), 1983 v N, Y, Bul; 1984 v N, Bul, Y (6)
Speed, G. A. (Leeds U), 1990 v Pol; 1991 v E, Pol (3)
Stevenson, N. (Swansea C), 1982 v F, Ho (2)
Stevenson, W. B. (Leeds U), 1977 v E, S; 1978 v S (3)
Symons, K. (Portsmouth), 1991 v E, Pol (2)

Taylor, G. K. (Bristol R), 1995 v Ge, Bul (2) (3)
Thomas, Martin R. (Bristol R), 1979 v E; 1981 v Ho (2)
Thomas, Mickey R. (Wrexham), 1977 v E; 1978 v S (2)
Thomas, D. G. (Leeds U), 1977 v E; 1979 v E; 1984 v N (3)
Tibbott, L. (Ipswich T), 1977 v E, S (2)
Twiddy, C. (Plymouth Arg), 1995 v Mol, Ge (2)

Vaughan, N. (Newport Co), 1982 v F, Ho (2)

Walsh, I. P. (C Palace), 1979 v E; (with Swansea C), 1983 v Bul (2)
Walton, M. (Norwich C.), 1991 v Pol (sub) (1)
Williams, D. (Bristol R), 1983 v Y (1)
Williams, G. (Bristol R), 1983 v Y, Bul (2)
Williams, S. J. (Wrexham), 1995 v Mol, Ge, Bul (2) (4)
Wilmot, R. (Arsenal), 1982 v F (2), Ho; 1983 v N, Y; 1984 v Y (6)

International Records

MOST GOALS IN AN INTERNATIONAL

England	Malcolm Macdonald (Newcastle U) 5 goals v Cyprus, at Wembley	16.4.1975
	Willie Hall (Tottenham H) 5 goals v Ireland, at Old Trafford	16.11.1938
	G. O. Smith (Corinthians) 5 goals v Ireland, at Sunderland	18.2.1899
	Steve Bloomer (Derby Co) 5 goals* v Wales, at Cardiff	16.3.1896
	Oliver Vaughton (Aston Villa) 5 goals v Ireland, at Belfast	18.2.82
Scotland	Charles Heggie (Rangers) 5 goals v Ireland, at Belfast	20.3.1886
Ireland	Joe Bambrick (Linfield) 6 goals v Wales, at Belfast	1.2.1930
Wales	James Price (Wrexham) 4 goals v Ireland, at Wrexham	25.2.1882
	Mel Charles (Cardiff C) 4 goals v Ireland, at Cardiff	11.4.1962
	Ian Edwards (Chester) 4 goals v Malta, at Wrexham	25.10.1978

* There are conflicting reports which make it uncertain whether Bloomer scored four or five goals in this game.

MOST GOALS IN AN INTERNATIONAL CAREER

		Goals	Games
England	Bobby Charlton (Manchester U)	49	106
Scotland	Denis Law (Huddersfield T, Manchester C, Torino, Manchester U)	30	55
	Kenny Dalglish (Celtic, Liverpool)	30	102
Ireland	Colin Clarke (Bournemouth, Southampton, QPR, Portsmouth	13	38
Wales	Ian Rush (Liverpool, Juventus)	28	71
	Ivor Allchurch (Swansea T, Newcastle U, Cardiff C)	23	68
Republic of Ireland	Frank Stapleton (Arsenal, Manchester U, Ajax, Derby Co, Le Havre, Blackburn R)	20	70

HIGHEST SCORES

World Cup Match	New Zealand	13	Fiji	0	1981
European Championship	Spain	12	Malta	1	1983
Olympic Games	Denmark	17	France	1	1908
	Germany	16	USSR	0	1912
International Match	Germany	13	Finland	0	1940
	Spain	13	Bulgaria	0	1933
European Cup	Feyenoord	12	K R Reykjavik	2	1969
European Cup-Winners' Cup	Sporting Lisbon	16	Apoel Nicosia	1	1963
Fairs & UEFA Cups	Ajax	14	Red Boys	0	1984

GOALSCORING RECORDS

World Cup Final	Geoff Hurst (England) 3 goals v West Germany	1966
World Cup Final tournament	Just Fontaine (France) 13 goals	1958
Major European Cup game	Lothar Emmerich (Borussia Dortmund) v Floriana in Cup-Winners' Cup – 6 goals	1965
Career	Arthur Friedenreich (Brazil) 1329 goals	1910–30
	Pelé (Brazil) 1281 goals	*1956–78
	Franz 'Bimbo' Binder (Austria, Germany) 1006 goals	1930–50

**Pelé subsequently scored two goals in Testimonial matches making his total 1283.*

MOST CAPPED INTERNATIONALS IN BRITISH ISLES

England	Peter Shilton	125 appearances	1970–90
Northern Ireland	Pat Jennings	119 appearances	1964–86
Scotland	Kenny Dalglish	102 appearances	1971–86
Wales	Neville Southall	81 appearances	1982–95
Republic of Ireland	Paddy Bonner	78 appearances	1981–95

TRANSFERS

Record British moves (UK only)

£8,500,000 Stan Collymore, Nottingham F to Liverpool, June 1995
£6,250,000 Andy Cole, Newcastle U to Manchester U, January 1995
£6,000,000 Les Ferdinand, QPR to Newcastle U, June 1995
£5,000,000 Chris Sutton, Norwich to Blackburn R, July 1994
£5,000,000 Andrei Kanchelskis, Manchester U to Everton, July 1995
£4,500,000 Chris Armstrong, Crystal Palace to Tottenham H, June 1995
£4,000,000 Duncan Ferguson, Dundee U to Rangers, July 1993
£4,000,000 Duncan Ferguson, Rangers to Everton, December 1994
£4,000,000 Warren Barton, Wimbledon to Newcastle U, June 1995
£3,750,000 Roy Keane, Nottingham F to Manchester U, July 1993

Other British moves

£7,000,000 Paul Ince, Manchester U to Internazionale, June 1995
£6,500,000 David Platt, Bari to Juventus, May 1992
£5,500,000 David Platt, Aston Villa to Bari, July 1991
£5,500,000 Paul Gascoigne, Tottenham H to Lazio, May 1992
£5,200,000 David Platt, Juventus to Sampdoria, July 1993
£5,000,000 Trevor Steven, Rangers to Marseille, August 1991
£4,750,000 David Platt, Sampdoria to Arsenal, July 1995
£4,500,000 Chris Waddle, Tottenham H to Marseille, July 1989
£4,300,000 Paul Gascoigne, Lazio to Rangers, July 1995
£3,200,000 Ian Rush, Liverpool to Juventus, June 1987
£2,800,000 Ian Rush, Juventus to Liverpool, August 1988
£2,750,000 Gary Lineker, Everton to Barcelona, June 1986

World records

£13,000,000 Gianluigi Lentini, Torino to AC Milan, June 1992
£12,000,000 Gianluca Vialli, Sampdoria to Juventus, June 1992
£10,000,000 Jean-Pierre Papin, Marseille to AC Milan, June 1992

INTERCONTINENTAL CUP

Group A
Saudi Arabia 0, Mexico 2
Saudi Arabia 0, Denmark 2
Denmark 1, Mexico 1

Group B
Japan 0, Nigeria 3
Argentina 5, Japan 1
Argentina 0, Nigeria 0

Third Place
Mexico 1, Nigeria 1
(*Mexico won 5-4 on penalties*)

Final
Denmark 2, Argentina 0

FA SCHOOLS AND YOUTH GAMES 1994–95

ENGLAND UNDER-16

26 Feb

Greece 0

England 4 *(Morris, Wright, Ormerod, Wicks)*

England: Heritage (Sheffield U); Dickman (Manchester U), Crowe (Arsenal), Curtis (Manchester U), Wicks (Arsenal), Gower (Tottenham H), O'Connor (Wimbledon) [Brightwell (Manchester U)], Staton (Blackburn R) [Ormerod (Middlesbrough)], Branch (Everton), Morris (Chelsea), Wright (Leeds U).

28 Feb

Romania 2

England 3 *(Branch 3)*

England: Heritage (Sheffield U); Dickman (Manchester U), Crowe (Arsenal), Curtis (Manchester U), Wicks (Arsenal), Gower (Tottenham H), Brightwell (Manchester U) [O'Connor (Wimbledon)], Staton (Blackburn R), Branch (Everton), Morris (Chelsea), Wright (Leeds U) [Clement (Chelsea)].

17 Sept

Holland 1

England 1 *(Wilson)*

England: Weaver (Leyton Orient) [Heritage (Sheffield U)]; Dickman (Manchester U), Clement (Chelsea), Curtis (Manchester U) [Wicks (Arsenal)], Perry (QPR), Morris (Chelsea), Brightwell (Manchester U), Gower (Tottenham H), Bunn (Tottenham H) [Smith (Crewe Alex)], Wilson (Manchester U) [Ormerod (Middlesbrough)], Platts (Sheffield W) [Wright (Leeds U)].

19 Nov

Turkey 3

England 2 *(Morris 2 (1 pen))*

England: Heritage (Sheffield U); [Weaver (Leyton Orient)]; Dickman (Manchester U), Clement (Chelsea) [Wicks (Manchester U)], Curtis (Manchester U), Perry (QPR), Gower (Tottenham H), Brightwell (Manchester U) [Ormerod (Middlesbrough)], Morris (Chelsea), Branch (Everton), Platts (Sheffield W) [Wilson (Manchester U)], Wright (Leeds U) [Smith (Crewe Alex)].

21 Jan

Portugal 0

England 0

England: Heritage (Sheffield U); Dickman (Manchester U), Crowe (Arsenal), Curtis (Manchester U), Wicks (Manchester U), Gower (Tottenham H), O'Connor (Wimbledon) [Brightwell (Manchester U)], Morris (Chelsea), Branch (Everton) [Burgess (Aston Villa)], Staton (Blackburn R) [Ormerod (Middlesbrough)], Wright (Leeds U) [Platts (Middlesbrough)].

24 Apr

England 1 *(Branch)*

Scotland 1

England: Heritage (Sheffield U); Dickman (Manchester U), Crowe (Arsenal) [Clement (Chelsea)], Curtis (Manchester U), Wicks (Manchester U), Morris (Chelsea), Brightwell (Manchester U), Gower (Tottenham H) [Ormerod (Middlesbrough)], Branch (Everton), Staton (Blackburn R), Wright (Leeds U).

26 Apr

England 2 *(Wicks, Curtis)*

Slovakia 1

England: O'Toole (Everton); Dickman (Manchester U), Crowe (Arsenal), Curtis (Manchester U), Wicks (Manchester U) [Clement (Chelsea)], Morris (Chelsea), Ormerod (Middlesbrough), Bunn (Tottenham H), Branch (Everton), Staton (Blackburn R), Wright (Leeds U).

28 Apr

England 3 *(Morris, Clement, Wright)*

Portugal 1

England: O'Toole (Everton); Dickman (Manchester U), Crowe (Arsenal), Curtis (Manchester U), Clement (Chelsea), Morris (Chelsea), Ormerod (Middlesbrough) [Wright (Leeds U)], Gower (Tottenham H), Branch (Everton), Staton (Blackburn R), Bunn (Tottenham H) [Smith (Crewe Alex)].

1 May

England 0

France 1

England: Heritage (Sheffield U); Dickman (Manchester U), Crowe (Arsenal), Curtis (Manchester U), Clement (Chelsea), Morris (Chelsea), Ormerod (Middlesbrough) [Brightwell (Manchester U)], Gower (Tottenham H), Branch (Everton), Staton (Blackburn R), Wright (Leeds U) [Bunn (Tottenham H)].

23 May

England 2 *(Branch, Clement)*

Oman 3

England: O'Toole (Everton) [Heritage (Sheffield U)]; Culshaw (Liverpool), Clement (Chelsea), Curtis (Manchester U), Gower (Tottenham H), Morris (Chelsea), Brightwell (Manchester U), Marshall (Everton) [Smith (Crewe Alex)], Branch (Everton), Wilson (Manchester U), Wright (Leeds U) [Johnson (Crewe Alex)].

26 May

England 1 *(Wright)*

Oman 1

England: Heritage (Sheffield U) [O'Toole (Everton)]; Brightwell (Manchester U), Clement (Chelsea), Curtis (Manchester U), Culshaw (Liverpool) [Brown (Manchester U)], Morris (Chelsea), Gower (Tottenham H), Marshall (Everton) [Haslam (Sheffield W)], Branch (Everton), Wilson (Manchester U) [Wright (Leeds U)], Smith (Crewe Alex) [Owen (Liverpool)].

ENGLAND UNDER-18

22 Feb

England 5 *(Bowyer, Moore 3, Davies)*

Denmark 6

England: Cutler (WBA); Allen (Everton), Aljofrey (Bolton W) [Millett (Wigan Ath)], Ashbee (Derby Co) [Hendrie (Aston Villa)], Mills (Norwich C), O'Connor (Everton), Thompson (Liverpool), Bowyer (Charlton Ath), Cooke (Manchester U), Davies (Chesterfield [Beresford (Oldham Ath)], Moore (Tranmere R).

24 July

Norway 3

England 3 *(Cooke 2, Murphy)*

England: Cutler (WBA); Neville (Manchester U), Power (QPR), Howell (Arsenal) [Murphy (Crewe Alex)], O'Connor (Everton), Mills (Norwich C), Bowyer (Charlton Ath), Beresford (Oldham Ath) [Spencer (Tottenham H)], Davies (Chesterfield), Hughes (Arsenal), Cooke (Manchester U).

26 July

Norway 2

England 3 *(Hughes, Davies, Bowyer)*

England: Tyler (Peterborough U); Neville (Manchester U), Power (QPR) [Mills (Norwich C)], Bowyer (Charlton Ath), O'Connor (Everton), Allen (Everton), Murphy (Crewe Alex) [Howell (Arsenal)], Spencer (Tottenham H), Davies (Chesterfield) [Cooke (Manchester U)], Hughes (Arsenal), Walley (Nottingham F).

6 Sept

England 2 *(Murphy 2)*

France 3

England: Cutler (WBA); Neville (Manchester U), Taylor (Arsenal) [Power (QPR)], Thompson (Liverpool) [Beresford (Oldham Ath)], Plummer (QPR), Allen (Everton) [O'Connor (Everton)], Bowyer (Charlton Ath), Hughes (Arsenal), Murphy (Crewe Alex), Davies (Chesterfield) [Furnell (Peterborough U)], Cooke (Manchester U).

13 Nov

England 3 *(Murphy 2, Beresford)*

Slovenia 0

England: Cutler (WBA); Murray (Carlisle U) [Allen (Everton)], Taylor (Arsenal), Thompson (Liverpool), Hodges (Wimbledon), O'Connor (Everton), Beresford (Oldham Ath) [Hendrie (Aston Villa)], Bowyer (Charlton Ath), Davies (Chesterfield), Murphy (Crewe Alex), Cooke (Manchester U).

17 Nov

England 0

Latvia 0

England: Cutler (WBA); Allen (Everton), Taylor (Arsenal), Thompson (Liverpool), Hodges (Wimbledon), O'Connor (Everton), Cooke (Manchester U), Bowyer (Charlton Ath), Davies (Chesterfield) [Woodsford (Luton T)], Murphy (Crewe Alex), Hendrie (Aston Villa) [Hughes (Arsenal)].

29 Mar

Hungary 0

England 1 *(Moore)*

England: Davis (Luton T); Neville (Manchester U), Stuart (Charlton Ath), O'Connor (Everton), Westwood (Manchester U), Beresford (Oldham Ath) [Ducros (Coventry C)], Murphy (Crewe Alex), Clemence (Tottenham H), Cooke (Manchester U), Davies (Chesterfield), Moore (Tranmere R).

25 Apr

England 0

Hungary 2 *(aet)*

England: Davis (Luton T); Neville (Manchester U), Westwood (Manchester U), O'Connor (Everton), Stuart (Charlton Ath) [Broomes (Blackburn R)], Piper (Wimbledon), Beresford (Oldham Ath) [Ducros (Coventry C)], Clemence (Tottenham H), Moore (Tranmere R), Murphy (Crewe Alex), Cooke (Manchester U).

FA WOMEN'S PREMIER LEAGUE

National Division

	P	W	D	L	F	A	Pts
Arsenal	18	17	1	0	60	8	52
Liverpool	18	12	3	3	58	17	39
Doncaster Belles	18	12	2	4	56	24	38
Croydon	18	9	2	7	42	24	29
Wembley	18	8	3	7	34	17	27
Leasowe Pacific	18	5	3	10	36	47	18
Ilkeston Town Rangers	18	4	3	11	20	49	15
Millwall Lionesses	18	4	3	11	25	60	15
Wolverhampton Wanderers	18	4	1	13	23	66	13
Red Star Southampton	18	3	3	12	23	65	12

Northern Division

	P	W	D	L	F	A	Pts
Villa Aztecs	18	11	4	3	59	22	37
Cowgate Kestrels	18	11	3	4	63	30	36
St Helens/Garswood	18	11	3	4	44	26	36
Sheffield Wednesday	18	9	4	5	38	27	31
Ipswich Town	18	8	4	6	33	29	28
Bronte	18	8	3	7	42	28	27
Langford	18	8	0	10	30	40	24
Kidderminster Harriers	18	4	2	12	24	57	14
Nottingham Argyle	18	3	2	13	22	66	11
Solihull Borough	18	4	1	13	22	52	10*

*3 points deducted

Southern Division

	P	W	D	L	F	A	Pts
Maidstone Tigresses	14	10	2	2	34	10	32
Berkhamsted & Hemel	14	8	4	2	28	13	28
Oxford United	14	7	3	4	28	28	24
Wimbledon	14	6	2	6	28	20	20
Brighton & Hove Albion	14	6	1	7	20	30	19
Town & Country	14	5	3	6	22	25	18
Brentford	14	3	4	7	29	41	13
Horsham	14	0	3	11	16	38	3

FA WOMEN'S CHALLENGE CUP 1994–95

First Round

Blackburn Rovers v Brighouse	3-0
Middlesbrough v Wakefield	3-0
Huddersfield Town v Newcastle	12-0
Wigginton Grasshoppers v Oakland Rangers	2-3
Grimsby withdrew v Bradford City w.o.	
City Roses v Barnsley	2-5
Preston Rangers v Kilnhurst	6-1
South Lakes v South Shields	0-6
Sheffield Hallam United v Vernon-Carus	5-0
Amble Town v Cleveland	0-1
Manchester Belle Vue v Manchester City	4-1
Bolton v Manchester United	1-4
Rochdale v Wigan	1-7
Stockport v Tranmere Rovers	1-5
Liverpool Feds v Warrington Town	2-5
Stockport County v Colls	7-0
Oldham Athletic v Port Vale	7-2
Bangor City Girls v Leek Town	1-3
Radcliffe Borough v Chester City	7-0
Haslingden v Wrexham	5-1
Leicester City v Birmingham City	3-4
Derby City v Chesterfield	4-5
Derby County v Rugby	3-1
Pye v Calverton MW	0-2
Nettleham v Sparta Nottingham	5-0
Rainworth Miners Welfare v Notts County	0-2
Peterborough Diamonds v Highfield Rangers	0-11
Milton Keynes Athletic v Leyton Orient	0-7
Enfield v St Germaine	3-3, 3-2
Charlton v Milton Keynes United	11-1
Dunstable v Mill Hill United	4-6
Queens Park Rangers v Redbridge Wanderers	8-1
Fulham v Leighton Linsdale	7-1
Clapton Orient v Slough Town	3-4
Barnet v Bedford Bells	1-5
Harlow Town v Clacton	3-1
Watford v Wycombe Wanderers	6-0
Collier Row v Colchester	5-1
Farnborough v Teynham Gunners	9-1
Havant v St Georges	2-6
Abbey Rangers v Binfield	0-7
Pagham v Hassocks	4-3
Carterton Town v Crowborough Athletic	0-2

Gosport Borough v Sutton Athletic	7-2
Comets v Eastleigh	0-9
Sittingbourne v Reading Royals	3-3, 3-3
(Reading Royals won 4-2 on penalties)	
Isle of Wight v Surbiton Town	0-6
Chailey Mavericks w.o. v Chislehurst United amalgamated with Charlton	
Edenbridge Town v Newbury	0-7
Whitehawk v Palace Eagles	5-0
Worthing v Portsmouth	0-4
Gillingham Girls v Lambeth	1-6
Plymouth Pilgrims v Cheltenham YMCA	4-2
Swindon Town Spitfires v Bournemouth	3-1
Yate Town v Torquay United	0-6
Worcester City v Exeter Rangers	8-2
Clevedon Town v Gloucester Greyhounds	8-1
Dorchester withdrew v Truro City w.o.	
Brislington v Southampton	1-6
Frome v Sturminster Newton	10-1
Bristol Rovers withdrew v Bristol City w.o.	
Swindon Town v Weymouth	8-0
Cardiff Institute v Tongwynlais	1-3

Second Round

Huddersfield Town v Barnsley	16-0
Haslingden v Bronte	0-5
Wigan v Bradford City	2-0
Preston Rangers v Middlesbrough	5-2
Oaklands Rangers v Radcliffe Borough	1-7
Oldham Athletic v Blackburn Rovers	5-1
South Shields v Manchester Belle Vue	0-11
Sheffield Hallam United v Cowgate Kestrels	2-6
Newsham v St Helens/Garswood	3-4
Tranmere Rovers v Cleveland	8-0
Warrington Town v Manchester United	3-4
Wilford withdrew v Birmingham City w.o.	
Stockport County v Calverton MW	1-2
Leek Town v Nottingham Argyle	1-4
Bedford Bells v Sheffield Wednesday	0-2
Highfield Rangers v Solihull Borough	2-3
Chesterfield v Villa Aztecs	2-5
Nettleham v Kidderminster Harriers	1-6
Notts County v Derby County	7-0
Brighton & Hove Albion v Reading	14-0
St Georges v Surbiton Town	1-2
Colchester Royals v Pagham	3-1
Whitehawk v Queens Park Rangers	7-0
Harlow Town v Watford	2-0
Berkhamsted & Hemel v Epsom & Ewell	9-1
Reading Royals v Langford	2-4
Leyton Orient v Slough Town	25-0
Town & Country v Chailey Mavericks	22-0
Lambeth v Binfield	1-0
Collier Row v Enfield	0-2
Crowborough Athletic v Wimbledon	0-7
Mill Hill United v Horsham	0-1
Fulham v Ipswich Town	2-5
Maidstone Tigresses v Charlton	2-1
Brentford v Farnborough	6-3
Bristol disbanded v Tongwynlais w.o.	
Clevedon Town v Oxford United	0-9
Inter Cardiff v Plymouth Pilgrims	2-4
Swindon Town v Southampton	2-1
Portsmouth v Newbury	2-3
Worcester City v Frome	4-3
Gosport Borough v Bristol City	1-8
Swindon Town Spitfires v Truro City	3-4
Torquay United v Eastleigh	4-1

Third Round

Villa Aztecs v Huddersfield Town	4-4, 0-4
(Replay ordered; Huddersfield Town fielded an ineligible player), 0-2	
Preston Rangers v Cowgate Kestrels	1-4
Notts County v Nottingham Argyle	4-2
Oldham Athletic v Birmingham City	2-1
Wigan v Manchester United	4-1
Tranmere Rovers v Sheffield Wednesday	5-5, 5-2
St Helens/Garswood v Bronte	4-2
Radcliffe Borough v Calverton MW	3-6
Manchester Belle Vue v Solihull Borough	3-1
Berkhamsted & Hemel v Wimbledon	3-4
Maidstone Tigresses v Langford	2-0
Town & Country v Brentford	3-4
Brighton & Hove Albion v Whitehawk	5-1
Leyton Orient v Lambeth	6-1
Enfield v Colchester Royals	6-1
Harlow Town v Surbiton Town	0-1
Ipswich Town v Horsham	0-0, 5-0
Plymouth Pilgrims v Tongwynlais	3-1
Oxford United v Torquay United	8-1
Bristol City v Kidderminster Harriers	7-1
Truro City v Worcester City	2-2, 5-2
Swindon Town v Newbury	3-4

Fourth Round

Brentford v Red Star Southampton	2-2, 1-2
Huddersfield Town v Ipswich Town	7-3
Tranmere Rovers v Leasowe Pacific	1-3
Newbury v Notts County	1-2
St Helens/Garswood v Oxford United	2-1
Leyton Orient v Enfield	7-0
Wolverhampton Wanderers v Millwall Lionesses	0-2
Doncaster Belles v Truro City	6-0
Liverpool v Surbiton Town	8-0
Wimbledon v Cowgate Kestrels	2-0
Ilkeston Town Rangers v Brighton & Hove Albion	5-1
Oldham Athletic v Croydon	1-7
Manchester Belle Vue v Wigan	2-3
Bristol City v Plymouth Pilgrims	6-2
Arsenal v Maidstone Tigresses	3-0
Calverton MW v Wembley	0-12

Fifth Round

Arsenal v Leasowe Pacific	3-1
Liverpool v Notts County	5-0
Huddersfield Town v Ilkeston Town Rangers	3-1
Leyton Orient v Red Star Southampton	3-1
Bristol City v Millwall Lionesses	3-2
Wimbledon v Croydon	0-5
Wembley v Doncaster Belles	3-3, 1-2
Wigan v St Helens/Garswood	1-3

Sixth Round

Liverpool v Croydon	3-0
Leyton Orient v Arsenal	1-8
Bristol City v Huddersfield Town	4-3
Doncaster Belles v St Helens/Garswood	4-0

Semi-finals

Doncaster Belles v Arsenal	1-3
Bristol City v Liverpool	0-5

Final at Tranmere Rovers FC

Arsenal (1) 3 *(Lonergan 2, Spacey)*

Liverpool (2) 2 *(Burke 2)* 3000

Arsenal: Cope; Pealing, Slee, Wylie, Spry, Churchman (Ball), Williams, Spacey, Kurley (Few), Lonergan, Britton. *Scorers: Lonergan 2, Spacey.*
Liverpool: Davidson; Taylor, Ryde, Thomas (Griffiths), Oldham, Burke, Easton, Murray, Gallimore, Harper, Hewitt (McQuiggan). *Scorer:* Burke 2.
Referee: J. Winter.

2ND WOMEN'S WORLD CHAMPIONSHIP

Group A
Germany 1, Japan 0
Brazil 1, Sweden 0
Japan 2, Brazil 1
Sweden 3, Germany 2
Sweden 2, Japan 0
Germany 6, Brazil 1

	P	*W*	*D*	*L*	*F*	*A*	*Pts*
Germany	3	2	0	1	9	4	6
Sweden	3	2	0	1	5	3	6
Japan	3	1	0	2	2	4	3
Brazil	3	1	0	2	3	8	3

Group B
Norway 8, Nigeria 0
England 3, Canada 2
Nigeria 3, Canada 3
Norway 2, England 0
Norway 7, Canada 0
England 3, Nigeria 2

	P	*W*	*D*	*L*	*F*	*A*	*Pts*
Norway	3	3	0	0	17	0	9
England	3	2	0	1	6	6	6
Canada	3	0	1	2	5	12	1
Nigeria	3	0	1	2	5	14	1

Group C
USA 3, China 3
Denmark 5, Australia 0
USA 2, Denmark 0
China 4, Australia 2
USA 4, Australia 1
China 3, Denmark 1

	P	*W*	*D*	*L*	*F*	*A*	*Pts*
USA	3	2	1	0	9	4	7
China	3	2	1	0	10	6	7
Denmark	3	1	0	2	6	5	3
Australia	3	0	0	3	3	13	0

Quarter-finals
USA 4, Japan 0
Norway 3, Denmark 1
China 1, Sweden 1
(*aet; China won 4-3 on penalties*)
Germany 3, England 0

Semi-finals
Norway 1, USA 0
Germany 1, China 0

Third Place
USA 2, China 0

Final: Stockholm, 18 June 1995, 17,158
Norway (2) 2 (*Riise, Pettersen*)
Germany (0) 0
Norway: Nordby; Svensson, Andersen N, Espeseth, Myklebust, Riise, Haugen, Andersen A, Pettersen, Aarones, Medalen.
Germany: Goller; Bernhard, Austermuhl, Lohn, Mohr, Neid, Wiegmann, Voss, Pohlman (Wunderlich), Meinert (Smisek), Prinz.

EUROPEAN CUP

EUROPEAN CUP FINALS 1956–95

Year	Winners	Runners-up	Venue	Attendance	Referee
1956	Real Madrid 4	Reims 3	Paris	38,000	Ellis (E)
1957	Real Madrid 2	Fiorentina 0	Madrid	124,000	Horn (Ho)
1958	Real Madrid 3	AC Milan 2 *(aet)*	Brussels	67,000	Alsteen (Bel)
1959	Real Madrid 2	Reims 0	Stuttgart	80,000	Dutsch (WG)
1960	Real Madrid 7	Eintracht Frankfurt 3	Glasgow	135,000	Mowat (S)
1961	Benfica 3	Barcelona 2	Berne	28,000	Dienst (Sw)
1962	Benfica 5	Real Madrid 3	Amsterdam	65,000	Horn (Ho)
1963	AC Milan 2	Benfica 1	Wembley	45,000	Holland (E)
1964	Internazionale 3	Real Madrid 1	Vienna	74,000	Stoll (A)
1965	Internazionale 1	Benfica 0	Milan	80,000	Dienst (Sw)
1966	Real Madrid 2	Partizan Belgrade 1	Brussels	55,000	Kreitlein (WG)
1967	Celtic 2	Internazionale 1	Lisbon	56,000	Tschenscher (WG)
1968	Manchester U 4	Benfica 1 *(aet)*	Wembley	100,000	Lo Bello (I)
1969	AC Milan 4	Ajax 1	Madrid	50,000	Ortiz (Sp)
1970	Feyenoord 2	Celtic 1 *(aet)*	Milan	50,000	Lo Bello (I)
1971	Ajax 2	Panathinaikos 0	Wembley	90,000	Taylor (E)
1972	Ajax 2	Internazionale 0	Rotterdam	67,000	Helies (F)
1973	Ajax 1	Juventus 0	Belgrade	93,500	Guglovic (Y)
1974	Bayern Munich 1	Atletico Madrid 1	Brussels	65,000	Loraux (Bel)
Replay	Bayern Munich 4	Atletico Madrid 0	Brussels	65,000	Delcourt (Bel)
1975	Bayern Munich 2	Leeds U 0	Paris	50,000	Kitabdjian (F)
1976	Bayern Munich 1	St Etienne 0	Glasgow	54,864	Palotai (H)
1977	Liverpool 3	Moenchengladbach 1	Rome	57,000	Wurtz (F)
1978	Liverpool 1	FC Brugge 0	Wembley	92,000	Corver (Ho)
1979	Nottingham F 1	Malmo 0	Munich	57,500	Linemayr (A)
1980	Nottingham F 1	Hamburg 0	Madrid	50,000	Garrido (P)
1981	Liverpool 1	Real Madrid 0	Paris	48,360	Palotai (H)
1982	Aston Villa 1	Bayern Munich 0	Rotterdam	46,000	Konrath (F)
1983	Hamburg 1	Juventus 0	Athens	75,000	Rainea (R)
1984	Liverpool 1	Roma 1	Rome	69,693	Fredriksson (Se)
	(aet; Liverpool won 4–2 on penalties)				
1985	Juventus 1	Liverpool 0	Brussels	58,000	Daina (Sw)
1986	Steaua Bucharest 0	Barcelona 0	Seville	70,000	Vautrot (F)
	(aet; Steaua won 2–0 on penalties)				
1987	Porto 2	Bayern Munich 1	Vienna	59,000	Ponnet (Bel)
1988	PSV Eindhoven 0	Benfica 0	Stuttgart	70,000	Agnolin (I)
	(aet; PSV won 6–5 on penalties)				
1989	AC Milan 4	Steaua Bucharest 0	Barcelona	97,000	Tritschler (WG)
1990	AC Milan 1	Benfica 0	Vienna	57,500	Kohl (A)
1991	Red Star Belgrade 0	Marseille 0	Bari	56,000	Lanese (I)
	(aet; Red Star won 5–3 on penalties)				
1992	Barcelona 1	Sampdoria 0 *(aet)*	Wembley	70,827	Schmidhuber (G)
1993	Marseille* 1	AC Milan 0	Munich	64,400	Rothlisberger (Sw)
1994	AC Milan 4	Barcelona 0	Athens	70,000	Don (E)
1995	Ajax 1	AC Milan 0	Vienna	49,730	Craciunescu (Ro)

**Subsequently stripped of title.*

EUROPEAN CUP 1994–95

Preliminary Round, First Leg

AEK Athens (1) 2 *(Saravakos 44, 70)*, Rangers (0) 0 35,000

Avenir Beggen (0) 1 *(Zaritski 50)*, Galatasaray (2) 5 *(Turkyilmaz 30, Saffet 35, Hakan 69, Arif 76, 89)* 6200

Legia Warsaw (0) 0, Hajduk Split (1) 1 *(Rapajic 22)* 18,000

Maccabi Haifa (0) 1 *(Revivo 47 (pen))*, Salzburg (0) 2 *(Hutter 82, Mladenovic 88 (pen))* 10,000

Paris St Germain (1) 3 *(Ricardo 30, Weah 48, Roche 82)*, Vac (0) 0 25,000

Silkeborg (0) 0, Dynamo Kiev (0) 0 4298

Sparta Prague (0) 1 *(Budka 89)*, IFK Gothenburg (0) 0 9600 *(in Jablonec)*

Steaua (3) 4 *(Ilie 1, Stan 17 (pen), Parvu 26, Lacatus 51)*, Servette (0) 1 *(Neuville 72)* 15,000

Preliminary Round, Second Leg

Dynamo Kiev (2) 3 *(Skatchenko 21, Kovalets 28, Kossovski 90)*, Silkeborg (0) 1 *(Fernandez 74)* 24,000

Galatasaray (0) 4 *(Hakan Sukur 52, 70, 83 (pen), Saffet 63)*, Avenir Beggen (0) 0 20,000

IFK Gothenburg (1) 2 *(Blomqvist 22, Lindqvist 63)*, Sparta Prague (0) 0 8000

Hajduk Split (0) 4 *(Asanovic 50, Vulic 64, Rapajic 80, Erceg 89)*, Legia Warsaw (0) 0 7500

Rangers (0) 0, AEK Athens (0) 1 *(Savevski 43)* 44,789

Salzburg (0) 3 *(Mladenovic 49, 53, Jurcevic 78)* Maccabi Haifa (0) 1 *(Hazan 89)* 9000

Servette (1) 1 *(Schepull 15)*, Steaua (0) 1 *(Parvu 62)* 7250

Vac (1) 1 *(Fule 31)*, Paris St Germain (1) 2 *(Mboma 19, 66)* 1800

CHAMPIONS LEAGUE

Group A

Manchester U (1) 4 *(Giggs 33, 65, Kanchelskis 48, Sharpe 70)*, IFK Gothenburg (1) 2 *(Petterson 27, Rehn 50)* 33,625

Barcelona (1) 2 *(Koeman 30, Amor 50)*, Galatasaray (1) 1 *(Turkyilmaz 14)* 76,000

IFK Gothenburg (0) 2 *(Erlingmark 74, Blomqvist 89)*, Barcelona (1) 1 *(Stoichkov 10)* 32,215

Galatasaray (0) 0, Manchester U (0) 0 35,000

Manchester U (1) 2 *(Hughes 18, Sharpe 80)*, Barcelona (1) 2 *(Romario 34, Bakero 49)* 40,064

IFK Gothenburg (0) 1 *(Erlingmark 76)*, Galatasaray (0) 0 26,412

Barcelona (2) 4 *(Pallister 9 (og), Romario 45, Stoichkov 52, Ferrer 88)*, Manchester U (0) 0 114,432

Galatasaray (0) 0, IFK Gothenburg (0) 1 *(Nilsson 86)* 30,000

IFK Gothenburg (1) 3 *(Blomqvist 10, Erlingmark 64, Kamark 71 (pen))*, Manchester U (0) 1 *(Hughes 64)* 36,350

Galatasaray (0) 2 *(Hakan 72 (pen), Arif 88)*, Barcelona (1) 1 *(Romario 15)* 30,000

Manchester U (2) 4 *(Davies 2, Beckham 37, Keane 48, Bulent (og))*, Galatasaray (0) 0 39,220

Barcelona (0) 1 *(Bakero 81)*, IFK Gothenburg (0) 1 *(Rehn 90)* 75,000

Final table

	P	*W*	*D*	*L*	*F*	*A*	*Pts*
IFK Gothenburg	6	4	1	1	10	7	9
Barcelona	6	2	2	2	11	8	6
Manchester United	6	2	2	2	11	11	6
Galatasaray	6	1	1	4	3	9	3

Group B

Dynamo Kiev (0) 3 *(Leonenko 48, 76, Rebrov 86)*, Spartak Moscow (2) 2 *(Pisarev 12, Tichonov 39)* 93,000

Paris St Germain (1) 2 *(Weah 41, Bravo 83)*, Bayern Munich (0) 0 36,924

Bayern Munich (1) 1 *(Scholl 9)*, Dynamo Kiev (0) 0 26,000

Spartak Moscow (1) 1 *(Rachimov 38)*, Paris St Germain (0) 2 *(Le Guen 56, Valdo 60)* 30,000

Spartak Moscow (0) 1 *(Pisarev 78)*, Bayern Munich (0) 1 *(Babbel 90)* 25,000

Dynamo Kiev (1) 1 *(Leonenko 32 (pen))*, Paris St Germain (1) 2 *(Guerin 26, Weah 76)* 60,000

Bayern Munich (2) 2 *(Nerlinger 29, Kuffour 36)*, Spartak Moscow (2) 2 *(Tikhonov 4, Alenichev 32)* 25,000

Paris St Germain (0) 1 *(Weah 68)*, Dynamo Kiev (0) 0 33,741

Spartak Moscow (0) 1 *(Mukhamadiyev 52)*, Dynamo Kiev (0) 0 40,000

Bayern Munich (0) 0, Paris St Germain (0) 1 *(Weah 81)* 35,000

Dynamo Kiev (1) 1 *(Shevchenko 35)*, Bayern Munich (1) 4 *(Nerlinger 45, Papin 56, 82, Scholl 87)* 60,000

Paris St Germain (2) 4 *(Weah 28, 52, Ginola 42, Rai 59)*, Spartak Moscow (0) 1 *(Rodionov 66)* 31,461

Final table

	P	*W*	*D*	*L*	*F*	*A*	*Pts*
Paris St Germain	6	6	0	0	12	3	12
Bayern Munich	6	2	2	2	8	7	6
Spartak Moscow	6	1	2	3	8	12	4
Dynamo Kiev	6	1	0	5	5	11	2

Group C

Hajduk Split (0) 0, Benfica (0) 0 38,000

Anderlecht (0) 0, Steaua (0) 0 16,000

Steaua (0) 0, Hajduk Split (0) 1 *(Asanovic 88)* 24,000

Benfica (2) 3 *(Caniggia 27, 40, Tavares 72)*, Anderlecht (0) 1 *(Madeira 85 (og))* 32,000

Benfica (1) 2 *(Caniggia 44 (pen), Joao Pinto II 60)*, Steaua (0) 1 *(Militaru 89)* 18,100

Hajduk Split (1) 2 *(Pralija 34, Butorovic 86)*, Anderlecht (0) 1 *(Weber 88)* 38,000

Steaua (1) 1 *(Panduru 27)*, Benfica (0) 1 *(Helder 64)* 22,000

Anderlecht (0) 0, Hajduk Split (0) 0 21,000

Benfica (1) 2 *(Isaias 33, Joao Pinto 76)*, Hajduk Split (0) 1 *(Andrijasevic 72)* 45,000

Steaua (0) 1 *(Dobos 52)*, Anderlecht (1) 1 *(Bosman 42)* 12,000

Hajduk Split (0) 1 *(Andrijasevic 48)*, Steaua (3) 4 *(Ille 11, 32, Lacatus 21, Galca 90)* 15,000

Anderlecht (0) 1 *(Rutjes 49)*, Benfica (0) 1 *(Edilson 83)* 22,000

Final table

	P	*W*	*D*	*L*	*F*	*A*	*Pts*
Benfica	6	3	3	0	9	5	9
Hajduk Split	6	2	2	2	5	7	6
Steaua	6	1	3	2	7	6	5
Anderlecht	6	0	4	2	4	7	4

Group D

Salzburg (0) 0, AEK Athens (0) 0 *in Vienna* 22,500

Ajax (0) 2 *(Ronald de Boer 51, Litmanen 65)*, AC Milan (0) 0 42,000

AC Milan (1) 3 *(Stroppa 39, Simone 59, 63)*, Salzburg (0) 0 22,475
AEK Athens (1) 1 *(Savevski 30)*, Ajax (1) 2 *(Litmanen 29, Kluivert 63)* 30,000
AEK Athens (0) 0, AC Milan (0) 0 30,000
Salzburg (0) 0, Ajax (0) 0 18,200
AC Milan (0) 2 *(Panucci 68, 74)*, AEK Athens (1) 1 *(Savevski 16)* 17,264
Ajax (0) 1 *(Litmanen 85)*, Salzburg (0) 1 *(Kocljan 62)* 40,000
AEK Athens (1) 1 *(Vlachos 29)*, Salzburg (2) 3 *(Pfeifenberger 6, 8, Hasenhuttl 76)* 20,000
AC Milan (0) 0, Ajax (1) 2 *(Litmanen 2, Baresi 65 (og))* *in Trieste* 29,764
Salzburg (0) 0, AC Milan (1) 1 *(Massaro 29)* 47,500
Ajax (1) 2 *(Oulida 7, 78)*, AEK Athens (0) 0 42,000

Final table

	P	*W*	*D*	*L*	*F*	*A*	*Pts*
Ajax	6	4	2	0	9	2	10
AC Milan	6	3	1	2	6	5	5
Salzburg	6	1	3	2	4	6	5
AEK Athens	6	0	2	4	3	9	2

AC Milan deducted 2 pts for crowd trouble.

Quarter-finals, first leg

Bayern Munich (0) 0, IFK Gothenburg (0) 0 45,000
Hajduk Split (0) 0, Ajax (0) 0 35,000
AC Milan (0) 2 *(Simone 63, 75)*, Benfica (0) 0 48,858
Barcelona (0) 1 *(Korneev 48)*, Paris St Germain (0) 1 *(Weah 54)* 114,700

Quarter-finals, second leg

Ajax (2) 3 *(Kanu 39, Frank De Boer 43, 68)*, Hajduk Split (0) 0 42,000
Benfica (0) 0, AC Milan (0) 0 70,000
IFK Gothenburg (0) 2 *(Lilienberg 75, Martinsson 90)*, Bayern Munich (0) 2 *(Zickler 63, Nerlinger 71)* 36,525
Paris St Germain (0) 2 *(Rai 73, Guerin 83)*, Barcelona (0) 1 *(Bakero 49)* 45,700

Semi-finals, first leg

Bayern Munich (0) 0, Ajax (0) 0 60,000
Paris St Germain (0) 0, AC Milan (0) 1 *(Boban 90)* 45,000

Semi-finals, second leg

Ajax (3) 5 *(Litmanen 10, 46, George 40, Ronald de Boer 43, Overmars 88)*, Bayern Munich (1) 2 *(Witeczek 36, Scholl 76)* 41,000
AC Milan (1) 2 *(Savicevic 21, 68)*, Paris St Germain (0) 0 79,855

Final: Ajax (0) 1, AC Milan (0) 0

(in Vienna, 24 May 1995, 49,730)

Ajax: Van der Sar; Reiziger, Blind, Frank de Boer, Rijkaard, Seedorf (Kanu 53), Davids, Litmanen (Kluivert 68), George, Ronald de Boer, Overmars.

Scorer: Kluivert 85.

AC Milan: Rossi; Panucci, Baresi, Costacurta, Maldini, Desailly, Donadoni, Albertini, Boban (Lentini 85), Massaro (Eranio 90), Simone.

Referee: Craciunescu (Romania).

Patrick Kluivert (No. 15) scores the only goal of the European Cup Final for Ajax against AC Milan. (Colorsport)

EUROPEAN CUP 1994–95 – BRITISH AND IRISH

Manchester United's Steve Bruce is challenged by Galatasaray No. 2 Ergun at Old Trafford. (Action Images)

Preliminary Round, First Leg

10 AUG

AEK Athens (1) 2 *(Saravakos 2)*

Rangers (0) 0 35,000

AEK Athens: Atmatsidis; Vlachos, Manolas, Papadopoulos, Kostis, Sabanadzovic, Savevski, Kassapis, Tsartas, Saravakos, Ketspajia (Dimitriades) (Agorogiannis).
Rangers: Goram; Pressley, Gough, Stevens, Murray, Ferguson, Durie (Durrant), McCall, Robertson, Hateley, Laudrup.

Preliminary Round, Second Leg

24 AUG

Rangers (0) 0

AEK Athens (1) 1 *(Savevski)* 44,789

Rangers: Goram; Boli, Gough, McPherson, Robertson, Durie (Durrant), Ferguson I, McCall, Laudrup, Hateley, Ferguson D.
AEK Athens: Atmatsidis; Agorogiannis, Vlachos, Manolas, Papadopoulos, Kassapis, Saravakos, Sabanadzovic, Savevski (Stamatis), Kostis, Tsartas (Kopitsis).

Group A

14 SEPT

Manchester U (1) 4 *(Giggs 2, Kanchelskis, Sharpe)*

IFK Gothenburg (1) 2 *(Pettersson, Rehn)* 33,625

Manchester U: Schmeichel; May, Irwin, Bruce, Sharpe, Pallister, Kanchelskis, Ince, Butt, Hughes, Giggs.
IFK Gothenburg: Ravelli; Kaamark, Johansson, Olsson (Rehn), Bjorklund, Nilsson, Martinsson, Lindqvist, Erlingmark, Blomqvist, Pettersson.

28 SEPT

Galatasaray (0) 0

Manchester U (0) 0 35,000

Galatasaray: Stauce; Mert, Bulent, Sedat, Yusuf, Tugay (Arif), Mapeza, Hamza, Turkyilmaz, Saffet (Osman), Hakan.
Manchester U: Schmeichel; May, Bruce, Pallister, Sharpe, Kanchelskis, Butt, Keane, Ince, Giggs (Parker), Hughes.

19 OCT

Manchester U (1) 2 *(Hughes, Sharpe)*

Barcelona (1) 2 *(Romario, Bakero)* 40,064

Manchester U: Schmeichel; May (Bruce), Irwin, Parker, Sharpe, Pallister, Kanchelskis, Ince, Keane, Hughes, Butt (Scholes).
Barcelona: Busquets; Abelardo, Koeman, Sergi, Guardiola, Nadal, Luis (Uesebio), Bakero, Beguristain (Jordi), Stoichkov, Romario.

2 NOV

Barcelona (2) 4 *(Pallister (og), Romario, Stoichkov, Ferrer)*

Manchester U (0) 0 114,432

Barcelona: Busquets; Abelardo, Koeman, Sergi, Ferrer, Amor, Guardiola, Bakero (Sanchez Jara), Stoichkov, Romario, Jordi (Iglesias).
Manchester U: Walsh; Parker, Irwin, Bruce, Kanchelskis, Pallister, Butt, Ince, Keane, Hughes, Giggs (Scholes).

23 NOV

IFK Gothenburg (1) 3 *(Blomqvist, Erlingmark, Kamark (pen))*

Manchester U (0) 1 *(Hughes)* 36,350

IFK Gothenburg: Ravelli; Kamark, Johansson, Bjorklund, Nilsson, Martinsson (Wahlstedt), Rehn, Lindqvist, Blomqvist, Erlingmark, Pettersson (Andersson).
Manchester U: Walsh; May (Neville), Irwin, Bruce, Kanchelskis, Pallister, Cantona, Ince, McClair, Hughes, Davies (Butt).

7 DEC

Manchester U (2) 4 *(Davies, Beckham, Keane, Bulent (og))*

Galatasaray (0) 0 39,220

Manchester U: Walsh; Neville, Irwin, Bruce, Keane, Pallister, Cantona, Beckham, McClair, Butt, Davies.
Galatasaray: Stauce; Sedat, Bulent, Mert, Suat, Tugay (Yusuf), Hamza (Ugar), Ergun, Arif, Turkyilmaz, Hakan.

EUROPEAN CUP-WINNERS' CUP

EUROPEAN CUP-WINNERS' CUP FINALS 1961–95

Year	Winners	Runners-up	Venue	Attendance	Referee
1961	Fiorentina 2	Rangers 0 *(1st Leg)*	Glasgow	80,000	Steiner (A)
	Fiorentina 2	Rangers 1 *(2nd Leg)*	Florence	50,000	Hernadi (H)
1962	Atletico Madrid 1	Fiorentina 1	Glasgow	27,389	Wharton (S)
Replay	Atletico Madrid 3	Fiorentina 0	Stuttgart	45,000	Tschenscher (WG)
1963	Tottenham Hotspur 5	Atletico Madrid 1	Rotterdam	25,000	Van Leuwen (Ho)
1964	Sporting Lisbon 3	MTK Budapest 3 *(aet)*	Brussels	9000	Van Nuffel (Bel)
Replay	Sporting Lisbon 1	MTK Budapest 0	Antwerp	18,000	Versyp (Bel)
1965	West Ham U 2	Munich 1860 0	Wembley	100,000	Szolt (H)
1966	Borussia Dortmund 2	Liverpool 1 *(aet)*	Glasgow	41,657	Schwinte (F)
1967	Bayern Munich 1	Rangers 0 *(aet)*	Nuremberg	69,480	Lo Bello (I)
1968	AC Milan 2	Hamburg 0	Rotterdam	60,000	Ortiz (Sp)
1969	Slovan Bratislava 3	Barcelona 2	Basle	40,000	Van Ravens (Ho)
1970	Manchester C 2	Gornik Zabrze 1	Vienna	10,000	Schiller (A)
1971	Chelsea 1	Real Madrid 1 *(aet)*	Athens	42,000	Scheurer (Sw)
Replay	Chelsea 2	Real Madrid 1 *(aet)*	Athens	24,000	Bucheli (Sw)
1972	Rangers 3	Moscow Dynamo 2	Barcelona	35,000	Ortiz (Sp)
1973	AC Milan 1	Leeds U 0	Salonika	45,000	Mihas (Gr)
1974	Magdeburg 2	AC Milan 0	Rotterdam	5000	Van Gemert (Ho)
1975	Dynamo Kiev 3	Ferencvaros 0	Basle	13,000	Davidson (S)
1976	Anderlecht 4	West Ham U 2	Brussels	58,000	Wurtz (F)
1977	Hamburg 2	Anderlecht 0	Amsterdam	65,000	Partridge (E)
1978	Anderlecht 4	Austria/WAC 0	Paris	48,679	Adlinger (WG)
1979	Barcelona 4	Fortuna Dusseldorf 3 *(aet)*	Basle	58,000	Palotai (H)
1980	Valencia 0	Arsenal 0	Brussels	40,000	Christov (Cz)
	(aet; Valencia won 5-4 on penalties)				
1981	Dynamo Tbilisi 2	Carl Zeiss Jena 1	Dusseldorf	9000	Lattanzi (I)
1982	Barcelona 2	Standard Liege 1	Barcelona	100,000	Eschweiler (WG)
1983	Aberdeen 2	Real Madrid 1 *(aet)*	Gothenburg	17,804	Menegali (I)
1984	Juventus 2	Porto 1	Basle	60,000	Prokop (EG)
1985	Everton 3	Rapid Vienna 1	Rotterdam	30,000	Casarin (I)
1986	Dynamo Kiev 3	Atletico Madrid 0	Lyon	39,300	Wohrer (A)
1987	Ajax 1	Lokomotiv Leipzig 0	Athens	35,000	Agnolin (I)
1988	Mechelen 1	Ajax 0	Strasbourg	39,446	Pauly (WG)
1989	Barcelona 2	Sampdoria 0	Berne	45,000	Courtney (E)
1990	Sampdoria 2	Anderlecht 0	Gothenburg	20,103	Galler (Sw)
1991	Manchester U 2	Barcelona 1	Rotterdam	45,000	Karlsson (Se)
1992	Werder Bremen 2	Monaco 0	Lisbon	16,000	D'Elia (I)
1993	Parma 3	Antwerp 1	Wembley	37,393	Assenmacher (G)
1994	Arsenal 1	Parma 0	Copenhagen	33,765	Krondl (Czr)
1995	Zaragoza 2	Arsenal 1	Paris	42,424	Ceccarini (I)

EUROPEAN CUP-WINNERS' CUP 1994–95

Preliminary Round, First Leg

Pirin (2) 3 *(Orachev 18, Yanev 28, Petrov 60 (pen))*, Schaen (0) 0 2000
Norma Tallinn (0) 1 *(Rychkov 83)*, Branik Maribor (0) 4 *(Galic 54, Milevski 63, Djurovski 78, Simundza 90)* 1000
Fandok (2) 4 *(Yeryomko 1, 5, Khripach 65, Savostikov 72)*, SK Tirana (0) 1 *(Prenga 90)* 5000
Tiligul (0) 0, Omonia (1) 1 *(Gogrichiani 16)* 3000
Ferencvaros (3) 6 *(Neagoe 3, Szekeres 17, 76, Paling 45, Lipcsei 57, Albert 78)*, Dudelange (0) 1 *(Fanelli 82)* 10,000
Floriana (0) 2 *(Stefanovic 53, 90)*, Sligo Rovers (2) 2 *(Moran 12, Reid 31)* 1500
Barry Town (0) 0, Zalgiris Vilnius (0) 1 *(Vencevicius 77)* 1914
Bodo Glimt (2) 6 *(Berstad 5, Berg 53, 89, Bjorkan 70, Johnsen 35, 82)*, Olimpija (0) 0 2290
Viktoria Zizkov (0) 1 *(Poborsky 72)*, Norrkoping (0) 0 1905
B71 Sandur (0) 0, HJK Helsinki (2) 5 *(Yanitalu 3, 86, Lius 20, 68, Heinola 80)* 462
Bangor (0) 0, Tatran Presov (0) 1 *(Nenadic 72)* 1100
IB Keflavik (0) 1 *(Tanasic 75)*, Maccabi Tel Aviv (1) 2 *(Klinger 36, Nimny 83)* 500

Preliminary Round, Second Leg

Branik Maribor (8) 10 *(Djurovski 5, 8, Gutalj 20, 45, Bozgo 22, 24, 42, 82, Simundza 40, 86)*, Norma Tallinn (0) 0 4500
Dudelange (1) 1 *(Morgante 21)*, Ferencvaros (3) 6 *(Lisztes 5, Paling 18, Lipcsei 38, 68, Kristiansen 55, Zavadszky 88)* 750
HJK Helsinki (1) 2 *(Kottila 1, Suokonautio 80)*, B71 Sandur (0) 0 2000
Maccabi Tel Aviv (3) 4 *(Brumer A 13, Brumer G 16 (pen), Klinger 25, Kriks 68)*, IB Keflavik (1) 1 *(Tanasic 36)* 8125
Norrkoping (1) 3 *(Hansson 41, 71, Vaattovaara 90 (pen))*, Viktoria Zizkov (0) 3 *(Trval 54, Kordule 57, Vrabec 88 (pen))* 6500
Olimpija (0) 0, Bodo Glimt (0) 0 2500
Omonia (2) 3 *(Kantilos 5 (pen), Tutic 45, Savvides 89)*, Tiligul (0) 1 *(Belous 51)* 6500
Schaen (0) 0, Pirin (1) 1 *(Jankov 2)* 800
Sligo Rovers (0) 1 *(Brennan 72)*, Floriana (0) 0 6000
SK Tirana (1) 3 *(Fortuzi 45, 75, 90)*, Fandok (0) 0 6000
Tatran Presov (2) 4 *(Kocis 13, 48, Matta 42, Hoger 52)*, Bangor (0) 0 5450
Zalgiris Vilnius (2) 6 *(Karvelis 18, 50, Baltusnikas 40, Poderis 48, Maciulevicius 68, Jankauskas 89)*, Barry Town (0) 0 2900

First Round, First Leg

Besiktas (2) 2 *(Oktay 28, Ertugrul 36)*, HJK Helsinki (0) 0 37,500
Bodo Glimt (2) 3 *(Staurvik 3, Johnsen 33, 58)*, Sampdoria (0) 2 *(Bertarelli 47, Platt 69)* 2015
Branik Maribor (0) 1 *(Bozgo 46 (pen))*, FK Austria (1) 1 *(Prosenik 23)* 4000
Brondby (1) 3 *(Jensen 19 (pen), Hansen B 56, Bjur 66)*, SK Tirana (0) 0 6035
Chelsea 2) 4 *(Furlong 2, Sinclair 4, Rocastle 52, Wise 69)*, Viktoria Zizkov (2) 2 *(Majoros 35, 41)* 22,036
Croatia Zagreb (2) 3 *(Jelicic 1, Soldo 40, Pamic 65)*, Auxerre (1) 1 *(Diomede 20)* 18,000
CSKA Moscow (0) 2 *(Mamchur 50, Sergeyev 73)*, Ferencvaros (0) 1 *(Christiansen 58)* 6000
Dundee U (1) 3 *(Petric 16, Nixon 66, Hannah 69)*, Tatran Presov (2) 2 *(Skalka 10, Zvara 41 (pen))* 9454
Gloria Bistrita (0) 2 *(Raduta 51, Lungu 54)*, Zaragoza (1) 1 *(Esnaider 43)* 13,000
Grasshoppers (1) 3 *(Bickel 41, Koller 52, Subiat 85)*, Odessa (0) 0 3600
Maccabi Tel Aviv (0) 0, Werder Bremen (0) 0 10,000
Omonia (0) 1 *(Malekos 72)*, Arsenal (1) 3 *(Merson 37, 80, Wright 50)* 14,500
Pirin (0) 0, Panathinaikos (0) 2 *(Nioblias 70, Alexoudis 83)* 25,000
Porto (0) 2 *(Domingos 72, Rui Barros 77)*, LKS Lodz (0) 0 25,000
Sligo Rovers (1) 1 *(Kenny 44)*, FC Brugge (1) 2 *(Vermant 10, Verheyen 63)* 6000
Zalgiris Vilnius (0) 1 *(Tereskinas 88 (pen)*, Feyenoord (1) 1 *(Larsson 9)* 7000

First Round, Second Leg

Arsenal (2) 3 *(Wright 9, 70, Schwarz 31)*, Omonia (0) 0 24,265
FK Austria (1) 3 *(Flogel 21, Kubica 53, 56)*, Branik Maribor (0) 0 10,000
Auxerre (1) 3 *(Diomede 41, Mahe 75, Lamouchi 90)*, Croatia Zagreb (0) 0 20,000
FC Brugge (2) 3 *(Staelens 4, 45 (pen), Eykelkamp 58)*, Sligo Rovers (1) 1 *(Rooney 7)* 5500
Ferencvaros (2) 2 *(Sinov 36 (og), Neagoe 45)*, CSKA Moscow (1) 1 *(Radimov 15)* 20,000 *Ferencvaros won 7-6 on penalties*
Feyenoord (0) 2 *(Larsson 54, Heus 66 (pen)*, Zalgiris Vilnius (0) 1 *(Vencevicius 89)* 17,500
HJK Helsinki (0) 1 *(Rantanen 67)*, Besiktas (0) 1 *(Derelioglu 86)* 3000
LKS Lodz (0) 0, Porto (1) 1 *(Drulovic 45)* 7000
Odessa (1) 1 *(Guseynov 9)*, Grasshoppers (0) 0 12,000
Panathinaikos (3) 6 *(Alexoudis 6, 17, Warzycha 30, 87, 90, Borelli 64)*, Pirin (1) 1 *(Orachev 44)* 21,000
Sampdoria (2) 2 *(Platt 13, Lombardo 37)*, Bodo Glimt (0) 0 35,000
Tatran Presov (2) 3 *(Zvara 10, 71, Kocis 18)*, Dundee U (1) 1 *(Nixon 2)* 8184
SK Tirana (0) 0, Brondby (1) 1 *(Strudal 31)* 3500
Viktoria Zizkov (0) 0, Chelsea (0) 0 *in Jablonec* 6000
Werder Bremen (0) 2 *(Bode 55, Basler 80)*, Maccabi Tel Aviv (0) 0 22,431
Zaragoza (2) 4 *(Pardeza 11, Aguado 42, Poyet 49, 55)*, Gloria Bistrita (0) 0 *in Valencia* 5000

Second Round, First Leg

Besiktas (2) 2 *(Mehmet 42, Ertugrul 44)*, Auxerre (0) 2 *(Saib 50, Martins 56)* 20,900
Brondby (0) 1 *(Strudal 53)*, Arsenal (2) 2 *(Wright 16, Smith 18)* 13,406
FC Brugge (1) 1 *(Staelens 4 (pen))*, Panathinaikos (0) 0 18,000
Chelsea (0) 0, FK Austria (0) 0 22,560
Feyenoord (0) 1 *(Larsson 65)*, Werder Bremen (0) 0 39,000
Porto (3) 6 *(Jorge Costa 17, Rui Barros 19, Drulovic 40, 58, Domingos 86, Aloisio 89)*, Ferencvaros (0) 0 16,000
Sampdoria (1) 3 *(Melli 45, Mihajlovic 76, Maspero 83)*, Grasshoppers (0) 0 25,000
Tatran Presov (0) 0, Zaragoza (2) 4 *(Poyet 26, Varga 44 (og), Esnaider 49, 88)* 12,105

Second Round, Second Leg

Arsenal (1) 2 *(Wright 25 (pen), Selley 46)*, Brondby (1) 2 *(Hansen B 2, Eggen 69)* 32,290
FK Austria (0) 1 *(Narbekovas 73)*, Chelsea (1) 1 *(Spencer 40)* 25,000
Auxerre (1) 2 *(Lamouchi 45, 49)*, Besiktas (0) 0 20,000

Ferencvaros (1) 2 *(Zavatsky 26, Neagoe 59)*, Porto (0) 0 15,000
Grasshoppers (1) 3 *(Willems 12, Bickel 51, Koller 55)*, Sampdoria (2) 2 *(Melli 17, Lombardo 40)* 12,100
Panathinaikos (0) 0, FC Brugge (0) 0 70,000
Werder Bremen (1) 3 *(Bestchastnich 12, 60, Basler 90)*, Feyenoord (2) 4 *(Larsson 20, 34, 66 (pen), Heus 56 (pen))* 31,118
Zaragoza (1) 2 *(Esnaider 5, Celada 56)*, Tatran Presov (1) 1 *(Kocis 38)* 9000 *In Valencia*

Quarter-finals, First Leg

FC Brugge (0) 1 *(Verheyen 83)*, Chelsea (0) 0 18,021
Arsenal (0) 1 *(Wright 59 (pen))*, Auxerre (0) 1 *(Verlaat 62)* 35,508
Feyenoord (0) 1 *(Larsson 62)*, Zaragoza (0) 0 47,000
Sampdoria (0) 0, Porto (0) 1 *(Yuran 64)* 31,000

Quarter-finals, Second Leg

Auxerre (0) 0, Arsenal (1) 1 *(Wright 16)* 22,000
Chelsea (2) 2 *(Stein 16, Furlong 38)*, FC Brugge (0) 0 28,661
Porto (0) 0, Sampdoria (0) 1 *(Mancini 48)* 43,000 *Sampdoria won 5-3 on penalties.*
Zaragoza (0) 2 *(Pardeza 58, Esnaider 72)*, Feyenoord (0) 0 36,800

Semi-finals, First Leg

Arsenal (2) 3 *(Bould 34, 36, Wright 68)*, Sampdoria (0) 2 *(Jugovic 51, 77)* 38,809
Zaragoza (2) 3 *(Pardeza 8, Esnaider 26, 57)*, Chelsea (0) 0 35,000

Semi-finals, Second Leg

Chelsea (1) 3 *(Furlong 30, Sinclair 62, Stein 86)*, Zaragoza (0) 1 *(Aragon 54)* 26,456
Sampdoria (1) 3 *(Mancini 13, Bellucci 82, 84)*, Arsenal (0) 2 *(Wright 60, Schwarz 87)* 35,000 *Arsenal won 3-2 on penalties.*

Final: Arsenal (0) 1, Zaragoza (0) 2 aet

(in Paris, 10 May 1995, 42,424)

Arsenal: Seaman; Dixon, Winterburn (Morrow 47), Schwarz, Linighan, Adams, Keown (Hillier 46), Wright, Hartson, Merson, Parlour.

Scorer: Hartson 76.

Zaragoza: Cedrun; Belsue, Aguado, Caceres, Solana, Poyet, Aragon, Nayim, Higuera (Sanjuan 67) (Geli 114), Pardeza, Esnaider.

Scorers: Esnaider 68, Nayim 120. *Referee:* Ceccarini (Italy).

Zaragoza players celebrated after the Cup-Winners' Cup Final victory over Arsenal. (Action Images)

EUROPEAN CUP-WINNERS' CUP 1994–95 – BRITISH AND IRISH

Preliminary Round, First Leg

11 AUG

Barry Town (0) 0

Zalgiris Vilnius (0) 1 *(Vencevicius)* 1914

Barry Town: Livingstone; Griffiths, Williams, Boyle, Davies (Leask), Ellis, Giles, Wright (Mitchell), D'Auria, Jones, Scott.
Zalgiris Vilnius: Spetyla; Suliauskas, Maciulevicius, Baltusnikas, Stonkus, Novikovas, Karvelis (Vencevicius), Tereskinas, Preiksaitis, Jankauskas, Poderis (Rimkus).

Bangor (0) 0

Tatran Presov (0) 1 *(Nenadic)* 1100

Bangor: Dalton; Glendining, Ferguson (Dornan), McCaffrey, Brown, Melly, Hill, Batey, McCallan, Magee (Wilkinson), McEvoy.
Tatran Presov: Jakubech; Bajtos, Kocis, Varga, Nenadic, Hlusko, Skalka, Hoger, Kantos, Zvara, Matta.

Floriana (0) 2 *(Stefanovic 2)*

Sligo Rovers (2) 2 *(Moran, Reid)* 1500

Floriana: Cluett; Cauchi, Wright (Marlow), Delia, Farrugia, Buttigieg, Busuttil, Stefanovic, Scriberras, Carvana, Buhagiar R.
Sligo Rovers: McLean; Reid D, Brunton, Boyle, Dykes, Kenny, Hastie, Carr, Brennan, Reid M, Moran (McDonnell).

Preliminary Round, Second Leg

25 AUG

Sligo Rovers (0) 1 *(Brennan)*

Floriana (0) 0 6000

Sligo Rovers: McLean; Reid D, Boyle, Dykes, McDonnell, Hastie, Kenny (Rooney), Moran, Brennan, Reid M, Brunton.
Floriana: Cluett; Cauchi, Farrugia (Carvana), Delia, Brincat, Buttigieg, Busuttil, Stefanovic, Scriberras, Marlow (Buhagiar J), Buhagiar R.

Tatran Presov (2) 4 *(Kocis 2, Matta, Hoger)*

Bangor (0) 0 4972

Tatran Presov: Jakubech; Bajtos, Kantos, Varga, Hlusko, Matta, Zvara, Shulka (Chihuri), Hoger, Kocis, Nenadic.
Bangor: Dalton; Glendinning, Ferguson, McCaffrey, Brown (Spiers), Melly, Hill, Wilkinson (Surgeon), McCallan, Magee, McEvoy.

Zalgiris Vilnius (2) 6 *(Karvelis 2, Baltusnikas, Poderis, Maciulevicius, Jankauskas)*

Barry Town (0) 0 2900

Zalgiris Vilnius: Spetyla (Koncevicius), Novikovas, Maciulevicius, Baltusnikas, Stonkus, Vencevicius, Suliauskas, Tereskinas, Preiksaitis (Urbonas), Karvelis (Jankauskas), Poderis.
Barry Town: Livingstone; Threlfall (Scott), Griffiths, Leask, Boyle, Ellis, Curtis, Sanderson, Mitchell, Jones, Giles.

First Round, First Leg

15 SEPT

Chelsea (2) 4 *(Furlong, Sinclair, Rocastle, Wise)*

Viktoria Zizkov (2) 2 *(Majoros 2)* 22,036

Chelsea: Kharine; Minto, Sinclair, Newton, Johnsen, Spackman, Rocastle (Rix), Spencer, Furlong, Peacock, Wise.
Viktoria Zizkov: Zitka; Kordule, Casko, Gabriel, Petrous, Poborsky, Bilek, Majoros, Vrabec, Jancula (Masek), Trval (Krejcik).

Dundee U (1) 3 *(Petric, Nixon, Hannah)*

Tatran Presov (2) 2 *(Skalka, Zvara (pen))* 9454

Dundee U: Main; McInally, Malpas, Hannah, Petric, Welsh, Bowman, McKinlay, Ristic (McLaren), Brewster (Dailly), Nixon.
Tatran Presov: Jakubech; Bajtos, Chihuri (Kocis), Varga, Menadic, Hlusko, Skalka, Hoger, Kentos (Pertus), Zvara, Matta.

Omonia (0) 1 *(Malekos)*

Arsenal (1) 3 *(Merson 2, Wright)* 14,500

Omonia: Christou; Constantinou, Panagiotou, Christophi, Christodoulou, Malekos, Savvides, Xiourouppas (Kaifas), Kantilos (Kizilasvili), Andreou, Gogritsiani.
Arsenal: Seaman; Dixon, Winterburn, Schwarz (Morrow), Keown, Linighan, Jensen, Wright, Smith, Merson, Parlour.

Sligo Rovers (1) 1 *(Kenny)*

FC Brugge (1) 2 *(Vermant, Verheyen)* 6000

Sligo Rovers: McLean; Kelly, Brunton, Boyle, Dykes, Kenny, Hastie, Carr, Houlihan, Annand, Moran.
FC Brugge: Verlinden; Medved, Van der Elst, Verheyen, Borkelmans, Van der Heyden, Okon, Vermant, Staelens, Eykelkamp, Plovie.

First Round, Second Leg

29 SEPT

Arsenal (2) 3 *(Wright 2, Schwarz)*

Omonia (0) 0 24,265

Arsenal: Seaman; Dixon, Winterburn, Schwarz, Linighan, Adams, Jensen (Hillier), Wright, Smith, Merson (Campbell), Parlour.
Omonia: Christou; Christodoulou, Christophi, Constantinou, Panagiotou, Savvides, Kalotheou, Andreou, Kantilos (Kaiafas), Malekos, Xiourouppas (Tutic).

Viktoria Zizkov (0) 0

Chelsea (0) 0 6000

Viktoria Zizkov: Silhavy; Notin, Kordule, Gabriel, Bileck, Petrous, Poborsky, Majoros (Trval), Vrabec (Masek), Casko, Jancula.
Chelsea: Kharine; Clarke, Johnsen, Sinclair, Barness, Wise, Rocastle, Newton, Rix, Peacock, Furlong.

Tatran Presov (2) 3 *(Zvara 2, Kocis)*

Dundee U (1) 1 *(Nixon)* 8184

Tatran Presov: Jakubech; Bajtos, Kentos, Lukac, Ptreus, Hlusko, Skalka, Hoger, Kocis (Lesko), Zvara, Matta (Pukah).
Dundee U: Main; Cleland (Craig), Malpas, Hannah, Petric, Welsh, Dailly, McKinlay, McLaren (Brewster), McInally, Nixon.

FC Brugge (2) 3 *(Staelens 2 (1 pen), Eykelkamp)*

Sligo Rovers (1) 1 *(Rooney)* 5500

FC Brugge: Belpaire; Medved, Van der Elst, Verheyen, Borkelmans, Van der Heyden, Okon, Vermant (Vrul), Staelens, Eykelkamp, Plovie.
Sligo Rovers: McLean; Kelly, Lynch, Boyle, Dykes, Kenny, Hastie, Carr, Houlihan (Annand), Rooney, McDonnell (Moran).

Second Round, First Leg

20 OCT

Brondby (0) 1 *(Strudal)*

Arsenal (2) 2 *(Wright, Smith)* 13,406

Brondby: Krogh; Colding (Hogh), Rieper, Eggen, Risager, Bjur, Vilfort, Jensen (Kristensen), Thogersen, Strudal, Hansen.
Arsenal: Seaman; Dixon, Winterburn, Schwarz, Bould, Adams, Jensen, Wright, Smith, Campbell, Parlour.

Chelsea (0) 0

FK Austria (0) 0 22,560

Chelsea: Kharine; Newton, Sinclair (Barness) (Rix), Kjeldbjerg, Johnsen, Spackman, Rocastle, Shipperley, Furlong, Peacock, Wise.
FK Austria: Wohlfahrt; Belaic, Kogler, Pfeffer, Sekerlioglu, Zsak, Schmid, Prosenik, Flogel, Mjelde (Zechner), Ogris (Kubica).

Quarter Finals, First Leg

28 FEB

FC Brugge (0) 1 *(Verheyen)*

Chelsea (0) 0 18,000

FC Brugge: Verlinden; Medved, Okon, Van der Elst (De Broule), Renier, Borkelmans, Verheyen, Vernant, Staelens, Buelinckx, Eijkelkamp.
Chelsea: Hitchcock; Clarke, Minto, Spackman, Johnsen, Sinclair, Newton, Spencer, Furlong, Peacock, Wise (Rocastle).

2 MAR

Arsenal (0) 1 *(Wright (pen))*

Auxerre (0) 1 *(Verlaat)* 35,508

Arsenal: Seaman; Dixon, Winterburn, Schwarz, Bould, Adams, Jensen, Wright, Kiwomya (Parlour), Merson, McGoldrick (Hartson).
Auxerre: Cool; Verlaat, Goma, West, Mahe, Rabarivony (Remy), Lamouchi, Violeau, Martins, Vahirua (Baticle), Laslandes.

Quarter Finals, Second Leg

14 MAR

Chelsea (2) 2 *(Stein, Furlong)*

FC Brugge (0) 0 28,661

Chelsea: Hitchcock; Clarke, Minto (Hall), Spackman, Johnsen, Sinclair, Rocastle (Lee), Furlong, Stein, Peacock, Burley.
FC Brugge: Verlinden (Belpaire); Medved (Vermant), Okon, Renier, Verheyen, Van Der Elst, Borkelmans, De Brul, Staelens, Buelinckx (Van Der Hayden), Eykelkamp.

16 MAR

Auxerre (0) 0

Arsenal (1) 1 *(Wright)* 22,000

Auxerre: Cool; Goma, Verlaat, Silvestre, Mahe, Saib, Martins, Rabarivony (Cocard), Lamouchi, Vahirua (Baticle), Laslandes.
Arsenal: Seaman; Dixon, Winterburn, Schwarz, Bould, Adams, Keown, Wright, Hartson (Morrow), Merson, Parlour.

Semi-Finals, First Leg

6 APR

Arsenal (2) 3 *(Bould 2, Wright)*

Sampdoria (0) 2 *(Jugovic 2)* 38,809

Arsenal: Seaman; Dixon, Winterburn, Schwarz, Bould, Adams, Hillier, Wright (Kiwomya), Hartson, Merson (Morrow), Parlour.
Sampdoria: Zenga; Sacchetti, Rossi, Mannini, Invernizzi (Maspero), Evani, Jugovic, Serena, Mancini, Salsano, Lombardo.

Zaragoza (2) 3 *(Pardeza, Esnaider 2)*

Chelsea (0) 0 35,000

Zaragoza: Juanmi; Belsue, Aguado, Caceres, Solana, Aragon (Sanjuan), Poyet, Nayim, Higuera, Esnaider, Pardeza (Oscar).
Chelsea: Hitchcock; Clarke, Minto, Myers, Johnsen, Sinclair, Rocastle (Hoddle), Spencer (Stein), Furlong, Peacock, Spackman.

Semi-Finals, Second Leg

20 APR

Chelsea (1) 3 *(Furlong, Sinclair, Stein)*

Zaragoza (0) 1 *(Aragon)* 26,456

Chelsea: Hitchcock; Clarke, Minto, Lee, Johnsen (Hoddle), Sinclair, Rocastle (Spencer), Furlong, Stein, Peacock, Spackman.
Zaragoza: Juanmi; Belsue, Caceres, Solana, Cafu, Higuera (Jeli), Aragon, Oscar, Nayim, Esnaider (Rodriguez), Pardeza.

Sampdoria (1) 3 *(Mancini, Bellucci 2)*

Arsenal (0) 2 *(Wright, Schwarz)* 35,000

Sampdoria: Zenga; Mannini, Ferri (Bellucci), Vierchowod, Serena, Evani (Invernizzi), Jugovic, Maspero, Lombardo, Mihajlovic, Mancini.
Arsenal: Seaman; Dixon, Winterburn, Schwarz, Bould, Adams, Keown, Wright (Kiwomya), Hartson, Merson, Hillier (McGoldrick).

Final

10 MAY

Arsenal (0) 1 *(Hartson)*

Zaragoza (0) 2 *(Esnaider, Nayim) aet* 42,424

Arsenal: Seaman; Dixon, Winterburn (Morrow), Schwarz, Linighan, Adams, Keown (Hillier), Wright, Hartson, Merson, Parlour.
Zaragoza: Cedrun; Belsue, Aguado, Caceres, Solana, Poyet, Aragon, Nayim, Higuera (Sanjuan) (Geli), Pardeza, Esnaider.

INTER-CITIES FAIRS & UEFA CUP

FAIRS CUP FINALS 1958–71

(Winners in italics)

Year	First Leg	Attendance	Second Leg	Attendance
1958	London 2 Barcelona 2	45,466	*Barcelona* 6 London 0	62,000
1960	Birmingham C 0 Barcelona 0	40,500	*Barcelona* 4 Birmingham C 1	70,000
1961	Birmingham C 2 Roma 2	21,005	*Roma* 2 Birmingham C 0	60,000
1962	Valencia 6 Barcelona 2	65,000	Barcelona 1 *Valencia* 1	60,000
1963	Dynamo Zagreb 1 Valencia 2	40,000	*Valencia* 2 Dynamo Zagreb 0	55,000
1964	*Zaragoza* 2 Valencia 1	50,000	(in Barcelona)	
1965	*Ferencvaros* 1 Juventus 0	25,000	(in Turin)	
1966	Barcelona 0 Zaragoza 1	70,000	Zaragoza 2 *Barcelona* 4	70,000
1967	Dynamo Zagreb 2 Leeds U 0	40,000	Leeds U 0 *Dynamo Zagreb* 0	35,604
1968	Leeds U 1 Ferencvaros 0	25,368	Ferencvaros 0 *Leeds U* 0	70,000
1969	Newcastle U 3 Ujpest Dozsa 0	60,000	Ujpest Dozsa 2 *Newcastle U* 3	37,000
1970	Anderlecht 3 Arsenal 1	37,000	*Arsenal* 3 Anderlecht 0	51,612
1971	Juventus 0 Leed U 0 *(abandoned 51 minutes)*	42,000		
	Juventus 2 Leeds U 2	42,000	*Leeds U* 1* Juventus 1	42,483

UEFA CUP FINALS 1972–95

(Winners in italics)

1972	Wolverhampton W 1 Tottenham H 2	45,000	*Tottenham H* 1 Wolverhampton W 1	48,000
1973	Liverpool 0 Moenchengladbach 0 *(abandoned 27 minutes)*	44,967		
	Liverpool 3 Moenchengladbach 0	41,169	Moenchengladbach 2 *Liverpool* 0	35,000
1974	Tottenham H 2 Feyenoord 2	46,281	*Feyenoord 2* Tottenham 0	68,000
1975	Moenchengladbach 0 Twente 0	45,000	Twente 1 *Moenchengladbach* 5	24,500
1976	Liverpool 3 FC Brugge 2	56,000	FC Brugge 1 *Liverpool* 1	32,000
1977	Juventus 1 Athletic Bilbao 0	75,000	Athletic Bilbao 2 *Juventus* 1*	43,000
1978	Bastia 0 PSV Eindhoven 0	15,000	*PSV Eindhoven* 3 Bastia 0	27,000
1979	Red Star Belgrade 1 Moenchengladbach 1	87,500	*Moenchengladbach* 1 Red Star Belgrade 0	45,000
1980	Moenchengladbach 3 Eintracht Frankfurt 2	25,000	*Eintracht Frankfurt* 1* Moenchengladbach 0	60,000
1981	Ipswich T 3 AZ 67 Alkmaar 0	27,532	AZ 67 Alkmaar 4 *Ipswich T* 2	28,500
1982	Gothenburg 1 Hamburg 0	42,548	Hamburg 0 *Gothenburg* 3	60,000
1983	Anderlecht 1 Benfica 0	45,000	Benfica 1 *Anderlecht* 1	80,000
1984	Anderlecht 1 Tottenham H 1	40,000	*Tottenham H* 1[1] Anderlecht 1	46,258
1985	Videoton 0 Real Madrid 3	30,000	*Real Madrid* 0 Videoton 1	98,300
1986	Real Madrid 5 Cologne 1	80,000	Cologne 2 *Real Madrid* 0	15,000
1987	Gothenburg 1 Dundee U 0	50,023	Dundee U 1 *Gothenburg* 1	20,911
1988	Espanol 3 Bayer Leverkusen 0	42,000	*Bayer Leverkusen* 3[2] Espanol 0	22,000
1989	Napoli 2 Stuttgart 1	83,000	Stuttgart 3 *Napoli* 3	67,000
1990	Juventus 3 Fiorentina 1	45,000	Fiorentina 0 *Juventus* 0	32,000
1991	Internazionale 2 Roma 0	68,887	Roma 1 *Internazionale* 0	70,901
1992	Torino 2 Ajax 2	65,377	*Ajax** 0 Torino 0	40,000
1993	Borussia Dortmund 1 Juventus 3	37,000	*Juventus* 3 Borussia Dortmund 0	62,781
1994	Salzburg 0 Internazionale 1	47,500	*Internazionale* 1 Salzburg 0	80,326
1995	Parma 1 Juventus 0	23,000	Juventus 1 *Parma* 1	80,750

**won on away goals* [1]*Tottenham H won 4-3 on penalties aet* [2]*Bayer Leverkusen won 3-2 on penalties aet*

UEFA CUP 1994–95

Preliminary Round, First Leg

Slavia Prague (1) 2 *(Smicer 37, Suchoparek 68)*, Cork City (0) 0 3690
Motherwell (2) 3 *(Coyne 20, McGrillen 34, Kirk 83)*, Havnar (0) 0 7517
FC Copenhagen (0) 0, Jazz (1) 1 *(Ruhanen 33)* 4390
Portadown (0) 0, Slovan Bratislava (0) 2 *(Timko 58, Rosnak 75)* 2000
Bangor City (1) 1 *(Mottram 23)*, IA Akranes (1) 2 *(Reynisson 42, Jonsson 47)* 3426
Inter Bratislava (0) 0, MyPa (2) 3 *(Kolkka 11, 30, Rajamaki 49)* 2007
Odense (1) 3 *(Thorup 13, Schonberg 58, Madsen 89)*, Flora Tallinn (0) 0 2834
Lillestrom (2) 4 *(Hedman 2, Johnsen 42, Gulbrandsen 49, Pedersen 68)*, Donetsk (0) 1 *(Petrov 58)* 2779
GI Gotu (0) 0, Trelleborgs (1) 1 *(Karlsson 44)* 814
Gornik Zabrze (2) 7 *(Szemonski 30, 83, Baluszynski 35 (pen), Kosela 52, Kubik 61, 80, Orzeszek 78)*, Shamrock Rovers (0) 0 7001
Romar (0) 0, AIK Stockholm (1) 2 *(Johansson 26, Simpson 60)* 4000
Inter Cardiff (0) 0, Katowice (0) 2 *(Sermak 84 (pen), 89)* 1115
Aarau (0) 1 *(Kucharski 71)*, Mura Sobota (0) 0 4800
Anorthosis (2) 2 *(Charalambous 19, Nicolic 40)*, Shumen (0) 0 6000
Dynamo Tbilisi (1) 2 *(Kinkladze 27, Arveladze S 59)*, Uni Craiova (0) 0 45,000
Vardar Skopje (1) 1 *(Milosevski 38)*, Bekescsaba (1) 1 *(Nracko 44)* 20,000
Fenerbahce (2) 5 *(Uygun 15, Aykut 44, 66, 88, Nielsen 81)*, Turan Tauz (0) 0 30,000
Valletta (1) 2 *(Agius 16, Zerafa 68)*, Rapid Bucharest (2) 6 *(Chebac 5, Vladoiu 14, 46, Kira 74, Chirita 78, Voinea 84)* 3000
Kispest Honved (1) 4 *(Illes 27, 68, Pisont 60, Hamar 76)*, Zimbru (0) 1 *(Timbur 58)* 5000
CSKA Sofia (2) 3 *(Tanev 21 (pen), Koilov 44, 74)*, Ararat Erevan (0) 0 4000
Dynamo Minsk (0) 3 *(Kashentsev 69, Kachuro 78, Yaskovich 85)*, Hibernians (1) 1 *(Lawrence 6)* 7000
Teuta (1) 1 *(Fraholli 12)*, Apollon (0) 4 *(Spoliaric 57, Krcmarevic 80, 84, Cepovic 82)* 14,000
Aris Salonika (1) 3 *(Sapountzis 8, 64, (pen) Ivan 89)*, Hapoel Beer Sheba (1) 1 *(Guseyev 14)* 19,000
Hafnafjordur (0) 1 *(Magnusson 74)*, Linfield (0) 0 700
Skonto Riga (0) 0, Aberdeen (0) 0 2300
Grevenmacher (0) 1 *(Silva 83)*, Rosenborg (1) 2 *(Leonhardsen 4, Loken 89 (pen))* 500
Olimpija Ljubljana (2) 3 *(Dosti 35, 37, 73)*, Levski Sofia (0) 2 *(Sirakov 57, 72)* 4000

Preliminary Round, Second Leg

Aberdeen (0) 1 *(Kane 90)*, Skonto Riga (0) 1 *(Semenov 55)* 8500
AIK Stockholm (1) 2 *(Lidman 21, 63)*, Romar (0) 0 4000
IA Akranes (2) 2 *(Ingolfsson 8, Thordarson 21)*, Bangor City (0) 0 800
Apollon (2) 4 *(Cepovic 24, 29, Hadjiloizou 60, Pittas 89)*, Teuta (0) 2 *(Citsa 73, Ampazi 78)* 5000
Ararat Erevan (0) 0, CSKA Sofia (0) 0 7000
Bekescsaba (0) 1 *(Csato 61)*, Vardar Skopje (0) 0 3500
Cork City (0) 0, Sparta Prague (1) 4 *(Hogen 33, 50, Vaura 49, Berger 90)* 3200
Flora Tallinn (0) 0, Odense (1) 3 *(Hemmingsen 19, 49, Tchami 68)* 1000
Havnar Boltfelag (0) 1 *(Hansen 59)*, Motherwell (1) 4 *(Kirk 13, 69, Davies 20, Burns 88)* 750
Hibernians (1) 4 *(Ostrovsky 55 (og), Xerri 71, Spiteri 90, Miller 109)*, Dynamo Minsk (1) 3 *(Yuravin 44 (pen), Plaskevic 94, Spiteri 105 (og))* 2400
Hapoel Beer Sheba (0) 1 *(Madar 46)*, Aris Salonika (1) 2 *(Bouyouklis 30, Milojevic 55)* 6800
Jazz (0) 0, FC Copenhagen (0) 4 *(Johansen 54, Nielsen M. 81, Frandsen 83, Nielsen A. 87)* 1800
Katowice (3) 6 *(Walcsak 25, 83, Maciejewski 33, 45 (pen), Jojko 75 (pen), Wolny 89)*, Inter Cardiff (0) 0 4500
Linfield (3) 3 *(Beatty 15, Gorman 31, Peebles 36)*, Hafnarfjordur (1) 1 *(Podunavac 21)* 3201
Levski Sofia (1) 1 *(Stoilov 2)*, Olimpija Ljubljana (1) 2 *(Novak 24, Paulin 89)* 6800
MyPa (0) 0, Inter Bratislava (1) 1 *(Rupec 3)* 800
Mura Sobota (0) 0, Aarau (1) 1 *(Skrzypczak 17)* 1800
Rosenborg (2) 6 *(Strand 37, 87, Bergersen 45, Jakobsen 62, Brattbakk 77, 84)*, Grevenmacher (0) 0 11,000
Rapid Bucharest (1) 1 *(Tira 32)*, Valletta (1) 1 *(Agius 22)* 5000
Donetsk (0) 2 *(Orbu 49, Petrov 58)*, Lillestrom (0) 0 14,000
Shamrock Rovers (0) 0, Gornik Zabrze (0) 1 *(Baluszynski 49)* 5000
Shumen (1) 1 *(Iskrenov 43 (pen))*, Anorthosis (0) 2 *(Ashiotis 61, Kokich 82)* 4750
Slovan Bratislava (2) 3 *(Faktor 15, Tittel 33, Rusnak 65)*, Portadown (0) 0 6500
Turan Tauz (0) 0, Fenerbahce (0) 2 *(Ali 83 (pen), Bulent 87)* 1000
Trelleborg (2) 3 *(Karlsson 6 (pen), Eriksson 12, Rasmusson 48)*, GI Goto (0) 2 *(Jarnskor H. 55, Jarnskor M. 83)* 5500
Uni Craiova (0) 1 *(Pigulea 59)*, Dynamo Tbilisi (1) 2 *(Kavelasvili 3, Kinkladze 83)* 13,000
Zimbru (0) 0, Kispest Honved (0) 1 *(Orosz 83)* 3000

First Round, First Leg

Aarau (0) 0, Maritimo (0) 0 5400
Admira Wacker (2) 5 *(Gager 7 (pen), 60 (pen), Schiener 18, Klausz 66, Waldoch 90 (og))*, Gornik Zabrze (2) 2 *(Szemonski 26, Orzeszek 35)* 1500
AIK Stockholm (0) 0, Slavia Prague (0) 0 3190
IA Akranes (0) 0, Kaiserslautern (2) 4 *(Hamann 33, Anders 44, Kuntz 53, Kuka 59)* 4000
Anorthosis (2) 2 *(Gogic 6, Tamboris 41)*, Athletic Bilbao (0) 0 3000
Antwerp (0) 0, Newcastle U (3) 5 *(Lee 1, 9, 51, Sellars 40, Watson 78)* 15,000
Apollon (1) 1 *(Krcmarevic 36)*, Sion (0) 3 *(Bonvin 70, Marin 82, 85)* 4000
Bayer Leverkusen (4) 5 *(Kirsten 6, 16, 41, Dooley 14, Schuster 73)*, PSV Eindhoven (2) 4 *(Ronaldo 11 (pen), 45, 61, Nilis 87)* 16,000
Blackburn R (0) 0, Trelleborg (0) 1 *(Sandell 71)* 13,775
Boavista (1) 2 *(Artur 2, Gomes 62)*, MyPa (1) 1 *(Laaksonen 42)* 2000
Bordeaux (2) 3 *(Dugarry 4, Johnsen 38 (og), Witschge 85)*, Lillestrom (1) 1 *(Huard 6 (og))* 15,000
Borussia Dortmund (0) 1 *(Moller 57)*, Motherwell (0) 0 35,420
Cannes (0) 4 *(Durix 49 (pen), Kozniku 56, 80, Horlaville 67)*, Fenerbahce (0) 0 7500
CSKA Sofia (1) 3 *(Mihtarski 44, 82, Radukanov 70)*, Juventus (1) 2 *(Porrini 39, Del Piero 76)* 22,000
Dynamo Minsk (0) 0, Lazio (0) 0 20,000
Dynamo Tbilisi (1) 1 *(Arveladze 40 (pen)*, Tirol Innsbruck (0) 0 45,000
Internazionale (0) 1 *(Bergkamp 75 (pen)*, Aston Villa (0) 0 22,639
Kamyshin (1) 6 *(Goessakov 38, Polstyanov 55, 90, Volgin 58, Filipov 80, 90)*, Bekescsaba (1) 1 *(Szarvas 14)* 1500

Katowice (1) 1 *(Maciejewski 20 (pen))*, Aris Salonika (0) 0 8000
Linfield (0) 1 *(Anderson 86)*, Odense (0) 1 *(Schjonberg 46)* 3585
Napoli (1) 2 *(Carbone 30 (pen), 49)*, Skonto Riga (0) 0 12,000
Olimpija Ljubljana (1) 1 *(Siljak 3)*, Eintracht Frankfurt (0) 1 *(Legat 84)* 3500
Olympiakos (0) 1 *(Ivic 57)*, Marseille (1) 2 *(Ferrer 31, Marquet 79)* 40,000
Rapid Bucharest (1) 2 *(Chirita 18, Vladoiu 73)*, Charleroi (0) 0 7000
Real Madrid (1) 1 *(Vazquez 11)*, Sporting Lisbon (0) 0 80,000
Rosenborg (0) 1 *(Loken 52)*, La Coruna (0) 0 5281
Seraing (0) 3 *(Wamberto 67, Schaessens 75, Edmilson 90)*, Dynamo Moscow (3) 4 *(Smirnov 17, Tsjerisjev 26, 61, Simutenkov 44)* 3750
Slovan Bratislava (0) 1 *(Tomaschek 76)*, FC Copenhagen (0) 0 7570
Trabzonspor (2) 2 *(Orhan K 7, Soner 19)*, Dynamo Bucharest (1) 1 *(Ivan 29)* 20,000
Twente (1) 1 *(Mols 38)*, Kispest Honved (1) 4 *(Kovacs 19, 52, 75, Hamar 88)* 6000
Vitesse (0) 1 *(Gillhaus 51)*, Parma (0) 0 9200
Volgograd (1) 3 *(Gerasimenko 42, Nechayev 63, Veretennikov 75)*, Nantes (1) 2 *(Ouedec 28, N'Doram 81)* 19,000

First Round, Second Leg

Aris Salonika (1) 1 *(Sapountzis 47)*, Katowice (0) 0 8000 *Katowice won 4-3 on penalties*
Aston Villa (1) 1 *(Houghton 41)*, Internazionale (0) 0 30,533 *Villa won 4-3 on penalties*
Athletic Bilbao (2) 3 *(Guerrero 17, Panayiotou 24 (og), Andrinua 89)*, Anorthosis (0) 0 29,000
Bekescsaba (0) 1 *(Csato 77 (pen))*, Kamyshin (0) 0 2000
Charleroi (0) 2 *(Balog 89, Misse 90)*, Rapid Bucharest (0) 1 *(Tira 48)* 7000
FC Copenhagen (1) 1 *(Nielsen 45 (pen))*, Slovan Bratislava (1) 1 *(Negro 24)* 4232
Dynamo Bucharest (1) 3 *(Ceausila 6, Niculescu 51, Lica 82)*, Trabzonspor (2) 3 *(Orhan K 21, Orhan B 23, Soner 78)* 7000
Dynamo Moscow (0) 0, Seraing (0) 1 *(Schaessens 87)* 7000
Eintracht Frankfurt (1) 2 *(Dickhaut 9, Yeboah 84)*, Olimpija Ljubljana (0) 0 11,500
Fenerbahce (0) 1 *(Bulent 58)*, Cannes (2) 5 *(Tayfur 21 (og), Horlaville 25, 62, Micoud 50, Vieira 77)* 31,000
Gornik Zabrze (1) 1 *(Baluszynski 30)*, Admira Wacker (1) 1 *(Litovchenko 45)* 8500
Juventus (1) 5 *(Ravanelli 9, 75, 79, 81, 86)*, CSKA Sofia (0) 1 *(Mihtarski 90)* 22,000
Kaiserslautern (0) 4 *(Kuka 56, 84, Wagner 59, Haber 81)*, IA Akranes (0) 1 *(Gislason 88)* 23,070
Kispest Honved (0) 1 *(Illes 58 (pen))*, Twente (1) 3 *(Vurens 34, Ellerman 67, Boerebach 87)* 7000
Lazio (1) 4 *(Ostrovski 45 (og), Favalli 61, Boksic 74, Fuser 84)* Dynamo Minsk (1) 1 *(Kachuro 9)* 37,000
La Coruna (0) 4 *(Bebeto 81, 98, 114, Donato 107 (pen))*, Rosenborg (0) 1 *(Brattbakk 92)* 21,000
Lillestrom (0) 0, Bordeaux (2) 2 *(Zidane 2, Fournier 15)* 2003
Maritimo (0) 1 *(Paulo Alves 63)*, Aarau (0) 0 8500
Marseille (0) 3 *(Cascarino 53, 89, Ferreri 85)*, Olympiakos (0) 0 40,000
Motherwell (0) 0, Borussia Dortmund (0) 2 *(Riedle 54, 64)* 9362
MyPa (0) 1 *(Gronholm 75)*, Boavista (0) 1 *(Artur 89 (pen))* 3616
Nantes (1) 3 *(Ouedec 29, 61, Loko 75)*, Volgograd (0) 0 26,000
Newcastle U (4) 5 *(Lee 11, Cole 26, 39, 88, Beardsley 38 (pen)*, Antwerp (0) 2 *(Kiekens 75, Severeyns 77)* 29,737
Odense (4) 5 *(Nedergaard 5, 85, Schjonberg 25, 42 (pen), Thorup 40)*, Linfield (0) 0 4518
Parma (1) 2 *(Zola 23, 73)*, Vitesse (0) 0 9081
PSV Eindhoven (0) 0, Bayer Leverkusen (0) 0 21,500
Sion (0) 2 *(Marin 89, Orlando 101)*, Apollon (0) 3 *(Krcmarevic 49, Spoljaric 66, Cepovic 77)* 5000
Slavia Prague (1) 2 *(Suchoparek 26, Bejbl 57)*, AIK Stockholm (1) 2 *(Lidman 35, Sundgren 81)* 6329
Skonto Riga (0) 0, Napoli (1) 1 *(Buso 31)* 2589
Sporting Lisbon (2) 2 *(Joao Pinto 3, Oceano 31)*, Real Madrid (1) 1 *(Laudrup 14)* 58,000
Tirol Innsbruck (3) 5 *(Cerny 4, Stoger 32, Danek 35, 56, Janeschitz 89)*, Dynamo Tbilisi (1) 1 *(Arveladze S 38)* 7000
Trelleborg (0) 2 *(Karlsson J 50, 85)*, Blackburn R (1) 2 *(Sutton 18, Shearer 84)* 6730

Second Round, First Leg

Admira Wacker (1) 1 *(Gager 36 (pen))*, Cannes (0) 1 *(Bedrossian 66)* 4000
AIK Stockholm (0) 0, Parma (0) 1 *(Crippa 72)* 18,146
Boavista (1) 1 *(Sanchez 26)*, Napoli (0) 1 *(Carbone 57)* 7000
Dynamo Moscow (0) 2 *(Simutenkov 65, Cheryshev 69)*, Real Madrid (1) 2 *(Sandro 21, Zamorano 73)* 7000
Kaiserslautern (0) 1 *(Sforza 75)*, Odense (0) 1 *(Hemmingsen C 71)* 19,872
Katowice (0) 1 *(Strojek 88)*, Bordeaux (0) 0 6000
Kispest Honved (0) 0, Bayer Leverkusen (1) 2 *(Munch 16, Sergio 80)* 8500
Maritimo (0) 0, Juventus (0) 1 *(Ravanelli 78)* 15,500
Nantes (1) 2 *(Ouedec 32 (pen), 61)*, Kamyshin (0) 0 34,000
Newcastle U (2) 3 *(Fox 9, Beardsley 34 (pen), Cole 56)*, Athletic Bilbao (0) 2 *(Ziganda 71, Suances 79)* 32,140
Rapid Bucharest (0) 2 *(Vladoiu 67, Voinea 74)*, Eintracht Frankfurt (0) 1 *(Furtok 64)* 10,000
Sion (2) 2 *(Wicky 25, Kunz 41)*, Marseille (0) 0 15,500
Slovan Bratislava (0) 2 *(Rusnak 49, 60)*, Borussia Dortmund (1) 1 *(Tomacek 18 (og))* 18,060
Tirol Innsbruck (1) 2 *(Sane 30, Stoger 56)*, La Coruna (0) 0 11,800
Trabzonspor (0) 1 *(Orhan K 78)*, Aston Villa (0) 0 27,500
Trelleborg (0) 0, Lazio (0) 0 7303

Second Round, Second Leg

Aston Villa (0) 2 *(Atkinson 77, Ehiogu 90)*, Trabzonspor (0) 1 *(Orhan K 90)* 23,858
Athletic Bilbao (0) 1 *(Ziganda 67)*, Newcastle U (0) 0 47,000
Bayer Leverkussen (2) 5 *(Kirsten 28, 65, 68, Hapal 32, Tolkmitt 60)*, Kispest Honved (0) 0 14,900
Bordeaux (1) 1 *(Histilloes 18)*, Katowice (0) 1 *(Walczak 70 (pen))* 20,000
Borussia Dortmund (1) 3 *(Moller 15, Riedle 46, 68)*, Slovan Bratislava (0) 0 32,534
Cannes (0) 2 *(Kozniku 48, Charvel 87)*, Admira Wacker (3) 4 *(Mayrieb 7, Klausz 16, 56, Schiener 23)* 9000
Eintracht Frankfurt (3) 5 *(Bommer 10, Yeboah 13, 17, Furtok 65, 67)*, Rapid Bucharest (0) 0 12,000
Juventus (1) 2 *(Ravanelli 33, 51)*, Maritimo (0) 1 *(Paulo Alves 79)* 4254
Kamyshin (0) 1 *(Polstyanov 67)*, Nantes (0) 2 *Ouedec 47, 63) in Moscow* 1000
La Coruna (3) 4 *(Claudio 35, 37, Donato 40 (pen), Manjarin 71)*, Tirol Innsbruck (0) 0 25,000
Lazio (0) 1 *(Boksic 90)*, Trelleborg (0) 0 45,000
Napoli (2) 2 *(Agostini 18, 36)*, Boavista (0) 1 *(Luciano 76)* 45,000
Marseille (0) 3 *(Libbra 47, 65, Ferreri 73)*, Sion (1) 1 *(Kunz 5)* 40,000
Odense (0) 0, Kaiserslautern (0) 0 14,192
Parma (2) 2 *(Minotti 4, 16)*, AIK Stockholm (0) 0 5301
Real Madrid (0) 4 *(Zamorano 48, Redondo 76, Dani 89, 90)*, Dynamo Moscow (0) 0 60,000

Third Round, First Leg

Admira Wacker (0) 1 *(Binder 56)*, Juventus (3) 3 *(Conte 9, Roberto Baggio 14, 43)* 8000

Athletic Bilbao (0) 1 *(Ziganda 48)*, Parma (0) 0 45,000

Eintracht Frankfurt (0) 1 *(Buso 55 (og))*, Napoli (0) 0 42,000

Katowice (0) 1 *(Nikodem 54)*, Bayer Leverkusen (3) 4 *(Kirsten 29, 44, Lehnhoff 41, 64)* 8000

La Coruna (1) 1 *(Bebeto 23)*, Borussia Dortmund (0) 0 25,000

Nantes (2) 4 *(Loko 16, Ferri 33, N'Doram 54, Makelele 79)*, Sion (0) 0 34,000

Odense (1) 2 *(Schjonberg 45, Hjorth 79)*, Real Madrid (0) 3 *(Zamorano 66, Amavisca 69, Laudrup 90)* 15,000

Trabzonspor (0) 1 *(Unal 67)*, Lazio (0) 2 *(Rambaudi 59, Negri 61)* 25,000

Third Round, Second Leg

Bayer Leverkusen (4) 4 *(Schuster 11, Thom 13, Scholz 15, Hapal 28)*, Katowice (0) 0 24,000

Borussia Dortmund (0) 3 *(Zorc 50, Riedle 115, Ricken 118)*, La Coruna (0) 1 *(Alfredo 102) aet* 35,800

Juventus (1) 2 *(Ferrara 17, Vialli 86)*, Admira Wacker (0) 1 *(Wimmer 73)* 5732

Lazio (1) 2 *(Cravero 27, Di Vaio 75)*, Trabzonspor (0) 1 *(Soner 73)* 24,000

Napoli (0) 0, Eintracht Frankfurt (0) 1 *(Falkenmayer 56)* 25,000

Parma (2) 4 *(Zola 20, Dino Baggio 38, 47, Fernando Couto 64)*, Athletic Bilbao (0) 2 *(Vales 65, Guerrero 75)* 14,600

Real Madrid (0) 0, Odense (0) 2 *(Pedersen 71, Bisgaard 92) aet* 50,000

Sion (0) 2 *(Herr 76, Marin 82)*, Nantes (2) 2 *(Loko 30, N'Doram 31)* 12,000

Quarter-finals, First Leg

Eintracht Frankfurt (0) 1 *(Furtok 73)*, Juventus (1) 1 *(Marocchi 36)* 42,000

Bayer Leverkusen (2) 5 *(Lehnhoff 9, Kirsten 18, 89, Sergio 79, 84)*, Nantes (0) 1 *(Ouedec 64 (pen))* 21,400

Lazio (0) 1 *(Freund 69 (og))*, Borussia Dortmund (0) 0 50,000

Parma (0) 1 *(Zola 49 (pen))*, Odense (0) 0 6300

Quarter-finals, Second Leg

Borussia Dortmund (1) 2 *(Chapuisat 11 (pen), Riedle 90)*, Lazio (0) 0 35,400

Juventus (0) 3 *(Conte 77, Ravanelli 88, Del Piero 89)*, Eintracht Frankfurt (0) 0 20,000

Nantes (0) 0, Bayer Leverkusen (0) 0 34,210

Odense (0) 0, Parma (0) 0 13,000

Semi-finals, First Leg

Bayer Leverkusen (1) 1 *(Sergio 20)*, Parma (0) 2 *(Dino Baggio 48, Asprilla 53)* 21,500

Juventus (1) 2 *(Roberto Baggio 25 (pen), Kohler 88)*, Borussia Dortmund (1) 2 *(Reuter 7, Moller 70)* 80,000

Semi-finals, Second Leg

Borussia Dortmund (1) 1 *(Cesar 10)*, Juventus (2) 2 *(Porrini 7, Roberto Baggio 31)* 35,400

Parma (1) 3 *(Asprilla 3, 55, Zola 67)*, Bayer Leverkusen (0) 0 16,000

Final, First Leg: Parma (1) 1, Juventus (0) 0

(in Parma, 3 May 1995, 22,062)

Parma: Bucci; Benarrivo (Mussi 9), Minotti, Apolloni, Fernando Couto, Di Chiara, Pin, Dino Baggio, Sensini, Zola (Fiore 89), Asprilla. *Scorer:* Dino Baggio 5.

Juventus: Rampulla; Fusi (Del Piero 72), Tacchinardi, Carrera (Marocchi 46), Jarni, Paulo Sousa, Di Livio, Deschamps, Vialli, Roberto Baggio, Ravanelli. *Referee:* Lopez Nieto (Spain).

Final, Second Leg: Juventus (1) 1, Parma (0) 1

(in Milan, 17 May 1995, 80,750)

Juventus: Peruzzi; Ferrara, Torricelli, Porrini, Jarni, Paulo Sousa, Di Livio (Carrera 82), Marocchi (Del Piero 75), Roberto Baggio, Vialli, Ravanelli. *Scorer:* Vialli 33.

Parma: Bucci; Benarrivo (Mussi 46), Minotti, Susic, Fernando Couto, Di Chiara (Castellini 81), Dino Baggio, Fiore, Crippa, Zola, Asprilla. *Scorer:* Dino Baggio 53. *Referee:* Van den Wijngaert (Belgium).

Gianluca Vialli (striped shirt) eludes several Parma defenders as Juventus are held by their Italian opponents. (Action Images)

UEFA CUP 1994–95 – BRITISH AND IRISH

Preliminary Round, First Leg

9 AUG

Bangor City (1) 1 *(Mottram)*
IA Akranes (1) 2 *(Reynisson, Jonsson)* 3426
Bangor City: Adkins; Jones, Rutter, Wiggins, Middleton, Humphries, Evans, Noble, Mottram, Lloyd-Williams (McClelland), Barnett.
IA Akranes: Thordarsson T; Adolfsson, Miljhovic, Hervasson, Haraldsson S, Haraldsson P, Jonsson, Thordarsson O, Ingolfsson, Reynisson (Tordarsson), Bibercic (Petursson).

Gornik Zabrze (2) 7 *(Szemonski 2, Baluszynski 1 (pen), Kosela, Orzeszek, Kubik 2)*
Shamrock Rovers (0) 0 7001
Gornik Zabrze: Klak; Jegor, Waldoch, Brzoza, Zadylak, Grembocki (Orzeszek), Kosela, Brzeczek, Kubik, Szemonski, Baluszynski (Jarosz).
Shamrock Rovers: O'Neill; Burke, Brazil, Whelan, Nolan, McGrath, Mullen, Dodd, Toal, Bacon (Gannon), Eviston (Giles).

Hafnafjordur (0) 1 *(Magnusson)*
Linfield (0) 0 700
Hafnafjordur: Arnarson S; Racnarsson, Podunavic, Vikingsson, Mrazek, Jonsson, Helgason, Marteinsson, Magnusson, Arnarson H, Kirstjansson K.
Linfield: Lamont; Dornan, Easton, Peebles, Spires, Beatty, Campbell, McCoosh (McIlroy), Haylock, Fenlon, Bailie.

Inter Cardiff (0) 0
Katowice (0) 2 *(Sermak 2 (1 pen))* 1115
Inter Cardiff: Wood; Knight, Batchelor, Lewis, John, Jones L, Beattie, Thomas, O'Brien, Evans P (Williams), Taylor (Burrows).
Katowice: Jojko; Wegrzyn, Swierczewski, Maciejewski, Strojek, Widuch, Sermak, Borawski, Wolny, Janoszka (Walczak), Kucz (Nikodem).

Motherwell (2) 3 *(Coyne, McGrillen, Kirk)*
Havnar Boltfelag (0) 0 7517
Motherwell: Woods; Shannon, McKinnon, Philliben, Martin, McCart, Lambert, Dolan, McGrillen (Kirk), O'Donnell (Davies), Coyne.
Havnar Boltfelag: Johannesen; Jakobsen, Dahl, Hansen, Wang, Dam J, Nolsoe, Thomasson, Johnsson, Mohr, Dam J H (Eydun).

Portadown (0) 0
Slovan Bratislava (0) 2 *(Timpko, Rosnak)* 2000
Portadown: Keenan; Major, Murray, Mills, Sloan, Stewart, Cunningham, Shepherd, Casey, Smith, Russell.
Slovan Bratislava: Molnar; Seman, Chvila, Tomaschek, Kinder, Tittel, Pecko, Lancz, Faktor, Maixner (Rusnaik), Timko (Klinovsky).

Skonto Riga (0) 0
Aberdeen (0) 0 2300
Skonto Riga: Laizans; Troytsky, Zemlinsky, Mikutsky, Shevlykakov, Monyak, Semenov, Blagomadezhdin, Stepanov, Babichev, Yeliseyez.
Aberdeen: Snelders; McKimmie, Woodthorpe, Grant, Irvine, Wright, Robertson, Shearer (Booth), McKinnon, Dodds, Winnie.

Slavia Prague (1) 2 *(Smicer, Suchoparek)*
Cork City (0) 0 3690
Slavia Prague: Stejskal; Vaura, Suchoparek, Bejbl, Smejkal, Korel, Smicer, Penicka, Kristofik, Berger, Knoflicek (Hogen).
Cork City: Harrington; Daly, Smith, O'Donoghue (Cotter), Napier, Caulfield (Woods), Barry, Hyde, Murphy, Gaynor, Morley.

Preliminary Round, Second Leg

23 AUG

Aberdeen (0) 1 *(Kane)*
Skonto Riga (0) 1 *(Semenov)* 8500
Aberdeen: Snelders; Irvine (Miller), McKimmie, Winnie, Wright, McKinnon, Kane, Hetherston (Shearer), Woodthorpe, Dodds, Booth.
Skonto Riga: Laizan; Troitski, Monyak, Shevlyakov, Mikutsky, Lobanev, Stepanov, Babichev, Blagonadazhdin, Yeliseyev, Semenov.

Cork City (0) 0
Slavia Prague (1) 4 *(Hogen 2, Vaura, Berger)* 3200
Cork City: Harrington; Daly, Smith, O'Donoghue, Napier, Murphy, Barry, Hyde (Cotter), Caulfield, Gaynor, Morley.
Slavia Prague: Stejskal; Vaura, Suchoparek, Bejbl, Smejkal, Kozel, Hogen, Penicka, Kristofik (Vesely), Berger, Knoflicek (Lerch).

Katowice (3) 6 *(Walczak 2, Maziejewski 2 (1 pen), Jojko (pen), Wolny)*
Inter Cardiff (0) 0 4000
Katowice: Jojko; Maciejewski, Borawski, Wegrzyn, Nikodem (Szala), Wolny, Kucz (Szczygiel), Strojek, Walczak, Swierczewski, Sermak.
Inter Cardiff: Wood (Fisher); Knight, Jones V, Batchelor, O'Brien, Lyons, Burrows, Jones D, Hunter, Beattie, Taylor (Jones W).

Havnar Boltfelag (0) 1 *(Hansen)*
Motherwell (1) 4 *(Kirk 2, Davies, Burns)* 750
Havnar Boltfelag: Johannesen K; Jakobsen, Dahl, Hansen, Johannesen N, Dam, Nolsoe, Wang, Jonsson, Mohr, Clementsen.
Motherwell: Woods; Shannon, Philliben, Martin, McLeish, McCart, Burns, Dolan, Kirk, Davies, McGrillen.

Linfield (3) 3 *(Beatty, Gorman, Peebles)*
Hafnafjordur (1) 1 *(Podunavac)* 3201
Linfield: Lamont; Dornan, Easton, Peebles, Spires, Beatty, Knell, Gorman (McCoosh), Anderson, Fenlon, Bailie.
Hafnafjordur: Arnarson S; Podunavic, Halldorsson (Einarsson), Vikingsson, Mrazek, Arnarson H, Helgason, Marteinsson, Magnusson, Jonsson (Ragnarsson), Kristjansson H.

Shamrock R (0) 0
Gornik Zabrze (0) 1 *(Baluszynski)* 5000
Shamrock R: O'Neill; Burke (Giles), O'Duchon, Brazil, Whelan, Toal, McCormack, McGrath, Gannon (Greene), Bacon, Mullen.
Gornik Zabrze: Klytta; Zadylak, Brzoza, Jegor, Waldoch, Agafon, Kubik (Grembocki), Kosela, Orzeszek (Jarosz), Brzeczek, Baluszynski.

Slovan Bratislava (2) 3 *(Faktor, Tittel, Rusnak)*
Portadown (0) 0 6500
Slovan Bratislava: Molnar (Kakas); Seman (Pecko), Tittel, Chvila, Kinder, Faktor, Tomaschek (Demo), Negro, Lancz, Maixnor, Rusnak.
Portadown: Keenan; Major, Strain (Evans), Stewart, Mills (Gray), Cunningham, Shepherd, Casey, Russell, Murray, Frazer.

24 AUG

IA Akranes (2) 2 *(Ingolfsson, Thordarson O)*
Bangor City (0) 0 1200
IA Akranes: Thordarson T; Haraldsson S (Thordarson S), Haraldsson P, Jonsson, Hervarsson, Miljkovic, Hognason, Gislason, Bibercic (Petursson), Thordarson O, Ingolfsson.
Bangor City: Adkins; Jones, Middleton, Evans, Rutter, Humphries (Hughes), Wiggins, Barnett, Mottram, Williams (Barry), Noble.

First Round, First Leg

13 SEPT

Antwerp (0) 0
Newcastle U (3) 5 *(Lee 3, Sellars, Watson)* 19,700
Antwerp: Svilar; Broeckaert, Kulcsar, Emmerechts, Smidts, Porte, Kiekens, Godfroid, Zohar (Monteiro), Severeyns, Vangompel.
Newcastle U: Srnicek; Hottiger, Beresford, Venison, Peacock, Albert, Lee, Beardsley (Watson), Cole (Jeffrey), Fox, Sellars.

Blackburn R (0) 0
Trelleborg (0) 1 *(Sandell)* 13,775
Blackburn R: Flowers; Berg, Le Saux, Slater (Atkins), Hendry, Gale, Ripley, Sherwood (Makel), Shearer, Sutton, Wilcox.
Trelleborg: Jankowski; Brorsson, Andersson, Karlsson C, Mattsson, Hansson, Engqvist, Severin, Blixt (Larsson), Sandell, Karlsson J.

Borussia Dortmund (0) 1 *(Moller)*
Motherwell (0) 0 35,420
Borussia Dortmund: Klos; Schmidt, Julio Cesar, Kree (Povlsen), Reuter, Zorc, Sammer, Reinhardt, Moller, Chapuisat, Riedle (Ricken).
Motherwell: Woods; Shannon, McCart, Philliben, Martin, McKinnon, Lambert, Dolan, Davies (McGrillen), Coyne, Arnott (Kirk).

Linfield (0) 1 *(Anderson)*
Odense (0) 1 *(Schjonberg)* 3585
Linfield: Lamont; Dornan, Easton, Peebles, McConnell, Beatty, Campbell, Knell (Anderson), Haylock, Fenlon, Bailie.
Odense: Hogh; Nedergaard, Hemmingsen M, Hansen, Schjonberg, Hemmingsen C, Melvang, Dethefsen, Bisgaard (Petterson), Tchami (Madson), Thorup.

15 SEPT

Internazionale (0) 1 *(Bergkamp (pen))*
Aston Villa (0) 0 22,639
Internazionale: Pagliuca; Bergomi, Festa, Bia (Paganin), Conte, Bianchi, Berti, Seno, Jonk, Bergkamp, Sosa (Del Vecchio).
Aston Villa: Spink; Barrett, King, Ehiogu, McGrath, Richardson, Townsend, Fashanu (Houghton), Saunders, Atkinson, Staunton.

First Round, Second Leg

27 SEPT

Newcastle U (4) 5 *(Lee, Cole 3, Beardsley (pen))*
Antwerp (0) 2 *(Kiekens, Severeyns)* 29,737
Newcastle U: Srnieck; Hottiger, Beresford, Howey, Peacock, Albert, Lee (Watson), Beardsley (Clark), Cole, Fox, Sellars.
Antwerp: Van der Straeten; Emmerechts (Moukram), Smidts, Taeymans, Godfroid, Kiekens, Porte, Kulcsar, Vangompel (Nilson), Zohar, Severeyns.

Odense (4) 5 *(Nedergaard 2, Schjonberg 2 (1 pen), Thorup)*
Linfield (0) 0 4518
Odense: Hogh; Nedergaard, Hemmingsen M, Hansen, Schjonberg, Hemmingsen C, Melvang, Dethlefsen, Bisgaard (Pederson), Tchami, Thorup (Madsen).
Linfield: Lamont; Dornan, Easton, Peebles, McConnell, Beatty, Campbell, Gorman, Haylock, McCoosh, Bailie.

Trelleborg (0) 2 *(Karlsson 2)*
Blackburn R (1) 2 *(Sutton, Shearer)* 6730
Trelleborg: Jankowski; Mattasson, Karlsson C, Brorsson M, Andersson M, Severin, Palmer (Eriksson), Engqvist, Karlsson J, Hansson, Sandell.
Blackburn R: Flowers; Berg, Le Saux, Sherwood, Hendry, Gale (Pearce), Ripley, Atkins (Warhurst), Shearer, Sutton, Wilcox.

28 SEPT

Motherwell (0) 0
Borussia Dortmund (0) 2 *(Riedle 2)* 9362
Motherwell: Woods; Shannon, McKinnon, Philliben, Martin, McCart, Lambert (Kirk), Dolan, Coyne, Arnott, Davies (Burns).
Borussia Dortmund: Klos; Reinhardt (Tanko), Julio Cesar, Sammer, Schmidt, Reuter, Freund, Moller, Zorc, Chapuisat, Riedle (Ricken).

29 SEPT

Aston Villa (1) 1 *(Houghton)*
Internazionale (0) 0 30,533
Aston Villa: Spink; Barrett, King, Ehiogu, McGrath, Richardson (Parker), Houghton, Townsend, Saunders (Whittingham), Atkinson, Staunton.
Internazionale: Pagliuca; Bergomi, Festa, Paganin, Bia, Conte (Orlandini), Berti, Bergkamp, Seno, Pancev (Fontolan), Sosa.

Second Round, First Leg

18 OCT

Newcastle U (2) 3 *(Fox, Beardsley (pen), Cole)*
Athletic Bilbao (0) 2 *(Ziganda, Suances)* 32,140

Newcastle U: Srnicek; Hottiger, Beresford, Howey, Peacock, Albert, Clark, Beardsley, Cole, Fox, Sellars.
Athletic Bilbao: Valencia; Trabuenca (Suances), Adrinua, Karanka, Larrazabal, Estibariz (Konno), Vales, Alkiza, Garitano, Mendiguren, Ziganda.

Trabzonspor (0) 1 *(Orhan)*
Aston Villa (0) 0 27,500

Trabzonspor: Grishko; Ogon, Lemi, Kernal, Chengiz, Abdullah, Soner, Tolunay, Unal, Hami (Hamdi), Orhan (Katcharava).
Aston Villa: Spink; Barrett, King, Ehiogu, McGrath, Richardson, Houghton, Townsend, Saunders, Whittingham, Staunton.

Second Round, Second Leg

1 NOV

Aston Villa (0) 2 *(Atkinson, Ehiogu)*
Trabzonspor (0) 1 *(Orhan)* 23,858

Aston Villa: Spink; Barrett, King, Ehiogu, McGrath, Richardson (Parker), Houghton, Townsend, Saunders, Atkinson, Staunton.
Trabzonspor: Grisco; Ogun, Cengiz, Kemal, Hamdi, Soner, Tolunay, Unal, Abdullah, Hami (Katcharava), Orhan (Osman).

Athletic Bilbao (0) 1 *(Ziganda)*
Newcastle U (0) 0 47,000

Athletic Bilbao: Valencia; Tabuenka, Andrinua, Karanka, Larrazabal, Larrainzar (Urrutia), Garitano, Mendiguren (Kortina), Alkiza, Suances, Ziganda.
Newcastle U: Srnicek; Hottiger, Beresford, Howey, Peacock, Albert, Watson, Beardsley, Lee, Fox (Jeffrey), Sellars (Clark).

EUROPEAN CUP DRAWS 1995–96

EUROPEAN CUP
Preliminary Round
Grasshoppers Zurich v Maccabi Tel Aviv, Rangers v Famagusta (Cyprus), Legia Warsaw v IFK Gothenburg, Salzburg (Austria) v Steaua Bucharest, Dynamo Kiev (Ukraine) v Aalborg (Denmark), Rosenborg (Norway) v Besiktas (Turkey), Anderlecht v Ferencvaros (Hungary), Panathinaikos (Greece) v Hajduk Split (Croatia).

EUROPEAN CUP-WINNERS' CUP
Preliminary Round
Tiligul Tiraspol (Moldova) v Sion (Switzerland), VAC Samsung (Hungary) v FC Sileks (Macedonia), Turku (Finland) v FC Teuta (Albania), FC Vaduz (Liechtenstein) v Hradec Kralove (Czech Republic), Hapoel Nicosia (Cyprus) v Nefski Baku (Azerbaijan), Wrexham v Petrolul Ploesti (Romania), Valletta (Malta) v Inter Bratislava (Slovakia), Shakytyor (Ukraine) v Linfield, Zalgiris Vilnius (Lithuania) v NK Mura (Slovenia), Katowice (Poland) v Ararat Erevan (Armenia), FC Obilic (Yugoslavia) v Dinamo Batumi (Georgia), Lokomotiv Sofia (Bulgaria) v Derry City, Maccabi Haifa (Israel) v Klakksvikar (Faeroes), Dinamo-93 Minsk (Belarus) v Molde FK (Norway), Grevenmacher (Luxembourg) v Reykjavik (Iceland), Dag-Liepaja (Latvia) v FC Lantana (Estonia).

UEFA CUP
Preliminary Round
Orebro SK (Sweden) v Beggen (Luxembourg), Tampere (Finland) v Viking FK (Norway), Bangor City (Wales) v Widzew Lodz (Poland), Shelbourne v Akranes (Iceland), Glenavon v FC Hafnarfjordur (Iceland), Brondby (Denmark) v Inkaras-Grifas (Lithuania), Lillestroem (Norway) v Flora Tallinn (Estonia), Motherwell v MyPa-47 (Finland), Skonto Riga (Latvia) v Maribor Branik (Slovenia), Sturm Graz (Austria) v Slavia Prague (Czech Republic), Jeunesse d'Esch (Luxembourg) v FC Lugano (Switzerland), Slovan Bratislava (Slovakia) v NK Osijek (Croatia), Dundalk v Malmo (Sweden), Crusaders v Silkeborg (Denmark), Afan Lido v RAF Riga (Latvia), Raith Rovers v Gotu Itrottarfelag (Faeroes), Slavia Sofia (Bulgaria) v Olympiakos (Greece), Zimbru Chisinau (Moldova) v Hapoel Tel Aviv (Israel), Sparta Prague (Czech Republic) v Galatasaray (Turkey), Omonia Nicosia (Cyprus) v Sliema Wanderers (Malta), FC Kosice (Slovakia) v Ujpest Egylet (Hungary), Universitatea Craiova (Romania) v Dinamo Minsk (Belarus), Fenerbahce (Turkey) v FC Partizan (Albania), FC Varda (Macedonia) v FC Samtredia (Georgia), Botev Plovdiv (Bulgaria) v Dinamo Tbilisi (Georgia), Apollon Athens (Greece) v Olimpija Ljublijana (Slovenia), Red Star Belgrade (Yugoslavia) v Neuchatel Xamax (Switzerland), Hibernians FC (Malta) v Chernomorets (Ukraine), Kapaz Ganja (Azerbaijan) v FK Austria Memphis, FC Tirana (Albania) v Hapoel Beer Sheva (Israel), Levski Sofia (Bulgaria) v Dinamo Bucharest (Romania), Zaglebie Lubin (Poland) v Shirak Erevan (Armenia).

Summary of Appearances

EUROPEAN CUP (1955–95)

English clubs
12 Liverpool
7 Manchester U
3 Nottingham F, Leeds U
2 Derby Co, Wolverhampton W, Everton, Aston Villa, Arsenal
1 Burnley, Tottenham H, Ipswich T, Manchester C

Scottish clubs
16 Rangers
15 Celtic
3 Aberdeen
2 Hearts
1 Dundee, Dundee U, Kilmarnock, Hibernian

Welsh clubs
1 Cwmbran

Clubs for Northern Ireland
18 Linfield
8 Glentoran
2 Crusaders, Portadown
1 Glenavon, Ards, Distillery, Derry C, Coleraine

Clubs for Eire
7 Shamrock R, Dundalk
6 Waterford
3 Drumcondra
2 Bohemians, Limerick, Athlone T, Shelbourne
1 Cork Hibs, Cork Celtic, Cork City, Derry C*, Sligo Rovers, St Patrick's Ath

Winners: Celtic 1966–67; Manchester U 1967–68; Liverpool 1976–77, 1977–78, 1980–81, 1983–84; Nottingham F 1978–79, 1979–80; Aston Villa 1981–82

Finalists: Celtic 1969–70; Leeds U 1974–75; Liverpool 1984–85

EUROPEAN CUP-WINNERS' CUP (1960–95)

English clubs
6 Tottenham H
5 Manchester U
4 West Ham U, Liverpool
3 Arsenal, Chelsea
2 Everton, Manchester C
1 Wolverhampton W, Leicester C, WBA, Leeds U, Sunderland, Southampton, Ipswich T

Scottish clubs
10 Rangers
8 Aberdeen
7 Celtic
3 Dundee U
2 Dunfermline Ath
1 Dundee, Hibernian, Hearts, St Mirren, Motherwell, Airdrie

Welsh clubs
14 Cardiff C
7 Wrexham, Swansea C
2 Bangor C
1 Borough U, Newport Co, Merthyr Tydfil, Barry T

Clubs from Northern Ireland
7 Glentoran
4 Ballymena U, Coleraine, Glenavon
3 Crusaders
2 Ards, Bangor, Linfield
1 Derry C, Distillery, Portadown, Carrick Rangers, Cliftonville

Clubs from Eire
6 Shamrock R
3 Limerick, Waterford, Dundalk, Bohemians
2 Cork Hibs, Galway U, Shelbourne, Sligo Rovers
1 Cork Celtic, St Patrick's Ath, Finn Harps, Home Farm, University College Dublin, Derry C*, Cork City, Bray Wanderers

Winners: Tottenham H 1962–63; West Ham U 1964–65; Manchester C 1969–70; Chelsea 1970–71; Rangers 1971–72; Aberdeen 1982–83; Everton 1984–85; Manchester U 1990-91; Arsenal 1993–94

Finalists: Rangers 1960–61, 1966–67; Liverpool 1965–66; Leeds U 1972–73; West Ham U 1975–76; Arsenal 1979–80, 1994–95

EUROPEAN FAIRS CUP & UEFA CUP (1955–95)

English clubs
8 Leeds U, Ipswich T
7 Liverpool
6 Everton, Arsenal, Manchester U, Aston Villa
5 Southampton, Tottenham H, Newcastle U
4 Manchester C, Birmingham C, Nottingham F, Wolverhampton W, WBA
3 Chelsea, Sheffield W
2 Stoke C, Derby Co, QPR
1 Burnley, Coventry C, Norwich C, London Rep XI, Watford, Blackburn R

Scottish clubs
17 Dundee U
14 Hibernian
11 Aberdeen
9 Celtic, Hearts
8 Rangers
5 Dunfermline Ath
4 Dundee
3 St Mirren, Kilmarnock
2 Partick Th
1 Morton, St Johnstone, Motherwell

Welsh Clubs
1 Inter Cardiff, Bangor C

Clubs from Northern Ireland
11 Glentoran
6 Coleraine
5 Linfield
3 Glenavon, Portadown
1 Ards, Ballymena U, Bangor, Crusaders

Clubs from Eire
8 Bohemians
4 Dundalk, Shamrock R
3 Finn Harps
2 Shelbourne, Drumcondra, St Patrick's Ath, Derry C*, Cork City
1 Cork Hibs, Athlone T, Limerick, Drogheda U, Galway U

Winners: Leeds U 1967–68, 1970–71; Newcastle U 1968–69; Arsenal 1969–70; Tottenham H 1971–72, 1983–84; Liverpool 1972–73, 1975–76; Ipswich T 1980–81

Finalists: London 1955–58, Birmingham C 1958–60, 1960–61; Leeds U 1966–67; Wolverhampton W 1971–72; Tottenham H 1973–74; Dundee U 1986–87

* *Now play in League of Ireland.*

WORLD CLUB CHAMPIONSHIP

Played annually up to 1974 and intermittently since then between the winners of the European Cup and the winners of the South American Champions Cup — known as the Copa Libertadores. In 1980 the winners were decided by one match arranged in Tokyo in February 1981 and the venue has been the same since. AC Milan replaced Marseille who had been stripped of their European Cup title in 1993.

1960 Real Madrid beat Penarol 0-0, 5-1
1961 Penarol beat Benfica 0-1, 5-0, 2-1
1962 Santos beat Benfica 3-2, 5-2
1963 Santos beat AC Milan 2-4, 4-2, 1-0
1964 Inter-Milan beat Independiente 0-1, 2-0, 1-0
1965 Inter-Milan beat Independiente 3-0, 0-0
1966 Penarol beat Real Madrid 2-0, 2-0
1967 Racing Club beat Celtic 0-1, 2-1, 1-0
1968 Estudiantes beat Manchester United 1-0, 1-1
1969 AC Milan beat Estudiantes 3-0, 1-2
1970 Feyenoord beat Estudiantes 2-2, 1-0
1971 Nacional beat Panathinaikos* 1-1, 2-1
1972 Ajax beat Independiente 1-1, 3-0
1973 Independiente beat Juventus* 1-0
1974 Atlético Madrid* beat Independiente 0-1, 2-0
1975 Independiente and Bayern Munich could not agree dates; no matches.
1976 Bayern Munich beat Cruzeiro 2-0, 0-0
1977 Boca Juniors beat Borussia Moenchengladbach* 2-2, 3-0
1978 Not contested
1979 Olimpia beat Malmö* 1-0, 2-1
1980 Nacional beat Nottingham Forest 1-0
1981 Flamengo beat Liverpool 3-0
1982 Penarol beat Aston Villa 2-0
1983 Gremio Porto Alegre beat SV Hamburg 2-1
1984 Independiente beat Liverpool 1-0
1985 Juventus beat Argentinos Juniors 4-2 on penalties after a 2-2 draw
1986 River Plate beat Steaua Bucharest 1-0
1987 FC Porto beat Penarol 2-1 after extra time
1988 Nacional (Uru) beat PSV Eindhoven 7-6 on penalties after 1-1 draw
1989 AC Milan beat Atletico Nacional (Col) 1-0 after extra time
1990 AC Milan beat Olimpia 3-0
1991 Red Star Belgrade beat Colo Colo 3-0
1992 Sao Paulo beat Barcelona 2-1
1993 Sao Paulo beat AC Milan 3-2

*European Cup runners-up; winners declined to take part.

1994

1 December in Tokyo

Velez Sarsfield (0) 2 *(Trotta 50 (pen), Asad 57)*

AC Milan (0) 0 55,860

Velez Sarsfield: Chilavert; Trotta, Cardozo, Almandoz, Gomez, Sotomayor, Bassedas, Basualdo, Asad, Pompei, Flores.

AC Milan: Rossi; Tassotti, Maldini, Albertini, Costacurta, Baresi, Bonadoni, Desailly, Boban, Savicevic (Simone 60), Massaro (Panucci 86).
Referee: Torres (Colombia).

EUROPEAN SUPER CUP

Played annually between the winners of the European Champions' Cup and the European Cup-Winners' Cup. AC Milan replaced Marseille in 1993–94.

Previous Matches

1972 Ajax beat Rangers 3-1, 3-2
1973 Ajax beat AC Milan 0-1, 6-0
1974 Not contested
1975 Dynamo Kiev beat Bayern Munich 1-0, 2-0
1976 Anderlecht beat Bayern Munich 4-1, 1-2
1977 Liverpool beat Hamburg 1-1, 6-0
1978 Anderlecht beat Liverpool 3-1, 1-2
1979 Nottingham F beat Barcelona 1-0, 1-1
1980 Valencia beat Nottingham F 1-0, 1-2
1981 Not contested
1982 Aston Villa beat Barcelona 0-1, 3-0
1983 Aberdeen beat Hamburg 0-0, 2-0
1984 Juventus beat Liverpool 2-0
1985 Juventus v Everton not contested due to UEFA ban on English clubs
1986 Steaua Bucharest beat Dynamo Kiev 1-0
1987 FC Porto beat Ajax 1-0, 1-0
1988 KV Mechelen beat PSV Eindhoven 3-0, 0-1
1989 AC Milan beat Barcelona 1-1, 1-0
1990 AC Milan beat Sampdoria 1-1, 2-0
1991 Manchester U beat Red Star Belgrade 1-0
1992 Barcelona beat Werder Bremen 1-1, 2-1
1993 Parma beat AC Milan 0-1, 2-0

1994-95

First Leg, 1 February 1995, Highbury

Arsenal (0) 0

AC Milan (0) 0 38,044

Arsenal: Seaman; Dixon, Winterburn, Schwarz, Bould, Adams, Jensen, (Hillier 85), Wright, Hartson, Selley, Campbell (Merson 74).
AC Milan: Rossi; Tassotti, Maldini, Albertini, Costacurta, Baresi, Donadoni, Desailly, Simone, Savicevic (Dir Canio 89), Massaro.
Referee: Van der Ende (Holland).

Second Leg, 8 February 1995, Milan

AC Milan (1) 2 *(Boban 41, Massaro 67)*

Arsenal (0) 0 23,953

AC Milan: Rossi; Tassotti, Albertini, Costacurta, Baresi, Donadoni, Desailly, Savicevic (Eranio 89), Boban, Massaro (Di Canio 80).
Arsenal: Seaman; Dixon (Keown 66), Winterburn, Schwarz, Bould, Adams, Campbell (Parlour 76), Wright, Hartson, Merson, Selley.
Referee: Krug (Germany).

SOUTH AMERICA

COPA LIBERTADORES 1994
(Results continued from last edition)

Quarter-Finals, First Leg
Olimpia 1, Bolivar 0
Indep. Medellin 0, Junior 2
Minerven 0, Velez Sarsfield 0
Union Espanola 1, Sao Paulo 1

Quarter-Finals, Second Leg
Bolivar 0, Olimpia 2
Junior 0, Indep. Medellin 0
Velez Sarsfield 2, Minerven 0
Sao Paulo 4, Union Espanola 3

Semi-Finals, First Leg
Junior 2, Velez Sarsfield 1
Sao Paulo 2, Olimpia 1

Semi-Finals, Second Leg
Velez Sarsfield 2, Junior 1
(aggregate 3-3; Velez Sarsfield won 5-4 on penalties)
Olimpia 1, Sao Paulo 0
(aggregate 2-2; Sao Paulo won 4-3 on penalties)

Final First Leg
Velez Sarsfield 1, Sao Paulo 0

Final Second Leg
Sao Paulo 1, Velez Sarsfield 0
(aggregate 1-1; Velez Sarsfield won 5-3 on penalties)

SOUTH AMERICAN SUPER CUP

First Round, First Leg
Flamengo 0, Estudiantes 0
River Plate 2, Nacional (U) 2
Santos 1, Independiente 0
Olimpia 2, Cruzeiro 0
Penarol 1, Boca Juniors 0
Gremio 1, Racing Club 1
Colo Colo 4, Argentinos Juniors 1
At. Nacional 0, Sao Paulo 2

First Round, Second Leg
Cruzeiro 4, Olimpia 0
Nacional (U) 0, River Plate 1
Independiente 4, Santos 0
Estudiantes 2, Flamengo 0
Sao Paulo 1, At. Nacional 1
Argentinos Juniors 1, Colo Colo 1
Boca Juniors 4, Penarol 1
Racing Club 1, Gremio 2

Quarter Finals, First Leg
Colo Colo 2, Sao Paulo 1
Estudiantes 1, Cruzeiro 0
Gremio 1, Independiente 1
River Plate 0, Boca Juniors 0

Quarter Finals, Second Leg
Independiente 2, Gremio 0
Cruzeiro 3, Estudiantes 0
Sao Paulo 4, Colo Colo 1
Boca Juniors 1, River Plate 1
(aggregate 1-1; Boca Juniors won 5-4 on penalties)

Semi-finals, First Leg
Boca Juniors 2, Sao Paulo 0
Cruzeiro 1, Independiente 0

Semi-Finals, Second Leg
Independiente 4, Cruzeiro 0
Sao Paulo 1, Boca Juniors 0

Final First Leg
Boca Juniors 1, Independiente 1

Final Second Leg
Independiente 1, Boca Juniors 0

COPA LIBERTADORES 1995

First Round

Group 1

	P	*W*	*D*	*L*	*F*	*A*	*Pts*
River Plate	6	3	3	0	11	3	12
Penarol	6	2	3	1	9	7	9
Independiente	6	2	1	3	5	7	7
Cerro	6	1	1	4	5	13	4

Group 2

	P	*W*	*D*	*L*	*F*	*A*	*Pts*
Cerro Porteno	6	4	2	0	16	6	14
Olimpia	6	3	3	0	16	7	12
Caracas	6	2	0	4	8	18	6
Trujillanos	6	0	1	5	8	17	1

Group 3

	P	*W*	*D*	*L*	*F*	*A*	*Pts*
Millonarios	6	3	1	2	11	8	10
At. Nacional	6	2	3	1	5	4	9
Univ de Chile	6	2	1	3	7	7	7
Univ Catolica	6	2	1	3	10	14	7

(Play-off: Univ Catolica 4, Univ de Chile 1)

Group 4

	P	*W*	*D*	*L*	*F*	*A*	*Pts*
Palmeiras	6	4	1	1	15	5	13
Gremio	6	3	2	1	12	7	11
Emelec	6	1	2	3	8	12	5
Nacional	6	1	1	4	3	14	4

Group 5

	P	*W*	*D*	*L*	*F*	*A*	*Pts*
Sporting Cristal	6	3	3	0	15	4	12
Bolivar	6	2	3	1	8	5	9
Alianza	6	1	2	3	10	11	5
Wilsterman	6	1	2	3	6	19	5

Second Round, First Leg
Olimpia 0, Gremio 3
Emelec 2, Cerro Porteno 0
Alianza 1, Millonarios 1
Bolivar 1, Palmeiras 0
Caracas 2, Sporting Cristal 2
At. Nacional 3, Penarol 1
Velez Sarsfield 3, Independiente 0
Univ Catolica 2, River Plate 1

Second Round, Second Leg
River Plate 3, Univ Catolica 1
Cerro Porteno 2, Emelec 0
(aggregate 2-2; Emelec won 5-4 on penalties)
Millonarios 2, Alianza 0
Palmeiros 3, Bolivar 0
Penarol 1, At. Nacional 3
Gremio 2, Olimpia 0
Velez Sarsfield 2, Independiente 2
Sporting Cristal 6, Caracas 3
Tournament still being completed

COPA AMERICA 1995

Uruguay won the Copa America for the South American Championship, the oldest international competition still being played in the world. Their record of never having lost a tournament played on their own territory held good, though they needed an immaculate series of penalties after the normal 90 minutes, to defeat World Cup holders Brazil.

Group A
Uruguay 4, Venezuela 1
Mexico 1, Paraguay 2
Uruguay 1, Paraguay 0
Mexico 3, Venezuela 1
Paraguay 3, Venezuela 2
Uruguay 1, Mexico 1

Group B
Colombia 1, Peru 1
Brazil 1, Ecuador 0
Colombia 1, Ecuador 0
Peru 0, Brazil 2
Peru 1, Ecuador 2
Brazil 3, Colombia 0

Group C
USA 2, Chile 1
Argentina 2, Bolivia 1
USA 0, Bolivia 1
Chile 0, Argentina 4
Bolivia 2, Chile 2
Argentina 0, USA 3

Quarter-finals
Paraguay 1, Colombia 1
Colombia won 5-4 on penalties.
Uruguay 2, Bolivia 1
USA 0, Mexico 0
USA won 4-1 on penalties.
Brazil 2, Argentina 2
Brazil won 4-2 on penalties.

Semi-finals
Uruguay 2, Colombia 0
USA 0, Brazil 1

Third place
Colombia 4, USA 1

Uruguay (0) 1 *(Bengoechea)*
Brazil (1) 1 *(Tulio) in Montevideo* 70,000
Uruguay: Alvez; Mendez, Moas, Herrera, Silva (Adinolfi), Dorta (Bengoechea), Gutierrez, Poyet, Francescoli, Otero, Fonseca (Martinez).
Brazil: Taffarel; Jorghino, Aldair, Cruz, Roberto Carlos, Sempao, Dunga, Juninho (Beto), Zinho, Edmundo, Tulio.
Referee: Brizio (Mexico).
Uruguay won 5-3 on penalties.

Conmebol Cup
Final first leg
Sao Paulo 6, Penarol 1

Final second leg
Penarol 3, Sao Paulo 0

Masters Cup (for super Cup Winners)
Final first leg
Olimpia 0, Cruzeiro 0

Final second leg
Cruzeiro 1, Olimpia 0

PANAMERICAN GAMES
Final
Argentina 0, Mexico 0
(*Argentina won 5-4 on penalties*)

American Airlines Cup 1994
Final
Cartagines (Costa Rica) 3, Atlante (Mexico) 2

AFRICA

East and Central African Cup
Final
Tanzania 2, Uganda 2
(*Tanzania won 4-3 on penalties*)

East and Central African Club Championship
Final
SC Simba 1, Express 1
(*Simba won 4-2 on penalties*)

Four Nations Cup

	P	*W*	*D*	*L*	*F*	*A*	*Pts*
Ivory Coast	3	1	2	0	3	2	5
South Africa	3	1	2	0	3	2	5
Ghana	3	1	1	1	3	3	4
Cameroon	3	0	1	2	2	4	1

ASIA

Gulf Cup

	P	*W*	*D*	*L*	*F*	*A*	*Pts*
Saudi Arabia	5	4	1	0	10	4	9
UAE	5	3	2	0	7	1	8
Bahrain	5	1	3	1	5	6	5
Qatar	5	1	1	3	6	8	3
Kuwait	5	1	1	3	2	6	3
Oman	5	0	2	3	4	9	2

ASIAN GAMES
Final
Uzbekistan 4, China 2

South Asian Gold Cup
Final
Sri Lanka 1, India 0
(*sudden-death extra time*)

Dynasty Cup
Final
Japan 2, South Korea 2
(*Japan won 5-3 on penalties*)

VAUXHALL CONFERENCE 1994-95

VAUXHALL CONFERENCE TABLE 1994–95

		Home			Goals		Away			Goals		
	P	W	D	L	F	A	W	D	L	F	A	Pts
Macclesfield Town	42	14	3	4	39	18	10	5	6	31	22	80
Woking	42	11	8	2	46	23	10	4	7	30	31	75
Southport	42	13	4	4	46	21	8	5	8	22	29	72
Altrincham	42	10	3	8	34	27	10	5	6	43	33	68
Stevenage Borough	42	10	4	7	40	27	10	3	8	28	22	67
Kettering Town	42	12	5	4	40	25	7	5	9	33	31	67
Gateshead	42	12	4	5	28	13	7	6	8	33	40	67
Halifax Town	42	11	6	4	46	20	6	6	9	22	34	63
Runcorn	42	11	7	3	39	28	5	3	13	20	43	58
Northwich Victoria	42	7	8	6	39	30	7	7	7	38	36	57
Kidderminster Harriers	46	6	5	10	28	29	10	4	7	35	32	57
Bath City	42	10	6	5	35	26	5	6	10	20	30	57
Bromsgrove Rovers	42	9	7	5	42	35	5	6	10	24	34	55
Farnborough Town	42	8	5	8	23	31	7	5	9	22	33	55
Dagenham & Redbridge	42	8	5	8	28	32	5	8	8	28	37	52
Dover Athletic	42	6	10	5	28	25	5	6	10	20	30	49
Welling United	42	9	3	9	31	33	4	7	10	26	41	49
Stalybridge Celtic	42	9	6	6	29	27	2	8	11	23	45	47
Telford United	42	9	9	3	30	20	1	7	13	23	42	46
Merthyr Tydfil	42	10	4	7	37	27	1	7	13	16	36	44
Stafford Rangers	42	5	5	11	29	34	4	6	11	24	45	38
Yeovil Town	42	5	8	8	29	31	3	6	12	21	40	37

Note: Yeovil Town deducted 1 point

ATTENDANCES BY CLUB 1994–95

	Aggregate Attendance 1994–95	Average Attendance 1994–95	Average Attendance 1993–94	% Change
Altrincham	21,050	1002	751	+33
Bath City	13,579	647	683	–5
Bromsgrove Rovers	23,738	1130	1139	0
Dagenham & Redbridge	19,935	949	952	0
Dover Athletic	23,119	1101	1347	–18
Farnborough Town	16,766	798	513	+55
Gateshead	14,548	693	477	+45
Halifax Town	20,455	974	1035	–6
Kettering Town	38,584	1837	2025	–9
Kidderminster Harriers	41,129	1959	2250	–13
Macclesfield Town	26,458	1260	853	+48
Merthyr Tydfil	12,621	601	581	+3
Northwich Victoria	19,821	944	933	+1
Runcorn	9,818	468	594	–21
Southport	22,649	1079	1293	–17
Stafford Rangers	14,953	712	949	–25
Stalybridge Celtic	14,916	710	615	+15
Stevenage Borough	29,909	1424	1064	+34
Telford United	17,029	811	929	–13
Welling United	15,525	739	967	–24
Woking	38,122	1815	1712	+6
Yeovil Town	36,659	1746	2495	–30

HIGHEST ATTENDANCES 1994–95

4347	Kidderminster Harriers v Bromsgrove Rovers	26.12.94
3267	Bromsgrove Rovers v Kidderminster Harriers	2.1.95
3049	Kettering Town v Kidderminster Harriers	23.8.94
2734	Gateshead v Yeovil Town	3.9.94
2650	Kettering Town v Runcorn	5.11.94
2532	Kettering Town v Stevenage Borough	26.12.94
2406	Woking v Dagenham & Redbridge	26.12.94
2386	Macclesfield Town v Altrincham	25.2.95
2368	Woking v Kidderminster Harriers	5.11.94
2351	Yeovil Town v Bath City	6.9.94
2340	Kettering Town v Woking	19.11.94
2325	Woking v Macclesfield Town	25.4.95

VAUXHALL CONFERENCE LEADING GOALSCORERS 1994–95

Conf.			FAC	BLT	FAT
25	Paul Dobson *(Gateshead)*	+	2	2	3
23	Carl Alford *(Kettering Town)*	+	1	3	—
21	Leroy May *(Stafford Rangers)*	+	—	1	—
19	Andy Green *(Altrincham)*	+	2	—	—
	Clive Walker *(Woking)*	+	1	—	5
18	Recky Carter *(Bromsgrove Rovers)*	+	—	12	—
	David Leworthy *(Dover Athletic)*	+	5	2	—
	Phil Power *(Macclesfield Town)*	+	—	2	3
	Malcolm O'Connor *(Northwich Victoria)*	+	4	—	1
17	Darran Hay *(Woking)*	+	—	—	—
16	Dean Birkby *(Bath City)*	+	—	2	—
	Mark Hughes *(Runcorn)*	+	—	1	2
15	Paul Wilson *(Yeovil Town)*	+	—	—	—

CLUB REVIEW

	VC	FAT	BLT	FAC
Altrincham	4	QF	QF	3
1993–94	10	1	1	4q
Bath City	12	2	2	1
	12	2	2	3
Bromsgrove Rovers	13	1	W	4q
	18	3	SF	3
Dagenham & Red.	15	1	SF	2q
	6	2	QF	4q
Dover Athletic	16	1	QF	4q
	8	3	2	1q
Farnborough Town	14	2	2	4q
	21	2	2	1
Gateshead	7	3	1	2q
	11	QF	3	3q
Halifax Town	8	1	1	2
	13	3	QF	2
Kettering Town	6	2	F	1
	2	2	1	1
Kidderminster H.	11	F	2	1
	1	1	QF	5
Macclesfield Town	1	QF	SF	4q
	7	3	W	2
Merthyr Tydfil	20	3	1	2q
	20	3	1	4q
Northwich Victoria	10	1	2	1
	15	1	SF	1q
Runcorn	9	3	2	1
	5	F	2	1
Southport	3	1	2	1
	4	3	1	4q
Stafford Rangers	21	1	2	4q
	9	2	2	4q
Stalybridge Celtic	18	1	QF	4q
	14	1	2	2
Stevenage Borough	5	3	1	2q
	22	1	1	1
Telford United	19	2	1	4q
	17	2	1	1
Welling United	17	2	1	2q
	16	2	QF	1q
Woking	2	W	QF	2
	3	W	2	2
Yeovil Town	22	2	2	4q
	19	1	F	2

HIGHEST SCORERS

4 David Leworthy *DOVER ATHLETIC* v Molesey (FA Cup 24.9.94)
4 Terry Robbins *WELLING UNITED* v Marlow (FA Trophy 30.1.95)

HIGHEST AGGREGATE SCORES

Bromsgrove Rovers 5–5 Woking 14.1.95
Dagenham & Redbridge 5–3 Woking 26.12.94
Farnborough Town 5–3 Telford United 1.4.95
Yeovil Town 4–4 Northwich Victoria 6.5.95
Bath City 3–5 Kidderminster Harriers 24.9.94

LARGEST HOME WINS

Halifax Town 6–0 Stafford Rangers 5.11.94
Bromsgrove Rovers 5–0 Yeovil Town 27.9.94
Northwich Victoria 5–0 Dagenham & Redbridge 3.9.94
Southport 5–0 Gateshead 23.8.94
Southport 5–0 Runcorn 26.12.94
Stevenage Borough 5–0 Yeovil Town 17.12.94

LARGEST AWAY WINS

Welling United 1–5 Northwich Victoria 19.11.94
Welling United 1–5 Bath City 28.1.95
Dagenham & Redbridge 0–4 Altrincham 4.2.95
Dagenham & Redbridge 0–4 Macclesfield Town 19.11.94
Telford United 0–4 Dagenham & Redbridge 18.2.95
Farnborough Town 0–4 Runcorn 24.9.94

MATCHES WITHOUT DEFEAT

13 Macclesfield Town
11 Woking
10 Southport
9 Northwich Victoria, Southport

MATCHES WITHOUT SUCCESS

11 Dover Athletic
10 Telford United
9 Bath City, Stafford Rangers, Stalybridge Celtic, Yeovil Town (twice)
8 Northwich Victoria, Stafford Rangers, Stalybridge Celtic, Stevenage Borough

CONSECUTIVE CONFERENCE VICTORIES

10 Macclesfield Town (Conference Record)
5 Woking
4 Altrincham, Farnborough Town, Halifax Town, Northwich Victoria, Southport, Stevenage Borough

CONSECUTIVE CONFERENCE DEFEATS

6 Stafford Rangers, Yeovil Town
5 Bath City, Farnborough Town, Stalybridge Celtic
4 Kidderminster Harriers, Merthyr Tydfil, Northwich Victoria, Stafford Rangers, Welling United, Yeovil Town

VAUXHALL CONFERENCE 1994–95

APPEARANCES AND GOALSCORERS

Altrincham
Vauxhall Appearances: Bolland, P. 0(1); Butler, B. 25(7); Carmody, M. 36; Cockram, D. 2(4); Collings, P. 42; Constable, S. 5(14); Cox, P. 0(2); Cross, S. 42; France, P. 41; Green, A. 35(1); Harris, R. 16; Hatton, B. 0(3); Heesom, D. 41; Martindale, D. 2; Morton, N. 27(1); O'Neill, S. 18(7); Ramoon, L. 0(2); Reid, A. 34(1); Sharratt, C. 39; Shaw, N. 10(5); Terry, S. 34; Whalley, N. 8
Goals (77): Green 19, Terry 12, Morton 10, Sharratt 6, France 6, Harris 5, O'Neill 4, Constable 3, Reid 3, Shaw 3, Cross 2, Butler 1, Cockram 1, Heesom 1, Ramoon 1.

Bath City
Vauxhall Appearances: Adcock, P. 26; Adekola, D. 7; Baldwin, D. 5; Birkby, D. 37; Birks, S. 22; Brooks, N. 25; Chenoweth, P. 34; Clements, S. 1; Cousins, R. 36; Crocker, M. 3; Crowley, R. 14; Dicks, G. 27; Forbes, D. 16; Gill, J. 40; Hedges, I. 32; Hervin, M. 4; Hewlett, M. 3; Jackson, D. 8; James, L. 3; Jones, V. 7; Loss, C. 5; Lucas, J. 4; McLoughlin, P. 14; Mings, A. 22; Mogg, D. 38; Ricketts, A. 12; Smart, G. 30; Spencer, M. 7; Taylor, C. 13; Tilley, D. 3; Vernon, D. 18; Walsh, A. 8.
Goals (55): Birkby 16, Adcock 10, Smart 7, Brooks 4, Chenoweth 3, Mings 3, Adekola 2, Crocker 2, McLoughlin 2, Birks 1, Cousins 1, Crowley 1, Dicks 1, Vernon 1, og 1.

Bromsgrove Rovers
Vauxhall Appearances: Bayliss, S. 0(1); Booth, S. 0(2); Boston, K. 1(3); Brain, S. 1(1); Brighton, S. 1(3); Burgher, S. 11; Carter, R. 33; Clarke, N. 34; Crane, S. 0(2); Daly, T. 0(2); Devery, B. 17(5); Gaunt, C. 41; Glasser, N. 17(3); Gray, A. (1); Gray, B. 18(8); Gray, M. 12(3); Grealish, T. 3(1); Green, R. 21(20); Greenman, C. 2(1); Humphrey, P. 4(3); Judge, A. 21(9); Marlowe, A. 10(4); Morley, T. 0(1); Pearce, C. 7(4); Power, A. 29(4); Radburn, C. 1; Richardson, K. 27; Shilvock, R. 12(17); Skelding, J. 38; Smith, A. 16(7); Stott, S. 39; Taylor, C. 0(2); Taylor, S. 30(1); Walker, R. 0(3); Warner, A. 4(1); Whitehead, S. 0(3); Young, L. 2(3).
Goals (66): Carter 18, Stott 9, Taylor 9, Skelding 6, Gray B 5, Pearce 4, Devery 2, Gaunt 2, Gray M 2, Brain 1, Brighton 1, Clarke 1, Marlow 1, Power 1, Shilvock 1, Smith 1, Warner 1, Young 1.

Dagenham & Redbridge
Vauxhall Appearances: Bennett, G. 8; Bolder, B. 29(3); Boyle, G. 2; Broom, J. 31; Cavell, P. 14(3); Conner, S. 26(1); Cook, J. 19; Cooper, W. 0(5); Culverhouse, D. 23(7); Devereux, J. 6(7); Dunphy, N. 6; Emery, N. 0(2); Forbes, R. 7(3); Fowler, L. 5(2); Gammons, R. 3(12); Gothard, P. 4(17); Greene, D. 33(6); Groves, P. 6; Haag, K. 12(1); Jones, D. 6(1); Kalogeracos, V. 1; Kimble, G. 2(4); Livett, S. 6; Martin, D. 3(4); McDonough, R. 23; McPherson, M. 4(1); Moore, C. 10(1); Moore, M. 0(2); O'Sullivan, J. 0(3); Oliver, S. 2(10); Pettinger, P. 7; Philip, R. (1); Richardson, I. 36; Risley, M. 2(3); Roberts, B. 7(12); Shipp, D. 9; Sinclair, R. 0(1); Sorrell, T. 15(1); Steam, M. 0(5); Stebbing, G. 41; Tomlinson, D. 1; Wallace, A. 9(1); Watts, P. 33; Wordsworth, D. 10(3).
Goals (56): Richardson 10, McDonough 7, Haag 6, Shipp 6, Greene 5, Wordsworth 4, Bennett 3, Broom 3, Cavell 3, Conner 2, Stebbing 2, Cook 1, Cooper 1, Jones 1, Martin 1, Sorrell 1.

Dover Athletic
Vauxhall Appearances: Barlett, J. 7; Blewden, C. 18(7); Bond, K. 7; Browne, C. 26(2); Budden, J. 38; Carruthers, M. 0(12); Carter, I. 17; Chambers, P. 5(7); Costello, P. 3(5); Darlington, J. 9(14); Dixon, A. 35; Donn, N. 25(11); Ebbli, E. 13; Eeles, A. 10(8); Embery, J. 0(3); Fox, L. 0(2); Hall, M. 10; Lewis, J. 30(7); Leworthy, D. 35(2); Lillis, J. 4; Livett, S. 4; Milton, R. 31; Munden, M. 6(4); O'Brien, P. 13(10); O'Connell, I. 15(2); Omogbehin, C. 1(2); Partner, L. 0(1); Restarick, S. 9(1); Scott, D. 26; Strouts,J. 5(1); Walker, D. 37(3); Williams, D. 23(3); Wilks, M. 0(9).
Goals (48): Leworthy 18, Lewis 5, Chambers 4, Blewden 3, Budden 2, Browne 2, Darlington 2, Eeles 2, Hall 2, Restarick 2, Carruthers 1, Carter 1, Costello 1, Lillis 1, Scott 1, og 1.

Farnborough Town
Vauxhall Appearances: Baker, K. 10; Baker, S. 37; Boothe, C. 39; Coney, D. 30; Day, K. 34(1); Denny, R. 12(8); Dobson, R. 3(1); Harlow, D. 20; Hayward, D. 0(1); Horton, J. 16(4); Jones, Mark 26; Jones, Murray 17(2); Juryeff, I. 3; Pratt, B. 36; Read, S. 11(3); Rowe, A. 6; Rowe, D. 1(1); Savage, I. 3(5); Steadman, C. 2; Stemp, W. 30; Stevens, G. 1(2); Taylor, M. 36; Terry, P. 26(5); Thompson, N. 11(2); Turkington, M. 29(1); Underwood, J. 11(5); Walters, D. 12(1).
Goals (45): Boothe 14, Denny 9, Read 5, Turkington 5, Harlow 3, Jones Murray 2, Baker S 1, Day 1, Horton 1, Pratt 1, Terry 1, Thompson 1, og 1.

Gateshead
Vauxhall Appearances: Cavell, P. 15(2); Copeland, L. 2; Corner, D. 5(1); Cramman, K. 38(2); Dobson, P. 39; Dowson, A. 37; Farrey, M. 30(3); Hine, M. 37(1); Lacey, N. 9; Lamb, A. 12(18); Musgrave, S. 9; Nobbs, K. 28(5); Parkinson, G. 39; Proudlock, P. 21(11); Robinson, D. 6(12); Rowe, B. 31(3); Rowntree, P. 0(1); Smith, S. 1; Stephenson, N. 0(2); Sweeney, P. 0(4); Taylor, I. 31; Watson, J. 31(3); Wrightson, J. 40(2).
Goals (61): Dobson 25, Cramman 6, Lamb 6, Hine 5, Proudlock 4, Cavell 3, Dowson 2, Farrey 2, Robinson 2, Corner 1, Lacey 1, Watson 1, og 3.

Halifax Town
Vauxhall Appearances: Beddard, E. 6(10); Boardman, C. 32(1); Circuit, S. 1; Dunphy, S. 2(2); Flemming, P. 23; Flounders, A. 9(8); Ford, S. 5(7); Fowler, L. 12(7); German, D. 22(6); Gray, R. 0(2); Hall, D. 4(5); Hanson, D. 26(5); Heyes, D. 28(14); Horner, N. 1(2); Johnson, S. 3; Jones, A. 39; Kiwomya, A. 29(1); Lambert, C. 38(1); Lancaster, D. 21(3); Langley, K. 13(1); Leitch, G. 11(6); Martin, D. 5(1); Patterson, J. 13(3); Pettinger, P. 7(1); Prindiville, S. 39; Rathbone, M. 5(1); Sunley, M. 7(2); Trotter, M. 18(4); Wilmot, R. 2(21); Worthington, G. 29(8).
Goals (68): Kiwomya 13, Hanson 11, Worthington 9, Lancaster 7, Patterson 5, Prindiville 5, German 3, Lambert 3, Beddard 2, Jones 2, Flemming 1, Flounders 1, Ford 1, Johnson 1, Leitch 1, Rathbone 1, Wilmot, og 1.

Kettering Town
Vauxhall Appearances: Alford, C. 38(2); Arnold, I. 22; Ashby, N. 34; Ashdjian, J. 0(2); Barnes, R. 4(5); Benstead, G. 22; Brown, P. 40(1); Chard, P. 6(1); Clarke, S. 29(5); Donald, W. 19(2); Dunphy, S. 1; Gleasure, P. 15(10); Graham, J. 8(13); Holden, S. 32; Howe, S. 6; Magee, J. 0(2); Martin, D. 9(4); Oxbrow, D. 12; Pettinger, P. 5; Price, G. 12(4); Reed, G. 18; Saddington, J. 25; Smith, P. 8; Stringfellow, I. 31(2); Taylor, R. 27(1); Thomas, A. 30(6); Wright, O. 8(6).
Goals (73): Alford 23, Arnold 11, Brown 10, Thomas 8, Stringfellow 6, Graham 4, Taylor 4, Holden 3, Clarke 2, Howe 1, og 1.

Kidderminster Harriers
Vauxhall Appearances: Bancroft, P. 20; Brindley, C. 26; Cartwright, N. 26; Casey, K. 7; Davies, D. 1; Davies, P. 6; Deakin, J. 16; Dearlove, M. 5; Eades, G. 2; Forsyth, R. 42; Grainger, P. 19; Hodson, S. 42; Hughes, L. 35; Humphreys, D. 34; Langford, T. 3; Palmer, L. 16; Phillips, R. 2; Powell, J. 19; Purdie, J. 18; Rose, K. 28; Steadman, D. 16; Webb, P. 42; Weir, M. 21; Yates, M. 42
Goals (63): Forsyth 13, Davies Paul 11, Yates 10, Hughes 9, Humphreys 8, Brindley 2, Casey 2, Webb 2, Dearlove 1, Palmer 1, Phillips 1, Weir 1, og 2.

Macclesfield Town
Vauxhall Appearances: Allen, G. 2(1); Askey, J. 30; Bimson, S. 21; Bradshaw, M. 15; Crisp, M. 4(4); Farrelly, S. 42; Howarth, N. 39; Kendall, P. 11(2); Lillis, M. 0(1); Locke, S. 16(2); Lyons, D. 20(8); McDonald, M. 38; Marginson, K. 7; Midwood, M. 7; Monk, I. 16(7); Murray, M. 20; Norman, D. 13(1); Payne, S. 33; Power, P. 37; Shepherd, G. 12; Sorvel, N. 38(2); Tobin, S. 14(10); Wright, P. 4(4); Wood, S. 35(2).
Goals (70): Power 18, Howarth 11, Askey 9, Wood 9, Sorvel 5, Lyons 4, McDonald 3, Monk 3, Midwood 2, Tobin 2, Marginson 1, Payne 1, Shepherd 1, Wright 1.

Merthyr Tydfil

Vauxhall Appearances: Abraham, G. 24(1); Adebowle, A. 10; Beattie, A. 8(1); Boyle, T. 7(1); Costa, L. 3(2); David, R. 2(1); Davies, M. 13(1); Downs, G. 8; Dyer, S. 29(6); French, I. 11(5); Holtam, M. 29(6); Hopkins, A. 13(1); Hunter, P. 2; James, Rob1; James, Ryan4; Jenkins, A. 20(7); Jones, Lee2(3); Jones, Nathan36(2); Loss, C. 11; Mitchell, I. 20(7); Morris, S. 1; Narbett, J. 1; Needs, A. 7(2); O'Brien, N. 13; Popham, P. 3(2); Rogers, K. 38(1); Sanderson, P. 4(1); Scott, M. 15(5); Threlfall, D. 0(2); Vowles, P. 3(1); Wager, G. 41; Walton, M. 0(1); Webley, D. 28(4); Williams, M. 19; Woolgar, M. 3; York, A. 33.

Goals (53): Webley 12, Dyer 9, Mitchell 6, Rogers 6, Jones N 4, Jenkins 3, Abraham 2, Holtam 2, Hunter 2, Scott 2, Adebowle 1, French 1, York 1, og 2.

Northwich Victoria

Vauxhall Appearances: Abel, G. 33(1); Adams, C. 0(4); Baab, P. 5; Boyd, C. 30(1); Bullock, A. 0(1); Butler, B. 37(1); Cooke, I. 25(9); Deeley, N. 0(1); Duffy, C. 28; Gallagher, J. 22(4); Greygoose, D. 42; Hardy, N. 11(9); Hilton, R. 2; Jones, M. 33(2); Mitten, P. 0(2); Nesbitt, C. 2; Norman, D. 9(1); O'Connor, M. 31(7); Oghani, G. 29(8); Parker, J. 31; Radcliffe, R. 0(4); Snowden, T. 9(1); Tinson, D. 34(2); Turpin, S. 3; Vicary, D. 10(1); Walters, S. 16; Williams, C. 24(5).

Goals (77): O'Connor 18, Cooke 13, Oghani 12, Williams 11, Butler 7, Vicary 4, Hardy 3, Abel 2, Boyd 1, Duffy 1, Norman 1, Parker 1, Snowden 1, Turpin 1, Walters 1.

Runcorn

Vauxhall Appearances: Anderson, G. 30; Bates, J. 39; Brady, I. 16(1); Byrne, P. 34; Connor, J. 31; Curtis, R. 2(1); Doherty, N. 10(11); Ellis, P. 6; Finley, A. 25; Godfrey, W. 0(2); Hill, G. 26; Hughes, M. 39(1); Lee, A. 13(1); McInerney, I. 30(5); Morris, M. 40; Murphy, C. 2; Pugh, S. 4(3); Robertson, P. 35; Ruffer, C. 16(5); Shaw, N. 6; Smith, M. 24(15); Taylor, C. 0(3); Thomas, K. 34(1).

Goals (59): Hughes 16, Thomas 11, Anderson 6, Brady 4, Connor 4, McInerney 4, Smith 3, Shaw 3, Bates 2, Byrne 1, Doherty 1, Finley 1, Hill 1, Pugh 1, og 1.

Southport

Vauxhall Appearances: Blackhurst, J. 15(11); Challender, G. 5(1); Clark, M. 37; Comstive, P. 24(5); Cooper, L. 0(1); Cunningham, H. 27(6); Dove, L. 36; Edwards, E. 5; Fuller, D. 30; Gamble, D. 31(6); Goulding, D. 38; Haw, S. 30(5); Lodge, P. 38; McDonald, A. 17(7); McKenna, J. 42; McNally, J. 1; Penman, J. 9(11); Pritchard, B. 8; Quinlan, P. 0(1); Simms, M. 11; Sloan, M. 0(2); Symons, P. 1; Thomas, G. 24(5); Ward, D. 33.

Goals (68): Gamble 12, Haw 12, Comstive 9, Blackhurst 6, Thomas 6, Cunningham 5, Clark 3, Dove 3, Goulding 3, McDonald 3, Penman 2, Ward 2, Challender 1, Lodge 1.

Stafford Rangers

Vauxhall Appearances: Abbishaw, D. 2(1); Berry, George6(6); Berry, Gwynne4; Boughey, D. 34(2); Bradshaw, M. 27; Brown, G. 6(2); Cooke, J. 1(1); Corbett, S. 1(1); Crisp, M. 6; Crowley, D. 8(2); Davies, M. 13; Dawson, D. 7(1); Drewitt, I. 29; Duffin, S. 13; Edensor, J. 1; Foy, D. 10; Griffiths, A. 17(6); Hassall, J. 23(4); Harrison, M. 2; Hawkins, R. 0(2); Hicks, N. 1(2); Kilbane, F. 13; Law, M. 5; Leeming, D. 8; Luby, S. 1; Mackenzie, S. 16(2); Mardenborough, S. 10; May, L. 35(1); Mee, A. 2(4); Milson, P. 6; Molloy, P. 8(1); O'Toole, P. 14; Penny, A. 10(1); Rees, M. 3(2); Shepstone, P. 3; Simpson, W. 29; Smith, Mark2; Smith, Robert9(1); Squires, J. 8; Timons, C. 5; Walker, G. 19; Williams, D. 31(3); Woodward, A. 2(1); Wright, E. 1(1).

Goals (53): May 21, Duffin 6, Mardenborough 5, Drewitt 4, Kilbane 3, Crisp 2, Milsom 2, Williams 2, Berry George 1, Bradshaw 1, Griffiths 1, Mackenzie 1, Shepstone 1, Simpson 1, og 2.

Stalybridge Celtic

Vauxhall Appearances: Anderson, S. 26(8); Bauress, G. 33(6); Bennett, P. 9(4); Booth, K. 6(7); Burke, B. (21); Clayton, P. 34(2); Coathup, L. 38(1); Cooksey, S. 13; Dixon, P. 11; Edmonds, N. 28(3); Ellis, N. 2(3); Frain, D. 7; Hall, D. 12; Hughes, R. 26; Jackson R. 11; Leicester, S. 1(2); Livingstone, R. 2(1); Megson, K. 25(6); Ogley, M. 35; O'Shaughnessy, S. 11; Patterson, I. 19; Robinson, P. 22; Ryan, J. 31; Shaughnessy, S. 29(9); Sunley, M. 2; Wheeler, P. 27(13); Zelem, A. 1.

Goals (52): Shaughnessy 7, Wheeler 7, Clayton 6, Jackson 6, Bauress 5, Ryan 4, Burke 3, Megson 3, Anderson 2, Dixon 2, Edmonds 2, Frain 2, Hall 1, Leicester 1, og 1.

Stevenage Borough

Vauxhall Appearances: Allinson, K. 0(3); Bates, M. 0(3); Bedrossian, A. 5; Beevor, S. 24(4); Brock, K. 5(2); Case, S. 5; Conroy, S. 3(2); Crawshaw, G. 5; Cretton, S. 0(3); Dillon, K. 12; Fortune-West, L. 13(4); Gallagher, D. 29(13); Gittings, M. 10(3); Hayles, B. 35;Hedman, R. 31(3); Joyce, T. 2; Kalogeracos, V. 2(1); Lomas, A. 12(12); Luque, M. 4(12); Lynch, A. 28(10); Manual, W. 2; Neville, C. 0(11); Nugent, R. 27(2); Nyamah, K. 6; Omogbehin, C. 1(1); Parker, A. 7(11); Pennyfather, G. 3(1); Phillips, M. 1(1); Rattle, J. 20; Roberts, G. 11; Rudgley, S. 1(3); Simpson, P. 22(1); Sodje, P. 22(9); Smart, G. 18(2); Smith, M. 41; Venables, D. 37; Webster, K. 13(1); Whitmarsh,P. 0(5); Williams, D. 4(3).

Goals (68): Hayles 13, Lynch 8, Venables 8, Fortune-West 7, Smith 4, Beevor 3, Williams 3, Dillon 2, Gittings 2, Hedman 2, Nugent 2, Simpson 2, Bates 1, Brock 1, Conroy 1, Crawshaw 1, Kalogeracos 1, Nyamah 1, Omogbehin 1, Rattle 1, Roberts 1, Sodje 1, Smart 1, og 1.

Telford United

Vauxhall Appearances: Adams, C. 13(6); Bignot, M. 37; Brough, J. 6(1); Carr, D. 17(2); Castledine, G. 3(3); Costello, P. 4(1); Crisp, R. 27(4); Crookes, D. 24(10); Davidson, J. 15(2); Donnelly, S. 3(1); Dougherty, P. 2; Ford, G. 13; Foster, S. 34(2); Fowler, L. 8(1); Goodwin, N. 39; Griffiths, B. 16(1); Holden, M. 5(1); Howell, P. 9(5); Hughes, K. 3; Kearney, M. 38; Myers, M. 35(1); Niblett, N. 24; Roberts, D. 10; Taylor, C. 4; Treharne, J. 1(2); Warner, A. 11(3); Wilcox, B. 25(3); Wilson, L. 33(4); Winstone, S. 3; Wood, J. 0(2).

Goals (53): Wilson 9, Myers 6, Warner 6, Roberts 5, Kearney 4, Bignot 3, Crookes 2, Donnelly 2, Griffiths 2, Howell 2, Niblett 2, Brough 1, Costello 1, Ford 1, Foster 1, Fowler 1, Holden 1, Taylor 1, og 1.

Welling United

Vauxhall Appearances: Barnes, S. 24(11); Barrett, C. 14(1); Brown, W. 38; Burgess, R. 0(1); Cleevely, L. 10; Collins, P. 2(3); Copley, P. 28; Cooksey, S. 5; Farley,J. 26(2); Finnan, S. 14(5); Gamble, B. 0(1); Gorman, P. 17; Hales, K. 28(2); Hancock, D. 5(1); Hopping, A. 12; Horton, D. 25(1); Kimble, G. 11; Martin, D. 3; Napier, M. 1; Quamina, M. 31(4); Ransom, N. 34; Reynolds, A. 2; Robinson, S. 32; Robbins, T. 42; Rutherford, M. 23; Smith, D. 5(12); Wastell, J. 3; White, S. 15; Williams, D. 12.

Goals (57): Gorman 13, Robbins 10, Copley 6, Barnes 5, Ransom 5, Brown 3, Farley 3, Robinson 3, Quamina 2, Smith 2, White 2, Finnan 1, Reynolds 1, og 1.

Woking

Vauxhall Appearances: Alexander, T. 7(1); Batty, L. 38; Benton, J. 2; Berry, G. 5(1); Brooks, S. 0(1); Brown,D. 12(3); Brown, K. 37; Crumplin, J. 11(1); DeGaris, P. 1; Dennis, L. 14(9); Ellis, A. 26(1); Fielder, C. 41; Girdler, 1(1); Greene, D. 4(1), Hay, D. 25; Newberry, R. 3(4); Payne, G. 6(1); Rattray, K. 21(9); Ravenscroft, C. 1(2); Read, T. 3(1); Steele, S. 37(2); Tierling, L. 21(2); Timothy, D. 1(1); Tucker, M. 42; Wye, L. 40; Wye, S. 28.

Goals (76): Walker 19, Hay 17, Dennis 8, Steele 6, Rattray 5, Payne 4, Ellis 3, Fielder 3, Greene 3, Tucker 2, Crumplin 1, Newberry 1, Wye L 1, Wye S 1, og 2.

Yeovil Town

Vauxhall Appearances: Benbow, I. 13(8); Black, S. 10(1); Brock, K. 16(1); Burwood, D. 0(2); Cleeveley, L. 1; Coates, M. 11(13); Coll, O. 2; Conning, P. 26(2); Cooper, R. 18(3); Cordice, N. 34(1); Dillon, K. 13; Dobbins, W. 8(5); Evans, R. 21(9); Ferns, P. 18; Flory, A. 4(2); Groves, L. 3(4); Hornby, L. 12; LeBihan, N. 6; Leonard, M. 0(1); Lowe, T. 1; Llewellyn, A. 13; Mason, P. 41; McClelland, J. 20(1); Morris, D. 16(3); Powell, L. 3(8); Sherwood, J. 16; Spencer, M. 20(5); Wallace, A. 21; Whale, L. 10(1); White, C. 29; Williams, N. 7(1); Wilson, P33(1); Wratten, A. 0(1).

Goals (50): Wilson 15, Coates 5, Black 4, Spencer 4, Evans 3, Groves 3, Brock 2, Dillon 2, Morris 2, Wallace 2, Whale 2, Cooper 1, Dobbins 1, McClelland 1, White 1, og 2.

VAUXHALL CONFERENCE: MEMBERS CLUBS SEASON 1995–96

Club: ALTRINCHAM
Colours: Red and white striped shirts, black shorts
Ground: Moss Lane, Altrincham, Cheshire WA15 8AP
Tel: 0161-928 1045
Year Formed: 1903
Record Gate: 10,275 (1925 v Sunderland Boys)
Nickname: The Robins
Manager: John King
Secretary: Graham Heathcote

Club: BATH CITY
Colours: Black and white striped shirts, black shorts
Ground: Twerton Park, Bath BA2 1DB
Tel: 01225 423087 and 313247
Year Formed: 1889
Record Gate: 18,020 (1960 v Brighton)
Nickname: City
Manager: Tony Ricketts
Secretary: Bob Twyford

Club: BROMSGROVE ROVERS
Colours: Green and white striped shirts, black shorts
Ground: Victoria Ground, Birmingham Road, Bromsgrove, Worcs. B61 0DR
Tel: 01527 876949
Year Formed: 1885
Record Gate: 7563 (1957–58 v Worcester City)
Nickname: Rovers
Manager: Brian Kenning
Secretary: Brian Hewings

Club: DAGENHAM & REDBRIDGE
Colours: Red shirts, red shorts
Ground: Victoria Road Ground, Victoria Road, Dagenham, Essex RM10 7XL
Tel: 0181-592 7194
Year Formed: 1992
Record Gate: 5300 v Leyton Orient (1992)
Nickname: The Daggers
Manager: David Cusack
Secretary: Derek Almond

Club: DOVER ATHLETIC
Colours: White shirts, black shorts
Ground: Crabble Athletic Ground, Lewisham Road, River, Dover, Kent CT17 0PB
Tel: 01304 822373
Year Formed: 1983
Record Gate: 4035 versus Bromsgrove Rovers (1992)
Nickname: The Lilywhites
Manager: John Ryan
Secretary: John Durrant

Club: FARNBOROUGH TOWN
Colours: Yellow and royal blue shirts, yellow shorts
Ground: Cherrywood Road, Farnborough, Hampshire GU14 8UD
Tel: 01252 541469
Year Formed: 1967
Record Gate: 3069 (1991 v Colchester U)
Nickname: Boro
Manager: Alan Taylor
Secretary: Terry Parr

Club: GATESHEAD
Colours: Black and white halved shirts, black shorts
Ground: International Stadium, Neilson Road, Gateshead NE10 0EF
Tel: 0191-478 3883
Year Formed: 1977 (Reformed)
Record Gate: 20,752 (1937 v Lincoln C)
Nickname: Tynesiders
Manager: Colin Richardson
Secretary: Mark Donnelly

Club: HALIFAX TOWN
Colours: Blue and white shirts, white shorts
Ground: Shay Ground, Halifax HX1 2YS
Tel: 01422 345543 (330383 Match Days Only)
Year Formed: 1911
Record Gate: 36,885 versus Tottenham Hotspur (1953)
Nickname: The Shaymen
Manager: John Bird
Secretary: Derek Newiss

Club: HEDNESFORD TOWN
Colours: White and black shirts with red trim, black shorts with red and white trim
Ground: Keys Park, Hill Street, Hednesford, Staffordshire
Tel: tba
Year Formed: 1880
Record Gate: 10,000 (1927 v Walsall)
Nickname: The Pitmen
Manager: John Baldwin
Secretary: Richard Murning

Club: KETTERING TOWN
Colours: Red and white striped shirts, red shorts
Ground: Rockingham Road, Kettering, Northants NN16 9AW
Tel: 01536 83028/410815
Year Formed: 1875
Record Gate: 11,536 (1947 v Peterborough)
Nickname: The Poppies
Manager: Gary Johnson
Secretary: Gerry Knowles

Club: KIDDERMINSTER HARRIERS
Colours: Red and white shirts, red shorts
Ground: Aggborough, Hoo Road, Kidderminster DY10 1NB
Tel: 01562 823931
Year Formed: 1886
Record Gate: 9155 (1948 v Hereford)
Nickname: The Harriers
Manager: Graham Allner
Secretary: Ray Mercer

Club: MACCLESFIELD TOWN
Colours: Royal blue shirts, white shorts
Ground: Moss Rose Ground, London Road, Macclesfield, Cheshire SK10 3JH
Tel: 01625 424324/511113
Year Formed: 1875
Record Gate: 8900 (1968 v Stockport Co)
Nickname: The Silkmen
Manager: Sammy McIlroy
Secretary: Colin Garlick

Club: MORECAMBE
Colours: Red and white striped shirts, black shorts
Ground: Christie Park, Lancaster Road, Morecambe, Lancashire LA4 5TJ
Tel: 01524 411797
Year Formed: 1920
Record Gate: 9326 (1962 FA Cup Third Round Proper v Weymouth)
Nickname: The Shrimps
Manager: Jim Harvey
Secretary: Neil Marsdin

Club: NORTHWICH VICTORIA
Colours: Green and white shirts, white shorts with green trim
Ground: The Drill Field, Northwich, Cheshire CW9 5HN
Tel: 01606 41450
Year Formed: 1874
Record Gate: 11,290 (1949 v Witton A) 12,000 (1977 v Watford FAC4)
Nickname: The Vics
Manager: Brian Kettle
Secretary: Derek Nuttall

Club: RUNCORN
Colours: Yellow shirts, green shorts
Ground: Canal Street, Runcorn, Cheshire WA7 1RZ
Tel: 01928 560076
Year Formed: 1919
Record Gate: 10,011 (1939 v Preston NE)
Nickname: The Linnets
Manager: John Carroll
Secretary: Graham Ost

Club: SLOUGH TOWN
Colours: Amber shirts, navy blue shorts
Ground: Wexham Park Stadium, Wexham Road, Slough, Berkshire SL2 5QR
Tel: 01753 523358
Year Formed: 1980
Record Gate: 5000 (1982 v Millwall at Wexham Park Stadium)
Nickname: The Rebels
Manager: David Russell
Secretary: David Stanley

Club: SOUTHPORT
Colours: Old gold shirts, black shorts
Ground: Haig Avenue, Southport PR8 6JZ
Tel: 01704 533422
Year Formed: 1881
Record Gate: 20,010 (1932 v Newcastle United)
Nickname: The Sandgrounders
Manager: Billy Ayre
Secretary: Roy Morris

Club: STALYBRIDGE CELTIC
Colours: Blue shirts, blue shorts
Ground: Bower Ford, Mottram Road, Stalybridge, Cheshire SK15 2RT
Tel: 0161-338 2828
Year Formed: 1911
Record Gate: 9753 (1992–23 v West Bromwich Albion)
Nickname: Celtic
Manager: Peter Wragg
Secretary: Martyn Torr

Club: STEVENAGE BOROUGH
Colours: Red and white shirts, white shorts
Ground: Broadhall Way, Stevenage, Herts SG2 8RH
Tel: 01438 743322
Year Formed: 1976
Record Gate: 3005 (1994 v Harrow Borough)
Nickname: The Boro
Manager: Paul Fairclough
Secretary: Janice Hutchings

Club: TELFORD UNITED
Colours: White shirts, white shorts
Ground: Bucks Head, Watling Street, Telford TF1 2NJ
Tel: 01952 223838
Year Formed: 1877
Record Gate: 13,000 (1935 v Shrewsbury)
Nickname: The Lillywhites
Manager: Wayne Clarke
Secretary: Mike Ferriday

Club: WELLING UNITED
Colours: Red shirts, red shorts
Ground: Park View Road Ground, Welling, Kent DA16 1SY
Tel: 0181-301 1196
Year Formed: 1963
Record Gate: 4020 (1989 v Gillingham)
Nickname: The Wings
Manager: Kevin Hales
Secretary: Barrie Hobbins

Club: WOKING
Colours: Red and white halved shirts, black shorts
Ground: Kingfield Sports Ground, Kingfield, Woking, Surrey GU22 9AA
Tel: 01483 772470
Year Formed: 1889
Record Gate: 6000 (1978–79 v Swansea)
Nickname: The Cardinals
Manager: Geoff Chapple
Secretary: Phil Ledger, JP

VAUXHALL CONFERENCE RESULTS 1994–95

	Altrincham	Bath City	Bromsgrove Rovers	Dagenham & Redbridge	Dover Athletic	Farnborough Town	Gateshead	Halifax Town	Kettering Town	Kidderminster Harriers	Macclesfield Town	Merthyr Tydfil	Northwich Victoria	Runcorn	Southport	Stafford Rangers	Stalybridge Celtic	Stevenage Borough	Telford United	Welling United	Woking	Yeovil Town
Altrincham	—	1-0	1-1	0-1	3-0	2-0	1-3	3-1	2-4	2-0	1-2	1-0	1-3	3-2	0-0	5-1	1-0	1-2	3-1	1-1	1-2	1-3
Bath City	0-3	—	1-1	3-0	0-0	2-0	0-2	0-0	2-0	3-5	1-0	1-0	2-2	4-3	1-2	3-3	2-3	2-1	1-1	2-0	2-0	3-0
Bromsgrove Rovers	0-3	1-1	—	2-2	2-0	2-2	2-2	0-1	2-4	4-3	2-2	2-0	1-4	1-0	1-1	2-1	2-1	2-1	0-1	4-1	5-5	5-0
Dagenham & Redbridge	0-4	1-0	2-0	—	2-0	0-1	0-0	1-4	2-1	1-2	0-4	2-1	1-2	3-2	5-1	3-3	2-2	0-1	3-2	0-0	0-2	0-0
Dover Athletic	1-3	3-0	0-2	1-1	—	1-1	2-2	1-1	0-2	1-0	0-0	2-2	3-1	1-1	1-2	3-2	0-0	2-0	2-0	1-1	2-3	1-1
Farnborough Town	2-3	0-0	0-3	1-3	1-0	—	3-1	2-0	0-0	1-0	1-0	2-1	2-1	0-4	1-4	0-0	0-0	1-1	5-3	1-2	0-2	0-3
Gateshead	1-0	0-1	2-1	2-1	1-0	2-0	—	1-2	0-0	1-0	2-1	2-0	4-0	4-0	0-1	1-1	0-0	1-2	0-0	2-0	2-0	0-3
Halifax Town	1-1	4-2	4-2	1-1	4-0	0-1	3-2	—	2-1	1-2	0-1	2-2	0-0	4-0	2-0	6-0	1-1	0-2	1-1	4-0	4-0	2-1
Kettering Town	2-2	0-0	0-1	2-2	1-0	4-1	2-4	5-1	—	0-0	1-0	4-1	3-3	3-0	1-0	1-0	1-0	0-2	3-2	4-3	0-1	3-2
Kidderminster Harriers	2-2	2-1	0-1	1-1	0-0	0-1	2-3	3-0	1-3	—	1-2	2-0	1-2	1-1	0-1	1-2	3-2	0-3	1-1	3-0	1-3	3-0
Macclesfield Town	4-2	1-0	2-2	2-0	3-0	4-1	2-1	1-1	1-0	1-3	—	0-0	3-1	0-1	3-0	1-2	3-0	0-3	2-0	3-1	2-0	1-0
Merthyr Tydfil	2-5	2-0	2-1	2-0	2-3	1-1	1-2	2-0	2-1	0-1	1-2	—	2-0	3-0	1-2	4-1	4-2	2-2	3-1	0-2	1-1	0-0
Northwich Victoria	1-1	1-1	3-1	5-0	1-3	1-2	1-1	3-0	3-2	3-4	1-3	2-0	—	4-1	2-1	0-1	2-2	0-1	1-1	1-1	2-2	2-2
Runcorn	3-0	1-1	3-1	0-0	3-3	1-0	3-2	0-3	1-2	2-2	2-2	0-0	2-2	—	2-1	3-1	0-3	3-1	4-1	3-2	1-0	2-1
Southport	1-4	3-1	2-1	1-1	2-2	0-1	5-0	4-0	1-1	4-1	2-3	3-1	0-2	5-0	—	3-0	3-1	2-1	2-1	1-0	2-0	0-0
Stafford Rangers	0-1	0-2	1-1	1-2	1-0	1-1	3-1	0-1	2-3	1-2	0-3	2-1	1-3	1-2	1-1	—	5-0	0-3	2-2	1-1	2-3	4-1
Stalybridge Celtic	2-1	0-1	1-1	1-0	2-1	4-1	0-1	1-0	1-4	1-3	2-2	1-1	2-1	0-0	1-1	2-3	—	1-0	1-0	1-3	2-1	3-1
Stevenage Borough	4-2	3-0	1-0	3-1	0-3	3-1	2-3	1-0	2-2	2-3	1-1	0-0	1-1	0-1	1-2	1-0	5-1	—	4-3	1-2	0-1	5-0
Telford United	2-3	3-0	2-2	0-4	1-1	1-1	3-1	1-1	1-0	3-1	2-0	1-1	1-0	2-0	0-0	0-0	1-1	1-2	—	4-2	0-0	1-0
Welling United	0-0	1-5	1-2	4-1	0-1	1-3	3-0	1-1	2-1	0-2	0-1	2-1	1-5	1-2	3-1	3-1	3-3	1-0	1-0	—	1-2	2-1
Woking	4-0	2-2	4-0	3-5	0-0	3-2	1-1	1-3	3-1	0-0	1-0	4-1	1-1	2-0	3-0	2-2	4-1	3-0	2-1	1-1	—	2-2
Yeovil Town	1-3	1-2	2-0	2-2	1-3	0-1	1-1	3-1	1-1	1-1	1-2	1-3	4-4	1-0	0-1	1-0	3-0	0-0	1-1	3-3	1-2	—

BOB LORD TROPHY 1994–95

First Round (*two legs*)
Altrincham 1(*O'Neill*)
Telford 1 (*Brough*) 671

Telford 0
Altrincham 3 (*Terry, Carmody, O'Neill*) 604

Bath City 3 (*Vernon, Smart, Adcock*)
Welling United 1 (*Gorman*) 323

Welling United 2 (*Rutherford, og*)
Bath City 6 (*Mings, Smart, McLoughlin, Adcock, Birkby 2*) 226

Gateshead 2 (*Dobson 2*)
Stalybridge Celtic 3 (*Clayton, Wheeler 2*) 296

Stalybridge Celtic 3 (*Shaughnessy 2, Edmonds*)
Gateshead 2 (*Lamb, Robinson*) 261

Halifax Town 0
Northwich Victoria 1 (*Butler*) 476

Northwich Victoria 1 (*Williams*)
Halifax Town 1 (*Lambert*) 780

Merthyr Tydfil 2 (*Rogers, Williams*)
Bromsgrove Rovers 1 (*B Gray*) 306

Bromsgrove Rovers 4 (*Glasser, Carter, Stott, Burgher*)
Merthyr Tydfil 1 (*Scott*) 941

Stevenage Borough 1 (*Whitmarsh*)
Farnborough Town 2 (*Baker, Boothe*) 673

Farnborough Town 3 (*Boothe 2, Baker*)
Stevenage Borough 1 (*Gittings*) 504

Byes to Second Round
Dagenham & Redbridge, Dover Athletic, Kettering Town, Kidderminster Harriers, Macclesfield Town, Runcorn, Southport, Stafford Rangers, Woking, Yeovil Town

Second Round
Altrincham 3 (*Terry 2, Morton*)
Northwich Victoria 2 (*Williams, Oghani*) 811

Bath City 0
Dover Athletic 1 (*Hall*) 276

Kidderminster Harriers 1 (*Humphreys*)
Kettering Town 5 (*og, Stringfellow, Magee, Martin, Brown*) 914

Macclesfield Town 4 (*Power, McDonald, Askey, Tobin*)
Runcorn 2 (*Anderson, Hughes*) 441

Stalybridge Celtic 3 (*Clayton 2, Ryan*)
Southport 1 (*Blackhurst*) 326

Stafford Rangers 1 (*May*)
Bromsgrove Rovers 4 (*Carter 3, Taylor*) 356

Woking 0
Farnborough Town 0 1375

Farnborough Town 0
Woking 1 (*Rattray*) 935

Yeovil Town 2 (*Cooper, Ferns*)
Dagenham & Redbridge 4 (*Bennett 3, Wordsworth*) 719

Quarter-Finals
Dagenham & Redbridge 4 (*Greene, Bennett 2, Conner*)
Dover Athletic 3 (Scott, Leworthy 2) 399

Kettering Town 2 (*Arnold, Alford*)
Woking 1 (*Rattray*) 964

Macclesfield Town 2 (*Sorvel, Midwood*)
Altrincham 1 (*Sharratt*) 853

Stalybridge Celtic 3 (*Ryan, Jackson, Coathup*)
Bromsgrove Rovers 3 (*Gaunt, Carter, Taylor*) 427

Bromsgrove Rovers 2 (*Taylor, Stott*)
Stalybridge Celtic 0 765

Semi-Finals (*two legs*)
Kettering Town 0
Dagenham & Redbridge 2 (*Richardson, Haag*) 1033

Dagenham & Redbridge 2 (*McPherson, Haag*)
Kettering Town 4 (*Alford, Brown, Arnold, Thomas*) 750

Macclesfield Town 2 (*Lyons, Power*)
Bromsgrove Rovers 1 (*Carter*) 660

Bromsgrove Rovers 4 (*Carter 2, Taylor, Burgher*)
Macclesfield Town 1 (*Midwood*) 1118

Final (*two legs*)
Bromsgrove Rovers 4 (*Carter 2, Taylor, og*)
Kettering Town 1 (*Clarke*) 1393

Kettering Town 1 (*Alford*)
Bromsgrove Rovers 6 (*Stott, Taylor 3, Carter 2*) 1311

UNIBOND LEAGUE

PREMIER DIVISION

		Home					*Away*					*Total*
	P	W	D	L	F	A	W	D	L	F	A	Pts
Marine	42	17	3	1	43	15	12	8	1	40	12	98
Morecambe	42	14	5	2	56	20	14	5	2	43	14	94
Guiseley	42	16	4	1	54	22	12	5	4	42	28	93
Hyde United	42	14	2	5	57	30	8	8	5	32	29	76
Boston United	42	11	5	5	50	25	9	6	6	30	18	71
Spennymoor United	42	12	6	3	41	24	8	5	8	25	28	71
Buxton	42	9	5	7	34	27	9	4	8	31	35	63
Gainsborough Trinity	42	9	8	4	34	25	7	5	9	35	36	61
Bishop Auckland (3)	42	6	8	7	26	26	10	4	7	42	29	57
Witton Albion	42	6	7	8	27	31	8	7	6	27	25	56
Barrow	42	10	4	7	37	29	7	1	13	31	42	56
Colwyn Bay	42	8	5	8	33	32	8	3	10	38	48	56
Emley	42	9	7	5	32	26	5	6	10	30	42	55
Matlock Town	42	7	4	10	34	31	8	1	12	28	41	50
Accrington Stanley	42	6	5	10	29	42	6	8	7	26	35	49
Knowsley United	42	7	6	8	32	36	4	8	9	32	47	47
Winsford United	42	6	5	10	34	37	4	6	11	22	38	41
Chorley	42	5	1	15	28	45	6	6	9	36	42	40
Frickley Athletic	42	4	7	10	29	38	6	3	12	24	41	40
Droylsden	42	7	3	11	30	43	3	5	13	26	50	38
Whitley Bay	42	4	5	12	20	39	4	3	14	26	58	32
Horwich RMI	42	4	3	14	25	47	5	1	15	24	47	31

FIRST DIVISION

		Home					*Away*					*Total*
	P	W	D	L	F	A	W	D	L	F	A	Pts
Blyth Spartans	42	14	5	2	54	27	12	4	5	41	28	87
Bamber Bridge	42	14	5	2	56	19	11	5	5	45	32	85
Warrington Town	42	14	5	2	42	19	11	4	6	32	21	84
Alfreton Town	42	15	3	3	53	24	10	4	7	41	25	82
Lancaster City	42	13	4	4	44	18	10	6	5	37	26	79
Worksop Town	42	15	2	4	63	29	4	12	5	32	39	71
Radcliffe Borough	42	8	5	8	37	37	10	5	6	39	33	64
Ashton United	42	12	4	5	44	25	6	4	11	36	45	62
Netherfield	42	9	5	7	33	30	8	2	11	21	26	58
Eastwood Town	42	9	7	5	40	26	5	6	10	27	35	55
Gretna	42	6	8	7	36	36	8	5	8	28	30	55
Atherton LR	42	8	5	8	33	27	6	3	12	27	40	50
Harrogate Town	42	10	1	10	35	40	4	7	10	22	38	50
Caernarfon Town	42	6	6	9	26	29	7	4	10	32	33	49
Curzon Ashton	42	8	8	5	39	33	2	8	11	25	47	46
Great Harwood Town	42	7	6	8	37	50	4	7	10	29	37	46
Congleton Town	42	3	7	11	22	38	8	6	7	30	37	46
Fleetwood (3)	42	9	5	7	27	21	3	6	12	24	53	44
Farsley Celtic	42	7	5	9	36	38	5	2	14	30	62	43
Workington	42	6	3	12	31	41	6	3	12	30	50	42
Goole Town	42	7	5	9	30	36	4	2	15	16	45	40
Mossley (1)	42	7	3	11	25	29	4	2	15	27	61	37

(-) points deducted for breach of rule

Leading goalscorers

Premier Division

Lge	*Cup*	*Tot*	
31	15	46	John Coleman (Morecambe)
31	5	36	Andy Whittaker (Barrow)
29	10	39	Jim McCluskie (Morecambe)
24	9	33	Ged Kimmins (Hyde United)
23	7	30	Brian Ross (Marine)
22	10	32	Geoff Horsfield (Guiseley)
21	14	35	David Laws (Bishop Auckland)
20	15	35	Colin Little (Hyde United)
20	6	26	Tony McDonald (Chorley)
19	4	23	Darren Hunton (Boston United)
17	5	22	David Nolan (Hyde United)
17	4	21	Paul Beck (Accrington Stanley)
16	4	20	Colin Bishop (Gainsborough Trinity)
16	1	17	Grant Morrow (Gainsborough Trinity)

First Division

Lge	*Cup*	*Tot*	
36	21	57	Kenny Clark (Worksop Town)
30	6	36	Keith Evans (Ashton United)
24	10	34	Robbie Whellans (Farsley Celtic)
23	6	29	Tony Carroll (Barber Bridge–12 + 1 for Radcliffe Borough)
21	11	32	Stephen Pyle (Blyth Spartans)
21	8	29	Richie Bond (Blyth Spartans)
20	4	24	Mark Edwards (Bamber Bridge–15 + 2 for Horwich RMI/Ashton Utd)
20	1	21	Martin Henderson (Workington)
20	1	21	John McFadzean (Alfreton Town)
18	15	33	Stuart Diggle (Lancaster City)
17	7	24	Chris Shaw (Ashton United)
17	5	22	Ian Lunt (Radcliffe Borough)
17	4	21	Paul Heavey (Warrington Town)

UNIBOND LEAGUE—PREMIER DIVISION RESULTS 1994–95

	Accrington Stanley	Barrow	Bishop Auckland	Boston United	Buxton	Chorley	Colwyn Bay	Droylsden	Emley	Frickley Athletic	Gainsborough Trinity	Guiseley	Horwich RMI	Hyde United	Knowsley United	Marine	Matlock Town	Morecambe	Spennymoor United	Whitley Bay	Winsford United	Witton United
Accrington Stanley	—	5-2	1-4	0-4	1-0	1-1	1-3	2-1	1-1	1-1	1-2	1-4	3-0	1-0	2-2	1-5	0-2	0-4	0-1	4-1	2-2	1-2
Barrow	2-2	—	2-1	2-5	4-2	2-1	5-0	1-1	1-0	1-2	1-0	2-3	1-0	1-1	2-3	0-3	3-1	0-1	1-1	4-0	2-1	0-1
Bishop Auckland	2-0	3-0	—	0-0	2-2	2-2	3-3	0-1	2-2	2-0	1-1	0-1	2-1	0-2	0-2	0-1	3-1	0-3	0-0	2-2	2-1	0-1
Boston United	4-2	3-1	1-2	—	0-1	2-0	5-2	5-1	1-2	5-0	2-2	2-2	4-0	2-1	6-1	1-1	2-0	0-2	2-3	2-1	0-0	1-1
Buxton	0-1	1-0	2-2	0-0	—	1-2	4-2	2-2	0-1	3-2	0-4	3-2	4-0	1-2	1-0	0-2	4-0	1-2	3-0	2-1	1-1	1-1
Chorley	1-2	3-1	1-1	0-1	0-1	—	3-2	2-4	2-3	2-3	0-2	2-4	2-3	1-0	3-1	1-4	0-1	1-4	1-2	1-4	2-0	0-2
Colwyn Bay	3-3	1-2	1-3	0-1	1-2	3-2	—	3-2	3-0	1-2	0-0	2-4	3-1	1-0	1-1	0-1	0-4	0-0	2-1	5-1	1-0	2-2
Droylsden	1-3	1-0	1-4	1-0	1-2	0-0	1-3	—	0-0	2-1	2-6	1-3	2-1	3-3	1-3	1-4	3-2	3-2	1-2	0-1	5-1	0-2
Emley	0-0	2-1	1-4	1-4	2-0	1-4	1-0	3-1	—	2-0	3-2	1-0	1-1	1-3	3-3	0-0	0-1	0-0	5-1	4-0	1-1	0-0
Frickley Athletic	1-1	1-2	2-2	1-1	1-1	3-3	1-2	2-0	3-2	—	1-2	2-1	1-2	1-2	2-2	0-1	0-1	1-4	0-2	1-5	3-0	2-2
Gainsborough Trinity	0-1	4-3	2-2	2-0	0-2	3-2	6-1	2-2	3-0	1-1	—	0-1	1-0	1-1	2-1	0-0	3-2	0-0	0-3	2-2	1-1	1-0
Guiseley	4-0	2-1	2-1	2-1	3-1	2-1	3-2	2-0	2-0	2-1	1-0	—	1-2	3-3	5-0	2-1	3-0	2-2	1-1	6-3	5-1	1-1
Horwich RMI	1-5	1-6	0-2	0-4	4-1	6-0	0-1	2-2	4-4	0-3	2-1	0-2	—	0-1	1-2	1-4	0-3	0-2	0-0	2-3	1-0	0-1
Hyde United	4-1	3-1	1-0	1-0	4-2	2-3	4-3	5-2	1-1	6-0	5-1	1-2	2-1	—	3-0	1-2	6-3	1-4	1-1	3-0	1-2	2-1
Knowsley United	0-0	0-2	2-3	2-2	1-3	1-2	2-2	3-0	4-2	0-3	4-2	2-1	2-1	1-2	—	1-1	0-0	1-1	2-0	3-0	0-5	1-4
Marine	2-1	4-0	2-0	2-1	1-1	3-1	1-0	4-1	2-1	2-0	1-4	1-1	2-0	1-1	1-0	—	3-0	2-1	1-0	2-0	2-1	4-1
Matlock Town	0-1	1-1	4-0	0-1	2-1	2-2	1-2	3-2	5-1	0-2	2-1	2-3	3-2	0-1	3-3	0-0	—	0-2	1-2	5-1	0-2	0-1
Morecambe	3-0	1-3	1-0	2-1	1-1	2-0	1-1	4-0	2-1	3-1	4-0	2-2	7-1	1-3	1-1	0-0	5-0	—	3-2	2-0	6-1	5-2
Spennymoor United	5-1	0-1	1-0	1-1	4-1	2-2	5-2	2-1	2-1	2-0	1-1	1-1	2-1	1-1	2-1	0-3	2-1	1-3	—	4-0	1-1	2-1
Whitley Bay	0-0	3-1	1-4	0-1	1-3	2-1	0-2	0-1	0-3	2-2	2-2	0-1	0-3	2-2	5-3	0-4	0-2	0-2	1-0	—	0-1	1-1
Winsford United	2-2	3-0	0-4	1-2	1-2	1-3	0-1	2-1	2-3	2-0	2-0	2-2	2-3	5-1	2-2	2-2	2-4	0-2	1-2	1-1	—	1-0
Witton Albion	0-0	0-3	1-3	0-0	1-2	1-4	1-4	1-1	2-2	2-0	1-2	1-2	2-1	2-2	1-1	1-1	2-0	1-2	2-1	3-0	2-0	—

UNIBOND CHALLENGE CUP

First Round
Alfreton Town 0, Worksop Town 0
(*after 2-2 draw; aet, Worksop won 4-3 on penalties*)
Ashton United 1, Congleton Town 2
Atherton LR 3, Radcliffe Borough 0
Blyth Spartans 1, Bamber Bridge 2
Caernarfon Town 3, Mossley 0
Eastwood Town 3, Harrogate Town 0
Goole Town 1, Farsley Celtic 2
Great Harwood Town 5, Horwich RMI 2
Guiseley 2, Fleetwood 1
Lancaster City 4, Gretna 0 (*after 2-2 draw*)
Warrington Town 3, Curzon Ashton 0
Workington 4, Netherfield 1

Second Round
Accrington Stanley 2, Hyde United 0
Atherton LR 0, Barrow 1 (*after 2-2 draw*)
Bamber Bridge 2, Whitley Bay 1
Bishop Auckland 5, Frickley Athletic 2
Boston United 2, Matlock Town 1
Buxton 1, Droylsden 0
Caernarfon Town 0, Warrington Town 1 (*aet and a 1-1 draw*)
Chorley 3, Guiseley 2
Colwyn Bay 2, Congleton Town 1
Emley 3, Spennymoor United 0
Farsley Celtic 1, Gainsborough Trinity 0
Great Harwood Town 0, Marine 1
Knowsley United 3, Morecambe 1
Lancaster City 3, Workington 0
Witton Albion 3, Winsford United 1
Worksop Town 2, Eastwood Town 1

Third Round
Accrington Stanley 4, Farsley Celtic 2
Bamber Bridge 2, Marine 1 (*after 2-2 draw*)
Chorley 1, Lancaster City 0
Colwyn Bay 1, Knowsley United 4
Emley 2, Bishop Auckland 3 (*after 2-2 draw*)
Matlock Town 3, Worksop Town 2
Warrington Town 2, Barrow 1
Witton Albion 2, Buxton 3

Fourth Round
Accrington Stanley 3, Bishop Auckland 5 (*aet and a 1-1 draw*)
Bamber Bridge 3, Knowsley United 2
Buxton 0, Matlock Town 4
Chorley 2, Warrington Town 0 (*after 0-0 draw*)

Semi-finals (two legs)
Bamber Bridge 7, Chorley 2
Chorley 2, Bamber Bridge 0
(*Bamber Bridge won 7-4 on aggregate*)
Bishop Auckland 0, Matlock Town 2
Matlock Town 1, Bishop Auckland 4

Final
Bamber Bridge 2, Bishop Auckland 1 (*at Bolton Wanderers*)

UNIBOND PRESIDENT'S CUP

First Round
Barrow 1, Lancaster City 3
Bishop Auckland 0, Ashton United 2
Frickley Athletic 1, Boston United 2
Hyde United 3, Alfreton Town 0 (*after 2-2 draw*)
Marine 3, Warrington Town 0
Morecambe 3, Netherfield 2
Spennymoor United 3, Guiseley 1
Witton Albion 8, Colwyn Bay 1

Second Round
Boston United 3, Hyde United 0
Marine 0, Lancaster City 1
Morecambe 3, Witton Albion 5
Spennymoor United 2, Ashton United 1

Semi-finals
Boston United 1, Witton Albion 1
Witton Albion 2, Boston United 1
Lancaster City 3, Spennymoor United 1
Spennymoor United 2, Lancaster City 1
(*Lancaster City won 4-3 on aggregate*)

Final (two legs)
Witton Albion 0, Lancaster City 0
Lancaster City 3, Witton Albion 2
(*aet; Lancaster City won 3-2 on aggregate*)

UNIFILLA FIRST DIVISION CUP

First Round
Blyth Spartans 2, Workington 0
Congleton Town 0, Caernarfon Town 3
Harrogate Town 0, Farsley Celtic 1
Mossley 0, Curzon Ashton 2 (*after 2-2 draw*)
Radcliffe Borough 2, Gretna 0 (*after 2-2 draw*)
Worksop Town 5, Goole Town 1

Second Round
Bamber Bridge 1, Great Harwood Town 3
Blyth Spartans 3, Radcliffe Borough 2
Caernarfon Town 2, Warrington Town 0 (*after 0-0 draw*)
Curzon Ashton 0, Ashton United 3 (*after 1-1 draw*)
Eastwood Town 1, Alfreton Town 2
Fleetwood Town 3, Atherton LR 2
Lancaster City 2, Netherfield 4
Worksop Town 6, Farsley Celtic 1

Third Round
Blyth Spartans 2, Ashton United 0
Caernarfon Town 4, Netherfield 3
Great Harwood Town 4, Fleetwood 0
Worksop Town 2, Alfreton Town 5 (*after 2-2 draw*)

Semi-finals (two legs)
Great Harwood Town 3, Caernarfon Town 4
Caernarfon Town 0, Great Harwood Town 3
(*Great Harwood Town won 6-4 on aggregate*)
Blyth Spartans 3, Alfreton Town 3
Alfreton Town 1, Blyth Spartans 3
(*Blyth Spartans won 6-4 on aggregate*)

Final (two legs)
Great Harwood Town 0, Blyth Spartans 1
Blyth Spartans 4, Great Harwood Town 2
(*Blyth Spartans won 5-2 on aggregate*)

BEAZER HOMES LEAGUE 1994–95

Premier Division

	P	W	D	L	F	A	Pts
Hednesford Town	42	28	9	5	99	49	93
Cheltenham Town	42	25	11	6	87	39	86
Burton Albion	42	20	15	7	55	39	75
Gloucester City	42	22	8	12	76	48	74
Rushden & Diamonds	42	19	11	12	99	65	68
Dorchester Town	42	19	10	13	84	61	67
Leek Town	42	19	10	13	72	60	67
Gresley Rovers	42	17	12	13	70	63	63
Cambridge City	42	18	8	16	60	55	62
Worcester City	42	14	15	13	46	34	57
Crawley Town	42	15	10	17	64	71	55
Hastings Town	42	13	14	15	55	57	53
Halesowen Town	42	14	10	18	81	80	52
Gravesend & Northfleet	42	13	13	16	38	55	52
Chelmsford City	42	14	6	22	56	60	48
Atherstone United	42	12	12	18	51	67	48
VS Rugby	42	11	14	17	49	61	47
Sudbury Town	42	12	10	20	50	77	46
Solihull Borough	42	10	15	17	39	65	45
Sittingbourne	42	11	10	21	51	73	43
Trowbridge Town	42	9	13	20	43	69	40
Corby Town*	42	4	10	28	36	113	21

(*Corby Town—one point deducted—ineligible player[s])

Midland Division

	P	W	D	L	F	A	Pts
Newport AFC	42	29	8	5	106	39	95
Ilkeston Town	42	25	6	11	101	75	81
Tamworth	42	24	8	10	98	70	80
Moor Green	42	23	8	11	105	63	77
Bridgnorth Town	42	22	10	10	75	49	76
Buckingham Town	42	20	14	8	55	37	74
Nuneaton Borough	42	19	11	12	76	55	68
Rothwell Town	42	19	7	16	71	71	64
King's Lynn	42	18	8	16	76	64	62
Racing Club Warwick	42	17	11	14	68	63	62
Dudley Town	42	17	10	15	65	69	61
Bilston Town	42	17	8	17	73	64	59
Bedworth United	42	17	7	18	64	68	58
Evesham United	42	14	10	18	57	56	52
Hinckley Town	42	14	10	18	61	76	52
Stourbridge	42	15	7	20	59	77	52
Sutton Coldfield Town	42	12	10	20	62	72	46
Forest Green Rovers	42	11	13	18	56	76	46
Redditch United	42	8	14	20	47	64	38
Leicester United	42	10	8	24	51	99	38
Grantham Town	42	8	9	25	55	93	33
Armitage	42	2	5	35	35	116	11

Southern Division

	P	W	D	L	F	A	Pts
Salisbury City	42	30	7	5	88	37	97
Baldock Town	42	28	10	4	92	44	94
Havant Town	42	25	10	7	81	34	85
Waterlooville	42	24	8	10	77	36	80
Ashford Town	42	21	12	9	106	72	75
Weston-Super-Mare	42	18	13	11	82	54	67
Bashley	42	18	11	13	62	49	65
Weymouth	42	16	13	13	60	55	61
Newport IOW	42	17	10	15	67	67	61
Witney Town	42	14	14	14	57	57	56
Clevedon Town	42	14	13	15	73	64	55
Tonbridge Angels	42	14	12	16	74	87	54
Margate	42	15	7	20	60	72	52
Braintree Town	42	12	13	17	64	71	49
Wealdstone	42	13	8	21	76	94	47
Yate Town	42	11	13	18	57	75	46
Fisher 93	42	9	16	17	54	70	43
Bury Town	42	11	8	23	59	86	41
Erith & Belvedere	42	10	9	23	49	94	39
Poole Town	42	10	8	24	53	79	38
Fareham Town	42	10	8	24	46	91	38
Burnham	42	7	7	28	40	89	28

LEADING GOALSCORERS

(LEAGUE AND CUP)

Premier Division

J. O'Connor (Hednesford Town)	35
O. Pickard (Dorchester Town)	29
I. Wheaton (Leek Town)	27
D. Watkins (Rushden & Diamonds)	26
S. Lovell (Sittingbourne)	21
J. Smith (Cheltenham Town)	21

Midland Division

P. Davies (Moor Green)	38
D. Taylor (Ilkeston Town)	35
C. Williams (Newport AFC)	33
G. Piggott (Dudley Town)	29
R. Straw (Nuneaton Borough)	26
J. Symonds (Bedworth United)	24

Southern Division

D. Arter (Ashford Town)	37
S. Cuggy (Margate)	36
S. Devine (Fisher 93)	30
S. Lovell (Salisbury City)	26
S. Penny (Clevedon Town)	26
M. Stanton (Ashford Town)	25
E. Fearon (Newport IOW)	23
N. Selby (Waterlooville)	23

ATTENDANCES

Premier Division

Aggregate: 293,435
Highest individual: Rushden & Diamonds 1521.

Midland Division

Aggregate: 146,951
Highest individual: Newport AFC 1191.

Southern Division

Aggregate: 116,731
Highest individual: Weymouth 796.

BEAZER HOMES PREMIER DIVISION RESULTS 1994–95

	Atherstone United	Burton Albion	Cambridge City	Chelmsford City	Cheltenham Town	Corby Town	Crawley Town	Dorchester Town	Gloucester City	Gravesend & Northfleet	Gresley Rovers	Halesowen Town	Hastings Town	Hednesford Town	Leek Town	Rushden & Diamonds	Sittingbourne	Solihull Borough	Sudbury Town	Trowbridge Town	VS Rugby	Worcester City
Atherstone United	—	1-2	0-2	1-1	2-4	4-0	0-0	0-1	1-0	3-0	1-2	1-1	1-3	1-3	1-1	1-7	3-1	2-0	3-0	1-2	1-1	0-0
Burton Albion	1-1	—	0-0	2-1	2-0	3-2	1-0	1-1	0-1	2-1	2-1	0-0	1-1	2-4	1-1	2-2	1-0	2-0	1-1	2-0	3-1	0-1
Cambridge City	0-2	2-0	—	1-0	0-1	2-1	2-1	2-1	0-1	1-0	0-1	2-2	1-0	1-1	5-1	2-3	4-1	2-4	1-1	4-0	2-0	0-2
Chelmsford City	4-1	0-4	2-0	—	1-2	5-0	1-2	3-1	0-2	1-2	2-4	4-3	0-0	1-2	2-2	2-2	2-1	3-1	1-0	0-1	3-2	1-0
Cheltenham Town	2-2	1-2	1-1	1-0	—	8-0	1-2	1-1	1-1	2-0	1-1	3-0	6-0	2-0	1-0	3-0	2-1	2-0	3-0	3-2	1-0	1-1
Corby Town	0-0	1-1	1-2	1-4	2-2	—	1-1	2-4	0-6	0-2	1-2	0-2	1-1	3-1	0-1	0-4	2-1	1-2	3-4	1-1	1-0	2-1
Crawley Town	2-1	3-4	1-0	1-0	1-1	2-2	—	2-1	0-1	1-2	1-1	5-1	5-2	2-4	0-1	2-4	2-0	0-1	2-0	4-2	1-0	1-0
Dorchester Town	2-3	0-1	0-1	1-0	1-4	5-0	5-2	—	4-2	4-5	1-1	3-1	3-1	0-0	2-1	4-2	3-1	1-1	3-0	1-3	3-1	1-1
Gloucester City	4-0	1-0	5-1	2-0	1-2	2-2	4-1	0-3	—	3-3	3-3	1-2	1-0	2-2	2-0	1-0	0-0	1-2	3-0	2-0	3-0	1-2
Gravesend & Northfleet	2-1	0-1	1-1	1-0	0-1	1-0	0-2	2-1	1-0	—	1-0	1-1	0-0	0-0	1-1	0-1	1-1	0-0	3-0	0-0	0-0	0-0
Gresley Rovers	1-2	1-1	3-1	1-0	1-4	1-0	2-4	1-3	3-2	0-0	—	3-2	3-2	1-2	2-1	4-3	1-1	5-1	0-1	5-1	2-2	0-0
Halesowen Town	3-0	0-1	1-0	3-2	1-1	4-1	2-2	2-5	1-1	4-1	1-4	—	1-2	1-2	4-5	2-4	3-0	4-2	5-1	2-0	5-0	0-3
Hastings Town	3-1	1-1	4-3	0-1	3-1	1-1	2-2	2-1	2-1	1-2	2-0	3-1	—	0-0	1-2	0-2	1-1	3-0	4-1	1-0	1-1	1-1
Hednesford Town	6-1	5-1	2-1	2-1	3-1	4-1	2-1	0-0	1-3	5-1	2-1	3-2	2-1	—	3-0	5-2	2-1	5-0	1-1	4-1	2-0	1-1
Leek Town	2-1	0-1	4-1	0-3	1-3	6-1	3-0	4-5	3-1	2-0	1-1	3-0	1-0	1-3	—	3-3	2-0	0-1	4-1	3-0	0-0	0-0
Rushden & Diamonds	2-2	2-2	2-1	3-1	0-2	6-1	5-0	2-1	1-2	6-2	0-1	1-1	3-1	2-3	5-0	—	5-0	3-1	2-2	2-1	4-1	1-1
Sittingbourne	1-0	0-2	1-1	2-3	0-3	4-0	3-1	1-2	2-1	4-0	0-0	3-2	2-1	3-2	0-0	3-1	—	2-1	0-4	4-1	1-1	1-2
Solihull Borough	0-1	1-1	0-2	1-1	0-0	0-0	1-1	2-4	1-2	0-0	0-0	2-2	1-3	2-2	1-2	0-0	2-1	—	1-1	1-0	0-3	1-0
Sudbury Town	0-2	0-1	1-2	1-0	1-5	5-1	0-0	1-1	0-1	2-0	2-1	0-4	1-0	3-2	1-3	1-0	2-2	0-1	—	2-4	3-1	0-0
Trowbridge Town	0-0	0-0	1-2	1-0	1-2	2-0	1-1	1-1	1-2	2-0	3-2	2-2	0-0	1-2	1-1	1-1	1-1	0-0	4-3	—	1-3	0-1
VS Rugby	1-1	0-0	1-1	0-0	2-0	3-0	3-1	1-0	3-3	0-2	6-3	0-2	0-0	0-3	1-3	2-0	2-0	2-3	2-2	0-0	—	2-0
Worcester City	0-1	1-0	1-3	3-0	2-2	3-0	4-2	0-0	0-1	1-0	0-1	3-1	1-1	0-1	1-3	1-1	4-0	1-1	0-1	3-0	0-1	—

DR. MARTENS CUP

Preliminary Round First Leg
Tonbridge 1, Margate 4
Armitage 1, Racing Club Warwick 1

Preliminary Round Second Leg
Margate 3, Tonbridge 1
Racing Club Warwick 2, Armitage 1

First Round First Leg
Hastings Town 2, Gravesend & Northfleet 1
Ashford Town 2, Erith & Belvedere 1
Fisher 93 1, Margate 5
Sittingbourne 0, Crawley Town 1
Cambridge City 2, Grantham Town 1
Sudbury Town 3, Wealdstone 3
Chelmsford City 3, Buckingham Town 1
King's Lynn 3, Corby Town 1
Newport AFC 0, Forest Green 2
Yate Town 0, Cheltenham Town 1
Salisbury City 2, Bashley 2
Dorchester Town 2, Newport IOW 0
Tamworth 2, Witney Town 1
Poole Town 0, Waterlooville 3
Fareham Town 2, Havant Town 0
Trowbridge 0, Weymouth 2
Dudley Town 1, Redditch United 1
Nuneaton Borough 3, VS Rugby 3
Weston-Super-Mare 0, Worcester City 2
Clevedon Town 0, Gloucester City 1
Rushden & Diamonds 0, Rothwell Town 0
Halesowen Town 1, Bedworth United 2
Burnham 0, Baldock Town 3
Bury Town 1, Braintree Town 1
Bilston Town 1, Ilkeston Town 0
Atherstone United 2, Hednesford Town 0
Solihull Borough 1, Burton Albion 1
Stourbridge 0, Bridgnorth Town 0
Hinckley Town 1, Gresley Rovers 0
Moor Green 0, Evesham United 1
Leicester United 3, Sutton Coldfield Town 3
Racing Club Warwick 1, Leek Town 2

First Round Second Leg
Gravesend & Northfleet 2, Hastings Town 2
Erith & Belvedere 1, Ashford Town 6
Margate 2, Fisher 93 2
Crawley Town 1, Sittingbourne 2
Grantham Town 1, Cambridge City 3
Wealdstone 1, Sudbury Town 2
Buckingham Town 2, Chelmsford City 1
Corby Town 0, King's Lynn 3
Forest Green 0, Newport AFC 3
Cheltenham Town 2, Yate Town 0
Bashley 2, Salisbury City 0
Newport IOW 2, Dorchester Town 1
Witney Town 3, Tamworth 1
Waterlooville 4, Poole Town 0
Havant Town 4, Fareham Town 0
Weymouth 1, Trowbridge 2
Redditch United 1, Dudley Town 5
VS Rugby 0, Nuneaton Borough 0
Worcester City 2, Weston-Super-Mare 1
Gloucester City 2, Clevedon Town 1
Rothwell Town 1, Rushden & Diamonds 2
Bedworth United 1, Halesowen Town 1
Baldock Town 0, Burnham 0
Braintree Town 3, Bury Town 1
Ilkeston Town 2, Bilston Town 3
Hednesford Town 1, Atherstone United 1
Burton Albion 1, Solihull Borough 2
Bridgnorth Town 3, Stourbridge 1
Gresley Rovers 1, Hinckley Town 3
Evesham United 1, Moor Green 0
Sutton Coldfield Town 1, Leicester United 2
Leek Town 4, Racing Club Warwick 0

Second Round
Hastings Town 3, Ashford Town 0
Margate 1, Sittingbourne 0
Cambridge City 2, Sudbury Town 3
Chelmsford City 3, King's Lynn 1
Newport AFC 2, Cheltenham Town 3
Bashley 2, Dorchester Town 2
Replay: Dorchester Town 2, Bashley 0
Witney Town 0, Waterlooville 1
Havant Town 2, Weymouth 2
Replay: Weymouth 2, Havant Town 1
Dudley Town 1, VS Rugby 1
Replay: VS Rugby 3, Dudley Town 0
Worcester City 2, Gloucester City 1
Rushden & Diamonds 4, Bedworth United 2
Baldock Town 3, Braintree Town 1
Bilston Town 0, Atherstone United 0
Replay: Atherstone United 3, Bilston Town 1
Solihull Borough 3, Bridgnorth Town 1
Hinckley Town 3, Evesham United 0
Leicester United 1, Leek Town 4

Third Round
Hastings Town 0, Margate 0
Replay: Margate 1, Hastings Town 3
Sudbury Town 1, Chelmsford City 2
Cheltenham Town 1, Dorchester Town 1
Replay: Dorchester Town 1, Cheltenham Town 2
Waterlooville 5, Weymouth 1
VS Rugby 1, Worcester City 3
Rushden & Diamonds 3, Baldock Town 0
Atherstone United 4, Solihull Borough 0
Hinckley Town 0, Leek Town 2

Fourth Round
Hastings Town 2, Chelmsford City 0
Cheltenham Town 0, Waterlooville 1
Worcester City 0, Rushden & Diamonds 0
Replay: Rushden & Diamonds 3, Worcester City 1
Atherstone United 0, Leek Town 1

Semi-final First Leg
Hastings Town 7, Waterlooville 2
Rushden & Diamonds 0, Leek Town 4

Semi-final Second Leg
Waterlooville 0, Hastings Town 1
Leek Town 0, Rushden & Diamonds 2

Final First Leg
Hastings Town 1, Leek Town 0

Final Second Leg
Leek Town 1, Hastings Town 2

DIADORA FOOTBALL LEAGUE 1994–95

Premier Division

		Home			Away			Totals			Goals		
	P	*W*	*D*	*L*	*W*	*D*	*L*	*W*	*D*	*L*	*F*	*A*	*Pts*
Enfield	42	14	5	2	14	4	3	28	9	5	106	43	93
Slough Town	42	13	6	2	9	7	5	22	13	7	82	56	79
Hayes	42	12	6	3	8	8	5	20	14	8	66	47	74
Aylesbury United	42	14	5	2	7	1	13	21	6	15	86	59	69
Hitchin Town	42	9	7	5	9	5	7	18	12	12	68	59	66
Bromley	42	10	5	6	8	6	7	18	11	13	76	67	65
St Albans City	42	13	5	3	4	8	9	17	13	12	96	81	64
Molesey	42	9	5	7	9	3	9	18	8	16	65	61	62
Yeading	42	7	8	6	7	7	7	14	15	13	60	59	57
Harrow Borough	42	10	2	9	7	4	10	17	6	19	64	67	57
Dulwich Hamlet	42	9	4	8	7	5	9	16	9	17	70	82	57
Carshalton Athletic	42	7	6	8	9	3	9	16	9	17	69	84	57
Kingstonian	42	10	2	9	6	6	9	16	8	18	62	57	56
Walton & Hersham	42	9	5	7	5	6	10	14	11	17	75	73	53
Sutton United	42	8	5	8	5	7	9	13	12	17	74	69	51
Purfleet	42	6	6	9	7	6	8	13	12	17	76	90	51
Hendon	42	8	7	6	4	7	10	12	14	16	57	65	50
Grays Athletic	42	4	8	9	7	8	6	11	16	15	57	61	49
Bishop's Stortford	42	8	5	8	4	6	11	12	11	19	53	76	47
Chesham United	42	7	5	9	5	4	12	12	9	21	60	87	45
Marlow	42	7	6	8	3	3	15	10	9	23	52	84	39
Wokingham Town	42	4	5	12	2	4	15	6	9	27	39	86	27

Division One

		Home			Away			Totals			Goals		
	P	*W*	*D*	*L*	*W*	*D*	*L*	*W*	*D*	*L*	*F*	*A*	*Pts*
Boreham Wood	42	17	3	1	14	2	5	31	5	6	90	38	98
Worthing	42	13	6	2	8	7	6	21	13	8	93	49	76
Chertsey Town	42	12	4	5	9	7	5	21	11	10	109	57	74
Aldershot Town	42	14	2	5	9	3	9	23	5	14	80	53	74
Billericay Town	42	9	5	7	11	4	6	20	9	13	68	52	69
Staines Town	42	8	6	7	9	6	6	17	12	13	83	65	63
Basingstoke Town	42	7	8	6	10	2	9	17	10	15	81	71	61
Tooting & Mitcham United	42	6	10	5	9	4	8	15	14	13	58	48	59
Wembley	42	8	4	9	8	7	6	16	11	15	70	61	59
Abingdon Town	42	10	6	5	6	5	10	16	11	15	67	69	59
Whyteleafe	42	11	4	6	6	3	12	17	7	18	70	78	58
Maidenhead United	42	11	3	7	4	9	8	15	12	15	73	76	57
Uxbridge	42	9	4	8	6	7	8	15	11	16	54	62	56
Leyton	42	8	6	7	7	4	10	15	10	17	67	66	55
Barking	42	8	4	9	8	3	10	16	7	19	74	77	55
Heybridge Swifts	42	9	4	8	7	2	12	16	6	20	73	78	54
Ruislip Manor	42	10	5	6	4	6	11	14	11	17	70	75	53
Bognor Regis Town	42	8	6	7	5	8	8	13	14	15	57	63	53
Berkhamsted Town	42	8	5	8	6	5	10	14	10	18	54	70	52
Newbury Town	42	7	6	8	5	9	7	12	15	15	58	71	51
Wivenhoe Town	42	6	4	11	2	3	16	8	7	27	47	94	31
Dorking	42	1	2	18	2	1	18	3	3	36	40	163	12

Division Two

		Home			Away			Totals			Goals		
	P	*W*	*D*	*L*	*W*	*D*	*L*	*W*	*D*	*L*	*F*	*A*	*Pts*
Thame United	42	17	1	3	13	2	6	30	3	9	97	49	93
Barton Rovers	42	13	4	4	12	3	6	25	7	10	93	51	82
Oxford City	42	10	6	5	14	2	5	24	8	10	86	47	80
Bracknell Town	42	10	4	7	13	5	3	23	9	10	86	47	78
Metropolitan Police	42	12	3	6	7	9	5	19	12	11	81	65	69
Hampton	42	11	3	7	9	6	6	20	9	13	79	74	69
Croydon	42	13	3	5	7	2	12	20	5	17	85	65	65
Banstead Athletic	42	10	4	7	8	6	7	18	10	14	73	59	64
Saffron Walden Town	42	12	6	3	5	7	9	17	13	12	64	59	64
Chalfont St Peter	42	8	6	7	9	6	6	17	12	13	67	54	63
Witham Town	42	10	4	7	8	5	8	18	9	15	75	64	63
Leatherhead	42	12	4	5	4	8	9	16	12	14	71	75	60
Edgware Town	42	8	5	8	8	5	8	16	10	16	70	66	58
Tilbury	42	10	8	3	5	1	15	15	9	18	62	82	54
Cheshunt	42	7	8	6	6	5	10	13	13	16	66	81	52
Ware	42	10	2	9	4	5	12	14	7	21	61	81	49
Egham Town	42	7	6	8	4	8	9	11	14	17	60	65	47
Hemel Hempstead	42	6	7	8	4	4	13	10	11	21	45	76	41
Hungerford Town	42	8	2	11	3	5	13	11	7	24	55	81	40
Windsor & Eton	42	6	5	10	4	3	14	10	8	24	58	84	38
Aveley	42	4	5	12	5	0	16	9	5	28	48	95	32
Maiden Vale	42	3	5	13	2	4	15	5	9	28	46	108	24

Division Three

		Home			Away			Totals			Goals		
	P	*W*	*D*	*L*	*W*	*D*	*L*	*W*	*D*	*L*	*F*	*A*	*Pts*
Collier Row	40	15	4	1	15	1	4	30	5	5	86	23	95
Canvey Island	40	14	4	2	14	0	6	28	4	8	88	42	88
Bedford Town	40	9	7	4	13	4	3	22	11	7	90	50	77
Northwood	40	12	4	4	10	4	6	22	8	10	80	47	74
Horsham	40	11	3	6	11	3	6	22	6	12	84	61	72
Southall	40	10	5	5	11	3	6	21	8	11	87	59	71
Leighton Town	40	9	4	7	11	4	5	20	8	12	66	43	68
Camberley Town	40	9	5	6	10	3	7	19	8	13	59	39	65
Kingsbury Town	40	10	4	6	8	7	5	18	11	11	72	54	65
Hornchurch	40	8	3	9	9	5	6	17	8	15	64	63	59
Clapton	40	8	6	6	6	5	9	14	11	15	69	61	53
Tring Town	40	9	4	7	4	8	8	13	12	15	68	69	51
East Thurrock United	40	8	2	10	6	6	8	14	8	18	60	79	50
Epsom & Ewell	40	5	6	9	8	4	8	13	10	17	58	62	49
Harlow Town	40	7	2	11	6	6	8	13	8	19	53	83	47
Harefield United	40	6	4	10	6	4	10	12	8	20	51	79	44
Hertford Town	40	8	3	9	3	7	10	11	10	19	56	78	43
Feltham & Hounslow	40	6	3	11	7	1	12	13	4	23	64	87	43
Flackwell Heath	40	6	2	12	2	2	16	8	4	28	50	99	28
Lewes	40	4	3	13	2	2	16	6	5	29	34	104	23
Cove	40	3	3	14	0	2	18	3	5	32	37	94	14

LEADING GOALSCORERS

Premier Division		*Lge*	*Lge Cup*	*Carlsberg*
34	Gary Abbott (Enfield)	34		
32	Shaun Marshall (Hitchin Town)	27	1	4
31	Mark West (Slough Town)	21	8	2
30	Steve Clark (St Albans City)	28	2	
29	David Crown (Purfleet)	28	1	
	Jim Bolton (Carshalton Athletic)	19	8	2
28	Neil Fraser (Harrow Borough)	25	1	2
	Brian Stein (Enfield)	22	2	4
	(Includes 16 League, 2 League Cup & 4 Carlsberg Cup for St Albans City)			
27	Dean Williams (Aylesbury United)	21	5	1
25	Ansil Bushay (Slough Town)	17	6	2
Division One				
34	Lee Charles (Chertsey Town)	30		4
26	Paul Coombs (Basingstoke Town)	23	1	2
25	Jeff Wood (Barking)	24	1	
	Mark Butler (Aldershot Town)	21	3	1
24	Mark Hynes (Whyteleafe)	23	1	
23	Steve Darlington (Staines Town)	16	2	5
20	Paul Battram (Billericay Town)	19		1
	Tony Samuels (Boreham Wood)	18		2
	(Includes 1 League for Leyton)			
Division Two				
32	Damon Miles (Ware)	31		1
28	Gordon Guile (Barton Rovers)	28		
24	Nigel Mott (Thame United)	24		
	Andy Shildrick (Thame United)	22		2
	Justin Day (Bracknell Town)	21		3
23	Micky Waite (Witham Town)	21	2	
Division Three				
36	Steve Fraser (Southall)	29	1	6
26	Andy Jones (Canvey Island)	23	2	1
25	Gary Sealey (Tring Town)	25		
24	Jason Reed (Bedford Town)	23	1	
23	Marc Salmon (Harlow Town)	21	1	1
21	Mark Ivers (Kingsbury Town)	21		

ATTENDANCES

Premier Division
Aggregate: 207,869
Highest Individual average: Enfield 894
Division One
Aggregate: 132,201
Highest Individual average: Aldershot Town 1853
Division Two
Aggregate: 46,113
Highest Individual average: Oxford City 194
Division Three
Aggregate: 47,520
Highest Individual average: Bedford Town 390

DIADORA FOOTBALL LEAGUE PREMIER DIVISION 1994–95

	Aylesbury United	Bishop's Stortford	Bromley	Carshalton Athletic	Chesham United	Dulwich Hamlet	Enfield	Grays Athletic	Harrow Borough	Hayes	Hendon	Hitchin Town	Kingstonian	Marlow	Molesey	Purfleet	St Albans City	Slough Town	Sutton United	Walton & Hersham	Wokingham Town	Yeading
Aylesbury United	—	3-0	3-2	5-0	5-1	5-3	3-3	2-0	3-0	2-0	1-0	2-1	2-0	0-0	2-4	1-1	0-0	3-3	3-0	4-0	4-1	1-2
Bishop's Stortford	2-1	—	2-1	3-4	0-3	3-3	1-1	0-1	0-2	2-2	1-2	1-0	2-1	2-0	3-1	2-5	1-2	2-2	1-1	0-2	5-1	2-0
Bromley	3-2	0-1	—	0-1	1-3	0-2	2-0	2-1	1-0	2-0	1-1	0-2	3-1	0-6	4-3	2-2	2-2	1-1	4-4	5-0	3-1	3-1
Carshalton Athletic	1-3	1-2	0-3	—	1-1	2-1	1-3	0-1	3-4	0-0	3-0	2-4	0-0	3-1	2-0	2-2	2-0	1-3	2-1	1-0	2-2	1-1
Chesham United	0-2	1-1	0-3	6-2	—	2-1	0-3	1-1	2-0	2-3	3-1	2-2	0-5	1-0	0-3	1-1	1-6	0-1	1-3	1-0	5-1	1-1
Dulwich Hamlet	4-3	0-2	2-2	1-2	1-0	—	1-2	1-1	2-3	4-2	1-0	0-1	1-5	3-2	3-2	2-2	4-1	0-2	4-2	4-3	1-1	1-3
Enfield	2-2	1-0	3-1	2-1	1-1	8-1	—	2-1	3-0	0-1	5-1	4-1	1-1	5-0	1-1	3-1	3-1	0-1	2-1	1-1	6-0	3-0
Grays Athletic	0-2	2-3	0-3	3-4	5-0	0-0	2-3	—	1-1	0-3	2-1	1-3	0-0	2-1	0-0	1-2	2-2	3-3	2-2	1-1	2-0	1-3
Harrow Borough	3-0	2-0	2-0	2-1	1-0	1-2	0-1	1-2	—	0-1	2-4	2-4	1-1	3-1	5-2	3-5	2-1	0-3	1-3	4-2	3-0	1-1
Hayes	2-0	1-0	2-2	5-0	2-0	1-1	1-4	1-2	1-1	—	1-1	0-0	1-0	2-0	3-2	4-1	1-1	3-1	2-1	2-0	1-0	1-3
Hendon	2-1	1-1	1-1	0-1	2-1	4-0	1-3	3-3	1-2	0-0	—	4-1	0-0	3-0	3-1	1-0	1-1	1-2	0-1	1-6	2-0	2-2
Hitchin Town	3-1	1-1	3-3	0-1	4-3	0-1	0-3	0-0	0-0	0-0	2-0	—	1-1	4-2	1-3	3-2	2-0	1-0	1-1	3-1	1-0	1-3
Kingstonian	2-0	1-0	1-0	0-1	5-1	0-1	3-2	1-0	3-1	1-1	1-2	3-1	—	2-1	0-1	0-1	3-5	0-3	1-1	2-5	5-0	0-1
Marlow	3-2	3-1	1-2	1-1	1-4	0-4	2-2	1-4	2-0	1-3	0-0	0-4	1-0	—	3-0	1-0	4-4	0-2	1-3	2-2	1-1	1-0
Molesey	1-3	4-0	1-1	4-1	1-2	1-0	0-2	1-1	2-0	0-2	1-1	0-0	1-2	2-1	—	1-2	3-2	0-2	1-1	2-1	1-0	1-0
Purfleet	0-3	3-3	2-1	4-4	3-1	1-2	2-2	0-3	4-2	1-2	3-3	1-3	0-3	3-1	0-1	—	0-4	3-0	2-2	2-5	4-3	2-2
St Albans City	2-1	5-0	1-2	3-1	4-2	3-2	1-2	1-1	1-0	1-1	3-2	3-3	8-3	3-2	0-2	2-0	—	3-1	3-2	2-2	6-2	1-1
Slough Town	1-0	1-0	4-1	3-3	5-2	1-1	1-4	2-0	1-1	3-1	2-2	3-2	2-1	4-0	3-1	2-4	1-1	—	3-2	0-0	1-0	5-3
Sutton United	1-3	5-0	1-2	3-2	1-2	4-2	0-2	2-2	2-1	3-3	3-1	0-0	4-1	1-2	2-3	1-2	5-1	1-1	—	0-0	0-2	2-0
Walton & Hersham	2-0	5-2	2-3	2-4	1-1	4-1	1-3	2-1	1-2	3-1	2-0	4-1	0-2	1-1	1-2	2-2	3-2	3-3	1-0	—	0-1	1-1
Wokingham Town	0-1	0-0	1-1	2-3	2-1	0-1	0-3	0-1	0-2	1-2	1-1	1-3	0-1	1-2	1-1	5-1	2-2	2-0	0-1	3-2	—	0-3
Yeading	4-2	1-1	1-3	3-2	1-1	1-1	4-2	1-1	0-3	1-1	0-1	0-1	1-0	0-0	0-4	1-0	7-2	0-0	2-1	0-1	1-1	—

DIADORA FOOTBALL LEAGUE CUP 1994–95

Preliminary Round
Aldershot Town 3, Bracknell Town 1
Barton Rovers 2, Egham Town 4
Chalfont St Peter 4, Kingsbury Town 1
Chertsey Town 2, Oxford City 3
Cheshunt 0, Ware 1
Clapton 2, Hemel Hempstead 3 *aet*
East Thurrock United 2, Banstead Athletic 0 *aet*
Epsom & Ewell 0, Hornchurch 0 *aet*
Feltham & Hounslow Borough 0 Leighton Town 0 *aet*
Hampton 1, Edgware Town 3
Harefield United 1, Hungerford Town 2
Hertford Town 1, Camberley Town 3
Horsham 2, Cove 0
Leatherhead 1, Canvey Island 2 *aet*
Lewes 1, Aveley 1 *aet*
Malden Vale 2, Harlow Town 4
Newbury Town 3, Metropolitan Police 0
Northwood 0, Bedford Town 1
Southall 2, Saffron Walden Town 6
Tilbury 1, Flackwell Heath 1 *aet*
Tring Town 1, Collier Row 3 *aet*
Windsor & Eton 3, Croydon 1
Witham Town 5, Thame United 4 *aet*

Replays
Aveley 1, Lewes 1 *aet*
(*Lewes won 5-4 on penalties*)
**Lewes removed from competition for playing an ineligible player.*
Flackwell Heath 3, Tilbury 0
Hornchurch 3, Epsom & Ewell 0
Leighton Town 1, Feltham & Hounslow Borough 1 *aet*
(*Leighton Town won 3-2 on penalties*)

First Round
Aldershot Town 4, Basingstoke 2
Aylesbury United 4, Whyteleafe 2
Barking 2, Wokingham Town 0
Bedford Town 2, Dulwich Hamlet 3 *aet*
Billericay Town 1, Purfleet 2
Bishop's Stortford 2, Marlow 6
Bognor Regis Town 4, Hemel Hempstead 1
Bromley 0, Oxford City 1
Carshalton Athletic 6, Flackwell Heath 0
Chalfont St Peter 2, Saffron Walden Town 3
Chesham United 2, Aveley 1 *aet*
Collier Row 2, Yeading 0
Dorking 1, Ware 0
East Thurrock United 2, Uxbridge 0
Edgware Town 3, Enfield 4
Egham Town 1, Wembley 2
Grays Athletic 2, Harlow Town 1
Hayes 0, Slough Town 1
Heybridge Swifts 2, Boreham Wood 0
Hitchin Town 3, Berkhamsted Town 1
Kingstonian 1, Abingdon Town 2
Leighton Town 0, Staines Town 2
Leyton 4, Camberley Town 0
Maidenhead United 0, Walton & Hersham 2
Molesey 1, Newbury Town 2
Ruislip Manor 2, Horsham 1 *aet*
St Albans City 2, Harrow Borough 1
Sutton United 1, Canvey Island 1 *aet*
Tooting & Mitcham United v Hornchurch
Witham Town 3, Windsor & Eton 1
Wivenhoe Town 0, Hungerford Town 2
Worthing 3, Hendon 3 *aet*

Replays
Canvey Island 2, Sutton United 4 *aet*
Hendon 2, Worthing 2 *aet*
(*Hendon won 3-1 on penalties*)

Second Round
Abingdon Town 2, St Albans City 3
Aldershot Town 2, Walton & Hersham 1 *aet*
Carshalton Athletic 7, Dorking 0
Grays Athletic 5, Saffron Walden Town 1
Heybridge Swifts 1, Aylesbury United 2
Hungerford Town 0, Dulwich Hamlet 6
Leyton 2, Hendon 1 *aet*
Marlow 2, Newbury Town 1 *aet*
Oxford City 2, Chesham United 1
Purfleet 2, East Thurrock United 0
Ruislip Manor 1, Sutton United 3
Slough Town 4, Collier Row 0
Staines Town 4, Barking 1
Tooting & Mitcham United 1, Hitchin Town 2
Wembley 2, Bognor Regis Town 1
Witham Town 0, Enfield 5

Third Round
Aldershot Town 3, Staines Town 2
Aylesbury United 2, Grays Athletic 0
Carshalton Athletic 3, Enfield 1
Dulwich Hamlet 3, Wembley 2
Leyton 1, Marlow 2
Oxford City 1, St Albans City 2
Purfleet 1, Hitchin Town 2 *aet*
Slough Town 5, Sutton United 1

Fourth Round
Aldershot Town 1, Aylesbury United 2
Carshalton Athletic 1, Dulwich Hamlet 1 *aet*
Marlow 2, Hitchin Town 0
St Albans City 3, Slough Town 4

Replay
Dulwich Hamlet 5, Carshalton Athletic 1

Semi-finals First Leg
Aylesbury United 4, Marlow 0
Slough Town 3, Dulwich Hamlet 1

Semi-finals Second Leg
Dulwich Hamlet 1, Slough Town 2
(*Slough Town won 5-2 on aggregate*)
Marlow 2, Aylesbury United 2
(*Aylesbury United won 6-2 on aggregate*)

Final
Aylesbury United 1, Slough Town 1 *aet*
(*Aylesbury United won 7-6 on penalties*)
(*at Marlow FC*)

CARLSBERG CUP 1994–95

First Round
Billericay Town 2, Barking 0
Bognor Regis Town 1, Aldershot Town 2
Boreham Wood 2, Wivenhoe Town 1
Chertsey Town 1, Newbury Town 0
Chesham United 3, Grays Athletic 1
Dorking 3, Dulwich Hamlet 1
Hitchin Town 2, Enfield 1
Maidenhead United 1, Tooting & Mitcham United 3
Uxbridge 1, St Albans City 5
Walton & Hersham 5, Marlow 1
Whyteleafe 0, Basingstoke Town 3
Yeading 2, Wembley 1

Second Round
Berkhamsted Town 1, Bishop's Stortford 1 *aet*
(*Berkhamsted Town won 6-5 on penalties*)
Billericay Town 2, Heybridge Swifts 1 *aet*
Boreham Wood 3, Purfleet 1
Carshalton Athletic 2, Tooting & Mitcham United 0
Chertsey Town 2, Aldershot Town 0
Chesham United 1, Harrow Borough 5
Hendon 5, Aylesbury United 1
Hitchin Town 3, Leyton 1
Kingstonian 1, Sutton United 3
Molesey 3, Bromley 3 *aet*
(*Molesey won 4-3 on penalties*)

St Albans City 1, Ruislip Manor 1 *aet*
(*Ruislip Manor won 4-2 on penalties*)
Staines Town 6, Dorking 0
Walton & Hersham 5, Abingdon Town 4 *aet*
Wokingham Town 1, Basingstoke Town 4
Worthing 3, Slough Town 6
Yeading 2, Hayes 3

Third Round
Basingstoke Town 3, Sutton United 5 *aet*
Berkhamsted Town 1, Billericay Town 1 *aet*
(*Berkhamsted Town won 5-4 on penalties*)
Chertsey Town 3, Slough Town 2 *aet*
Hendon 0, Boreham Wood 2
Hitchin Town 3, Harrow Borough 1
Molesey 1, Walton & Hersham 0
Ruislip Manor 1, Hayes 4
Staines Town 5, Carshalton Athletic 1

Fourth Round
Berkhamsted Town 0, Boreham Wood 1
Hitchin Town 2, Hayes 2 *aet*
(*Hayes won 4-3 on penalties*)
Staines Town 3, Molesey 0
Sutton United 2, Chertsey Town 1

Semi-finals
Hayes 1, Boreham Wood 2
Sutton United 2, Staines Town 3 *aet*

Final
Staines Town 3, Boreham Wood 3 *aet*
(*Staines Town won 4-2 on penalties*)
(*at Harrow Borough FC*)

CARLSBERG TROPHY 1994–95

First Round
Cheshunt 1, East Thurrock United 1 *aet*
(*East Thurrock United won 3-2 on penalties*)
Croydon 3, Leatherhead 1
Hampton 2, Metropolitan Police 3
Hertford Town 2, Barton Rovers 1
Horsham 1, Bracknell Town 2
Leighton Town 2, Tring Town 1
Lewes 5, Banstead Athletic 2 *aet*
Oxford City 4, Epsom & Ewell 1
Saffron Walden Town 1, Collier Row 3
Southall 4, Clapton 2
Windsor & Eton 0, Camberley Town 2

Second Round
Canvey Island 2, Witham Town 2 *aet*
Chalfont St Peter 1, Hungerford Town 1 *aet*
(*Hungerford Town won 3-1 on penalties*)
Croydon 3, Oxford City 1
(*Croydon removed from competition for playing an ineligible player*)
Edgware Town 3, Collier Row 5 *aet*
Feltham & Hounslow Borough 1, Bracknell Town 3
Flackwell Heath 6, Cove 1
Harefield United 1, Egham Town 3
Harlow Town 3, Hertford Town 1
Hemel Hempstead 1, Kingsbury Town 1 *aet*
(*Hemel Hempstead won 5-4 on penalties*)
Leighton Town 1, Bedford Town 1 *aet*
(*Leighton Town wn 4-1 on penalties*)
Lewes 3, Malden Vale 1
Northwood 0, Metropolitan Police 1
Southall 3, East Thurrock United 0
Thame United 4, Camberley Town 1
Tilbury 3, Aveley 0
Ware 2, Hornchurch 5 *aet*

Replay
Witham Town 4, Canvey Island 2 *aet*

Third Round
Flackwell Heath 1, Egham Town 0
Harlow Town 1, Leighton Town 3
Hornchurch 0, Collier Row 2
Hungerford Town 1, Bracknell Town 0
Metropolitan Police 5, Lewes 3
Southall 0, Witham Town 0 *aet*
(*Southall won 6-5 on penalties*)
Thame United 2, Oxford City 1
Tilbury 1, Hemel Hempstead 4

Fourth Round
Flackwell Heath 2, Hungerford Town 2 *aet*
(*Hungerford Town won 3-2 on penalties*)
Hemel Hempstead 1, Collier Row 2
Leighton Town 1, Southall 3
Thame United 1, Metropolitan Police 2 *aet*

Semi-finals
Hungerford Town 0, Collier Row 3
Metropolitan Police 2, Southall 2 *aet*

Replay
Southall 1, Metropolitan Police 2

Final
Metropolitan Police 1, Collier Row 1 *aet*
(*Metropolitan Police won 4-3 on penalties*)
(*at Boreham Wood FC*)

NEW SPONSOR FOR ISTHMIAN LEAGUE

ICIS (pronounced 'eye-siss'), which manufactures football strips, takes over from Diadora as sponsor of the Isthmian Football League.

ICIS Sportswear Limited is based on the fringe of the Lake District. In addition to football clothing they make leisurewear for the sport and corporate markets. They are a subsidiary of one of the UK's leading sales promotion companies—ICIS Limited—Innovative Consumer Incentive Services—who have a variety of 'blue chip' clients.

Although ICIS acquired the sportswear company less than 12 months ago, it has a 20 year history of manufacturing football clothing under the name of New Olympic.

The new management has restructured the business to cater for larger clubs and the corporate sector. They sell direct to football clubs—providing both 'off-the-shelf' and 'bespoke' designs.

For 1995/96 the company has introduced new fabrics and shirt designs—from traditional to modern.

FA UMBRO TROPHY 1994–95

Preliminary Round

Chester-le-Street Town v Tow Law Town	2-4
Fisher 93 v Whyteleafe	1-1, 0-1
Poole Town v Havant Town	1-2
(at Havant Town)	

First Qualifying Round

Whitley Bay v Bamber Bridge	0-4
Bedlington Terriers v Peterlee Newtown	2-1
West Auckland Town v Shildon	5-0
Harrogate Town v Eppleton CW	4-0
Tow Law Town v Lancaster City	2-3
Consett v RTM Newcastle	0-0, 0-2
Guisborough Town v Murton	2-0
Hebburn v Prudhoe Town	2-1
Accrington Stanley v Emley	1-0
Workington v Great Harwood Town	2-2, 2-4
Dunston Federation Brewery v Netherfield	2-0
Bridgnorth Town v Sutton Coldfield Town	2-0
Leicester United v Caernarfon Town	2-2, 2-1
Goole Town v Knowsley United	1-1, 2-6
Gresley Rovers v Congleton Town	3-1
Chorley v Bilston Town	2-0
Redditch United v Eastwood Town	0-1
Mossley v Dudley Town	2-2, 5-4
Farsley Celtic v Droylsden	1-1, 3-6
Fleetwood v Radcliffe Borough	3-0
Horwich RMI v Nuneaton Borough	0-3
Hinckley Town v Ilkeston Town	3-3, 0-1
Matlock Town v Buxton	2-1
Armitage v Curzon Ashton	1-4
Stourbridge v Gainsborough Trinity	3-6
Solihull Borough v Atherton LR	1-0
Burton Albion v Ashton United	1-1, 0-3
Moor Green v Worksop Town	8-4
Alfreton Town v Bedworth United	2-4
Kings Lynn v Burnham	3-3, 0-2
Leyton v Purfleet	0-1
Berkhamsted Town v Boreham Wood	0-2
Wivenhoe Town v Rothwell Town	1-2
Hayes v Tamworth	1-0
Racing Club Warwick v Harrow Borough	1-3
(Harrow Borough played ineligible player; match replayed:	*2-5)*
Heybridge Swifts v Billericay Town	2-0
Rushden & Diamonds v Hendon	0-0, 4-1
Wembley v Bury Town	5-2
Aylesbury United v Barking	5-0
Cambridge City v Bishops Stortford	6-1
Ruislip Manor v Baldock Town	0-3
Sudbury Town v Corby Town	5-0
VS Rugby v Braintree Town	4-3
Hastings Town v Gravesend & Northfleet	0-2
Chertsey Town v Tonbridge	3-1
Whyteleafe v Uxbridge	1-2
Dulwich Hamlet v Dorking	3-1
Ashford Town v Bognor Regis Town	3-4
Molesey v Sittingbourne	1-0
Wealdstone v Bromley	3-0
Tooting & Mitcham United v Walton & Hersham	0-2
Margate v Yeading	0-2
Erith & Belvedere v Staines Town	0-1
Gloucester City v Weymouth	1-0
Newbury Town v Buckingham Town	0-0, 1-1, 2-0
Maidenhead United v Fareham Town	0-1
Yate Town v Forest Green Rovers	0-2
Havant Town v Waterlooville	3-0
Evesham United v Basingstoke Town	0-1
Newport AFC v Aldershot Town	1-3
Abingdon Town v Witney Town	1-1, 0-1
Dorchester Town v Wokingham Town	2-0
Newport (IW) v Salisbury City	2-4
Clevedon Town v Bashley	1-1, 0-1

Second Qualifying Round

Droylsden v Hebburn	2-2, 4-0
RTM Newcastle v Dunston Federation Brewery	0-2
Curzon Ashton v Harrogate Town	4-2
Guisborough Town v Bedlington Terriers	2-1
Chorley v Bamber Bridge	1-2
Lancaster City v Knowsley United	1-1, 1-2
Great Harwood Town v Fleetwood	1-2
Accrington Stanley v West Auckland Town	2-2, 1-3
Baldock Town v Matlock Town	2-0
Nuneaton Borough v Ashton United	1-2
Rothwell Town v Eastwood Town	5-4
Ilkeston Town v Leicester United	6-1
Bedworth United v Bridgnorth Town	2-0
Mossley v Moor Green	1-3
Solihull Borough v VS Rugby	0-1
Gainsborough Trinity v Gresley Rovers	1-1, 0-1
Yeading v Burnham	0-0, 4-0
Heybridge Swifts v Chertsey Town	1-1, 1-3
Sudbury Town v Hayes	2-0
Dulwich Hamlet v Aylesbury United	1-2
Walton & Hersham v Cambridge City	2-1
Wealdstone v Purfleet	0-3
Boreham Wood v Uxbridge	1-1, 2-1
Rushden & Diamonds v Wembley	2-1
Molesey v Staines Town	4-2
Gravesend & Northfleet v Harrow Borough	1-1, 1-5
Basingstoke Town v Aldershot Town	0-1
Havant Town v Dorchester Town	1-3
Salisbury City v Bognor Regis Town	0-0, 2-4
Forest Green Rovers v Newbury Town	1-1, 1-2
Witney Town v Bashley	1-2
Gloucester City v Fareham Town	3-0

Third Qualifying Round

Northallerton v Blyth Spartans	0-2
Warrington Town v Colwyn Bay	1-1, 0-3
Knowsley United v Ashton United	1-4
Fleetwood v Spennymoor United	1-1, 0-3
Curzon Ashton v Gresley Rovers	0-1
Barrow v Winsford United	1-1, 2-4
Frickley Athletic v Whitby Town	1-2
Guisborough Town v West Auckland Town	1-2
Hyde United v Boston United	1-0
Dunston Federation Brewery v Ilkeston Town	2-3
Bamber Bridge v Grantham Town	3-1
Droylsden v Leek Town	0-1
Gretna v Seaham Red Star	2-1
Rushden & Diamonds v Crawley Town	2-1
Cheltenham Town v Worthing	4-0
Aldershot Town v Rothwell Town	1-1
(tie awarded to Rothwell Town; Aldershot included an ineligible player)	
Sudbury Town v Carshalton Athletic	6-1
Gloucester City v Chelmsford City	0-2
Grays Athletic v Chertsey Town	0-0, 1-1, 3-1
Hednesford Town v Trowbridge Town	2-1
Bedworth United v Boreham Wood	0-1
Worcester City v Molesey	2-2, 0-2
Moor Green v Marlow	0-0, 0-1
Bashley v Yeading	1-1, 0-1
St Albans City v Purfleet	4-3
Baldock Town v Walton & Hersham	1-1, 1-2
Halesowen Town v Hitchin Town	4-0
Aylesbury United v Dorchester Town	2-1
Weston-Super-Mare v Chesham United	1-3
Kingstonian v Harrow Borough	3-1
VS Rugby v Bognor Regis Town	2-1
Atherstone United v Newbury Town	1-2

First Round

Runcorn v Northwich Victoria	2-1
Leek Town v Durham City	2-1
Gretna v Halesowen Town	1-1, 1-4
Telford United v Southport	2-0
Witton Albion v Guiseley	0-0, 2-2, 1-2
Gresley Rovers v Stafford Rangers	2-0

Bamber Bridge v Halifax Town	1-0
Hednesford Town v Altrincham	1-2
Stalybridge Celtic v Hyde United	3-3, 1-3
Billingham Synthonia v Ashton United	1-2
Bishop Auckland v Gateshead	0-1
West Auckland Town v Macclesfield Town *(at Macclesfield)*	1-2
Colwyn Bay v Blyth Spartans	1-1, 2-2, 2-1
Marine v Whitby Town	3-1
Spennymoor United v Morecambe	0-3
Ilkeston Town v Winsford United	4-2
Newbury Town v Rothwell Town	1-2
Boreham Wood v Grays Athletic	1-0
VS Rugby v Aylesbury United	2-1
Woking v Chesham United	3-0
Molesey v Cheltenham Town	0-2
Chelmsford City v Yeovil Town	2-4
Merthyr Tydfil v Slough Town	3-2
Rushden & Diamonds v Sudbury Town	3-1
Stevenage Borough v Dagenham & Redbridge	2-1
St Albans City v Kidderminster Harriers	2-3
Kingstonian v Yeading	3-2
Welling United v Marlow	2-2, 5-1
Farnborough Town v Dover Athletic	1-0
Sutton United v Bath City	1-1, 0-1
Bromsgrove Rovers v Enfield	1-3
Walton & Hersham v Kettering Town	2-2, 0-1

Second Round

Farnborough Town v Rushden & Diamonds	0-1
Halesowen Town v Guiseley	2-1
Bath City v Marine	1-2
Runcorn v Leek Town	4-2
Ashton United v Macclesfield Town	0-5
Altrincham v VS Rugby	1-1, 2-1
Colwyn Bay v Enfield	1-2
Gresley Rovers v Morecambe	2-3
Merthyr Tydfil v Bamber Bridge	2-1
Gateshead v Rothwell Town	6-1
Hyde United v Telford United	2-0
Woking v Cheltenham Town	3-1
Welling United v Ilkeston Town	1-1, 0-3
Yeovil Town v Stevenage Borough	1-1, 0-2
Kingstonian v Kidderminster Harriers	0-0, 0-1
Boreham Wood v Kettering Town	2-1

Third Round

Marine v Boreham Wood	2-0
Runcorn v Hyde United	0-0, 0-4
Gateshead v Macclesfield Town	0-1
Rushden & Diamonds v Halesowen Town	6-1
Ilkeston Town v Kidderminster Harriers	2-2, 1-2
Stevenage Borough v Woking	0-3
Morecambe v Altrincham	2-3
Enfield v Merthyr Tydfil	1-1, 1-1 (abandoned), 1-0

Fourth Round

Marine v Hyde United	1-3
Enfield v Rushden & Diamonds	1-1, 3-4
Kidderminster Harriers v Altrincham	5-0
Macclesfield Town v Woking	0-1

Semi-finals (two legs)

Kidderminster Harriers v Hyde United	2-0, 0-1
Rushden & Diamonds v Woking	1-0, 0-2

FA Umbro Trophy Final at Wembley

14 May

Kidderminster Harriers (0) 1 *(Davies)*

Woking (1) 2 *(Steele, Fielder) aet* 17,815

Kidderminster Harriers: Rose; Hodson, Bancroft, Webb, Brindley (Cartwright), Forsyth, Deakin, Yates, Humphreys (Hughes), Davies, Purdie.
Woking: Batty; Tucker, Wye L, Fielder, Brown, Crumplin (Rattray), Wye S, Ellis, Steele, Hay (Newbery), Walker.
Referee: D. Gallagher (Oxfordshire).

Woking captain Colin Fielder (left) with the FA Umbro Trophy at Wembley following the team's success against Kidderminster Harriers. (Action Images).

FA CARLSBERG VASE 1994–95

Extra Preliminary Round

Cleator Moor Celtic v Norton & Stockton Ancients 1-2
Morpeth Town v Horden CW 4-3
Langley Park S & S United v Shotton Comrades 3-1
Marske United v Seaton Delaval Amateurs 4-3
Ponteland United v North Shields 8-1
Sunderland Kennek Roker v Annfield Plain 4-1
Waterloo Dock v Kimberley Town 3-0
Maghull v Merseyside Police 1-2
South Normanton Athletic v Long Eaton United 3-0
Staveley MW v Daisy Hill 3-1
Rainworth MW v Wythenshawe Amateur 3-1
Heswall v Cheadle Town 2-1
Borrowash Victoria v Nuthall 2-2, 1-1, 2-2, 1-0
Shirebrook Town v Grove United 1-2
Vauxhall v Lucas Sports 6-3
Nettleham v Glapwell 0-2
Garforth Town v Oakham United 0-1
Harworth CI v Castleton Gabriels 4-3
Ashville v Hall Road Rangers 0-1
Clipstone Welfare v Poulton Victoria 1-3
Holwell Sports v Birstall United 4-3
Friar Lane OB v St Andrews 1-2
Cradley Town v Westfields 1-1, 1-5
Knowle v Pegasus Juniors 4-0
Northfield Town v Darlaston 4-1
Kings Heath v Meir KA 0-1
Lutterworth Town v Bloxwich Town 0-0, 0-0, 0-2
Gedling Town v Coleshill Town 4-2
Brantham Athletic v Mildenhall Town 4-1
Great Wakering Rovers v Clacton Town 2-0
Swaffham Town v Somersham Town 1-1, 2-1
Downham Town v Stanway Rovers 4-1
(at Long Sutton Athletic)
Warboys Town v Hullbridge Sports 5-1
Southend Manor v Maldon Town 1-2
Milton Keynes v Shillington 0-5
Stansted v Potters Bar Town 0-1
East Ham United v Leverstock Green 0-3
Rayners Lane v Eton Wick 0-3
St Margaretsbury v Cockfosters 1-2
(at Hertford Town)
Harpenden Town v Brentwood 1-0
Beaconsfield SYCOB v Eton Manor 4-1
London Colney v Waltham Abbey 4-0
Tower Hamlets v Totternhoe 9-1
West Wickham v Cobham 0-4
Worthing United v East Grinstead 2-1
Stamco v Furness 2-1
Thamesmead Town v Eastbourne United 2-1
Cranleigh v Broadbridge Heath 0-2
Greenwich Borough v Mile Oak 3-4
Sherborne Town v North Leigh 0-3
Flight Refuelling v Peppard 2-1
Petersfield Town v Hamworthy United 6-0
Sandhurst Town v Carterton Town 1-2
Bridgwater Town v Dawlish Town 4-1
Chard Town v Bishop Sutton 1-2
Cadbury Heath v Brislington 1-5
Cirencester Town v DRG AFC 3-2
Bristol Manor Farm v Almondsbury Town 1-3
(at Almondsbury Town)
Crediton United v Clyst Rovers 0-1
Wotton Rovers v Old Georgians 2-2, 2-0

Preliminary Round

Alnwick Town v Esh Winning 3-0
Ponteland United v West Allotment Celtic 2-2, 1-0
Penrith v Billingham Town 7-0
Walker v Washington 3-4
Morpeth Town v Ryhope CA 1-0
Crook Town v Langley Park S & S United 9-0
Pickering Town v Harrogate Railway 4-0
Darlington Cleveland Soc v Wolviston 3-5
Marske United v Willington 3-4
Easington Colliery v Evenwood Town 1-2
Norton & Stockton Ancients v Sunderland Kennek Roker 4-2
Armthorpe Welfare v North Ferriby United 2-3
Salford City v Skelmersdale United 1-1, 1-1, 2-0
Hucknall Town v Formby 5-1
Chadderton v Sheffield 4-1
Maltby MW v Blackpool (Wren) Rovers 1-4
Borrowash Victoria v Blidworth MW 3-1
Heanor Town v Kidsgrove Athletic 2-1
Rossendale United v St Helens Town 1-2
Tadcaster Albion v Glapwell 3-1
Ashfield United v Harworth CI 3-0
Heswall v Darwen 1-0
Ossett Town v Grove United 1-1, 0-1
Oakham United v Merseyside Police 2-1
Worsbro Bridge MW v Prescot AFC 3-2
Priory (Eastwood) v Trafford 0-7
Louth United v Hallam 2-1
Bradford (Park Avenue) v South Normanton Ath 6-4
Clitheroe v Waterloo Dock 3-4
Winterton Rangers v Newcastle Town 0-1
Lincoln United v Poulton Victoria 4-5
RES Parkgate v Denaby United 2-0
Staveley MW v Bootle 0-2
Maine Road v Immingham Town 1-0
Bacup Borough v Glasshoughton Welfare 2-4
Yorkshire Amateur v Rainworth MW 0-2
Atherton Collieries v Hatfield Main 0-1
Liversedge v Hall Road Rangers 2-4
Pontefract Collieries v Ossett Albion 1-5
Oldham Town v Rossington Main 1-1, 4-0
Vauxhall v Eccleshill United 3-2
Knowle v Willenhall Town 0-2
Stourport Swifts v Bolehall Swifts 3-2
Highgate United v St Andrews 1-5
Brierley Hill Town v Barwell 0-1
Meir KA v Chasetown 4-2
Shepshed Dynamo v Holwell Sports 2-3
Halesowen Harriers v Stewarts & Lloyds 1-2
Stapenhill v Gedling Town 2-3
Oldbury United v Shifnal Town 4-2
Knypersley Victoria v Westfields 4-1
Blakenall v Rocester 2-1
Lye Town v Stratford Town 3-1
Paget Rangers v Boldmere St Michaels 2-1
Long Buckby v Wellingborough Town 3-0
Sandwell Borough v Northampton Spencer 0-1
Northfield Town v Bloxwich Town 0-1
Rushall Olympic v Newport Pagnell Town 1-2
Desborough Town v Wednesfield 1-5
Brantham Athletic v Cornard United 2-0
Harwich & Parkeston v Stowmarket Town 0-2
Holbeach United v Eynesbury Rovers 0-4
Sudbury Wanderers v Haverhill Rovers 2-2, 2-2, 0-1
Swaffham Town v Long Sutton Athletic 4-1
Burnham Ramblers v Gorleston 1-1, 0-5
Watton United v Wroxham 0-4
Warboys Town v Downham Town 1-0
Ipswich Wanderers v Felixstowe Town 0-2
Norwich United v Newmarket Town 0-3
Stamford AFC v Sawbridgeworth Town 1-0
Bowers United v Great Yarmouth Town 1-0
Woodbridge Town v Maldon Town 0-1
Hadleigh United v March Town United 4-3
Chatteris Town v Witham Town 1-6
Great Wakering Rovers v Fakenham Town 2-2, 4-2
Ely City v Tiptree United 1-4
Histon v Spalding United 2-3
Bourne Town v Mirrlees Blackstone 2-1
Ashford Town (Middx) v Stotfold 1-2
Harlow Town v Hanwell Town 0-0, 2-0
Haringey Borough v Wootton Blue Cross 1-1, 3-1
Hampton v Viking Sports 0-1
Northwood v Ford United 2-0
East Thurrock United v Leverstock Green 5-2
London Colney v Harpenden Town 1-0
Harefield United v Langford 6-1

Kingsbury Town v Royston Town 0-2
Cockfosters v Edgware Town 3-0
Southall v Eton Wick 3-4
Brook House v Biggleswade Town 7-5
Potton United v Hemel Hempstead 1-3
Kempston Rovers v Concord Rangers 1-2
Beaconsfield SYCOB v Tower Hamlets 1-2
Tilbury v Shillington 3-1
Welwyn Garden City v Wingate & Finchley 3-5
Leighton Town v Bedford Town 2-1
Letchworth Garden City w.o. v Dunstable removed from competition
Ware v Hertford Town 1-2
Hornchurch v Flackwell Heath 5-0
Clapton v Hillingdon Borough 0-1
Cheshunt v Romford 0-3
Potters Bar Town v Feltham & Hounslow Borough 2-1
Croydon Athletic v Whitstable Town 2-7
Southwick v Chichester City 8-0
Sheppey United v Stamco 2-4
Burgess Hill Town v Chipstead 1-0
Corinthian v Canterbury City 4-3
Camberley Town v Ramsgate 3-2
Cobham v Epsom & Ewell 0-0, 1-0
Newhaven v Chatham Town 1-4
Three Bridges v Slade Green 2-1
Wick v Eastbourne Town 3-0
Deal Town v Arundel 5-2
Selsey v Broadbridge Heath 2-0
Redhill v Leatherhead 3-4
Mile Oak v Thamesmead Town 1-4
Corinthian-Casuals v Bracknell Town 1-4
Steyning Town v Dartford 1-3
Worthing United v Horsham 0-4
Langney Sports v Ash United 3-0
Ringmer v Shoreham 0-3
Bedfont v Beckenham Town 1-3
Folkestone Invicta v Horsham YMCA 5-1
Cray Wanderers v Merstham 1-1, 1-2
Crowborough Athletic v Pagham 2-1
Portfield v Oakwood 2-0
Lancing v Egham Town 0-3
Godalming & Guildford v Littlehampton Town 3-4
Bemerton Heath Harlequins v Eastleigh 2-2, 0-3
Gosport Borough v Hungerford Town 2-3
Thatcham Town v First Tower United 2-5
Totton AFC v Abingdon United 1-3
Swanage Town & Herston v Westbury United 0-4
Cove v Carterton Town 4-3
Flight Refuelling v Lymington AFC 1-2
Swindon Supermarine v Brockenhurst 1-2
Wantage Town v Fleet Town 2-1
Kintbury Rangers v Bournemouth 2-3
Bicester Town v Milton United 1-2
Christchurch v Petersfield Town 2-3
North Leigh v Calne Town 3-3, 3-0
Banbury United v Ryde 3-0
Cirencester Town v Tuffley Rovers 1-3
Porthleven v Fairford Town 6-1
Cinderford Town v Bishop Sutton 3-1
(at Bishop Sutton)
Frome Town v Devizes Town 2-2, 1-2
Clyst Rovers v Glastonbury 3-2
Torrington v Bridgwater Town 3-1
Ilfracombe Town v Odd Down 3-2
Bridport v Backwell United 2-1
Melksham Town v Barnstaple Town 1-2
Chippenham Town v Brislington 3-1
Elmore v Warminster Town 5-1
Larkhall Athletic v Saltash United 1-3
Minehead v Exmouth Town 0-4
Keynsham Town v St Blazey 5-3
Newquay v Mangotsfield United 1-3
Almondsbury Town v Wotton Rovers 1-2
Wellington Town v Liskeard Athletic 1-3
Hallen v Shortwood United 1-2

First Round
Ponteland United v Washington 1-2
Crook Town v Willington 0-1
Ossett Albion v Wolviston 8-0
Whickham v Norton & Stockton Ancients 3-1
Pickering Town v Evenwood Town 1-0
Thackley v Morpeth Town 4-0
Blackpool (Wren) Rovers v Waterloo Dock 0-2
Alnwick Town v South Shields 1-4
North Ferriby United v Penrith 2-1
Oldham Town v Tadcaster Albion 3-0
Bootle v Newcastle Town 7-6
Hall Road Rangers v Trafford 0-1
Grove United v Hatfield Main 1-1, 2-4
Borrowash Victoria v Chadderton 3-1
Poulton Victoria v Parkgate 4-1
Bradford (Park Avenue) v St Helens Town 3-0
Ashfield United v Stocksbridge Park Steels 1-2
Rainworth MW v Vauxhall 1-0
Hucknall Town v Nantwich Town 2-1
Oakham United v Louth United 2-0
Worsbro Bridge MW v Glossop North End 2-4
Heanor Town v Salford City 2-1
Maine Road v Glasshoughton Welfare 5-2
Flixton v Heswall 8-1
St Andrews v Bloxwich Town 2-0
Paget Rangers v Barwell 2-3
Lye Town v Wednesfield 1-3
Meir KA v Gedling Town 1-1, 4-2
Arnold Town v Long Buckby 2-0
Knypersley Victoria v Oldbury United 0-1
Stewarts & Lloyds v Raunds Town 1-5
Cogenhoe United v Bourne Town 4-1
Holwell Sports v West Midlands Police 1-1, 0-2
Pershore Town v Willenhall Town 0-2
Northampton Spencer v Blakenall 1-2
Spalding United v Stamford 2-1
Stourport Swifts v Newport Pagnell Town 0-2
Northwood v Tiptree United 6-3
Potters Bar Town v Hadleigh United 3-4
Harefield United v Tring Town 0-2
Hertford Town v Swaffham Town 2-0
Newmarket Town v Brimsdown Rovers 2-0
Maldon Town v Haringey Borough 5-1
Letchworth Garden City v Aveley 1-2
(Aveley included ineligible player; Letchworth Garden City re-instated)
Barton Rovers v Felixstowe Town 2-1
Collier Row v Concord Rangers 3-1
Cockfosters v Halstead Town 0-1
Stotfold v Witham Town 0-0, 2-0
Viking Sports v Tower Hamlets 3-4
Gorleston v Harlow Town 5-1
Hornchurch v East Thurrock United 1-2
Great Wakering Rovers v Tilbury 4-2
Wroxham v Brantham Athletic 2-2, 1-0
Royston Town v Brook House 1-1, 2-2, 2-0
Eynesbury Rovers v Hemel Hempstead 1-0
Hillingdon Borough v Stowmarket Town 4-2
Basildon United v Haverhill Rovers 3-0
Bowers United v Wingate & Finchley 2-5
Leighton Town v Soham Town Rangers 2-0
Warboys Town v London Colney 3-2
Lowestoft Town v Romford 5-0
Littlehampton Town v Camberley Town 2-2, 0-4
Cobham v Horsham 2-3
North Leigh v Lewes 3-2
Shoreham v Bracknell Town 2-1
Wantage Town v Hailsham Town 1-4
Crowborough Athletic v Cove 1-5
Milton United v Langney Sports 6-2
Eton Wick v Andover 6-4
Hungerford Town v Portfield 4-1
Bournemouth v Beckenham Town 5-0
Stamco v Whitstable Town 4-2
Burgess Hill Town v Wick 0-3
Oxford City v Herne Bay 4-1
Abingdon United v Selsey 0-2
Thame United v Leatherhead 1-2
Deal Town v Dartford 3-2
Three Bridges v Thamesmead Town 1-3

Eastleigh v Banbury United	2-1
Egham Town v Brockenhurst	6-2
Chatham Town v Merstham	4-0
Southwick v Petersfield Town	1-2
Folkestone Invicta v Corinthian	1-2
First Tower United v Lymington AFC	3-4
Mangotsfield United v Moreton Town	2-0
Torrington v Welton Rovers	3-0
Elmore v Clyst Rovers	4-0
Ilfracombe Town v Falmouth Town	1-9
Tuffley Rovers v Wotton Rovers	2-1
Bridport v Shortwood United	6-0
Chippenham Town v Cinderford Town	3-4
Westbury United v Devizes Town	0-0, 2-1
Barnstaple Town v Keynsham Town	3-1
Liskeard Athletic v Bideford	2-1
Torpoint Athletic v Exmouth Town	4-1
Saltash United v Porthleven	6-3

Second Round

Heanor Town v Hatfield Main	2-4
South Shields v Flixton	3-2
Cammell Laird v Meir KA	2-2, 2-0
Whickham v Pickering Town	0-0, 2-3
Brandon United v Dunkirk	2-1
Arnold Town v Trafford	2-1
North Ferriby United v Thackley	0-3
Waterloo Dock v Hucknall Town	1-2
Burscough v Brigg Town	2-0
Rainworth MW v Poulton Victoria	0-4
Stocksbridge Park Steels v Oakham United	2-1
Glossop North End v Bootle	2-0
Eastwood Hanley v Bradford (Park Avenue)	3-1
Ossett Albion v Stockton	2-0
Maine Road v Borrowash Victoria	2-1
Belper Town v Washington	5-0
Oldham Town v Willington	1-2
Great Wakering Rovers v Raunds Town	1-2
Diss Town v Cogenhoe United	3-2
Hoddesdon Town v Arlesey Town	0-2
Boston Town v Walthamstow Pennant	1-0
Tower Hamlets v West Midlands Police	2-2, 0-1
Letchworth Garden City v Hadleigh United	0-3
Stotfold v Warboys Town	3-1
St Andrews v Willenhall Town	3-1
Oadby Town v Wednesfield	5-4
Collier Row v Newport Pagnell Town	7-0
Wisbech Town v Blakenall	3-1
Halstead Town v Saffron Walden Town	4-2
East Thurrock United v Canvey Island	0-2
Wroxham v Pelsall Villa	0-1
Royston Town v Basildon United	0-1
Eynesbury Rovers v Spalding United	2-0
Newmarket Town v Tring Town	2-1
Lowestoft Town v Maldon Town	3-1
Gorleston v Barton Rovers	0-4
Leighton Town v Wingate & Finchley	0-3
Barwell v Hertford Town	2-1
Oldbury United v Hinckley Athletic	1-2
Wick v Chalfont St Peter	2-1
Horsham v Malden Vale	1-1, 3-1
Cove v Hailsham Town	2-3
Hillingdon Borough v Northwood	0-1
Stamco v Leatherhead	4-0
Corinthian v Egham Town	4-3
Windsor & Eton v Shoreham	2-3
Metropolitan Police v Eton Wick	3-1
Camberley Town v Banstead Athletic	0-2
Thamesmead Town v Croydon	1-6
Peacehaven & Telscombe v Deal Town	3-0
Whitehawk v Chatham Town	1-0
Selsey v Tunbridge Wells	0-1
Eastleigh v Lymington AFC	6-3
Milton United v Oxford City	1-4
Bridport v Falmouth Town	1-3
Liskeard Athletic v Cinderford Town	3-1
Petersfield Town v Taunton Town	0-7
Bournemouth v Torpoint Athletic	4-3
North Leigh v Elmore	0-4
Tiverton Town v Saltash United	9-0
Westbury United v Tuffley Rovers	4-1
Wimborne Town v Torrington	4-2
Barnstaple Town v Hungerford Town	3-1
Mangotsfield United v Paulton Rovers	3-2

Third Round

Oadby Town v Ossett Albion	0-6
Hatfield Main v Maine Road	0-1
Barwell v Brandon United	0-1
Thackley v Cammell Laird	1-1, 1-1, 1-2
Eastwood Hanley v Pickering Town	3-1
Poulton Victoria v St Andrews	2-3
Arnold Town v Burscough	2-3
Glossop North End v Stocksbridge Park Steels	0-5
South Shields v Hucknall Town	3-1
Belper Town v Willington	6-4
Wisbech Town v Stotfold	3-4
Hadleigh United v Corinthian	3-1
Newmarket Town v Canvey Island	0-5
Wingate & Finchley v Basildon United	1-2
Diss Town v Barton Rovers	3-1
Lowestoft Town v Raunds Town	1-3
Metropolitan Police v Collier Row	2-1
Eynesbury Rovers v Halstead Town	2-3
Hinckley Athletic v Pelsall Villa	1-2
Boston Town v Arlesey Town	1-2
West Midlands Police v Northwood	3-2
Bournemouth v Croydon	1-2
Hailsham Town v Eastleigh	0-4
Taunton Town v Westbury United	4-2
Wick v Elmore	4-4, 1-4
Tiverton Town v Horsham	4-1
Banstead Athletic v Falmouth Town	3-5
Mangotsfield United v Whitehawk	4-0
Stamco v Shoreham	5-3
Oxford City v Peacehaven & Telscombe	1-0
Wimborne Town v Barnstaple Town	1-4
Tunbridge Wells v Liskeard Athletic	1-1, 0-2

Fourth Round

Burscough v Brandon United	3-0
Stocksbridge Park Steels v Eastwood Hanley	1-1, 1-3
Pelsall Villa v Cammell Laird	1-2
Halstead Town v Hadleigh United	5-5, 2-3
West Midlands Police v Raunds Town	0-2
Ossett Albion v Diss Town	1-1, 1-1, 0-3
St Andrews v Maine Road	2-1
Belper Town v South Shields	4-0
Liskeard Athletic v Falmouth Town	0-2
Stotfold v Basildon United	0-4
Mangotsfield United v Canvey Island	1-5
Barnstaple Town v Arlesey Town	0-2
Croydon v Oxford City	1-2
Taunton Town v Elmore	2-1
Eastleigh v Metropolitan Police	1-3
Stamco v Tiverton Town	4-3

Fifth Round

Raunds Town v St Andrews	3-0
Arlesey Town v Diss Town	1-0
Falmouth Town v Belper Town	1-5
Taunton Town v Oxford City	0-3
Canvey Island v Stamco	3-0
Cammell Laird v Burscough	4-2
Metropolitan Police v Hadleigh United	4-1
Eastwood Hanley v Basildon United	2-3

Sixth Round

Arlesey Town v Cammell Laird	3-0
Oxford City v Canvey Island	2-0
Metropolitan Police v Belper Town	0-1
Basildon United v Raunds Town	0-2

Semi-finals (two legs)

Raunds Town v Arlesey Town	3-0, 0-5
Belper Town v Oxford City	1-0, 1-3

Vase Final at Wembley

13 May

Arlesey Town (1) 2 *(Palma, Gyalog)*

Oxford City (0) 1 *(Fontaine S)* 13,670

Arlesey Town: Young; Cardines, Hull, Gonsalves, Bambrick, Gyalog, Cox, O'Keefe, Marshall (Nicholls), Palma (Ward), Kane.

Oxford City: Fleet; Brown (Fisher), Hume, Shepherd, Muttock, Hamilton (Kemp), Thomas, Spittle, Fontaine C, Sherwood, Fontaine S.

Referee: G. Willard (Worthing).

FA COUNTY YOUTH CHALLENGE CUP 1994–95

First Round

Lancashire v East Riding	0-3
Westmorland v Sheffield & Hallamshire	1-2
Liverpool v Nottinghamshire	3-2
North Riding v Lincolnshire	0-3
Herefordshire v Northamptonshire	0-2
Leicestershire & Rutland v Worcestershire	3-3, 3-1
Hertfordshire v Cambridgeshire	4-1
Bedfordshire v London	2-1
Berks & Bucks v Surrey	0-1
Dorset v Devon	2-3
Wiltshire v Somerset & Avon	3-3, 1-3
Hampshire v Army	3-1

Second Round

Shropshire v West Riding	1-3
Cumberland v East Riding	1-1, 1-0
Northumberland v Sheffield & Hallamshire	3-1
Durham v Liverpool	0-1
Manchester v Lincolnshire	4-1
Derbyshire v Northamptonshire	6-0
Cheshire v Leicestershire & Rutland	2-1
Birmingham v Hertfordshire	1-4
Huntingdonshire v Staffordshire	3-2
Norfolk v Bedfordshire	3-2
Suffolk v Surrey	1-2
Gloucestershire v Sussex	3-1
Kent v Essex	3-4
Oxfordshire v Devon	4-2
Middlesex v Somerset & Avon (South)	1-3
Cornwall v Hampshire	5-0

Third Round

Derbyshire v Liverpool	2-4
West Riding v Cheshire	4-2
Hertfordshire v Northumberland	1-1, 1-2
Manchester v Cumberland	2-1
Oxfordshire v Essex	1-2
Huntingdonshire v Somerset & Avon (South)	2-4
Cornwall v Surrey	3-2
Gloucestershire v Norfolk	2-3

Fourth Round

Liverpool v Norfolk	2-2, 1-0
Somerset & Avon (South) v Essex	1-3
Manchester v Northumberland	0-1
West Riding v Cornwall	1-2

Semi-finals

Liverpool v Cornwall	2-2, 3-0
Northumberland v Essex	0-2

Final

Liverpool v Essex	3-2

FA XI MATCHES

18 Oct

FA XI 1 *(Genovese)*
Huntingdonshire FA 1 120
FA XI: Ladley (Holbeach United) [Crane (Rushden & Diamonds)]; Mountain (Spalding United), Fuff (Rushden & Diamonds), Quow (Sudbury Town) [Genovese (Holbeach United)], Gray (Holbeach United), Rhule (Stamford), Crunkhorn (Holbeach United), Carr (Raunds Town), Keeble (Raunds Town), Boon (Stotfold), Fortune (Holbeach United).

15 Nov

FA XI 2 *(Connor, Green)*
Northern Premier League 2 137
FA XI: Farrelly (Macclesfield Town); Cross (Altrincham), Bimson (Macclesfield Town), France (Altrincham), Reid (Altrincham), Connor (Runcorn) [Anderson (Stalybridge Celtic)], Thomas (Runcorn) [Terry (Altrincham)], McDonald (Macclesfield Town) [Sorvel (Macclesfield Town)], Green (Altrincham), Carmody (Altrincham), Shrratt (Altrincham).

7 Dec

FA XI 1 *(Rattray)*
Isthmian League 0 250
FA XI: Williams (Dover Athletic) [Batty (Woking)]; Tucker (Woking), Brown (Welling United), Brown K (Woking), Wye (Woking), Brown D (Woking), Browne (Dover Athletic) [Boothe (Farnborough Town)], Lewhorthy (Dover Athletic), Robbins (Welling United) [Rattray (Woking)], Broom (Dagenham & Redbridge).

10 Jan

FA XI 4 *(Carter, Stott, May, Forsyth)*
British Students 0 140
FA XI: Goodwin (Telford United) [Steadman (Kidderminster Harriers); Bignot (Telford United) [Skelding (Bromsgrove Rovers)], Bancroft (Kidderminster Harriers), Yates (Kidderminster Harriers), Foster (Telford United) [Weir (Kidderminster Harriers)], Forsyth (Kidderminster Harriers), Snape (Halesowen Town), Stott (Bromsgrove Rovers), May (Stafford Rangers) [Burton (Westfields)], Carter (Bromsgrove Rovers) [O'Connor (Hednesford Town)], Coogan (Solihull Borough).

17 Jan

FA XI 2 *(Terry, Dove)*
Combined Services 0 100
FA XI: Morris (Runcorn); Norman (Macclesfield Town), Robertson (Runcorn), Ruffer (Runcorn), Howarth (Macclesfield Town)], Bimson (Macclesfield Town), Bimson (Macclesfield Town), Terry (Altrincham), Dove (Southport), Burke (Stalybridge Celtic), Power (Macclesfield Town), Sorvel (Macclesfield Town).

19 May

FA XI 3 *(Richardson 1, May, Hayles)*
Highland League 4 450
FA XI: Williams (Dover Athletic) [Mogg (Bath City)]; Webb (Kidderminster Harriers), Ashby (Kettering Town), Brown K (Woking), Reid (Altrincham) [Richardson (Bromsgrove Rovers)], Richardson I (Dagenham & Redbridge), Venables (Stevenage Borough) [Pye (Enfield)], Forsyth (Kidderminster Harriers), Stott (Bromsgrove Rovers), Bolton (Kingstonian) [Hayles (Stevenage Borough)], May (Stafford Rangers) [Taylor (Bromsgrove Rovers)].

FA SUNDAY CUP 1994–95

First Round

Dock v Newfield	1-3
Croxteth & Gilmoss RBL v Humbledon Plains Farm	1-3
BRNESC v Albion Sports	2-2, 3-1
A3 v Dudley & Weetslade	1-0
Lobster v Nenthead	4-1
Baildon Athletic v Mode Force Boulevard	1-1, 0-1
Northwood v SDV	5-0
Clubmoor Nalgo v Etnaward	0-0, 0-3
East Bowling Unity v Mitre	1-2
Boundary w.o. v Iron Bridge withdrew	
Sandon v Hartlepool Staincliffe Hotel	3-2
Waterloo Social Club Blyth v Littlewoods Athletic	2-3
Seaton Sluice SC v Britannia	1-1, 2-3
Queens Park v Stockton Roseworth Social	3-2
Salerno v Fiddlers Horse 93	7-2
Townley v Bolton Woods	5-0
Cork & Bottle v Walford Maritime	3-1
Almithak v Poets Corner	2-0
Egerton Boys v Norwich Busmen	1-1, 3-0
Slade Celtic v Clifton Albion	2-1
Elliott Bull & Tiger v Poringland Wanderers	5-1
Capel Plough v Grosvenor Park	2-1
Greyhound 83 v Hammer	0-4
Dereham Hobbies v Brookvale Athletic	0-1
Leavesden Sports & Social v Melton Youth Old Boys	2-2, 0-2
Hundred Acre v Leicester City Bus	0-1
Sawston Keys v Continental	2-1
St Joseph's (Sth Oxhey) v Altone Steels	0-2
Collier Row Supporters withdrew v London Boys w.o.	
Sandwell v Kenwick Dynamo	0-3
Forest Athletic v Oakwood Sports	0-2
Fryerns Community v Caversham Park	10-0
Courage v BRSC Aidan	0-4
Olympic Star v Erdington Cosmos	0-2
Sheerness Steel United v Charlton Royal 89	3-0
Inter Royale v Shell Club	2-3
Somersett Ambury V&E v Oxford Road Social	4-1
Hartley Wintney Sunday v Hanham Sunday	0-4
Biddestone (Sun) v Evergreen	3-4
Chequers (Herts) v Pitsea	2-3
Poole Town Social v British Rail SA	2-3
Park Royals v St Joseph's AFC (Bristol)	1-1, 1-0
Coach & Horses v Gracelands	4-4, 4-3
Vosper Sunday v Watford Labour Club	2-3

Second Round

Allerton v Cork & Bottle	4-2
Newfield v Boundary	2-1
Littlewoods Athletic v B&A Scaffolding	0-1
Mode Force Boulevard v A3	2-1
Sandon v Mitre	5-4
Hartlepool Lion Hotel v Salerno	2-0
Nicosia v Townley	3-4
Northwood v Queens Park AFC	2-4
Lobster v BRNESC	1-0
Etnaward v Humbledon Plains Farm	1-2
Britannia v Lion Hotel	0-3
Almithak v Oakenshaw	2-4
Seymour v Manfast Kirkby	3-2
Leicester City Bus v Hammer	0-2
Brookvale Athletic v Egerton Boys	2-0
Heathfield v London Boys	2-3
Ouzavich v Sacred Heart	0-4
Lodge Cottrell v Fryerns Community	4-0
Marston Sports v Slade Celtic	1-3
St Clements Hospital v Capel Plough	1-1, 2-4
Melton Youth Old Boys v St Josephs (Luton)	2-3
Erdington Cosmos v Kenwick Dynamo	1-4
Sawston Keys v Altone Steels	1-3
Oakwood Sports v Elliott Bull & Tiger	2-3
BRSC Aidan v Pitsea	0-0, 1-0
Shell Club v Park Royals	2-0
British Rail SA v Lebeq Tavern	1-3
Coach & Horses v Bedfont Sunday	2-1
Evergreen v Watford Labour Club	2-0
Theale Sunday v Hanham Sunday	3-0
Reading Borough v Somersett Ambury V&E	6-2
bye: Sheerness Steel United	

Third Round

Allerton v Townley	4-0
Oakenshaw v Altone Steels	2-4
B&A Scaffolding v Slade Celtic	3-1
Brookvale Athletic v Humbledon Plains Farm	0-4
Lion Hotel v Newfield	0-2
Seymour v Mode Force Boulevard	1-3
Lobster v Hartlepool Lion Hotel	0-2
Sandon v Queens Park AFC	0-2
Hammer v Kenwick Dynamo	3-0
Coach & Horses v Reading Borough	7-0
Sacred Heart v Theale Sunday	3-0
Sheerness Steel United v Shell Club	1-0
Lebeq Tavern v London Boys	4-1
Evergreen v Lodge Cottrell	0-2
BRSC Aidan v St Josephs (Luton)	1-2
Capel Plough v Elliott Bull & Tiger	3-0

Fourth Round

Hartlepool Lion Hotel v Allerton	0-1
Newfield v Altone Steels	6-1
Queens Park AFC v Humbledon Plains Farm	1-2
B&A Scaffolding v Mode Force Boulevard	4-2
Sheerness Steel United v Coach & Horses	2-0
Lebeq Tavern v Lodge Cottrell	1-0
Hammer v Capel Plough	1-2
Sacred Heart v St Josephs (Luton)	0-1

Fifth Round

Allerton v Newfield	3-1
B&A Scaffolding v Humbledon Plains Farm	4-0
Lebeq Tavern v St Josephs (Luton)	1-3
Capel Plough v Sheerness Steel United	3-2

Semi-finals

Allerton v B&A Scaffolding	0-2
Capel Plough v St Josephs (Luton)	0-0, 1-1
(St Josephs (Luton) won 4-2 on penalties)	

Final

St Josephs (Luton) v B&A Scaffolding	2-1

FA YOUTH CHALLENGE CUP 1994–95

Extra Preliminary Round

Atherton LR withdrew v Warrington Town w.o.	
Mansfield Town v Wrexham	1-4
Worksop Town v Redditch United	1-2
Bedworth United v Stourport Swifts	3-1
Corby Town v Wednesfield	2-1
Barkingside v Stevenage Borough	0-4
Eaton Manor v Hemel Hempstead	1-2
(at Hemel Hempstead)	
Ruislip Manor v Wingate & Finchley	2-4
Bromley v Sittingbourne	1-2
Bracknell Town v Kingstonian	0-2
Farnborough Town v Windsor & Eton	3-2
Newhaven withdrew v Basingstoke Town w.o.	
Fleet Town v Southwick	4-0
Wokingham Town v Newbury Town	1-1, 0-2
Oxford City v Maidenhead United	4-4, 6-0
Thatcham Town v Banbury United	1-2
Chippenham Town v Abingdon Town	1-4
Dorchester Town v Bashley	2-2, 0-1
Weymouth v Weston-Super-Mare	1-2
Yeovil Town v Romsey Town	7-0
Clevedon Town withdrew v Eastleigh w.o.	
Cheltenham Town v Yate Town	4-0
Forest Green Rovers v Gloucester City	3-3, 4-5
Hereford United v Worcester City	6-0
Mangotsfield United v Bristol Rovers	0-3

Preliminary Round

Harrogate Town v Darlington	4-2
Hartlepool United v Lancaster City	1-0
Chorley v Carlisle United	0-7
Morecambe v Guisborough Town	2-0
Chadderton v Bolton Wanderers	1-1, 2-4
Chesterfield v Huddersfield Town	0-2
Lincoln City v Warrington Town	7-5
Wigan Athletic v Bury	0-1
Port Vale v Marine	3-1
Rochdale v Southport	2-1
Stalybridge Celtic v Wrexham	1-10
Stockport County v Oldham Town	3-1
Hinckley Athletic v Burton Albion	1-2
Hinckley Town v Lutterworth Town	2-1
Hednesford Town v Redditch United	2-0
Pelsall Villa v Birstall United	2-3
Bridgnorth Town v Bilston Town	1-4
Brierley Hill Town v Chasetown	0-1
Nuneaton Borough v Bedworth United	1-1, 1-0
Oldbury United v Boldmere St Michaels	2-4
Lye Town v Daventry Town	2-2, 4-0
Northampton Spencer v Rushden & Diamonds	0-6
Stratford Town v Corby Town	1-0
VS Rugby v Kettering Town	3-3, 1-7
Halstead Town v Braintree Town	1-5
March Town United v Saffron Walden Town	1-2
Wivenhoe Town v Bishops Stortford	0-0, 0-2
Concord Rangers v Chatteris Town	4-4, 5-2
Enfield v Baldock Town	6-1
Barnet v Royston Town	12-1
St Albans City v Canvey Island	0-1
Letchworth Garden City v East Thurrock United	1-8
Edgware Town v Brook House	4-4, 1-6
Hillingdon Borough v Kempston Rovers	4-0
Kingsbury Town v Stevenage Borough	3-3, 2-5
Leighton Town v Clapton	1-0
Hampton v Feltham & Hounslow Borough	1-4
Hanwell Town withdrew v Harefield United w.o.	
Harlow Town v Hemel Hempstead	2-6
Hayes v Flackwell Heath	1-1, 2-1
Viking Sports did not enter v Staines Town w.o.	
Waltham Abbey v Welwyn Garden City	1-3
Wembley v Wingate & Finchley	1-2
Bedfont v Uxbridge	1-0
Corinthian v Ashford Town	2-0
(match abandoned 50 minutes; floodlit failure)	4-1
Dover Athletic v Gillingham	0-3
Herne Bay v Sittingbourne	0-4
Dartford v Chatham Town	6-1
Crawley Town v Chertsey Town	4-2
Marlow v Croydon Athletic	1-2
Dorking v Kingstonian	1-3
Egham Town withdrew v Chipstead w.o.	
Thamesmead Town v Welling United	1-1, 1-3
Tonbridge v Malden Vale	0-1
Redhill v Farnborough Town	0-3
Whyteleafe v Whitstable Town	3-6
Three Bridges v Ringmer	6-1
Whitehawk v Woking	2-2, 1-3
Aldershot Town v Basingstoke Town	3-0

First Qualifying Round

Morecambe v Harrogate Town	6-0
Carlisle United v Hartlepool United	7-2
Bury v Bolton Wanderers	4-0
Lincoln City v Huddersfield Town	1-10
Stockport County v Port Vale	0-1
Wrexham v Rochdale	2-1
Birstall United v Burton Albion	2-2, 0-1
Hednesford Town v Hinckley Town	0-4
Boldmere St Michaels v Bilston Town	3-0
Nuneaton Borough v Chasetown	3-1
Kettering Town v Lye Town	1-1, 1-1
(Kettering Town won 5-4 on penalties)	
Stratford Town v Rushden & Diamonds	1-1, 2-3
Concord Rangers v Braintree Town	0-7
Bishops Stortford v Saffron Walden Town	3-2
East Thurrock United v Enfield	2-2, 0-1
Canvey Island v Barnet	0-3
Leighton Town v Brook House	8-0
Stevenage Borough v Hillingdon Borough	2-3
Hayes v Feltham & Hounslow Borough	1-5
Hemel Hempstead v Harefield United	1-2
Bedfont v Staines Town	3-4
Wingate & Finchley v Welwyn Garden City	2-4
Dartford v Corinthian	3-1
Sittingbourne v Gillingham	2-2, 1-2
Chipstead v Crawley Town	1-3
Kingstonian v Croydon Athletic	0-0, 1-4
Whitstable Town v Welling United	1-3
Farnborough Town v Malden Vale	2-0
Fleet Town v Three Bridges	1-2
Aldershot Town v Woking	2-3
Abingdon Town v Newbury Town	2-5
Banbury United v Oxford City	2-3
Eastley v Bashley	0-1
Yeovil Town v Weston-Super-Mare	8-2
Bristol Rovers v Cheltenham Town	3-0
Hereford United v Gloucester City	2-0

Second Qualifying Round

Morecambe v Carlisle United	1-8
Bury v Huddersfield Town	2-0
Port Vale v Wrexham	0-5
Burton Albion v Hinckley Town	1-0
Boldmere St Michaels v Nuneaton Borough	2-1
Kettering Town v Rushden & Diamonds	3-4
Braintree Town v Bishops Stortford	2-4
Enfield v Barnet	0-3
Leighton Town v Hillingdon Borough	1-0
Feltham & Hounslow Borough v Harefield United	4-1
Staines Town v Welwyn Garden City	2-1
Dartford v Gillingham	0-3
Crawley Town v Croydon Athletic	2-2, 2-2
(Croydon Athletic won 4-3 on penalties)	
Welling United v Farnborough Town	3-0
Three Bridges v Woking	1-2
Newbury Town v Oxford City	1-2
(at Oxford City)	
Bashley v Yeovil Town	2-3
Bristol Rovers v Hereford United	2-2, 3-1

First Round

Doncaster Rovers v Scunthorpe United	2-0
Hull City v Blackburn Rovers	0-3
Carlisle United v Sunderland	0-2
Preston North End v Rotherham United	4-1
Newcastle United v Everton	0-2
Oldham Athletic v Bury	3-0
Grimsby Town v Sheffield Wednesday	1-3
Tranmere Rovers v Burnley	5-0
Barnsley v Blackpool	1-3
Leicester City v Kidderminster Harriers	4-1
Northampton Town v Walsall	1-2
Peterborough United v Rushden & Diamonds	7-1
Shrewsbury Town v Birmingham City	1-2
Aston Villa v Derby County	1-1, 3-0
Boldmere St Michaels v Cambridge City	2-1
Wrexham v Burton Albion	8-0
Wolverhampton Wanderers v Cambridge United	1-1, 6-2
Woking v Charlton Athletic	0-8
Bishops Stortford v Ipswich Town	0-2
Wycombe Wanderers v Gillingham	2-1
Luton Town v Staines Town	5-0
Lewes v Croydon Athletic	0-2
Enfield v Fulham	1-2
Leighton Town v Sutton United	4-2
Watford v Welling United	0-0, 1-2
Witney Town v Boreham Wood	1-3
Dulwich Hamlet v Feltham & Hounslow Borough	4-1
Cardiff City v Torquay United	3-1
Exeter City v Plymouth Argyle	0-2
Bournemouth AFC v Swansea City	5-0
Bristol Rovers v Oxford United	0-2
Oxford City v Yeovil Town	0-2
Southampton v Reading	1-0
Colchester United w.o. v Epsom & Ewell withdrew	

Second Round

Peterborough United v Everton	0-1
Liverpool v Tranmere Rovers	1-2
Stoke City v Notts County	1-0
Crewe Alexandra v Blackburn Rovers	3-0
Nottingham Forest v Leicester City	2-1
Aston Villa v Leeds United	1-0
Manchester United v Wrexham	4-1
Sunderland v Sheffield Wednesday	1-1, 1-0
York City v Birmingham City	0-0, 2-0
Middlesbrough v Oldham Athletic	4-3
Manchester City v Walsall	1-1, 1-1
(Manchester City won 4-1 on penalties)	
West Bromwich Albion v Doncaster Rovers	0-1
Preston North End v Blackpool	1-2
Bradford City v Sheffield United	1-1, 0-3
Arsenal v Brighton & Hove Albion	5-0
West Ham United v Wimbledon	2-2, 2-4
Wycombe Wanderers v Luton Town	1-0
Leyton Orient v Chelsea	0-0, 2-0
Tottenham Hotspur v Boldmere St Michaels	10-0
Norwich City v Millwall	2-1
Ipswich Town v Croydon Athletic	3-0
Wolverhampton Wanderers v Brentford	2-0
Bournemouth AFC v Bristol City	0-0, 1-3
Colchester United v Yeovil Town	3-0
Dulwich Hamlet v Welling United	1-1, 3-1
Oxford United v Leighton Town	6-0
Fulham v Boreham Wood	5-0
Portsmouth v Swindon Town	0-0, 1-1
(Portsmouth won 11-10 on penalties)	
Charlton Athletic v Cardiff City	2-1
Southend United v Crystal Palace	2-1
Queens Park Rangers v Plymouth Argyle	3-1
Southampton v Coventry City	0-5

Third Round

Bristol City v Nottingham Forest	0-0, 1-0
Crewe Alexandra v Oxford United	1-0
Sheffield United v York City	1-0
Wycombe Wanderers v Colchester United	0-5
Sunderland v Doncaster Rovers	0-0, 2-0
Stoke City v Norwich City	0-0, 1-0
Dulwich Hamlet v Fulham	0-2
(Tie awarded to Dulwich Hamlet; Fulham included an ineligible player)	
Manchester City v Portsmouth	2-2, 1-0
Aston Villa v Leyton Orient	1-0
Tottenham Hotspur v Wolverhampton Wanderers	4-2
Southend United v Tranmere Rovers	4-3
Queens Park Rangers v Arsenal	0-2
Wimbledon v Ipswich Town	4-0
Everton v Blackpool	6-5
Manchester United v Charlton Athletic	1-1, 5-2
Coventry City v Middlesbrough	2-2, 6-2

Fourth Round

Aston Villa v Colchester United	4-0
Tottenham Hotspur v Southend United	1-1, 2-1
Dulwich Hamlet v Bristol City	2-3
Manchester United v Arsenal	2-1
Sunderland v Crewe Alexandra	3-1
Everton v Sheffield United	1-3
Coventry City v Manchester City	2-3
Stoke City v Wimbledon	1-2

Fifth Round

Sunderland v Manchester City	2-2, 1-3
Bristol City v Tottenham Hotspur	1-2
Aston Villa v Manchester United	2-3
Wimbledon v Sheffield United	3-3, 3-2

Semi-finals (two legs)

Manchester City v Tottenham Hotspur	0-5, 1-2
Manchester United v Wimbledon	2-1, 3-0

FA Youth Cup Final, first leg

11 May

Tottenham H (1) 2 *(Wormull, Allen)*

Manchester U (0) 1 *(Cooke)* 8213

Tottenham H: Brown; Carr, Maher, Darcy, Arber, Wormull, Clemence, Spencer, Gain, Allen (Bunn), Fenn.

Manchester U: Gibson; Neville P, Westwood, Clegg, Wallwork, Mulryne (Gordon), Mustoe, Hall, Baker (Curtis), Johnson, Cooke.

Referee: P. Vanes (Birmingham).

FA Youth Cup Final, second leg

15 May

Manchester U (0) 1 *(Cooke)*

Tottenham H (0) 0 20,190

Manchester U: Gibson; Neville P, Westwood, Curtis, Wallwork, Mulryne (Hilton), Mustoe, Hall (Gardner), Baker, Brebner, Cooke.

Tottenham H: Brown; Carr, Maher, Darcy, Arber, Wormull (Clemence), Brady, Spencer, Gain, Allen (Winston), Fenn.

aet; Manchester U won 4-3 on penalties.

Referee: P. Vanes (Birmingham).

SCHOOLS FOOTBALL 1994–95

ESFA FUJI FILM TROPHY

SEMI-FINALS:
South Tyneside v Manchester 2-0
Newport v Islington & Camden 1-2

FINAL: 1ST LEG
South Tyneside v Islington & Camden 1-1
Played at Sunderland FC on 4 May

FINAL: 2ND LEG
Islington & Camden v South Tyneside 3-0
Played at Arsenal FC on 12 May

ESFA SNICKERS U.16 COMPETITION

SEMI-FINALS
Mount St Marys, Leeds v Cardinal Heenan, Liverpool 0-0, 1-2
Denefield, Reading v St. Michaels, Watford 2-2, 0-3

FINAL
Cardinal Heenan, Liverpool v St Michaels, Watford 0-0
Played at Tranmere Rovers FC on 18 May

ESFA SNICKERS U.19 COMPETITION

SEMI-FINALS
Swindon College v Northgate High, Ipswich 3-3, 1-2
Winstanley College, Manchester v Preston College* 0-0, 3-3
**Preston College won on penalties*

FINAL
Northgate High, Ipswich v Preston College 1-2
Played at Ipswich Town FC on 10 May

ESFA ADIDAS U.16 INTER COUNTY COMPETITION

SEMI-FINALS
Staffordshire v Greater Manchester 1-3
Avon v Kent 1-2

FINAL
Greater Manchester v Kent 2-1
Played at Rochdale FC on 21 October

ESFA PREMIER LEAGUE U.16 COUNTY COMPETITION

SEMI-FINALS
Greater Manchester v West Midlands 0-0, 2-2, 2-1
Essex v Sussex 3-5

FINAL
Greater Manchester v Sussex 0-1
Played at Ashton United FC on 27 May

ESFA PREMIER LEAGUE U.19 INTER COUNTY COMPETITION

SEMI-FINALS
Humberside v Hampshire 1-1, 2-4
West Yorkshire v Essex 3-2

FINAL
West Yorkshire v Hampshire 0-0
Played at Bradford City FC on 15 May

ESFA PREDATOR PREMIER 7-A-SIDE TROPHY

SEMI-FINALS
Swindon* v Stevenage 0-0
Wirral* v Telford 0-0
**Won on corners gained*

THIRD PLACE
Telford v Stevenage 1-0

FINAL
Wirral v Swindon 2-0
Played at Wembley Stadium on 11 March

ESFA PREDATOR 6-A-SIDE TROPHY

SEMI-FINALS
Priestmead Middle School, Harrow v Broadstone Middle School, Poole 2-1
Ling Moor Primary School, Lincoln* v St Aidan's Primary, Hartlepool 0-0
**Won on corners gained*

THIRD PLACE
Broadstone v St. Aidan's 3-2

FINAL
Priestmead v Ling Moor 0-0
Played at Wembley Stadium on 10 June

BOODLE & DUNTHORNE INDEPENDENT SCHOOLS FA CUP 1994–95

FIRST ROUND
Bye–Wellingborough
Latymer Upper 1, Manchester GS 5
Bradfield 3, Aldenham 1
QEGS, Blackburn 3, Kimbolton 1
Wolverhampton GS 2, Lancing 0
Bury GS 0, Hampton 1
Ardingly 2, Bolton 1
St Bede's 4, Charterhouse 0
Malvern 1, King's School, Chester 4
Shrewsbury 1, Eton 2
KES, Witley 0, Chigwell 1
Hulme GS 0, Forest 0 *aet* (*Forest won 3-1 on penalties*)
Alleyn's 2, Repton 2 *aet* (*Alleyn's won 5-4 on penalties*)
Batley GS 5, Oswestry 1
Westminster 1, Brentwood 4
John Lyon 7, Highgate 1

SECOND ROUND
Chigwell 2, Forest 1
Brentwood 2, King's School, Chester 0
Ardingly 6, John Lyon 2
St Bede's 3, Alleyn's 0
Eton 1, Batley GS 3 *aet*
QEGS, Blackburn 2, Hampton 1
Bradfield 5, Wellingborough 0
Wolverhampton GS 3, Manchester GS 2

THIRD ROUND
Wolverhampton GS 7, Bradfield 1
Ardingly 4, Brentwood 0
QEGS, Blackburn 3, St Bede's 3 *aet* (*St Bede's won 5-3 on penalties*)
Batley GS 2, Chigwell 1 *aet*

SEMI-FINALS
Wolverhampton GS 1, St Bede's 2
Ardingly 3, Batley GS 0

FINAL
St Bede's 3, Ardingly 2 *aet* (*at Craven Cottage*)

INTERNATIONAL PROGRAMME 1994–95

UNDER 15
England 2, Wales 2–Newport, 10 February
England 7, Belgium 0–Plymouth, 3 March
England 1, Brazil 0–Wembley, 11 March
England 1, N. Ireland 0–Newtownards, 24 March
England 2, Scotland 1–Newcastle, 28 April
England 5, Austria 0–Salzburg, 10 May
England 0, Eire 2–Dublin, 23 May
England 2, Germany 4–Wembley, 10 June
Overall Record....Played 8, Won 5, Drawn 1, Lost 2, Goals For 20 Goals Against 9
Goals: Owen (12), Hibburt (2), Jones (2), Ball, Burt, Kell, O'Brien

UNDER 18
England 0, France 5–Armenttieres, 15 February
England 1, Holland 3–Bodegraven, 28 February
England 4, Wales 4–Mansfield, 27 March
England 0, Switzerland 0–Nottingham, 31 March
England 0, Eire 0–Huddersfield, 10 April
Overall Record....Played 5, Won 0, Drawn 3, Lost 2, Goals For 5 Goals Against 12
Goals: Miles (3), Pierson, Ward

VICTORY SHIELD 1994–95

Wales 2, England 2–Newport, 10 February
N. Ireland 1, Wales 3–Belfast, 24 February
Scotland 5, N. Ireland 1–East Fife, 10 March
Scotland 7, Wales 3–Dumbarton, 16 March
N. Ireland 0, England 1–Newtownards, 24 March
England 2, Scotland 1–Newcastle, 28 April

	P	W	D	L	F	A	Pts
England	3	2	1	0	5	3	5
Scotland	3	2	0	1	13	6–	4
Wales	3	1	1	1	8	10	3
N. Ireland	3	0	0	0	2	9	0

CENTENARY SHIELD 1994–95

England 4, Wales 4–Mansfield, 27 March
Wales 0, Switzerland 1–Nottingham, 29 March
England 0, Switzerland 0–Nottingham, 31 March

	P	W	D	L	F	A	Pts
Switzerland	2	1	1	0	1	0	3
England	2	0	2	0	4	4	2
Wales	2	0	1	1	4	5	1

England photographed before a coaching weekend at Lilleshall National Sports Centre
Back Row (left to right): Ian Foster, Sufyan Ghazghazi, Richard Ward, Nicholas Miles, Richard Cort, David Gee, Graham Knight
Centre Row: Paul Bracknell (Team Manager), David Cook (Assistant Manager), Andrew Fotiadis, Lee Bray, David Diggle, Christopher Jones, Dr Daniel Baron (Team Doctor), Frank Melia (Physiotherapist)
Front Row: Dean Tallentire, Richard Fidler (Captain), David Willacy (Chairman), Gregg Dalley, Christopher Pedrick

THE AVON INSURANCE COMBINATION

Division One

	P	W	D	L	F	A	Pts
Tottenham Hotspur	38	19	13	6	67	34	70
Southampton	38	21	7	10	78	54	70
Charlton	38	20	9	9	71	46	69
QPR	38	19	9	10	68	34	66
Chelsea	38	17	13	8	76	53	64
Ipswich Town	38	14	13	11	65	50	55
Crystal Palace	38	15	10	13	50	40	55
West Ham United	38	16	6	16	49	39	54
Watford	38	15	9	14	48	49	54
Norwich City	38	13	12	13	62	58	51
Luton Town	38	14	7	17	57	66	49
Millwall	38	14	6	18	51	62	48
Wimbledon	38	11	14	13	55	56	47
Arsenal	38	11	14	13	61	69	47
Bristol City	38	12	10	16	61	65	46
Bristol Rovers	38	10	10	18	50	81	40
Swindon Town	38	9	12	17	34	60	39
Brighton & HA	38	10	9	19	54	84	39
Portsmouth	38	11	6	21	31	72	39
Oxford United	38	9	11	18	50	66	38

Division Two

	P	W	D	L	F	A	Pts
Swansea City	20	12	6	2	42	27	42
Birmingham City	20	11	5	4	42	20	38
Cardiff City	20	12	1	7	47	27	37
Torquay United	20	11	2	7	49	37	35
Exeter City	20	10	4	6	40	36	34
Plymouth Argyle	20	10	1	9	33	26	31
AFC Bournemouth	20	8	4	8	36	33	28
Bath City	20	7	2	11	32	47	23
Cheltenham Town	20	4	5	11	22	46	17
Hereford United	20	3	4	13	27	45	13
Yeovil Town	20	3	4	13	27	53	13

League Cup Tables

Group A

	P	W	D	L	F	A	Pts
Torquay United	8	4	3	1	22	15	15
AFC Bournemouth	8	4	2	2	22	19	14
Plymouth Argyle	8	2	4	2	19	16	10
Exeter City	8	2	4	2	11	13	10
Yeovil Town	8	1	1	6	9	20	4

Group B

	P	W	D	L	F	A	Pts
Swansea City	10	8	1	1	36	7	25
Birmingham City	10	5	3	2	29	15	18
Cardiff City	10	4	1	5	18	18	13
Hereford United	10	3	3	4	13	18	12
Cheltenham Town	10	3	1	6	13	35	10
Bath City	10	1	3	6	8	24	6

THE CENTRAL LEAGUE

Division One

	P	W	D	L	F	A	Pts
Bolton Wanderers	34	22	5	7	69	46	71
Everton	34	17	10	7	63	32	61
Leeds United	34	19	4	11	53	37	61
Sheffield United	34	17	8	9	49	36	59
Tranmere Rovers	34	16	9	9	65	53	57
Derby County	34	15	7	12	51	52	52
Notts County	34	15	6	13	46	48	51
West Bromwich Albion	34	13	8	13	53	54	47
Wolverhampton Wanderers	34	12	11	11	40	52	47
Manchester United	34	12	9	13	45	45	45
Stoke City	34	12	7	15	46	44	43
Blackburn Rovers	34	10	12	12	31	37	42
Liverpool	34	11	9	14	41	48	42
Nottingham Forest	34	9	11	14	45	46	38
Sunderland	34	10	8	16	49	56	38
Aston Villa	34	11	4	19	41	53	37
Coventry City	34	8	7	19	30	45	31
Rotherham United	34	7	5	22	34	67	26

Division Two

	P	W	D	L	F	A	Pts
Newcastle United	34	22	4	8	68	38	70
Birmingham City	34	21	5	8	74	39	68
Sheffield Wednesday	34	20	6	8	74	40	66
Oldham Athletic	34	20	6	8	73	51	66
Leicester City	34	20	4	10	72	42	64
Middlesbrough	34	17	7	10	84	48	58
Barnsley	34	17	7	10	68	45	58
Manchester City	34	17	5	12	52	40	56
Burnley	34	15	6	13	67	68	51
Port Vale	34	12	11	11	58	52	47
Preston North End	34	10	12	12	51	57	42
Grimsby Town	34	10	7	17	47	62	37
York City	34	10	7	17	39	53	37
Blackpool	34	10	3	21	41	59	33
Mansfield Town	34	8	5	21	42	87	29
Huddersfield Town	34	7	7	20	38	67	28
Hull City	34	7	5	22	26	80	26
Bradford City	34	6	7	21	32	78	25

THE FEDERATION BREWERY NORTHERN LEAGUE

Division One

	P	W	D	L	F	A	Pts
Tow Law Town	38	28	6	4	105	39	90
Billingham Synthonia	38	23	7	8	99	35	76
Whitby Town	38	22	10	6	88	45	76
Bedlington Terriers	38	21	12	5	72	35	75
RTM Newcastle	38	21	9	8	93	42	72
Guisborough Town	38	19	11	8	79	48	68
Durham City	38	17	12	9	75	45	63
Dunston FB	38	16	12	10	70	62	60
Consett	38	15	11	12	74	55	56
Shildon	38	12	13	13	57	63	49
Hebburn*	38	14	9	15	57	68	48
West Auckland	38	13	8	17	47	61	47
Seaham Red Star*	38	14	6	18	72	72	45
Peterlee Newtown	38	12	9	17	62	80	45
Murton	38	10	5	23	48	89	35
Chester Le Street	38	8	7	23	57	99	31
Ferryhill Athletic*	38	9	6	23	34	80	30
Eppleton CW	38	8	4	26	38	97	28
Northallerton*	38	9	3	26	35	93	27
Prudhoe Town	38	6	6	26	39	93	24

Division Two

	P	W	D	L	F	A	Pts
Whickham	38	26	10	2	103	37	88
Crook Town	38	26	6	6	102	40	84
Stockton**	38	26	5	7	116	49	77
Brandon United	38	21	9	8	77	39	72
Billingham Town*	38	23	4	11	95	50	70
Hartlepool Town**	38	22	9	7	91	50	69
Ashington	38	19	2	17	77	66	59
Evenwood Town	38	17	8	13	72	63	59
Washington*	38	17	9	12	74	55	57
Easington Colliery	38	15	10	13	55	51	55
Willington	38	17	3	10	62	61	54
Shotton Comrades	38	15	8	15	86	83	53
Esh Winning	38	15	7	16	78	88	52
Morpeth Town	38	13	6	19	69	67	45
Ryhope CA	38	12	9	17	55	62	45
Norton	38	13	4	21	71	83	43
Alnwick Town	38	10	6	22	60	87	33
Darlington CS	38	4	5	29	37	140	17
Hordern CW	38	3	3	32	42	151	12
Langley Park*	38	3	3	32	40	140	9

*Three points deducted

**Six points deducted

SKOL MIDLAND FOOTBALL COMBINATION

Premier Division

	P	W	D	L	F	A	Pts
Northfield Town	33	27	3	3	96	37	84
Bloxwich Town	32	21	8	3	103	36	71
Wellesbourne	32	20	4	8	60	40	64
Alvechurch Villa	32	14	11	7	64	37	53
Handrahan Timbers	32	14	9	9	60	43	51
Olton Royale	31	15	5	11	62	66	50
Meir KA	30	13	8	9	68	52	47
Shirley Town	33	13	6	14	56	64	45
Studley BKL	31	12	8	11	59	48	44
West Midland Fire	33	11	10	12	38	44	43
Chelmsley Town	32	9	10	13	49	60	37
Knowle	33	9	10	14	40	60	37
Coleshill Town	33	9	9	15	45	59	36
Kings Heath	32	8	7	17	44	67	31
Ansells	31	9	4	18	35	58	31
Sherwood Celtic	31	8	5	18	46	71	29
Upton Town	34	7	7	20	45	68	28
Highgate United	33	6	4	23	34	94	22

Division One

	P	W	D	L	F	A	Pts
Southam United	31	20	3	8	71	42	63
Sphinx	28	19	5	4	68	24	62
Bilston Community College	32	19	4	9	86	40	61
Massey Ferguson	26	17	7	2	62	22	58
GPT (Coventry)	30	18	3	9	86	53	57
Jaguar-Daimler	30	16	5	9	54	39	53
Kenilworth Town	30	11	9	10	55	46	42
Hams Hall	29	11	5	13	38	48	38
Polesworth North Warwick	31	11	5	15	65	78	38
Dudley Sports	29	10	7	12	50	57	37
Colletts Green	32	10	7	15	54	65	37
Monica Star	31	8	12	11	39	49	36
Wilmcote	31	9	5	17	45	79	32
Badsey Rangers	29	8	6	15	42	58	30
Kings Norton Ex Service	31	7	7	17	44	73	28
Barlestone St Giles	32	7	7	18	48	82	28
Thimblemill REC	32	6	3	23	40	92	21

Division Two

	P	W	D	L	F	A	Pts
Richmond Swifts	28	23	2	3	91	22	71
Alveston	28	17	5	6	56	27	56
Fairfield Villa	30	15	8	7	58	43	53
Holly Lane 92	30	16	4	10	81	47	52
Albright & Wilson	30	14	9	7	65	46	51
Rugby Town	30	14	6	10	61	57	48
Continental Star	30	14	4	12	57	47	46
Alvis SGL	29	14	3	12	43	35	45
Earlswood Town	30	11	10	9	54	40	43
Enville Athletic	30	12	6	12	53	56	42
Blackheath Electrodrives	30	10	8	12	43	49	38
Ledbury Town '84	30	9	3	18	54	73	30
Coleshill Town Res	30	8	6	16	38	85	30
Archdale '73	30	8	4	18	42	66	28
Burntwood	30	6	3	21	28	80	21
Studley BKL Res	29	2	7	20	26	77	13

LANCASHIRE LEAGUE

Division One

	P	W	D	L	F	A	Pts
Manchester United A	22	15	5	2	65	24	50
Crewe Alexandra Reserve	22	13	5	4	65	40	44
Burnley A	22	14	2	6	52	33	44
Everton A	22	12	0	10	49	34	36
Blackburn Rovers A	22	11	3	8	38	35	36
Tranmere Rovers A	22	10	5	7	46	33	35
Liverpool A	22	10	4	8	41	28	34
Oldham Athletic A	22	8	4	10	34	40	28
Bury A	22	7	5	10	28	44	26
Blackpool A	22	6	3	13	36	50	21
Marine Reserve	22	4	1	17	29	64	13
Morecambe Reserves	22	2	3	17	14	72	9

Division Two

	P	W	D	L	F	A	Pts
Manchester City A	36	25	5	6	89	34	80
Blackburn Rovers B	36	24	6	6	84	33	78
Manchester United B	36	21	6	9	93	47	69
Preston North End B	36	20	7	9	90	54	67
Liverpool B	36	21	4	11	80	52	67
Crewe Alexandra A	36	17	5	14	73	62	56
Tranmere Rovers B	36	16	7	13	64	49	55
Everton B	36	15	9	12	67	61	54
Burnley B	36	16	6	14	61	66	54
Wigan Athletic A	36	16	6	14	65	73	54
Oldham Athletic B	36	15	5	16	54	54	50
Bolton Wanderers A	36	13	10	13	43	45	49
Blackpool B	36	15	3	18	70	66	48
Carlisle United A	36	12	8	16	61	63	44
Stockport County A	36	10	6	20	66	94	36
Chester City A	36	9	6	21	49	95	33
Rochdale A	36	8	6	22	44	94	30
Bury B	36	7	6	23	47	92	27
Marine Youth	36	4	5	27	25	91	17

CARLING NORTH WEST COUNTIES LEAGUE

Division One

	P	W	D	L	F	A	Pts
Bradford Park Avenue	42	30	4	8	98	43	94
Clitheroe	42	27	9	6	104	49	90
St Helens Town	42	27	8	7	86	42	89
Trafford	42	27	5	10	98	52	86
Newcastle Town	42	24	7	11	75	57	79
Glossop North End	42	23	8	11	88	59	77
Blackpool Rovers	42	22	7	13	81	64	73
Burscough	42	19	15	8	102	65	72
Prescot	42	16	8	18	47	47	56
Penrith	42	16	7	18	72	71	55
Chadderton	42	15	7	20	56	70	52
Maine Road	42	14	9	19	68	83	51
Holker Old Boys	42	13	11	18	61	69	50
Kidsgrove Athletic	42	14	8	20	66	78	50
Eastwood Hanley	42	14	8	20	74	81	50
Nantwich Town	42	14	6	21	84	82	49
Darwen	42	14	5	19	65	82	47
Rossendale United	42	12	11	19	60	82	47
Bootle	42	11	9	21	45	67	43
Skelmersdale United	42	10	7	25	67	118	37
Salford City	42	9	9	24	45	85	36
Bacup	42	3	6	33	35	132	15

Division Two

	P	W	D	L	F	A	Pts
Flixton	30	21	6	3	98	32	69
Oldham Town	30	20	6	4	83	34	66
Tetley Walker	30	18	5	7	75	46	59
Atherton Collieries	30	18	4	8	67	41	58
Stantondale	30	18	3	9	58	43	57
Nelson	30	13	8	9	64	44	47
Haslingden	30	14	4	12	76	64	46
Blackpool Mechanics	30	12	8	10	72	57	44
Maghull	30	11	8	11	58	46	41
Formby	30	11	6	13	57	53	39
Cheadle Town	30	10	7	13	48	52	37
Castleton Gabriels	30	9	9	12	56	75	36
Daisy Hill	30	6	8	16	53	73	26
Ashton Town	30	6	2	22	39	92	20
Irlam Town	30	5	3	22	30	98	18
Squires Gate	30	2	5	23	30	114	11

VAUX WEARSIDE LEAGUE

Division One

	P	W	D	L	F	A	Pts
South Shields	34	28	2	4	116	44	86
Marske United	34	24	8	2	109	44	80
Jarrow Roofing	34	21	5	8	104	40	68
Nissan	34	20	6	8	84	36	66
Annfield Plain	34	20	6	8	81	63	66
Windscale	34	17	8	9	89	58	59
Kennek Roker*	34	19	4	11	71	52	58
Ryhope CW	34	15	7	12	67	56	52
Boldon CA	34	15	5	14	66	53	50
North Shields	34	14	6	14	52	60	48
Cleadon SC	34	14	5	15	53	52	47
Jarrow*	34	13	4	17	66	71	40
Wolviston	34	10	6	18	65	90	36
Herrington CW	34	8	8	18	44	76	32
Hartlepool BWOB*	34	7	6	21	48	70	24
North Ormesby	34	6	4	24	47	99	22
Cleator Moor	34	4	7	23	28	118	19
Silksworth	34	0	5	29	31	129	5

Division Two

	P	W	D	L	F	A	Pts
Birtley Town	24	18	2	4	84	29	56
Brinkburn CA	24	14	4	6	71	40	46
SC Fulwell	24	12	9	3	47	22	45
Murton Inter	24	13	5	6	61	42	44
Whitehaven Ams*	24	13	6	5	69	43	42
Harton & Westoe CW	24	12	4	8	56	47	40
Stanley United	24	10	8	6	65	44	38
Wingate	24	7	7	10	53	48	28
Guisborough Priory	24	7	7	10	42	49	28
Chilton Moor	24	8	2	14	41	64	26
Northallerton TS*	24	4	4	16	37	76	16
Washington Glebe	24	3	5	16	34	82	14
Prudhoe Swinton	24	1	3	20	24	96	6

*3 points deducted

THE JEWSON SOUTH-WESTERN FOOTBALL LEAGUE

	P	W	D	L	F	A	Pts
Launceston	34	26	8	2	115	24	84
Bodmin Town	34	25	4	5	89	36	79
Truro City	34	23	4	7	93	45	73
Falmouth Town	34	22	5	7	106	45	71
Torpoint Athletic	34	21	5	8	79	40	68
Porthleven	34	16	9	9	84	54	57
Millbrook	34	14	11	9	68	58	53
Holsworthy	34	14	9	11	44	44	51
Wadebridge Town	34	14	7	13	66	75	49
Tavistock*	34	12	8	14	46	71	43
Appledore/BAAC	34	10	4	20	55	79	34
Mullion	34	8	10	16	46	77	34
Newquay	34	9	6	19	66	86	33
St Blazey	34	9	6	19	60	70	33
Okehampton Argyle	34	8	4	22	49	102	28
Devon/Cornwall Police	34	8	3	23	52	93	27
Penzance	34	6	7	21	35	79	25
St Austell	34	4	6	24	31	96	18

*One point deducted

NORTHERN ALLIANCE LEAGUE

Premier Division

	P	W	D	L	F	A	Pts
Benfield Park	28	20	4	4	76	32	64
West Allotment Celtic	28	20	2	6	78	34	62
Gillford Park	28	19	4	5	74	30	61
Seaton Delaval Amateurs	28	18	6	4	72	38	60
Carlisle City	28	18	5	5	93	39	59
Ponteland United	28	15	6	7	64	43	51
Westerhope	28	11	9	8	61	53	42
Winlaton*	28	13	5	10	69	55	41
Blyth Seahorse	28	9	7	12	53	60	34
Spittal Rovers	28	9	6	13	54	47	33
Heaton Stannington	28	7	2	19	46	80	23
Walker**	28	8	3	17	57	72	21
Longbenton*	28	5	4	19	40	92	16
Haltwhistle Crown Paints	28	2	3	23	21	102	9
Wark	28	2	2	24	20	101	8

Division One

	P	W	D	L	F	A	Pts
Amble Town*	30	25	0	5	108	46	72
North Shields St Columbas	30	19	4	7	77	46	61
Hexham Swinton	30	16	8	6	59	40	56
Orwin Rosehill*	30	18	4	8	96	51	55
Ashington Hirst	30	16	4	10	98	64	52
Percy Main Amateurs	30	13	9	8	60	37	48
Hebburn Reyrolle	30	13	6	11	90	64	45
Newbiggin Central Welfare*	30	14	4	12	70	72	43
Dudley Welfare	30	13	4	13	64	75	43
Forest Hall	30	12	6	12	49	52	42
Gosforth Bohemians	30	10	5	15	55	68	35
Swalwell*	30	8	10	12	63	76	31
Procter and Gamble	30	8	2	20	54	90	26
Ryton	30	6	6	18	51	86	24
Northern Counties	30	5	5	20	46	122	20
Wylam	30	4	3	23	53	104	15

Division Two

	P	W	D	L	F	A	Pts
Walker Ledwood	30	24	2	4	118	43	74
Shankhouse	30	21	1	8	108	44	64
Rutherford	30	20	3	7	98	42	63
Newcastle University	30	18	5	7	77	57	59
Monkseaton Kosa	30	13	6	11	66	65	45
Otterburn	30	12	8	10	51	43	44
Highfields United	30	13	2	15	71	65	41
Heddon Institute	30	11	7	12	67	68	40
Wheelcroft	30	11	5	14	56	71	38
Throckley†	30	16	1	13	82	65	37
Stobswood Welfare	30	11	4	15	55	71	37
Hexham Border Counties*	30	12	4	14	66	91	37
Marden Athletic	30	10	4	16	66	78	34
Aydon Forest	30	9	4	17	63	83	31
Shilbottle Col/Welfare	30	7	5	18	52	87	26
Norgas United*	30	0	3	27	29	152	0

*Three points deducted
**Six points deducted
†Twelve points deducted

INTERLINK EXPRESS MIDLAND FOOTBALL ALLIANCE

	P	W	D	L	F	A	Pts
Paget Rangers	38	24	9	5	65	32	81
Hinckley Athletic	38	20	9	9	76	49	69
Stratford Town	38	19	9	10	69	46	66
Shepshed Dynamo	38	18	10	10	63	51	64
Halesowen Harriers	38	19	6	13	87	55	63
Shifnal Town	38	16	14	8	65	45	62
Boldmere St Michael	38	18	8	12	65	48	62
Oldbury United	38	18	8	12	58	47	62
Knypersley Victoria	38	15	12	11	82	54	57
Willenhall Town	38	15	7	16	55	58	52
West Midlands Police	38	14	8	16	53	51	50
Stapenhill	38	15	5	18	60	80	50
Rocester	38	12	12	14	48	50	48
Sandwell Borough	38	12	12	14	62	69	48
Barwell	38	12	9	17	58	69	45
Pershore Town	38	12	9	17	49	71	45
Chasetown	38	8	13	17	52	72	37
Rushall Olympic	38	9	10	19	60	85	37
Bolehall Swifts	38	9	9	20	45	60	36
Brierley Hill Town	38	3	5	30	27	107	14

MANCHESTER LEAGUE

Premier Division

	P	W	D	L	F	A	Pts
Abbey Hey	30	20	5	5	79	39	65
Mitchell Shackleton	30	17	5	8	72	45	56
East Manchester	30	17	4	9	56	49	55
Wythenshawe Town	30	16	6	8	55	40	54
Woodley SC	30	16	5	9	73	53	53
Wythenshawe Amateurs	30	14	7	9	56	37	49
Ramsbottom United	30	12	8	10	55	48	44
Atherton Town	30	14	1	15	71	62	43
BTCL	30	11	8	11	47	49	41
Dukinfield Town	30	11	7	12	50	56	40
Prestwich Heys	30	10	5	15	56	61	35
Stockport Georgians	30	10	4	16	43	62	34
Little Hulton United	30	9	6	15	41	53	33
Springhead	30	9	5	16	47	60	32
Sacred Heart	30	8	5	17	39	71	29
Monton	30	4	3	23	40	95	15

Division One

	P	W	D	L	F	A	Pts
Highfield United	30	23	4	3	102	31	73
Avro	30	19	9	2	73	28	66
Hollinwood	30	17	9	4	77	38	60
Stand Athletic	30	17	5	8	73	42	56
Milton	30	15	5	10	63	45	50
Manchester Royal	30	15	3	12	56	62	48
Breightmet United	30	12	9	9	54	48	45
Whitworth Valley	30	11	10	9	60	51	43
Pennington	30	11	8	11	62	53	41
Coldhurst United	30	12	2	16	61	81	38
Old Alts	30	10	5	15	65	80	35
Whalley Range	30	10	1	19	46	73	31
New Mills	30	8	6	16	49	82	30
Zeneca	30	7	3	20	34	79	24
GMP	30	7	2	21	54	80	23
Ashton Athletic	30	4	3	23	32	88	15

WINSTONLEAD KENT LEAGUE

Division One

	P	W	D	L	F	A	Pts
Sheppey United	40	29	9	2	118	32	96
Chatham Town	40	26	10	4	117	41	88
Furness	40	24	9	7	81	33	81
Folkestone Invicta	40	21	11	8	107	51	74
Ramsgate	40	21	11	8	91	45	74
Thamesmead Town	40	21	10	9	87	52	73
Herne Bay	40	19	13	8	68	35	70
Deal Town	40	18	10	12	87	62	64
Whitstable Town	40	17	11	12	83	61	62
Beckenham Town	40	15	11	14	61	61	56
Dartford	40	14	11	15	61	51	53
Corinthian	40	15	8	17	50	63	53
Canterbury City	40	14	6	20	66	80	48
Tunbridge Wells	40	12	11	17	48	66	47
Greenwich Borough	40	13	6	21	71	94	45
Crockenhill	40	10	12	18	45	62	42
Slade Green	40	10	12	18	49	73	42
Faversham Town	40	9	8	23	49	118	35
Cray Wanderers	40	6	14	20	45	76	32
Darenth Heathside	40	3	4	33	32	137	13
Kent Police	40	4	1	35	30	153	13

Division Two

	P	W	D	L	F	A	Pts
Thamesmead Town	28	19	5	4	74	31	62
Dover Athletic	28	18	5	5	73	44	59
Tonbridge FC	28	16	4	8	67	40	52
Herne Bay	28	15	2	11	69	47	47
Ramsgate	28	13	8	7	46	39	47
Hastings Town	28	11	9	8	59	42	42
Chatham Town*	28	12	5	11	57	54	40
Furness	28	11	7	10	40	37	40
Folkestone Invicta	28	11	6	11	60	54	39
Beckenham Town	28	8	8	12	48	56	32
Corinthian	28	8	6	14	37	56	30
Whitstable Town	28	6	9	13	49	56	27
Faversham Town**	28	7	5	16	31	61	23
Deal Town	28	6	4	18	40	78	22
Canterbury City	28	5	5	18	26	81	20

*One point deducted

**Three points deducted

GREAT MILLS LEAGUE

Premier Division

	P	W	D	L	F	A	Pts
Tiverton Town	34	28	3	3	128	23	87
Elmore	34	27	5	2	94	39	86
Taunton Town	34	15	12	7	59	28	57
Barnstaple Town	34	16	8	10	58	48	56
Westbury United	34	16	6	12	71	53	54
Mangotsfield United	34	16	6	12	51	50	54
Paulton Rovers	34	15	7	12	62	71	52
Chippenham Town	34	14	9	11	54	54	51
Bristol Manor Farm	34	14	6	14	51	48	48
Liskeard Athletic	34	12	9	13	59	55	45
Saltash United	34	12	9	13	38	43	45
Odd Down	34	11	9	14	47	53	42
Bridport	34	11	6	17	44	59	39
Calne Town	34	11	3	20	36	68	36
Bideford	34	10	5	19	48	69	35
Crediton United	34	8	6	20	43	77	30
Torrington	34	6	10	18	49	89	28
Frome Town	34	3	3	28	36	101	12

First Division

	P	W	D	L	F	A	Pts
Brislington	40	30	7	3	113	25	97
Glastonbury	40	26	8	6	91	35	86
Backwell UnitEd	40	26	8	6	75	33	86
Warminster Town	40	26	7	7	93	42	85
Chard Town	40	25	10	5	74	35	85
Bridgwater Town	40	18	13	9	62	47	67
Keynsham Town	40	17	11	12	73	62	62
Bishop Sutton	40	17	7	16	61	61	58
Exmouth Town	40	16	6	18	55	63	54
Melksham Town	40	14	10	16	62	61	52
Clyst Rovers	40	15	5	20	60	84	50
Amesbury Town	40	14	7	19	67	61	49
Wellington	40	14	7	18	55	59	49
Ilfracombe Town	40	13	8	19	64	58	47
Heavitree United	40	12	7	21	52	94	43
Welton Rovers	40	11	9	20	50	62	42
Devizes Town	40	11	7	22	57	82	40
Pewsey Vale	40	10	8	22	52	77	38
Larkhall Athletic	40	8	8	24	39	89	32
Dawlish Town	40	8	8	24	41	92	32
Minehead	40	5	7	28	24	98	22

JEWSON (EAST COUNTIES) LEAGUE

Premier Division

	P	W	D	L	F	A	Pts
Halstead Town	42	31	8	3	129	35	101
Wroxham	42	29	7	6	96	44	94
Wisbech Town	42	28	7	7	108	46	91
Diss Town	42	27	6	9	114	49	87
Harwich & Parkeston	42	24	8	10	130	77	80
Fakenham Town	42	22	7	13	80	53	73
Lowestoft Town	42	20	12	10	77	56	72
Newmarket Town	42	20	8	14	69	57	68
Sudbury Wanderers	42	19	10	13	77	63	67
Woodbridge Town	42	17	11	14	66	58	62
Stowmarket Town	42	15	11	16	77	72	56
Tiptree United	42	17	5	20	76	86	56
Felixstowe Town	42	17	4	21	54	70	55
March Town United	42	13	14	15	51	56	53
Hadleigh United	42	12	10	20	64	80	46
Great Yarmouth Town	42	11	8	23	44	69	41
Haverhill Rovers	42	11	7	24	52	82	40
Soham Town Rangers	42	9	11	22	60	99	38
Watton United	42	10	6	26	44	87	36
Cornard United	42	8	10	24	46	99	34
Histon	42	10	3	29	54	127	33
Chatteris Town	42	2	7	33	30	133	13

Division One

	P	W	D	L	F	A	Pts
Clacton Town	36	25	5	6	86	39	80
Sudbury Town Reserves	36	23	6	7	102	49	75
Warboys Town	36	23	5	8	82	45	74
Gorleston	36	21	10	5	101	44	73
Downham Town	36	20	9	7	99	43	69
Ely City	36	21	5	10	87	45	68
Brightlingsea United	36	20	5	11	69	46	65
Ipswich Wanderers	36	18	8	10	85	62	62
Somersham Town	36	16	5	15	61	61	53
Swaffham Town	36	15	7	14	69	59	52
Mildenhall Town	36	15	5	16	57	60	50
King's Lynn Reserves	36	14	6	16	66	67	48
Norwich United	36	8	13	15	48	59	37
Stanway Rovers	36	11	4	21	60	89	37
Thetford Town	36	9	7	20	38	76	34
Long Sutton Athletic	36	9	3	24	47	91	30
Cambridge City Res	36	7	9	20	37	83	30
Brantham Athletic	36	6	5	25	45	82	23
Bury Town Reserves	36	2	1	33	33	172	7

JOHN SMITH'S BITTER CENTRAL MIDLANDS LEAGUE

Supreme Division

	P	W	D	L	F	A	Pts
Heanor Town	32	26	1	5	92	34	79
Oakham United	32	23	2	6	84	36	71
Priory (Eastwood)	32	21	6	5	73	32	69
Kimberley Town	32	15	9	8	60	48	54
Glapwell	32	15	8	9	63	45	53
Borrowash Victoria	32	13	13	6	43	27	52
Kiveton Park	32	15	5	12	60	45	50
Harworth CI	32	12	9	11	55	56	45
Sandiacre Town	32	11	10	11	58	61	43
Gedling Town	32	12	5	15	62	54	41
Shirebrook Town	32	11	5	16	43	68	38
Staveley MW	32	8	7	17	40	64	31
Sheffield Aurora	32	7	8	17	47	88	29
South Normanton Ath	32	7	7	18	45	72	28
Nettleham	32	5	10	17	31	57	25
Long Eaton United	32	6	7	19	43	71	25
Rossington	32	4	10	18	45	86	22

Premier Division

	P	W	D	L	F	A	Pts
Clipstone Welfare	32	23	4	5	88	28	73
Case Sports	32	21	7	4	97	37	70
Thorne Colliery	32	20	7	5	82	30	67
Mickleover Sports	32	20	4	8	84	51	64
Nuthall	32	18	7	7	62	34	61
Derby C&WR	32	18	3	11	73	44	57
Radford	32	16	6	10	57	43	54
Shardlow St. James	32	14	7	11	46	43	49
Askern Welfare	32	13	7	12	80	57	46
Derby Rolls Royce	32	13	4	15	51	69	43
Holbrook MW	32	9	8	15	47	65	35
Newhall United	32	9	7	16	56	82	34
Mexborough Athletic	32	9	5	18	59	80	32
Killamarsh Athletic	32	7	6	19	52	82	27
Stanton Ilkeston	32	5	10	17	42	74	25
Mickleover RBL	32	4	9	19	33	82	21
Blackwell MW	32	1	3	28	22	130	6

LONDON SPARTAN FOOTBALL LEAGUE

Premier Division

	P	W	D	L	F	A	Pts
Croydon	30	23	3	4	87	31	72
St Margaretsbury	30	21	5	4	77	38	68
Barkingside	30	18	4	8	58	47	58
Brimsdown Rovers	30	17	5	8	56	39	56
Corinthian Casuals	30	16	4	10	70	45	52
Willesden	30	12	9	9	55	36	45
Brook House	30	13	5	12	69	52	44
Cockfosters	30	10	11	9	52	45	41
Hillingdon Borough	30	10	7	13	43	66	37
Tower Hamlets*	30	11	4	15	58	67	34
Beaconsfield	30	9	6	15	31	51	33
Waltham Abbey	30	8	7	15	39	59	31
Harringey Borough*	30	10	3	17	37	49	30
Hanwell Town	30	6	12	12	37	60	30
Walthamstow Pennant	30	8	5	17	43	56	29
Amersham Town	30	2	2	25	46	84	8

*Three points deducted – ineligible player

ESSEX SENIOR LEAGUE

Premier Division

	P	W	D	L	F	A	Pts
Great Wakering Rovers	28	23	2	3	82	14	71
Sawbridgeworth Town	28	23	2	3	73	20	71
Romford	28	18	7	3	54	30	61
Maldon Town	28	16	6	6	58	33	54
Ford United	28	13	6	9	48	30	45
Bowers United	28	12	3	13	41	45	39
Burnham Ramblers	28	12	3	13	42	47	39
Basildon United	28	10	8	10	57	35	38
East Ham United	28	9	9	10	28	32	36
Brentwood	28	7	11	10	39	37	32
Concord Rangers	28	9	5	14	32	42	32
Stansted	28	8	7	13	40	57	31
Southend Manor	28	3	8	17	32	80	17
Hullbridge Sports	28	4	1	23	17	67	13
Eton Manor	28	2	4	22	19	93	10

NORTHERN COUNTIES EAST LEAGUE

Premier Division

	P	W	D	L	F	A	Pts
Lincoln United	38	29	5	4	116	49	92
Arnold Town	38	25	7	6	98	46	82
Stockbridge PS	38	21	6	11	74	46	69
Belper Town	38	19	8	11	78	44	65
Ashfield United	38	18	11	9	65	48	65
Pickering Town	38	19	7	12	89	63	64
North Ferriby United	38	18	8	12	68	60	62
Armthorpe Welfare	38	13	18	7	56	41	57
Thackley	38	15	11	12	76	56	56
Ossett Albion	38	15	9	14	48	57	54
Brigg Town	38	14	10	14	49	57	52
Ossett Town	38	12	10	16	50	56	46
Maltby MW	38	13	7	18	59	71	46
Denaby United	38	12	9	17	48	77	45
Hucknall Town	38	9	13	16	47	60	40
Glasshoughton Welfare	38	10	9	19	60	68	39
Hallam	38	9	8	21	46	76	35
Sheffield	38	6	12	20	45	87	30
Liversedge	38	7	8	23	48	81	29
Pontefract Collieries	38	3	10	25	30	107	19

Division 1

	P	W	D	L	F	A	Pts
Hatfield Main	30	25	2	3	88	32	77
Worsborough Bridge	30	19	4	7	66	40	61
Immingham Town	30	18	4	8	66	43	58
Selby Town	30	16	9	5	62	38	57
Yorkshire Amateurs	30	15	8	7	53	29	53
Hall Road Rangers	30	15	7	8	57	44	52
Harrogate Railway	30	16	4	10	64	52	52
Eccleshill United	30	13	5	12	62	47	44
Garforth Town	30	11	8	11	58	49	41
Louth United	30	9	8	13	39	50	35
Rossington Main	30	9	7	14	48	63	34
Tadcaster Albion	30	6	8	16	36	59	26
Blidworth Welfare	30	7	5	18	39	63	26
Winterton Rangers	30	7	3	20	44	72	24
Parkgate*	30	5	5	20	47	84	18
Brodsworth MW	30	2	7	21	15	79	13

*Two points deducted

SOUTH EAST COUNTIES LEAGUE

Division One

	P	W	D	L	F	A	Pts
Tottenham Hotspur	30	21	4	5	67	32	46
Chelsea	30	17	6	7	66	45	40
Arsenal	30	18	3	9	72	39	39
Watford	30	16	5	9	53	48	37
Fulham	30	15	5	10	59	44	35
Norwich City	30	15	5	10	56	44	35
West Ham United	30	11	10	9	57	48	32
Gillingham	30	11	8	11	35	40	30
Millwall	30	11	7	12	44	55	29
Cambridge United	30	11	4	15	53	54	26
Charlton Athletic	30	7	12	11	39	46	26
Queens Park Rangers	30	9	7	14	44	57	25
Ipswich Town	30	8	8	14	31	43	24
Leyton Orient	30	6	9	15	26	40	21
Southend United	30	7	7	16	35	54	21
Portsmouth	30	5	4	21	32	80	14

Division Two

	P	W	D	L	F	A	Pts
Crystal Palace	28	20	5	3	68	26	45
Wimbledon	28	19	5	4	97	45	43
Bristol City	28	16	5	7	64	29	37
Swindon Town	28	16	3	9	57	35	35
Oxford United	28	12	11	5	49	33	35
AFC Bournemouth	28	13	7	8	57	57	33
Brentford	28	12	8	8	40	38	32
Tottenham Hotspur	28	12	4	12	58	59	28
Southampton	28	9	8	11	39	40	26
Brighton & Hove Albion	28	11	4	13	51	67	26
Luton Town	28	9	4	15	49	47	22
Colchester United	28	8	6	14	43	59	22
Reading	28	5	6	17	30	73	16
Bristol Rovers	28	1	11	16	28	54	13
Wycombe Wanderers	28	2	3	23	24	92	7

HELLENIC LEAGUE

Premier Division

	P	W	D	L	F	A	Pts
Cinderford Town	30	23	4	3	118	24	73
Fairford Town	30	21	4	5	73	25	67
Swindon Supermarine	30	16	4	10	76	44	52
North Leigh	30	15	7	8	55	39	52
Shortwood United	30	16	3	11	60	53	51
Cirencester Town	30	15	5	10	56	43	50
Tuffley Rovers	30	14	7	9	65	44	49
Banbury United	30	12	7	11	44	44	43
Pegasus Juniors	30	11	9	10	49	43	42
Bicester Town*	30	12	6	12	70	60	40
Abingdon United	30	11	5	14	55	58	38
Almondsbury Town	30	10	7	13	49	53	37
Carterton Town	30	7	9	14	36	60	30
Brackley Town	30	7	5	18	42	80	26
Highworth Town	30	2	6	22	30	93	12
Kintbury Rangers*	30	3	2	25	30	145	9

*Two points deducted

THE WASHINGTON AND DISTRICT LEAGUE

	P	W	D	L	F	A	Pts
Cabplant	26	19	3	4	55	30	60
Deneside	26	19	2	5	102	34	59
Belford House	26	18	3	5	84	46	57
Jig Net	26	17	2	7	73	47	53
Springwell	26	14	3	9	63	50	45
Easington Mechanics*	26	12	8	6	78	42	41
Throston	26	11	8	7	67	40	41
Dawdon	26	10	7	9	61	59	37
Simonside	26	8	6	12	49	62	30
Westwood	26	6	6	14	43	78	24
Mallard	26	6	4	16	43	72	22
Boldon Rossi	26	6	2	18	45	73	21
Whitehill	26	6	2	18	49	77	20
Wearmouth	26	1	1	24	27	165	4

**Points deducted*

MINERVA FOOTBALLS SOUTH MIDLANDS LEAGUE

Premier Division

	P	W	D	L	F	A	Pts
Arlesey Town	45	34	5	6	90	32	107
Wingate & Finchley	45	25	13	7	97	49	88
Brache Sparta	45	23	15	7	85	61	84
Royston Town	45	24	11	10	77	42	83
Shillington	45	22	11	12	64	38	77
Potters Bar Town	45	19	7	19	75	70	64
Biggleswade Town	45	17	10	18	65	71	61
Langford	45	15	15	15	61	64	60
Milton Keynes	45	15	14	16	71	77	59
Hoddesdon Town	45	15	11	19	56	57	56
Hatfield Town	45	14	12	19	66	80	54
Welwyn Garden City	45	11	13	21	53	72	46
Buckingham Athletic	45	10	13	22	51	88	43
Dunstable United	45	11	10	24	39	77	43
Harpenden Town	45	9	12	24	60	72	39
Letchworth Garden City	45	5	10	30	58	118	25

Senior Division

	P	W	D	L	F	A	Pts
London Colney	26	22	2	2	87	20	68
Toddington Rovers	26	16	4	6	80	30	52
New Bradwell St Peter	26	15	6	5	90	32	51
Leverstock Green	26	14	8	4	50	21	50
Stony Stratford Town	26	16	1	9	60	37	49
ACD FC	26	14	3	9	56	39	45
Tring Athletic	26	10	6	10	44	38	36
Bedford United	26	9	7	10	30	47	34
Ampthill Town	26	7	7	12	57	66	28
Winslow United	26	7	6	13	45	65	27
Totternhoe	26	8	2	16	40	64	26
Risborough Gardens	26	6	6	14	47	68	24
The 61 FC (Luton)	26	6	4	16	33	69	22
Pitstone & Ivinghoe	26	0	2	24	22	145	2

Division One

	P	W	D	L	F	A	Pts
Houghton Town	26	20	3	3	82	17	63
Kent Athletic	26	16	7	3	68	31	55
Walden Rangers	26	17	4	5	57	37	55
Eaton Bray	26	16	3	7	48	25	51
De Havilland	26	10	10	6	44	30	40
Bow Brickhill	26	10	7	9	47	44	37
Scot	26	9	6	11	42	52	33
Cranfield United	26	9	5	12	42	64	32
Caddington	26	8	7	11	50	45	31
Flamstead	26	9	2	15	27	48	29
Abbey National (MK)	26	6	5	15	32	65	23
Mercedes Benz	26	4	10	12	27	46	22
Emberton	26	5	7	14	31	52	22
Clifton Old Boys	26	2	6	18	20	61	12

TYNE WEAR THORPE LEAGUE

	P	W	D	L	F	A	Pts
Freeman	24	21	2	1	100	33	65
Grange Athletic	24	18	3	3	97	41	57
Fort	24	18	2	4	88	41	56
Crown Photo	24	17	1	6	94	64	52
Dunsfords	24	12	2	10	82	54	38
Rolls Royce*	24	11	3	10	74	54	36
Chowdene	24	10	2	12	57	73	32
Weardale*	24	10	4	10	63	69	28
Low Fell	24	8	1	15	47	78	25
New Ship	24	4	4	16	45	88	16
East North	24	5	1	18	42	87	13
251 Field*	24	5	3	16	32	89	12
Ivy House	24	8	2	14	29	96	11

**Points deducted*

HEREWARD SPORTS UNITED COUNTIES FOOTBALL LEAGUE

Premier Division

	P	W	D	L	F	A	Pts
Boston	36	25	5	6	92	36	80
Raunds	36	23	11	2	82	42	80
Cogenhoe	36	24	5	7	90	37	77
Holbeach	36	18	9	9	56	39	63
Northampton Spencer	36	17	8	11	69	47	59
Eynesbury	36	15	11	10	53	41	56
Mirrless Blackstone	36	14	10	12	53	52	52
Bourne	36	14	9	13	53	68	51
Stotfold	36	12	13	11	50	41	49
Spalding	36	11	12	13	57	54	45
Desborough	36	11	12	13	53	60	45
Long Buckby	36	9	16	11	58	61	43
Wootton	36	10	10	16	47	59	40
Potton	36	11	6	19	46	69	39
Stamford	36	9	9	18	50	69	36
Newport Pagnell	36	8	12	16	31	54	36
S & L Corby	36	8	10	18	40	65	34
Wellingborough	36	5	10	21	40	84	25
Kempston	36	4	10	22	46	88	22

Division One

	P	W	D	L	F	A	Pts
St Neots	36	28	3	5	119	41	87
Higham	36	27	4	5	92	31	85
Thrapston	36	25	7	4	107	44	82
Northampton Vanaid	36	24	4	8	132	51	76
Whitworths	36	23	5	8	115	45	74
Bugbrooke	36	22	6	8	84	43	72
St Ives	36	17	10	9	92	53	61
Olney	36	16	8	12	75	60	56
O N Chenecks	36	15	9	12	76	57	54
Blisworth	36	13	7	16	74	81	46
Ford Sports	36	13	6	17	86	81	45
Ramsey	36	12	7	17	66	76	43
Burton P W	36	12	4	20	59	91	40
Sharnbrook	36	11	6	19	46	79	39
British Timken	36	7	8	21	38	92	29
Irchester	36	6	9	21	40	86	27
Cottingham	36	5	6	25	44	84	21
Harrowby	36	5	2	29	24	171	17
Daventry	36	3	5	28	34	137	14

JEWSON WESSEX FOOTBALL LEAGUE

	P	W	D	L	F	A	Pts
Fleet Town	42	32	4	6	116	43	100
Bournemouth	42	31	5	6	109	33	98
Thatcham Town	42	29	9	4	104	44	96
Wimborne Town	42	22	14	6	102	52	80
Bemerton Heath Har	42	24	8	10	75	48	80
Brockenhurst	42	24	4	14	87	59	76
Andover	42	23	5	14	122	69	74
AFC Lymington	42	17	10	15	85	67	61
AFC Totton	42	18	6	18	69	70	60
Gosport Borough	42	17	6	19	83	66	57
Portsmouth RN	42	16	8	18	65	64	56
Ryde	42	16	6	20	81	88	54
BAT	42	15	8	19	62	82	53
Eastleigh	42	14	9	19	66	73	51
Cowes Sports	42	14	8	20	61	87	50
East Cowes Vics	42	13	10	19	65	72	49
Aerostructures S&S	42	12	10	20	60	77	46
Christchurch	42	12	8	22	58	95	44
Swanage & Herston	42	11	6	25	49	112	39
Downton	42	7	11	24	45	86	32
Petersfield Town	42	7	5	30	56	161	26
Horndean	42	6	4	32	49	121	22

HIGHLAND LEAGUE

	P	W	D	L	F	A	Pts
Huntly	30	24	2	4	102	30	74
Cove Rangers	30	18	3	9	69	38	57
Lossiemouth	30	17	3	10	75	53	54
Keith	30	16	5	9	59	32	53
Brora Rangers	30	15	7	8	63	41	52
Peterhead	30	15	7	8	64	43	52
Fraserburgh	30	16	4	10	56	43	52
Elgin City	30	15	3	12	52	42	48
Deveronvale	30	14	5	11	58	49	47
Buckie Thistle	30	12	8	10	50	52	44
Forres Mechanics	30	12	5	13	46	56	41
Fort William	30	11	4	15	46	57	37
Clachnacuddin	30	7	5	18	37	61	26
Wick Academy	30	7	4	19	32	77	25
Rothes	30	2	5	23	27	77	11
Nairn County	30	3	2	25	20	105	11

MIDLAND AMATEUR ALLIANCE

Division One	P	W	D	L	F	A	Pts
Sherwood Amateurs	20	17	3	0	77	20	37
Magdala Amateurs	20	13	3	4	81	28	29
Lady Bay	20	13	3	4	72	35	29
Old Elizabethans	20	8	7	5	47	37	23
Peoples College	20	7	6	7	44	39	20
Old Bemrosians	20	8	4	8	37	44	20
Bassingfield	20	7	4	9	57	55	18
F.C. Toton	20	6	2	12	39	67	14
Brunts Old Boys	20	3	6	11	17	54	12
Derbyshire Amateurs	20	2	7	11	31	66	11
Kirton B. W.	20	2	3	15	26	83	7
Division Two							
Old Elizabethans Res.	22	13	7	2	67	46	33
Magdala Amateurs Res.	22	10	8	4	47	32	28
Sherwood Amateurs Res.	22	10	7	5	63	33	27
County Nalgo	22	10	4	8	66	49	24
Chilwell	22	9	6	7	48	41	24
Bassingfield Res.	22	8	8	6	46	48	24
Nottingham Univ. Postgraduates	22	9	5	8	62	62	23
Nottinghamshire	22	10	2	10	49	43	22
Keyworth A.F.C.	22	8	3	11	36	54	19
Woodborough United	22	6	5	11	33	63	17
Ilkeston Electric	22		4	14	32	49	12
Tibshelf Old Boys	22	3	5	14	32	68	11
Division Three							
Beeston Old Boys Assn.	18	13	4	1	64	25	30
Ilkeston Rangers	18	12	4	2	62	30	28
Lady Bay Res.	18	9	4	5	48	37	22
Old Elizabethans 3rd	18	9	3	6	55	33	21
West-Clif	18	7	5	6	45	47	19
Peoples College Res.	18	7	1	10	43	41	15
Derbyshire Amateurs Res.	18	5	3	10	42	51	13
Nottingham Res.	18	4	4	10	27	53	12
Old Bemrosians Res.	18	3	5	10	19	48	11
Tibshelf Old Boys Res.	18	1	7	10	24	65	9
Division Four							
Brunts Old Boys Res.	20	18	0	2	85	24	36
South Forest	20	17	0	3	95	27	34
Magdala Amateurs 3rd	20	15	2	3	80	35	32
Beeston O.B. Assn. Res.	20	9	3	8	55	45	21
Derbyshire Amateurs 3rd	20	8	4	8	47	37	20
Peoples College 3rd	20	6	4	10	37	70	16
Old Elizabethans 4th	20	6	2	12	37	82	14
Ilkeston Rangers Res.	20	6	1	13	45	69	13
Nottinghamshire 3rd	20	5	2	13	32	63	12
Old Bemrosians 3rd	20	5	2	13	29	63	12
West-Clif Res.	20	5	0	15	39	66	10

Senior Cup–won by Sherwood Amateurs
Intermediate Cup–won by Sherwood Amateurs Res.
Minor Cup–won by A.C. College 3rd
Challenge Trophy–won by Magdala Amateurs
Division Two Challenge Cup–won by Old Elizabethans Res.
Division Three Challenge Cup–won by Derbyshire Amateurs Res.
Division Four Challenge Cup–Brunts Old Boys Res.
Division Three Supplementary Cup–Beeston O.B.A.
Division Four Supplementary Cup–South Forest
H.B. Poole Trophy–won by Sherwood Amateurs

AMATEUR FOOTBALL ALLIANCE 1994–95

AFA SENIOR CUP

1st Round Proper
Witan 2, Carshalton 3
Hale End Athletic 1, West Wickham 2
Old Owens 1, Civil Service 3
Old Suttonians 2, City of London 1
Old Danes 0, Old Salvatorians 2
Old Lyonian 0, Old Ignatians 3
Old Dorkinian 1*:0, Norsemen 1*:4
Old Esthameians 4, Old Aloysians 1
Old Parkonians 0, Old Chigwellians 1
Old Malvernian 3, Wandsworth Borough 2
Old Wokingians 1, South Bank 3
UCL Academicals 0, Old Salesians 6
Alexandra Park 1, Old Foresters 4
Ealing Association 3, Old Woodhouseians 2
Winchmore Hill 1, Old Latymerians 2
Bank of England 1, Old Kingsburians 3
Old Camdenians 0, Cuaco 7
Merton 1, Cardinal Manning OB 4
Old Hamptonians 4, Polytechnic 0
Old Grocers 1*:0, Old Isleworthians 1*:1
Westerns 3, Midland Bank 2
William Fitt 0, Duncombe Sports 5
Old Wilsonians 0, Crouch End Vampires 1
Old Michendenians 1, Old Manorians 3
Old Reptonian 3*:1, Wake Green 3*:3
Mill Hill Village 0, Glyn Old Boys 2
Broomfield 4, Old Westhamians 0
St Mary's College 1*:5, Southgate County 1*:1
E. Barnet Old Grammarians 2, Old Stationers 1
Nottsborough 1*:2, Old Meadonians 1*:4
Kew Association 3, Old Grammarians 4
National Westminster Bank 3, Old Tenisonians 0

2nd Round Proper
Carshalton 2, West Wickham 1
Civil Service 3, Old Suttonians 1
Old Salvatorians 2:0, Old Ignatians 2:3
Norsemen 1, Old Esthameians 5
Old Chigwellians 5, Wandsworth Borough 0
South Bank 8, Old Salesians 0
Old Foresters 3, Ealing Association 1
Old Latymerians 5, Old Kingsburians 0
Cuaco 4, Cardinal Manning OB 3
Old Hamptonians 0, Old Isleworthians 2
Westerns 5, Duncombe Sports 4
Crouch End Vampires 2, Old Manorians 1
Wake Green 3, Glyn Old Boys 1
Broomfield 2, St Mary's College 3
E. Barnet Old Grammarian 2, Old Meadonians 1
Old Grammarians 1, National Westminster Bank 3

3rd Round Proper
Carshalton 2, Civil Service 5
Old Ignatians 4, Old Esthameians 2
Old Chigwellians 1, South Bank 3
Old Foresters 2*:1, Old Latymerians 2*:0
Cuaco 0*:0, Old Isleworthians 0*:1
Westerns 2, Crouch End Vampires 1
Wake Green 2, St Mary's College 3
E. Barnet Old Grammarians 3, National Westminster Bank 4

4th Round Proper
Civil Service 2, Old Ignatians 1
South Bank 2, Old Foresters 1
Old Isleworthians 4, Westerns 1
St Mary's College 3, National Westminster Bank 4

Semi-finals
Civil Service 2, South Bank 1
Old Isleworthians 1, National Westminster Bank 2
**after extra time*

Final
National Westminster Bank 3, Civil Service 1

ARTHUR DUNN CUP

Final
Old Salopians (1) 2 (*Honychurch 2*)
Old Foresters (1) 1 (*Pratt*)
Old Salopians: J. Skelton; A. Pollock, T. Cooke, P. Deans, H. Raven, M. Lascelles, R. Cooke, S. Ellis, D. Honychurch, D. Arthur, P. Dyke.
Old Foresters: M. Butler; C. Hossain, A. Heyes, J. Banks, M. Sheppard, D. Pratt, R. Harnack, L. Douris, B. Barnet, N. Francis, C. Elliott.
Referee: B. Harvey (Surrey).

OTHER AFA CUP RESULTS 1994–95

Intermediate
Polytechnic Res. 3*:1, Civil Service Res. 3*:2
Junior
Norsemen 3rd 1*, National Westminster Bank 3rd 2*
Minor
Norsemen 4th 3, Kew Association 4th 0
Senior Novets
Cardinal Manning OB 5th 2*, Old Finchleians 5th 1*
Intermediate Novets
Civil Service 6th 1, Polytechnic 6th 0
Junior Novets
Old Parmiterians 8th 0, Old Parmiterians 11th 1
Veterans
Old Chigwellian Veterans 8, Broomfield Veterans 2
Open Veterans
Toby Veterans 0, Port of London Authority Veterans 2
Essex Senior
Old Foresters 2, Old Parmiterians 0

Middlesex Senior
Old Actonians Association 2, St Mary's College 1

Surrey Senior
National Westminster Bank 3*, South Bank 4*

Essex Intermediate
Old Buckwellians 1st 2, Old Parmiterians Res. 3

Kent Intermediate
Cuaco Res. 4*:1, Old Sedcopians 1st 4*:2

Middlesex Intermediate
Old Latymerians Res. 2, Latymer Old Boys Res. 1

Surrey Intermediate
National Westminster Bank Res. 3, Nottsborough Res. 1

W E Greenland Memorial
South Bank 3, Old Ignatians 1
**after extra time*

LONDON OLD BOYS' CUPS

Senior
Old Parmiterians 3*, Old Meadonians 1*

Intermediate
Old Danes Res. 4, Phoenix Old Boys Res. 2

Junior
Old Tollingtonians 3rd 2, Clapham O. Xaverians 3rd 1

Minor
Old Actonians 4th 2, Old Southallians 4th 0

Novets
Old Actonians 5th 1, Old Salvatorians 5th 0
Drummond Cup
Old Salesians 6th 3, Old Suttonians 6th 2
Nemean Cup
Latymer Old Boys 7th 2, Old Parmiterians 11th 4
Veterans' Cup
Old Kingsburians Veterans 2, City of London Veterans 4
**after extra time*

OLD BOYS' INVITATION CUPS

Senior
Old Esthameians 3, Old Tenisonians 0
Junior
Old Tenisonians Res 1, Old Lyonians 2
Minor
Old Latymerians 3rd 2, Glyn Old Boys 3rd 3
4th XI
Old Stationers 4th 6, Old Finchleians 4th 2
5th XI
Old Finchleians 5th 3, Old Stationers 5th 2
6th XI
Old Suttonians 6th 2, Old Stationers 6th 1
7th XI
Old Latymerians 7th 3, Old Stationers 7th 2
Veterans' XI
Old Stationers Veterans 3, Old Esthameians Veterans 1

SOUTHERN OLYMPIAN LEAGUE

Senior Section

Division One	*P*	*W*	*D*	*L*	*F*	*A*	*Pts*
Witan	18	14	0	4	53	26	28
Old Owens	18	12	3	3	47	23	27
Nottsborough	18	10	4	4	52	24	24
Ulysses	18	7	7	4	33	25	21
Old Grammarians	18	7	4	7	29	44	18
St Mary's College	18	5	6	7	31	29	16
Parkfield	18	5	5	8	33	42	15
Southgate County	18	4	6	8	22	28	14
Wandsworth Borough	18	2	4	12	22	49	8
Mill Hill Village	18	4	1	13	21	53	7*

Division Two	*P*	*W*	*D*	*L*	*F*	*A*	*Pts*
Hale End Athletic	20	14	3	3	66	25	31
Albanian	19	13	3	3	46	17	29
Ealing Association	20	10	6	4	38	30	26
Honourable Artillery Company	19	11	2	6	39	21	24
UCL Academicals	20	9	4	7	34	29	22
Old Bealonians	20	6	7	7	43	42	19
Corinthians-Casuals "A"	20	6	5	9	21	37	17
Old Finchleians	20	8	0	12	46	59	16
Hadley	20	5	5	10	20	30	15
Old Fairlopians	20	3	4	13	26	54	10
Duncombe Sports	20	3	3	14	20	55	8*

Division Three	*P*	*W*	*D*	*L*	*F*	*A*	*Pts*
City of London	20	14	2	4	58	29	29*
Old Woodhouseians	20	13	3	4	66	38	29
BBC	20	13	1	6	74	43	27
Fulham Compton Old Boys	20	12	3	5	60	33	27
Pollygons	20	9	2	9	46	62	20
Old Monovians	20	9	1	10	45	71	19
Westerns	20	9	0	11	46	54	18
London Welsh	20	7	3	10	43	46	17
Birkbeck College	20	6	4	10	36	50	16
Old Colfeians	20	3	5	12	30	52	11
Brent	20	2	2	16	23	49	6

Division Four	*P*	*W*	*D*	*L*	*F*	*A*	*Pts*
Broadfields United	20	17	1	2	95	23	35
Old Simmarobians	20	14	4	2	73	23	32
Hampstead Heathens	20	13	3	4	44	28	29
Cardinal Pole Old Boys	20	11	4	5	52	44	26
Inland Revenue	20	9	3	8	49	35	21
London Airways	20	10	1	9	45	45	21
Pegasus (Inner Temple)	20	7	5	8	43	40	19
Centymca	20	7	2	11	37	55	16
Economicals	20	3	2	15	32	74	8
Mayfield Athletic	20	3	2	15	29	59	6*
Bourneside	20	1	3	16	21	94	5

**points deducted for breach of rule*

Intermediate Section
Division One:–10 Teams–won by Old Owens Res.
Division Two:–10 Teams–won by Hampstead Heathens Res.
Division Three:–11 Teams–won by St Mary's College Res.
Division Four:–11 Teams–won by Centymca Res.

Junior Section
Division One:–10 Teams–won by Albanian 3rd
Division Two:–10 Teams–won by Old Owens 3rd
Division Three:–9 Teams–won by Old Finchleians 5th
Division Four:–10 Teams–won by City of London 5th

Minor Section
Division "A":–10 Teams–won by Ealing Association 4th
Division "B":–10 Teams–won by Broadfields United 4th
Division "C":–10 Teams–won by Broadfields United 5th
Division "D":–10 Teams–won by Broadfields United 6th
Division "E":–10 Teams–won by Old Owens 6th
Division "F":– 8 Teams–won by Broadfields United 8th
Senior Challenge Bowl:–won by Nottsborough
Senior Challenge Shield:–won by Old Owens
Intermediate Challenge Cup:–won by Old Owens Res.
Intermediate Challenge Shield:–won by Nottsborough Res.
Junior Challenge Cup:–won by Old Owens 3rd
Junior Challenge Shield:–won by Old Woodhouseians 3rd
Mander Cup:–won by City of London 4th
Mander Shield:–won by Broadfields 4th
Burntwood Trophy:–won by Albanian 5th
Burntwood Shield:–won by Old Finchleians 5th
Thomas Parmiter Cup:–won by Albanian 6th
Thomas Parmiter Shield:–won by Broadfields 7th
Veterans' Challenge Cup:–won by City of London Veterans
Veterans' Challenge Shield:–won by Parkfield Veterans

ARTHURIAN LEAGUE

Premier Division	*P*	*W*	*D*	*L*	*F*	*A*	*Pts*
Old Chigwellians	16	14	2	0	51	7	30
Lancing Old Boys	16	9	2	5	30	18	20
Old Carthusians	16	8	3	5	29	19	19
Old Reptonians	16	6	4	6	21	35	16
Old Aldenhamians	16	7	1	8	26	35	15
Old Etonians	16	5	4	7	28	31	14
Old Malvernians	16	4	5	7	20	30	13
Old Brentwoods	16	3	4	9	28	32	10
Old Wellingburians	16	1	5	10	15	41	7

Division One	*P*	*W*	*D*	*L*	*F*	*A*	*Pts*
Old Foresters	18	18	0	0	78	19	36
Old Cholmeleians	18	14	1	3	61	22	29
Old Harrovians	18	9	3	6	43	32	21
Old Wykehamists	18	9	3	6	43	46	21
Old Salopians	18	8	4	6	50	38	20
Old Bradfieldians	18	5	4	9	41	58	14
Old Haileyburians	18	4	3	11	39	54	11
Old Witleians	18	4	3	11	34	54	11
Old Westminsters	18	3	4	11	30	49	10
Old Ardinians	18	1	5	12	22	69	5*

Division Two	*P*	*W*	*D*	*L*	*F*	*A*	*Pts*
Old Haberdashers	18	13	1	4	55	35	27
Old Carthusians Res.	18	10	4	4	46	26	24
Old Cholmeleians Res.	18	10	4	4	32	27	24
Old Chigwellians Res.	18	9	3	6	56	30	21
Old Chigwellians 3rd	18	9	2	7	43	33	20
Old Etonians Res.	18	6	5	7	47	38	17
Lancing Old Boys Res.	18	6	3	9	35	44	15
Old Foresters Res.	18	5	3	10	34	45	13
Old Aldenhamians Res.	18	3	1	11	34	64	13
Old Reptonians Res.	18	2	2	14	23	63	6

Division Three	*P*	*W*	*D*	*L*	*F*	*A*	*Pts*
Old Cholmeleians 3rd	16	10	5	1	50	24	25
Old Salopians Res.	16	9	1	6	36	31	19
Old Brentwoods Res.	16	6	5	5	45	41	17
Old Harrovians Res.	16	6	3	7	39	36	15
Old Westminsters Res.	16	5	5	6	34	36	15
Old Malvernians Res.	16	4	6	6	38	41	14
Old Etonians 3rd	16	4	6	6	32	41	14
Old Wellingburians Res.	16	6	1	9	30	37	13
Old Bradfieldians Res.	16	4	4	8	31	48	12

**2 points deducted breach of rule*

Division Four–won by Old Haberdashers Res.
Division Five–won by Old Cholmeleians 5th
Junior League Cup: Old Chigwellians Res. 0*:4p, Old Cholmeleians Res. 0*:1p
Derrik Moore Veterans' Cup: Old Chigwellians Vets 0, Old Carthusians Vets 3
(**p–after extra time & penalties*)

LONDON LEGAL LEAGUE

Division One	P	W	D	L	F	A	Pts
Grays Inn	18	15	0	3	63	25	30
Wilde Sapte	18	13	2	3	78	26	28
Nabarro Nathanson	18	9	2	7	43	32	20
Linklaters & Paines	18	9	2	7	42	43	20
Pegasus (Inner Temple)	18	6	5	7	38	39	17
Slaughter & May	18	7	2	9	41	43	16
D. J. Freeman & Co	18	4	6	8	33	41	14
Cameron Markby Hewitt	18	5	3	10	37	66	13
Freshfields	18	4	4	10	35	56	12
Herbert Smith	18	4	2	12	24	63	10

Division Two	P	W	D	L	F	A	Pts
Clifford Chance	18	14	1	3	54	17	29
Gouldens	18	12	3	3	53	28	27
Norton Rose	18	12	3	3	52	33	27
Lovell White Durrant	18	8	4	6	47	38	20
Stephenson Harwood	18	9	1	8	50	51	19
S. J. Berwin	18	8	3	7	32	38	19
Watson Farley & Williams	18	6	4	8	33	39	16
Allen & Overy	18	4	3	11	21	41	11
Taylor Joynson Garrett	18	3	1	14	23	47	7
Simmons & Simmons	18	1	3	14	13	52	5

Division Three	P	W	D	L	F	A	Pts
Macfarlanes	14	12	0	2	62	20	24
Rosling King	14	9	3	2	47	22	21
Denton Hall	14	9	1	4	48	25	19
McKenna & Co	14	8	1	5	27	32	17
Oyez	14	6	2	6	40	33	14
Baker & McKenzie	14	3	2	9	34	40	8
Richards Butler	14	1	3	10	17	42	5
Rowe & Maw	14	2	0	12	13	74	4

League Challenge Cup:–Gray's Inn 1, Nabarro Nathanson 3
Weavers Arms Cup:–Gouldens 2, Freshfields 4
Invitation Cup:–Norton Rose 5, Stephenson Harwood 3
Division 3 Cup:–Macfarlanes 2, Baker & McKenzie 5

LONDON FINANCIAL FA

Senior Section

Division One	P	W	D	L	F	A	Pts
Coutts	16	9	3	4	43	23	21
Royal Bank of Scotland	16	10	1	5	43	32	21
Bank America	16	9	2	5	52	23	20
Temple Bar	16	7	4	5	31	42	18
Sun Alliance	16	6	4	6	34	33	16
Liverpool Victoria	16	6	2	8	31	42	14
Hong Kong Bank	16	7	1	8	50	43	13*
Kleinwort Benson	16	4	2	10	33	46	10
Chemical Bank	16	4	1	11	31	64	9

Division Two	P	W	D	L	F	A	Pts
Citibank	18	15	2	1	48	18	32
Morgan Stanley International	18	12	2	4	53	28	26
Allied Irish Bank	18	9	3	6	34	27	21
Sedgwick	18	8	3	7	40	27	18*
Bardhill	18	7	3	8	23	34	17
Granby	18	6	4	8	32	36	16
Invesco	18	6	2	10	38	40	14
Eagle Star	18	4	5	9	37	52	13
Salomon Brothers	18	6	1	11	28	49	13
Royal Bank of Scotland Res.	18	3	3	12	18	40	9

Division Three	P	W	D	L	F	A	Pts
Morgan Guaranty	18	12	5	1	71	21	29
Churchill Insurance	18	12	5	1	60	27	29
Union Bank of Switzerland	18	11	1	6	51	24	23
Bowring	18	10	3	5	58	40	23
Direct Line Insurance	18	8	4	6	38	41	20
Coutts Res.	18	7	3	8	43	45	17
Sedgwick Noble Lowndes	18	2	10	6	27	37	14
United Bank of Kuwait	18	4	3	11	47	56	11
Temple Bar Res.	18	3	3	12	25	69	9
Gaflac	18	1	3	14	23	83	5

Division Four	P	W	D	L	F	A	Pts
Chase Manhattan Bank	18	13	4	1	63	25	30
ANZ Banking Group	18	8	5	5	38	26	21
Lincoln National	18	8	5	5	40	35	21
Granby Res.	18	6	7	5	41	38	19
Asphalia	18	9	0	9	41	48	18
U C B Bank	18	7	3	8	43	39	17
Royal Bank of Scotland 3rd	18	7	3	8	26	34	17
Citibank Res.	18	6	4	8	36	44	16
Sun Alliance Res.	18	3	5	10	37	55	11
Liverpool Victoria Res.	18	4	2	12	34	55	10

**points deduction breach of rule*

Division Five:–11 Teams–won by Bank America Res.
Division Six:–10 Teams–won by Credit Suisse Financial Res.
Sportsmanship Trophy:–won by Asphalia

OLD BOYS' LEAGUE

Premier Division	P	W	D	L	F	A	Pts
Old Ignatians	20	14	3	3	52	27	31
Old Meadonians	20	13	5	2	46	22	31
Glyn Old Boys	20	13	3	4	49	20	29
Cardinal Manning Old Boys	20	11	2	7	46	29	24
Old Tenisonians	20	10	3	7	44	35	23
Old Hamptonians	20	8	3	9	31	45	19
Old Aloysians	20	8	1	11	29	32	17
Clapham Old Xaverians	20	5	5	10	37	65	15
Old Danes	20	4	6	10	38	54	14
Old Wilsonians	20	4	3	13	28	43	11
Chertsey Old Salesians	20	2	2	16	31	59	6

Senior Division One	P	W	D	L	F	A	Pts
Latymer Old Boys	20	15	2	3	61	22	32
Old Isleworthians	20	12	1	7	47	36	25
Phoenix Old Boys	20	9	6	6	42	42	22
Old Tiffinians	20	9	3	8	61	37	21
Shene Old Grammarians	20	9	3	8	35	31	21
Old Tenisonians Res.	20	9	3	8	29	48	21
Old Suttonians	20	9	2	9	52	38	20
Old Kingsburians	20	9	1	10	53	44	19
Old Salvatorians	19	7	4	8	35	32	18
Old Wokingians	20	7	3	10	38	50	17
Old Edmontonians	19	0	2	17	26	99	0*

Senior Division Two	P	W	D	L	F	A	Pts
Old Manorians	22	16	4	2	82	20	36
Old Vaughanians	22	17	2	3	56	27	36
Old Michendenians	22	13	2	7	61	31	28
Old Meadonians Res.	22	13	2	7	66	53	28
Old Tollingtonians	22	11	2	9	55	45	24
Enfield Old Grammarians	22	11	0	11	76	49	22
Old Westhamians	22	10	2	10	51	48	22
Mill Hill County Old Boys	22	8	4	10	49	59	20
Old Southallians	22	7	3	12	49	62	17
Old Camdenians	22	8	1	13	40	66	17
John Fisher Old Boys	22	5	1	16	29	85	11
Old Ignatians Res.	22	1	1	20	21	90	3

Senior Division Three	P	W	D	L	F	A	Pts
Latymer Old Boys Res.	20	15	2	3	66	25	32
Phoenix Old Boys Res.	20	11	4	5	58	33	26
Old Grocers	20	10	6	4	54	38	26
Old Salvatorians Res.	20	9	3	8	30	35	21
Old Vaughanians Res.	20	8	4	8	45	37	20
Glyn Old Boys Res.	20	8	4	8	40	51	20
Old Hamptonians Res.	20	8	4	8	36	47	20
Chorley Wood Danes Old Boys	20	6	6	8	35	41	18
Leyton County Old Boys	20	5	6	9	32	48	16
Old Greenfordians	20	3	8	9	31	49	14
Old Alpertonians	20	2	3	15	28	51	7

**–points deducted for breach of rule*

Intermediate Division North:–12 Teams–won by Old Buckwellians
Intermediate Division South:–12 Teams–won by Old Dorkinians
Division One North:–11 Teams–won by Queen Mary College Old Boys
Division One South:–12 Teams–won by Old St Mary's

Division One West:–11 Teams–won by Old Kingsburians Res.
Division Two North:–10 Teams–won by Wood Green Old Boys Res.
Division Two South:–11 Teams–won by Glyn Old Boys 3rd
Division Two West:–10 Teams–won by Old Manorians 3rd
Division Three North:–11 Teams–won by Old Grocers Res.
Division Three South:–12 Teams–won by Chertsey Old Salesians 3rd
Division Three West:–10 Teams won by Old Manorians 4th
Division Four North:–11 Teams–won by Davenant Wanderers
Division Four South:–11 Teams–won by Old Meadonians 5th
Division Four West:–9 Teams–won by Shene Old Grammarians 4th
Division Five North:–9 Teams–won by Old Camdenians 5th
Division Five South:–10 Teams–won by Old Reigatians 4th
Division Five West:–10 Teams–won by Cardinal Manning OB 4th
Division Six North:–9 Teams–won by Old Tollingtonians 6th
Division Six South:–9 Teams–won by Old Wilsonians 5th
Division Six West:–9 Teams–won by Phoenix Old Boys 5th
Division Seven North:–8 Teams–won by Ravenscroft Old Boys 3rd
Division Seven South:–10 Teams–won by Old Sinjuns 4th
Division Seven West:–11 Teams–won by Cardinal Manning O.B. 5th
Division Eight South:–9 Teams–won by Old Suttonians 8th
Division Eight West:–11 Teams–won by Old Southallians 5th
Division Nine South:–8 Teams–won by Old Sedcopians 5th

SOUTHERN AMATEUR LEAGUE

Senior Section

First Division	*P*	*W*	*D*	*L*	*F*	*A*	*Pts*
South Bank Polytechnic	22	17	3	2	48	17	37
Old Esthameians	22	13	3	6	47	30	29
East Barnet Old Grammarians	22	11	4	7	47	42	26
Old Actonians Association	22	9	6	7	39	37	24
Civil Service	22	10	3	9	32	35	23
Norsemen	22	7	6	9	26	26	20
Crouch End Vampires	22	6	8	8	34	35	20
West Wickham	22	7	6	9	26	30	20
Winchmore Hill	22	4	10	8	29	38	17*
National Westminster Bank	22	7	3	12	32	43	17
Midland Bank	22	5	5	12	28	38	15
Old Latymerians	22	6	3	13	33	49	15

Second Division	*P*	*W*	*D*	*L*	*F*	*A*	*Pts*
Carshalton	22	15	2	5	47	29	32
Kew Association	22	14	3	5	55	26	31
Polytechnic	22	13	4	5	49	31	30
Lloyds Bank	22	13	3	6	48	34	29
Old Parkonians	22	9	7	6	35	27	25
Old Parmiterians	22	9	4	9	40	34	22
Alexandra Park	22	6	10	6	38	39	22
Old Bromleians	22	7	4	11	33	36	18
Lensbury	22	7	3	12	34	45	17
Old Stationers	22	7	1	14	26	43	15
Broomfield	22	5	4	13	33	50	14
Old Westminster Citizens	22	4	1	17	27	71	9

Third Division	*P*	*W*	*D*	*L*	*F*	*A*	*Pts*
Old Lyonians	20	15	4	1	62	21	34
Barclays Bank	20	15	3	2	73	22	33
Southgate Olympic	20	9	6	5	39	31	24
Old Salesians	20	10	3	7	46	32	23
Cuaco	20	10	3	7	39	36	23
Brentham	20	10	0	10	64	51	20
Bank of England	20	8	3	9	31	28	19
Alleyn Old Boys	20	7	5	8	41	44	19
Ibis	20	5	2	13	31	56	12
Merton	20	4	3	13	29	65	11
Reigate Priory	20	0	2	18	17	86	2

**1 point deducted–breach of rule*

Reserve Teams Section
First Division:–12 Teams–won by Polytechnic Res.
Second Division:–12 Teams–won by Old Latymerians Res.
Third Division:–11 Teams–won by Cuaco Res.
3rd Teams Section:
First Division:–12 Teams–won by Civil Service 3rd
Second Division:–12 Teams–won by Crouch End Vampires 3rd
Third Division:–11 Teams–won by Cuaco 3rd
4th Teams Section:
First Division:–12 Teams–won by Winchmore Hill 4th
Second Division:–12 Teams–won by Barclays Bank 4th
Third Division:–11 Teams–won by Merton 4th
5th Teams Section:
First Division:–10 Teams–won by Polytechnic 5th
Second Division:–10 Teams–won by Civil Service 5th
Third Division:–10 Teams–won by Old Salesians 5th
6th Teams Section:
First Division:–9 Teams–won by Civil Service 6th
Second Division:–9 Teams–won by Old Parmiterians 6th
Third Division:–9 Teams–won by Carshalton 6th
7th Teams Section:
First Division:–8 Teams–won by National Westminster Bank 7th
Second Division:–9 Teams–won by Old Actonians Association 7th
8th Teams Section:
First Division:–9 Teams–won by Old Parmiterians 8th
9th, 10th & 11th Teams Sections:
First Division:–9 Teams–won by Old Parmiterians 9th
Second Division:–8 Teams–won by Old Parmiterians 11th

UNIVERSITY FOOTBALL 1994–95

111TH UNIVERSITY MATCH

(at Craven Cottage, Fulham)

Oxford 1, Cambridge 0

Oxford: Novy; Prest, Campbell, Washington, Smith A, Smith M, Mills, Worthington, Kraft, Hanssen (D'Andrea), Seymour (Cotton). *Scorer:* Washington.

Cambridge: Park; Budd (Batstone), Bullmore, White, Thompson, Collins, Pett, Luke, Millar, Smart, Morrow (McMurray).

Referee: M. Halsey (Herts).

Cambridge have not won the fixture for seven years, but still lead Oxford by 45 wins to 41 with 25 drawn.

UNIVERSITY OF LONDON INTER-COLLEGIATE LEAGUE

Premier Division

	P	*W*	*D*	*L*	*F*	*A*	*Pts*
Royal Holloway College	14	12	1	1	63	14	25
Imperial College	14	11	2	1	47	20	24
London School of Economics	14	7	2	5	35	28	16
Goldsmiths' College	14	5	1	8	28	40	11
University College	14	5	1	8	23	37	11
Queen Mary Westfield College	14	4	2	8	25	34	10
King's College	14	3	2	9	19	42	8
R. Free Hospital Sch. of Medicine	14	2	3	9	18	43	7

Division One

	P	*W*	*D*	*L*	*F*	*A*	*Pts*
Ch. Cross & W'min. Hosp. Med. Sch.	18	13	3	2	45	19	29
Royal Holloway College Res.	18	11	4	3	54	25	26
University College Res.	18	8	8	2	41	22	24
Queen Mary Westfield College Res.	18	10	1	7	41	38	21
St. Bartholomew's Hosp. Med. Sch.	18	7	2	9	42	43	16
London Sch. Economics Res.	18	6	4	8	31	40	16
Univ. Coll. & Middx. Hosp. Med. Sch.	18	6	3	9	29	28	15
St George's Hospital Med. Sch.	18	4	6	8	31	40	14
U.M.D.S.	18	5	4	9	19	40	14
King's College Hosp. Med. Sch.	18	2	1	15	22	60	5

Division Two

	P	*W*	*D*	*L*	*F*	*A*	*Pts*
Royal London Hosp. Med. College	18	13	3	2	83	32	29
Royal Holloway College 3rd	18	13	1	4	65	31	27
Imperial College Res.	18	11	3	4	64	39	25
St Mary's Hospital Med. Sch.	18	8	2	8	49	41	18
King's College Res.	18	8	2	8	38	43	18
Sch. Slavonic & East European Studies	18	7	3	8	32	42	17
University College 3rd	18	6	1	11	47	46	13
Imperial College 3rd	18	5	3	10	40	52	13
Royal School of Mines (IC)	18	5	0	12	25	71	10
Goldsmiths' College Res.	18	4	0	13	17	63	8

Division Three

	P	*W*	*D*	*L*	*F*	*A*	*Pts*
Royal Holloway College 4th	16	10	4	2	42	26	24
London Sch. Economics 3rd.	16	9	4	3	45	28	22
Royal Veterinary College	16	9	3	4	61	26	21
King's College 3rd	16	9	2	5	43	34	20
University College 4th	16	6	2	8	47	51	14
Queen Mary Westfield College 3rd	16	6	1	9	59	42	13
Goldsmiths' College 3rd	16	5	2	9	40	61	12
Ch. Cross & W'min Hosp. Med. Sch. Res.	16	5	1	10	28	54	11
St George's Hospital Medical School Res.	16	2	3	11	26	69	7

Division Four—10 Teams–won by London School of Economics 4th.
Division Five—10 Teams–won by Royal Holloway College 5th.
Division Six— 8 Teams–won by Royal London Hospital Med. College Res.
Challenge Cup: R. Holloway College 3, Goldsmiths' College 1
Upper Reserves Cup: R. Holloway Res. 4, University College Res. 0
Lower Reserves Cup: King's College 4th 2*, UC & Middx. Hosp. M.S. 5th 4*
(**–after extra time & penalties*)
United Hospitals:
Senior Cup: Charing Cross & Westminster Hospital Medical School 3, University College & Middlesex Hospital Medical School 2
Junior Cup: Royal Free Hospital Sch. of Medicine Res. 1, St. Georges's Hospital Medical School Res. 0 *aet*

BRITISH UNIVERSITIES SPORTS ASSOCIATION CHAMPIONSHIP

First XI Final
Greenwich 2, Crewe 2 (*at Walsall FC*)
(*Greenwich won 5-4 on penalties*)

Second XI Final
Leeds 1, Loughborough (*at Crewe & Alsager*)

Third XI Final
Nottingham Trent 3, West Sussex 4 (*at Birmingham*)

Fourth XI Final
Loughborough 3, De Montfort (Beds) 2 *aet* (*at Warwick*)

Women's Final
De Montfort (Beds) 3, Crewe & Alsager 2 *aet* (*at Loughborough*)

ENGLISH UNIVERSITIES FOOTBALL (MEN)

English Universities 2, Stoke City 2
English Universities 2, Royal Navy 2
English Universities 1, Bradford City 1
English Universities 0, Irish Universities 0

HOME NATIONS TOURNAMENT

English Universities 2, N. Ireland 2
English Universities 2, Scottish Universities 0
English Universities 4, Welsh Universities 0
N. Ireland 3, Scottish Universities 1
N. Ireland 2, Welsh Universities 0
Scottish Universities 5, Welsh Universities 1

Positions 1. English Universities
2. N. Irish Universities
3. Scottish Universities
4. Welsh Universities

ENGLISH UNIVERSITIES (WOMEN)

English Universities 3, Welsh Universities 0
English Universities 4, Scottish Universities 2

CAMBRIDGE UNIVERSITY 1994–95

Amateur Football Alliance	Lost	0-2
Old Blues	Won	5-3
Army Crusaders	Lost	0-2
U.C.W. College Cardiff	Lost	0-2
Ipswich Town XI	Lost	1-12
Royal Navy F.A.	Won	2-1
Tottenham Hotspur XI	Lost	0-6
Royal Air Force U-21	Lost	0-3
Luton Town XI	Lost	1-5
Loughborough University	Drawn	0-0
Lloyds Select XI	Won	3-2
Arthurian League	Drawn	0-0
London Legal League	Won	5-1
Leicester University	Won	4-2
Southern Amateur League	Drawn	0-0
London University	Won	3-2
C.U. "Falcons"	Lost	2-3
Territorial Army	Won	3-2
Honourable Artillery Company	Won	2-1
Lloyds Select XI	Won	3-2
London Legal League	Won	2-1
Oxford University	Lost	0-1

LONDON UNIVERSITY 1994–95

United Hospitals	Won	3-1
Ulysses	Won	2-1
Old Boys' League	Won	4-0
Barnet XI	Won	4-2
Southern Amateur League	Lost	3-4
Royal Navy	Lost	2-4
Fulham XI	Lost	2-3
Charlton XI	Won	5-1
Arthurian League	Won	3-2
Royal Air Force U-21	Won	1-0
London Legal League	Won	3-2
Army Crusaders	Won	5-1
Metropolitan Police	Lost	1-2
Oxford University	Won	2-0
Cambridge University	Lost	2-3
Amateur Football Alliance	Drawn	1-1
Crystal Palace XI	Lost	0-1
Millwall XI	Won	3-1

RECORDS

Major British Records

HIGHEST WINS

First-Class Match		Arbroath (*Scottish Cup 1st Round*)	36	Bon Accord	0	12 Sept 1885
International Match		England	13	Ireland	0	18 Feb 1882
FA Cup		Preston NE (*1st Round*)	26	Hyde U	0	15 Oct 1887
League Cup		West Ham U (*2nd Round, 2nd Leg*)	10	Bury	0	25 Oct 1983
		Liverpool (*2nd Round, 1st Leg*)	10	Fulham	0	23 Sept 1986
FA PREMIER LEAGUE						
	(*Home*)	Manchester U	9	Ipswich T	0	4 March 1995
FOOTBALL LEAGUE						
Division 1	(*Home*)	WBA	12	Darwen	0	4 April 1892
		Nottingham F	12	Leicester Fosse	0	21 April 1909
	(*Away*)	Newcastle U	1	Sunderland	9	5 Dec 1908
		Cardiff C	1	Wolverhampton W	9	3 Sept 1955
Division 2	(*Home*)	Newcastle U	13	Newport Co	0	5 Oct 1946
	(*Away*)	Burslem PV	0	Sheffield U	10	10 Dec 1892
Division 3	(*Home*)	Gillingham	10	Chesterfield	0	5 Sept 1987
	(*Away*)	Halifax T	0	Fulham	8	16 Sept 1969
Division 3(S)	(*Home*)	Luton T	12	Bristol R	0	13 April 1936
	(*Away*)	Northampton T	0	Walsall	8	2 Feb 1947
Division 3(N)	(*Home*)	Stockport Co	13	Halifax T	0	6 Jan 1934
	(*Away*)	Accrington S	0	Barnsley	9	3 Feb 1934
Division 4	(*Home*)	Oldham Ath	11	Southport	0	26 Dec 1962
	(*Away*)	Crewe Alex	1	Rotherham U	8	8 Sept 1973
Aggregate Division 3(N)		Tranmere R	13	Oldham Ath	4	26 Dec 1935
SCOTTISH LEAGUE						
Premier	(*Home*)	Aberdeen	8	Motherwell	0	26 March 1979
Division	(*Away*)	Hamilton A	0	Celtic	8	5 Nov 1988
Division 1	(*Home*)	Celtic	11	Dundee	0	26 Oct 1895
	(*Away*)	Airdrieonians	1	Hibernian	11	24 Oct 1950
Division 2	(*Home*)	Airdrieonians	15	Dundee Wanderers	1	1 Dec 1894
	(*Away*)	Alloa Ath	0	Dundee	10	8 March 1947

LEAGUE CHAMPIONSHIP HAT-TRICKS

Huddersfield T	1923–24 to 1925–26
Arsenal	1932–33 to 1934–35
Liverpool	1981–82 to 1983–84

MOST GOALS FOR IN A SEASON

FA PREMIER LEAGUE		*Goals*	Games	Season
	Newcastle U	82	42	1993–94
FOOTBALL LEAGUE				
Division 1	Aston V	128	42	1930–31
Division 2	Middlesbrough	122	42	1926–27
Division 3(S)	Millwall	127	42	1927–28
Division 3(N)	Bradford C	128	42	1928–29
Division 3	QPR	111	46	1961–62
Division 4	Peterborough U	134	46	1960–61
SCOTTISH LEAGUE				
Premier Division	Rangers	101	44	1991–92
	Dundee U	90	36	1982–83
	Celtic	90	36	1982–83
	Celtic	90	44	1986–87
Division 1	Hearts	132	34	1957–58
Division 2	Raith R	142	34	1937–38
New Division 1	Dunfermline Ath	93	44	1993–94
	Motherwell	92	39	1981–82
New Division 2	Ayr U	95	39	1987–88
New Division 3	Montrose	69	36	1994–95

FEWEST GOALS FOR IN A SEASON

FA PREMIER LEAGUE		*Goals*	Games	Season
	Crystal Palace	34	42	1994–95
FOOTBALL LEAGUE	(minimum 42 games)			
Division 1	Stoke C	24	42	1984–85
Division 2	Watford	24	42	1971–72
	Leyton Orient	30	46	1994–95
Division 3(S)	Crystal Palace	33	42	1950–51
Division 3(N)	Crewe Alex	32	42	1923–24
Division 3	Stockport Co	27	46	1969–70
Division 4	Crewe Alex	29	46	1981–82
SCOTTISH LEAGUE	(minimum 30 games)			
Premier Division	Hamilton A	19	36	1988–89
	Dunfermline Ath	22	44	1991–92
Division 1	Brechin C	30	44	1993–94
	Ayr U	20	34	1966–67
Division 2	Lochgelly U	20	38	1923–24
New Division 1	Stirling Alb	18	39	1980–81
New Division 2	Berwick R	22	36	1994–95
New Division 3	Albion R	27	36	1994–95
	Berwick R	32	39	1987–88

MOST GOALS AGAINST IN A SEASON

FA PREMIER LEAGUE		*Goals*	Games	*Season*
	Swindon T	100	42	1993–94
FOOTBALL LEAGUE				
Division 1	Blackpool	125	42	1930–31
Division 2	Darwen	141	34	1898–99
Division 3(S)	Merthyr T	135	42	1929–30
Division 3(N)	Nelson	136	42	1927–28
Division 3	Accrington S	123	46	1959–60
Division 4	Hartlepools U	109	46	1959–60
SCOTTISH LEAGUE				
Premier Division	Morton	100	36	1984–85
	Morton	100	44	1987–88
Division 1	Leith Ath	137	38	1931–32
Division 2	Edinburgh C	146	38	1931–32
New Division 1	Queen of the S	99	39	1988–89
	Cowdenbeath	109	44	1992–93
New Division 2	Meadowbank T	89	39	1977–78
New Division 3	Albion R	82	36	1994–95

FEWEST GOALS AGAINST IN A SEASON

FA PREMIER LEAGUE		*Goals*	Games	*Season*
	Arsenal	28	42	1993–94
	Manchester U	28	42	1994–95
FOOTBALL LEAGUE	(minimum 42 games)			
Division 1	Liverpool	16	42	1978–79
Division 2	Manchester U	23	42	1924–25
	West Ham U	34	46	1990–91
Division 3(S)	Southampton	21	42	1921–22
Division 3(N)	Port Vale	21	46	1953–54
Division 3	Middlesbrough	30	46	1986–87
Division 4	Lincoln C	25	46	1980–81
SCOTTISH LEAGUE	(minimum 30 games)			
Premier Division	Rangers	19	36	1989–90
	Rangers	23	44	1986–87
	Celtic	23	44	1987–88
Division 1	Celtic	14	38	1913–14
Division 2	Morton	20	38	1966–67
New Division 1	Hibernian	24	39	1980–81
	Falkirk	32	44	1993–94
New Division 2	St Johnstone	24	39	1987–88
	Stirling Alb	24	39	1990–91
New Division 3	Montrose	32	36	1994–95

MOST POINTS IN A SEASON

FOOTBALL LEAGUE	(under old system of two points for a win)	*Points*	Games	*Season*
Division 1	Liverpool	68	42	1978–79
Division 2	Tottenham H	70	42	1919–20
Division 3	Aston V	70	46	1971–72
Division 3(S)	Nottingham F	70	46	1950–51
	Bristol C	70	46	1954–55
Division 3(N)	Doncaster R	72	42	1946–47
Division 4	Lincoln C	74	46	1975–76
SCOTTISH LEAGUE				
Premier Division	Aberdeen	59	36	1984–85
	Rangers	73	44	1992–93
Division 1	Rangers	76	42	1920–21
Division 2	Morton	69	38	1966–67
New Division 1	St Mirren	62	39	1976–77
	Falkirk	66	44	1993–94
New Division 2	Forfar Ath	63	39	1983–84
FA PREMIER LEAGUE	(three points for a win)			
	Manchester U	92	42	1993–94
FOOTBALL LEAGUE				
Division 1	Everton	90	42	1984–85
	Liverpool	90	40	1987–88
Division 2	Chelsea	99	46	1988–89
Division 3	Bournemouth	97	46	1986–87
Division 4	Swindon T	102	46	1985–86
SCOTTISH LEAGUE				
Premier Division	Rangers	69	36	1994–95
New Division 1	Raith R	69	36	1994–95
New Division 2	Morton	64	36	1994–95
New Division 3	Forfar Ath	80	36	1994–95

FEWEST POINTS IN A SEASON

FA PREMIER LEAGUE		*Points*	Games	Season
	Ipswich T	27	42	1994–95
FOOTBALL LEAGUE	(minimum 34 games)			
Division 1	Stoke C	17	42	1984–85
Division 2	Doncaster R	8	34	1904–05
	Loughborough T	8	34	1899–1900
	Walsall	31	46	1988–89
Division 3	Rochdale	21	46	1973–74
	Cambridge U	21	46	1984–85
Division 3(S)	Merthyr T	21	42	1924–25 & 1929–30
	QPR	21	42	1925–26
Division 3(N)	Rochdale	11	40	1931–32
Division 4	Workington	19	46	1976–77
SCOTTISH LEAGUE	(minimum 30 games)			
Premier Division	St Johnstone	11	36	1975–76
	Morton	16	44	1987–88
Division 1	Stirling Alb	6	30	1954–55
Division 2	Edinburgh C	7	34	1936–37
New Division 1	Queen of the S	10	39	1988–89
	Cowdenbeath	13	44	1992–93
New Division 2	Berwick R	16	39	1987–88
	Stranraer	16	39	1987–88

MOST WINS IN A SEASON

FA PREMIER LEAGUE		*Wins*	Games	Season
	Manchester U	27	42	1993–94
	Blackburn R	27	42	1994–95
FOOTBALL LEAGUE				
Division 1	Tottenham H	31	42	1960–61
Division 2	Tottenham H	32	42	1919–20
Division 3(S)	Millwall	30	42	1927–28
	Plymouth Arg	30	42	1929–30
	Cardiff C	30	42	1946–47
	Nottingham F	30	46	1950–51
	Bristol C	30	46	1954–55

Division 3(N)	Doncaster R	33	42	1946–47
Division 3	Aston Villa	32	46	1971–72
Division 4	Lincoln C	32	46	1975–76
	Swindon T	32	46	1985–86
SCOTTISH LEAGUE				
Premier Division	Aberdeen	27	36	1984–85
	Rangers	33	44	1991–92
	Rangers	33	44	1992–93
Division 1	Rangers	35	42	1920–21
Division 2	Morton	33	38	1966–67
New Division 1	Motherwell	26	39	1981–82
New Division 2	Forfar Ath	27	39	1983–84
	Ayr U	27	39	1987–88
New Division 3	Forfar Ath	25	36	1994–95

RECORD HOME WINS IN A SEASON

Brentford won all 21 games in Division 3(S), 1929–30

UNDEFEATED AT HOME

Liverpool 85 games (63 League, 9 League Cup, 7 European, 6 FA Cup), Jan 1978–Jan 1981

RECORD AWAY WINS IN A SEASON

Doncaster R won 18 of 21 games in Division 3(N), 1946–47

FEWEST WINS IN A SEASON

FA PREMIER LEAGUE		*Wins*	Games	*Season*
	Swindon T	5	42	1993–94
FOOTBALL LEAGUE				
Division 1	Stoke C	3	22	1889–90
	Woolwich Arsenal	3	38	1912–13
	Stoke C	3	42	1984–85
Division 2	Loughborough T	1	34	1899–1900
	Walsall	5	46	1988–89
Division 3(S)	Merthyr T	6	42	1929–30
	QPR	6	42	1925–26
Division 3(N)	Rochdale	4	40	1931–32
Division 3	Rochdale	2	46	1973–74
Division 4	Southport	3	46	1976–77
SCOTTISH LEAGUE				
Premier Division	St Johnstone	3	36	1975–76
	Kilmarnock	3	36	1982–83
	Morton	3	44	1987–88
Division 1	Vale of Leven	0	22	1891–92
Division 2	East Stirlingshire	1	22	1905–06
	Forfar Ath	1	38	1974–75
New Division 1	Queen of the S	2	39	1988–89
	Cowdenbeath	3	44	1992–93
New Division 2	Forfar Ath	4	26	1975–76
	Stranraer	4	39	1987–88
New Division 3	Albion R	5	36	1994–95

MOST DEFEATS IN A SEASON

FA PREMIER LEAGUE		*Defeats*	Games	*Season*
	Ipswich T	29	42	1994–95
FOOTBALL LEAGUE				
Division 1	Stoke C	31	42	1984–85
Division 2	Tranmere R	31	42	1938–39
	Chester C	33	46	1992–93
Division 3	Cambridge U	33	46	1984–85
Division 3(S)	Merthyr T	29	42	1924–25
	Walsall	29	46	1952–53
	Walsall	29	46	1953–54

Division 3(N)	Rochdale	33	40	1931–32
Division 4	Newport Co	33	46	1987–88

SCOTTISH LEAGUE

Premier Division	Morton	29	36	1984–85
Division 1	St Mirren	31	42	1920–21
Division 2	Brechin C	30	36	1962–63
	Lochgelly	30	38	1923–24
New Division 1	Queen of the S	29	39	1988–89
	Cowdenbeath	34	44	1992–93
New Division 2	Berwick R	29	39	1987–88
New Division 3	Albion R	28	36	1994–95

HAT-TRICKS

Career 34 Dixie Dean (Tranmere R, Everton, Notts Co, England)
Division 1 (one season post-war) 6 Jimmy Greaves (Chelsea), 1960–61
Three for one team one match
West, Spouncer, Hooper, Nottingham F v Leicester Fosse, Division 1, 21 April 1909
Barnes, Ambler, Davies, Wrexham v Hartlepools U, Division 4, 3 March 1962
Adcock, Stewart, White, Manchester C v Huddersfield T, Division 2, 7 Nov 1987
Loasby, Smith, Wells, Northampton T v Walsall, Division 3S, 5 Nov 1927
Bowater, Hoyland, Readman, Mansfield T v Rotherham U, Division 3N, 27 Dec 1932

FEWEST DEFEATS IN A SEASON

(*Minimum 20 games*)

FA PREMIER LEAGUE		*Defeats*	Games	*Season*
	Manchester U	4	42	1993–94
FOOTBALL LEAGUE				
Division 1	Preston NE	0	22	1888–89
	Arsenal	1	38	1990–91
	Liverpool	2	40	1987–88
	Leeds U	2	42	1968–69
Division 2	Liverpool	0	28	1893–94
	Burnley	2	30	1897–98
	Bristol C	2	38	1905–06
	Leeds U	3	42	1963–64
	Chelsea	5	46	1988–89
Division 3	QPR	5	46	1966–67
	Bristol R	5	46	1989–90
Division 3(S)	Southampton	4	42	1921–22
	Plymouth Arg	4	42	1929–30
Division 3(N)	Port Vale	3	46	1953–54
	Doncaster R	3	42	1946–47
	Wolverhampton W	3	42	1923–24
Division 4	Lincoln C	4	46	1975–76
	Sheffield U	4	46	1981–82
	Bournemouth	4	46	1981–82
SCOTTISH LEAGUE				
Premier Division	Celtic	3	44	1987–88
Division 1	Rangers	0	18	1898–99
	Rangers	1	42	1920–21
Division 2	Clyde	1	36	1956–57
	Morton	1	36	1962–63
	St Mirren	1	36	1967–68
New Division 1	Partick T	2	26	1975–76
	St Mirren	2	39	1976–77
	Raith R	4	44	1992–93
	Falkirk	4	44	1993–94
New Division 2	Raith R	1	26	1975–76
	Clydebank	3	26	1975–76
	Forfar Ath	3	39	1983–84
	Raith R	3	39	1986–87
New Division 3	Forfar Ath	6	36	1994–95

MOST DRAWN GAMES IN A SEASON

FA PREMIER LEAGUE		*Draws*	Games	*Season*
	Manchester C	18	42	1993–94
	Sheffield U	18	42	1993–94
	Southampton	18	42	1994–95
FOOTBALL LEAGUE				
Division 1	Norwich C	23	42	1978–79
Division 4	Exeter C	23	46	1986–87
SCOTTISH LEAGUE				
Premier Division	Aberdeen	21	44	1993–94
New Division 1	East Fife	21	44	1986–87

MOST GOALS IN A GAME

FA PREMIER LEAGUE	Andy Cole (Manchester U) 5 goals v Ipswich T	4 Mar 1995
FOOTBALL LEAGUE		
Division 1	Ted Drake (Arsenal) 7 goals v Aston Villa	14 Dec 1935
	James Ross (Preston NE) 7 goals v Stoke	6 Oct 1888
Division 2	Tommy Briggs (Blackburn R) 7 goals v Bristol R	5 Feb 1955
	Neville Coleman (Stoke C) 7 goals v Lincoln C (away)	23 Feb 1957
Division 3(S)	Joe Payne (Luton T) 10 goals v Bristol R	13 April 1936
Division 3(N)	Bunny Bell (Tranmere R) 9 goals v Oldham Ath	26 Dec 1935
Division 3	Steve Earle (Fulham) 5 goals v Halifax T	16 Sept 1969
	Barrie Thomas (Scunthorpe U) 5 goals v Luton T	24 April 1965
	Keith East (Swindon T) 5 goals v Mansfield T	20 Nov 1965
	Alf Wood (Shrewsbury T) 5 goals v Blackburn R	2 Oct 1971
	Tony Caldwell (Bolton W) 5 goals v Walsall	10 Sept 1983
	Andy Jones (Port Vale) 5 goals v Newport Co	4 May 1987
	Steve Wilkinson (Mansfield T) 5 goals v Birmingham C	3 April 1990
Division 4	Bert Lister (Oldham Ath) 6 goals v Southport	26 Dec 1962
FA CUP	Ted MacDougall (Bournemouth) 9 goals v Margate (*1st Round*)	20 Nov 1971
LEAGUE CUP	Frankie Bunn (Oldham Ath) 6 goals v Scarborough	25 Oct 1989
SCOTTISH LEAGUE CUP	Jim Fraser (Ayr U) 5 goals v Dumbarton	13 Aug 1952
SCOTTISH LEAGUE		
Premier Division	Paul Sturrock (Dundee U) 5 goals v Morton	17 Nov 1984
Division 1	Jimmy McGrory (Celtic) 8 goals v Dunfermline Ath	14 Sept 1928
Division 2	Owen McNally (Arthurlie) 8 goals v Armadale	1 Oct 1927
	Jim Dyet (King's Park) 8 goals v Forfar Ath	2 Jan 1930
	John Calder (Morton) 8 goals v Raith R	18 April 1936
	Norman Hayward (Raith R) 8 goals v Brechin C	20 Aug 1937
SCOTTISH CUP	John Petrie (Arbroath) 13 goals v Bon Accord (*1st Round*)	12 Sept 1885

MOST LEAGUE GOALS IN A SEASON

		Goals	Games	*Season*
FA PREMIER LEAGUE	Andy Cole (Newcastle U)	34	40	1993–94
	Alan Shearer (Blackburn R)	34	42	1994–95
Division 1	Dixie Dean (Everton)	60	39	1927–28
Division 2	George Camsell (Middlesbrough)	59	37	1926–27
Division 3(S)	Joe Payne (Luton T)	55	39	1936–37
Division 3(N)	Ted Harston (Mansfield T)	55	41	1936–37
Division 3	Derek Reeves (Southampton)	39	46	1959–60
Division 4	Terry Bly (Peterborough U)	52	46	1960–61
FA CUP	Sandy Brown (Tottenham H)	15	8	1900–01
LEAGUE CUP	Clive Allen (Tottenham H)	12	9	1986–87
SCOTTISH LEAGUE				
Division 1	William McFadyen (Motherwell)	52	34	1931–32
Division 2	Jim Smith (Ayr U)	66	38	1927–28

MOST LEAGUE GOALS IN A CAREER

FOOTBALL LEAGUE		*Goals*	Games	*Season*
Arthur Rowley	WBA	4	24	1946–48
	Fulham	27	56	1948–50
	Leicester C	251	303	1950–58
	Shrewsbury T	152	236	1958–65
		434	619	
SCOTTISH LEAGUE				
Jimmy McGrory	Celtic	1	3	1922–23
	Clydebank	13	30	1923–24
	Celtic	396	375	1924–38
		410	408	

MOST CUP GOALS IN A CAREER

FA CUP (post-war)

Denis Law 41 (Huddersfield T, Manchester C, Manchester U)
Ian Rush 41 (Chester, Liverpool)
Pre-war: Henry Cursham 48 (Notts Co)

A CENTURY OF LEAGUE AND CUP GOALS IN CONSECUTIVE SEASONS

George Camsell	Middlesbrough	59 Lge	5 Cup	1926–27
(101 goals)		33	4	1927–28
Steve Bull	Wolverhampton W	34 Lge	18 Cup	1987–88
(102 goals)		37	13	1988–89

(Camsell's cup goals were all scored in the FA Cup; Bull had 12 in the Sherpa Van Trophy, 3 Littlewoods Cup, 3 FA Cup in 1987–88; 11 Sherpa Van Trophy, 2 Littlewoods Cup in 1988–89.)

LONGEST SEQUENCE OF CONSECUTIVE SCORING (Individual)

FA PREMIER LEAGUE		
Mark Stein (Chelsea)	9 in 7 games	1993–94
FOOTBALL LEAGUE RECORD		
Dixie Dean (Everton)	23 in 12 games	1930–31

LONGEST WINNING SEQUENCE

FOOTBALL LEAGUE		*Games*	*Season*
Division 1	Everton	12	1893–94 (4) and 1894–95 (8)
Division 2	Manchester U	14	1904–05
	Bristol C	14	1905–06
	Preston NE	14	1950–51
Division 3	Reading	13	1985–86
From *Season's start*			
Division 1	Tottenham H	11	1960–61
Division 3	Reading	13	1985–86

LONGEST WINNING SEQUENCE IN A SEASON

FOOTBALL LEAGUE		*Games*	*Season*
Division 1	Tottenham H	11	1960–61
Division 2	Manchester U	14	1904–05
Division 2	Bristol C	14	1905–06
Division 2	Preston NE	14	1950–51
SCOTTISH LEAGUE			
Division 2	Morton	23	1963–64

LONGEST UNBEATEN SEQUENCE

FOOTBALL LEAGUE		Games	*Seasons*
Division 1	Nottingham F	42	Nov 1977–Dec 1978

LONGEST UNBEATEN CUP SEQUENCE

Liverpool 25 rounds League/Milk Cup 1980–84

LONGEST UNBEATEN SEQUENCE IN A SEASON

FOOTBALL LEAGUE		*Games*	*Season*
Division 1	Burnley	30	1920–21

LONGEST UNBEATEN START TO A SEASON

FOOTBALL LEAGUE		Games	*Season*
Division 1	Leeds U	29	1973–74
Division 1	Liverpool	29	1987–88

LONGEST SEQUENCE WITHOUT A WIN IN A SEASON

FOOTBALL LEAGUE		Games	*Season*
Division 2	Cambridge U	31	1983–84

LONGEST SEQUENCE WITHOUT A WIN FROM SEASON'S START

Division 1	Manchester U	12	1930–31

LONGEST SEQUENCE OF CONSECUTIVE DEFEATS

FOOTBALL LEAGUE		Games	*Season*
Division 2	Darwen	18	1898–99

GOALKEEPING RECORDS (without conceding a goal)

British record (all competitive games)
Chris Woods, Rangers, in 1196 minutes from 26 November 1986 to 31 January 1987.

Football League
Steve Death, Reading, 1103 minutes from 24 March to 18 August 1979.

PENALTIES

Most in a *Season (individual)*		*Goals*	*Season*
Division 1	Francis Lee (Manchester C)	13	1971–72
Most awarded in one game			
Five	Crystal Palace (4 – 1 scored, 3 missed) v Brighton & HA (1 scored), Div 2		1988–89
Most saved in a *Season*			
Division 1	Paul Cooper (Ipswich T)	8 (of 10)	1979–80

MOST LEAGUE APPEARANCES

996 Peter Shilton (286 Leicester City, 110 Stoke City, 202 Nottingham Forest, 188 Southampton, 175 Derby County, 34 Plymouth Argyle, Bolton Wanderers) 1966–95
824 Terry Paine (713 Southampton, 111 Hereford United) 1957–77
795 Tommy Hutchison (165 Blackpool, 314 Coventry City, 46 Manchester City, 92 Burnley 178 Swansea City, also 68 Alloa 1965–68) 1968–91
777 Alan Oakes (565 Manchester City, 211 Chester City, 1 Port Vale) 1959–84
770 John Trollope (all for Swindon Town) 1960–80†
764 Jimmy Dickinson (all for Portsmouth) 1946–65
762 John Burridge (27 Workington, 134 Blackpool, 65 Aston Villa, 6 Southend U (loan), 88 Crystal Palace, 39 QPR, 74 Wolverhampton W, 6 Derby Co (loan), 109 Sheffield U, 62 Southampton, 67 Newcastle U, 65 Hibernian, 3 Scarborough, 4 Lincoln C, 3 Aberdeen, 3 Dumbarton, 3 Falkirk, 4 Manchester C) 1968–96
761 Roy Sproson (all for Port Vale) 1950–72
758 Ray Clemence (48 Scunthorpe United, 470 Liverpool, 240 Tottenham Hotspur) 1966–87
757 Pat Jennings (48 Watford, 472 Tottenham Hotspur, 237 Arsenal) 1963–86
† record for one club

Consecutive
401 Harold Bell (401 Tranmere R; 459 in all games) 1946–55

FA CUP
88 Ian Callaghan (79 Liverpool, 7 Swansea C, 2 Crewe Alex)

Most Senior Matches
1379 Peter Shilton (996 League, 86 FA Cup, 102 League Cup, 125 Internationals, 13 Under-23, 4 Football League XI, 53 others including European Cup, UEFA Cup, World Club Championship, various domestic cup competitions)

MOST FA CUP FINAL GOALS

Ian Rush (Liverpool) 5: 1986(2), 1989(2), 1992(1)

MOST LEAGUE MEDALS

Phil Neal (Liverpool) 8: 1976, 1977, 1979, 1980, 1982, 1983, 1984, 1986

OTHER RECORDS

YOUNGEST PLAYERS
FA Premier League Andy Turner, 17 years 145 days, Tottenham H v Southampton, 15.8.92
FA Premier League Scorer Andy Turner, 17 years 166 days, Tottenham H v Everton, 5.9.92.
Football League Albert Geldard, 15 years 158 days, Bradford Park Avenue v Millwall, Division 2, 16.9.29; and Ken Roberts, 15 years 158 days, Wrexham v Bradford Park Avenue, Division 3N, 1.9.51
Football League scorer
Ronnie Dix, 15 years 180 days, Bristol Rovers v Norwich City, Division 3S, 3.3.28.
Division 1
Derek Forster, 15 years 185 days, Sunderland v Leicester City, 22.8.84.
Division 1 scorer
Jason Dozzell, 16 years 57 days as substitute Ipswich Town v Coventry City, 4.2.84
Division 1 hat-tricks
Alan Shearer, 17 years 240 days, Southampton v Arsenal, 9.4.88
Jimmy Greaves, 17 years 10 months, Chelsea v Portsmouth, 25.12.57
FA Cup (any round)
Andy Awford, 15 years 88 days as substitute Worcester City v Borehamwood, 3rd Qual. rd, 10.10.87
FA Cup proper
Scott Endersby, 15 years 288 days, Kettering v Tilbury, 1st rd, 26.11.77
FA Cup Final
James Prinsep, 17 years 245 days, Clapham Rovers v Old Etonians, 1879
FA Cup Final scorer
Norman Whiteside, 18 years 18 days, Manchester United v Brighton & Hove Albion, 1983
FA Cup Final captain
David Nish, 21 years 212 days, Leicester City v Manchester City, 1969
League Cup Final scorer
Norman Whiteside, 17 years 324 days, Manchester United v Liverpool, 1983
League Cup Final captain
Barry Venison, 20 years 7 months 8 days, Sunderland v Norwich City, 1985

OLDEST PLAYERS

Football League

Neil McBain, 52 years 4 months, New Brighton v Hartlepools United, Div 3N, 15.3.47 (McBain was New Brighton's manager and had to play in an emergency)

Division 1

Stanley Matthews, 50 years 5 days, Stoke City v Fulham, 6.2.65

FA Cup Final

Walter Hampson, 41 years 8 months, Newcastle United v Aston Villa, 1924

FA Cup

Billy Meredith, 49 years 8 months, Manchester City v Newcastle United, 29.3.24

International debutant

Leslie Compton, 38 years 2 months, England v Wales, 15.11.50

International

Billy Meredith, 45 years 229 days, Wales v England, 15.3 20

SENDINGS-OFF

Season	314 (League alone)	1994–95
Day	15 (3 League, 12 FA Cup*) **worst overall FA Cup total*	20 Nov 1982
League	13	14 Dec 1985
Weekend	15	22/23 Dec 1990
FA Cup Final	Kevin Moran, Manchester U v Everton	1985
Wembley	Boris Stankovic, Yugoslavia v Sweden (Olympics)	1948
	Antonio Rattin, Argentina v England (World Cup)	1966
	Billy Bremner (Leeds U) and Kevin Keegan (Liverpool), Charity Shield	1974
	Gilbert Dresch, Luxembourg v England (World Cup)	1977
	Mike Henry, Sudbury T v Tamworth (FA Vase)	1989
	Lee Dixon, Arsenal v Tottenham H (FA Cup semi-final)	1993
	Peter Swan, Port Vale v WBA (play-offs)	1993
	Michael Wallace and Chris Beaumont (both Stockport Co) v Burnley (play-offs)	1994
Quickest	Mark Smith, Crewe Alex v Darlington (away) Div 3: 19 secs	12 March 1994
Division 1	Liam O'Brien, Manchester U v Southampton (away): 85 secs	3 Jan 1987
World Cup	Jose Batista, Uruguay v Scotland, Neza, Mexico (World Cup): 55 secs	13 June 1986
Most one game	Four: Northampton T (0) v Hereford U (4) Div 3	11 Nov 1992
	Four: Crewe Alex (2) v Bradford PA (2) Div 3N	8 Jan 1955
	Four: Sheffield U (1) v Portsmouth (3) Div 2	13 Dec 1986
	Four: Port Vale (2) v Northampton T (2) Littlewoods Cup	18 Aug 1987
	Four: Brentford (2) v Mansfield T (2) Div 3	12 Dec 1987

RECORD ATTENDANCES

FA Premier League	45,347	Aston Villa v Liverpool, Villa Park	7.5.1994
Football League	83,260	Manchester U v Arsenal, Maine Road	17.1.1948
Scottish League	118,567	Rangers v Celtic, Ibrox Stadium	2.1.1939
FA Cup Final	126,047*	Bolton W v West Ham U, Wembley	28.4.1923
European Cup	135,826	Celtic v Leeds U, semi-final at Hampden Park	15.4.1970
Scottish Cup	146,433	Celtic v Aberdeen, Hampden Park	24.4.37
World Cup	199,854†	Brazil v Uruguay, Maracana, Rio	16.7.50

* It has been estimated that as many as 70,000 more broke in without paying.

† 173,830 paid.

ADDRESSES

The Football Association: R. H. G. Kelly, F.C.I.S., 16 Lancaster Gate, London W2 3LW

Scotland: J. Farry, 6 Park Gardens, Glasgow G3 7YE. *0141-332 6372*

Northern Ireland (Irish FA): D. I. Bowen, 20 Windsor Avenue, Belfast BT9 6EG. *01232 669458*

Wales: A. Evans, 3 Westgate Street, Cardiff, South Glamorgan CF1 1JF. *01222 372325*

Republic of Ireland (FA of Ireland): S. Connolly, 80 Merrion Square South, Dublin 2. *003531 766864*

International Federation (FIFA): S. Blatter, FIFA House, Hitzigweg 11, CH-8032 Zurich, Switzerland. *00 411 384 9595. Fax: 00 411 384 9696*

Union of European Football Associations: G. Aigner, Chermin de la Redoute 54, Case Postale 303 CH-1260 Nyon, Switzerland. *0041 22 994 44 44. Fax: 0041 22 994 44 88*

THE LEAGUES

The Premier League: R. N. Parry, 16 Lancaster Gate, London W2 3LW. *0171-262 4542.*

The Football League: J. D. Dent, F.C.I.S., The Football League, Lytham St Annes, Lancs FY8 1JG. *01253-729421. Telex 67675*

The Scottish League: P. Donald, 188 West Regent Street, Glasgow G2 4RY. *0141-248 384415*

The Irish League: H. Wallace, 87 University Street, Belfast BT7 1HP. *01232 242888*

Football League of Ireland: E. Morris, 80 Merrion Square South, Dublin 2. *003531 765120*

Vauxhall Conference: J. A. Moules, 24 Barnehurst Road, Bexleyheath, Kent DA7 6EZ. *01322 521116*

Central League: A. Williamson, The Football League, Lytham St Annes, Lancs FY8 1JG. *01253 729421*

North West Counties League: M. Darby, 87 Hillary Road, Hyde, Cheshire SK14 4EB.

Eastern Counties League: C. Lamb, 26 Dunthorpe Road, Clacton, Essex CO12 8UJ. *01255 436398*

Football Combination: N. Chamberlain, 2 Vicarage Close, Old Costessey, Norwich NR8 5DL. *01603 743998*

Hellenic League: M. J. Jenkins, 3 Leamington Drive, Faringdon, Oxon SN7 7JZ. *01367 240042*

Kent League: R. Vinter, The Thatched Barn, Lower Hardres, Canterbury, Kent CT4 5PG

Lancashire Amateur League: R. G. Bowker, 13 Shores Green Drive, Wincham, Northwich, Cheshire CW9 6EE. *0161-480 7723*

Lancashire Football League: J. W. Howarth, 465 Whalley Road, Clapton-le-Moors, Accrington, Lancs BB5 5RP. *01254 398957*

Leicestershire Senior League: D. Jamieson, 48 King Georges Road, Loughborough, Leics LE11 2PA. *01509 263411*

London Spartan: D. Cordell, 44 Greenleas, Waltham Abbey, Essex EN9 1SZ. *01992 712428*

Manchester League: F. J. Fitzpatrick, 102 Victoria Road, Stretford, Manchester M32 0AD. *0161-865 2726*

Midland Combination: N. Harvey, 115 Millfield Road, Handsworth Wood, Birmingham B20 1ED.

Mid-Week Football League: N. A. S. Matthews, Cedar Court, Steeple Aston, Oxford. *01869 40347*

Northern Premier: R. D. Bayley, 22 Woburn Drive, Hale, Altrincham, Cheshire WA15 8LZ. *0161-980 7007*

Northern Intermediate League: G. Thompson, Clegg House, 253 Pitsmoor Road, Sheffield S3 9AQ. *01742 27817*

Northern League: T. Golightly, 85 Park Road North, Chester-le-Street, Co Durham DH3 3SA. *0191-388 2056*

North Midlands League: G. Thompson, 7 Wren Park Close, Ridgway, Sheffield.

Peterborough and District League: M. J. Croson, 44 Storrington Way, Werrington, Peterborough, Cambs PE4 6QP.

Isthmian League: N. Robinson, 226 Rye Lane, Peckham SE15 4NL. *0181-653 3903*

Southern Amateur League: S. J. Lucas, 23 Beaufort Close, North Weald Bassett, Epping, Essex CM16 6JZ. *0137882 3932*

South-East Counties League: A. Leather, 66 Green Acres, Chichester Road, Croydon, Surrey CR0 5UX. *0181-681 7100*

Southern League: D. J. Strudwick, 11 Welland Close, Durrington, Worthing, West Sussex BN13 3NR. *01903 67788*

South Midlands League: M. Mitchell, 26 Leighton Court, Dunstable, Beds LU6 1EW. *01582 67291*

South Western League: M. Goodenough, Rose Cottage, Horrels Ford, Milton Damerel, Holsworthy, Devon EX22 7NJ. *01409 261402*

United Counties League: R. Gamble, 8 Bostock Avenue, Northampton. *01604 37766*

Wearside League: B. Robson, 12 Deneside, Howden-le-Wear, Crook, Co. Durham DL15 8JR. *01388 762034*

Western League: M. E. Washer, 16 Heathfield Road, Nailsea, Bristol BS19 1EB.

The Welsh League: K. J. Tucker, 16 The Parade, Merthyr Tydfil, Mid Glamorgan CF47 0ET. *01685 723884*

West Midlands Regional League: N. R. Juggins, 14 Badger Way, Blackwell, Bromsgrove, Worcs B60 1EX.

West Yorkshire League: W. Keyworth, 2 Hill Court Grove, Bramley, Yorks L13 2AP. *0113 74465*

Northern Counties (East): B. Wood, 6 Restmore Avenue, Guiseley, Nr Leeds LS20 9DG. *01943 874558 (home); 01274 29595 (9 a.m. to 5 p.m.)*

COUNTY FOOTBALL ASSOCIATIONS

Bedfordshire: P. D. Brown, Century House, Skimpot Road, Dunstable, LU5 4JU. *01582 565111*

Berks and Bucks: W. S. Gosling, 15a London Street, Faringdon, Oxon SN7 8AG. *01367 242099*

Birmingham County: M. Pennick, County FA Offices, Rayhall Lane, Great Barr, Birmingham B43 6JE. *0121-357 4278*

Cambridgeshire: A. K. Pawley, 3 Signet Court, Swanns Road, Cambridge CB5 8LA. *01223 277290*

Cheshire: A. Collins, The Cottage, Hartford Moss Rec Centre, Winnington, Northwich CW8 4BG.

Cornwall: J. M. Ryder, Penare, 16 Gloweth View, Truro, Cornwall TR1 3JZ.

Cumberland: R. Johnson, 72 Victoria Road, Workington, Cumbria CA14 2QT. *01900 3979*

Derbyshire: K. Compton, The Grandstand, Moorways Stadium, Moor Lane, Derby DE2 8FB. *01332 361422*

Devon County: C. Squirrel, County HQ, Coach Road, Newton Abbot, Devon TQ12 1EJ. *01626 332077*

Dorset County: P. Hough, County Ground, Blandford Close, Hamsworthy, Poole, Dorset BH15 4BF. *01202 682375*

Durham: J. R. Walsh, 'Codeslaw', Ferens Park, Durham DH1 1JZ. *01385 48653*

East Riding County: D. R. Johnson, 52 Bethune Ave, Hull HU4 7EJ. *01482 641458*

Essex County: T. Alexander, 31 Mildmay Road, Chelmsford, Essex CM2 0DN. *01245 357727*

Gloucestershire: P. Britton, Fernleigh House, South Road, Kingswood, Bristol BS15 2JL. *0117 940 7700*

Guernsey: D. Dorey, Haut Regard, St. Clair Hill, St. Sampson's, Guernsey, GY2 4DT, CI. *01481 46231*

Hampshire: R. G. Barnes, 8 Ashwood Gardens, off Winchester Road, Southampton SO9 2UA. *01703 766884*

Herefordshire: E. R. Prescott, 7 Kirkland Close, Hampton Park, Hereford HR1 1XP. *01432 51134*

Hertfordshire: R. G. Kibble, Marquis House, 68 Great North Road, Hatfield, Herts AL9 5ER.
Huntingdonshire: M. M. Armstrong, 1 Chapel End, Great Giddings, Huntingdon, Cambs PE17 5NP. *018323 262*
Isle of Man: Mrs A. Garrett, 60 Ballagarey Road, Glen Vine, IOM. *01624 676349*
Jersey: D. G. Speed, 93 Les Cinq Chenes, Five Oaks, St. Saviour, Jersey JE2 7UE.
Kent County: K. T. Masters, 69 Maidstone Road, Chatham, Kent ME4 6DT. *01634 43824*
Lancashire: J. Kenyon, 31a Wellington St, St John's, Blackburn, Lancs BB1 8AU. *01254 64333*
Leicestershire and Rutland: R. E. Barston, Holmes Park, Dog and Gun Lane, Whetstone, Leicester LE8 3LJ. *01533 867828*
Lincolnshire: F. S. Richardson, PO Box 26, 12 Dean Road, Lincoln LN2 4DP. *01522 24917*
Liverpool County: F. L. J. Hunter, 23 Greenfield Road, Old Swann, Liverpool L13 3EN. *0151-526 9515*
London: R. S. Ashford, Aldworth Grove, London SE13 6HY. *0181-690 9626*
Manchester County: F. Brocklehurst, Sports Complex, Brantingham Road, Chorlton, Manchester M21 1TG. *0161-881 0299*
Middlesex County: P. J. Clayton, 39 Roxborough Road, Harrow, Middx HA1 1NS. *0181-424 8524*
Norfolk County: R. Kiddell, 153 Middleton Lane, Hellesdon, Norwich, Norfolk NR6 5SF. *01603 488222*
Northamptonshire: B. Walden, 2 Duncan Close, Red House Road, Moulton Park, Northampton NN3 1WL. *01604 670741*
North Riding County: P. Kirby, 284 Linthorpe Road, Middlesbrough TS1 3QU. *01642 224585*
Northumberland: R. E. Maughan, Seymour House, 10 Brenkley Way, Blezard Bus Park, Seaton Burn, Newcastle upon Tyne NE13 6DT. *0191-297 0101*
Nottinghamshire: W. T. Annable, 7 Clarendon Street, Nottingham NG1 5HS. *01602 418954*
Oxfordshire: P. J. Ladbrook, 3 Wilkins Road, Cowley, Oxford OX4 2HY. *01865 775432*
Sheffield and Hallamshire: G. Thompson, Clegg House, 5 Onslow Road, Sheffield S11 7AF. *01142 670068*
Shropshire: A. W. Brett, 5 Ebnal Road, Shrewsbury SY2 6PW. *01743 56066*
Somerset & Avon (South): Mrs H. Marchment, 30 North Road, Midsomer Norton, Bath BA3 2QQ. *01761 413176*
Staffordshire: G. S. Brookes, County Showground, Weston Road, Stafford ST18 0DB. *01785 56994*
Suffolk County: W. M. Steward, 2 Millfields, Haughley, Suffolk IP14 3PU. *01449 673481*
Surrey County: A. P. Adams, 321 Kingston Road, Leatherhead, Surrey KT22 7TU. *01372 373543*
Sussex County: D. M. Worsfold, County Office, Culver Road, Lancing, Sussex BN15 9AX. *01903 753547*
Westmorland: J. B. Fleming, 101 Burneside Road, Kendal, Cumbria LA9 4RZ. *01539 730946*
West Riding County: R. Carter, Fleet Lane, Woodlesford, Leeds LS26 8NX. *0113 2821222*
Wiltshire: E. M. Parry, 44 Kennet Avenue, Swindon SN2 3LG. *01793 29036*
Worcestershire: M. R. Leggett Fermain, 12 Worcester Road, Eyesham, Worcs WR11 4JV. *01905 612336*

OTHER USEFUL ADDRESSES

Amateur Football Alliance: W. P. Goss, 55 Islington Park Street, London N1 1QB. *0171-359 3493*
English Schools FA: M. R. Berry, 1/2 Eastgate Street, Stafford ST16 2NN. *01785 51142*
Oxford University: M. H. Matthews, University College, Oxford OX1 4BH.
Cambridge University: Dr A. J. Little, St Catherine's College, Cambridge CB2 1RL.
Army: Major T. C. Knight, Clayton Barracks, Aldershot, Hants GU11 2BG. *01252 24431 Ext 3571*
Royal Air Force: Group Capt P. W. Hilton, 15 Western Court, Western Road, Cheltenham, Glos GL50 3RH. *01242 255215*
Royal Navy: Lt-Cdr J. Danks, R.N. Sports Office, H.M.S. Temeraire, Portsmouth, Hants PO1 4QS. *01705 822351 Ext 2271*
British Universities Sports Association: G. Gregory-Jones, Chief Executive: BUSA, 8 Union Street, London SE1 1SZ. *0171-357 8555*
Central Council of Physical Recreation: General Secretary, 70 Brompton Road, London SW3 1HE. *0171-584 6651*
British Olympic Association: 6 John Prince's Street, London W1M 0DH. *0171-408 2029*
National Federation of Football Supporters' Clubs: Chairman: Tony Kershaw, 87 Brookfield Avenue, Loughborough, Leicestershire LE11 3LN. *01509 267643 (and fax)*. National Secretary: Mark Agate, "The Stadium", 14 Coombe Close, Lordswood, Chatham, Kent ME5 8NU. *01634 863520 (and fax)*
National Playing Fields Association: Col R. Satterthwaite, O.B.E., 578b Catherine Place, London, SW1.
The Scottish Football Commercial Managers Association: J. E. Hillier (Chairman), c/o Keith FC Promotions Office, 60 Union Street, Keith, Banffshire, Scotland.
Professional Footballers' Association: G. Taylor, 2 Oxford Court, Bishopsgate, Off Lower Mosley Street, Manchester M2 3W2. *0161-236 0575*
Referees' Association: W. J. Taylor, Cross Offices, Summerhill, Kingswinford, West Midlands DY6 9JE. *01384 288386*
Women's Football Alliance: Miss H. Jeavons, 9 Wyllyotts Place, Potters Bar, Herts EN6 2JB. *01707 651840*
The Association of Football League Commercial Managers: G. H. Dimbleby, Secretary WBA FC, The Hawthorns, Halford Lane, West Bromwich B71 4LF.
The Association of Football Statisticians: R. J. Spiller, 22 Bretons, Basildon, Essex SS15 5BY. *01268 416020*
The Football Programme Directory: David Stacey, 'The Beeches', 66 Southend Road, Wickford, Essex SS11 8EN.
England Football Supporters Association: Publicity Officer, David Stacey, 66 Southend Road, Wickford, Essex SS11 8EN.
The Football League Executive Staffs Association: PO Box 52, Leamington Spa, Warwickshire.
The Ninety-Two Club: 104 Gilda Crescent, Whitchurch, Bristol BS14 9LD.
Scottish 38 Club: Mark Byatt, 6 Greenfields Close, Loughton, Essex IG10 3HG. *0181-508 6088*
The Football Trust: Second Floor, Walkden House, 10 Melton Street, London NW1 2EJ. *0171-388 4504*
The Football Supporters Association: PO Box 11, Liverpool L26 1XP. *0151-709 2594*
Association of Provincial Football Supporters' Clubs in London: Tina A. Robertson, 45 Durham Avenue, Heston, Middlesex TW5 0HG. *0181-843 9854*
World Association of Friends of English Football: New St 25A, Dk 6330 Pattburg, Denmark. *0045 467 4911*
Football Postcard Collectors Club: PRO: Bryan Horsnell, 275 Overdown Road, Tilehurst, Reading RG3 6NX. *01734 424448*

OTHER AWARDS 1994–95

FOOTBALLER OF THE YEAR

The Football Writers' Association Award for the Footballer of the Year went to Jurgen Klinsmann of Tottenham Hotspur and Germany.

Past Winners

1947–48 Stanley Matthews (Blackpool), 1948–49 Johnny Carey (Manchester U), 1949–50 Joe Mercer (Arsenal), 1950–51 Harry Johnston (Blackpool), 1951–52 Billy Wright (Wolverhampton W), 1952–53 Nat Lofthouse (Bolton W), 1953–54 Tom Finney (Preston NE), 1954–55 Don Revie (Manchester C), 1955–56 Bert Trautmann (Manchester C), 1956–57 Tom Finney (Preston NE), 1957–58 Danny Blanchflower (Tottenham H), 1958–59 Syd Owen (Luton T), 1959–60 Bill Slater (Wolverhampton W), 1960–61 Danny Blanchflower (Tottenham H), 1961–62 Jimmy Adamson (Burnley), 1962–63 Stanley Matthews (Stoke C), 1963–64 Bobby Moore (West Ham U), 1964–65 Bobby Collins (Leeds U), 1965–66 Bobby Charlton (Manchester U), 1966–67 Jackie Charlton (Leeds U), 1967–68 George Best (Manchester U), 1968–69 Dave Mackay (Derby Co) shared with Tony Book (Manchester C), 1969–70 Billy Bremner (Leeds U), 1970–71 Frank McLintock (Arsenal), 1971–72 Gordon Banks (Stoke C), 1972–73 Pat Jennings (Tottenham H), 1973–74 Ian Callaghan (Liverpool), 1974–75 Alan Mullery (Fulham), 1975–76 Kevin Keegan (Liverpool), 1976–77 Emlyn Hughes (Liverpool), 1977–78 Kenny Burns (Nottingham F), 1978–79 Kenny Dalglish (Liverpool), 1979–80 Terry McDermott (Liverpool), 1980–81 Frans Thijssen (Ipswich T), 1981–82 Steve Perryman (Tottenham H), 1982–83 Kenny Dalglish (Liverpool), 1983–84 Ian Rush (Liverpool), 1984–85 Neville Southall (Everton), 1985–86 Gary Lineker (Everton), 1986–87 Clive Allen (Tottenham H), 1987–88 John Barnes (Liverpool), 1988–89 Steve Nicol (Liverpool), 1989–90 John Barnes (Liverpool), 1990–91 Gordon Strachan (Leeds U), 1991–92 Gary Lineker (Tottenham H), 1992–93 Chris Waddle (Sheffield W), 1993–94 Alan Shearer (Blackburn R).

THE PFA AWARDS 1995

Player of the Year: Alan Shearer (Blackburn R).

Previous Winners: 1974 Norman Hunter (Leeds U); 1975 Colin Todd (Derby Co); 1976 Pat Jennings (Tottenham H); 1977 Andy Gray (Aston Villa); 1978 Peter Shilton (Nottingham F); 1979 Liam Brady (Arsenal); 1980 Terry McDermott (Liverpool); 1981 John Wark (Ipswich T); 1982 Kevin Keegan (Southampton); 1983 Kenny Dalglish (Liverpool); 1984 Ian Rush (Liverpool); 1985 Peter Reid (Everton); 1986 Gary Lineker (Everton); 1987 Clive Allen (Tottenham H); 1988 John Barnes (Liverpool); 1989 Mark Hughes (Manchester U); 1990 David Platt (Aston Villa); 1991 Mark Hughes (Manchester U); 1992 Gary Pallister (Manchester U); 1993 Paul McGrath (Aston Villa); 1994 Eric Cantona (Manchester U).

Young Player of the Year: Robbie Fowler (Liverpool).

Previous Winners: 1974 Kevin Beattie (Ipswich T); 1975 Mervyn Day (West Ham U); 1976 Peter Barnes (Manchester C); 1977 Andy Gray (Aston Villa); 1978 Tony Woodcock (Nottingham F); 1979 Cyrille Regis (WBA); 1980 Glenn Hoddle (Tottenham H); 1981 Gary Shaw (Aston Villa); 1982 Steve Moran (Southampton); 1983 Ian Rush (Liverpool); 1984 Paul Walsh (Luton T); 1985 Mark Hughes (Manchester U); 1986 Tony Cottee (West Ham U); 1987 Tony Adams (Arsenal); 1988 Paul Gascoigne (Tottenham H); 1989 Paul Merson (Arsenal); 1990 Matthew Le Tissier (Southampton); 1991 Lee Sharpe (Manchester U); 1992 Ryan Giggs (Manchester U); 1993 Ryan Giggs (Manchester U); 1994 Andy Cole (Newcastle U).

Merit Award: Gordon Strachan.

Previous Winners: 1974 Bobby Charlton CBE, Cliff Lloyd OBE; 1975 Denis Law; 1976 George Eastham OBE; 1977 Jack Taylor OBE; 1978 Bill Shankly OBE; 1979 Tom Finney OBE; 1980 Sir Matt Busby CBE; 1981 John Trollope MBE; 1982 Joe Mercer OBE; 1983 Bob Paisley OBE; 1984 Bill Nicholson; 1985 Ron Greenwood; 1986 The 1966 England World Cup team, Sir Alf Ramsey, Harold Shepherdson; 1987 Sir Stanley Matthews; 1988 Billy Bonds MBE; 1989 Nat Lofthouse; 1990 Peter Shilton; 1991 Tommy Hutchison; 1992 Brian Clough; 1993 the 1968 Manchester United team; 1994 Billy Bingham.

THE SCOTTISH PFA AWARDS 1995

Player of the Year: Brian Laudrup (Rangers).

Previous Winners: 1978 Derek Johnstone (Rangers); 1979 Paul Hegarty (Dundee U); 1980 Davie Provan (Celtic); 1981 Sandy Clark (Airdrieonians); 1982 Mark McGhee (Aberdeen); 1983 Charlie Nicholas (Celtic); 1984 Willie Miller (Aberdeen); 1985 Jim Duffy (Morton); 1986 Richard Gough (Dundee U); 1987 Brian McClair (Celtic); 1988 Paul McStay (Celtic); 1989 Theo Snelders (Aberdeen); 1990 Jim Bett (Aberdeen); 1991 Paul Elliott (Celtic); 1993 Ally McCoist (Rangers); 1993 Andy Goram (Rangers); 1994 Mark Hateley (Rangers).

Young Player of the Year: Charlie Miller (Rangers).

Previous Winners: 1978 Graeme Payne (Dundee U); 1979 Graham Stewart (Dundee U); 1980 John MacDonald (Rangers); 1981 Francis McAvennie (St Mirren); 1982 Charlie Nicholas (Celtic); 1983 Pat Nevin (Clyde); 1984 John Robertson (Hearts); 1985 Craig Levein (Hearts); 1986 Craig Levein (Hearts); 1987 Robert Fleck (Rangers); 1988 John Collins (Hibernian); 1989 Bill McKinlay (Dundee U); 1990 Scott Crabbe (Hearts); 1991 Eoin Jess (Aberdeen); 1992 Phil O'Donnell (Motherwell); 1993 Eoin Jess (Aberdeen); 1994 Phil O'Donnell (Motherwell).

SCOTTISH FOOTBALL WRITERS' ASSOCIATION

Player of the Year 1995 – Brian Laudrup (Rangers)

1965 Billy McNeill (Celtic)
1966 John Greig (Rangers)
1967 Ronnie Simpson (Celtic)
1968 Gordon Wallace (Raith R)
1969 Bobby Murdoch (Celtic)
1970 Pat Stanton (Hibernian)
1971 Martin Buchan (Aberdeen)
1972 Dave Smith (Rangers)
1973 George Connelly (Celtic)
1974 Scotland's World Cup Squad
1975 Sandy Jardine (Rangers)
1976 John Greig (Rangers)
1977 Danny McGrain (Celtic)
1978 Derek Johnstone (Rangers)
1979 Andy Ritchie (Morton)
1980 Gordon Strachan (Aberdeen)
1981 Alan Rough (Partick Th)
1982 Paul Sturrock (Dundee U)
1983 Charlie Nicholas (Celtic)
1984 Willie Miller (Aberdeen)
1985 Hamish McAlpine (Dundee U)
1986 Sandy Jardine (Hearts)
1987 Brian McClair (Celtic)
1988 Paul McStay (Celtic)
1989 Richard Gough (Rangers)
1990 Alex McLeish (Aberdeen)
1991 Maurice Malpas (Dundee U)
1992 Ally McCoist (Rangers)
1993 Andy Goram (Rangers)
1994 Mark Hateley (Rangers)

EUROPEAN FOOTBALLER OF THE YEAR 1994

Hristo Stoichkov (Barcelona) became the first Bulgarian to be honoured as European Footballer of the Year in the annual *France Football* award. He was also runner-up in FIFA's World Player of the Year for 1994 behind the winner Romario of Brazil.

Past winners

1956 **Stanley Matthews** (Blackpool
1957 **Alfredo Di Stefano** (Real Madrid)
1958 **Raymond Kopa** (Real Madrid)
1959 **Alfredo Di Stefano** (Real Madrid)
1960 **Luis Suarez** (Barcelona)
1961 **Omar Sivori** (Juventus)
1962 **Josef Masopust** (Dukla Prague)
1963 **Lev Yashin** (Moscow Dynamo)
1964 **Denis Law** (Manchester United)
1965 **Eusebio** (Benfica)
1966 **Bobby Charlton** (Manchester United)
1967 **Florian Albert** (Ferencvaros)
1968 **George Best** (Manchester United)
1969 **Gianni Rivera** (AC Milan)
1970 **Gerd Muller** (Bayern Munich)
1971 **Johan Cruyff** (Ajax)
1972 **Franz Beckenbauer** (Bayern Munich)
1973 **Johan Cruyff** (Barcelona)
1974 **Johan Cruyff** (Barcelona)
1975 **Oleg Blokhin** (Dynamo Kiev)
1976 **Franz Beckenbauer** (Bayern Munich)
1977 **Allan Simonsen** (Borussia Moenchengladbach)
1978 **Kevin Keegan** (SV Hamburg)
1979 **Kevin Keegan** (SV Hamburg)
1980 **Karl-Heinz Rummenigge** (Bayern Munich)
1981 **Karl-Heinz Rummenigge** (Bayern Munich)
1982 **Paolo Rossi** (Juventus)
1983 **Michel Platini** (Juventus)
1984 **Michel Platini** (Juventus)
1985 **Michel Platini** (Juventus)
1986 **Igor Belanov** (Dynamo Kiev)
1987 **Ruud Gullit** (AC Milan)
1988 **Marco Van Basten** (AC Milan)
1989 **Marco Van Basten** (AC Milan)
1990 **Lothar Matthaus** (Inter-Milan)
1991 **Jean-Pierre Papin** (Marseille)
1992 **Marco Van Basten** (AC Milan)
1993 **Roberto Baggio** (Juventus)

THE CARLING AWARDS WINNERS 1994–95

Carling is the first football sponsor to include fans on its Awards panel which judges the Carling Manager of the Month, Carling Player of the Month and Carling No.1 Awards. The Carling Panel represents all sides of the game. **Gordon Taylor** Chief Executive, Professional Footballers Association; **Jim Smith** Chief Executive, League Managers Association; **Rick Parry** Chief Executive, The FA Premier League; **Graham Kelly** Chief Executive, The Football Association; **Neil Midgley** President, Referees Association; **Brian Barwick** Editor, Sportsnight/Match of the Day BBC TV; **Vic Wakeling** Head of Sport, BSkyB; **Trevor East** Deputy Controller, ITV Sport; **Alex Montgomery** Chairman, Football Writers Association; **Terry Venables** England Coach; **Tim Crabbe** Chairman, Football Supporters Association; **Tony Kershaw** Chairman, The National Federation of Supporters Clubs; **Paul Hughes** Sponsorship Director, Bass Brewers Ltd.

Carling Manager of the Month

August	Kevin Keegan	Newcastle United
September	Frank Clark	Nottingham Forest
October	Alex Ferguson	Manchester United
November	Kenny Dalglish	Blackburn Rovers
December	Gerry Francis	Tottenham Hotspur
January	Brian Little	Aston Villa
February	Kevin Keegan	Newcastle United
March	Ron Atkinson	Coventry City
April	Howard Wilkinson	Leeds United

Each winner receives a Carling Manager of the Month trophy, a cheque for £750 and a magnum of champagne.

Carling Manager of the Season	**Kenny Dalglish**	**Blackburn Rovers**
Carling No.1 of the Season	**Frank Clark**	**Nottingham Forest**

Carling Player of the Month

August	**Jürgen Klinsmann**	Tottenham Hotspur
September	**Robert Lee**	Newcastle United
October	**Paul Ince**	Manchester United
November	**Alan Shearer/Chris Sutton**	Blackburn Rovers
December	**Matthew Le Tissier**	Southampton
January	**Chris Waddle**	Sheffield Wednesday
February	**Duncan Ferguson**	Everton
March	**Anthony Yeboah**	Leeds United
April	**David Seaman**	Arsenal
Carling Player of the Season	**Alan Shearer**	**Blackburn Rovers**

Carling No.1 Awards

The Carling No.1 Award goes to the person or people who make the most outstanding contribution to the domestic game.

August 1994	**Match of the Day** As a salute to its 30 years on the air.
September 1994	**Chelsea Independent Supporters Association** Organising a trip of a lifetime for a seriously ill young fan from Canada to see his heroes at Stamford Bridge.
January 1995	**Sir Stanley Matthews** The 80th birthday of an English football legend.

November was clearly a good month for Blackburn Rovers. Left to right: Alan Shearer, Manager Kenny Dalglish and Chris Sutton.

FROM THE CHAPLAIN

There are perhaps seven questions often asked about football club chaplaincy. This article raises these questions, and tries to answer them.

1. *What is a football chaplain?*
He is similar to a chaplain in industry, education or the armed forces—in other words, he is a clergyman working in a secular situation. Usually he is a minister or vicar in a local church who, as part of his ministry, gives time to working with his local football club. This involvement varies from usually between 3–4 hours up to a whole day or more per week in certain situations.

2. *What does he do?*
The club and chaplain together agree on the precise nature of the chaplain's involvement, but essentially he is available as a pastoral and spiritual safety-net at the club. He visits the club regularly and tries to get to know its employees—players and non-playing staff alike. With all of them he tries to build friendship, offer his availability and support, functions as a listening ear, a counsellor, a source of advice when asked and is generally a confidential and trustworthy source of care and spiritual input.

3. *Why do clubs need chaplains?*
Football clubs need chaplains because the chaplain's role is to help people, and at clubs there are many sorts of people. He is available to all at the club: directors and cleaners, YTS trainees and superstars, office workers and management. He offers his unique input when crises arise: when people face hospitalisation, major surgery, serious family illness or bereavement. He is a trusted listener when personal problems or family difficulties arise. He can be available to listen and offer counsel when there may be difficulties over money, relationships, the police, drugs or a career. He doesn't impose himself on folk; he must be absolutely confidential, and must always remain 'neutral'. He is part of the club, but is not there to represent the club line—or indeed, any other line. Sometimes he is required for the more formal side of his professional services: taking wedding, funeral, christening or thanksgiving services, or being involved on behalf of the club in a memorial service, a centenary or other anniversary service or a service of remembrance.

4. *Do chaplains pray for success?*
Chaplains pray for people but they aren't witch-doctors! They are not involved in offering up incantations to ensure the club will be successful, or will win crucial matches. It is players, managers and coaches who deserve credit for success, and I hope no chaplain ever claims he or his prayers are the reason for his club's victories.

However, some players and managers have used the chaplain as a source of help and inspiration at times of stress and significance. More than once, a chaplain has been asked by a player before a big match, 'Rev, can we find a quiet corner—I need you to pray for me. This is a big game, and I've got responsibilities—I need God's help today', or some such.

So in specific situations, and as part of their routine prayer commitment, chaplains pray for their clubs. It is not so that God will bring instant success—we can't really pray for the opposing defence to open up *à la* Red Sea before Moses—but so that people will know the reality of God's love, His help, His strength, His closeness.

5. *Do chaplains preach to their clubs?*
The chaplain's role is different from that of a minister in his church. There, he has every freedom to preach from the pulpit. His job in football is not that of a preacher. He doesn't go around threatening people with sermons or imposing his beliefs on unwilling listeners. The chaplain must have the freedom to speak about spiritual matters and, if asked, would be expected to explain his faith. However, such input is broadly reactive, not proactive. He responds to questions and discussions, but is not there to impose such debate on an audience which does not wish to hear or listen.

People have to feel 'safe' with the chaplain about. They have to feel they can introduce spiritual issues into a conversation, and that these will be taken seriously. Equally, they may seek to discuss other issues, or just simply have a normal, friendly conversation, without being 'Bible-bashed'.

6. *Do all clubs have chaplains?*
No—but chaplaincy in football is a relatively recent development. In the mid-1970s there were perhaps half a dozen with chaplains; now, throughout the league, there are around 45. So this is a growing movement. Yet, if a club decides it doesn't want a chaplain, it is quite entitled to that opinion. Obviously, we believe that a right understanding of football chaplaincy, combined with the right man for the job, will bring real benefits to a club and its staff.

7. *How do we find out more about chaplaincy?*
The chaplains, contactable at their clubs, will explain their individual involvements. Otherwise contact with the following organisations may be helpful:

SCORE (Sports Chaplaincy Offering Resources and Encouragement), PO Box 123, Sale, Manchester M33 4ZA

Christians in Sport, PO Box 93, Oxford OX2 7YP

Continued on Page 936

STOP PRESS

George Graham banned for a year... Graham Kelly becomes FA's 'El Supremo'... PFA to help ex-players become referees... Peter Beardsley MBE, Harry Gregg MBE... Bruce Grobbelaar, John Fashanu and Hans Segers to face charges in October... Peter Shilton joins Coventry at 45... Italian exiles David Platt and Paul Gascoigne come back... Foreign imports soar... transfer spending continues and tops £100 million.

June moves: Warren Barton, Wimbledon to Newcastle U £4 million (Dons record); Tom Bennett, Wolverhampton W to Stockport Co; John Butler, Stoke C to Wigan Ath; Darren Carter, Leyton Orient to Peterborough U; Marc Edworthy, Plymouth Arg to Crystal Palace; Les Ferdinand, QPR to Newcastle U, £6 million (record fees for both clubs); Steve Finney, Manchester C to Swindon T; Neil Fisher, Bolton W to Chester C; Paul Holland, Mansfield T to Sheffield U; Mike Jeffrey, Newcastle U to Rotherham U; Ian Muir, Tranmere R to Birmingham C; Alan Neilson, Newcastle U to Southampton; Dean Richards, Bradford C to Wolverhampton W; Mark Seagraves, Bolton W to Swindon T; Lee Turnbull, Wycombe W to Scunthorpe U; Jason White, Scarborough to Northampton T; Steve Wilkinson, Mansfield T to Preston NE; Clive Wilson, QPR to Tottenham H.

Major Moves

Stan Collymore, Nottingham F to Liverpool, £8.5m; **Dennis Bergkamp,** Inter to Arsenal, £7.5m; **Les Ferdinand,** QPR to Newcastle U; **Paul Ince,** Manchester U to Inter, £7m; **Andrei Kanchelskis,** Manchester U to Everton, £5m; **David Platt,** Sampdoria to Arsenal, £4.7m (taking his total to £22.15m); **Chris Armstrong,** Crystal Palace to Tottenham H, £4.5m; **Warren Barton,** Wimbledon to Newcastle U, £4m; **Savo Milosevic,** Partizan Belgrade to Aston Villa, £3.5m; **Mark Draper,** Leicester C to Aston Villa, £3.25m; **Gica Popescu,** Tottenham H to Barcelona, £3m; **David Ginola,** Paris St Germain to Newcastle U, £2.5m; **Stefan Schwarz,** Arsenal to Fiorentina, £2.5m; **Gareth Southgate,** Crystal Palace to Aston Villa, £2.5m; **Craig Short,** Derby Co to Everton, £2.4m; **Georgi Kinkladze,** Dynamo Tbilisi to Manchester C, £2m; **Dean Richards,** Bradford C to Wolverhampton W, £1.85m; **Andy Roberts,** Millwall to Crystal Palace, £1.8m; **Andrea Silenzi,** Torino to Nottingham F, £1.8m; **Jurgen Klinsmann,** Tottenham H to Bayern Munich, £1.7m; **Marc Degryse,** Anderlecht to Sheffield W, £1.5m; **Mark Hughes,** Manchester U to Chelsea, £1.5m; **Dean Saunders,** Aston Villa to Galatasaray, £1.5m; **Simon Osborn,** Reading to QPR, £1.1m; **Marco Boogers,** Sparta Rotterdam to West Ham U, £1m; **Ruud Gullit,** Sampdoria to Chelsea – free!

OFFICIAL CHAPLAINS TO FA PREMIERSHIP AND FOOTBALL LEAGUE CLUBS

Rev John Bingham—Chesterfield
Rev Richard Chewter—Exeter C
Rev Michael Lowe—Bournemouth
Rev Andrew Taggart—Torquay U
Rev David Jeans—Sheffield W
Rev Nigel Sands—Crystal Palace
Rev Graham Spencer—Leicester C
Rev Phillip Miller—Ipswich T
Rev Allen Bagshawe—Hull C
Rev David Tully—Newcastle U
Rev Derek Cleave—Bristol C
Rev Brian Rice—Hartlepool U
Rev Ken Sykes—Watford
Rev Michael Chantry—Oxford U
Rev Michael Futens—Derby C
Very Rev Brandon Jackson—Lincoln C
Rev Paul Bennett—Swindon T
Rev Ken Hawkins—Birmingham C
Rev Simon Stevenette—Bristol R
Rev Michael Hunter—Grimsby T
Rev Dick Syms—York City
Rev Dennis Hall—Wigan Ath
Rev William Hall—Middlesbrough
Rev Canon John Hestor—Brighton & HA
Rev Mervyn Terrett—Luton T
Rev Jim Rushton—Carlisle U
Rev Robert de Berry—Queen's Park Rangers
Rev Gary Piper—Fulham
Rev Charlie Mackenzie—Barnsley
Rev Barry Kirk—Reading
Rev Martin Short—Bradford C
Rev John Boyers—Manchester U
Rev Martin Butt—Walsall
Rev Steve Riley—Leeds U
Revs Alan Poulter and Gerald Courell—Tranmere R
Rev Mark Kichenside—Charlton Ath
Rev Owen Beament—Millwall
Rev Elwin Cockett—West Ham U
Rev Mike Woodhead—Sheffield U
Rev Jim Pearce—Southampton
Rev Alan Comfort—Leyton Orient
Rev John Hall-Matthews—Wolverhampton Wanderers
Rev Mark Cockayne—Doncaster Rovers

The chaplains hope that those who read this article will see the value and benefit of chaplaincy work in sport, and will take appropriate steps to spread the word where this is possible. They would also like to thank the editor of the Rothmans Yearbook for his continued support for this specialist and growing area of work.

OBITUARIES

Adie, John 'Jock' (b. 1925; d. 1995). A full-back with Hearts who joined East Fife in the mid-fifties, making 49 appearances.

Anders, Harry (b. St Helens 26.11.26; d. 10.94). A diminutive winger who, with his younger brother Jimmy, signed for Preston North End in 1945 and made 69 League appearances, often as an understudy to Tom Finney. Joined Manchester City in March, 1953, and had 32 outings before a move to Port Vale in July, 1956. After only three League matches he was signed by Accrington Stanley, where he linked up once more with his brother. There he hit 18 goals in 114 games before completing his career with Workington in the 1960–61 season.

Anderson, John (b. Newcastle 9.11.24; d. 14.11.94). Goalkeeper who joined Middlesbrough in November, 1945, but only made one League appearance. Had a spell with Blackhall Colliery before returning to League football with Crystal Palace in 1951. After 38 games, he moved to Bristol Rovers where he won a Third Division (South) Championship medal in 1954 and repeated the feat a year later following a transfer to neighbours Bristol City.

Armstrong, William (b. Newcastle 3.7.12; d. 9.1.95). A half-back, he signed for Rochdale in 1931 from Brockley and then had spells with Aston Villa and Swindon Town before skippering Gillingham in the late thirties.

Auld, Robert (b. Aberdeen 1923 d. 4.95). Played League football with Dundee in the 1940s before moving on to Fraserburgh.

Bacuzzi, Joe (b. London 25.9.16; d. 1.2.95). A fine Fulham full-back who made 70 pre-war League appearances before the Second World War, then a further 213 games for the Cottagers until the mid-fifties. He won a Second Division Championship medal in 1949 and represented England on 13 occasions during war-time internationals.

Baxter, Jim C. (b. Hill of Beath 8.11.25; d. 5.94). Joined Barnsley from Dunfermline for £3000 in 1945 and went on to make 224 League appearances for the Tykes, scoring 56 goals. A talented inside-forward, Jim was snapped up by Preston North End in 1952 and had 245 outings (65 goals) before returning to Barnsley in 1959 where he completed his League career.

Bell, Harold (b. Liverpool 22.11.24; d. 7.94). Began as a centre-forward, but converted to a centre-half by Tranmere Rovers, for whom he signed professionally in 1941. Harold went on to make 401 consecutive League appearances for Rovers between 1946 and 1955—a record which is likely to stand forever. He retired at the end of the 1959–60 season after giving sterling service to his one and only club and amassing 595 League games in the process.

Berry, Johnny (b. Aldershot 1.6.26; d. 9.94). A skilful winger who began with Birmingham City in 1944 and played 103 League games between 1946 and 1951 before joining Manchester United for £25,000. With the Red Devils he won Championship medals in 1952, 1956 and 1957 and won an FA Cup runners-up medal in 1957. He was injured in the Munich air disaster of 1958, which forced a premature retirement at 31. In a wonderful career, Johnny made 247 League appearances for United and scored 37 times. He also represented England on four occasions.

Bicknell, Charlie (b. New Tupton 6.11.05; d. 6.9.94). A full-back who signed for local club Chesterfield in 1927, he had 79 League outings before joining Bradford City in 1930. At City he didn't miss a match for 5½ years and amassed 240 League games, eventually becoming skipper. In 1936 he departed for West Ham United and combined playing for the Hammers during war time (210 games) with his job as a policeman. Was captain when the Hammers beat Blackburn in the Football League War Cup at Wembley. He was still skipper at 41 and continued playing after hostilities, making a further 19 League appearances in 1946–47.

Blakeman, Alec (b. Headington 11.6.18; d. 12.94). An inside-forward who started out with local club Oxford City in 1945 and moved to Brentford the following year. Scored seven goals in 42 League outings for the Bees before joining Sheffield United in November, 1948. Five games later he was transferred to Bournemouth in February, 1949, where he hit eight goals in 25 games.

Bradford, Geoff (b. Bristol 18.7.27; d. 31.12.94). A one club man with Bristol Rovers, who made 461 League appearances and scored a phenomenal 245 goals, which included many hat-tricks. Geoff holds both club records for total aggregate goals, plus the highest number of League goals in a season. In 1952–53 when Rovers won the Third Division (South) Championship, he hit the target 33 times. An England cap was celebrated in 1955, with a goal in the 5-1 win over Denmark.

Frank Broome (left) and Raich Carter

Broome, Frank (b. Berkhamsted 11.6.15; d. 9.94). A versatile forward who joined Aston Villa in 1934. Four years later he won a Second Division championship medal and made his England debut, scoring against Germany. It was one of seven international appearances before the Second World War when he hit 77 goals in 132 League appearances. During hostilities Frank scored 68 goals in 112 games as well as making guest appearances for Birmingham, Northampton, Chesterfield, Nottingham Forest, Notts County, Watford and Wolves. He left Villa for Derby after just one League game following the war and at the Baseball Ground he hit 45 goals in 112 games. In 1949 he moved to Notts County, where he scored a further 35 goals in 105 matches. Frank had a short spell with Brentford in 1953 before completing his playing career with Crewe (16 goals in 36 games). Managerial appointments followed with Notts County, Exeter City and Southend United.

Brown, Hugh (b. Carmyle 7.12.21; d. 7.94). Scotland international half-back with three caps who was signed by Torquay United in November 1950 from Partick Thistle. He made 55 League appearances for the Plainmoor Club before leaving the game in 1952.

Brown, James (b. Kilmarnock 31.12.08; d. 9.1.94). Moved to America as a teenager, where he took up soccer, and was a member of the 1930 United States World Cup side. John came to England following the Wall Street crash and joined Manchester United as a forward, for whom he played 40 matches between 1932 and 1934, scoring 17 goals. He had short spells with Brentford and Tottenham, but returned to the States following the war.

Burgon, Archie (b. 29.3.12; d. 9.94). A forward, Archie signed for Notts County in 1932, but was snapped up by Spurs three years later. After only four matches, he joined Wrexham in October, 1935, where he enjoyed great success as a winger. He left the Racecourse Ground for Carlisle United in the summer of 1939, but his only two appearances for the Cumbrians were deleted at the outbreak of war and he never played League soccer again.

Cabrielli, Peter (b. 1909; d. 14.12.94). Of Italian extraction, Peter had trials with Inter Milan and Genoa, before playing for Dundee United, Forfar Athletic, Falkirk, Raith Rovers and Montrose.

Campbell, William (b. 26.7.20; d. 7.12.94). A fine half-back who signed for Morton in 1942 and won a Scottish Cup runners-up medal in 1948. Billy also won five full caps for Scotland before retiring through ill health in 1949.

Cape, Jackie (b. Carlisle 16.11.10; d. 6.6.94). John joined his local club, Carlisle United, in 1929, but after 15 League games, he left for Newcastle. At United the winger scored 18 goals in 51 games and, on 3rd September, 1930, he played in front of Newcastle's record attendance—68,386—and scored the only goal against Chelsea. He also scored twice n the Magpies' record Cup victory—a 9-0 win over Southport in 1932. Jackie signed for Manchester United in 1934 and won a Second Division Championship medal in 1936. A year later he moved on to QPR and played in the club's record Cup win over Bristol Rovers. In 1939, he returned to Air Ministry work in Carlisle and after the war rejoined his local club.

Carter, Raich (b. Sunderland 21.12.13; d. 9.10.94). A wonderfully accomplished inside-forward whose career was unfortunately interrupted by the war, but he still managed to win England caps either side of hostilities (only Tommy Lawton and Stanley Matthews achieved a similar feat). Was overlooked by Leicester in 1930 and joined Sunderland the following year. He skippered the Rokerites to the First Division Championship in 1936 and to victory in the 1937 FA Cup final. Raich hit a remarkable 118 goals in 246 League games for the club before joining Derby, whom he helped win the Cup in 1946. He scored 34 goals in 63 games for the Rams and then moved on to Hull City in April, 1948, as player-manager. He led the Tigers to the Third Division (North) Championship the following year and scored 56 goals in 136 League matches. Two years later he resigned as player-manager but continued playing for Hull until 1952. Managerial posts with Leeds (1953–58), Mansfield (1960–63) and Middlesbrough (1963–66) followed. He also played first-class cricket for Derbyshire in 1946.

Chadder, Alwyn (b. 1903; d. 23.12.94). A centre-half with Corinthians, he won six England amateur caps. He was also a founder of Pegasus, the joint Oxford-Cambridge amateur club.

Cooper, Davie (b. Hamilton 25.2.56; d. 2.95). A supremely skilful winger who joined Clydebank in 1974 and won the first of six Scotland Under-21 caps in 1977. That same year he moved to Rangers after hitting 28 goals in 90 League games. A year later he was part of the side who won the Championship, Scottish Cup and League Cup, scoring in the final of the latter against Celtic. In 1979, Davie won the first of his 22 full caps and won another Scottish Cup medal. Two years later he scored in the replayed Scottish Cup Final against Dundee United and hit another goal against United the following year as Rangers won the League Cup. Further League Cup success came in 1986 when he scored a penalty in a 2-1 win over Celtic. That summer he was in the Scotland World Cup party for Mexico. He won further titles with Rangers in 1987 and 1989 and in between helped the club beat Aberdeen on penalties in the League Cup. Following 377 games he moved to Motherwell in 1989 and won a Scottish Cup medal in 1991 after a thrilling 4-3 win over Dundee United. In 1993, he rejoined Clydebank.

Cooper, George (b. Kingswinford 1.10.32; d. 5.94). Industrious inside-forward signed by Crystal Palace from Brierly Hill in 1955. Top scorer in 1957-58 with 17 goals from 25 appearances. Subsequently had two seasons with Rochdale.

Cooper, William (b. 1910; d. 5.94). Willie signed for Aberdeen in 1927, having represented Scotland at schoolboy level. A consistent right-back throughout the thirties, he continued playing after the war and scored the goal that put the Dons into the 1947 Scottish Cup Final, which he unfortunately missed through injury. Set a club record between 1932 and 1936 of 162 consecutive appearances. Twenty-nine years after signing for Aberdeen, he left Pittodrie to become player-manager of Huntly.

Dare, Billy (b. Willesden 14.2.27; d. 8.5.94). Billy began at Brentford in 1948 and scored 61 goals in 208 games as a centre-forward. He joined West Ham in January, 1955, and became the first player to be filmed for television signing a contract. In 1958, he won a Second Division Championship medal and scored 44 times in 111 League games for the Hammers.

Drake, Ted (b. Southampton 16.8.12; d. 31.5.95). A life president of Fulham, Ted Drake was a brave, uncompromising centre-forward, who scored 150 goals for Arsenal before the war and also played cricket for Hampshire between 1931 and 1936. Ted started out at Southampton, whom he joined from Winchester City in 1931. He scored 48 goals in 72 League games for the Saints, but in 1934, a £6500 fee took him to Arsenal, where he won League Championship medals in 1935 and 1938. He hit the winner for Arsenal in the 1936 FA Cup final against Sheffield United and he holds two records from the thirties; on 14th December, 1935, he scored the most goals ever in an away game—all seven at Aston Villa and an Arsenal club record of 42 goals in 41 appearances, also during 1934–35. Added to that Ted hit six goals in as many international appearances for England, but in 1944 was forced to retire from playing through injury. From 1947 to 1952, he took charge of Reading, then in the summer of 1952 he became boss at Chelsea. He became the first man to play in, and manage a title-winning side (1955). The likes of Jimmy Greaves, Peter Bonetti, Bobby Tambling and Terry Venables came through his youth scheme. He left Stamford Bridge in 1961, joined the Fulham backroom staff in 1965, then became assistant manager of Barcelona in 1970. He returned to Craven Cottage as reserve team manager, before a Chief Scout post followed in 1975 and then, on retirement, Ted joined the board at Fulham.

Dyson, Barry (b. Oldham 6.9.42; d. 26.2.95). Barry started out with Bury in 1960, but left two years later to join Tranmere Rovers. He was a great success at Prenton Park, scoring 99 goals in 174 League games. In 1966, the talented inside-forward moved to Crystal Palace, but a couple of years later he was on his travels again—to Watford. There he notched 19 goals in 38 games and was snapped up by Orient in December, 1968, as a consequence. There he was involved in a more midfield role and had great success, helping the O's to the Third Division title in 1970. After 160 games and 28 goals, he moved to Colchester where he ended his first class career.

Edwards, Don (b. Wrexham 2.8.30; d. 3.95). Signed for Norwich City in September, 1947 and became their youngest ever goalkeeper when he played against Torquay United that same month as a 17-year-old. He made two appearances for the club before being transferred to Gorleston in 1953.

Ted Drake (left) and Len Goulden

Feehan, Ignatius 'Sonny' (b. Dublin 17.9.26; d. 11.3.95). A goalkeeper who joined Manchester United from Waterford in 1948 and helped them finish fourth in the League. But after making 12 League appearances he signed for Northampton Town in 1950, where he had 39 outings. Four years later, he was off to Brentford where he completed his career, retiring in 1959.

Frodsham, Ian (b. 27.12.75; d. 2.1.95). Signed for Liverpool as a junior aged 14 and joined the professional ranks three years later. A regular in the Reds' reserve team, he played for the England Youth team, making his debut in 1993. Ian fought bravely against cancer.

Garrett, Archie (b. Lesmahagow 17.6.19; d. 10.4.94). A forward who joined Preston North End from Hearts in 1938, but played for Bristol City during hostilities. After the war he signed for Northampton Town and hit 35 goals in only 51 League games, prompting interest from Birmingham. But after only 18 games he went back to Northampton where he completed his playing career in 1950.

Gilbert, Tim (b. South Shields 28.8.58; d. 31.5.95). A defender who signed for Sunderland in August, 1976 and went on to make 36 appearances for the Rokerites, scoring three times. In February, 1981, Tim moved on to Cardiff City where he had 33 League outings, scoring once. August, 1982, saw him transferred to Darlington, for whom he made 65 League appearances, with three goals to his credit.

Greenwood, John (b. Manchester 22.1.21; d. 25.11.94). Signed for Manchester City in September, 1946, but only made one League appearance before moving to Exeter City three years later. A half-back, John had 31 League outings for the Grecians, then in 1951 he was transferred to Aldershot. After 12 League matches, he joined Halifax Town later that year.

Goulden, Len (b. West Ham 16.7.12; d. 14.2.95). Cultured inside-forward with West Ham and Chelsea, his career spanning the war years in which he guested for Chelsea. A former schoolboy international he later won 14 full caps, another five in wartime internationals and played for the Football League. Subsequently coach at Chelsea and manager at Watford in 1952, where ironically he had made his professional debut for the Hammers in a London Combination game.

Guest, William (b. Birmingham 26.6.17; d. 11.94). A winger who joined the Birmingham City groundstaff in 1928 and scored 15 goals in 76 League appearances for the Blues. Signed for Blackburn Rovers in 1937 and played against West Ham in the 1940 Wartime Cup final. Bill hit 30 goals in only 88 League games for the Rovers and continued playing for them until August, 1947 when he joined Walsall, where he saw out his first-class career.

Hair, George (b. Ryton 28.4.25; d. 24.10.94). George was an outside-left who signed for Newcastle United during the war and played 23 games (7 goals) when League football resumed after hostilities. He joined Grimsby Town in February, 1949, for £6000 and hit a further 9 goals in 68 League games for the Mariners. Left for Peterborough United in 1951 when the Posh were in the Midland League.

Hall, Almerick (b. Hove 12.11.12; d. 11.94); An inside-forward, he joined his local side, Brighton and Hove Albion in 1931, but moved on to Spurs two years later for whom he scored three goals in 10 outings. Signed for Southend in 1937 and hit 10 goals in 37 games before a transfer to Bradford City in June, 1939. After hostilities Almer moved to West Ham where he scored 11 goals in 50 appearances. He became manager of Margate Town on retiring from first-class football and spent 30 years at the helm of the Kent club.

Harkness, Willie CBE (b. Dumfries 1919; d. 14.1.95). Played for his local club, Queen of the South, for whom he later became a scout, Director and chairman. He was appointed president of the Scottish Football Association in 1978 and stayed to lead Scotland to the 1982 World Cup finals.

Heaton, Mick (b. Sheffield 15.1.47; d. 11.4.95). A full-back who began with Sheffield United, signing in November, 1964. Then, after 33 games, he joined Blackburn Rovers for £7000 and played 171 matches for the Rovers between 1971 and 1975, when he was forced to retire through injury. After a spell out of the game, he returned to Rovers as first-team coach in 1978. When manager Howard Kendall went to Everton, Mick joined him and enjoyed Championship, FA Cup and Cup-Winners' Cup success at Goodison. When Kendall left for Athletic Bilbao, Mick managed Workington before the pair reunited at Manchester City in 1990. Mick's untimely death earlier this year occurred in a road accident.

Hibbitt, Terry (b. Bradford 1.12.47; d. 5.8.94). Terry signed for Leeds United in 1964 and played 47 League games, scoring nine times from midfield. In 1968, he won a European Inter-Cities Cup medal. Three years later he was off to Newcastle United, where he stayed until 1975, making 138 League appearances. In August of that year a move to Birmingham ensued, but following 110 outings and 11 goals he was back at Newcastle, where he finished his first-class career with a further 90 League matches and five goals.

Hill, Frank (b. Forfar 21.5.06; d. 1994). Originally a half-back with Forfar Athletic in 1924, Frank was transferred to Aberdeen where he won the first of three Scotland caps in 1930–31. Transferred to Arsenal in 1932, he won Championship medals in 1933 and again in 1934, but only had nine outings in the title winning team of 1935. Joined Blackpool in 1936, but left for Southampton a year later. Frank departed The Dell in 1938–39 to become assistant-trainer at Preston, but in 1944 he went to Crewe as player-manager. He continued playing after the war, finally hanging up his boots in his 41st year. In 1948, he took over at Burnley where he remained until 1954, laying great foundations. A spell at Preston followed, then in 1958 he became boss at Notts County and discovered Tony Hateley. He later managed Charlton Athletic in the 1960s.

Hindmarsh, Billy (b. Crook 26.12.19; d. 28.11.94). Signed by Portsmouth in 1939, he had to wait until 1946 to make his debut. Billy was a full-back in the Pompey side who won the Championship in 1948–49, but his 10 League appearances at the end of the campaign did not constitute a medal. When Pompey repeated the feat the following season, he amassed 34, coming in for the fourth match of the season and being a consistent member of a reaguard which only conceded 38 goals. He was transferred to Swindon in 1951, but after 11 matches he left the professional game.

Holt, Arthur (b. Southampton 8.4.11; d. 28.7.94). Arthur joined his local club, Southampton, in 1932 and made his debut at Manchester United the following year, deputizing for Ted Drake. An inside-forward, he scored 206 goals in 206 League matches and also played cricket for Hampshire between 1935 and 1948.

Hopkins, Idris 'Dai' (b. Merthyr Tydfil 11.10.07; d. 9.10.94). Idris had spells for Sheffield Wednesday and Crystal Palace before he signed for Brentford in 1932 and was a key member of the side who lifted the Third Division Championship a year later. He won 12 caps on the wing for Wales and played in nine wartime internationals. In 1942, he was a member of the Brentford side that defeated Pompey 1-0 to win the London Cup at Wembley. He made 290 League appearances for the Bees and scored 75 goals. A move to Bristol City came in May, 1947, where he made 24 appearances, scoring once.

Houghton, Frank (b. Preston 15.2.26; d. 19.8.94). Joined his local club, North End, as an amateur in 1942–43. He was then transferred to Ballymena, before signing for Newcastle for a club record fee of £5500. A half-back, Frank scored 10 goals in 55 League games. After injury and illness which appeared to have ended his career, he bravely came back with Exeter City in 1954. He hit 11 goals in 28 games to complete his first-class career.

Houldsworth, Freddie (b. Henley-on-Thames 29.5.11; d. 1994). A goalkeeper who played for Stoke City, Swindon Town, Ipswich Town and Reading.

Jarvis, Syd (b. 1905; d. 24.6.94). Syd signed for Middlesbrough as a full-back in 1927 and made his debut the following year. He won a Second Division Championship medal in 1929 and played 86 League games, scoring once. He finished his professional career at Darlington.

Jessop, William (b. Preston 2.4.22; d. 5.94). Outside-left Billy signed for his local club, North End, in 1940, and played 25 war-time games. Following hostilities, he made a further four League apearances before joining Stockport County in April, 1947. There he had 17 outings and scored four times. The following year he moved on to Oldham, where in 94 games, he hit the target 16 times. He completed his first-class career at Wrexham, for whom he scored twice in 14 matches.

Jones, John (b. Bromborough 3.7.13; d. 26.1.95). A full-back who joined Everton in 1932 and made 90 League appearances. After the war, he signed for Sunderland, where he had 24 League outings.

Lattimer, Frank (b. Durham 3.10.23; d. 11.94). A half-back for Brentford between 1945 and 1956. He made 171 League appearances for the Bees, scoring three times.

Liddle, Jimmy (b. Felling 7.12; d. 7.10.94). Jimmy played on the right wing for Reading and Crystal Palace in the thirties, amassing 34 goals in 66 League appearances for the Elm Park club. At Palace he had 13 League outings, scoring once.

Little, Barry (b. Greenwich 25.8.64; d. 9.94). An England Youth international who signed for Charlton in July, 1982, following his apprenticeship with the Valiants. He scored on his debut against Queens Park Rangers, but made only one further League appearance for Charlton. A talented midfielder, Barry went on to have spells with Dagenham, Barnet and Fisher Athletic, before helping Dover Athletic to win the Beazer Homes League Championship in 1993.

Loughran, Joe (b. Consett 12.8.15; d. 23.8.94). Joe joined Birmingham City in 1935, but after 35 League games and two goals he left for Luton two years later. On the eve of the Second World War he was transferred to Burnley, following 25 games for the Hatters. Joe then had to wait until September, 1946, before he was able to make his League debut at full-back. He made 65 League appearances for the Clarets before he moved to Southend United, where he had 147 outings, scoring once.

Low, Norman (b. Newcastle 23.3.14; d. 1994). A centre-half who began his career with Liverpool in 1933. Norman moved on to Newport County three years later, whom he helped win the Third Division (South) title in 1939. He resumed playing for County after the war, but Norwich City ended his 112 match association by signing him for £750. He made 150 League appearances before becoming manager at Carrow Road in 1950. He stayed until 1955, before taking further posts at Workington and Port Vale.

Malkin, John (b. Stoke 9.11.25; d. 19.5.94). A small, but effective winger, John signed for his local club in July, 1947, and took over from Stanley Matthews when the great man left for Blackpool. He went on to make 175 League appearances for the Potters and scored 23 goals. In 1956, he received a serious knee injury, which forced his early retirement.

March, Zechariah (b. Chichester 25.10.1892; d. 9.94). Zechariah died in Bognor Regis just weeks before his 102nd birthday. He started out at Brighton in 1913, but his career was disrupted by the First World War. He made 29 appearances in the Southern League for Brighton and a further 56 League games before a move along the coast to Pompey, then in the Third Division. In 1922–23, he made four appearances, three in the No. 7 shirt and once wearing No. 11. Before his death, he was believed to have been Britain's oldest surviving professional footballer.

McBennett, James (Seamus) (b. Newcastle, Northern Ireland 16.11.25; d. 23.2.95). Joined Cardiff City from Belfast Celtic in September, 1947. Scored twice in four League games for City and then in November, 1948, he moved to Tranmere. At Rovers, the right-winger had 12 outings and scored once.

McDonald, Gordon (b. Hampstead 7.2.32 d. 2.1995). Full-back with Crystal Palaceand later Swindon Town. After making 13 League appearances with Palace he was transferred in July 1957 and added a further ten matches at the County Ground.

Millar, Gordon (b. 1948; d. 9.6.94). A goalkeeper who saw service with Hearts, Morton and Stirling Albion. He also played in South Africa but returned to coach Cowdenbeath, Montrose and Rossyth.

Mochan, Neil (b. 6.4.27; 28.8.94). A centre-forward, Neil started out with Morton in 1944, before moving to Middlesbrough in 1951 for £14,000 and scored 14 times in 38 League games. Two years later he was on his way to Celtic for £8000. There he helped the club win the League and Cup double (1954) and League Cup in 1958. Won a Scotland 'B' cap in March, 1954, then went on to win three full internationals. He joined Dundee United in 1960 and ended his first class playing career with Raith Rovers. Neil, nicknamed 'Smiler', became head trainer at Celtic, being with the side throughout the late 1960s until his death last August.

Morgan, Billy (b. Burnley 16.12.1896; d. 4.11.93). Billy began at his local club in 1920, making his League debut the following year. A wing-half, his career came to a sad end when he was badly injured in 1924, enforcing his retirement from first-class football with 28 League appearances to his name.

Moulson, George (b. Clogheen 6.8.14; d. 11.11.94). A goalkeeper, George was bought out of the Army to sign for Grimsby Town in 1936, but did not make his League debut until 1947. It was his only League appearance before a move to Lincoln City in June, 1947. He proved a great success, helping the club to win the Third Division (North) Championship and was selected for the Republic of Ireland on three occasions by virtue of many superb performances. After 60 League outings, he left to join Peterborough United.

Moyse, Alec (b. Mitcham 5.8.35; d. 1994). Alec played on the wing, signing for Crystal Palace in 1956, and scored once in four League games. In August, 1958, he joined Swindon, but after only a month and four matches he signed for Millwall. There he scored three times in 22 League games. Cambridge City then benefited from his talent and he was converted to a defender during a five-year stay.

Mullett, Joe (b. Birmingham 2.10.36; d. 3.94). A full-back who joined Norwich City in February, 1959, having spent four years at Birmingham City, where he made three League appearances. At Norwich he had 213 League outings and scored twice before bringing his professional playing career to a close in 1968.

Munnings, Charles (b. 1907; d. 10.3.95). Began as a winger at Boston United and moved on to Grimsby, but he was unable to make a first team appearance for the Mariners. He had subsequent moves to Swindon Town and Hull City in 1930 and 1931 respectively. Returned to Swindon in 1932 and completed his first-class career with Mansfield Town in 1934.

Nicholls, Johnny (b. Wolverhampton 3.4.31; d. 1.4.95). An inside-forward, Johnny signed for West Bromwich Albion in 1950 and went on to make 131 League appearances for the Baggies, scoring 58 goals. He won an FA Cup medal in 1954 and two full caps, scoring against Scotland on his debut. In 1957, he joined Cardiff City, but after only eight games and two goals he was off to Exeter City, which made him one of the first to play in all four Divisions of the Football League. At Exeter, he hit an impressive 23 goals in 56 League matches but, in 1959, four seasons after playing in the top Division, he found himself in the Southern League with Worcester City.

Nicholls, Ron (b. Sharpness 4.12.33; d. 7.94). A goalkeeper who began as an amateur with Fulham before signing for Bristol Rovers in November, 1954. He made 71 League appearances for the then Eastville club before a move to Cardiff City in 1958. At Ninian Park he had 51 League outings and then saw out his first-class football career with Bristol City, playing 39 League games. An opening batsman for Gloucestershire, Ron played 534 Championship matches in his 24-year county career.

Oliver, Ken (b. Loughborough 10.8.24; d. 13.5.94). A dominating centre-half, who began as a forward. Ken started out with Sunderland in 1946, but after nine League games and one goal he left for Derby County three years later. At the Baseball Ground he made 184 League appearances, before completing his playing career with Exeter City in 1960 following 92 League matches.

Page, Albert (b. Walthamstow 18.3.16; d. 10.1.95). Joined Spurs from Leyton as an amateur in 1935 and turned professional the following year. He played 56 League matches for Tottenham as a half-back before signing for Colchester United in 1947.

Parker, Stan (b. Worksop 31.7.20; d. 14.11.94). An inside-forward, Stan signed for Ipswich Town in May, 1946 and hit 48 goals in 126 League games. Joined Norwich in August, 1951, but did not play any first team matches for the Canaries.

Pearson, Harold (b. Tamworth 5.08; d. 2.11.94). A reliable goalkeeper, he began with WBA in 1925 and eventually made 281 League appearances for the Baggies. In 1932 he won an England cap (replacing his cousin Harry Hibbs between the posts). In 1937, he moved to Millwall and collected a Third Division (South) Championship medal in his first season. He went on to have 39 League outings before retiring.

Penman, Andy (b. . . . ; d.20.7.94). A wonderfully gifted inside-forward who starred for Dundee in the 1960s, having signed, originally as an amateur in 1959. He was capped at youth and four times for Scotland Under-23's. Andy's one full cap came in May, 1966. He won a Championship medal with Dundee in 1962 and moved to Rangers five years later for £35,000. He completed his professional career with Arbroath in the 1970s.

Reeves, Derek (b. Parkstone 27.8.34; d. 25.5.95). Centre-forward Derek was holder of the Third Division post-war goalscoring record—39 goals in only 46 games for Southampton in 1959–60. He signed for the Saints in December, 1962, and in 273 League outings he hit a remarkable 145 goals. Moved on to Bournemouth in 1962, where he managed 11 goals in 35 games before completing his professional career.

Russell, Sid (b. Feltham 4.10.37; d. 6.94). Played cricket for both Middlesex and Gloucestershire, winning his county cap for the latter. A full-back with Brentford, whom he joined in 1956. Sid made 54 League appearances for the Bees, but quit to concentrate on cricket. In all he hit 5,464 first class runs.

Rutherford, Joe (b. Chester-le-Street 20.9.14; d. 12.94). Joe was a former blacksmith who had an unsuccessful trial with West Ham, but went on to join Southport where he made 88 League appearances between 1936 and 1939. In March, 1939, he signed for Aston Villa for £2500 and played eleven games in goal before the outbreak of war and a further 137 matches following hostilities.

Seed, Trevance (b. Preston 3.9.23; d. 12.94). A centre-half who signed for his local club, North End, in July, 1946, but before he had made a League debut he moved to Carlisle at the end of the year. Trevance made 81 League games for the Cumbrians and in 1950 he joined Accrington Stanley. Unfortunately, he was only able to play one League match, injury curtailing his career.

Stokes, Bobby (b. Portsmouth 30.1.51; d. 31.5.95). Bobby joined Southampton in February, 1968, playing in 218 League games for the Saints, and scoring 40 goals in a hard grafting inside-forward role. But the goal he will always be remembered for was the stunning solo effort that beat Alex Stepney and Manchester United in the 1976 FA Cup final. The Saints were then in the Second Division and produced one of the great Cup upsets. In August, 1977, Bobby joined his home town club, Pompey, where he made 24 appearances, scoring twice, before seeing out his career with Washington Diplomats.

Streten, Bernard (b. Gillingham 14.1.21; d. 5.94). An excellent goalkeeper who had spells with Notts County and Shrewsbury Town before settling at Luton Town, whom he joined in January, 1948. In all Bernard played 276 League games for the Hatters and played for England in their 9-2 victory over Northern Ireland in November, 1949. A wonderful character who had a great rapport with fans behind his goal. Bernard retired from the first-class game in 1957.

Sykes, Albert (b. 1900; d. 12.94). A left-half with Brighton in the Third Division (South) between 1926 and 1928, making 16 League outings.

Tadman, George (b. Rainham, Kent 5.5.14; d. 29.9.94). Started out with Gillingham in 1932, but joined Bristol Rovers a year later without making a League debut for the Gills. George scored on his debut in April, 1934, but after two goals in five League games, he rejoined Gillingham and finished top scorer with 18 goals in 40 League outings. George then signed for Charlton Athletic for £1000 in 1936 where he led the Valiants' goalscoring three seasons in succession to finish with 46 League goals in 87 games. Unfortunately, the Second World War terminated a fine career.

Tadman, Maurice (b. Rainham, Kent 28.6.21; d. 11.94). The younger brother of George who started his professional career with Charlton Athletic, but after only three League games he was sold to Plymouth Argyle for £4000. At Home Park, he became a real favourite, scoring 107 goals in 240 League matches and helped the club win the Third Division (South) in 1951–52. That season he amassed 27 goals which is still Argyle's post-war scoring record. He was the club's top marksman on five occasions before leaving in 1955.

Taylor, Richard (b. Wolverhampton 9.4.18; d. 28.1.95). A centre-half who began with Grimsby Town in 1935, making his debut three years later. After 38 League games (four prior to the war), he joined Scunthorpe in May, 1948. Then in the Midland League, Dick made 131 appearances, scoring twice, before becoming trainer-coach at the club. He later assisted Joe Mercer at Sheffield United and Aston Villa, then took over the helm at Villa Park in 1964, staying until 1967.

Timmins, Arnold (b. Whitehaven 29.1.40; d. 14.5.94). Scored on his League debut for Workington in the 1960–61 season and in total he made 44 League appearances, scoring 10 goals. An inside-forward, he left the club in August, 1964, to play non-league football.

Walter, Joe (b. 1896; d. 24.5.95). One of the Huddersfield Town Legends who helped the club to win the First Division Championship in 1923, 1924 and 1925 died in his 99th year. An outside-right, he made 55 League appearances and scored five goals.

White, Len (b. Skellow 23.3.30; d. 6.94). A goalscoring inside-forward and one of four brothers who played League football. Len began with Rotherham United in May, 1948 and hit 14 goals in 43 League games for the Millers. In February, 1953, came a big move to Newcastle United, where he was a great success, scoring 142 goals in 243 League games. It made him the Magpies' second highest goalscorer of all time, behind Jackie Milburn, whom he succeeded at St. James' Park. In the 1955 FA Cup final, he provided the corner-kick from which Milburn scored after 45 seconds, to eventually beat Manchester City 3-1. After nearly ten years at the club, he left for Huddersfield in February, 1962, where he scored another 39 goals in 105 League games. A superb career in the top flight was completed with 22 goals in 53 games for Stockport between 1965 and May 1966.

White, Ron (b. Bethnal Green 9.11.31; d. 12.8.94). A forward with Charlton Athletic who joined the club in March, 1954 and played 165 League games, scoring eight times. He completed his career at The Valley in 1962.

Wright, Ken DFC (b. Lode 16.5.22; d. 6.6.94). Ken was a bomber pilot who won the Distinguished Flying Cross for his heroism during the Second World War. On leave from the RAF in 1943, he guested for West Ham and in 1945–46 scored five goals in five games. After the war the Flight-Lieutenant hit a further 20 goals in 51 League games for the Hammers, but retired from first-class football in 1950, then saw active service in Korea. Ken passed away on the 50th anniversary of D-Day 1994.

Wright, Billy CBE (b. Ironbridge 6.2.24; d. 3.9.94). A pillar of the Wolves and England defence, he was the inspirational skipper of both in the immediate post-war years. Billy captained Wolves to three Championships in 1954, 1958 and 1959 and FA Cup success in 1949. He began on the groundstaff at Molineux, but was originally sent home for being too small! He made his international debut against Belgium and went on to make 105 appearances for England, 90 as captain, a record he shares with Bobby Moore. He was footballer of the Year in 1952 and amassed 491 League games for his beloved Wolves, scoring 13 times. On his retirement he was awarded the CBE and appointed manager of the England Youth side, eventually taking over the Under-23 team. He also had a spell as manager of Arsenal in 1962 and left four years later to enjoy a successful career in television with ATV. A player to whom so many football-mad children of the day wished to aspire, he was an astute passer of the ball, a solid, but fair tackler, and a thorough gentleman, on and off the pitch. In 1990, he became a director of Wolverhampton Wanderers and a superb, new stand at Molineux was appropriately named in his honour.

Billy Wright (white shirt) leading out Wolverhampton Wanderers against Honved in 1954, with Ferenc Puskas on his left.

THE FA CARLING PREMIERSHIP and ENDSLEIGH INSURANCE LEAGUE FIXTURES 1995–96

Saturday 12 August 1995

Endsleigh League Division 1
Birmingham C v Ipswich T
Crystal Palace v Barnsley
Millwall v Grimsby T
Oldham Ath v Huddersfield T
Portsmouth v Southend U
Stoke C v Reading
Sunderland v Leicester C
Tranmere R v Wolverhampton W
Watford v Sheffield U
WBA v Charlton Ath

Endsleigh League Division 2
Bradford C v AFC Bournemouth
Bristol C v Blackpool
Burnley v Rotherham U
Carlisle U v Bristol R
Hull C v Swindon T
Oxford U v Chesterfield
Peterborough U v Brighton & HA
Swansea C v Shrewsbury T
Walsall v Stockport Co
Wrexham v Notts Co
Wycombe W v Crewe Alex
York C v Brentford

Endsleigh League Division 3
Chester C v Hartlepool U
Colchester U v Plymouth Arg
Doncaster R v Scarborough
Exeter C v Darlington
Fulham v Mansfield T
Gillingham v Wigan Ath
Hereford U v Barnet
Leyton Orient v Torquay U
Northampton T v Bury
Preston NE v Lincoln C
Rochdale v Cardiff C
Scunthorpe U v Cambridge U

Sunday 13 August 1995

Endsleigh League Division 1
Derby Co v Port Vale
Luton T v Norwich C

Saturday 19 August 1995

FA Carling Premiership
Aston Villa v Manchester U
Blackburn R v QPR
Chelsea v Everton
Liverpool v Sheffield W
Manchester C v Tottenham H
Newcastle U v Coventry C
Southampton v Nottingham F
West Ham U v Leeds U
Wimbledon v Bolton W

Endsleigh League Division 1
Barnsley v Oldham Ath
Charlton Ath v Birmingham C
Grimsby T v Portsmouth
Huddersfield T v Watford
Ipswich T v Crystal Palace
Leicester C v Stoke C
Norwich C v Sunderland
Port Vale v Millwall
Reading v Derby Co
Sheffield U v Tranmere R
Southend U v Luton T

Endsleigh League Division 2
AFC Bournemouth v Peterborough U
Blackpool v Wrexham
Brentford v Oxford U
Brighton & HA v Bradford C
Bristol R v Swansea C
Chesterfield v Carlisle U
Notts Co v Wycombe W
Rotherham U v Hull C
Shrewsbury T v Walsall
Stockport Co v Burnley
Swindon T v York C

Endsleigh League Division 3
Barnet v Colchester U
Bury v Chester C
Cambridge U v Hereford U
Cardiff C v Northampton T
Darlington v Rochdale
Hartlepool U v Exeter C
Lincoln C v Gillingham
Mansfield T v Leyton Orient
Plymouth Arg v Preston NE
Scarborough v Fulham
Torquay U v Doncaster R
Wigan Ath v Scunthorpe U

Sunday 20 August 1995

FA Carling Premiership
Arsenal v Middlesbrough

Endsleigh League Division 1
Wolverhampton W v WBA

Monday 21 August 1995

FA Carling Premiership
Leeds U v Liverpool

Tuesday 22 August 1995

FA Carling Premiership
Bolton W v Newcastle U

Wednesday 23 August 1995

FA Carling Premiership
Coventry C v Manchester C
Everton v Arsenal
Manchester U v West Ham U
Nottingham F v Chelsea
QPR v Wimbledon
Sheffield W v Blackburn R
Tottenham H v Aston Villa

Saturday 26 August 1995

FA Carling Premiership
Bolton W v Blackburn R
Coventry C v Arsenal
Everton v Southampton
Leeds U v Aston Villa
Manchester U v Wimbledon
Middlesbrough v Chelsea
Nottingham F v West Ham U
QPR v Manchester C
Tottenham H v Liverpool

Endsleigh League Division 1
Birmingham C v Norwich C
Crystal Palace v Charlton Ath
Derby Co v Grimsby T
Luton T v Leicester C
Millwall v Southend U
Oldham Ath v Sheffield U
Portsmouth v Reading
Stoke C v Port Vale
Sunderland v Wolverhampton W
Tranmere R v Huddersfield T
Watford v Barnsley
WBA v Ipswich T

Endsleigh League Division 2
Bradford C v Shrewsbury T
Bristol C v Stockport Co
Burnley v Brentford
Carlisle U v Swindon T
Hull C v Blackpool
Oxford U v Rotherham U
Peterborough U v Notts Co
Swansea C v Chesterfield
Walsall v Bristol R
Wrexham v Brighton & HA
Wycombe W v AFC Bournemouth
York C v Crewe Alex

Endsleigh League Division 3
Chester C v Plymouth Arg
Colchester U v Lincoln C
Doncaster R v Cardiff C
Exeter C v Scarborough
Fulham v Torquay U
Gillingham v Cambridge U
Hereford U v Bury
Leyton Orient v Darlington
Northampton T v Mansfield T
Preston NE v Wigan Ath
Rochdale v Hartlepool U
Scunthorpe U v Barnet

Sunday 27 August 1995

FA Carling Premiership
Sheffield W v Newcastle U

Monday 28 August 1995

FA Carling Premiership
Blackburn R v Manchester U

Endsleigh League Division 3
Lincoln C v Scunthorpe U

Tuesday 29 August 1995

FA Carling Premiership
Arsenal v Nottingham F

Endsleigh League Division 1
Barnsley v Tranmere R
Charlton Ath v Watford
Grimsby T v Luton T
Ipswich T v Stoke C
Port Vale v Sunderland
Reading v Millwall
Sheffield U v Crystal Palace
Southend U v WBA

Endsleigh League Division 2
AFC Bournemouth v Wrexham
Blackpool v Peterborough U
Brentford v Hull C
Brighton & HA v Wycombe W
Bristol R v Burnley
Chesterfield v York C
Crewe Alex v Walsall
Notts Co v Bradford C
Rotherham U v Carlisle U
Shrewsbury T v Bristol C
Stockport Co v Swansea C

Endsleigh League Division 3
Barnet v Gillingham
Bury v Preston NE
Cambridge U v Colchester U
Cardiff C v Exeter C
Darlington v Fulham
Hartlepool U v Northampton T
Mansfield T v Doncaster R
Plymouth Arg v Hereford U
Torquay U v Rochdale
Wigan Ath v Chester C

Wednesday 30 August 1995

FA Carling Premiership
Aston Villa v Bolton W
Chelsea v Coventry C
Liverpool v QPR
Manchester C v Everton
Newcastle U v Middlesbrough
Southampton v Leeds U
West Ham U v Tottenham H
Wimbledon v Sheffield W

Endsleigh League Division 1
Huddersfield T v Birmingham C
Leicester C v Portsmouth
Norwich C v Oldham Ath
Wolverhampton W v Derby Co

Endsleigh League Division 2
Swindon T v Oxford U

Endsleigh League Division 3
Scarborough v Leyton Orient

Saturday 2 September 1995

Endsleigh League Division 1
Barnsley v Birmingham C
Charlton Ath v Huddersfield T
Crystal Palace v Tranmere R
Grimsby T v Watford
Ipswich T v Sunderland
Leicester C v Wolverhampton W
Luton T v Derby Co
Norwich C v Port Vale
Portsmouth v Millwall
Southend U v Reading
Stoke C v Oldham Ath
WBA v Sheffield U

Endsleigh League Division 2
AFC Bournemouth v Rotherham U
Bradford C v Wycombe W
Brentford v Swindon T
Brighton & HA v Notts Co
Bristol R v Wrexham
Burnley v Walsall
Chesterfield v Hull C
Oxford U v York C
Peterborough U v Bristol C
Shrewsbury T v Blackpool
Stockport Co v Crewe Alex
Swansea C v Carlisle U

Endsleigh League Division 3
Barnet v Lincoln C
Bury v Plymouth Arg
Chester C v Hereford U
Darlington v Cardiff C
Doncaster R v Hartlepool U
Exeter C v Scunthorpe U
Gillingham v Colchester U
Leyton Orient v Fulham
Preston NE v Cambridge U
Rochdale v Northampton T
Scarborough v Wigan Ath
Torquay U v Mansfield T

Saturday 9 September 1995

FA Carling Premiership
Blackburn R v Aston Villa
Bolton W v Middlesbrough
Coventry C v Nottingham F
Everton v Manchester U
QPR v Sheffield W
Southampton v Newcastle U
Tottenham H v Leeds U
Wimbledon v Liverpool

Endsleigh League Division 1
Birmingham C v Crystal Palace
Derby Co v Leicester C
Huddersfield T v Ipswich T
Millwall v Barnsley
Oldham Ath v WBA
Port Vale v Portsmouth
Reading v Luton T
Sheffield U v Norwich C
Sunderland v Southend U
Tranmere R v Charlton Ath
Watford v Stoke C
Wolverhampton W v Grimsby T

Endsleigh League Division 2
Blackpool v Stockport Co
Bristol C v Brighton & HA
Carlisle U v Burnley
Crewe Alex v Shrewsbury T
Hull C v Oxford U
Notts Co v AFC Bournemouth
Rotherham U v Brentford
Swindon T v Chesterfield
Walsall v Swansea C
Wrexham v Bradford C
Wycombe W v Peterborough U
York C v Bristol R

Endsleigh League Division 3
Cambridge U v Barnet
Cardiff C v Torquay U
Colchester U v Chester C
Fulham v Doncaster R
Hartlepool U v Darlington
Hereford U v Preston NE
Lincoln C v Rochdale
Mansfield T v Scarborough
Northampton T v Exeter C
Plymouth Arg v Leyton Orient
Scunthorpe U v Gillingham
Wigan Ath v Bury

Sunday 10 September 1995

FA Carling Premiership
Manchester C v Arsenal

Monday 11 September 1995

FA Carling Premiership
West Ham U v Chelsea

Tuesday 12 September 1995

FA Carling Premiership
Middlesbrough v Southampton

Endsleigh League Division 1
Birmingham C v Stoke C
Huddersfield T v Barnsley
Oldham Ath v Ipswich T
Port Vale v Leicester C
Reading v Grimsby T
Sheffield U v Charlton Ath
Sunderland v Portsmouth
Tranmere R v WBA
Watford v Crystal Palace

Endsleigh League Division 2
Blackpool v AFC Bournemouth
Bristol C v Brentford
Carlisle U v Peterborough U
Crewe Alex v Brighton & HA
Hull C v Swansea C
Notts Co v Stockport Co
Rotherham U v Bristol R
Walsall v Oxford U
Wrexham v Shrewsbury T
Wycombe W v Chesterfield
York C v Burnley

Endsleigh League Division 3
Cambridge U v Exeter C
Cardiff C v Scarborough
Colchester U v Preston NE
Fulham v Rochdale
Hartlepool U v Torquay U
Hereford U v Gillingham
Lincoln C v Bury
Mansfield T v Darlington
Northampton T v Leyton Orient
Plymouth Arg v Doncaster R
Scunthorpe U v Chester C
Wigan Ath v Barnet

Wednesday 13 September 1995

Endsleigh League Division 1
Derby Co v Southend U
Millwall v Luton T
Wolverhampton W v Norwich C

Endsleigh League Division 2
Swindon T v Bradford C

Saturday 16 September 1995

FA Carling Premiership
Arsenal v West Ham U
Aston Villa v Wimbledon
Chelsea v Southampton
Leeds U v QPR
Liverpool v Blackburn R
Manchester U v Bolton W
Middlesbrough v Coventry C
Newcastle U v Manchester C
Sheffield W v Tottenham H

Endsleigh League Division 1
Barnsley v Sheffield U
Charlton Ath v Oldham Ath
Crystal Palace v Huddersfield Town
Grimsby T v Port Vale
Ipswich T v Watford
Leicester C v Reading
Luton T v Sunderland
Norwich C v Millwall
Portsmouth v Derby Co
Southend U v Wolverhampton W
Stoke C v Tranmere R
WBA v Birmingham C

Endsleigh League Division 2
AFC Bournemouth v Crewe Alex
Bradford C v Bristol C
Brentford v Walsall
Brighton & HA v Blackpool
Bristol R v Swindon T
Burnley v Hull City
Chesterfield v Rotherham U
Oxford U v Carlisle U
Peterborough U v Wrexham
Shrewsbury T v Notts Co
Stockport Co v Wycombe W
Swansea C v York C

Endsleigh League Division 3
Barnet v Plymouth Arg
Bury v Cambridge U
Chester C v Lincoln C
Darlington v Colchester U
Doncaster R v Northampton T
Exeter C v Fulham
Gillingham v Cardiff C
Leyton Orient v Hartlepool U
Preston NE v Scunthorpe U
Rochdale v Mansfield T
Scarborough v Hereford U
Torquay U v Wigan Ath

Sunday 17 September 1995

FA Carling Premiership
Nottingham F v Everton

Saturday 23 September 1995

FA Carling Premiership
Arsenal v Southampton

Aston Villa v Nottingham F
Blackburn R v Coventry C
Liverpool v Bolton W
Manchester C v Middlesbrough
Sheffield W v Manchester U
West Ham U v Everton
Wimbledon v Leeds U

Endsleigh League Division 1
Barnsley v Derby Co
Grimsby T v Norwich C
Huddersfield T v Sheffield U
Ipswich T v Charlton Ath
Leicester C v Southend U
Millwall v Sunderland
Oldham Ath v Crystal Palace
Portsmouth v Tranmere R
Reading v Port Vale
Stoke C v WBA
Watford v Birmingham C
Wolverhampton W v Luton T

Endsleigh League Division 2
AFC Bournemouth v Brighton & HA
Blackpool v Crewe Alex
Bristol R v Brentford
Carlisle U v Hull C
Chesterfield v Burnley
Notts Co v Bristol C
Peterborough U v Bradford C
Shrewsbury T v Stockport Co
Swansea C v Oxford U
Swindon T v Rotherham U
Wycombe W v Wrexham
York C v Walsall

Endsleigh League Division 3
Bury v Barnet
Chester C v Gillingham
Colchester U v Hereford U
Darlington v Scarborough
Doncaster R v Rochdale
Exeter C v Leyton Orient
Fulham v Preston NE
Hartlepool U v Cardiff C
Lincoln C v Cambridge U
Mansfield T v Scunthorpe U
Torquay U v Northampton T
Wigan Ath v Plymouth Arg

Sunday 24 September 1995

FA Carling Premiership
Newcastle U v Chelsea

Monday 25 September 1995

FA Carling Premiership
QPR v Tottenham H

Saturday 30 September 1995

FA Carling Premiership
Bolton W v QPR
Chelsea v Arsenal
Coventry C v Aston Villa
Leeds U v Sheffield W
Middlesbrough v Blackburn R
Nottingham F v Manchester C
Southampton v West Ham U
Tottenham H v Wimbledon

Endsleigh League Division 1
Birmingham C v Oldham Ath
Charlton Ath v Barnsley
Crystal Palace v Stoke C
Derby Co v Millwall
Luton T v Portsmouth
Norwich C v Leicester C
Port Vale v Wolverhampton W
Sheffield U v Ipswich T
Southend U v Grimsby T
Sunderland v Reading
Tranmere R v Watford
WBA v Huddersfield T

Endsleigh League Division 2
Bradford C v Blackpool
Brentford v Chesterfield
Brighton & HA v Shrewsbury T
Bristol C v Wycombe W
Burnley v Swansea C
Crewe Alex v Notts Co
Hull C v York C
Oxford U v Bristol R
Rotherham U v Peterborough U
Stockport Co v AFC Bournemouth
Walsall v Carlisle U
Wrexham v Swindon T

Endsleigh League Division 3
Barnet v Darlington
Cambridge U v Hartlepool U
Cardiff C v Mansfield T
Gillingham v Bury
Hereford U v Wigan Ath
Leyton Orient v Doncaster R
Northampton T v Fulham
Plymouth Arg v Lincoln C
Preston NE v Chester C
Rochdale v Exeter C
Scarborough v Torquay U
Scunthorpe U v Colchester U

Sunday 1 October 1995

FA Carling Premiership
Everton v Newcastle U
Manchester U v Liverpool

Saturday 7 October 1995

Endsleigh League Division 1
Barnsley v Leicester C
Birmingham C v Southend U
Charlton Ath v Grimsby T
Crystal Palace v Sunderland
Huddersfield T v Port Vale
Ipswich T v Wolverhampton W
Oldham Ath v Portsmouth
Sheffield U v Derby Co
Stoke C v Norwich C
Tranmere R v Luton T
Watford v Millwall
WBA v Reading

Endsleigh League Division 2
Brentford v Blackpool
Bristol R v AFC Bournemouth
Burnley v Wycombe W
Carlisle U v Notts Co
Chesterfield v Crewe Alex
Hull C v Shrewsbury T
Oxford U v Stockport Co
Rotherham U v Brighton & HA
Swansea C v Bradford C
Swindon T v Bristol C
Walsall v Peterborough U
York C v Wrexham

Endsleigh League Division 3
Barnet v Exeter C
Bury v Leyton Orient
Cambridge U v Cardiff C
Chester C v Doncaster R
Colchester U v Hartlepool U
Gillingham v Rochdale
Hereford U v Torquay U
Lincoln C v Darlington
Plymouth Arg v Fulham
Preston NE v Scarborough
Scunthorpe U v Northampton T
Wigan Ath v Mansfield T

Tuesday 10 October 1995

Endsleigh League Division 2
Crewe Alex v Bristol C

Saturday 14 October 1995

FA Carling Premiership
Aston Villa v Chelsea
Blackburn R v Southampton
Bolton W v Everton
Leeds U v Arsenal
Liverpool v Coventry C
Manchester U v Manchester C
QPR v Newcastle U
Tottenham H v Nottingham F

Endsleigh League Division 1
Derby Co v Ipswich T
Grimsby T v Oldham Ath
Leicester C v Charlton Ath
Luton T v WBA
Millwall v Tranmere R
Norwich C v Barnsley
Port Vale v Crystal Palace
Portsmouth v Birmingham C
Reading v Huddersfield T
Southend U v Sheffield U
Sunderland v Watford
Wolverhampton W v Stoke C

Endsleigh League Division 2
AFC Bournemouth v Burnley
Blackpool v Chesterfield
Bradford City v Bristol R
Brighton & HA v Swindon T
Bristol C v Hull C
Crewe Alex v Carlisle U
Notts Co v Rotherham U
Peterborough U v Swansea C
Shrewsbury T v York C
Stockport Co v Brentford
Wrexham v Oxford U
Wycombe W v Walsall

Endsleigh League Division 3
Cardiff C v Barnet
Darlington v Gillingham
Doncaster R v Hereford U
Exeter C v Wigan Ath
Fulham v Bury
Hartlepool U v Scunthorpe U
Leyton Orient v Chester C
Mansfield T v Plymouth Arg
Northampton T v Cambridge U
Rochdale v Colchester U
Scarborough v Lincoln C
Torquay U v Preston NE

Sunday 15 October 1995

FA Carling Premiership
Sheffield W v Middlesbrough

Monday 16 October 1995

FA Carling Premiership
Wimbledon v West Ham U

Saturday 21 October 1995

FA Carling Premiership
Arsenal v Aston Villa
Chelsea v Manchester U
Coventry C v Sheffield W
Everton v Tottenham H
Manchester C v Leeds U
Middlesbrough v QPR
Newcastle U v Wimbledon
Nottingham F v Bolton W
West Ham U v Blackburn R

Endsleigh League Division 1
Barnsley v Port Vale
Birmingham C v Grimsby T
Charlton Ath v Norwich C
Crystal Palace v Millwall
Huddersfield T v Sunderland
Ipswich T v Luton T
Oldham Ath v Reading
Sheffield U v Leicester C
Stoke C v Derby Co
Tranmere R v Southend U
Watford v Wolverhampton W
WBA v Portsmouth

Endsleigh League Division 2
Brentford v Peterborough U
Bristol R v Notts Co
Burnley v Brighton & HA
Carlisle U v Bradford C
Chesterfield v Shrewsbury T
Hull C v Stockport Co
Oxford U v Wycombe W
Rotherham U v Blackpool
Swansea C v AFC Bournemouth
Swindon T v Crewe Alex
Walsall v Wrexham
York C v Bristol C

Endsleigh League Division 3
Barnet v Rochdale
Bury v Scarborough
Cambridge U v Darlington
Chester C v Fulham
Colchester U v Northampton T
Gillingham v Doncaster R
Hereford U v Exeter C
Lincoln C v Cardiff C
Plymouth Arg v Torquay U
Preston NE v Mansfield T
Scunthorpe U v Leyton Orient
Wigan Ath v Hartlepool U

Sunday 22 October 1995

FA Carling Premiership
Southampton v Liverpool

Saturday 28 October 1995

FA Carling Premiership
Aston Villa v Everton
Blackburn R v Chelsea
Leeds U v Coventry C
Liverpool v Manchester C
Manchester U v Middlesbrough
QPR v Nottingham F
Sheffield W v West Ham U
Wimbledon v Southampton

Endsleigh League Division 1
Derby Co v Oldham Ath
Grimsby T v Stoke C
Leicester C v Crystal Palace
Luton T v Charlton Ath
Millwall v WBA
Norwich C v Tranmere R
Port Vale v Birmingham C
Portsmouth v Watford
Reading v Ipswich T
Southend U v Huddersfield T
Sunderland v Barnsley
Wolverhampton W v Sheffield U

Endsleigh League Division 2
AFC Bournemouth v Carlisle U
Blackpool v Oxford U
Bradford C v Burnley
Brighton & HA v Bristol R
Bristol C v Walsall
Crewe Alex v Brentford
Notts Co v Swindon T
Peterborough U v York C
Shrewsbury T v Rotherham U
Stockport Co v Chesterfield
Wrexham v Swansea C
Wycombe W v Hull C

Endsleigh League Division 3
Cardiff C v Colchester U
Darlington v Plymouth Arg
Doncaster R v Preston NE
Exeter C v Lincoln C
Fulham v Hereford U
Hartlepool U v Gillingham
Leyton Orient v Wigan Ath
Mansfield T v Bury
Northampton T v Barnet
Rochdale v Cambridge U
Scarborough v Chester C
Torquay U v Scunthorpe U

Sunday 29 October 1995

FA Carling Premiership
Tottenham H v Newcastle U

Monday 30 October 1995

FA Carling Premiership
Bolton W v Arsenal

Endsleigh League Division 3
Doncaster R v Cambridge U

Tuesday 31 October 1995

Endsleigh League Division 2
AFC Bournemouth v Swindon T
Blackpool v Bristol R
Bradford C v Walsall
Brighton & HA v Swansea C
Bristol C v Chesterfield
Crewe Alex v Hull C
Notts Co v Brentford
Peterborough U v Burnley
Shrewsbury T v Oxford U
Stockport Co v Rotherham U
Wrexham v Carlisle U
Wycombe W v York C

Endsleigh League Division 3
Cardiff C v Scunthorpe U
Darlington v Wigan Ath
Exeter C v Gillingham
Fulham v Colchester U
Hartlepool U v Barnet
Leyton Orient v Hereford U
Mansfield T v Lincoln C
Northampton T v Preston NE
Rochdale v Chester C
Scarborough v Plymouth Arg
Torquay U v Bury

Saturday 4 November 1995

FA Carling Premiership
Arsenal v Manchester U
Chelsea v Sheffield W
Coventry C v Tottenham H
Manchester C v Bolton W
Middlesbrough v Leeds U
Newcastle U v Liverpool
Nottingham F v Wimbledon
Southampton v QPR
West Ham U v Aston Villa

Endsleigh League Division 1
Barnsley v Wolverhampton W
Birmingham C v Millwall
Charlton Ath v Sunderland
Crystal Palace v Reading
Huddersfield T v Norwich C
Ipswich T v Grimsby T
Oldham Ath v Port Vale
Sheffield U v Portsmouth
Stoke C v Luton T
Tranmere R v Derby Co
Watford v Southend U
WBA v Leicester C

Endsleigh League Division 2
Brentford v Shrewsbury T
Bristol R v Peterborough U
Burnley v Notts Co
Carlisle U v Brighton & HA
Chesterfield v Bradford C
Hull C v Wrexham
Oxford U v Bristol C
Rotherham U v Crewe Alex
Swansea C v Wycombe W
Swindon T v Blackpool
Walsall v AFC Bournemouth
York C v Stockport Co

Endsleigh League Division 3
Barnet v Doncaster R
Bury v Darlington
Cambridge U v Scarborough
Chester C v Torquay U
Colchester U v Exeter C
Gillingham v Northampton T
Hereford U v Mansfield T
Lincoln C v Hartlepool U
Plymouth Arg v Cardiff C
Preston NE v Leyton Orient
Scunthorpe U v Rochdale
Wigan Ath v Fulham

Sunday 5 November 1995

FA Carling Premiership
Everton v Blackburn R

Wednesday 8 November 1995

FA Carling Premiership
Newcastle U v Blackburn R

Saturday 11 November 1995

Endsleigh League Division 1
Derby Co v WBA
Grimsby T v Barnsley
Leicester C v Watford
Luton T v Oldham Ath
Millwall v Ipswich T
Norwich C v Crystal Palace
Port Vale v Sheffield U
Portsmouth v Huddersfield T
Reading v Birmingham C
Southend U v Stoke C
Sunderland v Tranmere R
Wolverhampton W v Charlton Ath

Saturday 18 November 1995

FA Carling Premiership
Aston Villa v Newcastle U
Blackburn R v Nottingham F
Bolton W v West Ham U
Leeds U v Chelsea
Liverpool v Everton
Manchester U v Southampton
Sheffield W v Manchester C
Tottenham H v Arsenal
Wimbledon v Middlesbrough

Endsleigh League Division 1
Derby Co v Charlton Ath
Grimsby T v WBA
Leicester C v Tranmere R
Luton T v Birmingham C
Millwall v Huddersfield T
Norwich C v Ipswich T
Port Vale v Watford
Portsmouth v Stoke C
Reading v Barnsley
Southend U v Crystal Palace
Sunderland v Sheffield U
Wolverhampton W v Oldham Ath

Endsleigh League Division 2
AFC Bournemouth v Brentford
Blackpool v York C
Bradford C v Hull C
Brighton & HA v Walsall
Bristol C v Carlisle U
Crewe Alex v Swansea C
Notts Co v Chesterfield
Peterborough U v Oxford U
Shrewsbury T v Burnley
Stockport Co v Swindon T
Wrexham v Rotherham U
Wycombe W v Bristol R

Endsleigh League Division 3
Cardiff C v Bury
Darlington v Scunthorpe U
Doncaster R v Colchester U
Exeter C v Preston NE
Fulham v Barnet
Hartlepool U v Plymouth Arg
Leyton Orient v Cambridge U
Mansfield T v Chester C
Northampton T v Wigan Ath

Rochdale v Hereford U
Scarborough v Gillingham
Torquay U v Lincoln C

Sunday 19 November 1995

FA Carling Premiership
QPR v Coventry C

Monday 20 November 1995

FA Carling Premiership
Southampton v Aston Villa

Tuesday 21 November 1995

FA Carling Premiership
Arsenal v Sheffield W
Middlesbrough v Tottenham H

Endsleigh League Division 1
Barnsley v Portsmouth
Birmingham C v Derby Co
Charlton Ath v Reading
Crystal Palace v Wolverhampton W
Huddersfield T v Leicester C
Ipswich T v Southend U
Oldham Ath v Millwall
Sheffield U v Grimsby T
Tranmere R v Port Vale
Watford v Luton T
WBA v Norwich C

Wednesday 22 November 1995

FA Carling Premiership
Chelsea v Bolton W
Coventry C v Manchester U
Everton v QPR
Manchester C v Wimbledon
Nottingham F v Leeds U
West Ham U v Liverpool

Endsleigh League Division 1
Stoke C v Sunderland

Saturday 25 November 1995

FA Carling Premiership
Chelsea v Tottenham H
Coventry C v Wimbledon
Everton v Sheffield W
Manchester C v Aston Villa
Middlesbrough v Liverpool
Newcastle U v Leeds U
Nottingham F v Manchester U
Southampton v Bolton W
West Ham U v QPR

Endsleigh League Division 1
Barnsley v Luton T
Birmingham C v Leicester C
Charlton Ath v Port Vale
Crystal Palace v Derby Co
Huddersfield T v Wolverhampton W
Ipswich T v Portsmouth
Oldham Ath v Southend U
Sheffield U v Reading
Stoke C v Millwall
Tranmere R v Grimsby T
Watford v Norwich C
WBA v Sunderland

Endsleigh League Division 2
Brentford v Bradford C
Bristol R v Stockport Co
Burnley v Wrexham
Carlisle U v Wycombe W
Chesterfield v AFC Bournemouth
Hull C v Peterborough U
Oxford U v Crewe Alex
Rotherham U v Bristol C
Swansea C v Notts Co
Swindon T v Shrewsbury T
Walsall v Blackpool
York C v Brighton & HA

Endsleigh League Division 3
Barnet v Leyton Orient
Bury v Exeter C
Cambridge U v Torquay U
Chester C v Darlington
Colchester U v Mansfield T
Gillingham v Fulham
Lincoln C v Northampton T
Plymouth Arg v Rochdale
Preston NE v Hartlepool U
Scunthorpe U v Scarborough
Wigan Ath v Doncaster R

Sunday 26 November 1995

FA Carling Premiership
Arsenal v Blackburn R

Endsleigh League Division 3
Hereford U v Cardiff C

Saturday 2 December 1995

FA Carling Premiership
Aston Villa v Arsenal
Blackburn R v West Ham U
Bolton W v Nottingham F
Leeds U v Manchester C
Liverpool v Southampton
Manchester U v Chelsea
QPR v Middlesbrough
Tottenham H v Everton

Endsleigh League Division 1
Derby Co v Sheffield U
Grimsby T v Charlton Ath
Leicester C v Barnsley
Luton T v Tranmere R
Millwall v Watford
Norwich C v Stoke C
Port Vale v Huddersfield T
Portsmouth v Oldham Ath
Reading v WBA
Southend U v Birmingham C
Sunderland v Crystal Palace
Wolverhampton W v Ipswich T

Sunday 3 December 1995

FA Carling Premiership
Wimbledon v Newcastle U

Monday 4 December 1995

FA Carling Premiership
Sheffield W v Coventry C

Tuesday 5 December 1995

Endsleigh League Division 1
Millwall v Charlton Ath

Saturday 9 December 1995

FA Carling Premiership
Bolton W v Liverpool
Chelsea v Newcastle U
Coventry C v Blackburn R
Everton v West Ham U
Leeds U v Wimbledon
Manchester U v Sheffield W
Middlesbrough v Manchester C
Southampton v Arsenal
Tottenham H v QPR

Endsleigh League Division 1
Birmingham C v Watford
Charlton Ath v Ipswich T
Crystal Palace v Oldham Ath
Derby Co v Barnsley
Luton T v Wolverhampton W
Norwich C v Grimsby T
Port Vale v Reading
Sheffield U v Huddersfield T
Southend U v Leicester C
Sunderland v Millwall
Tranmere R v Portsmouth
WBA v Stoke C

Endsleigh League Division 2
Bradford C v Peterborough U
Brentford v Bristol R
Brighton & HA v AFC Bourne-
mouth
Bristol C v Notts Co
Burnley v Chesterfield
Crewe Alex v Blackpool
Hull C v Carlisle U
Oxford U v Swansea C
Rotherham U v Swindon T
Stockport Co v Shrewsbury T
Walsall v York C
Wrexham v Wycombe W

Endsleigh League Division 3
Barnet v Bury
Cambridge U v Lincoln C
Cardiff C v Hartlepool U
Gillingham v Chester C
Hereford U v Colchester U
Leyton Orient v Exeter C
Northampton T v Torquay U
Plymouth Arg v Wigan Ath
Preston NE v Fulham
Rochdale v Doncaster R
Scarborough v Darlington
Scunthorpe U v Mansfield T

Sunday 10 December 1995

FA Carling Premiership
Nottingham F v Aston Villa

Saturday 16 December 1995

FA Carling Premiership
Arsenal v Chelsea
Aston Villa v Coventry C
Blackburn R v Middlesbrough
Manchester C v Nottingham F
Newcastle U v Everton
QPR v Bolton W
Sheffield W v Leeds U
West Ham U v Southampton
Wimbledon v Tottenham H

Endsleigh League Division 1
Barnsley v Charlton Ath
Grimsby T v Southend U
Huddersfield T v WBA
Ipswich T v Sheffield U
Leicester C v Norwich C
Millwall v Derby Co
Oldham Ath v Birmingham C
Portsmouth v Luton T
Reading v Sunderland
Stoke C v Crystal Palace
Watford v Tranmere R
Wolverhampton W v Port Vale

Endsleigh League Division 2
AFC Bournemouth v Stockport Co
Blackpool v Bradford C
Bristol R v Oxford U
Carlisle U v Walsall
Chesterfield v Brentford
Notts Co v Crewe Alex
Peterborough U v Rotherham U
Shrewsbury T v Brighton & HA
Swansea C v Burnley
Swindon T v Wrexham
Wycombe W v Bristol C
York C v Hull C

Endsleigh League Division 3
Bury v Gillingham
Chester C v Preston NE
Colchester U v Scunthorpe U
Darlington v Barnet
Doncaster R v Leyton Orient
Exeter C v Rochdale
Fulham v Northampton T
Hartlepool U v Cambridge U
Lincoln C v Plymouth Arg
Mansfield T v Cardiff C

Torquay U v Scarborough
Wigan Ath v Hereford U

Sunday 17 December 1995

FA Carling Premiership
Liverpool v Manchester U

Tuesday 19 December 1995

Endsleigh League Division 2
Peterborough U v Stockport Co

Endsleigh League Division 3
Hereford U v Scunthorpe U

Wednesday 20 December 1995

Endsleigh League Division 1
Southend U v Port Vale
Stoke C v Sheffield U

Friday 22 December 1995

Endsleigh League Division 1
Ipswich T v Barnsley

Endsleigh League Division 2
Brighton & HA v Chesterfield
Carlisle U v York C
Notts Co v Blackpool
Wrexham v Brentford

Endsleigh League Division 3
Doncaster R v Exeter C
Leyton Orient v Rochdale

Saturday 23 December 1995

FA Carling Premiership
Coventry C v Everton
Liverpool v Arsenal
Manchester C v Chelsea
Middlesbrough v West Ham U
Newcastle U v Nottingham F
QPR v Aston Villa
Sheffield W v Southampton
Tottenham H v Bolton W
Wimbledon v Blackburn R

Endsleigh League Division 1
Birmingham C v Tranmere R
Derby Co v Sunderland
Grimsby T v Leicester C
Luton T v Huddersfield T
Oldham Ath v Watford
Portsmouth v Norwich C
Reading v Wolverhampton W
WBA v Crystal Palace

Endsleigh League Division 2
AFC Bournemouth v Hull C
Bradford C v Oxford U
Bristol R v Crewe Alex
Burnley v Bristol C
Swansea C v Rotherham U
Walsall v Swindon T
Wycombe W v Shrewsbury T

Endsleigh League Division 3
Bury v Colchester U
Chester C v Barnet
Fulham v Cardiff C
Mansfield T v Hartlepool U
Plymouth Arg v Cambridge U
Preston NE v Gillingham
Scarborough v Northampton T
Torquay U v Darlington
Wigan Ath v Lincoln C

Sunday 24 December 1995

FA Carling Premiership
Leeds U v Manchester U

Tuesday 26 December 1995

FA Carling Premiership
Arsenal v QPR
Aston Villa v Liverpool
Blackburn R v Manchester C
Chelsea v Wimbledon
Everton v Middlesbrough
Manchester U v Newcastle U
Nottingham F v Sheffield W
Southampton v Tottenham H
West Ham U v Coventry C

Endsleigh League Division 1
Barnsley v Stoke C
Charlton Ath v Portsmouth
Crystal Palace v Luton T
Huddersfield T v Derby Co
Leicester C v Ipswich T
Norwich C v Southend U
Port Vale v WBA
Sheffield U v Birmingham C
Sunderland v Grimsby T
Tranmere R v Oldham Ath
Watford v Reading
Wolverhampton W v Millwall

Endsleigh League Division 2
Blackpool v Burnley
Brentford v Brighton & HA
Bristol C v Swansea C
Chesterfield v Peterborough U
Crewe Alex v Wrexham
Hull C v Notts Co
Oxford U v AFC Bournemouth
Rotherham U v Walsall
Shrewsbury T v Bristol R
Stockport Co v Carlisle U
Swindon T v Wycombe W
York C v Bradford C

Endsleigh League Division 3
Barnet v Mansfield T
Cambridge U v Wigan Ath
Cardiff C v Chester C
Colchester U v Leyton Orient
Darlington v Doncaster R
Exeter C v Torquay U
Gillingham v Plymouth Arg
Hartlepool U v Scarborough
Lincoln C v Fulham
Northampton T v Hereford U
Rochdale v Preston NE
Scunthorpe U v Bury

Wednesday 27 December 1995

FA Carling Premiership
Bolton W v Leeds U

Saturday 30 December 1995

FA Carling Premiership
Arsenal v Wimbledon
Aston Villa v Sheffield W
Blackburn R v Tottenham H
Bolton W v Coventry C
Chelsea v Liverpool
Everton v Leeds U
Manchester U v QPR
Nottingham F v Middlesbrough
Southampton v Manchester C
West Ham U v Newcastle U

Endsleigh League Division 1
Barnsley v WBA
Charlton Ath v Southend U
Crystal Palace v Grimsby T
Huddersfield T v Stoke C
Leicester C v Oldham Ath
Norwich C v Reading
Port Vale v Luton T
Sheffield U v Millwall
Sunderland v Birmingham C
Tranmere R v Ipswich T
Watford v Derby Co
Wolverhampton W v Portsmouth

Endsleigh League Division 2
Blackpool v Swansea C
Brentford v Wycombe W
Bristol C v Bristol R
Chesterfield v Walsall
Crewe Alex v Peterborough U
Hull C v Brighton & HA
Oxford U v Notts Co
Rotherham U v Bradford C
Shrewsbury T v Carlisle U
Stockport Co v Wrexham
Swindon T v Burnley
York C v AFC Bournemouth

Endsleigh League Division 3
Barnet v Torquay U
Cambridge U v Fulham
Cardiff C v Wigan Ath
Colchester U v Scarborough
Darlington v Preston NE
Exeter C v Chester C
Gillingham v Mansfield T
Hartlepool U v Hereford U
Lincoln C v Leyton Orient
Northampton T v Plymouth Arg
Rochdale v Bury
Scunthorpe U v Doncaster R

Monday 1 January 1996

FA Carling Premiership
Coventry C v Southampton
Leeds U v Blackburn R
Liverpool v Nottingham F
Manchester C v West Ham U
Middlesbrough v Aston Villa
Sheffield W v Bolton W
Tottenham H v Manchester U
Wimbledon v Everton

Endsleigh League Division 1
Birmingham C v Wolverhampton W
Derby Co v Norwich C
Grimsby T v Huddersfield T
Ipswich T v Port Vale
Luton T v Sheffield U
Millwall v Leicester C
Oldham Ath v Sunderland
Portsmouth v Crystal Palace
Reading v Tranmere R
Southend U v Barnsley
Stoke C v Charlton Ath
WBA v Watford

Endsleigh League Division 2
AFC Bournemouth v Shrewsbury T
Bradford C v Crewe Alex
Brighton & HA v Stockport Co
Bristol R v Chesterfield
Burnley v Oxford U
Carlisle U v Blackpool
Notts Co v York C
Peterborough U v Swindon T
Swansea C v Brentford
Walsall v Hull C
Wrexham v Bristol C
Wycombe W v Rotherham U

Endsleigh League Division 3
Bury v Hartlepool U
Chester C v Northampton T
Darlington v Hereford U
Doncaster R v Lincoln C
Fulham v Scunthorpe U
Hereford U v Darlington (*postponed*)
Leyton Orient v Gillingham
Mansfield T v Cambridge U
Plymouth Arg v Exeter C
Preston NE v Cardiff C
Scarborough v Barnet
Torquay U v Colchester U

Tuesday 2 January 1996

FA Carling Premiership
Newcastle U v Arsenal

QPR v Chelsea

Endsleigh League Division 3
Wigan Ath v Rochdale

Saturday 6 January 1996

Endsleigh League Division 2
AFC Bournemouth v Bristol C
Blackpool v Wycombe W
Brentford v Carlisle U
Brighton & HA v Oxford U
Bristol R v Hull C
Chesterfield v Wrexham
Crewe Alex v Burnley
Notts Co v Walsall
Rotherham U v York C
Shrewsbury T v Peterborough U
Stockport Co v Bradford C
Swindon T v Swansea C

Endsleigh League Division 3
Barnet v Preston NE
Bury v Doncaster R
Cambridge U v Chester C
Cardiff C v Leyton Orient
Darlington v Northampton T
Hartlepool U v Fulham
Lincoln C v Hereford U
Mansfield T v Exeter C
Plymouth Arg v Scunthorpe U
Scarborough v Rochdale
Torquay U v Gillingham
Wigan Ath v Colchester U

Saturday 13 January 1996

FA Carling Premiership
Bolton W v Wimbledon
Coventry C v Newcastle U
Everton v Chelsea
Leeds U v West Ham U
Manchester U v Aston Villa
Middlesbrough v Arsenal
Nottingham F v Southampton
QPR v Blackburn R
Sheffield W v Liverpool
Tottenham H v Manchester C

Endsleigh League Division 1
Birmingham C v Charlton Ath
Crystal Palace v Ipswich T
Derby Co v Reading
Luton T v Southend U
Millwall v Port Vale
Oldham Ath v Barnsley
Portsmouth v Grimsby T
Stoke C v Leicester C
Sunderland v Norwich C
Tranmere R v Sheffield U
Watford v Huddersfield T
WBA v Wolverhampton W

Endsleigh League Division 2
Bradford C v Brighton & HA
Bristol C v Crewe Alex
Burnley v Stockport Co
Carlisle U v Chesterfield
Hull C v Rotherham U
Oxford U v Brentford
Peterborough U v AFC Bournemouth
Swansea C v Bristol R
Walsall v Shrewsbury T
Wrexham v Blackpool
Wycombe W v Notts Co
York C v Swindon T

Endsleigh League Division 3
Chester C v Bury
Colchester U v Barnet
Doncaster R v Torquay U
Exeter C v Hartlepool U
Fulham v Scarborough
Gillingham v Lincoln C
Hereford U v Cambridge U
Leyton Orient v Mansfield T
Northampton T v Cardiff C
Preston NE v Plymouth Arg
Rochdale v Darlington
Scunthorpe U v Wigan Ath

Saturday 20 January 1996

FA Carling Premiership
Arsenal v Everton
Aston Villa v Tottenham H
Blackburn R v Sheffield W
Chelsea v Nottingham F
Liverpool v Leeds U
Manchester C v Coventry C
Newcastle U v Bolton W
Southampton v Middlesbrough
West Ham U v Manchester U
Wimbledon v QPR

Endsleigh League Division 1
Barnsley v Crystal Palace
Charlton Ath v WBA
Grimsby T v Millwall
Huddersfield T v Oldham Ath
Ipswich T v Birmingham C
Leicester C v Sunderland
Norwich C v Luton T
Port Vale v Derby Co
Reading v Stoke C
Sheffield U v Watford
Southend U v Portsmouth
Wolverhampton W v Tranmere R

Endsleigh League Division 2
AFC Bournemouth v Bradford C
Blackpool v Bristol C
Brentford v York C
Brighton & HA v Peterborough U
Bristol R v Carlisle U
Chesterfield v Oxford U
Crewe Alex v Wycombe W
Notts Co v Wrexham
Rotherham U v Burnley
Shrewsbury T v Swansea C
Stockport Co v Walsall
Swindon T v Hull C

Endsleigh League Division 3
Barnet v Hereford U
Bury v Northampton T
Cambridge U v Scunthorpe U
Cardiff C v Rochdale
Darlington v Exeter C
Hartlepool U v Chester C
Lincoln C v Preston NE
Mansfield T v Fulham
Plymouth Arg v Colchester U
Scarborough v Doncaster R
Torquay U v Leyton Orient
Wigan Ath v Gillingham

Saturday 27 January 1996

Endsleigh League Division 2
Bradford C v Notts Co
Bristol C v Shrewsbury T
Burnley v Bristol R
Carlisle U v Rotherham U
Hull C v Brentford
Oxford U v Swindon T
Peterborough U v Blackpool
Swansea C v Stockport Co
Walsall v Crewe Alex
Wrexham v AFC Bournemouth
Wycombe W v Brighton & HA
York C v Chesterfield

Endsleigh League Division 3
Chester C v Wigan Ath
Colchester U v Cambridge U
Doncaster R v Mansfield T
Exeter C v Cardiff C
Fulham v Darlington
Gillingham v Barnet
Hereford U v Plymouth Arg
Leyton Orient v Scarborough
Northampton T v Hartlepool U
Preston NE v Bury
Rochdale v Torquay U
Scunthorpe U v Lincoln C

Saturday 3 February 1996

FA Carling Premiership
Arsenal v Coventry C
Aston Villa v Leeds U
Blackburn R v Bolton W
Chelsea v Middlesbrough
Liverpool v Tottenham H
Manchester C v QPR
Newcastle U v Sheffield W
Southampton v Everton
West Ham U v Nottingham F
Wimbledon v Manchester U

Endsleigh League Division 1
Barnsley v Watford
Charlton Ath v Crystal Palace
Grimsby T v Derby Co
Huddersfield T v Tranmere R
Ipswich T v WBA
Leicester C v Luton T
Norwich C v Birmingham C
Port Vale v Stoke C
Reading v Portsmouth
Sheffield U v Oldham Ath
Southend U v Millwall
Wolverhampton W v Sunderland

Endsleigh League Division 2
AFC Bournemouth v Wycombe W
Blackpool v Hull C
Brentford v Burnley
Brighton & HA v Wrexham
Bristol R v Walsall
Chesterfield v Swansea C
Crewe Alex v York C
Notts Co v Peterborough U
Rotherham U v Oxford U
Shrewsbury T v Bradford C
Stockport Co v Bristol C
Swindon T v Carlisle U

Endsleigh League Division 3
Barnet v Scunthorpe U
Bury v Hereford U
Cambridge U v Gillingham
Cardiff C v Doncaster R
Darlington v Leyton Orient
Hartlepool U v Rochdale
Lincoln C v Colchester U
Mansfield T v Northampton T
Plymouth Arg v Chester C
Scarborough v Exeter C
Torquay U v Fulham
Wigan Ath v Preston NE

Saturday 10 February 1996

FA Carling Premiership
Bolton W v Aston Villa
Coventry C v Chelsea
Everton v Manchester C
Leeds U v Southampton
Manchester U v Blackburn R
Middlesbrough v Newcastle U
Nottingham F v Arsenal
QPR v Liverpool
Sheffield W v Wimbledon
Tottenham H v West Ham U

Endsleigh League Division 1
Birmingham C v Huddersfield T
Crystal Palace v Sheffield U
Derby Co v Wolverhampton W
Luton T v Grimsby T
Millwall v Reading
Oldham Ath v Norwich C
Portsmouth v Leicester C
Stoke C v Ipswich T
Sunderland v Port Vale
Tranmere R v Barnsley

Watford v Charlton Ath
WBA v Southend U

Endsleigh League Division 2
Bradford C v Stockport Co
Bristol C v AFC Bournemouth
Burnley v Crewe Alex
Carlisle U v Brentford
Hull C v Bristol R
Oxford U v Brighton & HA
Peterborough U v Shrewsbury T
Swansea C v Swindon T
Walsall v Notts Co
Wrexham v Chesterfield
Wycombe W v Blackpool
York C v Rotherham U

Endsleigh League Division 3
Chester C v Cambridge U
Colchester U v Wigan Ath
Doncaster R v Bury
Exeter C v Mansfield T
Fulham v Hartlepool U
Gillingham v Torquay U
Hereford U v Lincoln C
Leyton Orient v Cardiff C
Northampton T v Darlington
Preston NE v Barnet
Rochdale v Scarborough
Scunthorpe U v Plymouth Arg

Saturday 17 February 1996

FA Carling Premiership
Arsenal v Manchester C
Aston Villa v Blackburn R
Chelsea v West Ham U
Leeds U v Tottenham H
Liverpool v Wimbledon
Manchester U v Everton
Middlesbrough v Bolton W
Newcastle U v Southampton
Nottingham F v Coventry C
Sheffield W v QPR

Endsleigh League Division 1
Barnsley v Huddersfield T
Charlton Ath v Sheffield U
Crystal Palace v Watford
Grimsby T v Reading
Ipswich T v Oldham Ath
Leicester C v Port Vale
Luton T v Millwall
Norwich C v Wolverhampton W
Portsmouth v Sunderland
Southend U v Derby Co
Stoke C v Birmingham C
WBA v Tranmere R

Endsleigh League Division 2
AFC Bournemouth v Blackpool
Bradford C v Swindon T
Brentford v Bristol C
Brighton & HA v Crewe Alex
Bristol R v Rotherham U
Burnley v York C
Chesterfield v Wycombe W
Oxford U v Walsall
Peterborough U v Carlisle U
Shrewsbury T v Wrexham
Stockport Co v Notts Co
Swansea C v Hull C

Endsleigh League Division 3
Barnet v Wigan Ath
Bury v Lincoln C
Chester C v Scunthorpe U
Darlington v Mansfield T
Doncaster R v Plymouth Arg
Exeter C v Cambridge U
Gillingham v Hereford U
Leyton Orient v Northampton T
Preston NE v Colchester U
Rochdale v Fulham
Scarborough v Cardiff C
Torquay U v Hartlepool U

Tuesday 20 February 1996

Endsleigh League Division 1
Birmingham C v Barnsley
Huddersfield T v Charlton Ath
Oldham Ath v Stoke C
Port Vale v Norwich C
Reading v Southend U
Sheffield U v WBA
Sunderland v Ipswich T
Tranmere R v Crystal Palace
Watford v Grimsby T

Endsleigh League Division 2
Blackpool v Shrewsbury T
Bristol C v Peterborough U
Carlisle U v Swansea C
Crewe Alex v Stockport Co
Hull C v Chesterfield
Notts Co v Brighton & HA
Rotherham U v AFC Bournemouth
Walsall v Burnley
Wrexham v Bristol R
Wycombe W v Bradford C
York C v Oxford U

Endsleigh League Division 3
Cambridge U v Preston NE
Cardiff C v Darlington
Colchester U v Gillingham
Fulham v Leyton Orient
Hartlepool U v Doncaster R
Hereford U v Chester C
Lincoln C v Barnet
Mansfield T v Torquay U
Northampton T v Rochdale
Plymouth Arg v Bury
Scunthorpe U v Exeter C
Wigan Ath v Scarborough

Wednesday 21 February 1996

Endsleigh League Division 1
Derby Co v Luton T
Millwall v Portsmouth
Wolverhampton W v Leicester C

Endsleigh League Division 2
Swindon T v Brentford

Saturday 24 February 1996

FA Carling Premiership
Blackburn R v Liverpool
Bolton W v Manchester U
Coventry C v Middlesbrough
Everton v Nottingham F
Manchester C v Newcastle U
QPR v Leeds U
Southampton v Chelsea
Tottenham H v Sheffield W
West Ham U v Arsenal
Wimbledon v Aston Villa

Endsleigh League Division 1
Birmingham C v WBA
Derby Co v Portsmouth
Huddersfield T v Crystal Palace
Millwall v Norwich C
Oldham Ath v Charlton Ath
Port Vale v Grimsby T
Reading v Leicester C
Sheffield U v Barnsley
Sunderland v Luton T
Tranmere R v Stoke C
Watford v Ipswich T
Wolverhampton W v Southend U

Endsleigh League Division 2
Blackpool v Brighton & HA
Bristol C v Bradford C
Carlisle U v Oxford U
Crewe Alex v AFC Bournemouth
Hull C v Burnley
Notts Co v Shrewsbury T
Rotherham U v Chesterfield
Swindon T v Bristol R
Walsall v Brentford
Wrexham v Peterborough U
Wycombe W v Stockport Co
York C v Swansea C

Endsleigh League Division 3
Cambridge U v Bury
Cardiff C v Gillingham
Colchester U v Darlington
Fulham v Exeter C
Hartlepool U v Leyton Orient
Hereford U v Scarborough
Lincoln C v Chester C
Mansfield T v Rochdale
Northampton T v Doncaster R
Plymouth Arg v Barnet
Scunthorpe U v Preston NE
Wigan Ath v Torquay U

Monday 26 February 1996

Endsleigh League Division 3
Doncaster R v Fulham

Tuesday 27 February 1996

Endsleigh League Division 1
Barnsley v Millwall
Charlton Ath v Tranmere R
Crystal Palace v Birmingham C
Grimsby T v Wolverhampton W
Ipswich T v Huddersfield T
Luton T v Reading
Southend U v Sunderland
WBA v Oldham Ath

Endsleigh League Division 2
AFC Bournemouth v Notts Co
Bradford C v Wrexham
Brentford v Rotherham U
Brighton & HA v Bristol C
Bristol R v York C
Burnley v Carlisle U
Chesterfield v Swindon T
Oxford U v Hull C
Peterborough U v Wycombe W
Shrewsbury T v Crewe Alex
Stockport Co v Blackpool
Swansea C v Walsall

Endsleigh League Division 3
Barnet v Cambridge U
Bury v Wigan Ath
Chester C v Colchester U
Darlington v Hartlepool U
Exeter C v Northampton T
Gillingham v Scunthorpe U
Leyton Orient v Plymouth Arg
Preston NE v Hereford U
Rochdale v Lincoln C
Scarborough v Mansfield T
Torquay U v Cardiff C

Wednesday 28 February 1996

Endsleigh League Division 1
Leicester City v Derby Co
Norwich C v Sheffield U
Portsmouth v Port Vale
Stoke C v Watford

Saturday 2 March 1996

FA Carling Premiership
Coventry C v West Ham U
Leeds U v Bolton W
Liverpool v Aston Villa
Manchester C v Blackburn R
Middlesbrough v Everton
Newcastle U v Manchester U
QPR v Arsenal
Sheffield W v Nottingham F
Tottenham H v Southampton
Wimbledon v Chelsea

Endsleigh League Division 1
Birmingham C v Sheffield U
Derby Co v Huddersfield T
Grimsby T v Sunderland
Ipswich T v Leicester C
Luton T v Crystal Palace
Millwall v Wolverhampton W
Oldham Ath v Tranmere R
Portsmouth v Charlton Ath
Reading v Watford
Southend U v Norwich C
Stoke C v Barnsley
WBA v Port Vale

Endsleigh League Division 2
AFC Bournemouth v Oxford U
Bradford C v York C
Brighton & HA v Brentford
Bristol R v Shrewsbury T
Burnley v Blackpool
Carlisle U v Stockport Co
Notts Co v Hull C
Peterborough U v Chesterfield
Swansea C v Bristol C
Walsall v Rotherham U
Wrexham v Crewe Alex
Wycombe W v Swindon T

Endsleigh League Division 3
Bury v Scunthorpe U
Chester C v Cardiff C
Doncaster R v Darlington
Fulham v Lincoln C
Hereford U v Northampton T
Leyton Orient v Colchester U
Mansfield T v Barnet
Plymouth Arg v Gillingham
Preston NE v Rochdale
Scarborough v Hartlepool U
Torquay U v Exeter C
Wigan Ath v Cambridge U

Saturday 9 March 1996

FA Carling Premiership
Arsenal v Liverpool
Aston Villa v QPR
Blackburn R v Wimbledon
Bolton W v Tottenham H
Chelsea v Manchester C
Everton v Coventry C
Manchester U v Leeds U
Nottingham F v Newcastle U
Southampton v Sheffield W
West Ham U v Middlesbrough

Endsleigh League Division 1
Barnsley v Ipswich T
Charlton Ath v Millwall
Crystal Palace v WBA
Huddersfield T v Luton T
Leicester C v Grimsby T
Norwich C v Portsmouth
Port Vale v Southend U
Sheffield U v Stoke C
Sunderland v Derby Co
Tranmere R v Birmingham C
Watford v Oldham Ath
Wolverhampton W v Reading

Endsleigh League Division 2
Blackpool v Notts Co
Brentford v Wrexham
Bristol C v Burnley
Chesterfield v Brighton & HA
Crewe Alex v Bristol R
Hull C v AFC Bournemouth
Oxford U v Bradford C
Rotherham U v Swansea C
Shrewsbury T v Wycombe W
Stockport Co v Peterborough U
Swindon T v Walsall
York C v Carlisle U

Endsleigh League Division 3
Barnet v Chester C
Cambridge U v Plymouth Arg
Cardiff C v Fulham
Colchester U v Bury
Darlington v Torquay U
Exeter C v Doncaster R
Gillingham v Preston NE
Hartlepool U v Mansfield T
Lincoln C v Wigan Ath
Northampton T v Scarborough
Rochdale v Leyton Orient
Scunthorpe U v Hereford U

Saturday 16 March 1996

FA Carling Premiership
Coventry C v Bolton W
Leeds U v Everton
Liverpool v Chelsea
Manchester C v Southampton
Middlesbrough v Nottingham F
Newcastle U v West Ham U
QPR v Manchester U
Sheffield W v Aston Villa
Tottenham H v Blackburn R
Wimbledon v Arsenal

Endsleigh League Division 1
Birmingham C v Sunderland
Derby Co v Watford
Grimsby T v Crystal Palace
Ipswich T v Tranmere R
Luton T v Port Vale
Millwall v Sheffield U
Oldham Ath v Leicester C
Portsmouth v Wolverhampton W
Reading v Norwich C
Southend U v Charlton Ath
Stoke C v Huddersfield T
WBA v Barnsley

Endsleigh League Division 2
AFC Bournemouth v York C
Bradford C v Rotherham U
Brighton & HA v Hull C
Bristol R v Bristol C
Burnley v Swindon T
Carlisle U v Shrewsbury T
Notts Co v Oxford U
Peterborough U v Crewe Alex
Swansea C v Blackpool
Walsall v Chesterfield
Wrexham v Stockport Co
Wycombe W v Brentford

Endsleigh League Division 3
Bury v Rochdale
Chester C v Exeter C
Doncaster R v Scunthorpe U
Fulham v Cambridge U
Hereford U v Hartlepool U
Leyton Orient v Lincoln C
Mansfield T v Gillingham
Plymouth Arg v Northampton T
Preston NE v Darlington
Scarborough v Colchester U
Torquay U v Barnet
Wigan Ath v Cardiff C

Saturday 23 March 1996

FA Carling Premiership
Arsenal v Newcastle U
Aston Villa v Middlesbrough
Blackburn R v Leeds U
Bolton W v Sheffield W
Chelsea v QPR
Everton v Wimbledon
Manchester U v Tottenham H
Nottingham F v Liverpool
Southampton v Coventry C
West Ham U v Manchester C

Endsleigh League Division 1
Barnsley v Southend U
Charlton Ath v Stoke C
Crystal Palace v Portsmouth
Huddersfield T v Grimsby T
Leicester C v Millwall
Norwich C v Derby Co
Port Vale v Ipswich T
Sheffield U v Luton T
Sunderland v Oldham Ath
Tranmere R v Reading
Watford v WBA
Wolverhampton W v Birmingham C

Endsleigh League Division 2
Blackpool v Carlisle U
Brentford v Swansea C
Bristol C v Wrexham
Chesterfield v Bristol R
Crewe Alex v Bradford C
Hull C v Walsall
Oxford U v Burnley
Rotherham U v Wycombe W
Shrewsbury T v AFC Bournemouth
Stockport Co v Brighton & HA
Swindon T v Peterborough U
York C v Notts Co

Endsleigh League Division 3
Barnet v Scarborough
Cambridge U v Mansfield T
Cardiff C v Preston NE
Colchester U v Torquay U
Darlington v Hereford U (*postponed*)
Exeter C v Plymouth Arg
Gillingham v Leyton Orient
Hartlepool U v Bury
Hereford U v Darlington
Lincoln C v Doncaster R
Northampton T v Chester C
Rochdale v Wigan Ath
Scunthorpe U v Fulham

Saturday 30 March 1996

FA Carling Premiership
Aston Villa v West Ham U
Blackburn R v Everton
Bolton W v Manchester C
Leeds U v Middlesbrough
Liverpool v Newcastle U
Manchester U v Arsenal
QPR v Southampton
Sheffield W v Chelsea
Tottenham H v Coventry C
Wimbledon v Nottingham F

Endsleigh League Division 1
Derby Co v Stoke C
Grimsby T v Birmingham C
Leicester C v Sheffield U
Luton T v Ipswich T
Millwall v Crystal Palace
Norwich C v Charlton Ath
Port Vale v Barnsley
Portsmouth v WBA
Reading v Oldham Ath
Southend U v Tranmere R
Sunderland v Huddersfield T
Wolverhampton W v Watford

Endsleigh League Division 2
AFC Bournemouth v Bristol R
Blackpool v Brentford
Bradford C v Swansea C
Brighton & HA v Rotherham U
Bristol C v Swindon T
Crewe Alex v Chesterfield
Notts Co v Carlisle U
Peterborough U v Walsall
Shrewsbury T v Hull C
Stockport Co v Oxford U
Wrexham v York C
Wycombe W v Burnley

Endsleigh League Division 3
Cardiff C v Cambridge U
Darlington v Lincoln C
Doncaster R v Chester C
Exeter C v Barnet
Fulham v Plymouth Arg
Hartlepool U v Colchester U
Leyton Orient v Bury
Mansfield T v Wigan Ath
Northampton T v Scunthorpe U
Rochdale v Gillingham
Scarborough v Preston NE
Torquay U v Hereford U

Tuesday 2 April 1996

Endsleigh League Division 1
Barnsley v Norwich C
Birmingham C v Portsmouth
Charlton Ath v Leicester C
Crystal Palace v Port Vale
Huddersfield T v Reading
Ipswich T v Derby Co
Oldham Ath v Grimsby T
Sheffield U v Southend U
Tranmere R v Millwall
Watford v Sunderland
WBA v Luton T

Endsleigh League Division 2
Brentford v Stockport Co
Bristol R v Bradford C
Burnley v AFC Bournemouth
Carlisle U v Crewe Alex
Chesterfield v Blackpool
Hull C v Bristol C
Oxford U v Wrexham
Rotherham U v Notts Co
Swansea C v Peterborough U
Walsall v Wycombe W
York C v Shrewsbury T

Endsleigh League Division 3
Barnet v Cardiff C
Bury v Fulham
Cambridge U v Northampton T
Chester C v Leyton Orient
Colchester U v Rochdale
Gillingham v Darlington
Hereford U v Doncaster R
Lincoln C v Scarborough
Plymouth Arg v Mansfield T
Preston NE v Torquay U
Scunthorpe U v Hartlepool U
Wigan Ath v Exeter C

Wednesday 3 April 1996

Endsleigh League Division 1
Stoke C v Wolverhampton W

Endsleigh League Division 2
Swindon T v Brighton & HA

Saturday 6 April 1996

FA Carling Premiership
Arsenal v Leeds U
Chelsea v Aston Villa
Coventry C v Liverpool
Everton v Bolton W
Manchester C v Manchester U
Middlesbrough v Sheffield W
Newcastle U v QPR
Nottingham F v Tottenham H
Southampton v Blackburn R
West Ham U v Wimbledon

Endsleigh League Division 1
Barnsley v Sunderland
Birmingham C v Port Vale
Charlton Ath v Luton T
Crystal Palace v Leicester C
Huddersfield T v Southend U
Ipswich T v Reading
Oldham Ath v Derby Co
Sheffield U v Wolverhampton W
Stoke C v Grimsby T
Tranmere R v Norwich C
Watford v Portsmouth
WBA v Millwall

Endsleigh League Division 2
Brentford v Crewe Alex
Bristol R v Brighton & HA
Burnley v Bradford C
Carlisle U v AFC Bournemouth
Chesterfield v Stockport Co
Hull C v Wycombe W
Oxford U v Blackpool
Rotherham U v Shrewsbury T
Swansea C v Wrexham
Swindon T v Notts Co
Walsall v Bristol C
York C v Peterborough U

Endsleigh League Division 3
Barnet v Northampton T
Bury v Mansfield T
Cambridge U v Rochdale
Chester C v Scarborough
Colchester U v Cardiff C
Gillingham v Hartlepool U
Hereford U v Fulham
Lincoln C v Exeter C
Plymouth Arg v Darlington
Preston NE v Doncaster R
Scunthorpe U v Torquay U
Wigan Ath v Leyton Orient

Monday 8 April 1996

FA Carling Premiership
Aston Villa v Southampton
Blackburn R v Newcastle U
Bolton W v Chelsea
Leeds U v Nottingham F
Liverpool v West Ham U
Manchester U v Coventry C
QPR v Everton
Sheffield W v Arsenal
Tottenham H v Middlesbrough
Wimbledon v Manchester C

Endsleigh League Division 1
Derby Co v Tranmere R
Grimsby T v Ipswich T
Norwich C v Huddersfield T
Port Vale v Oldham Ath
Portsmouth v Sheffield U
Reading v Crystal Palace
Southend U v Watford
Sunderland v Charlton Ath
Wolverhampton W v Barnsley

Endsleigh League Division 2
Blackpool v Rotherham U
Bradford C v Carlisle U
Bristol C v York C
Crewe Alex v Swindon T
Peterborough U v Brentford
Stockport Co v Hull C
Wrexham v Walsall
Wycombe W v Oxford U

Endsleigh League Division 3
Cardiff C v Lincoln C
Darlington v Cambridge U
Doncaster R v Gillingham
Exeter C v Hereford U
Fulham v Chester C
Hartlepool U v Wigan Ath
Leyton Orient v Scunthorpe U
Mansfield T v Preston NE
Northampton T v Colchester U
Rochdale v Barnet
Torquay U v Plymouth Arg

Tuesday 9 April 1996

Endsleigh League Division 1
Leicester C v WBA
Luton T v Stoke C

Endsleigh League Division 2
AFC Bournemouth v Swansea C
Brighton & HA v Burnley
Notts Co v Bristol R
Shrewsbury T v Chesterfield

Endsleigh League Division 3
Scarborough v Bury

Wednesday 10 April 1996

Endsleigh League Division 1
Millwall v Birmingham C

Saturday 13 April 1996

FA Carling Premiership
Arsenal v Tottenham H
Chelsea v Leeds U
Coventry C v QPR
Everton v Liverpool
Manchester C v Sheffield W
Middlesbrough v Wimbledon
Newcastle U v Aston Villa
Nottingham F v Blackburn R
Southampton v Manchester U
West Ham U v Bolton W

Endsleigh League Division 1
Barnsley v Reading
Birmingham C v Luton T
Charlton Ath v Derby Co
Crystal Palace v Southend U
Huddersfield T v Millwall
Ipswich T v Norwich C
Oldham Ath v Wolverhampton W
Sheffield U v Sunderland
Stoke C v Portsmouth
Tranmere R v Leicester C
Watford v Port Vale
WBA v Grimsby T

Endsleigh League Division 2
Brentford v Notts Co
Bristol R v Blackpool
Burnley v Peterborough U
Carlisle U v Wrexham
Chesterfield v Bristol C
Hull C v Crewe Alex
Oxford U v Shrewsbury T
Rotherham U v Stockport Co
Swansea C v Brighton & HA
Swindon T v AFC Bournemouth
Walsall v Bradford C
York C v Wycombe W

Endsleigh League Division 3
Barnet v Hartlepool U
Bury v Torquay U
Cambridge U v Doncaster R
Chester C v Rochdale
Colchester U v Fulham
Gillingham v Exeter C
Hereford U v Leyton Orient
Lincoln C v Mansfield T
Plymouth Arg v Scarborough
Preston NE v Northampton T
Scunthorpe U v Cardiff C
Wigan Ath v Darlington

Saturday 20 April 1996

Endsleigh League Division 1
Derby Co v Birmingham C
Grimsby T v Sheffield U
Leicester C v Huddersfield T
Luton T v Watford
Millwall v Oldham Ath
Norwich C v WBA
Port Vale v Tranmere R
Portsmouth v Barnsley
Reading v Charlton Ath
Southend U v Ipswich T
Sunderland v Stoke C

Wolverhampton W v Crystal Palace

Endsleigh League Division 2
AFC Bournemouth v Walsall
Blackpool v Swindon T
Bradford C v Chesterfield
Brighton & HA v Carlisle U
Bristol C v Oxford U
Crewe Alex v Rotherham U
Notts Co v Burnley
Peterborough U v Bristol R
Shrewsbury T v Brentford
Stockport Co v York C
Wrexham v Hull C
Wycombe W v Swansea C

Endsleigh League Division 3
Cardiff C v Plymouth Arg
Darlington v Bury
Doncaster R v Barnet
Exeter C v Colchester U
Fulham v Wigan Ath
Hartlepool U v Lincoln C
Leyton Orient v Preston NE
Mansfield T v Hereford U
Northampton T v Gillingham
Rochdale v Scunthorpe U
Scarborough v Cambridge U
Torquay U v Chester C

Saturday 27 April 1996

FA Carling Premiership
Aston Villa v Manchester C
Blackburn R v Arsenal
Bolton W v Southampton
Leeds U v Newcastle U
Liverpool v Middlesbrough
Manchester U v Nottingham F
QPR v West Ham U
Sheffield W v Everton
Tottenham H v Chelsea
Wimbledon v Coventry C

Endsleigh League Division 1
Derby Co v Crystal Palace
Grimsby T v Tranmere R
Leicester C v Birmingham C
Luton T v Barnsley
Millwall v Stoke C
Norwich C v Watford
Port Vale v Charlton Ath
Portsmouth v Ipswich T
Reading v Sheffield U
Southend U v Oldham Ath
Sunderland v WBA
Wolverhampton W v Huddersfield T

Endsleigh League Division 2
AFC Bournemouth v Chesterfield
Blackpool v Walsall
Bradford C v Brentford
Brighton & HA v York C
Bristol C v Rotherham U
Crewe Alex v Oxford U
Notts Co v Swansea C
Peterborough U v Hull C
Shrewsbury T v Swindon T
Stockport Co v Bristol R
Wrexham v Burnley
Wycombe W v Carlisle U

Endsleigh League Division 3
Cardiff C v Hereford U
Darlington v Chester C
Doncaster R v Wigan Ath
Exeter C v Bury
Fulham v Gillingham
Hartlepool U v Preston NE
Leyton Orient v Barnet
Mansfield T v Colchester U
Northampton T v Lincoln C
Rochdale v Plymouth Arg
Scarborough v Scunthorpe U
Torquay U v Cambridge U

Saturday 4 May 1996

FA Carling Premiership
Arsenal v Bolton W
Chelsea v Blackburn R
Coventry C v Leeds U
Everton v Aston Villa
Manchester C v Liverpool
Middlesbrough v Manchester U
Newcastle U v Tottenham H
Nottingham F v QPR
Southampton v Wimbledon
West Ham U v Sheffield W

Endsleigh League Division 1
Barnsley v Grimsby T
Birmingham C v Reading
Charlton Ath v Wolverhampton W
Crystal Palace v Norwich C
Huddersfield T v Portsmouth
Ipswich T v Millwall
Oldham Ath v Luton T
Sheffield U v Port Vale
Stoke C v Southend U
Tranmere R v Sunderland
Watford v Leicester C
WBA v Derby Co

Endsleigh League Division 2
Brentford v AFC Bournemouth
Bristol R v Wycombe W
Burnley v Shrewsbury T
Carlisle U v Bristol C
Chesterfield v Notts Co
Hull C v Bradford C
Oxford U v Peterborough U
Rotherham U v Wrexham
Swansea C v Crewe Alex
Swindon T v Stockport Co
Walsall v Brighton & HA
York C v Blackpool

Endsleigh League Division 3
Barnet v Fulham
Bury v Cardiff C
Cambridge U v Leyton Orient
Chester C v Mansfield T
Colchester U v Doncaster R
Gillingham v Scarborough
Hereford U v Rochdale
Lincoln C v Torquay U
Plymouth Arg v Hartlepool U
Preston NE v Exeter C
Scunthorpe U v Darlington
Wigan Ath v Northampton T

FA CARLING PREMIERSHIP FIXTURES 1995–96

	Arsenal	Aston Villa	Blackburn R	Bolton W	Chelsea	Coventry C	Everton	Leeds U	Liverpool	Manchester C	Manchester U	Middlesbrough	Newcastle U	Nottingham F	QPR	Sheffield W	Southampton	Tottenham H	West Ham U	Wimbledon
Arsenal	—	21.10	26.11	4.5	16.12	3.2	20.1	6.4	9.3	17.2	4.11	20.8	23.3	29.8	26.12	21.11	23.9	13.4	16.9	20.12
Aston Villa	2.12	—	17.2	30.8	14.10	16.12	28.10	3.2	26.12	27.4	19.8	23.3	18.11	23.9	9.3	30.12	8.4	20.1	30.3	16.9
Blackburn R	27.4	9.9	—	3.2	28.10	23.9	30.3	23.3	24.2	26.12	28.8	16.12	8.4	18.11	19.8	20.1	14.10	30.12	2.12	9.3
Bolton W	30.10	10.2	26.8	—	8.4	30.12	14.10	27.12	9.12	30.3	24.2	9.9	22.8	2.12	30.9	23.3	27.4	9.3	18.11	13.1
Chelsea	30.9	6.4	4.5	22.11	—	30.8	19.8	13.4	30.12	9.3	21.10	3.2	9.12	20.1	23.3	4.11	16.9	25.11	17.2	26.12
Coventry C	26.8	30.9	9.12	16.3	10.2	—	23.12	4.5	6.4	23.8	22.11	24.2	13.1	9.9	13.4	21.10	1.1	4.11	2.3	25.11
Everton	23.8	4.5	5.11	6.4	13.1	9.3	—	30.12	13.4	10.2	9.9	26.12	1.10	24.2	22.11	25.11	26.8	21.10	9.12	23.3
Leeds U	14.10	26.8	1.1	2.3	18.11	28.10	16.3	—	21.8	2.12	24.12	30.3	27.4	8.4	16.9	30.9	10.2	17.2	13.1	9.12
Liverpool	23.12	2.3	16.9	23.9	16.3	14.10	18.11	20.1	—	28.10	17.12	27.4	30.3	1.1	30.8	19.8	2.12	3.2	8.4	17.2
Manchester C	10.9	25.11	2.3	4.11	23.12	20.1	30.8	21.10	4.5	—	6.4	23.9	24.2	16.12	3.2	13.4	16.3	19.8	1.1	22.11
Manchester U	30.3	13.1	10.2	16.9	2.12	8.4	17.2	9.3	1.10	14.10	—	28.10	26.12	27.4	30.12	9.12	18.11	23.3	23.8	26.8
Middlesbrough	13.1	1.1	30.9	17.2	26.8	16.9	2.3	4.11	25.11	9.12	4.5	—	10.2	16.3	21.10	6.4	12.9	21.11	23.12	13.4
Newcastle U	2.1	13.4	8.11	20.1	24.9	19.8	16.12	25.11	4.11	16.9	2.3	30.8	—	23.12	6.4	3.2	17.2	4.5	16.3	21.10
Nottingham F	10.2	10.12	13.4	21.10	23.8	17.2	17.9	22.11	23.3	30.9	25.11	30.12	9.3	—	4.5	26.12	13.1	6.4	26.8	4.11
QPR	2.3	23.12	13.1	16.12	2.1	19.11	8.4	24.2	10.2	26.8	16.3	2.12	14.10	28.10	—	9.9	30.3	25.9	27.4	23.8
Sheffield W	8.4	16.3	23.8	1.1	30.3	4.12	27.4	16.12	13.1	18.11	23.9	15.10	27.8	2.3	17.2	—	23.12	16.9	28.10	10.2
Southampton	9.12	20.11	6.4	25.11	24.2	23.3	3.2	30.8	22.10	30.12	13.4	20.1	9.9	19.8	4.11	9.3	—	26.12	30.9	4.5
Tottenham H	18.11	23.8	16.3	23.12	27.4	30.3	2.12	9.9	26.8	13.1	1.1	8.4	29.10	14.10	9.12	24.2	2.3	—	10.2	30.9
West Ham U	24.2	4.11	21.10	13.4	11.9	26.12	23.9	19.8	22.11	23.3	20.1	9.3	30.12	3.2	25.11	4.5	16.12	30.8	—	6.4
Wimbledon	16.3	24.2	23.12	19.8	2.3	27.4	1.1	23.9	9.9	8.4	3.2	18.11	3.12	30.3	20.1	30.8	28.10	16.12	16.10	—

ENDSLEIGH INSURANCE FIXTURES 1995–96

DIVISION ONE

	Barnsley	Birmingham C	Charlton Ath	Crystal Palace	Derby Co	Grimsby T	Huddersfield T	Ipswich T	Leicester C	Luton T	Millwall	Norwich C	Oldham Ath	Port Vale	Portsmouth	Reading	Sheffield U	Southend U	Stoke C	Sunderland	Tranmere R	Watford	WBA	Wolverhampton
Barnsley	—	2.9	16.12	20.1	23.9	4.5	17.2	9.3	7.10	25.11	27.2	2.4	19.8	21.10	21.11	13.4	16.9	23.3	26.12	6.4	29.8	3.2	30.12	4.11
Birmingham C	20.2	—	13.1	9.9	21.11	21.10	10.2	12.8	25.11	13.4	4.11	26.8	30.9	6.4	2.4	4.5	2.3	7.10	12.9	16.3	23.12	9.12	24.2	1.1
Charlton Ath	30.9	19.8	—	3.2	13.4	7.10	2.9	9.12	2.4	6.4	9.3	21.10	16.9	25.11	26.12	21.11	17.2	30.12	23.3	4.11	27.2	29.8	20.1	4.5
Crystal Palace	12.8	27.2	26.8	—	25.11	30.12	16.9	13.1	6.4	26.12	21.10	4.5	9.12	2.4	23.3	4.11	10.2	13.4	30.9	7.10	2.9	17.2	9.3	21.11
Derby Co	9.12	20.4	18.11	27.4	—	26.8	2.3	14.10	9.9	21.2	30.9	1.1	28.10	13.8	24.2	13.1	2.12	13.9	30.3	23.12	8.4	16.3	11.11	10.2
Grimsby T	11.11	30.3	2.12	16.3	3.2	—	1.1	8.4	23.12	29.8	20.1	23.9	14.10	16.9	19.8	17.2	20.4	16.12	23.10	2.3	27.4	2.9	18.11	27.2
Huddersfield T	12.9	30.8	20.2	24.2	26.12	23.3	—	9.9	21.11	9.3	13.4	4.11	20.1	7.10	4.5	2.4	23.9	6.4	30.12	21.10	3.2	19.8	16.12	25.11
Ipswich T	22.12	20.1	23.9	19.8	2.4	4.11	27.2	—	2.3	21.10	4.5	13.4	17.2	1.1	25.11	6.4	16.12	21.11	29.8	2.9	16.3	16.9	3.2	7.10
Leicester C	2.12	27.4	14.10	28.10	28.2	9.3	20.4	26.12	—	3.2	23.3	16.12	30.12	17.2	30.8	16.9	30.3	23.9	19.8	20.1	18.11	11.11	9.4	2.9
Luton T	27.4	18.11	28.10	2.3	2.9	10.2	23.12	30.3	26.8	—	17.2	13.8	11.11	16.3	30.9	27.2	1.1	13.1	9.4	16.9	2.12	20.4	14.10	9.12
Millwall	9.9	10.4	5.12	30.3	16.12	12.8	18.11	11.11	1.1	13.9	—	24.2	20.4	13.1	21.2	10.2	16.3	26.8	27.4	23.9	14.10	2.12	28.10	2.3
Norwich C	14.10	3.2	30.3	11.11	23.3	9.12	8.4	18.11	30.9	20.1	16.9	—	30.8	2.9	9.3	30.12	28.2	26.12	2.12	19.8	28.10	27.4	20.4	17.2
Oldham Ath	13.1	16.12	24.2	23.9	6.4	2.4	12.8	12.9	16.3	4.5	21.11	10.2	—	4.11	7.10	21.10	26.8	25.11	20.2	1.1	2.3	23.12	9.9	13.4
Port Vale	30.3	28.10	27.4	14.10	20.1	24.2	2.12	23.3	12.9	30.12	19.8	20.2	8.4	—	9.9	9.12	11.11	9.3	3.2	29.8	20.4	18.11	26.12	30.9
Portsmouth	20.4	14.10	2.3	1.1	16.9	13.1	11.11	27.4	10.2	16.12	2.9	23.12	2.12	28.2	—	26.8	8.4	12.8	18.11	17.2	23.9	28.10	30.3	16.3
Reading	18.11	11.11	20.4	8.4	19.8	12.9	14.10	28.10	24.2	9.9	29.8	16.3	30.3	23.9	3.2	—	27.4	20.2	20.1	16.12	1.1	2.3	2.12	23.12
Sheffield U	24.2	26.12	12.9	29.8	7.10	21.11	9.12	30.9	21.10	23.3	30.12	9.9	3.2	4.5	4.11	25.11	—	2.4	9.3	13.4	19.8	20.1	20.2	6.4
Southend U	1.1	2.12	16.3	18.11	17.2	30.9	28.10	20.4	9.12	19.8	3.2	2.3	27.4	20.12	20.1	2.9	14.10	—	11.11	27.2	30.3	8.4	29.8	16.9
Stoke C	2.3	17.2	1.1	16.12	21.10	6.4	16.3	10.2	13.1	4.11	25.11	7.10	2.9	26.8	13.4	12.8	20.12	4.5	—	22.11	16.9	28.2	23.9	3.4
Sunderland	28.10	30.12	8.4	2.12	9.3	26.12	30.3	20.2	12.8	24.2	9.12	13.1	23.3	10.2	12.9	30.9	18.11	9.9	20.4	—	11.11	14.10	27.4	26.8
Tranmere R	10.2	9.3	9.9	20.2	4.11	25.11	26.8	30.12	13.4	7.10	2.4	6.4	26.12	21.11	9.12	23.3	13.1	21.10	24.2	4.5	—	30.9	12.9	12.8
Watford	26.8	23.9	10.2	12.9	30.12	20.2	13.1	24.2	4.5	21.11	7.10	25.11	9.3	13.4	6.4	26.12	12.8	4.11	9.9	2.4	16.12	—	23.3	21.10
WBA	16.3	16.9	12.8	23.12	4.5	13.4	30.9	26.8	4.11	2.4	6.4	21.11	27.2	2.3	21.10	7.10	2.9	10.2	9.12	25.11	17.2	1.1	—	13.1
Wolverhampton	8.4	23.3	11.11	20.4	30.8	9.9	27.4	2.12	21.2	23.9	26.12	13.9	18.11	16.12	30.12	9.3	28.10	24.2	14.10	3.2	20.1	30.3	20.8	—

ENDSLEIGH INSURANCE FIXTURES 1995–96

DIVISION TWO

	Blackpool	Bournemouth	Bradford C	Brentford	Brighton & HA	Bristol C	Bristol R	Burnley	Carlisle U	Chesterfield	Crewe Alex	Hull C	Notts Co	Oxford U	Peterborough U	Rotherham U	Shrewsbury T	Stockport Co	Swansea C	Swindon T	Walsall	Wrexham	Wycombe W	York C
Blackpool	—	12.9	16.12	30.3	24.2	20.1	31.10	26.12	23.3	14.10	23.9	3.2	9.3	28.10	29.8	8.4	20.2	9.9	30.12	20.4	27.4	19.8	6.1	18.11
Bournemouth	17.2	—	20.1	18.11	23.9	6.1	30.3	14.10	28.10	27.4	16.9	23.12	27.2	2.3	19.8	2.9	1.1	16.12	9.4	31.10	20.4	29.8	3.2	16.3
Bradford C	30.9	12.8	—	27.4	13.1	16.9	14.10	28.10	8.4	20.4	1.1	18.11	27.1	23.12	9.12	16.3	26.8	10.2	30.3	17.2	31.10	27.2	2.9	2.3
Brentford	7.10	4.5	25.11	—	26.12	17.2	9.12	3.2	6.1	30.9	6.4	29.8	13.4	19.8	21.10	27.2	4.11	2.4	23.3	2.9	16.9	9.3	30.12	20.1
Brighton & HA	16.9	9.12	19.8	2.3	—	27.2	28.10	9.4	20.4	22.12	17.2	16.3	2.9	6.1	20.1	30.3	30.9	1.1	31.10	14.10	18.11	3.2	29.8	27.4
Bristol C	12.8	10.2	24.2	12.9	9.9	—	30.12	9.3	18.11	31.10	13.1	14.10	9.12	20.4	20.2	27.4	27.1	26.8	26.12	30.3	28.10	23.3	30.9	8.4
Bristol R	13.4	7.10	2.4	23.9	6.4	16.3	—	29.8	20.1	1.1	23.12	6.1	21.10	16.12	4.11	17.2	2.3	25.11	19.8	16.9	3.2	2.9	4.5	27.2
Burnley	2.3	2.4	6.4	26.8	21.10	23.12	27.1	—	27.2	9.12	10.2	16.9	4.11	1.1	13.4	12.8	4.5	13.1	30.9	16.3	2.9	25.11	7.10	17.2
Carlisle U	1.1	6.4	21.10	10.2	4.11	4.5	12.8	9.9	—	13.1	2.4	23.9	7.10	24.2	12.9	27.1	16.3	2.3	20.2	26.8	16.12	13.4	25.11	22.12
Chesterfield	2.4	25.11	4.11	16.12	9.3	13.4	23.3	23.9	19.8	—	7.10	2.9	4.5	20.1	26.12	16.9	21.10	6.4	3.2	27.2	30.12	6.1	17.2	29.8
Crewe Alex	9.12	24.2	23.3	28.10	12.9	10.10	9.3	6.1	14.10	30.3	—	31.10	30.9	27.4	30.12	20.4	9.9	20.2	18.11	8.4	29.8	26.12	20.1	3.2
Hull C	26.8	9.3	4.5	27.1	30.12	2.4	10.2	24.2	9.12	20.2	13.4	—	26.12	9.9	25.11	13.1	7.10	21.10	12.9	12.8	23.3	4.11	6.4	30.9
Notts Co	22.12	9.9	29.8	31.10	20.2	23.9	9.4	20.4	30.3	18.11	16.12	2.3	—	16.3	3.2	14.10	24.2	12.9	27.4	28.10	6.1	20.1	19.8	1.1
Oxford U	6.4	26.12	9.3	13.1	10.2	4.11	30.9	23.3	16.9	12.8	25.11	27.2	30.12	—	4.5	26.8	13.4	7.10	9.12	27.1	17.2	2.4	21.10	2.9
Peterborough U	27.1	13.1	23.9	8.4	12.8	2.9	20.4	31.10	17.2	2.3	16.3	27.4	26.8	18.11	—	16.12	10.2	19.12	14.10	1.1	30.3	16.9	27.2	28.10
Rotherham U	21.10	20.2	30.12	9.9	7.10	25.11	12.9	20.1	29.8	24.2	4.11	19.8	2.4	3.2	30.9	—	6.4	13.4	9.3	9.12	26.12	4.5	23.3	6.1
Shrewsbury T	2.9	23.3	3.2	20.4	16.12	29.8	26.12	18.11	30.12	9.4	27.2	30.3	16.9	31.10	6.1	28.10	—	23.9	20.1	27.4	19.8	17.2	9.3	14.10
Stockport Co	27.2	30.9	6.1	14.10	23.3	3.2	27.4	19.8	26.12	28.10	2.9	8.4	17.2	30.3	9.3	31.10	9.12	—	29.8	18.11	20.1	30.12	16.9	20.4
Swansea C	16.3	21.10	7.10	1.1	13.4	2.3	13.1	16.12	2.9	26.8	4.5	17.2	25.11	23.9	2.4	23.12	12.8	27.1	—	10.2	27.2	6.4	4.11	16.9
Swindon T	4.11	13.4	13.9	21.2	3.4	7.10	24.2	30.12	3.2	9.9	21.10	20.1	6.4	30.8	23.3	23.9	25.11	4.5	6.1	—	9.3	16.12	26.12	19.8
Walsall	25.11	4.11	13.4	24.2	4.5	6.4	26.8	20.2	30.9	16.3	27.1	1.1	10.2	12.9	7.10	2.3	13.1	12.8	9.9	23.12	—	21.10	2.4	9.12
Wrexham	13.1	27.1	9.9	22.12	26.8	1.1	20.2	27.4	31.10	10.2	2.3	20.4	12.8	14.10	24.2	18.11	12.9	16.3	28.10	30.9	8.4	—	9.12	30.3
Wycombe W	10.2	26.8	20.2	16.3	27.1	16.12	18.11	30.3	27.4	12.9	12.8	28.10	13.1	8.4	9.9	1.1	23.12	24.2	20.4	2.3	14.10	23.9	—	31.10
York C	4.5	30.12	26.12	12.8	25.11	21.10	9.9	12.9	9.3	27.1	26.8	16.12	23.3	20.2	6.4	10.2	2.4	4.11	24.2	13.1	23.9	7.10	13.4	—

ENDSLEIGH INSURANCE FIXTURES 1995–96

DIVISION THREE

	Barnet	Bury	Cambridge U	Cardiff C	Chester C	Colchester U	Darlington	Doncaster R	Exeter C	Fulham	Gillingham	Hartlepool U	Hereford U	Leyton O	Lincoln C	Mansfield T	Northampton T	Plymouth Arg	Preston NE	Rochdale	Scarborough	Scunthorpe U	Torquay U	Wigan Ath
Barnet	—	9.12	27.2	2.4	9.3	19.8	30.9	4.11	7.10	4.5	29.8	13.4	20.1	25.11	2.9	26.12	6.4	16.9	6.1	21.10	23.3	3.2	30.12	17.2
Bury	23.9	—	16.9	4.5	19.8	23.12	4.11	6.1	25.11	2.4	16.12	1.1	3.2	7.10	17.2	6.4	20.1	2.9	29.8	16.3	21.10	2.3	13.4	27.2
Cambridge U	9.9	24.2	—	7.10	6.1	29.8	21.10	13.4	12.9	30.12	3.2	30.9	19.8	4.5	9.12	23.3	2.4	9.3	20.2	6.4	4.11	20.1	25.11	26.12
Cardiff C	14.10	18.11	30.3	—	26.12	28.10	20.2	3.2	29.8	9.3	24.2	9.12	27.4	6.1	8.4	30.9	19.8	20.4	23.3	20.1	12.9	31.10	9.9	30.12
Chester C	23.12	13.1	10.2	2.3	—	27.2	25.11	7.10	16.3	21.10	23.9	12.8	2.9	2.4	16.9	4.5	1.1	26.8	16.12	13.4	6.4	17.2	4.11	27.1
Colchester U	13.1	9.3	27.1	6.4	9.9	—	24.2	4.5	4.11	13.4	20.2	7.10	23.9	26.12	26.8	25.11	21.10	12.8	12.9	2.4	30.12	16.12	23.3	10.2
Darlington	16.12	20.4	8.4	2.9	27.4	16.9	—	26.12	20.1	29.8	14.10	27.2	1.1	3.2	30.3	17.2	6.1	28.10	30.12	19.8	23.9	18.11	9.3	31.10
Doncaster R	20.4	10.2	30.10	26.8	30.3	18.11	2.3	—	22.12	26.2	8.4	2.9	14.10	16.12	1.1	27.1	16.9	17.2	28.10	23.9	12.8	16.3	13.1	27.4
Exeter C	30.3	27.4	17.2	27.1	30.12	20.4	12.8	9.3	—	16.9	31.10	13.1	8.4	23.9	28.10	10.2	27.2	23.3	18.11	16.12	26.8	2.9	26.12	14.10
Fulham	18.11	14.10	16.3	23.12	8.4	31.10	27.1	9.9	24.2	—	27.4	10.2	28.10	20.2	2.3	12.8	16.12	30.3	23.9	12.9	13.1	1.1	26.8	20.4
Gillingham	27.1	30.9	26.8	16.9	9.12	2.9	2.4	21.10	13.4	25.11	—	6.4	17.2	23.3	13.1	30.12	4.11	26.12	9.3	7.10	4.5	27.2	10.2	12.8
Hartlepool U	31.10	23.3	16.12	23.9	20.1	30.3	9.9	20.2	19.8	6.1	28.10	—	30.12	24.2	20.4	9.3	29.8	18.11	27.4	3.2	26.12	14.10	12.9	8.4
Hereford U	12.8	26.8	13.1	26.11	20.2	9.12	23.3	2.4	21.10	6.4	12.9	16.3	—	13.4	10.2	4.11	2.3	27.1	9.9	4.5	24.2	19.12	7.10	30.9
Leyton O	27.4	30.3	18.11	10.2	14.10	2.3	26.8	30.9	9.12	2.9	1.1	16.9	31.10	—	16.3	13.1	17.2	27.2	20.4	22.12	27.1	8.4	12.8	28.10
Lincoln C	20.2	12.9	23.9	21.10	24.2	3.2	7.10	23.3	6.4	26.12	19.8	4.11	6.1	30.12	—	13.4	25.11	16.12	20.1	9.9	2.4	28.8	4.5	9.3
Mansfield T	2.3	28.10	1.1	16.12	18.11	27.4	12.9	29.8	6.1	20.1	16.3	23.12	20.4	19.8	31.10	—	3.2	14.10	8.4	24.2	9.9	23.9	20.2	30.3
Northampton T	28.10	12.8	14.10	13.1	23.3	8.4	10.2	24.2	9.9	30.9	20.4	27.1	26.12	12.9	27.4	26.8	—	30.12	31.10	20.2	9.3	30.3	9.12	18.11
Plymouth Arg	24.2	20.2	23.12	4.11	3.2	20.1	6.4	12.9	1.1	7.10	2.3	4.5	29.8	9.9	30.9	2.4	16.3	—	19.8	25.11	13.4	6.1	21.10	9.12
Preston NE	10.2	27.1	2.9	1.1	30.9	17.2	16.3	6.4	4.5	9.12	23.12	25.11	27.2	4.11	12.8	21.10	13.4	13.1	—	2.3	7.10	16.9	2.4	26.8
Rochdale	8.4	30.12	28.10	12.8	31.10	14.10	13.1	9.12	30.9	17.2	30.3	26.8	18.11	9.3	27.2	16.9	2.9	27.4	26.12	—	10.2	20.4	27.1	23.3
Scarborough	1.1	9.4	20.4	17.2	28.10	16.3	9.12	20.1	3.2	19.8	18.11	2.3	16.9	30.8	14.10	27.2	23.12	31.10	30.3	6.1	—	27.4	30.9	2.9
Scunthorpe U	26.8	26.12	12.8	13.4	12.9	30.9	4.5	30.12	20.2	23.3	9.9	2.4	9.3	21.10	27.1	9.12	7.10	10.2	24.2	4.11	25.11	—	6.4	13.1
Torquay U	16.3	31.10	27.4	27.2	20.4	1.1	23.12	19.8	2.3	3.2	6.1	17.2	30.3	20.1	18.11	2.9	23.9	8.4	14.10	29.8	16.12	28.10	—	16.9
Wigan Ath	12.9	9.9	2.3	16.3	29.8	6.1	13.4	25.11	2.4	4.11	20.1	21.10	16.12	6.4	23.12	7.10	4.5	23.9	3.2	2.1	20.2	19.8	24.2	—

OTHER FIXTURES—SEASON 1995–96

August

9 Wed Euro Comps Prel Rd–1st Leg
12 Sat Commencement of Football League season
13 Sun Littlewoods Pools FA Charity Shield—Wembley Stadium
16 Wed International Date
FL Coca-Cola Cup—1st Rd–1st Leg
19 Sat Commencement of FA Premier League season
23 Wed Euro Comps Prel Rd–2nd Leg
FL Coca-Cola Cup—1st Rd–2nd Leg
26 Sat FA Cup Sponsored by Littlewoods Pools—Prel Rd

September

2 Sat + FA Carlsberg Vase—1st Rd Qual (*ex-Extra Prel Rd*)
Portugal v England (U21)
6 Wed International Date England v Croatia (F)
9 Sat FA Cup Sponsored by Littlewoods Pools—1st Rd Qual
FA Youth Cup—Extra Prel Rd*
13 Wed Euro Comps 1st Rd–1st Leg
16 Sat FA Umbro Trophy—Prel Rd (*if required*)
FA Youth Cup—Prel Rd
17 Sun FA Women's Cup—1st Rd
20 Wed FL Coca-Cola Cup—2nd Rd–1st Leg
23 Sat FA Cup Sponsored by Littlewoods Pools—2nd Rd Qual
24 Sun FA Sunday Cup—Prel Rd (*if required*)
27 Wed Euro Comps 1st Rd–2nd Leg
FL Auto Windscreens Shield—1st Rd–1st Leg
30 Sat FA Carlsberg Vase—2nd Rd Qual (*ex-Prel Rd*)

October

4 Wed FL Coca-Cola Cup—2nd Rd–2nd Leg
7 Sat + FA Cup Sponsored by Littlewoods—3rd Rd Qual
FA Youth Cup—1st Rd Qual
10 Tue Norway v England (U21)
11 Wed Norway v England (F)
14 Sat FA Umbro Trophy—1st Rd Qual
FA County Youth Cup—1st Rd*
15 Sun FA Women's Cup—2nd Rd
18 Wed Euro Comps 2nd Rd–1st Leg
FL Auto Windscreens Shield–1st Rd–2nd Leg
21 Sat FA Cup Sponsored by Littlewoods Pools—4th Rd
FA Youth Cup—2nd Rd Qual*
25 Wed FL Coca-Cola Cup—3rd Rd
28 Sat FA Carlsberg Vase—1st Rd Proper
29 Sun FA Sunday Cup—1st Rd

November

1 Wed Euro Comps 2nd Rd–2nd Leg
4 Sat FA Umbro Trophy—2nd Rd Qual
8 Wed FL Coca-Cola Cup—3rd Rd Poss Replays
FL Auto Windscreens Shield—1st Rd–3rd Leg
11 Sat + FA Cup Sponsored by Littlewoods Pools—1st Rd Proper
12 Sun FA Women's Cup—3rd Rd
14 Tue England v Austria (U21)
FA XI v Northern Premier League
15 Wed England v Switzerland (F)
18 Sat FA Carlsberg Vase—2nd Rd Proper
FA Youth Cup—1st Rd Proper*
19 Sun FA Sunday Cup—2nd Rd
22 Wed Euro Comps 3rd Rd–1st Leg
FA Cup Sponsored by Littlewoods Pools—1st Rd Poss Replays
25 Sat FA Umbro Trophy—3rd Rd Qual
FA County Youth Cup—2nd Rd*
29 Wed FL Coca-Cola Cup—4th Rd
FL Auto Windscreens Shield–2nd Rd

December

2 Sat FA Cup Sponsored by Littlewoods Pools—2nd Rd Proper
3 Sun FA Women's Cup—4th Rd
5 Tue FA XI v Isthmian League
6 Wed Euro Comps 3rd Rd–2nd Leg
9 Sat FA Carlsberg Vase—3rd Rd Proper
FA Youth Cup—2nd Rd Proper*
10 Sun FA Sunday Cup—3rd Rd
12 Tue Draw for Qualifying Competition of 1998 World Cup
13 Wed International Date
FA Cup Sponsored by Littlewoods Pools—2nd Rd Poss Replays
17 Sun Euro '96 Draw
20 Wed FL Coca-Cola Cup—4th Rd Replays

January 1996

6 Sat FA Cup Sponsored by Littlewoods Pools—3rd Rd Proper
9 Tues FA XI v British Students
10 Wed FL Coca-Cola Cup—5th Rd
FL Auto Windscreens Shield—Area Quarter Finals
13 Sat FA Carlsberg Vase—4th Rd Proper
FA Youth Cup—3rd Rd Proper*
FA County Youth Cup—3rd Rd*
14 Sun FA Sunday Cup—4th Rd
16 Tue FA XI v Combined Services
17 Wed FA Cup Sponsored by Littlewoods Pools—3rd Rd Poss Replays
20 Sat FA Umbro Trophy—1st Rd Proper
21 Sun FA Women's Cup—5th Rd
24 Wed International Date (*not UEFA*)
FL Coca-Cola Cup—5th Rd Poss Replays
27 Sat FA Cup Sponsored by Littlewoods Pools—4th Rd Proper
31 Wed FL Auto Windscreens Shield—Area Semi-Finals

February

3 Sat FA Carlsberg Vase—5th Rd Proper
7 Wed International Date (*not UEFA*)
FA Cup Sponsored by Littlewoods Pools—4th Rd Poss Replays
10 Sat FA Umbro Trophy—2nd Rd Proper
11 Sun FA Sunday Cup—5th Rd
FL Coca-Cola Cup—Semi-Final–1st Leg
14 Wed FL Coca-Cola Cup—Semi-Final–1st Leg
17 Sat FA Cup Sponsored by Littlewoods Pools—5th Rd Proper
FA Youth Cup—4th Round Proper*
FA County Youth Cup—4th Rd*
18 Sun FA Women's Cup—6th Rd
21 Wed FL Coca-Cola Cup—Semi Final–2nd Leg
24 Sat FA Carlsberg Vase—6th Rd Proper
25 Sun FL Coca-Cola Cup—Semi Final–2nd Leg
28 Wed FA Cup Sponsored by Littlewoods Pools—5th Rd Poss Replays

March

2 Sat FA Umbro Trophy—3rd Rd Proper
6 Wed Euro Comps Quarter Finals–1st Leg
FL Auto Windscreen Shield—Area Final–1st Leg
9 Sat FA Cup Sponsored by Littlewoods Pools—6th Rd Proper
FA Youth Cup—5th Rd Proper*
13 Wed FL Auto Windscreens Shield—Area Final–2nd Leg
16 Sat FA Carlsberg Vase—Semi-Final–1st Leg
FA County Youth Cup—Semi-Final*
17 Sun FA Sunday Cup—Semi-Finals
20 Wed Euro Comps Quarter Finals–2nd Leg
FA Cup Sponsored by Littlewoods Pools—6th Rd Poss Replays
23 Sat FA Umbro Trophy—4th Rd Proper
FA Carlsberg Vase—Semi-Final–2nd Leg
24 Sun FL Coca-Cola Cup—Final Tie—Wembley Stadium
FA Women's Cup—Semi-Finals
27 Wed International Date
FA Carlsberg Vase—Semi-Final Poss Replays (*prov*)
31 Sun FA Cup Sponsored by Littlewoods Pools—Semi-Finals

April

3 Wed Euro Comps Semi-Finals–1st Leg
FA Cup Sponsored by Littlewoods Pools—Semi-Finals Poss Replays
6 Sat FA Youth Cup—Semi-Final*
13 Sat FA Umbro Trophy—Semi-Final–1st Leg
14 Sun FL Auto Windscreens Shield—Final Tie—Wembley Stadium
17 Wed Euro Comps Semi Finals–2nd Leg
20 Sat + FA Umbro Trophy—Semi-Final–2nd Leg
24 Wed International Date
FA Umbro Trophy—Semi-Final Poss Replays (*prov*)
27 Sat FA County Youth Cup Final (*fixed date*)
28 Sun FA Women's Cup—Final Tie (*venue to be decided*)

May

1 Wed UEFA Cup–1st Leg
4 Sat Final matches in FA Premier & Football League
5 Sun FA Sunday Cup—Final Tie (*venue to be decided*)
8 Wed European Cup Winners Cup Final (*venue to be decided*)
11 Sat FA Cup Sponsored by Littlewoods Pools—Final Tie—Wembley Stadium
FA Youth Cup—Final*
12 Sun FA Carlsberg Vase—Final Tie—Wembley Stadium
FL Play-Off Semi-Final–1st Leg
14 Tue FA Carlsberg Vase—Final Tie Poss Replay
15 Wed UEFA Cup Final–2nd Leg
FL Play-Off Semi-Final–2nd Leg
16 Thu FA Cup Sponsored by Littlewoods Pools—Final Tie Poss Replay
18 Sat Possible England International
19 Sun FA Umbro Trophy—Final Tie—Wembley Stadium
22 Wed European Champion Clubs' Cup Final
23 Thu FA Umbro Trophy—Final Tie Poss Replay
25 Sat FL Third Division Play-Off Final–Wembley Stadium
26 Sun FL Second Division Play-Off Final–Wembley Stadium
27 Mon FL First Division Play-Off Final–Wembley Stadium

REFEREEING AND THE REFEREES

The most fundamental change in the Laws of the Game for the 1995/96 Season is to alter the number of players allowed to take part in a match. Instead of two substitutes plus a goalkeeper (at any time) being available there is to be a switch to a fourteen man game with any three named substitutes taking part. This means that a team can choose in their absolute discretion either three outfield players or two outfield players and a goalkeeper. All competitions must now stipulate whether 3, 4, or 5 substitutes may be nominated.

As far as the field of play is concerned, a new mark *may* be made off the field of play eleven yards from the corner flag to ensure that distance is observed at the taking of a corner. Publicity may not be allowed on the field especially advertising on nets, corner flags, or goal posts. Finally it is recommended that actual markings be used to define the "Technical Area" when it is desired to incorporate such an area.

For the first time spitting has become a separate section under Fouls and Misconduct. There are now 10 penal offences rather than nine and at the taking of a penalty kick all players must now stand behind the penalty spot at a distance of 10 yards rather than merely standing 10 yards away from the penalty spot which has caused problems in the past.

Finally two existing practical situations are now officially incorporated into the Laws. Following on from last season's change in the Off-side Law a player will only be penalised for being in an off-side position if in the referee's opinion he is "involved in active play". The second inclusion is that the fourth match referee becomes officially recognised as it is now stated "the fourth official will assist the referee at all times".

The National List of Referees for the forthcoming Season consists of 67 men of whom the most senior is Mr David Allison of Lancaster. In all 15 officials left the List last Season of whom perhaps the most notable were FIFA referee Phil Don (retired through work commitments) ex-FIFA men Joe Worrall and Brian Hill and such stalwarts as Terry Holbrook, Kelvin Morton, Peter Fowkes and last season's Coca-Cola Cup Final fourth official Jim Parker.

The new men on the List are Messrs. Baines, Bennett, Fletcher, Frankland, Knight, Laws, Leake, Pearson, Stretton, Taylor and Wiley.

KEN GOLDMAN

The full List is as follows:

NATIONAL LIST OF REFEREES FOR SEASON 1995–96

Paul Alcock, (Redhill, Surrey)
David Allison, (Lancaster)
Gerald Ashby, (Worcester)
Mick Bailey, (Impington, Cambs.)
Steve Baines, (Chesterfield)
Graham Barber, (Warwick)
Neale Barry, (Scunthorpe)
Steve Bennett, (Dartford)
Martin Bodenham, (Looe, Cornwall)
John Brandwood, (Lichfield, Staffs.)
Kevin Breen, (Liverpool)
Keith Burge, (Tonypandy)
Bill Burns, (Scarborough)
Alan Butler, (Sutton-in-Ashfield)
George Cain, (Bootle)
Keith Cooper, (Pontypridd)
Keith A. Cooper, (Swindon)
Ian Cruikshanks, (Hartlepool)
Paul Danson, (Leicester)
Roger Dilkes, (Mossley, Lancs.)
Stephen Dunn, (Bristol)
Paul Durkin, (Portland, Dorset)
Andy D'Urso, (Billericay, Essex)
David Elleray, (Harrow-on-the-Hill)
Mick Fletcher, (Warley, West Midlands)
Graham Frankland, (Middlesbrough)
Roger Furnandiz, (Doncaster)
Dermot Gallagher, (Banbury, Oxon.)
Rodger Gifford, (Llanbradach, Mid. Glam.)
Bob Harris, (Oxford)
Robbie Hart, (Darlington)
Terry Heilbron, (Newton Aycliffe)
Ian Hemley, (Ampthill, Beds.)
Peter Jones, (Loughborough)
John Kirkby, (Sheffield)
Barry Knight, (Orpington)
David Laws, (Whitley Bay)
Ken Leach, (Brewood, Staffs.)
Tony Leake, (Darwen, Lancs.)
John Lloyd, (Wrexham)
Steve Lodge, (Barnsley)
Eddie Lomas, (Manchester)
Terry Lunt, (Ashton-in-Makerfield, Lancs.)
Kevin Lynch, (Knaresborough)
Scott Mathieson, (Stockport)
David Orr, (Iver, Bucks.)
Roy Pearson, (Peterlee, Durham)
Mick Pierce, (Portsmouth)
Graham Poll, (Tring, Hertfordshire)
Graham Pooley, (Bishops Stortford)
Richard Poulain, (Huddersfield)
Mike Reed, (Birmingham)
Paul Rejer, (Tipton, West Midlands)
Uriah Rennie, (Sheffield)
Phil Richards, (Preston)
Mike Riley, (Leeds)
Jim Rushton, (Stoke-on-Trent)
Gurnam Singh, (Wolverhampton)
Frazer Stretton, (Nottingham)
Paul Taylor, (Cheshunt, Hertfordshire)
Trever West, (Hull)
Alan Wiley, (Walsall)
Clive Wilkes, (Gloucester)
Alan Wilkie, (Chester-le-Street)
Gary Willard, (Worthing, W. Sussex)
Jeff Winter, (Stockton-on-Tees)
Eddie Wolstenholme, (Blackburn)